THE YEAR'S WORK IN
MODERN LANGUAGE
STUDIES

THE
YEAR'S WORK IN
MODERN LANGUAGE
STUDIES

EDITED BY

DAVID A. WELLS, M.A., Ph.D.
Professor of German, Birkbeck College, London

GLANVILLE PRICE, M.A., Doct. de l'Univ.
Professor of French,
University of Wales, Aberystwyth

STEPHEN PARKINSON, M.A., Ph.D.
Lecturer in Portuguese Language and Linguistics
University of Oxford

JOHN M. A. LINDON, M.A.
Senior Lecturer in Italian,
University College London

AND

PETER J. MAYO, M.A., Ph.D.
Senior Lecturer in Russian and Slavonic Studies,
University of Sheffield

VOLUME 53

1991

THE MODERN HUMANITIES
RESEARCH ASSOCIATION
1992

The Year's Work in Modern Language Studies may be ordered from the Hon. Treasurer, MHRA, King's College, Strand, London WC2R 2LS, England.

ISBN 0 947623 51 5

ISSN 0084-4152

Printed in Great Britain by
W. S. MANEY & SON LIMITED
HUDSON ROAD LEEDS LS9 7DL

CONTENTS

PREFACE
page xi

1 LATIN
    I   MEDIEVAL LATIN   1
        by PROFESSOR C. J. MCDONOUGH, M.A., PH.D.

    II NEO-LATIN, Postponed

2 ROMANCE LANGUAGES
    I   ROMANCE LINGUISTICS   11
        by PROFESSOR J. N. GREEN, M.A., D.PHIL.

    II FRENCH STUDIES
        Language,   25
            by PROFESSOR GLANVILLE PRICE,
            M.A., DOCT. DE L'UNIV.
        Early Medieval Literature,   50
            by MARIANNE J. AILES, M.A., PH.D.
        Late Medieval Literature,   68
            by KAREN PRATT, M.A., PH.D.
        The Sixteenth Century,   78
            by JOHN O'BRIEN, M.A., D.PHIL.
        The Seventeenth Century,   97
            by ELIZABETH M. M. WOODROUGH, M.A., D.PHIL.
        The Eighteenth Century,   131
            by T. C. NEWLAND, M.A.,
            and SIMON HARVEY, M.A., PH.D.
        The Romantic Era,   161
            by MYRTO KONSTANTARAKOS, L.ÈS L., M.ÈS L.
        The Nineteenth Century (Post-Romantic),   180
            by JANINE R. DAKYNS, M.A., D.PHIL.
        The Twentieth Century, 1900–45,   208
            by SUSAN R. HARROW, M.A., PH.D.
        The Twentieth Century, since 1945,   233
            by H. G. MCINTYRE, B.A., PH.D.
        French Canadian Literature, Postponed
        African and Caribbean Literature, Postponed

III OCCITAN STUDIES

Language,   245
  by PETER V. DAVIES, B.A., PH.D.

Literature,   260
  by MICHAEL J. ROUTLEDGE, B.A., PH.D.

IV SPANISH STUDIES

Language,   266
  by JOHN ENGLAND, B.A., PH.D.,
  and CHRISTOPHER LYONS, M.A., PH.D.

Medieval Literature,   287
  by B. BUSSELL THOMPSON, B.A., M.A., PH.D.,
  MERCEDES VAQUERO, M.A., PH.D.,
  and CARLOS ALBERTO VEGA, B.A., M.A., M.A., PH.D.

Aljamiado Literature,   300
  by CONSUELO LÓPEZ-MORILLAS, PH.D.

Literature, 1490–1700 (Prose and Poetry),   304
  by J. A. JONES, B.A., PH.D.

Literature, 1490–1700 (Drama),   314
  by PROFESSOR WILLIAM R. BLUE, M.A., PH.D.

Literature, 1700–1823, Postponed

Literature, 1823–1898,   326
  by CATHERINE DAVIES, LIC. FIL., PH.D.

Literature, 1898–1936,   341
  by K. M. SIBBALD, M.A., PH.D.

Literature, 1936 to the Present Day,   362
  by STEPHEN M. HART, M.A., PH.D.,
  and ABIGAIL E. LEE SIX, M.A., PH.D.

V CATALAN STUDIES

Language,   375
  by BLANCA PALMADA, LLIC.FIL., PH.D.,
  VICENT DE MELCHOR, LLIC.FIL.,
  ALBERT TURULL, LLIC.FIL.,
  and JORDI BAÑERES, LLIC.HIST.

Literature, Postponed

VI PORTUGUESE STUDIES

Language,   388
  by STEPHEN PARKINSON, MA., PH.D.

Medieval Literature, Postponed

Literature, 1500 to the Present Day, Postponed

VII   LATIN AMERICAN STUDIES

Spanish-American Literature: The Colonial Period, 406
by PETER T. BRADLEY, B.A., PH.D.

The Nineteenth Century, 410
by ANNELLA MCDERMOTT, M.A.

The Twentieth Century, 412
by PROFESSOR D. L. SHAW, M.A., PH.D.,
and PROFESSOR G. M. MARTIN, B.A., PH.D.

Brazilian Literature, Postponed

VIII   ITALIAN STUDIES

Language, 424
by M. MAIR PARRY, M.A., PH.D.

Duecento and Trecento I (Dante), Postponed
Duecento and Trecento II (excluding Dante), 447
by JENNIFER PETRIE, M.A., M.LITT.

Humanism and the Renaissance, 453
by E. HAYWOOD, M.A., M.A., PH.D.,
and P. L. ROSSI, M.A.

Seicento, 490
by MAURICE SLAWINSKI, M.A.

Settecento, 511
by G. W. SLOWEY, M.A.

Ottocento, Postponed
Novecento, 525
by BRUCE MERRY, M.A., PH.D.

IX   ROMANIAN STUDIES

Language, 550
by PROFESSOR GLANVILLE PRICE,
M.A., DOCT. DE L'UNIV.

Literature, Postponed

X   ROMANSH STUDIES 555
by PROFESSOR KENNETH H. ROGERS, M.A., PH.D.

3   CELTIC LANGUAGES

I   WELSH STUDIES

Language, 559
by DAVID THORNE, M.A., PH.D.

Early and Medieval Literature, Postponed
Literature since 1500, 563
by DAVID R. JOHNSTON, M.A., PH.D.

II   BRETON AND CORNISH STUDIES   568
     by HUMPHREY LLOYD HUMPHREYS, B.A., D. ÈS L.

III IRISH STUDIES
     Early Irish, Postponed
     Modern Irish,   572
     by NOLLAIG MAC CONGÁIL, PH.D.

IV   SCOTTISH GAELIC STUDIES   584
     by PROFESSOR DERICK S. THOMSON, M.A.

4 GERMANIC LANGUAGES
   I   GERMAN STUDIES
       Language,   589
       by CHARLES V. J. RUSS, M.A., M.LITT., PH.D.
       Medieval Literature,   610
       by PROFESSOR DAVID A. WELLS, M.A., PH.D.
       The Sixteenth Century, Postponed
       The Seventeenth Century,   665
       by JILL BEPLER, B.A., PH.D.
       The Classical Era,   679
       by M. L. DAVIES, M.A.
       The Romantic Era,   735
       by NICHOLAS SAUL, M.A., PH.D.
       Literature, 1830–1880,   774
       by JOHN GUTHRIE, B.A., PH.D.
       Literature, 1880–1945,   807
       by MALCOLM HUMBLE, M.A., PH.D.
       Literature from 1945 to the Present Day,   830
       by MARGARET LITTLER, B.A., PH.D.

   II DUTCH STUDIES
       Language,   876
       by R. VISMANS, M.A.
       Literature,   885
       by ELSA STRIETMAN, DRS.

   III DANISH STUDIES   901
       by BENTE ELSWORTH, B.A.

   IV NORWEGIAN STUDIES
       Language and Early Literature,   914
       by E. G. LARSEN, CAND.PHILOL.
       Literature since the Reformation, Postponed

V SWEDISH STUDIES
Language, 923
  by KERSTIN PETERSSON, FIL.KAND., FIL.MAG., M.A.
Literature, 929
  by PETER GRAVES, M.A.

5 SLAVONIC LANGUAGES

I CZECH STUDIES
Language, Postponed
Literature, 937
  by K. BRUŠÁK, M.A.

II SLOVAK STUDIES
Language, 946
  by JAMES D. NAUGHTON, M.A., PH.D.
Literature, 952
  by K. BRUŠÁK, M.A.

III POLISH STUDIES
Language, 957
  by NIGEL GOTTERI, M.A.
Literature, 972
  by URSULA PHILLIPS, B.A., B.A., DIP.LIB.

IV RUSSIAN STUDIES
General, 984
  by D. L. L. HOWELLS, M.A.
Language, 990
  by P. J. MAYO, M.A., PH.D.
Literature from the Beginning to 1700, 997
  by R. M. CLEMINSON, M.A., D.PHIL.
Literature, 1700–1820, 1002
  by NICHOLAS J. CROWE, M.A., PH.D.
Literature, 1820–1880, Postponed
Literature, 1880–1917, 1012
  by D. N. WELLS, M.A., D.PHIL.
Literature from 1917 to the Present Day, 1026
  by DAVID C. GILLESPIE, B.A., PH.D.

V UKRAINIAN STUDIES 1052
  by V. SWOBODA, M.A.

VI BELORUSSIAN STUDIES 1063
  by J. DINGLEY, B.A.

VII   SERBO-CROAT STUDIES
      Language,   1070
         by TREVOR PRESTON, B.A.
      Literature,   1072
         by DAVID A. NORRIS, B.A., PH.D.

VIII BULGARIAN STUDIES   1078
         by T. HENNINGER, M.A., PH.D.

ABBREVIATIONS

  I   ACTA, FESTSCHRIFTEN AND OTHER   1085
      COLLECTIVE AND GENERAL WORKS

 II   GENERAL   1098

III   PLACE NAMES   1099

IV   PERIODICALS, INSTITUTIONS, PUBLISHERS   1099

INDEXES

  I   SUBJECTS   1141

 II   NAMES   1178

PREFACE

This volume surveys work, published in 1991 unless otherwise stated, in the fields of Romance, Celtic, Germanic, and Slavonic languages and literatures.

The new policy of collective editorship authorized by the Committee of the Modern Humanities Research Association is now almost fully implemented. Stephen Parkinson joins the editorial team with responsibility for the Spanish, Catalan, Portuguese, and Latin American sections. At the conclusion of a twenty-year period in which he has worked as an Editor Glanville Price is responsible for the Latin, Romance Linguistics, French, Occitan, and Celtic sections. David Wells serves as General Editor for the last time but will retain his editorial responsibility for the Germanic languages and literatures. John Lindon continues in office as Editor of the Italian, Romanian, and Romansh sections, and Peter Mayo remains responsible for the Slavonic sections.

The attention of users is drawn to the lists of abbreviations at the end of the volume. It should be noted, however, that abbreviations for *Acta*, *Festschriften*, and other collective and general works that relate only to one section of the volume are sometimes given in the relevant section (usually in an introductory 'General' subsection) rather than in the list at the end of the volume. An asterisk before a title indicates that the item in question has not been seen by the contributor.

Many authors, editors, and publishers supply review copies and offprints of their publications. To these we and our contributors are grateful and we invite others to follow their example, especially in the case of work issuing from an unusual or unexpected source of publication. We would ask that, whenever possible, items for review be sent directly to the appropriate contributor rather than to one of the Editors. However, items relating to a number of fields are best sent to one of the Editors who will then take appropriate steps.

We record with sorrow the death while in office of our longest-serving contributor. Mr Victor Swoboda introduced Ukrainian Studies into *The Year's Work* in Volume 24 (report year 1962) and, apart from only three postponements, during his thirty years in office contributed the Ukrainian Studies section in every volume to the present. With additional contributions in Volumes 25 and 26 (1963 and 1964) he also introduced Belorussian (White Russian) Studies into the publication. Among contributors retiring this year special mention must be made of Dr Peter Bradley, who has contributed the section on the Colonial Period of Spanish-American literature in twenty-three successive volumes without interruption.

The Editors often receive the comment that the volume is the first work of reference consulted by scholars embarking on a new research topic in our field. Through the Committee of the Modern Humanities Research Association we continue to represent both to the Universities Funding Council and to those having authority in some university institutions the fundamental importance of bibliography in the assessment of the research performance of individuals and in the maintenance of scholarly standards generally. We again express our thanks to our authors, who work in varying and often difficult conditions, to the institutions which have made research grants to contributors, to many librarians for their patient supply of both literature and information, to those who have provided technical and secretarial assistance, to Julia McVaugh who has compiled both the subject index and the name index, to Dorothy Evans who concludes her work as secretary after many years, and to our printers, W. S. Maney & Son Ltd, and especially Derek Brown with whom it is an unfailing pleasure to collaborate.

22 October 1992   D.A.W., G.P., S.R.P., J.M.A.L., P.J.M.

1

LATIN

I. MEDIEVAL LATIN

By C. J. McDonough, *Professor of Classics, University of Toronto*

1. General

Elizabeth Archibald, *Apollonius of Tyre: Medieval and Renaissance Themes and Variations, including the Text of the 'Historia Apollonii Regis Tyri' with an English Translation*, Cambridge, D. S. Brewer, xiii 1 250 pp., is a rich resource of information on the bibliography, versions, adaptations, and sources of a tale whose influence extended to Shakespeare's *Pericles*. *The Theatre of Medieval Europe: New Research in Early Drama*, ed. Eckehard Simon, CUP, xxii + 311 pp., contains two items that stress the need for an interdisciplinary approach: C. C. Flanigan, 'Medieval Latin music-drama' (21–41), isolates theoretical and historical issues surrounding the *Visitatio Sepulchri*, some Christmas texts, and other items in the repertory, and concludes with remarks on specific plays, the *Ludus Danielis* among them; A. Hughes, 'Liturgical drama: falling between the disciplines' (42–62), concentrates on the liturgy, music, the dating, provenance, and the transmission of MSS. *Aevum inter Vtrumque: Mélanges offerts à Gabriel Sanders*, ed. Marc Van Uytfanghe and Roland Demeulenaere, The Hague, Steenbrugis, xli + 537 pp., includes the following: J. Fontaine, 'Une épitaphe rythmique d'un contemporain d'Isidore de Séville: l'éloge funèbre du Visigot Oppila' (163–86), presents a line-by-line commentary on the language, style, rhythm, and contents of a short epitaph and draws attention to its debt to classical poetic culture and to the accentual prose *cursus*; G. de Nie, 'Le corps, la fluidité et l'identité personnelle dans la vision du monde de Grégoire de Tours' (75–87), weighs the possible meanings of bodily decomposition and secretions for Gregory and points to the association of the latter with the devil; M. Heinzelmann, 'Hagiographischer und historischer Diskurs bei Gregor von Tours?' (237–58), compares texts on the same subject from the *Historiarum libri decem* and from hagiographical works to identify the kinds of discourse used in the different genres; M. Van Uytfanghe, 'Les *Visiones* du très haut moyen âge et les récentes "experiences de mort temporaire". Sens ou non-sens d'une comparaison, Première partie' (447–81), investigates pre-Carolingian vision literature, some with hagiographic overtones, and compares it with the so-called 'near-death experiences' documented over the last 20 years; É. Évrard, 'Les *Enigmata* de saint Boniface. Étude de métrique quantitative' (153–61), discusses several textual problems in Boniface's poem on the virtues and vices and then tests the information derived from a detailed metrical analysis of the hexametrical schemata against the theoretical pronouncements of the period; B. Janssens, 'L'étude de la langue et les citations bibliques dans le *Liber manualis* de Dhuoda: un sondage' (259–75), notes the Bible's influence on Dhuoda's style and language and distinguishes several types of modifications to the biblical citations; P. G. Schmidt, 'Eine metrische Fassung der "Vita Gregorii" des Johannes Hymmonides. (MS Brügge 406; BHL 3644 a)' (379–83), publishes a first edition of a prose prologue between a master and a pupil, possibly named Sigeboto and Luitold respectively, as an aid in locating the date and provenance of the metrical life of John in the 10th or 11th c.

A new journal devoted to medieval Latin includes the following: D. Norberg, 'Dyname Patrice de Marseilles', *JMLat*, 1:46–51, examines the rhetoric of two letters contained in the 7th-c. *Epistulae Austrasicae* and emends the text in several places; H. J. Westra, 'Literacy, orality and medieval patronage: a phenomenological approach', *ib.*, 52–59, re-examines patronage from Charlemagne to the 12th c. and suggests that the conventional polarities of orality and literacy, vernacular and Latin, and popular and high culture tended to break down through the interaction of patron and the *literati*. The first topic is also broached by P. von Moos, 'Zwischen Schriftlichkeit und Mundlichkeit: Dialogische Interaktion im lateinischen Hochmittelalter (Vorstellung des neuen Teilprojekts H im SFB 231)', *FmSt*, 25:300–14, who outlines his methodological principles before he attempts to reconstruct the *ars dialogica* of the Middle Ages. V. Law, 'Fragments from the lost portions of the *Epitomae* of Virgilius Maro Grammaticus', *CMCS*, 21:113–23, argues from style, content, attribution and position within sections that the 14 fragments from the anonymous *Florilegium Frisingense* and Sedulius Scottus's *Collectaneum Miscellaneum* contain features that suggest they originated from the *Epitomae* of Virgilius. L. Löfstedt, 'Les neveux de Charlemagne — notule sur la Nota Emilianense', *NMi*, 91, 1990:487–89, notes regarding the meaning of *neptis* in the *Nota* that medieval Ireland knew the word 'nia' as 'warrior' and 'nephew', a finding that has broader implications for uncle–nephew relationships in OF literature, such as Charlemagne and Roland.

P. Meyvaert, '"Rainaldus est malus scriptor Francigenus" — voicing national antipathy in the Middle Ages', *Speculum*, 66:743–63, surveys the literary tradition which transmitted to the Middle Ages the national characteristics of different peoples and illuminates the often antagonistic attitudes of different nationalities to the languages of other groups. A. Punzi, 'Sulle fonti dell' *Excidium Troiae*', *CN*, 51:5–26, concentrates on Statius's *Achilleid* and its glossular tradition, and Servius's commentary on Virgil's *Aeneid*. R. Martin, '"Vinum dulce, gloriosum . . ." Le thème du vin dans la poésie latine médiévale', *Bulletin de l'Association Guillaume Budé*, 49, 1990:356–70, looks at the attitudes to wine expressed by Alcuin and Theodulf of Orleans before he compares and contrasts two debate poems on the theme of the conflict between water and wine by Walter Map and the anonymous *Denudata ueritate*. A. Garnier, 'Thèmes et variations sur la pie dans le monde médiéval', *MA*, 97:47–78, sketches the image of the *pica* from antiquity to its treatment by medieval exegetes, who demonized it as a symbol of duplicity. H. Needler, 'The animal fable among other medieval literary genres', *NLH*, 22:423–39, surveys the beast epic, chivalric romance, feudal epic and fable to uncover what the texts of fable say about the generation of literary form itself.

2. ANGLO-SAXON ENGLAND

C. A. Ireland, 'Some analogues of the OE *"Seafarer"* from Hiberno-Latin sources', *NMi*, 92:1–14, looks at late-7th-c. texts by Adomnán, Muirchú, and Tirechán to argue that early Church contacts mediated the Irish tradition of *peregrinatio*, which offers analogues that help in understanding *Seafarer*. T. N. Hall, 'The cross as green tree in the *Vindicta Salvatoris* and the green rod of Moses in *Exodus*', *ESt*, 72:297–307, uses a passage from the Latin and OE versions of the *Vindicta Salvatoris* to assess the implications for a crux in OE *Exodus*, where Moses parts the Red Sea with a *grene tacen*. W. T. Whobrey, 'King Alfred's metrical epilogue to the *Pastoral Care*', *JEGP*, 90:175–86, investigates the epilogue's sources, the question of Alfred's authorship, and his intentions in translating Gregory's work. R. Marsden, 'Aelfric as translator: the Old English prose *Genesis*', *Anglia*, 109:319–58, examines the translation methods of Aelfric and Jerome and concludes from a discussion of Genesis 2. 3 and 17. 4 that critics have misjudged the nature and degree of Aelfric's 'literalism'. J. McGowan, 'Notes on the OE version of the *Vita Sancti Christophori*', *Neophilologus*, 75:451–55, emends six passages in the fragmentary OE text from the Latin version. J. E. Cross, 'Wulfstan's *De Anticristo* in a twelfth-century Worcester manuscript', *Anglo-Saxon England*, 20:203–20, has uncovered in Cambridge, St John's College 42 (B. 20), a new text of Wulfstan's work and his association of the anonymous texts with Worcester allows him to formulate a hypothesis about Wulfstan's Latin writings; M. F. Wack and C. D. Wright, 'A new Latin source for the Old English "Three Utterances" exemplum', *ib.*, 187–202, have identified more than 20 additional Latin MSS of the

4 *Medieval Latin*

exemplum. P. P. O'Neill, 'Latin learning at Winchester in the early eleventh century: the evidence of the Lambeth Psalter', *ib.*, 143–66, describes London, Lambeth Palace Library 427, and speculates that it served private, devotional, and pedagogical functions. J. I. McEnerney, 'The dream of Aedilvulf', *MJ*, 23, 1988 (1991): 28–36, analyses the contents of part of the 9th-c. poem on the holy men of Lindisfarne and comments on metrics, style, grammar, and sources.

3. The Carolingian and Ottonian Period

Aspects of Alcuin's work are discussed in the following: M. Forthomme-Nicholson, 'Pélage et Alcuin', *ECla*, 59:43–51, points to the similarities between the traditions and pedagogical methods of the two; M. Alberi, 'Jerome, Alcuin and Vergil's "Old Entellus"', *JMH*, 17:103–13, discusses Alcuin's citations from Jerome in a polemical academic debate as evidence of the competitive struggle at Charlemagne's court, which ruptures Alcuin's attempts elsewhere to idealize curial life; V. Serralda, 'Étude comparée de la "Confessio Fidei" attribuée à Alcuin et de la "Confessio Theologica" de Jean de Fécamp', *MJ*, 23, 1988 [1991]:7–27, shows that the former work contains many attitudes that are present in Alcuin's correspondence, and that it imitates Alcuin's liberty in adapting canonical texts to express his own personality; on these grounds he thinks Alcuin wrote the *Confessio Fidei*; J. Pucci, 'Alcuin's cell poem: a Virgilian reappraisal', *Latomus*, 49, 1990:839–49, underlines the novel features of genre and style in the appropriation of the classical material. K. Heene, 'Female saints and their lives. The geographical distribution of the Carolingian *vitae feminarum*', *Aevum inter Vtrumque*, 205–26, explains why almost all the texts of the lives and miracles of female saints originated north of the Loire. M. W. Herren, 'The "De imagine tetrici" of Walahfrid Strabo: edition and translation', *JMLat*, 1:118–39, points to Strabo's anxiety about the empire's future; the edition presents a different line order and several departures from Dümmler's edition. D. R. Bradley, 'Variations on some Cambridge songs', *MAe*, 59, 1990:260–75, offers textual and interpretive comments on some eighteen passages. J. L. van Dieten, 'Plastes Ke Piitis. Die "versiculi greci" des Bischofs Reginold von Eichstätt', *SM*, 31, 1990:357–416, exhaustively studies the Greek component in *Terminus et idem interminus* with a full discussion of authorship, earlier editions, the MS tradition, orthography, textual problems, sources, and an edition of the Latin and Greek texts. C. Manning, '"Waltharius" 1441: "Lardatam pultam"', *ib.*, 259–64, uses a passage from Anthimus, *De observatione ciborum*, to explain the significance of bacon in the epic, and emends *pulpam* to *pultam*; I. Deug-Su, 'La "Vita Rictrudis" di Ubaldo di Saint-Amand: un'agiografia intellettuale e i santi imperfetti', *ib.*, 545–82, observes two strains in Ubaldo's hagiography, one traditional, the other critical, and demonstrates how these opposing trends are integrated. U. Kindermann, 'Der Satiriker Wilchard von Lyon', *MJ*, 23, 1988 [1991]: 37–45, starts from Bernard of Morval's statement that only two poets before him had written *hexametri tripertiti*, of whom one, Wilchard, had written about 30 verses, to identify the anti-monastic poem *Ordo monasticus* as the work of Wilchard written around 1080. J. M. Ziolkowski, 'Eupolemius', *JMLat*, 1 : 1–45, offers a full introduction on the dating, literary influences, and a literal translation for use with Manitius's edition. J. R. E. Bliese, 'The courage of the Normans — a comparative study of battle rhetoric', *NMS*, 35 : 1–26, isolates what was particular to the Norman concept of courage by examining 331 battle speeches from 91 chronicles composed between 1000 and 1250 and constructs a typology of 16 recurrent motifs. D. Townsend, 'Anglo-Latin hagiography and the Norman transition', *Exemplaria*, 3 : 385–433, applies reader-response criticism and other modern theoretical approaches in a close reading of two hagiographies of Dunstan. E. Nègre, 'Un refrain en langue d'oc', *RLiR*, 55 : 487–96, re-examines the linguistic difficulties in the bilingual *aube Phebi claro nondum orto jubare* and contends that it concerns the waking of a troop of soldiers in the countryside. P. Walter, 'Der Bär und der Erzbischof. Masken von Reims und Adalbero von Laon', *Symposion* (Paderborn), 377–88, uses literary and non-literary texts to detect traces of a carnivalesque myth, central to which was the figure of a wild man, who was associated with a bear.

4. THE TWELFTH CENTURY

M. D. Reeve sifts a very large number of MSS in 'The transmission of the *Historia Regum Britannie*', *JMLat*, 1 : 73–117. J. Fried, 'Der Archipoeta — ein Kölner Scholaster?', *Fest. Zimmermann*, 85–90, identifies the Archpoet with the younger of the two cathedral scholars at Cologne called Rudolf, who was active between 1176 and 1201. B. Löfstedt, '*cauma* bei Pseudo-Beda', *Eranos*, 89 : 61–62, proposes that *cauma* derived its meaning from the Greek loan word for 'heat' and shows how the word attained the sense of 'cold' or 'cold wind'. G. W. Olsen, 'Twelfth-century humanism reconsidered: the case of St Bernard', *SM*, 31, 1990 : 27–53, assesses the writings of modern scholars on humanism and uses St Bernard to evaluate each different approach; C. J. McDonough, 'Orpheus, Ulysses and Penelope in a twelfth-century setting', *ib.*, 85–121, suggests that an Orpheus poem may have been constructed as a begging poem for delivery at a court and points out that the themes of begging, hunger, clothing, and destitution in a poem on Ulysses's return connect it with other Goliardic poems in the same miscellany; A. Simonetti, 'Rufino di Assisi e il cod. C 30 Sup. dell'Ambrosiana', *ib.*, 125–42, identifies two sermons as the work of a French homilist and concludes that the collection was not by Rufinus; P. Godman, 'Ambiguity in the "Mathematicus" of Bernardus Silvestris', *ib.*, 583–648, presents Bernard as a champion of a shift from conventional mannerism to an experimental classicism, in which he explored the issue of ambiguity; P. Garbini, 'Sulla "Vita scolastica" di Bonvesin de la Riva', *ib.*, 705–37, outlines the literary debts of this popular manual to the *Floretus*, and to Matthew of Vendôme's *Tobias* among others. T. A.-P. Klein, 'Der "Ernestus" des Odo von Magdeburg: Studien zur Textkritik und Interpretation', *ib.*, 907–23, suggests textual corrections, together with second thoughts.

P. von Moos, 'Das 12. Jahrhundert — eine "Renaissance" oder ein "Aufklärungszeitalter"?', *MJ*, 23, 1988 [1991]:1–10, surveys the history of the concept from Charles Homer Haskins onwards and finds that the word can be used as a metaphor of the medieval rediscovery of important ancient texts, which were chiefly academic and scientific, not literary; C. A. Cioffi, 'The epistolary style of Odo of Deuil in his "De profectione Ludovici VII in orientem"', *ib.*, 76–81, shows that the account of the second Crusade was written in rhythmic prose, a useful discovery for future editors and of interest to students of medieval Latin style; P. G. Schmidt, '*Magnificus Cisterciensium ordo*. Ordenskritik in einer Jenseitsvision', *ib.*, 82–90, edits from Paris B. N. lat. 18201 a vision that describes the fate awaiting Cistercians after their death; R. Levine, 'How to read Walter Map', *ib.*, 91–105, rescues the *De nugis curialium* from trivializing critics and highlights the darker elements of sex and violence; J. C. Eade, 'Astrological compression in "Iove cum Mercurio" (CB 88/88a)', *ib.*, 152–53, elaborates on the poetic associations of an astrological reference to a girl's supposed horoscope; R. E. Pepin, 'Fulgentius — the enigmatic *Furvus* in John of Salisbury's "Entheticus"', *ib.*, 119–25, speculates that the writer designated as *Furvus* is not Macrobius or Seneca, but Fulgentius; D. A. Traill, 'Notes on "Dum Diane vitrea" (CB 62) and "A globo veteri" (CB 67)', *ib.*, 143–51 discusses problematic readings in CB 62, and the order and authenticity of stanzas 5–8; in CB 67 the debt to Bernard Silvestris's *Cosmographia* provides the key to a crux in stanza 1a. 4.

J. W. Baldwin, 'Five discourses on desire: sexuality and gender in Northern France around 1200', *Speculum*, 66:797–819, discusses the theme of sexual desire as treated by Peter the Chanter, an anonymous physician, Jean Bodel of Arras, Andreas Capellanus, and Jean Renart, and finds that only in Peter does the Augustinian view of

Medieval Latin 7

desire as concupiscence survive. K. B. Wolf, 'Crusade and narrative: Bohemond and the *Gesta Francorum*', *JMH*, 17:207–16, examines historiographical questions of narrative patterns and structures and the consequences of casting Bohemond as the protagonist in the story. C. J. Nederman and A. Feldwick, 'To the court and back again: the origins and dating of the *Entheticus de dogmate entheticorum* of John of Salisbury', *JMRS*,21:129–45, date the work before 1156–57 and argue that it was written as an instructional manual addressed to Thomas Becket after his appointment as royal chancellor. A. Groos, 'Cundrie's announcement ("Parzival" 781–782)', *BGDSL*, 113:384–414, finds parallels to the mythic dimension of Cundrie's announcement in Bernard Silvestris's *Cosmographia* and Alain of Lille's *Anticlaudianus*. H. C. R. Laurie, 'Cligès and the legend of Abelard and Heloise', *ZRP*, 107:324–42, proposes that Chrétien was the first vernacular poet to be inspired by the famous love story in his depiction of Cligès's relationship with Fénice. P. G. Schmidt, 'Jubel and Resignation. Amtjubiläen und Amtsniederlegungen von Bischöfen und Abten in literarischen Texten des Mittelalters', *IIZ*, 252:541–57, deals with the genre of poems composed on the selection and enthronement of a bishop; one which survives celebrates the choice of Albertus Magnus of Regensburg. F. C. Coulson and L. C. Jones, 'A newly acquired manuscript of the *De planctu naturae* of Alan of Lille in the Ohio State University (Columbus, Ohio)', *Scriptorium*, 45:84–88, point to the importance of the MS's glosses and the two running commentaries on the text, while R. Sharpe, 'London, British Library MS Royal 15 C. XI and Osbern of Gloucester's use of Plautus', *ib.*, 93–98, concludes from Osbern's citation of Plautus, *Aul.* 508–16, that Osbern's text differs from that in the Royal MS and points to the deficiencies in Osbern's use of Plautus for lexicographical purposes. S. Bordier, 'Aenigma somniorum', *Bulletin de l'Association Guillaume Budé*, 50:306–14 shows from John of Salisbury's *Policraticus* that the dream, allegory, riddle, and other fictional devices function according to the same rules, and this finding can be useful in interpreting OFr poetry. L. van Acker, 'Der Briefwechsel zwischen Elisabeth von Schönau und Hildegard von Bingen', *Aevum inter Vtrumque*, 409–17, questions the attribution of a letter to Hildegard and edits a previously unpublished letter of Hildegard.

5. THE THIRTEENTH CENTURY

Neil Wright, *The Historia regum Britannie of Geoffrey of Monmouth. v. Gesta regum Britannie*, Cambridge, D. S. Brewer, cxvi + 340 pp., has edited from three MSS a metrical paraphrase of Geoffrey's history, with a full introduction and followed by three indexes. D. Townsend,

'The "Versus de corona spinea" of Henry of Avranches', *MJ*, 23, 1988 [1991]: 154–70, offers a first edition of Henry's poem on the Incarnation and Passion, which survives uniquely in Cambridge, U. L., MS Dd. X1. 78. K. Bund, 'Die "Prophetin", ein Dichter und die Niederlassung der Bettelorden in Köln. Der Brief der Hildegard von Bingen an der Kölner Klerus und das Gedicht "Prophetia sancte Hyldegardis de novis fratribus" des Magisters Heinrich von Avranches', *ib.*, 171–260, edits Henry's versification of *Ep.* 48 of Hildegard, which provides evidence for Hildegard's literary reception and for the beginnings of the spread of the mendicant orders. D. L. D'Avray, 'Sermons on the dead before 1350', *SM*, 31, 1990:207–23, sets out the distinctive features of memorial preaching with their insights into social attitudes to kings, popes, nobility, and secular learning. D. Britton, 'The sources of lines 3562–3939 of the *Prick of Conscience*', *Anglia*, 109:87–93, notes John of Freiburg's *Summa confessorum* Book 3 as a source, and finds that it also provided the author with knowledge of Raymund, Hostiene, and Innocent. U. Kühne, '. . . Ex opere dicuntur Paulite. Zu Marner CB 9*', *BGDSL*, 113:251–56, interprets the word 'Paulite' not as a reference to the order of Pauline hermits or as a hit against the Franciscans, but as an allusion to the apostle Paul, who would naturally be associated with the Dominicans' main activity, preaching. P. Binkley, 'The date and setting of Michael of Cornwall's *Versus contra Henricum Abrincensem*', *MAe*, 60:76–84, dates the performance of the mock-trial to 5 February 1255, through identifying some of the judges. A. G. Rigg, 'Henry of Huntingdon's metrical experiments', *JMLat*, 1:60–72, analyses Henry's metrical and accentual poetry and his translation of an OE poem, while in 'Richard Pluto's *Equiuoca*: an edition', *Latomus*, 50:563–80, he edits from Oxford, Bodleian Library, Laud. misc. 363, a school text that helped learners of Latin to determine the quantity of a word's first syllable. H. Meyer, 'Ordo rerum und Registerhilfen in mittelalterlichen Enzyklopädiehandschriften', *FmSt*, 25:315–39, uses as the material basis for his study Bartholemeus Anglicus, *De proprietatibus rerum*, Thomas of Cantimpré, *Liber de natura rerum*, and Vincent of Beauvais, *Speculum maius*. C. Burnett and P. G. Dalché, 'Attitudes towards the Mongols in medieval literature: the xxii kings of Gog and Magog from the court of Frederick II to Jean de Mandeville', *Viator*, 22:153–67, use the *Mirabilia mundi* to illustrate the interpenetration of myth and historical fact and to chart the shifting attitudes in the West toward the Mongols. P. Eley, 'The myth of Trojan descent and perceptions of national identity: the case of *Eneas* and the *Roman de Troie*', *NMS*, 35:27–40, finds that the vernacular poems depicted the Trojans so that they reflected the growing sense of national identity that was consciously fostered by medieval rulers. T. A.-P. Klein, 'Eine Jungfrau aus Korinth am südlichen Nachthimmel im "Ernestus" des Odo von Magdeburg', *Hermes*, 119:127–28, deduces that *Chorinthia* in *Ernestus* 240 is an adjective from *corytus* and alludes to the goddess *Diana*. U. Kindermann, 'A la feste sui venuz, et ostendam quare: Ein Gegenfest schafft lateinische Literatur', *Symposion* (Paderborn), 349–58, explicates a satire, which he associates with the so-called *Bakelfest* of the medieval clergy.

6. THE FOURTEENTH AND FIFTEENTH CENTURIES

J. W. Marchand, 'An unidentified Latin quote in Piers Plowman', *MP*, 88:398–400, traces a quotation from Pseudo-Ezekiel 33. 12 through selected Latin sermons. C. D. Eckhardt, 'The presence of Rome in the Middle English chronicles of the fourteenth century', *JEGP*, 90:187–207, uncovers the influence of Geoffrey of Monmouth's Latin chronicle on the few chronicles written in English. R. F. Green, 'Jack Philipot, John of Gaunt, and a poem of 1380', *Speculum*, 66:330–41, redates a bilingual poem to 1380, just before the Peasants' Revolt, and adverts briefly to the interlingual mix. R. R. Edwards, 'Narration and doctrine in the Merchant's Tale', *ib.*, 66:342–67, draws on the *artes rhetoricae* of Matthew of Vendôme, Geoffrey of Vinsauf, and John of Garland to examine Chaucer's portrayal of the merchant as narrator. G. Silagi, 'Das Urteil des Paris: eine Revision', *SM*, 31, 1990:417–32, presents a complete edition of a poem in *Vagantenstrophen*, which he places in the 14th or 15th c., a view contested by G. Orlandi, 'A proposito del "Rhythmus de iuditio Paridis"', *ib.*, 901–06, who also offers several emendations. P. Brockmeier, 'Imitatio und ingenium in der Lyrik, Quellen und Variationen von Petrarcas Sonett', *Arcadia*, 26:33–49, re-examines Petrarch's thoughts on literary appropriation and studies the concepts and images in *Canzoniere* 189, finding debts to Virgil and Ovid. Martin Camargo, 'The consolation of Pandarus', *The Chaucer Review*, 25:214–28, discovers that in his translation of *Filostrato* Chaucer was influenced by Boethius's *Consolation of Philosophy* to develop the role of Pandarus in a dramatic way. H. Linke, 'Das angebliche Vorauer Osterspiel', *BGDSL*, 113:415–25, demonstrates that Vorau, Stiftsbibliothek MS 90 fols. 180V/181R, contains not a hitherto unknown German Easter play but two texts, which are here edited. J. Hoy, 'Chaucer and Dictys', *MAe*, 59, 1990:288–91, shows that an analogue between *Troilus* 4. 176–82 and Dictys *Ephemeris belli Troiani* suggests Chaucer was aware of the Latin work. J. Monfasani, 'Hermes Trismegistus, Rome, and the myth of Europa: an unknown text of Giles of Viterbo', *Viator*, 22:311–42, has edited from Naples,

Biblioteca nazionale MS V F 14, a fragment of a fictive dialogue between the archangel Michael and Saint Lorenzo Maiorano of Siponto, in which the Europa myth is seen as an allegory about Italy's corruption. P. Weinig, 'Aeneas Silvius Piccolominis "De curialium miseriis" Deutsch. Eine unbekannte Übersetzung aus dem 15. Jahrhundert', *ZDA*, 120:73–82, describes Innsbruck, Ferdinandeum Cod. F. B. 1050, which contains an anonymous translation of Aeneas's satire on court life, and discusses Wilhelm of Hirnkofen's different working methods. I. Thomson, 'The scholar as hero in Ianus Pannonius' panegyric on Guarinus Veronensis', *RQ*, 44:197–211, underlines the originality of presenting scholarship as a heroic virtue. J. Hankins, 'The myth of the Platonic Academy of Florence', *ib.*, 429–75, looks again at Ficino's letters and the *Declamationes* of Benedetto Colucci to conclude that Ficino's 'academy' was a private gymnasium located within Florence, that there are no strong reasons to qualify it as Platonic, nor to assume that it was patronized by the Medici. M. Stevens, 'The intertextuality of late medieval art and drama', *NLH*, 22:317–37, argues the merits of looking at the relationship between art and drama less in causative terms than on grounds of their intertextuality.

II. NEO-LATIN

POSTPONED

2

ROMANCE LANGUAGES

I. ROMANCE LINGUISTICS

By JOHN N. GREEN, *University of Bradford*

1. ACTA, FESTSCHRIFTEN

The publication of two more imposing tomes of *Actes* (Trier), II devoted to theoretical and synchronic linguistics and III mainly to historical grammar and dialectology (both discussed in the relevant sections below), almost concludes the Herculean task of editor Dieter Kremer. Two Congresses later, however, one really must ask whether the monumental effort, cost, and air of permanence are still justified by *all* the contents, among which conference ephemera and 'discussion' that is sometimes embarrassingly jejune and partisan jostle with a minority of items of real substance. More compact and no less scholarly are the records of a lively series of international colloquia on Latin linguistics that have revitalized the discipline: *Papers* (Cambridge), the fourth, assembles 29 articles on most structural aspects of Latin, including textual cohesion, but with special emphasis on word order typology — items which, in the balanced view of editor R. Coleman (vii–x), serve to correct earlier hasty and flawed conclusions.

Linguistica (Ljubljana), no. 31, marking the 60th birthday of Paulo Tekavčić, contains a bibliography of his writings (11–24) and 40 articles mainly on aspects of eastern Romance; items with a wider focus include: H. Ludtke, 'Überlegungen zur Entstehung des bestimmten Artikels im Romanischen' (81–98), and E. Roegiest, 'Typologie romane et position des pronoms personnels clitiques en roumain' (133–39), arguing that Romanian favours proclisis (there are special factors governing fem. -*o* arising naturally from its phonology) and adheres quite closely to the Romance type. In similar vein, *RRL*, 35. 4–6: 1990, ed. M. Sala, appears as a tribute to Iorgu Iordan, with 21 short, and mostly contrastive, articles under the general title 'Le roumain, idiome roman', including: A. Avram, 'Sur le rapport entre la force d'articulation et la palatalisation des dentales nasales' (257–63), I. Baciu, 'Les subordonnées à deux régissantes non coordonnées' (265–70), T. Cristea, 'Ellipse et négation en français et en roumain' (285–93), A. Cuniţă, 'Contrastivité et traduction: les augmentatifs en roumain et en français' (295–301), A. Kovačec,

'Sobre una innovación común al rumano y a las lenguas iberor-románicas' (313–22) (on spatial adverbials), L. Mourin, 'Les verbes irréguliers roumains dans la perspective romane' (341–46; see also p. 16), C. Pensado, 'Sobre el debilitamiento de las consonantes nasales en portugués y en rumano' (347–52), J. L. Pensado, 'Concordancias léxicas entre el gallego y el rumano' (353–56), J. Pohl, 'Économie et computation. Essai sur l'expression numérique dans huit langues' (357–63), S. Reinheimer-Rîpeanu, 'Mots latins hérités face aux emprunts de substrat et de superstrat' (365–69), T. Repina, 'Essai d'une typologie comparée des systèmes de la déclinaison des substantifs en latin, en ancien français et en roumain' (371–74), L. Tasmowski-De Ryck, 'Les pronoms démonstratifs français et roumains' (375–82), M. Tuțescu, 'L'énoncé conditionnel roman: continuité et innovation' (383–88), and L. Wald, 'Some observations concerning the plural of abstract nouns in Roumanian and other Romance languages' (389–93), which shows that French has the largest number of pluralized/pluralizable abstract nouns — usually in the sense of 'an act of, an instance of' as in *effronteries*, *illégalités, incorrectitudes, lassitudes* — and Spanish the smallest; for items exclusively on Romanian, see p. 550 below.

2. GENERAL ROMANCE

It has been a good ·year for reference works. The authoritative, four-volume *International Encyclopedia of Linguistics*, ed. William Bright, NY — Oxford, OUP, proffers a helpful and balanced entry on 'Romance languages' by S. Fleischman (3:337–43, with map, family tree, and list of languages and varieties), and another on 'Italic languages' by R. Coleman (2:242–44), complemented by individual entries on 'French' by M. B. Harris (2:25–31), 'Italian' by N. B. Vincent (2:236–42), 'Portuguese' by S. Parkinson (3:252–56), 'Rumanian' [*sic*] by G. Mallinson (3:346–50), and 'Spanish' by J. N. Green (4:58–64), but relegating the 'minor' Romance languages to patchy coverage under their nearest national standard. Ironically, Campbell's *Compendium*, a work addressed to a less specialized readership, with a thumb-nail sketch and illustrative text of some thousand languages, eschews a comparative Romance entry but offers equal status to Catalan and Occitan alongside the five national standards. Appropriately, vol. v.2, of the *Lexikon der romanistischen Linguistik* (*YWMLS*, 50:16, 51:20, 52:18) is devoted to intrasystemic and sociolinguistic aspects of *Okzitanisch und Katalanisch*, ed. Günter Holtus *et al.*, Tübingen, Niemeyer, xxii + 310 pp. — compact by the standards of the series and easy to negotiate. *The Legacy of Rome. A New Appraisal*, ed. Richard Jenkyns, OUP, xii + 479 pp., is a complete remake of Cyril Bailey's companion volume of 1923, tracing the pervasive influence of Roman civilization through two millennia; among its 15 readable and learned chapters we should mention: R. Jenkins, 'The legacy of Rome' (1–35), R. H. Rouse, 'The transmission of the texts' (37–59), and R. Posner, 'Language' (367–98), which examines dates of romanization, Romance phonological and morphosyntactic innovations, lexical borrowings, and the influence of Latin models of style and of grammatical analysis, along with their less welcome concomitants of purism and prescriptivism.

A symposium held at Rutgers in 1989 to tease out the implications of R. Wright's *Late Latin* (*YWMLS*, 44:14, 45:15, 46:36, 49:16), has resulted in a thought-provoking collection of 18 papers: Wright, *Latin*, arranges its material in three chronological sections with good editorial overviews ('Latin' and 'Romance' before AD 800; in 9th-c. France; and in Iberia and Italy from the mid 10th c.). The book includes an update of W.'s own thesis, 'The conceptual distinction between Latin and Romance: invention or evolution?' (103–13), and noteworthy contributions to the early period from P. M. Lloyd, 'On the names of languages (and other things)' (9–18), and T. Janson, 'Language change and metalinguistic change' (19–28), both of which argue that consciousness of a linguistic split is recognized by the act of adopting a new language name, and from J. Herman, 'Spoken and written Latin in the last centuries of the Roman Empire' (29–43), who suggests that the dominant feeling in western Romania of linguistic unity was probably an illusion, and A. Vàrvaro, 'Latin and Romance: fragmentation or restructuring' (44–51), who views fragmentation as a delayed consequence of a profound sociolinguistic restructuring when centripetal forces gave way before emergent local identities (see also below). Meanwhile, M. Alinei, 'Il problema della datazione in linguistica storica', *QS*, 12:5–19 — a discussion paper followed by comments from R. Ambrosini, G. Giacomelli, A. Stassi, P. Swiggers, P. Tekavčić, and E. F. Tuttle (21–46) with a summing up by A. (47–51) — concludes that the types of surviving written evidence and the methods developed for reconstruction conspire to produce datings which are almost invariably too late, an assertion reiterated to slightly different effect in A.'s 'New hypotheses on the linguistic origins of Europe', *ib.*, 187–203.

*Du latin aux langues romanes. Choix de textes traduits et commentés (du II*e *siècle avant J.C. jusqu'au X*e *siècle après J.C.),* ed. Maria Iliescu and Dan Slusanski, Wilhelmsfeld, Egert, xx + 301 pp., aims to guide the neophyte through the early history of Romance via its surviving texts, with commentaries designed to mesh with Väänänen's *Introduction*; the texts are judiciously chosen and well set out, with reliable linguistic annotations (but sparser notes on textual/editorial cruces)

and the section on Latin grammarians is a useful innovation. *Actes*
(Trier), III, reports on a round table on the editing of non-literary
texts, with an overview by A. Castellani, 'Problèmes concernant la
notion de *scripta* et problèmes concernant le rapport entre graphèmes
et phonèmes' (695–99), and contributions by A. Dees, 'Ancien
français écrit et ancien français parlé' (700–05), H. Goebl, 'Quelques
réflexions sur la *scriptologie*' (706–09), and A. Vàrvaro, 'Sull'origine
della polimorfia nella *scripta*' (710–15). A special theme issue of *RPh*,
45. 1, is devoted to 'Textual philology', with individual consideration
of the main areas of western Romance, a prospectus for 'Computers
and text editing' by F. Marcos Marín (102–22), and an interesting
editorial by C. B. Faulhaber and J. Craddock (1–5) on the oscillation
in textual scholarship between Lachmann's 'comparative method'
and the conscious 'non-method' of Bédier, concluding that computer-
aided matching and retrieval may now be the best way forward. A
plea for minimal intervention comes from R. Wright, 'On editing
"Latin" texts written by Romance-speakers', *Linguistic Studies in
Medieval Spanish*, ed. R. Harris-Northall and T. D. Cravens, Madison,
Hispanic Seminary of Medieval Studies, 191–208; homogenizing
graphemic variants, or expanding abbreviations that were meant to
be recognized as lexemes not pronunciations, can result in danger-
ously misleading texts.

Witold Mańczak, *La Classification des langues romanes*, Kraków U.P.,
134 pp., rejects previous schemata based on shared grammatical
features in favour of one relying on lexical correspondences in
comparable running text. M.'s method is illustrated by the analysis of
translations of the Gospel of St Matthew in nine Romance varieties,
from which it emerges: (a) that Romanian and Sardinian are aberrant
languages, while all other varieties constitute *Romania continua*; (b)
that the resulting scale (Italian > Ibero-Romance > Gallo-Romance
> Romansh > Sardinian > Romanian) defines Italian as the 'most
Romance' language and Romanian as the least; (c) that the new
classification roughly matches the known dates of Romanization; (d)
that Bartoli's norms and Meillet's belief in the stability of morphology
are wrong and should be discarded; and (e) that the method has
universal application. A companion piece by M., 'Nouvelle classification des langues romanes', *RevR*, 26:14–24, exonerates Diez from
advocating a two-way split (a popular misconception, but it was
three-way), and attacks the taxonomic precedence accorded to
grammar over vocabulary, for which he blames the 17th-c. orientalist
J. Ludolf. Returning to an older tune (*YWMLS*, 39:27, 41:30, 43:32,
50:16), M.'s 'Origine des langues romanes', *RLaR*, 95:159–70,
restates his view that the concept of linguistic evolution was not
understood before the 19th c. and that changes occurring between

Classical and Vulgar Latin parallel those between VL and Old French; M. goes on to inveigh against anyone holding contrary opinions — Väänänen, Lloyd, and the contributors to Harris and Vincent, *The Romance Languages* (*YWMLS*, 50:15–16), here arraigned for their 'stupéfiant' silence on the origin of Romance and for wishing to make a taboo of the topic. Oh dear!

3. HISTORY OF ROMANCE LINGUISTICS

H. H. Christmann, 'Romanische Philologie an den Akademien der Wissenschaften des deutschen Sprachgebietes im 19. Jahrhundert', *ZPSK*, 44:4–16, documents a long struggle for disciplinary recognition and independence from Classical Philology, culminating in the election of Adolf Tobler to the Prussian Academy in 1882; fortuitously, this coincided with the movement to reform language teaching, which inevitably reoriented Modern (and Romance) Philology away from classical models. J. Herman, 'La démarche comparative en linguistique romane — problèmes et perspectives', *Actes* (Trier), III, 3–9, reflects sagely on the antagonism between attestation-based chronological evolution and comparative reconstruction, tracing the split back to Diez (who did not aim for methodological innovation, but probably underestimated his debt to Bopp, filtered via his friend Grimm), and averring that we should not strive to steamroller into equivalence two approaches with valid but differing ontological status. Y. Malkiel corrects 'Two issues of authorship and influence in turn-of-the-century French linguistics', *Lingua*, 83:249–54, giving due recognition to É. Littré, who co-founded French semantics with Bréal and Darmsteter, and who, in a brilliant but forgotten essay, invented the pathological metaphor erroneously ascribed to Gilliéron. Two items venture into earlier and more treacherous terrain: M. Danesi, 'Latin vs Romance in the Middle Ages: Dante's *De vulgari eloquentia* revisited', Wright, *Latin*, 248–58, refutes interpretations of *DVE* as a textbook in Romance philology or historical linguistics, seeing instead an eloquent but isolated treatise on poetic language; while P. Pierini, 'La teoria linguistica di Juan de Valdés', *LS*, 26:3–16, examines V.'s concepts of language, norm, register, and change, in comparison with those of his nearest counterparts in Italy and France — Speroni and Du Bellay.

4. PHONOLOGY

Two articles by J.-L. Moralejo refine the input to later Romance developments: '*Qui, cui* y la interpretación fonológica de las labiovelares latinas', *Excerpta Philologica* (Cádiz), 1:521–27, sees the labiovelars as temporarily bolstered by reductive change in neigh-bouring forms which must be kept distinct (bisyllabic QUOIEI gives way to monosyllabic CUI [kuj]); while 'Vocalis ante uocalem: corripitur an distrahitur?', *Papers* (Cambridge), 35–45, treats long vowels in hiatus as diphonematic, leading to glide formation and eventual resyllabification ([u:A] > [u–wA]). A. Castellani, 'Sulla scomparsa dell'opposizione di quantità vocalica in latino volgare', *Actes* (Trier), III, 10–21, believes the explanation lies with accentual factors, often overlooked, coupled with morphological changes away from inflection which led to different accent locations and rhythms. When did lenition begin, and when did allophonic variation consoli-date into restructuring? Early, according to T. D. Cravens, whose 'Phonology, phonetics, and orthography in Late Latin and Romance: the evidence for early intervocalic sonorization', Wright, *Latin*, 52–68, plausibly reconstructs early variation from frequent misspellings in inscriptions, papyri, and ostraca, together with modern attestations of unsystematic voicing in conservative dialectal areas.

5. MORPHOLOGY

Maria Iliescu and Louis Mourin join forces to offer a vast and trustworthy *Typologie de la morphologie verbale romance. 1. Vue synchronique*, Innsbruck, Institut für Sprachwissenschaft, x + 584 pp., arranged by paradigm and degree of regularity, and shorn of superfluous theoreti-cal assumptions (forms are analysed solely in terms of roots, flexions, and expansions); though modest about their aims ('limited' typology, *à la* Ineichen), the authors have produced a valuable reference work from which others can theorize with confidence. Sharper in concep-tual focus is Martin Maiden's *Interactive Morphonology. Metaphony in Italy*, London, Routledge, xii + 295 pp., which has implications far beyond its title and reveals in loving detail the (often overlooked) effects of metaphony on inflectional paradigms and their consequent vulnerability to restructuring. Competitive morphosyntactic innova-tion is investigated empirically by Catherine E. Harre, *TENER + Past Participle. A Case Study in Linguistic Description, ib.*, viii + 213 pp., who finds that the acceptability of TENERE as a perfect auxiliary varies, in Spain and elsewhere, along a scale which mirrors the phases of its historical development. An alternative approach to the structure of verb systems, stressing the conceptual shape within which morphological choices are made, is sketched by P. Demarolle, 'Pour une approche "topologique" de la morphologie verbale', *ZRP*, 107 : 1–12.

A valuable and well-documented study by J. N. Adams of 'Some neglected evidence for Latin HABEO with infinitive: the order of the constituents', *TPS*, 89:131–96, draws on a dictated treatise of the 5th-c. grammarian Pompeius to demonstrate the circuitous evolution of the new Romance future paradigm and to challenge the chronology assumed by Fleischman (*YWMLS*, 44:17) and Pinkster (*YWMLS*, 49:18). Reviewing some changes whose morphological aspect is fairly well studied (the loss of the synthetic passive and of deponent verbs, the emergence of HABERE as a perfective auxiliary, and the retreat of the subjunctive from factual subordinate clauses), S. Kiss, 'A la recherche d'un nouvel équilibre: les modifications de la syntaxe du verbe en préroman', *Actes* (Trier), III, 34–42, argues that the disparate changes have a common motivation in correcting earlier asymmetries and semantic anomalies. Less inclined to take the data at face value, J. N. Green, 'The collapse and replacement of verbal inflection in Late Latin/Early Romance: how would one know?', Wright, *Latin*, 83–99, charts the persistence of the synthetic passive in written Late Latin centuries after its probable disappearance from the spoken language, and examines the awkward consequences for those required to read aloud high-register texts containing potentially unintelligible forms.

6. SYNTAX AND SEMANTICS

Actes (Trier), II, opens with a round table discussion 'Qu'est-ce qu'*expliquer* en linguistique?' (3–36), and has coherent later sections on: determiners and problems of reference; mood and modality; negation; clitics; configuration and diathesis; and relatives. There are also a number of comparative items, notably: D. Copceag, 'Sobre la oposición "inesivo"/"ilativo"' (582–88), on the apparent neutralization in Romance of an opposition maintained in other Indo-European languages (*Jean est/entre dans le jardin*); and T. Stolz, 'Il passivo, la negazione e una tipologia nuova' (542–50), against the linked passive/negative classificatory feature proposed by Körner (*YWMLS*, 46:39, 47:32–33, 49:19). Focus constructions are treated by G. Serbat, 'Intégration à la phrase latine d'un groupe nominal sans fonction syntaxique', *Langages*, 104:22–32, on the so-called *nominativus pendens*, here likened to left dislocation; and by R. Sornicola, 'Origine e diffusione della frase scissa nelle lingue romanze', *Actes* (Trier), III, 43–54, on the Ascoli/Wagner claim that clefting was calqued on Gaulish Celtic; the evidence is inconclusive, and mismatch of tense usage tips the balance towards coincidence.

*Connexiones romanicae. Dependez und Valenz in romanischen Sprachen, ed. Peter Koch and Thomas Krefeld (LA, 268), viii + 384 pp., covers both theoretical and practical applications of valency theory, with special reference to information structure, diathesis, and reflexivity.

The contributors to *Romanistische Computerlinguistik*, ed. Jürgen Rolshoven and Dieter Seelbach (LA, 266), vi + 229 pp., for the most part deal with the computational modelling of linguistic theories (principally GB and LFG [Lexical Functional Grammar]) applied in a monolingual context, but there is also a welcome sprinkle of items on machine translation. Similarly inspired is E.-P. Kester's 'Adnominal infinitives in Germanic and Romance languages', *RLFRU*, 10:13–22, a GB treatment — via movement rules and traces — of constructions in which Spanish and Italian more or less match the possibilities of Germanic languages but French has a restricted range (**un homme pour réparer ma voiture*). Aspects of noun-phrase syntax are also addressed by M. Iliescu, 'Les correspondants roumains du syntagme nominal français: N1 + de + N2', *ASNS*, 228:52–63, who identifies more than 60 structural subtypes like *les jeux olympiques de Grenoble*, and by A. Battye, who uses 'La quantificazione nominale: il veneto e l'italiano a confronto con il genovese e il francese', *Annali di Ca' Foscari*, 29, 1990:27–44, to demonstrate that the apparently divergent surface structures can be unified at a more abstract level by the setting of one simple parameter (whether the language makes use of nominal quantifiers and/or empty adjectivals).

  J. N. Falk, 'Causativization', *JL*, 27:55–79, makes prominent use of Romance data to argue against Zubizarreta's affixal analysis of *faire/fare* (*YWMLS*, 47:33), in favour of a return to a variant of clause-union — although E. Roegiest, 'La redondance fonctionnelle dans la construction factitive', *Actes* (Trier), II, 559–70, documents some problems with extraction sites that have been overlooked in previous accounts of causatives and may well continue to prove troublesome. A rewarding technical piece by R. S. Kayne, 'Romance clitics, verb movement, and PRO', *LI*, 22:647–86, after pointing to some differences in clitic behaviour between French and Italian, claims that clitics invariably left-adjoin to their functional head, so that deceptive instances of enclisis on to a verb are to be treated as leftward movement of the verb past its functional head. The thorny issue of the 'impersonal' function of *se* is now ably tackled by A. Mendikoetxea and A. Battye, 'Arb *se/si* in transitive contexts', *RGG*, 15, 1990 [1991]:161–95, who draw on comparative data to establish a distinction between ARB and ergative *se*, and conclude that the ARB variety is not base-generated but is rather the head of a functional projection outside the VP.

  In 'The morphological basis of anaphora', *JL*, 27:81–105, L. Burzio identifies a divergence in Romance (*Jean$_i$ a honte de lui$_i$/*soi$_i$* versus *Gianni$_i$ ha vergogna di *lui$_i$/se$_i$*) and proposes a new hierarchy — anaphors > pronouns > R-expressions — to replace Chomsky's three binding principles. Likewise on pronominal anaphora, A. Orlandini,

'Les pronoms possessifs et personnels en latin', *IF*, 94, 1989[1990]:177–89, illustrates three unusual types of co-reference and transfer that have not survived into Romance, and M. Cennamo, '*Se, sibi, suus* nelle *Inscriptiones latinae christianae veteres* ed i successivi sviluppi romanzi', *MedRom*, 16:3–20, sees in some grammaticalized pleonastic uses the origins of Romance 'ethic' datives. A comparative study by E. Roegiest and A.-M. Spanoghe, 'Relation de possession inaliénable et quantification en français et en espagnol', *RLiR*, 55:81–94, finds that the presence of a qualifying adjective affects the choice of predeterminer, the important pragmatic factor being the degree of individualization of the noun and the participative autonomy of the body part.

7. PRAGMATICS AND DISCOURSE

The nine stimulating essays comprising *Discourse Pragmatics and the Verb. The Evidence from Romance*, ed. Suzanne Fleischman and Linda R. Waugh, London, Routledge, viii + 220 pp., apply to good effect variants of the functional perspective, grounded in real discourse, for which the editors are already well known (*YWMLS*, 49:32, 51:26, 52:23), and here typified by F.'s 'Verb tense and point of view in narrative' (26–54) — one of only two items (despite the subtitle) to draw on comparative Romance data. The book's recurrent themes are: alternating past tenses, the shifting pragmatic values of verb inflections, including the notorious Spanish -*ra*, and the meaning of grammatical categories, while new ground is broken in the comparative study by B. Lamiroy and P. Swiggers of 'The status of imperatives as discourse signals' (120–46). In a complementary tradition, J. Schmidely, '*Être* et *avoir*: de la sémantique à la syntaxe ou de la syntaxe à la sémantique', *RLaR*, 95:147–57, compares the frequency and functional/relational roles of the BE and HAVE verbs in French and Spanish, arguing that BE is the more neutral and that HAVE implies hierarchization of the constituents.

Analyse et synthèse dans les langues romanes et slaves, ed. Harro Stammerjohann (TBL, 347), 266 pp., records a 1989 symposium where long-established ideas were reassessed in the light of pragmatic and discourse perspectives; an overview by S., 'En guise d'introduction: analyse et synthèse, oralité et écriture, restriction et élaboration' (9–20), leads into twenty largely monolingual papers, including B. Schlieben-Lange's interesting historiographic approach to 'Les conjonctions dans les langues romanes' (27–40). D. Dumitrescu, 'General considerations about echo questions in Spanish and Romanian', *RRL*, 36:141–67, finds few differences in exponency between the two languages, but significant problems both in applying

Quirk's 'recapitulatory versus explicatory' classification, and in resolving the pragmatic function of echo questions.

M. Manoliu-Manea, 'Dynamisme communicatif, dynamisme actanciel et ordre des mots en roman', *Actes* (Trier), II, 228–38, compares texts in Italian, Romanian and Spanish in terms of information structure and subject prominence, finding a strong preference for SVO order but also some apparent anomalies, which are best explained by the precedence accorded to [+ human] participants. Four items on Latin also make illuminating use of the concept of information structure. J. Herman, 'On the grammatical subject in Late Latin', *Papers* (Cambridge), 415–25, detects a shift in Merovingian texts in the expression of third-person subjects (which, unlike first or second persons, are chosen and so necessarily informative) towards the grammaticalization of demonstratives and the automatic filling of the subject slot. R. Risselada, 'Passive, perspective and textual cohesion', *ib.*, 401–14, sees the purpose of the agentive personal passive as being to present events from the viewpoint of the patient; while D. Pennell Ross, 'The role of displacement in narrative prose', *ib.*, 453–66, contrasts two pragmatic approaches to prolepsis, concluding that displaced elements are best characterized as non-new information. The last word must go to H. Pinkster, whose 'Evidence for SVO in Latin?', Wright, *Latin*, 69–82, consists of valuable new statistics on variant word orders (VS is quite common in all-new contexts), and the cautious conclusion that we should not assume a basic SOV order for Classical Latin, or its replacement by a basic SVO order by AD 400.

8. LEXIS

Publication has begun of a valuable new thesaurus of all major Romance varieties arranged by conceptual fields: the attractively presented first volume of Henri Vernay's ambitious *Dictionnaire onomasiologique des langues romanes (DOLR)*, Tübingen, Niemeyer, xxiii + 244 pp., deals with the human person, in physical, socio-organizational and philosophical dimensions. The earlier PATROM project (*YWMLS*, 52:25) seems to have spawned an annual symposium and a series of subplots, of which the latest to be announced are: *Dictionnaire historique des noms de famille romans III. Actes del III col·loqui (Barcelona, 19–21 juny 1989)*, ed. Antoni M. Badia i Margarit, *ib.*, 262 pp., and *Anthroponymie afro-romane. Esquisse d'un projet*, ed. Willy Bal *et al.*, *ib.*, vii + 70 pp. Another major reference survey, Gvozdanović, *Numerals*, sees the light of day more than twenty years after it was launched by the late A. S. C. Ross; the editorial vicissitudes have left some inevitable blemishes, but Romanists are still well served by the substantial and authoritative chapters by R. Coleman on 'Italic' (389–445) and by G. Price on 'Romance' (447–96); the latter presents the main synchronic sets in helpful tabular form, but includes many minor variants, with phonetic and etymological annotations where appropriate — overall, one is struck by the sheer range of systems in operation. The methodology for investigating pre-Romance survivals is debated in a friendly exchange between R. Bracchi, 'Sopravvivenze alpine di origine indoeuropea', *RLiR*, 55:5–15, and J. Hubschmid, 'Sopravvivenze di parole alpine preromane di origine indoeuropea e preindoeuropea; suffissi di origine preindoeuropea e rapporti gallo-germanici', *ib.*, 17–41. H. E. Wilkinson, 'The Latin neuter plurals in Romance, VII', *Ronshu* (Tokyo), 32:35–49, concludes a substantial and revealing study of a sizeable group of words not usually treated as a discrete category in modern Romance (*YWMLS*, 48:28, 50:19, 51:29, 52:21); inevitably, the final batch is something of a residue, but it does include intriguing examples of 'collective singulars' (Romansh *greppa* 'rocks') and of back-formed masculines.

Birte Stengaard, *Vida y muerte de un campo semántico. Un estudio de la evolución semántica de los verbos latinos* STARE, SEDERE *e* IACERE *del latín al romance del s. XIII* (*ZRP*, Beiheft 234), xii + 414 pp., brilliantly applies the componential method to an originally lexical field where the primary semes of [position], [location], and [duration] intersected with the features [vertical], [horizontal], and [medial], but where the lexico-semantic evolution was overtaken by creeping syncretism between ESSE and SEDERE (traced back to at least the 10th c. in Ibero-Romance) and grammatical processes of auxiliarization which promoted STARE, but at the expense of its lexical content. Two verbs that have so far resisted grammaticalization, but have aligned themselves firmly with 'here/there' deixis, are studied by D. Ricca, '*Andare* e *venire* nelle lingue romanze e germaniche: dall'*Aktionsart* alla deissi', *AGI*, 76:159–92. *Discours étymologiques. Actes du colloque international organisé à l'occasion du centenaire de la naissance de Walther von Wartburg*, ed. Jean-Pierre Chambon and Georges Lüdi, Tübingen, Niemeyer, vi + 324 pp., brings together 22 eminent practitioners to reflect — in the shadow of the master, as it were — on the origins of etymology, its position within 20th-c. linguistics, its role as a bridge between popular and scientific views of language, and the nature of the enterprise from now on. A reminder that etymology can be contentious comes from G. Colón, 'És *volcá* un lusisme international?', *RLiR*, 55:319–37, favouring a straightforward metaphorical development of VULCANUS and adducing evidence, against Corominas (with whom an acrimonious dispute threatens to erupt), that the word was not even known in Portuguese at the relevant date, and B. Peeters,

'Esp./port. *matar*: explication interne ou externe?', *RF*, 103:71–75, who appears to be recanting his earlier support for Menocal's Arabic hypothesis (*YWMLS*, 46:40) in favour of the Diez/Lodares derivation from MACTARE 'to slaughter, sacrifice', perhaps with reinforcement from the Arabic *māt*.

In his second richly documented monograph within four years (*YWMLS*, 48:307), David A. Pharies, *The Origin and Development of the Ibero-Romance –NC-/-NG– Suffixes* (*ZRP*, Beiheft 228), 1990, xii + 235 pp., homes in on the phonological and semantic variants of a productive suffix whose primary function is to derive adjectives that express pertinence to their nominal roots. Ever prolific, Y. Malkiel continues to hew away at blended word families and apparently simple etymologies concealing derivational stages: 'Some erratic developments of Romance words for "rancor"', *NMi*, 91:491–99, continues his investigations into the pressure exerted by RINGĪ (*YWMLS*, 51:28); 'Vowel gamuts in Romance derivational suffixation', *Papers* (Leningrad), 39–56, allows M. to expand laterally an idea he first applied to French (*YWMLS*, 52:42); 'The transmutation of Church Latin *(Diēs) Nātālis* "birthday" into French *Noël* "Christmas"', *Neophilologus*, 75:21–30, unites both strands in resolving an unusual vocalic development analogous to that of *noyer* < NĀTĀRE. More historiographical — and no less interesting for that — is M.'s 'An imported derivative in search of a missing primitive. The near-antonyms OProv., Cat. *avinenteza* "composure, charm" vs. OSp. *avin-, avil-entez(a)* "boisterous arrogance"', *RoQ*, 38, 449–70, eventually plumps for unacceptable ambiguity as the main explanation of a lexical loss that may also have been hurried along by anti-Catalan xenophobia (as, M. assures us, in the case of *ávol*; see *YWMLS*, 52:26).

Detective work by A. J. L. van Hooff, 'A longer life for "suicide"', *RF*, 102, 1990[1991]:255–59, shows that the word cannot go back to Latin (the Classical suffixes -CĪDIUM/-CĪDA could only combine with nominals, so that Cicero would have understood *suicidium* as 'pig-slaying'), and produces a 12th-c. attestation which seems to be a new coinage, by analogy with *fratricida*. G. Serbat, 'Structure des noms d'agent en *-TOR', *LInv*, 14, 1990:343–48, reports briefly on a very large study of Latin agentives, concluding that the productivity of -TOR and near cognates remains high and remarkably stable over a millennium, and that though it acts principally as a deverbal agentive, denominals can also be found, as in *aleātor* 'dice-thrower, gambler', *arborātor* 'tree pruner', *fistulātor* 'flautist'. D. Langslow, 'The formation of Latin technical vocabulary with special reference to medicine', *Papers* (Cambridge), 187–200, finds a strong correlation between derivational type and semantic field, with diminutives a favoured quarry for names of new ailments (*auricula* 'mumps'; see also *YWMLS*, 51:27). M. Fruyt, 'L'agglutination des mots en latin', *BSLP*, 85, 1990:173–209, examines a productive range of syntagmatic compounds (*animadvertĕre* 'to notice', *respublica* 'state') and the stages by which they were reanalysed as single lexemes, with no internal morpheme boundary. H. D. Bork, 'L'origine des composés romans verbe–nom', *Actes* (Trier), III, 61–67, sets out to dispel the twin misapprehensions that compounds such as It. *battiloro*, Fr. *perce-neige*, or Sp. *matacán* represent Romance innovations dating from the medieval period, and that they were virtually confined to animate concepts; rather, inanimates predominate in medieval Romance, and the pattern (if not its individual products) has a continuous pedigree from Greek-inspired coinings in Latin.

9. DIALECTOLOGY AND CONTACT

Actes (Trier), III, incorporates a long section on dialectology (331–692), starting with a round table on methodological innovation, to which contributed: H. Goebl, 'La dialectométrie — pourquoi faire?' (332–41), on the equivalence within Euclidean geometry of the concepts of similarity and distance; S. Verlinde and P. Derynck, 'La dialectométrie de la délimitation des zones dialectales' (342–51; see also *YWMLS*, 52:27), on the superiority of normal-distribution testing for revealing morphological divergence; and H. Guiter, 'Applications d'une méthode géolinguistique en galloroman et ibéroroman' (352–61), on the triangulation mechanism within the *méthode globale* whose application G. insists is original — despite Goebl's contention that it was invented by the German dialectologist Carl Haag in 1898. Among the numerous areal studies which follow, we should single out two: M. Contini *et al.*, 'Les traits "strident ∼ mat" et "tendu ∼ lâche"' dans les systèmes consonantiques des parlers romans' (*ib.*, 465–77), a complex study resulting in several useful pan-Romance maps of sibilant distributions; and R. de Dardel, 'Types d'isoglosse en roman commun' (478–84), which establishes terminological distinctions between monolingual versus bilingual and organic versus inorganic isoglosses, before arguing, on the basis of the distribution of the conjunction types KA < QUIA, QUOMODO, KO < QUOD, and KE (see *YWMLS*, 45:17), that inorganic frontiers began to gel in common Romance and long pre-date the now more common organic/bilingual ones. D.'s recent work on pan-Romance toponymic patterns, reported in 'La place de l'adjectif qualifiant dans les toponymes romands', *RLiR*, 55:43–79, lends support to the theory that differential waves of romanization were largely responsible for early dialectalization.

An alternative round table, called by M. Alinei and 21 co-discussants to debate the crisis of identity in dialectology and whether it should be allowed to merge into sociolinguistics, is reported in 'Whither dialectology?', *QS*, 12:207–333, ending with a vigorous assertion from A. (not always chiming with his discussants) that dialectology is 'an autonomous, independent, and intensely growing discipline'. As examples of newer approaches, we should mention: Joshua A. Fishman, *Reversing Language Shift. Theoretical and Empirical Foundations of Assistance to Threatened Languages*, Clevedon, Multilingual Matters, xiv + 431 pp., which cites Catalan and Quebec French as two of only three success stories in language rehabilitation; and G. Kremnitz, 'Y a-t-il des "diglossies neutres"?', *Lengas*, 30:29–36, which answers negatively, claiming that in acute diglossic situations speakers cannot 'innocently' switch from one variety to the other, although open and liberal policies can avert the worst kinds of linguistic conflict. Which, of course, places bilinguals in a political front line not of their own making. Less stressful interactions are reported by Martine Krämer, *L'Interlocution exolingue: hispanophones et Français en conversation informelle*, Wilhelmsfeld, Egert, iv + 210 pp., and by F. Grosjean and B. Py, 'La restructuration d'une première langue: l'intégration de variantes de contact dans la compétence de migrants bilingues', *La Linguistique*, 27.2:35–60, which shows how long-term Spanish-speaking immigrants in the Neuchâtel area have accommodated to their new environment to the extent of editing out salient 'Spanish' features from their mother tongue.

II. FRENCH STUDIES*

LANGUAGE

By GLANVILLE PRICE, University of Wales, Aberystwyth

1. GENERAL

We welcome the appearance of CUP's new twice-yearly periodical *Journal of French Language Studies* (hereafter *JFLS*). Items appearing in vol. 1 are noted under appropriate sections below. Willy Bal, Jean Germain, Jean Klein, and Pierre Swiggers, *Bibliographie sélective de linguistique romane et française*, Louvain-la-Neuve, Duculot, 268 pp., is likely to prove indispensable; the classification is sensible and thorough (French has 48 subsections) and the selection, on the whole, judicious; articles, with some exceptions, are excluded, but the section on French nevertheless lists some 850–900 items. Marina Yaguello, *En écoutant parler la langue*, Seuil, 128 pp., consists of 25 perspicacious essays combining erudition with readability, prompted by the author's reflections on points of grammar, vocabulary, pronunciation, and spelling that she had picked up *sur le vif* and that she comments on 'sous l'angle de la créativité linguistique'. [René] Étiemble, *Parlez-vous franglais? Fol en France. Mad in France. La belle France. Label France*, Gallimard, 438 pp., reprints the text of the (already revised and twice expanded) 1980 edn of *P.-v. f.*, with a new preface, 'Un quart de siècle plus tard'. J.-C. Bouvier and C. Martel (eds), **Les Français et leurs langues*, Univ. of Provence, 550 pp. R. A. Lodge, 'Authority, prescriptivism and the French standard language', *JFLS*, 1:93–111, applies to French E. Haugen's model of language standardization 'in the light of the notion of "standard ideology" proposed by J. and L. Milroy'. The contributions to *LaF*, no. 89 (Feb.), 'L'oral dans l'écrit', ed. Daniel Luzzati, are in general marginal to, or outside the scope of, this section; eligible for mention here are: J. Pinchon and M.-A. Morel, 'Rapport de la ponctuation à l'oral dans quelques dialogues de romans contemporains' (5–19); C. Vigneau-Rouayrenc, 'L'oral dans l'écrit: histoire(s) d'e' (20–24), on the omission in writing of a genuinely mute *e* (e.g. *c'que*); G. Petiot, 'L'oral dans l'écrit politique' (72–85); D. Delomier and M. Esquenet-Bernaudin, 'L'écrit dans le sillage de l'oral, mais encore?' (86–98); F. Gadet, 'Le parlé coulé dans l'écrit: le traitement du détachement par les grammaires du XXᵉ siècle' (110–24). Pierre Bourgeade, *Chronique du français quotidien*, Belfond (Coll. 'La vie des mots'), fits somewhat uneasily into the collection; it reproduces about a hundred of B.'s

*The place of publication of books is Paris unless otherwise stated.

lively but often superficial comments (originally published in *Le Figaro Magazine*), on points of syntax, lexicon and style, each followed by one or more readers' responses. (On a better volume in the same series, see p. 38.)

Xavier Deniau, *La Francophonie* (Que sais-je?, 2111), PUF, 126 pp., a completely up-dated version of a work first published in 1983, covers authoritatively both the concept of *francophonie* and what it means in practice, and envisages its likely future. Robert Chaudenson (ed.). *La Francophonie, représentations, réalités, perspectives,* Didier-Érudition, 218 pp. Haut Conseil de la Francophonie, *État de la francophonie dans le monde*, Documentation française, 414 pp. D. de Robillard, *Aménagement linguistique et développement dans l'espace francophone: bibliographie sélective*, ACCT/CIRELFA, 1989, 218 pp. P. Dumont, 'Francophonie, francophonies', *LaF*, no. 85 (Feb. 1990): 35–47, shows that his use of the plural is justified.

2. HISTORY OF GRAMMAR AND OF LINGUISTIC THEORY

P. Swiggers, 'Chronique de linguistique générale et française (III)' (see *YWMLS*, 51:31 and 52:30), *Trl*, 22:131–57, is devoted to work on the history of linguistics, including Romance linguistics (but, despite one of its subheadings, has nothing on the history of French linguistics).

CFS, 44, 1990 [1991], has a wide-ranging selection of articles including (in addition to items specifically on Korean and German respectively): P. Villani, 'Documenti saussuriani conservati a Lipsia e a Berlino' (3–33), which consists mainly of letters (some of them of only minor importance) from Saussure, his widow, and K. Brugmann to W. Streitberg; A. L. Prosdocimi and A. Marinetti, 'Saussure e il saturnio. Tra scienza, biografia e storiografia' (37–71); D. Di Cesare. 'Pour une herméneutique du langage. Épistémologie et méthodologie de la recherche linguistique d'après Humboldt' (123–40); and R. Rohrbach's 'Glossaire des termes spéciaux de Damourette et Pichon' (141–93) which, though covering only terms in the field of subordination, is most welcome as an aid to crossing the terminological barrier erected by D. and P. *La Licorne*, 19, includes *inter alia*: W. Ayres-Bennett, '*Observations* et *Remarques sur la langue française*: histoire d'un genre' (1–24); J. de Clercq, 'Les *Mémoires de Trévoux* (1701–1762) et la réception de la grammaticographie française' (25–44); B. Nerlich, 'De la phonétique à la phonologie. Éléments pour une histoire de la "science des sons"' (45–70) (covering, among others, Passy, Rousselot and Saussure); S. Mellet, 'Élaboration progressive d'une catégorie grammaticale: à propos du temps verbal' (87–97) (dealing with, among others, Beauzée and Port-Royal); C. Lecointre, 'Les turbulences du signifiant: ellipse et sous-entendu dans la tradition grammaticale de Despautère à Port-Royal' (99–113); P. Swiggers, 'Creuser dans l'histoire des sciences du langage: vers une archéologie du savoir linguistique' (115–34); and D. Baggioni, 'Linguistique fantastique ou théorie prophétique? Le cas Gustave Fallot' (193–212) (F. died in 1836 at the age of 29, leaving an almost completed monograph on Old French morphology and dialectology, published in 1839).

P. van Reenen and L. Schøsler discuss (specifically with reference to Old French, but the argument has general applicability) 'Le problème de la prolifération des explications', *TLP*, 28, 1990:221–38. W. Ayres-Bennett, '"Influence" in linguistic historiography: some examples from seventeenth-century France', Niederehe, *Linguistics*, 1, 367–79, concludes that, despite the difficulty of 'grasp[ing] hold of the elusive notion of genuine influence', the quest is a valid one. F. Hartweg, 'Jérémie-Jacques Oberlin et le débat rèvolutionaire [sic] sur la politique des langues', *ZPSK*, 44:454–63. J. de Clercq and P. Swiggers, 'Le terme "complément" au XVIIIe siècle: remarques sur un concept grammatical', *TLP*, 28, 1990:55–61; J. Roelandt and P. Swiggers, 'La "modification" comme relation sémantico-syntaxique chez Claude Buffier', *ib.*, 63–70. Y. Malkiel, 'Two issues of authorship and influence in turn-of-the-century French linguistics', *Lingua*, 83:249–54, stresses Littré's role in the history of the study of semantics and the use of medical metaphors (i.e. before Gilliéron) in developmental linguistics. Hélène Huot (ed.), *La Grammaire française entre comparatisme et structuralisme, 1870–1960*, Colin, 313 pp., contains surveys, each with an extensive bibliography, of a number of French linguists, viz.: J. Bourquin, 'Léon Clédat (1850–1930) et la *Revue de philologie française*' (25–72); J.-Cl. Chevalier, 'Ferdinand Brunot (1860–1937), *La Pensée et la Langue*' (73–114); R. Amacker, 'Charles Bally (1865–1947) et la "Stylistique"' (115–54); H. Huot, 'Jacques Damourette (1873–1943) et Édouard Pichon (1890–1940), *Des mots à la pensée: essai de grammaire de la langue française*' (155–200); M. Wilmet, 'Gustave Guillaume (1883–1960) et la psychomécanique du langage' (201–25); F. Corblin, 'Lucien Tesnière (1873–1954), *Éléments de syntaxe structurale*' (227–56); J. Pichon, 'Georges Gougenheim (1900–1972), traditionalisme et modernité' (257–311). L. Melis, 'Variations sur une typologie: le classement des tours pronominaux dans la tradition grammaticale française des XIXe et XXe siècles', *TLP*, 28, 1990:37–53. The scope of François Tollis, *La Parole et le sens: le guillaumisme et l'approche contemporaine du langage*, Colin, xii + 495 pp., is clearly defined by its subtitle; it traces the development of the linguistic theories of the best known followers and successors of

Gustave Guillaume, including (among others) Roch Valin, Maurice Toussaint, K. Mantchev, Robert Lafont, A. Joly, and J.-Cl. Chevalier, and, what is more, T. writes much more lucidly than some of the practitioners themselves. P. Bourdin, 'Some issues in the metalinguistic representation of French tense and aspect', *CanJL*, 36:269–94, is largely (but not solely) a critique of C. Fuchs and A.-M. Léonard, *Vers une théorie des aspects* (1979), and A. Joly and M.-J. Lerouge, 'Problèmes de l'analyse du temps en psychoméchanique' (1980).

3. HISTORY OF THE LANGUAGE

Apart from a few pages here and there, Bernard Cerquiglini, *La Naissance du français* (Que sais-je?, 2576), PUF, 127 pp., disappoints; whereas many contributors to this admirable series find the format restrictive, C. spins out his potentially interesting, but limited, substance (*de quoi faire un long article, mais pas plus*) to the point of tediousness. C. Holm, 'Le maintien de la voyelle finale en galloroman dans les proparoxytons latins', *Actes* (Trier), iii, 118–28, challenges some well established views. Rika Van Deyck, *TrL*, 22:93–102, discusses the value of the diphthongs [jɛ] and [aj] in the *Roland*. J.-P. Y. Montreuil, *'Old French stress patterns and closed syllable adjustment', Wanner and Kibbee, *New Analyses*, 49–76. H. Jacobs offers 'A nonlinear analysis of the evolution of consonant + yod sequence in Gallo-Romance', *CanJL*, 36:27–64. F. de la Chaussée, 'Les dépalatalisations consonantiques de l'ancien français sont-elles datables?', *Actes* (Trier), iii, 129–34, assumes more than we can really know about subtle differences in pronunciation from the 3rd to the 12th c. A. Dees, 'Ancien français écrit et ancien français parlé', *ib.*, 700–05, constitutes a positive approach to the problem presented by the multiplicity of spellings that occur in OFr texts. A. Meiller has two notes on OFr verb endings: (i) 'L'origine de la désinence *-ons*', *Romania*, 109, 1988 [1991]:433–42, is an unconvincing attempt to rehabilitate *sumus* as the etymon; (ii) 'La double issue de la finale latine atone *-at*', *ib.*, 442–44, advances a hypothesis that is at least worth considering. W. Ashby, 'When does variation indicate linguistic change in progress?', *JFLS*, 1:1–19, which takes us back as far as Old French, looks at the deletion of /l/ in the pronouns *il(s)*, *elle(s)* and the deletion of *ne* (but in this case, like many others before him, he misinterprets the Old and Middle French data).

Douglas A. Kibbee, *For to Speke Frenche Trewely. The French Language in England, 1000–1600: Its Status, Description and Instruction* (Studies in the History of the Language Sciences, 60), Amsterdam, Benjamins, viii + 268 pp., is an important, well researched and highly informative work, of interest to scholars in a number of fields (the history of

French and English languages, sociolinguistics, the history of linguistic ideas, the history of England, the history of education, and the list is not exhaustive); the useful bibliography includes a list of primary sources, covering both medieval MSS and printed works of the Renaissance.

Actes du 6ᵉ colloque international sur le moyen français, ed. S. Cigada and A. Slerca, 3 vols, Milan, Vita e pensiero. Y.-Ch. Morin and G. Desaulniers, *Actes* (Trier), III, 211–21, conclude that P. de Lanoue's representation in his rhyming dictionary of French (1596) of vowel length in the morphology of plural nouns and adjectives 'correspond à un état de langue authentique'. Louise Dagenais, 'De la phonologie du français vers 1700: les systèmes vocaliques de Hindret (1687, 1696) et de Vaudelin (1713, 1715)', *La Linguistique*, 27.2:75–89, is thorough and does not attempt to go further than the evidence allows. L. Dagenais, 'Évolution du vocalisme en français moderne: la place de Féraud (fin XVIIIᵉ siècle)', *Actes* (Trier) III, 222–31, argues that 'la variété décrite par [F.] doit sûrement être comprise comme représentation du français général de l'époque'.

Georges Molinié, *Le Français moderne* (Que sais-je, 392), 128 pp., is a disappointing addition to a generally useful series — too much verbiage and too little hard information.

4. PHONETICS AND PHONOLOGY

E. Eggs and I. Mordellet, *Phonétique et phonologie du français: théorie et pratique* (RA, 34), 1990, 135 pp. Glanville Price, *An Introduction to French Pronunciation*, Oxford, Blackwell, ix + 176 pp., is what it says it is.

P. Scherfer, *'A propos des élisions en français: le cas du /l/', GLS, 3, 1989:101–20. Y.-Ch. Morin, 'La prononciation de [t] après *quand*', *Linv*, 14, 1990:175–89, takes a historical perspective. W. Bennett, 'Liaison in French', *Word*, 42:57–88. J. Fletcher, 'Rhythm and final lengthening in French', *JPh*, 19, 1989:193–212, is experimentally based. C. Laeufer, *'Syllabification and resyllabification in French', Wanner and Kibbee, *New Analyses*, 19–36. G. Bailly, *'Integration of rhythmic and syntactic constraints in the model of generation of French prosody', *SpC*, 8, 1989:137–46.

5. ORTHOGRAPHY

H. Hermans's study of 'La critique de l'orthographe française au 16ᵉ siècle et la *Declaration des abus* d'Honorat Rambaud', *Actes* (Trier), III, 190–201, is, inevitably, much more thorough than L. Pasques's attempt to trace in too little space 'Les grands courants orthographiques au XVIIᵉ siècle et la formation de l'orthographe moderne', *ib.*, 202–10. M. Keller, *Ein Jahrhundert Reformen der französischen Orthographie: Geschichte eines Scheiterns, 1886–1900*, Tübingen, Stauffenburg, 1990, 250 pp.

Conseil Supérieur de la Langue Française, *Les Rectifications de l'orthographe*, Journal Officiel, 1990, 24 pp., is the official text. André Goosse, *La 'nouvelle' orthographe*. Louvain-la-Neuve, Duculot, 136 pp., provides an authoritative exposition of and commentary on what now seems to be the *réformette* that never was (the text of the 'Rapport du Conseil supérieur de la langue française', published in the *Journal officiel*, is given, pp. 109–32). Michel Masson, *L'Orthographe: guide pratique de la réforme*, Seuil, 190 pp.

Jacques Drillon, *Traité de la ponctuation française*, Gallimard, 473 pp., meets a need; an exhaustive treatment of the use of each punctuation mark is preceded by a lengthy historical survey (19–126) of the theory and practice of punctuation.

6. GRAMMAR

OLD AND MIDDLE FRENCH

Lene Schøsler, 'Les causes externes et internes des changements morphosyntaxiques', *ALHa*, 23:83–112, is based on OFr data but is of more general applicability; the conclusion is that changes are triggered by internal factors but spread by external factors. Suzanne Fleischman, 'Discourse pragmatics and the grammar of Old French: a functional reinterpretation of *si* and the personal pronouns', *RPh*, 44:251–83, argues that '*si* functions as a marker of *subject/topic continuity*, while subject pronouns [. . .] function as markers of *switch reference* and *topic discontinuity*'. P. van Reenen and L. Schøsler, '*La maison(s) et li charbons*. La forme du nominatif singular féminin et masculin', *Actes* (Trier), III, 135–66, is characteristically well documented and argued. M. Horne, 'The clitic group as a prosodic category in Old French', *Lingua*, 82, 1990:1–13. Elizabeth Pearce, *Parameters in Old French Syntax: Infinitival Complements*, Dordrecht, Kluwer, 1990, ix + 327 pp., analyses Old French infinitival complement constructions within a GB framework; a brief introductory chapter is followed by two in which the OFr constructions are purportedly set within a wider Romance context (though, in reality, there is relatively little on languages other than Italian), and two specifically on Old French, viz. 'Causatives in Old French' and 'Non-causative infinitival complements in Old French'. F. Martineau, *'Clitic climbing in infinitival constructions of Middle French', Wanner and Kibbee, *New Analyses*, 235–52. M. D. Sánchez Palomino discusses the use of the article in comparative sentences in the *Cent nouvelles nouvelles*, Actes (*Trier*), II, 372–79. C. Brucker,

'Aspects de la structure de la phrase en moyen français', *ib.*, III, 176–89, attempts too much within the scope of one paper.

MODERN FRENCH AND GENERAL

Joëlle Gardes-Tamine, *La Grammaire*, 2 vols (see *YWMLS*, 50:25), has appeared in a 2nd edn 'revue et corrigée', Colin, 1990, 152 + 159 pp. William Rowlinson, *Oxford Reference French Grammar*, OUP, 1990, xiii + 288 pp., which, apart from format, is identical with the author's *Oxford Minireference French Grammar*, OUP, 1990, offers a clear summary of much of 'the basic grammar of French' but its claim to cover 'all the grammar used in modern French' is untenable. Claire Blanche-Benveniste and others, *Le Français parlé: études grammaticales*, CNRS, 1990, 272 pp., is not (and specifically is not) a grammar of spoken French but a series of studies of syntax or of 'macro-syntax', i.e. of '[les] relations qu'on ne peut pas décrire à partir des rections de catégories grammaticales', with additional chapters on intonation, 'configurations' (structures corresponding to some extent to oral 'paragraphs'), and 'Quelques applications'; all in all, a volume of considerable interest from a theoretical standpoint and also, given its wealth of examples, useful for its documentary value. H. Werner, 'Wie komplex ist das Französische?', *LBer*, 132:133–56, is pessimistic about the prospects for formal linguistics. J.-P. Sueur, 'Sur la syntaxe du récit oral', *LInv*, 14, 1990:95–148.

J. Eschmann, 'La syntaxe des noms de saisons en français', *ZFSL*, 101:1–9, studies current usage, especially in *L'Express* and *Le Monde*. Two of the contributions to *LaF*, 92 (Dec. 1991) (see also p. 42) bear specifically on grammatical aspects of the use of proper names in French, viz. G. Kleiber, 'Du nom propre non modifié au nom propre modifié: le cas de la détermination des noms propres par l'adjectif démonstratif' (82–103), and M. Noailly, '"L'énigmatique Tombouctou": nom propre et position de l'épithète' (104–12). M.-M. de Gaulmyn and S. Remi-Giraud (eds), *A la recherche de l'attribut*, Lyons U.P., 319 pp. E. Schepper, *Das Mikrosystem der französischen Artikel im Blickfeld theoretischer Ansätze: eine kritische Synthese als Beitrag zur grammatischen Semantik* (EH, XIII. 156), 1990, xlvi + 798 pp. G. Kleiber, 'Sur les emplois anaphoriques et situationnels de l'article défini et de l'adjectif démonstratif [en français]', *Actes* (Trier), II, 294–307, makes clear distinctions. H. Blank, 'Der französische Teilungsartikel', *ASNS*, 227, 1990:61–95, is a diachronic and synchronic survey with a useful bibliography. D. Gaatone, 'Les déterminants de la quantité peu élevée en français. Remarques sur les emplois de *quelques* et *plusieurs*', *RevR*, 26:2–13, distinguishes between them lucidly (but, rather than being, as the author suggests, a 'trop rapide étude', could have been more succinctly expressed). A. Henry, '*Tel* en français moderne', *RLiR*, 55:339–426, is an abundantly illustrated and subtly analysed study. The interest and value of P. Gardner-Chloros, 'Ni *tu* ni *vous*: principes et paradoxes dans l'emploi des pronoms d'allocution en français contemporain', *JFLS*, 1:139–55, would have been greatly enhanced had the fieldwork on which it is based been carried out in a monolingual French area rather than in Alsace. K. Hunnius, '*T'as vu?* — Die Deklination der klitischen Personalpronomina im Französischen', *ZFSL*, 101:113–24, argues that the fact that the pronouns vary paradigmatically makes for syntagmatic economy. L. Kupferman, 'Le pronom réfléchi non-clitique existe-t-il en français?', *Actes* (Trier), II, 485–94, suggests himself that his 'solution toute technique' may create an 'impression d'artificialité', and who am I to argue? Co Vet, 'Les constructions causatives et réfléchies en français', *ib.*, 571–81, is an exercise in Functional Grammar. F. Cornish, 'Non-discrete reference, discourse construction, and the French neuter clitic pronouns', *JFLS*, 1:123–38, considering the clitics *le*, *y*, *en* 'from the point of view of their discourse motivation', is a well argued and rewarding study that could have been expanded to advantage. N. Ruwet's article, '*En* et *y*: deux clitiques pronominaux antilogophoriques', *Langages*, 97, 1990:51–82, gives rise to a Chomskyan rejoinder by B. Lamiroy, 'Coréférence et référence disjointe: les deux pronoms *en*', *TrL*, 22:41–65, which is itself followed by a brief postscript by Ruwet, *ib.*, 66–67. Édith Le Bel, 'Le statut remarquable d'un pronom inaperçu', *La Linguistique*, 27.2:91.109, is mainly of interest as a survey of the syntactical history of *on* and of the 'grande hétérogénéité des classifications et des descriptions dont *ON* a fait l'objet'.

L. Zaring, *'Deriving expletives as complements: French *ce*', Wanner and Kibber, *New Analyses*, 371–88. M. Pierrard returns to the problem of the status of the pronouns *celui*, etc. (see *YWMLS*, 52:34 and 36), with 'Observations sur le statut syntaxique et sémantique de "*celui* + relative"', *TrL*, 22:69–91. J. Rooryck, '*Que* et *qui*: pronoms relatifs ou complémenteurs?', *Actes* (Trier), II, 638–46, argues against an analysis proposed by R. Kayne. M. Pierrard, 'Relative sans antécédent et interrogative indirecte: détermination et interprétation d'une classe propositionnelle', *ib.*, 647–59, is specifically on French. L. Gosselin, 'L'interprétation des relatives: le rôle des déterminants', *LInv*, 14, 1990:1–30. M.-A. Friedemann discusses 'Le pronom interrogatif *que* et la montée de verbe en C°', *RGI*, 15, 1990:123–39. William Rowlinson, *Oxford Reference French Verbs*, OUP, xxiii + 273 pp., is a physically enlarged but textually unchanged version of his handy little guide to the formation of French verbs, *Oxford Minireference French Verbs*. Hervé Curat, *Morphologie verbale et* *référence temporelle en français moderne: essai de sémantique grammaticale* (Langues et cultures, 24), Geneva, Droz, 340 pp., is theory-oriented and in the Guillaumian tradition, but well enough documented and clearly enough presented to have much to offer even to those who are less than fully familiar with or sympathetic to the psychosystematic school. Bettina Lorenz, *Die Konkurrenz zwischen dem futur simple und dem futur périphrastique im gesprochenen Französisch der Gegenwart* (MBRP, 2), 1989, xiii + 200 pp., and Sabine Lorenz, *Die Konkurrenz zwischen dem futur simple und dem futur périphrastique im geschriebenen Französisch der Gegenwart* (MBRP, 3), 1989, xii + 252 pp., are two thorough, well documented theses, taking account of a number of variables. The former is based both on a pre-existing corpus (including the *Français fondamental* material) and on the author's questionnaire-derived data, the latter both on pre-existing written material (literary texts, newspapers, comic strips, etc.) and on written answers to the same questionnaire as that used by the author's twin sister for her work on spoken French. The two theses, taken together, provide an abundance of useful and interesting information; one can only regret that there is not (and perhaps could not have been) more cross-referencing between the two. B. Stankova, *'Sur les fonctions modales du futur périphrastique français', ConL,* 14, 1989:65–70. The scope of K. Bogacki, 'Représentations sémantiques et contraintes de surface en français', *Actes* (Trier), II, 53–62, is far more restricted than the title suggests; it deals with semantic contexts in which an object noun clause cannot take the future tense when the main clause has present reference. Cercle linguistique du centre et de l'ouest, **L'Auxiliaire en question,* Rennes U.P., 1990, 251 pp. M. Wilmet, 'L'aspect en français: essai de synthèse', *JFLS,* 1:209–22, is a clear and persuasive contribution to the debate on this controversial subject. Brigitte Kampers-Manhe, *L'Opposition subjonctif/indicatif dans les relatives,* Amsterdam, Rodopi, |xi| + 239 pp., is an admirably thorough and much needed contribution to the study of an inadequately understood (and often misunderstood) aspect of modern French grammar. After surveying the views expressed by a number of other (in many cases eminent) grammarians, the author concludes, with every justification, that 'la description faite jusqu'ici de l'emploi du subjonctif dans la relative reste insuffisante'. She proceeds by evaluating the acceptability of the subjunctive and the indicative respectively in otherwise identical contexts and, despite operating mainly with invented examples, arrives at persuasive and instructive conclusions. Wolfgang J. Meyer, *Modalität und Modalverb* (= *ZFSL,* Beiheft 19), Stuttgart, Steiner, 152 pp., subtitled 'Kompetenztheoretische Erkundungen zum Problem der Bedeutungsbeschreibung modaler Ausdrücke am Beispiel von *devoir* und *pouvoir* im heutigen

Franzosisch', is a good example of the type of well devised and well documented book that ought to be made available in a French translation. N. Rivière asks, in a well documented article, 'Le participe passé est-il verbe ou adjectif?', *TLP*, 28, 1990:131–69, and concludes that it is not really either.

Claude Muller, *La Négation en français: syntaxe sémantique et éléments de comparaison avec les autres langues romanes* (PRF, 198), 470 pp., is a wide-ranging and thorough study, which has the further inestimable advantage of being both convincingly structured and clearly expressed.

M. Forsgren proposes 'Éléments pour une typologie de l'apposition en linguistique française', *Actes* (Trier), II, 597–612, while S. Hanon, *ib.*, 613–24, studies absolute expressions of the type *les yeux fermés* in spoken French, and K.-H. Körner, *ib.*, 625–29, contests the view that the absolute use of the present participle is on its way out. W. A. Bennett, *ZPSK*, 44:565–87, argues that Exceptional Case Marking occurs in French with some verbs of perception. *LaF*, no. 88 (Dec., 1990), contains four articles of general import, viz.: J. Cervoni, 'La partie du discours nommée adverbe' (5–11); P. Blumenthal, 'Classement des adverbes: Pas la couleur, rien que la nuance' (41–50); F. Nef, 'Problèmes de classification des adverbes d'un point de vue logique' (51–59); and H. Nølke, 'Recherches sur les adverbes: bref aperçu historique des travaux de classification' (117–27) (which includes a useful bibliography); two items largely or specifically on adverbs in *-ment*: H. Nølke, 'Les adverbiaux contextuels: problèmes de classification' (12–27) (also takes in 'les adverbiaux contextuels'), and C. Molinier, 'Une classification des adverbes en *-ment*' (28–40); and three more specific studies: H. Korzen, 'Pourquoi *pourquoi* est-il différent? L'adverbial de cause et la classification des adverbes en général' (60–79), R. Martin, 'Pour une approche véraconditionnelle de l'adverbe *bien*' (80–89), and J.-C. Anscombre, 'L'opposition *longtemps/longuement*: durée objective et durée subjective' (90–116). Thanh Nyan, '*Maintenant*: emploi pragmatique', *JFLS*, I:157–77, is conceived in terms of O. Ducrot's 'Théorie de l'Argumentation'. D. Maurel, 'Adverbes de date: étude préliminaire à leur traitement automatique', *LInv*, 14, 1990:31–63.

Jürgen Lang, *Die französischen Präpositionen: Funktion und Bedeutung*, Heidelberg, Winter, 516 pp., proceeds from a general chapter on the problem of delimiting the preposition as a part of speech, via others ranging over (inter alia) prepositional word-groups, the preposition in relation to participant roles, government, word-formation, the preposition as defined by other linguists, to a lengthy study of the meaning of individual French prepositions. Jean Cervoni, *La préposition. Étude sémantique et pragmatique*, Duculot, 309 pp., the second volume in the important new 'Champs linguistiques' series (see *YWMLS*, 52:35), is a thorough-going and far-reaching 'neo-Guillaumian' study. *LaF*, no. 91 (Sept.), ed. A.-M. Berthonneau and P. Cadiot, is devoted to 'Prépositions, représentations, référence' and includes: P. Cadiot, '*A la hache* ou *avec la hache*? Représentation mentale, expérience située et donation du référent' (7–23) — more wide-ranging than the title might suggest; J.C. Anscombre, 'L'article zéro sous préposition' (24–39); B. I. Bosredon-Tamba, '*Verre à pied, moule à gaufres*: préposition et noms composés de sous-classe' (40–55); J.-J. Franckel and D. Lebaud, 'Diversité des valeurs et invariance du fonctionnement de *en* préposition et préverbe' (56–70) — rather long-drawn-out; D. Leeman, '*Hurler de rage, rayonner de bonheur*: remarques sur une construction en *de*' (80–101) — identifies three overlapping types and provides in an appendix a list of verbs taking a complement of the type *de* + noun; A. M. Berthonneau, '*Pendant* et *pour*, variations sur la durée et donation de la référence' (102–24). Pierre Cadiot, **De la grammaire à la cognition, la préposition 'pour'*, CNRS, 290 pp. Id., *CLe*, 58:63–79, studies the use of prepositions that introduce either the word *train* (*par train, dans le train*, etc.) or its complement (*le train de/pour Genève*, etc.). *LaF*, no. 86 (May 1990), 'Sur les compléments circonstanciels', ed. Danielle Leeman, includes as language-specific items, together with several others that are beyond the scope of *YWMLS*: C. Molinier, 'Les quatre saisons — à propos d'une classe d'adverbes temporels' (46–50); P. Cadiot, 'A propos du complément circonstanciel de but' (51–64), on infinitives introduced by *pour* or *afin de* respectively; A. Balibar-Mrabti, 'Analyse d'adverbes en *dans*' (65–74); A. Borielo, 'A propos de la localisation spatiale' (75–84); J. Cervoni, 'Prépositions et compléments prépositionnels' (85–89); M. Gross, 'La caractérisation des adverbes dans un lexique-grammaire' (90–102); and J.-C. Anscombre, 'Pourquoi un moulin à vert n'est pas un ventilateur' (103–25), insightful survey of syntactical, semantic and pragmatic aspects of compound nouns of the type N *à* N. V. Roglic, *'Les différences dans l'emploi de la construction possessive N_1 *de* + N_2 entre le XIX et le XX s. dans la prose littéraire française', *RILA*, 23.3:169–75. C. Molinier, 'Les compléments adverbiaux du français de type *avec N*', *LInv*, 15:115–40, is a thorough and useful study. A. Battye, 'Partitive and pseudo-partitive revisited: reflections on the status of *de* in French', *JFLS*, 1:21–43, argues within the framework of GB theory that the widely accepted structural distinction between partitive (e.g. *beaucoup des problèmes épineux*) and pseudo-partitive (e.g. *beaucoup de problèmes*) constructions is based on too restrictive an interpretation of the structure of French NPs. Catherine Kerbrat-Orecchioni (ed.), *La Question, Lyons U.P., 377 pp. M. Helkkula-Lukkarinen,

'L'organisation thématique de l'énoncé', *NMi*, 92:371–90, offers some 'considerations générales et remarques particulières sur le français'. Olof Eriksson, *Coordination et subordination dans quelques séquences narratives du français actuel* (Romania Gothoburgensia, 38), Univ. of Göteborg, 1989, 99 pp., is a useful, fully accessible study of bipartite and tripartite structures involving co-ordinate clauses, relative clauses, other subordinate clauses, and 'narrative participial clauses' (types *(en) levant la tête*) in novels by Julien Green, Bernard Clavel, and Michel del Castillo. Els Verheugd-Daatzelaar, *Subject Arguments and Predicate Nominals: A Study of French Copular Sentences with Two NPs*, Amsterdam, Rodopi, 1990, 304 pp., works within the framework of GB theory, and will be hard going for those who are not familiar with that theory; those who are are likely to find it illuminating. D. Gaatone, 'Note sur la pseudo-synonymie de *Il s'agit* et *Il est question*', *CLe*, 58:81–91, shows that they are neither syntactically nor semantically equivalent. Id., 'Un calembour syntaxique en français', *JFLS*, 1:45–53, looks at the extension (usually for humorous effect) of the construction *elle a les yeux verts* to such utterances as *j'ai le geste éloquent*. M.-T. Vinet, *'French non-verbal exclamative constructions', *Probus*, 3:77–100. L. Stage, 'Analyse syntaxique et sémantique de la conjonction *si* dans les propositions factuelles', *RevR*, 26:163–205, is based, like so much Scandinavian work of its kind, on an abundance of data and a clear and thorough analysis thereof. H. Pijnenburg and A. Hulk, *'Datives in French causatives', *Probus*, 1, 1989:259–82. Dominique Maingueneau, *L'Énonciation en linguistique française: embrayeurs, temps discours rapporté*, new edn, Hachette-Classique, 126 pp. Christine Tellier, *Licensing Theory and French Parasitic Gaps*, Dordrecht, Kluwer, 224 pp. C. Tellier, *'Subjacency and subject condition violations in French', *LI*, 21, 1990:306–11. Junji Kawaguchi, *'Avoir' et les problèmes de la localisation en français*, French-Tosho, 199 pp.

7. LEXICOGRAPHY

The *FEW* has reached fasc. 151, constituting t. xxv, pp. 481–576, covering ASPERGERE–*ASSULARE. R. Arveiller, 'Addenda au *FEW* XIX (Orientalia), 20ᵉ article', *ZRP*, 107:363–97, run from SUKKAR to ŠAH. M.-G. Boutier and others discuss 'Cas d'étymologie douteuse dans le *FEW*', *TLP*, 27, 1989:151–79, and 28, 1990:25–36. T. R. Wooldridge, in an important article, *ib.*, 28, 1990:239–316, compares the *FEW*'s references to the dictionaries of R. Estienne and J. Nicot with the originals, and argues that the comparison 'aboutit à un constat de deux ensembles difficilement conciliables': worrying. The happily resurrected Tobler–Lommatzsch, *Altfranzösisches Wörterbuch*, now edited by H. H. Christmann (see *YWMLS*, 49:43), continues with fasc. 89, Wiesbaden, Steiner, which constitutes vol. xi, cols 193–384, covering VENTELER–VÏAIRE. Christmann contributes an informative article, 'Philologie oder Sprachwissenschaft? Zum altfranzösischen Wörterbuch (Tobler–Lommatzsch)', to *Fest. Flasche*, 572–84. W. Kesselring. *Dictionnaire chronologique de la langue française: le XVIIᵉ siècle*, I, *1601–1606*, Heidelberg, Winter, 1989, xxix + 417 pp., is the first volume of what will inevitably prove to be a major reference work that continues the author's earlier and comparable work on the 16th c. In it we find, itemized year by year, 'les mots nouveaux du XVIIᵉᵐᵉ siècle — néologismes formels et sémantiques', with, for each, not merely definitions, etymological notes, and references to the earliest attestations, but comments on the relevant semantic field and, where necessary, on such matters as register, pragmatics, and grammatical notes. The title of F. Möhren's review article, 'Theorie und Praxis in Stones *Anglo-Norman Dictionary*', *ZRP*, 107:418–42, will unfortunately serve to give wider currency to a misconception as to the editorship of the *AND*. C. Buridant, 'En passant par le *Glossaire des glossaires du moyen français*', *RLiR*, 55:427–78, is well enough indicated by its subtitle, 'Les glossaires des éditions de textes de moyen français et l'élaboration du *Dictionnaire de moyen français*: essai d'analyse critique'.

Daniel Péchoin (ed.), *Thésaurus Larousse*, Larousse, xxi + 1146 pp., is an indispensable reference work, inspired by Roget's *Thesaurus* which, one is astonished to learn, had, up until the appearance of this book, no real equivalent for French; some 100,000 words are classified in 873 sections, each with, in most cases, between ten and thirty subsections but in some cases many more. Bruno Lafleur, *Dictionnaire des locutions idiomatiques françaises*, Louvain-la-Neuve, Duculot, xlvii + 669 pp., is yet another fine reference work from this publisher; over 2300 idiomatic expressions are listed (to take *panier* as an example, we have *faire danser l'anse du panier, le dessus du panier, le panier à salade, ne pas mettre tous ses œufs dans le même panier, un panier percé*) with, for each, a definition, a made-up example bringing out clearly its use, and a 20th-c. literary example; there are indexes of key-words and of authors. John Humbley and Jacques Boissy, *Cahier des termes nouveaux, 1990*, CILF, 1990, 187 pp., list, with definitions, examples (mainly from newspapers and periodicals), and comments, some 700 new terms (including acronyms) noted by the Centre de Terminologie et de Néologie in 1988–89; there is no doctrinaire exclusion of anglicisms (e.g. *big bang*, WYSIWYG). *Aberystwyth Word Lists* (see *YWMLS*, 52:41) have reached nos 11 (May), 17 pp., and 12 (Nov.), 19 pp., the latter containing an English–French index to both. J. Cellard and A. Rey, *Dictionnaire du français non conventionnel*, Hachette, xx + 909 pp., a revised and expanded edition of a work first published in 1980, is an indispensable reference work for anyone with any kind of interest in the modern French language (or, indeed, modern French literature); covering the period 1880–1990, it has some 3500 main entries, each accompanied by full definitions and historical notes, and illustrated by at least one, and in many cases several, literary examples. There is also a 'Glossaire français conventionnel–non conventionnel'.

Henriette Walter and Gérard Walter, *Dictionnaire des mots d'origine étrangère*, Larousse, 413 pp., lists some 4000 words, with a substantial introductory essay, 'Les couches lexicales au cours des siècles' (17–115). This year has seen two additions to the series 'La Vie des mots' published by Belfond (see *YWMLS*, 51:43–44); Jean-Pierre Colin, *Califoutis, gourgandine et vilebrequin: les mots des provinces de France*, 192 pp., covers not — as the title might perhaps suggest — words of *français régional* but words of provincial origin 'qui se sont parfaitement intégrés dans notre lexique national'; some 500 such words, grouped under fourteen thematic headings, are defined, with etymological and historical notes and illustrations from literary texts; for the other recent addition to the series, see Bourgeade (p. 25). Other additions since 1989 are: J.-P. Colin, *Le Dico du cul*, 1989; P. Éluerd, *Le Dico du cœur*, 1989; J. Cellard, *Godillot, silhouette et cie*, 1990; and René Droin, *Dictionnaire extraordinaire des mots ordinaires*, 1990. Émile Littré, *Comment j'ai fait mon dictionnaire*, with a 'postface' by J. Cellard, Arles, Coutaz, 100 pp. *Lexique*, 9, 1990, 'Les marques d'usage dans les dictionnaires (XVIIᵉ – XVIIIᵉ siècles)', ed. M. Glatigny, includes: M. Glatigny, 'Présentation: l'importance des marques d'usage' (7–16); A. Rey, 'Les marques d'usage et leur mise en place dans les dictionnaires du XVIIᵉ siècle: le cas Furetière' (17–29); B. von Gemmingen, 'Recherches sur les marques d'usage dans le *Tesoro de las dos lenguas francesa y española* de Cesar Oudin (1607)' (31–41); L. Bray, 'Les marques d'usage dans le *Dictionnaire françois* (1680) de César-Pierre Richelet' (43–59); B. Lépinette, 'Trois dictionnaires du XVIIᵉ siècle, trois traitements différents d'étymologie: *Richelet* (1680), *Furetière* (1690), *Académie* (1694)' (61–79); A. Collinot, 'L'usage des mots, l'institution du sens dans le *Dictionnaire de l'Académie*' (81–88); F. Mazière, 'Les marques de *fabrique*. Marquage et marques de domaine dans les dictionnaires classiques, du *Furetière* aux *Trévoux*' (89–111); S. Branca-Rosoff, 'Deux éditions du *Trévoux*, 1732 et 1771: des dictionnaires jésuites' (113–28); J.-P. Seguin *et al.*, 'Les marqueurs de mauvais usage dans le *Dictionaire critique* de Féraud' (129–51); J.-P. Saint-Gérand, 'Usage, emplois, stéréotypie dans les éditions du *Dictionnaire universel* de Boiste: note sur le cas des marqueurs d'usage et leur fonction' (153–64). *CLe*, 56–57 (1990, 1–2), publishes the 'Actes du colloque franco-danois de lexicographie'; the items of greatest relevance to this section of *YWMLS* seem to be P. Corbin, 'Logique linguistique et logique botanique: problèmes posés par la définition d'une classe de mots dérivés français' (75–108), G. Gorcy, 'La polysémie verbale ou le traitement de la polysémie de sens dans le *Trésor de la langue française*' (109–22), P. Rézeau, 'Pour une étude des variantes géographiques et de la phraséologie du français' (131–39), and F. Henry, 'Informatisation du *Trésor de la langue française*: problèmes et perspectives' (201–12). *LaF*, no. 87 (Sept. 1990), 'Dictionnaires électroniques du français', ed. Blandine Courtois and Max Silberzstein, includes: J. Dubois and F. Dubois-Charlier, 'Incomparabilité des dictionnaires' (5–10); B. Courtois, 'Un système de dictionnaires électroniques pour les mots simples du français' (11–22); A. Dugas, 'La création lexicale et les dictionnaires électroniques' (23–29); D. Leeman and S. Meleuc, 'Verbes en tables et adjectifs en *-able*' (30–51); A. Guillet, 'Reconnaissance des formes verbales' (52–58); E. Laporte, 'Le dictionnaire phonémique DELAP' (59–70); M. Silberzstein, 'Le dictionnaire électronique des mots composés' (71–83); G. Gross, 'Définition des mots composés dans un lexique-grammaire' (84–90); R. Jung, 'Remarques sur la constitution du lexique des noms composés' (91–97); R. Vivès, 'Les composés nominaux par juxtaposition' (98–103); M. Mathieu-Colas, 'Ortho-graphe et informatique: établissement d'un dictionnaire électronique des variantes graphiques' (104–11); C. Leclère, 'Organisation du lexique-grammaire des verbes français' (112–22); M. Gross, 'Le programme d'extension des lexiques électroniques' (123–27). *TeN*, no. 5 (June 1991), includes, *inter alia*: C. Leonhardt, 'Les nouvelles technologies et la terminologie au Secrétariat d'État du Canada' (5–7); C. de Schaetzen, 'Une banque de troisième génération' (on a Belgian multilingual terminological databank, *Belgoterm*) (8–10); and a 'Bibliographie de la néologie' (31–35).

To the Larousse collection 'Le Souffle des mots' (see *YWMLS*, 50:33 and 52:40) can now be added the following: Jean-Claude Bologne, *Les Allusions bibliques*, 336 pp., which is, as its subtitle states, a 'dictionnaire commenté des expressions d'origine biblique'; it not only quotes and comments on the words and expressions listed but gives for each one or more literary references (many of them as recent as 1990); Id., **Les Allusions littéraires*, new edn, 335 pp.; Patricia Vigerie, *La Symphonie animale: les animaux dans les expressions de la langue française*, xvii + 241 pp., which presents an abundant harvest of idioms (including many specifically designated as obsolete or regional) based on the names of some 250 animals, birds, insects, and fish, together with definitions and, in many cases, literary examples; an appendix lists proverbs and sayings from languages from all over the world. C. Duneton and S. Claval, **Le Bouquet des expressions*

imagées: encyclopédie thématique des locutions figurées de la langue française,
Seuil, 1990, xv + 1380 pp.

8. LEXICOLOGY

GENERAL

TrL, 23, 'Où en sont les études sur le lexique? Bilan et perspectives',
includes C. Muller, 'Lexicologie et informatique' (11–16), B. Quemada, 'Acquis et perspectives de l'informatique' (17–21), P. Tombeur, 'Pour une informatique qui ferait de nous des serviteurs du texte
et du "saint langage"' (23–29), D. Corbin, 'La morphologie lexicale:
bilan et perspectives' (33–56), J. Thiele, 'La structuration du lexique'
(57–61), M. Plénat, 'Commentaire sur la contribution de Danielle
Corbin' (63–65), J.-P. Chambon, 'Étymologie française (et gallo-
romane): un bilan (1971–1991)' (69–89), G. Roques, 'L'articulation
entre étymologie et histoire de la langue' (91–95), P. Swiggers,
'L'étymologie (g)allo-romane: perspectives et points de vue'
(97–103), M. Gross, 'Lexique et syntaxe' (107–32), B. Lamiroy, 'Où
en sont les rapports entre les études de lexique et de syntaxe?'
(133–39), J. Dubois, 'A propos des dictionnaires électroniques des
verbes' (141–42), J. Rey-Debove, 'La lexicographie moderne'
(145–59), P. Corbin, 'La lexicographie moderne: contrepoint. Réflexions sur la contribution de Josette Rey-Debove' (161–69), P. Rézeau,
'Simples prolongements et suggestions concrètes à la suite de l'exposé
de Josette Rey-Debove' (171–74), A. Lehman, 'A propos du *Petit
Robert des enfants*' (175–76), A. Rey, 'A propos de la sémantique
lexicale' (179–93), P. Lerat, 'Le sens lexical comme jeu de relations
entre des concepts' (195–200), J. Picoche, 'Septs motifs d'éton-
nement' (201–03). Otto Jänicke, *Französische Etymologie: Einführung
und Überblick* (RA, 35), 92 pp., reviews the history of French etymological studies from the 16th c. onwards, surveys the four main early
sources of the French lexicon (Vulgar Latin, Celtic, Germanic (i.e.
Frankish), and specifically Romance creations), and provides four
detailed case-studies (*aune, son* 'bran', *donjon*, and Franco/Provencal/
Occitan *brogì/broujà* 'to brood'); a French translation would be useful.
Michèle Lenoble-Pinson, *Anglicismes et substituts français*, Louvain-la-
Neuve, Duculot, 182 pp., is a worthy companion to the many
excellent books on the French language (foremost among them, of
course, Grevisse's *Le Bon Usage*) that we already owe to this publisher;
no mere dictionary, it provides highly informative comments on the
anglicisms in question (some 120 of them), and on the suggested
equivalents (in many cases three or more). P. Enckell, **Français
familier, populaire et argotique, début XVIe s. — vers 1870* (= Matériaux
pour l'histoire du vocabulaire français, 2e série: datations et

Language

41

documents lexicolographiques, 38), Klincksieck, xxxvi + 387 pp.
Graciela Christ, *Arabismen im Argot* (EH, xiii. 160), 632 pp., deals
with the second half of the 19th c.

SEMANTIC FIELDS

B. Lhoest, 'Les dénominations de la femme en moyen français:
approche lexicale et anthropologique', *ZRP*, 107:343–62, lists and
comments on 74 items. M.-R. Simoni-Aurembou, 'L'éducation des
arbres et des hommes sous Louis XIV et sous Louis XV', *Actes*
(Trier), iii, 667–87, is a lexicological study based on the horticultural
treatises of Jean de La Quintine (1690) and Roger Schabol (1767).
The real scope of S. Branca-Rosoff, 'De la culture de la vigne à la
cueillette des fleurs des champs', *LaF*, no. 85 (Fcb. 1990):48–47, is
indicated by the subtitle, 'Les noms de la langue dans la dialectologie
française du XIXᵉ siècle' — the *abbé* Grégoire, G. Paris, P. Meyer,
and P. Rousselot figure prominently. Laure Azem, *Das Wortfeld der
Sauberkeitsadjektive im heutigen Französisch* (MBRP, 4), 1990,
xii + 379 pp., recognizes a debt to the work of E. Coseriu and H.
Geckeler; some sixty adjectives are classified, analysed, and exemplified. C. Schmitt, 'Religion und Sprache: zum Gebrauch christlicher
Metaphorik und religiös markierten Wortschatzes in der französischen Pressesprache', *Fest. Flasche*, 654–73, tackles a subject that
merits fuller treatment; bibliographically useful. G. Costa, *Sein: les
mots pour (ne pas) le dire: étude onomasiologique*, Agnano Pisano, Giardini,
1990, 111 pp. C. Vandeloise, *L'expression linguistique de la relation
de suspension', *CLe*, 55, 1989:101–33. M. Grimaud, 'Nature et
classification des sobriquets honorifiques', *TrL*, 22:21–40, classifies
expressions of the type 'Monsieur 50%', 'Madame Touchatout'.

WORD FORMATION

A. Čaušev, 'De quelques caractéristiques de la composition nominale
en français', *ConL*, 14, 1989:13–15. M. H. Offord, 'Words ending in -o
in French', *SN*, 63:95–105, discusses origin, word-class, gender,
register, and compares the treatment of the 680-odd items he has
gathered (not all of them listed) in various dictionaries. J.-P. Boons,
'Morphosyntaxe comparée des verbes dénominaux préfixés par *en-*
dans le français d'avant 1600 et d'après 1900', *Actes* (Trier), ii,
91–103. C. Muller, 'Contraintes de perception sur la productivité de
la préfixation verbale en *dé-* négatif', *TLP*, 28, 1990–171–92.

WORD STUDIES

Y. Malkeil trains a powerful magnifying glass on 'The transmutation
of Church Latin (*dies*) *nātālis* "birthday" into French *Noël* "Christmas"', *NMi*, 75:21–30. K. Baldinger, 'Mfr. *pallesin*, la dialectologie et

la vieillesse', *RLiR*, 55 : 95–99, has erudite fun with an obscene 15th-c. riddle. F. Lecoy, '*Ortière*, subst. fem., "ornière",' *Romania*, 109, 1988 [1991] : 561–62, shows that the word is misinterpreted in the dictionaries. D. L. Gold, *RPh*, 44 : 425–28, casts considerable doubt on the alleged Russian origin of *bistro(t)*. U. L. Figge, 'Die Bedeutungen von *concevoir*. Eine kognitiv-semantische Analyse', *Fest. Flasche*, 598–619, is strictly synchronic. M.-J. Gerecht, '*Alors*: unicité et multiplicité', *Actes* (Trier), II, 120–26, shows that, in addition to contexts in which the value of *alors* is either wholly temporal or wholly consecutive, there are those which combine both values.

9.   ONOMASTICS

Ernest Nègre, *Toponymie générale de la France: étymologie de 35 000 noms de lieux* (see *YWMLS*, 52 : 42), is completed with vols II, *Formations non-romanes*; *formations dialectales* (pp. 711–1381), and III, *Formations dialectales (suite) et françaises* (pp. 1399–1855) ('Index', pp. 1747–1852) (PRF, 194 and 195). In reality, this magnificent *magnum opus* is more extensive even than the figure of 35,000 mentioned in the subtitle suggests — that figure relates specifically to 'noms de lieux', whereas, since different places of the same name (e.g. the five *(Le) Châtel* or the nine *Villedieu*) are grouped under the same number, the total of *places* listed is nearly 42,000. Each main etymologically based section is extensively subcategorized on the basis of onomasiological criteria — names of tribes, names of individuals, reference to geographical features, agricultural activities, man-made constructions, etc., etc. L. Palm, * '*On va à la Mouff?*': étude sur la syntaxe des noms de rues en français contemporain* (SRU, 45), 1989, 123 pp. Marie-Thérèse Morlet, *Dictionnaire étymologique des noms de famille*, Perrin, 1120 pp. While the majority of the contributions to *LaF*, 92 (Dec. 1991), 'Syntaxe et sémantique des noms propres', are not language-specific (but see also p. 31), they are illustrated exclusively from French: M.-N. Gary-Prieur, 'Le nom propre constitue-t-il une catégorie linguistique?' (4–25), and 'La modalisation du nom propre' (46–63); N. Flaux, 'L'antonomase du nom propre ou la mémoire du référent' (26–45); K. Jonasson, 'Les noms propres métaphoriques: construction et interprétation' (64–81); and M. Wilmet, 'Nom propre et ambiguïté' (113–24).

10.   DIALECTS AND REGIONAL FRENCH

P. van Reenen, 'Comment distinguer les espaces dialectaux?', *RLiR*, 55 : 479–86, takes issue with the main thesis (viz. the existence of a north-eastern French dialectal area, as distinguished from a central area) of Alf Monjour, *Der nordostfranzösische Dialektraum*, Frankfurt, Lang, 1989, 404 pp., while nevertheless paying tribute to M.'s erudition. M. Francard, 'Français régional et francisation d'un dialecte. De la déviance à la variation', *Actes* (Trier), III, 370–82, constitutes an important reassessment, and indeed a rehabilitation, of regional French as an object of linguistic study. Specific papers within the general field of regional French are presented by P. Boissel, '"De l'eau sur du lait." Étude du parler ordinaire rural de la région de Bayeux en 1985: français dialectal ou dialecte francisé?', *ib.*, 383–92, B. Rochet, 'Tendances de coupe syllabique en français régional de Bordeaux et en français standard', *ib.*, 393–405, and G. Salmon, 'État du français d'origine dialectale en Lyonnais', *ib.*, 406–26. P. Gardy, 'Aux origines du discours francophoniste: le meurtre des patois et leur rachat par le français', *LaF*, no. 85 (Feb. 1990): 22–34, is (as the word 'francophoniste' suggests) hard-hitting — and says much that needed saying. H. Boyer, 'Matériaux pour une approche des représentations sociolinguistiques. Éléments de définition et parcours documentaire en diglossie', *ib.*, 102–24, considers among others R. Lafont, the *abbé* Grégoire, and the *abbé* de Sauvages. H. Walter, 'Les témoignages graphiques permettent-ils une interprétation phonologique?', *Actes* (Trier), III, 561–70, assesses the value of the unpublished material obtained by G. Dottin in 1899 in response to 200 written responses to a lengthy questionnaire addressed to schoolmasters in the Gallo part of Brittany. Publication of the *Atlas linguistique de la Wallonie*, based on the material gathered by Jean Haust (who died in 1946), supplemented by later field-work, continues with *vol. 5, *La Maison et le Ménage*, pt II, ed. Jean Lechanteur, Univ. of Liège, 372 pp. The first fascicule of a *Petit atlas linguistique de la Wallonie*, derived from the main atlas, appeared in 1990. Lucien Dondaine, *Atlas linguistique et ethnologique de la Franche-Comté*, t.4, CNRS, 244 pp., is mainly devoted to grammar.

François Beauvy, *Dictionnaire des parlers et traditions du Beauvaisis*, published by the author, 1990, 359 pp., has a preface by R. Debrie. Jacques-Marie Rougé, *Petit dictionnaire du parler de Touraine*, Chambray les Tours, CLD, 92 pp., is, in fact, a most welcome re-issue of the glossary of some 4000 words appended to the author's pre-war *Folklore de la Touraine*. S. Verlinde and P. Derynck, 'La dialectométrie et la délimitation des zones dialectales. Application au domaine Wallon', *Actes* (Trier), III, 342–51, avoid the detailed technicalities that make so much dialectometrical work unreadable. L. Baugnet, 'Identité culturelle et représentations de la langue', *TrL*, 22:103–20, looks at attitudes towards Walloon. T. Pooley, 'Le recul du patois roubaisien — le cas de deux variantes stéréotypées', *RevR*, 26:54–68, provides statistical evidence for the decline of [ʃ] for [s] and of [ɛ̃] for [ɑ̃] which, in so far as they remain, are now largely restricted to relatively uneducated speakers aged over 45. A. Liddicoat, 'Le traitement de l'*r* intervocalique en sercquiais', *RLiR*, 55: 119–24, highlights a feature not found in Jersey French, viz. the affrication of *r* when, after the loss of [ə], it comes into contact with a previous consonant, e.g. [kɔptʃɛ] *couperai*, [truvdʒa] *trouvera* (but he does not specify the source of his data).

Bonneton's admirable series of 'Dictionnaires du français régional' (see *YWMLS*, 52: 42–43) continues with Fernand Carton and Denise Poulet, *Dictionnaire du français régional du Nord-Pas-de-Calais*, 125 pp., Philippe Blanchet, *Dictionnaire du français régional de Provence*, 157 pp., Christian Camps, *Dictionnaire du français régional du Languedoc (Aude, Gard, Hérault, Lozère)*, 157 pp.; and Jacques Boisgontier, *Dictionnaire du français régional des Pays Aquitains (Bordelais, Agenais, Périgord, Landes, Gascogne, Pays Basque, Béarn, Bigorre)*, 157 pp., all of them by authorities on the respective areas and worthy companions to earlier vols in the series. It is now clear that, once all fifteen volumes in the series are available, we shall have here a most useful lexical corpus.

Gilbert-Lucien Salmon (ed.), *Variétés et variantes du français: états de l'est de la France*, Champion — Geneva, Slatkine, xvi + 346 pp., includes: J. Bourguignon, 'Quelques aspects du français parlé à Lyon' (9–24); G. Salmon, 'Une cohabitation réussie. Français de France et régionalismes du français à Lyon aux XIXe et XXe siècles' (25–63); a linguistic study by C. Dondaine of L. Semonin's TV monologue *La Madeleine Proust en forme* (written in the regional French of Morteau, in the Doubs) (65–80); C. Rittaud-Hutinet, 'Variétés du français de Besançon et grammaire polylectale' (81–98); Y. Baradel, 'Belfort et sa région au contact des mondes roman at germain, XVIIe–XIXe siècles' (99–111); C. Girardot-Soltner, 'Variétés de comportement dans le pancartage mulhousien' (113–26); R. Matzen, 'Le *franglais* en Alsace et les anglicismes alsaciens' (127–37); D. Crévenat-Werner, 'Étude quantitative et qualitative des lexèmes français en strasbourgeois contemporain' (139–57); G. Roques, 'Commentaires philologiques sur quelques régionalismes de Nancy' (159–69); F. Carton, 'Besançon, Lille, Nancy: quelques données de prosodie comparée' (171–83); D. Willems, 'Les francophones de Gand: éléments d'une analyse linguistique et sociolinguistique' (185–99); A. Goosse, 'La part du substrat dialectal dans le français de Belgique' (201–09); C. Blanche-Benveniste, 'La difficulté à cerner les régionalismes en syntaxe' (211–20); L. Wolf, 'La description des variantes géographiques' (221–28); and, under the overall title 'Le français des villes dans l'est de la France: Lyonnais, Alsace', five papers by the editor, viz. 'Lorsque le *Littré de la Grand-Côte* eut les cent ans ou le français de Lyon un siècle après' (231–56), 'Les idées linguistiques de Nizier du Puitspelu, chantre du parler lyonnais (1827–1898)' (257–73), 'La diglossie au quotidien: disponibilité et réalisations d'après l'exemple mulhousien' (with C. Girardot-Soltner) (275–85), 'Mélange alsacien ou De quelques essais de transcription du français d'Alsace et de quelques autres textes en langue alternée (1895–1934)' (287–316), and 'Alsacianismes: néologismes, antidates, attestations, citations (lettres *a–d*)' (317–44).

T. J. Nadasdi, *'Déviation et simplification linguistique dans le français bruxellois', *JAPLA*, 11, 1989:1–18. J.-P. Watbled, 'Les processus de sandhi externe en français de Marseille', *JFLS*, 1:71–91, is concerned with contexts in which elision and liaison are blocked in the case of words with an initial vowel or semi-vowel.

11. FRENCH IN CANADA AND THE UNITED STATES

Brigitte Horiot (ed.), *Français du Canada — français de France* (Canadiana Romanica, 6), Tübingen, Niemeyer, vi + 236 pp., constitutes the 'Actes du deuxième Colloque international de Cognac' of 1988 (for the *Actes* of the first colloquium, Trier, 1985, see *YWMLS*, 50:38–39); with the exception of G. Roques, 'La mer dans la *Chronique des ducs de Normandie*' (7–15), which, despite being devoted in part to maritime vocabulary, seems somewhat out of place in this volume, the contributions are specifically geared to linguistic topics; they include (in addition to the verbatim record, 79–111, which should have been abridged, of a 'table ronde' on 'Recherches en cours et projetés'), a number of useful and in some cases important studies: M. Juneau, 'Le vocabulaire maritime dans la langue commune au Québec: apport gallo-roman' (17–23), comments on over thirty words attested both in France and in Canada; G. Dulong, 'L'emploi du vocabulaire maritime dans des domaines non maritimes dans le français du Canada' (25–28), is too sketchy to be of much value; L. Péronnet, 'Atlas linguistique des côtes francophones de l'Atlantique (état des recherches au Canada)' (29–46), is both well informed and informative, and is usefully complemented by P. Brasseur's more specific study, 'L'Atlas linguistique des côtes de l'Atlantique: l'exemple du casier à crustacés' (47–56); A. Geistdoerfer, 'Parler poisson — de l'astuce des pêcheurs saint-pierrais et madelinots' (57–65), has some sociolinguistic interest; M.-R. Simoni-Aurembou, 'Mirages génétiques' (69–76), demonstrates, in a persuasive paper that one wishes were more fully developed, that the contribution of the *parlers* of the Île-de-France to the lexicon of Canadian French has been consistently underestimated; L. Wolf, 'Le langage de la Cour et le français canadien. Exemples de morphologie et de syntaxe' (115–23), looks at a number of Canadianisms in the light of Vaugelas's *Remarques*; L. Jagueneau, 'Les prépositions dans le français parlé au Canada et en poitevin-saintongeais' (125–36), recognizes that a more thorough study is necessary before firm conclusions can be reached; N. Maury, 'De l'interrogation en Normandie et au Canada francophone' (137–59), is well documented and argued; L. Rodriguez, 'De l'Atlantique français à la prairie canadienne: aspects morphologiques et syntaxiques du parler franco-manitobain' (161–72), and G. Richard and B. E. Gesner, 'Les pronoms personnels sujets de la première personne dans deux parlers acadiens de la Nouvelle-Écosse et comparaison avec les parlers de l'ouest de la France' (173–93), though having little else in common, are both (as their titles suggest) of strictly limited interest; K. Flikeid, 'Les parlers acadiens de la Nouvelle-Écosse (Canada): diversification ou origines diverses?' (195–214), shows that there is no simple answer; H.-J. Niederehe, 'Quelques aspects de la morphologie du franco-terreneuvien' (215–33), is largely data-oriented, ranging over nouns, articles, personal pronouns, and a number of parts of the verb.

N. Beauchemin discusses, with the aid of nine maps, 'Aires linguistiques au Québec d'après l'*ALEC*', *Actes* (Trier), III, 436–51. K. Connors, 'The norm vs. the reality in Quebec French: three studies in phonology and lexicon', *RPh*, 44:429–41, reviews D. C. Walker, *The Pronunciation of Canadian French* (1984), C. Poirier (ed.), *Dictionnaire du français québécois: volume de présentation* (1985), and L. Boisvert *et al.* (eds), *La Lexicographie québécoise* (1986) (see *YWMLS*, 47:54 and 48:51). D. Bossé and A. Dugaş, 'Les deux "A" du français québécois', *LInv*, 14, 1990:217–43, propose a new analysis of the phonetic features of the phonemes in question.

Readers of C. A. Fox, 'A discriminant analysis of Yes–No questions in Quebec French', *Word*, 42:277–93, may find that the effort needed to understand the statistical methodology is not repaid by the benefit derived; however, if applied to a much greater and wider corpus of data, maybe the method could lead somewhere interesting. Ruth King studies '*Wh*-words, *wh*-questions and relative clauses in Prince Edward Island Acadian French', *CanJL*, 36:65–85. M. Picard, 'Clitics, affixes, and the evolution of the question marker *tu* in Canadian French', *JFLS*, 1:179–87, argues that *tu* (from *ti* – e.g. *il vient-tu?*) should be classified as an affix rather than as a clitic or a particle. R. King and Y. Roberge, *'Preposition stranding in Prince Edward Island French', *Probus*, 2, 1990:351–69. P. Brasseur, 'Synonymie et usage dans le français de Saint-Pierre-et-Miquelon', *Actes* (Trier), III, 452–59, presents two case-studies, of words for 'whelk' and 'le matériel qui sert à l'échouage' respectively. A. Paquot, 'Les canadianismes: usage, valeur et statut', *ib.*, 427 35, is too brief to be other than very general.

Raymond Mougeon and Édouard Beniak, *Linguistic Consequences of Language Contact and Restriction: The Case of French in Ontario, Canada* (Oxford Studies in Language Contact), Oxford, Clarendon, viii + 247 pp., is likely to be of considerable general interest for those concerned with language-contact situations in that it deals with a context in which one of the world's major languages finds itself in the position of a threatened minority language. The basis of the study is the language of four relatively recently established (i.e. 1840 +) Francophone communities in predominantly English-speaking Ontario. The survey ranges over both negative and positive aspects of the societal situation while over half the book is devoted to internal changes (morphological, syntactical, lexical, and idiomatic) in the French of the communities in question. H.-M. Militz, 'Joual contre Norm. Zur sprachlichen Situation in Quebec', *ZPSK*, 43, 1990:805–09. Neil Corbett (ed.), *Langue et identité: le français et les francophones d'Amérique du Nord*, Quebec, Laval U.P., 1990, xxxiii + 398 pp.

J. Maurais makes 'A sociolinguistic comparison between Québec's charter of the French language and the 1989 language laws of five Soviet republics', *JMMD*, 12:117–25. P.-É. Laporte and J. Maurais compare 'Quelques aspects de l'aménagement linguistique au Québec et en Finlande', *BFF*, no. 3 (Autumn):59–69.

P. Sérant, *Les Enfants de Jacques Cartier: du Grand Nord au Mississippi, les Américains de langue française*, Laffont, 290 pp.

12. FRENCH IN AFRICA

Ambroise Queffélec and Augustin Niangouna, *Le Français au Congo*, Aix-en-Provence, 1990, 333 pp., is basically a dictionary with examples. J. Schmidt, 'Phénomènes d'interférences: les emprunts à l'anglais dans le français parlé en Afrique noire', *CILL*, 16.2–4, 1990:139–70, spins out his material at inordinate length.

13. FRENCH CREOLES

Marie-Christine Hazaël-Massieux, *Bibliographie des études créoles: langues, cultures, sociétés*, Didier Érudition, 254 pp., is necessarily selective but nevertheless lists over a thousand items (books and articles) with, in each case, scope-notes and, in many cases, a brief summary; presentation is alphabetical by author but the lack of thematic classification is well compensated for by a subject index running to nearly 400 headings. *Études créoles*, *2, 1990 [1991], is devoted to French Guyana. R. Ludwig (ed.), *Les Créoles français entre l'oral et l'écrit*, Tübingen, Narr, 1989, 305 pp.

J. S. Lumsden, 'On the argument structure of certain Haitian predicates — *rete* "to remain", *posib* "possible"', *JPCL*, 6:59–72. M. M. Marshall, 'The Creole of Mon Louis Island, Alabama, and the Louisiana connection', *ib.*, 73–87. C. Lefebvre and E. Ritter, *ib.*, 279–83, discuss three types of causal clauses in Haitian Creole.

14. PRAGMATICS AND SOCIOLINGUISTICS

D. Duez, *La Pause dans la parole de l'homme politique*, CNRS, 168 pp. *CLF*, 12, 'Analyse du discours et l'interaction: modèles théoriques, études et ouvertures', includes (in addition to other items not relating to French): J. Moeschler, 'L'analyse pragmatique des conversations' (7–30); M. de Fornel, 'Gestes, processus de contextualisation et interaction verbale' (31–51); E. Roulet, 'Vers une approche modulaire de l'analyse du discours' (53–81); T. Jeanneret, 'Fabrication du texte conversationnel et conversation pluri-locuteurs' (103–26); and A. Reboul, 'Le plaisir dans la langue: les formes linguistiques de la jubilation' (127–52). Than Nyan, '*Maintenant*: emploi pragmatique', *JFLS*, 1:157–77, is inspired by O. Ducrot's 'Théorie de l'Argumentation'.

Penelope Gardner-Chloros, *Language Selection and Switching in Strasbourg* (Oxford Studies in Language Contact), Oxford, Clarendon, xvi + 218 pp., is based on three surveys conducted in, respectively, three socially differentiated department stores, an insurance office, and a variety of other situations (small shops, a village, nursery, and primary schools), and on the analysis of six hour-long conversations; the result is a considerable body of highly informative quantifiable data on code-switching, all the more valuable in that it is presented in such a way that the human reality encompassing it is never lost sight of.

Among items relating specifically to French, *LaF*, no. 85 (Feb. 1990), 'Les représentations de la langue: approches sociolinguistiques', includes J.-M. Marconot, 'Le français parlé dans un quartier HLM' (68–81), and D. Bourgain, 'Des représentations sociales de la norme dans l'ordre scriptural' (82–101) (see also pp. 26 and 41 above). *Langages*, no. 101 (March), ed. Marc Plénat, is devoted to 'Le javanais', a title adopted (perhaps ill-advisedly?) instead of 'Les langages secrets' as originally intended. 'Le javanais' in the strict sense of the word, i.e. 'un codage procédant par insertion de *-av-*' in each syllable (see M. Plénat, 'Présentation des javanais', 5–10) is the subject of the editor's own article, 'Le javanais: concurrence et haplologie' (95–117), while what may be the mostly widely known (in the sense of 'known of') French-based 'secret language' is studied by V. Méla, 'Le verlan ou le langage du miroir' (73–94). The editor also contributes a useful 'Bibliographie des javanais' (118–25). The remaining three items do not relate to French. *LaF*, no. 90 (May), 'Parlures argotiques', includes: D. François-Geiger, 'Panorama des argots contemporains' (5–9); J.-P. Goudaillier, 'Argotolâtrie et argotophobie' (10–12); M. Sourdot, 'Argot, jargon, jargot' (13–27); J.-P. Colin and A. Carnel, 'Argot, dicos, tombeaux?' (28–39); L.-J. Calvet, 'L'argot comme variation diastratique, diatopique et diachronique (autour de Pierre Guiraud)' (40–52); H. Walter, 'Où commencent les innovations lexicales?' (53–64); M. Verdelhan-Bourgade, 'Procédés sémantiques et lexicaux en français branché' (65–79); G. Bensimon-Choukroun, 'Les mots de connivence des jeunes en institution scolaire' (80–94); S. Lafage, 'L'argot des jeunes Ivoiriens, marque d'appropriation du français?' (95–105); F. Mandelbaum-Reiner, 'Suffixation gratuite et signalétique textuelle d'argot' (106–12); and F. Robert l'Argenton, 'Larpélem largomuche de louchébem. Parler l'argot du boucher' (113–25).

A. Lodge, 'Molière's peasants and the norms of spoken French', *NMit*, 92:485–99, shows that, in representing peasant speech in *Dom Juan*, M. picks on stereotypically stigmatized lexical, morphosyntactic, and phonetic features. F. Hartweg follows up an earlier article (see *YWMLS*, 47:55) with 'Sprachen und Hugenottische Identität in der französisch-reformierten Kirche Preussens (1814–1817)', *BRP*, 29, 1990:97–103.

15. Contrastive Studies

M.-P. Péry-Woodley analyses 'French and English passives in the construction of text', *JFLS*, 1:55–70. Jean-Paul Confais, **Temps, mode, aspect: les approches des morphèmes verbaux et leurs problèmes à l'exemple du français et de l'allemand*, Mirail–Toulouse U.P., 355 pp. E. Lavric, 'Analyse sémantique et analyse contrastive: quelques réflexions méthodologiques à propos de leur combinaison (à l'occasion d'une étude sur les déterminants en français et en allemand)', *Actes* (Trier), II, 336–46, draws both on translations and on commutation tests. Z. Guentchéva, 'Implications aspecto-temporelles en français et en bulgare', *ConL*, 14, 1989:26–37. A. Vasileva, 'Notes sur l'interjection en français et en bulgare', *ib.*, 77–82.

EARLY MEDIEVAL LITERATURE

By MARIANNE J. AILES, *Wadham College, Oxford*

1. GENERAL

ABHL, 75, Section III (27–31), deals with the Central Middle Ages (900–1200). *BSSCLE*, 11, includes a useful bibliography of recent and forthcoming publications on all matters concerning the crusades; a list of work in process and another of recently completed theses are also given. *Médiévales*, 18, 1990, **Espaces de Moyen âge*; 19, 1990, **Liens de famille: Vivre et choisir sa parenté*; 20, *Sagas et chroniques du Nord*, contains, in addition to articles on the Northern chronicles, A. Bratu, 'L'ici-bas et l'au-delà en image: formes de representation de l'espace et du temps' (75–90), an iconographical study of heaven, hell, and purgatory in the later Middle Ages; of wider interest and greater controversy is 21, *L'an mil: rhythmes et acteurs d'une croissance*, which has a number of articles showing divers reactions to Guy Bois's book, *La Mutation de l'an mil*, and a reply by Bois. J. W. Baldwin, 'Five discourses on desire: sexuality and gender in northern France around 1200', *Speculum*, 69: 797–819, examines examples of five very different genres with respect to their attitudes about sexuality and gender. The five writers are the theologian Peter the Chanter, one of the physicians who composed the *Prose Salernitan Questions* (written in northern France, not Salerno), Jean Bodel as a writer of fabliaux, Andreas Capellanus, and Jean Renart. Each is analysed in turn with due consideration being paid to the conventions of the genre. Jean Renart's work is examined in most detail. Points of agreement (e.g. the unacceptability of homosexuality) and of discord among the five are then brought out. B. points out that changes took place at the beginning of the 13th c., with the Aristotelian model of the single seed in procreation becoming more dominant, which make the turn of the century a unique period in this respect. E. J. Benkov, 'Language and women from silence to speech', Wasserman, *Sign*, 245–65, examines the idea that female discourse was seen as a potential threat to the established order. B. looks first at ideals as set out in the didactic treatises and courtesy lit. and finds the ideal of speaking little but wisely. B. then shows the use made by fabliaux of these conventions, e.g. for comic ends, particularly in the use of sexual language and sometimes by a disassociation between the sign and the object, first with women as victims then with women as verbal manipulators. Finally, B. turns to women of higher social status in romance and fabliaux and women's use of deceptive language to cover up sin. R. E. Brown, 'Pregnancy in classical and medieval literature',

Neophilologus, 75:321–26, is a brief analysis of the lack of pregnancy in medieval courtly lit., paying particular attention to Tristan and Isolde and the parallel with heroic lit. of the classical period, except when gods have relationships with mortal women. Ursula Ernst, **Studien zur altfranzosischen Vers-Legende (10.–Anfang 13. Jahrhunderts): Die Legende im Spannungsfeld von Chanson de gest und Roman*, NY, Lang, 1989, 280 pp. A. Garnier, 'Thèmes et variations sur la pie dans le monde médiéval', *MA*, 97:77–81, looks at the presence and treatment of this bird in Latin and Old French texts incl. Conon de Béthune and Gautier de Coinci. Aron Gurevich, *Medieval Popular·Culture: Problems of Belief*, CUP, 275 pp., trans. Janos M. Bak and Paul A. Hollingsworth, is a translation of the Russian text of 1981. It is of particular interest with regard to religious material and hagiography. The discussion is linked directly to Latin lit. but is relevant for an understanding of all medieval lit. Douglas Kelly, *The Arts of Poetry and Prose*, Turnhout, Brepols, 194 pp., is an evaluation and discussion of the genre, concentrating on the Latin sources but listing vernacular sources which are discussed in an important appendix (146–79). The main body of the book is useful for all medievalists in placing rhetoric in the context of the medieval outlook, e.g. philosophy, pedagogy, and artistry. Muriel Lahurie, *La Folie au Moyen Âge XIe – XIIIe siecles*, Le Léopard d'Or, 308 pp. + 82 pl., is a detailed study looking first at supernatural madness (the possessed and the 'Fous de Dieu'), then at natural madness. Literary and iconographic stereotypes of madness are examined. The second part of the study looks at how feudal society dealt with madness. Literary models include Perceval and Yvain. Hagiography is an important source with saints as miracle-workers discussed and listed comprehensively. B. A. Masters, 'The distribution, destruction and dislocation of authority in medieval literature and its modern derivatives', *RR*, 82:270–85, takes us back to an important recognition of the uniqueness of MSS, looking again at the whole problem of edited texts and the concept of an original author. The concept of *auctoritas* is looked at in respect not only of literary texts but also of the visual arts, which are taken to some degree as models for the literary texts. M. Moulis, '"Sang du cœur qui monte as yeulx faut larmes"', *Le 'Cuer'*, 225–32, after a brief survey of the different attributions of the heart in lit. (e.g. the *Couronnement de Louis*, *Cligès*, *La Prise d'Orange*, prose *Lancelot*), goes on to examine the relationship between courtly lit. and medical lit. around the concept of 'illness of love' and the passion/humours/heart link. S. G. Nichols, 'Seeing food: an anthropology of ekphrasis and still life in classical and medieval examples', *MLN*, 106:818–51, is a detailed study of the subject through a variety of texts as part of an issue on 'cultural presentations of food'. C. Raynaud, *La Violence au* *moyen âge (XIIIᵉ–XVᵉ siècles*, Le Léopard d'Or, 378 pp. + 87 pls, is an iconographical study of violence as depicted in the MSS of French vernacular historical writings. Many of these texts deal with subjects which are inherently violent. B. Ribemont, ' "Le Cuer del Ventre li as trais": cœur arraché, cœur mangé, cœur envolé: un regard medico-théologique sur quelques thèmes littéraires', *Le 'Cuer'*, 344–61, examines the motifs and concepts of heart, soul, and spirit in the context of medical and theological writings. J. E. Salisbury, *Medieval Sexuality: A Research Guide* (Garland Medieval Bibliographies, 5), NY, Garland, 1990, 200 pp., provides a list of primary and secondary sources on the subject with a brief summary of the contents of each. The primary sources are divided into history, law, literature, and science. A. Taylor, 'The myth of the minstrel manuscript', *Speculum*, 66:43–73, subjects a number of MSS to scrutiny, questioning whether these are really 'working MSS'. The study incl. MSS containing *chansons de geste*, e.g. Digby 23, and Middle English romances. T. raises issues of our stereotype of the minstrel. He concludes that it is difficult, even meaningless, to attempt to distinguish minstrel MSS from library or commercial texts. C. Thornasset, 'La chevalerie et l'ostentation dans l'évocation de la fête', *Symposion* (Paderborn), 181–91, is a semantic study looking at lit. through the words *fête* and *joie*. Certain elements are seen as essential to evoke a festive atmosphere. The use of the words *joie* and *fête* is examined through a number of texts, mostly *chansons de geste* but also others, e.g. Robert de Clari and the *Châtelaine de Vergy*. First examined are informal occasions with a festive mood, then more organized *fêtes*. T. concludes that the terms are virtually interchangeable. J.-J. Vincensini, 'Figure de l'imaginaire et figure de discours. Le motif du "cœur mangé" dans la narration médiévale', *Le 'Cuer'*, 439–59, is a wide-ranging anthropomorphic study. Michel Zink, *Littérature fran-çaise: le moyen âge*, Nancy U.P., 1990, is an introductory chronological study of Old French lit. The chapter division is by genres. As well as examining trends and texts, Z. explains such issues as the relationship between Latin and the vernacular and between written and oral.

2. EPIC

P. Bennett, 'Le refus d'aide, déni de justice', *Actes* (Barcelona), 53–64, studies the motif of the king who refuses to come to the aid of a vassal, beginning with *Aliscans* (which B. suggests in this case is closer to the common original than G_2). The versions of *Aliscans* and G_2 are compared. B. turns his attention to *Garin le Loherin*, then the *Enfances Vivien*. B. questions whether the motif in the *E.V.* is really a reflection of the attitude of the great feudatories but sets it in a quite different political context, that of the antagonism between Philippe Auguste and John of England. G. J. Brault, 'The religious content of the *chansons de geste*: some recent studies', *Grigsby Vol.*, 175–86, reviews recent findings on the religious matter in *chansons de geste*. J. Flori, '"Pur eshalcier sainte crestienté."' Croisade, guerre sainte et guerre juste dans les anciennes chansons de geste françaises', *MA*, 97:171–88, examines the ethos of the *chansons de geste* in terms of what were the major characteristics of a crusade and whether these are found in the *chansons de geste*, showing that generally they are not. Religious motives are, however, clearly important in the *chansons*. F. shows the crusading elements present to be the struggle against the Saracens and the indulgences. F. looks at the integration of the values of a Holy War with an aristocratic ideal, serving God through the service of a monarch. A useful study applying the work of medieval crusade historians to the lit. E. A. Heinemann, 'Rythmes sémantiques de la chanson de geste: types grammaticaux du vers et pulsions à la césure', *Romania*, 109, 1988 [1991]:145–82, is to a large extent a synthesis of the work of Rychner and Zumthor, a recognition of the metrical and grammatical use of rhythm in *chansons de geste*. Rychner's classifications of line structure and caesura are *retouché*. A detailed classification of lines or line-types by grammar is given. E. A. Heinemann, 'On the metric artistry of the *chanson de geste*', *Olifant*, 16:5–60, studies the art of repetition, looking at what H. calls 'disjunctive echoes', i.e. the use of formulae within a text, 'external echoes', i.e. formulae referring to outside the text, found in a number of *chansons*, 'consecutive echoes', in consecutive verses, and at the metric repetitions of verse and laisse. Four components of measure are also discerned: internal cohesion, length, position, and thrust. The analysis builds on, but does not much refer to, Rychner and nuances our understanding of the role of repetition and rhythm or metre in the *chanson de geste*. The analysis uses a number of *chansons de geste* but concentrates on the *Charroi de Nîmes*. M. Heintze, *König, Held und Sippe: Untersuchungen zur Chanson de geste des 13. und 14. Jahrhunderts und ihrer Zyklenbildung* (Studia Romanica, 76), Heidelberg, Winter, 724 pp., is a comprehensive study of the development of the *chanson de geste* in four parts: I, on the career of the hero, birth, childhood, and youth; II, on the king and vassal; III, on family structures, 'lignage'; IV, on the formation of cycles. The texts used for the study are all the published *chansons de geste* but H. sees the work of Bertrand de Bar-sur-Aube as crucial to the development of the genre so this is given particular emphasis. Certain other texts, such as *Jehan de Lanson* and *Hervis de Metz*, are also given more detailed analysis. One of the most interesting aspects of the study is the examination of the role of the king(s) through the period. Overall H. sets out to show the continuity of the genre through its development.

LA CHANSON DE ROLAND.   R.-J. Bery, 'Les deux scènes du cor dans la *Chanson de Roland*', *RoN*, 30, 1989–1990:115–24, is a sensible reappraisal of the critical interpretations of these scenes. B. concentrates on what Roland actually says, on what is written in the text, in accordance with what we know about epic narrative technique which is dramatic and externalizing rather than analytical and implicit. *The Song of Roland*, trans. Glyn Burgess, 1990, Harmondsworth, Penguin, 219 pp., has large sections of the Old French in an appendix, following the format of the Penguin translation of the *Lais* of Marie de France (1986), an alternative to the parallel text format. A glossary of unusual terms, e.g. feudal terms or items of armour, is appended. The wide-ranging introduction, clearly aimed at the general reader, incl. many of the major issues surrounding the *Roland*: origins of epic, nature of the discourse and structure of the text, integrality of the Baligant episode etc. A. Clej, 'Le miroir du roi: une réflexion sur la *Chanson de Roland*', *RPh*, 44, 1990:36–53, analyses *laisse* 155 (Bédier edn) as a springboard for a new discussion of the origins of the poem, looking in particular at the relationship between Charlemagne and Roland. P. Haidu, 'Funerary rituals in the *Chanson de Roland*', *Grigsby Vol.*, 187–202, analyses in some detail the lament for the dead, the revenge upon the retreating saracens, the discovery, collection, evisceration and burial of the heroes' bodies, bringing out the implications of this analysis for the question of the integrality of the Baligant episode. H. then studies the Aude episode, giving it the importance and value it deserves, as this episode has often been rather summarily dismissed. Aude's reaction to Roland's death is seen in the light of the value systems of the Middle Ages. W. W. Kibler, 'The prologue to the Lyon MS of the *Chanson de Roland*', *ib.*, 217–28, studies the twelve lines (ten of them from the beginning of Chrétien's *Yvain*) which precede the *Roland* in this MS, considered in conjunction with the other modifications of the text, and with similar apparently unrelated opening lines in other MSS of different texts. K. argues that these lines in *LY* are integral to the writer's conception of the text. E. J. Michel, *Ganelon, Treason and the 'Chanson de Roland'*, Penn State Press, 1989, 184 pp., is an important and detailed analysis of the trial and punishment of Ganelon. M. is not the first to set Ganelon's trial in the context of medieval law, but his examination of what can be established about medieval law and the implications of this for our interpretations of the *Roland* is the most thorough to date. Many medieval documents and legal treatises are used and a number of issues examined, incl. Charlemagne's role and Ganelon's defence. The important variants of the Chateauroux MS are taken into consideration. Finally the dating implications of his perceptions are discussed. J. Reed, 'The "bref" in the *Chanson de Roland*', *FSB*, 39:3–7, is a brief but important note on the problems of the *bref*: when could it have been written? what were its contents? R. argues that Charlemagne wrote it and that Marsile honestly divulges its contents. The question of the order of the *laisses* and the reliability of the Oxford text is brought up. R.'s suggestion that Ganelon knew the contents and that their purpose was partly to protect Ganelon in demanding the *algalife* as hostage is one that could alter our perception of Charlemagne and of the value of Ganelon to the Franks.

OTHER EPICS. W. Calin, 'Women and their sexuality in *Ami et Amile*: an occasion to deconstruct', *Olifant* 16:77–89, is a response to S. Kay's feminist analysis of the poem (*FS*, 44, 1990:129–42). C. insists his conclusions must be taken alongside K.'s. He argues that Amile and Belissant are not punished for defying patriarchal feudal order and sees this part of the poem as a wish-fulfilment fantasy. C. goes on to look again at Lubias, almost sympathetically, suggesting elements of reality and a level of communication in the marriage between Ami and Lubias. C. sees the conflict as less male/female and more clerical/lay. It is not easy to reconcile C.'s ideas with those of K., but perhaps, as C. himself states, we need to hold both interpretations in mind. S. Gregory, 'Pour un commentaire d'un passage obscur du *Charroi de Nîmes*', *Romania*, 109, 1988 [1991]:381–83, concerning ll. 908–17 (McMillan edn) is a note on the puns and humour of the passage. W. L. Hendrickson, '*Garin de Monglane* and *La Chanson de la croisade albigeoise*: a comparative Old French–Occitan study', *Grigsby Vol.*, 203–17, suggests parallels between Garin de Monglane and Simon de Montfort. A. Labbé, 'Corps et cœur dans *Girart de Roussillon*', *Le 'Cuer'*, 161–86, through a detailed lexical analysis shows a unity underlying the diversity of this poem. K. V. Sinclair, 'Un fragment inédit de la chanson de geste d'*Auberi le Bourguignon*', *AJFS*, 26, 1989:115–24, edits a short fragment of some 120 lines with a brief introduction. I. Weill, 'Les syntagmes du cœur dans la geste des Lorrains', *Le 'Cuer'*, 461–70, examines the function of 'cuer' in *Garin le Loherin*, *Gerbert de Mez*, and *Anseys de Mes*, its meaning, position in the line, position at the rhyme, its grammatical function.

3. ROMANCE

GENERAL AND GENERAL ARTHURIAN. R. H. Bloch, 'The Arthurian fabliau and the poetics of virginity', *Grigsby Vol.*, 231–50, examines the feminine chastity testing motif in the *First Continuation of Perceval*, the *Livre de Caradoc*, the *Vengeance Raguidel*, the *Prose Tristan*, and the ordeal of the mantel and horn in 'Du mantel mautaillie', and the 'Lai du cor'. Attitudes to women are studied in the context of Christian writings and the Bible. M. Combarieau du Gres, '"Un cœur gros comme ça":

(le cœur dans le Lancelot-Graal)', *Le 'Cuer'*, 77–105, examines the divers meanings of 'cuer' in the Grail cycle, first as a vital organ, damage to which can cause death or loss of consciousness. This may be caused by strong emotion as well as injury, thus linking the heart as seat of the emotions to the heart as organ. C. goes on to analyse the complex relationship between 'heart' and 'body'. The heart is also seen as the seat of moral life. C. shows the diversity and degree of unity between the texts. J. M. Dornbush, *Pygmalion's Figure: Reading Old French Romance*, Lexington, KY, French Forum, 1990, 153 pp., is an excellent study exploring issues of interpretation of Old French Romance in the 12th and 13th cs, largely through studies of Thomas's *Tristan*, Jean de Meun's *Roman de la Rose*, and the *Prose Lancelot*, concentrating on passages on image-making. D. calls us back to medieval literary concepts with an emphasis on rhetoric and the rhetorical training of the Middle Ages. Quotations from Latin and Old French are translated. J. J. Duggan, 'Oral performance of romance in Medieval France', *Grigsby Vol.*, 51–61, after reminding us of the textual evidence for romances being read aloud, sets out other evidence of courtly material being part of jongleurs' performances. R. A. Dwyer, 'Scriveners' tales: scribal versions of the French prose romances', Lagorio and Day, *Arthur*, 1, 99–109, surveys Palamedes, the Compilation of Rusticiano da Pisa, the *Prophecies de Merlin*, the Compilation of Michel Gonnot, *Le Chevalier du Papegau*. E. Kennedy, 'Failure in Arthurian romance', *MAe*, 60: 16–32, examines how failure is presented, as the inability of a character or with emphasis on the striving. K. shows how the failure of one knight may enhance the success of another. The place of failure in the romance pattern is demonstrated. The Grail poems are studied in detail, beginning with Chrétien, particularly in terms of the readers' expectations and whether they are fulfilled. C. Moorman, 'Literature of defeat and conquest: the Arthurian revival of the twelfth century', Lagorio and Day, *Arthur*, 1, 22–43, asks why there is an outburst of Arthurian literature in the period 1050–1180, looking at certain Celtic texts, Geoffrey of Monmouth, and Chrétien. M. suggests that all of these are different reactions to the Norman invasion of England. L. Morin, 'La naissance du roman médiéval', *DFS*, 16, 1989: 3–14, sets the beginnings of romance in the context of the 12th c. which M. sees as a period full of change and of new things, while the society of the time sought continuity and permanence. The romance is presented as lit. impinging on reality attempting to reconcile the new with the old. M. Plouzeau, 'Si n'aies pas le cuer parfont! lexique et syntaxe', *Le 'Cuer'*, 273–96, examines parfont/par font in *Raguidel* P.2522 in the context of similar expressions in a number of other texts from the end of the 12th to the end of the 13th c. E. H. Ruck, *An Index of Themes and Motifs in*

12th-Century French Arthurian Poetry, Woodbridge, Boydell and Brewer, 192 pp., covers Arthurian material up to and including the beginning of the 13th c. R. limits herself to Arthurian material, and therefore in Wace to the Arthurian sections and in Marie de France to the Arthurian *Lais* (although reference to non-Arthurian lais and parts of Wace can be found in the notes). The *Index* is easy to use and most comprehensive, covering not only recognized literary motifs and *topoi* such as the Faithless Wife or the Rash Boon, but a wider range of motifs from heraldry to the spoils of tournaments, from Fate to religious motifs, and from the hero's accomplishments to the use of *tu*. D. Régnier-Bohler (ed.), *La Légende arthurienne: le Graal et la Table Ronde*, Laffont, 1989, lix + 1206 pp., contains in modern French trans. Chrétien's *Perceval*, *Perlesvaus*, *Robert de Boron*, *Merlin*, *Hunbaut*, *Glilois*, *Blandin de Cornouille*, *Les Merveilles de Rigomer*, *Le Chevalier de Papegau*, and others. P. Zumthor, 'De Perceval à Don Quichotte', *Poétique*, 89:259–69, examines the concept of the knight errant in the Middle Ages and how that eventually led to Don Quixote. Z. starts with the examples of Calogrenant and Perceval which he links to the problem of space in the 12th c. Wm. Calin, '*Amadas et Ydoine*: the problematic world of an idyllic romance', *Grigsby Vol.*, 39–50, studies the use of a number of love conventions, pushed to their limits within the text. C. looks at the interplay of illusion and reality in the text. The author's use of the material of *Tristan* and *Cligès* is seen through this analysis. H.-E. Keller, 'De l'amour dans le *Roman de Brut*', *ib.*, 63–82, studies the presentation of sexuality, eroticism, and love in Wace's *Brut*, showing that W. gives different picture of 'real' love and relegates 'fin' amor' to the fictitious world of Arthur. D. Kelly, 'Description and narrative in romance: the contextual co-ordinates of *Meraugis de Portllesguez* and the *Bel Inconnu*', *ib.*, 83–94, examines the place of description in medieval narrative through a study of these two texts. S. Aronstein, 'Prize or pawn: homosocial order, marriage and the redefinition of women in the *Gawain Continuation*', *RR*, 82:115–26, studies the text within the context of anthropological and feminist criticism. The question of how and why the romance woman is redefined in the *Continuation* is asked and convincingly answered. G. Torrini-Roblin, 'Oral or written model? Description, length and unity in the *First Continuation*, *Grigsby Vol.*, 145–62, examines the different redactions of the *First Continuation*. F. Dubost, 'Procédures d'initialité dans la littérature du Graal', *Actes* (Montpellier), 16–33, first classifies the *exordia*; considerable attention is paid to the *Estoire del Saint Graal*; D. suggests that all forms reveal the ambiguous nature of the relationship between the writer and text: '*écrivain ou écrivant*'; the continuations are a special case given separate treatment; a study of one particular *topos* of the opening phase then follows: the arrival of a character. A. L. Furtado, 'Geoffrey of Monmouth: a source of the Grail stories', *Quondam et Futurus*, 1:1–14, looks at the relationship between Chrétien, *Peredur* in the *Mabinogion*, and Geoffrey of Monmouth. This link is seen as a key to understanding some of the problems in Chrétien's text, such as the role of Gawain or the advice of Gornemant. N. J. Lacy, 'The design of the *Didot-Perceval*', *Grigsby Vol.*, 95–106, is a re-appraisal of the structure of this text. While acknowledging its limitations, L. makes out a good case for the revaluation of the *Didot-Perceval*. The preface to *La Mort le Roi Arthur*, trans. Monique Santucci, Champion, 255 pp., a trans. of Frappier's edn, places the *Mort* in its literary context and the narrative is analysed in some detail. A. Henry, 'Enchises, un mot-fantome', *Romania*, 109, 1988 [1991]:379–81, examines the meaning of *enchises* in the Prose *Lancelot*. R. Hyatte, 'Recoding ideal male friendship as *fine amor* in the prose Lancelot', *Neophilologus*, 75:505–18, studies the relationship between Galehout and Lancelot. H. takes as a model Ciceronian perfect friendship, the *fine amor* of Tristan and Iseut in Thomas, and that of Lancelot and Guinevere in the prose *Lancelot*. J. F. Plummer, 'The quest for significance in *La Queste del Saint Graal* and Malory's *Tale of the Sankgreal*', *Grigsby Vol.*, 107–19, examines how Malory has adapted the *Queste* in semiotic terms. P. suggests that understanding (through the sign, the glass, the commentary) is more important in the *Queste* than in Malory. M. Szkilnik, *L'Archipel du Graal: étude de l'Estoire del Saint Graal*, Geneva, Droz, presents a very positive view of the text, suggesting that through the images of the sea-voyage the text is tightly knit. The images and stages of the sea-journey in the text are shown to be also images of the composition of the text. Analysis of themes, images and concepts is firmly within the context of the use of similar themes in other medieval texts. C.-A. van Coolput, 'La Poupee d'Evalac ou la conversion tardive du roi Mordrain', *Grigsby Vol.*, 163–72, examines the *Estoire*, particularly in the light of the *Quete*.

CHRÉTIEN DE TROYES.   B. Aguirano, 'Le cœur dans Chrétien', *Le 'Cuer'*, 10–25, looks first at 'cœur' and 'corage' in the secondary characters, acknowledging the difficulty in defining these, then analyses the 'cœur' of the hero and his lady. J. T. Grimbert, 'Misrepresentation and misconception in Chrétien de Troyes; non-verbal and verbal semiotics in *Erec en Enide* and *Perceval*', Wasserman, *Sign*, 50–79, extends G.'s semiotic study of *Yvain* to *Erec et Enide* and *Perceval*, showing the treatment of the problem of the discrepancy between reality and the signs used to represent it. G. looks first at non-verbal signs in *Perceval* then turns to verbal signs, which can clear up ambiguous non-verbal signs but can also be themselves misunderstood or misleading. The use of language and silence in the two texts is also crucial and is studied in some detail. S. Kay, 'Commemoration, memory and the role of the past in Chretien de Troyes: retrospection and meaning in *Erec et Enide*, *Yvain* and *Perceval*', *RMS*, 17:31–50, defines commemoration as the retelling of events by the characters within the text. Past time is a theme, one aspect of whose treatment is commemorative discourse in which the hero's exploits are reviewed. The romances are then studied in turn. The conclusion shows how commemoration, memory, and forgetfulness and the role of the past change through these three texts. Past time remains important but K. sees increasing pessimism about our ease of access, the erasability of past error and the value of retrospection as a key to understanding. H. R. Runte, 'Initial readers of Chrétien de Troyes', *Grigsby Vol.*, 121–32, examines indices in the MSS of how Chrétien's texts were read. These indices may be subdivisions of the text by initials or the use of miniatures, providing 'visual structuring' of the text. N. Bradley-Croney, 'The "recreantise" episode in Chrétien's *Erec et Enide*', Chickering, *Chivalry*, 449–71, sets out first the understanding of chivalry in the *Chanson de Roland*, then the shifts in emphasis by *c.* 1170. From this context B. turns to a definition of *recreantise*. J. A. Nightingale, 'Chrétien de Troyes and the mythographical tradition: the couple's journey in *Erec et Enide* and Martianus' *De Nuptis*', Lagorio and Day, *Arthur*, I, 56–79, is an intertextual analysis of Chrétien and his intentions in *Erec et Enide* with particular reference to the meaning of *conjointure* and *coniunctura* as used by Alain de Lille, who makes considerable use of Martianus in *De Plancta Naturae*. G. Paoli, 'La relation œil–cœur: recherches sur la mystique amoureuse de Chrétien de Troyes dans *Cligès*', Le *'Cuer'*, 233–44, examines the *œil–cœur* relationship in the light of concepts found in the Old Testament, in the New Testament, and in Islam, which are presented as possible influences on Chrétien, although P. acknowledges that the apparent knowledge of Islam seen in *Cligès* may be no more than a coincidence of images. Z. P. Zaddy, 'Les castors ichthyophages de Chrétien de Troyes', *MA*, 97:41–46, looks at the meaning of *bievre* in *Cligès*, 3850, with possible interpretations supported by medieval and 16th-c. texts. H. Arden, 'Chrétien de Troyes's *Lancelot* and the structure of twelfth-century French romance', Lagorio and Day, *Arthur*, I, 80–98, opens with a review of some of the structural analyses of Chrétien, then concentrates on the problems of structure in the *Lancelot*. Chrétien's other romances are also used as 'clues' to try to unravel this most complex romance. L. D. Wolfgang, 'Chrétien's Lancelot: love and philology', *RMS*, 17:3–18, is to a degree a defence of Lancelot but also raises important methodological questions. The MS problems are set out and six passages then examined in some detail. B. N. Sargent-Baur, '"Avis li fu": vision and cognition in the

Conte du Graal', Grigsby *Vol.*, 133–44, examines the techniques of characterization in Chrétien's *Conte du Graal*. Y. G. Lepage, 'Encore les trois cents pucelles (Chrétien de Troyes, *Yvain* v. 5298–5324)', *CCM*, 133:159–66, is a reassessment (with an examination of previous scholarship) revolving round the meaning of *gaegnier*. R. Rosenstein, '"Celi que del cuer voit": le don du cœur, d'*Yvain* à la chanson de Croisade', *Le 'Cuer'*, 363–74, shows the motif to be something of a *topos* before Chrétien's use of it in *Yvain*. R. widens the whole idea of the source for Chrétien. R. examines in detail its meaning in the Chanson de Croisade.

TRISTAN. C. Chocheyras, 'Sur les sources livresques possibles de quelques motifs tristaniens', *Pris MA*, 7:27–42, looks at sources for (i) the name and character of Andret, (ii) St Andrew and his legend, (iii) Tristan and Theseus, from which C. draws general conclusions on the development of the legend. R. Colliot, 'Messages d'amour et de mort dans la legende de Tristan: anneaux et lais', *ib.*, 43–56 looks at the object, in this case in particular the ring as signifier, as message, particularly in the verse texts, then at the use in the *Prose Tristan* of poems as a means of communication. The two symbols, carriers of death, are brought together at the end of the *Prose Tristan*. R. Hyatt, 'Arthur as Marc's and Tristan's double in the French *Tristan* fragments by Béroul and Thomas', Lagorio and Day, *Arthur*, I, 110–26, looks at the 'Arthurianization' of the Tristan legend. H. suggests that in Béroul Arthur is Mark's counterpart and in Thomas he is Tristan's. The parallels are analysed in some detail. H. sees B.'s Mark as very unsympathetic. Arthur is his antithesis. K. Busby, 'Le Tristan de Béroul en tant qu'intertexte', *Grigsby Vol.*, 19–38, relates the adulterous love to the lyric, looking at e.g. B.'s vocabulary. The three barons and other aspects are shown to have echoes of epic, but elements of parody of epic are also discerned and the use of epic techniques discussed. Fabliau elements in B. are then examined. Busby finally looks at the all-important romance nature of the poem. The study raises the whole question of genre and intertextuality with regard to medieval texts. A. Saly, 'Images récurrentes dans le *Tristan* de Béroul', *Pris MA*, 7:107–18, deals with the coherence of the text and in this context studies the motifs and images within a number of episodes. The study does not claim to be comprehensive but rather to call attention to Beroul's method of composition. M. R. Blakeslee, 'Misogynie, "fin' amur" et ambiguïté dans le *Tristan* de Thomas', *ib.*, 1–16, questions the traditional, sometimes simplistic, view of Thomas as courtly and seeks to show an essential ambivalence in the text in the attitude to love. F. Lecoy, 'Sur l'étendue probable du *Tristan* de Thomas', *Romania*, 109, 1988 [1991]:378–79, is a recalculation of the possible length of Thomas's *Tristan* on the basis of the lacuna in the

Sneyd fragment; L. concludes that it was *c.* 12,082 lines. P. M. Thomas, 'Nuances of chastity: the *Tristan* of Thomas', *FSB*, 41 : 1–3, looks at the question of mental and physical chastity with regard to the four main characters, Ysolt of the White Hands, Tristan, Ysolt the Fair and, Mark, *vis-à-vis* each other. M.-L. Chenerie, 'Le sénéchal Keu dans le *Tristan en prose*', *Pris MA*, 7 : 17–26, analyses the role and character of Kay in the prose *Tristan*, showing what this character owes to the prose *Lancelot* and how different he is from the depiction of Kay in other Tristan texts. Finally C. shows his importance thematically particularly through his relationship with Kahedrin. F. Dubost, 'Trois géants, trois époques, un "roman": le géant poseur d'énigmes, le géant de Cornouailles at Taulas de la Montagne dans le *Tristan en prose*', *ib.*, 57–72, suggests that the 'giant' of the *Prose Tristan* is so only in name. This thesis is supported by a study of each of the giants in turn. D. concludes that the presentation of the giants represents three periods, three types of writing. The study is firmly set in the context of the treatment of the *merveilleux* in general and in the historical and, crucially, religious context. P. Walter, 'Un archétype mythologique du *Tristan en prose*: le géant', *ib.*, 119–31 works from the basis of the intertextuality of this work. The figure of the giant is chosen as an important one in Tristan lit. and in human mythology. The prehistory of Arthurian tradition is also examined and the giant seen as the possible intermediary in the 'Arthurianization' of the Tristan legend.

LAIS. Marie de France, *Les Fables*, ed. Charles Bruchner, Louvain, Peeters, 402 pp., is an edn with parallel modern French trans. The introduction gives the *Fables* the treatment normally given to the *Lais*, looking at sources, literary merit, MS tradition, etc. A useful glossary and index complete the edn. M. T. Bruckner, 'Of men and beasts in *Bisclavret*', *RR*, 82 : 251–69, examines Marie's *lai* in terms of the duality of human nature (man/beast) beginning from the problematic opening and closing lines. The other major dualities discussed are the marvellous/nature and male/female. Parallels with Adam and Eve, briefly noted, are interesting. The importance of the interrelationships of characters in the humanity of an individual is stressed. Bisclavret may unite the man and beast but in the conclusion the male/female couple is split. M. T. Bruckner, 'Strategies of naming in Marie de France's *Lais*: at the crossroads of gender and genre', *Neophilologus*, 75 : 31–40, examines patterns of naming and not naming of characters, the names of the *lais* and her naming of herself. J.-C. Bibolet, '"Guillaume, as-tu du cuer?" ou "cuer" dans *Le vair palefroi*', *Le 'Cuer'*, 43–53, treats the text as a *lai* and 'histoire d'amour', rather than a *fabliau*. B. examines in detail the occurrences of 'cuer' and 'corage' in the text. Lenora D. Wolfgang,

Le Lai de l'Oiselet: An Old French Poem of the Thirteenth Century,
(transactions of the American Philosophical Society, 80, part 5,
1990), Philadelphia, American Pilosophy Society, uses MS *B* as a
base MS with a list of rejected readings. The texts of the other MSS
are given in full in diplomatic and synoptic texts. W. gives a very
detailed textual study and examines e.g. sources and analogues,
making interesting generic and stylistic observations.

OTHER COURTLY LITERATURE.   *The Romances of Alexander*, ed. D. M.
Kratz, NY, Garland, 1990, 175 pp., translates the Latin texts *Iter ad
Paradisum* and *Epistula Alexandri ad Aristotelem* which are so important
to an understanding of the development of the Alexander legend in
western Europe in the Middle Ages. L. C. Brook, 'The continuators
monologue: Godefroy de Lagny and Jean de Meun', *FS*, 45:1–16,
compares Godefroy's use of monologue to Chrétien's. Jean de Meun's
approach as a continuator is different to that of G., and B. shows that
while he links his monologue to the text of his predecessor he actually
subverts it. H. Kluppelholz, 'The continuation within the model:
Godefroi de Lagny's "solution" to Chrétien de Troyes' *Chevalier de la
Charrette*', *Neophilologus*, 75:342–44, while unfortunately incomplete
due to a printing error, looks at the way Godefroy alters what appears
to have been Chrétien's intention while profiting from Chrétien's
reputation. *Guillaume le Clerc, Fergus of Galloway: Knight of King Arthur*,
trans. D. D. R. Owen, London, Wiedenfeld and Nicolson (Every-
man), is a trans. with introduction and notes of this little known
Arthurian text of the late 12th and early 13th c. The introduction is
helpful, placing Guillaume in the context of the lit. of the period and
outlining his use of Chrétien. An appendix offers a possible identification of the author and suggests the literary value of the text has been
underrated. L. de Looze, 'The gender of fiction: womanly poetics in
Jean Renart's *Guillaume de Dole*', *FR*, 64:596–606, links the real/
fictional dichotomy of the work with gender, showing that in
Guillaume de Dole, exceptionally, it is the men who seek or inhabit the
fictional world and women the real world. The men reduce the
women to the narrative level. Narrative and reality are expressed in
the verbs *oir*, *dire*, and *veoir*. The difference between the sign and what
it signifies is brought out and Lienor's disguise seen as a synthesis of
masculine and feminine. H. Braet, '*Le Roman de la Rose*: espace du
regard', *SFr*, 103:1–12, studies the iconography of the *Roman de la
Rose*, its representation in MSS. F. Vieillard, 'Sain Cicaut', *Romania*,
109, 1988 [1991]:383–92, finds other references to this saint, mentioned in the *Roman des Sept Sages de Rome*, and suggests his possible
identity as Sigibaldus, Bishop of Metz. P. Gallais and J. Thomas,
'L'arbre et la forêt dans l'*Énéide* et l'*Énéas*: de la psyché antique à la
psyché mediévale. III. Condensation et mutation des symboles: l'*Énéas*

ou l'unité édifiée', *Pris MA*; 6, 1990:209–36, is a comparative analysis of the 12th-c. text and its source, going beyond looking at the symbolism of trees and attitude to nature. From a description of the tomb of Camille G. and T. go on to give a brief survey of impossible structures in medieval French lit. using a wide range of texts. A. Paupert, 'L'arbre, l'amour et la mort: à propos de *Floire et Blancheflor* et *Piramus et Thisbe*', *ib.*, 75–88, concentrates on four passages in *F. et B.*, looking in the symbolism of the tree for the 'senefiance' of the narrative. P. Eley, 'The myth of Trojan descent and perceptions of national identity: the case of *Énéas* and the *Roman de Troie*', *NMS*, 35:27–40, examines such factors as are linked to national groupings: language, territory, kinship, social and political institutions, and culture, with the aim of determining whether the two texts show a common sense of 'Trojanness'. The sources of the texts (Dares Phrygius and Virgil) are taken into account. The degree of consensus between the texts is shown to be remarkable, although there are differences. H. B. Teunis, *'Benoit of St Maure and William the Conqueror's "amor"'*, *Proceedings of the Battle Conference*, 1989, ed. M. Chibnall, Woodbridge, Boydell and Brewer, 1990, 199–209. F. Vieilliard, 'Le Roman de Troie en prose dans la version du MS Rouen, Bibl. mun. o.33, "Membra Disjecta", d'un MS plus ancien?', *Romania*, 109, 1988 [1991]:502–39, describes the MS in detail and summarizes its content extensively.

4. RELIGIOUS LITERATURE

B. B. Burnam, 'An unedited Anglo-Norman prologue to the *Passion des Jongleurs* and its relation to the *Passio Christi* of Clermont Ferrand', *MAe*, 60:197–206, is an edn with introduction and linguistic analysis of this short prologue, dated around the first half of the 13th c. Parallel lines from the 10th-c. *Passio Christi*, close links with which are shown, are printed alongside. B. Cazelles, *The Lady as Saint: A Collection of French Hagiographic Romances of the Thirteenth Century*, Pennsylvania U.P., 334 pp. is a fascinating anthology of translations of thirteen hagiographies, although unfortunately the original Old French is not given and many of the edns of these texts are old and not widely available. The study which forms the first part of the vol. examines ideals of femininity and sanctity in the texts. G. Gros, 'La semblance de la verrine, description et interprétation d'une image mariale', *MA*, 97:217–57, examines this symbol in secular (e.g. Chrétien de Troyes and Wace) and religious texts in Old French and Latin, throughout the medieval period. H. E. Keller and W. Meiden, 'Le Roman de Saint Paul', *ib.*, 189–216 is an edition with a short introduction of this 13th-c. verse account of the dream of St Paul. A. Lupin, '"Arte callidissima et occulta": *La Séquence de Sainte Eulalie* en ancien français', *Romania*, 109, 1988 [1991]:447–71, gives first the linguistic context of this text followed by a reinterpretation of its literary aspect. The sources of the *Séquence* are brought into consideration. L. presents a very positive reassessment of the text. G. Milin, 'La *Vita Ronani* et les contes de loup-garou aux XIIe et XIIIe siècles', *MA*, 97:259–73, beginning with a study of the 'loup-garou' episode in the Latin Life goes on to consider other treatments of the theme. M. A. Polo de Beaudieu, 'La légende du cœur inscrit dans la littérature religieuse et didactique', *Le 'Cuer'*, 297–312, examines the *topos* of the heart inscribed with the name of Christ, concentrating on St Ignatius, the first to whom the miracle is ascribed. P. looks at the development of the *topos*, variants and other saints. J. R. Smeets (ed.), *La Chevalerie de Judas Macchabée de Gautier de Belleperche (et de Pieros du Ries)*, Assen, van Gorcum, 2 vols, 413 + 557 pp. Vol. I is the introduction and critical apparatus, including the variants. The authors are discussed as well as date, sources, MSS, etc. The text (vol. II) of this 13th-c. poem is based on MS *B* with a minimum of corrections. J. Wogan-Browne, 'Saints' lives and the female reader', *FMLS*, 27:314–32, looks at 12th- and 13th-c. vernacular (Anglo-Norman and Middle English) texts asking about the use of these texts. W. examines a historic case, 12th-c. Christina, of whom we have a Latin 'Life' written within a few years of her death. W. suggests that violence as a response to a girl's choice of virginity was at least credible. The place of hagiographic convention is acknowledged. The text is linked to the social context. W. looks also at the use of hagiography in the composition of *Cligès*.

5.   OTHER GENRES

LYRIC.   M. Abramowicz, 'Le lieu commun et l'imaginaire: exordes des pastourelles et des chansons de toile', *Romania*, 109, 1988 [1991]:472–501, despite the difficulties in treating these genres together, does so successfully. The formulae of the *exordia* are classified into two groups. The structures in the pastourelles are examined first, then the *chansons de toile*. The *exordium* is the feature which both subgenres contain. Conclusions are drawn on both groups together. Deborah Hubbard Nelson (ed.); *The Songs Attributed to Andrieu Contredit D'Arras, with a Translation into English and the Extant Melodies*, Amsterdam, Rodopi, 207 pp.; the lyrics are trans. and ed. by D. H. N. and the melodies are edited by Hendrick van der Werf. This is an exceptionally comprehensive edn and trans. with the music. Each lyric is preceded by a brief introduction giving details of the MSS, edns, structure, and MS variations. A literary introduction by D. H. N. covers the literary milieu of Arras, the poet, the MS tradition, language and the form of the songs. The unusual feature of a musical introduction by H. van der W. gives a valuable insight into the musical background, tradition, rhythm, rhyme, and metre and MSS with a detailed discussion of three songs.

DRAMA. A. E. Knight, 'France', Simon, *Theatre*, 151–68, begins with a brief glance at the paucity of much earlier criticism then gives a detailed examination of more recent work. K. divides the drama into two periods: 11th – end 13th c., 13th – mid-16th c., but first reviews some of the recent studies covering medieval theatre generally. An optimistic view of where things are going in drama studies is given. D. Maddox, 'Rewriting recognition in early medieval veridictory drama', *Grigsby Vol.*, 277–98, studies a range of medieval texts in the light of the Aristotelian concept of recognition. M. first justifies the use of a concept which was not itself well known in the Middle Ages, then examines the texts, beginning with Latin liturgical plays and including Jean Bodel's *Jeu de saint Nicolas* and the *Jeu de la Feuillée*, both of which are examined at length.

HISTORY AND CHRONICLE. J. R. E. Bliese, 'The courage of the Normans: a comparative study of battle rhetoric', *NMS*, 35:1–26, gives an analysis of battle speeches in the chronicles in terms of what they tell us about the self-image of the Normans. The chronicles dating *c.* 1000 — *c.* 1250 are mostly in Latin but B. includes Wace who is discussed in some detail. S. Lloyd, 'William Longuespee II: the making of an English crusading hero', *NMS*, 35:41–69, is the first part of a longer study. L. examines how a historical defeat is turned into a moral victory (something which is almost a *topos* of medieval literature). L. is concerned more with the creation of a myth about Longuespee than establishing historical accuracy and to this end examines the chronicles, e.g. Matthew Paris and Joinville.

ROMAN DE RENARD. F. de la Breteque, 'La place de Noble dans l'imaginaire du *Roman de Renart*', *Pris MA*, 7:171–82, studies the different manifestations of Noble. The *branches* are looked at in three groups: I, 'Le roi lointain', *branches* II and VA; II, 'Le plaid et le siege', *branches* I, IA, IB; III, 'Le lion declinant', *branches* X and XI. Concluding that the character of Noble is not a coherent, unified one, B. still shows that either simultaneously or sequentially Noble can fulfil various functions. One is left with an appreciation of the richness of the texts. M. de Combarieu, '"Faire la morte vielle": la ruse de la mort feinte dans le *Roman de Renart*', *ib.*, 153–70, first surveys this ruse in the different *branches* , classified by purpose: why is the animal pretending to be dead? C. shows the motif to have its roots in the observation of the *Bestiaries* and brings out the dramatic and often comic elements of the motif. P. Gallais, 'Et si Chrétien était l'auteur de Lietart? L'argument de la versification', *ib.*, 7:229–55, readdresses the question of the authorship of *branche* IX, first questioning the major assumption which has generally led to Chrétien being dismissed as the author, i.e. the date, largely based on the identification of the 'conte Thibaut'. G. goes on to analyse in detail the quality and nature of the versification, throughout this analysis making comparisons with Chrétien's known works and, by way of control, with other courtly texts. He concludes that either Chrétien had at least a hand in the composition of this text or one of his friends or disciples was responsible for it. K. Gravdal, 'Law and literature in the French middle ages: rape law on trial in *Le Roman de Renart*', *RR*, 82:1–24, examines the complex interweaving of literary and legal models in the *Roman de Renart*, classified under four interrelations: subversion, literary mimesis — a critique of actual practices, faithful reproduction, undermining of literary or cultural discourse of courtly love. A detailed analysis of the relevant *branches* is set in the context of medieval law and the legal question of rape is presented as a vehicle for wider issues. G. Gros, 'Au plaisir des noms: le *Roman de Renart* branche x (éd. M. Roques): essai d'onomastique littéraire', *Pris MA*, 7:205–28, examines in turn the names in this *branche* giving most space to Lietart and Bruntamin, working from the premise that names in lit. are not chance but may tell us much about the intentions of the writer. The name itself is shown as a possible vehicle of satire. Anthony Lodge and Kenneth Varty, *The Earliest Branches of the 'Roman de Renart'*, New Alyth, Lochee Publications, 1989, is an edition of *branches* ii and va. The literary context and critical background of these *Branches* are clearly explained. The writers disagree with the commonly held belief that the texts were written by one man. A detailed analysis of the text is given. M. Pastoureau, 'Entre chien et loup: introduction à l'étude du goupil', *Pris MA*, 7:133–46, the first study in a fascicule given over to the study of 'les Romans de Renart', serves as an introduction to the others, looking first at where the fox fits into the animal kingdom. The naturalists' view is presented within a historical perspective. The etymological links between *Goupil*, *vulpes* and *lupus* are set out and attitudes and treatment of the fox examined. J. Subrenat, 'Renart en son château', *ib.*, 7:183–94, notes first that only Renart comes from a specific named place, the château de Maupertuis. S. looks at the residence of the other animals, Noble's palace, but the *lovere* of Ysengrin. The king lives in a totally 'human' environment, the wolf in a largely animal one. S. then studies the various descriptions of the château de Maupertuis as a well-fortified castle with all the trappings of a feudal seat, and as a *fosse* or *tesnere*, both descriptions coming from the oldest *branche* through the tradition. Renart, when vulnerable, is seen in his *fosse*, Renart invincible in his château. The man/beast dichotomy is seen united in the fox. S. draws from this study conclusions which are helpful for an understanding of the complexity of the way the anthromorphization occurs in the texts as a whole.

FABLIAUX.   L. S. Crist, 'Gastrographie et pornographie dans les fabliaux', *Grigsby Vol.*, 251–60, examines the link between eating and sex in the *fabliau*. E. Suomela-Harma, 'Le cœur, le corps et le cul: variationa lexicales dans les fabliaux', *Le 'Cuer'*, 393–408, is a detailed lexical analysis based on an examination of the use of 'cuer' and variants in all the published fabliaux. L. D. Wolfgang, '*Les Trois Savoirs* in Phillipps Manuscript 25970', *Grigsby Vol.*, 311–22, gives the lines of this fabliau not transcribed by P. Meyer (*Romania*, 37) from a MS hitherto believed to have been lost. W.'s main concern is with the parallels with the *Lai de l'oiselet*. A brief introduction gives examples of Anglo-Norman features in the text.

LATE MEDIEVAL LITERATURE

By KAREN PRATT, *University of London, Goldsmiths' College*

1. NARRATIVE GENRES

EPIC. K. Sinclair, 'Un fragment inédit de la chanson de geste d'*Auberi le Bourguignon*', *A JFS*, 26, 1989: 115–24, publishes a fragment found in Cardiff Central Library containing significant variants from the other extant MSS. I. Weill, '"Sin a un ris jeté", rire et énonciation dans *Auberi le Bourgoin*', Bouché, *Le Rire*, 357–67, concentrates on the narrator's references to laughter and on the episodes providing light relief in this tragic epic.

ROMANCE. Françoise Clier-Colombani, *La Fée Mélusine au moyen âge: images, mythes et symboles*, Le Léopard d'Or, 276 pp., discusses in this richly illustrated book the symbiotic relationship between text and image in MSS and early printed editions of the *Roman de Mélusine* and tries to identify those characteristics which distinguish M. iconographically from other sirens. A. Berthelot, 'Des fêtes arthuriennes classiques aux fêtes ritualisées du *Roman de Perceforest*', *Symposion* (Paderborn), 433–40, examines the role of *fêtes* in structuring the romance and in conveying its ideology and shows how this masculine system for imposing order is dependent upon the feminine *merveilleux*. J.-M. Fritz, 'Daguenet ou le bouffon amoureux', Poirion, *Styles*, 37–73, demonstrates how in *Guiron le Courtois* and the *Prophécies de Merlin* D. embodies in different ways the traits of the fool in Arthurian romance. An edition of the D. episode in the *Prose Tristan* is appended. N. Lacy, 'The margins of romance: art and artifice in *Joufroi de Poitiers*', *Symposium*, 44: 264–71, denies that the romance is a parody whose hero gradually disintegrates, claiming instead that J. adapts successfully as the work evolves from courtly romance through epic to fabliau, thus reflecting the narrator's shift from erotic idealism to cynical disillusionment. P. Allen, 'The ambiguity of Silence: gender, writing, and *Le Roman de Silence*', Wasserman, *Sign*, 98–112, discusses the romance's MS context, illuminations and use of language, which all contribute to its ambiguity as a *texte de jouissance*. Heldris de Cornüälle. *Le Roman de Silence*, trans. Regina Paski, NY, Garland, 1989, xlii + 182 pp., provides a fairly literal and timely translation of this fascinating romance. R. Colliot, 'Les états du *cuer* dans le *Cleomadès* d'Adenet le Roi', *Le 'Cuer'*, 55–76, argues that the heart provides the moral code for an aristocratic society with no religious beliefs. N. Durling, *'Rewriting gender: *Yde et Olive* and Ovidian myth', *RLA*, 1, 1989:256–62. R. Dubuis, 'Le mot *nouvelle* au moyen âge: de la nébuleuse au terme générique', Alluin, *Nouvelle*, 13–27, argues that, although the author of the *Cent nouvelles nouvelles* translates the generic term from the Italian, the word *nouvelle* in Old French already meant 'le récit d'une aventure'. M. Léonard, 'Les *dits* aux origines de la *nouvelle*', *ib.*, 29–42, analyses a group of 27 *dits* from the 13th to the 15th c. which were called 'nouveaux', suggesting that the more narrative forms of this didactic genre were the forerunners of the less moralistic *nouvelle*. F. Suard, '*Floridan et Elvide* aux XVème et XVIème siècles', *ib.*, 163–79, traces this tragic yet exemplary story of rape and death from the French translation by Nicolas de Clamanges of the Latin tale, through no. 98 of the *Cent nouvelles*, to two 16th-c. *nouvelles*, highlighting the original contribution made by each *remanieur*. R. Stuip, '*La Châtelaine de Vergy* du XIIème au XVIIIème siècles', *ib.*, 151–61, surveys the generic classification of this story in the Middle Ages. D. Quéruel, 'L'histoire de la *Fille du Comte de Ponthieu*: distorsions et avatars d'une nouvelle', *ib.*, 139–50, discusses the transformations of this story from 13th-c. *nouvelle* through 15th-c. historical romance to 20th-c. Japanese film. M. Baker, 'The image of the woman in tales 26 and 99 of the *Cent nouvelles nouvelles*', *MoyFr*, 24–25, 1990:242–50, employs the Jungian concepts of *animus* and *anima* to analyse the problem of self-individuation for the two very different heroines of these *nouvelles*. *The One Hundred New Tales*, trans. Judith B. Diner, NY, Garland, 1990, xl + 348 pp., is based on Sweetser's edition and contains a short introduction and select bibliography. A. Kelly, 'Jehan de Saintré and the Dame des Belles Cousines: problems of a medieval tale', *FrF*, 14, 1989:447–57, claims that the heroine's centrality to the work and the MS evidence point to the inappropriateness of the modern title. M. Santucci, '*Rire* et *ire* dans *Jean de Saintré*', Bouché, *Le Rire*, 299–307, investigates the meaning of *ire* in this work and shows that laughter can be either positive or negative, often a sign of complicity.

2. POETRY

François Villon: Bibliographie und Materialen (1498–1988), ed. Rudolf Sturm, 2 vols, Munich, Saur, 1990, 344 + 347 pp., is a lavish book with beautiful illustrations. Vol. I's introductory essays and the sectional headings of the bibliography are in French and German; vol. II contains studies in German on V. reception throughout the ages. W. Pöckl, *Formen produktiver Rezeption François Villons im deutschen Sprachraum* (SAG, 234), 1990, 416 pp., includes reception in France, England, US. Barbara N. Sargent-Baur, *Brothers of Dragons: 'Job dolens' and François Villon*, NY, Garland, 1990, xvi + 170 pp., examines V.'s debt to the Job tradition. *Villon: Œuvres*, ed. and trans. André Lanly, Champion, 315 pp., offers the *Lais*, *Testament*, and *Poésies diverses* in the revised Longnon–Foulet edition. R. Peckham, 'The current state of Villon studies', *FCS*, 18:187–200. Id, 'Oral textuality — textual orality: patterns of ambiguity in François Villon's *Testament*', *FCS*, 17, 1990:291–98, analyses those elements which draw attention to the work as written document and those which emphasize the dictation process and the text's dependence on orality for its transmission. J. Dufournet, 'Les jeux de l'autoréécriture dans le *Testament* de Villon', *ib.*, 81–92, explores the many levels of meaning in *huitain* CV and compares the *ballade de la Grosse Margot* with the *ballade pour prier Notre Dame*, showing how the former subverts the latter. G. Pinkernell, 'La *Ballade contre les ennemis de la France* de François Villon. Un remerciement poétique à Louis XI (octobre 1461)', *RZLG*, 14, 1990:11–24, attempts to situate the composition of this ballad within V.'s biography. R. Van Deyck, 'Exploitation syntaxique et pragmatique de la coordination par François Villon', *MoyFr*, 24–25, 1990:71–92. O. Dull, 'Tradition et renouveau dans la *Ballade pour prier Notre dame* de Villon', *RoQ*, 38:387–97, summarizes what we already know about V.'s original use of topoi and voice. D. Hue, 'Propos cordiaux: le cœur dans les poèmes dialogués', *Le 'Cuer'*, 121–43, investigates the significance of the heart when it is personified in poetic dialogues, notably V.'s *débat*. *Rutebeuf: Œuvres complètes*, ed. Michel Zink, vol. II, Garnier, 1990, 535 pp., offers texts based on a different MS from that used by Faral–Bastin, a translation and notes for various *dits*, the *Miracle de Théophile* and the *Miracle du Sacristain*, ordered chronologically rather than thematically. *Rutebeuf et les frères mendiants: poèmes satiriques*, ed. and trans. Jean Dufournet, Champion, 192 pp. Leonard Johnson, *Poets as Players: Theme and Variation in Late Medieval French Poetry*, Stanford U.P., 1990, 357 pp. Albrecht Classen, *Die autobiographische Lyrik des europäischen Spätmittelalters: Studien zu Hugo von Montfort, Oswald von Wolkenstein, Antonio Pucci, Charles d'Orléans, Thomas Hoccleve, Michel Beheim, Hans Rosenplüt und Alfonso Alvarez de Villasandino*, Amsterdam, Rodopi, 674 pp. L. Porter, 'The problematics of embedded poems from *Aucassin* to Artaud', *FLS*, 18:26–41, surveys the function of the embedded lyric in literature from the Middle Ages to the present day, concluding that medieval, 19th- and 20th-c. examples emphasize opposition intratextually, while those from the intervening periods emphasize intertextual relationships. J. Cerquiglini-Toulet, 'Fullness and emptiness: shortages and storehouses of lyric treasure in the fourteenth and fifteenth centuries', Poirion, *Contexts*, 224–39, situates the lyrics of Machaut and Froissart in an exchange economy in which the poet needs to have a supply of poems at hand, the image of the coffer suggesting a storehouse of written currency waiting to be put into circulation. S. Huot, 'The daisy and the laurel: myths of desire and creativity in the poetry of Jean Froissart', *ib.*, 240–51, shows how F. established a mythographic basis for his self-presentation as intellectual love poet by reworking Ovidian myths and inventing some of his own. P. Bennett, 'The mirage of fiction: narration, narrator, and narratee in Froissart's lyrico-narrative *dits*', *MLR*, 86:285–97, explores F.'s debt to Machaut and the different fictive levels in F.'s work through which he investigates the process of literary creation. R. Mullally, 'Dance terminology in the works of Machaut and Froissart', *MAe*, 59, 1990:248–59, traces the development in meaning of *carole, danse*, and related dance and musical terms from 13th to 15th c. B. Ribémont, 'Rire et sourire chez Froissart: l'exemple de l'*Espinette amoureuse* et du *Joli Buisson de Jonece*', Bouché, *Le Rire*, 269–81, claims that apart from the prayer to the Virgin at the end of the *Joli Buisson* the tone of these two works is comic and ironic. G. Roccati, 'Sur quelques textes d'Eustache Deschamps témoignant de la fonction comique du poète de cour', *ib.*, 283–97, identifies the historical contexts of those poems in which D. is the butt of his humour and shows that their comic effect resides in their exaggeration of real events, their parody of court encomia and their portrayal of D. as buffoon. A. Strubel, '"Dans la foret de longue actente": réflexions sur le style allégorique de Charles d'Orléans', Poirion, *Styles*, 167–86, investigates the syntactical ambiguity of expressions containing a concrete and an abstract noun linked by *de*. A. Harrison, 'Reflections of theater in Charles d'Orléans', *FCS*, 17, 1990:147–56, examines *ballades* and *rondeaux* which show the influence of theatre in their use of monologue, dialogue or *fractionnement*. P. Uhl, 'Les *sotes chançons* du *Roman de Fauvel* (MS *E*): la symptomatique indécision du rubricateur', *FS*, 45:385–402, argues that the lyrics inserted into the MS in 1316 are not *sotes chansons* (*pace* the rubricator), but nonsense poems providing a chronological link between the *Fatrasies d'Arras* and the *Fatras* of Watriquet de Couvin.

3. DRAMA

Nicholas of Verona. La Passion (cod. marc. franc. app. XXXIX = 272), ed. Virginio Bertolini, Verona U.P., 1989, 109 pp., is an interesting example of Franco-Italian literature, a mid-14th-c. translation in 35 Alexandrine *laisses monorimes* by N. of a Latin passion play. *La Passion d'Isabeau: une édition du MS Fr. 966 de la Bibliothèque Nationale de Paris*, ed. E. Dubruck, NY, Lang, 1990, viii + 234 pp. André Tissier, *Recueil de farces (1450–1550)*, vol. 6 (TLF, 391), 472 pp., contains *L'Obstination des femmes, Le Pont aux ânes, Les Femmes qui font refondre leurs maris, Frère Guillebert, Lucas, sergent boîteux et borgne, et le bon payeur, Le Galant qui a fait le coup*, and *La Confession Margot*. Graham A. Runnalls, *Le Mystère de la Passion à Amboise au moyen âge: représentations théâtrales et texte,*

Montreal, Ceres, 86 pp., offers a corrected, less interventionist edition of the fragments than Picot's, allows us a fascinating insight into theatrical productions at Amboise in the late Middle Ages, and concludes that the *Passion* referred to in the account book was a different work, now lost, from the one published here. Marcel Couturier and Graham A. Runnalls, *Compte du Mystère de la Passion, Châteaudun. 1510*, Chartres, Société archéologique d'Eure-et-Loir, 182 pp., makes another important contribution to our knowledge of the practicalities of staging passion plays and enables us to reconstruct to some extent the play performed in C. in 1510, whose source was a *Passion d'Amboise*. Id., 'Le *Mystère de la Passion* joué à Châteaudun en 1510: le *Compte* de Jehan Brebier', *FCS*, 18:201–10, discusses more fully the information in the account book concerning the MSS (now lost) used for performance and with which one can verify the MS typologies proposed by R. and others. G. Runnalls, 'Un siècle dans la vie d'un mystère: le *Mystère de saint Denis*', *MA*, 97:407–30, reinterprets the MS evidence in order to trace the development of this *mystère* from a hypothetical *cycle original* containing *c*. 3500 lines to a *Mystère de St Denis* (*c*. 30,000 lines), into which had been incorporated an Assumption of the Virgin Mary. G. Gros, 'Du registre de confrérie à l'anthologie mariale. (Étude sur la conception du manuscrit de Cangé, Paris, Bibl. nat., fr. 819 et 820)', Poirion, *Styles*, 75–100, explains the erasure of many references to the performance of the *Miracles de Nostre Dame par personnages* and of the rubrics introducing the *serventois* which follow the *miracles* as an attempt to turn a register of the activities of the Confrérie des Orfèvres in Paris into a presentation anthology. **Nicolas de la Chesnaye, La Condamnation de Banquet*, ed. Jelle Koopmans and Paul Verhuyck (TLF, 395), 328 pp. J. Koopmans, 'Une pièce parodique à trois codes implicites: la moralité de la *Condamnation de Banquet* de Nicolas de la Chesnaye', *FCS*, 18:159–74, highlights the problem of generic attribution, for the *Condamnation* contains a parody of a *mystère*, a carnival play and a *morisque*. P. Verhuyck, 'Fatras et Sottie', *ib.*, 285–99, finds elements of nonsense poetry in the *sotties*, especially in the *Sottie des cris de Paris*, where the *fatras* is 'fractured', i.e. spoken by three characters. S. Hendrup, 'Une sottie méconnue: la *Moralité de Chascun, Plusieurs, le Temps-qui-court, le Monde* du manuscrit La Vallière', *RevR*, 25, 1990:331–40, compares and contrasts *Chascun* with *Le Moral de Tout le Monde*, concluding that the former is a *Grenzform* of the *sottie*, while the latter is a *Nebenform*, which could have become a *sottie* if performed by fools. G. McGregor, **The Broken Pot Restored: 'Le Jeu de la Feuillée' of Adam de la Halle*, Kentucky, French Forum, 187 pp. R. Dragonetti, 'Le dervé-roi dans le *Jeu de la Feuillee* d'Adam de la Halle', *RLaR*, 95:115–35, analyses the symbolic significance of the madman's words and actions for the author's own project. K. Brownlee, 'Transformations of the couple: genre and language in the *Jeu de Robin et Marion*', *FrF*, 14, 1989:419–33, notes Marion's verbal sparring with the *chevalier* and her linguistic education of Robin, concluding that once the *pastourelle* has become a play the authorial *je* no longer corresponds to the knight's voice, but privileges instead the heroine. E. Benkov, 'The code revealed: subversion of discourse in *Le Cuvier*', *MoyFr*, 24–25, 1990:271–82, focuses on gender politics in this misogynistic farce. H. Carpenter, 'Le rire et le comique dans *Le Mistére du Viel Testament*', Bouché, *Le Rire*, 107–35, studies the theme of laughter and the humorous interludes in this collection of *mystères*. T. Sankovitch, 'Georges Chastellain and the celebratory morality play', *FCS*, 17, 1990:371–79, claims that the mythic character of three *moralités* by C. enables him to present the house of Burgundy as transcending temporal history in its importance. M. Newels, 'From narrative style to dramatic style in *Les Moralités*', Poirion, *Contexts*, 252–68, assesses a group of *Voies d'Enfer et de Paradis* texts (which she is editing), using the scholastic categories of *auctor*, *materia*, *forma*, and *effectus*. J. Taylor, 'Que signifiait *danse* au quinzième siècle? Danser la *Danse macabré*', *FCS*, 18:259–77, studies the function and connotations of dance both in the title and as the central metaphor of the work, arguing that the reader/spectator would appreciate the ironic equation of dancing with death and the privileging of dancing's coercive and dangerous qualities over its delights. J.-C. Aubailly, 'Pyrame et Tisbé au théâtre: légende et idéologie', *ib.*, 1–15, shows how the Ovidian tale is transformed into a 16th-c. morality play in which P. symbolizes Christ and T. the human soul separated from him by original sin (the wall).

4. HISTORICAL LITERATURE

Christine Raynaud, *La Violence au moyen âge (XIIIe–XVe siècle) d'après les livres d'histoire en français*, Le Léopard d'Or, 1990, 378 pp. *Georges Chastellain. Chronique. Les Fragments du Livre IV révélés par l'Add. Ms 54156 de la Brit. Library*, ed. J.-C. Delclos (TLF, 394), 376 pp., provides us with a more complete text than the edition by de Lettenhove, supplying information for 1456–57 and 1458–61. *Jean Froissart. Chroniques. Le Manuscrit d'Amiens, Livre I (1307–40)*, ed. George T. Diller (TLF, 407), lv + 329 pp., supplements D.'s earlier edition of the Rome MS. D. Poirion, 'La fête dans les *Chroniques* de Froissart', *Symposion* (Paderborn), 95–107, focusing on Book IV of the *Chroniques*, examines the dialectical relationship between order and disorder produced by *fêtes*. B. Ribémont, 'L'entrée d'Isabeau de Bavière à Paris: une fête textuelle pour Froissart', *ib.*, 515–22, shows how F.'s account of this historical event is conveyed from the point of view of the queen, who is both spectator and participant, and how the *fête* is used to promote the notion of a chivalric and courtly monarchy. M. Zink, 'The time of plague and the order of writing: Jean le Bel, Froissart, Machaut', Poirion, *Contexts*, 269–80, notes differences in the ordering of historical events connected with the plague in chronicle and poetry which reveal their authors' different hierarchies of values. H. Williams, '*Le Pas de la bergère*. A critical edition', *FCS*, 17, 1990:485–513, provides a new edition with glossary and description of MSS of this stylized, theatrical tournament held in Tarascon in 1449. A. Annunziata, 'Teaching the *Pas d'Armes*', Chickering, *Chivalry*, 557–82, discusses the *pas d'armes* as a ritualized re-enactment of the one-to-one combats of Arthurian romance and includes translated extracts from *Le Pas de la bergère*, *L'Histoire du Maréchal de Boucicaut* and Chastellain's *Chronique de Jacques de Lalaing*. G. Orgelfinger, 'The vows of the pheasant and late chivalric ritual', *ib.*, 611–43, surveys the literary and historical antecedents for Philip the Good's vow on a pheasant in 1454 and appends translated extracts from Olivier de la Marche's *Mémoires*. J. Blanchard, 'Écrire la guerre au XVe siècle', *MoyFr*, 24–25, 1990:7–21, analyses *Le Jouvencel* as a work of compilation, structured according to Aristotelian categories, and Tringant's *Exposition* as an attempt to simplify its message.

5. RELIGIOUS, MORAL, AND DIDACTIC LITERATURE

Eric Hicks, *La Vie et les epistres Pierre Abaelart et Heloys sa fame: traduction du XIII siècle attribuée à Jean de Meun, avec une nouvelle édition des textes latins d'après le ms Troyes Bib. mun. 802*, vol. 1, *Introduction et textes*, Champion, lix + 161 pp., offers a useful facing page edition of Latin and French texts. T. Bouché, 'L'obscène et le sacré ou l'utilisation paradoxale du rire dans le *Roman de la Rose* de Jean de Meun', Bouché, *Le Rire*, 83–95, analyses Genius's sermon, the *exemplum* of Pygmalion and the conquest of the rose and claims that J. is able to refine his definition of the sacred by contrasting it provocatively with the obscene, using the reader's laughter positively to glorify the act of procreation. L. Friedman, 'La mesnie Faux Semblant: homo interior =/= homo exterior', *FrF*, 14, 1989:435–45, discusses passages in the works of Joinville and Olivier de la Marche where a person appears to be acting out a part, then analyses the term *personnage* in the *querelle de la Rose*, showing that Christine de Pizan accepts a difference of opinion between author and character in her own case more readily than in that of Jean de Meun. S. Gallarati, '"Mots sous les mots": una firma per il *Testament*', *MedRom*, 15, 1990:259–76, claims to have found in ll. 5–8, 241–56, 2117–20 anagrams proving that Jean de Meun was the author of the *Testament*. T. Scully, 'Les modifications du *Viandier* dit de Taillevent dans le quinzième siècle', *FCS*, 18:211–19, shows how cookery books evolved from the 13th to the 15th c. reflecting the tastes and needs of French aristocratic families. Id., 'The menus of the *Menagier de Paris*', *MoyFr*, 24–25, 1990:215–31, concentrates on the eating habits of a late 14th-c. affluent bourgeois household, demonstrating that each dish had its preordained position in the menu, and that medical considerations influenced the choice of dishes. A. de Wolf, 'L'allégorie en contexte: la mise en œuvre des personnifications dans le *Songe du Viel Pelerin*', *ib.*, 251–63, offers a statistical analysis of personification in the *Songe*, indicating how Philippe de Mézières distinguishes it from *abstractum agens*. H. Solterer, 'Figures of female militancy in medieval France', *Signs*, 16:522–49, focuses on a group of four 13th-c. narratives, *Li Tournoiement as dames*, which depict women participating in tournaments under the gaze of the male narrator, and considers the reaction of female and male readers to this ambiguous text and its illuminations. **Le Chevalier des Dames du Dolent Fortuné: allégorie en vers de la fin du XVe siècle*, ed. Jean Miquet, Ottawa U.P., 254 pp. P. Dembowski, 'Martin le Franc, Fortune, Virtue, and 15th-c. France', *Grigsby Vol.*, 261–76, argues that M.'s rhetorically sophisticated *prosimetrum L'Estrif de Fortune et Vertu* (still unpublished) deserves wider study, not just as a historical record but as an early humanist discussion of the roles of fortune, providence, and virtue in history. G. Gros, 'Préférer la Vierge à l'autre Marie (étude sur le miracle XXIII de Jean Le Marchant)', *Le 'Cuer'*, 145–60, compares this *conte* about an English knight who turns from *fole amour* to devotion to the Virgin with Marie de France's *Lanval*, claiming that the *miracle* represents a Christian alternative to Celtic myth. C. Raynaud, 'La mise en scène du cœur dans les livres religieux de la fin du moyen âge', *ib.*, 315–43, includes *Le Mortifiement de vaine plaisance*. J. Arrouye, 'Le cœur et son paysage', *ib.*, 27–42, shows how the illuminations by Barthélémy d'Eyck in the Vienna MS of René d'Anjou's *Le Cœur d'amour épris* enhance the meaning of the text. H. Williams, 'Joan of Arc, Christine de Pizan, and Martin le Franc,' *FCS*, 16, 1990:233–37, claims that C. in her *Ditié* was keen to preserve J.'s exploits for posterity, while M. was trying to counteract the criticisms of J. made by her male contemporaries. C. Willard, 'Women and marriage around 1400: three views', *FCS*, 17, 1990:475–84, examines the attitudes towards woman's role within marriage in the *XV Joies de mariage* and in the works of Christine de Pizan and Deschamps, placing them in their historical context. P. Gilli, 'Politiques italiennes, le regard français (*c.* 1375–1430)', *Médiévales*, 19, 1990:109–23, describes the nuanced attitude of French writers such as Christine de Pizan, Philippe de Mézières, Alain Chartier, Froissart, and

Commynes towards Italy, its people and politics, noting their approval of Venice as an ideal city state.

CHRISTINE DE PIZAN (DIDACTIC AND POETIC WORKS). *Poems of Cupid, God of Love: Christine de Pizan's 'Epistre au dieu d'Amours' and 'Dit de la Rose', Thomas Hoccleve's 'The Letter of Cupid' with George Sewell's 'The Proclamation of Cupid'*, ed. and trans. Thelma S. Fenster and Mary Carpenter Erler, Leiden, Brill, 1990, vii + 237 pp., contains a new edition of C.'s works based, unlike that of Roy, not on the oldest extant version but, in the case of the *Epistre*, on Harley 4431, probably revised by C. herself. The welcome English translation respects the rhythm and style of the original as well as the content, and the introduction deals thoroughly with the *querelle de la Rose*. Christine de Pizan, *A Medieval Woman's Mirror of Honor: the Treasury of the City of Ladies*, trans. Charity C. Willard, NY, Persea, 1989, 266 pp., contains introductory essays by W. and M. Cosman. E. Hicks, 'Le Livre des trois vertus of Christine de Pizan: Beinecke MS 427', Poirion, *Contexts*, 57–71, comments on problems of editing a text revised by its author, on the relationship between the text and image, and between the *Mirror of Honour* and the *City of Ladies*. M. Zimmermann, '"Sages et prudentes mainagieres" in Christine de Pizan's *Livre des trois vertus* (1405)', Ehlert, *Haushalt*, 193–206, compares C.'s practical advice to women of all classes, whose activities reach far beyond the domestic, with that given in male-authored texts. A. Kennedy, 'Christine de Pizan, Victor de Saint-Genis et le manuscrit de Châtellerault', *Romania*, 109, 1988 [1991] : 540–60, publishes the transcription of C.'s *Epistre à la reine* made by Saint-Genis and concludes that the Châtellerault MS he referred to survives in fragmentary form in Brussels, Bibl. Royale, IV 1176, that the part containing Book VII of the *Mutacion* has been lost, and that Paris, Bibl. nat. fr. 25430 (Books IV and V of the *Mutacion*) formed part of this multi-volume MS copy of the *Mutacion* and the *Epistre*. K. Brownlee, 'The image of history in Christine de Pizan's *Livre de la Mutacion de Fortune*', Poirion, *Contexts*, 44–56, analyses C.'s reworking of the *Aeneid*, the *Roman de la Rose*, the *Prose Lancelot* and the *Divine Comedy* and shows that C., the post-erotic widow turned detached clerkly historian, acquires authority for her narrative through the contrast with her male predecessors, who were personally involved as lovers in the histories they recounted. L. Dulac, 'Les ouvertures closes dans le *Livre de la Cité des Dames* de Christine de Pizan: le topos du "veuvage qualifiant"', *Actes* (Montpellier), 35–45, demonstrates that widowhood as a prerequisite for women to adopt active, masculine roles in world affairs is a topos which C. uses to introduce many of the exemplary *récits* in the *Cité*. K. Sullivan, 'At the limit of feminist theory: an architectonics of the *Querelle de la Rose*', *Exemplaria*, 3:435–66,

approaches C.'s *Epistre* and her correspondence on the *Rose* from a
feminist perspective, using the metaphors of the crypt, the *secretum*,
and the castle to describe respectively Jean de Montreuil's relationship to Jean de Meun, C.'s access to the truth about women, and her
ambiguous position as both object of conquest/study and commentator on her sex. R. Blumenfeld-Kosinski, 'Christine de Pizan and the
misogynistic tradition', *RR*, 81, 1990:279–92, explores C.'s treatment
of reason, experience, and writing, her attitude towards her mother
and her redefinition of the natural/unnatural woman. D. Nelson,
'Christine de Pizan and courtly love', *FCS*, 17, 1990:281–89, analyses
the woman's voice in the *Cent ballades d'amant et de dame* arguing that C.
presents the lady more sympathetically than Chrétien and gives her
more scope to express her feelings than do the *trouvères*. C. Willard,
'Christine de Pizan on chivalry', Chickering, *Chivalry*, 511–28, looks
at C.'s advice to rulers concerning the military and moral aspects of
chivalry.

6. Miscellaneous

Denyse Delcourt, **L'Éthique du changement dans le roman français du 15e
siècle*, Geneva, Droz, 1990, 170 pp. **Rauf de Lenham. Art de kalender:
poème anglo-normand de l'année 1256*, ed. Ö. Södergård, Stockholm,
Almquist and Wiksell, 1990, 71 pp. J. Dufournet, 'La génération de
Louis XI: quelques témoins littéraires', *FCS*, 18:49–81, concludes
that materialism, deceit and the ambiguity of language are the themes
that characterize the literature of late 15th-c. France (notably the
poetry of Villon, the farce of *Pathelin*, the *Cent nouvelles nouvelles* and
Commynes's *Mémoires*). P. Mason, 'The pronouns of address in
Middle French', *SN*, 62, 1990:95–100, challenges the view that *tu* and
vous were used arbitrarily in the 14th and 15th c. by examining their
use in *Les XV Joies de mariage, Jehan de Saintré* and the *Cent nouvelles
nouvelles*. B. Lhoest, 'Les dénominations de la femme en moyen
français: approche lexicale et anthropologique', *ZRP*, 107:343–62,
shows that in 74 nouns denoting women the most common seme is
lust, then in descending order: frivolity, ugliness, weakness, stupidity,
deceit, bestiality, loquaciousness, virginity, magic. L. concludes that
woman was in an anthropological no man's land between animal and
human, nature and culture.

THE SIXTEENTH CENTURY

By JOHN O'BRIEN, *University of Liverpool*

I. GENERAL

HUMANISM, THOUGHT

Robert Aulotte (ed.), *Précis de littérature française du XVIe siècle*, PUF, 458 pp., contains: 'Vue panoramique — Humanisme et Renaissance' (R. Aulotte), 'Le théâtre' (M. Lazard), 'Narrations' (N. Cazauran and M. Simonin), 'Formes discursives' (J. Céard), 'La poésie' (G. Mathieu-Castellani and J. Pineaux), 'Langues et signes' (M. Huchon), 'Littérature et spiritualité' (F. Joukovsky), 'Littérature et politique: la cité' (D. Ménager), 'Arts et littérature' (F. Lecercle), 'Littérature et imaginaire' (C.-G. Dubois). The last few essays in particular are excellent. Generally speaking, a scholarly and helpful collection of material, but more likely to appeal to *agrégatifs* or American Graduate School than the normal run of undergraduates. Stephen Bamforth and Jean Dupèbe (eds), *Francisci Francorum Regis et Henrici Anglorum Colloquium*, *RenS*, 5 (Special Number), x + 237 pp., an excellent edition with full notes and translation of a text by Sylvius (better known as Jacques Dubois, the doctor and grammarian) which gives new and important details about the meeting of Francis I and Henry VIII on the Field of the Cloth of Gold. *Actes* (Mulhouse) includes several papers on humanist topics: A. Dufour, 'La notion de liberté de conscience chez les Réformateurs' (15–20), deals principally with Bèze and Calvin; O. Millet, 'Le thème de la conscience libre chez Calvin' (21–37), attends to the political as well as theological dimensions of this aspect of Calvin's thought; M.-D. Legrand, 'Michel de l'Hospital: éléments pour une poétique de la liberté de conscience' (85–96), looks at the *Harangues* and *Mémoires*; G. Roellenbleck, 'Jean Bodin et la liberté de conscience' (97–106), concentrates on the *Six Livres de la République* of 1576; K. F. Faltenbacher, 'Examen de conscience à Venise: le *Colloquium Heptaplomeres*' (107–13), interprets the *Colloquium* as a step along the road to tolerance rather than a treatise on tolerance as such; P. Desan, 'La conscience et ses droits: les *Vindiciae contra Tyrannos* de Du Plessis-Mornay et Hubert Languet' (115–33), emphasizes that for the *Vindiciae* freedom of conscience is a necessity, a duty owed to God, and examines practical implications of its application in the social and political sphere; F. Berriot, 'Islam et liberté de conscience à la Renaissance' (173–90), excellent *essai de synthèse* of this topic in relation to France. F. Higman, '"Il serait trop plus decent respondre en latin": les controversistes catholiques du XVIe siècle face aux

écrits réformés', Jones-Davies, *Renaissance*, 189–212, a richly documented piece showing that Catholics and Protestants alike saw the
advantages of the French vernacular in theological polemic and
controversy. Desan, *Humanism*, includes the following of relevance to
our period: P. Desan, 'The worm in the apple: the crisis of humanism'
(11–34), an excellent overview; J. J. Supple, 'The failure of humanist
education: David de Fleurance-Rivault, Anthoine Mathé de Laval
and Nicolas Faret' (35–53), takes three case-studies which extend
into the seventeenth century; G. Huppert, 'Ruined schools: the end of
the Renaissance school system in France' (55–67), is a more general
essay on the same topic as the previous paper; Z. S. Schiffman,
'Humanism and the problem of relativism' (69–83), examines the
varying attitudes of lawyers, historians, Montaigne, and Descartes;
T. J. Reiss, 'The idea of meaning and practice of method in Peter
Ramus, Henri Estienne and others' (125–51), a detailed piece which
detects in its selected authors 'the ambivalence of their effort to
ground reason and its judgement'; J. Céard, 'The crisis of the science
of monsters' (181–205) relates the crisis in teratology to changes in the
idea of Nature; C.-G. Dubois, 'The erosion of the eschatological myth
(1597–1610)' (207–22), confines himself to the myth of the Antichrist;
M. E. Blanchard, 'Fin de siècle living: writing the daily at the end of
the Renaissance' (223–57), selects Gilles de Gouberville, Pierre de
l'Estoile and Blaise de Monluc; B. Crampé, '*De arte rhetorica*: the
gestation of French classicism in Renaissance rhetoric' (259–77), is on
Soarez's *Rhetoric*, published in 1562.

In travel literature, it goes without saying that the indefatigable
Frank Lestringant has been busy again this year, publishing more of
his thesis. This has resulted in two volumes, the first of which is *André
Thevet, cosmographe des derniers Valois* (THR, 251), Geneva, Droz,
427 pp. This follows the life of the cosmographer by stages, in
sumptuous detail, including a final chapter on 'Fortunes et infortunes
(1592–1800)' and an amusing yet instructive epilogue on 'Les oiseaux
de Flaubert'. Id., *L'Atelier du cosmographe ou l'image du monde à la
Renaissance*, Albin Michel, 270 pp., is again on Thevet, but the
chapters are organized according to themes, e.g. 'Le monde cos-
mographique', 'Mythologiques: l'invention du Brésil'. In some ways
even more attractive than its larger companion volume, because more
attractively laid out; but both are indispensable reading. Id., 'The
crisis of cosmography at the end of the Renaissance', Desan,
Humanism, 153–79, locates this crisis in the dichotomy between
scholarly and practical cartography, and in the overriding importance of independent analysis contrasted with received truths.

Women's writing has similarly attracted interest. Evelyne Berriot-
Salvadore, *Les Femmes dans la société française de la Renaissance*, Geneva,

Droz, 1990, 592 pp., is an extended overview of woman's position and role in 16th-c. society, divided into four sections beginning with the legal status of the married woman, then dealing with the housewife, the woman as helpmeet (nurse, religious, teacher), and a final section dealing with the women writers. Useful and solid but still very much a thesis; little literary enlightenment in the section on women writers. C. M. Bauschatz, 'Marie de Gournay and the crisis of humanism', Desan, *Humanism*, 279–94, looks at the 'Deffence de la poësie et du langage des poëtes', and in '"L'horreur de mon exemple" in Marie de Gournay's *Proumenoir de Monsieur de Montaigne* (1594)', *EsC*, 30, 1990:97–105, finds that G. tries to determine her role as a woman writer 'in treating the gender-marked heritage of exemplary fiction'. Interesting idea but too short. A. R. Larsen '"Un honneste passe-tems": strategies of legitimation in French Renaissance women's prefaces', *ib.*, 11–22, a succinct and ideologically pointed account. In a similar line of country is Lawrence D. Kritzman, *The Rhetoric of Sexuality and the Literature of the French Renaissance* (Cambridge Studies in French), CUP, xii + 260 pp. This post-modernist account deals with sexual differentiation and gender positioning and stereotyping, as well as questions of the self and authorship, in a number of Renaissance writers: Pernette du Guillet, Marguerite de Navarre, Rabelais, Montaigne, Scève, Ronsard. The writing is extremely dense and makes no allowance for those who do not have close acquaintance with the vocabulary of psychoanalysis.

A few items on philosophical approaches to literature. N. Kenny, '"Curiosité" and philosophical poetry in the French Renaissance', *RenS*, 5:263–76, explores the different attitudes towards *curiosité*, which the author regards as a form of desire; solid Renaissance scholarship with a dash of Lacan. I. Maclean, 'The readership of philosophical fictions: the bibliographical evidence', Kenny, *Fictions*, 7–15, examines the tripartite readership of philosophy as a genre (students, specialists, general readers); paradoxically broad and flexible as well as specific and precise as a genre, with wide as well as narrow appeal. R. Cooper, 'The philosophical phoenix', *ib.*, 71–87, looks at the political, religious, and philosophical implications of the phoenix theme in the work of (among others) La Garde, Du Monin, and Béroalde de Verville. The most unusual contribution on philosophy comes from Françoise Joukovsky, *Le Feu et le Fleuve. Héraclite et la Renaissance française* (THR, 249), Geneva, Droz, 150 pp., which has sections on fire, water, becoming and knowing. The author has little difficulty in demonstrating interest in Heraclitus, to varying degrees, on the part of Renaissance editors and some philosophers. However, there is a striking absence of discernible influence in vernacular writers, apart from scattered references (notably in

Montaigne) and the topos of the laughter of Democritus and the tears of Heraclitus. 'Negative capability' seems the appropriate phrase, even though Joukovsky tries to persuade us otherwise.

Emblems seem to have gained rather less attention this year than last. I. Bergal, 'Pierre Coustau's *Pegme*: from emblem to essay', *Stone Vol.*, 113–22. D. Russell, 'Emblematics in the French provinces: the case of Loys Papon and Anne d'Urfé in the Forez', *ib.*, 123–37, is an illustrated discussion.

INDIVIDUAL WORKS OR WRITERS

M. M. Fontaine, '*Alector* de Barthélemy Aneau: la rencontre des ambitions philosophiques et pédagogiques avec la fiction romanesque en 1560', Kenny, *Fictions*, 29–43, investigates instructively the example of the 'histoire fabuleuse'. J. C. Nash, '"Exerçant œuvres viriles": feminine anger and feminist (re)writing in Hélisenne de Crenne', *EsC*, 30, 1990:38–48, focuses on H.'s treatment of female heroines in the *Epistres*, which challenge 'the principle that define human wisdom, strength and action as male'. D. S. Wood, 'The evolution of Hélisenne de Crenne's persona', *Symposium*, 45:140–51, examines both the *Angoisses* and the *Epistres* in order to demonstrate how H. gives us a psychological profile in the novel, a sociological one in the *Epistres familieres*, and finally finds in the *Epistres invectives* a voice with which to defend herself and her sex. Worthy without being inspired. D. Fenoaltea, 'Doing it with mirrors: architecture and textual construction in Jean Lemaire's *La Concorde des deux langages*', *Stone Vol.*, 21–32, is a sophisticated account, averring that despite the differentiated architecture of the Temples, the processes of fiction make such differentiation equivocal. A. Moss, 'Fabulous narrations in the *Concorde des deux langages* of Jean Lemaire de Belges', Kenny, *Fictions*, 17–28, suggests that man's spiritual and moral progress, according to the *Concorde*, depends first on rejecting the Temple of Venus and then on rejecting the allurements of poetic fiction itself, in favour of the realities of history. M. C. Smith, 'A sixteenth-century anti-theist (on the *Cymbalum Mundi*)', *BHR*, 53:593–618, contends that Hylactor is Dolet, and Pamphagus Rabelais; he adds that the work can with certainty be ascribed to P., before concluding against Screech, Nurse, and Saulnier that *Cymbalum Mundi* is an irreligious work. M. M. Fragonard, 'La liberté de conscience chez Du Plessis-Mornay (1576–1598)', *Actes* (Mulhouse), 135–52, concentrates on P.'s views in respect of the conversion of Henri IV. J.-C. Arnould (ed.), Claude de Taillemont, *Discours des champs faëz* (TLF, 401), Geneva, Droz, 304 pp. + 2 figs, is an edition of a work by an author who is gradually becoming better known. The notes are succinct, indeed even spare. Neil Kenny, *The Palace of Secrets: Béroalde de Verville and Renaissance Conceptions of Knowledge*, Clarendon, xii + 305 pp., deals with the whole range of V.'s work (not just *Le Moyen de parvenir*) in relation to competing conceptions of knowledge. This is an excellent contribution to its subject and will quickly become a standard work.

2. RABELAIS AND THE CONTEURS

Richard Cooper, *Rabelais et l'Italie* (THR, 245 = *ERab*, 24), Geneva, Droz, 299 pp., contains an excellent introduction of 85 pages and, starting with the *dédicace* to the introduction to Manardi, a scholarly edition of R.'s correspondence with full notes and variant readings. Vatican MS material concerning 'la supplique de Rabelais' is given at the end. Very full and helpful *index nominum* and *index verborum* round off this outstanding contribution to Rabelais studies. Guy Demerson, *Rabelais*, Fayard, 350 pp., is a revised and updated version of his 1986 book with the same title. The new version remains as useful as the previous edition, but is more helpfully organized. This is a book which works well all round. Edwin M. Duval, *The Design of Rabelais's 'Pantagruel'*, Yale U.P., xviii + 206 pp. — the design in question being Christian-humanist. Duval takes a number of episodes in *Pantagruel* (Loup-Garou, Panurge, Anarche) and sees in them evidence of a redemptive process culminating in Pantagruel's creation of the Kingdom of God on earth. This leads to difficult or controversial interpretations e.g. that Panurge is 'a crafty, ironic, Pauline agent of God'. Serious intentions, but over-zealous, and the laughter tends to evaporate in the process. Carla Freccero, *Father Figures. Genealogy and Narrative Structures in Rabelais*, Ithaca and London, Cornell U.P., xiii + 213 pp., concentrates principally on *Gargantua* and *Pantagruel*, claiming that sons (variously interpreted) cut themselves free from the authority of the Father. The argument is most controversially embodied in the chapter on Thélème which sees Thélème as initiating a new type of (modernist) narrative, free from authorial control, adrift from origins. Some *aperçus* amid the tendentiousness. Kathleen Hall, *Rabelais: 'Pantagruel' and 'Gargantua'* (CGFT, 88), 84 pp., emphasizes laughter, entertainment, friendship as the basis for the books and keeps these firmly in view when dealing with important episodes (e.g. the first meeting with Panurge; Thélème). Some thorny issues (e.g. the Prologue to *Gargantua*) are too quickly dealt with. Without underestimating the scholarly side, Hall prefers a cheery view of Rabelais, based on common sense and laughter. Useful but is unlikely to replace the little guides by Ménager and Charpentier. C.-G.

Dubois, 'Enfants trouvés et langue perdue (deux cas d'esthétisme polyglossique chez Rabelais)', *Corps écrit*, 36, 1990: 107–13, claims in respect of Pantagruel's meeting with Panurge and the Écolier limousin that 'les parades de virtuosité linguistique recouvrent une problématique en rapport avec les modes de construction d'un sujet'. A. F. Berry, '"L'isle Medamothi": Rabelais's itineraries of anxiety', *PMLA*, 106: 1040–53, reads Medamothi as the *espace littéraire* in which Rabelais needs to read and transumpt his precursors before launching once more into an uncertain future, subject to the revisionary powers of his own readers. Phew! B. C. Bowen, 'Rabelais and the library of Saint Victor', *Stone Vol.*, 159–70, demonstrates the scholarship and fun in the Catalogue of Books. T. Cave, 'Panurge, Pathelin and other polyglots', *ib.*, 171–82, as usual, a subtle and perceptive piece on the changes to the linguistic map of France and Europe which make Panurge an early modern linguist. N. Cazauran, 'En marge du *Tiers Livre*: le coq de Panurge', *NRSS*, 9: 41–44, uses Amaury Bouchard's manuscript *Traité de l'ame* to argue that Panurge's gift of a white cock to Raminogrobis is a Neoplatonic symbol of the poet's soul. H. H. Glidden, 'Childhood and the vernacular in Rabelais's *Gargantua*', *Stone Vol.*, 181–94, reads the account of Gargantua's childhood against a variety of *intertextes*, including the *Roman de la rose*. F.-R. Hausmann, 'Rabelais' *Gargantua et Pantagruel* als Quelle mittelaltericher Fest- und Spieltradition', *Symposion* (Paderborn), 335–48, is a Bakhtin-inspired analysis of episodes dealing with religion and politics (the episodes are *not* confined to the books named in the title). R. C. La Charité, 'Narrative strategy in Rabelais's *Quart Livre*', *Stone Vol.*, 195–205, despite its title, is in fact an essay about the nature and status of the narrator in the *Quart Livre*. Id., 'Par où commencer? Histoire et récit dans le *Pantagruel* de Rabelais', Kritzman, *Signe*, 79–89, compares framing devices in *Pantagruel* and *Genesis*. P. Sommers, 'The cradle and beyond: psychological implications of *Pantagruel* iv', *Stone Vol.*, 149–58, is really a Lacanian psychoanalytical interpretation (and so not just psychological) about the Oedipus complex. A particularly welcome addition to critical works about *conteurs* this year is Catherine Magnien-Simonin (ed.), *Noël du Fail écrivain* (L'Oiseau de Minerve), Vrin, 204 pp., which contains: J.-M. Constant, 'Un groupe social ouvert et dynamique: la noblesse provinciale de l'ouest au XVIe siècle' (11–22); M. Simonin, 'Le propos de Noël du Fail' (23–33), gives bibliographical information behind the printing of F.'s work; N. Cazauran, 'La première manière de Noël du Fail' (35–47), investigates the art of the *conteur* in *Les Propos rustiques*; A. Leclercq-Magnien, '*Propos rustiques*: caractérisation des devisants et statut du texte' (49–61), after describing the interlocutors, relates the text to the symposium tradition; A. Comparot, 'La réception de Rabelais dans les *Propos rustiques*' (63–72), draws comparisons; M. Bideaux, 'Les *Baliverneries d'Eutrapel*: Du Fail entre deux livres' (73–85), explores the 'statut inconfortable' of the book, which he considers 'insuffisamment personnalisé pour accueillir et s'approprier un contenu disparate'; G.-A. Pérouse, 'A propos de Lupolde: un mot sur les personnages de Noël de Fail' (87–95), is a well-judged piece from an expert on the *genre*; M.-C. Bichard, 'Comparaisons et métaphores animales dans l'œuvre narrative de Noël du Fail' (97–110), illuminating; M. Huchon, 'Le propos linguistique de Noël du Fail' (111–25), analyses morphology; M. Rousse, 'Noël du Fail et le théâtre: de l'art de voir à l'art d'écrire' (127–43), speculates on possible connections and tries to discern some influences in F.'s work; J. Barbier, 'Noël du Fail et la musique' (145–60), helpfully lists and analyses the songs and musical quotations in F.; K. Cameron, 'Noël du Fail et "l'aage doré"' (161–72), regards F.'s nostalgia for a Golden Age as a plea for the restitution of the fortunes of the nobles, as well as the restoration of public order and peace in a time of Civil War; J. Rohou, 'L'avidité, l'amour de soi et la générosité chez Noël du Fail et ses contemporains' (173–84), on F. and social pretentiousness (= *amour de soi*), as contrasted with the *générosité* of the nobles; H. Baudry, 'Noël du Fail préfacier du *Demosterion* de Roch le Baillif (1578)' (185–201), an interesting document which casts a sidelight on Fail. F. Charpentier, 'A l'épreuve du miroir: narcissisme, mélancolie et "honneste amour" dans la XXIVe nouvelle de l'*Heptaméron*', *EsC*, 30, 1990:23–37, thinks that 'avec Elisor on est porté à se demander si le monde masculin n'enferme pas le féminin dans une projection de sa propre cruauté ou de ses propres fantasmes'. R. Esclapez, 'Des contes "plaisans à escripre": fonctions des images dans l'*Heptaméron*', *ChS*, 2:107–22, studies images of earth, fire, air, and water, concluding (unremarkably) that Marguerite de Navarre's images 'renforcent la leçon tout en agrémentant le récit'. C. Giardina, 'La parole dans l'*Heptaméron* de Marguerite de Navarre', *IL*, 43:3–6, is a rather too brief study emphasizing that 'le don de la voix' is 'lié au désir ou à l'amour'; needs more detailed examination. P. de Lajarte, 'Christianisme et liberté de pensée dans les *Nouvelles* de Marguerite de Navarre', *Actes* (Mulhouse), 55–63, argues that, despite the absence of theoretical statements about freedom of conscience, it effectively exists in the form of a challenge on the part of some *devisants* to the predominantly Christian ethics of the *Nouvelles*. G. Mathieu-Castellani, 'Pour une poétique de la nouvelle', *CRCL*, special issue, 167–78, usefully situates the *Heptaméron* in respect of the *nouvelle* as genre and discusses theoretical implications.

3. POETRY

PRE-PLÉIADE

Jennifer Britnell (ed.), Jean Bouchet, *La Déploration de l'église militante* (TLF, 405), Geneva, Droz, 165 pp., is a welcome edition, which, in addition to the principal text, contains the variants of the *Déploration* for 1525, 1526, and 1545. F. Charpentier, 'Les voix du désir: le *Debat de folie et d'amour* de Louise Labé', Kritzman, *Signe*, 27–38. F. Rigolot, 'Louise Labé et les "Dames Lionnoises": les ambiguïtés de la censure', *ib.*, 13–25, offers the hypothesis that L.L. escapes masculine and feminine censorship in order to reconcile individual and group in shared values. J. Jones Wright and F. Rigolot, 'Les irruptions de Folie: fonction idéologique du *porte-parole* dans les *Œuvres* de Louise Labé', *EsC*, 30, 1990:72–84, studies the semiotic 'agrammaticalities', notably in the *Débat*, by which L.L. contests the dominance of the 'parole masculine'. Jean-Luc Déjean (ed.), *Clément Marot*, Fayard, 1990, 439 pp., is rather *haute vulgarisation*, written almost entirely in the graphic present, with plenty of rhetorical questions to cover difficult moments and lavish use of the poetry to illustrate the life, as though the poetry were no more than versified biography. Gérard Defaux (ed.), Clément Marot, *Œuvres poétiques, 1: L'Adolescence clementine, Suite de l'Adolescence clementine* (Classiques Garnier), Bordas, 1990, clxxxviii + 855 pp. The hefty introduction is a life of Marot. The notes are up to date and challenge previous interpretations. Despite the problems of overlap and indebtedness to previous editions, this edition will appeal, as being easier to handle than Mayer and infinitely more detailed than Lestringant. R. D. Cottrell, 'The poetics of transparency in evangelical discourse: Marot, Briçonnet, Marguerite de Navarre, Héroët', *Stone Vol.*, 33–44, takes an implicitly anti-Derrida line about the relationship of speech to writing, by claiming that the evangelical writers under discussion believe in the transparency of their poetic voice. G. Ferguson, 'Now in a glass darkly: the textual status of the *je parlant* in the *Miroirs* of Marguerite de Navarre', *RenS*, 5:398–411, is a post-modernist interpretation, offering some predictable remarks. B. Marczuk-Szwed, 'Marguerite de Navarre à la recherche du sens spirituel de la Bible', *RHR*, 33:31–42, holds that, in commenting on the Bible in *Miroirs, Prisons*, and *Discord*, 'Marguerite n'adopte jamais le point de vue d'un théologien savant, mais met l'explication à la bouche de protagonistes, selon différentes perspectives'. In 'Le *Discord* de Marguerite de Navarre: "annotation" poétique de la Bible', *NRSS*, 9:5–13, the same author claims that M. glosses, and in so doing modifies, St Paul. J. Boney, '"Ardeur de veoir": reading knowledge in Pernette du Guillet's *Rymes*', *EsC*, 30, 1990:49–60, interprets the *Rymes* as P.'s personal interpretation of Scève and links reading with seeing knowledge. G. Mathieu-Castellani, 'Parole d'Écho? Pernette au miroir des *Rymes*', *EsC*, 30, 1990:61–71, confirms previous investigations rather than breaks new ground by looking for *marques du féminin* and finding them in a text which emphasizes the voice and gives the body *its* voice. S. Murphy, 'The death of Actaeon as petrarchist topos', *CLS*, 28:137–55, contains material on this theme from P. and Scève. Jerry C. Nash, *The Love Aesthetics of Maurice Scève: Poetry and Struggle* (Cambridge Studies in French), CUP, xii + 205 pp., develops a phenomenological view of the *Délie*, in which he claims controversially that Scève's depiction of spiritual darkness is part and parcel of an ultimate experience of light. The collection is finally optimistic and tends towards the 'diaphanous' by means of *difficulté vaincue* (a favourite expression of Nash's). Some interesting readings of *dizains*, but on the whole not a point of view with which very many will nowadays be in agreement. A. Glauser, '"Souffrir non souffrir": formule de l'écriture scévienne', Kritzman, *Signe*, 39–48, treats the impossible yearning for a fully reciprocated love in *Délie* as an allegory of the impossible search for meaning. J. F. Pestureau, 'Théologie et stylistique: à propos du *Microcosme* de M. Scève', *NRSS*, 9:55–72, is a presentation. F. Cornilliat, 'Quelques enjeux de la rime équivoque', *RHR*, 33:5–30, deals with this issue in respect of the Grands Rhétoriqueurs.

RONSARD AND THE PLÉIADE

Michel Simonin, *Pierre de Ronsard*, Fayard, 1990, 425 pp., is an excellent and very readable biography. It is based on solid historical research and is unsurpassed in its command of detail. Simonin sets the poetry in an historical context without assuming that the poet's life is at every point reflected in his work. The book is aimed at the intelligent reading public and scholars alike, but the latter should observe that the volume contains no notes. Marcel Tetel (ed.), *Sur des vers de Ronsard, 1585–1985. Actes du colloque international, Duke University, 11–13 April 1985*, Aux Amateurs de Livres, 1990, 186 pp., contains the following: R. Aulotte, 'Paroles émues, paroles élues dans les *Amours de Marie* et les *Sonnets pour Hélène*' (9–15), tries to ascertain the relationship between words and feelings; a slight piece; M. Beaujour, 'La pragmatique des incipits dans les *Sonnets pour Hélène*' (17–27), makes one or two useful remarks about the interplay of incipits and 'real life' events; C. Blum, 'Peinture de la souffrance et représentation du moi dans la poésie amoureuse de Ronsard' (29–36), as usual an intelligent essay, proposing that 'le plaisir de la souffrance se confond [...] avec le plaisir d'écrire'; J. Céard, 'Muret, commentateur des

Amours de Ronsard' (37–50), elucidates Muret's theory of fable, as manifested in his Ronsard Commentaries; M. Dassonville, 'Pour une poétique de l'illusion' (51–59), illustrates this theme in respect of politics and love; M. Jeanneret, 'Les *Amours de Marie*: inscription de la deuxième personne et stratégies dialogiques' (60–70), notes the greater number of dialogic forms in the *Amours de Marie* and relates this ultimately to R.'s endeavours to seduce the reader; perceptive; L. D. Kritzman, 'Le corps de la fiction et la fiction du corps chez Ronsard' (71–83), is a Lacanian analysis; G. Mathieu-Castellani, 'La main dextre et l'autre, ou la rhétorique détournée' (85–92), examines the tensions of hand, heart, and writing in R.; R. Melançon, 'La fureur amoureuse' (93–104), an analysis of the 1552 *Amours* in a Neoplatonic light, adding little that is new; D. Ménager, 'L'amour au féminin' (105–16), on the ways R. hands his poetic voice to women, especially in the *Franciade*; well observed; R. Regosin, 'Poétique et rhétorique de l'amour: le propre et l'impropre de la lecture de Ronsard' (117–26), considers the question of 'true' interpretation; M. Simonin, 'Hélène avant Surgères: pour une lecture humaniste des *Sonnets pour Hélène*' (127–43), is on the Helen legend and R.'s treatment of it; W. Theile, 'Ronsard et la poétique du "variant penser"' (145–58), on poetry and painting; N. Vickers, 'Les métamorphoses de la Méduse: pétrarquisme et pétrification chez Ronsard' (159–70), sees R. as wishing to free himself from the rigidity of Petrarchist and Gorgiastic rhetoric; H. Weber, 'La circonstance et le symbole dans les *Sonnets pour Hélène*' (171–80), self-explanatory. T. Conley, 'Ronsard, le sonnet et la lettre: amorces de "Soit que son or se crespe lentement"', Kritzman, *Signe*, 117–30, compares this poem with 'Quand vous serez bien vieille' in one of those intense semiotic analyses for which Conley is famous. D. Cowling, 'Ronsard, Du Bellay et Ennius; l'image du vol dans une ode de Ronsard', *NRSS*, 9:45–53, suggests Ennius's 'volito vivos per ora virûm' as the source for 'Je volerai vif par l'univers' in Ronsard's ode 'A sa Muse' (= Laumonier II, 152). P. Desan, '"Le labeur de mes dois": Ronsard et la création poétique', *Revue des Amis de Ronsard du Japon*, 4:53–68, stresses that poetic creation for R. is connected with physical labour and expects a suitable level of financial reward. A corrective to any lingering ideas about the transcendence of inspiration in R. and an interesting materialist view of his work. P. Eichel, 'Quand le poète-*fictor* devient *pictor* . . . Lecture de l'ode II, 28 de Ronsard, "Des peintures contenues dedans un tableau" (fin 1549)', *BHR*, 53:619–43, sees this ode as a tension between R.'s belief in the return of a political Golden Age under Henri II and his awareness that international relations, like the order of nature, are uncertain and fragile. P. Ford, 'Neoplatonic fictions in the *Hymnes* of Ronsard', Kenny,

Fictions, 45–55, analyses the role of Proclus's commentary on the *Timaeus* and Eusebius's *Praeparatio evangelica* in R.'s Seasonal Hymns. L. M. Heller and C. G. Brown, 'Ronsard, Horace et la rage des frères', *BHR*, 53:123–26, prove definitively that the phrase 'des freres la rage' in *Odes* IV, 18 (= Laumonier II, 152) refers to Calais and Zetes and not the Dioscuri, as Laumonier claims. J. O'Brien, 'Theatrum Catopticum: Ronsard's *Les Amours de Cassandre*', *MLR*, 86:298–309, looks at this collection from the standpoint of effects of perspective. F. Rigolot, 'Writing the crisis differently: Ronsard's *Discours* and Montaigne's *Essais*', Desan, *Humanism*, 107–23, maintains that 'the *essai* distinguishes itself from the *discours* to the extent that the first form accommodates the general deliberations of a private subject, the "individual", whereas the second can only allow the individual expression of public subjectivity'. M. Simonin, 'Ronsard et l'exil de l'âme', *CAIEF*, 43:25–44, makes an interesting argument for regarding some of R.'s poetry as forms of spiritual exile. F. M. Weinberg, 'Double Dido: patterns of passion in Ronsard's *Franciade*', *Stone Vol.*, 73–85, does some solid work on the problem of Hyante and Clymène.

François Joukovsky, *Le Bel Objet. Les Paradis artificiels de la Pléiade*, Champion, 225 pp., is a thorough examination of the Pleiade's attitudes to the plastic arts, emphasizing throughout that they had very clear ideas of beauty. M. Riffaterre, 'Un faux problème: l'érosion intertextuelle', Kritzman, *Signe*, 51–59, uses *Le Premier des meteores* to contend that intertextuality need not assume a reader highly equipped to spot all the allusions. Stimulating, but needs more work in order to substantiate its case. E. Ahmed, 'Du Bellay, Sébillet and the problematic identity of the French humanist', *Neophilologus*, 75:185–93, says that whereas S. held a divinely inspired view of the poet's identity, B. valued the actual labour of poetic creativity; too clear-cut. J. Debu, 'De l'ordonnance de Villers-Cotterêts à la *Deffence et illustration de la langue françoise*: affirmation poétique et revendication littéraire', Jones-Davies, *Renaissance*, 137–51, is an inconclusive attempt to see the *Deffence* as the continuation of the *Ordonnance*. J. C. Nash, 'The poetics of seeing and showing: Du Bellay's love lyrics', *Stone Vol.*, 45–59, claims that *L'Olive* illustrates 'the seeing and showing of bright metaphorical presence, even of metaphysical essences'. Perhaps. M. Quainton, 'Du Bellay and Janus Vitalis', *FSB*, 38:12–15, compares and contrasts B.'s 'Nouveau venu, qui cherches Rome en Rome' with Vitalis's 'original', to the advantage of the former. J. Schwartz, 'The poet in bivio: Du Bellay's spiritual itinerary in *Les Regrets*', *Stone Vol.*, 61–71, characterizes the poet's desire for his homeland as a movement out of irony and satire, and towards the reclaiming of virtue. J. Braybrook, 'Science and myth in the poetry of Remy Belleau', *RenS*, 5:277–87, describes *Les Amours et nouveaux eschanges des pierres precieuses* (1576) and concludes that it ultimately contains a religious message. Robert Melançon (ed.), Étienne Jodelle, *L'Amour obscur, Orphée*, 192 pp., is a selection principally from the *Amours, Contr'Amours*, and *Album de la maréchale de Retz*. There are sparse notes and a glossary of the most difficult lexical terms. Its *abordable* price makes this edition obviously useful at undergraduate level, but the absence of line numbers for the poems turns quick referencing into a problem and the modernization of the Renaissance spelling will not meet with everyone's approval. M. Tetel, 'L'effacement du *tu* chez Jodelle', Kritzman, *Signe*, 61–76, demonstrates how *je* highlights its own position at the expense of the *tu* in J.'s love poetry.

AFTER THE PLÉIADE

Placing books II and III of d'Aubigné's *Les Tragiques* on the list of *agrégation* set texts for 1991 has had the effect of provoking a tidal wave of publications. Jean-Raymond Fanlo, *Tracés, ruptures. La Composition instable des 'Tragiques'*, Champion, 1990, 493 pp., traces problems of representation especially in the first five books, contrasting the thrust and organization of the poem with the interruptions, digressions, and disruptive pluralities of meaning which occur along the way. This work accords extraordinary and painstaking attention to even the smallest details; this is far from being an asset, however, and the argument would have gained from greater streamlining. Marie-Madeleine Fragonard, Frank Lestringant, and Gilbert Schrenck, *La Justice des Princes. Commentaires des 'Tragiques', livres II et III*, Mont-de-Marsan, Éditions InterUniversitaires, 1990, 230 pp., contains: M. M. Fragonard, F. Lestringant, G. Schrenck, 'Pour une poétique des *Tragiques*' (11–60) — basic information about title, genre and structure (with tabulations); G. Schrenck, 'La généalogie du mal: la mère et ses trois fils' (63–113), on *Princes*, ll. 755–930; F. Lestringant, 'Ciel ouvert' (117–78), on *Chambre Dorée*, ll. 1–160; M. M. Fragonard, 'Figures d'injustice' (181–208), on *Chambre Dorée*, ll. 233–510. Marie Madeleine Fragonard, *Essai sur l'univers religieux d'Agrippa d'Aubigné*, Mont-de-Marsan, Éditions InterUniversitaires, 207 pp., is overtly designed for student requirements, but is less pedestrian than many of its kind. The subject is thoughtfully and helpfully explored (with sections on e.g. 'Textes croisés et formulation du sacré', 'Dogmatique, pragmatique, tradition', 'L'unité en jeu de miroirs') and is well elucidated. Frank Lestringant, *La Cause des martyrs dans 'Les Tragiques' d'Agrippa d'Aubigné*, Mont-de-Marsan, Éditions InterUniversitaires, 117 pp., is really three essays aimed at *agrégatifs*, in theory centring on the paradoxical idea that a return to the principles of the Gospel brought about increased blood-letting. In reality only the last two essays hang together, as comparisons between A. and Crespin and then A. and classical writing on martyrs. Three useful articles rather than a substantial book. Gisèle Mathieu-Castellani, *Agrippa d'Aubigné. Le Corps de Jézabel*, PUF, 125 pp. Psychoanalytical approach to A., taking as its theme the ambiguous sado-masochistic attitudes towards the mother's body (symbolic of the female body in general). The author traces the thematics of blood, wounding, *déchirement*, sacrifice in the Diane–Hécaté cycle of *Le Printemps* as well as in the mother figures in *Les Tragiques*, ending with 'le corps obscène' of Jézabel–Cathérine de Médicis. Despite the title, she spends at least as much time on *Le Printemps* as on *Les Tragiques*, but an intelligent study very well brought off. André Thierry (ed.), Agrippa d'Aubigné, *Histoire universelle*, vol. 5 (TLF, 399), Geneva, Droz, 381 pp., continues the critical edition from Books VII, chap. 20, up to Book IX, chap. 5, covering the years 1576–1579. Marie Madeleine Fragonard and Madeleine Lazard (eds), *'Les Tragiques' d'Agrippa d'Aubigné* (Unichamp, 24), Champion, 1990, 176 pp., contains the following: J.-R. Fanlo, '"Encor pour l'advenir": les dates de *Princes* et de la *Chambre Dorée*' (11–34), sifts through these two books, dating the historical events and persons alluded to, and concluding that more of the poem than was previously imagined achieved its final form in the reign of Henri IV; M.-H. Prat, 'Le discours de l'analogie dans *Les Tragiques* et les problèmes du langage véridique' (35–61), examines analogical language as part of the discourse of truth; F. Lestringant, 'L'œil de Scipion. Point de vue et style dans *Les Tragiques*' (63–86), looks at the influences of the *Somnium Scipionis* particularly in relation to Coligny and sees this as part of an overall upward movement in *Les Tragiques*; C.-G. Dubois, '"Dieu descend". Figuration et transfiguration dans *Les Tragiques*, III, 139–232' (87–111); in the course of this paper the author has the exotic idea of comparing God's descent to *Blitzkrieg* and *Nacht und Nebel*. A. Tournon, 'La prophétie palimpseste' (113–24), as usual an intelligent and stimulating piece, suggesting how prophecy in *Les Tragiques* 'travaille contre l'évidence des échecs et des deuils à une difficile transfiguration'; G. Schrenck, 'Ubris et Themis. La justice dans les livres II et III des *Tragiques*' (125–44); M.-M. Fragonard, 'La tragédie universelle. Image des relations entre les nations' (145–65), a fresh and original look at how the Civil War affects A.'s view of other nations. *Albineana*, 3, 1990, contains the following: Y. Delègue, 'L'écriture de la vérité dans *Les Tragiques*' (7–17), argues that Truth lies in seeing, an interesting idea which is too embryonic and needs greater substance than ten pages; A. Thierry, '*Les Tragiques* et *L'Histoire universelle*, de Melpomène eschevelée à Clio astorge?' (19–31), compares and contrasts parallel episodes from these two works — useful rather than gripping; E. Kotler, 'De la poésie à la prose. L'écriture du travestissement des livres II et III des *Tragiques* aux pamphlets d'A. d'Aubigné (*Confession du Sieur de Sancy, Avantures du Baron de Faeneste*)' (33–52), draws on a variety of material in an interesting presentation of this theme; M. Soulié, 'Agrippa d'Aubigné. Étude de l'*Elégie* no. v' (53–61), reads the poem in the light of A.'s break with Henri of Navarre in the 1570s and his withdrawal to his estates at Landes-Guinemer; M.-D. Legrand, 'Le moment de la métamorphose: instant rhétorique dans *Le Printemps* d'Agrippa d'Aubigné' (63–77), a study of 'Baroquisme' in semi-lyrical style and with stylized, formalist personifications (e.g. *Élan, Retenue, Fuite*). Baroque indeed; C.-G. Dubois, '"L'Espagne au front". Remarques sur quelques occurrences des affaires d'Espagne dans les œuvres d'Agrippa d'Aubigné datées de 1616' (79–94); good collection of material about a little-studied subject; K. A. Perry, 'D'Aubigné, père et fils: paternité, continuité et discontinuité historique et narratologique dans l'œuvre albinéenne' (95–107), traces the self-destructiveness and cruelty of *Les Tragiques* and *Le Printemps* back to A.'s tortured relationship with his father; an article on an aspect of A. which has attracted a certain quantity of recent work; M. Walzer, 'Rapports de l'écrit à l'histoire et au "politique": l'image d'Henri IV dans l'œuvre d'Agrippa d'Aubigné' (109–31), focuses on *Les Tragiques, Histoire Universelle* and *Sa vie à ses enfants*, shows how the mythic status of Henri IV increases and diminishes according to context. Françoise Charpentier (ed.), *'Les Tragiques' d'Agrippa d'Aubigné. Actes de la journée d'étude Agrippa d'Aubigné, 9 novembre 1990*, Université de Paris–VII, 116 pp., contains: F. Lestringant, 'Les *Tragiques* et les *Hymnes*: la cosmologie de Ronsard et de d'Aubigné' (7–23), concludes his comparison by stating 'on peut donc lire [...] l'ensemble des *Tragiques* comme une hymne chrétienne'; M. Soulié, 'De l'éloquence à la Parole' (27–37), a close reading of *Princes* 1486 ff. and *Chambre Dorée* 1003 f., comparing A.'s phraseology with the Hebrew original; M.-M. Fragonard, 'L'éloge d'Elisabeth' (39–52), self-explanatory; good, logical paper, however; G. Schrenck, 'Agrippa d'Aubigné et la vérité dans le livre II des *Tragiques*' (53–63); A. Tournon, 'La mémoire de l'enfer' (65–77), examines curses and imprecations as a means of keeping memories of hell firmly present in the sinner's consciousness; J.-R. Fanlo, 'Enthousiasme et colère dans les livres II et III des *Tragiques*' (79–89), argues that the combination of enthusiasm and anger defies all prescriptive norms and finds its logical expression in the expectation of apocalypse; G. Mathieu-Castellani, 'La scène judiciaire dans *Les Tragiques*' (91–102), on A.'s fascination with legal terminology and particularly the courtroom scene; S. Perrier, 'L'écrit et la voix dans *Les Tragiques* (livres II et III)' (103–16). S. Bokoam,

'Histoire et eschatologie dans les livres II et III des *Tragiques*', *IL*, 43 : 9–13, argues that *Les Tragiques* do not reconcile present and origin; interesting argument if rather brief. J.-R. Fanlo, 'Fiction poétique et prière dans le livre III des *Tragiques*', *RHR*, 32 : 5–15, claiming that 'l'invention poétique se garantit sur une pratique presque liturgique, elle s'agrège la voix de la prière'. M. Jeanneret, '*Les Tragiques*: mimesis et intertexte', Kritzman, *Signe*, 101–13, demonstrates eloquently the imbrication of the real and the written in *Les Tragiques*. Excellent quality, as usual. J. O'Brien, 'Les seuils de d'Aubigné', *RR*, 82 : 286–96, shows how the theme of the threshold in *Les Tragiques* is related to ideas of pollution and crime. M. Quainton, 'Alchemical reference and the making of poetry in d'Aubigné's *Les Tragiques*', Kenny, *Fictions*, 57–69, detects a persistent pattern of alchemical allusion in *Les Tragiques* (*circulatio*, the celestial smith, transmogrification of the *massa confusa*). G. Schrenck, 'Agrippa d'Aubigné et la liberté de conscience, d'après ses écrits politiques', *Actes* (Mulhouse), 153–69, deals with *Le Caducée*, the *Traitté sur les guerres civiles* and the *Debvoir mutuel*.

Yvonne Bellenger, James Dauphiné, Claude Faisant, Frank Lestringant, Isabelle Pantin, Josianne Rieu, Françoise Roudaut and Gilbert Schrenck (eds), Du Bartas, *La Seconde Semaine (1584)* (STFM, 193), vol. I, Klincksieck, lix + 254 pp., contains the four books of the *Premier Jour*, with an average-length introduction and extensive quotation throughout in the footnotes from Simon Goulart's commentary. Y. Bellenger, 'Le temps de la création et le temps des créatures dans *Les Semaines* de du Bartas', *Stone Vol.*, 87–100, is an analysis of the interplay between present and past tenses. N. Heather, 'Number, symmetry and order in Du Bartas's *Semaines*: reform of church *and* sky?', *RenS*, 5 : 288–300. E. S. Miller, 'La Ceppède's *Théorèmes*: parts and wholes, St Peter in context and rhetorical structure', *BHR*, 53 : 33–47, begins by using the example of St Peter to emphasize that the *Théorèmes* must be read as a whole in order to appreciate thematic developments, but then loses sight of St Peter and concentrates on rhetorical structure instead. Two articles in one. R. Guillot, ' "Un langage à deux versants" dans *Le mespris de la vie et la consolation contre la mort* de J. B. Chassignet', *RHR*, 32 : 17–36, studies in detail C.'s use of images to communicate directly with the reader by embodying abstract concepts in concrete form. Guy Demerson with J.-P. Labrousse (eds), Jean de la Gessée, *Les Jeunesses* (STFM, 194), cxxv + 328 pp., has a careful introduction (including biography and bibliography), notes and glossary. R. Patterson, ' "Politique" propaganda and the Paris Parlement: Jacques de la Guesle's *Polimetrie* of 1588', *FS*, 45 : 257–67, construes this poem as both a defence of Harlay and in praise of moderation 'as an affirmation of the political rallying call of [. . .] "moyenneurs" in support of their legitimate sovereign'. S. Perrier, 'La circulation du sens dans les *Emblemes chrestiens* de Georgette de Montenay (1571)', *NRSS*, 9:71–89, uses facsimiles of the *Emblemes* to study how theological meaning arises from the interplay between picture, motto, and *huitain*. M. Lazard, 'Deux féministes poitevines au XVIe siècle: les dames Des Roches', *Albineana*, 3, 1990:143–53, examines their attitude to issues such as learning, literary creation, and marriage, without making over-exaggerated claims for the effects of their feminism.

4. DRAMA

Jelle Koopmans and Paul Verhuyck (eds), Nicolas de la Chesnaye, *La Condemnation de banquet* (TLF, 395), Geneva, Droz, 321 pp., is a scholarly edition of this early drama with an assiduous introduction and notes. There is a glossary of uncommon words, a list of authorities quoted in the course of the play and a bibliography. C. E. Campbell, '"Medieval" and "Renaissance" in French Renaissance comedies', *Stone Vol.*, 103–11, contests the importance of 1552 as marking the appearance of French Comedy and wishes to adopt a broader perspective. A. Billault, 'Jean-Antoine de Baïf, traducteur d'*Antigone*', *RHT*, 43:76–84, is a brief presentation. Y. Loskoutoff, 'Magie et tragédie: la *Cléopâtre captive* d'Étienne Jodelle', *BHR*, 53:65–80, makes a persuasive case for regarding the play as an instance of Renaissance Egyptomania. J. T. Mann, 'Character development in French Renaissance comedy: Larivey's unreasonable Severin', *RoN*, 31, 1990:73–80, argues that Severin has the potential to hold *Les Esprits* together, but that L. fails to exploit this potential to the full. P. Servet, 'La *Résurrection abrégée* (inédite) d'Eloy du Mont, dit Costentin: mystère ou tragédie?', *NRSS*, 9:15–40, is a very thorough presentation of the play, concluding (rather flatly) that it is half-way between tragedy and *mystère*. L. Marmin, 'A neglected piece of evidence in the dating of Jean de la Taille's *La Famine ou les Gabéonites*', *FSB*, 40:7–8, proposes that we re-date the play to 1571 (i.e. *preceding Saül*).

5. MONTAIGNE

Interest in M. continues unabated, especially as we approach the quatercentenary of his death. Floyd Gray, *Montaigne bilingue: le latin des 'Essais'* (Études montaignistes, 7), Champion, 156 pp., is a helpful examination, starting from the premise that the quotations are an integral part of the *Essais* and cannot simply be neglected. Emphasizes the great range and variety of M.'s Latin quotations.

Particularly good is the section dealing with 'Citations réalistes et obscènes' — which quickly disposes of the coyness of Villey and Thibaudet — followed by very pertinent remarks on 'Éros et l'écriture'. These chapters have the effect of restoring to Montaigne the full force of his thinking and writing about sex. Pierre Leschemelle, *Montaigne ou le Mal à l'âme*, Imago, 216 pp., sees Michel de Montaigne as arising out of Michel Eyquem by the slaying of the biological father (Pierre Eyquem) and the spiritual father (La Boétie). Regards M.'s sex life as subject to repression and hang-ups; these then give rise to melancholy, which M. later converts into *gaie sagesse*. A mixture of the zany and the unconvincing. Malcolm C. Smith, *Montaigne and Religious Freedom, The Dawn of Pluralism*, Geneva, Droz, 257 pp., makes comparisons between M.'s concept of freedom and that of his friend, La Boétie. Argues that M. began by sharing La Boétie's attitude but, over the course of time, evolved his own views. Builds not only on the *Discours de la servitude volontaire*, but also on the *Mémoire sur la pacification des troubles* which Smith believes can be securely attributed to La Boétie. A piece of historical and religious detection work, the book sees certain passages in *Essais* as a direct reference to the political and religious situation of their time. Blum, *Montaigne*, includes the following: M. Simonin, 'La préhistoire de l'*Apologie de Raimond Sebond*' (85–116), emphasizes the mediocre fortunes of the *Theologia naturalis* before its take-up by M. and concludes with the bold suggestion that M. had invented detractors 'afin de pouvoir ensuite feindre de les réfuter, pour mieux enfin les servir'; P. Hendrick, 'Traduttore traditori: Montaigne et Sebond' (139–65), studies M. as a translator of Sebond, showing that M.'s cuts and adaptations reduce the role played by reason in Sebond's work; M. McKinley, 'Traduire/écrire/croire: Sebond, les anciens et Dieu dans le discours des *Essais*' (167–86), looks at the *Apologie* through the optic of translation and concludes that what can never be translated is God; J. C. Pons, 'Sur le second degré de l'*Apologie*' (187–200), concerns two types of reason from a philosophical viewpoint inspired by Kant; too clever by half; R. Esclapez, 'L'échelle de Nature dans la *Théologie naturelle* et dans L'*Apologie de Raimond Sebond*' (201–26), sees in M. a subversive who overthrows the natural order symbolized by the *échelle de Nature*, substituting an anthropological and zoological discourse for Sebond's theological outlook; E. Limbrick, 'Métamorphose d'un philosophe en théologien' (229–46), argues that M. attempts to set Christian truths beyond the reach of reason by invoking the necessity of faith and grace; D. Ménager, 'L'ironie dans L'*Apologie*' (247–60); F. Rigolot, 'D'une *Théologie* "pour les dames" à une *Apologie* "per le donne"' (261–90), interprets the *Apologie* as a pro-feminist tract directed against *l'homme* (= 'man' rather than 'mankind'); provocative. *Actes* (Dakar) includes the following: R. Aulotte, 'Montaigne et l'humanisme' (7–15), a humanist's defence of M. the humanist, restating the case without breaking any new ground; J.-Y. Pouilloux, 'Comment commencer à penser véritablement?' (19–30), at the end of which we still don't know how; Z. Samaras, 'Montaigne et Platon: la philosophie du langage' (31–43), a modest study with parallels and contrasts; J. C. Pons, 'Trois incursions de Montaigne dans la métaphysique' (45–52), for whom M.'s metaphysics is the 'histoire pragmatique de la conscience instable d'un demi-être' — a hard-hitting, un-Sorbonne line ('M. nie la métaphysique') but strongly argued; P. Gueye, 'Montaigne philosophe politique: l'écho de la polémique ligueuse dans les *Essais* autour des années 1588: religion, politique et morale sociale' (61–71), provides an overview of M.'s disagreement with the Ligue, but argues (too feebly) that M. resigned himself to the current political situation; M. Tetel, 'Le conte du philosophe' (73–87), a much-needed study of M.'s role as a *conteur*; E. Balmas, 'Tradition et invention dans l'idéologie des "Cannibales"' (89–100), considers that M. uses the cannibals in order to challenge the Christian culture of the West; unexceptional; A. Diane, 'Rabelais et Montaigne. De la chronique gigantale à l'essai infini: réécriture kaléidoscopique d'un parcours' (101–12), compares and contrasts these writers on theme of the journey of self-discovery; neat; A. Toure, 'Montaigne: écrire baroque' (113–28), studies the rhetorical and stylistic features which he claims make M. a baroque writer; C . Blum, 'L'être et le néant. Les *Essais*, voyage au bout de la métaphysique' (129–39), is a carefully argued, well constructed essay which shows how M. alters the received notion of man as *néant*. *BSAM*, 7e série, 23–24, contains: C. Lafon and J. Saint-Martin, 'Iconographie de Montaigne' (1–44, with special pagination), a reprint of an old document which has not been bettered; S. Farquhar, 'Les tactiques du scepticisme dans l'*Apologie de Raimond Sebond*' (19–43), purpose: how M. breaks free of divine authority which inspired Sebond and finds his own autonomy as a writer; R. Esclapez, 'Le nom de Montaigne dans les *Essais*: mythe, réalité, littérature' (45–61), quasi-semiotic study of the name 'M.' solidifying into the place 'M.' and achieving substantial form in literature; 'M.' equals a place, an author and a work fused together; P. Venesoen, 'Montaigne et *L'Égalité des hommes et des femmes*' (65–71), compares and contrasts the views of M. and Mlle de Gournay on the position of women; P. Leschemelle, '"Je n'ai point autre passion qui me tienne en haleine" (Montaigne, l'amour, l'impuissance et les *Essais*)' (73–83), speculates that M. suffered from impotence and attempts to evaluate the effect of this on his work; a bad case of 'flux de caquet'. C. Blum, 'L'*Apologie de Raimond Sebond* et le déplacement de l'apologétique traditionnelle à la fin du XVIe siècle', Kritzman, *Signe*, 161–73, contends that the contradiction between M.'s aims in the *Apologie* and his achievements are the product of a transformation of the concept of the *Apologia* genre; a very worthwhile piece. R. D. Cottrell, 'Gender imprinting in the *Essais*', *EsC*, 30, 1990:85–96, is all about M. liberating himself from the strait-jacket of patriarchal discourse. P. Desan, '"Pour clore nostre conte": la comptabilité de Montaigne', *Littérature*, 82:28–42, makes an interesting and well argued case for seeing M. as a book-keeper and the *Essais* as a rendering of account. F. Gray, 'Montaigne et le langage des animaux', Kritzman, *Signe*, 149–59, considers M.'s humanization of animals in the *Apologie*, in the light of his debt to Plutarch and in contrast to Descartes. T. Hampton, 'Unreadable signs: Montaigne, virtue and the interpretations of history', Desan, *Humanism*, 85–106, traces the collapse of French humanism through M.'s meditation on the difficulty of taking heroic figures as models of right conduct. A partial reading, but very worthwhile and challenging. J. Holyoake, '"Montaigne is meaningless" — official', *FSB*, 41:3–5, has just read *The Cornucopian Text*, over ten years after its publication, and takes issue with what he mistakenly believes is its view about Montaigne. S. Neumeister, 'Montaigne: von der Adelsrolle zur schriftstellerischen Autonomie', Haug, *Autorentypen*, 164–76, attempts to highlight M.'s uniqueness as a writer by contrasting him with early-modern notions of the self. Worthy. R. Regosin, 'Les figures de l'interpretation: moi/texte/contextes dans les *Essais* de Montaigne', Kritzman, *Signe*, 175–87, focuses on 'De la phisionomie' where he finds that M.'s efforts to keep Nature clear of the 'dangéreux suppléments' of knowledge and writing only end in their further entanglement. J. Supple, '"Excusions icy ce que je dy souvent": the relationship between "Du repentir" and "De l'utile et de l'honneste"', *MLR*, 86:567–72, capitalizing on the work of Marianne Meijer argues that 'III.1 and III.2 not only provide parallel explorations of the conflict between *l'utile* and *l'honnête* but jointly expose the hypocrisy of those who appeal to legitimate moral concepts (*l'honnête*, repentance) in order to disguise [. . .] their moral failings'.

THE SEVENTEENTH CENTURY

By Elizabeth Woodrough, *Lecturer in French, University of Exeter*

1. General

The shifting ground of the baroque again provides material for exciting debate: *YFS*, 80, subtitled 'Baroque topographies: literature/history/philosophy', contains the following general papers: L. Marin, 'Classical, baroque: Versailles, or the architecture of the Prince' (167–82), considers 'the palace of the Monarch, the French "classic" replacement of the baroque powers of Berninian architecture'; C. Jouhaud, 'Richelieu, or "baroque" power in action' (183–201), re-examines, among other affairs, the *Querelle du Cid* in relation to the challenging idea that the 'energy captured from power by the dramatic author or the critic is returned to it [. . .] in a game of mirrors which it will perhaps *please* the minister to practice in the intimacy of private performances'; O. Ranum, 'Encrustation and power in early modern French baroque culture' (202–26), draws up a vast inventory of baroque places in order to restore 'analytical force' to the term and 'to enhance the possibility of writing baroque history', and includes as adjuncts to artistic landmarks references to *Télémaque* and *La Place Royale*. A. B. Baccar, *La Mer, source de création littéraire en France au XVIIe siècle (1640–1671)*, PFSCL, 299 pp., charts the ebb and flow of sea imagery omnipresent in novels, plays, poetry and other texts from Gomberville's *Cythérée* and Mairet's *L'Illustre Corsaire* to *Psyché* and the *Entretiens d'Ariste et d'Eugène* (appearing to date *Zaïde* in the same year), as it changes form within Baroque lit. and achieves a new calm in Classical lit. when 'nous assistons au rétrécissement de ce thème qui n'est plus mentionné qu'avec sobriété'.

Memoirs provide an increasingly stable bridge between historical periods, and between lit. and history. As with the novel, the compilation of *banques de données* seems set to revolutionize our knowledge of the period.

Actes (Strasbourg) explores 'La cour au miroir des mémorialistes (1530–1682)' and contains the following papers on 17th-c. matters: M. Bertaud, 'Images de Louis XIII' (77–88), finds the material much harder to come by and to exploit than she had expected and that, beyond a certain minimalist portrait, 'tout le reste est subjectivité'; S. Bertière, 'Faire sa cour sous la Fronde: enjeux et périls' (147–62), studies the question: 'Comment faire sa cour au Roi et à la Reine, sans la faire en même temps à Mazarin?'; M. Cuénin-Lieber, 'L'expérience de la disgrâce sous Louis XIII et sous la Régence' (11–22), examines the attitudes of among others, Bassompierre, La

Châtre, and Pontis to an experience '[qui] n'est pas source d'enseignement pour le courtisan'; C. Douvier, 'Les portraits du Grand
Condé dans les Mémoires de P. Lenet et de N. Goulas' (175–82),
contrasts the two styles right down to their use of tenses, observing
that 'si le premier dépeint un idéal, le second [. . .] décrit un homme';
L. Godard de Donville, 'L'art de plaire chez les dames de cour au
temps de la régence d'Anne d'Autriche' (147–62), takes evidence
from the Memoirs of Mme de Motteville and Goulas to show that 'la
vertu qui plaît à la Cour doit plus à l'art qu'à la nature'; J.
Hennequin, 'La conjuration à la Cour de Henri IV et de Louis XIII'
(89–93), offers itself as a partial study of a phenomenon of which a
computer-aided analysis should eventually give the complete picture;
N. Hepp, 'Peut-on être homme de bien à la Cour: le débat sous
Louis XIII' (163–74), concludes that 'le destin de l'homme de bien
est d'être acculé à la retraite s'il veut devancer les orages que sa belle
conduite lui a préparés'; Id., 'L'étude du phénomène de la Cour par le
traitement informatique des notions' (207–13), presents a *feuille de
dépouillement* for the systematic study of the genre; C. Lauvergnat-
Gagnière, 'La Cour, lieu de pouvoir sous Henri IV' (55–68), compiles
evidence to show that this was a court 'qu'Henri IV sait faire briller
quand il le juge nécessaire' and no less full of intrigue than all the
others; E. Lesne-Jaffro, 'La question du genre des Mémoires chez
Bussy-Rabutin, Mlle de Montpensier et l'abbé Arnauld' (193–206),
suggests that these three authors of the 1660 generation 'confondent
la marginalité théorique du genre avec une liberté qui s'avère à
l'expérience illusoire'; M. McGowan, 'La fonction des fêtes dans la
vie de cour au XVIIe siècle' (43–54), locates descriptions of festivals
in the memoires of Bassompierre, Mlle de Montpensier, Louis XIV
and others and notes the primary importance of such occasions which
'offraient la possibilité à la fois de se donner en spectacle et de se
contempler soi-même'; M. Pernot, 'La Journée des Dupes: la leçon
des mémorialistes' (95–110), assesses the impact of *le grand orage* in the
work of nine memorialists and considers that the King made the right
choice; D. A. Watts, 'Jugements sur la Cour chez Retz et quelques
contemporains' (135–46), confronts the memoirs of Retz, Mme de
Motteville, and the *grande Mademoiselle* in particular and concludes
that 'les mémoralistes, lorsqu'ils jugent la Cour, préparent la voie à
La Bruyère et à Saint-Simon'; H. Zuber, 'La faveur et la disgrâce:
comparaison des cours d'Henri III et d'Henri IV' (69–76), observes
that 'les deux Rois, s'ils ont différé dans leur attitude à l'égard de la
haute noblesse de cour, n'en ont pas moins su pratiquer la faveur au
service de l'État'.

'Enfance et littérature au XVIIe siècle' is the theme of *LitC*, 14,
which contains the following general articles: D. Dupont-Escarpit,

'De la littérature populaire à la littérature d'enfance et de jeunes' (9–21), examines the status of childhood and finds that most of the texts accessible to children and young people were not written specially for them; A. Franchetti, 'L'enfant dans l'art: présences et absences' (21–33), considers the gallery of images of childhood in 'great' literature disappointing, when compared to art, where the desire to preserve 'l'aspect fugace de l'enfance' springs in part from the influence of religious iconography.

OC, 16, devoted to 'Critique contemporaine et littérature du XVIIe siècle', contains the following: J. M. Apostolidès, 'Portrait de l'auteur en dix-septiémiste' (11–31), examines the author's intellectual career in relation to the idea that it is not possible to understand French society in the classical period unless one is prepared at the same time to analyse the contemporary world and our own place in it; M. M. Houle, 'On reading Louis Marin' (95–113), explores Marin's experience as a reader of 17th-c. writings and particularly those of Perrault, concluding that his judgement of texts in non-canonical, but that his 'classicism is still constructed by the King's gaze'; O. Hullot-Kentor, 'Adorno in the seventeenth century' (97–103), suggests that 'what makes Adorno's work relevant to the contemporary discontents of theory and the study of 17th-c. literature is — to put it as provocatively as possible — just its inapplicability'; C. Spencer, 'Nouvelles voies/voix de l'analyse textuelle: entre sémiotique et stylistique, l'énonciation' (73–86), is a brief inventory of recent studies of Racine, Corneille, and 17th-c. fiction with a marked methodological allegiance, which proposes 'l'analyse énonciative' as the 'voie royale, susceptible d'ouvrir de nouveaux accès au texte en en libérant la polyphonie'.

K.-A. Jensen, 'La Nouvelle Querelle des Femmes: feminist criticism and seventeenth-century literature' (87–94), offers an overview of some representative readings of the 17th c. from D. Stanton's *Fiction of Préciosité* to M. L. Farrell's *Grandmother Sévigné*, arguing that 'the plurality of critical strategies is representative of feminist criticism in general'. J. DeJean, 'Classical reeditions: decanonizing the feminine', in *Displacements, Women, Tradition, Literatures in France*, ed. J. DeJean and N. K. Miller, Johns Hopkins Press, 336 pp., pp. 22–36, goes in search of an explanation for the exclusion of women from classic status and considers among other authors M. Buffet's *Nouvelles observations sur la langue française*. J. DeJean, *Tender Geographies: Women and the Origin of the Novel in France*, NY, Columbia U.P., xii + 279 pp., has a section on *La Princesse de Clèves*. E. Harth, 'Cartesian women', *YFS*, 80: 146–64, concentrates on the reflections on Descartes of Anne de la Vigne, Marie Dupré, and Catherine Descartes, the philosopher's niece. B. Krajewska, 'Encore autour des lettres du XVIIe siècle. La femme et son univers précieux à travers le prisme des lettres des contemporains', *SF*, 35:13–23, surveys the 'douce manie' of letter-writing theory and practice from a feminine perspective.

G. Couton, **Écritures codées. Essais sur l'allégorie au XVIIe siècle*, Aux Amateurs des Livres, 185 pp. *De Gaulle et les écrivains*, ed. J. Serroy, Grenoble U.P., 208 pp., gives substantial attention to 17th-c. writers in three papers: R. Bourgeois, 'Le Cardinal de Retz et de Gaulle mémorialistes' (113–20), discusses *grandeur* as an ideal and a leitmotif in both sets of Memoirs, and theatrical metaphor; J. Chocheyras (121–39) draws a parallel between the maxims in the Memoirs and in La Rochefoucauld; J. Serroy, 'De Gaulle et la tragédie: Corneille' (141–60), takes as its point of departure the quotation from *Le Cid* which was the climax of the 1942 speech and again emphasizes the obsessive recurrence of theatrical metaphor in De Gaulle's writings. G. Dotoli, **Letteratura per il populo in Francia (1600–1750). Proposte di lettura della 'Bibliothèque bleue'*, Fasano, Schena, Biblioteca della Ricerca, Mentalità e Scrittura, 405 pp. + 96 illus. W. Gibson, 'Attitudes towards obesity in seventeenth-century France', *SCFS*, 13:215–29, is 'a brief tour round 17th-century French contours' with over 70 refs to contemporary views on diet and its consequences. R. Horville, **Histoire de la littérature française: XVIIe siècle*, Hatier, 416 pp. A. Mercier, *La Littérature facétieuse sous Louis XIII (1610–1643)*, Droz, 355 pp., is a critical bibliography of the first edn of 812 texts ranging from monologues, dialogues, *récits* and *nouvelles*, to songs, farces and poetic forms, which aims 'de faire revivre toute une littérature généralement oubliée ou méconnue que son abondance met pourtant au rang d'un phénomène d'édition notable'. P.-J. Salazar, 'Les pouvoirs de la fable: mythologie, littérature et tradition (1650–1725)', *RHLF*, 91:878–90, moves from F. Pomey's *Pantheum mythicum seu fabulosa deorum historia* (1658) to the work of Père de Tonnemine which 'dépouille la Fable de sa dimension hermèneutique, de sa séduisante présence et de son statut littéraire'. V. Worth, 'Optimism and misanthropy: some seventeenth-century models in a late eighteenth-century debate', *SFCS*, 13:163–78, seeks to draw attention to the significance of Molière, La Fontaine and possibly La Bruyère in the Enlightenment debate centred around C. d'Harleville's *L'Optimiste*.

Wentzlaff-Eggebert, *Langage*, includes M. O. Sweetser, 'La littérature et les femmes' (51–66), which illustrates with particular relevance to Mlle Desjardins, *La Princesse de Clèves* and Mme de Sévigné how 'l'art de la parole pouvait s'appliquer, *mutatis mutandis*, aux nouveaux venus dans la littérature au XVIIe siècle', and the following general studies: B. Bray, 'Art épistolaire et art poétique: Théophile, Maynard, Tristan' (119–33), aims to extract some of the secrets of letter writing by comparing these three authors' *recueil épistolaire* with their other poetic works; R. Duchêne, 'De Sorel à Molière, ou la rhétorique des Précieuses' (135–45), tests the theory that the *Recueil de pièces en prose* was one of the twin sources of *Les Précieuses ridicules*; Y. Giraud, 'Le goût classique et la pointe' (95–108), surveys definitions, recommendations and usage in 17th-c. authors of 'un abus de la rhétorique' which should only be employed as a musician would use dissonance'; A. Kibédi-Varga, 'Rhétorique et narration' (279–86), discusses the *rhétorisation* and '*dérhétorisation*' of a range of narrative forms; W. Leiner, 'L'apostrophe à un destinataire fictif. De l'emploi d'un artifice rhétorique chez les auteurs du XVIIe siècle' (35–50), considers its frequency a further sign that 'L'éloquence n'est pas venue de l'artifice, mais au contraire celuy-ci est né de l'éloquence, qui l'a précédé'; A. Steffenelli, '"Mots vieux" et bon usage au XVIIe siècle' (81–94), follows F. Brunot (*HLF*, 1939/40), and traces the *Renaissance* of archaisms in 17th-c. French, concluding with an examination of 'le bon usage littéraire' in Racine; L. Van Delft, 'Les caractères des nations: de la topique à la création littéraire' (67–80), considers English authors particularly instructive on this point. Other contributions are noted below.

I. Landy-Houillon, 'Usage et raison aux siècles classiques', *DSS*, 173:359–73, is a rational synthesis of ideas gleaned from theoretical grammars from Meigret to Féraud's *Dictionnaire critique* and the views of *Remarqueurs* on current usage. O. Pot, 'La question de l'obscénité à l'âge classique', *ib.*, 403–36, proceeds from the first instance of the term in *L'École des femmes*, through *la scène de l'obscène* to *l'obscène de la cène* and *l'obscène en scène*, to suggest, among other things, that in Molière's play 'l'obscène n'est pas dans la représentation (les mots), mais dans *l'irreprésentable* du discours'.

2. POETRY

G. Mathieu-Castellani, *La Poésie amoureuse de l'âge baroque: vingt poètes maniéristes et baroques*, LGF. J.-P. Chauveau, 'Les avatars de l'élégie au XVIIe siècle', Wentzlaff-Eggebert, *Langage*, 209–22, finds there is life still in the anti-Petrarchism of a poetic genre that was ever the poor relation of tragic drama, which 17th-c. poets used as a kind of 'experimental laboratory' for new forms. J.-P. Collinet, 'La Fontaine et Théophile', *Actes* (Marseille), 151–70, observes among numerous other affinities, the deep bond in their individual attitudes to friendship. R. Guichemerre, *Quatre poètes du XVIIe siècle. Malherbe — Tristan l'Hermite — Saint-Amant — Boileau*, SEDES, 249 pp., not unsurprisingly devotes more space to the first and last of the four (giving full coverage to Malherbe and the *Satires* I–IX, and virtually ignoring *la poésie galante*), and moves deftly between the gravity of Tristan and the facetious burlesque of Saint-Amant, allowing readers to draw their own conclusions. T. Marcus, 'L'Innocence persécutée (*c.* 1665): one polemicist's perception of contemporary politics', *SCFS*, 13:71–89, considers this anon. pro-Fouquet verse satire 'of exceptional historical and literary interest'. A. Niderst, 'La querelle de la pastorale', Niderst, *Pastorale*, 99–109, enters into the debate which developed, 'et parfois avec violence' between 1685 and 1730, as an extension of the *Querelle des Modernes*. G. Nondier, '"Eglogues en sabots . . .". Quelques aspects de la pastorale normande', *ib.*, 51–68, discusses this phenomenon in the Norman poets Pierre de Marbeuf, Vauquelin de La Fresnaye, and Louis Le Petit, among others. B. Papasogli, '"Cet océan vit en moy". Figure dello spazio interiore nel Seicento Francese', *SF*, 102:373–91, views the sea imagery in Le Moyne and other poets as a kind of vast 'mer spirituelle'.

    LA FONTAINE.   M. Beynel, 'Iconographies du XIXe siècle: comment interpréter les *Fables* de La Fontaine', *DSS*, 173:437–48, judges Gustave Moreau's work more sensitive to La F.'s poetry, while Gustave Doré remains 'prisonnier de la tradition classique, plus particulièrement de celle du XVIIIe siècle'. J.-P. Collinet, *Les Fables*, Gallimard, 582 pp., reproduces the original 1668 edn of Books 1–6, 1678–79 edn of Books VII–XI, and the 1693 edn of the *Fables choisies* of Book XII. Id., 'La Fontaine et l'enfance', *LitC*, 14:123–34, examines La F.'s ideas on child psychology and education. Id., J.-P. Collinet, 'Métamorphoses de La Fontaine', *Littératures*, 25:29–40, examines Ovidian metamorphoses in the *Fables*. Id., *Œuvres complètes*, vol. I, *Contes et Fables*, ed. J.-P. Collinet, Gallimard, Pléiade, clxxxii + 1544 pp., replaces the Pilon/Groos/Schiffrin edition of 1954, and is itself a work of monstrous and marvellous erudition with 700 pages of paratextual information, which deliberately ignores some more recent trends in La F. criticism, includes all the *Contes* and *Fables* and examples of the work of all the different generations of illustrators, as well as reproducing the Chauveau *vignettes* at the head of each fable. This edn reproduces the 1692 D. Thierry and C. Barbin edn of Books I–XI of the *Fables*, the C. Barbin 1693 edn of Book XII and the 1669 edn of the first two parts of the *Contes et nouvelles*, the 1671 edn of part III (by the same publishers) and the 1674 edn of the *Nouveaux contes* publ. by G. Migeon. P. Dandrey, *La Fabrique des Fables. Essai sur la poétique de La Fontaine*, Klincksieck, 280 pp., elaborates the idea of the *Fables* as a new '"art de conter" l'apologue' and devotes chapters to the *manière* of the fabulist and the *matière* of the fable. W. Drost, **Jean de La Fontaine dans l'univers des arts: richesses inconnues et inédites du Musée de La Fontaine à Château-Thierry*, Heidelberg, Winter, 92 pp. R. Garapon,

'A propos d'un opéra oublié de La Fontaine', Niderst, *Pastorale*, 93–98, takes another look at the *tragédie lyrique, Astrée*. F.-C. Gaudrard, 'La versification chez La Fontaine', *ChS*, 2 : 149–80, considers that as 'la critique selon Saint-Beuve' and the semioticians alike have conspired to study the poetic universe of the *Fables* with insufficient attention to versification, his detailed analysis of La F.'s freedom of interpretation of the *règles classiques* is long overdue. J. Grimm, *'Plus fait douceur que violence.* La rhétorique indirecte dans les *Fables* de La Fontaine', Wentzlaff-Eggebert, *Langage*, 109–18, takes as his point of departure the thesis that La F.'s choice of this form was directly influenced by Foucquet's arrest. C. Grisé, 'Under the pear tree: cognitive space and deceit structures in five "magical" *contes* of La Fontaine', *FrF*, 16:21–38, argues that structures of deceit constitute the major diegetic framework of the *Conte*. **Les Amours de Psyché et de Cupidon*, ed. J. C. Lambert, Castor Astral, 221 pp. F. Luoni, 'Un nouveau monde pour Psyché (Marino et La Fontaine)', *DSS*, 171 : 143–60, compares *Adone* and *Les Amours de Psyché et de Cupidon* and finds that in general 'la fidélité de Marino au texte d'Apulée est grande', whereas La F. 'a partout humanisé [...] l'aspect de la légende ancienne'. G. Maurand, 'Les "enfants" des *Fables* de La Fontaine: essai d'analyse actantielle d'un personnage', *LitC*, 14:135–50, examines all the fables which include children, however fleetingly, and seeks to establish their thematic coherence. H. Mazaheri, 'Les obsèques de la lionne ou l'art de survivre sous le despotisme', *LR*, 45:3–11, seeks to persuade that this centrally located fable is a prime example of La F.'s Machiavellian politics and of the art of survival. A. Niderst, 'Sur la composition des *Fables* de La Fontaine', *FR*, 65:187–95, discusses order in the second and richer *recueil* (1678) and suggests that, like the *Caractères*, 'les *Fables* n'offrent qu'un faux désordre'. D. L. Rubin, *A Pact with Silence: Art and Thought in the Fables of Jean de La Fontaine*, Columbus, Ohio State U.P., 125 pp., seeks to redefine the fable according to three types (assertive, dialectic, and problematic) and observes how, through his solutions to the poetic problems of his time, La F. anticipates the best of 19th- and 20th-c. French poets. M. Slater, 'La Fontaine's view of animals in his *Fables*', *SCFS*, 13:179–94, finds that La F.'s animals are not just emblematic of human psychology, but 'vivid, unexpected and exciting in their own right'.

*Le Fablier, 2, 'La Fontaine et la tradition européenne de la fable', 78 pp.; 3, 75 pp., sub-titled *Jean de La Fontaine, Bibliographie décennale (1980–1989)*, contains the following: T. Allott, 'Une décennie d'éditions et de traductions des œuvres de La Fontaine' (17–24), is happily able to report, following the sumptuous editions of the *Fables* by M. Fumaroli and J.-P. Collinet and others, that the autumnal

decade of this century has been one of 'mellow fruitfulness' in La F.
studies; P. Dandrey, 'Bibliographie analytique' (45–64), lists 307
articles, books and editions and gives a brief summary of each; M.
Schmitt, 'La place et l'image de La Fontaine dans l'enseignement
durant la décennie' (33–44), draws up a series of 'popularity' tables to
reflect the use and abuse of the *Fables* in French schools; M.-O.
Sweetser, 'Une décennie d'éditions critiques des œuvres de La
Fontaine' (25–32), observes that linguistic studies of La F. have been
rather thin on the ground, and that the newest and most fruitful
directions for research attempt to relate 'l'œuvre lafontainienne et les
réalités historiques, politiques, sociales' and to expose 'les couches
multiples de signification des *Fables* et autres œuvres'; P. Dandrey,
'Actualité de La Fontaine' (71–73), reviews two of the latest studies of
La F.

MALHERBE.   H. de B. Racan, *Vie de Monsieur de Malerbe*, ed. M.-F.
Quignard, Le Promeneur, 76 pp.

MALLEVILLE.   E. Verroul, 'Les épigrammes de Claude Malleville
ou la rhétorique des passions', Wentzlaff-Eggebert, *Langage*, 231–40,
declares that with M. the madrigal becomes 'un genre prédestiné à
vivre de l'effet de plaire'.

LE MOYNE.   T. Logé, 'Baroque et classicisme: le XVIIIe siècle face
au Père Le Moyne', *SF*, 103:24–34, is concerned with the kind of
attraction and repulsion which 18th-c. readers felt for a writer and 'le
dynamisme d'une poésie qui, dans sa profusion, ne cesse de chanter
les métamorphoses de la nature, la sauvagerie des éléments et la
puissance créatrice de la lumière'.

G. DE SCUDÉRY, *Le Cabinet de Monsieur de Scudéry*, ed. C. Biet and D.
Moncond'huy, Klincksieck, 372 pp., is only the second edn of this
splendid example of 'le regard de la poésie sur l'illusion picturale',
which constitutes both 'une promenade dans les formes poétiques'
and 'une promenade apparemment sans ordre dans les formes
esthétiques'. E. Dutertre, *Scudéry théoricien du classicisme*, PFSCL,
73 pp., evaluates S.'s critical judgement in diverse domains and finds
that — though he may have little really new to say on any subject —
'[il] a contribué grandement à éclairer certains problèmes doctrinaux
latents, et à conforter certaines notions mal établies comme celle de la
bienséance'. Id., 'Un précurseur de la critique d'art: Georges de
Scudéry, *Le Cabinet* et autres œuvres', *TLit*, 4:101–16, would
persuade us that 'un jugement motivé par les grands principes qui
seront ceux du classicisme' is what distinguishes S.'s catalogue of his
supposed artistic possessions from the *Galeria del Cavalier Marino*
(1620), an acknowledged influence.

THÉOPHILE DE VIAU.   *Actes* (Las Vegas) devotes its middle section
to T. and includes the following papers (with responses where

appropriate): K. Collins, 'Théophile de Viau and the echoes of distant voices' (109–14), pursues comparisons with Propertius, Virgil, and Lucretius to suggest that 'Théophile's use of classical models produces an expanding text'; N. Ekstein, 'Pyrame and Thisbé: lost in a "minimalist" world' (131–38), concentrates on 'the dramatic world in which the lovers' tragedy unfolds'; J. Leva, 'Latency and metamorphosis in Théophile de Viau's *La Solitude*' (115–19), contends that 'the myths which pervade [the poem] are to be taken seriously and explored a part of [its] "substantificque mouelle"'; D. Roberts, 'Théophile's Cygnus and the vulnerable *locus amoenus*' (123–27), finds that 'Théophile's subversions of the ode form involves an entry into a profound artistic dialogue with another persecuted poet of dubious morals' — Ovid; G. Saba, 'Situation de Théophile de Viau' (83–99), revs critical opinion from Racan to R. Sabatier and insists that, if T. is still denied the reputation he deserves, 'cela est dû tout simplement au fait qu'il est mort trop jeune'; C. Wentzlaff-Eggebert, 'Les "couleurs" de Théophile dans les premières versions de l'ode *Le Matin*' (101–08), calls for the correction of the 1619 version and comparison with contemporary Italian poetry and, amongst others, G. Marino.

Actes (Marseille) begins with a general paper: G. Saba, 'Sur la modernité de Théophile de Viau' (21–44), suggests that T.'s view of the originality of the writer coincides with our own today. It also includes the following on T. the poet: 'B. Beugnot, 'L'imaginaire de l'espace privé dans l'œuvre de Théophile' (111–23), tackles the question: 'quelle place peut ou doit occuper Théophile dans une étude historique et littéraire du discours de la retraite au XVIIe siècle?'; R. T. Corum, Jr, 'La quête de l'autre dans la poésie amoureuse de Théophile' (63–74), argues that 'le pessimisme de Théophile est d'autant plus profond qu'il se rendait compte lui-même de l'inadé-quation entre le discours et le désir'; Y. Giraud, 'La facture des vers chez Théophile' (75–88), after close observation of T.'s verses 'dans le détail de leur texture et de leur combinaison' is forced to comply with the general view that our admiration should be reserved for other aspects of T.'s work; G. Mathieu-Castellani, 'Théophile de Viau: une poétique du discontinu' (89–100), regards T. as representative of literary mannerism, and the theorist and herald of 'la discontinuité maniériste'; J. Pedersen, 'Images et figures dans la poésie de Théophile de Viau' (101–10), adds a study of the *Stances* (xxxi, Première Partie), which have always fascinated him, to remarks on the twin constants of *Le Matin* and *La Solitude*. G. Saba, 'Des "impossibilia" au "monde renversé"', Wentzlaff-Eggebert, *Langage*, 195–208, is concerned to show that T.'s work on these traditional themes is amongst the most remarkable of the century.

3. PROSE

LitC, 15, on 17th-c. novelists, includes *inter alia* the following: H. Coulet, 'Vers le dix-huitième siècle' (303–11), examines the question: 'Qu'est-ce qu'une époque de transition?' in relation to the *Querelle des Anciens et des Modernes, fin-de-siècle nouvelles,* the omnipresent C. de Sandras, *Télémaque,* and R. Challe, concluding that 'la fin du grand règne [. . .] paradoxalement produit une littérature romanesque fourmillante de promesses et de nouveautés'; M. Lever, 'Au seuil du XVIIe siècle' (9–13), re-examines the genesis of the French novel and notes that at the beginning of the 17th c. 'le romanesque n'est pas propre au roman, il est partout à la fois'; S. Poli, 'Autour de Rosset et de Camus: l'histoire tragique, ou le bonheur impossible' (29–39), examines the uniformity, violence, deep structure, and evolution of 'la forêt encore vierge' of the *histoire tragique*; P. Ronzeaud, 'Foigny, Veiras, romanciers intégristes, où les dérives d'un genre' (246–59), is a critical survey and interpretation of 'le territoire maintenant bien exploré' of French Utopian literature, which suggests that 'les utopies de Veiras et de Foigny contiennent en germes leurs propres dystopies'. F. Gevrey, 'L'enfance du héros dans la nouvelle classique', *LitC*, 14 : 151–59, charts the progressive introduction of children and descriptions of the state of childhood from birth to the first wakings of romantic feelings in such texts as *La Princesse de Clèves, La Duchesse d'Estramène, Gage touché,* and *Les Illustres Françaises*.

Colloque (Fordham) examines the findings of the team of researchers evaluating an *IT* approach to *Le Roman Comique* (1–24); as well as those of the 'Methodology' team (35–52); the 'Mariage contrarié du couple amoureux' team (57–88); the 'Interventions du narrateur-auteur' team (89–138); the team working on 'Le Secret' (139–66); the 'Les textes parodiques' team (167–86). *Actes* (Montpellier) has the following general papers on the *incipit* of 17th-c. narrative fictions: G. Abreu, 'Le piège de l'avertissement: l'ironie et la vérité à l'enjeu de la persuasion' (81–90), discusses comic and epistolary fiction; D. Godwin, 'Les indices de ton et de dénouement dans l'ouverture des nouvelles de 1657 à 1713' (185–98), tentatively concludes that 'le genre d'ouverture décrit et conseillé par Du Plaisir [a] été répandu tout au long de la deuxième moitié du XVIIe siècle, et qu'il relie [. . .] l'ouverture au dénouement'. D. Kuizenga, 'Les autres *incipit*: ouvertures des récits intercalés chez Lafayette, Scudéry et d'Urfé (199–216), observes that 'le moment de transition entre la fiction au premier degré et le récit intercalé est un moment privilégié de la fiction narrative' and that *La Princesse de Clèves* is the best example; G. Verdier, 'De la rhétorique au roman: contrats narratifs dans les romans d'amour (1600–1625)' (257–78), discusses this theme in almost thirty texts.

The fairy-tale is proving increasingly popular with adults: A. Niderst, 'Au début des contes de fées', *ib.*, 232–40, distinguishes two types of topoi: of content and expression. The third section of *Actes* (Las Vegas) is concerned with this genre and has the following: P. Gethner, 'The emergence of fairies in French comedy' (167–78), looks mainly at 18th-c. plays, but also includes references to *fin-de-siècle* 'fairy comedies' by Dancourt and Dufresny; A. Niderst, 'Quelques topoi des contes de fées de la fin du XVIIe siècle' (147–57), admits in the first sentence that he will not be able to speak to his subject: 'il est trop de contes, et trop de topoi'; L. C. Seifert, 'Tales of difference: infantilisation and the recuperation of class and gender in 17th-century *Contes de fées*' (177–94), would argue that such tales represent 'a reaffirmation of phantasmic class identity, [and] the (re)initiation of their storytellers and readers into a cultural symbolic of distinction and dominance'; G. Verdier, 'Approaches to the literary fairy tale: questions of genre and gender' (141–46), which in addition to an account of other papers reprints the bibliography of *Contes de fées* (1690–1715) from R. Robert's *le Conte de fées littéraire*. Other contributions are reviewed below. F. Assaf, 'Le miroir dans le labyrinthe: préfaces d'histoires comiques', *PFSCL*, 18:283–302, finds that what really links *Le Gascon extravagant* (1637), *Le Page disgracié* (1643) and *L'Orphelin infortuné* (1660), 'c'est leur volonté baroque de brouiller les pistes'. G. Berger, 'Préfaces et vérité: la théorie romanesque du XVIIe siècle entre la contrainte à l'apologie et la tentation de l'histoire', *ib.*, 275–82, surveys divergent attitudes to 'true fiction' in comic fiction, epic novels, and historical *nouvelles*.

The idea of the 17th c. as a Republic of *Letters* is still taken literally: G. Haroche-Bouzinac, 'Quelques métaphores de la lettre dans la théorie épistolaire au XVIIe siècle: flèche, miroir, conversation', *DSS*, 172:243–57, has consulted forty theoretical works from 1626 to 1751 and studies metaphors relating to the despatch and content of the letter. *La Correspondance entre Gabriel Naudé et le Cardinal Mazarin*, ed. K. W. Wolfe and P. J. Wolfe, PFSCL, 215 pp., is a complete edition of the 53 letters exchanged, which draws attention to a difference in style in this part of the Naudé correspondence, as their author insistently offered his patron advice which, through force of circumstance, Mazarin could not immediately put into effect. Histories, historical memoirs, and biographies, and the evolving genre of the historical novel continue to attract attention, and occasionally such interest branches out into other genres: F. Assaf, 'L'histoire vue à travers la presse: 1680–85', *SCFS*, 13:55–70, assesses consumption rather than production of history from a survey of 79 articles in the *Journal des Savants*; M. Bannister, ' "Imagination et jugement": history and the novel in mid-seventeenth-century

France', *ib*., 19–32, traces the historical sources of Guérin de Bouscal's *Antiope* (1644), Segrais's *Bérénice* (1648–49), and *Axiane* (1647); J. Davies, 'History, biography, propaganda and patronage in early seventeenth-century France', *ib*., 5–17, reminds us that 'no clear distinction seems necessarily to have been drawn between the recollections of an individual or the compilations of someone who may have been [...] close to the subject of study', and looks more closely at the work of, among others, Simon du Cros and the comte de Brissac. L. Lobbes, 'Les sentences de Pierre Matthieu: un *AntiMachiavel* méconnu', *TLit*, 4:91–100, sees continuity between Matthieu's early 17th-c. *Histoire du roi* and *Histoire de Louis XI* and his late 16th-c. career as a dramatist.

D'AUBIGNÉ. E. M. Duval, 'The place of the present: Ronsard, d'Aubigné, and the "Misères de ce Temps"', *YFS*, 80:13–29, is primarily concerned to demonstrate that 'in its spatial organisation [...] *Les Tragiques* mimic the *Discours* in such a way as to make 1562 signify precisely the opposite of what it had signified for Ronsard'.

MME D'AULNOY. P. Hannon, 'Out of the kingdom: Madame d'Aulnoy's *Finette Cendron*', *Actes* (Las Vegas), 201–08, would persuade us that the greater length of female-authored texts 'tends to subvert rather than consolidate the story'.

JOHN BARCLAY. J. Desjardins-Daude, 'John Barclay, ou les derniers feux de l'humanisme', *LitC*, 15:68–83, classifies B. as practically the inventor of the *roman à clef*, who would have today have used names like Jacques Chirac, François Mitterrand, Giscard D'Estaing, Madame Thatcher, Gorbatchev for his characters, and concludes that his Latin novels were one of the most representative examples of international European culture in the 17th century.

BÉROALDE DE VERVILLE. N. Kenny, *The Palace of Secrets: Béroalde de Verville and Renaissance Conceptions of Knowledge*, Oxford, Clarendon, x + 305 pp., does not try to rehabilitate B., presents his work as 'an arena' in which we may view two conceptions of knowledge, and includes reference to his early 17th-c. texts.

BOILEAU. R. Zuber, 'Boileau traducteur: de la rhétorique à la littérature', Wentzlaff-Eggebert, *Langage*, 287–94, considers that, in his work on the translation of Longinus, B. is an excellent example of *Rhétorique adulte*.

BOSSUET. G. Ferreyrolles, 'Les bergers de Bossuet', Niderst, *Pastorale*, 69–82, argues that shepherds are present in his work, as they are in the Bible, 'à la fois proches et infiniment distants des Céladons fabuleux, il s'attache à leur mode de vie une valeur morale'.

BOURGEOIS. W. Perkins, 'Louise Bourgeois's *Recueil des secrets*', *SFCS*, 13:199–214, finds that the 280 or so 'recipes for conditions ranging from colds [...] to cancer' are 'close to the thinking of medical men'.

BUSSY-RABUTIN. D. Plaisance, 'Bussy-Rabutin et les *Maximes*', *Littératures*, 24:7–13, studies in B.'s text the 'double appartenance — aux vers mondains et (moins fidèlement!) à la forme brève qui a fait le succès des Maximes de La Rochefoucauld'.

J.-P. CAMUS. E. Henein, 'J.-P. Camus ou l'épigone téméraire', *LitC*, 15:41–58, discusses C.'s 'prodigieuse fécondité' and proposes that no French writer before Voltaire has published as many pages in as many different genres, nor shown such 'coquetterie d'auteur', concluding with an examination of the relationship between C. and d'Urfé, suggesting that the publication of *Alexis* (1622) may have influenced d'Urfé's decision to cease writing *l'Astrée*. M. Vernet, 'Les entrées en récit dans les nouvelles de J.-P. Camus', *Actes* (Montpellier), 279–96, discovers a dozen common elements in C.'s openings, which form a kind of rite through which the reader and the author have to pass.

CHALLE. M. Weil, *Robert Challe romancier*, Droz, 1991, 340 pp., is a profound study of C.'s imaginary universe, which explores through the notion of the *dispositif dialogique* a new alliance between his conceptions of fiction and the world.

CHAMPLAIN. N. Doison, 'Songe et mensonge dans le *Quatrième voyage du Seigneur de Champlain* (1613). Étude d'un lieu commun baroque', *SF*, 35:227–49, maintains that this two-part text justifying the failure of C.'s mission conforms in detail to the rule of 'l'onirisme baroque' in its illustration and denunciation of the dream of finding the North passage.

CHOISY. M. M. Rowan, 'Crossing borders: tales of the Abbé de Choisy', *Actes* (Las Vegas); 225–30, has little difficulty in presenting C. as one of the 'more amusing challenges to all preconceptions and prejudiced thinking about the divisions of genre and the boundaries of gender'.

CYRANO DE BERGERAC. J. Prévot, 'Cyrano de Bergerac, ou l'homme qui avait le tête dans les étoiles', *LitC*, 15:145–59, rethinks the theory of J. Prévot, *Cyrano de Bergerac romancier* (1977), presents *L'Autre Monde* as the first epistemological novel, replaces it in the context of the history of ideas and gives an ample bibliography.

DES ESCUTEAUX. E. Henein, 'Des Escuteaux et cie, ou les victimes de la renommée, *LitC*, 15:15–28, observes that, like Guillaume Coste and Jean du Mélezet, D.E. 'démontre la richesse des inclassables', though it would be an exaggeration to describe him as the Queneau or San Antonio of his century.

DU BAIL. A. Niderst, 'Le contexte dans les livres du XVIIe siècle', *PFSCL*, 18:265–73, makes an arbitrary choice of D.B.'s fourteen novels published between 1622 and 1646 as an illustration of the particularly 'heavy' contextual paraphernalia associated with 17th-c. texts.

J. DU BOSCQ.   N. Mallet, 'Aspects, leçons et messages du discours préfaciel: l'exemple de L'*Honnête Femme* de Jacques Du Boscq', *PFSCL*, 18:303–30, feels, extending the Genettian metaphor, that this preface forms 'un seuil majestueux et initiatique qui conduit et oriente le lecteur/la lectrice vers la somme des traités et discours de Du Boscq'.

FÉNELON.   D. Bertrand, 'L'éducation chez Fénelon, ou l'enfant et le pédagoge à l'épreuve du rire et de la gaité', *LitC*, 14:203–25, puzzles over the allusions to laughter and gaiety in the text of the *Traité de l'éducation des filles*, with which F. hoped to create a climate of confidence which would facilitate the child's spontaneous thirst for knowledge. C. Cavaillac, 'Fénelon et le mythe de l'origine des arts', *Poétique*, 85:17–34, argues that in *Télémaque*, F. tries to ' "se désapproprier", de se fondre dans un ordre poétique millénaire en intégrant à la forme d'expression la plus commune: la prose, une écriture *consacrée*'.

FURETIÈRE.   F. Assaf, 'Furetière, ou l'esthétique du contraire', *LitC*, 15:163–68, catalogues thirty-five European and American studies of *Le Roman bourgeois*, illustrating the complexity of the novel and the possibility of *relectures* and suggests a number of new directions for new criticism and gives a comprehensive bibliography. A. P. Morais, 'La mise en préface du roman: les déguisements de l'auteur dans *Le Roman Bourgeois*', *Actes* (Montpellier), 225–30, notes 'la tension oppositive entre d'une part la tradition de l'effacement de l'auteur et la pratique de l'anonymat, et d'autre part la tentation d'apparaître'. F. P. Weber, 'Realistiches Sittenbild — Standpunktlose Intransigenz — Antiroman? Der *Roman bourgeois* (1666) von Antoine Furetière im Spiegel der literaturwissenschafftlichen Forschung', *PFSCL*, 35:425–42, surveys 'world' criticism of *Le Roman bourgeois* from 1852. J.-C. Darmon, 'Furetière et l'universel', *SFR*, 14, 1990:15–46, finds a Foucauldian 'forme intermédiaire d'universalité' in F.'s dictionary, which provides an early example of a type of universal which 'donne moins licu à un tableau exhaustif, sereinement ordonné du savoir qu'à une ouverture critique indéfinie, non géométrisable, des plages de sens et des lieux de vérité'.

C. GILBERT.   *Histoire de Clejava ou de l'Isle des hommes raisonnables*, ed. M.-S. Rivière, Univ. of Exeter, 1990, xxiv + 115 pp., reproduces the only copy of the 1700 Dijon edn of this didactic and utopian text, which the author hoped would reform both men and society.

MARIN LE ROY GOMBERVILLE.   A. Zotos, 'Gomberville, ou l'ambition du roman total', *LitC*, 15:99–118, speculates as to whether, in G.'s novel of the sea, it is possible to detect 'la volonté de l'auteur d'accuser la paternité de son livre, en le donnant comme l'illustration de tous les sens du mot, de son nom et prénom'.

GOURNAY. C. Venesoen, 'Le *Proumenoir de M. de Montaigne*: de l'original (1594) à la refonte (1626)', *DSS*, 172:229–42, finds both edns equally favourable to the cause of 'celle qui écrit', but that there is greater aesthetic value in the 17th-c. edition.

GUILLERAGUES. F. Deloffre, 'Guilleragues et les *Lettres portugaises*, ou de l'œuvre à l'auteur', *LitC*, 15:259–70, surveys the current critical position and takes up many of the points discussed in the preface to his 1990 edition of the text (see *YWMLS*, 52:110), and concludes 'cette combinaison d'une forme originale et d'un esprit unique [sont ce] qu'il faut reconnaître dans les *Lettres portugaises*, au lieu d'y rechercher l'exemple appliqué d'un rhétoricien à court d'inspiration'. Id., 'La rhétorique des *Lettres portugaises*', Wentzlaff-Eggebert, *Langage*, 147–52, is persuaded that 'la rhétorique de Guilleragues a précisément pour objet de créer l'*impression* du naturel'. P. Hartmann, 'Réflexion et communication dans la monodie épistolaire: à propos d'une nouvelle édition des *Lettres portugaises*', *DSS*, 172:275–86, takes to task the view of F. Deloffre and L. Spitzer that the text has 'une conclusion univoque et sans appel'.

LA BRUYÈRE. *LitC*, supplement to 13 is a slim vol. on La B. devoted to the principle that 'less is more' and containing the following: E. Bury, 'La Bruyère et la tradition des *Caractères*' (7–25), inscribes *Les Caractères* in the rhetorical tradition of Theophrastian moral discourse, showing how his free interpretation of sources allowed La B. to demonstrate his originality and modernity; J. Dagon, 'Le clair-obscur de La Bruyère' (25–43), uses an aesthetic analogy with Caravaggio's *chiaroscuro* to study how the moralist's style of writing 'par lopins' exposes 'l'artifice des taxinomies simplistes', enabling him to imitate the real; R. Garapon, 'La chronologie de la composition des *Caractères* et l'évolution de la pensée de La Bruyére' (143–55), offers a *vue d'ensemble* of La B.'s preoccupations in the period 1670–94; J. Morel, 'La Bruyère écrivain ironique' analyses the indirect character of La B.'s expression, noting the 'nuance destructrice' of La B.'s irony; L. Van Delft, 'Les *Caractères*: du monde clos à l'œuvre ouverte' (63–87), seeks by its title to link *Les Caractères* with A. Koyré, *Du monde clos à l'univers infini* (1957), and Umberto Eco's *Œuvre ouverte* in an effort to illuminate the 'structure éclatée' and 'clarté inépuisable' of the work.

LA CALPRENÈDE. G. Molinié, 'La Calprenède, ou l'héroïsme à la question', *LitC*, 15:111–18, discusses 'l'abondance quantitative, et la délicatesse qualitative' of *Cassandre* and *Cléopâtre*, considers the differing role of two characters both named Artaban, and concludes that, unlike the novels of Mlle de Scudéry, the *romanesque* remains dominant in L.C.'s novels.

LA FAYETTE. B. Bray, 'L'introduction des récits secondaires dans *La Princesse de Clèves*', *Actes* (Montpellier), 145–54, sheds new light on the 'procédure d'insertion' of the 'digressions' in the primary narrative. E. Chapco, 'L'*incipit* narratif et l'entrée en scène: trois œuvres de Mme de La Fayette', *ib.*, 169–76, despite identifying six constants in 'une configuration narrative presque identique, still finds the gulf between *La Princesse de Clèves* and the *nouvelles* just as impossible to bridge. **Mme de Lafayette: La Princesse de Clèves*, ed. H.-P. Blottier and C. Vandel, Hatier, 96 pp. M. Laugaa, 'Mme de Lafayette, ou l'intelligence du cœur', *LitC*, 15:195–226, surveys criticism of L. from 1971 to 1990, listing some ninety books and articles and notes, despite the divergence of certain critical directions, 'un retour incessant vers le double foyer de l'aveu et de la retraite'.

LA FORCE. M. M. Welch, 'L'éros féminin dans les contes de fées de Mlle de la Force', *Actes* (Las Vegas), 217–23, suggests that L.F. 'a mis en place un système de valeurs qui élevait la féminité au rang de qualité forte sans tomber dans le piège de l'imitation héroïque'.

LA MOTHE LE VAYER. P.-J. Salazar, 'La Mothe le Vayer ou l'impossible métier d'historien', *SCFS*, 13:55–70, finds that 'le métier d'historien [. . .] ne se concevait pas sans une certain réticence, laquelle apparaît au grand jour dans l'œuvre de La Mothe Le Vayer'.

LA ROCHEFOUCAULD. J. Brody, 'Les *Maximes* de La Rochefoucauld: essai de lecture rhétorique', Wentzlaff-Eggebert, *Langage*, 153–80, finds that the *Maximes* are never quite what they seem.

E. LE NOBLE. P. Hourcade, **Entre Pic et Rétif: Eustache Le Noble (1643–1711)*, Aux amateurs des livres, 604 pp. Id., 'Eustache Le Noble, ou le romancier de passage', *LitC*, 15:291–301, questions 'pourquoi et comment un Eustache Le Noble, nourri d'érudition gallicane et humaniste, ancien haut magistrat, a pu se mettre au roman' (a decision here portrayed as a prolongation of his career as historiographer royal), and finishes with a brief glimpse of the later works (1707–10) which complemented the 'grand Œuvre' of 1694–99 without contributing much to his reputation.

MAILLY. C.-L. Malarte, '*Le prince Guérini* du Chevalier de Mailly', *Actes* (Las Vegas), 209–15, examines the differences between the literary fairy tale and folklore.

J. DE PRÉCHAC. J. Chupeau, 'J. de Préchac, ou le romancier courtisan', *LitC*, 15:271–91, explores the biography of the recently ennobled P. family, maintains that for P., with his talent for celebrating the virtues of the King, writing was 'un des leviers de la réussite', and that it is possible to 'détacher de cette production abondante et souvent médiocre quelques récits de meilleure venue'.

MOLIÈRE D'ESSERTINE. J.-C. Brunon, 'L'ouverture de *Polyxène*: forme et signification d'une procédure d'initialité inversée', *Actes*

(Montpellier), 155–68, argues that the 'maladresse apparente' of the opening 'n'est qu'une finesse nouvelle'.

PERRAULT. J. Barchilon, 'Souvenirs et réflexions sur le conte merveilleux', *LitC*, 14:231–47, is a mainly autobiographical account of the author's discovery of the only contemporary manuscript of P.'s *Cendrillon*, which comments on the essential ambiguity of the *conte merveilleux*, that at one and the same time the audience both believes and does not believe; P. Lewis, 'Food for sight: Perrault's "Peau d'âne"', *MLN*, 106:215–24, takes as its starting point Lévi-Strauss's theory of food as an articulation of nature and culture, examines the 'dialectic of the edible and the consumed' in Perrault's tales, and concludes that though the *Peau d'âne* may invite us 'to grasp a certain writing in or with the mouth or the voice, the tale itself invites us to apprehend a scopic culture, given over to eating with the eyes'. C. Magnien-Simonin, 'Perrault entre légende et histoire: les héros de l'"Epistre à Mademoiselle" des *Histoires ou Contes du temps passé* (1697)', *DSS*, 171:133–42, deduces that it is indeed to the debonnaire Henri IV that P. alludes in the *Epistre* 'avec une discrétion dont on doit trouver les raisons dans la conjoncture politique du royame en ce XVIIe siècle finissant'. J. M. McGlathery, **Fairy Tale Romance: The Grimms, Basile, and Perrault*, Illinois U.P., xii + 227 pp. J. Miel, 'Perrault's *Cendrillon*', *Actes* (Las Vegas), 197–99, takes 'an ahistorical approach' 'to why, after nearly three hundred years, we still read and enjoy a story like this'. M.-J. Muratore, 'Mimesis annulled: modes of fictionalization in Perrault's *Contes*', *RoN*, 31, 1990:111–18, examines 'anti-mimetic tendencies both at the thematic and the stylistic levels'. F. Népote-Desmarres, 'Parole et sacrifice: l'enfant dans les contes de Perrault', *OC*, 14:47–59, considers them as the 'achèvement de l'interrogation de Perrault sur l'ordre du monde'; G. Ottevaere-van Praag, 'A l'aube de la littérature enfantine: formes narratives de la mise en garde à l'usage des jeunes', *ib.*, 107–22, compares Catholic and Protestant attitudes to childhood and P.'s version of Aesop's *Fables* with those of Sir Roger L'Estrange; R. Robert, 'L'infantalisation du conte merveilleux au XVIIe siècle', *ib.*, 34–46, compares the *Histoires ou contes du temps passé* with the work of Mme d'Aulnoy among others, distinguishing P. as a quasi-Machiavellian author, who alone of the writers of fairy tales offers a 'savant dosage d'ironie et de simplicité' in a publication which was actually intended for adults. M. Soriano, 'L'enfant du XVIIe siècle à travers les proverbes', *ib.*, 59–67, tries to identify the characteristics that 'la sagesse populaire' attributes to children, and finds the whole century and P. caught between two images of the child and two images of education. W. Troubetzkoy, 'De l'art d'accommoder les grands-mères: la Belle et le Chaperon', *Littératures*, 24:28–49, suggests that such tales tell 'l'histoire dramatique des générations, le drame de la passation des pouvoirs entre femmes, l'élimination inéluctable des vieilles par les jeunes, leur entre-dévoration'.

SABLÉ. H. Wentzlaaf-Eggebert, 'Montaigne, Grecián, La Rochefoucauld, La Bruyère, et les *Maximes de Mme de Sablé*', Wentzlaff-Eggebert, *Langage*, 181–94, argues that despite 'des parallèles surprenants, la Marquise n'a imité aucune des attitudes des moralistes antérieurs'.

SAINT-RÉAL. A. Mansau, 'Saint-Réal, ou les miroirs brisés', *LitC*, 15:227–38, gives a double interpretation of the mirror images in S.-R.'s works of fiction and history, and suggests that the former reflects the political and moral thought of the time, concluding with an analysis of his attempt to renew his style in *Césarion*.

SAINT-SIMON. Two articles which must be read together: Y. Coirault, 'Saint-Simon sans Proust ou le mémorialiste avant le déluge' *RLMC*, 43, 1990:275–86, reproduces the text of an unpublished and unfinished letter by the young P. on the delights of reading extracts from S.-S., and acknowledges that for the modern reader 'les personnages de Saint-Simon deviennent vaguement proustiens', though the researcher's duty is to try to read the *Mémoires* 'comme si la *Recherche* n'existait pas'; Id., 'Proust pasticheur de Saint-Simon: technique ou vision', *TLit*, 4:231–43, pursues these ideas through a fascinating if *insaisissable* series of reflections, written *en marge* of other studies of Proustian pastiche by a critic who, no less than Proust, has accepted that 'pour bien le *rendre*, il fallait sentir, sinon vivre, avec Saint-Simon; continuer d'écrire, le jour ou la nuit, qu'importe?'

SCARRON. C. Spencer, 'Aux marges du texte; *Le Roman Comique*: des titres à la page', *Actes* (Montpellier), 245–55, argues that 'Les intitulés font ici exactement ce qu'un texte n'est pas supposé faire: c'est à *nous*, lecteurs, de sélectionner, filtrer, hiérarchiser les informations pour les emmagasiner à différents niveaux.' R. Guichemerre 'Scarron, ou le romanesque contenu', *LitC*, 15:137–44, surveys the duality of comic and novelistic inspiration in S.'s *romans* and *nouvelles*.

M. DE SCUDÉRY. N. Boursier, 'Le renouvellement des *topoi* d'ouverture et le passage du grand roman à la nouvelle chez Madeleine de Scudéry', *Actes* (Montpellier), 125–30, discovers that from *Clélie* to *Célinte* and *La Promenade de Versailles*, 'le renouvellement est plus apparent que réel et plus structural que topique'. M. Madureira, 'La représentation de la fiction dans le Prologue de *Célinte*', *ib.*, 217–24, shows how this type of metadiscourse 'exalte la dignité de la fiction romanesque, mise en question par les doctrines poétiques du XVIIe siècle'. *Les Femmes illustres ou Les Harangues héroïques*, ed. C. Maignien, Côté femmes, 165 pp. A. Niderst, 'Madeleine de Scudéry ou du Tasse à Balzac, de Balzac à Proust', *LitC*,

15:119–26, reads S.'s *romans à clef* as the *Comédie Humaine* of the 17th c., which includes 'toutes sortes de pensées, [et des] allusions à toutes les connaissances'.

SEGRAIS. R. Guichemerre, 'Segrais ou la diversité romanesque', *LitC*, 15:185–93, observes that S. does not apply his theories of new fiction systematically in *Les Nouvelles françaises*.

SÉVIGNÉ. T. Lassalle, 'Une grand-mère au XVIIe siècle. Mme de Sévigné', *LitC*, 14:161–77, addresses the double question: 'Mme de Sévigné pourrait-elle s'intéresser à ses petits-enfants, [. . .] pourrait-elle entretenir avec eux?' The answer is affirmative.

SOREL. M. Bideaux, 'Les ouvertures narratives dans *Les Nouvelles françoises* de Charles Sorel', *Actes* (Montpellier), 111–23, considers three familles of *topoi* in this text: narrative, discursive, and metanarrative. D. Bertrand, 'Les figures du songe ou les arcanes de la fiction', *PFSCL*, 18:411–23, traces the parabola of the *récit onirique* in the *Histoire comique de Francion*. J. A. Frazao, '*Francion* — les Avertissements: une rhétorique de la certitude', *Actes* (Montpellier), 177–84, studies the modifications to the Preface in the 1626 and 1633 edns; D. Godwin, 'Les indices de ton et de dénouement dans l'ouverture des nouvelles de 1657 à 1673', *ib.*, 185–98; M. Paixao, 'La préface du roman comique Francion de Sorel: ordre vs chaos', *ib.*, 241–44, is of the opinion that the ambiguity of the story to follow is already a feature of the preface itself. G. Verdier, 'Charles Sorel ou le roman en procès', *LitC*, 15:85–97, reviews criticism and critical editions of S.'s fiction and lists the major questions that his 'textes protéiformes' have posed over the last twenty years, concluding that S.'s mission is 'de nous faire exercer nos facultés créatrices' by offering us 'les feintes et les déguisements [. . .] la représentation des personnages qui jouent et qui racontent des histoires mensongères [. . .] et ainsi la figure récurrente du narrateur-auteur qui mystifie ses lecteurs'. W. de Vos, 'La théorie littéraire de Sorel dans les préfaces de *Francion*, du *Berger extravagant* et de *Polyandre*', *Actes* (Montpellier), 297–312, discusses three problems in the three prefaces under the rubrics: *la langue, l'histoire, personnages*.

THÉOPHILE DE VIAU. B. Bray, 'Effets d'écriture, image du moi dans l'œuvre en prose de Théophile', *Actes* (Marseille), 129–38, studies this subject in T.'s surviving correspondence and in the *Epître d'Actéon à Diane*. B. Ching, 'Théophile de Viau and the dawn of burlesque narrative', *FS*, 45:403–16, questions Bakhtin's placing of the *Fragments d'une histoire comique* 'within the comic heritage of Rabelaisian narratives' and contends that 'ultimately these books narrate why they are not fully what they set out to be'. C. Rizza, 'L'art de Théophile de Viau polémiste', *Actes* (Marseille), 139–49, finds 'des accents polémiques d'une extrême violence' in T.'s earliest works.

T. L'HERMITE. J. Serroy, 'Tristan l'Hermite, ou les vertus de l'infortune', *LitC*, 15:127–35, offers a synthesis of the study of *Le Page disgracié* over the past forty years and regrets that 'cet auteur enfin sorti des limbes [n'ait] pas encore suscité le travail de fond qui pourrait apporter l'éclairage nouveau qu'autorisent tant d'études partielles', which might answer the question: 'quel rapport une œuvre entretient-elle avec la vie?'. 'Tristan et le comique', *CTH, no. 13, 64 pp.

D'URFÉ. S. Kevorkian, *Thématique de l''Astrée' d'Honoré d'Urfé*, Champion–Slatkine, 206 pp., aims to prevent readers from getting lost in the vast detours of the novel, and includes over four thousand references, sub-divided into forty-two 'families' and listed alphabetically. B. Yon, 'Honoré d'Urfé, ou le conseiller des vrais amants', *LitC*, 15:59–67, observes that 'il est significatif qu'Honoré d'Urfé ait laissé sans remède la séparation des amants', and questions whether Gomberville's VIth Part (1626) and Baro's conclusion (1628) represent faithful interpretations of the author's intentions.

VILLEDIEU. M. Cuénin, 'Mme de Villedieu, ou la gerbe romanesque', *LitC*, 15:239–45, imputes in large part 'la fécondité romanesque qui caractérise la seconde moitié du XVIIe siècle' to Mme de Villedieu and gives a brief history of her successful novelistic career.

4. THOUGHT

DSS, 170, is devoted to 'Aspects de la spiritualité en France au XVIIe siècle' and begins in the late 16th c. with a comparison of Bèze and S. François de Sales, and also contains the following: H. Bordès, 'Charité et humilité dans l'œuvre de François de Sales' (15–26), analyses the relationship between these two virtues and shows that for the author of the *Traité de l'amour de Dieu*, they are founded on 'la vie trinitaire d'un Dieu "diffusif en lui-même"'; B. Chédozeau, 'Port-Royal et le jansénisme: la revendication d'une autre forme de tridentisme' (119–25), tries to distinguish between these twin notions which are too often amalgamated; M. Chevallier, 'Spiritualité réformée de la communion au XVIIe siècle' (61–76), is a selection of readings from long forgotten sacred texts which served 'ce pauvre peuple réformé, resté en France, étouffé, [. . .] pendant tout un siècle de clandestinité'. Other contributions are rev. below. K. P. Luria, **Territories of Grace. Cultural Change in the Seventeenth-Century Diocese of Grenoble*, Berkeley, Univ. of California Press, 267 pp. F. Mariner, 'Gender and authority in Jansenist memoir writing', *PFSCL*, 18:443–60, assesses Jansenist sensitivity 'to the contradiction implied in first-person narrative' in the work of Claude Lancelot and Angélique de Saint-Jean. P. D. Laude, *Approches du quiétisme*, *PFSCL*, 145 pp., brings together two complementary studies of La Bruyère's *Dialogues posthumes* and the conflicting opinions of Bossuet and Fénelon on this subject, by way of introduction to a reproduction of the 1685 text of Mme de la Mothe Guyon's *Moyen court et très facile pour l'oraison*. J. Mesnard, 'Langage littéraire et philosophie au XVIIe siècle', Wentzlaff-Eggebert, *Langage*, 241–64, analyse the lit. formulation and modernization of the language of scholastic philosophy by, among others, S. Dupleix, La Mothe Le Vayer, Descartes, and Pascal. C. Strosetzki, 'Entre l'esprit de géométrie et l'esprit de finesse'. *ib.*, 265–74, discusses these twin concepts in Descartes and Pascal, Fontenelle and Saint-Évremond and 18th-c. views thereof. A. Niderst, 'Il n'y a ni subconscient ni inconscient au XVIIe siècle', *LitC*, 16:43–50, takes to task teachers who 's'autorisant de quelques lignes des *Pensées* et des *Maximes*, ont durant des générations confondu l'explication de texte et l'analyse psychologique', questions the use of psychoanalysis in 17th-c. studies, and recommends instead a close study of the mentalities of the age. Y. Durand, 'Mystique et politique au XVIIe siècle: l'influence du Pseudo-Denys', *DSS*, 172:323–50, assesses the impact of these writings on early 17th-c. thought. M. Cook, 'Malebranche versus Arnauld', *JHP*, 29:183–99, finds that the two disagree about the nature of ideas 'but agree in believing that we mediately see external objects only by immediately seeing ideas', and is of the opinion that Malebranche's theory is incomplete at this crucial point. M. Le Guern, 'Sur une collaboration probable entre Pascal et Arnauld', *DSS*, 172:351–58, proceeds from textual comparisons of the *Réflexions* and the *Logique* to suggest that, if Pascal contributed to the former, he may also have written *De l'esprit géométrique after* May 1657 as a response to Arnauld's invitation to collaborate with him on the latter.

La liberté de conscience (XVIe — XVIIe siècles), ed. H. R. Guggisberg *et al.*, Droz, 375 pp., is mainly concerned with the situation in the 16th c. and elsewhere in Europe, but also includes: M. Turchetti, 'La liberté de conscience et l'autorité du magistrat au lendemain de la Révocation' (289–367), which aims to demonstrate with reference to the work of, among others N. A. de Versé, P. Jurieu, J. Philipot and E. Saurin, that it is not correct to suggest that 'les protestants français proprement dits [. . .] ont contribué de manière décisive à l'essor et à l'affirmation de la *liberté de conscience*', other than the *liberté de la conscience réformée*. P. Oppici, 'L'enfant modèle et le modèle de l'enfance dans la littérature religieuse du XVIIe siècle', *LitC*, 14:202–13, explores the 'image ambiguë et bivalente de l'enfance' in writers such as Bourdaloue and F. de Sales.

AGNÈS ARNAULD. J.-R. Armogathe, '*Le Chapelet secret* de Mère Agnès Arnauld', *DSS*, 170:77–83, examines in detail this rare and difficult text, reprinted here in an annex, which helps us to understand the state of mind of the nuns of Port-Royal.

ANGÉLIQUE ARNAULD. P. Bugnion-Secretan, *La Mère Angelique Arnauld, 1591–1661, abbesse et réformatrice de Port-Royal*, Cerf, 274 pp., is the first biography of its kind.

ANTOINE ARNAULD. A. R. Ndiaye, **La Philosophie d'Antoine Arnauld*, Bibliothèque d'Histoire de la Philosophie, 376 pp.

JACQUES BASNAGE. R. Whelan, 'Huguenot conceptions of the past: the case of Jacques Basnage', *SCFS*, 13:91–95, appeals for more studies of 'second-rate Huguenot thinkers' like B. 'to break the old moulds of pre-Enlightenment and early-Enlightenment thought'.

BERULE. M. Dupuy, 'Bérulle et la grâce', *DSS*, 170:39–50, shows how B. moved gradually from Molinism to Jansenism, partly under the influence of his friend and confident Duvergier.

CANTENAC. G. Turbet-Delof, 'État présent des études sur Cantenac: Bibliographie (1980–1990)', *DSS*, 171:161–65, lists 14 works and analyses five different stages in C. studies.

LA CEPPÈDE. Y. Quenot, 'La vierge dans les *Théorèmes* de La Ceppède', *DSS*, 170:27–38, underlines 'le côté tout à la fois rigoureux et tendre de sa piété mariale'.

CHARRON. M. Adam, **Études sur Pierre Charron*, Bordeaux U.P., 238 pp.

DESCARTES. **Philosophical Writings*, vol. 3: *The Correspondence*, J. Cottingham *et al.*, CUP. **Metaphysics of Science and Freedom*: *From Descartes to Kant to Hegel*, W. Cristando (ed.), Avebury. **Central Readings in the History of Modern Philosophy: Descartes to Kant*, ed. R. Cummins and D. Owen, Wadsworth Publishing Company, D. C. Dennett, *Consciousness Explained*, Allen Lane, 511 pp., claims we must abandon not just the dualism of the mind and body that is our legacy from Descartes, but also what he dubs the Cartesian Theatre, the mythical place in the brain 'where it all comes together'. Appendix A is philosophical; Appendix B, scientific. K. Dunn, '"A great city is a great solitude": Descartes's urban pastoral', *YFS*, 80:93–107, reads the *Discourse on Method* as 'the register of [. . .] social and ideological commuting' to and from Amsterdam and the country. J.-L. Marion, **Questions cartésiennes: méthode et métaphysique*, PUF, 264 pp. E. R. Grosholz, *Cartesian Method: The Problem of Reduction*, OUP, 170 pp. S. Priest, *Theories of the Mind*, Penguin, xi + 233 pp., compares in the first part Plato's and D.'s view of Dualism, and claims that 'we may learn from his insights and argument, even if in the end we should wish to repudiate his strict mind–body dualism'. T. J. Reiss, 'Descartes, the Palatinate, and the Thirty Years War: political theory and political practice', *YFS*, 80:108–45, discusses amongst other things the correspondence between certain aspects of Descartes's early thinking and 'the political context in which he lived', *René Descartes: Critical Assessments*, ed. J. D. Moyal, Routledge, 4 vols, 1696 pp., collects together 116 of the most important articles: vol. I, 'The Method, Belief and Knowledge'; vol. II, 'The *Meditations* and Metaphysics'; vol. III, 'The *Meditations* and Metaphysics (continued)'; vol. IV, 'The Sciences: from Physics to Ethics'. J. Vance Buroker, 'Descartes on sensible qualities', *JHP*: 585–612, hopes 'to show that D.'s analysis of sensation in the *Rules* is the key to the epistemology underlying his physics'. F. P. Van de Pitte, 'The dating of rule IV–B in Descartes's *Regulae ad directionem ingenii*', *ib.*, 375–96, is an extended demonstration of the argument that 'IV–B is *later* than IV–A, rather than *earlier*' which concludes that the period '1639–40 has much to recommend it', so that the *Mathesis universalis* may be regarded as 'an insight' achieved at the exact moment when D. was 'concerned with the details of his *Meditations*'.

S. PIERRE FOURIER. J. Hennequin, 'La pastorale de saint Pierre Fourier d'après sa *Correspondance* (1598–1640)', *DSS*, 170:51–60, which is based on Mère Hélène Derréal's edition of the correspondence, shows how the curate of Matincourt, while respecting 'les charismes et les cheminements spirituels de chacun', managed to develop a 'pastorale de la communication'.

MALEBRANCHE. *Nicolas Malebranche: His Philosophy, Critics and Successors*, ed. S. Brown, Assen, Van Gorcum, 173 pp., contains eight scholarly papers, also discusses Arnauld, Locke, Berkeley, and Hume. J. Cottingham, 'Nicolas Malebranche: illumination and rhetoric', *SCFS*, 13:239–45, reviews our understanding of this 'largely unknown and neglected figure' following the publ. of N. Jolley, *The Light of the Soul. Theories of Ideas in Leibniz, Malebranche and Descartes* (*YWMLS*, 52:120) S. Nadler, 'Malebranche and the vision in God: a note on the *Search After Truth*, iii, 2, iii', *JHI*, 52:309–14, suggests that in this text, 'the theory under attack is a Cartesian one [. . .] and that Malebranche intends his critique to be understood in this way'.

PASCAL. J. A. Galluci, 'Faith and language: allegories of interpretation in Pascal', *FrF*, 16:149–76, discovers 'that as soon as one has opened up the question of allegory in Pascal, it is impossible not to see it at every turn', and discusses in detail two enigmatic *pensées* and the texts relating to P.'s controversy with Père Noël. E. James, 'Pascal's art of polemic', *SCFS*, 13:231–37, revs R. Parish's study of the *Provinciale* (see *YWMLS*, 52:128). *Œuvres complètes*, ed. J. Mesnard, vol. 3, *Œuvres diverses*, 1654–1657, Bibliothèque européenne, Desclée de Brouwer, 1214 pp. *Pensées*, ed. P. Sellier, Classiques Garnier, Bordas, 657 pp. G. Oppy, 'On Rescher on Pascal's wager', *International Journal for the Philosophy of Religion*, 30:159–68, defends the traditional view that Pascal's wager argument is almost entirely worthless — at least from the theological standpoint, and explains why Rescher's defence fails.

s.-j. BAPTISTE DE LA SALLE. H. Bordès, 'Charité et humilité dans l'œuvre de François de Sales', *DSS*, 170:15–26, finds in the 'l'union des deux vertus un fondement théologique, et la contemplation de cette union est chez lui liée à la contemplation de Dieu' in the *Traitté de l'amour de Dieu* and the sermon for the Visitation of 1621. Y. Poutet, 'L'éducation du caractère et des mœurs des enfants du peuple d'après les écrits de saint Jean-Baptiste de la Salle', *LitC*, 14:178–201, finds that the 'méthodologie lasallienne' relies more on the quality of the teacher than pedagogical method and leaves God to do the rest.

THÉOPHILE DE VIAU. J.-P. Chauveau, 'Le *Traicté de l'Immortalité de l'Ame ou la mort de Socrate*', *Actes* (Marseille), 45–61, is persuaded that with this text, to which not even the most recent studies of 17th-c. classical translation refer, 'nous avons affaire à une véritable, attentive, et scrupuleuse traduction de Platon'. L. Godard de Donville, 'Théophile et son milieu dans les années précédant son procès', *ib.*, 31–44, investigates the arguments of Jesuit tracts and 'les rapports possibles entre le milieu de Sully et Théophile'.

5. DRAMA

E. J. Campion, 'Representation of history and mythology by Quinault and Racine', *SFCS*, 13:115–27, 'analyses the representation and modification of sources' in *Astrate*, *Bellérephon*, and *Andromaque*. J. Emelina, *Le Comique. Essai d'interprétation générale*, SEDES, 209 pp., goes one stage further than Bergson, by looking at the cause rather than the effect of laughter, abounds in explanatory formula, and considers most of the traditional questions about the genre, without making Molière a more important reference than *les B.D.*, *Le Bébête Show* or *Le Canard enchaîné*. Ib., 'L'enfant dans le théâtre du XVIIe siècle', *LitC*, 14:94–106, examines the role of the child in Montchrestien, Rotrou, Corneille, Racine, and Molière, and finds that real children were already present on the stage at the beginning of the c. J. Morel, 'Pastorale et tragédie', Niderst, *Pastorale*, 47–50, finds aspects of this elevated genre, 'à des degrés différents et sous des perspectives divers [*sic*]', in Théophile's *Pyrame*, and in *Clitandre*, *Saint Genest*, *Britannicus*, and *Phèdre*. P. Pasquier, 'Les apartés d'Icare: éléments pour une théorie de la convention classique', *PFSCL*, 18:331–58, re-examines the premisses of the conventions formalized by La Mesnardière, Sarrasin, and d'Aubignac. I. Pilström, *Le Médecin et la médecine dans le théâtre comique français du XVIIe siècle*, (SRU, 47), Almqvist and Wiksell, 153 pp. A. Stegmann, 'Le théâtre jésuite à La

Flèche: analyse et mise en perspective', *RHT*, 170:95–105, considers theatrical productions at La Flèche (1608–26), tracing the influence of the tragedies performed there on the French theatre in general, and gives a history of contemporary Jesuit theatre elsewhere in Europe (1600–30), noting that the brief apogee of the theatre at La Flèche was only part of a long tradition with no equivalent outside Pont-à-Moussin. J. Supple, 'Pommier versus Barthes: vérités et con-trevérités', *SFCS*, 13:153–61, judges that, while not without value, Pommier's criticism of *Sur Racine* as a means of destroying Barthes's reputation as a critic is misguided.

Actes (Las Vegas) devotes the first section to dramatic theory and includes: W. S. Brooks, 'Quinault criticism, Boileau, and the problem of Racine' (37–51), challenges 'the persistent commonplace that Quinault's plays are about love', and presents him as the victim *par excellence* of 'l'habitude de juger tout le théâtre du XVIIe siècle d'après Racine et à travers lui'. J. Morel, 'Les conditions de la critique théâtrale au XVIIe siècle' (13–18), looks at a variety of sources for evidence of the classical vision of the theatre and tries to define the common ground of doctrinal disputes. R. Garapon, 'Le langage de la comédie au XVIIe siècle: de la rhétorique à la littérature', Wentzlaff-Eggebert, *Langage*, 13–22, looks at the adaptation of language to character in Corneille and Molière. J. Morel, **Agréables mensonges. Essais sur le théâtre français au XVIIe siècle*, Klincksieck, 382 pp.

Comparative studies are not quite so common: N. Hepp. 'De la littérature à la rhétorique (*Andronic*, 1,7. *Phèdre*, 1,1)', *ib.*, 295–306, finds all her material in the unequal inspiration of the two dramatists. A. Niderst, 'Ronsard, *Andromaque* et *Attila*', *TLit*, 4:117–26, wonders whether the origins of Racine's play are to be found in the *Franciade* or *Clovis*, and perceives in *Andromaque* a human vision of history and in *Attila* a divine vision of the past — 'sans perspective, sans ombre, presque sans durée'.

BROSSE. M. Wuillermoz, 'Les mythes de l'amour à l'épreuve de la comédie dans *Les songes des hommes esveillez* de Brosse', *SF*, 102:391–402, suggests that the lovers of the play are 'prisonniers d'un discours amoureux accaparant qui, ne laissant que très peu de marge à ceux qui le parlent, s'avère profondément inapte à traduire la réalité du sentiment'.

CORNEILLE. H. Curial, **Corneille: Le Cid*, Profil d'une œuvre, Hatier, 80 pp. S. Read Baker, 'The problematic of exemplarity in Corneille's theoretical texts', *Actes* (Las Vegas), 53–61, discusses the concept of exemplary action as it relates to rhetoric and history. J. Bem, **Le Texte à travers: Corneille, Prévost, Marivaux, Musset, Dumas, Nerval*, Champion, 210 pp. C. Kinzler, *Poétique de l'opéra français: de Corneille à Rousseau*. Minerve, 582 pp., examines three moments (*lullyste, ramiste, rousseauiste*) in the history of French opera and distinguishes between Perrin's views of the cardinal virtues of opera and 'la conception cornélienne d'après laquelle la musique au théâtre ne doit être qu'une musique d'agrément, d'avant scène, une sorte de hors d'œuvre'. R. C. Knight, *Corneille's Tragedies. The Role of the Unexpected*, Cardiff, Univ. of Wales Press, vi + 134 pp., is an economic study which evaluates the plays in relation to firmly held dramaturgical values, paying little attention to historico-political criticism, and is at its most incisive in the analysis of the 'tragedies without heroes' from *Sertorius* onwards. J. Krau, 'L'esthétique et l'éthique dans la tragédie cornélienne', *Actes* (Las Vegas), 65–78, would persuade us that exemplarity functions in the plays in an ambiguous fashion and that 'l'esthétique modifie sans cesse une éthique idéale, conçue en vertu de son pouvoir dramatique, pour divertir et non pour édifier'. J. Lichtenstein, 'What is the subject of *La Place Royale*', *YFS*, 80: 41–69, proposes that the title of C.'s play refers to a space that is not merely geographical, but also political, philosophical, and politico-philosophical 'in which the subject discovers himself as master'. J. D. Lyons, 'Unseen space and theatrical narrative: the "récit de Cinna"', *ib.*, 70–90, notes that 'as an illusory window onto the world offstage, Cinna's narrative is reminiscent of the architectural illusions of its day'. M.-O. Sweetser, 'Nouvelles réflexions sur la dramaturgie cornélienne', *Actes* (Las Vegas), 71–78, reminds us of the limitations of 'les textes théoriques [. . .] peu nombreux après 1660 [. . .] — mais que la création a continué et a produit des chefs-d'œuvre jusqu'au bout'. J. Trethewey, *Corneille: 'L'Illusion comique' and 'Le Menteur'*, Grant and Cutler, 97 pp., is convinced that the early period of C.'s career is not to be viewed as an apprenticeship and that in terms of plot, themes, and characterization, *Mélite* 'is a very professional piece of work'. C. Venosoen, '*Cinna* et les avatars de l'héroïsme cornélien', *PFSCL*, 18: 359–81, provocatively suggests that 'l'héroïsme d'Auguste n'était [. . .] qu'un leurre, une illusion de grandeur. C'est par la sensibilité *féminine* [. . .] qu'il obtient son salut.'

N.-CHRÉTIEN DES CROIX. *Les Portugaiz infortunez* (1608), ed. A. Maynor Hardee (TLF 397), 181 pp., is distinguished as the first French tragedy to have incorporated 'les matériaux exotiques des cultures primitives ainsi que le mélange de sentiments suscités dans la connaissance européenne au contact de ses cultures'.

GUÉRIN DE LA PINELIÈRE. J. Pineau, 'Un jeune dramaturge qui se dit angevin: Pierre Guérin de la Pinelière', *RHT*, 170: 85–94, reconsiders the work of this rare dramatist from Anjou, who died young and whose *Hippolyte* (1635) may be regarded as an early *Phèdre*.

HARDY. M.-F. Hilgar, 'Les pastorales d'Alexandre Hardy: tradition et innovation', Niderst, *Pastorale*, 37–50, discusses this much neglected aspect of H.'s five published pastorals, and notes the difficulty of dating them, and that among the many aspects they have in common is the importance which they accord to female characters.

MAHELOT. J. Golder, 'An unidentified sketch of the Mahelot *mémoire*, at folio 81 recto', *SCFS*, 13:129–38, 4 pls, feels impelled towards the conclusion 'that the folio 81 recto sketch is the work of Laurent [...] and dates from the 1670s [...] and inspired, consciously or unconsciously, by a ... design for Corneille's *Polyeucte*'.

MOLIÈRE. *Le Bourgeois gentilhomme: problèmes de la comédie-ballet*, ed. V. Kapp, PFSCL, 223 pp., vaunts the merits of an interdisciplinary study of this model of the genre which integrates dance and music perfectly: L. E. Auld, 'Une rivalité sournoise: Molière contre Pierre Perrin' (123–39), suggests that M. was trying to protect 'comédie mêlée de musique et de danse' from the new form of 'comédie-en-musique' sung from beginning to end promoted by P.; D. Fricke, 'Deux mises en scène cinématographiques récentes du *Bourgeois gentilhomme* de Molière: Roger Coggio, 1982; Jérôme Savary, 1981/2' (115–23), contrasts Coggio's version made in the sacrosanct tradition of the Comédie-Française with Savary's more adventurous style for which he received no support from 'la mafia théâtreuse parisienne'; G. C. Gerhardi, 'Circulation monétaire et mobilité sociale dans le *Bourgeois gentilhomme*' (23–35), views the text as a 'pièce à conviction dans un procès intenté, en dernière analyse, au roi lui-même'; C. Jeschke, 'Vom *Ballet de Cour* zum *Ballet d'action*. Über den Wandel des Tanzverständnisses im ausgehenden 17. und beginnenden 18. Jahrhundert' (185–233), gives a history of the *ballet de cour* and choreography from the *Ballet comique de la reine* (1581) to Weaver's *Essay towards an History of Dancing* (1712) and his *Loves of Mars and Venus* (1717), only considers dance *praxis* in so far as it illustrates theory, and concludes with a brief section on M. and Lully's 'Art Gesamt-kunstwerk — oder salopper: "Multi-media Show"'; V. Kapp, 'Langage verbal et langage non-verbal dans le *Bourgeois gentilhomme*' (95–115), considers that dramatic literature and the actor's art are both based on ancient rhetoric and oratory which also determine the codification of social behaviour in 17th-c. treatises on civility, and concludes: 'Dans le *Bourgeois gentilhomme*, M. se moque avec l'aristocratie de l'intrus bourgeois et il s'allie avec le Bourgeois pour démasquer les mécanismes de communication non-verbale qui protègent l'élite politique de ses concurrents du Tiers-État'; F. Karro, 'La cérémonie turque du *Bourgeois gentilhomme*: mouvance temporelle et spirituelle de la foi' (35–95), is an extensive examination of two contemporary pamphlets (*Apologie pour les Français* (anon.) and F.-P. de Lisola's *La France démasquée*) which attempts 'de relativiser et de replacer [la pièce] dans une politique orientale plus complète que des

querelles de cérémonial', contains sub-sections on diplomatic cere-
monial and the theatricalization of Turkish rites and Simon Arnauld,
marquis de Pomponne, and confirms the importance of the Chevalier
d'Arvieux in the elaboration of the Turkish ceremony in the play,
concluding with a comparison of the text of Arvieux's letter to H. de
Lionne concerning his interview with Soliman Aga and his Memoirs;
M. McGowan, 'La danse: son rôle multiple' (163–85), presents dance
as the *maître de cérémonie* of the entire play and turns to the theorist
Menestrier's *Des ballets anciens et modernes* (1682) for confirmation of
the supreme significance of this art form in the theatre, and also
considers the views of Chappuzeau, Beauchamps, and Louis XIV on
this kind of 'divertissement propre au roi'; H. Schneider, 'Die
Serenade im *Bourgeois gentilhomme*' (139–63), following in the tradition
of Böttgers and Fricke, is less a study of the play than of the genre of
the '*Air pour une sérénade*' and its semantics and includes tabular
comparisons of the timing, form, key, and expression of serenades in
three of M.'s plays and other contemporary *ballets de cour*; H. Stenzel,
'Projet critique et divertissement de cour. Sur la place de la
comédie-ballet et du *Bourgeois gentilhomme* dans le théâtre de Molière'
(9–23), suggests that 'dans le domaine de l'art, et à plus forte raison
au XVIIe siècle, il n'existe pas de divertissement innocent' but that
any social criticism is deflected by the culmination of the action in the
final ballet-spectacle.

　　*Amphytrion, ed. M. Autrand, Bordas, 127 pp. *Amphytrion*, ed. J.
Bénazraf, Classiques Larousse, 227 pp. A. Boviatsis, 'Le politique et
la politesse chez Molière: sur certains *topoi* d'exposition narrative
comme indicateurs de relations civiles', *Actes* (Montpellier), 131–45,
would persuade us of 'une correspondance bi-univoque' in the play
between Topos I (la part de Philinte qu'il y a dans Alceste) and
Topos II (le reste du *complexe Alceste*); P. Dandrey, 'Le *Dom Juan* de
Molière et la tradition de l'éloge paradoxal', *DSS*, 172:211–27, moves
from the *registre épidéitique* of pseudo-encomium to street farce and
discovers in the play a 'culture mêlée, complexe et déroutante'; Id.,
*'Tartuffe, Narcisse et la mélancolie', *Théâtre public*, 97:71–74. **Dom
Juan*, ed. J.-J. Robrieux, Nathan, 64 pp. **Dom Juan ou le festin de pierre*,
ed. G. Ferreyrolles, Classiques Larousse, 176 pp. **École des femmes*, ed.
F. Hinard, Hachette, 175 pp. S. Kofman, **Dom Juan ou le refus de la
dette*, Gallilé, 159 pp. **Le Médecin malgré lui*, ed. S. Speiss, Classiques
Hachette, 96 pp. **Les Fourberies de Scapin*, ed. E. Bonetto, Hachette,
128 pp. **Le Misanthrope*, ed. A. Pelletier, Bordas, 96 pp. **The Miser*,
trans. J. Sams, Methuen, vi + 83 pp., reproduces the text of the
version premièred at the National Theatre in May 1991. A. Forti-
Lewis, 'Virtuosismo linguistico del *Dom Juan* di Molière', *SF*,
35:59–66, examines speech patterns in the dialogue of Sganarelle and

Dom Juan as a reflection of the structural and thematic conflict between oppressive authority and rebellious individualism, classifying M.'s hero as 'l'esempio più estremo dell'ambiguità semiologica del periodo'. A. Greive, 'Les vers mêlés dans *Amphytrion* de Molière', Wentzlaff-Eggebert, *Langage*, 23–34, offers a micro- and macrostructural examination of the exceptional use of metrical variation in this play. E. James, 'Molière moralized: the *Lettre sur la comédie de l'Imposteur*', *SCFS*, 13:105–13, is intended as a criticism of W. G. Moore's 'now somewhat outdated *New Criticism*', which argues that 'the pedantically moralistic character of the doctrine has no bearing on the quality of Molière's achievement as a practising writer of comedies'. D. F. Jones, 'Daily bread in *Les Femmes savantes*', *RoN*, 31:215–24, takes as its point of departure F. Seigner's 1986 staging of the play in Boulogne Billancourt and considers the 'disquieting impact of the traditional nuptial feast in the context of *Les Femmes savantes*'. H. Knutson, 'Molière et la satire contre la médecine: hargne personnelle ou décision de métier', *DSS*, 171:127–31, examines M.'s decision to return to Italian theatrical practice following the difficult year 1664–65, embracing the arguments of J. Cairncross to refute G. Michaut's view that the principal reasons were related to M.'s health. Id., 'A prolegomenon for a Marxist study of Molière', *Actes* (Las Vegas), 19–28, feels that 'it is probably anachronistic to see M.'s theatre in class terms'. P. H. Nurse, *Molière and the Comic Spirit*, Droz, 144 pp., is dedicated to the thesis that moral questions underlie all the comedies, including the earliest farces, and opens M. up to the world of English literature by a system of literary references, which places Shakespeare and Shelley above the French critics of today. R. Parish, 'Le Misanthrope: des raisonneurs aux rieurs', *FS*, 45:17–35, identifies Damon as the real *raisonneur* of the play and elaborates G. Defaux's view of *Le Misanthrope* as neither 'une pièce totalement sérieuse' nor 'une pièce totalement comique'. R. Pommier, 'Argan et le "danger de contrefaire le mort"', *RHLF*, 91:927–31, reconsiders R. Garapon's view in *Le Dernier Molière* that Argan's readiness to pretend to be dead detracts from the coherence of the character in relation to three points: Toinette's dexterity, the complexity of Argan's psychology, and little Louison's reassuring demonstration of her own *fausse mort*. B. Schlossman, 'Disappearing acts: style, seduction, and performance in *Dom Juan*', *MLN*, 106:1030–47, finds that Dom Juan's 'ultimate role' is as a 'literary stylist' and that Sganarelle 'offers an oblique representation of Dom Juan's fictions, his beautiful rhetoric, and his stylistic effects'. D. Shaw, 'Moliere's temporary happy endings', *FS*, 45:129–42, questions 'the tyranny of the "happy marriage" convention' and concludes that 'Molière's dénouements are as rich and varied a feature of his plays as any other'. Id.,

'Theatrical self-consciousness in Molière', *NFS*, 30:1–13, surveys M.'s 'willingness to explore dramatic illusion for comic effect', from the minor farces to *Le Malade imaginaire*, giving particular attention to the moments when critical opinion was against him, concluding that 'instances of self-consciousness in his work are numerous, varied and brief and occur in the unlikely places'. A. Stäuble, 'Gli antenati italiani di un pedante du Molière', *BHR*, 53:423–29, supports the view that *Monsieur de Pourceaugnac* is more reminiscent of two comedies by G. Della Porte than Tessonerie's *Desniaisé*. J. Sylvester, 'Molière's *Dom Juan*: charity's prodigal son', *RoN*, 32:23–28, presents Dom Juan as a negative force, incapable of either charity or love; M. Vernet, 'Économie, histoire, littérature', *OC*, 16:61–72, analyses the *scène du pauvre* in *Dom Juan* and concludes that 'il y a chez Molière méconnaissance presque totale de ce qui se passe en matière d'économie dans sa société, tant dans les faits que dans le discours qui se tient sur eux'. Id., *Molière: côté jardin, côté cour*, Nizet, 381 pp., is a challenging study, determined to offer a new approach, which takes issue with the *Comédie française* productions which perpetuate the tradition of the théâtre de la ville' and '"oublie" la Cour et le roi', and develops a new category — the *Ucomique*. D. Whitton, *Molière: Le Misanthrope*, GUPGFL, 88 pp., aims to demonstrate to students 'how the play works as a piece of theatre' and 'not a dramatisation of a moral thesis'. K. Willis Wolfe, 'Le caractère polémique de la *Lettre sur la comédie de l'Imposteur*', *Actes* (Las Vegas), 29–35, pronounces the letter 'sans conteste une réussite parmi les textes qui s'engagent dans la politique verbale'.

PICHOU. *L'Infidèle Confidente*, ed. J.-P. Leroy, Droz, 223 pp., is an interesting example of how a dramatist sets about turning a *nouvelle* full of incidents into a play, much of the surprising success of which may be attributed to 'dynamisme, technique de la surprise, effets spectaculaires'.

RACINE. R.-L. Barnett, 'L'hyper-auto-représentation racinienne', *EsC*, 31:14–21, detects the 'parole ici iphigénieuse, là bérénicienne, encore et parfois hyppolytique' engaged in 'la poursuite irrévocable, vampirique d'elle même'; J. Campbell, 'The unity of time in *Athalie*', *MLR*, 86:572–79, considers the 'foreign convention of time' from the perspective of 'an Anglo-Saxon man of common sense and no nonsense', but is impressed by 'the mysterious union between the spectator's time, biblical time and Racine's own time'; A. Couprié, 'La notion de justice dans le théâtre de Racine', *TLit*, 4:127–38, argues that, with few exceptions, the Racinian universe has no notion of justice 'non qu'elle soit absente, mais parce que la pluralité des notions de justice empêche l'une d'elles de devenir la norme'. J. Dubu, 'Esther: Bible et poésie dramatique' *FR*, 64:607–20, keeps one

eye on the *supplice d'Aman* in the Sistine Chapel as he examines R.'s
exploitation of the original version of the story of Esther and the most
important of the thirteen other tragedies on the subject published
between 1543 and 1689; Id., (ed.), *Racine. Lettres d'Uzès*, Nîmes,
Lacour, 119 pp.; X. Galmiche, *Récits d'agonie: Racine, Chateaubriand,
Blanchot*, Quintette, 1990, 79 pp., considers the *récit de Théramène* as an
example of a 'genre subversif', and develops the *explication de texte*
which follows accordingly. F. Garette, 'Joas: âge et langage dans le
théâtre du XVIIe siècle', *LitC*, 14:79–93, attempts to show, through
the statistical method inspired by the works of C. Muller, that stylistic
variation in the role distinguishes Joas's character from others in the
play, but is not distinctively childlike. S. Guénoun, 'Psychanalyse et
critique littéraire: un sujet classique?', *LitC*, 16:21–42, agrees that R.
'pourrait s'étonner des destins critiques qui gèrent son œuvre à partir
de l'analyse psychanalytique', but goes on to consider 'la transformation racinienne de la notion du destin' in *Iphigénie*, in semi-Freudian
terms intended ultimately to place the Racinian literary machine in
the tradition of Cartesian reflexion; M. Pittas-Herschbach, *Time and
Space in Euripides and Racine: The 'Hippolytos' of Euripides and Racine's
'Phèdre'* (AUS, III.32), 1990, 344 pp., aims 'to explore the relationship
between theatrical architecture and drama', and traces the influence
of classical theatre through medieval religious drama. I. J.-F. de Jong,
*'Verhaal en drama: het bodeverhaal in de Griekse tragedie', *Forum
der Letteren*, 32:208–20. J. Kirkness, 'The language of choice in
Racine's *Britannicus*', *PFSCL*, 18:383–408, inspired by a 1975 paper
by M.-O. Sweetser 'illustrates the predominance of "Cornelian"
terms on a specific aspect of the characteristic vocabulary of
Britannicus'. H. Knutson, 'Marx in the century of Louis XIV:
Goldmann and Racine revisited', *LitC*, 16:51–59, questions whether
a dozen or so tragedies can be put on the same plane of ideological
relevance as the writings of Pascal, and concludes that 'if *Phèdre* can
continue to move us as members of a largely capitalist, consumer
society of the late twentieth century, it has obviously done more than
speak for Jansenism and the momentary grievances of a vanished
subclass against a cavalier King'. *Landmarks of French Classical Drama:
Corneille, 'The Cid'; Racine, 'Phedra'; Molière, 'Tartuffe'*, introd. by D.
Bradby, Methuen, 393 pp., brings together the trans. of *The Cid* used
by the Cheek by Jowl Theatre Company, R. D. MacDonald's
translation of *Phedra* with Glenda Jackson in the title role, and the
translation of *Tartuffe* used by the Royal Shakespeare Company of
Anthony Sher fame. L. Mall, 'Dire le départ, ou comment faire
quelque chose de rien: étude sur Bérénice', *Poétique*, 75:41–55, is
fascinated by the essential artificiality (time and space) of theatrical
convention 'qui force la présence à se dire entre [...] l'avant- et

l'après-pièce' and by R.'s wager of Beckettian proportions to write a play where nothing much happens. D. Maskell, *Racine: A Theatrical Reading*, Oxford, Clarendon, viii + 272 pp., is about reading the text for what it offers to the mind's eye and 'shows how particular performances [from the 17th c. to the present day] accord with the theatrical implications of Racine's texts'. N. M. McElveen, 'The labyrinth as the mimesis of absence in *Phédre*', *RoN*, 31, 1990:3–10, enters the labyrinth by way of 'the Derridean pathway of *différance*, supplement, and deconstruction and considers Act II, scene V, as an example of 'acting by proxy'. J. Morel, 'Des tragédies "profanes" aux "tragédies sacrées" dans le théâtre', *FR*, 65:30–35, is convinced that the first are a preparation for the second and traces five *lignées* of characters. R. Morel, 'Narcisse mortifié et mortifère: le regard chez Racine', *FR*, 64, 921–33, looks at multiple aspects of the *focalisation obsessionnelle* of the private and the public eye in the most famous of the profane tragedies. H. Phillips, 'Racinian letters', *FMLS*, 27:35–42, proceeds from a discussion of the use of the letter in *Bérénice*, *Bajazet*, *Iphigénie*, and *Phèdre* 'to suggest some directions we might take in an examination of the status of the written as a whole in Racinian tragedy'. J. Rohou, *L'Évolution du tragique racinien*, SEDES, 386 pp., analyses the plays in chronological order and traces a four-stage dramatic evolution in relation to attitudes to the Father, culminating in his transfiguration as God the Father in *Esther* and *Athalie*. M. Slater, 'Racine's *Bajazet*: the language of violence and secrecy', *Themes in Drama*, 13: *Violence in Drama*, ed. J. Redmond, CUP, 142–50, suggests that R.'s 'obsessive use' of such language 'is a practical device for making the play acceptable to an audience'; G. Snaith, 'Andromache, Annette and *Andromaque*: a look at two recent translations', *SCFS*, 13:139–52, compares two Radio 3 1990 productions: D. Dunn's *Andromaque* and C. Raine's 1953. *Racine: théâtre et poésie*, ed. C. M. Hill, Leeds, Cairns, 222 pp., contains the following: C. Abraham, '*Phèdre*: lyrisme et théâtralité' (37–48), believes with J.-L. Barrault that 'Racine est le plus musicien de tous les dramaturges français', but warns against the temptation to reduce R.'s theatre to nothing more than musicality; C. Delmas, 'Bérénice comme rituel' (191–203), insists that in this play 'c'est le sacrifice, et plus précisément le rituel sacrificiel, qui se fait drame et action, dans le même temps que la poésie [. . .] se fait liturgie'; M. Defrenne, 'Formes scéniques et création des personnages dans le *Mithridate* de Racine' (107–35), offers a tripartite portrait of Monime and Mithridate in relation to *qualification*, *déplacements scéniques*, and *structure des dialogues*; M. Delcroix, 'La poétique du monstre dans le théâtre de Racine' (175–90), takes to task L. Van Delft's view 'que le monstre soit partout et de manière égale', suggesting that the monster-motif is in

fact only to be found in *Phèdre* and even then only in the rich
expressivity of the *textual moment*; J. Dubu, 'La prosodie de Racine'
(3–23), examines R.'s 'skill in metres other than the alexandrine', and
illustrates vocalic, phonetic and other elements indicative of 'the
dramatist's sensitivity to sound'; P. France, 'L'hyperbole chez
Racine' (23–35), traces the different modalities of this aspect of R.'s
verbal strategy, which combines the sublime and the ridiculous to
effect; J. Gaudon, 'Fantasmes' (205–17), recalls the lasting impact of
his first meeting with E. Vinaver by way of introduction to a study of
the *scénario fantasmatique* in *Phèdre* the play rather than of the heroine or
the dramatist; D. Maskell, 'La précision du lieu dans les tragédies de
Racine' (151–71), gives the lie once and for all to the idea of R.'s
recourse to a *palais à volonté*, by offering abundant evidence of the
indications in the plays which allow us 'de visualiser et de recon-
struire ces lieux très précis où l'action se déroule'; R. Parish, 'Racine:
scène et vers' (139–50), concludes that for R. there is no question of
adaptation of one to the other, since 'le vers [. . .] est le seul véhicule
qui puisse convenir à sa conception scénique'; J. Morel, 'Le
personnage sacrifié dans l'œuvre de Racine' (83–90), looks at Hémon,
Andromaque, Junie, Antiochus, Atalide, and proceeds to argue that,
from *Mithridate* onwards, such characters become the rule; J.-C.
Ranger, 'Fureurs raciniennes' (59–80), finds a total of 179 instances of
fureur(s)/furie/furieux in the plays, but, unimpressed by statistics,
argues that the full force of the Greek is only expressed in 'cette fureur
qui chez Racine ne dit jamais son nom: la poésie'; J.-P. Short,
'Passion: source of action in the tragedies of Racine?' (93–106), warns
of the dangers of 'fitting theory to practice' in *Britannicus* and *Bérénice*
and suggests a modified reading of *Iphigénie* and *Andromaque*; R.
Tobin, 'Le plaisir chez Racine' (49–58), has been struck by the
recurrence of the two terms *plaisir* and *plaire* in the tragedies from
Andromaque to *Bajazet* and considers that this authorizes a study of
certain comic aspects in *Britannicus*.

Racine: Appraisal and Re-appraisal, ed. E. B. Forman, Univ. Bristol,
120 pp., includes the following: P. Bayley, 'Aricie' (54–66), injects life
into this impassive creature by provocatively suggesting that her
presence on stage resolves the problem of 'How to get the heroine off
[it]', as well as providing the 'glue which makes the parts [of the play]
cohere'; E. Forman, '"En un mot, elle est femme": Racine and
feminist criticism' (95–112), argues against extreme interpretations
and suggests that 'the two genders of investigation will have no choice
but to get together'; B. Kite, 'The guilt of Phèdre: the play and its
sources' (67–82), justifies its title in the comparisons he draws with
Euripides and Seneca and further suggests that this character may
represent R.'s feelings of remorse; J. O'Brien, 'Characterizing the

past: Racine's *Andromaque*' (38–53), credits the 'dramatic text with prescience in respect of its potential interpretations, and with the property of refusing collusion with these'; H. Phillips, 'Text as theatre' (25–37), is basically an *analyse énonciative*, which argues for the 'theatrical dimension' of speech with reference mainly to Anne Ubersfeld's *Lire le théâtre* (1977); P. Thody, 'Barthes v. Picard, twenty years on' (5–24), is more Picardian than Barthesian; Id., 'Barthes v. Picard, twenty years on: second thoughts' (113–20), extends the argument of the initial paper with a mildly self-critical apology for having been too long-winded; J. Trethewey, 'Biblical and classical thematic elements in *Athalie*: liaisons dangereuses' (83–94), believes that the play 'involves the revelation of the will of God [. . .], in ways beyond the comprehension of *all* the characters in the play', including Joas and Athalie.

REGNARD. *'Attendez-moi sous l'orme'*, *'La Sérénade'*, et *'Le Bal'*: *Comédies*, ed. C. Mazouer TLF, 396, Droz, 600 pp., brings together the texts of three little one-act plays which, unusually, R. wrote between 1694 and 1696 for French actors rather than the Italian troupes, which are all 'du meilleur Regnard'.

ROTROU. *Venceslas*, ed. D. Watts, Univ of Exeter, 1990, xxxii + 105 pp., more than succeeds in its aim of making this play, which may be described as either 'un chef d'œuvre méconnu' or 'une rareté recherchée par les bibliophiles', easily affordable again for all.

THÉOPHILE DE VIAU. J. Morel, *'Pyrame et Thisbé'*, *Actes* (Marseille), 123–28, offers a summary of the play that Corneille would take up and correct in *Clitandre* and considers the dominating feature a kind of naturalistic or tragic scepticism reminiscent of Montaigne.

THE EIGHTEENTH CENTURY

By T. C. NEWLAND, *Senior Lecturer in French, Coventry Polytechnic*, and
S. HARVEY, *Lecturer in French, Queen Mary and Westfield College,
University of London*

I. GENERAL

CULTURE AND THOUGHT. R. A. Nablow, *The Addisonian Tradition in France: Passion and Objectivity in Social Observation*, Fairleigh Dickinson U.P., 1990, 278 pp., keeps closely to its title and covers Marivaux, Montesquieu, Prévost, Rétif, and Mercier. B. Cottret, *Le Christ des Lumières: Jésus de Newton à Voltaire (1680–1760)*, Cerf, 1990, 189 pp. J. W. Yolton, *Locke and French Materialism*, Oxford, Clarendon, 239 pp., is clearly a major contribution to our understanding of its subject. Explores the whole area of how the British debate relates to that of the *philosophes*, and effectively demolishes the simplistic notion of L. as the precursor of Condillac's so-called school of sensualism. Contains sections on Voltaire, La Mettrie, Holbach, Diderot and many lesser writers. R. Hutchison, *Locke in France (1688–1734)*, StV, 290, ix + 251 pp., neatly complements Yolton's work on materialism since the stress is put on L.'s personal contacts with the French and on the overall complexity of the intellectual debate at the turn of the century. L. is seen to fit into the context of several discussions of great significance at this time. C. M. Northeast, *The Parisian Jesuits and the Enlightenment (1700–62)*, StV, 288, 261 pp., sheds light on the relationship between believers and non-believers in the first half of the century. Concentrates on the nature of Enlightenment irreligion and isolates the key problems for the Jesuits in their account of Christianity.

J.-M. Racault, *L'Utopie narrative en France et en Angleterre (1675–1761)*, StV, 280, 830 pp., is an exceptionally rich study of magisterial proportions which ranges over a vast field. Tackles not only the major models of the genre but also many subtle variations, as well as the whole corpus of imaginary voyages and the Utopianism of the principal novelists such as Prévost, Voltaire, and Rousseau. Likely to serve as an indispensable work of reference for many years it has a particularly erudite section on social experimentation and ideal communities. I. Brouard-Arends, *Vies et images maternelles dans la littérature française du dix-huitième siècle*, StV, 291, 465 pp., presents a large topic somewhat disappointingly, partly through a lack of a proper organizing principle for so much material. Reads at times like a catalogue of appearances of the mother figure and indeed concludes with an inventory of themes and types. The confident section on background gives way to a meandering study of works treated rather indiscriminately and with little or no *esprit de synthèse*. A. Gunny, 'Images of Islam in some French writings of the first half of the eighteenth century', *BJECS*, 14: 191–201, concludes that most writers offer stereotyped views of the Moslem religion. R. Rosbottom, 'Narrating the Regency', *RoQ*, 38: 341–53, tries to show a relationship between political structures, narrative (Marivaux's *journaux*) and painting (Watteau's *L'Enseigne de Gersaint*). M. Gilot, 'Quelques aspects du sentiment de la solitude au XVIIIe siècle', *Mélanges Deloffre*, 623–33, distinguishes three separate periods for this theme and evokes an awakening of narcissism that culminates in Prévost, followed by an absorption with salvation and perdition, then finally the golden age of landscape after 1770.

International Directory of Eighteenth-Century Studies 1991, ed. Andrew Brown, Oxford, Voltaire Foundation, xii + 207 pp. is the seventh and latest edition of this (hopefully) comprehensive list of scholars working on different aspects of the 18th c. (cf. *YWMLS*, 50: 148). *DhS*, 23, in a special issue on Enlightenment physiology and medicine includes *inter alia*: R. Rey, 'La théorie de la sécrétion chez Bordeu, modèle de la physiologie et de la pathologie vitalistes' (45–58); M. D. Grmek, 'La réception du *De Sedibus* de Morgagni en France au 18e siècle' (59–73); G. Rudolph, 'La méthode hallérienne en physiologie' (75–84), on the work of the Swiss scientist Albrecht von Haller; C. Castellani, 'La réception en Italie et en Europe du *Saggio di Observazioni microscopiche* de Spallanzani (1765)' (85–95); P. di Pietro, 'La méthode de Spallanzani à travers sa correspondance' (97–105); F. Azouvi, 'Magnétisme animal. La sensation infinie' (107–18), on the work of Mesmer and the Mesmerians; J.-P. Goubert, 'Entre Ancien Régime et Révolution: les chirurgiens vus par eux-mêmes (1790–1791)' (119–28), on an investigation into the practice of surgery in France carried out at the end of 1790; N. Pellegrin, 'L'uniforme de la santé: les médecins et la réforme du costume' (129–40); J.-L. Fischer, 'La callipédie, ou l'art d'avoir de beaux enfants' (141–58), on a Latin poem by Claude Quillet translated into French in 1749; D. Teysseire, 'Une étape dans la constitution de la pédiatrie: l'*Encyclopédie méthodique*' (159–69); and C. Milanesi, 'La mort-instant et la mort-processus dans la médecine de la seconde moitié du siècle' (171–90). On a related subject *Les Savants et la politique à la fin du XVIIIe siècle*, ed. Gisèle Van de Vyver and Jacques Reisse, Brussels U.P., 96 pp., includes R. Devleeshouwer, 'L'heureux XVIIIe siècle' (11–21); J. Dhombres, 'Savants en politique, politique des savants. Les expériences de la Revolution française' (23–41), which shows the far from unanimous reaction of scientists to the French Revolution; B. Mattie, 'L'enseignement des sciences'

(43–55); J.-B. Robert, 'L'itinéraire d'un savant: Joseph Fourier' (57–68); H. Hasquin, 'La Révolution et les sciences. La passion de l'Universel' (69–83), which shows the desire among scientists at the end of the c. to reduce all phenomena, thought, and behaviour to unitary norms; C. Sorgeloos, 'Les savants à l'école. Le cas de Hainaut' (85–88), which shows Belgium was not excluded from the teaching of science at this period. Studies on different aspects of the Revolution continue to predominate. Roger Chartier, *The Cultural Origins of the French Revolution*, trans. Lydia G. Cochrane, Durham, Duke U.P., xix + 239 pp., is a translation of his *Les Origines culturelles de la Révolution française, Seuil, 1990, 249 pp. Chartier aims firstly to synthesize the vast amount of new research which has been carried out on the subject since the publication of Daniel Mornet's classic study in 1935. Secondly he enters the controversial debate about the relationship between the profound cultural changes of the 18th c. and the events of 1789. It is clearly a major contribution to the field, although probably best read in the French original. *Mythe et Révolutions*, ed. Yves Chalas, Grenoble U.P., 1990, 330 pp., includes R. Alleau, 'Epistémologie du mythique et du symbolique dans les discours politiques de la Terreur' (23–43); Y. Barrel, 'Le mythe et le sens: esquisse d'un mythe du mythe' (45–96); J.-P. Sironneau, 'Les équivoques de la religion révolutionnaire' (99–132); C. Rivière, 'La ritualisation des mythes révolutionnaires' (133–49); F. Berthier, 'Jean-Baptiste Davaux, une symphonie déconcertante' (153–83); A Verjat, 'L'imaginaire de Sade et la Révolution (185–97); S. Bernard-Griffiths, 'Révolution française et mythe du héros dans l'imaginaire d'Edgar Quinet' (199–225); R. Bellet, 'Mythe jacobin et mythe révolutionnaire chez Jules Vallès de 93 à la Commune de Paris' (227–44); R. Karst-Matausch, 'La légende des femmes révolutionnaires au XIXᵉ siècle' (247–67); A. Pessin, 'Mythe du peuple et révolution' (269–87); A. Girardet, 'Le mythe de la révolution fasciste chez les intellectuels français de l'entre-deux-guerres' (289–96); P. Sansot, 'Pour une révolution sans mythes' (299–304); P. Sansot, 'Du bon et du moins bon usage de la commémoration' (305–12); L. Sfez, 'Deux mots provisoires sur la question du Bicentenaire' (313–18) — a series of conference papers by sociologists, ethnologists, and his-torians as well as literary specialists on the importance of myth in particular in the French Revolution of 1789. *L'Espace et le temps reconstruits: la Révolution française, une révolution des mentalités et des cultures*, ed. Philippe Joutard, Aix-en-Provence, Univ. de Provence, 1990, x + 389 pp., includes *inter alia* J. Guilhamou, 'La formation d'un nouvel espace de relations politiques: "Les missionnaires patriotes"', créateurs de la civilité en Provence (1792)' (77–84); H.-J. Lüsebrink, 'L'exportation de la "flamme nationale" — rhétoriques et lectures du quatorze juillet aux frontières de la République' (85–96); C. Labrosse, 'Le temps immédiat dans la presse parisienne de 1789' (109–20); P. Retat, 'Représentation du temps révolutionnaire (d'après les journaux de 1789)' (121–29); J. Giordani, 'L'antiquité imaginée à travers certains projets d'éducation' (131–41); M.-C. Grassi, 'La Révolution à l'œuvre dans le discours intime nobiliaire' (143–52); E. Pommier, 'Boissy d'Anglas: culture et conscience de l'Histoire en l'An II' (153–67); B. Didier, 'Nouvel espace, nouvelle temporalité dans la fiction romanesque de la Révolution Française' (217–27). *La Pensée économique pendant la Révolution française*, ed. G. Faccarello and Ph. Steiner, Grenoble U.P., 1990, 559 pp., contains the 'Actes du Colloque International de Vizille (6–8 septembre 1989)' and includes *inter alia* G. Faccarello and Ph. Steiner, 'Prélude: une génération perdue?' (9–56); C. Théré, 'L'édition économique et ses auteurs en 1789' (59–65); G. Faccarello, 'Le legs de Turgot: aspects de l'économie politique sensualiste de Condorcet à Roederer' (67–107); S. Meysonnier, 'Deux économistes sous la Révolution: François Véron de Fourbonnais et l'abbé Morellet' (109–21); B. Delmas and T. Demals, 'Du Pont et les "éclectiques": la controverse sur la stérilité pendant la période révolutionnaire' (123–39); Y. Breton, 'Germain Garnier, l'économiste et l'homme politique' (141–50); R. Tortajada, 'Produit net et latitude: Nicolas-François Canard 1754–1833' (151–72); P. Steiner, 'Comment stabiliser l'ordre social moderne? J.-B. Say, l'économie politique et la Révolution française' (173–93); J.-P. Joubert, 'Turgot et Condorcet: droits de l'homme, droit de vote et propriété (197–209); F. Hincker, 'Y eut-il une pensée économique de la Montagne?' (211–24); J.-J. Gislain, 'Le garantisme de la Révolution française' (225–60); G. Caire, 'D'une révolution à l'autre: Gracchus Babeuf et la question sociale' (261–80); F. Démier, 'Les "économistes de la nation" contre l' "économie-monde" du XVIIIe siècle' (281–303); J.-L. Billoret, 'L'affirmation et les polémiques du modèle consulaire' (305–21); C. Schmidt, 'L'économie de la force publique selon Guibert' (323–35); P. Crépel, 'Les calculs économiques et financiers de Condorcet pendant la Révolution' (339–50); F. Etner, 'Le calcul économique: 1789–1815' (351–61); O. Arkhipoff, 'Une révolution dans la Révolution: Condorcet, Lavoisier et Peuchet' (363–70); H. Duprat, 'Théorie et pratique en économie: 1791, année cruciale' (371–77); P.-H. Derycke, 'La Révolution française et le maillage territorial' (379–89). *L'Écrivain devant la Révolution: 1780–1800*, ed. Jean Sgard, Univ. Stendhal de Grenoble, 1990, 328 pp., includes *inter alia* D. Masseau, 'L'offensive des romanciers à la veille de la Révolution' (3–15); P. Rétat, 'L'ébranlement de la littérature en 1789' (17–29); C. Labrosse, 'Missions et figures de l'homme de lettres à l'aube de la Révolution'

(31–41); B. Consarelli, 'Babeuf, Maréchal e Buonarotti: testimonianze e rifflessioni' (75–87); H.-J. Lüsebrink, 'La chute d'un écrivain-philosophe, l'abbé Raynal devant les événements révolutionnaires (1789–1796)' (89–105); E. Di Rienzo, 'Morellet e la Rivoluzione' (107–20); C. Albertan, 'Lumières et Révolution, le point de vue de Morellet' (121–30); E. Boggio Quallio, 'Sabatier de Castres e la liberta di stampa' (131–38); P. Roger, 'Sade et le Révolution' (139–54); R. Granderoute, 'Senac de Meilhan et la Révolution' (171–80); S. Albertan-Coppola, 'La réaction de l'apologiste Barruel à la Révolution française' (181–91); H. Hofer, 'Mercier devant la Révolution' (205–16); M.-L. Girou-Swiderski, 'Les "Montagnards" de Mme Monnet' (237–49); J.-C. Bonnet, 'La gloire de l'homme de lettres dans le Panthéon révolutionnaire' (265–78); B. Craveri, 'La poesia di Chenier e il mito della rivoluzione' (279–89); M. Gilot and J. Oudart, 'L'écrivain en question: de l'an I à l'an III' (291–304); G. and M.-T. Bourez and J. Sgard, 'La Révolution devant l'écrivain (305–13); P. Jager and M.-F. Luna, 'L'iconographie de l'écrivain sous la Révolution' (315–26). H. Boyer *et al.*, *Le texte occitan de la période révolutionnaire (1788–1800): inventaire, approches, lectures,* Montpellier, SFAIED, 1989, 517 pp. includes, in addition to the inventory of both printed and manuscript texts in Occitan during these years, P. Martel, 'Les textes occitans de la période révolutionnaire' (219–45); R. Merle, 'Le texte occitan et francoprovençal du grand Sud-Est (Provence, Bas-Languedoc oriental, Avignon et Comtat, Comté de Nice, Dauphiné, Forez, Lyonnais, Savoie, Suisse romande)' (247–365); G. Fournier, 'La production toulousaine' (367–423); P. Gardy, 'Autour de Pierre Bernadan: le silence bordelais ou la traduction impossible' (425–40); H. Boyer, 'Le "patois" efficace? Une approche sociopragmatique des mises en texte de la Révolution en langue minorée' (443–72); P. Gardy, 'Les modèles d'écriture: ruptures et continuités' (473–516). *Dictionnaire des Constituants 1789–1791,* Oxford, Voltaire Foundation, vii + 1023 pp., 2 vols., includes a detailed chronology of the Assembly, a list of the parliamentary committees and their members, an index of the deputies by constituency and a thematic index of the major subjects debated by the Assembly. Useful as a work of reference. Jean Sgard, *Les trente récits de la Journée des Tuiles,* Grenoble U.P., 1988, 141 pp., uses a wide range of contemporary accounts of 7 June 1788 (when the population of Grenoble took up arms to prevent the exile of the Dauphiné Parlement) to carry out his literary analysis of these 30 texts. B. Durruty, 'Les auteurs des catéchismes révolutionnaires (1789–1799)', *AHRF*, 283:1–18, on the basis of an examination of some 200 revolutionary catechisms aims to trace a typology of their authors whom he presents in their sociological context; M. Biard, 'L'almanach du Père Gérard un exemple de diffusion des idées jacobines', *ib.*, 19–29, underlines the direct or roundabout references through which Collot d'Herbois states his convictions in this work; and M. Middell, 'La Révolution Française vue par les contre-révolutionnaires à l'Assemblée Nationale de 1789 à 1791', *ib.*, 67–77, is based on the systematic analysis of the speeches and stands taken within the National Assembly during these years, and attempts to establish the formative stages of a counter-revolutionary party and its strategies at the beginning of the Revolution. J. Guilhamou, 'Les porte-parole et le moment républicain (1790–1793)', *AESC*, 46:949–70, is part of the author's current investigation into the various types of spokesmen identifiable during these years; while D. Nicolaidis, 'La France et les Grecs sous la Révolution et l'Empire, étude d'une représentation à l'échelle de peuples', *AHRF*, 286:515–37, analyses the collective discourse of Frenchmen — consular agents, traders, travellers — concerning the people of Greece during the Revolution and the Empire. R. Favre, 'La Révolution: mort et régénération, ou la France "phénix"?', *DhS*, 23:331–44 studies the frequent use of the word 'regeneration' in 1789 and the revolutionary years, and particularly by André Chénier; and J.-L. Quantin, 'Sur l'histoire religieuse du mot "Révolution" au XVIIIe siècle', *HES*, 10:79–111, shows that most religious writers of the period used the word 'revolution' to describe the redemption of sinning humanity rather than in the modern sense of the word. Jack Hayward, *After the French Revolution: Six Critics of Democracy and Nationalism*, NY, Harvester Wheatsheaf, xvi + 366 pp., while being primarily concerned with studies of Maistre, Saint-Simon, Constant, Toqueville, Proudhon, and Blanqui, begins with a useful study of their ideological precursors (including Montesquieu, Rousseau, Condorcet, and Sieyès) and the political protagonists (notably Robespierre and the Idéologues) who set the scene for 19th-c. debate and action. P. H. Kaufman, 'Soviet perspectives on the French Enlightenment and Revolution', *SECC*, 20, 1990:115–29, examines changing attitudes as a result of glasnost and perestroika. The article already seems dated. **Révolution, restauration et les jeunes 1789–1848. Écrits et images*, ed. G. van de Loeuw and E. Genton, Didier, 1989, 181 pp. Two other articles to note are J. Lough, 'Lemonnier's painting "Une soirée chez Madame Geoffrin en 1755"', *FS*, 45:268–78, who concludes bluntly after an interesting discourse on the painting that it has no documentary value whatsoever and nothing can be deduced from it about the place of the writer in the society of the time; and G. Beale, 'Early French members of the Linnean Society of London, 1788–1802: initial encounters', *StV*, 292:129–38, which is concerned in particular with the correspondence of A.-L. de Jussieu, P.-M.-A. Broussonet and C.-L. L'Héritier.

LITERARY HISTORY, PUBLISHING, AND JOURNALISM. F. Bléchet, *Les ventes publiques de livres en France (1630–1750)*, Oxford, Voltaire Foundation, 156 pp., is an important source of material for the history of book collecting. These sale catalogues give precious information about prices, the size and nature of private libraries. Id., 'Un exemple d'échanges franco-anglais privilégiés: la correspondance entre Hans Sloane et l'abbé Bignon', *StV*, 292 : 119–28, reports on the results of a fruitful collaboration between the two presidents of the leading societies of their day. J. Lonbard, 'Les rédacteurs du *Mercure historique et politique* de La Haye', *Mélanges Deloffre*, 295–307, identifies only three authors with any certainty between 1686 and 1782: Courtilz de Sandras, Rousset, and Le Fibure. A. Kleinert, 'L'histoire du *Journal de Berlin* (1740–41), magazine politique et culturel', *StV*, 284 : 225–33. *Textologie du journal*, ed. P. Rétat, Minard, 1990, 173 pp., includes J. Sgard, 'La presse militante au 18e siècle: les gazettes ecclésiastiques' (7–34), which is a very scholarly and detailed account of the Jesuit and Jansenist press up to 1735, and M. Gilot, 'Un esprit et une forme: le lancement des feuilles de Spectateur' (35–49), which underlines the very different aims and character of each of Marivaux's three journals. Pierre M. Conlon, *Le Siècle des Lumières: Bibliographie chronologique*, vol. VIII, *1757–1760*, Geneva, Droz, xxix + 587 pp., is the latest vol. to appear in what has become established as a standard reference work (cf. *YWMLS*, 52 : 152). *Dictionnaire des journaux 1600–1789*: A–I and J–V, ed. Jean Sgard, Oxford, Voltaire Foundation, xi + 1211 pp., provides all the essential bibliographical information in this comprehensive guide to the French-language press during this period, a subject which continues to arouse considerable interest as shown by *The Press in the French Revolution (StV*, 287), ed. Harvey Chisick, Oxford, Voltaire Foundation, which includes D. Richet, 'Les canaux de la propagation des idées contestataires avant la presse révolutionnaire' (19–24); J. Sgard, '"On dit"' (25–32); J. Wagner, 'Peuple et pouvoir dans le *Journal encyclopédique* à la veille de la Révolution française' (33–57); R. Birn, 'The pamphlet press and the Estates-General of 1789' (59–69); P. Rétat, 'Pamphlet numéroté et journal en 1789' (71–82); J. D. Popkin, 'The élite press in the French Revolution: the *Gazette de Leyde* and the *Gazette universelle*' (85–98); J. Lenardon, 'The paradox of revolution within an *étatiste* mentality' (99–117); H. Chisick, 'The disappearance of a great Enlightenment periodical: the *Année littéraire*, 1789–1790' (119–30); J. Black, 'The challenge of the Revolution and the British press' (131–41); E. L. Eisenstein, 'The tribune of the people: a new species of demagogue' (145–59); W. J. Murray, 'Journalism as a career choice in 1789' (161–88); J. R. Censer, 'Robespierre the journalist' (189–96); F. Malino, 'Zalkind Hourwitz, the Jews and the revolutionary press'

138   *French Studies*

(197–207); M. Yardeni, 'Paradoxes politiques et persuasions dans les *Annales* de Linguet' (211–19); J.-P. Bertaud, '*L'Ami du roi* de l'abbé Royon' (221–27); S. Tucoo-Chala, 'Un *Moniteur universel* idéal: le *Supplément historique* de l'An IV' (229–34); M. Edelstein, '*La Feuille villageoise* and rural political modernisation' (237–60); A. de Baecque, 'La dénonciation publique dans la presse et le pamphlet (1789–1791)' (261–79); O. Elyada, 'Les récits de complot dans la presse populaire parisienne (1790–1791)' (281–92); E. Ducoudray, 'De la presse d'opinion aux groupes de pression: les clubs électoraux parisiens en 1791–1792' (293–307); D. Lenardon, 'The genesis of revolutionary language and vocabulary in the *Journal encyclopédique*' (311–17); R. Koren, 'Violence verbale et argumentation dans le presse révolutionnaire et contre-révolutionnaire' (319–34); H. Mitchell, 'Edmund Burke's language of politics and his audience' (335–60); S. Maza, 'L'image de la souveraine: féminité et politique dans les pamphlets de l'affaire du Collier' (363–78); M. Vovelle, 'L'altération de l'image royale à travers l'estampe et la chanson (1788–1794)' (379–94); C. Gaudelman, 'Appropriation et fécalisation: le rôle de la scatologie dans l'imagerie et le langage sans-culotte' (395–408). Other articles on the press include J.-P. Bertaud, 'Histoire de la presse et Révolution', *AHRF*, 285 : 281–98, which describes the current state of research on the revolutionary press and has the merit of not only making an inventory of recent historiography and of classic studies but also emphasizing the areas of research still to be prospected; M.-A. Guidicelli, 'Le journal de Louis XVI et de son peuple ou le défenseur de l'autel, du trône et da la patrie', *ib.*, 299–324, which examines this anonymous counter-revolutionary newspaper published between 1790–92 typical of many at the time although now little known; C. Paliersi, 'La Révolution du droit naturel dans *Les Révolutions de Paris* (juillet 1789 — septembre 1790)', *ib.*, 353–75, which studies the characteristics of the ideology reflected in this newspaper during the period that coincided with Élysée Loustallot's work on the paper, demonstrating the unity around the theme of natural law; B. Murray, '1789: the press, the revisionists and the bourgeois revolution', *AJFS*, 26, 1986 : 260–71, who suggests in a somewhat polemical study that there are severe limits to the 'revisionist' interpretations of 1789 while conceding that recent works on the press and the Revolution have added greatly to our knowledge of a previously underestimated aspect of the Revolution; and M. Foisil, F. de Noirfontaine and I. Flandrois, 'Un journal de polémique et de propagande. Les *Nouvelles ecclésiastiques*', *HES*, 10 : 399–420, who analyse the contents and vocabulary of this periodical which played a fundamental role in the diffusion of Jansenist views in the 18th c. Ouzi Elyada, **Presse populaire et feuilles volantes de la Révolution à Paris*

1789–1792, Soc. des Études Robespierristes. On a related topic D. K. Van Kley, 'New wine in old wineskins: continuity and rupture in the pamphlet debate of the French prerevolution, 1787–1789', *FHS*, 17:447–65, argues that competitive parlementary and royalist versions of the French past had opposed each other throughout the 18th c. and had origins as far back as in the literature of the 16th-c. wars of religion; while R. L. Dawson, 'Books printed in France: the English connection', *StV*, 292:139–67, provides some useful bibliographical information about books in English printed in France particularly in the latter part of the c. More broadly Robert Darnton, *Édition et sédition: l'univers de la littérature clandestine au XVIIIe siècle*, Gallimard, 281 pp., is an attempt to study in a broad canvas the vast amount of illegal literature written by authors who are now largely unknown but who at the time enjoyed considerable success as popularizers of the philosophical ideas of the period. Despite the wide number of texts studied and the detailed bibliographical information contained in the appendices this is a highly readable and stimulating survey. *Französische Übersetzervorreden des 18. Jahrhunderts*, ed. Wilhelm Grader, Frankfurt am Main, Lang, 1990, 197 pp., provides useful details of French translations of some 9 Spanish, 13 Italian, 54 English and 11 German texts mostly from well-known authors of the period. C. Hesse, *Publishing and Cultural Politics in Revolutionary Paris, 1789–1810*, Berkeley, California U.P., 256 pp. *Les Orateurs de la Révolution française: choix de textes*, ed R. Garaudy, Larousse, 1989, 240 pp. A. Criscenti Grassi, *Gli Idéologues: il dibattito sulla pubblica istruzione nella Francia rivoluzionaria*, Rome, Gangemi, 1990, 160 pp.

2. NON-FICTION

INDIVIDUAL AUTHORS

D'ANTRAIGUES. Roger Barny, *Le Comte d'Antraigues: disciple de J.-J. Rousseau (StV*, 281), Oxford, Voltaire Foundation, 261 pp., is a second and meticulous piece of research which traces the origins of d'A.'s political thought before he became a public figure and in particular the influence of J.-J. Rousseau. It is none the worse for being a 'traditional' thematic study of influences.

D'ARGENS. *Le Marquis d'Argens*, ed. J.-L. Vissière, Univ. de Provence, 1990, 208 pp., is a collection of papers given at a conference in Aix in 1988.

BASIRE. Y. Benot, 'Lettres inédites de C. Basire', *AHRF*, 283:105–11, contains three letters from B. dating from 1792, plus a fourth from a certain Maldaut written in 1793, all sent to the lawyer Claude Chaussier.

BATTEUX. *La Leçon de lecture*, ed. Sonia Branca-Rosoff, Cendres, 1990, 158 pp., publishes extensive extracts from B.'s *Beaux-Arts réduits à un même principe, Cours de belles lettres* and *Traité de la construction oratoire*, works which had a major influence on literary criticism and the teaching of literature when they first appeared in the mid 18th c.

BILLAUD-VARENNE. F. Brunel, 'L'acculturation d'un révolutionnaire: l'exemple de Billaud-Varenne (1786–1791)', *DhS*, 23:261–74, studies the particular cultural education of this notorious but insufficiently known revolutionary.

BRISSOT. L. Loft, '*La Théorie des loix criminelles*: Brissot and legal reform', *AJFS*, 26, 1989:242–59, reviews B.'s ideas for reform of the criminal code as detailed in both his prize essay *Les Moyens d'adoucir la rigueur des loix pénales en France, sans nuire à la sûreté publique* and *La Théorie*.

CHAMFORT. D. Conejo, 'Chamfort en Italie: note bibliographique', *StV*, 284:343–62, aims to supplement John Renwick, *Chamfort devant la postérité* (see *YWMLS*, 49:145), by providing on the same criteria bibliographical information about works which have been published in Italy.

CHARRIÈRE. I. de Charrière, *Lettres neuchâteloises, ed. I. and J.-L. Vissière, La Différence, 110 pp. I. de Charrière, *Une liaison dangereuse: correspondance avec Constant d'Hermenches (1760–1776), ed. I. and J.-L. Vissière, La Différence, 606 pp.

COCHIN. *Le Voyage d'Italie de Charles-Nicolas Cochin, ed. C. Michel, Rome, Boccard, viii + 510 pp.

CONDILLAC. F. Moureau, 'Condillac et Mably: dix lettres inédites ou retrouvées', *DhS*, 23:193–200, concerns seven letters by C. which had been lost since the end of the 19th c., two other unpublished ones, and an unpublished letter by Mably.

CONDORCET. Elisabeth and Robert Badinter, *Condorcet (1743–1794): un intellectuel en politique*, Fayard, 1989, 672 pp., is a revised edition of the biography first published in 1988 (see *YWMLS*, 50:155–56) which enables the authors to take into account the unpublished correspondence between C. and Franklin as well as some recent studies on C.'s life. J. Pappas, 'Condorcet le "seul" et le "premier" féministe du 18e siècle?', *DhS*, 23:441–43, points out that, 14 years before C., D'Alembert had written a similar essay 'On Women', quoted here at length, and argues D'Alembert's example influenced C.'s own position on women. D. Grimaldi, *Scienza, morale e politica in Condorcet, L'Aquila, Japadre, 179 pp.

FONTENELLE. *Œuvres complètes*, vol. 2, Fayard, 439 pp. A. Niderst, *Fontenelle*, Plon, 339 pp., follows in great detail the different stages of F.'s long career and is perhaps a definitive biography.

FRÉMONT. M. Porret, 'Rêver de s'enrichir ou s'enrichir en rêvant. Les "pensées nocturnes" du Genevois Pierre Frémont, 1774', *RHMC*, 38:22–50, was made possible by the discovery of the MS of F.'s work which reveals in particular his fear of poverty.

GRÉGOIRE. Pierre Fauchon, *L'Abbé Grégoire, le prêtre-citoyen*, Tours, Nouvelle République, 1989, 141 pp., is important in so far as it provides the only complete biography of this neglected figure, although this edition does not provide the annotation one would wish for in a serious critical study.

HELVÉTIUS. *Correspondance générale d'Helvétius*, vol. III: *1761–1774/ Lettres 465–720*, ed. Peter Allen *et al.*, Toronto U.P. — Oxford, Voltaire Foundation, xxii + 483 pp., finally completes this edition whose first two vols appeared to much critical acclaim in 1981 and 1984. This vol. covers his travels to England and Prussia and his final years in Paris troubled by gout.

D'HOLBACH. K. Muller, 'D'Holbach, determined fatalist', *StV*, 284:291–308, examines the dichotomy between determinism and fatalism found in the *Système de la nature*; while Shirley A. Roe, 'Metaphysics and materialism: Needham's response to d'Holbach', *ib.*, 309–42, publishes the text of the last edition of Needham's *Idée sommaire*, written in part as a reply to D'H.'s *Système de la nature*, but also to set out Needham's final thoughts on how his metaphysics and biology could combine together to refute materialism. This provides a clear exposition of the debate. P. Lurbe, 'D'Holbach et le "whig canon"', *DhS*, 23:321–30, shows how D'H. changed the meaning of many of the English thinkers whose work influenced him.

KANT. F. Azouvi and D. Borel, **De Königsberg à Paris: la réception de Kant en France, 1788–1804*, Vrin, 290 pp.

MME DE LAMBERT. R. Marchal, *Madame de Lambert et son milieu*, *StV*, 289, xvii + 798 pp., is a definitive study of the life and works of Mme de L. which breaks new ground by its serious consideration of *lambertinage*. The affinity with Marivaux is made quite apparent as is her contribution to a new wave of *préciosité*. A very relevant and revealing section on feminism clinches the case for a much needed re-evaluation of this writer.

LA METTRIE. S. Dressler, 'La Mettrie's death, or: the nonsense of an anecdote', *Neophilologus*, 75:194–99, examines some contemporary accounts of La M.'s death.

LEROUX. M. Manson, 'Être enseignant en France, 1750–1800: C.-J. Leroux et le "Journal d'Éducation"', *RHMC*, 38:462–72, studies this periodical between 1768 and 1790 to see how far enlightenment ideas were influencing teaching methods particularly for very young children. The results are not particularly original, although the existence at this time of a journal dedicated to educational issues is of itself significant.

MARAT. O. Coquard, 'La politique de Marat', *AHRF*, 285:325–51, breaks with the traditional view of M. as both muddle-headed and inconsistent. He also publishes, *ib.*, 277–79, a letter from M. to 'Monsieur Lablée, auteur du *Réclamateur*' dating from January 1790. L. L. Albina, '*De l'homme*: Marat lu par Voltaire', *RHLF*, 91:932–36, gives an account of V.'s review of this work by Marat. J. de Cock, **Marat et la lumière*, Brussels, Pôle Nord, 109 pp.

MARIVAUX. M. Matucci, 'De l'*Arlequin sauvage* à *L'Indigent Philosophe*', *Mélanges Deloffre*, 381–92, assesses the influence of Delisle de la Drévetière on M.'s social thought. F. Moureau, 'Marivaux contre Voltaire: une lettre retrouvée', *ib.*, 405–09, contains a criticism of V.'s *Temple du Goût*. O. A. Haac, 'Marivaux: de l'utopie à la perspective du moraliste', *ib.*, 415–21, reviews briefly the contrast between realism and idealism in M.

MAUPERTUIS. M. G. Di Domenico, **L'inquietudine della ragione: scienza e metafisica in Maupertuis*, Naples, Morano, 1990, 210 pp.

MORELLET. *Lettres d'André Morellet*: I. *1759–1785, lettres 1–262*, ed. Dorothy Medlin, Jean-Claude David, and Paul Leclerc, Oxford, Voltaire Foundation, xlvi + 624 pp., provides the first complete edition of his correspondence. Two further vols are planned.

MORELLY. A. Labib, '*La Basiliade*: une utopie orientale?', *DhS*, 23:307–20, summarizes M.'s borrowings from oriental tales.

NEUHOFF. J. Viviès, 'Fortune et infortunes d'un roi: de quelques traces de Théodore de Neuhoff dans la littérature du dix-huitième siècle', *StV*, 284:235–40, includes *inter alia* references to Voltaire and the marquis d'Argens.

QUESNAY. F. Quesnay, **Physiocratie: Droit naturel, Tableau économique et autres textes*, ed. J. Cartelier, Bordas, 449 pp.

RAYNAL. *Lectures de Raynal: L'"Histoire des deux Indes" en Europe et en Amérique au XVIIIᵉ siècle* (*StV*, 286), ed. Hans-Jürgen Lüsebrink and Manfred Tietz, Oxford, Voltaire Foundation, viii + 399 pp., includes: M. Duchet, 'L'*Histoire des deux Indes*: sources et structure d'un texte polyphonique' (9–15); G. Goggi, 'Quelques remarques sur la collaboration de Diderot à la première édition de l'*Histoire des deux Indes*' (17–52); M. Delon, 'L'appel au lecteur dans l'*Histoire des deux Indes*' (53–66); H. Guénot, 'La réception de l'*Histoire des deux Indes* dans la presse d'expression française (1772–1781)' (67–84); H.-J. Lüsebrink, 'Le rôle de Raynal et la réception de l'*Histoire des deux Indes* pendant la Révolution française' (85–97); M. Tietz, 'L'Espagne et l'*Histoire des deux Indes* de l'abbé Raynal' (99–130); Y.-G. Mix, 'L'*Histoire des deux Indes* au Danemark: un portrait de l'esclavagiste et abolitionniste Heinrich Ernst Graf von Schimmelmann' (131–40); Y. Benot, 'Traces de l'*Histoire des deux Indes* chez les anti-esclavagistes sous la Révolution' (141–54); M. Fontius, 'L'*Histoire des deux Indes* de

Raynal vue par les Allemands' (155–87); J. Mondot, 'La réception de Raynal en Allemagne: l'exemple de Wekhrlin' (189–204); D. Droixhe, 'Raynal à Liège: censure, vulgarisation, révolutions' (205–33); G. Imbruglia, 'Les premières lectures italiennes de l'*Histoire philosophique et politique des deux Indes*: entre Raynal et Robertson' (235–51); A. Strugnell, 'La réception de l'*Histoire des deux Indes* en Angleterre au dix-huitième siècle' (253–63); O. Penke, 'L'*Histoire des deux Indes* en Hongrie au siècle des Lumières' (265–85); M. Skrzypek, 'La réception de l'*Histoire des deux Indes* en Pologne et en Russie au dix-huitième siècle' (287–303); E. Tortarolo, "La réception de l'*Histoire des deux Indes* aux États-Unis' (305–28); D. Eisermann, 'La "Raynalisation" de l'*American farmer*: la réception de l'*Histoire des deux Indes* par Crèvecœur' (329–39); R. Ventura, 'Lectures de Raynal en Amérique latine aux XVIIIe et XIXe siècles' (341–59); G. Vidan, 'Une réception fragmentée: le cas de Raynal en terres slaves du Sud' (361–71); J. Chouillet, 'Postface: Raynal face à l'horizon d'attente des Lumières' (373–83).

MME DE SABRAN. A. Sokalski, 'Madame de Sabran: cinq lettres, un poème et un cul-de-lampe', *StV*, 284:241-57, includes the texts of three letters which have not been published previously.

SAINT-JUST. B. Vinot, 'Un inédit de Saint-Just: la Raison à la morne', *AHRF*, 284:233–41, publishes for the first time one of S.-J.'s early essays probably written in the spring of 1789.

MME DE STAËL. J. M. Kaplan, 'Some unpublished letters relating to the marriage of Mme de Staël found in Swedish collections', *StV*, 292:347–53, includes a letter from the baron de Staël to Gustav III of Sweden and two from Necker to Gustav Philip Creutz. B. Durand-Sendrail, 'Madame de Staël et la condition post-révolutionnaire', *RR*, 82:36–48, examines the way four texts by Mme de S. written before 1800 (*Réflexions sur le Procès de la Reine*, *Essai sur les fictions*, *De l'influence des passions*, and *Circonstances pour terminer la Révolution*) were profoundly marked by the events of the French Revolution and in particular by the Terror.

SUARD. J.-C. David, 'Un voyage en Suisse en 1784: quatorze lettres inédites de Jean Baptiste Antoine Suard et de sa femme', *StV*, 292:367–422, contains an exchange of letters written during a visit to Switzerland by S., plus a useful introduction to this minor figure of the Enlightenment.

VALINCOUR. C. G. S. Williams, *Valincour: The Limits of 'honnêteté'*, Catholic Univ. of America Press, ix + 338 pp., is a carefully researched study of the life and works of V., whose writings are shown to shift in focus from the rituals of polite society to Christian humanism and even suggest an openness to the critical spirit of the Enlightenment.

VAUVENARGUES. J.-L. Boucherie, 'Vauvenargues: de l'inquiétude vécue à l'expérience du savoir', *DhS*, 23 : 369–81, discusses the conflict between reason and passion in V. whose maxims represent the harnessing of a spirit of energy.

VOLNEY. A. and H. Denys, 'Six lettres inédites de Volney à Grégoire', *DhS*, 23 : 233–45, contains three letters written by V. during his stay in America from 1795 to 1798, and three from Sarcelles in 1805–07.

DIDEROT AND THE ENCYCLOPÉDIE

*Œuvres complètes, vol. 16, ed. E. M. Bukdahl, M. Delon, and A. Lorenceau, Hermann, 1990, xii + 681 pp., contains the *Salons* of 1767 and 1769. F. Moureau, *Le Roman vrai de l'Encyclopédie*, Gallimard, 1990, 224 pp., is in appearance a lavishly illustrated pocket-size version of a coffee-table book, but nevertheless puts together a great deal of relevant information with an expertise of judgement. J.-M. Apostolidès, 'Le paradoxe de l'*Encyclopédie*', *SFR*, winter 1990 : 47–63, is an elegantly written piece drawing interesting comparisons between the actor's role in the theatre and the *Encyclopédie*'s function in the systematization of knowledge. R. Pomeau, 'Les philosophes et l'Islam, ou de la lettre A à la lettre M de l'*Encyclopédie*', *Sareil Vol.*, 203–14, concentrates on two articles which veer from routine prejudice in the first to total sympathy in the second: the latter is by Jaucourt and unashamedly plagiarizes Voltaire's *Essai sur les mœurs*. K.-L. Selig, '*Le Neveu de Rameau* and the story of the Jew and the renegade of Avignon', *ib.*, 253–60, makes some observations about literary devices in this segment of the text. W. Anderson, *Diderot's Dream*, Baltimore, Johns Hopkins U.P., 1990, 259 pp., wrestles with the old problem of coherence in D. and starts by looking at the literariness of theoretical texts and the link posited by D. between natural science and poetics. The argument is not an easy one to present but we are given here an exceptionally clear exposition of D.'s very idiosyncratic materialism. The second part, under the heading of humanism, shifts the focus to the social side with a study of programmatic works and demonstrates the interdependence of the political and aesthetic. Stress is laid on the experimental, provocative cast of D.'s mind which places him in a very particular strain of Enlightenment thought. R. Pellerey, 'Diderot: il teatro del teatro. Un' analisi del *Paradoxe sur le comédien*', *SFr*, 102, 1990 : 403–16, reconsiders the question of theatrical reform and that of nervous sensibility. A. Vilar, 'Sensible diagnostics in Diderot's *La Religieuse*', *MLN*, 105, 1990 : 775–99, by examining the peculiarly clinical language used in this novel argues that D. transformed the standard fiction of sensibility into a far more experimental genre. Cogent and perceptive. M. Hobson, 'Genres and limits: Fielding, Sterne, Diderot', *RLMC*, 43, 1990:109–28, is a characteristically subtle analysis of D.'s ideal of beauty in relation to the issue of high and low styles. H. Mason, 'Diderot lecteur des œuvres en prose de Voltaire', *Mélanges Deloffre*, 515–25, shows that D.'s interest is primarily in V.'s historical writings. R. Pomeau, 'Le cas de Rameau le neveu: éthique et esthétique', *ib.*, 527–34, represents another attempt to arbitrate in the Moi/Lui dispute and to locate the 'real' meaning of the dialogue, pointing out an essential link between immorality and artistic failure. V. Mylne, 'Madame de la Pommeraye retraduite: étude stylistique', *ib.*, 535–45, compares two versions of the Pommeraye episode, D.'s original and a French translation of Schiller's text. P. Vernière, 'Diderot et la réalité russe', *ib.*, 555–65, underlines D.'s ignorance of Russia. R. Mortier, 'Diderot et la propriété privée', *ib.*, 547–53, demonstrates that liberty and property rights are closely associated in D. *Présence de Diderot*, ed. S. Juettner, Frankfurt, Lang, 1990, 316 pp., contains a number of papers, originally given at a conference in 1984, including J. Chouillet, 'Passéisme et futurisme dans l'œuvre de Diderot' (1–12); R. Desné, 'Faut-il utiliser le dictionnaire de Furetière pour lire *Jacques le fataliste*?' (13–32); D. Fricke, 'Les rapports entre la musique et la politique dans le *Neveu de Rameau*' (58–70); H.-G. Funke, 'Diderots *Supplément au Voyage de Bougainville* und die Tradition der literarischen Utopie' (71–91); R. Galle, 'Zur Dimension der Aufklärung in *Les Bijoux indiscrets*' (92–103); P. Knabe, 'Diderots Artikel "Acier" der *Encyclopédie*' (126–37); S. Lecointre, 'Diderot, un aspect de l'écriture: humour et persiflage' (138–51); E. Mass, 'Aesthetik der Transformation. Diderots *Analyse d'un petit roman* (1760)' (171–90); R. Mortier, 'Diderot devant la peinture de batailles' (202–09); F. Moureau, 'Les paradoxes de Lampédouse' (210–20); J. von Stackelburg, 'Diderot und der Spieler. Zum Pathos im bürgerlichen Trauerspiel' (238–50); J. Varloot, 'Buffon et Diderot' (298–315). *RDE*, 10, has five major articles on D., one on the E., and a presentation of some previously unpublished correspondence: J. Varloot, 'Vrais ou faux amis. L'original des *Eleuthéromanes*' (9–20), gives a detailed study of the original version of D.'s poem first published in 1796; R. Mortier, 'Didier Diderot lecteur de Denis: ses *Réflexions sur l'Essai sur le mérite et la vertu*' (21–39), shows D.'s brother's hostility towards both D. and Shaftesbury deriving from a concern to subordinate morality to religion; D. Malo, 'Diderot et la librairie: l'impensable propriété' (57–90), analyses the *Lettre sur le commerce de la librairie* and brings out its internal contradictions; A. Ibrahim, 'Sur l'expression chez Diderot autour du *Paradoxe sur le comédien* et des *Pensées sur l'interprétation de la nature*' (91–106), discusses D.'s treatment of the question of disorder and monsters in nature with regard to a generalized aesthetics; M. Wachs, 'L'identité de quatre interlocuteurs de la *Satire première*' (107–11), identifies three hitherto unknown authors of quotations and confirms a fourth; F. A. Kafker, 'Les encyclopédistes et le Paris du dix-huitième siècle' (113–21), studies the number of collaborators on the *E.* who were attracted to the capital; 'Lettres inédites de Grimm à Catherine II', ed. S. Karp, S. Iskul, G. Dulac, N. Plavinskaya (41–55), provide information concerning D.'s widow's pension, his daughter, the copies made of D.'s manuscripts and Naigeon's plans for an edition of his works. *DS*, 24, contains seven articles on D., one on the *E.*, and a bibliographical essay: M.-H. Chabut, 'Le *Supplément au Voyage de Bougainville*: une poétique du déguisement' (11–23), uses Bakhtinian methods to highlight internal contradictions in this dialogue, which is seen not so much as an anti-colonialist tract as a reflection on writing; H. Cohen, 'Diderot et les limites de la littérature dans les *Salons*' (25–45), ponders on the change of orientation after the 'Promenade de Vernet' of 1767 and analyses the abandonment of art criticism as a literary project; P. V. Conroy, 'Gender issues in Diderot's *La Religieuse*' (47–66), examines the latent tensions contained in D.'s presentation of Suzanne's femininity, especially in relation to lesbianism; T. Durand, 'Diderot et Heidegger: la poétique du bavardage dans *Jacques le fataliste*' (67–84), offers an existentialist reading of D.'s novel to illuminate problems of language; B. Durand-Sendrail, 'Diderot and Rameau: archéologie d'une polémique' (85–104), considers D.'s ideas on music in his *Mémoires de mathématiques*; R. Niklaus, 'Le *Plan d'une université* et le plan d'instruction publique de Condorcet mis en regard' (105–19), stresses the similarities in D. and C., both of whose theories are poised between freedom and interventions; B. A. Robb, 'The making of Denis Diderot: translation as apprenticeship' (137–54), is a rather loose examination of some aspects of D.'s practice as a writer; E. Potulicki, '*Éclairé, Clairvoyant, adj.* (Gramm.), un article de l'*Encyclopédie*, ou la présence dialogique de Diderot' (121–36), throws light on the intertextual dimension of the *E.*; F. Spear, 'Bibliographie de Diderot, supplément no. 4' (155–73), continues the work done in *DS*, 22, and covers material published in 1987 and 1988. J.-F. Bianco, **Diderot: Le Neveu de Rameau*, Bordas, 96 pp. J. Floch, **Denis Diderot, le bonheur en plus*, Édns Ouvrières, 139 pp. P. Lepape, **Diderot*, Flammarion, 445 pp. *Autour du 'Neveu de Rameau' de Diderot*, ed. A.-M. Chouillet, Champion, 112 pp., contains the following: S. Albertan-Coppola, 'Rira bien qui rira le dernier' (15–36), which concentrates on the aspect of satire; M. Buffat, 'La loi de l'appétit' (37–57), which analyses Rameau's outlook on life; R. Rey, 'La morale introuvable' (59–87), which considers the confrontation of different viewpoints in the dialogue. M. Vidal, 'La pantomime comme argument', *ChS*, 2:181–89, concerns D.'s art of composition in *Le Neveu*. J. O. Lowrie, 'Diderot's Quentin de la Tour and Balzac's Frenhofer', *RoN*, 31:267–73, argues that a thumb-nail sketch in D. accounts for Balzac's revisions to two of his stories. A. Ages, 'A gift for maxims, Diderot as moralist: the testimony of the correspondence', *NZJFS*, 12:5–14, sees D. as a spiritual descendant of Montaigne and the 17th-c. *moralistes*. Id., 'Diderot and religion: Didier-Pierre as catalyst. The record of the correspondence', *StV*, 292:243–58, claims that letters reveal how some of D.'s ideas originated as reactions to his brother's religious convictions. Id., 'Diderot's personal credo: the testimony of the correspondence', *RR*, 82:25–35, uses letters once again to fill out knowledge of some of D.'s anxieties. M. Wachs, '"Mon ami tomba malade, je le traitai, il mourut, je le disséquai" (Diderot, *Satire première*)', *FS*, 45:143–51, examines the doctor's statement and the circumstances surrounding D.'s use of it, and attempts to situate it in its social context. L. Gasbarrone, 'Voices from nature: Diderot's dialogues with women', *StV*, 292:259–91, concentrates on Julie de l'Espinasse, the Maréchale, D.'s own sister and Polly Baker to show very cogently how the feminine point of view brings out the conflict in D. between natural dictates and social codes. M.-H. Chabut, '*Topoi* d'intervention narrative dans les ouvertures de quelques récits de Diderot', *Actes* (Montpellier), 313–23, covers three texts (*Les Bijoux indiscrets, Ceci n'est pas un conte, Madame de la Carlière*) and discusses the ambiguity of the narratorial voice.

MONTESQUIEU

C. Dédéyan, *Montesquieu ou les lumières d'Albion*, Nizet, 1990, 239 pp., is very knowledgeable and traditional in approach. Catalogues every available association of M. with England in his career and thought but without reaching any new conclusions. P. Grenaud, **Montesquieu*, Lettres du Monde, 1990, 343 pp. L. Versini, 'La phrase miroitante de Montesquieu dans les *Lettres persanes*', *Mélanges Deloffre*, 357–65, gives an analysis of M.'s style as a mixture of the simple and the complex. G. Gargett, 'Jacob Vernet éditeur de Montesquieu', *RHLF*, 91:890–900, is concerned with the first edition of the *Esprit des lois* and M.'s anger at the delays and number of errors. S. Romanowski, 'La quête du savoir dans les *Lettres persanes*', *ECentF*, 3:93–111, presents a deconstructionist reading. Argues for two movements in the text, one critical of the notion of knowledge (relativist), the other recapturing at the end an earlier idealism. Stress laid on the enigmatic and ambivalent nature of the work. S. Mason, 'Montesquieu and the

148 *French Studies*

Dutch as a maritime nation', *StV*, 292:169–86, shows how M.'s writing about Holland offers a microcosm of his work and methods. M.-C. Vallois, 'Rêverie orientale et géopolitique du corps féminin chez Montesquieu', *RoQ*, 38:363–72, provides a careful study of M.'s biased observations on the oriental mode, especially with regard to sexual difference. F. Herdmann, *Montesquieurezeption in Deutschland im 18. und beginnenden 19. Jahrhundert*, Olms, 1990, 314 pp. S. Viselli, 'Les ouvertures narratives chez Montesquieu: voyage et traduction', *Actes* (Montpellier), 403–11, discusses the question of the artist in M. and the problem of truth/fiction in *Lettres persanes*, *Temple de Gnide*, *Céphise et l'Amour*, *Histoire véritable*, and *Arsace et Isménie*.

ROUSSEAU

CORRESPONDENCE, WORKS, BIOGRAPHY. *Correspondance complète de Jean Jacques Rousseau*: 50, ed. R. A. Leigh, Oxford, Voltaire Foundation, 618 pp., contains the first vol. of the indexes, ed. Janet Laming, and includes 'Tableau chronologique des lettres et autres documents' (1–256): 'Tableau alphabétique des correspondants' (257–462); 'Tableau chronologique des lettres citées dans les notes' (463–508); 'Tableau alphabétique des lettres citées dans les notes' (509–84); 'Listes des appendices' (585–618). Three further vols are to follow. Jean-Jacques Rousseau and Chrétien-Guillaume de Lamoignon de Malesherbes, *Correspondance*, ed. Barbara de Negroni, Flammarion, 370 pp. *Les Confessions*, ed. Françoise Lavocat (Balises, 18), Nathan, 1990, 128 pp., provides the kind of basic critical information typical of this series designed for the *lycéen*. Two other new editions are firstly *Discours sur l'origine et les fondements de l'inégalité parmi les hommes*, ed. Claude Habib, Presses Pocket, 1990, 313 pp., which contains a good introduction, a reliable text and a lot of supplementary material about the work; and secondly *Du contrat social*, Livres I et II, Nathan, 96 pp., which contains the basic text but the critical material is clearly designed for students preparing for the Baccalauréat. *Émile*, ed. A. Bloom, Harmondsworth, Penguin, ix + 501 pp. *Rousseau on International Relations*, ed. S. Hoffmann and D. P. Fidler, OUP, lxxix + 214 pp. Maurice Cranston, *The Noble Savage: Jean-Jacques Rousseau 1754–1762*, Allen Lane, xiv + 399 pp., is the long-awaited second vol. of Professor Cranston's new biography of R. which began in 1983 with the publication of *Jean-Jacques Rousseau: The Early Life and Work of Jean-Jacques Rousseau* to much critical acclaim. A final vol. is to follow. Apart from being eminently readable the main value of this new study lies in the use of hitherto neglected sources. Mireille Vedrine, *Les Jardins secrets de Jean-Jacques Rousseau*, Chambéry, Agraf, 1990, 196 pp., provides an anthology of the various landscapes which inspired R.'s work, but is interesting largely because of the superb illustrations of places associated with R.'s life and work.

THOUGHT AND INTELLECTUAL RELATIONSHIPS. A. O. Rorty, 'Rousseau's therapeutic experiments', *Philosophy*, 66:413–34, re-examines R.'s understanding of the role of the passions for natural man, man as the social subject and the self as autonomous citizen, three stages in man's development in what are called here R.'s therapeutic experiments; while R. Trousson, 'Jean-Jacques et "les derniers des hommes"', *SFr*, 35:249–59, studies R.'s relationships with servants both in his personal life and in his works, arguing that in spite of his theories hierarchical structures are retained and servants are not prepared for the society of the *Contrat social.* J. Simon-Ingram, 'Expanding the social contract: Rousseau, gender and the problem of judgment', *CL*, 43:134–49, raises in particular the issue of the exclusion of women from both the 'civil public' of social contract and philosophical dialogue; and H. A. Lloyd, 'Sovereignty: Bodin, Hobbes, Rousseau', *RIP*, 45:353–79, argues that, despite the safe-guards R. built into his account of sovereignty and the state, the message of the *Contrat social* is ultimately pessimistic — but this is also true of Bodin and Hobbes. James F. Jones, Jr, *Rousseau's 'Dialogues':* *An Interpretative Essay*, Geneva, Droz, 211 pp., begins by tracing the work's convoluted history before studying in turn its formal traits, the argument proposed by R. as a defence of himself, and the end of the work as a non-ending. N. Schippa, '*La Nouvelle Héloïse* et l'aristocra-tie', *StV*, 284:1–71, examines how far this work is linked to the feelings and ideas of the aristocracy of the time (as opposed to those of the bourgeoisie) by studying in turn its economic, cultural, social, and literary relationships with the ideology of the nobility; L. Spaas, 'D'un Clarens à l'autre: structures du désir sexuel dans *La Nouvelle Héloïse*', *ib.*, 73–82. P. Jimack, 'Some eighteenth-century imitations of Rousseau's *Émile*', *ib.*, 83–105, studies in particular G. Grivel, *L'Ami des jeunes gens*; Chiniac de la Bastide, *Miroir fidèle*; A. de Serres de La Tour, *Du bonheur*; La Fare, *Le Gouverneur*; Philippe Sérane, *Théorie de J. J. Rousseau sur l'éducation corrigée et réduite en pratique* — works which often attempted to conceal their debt to R. but on occasions came close to plagiarizing his theories. M. Trouille, 'A bold new vision of woman: Staël and Wollstonecraft respond to Rousseau', *StV*, 292:293–336, examines the responses of these two women literary figures to R. arguing both were passionate admirers of R. yet, at the same time, strong critics of him and strangely unaware of their own ambivalence. Françoise Barguillet, *Rousseau ou l'illusion passionnée: Les Rêveries du promeneur solitaire*, PUF, 188 pp., examines R.'s contradic-tory attitudes towards solitude as found in his final work, and questions how he can both deplore the solitude imposed upon him by his contemporaries and at the same time praise the occupations of a solitary life.

LITERARY. A. Rosenberg, '*Julie ou la Nouvelle Héloïse* today', *UTQ*, 60:265–73, suggests reasons why this has not become a popular novel today through the cinema or television in the way other 18th-c. classics have; while C. Weiand, 'Liebessemantik zwischen Paradox und Autonomie: Jean-Jacques Rousseaus "Les Amours de Milord Edouard Bomston" im Amhang zur *Nouvelle Héloïse*', *ZFSL*, 101:266–74, attempts to explain R.'s uncertainty over this appendix to the *Nouvelle Héloïse* by arguing it is because R. is a spokesman for pre-romanticism while his philosophy of man is still rooted in the classical period. R. Gautier, 'Les idées sociales et politiques dans le théâtre de Jean-Jacques Rousseau', *RHT*, 43:305–11, tries to show that R.'s theatrical work should be taken more seriously.

VOLTAIRE

CORRESPONDENCE, WORKS, BIOGRAPHY. *1737* (*Œuvres complètes de Voltaire*, 17), Oxford, Voltaire Foundation, xxiii + 585 pp., is the latest vol. in this edition to appear (cf. *YWMLS*, 51:132–33) and includes *Essai sur la nature du feu, et sur sa préparation*, ed. W. A. Smeaton and R. L. Walters (1–89); *Mérope tragédie*, ed. J. R. Vrooman and J. Godden (91–387); *Discours en vers sur l'homme*, ed. H. T. Mason (389–535); *Le Songe de Platon*, ed. J. Van den Heuvel (537–49); *Minor verse 1737*, ed. R. A. Nablow (551–56), although none of these works was published in 1737, a year in which no new separate works by V. appeared. As always from the Voltaire Foundation, this vol. contains all that one would expect from a modern critical edition. **Candide*, ed. X. Darcos, Hachette, 224 pp. M. Wachs, 'Voltaire's "Regnante puero": the date, the title, and the French original', *StV*, 284:107–13, is concerned with these bibliographical issues; and S. Davies, 'Voltaire et le *Voltaire*', *RHLF*, 91:756–61, concerns V.'s *Épitre à mon vaisseau* written in 1768. R. Desné and A. Maudich, 'Une lettre oubliée de Voltaire sur le Messie. Entre Polier de Bottens et l'*Encyclopédie*', *DhS*, 23:201–12, studies a copy of a letter by V., dated 21 October 1758, which has come to light in the Parma historical archives. C. Mervaud, **Voltaire en toutes lettres*, Bordas, 192 pp. René Pomeau and Christine Mervaud, *De la Cour au Jardin, 1750–1759* (*Voltaire en son temps*, 3), Oxford, Voltaire Foundation, vii + 416 pp., is the latest vol. in this new biography of V. to appear (see *YWMLS*, 50:161) and follows the same editorial principles as the earlier vols. Two further vols are awaited to complete the series. N. Perry, 'Voltaire's first months in England: another look at the facts', *StV*, 284:115–38, completes her earlier studies (cf. *YWMLS*, 50:161) with additional material which enables her to establish a reliable chronology of the first few months of V.'s stay in England.

THOUGHT AND INFLUENCE. F. Bessire, 'Voltaire lecteur de dom Calmet', *StV*, 284:139–77, analyses in particular the notes V. made on the copies of Dom Calmet's works he consulted at Cirey, notes which have been made available through the publication of the *Corpus des notes marginales* of which they form a substantial part; S. Rivière, 'Voltaire's concept of dramatic history in *Le Siècle de Louis XIV*', *ib.*, 179–98, builds on his earlier articles to argue that what sets V.'s historical work apart from his predecessors was not so much the new historical material he uncovered but the way in which he fused the borrowed secondary material into a work of art; while M. S. Rivière, 'The reactions of the anti-Voltaire lobby to *Le Siècle de Louis XIV*: Guyon, Nonnotte, Berthier and Fréron', *StV*, 292:217–42, argues the reactions of these traditionalists to V. reflect widespread views of the establishment and its responses to V.'s histories, some of whom were historians in their own right. C. Mervaud, 'De Westminster Abbey au Panthéon: le statut des "gens de lettres" dans les *Lettres philosophiques*', *RHLF*, 91:177–95, argues that according a proper status to writers is a key theme in the *Lettres philosophiques* as V. reflects on the English example which he idealizes; J. Goldzink, 'La religion dans les *Lettres philosophiques* ou l'art du désordre', *StV*, 292:187–200, concludes it is impossible to define the letters in terms of their anticlericalism because the religious problem is much more complex, and thus raises again the famous question of the work's unity; and J.-M. Warnet, 'La vingt-cinquième *Lettre philosophique* de Voltaire "Sur les *Pensées* de M. Pascal"': une réfutation en règle', *ib.*, 201–16, provides a detailed analysis of V.'s argument. G. Gargett, 'Jacob Vernet's *Lettre à Monsieur le Premier Syndic*: a reply to Voltaire and the *Dialogues Chrétiens*', *MLR*, 86:35–48, argues on the basis of a close examination of V.'s attacks on Vernet that the allegations were not 'pure calomnie'; and E. D. James, 'The concept of emanation in the later philosophy of Voltaire', *StV*, 284:199–209, in a brief but stimulating article argues V.'s adoption of the principle of emanation will seem less strange if we remember the largely Neoplatonic sources of the theory. T. Erwin, 'Voltaire and Johnson again: the *Life of Savage* and the Sertorius letter (1744)', *ib.*, 211–23, believes that in writing the *Life of Savage* Johnson looked to V. for his biographical model, and the article is therefore primarily concerned with Johnson; while I. H. Burchall, 'Voltaire and Brecht', *BJECS*, 14:1–12, examines Brecht's comments on V. emphasizing the similar polemical preoccupations of the two men.

LITERARY. Xavier Darcos, *Voltaire 'Candide': dossier du professeur*, Hachette, 96 pp., provides condensed notes for the busy teacher but is of little interest otherwise. M. Mougenot, *_Voltaire: Candide_, Bertrand-Lacoste, 127 pp.

3. PROSE FICTION

GENERAL

A. Pizzorusso, *_Letture di romanzi: saggi sul romanzo francese del Settecento_, Il Mulino, 1990, 223 pp. C. Cazenobe, _Le système du libertinage de Crébillon à Laclos_, StV, 282, 461 pp., offers three quite separate studies of 18th-c. novelists, arguing that there are distinct types of libertinism at work in each: intellect predominates in Crébillon, passion in Prévost's translation of Richardson, and reason in Laclos. Covers somewhat verbosely the ground already well researched by L. Versini without advancing much further. Alcibiade, Lovelace, and Valmont are the key figures whose seductiveness sets them apart from the heroes of Sade deliberately excluded from the discussion. A. Rivara, _Les sœurs de Marianne: suites, imitations, variations (1731–61)_, StV, 285, 499 pp., traces the development of the female social climber in the wake of Marivaux's novel and thereby raises some interesting questions about the relationship between literature and society. Emphasizes the inadequacy of the fictional representation of the outsider both in the continuations of the story of Marianne and in the numerous imitators. An attachment to aristocratic values (in spite of much bourgeois moralizing and sentimental cliché) together with a superficial realism are seen to characterize these works of mere entertainment. More significant, less conventional directions are found in the low-grade _littérature poissarde_. W. F. Edmiston, _Hindsight and Insight: Focalization in Four Eighteenth-Century French Novels_, Pennsylvania State U.P., xii + 208 pp., covers the first-person narrative in Crébillon, Marivaux, Prévost, and Diderot, using Genette's term for the function of point of view. There is an irritating use of abbreviations to designate narrator/character distance in the theoretical introduction which increases to a thicket of formulae in the long appendix on the evolution of the concept. Sandwiched between these are some important discussions of the novels along very relevant if not altogether unfamiliar lines (temporal ambiguity in _Le Paysan_ and narratorial reliability in _Manon_). _Exoticism in the Enlightenment_, ed. G. S. Rousseau and R. Porter, Manchester U.P., 1990, 230 pp., includes S. R. Pucci, 'The discrete charms of the exotic: fictions of the harem in eighteenth-century France' (145–74), which tries to uncover rhetorical strategies in the oriental tales of Galland, Montesquieu, and Diderot. R. Godenne, 'Turcs et Africains dans les nouvelles de la première moitié du XVIIIe siècle', _Mélanges Deloffre_, 609–22, deals with historical shortcomings, exoticism, religion, and racism. P.

Brady, 'Théorie du chaos et structure narrative', *ECentF*, 4:43–51, sounds familiar, revisiting ideas about the Rococo style of Enlightenment literature with reference to *La Vie de Marianne*, *Le Neveu*, and *Les Liaisons*. J. M. Goulemot, **Ces livres qu'on ne lit que d'une main: lecture et lecteurs de livres pornographiques au XVIIIe siècle*, Alinéa, 171 pp. *La Fin de l'Ancien Régime: Sade, Rétif, Beaumarchais, Laclos* (Manuscrits de la Révolution, 1), ed. Béatrice Didier and Jacques Neefs, Saint-Denis, Vincennes U.P., 206 pp., includes: A. Angremy, 'Les manuscrits de Sade à la Bibliothèque Nationale' (9–38), who gives a fairly detailed description of these MSS many of which have only recently been used by those working on Sade; M. Lever, 'Sade, papiers de famille et correspondance' (39–44), who describes his work in establishing a forthcoming critical edition of Sade's correspondence; P. Roger, 'Note conjointe sur Sade épistolier' (45–53); G. Festa, '*Le Voyage d'Italie* de Sade: genèse d'un matérialisme visionnaire' (55–72), who outlines his new critical edition of this text; J.-J. Pauvert, 'Éditer Sade, histoire d'un combat de deux siècles' (73–93), who traces the attempts to establish a definitive bibliography of Sade; M. Delon, 'Sade dans la Bibliothèque de la Pléiade' (95–102), who describes the editorial principles of this new edition; P. Testud, 'Les manuscrits de Rétif, écrivain typographe' (105–17), who aims to establish the rare MSS which are extant; P. Bourguet, 'A la recherche de *L'Enclos et les Oiseaux*: le manuscrit des *Revies* retrouvé' (119–32), who picks his way through the complexities of the MS involved; G. von Proschwitz, '"Une affaire politico-commerçante": les manuscrits de Beaumarchais aux Archives du Ministère des Affaires étrangères' (135–49), which contain about 150 letters and a few *mémoires* written between 1775 and 1786; P. Larthomas, 'Les manuscrits des œuvres dramatiques de Beaumarchais' (159–65), who can do no more than raise a few problems; R. Pomeau, 'Le manuscrit du *Sacristain*' (167–72), who gives a brief description; L. Versini, 'Le cas Laclos' (175–89), who gives a brief introduction to the MS of Laclos; and R. Pomeau, 'Le manuscrit des *Liaisons dangereuses*' (191–96), which despite the title is concerned primarily with one particular MS owned by Pomeau. An essential source of reference for anyone working on these four authors. J. Lacroix, 'A l'ouverture des contes: simple amorce ou programme narratif? De Marmontel à Sade', *Actes* (Montpellier), 353–69, studies briefly a number of 'contes' from the latter half of the 18th c.

INDIVIDUAL AUTHORS

BERNARDIN DE SAINT-PIERRE. Alain Boissinot, **Paul et Virginie de Bernardin de Saint-Pierre* (Parcours de Lecture), Bertrand Lacoste, 1988, 112 pp.

CASANOVA.　Jean-Didier Vincent, **Casanova: La contagion du plaisir*, Odile Jacob, 1990, 231 pp.

CAZOTTE.　*The Devil in Love*, trans. Judith Landry, Sawtry, Dedalus, 109 pp., provides a new translation of *Le Diable amoureux* together with a brief introduction by Brian Stableford.

CHALLE.　**Les Illustres Françaises*, ed. F. Deloffre and J. Cormier, Geneva, Droz, lxxxii + 710 pp., is a new edition. M. Weil, *Robert Challe romancier*, Geneva, Droz, 340 pp., is quite outstanding in its combination of erudition and critical finesse. C.'s fictional world is explored in such a way as to establish an entirely new understanding of the relationship between literary form and philosophical outlook in this author. The originality of C. is fully brought out in this subtle and elegant analysis of his work. J. Popin, 'L'an 1713, ou le style et la fortuité', *Mélanges Deloffre*, 321–30, offers a detailed stylistic comparison of C.'s novel with Marivaux's early works. J. Mesnard, 'Robert Challe et son double François Martin', *ib.*, 331–45, studies C.'s encounter as related in the *Journal d'un voyage*. R. Francillon, 'Le prix de l'honneur. Valeurs aristocratiques et valeurs bourgeoises dans l'univers des *Illustres françaises*', *ib.*, 347–56, concentrates on the theme of money and social class in early 18th-c. society.

CONSTANT.　**The Affair of Colonel Juste de Constant and Related Documents (1787–1796)*, ed. C. P. Courtney, Daemon Press, 1990, lviii + 304 pp.

FLORIAN.　J.-P.-C. Florian, *Fables complètes, Étoile-sur-Rhône, Nigel Gauvin, 160 pp.

GALLAND.　G. May, 'Style oral et style écrit dans *Les Mille et une Nuits* de Galland', *Mélanges Deloffre*, 309–20, shows G.'s brilliance at converting an oral tradition into a written one.

MME DE GENLIS.　M. Cook, '*Adèle et Théodore* ou les liaisons dangereuses', *StV*, 284:371–83, speculates that Laclos may have had this novel by G. in mind when he wrote his masterpiece by showing a number of thematic, stylistic, and lexical similarities between the two works; and C. Piau, 'Questions à propos de l'épitre dédicatoire des *Vœux Téméraires* de Mme de Genlis (Hambourg, 1799)', *Actes* (Montpellier), 391–95, raises a number of questions relating to this minor work.

GILBERT.　*Histoire de Caléjava*, ed. M. S. Rivière, Exeter U.P., 1990, xxxiv + 115 pp., provides a useful critical edition of this little-known work.

GOUGES.　**L'Esclavage des noirs, ou l'Heureux Naufrage*, ed. Eléni Varikas, Côté-femmes, 1989, 140 pp.

GRAFFIGNY.　J. G. Altman, 'A woman's place in the Enlightenment sun: the case of F. de Graffigny', *RoQ*, 38:261–72, charts the rise and fall of G.'s reputation and notes the power of cultural effacement.

LACLOS.   *Analyses et réflexions sur Laclos, 'Les Liaisons dangereuses': la passion amoureuse*, ed. D. Giovacchini *et al.*, Édition Marketing, 128 pp., includes *inter alia*: G. Benrekassa, 'La légende du libertinage: autonomie du sujet et passion amoureuse' (9–15); J. Askénazi, 'La passion démystifiée' (16–20); D. Prost, 'Le malheur d'individuation' (21–24); A. Ughetto, 'Le roman par lettres: une forme sens' (25–30); B. Caillet, 'Une saison en enfer?' (31–34); P. Bounin, 'Étude sur l'Avertissement de l'éditeur et la Préface du rédacteur' (35–39); G. Farasse, 'Du libertinage considéré comme un des beaux-arts' (40–44); C. Rommeru, 'La revanche de la nature' (45–48); J.-J. Jaunet, 'L'amour dans *Les Liaisons dangereuses*: "Un jeu de société dramatique"' (49–54); J. Picano, 'La transgression généralisée' (55–58); P. Villani, 'Le miroir: la séduction vertigineuse' (59–63); M. Buffard, 'Laclos moraliste' (64–67); G. Bafaro, 'Des hommes d'Église face à la passion' (68–73); B. Bonhomme, 'Commentaire de la Lettre XLVIII' (74–77); B. Urbani, 'Le couple libertin; Valmont, Merteuil' (78–81); C. Cazenobe, 'Le couple infantin: Cécile et Danceny' (82–85); J. Villani, 'Mme de Tourvel ou l'innocence et son double' (86–89); J. Labesse, 'La passion amoureuse comme stratégie' (90–96); M. Borrut, 'La guerre des sexes' (97–103); P. Malville, 'Raison et passion: Laclos, le libertin et le philosophe' (104–09); L. Rioual, 'Commentaire de la Lettre LXXVI' (110–12); P.-L. Assoun, 'Mensonge passionné et vérité inconsciente' (113–19); and E. Seknadje-Askénazi, '*Les Liaisons dangereuses*: filmographie' (120–22). With one or two exceptions the studies are basically of an introductory nature. Anne-Marie Brinsmead, *Strategies of Resistance in 'Les Liaisons dangereuses': Heroines in Search of 'Author-ity'*, Lewiston, Edwin Mellen, 1989, vii + 197 pp., examines in turn the three major female characters in the novel emphasizing the strategies they adopt to resist masculine control; and J. Herman, 'Miroitements intertextuels et structure métaphorique dans *Les Liaisons dangereuses*', *StV*, 292:337–46, selects a few passages from the novel to demonstrate his thesis about the 'mirror' effect of the libertine discourse. M. Barguillet, '*Les Liaisons dangereuses*. Commentaire de la Lettre LXXXI', *IL*, 43.5:11–16. P. Messière, **Laclos: Les Liaisons dangereuses*, Bordas, 96 pp.

LA MORLIÈRE.   R. Trousson, 'Le chevalier de la Morlière, un aventurier des lettres au XVIIIe siècle', *BARLLF*, 68:218–99, gives a useful outline of La M.'s career and offers some judicious criticism of his work.

MARIVAUX.   C. Bonfils, 'Une image de la mort dans *La Vie de Marianne*', *RHLF*, 90, 1990:77–81, analyses the swooning of Mlle Varthon in Part 7. F. Rubellin, 'A propos des gravures de *La Voiture embourbée* de Marivaux', *Mélanges Deloffre*, 367–79, shows how the engraver renders the originality of the author's parody.

P. Saint-Amand, 'Les parures de Marianne', *ECentF*, 4:15–26, concentrates on Marianne as a sex object and shifts from a feminist to a Freudian perspective. *Marivaux d'hier, Marivaux d'aujourd'hui*, ed. H. Coulet, J. Ehrard, and F. Rubellin, CNRS, 228 pp., contains a preponderance of articles concentrating on M.'s novels and journalism, with the main emphasis upon their importance for an understanding of his general outlook and view of society, and includes: H. Coulet, 'Hypothèses sur l'apparentement politique et religieux de Marivaux' (37–44); F. Rubellin, 'Le mode de vie dans les romans de jeunesse de Marivaux' (45–52); M. S. Ansalone, 'L'indigent Marivaux: le jeu des apparences et la société de l'argent' (53–64); M. Matucci, 'De la vanité à la coquetterie' (65–72); B. Didier, 'La société au miroir de Marianne' (73–86); G. Bonaccorso, 'Coutumes et langage populaires dans *Le Paysan parvenu*' (87–96); M. Gilot, 'Toutes les âmes se valent' (97–106); W. Trapnell, 'Identité et sympathie chez Marivaux' (107–20).

PIGAULT-LEBRUN. F. Larsson, 'Les ouvertures narratives des romans de Pigault-Lebrun', *Actes* (Montpellier), 379–89, concentrates in particular on the form of the 'topoi'.

POTOCKI. D. Triaire, 'Les ouvertures narratives dans le *Manuscrit trouvé à Saragosse* de Jean Potocki', *Actes* (Montpellier), 397–401, concerns a work dating probably from 1797.

PRÉVOST. S. Lamothe, 'Lucide mais amoureux: un portrait de Manon par le chevalier des Grieux', *Mélanges Deloffre*, 435–44, is a close textual commentary of a short passage from P.'s novel. M. Wellington, 'Unity and symmetry in the character of Tiberge', *RoQ*, 38:27–37, is a very full statement of the thesis that P.'s novel dramatizes the struggle for the control of its central character. E. Stockwell, 'The importance of the Channel in Prévost's life and work', *StV*, 292:43–54, detects in P.'s travel descriptions an early use of the pathetic fallacy. R. Dufeu, **L'Abbé Prévost: Manon Lescaut*, Nathan, 1990, 127 pp. S. Pailloux, **Prévost; Manon Lescaut*, Bordas, 96 pp.

RESTIF DE LA BRETONNE. David Coward, *The Philosophy of Restif de la Bretonne* (*StV*, 283), Oxford, Voltaire Foundation, x + 878 pp., fills an important gap because to date there has been no systematic study of R.'s philosophy. Coward argues that if you reassemble R.'s ideas into an orderly synthesis they acquire a complex but cohesive unity. This study also includes some useful biographical background, and will clearly become a seminal work for those wishing to study R.'s thought. H. Lafon, 'L'incipit dans les *Nuits révolutionnaires* de Rétif de la Bretonne', *Actes* (Montpellier), 371–78, studies the 'incipit' in vols XV and XVI; and D. A. Williams, 'Une chanson de Rétif réécrite par Flaubert', *RHLF*, 91:239–42, concerns a song from vol. I of R.'s *L'Année des dames nationales* which reappears in *Madame Bovary*.

MME RICCOBONI. *Histoire d'Ernestine,* ed. Colette Piau-Gillot, Côté-Femmes.

SADE. *Œuvres Complètes,* 12, ed. A. Le Brun and J.-J. Pauvert, Pauvert, 446 pp. (see *YWMLS*,49:164), contains *Histoire secrète d'Isabelle de Bavière, reine de France* and *Adélaïde de Brunswick, princesse de Saxe.* The edition aims as far as possible to follow the chronological order in which S.'s works were written, but this is not a new critical edition and so is useful only if the texts are not otherwise available. *Vol. 10 contains *Préface à Pauline et Belval, Lettres à des journaux, Les Crimes de l'amour, Projet d'avertissement,* and *L'Auteur des Crimes de l'amour à Villeterque, folliculaire;* *vol. 11 contains *Notes littéraires, Couplets et Pièces de circonstance, Notes pour les Journées de Florbelle, Journal de Charenton, Lettres de Charenton et Testament,* and *La Marquise de Gange.* Annie Le Brun, *Sade: A Sudden Abyss,* trans. Camille Naish, San Francisco, City Light Books, 1990, xvii + 220 pp., is a translation of the vol. published originally as the introduction to the new Pauvert edn of S.'s works in 1986 (see *YWMLS*, 48:186). M. Lever, 'Quatre lettres inédites d'Ange Goudar au marquis de Sade', *DhS*, 23:223–32, contains four letters from the S. family archives; and P. Roger, 'Rousseau selon Sade, ou Jean-Jacques travesti', *ib.*, 383–405, shows how R.'s philosophy, when mentioned in S.'s works, is always deformed or denigrated. G. Festa, 'D'Argens/Sade: convergences d'une esthétique', *StV*, 284:363–69, traces some of the aesthetic concepts from the *Mémoires secrets de la république des lettres* which are re-used by S., particularly in the *Voyage d'Italie;* while C. Thomas, 'Rencontres entre Sade et l'univers des pamphlets ou le mal comme unique programme politique', *Littérature,* 84:14–22, argues S. balances his use of pamphleteer rhetoric in *Isabelle de Bavière* with his poetics and logic. Lucienne Frappier-Mazur, *Sade et l'écriture de l'orgie: pouvoir et parodie dans l'"Histoire de Juliette',* Nathan, 254 pp., argues the *Histoire de Juliette* written after the French Revolution shows a new political consciousness for S., with the orgies at the heart of the work playing a subversive role so that sexual representation also becomes social representation; and S. Carpenter, 'Sade and the problem of closure: keeping philosophy in the bedroom', *Neophilologus,* 75:519–28, argues that S. made a career out of upsetting the notions of closure and enclosure that were so essential to the Classical age. *Lettres inédites et documents,* ed. J.-L. Debauve and A. Le Brun, Ramsay, 1990, x + 641 pp. *Sade: seltene Sadiana, analytische Bibliographie 1768–1990,* ed. M. Farin and H.-U. Seifert, Bonn, Bouvier, 500 pp. J.-J. Pauvert, *Sade vivant,* vol. 3, 'Cet écrivain à jamais célèbre . . .' (1793–1814), Laffont, v + 593 pp. (see *YWMLS*, 52:167). Maurice Lever, *Donatien Alphonse François, marquis de Sade,* Fayard, 912 pp.

VIVANT-DENON. J. Herman, 'Topique et incipit. — Le cas de *Point de Lendemain* de Vivant-Denon', *Actes* (Montpellier), 345–52, argues that the 'opening' of this text has to be looked for elsewhere than at the beginning.

WOLLSTONECRAFT. G. E. Bentley, Jr, 'Marie Wollstonecraft, Godwin and William Blake in France: the first foreign engravings after Blake's designs', *AJFS*, 26, 1989:125–47, contains a bibliographical description of a recently discovered French translation of W.'s *Original Stories* which appeared in Paris in 1799, as well as reproductions of the engravings.

4. THEATRE

GENERAL

J. C. Hayes, *Identity and Ideology: Diderot, Sade and the Serious Genre*, *PUMRL*, 35, xiv + 186 pp., divides almost equally between consideration of the general context and close readings of two representatives of the *drame*. Attempts on the one hand to discuss the social significance of the cult of sensibility and the critical debates surrounding bourgeois theatre, on the other to analyse Diderot's *Le Fils naturel* and the *Entretiens avec Dorval* in terms of 'selfhood' and to link Sade's plays to the themes of his other writings. Disappointingly disjointed and sketchy. S. S. Bryson, *The Chastised Stage: Bourgeois Drama and the Exercise of Power*, *SFIS*, 70, 125 pp., is heavily influenced by Foucault's writings on punishment and power and presents a chilling interpretation of the aims of the theorists of *drame bourgeois*, arguing that theatre reforms closely mirror new modes of policing in society. A political (rather than moral) programme is discussed here, along with various techniques proposed to control audiences and manipulate actors. There are some telling illustrations from the works of Diderot, Beaumarchais, Mercier, and Rétif. A compelling and original study.

Noëlle Guibert and Jacqueline Razgonnikoff, *Le Journal de la Comédie-Française 1787–1799: la comédie aux trois couleurs*, Antony, SIDES, 1989, 389 pp., attempts to provide a chronological history of the theatre during these years as far as possible on a day-by-day basis. The work is lavishly illustrated. *RHT*, 43, includes *inter alia*: J. Maillard, 'Le théâtre à Angers au XVIIIe siècle' (107–18); M. Biard, 'La scène angevine dans la carrière théâtrale de Jean-Marie Collot d'Herbois (1774–1776)' (119–27); A. Bendjebbar, 'Le théâtre angevin pendant la Révolution (1787–1799)' (136–46); A. Gomez and M.-H. Duracher, 'L'art dramatique et la mort de Beaurepaire à Verdun 1792–1873' (147–61); A. Bouysse, 'Les habits de Persée, 1770' (231–41) on the production of this work by Lully for the opening of the theatre at Versailles; and R. Gautier, 'Les idées sociales et politiques dans le théâtre de Jean-Jacques Rousseau' (305–11), which gives a brief introduction to this little-known side of Rousseau's work. D. Quéro, 'Le triomphe des Pointu', *CAIEF*, 43:153–67, studies the characteristics of these popular theatrical productions not normally recognized for their literary value in which a collection of plays portray the different members of the same family, and which flourished in the latter half of the 18th c. I. Guitton, 'Un avatar de l'oratorio en France à la veille de la Révolution: l'hiérodrame', *DhS*, 23:407–19, gives a useful introduction to this ephemeral genre. G. Radicchio and M. Sajous d'Oria, **Les Théâtres de Paris pendant la Révolution*, Milan, Elemond Periodici, 1990, 127 pp.

INDIVIDUAL AUTHORS

BEAUMARCHAIS. *Le Mariage de Figaro*, ed. Sylvie Puech (Balises, 17), Nathan, 1990, 127 pp., provides the kind of basic critical material you apparently need for your *bactalauréat* examination, and is to be read in conjunction with the text; *Le Mariage de Figaro*, ed. Bernard Combeaud, Hachette, 288 pp., on the other hand adopts a more traditional approach by providing the full text along with brief studies of B.'s life, work, and ideas; while John Dunkley, *Beaumarchais: 'Le Barbier de Séville'* (CGFT, 86), 92 pp. is written according to the format for the series, and provides a clear and succinct introduction to the play which takes into account recent research. R. Bismut, 'Recherche d'un "état-civil" des préfaçons d'Amsterdam (sic) de *La Folle Journée ou Le Mariage de Figaro*', *LR*, 45:13–42 and 'Sur une transcription manuscrite du *Mariage de Figaro* (suite)', *ib.*, 329–43, provides a long list of minor differences between the Amsterdam edns of this work and a recently discovered MS version in Brussels which shows many similarities with the Amsterdam edns, and raises a number of issues relating to the genesis of B.'s masterpiece. S. R. Pucci, 'The currency of exchange in Beaumarchais' *Mariage de Figaro*', *ECS*, 25:57–84, argues the importance of the *droit de seigneur* in this play lies in its staging as an avowed anachronism and simultaneous translation from ritual act into an economy of monetary exchange.

DUCIS. Jean-François Ducis, *Othello*, ed. Christopher Smith, Exeter U.P., xxi + 97 pp., in the tradition of this series provides a useful function by publishing a reliable edn of a little-known work of literature.

LAMARTELIÈRE. F. Labbé, 'Jean-Henri-Ferdinand Lamartelière (1761–1830), l'introducteur de Schiller en France, l'annonciateur du mélodrame, l'auteur révolutionnaire', *StV*, 284:259–89, examines the importance to the theatre of the time of this now largely forgotten figure.

MARIVAUX.   A. Spacagna, 'Le jeu linguistique et l'épreuve dans *L'Épreuve*', *Mélanges Deloffre*, 393–404, discusses the play as a 'rite de passage' which involves risks for both hero and heroine. R. J. Howells, 'Structure and meaning in the *Incipit* of Marivaux's comedies', *MLR*, 86:839–51, examines very thoroughly, under a number of rather familiar headings (duo, affinity, test, disguise), the main features of the opening scenes in the majority of M.'s plays. J. L. Caplan, 'Love on credit: Marivaux and law', *RoQ*, 38:289–99, is a clever attempt to link economics with the economy of passion in an analysis of M.'s *Le Jeu de l'amour*. J. Vassevière, *Marivaux: La Double Inconstance*, Nathan, 1990, 128 pp. J. Jordy, *L'Ile des esclaves de Marivaux*, Bertrand-Lacoste, 1990, 128 pp.

RESTIF DE LA BRETONNE.   *Le Drame de la vie, contenant un homme tout entier*, ed. Jean Goldzink, Imprimerie Nationale, 517 pp., contains the first edn of this strange work since it first appeared in 1793. It is composed of a series of short plays which are at least in part autobiographical, and while this is not a full critical edn it provides an interesting work to study alongside *Monsieur Nicolas*.

SAURIN.   *Beverlei, tragédie bourgeoise imitée de l'anglois*, ed. Derek F. Connon, Exeter U.P., 1990, xlv + 99 pp., provides a sound critical introduction to this play and the first edn to be published this century.

5.   POETRY

GENERAL

M. Condé, 'Note sur la poésie française au XVIIIe siècle', *EF*, 27:25–47, aims to rehabilitate 18th-c. French poetry arguing that 'la conception ornementale de la poésie est liée à la structure hiérarchisée de la société d'Ancien Régime'. T. Logé, 'Baroque et classicisme: le XVIIIe siècle face au Père Le Moyne', *SFr*, 103:25–34, traces the reception and reputation of a 17th-c. poet among 18th-c. critics.

THE ROMANTIC ERA

By MYRTO KONSTANTARAKOS, *Lecturer at Royal Holloway and Bedford New College, London*

1. GENERAL

Littérature et révolutions en France, ed. G. T. Harris and P. M. Wetherill, Amsterdam–Atalanta, Rodopi, 308 pp., includes: G. Gengembre, 'Pour une littérature républicaine: des idéologues à Mme De Staël' (13–39) (analyses S.'s political proximity to, and stylistic divergence from, the *Idéologues* in the 1800s); V. Kapp, 'Madame Roland ou l'autothémisation comme moyen de combat dans la France révolutionnaire' (41–59) (the first attempt to link historiography and R.'s conception of literature, discussing how, in prison, she chose to devote herself to writing rather than living the last moments of her life); N. Mozet, 'La bande noire ou un morceau d'histoire post-revolutionnaire dont la littérature n'a pas raconté l'histoire' (61–75) (examines links between the economic and aesthetic revolution around 1830, the violence inherent in the *bande noire*, and the creation of the French and especially the Balzacian novel); A. R. W. James, 'Le "Bonnet rouge" de Victor Hugo' (133–53) (reveals how H. changed the function of poetic language, rather than its nature by making speech coincide with action). *Juden Vol.* includes: D. Adamson, 'The priest in Balzac's fiction: secular and sacred aspects of the Church' (1–22) (considers how the figure of the priest evolves from negative to positive throughout the writing of the *Comédie Humaine*); S. Balayé, 'Un journaliste français à Londres: deux notes inédites de Fiévée à Bonaparte, Premier Consul' (49–68) (presents the texts in which F. warns B. against the Anglomania of France); H. Cockerham, 'Idéalisme, matérialisme et la femme chez Gautier' (95–110) (ingeniously shows how G. hesitated all his life between the North and the South: the English blonde embodying mystery and pure and absolute love, and the Mediterranean brunette representing profane and impure love); P. Deguise, 'Albertine de Staël, Duchesse de Broglie et Prosper de Barante. Amitié, politique et religion' (111–32) (reveals the disagreement between A. on one side and S. and Constant on the other in their correspondence relating to the importance of the love of God in religion); P. Delbouille, 'Note sur la date du *Cahier rouge* de Benjamin Constant' (133–38) (tries to determine when C. started writing about his life and uncovers an authorial mistake); E. Harpaz, 'Un texte inconnu de Benjamin Constant: *De la souveraineté*' (173–80) (provides the text and gives its political background); O. Heathcote, 'History, narrative position and the subject in Balzac: the example of *La Paix du ménage*' (181–200) (shows how the autonomy and authenticity of the subject is achieved); D. Kinloch, 'The status of art in Joubert's *Carnets* (1754–1824)' (241–62) (suggests that one of the reasons why J. wrote as he did and never published is his enthusiasm for the creative process itself as distinct from the actual production of finished specimens of style); L. Omacini, 'Madame de Staël, *Delphine*: du roman polyphonique au roman pluriel' (285–304) (refuses the feministic interpretation of the novel and instead concentrates on S.'s political and social questioning of the notion of power); M. Spencer, 'L'Utopie éclatée: lecture spatiale de Fourier' (327–46) (considers the spatial components of F.'s work in relation to the social system, and in the light of Mole's and Fischer's psychology). Wil Munsters, *La Poétique du pittoresque en France, de 1700 à 1830*, Geneva, Droz, 240 pp., shows how Romanticism moved with Sainte-Beuve from opposing the 'picturesque' to (first) Delille's 'école descriptive' and (secondly) the reconciliation of the two notions. **Romantik — Aufbruch zur Moderne*, ed. Karl Maurer and Winfried Wehle, Reihe: Romanistisches Kolloquium v, Munich, Wilhelm Fink Vlg, 567 pp., finds French Romanticism more vehement than German or English and closer to Italian and Spanish models. T. Ungvari, 'Revolution: a textual analysis', *NCFS*, 19:1–21, is a historical review of the changing meaning of the concept through the Hegelian interpretation of Enlightenment. *Romantisme*, no. 71, 'La critique d'art du XIXe siècle', includes: D. Gamboni, 'Propositions pour l'étude de la critique d'art du XIXe siècle' (9–17) (shows how critics and artists were mutually dependent even when antagonistic to each other); N. William, 'Opinions professionnelles: critique d'art et économie de la culture sous la Monarchie de Juillet' (19–30) (shows how, around 1830, culture became increasingly commercialized and how, as a result, art criticism acted as an intermediary between Salon and audience); P. Grate, 'Art, idéologie et politique dans la critique d'art' (31–38) (seeks to demonstrate that art critics had a background that was literary and that they generated an audience for art by use of polemics and vituperation); D. Bouverot, 'L'"expression" en peinture et en musique (1830–1850)' (69–84) (examines the occurrences of the word in literature, dictionaries, and articles on art and concludes that its range of different meanings synthesizes Romantic ideas on art). J.-P. Leduc-Adine, 'Des règles d'un genre: la critique d'art' (93–100) (usefully defines art criticism in terms of external and internal criteria and shows how art became a commercial product, which, to be marketed, required intermediaries between the artists and the ever-increasing body of consumers). J.-L. Diaz, 'Le dandysme littéraire après 1830, ou la badine et le parapluie', *ib.*, no. 72:31–47, explains how aristocrats and writers changed their relationship. *Romantisme*, no. 73, is a special issue on 'France–Allemagne, Passages–Partages' and includes: M. Espagne, 'Claude Fauriel en quête d'une méthode, ou l'Idéologie à l'écoute de l'Allemagne' (7–18) (identifies F. as a marginal *Idéologue* but at the centre of the cultural exchanges between Germany and the *Idéologie*, who contributed to the elevation of history to the status of a dominant human science); M.-C. Hoock-Demarie, 'Un lien d'interculturalité franco-allemande: le réseau épistolaire de Coppet' (19–28) (maintains that, ten years after the Revolution, Mme de Staël acted as an intercultural mediator, and Coppet became a place of circulation of people and ideas); P. Régnier, 'La question romantique comme enjeu national: critique française et littérature allemande autour de 1830' (29–42) (discusses translations and imitations of the German models of Romanticism in drama and poetry); M. Werner, 'Heine interprète en France de l'Allemagne intellectuelle. Conflits autour d'un cas modèle de transfert culturel' (43–55) (emphasizes the role of the Revolution of 1830 in the cultural exchanges between the two countries); J. Le Rider, 'Hugo von Hofmannsthal: rêve d'une rencontre avec le Booz de Victor Hugo' (81–91) (investigates how Hugo's poem, and in particular his use of colours, allows Hofmannsthal to come to terms with his homosexuality and his Jewishness); P. Vaisse, 'Sur les rapports artistiques franco-allemands au XIXe siècle' (93–102) (explores how German attempts to proclaim national identity through art alienated French artists). *Elseneur*, Centre des publications de l'Université de Caen, no. 6 is a special issue on 'La Révolution vue de 1800', Actes du Colloque de Caen 1988, on how, before the historians, Stendhal, Chateaubriand, Necker, and Sade gave their account of the French Revolution. Pierre Pachet, *Les Baromètres de l'âme. Naissance du journal intime*, Hatier, 146 pp., uses Keats's definition of the genre to distinguish between real intimate journals (Constant, Amiel) and false ones (Michelet, Hugo). Michel Orcel and François Boddaert, *Ces imbéciles de liberté, 1815–1852*, Hatier, 178 pp., is a chronicle of love affairs and literary events year by year which does not pretend to be objective (as the authors' idiosyncratic dislike of Hugo demonstrates). Claude Mouchard, *Un grand désert d'hommes, 1851–1885*, Hatier, 342 pp., selects texts in which Baudelaire responds to Nerval and Hugo. André Suarès, *Portraits et préférences (Âmes et visages*, t. II) *De Benjamin Constant à Arthur Rimbaud*, ed. Michel Drouin, NRF, 372 pp., is an unpublished and unfinished text which attempts to elevate criticism to the level of art, showing Suarès's dislikes (e.g. Hugo too much an orator, Balzac too much a historian, and Sand mediocre) and likes (e.g. Stendhal). J.-L. Diaz, 'Écrire la vie du poète. La biographie d'écrivain entre Lumières et

Romantisme', *RSH*, 224:215–33, asserts that the Romantics (after Byron) believed that a man's life explained — and was even more important than — his work. Max Milner, *On est prié de fermer les yeux*, NRF, 285 pp., applies psychoanalytic investigation to the role played by sight in mythology, and in Gautier (the importance of depiction takes its root in the fear of the female sex), in Stendhal (when in love, happiness and seeing are incompatible) and in Hugo (the poet sees the invisible like the blind man, attempting to rival God). A. H. Pasco, 'The unrocked cradle and the birth of the Romantic hero', *JES*, 21:95–110, investigates the social reasons for the strange and unpleasant Romantic hero.

2. CONSULATE AND EMPIRE WRITERS

CHATEAUBRIAND. Alexandre Vinet, *Chateaubriand*, Lausanne, Âge d'homme, 353 pp., includes most of the texts, articles, and lectures on literature of the first volume of *Études sur la littérature française au XIXe siècle*. Jean Salesse, 'Chateaubriand: le récit d'enfance dans les trois premiers livres des *Mémoires d'Outre-Tombe*', *RSH*, 222:9–34, shows how, for the adult C., the writing of his '*mémoires*' represented a 'mimesis' of life — investigating the self — in a 'poiesis' of death. H. Redman, 'Jusqu'à ce que la preuve irrécusable paraisse: l'Amérique, Washington et Chateaubriand', *NCFS*, 20:1–4, investigates, in the light of inconclusive evidence, whether C. actually visited certain places in America. B. Didier, 'De l'émigration à l'exil intérieur. Chateaubriand, *Les Mémoires d'Outre-tombe*', *CAIEF*, 43:59–80, maintains that writing about exile is not simply 'literary', but allowed him to overcome his interior exile. J. Aubert, *'From history to memoires: Joyce's Chateaubriand as Celtic Palampcestor', *Joyce Studies Annual*, 2:177–200.

CHÉNIER, MARIE-JOSEPH. J. L. Burkhart and and E. R. Farrel, 'Marie-Joseph Chénier and the subversion of myth and tradition', *NCFS*, 20:15–26, shows how C. augmented traditional narratives with revolutionary images.

CONSTANT. *Fragments d'un ouvrage abandonné sur la possibilité d'une constitution républicaine dans un grand pays*, ed. Henri Grange, Aubier, 506 pp., is the hitherto unpublished result of a collaboration with Mme de Staël, interrupted in 1798 and finished by him in 1810. *Ma vie (Le Cahier rouge)*, ed. C. P. Courtney, Cambridge, Dæmon Press, xl + 90 pp., differs from many other editions in reproducing Constant's text with its original spelling and punctuation and in providing much fuller annotation than has hitherto been available. D. Turton, 'First love: Benjamin Constant's recollection of Madame Johannot in *Le Cahier rouge*', *NCFS*, 19:187–202, argues that in this account (unlike an earlier one) C. oscillates between immediate narrative and narratorial comments upon that memory. T. argues that the textual equilibrium thus achieved is a substitute for peace of mind, and that it provides a linguistic resolution to an unresolved love. *Annales Benjamin Constant*, no. 12, Lausanne, *Actes* (Maryland), ed. Beatrice Fink includes: P. Thompson, 'Benjamin Constant: l'allégorie du polythéisme' (7–18) (explains the failure of *Recherches sur les religions de l'Antiquité* by suggesting that C. did not contrast two ideologies but two conceptions of duration — the first negating history and the second creating it); P. Deguise, 'La religion de Benjamin Constant et l'Unitarisme américain' (19–27) (compares two religious attitudes, both of extreme liberalism); S. Holmes, 'Constant and Tocqueville: an unexplored relationship' (29–41) (accentuates C.'s radicalism and T.'s emotional allegiance to the past, by comparing their attitude to egalitarism, freedom, and religion); E. Harpaz, 'Benjamin Constant entre la République et la Monarchie' (43–52) (explains how the disillusioned C. became an enemy of the Republic: he favoured a mixed system with separation of powers in a constitutional monarchy where morals and freedom take the place of equality); B. Fontana, 'Publicity and the "Res publica": the concept of public opinion in Benjamin Constant's writings' (53–63) (links this concept as pre-political force to C.'s constitutional model, his religious thinking and the individual experiment presented in *Adolphe*); C. P. Courtney, 'The correspondence of Benjamin Constant: an overview' (65–88) (on the critical edition being prepared: a collection of 4000 letters from C. and many to him, from 1774 to 1830); K. Kloocke, 'Les lettres de Benjamin Constant à Juliette Récamier ou la présence de la fiction dans la vie' (89–97) (reveals C.'s romantic conception of love through a discrepancy between the *Journal intime* and his letters to R.); M. de Rougemont, 'Benjamin Constant critique littéraire' (99–107) (discerns in texts published from 1803 to 1818 a union of 'concrete idealism' and socio-liberalism); L. Spaas, 'Constant's *Adolphe*: from implied to actual reader' (109–17) (examines the ironic game created by the confrontation of imagined and real readers in — or of — *Adolphe*; the network of readings becomes a polyphony, in which an increasing irony develops); C. A. Mossman, 'The semiotics of overkill: time and letters in *Adolphe*' (119–27) (defines a 'semiotic of residuals'); J.-D. Candaux, 'Revue des manuscrits de Benjamin Constant vendus sur le marché des autographes de 1976 à 1989' (131–62); S. Colbois, 'Benjamin Constant: parutions récentes 1986–1990' (163–81). Wardy Poelstra, *'Romantiek en deconstructie: Abrams versus Constant', Forum der Letteren*, 32:173–89.

MAISTRE, JOSEPH DE. *De la souveraineté du peuple*, ed. Jean-Louis Darcel, PUF, 294 pp., discusses M. and Revolution.

STAËL. *De la littérature*, ed. Gérard Gengembre and Jean Goldzink, Flammarion, 445 pp. B. Durand-Sendrail, 'Mme de Staël et la condition post-révolutionnaire', *RR*, 82:36–48, shows how history imposed on S. a rereading of the Enlightenment in terms of the Revolution that followed it; since the limitations of the rationalistic political agenda lie in an inability to make man sociable, she proposed two solutions: collective psychology or individual culture (literature). J. Isbel, 'The first French *Faust*: *De l'Allemagne*'s *Faust* chapter, 1810/1814', *FS*, 45:417–34, analyses S.'s distortions, which are commonly attributed to ignorance, and argues that she voluntarily pushed *Faust* towards neoclassicism. F. Schuerewegen, 'Volcans: Mme de Staël, Gobineau, Gautier', *LR*, 45:319–28, applies Freud's interpretation of volcanoes in *Gradiva* to the eruption of repressed desires in S. and to Gautier's 'engine' of memories.

3. POETRY

DESBORDES-VALMORE. W. Greenberg, 'L'exil et la nostalgie chez Marceline Desbordes-Valmore', *CAIEF*, 43:81–93, argue on the basis of a study of her relationships that physical exile was easier to bear than interior exile. G. M. Schultz, *'Gender and the sonnet: Marceline Desbordes-Valmore and Paul Verlaine', *CRR*, 10:190–99. M. Danahy, 'Marceline Desbordes-Valmore et la fraternité des poètes', *NCFS*, 19:386–93, reveals how D.-V.'s distinctive voice subverts unconscious habits of reading female poetry as addressed to men.

GAUTIER. R. Lloyd, 'Mirroring difference, figuring frames', *ib.*, 343–53, examines two lesser-known poems in which the representation of death and sex are twin aspects of the same female impulse which contains the inadmissible desire for G. to be other than he is. E. J. Lien, 'The prefatory poetics of Théophile Gautier', *RoN*, 32:47–54, comments on G.'s struggle in his earlier poetry to reconcile sentiment and well-crafted art. C. Gosselin Schick, 'Théophile Gautier's poetry as *Coquetterie Posthume*', *NCFS*, 20:74–84, reads the poem according to its allegorical rhetoric of paradoxical juxtaposition of seductive charm and death.

HUGO. J. C. Kessler, '"Cette babel du monde". Visionary architecture in the poetry of Victor Hugo', *NCFS*, 19:417–31, explores how H.'s imaginary architecture in his drawings and poetry takes on the lineaments of the mythic tower of Babel as ambivalent metaphor of history. D. M. Betz, 'Victor Hugo, Juliette Drouet, and an unpublished anniversary letter from 1851', *ib.*, 432–37, argues D.'s letter, with its self-denigratory prose style and use of recurring elements of private significance for the two correspondents, demonstrates a double talent for love and literature. F. Bassan, 'La poésie de Victor Hugo jugée par Paul Claudel', *ib.*, 536–40, notices that C., who often criticized H.'s poetry for its monotonous rhythms, melancholia, violence, religion, and meaningless (though beautiful) lines, seemed to become reconciled to it in old age. J. Malavie, 'Le saint et le sacré dans l'œuvre de Victor Hugo', *IL*, no. 3:17–29, distinguishes the sacred from the saintly in H., paying particular attention to concepts such as love, in which the distinction between these two terms is clearer, and concludes that H., unlike his contemporaries, is a religious man. R. Bach, '*Les Contemplations* or paternity regained', *RR*, 82:297–316, deals with H.'s exile, describing it as separation which re-enacts his daughter's death, and which leads him to assume a paternal role towards society in general. P. Laforgue, 'Poésie et poétique de l'exil: le livre cinquième des *Contemplations*', *CAIEF*, 43:95–111, shows how even H.'s pure poetry can be committed. Yvan Leclerc, *'L'idylle-Hugo: le groupe des idylles dans *La Légende des siècles*', in Niderst, *Pastorale*, 149–56. T. M. Pratt, 'Victor Hugo à la lumière de Roland Barthes', *SFr*, 101:253–57, is an ingenious close reading of *Demain, dès l'aube* in the new light of *S/Z* literary codes, revealing its complexity, extraordinary polysemy and modernity.

LAMARTINE. A. Abou Ghannam, 'Lamartine et la poésie de la répétition', *LR*, 45:43 51, investigates the link between poetic structures and meaning in *La Branche de l'amandier*. P. Laude, 'Sur l'imaginaire métaphysique du paysage chez Lamartine', *RoN*, 32:67–77, analyses the symbolic structures in *L'Isolement* and *Le Vallon* as movements respectively of elevation and integration. Mireille Vedrire, *Lamartine retrouvé*, Chambéry, Agnaf, 288 pp., is an illustrated anthology of L. based upon locations mentioned in the poems.

MUSSET. J. F. Hamilton, 'Reversed polarities in the *Nuits*: anatomy of a cure', *NCFS*, 20:65–73, on the confluence of personal time and of history.

SAINTE-BEUVE. P. Laude, 'Le poète à sa fenêtre: dualisme et errance métaphysique dans la poésie française du dix-neuvième siècle', *NCFS*, 19:354–68, analyses how windows enclose the poets' personal dreams.

VIGNY. **Correspondance d'Alfred de Vigny*, 2. *Août 1830 — septembre 1835*, ed. Madeleine Ambrière, PUF, 576 pp. M. Cambien, 'Alfred de Vigny dans le texte', *NCFS*, 19:369–80, shows how V. defines his text and himself in relation to previous texts and utterances. M. McGoldrick, *'The setting of Vigny's *La Mort du Loup*', *LQ*, 29:104–14.

4. THE NOVEL

BALZAC

ABa, n.s. 12, 538 pp., includes unpublished documents: M. Ambrière and D. Langlois-Berthelot, 'Un beau rêve dans la France littéraire de 1831–1832' (7–21) (introduces and gives the recently discovered text of Silvestre's *Prospectus* signed by most Romantics); R. Guise, 'Un texte inconnu de Balzac: *Du contrat social, par J.-J. Rousseau*' (23–28); R. Pierrot, 'Vingt-huit lettres' (from 1828 to 1848) (29–51); R. De Cesare, 'Encore une lettre inédite de Balzac à Alessandro Mozzoni-Frosconi' (53–57); A. D. Mikhaïlov, 'Une lettre inédite de Balzac' (to Prince Henri Lubomiriski) (59–61); papers of the 'Journée de Saché', 6 October 1990, on 'Balzac et les pouvoirs' comprise: J. Tulard, 'Balzac et la police' (65–69) (shows B.'s deep knowledge of the police); M. Leroy, 'Balzac et les Jésuites' (71–89) (on the evolution of his depiction of Jesuits); R. Chollet, 'Autour de la publication de l'*Histoire impartiale des Jésuites*' (91–109) (discusses B.'s moderation); R. Butler, 'Balzac et Louis XVIII' (111–34) (assesses B.'s depiction of the King and his criticism of him after 1830); G. Woollen, 'Balzac et le prix Montyon (suite)' (135–59) (devoted to B.'s reaction to his failure to win this prize); C. Galantaris, 'Balzac bibliophile' (161–83); A. Michel, 'Le pouvoir féminin dans *La Comédie humaine*' (185–99) (on strengths and weaknesses of women as portrayed by B.); 'Études historiques et littéraires' include: A.-M. Baron, 'Le rêve balzacien: théorie et mise en œuvre' (203–24) (attempts to interpret Balzacian dreams); R. de Smirnoff, 'Balzac peintre de l'instant' (225–43) (investigates B.'s representation of time); M. Le Yaouanc, 'En relisant *Le Lys dans la Vallée* (suite)' (245–85); S. Vachon, 'Nouvelles précisions bibliographiques sur quelques ouvrages de Balzac' (287–331); 'Lectures de Balzac' includes reactions to B. by Flaubert (A. Raitt: admiration but desire to be independent of him, 335–61); Taine (J.-T. Nordmann: B. as model novelist, 363–81); Paul Bourget (M. Raimond: esteem, 383–94); Barrès (V. Rambaud: strong interest, 393–408); Giono (P. Citron uses an unpublished journal to reveal G.'s unsuspected keenness on B. in 1943 and 1944, 409–24); the 'Notes' comprise: C. Dédéyan, 'Une anecdote de Henry Murger sur Balzac' (425–27); V. Miltchina, 'Balzac en 1845 vu par un Russe' (428–31); A. H. Armstrong, 'Balzac et *Marie Stuart*' (432–40) (discusses the participation of B. in Horace Raissen's historical novel and interestingly concludes that B. had written, well before 1828, the equivalent of a volume of this work); H. Sussmann, 'A propos des dédicaces de *La Comédie Humaine*' (441–46) (thinks B. borrowed them from Bandello); H. Kieffer, 'Précisions sur le peintre Drölling' (447–54) (a discussion of the hitherto unknown artist); J. Meyer-Petit, 'Le Balzac de

Granville: un "éventail" de lectures' (455–61) (explores the link between B.'s portrait and his work).

GENERAL STUDIES. Allan H. Pasco, *Balzacian Montage, Configuring 'La Comédie humaine'*, Toronto U.P., 192 pp., disputes the view that the *Comédie humaine* is fragmented by analysing the unifying elements (subordination of narrative to description, use of repetition and of coherent frames); he concludes that B. is the master not of collage but of montage. André Mauprat, *Honoré de Balzac, un cas*, Lyons, La Manufacture, 1990, 297 pp., argues that B. took refuge from reality in his imagination, in an attempt to overcome a lack of love. Georges Simenon, *Portrait-souvenir de Balzac et autres textes sur la littérature*, ed. Francis Lacassin and Christian Bourgois, 272 pp., shows the many points of similarity between Simenon's and B.'s lives. Juliette Frølich, *Au parloir du roman de Balzac et de Flaubert*, Oslo, Solum Forlag, 131 pp., uses Bakhtin's distinction to contrast B.'s effective utterance with Flaubert's powerless and 'in-significant' one. M. Hannoosh, 'La femme, la ville, le réalisme: fondements épistémologiques dans le Paris de Balzac', *RR*, 82:127–45, asserts that B. represents Paris as feminine to reveal its fantastic structure.

INDIVIDUAL WORKS. S. Stary, 'The erosion of morality in Balzac's *Un début dans la vie*', *NCFS*, 19:210–22, sees this novel as the beginning of B.'s investigation of the 'moral decrepitude' of bourgeois avarice. L. Kamm, 'Balzac's *La Peau de chagrin* and Zola's *Germinal*: points of contact', *ib.*, 223–30, explores the economic and geological link between the two novels. W. Paulsin, 'Pour une analyse dynamique de la variation textuelle: *Le Chef-d'œuvre* trop *connu*', *ib.*, 404–16, notes how B. only evokes woman as a real human being in order to hide her behind the creator's fantasy. L. A. Boldt, 'The framed image: the chain metaphors in Balzac's *Le Père Goriot*', *ib.*, 517–35, reveals B.'s desire both to recede as an authorial presence (allowing reader involvement in the narrative) and to emerge in framing and metaphors which are metonymically linked. C. Barry, 'Camille Maupin: Io to Balzac's Prometheus', *ib.*, 20:11–52, examines B.'s portrayal in the light of Zeus, Prometheus, and Io myths. A. Armstrong, 'One of Balzac's sources for *L'Excommunié*', *FSB*, 37:8–10, expertly reveals the influence of Walter Scott's *Quentin Durward* on the gipsy episode in the manuscript. M.-A. Hutton, 'Bleich seen through Balzac', *MLR*, 86:49–56, discusses how the concept of community in Bleich's epistemology, by emphasizing the role of the individual's reflective capacity, neglects the part played by the unconscious as a powerful source of motivation, something B. is careful not to do in *Le Colonel Chabert* and *Adieu*. B. Henmerdinger, 'La révolution agraire en France et en Russie', *Belfagor*, 1:76–77, explores the similarities between Rosa Luxembourg's and Montlosier's views on the French and Russian Revolutions (as shown in *L'Usurier des campagnes*). V. Carofiglio, 'La mort, le culte et la parole dans le *Médecin de campagne*', *RSH*, 221:105–19, analyses the variations on the theme of death in this novel, revealing how B. alternates ideas and narrative. J. O. Lowrie, 'The artist, real and imagined: Diderot's Quentin de la Tour and Balzac's Frenhofer', *RoN*, 31:267–73, explains the substantial changes B. made in his six editions from 1831 to 1847 under Diderot's influence. T. Unwin, 'Les Maximes de Balzac: l'exemple d'*Illusions perdues*', *ib.*, 32:55–61, assesses how far the exceptionally high concentration of maxims reflects B.'s thought, by examining their function rather than their content. F. Schuerewegen, 'De la nécessité préfacielle (Balzac, Zola)', *FrF*, 16:177–86, maintains prefaces compensate for the absence of the author in realistic novels. *EsC*, no. 3, 'Reading Balzac', includes: R. Chambers, 'Misogyny and cultural denial (Balzac's *Autre étude de femme*)' (5–14) (contends this novel, far from being the atypical text it has been taken for, is one of the keys to B.'s universe); A. Fischler, 'Distance and narrative perspective in Balzac's *Facino cane*' (15–25) (argues against the common identification of the young narrator with the author); A. K. Mortimer, 'Writing *Modeste Mignon*' (26–37) (asserts the novel forges a new alliance between the cynical social realism of marriage and the idealistic romanticism of love); J. T. Booker, 'Starting at the end of *Eugénie Grandet*' (38–48) (argues against the linearity of the novel by showing the many similarities between the beginning and the end); C. L. Thomas, '*La Cousine Bette* and the house divided' (49–59) (shows how mythological and biblical allusions produce a network of comparisons and oppositions revealing a hidden significance in the narrative); A. R. Pugh, 'Balzac's *La Muse du département*: the status of fiction' (60–66) (emphasizes the unity of this text, despite the textual history of B.'s multiple rewritings); A. H. Pasco, 'Balzac's second-rate muse' (67–77) (presents B.'s use of Dinah's framework to decry journalism); L. R. Schehr, 'Quoin of the realm: *La Muse du département*' (78–87) (explores the ramifications of over and undervaluing the figures of printing, reading, and writing). R. De Cesare, 'Quando Balzac riceveva una lettera . . . (A proposito di Balzac e Leonardo da Vinci)', *SFr*, 104:305–09, on the knowledge and opinion B. had of da Vinci's work.

STENDHAL

Jean-Jacques Hamm and Gregory Lessard, *Concordance to Stendhal's 'Armance'*, Edwin Mellen Press, 580 pp., lists all textual aspects, including proper names, italicized words, footnoted words. Martine Reid, *Stendhal en images. Réflexions sur la 'Vie de Henry Brulard'*, Geneva,

Droz, 212 pp., analyses the failure of S. to describe, by means of words and drawings, events in his own life. Gabrielle Pascal, *Rires, sourires et larmes chez Stendhal: une initiation poétique*, Geneva, Droz. Louis Marin, 'Écritures, images, gravures dans la représentation de soi chez Stendhal', in *La résurrection de l'auteur*, ed. Michel Contat, PUF, 197 pp., pp. 119–41, maintains the pictures in *Vie de Henry Brulard* are ambivalent and that autobiography represents S.'s attempts to compensate for the separation from his mother. M. Melara, 'Nominal intersections: pseudonymity and generic boundaries in Stendhal's *Vie de Henry Brulard*', *NCFS*, 19:247–61, claims that S. seeks to regain self-possession by re-naming himself. M. Peled Ginsburg, 'Stendhal's exemplary stories', *ib.*, 394–403, studies S.'s discrepancies. M. Melara, 'Money matters: identity and its values in Stendhal's definition of self', *NFS*, 30:13–22, draws a parallel between pseudo-nyms and money for S. as they both offer him freedom from his father. Dieter Dienfenbach, *Stendhal und die Freimaurerei*, Tübingen, Narr, 200 pp., deals with the influence of S.'s Masonic experience, which reaches its climax in *La Chartreuse*. *SCl*, 130, includes: Y. Ansel, 'Le savant et la mort du dilettante' (105–14) (S. hated scientists because they prevented him from enjoying art); E. Williamson, 'Stendhal inspecteur du Mobilier de la Couronne: administrateur ou artiste? Lettres et documents inédits, III' (115–33) (points out a mistaken date in a S. letter, and reveals that when the usually conscientious S. returned from Italy, he realized he could not compete with ambitious administrators); D. Bryant, 'Deux batailles qui ne font qu'une: *l'Enlèvement de la redoute* de Mérimée et Waterloo dans *La Chartreuse de Parme*' (134–44) (notices that the battle scenes from the two friends' works have much in common, in particular, the subjective first person narratorial perspectives); S. Esquier, '*Féder*: un "conte léger"' (145–58) (argues this so-called 'unfinished' novel is S.'s last attempt to realize a comic novel with a simple narrative structure; lightness is an aesthetic and existential choice, and the ending reminds the reader man is the prisoner of his limitations); V. Del Litto, 'Textes et documents inédits' (159–64): '1. Henri Beyle secrétaire de Pierre Daru' (gives a letter S. wrote for his cousin to Mathieu Dumas), '2. Grenoble 1814' (the correspondance of Joseph Fourier in the Isère Archives in 1814, year of the definite breakdown of relations between S. and his town, shows that, as the Empire was collapsing, S. was only thinking of saving his country), '3. La "calomnie"' (reveals the incomprehension that surrounded S. at the time), '4. Mareste, Luigi Buzzi et Romain Colomb' (publishes letters showing the link between the two men); J.-J. Hamm and G. Lessard, 'Concordances et études littéraires: le cas d'*Armance*' (170–76) (explaining why they chose this novel as a starting point for their concordance). *SCl*, 131, includes: V.

Del Litto, 'La source (à découvrir) d'un épisode de *Rouge et Noir*' (193–98) (provides the text of Coston's 'Grotte de Milleli' as a possible unknown source of S.); A. Pillepich, 'Nouvelles précisions sur Stendhal et Milan' (199–204) (an account of whom he met); G. De Wulf, 'Récit d'une germination: Frédérick Tristan et Stendhal autour d'un kaléidoscope culturel' (205–10) (examines the relation between text and epigraph in an attempt to define S.'s notion of culture and to assess if it is acquired by the characters of *Le Rouge et le Noir*); F. Claudon, 'Le dialogisme dans la *Vie de Henry Brulard*. Quelques remarques sur S. et la Révolution' (211–20) (applies Bakhtinian ideas to S.'s writing of Revolution as, although political commitment is absent, truth is sought through many voices); P. Hamon, 'Quelques visages de parlementaire au temps de la *Vie de Henry Brulard*' (221–31) (gives an annotated list of magistrates S. mentioned in *Brulard*); B. Bergerot, 'Stendhal rue Chaptal' (232–40) (considers a superficial one-way debate between the two men — one being realistic and the other idealistic — about the Revolution and the use of science to benefit the human race); a debate transcribed by M. Jarnet, 'Stendhal reçoit Balzac' (241–47) (on B.'s admiration for *La Chartreuse*, for he saw in it the novel he would have liked to have written). *SCl*, 132, includes: V. Del Litto, 'Contribution à l'histoire du stendhalisme. Stryienski, Paupe, Martineau en 1912 (avec des lettres inédites)' (265–74) (gives Paupe's 'Notice sur *Le Rouge et le Noir*', a response to Stryienski's hostile first introduction to the novel; also Martineau's letters to Paupe showing he was not concerned by the debate, as he was more interested in S.'s biography than in his work); P.-M. Neaud, 'Stendhal et Martial Daru (documents inédits). I. L'intendance de Vienne en 1809. II. Convocation à la Loge Caroline' (273–77) (reveals that like Daru, and because of him, S. became a Mason); P. Cova, '*La Chartreuse de Parme* et *le Guépard*' (280–86) (compares the two novels in terms of style and political disillusionment); M. Crouzet, 'La *Vie de Henry Brulard*. La moins "puante" des autobiographies?' (287–312) (the genre permits self-contradiction, and enables the narrator to go beyond mere facts to personal feelings); R. D. Berthet, 'La lumière de Julien' (313–17) (observes today's world in the light of S.'s portrayal of hypocrisy); A. Mansau and P. Rousseau, 'Michel Déon nomade sédentaire dans les pas du "Milanese"' (318–26) (showing how the novelist D. follows S.'s footsteps in Italy: for both, travel is a way of being confronted with oneself); J.-C. Augendre, 'Qui jouit? Foucault, Helvétius, Stendhal' (327–38) (argues S.'s love is aesthetic — linked to suffering and to creativity — and ethical). P. Berthier, 'Stendhal Club', *RSH*, 224: 139–59, contends that the accolade of professional scholars may be the end of the authentic S., as he wrote for the individual. N. Segal,

'The sick son: a motif in Stendhal and Flaubert', *RoS*, 19:7–19, is an astute essay on *Le Rouge et le Noir* and *L'Éducation sentimentale*, which concludes S. and F. work at a fantasy related to the Oedipal and the adulterous triangle. T. I. Eastridge, 'Tacitus and the portrait of Prince Ranuce-Ernest IV in *La Chartreuse de Parme*', *RoN*, 32:85–90, detects how S. has drawn on Tacitus to give impetus to his creative imagination, but in an unaffected style. A. H. Pasco, 'The unheroic mode: Stendhal's *La Chartreuse de Parme*', *PhilosQ*, 70:361–78, maintains that both Julien and Fabrice are overwhelmed by their environment, but that Fabrice alone represents the early stages of authorial revolt against the canonical Aristotelian character, since only he is defined by the action of the others. S. C. Witkin, 'Les lettres de rupture dans *Les Liaisons dangereuses* de Laclos et *La Chartreuse de Parme* de Stendhal', *NCFS*, 20:107–16, compares the fictional letter-writers' approaches to ending relationships. C. F. Danélan, 'La perception visuelle et le regard dans *Le Rouge et le Noir*', *ib.*, 117–27, shows how the initiation into visual perception reveals to Julien his identity. Dennis Porter, **Haunted Journeys: Desire and Transgression in European Travel Writing*, Princeton U.P., Lawrenceville, 341 pp., examines (amongst others things) S.'s aesthetic of the detour.

OTHER WRITERS

DESBORDES-VALMORE. *Les Petits Flamands*, ed. Marc Bertrand, Geneva, Droz, 280 pp. Detached from the *Contes*, this autobiography, reprinted for the first time since 1865, gives a detailed account of the daily life of a family in Douai.

GAUTIER. *Correspondance générale*, t. v (1852–53) and t. vi (1854–57), ed. P. Laubriet and Cl. Lacoste, Geneva, Droz, 474 pp., contains all letters from and to G., and indexes of all correspondents. *Bull. de la Soc. Théophile Gautier*, *no. 12: 'L'Orient de Théophile Gautier', *Actes*, 1990 (1991), 2 vols, 457 pp., includes 28 articles on ethnography, arts, music, Egyptians, Turks, and myth; no. 13 includes: P. Laubriet, 'Théophile Gautier, un annonciateur de l'esprit "fin de siècle"?' (7–34) (attempts to determine what is Romantic and what is no longer Romantic in G.); S. Zenkine, 'Le "chez soi" dans l'œuvre de Théophile Gautier' (35–60) (reveals the contradictions of G.'s predilection for domesticity); J. Lardoux, 'Découvrir les poésies libertines' (61–84) (discusses the quality of these inaccessible poems); P. Nogrette, 'Un pastiche – et autres – de Théophile Gautier' (85–90) (notices that G. had few imitators); C. Lacoste, 'Le Journal d'Eugénie Fort (suite)' (91–160); C. Brownson, 'Les traductions en langue anglaise des œuvres' (161–216).

HUGO. *Correspondance familiale et écrits intimes*, ed. Jean Gaudon, Laffont, Bouquins, 2 : 1828–39, xl + 1002 pp., gives equal status to letters between third parties and H.'s own correspondence, thus making this volume, like the first (published 1990), a very interesting historical compilation. *Le Rhin*, Nuée bleue, 430 pp. *Carnets d'écrivains*, 1, CNRS, 1990, 253 pp., include: L. Hay, 'L'amont de l'écriture' (7–22) (lists different types of *carnets*); J. Gaudon, 'Carnets, liasses, feuilles volantes' (73–98) (distinguishes between the relatively uninteresting chronological *carnets*, and the preliminary notes for poems and novels, in some cases elaborated many years later); G. Rosa, 'Outil de travail: les carnets des *Misérables*' (99–118) (notices that every note eventually found a place in the novel). *RLMod* is a special issue on 'Victor Hugo 3. Femmes', ed. Danièle Gasiglia-Laster. As the editor points out in her *Ouverture* (5–12), these essays share a feminine point of view and comprise: M. Fizaine, 'L'autre témoin ou le manchon de Juliette — étude à partir des textes autobiographiques de Juliette Drouet' (14–41) (examines how D., rejected by society, attempted to acquire a social role with the man she loved through writing, but failed); G. Malandain, 'Un regard à double voix — le Victor Hugo raconté par Adèle' (43–65) (shows how A. writes about H. with a 'double voice', appropriating his recollections); J. Archer, 'Situations et droits des femmes — discours et fiction chez Hugo' (67–88) (thinks H. goes further than his contemporaries in demanding women's rights and moves away from stereotypes in his fiction); N. Savy, 'De Notre-Dame aux Bénédictines — l'asile et l'exil' (89–98) (provides the counter-argument, elaborating H.'s alleged anti-feminism); A. Spiquel, 'Éponine ou le salut au féminin' (99–110) (shows that in *Les Misérables* and *La Fin de Satan*, females are redeemed by love); C. Habib, 'Le sadisme et la pitié' (111–23) (argues that, even if H. tends to defend women's right, he represents them suffering in order to provoke pity, which is not compatible with equality); C. Millet, 'Aspects du féminin dans *La Légende des siècles*' (125–58) (shows how allegories allow a 'feminine' history); C. Trévisan, 'Les avatars du féminin dans *L'Année terrible*' (159–67) (examines the ambivalence of women, arguing the absence of any 'real' one); A. Rosa, 'Jeanne, femme fatale' (169–94) (explains the happy representation of H.'s granddaughter by comparing the *Carnets* to his work); D. Gasiglia-Laster, 'La femme couronnée et la femme révoltée' (195–212) (argues that H. wanted to see women and children protected by laws, which implies he felt they were not inferior); F. Naugrette, 'Jany Gastaldi en Doña Sol, Nada Strancar en Lucrèce Borgia — les rayons et les ombres d'Antoine Vitez' (213–24) (investigates how V. emphasized the antitheses in H.'s texts by his choice of actresses); D. Gasiglia-Laster, '*Femmes*: bibliographie commentée' (225–41) (selected bibliography of less known works from 1843 to 1986). C. W. Thompson, 'Du rire romantique à l'espace éclaté: sur *L'Homme qui rit* et *Le Cœur du pitre* de Rimbaud', *RHLF*, 91:214–28, shows how both poets (like Lamartine) used the positive powers of dissolution of the Romantic laugh to destabilize space in order to subvert authority. G. D. Chaitin, 'Victor Hugo and the hieroglyphic novel', *NCFS*, 19:36–53, compares *Notre-Dame de Paris* to Walter Scott, arguing H.'s novel is dialogic and constructed according to the same principles that govern hieroglyphic writing. P. Gaitet, 'From the criminal's to the people's: the evolution of argot and popular language in the nineteeth century', *ib.*, 231–46, analyses H.'s *Le Dernier Jour d'un condamné* and *Les Misérables* and looks also into Balzac's *La Dernière Incarnation de Vautrin* to argue that the bourgeoisie barely conceals its anxiety in the face of the potential power of the working class. S. L. Arico, 'Mme Juliette Adam and Victor Hugo: a second and third unpublished souvenir', *SFr*, 102:437–41, introduces a recollection of H.'s political and love life. C. Karatsinidou, 'Le nid aérien dans *Les chansons des rues et des bois*', *ib.*, 456–63, underlines the feeling of freedom expressed by the images of openness. K. M. Grossman, 'Narrative space and androgyny in *Les Misérables*', *NCFS*, 20:97–106, uses Bachelard to argue that Jean Valjean transcends gender by combining the masculine linear space of law (of Javert) with the feminine tortuous space of lawlessness (of Thénardier). L. Bolzan, '*Quatre-vingt-treize* o gli equivoci della rappresentazione', *RLMC*, 44:223–40, concludes that the representations of reality are authentic, despite the focus on a particular point in time.

LAMARTINE. H. Redman, 'Lamartine en 1820: une lettre inédite', *RHLF*, 91:231–38, publishes a letter to Mme de La Pierre showing L. did not resent her trying to prevent his marriage. 'Hommage à Lamartine, Alphonse Daudet et Émile Zola', **Cahiers Ivan Tourueniev, Pauline Viardot, Maria Malibran*, n. 14, 184 pp., includes a dossier on L.'s Russian interests. **Mémoires de jeunesse, 1790–1815*, ed. Marie-Renée Morain, Tallandier, 290 pp., were published after his death.

NERVAL. Jean Senelier, *Bibliographie nervalienne 1981–1989*, Nizet, 108 pp. J. Bony, 'Nerval et le récit: une recherche des formes', *IL*, 1:15–17 (a summary of his 1989 thesis, shortly to be published by Corti), shows N.'s search for a narrative mode adapted to his personality finds fulfilment in autobiography. L. R. Schehr, 'Le Faust de Nerval: poésie et vérité', *RR*, 82:146–63, maintains this is the text which best illustrates the Nervalian theory of literature whilst revealing the unconscious psychological and linguistic constraints N. imposed on himself in his writings. M. Brix, 'Nerval et la "Léonore de Bürger"', *LR*, 45:183–94, explains that N. made eight versions of this translation because the text illustrated an obsession of his related to his childhood: the impossibility of finding happiness in marriage. Id., 'Les Illuminés de Nerval, ou le livre "parfaitement sensé sur les folies"', *SFr*, 102:464–71, shows N. achieves a subtle balance between biography and history. D. M. Betz, 'Nerval's *Voyage en Orient* and Baudelaire's imagined orient', *RoQ*, 38:399–406, asserts B.'s borrowing of a fragment of N.'s narrative (as a basis for his *Un Voyage à Cythère*) proves close affinities in their imaginary vision of exoticism.

NODIER.   M. Malibran, 'Model for Nodier's *Inès de las Sierras*, Eric Frederick Jensen', *NCFS*, 19:381–85, explores influences on Nodier. J. C. Kessler, 'Charles Nodier's demons: vampirism as metaphor in *Smarra*', *FrF*, 16:51–66, argues that N.'s vampirism was the emblem of an irrevocable fall from innocence: a burden of repressed anxiety and guilt which reached back into his adolescence and early manhood.

SAND.   *Agendas*, vol. 2, ed. Anne Chevereau, Touzot, 521 pp. *Correspondance*, ii: *avril 1852 — juin 1853*, ed. Georges Lubin, Garnier, 896 pp. S. and Champfleury, *Du réalisme*, ed. Luce Abélès, Cendres, 104 pp., S.'s letters are taken from the complete edition. S. Beyer and F. Kluck, 'George Sand and Gertrudis Gómez de Avellaneo', *NCFS*, 19:203–09, discusses the influence of *Indiana* on *Sab*'s representation of unrequited love; both novels emphasized the repressive nature of a European-male dominated society. R. B. Grant, 'George Sand's *Lélia* and the tragedy of dualism', *ib.*, 499–516, shows how the dualistic view of existence, which split 'higher' spiritual values off from the 'baser' material ones, is attacked in *Lélia*, a year after *Indiana*, in which dualism plays a key role. M. Reid, 'Flaubert et Sand en correspondance', *Poétique*, no. 85:53–68, argues that the 400 letters represent more a juxtaposition than a real 'correspondence', for the two writers are diametrically opposed. F. van Rossum-Guyon, 'La correspondance comme laboratoire de l'écriture: George Sand (1831–1832)', *RSH*, 221:87–104, explores how, by revealing her true self (and not the best side of it, as found in *Histoire de ma vie*), Aurore gets to know her personality in depth, assumes the name of Sand and, in this first transformation of real life into writing, finds her personal style. G. Seybert, 'L'écriture de l'enfermement chez D. A. F. de Sade et George Sand', *ib.*, 224:161–69, shows how the *Journal intime* makes a parallel between Sade's real imprisonment and the social one of the traditional role of women victims of love. G. Van Slyke, 'History in her story: historical referents in Sand's *La Petite Fadette*', *RR*, 82:49–69, explores the significance of the discontinuity between the preface and the tale. Jean Chalon, *Chère George Sand*, Flammarion, 478 pp., is a sentimental approach based upon Lubin's *Correspondance*. J. Golstein, *'The use of male hysteria: medical and literary discourse in nineteenth-century France', *Representations*, 34:134–65. G. Seybert and G. Stuhlmann, *'A life in one's own: the female image in the work of George Sand's *Anaïs*', *An International Journal*, 9:104–16. Michael Danaly, *The Feminization of the Novel*, University of Florida, 240 pp. *George Sand: une œuvre multiforme*, ed. Françoise van Rossum-Guyon, CRIN, 24.

VIGNY. L. M. Findlay, 'Reconstruing faith: Strauss, Vigny, and the Emperor Julian', *CL*, 43:246–59, observes that the effect of contact with Julian is to undermine the religious faith of S., whereas V. sees Julian as the precursor of his own Christianity.

5. DRAMA

L. Krugel, 'Attending (to) the national spectacle: instituting national (popular) theater in England and France', *Macropolitics of Nineteenth Century Literature. Nationalism, Exoticism, Imperialism*, ed. Jonathan Arac and Harriet Ritvo, Pennsylvania U.P., 311 pp., 243–67, argues that the popular theatre seems unable to escape the patronizing rhetoric of general edification.

HUGO. Frederick Burwick, *Illusion and the Drama. Critical Theory on the Enlightenment and Romantic Era*, Penn State Press, 326 pp., shows that H.'s characters do not merely play upon a decorative stage, they interact with the setting, which plays a role, as the place is a witness to the event and must reflect emotional atmosphere and personality. B. T. Cooper, 'Parodying Hugo', *ERR*:23–38, completes recent documents by revealing how audiences responded to *Hernani*; the author presents examples of parodies of H. in Boulevard theatre, in which comedy is used to object to H.'s violations of the neoclassicist conventions. E. F. Jasenas, 'La cohérence d'un texte: *William Shakespeare* de Victor Hugo', *NCFS*, 20:85–96, argues that the diversity within unity of this text adds to our knowledge of H.'s poetics.

MUSSET. *Textuel*, Paris 7, no. 8, ed. J.-L. Diaz, a special issue on *Lorenzaccio*, includes: A. Prassoloff, 'L'*Apologie* de Lorenzo de Médicis, ou Musset avec Machiavel' (9–23) (gives an Italian historical source with its translation); B. Masson, '*Lorenzaccio* manuscrit' (25–29) (discusses the atypical structure of the second act); A. Ubersfeld, 'Musset, l'art et l'artiste' (31–37) (compares the attitude of the intellectual towards freedom, money and power in France in 1830, with that of the Italian Renaissance); P. Laforgue, 'Œdipe à Florence' (39–55) (uses an Oedipal reading to argue against the same parallel); B. Diaz, 'Noces de sang' (57–79) (explores the erotic, existentialist, and symbolic dimensions of weddings); A. Ubersfeld, 'Mémoire de Lorenzo' (81–84) (on the fourth act); J.-L. Diaz, 'Le rêve du plongeur' (85–111) (analyses the recurrent theme of suffocation);

Y. Gohin, 'Le vin de la métaphore' (113–32) (sees metaphors as masks for unconscious desires); C. Duchet, 'Une dramaturgie de la parole' (133–43) (investigates the opposition between (i) words and (ii) action and silence); C. Derouin and N. Thevenin, '*Lorenzaccio*, ou les enfants de l'enfer' (145–49) (in defence of Huster's production); G. Rosa, 'Sur une représentation de *Lorenzaccio* de part et d'autre du mur' (151–53) (notices the difference in the actors' tone in Lavaudant's production); L. de Maynard, '*Un spectacle dans un fauteuil*, par M. Alf. de Musset (*Revue de Paris*, septembre 1834)' (161–74); H. Fortoul, '*Un spectacle dans un fauteuil*, par M. Alfred de Musset (*Revue des Deux Mondes*, septembre 1834)' (175–85). *Lorenzaccio, On ne badine pas avec l'amour*, ed. Jeanne Bem *et al.*, SEDES, 1990, 209 pp., emphasizes the union of the comic and the tragic in these two plays and comprises: B. T. Cooper, 'Congruences mussétistes' (3–24) (argues that Lorenzo and Camille are the two faces of the same opposition to tyranny, but that circumscribed revolts such as these are doomed to fail); L. Chotard, 'Le théâtre à l'essai' (25–42) (explains why M. was silent on drama theory and preferred to expose his views in critical texts from 1831 to 1839: he was torn between the nostalgia for classical rules and the temptation to transgress them); J. Bem, '*On ne badine pas avec l'amour*, ou le jeu du théâtre' (43–46) (discusses the opacity of the play); P. Berthier, 'Burlesque et tragique dans *On ne badine pas avec l'amour*' (57–71) (examines the quantity and the quality of the dosage of tragic and comedy); P. J. Siegel, '*On ne badine pas avec l'amour*, à vol d'oisieau' (73–95) (the history of critical texts on the play); B. Masson, 'Dramaturgie de la parole sociale dans *Lorenzaccio*' (97–112) (on the power of dialogue in the play); F. Court-Perez, 'La langage dans *Lorenzaccio*' (113–34) (notices that words are valueless and opposed to action, except in the case of Lorenzo and the Marquise); J.-M. Thomasseau, 'Le rapin démasqué et l'artiste en assassin' (135–54) (argues that the painter in *Lorenzaccio* stands for all the other arts, leading Romanticism towards Baudelaire and Rimbaud); S. Jeune, 'Le monologue dans *Lorenzaccio*' (155–75) (sees in the many monologues a confession of M. himself); M.-J. Whitaker, 'Lorenzaccio ou la force de la faiblesse' (177–208) (opposes Masson's Marxist, existentialist and psychoanalytic interpretations). 'Sur *Gamiani*', *RHLF*, n.6: 936–49, contains S. Jeune's and J.-P. Corsetti's answers to Gaujon (*RHLF* 1990: 217–26) on M.'s authorship of the play. G. Dessons, 'La parole du siècle dans les *Proverbes* de Musset', *TLit*, 4: 197–207, argues that M.'s attitude as a writer is political since his dialogues originate not in his characters but in society. A. Smith, 'Musset's *Les Caprices de Marianne*: a Romantic adaptation of a traditional comic structure', *NCFS*, 20: 53–64, shows that M.'s characters' failure to change from egotism to love leads to tragedy.

NODIER.   **Œuvres dramatiques*, II: *Bertram ou le Pirate; Le Monstre et le Magicien; Pantomimes et fragments*, ed. G. Picat-Guinoiseau, 296 pp.

6.   Writers in Other Genres

LACENAIRE.   **Mémoires et autres écrits*, ed. Jacques Simonelli, Corti, 3906 pp., includes archive material and testimonials.

LEROUX.   J. Viard, 'Pierre Leroux contre les Utopistes', *NCFS*, 19:541–53, reveals that L. fought 'absolute socialism' and that the fear he inspired in his enemies was the cause of the disappearance of his works.

MICHELET.   C. Colatrella, 'Representing liberty revolution, sexuality, and science in Michelet's histories and Zola's fiction', *ib.*, 20:27–43, tries to solve the apparent paradox that both writers reviled woman for the seductive nature of her sexuality, yet admired her for her political power.

NAPOLÉON.   B. Hemmerdinger, 'Homère vu par Napoléon et Victor Bérard', *Belfagor*, 77–78, investigates the similarities of views between the two men on the importance of Homer as military judge.

RABBE.   '*Album d'un pessimiste*' suivi de '*Portefeuille d'un pessimiste*', ed. Edouard Roditi and Jacques-Remi Dahan, Corti, 368 pp.

TALLEYRAND.   Georges Lacour-Gayet, *Talleyrand, Payot, 1488 pp.

TOCQUEVILLE.   *Œuvres complètes, t. VI (*Correspondance et conversations d'Alexis de Toqueville et Nassau William Senior*), H. Brogan and A. P. Kerr, trans. B. M. Wicks-Boisson, Gallimard, 544 pp. Contains all the letters and the notes Senior took of conversations with T. after 1848.

THE NINETEENTH CENTURY
(POST-ROMANTIC)

By JANINE DAKYNS, *Lecturer in French, University of East Anglia*

1. GENERAL

James Smith Allen, *In the Public Eye: A History of Reading in Modern France, 1800–1940*, Princeton U.P., xv + 356 pp., a valuable interdisciplinary study, offers fresh information, based on MS sources, on the relationship between authors and their readers, classified according to age and occupation. It includes substantial sections on the reception of *Madame Bovary*, *L'Assommoir*, France's *Le Lys rouge*, and Augier's *Le Fils de Giboyer*, as well as an analysis of images of readers in works by contemporary painters. Emelina, *Comique*, includes discussion of Baudelaire, Flaubert, Daudet, Heredia, Laforgue, Verlaine, Rimbaud, and Labiche. Christophe Prochasson, *Les Années électriques (1880–1910)*, La Découverte, 490 pp., offers a social and cultural history of Paris, with emphasis on distinct but interlinked *territoires* and very substantial and useful chronological tables. Yvan Leclerc, *Crimes écrits: la littérature en procès au dix-neuvième siècle*, Plon, 447 pp., is an important study of literary trials including those of Baudelaire and Flaubert. Patrick Wald Lasowski, *Les Échafauds du romanesque*, Lille U.P., 108 pp., examines the theme of the guillotine in 19th-c. French literature. Harry Redman, Jr, *The Roland Legend in Nineteenth-Century French Literature*, Lexington, Kentucky U.P., xii + 247 pp., furnishes an encyclopaedically authoritative account of treatments of this legend by major and minor authors. Special attention is drawn to the (unjustly, it is stated) forgotten poet and Protestant minister, Napoléon Peyrat. Catherine Millot, *La Vocation de l'écrivain*, Gallimard, 223 pp., subjects Flaubert and Mallarmé to Lacanian analysis. *Petit Bottin des lettres et des arts (1886)*, ed. René-Pierre Colin, Tusson, Du Lérot, 1990, 183 pp., reprints satirical pen-portraits of writers including Verlaine, Huysmans, and Zola. André Suarès, *Âmes et visages*, 11: *Portraits et préférences: de Benjamin Constant à Arthur Rimbaud*, ed. Michel Drouin, Gallimard, 360 pp., reprints subjective encounters between S.'s sensibility and a range of writers including Baudelaire, Flaubert, Taine, Huysmans, and Zola, with an essay on Rimbaud left unpublished for fear of offending Claudel. Jeanne Bem, *Le Texte traversé*, Champion, 211 pp., collects essays on Baudelaire, Flaubert, Verlaine, and Laforgue. Claude Mouchard, *Un grand désert d'hommes (1851–1885). Les équivoques de la modernité*, Hatier, 341 pp., offers personal re-readings of a range of writers. Chai, *Aestheticism*, an undemanding comparatist survey, includes a reading of Baudelaire's

Harmonie du soir as affirmation of 'the aesthetic nature of consciousness', appreciates the aestheticism of Renan, Huysmans, and Verlaine, but depreciates Leconte de Lisle's work (with the exception of
Midi). Marie-Christine Natta, **La Grandeur sans convictions: essai sur le
dandysme*, Félin, 232 pp. Henriette Levillain, **L'Esprit dandy, de
Brummell à Baudelaire: anthologie*, Corti, 269 pp. P. Laude, 'Dandysme
et mysticisme: de la subversion et de la conformité', *Symposium*,
45:356–69, explores parallels between 17th-c. quietism and the
aesthetic of dandyism elaborated by Baudelaire and Barbey
d'Aurevilly. Chris Bongie, **Exotic Memories: Literature, Colonialism and
the Fin de Siècle*, Stanford U.P., 262 pp., includes sections on Loti and
Verne. A special no. of *Europe* devoted to the *fin de siècle*, 69,
nos 751–52, incl.: H. Béhar, 'Les mots et les maux de la tribu' (38–47)
(using database to retrieve occurrences of terms such as *à rebours,
décadence, névrose,* and *fin de siècle* itself from a large corpus of literary
texts of the period); M. Clément, 'Un ésotérisme proliférant?' (69–75)
(exploring roots of *fin de siècle* esoterism and occultism); C. Dupuit,
'Presse et littérature à la fin du siècle' (111–21) (on conflict between
journalists and avant-garde writers), G. Peylet, 'Le mythe de Satan:
du romantisme au décadentisme', *La Licorne*, 18, 1990:123–36, sees
post-Romantic treatment of this myth as a process of impov-
erishment. C. Zissmann, 'Du Parnasse à la décadence: la lignée de
Baudelaire', Watson, *Patterns*, 178–86, links an ironic subtext discerned in B.'s *La Beauté* with texts by Banville, Mallarmé, Villiers de
l'Isle-Adam, Verlaine, and Rimbaud. R. Lloyd, 'Mirroring difference, figuring frames', *NCFS*, 19:343–53, discusses 'male fear of
female difference and female identity' in Banville, Flaubert, Fromentin, Mallarmé, and Zola. J. Matlock, 'Doubling out of the crazy
house: gender, autobiography, and the insane asylum system in
nineteenth-century France', *Representations*, 34:167–95, documents
the fate of Hersilie Rouy, author of *Mémoires d'une aliénée* (1883), a text
that raises questions about 'gender-based social control' in this
period. E. Apter, 'Splitting hairs: female fetishism and postpartum
sentimentality in the fin de siècle', Hunt, *Eroticism*, 164–90, focuses on
female mourning rituals and hair fetishism in Flaubert, Baudelaire,
Maupassant, Maeterlinck, and Rodenbach. A revised version of this
article forms a section of Apter, *Fetish*. *Romantisme*, 71, a special no. on
art criticism as literary genre, includes: D. Gamboni, 'Propositions
pour l'étude de la critique d'art du XIXe siècle' (9–17) (drawing
attention to increasing professionalism during second half of the
century); E. Schuck, 'La critique et la section d'architecture dans les
Salons de la seconde moitié du XIXe siècle' (49–56) (examining
reasons why contemporary critics and journalists neglected this
section); J. Newton, 'Whistler et ses critiques' (57–67) (documenting

W.'s hostile English reception in contrast with appreciation(and support from French critics including Mirbeau and Zola); J.-P. Leduc-Adine, 'Des règles d'un genre: la critique d'art' (93–100) (suggesting a typology of Salon criticism). J. Lalouette, 'Une rencontre oubliée: la libre pensée française et les savants matérialistes allemands (1863-1870)', *ib.*, 73:57–67, offers valuable information on French atheist and materialist thinkers under the Second Empire and their contacts with German counterparts.

2. Prose (Non-Fictional)

ALLAIS. J.-M. Defays, 'Mystification et démystification chez Alphonse Allais', *FS*, 45:279–94, treats this 'maître ès mystifications', currently enjoying a revival, as 'un écrivain à part entière', 'virtuose du texte court', whose work is 'une sorte de carrefour intertextuel', a parodic mirror of the impostures and illusions of the *fin du siècle*.

GOURMONT. *Chez les Lapons*, ed. Christian Mériot, Castor astral, 1990, 144 pp., is a facsimile of the 1890 edition, with a preface which discusses the mixture of exactitude and inexactitude in G.'s ethnographical exoticism.

LAPRADE. C. Crossley, 'Victor de Laprade as a cultural critic', Watson, *Patterns*, 17–31, maps the 'moral high ground' occupied by L., and ventures to compare him with Matthew Arnold.

MAUCLAIR. J. Newton, 'Camille Mauclair and Auguste Rodin', *NFS*, 30.1:39–55, surveys M.'s interpretative career, and retraces his relations with R., whose work 'offered the touchstone which proves his lasting validity as a critic'.

RENAN. Francis Mercury, **Renan*. Orban, 411 pp. H. Pfeiffer, *'Die Gegenwart der Spätantike, Christentum und Antike in Ernest Renans *Histoire des origines du christianisme*', *Poetica*, 22, 1990:323–54.

TAINE. **L'Ancien Régime*, ed. Daniel Dessert, Brussels, Complexe, xxvi + 320 pp. J.-T. Nordmann, 'Taine et Balzac', *ABa*, 12:363–81, identifies T.'s series of articles on Balzac published in 1858 as the first serious critical study of the *Comédie humaine*, and detects 'une irradiation balzacienne' throughout T.'s subsequent work.

3. Poetry

Robert Brécy, **La Chanson de la Commune: chansons et poèmes inspirés par la Commune de 1871*, Éds Ouvrières, 315 pp., is an album including texts and illustrations in facsimile. Quinones, *Cain*, includes pages on Baudelaire's and Leconte de Lisle's treatment of the theme of Cain. Marc Eigeldinger, *Le Soleil de la poésie: Gautier, Baudelaire, Rimbaud*, Neuchâtel, La Baconnière, 236 pp., collects in revised version articles already published, with a new chapter on Germain Nouveau. Bachelardian perspectives are applied to solar imagery in the work of each poet. Svetlana Boym, *Death in Quotation Marks: Cultural Myths of the Modern Poet*, Harvard U.P., 291 pp., explores modern cultural mythologies of the life and death of poets, including Mallarmé and Rimbaud. Michel Pierssens, *Savoirs à l'œuvre: essais d'épistémocritique*, Lille U.P., 187 pp., includes sections on Mallarmé and Lautréamont. Two important contributions to our understanding of the relationship between Parnassian poetry and the visual arts are made by J. Dalençon, 'Les croquis poétiques', *BEPar*, 1990, no. 5:3–45, who compares technical devices such as use of the frame in poetic and visual *croquis*, defended as stimulatingly modernist, rather than minor art; and D. Scott, 'La structure picturale du sonnet parnassien et symboliste: Heredia et Baudelaire', *ib.*, 55–67. Id., 'Pictorialist poetics: aspects of Parnassian prosodic theory and practice from Sainte-Beuve to Banville', Watson, *Patterns*, 85–99, points out how certain features of Sainte-Beuve's poetry anticipate Banville's theory and practice; P. J. Salazar, 'Le deuil de la voix: Baudelaire et le Parnasse', *ib.*, 3–16, assesses B.'s contribution to Parnassian ideology; G. Robb, 'Journalism and Parnassus', *ib.*, 171–77, explores interrelations between journalistic language and poetic inspiration in Baudelaire, Banville, and Mallarmé; M. Maclean, '"Such stuff as dreams are made on": the dream-work in Parnassian and anti-Parnassian poetry', *ib.*, 259–73, converts Rimbaud's *A une raison* into a semiotic rhizome; M. Pakenham, '*Sonnets et eaux-fortes*', *ib.*, 274–88, sheds new light on this anthology. P. Laude, 'Le poète à sa fenêtre: dualisme et errance métaphysique dans la poésie française du dix-neuvième siècle', *NCFS*, 19:354–68, views the window symbol in the poetry of Sainte-Beuve, Baudelaire, Mallarmé, and Rodenbach as an expression of 'la dualité chronique de la conscience occidentale'. J. Dalençon, 'Le parc nostalgique de la fête galante: Watteau et les poètes', *BEPar*, 1990, no. 6:21–74, discusses the cult of W. as practised by Verlaine and other post-Romantic poets. M. Giammarco, 'Dall'immaginario decadente alla poesia del crepuscolo: le metamorfosi del simbolismo', *Berenice*, 13:383–402, draws on texts by Belgian Symbolists. P. Baquiast, 'Un mystérieux cercle littéraire: le groupisme', *Littératures*, 24:181–83, publishes material shedding light on this group, all mention of which is confined to the year 1868.

BANVILLE. *La Mer à Nice. Lettres à un ami*, ed. François Brunet, Raphèle-les-Arles, Marcel Petit, 1990, 167 pp., reprints a travel narrative which illuminates aspects of B.'s aesthetic. 'Théodore de Banville: lettres inédites concernant son activité de journaliste', ed. Id., *BEPar*, 1990, no. 6:3–19, span the years 1854–87. E. Souffrin-Le Breton, 'Banville et l'image du laurier', Watson, *Patterns*, 32–57, is guided by this image towards a rewarding exploration of B.'s work; P. J. Edwards, 'La poétique du lieu commun: Théodore de Banville et la modernité', *ib.*, 58–70, focuses on the poetic renewal achieved by B. in *Odes funambulesques*; P. Andrès, 'Les frontispices de G. Rochegrosse et le texte de Théodore de Banville', *ib.*, 100–05; F. Brunet, 'Banville et la forêt fantastique de Rodolphe Bresdin', *ib.*, 120–35, moves from discussion of B.'s description of a lithograph by Bresdin to consideration of the forest as favourite theme in his poetry.

BAUDELAIRE. *Les Fleurs du mal*, ed. Jacques Dupont, Garnier-Flammarion, 373 pp., has digested into a remarkably comprehensive (and stimulating) preface, accompanied by over a hundred footnotes, complemented by notes and variants to individual poems, virtually all the important achievements of B. scholarship up to the late 1980s, including work published in English, for instance that of F. W. Leakey; extremely good value. 'Son activité lors de la révolution de 1848 importe peu à l'intelligence des *Fleurs*', states the editor, a view challenged by Richard D. E. Burton, *Baudelaire and the Second Republic*, Oxford, Clarendon, xv + 380 pp., who argues that B.'s commitment to radical republicanism survived beyond 1851. This thesis inspires provocative new readings of many poems as political allegory, against elaborately reconstructed contextual background. A *pavé dans la mare* of B. studies to which one awaits reaction with interest. Charles Asselineau, *Charles Baudelaire: sa vie et son œuvre, suivi de Baudelairiana*, Le temps qu'il fait, 1990, 135 pp. Henri Lecaye, *Le Secret de Baudelaire, suivi de Baudelaire et la modernité et de Baudelaire et Manet*, Place, 151 pp. Thomas Keck, *Der deutsche 'Baudelaire'*. I. *Studien zur übersetzerischen Rezeption der 'Fleurs du mal'*. II. *Materialien* (BNL, 111–12) Heidelberg, Winter, 244 + 210 pp., is an *outil de travail* of major importance, offering an impeccably documented history, encyclopaedic in scope, of the critical reception and translation of B. in Germany. It reprints the text (with detailed critical commentary) of each successive translation of a selection of poems, including *L'Albatros*, all four *Spleen* poems, and *Le Balcon*. Markus Preussner, *Poe und Baudelaire: ein Vergleich*, Bern, Lang, 232 pp. D. M. Betz, 'Nerval's *Voyage en Orient* and Baudelaire's imagined Orient', *RoQ*, 38:399–406, is a well crafted article which draws interesting parallels and contrasts. G. Robb, 'The poetics of the commonplace in *Les Fleurs du mal*', *MLR*, 86:57–65, offers a brilliantly illuminating account, rich in example, of ways in which B. revitalizes commonplaces dulled by usage, 'rendering the familiar strange and the strangeness of the altered image curiously familiar'. J. P. Houston, 'The two versions of *Les Fleurs du mal* and ideas of form', Fenoaltea, *Ladder*, 110–37, discusses B.'s work in relation to romantic literary theory based on the notion of organic form. T. A. Unwin, 'The "pseudo-narrative" of

Les Fleurs du mal', *OL*, 46:321–39, is concerned to show how each poem re-echoes, reflects, or anticipates other poems. P. Laude, 'Morsure et remords chez Baudelaire', *Neophilologus*, 75:346–57, argues that this constellation, in conjunction with 'mort', is the thematic centre of *Les Fleurs du mal*. J.-C. Le Boulay, '*Le Beau Navire*: composition et symboles', *Littératures*, 24:65–69, offers a commentary centred on the fifth and sixth stanzas. P. W. M. Cogman, 'The potential sonnet in Baudelaire', *FSB*, 37:10–13, contends that the creative imbalance between octave and sestet in the sonnet is preserved by B. in the structure of certain poems other than sonnets, which gain from being read in terms of two complementary parts. R. Killick, *ib.*, 40:13–15, seeks to enlarge this perspective with the suggestion that all the poems of *Les Fleurs du mal* bear the formal imprint of a dualistic cast of mind. R. D. E. Burton, 'The dead father: a note on *Le Cygne* and the *Iliad*', *ib.*, 38:7–9, points out that the body of B.'s father, like that of Hector, was denied a permanent, marked resting-place, and links this fact with the open-endedness of *Le Cygne*. G. Gasarian, 'La figure du poète hystérique ou l'allégorie chez Baudelaire', *Poétique*, 86:177–91, engages in a debate with Paul de Man and Ross Chambers on B.'s allegorical vision in *Le Cygne*. M. Levy-Bloch, 'Le mouvement de l'imagination baudelairienne: *Le Jet d'eau*', *DFS*, 16, 1989 (1991):37–63, maintains that this poem epitomizes B.'s distinctive imaginative dynamism. N. A. Haxell, '*Le Serpent qui danse*: woman as dancer in the works of Baudelaire, Mallarmé and Colette', *RoS*, 19:117–24, seeks to rescue B.'s snake-dancer and Mallarmé's evocation of Loïe Fuller from exploitative male-centred readings. B. Johnson, 'Gender and poetry: Charles Baudelaire and Marceline Desbordes-Valmore', De Jean, *Displacements*, 163–81, offers a feminist reading of B.'s article on D.-V., with a side-glance at 'the poetics of masochism' in *Le Vampire*. *The Prose Poems and 'La Fanfarlo'*, ed. and trans. Rosemary Lloyd, OUP (World's Classics), has an incisive introduction and helpful notes. R. Chambers, 'Irony and misogyny: authority and the homosocial in Baudelaire and Flaubert', *AJFS*, 26, 1989 [1992]:272–88, claims that B.'s and F.'s irony, in *La Fanfarlo* and *Un Cœur simple*, rests on a foundation of misogyny, directed towards 'the ideological production of motherliness as self-sacrifice'. S. Rubenstein, 'The figuration of genre: Baudelaire's prose poem *L'Horloge*', *RR*, 82:331–45, claims that 'vulgar sexual punning' is one of the devices that 'makes *L'Horloge* tick'. J. A. Hiddleston, 'Chacun son *Spleen*: some observations on Baudelaire's prose poems', *MLR*, 86:66–69, takes issue with A. Raitt's reading (see *YWMLS*, 52:193) in a bid to prove that the order of these poems is purely random. F.-C. Gaudard, 'De l'étude du style dans un texte littéraire: exercices', *ChS*, 1:67–83, offers schematic and somewhat hollow readings of *L'Étranger* and *Le Gâteau*. Y. Makino, 'Lafcadio Hearn's *Yuki-Onna* and Baudelaire's *Les Bienfaits de la lune*', *CLS*, 28:234–44, examines Hearn's debt to Baudelaire. M. Starke, *'Baudelaire Kritik der Freiheits- und Ordnungsparteien', *BRP*, 29:71–88. The 'psittacine debate', as one of the participants calls it, rages on unacrimoniously in *FSB* (for its inception, see *YWMLS*, 52:194). E. Souffrin-Le Breton (39:20–22), in an impressively well documented and ingenious contribution, drawing Ovid and Banville into the arena, would seem to have said the last word; but M. Pakenham and S. Vince (40:15–16; 16–17) point in the direction of further horizons, chromatic, artistic, linguistic, and (once more) ornithological. *Bull. baudelairien*, 26.1, is a bibliographical no., ed. J. S. Patty and R. R. Daniel, covering the years 1989 and 1990 with a supp. for 1988.

CORBIÈRE. J.-F. Ploquin, 'Étude sur *Les Amours jaunes* de Tristan Corbière: la poétique, la métrique, le chant', *BEPar*, 1990, no. 5:69–96, offers a careful study of metre, rhyme, and stanzaic form in C.'s work.

CROS. M. Pakenham, 'A propos de Charles Cros', *Littératures*, 24:185–90, adds further information to J.-L. Debauve's recent findings (see *YWMLS*, 52:194).

GIRAUD. R. Sorensen, 'Albert Giraud's *Pierrot lunaire*: a *mise en scène* of the Parnassian versus Symbolist polemic within the Jeunes Belgique', Watson, *Patterns*, 249–58, sees in this cycle of 50 rondels 'the challenge of the Parnassian Symbolist to the Decadent Symbolist'.

GLATIGNY. P. S. Hambly, 'Une œuvre "perdue" d'Albert Glatigny: *Les Angoisses d'un village*', *Littératures*, 25:187–203, retrieves and reprints, from the newspaper in which they were published in 1872, sketches of life in rural Normandy at the time of the Prussian invasion.

HEREDIA. S. Delaty, 'Gustave Moreau et José-Maria de Heredia: affinités esthétiques', Watson, *Patterns*, 136–52, draws on an unpublished correspondence between M. and H., spanning 25 years, and revealing shared preoccupations and mutual appreciation.

LAFORGUE. Two stimulating articles on L.'s poetic technique: J.-P. Bertrand, 'Enjeux et figurations de la coupe chez Laforgue', *EF*, 27.1:63–73 (bringing into crisp focus the 'dépeçage multidiscursif' of L.'s verse); J. McCann, 'Jules Laforgue: constructing the text', *OL*, 46:276–93 (on the revitalizing effect of L.'s 'atomization' of language). M. P. Caty, 'Poétique du spleen dans l'œuvre de Jules Laforgue', *FR*, 65:55–63, takes a tour round familiar territory. C. Giardina, 'Les renouvellements des clichés de langue dans *Les Moralités légendaires* de Jules Laforgue', *IL*, 43.4:7–13, offers a systematic study of L.'s playful subversion of cliché. E. F. Wilson,

'Fantasies of the other: the virgin as signifier in Jules Laforgue's *Derniers vers*', *NCo*, 9, 1990:139–48, views the female virgin in L.'s work as 'a confected projection who is an alter ego', 'a textual rather than sexual phenomenon'. A. Holmes, 'An Englishman's impression of Jules Laforgue at the German court', *FSB*, 39:17–18, prints a perceptive portrait of L. from an unpublished letter of the Wagnerian Houston Stewart Chamberlain.

LAUTRÉAMONT. *Les Chants de Maldoror. Poésies. Lettres*, ed. Louis Forestier, Imprimerie Nationale, 1990, 433 pp., has a substantial and stimulating preface and the unbecoming illustrations characteristic of these editions. G. Austin, '"Saisissant le conte": Lautréamont seizes upon Soulié's *Le Maître d'école*', *FSB*, 39:14–17, discovers an intriguing intertextual connection between a strophe of *Les Chants de Maldoror* and a *roman-feuilleton* published in 1841.

LECONTE DE LISLE. E. Pich, 'Leconte de Lisle et la musique', Watson, *Patterns*, 153–60, adopts a rewarding approach which sets L. de L.'s poetic evolution in a new perspective.

LOUŸS. *Les Chansons de Bilitis. Pervigilium Mortis, avec divers textes inédits*, ed. Jean-Paul Goujon, Gallimard, 1990, 343 pp., has a preface defending *Les Chansons de Bilitis* as creatively coherent literary achievement rather than mystificatory pastiche.

MALLARMÉ. *Villiers de l'Isle-Adam*, ed. Alan Raitt, Exeter U.P., xxxvii + 48 pp., makes available for the first time an impeccable critical edition (with a full account of variants) of this text, presented as M.'s most important aesthetic statement. Stefano Agosti, *Il Fauno di Mallarmé*, Milan, Feltrinelli, 189 pp., offers a word-by-word commentary. Robert Greer Cohn, *Vues sur Mallarmé*, trans. L. Holt and R. Coward, Nizet, pp. 324, reprints articles and reviews. Id., *Mallarmé's 'Divagations': A Guide and Commentary* (AUS, 144), Bern—NY, Lang, 1990, x + 411 pp. *Mallarmé's Text Database. 'Divagations'*. I. *Text*. II. *Word Index*., ed. Saburo Matsumuro, Nobuo Takeuchi, and Masakatsu Kaneko, 2 vols, Tokyo, Taga Shuppan, 377, iv + 644 pp. L. J. Austin, 'La correspondance de Stéphane Mallarmé: compléments et suppléments, IV', *FS*, 45:166–94, presents new gleanings since May 1988, among which are 14 unpublished letters including a finely tuned one to H. Fantin-Latour. Id., 'Verlaine et Mallarmé', *CAIEF*, 43:333–51, offers a rewarding *mise au point* of their personal and literary relationship. J.-L. Cornille, 'L'Épître châtiée', *RR*, 82:164–78, discerns complex epistolary subtexts in the two versions of this sonnet. D. Delacroix, 'Poe tel qu'en Mallarmé', *RLC*, 65:33–43, decodes intertextual allusions in *Le Tombeau d'Edgar Poe*. A. Viguier, 'Lexicologie et poétique: *Alchimie du Verbe*', *ChS*, 1:23–49, offers worthwhile readings of M.'s *Cantique de Saint Jean* and Rimbaud's *Voyelles* in the light of André Martinet's linguistic theory of connotation. S. Daniel, '*Hérodiade* [*sic*]: the bound book', Fenoaltea, *Ladder*, 138–49, applies modern theories of reading to the interpretation of this text that 'folds back upon itself in a series of *plis* and *replis*'. J. Mehlman, 'Mallarmé and "seduction theory"', *Paragraph*, 14:95–111, attempts to demonstrate that this theory is pertinent to a discussion of M.'s work. P. S. Hambly, 'Mallarmé et le Parnasse: lecture de *Toast funèbre*', Watson, *Patterns*, 207–34, pursues his quest for Banvillian echoes in Mallarmé. R. Killick, 'Les noms propres ou "the name of the game" chez les Parnassiens et chez Mallarmé', *ib.*, 235–48, compares these poets' exploitation of proper names with reference to Barthes's analysis of their functions. S. Saachi, '"Imiter le Chinois au cœur limpide et fin ..." La Chine en France aux environs de 1860', *ib.*, 161–70, discusses the myth of China, fashionable in the 1860s, as a source of inspiration for Mallarmé. G. Davies, 'Narrative thread in Mallarmé's *Igitur* drafts', *RLMC*, 44:45–58, uses his own transcription of M.'s MSS to trace the narrative development of this text. N. M. Huckle, 'Mallarmé and the strategy of transformation in *Igitur*', *NCFS*, 19:290–303, draws on alchemical processes and Sartre's philosophy. D. Reynolds, 'Mallarmé and Hegel: speculation and the poetics of reflection', *FrCS*, 2:71–89, fruitfully explores similarities and differences between the aesthetics of M. and Hegel. J.-F. Fourny, 'La passion de Stéphane Mallarmé', *FrF*, 16:317–28, offers a lively analysis of Sartre's posthumously published essay on M.

MIKHAËL. Y.-A. Favre, 'Éphraïm Mikhaël et le thème de l'automne en 1886', *Littératures*, 24:71–81, compares M.'s treatment of this theme with that of contemporary Symbolist poets.

RÉGNIER. R. A. Cardwell, 'Symbolist dream and difference: Henri de Régnier's *Allégorie*', *RoS*, 18:7–19, offers a Lacanian reading of this poem.

RIMBAUD. Celebration of R.'s life and work by *rimbaldiens* and *rimbaldolâtres* worldwide in the centennial year of his death has boosted productivity in a field never fallow even in an ordinary year. Pre-eminent publications are a superbly well documented and narrated new biography by Jean-Luc Steinmetz, *Arthur Rimbaud*, Tallandier, 491 pp., and Alain Borer, *Arthur Rimbaud: œuvre-vie: édition du centenaire*, Arléa, lxxxv + 1338 pp., a collective enterprise drawing on the labours of 'une pléiade de connaisseurs', which presents every word written by R. in a monumental chronological edition. Lost poems and letters are inserted in their due place, together with a facsimile of *Une Saison en enfer* including all its *pages blanches*. The aim is to give the reader 'tout Rimbaud, rien que Rimbaud, pour la première fois', disengaging his true face and voice from the parasitical *remplissage* of previous editions (notably the Pléiade), while

eliminating from his texts 'les bogues de Paterne Berrichon'. Id.,
Rimbaud d'Arabie: supplément au voyage, Seuil, 88 pp., complements
Rimbaud en Abyssinie (see *YWMLS*, 46:199–200) with a sequence of
biographical snapshots illustrated by contemporary engravings. Id.,
**Rimbaud: l'heure de la fuite*, Gallimard, 176 pp. **Rimbaud, portraits,
dessins et manuscrits 1854-1891*, ed. Hélène Dufour and André Guyaux,
Musée d'Orsay, 100 pp., is the catalogue of the principal centennial
exhibition. *Rimbaud Centenary: Plymouth 1991*, Plymouth Arts Centre,
65 pp., is an attractive compilation of short pieces and translations,
some very good, and most by creative writers. Jean Bourguignon and
Charles Houin, *Vie d'Arthur Rimbaud*, ed. Michel Drouin, Payot,
230 pp., reprints articles by R.'s first biographers published between
1896 and 1901 and not previously available in book form. Alain
Jouffroy, *Arthur Rimbaud et la liberté libre*, Rocher, 265 pp., conducts a
personal pilgrimage through time and space with R., who never
thought of anything but the future, but 's'est changé en air
indispensable à tous nos présents'. **Je suis ici dans les Gallas, lettres et
textes choisis*, ed. Id., Rocher, 138 pp. Pierre Michon, *Rimbaud le fils*,
Gallimard, 121 pp., is a subjective biography. André Guyaux,
Duplicités de Rimbaud, Paris, Champion — Geneva, Slatkine, 255 pp.,
collects in revised form essays published from the 1980s to the
present, with three new readings of *Marine*, *Mouvement*, and *H*. Steve
Murphy, **Rimbaud et la ménagerie impériale*, Paris, CNRS — Lyons
U.P., 246 pp. Olivier Bivort and André Guyaux, **Bibliographie des
'Illuminations' (1878-1990)*, Paris, Champion — Geneva, Slatkine,
xii + 458 pp. Claude Jeancolas, *Le Dictionnaire Rimbaud*, Balland,
428 pp., offers a glossary of rare, foreign, and obscure words and
proper names. Id., **Les Voyages de Rimbaud*, Balland, 318 pp., collects
more than 300 photographs of places associated with R. in France,
Africa, and Asia. **Rimbaud. Mots d'Europe*, ed. Agnès Rosenstiehl,
Seuil, 96 pp. Gabriel Bounoure, *Le Silence de Rimbaud: petite contribution
au mythe*, Fata Morgana, 50 pp., offers a personal meditation which
concludes: 'Le silence de Rimbaud est plus vivant que tout ce qu'il a
écrit.' **Parade sauvage, Colloque no. 2, Rimbaud 'à la loupe'*: Hommage à C.
A. Hackett, ed. Steve Murphy and George Hugo Tucker, Charleville
and Mézières, Musée–Bibliothèque Rimbaud, 1990, 245 pp., collects
contributions to a Cambridge conference of 1987 by a most impressive range of leading *rimbaldiens*, including the dedicatee. *Europe*, 69,
nos 746–47, dedicated to R., incl.: A. Jouffroy, 'Petite introduction à
un manifeste d'Aden' (5–14) (R.'s scientific ambitions of his later
years as affirmative project); A. Borer, 'De Arturi Rimbaldi latinis
carminibus' (18–26) (eloquently drawing attention to the premoni-
tory importance of R.'s Latin verse exercises); J.-L. Steinmetz,
'L'absence de Rimbaud' (40–49) (reflective overview of R.'s destiny

in the light of this writer's above-mentioned major biography); P. Brunel, 'Rimbaud et la tentation de l'Orient' (70–81) (continuity and complexity of this temptation in R.'s writing and in his life); M. Kacimi, 'Frédéric Rimbaud chef de bureau arabe' (82–87); E. Foucher, 'Arthur Rimbaud et la mission catholique de Harar' (88–97); A.-E. Berger, 'A vue de nez: fragment d'une esthétique du dégoût' (111–19) (on *Vénus Anadyomène*); S. Sacchi, 'Voici le temps des exégètes' (120–29) (on the compulsion to extract meanings and messages from R.'s poems, with particular reference to *Bottom*). *Parade sauvage*, 6, 1989 [1991] incl.: S. Murphy, 'La faim des haricots: la lettre de Rimbaud du 14 octobre 1875' (14–54) (facsimile of MS with detailed commentary); H. D. Saffrey, 'Analyse d'une lettre d'Arthur Rimbaud' (74–85) (shedding light on title of *Les Sœurs de charité*). *Ib.*, 7, incl.: A. Henry, 'Sur quelques régionalismes des *Poésies*' (3–7); N. Cordonier, 'Ouverture du *Buffet*' (8–15) (persuasive defence of this sonnet); E. Laurent, 'Le "pleur qui chante": sur la chanson des *Derniers vers*' (16–30) (inspiration derived from 18th-c. operatic *ariettes*); B. Meyer, '*L'Éternité* de Rimbaud' (31–47); A. W. G. Kingma-Eijgendaal, 'Structuralisme et motivation du signe poétique' (48–61) (on *Illuminations*); S. Sacchi, '"La stupeur qui vous attend": lecture de *Vies*' (62–74); O. Bivort, 'Un problème référentiel dans les *Illuminations*: les syntagmes nominaux démonstratifs' (89–102). *Parade Sauvage (bull.)*, 5, 1989 [1991], incl.: J.-P. Chambon, 'Annuaire des études rimbaldiennes (1988)' (7–51) (directory of publications and projects of R. scholars); P. Collier, 'Lire *Voyelles*' (56–102) (important contribution to debate provoked by this sonnet, with useful *mise au point* of previous interpretations); L. Gemenne, 'En finir avec le sonnet des *Voyelles*?' (103–10) (calling it 'une machine à produire une pluralité de sens'). *Ib.*, 6, 1990 [1991], incl.: J. Plessen, 'Pour en finir avec Faurisson' (12–19) (another vigorous contribution to the interpretation of *Voyelles*); J.-J. Lefrère and M. Pakenham, 'Rimbaud dans le journal de l'Abbé Mugnier' (20–27) (documenting R.'s friendship with Forain); S. Murphy, '"J'ai tous les talents!" Rimbaud harpiste et dessinateur' (28–49); J.-J. Lefrère, 'De Paul Soleillet à Georges Richard' (50–80) (on various associates of R. in Ethiopia). *Rimbaud vivant*, 30, is a special centennial no. devoted to the critical reception and creative influence of R. in countries from Chile to Japan. It includes a useful survey by J.-F. Laurent, 'Rimbaud en France' (53–72). J. Plessen, 'The tribulations of the alexandrine in the work of Rimbaud: a contest between innovation and convention', D'haen, *Convention*, 253–72, conducts a rigorous technical examination of R.'s innovations in this domain. A.-E. Berger, 'Lecture de quelques chants d'amour parisien de Rimbaud', *Romantisme*, 72:61–74, links *L'Orgie parisienne* with *Le Cœur du pitre*, reinterpreted in political terms as 'un chant de douleur parisien'. C. W. Thompson, 'Du rire romantique à l'espace éclaté: sur *L'Homme qui rit* et *Le Cœur du pitre* de Rimbaud', *RHLF*, 91:214–28, discerns Hugolian echoes in R.'s poem. J. Bellemin-Noël, 'Contrebande ou fausse monnaie: à propos de Rimbaud: *Sensation*', *TRCTL*, 10, 1990:109–20, verbosely decodes this poem to reveal an Œdipal subtext. C. Chadwick, 'Rimbaud's *volets*', *FSB*, 37:19, continuing a recently initiated discussion of a line from *Le Bateau ivre* (see *YWMLS*, 52:198), suggests that pragmatic expediency may have dictated R.'s choice of this word. R. Little, 'Rimbaud's *volets*', *ib.*, 39:19–20, persuasively argues that this is a reductive view. A. Cook, 'The transformation of "point": amplitude in Wordsworth, Whitman, and Rimbaud', *StRom*, 30:169–88, discusses R.'s subversion of conventional closure in *Une Saison en enfer*. G. Marcotte, 'Une ville appelée Rimbaud', *EF*, 27.1:49–61, reads *Ville*, *Villes I*, and *Villes II* as texts referring to new urban realities. B. Claisse, 'Les "bons Parnassiens" et *Promontoire* de Rimbaud', Watson, *Patterns*, 187–94, maintains that R. sarcastically subverts Parnassian themes in this poem. A. Fongaro, 'Quatre notes rimbaldiques', *Littératures*, 25:171–82, range from the unreliability of texts transmitted by Verlaine, to echoes from Gautier and Lautréamont in R.'s poetry and the absence or presence of the article in individual poems of *Illuminations*. C. Albert, *'Rimbaud vivant', *WB*, 37:1018–27. S. Murphy, 'Autour des "cahiers Demeny" de Rimbaud', *SFr*, 35:78–86, seeks to dismantle 'l'ordre factice' created by Paterne Berrichon's 'monumentale négligeance éditoriale' and restore something nearer to R.'s possible intentions.

VERLAINE. O. Bivort, 'Verlaine philologue', *CAIEF*, 43:249–69, reveals an erudite V., passionately attentive to all aspects of language. M. Décaudin, 'La tentation de la prose chez Verlaine', *ib.*, 271–79, assesses V.'s prose output, '*disjecta membra* d'un grand jeu que Verlaine ne parvient pas à rassembler'. G. Zayed, 'La tradition des fêtes galantes et le lyrisme verlainien', *ib.*, 281–99, contends that V.'s contribution to this long-established tradition was the last and the most brilliant, as well as 'le plus représentatif de son génie', and an act of disguised homage to his cousin, Élisa Moncomble. M. Pakenham, 'Pour une correspondance générale de Paul Verlaine', *ib.*, 301–14, gives an historical outline of editorial work already carried out, defectively in many cases, and calls upon *verlainiens* to form themselves into a team in order to fill 'la seule lacune importante qui reste parmi les correspondances littéraires du XIXe siècle'. P. Fortassier, 'L'évocation du chant des oiseaux indécis et précis dans la poésie verlainienne', *ib.*, 315–31, argues convincingly that V.'s ventures in this domain were the product of conscious poetic design rather than ornithological ignorance or enslavement to convention. *Nord'*, 18, a special no. devoted to V., incl.: P. Querleu, 'Paul Verlaine: le Ciel et l'Enfer' (9–27) (biographical outline); Id., 'Le Nord/Pas-de-Calais vu par Verlaine' (25–29); M. Cordier, 'Le logement de Verlaine' (31–37); C. Habib, 'Verlaine ou la matière grise' (39–53) (V.'s use of devices, including 'la non-couleur', to express the instability of the self); G. Delomez, 'Verlaine et la prosodie' (55–62); M. Bertrand, 'Verlaine, *Sagesse* XXI: étude stylistique' (63–68); R. Robinet, 'A l'origine des relations Verlaine–Rimbaud: Paul-Auguste Bretagne' (69–72); P. Querleu, 'Gustave Vanwelkenhuyzen': *Verlaine en Belgique*' (73–78) (summary of a study publ. in 1945). G. Schultz, 'Lyric itineraries in Verlaine's *Almanach pour l'année passée*', *RoQ*, 38:139–55, reassembles some of the poems destined for *Cellulairement* and makes them the object of sensitive and rewarding analysis. A. Elliot, 'L'expérience de traduire: Verlaine's *Femmes/Hombres*', *CC*, 13:185–93, discusses the metaphorical resources of this text, in relation to his translation of it.

4. NOVEL

Roudaut, *Villes, discusses several novelists of the period, including Rodenbach and Verne. Richard Griffiths, *The Use of Abuse: The Polemics of the Dreyfus Affair and its Aftermath*, NY, Berg, xiv + 207 pp., includes chapters on Zola and Bloy. Didier, *Penser, includes articles by J. Neefs on Flaubert's dossiers for *Bouvard et Pécuchet* and by H. Mitterand on Zola's *Le Rêve*. Apter, *Fetish*, includes chapters written from a feminist perspective on 'fetichistic fiction' and male voyeurism, including Mirbeau's *Journal d'une femme de chambre* and the Goncourts' *Madame Gervaisais* and *La Femme au XVIIIe siècle*. Pelckmanns, *Monde*, devotes several pages to works by the Goncourts, Champfleury, and Maupassant, in a study of the theme of fanatical antiquarianism in European literature. *Littérature et révolutions en France, Amsterdam, Rodopi, 1991, ed. G. T. Harris and P. M. Wetherill, includes papers on Flaubert and Maupassant. *Europe*, 69, nos 751–52, devoted to the *fin de siècle*, incl.: R. Bozetto, 'Le fantastique fin de siècle, hanté par la réalité' (15–26) (theme of the double in Lorrain, Schwob, and R. L. Stevenson); B. Slama, 'Où vont les sexes? Figures romanesques et fantasmes "fin de siècle"' (27–37) (blurring of sexual boundaries, necrophilia, and symbolic slaying of women in fiction by both male and female authors); J.-P. Bertrand *et al.*, 'Les romans de la décadence' (76–83) (the 'nouveau roman' invented by Huysmans and Gourmont, with special emphasis on *A rebours* and *Sixtine*); A. Guillemin, '"Le réalisme éternel des champs": les campagnes françaises sous le regard des romanciers, 1881–1904' (99–110) (utopian pastoral yielding place to social

realism). L. H. Ginn, '"Il a vu les choses de trop haut": Henri
Chambige and his literary destiny', *NFS*, 30.1:23–32, documents
partisan passions aroused by the murder trial of C. in 1888, and
discusses fiction inspired by the issues it raised, culminating in
Bourget's *Le Disciple*. R. Mahieu, 'Les théâtres de la cognition',
Littérature, 82:57–71, is a cogently argued essay on the difficulties
experienced by writers of realist fiction in their representation of
scientists and institutions of higher education. Particular attention is
paid to Zola's *Le Docteur Pascal*. P. A. Meadows, 'The symbol's
symbol: spider webs in French literature', *Symposium*, 44:272–90,
discusses Schwob's and Zola's use of this polyvalent image. J. Dubois,
'Conversion du héros décadent en narrateur proustien', Glaudes,
Personnage, 107–21, offers a lucid account of how decadent novelists
portraying a single subjective consciousness 'font le lit de la
révolution proustienne'. J. Kelly, 'Photographic reality and French
literary realism: nineteenth-century synchronism and symbiosis', *FR*,
65:195–205, is poorly focused. D. Chaperon and J. Kaempfer, 'Les
couleurs de la littérature: romans avec figures de peintre à la fin du
XIXe siècle', *EDL*, no. 3:3–39, explore links and contrasts between
Balzac's *Le Chef d'œuvre inconnu* and texts by Barbey d'Aurevilly, Bloy,
the Goncourts, Huysmans, and Zola.

BARBEY D'AUREVILLY. *Le Chevalier des Touches*, ed. Patrick and
Roman Wald Lasowski, Livre de Poche, 223 pp., has a lively preface
on the symbolic detail planted all the way through this text, 'une
véritable chouannerie littéraire'. C. Scheel, '*Le Chevalier des Touches* de
Barbey d'Aurevilly: roman à thèse ou épopée don-quichottesque?',
NCFS, 19:583–99, asks why this is B.'s least popular novel, and
suggests persuasively that the reason is because it is 'décidément
monologique'. M. Watthee-Delmotte, '*Le Chevalier des Touches*: une
forme subtile d'imposture littéraire', *LR*, 45:53–62, contends that in
this novel B., in his determination to avoid mention of satanism, 'lui
donne paradoxalement son expression la plus efficace'. A. Guyon,
'Barbey d'Aurevilly et le genre policier: les leçons d'un précurseur
oublié', *TLit*, 4:217–30, conducts a useful generic discussion. F. C.
Mugnier, 'Dissimulation des classes sociales, de l'économie et de
l'histoire dans la fiction de Barbey d'Aurevilly', *NCFS*, 19:279–89, is
a well argued and illustrated essay on the reactionary subtext of B.'s
fiction. M. Reid, 'Question de genre: *Une vieille maîtresse* de Barbey
d'Aurevilly', *RLMC*, 44:149–60, shows in a lively essay how B. makes
use of all the literary clichés of his age to offer the reader 'une
figuration du désir des plus singulières'. C. J. Stivale, '"Like the
sculptor's *Diaboliques*', *RR*, 82:317–30, engages in an indigestibly
Bakhtinian discussion of 'the dialogical tug-of-war of voices' in these
stories. P. Dendale, 'Le saura-t-il? Le malaise du lecteur dans *La*

Vengeance d'une femme', *Neophilologus*, 75:56–65, demonstrates how this story invites the reader's participation. K. Falicka, 'Le jeu du double et de l'unique dans *Ce qui ne meurt pas* de Jules Barbey d'Aurevilly', *ALitH*, 32, 1990 [1991]:117–24, explores binary oppositions in this text.

BARRÈS. *Un jardin sur l'Oronte*, ed. Émilien Carassus, Gallimard (Folio), 1990, 218 pp. *Barrès: une tradition dans la modernité*, ed. André Guyaux, Joseph Jurt, and Robert Kopp, Champion, 334 pp., collects papers from a conference held in 1989. V. Rambaud, 'Barrès et Balzac', *ABa*, 12:395–408, documents B.'s rejection of Balzac at the time of *Le Culte du moi*, followed by renewal of sympathy for him later in his career. E. Carassus, 'De l'affaire Chambige au *Jardin de Bérénice*', *Littératures*, 24:115–25, sheds light on the genesis of two chapters of this novel.

BLOY. *Les Funérailles du naturalisme*, ed. Pierre Glaudes, Stendhal-Grenoble III U.P., 1990, 97 pp., reprints texts and notes of lectures given by B. in Denmark in 1891. W. Kidd, 'Influence and identification: a psychoanalytical study of Bernanos and Bloy', *MLR*, 86:580–91, examines Bernanos's debt to B. in *Sous le soleil de Satan* and later works. J.-P. Corsetti, 'Apocalypse?', *Europe*, 69, nos 751–52:48–55, draws thematic comparisons between Bloy and Huysmans.

BOURGET. M. Raimond, 'Le Balzac de Paul Bourget', *ABa*, 12:383–94, discusses B.'s intellectual and aesthetic debt to Balzac, and summarizes the respects in which he considered him superior to Zola.

CHAMPFLEURY. *Du réalisme: correspondance entre Champfleury et George Sand*, ed. Luce Abélès, Cendres, 107 pp.

DAUDET. *Lettres de mon moulin*, ed. Catherine Eugène, Presses Pocket, 1990, 272 pp. N. Araujo, 'Prosaic licence and the use of the literary past in Daudet's *La Chèvre de M. Séguin*', *FMLS*, 27:195–207, identifies voices and codes at work in this 'far from simple and anything but unambiguous' story.

DU CAMP. *Mémoires d'un suicidé*, ed. Rodolphe Fouano, Septembre, 270 pp.

FLAUBERT. The major event of the year, and probably of the decade (if the present gap between the appearance of volumes is maintained), in Flaubert studies is the third volume (two more to follow) of Jean Bruneau's superb edition of his *Correspondance*, III, *janvier 1859 — décembre 1868*, Gallimard (Pléiade), xii + 1729 pp. Even more exciting than 79 unpublished letters from F. (many of them short notes, or requests for information) is editorial material including over a thousand items of correspondence addressed to him, much of it unpublished, notably the remarkable lamentations of Mlle Leroyer de Chantepie, and a range of reactions to *Salammbô* (among other interesting documentation on the genesis and reception of this novel). Appendices contain extracts from Bouilhet's and Du Camp's correspondences with F., and all F.'s recorded appearances in the Goncourts' diary. *Voyage en Égypte*, ed. Pierre-Marc de Biasi, Grasset, 464 pp., restores the complete version, expurgated by F.'s niece, of this uniquely intimate autobiographical text, the MS of which has recently resurfaced, written at a furious pace in under five weeks. A substantial introduction on F. in the years before, during, and after his journey (including excellent pages on his unsentimental feeling for animals) matches in quality this editor's *Carnets de travail* (see *YWMLS*, 50:183). Another most welcome edition based on scrupulous re-reading of MSS (where available) is *Mémoires d'un fou, Novembre et autres textes de jeunesse*, ed. Yvan Leclerc, Garnier–Flammarion, 543 pp., with short but pithily pertinent general and individual prefaces, judicious footnotes, and excellent bibliography. Perhaps the very best feature of this selection is that it makes available in an inexpensive edition *Souvenirs, notes et pensées intimes*, filling in gaps and correcting misreadings of J.-P. Germain's edition (see *YWMLS*, 50:183–84). *Lettres d'Orient*, pref. Pierre Bergounioux, Bordeaux, L'Horizon chimérique, 1990, 336 pp., is no more than a selection of letters reproduced from the Pléiade edition, with an insubstantial preface. The most important new monograph devoted to F. is Yong-Eun Kim, '*La Tentation de Saint Antoine*', *version de 1849: genèse et structure*, pref. Jean Bruneau, Chuncheon, Korea, Kangweon U.P., 1990, 397 pp., which achieves a considerable advance in the understanding of this text. This editor is the first to apply professional scholarship to F.'s *liasse* of notes and plans, identifying the earliest scenario and following the work's germination through each of its successors. Detailed commentaries are supplied; new sources are identified; the relationship of this text with F.'s *Conte oriental* is clarified, in the impressive first stage of a promised critical edition of *La Tentation de Saint Antoine, dans tous ses états*. Timothy Unwin, *Art et infini: l'œuvre de jeunesse de Gustave Flaubert*, Amsterdam, Rodopi, 211 pp., undervalues *La Tentation de Saint Antoine* in an otherwise unexceptionable but unexciting study, portions of which have appeared as articles, focused on the evolution of F.'s philosophical thought. Id., 'Mysticisme et langage chez Flaubert de *Mémoires d'un fou* à *Novembre*', *EFL*, 26, 1989 [1991]:38–62, is a section from the above work, taking issue with Sartre on the narrative technique of *Novembre*. William VanderWolk, *Flaubert Remembers: Memory and the Creative Experience*, AUS, 1990, 204 pp., treats with clarity an important subject, memory as 'essential strategy in F.'s writing'. No mention is made of F.'s own contrast between the creative experience and his nervous illness as 'maladie de la mémoire'. The study follows

F.'s career up to *L'Éducation sentimentale*, for which a contestably optimistic interpretation is proposed, regarding the hero's ultimate success in 'dogged pursuit' of his ideal. Jacques Chessex, *Flaubert ou le désert en abîme*, Grasset, 283 pp., is a personal excursion, by a disciple of F., novelist and poet, around F.'s world and that of other writers inspired by him. From the initial affirmation, interestingly developed, that F.'s aim was to 'dresser l'écrit contre le vide', it divagates far and wide: F.'s name, for instance, turns into a *trou normand* ('ce phonème *au*, tellement lié à l'eau [. . .] qu'il plonge le nom tout entier dans un trou mouillé et suave'). A. W. Raitt, *Flaubert: 'Trois contes'*, CGFT, 86 pp., is an excellent introduction to this text, gathering a multiplicity of critical insights into a short space, respecting the integrity and individuality of each story, and concluding that 'each of them is an experimental work and represents a new departure'. By contrast, Aimée Israel-Pelletier, *Flaubert's Straight and Suspect Saints: The Unity of 'Trois contes'*, PUMRL, 36, 165 pp., promises a lively and fresh reading, but disappoints from the first paragraph with untenable generalizations and the determination to read a message into F.'s text: 'the victory of the individual over the system in power', achieved by 'deliberate and systematic subversion' through the exercise of illusion and imagination. André Versaille, *La Bêtise, l'art et la vie, en écrivant 'Madame Bovary'*, Brussels, Complexe, 122 pp., synthesizes extracts from F.'s letters to Louise Colet into one long epistle. Sandro Volpe, *Il Tornio di Binet: Flaubert, James e il punto di vista*, Rome, Bulzoni, 157 pp., is a well documented and well argued study of point of view in *Madame Bovary*. Juliette Frølich, **Au parloir du roman: de Balzac et de Flaubert*, Solum, 132 pp. Rainer Wannicke, **Sartres Flaubert: zur Misanthropie der Einbildungskraft*, Berlin, Reimer, 1990, 300 pp. Lisa Lowe, *Critical Terrains: French and British Orientalisms*, Ithaca, Cornell U.P., xii + 216 pp., attempts unconvincingly to draw a distinction between F.'s 'articulation of orientalist logics' in earlier texts and 'parodic destabilization of orientalism' in *L'Éducation sentimentale*. The same essay is to be found in Arac, *Macropolitics*, 213–42. C. Gothot-Mersch, 'Sur le renouvellement des études de correspondances littéraires: l'exemple de Flaubert', *Romantisme*, 72:5–39, is an important generic essay which surveys successive editions of F.'s correspondence with reference to modern editorial practice, and discusses its past and potential uses for *flaubertistes*. M. Reid, 'Flaubert et Sand en correspondance', *Poétique*, 85:53–68, explores the 'subtil mélange de divergences et de connivances' which made this exchange mutually supportive and enriching. R. B. Griffin, 'Flaubert's mother rite: paradigm lost', *NCFS*, 19:262–78, discusses manifestations of the Great Earth Mother in F.'s fiction. A. Raitt, 'Le Balzac de Flaubert', *ABa*, 12:335–61, offers a very helpful *mise au point* of F.'s ambivalent attitude to B. Porter, *Desire*, includes a chapter on 'The perverse traveler: Flaubert in the Orient' which is a slightly expanded version of an article published in 1989 (see *YWMLS*, 51:186). R. B. Leal, 'La réception critique de *La Tentation de Saint Antoine*', *OC*, 16.1:115–34, offers a useful survey of work accomplished and suggests further directions for future research. Y. Thomas, 'La Tour au rat: un épisode oublié de *La Tentation de Saint Antoine* de 1856', *RoN*, 32:19–22, links this tower (of which *flaubertistes* remain more aware than is claimed) with Hugo's 'trou aux rats' in *Notre-Dame de Paris*. P. Dufour, 'Le chaudron et la lyre', *Poétique*, 86:193–214, pays richly rewarding (and overdue) attention to the omniscient narrator's image of speech as a 'chaudron fêlé' in *Madame Bovary*. M. McNamara, 'La fabrication d'un paragraphe dans les brouillons de *Madame Bovary*', *NMi*, 92:145–57, offers a rigorous linguistic study of the description of Lagardy's operatic performance. J. Hamilton, 'The ideology of place: Flaubert's Yonville-l'Abbaye', *FR*, 65:206–15, offers an incisive analysis which holds no surprises for the specialist but would be of use to newcomers. D. A. Williams, 'Une chanson de Rétif et sa réécriture par Flaubert', *RHLF*, 91:239–42, interestingly reveals F.'s reworking of the original version of the blind beggar's song. P. Brooks, 'The body in the field of vision', *Paragraph*, 14:46–67, discusses narrative presentation of Emma Bovary in the light of Freud's notion of scopophilia. J. Goldstein, 'The uses of male hysteria: medical and literary discourse in nineteenth-century France', *Representations*, 34:134–65, is a richly documented interdisciplinary essay which discusses how the concept of hysteria 'became the springboard for free-ranging and unorthodox ruminations about gender definition'. Focusing on F.'s correspondence with Sand and on *Salammbô*, it draws on newly available MS notes for the latter. Three helpful and well crafted articles on *L'Éducation sentimentale*: P. Campion, 'Roman et histoire dans *L'Éducation sentimentale*', *Poétique*, 85:35–52, shows how F. frustrates the reader's desire for meaning and drama in a novel which parodies conventional historical fiction: C. de Grandpré, 'Sénécal et Dussardier: la république en effigie', *FR*, 64:621–31, makes use of F.'s drafts in a discussion of these characters as incarnations of liberty and dictatorship; M. Jameson, 'Métonymie et trahison dans *L'Éducation sentimentale*', *NCFS*, 19:566–82, demonstrates how the hero's 'metonymic vision' turns the world around him into a clutter of disparate objects. N. Segal, 'The sick son: a motif in Stendhal and Flaubert', *RoS*, 19:7–19, discusses Œdipal and adulterous triangles in *Le Rouge et le Noir* and *L'Éducation sentimentale*, both read as 'unremittingly patrilinear texts'. Bevan, *Génétique*, incl.: M.-T. Mathet: 'Une page de Flaubert: texte et manuscrits' (65–75) (illuminating study of F.'s revisions of the passage in which Frédéric waits for Mme Arnoux in the rue Tronchet); D.A. Williams, 'La structuration du récit dans les scénarios de *L'Éducation sentimentale*' (77–89) (comparing F.'s working methods with Zola's); P. Wille-mart, 'Une prise d'histoire dans le manuscrit' (91–98) (on the description of the citadel of Machaerus in *Hérodias*). Ferrer, *Écriture*, incl. A. Grésillon, J.-L. Lebrave and C. Fuchs, *'Ruminer *Hérodias*. Du cognitif-visuel au verbal-textuel' (27–109). J. Berchtold, 'L'œil et le vitrail (II): le regard de la fenêtre dans *La Légende de Saint Julien l'Hospitalier*', *Versants*, 19:31–57, completes a valuable study (see *YWMLS*, 49:202), of this story as 'texte-vitrail'. E. J. Gallagher, 'Heavenly bodies: dogmatic parody in Flaubert's *Un cœur simple*', *NZJFS*, 12.2:16–23, reads Félicité's final vision as parody of the Catholic doctrine of transubstantiation. G. G. Granger, 'Savoir scientifique et défaut de jugement dans *Bouvard et Pécuchet*', *Littérature*, 82:86–95, surveys B. and P.'s intellectual horizons without arriving at any new discovery. L. Schehr, 'Flaubert entre l'indécidé et l'indécidable', *LR*, 45:293–306, focuses on 'le figuration du flou' in *Bouvard et Pécuchet*. G. Kliebenstein, 'L'encyclopédie minimale', *Poétique*, 88:447–61, offers a lengthy commentary on its first sentence, not without interest but laden with unpalatable jargon.

FRANCE. *Œuvres*, III, ed. Marie-Claire Bancquart, Gallimard (Pléiade), 1600 pp. *Le Crime de Sylvestre Bonnard*, ed. Marie-Claire Bancquart, Gallimard (Folio), 309 pp., situates this text in the context of F.'s career. M.-C. Bancquart, 'Anatole France et l'esprit fin de siècle', *Europe*, 69, nos 751–52, 92–98, contests the popular image of F. as 'un sceptique aimable et un peu léger'.

FROMENTIN. B. Wright, 'L'osmose entre le mot et l'image dans l'œuvre d'Eugène Fromentin', Watson, *Patterns*, 71–84, shows how F.'s written and painted studies of Saharan landscapes and people mutually enrich each other. W. A. Guentner, 'Fromentin voyageur et la tradition de l'esquisse littéraire', *RHLF*, 91:901–12, discusses F.'s 'esthétique de l'esquisse' as reflected in his travel writings.

GAUTIER, JUDITH. I. Merollo, 'Due romanzi all'ombra dell Par-nasse: *Le Dragon impérial* e *Iskender* di Judith Gautier', *SFr*, 35:35–46, contends that these two early novels should be taken seriously.

GOBINEAU. *Ternove*, ed. Roger Béziau, Minard, 1990, xix + 370 pp., presents this work, excluded from the Pléiade edition, as 'un très bon roman du second rayon'. *Arthur de Gobineau et le Brésil: correspondance diplomatique du Ministre de France à Rio de Janeiro (1869–1870)*, ed. Jean-François de Raymond, PUG, 1990, 190 pp. *Arthur de Gobineau cent ans après, 1882–1982*, ed. Michel Crouzet, Minard, 1990, 238 pp., collects papers from a colloquium held in 1982. Sylvie André, *Gobineau: parcours mythique d'une œuvre*, Lettres modernes, 1990, 99 pp. F. Schuerewegen, 'Volcans: Mme de Staël, Gobineau, Gautier', *LR*,

45:319–28, discusses a sexually symbolic volcanic eruption in G.'s story *Akrivie Pharangopoulo.*

GONCOURT. *La Fille Élisa*, ed. Gérard Delaisement, Boîte à Documents, 1990, 189 pp., has a preface on the complexity and polemical *portée* of this novel. *L'Italie d'hier: notes de voyages (1855–1856)*, ed. Jean-Pierre Leduc-Adine, Brussels, Complexe, xxxiv + 286 pp. Elisabeth Launay, **Les Frères Goncourt collectionneurs de dessins*, Arthéna, 552 pp., offers an encyclopaedic wealth of documentation and illustration. D. Johnson, 'Reconsidering *japonisme*: the Goncourts' contribution', *Mosaic*, 24.2:59–71, traces the evolution of the brothers' appreciation of Japanese art, and subjects it to valuable critical analysis. J.-L. Cabanès, 'Les Goncourt et la morbidité: catégorie esthétique de *L'Art du XVIIIe siécle*', *Romantisme*, 71:85–92, discusses their aesthetic valorization of pathological states, which made them 'les initiateurs du décadentisme'. L. Chotard, 'Deux hommes de lettres en 18 ... (sur les débuts des Goncourt)', *Francofonia*, 20:75–84, evokes the early stages of their journalistic career. P. O'Donovan, 'De l'écriture au texte dans les romans des Goncourt', *ib.*, 85–103, rewardingly analyses self-consciously experimental features of their style. N. R. Cirillo, 'A girl need never go wrong, or the female servant as ideological image in *Germinie Lacerteux* and *Esther Waters*', *CLS*, 28:68–88, is a very incisive article which exposes the political underpinnings of this apparently apolitical novel, the heroine of which emerges as 'a squashed bug' at the mercy of her determinist creators. M. Respaut, 'Regards d'hommes/corps de femmes: *Germinie Lacerteux* des frères Goncourt', *FR*, 65:46–54, offers a more routinely feminist reading. M. Kaczynski, '*Les Frères Zemganno*, exemple de transposition autobiographique d'un couple de personnages', *ALitH*, 32, 1990:125–32, suggests parallelisms between the world of circus acrobats and that of artist-aesthetes.

HUYSMANS.   Jean Borie, *Huysmans, le diable, le célibataire et Dieu*, Grasset, 300 pp., views H. within a new frame of reference: 'la notion de personnage célibataire sous son double aspect, mythique et historique', a literary tradition in which H. takes his place between Flaubert and Céline. Hubert de Phalese, **Comptes 'A rebours': l'œuvre de Huysmans à travers les nouvelles technologies*, Nizet, 147 pp. Pierre Jourda, *Huysmans: 'A rebours': l'identité impossible*, Champion, 166 pp., offers a well crafted and stimulating introduction which brings out the contradictions and paradoxes inherent in this novel and in the decadent aesthetic. A useful appendix supplies a glossary and anthology of critical reactions to the text in the year of its publication. Knapp, *Exile*, includes a chapter, 'Huysmans's *Against the Grain*: the willed exile of the introverted decadent' (75–92), solemnly examining Des Esseintes as a case of a 'superficial and undeveloped psyche', suffering from 'poor adaptation to life in general'. Brian Banks, *The Image of Huysmans*, NY, AMS, 1990, xix + 276 pp. S. Jouve, 'La passion selon J.-K. Huysmans ou la descente au paradis', *Europe*, 69, nos 751–52:56–60, discusses the conflict between aestheticism and spirituality in H.'s work. A. Pagès, 'La réception d'*A rebours* (février–décembre 1884). Essai de bibliographie', *CN*, 65:105–11, takes as *point de départ* H.'s own press cuttings. R. Felski, 'The counterdiscourse of the feminine in three texts by Wilde, Huysmans, and Sacher-Masoch', *PMLA*, 106:1094–1105, includes *A rebours* in a discussion of novels with feminized male protagonists. G. Séginger, '*A rebours*: le roman de l'écriture', *Littératures*, 25:69–80, presents it as a novel in transition between two aesthetics. M. Banniard, 'Fleurs vénéneuses et corruption latine: érudition et illusion langagière dans *A rebours*', *ChS*, 2, 1992 (1991):191–207, assesses the originality of Des Esseintes's views on late Latin authors. E. Mosele, 'Joris–Karl Huysmans tra labirinti e mostri', *QLL*, 15, 1990:145–56, examines examples of 'mise en abyme' in *Là-bas*. Id., 'Itinerari onirici nel romanzo *En rade* di Joris–Karl Huysmans', *ib.*, 263–78, applies a Bachelardian perspective to the hero's daydreams and nightmares. P. Glaudes, '*En rade* et la conjugalité', *ALitH*, 32, 1990:79–89, has no difficulty in demonstrating that H. is interested exclusively in the malfunctioning of marital relationships.

JARRY. T. Bridgeman, 'Innovation and ambiguity: sources of confusion in personal identity in *Les Jours et les nuits*', *FS*, 45:295–307, discusses elements in this text which mark J. as a precursor of much 20th-c. novelistic prose, but which still, a century later, present problems for the reader. B. Fisher, 'The companion and the dream: delirium in Rachilde and Jarry', *RoS*, 18:33–41, explores intertextual relationships between *Les Jours et les nuits* and R.'s *La Princesse des ténèbres*.

LORRAIN. Thibaut d'Anthonay, *Jean Lorrain*, Plon, 232 pp. G. Ponnau, 'L'écriture dans les marges', *Europe*, 69, nos 751–52:84–91, presents *M. de Phocas* as a brilliantly ambiguous text at many levels.

LOTI. *Voyages (1872–1913)*, ed. Claude Martin, Laffont, 1562 pp., collects, with a useful preface, maps, and notes, those texts deemed by the editor to be most representative of L.'s vision. B. Vercier, 'Un papillon citron-aurore', *RSH*, 222:35–40, discusses *Le Roman d'un enfant* as an equivocally autobiographical text recording L.'s troubled relations with his family, and prefiguring Proust and Freud.

LOUŸS. J.-P. Goujon, 'Pierre Louÿs ou la subversion de la morale', *Europe*, 69, nos 751–52:61–67, discusses L.'s 'manie de la classification', put to the service of 'une morale de la permissivité', throughout his work, including his unpublished erotica.

MAUPASSANT. *Toine*, ed. Louis Forestier, Gallimard (Folio), 240 pp., presents M.'s short fiction as a world governed by 'une Providence à rebours'. *Boule de suif et autres histoires de guerre*, ed. Antonia Fonyi, Garnier–Flammarion, 319 pp., has useful editorial material and an introduction exploring sociopolitical issues raised by these stories. *Un réveillon: contes et nouvelles de Normandie*, ed. Bernard Valette, Larousse, 272 pp. *Pierrot et autres nouvelles*, ed. Joan and Joël Amour, Livre de Poche, 222 pp. *La Peur et autres contes fantastiques*, ed. Hélène Lefebvre, Larousse, 159 pp. Tuula Lehman, *Transitions savantes et dissimulées. Une étude structurelle des contes et nouvelles de Guy de Maupassant*, Helsinki, Societas Scientiarum Fennica, 1990, 246 pp., offers a formidable systematic study of formal devices, themes, and images in M.'s stories, which aims to put an end to the myth of M. as a stereotypical writer. The analysis of his formal resources (14 different types of frame are identified) is particularly valuable. Trevor A. Le V. Harris, *Maupassant et 'Fort comme la mort': le roman contrefait*, Nizet, 95 pp. J. Bem, 'Le travail du texte dans *Boule de suif*', *TRCTL*, 10, 1990 [1991]:97–108, revivifies this story, and links it with others, in a brilliantly illuminating psychocritical reading. J. Lintvelt, 'L'homme et l'animal dans les *Contes* de Guy de Maupassant', *ALitH*, 32, 1990:71–78, discusses M.'s use of animal imagery in his representation of love, sexuality, and marriage. N. H. Traill, 'Fictional worlds of the fantastic', *Style*, 25:196–210, views *Le Horla* within the context of a suggested typology of fantastic fiction. M. Calle-Gruber, 'Quand le mot d'ordre est: ne pas trahir. *Deux amis* de Guy de Maupassant', *RSH*, 221:121–46, offers detailed textual analysis of this story. M. Issacharoff, 'Description, séduction', *RLMC*, 44:113–20, draws attention to the ludic, antimimetic function of description in the tale *Un coq chanta*.

MÉRIMÉE. *La Vénus d'Ille*, ed. Françoise Rommelaere and Françoise Teyssandier-Pichon, Larousse, 136 pp. *La Vénus d'Ille, suivie de Il Viccolo di Madama Lucrezia*, ed. Jean Vivier-Boudrier, Nathan, 48 pp. *Colomba*, ed. Yann Le Lay, Larousse, 296 pp., offers a lively new presentation of this text. P. Glaudes, 'Cave amantem: la Carmen mythique de Prosper Mérimée', *La Licorne*, 18, 1990:99–121, contends that this pseudo-objective narrative is the vehicle for 'un narcissisme noir', 'une charge de négativité exceptionnelle'. D. Bryant, 'Deux batailles qui ne font qu'une: *L'Enlèvement de la redoute* de Mérimée et Waterloo dans *La Chartreuse de Parme*', *SCl*, 33:134–44, discerns a subtle 'chassé-croisé d'influences' at work in these two apparently contrastive narratives.

MIRBEAU. Pierre Michel and Jean-François Nivet edit four vols, *Correspondance avec Camille Pissarro*, Tusson, Du Lérot, 1990, 219 pp., *Lettres de l'Inde*, Caen, L'Échoppe, 117 pp., *Notes sur l'art*, Caen,

L'Échoppe, 1990, 83 pp. (which collects a selection of combative and perspicacious *chroniques* published in *La France* between 1884 and 1885), and *Sac au dos*, Caen, L'Échoppe, 45 pp. *Combats pour l'enfant*, ed. Pierre Michel, Vauchrétien, Ian Davy, 1990, 238 pp. Apter, *Fetish*, includes a chapter on *Le Jardin des supplices* reworked from an article published in 1988 (see *YWMLS*, 50: 191–92).

RACHILDE.　Claude Dauphiné, *Rachilde*, Mercure de France, 414 pp., is a substantially documented biography.

RODENBACH.　D. Dhuygelaere, 'La petite patrie: la Flandre dans les romans de Georges Rodenbach', *Yearbook of European Studies*, 4: 137–63, supplies useful political background against which R. is presented not merely as a decadent aesthete but as 'un observateur attentif et chroniqueur engagé de notre petite patrie'. D. Flanell-Friedman, 'A medieval city as underworld: Georges Rodenbach's *Bruges-la-Morte*', *RoN*, 31: 99–104, studies the novel in relation to the Orpheus myth and to representations of dead cities in medieval literature. B. Carrère, 'Envoûtements et sortilèges de la ville morte au tournant du siècle: *Bruges-la-Morte* et *Mort à Venise*', *Littératures*, 24: 105–13, draws thematic parallels between these novels.

SCHWOB.　R. Ziegler, 'Fictions of the forgotten in Marcel Schwob', *FMLS*, 27: 227–37, views S.'s historical fiction as an autobiographical project.

SÉGUR.　*Œuvres complètes*, pref. Jacques Laurent, 3 vols, Laffont, 1990, 1260 + 1320 + 1140 pp. Marie-France Doray, *La Comtesse de Ségur: une étrange paroissienne*, Rivages, 1990, 240 pp. Colette Misrahi, *La Comtesse de Ségur ou la mère médecin*, Denoël, 160 pp., reprints an essay privately printed in 1855, *La Santé des enfants*, with critical analysis from a specialist in this field.

VALLÈS.　Chantal Dentzer-Tatin, *Jules Vallès, les mots de l'enfance révoltée*, Neyzac, Roure, 190 pp., focuses on V.'s childhood environment and early work, offering valuable linguistic and topographical information from a local specialist. Gaston Cherpillod, *Jules Vallès, peintre d'histoire*, Lausanne, L'Âge d'Homme, 143 pp., is an act of personal homage to V. by a Swiss novelist and poet. J. Migozzi, 'Les portraits dans *L'Insurgé*: une alternative à la chronique historique?', *Romantisme*, 72: 75–85, reads this novel as 'un livre-tombeau de la Commune', in which fictional portraits, negative and positive, serve as substitute for explicit value-judgements.

VERNE.　Daniel Compère, *Jules Verne écrivain*, Droz, 185 pp. Bertrand Gervais, *Récits et actions*, Longueuil, Quebec, Préambule — -Paris, SEDES, 1990, 412 pp., is a study of adventure fiction which devotes a section to Verne. Hunter, *Topos*, includes S. Bygrave, *'The rhetoric of the commonplace: argumentation and ideology (Jules Verne and Émile Zola)'*. D. Meakin, 'Jules Verne's alchemical journey short-circuited', *FS*, 45:152–65, examines alchemical motifs in V.'s fiction, 'pre-scientific in that what takes precedence is not experiment and observation but text and interpretation'. W. Butcher, 'La poésie de l'arborescence chez Verne', *SFr*, 35:261–67, also takes the view that 'V.'s imagination is as poetic as it is scientific', in an examination of his predilection for branching structures in rivers, mountain ranges, social hierarchies, sciences, and fictional plots.

VILLIERS DE L'ISLE-ADAM. R. Scarcella, '*Isis* de Villiers de l'Isle-Adam: la fascination du regard et les sortilèges de l'ombre', *QLL*, 15, 1990:219–33, discusses mythical aspects of V.'s heroine Tullia Fabriana.

ZOLA. *Correspondance*, VIII (1893–97), ed. B. H. Bakker *et al.*, Montreal U.P. and Paris, CNRS, 482 pp., takes Z. from the aftermath of the Rougon-Macquart series, through the *Trois villes* and to the eve of the Dreyfus Affair. *Les Rougon-Macquart*, ed. Colette Becker, Gina Gourdin-Servenière, and Véronique Lavielle, Laffont, 2 vols, 1225 + 1373 pp., is accompanied by a wealth of documentation, including Z.'s two family trees on detachable sheets. Three more volumes, with a *Dictionnaire Zola*, will complete the edition. *Thérèse Raquin*, ed. Philippe Hamon, Presses Pocket, 340 pp., has useful editorial material, including the section on the Morgue from *Paris-Guide*, and documentation on the work's reception and theatrical adaptation. *La Fortune des Rougon. Épisode du coup d'état en province, décembre 1851*, ed. Gina Gourdin-Servenière, Geneva, Strategic Communication, 1990, cxx + 584 pp., makes available all the variants of this text, and has an important preface on the genesis and grand design of the R.-M. series. *La Faute de l'abbé Mouret*, Gallimard (Folio), 505 pp., ed. Henri Mitterand, has a lively preface by Jean-Philippe Arrou-Vignod, presenting this novel as a parenthetical work in the series, situated in 'quelque interstice de l'espace-temps'. *La Conquête de Plassans*, ed. Henri Mitterand, pref. Marc B. de Launay, Gallimard (Folio), 1990, 467 pp. *Pour une nuit d'amour*, reprints four narratives published in a Russian periodical in 1880. *Écrits sur l'art*, ed. Jean-Pierre Leduc-Adine, Gallimard, 523 pp., is an extremely valuable *outil de travail* which collects, with an invaluable bibliography, all Z.'s art criticism including two *Lettres de Paris* published in a Marseille newspaper in 1874 and 1876, and never before reprinted. The judicious preface concludes that Naturalist theory was not a strait-jacket for Z., '[qui] a distribué ses admirations et ses aversions avec assez de bonheur'. René-Pierre Colin, *Tranches de vie: Zola et le coup de force naturaliste*, Tusson, Du Lérot, 220 pp., surveys and defends the main tenets of Naturalist ethics and aesthetics. Henri Mitterand, *Zola, l'histoire et la fiction*, PUF, 1990, 294 pp. Alain Pagès, *Émile Zola, un intellectuel dans l'affaire Dreyfus*, Séguier, 397 pp. Patricia

Carles and Béatrice Desgranges, *Zola*, Nathan, 127 pp., is a well crafted and wide-ranging introduction to Z.'s work. Willi Hirdt, **Alkohol im französischen Naturalismus: Der Kontext des 'Assommoir'*, AKML, 183 pp. **Il terzo Zola. Émile Zola dopo i 'Rougon-Macquart*; ed. Gian Carlo Menichelli and Valeria de Gregorio Cirillo, Naples, Instituto Universitario Orientale, 1990, 672 pp., collects conference papers by numerous leading specialists on a wide range of topics. Newton, *Romance*, a stimulating comparatist study of 'the division between the spheres of spirit and society' in the work of Dickens, Manzoni, Zola, and James, reads *Germinal*, *La Débâcle*, and other R.-M. novels as 'dialectically dynamic novels in which the romance and the real are of equal strength'. Tindall, *Countries*, has a section on Z.'s Paris, with an excursion to Plassans, compared with Hardy's Casterbridge. Valerie Minogue, *Zola: 'L'Assommoir'*, CGFT, 100 pp., is a sensitive and readable introduction drawing particular attention to 'the subtlety and psychological skill that Zola is said sometimes to lack'. Bernice Chitnis, *Reflecting on 'Nana'*, London, Routledge, 90 pp., offers feminist criticism at its best: attentive to a range of characters, female and male, besides the main protagonist, and to textual detail beyond the well-known set pieces, in lively pursuit of a thesis that this is a novel about a beleaguered 'female sub-culture' which looks forward to an era which will recognize 'the essential androgyny of all biological males and females'. Daniela De Agostini, *Il Mito dell'Angelo: genesi dell'opera d'arte in Proust, Zola, Balzac*, Urbino, Quattroventi, 1990, xiv + 177 pp., includes a section on *L'Œuvre* in relation to Z.'s preparatory dossiers. R. M. Viti, 'A woman's time, a lady's place: *Nana* and *Au bonheur des dames*', *Symposium*, 44:291–300, finds plenty of examples of 'upsetting of orderly, clock-ruled [male] time' by women in these novels. R. Garguilo, 'L'obsession de la faute dans *Thérèse Raquin*: la laïcisation du remords', *La Licorne*, 20:113–22, shows how Thérèse's and Laurent's remorse reduces itself to 'un désordre organique'. W. E. McClendon, 'Red on gray: *Thérèse Raquin*', *NCFS*, 19:304–16, shows how Z. manipulates the quantity and quality of references to the colour red, and to what effect. A. Sonnenfeld, 'Zola: food and ideology', *ib.*, 600–11, seeks to demonstrate, with abundant example, how 'eating, in Zola's novels, if not in his life, is always an ideological statement'. R. Warning, **"Kompensatorische Bilder einer "wilden Ontologie"": Zolas Les Rougon-Macquart'*, *Poetica*, 22, 1990:355–83. C. Becker, 'Les Goncourt, modèles de Zola?', *Francofonia*, 20:105–13, arrives at a negative answer to her question; but A. Belgrand, 'Zola "élève des Goncourt"": le thème de l'hystérie', *ib.*, 115–31, contends that Z.'s treatment of this theme owes much to the Goncourts' fiction. L. Szakács, 'Les vivants et les morts dans *La Fortune des Rougon*', *ALitH*, 32, 1990 [1991]:91–95, discusses the relationship between these two halves of society in this novel. R. Lethbridge, 'Reading the songs of *L'Assommoir*', *FS*, 45:435–47, is a very illuminating article which rescues these 'textual segments habitually condemned to critical "silence"', puts them in their political context, and goes on to explore Z.'s use of musical imagery throughout the text. P. Gaitet, 'From the criminal's to the people's: the evolution of argot and popular language in the nineteenth century', *NCFS*, 19:231–46, includes Z. in a discussion of 'the bourgeoisie's strategies of representation of *le peuple*'. F. Schuerewegen, 'De la nécessité préfacielle (Balzac, Zola)', *FrF*, 16:177–86, adopts a theoretical approach to Z.'s essay on Balzac and to his preface to *Thérèse Raquin*, reading in the latter 'une sorte de trop-plein diégétique qui aurait débordé sur le paratexte'. L. Kamm, 'Balzac's *La Peau de chagrin* and Zola's *Germinal*: points of contact', *NCFS*, 19:223–30, pursues unconvincing parallels between these texts. R. M. Viti, 'Étienne Lantier and family: two-timing in *L'Assommoir* and *Germinal*', *Neophilologus*, 75:200–06, fruitfully examines disruptions of bourgeois sequential time in these novels. Another worthwhile article, D. F. Bell, 'Bifurcations: espace et pouvoir dans *Germinal*', *LR*, 45:307–17, portrays the landscape of this text as image of 'un certain désordre', recalcitrant to the 'schémas simplifiants' which a capitalist order seeks to impose on it. J.-P. Leduc-Adine, 'Aspects de la genèse d'un discours mythique dans *L'Œuvre* d'Émile Zola', *La Licorne*, 18, 1990:41–50, explores mythical patterns which determine the artist's destiny, and reprints Z.'s list of over 52 alternative titles for this novel. P. Brady, 'From transactional analysis to chaos theory: new critical perspectives', *AJFS*, 26, 1989 [1992]:176–93, summarizes his already published application of transactional analysis to *L'Œuvre*. Livingston, *Literature*, is an interdisciplinary study which includes a chapter on *La Joie de vivre* (150–78), applying M. Bratman's theory of planning and decision to Lazare Chanteau's 'complex transgression of norms of rational planning and deliberation'. *CN*, 65, is a no. mainly devoted to the reception and influence of Z.'s Naturalism in countries which include Russia, Argentina, Flemish-speaking Belgium, and Israel. Other articles incl.: P. Baudorre, 'Zola, 1929–1935, ou les ambiguïtés d'un *retour* de Zola' (7–23) (Z.'s return to favour in a climate favourable to proletarian literature, swiftly followed by Marxist depreciation of his work); H. Suwala, 'Zola et Maupassant lecteurs de Flaubert' (57–77) (contrasting M.'s aesthetic appreciation of F. with Z.'s attitude, in which a large measure of self-projection is discernible); M.-S. Inzé-Armstrong, '*Germinal*, ou les aventures de Zola au pays des merveilles' (79–97) (unconvincing attempt to prove influence of *Alice in Wonderland* and equate Jeanlin with the White Rabbit); C. Elkabas,

'Fonctions et significations de la *persona comica* dans *Les Rougon-Macquart*' (123–37) (rewarding typology of comic characters); R. Butler, 'L'étranger, personnage des *Rougon-Macquart*' (139–53) (less helpful); E. Cosset, 'La représentation de "l'acte de parole" des personnages dans *La Fortune des Rougon*' (155–68) (rigorous study of relative frequency of direct and indirect speech and *style indirect libre*); S. Woodward, 'Le sang de *L'Œuvre*' (169–76) (funereal subtext of this novel); M. Fol, 'Compulsion répétitive, rites et tabous: Jacques Lantier, Émile Zola dans *La Bête humaine*' (177–88) (Freudian essay); R. Lethbridge, 'Zola et ses livres' (191–97) (interesting information on the contents and fate of Z.'s library); J.-L. Lioult, 'Nouvelles précisions sur les années aixoises d'Émile Zola' (199–214) (fruits of research in local archives); J. B. Sanders, 'Onomastique zolienne: les listes inédites de noms dressées par l'écrivain' (215–51) (publishing for the first time Z.'s harvest from the *Bottin*); D. Coussot, 'Vingt lettres inédites de Zola à Émile Bruneau' (253–65) (on building works at Médan); C. Becker, 'Une comédie inédite d'Émile Zola (II)' (267–95) (see *YWMLS*, 52:214).

5. DRAMA

Jean Chothia, *André Antoine*, CUP, xviii + 212 pp., is an impeccably researched and most attractive study that re-creates and documents the achievements, evolution, and influence of Antoine's Théâtre Libre, with the help of sketches, posters, and photographs (including some dating from 1887 which are the first known photographs of a play in performance). Corvin, *Théâtre*, the first work of this scope published in France, includes movements as well as individual dramatists and supplies helpful bibliographies. Jurkowski, *Écrivains*, has richly informative chapters on puppet theatres and those who wrote for them (including Duranty and Maurice Sand) under the Second Empire, and on Symbolist *fin de siècle* theatre designed for performance by puppets. J. S. Patty, 'Trestles on Parnassus: a preliminary survey of Parnassian theatre', Watson, *Patterns*, 106–19, adopting a bibliographical and statistical approach to a neglected field, locates a substantial body of Parnassian drama and gives details on performances up to the Second World War.

COURTELINE. M. Mazzochi Doglio, 'Courteline peintre de la médiocrité humaine', *CAIEF*, 43:183–200, analyses *Boubouroche* as a representative example of C.'s characteristic blend of comedy, social realism, and pessimism.

FEYDEAU. Henry Gidel, *Georges Feydeau*, Flammarion, 285 pp., is an attractive and authoritative biography of 'notre plus grand auteur comique après Molière'. J. Blancart-Cassou, 'L'irréalisme comique de Georges Feydeau', *CAIEF*, 43:201–16, identifies different comic effects achieved by F., which produce a disturbing sense of life as surreal farce, accentuated in modern performances.

JUBIEN. L. Richer, 'Moyen âge et XIXe siècle: Alfred Jubien, *La Reine de Neustrie*', *RHT*, 43:162–67, exhumes a play performed in Angers in 1865 and analyses its political *portée*.

LABICHE. *Théâtre*, ed. Henry Gidel, Bordas (Classiques Garnier), 2 vols, lxxix + 792 + 865 pp., are the first two of three volumes containing most of L.'s own choice for his collected works published in 1878–79, with a few additions, and a substantial introduction and bibliography. *La Cagnotte*, ed. Robert Abirached, Larousse, 1990, 184 pp. F. Bassan, 'Eugène Labiche (1815–1888) et la comédie de boulevard au XIXe siècle', *CAIEF*, 43:169–81, retraces the evolution of this genre and seeks to explain the enduring success of L.'s plays. J. Best, 'Quiproquos et mondes possibles dans *Un chapeau de paille d'Italie*', *NCFS*, 19:554–65, analyses devices by which L. ensures the spectator's creative participation in this play.

ROSTAND. *Cyrano de Bergerac*, ed. Patrice Pavis, Larousse, 352 pp., has a less useful introduction than the Bordas edition (see *YWMLS*, 51:196).

SARDOU. M. Autrand, 'La censure au théâtre à la fin du XIXe siècle: *Thermidor* de Victorien Sardou', *FSSA*, 20:1–29, is a very well documented essay discussing S.'s modifications to this play, designed to outwit the censors, and suggesting that covert censorship may have prevented its revival in 1989.

THE TWENTIETH CENTURY, 1900–1945

By SUSAN R. HARROW, *Lecturer in French at the University College of Swansea*

1. ESSAYS AND STUDIES

Surrealism provides the raw material for one of the most highly productive industries in the 1900–45 sector. However, it is pleasing to record sustained output in other areas particularly Belle Époque and First World War literature, *écriture féminine*, and the study of the relationship between verbal and visual language. The selection offered here reflects the pluralist approach of much current research and the tendency to combine the study of literature with social science disciplines, in particular the history of social and political ideas, cultural studies, gender studies, and the trend towards cross-media studies (particularly poetry and the plastic arts). Frand Field, *British and French Writers of the First World War: Comparative Studies in Cultural History*, CUP, 292 pp., has, as its central concern, the history of ideas and the intellectual and spiritual climate of the war period, but offers insights into literature and literary history with two chapters of particular interest: 'Maurice Barrès, Charles Maurras, Charles Péguy: the defence of France' (33–85) aims to reappraise the positions and prophecies in a contextualized and thus more carefully nuanced light; 'Romain Rolland: above the battle' (179–210) charts the eschatology of R.'s view of European culture and civilization, and examines the controversy surrounding R.'s advocacy of independent thought among intellectuals, contrasting his Olympian standpoint with his anti-Nazi commitment and his increasing disillusionment with the Soviet system. Elizabeth A. Marsland, *The Nation's Cause: French, English, and German Poetry of the First World War*, London, Routledge, xii + 284 pp., rejects biography and textual analysis in favour of a discussion of poetry's social function and historical context. This important study draws out structural similarities and homogeneous approaches across the three-nation corpus. The inclusive, non-hierarchical conception of the study determines that the work of minor and relatively unknown poets receives equal attention with that of the literary greats: comprises chapters on patriotic verse and the concepts of nationhood and nationalism, protest poetry, the personal lyric of soldier-poets, the poetry of civilians, and includes reference to Nicolas Beauduin, Raymond De La Tailhède, Louis Texier, Alfred Droin, G. A. Fauré, Lois Cendré, Marcel Martinet, Georges Chennevière, as well as to Claudel, Verhaeren, Apollinaire, Vildrac, Arcos, Spire, Romains, Jouve, and Rolland. Richard Stamelman, *Lost Beyond Telling: Representations of Death and Absence in*

Modern French Poetry, Ithaca, Cornell U.P., 1990, xvi + 291 pp., has chapters on Apollinaire and Jouve: 'The fatal shadow of otherness: Guillaume Apollinaire' (70–92) is a psychothematic study of the search for self and the uncovering of difference represented by the centripetal and centrifugal forces powering A.'s poetry; this opens into a consideration of A.'s ambivalent treatment of alterity — alternately 'self-centred' (autotropic) and 'other'-focused (allotropic) — in poems drawn from *Alcools* and *Calligrammes*; 'The eros of love: Pierre Jean Jouve' (93–121) considers language as a crystallization of the absence of being, specifically the being of the Other ('l'Abolie', 'la Disparue'), and argues that it is this essential absence of Woman which defines beauty and makes possible the perfection of form through the pursuit of 'melancholic incorporation' and lyrical possession. John Richardson, *A Life of Picasso: 1881–1906*, London, Jonathan Cape, ix + 548 pp., dissects the complex relationship between poetry and painting in the years preceding the Cubist revolution, and has much to interest specialists in the early Modernist period. Chapter 21, 'The Apollinaire period' (327–49), begins by demystifying the circumstances of the first meeting of Picasso and Apollinaire and moves on to consider the cross-fertilization of circus and *commedia dell'arte* imagery (with special reference to the enigmatic 'Un fantôme de nuées'). N. M. Mosher, *Le Texte visualisé: le calligramme de l'époque alexandrine à l'époque cubiste*, NY, Lang, 1990, 179 pp. Adelia V. Williams, *The Double Cipher: Encounter between Word and Image in Bonnefoy, Tardieu and Michaux*, NY, Lang, 1990, 242 pp., extends the discussion of the interrelationship of poetry and the plastic arts with an appropriately delineated study of three 'independents', poets whose individual responses to the problematics of verbal and visual representation map the development from a traditional separation of literature and painting (the restoration of presence in Bonnefoy) to the post-modern erasure of difference (the negation of mimesis and the set towards abstraction in Tardieu and Michaux). A. Fongaro, 'Poétiques reverdienne, surréaliste et autres', *Littératures*, 23, 1990: 183–93, examines the theory and practice (poeticization) of the image, demonstrating that the production of the specifically Modernist image owes much to a traditional poetic grounded in values of culture and civilization. Helena Lewis, *Dada Turns Red: The Politics of Surrealism*, Edinburgh U.P., 1990, xi + 229 pp., unscrambles the relationship between the literary and artistic movement, and the revolutionary, political mainstream, and provides key reading on the positions of Breton, Aragon, and Eluard. J. H. Matthews, *The Surrealist Mind*, Selinsgrove, Susquehanna U.P. — London and Toronto, Associated University Presses, 233 pp., is a posthumously published examination of the logic of the illogical that puts the case for a coherent, and constant surrealist 'mind', distinct from Surrealist philosophy and Surrealist politics; addresses the specifically unitary nature of Surrealist thought and practice with reference to poetry and painting, reaffirming the duality of a Surrealist mind which is simultaneously self-reflexive in its theorization and anti-reflexive in its practice. Predictably, considerable attention is paid to Breton who, it is argued, was not the inflexible dogmatist that his legendary belligerence would imply, but an open-minded experimentalist. There are, in addition, assessments of verbal automatism, the mainstream critical response, the crucial relationship of pictorial and verbal modes of expression, and the relationship of Surrealism to the *avant-garde*. The importance of Paris as a cultural capital in the birth throes of Modernism is reflected in a number of studies. *Les Villes d'Europe inspiratrices des écrivains*, ed. Margaret Parry and Michel Bonte, Sarreguemines, Pierron, 1990, 119 pp., has Dom C.-J. Nesmy, 'Expérience et théologie de la ville chez Paul Claudel' and M. Bonte, 'La ville inspiratrice des romans de François Mauriac'. *Écrire Paris*, Seesam, 1990, 144 pp., has two essays relating to our period: P. Citti, 'Paris dans *Les Déracinés*' (121–30), looks at the dual status of Paris in Barrès's novel, the entropy-inducing cemetery-city and the 'carrefour de toutes les énergies'; J.-Y. Tadié, 'Le Paris de Marcel Proust' (133–43), concentrates on the place of intellectual institutions, of literary salons, and of the Paris *avant-garde* in P.'s novel. George Melly, *Paris and the Surrealists*, London, Thames and Hudson, 159 pp., is a more of a personal appreciation than a description or analysis; aimed at a general readership, it nevertheless succeeds in capturing in words and photographs the spirit of Surrealism's 'elective places'. Nancy Perloff, *Art and the Everyday: Popular Entertainment and the Circle of Erik Satie*, Oxford, Clarendon Press, 227 pp. Several important studies of the novel have appeared. Jean-Yves Tadié, *Le Roman du XXe siècle* (Dossiers Belfond), Pierre Belfond, 1990, 230 pp., sets out to 'think' the modern novel and to this end challenges the isolationist tendency of literary criticism by looking transtextually at the century's major novels; discerns, in the felicitous coexistence of works by Céline, Gide, Proust, and Bernanos, areas of conceptual and stylistic convergence; with chapters on narration, character, open and closed structure, the city, and the interrelationship of fiction and philosophy. Jennifer Waelti-Walters, *Feminist Novelists of the Belle Époque*, Bloomington, Indiana U.P., 1990, xi + 207 pp., is a readable socio-historical and literary scamper through the writings of Colette, Anna de Noailles, Rachilde, and neglected authors such as Miriam Harry, Jeanne Landre, and Marcelle Tinayre; considers, from a positive but not uncritical perspective, the projection of autonomous womanhood through treatments of love and marriage, maternity, and daughterhood. Nelly Wolf, *Le Peuple dans le roman français de Zola à Céline*, PUF, 1990, 264 pp., is a socio-cultural, linguistic, and literary study that considers the stylistic development of the portrayal of the working classes through representations of popular language. The author's particular concern is discourse 'misrepresented', that is (1) treated as deviance from the academic norm (and as such differentiated textually from the 'legitimate' discourse of the narrator); (2) de-authentified by the author who asserts the hegemony of elementary French as imposed by the Republican education system. From a study of the work of a host of authors of the 1900–45 period (Carco, Giono, Ramuz, Poulaille, Dabit, Péguy, Queneau), she concludes that it is with Céline that such tendencies are most radically subverted in the assimilation of 'le parler populaire' into the discourse of the narrator from *Mort à crédit* onwards. D. G. Bevan, 'La littérature paysanne du vingtième siècle: Arcadie, Anti-Destin ou Holocauste', *NZJFS*, 11.1, 1990:50–56, extols the universalist, humanist vision of Giono and Ramuz, and identifies in their work a form of literary resistance to the progressive alienation of modern man and, in the aftermath of the First World War, a response of a properly existential order. Anne-Marie Thiesse, **Écrire la France: le mouvement littéraire régionaliste de langue française entre la Belle Époque et la Libération* (Ethnologies), PUF, 1991, 314 pp. In *CCe*, no. 6, 1990, 126 pp., 'Légendaire et mythe dans le roman contemporain', A. Guyon, 'Proust et les Mille et une Nuits' (27–48), considers the role of the Arabian source from a philosophical and spiritual perspective and sees in the assimilation of the Oriental model an effort to rehumanize and, by countering pessimism, despair, and hopelessness, oppose the constraining forces of modernity; B. Duchatelet, 'Un roman d'amour et d'adultère, mais à ma façon: Béroul, Wagner et le *Tristan* de Romain Rolland' (103–20), considers *Jean-Christophe* and the parity/ disparity relationship between the tragic couples Christophe/Anna and Tristan/Iseut. The most pertinent observations emerging from this study of the alternating receptivity and resistance of R. to the medieval source concern those aspects against which R. militates in order to avoid the extremes of moralism and immoralism. Includes an appendix reproducing two letters from R. to Jacques Reboul that offer unambiguous evidence of R.'s commitment to the modernization of the Celtic corpus. *Juden Vol.* has essays on Gide and Ponge: M. Mein, 'Gide and the Seven "Last Words" from the Cross' (263–73), considers the discussion in 'Deux interviews imaginaires suivis de Feuillets' of the reporting of Christ's cry of dereliction in the gospels of Mark and Matthew, and concludes that G. neglects the ultimately positive and deity-affirming aspects of the two Apostles' emphasis on the theme of spiritual abandonment; K. Anderson, 'Towards a new reason: guilt, language and nature in the work of Roland Barthes and Francis Ponge' (23–48), assesses P.'s response to the chaos of consciousness in the Western world, particularly his perception of Self as an integral element in a vast, pre-Christian, mystical tradition; examines the Epicurean and Stoic influences on P.'s formulation of a new rationality founded on the principle of ecstatic contact of mind and material reality. *OC*, 16.2, 'Les dernières œuvres des auteurs devant la critique', is conceived as a reappraisal of the status and role of authors' concluding achievements and one that avoids the *fin de parcours* preoccupation of critics faced with authorial 'Last Testaments'. Three items are of particular interest to our period: C. Foucart, 'Le *Thésée* d'André Gide: œuvre d'un patriarche ou d'un éternel adolescent' (99–109), argues that the 'testament' label is reductive and limiting, and insists that the composition of *Thésée* is a product of the writer's double struggle against the inhumanity of the modern age and against the gradual waning of his own intellectual powers; M.-V. Nantet, 'La seconde œuvre de Claudel ou le continent inconnu' (111–21), looks at 'cette liasse en désordre', the mass of exegetical writings of the last thirty years of C.'s life, and suggests that the intellectual endeavour sinks under the weight of commentary, extrapolation, and cumbersome *explication de textes*; B. Beugnot, 'L'invention et la glane: l'autonomie de Ponge' (123–36), explores the difficulty of locating a proper *point d'orgue* for P.'s creativity, and decides that P.'s practice of rewriting and accumulation ensures that his work is more resistant to attempts to define and describe the phenomenon of 'last works'. Jean-Marc Varaut, *Poètes en prison: de Charles d'Orléans à Jean Genet*, Perrin, 1989, 286 pp., sets out to assess the impact of incarceration upon writing but delivers instead a sentimentalized, biography-bound overview of the penitentiary poets, Apollinaire, Desnos, Jacob, Brasillach, and Maurras.

2. THEATRE

Copeau: Texts on Theatre, ed. John Rudlin and Norman H. Paul, London, Routledge, 1990, xxi + 281 pp., draws on material published in vols 1–4 of *Registres*, as well as on numerous published and unpublished sources including the Fonds Copeau at the Bibliothèque de l'Arsénal, and the private collection of C.'s daughter, Marie-Hélène Dasté. Organized thematically, this three-part collection opens with 'The School' which gives due place to C.'s belief that the founding of the Theatre was but an expedient to his project for the education of actors; includes chapters on Gordon Craig, the early years of the School, the Burgundy experience, and Émile Jacques-Dalcroze and Rhythmic Gymnastics. Part 2 ('The Theatre') looks at stage and stagecraft, poetry in drama, the function of the director, the role of the audience, and the influence on C. of the musician and architect Adolphe Appia. Part 3 ('Past and Future Forms') takes in C.'s view of Molière as a model for the director, comedy and improvization, the centrality of the chorus, popular theatre, the regenerative function of drama, and C.'s mystical conception of his art. Appendices contain correspondence, citations, and observations relative to C. and André Antoine, Charles Dullin, Louis Jouvet, Michel Saint-Denis, and Constantin Stanislavsky. Illustrated with black and white plates, the book includes a chronology and bibliography.

3. AUTHORS

APOLLINAIRE. *Le 'Casanova' d'Apollinaire: 'Comédie parodique'*, ed. Michel Décaudin, Lettres Modernes, 169 pp. J.-P. Bobillot, 'L'élasticité métrico-prosodique chez Apollinaire', *Poétique*, 84, 1990:411–33, reveals how 'Les Colchiques' elicits three competing types of scansion. These are the 'horizon prosodique de vers' based on the traditional syllable count, the 'horizon prosodique de prose' which ignores traditional constraints, and the 'horizon métrique de vers' which exposes the isosyllabic (6 + 6) structure of the poem: three readings which produce three different texts and thus provide a foretaste of 'littérature potentielle'. Willard Bohn, *Apollinaire and the Faceless Man: The Creation and Evolution of a Modern Motif*, London — Toronto, Associated University Presses, 176 pp. Madeleine Boisson, *Apollinaire et les mythologies antiques*, Fasano, Schena — Paris, Nizet, 1989, 792 pp., is a study of encyclopedic scope and one that will prove an indispensable research tool. The clear and workmanlike organization of chapters and subsections makes for easy consultation and reference. However, this is no mere repository of erudition but a structured study which looks initially at the diversity of influences (Hellenistic, Egyptian, Babylonian, and Persian; 19th-c. interpretations), and subsequently at A.'s treatment of the mythology of origins (Merlin, Croniamantal, Macarée, the multiform figure of the Virgin). The work concludes with a study of the individual divinities figuring in A.'s corpus (Hermes, Amphion, Pan, Icarus, Orpheus, Ixion), and with in-depth analyses of some of the most hermetic texts notably 'Les Sept Epées' and 'Onirocritique'. *Du paysage apollinarien: Actes du colloque de Stavelot (ALM, 246)*, ed. Michel Décaudin, Minard, 125 pp., has six substantial articles: M. Décaudin, 'Le paysage dans la critique d'art' (5–16), discerns, in A.'s apparently asystematic approach to landscape, a body of aesthetic values centering on qualities of clarity, precision, truth, and the absolute power of the artistic imagination, in line with the poet's 1908 pronouncement *Les Trois Vertus plastiques*; N. Cailliot, 'L'imaginaire du paysage médiéval dans *L'Enchanteur pourrissant*' (17–36), is written against the exegetic tradition that once characterized the study of A.'s sources, as a computer-assisted analysis of the assimilation and transformation of the medieval-inspired motifs 'forêt' and 'verger'; C. Debon, 'Les paysages de guerre dans *Calligrammes* ou "L'art de l'invisibilité"' (37–49), examines the methodological difficulties of assessing descriptions of 'landscape' in poetry, surveys the generally isolated and fragmented nature of description in the war poems, and concludes with a typology of descriptive instances that reveals A.'s remaking of the personal landscape of war through techniques of transformation, dispersal, and ellipsis; F. Chenet, 'De Hugo à Apollinaire, le paysage rhénan: une symbolique et une poétique de la mort' (51–72), explores the role of landscape in the development of A.'s personal myth, working out from the Rhenish poems to 'Le Voyageur' and *Les Onze Mille Verges*, by way of a strikingly uninhibited exposure of the anal subtext of 'Les Colchiques'; M. Boisson, 'Paysages célestes' (73–97), discusses celestial and meteorological transformations of the terrestrial in A. with particular reference to schemata of ascent and descent, to aspects of echo and reflection, and to the alternately paradisiac, parodic, or enigmatic construction of a poetic skyscape; J. Burgos, 'La fabrique du paysage apollinarien' (99–123), points to the high incidence of spatio-temporal indicators ('ensembles paysagers') and to their role in triggering the processes of de-realization and elaboration instrumental in the construction of a new reality identified with the experience of asceticism, 'apprentissage', and initiation. G. J. Jones, *Apollinaire: la poésie de la guerre. Voyage d'aventure pour poète et lecteur*, Slatkine, 1990, 137 pp., focuses sympathetic attention on the still relatively neglected later years of A.'s production, and extends the discussion of the war poems beyond the familiar parameters of *Calligrammes*. However it is doubtful whether the flimsy structure of the study and thinness of the argument can support the excess weight of quotation. A. Whiteside, 'Apollinaire's ideogrammes: sound, sense ... and visible signs', *Word and Image*, 6, 1990: 163–79, is a substantial contribution to recent research into A.'s *calligrammes* and, in particular, into the critically neglected ideogrammes of the *Poèmes à Lou*, *Poèmes à Madeleine*, and *Poèmes à la Marraine* collections. Challenging a tradition which implies a static visual poem, the author emphasizes the constant dynamic interplay of semantic, phonic, and visual elements.

ARAGON. *Europe*, no. 745, is devoted to A.'s poetry: C. Dobzynski, 'Aragon, une poétique de la totalité' (3–15), situates A. in the development of modern poetry, with specific reference to prosody, and seeks the reason for the contradictory reactions to A.'s poetry; H. Béhar, 'La parenthèse dada' (34–44), reassesses A.'s claim that Dada was but a phase in his creative life, revealing both the poet's tendency to place a positive value on the import of Dada for his development as a writer, and his practice which, if initially and ultimately resistant to Dada as a movement, shares common ground with Dadaist aims and temper; M. Apel-Muller, 'Elsa dans le texte' (45–53), asks why, after ten years of textual silence, the name of Elsa is incorporated into the poem proper (as opposed to the paratext), in October 1940, in the concluding poem of *Crève-Cœur*, and suggests that the answer is to be found in the assimilation of a medieval intertext: A.'s evocation of the values of courtly civilization and of the humanist tradition at a time when French national integrity was threatened made love a supreme value and Elsa its personification; N. Martine, 'Contradiction et unité dans la poétique d'Aragon' (63–73), studies the development of A. after 1934 in terms of the convergence of poetry and politics, the return to a cultural heritage, the rehabilitation of the sonnet, and A.'s criticism of the pseudo-modernism of the manifold *avant-garde*. The unitariness of A.'s poetics with regard both to prose and verse production is given particular emphasis and stress is placed on A.'s struggle to have the poeticity of prose recognized; S. Ravis and L. Victor, 'Sur les trois "Proses" du *Roman inachevé*' (80–90), is a lucid stylistic and structural study that brings out the ambiguous status of the prose pieces, emphasizing their textual autonomy and their complicity with the macro-poem. Among the various short articles which complete this issue, the following are most noteworthy: H. Meschonnic, 'Tradéridéra comme personne' (74–79), on rhyme and rhythm; M.-N. Wucher, 'De l'influence d'une légende' (91–96), considering A.'s fascination with and rewriting of the legend of Majnûn in the wake of the classical Persian poet Jami; C. Haroche, 'Langage et styles dans *Le Fou d'Elsa*' (97–102); W. Babilas, 'D'une enclave: à propos du *Voyage de Hollande*' (103–11), focusing on the programmatic component of the collection of poems published in 1964; R. Bordier, 'L'inévitable rendez-vous: Aragon et Hugo' (112–17).

ARTAUD, Karl Blüher, **Antonin Artaud und das 'Nouveau Théâtre' in Frankreich*, Tübingen, Narr, 311 pp. C. Dumoulié, 'Artaud peintre de Van Gogh', *NRF*, 455, 1990:68–83, discusses 'Van Gogh, le suicidé de la société', A.'s analysis of a fellow *pharmakos* and the imperative of genius in awakening the violence and vengeance of society that are traditionally channelled through the 'sanitizing' myths of metaphysics, religion, psychiatry, and alchemy, myths which 'contain' and 'explain' the recalcitrant personalities of the age. *Artaud on Theatre*, ed. Claude Schumacher, London, Methuen, 1989, xxx + 210 pp., is an eight-part thematico-chronological presentation and translation of the seminal texts on theatre and the related issues of cinema, religion, and sexuality; with introduction, potted biography, name index, and superb reproductions of photographs of A. taken in 1947.

BATAILLE. G. Orlandi Cerenza, 'Un manuscrit inédit de Bataille: de nouvelles variantes du *Bleu du ciel*', *LR*, 45:77–86, compares the text of a 1935 typescript (Guy Lévis Mano collection) with that of the first published version (Pauvert) of 1957, confirming the importance of fragmentary writing and with it the function of the interlude as a textual equivalent of the Greek chorus. *On Bataille*, *YFS*, 78, 1990, responds to the sustained high level of interest in B., setting itself the task of discussing and, inevitably, rewriting B.'s philosophy from chosen aesthetic, ethical, economic, and political perspectives. The essays selected here are contained in the sections 'Detours of rewriting' and 'The "impossible" esthetic'. S. Guerlac, '"Recognition" by a woman!: a reading of Bataille's *L'Érotisme*' (90–105), examines the dual mechanism of interdiction and transgression at the centre of B.'s theory of eroticism, assessing the degrees of convergence and of discrepancy between B.'s version and the Hegelian concepts of mastery and recognition. The author centres on the function of Woman as the erotic, non-desiring object in the staging of a fiction which sets up a dialectical relationship between a female object and a male subject whose struggle for recognition succeeds only to the extent that the non-autonomous, 'object' status of Woman is permanent and unchanging. J. Strauss, 'The inverted Icarus' (106–23), explores B.'s tendency to invest his writing with terms which themselves jeopardize the very possibility of meaning, and instances 'hétérogène' as a recurrent signifier designating an alterity, unassimilable and radical, which, by giving purpose and direction to the homogeneous, thereby subordinates it: the instability and fragmentation of the heterogeneous corresponds to mutually exclusive but often coexisting states of being and non-being (the fall of Icarus as glorious self-sacrifice and self-destruction constituting a case in point).

BERNANOS. W. Kidd, 'Influence and identification: a psychoanalytical study of Bernanos and Bloy', *MLR*, 86:580–91, counters the claim of the critical mainstream that B.'s development as a writer involves a gradual shedding of the influence of Bloy and points, instead, to the sublimation of that influence. Extending the Kleinian identification/ambivalence model, the author puts the case for the Oedipification of the complex relationship of writer to a precursor alternately textually acknowledged and denied.

BRASILLACH. A. Franchetti, 'Drammaturgia di un romanza *Les Sept Couleurs* di Robert Brasillach', *RLMC*, 44:75–87.

BRETON. Henri Béhar, *André Breton: le grand indésirable*, Calmann-Lévy, 1990, 475 pp., surely qualifies as an epic amongst biographies. Maintaining a rigorous chronology, this six-part study follows B. in his search for the modern spirit, his flirtation with Dada, his adventure with Surrealism, and in so doing conveys something of the heady intellectual and artistic climate which inspired the century's iconoclasts. Despite the imposing proportions of the study, the author sustains a freshness of approach throughout. *Europe*, no. 743, includes N. Bandier, 'André Breton et la culture classique' (22–30), which considers the influence of a 'modern', non-humanist education on the ethical component of Surrealism in terms of B.'s rejection of the elitist, formalist assumptions of the traditional *lettrés*, and his espousal of a literary ethos based on Hegelian (and Heraclitean) dialectics and a belief in the moral and subversive imperative of the writer; J.-L. Steinmetz, 'Les *Manifestes*. Impressions tardives' (31–39), is a sympathetic reappraisal which explores the interface of poetry and polemic, hesitation and affirmation, mystery and lucidity; R. Amossy, 'Délire paranoïaque et poésie' (40–54), begins by looking at the mutual interest of B. and Dali in paranoia in the late '20s and early '30s, moves on to consider the disparities between their approaches in a comparative study of B.'s 'Essai de simulation du délire d'interpré-tation' and Dali's poem 'La Métamorphose de Narcisse', and concludes by highlighting B.'s affirmation of the rights of the irrational over Dali's attempt to impose aesthetic order by applying criteria of a critical, rational, and organizational nature; R. Antoine, 'La fée noire et la fée caraïbe' (55–63), assesses B.'s confrontations with francophone literature on his 1941 visit to Martinique, and his 1945 visit to Haiti: the first half considers B.'s reception of the work of Aimé Césaire, his attempt to claim Césaire's poetry for Surrealism, his consequent denial of the struggle for a properly ethnic identity, and his rejection of issues of cultural difference; the second half of the article follows B. in Haiti, underlining his solidarity with the Blacks but exposing his inability to break out of European resistance to questions of West Indian personality, primitive practices, and spiritual life; J.-M. Baude, 'Le "morale poétique" d'André Breton' (72–80), examines the engendering of an ethics through the practice of writing, and considers the specifically poetic nature of this ethics (a symbiotic 'poéthique'), with reference to B.'s emphasis on sudden illumination, spontaneity, transcendence of the temporal, and his corresponding rejection of values of effort, will, progress, limitation, and duration; H. Pastoureau, 'André Breton, les femmes et l'amour' (81–94), establishes a roll-call of the women in B.'s life between 1913 and 1946, from his cousin Manon to his third wife Elisa Bindhoff, and speculates on their possible textual appearances and transfigurations.

P. Powrie, 'Breton's vertical labyrinth. Towards a psycho-semiosis', *RR*, 81, 1990:455–65, complements a Riffaterriañ analysis of inter-text in 'Le 13 l'échelle a frôlé le firmament' by exposing the influence of Surrealist ideology, firstly in terms of the treatment of Apuleius's rendering of the myth of Cupid and Psyche, secondly at the level of the 'repressed' Flaubertian subtext ('Hérodias'), and thirdly in terms of the central dramatization of the fundamental conflict in automatic writing between visual image and verbal image represented and neutralized by the triumph of Iaokannan/Tower/Word over Salome/Psyche/Image.

CÉLINE.   H. Godard, * '*Voyage au bout de la nuit*' de Céline*, Gallimard, 224 pp. Jack Murray, *The Landscapes of Alienation: Ideological Subversion in Kafka, Céline, and Onetti*, Stanford U.P., xii + 264 pp., addresses the systematic violation of the realist canon and of the ideological value system that underpins realism. The study of *Voyage au bout de la nuit* centres on the pursuit of the dialectic between setting and plot, the role of satire in the production of an anti-axiomatic that targets the axiomatic of the dominant capitalist imperium, and the struggle for legitimacy as an antidote to alienation. T. Spear, 'Céline and "autofictional" first-person narration', *Studies in the Novel*, 23:357–70, begins by considering the debate over the description of autofiction (with reference to Doubrovsky and Lejeune), and opts for a description of autofiction which stresses the transgression of the traditional author–narrator contract; an examination of C.'s produc-tion reveals the setting-up of an alternative contract based on the transposition of reality and the production of a textual fiction that weaves complex, subtle, and variable links with extratextual reality.

CENDRARS.   D. Maggetti, 'Rétif par Cendrars', *Europe*, no. 732, 1990:96–102, traces the affinities — stylistic, thematic, and attitu-dinal — of two unexpectedly aligned transgressor-writers.

CHAR.   *RHLF*, 1990, has the following articles: C. Dupouy, 'Les Transparents, du mythe au poème' (3–18), considers the rewriting of the myth of the Transparents inherited from Novalis via Breton, and contrasts C.'s felicitous interpretation of the familiar spirits — the 'vagabonds luni-solaires' — with that of Breton's gloomy version, tracing the depoliticization of the Transparent symbol after *Le Soleil des eaux* and its progressive poeticization through the different versions of *Les Matinaux* where the Transparents represent the defiance of the free poet faced with the tyrannical Sédentaires; J.-C. Mathieu, 'Noces d'herbe, salves de vent' (19–31), addresses in *Fureur et mystère* and *Les Matinaux* the conjunction of contradictory forces — grass and wind — in the intimation of the figure of the 'Marcheur' and, beyond that, of the Poet; J.-L. Steinmetz, 'Les armes du poème'

(32–42), is a close and precise study of the calligrammatic conclusion of *Les Matinaux*, 'Toute vie . . .', one partner (with 'Fête des arbres et du chasseur') in a liminal pair which asserts poetry as a means of revolt and realization; L. Ray, 'L'écriture brève dans *Fureur et mystère*' (43–51), identifies three categories of utterance: lapidary utterance as an essentially demetaphorized, verbal condensing of thought and opinion; the properly poetic utterance and the pull towards image at the point where thought-sentence becomes thought-image; the utterance whose semantic indeterminacy produces a verbal object of irreducible mystery. Michael Bishop, *René Char: les dernières années*, Amsterdam — Atlanta, Rodopi, 1990, 110 pp., is a collection of short studies of poems selected from the volumes spanned by *Aromates chasseurs* (1975) and the posthumously published *Éloge d'une soup-çonneuse* (1988). G. Mary, 'Jeu d'espaces', *Poétique*, 86:215–20, demonstrates how the poem — in this case, 'Congé au vent' (in *Fureur et mystère*) — is inscribed between two 'spaces' or types of organization, the first structured and homogeneous (the space of semiotics), the second a delinearized, aleatory space (for which a semiotic treatment is inappropriate). This study looks at the tangential contact between the two spaces, in terms of the phonic group [vã], its unifying role in the first paragraph, and its shortcircuiting by the critical narrative sequence triggered by 'elle s'en va' (where the reversal of the phonemes [ã v] precipitates a shift from time-as-object to time-as-subject, and thus from narrated to narration). P. Veyne, *Renè Char en ses poèmes* (Essais), *NFR*, 1990, 537 pp.

CLAUDEL.   C. Flood, 'Apocalyptic and millenarian tendencies in the works of Paul Claudel', *FMLS*, 27:348–57, examines the utopia/dystopia dynamic in four works, beginning with the unambiguously dialectical structuring of *La Ville*, and moving on to the synthetic and essentially Utopian vision of the meditative dialogues *Conversations dans le Loir-et-Cher* that is contrasted with the shift to a markedly apocalyptic world-view in *Au milieu des vitraux*. The author shows how in *Paul Claudel interroge l'Apocalypse* C. achieves a unitary vision of the two contradictory and endlessly fertile imperatives which impel the poet and dramatist. M.-T. Killiam, **The Art Criticism of Paul Claudel* (AUS, 22), 1990, ix + 411 pp. *Lettres à son fils Henri et à sa famille*, ed. Michel Malicet, Lausanne, L'Âge d'Homme, 1990, 300 pp., contains 150 letters that reveal C. to be both a moral guide and a morale-raiser for his son Henri, as well as an indulgent patriarch for his extended family. Of greatest interest are those letters written from Brangues in 1940 and 1941, revealing C.'s shift in attitude towards Pétain ('le vieux crocodile'), his disgust at the arrest of the Jewish director of Gnôme et Rhône, and numerous insights into the workings of Vichy France.

COCTEAU. P. Bauschatz, '*Oedipus*: Stravinsky and Cocteau recompose Sophocles', *CL*, 43:150–70, moves from a consideration of the joint operatic production of *Oedipus-Rex* to a study of C.'s reworking of the myth in *Oedipe roi* and *La Machine infernale*, drawing special attention to elements of stagecraft and action which demonstrate C.'s pursuit of character individualization, reduction, and idiosyncracy as an alternative to tragedy, elevation, and amplification. Danielle Chaperon, **Jean Cocteau: La Chute des anges*, Lille U.P., 1990, 229 pp.

COLETTE. **Œuvres*, III (Pléiade), ed. Claude Pichois, Gallimard, lxxvii + 1984 pp. C. Adam *et al.*, **Analyses et réflexions sur Colette, Sido et 'Les Vrilles de la vigne': l'hymne à l'univers*, Éds du Marketing, 1990, 128 pp. Diana Holmes, *Colette*, Basingstoke, Macmillan, viii + 142 pp., sets out to counter the gender bias which has trivialized and disparaged C.'s writing. Placing equal stress on text and context, she considers the conflicting ideologies which informed C.'s early experience, then moves through a series of interconnected perspectives on social and economic realism, the representation of the body, and language and gender, to reveal C. as a complex and committed feminist writer. C. Slawysutton, '"Où sont les enfants?": aspects du silence dans *La Maison de Claudine*', *FR*, 64, 1990:299–308, aims to disprove the view that *La Maison de Claudine* is merely the poetic description of a childhood, arguing instead that the novel describes the adult experience of failed communication and demonstrating the limits of language and silence both as the expression of such a breakdown and as a palliative to it.

DAUMAL. Phil Powrie, *René Daumal. Étude d'une obsession*, Droz, 1990, 176 pp., devotes two chapters to D.'s theoretical discourse, in particular to his efforts to neutralize the harmful effects of automatic writing and waking dream experiments through the elaboration of a Hegelian, non-dualist system; the remaining chapters examine D.'s literary discourse in terms of triadic structuring and a developing problematics of allegorization, in poetry from *Le Contre-ciel* to the 1935–44 output and in narrative from the little-known *Mugle* through *La Grande Beuverie* to *Le Mont analogue*.

DRIEU LA ROCHELLE. L. Rasson, 'Colonialisme fasciste: Drieu, Brasillach', *RR*, 82:76–88, starts from the premise that exoticism is a politico-literary necessity for collaborator-authors in a situation where the colonial question dominates the relationship between occupied and occupier: D.'s *L'Homme à cheval* reveals that the failure of one Fascist project is merely a deferral of the realization of the total plan.

ELUARD. D. C. Potts, 'Poem and programme: Eluard's "Denise disait aux merveilles"', *FS*, 45:55–61, is a close and careful reading of the poem that concludes with some incisive comments on the metapoetic function of the title, and a vigorous repudiation of biographical interpretation.

GIDE.   Marie-Denise Boros Azzi, *Problématique de l'écriture dans 'Les Faux-Monnayeurs' d'André Gide (Archives André Gide, 6) (ALM,* 244), Lettres Modernes, 1990, 137 pp., is a semiotic study of the diegesis of G.'s novel that exposes the protean and polyvalent function of the 'phénomène scriptural', and concludes that G. is a precursor not only of the 'nouveau roman' but also of Derridean deconstructionism. P. Chartier, * *'Les Faux-Monnayeurs' d'André Gide* (Foliothèque), Gallimard, 256 pp. A. Goulet, 'Mystifier pour démystifier: le narrateur des *Faux-Monnayeurs'*, *Littératures*, 23, 1990:169–81, explores the subjective, relative, and at times disconcertingly unstable criteria which constitute the position of the explicit narrator ('ombre itinérante') and enable G. to problematize questions of literary production and reception, and in so doing engage the reader in an active, critical reading of the text. Pierre Masson, * *Lire 'Les Faux-Monnayeurs'*, Lyons U.P., 1990, 167 pp. L. MacKenzie, 'The language of excitation in Gide's *L'Immoraliste'*, *RoQ*, 37, 1990:309–19, confronts the 'modesty' of G.'s language and its coextensive power to tantalize the reader, in order to tease out meanings veiled in semantic suggestiveness, namely the erotic connotations of the terms 'alerte' (erta) and 'exaltation' (altus). D. Moutote, * *Réflexions sur 'Les Faux-Monnayeurs'* (Unichamp, 25), Slatkine, 1990, 227 pp. G. Pistorius, *André Gide und das Deutschland: eine internationale Bibliographie*, Heidelberg, Winter, 1990, xxii + 704 pp. Patrick Pollard, *André Gide: Homosexual Moralist*, Newhaven — London, Yale U.P., xvi + 498 pp., makes a major contribution to scholarship on two fronts, the history of ideas, specifically the philosophy of homosexuality, and the literary representation of the homosexual. It combines the study of G. the writer with an ambitious investigation of G. the reader. *Corydon* provides the foundation text for a three-part study which looks at the genesis, structure, and language of G.'s 'Four Socratic Dialogues', exposing the crucial moral distinction G. makes between the positive and negative poles of homosexuality as indicated by the lexical distinction between 'pédéraste' and 'inverti'. This is followed by a major reconstruction and discussion of the abundant material (philosophical, socio-political, legal, medical, biological, botanical) to which G. had access. Part 3 is devoted to G.'s vast literary culture and to certain sources and influences, ancient and modern, Western and Oriental, while Part 4 traces the changes in G.'s portrayal of homosexuality from the reticence of the earlier works to the amoral liberation represented in *Les Caves du Vatican*, the post-war humanitarian portrayal, and the ultimate assimilation of the homosexual issue to the search for authenticity in *Thésée*. Appendices reproduce the 1911 Introductions to Dialogues I and III, the 1911 Appendix to *Corydon*, and the 1920 proof-copy Introduction to Dialogue II. Dennis Porter, *Haunted Journeys: Desire and Transgression in European Travel Writing*, Princeton U.P., xi + 341 pp., has chapter 9 'Political witness: T. E. Lawrence and Gide' (223–45), which looks at *Retour de l'URSS, suivi de Retouches* and asserts that the geopolitical fascination of a novelist more obviously concerned with individual rather than collective codes represents not so much a new departure as the turning upon a new sphere of interest of the same sense of revulsion and revolt towards systems of moral and social organization based on control and repression that bursts forth in his earlier fiction. W. C. Putnam, *L'Aventure littéraire de Joseph Conrad et d'André Gide* (SFIS 67), Saratoga, Anma Libri, 1990, xiv + 261 pp., is a lucid study of the reciprocity of the two writers and one that draws a careful distinction between their affinities and parallel developments, on the one hand, and the degree of influence of Conrad on G., on the other, in the period spanning the writing of *Les Caves du Vatican* and the completion of *Les Faux-Monnayeurs*; focuses on G.'s engagement with aesthetic and ethical questions, his receptivity to Symbolism, and his analysis of the human issues raised by the colonialist system in the African continent. A comparative study of *Les Caves* and *Lord Jim* explores the subversion of the adventure novel, whilst the concluding chapter on *Les Faux-Monnayeurs* examines the presentation of reality, objectivization, and the textual development of character.

GIONO. Pierre Citron, *Giono, 1895–1970*, Seuil, 1990, 670 pp., is a meticulous and very readable biography which writes against the grain of other studies by seeking to differentiate between 'facts' and G.'s imaginative presentation of things, whilst teasing out the parallels, analogies, and correspondences between the author's life and the world of his texts. Christiane Kègle, *Fiction et scriptibilité: l'exemple de Giono*, Toronto, Paratexte, 1990, 141 pp.

GIRAUDOUX. E. Goulding, 'Bulles de bonheur et anges de bois. Deux inédits de Jean Giraudoux', *NZJFS*, 10.2, 1989: 5–47, presents the abandoned opening chapter of *Combat avec l'ange*, a complete story which prefigures some of the novel's key themes and ideas, and the text in which G. finally explores the Dreyfus question; the second fragment, intended as a transition between chapters two and three, introduces the character Amparo, and presents a further variation on the theme of the struggle with the angel. Id., 'Le Maître des pastiches. Giraudoux et Flaubert — un parallèle entre Monsieur de Fortranges et Saint Julien l'hospitalier', *NZJFS*, 10.2, 1989: 49–71. L. W. Leadbeater, 'Aristotelian inversion in Jean Giraudoux's *Electre*', *FrF*, 15, 1990: 315–27, is a cogently argued study that explodes the Sartrean myth of G.'s slavish espousal of Aristotelian formulae —

causality, potentiality, actuality — by exposing in *Électre* G.'s anti-determinism, his ironic subversion of 'becoming' and the consequent non-fulfilment of the archetypal telic scheme. Brenda J. Powell, *The Metaphysical Quality of the Tragic: A Study of Sophocles, Giraudoux and Sartre*, Berne — NY, Lang, 1990, 205 pp., has 'A cacophonous quest for harmony: Giraudoux's *Électre*' where the author works out from Roman Ingarden's theory of the tragic as a metaphysical quality, focusing on the struggle between two high positive values and the emergence of Électre as a tragic heroine when absolute truth asserts itself as supreme among the moral values presented and as the necessary basis for the development of the metaphysical and the transcendence of the time-bound, relative parameters of the values espoused by Égisthe. Susan Nagel, *The Influence of the Novels of Jean Giraudoux on the Hispanic Vanguard Novels of the 1920s–1930s*, London — Toronto, Associated University Presses, 150 pp.

GREEN.   P. Derivière, 'La genèse du roman selon Julien Green', *NRF*, 454, 1990:52–60, aims at a reappraisal of a misrepresented novelist and, to this end, considers the dilemmas facing the Catholic novelist, arguing that G., in rejecting the literary 'engagement' of fellow writers in the name of freedom and non-alignment, placed his absolute faith in literature as a source of inner truth, as a reflection of the external world, and as a means of registering the fluctuating and febrile nature of the modern sensibility; identifies in *Épaves* the consolidation of Green's conception of the novel thereby breaking with a critical tradition which sees the protagonist Philippe as the antithesis of previous Greenian characters.

JACOB.   *Poèmes de Morven le Gaëlique* (Poésie), Gallimard, 189 pp.

JOUVE.   *Nord*, 16, 1990, is a special issue which offers, amidst a clutch of biographical and thematic sketches, several more substantial articles: C. Blot-Labarrère, 'Pierre Jean Jouve et le roman' (19–26), is an attempt to understand the creative and human imperatives which led J. to a ten-year experiment with the novel form; Y. Baudel, '*Paulina 1900* (éloge de *Paulina*)' (27–48), for all its declared laudatory function, confronts the clichés and conventionalisms of J.'s novel, placing the temptations of romanticism in the wider context of a search for new narrative techniques and the achievement of an enduringly modernist work that reveals its stylistic 'parenté' with Stendhal; D. Viart, 'Pierre Jean Jouve: inconscient, spiritualité et fiction' (49–62), takes the second novel of *Aventure de Catherine Crachat*, *Vagadu*, and assesses the fertilizing role of clinical psychoanalysis for J.'s construction of a poetic unconscious, distinguishing J.'s procedure from that of the Surrealists in terms of the former's rejection of automatism, and his practice of 'creating' signs in order to construct an unconscious which is itself not the producer of signs but the product of signs; thus J.'s abandonment of the novel as a genre is explained by the incompatibility of the potentially disruptive effects of the psychoanalytical experiment which J. envisaged, and his enduring commitment to the representationalist and ideological aims of traditional narrative. Other articles include: B. Caramatie, 'Mort du roman et naissance de la poésie: *Dans les années profondes*' (63–70); D. Combe, 'Rhétorique et théâtre chez Pierre Jean Jouve' (79–86); J. Deguy, 'Jouve et l'opéra: le *Don Juan* de Mozart' (87–96). J. Starobinski, '"Vrai corps" de Pierre Jean Jouve', *NRF*, 462–63: 10–21, proceeds by a detailed comparison of the Latin prayer from Mozart's *Ave verum* motet, and the concluding poem of *Les Noces* (1931), and reveals how J.'s poem amplifies, aestheticizes, and ultimately transforms both the original inspirational text and the expression of mystical desire into a celebration of creative passion.

MARTIN DU GARD. J.-F. Massol, 'La nouvelle et le roman-fleuve: à propos de Martin du Gard', *Poétique*, 81, 1990: 63–75, is a narratological reappraisal of 'La Sorellina', the short story which gives its title to the fifth volume of *Les Thibault*, and 'Confidence africaine', written in 1931. It examines the intricate relationship between minor genre and massive *roman-fleuve*, mirrored through the theme of incest, and demonstrates how M. incorporates the enigma typical of the short story, yet attenuates the thetic function of the minor genre and counters its subjectivity by means of a shift from the first narrator/author identification in 'Confidence africaine' to narrator-absence in the 'La Sorellina' volume.

MAURIAC. Toby Garfitt, *Mauriac: Thérèse Desqueroux*, London, Grant and Cutler, 76 pp. G. Imhoff, 'Thérèse Desqueroux: un monstre parmi tant d'autres', *RoQ*, 38: 157–67, puts the case for the attenuation of monstrousness, and subsequently for a more nuanced portrait of Thérèse, using the thematic of earth–mud–dirt to justify a sympathetic reading of a soul itself floundering in the quagmire of monsters. Jean Touzot, *Mauriac sous l'Occupation*, Lyons, La Manufacture, 1990, 370 pp., is a fascinating exploration of the conscience of the journalist-writer examined against the background of the vicious 'querelle des mauvais maîtres' mounted by Brasillach and fellow collaborationists, and the persecution of the author and his latest novel *La Pharisienne*. The abundant documents dating from the 1938–46 period are presented in a systematic way. The first section of the book reproduces the *Paris-Soir* contributions of 1938–40 in which an impassioned M. probes the already very real threat to intellectual integrity posed by the Nazis prior to the events of June 1940. Further sections reproduce an extract from the *Livre de raison* written in occupied Malagar; the *Figaro* articles of Summer 1940 whose occasional 'maréchalisme' the biographer distinguishes from ideological 'pétainisme' and whose anglophobism (after Mers-el-Kébir) he explains as a momentary lapse in the conviction of the 'pélerin de l'espérance'; plus articles published in the *Gazette de Lausanne* of which the most significant are 'Évasion par la lecture', on the redemptive power of literature, and the poignant 'Épreuve du silence'. The text of the clandestinely published *Cahier noir* figures alongside articles which appeared in *Les Lettres françaises*, bitterly denouncing the collaborationist enemy, identified as the Maurras – Drieu – Brasillach trio ('l'important, M. Brasillach, n'est pas que vous ayez aimé un seul Allemand, c'est que vous les ayez servis tous'). The penultimate section includes a moving celebration of the resistance poets, particularly Aragon, Eluard, Jacob, Tardieu, and Cassou: good quality reproductions of photographs from M.'s family collections.

MICHAUX. Brigitte Ouvry-Vial, *Henri Michaux*, Lyons, La Manufacture, 1989, 254 pp.

MILOSZ. Leonard Nathan and Arthur Quinn, *The Poet's Work: An Introduction to Czeslaw Milosz*, Cambridge, Mass., Harvard U.P., xi + 178 pp., plots M.'s development along the Poland–Paris–Berkeley axis, identifying the contradictory influences of Witkiewicz and Simone Weil on the development of M.'s thought in the 1950s, the struggle between pantheism and Christianity and its reconciliation through Manicheanism, in the context of the tensions between pessimism and ecstasy which impel M.'s poetry

NIZAN. *Literature and Revolution*, ed. David Bevan, Amsterdam — Atlanta, Rodopi, 1989, 182 pp., has R. Thornberry, 'Paul Nizan: revolutionary in politics, conservative in aesthetics' (87–95), an essentially anti-Marxist critique which savages N. on grounds both literary and ideological, whilst recognizing his achievement as an ironist and a critic.

PAULHAN. J. Baetens, 'Jean Paulhan et le discours analogique', *EsC*, 31.2:30–8, considers the prevalence of analogy as a deliberate strategy of de-figuration that is stylistically consonant with the search for meaning reflected in the pursuit of 'le mot juste' in *Le Guerrier appliqué*. M. Crouzet, 'A propos des *Fleurs de Tarbes*: Jean Paulhan critique de la modernité', *RLMC*, 43, 1990:287–309, examines P.'s diagnosis of *avant-garde* 'terror', in a study of P.'s critique of Modernist anti-values that explores Rhetoric, P.'s antidote to the Modernist 'misology', and an esoteric alternative based on the simultaneous perception of language and idea.

PÉGUY. *RLMod, Charles Péguy*, 5. *L'Écrivain*, ed. S. Fraisse, Minard, 1990, 196 pp., contains two main types of article, one which considers the development of P.'s style and one which addresses questions of inspiration and influence: F. Gerbod, 'La constitution d'une écriture' (11–29), is a diachronic study of the development of P.'s style that sets out to rescue the writer from charges of verbal effusiveness by emphasizing his versatility; J. Onimus, 'Poésie et profondeur' (31–54), engages with the problematics of defining P.'s poetic style and concludes that in the *écart* between P.'s theory and his poetic practice lies an authentic, unfettered, organic classicism born of a desire to communicate reality freely and fully; S. Fraisse, ' "J'ai horreur de l'éloquence" ' (57–80), is a clear, informative discussion of P.'s writing that shows how there is, behind P.'s declared rejection of rhetoric and oratory, a driving concern with creating specific stylistic effects: by focusing attention on those aspects of P.'s style (dialogue, apostrophe, injunction, interrogatives, systolic and diastolic movements) which engage the reader's participation most directly, the study demonstrates that P. is a skilled exponent of the dialogical principle described by Bakhtin; R. Dadoun, 'De la répétition' (81–92), challenges critical assumptions that label P.'s style repetitious and aesthetically inept, and shows how repetition functions as a sign of the inadequacy of language, and of the mediation of language towards reality, and is thus strategically incorporated by P. into a metaphysical style which sees Creation as an act of continuous Re-creation; G. Fritz, 'Un mouvement essentiel à la prose de Péguy: de l'abstrait au concret' (93–105), identifies P.'s struggle as a writer in terms of his resistance to intellectualized language and his desire to adapt language to the expression of a concrete reality; highlights the strategy of repetition whereby meaning is amplified, or, indeed, metaphorized by P. as a means of transposing abstract truth into visible reality; M. Dufresne, 'Le paratexte: signatures et titres' (107–21), gives a Genettian guise to what is a rather traditional study of the inconsistency between the orientations announced in P.'s titles and the content of the texts which follow, and concludes that the title is often the intimation of a point of departure, an obsession, or a subject to be explored in a future text; R. Balibar, ' "O mère ensevelie hors du premier jardin". La poésie des écoliers républicains' (125–51), considers the impact on P.'s style in *Ève* of the grammar training dispensed by the Republican education system; S. Fraisse, 'De l'intertextualité à la réécriture' (153–61), considers P.'s assimilation and transformation of the writings of Ronsard, Molière, Corneille, Hugo, and Renan, through a few choice textual examples, and suggests that P.'s motive is to establish complicity with a cultivated readership; G. Lecomte, 'Péguy et la crise moderniste: une occasion manquée?' (169–94), in other words, why did P., normally so galvanized by crises, remain silent in the debate over the future of French Catholicism? The tentative answer is that he saw it as a debate between bourgeois intellectuals.

PONGE. D. Sears, 'The two-way text: Ponge's metapoctic "Fable"', *EsC*, 31.2:50–57, addresses, in the wake of Derrida and others, aspects of self-reflexivity in the *Proêmes* volume. A circuitous exposé of the text's polysemous possibilities, it centres on the enigmatic 'toléré', taking us via its Latin etymology and associations ('tolerare' and 'tolere') back to 'tôle' and then to the textual reference 'tain', and stops just short of 'tiré par les cheveux'. The concluding remark, 'If reading all these meanings into "toléré" seems unjustified . . .', is appropriately self-reflexive.

PROUST. *Sur la génétique textuelle*, ed. D. G. Bevan and P. M. Wetherill, Amsterdam, Rodopi, 1990, 205 pp., has A. Pugh, 'Proust's working methods: the importance of structure' (109–24), which begins with a brief history of the efforts of scholars to determine the exact development of *A la recherche*, then skilfully zigzags between the *Cahiers* in order to plot P.'s method of composition in structural terms, showing how that structure, once discovered, is constantly transformed, revised, and renewed through processes of insertion and displacement; concludes by putting the case for a shift of emphasis in genetic studies from thematic and stylistic perspectives to a broader structural approach. Other contributions include E. Nicole, 'Les notations marginales dans les *Cahiers Proust*' (125–32), and K. Hamer, 'Notes de lecture: Proust et Joannis Guigard, Le Nouvel Armorial du bibliophile' (133–43). B. Brun, 'L'enfance d'un roman: *Du côté de chez Swann*', *RSH*, 222:41–49, uses the critical tools of textual genesis and analysis of structures and sources in order to demonstrate the non-validity of the concept of an authentic 'récit d'enfance' where questions of transposition (whereby 'récit' becomes a literary genre) and transformation (processes of rewriting revealed by the study of textual genesis) are paramount. N. Diamant, 'Judaism, homosexuality, and other sign systems in *A la recherche du temps perdu*', *RR*, 82:179–92, considers how an initial, non-signifying code (Father as Enabler rather than Rival), inscribed in the biblical reference to the binding of Isaac at the beginning of *Combray*, triggers the collapse of codes of difference (social, cultural, sexual, gender) which are reconstructed in *A la recherche* in the relationship between limits and their transgression. T. M. Donnan, 'Vinteuil's music as central to Marcel's artistic calling', *RoQ*, 37, 1990:419–30, contrasts Swann's sentimental infatuation with Vinteuil's Sonata, with Marcel's appreciation of the cyclically-conceived Septet, and identifies the superior power of the Septet with the intimation of the mystery of art and the appeal to artistic realization. G. Genette, '"Un de mes écrivains préférés"', *Poétique*, 84, 1990:509–19, takes Riffaterre to task for failing to distinguish (in *Fictional Truth*, 1990) between structural and genetic approaches and thus arriving at an 'interpretation' of the

228 *French Studies*

reference ('un de mes écrivains préférés') that is determinist, partial, and ill-founded; in so doing he warns against 'la facilité de sauter sur un terrain dès que l'autre résiste, et par exemple, d'invoquer une lecture de Virgile en se gardant de préciser si le lecteur s'appelle Proust, Marcel — ou Riffaterre'. Richard E. Goodkin, *Around Proust*, Princeton U.P., x + 162 pp., is a three-part study which adds up to a composite picture of the novel's resistance to 'inwardness'. Chapters 1 and 2 deal with relations between P.'s novel and the genres of epic, lyric, and tragedy, in particular through explicit connections with the *Odyssey*, Mallarmé's sonnets, and *Phèdre*. However the reader is invited beyond the parameters of purely literary intertextuality in chapters 3 to 6 which address non-literary, artistic, and intellectual areas with studies of P.'s treatment of movement and time from perspectives both philosophical (Zeno of Elea) and cinematic (Hitchcock's *Vertigo*), and P.'s depictions of love and death and their affinities with Freud's *Mourning and Melancholia*, and with Wagner's *Tristan and Isolde* 'Prelude', specifically the unresolved 'Tristan' chord. A work of sustained clarity and certain interest, its aim is to link P.'s novel to other constellations, assessing the nature and degree of correspondence — be it explicit connections or subtle affinities. Juliette Hassine, *Ésotérisme et écriture dans l'œuvre de Proust*, Minard, 1990, 190 pp. Ronald Hayman, *Proust*, London, Heinemann, 1990, 564 pp., is likely to be warmly received by specialists and general readers alike, as a complement rather than a counterpoint to Painter's biography. Hayman researches the Proustian inner self (its contradictions, conflicts, and complexities), speaking directly, even informally, to his reader whilst avoiding popularization and trivialization. This is no mere chaptering of a life but a work which succeeds in combining anecdote with illuminating analysis. In Philip Kolb, *Marcel Proust: Correspondance*, Plon, xx + 857 pp., P. emerges, against a background of sporadic strikes in Paris, revolution in Mexico, and a near-debilitating obsession with his health, surprisingly ebullient (confirming Montesquiou's suspicion in letter 233) as he cajoles, castigates, and corrects the critics, when he is not pursuing, doggedly but with disarming ineptitude, public honours. What emerges more subtly from some of the letters is the struggle for a more profound, closer critical understanding of the objectives of his writing, of his preoccupation with composition, and with the unity and architecture of his novel (letters 30 and 161). The ingenuousness of Jacques Blanche's view quoted by P. in a letter to Jacques Rivière (letter 177) is not lost on P., nor is it likely to be lost on Proustians today: '*A la recherche du temps perdu* est un domaine spirituel où plusieurs générations de psychologues, de littérateurs, pourront travailler sans gêner leurs voisins et sans se disputer'. M. Lydon, 'Pli selon pli: Proust and

Fortuny', *RR*, 81, 1990:438–53, addresses the conflict between metaphor and metonymy, between object of desire (Venice metaphorized by Albertine's Fortuny gown) and desire (which is mediated through, and in the process blocked by, the literal body of Albertine); traces the 'couture'–'peinture' association from Elstir to Fortuny, and back to Carpaccio; with black and white plates. Yann Le Pichon, *Le Musée retrouvé de Marcel Proust*, Stock, 1990, 270 pp., between cork-look endpapers, is a collection of extracts from *A la recherche* and other writings sumptuously illustrated by high quality reproductions of the paintings to which P. refers: this textual gallery includes works by Vermeer, Frans Hals, Velasquez, Fra Angelico, Carpaccio, Gozzòli, Luini, Turner, Whistler, Chardin, Corot, and Bakst. Also included are a biography by Anne Borrel and a useful index of the artists referred to by P. Luz Pimentel, **Metaphoric Narration: Paranarrative Dimensions in 'A la recherche du temps perdu'*, Buffalo — London, Toronto U.P., 1990, xi + 217 pp. S. Ménager, 'Horticouture proustienne', *NFS*, 30.1 : 33–38, is a sensitive if rather slight thematic sketch which establishes, as the hybrid title suggests, the link between the floral and the sartorial in Proust. K. Newmark, 'Ingesting the mummy: Proust's allegory of memory', *YFS*, 79, 150–77, uses the Madeleine episode to demonstrate P.'s resistance to the Idealist component of Symbolism, and his pursuit of a materialist alternative based on a literal truth, rather than a speculative truth. The author sets out to show how the negativity at the heart of Symbolist poetics is subsumed by the positivity of the novel as an attempt to understand, the very existence of the text constituting in itself a recovery of what is lost: an article whose own meaning is at times obscured where it strains after metaphorical effect, and contracts in curious semantic obstetrics ('Memory as this power of turning in language is thus the unnatural and inhuman album(en) where an abortion of nature is written down and stored as the embryonic promise of a human subject that is not yet there'). T. de Praetere, 'Contradiction de Proust; logique(s) de Proust', *LR*, 45:63–76, examines aspects of peripaeteia and ambivalence: an initial discussion of the co-presence of contrasting values and their alternate triumphs focuses upon the functions of peripaetia as a form of resistance to neutrality and as a producer both of surprise and of predictability; subsequent discussion addresses the role of ambivalence in abolishing hierarchies and producing simultaneous states, thereby complementing the horizontality imposed by a system of successive reversals. Janet Stock, **Marcel Proust: A Reference Guide 1950–1970*, Boston, Mass., G. K. Hall, xxiv + 565 pp.

QUENEAU.   Jane Hale, **The Lyric Encyclopedia of Raymond Queneau*, Ann Arbor, Michigan U.P. — Manchester U.P., 1989, 189 pp. W. Motte, 'Raymond Queneau and the aesthetic of formal constraint',

RR, 82: 193–209, evaluates Q.'s repudiation of the Surrealist concepts of inspiration and chance, and his development of a counter-poetics of consciousness, will, and control, underpinned by formal values of symmetry, structure, and mathematical rigour; considers the various applications of Q.'s theory in *Le Chiendent, Cent Mille Milliards de poèmes*, and *Morale élémentaire*. Madeleine Velguth, *The Representation of Women in the Autobiographical Novels of Raymond Queneau*, NY, Lang, 1990, x + 340 pp., is a bland, rather slight study which begins with a socio-historical overview of attitudes towards women (in education and in the early Surrealist movement), and moves on to consider the development of the relationship of author to female Other, plotting this against the progress of the novels from pessimism to fulfilment. S. Winspur, 'Queneau's contexts of irony', *RR*, 82: 70–75, is an incisive article that looks at the textual production of irony in the *Pour un art poétique* series, showing how the debunking of the literary canon works not to negate poetry but to expose its structuring principles.

ROLLAND. *Correspondance entre Romain Rolland et Maxime Gorki (1916–1936) (Cahiers Romain Rolland, 28)*, ed. J. Pérus, Albin Michel, 546 pp., is a collection of over 200 letters that charts the tormented friendship between two socialist comrades; of primarily historical and political interest. M. Rogister, 'Romain Rolland: one German view', *MLR*, 86: 349–60, probes the relationship between R. and two of his commentator–admirers — Stefan Zweig and René Schichele — assessing their differing treatments of R. as a biographical subject; concludes by imputing to Schichele the role of plagiarist of Zweig's monograph albeit one with the creditable purpose of affirming the importance of R.'s ideas to the pursuit of the European ideal.

SAINT-EXUPÉRY. S. Beynon John, *'Vol de nuit' and 'Terre des hommes'*, London, Grant and Cutler, 1990, 93 pp., argues a carefully balanced view of S.-E. that insists on the poetic quality of his writing, and the energizing effect of his style, but also draws attention to lapses in narrative structure and plot, and inadequacies of characterization, and thus promotes an awareness of the limitations of S.-E.'s world-view. Luc Estang, **Saint-Exupéry*, Seuil, 1989, 186 pp. Jules Roy, **Saint-Exupéry*, Lyons, La Manufacture, 1990, 99 pp.

SEGALEN. J. Ferry, 'Les avatars du vieillard vénérable de Bougainville, chez Diderot et Segalen', *NZJFS*, 11.2, 1990: 35–51, sees the character Paofaï the High Priest in *Les Immémoriaux* as a product of S.'s meditation on the collective situation of the Polynesian people faced with the intrusive forces of European civilization. Thus S. emerges as a continuer and transformer of Bougainville and Diderot's studies of the reconciliation of nature and society in primitive cultures. O. Houbert, 'La Chine intérieure de Victor Segalen', *NRF*, 450–1, 1990: 80–103, uncovers the essentially dynamic vision of China through which S. opposes the sclerosis induced in civilization by forced modernity and characterized by the 'levelling' of cultures, the erosion of ethnic difference, and the standardization of diversity.

SIMENON.   A. Gabriel, 'Faire parler le mort: Simenon et le non-dit', *RoQ*, 37, 1990:175–85, studies Maigret's reticence and scepticism faced with the semantic component of language, and lists instances where non-verbal language (gesture, clothing, physionomy, movement) are sources of meaning: this is evidence of S. challenging the mainstream assumption of his day that verbal language pre-existed man, and giving proper place to pre-verbal communication as a more effective means of knowing the Other.

VALÉRY.   *Cahiers 1894–1913*, vol. III, ed. Nicole Celeyrette-Pietri and Judith Robinson-Valéry, Gallimard, 1990, 670 pp. *Paul Valéry: le cycle de 'Mon Faust' devant la sémiotique théâtrale et l'analyse textuelle* (Acta Romanica, 7), ed. K. A. Blüher and J. Schmidt–Radefelt, Tübingen, Narr, 283 pp. Elisabeth Howe, *Stages of Self: The Dramatic Monologues of Laforgue, Mallarmé and Valéry*, Athens, GA, Ohio U.P., 1990, x + 219 pp., examines a somewhat neglected genre in the French tradition — the dramatic monologue (as opposed to the preconscious *monologue intérieur* of Joyce) which the author differentiates from its Shakespearian counterpart (Browning, Eliot, and Laforgue). The chapter devoted to *La Jeune Parque* considers the struggle against referentiality, the construction of distance, and the centrality of voice, arguing that the dramatic nature of the Fate's monologue is a product of the 'conscience consciente' and that the inevitable split between 'parleur' and 'auditeur' implied by such self-consciousness transforms the monologue of the character into the dialogue of the psyche. *Paul Valéry* (Littérature moderne, 2), ed. James Lawler and André Guyaux, Champion — Geneva, Slatkine, xii + 225 pp. Florence de Lussy, *'Charmes' d'après les manuscrits de Paul Valéry: histoire d'une métamorphose*, Lettres Modernes, 1990, 388 + i + xiii pp. D. Oster, 'Valéry babélien', *CEcr*, 36, 1990:137–44, meditates on the limitations of V.'s application of a thermodynamic model to attempts to make sense of (and manage) the cultural hurly-burly and philosophical Babelism of the modern world in *La Crise de l'esprit*, *Monsieur Teste*, and *La Jeune Parque*. R. Pickering, *Genèse du concept valéryen 'pouvoir' et 'conquête méthodique' de l'écriture*, Lettres Modernes, 1990, 150 pp. P.-J. Quillien, 'Paul Valéry et la notion d'événement', *RHis*, 574, 1990:277–301, assesses the limitations of V.'s pronouncements on History — his critique of the content of History and of the procedures underpinning it, particularly the failure of History to expose the subjective and arbitrary mechanisms of its own production, and, as V. sees it, the reductionist tendency of historians to foreground 'sensational' events at the expense of 'functional' events

('Les événements sont l'écume des choses. Mais c'est la mer qui m'intéresse'); concludes that V. is not the precursor of New History but a continuer of the old debate over the rivalry between *Kulturgeschichte* and 'l'histoire-batailles'. S. Winspur, 'Valéry's meta-formalism', *EsC*, 31.2:39–49, challenges three commonplaces central to standard assessments of V.'s formalism, in particular the charge that V.'s poetry is divorced from 'real life'. He argues (1) that the poem cannot be dissociated from the reaction it produces in the reader and that this is an inevitable link with 'life'; (2) that poetic language replaces the 'exchange economy' of non-poetic language with an alternative economy of an intransitive, performative type capable of revealing the procedures whereby reality is constructed in transitive, constative discourse: thus poetry illuminates the subjective structures we use to construct 'reality'; (3) that the poem is less formal than meta-formal in that it produces in the reader not merely a sense of the 'formal necessity' of the text, but, more significantly, an awareness of the inexhaustible potential of 'form-making'.

THE TWENTIETH CENTURY SINCE 1945

By H. G. McIntyre, *Lecturer in French at the University of Strathclyde*

1. GENERAL

Zoë Boyer, 'French women writers: the forthright generation', *EFL*, 27:64–74, studies a generation of women writers — Rochefort, d'Eaubonne, Cardinal, and Groult — who, born in the twenties and coming to womanhood at the time of the Second World War, are sandwiched between Colette, Duras, de Beauvoir, etc., on the one hand and contemporary theorists of gender and language difference such as Cixous and Kristeva on the other. Boyer characterizes this intermediate generation as depicting direct female experience and distinguishes between 'écriture féminine' and feminist writing proper. Rather than tackling this idea on a broad front, however, the article consists of four separate sections, one on each author. Sophie Bertho, 'L'attente postmoderne: à propos de la littérature contempo-raine en France', *RHLS*, 4–5:735–43, considers the position of the anti-novel in these postmodernist, poststructuralist, post *nouveau roman* days and discerns, in the wake of disaffection with theory and the complete rout of committed literature, a return to the story and the subject, even if this latter can never again achieve the status of the Balzacien *moi*. The article cites Robbe-Grillet as a convert in his latest works and presages the re-emergence of a thirst for values and 'la volonté de redécouvrir les critères du bien et du mal'. Michael Issacharoff, 'Vox clamantis: l'espace de l'interlocution', *Poétique*, 87:315–26, addresses what he regards as an elementary but neglected question: what exactly is 'dialogue'? Drawing on Beckett, Sartre, Cocteau and Camus's *La Chute*, he attempts to define the distinction between dialogue and monologue. *La Voix humaine* and *Oh les beaux jours* are given as extreme examples. There are interesting comments but it is debatable that his conclusion — 'il faut une voix concrète actualisée et la conscience d'une présence auditive' — leaves us much the wiser. Most of the contributions to *YFS*, 79, 'Literature and the ethical question', are weighted more towards the ethical and philosophical than the directly literary and are therefore of only tangential interest to the literary specialist. Jean-Luc Nancy, 'The unsacrificeable' (20–38), studies the importance of the idea of sacrifice in Bataille, seen against the wider background of western tradition from Socrates to Christianity. Modern literature specialists might derive some profit from Jill Robbins, 'Visage, figure: reading Levinas' *Totality and Infinity*' (135–49), in an area where one is grateful for any guidance. Of more general interest is Vincent P.

Pecora, 'Ethics, politics and the middle voice' (203–30); borrowing the idea of 'la voix moyenne' from Derrida's 1968 essay, *La Différance*, he discusses the ideas of a number of contemporary French thinkers, notably Derrida himself, Foucault, and Bourdieu. The most readable contribution is that by Yves Bonnefoy, 'Poetry and liberty' (255–69), asking: 'What does the word liberty mean to us and what are its uses?' In the same theoretical domain but of more direct application to literary studies is Jean-Marie Schaeffer, 'Défense et illustration de la poétique', *Critique* 528:346–56, which greets the publication of Genette's *Fiction et diction*, this blueprint for a 'poétique élargie', as proof that the discipline founded by Aristotle is still alive and well in the self-consciously postmodernist eighties and nineties. *StLM*, 24.2, is devoted to Performance Theory and the theatre; the articles tend to be wide-ranging and contain numerous references to and discussions of the theory and practice of French figures like Artaud, Baudrillard, Derrida, Ionesco, Beckett, and Duchamp; in particular, a study by Marvin Carlson on the function of stage directions draws for illustration on a variety of French sources from Diderot to Ionesco and Beckett. Danièle de Ruyter-Tognotti, 'Théâtre et histoire: position critique dans 1789 du Théâtre du Soleil', *Neophilologus*, 75:367–78, analyses the various 'forms of denunciation' by which the Théâtre du Soleil creates a critical perspective on the Revolution and links them to the troupe's perceptions of the events of its own time. Examining the choice of scenes and the presentation of characters, and based on the video of the production as well as the text, the article also encompasses metatheatrical aspects such as the 'problématique elle-même de la transmission du message au public actuel'. In Samuel L. Leiter, *From Stanislavsky to Barrault: Representative Directors of the European Stage*, NY, Greenwood Press, 241 pp., French theatre is represented by Jacques Copeau and Jean-Louis Barrault. Leiter's partly biographical, partly analytical account of Barrault's work as actor and director describes his collaboration with various theatres, analyses his production style, the importance of movement and scenic techniques, how he approaches rehearsals and casting and how he relates to his actors. For reference there is a useful chronology of his activities up to the late eighties. Micheline Servin, 'Les ombrelles trouées d'Avignon', *TM*, 543:165–90, provides an account of the 1991 Avignon Theatre Festival for those unable to be there in person. For the modern theatre specialist, there is an account of an Armand Gatti production, *Ces empereurs aux ombrelles trouées*, which draws on the talents of young people from a deprived area and is not so much a 'spectacle exhibition' as an opportunity via the theatre for people to come together whose paths might not otherwise cross. Another update on recent theatre comes in the form of a new, enlarged edition of David Bradby's *Modern French Drama (1940-1990)*, CUP, xiii + 331 pp., which contains an additional chapter on the playwrights of the eighties, bringing what was already the most comprehensive survey in its field right up to date. In the poetic domain, Michael Bishop, 'Vérité et indicible dans la poésie francaise contemporaine', *EsC*, 31.2:58–67, takes on the challenge of surveying more or less the whole field of modern poetry from the Dadaists and Surrealists onwards, from which source contemporary poetry draws its 'dialectique fondamentale'. He achieves something of a *tour de force* within a very limited compass in managing to refer to all the significant figures.

2. AUTHORS

BARTHES. George H. Bauer, 'Met(s)atextualité poétique: les *biographèmes* de R. B.', *EsC*, 31.2:68–75, offers an interesting, if somewhat idiosyncratic, literary peregrination among the neologisms of B.'s *biographèmes*. Based on extended culinary metaphors and allusions which become tiresome ultimately, it is perhaps a case of making too much of a meal of things.

BECKETT. Ann Beer, 'B.'s "autography" and the company of languages', *SoRL*, 27:771–91, examines B.'s sense of 'aloneness' in old age and his 'autographic' quest for understanding of the self. Based on the late bilingual trilogy of novellas, *Company, Mal vu, mal dit, Worstward Ho*, it is an interesting study of B.'s relationship to both his creative languages and of the function of his deliberately chosen bilingualism in seeking and creating a sense of identity. Despite his sweeping title, Manfred Beyer, 'B.'s Dramen and Sartres Ontologie: die Absurdität der Freiheit', *ASNS*, 227, 1990:256–75, applies Sartrean notions of *soi, en soi*, and *pour soi* almost exclusively to *En attendant Godot*. Shira Wolosky, 'The negative way negated: S.B.'s *Texts for Nothing*', *NLH*, 22:213–30, finds behind B.'s generally assumed negativity and linguistic nihilism an equivocal axiology. Even in such as *Texts for Nothing*, one may discern a positive affirmation in the generation of a language which negates negation and denies self-denial. H. Porter Abbot, 'Reading as theatre: understanding defamiliarisation in B.'s art', *ModD*, 34.1:5–22, focuses on *Ohio Impromptu* and looks at the fusion or confusion of 'reading' and 'theatre', i.e. recited discourse and dramatic action in B.'s later work, in particular his blurring of genre distinctions and his fondness for 'making strange'. Hélène Merlin, 'Le chicot-crucifix et le texte vestige', *Littérature*, 83:31–42, sees *Malone meurt* as an 'ars moriendi en acte'. Although not always easy going perhaps, the analysis is a thoughtful and closely argued reading of the book. Angela Montgomery, 'B. and science: *Watt* and the quantum universe', *CC*, 13, *Literature and Science*, 171–81, seems at first sight to be engaged in an unprofitable enterprise. It appears less unwise in the light of documentary evidence in B.'s own hand from the thirties of his interest in the principles of physics. None the less, whether or not we need relate narrative discontinuity and uncertainty in *Watt* to the principles of quantum physics remains a moot point. **The World of S. B.*, ed. J. H. Smith, Johns Hopkins U.P., xxiv + 226 pp. P. Zard, *B. En attendant Godot*, Bordas, 96 pp., is an attractively presented student guide. *En attendant Godot & Fin de partie*, ed. R. Thibault, Nathan, 96 pp.

BLONDIN. Roger Grenier, 'A.B.', *NRF*, 464:63–64, offers us a biographical glimpse or reminiscence of B. in the fifties when they both worked together as journalists, pointing out the contrast between B.'s disorganized personal lifestyle and the grace and style of his writing.

BONNEFOY. Despite the title, Anja Pearre, 'Constable and B.: mirrors and reflections in *Ce qui fut sans lumière*', *FrF*, 16:91–105, deals not just with the important structural and emblematic function of Constable's influence but also that of Claude Lorrain and examines how the relationship between these two painters — symbolized by the mirrors of the title — acts as a vehicle for B.'s aesthetics. Michael Edwards, 'Yeats dans la traduction d'Y.B.', *Critique*, 535:915–30, is less interested in the accuracy of B.'s translations and more in how his approach to and rendering of Y.'s poems sheds light on his own work. Pierre Campion, 'Poésie et philosophie: étude du poème d'Y.B. *Aux arbres*', *IL*, 4:17–21, offers a straightforward but usefully detailed analysis of the poem in question, illustrating that the philosophical task of poetry is to 'constituer des médiations vraies'. Olivier Himy, *Y.B. Poèmes commentés*, Champion, 155 pp., is a good idea well executed. The format is prompted by a practical need since B.'s poetry figures for the first time on a *programme de concours*. The choice of only ten poems must inevitably be subjective but the commentaries are eminently clear and sensible and throw genuine light not just on the poems chosen but more generally on the ideas and practice of this 'difficult' writer. J. Naughton, **In the Shadow's Light*, Chicago U.P., ix + 179 pp., is a translation but contains an interview with B.

BUTOR. Jean-Charles Gateau, 'B. et Pfund en nécromants', *Littérature*, 81:70–84, shows how B. took his inspiration for *Voix d'outre-cuivre* from an exhibition of P. aquatints based on retouched old photographs. With the aid of diagrams and a detailed look at permutations of 'moules syntaxiques', Gateau shows B. imitating P.'s attempt to 'contraindre des morts à revenir' by giving them new voices.

CAMUS, A. Steven G. Kellman, '*La Peste*: infected by the bacillus of self-consciousness', *EsC*, 31.2:22–29, sees the novel as a supremely self-conscious fiction but one with a 'troubled conscience about its own reflexivity'. Evidence for the metatextual in *La Peste* is garnered from Fitch's work on references and allusions and the study as a whole is readable, clear and refreshingly jargon-free. Albert Mingelgrün, '*Caligula* ou comment s'écrit la maladie de la lune', *IL*, 4:14–16, points out an intellectual and/or esthetic paradox in that the failure of Caligula's attempt to come to terms with 'un royaume où l'impossible est roi' is highlighted all the more by the 'écriture lumineuse' of Camus's style. The metaphysical failure in the play is confirmed by the aesthetic success. *La Peste* is included in two new student guides; V. Anglard, *A. C. La Peste*, Nathan, 127 pp., and J. Lévi-Valensi, *La Peste d'A.C.*, Gallimard, 219 pp.

CAMUS, R. P. Jourde, 'Un exemple de création de pays imaginaire: "La Caronie" dans *Roman Roi* de R.C.', *IL*, 1:22–26, is a methodical examination of toponyms, with maps to help, demonstrating how C. goes about constructing the geography of his imaginary country.

DEBRAY. Bill Marshall, 'From Guevarra to Mitterand: the masks of R.D.', *NFS*, 30.1:72–83, is based on two novels, *L'Indésirable* and *La Neige brûle*, both read in the light of the autobiographical *Les Masques* (1987). The comparison helps highlight the problems of the relationship between the private and the political man which is the determining influence in D.'s writing.

DEGUY. Patrice Bougon, 'M.D.: un écrivain en voyage', *Critique*, 526:167–71, is a review of a recent D. collection *Arrêts fréquents* (1990). Reflecting on some characteristic elements of D.'s style and tone, Bougon suggests that the appearance of this 'polymorphous' work serves as a reminder that the poet in D. does not overshadow the thinker and trained philosopher. Michel Ballabriga, 'Étude sémantique d'un texte de M.D.: de la description à l'interprétation', *ChS*, 2:37–55, does what the title indicates: a detailed semantic study of a text from Quaternaire no. 2. The exercise needs no justification in itself since the D. text is far from obvious but it is not helped by persistent use of jargon and a somewhat obscure style.

DEPESTRE. Pierre Guy Lapaire. 'L'érotisme baroque, le télédial et les femmes-jardin de R.D.', *EFL*, 27:91–101, explores D.'s enthusiastic celebration of uninhibited sexuality, principally in his *Alléluia pour une femme-jardin*, where the luxuriousness and fertility of the garden serves as a symbol of the 'ideal' woman. The article demonstrates D.'s rejection of the various social, legal and religious taboos which constrain human relations.

DES FORÊTS. Focusing on des F.'s novella, *Une Mémoire démentielle*, Anthony Wall, 'La parole mystique est un prétexte: *Une mémoire démentielle* de L. R. des F.', *Poétique*, 88:419–29, sets out to demonstrate nothing, but 'a very significant nothing', i.e. the link between silence, *discours mystique*, and memory. This analysis of the tension between memory's efforts to retain all that is said and silence's frustration at the impossibility of saying all will appeal to those with a taste for paradox.

DU BOUCHET. Jacques Depreux, 'A. du B. ou l'approche du dehors', *Critique*, 524–25 : 71–82, tackles the theme of 'le dehors' in du B., which he explains as that 'espace de la parole' towards which any questioning of the origin and destination of things projects the questioner. Unfortunately, it is the kind of discussion which tends to leave the uninitiated on the outside as well.

DURAS. Carol J. Murphy, 'D.'s 'beast in the jungle': writing fear (or fear of writing) in *Emily L.*', *Neophilologus*, 75 : 539–47, identifies a number of Durassian constants such as reduplication and the tale-within-a-tale as sources of that fear and anxiety which transmit the characters' malaise to the traditional reader in search of a readable plot. Maryse Fauvel, '*Le Marin de Gibraltar* et *Détruire dit-elle* de D.: sous le signe de Dionysos', *FR*, 65 : 226–35, links two unlikely or dissimilar texts together by virtue of their common dedication to 'Dionys', an 'emasculated form' of Dionysus. The writing of both texts is defined as Dionysian since they rely more heavily on non-verbal than verbal signs. From then on, she is on familiar ground, detailing how the aural, the visual and the silences supplant the primacy of the verbal in D.

GARY. Leroy T. Day, 'Gary-Ajar and the rhetoric of non-communication', *FR*, 65 : 75–83, examines the role assigned to language in Gary's theory of fiction, more specifically the implications and applications of Gary's enforced adoption of a 'highly idiosyncratic style' to preserve his cover while writing the Ajar novels of the seventies.

GENET. Marc Guyon, 'La politesse de J.G.', *NRF*, 465 : 61–65, offers an affectionate and respectful, not to say effusive, homage to G. Meanwhile A. Dichy edits vol. 6 of his *Œuvres complètes; L'Ennemi déclaré: textes et entretiens*, ed. A. Dichy, Gallimard, vi + 425 pp.

GRACQ. Simone Grossman, 'J.G. et le merveilleux surréaliste urbain dans *La Forme d'une ville*', *IL*, 1 : 18–21, shows how the mature G. imbues the Nantes of his schooldays with an infusion of 'le merveilleux urbain' transforming it into a Proteiform place where dreams and reality intermingle. Perhaps the most interesting part of this study details the various quotes and allusions G. integrates into his text, evoking Nantes's different literary associations and turning his setting ultimately into an 'intertexte surréaliste'.

IONESCO. I. joins the Immortals in another sense with the inclusion of his *Théâtre complet* among the august tomes of the Bibliothèque de la Pléiade, ed. Emmanuel Jacquard, Gallimard, cxxiii + 1951 pp. There is the usual Pléiade apparatus criticus of preface, notices, notes, and variants as well as contributions from a range of individuals. François George, 'Angepain et Tudide au festile des rébulites', *Critique*, 533:786–99, is a loosely structured, not to say rambling, piece occasioned by the publication of I.'s *Théâtre complet* in which he takes the opportunity to unburden himself of his own divided loyalties between Sartre and I. Among the personal reminiscences are a number of perceptive comments on I.'s plays. I.'s theatre generally continues to be a fertile and profitable source for publishers, with three new students' guides: *E. I. Le Roi se meurt*, ed. R. Scemama, Nathan, 125 pp. is, in scope and format, very similar to Hatier's well established *Profil d'une œuvre* series, I. *Rhinocéros*, ed. J. Rougeon, Bordas, 96 pp., is intended for the same general undergraduate readership but is very clear and schematic in layout; the most ambitious is *La Cantatrice chauve et La Leçon d'E.I.*, ed. M. Bigot and M.-F. Savéan, Gallimard, Collection Foliothèque, 249 pp.; as well as general analysis and an 'éclaircissements et notes' section on the texts, it also reprints relevant material from *Notes et contrenotes*.

JABÈS. A piece by Olivier Houbert, 'Jabès éclaireur', *NRF*, 459:68–73, records its author's debt to J. and discusses the sense of double alienation in J.'s work which both men share from being Jewish and writers. Philippe de Saint-Chéron, 'Entretien avec E.J.', *NRF*, 464:65–75, is a fairly substantial interview with J. in which he speaks of his sense of Jewishness and his debt to the various hereditary and cultural influences on him, e.g. his family, his contacts with Islam, and the influence of the French poetic tradition, notably Baudelaire, Mallarmé and Max Jacob.

LE CLÉZIO. Didier Pobel, '"Un long voyage" dans l'immobilité du regard. Variations autour d'*Onitsha* de J.M.G. Le C.', *NRF*, 464:76–80, leafs through Le C.'s latest novel and half a dozen others in search of answers to questions such as: why does reading Le C. dispel the veil of darkness before our eyes and why, when it is lifted, do we have the strange feeling of slipping into a dream 'commencé le jour où nous aurions appris que les yeux servent à lire, que les yeux servent à vivre'? It is not certain that the discussion provides answers any clearer than the original questions.

MALRAUX. The appearance of the first tome of M.'s collected works in the Bibliothèque de la Pléiade series is the occasion for Alfred Cismaru, 'The anti-destiny of M.'s *Anti-Mémoires*', *DalR*, 70:526–34. This is a leisurely run through the *Anti-Mémoires* in pursuit of M.'s own answers to the questions raised at the outset. How much blood and sacrifice is it worth putting into the production of art? How can one glorify art when the consolation or catharsis it offers the elite are denied to the poor and downtrodden? Guy Talon, 'Un aspect original des *Anti-Mémoires* de M.: le retour du baron de Clappique', *RHLF*, 91:672–76, takes another look at the same book, this time studying the various reappearances or reincarnations of the baron, the character responsible for reintroducing the *farfelu* and the *dérisoire* into the *Anti-Mémoires*. E. Rosa da Silva, 'L'œuvre d'A.M.: un dialogue fascinant avec la mort', *IL*, 3:29–34, ranges more widely over a number of novels, but with particular reference to *Les Conquérants* and *La Voie royale*. The main concern is with the pervasiveness of the sentiment of death in M.'s work and his obsession with its 'force implacable'. It also embraces eroticism, however, since man experiences the same ambiguous feelings of attraction and repulsion before the sexual act as he does in the face of death.

MICHAUX. J.-P. Martin, 'L'écriture de soi traversée par l'histoire: *Épreuves, Éxorcismes* d'H.M.', examines this unusual or uncharacteristic work written in 1945 against the background of M.'s experiences of the war and the Resistance. The starting point for André Pierre Colombat, 'Le philosophe critique et poète: Deleuze, Foucault et l'œuvre de M.', *FrF*, 16:209–25, is Deleuze's definition: 'les grands philosophes sont aussi de grands stylistes' and his interest in the style of Foucault and M. There is enough comment on M.'s style to make the article of interest to the specialist.

PAULHAN. Jan Baetens, 'J.P. et le discours analogique', *EsC*, 31.2:30–38, deals with P.'s constant and unrelenting preoccupation with the secrets of language as an enigma to be penetrated and experienced. He looks principally at an early P. *récit*, *Le Guerrier appliqué*, to verify the principles set out, perhaps a bit tersely, in his first paragraph and argues that reading P. is an active participation with the author in the quest for the secrets of language. Baetens's article will suit the general reader but the P. specialist will be more interested no doubt in the publication of his *Correspondance J.P. — Roger Caillois (1934–1967)*, ed. O. Felgine and C.-P. Perez, Gallimard, 301 pp.

PINGET. Jean Kaempfer, 'R.P., la description dans quelques états', *Poétique*, 88:387–98, treats P.'s descriptive techniques, establishing a typological classification based on three states of description; an 'état heureux', an 'état malheureux', and an 'état rédimé'. This classification proves to be chronological as well since Kaempfer argues that they correspond to three stages in P.'s evolution. Whether or not one understands or agrees with the schema suggested, the article remains well written and thoughtful throughout.

PONGE. Shinji Jida, 'La figure de "lecteur" dans l'œuvre de F.P.', *ELLF*, 58:187–202, concentrates on the complex role of the 'je énonciateur' in P. and its relationship with the reader. We are advised however that the word *lecteur* does not designate the 'lecteur soi-même' but rather the 'lecteur comme réprésentation, comme figure'. The same applies to *auteur*. The article traces P.'s evolving sense of his own methodological originality after *Le Parti pris des choses* and his discovery by the public. Rosemarie Scullion, 'Zénon dans la cour pluvieuse de F.P.', *FrF*, 16:187–98, is inspired by the epistemology of Michel Serres in *Hermes V: Le Passage du nord-ouest*. Her article explores the 'dimension fractale' of objects in P., concentrating on the poem *Pluie* from *Le Parti pris des choses* which illustrates in an exemplary fashion the parallels between P.'s endeavours as poet and those of Serres as critic. More perhaps for the P. aficionado, it does not always make for light reading. Diane E. Sears, 'The two-way text: P.'s metapoetic *fable*', *EsC*, 31.2:50–57, starts from the conviction that every P. text can be read as both text and metatext. *Fable* offers particularly fertile ground for studying the poetics of metatextuality in P.'s work as a whole and is subjected to detailed examination making noticeable use of etymological evidence.

QUENEAU. Stephen Winspur, 'Q.'s contexts of irony', *RR*, 82.1:70–75, uses irony to demonstrate how the authorial voice in Q. 'dissolves' behind the rhetorical web of figures of speech, making it difficult if not impossible to define the author's intentions. Warren F. Motte, Jr, 'R.Q. and the aesthetic of formal constraint', *ib*., 193–209, examines Q.'s grapplings with 'constraint', choosing four key texts from different periods in which the notion of constraint plays a crucial role: *Le Voyage en Grèce* (1930), *Le Chiendent* (1933), *Cent mille milliards de poèmes*, (1961), and *Morale élémentaire* (1975). This wide chronological sweep from early essays to last novel supports the view of Q.'s work as a sustained meditation on the uses and abuses of formal constraint as an aid to artistic expression. The article is both fascinating in its detailed analysis of structure, e.g. of *Morale élémentaire*, and interesting for its more general application beyond Q. to the relationship of form to inspiration. Q. also figures among the new titles in the excellent and growing Collection Foliothèque series: *Les Fleurs bleues de R.Q.*, ed. J.-Y. Pouilloux, Gallimard, 253 pp. with an informative mixture of general and detailed analysis.

ROBBE-GRILLET. Gérard Bucher, 'L'au-delà du réel: à propos de *La Mauvaise Direction* d'A.R.-G.', *EsC*, 31.2:76–84, offers a detailed and systematic examination of the 'récit emblématique' *La Mauvaise Direction* which emphasizes the paradox between the apparently smooth objective surface of the text and the subjective intrusions which make of it a 'discours où rien n'est innocent'.

ROUBAUD. Susan Ireland, 'The comic world of J.R.', *EsC*, 31.4:22–31, reminds us that, as a member of Oulipo (Ouvroir de Littérature Potentielle), R. endorses the concept of literature as a form of play. Two recent novels, *La Belle Hortense* and *L'Enlèvement*

d'Hortense, are good examples of his interest in various forms of play
and experimentation. This article details the different ludic ingre-
dients, e.g. intertextual allusions, metaliterary comments, parody of
various novelistic styles and, oddly, the structural importance of the
number six which go to make up the carnavalesque world of J.R.

ROY.   Dennis Drummond, '*Alexandre Chenevert* and the *Book of Job*',
EFL, 27, 1990:40–45, is a straightforward comparison of the two texts
involved but the many parallels demonstrated make a convincing
case. **Un pays, une voix*, *G.R.*, Maison des Sciences de l'Homme
d'Aquitaine, 116 pp., is the proceedings of a G.R. conference held in
Bordeaux in 1987.

SARRAUTE.   Sandra Golopentia, 'L'histoire d'un verdict superlatif
— N.S.: Ich sterbe', *RR*, 82:346–61, compares S.'s terse version of
Chekhov's death and his famous 'Ich sterbe' in the first essay of her
volume *L'Usage de la parole* and the account given by Chekhov's
French biographer Henri Troyat. Under the guiding influence of J. L.
Austin, *How to do Things with Words*, the rest of the piece is devoted to
S.'s subsequent detailed analysis of Chekhov's motives for uttering
the phrase. Helen Watson-Williams, 'Quintessential S.: a reading of
L'Usage de la parole', *EFL*, 27, 1990:40–45, gives a brief account of the
content and style of the book, concluding that it is very much in the S.
tradition with a continuation of lifelong themes and preoccupations.

SARTRE.   Bruno Thibault, '*Dépaysement*: une nouvelle "manquée"
de J.-P. S.', *FrF*, 16:81–90, resurrects a forgotten short story based on
a visit by S. to Naples in 1936 and originally intended for inclusion in
Le Mur. Thibault addresses the question of why S. should have
abandoned this work which is in the *La Nausée* tradition of reflection
on *la contingence*. In response, he suggests S.'s aesthetic dissatisfaction
with structural weakness in the story, e.g. lack of unity, and his
intellectual dissatisfaction with an unresolved conflict between the
hero's objectivity and his authenticity. Denis Boak, 'S. and Malraux',
JES, 21:189–200, has a strong biographical and historical slant.
Against this background, he suggests certain affinities and differences
between the two in their work, outlook, and temperament. Given
their different backgrounds, the similarities Boak finds are perhaps
more surprising than the dissimilarities. Edouard Morot-Sir, 'Liberté
et totalité: le paradoxe sartrien de l'écriture', *RHLF*, 91:718–34,
tackles the 'problème du tout' in S.'s philosophy, in other words how
S. thinking becomes gradually more preoccupied with 'l'exigence de
totalité' and how he explores the notion of *totalité* in the consciousness
of existence. His discussion of some of the great paradoxes of Greek
philosophy, Achilles and the turtle or Zeno's heap for instance, make
this more of a study for the trained philosopher perhaps; but, as
Morot-Sir points out, it was for S. also a quest with literary

applications. There may well then be some interest in it for the student of literature or for anyone with an urgent need to 'surtotaliser les totalités totalisantes'. Yoseph Milman, 'The moral-esthetic imperative in literature: a study of the basic dualism of the poetics of S. in the forties', *OL*, 46:27–38, sets out to elucidate the premises underlying S.'s critical and poetic articles written between 1938 and 1948 and to link these to the principles laid down in the later *Psychology of the Imagination* and *What is Literature?* Despite the complexities of his subject, Milman's paper is well organized, clearly argued and readable. Charles D. Minahan, 'Crime: a floating signifier in S.'s *Les Mouches*', *Neophilologus*, 75:529–38, applies S. theory of language to one of his literary works. He scrutinizes the use of the word 'crime' in *Les Mouches* in order to highlight what he sees as a dual problem; the ethical connotations of the word and the distinction S. makes between *sens* and *signification*. All's well in the end however. When Oreste's act empties the sign 'crime' of the pseudo-significances that have corrupted it, new significations can emerge to fill the semantic void. If this is rephrased in Oreste's own words: 'tout est neuf ici, tout est à recommencer', it is hardly the most startling of conclusions. Marie Miguet-Ollagnier, 'La "saveur S." du *Livre brisé*', *TM*, 542:132–53, produces a systematic and well presented study of S.'s influence on Serge Doubrovsky's last *autofiction*, *Le Livre brisé*. There are two new student guides: *S.; Les Mouches & Huis clos*, ed. M. Cornud-Peyron, Nathan, 128 pp., and *Les Mains sales de J.-P. S.*, ed. M. Buffat, Gallimard, Collection Foliothèque, 253 pp.

SENAC. Dominique Combe, 'J.S., le roman impossible', *Critique*, 527:246–59, looks at *Ébauche du père*, the first part of a massive but unfinished novel project based on S.'s childhood and conceived in 1959–62. Despite the fact it was never completed, Combe argues that it plays a central role in S.'s work and inspiration and has close links with his poetry.

SIMON. Mireille Calle-Gruber, 'C.S.: le temps, l'écriture: à propos de *L'Acacia*', *Littérature*, 83:31–42, asks the question to what extent *L'Acacia* can be considered an autobiographical text. The question is possibly an interesting one but the phraseology is so jargon-filled and obscure in places that it is difficult to tell what the answer is. The same novel attracts the attention of Ralph Saronak, 'Un drôle d'arbre: *L'Acacia* de C.S.', *RR*, 82:210–32. The appearance of the novel in 1989 only serves to underline one of the constants of S.'s work, the concomitance of past and present. This is illustrated by a discussion of the various ramifications of the notion of arborescence in the novel with reference to earlier appearances of the acacia from *Le Tricheur* onwards. The argument is fascinating, if not downright inventive in places, in relating botanical attributes of the acacia to aspects of the novel and S.'s thinking but it does provide a substantial insight into the meaning and structure of the book.

SULIVAN. Patrick Gormally, 'Time and eternity in the works of J.S.', *FMLS*, 27: 169–75, is a clear and well documented analysis of S.'s preoccupation with the passage of time and the idea of eternity. Interestingly, despite S.'s training as a priest, this is not eternity in the traditional sense but rather a 'condensed intensity of life in the present, timeless, duration-less instant'. Of interest to the S. reader might be **Paroles du passant*, Albin Michel, 154 pp., a collection of texts first published separately in *Panorama aujourd'hui* between 1978 and 1980.

TOURNIER. Rachel Edwards, 'Initiation and menstruation: M.T.'s *Amandine ou les deux jardins*', *EFL*, 27:75–90, chronicles T.'s interest in the structure of initiation rituals, reading *Amandine ou les deux jardins* as a parable of the passage from childhood to adulthood and as an attempt to make 'the potentially traumatic experience of menstruation more accessible and palatable'. L. Korthals Altes, 'Un mythique en trompe-l'œil: *Le Roi des aulnes* de M.T.', *RHLF*, 91:677–90, owes a debt to Mieke Taat's view of T. as a 'romancier mythologue'. Arguing against the too facile view that *Le Roi des aulnes* is a traditional novel which does not reflect the spirit of its times, this study contends that T.'s use of myth and the mythical creates an uncertainty and 'mélange instable' in the book which makes it a thoroughly postmodernist text. Inge Degn, 'Les modèles d'évolution dans *Les Météores* de M.T.', *OL*, 46:240–56, targets ambiguity in T.'s novel. Examining each of the evolutionary models in the book, and the hero Paul's voyage of initiation in the light of these, she emphasizes the unresolved opposition and the 'caractère conflictuel' of the novel's ending. *Vendredi ou les limbes du Pacifique de M.T.*, ed. A. Bouloumié, Gallimard, 253 pp., follows the Collection Foliothèque pattern of helpful background information and useful analysis. It provides a good basis for discussion for a sometimes deceptively accessible novel.

FRENCH CANADIAN LITERATURE

POSTPONED

AFRICAN AND CARIBBEAN LITERATURE

POSTPONED

III. OCCITAN STUDIES

LANGUAGE

By PETER V. DAVIES, *Lecturer in French, University of Glasgow*

(This survey primarily covers the years 1988–1991)

1. BIBLIOGRAPHICAL AND GENERAL

Holtus, *Lexikon*, v/2, contains nine major articles on Occitan, incl. general histories of its grammar (1–18) and lexis (18–23) by R. Lafont, its 'Grammatikographie und Lexikographie' by B. Schlieben-Lange (105–26), and an outline of 'Externe Sprachgeschichte' by G. Kremnitz (69–80), who also gives a useful historical introd. and notes in his critical edn of Fabre d'Olivet's *La Langue d'oc rétablie: grammaire* (Wiener romanistische Arbeiten, 14), Vienna, Braumüller, 1988, xcii + 183 pp. This pioneering historical grammar is the hitherto unpubl. first vol. of a neglected tripartite study written *c.* 1820. The entire work, incl. an Occitan–French dictionary (nearly 10,000 entries) and a partly revised version of d'Olivet's *Le Troubadour* (first publ. 1804), has since appeared with a brief preface by David Steinfeld: Antoine Fabre d'Olivet, *La Langue d'oc rétablie dans ses principes: première édition intégrale d'après le manuscrit de 1820*, Ganges, Assoc. Fabre d'Olivet, 1989, xlvi + 941 pp. In an article submitted before the publ. of Steinfeld's edn, J.-M. Petit analyses 'L'œuvre lexicographique occitane de Fabre d'Olivet', *Mélanges Bec*, 443–53, noting *inter alia* the predominance of eastern Languedocian forms, an awareness of polymorphism and a normative tendency.

L'Identité occitane: réflexions théoriques et expériences. Actes du Colloque de Béziers (4,5 et 6 septembre 1986), réunis par François Pic, Montpellier, Section Française de l'AIEO, 1990, 229 pp., of mainly linguistic interest, gathers 17 of the 25 papers, the remainder having already appeared elsewhere (see *YWMLS*, 49:268). *Per Robert Lafont: estudis oferts a Robert Lafont per sos collègas e amics* [ed. Gaston Bazalgas, Felip Gardy, and Patric Sauzet], Montpellier, Centre d'Estudis Occitans, 1990, xiv + 313 pp., contains 21 articles including: P. Bec, 'Polimorfisme e volontat linguistica en cò del poèta gascon comengés Bertrand Larada' (17–36); H.-E. Keller, 'Recueil de poésies languedociennes tant anciennes que modernes en patois de Montpellier' (169–87); and B. Schlieben-Lange, 'Le glossaire provençal de Lacurne de Sainte-Palaye' (267–73). The Occitan section in vol. 1 of *Espaces romans: études de dialectologie et de géolinguistique offertes à Gaston Tuaillon*, Grenoble, Ellug, 1988–89, 2 vols, 304 pp. + 608 pp., includes: J. Allières, 'Quelques énigmes de la conjugaison gasconne ou le verdict de l'aire' (175–92); J.-P. Dalbera, 'Dans le sillage de la toupie nissarde. Notes d'étymologie et de géographie linguistique' (193–204); A. Genre, 'Dittongamenti condizionati e non in un'areola dell'occitano alpino' (215–28); J. Lescuyer, 'La porte de Villars à Châtillon-en-Dombes d'après les *Comptes de Syndics* (1375–1500)' (229–45); J.-C. Potte, '"L'électricité aux Garniers". Chanson commémorative de Prosper Dosgilbert' (246–55); X. Ravier, 'Battage, dépiquage: la carte III, 698, de l'*Atlas linguistique et ethnographique du Languedoc occidental*' (256–78); and L. Wolf, 'Les fichiers de Pierre Nauton' (279–81). *Les Édouard Privat, libraires-éditeurs à Toulouse: un siècle de bibliothèque familiale, 1849–1949. Catalogue thématique*, ed. Mme Suzanne-Pierre Privat, Toulouse, Privat, 223 pp., illus., gives publ. details of 3180 works, largely on Occitan history and culture, now held in the Archives départementales de la Haute-Garonne. The section on 'Langue et littérature méridionales' (159–72) includes 20 linguistic studies, some of them recondite.

2. MEDIEVAL PERIOD (TO 1500)

On general matters: François Zufferey's *Recherches linguistiques sur les chansonniers provençaux* (see *YWMLS*, 49:269) has attracted important reviews by G. Gouiran, *RLiR*, 52, 1988:290–94, M.-D. Glessgen, *RLaR*, 92, 1988:177–86, and Å. Grafström, *ZRP*, 106, 1990:182–90. 'Cantalausa' (alias L. Combes), *Aux racines de notre langue: les langues populaires des Gaules de 480 à 1080*, Rodez, Culture d'oc, Saint-Pierre, 1990, 607 pp., offers a convenient collection of 22 linguistic monuments from the period 750–1080. MS facs are reproduced with facing reprints of (sometimes outdated) critical edns and (sometimes questionable) authorial comments. S. Kudo, 'La naissance d'une langue nationale: réflexions politico–linguistiques sur les Serments de Strasbourg', *Mélanges Bec*, 273–84, explains the problematic, hybrid Gallo-Romance idiom of the Oaths by political factors. M. van Uytfanghe's study, 'Les expressions du type *quod vulgo vocant* dans des textes latins antérieurs au Concile de Tours et aux Serments de Strasbourg: témoignages lexicologiques et sociolinguistiques de la "langue rustique romaine"?' (see *YWMLS*, 51:2, 20), though primarily concerned with northern Gaul, is also of southern interest since, of the eight pre-Carolingian hagiographies examined, one was written in Guéret (Creuse) and two others refer to Gascony and Poitou.

On morphosyntax: K. Machida, 'La distribution des temps verbaux dans le texte en ancien provençal', *Gengo Kenkyu* (Tokyo), 91, 1987:56–83, examines the use of past tenses in *Fierabras* and *La Chanson de la croisade albigeoise*, distinguishing between verbs expressing state and other verbs. R. M. Medina Granda, 'La importancia sintáctica de la declinación bicasual en *Lo Codi*', *Verba* (Santiago de Compostela), 15, 1988:339–50, finds the declension system redundant though generally well maintained in 12th-c. MS *A*. F. Jensen, 'Quelques observations sur la parataxe en occitan médiéval', *Mélanges Bec*, 215–21, classifies types of parataxis and finds instances much more commonly in troubadour poetry than in medieval prose texts. Id., 'Sur les comparaisons proportionnelles en français et en occitan', *RLaR*, 95:351–58, notes similarities and differences in comparative structures in medieval texts. P. Swiggers comments on 'Les premières grammaires occitanes: les *Razos de trobar* de Raimon Vidal et le *Donatz proensals* d'Uc (Faidit)', *ZRP*, 105, 1989:134–47, and 'La méthode grammaticale d'Uc Faidit dans le *Donatz proensals*', *RLaR*, 95:343–50.

On lexis and lexicology: fascs 3, 1988, pp. 161–240, and 4, pp. 241–320, of the *DAO Supplément* (see *YWMLS*, 42:241) cover items 574 *arbre* to 699 *groseillier* and 700 *groseille* to 821 *endive* respectively. K. Baldinger, 'Lexicologie romane: dictionnaires en cours d'élaboration en R.F.A.', *Actes* (Trier), VII, 316–26, includes sections on the *DAO*, *DAG*, and the forthcoming *Dictionnaire étymologique de l'ancien provençal (DEAP)*. H. Stimm continues his 'Berichtigungen und Ergänzungen zur altprovenzalischen Lexikographie', *ZFSL*, 96, 1986:238–58 (cf. *YWMLS*, 46:262–63), by examining derivatives of Latin LAMINA/LAMNA (§5) and studying *lagui* 'fatigue, peine', *(se) laguïar* 'se fatiguer' (§6), and *galiar* 'tromper' (§7) and their derivatives. T. A. Malachova, 'St.-provans. *lauzengiers*: k istorii i etimologii termina', *Etimologija* (Moscow), 1985 (1988):138–46, includes study of cognate forms. G. M. Cropp, 'Les expressions *mas jonchas* et *a (de) genolhos* dans la poésie des troubadours', *Mélanges Bec*, 103–12, studies occurrences of these two associated images of feudal homage and Christian worship mainly in troubadour poetry. M. de Combarieu considers the affective quality of 'Le nom de la ville Toulouse dans la *Chanson de la Croisade albigeoise*', *Hommage Payen*, 133–49.

On Old Gascon: In 1988 the *DAG* (see *YWMLS*, 42:241) reached fasc. 6, pp. 401–80, covering items 541 *sapin* to 704 *fraise*. Juridical texts have received considerable attention. R. Cierbide Martinena, *Estudio lingüístico de la documentación medieval en lengua occitana de Navarra*, Bilbao, Servicio editorial de la Univ. del País Vasco/Argitarapen Zerbitzua Euskal Herriko Univ., 1988, 358 pp., sees a distinct idiom, 'Occitano-Navarrese' (p. 99), in 204 diverse documents written between 1232 and 1325 and here submitted to meticulous linguistic analysis. Critical reception has ranged from appreciation (M. Pfister, *ZRP*, 106, 1990:190–94) to scepticism (G. Gouiran, *RLaR*, 93, 1989:138–42). A more concise version of the graphological, phonological, and morphosyntactic sections of this study has also appeared: Id., 'La scripta administrativa en la Navarra medieval en lengua occitana: comentario lingüístico', *ZRP*, 105, 1989: 276–312. See also Id., *'Recogida, inventario y estudio histórico-lingüístico de la documentación medieval de Iparralde en lengua gascona', *Euskara biltzarra/Congreso de la lengua vasca*, Vitoria, Servicio central de publicaciones del gobierno vasco, 1988, vol. I, 381–88. Vincent-Raymond Rivière-Chalan, *Vocabulaire gascon d'après les minutes notariales de la vallée de Barèges (1175–1550)*, Tarbes, Soc. Acad. des Hautes Pyrénées (Archives départementales), 1989, 53 pp., lists, translates and comments generally upon 1700 terms found in vernacular notarial records. *La Coutume de Saint-Sever (1380–1480), édition et commentaire des textes gascon et latin*, ed. Michel Maréchal and Jacques Poumarède (Mémoires et documents d'histoire médiévale et de philologie, 2), Paris, Édns du CTHS, 1988, 139 pp., presents 132 extremely varied articles in a Latin copy of 1380 and a Landais translation made a century later. The lexical interest of the edn is shown by M. Pfister, 'Le vocabulaire de la coutume de Saint-Sever (1480)', *Mélanges Bec*, 455–63, who notes 98 mainly legal terms not found in the *FEW*. X. Ravier, 'Les actes en occitan du Cartulaire de l'abbaye de Lézat', *ib.*, 465–73, observes a total predominance of Gascon over Languedocien characteristics in five vernacular charters transcribed in Comminges between 1189 and 1242.

Two important theses on Old Provençal have been published: Angela Hug-Mander, *Die okzitanischen Urkunden im Departement Alpes-de-Haute-Provence: Untersuchung einiger graphischer, phonetischer und morphologischer Erscheinungen* (EH, XIII.148), 1989, vii + 297 pp., examines 201 documents written between 1331 and 1575 and publ. by P. Meyer in 1909; while *'Lo Thesaur del hospital de Sant Sperit': Edition eines Marseiller Urkundeninventars (1399–1511) mit sprachlichem und geschichtlichem Kommentar unter besonderer Berücksichtigung des Rechtswortschatzes*, ed. Martin-Dietrich Glessgen (*ZRP*, Beiheft 226), 1989, xi + 596 pp., is a scrupulous edn and analysis of an 80-folio register written in Provençal between 1399 and 1511 by three notaries working for the Hôpital du Saint-Esprit (now the Hôtel-Dieu) at Marseilles. The register summarizes the content of some 500 mostly extant documents from the period 1188–1503 concerning three Marseilles hospitals (rev.: D. Hauck, *RLiR*, 53, 1989: 534–47, J.-P. Chambon, *ZRP*, 106, 1990: 494–99, and G. Roques, *RLaR*, 94, 1990: 141–43). G. Gouiran, 'Le roi et la lettre: écrits politiques provençaux des XIVᵉ et XVᵉ siècles', *Actes* (Trier), III, 752–65, gives a graphological and phonological analysis of six sets of minutes of the États de Provence between 1390 and 1472 and is struck by the homogeneity and abstract quality of the administrative Provençal despite the heterogeneity of his source

Language 249

(Archives des Bouches-du-Rhône, registre B 49). E. Schulze-
Busacker, 'French conceptions of foreigners and foreign languages in
the twelfth and thirteenth centuries', *RPh*, 41, 1987–88:24–47,
provides a detailed study of attitudes in both the south and north of
France (see *YWMLS*, 49:45). B. Doumerc reproduces ten 'Documents commerciaux en langue d'oc enregistrés à Alexandrie par les
notaires vénitiens (fin XIVe – début XVe siècle)', *AMid*, 99, 1987:
227–44.

3. POST-MEDIEVAL PERIOD

M. W. Wheeler, 'Occitan' in Harris and Vincent, *Romance Languages*,
246–78, succinctly surveys phonology, morphology, and syntax, incl.
such topics as sandhi processes, structure of verb inflections and
stem-final consonant alternation, aspect, quasi-modals, topicalization and Gascon *enonciatus*. The superficial chapter on 'Occitan' in
Campbell, *Compendium*, 1049–53, in fact deals mainly with Provençal.
Reviving the Occitan/Provençal polemic, Henri Barthès, *Études
historiques sur la 'langue occitane'*, Saint-Geniès-de-Fontédit, H. Barthès,
1987, 461 pp., follows L. Bayle in denying the historical validity of the
linguistic and political concept of *Occitania*, which is seen as a 17th-c.
neologism that gained widespread currency only in the 19th and
20th cs. Orthographic standardization is rejected and respect for
dialectal diversity advocated (severe review: T. Meisenburg, *ZRP*,
106, 1990:194–98). F. Martel, 'Per una istòria del fach occitan', *EOc*,
6, 1989:5–10, and R. Teulat, 'Occitan e autonomia', *ib.*, 10:3–8,
dismiss these arguments by implication. P. Bec, 'Norme et standard'
in Holtus, *Lexikon*, v/2, 45–58, outlines post-medieval destandardi-
zation and restandardization, while F. P. Kirsch generally reviews
the history of 'Sprache und Literatur', *ib.*, 59–68. C. Camenisch and
A. M. Kristol study 'L'intercompréhension entre le gascon, le
languedocien et le catalan', *Langues en Béarn* (see below), 71–86. On
phonetics and phonology: P. Sauzet, 'Diasystème et paramètres. A
propos d'une contrainte phonologique de l'occitan', *Mélanges Bec*,
513–30, considers reasons for the general avoidance of the diphthong
[uw] in Occitan and advocates a revised classification of the Occitan
vowel system. On orthography: F. Martel, 'A l'entorn de la grafia:
quauques precursors dau segle XIX', *EOc*, 8, 1990:11–23, considers
the cases of Dessales (1838), Mma Juli Michelet (1867), Durand de
Gros (1878), P.-L. Caire (1884), Moutier (1886) and Henri de France
(1893), while R. Merle, 'Lengadòc-Provença: Yalta grafic d'ara e
causidas graficas de 1785 a 1853', *ib.*, 25–33, sees nothing new in the
interregional polemic. On morphosyntax: Q.I.M. Mok outlines an
approach to the question of the 'Concurrence de *tornar* + infinitif et *re-*

en occitan', *Actes* (Trier), II, 104–11. H. P. Kunert, '*Qu'es aquel lum ailà luènh?*': normative Grammatik und literarischer Sprachgebrauch im Bereich der okzitanischen Deiktika', *Energeia und Ergon*, II, 513–24, argues against Alibert's claim that Occitan has a three-term system of demonstratives; *aiceste, aqueste, aquel* (*aicí, aquí, ailà*) do not each have distinctive syntactic roles despite regional variation in use.

On lexis and lexicology: The first vol. of Cristian Rapin's useful *Diccionari francés–occitan segon lo lengadocian*, [Hautefage-la-Tour], IEO/Escòla Occitana d'Estiu, 409 pp., has appeared, covering the letters A–B very fully and indexing the 583 authors and 1029 works consulted. Some variant North Occitan, Provençal, and Gascon forms are given together with idiomatic expressions. Edmond Albi, *Los Peisses d'aiga doça* (Descobèrtas), Hautefage-la-Tour, Escòla Occitana d'Estiu, 1986, 144 pp., illus., lists 47 species, giving for each the various Occitan names, French equivalent and scientific term, description of appearance and habitat, fishing methods, and gastronomic qualities. J. R. Fernández Gonzáles, 'Los nombres de los días de la semana: el orden de elementos y resultados en occitano', in *Homenaje a Álvaro Galmés de Fuentes*, Oviedo U.P., III, 1987, 49–75, is meticulous and well documented. J. Rigosta surveys vocabulary of the occult arts in 'Sorcièrs, fachilhièrs, bruèishes e posoèrs', *EOc*, 8, 1990:3–9, supplementing the more geographically specific study by Jean-Pierre Piniès, *Figures de la sorcellerie languedocienne: brèish, endevinaire, armièr*, Paris, CNRS, 1983, ix + 324 pp.

P. Fabre surveys Occitan onomastics generally in Holtus, *Lexikon*, V/2, 23–33. There is much of southern interest in Marianne Mulon, *L'Onomastique française* (see *YWMLS*, 50:37) and in Ernest Nègre, 3-vol., *Toponymie générale de la France* (see *YWMLS*, 52:42, and p. 42 above). E. Nègre, 'Les toponymes *Marais, Marchais, Margastaut* en France' (see *YWMLS*, 51:47), likewise deals largely with Occitania as does R. Sindou, '*VITRINA* ou *VETERINA?*', *Actes* (Trier), IV, 653–64.

On general dialectology X. Ravier usefully surveys 'Les aires linguistiques' in Holtus, *Lexikon*, V/2, 80–105. H. Guiter takes a broad dialectometric overview when considering the 'Applications d'une méthode géolinguistique en galloroman et ibéroroman', *Actes* (Trier), III, 352–61. A more hermetic approach to study of the dialectal continuum is shown by J.-L. Fossat, 'Entre dictionnaire et atlas: base de données. Les mots en *moc-* dans une base de données lexicales', *ib.*, IV, 341–59.

G. Kremnitz continues his series of sociolinguistic studies with: 'Politische Einflüsse auf Sprachentwicklungen: zur aktuellen Situation des Okzitanischen in Frankreich und Katalonien', *Beiträge zum 4. Essener Kolloquium über 'Sprachkontakt, Sprachwandel, Sprachwechsel, Sprachtod' vom 9.10–10.10.1987 an der Universität Essen*, ed. N. Boretzky,

W. Enninger, and T. Stolz, Bochum, Brockmeyer, 1988, 175–91; *La Recherche (socio-)linguistique en domaine occitan*, *BAIEO*, 2, 1988:1–31, and 3, 1988:1–38; 'Remarques sur la situation sociolinguistique de l'occitan en 1989', *Mélanges Bec*, 259–72; and 'Soziolinguistik' in Holtus, *Lexikon*, v/2, 33–45. P. Cichon, 'Comment faire une enquête sur la conscience linguistique?', *BAIEO*, 8, 1990:13–28, advocates an empirical and interpretative approach. The future of Occitan and its culture is the subject of a discussion introd. by J.-P. Thibault-Delpuech, 'La politique des régions en faveur de la culture occitane et l'occitanisme d'aujourd'hui', *EOc*, 9:21–37. Marianne Gretz, *Die Ausbreitung des français commun im südosten Frankreichs nach den regionalen Sprachatlanten* (Heidelberger Beiträge zur Romanistik, 20), Frankfurt am Main, Lang, 1987, 467 pp., surveys not only Provence, but the Massif Central, Lyonnais, Burgundy, Jura, and northern Alps. The more narrowly focused diss. by Wolfgang Markhof, *Renaissance oder Substitution? Eine soziolinguistische Untersuchung zur Stellung des Okzitanischen im Département Cantal* (KRA, n.F., 64), 1987, [viii] + 308 + [xi] pp., analyses the decline in the use of Occitan at the Languedocien–Auvergnat interface in various age-groups, classes, and social contexts. One of the more solid chapters in a generally disappointing vol., Grillo, *Dominant Languages*, is devoted to 'Occitanie' (63–83). The 1789 bicentenary has prompted several studies with sociolinguistic implications, most notably H. Boyer *et al.*, *Le Texte occitan de la période révolutionnaire (1788–1800): inventaire, approches, lectures*, Montpellier, Section Française de l'AIEO, 1989, 517 pp. Less substantial though wider ranging are Y. Lavalade, *La Révolution et les langues en France (La Clau lemosina*, 74), Limoges, CLEOAP, 1989, 32 pp., and G. Barsòtti, 'Lengas e ideologia: de la revolution de 1789 a l'Euròpa de 1993', *EOc*, 6, 1989:35–43. Even more broadly A. Sakari notes 'Le parallélisme du réveil occitan et du réveil national finlandais, au XIX^{e}s.', *Mélanges Bec*, 507–12. *Amiras/Repères*, Aix-en-Provence, 13, 1986, 140 pp., and 21, 1990, 127 pp., are respectively devoted to *Les Fous de la langue: langue, littérature et idéologies occitanes au XIXe siècle* (9 articles) and *Enseigner l'occitan: le tableau est-il si noir?* (18 articles on the general teaching situation). M.-C. Viguier, 'Le judéo-occitan existe . . . : essai sur la *lenga juzieva*', *Juifs et source juive en Occitanie*, Valdariás, Vent Terral, 1988, 193–209, draws conclusions from a sketchy examination of the evidence.

GASCON AND BÉARNAIS. *Langues en Béarn*, ed. B. Moreux (Cahiers de l'Univ. de Pau et des pays de l'Adour, n.s. 15), Toulouse, Le Mirail U.P., 1989, 288 pp., comprises 15 articles. The more wide-ranging discussions include M. Grosclaude, 'Langue populaire, langue littéraire et langue administrative en Béarn du XIIIe siècle à nos jours' (11–29), and J.-M. Puyau, 'Le concept de langue et le discours régionaliste: le cas du béarnais et du gascon' (87–106). S. Auroux, 'L'*essay* sur l'origine de la langue gasconne de Court de Gébelin: un modèle non-latin pour l'origine des langues romanes', *Actes* (Trier), VII, 108–19. On phonetics and phonology: J. Allières, 'Note sur l'alternance *f-/h-* dans les parlers gascons du haut Couserans (Ariège) limitrophes du languedocien', *Mélanges Bec*, 27–31, tentatively suggests a phonotactic explanation for the unexpected but frequent retention of *f-* in this region. J.-L. Fossat, 'L'expression figée, la ganelha et le diasystème', *ib.*, 113–22, outlines rather abstrusely a general approach to the establishment of a Gascon phonological grammar. On morphosyntax: Jean-Pierre Birabent and Jean Salles-Loustau, *Memento grammatical du gascon*, [Pau], Escòla Gaston Febus — [Tarbes], Nosauts de Bigòrra, 1989, 151 pp., provide a straightforward, usefully indexed grammar. Jürgen Pilawa, *Enunziative: Eine sprachliche Neuerung im Spiegel der gaskognischen Schriftkultur*, Tübingen, Narr, 1989, 146 pp., details use and omission of enunciative *que* in clauses of various categories. T. T. Field examines 'L'auxiliaire en gascon pyrénéen', *Langues en Béarn*, 43–54, while R. Saint-Guilhem considers 'Le futur du passé en béarnais', *ib.*, 55–67. K. Baldinger, 'Das Begriffsfeld "während" im Südwesten Frankreichs auf Grund der altgaskognischen, mittellateinischen und regionalfranzösischen Urkunden', *Mélanges Bec*, 33–75, draws on extensive documentation. On lexis and lexicology: Joan-Pau Latrubesse *et al.*, *Petit Dictionnaire français-occitan (Béarn)*, Pau, La Civada — Orthez, Per Noste, 1984, 133 pp., though unpretentious, plugs a yawning gap with its coverage of 7000 words and 500 proper names. Dupleich's 1843 *Dictionnaire patois-français* [. . .] *à l'usage de l'arrondissement de Saint-Gaudens*, 157 pp., has been repr. with an appended *Dictionnaire français–patois pyrénéen* by Nicole and Christian Lacour, Nîmes, Lacour, 103 pp. André Hourcade's well-indexed *Dictionnaire bilingue des expressions gasconnes*, Oloron-Sainte-Marie, Assoc. éditrice Los Caminaires, 1990, 246 pp., gives the Gascon equivalents of idiomatic French expressions together with Gascon expressions that have no French equivalent. Comparisons are the subject of a third and final chapter. Francis Beigbeder, *Ausèths: les noms gascons des oiseaux sauvages*, Orthez, Per Noste — Tarbes, Nosauts de Bigòrra, 1986, 159 pp., illus., notes and comments on the various terms used in Gascony for 90 species, often with the appropriate *ALG* map. The vol. is completed by an anthology of written and oral Gascon literature of ornithological interest, a section on Gascon noun-formation and full indexes. G. Serbat, 'Survivance de *gallus* en gascon', *Études de lexicologie, lexicographie et stylistique offertes en hommage à Georges Matoré*, ed. I. Tamba, Paris, Soc. pour l'Information grammaticale, 1987, 193–99. A. Puig, 'De l'ethnographie comme matériau littéraire: l'exemple du Bassin d'Arcachon et des pratiques de pêche durant la première moitié du XXᵉ siècle chez E. Barreyre et R. Rougerie', *La Littérature régionale en langue d'oc et en français à Bordeaux et dans la Gironde, Actes du colloque du CECAES, 21 et 22 octobre, 1988*, Bordeaux U.P., 1989, 273–80, discusses maritime vocabulary. On toponymy: Michel Grosclaude, *Dictionnaire toponymique des communes du Béarn*, Pau, Escòla Gaston Febus, 416 pp., is a fine work of scholarship which systematically analyses 485 toponyms in 30 cantons, arranged alphabetically. Apparatus includes an index, full historical and bibliographical refs, and discussion of pronunciation and orthography, ethnological stratification, key suffixes, and hydronyms. New hypotheses are advanced with commendable caution. B. Boyrié-Fénié, 'Aperçu sur les voies romaines reliant Bordeaux à Dax, à la lumière de la toponymie', *Actes* (Trier), IV, 536–44, proposes etymologies, some of them dubious, for the names of stations mentioned in the Antonine itinerary. T. Peillen, 'Toponymie gasconne en Pays Basque et basque en Béarn limitrophe', *Langues en Béarn*, 107–28. On sub-dialects: Most attention has been focused on the Val d'Aran. Otto Winkelmann, *Untersuchungen zur Sprachvariation des Gaskognischen im Val d'Aran (Zentralpyrenäen)* (*ZRP*, Beiheft 224), 1989, x + 412 pp., and Joan Coromines, *El parlar de la Vall d'Aran: Gramàtica, diccionari i estudis lexicals sobre el gascó*, Barcelona, Curial Edicions Catalanes, 1990, 773 pp., provide comprehensive models of scholarship. Gerald Bernhard, *Die volkstümlichen Pflanzennamen im Val d'Aran (Zentralpyrenäen)* (Pro lingua, 1), Wilhelmsfeld, Egert, 1988, xi + 175 pp., publishes an extremely thorough Heidelberg Univ. diss. Alain Viaut, *L'Occitan gascon en Catalogne espagnole: le Val d'Aran. Du vernaculaire au formel*, Talence, Maison des Sciences de l'Homme d'Aquitaine, 1987, 193 pp., treats the external history of the sub-dialect and the local triglossia. More broadly, T. T. Field, 'La recherche de l'oralité en gascon pyrénéen à l'aube de l'époque moderne', *Actes* (Trier), V, 68–77, sensitively traces the development of three features of spoken Gascon visible in texts from Béarn and Bigorre. On sociolinguistics: *Drin de tot: travaux de sociolinguistique et de dialectologie béarnaises*, ed. Andres M. Kristol and Jakob T. Wüest, Bern, Lang, 1985, vii + 323 pp., presents the results of fieldwork done by Zurich university students in the Aspe valley. The approaches and data are interestingly diverse. *Langues en Béarn* contains six articles on the French–Béarnais interface: C. Desplat, 'Le béarnais, instrument de la critique sociale au XVIIIᵉ siècle' (171–83); B. Lépinette, 'L'*Essai sur les vices du langage* de B. Sajus (Pau, 1821): un lexique à visée corrective' (185–201); B. Moreux, 'L'*Essai* de B. Sajus: français régional et idéologie à Pau en 1821' (203–34); B. and C. Moreux, 'La transmission du béarnais en milieu rural aujourd'hui' (235–56); A.

Marchal and B. Moreux, 'La longueur des voyelles en béarnais et en français du Béarn' (257–80); and P. Delay, 'Des traces de béarnais dans le roman français' (281–88). F. Garavini, 'Je suis Gascon, et si ...', *Mélanges Bec*, 141–51, examines the linguistic position of Montaigne given his Gascon origins. P. Lavaud, 'La transmission de la littérature orale gasconne aujourd'hui en Gironde. L'exemple de la transmission familiale', *La Littérature régionale en langue d'oc et en français à Bordeaux et dans la Gironde* (see above), 281–91, finds oral tradition among 11–16 year-olds more lively in Bazadais than in Médoc. X. Ravier reviews the activity of 'Vastin Lespy, parémiologue béarnais', *Langues en Béarn*, 31–41.

SOUTHERN OCCITAN

Savinian's *Grammaire provençale: précis historique de la langue d'oc. Parties du discours pour les sous-dialectes marseillais, cévenol et montpelliérain* (1882) has been repr. (Collection Rediviva), Nîmes, C. Lacour, xl + 197 pp. LANGUEDOCIEN. On general matters: *Joseph Salvat (1889–1972): Actes du colloque de Rivel et Chalabre (6 et 7 mai 1989)*, Béziers, CIDO, 181 pp., contains a repr. of the 1973 bibliography of Salvat's writings by E. Nègre and C. Anatole (169–80) and 14 papers incl. R. Teulat, 'La *Gramatica* de Salvat coma esplech del renaissentisme lingüistic' (17–29) and J. Allières, 'Joseph Salvat grammairien' (31–38). R. Teulat's thoughtful *Uèi l'occitan*, Bedous, IEO Sector recèrca, 1985, 157 pp., a collection of 12 previously publ. articles, includes a critique of Alibert's 1935 *Gramatica* (11–36) and essays on the problems of establishing *l'occitan referencial*. X. Ravier, *Atlas linguistique et ethnographique du Languedoc occidental*, III, Paris, CNRS, 1986, 340 pp., gives maps 573–882. On morphosyntax: Q. I. M. Mok, 'Aspects de la construction des phrases chez Joan Bodon', *Mélanges Bec*, 361–76, notes oral influence in the author's use of extraposition and the narrative infinitive. On lexis and lexicology: André Lagarde, *Le Trésor des mots d'un village occitan: dictionnaire du parler de Rivel (Aude)*, Rivel, A. Lagarde, 281 pp., explains some 14,000 words, expressions, proverbs, and sayings with an introd. noting *inter alia* local deviations from *languedocien référentiel*. Works on particular semantic fields include: Danièl Descomps (vols I and 2 with Xavièr Descomps), *Ambe lo cotelon: joguets rustiques d'un còp èra (Avec mon couteau: jouets rustiques d'autrefois)*, Hautefage-la-Tour, Escòla Occitana d'Estiu, 1987–88–90–91, 4 vols, 48 + 48 + 50 + 47 pp., illus., a fascinating and amusing series; Paulona Duconquéré, *La Cosina occitana del país d'Agde* (Descobèrtas), Hautefage-la-Tour, Escòla Occitana d'Estiu, 1987, 158 pp., illus., 26 traditional recipes. Claudi Vaissièra, *Botanica occitana* (Descobèrtas), Béziers, Seccion regionala Lengadòc de l'IEO,

1985–89, 2 vols, *vol. 1 — De la garriga*; vol. 2 — *De la mar a la montanha*, 241 pp., illus., describes in Occitan and French the most common wild plants of Bas Languedoc. The index lists Occitan, French, and Latin names. More localized is Amada Lacomba's *Flora occitana*, [Hautefage-la-Tour], Escòla Occitana d'Estiu, 1988, 94 pp., illus., a study of the 220 commonest plants in the author's native Savignac (Lot-et-Garonne). On onomastics: Lucien Lescou, *Communes et lieux-dits du canton de Castillonnès: étymologie, histoire* (Groupe de Recherche Onomastique de l'IEO), Saint-Prix, L. Lescou, 171 pp., illus., modestly aimed at the non-specialist and lacking an index, nevertheless provides some insight into the history and toponymy of ten communes in Haut Agenais (Lot-et-Garonne). Marcel Barral, *Les Noms de rues à Montpellier du moyen âge à nos jours*, Montpellier, P. Clerc, 1989, 406 pp., includes a chapter on 'Les noms de rue en occitan' (367–69). J.-P. Chambon, 'Boudou entre onymique et lexique', *RLiR*, 52, 1988: 139–41, suggests that *ajuston*, 'tributary', an apparent *hapax* in Boudou's last, unfinished novel *Las Domaisèlas*, may exemplify a toponym resuming the function of a common noun. On sub-dialects: Christian Camps, *Atlas linguistique du Biterrois*, Béziers, IEO, 1985, xxxiii + 553 pp., supplements the *ALLOr* with an enquiry at 58 points in Aude and Hérault resulting in 551 maps. He also seeks to establish the 'Limites linguistiques en Languedoc oriental', *Actes* (Trier), III, 362–69, by subjecting 100 maps of the *ALLOr*, I, to dialectometric analysis. T. Meisenburg traces the history of 'L'occitan écrit et l'occitan parlé à Lacaune', *Actes*, (Trier), V, 78–90, reproducing four illustrative texts. Gérard Maruéjouls *et al.*, *En cò nostre: parler et coutumes du Pays des Vans et des régions environnantes*, Les Vans, La Faraça, 472 pp., illus., have produced an attractive bilingual collection of pieces celebrating *l'òme*, *las bèstias*, and *la natura* and incl. several specialized glossaries and lists of proverbs. Only a French index is given. On sociolinguistics: Henri Boyer, *Langues en conflit: études sociolinguistiques*, Paris, L'Harmattan, 274 pp., writes on diglossia, the 'folklorization' of Occitan, *francitan* and the *piche* sociolect of Bas Languedoc. Id., 'Usages propagandistes de l'occitan écrit en contexte urbain (XIXᵉ–XXᵉ siècles)', *Lengas*, 25, 1989: 163–80; Id., 'La lutte et le verbe. Une approche socio-pragmatique de "l'affaire du Larzac"', *ib.*, 21, 1987: 7–30. Waltraud Rogge, **Aspekte des Sprachwissens von Jugendlichen im Bereich der französisch-okzitanischen Diglossie*, Trier, Wissenschaftlicher Vlg, 1987, 353 pp. *La Batalha de la lenga*, filmé dans l'Aveyron, le Tarn et l'Hérault en octobre 1989 par R. Alexander, D. Bickerton et P. Davies, Univ. of Glasgow Language Centre, video cassette + transcript and introd., 36 pp., is a 30-minute documentary (with optional French subtitles) on the rearguard action to save *languedocien*. *Lenga e païs d'oc*, Montpellier, CRDP, 21, contains articles of pedagogic interest incl. A. Clément, 'Didactique d'une langue seconde minorisée: cycle des apprentissages premiers: bref résumé des propositions de J. M. Artigal' (10–17), and C. Torreilles, 'L'espròva escricha del Bac: elaboracion d'un subjècte' (47–54). It also contains two thematic anthologies: C. Torreilles, 'La fête en Languedoc au début du XIXᵉ siècle: récits de fêtes' (59–73); and M.-J. Verny, 'Le jeu dans la littérature occitane du XXᵉ siècle' (75–91).

PROVENÇAL.   On general matters: André Compan, *Illustration du nissart et du provençal*, Berre l'Étang, L'Astrado, 1990, 492 pp., conveniently gathers 159 short articles first publ. in *Nice Matin*, 1970–75, incl. several on onomastics, lexis and idiom and a few on grammar and pronunciation. René Merle's richly documented thesis *L'Écriture du provençal de 1775 à 1840: inventaire du texte occitan, publié ou manuscrit, dans la zone culturelle provençale et ses franges*, Béziers, CIDO, 1990, 2 vols, 1027 pp., while largely concerned with social history, contains much of linguistic interest; the alternation between enthusiasm for Provençal and its repression is traced under successive governments. On orthography: Philippe Blanchet, **Essai de description du système graphique de Michel Tronc*, Màrseilles, CIREP/Lou Prouvençau à l'Escolo, 1989, 45 pp. On morphosyntax: J.-P. Dalbera, 'Les pronoms personnels atones dans les parlers des Alpes-Maritimes. Champs et mécanismes de variation', *Actes* (Trier), III, 599–613, notes greatest dialectal variation in the accusative and dative forms of 3rd p. singular and plural pronouns and observes some differences in syntax between, on the one hand, Menton and the Haute-Roya and, on the other, the rest of the *département*. On lexis and lexicology: A repr. of the 1785 Marseilles edn of Claude-François Achard, **Vocabulaire français–provençal et provençal–français*, Geneva, Slatkine, 1983, 2 vols, 1425 pp., is still available. R. Caprini, 'I nomi della "montagna" tra Liguria e Provenza', *Actes* (Trier), III, 461–64, outlines the breadth of this semantic field. On onomastics: S. Kerner tentatively transliterates 27 Hebraic anthroponyms found in 18th-c. local records, 'Les surnoms des Juifs de Carpentras' in *Juifs et source juive en Occitanie* (see above), 173–92. On sociolinguistics: R. Merle, 'C. F. Achard et le bilinguisme provençal de la fin des Lumières', *Provence historique*, 38, 1988:285–302, documents the evolution in Achard's attitude to Provençal from enthusiasm to disenchantment by 1789 and affords glimpses of broader social attitudes on the language question. Barbara Nowakowski, *Zu Sprache und Sprachideologie bei Vertretern der okzitanischen Renaissance in der Provence: Ergebnisse einer Befragung*, Trier, Wissenschaftlicher Vlg, 1988, vii + 471 pp., studies the linguistic commitment of 20 informants (incl. 14 teachers) interviewed in Provence in 1985. F. Bronzat, **'Renaissença culturala* e grafia dins las valadas occitanas d'Italia', *Cahiers crit. du patrimoine*, 3, 1987:89–94. The fragmentary text of the first Provençal revolutionary song of 1789 to be discovered is reproduced with historical commentary by R. Merle, 'Données nouvelles sur le texte provençal et les émeutes de mars–avril 1789', *Provence historique*, 40, 1990:111–17. Georges Bonifassi, *Apprendre le provençal — avec 'Aprendissage de la vido' de Paul Ruat*, Marseille, Tacussel, 1990, 188 pp., somewhat misleadingly titled, is in fact a full critical edn of the 1910 novel by the *felibre* Ruat (1862–1938), a teacher in Marseilles, with linguistic and other notes.

NORTHERN OCCITAN

H. Guiter, 'Sur l'Atlas linguistique de l'Auvergne et du Limousin', *RLiR*, 55:101–17, broadly outlines degrees of dialectal variation in the Haute-Vienne, Creuse, Puy-de-Dôme, Corrèze, and Dordogne, using his triangulation method. Jean-Pierre Baldit, *Les Parlers creusois* (Culture populaire en Creuse), [Aubusson], IEO Marche-Combraille, 1980, 43 pp. + map, indicates the variations in Marchois, Limousin, and Auvergnat as spoken in the north, south-east, and south-west of the *département*. Use of IPA symbols would have clarified some points. For a more general survey of Creusois dialects and culture, see Id., 'Chabatz d'entrar', *'A tout bout d'champ'*, *Revue culturelle du Conseil Général de la Creuse*, Guéret, 6:10–17. A more systematic, prescriptive grammar intended for pedagogic purposes is Jacques Chauvin's *Petite grammaire des parlers occitans du sud de la Creuse*, [Aubusson], IEO Marche-Combraille, 1980, 130 pp., which unhelpfully lacks an index.

LIMOUSIN. Éliane Gauzit *et al.*, *Le Limousin et son patrimoine culturel: inventaire bibliographique*, Migne-Auxances, IEO de la Vienne, 1988, 88 pp., list the relevant holdings of ten Poitiers libraries. The section on 'Études linguistiques' (37–44) includes some unpubl. theses and studies. Margaret M. Marshall, *The Dialect of Notre-Dame-de-Sanilhac: A Natural Generative Phonology* (SFIS, 31), Saratoga, Anma Libri, 1984, viii + 112 pp., provides a thorough analysis of a Périgourdin subdialect applying NGP methodology. Yves Lavalade, *L'Accentuation occitane (Haut-Limousin)*, Limoges, La Clau lemosina, 1986, 65 pp., advocates some modification of standard written Occitan accentuation to accommodate the oxytonic tendency of Limousin, particularly marked in Haut-Limousin. After general remarks on standard Limousin morphology and syntax of the verb (and personal pronouns), Id., *La Conjugaison occitane (Limousin)*, Limoges, La Clau lemosina, 1987, 186 pp., gives paradigms of regular and irregular conjugations, noting variants found in Charente and Basse-Marche.

9

An appx includes a summary of Marchois adjectives, pronouns, articles, and negation. On lexis and lexicology: Pierre Barrier has edited and revised the previously unpubl. second part of the *Dictionnaire périgourdin* by landscape artist Jean-Louis Daniel (1861–1929) as *Dictionnaire périgourdin–français*, Périgueux, Le Bournat du Périgord, 1988, [ix] + 335 pp. Ives Lavalada (= Yves Lavalade), *Au païs de la metafòra: recueil d'expressions imagées limousines*, Limoges, La Clau lemosina, 2nd edn, 1985, 31 pp., contains *inter alia* sections on comparisons, nicknames, oaths and onomatopoeia. J.-P. Baldit, 'Dire des oiseaux en Haute Marche', *La Clau lemosina*, Limoges, 78, 1990:15–16, and 81, 1990:13–15. On onomastics: Yves Lavalade, *Toponymie de la commune de Miallet (Dordogne limousine)*, Limoges, La Clau lemosina, 1985, 32 pp. + map, and (with Pierre and Simone Vignaud), *Les Noms de lieux de Saint-Junien*, Limoges, La Clau lemosina, 20 pp. + 5 maps, which notes the French and Occitan forms of some 146 local toponyms, incl. a selection of 36 *noms cadastraux* and three river-names. Etymological comment here is minimal. Short articles in *La Clau lemosina* include: Y. Lavalade, 'Toponymie limousine: la finale *-eix*', 75, 1989:7–9; CLEO-AP, 'Une signalisation en occitan à Aixe' and 'Sentiers pedestres bilingues', 81, 1990:1–9, 10–11. On sub-dialects: Nicolas Quint, *Le Parler marchois de Saint-Priest-la-Feuille (Creuse)*, Limoges, La Clau lemosina, 52 pp., is mainly a short dictionary and grammar with some preliminary remarks on pronunciation and orthography which would benefit from use of IPA symbols. J. Monestier, **Le Dialecte du Périgord Noir* (Coll. Campanule), P.L.B., 1987. The video cassette by Lo Teatre dau Vent Folhos, *N'autres tanben la Revolucion/Nous aussi la Révolution, ou des chansons de l'abbé Richard … aux fables du citoyen Foucaud*, Limoges, Crédit Agricole Mutuel de la Haute-Vienne, 1989, 140 minutes, is accompanied by an explanatory booklet, [xxii pp.], reproducing contemporary documents and containing some transcripts with parallel French translation.

AUVERGNAT. A slim and far from exhaustive but nevertheless serviceable vol. on morphology comes from Pierre Bonnaud *et al.*, *Abrégé de grammaire des parlers du nord-est de l'Auvergne: Bassin Durollien, Bois Noirs, Forez septentrional, Varenne et territoires adjacents*, Clermont-Ferrand, Cercle Terre d'Auvergne, 1987, 74 pp. In an illuminating study J.-P. Chambon and T. R. Wooldridge, 'Une source méconnue pour l'étude de l'occitan d'Auvergne au XVIIᵉ siècle: le *Dictionnaire* de Marquis (Lyon 1609)', *RLiR*, 54, 1990:377–445, note and comment upon some 170 arvernisms among other dialectalisms added by Pierre Marquis in his revision of the *Grand dictionnaire françois–latin* (1603 edn). While one shares the authors' doubts about whether some of the forms should be classed as Occitan or as regional

French, the interest of such an early source of Auvergnat lexis is undeniable. J.-P. Chambon, 'A propos du bilhard et des argots de métiers du Massif Central', *La Clau lemosina*, Limoges, 78, 1990: 1–5. In a well-informed study, Christian Hérilier, *Les Noms des communes de l'arrondissement de Thiers (PdD)* (Arrestador, ser. Toponomia occitana), Thiers, Agència Carcular/Piaron Pinha, 1989, 48 pp., follows analysis of some 43 local toponyms by a more discursive section explaining particular points of etymology, syntax or derivative forms with cross-refs to other toponyms in Occitania. J.-C. Rivière, 'Problèmes et méthodes de la microtoponymie. Le cas de Vebret (Cantal)', *Actes* (Trier), IV, 644–52, analyses the various toponymical strata in a smaller locality. On dialectology: Guy Marcou, **Étude phonétique, morphologique, syntaxique et lexicale du parler occitan de Pradelles (Haute-Loire)*, Le Puy, IEO Haute-Loire, 1987, 2 vols, iv + 345 pp., 628 pp.

PROVENÇAL ALPIN. Joannès Dufaud, *L'Occitan nord-vivarais (région de La Louvesc)*, Davézieux, J. Dufaud, 1986, 327 pp., provides a welcome dictionary of *vivaro-alpin* terms, preceded by a succinct grammar (17–48) incl. general and phonological remarks, and followed by a short anthology of oral literature collected in and around La Louvesc (*ALLy*, point 74).

LITERATURE

By MICHAEL J. ROUTLEDGE, *Senior Lecturer in French, Royal Holloway and Bedford New College, University of London*

1. MEDIEVAL PERIOD

Pride of place must go to Angelica Rieger, *Trobairitz. Der Beitrag der Frau in der altokzitanischen höfischen Lyrik. Edition des Gesamtkorpus*, Tübingen, Niemeyer, xiv + 766 pp., a near-encyclopaedic edition including an extensive review of reception and scholarship, analysis of the *je lyrique* and of linguistic and rhetorical peculiarities, together with an account of the manuscript tradition. Other work on *trobairitz* by A. Rieger includes 'Beruf: *Joglaressa*. Die Spielfrau im okzitanischen Mittelalter', *Symposion* (Paderborn), 229–42, 'Alamanda de Castelnau — une *trobairitz* dans l'entourage des comtes de Toulouse?', *ZRP*, 107:47–57, and 'La *Poétesse de Carcassonne* de Paul Heyse ou: comment "moraliser" la *fin'amor*?', *Mélanges Bec*, 485–96. Katharina Städtler, *Altprovenzalische Frauendichtung (1150–1250). Historisch-soziologische Untersuchungen und Interpretationen*, Heidelberg, Winter (*GRM*, Beiheft 9), xii + 347 pp., is an important study of the status of the *trobairitz* and includes the text and translation of 19 pieces. I. de Riquer, 'El guante robado de Castelloza', *AF*, 14:49–60, shows how this *trobairitz* transforms the motif of the glove as love-token. U. Mölk, 'Chansons de femme, trobairitz et la théorie romantique de la genèse de la poésie lyrique romane', *LS*, 35, 1990:135–46 examines the poetics of feminine writing.

Amelia E. Van Vleck, *Memory and Re-creation in Troubadour Lyric*, Berkeley, California U.P., x + 283 pp., is a challenging study which, developing the notion of *mouvance*, rejects the idea of a 'perfect' or authentic written text as anachronistic and asserts the primacy of performance. Luciano Formisano, *La lirica*, Bologna, Il Mulino, 1990, 448 pp., is an anthology of critical writing on the troubadours in Italian translation. Mario Mancini, *Il punto su: i trovatori*, Rome, Laterza, viii + 258 pp., is a very similar collection but includes extracts from Stendhal, *De l'amour*, Nietzsche on 'Fröhliche Wissenschaft' and Lacan on courtly love and *jouissance*. Id., ' "Gay Saber": la questione dello stile', *Mélanges Bec*, 307–23, is a review of critical approaches. S. Gaunt, 'Poetry of exclusion: a feminist reading of some troubadour lyrics', *MLR*, 85, 1990:310–29, through readings of Guilhem IX, Marcabru, B. de Ventadorn, A. de Marueil, and R. de Vaqueiras, persuasively deconstructs the critical myth that troubadour poetry is about women. V. Fraser, 'Figures and tropes of erotic implication in the Occitan lyric', *Tenso*, 7:1–11, examines the function of *carientismos*, *diminutio*, and *aposiopesis* in poems by P. Vidal, the Comtessa de Dia and Castelloza. P. Wunderli, 'Réflexions sur le système des genres lyriques en ancien occitan', *Mélanges Bec*, 599–615, is a laborious reclassification, a departure from Köhler's system which gave centrality to the *canso*. D. Rieger, '"Chantar" und "faire"'. Zum Problem der trobadoresken Improvisation', *ZRP*, 106, 1990:423–35, weighs arguments for and against improvisation in *tensos* and *partimens*. A. Torres-Alcalá, 'Del libelo politico al sirventés provenzal: una analogia', *RoQ*, 38:49–57, takes issue with Karen W. Klein (*The Partisan Voice*, Paris, Mouton, 1971) regarding the function of the *sirventes* and argues that the analogy of the political pamphlet is valid. P. T. Ricketts, 'L'*estribot*: forme et fond', *Mélanges Bec*, 475–83, examines surviving examples (P. C. 315, 5 and 335, 64) to see whether the monorhymed alexandrine *laisse* is the standard form. G. M. Cropp, 'Les expressions *mans jonchas* et *a (de) genolhos* dans la poésie des troubadours', *ib.*, 103–12, catalogues these images and their connotations. G. Le Vot, 'Quelques indices du silence dans la *canso* des troubadours', *ib.*, 295–306, suggests means whereby melodic discontinuity may have been effected and indicated.

New editions of troubadours include Stefano Asperti (ed.), *Il trovatore Raimon Jordan, edizione critica*, Modena, Mucchi, 1990, 568 pp., and J. Gourc, *Azemar lo Negre, troubadour albigeois du XIIIe siècle*, Paris, CNRS, 109 pp. R. Taylor, 'Pons d'Ortaffa: images of exile and love', *Mélanges Bec*, 567–75, edits the two surviving songs and shows how this early 13th-c. poet renewed the dialectic of suffering and joy. U. Mölk, '"Quan vei les praz verdesir"', *ib.*, 377–84, is an edition and commentary on this *chanson de femme*. J. H. Marshall, 'Les jeunes femmes et les vieilles: une *tenso* (P. C. 88.2 = 173.5) et un échange de *sirventes* (P. C. 173.1a + 88.1)', *ib.*, 325–38, edits, translates, and identifies the participants in this unique cycle. G. Gouiran, 'Le cycle de la bataille des jeunes et des vieilles', *Estudis Lafont*, 109–33, addresses precisely the same subject and draws the same conclusions. L. Lazzerini, 'Marcabru, A l'*alena del vent doussa (BdT*, 293, 2): proposte testuali e interpretative', *Messana*, 4, 1990:47–87, is a new edition and translation of this problematic piece. G. Brunel-Lobrichon, 'Réflexions sur les manuscrits occitans médiévaux', *BAIEO*, 8:1–12, is a guide to the location of 60 manuscripts and fragments. G. D. B. Brunetti, 'Per la storia del manoscritto provenzale T', *CN*, 51:27–41, completes an earlier study (*CN*, 50:45–73).

Work on individual troubadours includes N. Pasero, 'Due passi controversi di Guglielmo IX: *Companho, farai un vers* [. . .] *convinen* (I, 1); *mandacarrei* (II, 8)', *Mélanges Bec*, 415–23, offering one solution based on intertextuality within G.'s own works and another relating to charivari. Ph. Ménard, 'Sens, contresens, non-sens, réflexions sur la pièce *Farai un vers de dreyt nien* de Guillaume IX', *ib.*, 339–48, looks for a simpler, more comprehensive explanation of the piece. F. Zambon, 'L'amante onirica du Guglielmo IX', *RZLG*, 15:247–61, argues that it is a *rêve amoureux* and points to the dream-lover in mozarabic tradition. P. Uhl, 'Un chat peut en cacher un autre: autour d'une interprétation "sans difficulté" de Henri Rey-Flaud et de Jean-Charles Huchet', *Neophilologus*, 85:178–84, warns against psychoanalytic approaches which take no account of the precise signifier. Id., *'Guillaume IX d'Aquitaine et la sorcellerie de Babel. A propos des vers arabes de la Chanson v (MS. C)', *Arabica*, 33:19–39, examines another aspect of this much discussed piece. M. L. Meneghetti, 'De l'art d'éditer Jaufre Rudel', *CCMe*, 34:166–75, compares approaches and in '*Qui non sap esser chantaire*: un'attribuzione possibile', *Mélanges Bec*, 349–60, suggests that P. C. 262, 7 might be the work of Bernart Marti. M. Heintze, 'Jaufre Rudel zwischen "*lunhatz d'amor*" und "*amor de lonh*"', *RZLG*, 15:11–46, sees the dedication of *Cortesamen vuoill comensar* to Rudel as evidence of a poetic debate and of Rudel's conversion to the Marcabrunian school. G. D. Economou, 'Marcabru, love's star witness: for and against', *Tenso*, 7:23–39, is a digest of recent work on Marcabru and includes the text and a translation of *Al son desviat, chantaire* (P. C. 293, 5). M. C. Corcoran, 'Ambiguous vocabulary and expression of emotion in Giraut de Bornelh's *Gen m'aten*', *MAe*, 59, 1990:275–88, is an elegant demonstration of how the poet exploits ambiguity to convey emotional conflict. M. Segarra, '*Can vei la lauzeta mover*; une analyse rythmique', *RLaR*, 95:139–46, successfully avoiding the subjectivism which often characterizes such approaches, applies Meschonnic's claim that 'le rythme est en interaction avec le sens dans tout discours' to show that the poem's structure depends on echo effects and expresses the struggle to overcome the passage of time. P. A. Thomas, 'La voyelle en miroir. La tapisserie vocalique de "Can vei la lauzeta mover"', *NMi*, 92:363–70, sees a system of reflecting tonic vowels in the same piece. R. Rosenstein, 'Latent dialogue and manifest role-playing in Bernart de Ventadorn', *NMi*, 91, 1990:357–68, develops the view that *Non es meravelha* (P. C. 70,31) expresses different lyric voices in a single persona. W. D. Paden, 'Bernart de Ventadour le troubadour devint-il abbé de Tulle?', *Mélanges Bec*, 401–13, returns to Rita Lejeune's hypothesis (*YWMLS*, 48:285) and makes adjustments to the chronology; the case remains open. D. A. Monson, 'Bernart de Ventadorn et Tristan', *ib.*, 385–400, examines the allusion in P. C. 70,44 and expresses doubts concerning the identification of 'Tristan' (*tornadas* of P. C. 70, 4, 29, 42, and 43) as

Raimbaut d'Aurenga. M. M. R. Vuijlsteke, 'Eléments de définition d'un mode de l'énoncé poétique. Raimbaut d'Orange et le *trobar clus*', *ib.*, 587–98, is a persuasive and coherent analysis of the debate with Guiraut de Bornelh (P. C. 389, 10a). M. Perugi, 'Modelli critico-testuali applicabili a un lessico dei trovatori del periodo classico (LTC)', *SM*, 31, 1990:481–544, illustrates, mainly with reference to R. d'Aurenga, linguistic problems which arise in the establishment of stemmata. C. Phan, 'La tornada et l'envoi: fonctions structurelles et poïetiques', *CCMe*, 34:57–61, discusses the privileged position of the *tornada*. The article is concerned with trouvères but includes reference to R. d'Aurenga and B. de Born. G. Straka, 'Bertran de Born, *Be.m platz lo gais temps de pascor*. En marge de deux nouvelles éditions', *Mélanges Bec*, 541–48, is a staunch defence of the traditional five-stanza version. P. Stäblein Harris, 'La genèse de la fureur: Bertran de Born, *Inferno* XXVIII, et *Gerusalemme Liberata* VIII', *ib.*, 193–205, traces the image of the poet through Dante and Tasso. R. Lafont, 'Un personnage textuel: Eble (d'Ussel?)', *ib.*, 285–94, offers a prudent but imaginative approach to identification and attribution. M. Switten, 'De la sextine: amour et musique chez Arnaut Daniel', *ib.*, 549–65, suggests that the poet was acquainted with Plato's *Timaeus*. D. Rieger, '"Lop es nomnat lo pes, e lop no es". Un *devinalh* sans solution?', *ib.*, 497–506, decodes the exchange between Guillem de Berguedan and Peire de Gauceran (P. C. 210, 10b = 342b, 1). M.-A. Bossy, 'Cyclical composition in Guiraut Riquier's book of poems', *Speculum*, 66:277–93, concludes that Guiraut collated his poems in such a way as to suggest both a 'love-life' and a poetic career.

On epic texts, Gérard Gouiran and Robert Lafont, *Le Roland occitan: Roland à Saragosse, Ronsasvals, édition et traduction*, Paris, UGE, 257 pp., are the first editions since those by Mario Roques (1956 and 1932). There is a facing translation and sparse notes but regrettably no glossary. Lafont's introduction lays emphasis on the texts as *épopées de la frontière* and is on the same lines as Id., *La Geste de Roland*, Paris, L'Harmattan, 2 vols, 344 + 294 pp. H.-E. Keller, 'Charlemagne et ses pairs dans le *Roman d'Arles*', *Mélanges Bec*, 235–47, studies the place of this text in the epic tradition. L. M. Paterson, 'L'épouse et la formation du lien conjugal selon la littérature occitane du XIe au XIIIe s.: mutations d'une institution et condition féminine', *ib.*, 425–42, studies economic, legal, and ritual aspects of marriage in epic and romance. G. Gouiran, 'Silhouettes de femmes dans les textes rolandiens occitans et franciens', *ib.*, 179–92, shows how the depiction of female characters translates differing ideologies. Id., 'Le jardin de Belauda', *Vergers et jardins*, 127–37, examines *Ronsasvals* and the *Jeu de sainte Agnès* to show the Occitan heroine to be less of a *femme d'intérieur* than her northern counterpart. A. Labbé, 'Nature et artifice dans quelques jardins épiques', *ib.*, 179–95, discusses the royal garden in *Girart de Roussillon*. W. Pfeffer, 'Rotten apples and other proverbs in "The Song of the Albigensian Crusade"', *Proverbium*, 8:147–58, suggests that the choice of proverbs and proverbial expressions reveals the two authors' ideological positions.

Jean-Charles Huchet, *Le Roman occitan médiéval*, Paris, PUF, 214 pp. investigates the case of the missing narrative texts. The clues point to the overwhelming prestige of the lyric, from which the romance draws its themes and structures. A. Serper, 'Giraut de Bornelh et *Jaufre*', *Mélanges Bec*, 531–39, a sequel to the article in *RLaR*, 86, 1982:293–304, argues that the 'Jaufre' whom the poet claims to resemble in P. C. 242, 53 is the hero of an early version of the romance. M.-R. Jung, '*Jaufre*: "E aiso son novas rials"', *ib.*, 223–34, perceives a critique of the ideology of the Arthurian verse romance. P. T. Ricketts, 'Plantes et recettes médicales dans le *Breviari d'Amor* de Matfre Ermengaud de Béziers', *Estudis Lafont*, 255–66, reproduces ll. 6903–7144, and identifies the species mentioned.

2. FROM 1500 ONWARDS

B. Schlieben-Lange, 'Le glossaire provençal de Lacurne de Sainte-Palaye', *Estudis Lafont*, 267–84, draws attention to the philological work of Sainte-Palaye and others. Ph. Gardy, 'Éloge du *chant royal* occitan', *Mélanges Bec*, 153–69, is an account of the reappearance of Occitan in the Jeux floraux in poems by Godolin and Bertrand Larada. 'L'edition des textes littéraires occitans (XVIe–XVIIIe siècles). Bilan et perspectives', *BAIEO*, 8:41–57, has contributions by Ph. Gardy, F. Pic, J.-Y. Casanova, and F. Garavini. H.-E. Keller, 'Recueil de poésies languedociennes tant anciennes que modernes en patois de Montpellier', *Estudis Lafont*, 169–87, includes texts from the anthology compiled by François Robert Martin in 1812. Ph. Martel, 'Félibres rouges ou rouges félibres', *ib.*, 209–22, assesses the extent to which political ideologies and groups were integral to the movement. *Oc*, 300:41–48, 49–53, 111–15, includes studies and appreciations by F. M. Castan, M. Roqueta, and R. Lafont of the work of Ismaël Girard (1898–1976), the effective founder of *occitanisme*. C. Camps, 'L'obra poética de J.-S. Pons', *ib.*, 237–57, is a statistical semantic analysis treating nature, sentiments, and movement. R. Teulat, 'Los poèmas en "vièlh romanç" a l'entorn de 1900', *Mélanges Bec*, 578–85, studies the language, content, and inspiration of these fake antiquities. *L'Astrado*, 26, is devoted to the work of Farfantello (Henriette Dibon) and includes examples of her writings, studies of her works and poems dedicated to her. F. P. Kirsch, 'A las raras del silenci. Sobre la pròsa narrativa de Max Roqueta', *Estudis Lafont*, 189–96, concludes that Rouquette's writing is characterized by a desire to express the inexpressible. Ph. Gardy, 'Roman de la langue ou langue du roman', *ib.*, 91–107, compares Lafont's *La Festa* with Canetti's *Histoire d'une jeunesse. La langue sauvée* and Régine Robin's *L'Amour du Yiddish.* H. Godinho, 'A poesia occitanica de Pierre Bec', *Mélanges Bec*, 171–78, is a brief thematic study. W. Calin, 'Les lettres d'Oc aujourd'hui: le cas Delavouët', *ib.*, 95–102, studies 9 poems from vols I and II of *Pouèmo.*

IV. SPANISH STUDIES

LANGUAGE

By JOHN ENGLAND, *Senior Lecturer in Spanish, University of Sheffield,* and
CHRISTOPHER LYONS, *Lecturer in Modern Languages, University of Salford*

1. GENERAL

The section on Spanish in Campbell, *Compendium*, II, 1264–70, gives
some basic information, although there is an unacceptably high
number of errors, both factual and typographical. The decision to
omit *vosotros* verb-forms from verb paradigms is bizarre. Aurelio
Guaita Martorell, *Lenguas de España y artículo 3° de la Constitución*, M,
Editorial Civitas, 1989, 207 pp., is in effect a series of short essays by a
specialist in administrative law, many dealing with education,
especially with legal cases involving the question of Castilian versus
other languages; his main concern is the rights of those wishing to use
Castilian. J. C. Herreras, 'Le panorama linguistique espagnol', *La
Linguistique*, 17:75–85, presents facts and figures on language use in
the media and education, etc.; analysis is slight, with a strongly
centralist view prevailing. B. García-Hernández, 'Español y castellano; pero no indistintamente', *EspA*, no. 56:53–61, attempts to
reduce the bitterness of the terminological debate; both terms should
continue to be used, they are distinct, although speakers need to
accept that they both refer to the same language.

2. HISTORY OF SPANISH LINGUISTICS

Juan M. Lope Blanch, *Estudios de historia lingüística hispánica*, M, Arco,
1990, 225 pp., contains revised versions of 14 articles: 'La lingüística
española del Siglo de Oro' (5–50); 'Notas sobre los estudios
gramaticales en la España del Renacimiento' (51–67); 'El *Diálogo de la
lengua* de Juan de Valdés' (69–102); 'Dos principios gramaticales de
Villalón' (103–09); 'El *Vocabulario de las dos lenguas toscana y castellana* de
Cristóbal de las Casas' (111–24); 'La *Gramática española* de Jerónimo
de Texeda' (125–42); 'Las gramáticas de Juan de Luna y de Jerónimo
de Texeda' (143–46); 'A vueltas con Jerónimo de Texeda y Juan de
Luna' (147–52); 'Los indoamericanismos en el *Tesoro* de Covarrubias'
(153–74); 'Sebastián de Covarrubias y el elemento germánico del
español' (175–83); 'El juicio de Ménage sobre las etimologías de
Covarrubias' (185–91); 'Otro aspecto de la relación entre Ménage y
Covarrubias' (193–200); 'Las fuentes americanas del *Tesoro* de
Covarrubias' (201–12); 'Bello y el concepto de oración' (213–24). J.
Perona, 'De rerum et verborum significatione: el Título XXXIII de

la Séptima Partida y la Suma Azonis', *Homenaje Lapesa*, 157–90, demonstrates how definitions and translations can lead writers to develop reflections on language. B. Müller, 'La paraphrase dans la lexicographie espagnole au Moyen-Âge', *CLHM*, 14–15, 1989– 90:235–45, is based on the premise that Spanish lexicography existed before the 16th c., and that the notion of paraphrase can be applied to non-literary texts; M. compares the techniques of single-word synonyms, multi-word explanations, etc. J.-C. Santoyo, 'Alonso de Madrigal: a medieval Spanish pioneer of translation theory', *Papers* (Trier), I, 219–31, shows that Madrigal, in his commentaries on St Jerome's observations on translation, was an important theorist of translation, who started from the premise that no language is intrinsically superior to any other. R. Recio, 'Alfonso de Madrigal (El Tostado): la traducción como teoría entre lo medieval y lo renacentista', *La Corónica*, 19:112–31, examines similar material against the background of 15th- and 16th-c. ideas on translation; R. picks up Madrigal's distinction between *defectos* and *errores*, and is particularly good on the tension between tradition and originality.

A useful reprint is: *Vocabulario español-latino de Elio Antonio de Nebrija. Facsímil de la primera edición, patrocinado por la Asociación de Amigos de la Real Academia Española*, M, RAE, 1989. The facsimile first appeared in 1951. J. Caravolas, 'Quatre anniversaires en 1992: Antonio de Nebrija, Juan Luis Vivès, Nicolas Clénard et Jan Amos Coménius', *HistL*, 18:407–18, gives some basic information on Nebrija, (407–09) and Vives, (409–11). A. Ramajo Caño, 'De Nebrija al Brocense', *AEF*, 13, 1990:331–47, explains that the latter preferred empirical rather than theoretical methods, whilst Nebrija built on his experience in Italy to write his *Introductiones*. J. M. Fórneas, 'Hitos en el estudio de los arabismos hasta el "Glossaire" de Engelmann-Dozy', *Homenaje Lapesa*, 127–55, provides an interesting survey, beginning with Nebrija, and ending with a brief analysis of recent studies. M. Breva-Claramonte, 'Translation in Pedro-Simón Abril's (1530– 1600) teaching method', *Papers* (Trier), I, 275–86, outlines Abril's use of translation for the teaching of Latin and Greek to Spanish-speakers. J. Calvo Pérez, 'La definición latina en el *Tesoro* de S. de Covarrubias', *Homenatge García Díez*, 299–312, points out that Covarrubias made use of Latin in a substantial minority of his definitions, and proceeds to examine the mix of Latin and Castilian. R. Sarmiento, 'Lorenzo Hervás y Panduro (1735–1809): entre la tradición y la modernidad', *Papers* (Trier), II, 461–82, is an interesting essay on a broad range of linguistic ideas, including the principles governing the evolution of languages. V. Vázquez, 'Algunos aspectos de la historia de las funciones sintácticas clausales en la gramática española', *Verba*, 17, 1990:427–38, covers the period 1771–1870. C.

Lleal, 'Reflexiones a propósito de un Probo decimonónico', *AEF*, 13, 1990: 161–65, describes an *Appendix Probi*-type booklet of 1865, listing 687 pronunciation errors (vowel quality, reduction of consonant clusters, etc.), but warns that such documents, though useful, must be handled with caution. Dealing with more recent matters are F. Abad, 'Positivismo e idealismo en la "escuela española" de Filología', *Homenaje Lapesa*, 15–29, and J. Muñoz Garrigós, 'La obra filológica de D. Rafael Lapesa', *ib.*, 31–41, which rightly highlights Lapesa's skill in handling texts and analysing language in its social and cultural contexts. Two items deal specifically with Latin America: H.-D. Paufler, 'Lexikbeschreibung und Lexicographie zum Spanischen in Amerika', *Papers* (Trier), 1, 329–36, and A. M. Barrenchea and E. Lois, 'El exilio y la investigación lingüística en la Argentina', *CHA*, no. 473–4, 1989: 81–91.

3. PRE-MODERN LANGUAGE

Bodo Müller's *Diccionario del español medieval* (see *YWMLS*, 51, 1989: 244–45) continues with the publication of fascicles IV, 1989, *ABREGO–ACABADO* (pp. 195–274), and V, 1990, *ACABADOR–ACEBUCHE* (pp. 275–354). Leopoldo Peñarroja Torrejón, *El mozárabe de Valencia: Nuevas cuestiones de fonología mozárabe*, M, Gredos, 1990, 514 pp., builds up via a close analysis of a vast quantity of materials a detailed description of one variety of *mozárabe*, which did not diphthongize stressed ĕ/ŏ, and reduced AI and AU to /e/ and /o/ respectively; the distinctive nature of this variety emerges, and a case is made for viewing it as an important factor in the creation of modern *valenciano*. N. Roth, 'La lengua hebrea entre los cristianos españoles medievales: voces hebreas en español', *RFE*, 71: 137–43, draws attention to borrowings previously not recorded, and gives more detailed information on those already noted in Corominas, etc. A. J. Meilán García, 'La expresión de la "denominación" en castellano medieval', *Verba*, 17, 1990: 331–41, examines different constructions with *dezir, llamar, poner nombre*, etc. B. Stengaard, 'The combination of glosses in the *Códice Emilianense 60 (Glosas Emilianenses)*', Wright, *Latin*, 177–89, examines alphabetical and grammatical glosses, and concludes that they formed part of a system of aids for producing an oral version of the text. C. Pensado, 'How was Leonese Vulgar Latin read?', *ib.*, 190–204, looks closely at the 'Leonese Vulgar Latin' texts, and in particular at the mis-spellings, concluding that the texts were read as Romance, but were probably felt to be Latin; the clarity of exposition is exemplary, as is the care taken not to draw conclusions beyond what the evidence will permit. A. Emiliano, 'Latin or Romance? Graphemic variation and scripto-linguistic change in medieval Spain', *ib.*, 233–47, examines 12th- and 13th-c. Leonese texts, tracing the emergence of Romance writing as the Latin veneer is gradually removed. F. Gómez Solís, 'Aspectos de toponimia mayor medieval cordobesa', *AEF*, 13, 1990:123–32, analyses Cordoban toponymy, as recorded in cartularies; he studies a variety of linguistic features (phonology, morphology, lexis), and finds a great diversity of contributory elements, many to do with the Reconquest and repopulation. There are three studies on 14th-c. texts: S. Repiso Repiso, '*Derecha*: arabismo semántico en el v. 256d del *Libro de buen amor*', *RFE*, 71:153–55, proposes a semantic borrowing (='[good] fortune'), rather than an unexplained use of *derecha* for *derecho*, 'right'; M. J. López Bobo, 'Sobre el leísmo en el *Libro de buen amor*', *Verba*, 17, 1990:343–61, presents a detailed analysis of the three principal MSS, though many readers will be wary of accepting that the conclusions based on an analysis of Corominas' reconstruction of the 'original' are reliable as a statement about Castilian in 1330; and I. C. Báez Montero, 'El predicativo del C. D. con verbos de percepción en *El Conde Lucanor*', Wotjak, *Verbo*, 23–32, is a descriptive study. A. Rubio Vela, 'Un topónimo inadvertido en la "Comedieta de Ponça". Apunte sobre la cultura histórica del Marqués de Santillana', *BRAE*, 70, 1990:53–64, explains that *valençia* of stanza xcix is not an abstract noun, but *Valençia*, believed in the Middle Ages to have been a name for Rome. M. Alvar, 'Valor fonético de las rimas en la *Gaya Ciencia* de Pedro Guillén de Segovia', *AnM*, 1, 1989:10–33, concludes that the writer, born in Seville but a resident of Segovia, did not distinguish /s/ and /z/, but did distinguish /b/ and /ß/, /ts/ and /dz/, and /ʃ/ and /ʒ/. Medical texts provide the data for M. Laín Martínez and D. Ruiz Otín, 'Estudio de los verbos derivados de adjetivos a través de los textos médicos del siglo XV', *BRAE*, 71:121–31, who discover an interesting diversity of forms (e.g. *blando > ablandar, ablandeçer, blandeçer, emblandeçer*). R. Penny, 'The stage jargon of Juan del Encina and the Castilianization of the Leonese dialect area', *Varey Vol.*, 155–66, finds that Encina's rustic characters do not speak *sayagués*, but a variety based on the speech of rural Salamanca, an area characterized by competing Leonese and Castilian forms; the evidence showing Castilianization in the late 15th and early 16th c. is strong. Jesús Terrón González, *Léxico de cosméticos y afeites en el Siglo de Oro*, Cáceres, Extremadura U.P., 1990, 233 pp., is based mainly on literary texts, and should be of interest to linguists, literary specialists, and social historians. J. L. Alonso Hernández, 'Notas sobre un lenguaje que nunca existió: la jerigonza', *BHi*, 92, 1990:29–44, takes issue with those who have claimed that *jerigonza* is the name of a specific language variety; the misunderstanding arises from a misreading of *Lazarillo de Tormes*. Eva María Bravo García, *Fonética de la crónica criolla de Baltasar Obregón (México, 1584)*, Zaragoza, Pórtico, 1990, 107 pp., takes advantage of archive materials in Seville to analyse the orthography, phonetics, and phonology of one example of 16th-c. American Spanish; there are no startling conclusions, but the analysis is sensible. Ramón Menéndez Pidal, *La lengua castellana en el siglo XVII*, M, Austral, 225 pp., was begun in 1938, and first appeared in 1986 as part of vol. xxvi of the *Historia de España*; the focus is very much on the literary language and how it influenced other types of language. F. Caimari Frau, 'Morfosintaxis histórica, siglo XVII. Historias peregrinas y ejemplares', *Caligrama*, 3:31–51, gives a basic description of a series of features of a work by Gonzalo de Céspedes y Meneses. M. Urdiales, 'Diferencias de lengua entre dos libros de cuentas de una misma parroquia leonesa de los siglos XVII y XVIII', *BRAE*, 70, 1990:171–200, compares the two texts rather unsystematically. Carlos González de Posada, *Diccionario de algunas voces del dialecto asturiano [1788] y otros papeles*, (Biblioteca de Filoloxia Asturiana, 4), Oviedo U.P., xxv + 63 pp., is a useful edition of this early dialectal witness. The only other 18th-c. item to record is an interesting one: G. de Granda, 'Galicismos léxicos en el español dominicano de la segunda mitad del siglo XVIII', *Lexis*, 14, 1990:197–219. The final items in this section all deal with the language of literary texts, and are long on examples, but short on analysis: A. B. Dellepiane, 'La lengua "gauchesca" de *Don Segundo Sombra*', *EspA*, no. 56:63–110; M. A. Rebollo Torío, 'Los extranjerismos en Antonio de Hoyos y Vinent', *AEF*, 13, 1990:349–53; A. I. Navarro Carrasco, 'Ortografía utilizada por los Alvarez Quintero para reflejar la pronunciación andaluza en *Las Flores*', *EspA*, no. 55:55–83.

4. DIACHRONIC STUDIES

GENERAL.   The outstanding work this year is Ralph Penny, *A History of the Spanish Language*, Cambridge U.P., xvi + 319 pp., which provides a clear, but not over-simplified, account of the internal history of the language. The emphasis is on the continuity from Latin to Spanish, a point conveyed by the organization of the material. As a manual this book is likely to stand the test of time. Coloma Lleal, *La formación de las lenguas romances peninsulares*, B, Barcanova, 1990, 383 pp., is full of good things on both the internal and external history of the language, but is too ambitious and imprecise in its aims; if it is intended as a basic manual, the lack of bibliography and index makes it difficult to use, and given that it does cover developments up to the present day, L. has relatively little to say on the 20th-c. language. Antonio Alatorre, *Los 1,001 años de la lengua española*, 2nd edn, Mexico City, Tezontle, 1989, 342 pp., is aimed at the general reader rather than the specialist; this works with external history, borrowings, etc., but will the interested layman be able to cope with historical phonology? Alain Milhou (ed.), *Langues et identités dans la Péninsule Ibérique* (Les Cahiers du CRIAR, 9), Rouen U.P., 1989, 146 pp., deals mainly with languages other than Castilian, but the editor's introduction, 'L'impérialisme linguistique: mythe et réalité' (7–21), is good on the manner of Castilian expansion, by prestige rather than by prohibition of other languages, until the *Decretos de Nueva Planta*. R. Eberenz, '*Castellano antiguo y español moderno*: reflexiones sobre la periodización en la historia de la lengua', *RFE*, 71:79–106, is a fascinating essay on the internal and external history of the language. On internal grounds he presents a strong case for dividing the history of the language into three periods: *castellano/español antiguo* (1200–1450); *medio* (1450–1650); *moderno* (1650–present). M. T. Echenique Elizondo, 'Vascos y vascuence en textos romances', *Homenaje Lapesa*, 121–26, covers too much material, and some of the cases need to be argued: for example, a few instances of OV in Old Spanish are not grounds for classifying it as an OV language. B. Cifuentes and D. Pellicer, 'Ideology, politics and national language: a study in the creation of a national language in 19th-century Mexico', *Sociolinguistics*, 18, 1989:7–17, divide American developments into two periods, the colonial period (16th–18th c.), and the national period (19th c.–present); the power and prestige associated with Spanish as a national language led to the decline of indigenous languages. A.–M. Bañón Hernández, 'Los preámbulos constitucionales españoles. Datos para su análisis semiolingüístico', *AFHis*, 5, 1990:255–79, analyses the texts of seven Spanish Constitutions (1812–1978).

PHONETIC. J. Brandão de Carvalho, '"Cantabrie" et "Mozarabie": de quelques divergences entre espagnol et portugais', *La Linguistique*, 27:61–73, interprets several features of historical phonology as evidence that the traditional view of the Reconquest as the determinant of the linguistic structure of the Iberian Peninsula needs to be modified, and proposes that some of the differences between north and south be seen as crucial. T. J. Walsh, 'Spelling lapses in early medieval Latin documents and the reconstruction of primitive Romance phonology', Wright, *Latin*, 205–18, continues to argue, against the views of the editor of this splendid volume, that Latin and early Romance were distinct languages; he uses 10th-c. texts to deduce some features of Leonese phonology, and concludes that not only had intervocalic /p/, /t/ and /k/ voiced, but they had become fricatives. M. Torreblanca, 'Sobre la evolución /ŭ/ latina > /ú/ en español: *junco, surco, ducho*', *JHispP*, 14, 1990:247–76, explains the non-appearance of /o/ in terms of the assumption that a velar or velarized consonant in syllable-final position prevented the lowering of Latin /ŭ/; the argument is elegantly made, although there is a high number of exceptions not satisfactorily accounted for. J. Rini, 'The diffusion of /-ee-/ > /-e-/ in Ibero-Romance infinitives: *creer, leer, veer, preveer, proveer, seer, poseer*', *NMi*, 92:95–103, proposes that the retardation of /-ee-/ > /-e-/ be treated as a case of lexical diffusion: *creer, leer, poseer, proveer*, remain because of the structure of their past participles, whereas *previsto, sido, visto*, could exert no such pressure. R. Penny, 'Labiodental /f/, aspiration and /h/ dropping in Spanish: the evolving phonemic value of the graphs *f* and *h*', *Harvey Vol.*, 157–82, challenges the assumption that medieval *h* could represent aspirate /h/, or that *f* indicated a labiodental, and argues persuasively that *h* was a phonologically void symbol prior to the Renaissance, and that *f* represented /h/, acquiring the value /f/ only in later Old Spanish. F. J. Herrero Ruiz de Loizaga, 'La aspiración de la "h": hiato y sinalefa en poetas de la Edad de Oro', *BRAE*, 70, 1990:111–70, painstakingly builds up a picture of the progressive loss of aspiration through the 16th c., with considerable regional variations. D. Eddington, 'Distancing as a causal factor in the development of /θ/ and /x/ in Spanish', *JHispP*, 14, 1990:239–45, accepts the functionalist approach of distancing for Castilian, but the chronology rules it out for *andaluz*; E's instinct is to ascribe it to the influence of Arabic guttural fricatives, but no evidence is produced. M. Ariza, 'Diacronía de las consonantes labiales sonoras en español', Anglada, *Cambio*, 11–26, examines the contradictory nature of written evidence from Latin to Golden-Age Spanish, especially for the possible existence of /v/ in Old Spanish; things are not made clearer by taking the orthography of late MSS to represent the speech of the original writers.

MORPHOSYNTACTIC. Catherine E. Harre, *'Tener' + Past Participle: A Case Study in Linguistic Description*, London, Routledge, viii + 213 pp., seeks via a historical and comparative analysis (particularly with Portuguese) to shed light on the use of *tener* + p.p. in modern Spanish, and to test theories concerning auxiliaries and periphrastic verbs; the approach is flexible (textual analysis and questionnaires), and H. draws conclusions on the nature of language variation and language change. R. Blake, 'Syntactic aspects of Latinate texts of the early Middle Ages', Wright, *Latin*, 219–32, examines documents from the 9th–11th cs, and finds in the dominant VO order support for the case for regarding them as Romance texts using a Latin writing-system. E. C. García, 'Morphologization: a case of reversible markedness?', *Probus*, 3:23–54, analyses the replacement of *ha* by *hay*, interested in particular in the replacement of a morphologically simpler item by a more complex innovation, whose increased use makes it the unmarked exponent of a function. K.

Ferreiro-Couso González, 'Precedentes mediatos e inmediatos de los adverbios en -mente', *AFHis*, 5, 1990:281–300, presents a huge number of examples with little commentary, and appears to trust the word-division of medieval scribes and modern editors. C. Company, 'La extensión del artículo en el español medieval', *RPh*, 44:402–24, examines the increasing use of the article in Old Spanish, and charts the development in detail according to the class of noun, function of the noun-phrase, etc. E. Ridruejo Alonso, 'Calcos, reanálisis y procesos analógicos en la sintaxis del español preclásico', *Homenaje Lapesa*, 205–26, has a good general introduction, followed by analysis of *como* + subjunctive, infinitive constructions, present participles, and hyperbaton; *Id.*, 'El cambio sintáctico', Anglada, *Cambio*, 91–111, is a general article on the nature of syntactic change, with almost all the illustrations taken from Spanish. E. Blasco Ferrer, 'L'evolució de l'ordre dels mots en francès, espanyol i català. Una anàlisi tipològica i comparativa', *ELLC*, 18, 1989:11–35, has interesting observations, although the topic is so broad that some of his comments are over-generalized, and avoid the difficulties created by 'real' examples. A. Líbano Zamalacárregui, 'Morfología diacrónica del español: las fórmulas de tratamiento', *RFE*, 71:107–21, is thorough, but comes up with few surprises. G. Bossong, 'El uso de los tiempos verbales en judeoespañol', Wotjak, *Verbo*, 71–96, analyses both *ladino* and modern spoken Judeo-Spanish; the latter is found to contain a mixture of archaic forms and innovations.

LEXICAL. Birte Stengaard, *Vida y muerte de un campo semántico: un estudio de la evolución semántica de los verbos latinos 'stare', 'sedere' e 'iacere' del latín al romance del s. XIII*, Tübingen, Niemeyer, xii + 414 pp., is excellent on the evolution of the semantic field of verbs of position, and their loss in Romance (or, at least, their loss of meaning). The largest section deals with the Romance languages of the Iberian Peninsula. M. A. Pastor Milán, *Indagaciones lexemáticas. A propósito del campo léxico 'asir'*, Granada U.P., 1990, 402 pp., is both descriptive and historical, including American Spanish. Y. Malkiel, 'Dos problemas complejos de etimología española', *VLet*, 1, 1990:3–17, looks at *alcurnia/alcuña* > American *cuña*, and FINIRE > *fenecer* (not *finecer*); M. shows that simple solutions are not always the best, as complex evolutions require complex explanations. Id., 'Español *juez*, portugués *juiz*: ¿otro caso de autoafirmación excesiva?', *Homenaje a Jorge A. Suárez. Lingüística indoamericana e hispánica*, Mexico City, Colegio de México, 1990, 335–46, seeks to explain the difference between the Portuguese and the Spanish; the likely cause is excessive self-assertion, with Portuguese-speakers hostile to the characteristic Castilian [wé] diphthong. Id., 'Erratic derivational or compositional designs as clues to word origins', *Proceedings of the Fifteenth Annual*

Meeting of the Berkeley Linguistics Society, February 18–20, 1989, Berkeley, Berkeley Linguistics Society, 379–90, gives imaginative explanations for three items which cannot be explained by conventional phonology: *vergüenza, conmigo* and related forms, and the suffix *-ilón*. Id., 'Some erratic developments of Romance words for "Rancor"', *NMi*, 91, 1990:491–99, explains the initial vowel of Spanish *rencor* (< *rancōre*) as a result of influence from *reñir* and related forms. Id., 'Esbozos de dos estudios de lexicología diacrónica', *EstL*, 6, 1990:9–21, examines the complex relationships (i) between *(a)rrematar, (a)rrebatar, (a)rremeter*, and (ii) between Sp. *menudencia*/ Port. *miudeza*. Id., 'An imported derivative in search of a missing primitive: the near-antonyms OProv., Cat. *avinenteza* "composure, charm" vs. OSp. *avin-, avil-entez(a)* "boisterous arrogance"', *RoQ*, 38:449–70, sees antonymy in its various guises as an interesting field of investigation, and demonstrates this by taking the reader through some derivatives of AD-VENĪRE; the borrowing in Castilian was especially vulnerable because of its isolation, as the primitive was not borrowed in. J. M. Chamorro Martínez, '*Kabsane* "manto", pseudoarabismo en un documento leonés del siglo X', *Homenaje Gallego Morell*, 1, 347–50, confirms that *kabsane* is of Latin origin. M. Alvar, 'Dos helenismos marineros: *jarcia* y *gánguil*', *VLet*, 1, 1990:19–32, traces the complex history of *jarcia*, first documented in Juan Manuel, with a brief aside on the infrequent *gánguil*. R. M. Espinosa Elorza, 'Posibles occidentalismos en castellano medieval: algunas expresiones de sentido colectivo o distributivo en la prosa jurídica y la lengua literaria', *Verba*, 17, 1990:315–29, suggests that expressions such as *de consuno* are western (Galician) in origin, although the case appears to be far from proven. C. I. Nepaulsingh, '*Mestureros*', *AnM*, 1, 1989:156–66, looks at *mesturar/mesturero* and their (not necessarily pejorative) meanings in Old Spanish; a blend of Hebrew *metsora* and Latin MIXTURA is the proposed origin. J. S. Turley, 'Hispano-Latin/ Mozarabic *escala* "goblet" and Old Spanish *(es)calescer* "to become warm"', *RPh*, 44:306–12, suggests that while the secondary meaning of *(es)calescer* (= 'to become inebriated') can be explained as a metaphorical extension, it was probably reinforced by partial homonymy with *escala*. J. W. Marchand and S. Baldwin, '*Quandoque Bonus Dormitat Homerus* — Old Spanish *echan* again', *RoN*, 32:63–66, feel the need to defend their honour, but have no new information or interpretation to offer; cf. *YWMLS*, 45:269. M. Morera, 'La preposición española *contra*: su evolución semántica', *Verba*, 17, 1990:287–313, works backwards (the modern language is the only one that the native-speaker can use his intuition for) to Latin; but is the way of working necessarily the best way of presenting findings? R. A. Verdonk, 'La importancia de las guerras de Flandes para la neología en los siglos de oro', Anglada, *Cambio*, 113–26, examines loan-words and calques in one clearly defined situation; the methodology and conclusions are exemplary. I. A. A. Thompson, '*Hidalgo* and *pechero*: the language of "estates" and "classes" in early-modern Castile', Corfield, *Language*, 53–78, is good on the relationship between social and linguistic change; during the period examined the terminology changed little, but its meanings did. E. Martinell, 'Visión del cambio léxico en las crónicas de Indias', Anglada, *Cambio*, 61–78, looks at writers' comments on loan-words over 250 years, and makes an interesting series of comments on the most frequently found borrowings, writers' awareness of their status, derivational productivity, etc. P. Alvarez de Miranda, 'El doblete "antojo"/"anteojo": cronología de una recomposición etimológica', *BRAE*, 71:221–44, is a magnificent demonstration of historical linguistics' need for reliable texts: editors' modernizations of texts have produced incorrect datings for the first appearance of reconstructed *anteojos*. D. Wasserstein, 'La primera aparición de la palabra *impronta* en castellano', *RFE*, 71:157, pushes the date of its first appearance back to 1893. J. R. Lodares, '*Les Muedas*: una hipótesis toponímica', *ib.*, 145–53, proposes Latin MŎDUS, with change of gender to contrast with MŎDIUS > *moyo*. E. Bédard, 'De *mandinga*, africanismo, a *mandinga*, ictiónimo', *RCEH*, 16:13–27, gives a historical account of a word which has lost its semantic motivation. M. Morreale, '"Yo fatigo sin rumbo los confines . . .": implicaciones verbales y lexicográficas de los latinismos semánticos y su incomprensión en la actualidad', Anglada, *Cambio*, 79–90, laments the Spanish-speakers' loss of ability to understand semantic latinisms.

5. PHONETICS AND PHONOLOGY

V. Marrero, 'Estudio acústico de la aspiración en español', *RFE*, 70, 1990:345 97, uses a spectrographic analysis to attempt to define aspiration, by which she means [h], as it occurs in varieties of Spanish; she finds it is friction, with laryngeal, pharyngeal or velar articulation, producing turbulence in the central area of the spectrogram. M. Halle, J. W. Harris and J.-R. Vergnaud, 'A reexamination of the Stress Erasure Convention and Spanish stress', *LI*, 22:141–59, argue, against earlier work by Harris (see *YWMLS*, 51:251), that the SEC is necessary to account for the facts of Spanish stress. M. Almeida, 'El timbre vocálico en español actual', *RFR*, 7, 1990:75–85, is based on articulatory and acoustic analysis of the Spanish of the Canaries. T. Berg, 'Phonological processing in a syllable-timed language with pre-final stress: evidence from Spanish speech error data', *Language and Cognitive Processes*, 6:265–301, suggests that it is because Spanish has these characteristics that, by contrast with English and German, slips of the tongue are concentrated in syllable-initial (rather than word-initial) consonants and stressed syllables are not more vulnerable than unstressed ones. T. A. Morgan and K. Arrieta, 'Sobre la pronunciabilidad de grupos consonánticos marginales. Evidencia empírica en español', *HisJ*, 11, 1990:171–84, are concerned with consonant clusters permitted by the language, though not occurring in native words; they test invented words containing word-initial orthographic clusters like *jl, mr* on speakers, and argue for a gradient between pronounceable and non-pronounceable. J. M. Lipski, 'Spanish taps and trills: phonological structure of an isolated opposition', *FLin*, 23, 1990:153–74, asks why [r] is the only consonant that can occur onset-initially in intervocalic position but not word-initially; he proposes that [r] maximizes the syllabic template, while intervocalic [ɾ] is pre-attached to the prosodic skeleton, non-pre-attached [ɾ] being expanded to a dual structure in appropriate contexts. D. Recasens, 'On the production characteristics of apicoalveolar taps and trills', *JPh*, 19:267–80, shows, by means of electropalatographic and acoustic analysis, that V–to–C effects are less for [r] than for [ɾ]; this means that the tongue is subject to greater constraint in the trill, which is not merely a series of taps. A. M. Pandolfi Burzio and M. O. Herrera Garbarini, 'Producción fonológica diastrática de niños menores de tres años', *RLTA*, 28, 1990:101–22, compare various aspects of the phonological production of children from different social groups. M. Cid Uribe and P. Roach, 'Spanish intonation: design and implementation of a machine-readable corpus', *JIPA*, 20, 1990:1–8, report on the preliminary results derived from a corpus: Spanish favours falls rather than rises, level tones are frequent, major tone units tend to be short, and the average number of syllables per word is 1.96.

6. Morphology

R. A. Núñez Cedeño, 'Análisis unitario de variantes sufijales: el caso de *-ico, -ático* y *-aico*', *His(US)*, 74:157–62, derives all three from a single suffix *-ico*; *-at-* is an infix, sometimes reduced to *-a-*. E.-P. Kester, 'Algunos sufijos nominalizadores del español', *EspA*, 55:5–21, examines nouns derived with apparent variants of the suffix *-ura* (*blanco-blancura, quemar-quemadura, crear-creatura*); she finds that *-ura* occurs most productively on participle or adjective bases. J. W. Harris, 'The exponence of gender in Spanish', *LI*, 22:27–62, argues that biological sex, grammatical gender and form class are interrelated but autonomous domains; *-o* and *-a* are not gender markers and have no meaning or function, though some rules are needed to capture the limited predictability existing between the above domains. A. Arias Barredo, 'Género gramatical y motivación semántica', *EstL*, 6, 1990: 107–21, limits himself to animate nouns and looks in semantic terms at the relationship between sex and gender. M. García-Page, 'Un aspecto de morfología flexiva del español actual: la presencia de morfemas alternantes en sustantivos unigéneros', *EspA*, 56:23–38, is about noun stems not showing gender variation (*rosa,**roso, by contrast with *niño, niña*), and the limited circumstances in which such variation can arise, for example in intensive expressions like *Me quedé sin coche ni cocha*. E. M. Bravo García, 'Anotaciones sobre el uso de las formas *el* y *este/ese/aquel* como femeninos', *EstL*, 6, 1990:123–27, shows, through a survey of usage, that there is quite a lot of variation and uncertainty about the form of determiners before feminine nouns beginning with stressed /a/. J. Jiménez Martínez and P. Sancho Cremades, 'Aspectos morfosintácticos del apodo', *Homenatge García Díez*, 375–86, is an interesting corpus-based study of the formal mechanisms by which nicknames are created. Wotjak, *Verbo*, includes: S. Alcoba, 'El morfema temático del verbo español' (9–22), A. Veiga, 'Planteamientos básicos para un análisis funcional de las categorías verbales en español' (237–57), B. Wotjak, 'Acerca de incorporaciones lexemáticas en verbos españoles' (259–64).

7. SYNTAX

Dwight Bolinger, *Essays on Spanish: Words and Grammar*, ed. Joseph H. Silverman, Newark, Delaware, Juan de la Cuesta, xii + 352 pp., gathers together his writings of the last half century on aspects of Spanish, based, he says, on his experiences of teaching the language; it includes such topics as the syntax of *parecer*, word order, *ser* and *estar* (and English analogues of this distinction), comparison, use of the subjunctive, and is highly recommended for students, teachers of Spanish language, and theoretical and descriptive linguists. José Manuel González Calvo, *Análisis sintáctico (comentario de cinco textos)*, Cáceres, Extremadura U.P., 1990, 120 pp., is intended as an aid to the teaching of text analysis. A. Briz, 'En los límites de la oración bipolar consecutiva', *Homenatge García Díez*, 291–98, looks at sentences with *tan, tal, de manera . . . que*; these consecutive clauses can undergo modifications which bring them close to other clause types (relative, causal, comparative, etc.), resulting in a kind of neutralization. D. Dumitrescu, 'El dativo posesivo en español y en rumano', *RELing*, 20, 1990:403–29, considers *Los ojos se le llenaron de lágrimas* as an alternative to *Sus ojos se llenaron de lágrimas* and claims the two are not equivalent in discourse terms; the dative of possession is a topicalizing device, conveying the involvement of the possessor in the event described. E. Roegiest and A.-M. Spanoghe, 'Relation de possession inaliénable et qualification en français et en espagnol', *RLiR*, 55:81–94, is concerned with the degree of adjectival qualification an inalienably possessed direct object needs in order to be predetermined by a weak possessive adjective rather than the definite article. J. Calvo Pérez, 'El problema no resuelto de a + objeto directo en español', *EspA*, 56:5–21, approaches the 'personal *a*' within a version of liminar grammar, and claims there is a constant projection of the world on to language and vice versa. M. Weissenrieder, 'A functional approach to the accusative *a*', *His(US)*, 74:146–56, is on the 'personal *a*' with inanimate direct objects, as in *Los gerundios modifican al sujeto*; she argues for a principle of noun salience, and discusses the factors which make a noun salient, that is, foregrounded in the discourse. C. Fuentes Rodríguez, 'La complejidad del artículo', *AEF*, 13, 1990:85–102, examines the category status of the article, and concludes it is not a pronoun, but that pronoun and article both belong to the larger class of grammatical words. A. Briz, 'El proceso de sustantivación y lexicalización de los adjetivos con artículo en español', *RFR*, 7, 1990:231–39, is about the use of adjectives as nouns. H. Campos, 'Preposition stranding in Spanish?', *LI*, 22:741–50, considers structures like *la señora de quien vivo encima* which seem to have stranding, resulting from the ability of one class of preposition to reanalyse with the verb; but it is not real preposition stranding, because the words in this class behave more like nouns and adjectives, and are to be assigned to a neutralized category [+ N]. H. Campos, M. Charnitski, and W. J. Woodward, 'Silent prepositional phrases and pro-PP in Spanish', *Probus*, 3:1–21, contrasts *¿Discrepa ese artículo de tus puntos de vista? — No, creo que no discrepa* with *¿La reunión consistió en un encierro? — *No, creo que no consistió*, and claims the grammatical example illustrates an empty PP complement, licensed by L-marking by the head verb and by the possibility of a zero topic.

José A. Padilla, *On the Definition of Binding Domains in Spanish*, Dordrecht, Kluwer, 1990, xviii + 163 pp., examines structures involving anaphora from a theoretical and experimental perspective, and seeks to determine the relative roles of innateness and experience in language acquisition. E. Mallén, 'A syntactic analysis of secondary predication in Spanish', *JL*, 27:375–403, base-generates secondary predicates inside VP, either as sisters to the verbal complement or as sisters to the subject; these positions account for asymmetries between object-oriented and subject-oriented secondary predicates. L. Gómez Torrego, 'Reflexiones sobre el "dequeísmo y el queísmo" en el español de España', *EspA*, 55:23–44, deals with the 'anomalous' insertion of *de* before *que* (*Opino de que no tiene razón*) and its omission (*Me acuerdo que era Navidad*), and is descriptively good, if rather prescriptive in attitude. L. Cortés Rodríguez, 'Usos anómalos del relativo en el español hablado', *RELing*, 20, 1990, 431–46, is a statistical study of structures differing from those considered correct in written Spanish, and covers such 'anomalies' as the omission of prepositions (*No es como otros sitios que vas*), non-standard agreement (*grupos de gente que vaya en vaqueros*), pronoun duplication (*quince días que me los pasé*). R. Trujillo, 'Sobre la supuesta despronominalización del relativo', *EstL*, 6, 1990:23–46, claims that not only relative *que* when followed by a resumptive pronoun (*Hay gente que le guste vivir*), but 'relative pronouns' in general are not pronouns, but determiners; they have no nominal content and do not stand for an antecedent. F. D'Introno *et al.*, 'Condiciones gramaticales sobre la alternancia', *His(US)*, 74:400–08, looks at constraints on code-switching among Spanish-English bilinguals, particularly in relation to interrogative and relative pronouns, which must be from the same lexicon as the element governing them. N. González, *Object and Raising in Spanish*, NY, Garland, 1988, 218 pp., is a relational grammar account, dealing with impersonal constructions, inversion and clause reduction as well as raising. M. Luján, 'Postposed subjects', *Texas Linguistic Forum*, 31, 1989:71–78, tries to explain why a postposed lexical subject cannot provide the reference of a pronominal clitic in a preposed adverbial clause (**Cuando no la invitan, se ofende Ana*), nor be bound by a wh-operator (**¿Quién cree que dijo que es inteligente él?*), and says postposed subjects are variables bound by a focus operator. R. Meyer-Hermann, 'Theorie und Empirie der Wortfolge im Spanischen (u.a. am Beispiel der *Primera Crónica General*)', *ZRP*, 107:58–103, offers a survey of theoretical work on word order and a statistical study of Spanish, and concludes there is no one basic word order; it depends on the structure of the sentence. F. Ocampo, 'Word order in constructions with a one-valency verb, a subject NP and a PP in spoken Rioplatense Spanish', *His(US)*, 74:409–16, considers pragmatic factors, verb type, and primary stress placement as determinants of word order in such sentences.

Wotjak, *Verbo*, includes: V. Báez San José and I. Penadés Martínez, 'Diccionario informatizado de construcciones oracionales y el proyecto *Esquemas sintáctico-semánticos del español*' (33–70), M. Fernández Pérez, 'Consideración del aspecto en español a partir de sus implicaciones sintácticas' (127–31), J. Garrido, 'El lugar teórico del verbo en la descripción del español' (133–39), J. de Kock and C. Gómez Molina, 'Verbos conjugados pronominalmente, acompañados de un complemento de agente' (167–74), V. Lamíquiz, 'Lexemática y sintaxis del verbo: funcionamiento interdependiente' (183–97), J. Lüdtke, 'Observaciones sobre el alcance del concepto de auxiliaridad en español' (199–206), M. V. Vázquez Rozas, 'Una aproximación al análisis de las cláusulas sujeto-predicado-complemento indirecto' (231–36). Bosque, *Indicativo* includes: I. Bosque, 'Las bases gramaticales de la alternancia modal. Repaso y balance' (13–65), N. Fukushima, 'Sobre la cláusula superregente' (164–79), M. Suñer and J. Padilla Rivera, 'Concordancia temporal y subjuntivo' (185–201), C. Picallo, 'El nudo FLEX y el parámetro del sujeto nulo' (202–33), C. R. Gonzalo, 'La alternancia modal en las relativas y los tipos de mención del SN complejo' (280–300). G. Latorre, 'La concordancia y los rasgos subcategoriales de IR_3', *RLTA*, 28, 1990:41–49, uses subcategorization to account for the structure in *Me va bien en el negocio*. A. Vera Luján, *Las construcciones pronominales pasivas e impersonales en español*, Murcia U.P., 1990, 195 pp., argues for a grammatical model in which differences of level are crucial and categories can be non-discrete, and claims the different *se* constructions are distinct at the clausal level but not at the monemic level. C. Hernández Sacristán, 'Configuración funcional y construcción refleja en español', *Iberoromania*, 33:16–27, believes the centrality of a reflexivized nominal expression in the configuration of arguments governed by a verb correlates with the degree of reorganization of the sentence induced by reflexivization.

8. SEMANTICS AND PRAGMATICS

Miguel Metzeltin, *Semántica, pragmática y sintaxis del español*, Wilhelmsfeld, Egert, 1990, xi + 194 pp., aims to show how the meanings of texts can be arrived at. R. Meyer-Hermann, 'Sobre algunas condiciones pragmáticas de la posición del sujeto en español', *EstL*, 6, 1990:73–88, argues that the concept of identifiability, as used in earlier pragmatic work, is inadequate to account for word order. G. Herrero Moreno, 'Procedimientos de intensificación-ponderación en el español coloquial', *EspA*, 56:39–51, shows how expressive devices used to intensify, in place of *muy*, *tanto*, etc, lead to changes in structure. A. M. Martín Rodríguez, 'La posición estructural de *entregar* en el campo semántico de "dar"', *ib.*, 55:45–53, applies Coseriu's lexical field theory, and distinguishes two values for *entregar*: *dar en mano* and *dar por entero*. J. Rösner, 'Konjunktionen als Eröffnungspartikeln im Dialog. Eine Untersuchung zum Spanischen', *RJ*, 41, 1990:262–89, is about *pues*, *y*, and *pero*. J. L. Girón Alconchel, 'Sobre la consideración del adverbio *ya* como un "conmutador"', *RELing*, 21:145–53, elaborates the pragmatic concept of 'shifter' and examines the contextual elements determining the meaning of *ya*. C. López Alonso, 'El discurso y el conector reformulativo: "es decir"', *RFR*, 7, 1990:87–97, is an illustration of discourse theory. H. Haverkate, 'Aspectos semióticos de la cortesía verbal',

Language

Language 281

RLTA, 28, 1990:27–40, is based on Spanish examples, and distinguishes symbolic, indexical, and iconic politeness. Manuel Leonetti Jungl, *El artículo y la referencia*, M, Taurus, 1990, 167 pp., is a useful introduction.

Gerhard Bauhr, *El futuro en -ré e ir a + infinitivo en español peninsular moderno*, Gothenburg U.P., 1989, ix + 410 pp., is a corpus-based account of the use of these two constructions, and finds significant pragmatic differences. D. García Padrón, 'En torno al llamado "proceso de desemantización"', *RFR*, 7, 1990:241–53, argues against the view that some verbs, like *andar*, are sometimes reduced to auxiliary status. Wotjak, *Verbo*, includes: M. Casas Gómez, 'Aspectos lingüísticos acerca de una pareja léxica verbal' (97–105), J. Dubský, 'El campo léxico de los verbos de introducción, de relación, de apoyo y verbos formemáticos' (107–11), C. Eggermont, 'La relación entre el sistema pronominal y la valencia verbal en español, francés y portugués' (113–20), M. Emsel, 'Estructura semántica de verbos complejos en el contexto técnico' (121–26), E. Gärtner, 'Predicados con argumentos proposicionales en español: problemas de una descripción basada en la teoría de valencias' (141–51), M. Ll. Hernanz, 'Personas generales y tiempo verbal' (153–62), G. Hilty, 'Análisis semántico de algunos verbos de movimiento' (163–66), W. Kutz, 'La semántica de la comprensión y el verbo' (175–82), E. Méndez García de Paredes, 'Tiempo verbal y subordinación temporal: la relación de simultaneidad' (207–20), A. Suñer, 'Características sintácticas y semánticas de los verbos afines a *lamentar*' (221–29), G. Wotjak, 'Fundamentos metodológicos para una descripción modular integrativa del potencial comunicativo de los verbos' (265–85). Bosque, *Indicativo*, includes: A. Bell, 'El modo en español: consideración de algunas propuestas recientes' (81–106), R. Navas Ruiz, 'El subjuntivo castellano. Teoría y bibliografía crítica' (107–41), J. Bybee and T. D. Terrell, 'Análisis semántico del modo en español' (145–63), J. M. Lope Blanch, 'Algunos usos de indicativo por subjuntivo en oraciones subordinadas' (180–82), P. Kempchinsky, 'Más sobre el efecto de referencia disjunta del subjuntivo' (234–58), M. L. Rivero, 'Especificidad y existencia' (261–79), F. Klein, 'Restricciones pragmáticas sobre la distribución del subjuntivo en español' (303–14), J. M. Guitart, 'Aspectos pragmáticos del modo en los complementos de predicados de conocimiento y de adquisición de conocimiento en español' (315–29), B. Lavandera, 'El cambio de modo como estrategia de discurso' (330–57).

9. Lexis

This section begins with five works on how to produce dictionaries. M. Alvar Ezquerra, 'La confección de diccionarios', *VLet*, 1,

1990:47–60, is a broad study. M. Trapero, 'Variantes e invariantes de contenido en las definiciones del "Diccionario" académico: sobre el(los) significado(s) de "canario"', *BRAE*, 71:247–73, uses *canario* and its definitions to criticize the Academia for its haphazard approach, with telling points (a dictionary is not an ornithology manual); whether T.'s ideal dictionary would be more user-friendly is open to debate. Carlos E. Granados González and Manuel López Rodríguez, *Las definiciones de los elementos químicos en el "Diccionario de la lengua española". Análisis de la sistemática actual, propuesta de una nueva y colección de definiciones acordes con ella*, M, RAE, 1989, 120 pp., make proposals to improve one particular set of definitions. I. Ahumada Lara, 'Localizaciones geográficas andaluzas y lexicografía española actual', *Homenaje Gallego Morell*, 1, 75–88, analyses seven words to show how dictionaries such as that of the RAE have failed to take advantage of detailed studies on *andaluz*. Luis Fernando Lara, **Dimensiones de la lexicografía. A propósito del Diccionario del español de México*, Mexico City, El Colegio de México, 1990, 249 pp., contains the following 10 articles by the director of the project: 'El objeto diccionario' (21–38); 'El diccionario, instrumento de la etnicidad' (39–50); 'La cuantificación en el *Diccionario del español de México*' (51–84); 'Caracterización metódica del *corpus* del *DEM*' (85–106); 'Sociolingüística del *DEM*' (107–31); 'El diccionario entre la tradición y la realidad' (133–56); 'La cuestión de la norma en el *DEM*' (157–93); 'Problemas y métodos del significado estereotípico' (195–212); 'Diccionario de lengua, enciclopedia y diccionario enciclopédico: el sentido de sus distinciones' (213–31); 'Lagunas y debilidades de la lexicografía hispánica' (233–37). C. Smith, 'The anglicism: no longer a problem for Spanish?', *Actas del XIII Congreso Nacional de AEDEAN*, Tarragona, 119–36, reduces the number of anglicisms by adopting a narrow definition, and considers the effects of loan-words to be mainly positive. S. Alvarado, 'Hebraísmos en español y búlgaro', *BRAE*, 71:133–56, is a list of loan-words in Spanish and Bulgarian; the purpose is not explained. A. Fajardo, 'La jerga juvenil española', *LebS*, 36:169–77, is similarly little more than a list of words, with nothing said about the informants. E. Náñez Fernández, 'La locución prepositiva en el lenguaje administrativo', *BRAE*, 71:383–95, draws our attention to the large number of prepositional phrases typical of bureaucratic language which are now entering the language at large. P. Barros García, 'Neología y periodismo', *Homenaje Gallego Morell*, 1, 163–81, looks at the neologisms in the work of one journalist; and also dealing with the language of the media is F. Rodríguez González, 'La composición por siglas', *BRP*, 29, 1990:105–16, who investigates the structures underlying *peceprofesor*, *GRAPOpreguntas*, etc. Miguel Ropero Núñez,

El léxico caló en el lenguaje del cante flamenco, Seville U.P., 2nd edn, 223 pp., contains a general historical essay, as well as the more specific subject-matter of the book. J. de Bruyne, 'Complementos de *Esbozo de una nueva gramática de la lengua española* — II (Nota sobre *devenir*)', *RJ*, 41, 1990:249–61, accepts that *devenir* is defective and belongs principally to the register of philosophy, but shows that it has a greater diversity of usage than has previously been recognized.

10. SOCIOLINGUISTICS AND DIALECTS

AMERICA. M. Hidalgo, 'The emergence of standard Spanish in the American Continent: implications for Latin American dialectology', *LPLP*, 14, 1990:47–63, is a wide-ranging essay, attempting to evaluate key factors in the establishment of a standard form of Spanish in America. Factors such as the urban nature of the Conquest and the attitudes of the *conquistadores* to their language are taken into account, and H. makes proposals on the future directions the study of American Spanish should take. J. Lüdtke, 'Geschichte des Spanischen in Übersee', *RJ*, 41, 1990:290–301, also deals with a variety of aspects of American Spanish, including historical ones. A. Torrejón, 'El castellano de América en el siglo XIX: creación de una nueva identidad lingüística', *EFil*, 25, 1990:39–53, examines the movement towards the establishment of national standards, particularly in Chile.

The remainder of this section is arranged in an approximate south to north direction. M. B. Fontanella de Weinberg, 'La evolución de las palatales en español bonaerense', *RLTA*, 27, 1989:67–80, makes good use of the data, and shows how two structural factors usually considered essential to phonological change have come together, namely low functional load, and the weak integration of the sounds in question within the BA phonological system. A. Bocaz, 'Los marcadores de expresión de la simultaneidad en el desarrollo de estructuras sintácticas y textuales complejas', *ib.*, 15–22, is based on Argentinian and Chilean speech, and charts clearly the development of linguistic markers of simultaneity to produce syntactic and textual packaging. A. M. Pandolfi, '-*illo*: ¿sufijo diminutivo?', *ib.*, 133–49, is based on Chilean usage, and concentrates on pejorative and lexicalized functions. A. Torrejón, 'Fórmulas de tratamiento de segunda persona singular en el español de Chile', *His(US)*, 74:1068–76, examines forms of address in a variety of social contexts, and concludes that there is a process of simplification of complex social structures taking place, with a more egalitarian system evolving. H. Valdivieso, J. Magaña, and G. Tassara, 'La variation du /s/ implosif dans l'espagnol du Chili', *La Linguistique*, 27:119–27, find that the pronunciation [h] is the most frequent, without significant variations according to sex or geography.

The linguistic situation in Peru is prominent this year. R. Cerrón-Palomino, 'Aspectos sociolingüísticos y pedagógicos de la motosidad en el Perú', Cerrón-Palomino, *Temas*, 153–80, presents a historical analysis, followed by proposals for the education system. The influence of L1 on L2 is natural, but disadvantages speakers of the low-prestige varieties, particularly those which use only a 3-vowel system; bilingual education is essential to help speakers keep the two languages separate. E. Gugenberger, 'Migración y desplazamiento lingüístico en Arequipa', *ib.*, 181–91, studies patterns of migration, and shows that migration to towns such as Arequipa is important in helping to increase the dominance of Castilian over Quechua. E. C. García, 'Bilingüismo e interferencia sintáctica', *Lexis*, 14, 1990:151–96, presents a strong case for accepting the substratum influence of Quechua on Andean varieties of Spanish, via an analysis of the usage of 3rd person singular object pronouns. C. Junquera, 'El mutilingüismo peruano: el caso de la lengua harakmbet', *CILL*, 16, 1990:171–98, contrasts the status of Castilian and Harakmbet. P. M. Harvey, 'Drunken speech and the construction of meaning: bilingual competence in the Southern Peruvian Andes', *LSo*, 20:1–36, describes in fascinating detail the changing roles played by Spanish and Quechua during drinking sessions, and comments on the social implications of language choice; a tape-recorder is presumably essential to allow the researcher to recall the data in this situation.

A. Correa Ramírez, 'Sobre una peculiaridad del español paisa', *Glotta*, 5, 1990:20–25, looks at the tendency to drop the first consonant in consonant clusters, and high levels of hypercorrection. M. Navarro, 'La alternancia -ra/-se y -ra/ría en el habla de Valencia (Venezuela)', *Thesaurus*, 45, 1990:481–88, finds that *-se* is little used, particularly in the speech of the young, poor, and ill-educated, and that *-ra* is used in the apodosis of conditional expressions (38%). A. Quilis, *'Notas sobre el español de Belice', *VLet*, 1, 1990:139–47. Five items deal with Mexico, including two books: Juan M. Lope Blanch, *Investigaciones sobre dialectología mexicana*, Mexico City, UNAM, 1990, 197 pp., and Raúl Avila, *El habla de Tamazunchale*, Mexico City, Colegio de México, 1990, 208 pp. J. A. Flores and L. Valiñas, 'Nahuatl–Spanish interferences: a sociolinguistic approach', *Sociolinguistics*, 18, 1989:19–32, examine language maintenance and shift, whilst J. A. Flores and G. López, 'A sociolinguistic perspective on Mexican multilingualism', *ib.*, 33–40, look at the variety of situations in Mexico. D. A. Rissel, 'Sex, attitudes, and the assibilation of /r/ among young people in San Luis Potosí, Mexico', *LVC*, 1, 1989:269–83, is an intriguing study of a change which originated in the speech of

middle- and upper-class females, and has now spread down the social
scale, but not to males; R. interprets this as a strategy to mark gender
differences. R. García Riverón, 'La entonación en el atlas lingüístico
de Cuba', *EspA*, no. 55:103–12, reports on work so far on the difficult
question of how to include intonation in the forthcoming linguistic
atlas. D. J. Heap, 'Les questions à sujet pronominal préposé dans les
dialectes de l'espagnol des Caraïbes', *JAPLA*, 12, 1990:13–38, looks
at the structure of '¿Qué tú haces?', rejects a language contact
explanation, and sees Caribbean Spanish as being in a state of
transition from a null-subject language to a clitic subject language. A.
Morales, 'Manifestaciones de pasado en niños puertorriqueños de
2–6 años', *RLTA*, 27, 1989:115–31, demonstrates via an analysis of
recorded speech that acquisition of aspect occurs before that of tense.
Also to be noted are M. Vaquero, *'Estudios fonológicos en Puerto
Rico: revisión crítica', *VLet*, 1, 1990:111–27, and H. López Morales,
*'En torno a la /s/ final dominicana: cuestiones teóricas', *ib.*, 129–37.

There are three books on Spanish in the United States: John J.
Bergen (ed.), *Spanish in the United States: Sociolinguistic Issues*, Wash-
ington DC, Georgetown U.P., 1990, ix + 166 pp.; John M. Lipski,
The Language of the Isleños: Vestigial Spanish in Louisiana, Baton Rouge,
Louisiana U.P., x + 148 pp.; and Juan M. Lope Blanch, *El español
hablado en el suroeste de los Estados Unidos. Materiales para un estudio*,
Mexico City, UNAM, 331 pp. A. Hurtado and R. Rodríguez,
'Language as a social problem: the repression of Spanish in South
Texas', *JMMD*, 10, 1989:401–19, analyse (i) the correspondence
which schools perceive between students' use of English and their
economic/social mobility, and (ii) the assertion that English is the
prestige language, and that Spanish should therefore be relegated to
the private domain; pressure is exerted on students to reduce their use
of Spanish. R. F. Stein, 'Closing the "achievement gap" of Mexican
Americans: a question of language, learning style, or economics?'.
JMMD, 11, 1990:405–19, concludes that economics, not language, is
the problem. A. J. Ramírez, 'Sociolingüística del español-inglés en
contacto entre adolescentes hispanos de Estados Unidos', *His(US)*,
74:1057–67, aims to cover Spanish-speakers of different origins and
in different parts of the USA, and provides an interesting snapshot of
attitudes, contexts, etc.

CISATLANTIC. Francisco Gimeno Menéndez, *Dialectología y sociolingüística españolas*, Alicante U.P., 1990, 188 pp., is a clear and
coherent manual, with most of the illustrative materials taken from
Spain. Manuel Alvar, *Estudios de geografía lingüística*, M, Paraninfo,
523 pp., contains the following revised versions of previously published materials: 'Atlas lingüísticos y diccionarios' (49–115); 'Cues-
tionarios de láminas (El ALM y las investigaciones en Gran

Canaria)' (116–25); 'Ictionimia y geografía lingüística (consideraciones sobre la nomenclatura oficial española de los animales de interés pesquero)' (126–81); 'El atlas lingüístico y etnográfico de Andalucía' (185–227); 'El cambio *-al, -ar* > *-e* en andaluz' (228–31); 'Modalidades fonéticas cordobesas en el "Atlas lingüístico y etnográfico de Andalucía"' (232–45); 'Portuguesismos en andaluz' (246–60); 'La terminología del *maíz* en Andalucía (ALEA I, 102, 103, 105, 107, 108)' (261–71); 'El atlas lingüístico y etnográfico de las Islas Canarias' (272–83); 'Dialectología y cultura popular en las Islas Canarias' (284–99); 'Originalidad interna en el léxico canario' (300–34); 'Proyecto de un atlas lingüístico de Aragón' (335–48); 'El atlas lingüístico y etnográfico de la provincia de Santander (España)' (349–78); 'Un ejemplo de atlas lingüístico automatizado: el ALES' (379–91); 'Atlas lingüístico de los marineros peninsulares' (392–402); 'La terminología canaria de los seres marinos' (403–38); 'Proyecto de un atlas lingüístico de Hispanoamérica' (439–56). G. de Granda, 'El español de Guinea Ecuatorial. Sobre un fenómeno sintáctico: la marcación en superficie de los pronombres personales sujeto', *Thesaurus*, 45, 1990:332–54, finds the influence of Niger–Congo languages to be the best explanation for the high usage of subject pronouns. José Antonio Samper Padilla, *Estudio sociolingüístico del español de Las Palmas de Gran Canaria*, Las Palmas de Gran Canaria, Pérez Galdós, 1990, 328 pp., follows Labov's methodology, and examines variables via an analysis of informants selected on the basis of the 1981 census; particular attention is paid to /-s/, /-r/, /-l/, /-n/, and /-d-/. M. Galeote, 'Léxico rural del treviño de Córdoba, Granada y Málaga', *RDTP*, 45, 1990:131–67, examines the diversity and instability of rural speech in the late 20th c. Federico Núñez Muñoz and Eduardo Caballero Escribano, *Diccionario del agropó*, Seville U.P., 44 pp., in contrast, set out to amuse rather than instruct. J. I. Hualde, 'Aspiration and resyllabification in Chinato Spanish', *Probus*, 3:55–76, examines this dialect in terms of its differences from 'typical' aspirating dialects of Spanish. Rosa María Castañer Martín, *Estudio del léxico de la casa en Aragón, Navarra y Rioja*, Zaragoza, Diputación General de Aragón, 1990, 466 pp., is based on the *Atlas lingüístico y etnográfico de Aragón, Navarra y Rioja*, and provides much detailed information. There is one major study of Judeo-Spanish: Max Leopold Wagner, **Judenspanisch*, 2 vols, Stuttgart, Steiner, 1990, 279, 244 pp.

MEDIEVAL LITERATURE

By B. Bussell Thompson, *Hofstra University*
Mercedes Vaquero, *Brown University*, and
Carlos Alberto Vega, *Wellesley College*

1. General

The ever-growing use of advanced technology in textual studies prompted several important articles, both on the use of computers themselves and on manual preparation of editions. C. B. Faulhaber, 'Textual Criticism in the 21st Century,' *RPh*, 45:123–48, reflects upon the past, present, and possible future state of computerized textual criticism. F. describes the *Archivo Digital de Manuscritos y Textos Españoles (ADMYTE)*, noting its relationship to parallel — although less inclusive — ventures in other languages, and gives an overview of the practical and theoretical implications of recent advances, particularly hypertext — a system by which links can be made between several bodies of information. F. Marcos Marín, 'Computers and Text Editing: A Review of Tools, and Introduction to UNITE and Some Observations Concerning its Application to Old Spanish Texts', *ib.*, 102–22, reviews several computer programs, paying particular attention to the UNITE program and its application for stanza 51 of the *Libro de Alexandre*. A. Blecua, *ib.*, 73–88, offers a succinct but thorough historical review of the editing of selected Castilian texts, paying particular attention to the traditional Lachmann-Bedier polarity and coming out in favour of a neo-Lachmannian methodology. B. notes how the small body of Castilian medieval texts *vis-à-vis* other languages, their limited transmission, and the fact that Spanish texts, libraries, and archives have lagged behind in terms of cataloguing and editing materials have meant that textual studies have until recently enjoyed less critical interest than would have been expected. G. Orduna, in 'Ecdótica hispánica y el valor estemático de la historia del texto', *ib.*, 89–101, offers an overview of editorial theory and practice in Spain and suggests individual steps and guidelines basic to the editorial process. The same author, in 'La "edición crítica"', *Incipit*, 10, 1990:17–43, studies various concepts of 'la edición crítica' from the time of Maas, Pasquali, Dom Quintin and Michel Barbi up to the present decade giving praise to the system of codification developed by HSMS and declares his reservations to the principles of certain French scholars. G. Avezona and G. Orduna, 'Registro de filigranas de papel en códices españoles (cont.)', *ib.*, 1–15, an instalment in the journal's ongoing watermark project (vols 1, 2, 5, 7), reproduces and describes eighteen watermarks. Carlos Alvar, Angel Gómez Moreno, and

Fernando Gómez Redondo, *La prosa y el teatro en la Edad Media*, M, Taurus, 286 pp., offer concise yet extremely thorough and reliable overviews of 'Historiografía medieval' (Gómez Redondo, 13–83), 'Prosa didáctica' (Alvar, 87–129), 'Prosa de ficción' (Gómez Redondo, 133–81) and 'Teatro medieval' (Gómez Moreno, 185–233), and bibliography (237–79). Of considerable note was the publication of *Historia y crítica de la literatura española*, vol. I/I, *Edad Media. Primer suplemento*, ed. Alan Deyermond, Editorial Crítica, xii + 451 pp., a collection of published essays by leading scholars with comments by D. on recent research in various fields and thorough bibliographies. A repertoire of names, dates, and works is found in J. M. Viña Liste, *Cronología de la literatura española*, M, Cátedra, 123 pp. V. Cirlot, 'La estética de lo monstruoso en la Edad Media', *RLMed*, 2, 1990:175–82, drawing from Aldhelmus of Malmesbury's *Liber monstrorum* and Thomas of Cantimpré's *De natura rerum*, emphasizes a concept of the monster as an entity not outside of, but within, nature; what becomes important is the placing of the monster at the limits of the natural order — primarily geographic (hence Baltrusaitis's observation of the relationship between location of monsters at the ends of the earth and in the margins of manuscripts) and the viewing of the monster — oftentimes a depiction of excess — within the totality of a text, image, or structure. J. L. Martín, 'El rey ha muerto. ¡Viva el rey!', *His*, 51:5–39, traces the evolution of the expression, reveals the particular symbolism of the monarch's death, and appends sample supporting texts. N. Roth, 'La lengua hebrea entre los cristianos españoles medievales: voces hebreas en español', *RFE*, 71:137–43, offers some brief notes on the study of Hebrew and gives samples of Hebrew words (and words found in Jewish texts and Christian writings about Jews that are of Arabic origin) in medieval Spain. Concentrating primarily on the *Embajada a Tamorlán*, J. A. Ochoa, 'El valor de los viajeros medievales como fuente histórica', *RLMed*, 2, 1990:85–102, offers a plan for the study of voyage accounts and suggests ways in which these can be used in historical investigation. A. L. Molina Molina offers an overview of 'Honor y honra en la España de los siglos XIII al XVII', *Homenaje Barceló Jiménez*, 399–410. B. Taylor, *Actas . . .* (Lisbon), 57–70, offers a succinct but encompassing review of voyage texts, paying particular attention to the pan-European scope of certain accounts and the role of translated versions. The ideological significance of Spain in French Medieval Literature is examined in D. Régnier-Bohler, 'L'Avènement de l'Espace Ibérique dans la Littérature Médiévale Française', *ib.*, 91–105. C. Chauchadis studies the implications of 'La figure de l'autre dans le duel chevaleresque' in some Castilian (*Partidas*, Diego de Valera, Cervantes) and Catalan texts, Ramond, *Figures*, 57–67.

L. P. Harvey, *Islamic Spain, 1250 to 1500*, Chicago U.P., 1990, xiv + 370 pp. A. Deyermond, 'Salamanca, ¿Centro de gravedad de la literatura castellana del siglo XV? (A propósito de *Amor y pedagogía*, de Pedro Cátedra)', *Insula*, 531 : 3–4, notes the importance of Salamanca to Spanish letters and intellectual life in the fifteenth century, paying particular attention to how various currents are traced in Cátedra's impressive 1989 study (University of Salamanca). Jerrilynn Denise Dodds, *Architecture and Ideology in Early Medieval Spain*, University Park, Pennsylvania State U.P., 1990, xiv + 174 pp. *Godfrey Goodwin, *Islamic Spain*, London, Viking, 1990, x + 150 pp. José García Pelegrín, *Studien zum Hochadel der Königreiche Leon und Kastilien im Hochmittelalter*, Münster, Aschendorff, 204 pp.

2. THE EARLY RECONQUEST AND HISPANO-LATIN LITERATURE

Kenneth Baxter Wolf, *Conquerors and Chronicles of Early Medieval Spain*, Liverpool U.P., 1990, xvii + 203 pp., offers introductory words, notes, and English translations of John of Biclaro, *Chronicle*, Isidore of Seville, *History of the Kings of the Goths*, *The Chronicle of 754*, and *The Chronicle of Alfonso III*.

3. EARLY LYRIC POETRY, EPIC, BALLADS

KHARJAS, LYRIC POETRY

Vicente Beltrán, *El estilo de la lírica cortés. Para una metodologia del análisis literario*, PPU, 1990, 142 pp., is a computer-aided lexical and syntagmatic study of 140 14th- and 15th-c. poems. Pilar Lorenzo Gradín, *La canción de mujer en la lírica medieval*, Santiago de Compostela U.P., 1990, 284 pp. R. Hitchcock, 'The Girls from Cádiz and the *Kharjas*', *JHispP*, 15:103–16, analyses pre-Islamic popular literary traditions dealing with the women of Cádiz. E. Tornero Poveda, 'La noética de Ibn Hazm', *Al-Qanṭara*, 11, 1990:527–34, studies I.H.'s brief treatise on the theory of knowledge and gives a Spanish translation. M. Frenk, 'Amores tristes y amores gozosos en la antigua lírica popular', *RCEH*, 15:377–84, points out how critics have ignored obscene songs, which constitute a considerable portion of the traditional lyric corpus, giving preference to the 'virginal' ones. M. J. Kelley, 'Virgins misconceived: Poetic voice in the Mozarabic *kharjas*', *La Corónica*, 19:1–23, investigates the relationship between the female voice of the *kharjas* and the male poets who wrote them. K. points out what she considers sexist prejudices in the readings of contemporary critics who turn "the *kharjas* into expressions . . . of female emotion to be admired by the male reader". B. Logan

Capuccio, '"Cómo es ancha y larga": la queja de la malmaridada en la poesía medieval española', *LF*, 17:1–14, protests against the discrimination of women in the Middle Ages and today. M. Frenk, 'Contra Devoto', *Criticón*, 49, 1990:7–19, blunts systematically the poisonous darts that Daniel Devoto had lanced against her *Corpus de la antigua lírica popular hispánica* (*YWMLS*, 49:299).

EPIC

Carlos Alvar, *Épica medieval española*, M, Cátedra, 413 pp., is divided in two parts: an introduction covering medieval romance epic, paying particular attention to the Castilian tradition; and editions undertaken together with Manuel Alvar of poems and/or reconstructions based on chronicles of *Mocedades de Rodrigo, Roncesvalles, Siete Infantes de Lara, Cantar de Sancho II, Campana de Huesca, Condesa Traidora, Romanz del Infant García, Mainete*, and *Bernardo del Carpio*. M. Vaquero, 'El rey don Alfonso, al que dixieron el Bravo e el de las partiçiones', *BRAE*, 70, 1990:265–88 rejects S. Martínez's view (*YWMLS*, 48:317) that Alfonso could not have been the hero of Latin and vernacular epic texts; V. argues in favour of Alfonso as protagonist of *Cantar de las Partiçiones*.

POEMA DE MIO CID

James F. Burke, **Structures from the Trivium in the 'Cantar de Mio Cid*, University of Toronto, vii + 239 pp. R. Moreno Castillo, 'El *Cantar del Cid* como obra poética', *RLit*, 53:19–48, studies *CMC* in relation to the *Chanson de Roland* and *Beowulf*. Th. Montgomery, 'Las palabras abstractas del *Poema del Cid*', *CLHM*, 16:123–40, examines in a general way selected lexical items, paying particular attention to concepts of honour in *CMC* as compared to usage in the *Poema de Fernán Gonzalez* and *Chanson de Roland*. The same author, 'Interaction of Factors in Tense Choice in the *Poema del Cid*', *BHS*, 68:355–69, believes *PMC* uses verb tenses as a poetic device: 'it fuses a grammatical convention with a metonymic perception of events, and at the same time turns that convention to great advantage toward the achievement of desired phonetic effects'. **El Cid en el valle del Jalón. El Simposio internacional. Ateca-Calatayud, 7–10 de octubre de 1989*, Calatayud, Centro de Estudios Bilbilitanos, 215 pp.

BALLADS

Alberto Barugel, *The 'Sacrifice of Isaac' in Spanish and Sephardic Balladry*, NY, Peter Lang, 1990, xi + 240 pp., is an important contribution to *romancero* studies, particularly his examination of the influence of *midrash* (biblical legends) on both Sephardic and Christian versions of the Isaac ballad. Mercedes Díaz Roig, *Romancero tradicional de América*, México, Colegio de México, Centro de Estudios Lingüísticos y Literarios, 1990, 328 pp. M. L. Escribano Pueo, *et al.*, *Romancero granadino de tradición oral. Primera Flor*, Granada U.P., 1990, 219 pp. S. G. Armistead, 'Gaiferos' Game of Chance: A Formulaic Theme in the *Romancero*', *La Corónica*, 19:132–44, argues convincingly that the gaming theme in *Gaiferos* 'fits perfectly into the story as a formulaic signal to the traditional audience that what is to come next is still part of the hero's *enfances*'. A.'s analysis of this same theme in the lost *Cantar de Bernardo del Carpio* and in the second redaction of *Los Infantes de Lara* is equally illuminating. The same author, 'Un nuevo romancerillo sefardí', *ib.*, 20:60–71, comments upon a heretofore unknown edition of the *Endeċas de Thiš āh bĕ- ʿĀb*. J. Seeger, 'Can a traditional ballad be myth? An exploration of heroism in *Count Claros*', *ib.*, 72–77, examines several variants of *CC* and finds in a Brazilian version its protagonists converted into mythic heroes. G. Orduna transcribes 'Una versión del "Romance de Don Bueso" en Buenos Aires (1991)', *Incipit*, 10, 1990:139–40. J. Gornall, 'Spanish Ballads: Rhyme and the Late Exploitation of Assonance', *RoN*, 31, 1990:65–72, argues that 'rhyme was not the exclusive property of learnèd poetry: the famed assonance of the *romancero viejo* also contained, unlike the new balladry, a considerable admixture of it'. M. Debax, 'Qui es(t)-tu? Où es(t)-tu? Figures de l'autre dans le *Romancero* de tradition orale', Ramond, *Figures*, 169–81, situates the role of the listener in the dynamics of the *romancero tradicional*. A. Soons, 'The *Romances* of the *Cancionero de Wolfenbüttel*', *BHS*, 68:305–09, transcribes the *romances* included in the *Cancionero de Peraza*.

4. THE THIRTEENTH AND FOURTEENTH CENTURIES
POETRY

M. C. Azuela, 'La *Razón de Amor* a la luz de la presencia musulmana en España', *La Corónica*, 20:16–31, argues that the enigmatic coupling of *RA* with *Debate entre el agua y el vino* can only be understood in an Arabic cultural context. J. W. Marchand and S. Baldwin, '*Quandoque bonus dormitat Homerus* — Old Spanish *Echan* again', *RoN*, 32:63–66, is a response to Y. Malkiel's comment on the authors' opinion regarding the word "echan" (cupbearer) in Berceo's *Duelo de la Virgen* 39d.

CUADERNA VÍA VERSE

In an important article, I. Uría, 'Una vez más sobre el sentido de la C.2 del *Alexandre*', *Incipit*, 10, 1990:45–63, criticizes earlier works on *mester de clerecía*, and argues that *mester* refers to the particular and new versification technique found in the *Libro de Alexandre* as well as other 13th-century works. A. Gómez Moreno, 'Nuevas reliquias de la cuaderna vía', *RLMed*, 2, 1990:9–34, studies new poetic fragments, mostly from Castilian *Libros de horas*, in connection with other European texts of the same genre. C. Soriano and A. Miranda offer a 'Nueva Descripción del Manuscrito 77 (*Miseria de omne*) de la Biblioteca Menéndez Pelayo de Santander', *La Corónica*, 20:32–39. J. Geary, 'The "tres monjes" of the *Poema de Fernán González*: Myth and History', *ib.*, 19:24–402, using for the most part a late medieval Benedictine chronicle by Gonzalo de Arrendondo, attempts to clarify the genesis and diffusion of the legend of the foundation of the monastery of San Pedro de Arlanza.

LIBRO DE ALEXANDRE

I. Uría (see CUADERNA VIA VERSE). Dana Nelson, **Gonzalo de Berceo y el "Alixandre": Vindicación de un estilo*, Madison, HSMS, xi + 505 pp.

GONZALO DE BERCEO

M. J. Kelley, 'Spinning Virgin Yarns: Narrative, Miracles, and Salvation in Gonzalo de Berceo's *Milagros de Nuestra Señora*', *His(US)*, 74:814–23, studies the Virgin's tales as circular narratives: from someone's experience of a miracle through others' narrations of it, to the listener's own miraculous experiences and subsequent narrations. E. J. Ardemagni studies in the context of 'La penitencia en las obras de Gonzalo de Berceo', *RLMed*, 2, 1990:131–40, a large number of penitential documents. G. P. Andrachuk, '*Extra qual nullus omnino salvatur*: The Epilogue of the *Vida de Santa Oria*', *La Corónica*, 19:43–56, proposes that Berceo may have chosen to add this polemical last section of the text to an already-completed poem for doctrinal reasons, inspired in the poet's own interest in the reforms dictated by the French Lateran Council. Nelson (see LIBRO DE ALEXANDRE).

LIBRO DE BUEN AMOR

M. Morreale, 'La fábula del caballo y el asno en el *Libro* del Arcipreste de Hita', *RFE*, 71:23–78, and '"Enxiemplo de la raposa e del cuervo" o "La zorra y la corneja" en el *Libro del Arcipreste de Hita* (1437–1443)', *RLMed*, 2, 1990:49–83, undertakes a detailed philological analysis of stanzas 237–45 and 1437–43 of *LBA*, paying special attention to sources, particularly *Romulus* or *Liber Aesopi*, *Romulus anglicus*, and other Aesopic medieval traditions. Jacques Joset offers a new edition of *LBA*, M, Taurus, 1990, 755 pp. M. Barra Jover, 'El *Libro de Buen Amor* como Cancionero', *RLMed*, 2, 1990:159–64, compares *LBA* and Chaillon de Pestain's *L'Hérésie de Fauvel*. L. O. Vasvari, 'The Battle of Flesh and Lent in the *Libro de Arçipreste*: Gastro-genital rites of reversal', *La Corónica*, 20:1–15, examines this episode in light of *carnival litteralisé*. J. Dagenais, '*Cantigas d'escarnho* and *serranillas*: The Allegory of Careless Love', *BHS*, 68:247–63, explores how some obscene *cantigas d'escarnho* and their narrative *razões* help to understand better the *LBA serranillas* and their narrative prologues in *cuaderna vía*. Th. L. Kassier, '"Ssabe de muchos pleitos é ssabe de lienda": The Law in the *Libro de Buen Amor*', *HispJ*, 11, 1990:7–31, examines legal aspects of *LBA*, particularly in the Doña Endrina episode, where he finds some autobiographical elements related to many other parts of the text. S. Repiso Repiso argues in '"Derecha": Arabismo semántico en el v. 256d del *Libro de Buen Amor*', *RFE*, 71:153–55, that the word "derecha" should be understood like the Arabic *yumn*, meaning, besides "derecha", "fortuna", "buena suerte", and "buena estrella". J. M. Fradejas Rueda, '*LBA* 801b: ¿Uñas o manos?', *JHispP*, 15:131–34, believes that the text should read "manos" and not "uñas". J. Gimeno Casalduero, 'La introducción del "Libro de buen amor"', *Homenaje Barceló Jiménez*, 249–58, studies the symbolism of the number three in *LBA* stanzas 11–19.

PROSE

ALFONSO X, EL SABIO

P. Sánchez-Prieto Borja, 'El modelo latino de la *General Estoria* (El Libro de la Sabiduría en GE3)', *RLMed*, 2, 1990:207–50, highlights the role of romance Biblical texts in the origins of Alfonso's efforts to validate Castilian and examines the relationship between A's text and Latin sources, suggesting a mid-13th century glossed Parisian student Bible. D. G. Pattison, 'The reign of Ordoño II in a new chronicle manuscript: More light on the Alfonsine *borrador*', *MAe*, 60:268–71, notes the significance of the Salamanca Caja de Ahorros *Crónica General Vulgata* for the dating and early textual history of the *CGV*. V. García Yebra, 'Traducciones (?) de Lucano en la *Primera Crónica General de España*', *RFE*, 71:5–22, examines the extent to which Latin texts were strictly translated or were altered or embellished, using as test case the use made in the *PCGE* of the *Farsalia*. Marilyn Stone, *Marriage and Friendship in Medieval Spain. Social Relations According to the Fourth Partida of Alfonso X*, NY, Peter Lang, 1990, vi + 187 pp., notes the significance of *FP* in Spanish and Spanish American life and law, and highlights the role of the text, particularly in the reasoning included as explanation of a given law, as a didactic work. She laments the relative lack of attention accorded *FP* in research; examines textual roots for *P*; profiles views on marriage, children, kinship, friendship; and suggests topics for future interdisciplinary research. R. Meyer-Hermann, 'Theorie und Empirie der Wortfolge im Spanischen (u.a. am Beispiel der *Primera Crónica General*)', *ZRP*, 107:58–103, proffers a study on historical Spanish syntax, using *PCG* as a base, with the further attempt to apply Hawkins' linguistic criteria (1983) to A.'s history. R. M. Garrido, 'Lectura alfonsí de las *Heroidas* de Ovidio', *RCEH*, 15:385–99, analyses the transformation of Ovid's letters in A.'s historiographic texts which prepare the way for the later medieval sentimental romance.

María Cecilia Ruiz, *Literatura y política: el 'Libro de los estados' y el 'Libro de las armas' de don Juan Manuel*, prologue by D. Catalán, Potomac, Maryland, Scripta Humanistica, xvi + 136 pp., analyses these texts and points out the historical and personal circumstances surrounding M's creation — including his insomnia. L. Funes and S.-M. Yoon, 'Motivación y verosimilitud en el relato-marco del *Libro de los estados*', contrast both narrative techniques and didactic goals in *LE* and *Barlaam and Josaphat* legend, calling attention to the intertextuality of the latter in the reception of the former. J. W. Marchand and S. Baldwin, 'A Note on the *Pia fraus* in Don Juan Manuel', *La Corónica*, 19:145–52, discuss a passage in the *Libro de los estados* which reviews the importance of Mary's being espoused (in that the Virgin birth could be hidden from the Devil), compare treatment of the theme in other (sometimes less explicit) authorities, and suggest its importance in determining influences in JM — Sancho and Gil de Zamora (whose *Liber Mariae* includes the motif). I. Urzainqui, 'Más sobre la novedad didáctica de Don Juan Manuel', *BH*, 92, 1990:701–28, discusses cogently JM's knowledge of theology in the secular and laic context of medieval spirituality. John England, ed., *El Conde Lucanor*, M, Editorial Everest, 285 pp., presents a student edition with copious notes on usage and bibliography for each *exemplum* and an introduction situating JM within the 13th and 14th centuries, analysing the work's composition, themes, and literary techniques. E. studies the manuscript tradition and details briefly the phonology, morphology, and syntax of the text.

J. N. Ferro, 'Intertexto político de las Crónicas de Ayala', *Incipit*, 10, 1990:65–89, gives an overview of A.'s politics (finding them more practical than theoretical) and didactic views, and situates these within A.'s historical setting. J. L. Moure, 'Las Cortes de Segovia de 1386 en la Crónica del Canciller Ayala: ¿omisión o composición?', *JHispP*, 14:231–38, noting A.'s omission of any reference to the Cortes of Sevilla, suggests that he did so, not solely because it was during his period of captivity, but so not to detract from the political aims of his patron. A. did, however, include material from the Cortes in another portion of *C*. P.A. Cavallero, 'Las concordancias de *Del soberano bien* y una aportación a la búsqueda de citas y fuentes por computadora en textos españoles medievales', *Incipit*, 10, 1990:121–26, reflects upon the special requirements of a concordance for the text — a translation attributed to Ayala based on Isidore's *Sententiae*, and offers suggestions for similar undertakings.

OTHER PROSE WORKS

C. Sainz de la Mata, 'Apuntes para la edición del tratado *Contra las hadas* atribuido a Alfonso de Valladolid (Abner de Burgos)', *Incipit*, 1990, 10:113–19, calls attention to the complexities of authorship, physical text, and doctrinal purpose that should inform a modern edition of the brief work. B. Taylor, 'An Old Spanish translation from the "Flores Sancti Bernardi" in British Library ADD. MS. 14040, ff. 111v–112v', *BLJ*, 16, 1990:58–65, notes the textual complexities of the manuscript as a whole and edits (with accompanying Latin source) the portion that contains the old Spanish text. Jane F. Connolly, *Los Miraglos de Santiago (Biblioteca Nacional de Madrid MS 10252)*, Salamanca U.P., 1990, 111 pp., presents an edition and study of the late 13th-c. Castilian translation of the Miracles included in a larger hagiographic collection. Carlos Alberto Vega, *La 'Vida de San Alejo': Versiones castellanas*, Salamanca U.P., 123 pp., offers the first lengthy study to date of Spanish versions of the St Alexis legend beginning in the late 14th century and includes three separate editions of the legend representing the three principal textual traditions. C. Heusch, 'Entre didacticismo y heterodoxia: Vicisitudes del estudio de la Etica aristotélica en la España Escolástica (siglos XIII y XIV)', *La Corónica*, 19:89–99, posits a sociological, cultural, and ideological reasoning to account for the fact that the study of *E* — despite the fact that it was indeed known — does not appear in Spanish universities until the 15th century. R. Recio, 'Alfonso de Madrigal (El Tostado): la traducción como teoría entre lo medieval y lo renacentista', *ib.*, 112–31, schematizes translation theory during the 15th and first 60 years of the 16th centuries. N. Fallows, 'Alfonso de Cartagena: An Annotated Tentative Bibliography', *ib.*, 20:78–93, covers both editions of, and studies on, C.'s works. C. Alvar, 'De

Samaria a Tiro: Navegaciones de Apolonio en el siglo XIII', *BH*, 93:5–12, in his adumbration of the figure of Apolonio in medieval literature, cites the *Fazienda de Ultramar* (before 1244), whose author confuses Apollonius, antagonist of Judas Maccabeus with the "rey de Tyr". T. A. Sears, 'Further Adventures: *El Caballero Cifar* and Variations on an Arthurian Theme', *Actas* . . . (Louvain), 204–12, suggests reading *C.* more in light of Arthurian texts than subsequent chivalric novels. John Cull and Brian Dutton edit with introduction, illustrations, and glossary, *Manuel básico de medicina medieval. Bernardo Gordoño. Lilio de medicina. Edición crítica de la versión española Sevilla 1495* (Medieval Spanish Medical Texts, 31), Madison, HSMS, xx + 415 pp.

5. THE FIFTEENTH CENTURY

POETRY

Of particular note was publication this year of *Cancionero del siglo XV c.1360–1520*, ed. Brian Dutton, (Biblioteca Española del Siglo XV), vols 3–7, Salamanca U.P., 517, 388, 578, 481, 671 pp. Volumes 3–6 complete Dutton's Herculean undertaking of editing every known *cancionero* text of that period, and volume 7 includes a thorough cross-indexing of materials. J. Weiss, '*La affeción poetal virtuosa*: Petrarch's Sonnet 116 as poetic manifesto for fifteenth-century Castile', *MLR*, 86:70–78, signals how a translation of the sonnet into Castilian, accompanied by an allegorical commentary giving emphasis to the concepts of *studium*, intellectual nobility, and poetics, shares the same ideological preoccupations as those of Mena, Santillana, and Villena.

SANTILLANA

Magnificent indeed is the two volume publication (facsimile and transcription) of Biblioteca Universitaria de Salamanca MS 26555, the *Cancionero del Marqués de Santillana*, by Pedro M. Cátedra and Javier Coca Senande, 2 vols, Salamanca U.P., 1990, xxxi + 371, [400] pp.; (facs. not paginated). J. Guadalajara Medina, 'Alvaro de Luna y el Anticristo: Imágenes apocalípticas en don Iñigo de Mondoza', *RLMed*, 2, 1990:183–206, uses both the rhetorical tradition of the Apocalypse and a true belief in the possibility of an imminent Apocalypse directed against the *privado* Alvaro de Luna. M. P. A. M. Kerkhof, 'Sobre la transmisión textual de algunas obras del Marqués de Santillana: doble redacción y variantes de autor', *ib.*, 35–47, synthesizes the textual traditions and how they bear on his works.

JUAN DE MENA

C. Smith, 'Notes: Mena's *Laberinto* and the Visual Arts', *BHS*, 68:297–303, proposes that episodes in *L* were inspired in actual iconographic images seen by M.

CANCIONEROS, OTHER POETS

Marcella Ciceri and Julio Rodríguez Puértolas edit in an important new edition and study, *Antón de Montoro. Cancionero* (Textos Recuperados 3–4), Salamanca U.P., 1990, 390 pp. M. Costa, 'Nuevas consideraciones sobre la muerte de los hermanos comendadores, la guerra cordobesa entre bandos y Antón de Montoro', *La Torre*, 5:385–427, points to 1459 as the date of the uxorcide by Fernando Alonso and examines various late renditions of the scandal. H. U. Gumbrecht, 'Intertextuality and Autumn/Autumn and the Modern Reception of the Middle Ages', Brownlee, *New Medievalism*, 301–30, argues for the study of *cancionero* poetry in light of textual pragmatics and in the context of 15th-c. literary historiography. Francisco Rico, **Texto y contextos. Estudios sobre la poesía española del siglo XV*, B, Crítica, 1990, 240 pp. M. García, 'Nuevas perspectivas para el estudio de la literatura medieval castellana', *Insula*, 534:3–4, surveys recent publications in cancionero poetry — particularly the *Cancionero de Baena* — including an important 1990 study by V. Beltrán, *El estilo de la lírica cortés* (see LYRIC POETRY). Dutton (see FIFTEENTH CENTURY. POETRY).

PROSE

MARTINEZ DE TOLEDO

R. J. González-Casanovas, 'Rhetorical Strategies in the Corbacho, Part III: From Scholastic Logic to Homiletic Example', *La Corónica*, 20:40–59, reads this portion of the text as a poetic microcosm of the work's typology, narratology, and ideology.

CHIVALRESQUE AND SENTIMENTAL FICTION

G. Serés, 'Ficción sentimental y humanismo: La *Sátira* de don Pedro de Portugal, *BH*, 93:31–60, traces, among other things, the importance of St. Isidore, Alonso de Madrigual, Rodríguez del Padrón, Cicero's *Rhetórica* (as translated by Alonso de Cartagena) in the formation of the *S*. J. Rodríguez Velasco, '"Yo soy de la Gran Bretaña, no sé si la oistes acá decir" (La tradición de Esplandián)', *RLit*, 53:49–61, revises the accepted interpretation of the *Esplandián* as a reaction against the worldly chivalresque ideal of fame, but instead sees the differences as a problem of narration and aesthetics rather than ideology. S. Miguel-Prendes, 'Las cartas de la *Cárcel de amor*', *Hispanófila*, 102:1–22, in concert with Whinnom's and Chorpenning's views that *Cárcel* is not merely of an epistolary structure, but that of the *oratio*, examines the tradition of the letter previous to San Pedro to show that in *Cárcel* it manipulates the intradiegetic addressee and extradiegetic reader both to accept the position defended in the *oratio*. P. García, 'La herencia del pecado en el *Lancelot en prose*', *MedRom*, 16:129–39, studies the philosophical effects of heredity, education, and environment in the characterizations of Mordret, Arthur, Lancelot, Helains, and Galaad. M. C. Marín Pina, 'Nuevos datos sobre Francisco Vázquez y Feliciano de Silva, autores de libros de caballerías', *JHispP*, 15:117–30, supplies information on a Francisco Vázquez who coincided with the well-known Feliciano de Silva in Ciudad Real, data which may have implications for the authorship of texts of the Palmerín cycle. Carlos Alvar, *El rey arturo y su mundo. Diccionario de mitología artúrica*, M, Alianza, 483 pp., includes important information on Spanish texts. M. S. Brownlee, 'Language and Incest in *Grisel y Mirabella*', Brownlee, *New Medievalism*, 157–82, examines this sentimental romance as a work in which the discourse established in its prefatory *carta* — the feminine figure here is an active intellect rather than a passive muse — is systematically undermined by the ensuing narrative.

OTHER PROSE WRITERS

R. Beltrán, 'El retorno a la "natura" como recuperación del linaje perdido: Actitudes mesiánicas en la biografía medieval del conde de Buelna', *MP*, 88:365–72, characterizing Gutiérrez Díaz de Games's *El Victorial* more a 'biografía novelesca' than a true chronicle and relating several concepts in the work to fictional works of chivalric and heroic dimensions, shows how the true focus of *V* is the revindication of the Niño family and how D. de G. emphasizes the Conde's behaviour as a reflection of the true and noble nature of this blood line. A. Vian Herrero, 'El *Libro de vita beata* de Juan de Lucena como diálogo literario', *BH*, 93:61–105, emphasizes Lucena's debt in writing dialogues in Castilian to those of Italian Humanism. D. M. Gitlitz, 'Hybrid conversos in the "*Libro llamado el Alboraique*"', *HR*, 60:1–17, concludes that this political pamphlet directed against *conversos*, though unflattering to them, shows that many of them in Castile and Aragon were sincere Christians; sees that *Alboraique* obliquely suggests that each person is responsible for his behaviour and, as such, is a distant textual cousin to *Celestina*. M. V. Amasuno Sárraga, 'Referencias literarias castellanas a una peste del siglo XV',

RLMed, 2, 1990: 115–29, points out references (Villena, Alvar García de Santa María, Pérez de Guzmán, Fernando Díaz de Toledo) to the plague outbreak of 1422 long overlooked by scholars. J. Weiss comments upon the importance of the gloss in fifteenth-century Castile as a reflection of literary taste and theory in 'Las *fermosas e peregrinas ystorias*: Sobre la glosa ornamental cuatrocentista', *ib.*, 103–12. W. points out that while the greater part of glosses were explanatory, the gloss could also be used to highlight the glosser's knowledge of history/mythology, and even serve as a springboard for an additional narrative note, development or argument. M. C. Marín Pina, 'Una Edición de la *Confesión del Amante* de John Gower', *Insula*, 536: 3, examines the 15th-c. Castilian translation of G's text in the light of an edition by Elena Alvar (introd. by Manuel Alvar, M, Anejos *BRAE* 1990).

6. THEATRE

The single most significant contribution to Spanish theatre studies was the publication of Angel Gómez Moreno, *El teatro medieval castellano en su marco románico*, M, Taurus, 195 pp. Other than discussing cogently the subject and relevant bibliography, G.M. includes significant and previously overlooked materials. R. Surtz offers a select guide to recent research in 'Spain: Catalan and Castilian Drama', Simon, *Theatre*, 189–206, Gómez Moreno (see GENERAL). A.-M. Álvarez Pellitero, 'La *Danza de la muerte* entre el sermón y el teatro', *BH* 93: 13–29 shows that the two Spanish manifestations — the printed *Dança* (Seville, 1520) and the manuscript (MS b IV, fol. 109r–129r) — derive separately from a hypothetical romance poem, the printed version of which is closer to the original poetical allegory than is the more popularized Escorial manuscript, that had been aimed toward preaching. A. Hermenegildo, 'Teatro, fantasía y catequesis en la Edad Media castellana', *RCEH*, 15: 429–51, studies *Auto de los Reyes Magos* and Gómez Manrique's *Nasçimiento de Nuestro Señor* in terms of their didactic and cataquistic functions and how these roles affect dramatic character of the works.

ALJAMIADO LITERATURE

By CONSUELO LÓPEZ-MORILLAS, *Associate Professor of Spanish,*
Indiana University

(This survey covers the years 1989–91)

G. Wiegers' meticulously researched "Isà b. Ŷābir and the origins of
Aljamiado literature', *al-Qantara*, 11, 1990:155–91, aside from re-
evaluating the life and work of this important figure, establishes once
and for all that Aljamiado was not the invention of the Segovian
alfaquí but goes back as far as the 13th c. Federico Corriente Córdoba
edits a lively series of *Relatos píos y profanos del manuscrito aljamiado de*
Urrea de Jalón, Zaragoza, Institución Fernando el Católico, 1990,
342 pp.; many are legends involving Biblical figures, Mohammed, or
heroes of early Islam. The codex was discovered in an Aragonese
village in 1984; M. J. Viguera provides the text with a wide-ranging
and informative introduction on Moriscos and Aljamiado. Alvaro
Galmés de Fuentes has edited *Dichos de los siete sabios de Grecia:*
Sentencias morales en verso, CLEAM, 8, M, Gredos, 182 pp., one of the
rare Morisco texts of European origin (from H. López de Yanguas'
Bocadillos de oro of 1549); the new, simplified transliteration system is
most welcome. A. Montaner Frutos disputes, in a series of articles,
Galmés' view of Aljamiado as 'literatura tradicional': 'Tradición,
oralidad y escritura en la literatura aljamiado-morisca', *SZ*, 10,
1989:171–81; 'En torno a la tradicionalidad de los textos aljamiados:
problemas de transmisión y criterios editoriales', Jauralde, *Actas*,
345–51; and (presumably) *'El concepto de oralidad y su aplicación a
la literatura española de los siglos XVI y XVII', *Criticón*, 45, 1989.

Actes (Zaghouan) contains two pieces of considerable interest: M.
T. Narváez, 'El Mancebo de Arévalo, lector morisco de *La Celestina*'
(267–77) finds that the author of the *Tafçira* incorporates a passage
from the prologue to F. de Rojas' 1502 edition, and sensitively
explores the solidarity between two *converso* writers, Jew and Muslim
respectively. A. V[espertino] Rodríguez, 'El Discurso de la Luz de
Mohamed Rabadan y la literatura aljamiada de los últimos moriscos
en España' (279–91) sees evidence of more Latin-letter, pre-expulsion
Morisco texts than heretofore realized; these reveal a degree of
syncretism and assimilation, and link up with Morisco writings from
North Africa. Other relevant contributions to the volume are M. N.
Ben Jemia, '"Almursida para kada mañana", comentario de un
fragmento del MS aljamiado no. 425 de la BN de Paris' (17–24); J. C.
Busto Cortina, 'Un cuento morisco en "El Conde Lucanor" y en
otros ejemplarios medievales: un caso más de sincretismo cultural
hispano-árabe' (61–72) (the story is 'La falsa beguina', the

framework narratological); M. J. Cervera Fras, 'Jaculatorias para toda la jornada en el MS 505 de Toledo' (100–10); M. J. Fernández [Fernández], 'La literatura del exemplus [*sic*] a luz de unos textos aljamiado-moriscos' (123–28) with links to other medieval *exempla* (see also her 'Análisis formal y comparado de un relato aljamiado-morisco', from the same MS J8, *al-Qantara*, 9, 1988:101–19, on an exemplary tale with Arabic and Christian analogues); A. Galmés de Fuentes, 'Literatura aljamiado-morisca y doble cultura' (143–48); O. Hegyi, 'En torno a la leyenda de Tamim Ad-dar' (167–74) (folk motifs, parallels in European literature); C. Mered, 'L'éducation religieuse des morisques à travers les écrits aljamiados' (263–66); and M. A. Vázquez, 'El sueño adoctrinador que soñó "Un Salih en la Sibdad de Tunes"' (317–23). (The Tunisian editors, though they have cleaned up their act somewhat, still appear oblivious to the existence of accent marks and *tildes* in Spanish.)

A charming piece on a slight subject is L. López-Baralt, 'La estética del cuerpo entre los moriscos del siglo XVI o de cómo la minoría perseguida pierde su rostro', *Colloque* (Sorbonne), 335–48: how the Moriscos represented their own appearance, with reference to Classical Arabic ideals of beauty. L.-B. also explores 'El extraño caso de un morisco "maurófilo"', *Homenaje Marichal*, 171–83, in which the anonymous author of MS S2 BRAH moves from Islamic doctrine to idealized romance, schizophrenically associating himself with some of the dominant Christian notions of *pureza de sangre*. The same MS yields a true literary and cultural sensation, announced by L.-B. as 'Un *Kama Sutra* español: el primer tratado erótico de nuestra lengua', *Vuelta*, 15:14–22: a treatise that celebrates the sexual act as a religious experience that brings the participants closer to God, and incorporates poetic quotations from Lope, Quevedo, and Góngora; an astonishing text of which we will hear much more.

A. Vespertino Rodríguez provides a general introduction to the field, 'Literatura aljamiada, literatura islámica', Mouillaud-Fraisse, *Littérature*, 121–48; A. Galmés de Fuentes, *Características literarias de los escritos aljamiado-moriscos', *Procs* (Teruel), 193–201. In L. P. Harvey, 'A Morisco collection of apocryphal *ḥadīths* on the virtues of al-Andalus', *al-Masāq*, 2, 1989:25–39, sayings spuriously attributed to the Prophet Mohammed encourage crypto-Muslims to remain strong in their faith. The MS is located in the British Library, and joins a number of other Morisco texts unearthed over the years in British collections by H.; in 'A second Morisco MS at Wadham College, Oxford: A 18.15', *al-Qantara*, 10, 1989:257–72, he describes a Latin-letter polemical treatise, unusual in its familiarity with Christianity, and evidently directed to Moriscos who had received some Christian upbringing. In Id., 'In Granada under the Catholic

Monarchs: a call from a doctor and another from a *curandera*', *Whinnom Vol.*, 71–75, the lady in question may be *la mora de Ubeda* known to us through the Mancebo de Arévalo. J. P. Hawkins, 'A Morisco philosophy of suffering: an anthropological analysis of an Aljamiado text', *Maghreb Review*, 13, 1988:199–217, argues that MS BN4953 (edited by O. Hegyi, see *YWMLS*, 47:315) constitutes a coherent treatise, not an anthology or miscellany, and presents its readers with an allegorical means of understanding their sorrows. M. J. Hermosilla continues her brief studies of Koranic texts with 'Una versión aljamiada sobre Job', *Sharq al-Andalus*, 8:211–14. The literal nature of Arabic-to-Aljamiado translation makes it an apt case study for machine translation in the view of U. Klenk, 'Die Koranverse in der Leyenda de Yusuf und die maschinelle Übersetzung', *Variatio Linguarum*, 135–48 (Aljamiado enters the 21st century!).

A variety of studies on aspects of the Moriscos' language will be of interest to students of their literature. L. F. Bernabé Pons and J. J. Martínez Egido, 'Estado de lengua de los MSS en carácteres latinos: el problema religioso', *Actes* (Zaghouan), 35–41, find much greater linguistic instability than in Christian texts of the period. L. Cardaillac, 'Les Morisques et leur langue', *CER*, 16, 1990:1–25, recalls the Moriscos' attachment to Arabic despite the official prohibitions of the 16th c. A controversial thesis is advanced by M. de Epalza, 'Le lexique religieux des morisques et la littérature aljamiado-morisque,' Cardaillac, *Morisques*, 51–64: that most Aljamiado literature dates from before the forced conversions (1502–26) or from after the expulsion, but that virtually no Islamic texts were written in Spanish between 1526 and 1609. The often-cited 'archaizing' nature of the language would thus be actually 'archaic'. But for evidence to the contrary see Vespertino, 'Aproximación', below. O. Hegyi, as in the past, places the Moriscos within an Islamic 'universe of discourse' that informs their language even after the loss of Arabic: two articles, 'Entorno y significación en los textos aljamiados', *Actas* (Berlin), 1, 125–30, and 'Tradition and linguistic assimilation among the Spanish Moriscos during the sixteenth century', Gervers, *Conversion*, 381–88. R. Kontzi covers familiar ground, 'Características lingüísticas de la literatura aljamiada', *Procs* (Teruel), 201–11. C. López-Morillas compares Aljamiado with Judeo-Spanish in their handling of the concept of translation, 'Hispano-Semitic calques and the context of translation', *BHS*, 67, 1990:111–28, and finds influence of Koranic diction in 'Aljamiado *desyerrar* "errar" y el prefijo *des-* intensivo en el nordeste peninsular', *Homenatge Roca-Pons*, 205–21.

R. Castrillo Márquez, **'Un MS de tema morisco en la Biblioteca del Palacio Real de Madrid', *Anaquel de Estudios Arabes*, 1, 1990:35–48.

M. J. Cervera Fras, *'Un tratado jurídico musulmán copiado por mudéjares aragoneses. Descripción de los MSS del Muḫtaṣar de al-Ṭulayṭuli', *Homenaje Ubieto Arteta*, 175–83. T. Fuente Cornejo, 'Las anotaciones en caracteres latinos de las guardas del MS aljamiado-morisco JXIII', *Sharq al-Andalus*, 8:137–52, unaccountably fails to cite a much more important earlier piece on the same MS: A. Montaner Frutos, 'El depósito de Almonacid y la producción de la literatura aljamiada (En torno al MS misceláneo XIII)', *AFA*, 41, 1988:119–52. M.F. dates the text to 1579–88, and explores the biographies of the scribe and his family; many implications here for the production and transmission of all Aljamiado literature. W. al-Ganabi discovers a unique Aljamiado work (with no known Arabic original) of al-Dānī on pronunciation of the Koran: 'Un MS aljamiado, último eslabón de la obra del Deniense en España', *Sharq al-Andalus*, 7, 1990:121–34.

A. Vespertino Rodríguez has taken a fresh look at MS dating in 'Una aproximación a la datación de los MSS aljamiado-moriscos', *Homenaje Rubio*, II, 1419–39. Though he has run a risk by relying wholly on catalogue information (rather than paper, watermarks, etc.), his conclusion that most MSS are of the mid- to late 16th c. merits serious consideration.

LITERATURE, 1490–1700
(PROSE AND POETRY)
By J. A. Jones, *Senior Lecturer in Hispanic Studies in the University of Hull*

1. General

Mary S. Gossy, *The Untold Story: Women and Theory in Golden Age Texts*, Ann Arbor, University of Michigan Press, 1989, vi + 142 pp., illuminates the role of women in texts such as *La Celestina* and Cervantes' *Novelas ejemplares*. A. Pallota, 'Venetian printers and Spanish literature in sixteenth-century Italy', *CL*, 43:20–42, and E. Seco, 'Historia de las traducciones literarias del italiano al español durante el Siglo de Oro (influencias)', *CILH*, 13, 1990:41–97, are useful complementary studies. A. Martín Vega, 'Cultura y creación literaria en el último tercio del siglo xvii', *DHA*, 8, 1989:91–109, is a further helpful illustration of literary activity in the period. Symbols and motifs of Golden Age literature are highlighted in M. R. Scaramuzzi Vidoni, 'Conquista de Granada y simbología del reino universal en textos españoles e italianos', Criado de Val, *Literatura*, 13–17; J. Caminero, 'El motivo del oro en la literatura española del siglo xvi', *ib.*, 57–72, and R. Hitchcock, 'La imagen literaria de los mozárabes en el Siglo de Oro', *Actas* (Berlin), i, 487–93. B. Ripoll and F. R. de la Flor, 'Los cien *Libros de novelas, cuentos, historias y casos trágicos* de Pedro Joseph Alonso y Padilla', *Criticón*, no. 51:75–97, deals with the reception of Golden Age works in the 18th c. *Homenaje Vilanova*, i, ii, contains over 30 articles on varied aspects of prose and poetry.

2. Thought

J. A. Parr, 'El renacimiento español: fortuna y futuro de una idea', Criado de Val, *Literatura*, 7–12, reflects on divergent views of the Spanish Renaissance. R. Sampayo Rodríguez, 'Antecedentes y precursores espirituales del erasmismo en la España de los Reyes Católicos', *ib.*, 21–31, identifies on-going spiritual currents. Anthony Pagden and Jeremy Lawrance, *Francisco de Vitoria: Political Writings*, C.U.P., xxxviii + 399 pp., is a valuable, scholarly edition and translation which makes widely accessible some key texts. Gordon Kinder, *Michael Servetus*, Baden-Baden & Bouxwiller, Valentin Koerner, 1989, 167 pp., is an indispensable research tool. Cipriano de la Huerga, *Prolegomenos y testimonios literarios, El sermón de los pendones*, ed. Gaspar Morocho Gayo *et al.*, León U.P., 1990, xv + 293 pp., shows the first impressive results of a well-directed research project aimed at publishing all of Cipriano de la Huerga's works. Arias Montano is studied in M. Pecellín Lancharro, 'La Naturae Historia de B. Arias Montano, *REE*, 45, 1989:269–80, and J. M. Ozaeta, 'Arias Montano, maestro de Fr. José de Sigüenza', *CiD*, 203:535–82. *La espiritualidad española del siglo XVI. Aspectos literarios y lingüísticos*, Salamanca U.P., 1990, 228 pp., contains nineteen articles on aspects of spirituality, including San Juan and Santa Teresa. *II Simposio sobre San Juan de la Cruz: ponencias*, Avila, Secretariado Diocesano Teresiano Sanjuanista, 1989, 210 pp., makes useful contributions on mysticism and San Juan, whose death is commemorated in *Insula*, 537, which contains the following background articles: T. Egido, 'Juan de la Cruz, un santo sin biografía' (3–4); L. E. Rodríguez-San Pedro Bezares, 'Atmósfera académica en la Salamanca de Fray Juan: 1564–1568' (4–6); J. C. Nieto, 'El bifrontismo Frayjuancruciano' (6–7); D. Ynduráin, 'San Juan, doctor de la Iglesia' (20); T. O'Reilly, 'San Juan de la Cruz y la lectura de la Biblia' (25–7); M. J. Mancho, 'Acerca de la "extrañez" Sanjuanista' (29–31); B. Sesé, 'Teoría y práctica del deseo según San Juan de la Cruz' (31–33). Another commemorative volume is Margaret A. Rees ed., *Leeds Papers on Saint John of the Cross: Contributions to a Quatercentenary Celebration*, Leeds, Trinity and All Saints, 237 pp., which contains the following items of background interest: M. E. Williams, 'The life and times of Saint John' (9–26); M. Wilson, 'St. John of the Cross and St. Teresa. Collaboration in Castile' (27–47); N. D. O'Donoghue, O.D.C., 'St. John of the Cross and the spiritual senses' (49–62); R. Cueto, 'The wilder shores of Carmelite spirituality. Ravens, deserts, clouds and prophecies in the Discalced Reform' (63–104); T. O'Reilly, 'St John of the Cross and the traditions of monastic exegesis' (105–26); J. Robson, 'Visions in St. John of the Cross: a twentieth-century psychologist's view' (161–98). San Juan's activities in the Carmelite order are also discussed in T. Sierra, 'La Consulta y San Juan de la Cruz', *Teresianum*, 41, 1990:543–87. Shirley du Boulay, *Teresa of Avila*, London, Hodder & Stoughton, xii + 258 pp., is an eminently readable and well-researched biography. Contextual material on St. Teresa is offered in M. Montero Vallejo, 'Apuntes sobre la circunstancia histórica de Teresa de Jesús', *CIH*, 12, 1989:123–67. St. Ignatius's spirituality is analysed in R. García-Mateo, 'S. Ignacio de Loyola y el humanismo', *Gregorianum*, 72:261–88, and, with clarity and sure grasp, in T. O'Reilly, '*The Spiritual Exercises* and the crisis of medieval piety', *The Way*, 70:101–13, and 'Ignatius of Loyola and the Counter-Reformation: the hagiographic tradition', *HeyJ*, 31, 1990:439–70. R. Hernández, 'La espiritualidad del Padre Granada, signo de contradicción', *CTh*, 116, 1989:3–32, contributes an extensive study in the context of the convent of San Esteban (Salamanca). A fitting tribute to fray Luis on the quatercentenary of his death is *El proceso inquisitorial de fray Luis de León*, ed. Angel Alcalá, Salamanca, Junta de Castilla y León, lxx + 737 pp., an impressive piece of research which gives us access to the trial documents. Fr. Luis's death is also commemorated in *Insula*, 539, which contains: R. Reyes Cano, 'Retrato de fray Luis de León por Francisco Pacheco' (1–3); C.Carrete Redondo, 'Acerca de la genealogía judaica de fray Luis de León: Elvira de Villanueva' (3–4); M. Durán, 'Fray Luis de León y Felipe II' (4–5); K. Hölz, 'Fray Luis de León y la Inquisición' (5–9); A. Alcalá, 'Hallazgos y enigmas literarios en el proceso de fray Luis de León' (9–12); C. Morón Arroyo, 'Imagen, teología, poesía' (13–14); J. San José Lera, 'Exégesis y filología en fray Luis de León' (14–16); J. Maristany, 'Sobre la dignidad del hombre. Breve noticia del documento de fray Luis' (18); A. Guy, 'Fama de Luis de León en Francia' (26–27); M. Morreale, 'Fray Luis de León al ras de la letra' (28). 'Homenaje a fray Luis de León, 1527–1591. IV Centenario de su muerte', *RA*, 32 : 3–436, also contains many valuable contributions. *El siglo de fray Luis de León: Salamanca y el Renacimiento*, Salamanca U.P. — Junta de Castilla y León, Ministerio de Cultura, 439 pp., includes scholarly articles on varied aspects of fray Luis's life and work.

3. Lyrical and Narrative Poetry

John Gornall, '*Ensaladas villanescas' associated with the 'Romancero nuevo'*, Exeter U.P., xxxv + 59 pp., contributes to our knowledge of early Spanish poetry. Other aspects are well treated in V. Infantes, 'Edición, literatura y realeza. Apuntes sobre los pliegos poéticos incunables', Criado de Val, *Literatura*, 85–98; J. Lluis Sirera, 'Una quexa ante el Dios de Amor . . . del Comendador Escrivá, como ejemplo posible de los autos de amores', *ib.*, 259–69; O. Anahory-Librowicz, 'Las mujeres no castas en el romancero', *Actas* (Berlin), 1, 321–30; F. J. Fuente Fernández, 'Pliegos sueltos góticos de Praga: las glosas de romances', *EHF*, 12, 1990 : 157–73. T. J. Dadson, 'El Conde de Salinas y la poesía cancioneril', Criado de Val, *Literatura*, 270–78, soundly studies the influence of *cancionero* poetry on Salinas. Material based on Miguel Sánchez de Lima, *Arte poética en romance Castellano*, Alcalá, 1580, is studied in M. G. Randel, 'El lenguaje de la conquista y la conquista del lenguaje en las poéticas españolas del Siglo de Oro', *Actas* (Berlin), 1, 469–75. P. Ruiz Pérez, 'Paradigmas genéricos en un romance de Rufo. "Los comendadores" y la épica culta', *RILCE*, 7 : 109–31, illustrates the transformation of the *romance* from the Renaissance to the Baroque.

garcilaso. G.'s reactíon to *cancionero* verse is considered in R. Boase, '*Rabia de amor*: Garcilaso's critique of the late-fifteenth century cult of amorous despair', *Varey Vol.*, 49–62, and P. Waley, 'Petrarch,

Garcilaso and the feral beloved', *ib.*, 227–31, offers a sound comparative study on the usage of *fiero/a*. The eclogues and elegies come under
scrutiny in O. T. Impey, 'El dolor, la alegría y el tiempo en la
Egloga III de Garcilaso', *Actas* (Berlin), I, 507–18, and A. Sánchez
Romeralo, 'La Elegía I de Garcilaso como pieza consolatoria', *ib.*,
611–17. I. Navarrete, 'Decentering Garcilaso: Herrera's attack on the
canon', *PMLA*, 106:21–33, focuses on Herrera's attempt to oust G.
from his established position in the poetic canon.

SAN JUAN. *Insula*, 537, contains: V. García de la Concha, 'Guía
estética de las ínsulas extrañas' (1–2, 35–36); P. Elia, 'La poesía de
San Juan de la Cruz: entre la oralidad y la escritura' (7–9); G.
Caravaggi, '"Vuelta a lo divino" y "misterio técnico" en la poesía de
San Juan de la Cruz' (9–10); C. P. Thompson, '"Aminadab tampoco
parecía": presencia y ausencia en el *Cántico* y en el *Cantar*' (10–11); L.
López-Baralt, 'El narcisismo sublime de San Juan de la Cruz; la
fuente mística del *Cántico espiritual*' (13–15); C. Morón Arroyo, 'Texto
de amor vivo' (15–17); N. Ly, 'Las liras del esposo' (17–19); E. Pacho,
'Instinto de integración sanjuanista en la segunda redacción del
Cántico espiritual' (20–23); C. Cuevas García, 'Perspectiva retórica
de la prosa de la *Llama de amor viva*' (23–25); G. Chiappini, 'Dios y la
voluntad (para un análisis semántico de la *Noche oscura* de San Juan de
la Cruz)' (27–29); J. Servera Baño, 'La crítica literaria de la
Generación del 27 sobre San Juan de la Cruz' (33–34). Another
contribution of note is C. Thompson, 'The metaphorical world of San
Juan', Rees, *Saint John*, 199–226. C. Bousoño, 'Poesía de San Juan de
la Cruz', *BRAE*, 70, 1990:467–74, emphasizes the modern aspects of
San Juan's verse, whilst I. Macpherson, '"Rompe la tela de este dulce
encuentro": San Juan's *Llama de amor viva* and the courtly context',
Wardropper Vol., 193–203, is a typically sharp study. An interesting
lexical contribution is M. J. Mancho Duque, 'El elemento aéreo en la
obra de San Juan de la Cruz', *Criticón*, no. 52:7–24. The poetic
context of San Juan is discussed in G. Hibbert, 'San Juan de la Cruz.
The poet and the theologian', Rees, *Saint John*, 127–59, and M. A.
Rees, 'A poet's world', *ib.*, 227–37. The relationship between
language and mystical experience is considered in J. Mandrell,
'Rending the "veils" of interpretation: San Juan de la Cruz and the
poetics of mystic desire', *RCEH*, 15, 1990:19–33, and L. J. Woodward, 'Verb tenses and sequential time in the *Cántico espiritual* of San
Juan de la Cruz', *FMLS*, 27:148–58.

LUIS DE LEON. C. Swietlicke, 'Desde la mitología clásica al
sincretismo renacentista: Apolo y Saturno en los versos originales de
Luis de León', *Actas* (Berlin), I, 645–53, continues her valuable work
on Renaissance literature with this study of L.'s syncretism. J. San

José Lera, 'El esfuerzo creador: unos versos de Horacio en la *Exposición del Libro de Job* de fray Luis de León', *Criticón*, no. 52:25–39, carefully examines the creative process of L. through the successive drafts of a translation of Horace in MS 219, Salamanca University Library. Another useful textual study is C. Cuevas, "Estilo del Espíritu Santo": crítica textual y polémica a propósito de un pasaje del *Cantar de los Cantares*', *Insula*, 539:16–18, whilst F. Garrote Pérez, 'El "ascenso platónico" y la unidad estructural de las *Odas*', *ib.*, 23–25, focuses on Platonic ascent as a unifying symbol.

GONGORA. K. H. Dolan, *Cyclopean Song: Aesthetics and Melancholy in Góngora's Fábula de Polifemo y Galatea*, North Carolina U.P., 1990, 140 pp., is a welcome consideration of the meditative quality of G.'s poem. G.'s bibliography is also enriched by: C. Chemris, 'Time, space and apocalypse in Góngora's *Soledades*', *Symposium*, 43, 1989:147–57; B. Taylor, 'Gongora's ballad "Quatro o seis desnudos ombros"', *Varey Vol.*, 215–26; M. Romanos, 'Las "Anotaciones" de Pedro Díaz de Rivas a los poemas de Góngora', *Actas* (Berlin), i, 583–89; A. S. Trueblood, 'Góngora visto por Picasso', *ib.*, 655–63.

OTHERS. G. Caravaggi, 'La "Nao de Amor" del Comendador Juan Ram de Escrivá', Criado de Val, *Literatura*, 248–58, examines some poems of the *Cancionero general*, whilst G. Mazzochi, 'Para la edición crítica de las "Coplas de la Pasión con la Resurrección" del Comendador Román', *ib.*, 285–96, illuminates a relatively unknown figure. Lope de Vega's poetic craft is discussed in E. I. Deffis de Calvo, 'La figura del pastor en dos sonetos místicos de Lope de Vega', *RILCE*, 5, 1989:273–84, and J. A. Martínez Comeche, 'La fundación de los Reales Estudios en la *Isagoge* de Lope: ¿testimonio o recreación literaria?', *Criticón*, no. 51:65–74. Items of note on Quevedo are I. Arellano, 'El soneto de Quevedo "Sulquivagante pretensor de Estolo": ensayo de interpretación', *Actas* (Berlin), i, 331–40, and J. M. González Fernández de Sevilla, 'La poesía metafísica de John Donne y Francisco de Quevedo', *Neophilologus*, 75:548–61. A. Laskier Martin, *Cervantes and the Burlesque Sonnet*, California U.P., ix + 295 pp., tackles a relatively neglected area of Cervantes' work. B. L. Lewis, '"Escalar pretendiendo las estrellas": "El sueño" de Sor Juana Inés de la Cruz y "Dios" de Justo Sierra', *RoN*, 32:3–10, interestingly compares poets and their contexts. J. M. Corominas, 'La Araucana en los comentarios a los Lusiadas (Camoens y Ercilla)', Criado de Val, *Literatura*, 457–66, is another comparative study which highlights aspects of European epic. Further useful work in this area is offered in M. Abad, 'La contextura estética de "La nave trágica": poema épico de Francisco de Contreras (1624)', *Actas* (Berlin), i, 281–89.

4. PROSE AND THE NOVEL

PICARESQUE. J. Iffland, 'El pícaro y la imprenta: algunas conjeturas acerca de la génesis de la novela picaresca', *Actas* (Berlin), 1, 495–506, relates the rise of the picaresque to the development of printing. J. L. Laurenti, *Catálogo bibliográfico de la literatura picaresca, siglos xvi–xx*, Kassel, Reichenberger, xi + 605 pp., is an essential research tool. J. R. Resina, '*Lazarillo de Tormes* y el lector', *ASNS*, 226, 1989:52–67, focuses on anonymity as an integrating element, whilst the relationship between reader and text is perceptively discussed in P. N. Dunn, 'Reading the text of *Lazarillo de Tormes*', *Wardropper Vol.*, 91–104. Aspects of interpretation and structure are examined in T. Herraiz de Tresca, '"Fortunas y adversidades": hacia una imagen del mundo en el *Lazarillo*', Criado de Val, *Literatura*, 467–75, and A. Hernández, 'El *Lazarillo de Tormes*: algunas observaciones sobre forma y estructuración de un ciclo gráfico', *Homenaje Porqueras Mayo*, 229–32. M. Ferrer-Chivite, 'Lázaro de Tormes y los godos', *Actas* (Berlin), 1, 449–56, offers interesting reflections on matters of caste and race, and A. Ruffinato, 'La *princeps* del *Lazarillo*, toda problemas', *RFE*, 70, 1990:249–96, grapples with textual problems. P. E. Beckman, *El valor literario del Lázaro de 1555: género, evolución y metamorfosis*, NY, Peter Lang, 171 pp., points to the merits of the anonymous continuation. N. Fallows, 'A note on the treatment of some popular maxims in the *Buscón*', *RoN*, 29, 1989:217–19, discusses the symbolic significance of specific episodes. P. Jauralde Pou, 'Errores de copia en los manuscritos de *El buscón*', *Varey Vol.*, 119–26, is a sound textual study. *Guzmán* criticism is well served by N. Cox Davis, 'Guzmán Swindles', *Symposium*, 43, 1989:194–208, and J. A. Whitenack, 'The *alma diferente* of Mateo Alemán's "Ozmín y Daraja"', *RoQ*, 38:59–73.

OTHERS. Various areas of prose writing are well treated in: P. Ruiz Pérez, 'Composiciones hispano-latinas del siglo xvi: los textos de Fernán Pérez de Oliva y Ambrosio de Morales', *Criticón*, no. 52:111–39; A. del Río Nogueras, 'Diálogo e historia en las *Batallas y Quinquagenas* de Gonzalo Fernández de Oviedo', *ib.*, 91–109; L. J. Peinador Marín, 'Un diálogo del siglo xvi español: *Eremitae*, de Juan Maldonado', *ib.*, 41–90; M. E. Venier, 'Los proverbios domésticos de Mal Lara', *Actas* (Berlin), 1, 681–86. J. J. Rodríguez Rodríguez, 'Literatura pastoril del s. xvi: acercamiento a su lengua poética', *CILH*, 13, 1990:107–22, and A. L. Baquero Escudero, 'La novela griega: proyección de un género en la narrativa española', *RILCE*, 6, 1990:19–45, are two sound studies on the respective forms of idealistic literature. E. Gallud Jardiel, 'La difusión de las novelas de caballería', Criado de Val, *Literatura*, 223–29, brings out elements of the reception of such works. Three useful additions in the same field are M. C. Marín Pina, 'Nuevos datos sobre Francisco Vázquez y Feliciano de Silva, autores de libros de caballería', *JHispP*, 15:117–30; J. B. de Avalle-Arce, 'La aventura caballeresca de Garci Rodríguez de Montalvo', *Wardropper Vol.*, 21–32; L. E. F. de Orduña, 'Heroes, troyanos y griegos en la "Hystoria del magnánimo, valiente e invencible cavallero don Belianís de Grecia (Burgos, 1547)', *Actas* (Berlin), I, 559–68. A. Cruz Casado, 'Los libros de aventuras peregrinas: nuevas aportaciones', *ib.*, 425–31, sheds light on this late Golden Age genre. J. F. Chorpenning, 'Santa Teresa's *Libro de la vida* as romance: narrative movements and heroic quest', *RCEH*, 14, 1989:51–64, emphasizes the narrative unity of this work, and Id., 'The pleasance, Paradise and Heaven: Renaissance cosmology and imagery in the "Castillo interior"', *FMLS*, 27:138–47, contends that the micro/macro comparison gives logical coherence to the imagery. Luis de León's prose comes under scrutiny in: Juventino Caminero, *La razón filológica en la obra de Fray Luis de León*, Kassel, Reichenberger, 1990, xiv + 194 pp.; A. S. Zamarreño, '*La perfecta casada*, ¿sólo un vademecum para ánimos flacos?', *Insula*, 539:19–20; J. A. Jones, 'Verdad, armonía y vocación: el sentido de plenitud en *La perfecta casada*', *ib.*, 21–23; J. San José Lera, 'Fray Diego de Zúñiga y fray Luis de León frente al "Libro de Job"', *CiD*, 204:967–83. E. Rhodes, 'Spain's misfired canon: the case of Luis de Granada's *Libro de la oración y meditación*', *JHispP*, 15, 1990:43–66, raises important issues concerning accepted views of Golden Age works. A further useful contribution is A. Gil, 'El predicador y el oyente: principios semióticos en la Rhetorica de Fray Luis de Granada', *Homenaje Porqueras Mayo*, 197–209. J. I. Tellechea Idígoras, *Léxico de la "Guía espiritual" de Miguel de Molinos*, M, FUE, xxxvi + 582 pp., is a valuable book both for the study of language and thought. L. Schwartz Lerner, 'Sátira y filosofía moral: el texto de Quevedo', *Actas* (Berlin), I, 619–27, is an interesting, semiotic study. S. G. Artal, 'La mujer que se pinta en *La hora de todos* y en *El mundo por de dentro*', *BHi*, 92, 1990:749–59, traces the evolution of Q.'s thought through comparisons of various texts in which women figure. Baroque writing and thought are further illuminated in J. C. Nanfito, '*El sueño*: the baroque imagination and the dreamscape', *MLN*, 106:423–31, and M. Etreros, 'La sátira política, discurso del barroco español', *BRAE*, 70, 1990:569–89. *Actas* (Berlin), I, contains the following items on Gracián: N. P. Wardropper, 'El discurso III de la "Agudeza y arte de ingenio" de Baltasar Gracián' (569–74); E. Hidalgo-Serna, 'Origen y causas de la "agudeza": necesaria revisión del "conceptismo" español' (477–86); A. Carreño, 'Gracián y sus lecturas en el romancero de Luis de Góngora' (395–403); S. Neumeister, 'El otro Gracián: la medítación xiii del *Comulgatorio* (1655)' (159–79). G.'s high regard for the Catholic Monarchs is emphasized in P. Montón Puerto, 'Isabel de Castilla y Fernando de Aragón como modelos en Luis Vives y Baltasar Gracián', Criado de Val, *Literatura*, 18–20. J. Checa, '"Oráculo manual": Gracián y el ejercicio de la lectura', *HR*, 59:263–80, focuses on textual pluralism. A. Madroñal Durán, 'Sobre el autobiografismo en las novelas de Gonzalo de Céspedes y Meneses a la luz de nuevos documentos', *Criticón*, no. 51:99–108, illuminates the life and works of this little known writer. K. A. Myers, 'Sor Juana's *Respuesta*: rewriting the *Vitae*', *RCEH*, 14, 1990:459–71, looks at aspects of the expression of the self. P. E. Grieve, 'Embroidering with saintly threads: María de Zayas challenges Cervantes and the Church', *RoQ*, 44:86–106, compares attitudes to women, and W. H. Clamurro, 'Locura y forma narrativa en "Estragos que causa el vicio" de María Zayas y Sotomayor', *Actas* (Berlin), I, 405–13, looks at problems of passionate love and morality.

CERVANTES

GENERAL. *Anales cervantinos*, M, CSIC, Instituto de Filología, 1990, vol. 28, 305 pp., contains fifteen articles on C.'s prose works, mainly on *D.Q.* J. Marías, 'Cervantes clave española', *BRAE*, 70, 1990:457–66, attempts to shed light on C.'s role in the Spain of his time. Substantial contributions to C. scholarship are made in D. Eisenberg, 'La teoría cervantina del tiempo', *Actas* (Berlin), I, 433–39; Id., 'Repaso crítico de las atribuciones cervantinas', *NRFH*, 38, 1990:477–92; Id., 'Cervantes' consonants', *Cervantes*, 10, 1990:3–14. *Insula*, 538, contains the following: J. B. de Avalle-Arce, 'Las voces del narrador' (4–6); F. Márquez Villanueva, 'Cervantes y el erotismo estudiantil' (26–28); M. Chevalier, 'Cervantes, Rousseau, Dostoievski' (15–16); E. C. Riley, 'Cervantes y Freud' (34–35). E. Garramiola Prieto, 'Un inédito documento cervantino', *JHispP*, 15:135–39, suggests contact between C. and Garcilaso de la Vega, El Inca.

DON QUIXOTE. Carroll B. Johnson, *Don Quixote. The Quest for Modern Fiction*, Boston, Twayne, 1990, 133 pp., is a readable, stimulating and perceptive book. H. P. Márquez, *La representación de los personajes femeninos en el Quijote*, M, Porrúa Turanzas, 1990, vii + 191 pp., focuses on the unifying role of female characters. *Insula*, 538, contains the following contributions: J. J. Allen, 'El duradero encanto del Quijote' (3–4); J. Canavaggio, 'La España del Quijote' (7–8); A. L. Cascardi, 'Orígenes de la novela' (9–11); L. Combet, 'Del libro al mito, o la cuarta salida de Don Quijote' (11–15); D. Eisenberg, 'Don Quijote, el Romanticismo y el renacimiento de lo caballeresco' (16–17); H. P. Endress, 'La paz, un ideal de Don

Quijote' (17–18); G. Guntert, '"En manos de Dios y del renegado": ambivalencia ideológica en la *Historia del cautivo* (*Don Quijote*, 1, 39–41)' (19–20); T. R. Hart, 'La novela y el romance en el *Quijote*' (21–23); M. Joly, 'De paremiología cervantina: una reconsideración del problema' (23–24); P. Lewis-Smith, 'Cervantes y los libros de caballería: los gustos del público, el gusto cervantino y el propósito del *Quijote*' (24–26); M. Moner, 'Los "Libros plúmbeos" de Granada y su influencia en el *Quijote*' (29–30); A. Redondo, 'Don Quijote "caballero" e "hijo" de ventero y rameras. Algunas calas en la parodia cervantina' (30–33); M. Socrate, 'Las formas digresivas y la unidad del *Quijote*' (35–38); F. Ayala, 'Toda ya en el *Quijote*' (38–40). L. Rodríguez Cacho, '*Don Olivante de Laura* como lectura cervantina: dos datos inéditos', *Actas* (Alcalá), 515–25, is a scholarly portrayal of the influence of *Olivante* on *D.Q.* Edward C. Riley, 'Romance, the picaresque and Don Quixote', *Wardropper Vol.*, 237–48, considers C.'s response to the picaresque. E. Urbina, 'La aventura guardada: Don Quijote como caballero desaventurado', *RoQ*, 37, 1990:431–40, studies the structuring role of this parodic motif. Interesting studies of individual episodes are found in: E. J. Ziolkowski, 'Don Quijote's windmill and Fortune's Wheel', *MLR*, 86:885–97; Y. Jehenson, 'The pastoral episode in Cervantes' *Don Quijote*: Marcela once again', *Cervantes*, 10, 1990:15–35; E. B. Kelley, 'En torno a la "maravillosa visión" de la pastora Marcela y otra ficción poética', *Actas* (Berlin), 1, 365–71; A. Rodríguez and M. M. Smeloff, '¿Dónde queda la espada mágica de don Quijote?', *Cervantes*, 11:119–24. E. Urbina, 'Tres aspectos de lo grotesco en el Quijote', *Actas* (Berlin), 1, 673–79, provides an analysis of this element. L. Lipson, '"Las Lenguas de las Gentes": gossip as a narrative device in selected works of Cervantes', *FMLS*, 27:268–83; C. Oriel, 'Narrative levels and the fictionality of *Don Quijote*, 1: Cardenio's story', *Cervantes*, 10, 1990:55–72; and K. L. Selig, '"Enumeratio"/enumeración en "Don Quijote"', *Actas* (Berlin), 1, 629–34, give insights into the various levels on which C.'s text operates. J. T. Cull, 'The "Knight of the Broken Lance" and his "Trusty Steed": on Don Quijote and Rocinante', *Cervantes*, 10, 1990:37–53, explores recurring symbols of D.Q.'s impotence as a knight. A. Egido, 'La memoria en el Quijote', *ib.*, 11:3–44, offers an extensive study of the relationship between memory and imagination. J. Amezcua, 'Seres de contacto y seres de no contacto: "Don Quijote", primera parte', *Actas* (Berlin), 1, 311–19, looks for physical manifestations of changes in D.Q. and Sancho. Studies of note on Sancho are M. Chevalier, 'Sancho Panza y la cultura escrita', *Wardropper Vol.*, 67–93, and A. Rodríguez and R. Chávez, 'La ambivalente caridad de Sancho Panza', *RoN*, 32:29–33. W. Rosenblat, 'Estructura y función de las novelas interpoladas en el *Quijote*',

Criticón, no. 51 : 109–16, illustrates the function of these stories within the novel as a whole. M. S. Gossy, 'Basilio's feminized body (*Don Quijote*, II, 20–21)', *RCEH*, 14, 1990:561–66, analyses influences on C.'s ideas on marriage. R. Ter Horst, 'In an echoing grove: Quijote II and a sonnet of Garcilaso', *Wardropper Vol.*, 335–46, and J. Canavaggio, 'El licenciado Márquez Torres y su aprobación a la Segunda Parte del *Quijote*: las lecturas cervantinas de unos caballeros franceses', *ib.*, 33–39, usefully illuminate aspects of Pt II. M. Molho, 'Para una lectura psicológica de los cuentecillos de locos del segundo *Don Quijote*', *Cervantes*, 11:87–98, aims to explain the anguish that sparked the 1615 text. G. San Román, 'Using OCP: a study of characterization in the two *Don Quijotes*', *LLC*, 5, 1990:314–18, succeeds in demonstrating how modern technology may be fruitfully applied to C.

OTHER WORKS. Daniel Eisenberg, *Las "Semanas del jardín" de Miguel de Cervantes*, Diputación de Salamanca, 1989, 194 pp., presents a persuasive case for accepting this fragment as C.'s work. An aspect of C.'s pastoral is found in V. Cabrera, 'La ironía cervantina en *La Galatea*', *His(US)*, 74:8–14. Interesting studies on *Novelas ejemplares* are: J. R. Resina, 'Laisser faire y reflexividad erótica en *La gitanilla*', *MLN*, 106:257–78; M. Nimetz, 'Genre and creativity in *Rinconete y Cortadillo*', *Cervantes*, 10:73–93; A. Sánchez, '*Rinconete y Cortadillo* y *El celoso extremeño*: claves narrativas en el contexto literario cervantino', *Homenaje Criado de Val*, 513–35; W. Schleiner, 'The Glass Graduate and the aphrodisiac that went wrong: new light from old texts', *FMLS*, 27:370–81; C. B. Johnson, 'Catolicismo, familia y fecundidad: el caso de "La española inglesa"', *Actas* (Berlin), I, 519–24; G. Stagg, 'The composition and revision of *La española inglesa*', *Wardropper Vol.*, 305–21; J. Alvarez Barrientos, 'Controversias acerca de la autoría de varias novelas de Cervantes en el siglo xviii: "El curioso impertinente", "Rinconete y Cortadillo", y "El celoso extremeño"' *Actas* (Berlin), I, 301–09. A. J. Cascardi, 'Reason and romance: an essay on Cervantes' *Persiles*', *MLN*: 106:279–93, is a sound attempt to relate C.'s work to its cultural context.

LITERATURE, 1490–1700
(DRAMA)

By WILLIAM R. BLUE, *Professor of Spanish, University of Kansas*

1. *LA CELESTINA*

J. T. Snow publishes another of his useful bibliographies of studies on *La Celestina* in *Celestinesca*, 15:79–100, to which the interested reader should refer. C. B. Faulhaber, '*Celestina* de Palacio: Rojas's holograph manuscript?', *ib.*, 3–52, in a detailed piece suggests that this MS is Rojas's transcription and thus a 'textual state prior to that of any of the printed editions'. He offers comparisons between that text and the printed ones. H. Okamura, 'Lucrecia en el esquema didáctico de Celestina', *ib.*, 53–62, examines Lucrecia as an example of the dangerous servant swayed by material gain to permit her mistress's downfall thus her role conforms to the warning with which the work begins against 'malos y lisonjeros sirvientes'. I. Lozano-Renieblas,' "Minerva con el can"', *ib.*, 75–78, tries to shed light on this line that has dogged critics for some time but her associative reading of the Minerva–Minos legend in which 'can' is a synecdoche for Escila strains at the leash. M. Morreale offers a number of entries in 'Apuntes bibliográficos para el estudio de la presencia de *La Celestina* en Italia' in *RLit*, 52:539–43. M. Garci-Gómez, 'El cabello de Melibea (Medusa): entre la petrificación y el emborricamiento', *Estudios Ruiz-Fornells*, 233–39, suggests that Calisto fetishizes Melibea's hair which can turn men to stone — like Medusa's hair which G.-G. sees as a terrifying castration symbol — or into asses, figuratively, 'enamorarse perdidamente'. For E. Gascón Vera, 'Visión y razón: elementos trágicos en *La Celestina*', *ib.*, 246–54, light equals reason, darkness stands for madness ('sin-razón'). While the principal characters move in the realm of darkness as the work progresses, none the less pessimism does not dominate at the end, since Sosia learns from Calisto's and the other servants' errors and, at Melibea's death, Pleberio sees the folly of materialism. E. Galán Font, 'La huella de *La Celestina* en *La casa de Bernarda Alba*', *RLit*, 52:203–14, believes the latter looked to the former for inspiration.

2. GENERAL

Catherine Larson publishes *Language and the comedia: theory and practice*, Lewisburg, Bucknell U.P., 181 pp., a study through the application of speech-act-theory of a number of Golden Age plays, *La dama boba*, *Entre bobos anda el juego*, *La verdad sospechosa*, *El caballero de Olmedo*, *La dama duende, Fuenteovejuna,* and *Cada uno para sí.* Throughout, L. stresses model building that incorporates critical intuitions about the role of language into a pre-existing form, speech-act, and the levels of communication that go on between characters, between the author and the audience, between the text/representation and the audience. J. E. Varey in 'Memory theaters, playhouses, and *corrales de comedias'*, Fothergill-Payne, *Drama,* 39–53, takes up the theory that both Spanish *corrales* and English theatres owe their design to memory theatres and thus have a similar source not due either to direct influence nor to separate but parallel evolution. While signalling the similarities between sixteenth-c. Spanish public theatres and their contemporary English counterparts, V. rejects the memory theatre thesis pointing out that the *corrales* were built according to the external constraints imposed by pre-existing buildings that surrounded the open spaces in which they were established. He then creates links between the sixteenth- and seventeenth-century commercial theatres and the structure of the medieval stage thereby emphasizing the continuity between the late middle age and the Golden Age stage. J. J. Allen, 'The disposition of the stages in the English and Spanish theaters', *ib.,* 54–72, concentrates on the stages, not the playhouses. A. divides Spanish stages into three groups but notes that the stage size is essentially the same with the ration of width to depth being 2 : 1. English stages vary much more. By looking at stage configuration, A. then suggests how that may be used to resolve doubts about design and staging. D. W. Cruickshank, 'Lisping and wearing strange suits: English characters on the Spanish stage and Spanish characters on the English stage, 1580–1680', *ib.,* 195–210, states that in none of the eleven plays by Lope in which English characters appear is there any rancour demonstrated, nor is there in Guillén de Castro nor Vélez. English dramatists, on the other hand, portray Spaniards as arrogant, vengeful, and duplicitous. J. Orrell, 'Spanish corrales and English theaters', *ib.,* 23–38, cautions against developmental notions based on mutual or one-directional influence of one theatre space on another, and thus against filling the gaps in knowledge about the development of Boar's Head by appeal to Madrid's *corrales* since neither stage was a fully worked-out design to begin with and both changed in fits and spurts mainly for economic reasons. The polygonal theatres, however, were essentially conceived as finished products from the outset. D. Dietz, 'England's and Spain's *corpus christi* theaters', *ib.,* 239–51, sees salvation history as the central feature of the Spanish *auto,* not the Eucharist as A. A. Parker maintained, and then signals the thematic and theological parallels between English and Spanish Eucharist theatres before the Reformation. D. then turns his attention to two post-Reformation moralities:

William Wager's *Enough is as good as a feast* and Calderon's *El gran mercado del mundo* as illustrations of the divergent paths taken: loss of dramatic force due to Calvinist notions of predestination in the English case, renewed vitality by insistent emphasis on free will in the Spanish. J. M. Ruano de la Haza, 'Unparallel lives: hagiographical drama in seventeenth-century England and Spain', *ib.*, 252–66, examines *The Virgin Martyr* in which, while there is a struggle between good and evil, there is no new insight into religion. In *El purgatorio de San Patricio* or *El esclavo del demonio*, on the other hand, the plot is essentially a signifier for the signified, namely a religious principle: in the first case, an invitation to the viewer to delve into the mysteries of the faith, in the second, to examine the role of reason in one's striving for salvation. C. Ganelin, 'Peter Brook: performance theory and the *comedia*', *BC*, 43:101–8, explores contemporary performances at the Chamizal Festival of Golden Age plays through Peter Brook's notion of shifting point, distance, and presence to defend 'modernized' versions of classical plays, namely, *El burlador de Sevilla* and *El gran mercado del mundo*. In 'Reworking the *comedia*: a prolegomenon to a study of the *refundición*', *His(US)*, 74:240–49, Ganelin continues his work on rewritings looking now at Calixto Boldún y Conde's *A secreto agavio, simulada venganza* showing its similarities to Calderón's play and its differences, among which is the 'shift away from a society that promulgates an oppressive honor code to an individual who betrays universal ethical laws'.

F. Ruiz Ramón, 'Reading Spanish classical theater (a case of cultural anomaly)', Fothergill-Payne, *Theater*, 15–22, stresses that the multiple thematic and theoretically based readings of *comedia* derive from its dramatic essence. Readers, critics, of classical theatre are cut off from the cultural well-spring of performance as disaffection between the world of the theatre and the world of the academy grows apace. R.R. argues eloquently for a renewed interest in performing the classics, seeing in the works not only meanings for modern times but also the vital, powerful links to the past. R. Lima, 'Supernatural fantasy in Spanish drama', *Estudios Ruiz-Fornells*, 389–95, looks briefly at miracles, devils, out-of-body experiences, etc., with references to *La Celestina* and *El caballero de Olmedo*, plus a short list of other Golden Age plays. C. Stern, 'A nativity play for the Catholic Monarchs', *BC*, 43:71–100, presents an informative and fascinating account of the complex vision presented in the play, describing the basic plot, the staging, and the tradition of such works along with their operatic qualities and certain practical details, such as payments. She concludes, 'So on Christmas Eve, 1487, the church of San Salvador in Zaragoza became concert hall and picture gallery, opera house and dance studio, a place where all the arts combined to render homage to

thè Almighty before an audience that included the Catholic Monarchs'. R. L. Hathaway, 'Dramatic variation in the pre-Lopean
theatre: Susanna and the elders', *ib.* 109–31, follows the story through
a number of playwrights showing its hoped-for effects on the
audiences and thus the changing dramaturgy. Among the dramatists
are Diego Sánchez, Pedraza, and Cairasco de Figueroa.

3. CALDERON DE LA BARCA

Margaret Rich Greer publishes *The play of power: mythological court
dramas of Calderón de la Barca*, Princeton U.P., xii + 256 pp. In this
study, G. incorporates some previously published material plus a
general introduction and a long chapter on Don Juan José into a
thoroughgoing examination of C.'s court plays. She investigates at
length *Las fortunas de Andrómeda y Perseo*, *El mayor encanto amor*, *La estatua
de Prometeo*, *Fieras afemnia Amor*, and *Hado y divisa de Leonido y Marfisa*,
among briefer references to others. The basic thesis is that court
drama combines highly developed theatrical art, well-written drama,
and commentary on contemporary politics into a court spectacle that,
while maintaining its contacts with popular theatrical traditions,
appealed to the sophisticated court audience, and, at the same time,
dealt, sometimes directly (*El mayor encanto amor*), sometimes subtly,
with synchronal political realities. G.'s efforts to contextualize C.'s
court plays on all three fronts — the dramatic, the theatrical, and the
historical/political — pay off in a handsomely presented and
altogether fascinating, informative study. Barbara Kurtz's *The play of
allegory in the autos sacramentales of Pedro Calderón de la Barca*, Washington
D.C., The Catholic Univ. of America Press, 250 pp., is a well-written,
often witty, examination of this sometimes resistant subgenre. After a
general introduction plus critical overview, K. turns to defining the
auto, to defining allegory, to a discussion of myth and truth, history
and time, and to *auto* as spiritual exercise. K. studies many of C.'s *autos*
— *El divino Orfeo*, *Andrómeda y Perseo*, *Psiquis y Cupido*, *El año santo en
Madrid*, and *El nuevo palacio del Retiro*, among others — as examples of
the foregoing headings. The theatrical qualities of the works are not
overlooked as K. insists that 'the metaphors of the *autos*' allegorical
discourse are . . . innately performative', 'performative' in both senses
of the word. Attempting to bridge the gap between seventeenth-c.
traditions and twentieth-c. reception, K. never discounts the 'reaction of doubt and denial' experienced by modern readers when
confronted by the sacramental nature of C.'s allegories. K. strives to
make these works accessible and interesting not only in terms of the
pertinence of contemporary literary theory to their study, but also in
terms of their historical, philosophical contexts and their consequent

cultural otherness, by means of which we can gauge what has been both won and lost through time.

C. Larson, 'La dama duende and the shifting characterization of Calderón's diabolical angel', Stoll, Women, 51–65, proposes to link, rather than oppose, a feminist perspective and traditional approaches to C. and, to do so, focuses on the subversive and the conventional in Angela's character. M. Martino Crocetti, 'La dama duende: spatial and hymeneal dialectics', ib., 51–65, sees the images of the door, window, and alacena as female, or hymeneal, spaces and la llave as a male marker. M.C. portrays Angela as distorting 'male space', or Manuel's room, but fails to note that that room was Angela's first. Not addressed in the hymeneal article is Angela as widow. T. A. O'Connor, 'The politics of rape and fineza in Calderonian myth plays', ib., 170–83, looks at seven myth plays in which rape occurs and then at the effect of that violence on the victims and their offspring. In 'Metamorphosis as challenge in the theater of Calderón', Fothergill-Payne, Drama, 269–79, O'C. sees transformation as tragic and thus emblematic of human suffering. Examining briefly a number of plays, O'C. offers the following taxonomy of metamorphosis: as outrage, escape, punishment, loss of personhood, and apotheosis. M. Welles, '"The Rape of Deineira" in Calderón's El pintor de su deshonra', Stoll, Women, 184–201, turns to the above-named painting in the belief that in its 'narrative' the play's action is mirrored. S. Rupp, 'Reason of state and repetition in The Tempest and La vida es sueño', CL, 42:289–318, presents a comparison of C.'s and Shakespeare's plays based on the struggle between Machiavellian and anti-Machiavellian thought and practice in England and Spain. He states, 'At the end of La vida es sueño Segismundo promises to restore due order to his divided realm. In his capacity for resolving political conflict he has become the counterpart of Ferdinand, and in both plays this resolution can occur because the princes themselves, along with the philosopher-kings who have attempted to direct their education, have accepted the human limits of royal authority'. None the less, Segismundo's final act — imprisoning the rebel soldier — and Antonio's unrepentance for his treachery call into question the presumed faith that Ferdinand and Segismundo exhibit for traditional values and laws. S. D. Voros, 'Thomas Kyd and Pedro Calderón: toward a semiotics of revenge drama', Fothergill-Payne, Drama, 108–24, examines The Spanish Tragedy and De un castigo, tres venganzas through A. Greimas and T. Pavel, that is to say, through a system of binary oppositions. S. Neumeister, in 'World picture and picture world in Shakespeare and Calderón', ib., 125–39, hoists up the 'great chain of being', long sunk by modern Shakespearian criticism, as emblematic of his, Shakespeare's, view of individual experience whereas C. adopts the attitude of a 'Catholic metaphysician'. In the final section, N. trots out the court-play-as-royal-flattery and narcissism routine saying that in the myth plays and the romances, C.'s theatre is little more than baroque spectacle, 'a royal toy'. G. P. Andrachuk, 'Calderón's view of the English schism', *ib.*, 224–38, asserts that a politico-religious reading of *La cisma de Inglaterra* is essential for its fuller understanding. C.'s sympathetic presentation of Henry — casting blame instead on Anne Boleyn and Wolsey — confers on the king the role of manipulated victim and, later, repentant sinner, yet unable in the final instance to bow to Rome's authority. S. L. Fischer, '"Bequeath to death your numbness, for from him/Dear life redeems you": Calderón, Shakespeare, and romance', *ib.*, 280–301, studies *Hado y divisa de Leonido y Marfisa* through romance conventions and by comparison to *The Winter's Tale*. As C. dramatizes the cyclical movements from birth to death to rebirth, he never fails to intertwine the polar views, reminding his spectators thus of death in life and life in death. In the final joyous scene of *Hado*, Polidoro's death, and Florante's undiscovered crime bring out romance's sense of loss in the midst of final triumph. In 'El garrote más bien dado o el alcalde de Zalamea: classical theatre as it ought to be performed', *Gestos*, 6:33–51, Fischer offers a detailed reading of José Luis Alonso's 1988 performance of C.'s play which, by collating acting, stagecraft, and character portrayal with what José Ruano de la Haza in his introduction to the 1988 edition of the play (*YWMLS*, 50:343), saw as the military caste's attempts to trample the inherent dignity of the individual, confirms Peter Brook's ideas about performing the classics. A. Hermenegildo continues his studies of the *pastor-bobo-gracioso* in 'Calderón's *El galán fantasma* and the characters of popular festivity', Fothergill-Payne, *Theater*, 49–66, with an actantial analysis of Candil's role in the carnivalesque space he creates, which brings into relief the schizophrenic behaviour of the nobles. H. offers several interesting observations on Candil's language. I. Benabu, 'Interpreting the *comedia* in the absence of a performance tradition: Gutierre in Calderón's *El médico de su honra*', *ib.*, 23–33, laments the absence of a performance tradition and offers, through reference and comparison to the Shakespearian tradition, to bridge the gap by presenting *El médico* as a true tragedy through its implicit staging and voicing inscriptions.

A. Valbuena Briones, 'A critique of Calderón's *Judas Macabeo*', *Estudios Ruiz-Fornells*, 658–65, shows that C. selected elements from the biblical story and re-organized them to suit his artistic-moral intentions. In 'El tratamiento del tema de Eco y Narciso de Calderón', *His(US)*, 74:250–54, A.V.B. insists on the moral message of C.'s mythological play: the eyes deceive and cause Narciso to fall into appearances' trap. In a footnote, he refers to C.'s possible warning to the court about the blinding enchantments of the Buen Retiro and of palace life in general. F. de Armas, 'The hippogryph as vehicle: layers of myth in *La vida es sueño*', *Estudios Ruiz-Fornells*, 18–26, follows up on his Astrea studies looking at the mythological beast whose equine characteristics belong to Rosaura while the gryphon — lion/eagle — pertains to Segismundo. He weaves into his mythological tapestry aspects of the Hercules (fury) and Saturn vs. Jupiter (self-control) stories. E. Engling, '*La aurora en Copacabana*: a Calderonian tapestry', *BC*, 43:133–45, sees this play as an adequate summary of themes and topics broached throughout his career by C. in his honour, philosophical, mythological, and religious plays. A. K. G. Paterson publishes his translation, *The painter of his dishonour*, *El pintor de su deshonra*, Warminster, Aris and Phillips, vi + 218. There is a good introduction that speaks of translation problems, date and performance, text, characters, and themes. Further commentary on individual scenes, words, or images is included at the end.

4. LOPE DE VEGA

Daniel Heiple, 'Profeminist reactions to Huarte's misogyny in Lope de Vega's *La prueba de los ingenios* and María de Zayas's *Novelas amorosas y ejemplares*', Stoll, *Women*, 121–34, says that both L. and Z., when seen in context of sixteenth- and seventeenth-c. thought portray woman as man's equal thereby rejecting Huarte de San Juan's biologically deterministic vision of woman's inherent inferiority. M. R. Hicks, 'Lope's other *dama boba*: the strategy of incompetence', *ib.*, 135–53, states that Diana's ingenuity, in *La boba para los otros y discreta para sí*, overturns received notions of feminine inferiority, but within established limits. M. D. McGaha, 'The sources and feminism of Lope's *Las mujeres sin hombres*', *ib.*, 157–69, discovers that Boccaccio's *Teseida della nozze d'Emilia* is the main source for L.'s play and that the dramatist adopts a 'feminist' stance because of his great passion for the intelligent and talented Marta de Nevares, with whom L. was deeply involved. The play thus demonstrates L.'s 'revisionist' view of women. L. Fothergill-Payne, 'Taming women on the Spanish stage: Lope on women, love, and marriage', Fothergill-Payne, *Theater*, 67–82, follows a similar path in this well-written, fascinating piece focusing on L.'s *La vengadora de las mujeres* and *Las mujeres sin hombres*. Setting both plays first within the on-going European debate on women's rights and women's roles, and then within the context of L.'s relationship with the well-educated, high-spirited Marta de Nevares, F.-P. clearly demonstrates how the playwright, while sympathetically addressing women's issues, balanced his plays so that spectators might receive many varying messages. T. Case, 'A time for heroines in Lope', Stoll, *Women*, 202–19, looks at *Las almenas de Toro* and *Las famosas asturianas* and endeavours both to analyse the works and tie them to their historical contexts. A. K. Stoll, 'Lope's *El anzuelo de Fenisa*: a woman for all seasons', in *ib.*, 245–58, ties the carnival-esque, world-upside-down elements in the play to commerce, focusing on the marginalized Fenisa and her shenanigans. S. then follows the play's fortunes through three later *refundiciones*. D. L. Smith, 'Text, stage, and public in Webster's *The Duchess of Malfi* and Lope's *El mayordomo de la Duquesa de Amalfi*', Fothergill-Payne, *Drama*, 75–90, begins with a consideration of stage dimensions and condi-tions in the Blackfriars and the two commercial theatres in Madrid in order to forward the idea that each playwright wrote his work based on perceptions of performance conditions and audience expectations, as well as on cultural differences and distinct socio-political contexts. C. Rodríguez-Badendyck, 'The neglected alternative: Shakespeare's *Romeo and Juliet* and Lope de Vega's *Castelvines y Monteses*', *ib.*, 91–107, re-evaluates L.'s play, questioning the presumed superiority of Shakespeare's and arguing in favour of the former. In the choice of the comedic ending in L.'s version, R.-B. affirms, he avoided many of the problems that nettle Shakespeare's 'experiment in tragedy'. T. J. Kirschner, 'The mob in Shakespeare and Lope de Vega', *ib.*, 140–51, points out that while the Bard portrays his mobs as a fickle and foul-smelling rabble, the *monstruo de la naturaleza* depicts his as a purposeful, consistent, political force to be reckoned with. K lists thirteen plays by L. wherein appear 'the baiting crowd'. A. Carreño, 'Las "causas que se silencian": *El castigo sin venganza* de Lope de Vega', *BC*, 43:5–19, states that L.'s play is an attack on J. Pellicer and a comment on the newer theatrical modes. L.'s desire to have the play printed so as to be read, C. takes up at some length in this interesting study that contains many useful footnotes. In 'La "sin venganza" como violencia: "El castigo sin venganza" de Lope de Vega', *HR*, 59:379–400, C. continues his study of L.'s play in a whirling, fascinating piece that investigates the complex system of symmetries, parallelisms, ambiguities, and inversions in this tragedy of 'ritual violence'. He studies the images, actions, themes, and staging as well. W. R. Blue, 'The politics of Lope's *Fuente Ovejuna*', *ib.*, 295–315, contextualizes this play within the period in which it was written, the middle of Philip III's reign, looking at the differing views of power and its uses expressed by the play's major characters. He studies the torture scene in light of Foucault's *Discipline and Punish* offering thus a different perspective on that central action. He shows that the play depicts a monarchial, socio-political model drawn from an idealized, fictionalized paradigm of the Catholic Monarchs against which L.'s contemporary audiences may measure the system in which they live.

C. D. Martínez, 'Alejandro y Diógenes: inversión e ironía en *El villano en su rincón* de Lope de Vega', *BC*, 43:21–30, reads the play through an inversion of the Alexander/Diogenes story and in reference to certain *bodegón* paintings as the monarch's correction of Juan Labrador's errors. Christian Andrés, 'Grandes mitos clásicos y utilización dramática en el teatro de Lope de Vega', *ib.*, 31–49, points out L.'s use of the myth of Icharus, Phaeton, Pygmalion, and Narcissus. E. J. Rodríguez Baltanás, 'Amor, honor y poder: tres valores renacentistas en el teatro trágico de Lope de Vega', *ib.*, 51–69, says that tragedy flourished in the Renaissance because it reflected the collision between decadent feudal values and emerging new class values. R.B. then shows how love, honour, and power function in L.'s 'egalitarian' plays. C. Larson, 'Lope de Vega and Elena Garro: the doubling of *La dama boba*', *His(US)*, 74:15–25, compares and contrasts the two plays, while highlighting the role of meta-drama in both. E. H. Friedman, 'Resisting theory: rhetoric and reason in Lope de Vega's *Arte nuevo*', *Neophilologus*, 75:86–93, examines L.'s rhetorical strategies in his defense of his own audience-sensitive writing practices addressed to an 'academic' group. The *Arte nuevo*, F. sees as an 'antitheoretical statement which documents his [Lope's] knowledge of theory'.

5. TIRSO DE MOLINA

J. A. Parr, 'Introducción a *El burlador de Sevilla y convidado de piedra*', 127–58, in *Confrontaciones calladas: el crítico frente al clásico*, Madrid, Editorial Orígenes, 1990, 190 pp., discusses characters, metaphors, symbols, structure, eroticism, genre, critical attitudes, and authorship, among other topics. In 'Erotismo y alimentación en *El burlador de Sevilla*: el mundo al revés', *Edad de Oro*, 9, 231–39, Parr writes about latent homosexuality, phallic images, appetite, sexual and eating images, and the transformation of the erotic into the scatological. M. D. Stroud, '"¿Y sois hombre o sois mujer?": sex and gender in Tirso's *Don Gil de las calzas verdes*', Stoll, *Women*, 67–82, sees the play as a working through of sexual roles, a passage from the Imaginary to the Symbolic. S. finds it surprising that characters cannot recognize that Gil is really Juana dressed as a man. This inability, he attributes, in part, to 'the fluid nature of pre-Symbolic sexual identity in general', making the play an anticipatory allegory of Lacan's structuralist ideas, which, in and of itself is an interesting reading, but it would be helpful at times to consider the work as also representative of its genre and remember that a fundamental dramatic convention in *comedia* is that nearly any disguise is, you should excuse the term, impenetrable. H. W. Sullivan, 'The incest motif in Tirsian drama: a Lacanian view',

Fothergill-Payne, *Drama*, 180–92, states that in T.'s plays desire frequently triumphs over law, as when a *dama* in man's clothing gets her man despite the social rules she breaks in the process. By pushing against *the* arbitrary law — incest prohibition — T. exerts subversive pressure against authority (Name of the Father) and thereby affects his audience powerfully by displaying, at the stage's remove, the Oedipal relationships. S. then proposes a Lacanian theory of the development (or lack of same) of comic and tragic genres. He says that for comedy and tragedy to flourish, 'a definite fountainhead of law in the spectator community is indispensable', therefore comedy and tragedy flourish under Phillip II and Elizabeth I, but not in France until Richelieu's ascendancy. J. V. Ricapito, 'A possible source of an episode in the life and loves of Tirso de Molina's Don Juan Tenorio: Bandello's XIV *novella* and Don Juan Tenorio's invasion of the wedding of Aminta and Batricio', *Estudios Ruiz-Fornells*, 530–38, the title is self explanatory. E. Canonica de Rochemonteix, 'Tirso contra Lope: imitación irónica de *La portuguesa y dicha del forastero* en *El amor médico*', *RLit*, 52:539–43, compares the two plays in terms of borrowings, rewriting, and attitude. C.R. details the parallelisms between L.'s earlier and T.'s later plays offering as well comments and analysis of *El vergonzoso en palacio* and ends with an interesting commentary on T.'s play as showing his growing disaffection for Lope. Gordon Minter publishes his *Tirso de Molina: Don Gil of the green breeches (Don Gil de las calzas verdes)*, Warminster, Aris and Phillips, viii + 311 pp., a facing-side translation of T.'s play with copious notes and a 47 page introduction.

6. OTHER WRITERS

ANA CARO. T. S. Soufas, 'Ana Caro's re-evaluation of the *mujer varonil* and her theatrics in *Valor, agravio y mujer*', Stoll, *Women*, 85–106, states that Caro uses role-playing to show 'a more just pattern for men and women in the patriarchal society in which she herself must live and write'. The play's protagonist, S. says, attempts to improve the system meting out justice intelligently, not violently, according to the characters' degree of guilt, but the point to which the new model the protagonist offers or the new values she stands for may take root in such a society is left questionable at the play's conclusion.

ENRÍQUEZ GOMEZ/FERNANDO DE ZARATE. M. Harris, 'A *marrano* in Montezuma's court: an oblique reading of *La conquista de México* by "Fernando de Zárate"', *BC*, 43:147–61, views the play as a captious look at Christian imperialism, more sympathetic to the *marrano* predicament than earlier believed. P. G. Martínez Domene and M. A. Pérez Sánchez add ninety entries on this writer in 'Addenda a Simón

Díaz: *Bibliografía de la literatura hispánica*: Antonio Enríquez Gómez', *LetD*, 20:65–80.

LUIS DE GONGORA. María Cristina Quintero, *Poetry as Play: gongorismo and the comedia*, Amsterdam, John Benjamins, PURML, xviii + 260 pp., studies *comedia* and *culto* poetry as exemplified by Góngora, relations between poetic discourse and dramatic convention, relations between Lope and Góngora, and the latter's influence on Calderón. In addition there is a detailed, forty-seven page analysis of *Las firmezas de Isabela* followed by a briefer treatment of the unfinished *El doctor Carlino*. These two analyses form the heart of the study and strive to establish G. as a force in the development of, and debate about, *comedia*. The analyses merit attention.

MIRA DE AMESCUA. A. R. Williamson, 'Sexual inversion: carnival and *la mujer varonil* in *La Fénix de Salamanca* and *La tercera de sí misma*', Stoll, *Women*, 259–71, situates the *mujer varonil* in a Bakhtinian carnival context to show up society's flaws. The two protagonists make fun of the love at first sight and unknown lover/beloved conventions. A. de la Granja, 'Sobre una comedia de Mira de Amescua vendida en 1603', *RILCE*, 7:193–202, offers an overview of the state of textual work on Mira and then turns his attention to the 'lost' *La bella poeta* which he subsequently identifies under its other title as *La hermosura de Fénix*, considered hitherto as an anonymous work. A. Biedma, 'El escenario y la escena en "El caballero sin nombre"', *ib.*, 203–15, takes us *cuadro* by *cuadro* through Mira's play signalling its theatrical force and its potential reception. A. Serrano, 'El espacio escénico en "La próspera fortuna de don Bernardo de Cabrera"', *ib.*, 217–36, focuses on the theatrical rejecting what he terms the 'literary'. He shows how both horizontal and vertical space could have been used on the *corral* stage and how and why Mira moved from exterior to interior spaces in this play. M. García Godoy, 'La lógica de las apariencias: duelo ficticio en "La adúltera virtuosa"', *ib.*, 237–48, examines the duel, its protocol and its relation to the honour question in the cited palace play. E. Hernández González, 'La naturaleza en "El palacio confuso"', *ib.*, 249–58, offers little more than a list of animals, flowers, plants, and stones he finds in the play. A. López Muñoz, 'Del disfraz y otras mañas en "El amparo de los hombres"', *ib.*, 259–66, presents the play as complying with the propagandistic notions established by, and attributed to the *comedia* by Maravall, and thus in this play, 'la solución de Mira es trasponer la lucha de clases a la lucha religiosa, refugiándose en lo sobrenatural'. C. Argente del Castillo, 'La confusión como apariencia fantástica', *ib.*, 267–79, believes that confusion is more than an effect achieved through complicated action and references to labyrinths, rather, behind the confusion there is a 'lógica profunda de la existencia, la confusión es solo una apariencia que se resolverá tras la intervención de un poder superior que devolverá cada personaje a su propio nivel' and is thus part of dominant 'baroque ideology'. N. Gómez López, 'La mujer en la obra "Examinarse de Rey"', *ib.*, 281–90, offers a brief overview of the aristocratic woman who not only participates in political questions but discovers truth in love as she chooses her future husband. Mira thereby highlights the dignity and equality of women. R. Morales Raya, 'Algunas fuentes y recursos dramáticos de "Las lises de Francia" de Antonio Mira de Amescua', *ib.*, 291–310, mentions two possible sources and shows the function of disguise, language play, echo, misunderstanding, *equívoco*, and stage technique in this play. M. Gallego Roca studies '"La rueda de la fortuna" de Mira de Amescua y la polémica sobre el "Heraclio" español', *ib.*, 311–24. Finally, I. Arellano, 'El teatro de Mira de Amescua, de la penúmbra a la luz', *ib.*, 177–92, offers a summary of the articles contained in this monographic issue, along with his personal intuitions of other directions the studies and the authors could, or should, have taken. He along with Agustín de la Granja, *ib.*, 383–93, cap this collection of studies with a most useful bibliography on Mira, 'Bibliografía esencial de estudios sobre el teatro de Mira de Amescua'.

SOR JUANA INÉS DE LA CRUZ. C. Wilkins, 'Subversion through comedy?: two plays by Sor Juana Inés de la Cruz and María de Zayas', Stoll, *Women*, 107–20, begins with the idea that authorial perspective depends on the author's gender and that comedy in the hands of the authors studied here is socially, politically, and literarily subversive. W. looks at *Los empeños de una casa* and *Traición en la amistad*.

VELEZ DE GUEVARA. R. Lundclius, 'Paradox and role reversal in *La serrana de la Vera*' in Stoll, *Women*, 220–44, finds V. used the *mujer varonil* in about one-fourth of his plays and that in this play, interpolates the ballad figure into the socio-psychological context of Golden Age Spain. L. concludes that Gila was too violent to be integrated into 'normal' society so, after expressions of compassion by others, receives merited punishment, and thus L. sees the play, in the final instance, as conformist.

LITERATURE 1700–1823

POSTPONED

LITERATURE, 1823–1898

By CATHERINE DAVIES, *Lecturer in Spanish, Queen Mary and Westfield College, University of London*

1. GENERAL

The indefatigable María Carmen Simón Palmer continues to rescue 19th-c. women writers from anonymity, hopefully providing the groundwork for future critical studies, in *Escritoras españolas del siglo XIX: manual bio-bibliográfico*, ed. María Carmen Simón Palmer, M, Castalia, 864 pp., and Id., 'Mil escritoras españolas del siglo XIX', *Crítica y ficción literaria: mujeres españolas contemporáneas*, ed. Aurora López and M. Angeles Pastor, Granada U.P., 1989, 39–60. In the essay she is able to share some important generalizations on the social status and material conditions of these authors, having studied one thousand of them. *Catálogo colectivo del patrimonio bibliográfico español. Impresos del siglo XIX. Vol. 4: Indices*, M, Biblioteca Nacional, 1990, 400 pp., and María P. Celma, *Literatura y periodismo en las revistas de fin de siglo. Estudios e índices (1888–1907)*, M, Júcar, 896 pp., are further impressive volumes. J. M. González-Herrán, '*Un drama nuevo* en San Petersburgo, en 1895', *RoQ*, 38:75–83, looks to Pavlovsky (see PÉREZ GALDÓS) for information on Russian translations of Tamayo y Baus. C. Menéndez Onrubia, 'El teatro clásico durante la Restauración y la Regencia (1875–1900)', *CTC*, 5, 1990:187–207, and M. J. Sánchez de León, 'El teatro español del Siglo de Oro y la preceptiva poética del siglo XIX', *ib.*, 77–98, engage with a theme which has become popular of late (see BRETON DE LOS HERREROS and PEREZ GALDOS). S. García Castañeda, '*La Tertulia* (1876–77), la *Revista Cantabro-Asturiana* (1877) y su aportación a las letras de Cantabria', *BBMP*, 66, 1990:295–341, gives a complete list of the contributors of these two important journals and focuses on the work of Menéndez Pelayo, Pereda, Gumersindo Laverde, and Amós de Escalante. *Teatro inédito gaditano del siglo XIX. Cinco sainetes*, ed. Rosario Martínez, M, Silex, 1990, 119 pp. M. de los Reyes Peña, 'El teatro mecánico de la Plaza de la Gavidia (Sevilla, 1859), *Homenaje Gallego Morell*, III, 109–25, gives all manner of details (from measurements to programmes) on this theatre brought from the Netherlands. I. Castro, *'Presencia de Heine en las imitaciones eruditas del cantar popular', *Epos*, 6, 1990:243–61.

2. ROMANTICISM

A. López-Casanova, *La poesía romántica*, M, Anaya, 96 pp., is for students but is visually interesting as it includes several useful reproductions of contemporary paintings and sketches. B. Dendle,

'Valentín de Llanos Gutiérrez's *Don Esteban* (1825): An anticlerical novel', *Estudios Ruiz-Fornells*, 142–48. Eduardo Iáñez, **El siglo XIX: literatura romántica*, B, Tesys Bosch, 235 pp. José García Templado, *El teatro romántico*, M, Anaya, 96 pp., is glossy. G. Ribbans, '*Renaixença/ Rexurdimento*: lírica catalana, lírica gallega', *Actas* (Brown), 35–58, gives a thoughtful comparative overview of the poetry of the two movements. J. Varela, 'The image of the people in Spanish Liberalism, 1808–1848', *IS*, 18, 1989: 1–24, looks at the political manipulation of the term 'pueblo' in an interesting survey of the press, referring briefly to the work of writers such as Galiano, Mora, Espronceda, and Ramón de la Sagra. M. Palenque, 'El romanticismo en Sevilla: *El nuevo paradiso* (1839)', *BHS*, 68:455–62, reviews the twelve numbers of this newspaper and shows how Sevilla, despite its allegiance to Neoclassicism, was as receptive to Romanticism as the rest of the country. D. Martínez Torrón, 'Algunas cartas inéditas de don Alberto Lista, y una felicitación de la Academia del Mirto', *Homenaje Gallego-Morell*, II, 375–87, publishes letters to Juan Gualberto González Bravo and other documents dated between 1829 and 1846. A. Salvador, 'Granada y su literatura durante la primera mitad del siglo XIX', *ib.*, III, 195–205, is a general overview.

3. REALISM

German Gullón, *La novela del XIX. Estudio sobre su evolución formal*, Amsterdam–Atlanta, Rodopi, 1990, 135 pp., covers the following key novels in the development of the genre from Romantic idealism to realism: *El caballero de las botas azules, El corte de Carlos IV, Doña Perfecta, La Regenta, Los Pazos de Ulloa*, and *Tristana*. Rafael Rodríguez Marín, *Realismo y naturalismo: la novela del siglo XIX*, M, Anaya, 96 pp. B. Wietelmann Bauer, 'Innovación y apertura: la novela realista del siglo XIX ante el problema del desenlace', *HR*, 59:187–203, considers narrative closure in a wide selection of novels and concludes that narrative experimentation, such as enigmatic endings, was very much part of the realist aesthetic. Similarly, Nicholas G. Round, *On Reasoning and Realism: Three Easy Pieces*, Manchester, Department of Spanish and Portuguese, 66 pp., in three keenly-argued essays ('Predictable fictions: reflections on Galdós and some others', 'Metacriticism and hypercriticism', and 'Overstepping the mark: *Rayuela* and *Lo prohibido*') reassesses and reinstates realism in the light of contemporary theoretical and anti-realist trends. Authors covered also include Borges and Goytisolo.

4. INDIVIDUAL WRITERS

ALARCÓN. *Insula*, 535, is a special issue commemorating the centenary of A.'s death and includes the following: R. de la Fuente

Ballesteros, 'Pedro Antonio de Alarcón, el "impresionable"' (1–2, 31), a general survey of life, works, and critical editions; L. Bonet, 'El "cuarteto ártico" de Pedro A. de Alarcón: hielo, nieve, fuego y ceniza' (11–13), an intriguing piece which studies imagery relating to frozen landscapes in four early texts and goes on to consider the symbolic bipolarity between dramatic paralysis and emotional fervour as a part of A.'s visionary world; M. D. Royo Latorre, 'Alarcón en sus relatos: el problema de la originalidad creadora' (13–15), looks at the influence of Poe on the early A., but concludes that oral traditions were as important; F. Gutiérrez Flórez, 'El inmarcesible romanticismo de Alarcón: *El final de Norma*' (15–16), searches for Romantic features in the novel; L. F. Cifuentes, 'Los viajes de Alarcón: "Shakespeare tiene la culpa . . ."' (16–17), surveys A.'s four travel books and shows how his views of the other were conservative and shortsighted; J. R. González García, 'Viajes y literatura. *La Alpujarra*, de Pedro Antonio de Alarcón' (18), examines the text as a fine example of heteroglossia; J. M. Martínez Cachero, 'Los *Escándalos* de Pedro Antonio de Alarcón' (19–20), considers the moral question; I. J. López, 'Alarcón y la "Guerra del Silencio": en torno a la recepción crítica del *Capitán veneno*' (20–21), reminds us how Alas urged A. to carry on writing despite the hostile reception of his adventure story and the fact that it compared unfavourably with Galdós's *La desheredada*, published only a few months previously; J. L. Calvo Carilla, '*La Pródiga*: entre Romanticismo y fin de siglo' (22), suggests A.'s naturalism was romantic; G. Gullón, 'La novela de Alarcón y el envés de la narrativa decimonónica' (31–32), is arguably the most substantial contribution. A case is made for appreciating A.'s view of the world (based on imagination, faith, and tradition) as the reverse side of the more well-known factual and rational view expressed by Galdós and Alas, and this is borne out by comparing *La Pródiga* (1882) with *La desheredada* (1881); the Pródiga's romantic imagination is her saving grace, while Isidoras Rufete's is her perdition. G. concludes that whereas Galdós, Alas, and Pardo Bazán are 'classical' realists preferring cognitive truth, Alarcón, Pereda, Valera, Coloma, Caballero, and Castro are 'castizo' authors preferring poetic truth. *El sombrero de tres picos*, ed. Arcadio López-Casanova, M, Cátedra, 173 pp., has a lengthy introduction and an excellent bibliography. *El sombrero de tres picos. El capitán veneno*, ed. Jesús Rubio Jiménez, M, Espasa Calpe, 231 pp. E. Cobo, 'Pedro Antonio de Alarcón en su centenario', *CHA*, 498:115–22, surveys life and works. J. Estruch Tobella, 'Revisión de Alarcón', *ib.*, 123–27, argues that A. has been hard done by because of his reactionary views. A. Soria, 'El *Diario de un testigo del la guerra de Africa* de Pedro Antonio Alarcón. Notas de lectura', *Homenaje Gallego Morell*, III, 251–63, discusses various approaches to the text and opts for a literary commentary. A. Sobejano-Morán, 'Recursos narrativos en *El sombrero de tres picos*', *Estudios Ruiz-Fornells*, 607–12.

ALAS. *'Malevolent insemination' and other essays on Clarín*, ed. Noel M. Valis, Michigan Romance Studies, X, Ann Arbor: Department of Romance Studies, University of Michigan, 1990, 220 pp., is an important collection of essays, although several have appeared previously (some in Spanish). The most illuminating contributions are, arguably: J. Mandrell, 'Malevolent insemination: *Don Juan Tenorio* in *La Regenta*' (1–28), where Freud and Lacan help situate Zorrilla's play as the explicit paradigmatic articulation of phallic desire, countered by the feminine 'jouissance' of Santa Teresa, and D. F. Urey, 'Writing Ana in Clarín's *La Regenta*' (29–45), which explores how both Ana, the product of her own discourse, and the novel slip the grasp of critical language; J. Rutherford published a previous version of 'On translating *La Regenta*: Sameness and Otherness' (47–66) in 1988 (see *YWMLS*, 51:332); H. S. Turner, 'From the verbal to the visual in *La Regenta*' (67–86), is an intelligent study of two story-telling techniques; S. Sieburth, 'Kiss and tell: the toad in *La Regenta*' (87–100), links toads, lips, kisses, language, and sex; E. D. Sánchez, 'Beyond the realist paradigm: subversive stratagems in *La Regenta* and *Madame Bovary*' (101–16), shows how both novels undermine their own realism; N. M. Valis, 'The perfect copy: Clarín's *Su único hijo* and the Flaubertian connection' (117–40), as the author points out, appeared in 1989 (see *YWMLS*, 51:334); F. Durand, 'Structure and the drama of role-playing in *La Regenta*' (141–54), considers the influence of theatre and fiction in Vetustan life; A. M. Gullón, 'Naming in Chapter XI of *La Regenta*' (155–66), studies forms of address and metaphors associated with de Pas; J. M. González Herrán, 'The structure and meaning of *Cuervo*' (167–82), C. Richmond, '*Juan Ruiz*, or Leopoldo Alas's literary apprenticeship' (183–92), D. M. Rogers, 'Language, image and the thought process in Clarín's *Pipá*' (193–204), and L. Rivkin, 'Clarín's musical ideal' (205–20), were all published in 1987 (see *YWMLS*, 51:334). *Su único hijo*, ed. Carolyn Richmond, M, Nueva Austral, 1990, 383 pp., and *Su único hijo*, ed. J. M. Martínez Cachero, M, Taurus, 391 pp., are good editions. S. Miller, 'Intertexts, contexts and the Clarinian canon: the place of 'El cura de Vericueto', *BHS*, 68:463–77, discusses C.'s literary tastes in the context of the *Cuentos morales*, finding it inconceivable (and rightly so) that C. should prefer Campoamor to Galdós; he suggests this might account for the unpopularity of the story in question. *Ensayos y revistas*, prol. A. Vilanova, B, Lumen, 336 pp. J. van Luxemburg, '*La Regenta*. Rhetoric and religion', *HisJ*, 11, 1990:71–89, argues that the ambiguous representation of bishop

Fortunato makes any judgement regarding A.'s religious views decidedly risky. M. Vidal Tibbits, 'El aislamiento del individuo en *Cuentos morales* de Clarín', *Estudios Ruiz-Fornells*, 688–93. J. Labanyi, 'Mysticism and hysteria in *La Regenta*: the problem of female identity', Condé, *Readings*, 37–46, is an excellent discussion of Ana as 'mysterical'. Using Irigaray and Cixous on Freud, the author argues that whether Ana breaks through the restraints of patriarchal discourse or simply reflects back her lack of boundaries, in the final instance her loss of self is her self. G. Sobejano, 'La inspiración de Ana Ozores', *AG*, 21, 1986 (1991):223–30, studies Ana as poet. Darío Villanueva, *El comentario de textos narrativos: La novela*, M, Júcar, 1989, 206 pp., includes a piece on *La Regenta*. A. Sotelo Vázquez, 'Clarín en torno a *Realidad* (1889)', *RHM*, 44:35–47, is a rehash of a previous article published in *LeD* (see *YWMLS*, 52). M. Vidal Tibbits, 'Ecos de las teorias de Emile Zola en la crítica teatral de Leopoldo Alas y Joseph Yxart', *RCEH*, 15:334–42, is instructive.

BÉCQUER. A. E. P. del Campo, 'Bécquer y Martí: populizadores de lo popular', *RILCE*, 7:9–24, goes over old ground, but reminds us how crucial the revival of popular poetry in the 1860s was for both poets. Antonio Carrillo Alonso, **Gustavo Adolfo Bécquer y los cantares de Andalucía*, M, Fundación Univ. Esp., 1990, 128 pp. G. A. Bécquer and V. Bécquer, **Obra Completa en el Moncayo y Veruela*, 3 vols, ed. M. Monsegur, Zaragoza, Diputación de Zaragoza, 423 pp. M. García Viño, *El esoterismo de Bécquer: su vida oculta*, Sevilla, Rodríguez Castillejo, 118 pp., is useful. *Rimas*, ed. Russell P. Sebold, M, Espasa Calpe, 371 pp. J. Estruch Tobella, 'El compromiso político de Bécquer', *CHA*, 496:101–08, examines B.'s contribution to five issues of González Bravo's *Los Tiempos* and recalls B.'s right-wing connections and opinions, despite posthumous portrayals of naïve woollymindedness. Eleazar Huerta, **El simbolismo de la mano en Bécquer*, Albacete, Diputación Provincial, 1990, 275 pp. A. F. Baker, 'Self-realization in the *Leyendas* of Gustavo Adolfo Bécquer', *RHM*, 44:191–206, divides the *Leyendas* into three groups according to the psychological development of the protagonists and engages in a Jungian analysis, and A. E. P. del Campo, 'Bécquer y Martí: poetas de la claridad/poetas de la vaguedad', *ib.*, 18–28, continues his comparison of these two poets (see above), this time focusing on dream/sleep and visions.

BRETÓN DE LOS HERREROS. G. A. Davies, 'The country cousin at Court. A study of Antonio de Mendoza's *Cada loco con su tema* and Manuel Bretón de los Herreros' *El pelo de la dehesa*', Rees, *Drama*, 43–60, believes B.'s play may have been inspired by M.'s (1630), the autograph manuscript of which was held in the Biblioteca Nacional when B. was there as director. The comparison is straightforward, but somewhat self-defeating; the author, while acknowledging resemblances, concludes that both plays are quite different. E. Caldera, 'Bretón o la negación del modelo', *CTC*, 5, 1990:141–53.

CAMPOAMOR. Kurt Spang, *"Colón" de Ramón de Campoamor. "Historia" e historia*, Kassel, Reichenberger, 1990, 36 pp.

CASTRO. *Rosalía de Castro: documentación biográfica y bibliografía crítica (1837–1988)*, 2 vols, ed. A. López and A. Pociña, La Coruña, Fundación P. Barrie de la Maza, 1680 pp., is exhaustive and commendable. *Follas Novas*, ed. M. Mayoral and B. Roig, Vigo, Edicions Xerais, 1990, 376 pp. *Crítica y ficción literaria: mujeres españolas contemporáneas*, ed. Aurora López and M. Angeles Pastor, Granada U.P., 1989, 146 pp., includes: A. Pociña, 'La crítica feminista ante la persona y la obra de Rosalía de Castro' (61–86), which attempts to explain the marked growth in Rosalian criticism in recent decades and provides a bibliography of (loosely) feminist critical works. *Flavio*, ed. Angel Abuin, La Coruña, Patronata Rosalía de Castro, 301 pp., is much needed. A. Pociña, A. López, 'Raros bibliográficos sobre Rosalía', *Homenaje Gallego Morell*, III, 57–75, brings to light 14 items including encyclopaedia entries and pieces from the review *Nós*. Carmen Blanco, *Literatura galega da muller*, Vigo, Edicións Xerais, 368 pp., has two sections dealing with feminist aspects of R.'s work and the model she set for 20th-c. female authors in Galicia. A. Carreño, 'El discurso de la tradición como diferencia: Rosalía de Castro en José Angel Valente', *ALEC*, 16:15–35, considers R. as the founder of modern Galician lyric poetry, the otherness of which is nevertheless a continuation of the traditional Galician canon. *Actas* (Brown), is an important volume, despite the annoying errata. It includes: C. Davies, '*El caballero de las botas azules*: narrative context and intertextual structure' (21–33), which discusses the novel as an 'illisible' parody consisting in incoherently conjoined subtexts; D. Conchado, '"O que perdéu Adán": ausencia y otredad en "As viudas dos vivos e as viudas dos mortos"' (177–86), a shrewd analysis of women, emigration, absence and lack; J. Coutreau, 'Rosalía's Sombra and the Modernists' (187–95), where the subject/object binary is deconstructed in the poem 'Negra sombra' and in other poems by Jiménez, Machado, and Pessoa; A. G. Loureiro, 'Sombra y (des)velos de Rosalía' (197–205), is a discerning analysis of prosopopeia in 'Dicen que no hablan las plantas' and 'Negra sombra'; M. Lafollette Miller, 'Mythical conceptualization of Galicia in Murguía and Pardo Bazán: aspects of Rosalian context' (267–76), is extremely interesting on the interrelated construction of myths of nationhood and gender. Murguía's angelic 'feminine myth' is contrasted to Pardo Bazán's more sexual 'feminine myth' as applied to the discursive construction of Galician identity and to Rosalía as its incarnation; M.

Albert Robato, 'Rosalía de Castro y Emilia Pardo Bazán: afinidades y contrastes' (295–312), is a comparative biographical survey. M. Lafollette Miller, *'Rosalía de Castro and her context', *Ensayos de literatura europea e hispanoamericana*, ed. Felix Menchacatorre, San Sebastián, Universidad del País Vasco, 1990, 605 pp., 325–29.
CORONADO. *Poesías*, ed. R. Navas Ruiz, M, Castalia, 740 pp.
CURROS ENRÍQUEZ. R. A. Cardwell, 'A significación de *Aires da miña terra* no contexto da literatura española finisecular', *Boletín Galego de Literatura*, 3, 1990:7–18, brings due attention to the work of this underrated poet by situating the socially radical *Aires* (1880) in its literary context. F. M. Mariño, 'Sobre la influencia de "The Raven" de Poe en el "Nouturnio" de Curros Enríquez', *Castilla*, 15, 1990:121–34, is competent but fails to come to a conclusion.
ESCOSURA. A. M. Freire López, 'Una carta inédita de Patricio de la Escosura y unas elecciones en la Real Academia', *Castilla*, 15, 1990:85–88, shows how E. wanted Romero Ortiz to fill the vacancy rather than Arnao.
ESPRONCEDA. *The student of Salamanca*, bilingual edition, translated by C. K. Davis and introd. by R. A. Cardwell, Warminster, Aris and Phillips, 152 pp., is a parallel text whose prefatory material includes a thorough introduction to Espronceda and his work. The annotated, rhyming translation manages to keep to metrical limitations and reads well, despite such formal complexity. J. Mandrell, 'The literary sublime in Spain: Meléndez Valdés and Espronceda', *MLN*, 106:294–313, is a perceptive discussion of concepts of sublimity (transcendence through elevated language and reader entrancement) applied to, *inter alia*, *El estudiante de Salamanca*. *Antología poética*, ed. Rubén Benítez, M, Taurus, 292 pp. has a substantial introduction and bibliography.
ESTÉBANEZ CALDERÓN. L. R. Scarano, 'La voluntad ficcional en *Escenas andaluzas* de Estébanez Calderón', *BBMP*, 66, 1990:139–54, reappraises this 1846 text as art rather than journalism by looking at the use of poetic language, imagery, character creation, intertextuality, and narrative techniques.
FERNÁN CABALLERO. K. Sabir, 'La novelistica de Fernán Caballero en Polonia en el siglo XIX', *AH*, 224, 1990:87–97.
GARCÍA ESCOBAR. Pedro Ojeda Escobar, *Ventura García Escobar (1817–1859). Biografía y obra dramática*, Valladolid, Ed. Provincial, 1990, 163 pp.
GIL Y CARRASCO. M. O'Byrne Curtis, 'La doncella de Arganza; la configuración de la mujer en *El señor de Bembibre*', *Castilla*, 15, 1990:149–59, is a fine feminist analysis (using N. Auerbach, S. Gilbert, and S. Gubar) of the protagonist, doña Beatriz, who is shown to subvert the masculinist dichotomy angel/monster.

GRIMALDI. D. T. Gies, 'Notas sobre Grimaldi y el "furor de refundir" en Madrid (1820–1833)', *CTC*, 5, 1990:111–24.

LARRA. J. Escobar, 'El teatro del Siglo de Oro en la controversia ideológica entre españoles castizos y críticos. Larra frente a Durán', *CTC*, 5, 1990:155–70. G. C. Martín, 'Larra, Borrego y Mendizábal: liberales o pícaros', *Estudios Ruiz-Fornells*, 403–09.

MENÉNDEZ PELAYO. A. H. Clarke and Biblioteca de Menéndez y Pelayo, 'Cartas de Pereda a Laverde', *BBMP*, 67:157–270, publishes and annotates 80 letters dated between 1864 and 1890. C. González Echegaray, 'Un texto autógrafo de las poesías amorosas de Menéndez Pelayo', *ib.*, 271–85, compares the original manuscripts with later published versions. M. de Riquer, 'Menéndez Pelayo de Santander a Barcelona', *ib.*, 389–98, provides anecdotes of the young M.P. (such as when, aged sixteen, he recited the *Iliad* in Greek backwards as a pastime) and his University studies.

PALACIOS VALDÉS. **La espuma. Cancionero tradicional*, ed. G. Gómez-Ferrer Morant, M, Castalia, 1990, 519 pp. *La aldea perdida*, ed. A. Ruiz de la Peña, M, 354 pp. G. Paolini, 'Resonancia armónica del mundo mágico creadora del porvenir regeneracional en *La alegría del capitán Ribot*', *Estudios Ruiz-Fornells*, 479–85.

PARDO BAZÁN. *Cartas inéditas a Emilia Pardo Bazán (1878–1883)*, ed. Ana María Freire López, La Coruña, Fundación P. Barrie de la Maza, 178 pp., includes references to·over one hundred individuals. Ana Rosa Rodríguez Rodríguez, *La cuestión feminista en los ensayos de Emilia Pardo Bazán*, La Coruña, Castro, 211 pp., is useful. *La Quimera*, ed. Marina Mayoral, M, Cátedra, 584 pp., has a fine introduction. D. Henn, 'Issues and individuals: Pardo Bazán's *La piedra angular*', *Forum*, 27:358–69, makes some keen observations on P.B.'s views on capital punishment and the execution of Higinia Balaguer. The analysis of the novel concentrates on the complementary and paradoxical relationship between the dignified executioner and the undignified doctor. M. S. Vásquez, 'Class, gender and parody in Pardo Bazán's *La tribuna*', *Estudios Ruiz-Fornells*, 679–87. M. Mayoral, 'Cartas inéditas de Emilia Pardo Bazan a Narcís Oller', *Homenaje Gallego Morell*, II, 389–410, publishes, with a brief summary of contents, 15 (annotated) letters from P. B. to Oller written between 1883 and 1890. J. Drinkwater, 'Emilia Pardo Bazán: *Un viaje de novios* and romantic fiction', Condé, *Feminist Readings*, 63–76, is a cogent discussion of the romantic features of this novel which, the author suggests, should not be considered flaws but rather part of a deliberate parodic strategy. E. Llácer, 'Análisis microestructural de *Los Pazos de Ulloa*', *RoQ*, 38:431–36, is pithy. After exploring the mock-Gothic features of chapter 20, the author argues that the chapter encapsulates the main themes and techniques of the novel as a whole. *Actas* (Brown) includes: B. A. González, 'From Pardo Bazán to Valle-Inclán: the case of the "falso marqués"' (261–65), which sees the *hidalgos* (of Ulloa and Bradomín) as representations of falsity and lack of legitimation, reading from this a poetics of absence; R. J. Quirk, 'Folklore and regional beliefs in Emilia Pardo Bazán' (289–93), is slight; A. R. Rodríguez, 'Emilia Pardo Bazán y el folklore gallego' (313–18), focuses on the short fiction, sanctuaries, and gastronomy. M. J. Hemingway, 'Emilia Pardo Bazán, Luis Vidart, and other friends: eight unpublished letters and two cards', *AG*, 21, 1986 (1991):263–73, is erudition at its best, revealing, among other things, how P.B. supported the Galicians Jesús Muruáis and Aureliano J. Pereira. *AG*, 22, 1986 (1991), has three good articles on *La madre naturaleza*: R. El Saffar, 'Mother nature's nature' (91–102), a canny analysis of androgyny as represented by the inextricable couple, Perucho and Manolita; M. Bieder, 'The female voice: gender and genre in *La madre naturaleza*' (103–16), examining the erudite narrative voice and the appeal to common consensus, and D. F. Urey, 'Incest and interpretation in *Los pazos de Ulloa* and *La madre naturaleza*' (117–31), which is excellent on incest and uses Derrida and de Man. M. Tasende-Grabowski, 'Otra vez a vueltas con el naturalismo . . .' *His(US)*, 74:26–35, goes against the grain in considering P.B. a fully fledged naturalist who differs from Zola only in her narrative techniques. (See CASTRO).

PEREDA. *Jose María de Pereda: antología*, ed. P. Beltrán de Heredia, Santander, Fundación Marcelino Botín, 160 pp. *Textos de Jose María Pereda*, M, Incafo, 207 pp. *Pedro Sánchez*, ed. José Manuel González Herrán, M, Espasa-Calpe, 1990, 361 pp. L. Litvak, 'Geología y metafísica: las montañas en *Peñas arriba* de Pereda', *AG*, 22, 1986 (1991):231–43, reviews P.'s descriptions of nature and considers them a means by which he communicates key ideas of the period to the reader; nature itself is a hieroglyphic text. *Peñas arriba*, ed. Enrique Miralles, B, Planeta, 366 pp. *Obras completas*, ed. José María del Cossío, M, Aguilar, 2 vols.

PÉREZ GALDÓS. Much welcomed is the appearance of three long-awaited issues of *AG*; fortunately, the delay has not impaired the high standard of scholarship. *AG*, 21, 1986 (1991), 'Homenaje a Rodolfo Cardona', includes 21 articles on Galdós, the majority by leading specialists: W. T. Pattison, 'Los Galdós en Cuba: la primera generación' (15–32), is full of useful facts; B. J. Dendle, 'Galdós in context: the Republican years, 1907–1914' (33–43), explores G.'s political activities; S. Gilman, '*El caballero encantado*: revolution and dream' (45–51), confers with J. López-Morillas, 'Galdós y la historia: los últimos años' (53–61); V. A. Chamberlin, 'A Cuban's reply to Galdós: *El caballero encantado* y *La moza esquiva*' (63–67), studies briefly Fernando Ortiz's intriguing version of G.'s novel; J. Beverley,

'Confusio's (his)story: Galdós after Liberalism' (69–78); G. Ribbans, 'The *Restauración* in the novels and *Episodios* of Galdós' (79–93), surveys historical events rendered in fiction; P. A. Bly, 'Las idiosin-crasias humanas y la estrategia narrativa en *Zumalacarregui*' (95–106), points to G.'s intellectual honesty; D. F. Urey, 'From monuments to syllables: the journey to knowledge in *Zumalacarregui*' (107–14), is a clever study of the journey as metaphor of life and Fago's divided self; D. M. Rogers, '"La novela en la tranvía" and the poetics of movement in Galdosian narrative' (115–26), looks at an early (1871) prose text; T. R. Franz, '*Doña Perfecta* and *Il Barbiere di Siviglia*' (127–33), see the roots of the novel's melodrama in the opera; R. H. Russell, 'La voz narrativa en *La de Bringas*' (135–40), is brief on the voice of disillusion; R. D. Pope, 'CGoarltdaozsar: el Galdós interca-lado en Cortazar en *Rayuela*' (142–46), was published in 1987 (see *YWMLS*, 51:342) and deals with the same theme as D. A. Castillo, 'Reading over her shoulder: Galdós/Cortazar' (147–60); H. S. Turner, 'Patterns of deception in the Galdós novel' (161–77), covers authenticity, modes of narrative and value systems; A. A. Andreu, '*Miau*: la escritura del poder o el poder de la escritura' (179–85), considers Villaamil, because of his writing, an influential cog in the bureaucratic wheel; E. Rodgers, 'Cristal o diamantes? La verdad de la mentira en *Misericordia*' (187–94), points to the fulfilment of spiritual values in a material world; R. G. Sánchez, 'Galdós y el oficio teatral: apuntes sobre *La de San Quintín*' (195–203); M. Z. Hafter, 'Galdós the playwright parodied' (204–13), focuses on the three good-natured parodies of *La de San Quintín*, the two of *Electra* and that of *Mariucha*; J. Lowe, '*Misericordia*: Galdós's novel and Mañas's play' (215–22), compares the novel to Alfredo Mañas's 1972 play; L. M. Willem, 'Catálogo de los manuscritos de Galdós y de las galeradas de sus obras en la casa-museo Pérez Galdós' (247–49); S. de la Nuez, '*Marianela* y los hermanos Alvarez Quintero: Epistolario' (251–62), brings to light 13 letters.

AG, 22, 1987 (1991), 'Centenario *Fortunata y Jacinta*. La madre naturaleza', includes: M. López-Baralt, '*Fortunata y Jacinta* en ges-tación: de la versión Alpha a la versión Beta del manuscrito galdosiano' (11–24); V. A. Chamberlin, 'Juan Valera and Galdós's characterization of Juanito Santa Cruz' (22–31), believes the latter is modelled on Juanito Valera; T. R. Franz, 'Galdós the pharmacist: Drugs and the Samaniego pharmacy in *Fortunata y Jacinta*' (33–46), lists the 33 medicines in the novel and suggests possible interpre-tations of these findings; V. Fuentes, 'La dimensión mítico-simbólico de Fortunata' (47–52); J. H. Sinnigen, 'Sexo y clase social en *Fortunata y Jacinta*: opresión, represión, expresión' (53–70), draws on Chodorow and Showalter; G. Ribbans, 'Feijóo: policeman, inventor, egotist, failure?' (71–87), offers a fifth reading of Part III, Chapter 4. *AG*, 23, 1988 (1991) includes: A. Tsuchiya, 'History as language in the first series of the *Episodios nacionales*: the literary self-creation of Gabriel de Araceli' (11–25), which follows Araceli's apprenticeship as semiotician, culminating in his written memoirs; V. A. Chamberlin, '"Vamos a ver las fieras": Animal imagery and the protagonist in *La desheredada* and *Lo prohibido*' (27–33), contrasts the naturalistic animalization of the former novel to the parodic techniques of the latter; J. P. Brownlow, 'Modes of figuration in *Miau*' (35–45), studies in depth the three chapters preceding Villaamil's suicide as *mise en abyme*; N. Malaret, 'El bestiario de *Miau*' (47–55), covers further animal imagery; M. Weber, 'Pragmatic ploys and cognitive processes in *La incógnita*' (57–65), is a perceptive analysis of the relationship between narrator and narratee; W. M. Sherzer, 'Narrative play and social context in *Torquemada en la hoguera*' (67–72), deals with T. as *converso* and narrative structure; D. J. O'Connor, 'The recurrence of images in *Angel Guerra*' (73–82), discloses breasts and masks; J. M. González Herrán, 'Un nihilista ruso en la España de la Restauración: Isaac Pavlovsky y sus relaciones con Galdós, Oller, Pardo Bazán y Pereda' (83–105), is informative; P. Ortiz Armengol, 'Hacia un texto depurado de *Fortunata y Jacinta*' (109–16), presses for a critical edition of the novel and makes the first move by raising a number of queries after having briefly consulted the manuscript; U. Aszyk, 'La obra de Benito Pérez Galdós en Polonia' (117–18); M. Kochiwa, 'Los estudios de Galdós en Japón' (119–20); M. L. Boo, 'Galdós: periodismo y novela (*La desheredada*, *La incógnito* y tres artículos de *La Prensa* de Buenos Aires)' (123–31); B. J. Dendle, 'Galdós, La Jeunesse and Oscar Wilde: Enrique Gómez Carrillos's tribute to Galdós' (133–36), provides the background to G.C.'s 1914 article 'Galdós en Europa'.

Edward Baker, *Materiales para escribir Madrid. Literatura y espacio urbano de Moratín a Galdós*, M, Siglo XXI, 152 pp., deals with Larra, Mesonero Romanos, and Galdós (*La fontana de oro*) among others. Estrella Molina Gete, *Claves de "Fortunata y Jacinta" de Pérez Galdós*, M, Ciclo, 112 pp. P. A. Bly, 'Galdós, Golden Age Theatre and Krausism', *Varey Vol.*, 39–48, is a lucid and convincing essay which uses G.'s early articles (1865–71) on Golden Age theatre to suggest that G. was guided by 17th-c. ideas on literature, particularly those of Calderón, as a basis for his own novelistic development. These ideas, echoed in Krausism, involve not only cultural chauvinism but also the view that art should reflect the daily customs of ordinary people as well as their idealistic aspirations. The *comedia* also served G. as a reference point against which he could contrast the poverty of 19th-c. theatre. Id., 'Putting nature's bonds to artistic use: sibling relationships in the contemporary social novels (1876–1897) of Benito Pérez Galdós', *Connecticut Review*, 12, 1990:55–68. Id., *Pérez Galdós: Nazarín*, (CGST 54), 113 pp. Two new editions of *La fontana de oro* have appeared: *La fontana de oro*, introduced by Pedro Ortiz Armengol, M, Hernando, 1990, 778 pp., is a facsimile, and *La fontana de oro*, ed. Y. Arencibia, Las Palmas, Cabildo Insular Gran Canaria, 1990. *Episodios nacionales*, introduced by Juan Ignacio Ferreras, M, Hernando, 1990, 219 pp. *The Campaign of the Maestrazgo*, trans. by Lila W. Guzmán, Wakefield, Longwood Academic, 1990, xvi + 236 pp. *Ocho cuentos de Galdós*, ed. Oswaldo Izquierdo Dorta, Tenerife, Cabildo Insular de Gran Canaria, 1990, 265 pp. Sebastián de la Nuez, *Biblioteca y archivo de la Casa Museo Pérez Galdós*, Las Palmas, Cabildo Insular de Gran Canaria, 1990, 356 pp. L. Behiels, 'Estabilidad e inestabilidad de los nombres de personajes galdosianos', *Hommage à Claude Dumas. Histoire et Création*, ed. Jacqueline Covo, Lille, U.P., 1990, 29–35 and B. Journeau, 'Histoire et création dans *Narváez* de Pérez Galdos', *ib.*, 67–74. L. Behiels, '"Marginales recuperados": Vicente Halconero y Segismundo García Fajardo (Quinta serie de *Episodios nacionales* de B. Pérez Galdós)', in *Minorités et marginalités en Espagne et en Amerique latine au XIXe siècle*, ed. Claude Dumas, Lille, U.P., 1990, 21–32 and B. Journeau, 'Nazarín, dissonance et consonance avec l'esprit d'un temps', *ib.*, 47–59. E. Penas, 'La ironía galdosiana. Apuntes sobre *La incógnita* y *Realidad*', *Castilla*, 15, 1990:161–67, explores various levels of irony and discovers that the former is an ironic hypotext of the latter. A. Navarro González, 'Viaje a Italia de don Benito Pérez Galdós', *Homenaje Gallego Morell*, II, 483–90, is a brief commentary of *Viaje a Italia*.

Galdós' House of Fiction, ed. Anthony H. Clarke and Eamonn J. Rodgers with the assistance of David Mackenzie, Oxford, Dolphin, 219 pp., is a substantial volume containing ten contributions from the 1986 Birmingham Galdós Coloquium: J. Whiston, '"Ficción verosímil" and "realidad documentada"' in the Second Series of Galdós' *Episodios nacionales*' (1–13), studies the role of Salvador Monsalud who manages to break out of socio-historical restrictions thanks to his artist's imagination; M. Hemingway, 'Narrative ambiguity and situational ethics in *La de Bringas*' (15–27), deals with G.'s pragmatic view of moral issues, his undermining of the narrator's authority, and the moral confusion implicit in the apparent justification of Rosalía's behaviour; K. Austin, 'Madness and madmen in Galdós's early fiction and in *La desheredada*' (29–40), considers madness as a warning by G. to his readers on the folly of uncontrolled character flaws; B. Dendle, '*El audaz*: historia de un radical de antaño' (41–53), reassesses the novel as an affirmation of the Romantic hero; G. Ribbans, 'Social document or narrative discourse? Some comments on recent aspects of Galdós criticism' (55–83), arbitrates between Blanco Aguinaga and Gilman and proposes an eclectic approach to *Fortunata y Jacinta*; P. Bly, '*El caballero encantado*: Galdós' ironic review of "Regeneracionistas"' (85–97), discovers three levels of irony aimed at Costa in particular and possibly at G. himself; L. Condé, 'Feminist imagery in Galdós' (99–125), looks at wing, doll and angel imagery in narrative and theatre from *Gloria* onwards; E. Rodgers, 'The unfinished anagorisis; the illness and death of José María Bueno de Guzmán in Galdós' *Lo prohibido*' (127–41), argues that José María's 'confesión' is confused and not self-enlightening; N. G. Round, 'The fictional plenitude of *Angel Guerra*' (143–67), considers the novel's flaws and suggests how the text itself overcomes them by appealing to its reader's value systems; A. Percival, 'Recent currents in Galdós studies' (169–219), covers 1975 to 1984, is thorough and includes a 33 pp. bibliography. P. puzzles over the incomprehensible indifference in Spain towards Galdós and reproaches the Spanish for such neglect.

　　La conjuración de las palabras. Cuentos de Galdós: antología, selection G. Gullón, B, Edhasa, 240 pp. Translations of G.'s work are always good news. Karen O. Austin has published two this year: *Angel Guerra*, Lewiston, Mellen Press, 744 pp., and *The Unknown/La incógnita*, Lewiston, Mellen Press, 252 pp. C. Alonso, *Galdós y los novelistas del 98*, Las Palmas, Cabildo Insular Gran Canaria, 1990, 196 pp. C. Ballester, *Grandes personajes: B. Pérez Galdós*, B, Labor, 1990, 238 pp. F. Carenas, *'La desalienación esquemocrática en *Nazarín*', *Iris*, 1990:15–24. C. M. Jaffe, *'Mothers and orphans in *La desheredada*', *Confluencia*, 5, 1990:27–38. J. M. Naharro-Calderón, 'Galdós y Baroja: caminos inter-textuales hacia la perfección', *Estudios Ruiz-Fornells*, 438–45. S. Sieburth, *'Galdós' *Tormento*: popular culture, politics and representation', *JILS*, 2, 1990:43–65. J. Whiston, '*El ideal de la humanidad para la vida* de Sanz del Río y *Lo prohibido* de Galdós', *BBMP*, 66, 1990:155–65, traces the admittedly vague influence of Krausism in G.'s novel but underlines the fact that for G. the true ideal for humanity is vitality, health and spontaneity, as personified by Camila and Constantino, in contrast to the corruption of Madrid. L. M. Willem, 'The narrative premise of Galdós's *Lo prohibido*', *RoQ*, 38:189–96, reminds us that the novel is conceived as memoirs which allows for narratorial flexibility. Id., 'The narrative voice presentation of Rosalía de Bringas in two Galdosian novels', *CH*, 12, 1990:75–87, compares the primarily external presentation of R. in *Tormento* with the more sympathetic internal focalization of *La de Bringas*. T. R. Franz, 'Who is responsible for the "text" in Galdós's *Tormento*?', *Hispanófila*, 101:1–13, sees the novel not as two or three novels in one (following Gullón *et al.*) but as the work of Ido alone, sole author and narrator. As F. acknowledges, this interpretation is not totally foolproof, despite convincing analyses of the text, but then neither are the alternative readings. A. Hoyle, 'El trasfondo irónico y económico de *Miau*', *RLit*, 53, 105:85–102, is solid and scholarly. H. reinstates the unfashionable notion of an author's intentions by placing G.'s novel in its immediate socio-economic context and giving much space to the thorny question of income tax. G.'s aim is to point out the madness of Spanish bureacracy. M. S. Collins, 'Levelling in Galdós's *La desheredada*: a blueprint for social change?', *Neophilologus*, 75:390–98, believes the novel posits a 'levelling' out of class inequalities, rather than a utopian solution to social injustice, which suggests the influence of Krausist ethics and underlines the importance of the middle class as the incarnation of such progressive harmony. L. P. Condé. 'The spread wings of Galdós' *mujer nueva*', Condé, *Feminist Readings*, 13–25, continues her enlightening study of wing/flight imagery in G.'s work from *Gloria* through to *Voluntad*. If the protagonist of the former has her wings clipped, Isidora, representing the 'new woman', is allowed to spread them and take control. C. Frank, 'Tragic relief. An intertextual reading of Galdós's *Fortunata y Jacinta* and Zola's *La joie de vivre*', *CL*, 43:209–29, is insightful. F. follows up the view that Fortunata escapes naturalistic determinism by contrasting G.'s more tragic novel (in the Nietzschean sense) to Z.'s sterner offering of 1884; the latter was more inspired by Schopenhauer and is lacking in notions of will and self-sacrifice. M. A. Schnepf, 'Galdós's *La desheredada* manuscript: a note on the creation of Isidora Rufete', *RoN*, 31:245–50, suggests the novel was originally more naturalistic. J. G. Kobylas, 'La función de la imagen ornitológica en *Doña Perfecta*', *RoN*, 32:79–83, makes rather trite observations on eagles, parrots, and similar winged creatures. G. Cabrejas, 'Galdós: una enciclopedia de hombres inútiles', *BH*, 93:157–82, proposes, true to the spirit of our times, a new type of Galdosian character: the 'useless man'. He substantiates this not unrealistic claim by studying in detail the bureaucrats, scientists, artists, politicians, dandys, orators and other mediocre, shortsighted, opportunist, selfish individuals of such ilk without, it must be said, dismissing the possibility of a category 'useless women'. The matter is not pursued. J. M. del Pino, 'El fracaso de los sistemas de orden en el cierre de *Fortunata y Jacinta*', *RHM*, 44:207–16, uses Kermode in a reading which sees in Fortunata a pre-modern person unable to adapt to her times and hence condemned to failure, death, or madness.

PICÓN. *La hijastra del amor*, ed. Noel M. Valis, B, PPU, 496 pp. Id., *Jacinto Octavio Picón, novelista*, B, Anthropos, 298 pp., is the Spanish translation of the earlier version (see *YWMLS* 52). Id., 'Más datos biobibliográficos sobre Jacinto Octavio Picón', *RLit*, 53:213–44, is extremely thorough and comprehensive and includes references to P.'s newspaper articles, prefaces and correspondence; the critical studies section even indicates forthcoming work in press.

RIVAS. C. Leal, 'Amor, honor y libertad en el *Don Alvaro* de Rivas', *Estudios Ruiz-Fornells*, 189–96, and J. P. Gabriele, *Don Alvaro o la fuerza del sino*: contradicción u ortodoxia', *ib.*, 226–32. M. J. Alonso Seoane, 'Sobre Don Alvaro y su verdadero origen (Presencia de la obra del Inca Garcilaso en el drama del duque de Rivas)', *Homenaje Gallego Morell*, I, 89–104, is refreshing. Don Alvaro is modelled not on the Inca Garcilaso himself, but on the imagined son of González Pizarro, who appears in a section of Garcilaso's *Comentarios reales* which, given the Cordoba link, Rivas is sure to have read. *Don Alvaro o la fuerza del sino*, ed. Carlos Ruiz Silva, M, Espasa-Calpe, 212 pp. **Homenaje al Duque de Rivas en el bicentenario de su nacimiento, 1791–1991*, Córdoba, Diputación Provincial, 127 pp.

ROS DE OLANO. M. Z. Hafter, 'Magnetism and corn plasters in *El doctor Lañuela*', *RoQ*, 38:175–88, draws attention to the metafictional aspects of this anarchic text. Much more could be done with its incoherencies.

VALERA. Several good new editions have appeared: *Doña Luz*, ed. Enrique Rubio Cremades, M, Espasa Calpe, 1990, 245 pp., *Pepita Jiménez*, ed. Enrique Rubio Cremades, M, Taurus, 220 pp., and *Pepita Jiménez*, ed. Leonardo Romero, M, Cátedra, 393 pp., whose lengthy and substantial introduction includes French (1874) and English (1886) reviews of the novel. *Las ilusiones del doctor Faustino*, introd. José Carlos Mainer, M, Alianza, 486 pp. M. Galera Sánchez, 'Don Juan Valera y Granada', *Homenaje Gallego Morell*, II, 9–25, is biographical and thematic. A. Rodríguez, S. Roll, '*Pepita Jiménez* y la creatividad de Pardo Bazán en *Insolación*', *RHM*, 44:29–34, is a comparative study. P.B. takes on board V.'s criticism of naturalism and uses his novel as a model for her own.

ZORRILLA. J. Mandrell, 'Nostalgia and the popularity of *Don Juan Tenorio*: reading Zorrilla through Clarín', *HR*, 59:37–55, reviews the lukewarm reception of the play received in the 1840s and argues that its inclusion in *La Regenta* was C.'s homage to a forgotten Z. The play's popularity was due to its nostalgic vision of a nobler and better past which Alas is able to insert in his contemporary reality. *Don Juan Tenorio*, ed. Enrique Llovet, M, Ayuntamiento, Concejalía de Cultura, 1990, 198 pp.

LITERATURE 1898–1936

By K. M. SIBBALD, *McGill University*

I. GENERAL

PERIODICAL PUBLISHING. Interest in periodical publications continues: María Pilar Celma Valero, *Literatura y periodismo en las revistas del fin de siglo. Estudio e índices (1888–1907)*, M, Júcar, 898 pp.; A. Sabugo Abril, 'Manuel Azaña y *La Pluma*', *CHA*, 492:65–72, is a useful introduction to this self-styled 'refugio contra la barbarie circundante', that documents the contents of the 34 issues, editorial policy and star-studded list of contributors; whilst T. Férriz, '*Romance*, una revista del exilio', *DHA*, 9, 1990:129–37, indicates that, since director Juan Rejano's principle objective was to provide a cultural bridge between 'la España peregrina' and Hispanoamerica, all 16 issues published between February and September 1940 revolved around the war against fascism, the defence of culture and the fraternization between some noted Spanish exiles and their equally famed *confrères* in the New World.

LITERARY AND CULTURAL HISTORY. Evelyn Picón Garfield and Ivan A. Schulman, *Las literaturas hispánicas. Introducción a su estudio*, Detroit, Wayne State U.P., 3 vols, is a general introduction to literary studies which contains some short commentaries on authors reviewed in this section, (I, 206–13 and II, 212–91, and 335–39). Interest centres on the revision of generational divisions: J. J. Gilabert, 'Valentí Almirall y la Generación del "98"', *RHM*, 44:217–25, rereads *España como es* (1872) in order to find similarities between the Catalan writer and Unamuno, Ortega, and the maverick Baroja, although A.'s disaffection for the 'trasnochado subjetivismo nerorromántico' so typical of the 1898 Generation is underscored; J. L. Abellán, 'El "27" fue un ambiente', *Insula*, 534:30–31, sets off the hare by arguing that the date itself hinders more than helps explain a poetics that is rooted in turn of the century crisis; whilst, zeroing in on the traditional date if not the traditional group, A. Soria Olmedo, 'Cubismo y creacionismo: matices del gris', *BFFGL*, 9:39–49, explores the intertextualities present in Gerardo Diego's *Revista de Occidente* article of that year, which links Juan Gris's painting, Huidobro's *creacionismo* and the poetic practice of the 1927 group, especially Juan Larrea. J. Servera Baño, 'La crítica literaria de la Generación del '27 sobre San Juan de la Cruz', *Insula*, 537:33–34, is a pedestrian compilation of writings by Diego, Salinas, Guillén, Moreno Villa, Dámaso Alonso, and Cernuda, that comes to the unsurprising conclusion that all share the same objective, namely, to identify a privileged *corpus* for their similar formalist criticism, which operates through text analysis that centres on the dialectic between signifier and signified. A more original approach is taken by H. T. Young, 'The Generation of 27 as translators', *ALEC*, 16:45–54, of translation as a cultural as well as linguistic activity whereby crosscurrents from the English romantics, Joyce, Manley Hopkins, and T. S. Eliot, or Paul Valéry and Wölfflin, inform the original poetry of Cernuda, Alonso, Guillén or Moreno Villa. Almost subversively, *Insula*, 529, dedicates a special number to those not usually counted among the super-stars. First, V. García de la Concha (3–4) introduces the dual concept here of commenting fully 'la década prodigiosa' (1920–30), and the rescue from (semi) oblivion of the 'other' members of the Group of 27, as a basis for J. M. Martínez Cachero, 'Examen de críticos: de "Andrenio" a Guillermo de Torre' (4–5), which traces the change from the negative destruction practised by Julio Casares and Luis Astraña Marín to an affirmative criticism attuned to the poetry and with Azorín and Ortega as models; A. Soria Olmedo (5–6) to examine the literary polemics of the 1920s and 1930s; I. Criado, 'De *El movimiento V.P.* a *Pero . . . ¿hubo alguna vez once mil vírgenes?*' (7–8), a list of novels published between those of Rafael Cansinos Assens (1921) and Enrique Jardiel Poncela (1931) of the title; J. M. Benet (9–10) to give an overview of art 'entre París y Vallecas', complemented by a similar documentation of the music of the period by A. Gallego (10–12); R. Utrera, 'Más literatura cinematográfica sobre aquel perro andaluz' (12–13), which examines the role of Rafael Porlán Merlo, co-founder of *Mediodía* (1926), as film critic in Seville; and timely reminders about the pluralistic nature of the 1920s within Spain itself, which come from E. Bou (13–14) describing the Catalan scene, and A. López-Casanova (14–16) concentrating on the Galician Generation of 1922. In the second part of this *homenaje* attention focuses on 'otros del 27', specifically: P. Carrero Eras (16–17) finds a place in the sun for Mauricio Bacarisse; J. Pérez Bazo (17–20) traces the trajectory of Juan Chabás from 'la deshumanización al compromiso'; A. de Paz (20–21) explores the Icarus–Dedalus relationship between Juan José Domenchina and Jiménez; a flurry of activity centres around Antonio Espina, G. Gullón (21–22) finds the semiotic pattern of the vanguard in *Signario* (1923), whilst J. Mas Ferrer (23–25) first substantiates Juan Ramón's *dictum*, 'mucho Larra natural en Espina' in his examination of E. as the romantic poet of the Spanish vanguard, and then Id. (25–27) also traces E.'s theory and practice as a novelist; J. Issorel (25–27) rescues Fernando Villalón from his own extravagant legend to show a poet imbued with a deep sense of the Andalusian landscape; E. G. de Nora (30–31) offers a brief introductory list the better to read Benjamín Jarnés today; C. Richmond (31–33) explores cinematographic techniques in Francisco Ayala's *Los usurpadores*; A. Rodríguez Fischer (33–35) finds evidence of metanovel and micropoetics in Rosa Chacel's early work; and M. de Paco (35–36) considers crisis and renovation in a long list of dramatists. Surrealism is singled out for special attention in some important new studies. A. Monegal, 'La "poesía nueva" de 1929: entre el álgebra de las metáforas y la revolución surrealista', *ALEC*, 16:55–72, makes eloquent use of Ricoeur, Riffaterre, Max Black, and Peter Bürger to concur with Apollinaire's original definition of surrealism as a new way of describing reality that is, paradoxically, more truthful than mere mimetic representation. Best read as a rich and informative sequel to the 1989 special issue of *Insula* (see *YWMLS*, 51:350) is *The Surrealist Adventure in Spain*, ed. C. Brian Morris, Ottawa, Dovehouse, 346 pp.: Id. provides an introduction (11–18) as well as a useful bibliography (320–42), which point up the relatively recent breaking of the 'strange conspiracy of silence' surrounding the movement in Spain; A. J. Bergero, 'Science, modern art and surrealism. The representation of imaginary matter' (19–39) discovers that surrealism and the new physics do have much in common; W. Bohn, 'Mirroring Miró: J. V. Foix and the surrealist adventure' (40–61) is a close reading of 'Presentació de Joan Miró', published in *L'Amic de les Arts* on 30 June 1928; I. Soldevila-Durante, 'Ramón Gómez de la Serna: *superrealismo* and *surrealismo*' (62–79) gives some precise definitions to characterize Ramón as the Apollinaire of the Spanish vanguard; N. Dennis, 'Ernesto Giménez Caballero and surrealism: a reading of *Yo, inspector de alcantarillas* (1928)' (80–100) examines the claim of first Spanish surrealist work but finds instead a carefully calculated exercise by an author soon enslaved by other fashions; J. Neira, 'Surrealism and Spain: the case of Hinojosa' (101–18) rescues the maladroit 'Poeta ya está' or 'Vil Colodra' from signal neglect and cruel misrepresentation to establish serious credentials for *La flor de California* (1928) as Spain's first surrealist work; P. Hernández-Pérez, 'Emilio Prados's contribution to Spanish surrealism' (114–44) throws light on the personal life of the ideologue of the surrealist group in Málaga and examines in detail the second *estampa* in *Seis estampas para un rompecabezas* (1925), a fragment of *Retratos* (1927), and 'Porque me voy cierro los ojos . . .' from *Cuerpo perseguido* (1928); J. Nantell, 'Irreconcilable differences: Rafael Alberti's *Sobre los ángeles*' (145–65) sees the text as 'a fathomless *mise en abîme*' and uses J. Hillis Miller for a close reading of 'Los ángeles muertos'; D. Harris, 'Hallucination and dream: imagery and language in Luis Cernuda's *Un río, un amor* and *Los placeres prohibidos*' (166–80) scrutinizes these functions at considerable length; A. L. Geist, '"Esas fronteras deshechas": sexuality, textuality, and ideology in Vicente Aleixandre's *Espadas como labios*' (181–90) argues that the text is paradigmatic of a particular and critical moment in Spanish cultural history; J. Cruz, 'Refuge and remorse: religion in Gutiérrez Albelo's *Enigma del invitado*' (191–204) explicates the 26 parts of the narrative poem written by this member of the Tenerife group centred around the *Gaceta de Arte*; A. Sánchez Vidal, 'Buñuel and the flesh' (205–24) documents the conflict between Calanda and Paris, or Jesuit discipline and surrealist freedom, that culminates in the antinomy between Christ and Sade articulated in the films; K. Ibsen, 'The illusory journey: García Lorca's *Viaje a la luna*' (225–39) is a useful textual analysis of the screen-play; A. A. Anderson, 'Bewitched, bothered, and bewildered: Spanish dramatists and surrealism, 1924–1936' (240–81) offers a splendid antidote to befuddlement in his guide to the *avant-garde* Spanish theatre of the 1920s and 1930s; whilst, by way of conclusion, C. B. Morris, 'Crucifying liberty' (295–319) ranges widely over the uninhibited voicing of attitudes that makes unlikely bedfellows of Lewis Carroll and the Marquis de Sade, brings together Granada, Seville, Málaga, Paris, and New York, couples Magritte and Tenerife, and juxtaposes Catholic rites and Fritz Lang's camera, all in constant excitement that is constant incitement. In complete contrast, although not without a certain complementarity, comes the special number dedicated to Manuel de Falla of *poesía*, 36–37, 303 pp., a lavishly illustrated collage of fragments of a long and full musical life (1876–1946) that touched many of the writers commented upon here.

2. POETRY

Zeroing in on the difficult compromise between poetry and revolution, C. Le Bigot, 'Les poètes entre le marteau et l'enclume', *Iris*, 1990:41–54, uses interviews, reviews and prologues to generate a politico-poetic text for some general remarks on Alberti, Arturo Serrano Plaja and Juan Gil-Albert. J. E. Serrano Asenjo, 'Las ruinas: poética y herencia modernista en *Imagen* de Gerardo Diego', *Hispanófila*, 101:37–48, corroborates through new readings D.'s autodefinition as 'poeta montañés, epígono del modernismo y, casi a la par, neófito y hasta inventor del Ultra y de la poesía de creación'. José María Barrera López, **Pedro Garfias. Poesía y soledad*, Seville, Alfar, 291 pp. E. Bou, 'Otro autorretrato de Manuel Machado: "Pintura", de *Ars moriendi*', *BFFGL*, 9:29–37, analyses painting as the theme of the last section of the collection. Francisco Chica selects, edits and introduces Emilio Prados, *Poesía extrema. Antología*, Seville, Andaluzas Unidas, 498 pp.; whilst R. C. Manteiga, 'En torno al binomio barco-mar en la poesía temprana de Emilio Prados', *ALEC*, 16:175–91, is painstakingly thorough but without flair.

INDIVIDUAL POETS

ALBERTI. Pedro Guerrero Ruiz, *Rafael Alberti. Arte y poesía de vanguardia*, Murcia U.P., 230 pp. B. A. González, 'Ekphrasis and autobiography', *ALEC*, 15, 1990:29–49, argues that *A la pintura* and *La arboleda perdida* constitute a single discourse; whilst L. García Montero, 'Rafael Alberti y la pintura', *BFFGL*, 9:51–64, indicates how painting played a humanizing, regenerative role during A.'s exile. José Monleón, **Tiempo y teatro de Rafael Alberti*, M, Primer Acto — Fundación de Rafael Alberti, 1990, 537 pp. L. S. Materna, *ALEC*, 15, 1990:83–95, juggles with semiotic intertextualities and marxist theory in the Venus-Adonis episode in *Noche de guerra en el Museo del Prado* (See LITERARY AND CULTURAL HISTORY above).

ALEIXANDRE. G. Morelli, 'De Vicente Aleixandre a Gerardo Diego ("mi vida es mía . . .")', *Insula*, 534:32, reproduces A.'s letter dated 14 March 1931 and written in response to Diego's request for biographical information for his *Antología de la poesía española*, in which A. comments on *Pasión de la tierra* as work in progress, stresses his retiring nature, gives good advice to future readers of his work, and knocks two years off his age. A. Poust, 'Antropología filosófica en *Sombra del paraíso* de Vicente Aleixandre', *RCEH*, 15:267–81, traces clearly the influence of Max Scheler; but C. García, 'Le parcours du personnage dans l'oeuvre de Vicente Aleixandre', *Iris*, 1990:33–39, gets lost along the way.

ALONSO, DÁMASO. *Insula*, 530, devotes most of the issue to a multi-voice discussion of A.'s impact on literary criticism in Spain: A. García Berrio, 'Dámaso Alonso y la crítica moderna' (1–2, 31–32) points out, like others here, how A. continues the line from Menéndez Pelayo, tempered by Menéndez Pidal, on to colleagueship with Américo Castro and Amado Alonso, and claims A. as the most spiritual critic of his generation, to be read with A. Chicharro Chamorro, 'La teoría literaria de Dámaso Alonso, de ayer a hoy. (Notas de una revisión historiográfica)' (13–15), who ponders at length on A.'s influence on criticism in Spain; A. Soria Olmedo, 'Dámaso Alonso en el epistolario de Salinas-Guillén' (11–12) quotes extensively from letters that tell as much about Salinas's theatre and Guillén's poetry as A., although there is a warmth here that evidently was completely lacking in A.'s relationship with Cernuda and F. Ruiz Noguera, 'Dámaso Alonso-Luis Cernuda. Crónica de un desafecto' (12–13) documents the virulent enmity Cernuda manifested for 'Alonso el Desamado', the 'pomposa nulidad' as a person, poet and critic; A. Orejudo, 'Dámaso Alonso: novela española y límites de la estilística' (15–16) shows A. in an unusual light, as a perspicacious if somewhat reluctant reader of prose; J. M. Cuesta Abad, 'La doctrina del nombre: poética y metafísica en Dámaso Alonso' (16–17) upholds A.'s poetic theorizing as a personalized example of the dialectic between divergent theories of Western aesthetics and modern criticism; J. A. Hernández Guerrero, 'Dámaso Alonso y el protagonismo del lector' (17–18) takes literally A.'s opinion that without a reader the poem is 'un pobre ser inexpresivo'; C. Piera, 'Sobre Dámaso Alonso y nuestro canon lírico' (18–19) is an interesting look at how A. both created and imposed the canon, particularly with reference to his own generation, whilst, more specifically, L. Bonet, 'Dámaso Alonso y la escuela de Barcelona: huellas, semillas, silencios' (19–22) examines the considerable influence A. exerted in the period from the funding of *Laye* (1950) to the publication of J. M. Castellet's first anthology (1960), on Castellet, Jaime Gil de Biedma and Juan Ferraté; and, oddly pertinent here, J. L. Cano, 'Retrato de Dámaso' (22) adds the finishing touch in poetry.

CERNUDA. A handy new edition, *La realidad y el deseo. Historial de un libro. (1924–1962), M, Alianza, 430 pp. J. L. Cano, 'Luis Cernuda y María Zambrano', *Insula*, 534:31–32, indicates C.'s role in the publication of 'Dos fragmentos sobre el amor', and quotes extensively from C.'s letter dated 11 January 1952 and Zambrano's later correspondence dated 21 July 1955 and May 1977. C. Real Ramos, *ALEC*, 15, 1990:109–27, shows how the poetry acquires an ethical dimension. A. Monegal, 'Pre-texto e intertexto en "Retrato de poeta", de Luis Cernuda', *BFFGL*, 9:65–75, explicates C.'s reaction to El Greco's portrait of Fray Hortensio Félix Paravicino in the Boston Museum of Fine Arts. (See ALONSO above).

GARCÍA LORCA. Hitherto unpublished material continues to appear. Manuel Fernández-Montesinos, *Nueva York en un poeta: recuerdos de García Lorca en América*, M, Tabapress, 34 pp., is a small collection of photographs and facsimile letters to the family that date from G.L.'s stay in New York. Interest, however, centres on G.L.'s drawings, or 'linear metaphors': Michael Mezzatesta prologues and Christopher Maurer translates into English, Mario Hernández, *Line of Light and Shadow. The Drawings of Federico García Lorca*, Durham, Duke U.P. — Duke Univ. Museum of Art, 273 pp., which makes more accessible the Spanish version. Id., *Libro de los dibujos de Federico García Lorca, M, Tabapress — Fundación Federico García Lorca, 1990. For this marvellously illustrated volume Id. writes a general introduction (15–34); eight interpretative essays on the distinct thematic series 'House and nature' (37–50), 'Half silver and shadow' (51–66), 'The melancholy of clowns' (67–86), 'Designs for the theatre' (87–96), 'A rustic book of saints' (97–110), 'Gypsies and sailors' (111–28), 'Sequence with self portraits in New York' (129–45), and 'Abstraction of the line' (146–72); and provides a useful 'Catalogue of the graphic work' (173–262), that updates and corrects the earlier catalogue, *Dibujos*, M, Ministerio de Cultura, 1986, 88 pp., put together to accompany the exhibition at the *Museo Español de Arte Contemporáneo* on the occasion of the *cincuentenario*. On a smaller scale, J. Yagüe Bosch, 'Aquí y allí de las barbas de Whitman: un dibujo de García Lorca', *BFFGL*, 9:77–117, comments upon the limited edition of the 'Oda de Walt Whitman' (1933) that was specially printed with space for G.L. to add drawings and dedications to his friends, and compares subtle differences between the drawings reproduced here from the first four such copies dedicated to Luis Rosales, José Caballero, Bebé Morla and Rafael Rodríguez Rapún, respectively; whilst A. Soria Olmedo, 'Federico García Lorca y el arte', *RHM*, 44:59–72, provides excellent background documentation to explicate the fruitful interaction between G.L. and the plastic arts. G. Celaya, 'Recordando a García Lorca', *BFFGL*, 9:163–65, republishes some personal reminiscing from *El País* of 10 June 1976; and J. M. Barrera López, 'Amistad y evocaciones: Pedro Garfias and Federico García Lorca', *ib.*, 167–73, gives details about a personal and literary friendship. Criticism from a particular perspective: Angel Sahuquillo, *Federico García Lorca y la cultura de la homosexualidad masculina. Lorca, Dalí, Cernuda, Gil-Albert, Prados y la voz silenciada del amor sexual*, Alicante, Instituto Juan Gil-Albert, 427 pp., makes more available his earlier study (see *YWMLS*, 48:387); and D. G. Walters, '"Comprendí. Pero no explico." Revelation and concealment in Lorca's *Canciones*', *BHS*, 68:255–79, offers close readings to interpret the pivotal nature of *Canciones* between the closure and secrecy about homosexuality in *Libro de poemas* and G.L.'s much more frank treatment in *Poeta en Nueva York*. Editorial activity continues unabated: Luis García Montero edits *Poema de cante jondo*, M, Espasa Calpe, 1990, 182 pp.; Christian de Paepe introduces with critical study *Primer romancero gitano*, M, Clásicos Castellanos, 315 pp., to be compared with Emilio de Miguel's edition of *Romancero gitano*, M, Espasa Calpe, 1990, 173 pp.; Luis Martínez Cuitiño provides useful critical apparatus for *Mariana Pineda*, M, Cátedra, 366 pp.; whilst details of other editions, translations and doctoral dissertations from between 1987–91 not given here are to be found in A. A. Anderson, 'Bibliografía lorquiana reciente IX', *BFFGL*, 9:177–87. Tadea Fuentes Vázquez, *El folclore infantil en la obra de Federico García Lorca*, Granada U.P., 1990, 240 pp. Some innovative criticism of the poetry: A. A. Anderson, 'Lorca at the crossroads: "imaginación, inspiración, evasión" and the "novísimas estéticas"', *ALEC*, 16:149–73, locates G.L. somewhere in the middle of controlled *creacionismo* and uncontrolled surrealism, revealing a sympathetic interpreter of Pierre Reverdy and Jean Epstein who yet maintained his status as an independent thinker in a complex mesh of tendencies and influences; D. Perri, 'Lorca's suite "Newton": the limits of science and reason', *Hispanófila*, 101 : 25–36, provides a close reading to combat the general currency of a facile characterization of the early 1920s as coldly cerebral; whilst Id., 'Lorca's suite "Palimpsestos": keeping the reader at bay', *RoQ*, 38 : 192–211, uses Bakhtin and Voloshinov to show how multiple layering, ellipses, and silences impede closure and possession of the text but encourage the reader to participate in the process of communication and exchange. Margaret A. Rees prologues a second, revised and expanded edition of *Leeds Papers on Lorca and on Civil War Verse*, Leeds U.P., 1990, 167 pp., for wider circulation than the 1988 collection of papers from the conference held at Trinity and All Saints College in 1987: R. Cueto, 'On the queerness rampant in *The House of Bernarda Alba*' (9–43) explicates well the parody of Cistercian silence and the rule of the *doctor mellifluus* and slyly wonders if 'a controlled, hieratic, drag version' from Lindsay Kemp and Nuria Espert would not do justice to the perversely adapted Bernardine imagery that permeates sets and text; R. G. Havard, '*Mariana Pineda*. Politics, poetry and periodization' (45–65) attempts the rescue of 'una obra debil de principiante' from 'minor' status by pointing up its strengths in language, theme, characterization, and creation of mood; P. McDermott, 'Lorca: crisis and commitment. An emerging "Theology of Liberation"' (67–84) depends heavily on previous work by Eutimio Martín (see *YWMLS*, 48 : 387) to explore the roots of G.L.'s religious politization and heterodox theology; M. A. Rees (85–95) characterizes G.L. as 'an Iberian Clay Jones' and explicates the role of flowers in the plays and poetry; a completely new essay in this edition, R. G. Havard, 'Dreams and nightmares in Lorca's *Poeta en Nueva York*' (115–43), uses Freud on wish-fulfilment, recollection and anxiety to interpret well G.L.'s oneiric poetic idiom; M. E. Williams, 'Roy Campbell, Lorca and the Civil War' (97–114) neutralizes the fanatically Catholic, pro-Franco content of the heroic couplets of *The Flowering Rifle* best known to most Hispanists through a comparison between G.L. and poems written before Campbell discovered either Spain or religion; all rather curiously rounded off by S. Hart, 'Some notes on the conventions of Spanish Civil War poetry: the *romance*' (145–67), which offers abundant quotation from the work of non-professional poets adept with both pen and grenade. María Encarnación Seco de Lucena Vázquez de Gardner, *Estética de lo pequeño y reducción espacial en la obra de Federico García Lorca*, Granada U.P., 1990, 196 pp. In time for the 55th anniversary of G.L.'s death Manuel Durán and Francesca Colecchia edit *Lorca's Legacy. Essays on Lorca's Life, Poetry, and Theatre*, New York, Peter Lang, 264 pp., containing some diverse and wide-ranging essays: J. Herrero (1–20) reprints his analysis of G.L.'s Christian vision (see *YWMLS*, 51:356); H. T. Young, 'Lorca and the afflicted monk' (21–29) dissects the layers of meaning of the anecdote of the confrontation between Beethoven and plainsong at the organ of the Monastery of Silos in 1917; R. Berroa with S. E. Morgan, 'Poetry and painting: García Lorca's dual manifestation of symbols and metaphor' (31–49) interprets the Derridean 'voice' of the metaphors that fill G.L.'s drawings and usefully reproduces 22 sketches (217–38); K. M. Sibbald, '*Catoblepas* and *putrefactos* in Antofagasta, or Lorca and a case of *serio ludere*' (51–69) traces the pedigree of three of the epithets that enjoyed favour during the polemics of the 1920s over what constitutes good literary taste and judgement; M. Donahue (71–81) merely piles up quotations in an identikit portrait; G. Correa, 'Nature and symbolism in the poetry of Federico García Lorca' (85–94) is replete with examples; A. Josephs, '"Don Perlimplín": Lorca's *amante-para-la-muerte*' (95–101) explores the ancient origins of G.L.'s modern version of the *Liebestod* theme and reads the play as an *auto sacrificial*; C. Maurer, 'Bach and *Bodas de sangre*' (103–14) unearths the various drafts of the English translation made by José Weissberger under G.L.'s supervision, the prompt-book of the Neighbourhood Playhouse production of 1935 in New York, and the music sent by G.L. to Irene Lewisohn for that production, to adduce a fascinating parallel between '¡Despierte la novia!' and 'Wachet auf, ruft uns die Stimme'; R. Lima, 'Toward the Dionysiac: pagan elements and notes in *Yerma*' (115–33) examines the substratum of pagan tradition beneath the veneer of the Christian ethos (see also *JDTC*, 4, 1990:62–82), whilst B. L. Knapp (135–45) views the same play as 'a woman's mystery'; A. Jiménez-Vera, 'The role of Spanish society in *Yerma*' (147–56) is an exercise in social work that delves into the married couple's point of view; D. Cañas, 'The poet of the city: Lorca in New York' (159–69) explicates how G.L.'s poetry 'became permeable to urban language'; unravelling the 'Stories of madness: the feminine in *Poeta en Nueva York*' (171–85), E. Gascón Vera uses the definition of Gilles Deleuze and Felix Guattari of the anti-oedipal man to unmask the female codes in G.L.'s writing; G. Durán, 'Conversation with Tulio Ossa, Director of United Theatre of the Americas, on *La casa de Bernarda Alba*' (187–93) records some inconsequential remarks on feminism and propaganda in general and, specifically, the play's unrealistic ending and lack of heroine; V. Higginbotham, 'Lorca's *Así que pasen cinco años*: a literary version of *Un chien andalou*' (195–204) traces the common elements of the elimination of the realistic, a fascination for the other as double, a lack of logical plot, the use of dreams, similar images of violence and emptiness, and a (sexual) identity crisis, that provided material for the genesis of G.L.'s rebuttal of 'una mierdesita así de pequeñita'; paying tribute to 'García Lorca's legacy: the live theatre at the battle front' (205–14); S. W. Byrd documents the activities during the Civil War of a revived *La barraca*, María Teresa León's *Arte y Propaganda*, the *Teatro de Guerra*, the PSOE's *Arte y Cultura*, the Tivoli and Apolo theatres in Valencia, and the front-line *Teatro de guerilla* and *Teatro de urgencia*; whilst F. M. Colecchia, 'Federico García Lorca: a selectively updated bibliography' (239–64) offers 'a selected sampling of Lorca scholarship' that might well be used in conjunction with the various instalments of the bibliography published in *BFFGL* since 1987. There are some fresh insights on the theatre: A. Vargas Churchill, 'Lorca's *Yerma* and divorce in the Spanish Republic', *JILS*, 2, 1990:67–75, argues that divided opinion about the play's merits reflected the left–right split over the contemporary divorce law since *Yerma* was viewed as advocating the destruction of archaic social canons and a decrepit civil code; tracing 'A genesis for García Lorca's *Bodas de sangre*', *His(US)*, 74:255–61, J. K. Walsh plausibly outlines the play's rapid composition in two weeks in September 1932, generated by G.L.'s re-reading of Antonio Machado's *La tierra de Alvargonzález*; S. G. Feldman, '*Perlimplín*: Lorca's drama about theatre', *Estreno*, 17.2:34–38, uses Patrice Pavis and Anne Ubersfeld to good effect in a characterization of the play as both semiotic object and semiotic analysis; Rosania Vitale, **El metateatro en la obra de Federico García Lorca*, M, Pliegos, 144 pp.; B. E. Weingarten, 'La estética de la farsa violenta lorquiana y el esperpento valleinclanesco', *HisJ*, 12:47–57, documents similarities between *La zapatera prodigiosa* and *Los cuernos de Don Friolera* in the trajectory from *deshumanización* or *esperpentización* to *fantochización*; and D. Ubaldo Gómez edits **Lecturas del texto dramático: variaciones sobre la obra de Lorca*, Oviedo U.P., 1990, 116 pp. Finally, for both students and scholars, Derek Harris edits and annotates *Romancero gitano*, London, Grant and Cutler, 160 pp.; and Andrew A. Anderson, *García Lorca: La zapatera prodigiosa*, ib., 114 pp., provides the critical guide. (See VALLE-INCLÁN below).

GUILLÉN. Francisco Quintana Docio, *La poesía urbana de Jorge Guillén*, Valladolid, Centro de Creación y Estudios Jorge Guillén — Diputación Provincial de Valladolid, 363 pp., is an ambitious analysis of the metaphors and symbols of G.'s urban poetic voice, densely written and coherently argued; as a postscript (329–60) Id. usefully contextualizes an historical revision of the incidence of urban poetry from Bécquer to G.'s contemporaries. Some intelligent rethinking of G.'s poetic practice: J. Mayhew, 'Jorge Guillén and the insufficiency of poetic language', *PMLA*, 106:1146–55, uses *Language and Poetry* to question accepted interpretations and point to G.'s contradictory definitions of 'sufficient language', thus to argue, unfashionably, that the highly structured autonomy of G.'s language does make difficult the communication of his vision; C. C. Soufas, Jr, 'Ideologizing form: anti-mimetic language theories in the early poetry of Jorge Guillén and Luis Cernuda', *ALEC*, 16:101–17, widens the debate by delicately picking his way between Bürger and Jameson to find serious divisions between G. and imagism (see also *YWMLS*, 51:357) and Cernuda and surrealism; whilst, narrowing the focus somewhat, M. C. Aldrich, 'Vehemencia incesante: configurando lecturas de la parte III de *Maremágnum* de Jorge Guillén', *ib.*, 91–100, neatly explicates the intertextual and intratextual relationships of the *treboles* to show a metaphysical dialectic on the Berceo–Baudelaire axis that also provides the context for the 'monumentality' of G.'s work; some fascinating inter-text discourse is interpreted by N. B. Mandlove, 'Dialogue of poets and poetry: intertextual patterns in the sonnets of Jorge Guillén', *ib.*, 73–89, which explores the metapoetic dimensions of the continuing dialogue with Mallarmé, Quevedo, and Lope on poetry, whilst H. T. Young, 'Texts and intertexts in Jorge Guillén's *Homenaje*', *CL*, 43:370–82, unravels intelligently the complex web of past readings and writings in resistance (Quevedo, Dámaso Alonso, Baudelaire), coincidence (Unamuno, Jiménez), glosses (Enrique Gil), translations and variations (Valéry, Rimbaud, Josep Carner, and, particularly, Wallace Stevens). (See ALONSO above and SALINAS below).

JIMÉNEZ. Valuable new material appears: Antonio Sánchez Romeralo edits and annotates *Ideolojía (1897–1957)*, B, Anthropos, 1990, cii + 761 pp., an enormously important *corpus* of previously unpublished writings fundamental to our understanding of J.'s poetics; Id. also reconstructs with study and notes **Mi Rubén Darío (1900–1956)*, Moguer, Fundación Juan Ramón Jiménez — Diputación Provincial de Huelva, 1990, 325 pp. (see also *YWMLS*, 50:370); and Graciela Palau de Nemes translates with introduction and notes Zenobia Camprubí, *Diario Vol. I: Cuba (1937–1939)*, M, Alianza, xxxvi + 356 pp., a necessary 'other' view of J. in exile (see also *YWMLS*, 49:360, and 50:371). For the initiated the fourth *Congreso de Literatura Española Contemporánea* generates ** Juan Ramón Jiménez. Poesía total y obra en marcha*, B, Anthropos, 398 pp. M. Juliá, 'Cosmovisión en el poema "Espacio" de Juan Ramón Jiménez', *La Torre*, 18:225–38, explores influence and intertextuality of precursors Walt Whitman and Albert Einstein; whilst J. M. Naharro-Calderón, 'Los descentrados espacios del exilio de Juan Ramón Jiménez (1939–1954)', *DHA*, 9, 1990:23–34, is a literary biopsy of J.'s exile as 'memoria elegíaca, heterotopía textual, soledad personal, lengua aislada, pérdida de manuscritos y recepción censurada'.

352   *Spanish Studies*

MACHADO, A.   Bernard Sesé, **Claves de Antonio Machado*, M, Espasa Calpe, 1990, 384 pp. A. Barbagallo Rolanía, **España, el paisaje, el tiempo y otros temas en la poesía de Antonio Machado*, Diputación Provincial de Soria, 1990, 172 pp. José Antonio García-Diego, **Antonio Machado y Juan Gris: (dos artistas masones)*, M, Castalia, 1990, 125 pp. A. Amorós, 'Antonio Machado y los toros', *CHA*, 487:121–32, looks at letters to brother Manuel and early journalism in *La Caricatura* to find details of Frascuelo, Lagartija and the legendary 'Carancha' (José Sánchez del Campo 1848–1925), that both explode the myth that A.M. was not interested in the national sport and explicate some poetic metaphors. P. Ontañón de Lope, 'Antonio Machado y el psicoanálisis: apreciaciones crítico-literarias', *La Torre*, 18:215–24, meanders through the *obra* looking for references that prove 'no todo/es prosa en la nueva ciencia/del psicoanálisis'. A. Castillo, 'Retorno de Machado', *ECon*, 4:103–08, rather obviously reviews the key dates celebrated in the 50 years since A.M.'s death as marking resistance to Francoist politics (1959), the return to democracy (1975), and revision and re-evaluation (1989). J. Butt, 'Embarrassed readings of Machado's "A orillas del Duero"', *MLR*, 86:322–36, is a polemical rereading of A.M. criticism of the 1960s and 1970s which avoids the usual distinction between 'poetic' and 'ideological' to allow for a new view of the uncertain, rather than linear, structure that complements the multiplicity of voices, shifts in tone, and central ambiguity that Butt so deftly indicates.

SALINAS.   The centenary has obviously stimulated critical interest. Francisco Javier Díez de Revenga edits with the earlier prologue by Jorge Guillén, **Poemas escogidos*, M, Espasa Calpe, 291 pp. *Insula*, 540, pays homage and S. Salinas, 'Más allá de la tierra' (1–2), leads off with some general remarks on the friendship and the poetry of S. and Rafael Alberti; J. González Muela, 'El mundo poético de Pedro Salinas' (3–4) combines broad outlines with close readings of 'La rosa pura' and 'Las ninfas', and throws in some comparisons with Guillén for good measure; C. Feal, 'Confianza y azar en la obra de Pedro Salinas' (4–7) uses Erik H. Erikson's 'sense of basic trust' to show how sure S. is of his own identity in the face of chaos and disintegration; M. Arizmendi, 'De *La voz a ti debida*. (Preliminares sobre un cancionero)' (7–8) explicates well the role of Garcilaso in the configuration of S.'s poetics; J. Crispin, 'Tres sonetos satíricos inéditos de Pedro Salinas' (9–11) indicates the historical background to three Quevedesque diatribes on Franco, 'Paca, la franca mona', and 'Plus proxeneta y archicelestinesco' Neville Chamberlain, the 'insigne pruto de la Gran Prutaña', composed in 1938; R. Katz Crispin, 'Salinas y el romanticismo inglés' (11–12) reads S. most convincingly by way of Coleridge;

G. Torres Nebrera, 'Hacia una lectura de *Víspera del gozo*' (13–14) is a balanced introduction to the context, structure, and reader reception of the prose; F. J. Díez de Revenga, 'Salinas ensayista: el espíritu en su letra' (15–16) emphasizes S.'s love of the Spanish language and ability to educate his public; S.'s correspondence yields new data, J. M. Barrera López, 'Salinas antes Bécquer. (Carta inédita a la revista *Mediodía*)' (17) reproduces a letter to Rafael Porlán Merlo dated 6 November 1928 that amply justifies S.'s unofficial title of 'mediador entusiasta, ministro plenipotenciario' of the younger Seville poets, A. Soria Olmedo, 'El Rubén Darío de Salinas, y sus cartas' (18–19) gives the background to S.'s attempt at 'vindicación de tantas superficialidades y extremosidades, ditirambos vacíos o desdenes pedantes' in his 1948 study, and F. Ruiz Ramón, 'Para una cronología del teatro de Pedro Salinas' (20–22) uses the S.-Guillén letters to document for the first time the genesis and chronology of S.'s 14 plays; while P. Moraleda, 'La vocación dramática de Pedro Salinas' (22–23) notes how S. combines traditional form and technical innovations that echo O'Neill and predate Buero Vallejo. D. L. Stixrude, 'Critical reception of the poetry of Pedro Salinas: 1969–1989', *ALEC*, 16:129–48, is criticism of criticism, dealing mainly with articles reviewed here, and concludes that these interpretations of S.'s literary text have involved little critical theorizing. A new leaf is, thus, turned collectively by J. Mayhew, '"Cuartilla": Pedro Salinas and the semiotics of poetry', *ib.*, 119–27, who finds in S. the fusion of poetic semiosis and metasemiosis for his critique of Riffaterre; by L. R. Scarano, 'La función del arte en el fin de siglo hispánico y su derivación en la obra de Pedro Salinas', *HisJ*, 12:97–108, who characterizes S. as a transition poet between modernism and postmodernity; by D. K. Benson, 'El amor contra la nada: Pedro Salinas, Francisco Brines y la tradición clásica española', *RCEH*, 15, 1990:1–18, who traces S. as an intertextuality in Brines's poetry; and, in a flurry of critical activity, by C. Feal, 'Lo visible y lo invisible en los primeros libros poéticos de Salinas', *BH*, 93:183–206, who rejects the usual Platonic basis sought for S.'s poetry and tries instead to connect S. with Heidegger and Merleau-Ponty, using a similar approach with the prose, Id., 'La amada de verdad y la incompleta en dos narraciones de Pedro Salinas', *RHM*, 44:48–58, endorses S.'s conclusion that love is 'vida, acción, movimiento, novedad en cada minuto', and continues on the psycho-philosophical plane in Id., 'Lo real, lo imaginario y lo simbólico en *Víspera del gozo* de Pedro Salinas', *MLN*, 106:314–29. After all this, Carmelo Guillén Acosta, * *Claves de la obra poética de Pedro Salinas*, M, Ciclo, 1990, 112 pp., comes rather as an anticlimax. (See ALONSO and GUILLÉN above).

3. PROSE

Susan Nagel, *The Influence of the Novels of Jean Giraudoux on the Hispanic Vanguard Novels of the 1920s–1930s*, Lewisburg, Bucknell U.P., 150 pp., views Giraudoux as the mentor of the younger writers Salinas, Jarnés, Max Aub, and Francisco Ayala; a useful Chapter 2 (57–74) traces Franco-Hispanic crosscurrents as background for the discussion in Chapter 3 (75–107) of metafiction, decharacterization and pneumatic imagery, as found in *Víspera del gozo* (1926), *El profesor inútil* (1926, 1933), *Geografía* (1929), and *El boxeador y un ángel* (1929). J. Bruner, 'A picture is worth a thousand words: ekphrasis in the contemporary Spanish novel', *JILS*, 3:71–90, has general comments on mutual compatibility between literature and the plastic arts, a good theoretical exposition of the phenomenon, and some interesting references to Ortega, Unamuno, Manuel Machado, Alberti, and Pérez de Ayala in the context of work by Carmen Laforet, Luis Martín-Santos, Carmen Martín Gaite, and Carlos Rojas. C. Malaxecheverría, 'Joaquín Arderíus y el nuevo romanticismo', *Hispanófila*, 102:47–56, argues that A. anticipates, in practice in his first novel *Así me fecundó Zaratustra* (1923) and by some seven years, Díaz Fernández's seminal theoretical definitions. Manuel María Pérez López edits with critical apparatus José Martínez Ruiz (Azorín), **Antonio Azorín*, M, Cátedra, 271 pp. V. Fuentes, 'Noticia de un fragmento inédito de *El profesor inútil*', *Insula*, 535:29, points out that a real jewel of vanguard writing has languished in the two issues of March 1927 of the *Revista Popular* (Cordoba), and rescues the text and sketches by Antonio López Obrero (29–30). José Miguel Fernández de Urbina, **La aventura intelectual de Ramiro de Maeztu*, Vitoria, Diputación Foral de Vizcaya, 1990, 101 pp. Noël Valis edits Jacinto Octavio Picón, **La hijastra del amor*, B, PPU, 1990, 491 pp.; and, by scouring the periodical literature, adds 'Más datos biobibliográficos sobre Jacinto Octavio Picón', *RLit*, 105:213–44, to be used with her earlier bibliographies of 1980 and 1985 (see *YWMLS*, 48:395).

INDIVIDUAL WRITERS

AYALA, F. In 'Todo ya con el *Quijote*', *Insula*, 538:38–40, an interview with Víctor García de la Concha, A. gives intelligent insights on Cervantes, and some even more telling comments on writing novels and the contemporary literary scene. The author is still the better critic: A. Martínez, 'Diálectica del poder y la libertad en *Los usurpadores* y *La Cabeza del cordero* de Francisco Ayala', *DHA*, 9, 1990:13–21, is little more than plot summary; and D. E. Gulstad, 'Homecoming and identity-quest in Ayala's *La cabeza del cordero*',

Hispanófila, 103:1–15, follows up the subliminal messages that run through the semiotic structure of the work. (See LITERARY AND CULTURAL HISTORY above).

AZAÑA. Enrique de Rivas edits with introduction and notes *Cartas 1917–1935*, V, Pre-Textos, 176 pp., A.'s hitherto unpublished letters to his brother-in-law, Cipriano de Rivas Cherif. J. M. Marco, *La creación de sí mismo. Ensayo sobre la literatura autobiográfica de Manuel Azaña*, M, Biblioteca Nueva, 177 pp.; and María Angeles Hermosilla Alvarez, *La prosa de Manuel Azaña*, Cordoba U.P., 255 pp. T. Feeny, *Hispanófila*, 103:33–46, separates fact and fiction in Carlos Rojas's *Azaña* (1973). Jesús Ferrer Sola, *Manuel Azaña: una pasión intelectual*, B, Anthropos, 332 pp. (See PERIODICAL PUBLISHING above).

BAROJA. Jesús María Lasagabaster edits *Paradox, rey*, M, Espasa Calpe, 218 pp. A. Sotelo Vázquez, 'Pío Baroja en 1901', *BH*, 92, 1990:856–80, provides the context for four forgotten articles published in April and May 1901 in *Las Noticias*; the first and the third derive from B.'s trip to Paris in 1899, whereby B. ostensibly writes on the Dreyfus affair but seizes the opportunity to criticize Spain as 'una especie de gelatina sin irritabilidad', and then venomously describes Madrid as 'un pueblo absceso que le ha salido a España en el vientre', but declines to take decadent Paris as a better model for Spain; the second is a version of Chapter 33 of *Camino de perfección*; and in the last B. denounces the cultural separatism practised by Madrid and praises the provincial artists Joaquín Mir, Zuloaga, Ruisiñol, and Regoyos. Matilde Sagaro Faci, *"La busca" de Pío Baroja*, M, Ciclo, 112 pp. is a student crib in the 'Claves' collection. (See UNAMUNO below).

GÓMEZ DE LA SERNA. *Nuevos retratos contemporáneos y otros retratos*, M, Aguilar, 1990, 736 pp. María del Carmen Serrano Vázquez, *El humor de las greguerías de Ramón. Recursos lingüísticos*, Valladolid U.P., 256 pp. J. E. Serrano Asenjo, 'Escritura para el túnel. (Acerca de *El hombre perdido* de Ramón Gómez de la Serna)', *ECon*, 4:23–45, shows how G. de la S. acts upon his own paradox that 'la vida sin novela no tiene ningún interés' by constructing a narrative in which language becomes the real protagonist. A. Rivero-Potter, 'Ramón Gómez de la Serna and Vicente Huidobro: intertextualidad', *HR*, 59:437–50, suggests that José María Romero is not the butt of G. de la S.'s attack, but defends Huidobro from Ramón's veiled charges of plagiarism.

ORTEGA. The correspondence brings a new dimension to O. studies. Soledad Ortega edits and Vicente Cacho Viu prologues *Cartas de un joven español (1891–1908)*, M, El Arquero, 785 pp., which contains some 200 letters written to parents, the woman who would become his wife, Rosa Spottorno, Francisco Navarro Ledesma, Julio Cejador, various publishers, and even Joaquín Costa, among others;

a veritable treasure trove of information about O.'s early intellectual growth from Jesuit schoolboy to the self-assured young man returning from studies in Germany and some fascinating insights into O.'s private life and relations with father and fiancée. Strong evidence of O.'s influence comes from 'Tres cartas de juventud a Ortega y Gasset', *RO*, 120 : 7–26, which presents the text and context of María Zambrano's letters (13–26), in which on 11 February 1930, in 'Carta de una joven a su maestro', Z. urges O. to action, on 13 November 1930 Z. defends herself from any charge of treachery because of Pablo de A. Cobos's article in *El Socialista* praising Z.'s act of distancing herself from O. in *Horizonte del liberalismo* (1930), and on 28 May 1932 Z. returns to the fold to tell of her disillusion with the lack of ideals and solidarity in her contemporaries. *RO*, 120, clusters a series of short studies: P. Cerezo Galán, 'Razón vital y liberalismo en Ortega y Gasset' (33–58) takes up an earlier study (V. Ouimette, 'Liberalismo e democrazia in Ortega y Gasset', *MondOperaio*, 11, 1989 : 99–107) to concur that the 'razón práctica' that motivates O. often sets him at odds with his socio-political context; Christian Pierre, 'Ortega en el ámbito cultural europea' (59–71), rather dramatically, hails the French translation of O.'s works begun in 1986 as a safeguard against empty theorizing, an antidote to polisemia, and a metaphysical talisman against the perpetual glossing according to the latest theory that has characterized French intellectual life recently, whilst Michel Pierre, '¿Por qué Ortega en Francia ahora?' (73–82) is merely a rhetorical question to justify enthusiastic acclaim; P. H. Dust, 'Ortega y Gasset y la destrucción del libro. (Hacia una hermenéutica del discurso orteguiano)' (83–95) virtually proves Christian Pierre's point by using the Derridean method against itself; R. Gibert (96–107) documents relations between the 'hermanos enemigos', O. and Eugenio D'Ors; J. Lasaga Medina, 'Don Juan o el héroe del esfuerzo inútil. (Sobre el Don Juan de Ortega y Gasset)' (108–26) considers O.'s interpretations of the 'maestro de afán y sed'; I. Sánchez Cámara, 'El integracionismo de Ferrater Mora y su impronta orteguiana' (127–42) traces the influence of O.'s *raciovitalismo*. Comparative studies are for the initiated: R. Fornet-Betancourt, 'Dos aproximaciones filosóficas al problema de la técnica: Ortega y Heidegger', *CA*, 29 : 200–35, examines O.'s conferences in Santander in 1935 and *Frage nach der Technik*; whilst, continuing her study, I. Ballano Olano, 'La obra de Stendhal bajo la mirada de José Ortega y Gasset. Segunda aproximación. Ensayos sobre el amor: *De l'Amour* y "Amor en Stendhal"', *LetD*, 49 : 35–51, shows how and how much O. influenced Stendhal's popularity in Spain.

SENDER. G. Gullón, 'La modernidad y la narrativa del exilio de 1939. (El *Requiem* de Ramón J. Sender)', *DHA*, 9, 1990 : 3–12, deftly contextualizes Spanish modernism in the novel and exemplifies the remodelling of the relationships between author and reader and narration and history. M. J. Schneider, '*La vida es sueño* remembered and dismembered: on Ramón J. Sender's *Los laureles de Anselmo*', *RCEH*, 15, 1990:65–79, argues that the 1958 novel is both a highly politicized *caveat* against fascism and an injunction against public tyranny and private egoism that uses Calderón as the ethical base for parody. A. A. Rodríguez, '*Imán*: la aventura mítica del héroe', *HisJ*, 12:147–57, is mainly plot summary and quotation. F. Lough, 'History and fiction in *Mister Witt en el Cantón*', *ALEC*, 16:275–90, tries to see both elements as equally important and complementary in the narrative form.

UNAMUNO. Important texts appear. A facsimile edition of **De Fuerteventura a París. Diario íntimo de confinamiento y destierro (París 1925)*, Puerto Rosario, Cabildo Insular de Fuerteventura, 169 pp.; **Epistolario íberico*, M, Orígenes, 110 pp., U.'s correspondence with Joaquim Teixeira de Pascoaes; G. W. Ribbans, 'Unamuno in England: four unpublished articles (1909)', *BHS*, 68:383–94 and 479–88, reproduces the text and context of U.'s articles published in *The Englishwoman* in November 1909, and should be read with R. Santervás, 'Polémica y romance en torno a los artículos de Unamuno en *The Englishwoman* (1909)', *RLit*, 103, 1990:193–202, which has some complementary information. A. de Frutos, 'Miguel de Unamuno, habitante del nombre', *CHA*, 490:93–98, is a circular disquisition on U.'s given name 'que hace una espada de su pluma, y se mete a pelear con el pandemónium'. N. Toscano, 'Unamuno, pintor', *ib.*, 492:89–96, emphasizes U.'s skill as both artist and art critic and reproduces four sketches (92), and catalogues U.'s preferences for Regoyos, Zuloaga, El Greco, Velázquez, and José Ribera as well as his antipathy for Picasso, whose painting U. detested as 'insincera, algebraica, cerebral, es decir, no pictórica'. Comparative studies abound: from the Hispanic context, Jesús Basañez, **Unamuno y Baroja. Un estudio conjunto*, Bilbao, Ekin, 340 pp., and Ana María Fernández, **Teoría de la novela en Unamuno, Ortega y Cortázar*, M, Pliegos, 158 pp.; and reaching out to English literature, Ofelia Hudson, **Unamuno y Byron: la agonía de Caín*, M, Pliegos, 128 pp., whilst María Asunción Alba Pelayo, *Unamuno y Greene. Un estudio comparativo*, Alicante U.P., 1989, 212 pp., which focuses on *San Manuel Bueno, mártir* and 'The Potting Shed', might well be read with J. S. Choi, **Greene and Unamuno: Two Pilgrims to La Mancha*, New York, Peter Lang, 1990, 216 pp. Modern criticism provides the tools: C. J. García, 'Vida y novela: postulados metanovelescos en *Cómo se hace una novela* de Unamuno', *RHM*, 44:226–37, uses Linda Hutcheon and Barbara Herrnstein-Smith to good effect; although A. A. Fox, 'Lo imaginario en Unamuno. El caso de *El otro*', *RCEH*, 16:61–72, prefers Lacan to explicate the drama as the portrayal of paranoia and alienation in the imaginary register. By looking at the early poetry, G. Jurkevich, 'Unamuno's gestational fallacy: *Niebla* and "escribir a lo que salga"', *ALEC*, 15, 1990:65–81, argues that *viviparismo* is by no means spontaneous generation but a lengthy mental gestation; whilst C. M. Strand, 'The dialectical treatment of life and death in Miguel de Unamuno's *Poesías*', *ALEC*, 16:37–44, is a close reading of 'La flor tronchada' and 'Elegía en la muerte de un perro', poems which exemplify U.'s 'agonic' and 'contemplative' attitudes. A. F. Baker, 'The God of Miguel de Unamuno', *His(US)*, 74:824–33, distinguishes between 'pantheism' and 'panentheism' to explain seeming contradictions and draws parallels with Teilhard de Chardin.

VALLE-INCLÁN. Much editorial activity. José M. García de la Torre prologues **El ruedo ibérico I: La corte de los milagros*, M, Espasa Calpe, 1990, 356 pp.; Antón Risco edits with introduction and notes, **Cara de plata. Aguila de blasón. Romance de lobos*, B, Círculo de lectores; Id. provides critical apparatus for *Cara de plata*, M, Espasa Calpe, 217 pp.; José Servera Baño, **Corte de amor. Cuento de abril. Voces de gesta*, B, Círculo de lectores; and Dominic Keown and Robin Warner both compile and collate the Spanish text and give a translation into English of *The Grotesque Farce of Mr Punch the Cuckold/Esperpento de Los cuernos de Don Friolera*, Warminster, Aris and Phillips, 131 pp., with a useful historical introduction that also points up V.-I.'s innovative theatrical techniques (1–17). M. Gil, **La epopeya en Valle-Inclán: trilogía de la desilusión*, M, Pliegos, 1990, 185 pp. Eliane Lavaud-Fage, *La singlatura narrativa de Valle-Inclán (1888–1915)*, Corunna, Fundación Pedro Barné de la Maza, 603 pp., updates in Spanish her earlier study (1979) (see *YWMLS*, 42:355). Rosa Alicia Ramos, **Las narraciones breves de Ramón del Valle-Inclán*, M, Pliegos, 242 pp. Luis T. González-del-Valle, *La ficción breve de Valle-Inclán. Hermenéutica y estrategias narrativas*, B, Anthropos, 1990, 376 pp., re-edits previous work on V.-I.'s narratology that uses Shlomith Rimmon-Kenan to provide new readings of the *relatos* (see *YWMLS*, 48:399, and 49:370); Id., 'Una nota olvidada sobre "Un cabecilla"', *ALEC*, 16:379–82, is an *addendum* on V.-I.'s selective use of Prosper Merimée and Alphonse Daudet in the short story of 1893. C. Nickel, 'Representation and gender in Valle-Inclán's "Rosita"', *REH*, 25:35–55, gives the publishing history and metamorphoses of the short story between 1899–1903, and reads 'Rosita' as an elaborate inscription of woman within the text; whilst C. Feal, 'Rivales amorosos y modelos masculinos en los *Sonatas* de Valle-Inclán', *ECon*, 4:47–64, concludes that, by leaving Bradomín without either father-figure or male rivals in contravention of the typical Oedipal model, V.-I. permits the character to act out a role that is both legitimist (or masculine) and anarchist (against the *status quo*). For the comparatists: Nicolás Miñambres Sánchez, * *Valle-Inclán y García Lorca en el teatro del siglo XX*, M, Anaya, 96 pp.; and R. W. Rotert, 'Monster in the mirror', *Estreno*, 17.2:39–42, which indicates parallels and differences between *Luces de Bohemia* and Buero Vallejo's *El sueño de la razón*, particularly in the characterization of Max Estrella and Don Francisco de Goya. Margarita Santos Zas organizes the monographic study in *Insula*, 531, and also writes the introductory 'Estéticas de de Valle-Inclán: balance crítico' (9–10), in which she takes account of previous criticism and presents: A. Risco, 'Leer a Valle-Inclán' (1–2), an appeal to abandon party politics and read V.-I. as 'postmoderne' in Jean-François Lyotard's sense; V. Milner Garlitz, '*La lámpara maravillosa*: humo y luz' (11–12) sums up the smoke and mirrors of criticism to date; L. Schiavo, 'La estética del recuerdo en Valle-Inclán' (12–14) distinguishes V.-I. from Proustian 'involuntary memory', whilst G. Allegra, 'La poesía de Valle-Inclán: *Claves líricas*' (14–15) reads *Aromas de leyendas* (1907) and *El pasajero* (1920) as stages in a 'biografía interior'; concentrating on genre, P. Cabañas Vacas, 'Teoría de los géneros dramáticos en Ramón del Valle-Inclán' (16–17), and L. Iglesias Feijoo, 'El concepto de tragicomedia en Valle-Inclán' (18–20), both argue that in *Divinas palabras* (1920) experiment culminates in the destruction of the model so that V.-I. might inaugurate the innovation of the *esperpento*, whilst in comparative vein, D. Dougherty, 'Valle-Inclán y la farsa' (17–18) seeks classic and contemporary, Spanish and European, and literary and stage parallels, and R. Cardona, 'El esperpento como género' (20–22) uses George H. Szanto's concept of 'dialectic propaganda' to suggest parallels between V.-I. and Ghelderode, Brecht and Kopit, or *The Cabinet of Dr. Caligari*, Lina Wertmüller's 1970–75 films, and Terry Gilliam's *Brazil* (1985); D. Villanova, 'El "modernismo" novelístico de Ramón del Valle-Inclán' (22–23) identifies *La medianoche* (1917) as the cornerstone of V.-I.'s narratological modernism; A. N. Zahareas, 'El esperpento como proyecto estético' (31–32) calls for a genuine synthesis of historical context and aesthetic form in any future critique of the *esperpento*; and, as a postscript, I. Soldevila-Durante, 'Valle, Bagaría, Ramón. (A propósito del estreno de *La Marquesa Rosalinda*)' (30–31) dishes the dirt on V.-I.'s reaction to Gómez de la Serna's harsh review and Bagaría's cartoon on the *estreno* that V.-I. did not attend.

ZAMBRANO. 'De los sueños y el tiempo', *BFFGL*, 9:11–16, are fragments reproduced from work in progress at Z.'s death; whilst A. Iglesias, 'Amor-Roma, itinerario de María Zambrano', *ib.*, 17–25, explains the axis of Z.'s work and gives substantial quotation. José O.

Jiménez, *Los senderos olvidados de la filosofía. Una aproximación al pensamiento de María Zambrano*, M, Religión y Cultura, 342 pp., analyses the Unamunian roots of 'antropología filosófica' and documents particularly well Z.'s concept of 'razón poética'. C. Maillard, 'María Zambrano y el Zen', *CHA*, 490:7–19, remarks on Z.'s many references to Buddhism but zeroes in on the underlying similarities between *satori* and Z.'s 'despertar', or realization of reality. (See ORTEGA above).

4. THEATRE

Critical work on the drama of the period is also noted above under LITERARY AND CULTURAL HISTORY, ALBERTI, GARCÍA LORCA, SALINAS, UNAMUNO, and VALLE-INCLÁN. Items not recorded here concerning work by Alberti, Bergamín, Casona, García Lorca, Muñoz Seca, and Valle-Inclán are documented in P. L. Podol and A. Vicente, 'El drama español del siglo XX: bibliografía selecta del año 1989', *Estreno*, 17.1:31–36; and in C. A. Carpenter, 'Modern drama studies; an annual bibliography', *MoD*, 34:171–311, see particularly section E: Hispanic (231–52), which ranges over the period 1987–90. L. R. Scarano, 'El modelo paródico como forma de enlace intertextual. (De Echegaray a Valle-Inclán)', *LetD*, 49:183–89, articulates very well Linda Hutcheon's notion of 'inter-art discourse' by showing how the cosmovision of Restoration Spain presented in *El gran galeoto* (1881) is examined critically in the successive parodies by Francisco Flores García. *Galeotito* (1883), and Valle-Inclán, *Los cuernos de Don Friolera* (1921). Dru Dougherty and María Francisca Vilches, *La escena madrileña entre 1918 y 1926. Análisis y documentación*, M, Fundamentos, 1990, 491 pp., debunks some cherished notions by giving chapter and verse to prove that Muñoz Seca, Arniches and the Quinteros (rather than Benavente) were most frequently performed, that the influence exercised on the great mass of the theatre-going public by the experimental offerings of Pío Baroja, Valle-Inclán, García Lorca, Azorín, and Unamuno was minimal, and that the comic genre reigned supreme at the box-office. The greater part of the study is taken up with the fleshing out of such conclusions with a welter of statistical information about the individual representations. Also part of the same picture, but with little interest in the bourgeois taste for comic light relief, C. Jerez-Ferrán, 'Decadencia y revitalización en el teatro español de los años 20', *Estreno*, 17.2:14, 25–33, is a basic overview that tries to synchronize innovations in Spain with European counterparts; whilst P. N. de la Paz, '"Teatros": página teatral de *El Sol* (1927–28)', *ALEC*, 16:291–319, documents the incisive reviews and thesis articles written between 29 September

1927 and 31 June 1928, mainly by Luis Araquistáin, Gómez
Baquero, Díez Canedo, and Pérez de Ayala, to educate and inform
public taste. Enrique de Rivas edits with an introduction Cipriano de
Rivas Cherif, *Cómo hacer teatro: apuntes de orientación profesional en las artes
y oficios del teatro español*, V, Pre-Textos, 376 pp., a fascinating
combination of theory and practice that subsumes R.C.'s personal
experience in the 1920s with the experimental theatres of the
vanguard (*Escuela Nueva, Mirlo Blanco, Cántaro Roto*, and *Caracol*), and
with the great spectacles of the early 1930s (Unamuno's *Medea* and
Electra, and the performance in the bullring of Madrid of *El alcalde de
Zalamea*), his view of Spanish actresses from María Guerrero to
Margarita Xirgu, and some sound financial advice for theatrical
directors. Written when R.C. was held as a political prisoner in El
Dueso gaol, it should be read together with M. Aznar Soler, 'Una
experiencia de teatro carcelario en la España franquista: Cipriano
Rivas Cherif y el Teatro-Escuela del Dueso (1943–1945)', *JILS*, 2,
1990:77–96, which documents fully another set of R.C.'s *apuntes*,
written between October and December 1945, tracing in useful detail
the history of the theatre school R.C. ran with and for the inmates, the
specific productions, scenic innovations and theoretical teaching.
(See AZAÑA above).

LITERATURE, 1936 TO THE PRESENT DAY

By STEPHEN M. HART, *Associate Professor at the*
University of Kentucky, and
ABIGAIL LEE SIX, *Lecturer at Queen Mary and Westfield College,*
University of London

1. GENERAL

The literary canon is expanding to accommodate other related expressive discourses (the fine and the visual arts, and film) and, in particular, women's writing, for which a new canon is now emerging which ranges between populist writers such as Rosa Montero and readerly writers such as Esther Tusquets. There now seems hardly any time-lag, if at all, between European discourse and Spanish discourse; Spain does not seem as 'different' as it used to and ideas flow in and out more rapidly than before (see discussion of postmodernism below). *RO*, 122–23, is a special number of the arts in contemporary Spain; of special interest is M. Vázquez Montalbán, 'La literatura española en la construcción de la ciudad democrática' (125–33), a wide-ranging piece on changes in the artistic horizon brought about by democracy. Other essays are treated separately below, while others on music, the media and the visual arts fall outside the scope of this essay. Some post-war journals are studied: T. Fèrriz, '*Romance*, una revista del exilio', *DH*, 9, 1990:129–37; J. P. González Martín, 'Una revista ilegal de poesía en la España franquista: *Si la píldora bien supiera no la doraran por defuera. Revista exterior de poesía hispana* (1967–1969)', *ib.*, 139–49; J. Gracia, 'Historia y descripción de una revista olvidada: *La jirafa* (1956–1959)', *ib.*, 151–67; J. Oskam, 'Falange e izquierdismo en *Indice* (1956–1962): el fin y los medios', *ib.*, 169–82; while M. J. Gallofré Virgili, '"Unidad precisa y duración segura": depuració, suspensió i prohibició (Barcelona, 1939)', *ib.*, 183–90, assesses Franco's anti-Catalan laws and implications for post-civil-war lit. González-del-Valle, *Essays*, contains essays which are covered separately below. B. J. Dendle, 'The second republic, the Spanish civil war and the *episodios nacionales*', *CH*, 13.1–2:141–55, is an intriguing analysis of how Galdós's novels were used both by the republicans and the nationalists in order to bolster up their respective political causes. E. Mateo, 'El escritor exiliado y el público', *CA*, 26.2:164–84, is on the intellectual victims of Franco's crusade who fled to Mexico; mentions Catalan as well as Castilian writers; well-informed. A. Sánchez Vázquez, 'Exilio y filosofía: la aportación de los exiliados españoles al filosofar latinoamericano', *CA*, 30.6:139–53, explores the integration of the work of Spanish thinkers such as José Gaos, Joaquín Xirau, and María Zambrano in the Mexican intellectual scene after the civil war. Of general background interest is R. J. Golsan, 'Spain and the lessons of history: Albert Camus and the Spanish civil war', *RoQ*, 38:407–16, which analyses Camus's theatre and essays which exemplify his anger at Franco's destruction of Spain. J. Kortazar & J. Rojo, 'La locura, camino de interpretación', *Insula*, 530:24, reviews creative madness in Felipe Juaristi's poetry and novels. J. C. Vidal, 'El milagro de las pequeñas cosas', *Quimera*, 97, 1990:24–29, is an interview with a contemporary travel-writer, Juan Eduardo Zúñiga. F. J. Higuero, 'Tres aproximaciones críticas al pensamiento postmoderno en el ensayo español actual: Subirats, Campillo y Albiac', *LPen*, 3, 1990:213–31, reviews the work of the three most significant Spanish inheritors of the Lyotard-Baudrillard-Vattimo brand of postmodernism. A. Sobejano-Morán, 'Poética de la postmodernidad', *REH*, 25.1:95–107, takes its point of departure from the work of Fredric Jameson and Gonzalo Sobejano, emphasizing the motif of disintegration of the subject, the fragmentation of the work and the enhanced role of discourse which, rather than a vehicle, becomes the aim of the postmodern work of art; the debate continues in P. J. Smith's discussion of postmodernity, *ib.*, 109–16, and Navajas's counter-response, *ib.*, 15.3:129–51. J. A. Alvarez Osés, 'El ensayo en España', *RFe*, 223:54–64, is a general overview which looks at some earlier writers. F. Javier Higuero, 'La argumentación autoafirmativa del altruísmo en *Humanismo impenitente*, de Fernando Savater', *Ojáncano*, 4, 1990:19–29, discusses humanism and essentialism in Savater's essays. G. Mariscal, 'An introduction to the ideology of hispanism in the US and Britain', in *Conflicts of Discourse*, ed. P. Evans, Manchester UP, 1990, 201 pp. (1–25) is a thoughtful though eclectic piece on the nineteenth-century roots of what we do. M. K. Reed, 'Writing in the institution: the politics of British hispanism', *JHP*, 15:140–48, is equally thoughtful; takes a neo-Marxian approach. *An Encyclopedia of Continental Women Writers*, New York — London, Garland, 2 vols., is an excellent, up-to-date reference manual containing a great deal of information on most of the women writers covered in this section; well worth consulting. M. del Carmen Simón, 'Información bibliografica', *RLit*, 133:277–354, is as always a very helpful bibliographical guide for criticism on 20th-c. work (324–51), listing items not mentioned here.

2. POETRY

N. Dennis, 'Creación y compromiso en la poesía de la guerra civil española', *RCEH*, 15:575–87, offers a good overview of civil war poetry. C. Le Bigot, 'Les poètes entre le marteau et l'enclume: le discours sur l'écriture engagée en Espagne dans les années trente', *Iris*, 1, 1990:41–54, discusses Republican poets and poetics before and during the civil war. M. López de Abiada, 'La ironía como rasgo generacional definidor en los comienzos del grupo del 50. Apostillas a tres poemas representativos de José Agustín Goytisolo, Jaime Gil de Biedma y Angel González', *DH*, 9, 1990:45–56, has the results of an intriguing survey on the ten best post-civil-war poems (Gil de Biedma's 'Contra Jaime Gil de Biedma' came top), and then proceeds to some critical analysis. J. Pont, 'Tres grupos poéticos de la inmediata posguerra: *Garcilaso, Postismo y Cántico* (estética e ideología)', *ib.*, 79–97, helpfully provides facts, figures, and themes of these three poetic journals. L. Bonet, 'Dámaso Alonso y la escuela de Barcelona: huellas, semillas, silencios', *Insula*, 530:19–22, delineates Alonso's presence among the poets grouped around *Laye*, and what ensued. *Insula* continues its annual audit of contemporary poetry; 'Poesía española 1990–1991', 534:11–22, has articles on Pablo García Baena, Juan Carlos Suñén, Diego Jesús Jiménez, Antonio Martínez Sarrión, and Luis Antonio de Villena, among others; informative. J. J. Lanz, 'La literatura como representación', *ib.*, 535:24–26, offers critical fine-tuning on Cuenca's anthology of contemporary Spanish poetry. J. Siles, 'Ultísima poesía española escrita en castellano: rasgos distintivos de un discurso en proceso y ensayo de una posible sistematización', *Iberoromania*, 34:8–31, is an important essay on the themes of the 80s poets; rejection of the *novísimos*, re-evaluation of the 1950 Generation, and their elusive postmodernity. A shortened version appears as 'Dinámica poética de la última década', *RO*, 122–23:149–69. J. L. Falcó, 'La poesía: vanguardia o tradición', *ib.*, 170–86, revalorizes motifs such as narrativity, the elegy, and minimalism, and proposes new groupings such as the 'outsiders', beat generation poetry, and women's writing. J. M. Calles, 'Una nueva sentimentalidad en la poesía española contemporánea', *ECon*, 4.1:85–96, applies Lyotard's theory of postmodernism to the poets of the 1980s, arguing that their work postulates the link between poetry and biography as indispensable but also theatrical; mentions Luis García Montero, Jon Juaristi, and Julio Llazamares, among others. A. Carreño, 'El discurso de la tradición como diferencia: de Rosalía de Castro a José Angel Valente', *ALEC*, 16:15–35, traces the Galician poetic tradition and has some mention of modern poets such as Valente and Luz Pozo Garza.

ARANGUREN. M. del Carmen Pallarés, '*Fuego Lento* — Gar Mantsoa de Jorge G. Aranguren', *Insula*, 536:30, makes a plea for greater recognition of A.'s poetry.

ARGAYA. I. Valverde Azula, 'Como luces de Gálibo en la noche (una poesía para espacios soñados)', *Insula*, 536:31, is an introduction to A.'s *intimista* poetry via his 1990 *Luces de Gálibo*.

BARRAL. C. Riera, 'Carlos Barral: la prehistoria literaria', *Quimera*, 98, 1990:28–31, is a useful introduction with special emphasis on B.'s role in the Escuela de Barcelona. M. Andueza, 'Carlos Barral: poeta, navegante y editor', *CA*, 26.2:185–89, is likewise a general introduction to B.'s various talents.

CARNERO. L. R. Scarano, 'La poesía de Guillermo Carnero: una estética de la negatividad', *ALEC*, 16:321–35, looks at C.'s postmodern debunking of poetry and language. J. Giordiano, 'Reflexiones sobre *Avila* de Guillermo Carnero: clausura del simbolismo', *ECon*, 3.2:69–78, is a close textual reading of the first poem from C.'s *Dibujo de la muerte*, emphasizing symbols.

CARVALHO GALERO. C. Blanco, 'Carvalho Calero o la nostalgia del edén', *Insula*, 530:25, reviews the poetry of an author more widely known for his lit. criticism.

CELAYA. J. A. Ascunce Arrieta, 'La poesía de Gabriel Celaya como forma y sonido: *Cantos Iberos*', *Ojáncano*, 4, 1990:3–18, is an in-depth analysis of metre and rhyme scheme in C.'s poetry; an intriguing way of looking at his work.

COLINAS. K. Pritchett, 'Antonio Colinas's *Larga carta a Francesca*: a Lacanian approach to its formal construction', *His(US)*, 74:262–68, is on the 1986 novel of a writer better known for his poetry; more 'explaining' of Lacan than of the novel, which concerns the life of a poet called Jano.

CUENCA. J. J. Lanz, *La poesía de Luis Alberto de Cuenca*, Córdoba, Trayectoria de navegantes, 79 pp., has a precise discussion of the various poetic generations of the post-war period, proposing C. as a poet of a so-called 'Generación del 68', followed by an analysis of the three stages of C.'s work; has balanced discussion (37–45) of C.'s most renowned work, *La caja de plata* (1985).

ENRIQUE. J. Lupiáñez, 'El mundo como un galeón atormentado', *Insula*, 535:27–28, looks at maritime imagery in E.'s *El galeón atormentado*.

FELIPE. J. Servera Baño, 'El mito en la poesía de León Felipe', *Caligrama*, 4:127–36, looks at role of images of utopia, biblical and classical topoi, Don Quixote and Shakespeare in F.'s poetry.

GIL-ALBERT. C. A. Bradford, 'Juan Gil-Albert and Jorge Guillén: the Apollonian and the Dionysian modes in contemporary Spanish poetry', *ECon*, 3.1, 1990:7–24, uses Nietzsche's theory of Dionysian/Apollonian dialectic to contrast G.-A.'s with Guillén's poetry.

GIMÉNEZ-FRONTÍN. J. F. Martín Gil, 'El compromiso del zorro', *Quimera*, 95, 1990:28–34, is an interview with the up-and-coming author of *Astrolabio*.

366 — *Spanish Studies*

GONZÁLEZ. *En homenaje a Angel González; ensayos, entrevista y poemas*, ed. A. P. Debicki & S. Keefe Ugalde, Boulder, Colorado, SSSAS, 139 pp., has an informative interview (111–25), some hitherto unpublished poems (127–31), and some good general essays on G.'s work; essential. S. Schumm, 'El aspecto alusivo de la poesía de Angel González', *HJ*, 12:133–45, mainly looks at religious irony. D. K. Benson, '*Heteroglossia* en la poesía de Angel González', González-del-Valle, *Essays*, 11–18, uses Bakhtin to elucidate the playful conflict of voices in G.'s poetry.

JANÉS. J. Pérez, 'The novels of a poet: Clara Janés', González-del-Valle, *Essays*, 197–207, begins with discussion of themes in J.'s poetry (alienation, being-toward-death), and then compares *Desintegración* (1969) with *Los caballos del sueño* (1989), the two novels J. talked about at the 1991 St Andrews conference on Hispanic women writers.

MANTERO. M. fictitiously interviews himself, 'Entrevista: Manuel Mantero', *Ojáncano*, 4, 1990:70–76; witty and interesting. *Ib.*, 77–82, provides a foretaste of M.'s forthcoming collection of poems entitled *Fiesta*.

PORPETTA. L. de Luis, 'Esplendor y ceniza en la poesía de Antonio Porpetta', *Insula*, 536:29–30, reviews the main trends of P.'s poetry in the 1980s.

RODRÍGUEZ FER. X. L. Axeitos, 'La poesía de Claudio Rodríguez Fer (Notas periféricas para su lectura)', *Insula*, 531:28–29, gives an introduction to R.F.'s readerly, metaphysical poetry. R.F. writes an authoritative 'Panorama de poesía galega', *Iberoromania*, 34:32–40.

ROSETTI. Y. Rosas & C. Hilde, 'La aproximación del lenguaje y de desmitificación de los códigos sexuales de la cultura de la poesía de Ana Rosetti', *ETL*, 20:1–12, looks at the representation of women in four of her poems from *Yesterday* (1989); concludes that her vision of womanhood is nearer to Cixous than to Kristeva.

SÁNCHEZ ROBAYNA. J. Malpartida, 'Cuerpo sumergido (Sobre Andrés Sanchez Robayna)', *CHA*, 498:41–47, looks at language, silence and depiction of the material universe in S.R.'s poetry; *ib.*: 49–52, prints some of his recent poems.

SILES. A. P. Debicki, 'Un clasicismo contemporáneo: la poesía reciente de Jaime Siles', *RHM*, 44:82–92, focuses on the classical turn of thought in S.'s *Música de agua* (1983) and *Columnae* (1987).

VALENTE. F. Rubio, 'Exiliado de la convención: la obra de José Angel Valente', *Quimera*, 106–07:62–67, is general; C. Rodríguez Fer, 'Un poeta europeo', *ib.*, 64–67, is on V.'s European sources. J. Mayhew, '"El signo de la femininidad": gender and poetic creation in José Angel Valente', *REH*, 25.2:123–33, points to the feminization of creativity in V.'s later work and addresses the problematics of a feminist reading.

3. NOVEL

This year has brought a large crop of work on gender. As well as items separately listed under authors, María Jesús Mayans Natal, *Narrativa feminista española de posguerra*, Madrid, Pliegos, 205 pp., focuses on the depiction of pre-adult women in the pre-feminist years in Spain up to the end of the 1960s and the symbolic significance of this frequent centre of interest for women writers. Elizabeth J. Ordóñez, *Voices of Their Own: Contemporary Spanish Narrative by Women*, Lewisburg: Bucknell U.P. — London: Associated U.P., 250 pp. is a broadly chronological study ranging from the forties to the eighties, informed by theory and looking in particular at the development of the maternal trope. Two articles by C. Davies have been published: 'Feminist writing in Spain since 1900: from political strategy to personal inquiry', Forsås-Scott, *Liberation*, 192–226, briefly surveys Laforet, Matute, Martín Gaite, Roig, Tusquets, and Montero, chiefly being pitched at non-Hispanist feminists but usefully placing the literature in its socio-political context. 'The Sexual Representation of Politics in Hispanic Feminist Narrative', Condé, *Readings*, 107–19, examines female subjectivity and desire in Roig, Montero, and Valenzuela. Two articles in *Actas* (Brown) study contemporary fiction from Galicia: R. Landeira, 'La novelística gallega actual' (357–65) is a general survey that makes special reference to Xohana Torres, *Adiós, María* (1965), Carlos Casares, *Xoguetes para un tiempo prohibido* (1975), and Xosé Luis Méndez Ferrín, *Antón e os inocentes* (1967); K. N. March, **'Prolegómenos a un estudio das novelistas galegas'*, (367–77) takes up the feminist theme again, looking at women's writing from the region. N. Torrents, **'Eine anachronistische Lektüre: Ana María Matute und Juan Marsé in der siebsiger Jahren'*, *Spanische Lektüre*, ed. by M. Strausfeld, Berlin, Surhkamp, 252–74. D. K. Herzberger has respectively two general articles with a certain amount of overlap and one more specific one: 'Narrating the past: history and the novel of memory in postwar Spain', *PMLA*, 106:34–45, concentrates on the interplay between characters' personal recollections and official history; 'Social realism and the contingencies of history in the contemporary Spanish novel', *HR*, 59:153–73, studies in more general terms how these novels undermined the official history promoted by the regime; 'History, apocalypse, and the triumph of fiction in the postwar Spanish novel', *RHM*, 44:247–58, explores, with reference to Juan Goytisolo and more briefly, Benet, Torrente Ballester, Martín Gaite, and Luis Goytisolo, the way in which history is framed within the vision of the apocalyptic in Francoist Spain and how Francoist historiography is rooted in a post-apocalyptic levelling of historical meaning. B. Jordan, 'Social realism in the 1950s: the contribution of *Revista Española*', *BHS*, 68:281–95, looks at this short-lived publication, highlighting the fiction it published by budding writers of the *generación de medio siglo*. F. Valls, 'La literatura erótica en España entre 1975 y 1990', *Insula*, 530:29–30, is pessimistic about the quality of such material.

BENET. M. Allen Compitello, 'Benet and Spanish postmodernism', *RHM*, 44:259–73, considers the elision of history and fiction in B.'s recent fiction and historiographical essays, concluding that they demonstrate that it is unfeasible to propose a Spanish postmodernism. J. Pérez Magallón, 'Tiempo y tiempos en *Volverás a Región*, de Juan Benet', *HR*, 59:281–94, considers the interlocking of the time of frame story with the time-spans evoked by memory and other devices in the novel.

CELA. Luis Blanco Vila, *Para leer a Camilo José Cela* (Clásicos del siglo XX, 3), Madrid, Atenea, 222 pp., is a conversational, somewhat anecdotal survey of C.'s life and works, eulogistic in tone. R. Manteiga, '"Das meigas, bruxas, e demos": superstition and violence in Cela's *Mazurca para dos muertos*', *Actas* (Brown), 421–29, is a general study of the novel which places it in the context of C.'s other writings. *Hispanística XX*, 8, 1990 (1991) is devoted to Cela: J. Alsina, 'El camino y la fuente. Campos léxicos en las primeras páginas del relato de Pascual Duarte' (7–24), argues that Pascual is self-consciously seeking a literary style for his discourse. C. Boix, 'Camilo José Cela: enunciación y estilística La colmena [*sic*]' (25–42), studies poliphony in this novel. A. Abuin, '"No una vez sino ciento": la frecuencia narrativa en *La colmena*' (43–51), applies Genette's distinction between singulative, iterative and repetitive narration, concluding that these devices contribute to a positive view of solidarity amongst the characters of the novel. D. Henn, 'El pesimismo en la narrativa celiana' (53–67), analyses C.'s pessimistic view of the human condition throughout his literary production. R. Kirsner, 'La persistente presencia de la guerra civil española en la obra de Camilo José Cela' (69–80), sees the legacy of the War as inseparable from Cela's depiction of Spain. A. Iglesias Ovejero, 'Cela onomaturgo: los nombres propios en el gallego y su cuadrilla' (81–101), considers the ludic element in Cela's invention of proper nouns. I. Soldevila-Durante, 'La creatividad léxica de Camilo José Cela' (103–17), adds to and partly contests S. Suárez Solí's 1969 study of C.'s lexicon. J. M. Martínez Cachero, 'Camilo José Cela, viajero por España' (119–32), juxtaposes C.'s travel writings with his actual travels. A. de Juan Bolufer, M. C. Luna Selles, and C. Sanfiz Fernández, 'Cela y el surrealismo: *Pisando la dudosa luz del día*' (133–53), argues that this early collection of C.'s poetry can properly be considered surrealist. J. Marín, 'Cela/Picasso: dibujos y retratos en torno a un encuentro y una colaboración' (155–73), documents Cela's writings on Picasso and the friendship between the two men. Two of the articles are on C.'s journal: J. M. Oltra, 'Significación de una aventura celiana: los *Papeles de Son Armadans* entre 1956 y 1966' (175–215), studies how he projects himself through it, whilst D. Villanueva, *'Papeles de Son Armadans* en la obra de Camilo José Cela', (217–28), concentrates more on the absolute value of the publication to Spanish culture. J. Costa Ferrandis, 'La difusión y recepción de Camilo José Cela en los años de la transición política española (el *Pascual Duarte* y *La colmena*)' (229–40), looks at the post-Franco film versions of these texts and the impact of modifications made in the process.

CHACEL. A. Lee Six, 'Perceiving the family: Rosa Chacel's *Desde el amanecer*', Condé, *Readings*, 79–90, maps C.'s use of voice and gaze in the text on to critical theory about these.

CONDE. V. Araguas, 'Abstracción de la colmena', *Insula*, 534:28, on *Los otros días* (1991), finds C. more relaxed when he writes in his native Gallego.

CUNQUEIRO. A. M. Dotras, *'Un hombre que se parecía a Orestes*, parodia moderna del mito helénico', *Actas* (Brown), 349–56, posits a reading of C.'s text that neither dismisses it as pure entertainment nor accords it mythical stature.

DELIBES. J. Lowe, 'Ironía e inversión en un relato de Miguel Delibes', *RILCE*, 7:62–68, analyses 'La mortaja' (1957) in terms of D.'s ironic focus on oppositions such as strength and weakness, woman and man, life and death, light and darkness, silence and noise.

GARCIA MORALES. E. J. Ordóñez, 'Writing ambiguity and desire: the works of Adelaida García Morales', in Brown, *Writers*, 258–77, draws on Lacanian and other theory.

JUAN GOYTISOLO. D. Henn, 'Two views of Almería: Juan Goytisolo and Gerald Brenan', *Revue de littérature comparée*: 429–46, argues that whilst G. sets out to explore and explain, Brenan simply seeks to inform and entertain, contrary to G.'s own view of Brenan's writings. Two articles by A. Lee Six have been published: 'Breaking Rules, Making History: A Postmodern Reading of Historiography in Juan Goytisolo's Fiction', *History and Post-war Writing*, ed. by Theo D'haen and Hans Bertens (Postmodern Studies, 3), Amsterdam, Rodopi, 1990 (1991), 33–60, argues that G.'s treatment of historiography can be classified as postmodern; 'Juan Goytisolo's portable *patria*: staying on home ground abroad', *ReMS*, 34:78–96, studies G.'s autobiographical texts and their attitude to his status as exile. M. Ruiz Lagos, *Propuestas de alcance del 'Pájaro Solitario'*, (Cuadernos del Mediodía, 4) Seville U.P., 44 pp. is the result of a seminar led by the author, structuralist in style and terminology.

GUERRA GARRIDO.   J. Cruz Mendizábal, 'El juego de los sentidos', *Insula*, 534:27–28, focuses on *Dulce objeto de amor* (1990), looking at the importance of G.G.'s use of sense of touch.

LAFORET.   G. Pérez Firmat, 'Carmen Laforet: the dilemma of artistic vocation', in Brown, *Writers*, 26–41, ingeniously argues that L.'s fading from the literary scene is foreshadowed in her fiction, which recurrently suggests that women's artistic creation is a sign of immaturity or sickness.

LANDERO.   J. L. Buendía López, 'Landero, al otro lado del espejo', *CHA*, 492:134–38, is a critical appreciation of *Juegos de la edad tardía* (1989).

MARSE.   J. M. Costas Goberno, 'La soledad se inventa espejos: sobre *El amante bilingüe*, de Juan Marsé', *Insula*, 534:25–27, looks at the treatment of time, memory, and the play of mirroring and masks in the text. C. Hernández García, 'El juego en *Historia de detectives* de Juan Marsé', *Hispanófila*, 101:49–60, analyses M.'s predilection for game-playing both directly with his readers and as theme within a novel about characters who resort to fantasy games. A. Rodríguez-Fischer, 'Entrevista a Juan Marsé', *Insula*, 534:23, 25, centres on *El amante bilingüe*. A. Sotelo Vázquez, 'Historia, discurso y polifonía en *El amante bilingüe* de Juan Marsé', *CHA*, 488:141–49, studies the text in the light of Bakhtinian and structuralist theories.

MARTIN GAITE.   J. L. Brown, 'Carmen Martín Gaite: reaffirming the pact between reader and writer', in Brown, *Writers*, 72–92, is a general survey that emphasizes the conversational element in M.G.'s fiction. Maria Vittoria Calvi, **Dialogo e conversazione nella narrativa di Carmen Martín Gaite*, Milan, Arcipelago, 1990, 180 pp. studies the opposition in her work between authentic communication and the social ritual of conversation. In appendix there is an interview with M.G. in Spanish.

MATUTE.   J. Pérez, 'The fictional world of Ana María Matute: solitude, injustice, and dreams', in Brown, *Writers*, 93–115, is a lucid survey which pinpoints major themes in M.'s fiction.

MAYORAL.   C. Alborg has published two articles on M.: 'Las artes plásticas en la narrativa de Marina Mayoral: de metaficción a metaarte', *RHM*, 44:144–49, categorizes the different uses to which M. puts the visual arts in her fiction; and 'Marina Mayoral's Narrative: old families and new faces from Galicia', in Brown, *Writers*, 179–97, is a general survey of her fiction. K. M. Glenn, 'Marina Mayoral's *La única libertad*: a postmodern narrative', *Actas* (Brown), 405–11, examines M.'s ironic rereading of earlier literary works, and the metafictionality of her narrative in this 1982 novel.

MEDIO.   M. E. W. Jones, 'Dolores Medio: chronicler of the contemporary Spaniard's interaction with society' in Brown, *Writers*,

59–71, sees her as heir to nineteenth-century naturalism and realism but in the postwar context and from a woman's angle.

MENDEZ FERRIN. E. Souto, '(A) mor(te) de Artur', *Actas* (Brown), 379–94, follows Campbell's theories in studying M.F.'s use of Arthurian tradition in *Amor de Artur* (1982).

MOIX. A. Bush, 'Ana María Moix's silent calling', in Brown, *Writers*, 136–58, studies M.'s fiction with ref. to woman's problematic relation with language and uses Lacan's theory of the imaginary.

MONTERO. J. L. Brown, 'Rosa Montero: from journalist to novelist', in Brown, *Writers*, 240–57, posits a gradual movement in M.'s fiction away from a journalistic style towards a more imaginative one.

ORTIZ. R. C. Spires, 'Lourdes Ortiz: mapping the course of postfrancoist fiction', in Brown, *Writers*, 198–216, situates each of O.'s novels on a scale running from writerly to readerly. L. K. Talbot, 'Lourdes Ortiz's *Urraca*: a re-vision/revision of history', *RoQ*, 38:437–48, studies the relationship between O.'s revision of the conventional historical view of the eponymous twelfth-century Spanish queen and the character's own re-vision of herself as she writes and tells her story.

POMBO. J. A. Masoliver Ródenas, 'La ironía de Alvaro Pombo', *Insula*, 531:27–28, is a laudatory commentary on *El metro de platino iridiado* (1990).

QUIROGA. M. C. Riddel, 'El elemento gallego en *Tristura* de Elena Quiroga' *Actas* (Brown), 413–19, despite its title is a general study of Q.'s technique in this novel. P. Zatlin, 'Writing against the current; the novels of Elena Quiroga', in Brown, *Writers*, 42–58, emphasizes Q.'s bold exploration of taboo subjects and her unrecognized status as ground-breaker.

ROJAS. T. Feeney, 'Fact and fiction in Rojas' *Azaña*', *Hispanófila*, 103:33–46, studies R.'s use of historical fact and the 'otro' motif in his fictionalized portrayal of Manuel Azaña.

SANCHEZ FERLOSIO. B. Jordan, 'Back to the future: recontextualising *El Jarama*', *RoQ*, 38:213–25, seeks to reconsider the novel in its 1950s context. J. Squires, 'Making sense of Rafael Sánchez Ferlosio's *El Jarama*', *MLR*, 86:602–12, uses structuralism to question both social realist and mythic readings of the novel, arguing that it centrally explores how we make sense of reality and experience. S. Sanz Villanueva, 'Ferlosio y *Alfanhuí*, o el gusto por contar historias' *CHA*, 492:39–54, is a general commentary on this understudied novel which also investigates the contrasts between it and *El Jarama*.

SENDER. Stephen M. Hart, *Sender: Réquiem por un campesino español* (Critical Guides to Spanish Texts, 49), London, Grant & Cutler–Támesis, 1990 (1991), 61 pp., is the helpful survey that is the hallmark of the series. A new scholarly edition by P. McDermott of *Réquiem por un campesino español*, MUP, III pp., contains critical introduction and extracts from *Contraataque* too.

TORRENTE BALLESTER. C. Urza, 'El contexto histórico-mítico de *La saga/fuga de J.B.*', *Hispanófila*, 102:57–76, studies the parodic relationship between the work and nineteenth-century regionalist histories of Galicia, concluding that T.B. is condemning the Galician obsession with creating a mythical past.

TUSQUETS. Nina L. Molinaro, *Foucault, Feminism, and Power: Reading Esther Tusquets*, Lewisburg, Bucknell U.P. — London, Associated U.P., 126 pp. focuses on intertextuality, simulation, temporal displacement, genre transgression, and retelling in T.'s novels. S. Hart, 'On the threshold: Cixous, Lispector, Tusquets', in Condé, *Readings*, 91–105, studies the concept of 'écriture féminine' with reference to T.'s fiction. M. Servodidio, 'Esther Tusquets's fiction: the spinning of a narrative web', in Brown, *Writers*, 159–78, looks at the recurrent themes of alienation, decision-making, and death in T.'s fiction in the light of feminist psychoanalytic theory.

ZAMBRANO. C. Maillard, 'María Zambrano y el Zen', *CHA*, 490:7–19 considers points of contact between Z.'s writings and Zen Buddhist philosophy.

4. DRAMA

J. P. Gabriele and C. Leonard, 'Perspectivas sobre el teatro español a los quince años de la democracia', *ALEC*, 15, 1990:253–73, has separate sections on Buero Vallejo, Fermín Cabal, Ana Diosdado, Lidia Falcón, Guillermo Heras, Jerónimo López Mozo, Antonio Martínez Ballesteros, Lauro Olmo, Pilar Pombo, María-José Rague-Arias, María Manuela Reina, and Carmen Resino; a useful who's who. U. Aszyk, 'Medio siglo de teatro: entre crisis y vanguardia', *DH*, 9, 1990:99–117, is a helpful overview that runs from pre-war theatre to 1984; clear demarcation of periods. P. W. O'Connor, 'The *Primer grupo de la democracia* and the return to the word', *Estreno*, 17.1:13–15, is on the new generation of dramatists in Spain, all in their twenties and thirties. V. F. Nigro, 'Contextualizing histories and historians of hispanic theatre', *REH*, 24.1, 1990:107–19, has some discussion of the canon of post-civil-war theatre. A. M. Pasquariello, 'The Madrid theater session of 1950: politics of the *premios*', González-del-Valle, *Essays*, 187–95, is a spirited introduction to the works of pro-Franco dramatists such as Ignacio Luca de Tena, José María Pemán, Joaquín Calvo Sotelo, José Antonio Giménez Arnau, *et al.*, now justifiably drowned in political oblivion. M. F. Vilches de Frutos, 'La temporada teatral española 1989–1990', *ALEC*, 16:337–60, provides, as ever, a nose-close-to-the-ground approach; essential reading. C. Oliva, 'Hacia un escenario muerto: teatro español de los ochenta', *Gestos*, 6:167–74, looks at the material effects of the state funding of national theatre after Franco's death, a topic also treated in A. L. Johnson, 'El teatro español: 1985–90 (presencias y ausencias en un lustro teatral)', *Estreno*, 17.1:7–11. A. Fernández Insuela, 'Entrevista: la generación realista ante el teatro español de 1985–1990', *ib.*, 17.2:5–9, publishes reactions from J. M. Rodríguez Méndez, José Martín Recuerda, Lauro Olmo, and Carlos Muñiz to recent Spanish theatre. M. J. Ragué, '*La cubana*, el gran éxito del teatro catalán en 1989', *ib.*, 17.1:26–30, is on the vibrancy of Castilian theatre in Catalunya. P. L. Podol, 'Sexuality and marital relationships in Paloma Pedrero's *La llamada de Lauren* and María Manuela Reina's *La cinta dorada*', *ib.*, 22–25, analyses plays by two of the most significant contemporary Spanish 'dramaturgas' according to Buero Vallejo; plays have female perspective. P. Zatlin, 'Two-character plays as "teatro último": examples from Díaz, Junyent and Salom', *ECon*, 4.1:97–102, compares Sebastián Junyent's *Hay que deshacer la casa* (1983) and Jaime Salom's *Una hora sin televisión* (1987) with a play by the Mexican dramatist, Jorge Díaz; centres on moment of crisis for two people who have been very close. Of bibliographical merit is P. C. Podol, 'El drama español del siglo XX: bibliografía selecta del año 1989', *Estreno*, 17.1:31–36.

BUERO VALLEJO. M. T. Halsey, 'Painters, painting and immersion: three tragedies of Buero Vallejo', *Atenea* (Puerto Rico), 10, 1990:71–82, analyses the role played by Velázquez's canvas in B.V.'s *Las meninas*, the art critic in *Diálogo secreto*, and Goya's Black Etchings in *El sueño de la razón*. M. Payeras Grau, 'Lectura parcial de *La detonación* (Visión retrospectiva sobre un drama de Antonio Buero Vallejo)', *Iris*, 1, 1990:55–65, is on the cathartic fusion of tragedy and social criticism in B.V.'s play. C. J. Harris, 'La mujer en el teatro de Buero Vallejo: una lectura femenina', *LPen*, 3, 1990:247–57, looks at female roles in *La tejedora de sueños*, *Madrugada*, and *Lázaro en el laberinto*. E. Pennington, 'Buero Vallejo's *Diálogo secreto*: the masks of mortals', *Hispanófila*, 103:17–32, looks for Jungian tropes of the unconscious in B.V.'s 1984 play. J. Cross Newman, 'Traumas de conciencia en el teatro de Buero Vallejo', *Estreno*, 17.2:15–19, is mainly on Tomás's guilt in *La fundación*. M. de Paco, 'La verdad, el tiempo y el recuerdo: *Lázaro en al laberinto y Música cercana*', *ib.*, 43–45, examines the ethical and metaphysical problems faced by protagonists of B.V.'s two recent plays. B.V. is interviewed in *ib.*, 17.1:9, and *ib.*, 17.2:20–24.

FERNÁN GÓMEZ. B. A. González, 'The civil war at a distance: space and the language of desire in *Las bicicletas son para el verano* by Fernando Fernán Gómez', *Gestos*, 6:71–84, is on F.G.'s popular play about the war, first staged in 1982.

MUÑIZ. A. Fernández Insuela, 'Nota previa a *El caballo del caballero*, de Carlos Muñiz', *Estreno*, 17.2:10, introduces M.'s recent play which is then printed (11–14).

OLMO. J. P. Gabriele, 'Conversación con Lauro Olmo', *ALEC*, 16:383–87, is a short interview focusing on O.'s views of the theatre.

ONETTI. E. Centeno, 'Antonio Onetti, la otra opción de la vanguardia', *Estreno*, 17.1:16, introduces an up-and-coming dramatist; O.'s play *La puñalá* follows (17–21).

PEDRERO. Interview in *Estreno*, 17.1:12.

SASTRE. J. Theophilis, 'Existential aspects of *Escuadra hacia la muerte*: the incorporation of the Sartrean-Camusian polemic', *DH*, 9, 1990:119–28, points to nodes of S.'s text which intersect with Existentialism. J. Estruch, '*Los últimos días de Emmanuel Kant*, de Alfonso Sastre: entre el realismo y la fantasía', *ECon*, 3.2:61–68, analyses what S. took from historical sources in his play which premiered on 21 February 1990 in Madrid; a horror play rather than a complex tragedy.

SEDANO. P. W. O'Connor, 'The "Dark Double" and the patriarch in *La diosa de arena*', González-del-Valle, *Essays*, 181–86, analyses progression in S.'s patriarchal play from woman as monster to woman as angel in the house.

V. CATALAN STUDIES

LANGUAGE*

By BLANCA PALMADA, *Lecturer at the Department of Catalan Philology of the Universitat Autònoma de Barcelona*, and
VICENT DE MELCHOR, *Lecturer at the Department of Catalan Philology of the Universitat Autònoma de Barcelona*, and
ALBERT TURULL, *Lecturer at the Department of Catalan Philology of the Universitat de Lleida*, and
JORDI BAÑERES, *Institut de Sociolingüística Catalana, Barcelona*

(This article covers the years 1989–91)

1. GENERAL AND HISTORICAL

The following works will be extensively referred to in this section: *Catalan Working Papers in Linguistics 1991*, B, Universitat Autònoma U.P., 351 pp. (*CWPL 1991*); Joan Solà, *Lingüística i normativa*, B, Empúries, 1990, 138 pp. (Solà, *Lingüística*); *Miscel.lània Joan Fuster. Estudis de llengua i literatura*, ed. Antoni Ferrando and Albert Hauf, 4 vols, I, 1989, II, 1990, IV, 1991, B, Abadia de Montserrat, 408, 442, 440 pp. (*Misc. Joan Fuster*). John Stevenson, *Catalán, gallego, vascuence: Ensayo bibliográfico de estudios lingüísticos publicados o realizados en España (1970–1986)*, Sydney, The University of New South Wales (School of Spanish and Latin American Studies), 1989, 235 pp., contains more than 2800 entries for the Catalan language. Joan Martí, *Gramàtica històrica. Problemes i mètodes*, Valencia U.P., 1990, 161 pp., provides a subject-based bibliography including about 500 items on the general history of Catalan from the 19th. c. until the end of 1988. The two bibliographies should be regarded as complementary as far as the historical perspective is concerned. Joan Coromines, *Diccionari etimològic i complementari de la llengua catalana*, vol. IX, B, Edicions 62, 623 pp. concludes this majestic work. Coromines handles a large number of sources, if not always accurately or diachronically balanced, with his characteristic vehement, idiosyncratic style, as well as many first-hand data from personal research. The latter has been reviewed by K. Baldinger, 'Kritische Würdigung des neuen katalanischen etymologischen Wörterbuches von Joan Coromines', *ZK*, 3, 1990: 130–37, with a large bibliography on the subject. The still much useful Francesc de B. Moll, *Gramàtica històrica catalana*, Valencia U.P., 288 pp., has been published in Catalan yet it has not been brought up to date. A. Ferrando, 'La formació històrica del valencià', *Segon*

*The editor wishes to thank Sílvia Coll-Vinent for her assistance in co-ordinating contributions to this article.

Congrés Internacional de la Llengua Catalana (1986), vol. VIII, V, Institut de Filologia Valenciana, 1989, pp. 399–428, discusses prior hypotheses based on the substratum and other linguistic strata and argues for the assimilation of the imported vernaculars onto the major dialect of Western Catalonia. Coloma Lleal, *La formación de las lenguas peninsulares*, B, Barcanova, 1990, 383 pp., may be regarded as an updated development of the classical work of W. J. Entwistle. Francesc Bernat and Jaume Torres, *Mapes per a l'estudi de la llengua catalana (Com ensenyar català als adults*, suppl. 6), B, Generalitat de Catalunya (Departament de Cultura), 1989, 62 pp., provides an outstanding general view on the history, dialectology, and sociolinguistics of Catalan with the inclusion of 76 maps and figures. A. Alsina, 'Un aspecte de la morfologia històrica catalana: la primera persona del singular del present d'indicatiu', *LlLi*, 3, (1988–1989):88–119, deals with this significant variant of dialect-division from a generative point of view. *Ib.*, 339–426, equally brings in full the *Col.loqui sobre el substrat lingüístic del català* (1985), with papers and discussions by linguists (such as Badia, Mariner, Moran) and archeologists on recent researches and trends. Nevertheless it remains difficult to relate particular features of Catalan to any specific substrata. *Jaume I, Libre dels feyts*, ed. Jordi Bruguera, 2 vols, B, Barcino, 333 + 395 pp., is the most authoritative edition, according to the oldest MS. It provides detailed linguistic features including a systematization of clitics and verbal inflection, and a copious range of selected linguistic variants found in other MSS and in the edition of 1557. Josep Moran, *Les homilies provençals de Tortosa*, B, Curial/Abadia de Montserrat, 1990, 244 pp., attempts to show, firstly, that the *Homilies d'Organyà*, which to the present have been considered as constituting the first literary text in Catalan, are not in fact original (or at least not entirely) but rather a cognate translation of those of Tortosa based on a common provençal source. Secondly the study in question puts forward the idea that by the end of the 12th c. it was felt necessary to translate these *Homilies* into Catalan (which may prove that both languages Catalan and Provençal were clearly distinguished). Giuseppe Tavani, Philip D. Rasico *et al.*, *Llibre Blanc sobre la unitat de la llengua catalana*, B, Barcino, 1989, 216 pp., collects evidence in favour of the unity amongst the different varieties of Catalan and against artificial controversy about its origin and characteristics. Moreover several non-Catalan scholars concentrate in particular on the history of the language (Tavani), on the appearance of more recent sounds in the language (Rasico), on morphology (M. W. Wheeler), on lexis (J. Gulsoy), on lexicography (J. A. Pascual), on sociolinguistics (G. Kremnitz), and on the linguistic unity within poetry (M. C. Zimmermann). *Actes de les Terceres Jornades d'Estudi de la*

Llengua Catalana [1987], B, Abadia de Montserrat, 1989, 288 pp., contains a critical survey by Albert Rico (pp. 75–112) of geosynonyms in current dictionaries in order to establish a standard variety. *Processos de normalització lingüística: L'extensió de l'ús social i la normativització*, ed. Joan Martí, B, Columna, pp. 231, includes the work of 12 scholars, mainly professors, and offers a multiple approach to these major polemical topics in the Catalan-speaking countries. Joan Bastardas, 'Quan es produí el pas del llatí al català?', *RCat*, 30, 1989:33–47, by comparing with other Romance languages, more particularly with French, postulates that the language of most Old Catalonia was a Romance language as early as *c.* AD 750, and that the linguistic awareness emerged by AD 800–850. B. convincingly criticizes Wright's theory on the late emergence of linguistic awareness amongst speakers of Romance languages. *A sol post*, 1, 1990, includes among other articles on the history of Catalan, J. Colomina, 'Bibliografia de dialectologia catalana', (75–131) which stands out as an excellent and comprehensive bibliography with more than 800 items ordered by regions, which goes from Milà i Fontanals to 1980.

2. PHONETICS AND PHONOLOGY

J. Mascaró, 'On the Form of Segment Deletion and Insertion Rules', *Probus*, 1, 1989:31–61, brings more of his research on rule constraints (cf. *YWMLS*, 47:407). The descriptive topics he deals with are epenthesis, cluster simplification and vowel deletion in Central Catalan. E. Farnetani and D. Recasens, 'Articulatory and acoustic properties of different allophones of /l/ in American English, Catalan and Italian', *Proceedings of the International Conference on Spoken Language Processing*, vol. II, Japan, Kobe, 1990, pp. 961–64, argue for the multivalued character of the velarization feature based on the observation that the velar character of American English and Catalan laterals is dependent on the context. D. Recasens and J. Martí, 'Perception of Unreleased nasal Consonants in Catalan', *Journal d'Acoustique*, 3, 1990:287–99, identify the most salient acoustic features in the perception of place distinctions in nasal stops in final position and they discuss the relevance of spectral discontinuity. D. Recasens, *Fonètica descriptiva del català (Assaig de caracterització de la pronúncia del vocalisme i consonantisme del català al segle XX)*, (Biblioteca filològica, XXI), B, IEC, 369 pp., is clearly a major work of synthesis, at the same time rich in detail. Recasens rediscusses some issues with acute observations and several interesting phenomena are brought to light. J. Mascaró, 'Iberian spirantization and continuant spreading', *CWPL 1991*, 167–79, argues for a phonetic treatment of the spirantization of voiced obstruents in Catalan and Spanish. Previous phonological analyses are evaluated. B. Palmada and P. Serra, 'On the specification of coronals', *ib.*, 181–99, account for assimilatory asymmetries in Central Catalan: laterals and stridents have a restricted pattern despite the general assimilation of coronals. Centralized Alguerese consonants are also considered and an explanation based on Feature Geometry is proposed.

3. LEXIS AND MORPHOLOGY

M. T. Cabré, 'La neologia efímera', *ELLC*, 18, 1989:37–58, contains clear reflections and in just a few pages provides a guide for neological research and a practical illustration. An important contribution is Joan Mascaró and Joaquim Rafel, *Diccionari català invers amb informació morfològica*, B, Abadia de Montserrat, 1990, lxvii + 1145 pp., a Catalan reverse dictionary with morphological information, the first to be effectively helpful (cf. *YWMLS*, 48:414). The basic source is the *Diccionari general de la llengua catalana* by Pompeu Fabra (4th edn, B, 1966) plus appendices. For every entry, there is information relating to the morphological class to which it belongs, the source where the word comes from and inflectional information. It also contains a useful English introduction. Joan Solà, 'Joan Coromines i el lèxic normatiu', *RCat*, 35, 1989:127–39, and Id. 'Joan Coromines i la llengua normativa' in Solà, *Lingüística*, 63–90, critically evaluates Coromines' criteria in his dictionary and provides many illustrations. Solà ends up summarizing Coromines' position as 'extremely meticulous as far as the linguistic wealth is concerned, but at the same time it reveals a remarkable flexibility in terms of presenting the current state of the language'. J. Viaplana, 'Sobre la flexió nominal en català', *ELLC*, 23:235–64, is a mainstream generative approach to final vowels in nominals; allomorphic variation is attributed to radicals.

4. SYNTAX, SEMANTICS, AND PRAGMATICS

There is much original research in syntax, mainly in the Generative Grammar framework. A. Bartra i Kaufmann, 'Reflexions sobre els pronoms febles predicatius', *Actes del vuitè Col.loqui Internacional de Llengua i Literatura Catalanes, Tolosa de Llenguadoc, 12–17 de setembre de 1988*, vol. I, B, Abadia de Montserrat, 1989, pp. 189–200, deals with the predicative pattern of weak pronouns *ho* and *hi* in Central Catalan. Id., 'Sobre unes frases relatives sense antecedent', *Caplletra*, 8, 1990:131–48, rejects the traditional analysis of certain free relatives, like *L'Eva no troba qui l'ajudi*, and argues that they are selected by a non-existential predicate. M. J. Cuenca, 'Els matisadors: connectors oracionals i textuals', *ib.*, 149–67 is an illuminating account of some connective expressions and their patterns in sentence and discourse levels. She establishes a semantic typology. Id., *Les oracions adversatives*, B, Abadia de Montserrat, 284 pp., represents an essential advance in the investigation of syntactic, semantic, and pragmatic properties of adversatives. In two complementary articles, M. T. Espinal expounds with clarity the results of her studies on adverbs. In 'Tipologia dels adverbis: El cas dels anomenats adverbis oracionals', *ELLC*, 19, 1989:21–49 and 'Nota sobre una tipologia dels adverbis en -ment', *Misc. Joan Fuster*, 1, 359–74, E. proposes a typology and critically reviews Fabra's previous classifications. Id., 'Negation in Catalan. Some remarks with regard to *no pas*', *CWPL 1991*, 33–63, presents a study of Catalan negative constructions. Since *pas* cannot occur alone it is interpreted as a morpheme inseparable from *no*. She characterizes *no pas* as a quantifier-like operator and discusses its focus nature. A. Gavarró, 'A note on Catalan clitics', *ib.*, 65–73, proposes an empty category *pro* with the feature [+ 3 person] to account for the absence of a one-to-one correspondence between theta roles and clitics in *L'hi dono*. No clear account of the distribution of this empty category is reported. Lluïsa Gràcia i Solé, *La teoria temàtica* (Sèrie Lingüística, 5), B, Universitat Autònoma de Barcelona U.P., 1989, 338 pp., publishes her dissertation, which is concerned with the relations between lexical properties and syntax. She shows convincingly that the best treatment is in terms of 'Thematic Roles' linked to canonical syntactic representations. Id., *Els verbs ergatius en català* (Col.lecció Premis Francesc de Borja Moll, 1) Maó, Institut Menorquí d'Estudis, 1989, 108 pp., follows up her analysis of the lexical projection requirements on syntax. M. Llinàs i Grau, 'The affix-like status of certain verbal elements', *CWPL 1991*, 129–47, is a serious and coherent account. She claims that *haver, va* and epistemic modals in Catalan have an affixal status in complex verb sequences and explains their syntactic behaviour as a function of the syntactic and morphological characteristics of V1 that morphologically subcategorizes V2. M. Pérez Saldanya, 'Notes sobre la categoria gramatical del temps', in *Misc. Joan Fuster*, IV, 425–34 and 'La categoria gramatical del temps i les relacions deíctiques i anafòriques', *Caplletra*, 8, 1990:117–29, considers the distinction between absolute/deictic and relative/anaphoric tenses and gives a convincing account of the way they are interpreted. Id., 'Imperfects are pronominals', *CWPL 1991*, 201–10, retakes the study of the pronominal behaviour of imperfects and shows that they are subject to the same restrictions that affect non-temporal pronominals. M. C. Picallo, 'Possessive pronouns in Catalan and the Avoid Pronoun Principle', *ib.*, 211–34, relates the possibility of having phonologically null subjects and the distribution and syntactic behaviour of possessive pronouns. She proposes that this parallelism follows from the application of a principle that restricts the lexical content of pronominal categories. G. Rigau, 'Prédication holistique et sujet nul', *RLaR*, 93, 1989:201–21, discusses what the ungrammaticality of **Amb en Pere nosaltres ens casarem demà* can tell us about the structure of Catalan grammar and Universal Grammar. From a more general perspective, Id., 'The semantic nature of some Romance prepositions', in Mascaró, *Grammar*, 363–73, argues that two transitive Romance prepositions *amb/con/avec* and *entre/fra* behave semantically as a logic operator and are reanalysed with the verb at the Logical Form level resulting in a semantic modification of the predicate. Northwestern Catalan *vindrà pluges* corresponds to Central Catalan *vindran pluges*, this evidence is considered to investigate the relation types between subject and verb triggered by person and number agreements in Id., 'On the functional properties of AGR', *CWPL 1991*, 235–60. Id., 'Les propietats d'*agradar*: estructura temàtica i comportament sintàctic', *Caplletra*, 8, 1990:7–19, elucidates the semantic and syntactic pattern of *agradar* and concludes that its subject does not behave like a derived subject as in the case of unaccusatives. Joan Solà, 'L'ordre de mots en català. Notes pràctiques', in Solà, *Lingüística*, 91–125, is careful and clear. S. combines theoretical, descriptive, and normative concerns. He adopts a functional sentence perspective to define the basic order and establishes the types of constructions that depart from it. The topics he deals with are the correctness of some clitic doublings and comma use. Id., '"Per" i "per a"'. Estat de la qüestió', *ib.*, 127–38, reconsiders the questions of *per/per a* alternations. S. sets the problem, gives a comprehensive account of Coromines-Solà proposal and recommends to avoid *per a* when possible, except in the Valencian area. His objections to Ruaix's recent work on the topic are correct and justified. An acute piece of work is J. Solà Pujols, 'Sobre la partícula *rai* i els tòpics', *Caplletra*, 8, 1990:55–67, which characterizes *rai* as a topic emphasizer and expounds the general properties of topics. J. Todolí, 'Les funcions pronominals en el català del País Valencià', *ELLC*, 21, 1990:253–61, makes some interesting remarks on Valencian weak pronouns. She claims that there is an internal explanation for the loss of some uses of *en* and *hi*. A. Viana, 'Sobre simetries: el cas de les finals i les causals', *Misc. Joan Fuster*, II, 371–91, considers the two complement types introduced by *per* and defines their different patterns. M. W. Wheeler, 'Dels quantitatius i altres elements especificadors', *Els Marges*, 43:25–49, demonstrates, conclusively, the adequacy of an explanation that makes use of the best mechanisms of both standard Generative Grammar and GPSG. He is concerned with prenominal specifiers. Feature marking and underspecification allow him to explain the syntactic distribution of some elements that can function as adjectives, adverbials or nouns.

5. DIALECTS AND TOPONYMY

Montserrat Alegre, *Dialectologia catalana*, Teide, 245 pp., is a didactic compendium of the basic aspects of general dialectology and a description of the Catalan dialects, but its contributions to the field are limited: in fact, it is insufficiently updated with regard to previous textbooks still on the market (especially of those of J. Veny). Joan Veny, *Mots d'ahir i mots d'avui*, B, Empúries, 151 pp., compiles five of his own papers, some of them previously published, on dialectal and lexical topics. In addition to the title essay the book contains a curious approach to the linguistic history of Catalan wines; a basic under-standing towards a typology of popular etymology starting from the adaptation of Buysens' proposals; an erudite study on Aragonese loanwords in the southern Catalan dialects, and other general works on aspects of Catalan geolinguistics. Another general study is D. Recasens, 'Tendències fonètiques i classificació dialectal al domini lingüístic català', *LlLi*, 4, 1990–91:277–310; after a detailed analysis of contextualized phonetic realizations (consonants and vowels, stressed and non-stressed) Recasens affirms the existence of six basic Catalan dialects, but concludes that their broad classification into two groups, Eastern and Western, is not completely justified from the perspective of synchronic phonetics rather that their central, lateral or isolated natures must be taken into account (cf. Bartoli). J. Viaplana, 'Comparació interdialectal i llengua', *ib.*, 215–42, investi-gates dialectal diversity and mutual intelligibility (based on certain Catalan verbal paradigms) and postulates a concept of language based on its di-systematic character. On another level, a number of descriptive studies on Catalan dialects and varieties have appeared, which has contributed substantially to an understanding of the panorama of Catalan dialectology. Noteworthy are Pep Coll, *El parlar del Pallars*, B, Empúries, 149 pp. and Jordi Colomina, *El valencià de la Marina Baixa*, V, Generalitat Valenciana, 416 pp., referring to the extreme northern and southern areas respectively of the Catalan territory; also Àngels Massip, *Aproximació descriptiva al parlar tortosí*, Tarragona, Diputació de Tarragona, 1989, 118 pp., on the linguistic frontier between the dialects of Lleida and the dialects of the Valencian country. As far as the Central and Northern-Western dialects are concerned, it is worth mentioning (in this order) Carme Vilà, *El parlar de la Plana de Vic*, Manresa, Caixa de Manresa, 1989, 102 pp., and the dossier compiled by R. Sistac *et al.*, 'Els parlars de Ponent', in *Ilerda Humanitats*, 48, 1990:191–215. An interesting sociolinguistic approach is found in Brauli Montoya, *La interferència lingüística al sud valencià*, V, Generalitat Valenciana, 1989 (1990), 202 pp., centred on the 'comarca' of Vinalopó which is co-inhabited by Catalan and Castilian populations, among whom Montoya observes an assymetry in favour of Spanish. Finally, examples of more peripheral topics of investigation in Catalan dialectology are: Carles Vega *et al.*, *La parla de la Ribera d'Ebre*. *Aspectes morfològics: la pronominalització àtona*, Centre d'Estudis de la Ribera d'Ebre, 1990, 128 pp.; M. S. González, 'El parlar de la Plana Baixa', in *Miscellània 91*, V, Generalitat Valenciana, 7–79; F. X. Serra 'Morfofonologia: *trencaclosques* i companyia', *Urtx* (Tàrrega), 2, 1990: 311–19; Ll. Gimeno, 'La pèrdua de la /d/ intervocàlica: casos de manteniment en tortosí meridional', *ELLC*, 19, 1989: 87–101; Id., 'La reducció vocàlica: /e/ àtona inicial', *Misc. Joan Fuster*, II, 393–430, also referring to what Gimeno calls 'tortosí meridional', that is, the variety spoken in the extreme north of the Valencian country.

Outstanding in the field of Onomastics is the publication of the first volume of a long-awaited seminal work, Joan Coromines, *Onomasticon Cataloniae*, I, B, Curial, 1989, xiii + 315 pp., on ancient toponomy of the Balearic Islands (in collaboration with J. Mascaró-Passarius). Approximately 500 toponyms are analysed, excluding those easily explained. Coromines himself has published a profound and controversial article, 'Etimology of *Reus*', *RCat*, 58: 55–64, the text of which is to be published in a future volume of the *Onomasticon*. Two other general books on the origin of Catalan toponyms have come out, but are not particularly significant: Pere Balañà, *Els noms de lloc de Catalunya*, Generalitat de Catalunya, 2nd edn, 1990, 298 pp., only deals with names of 'municipis', grouped by region, and is excessively inclined to adopt arabic-type solutions which are often unsuitable; Manuel Bofarull i Terrades, *Origen dels noms geogràfics de Catalunya*, Millà, 283 pp., is only a popular handbook. Bofarull tries to collect different opinions but is not critical enough in their selection and therefore holds untenable hypotheses. Albert Turull, *Els topònims de la Segarra*, Cervera, Centre Municipal de Cultura, 546 pp., focuses on one of the largest areas of Catalonia and with the systematic use of medieval data explains the origin and the meaning of approximately 400 place-names, also noting in an analytical way the previous hypotheses for each case. E. A. Llobregat, 'Hemeroscopium: un fals topònim', in *Misc. Joan Fuster*, II, 363–70, claims convincingly that the presumed existence of Greek toponym *Hemeroscopium* in the southern Valencian coast (corresponding to Dènia) is a result of a mistaken (perhaps intentional) interpretation of Strabo's text circulated in the beginning of this century. Another aspect is excellently presented by Ramon Amigó, *Sobre inventaris de noms de lloc. Introducció metodològica*, Reus, Centre de Lectura, 1989, 108 pp., an accurated and outstanding compendium of the elements and phases of toponymic research, written by one of the most renowned Catalan experts in this field; it includes a bibliography with the works on onomastics already published, which is completed by *Butlletí Interior de la Societat d'Onomàstica*, whose first 41 numbers are reviewed by M. A. Vidal-Collell, 'Deu anys d'una publicació lingüística', *Els Marges*, 44:104–08. In the field of anthroponymy it is important to mention D. Roigé, 'Sobre l'evolució dels noms de persona', *ib.*, 39, 1989:19–32, which includes a general introduction and an illustration (the village of Riudecanyes). It has served as a model for other studies on personal names from a diachronic point of view. Equally fundamental is Enric Moreu-rey, *Antroponímia. Història dels nostres prenoms, cognoms i renoms*, Barcelona U.P., 205 pp., which was published just before the death of the author (*alma mater* of the *Societat d'Onomàstica*) and which has to be placed within the tradition set by Paul Aebischer and Francesc de B. Moll; the latter puts together around twenty works previously published which in general combine at the same time a popular approach to the subject as well as philological rigour. Amongst these the studies on Catalan anthroponymy concerning the late Middle Ages deserve especial mention.

6. SOCIOLINGUISTICS

Beginning with general overviews, we must first mention the proceedings of the II International Conference of the Catalan Language: *Segon Congrés Internacional de la Llengua Catalana. III. Area 2. Sociologia de la llengua*, Girona, Diputació de Girona, 407 pp. An overall report containing up-to-date information on the situation of the Catalan language in all fields is Mireia Carulla, *The Catalan Language Today*, B, Generalitat de Catalunya, Institut de Sociolingüística Catalana, 1990, 46 pp. From an economic point of view, following Ferruccio Rossi-Landi, is Jesús Royo, *Una llengua és un mercat*, B, Ed. 62, 185 pp. Josep Inglés, *Els espais compartits en l'oferta lingüística: elements per a les bases d'un projecte de normalització*, B, El Llamp, 1990, 70 pp., contains some social indicators for the study of the process of normalization of Catalan. From an ethnolinguistic point of view is A. Woolard, *Double Talk: Bilingualism and the Politics of Ethnicity in Catalonia*, Stanford U.P., 1989, xiv + 183 pp. From a discourse analysis perspective, Ernest Querol, 'El procés de substitució lingüística: la comarca dels Ports com a exemple', in *Miscel.lània 89*, V, Generalitat Valenciana, Conselleria de Cultura, 1990, pp. 85–195. A polemical view is that of Henri Boyer, *Langues en conflict: études sociolinguistiques*, Paris, l'Harmattan, 1990, chapter III, 'Résistance et reconquête sociolinguistiques: aspects de la *normalisation* du catalan en Catalogne Autonomique'. Linguistic approaches are those of Brauli Montoya, *La interferència lingüística al sud valencià*, V, Generalitat

Valenciana, Gabinet d'Ús del Valencià, 1990, 200 pp., a Labovian study, and Toni Mollà, *La llengua als mitjans de comunicació*, Alzira, Bromera, 1990, 119 pp., which deals with linguistic standards for the Catalan media. Many general sociolinguistic studies of different areas in the Catalan territory have been published. Foremost among them is a study on the situation of one of the most important towns of Catalonia: *Simposi català a l'Hospitalet: 27, 28 i 29 de novembre de 1987*, L'Hospitalet de Llobregat, Centre d'Estudis de l'Hospitalet, 1989, 104 pp. On the situation in the Catalan speaking area of Aragon, *El català a Aragó*, ed. Artur Quintana, B, Curial, 1989, 245 pp., compiles the major texts written by different specialists while José R. Bada, *El debat del català a l'Aragó: 1983–1987*, Teruel, Associació Cultural del Matarranya, 1990, 207 pp., focuses on the political debate. In the field of demolinguistics, a great number of studies have been published. Regarding the Valencian country: D. Mollà *et al.*, *Enquesta sociolingüística al País Valencià*, Alicante U.P., 1989, xvii + 237 pp. (microfilm); and official publications such as *Coneixement del valencià: Anàlisi dels resultats del padró municipal d'habitants de 1986*, V, Generalitat Valenciana, Gabinet d'Ús del Valencià, 1990, 61 pp. A thorough study of the linguistic census of 1986 is that of Modest Reixach, *Difusió social del coneixement de la llengua catalana: anàlisi de les dades lingüístiques del padró d'habitants de 1986 de Catalunya, Illes Balears i País Valencià*, B, Generalitat de Catalunya, Departament de Cultura, 1990, vol. I, 151 pp., the contents of which are summarized in Jacqueline Hall, *Knowledge of the Catalan Language*, B, Generalitat de Catalunya, Institut de Sociolingüística Catalana, 1990, 50 pp. F. Hernández *et al.*, *La llengua catalana a Tarragona*, Tarragona, Diputació de Tarragona, 59 pp., deals with the south of Catalonia. Miquel Alenyar *et al.*, *Les migracions*, Palma de Mallorca, Ajuntament de Palma, 1989, 148 pp., treats the subject of the integration and assimilation of immigrants. On the language transmission from generation to generation in the metropolitan area of Barcelona an outstanding survey is Marina Subirats, *Enquesta metropolitana 1986: Transmissió i coneixement de la llengua catalana a l'àrea metropolitana de Barcelona*, B, Generalitat de Catalunya, Institut de Sociolingüística Catalana, x + 99 pp. On the language of the young people see *La joventut de Catalunya en xifres: 1991*, B, Generalitat de Catalunya, Direcció General de Joventut, especially pp. 159–71, and Raül Martínez, *Enquesta a la joventut de Catalunya 1990*, B, Generalitat de Catalunya, Gabinet d'Estudis Socials, especially pp. 105–62. For the subject of language rights a general view can be found in Josep M. Puig Salellas, *La situació jurídica de la llengua catalana avui: discurs llegit en la sessió inaugural del curs 1989–1990*, B, IEC, 1989, 21 pp. The position of Catalan within Spain is analysed in Aurelio Guaita, *Lenguas de*

Language 385

España y Artículo 3°. de la Constitución, M, Civitas, 1989, 207 pp., while its position in the European Community is discussed in *El català reconegut pel Parlament europeu*, B, Generalitat de Catalunya, 126 pp. The minutes of a monographic conference on language rights have been compiled in *Dret lingüístic: actes del Simposi sobre Dret Lingüístic. Barcelona, 1987*, B, Generalitat de Catalunya, Escola d'Administració Pública de Catalunya, 1989, 302 pp. Many sociolinguistic works on the situation of Catalan in different fields have been published. The situation in the Valencian autonomous administration is described in *L'ús del valencià en l'administració autonòmica*, V, Generalitat Valenciana, Gabinet d'Ús del Valencià, 94 pp. The situation in the field of Education is dealt with in many official reports. Particularly concerned with primary and secondary education is *Deu anys de normalització lingüística a l'ensenyament: 1978–1988*, B, Generalitat de Catalunya, Departament d'Ensenyament, 70 pp. and *Dades de la llengua a l'escola primària de Catalunya: 1989–1990*, B, Generalitat de Catalunya, Servei d'Ensenyament del Català, 281 pp. An outstanding piece of research — along the same lines as Wallace Lambert — on the experience of the Crash Course Programme (Programa d'Immersió) for Spanish-speaking students between 4 and 7 years old is Josep Maria Artigal, *La immersió a Catalunya: consideracions psicolingüístiques i sociolingüístiques*, Vic, Eumo, 1989, 122 pp. Less academic, yet written from a more official perspective, are the works of Joaquim Arenas: *Absència i recuperació de la llengua catalana a l'ensenyament a Catalunya (1970–1983)*, B, La Llar del Llibre, 1989, 103 pp.; *La catalaniat de l'ensenyament: un repte de la reforma educativa*, B, La Llar del Llibre, 1989, 71 pp.; and *Llengua i educació a la Catalunya d'avui*, B, La Llar del Llibre, 1990, 100 pp. Concerning the situation of Catalan in universities, see *L'ús del català a les universitats de Catalunya*, B, Generalitat de Catalunya, Departament d'Ensenyament, 93 pp. Many monographic studies have been published on this subject: *Coneixement i ús de la llengua catalana a la Universitat de Barcelona 1987–1989*, B, Universitat de Barcelona, 85 pp.; Enric Serra i Casals, *La llengua catalana a la UAB*, Bellaterra, Servei de publicacions de la Universitat Autònoma de Barcelona, 1989, 53 pp.; and Universitat Politècnica de Catalunya, *Anàlisi de les necessitats, els usos i els hàbits lingüístics del col.lectiu de professors de la UPC*, B, UPC, 133 pp. The problem of teaching Catalan to non-Catalan Spanish speaking adults has been the subject of a special conference: *Comunicacions del Segon Simposi sobre l'ensenyament del català a no-catalanoparlants. Vic, 4, 5 i 6 de setembre de 1991*, Vic, Eumo, 360 pp. The importance of the knowledge of foreign languages within the European Community is analysed in *El repte (socio)lingüístic de l'Acta Única: les llengües comunitàries a Catalunya*, ed. Jordi Bañeres, B, Generalitat de Catalunya, Institut de

13

Sociolingüística Catalana, 1990, 150 pp. In the field of the media, Josep M. Figueres describes the past history of the Catalan press in *La premsa catalana: apreciació històrica*, B, Rafael Dalmau, 1989, 120 pp., and its future is considered in *Informe sobre les perspectives de la premsa en català d'abast general a Catalunya*, B, El Llamp, 1990, 143 pp. An interesting piece of 'epilinguistic' research is that of Franz Lebsaneft, *Spanien und seine Sprachen in den Cartas al Director von El País: 1976–1987: Einfuhrung und Analytische Bibliographie*, Tübingen, Gunter Narr, 1990, 133 pp. Regarding the economic field, an outstanding study is *El valencià en el sector terciari avançat*, V, Generalitat Valenciana, Gabinet d'Ús del Valencià, 1990, 84 pp. Research on a variety of topics is reported in Jordi Bañeres, 'Els correlats macrosocials del multilingüisme igualitari. Assaig exploratori', in *Nous reptes en l'ensenyament de la llengua. Jornades de Didàctica de la llengua, Barcelona, del 3 al 7 de setembre de 1990*, Vic, Eumo, pp. 33–60; social and historical aspects of the autonomous and unionicist linguistic positions towards Catalan are dealt with in the collective work *Llibre blanc sobre la unitat de la llengua catalana*, B, Barcino, 1990, 216 pp. The history of the literary restoration of Catalan is studied eruditely by Irmela Neu-Altenheimer, *Sprach- und Nationalbewusstsein in Katalonien wehrend der Renaixença: 1833–1891*, B, IEC, 1987–89, 349 pp. Problems affecting aphasic bilinguals are studied by Carme Junqué, *Desorganització diferencial del català i el castellà en afàsics bilingües*, B, IEC, 1990, 74 pp. A series of works on militant linguistics have been published, some of which are of little methodological rigour but contain some interesting material. A history of the principal militant organization in favour of Catalan has been written by Enric Monné, *Història de la Crida a la Solidaritat en defensa de la llengua, la cultura i la nació catalanes*, B, La Campana, 165 pp. The IEC, the main official organization devoted to the linguistic corpus of the language has published two documents on the present status of the Catalan language: *Sobre l'estat actual de la normalització lingüística*, B, IEC, 1990, 4 ff. and *Debat sobre la normalització lingüística: ple de l'Institut d'Estudis Catalans*, B, IEC, 38 pp. Francesc Ferrer i Gironès has demonstrated his commitment in the following publications: *Lletres de batalla: cartes per la llengua catalana*, B, El Llamp, 1989, 414 pp.; *Insubmissió lingüística*, B, Ed. 62, 1990, 167 pp.; *Els drets lingüístics dels catalanoparlants*, B, Ed. 62, 1990, 328 pp. Taking as a starting point Friedrich Meinecke's distinction between cultural nation and political nation, Joan F. Mira has written *Cultura, llengües, nacions*, B, La Magrana, 1990, 212 pp. On the subject of the dialectical relationship between nation and language one can refer to *El nacionalisme català a la fi del segle XX. II Jornades*, B, Ed. 62, 1989, 125 pp. On the linguistic standards and the controversy surrounding them see: Maria-Lluïsa Pazos, *L'amenaça del català light*, B, Tibidabo,

1990, 122 pp. and Ernest Sabater, *Ni "heavy" ni "light"*: *Català modern*, B, Empúries, 130 pp. There has been much written about the future of the Catalan language. From a pessimistic point of view, there is a compilation of articles by Jordi Solé i Camardons, *Sobirania sociolingüística catalana*, B, La Llar del Llibre, 203 pp. and Modest Prats *et al.*, *El futur de la llengua catalana*, B, Empúries, 1990, 83 pp., which has prompted an opposite point of view in Francesc Vallverdú, *L'ús del català: un futur controvertit. Qüestions de normalització lingüística al llindar del segle XXI*, B, Ed. 62, 1990, 139 pp. Linguistic planning takes great importance — in concordance with the great political and economic effort devoted to the process of catalanization. A general view of this process is that of Albert Bastardas, *Fer el futur: sociolingüística, planificació i normalització del català*, B, Empúries, 107 pp. Isidor Marí, *Condicions per a la normalització lingüística*, Manacor, Patronat de l'Escola Municipal de Mallorquí, 1989, 13 pp. Many works on the linguistic planning in universities have been published. A useful summary is offered in *Els serveis lingüístics universitaris*, B, Promociones y Publicaciones Universitarias, 1990, 127 pp. Linguistic planning in the media is dealt with, in a committed way, in Josep Gifreu (dir.), *Construir l'espai català de comunicació*, B, Generalitat de Catalunya, Centre d'Investigació de la Comunicació, 295 pp.

LITERATURE

POSTPONED

VI. PORTUGUESE STUDIES

LANGUAGE
(INCLUDING BRAZILIAN PORTUGUESE AND GALICIAN)

(This survey covers the years 1989–91)

By STEPHEN PARKINSON, *Lecturer in Portuguese Language and Linguistics, Taylor Institution, Oxford University*

1. GENERAL AND HISTORICAL

Extensive reference will be made to the following: *Congresso sobre a situação actual da língua portuguesa no mundo. Actas*, II, L, ICALP, 1988, 573 pp. (*Congresso*, II); *Actas do 3° Encontro da Associação Portuguesa de Linguística*, L, APL, 1988, 681 pp. (*3° Encontro*); *Actas do 4° Encontro da Associação Portuguesa de Linguística*, L, APL, 1989, 330 pp. (*4° Encontro*); *Actas do 5° Encontro da Associação Portuguesa de Linguística*, L, APL, 1990, 399 pp. (*5° Encontro*); *Fotografias Sociolingüísticas*, ed. Fernando Tarallo, Campinas U.P., 1989, 332 pp. (Tarallo, *Fotografias*); *Português culto falado no Brasil*, ed. Ataliba Teixeira de Castilho, Campinas U.P., 1989, 322 pp. (Castilho, *Português culto*); *Diversidade do Português do Brasil*, ed. Carlota Ferreira *et al.*, Bahia U.P., 1988, 235 pp. (Ferreira, *Diversidade*).

Maria Helena Mira Mateus *et al.*, *Gramática da Língua Portuguesa*, 2nd edn, L, Caminho, 1989, 417 pp., is a much revised and expanded version of this important manual. Campbell, *Compendium*, II, 1132–37, has very basic information mainly on European Portuguese, distorted by wildly inconsistent transcription of vowels and a sample text in 17th-c. language and orthography. A. Santamarina, 'Estado e tarefas da lingüística galega', *Actes* (Trier), VII, 289–310, gives an overview and bibliography. J. A. Ferreira, *Bibliografia selectiva da língua portuguesa*, L, ICALP, 1989, xvi + 332 pp. is an extensive but far from complete bibliography of recent work, including unpublished dissertations, organized in useful subject sections. M. H. M. Mateus, 'Terminologia linguística', *5° Encontro*, 1–4, is an introduction to Maria Francisca Xavier and Maria Helena Mira Mateus, *Dicionário de Termos Linguísticos*, vol. I, L, APL — ILTEC — Cosmos, 423 pp., an invaluable reference tool listing a database of Portuguese terms and their equivalents, with sources. An electronic edition is promised. M. Ramsey, 'A utilização do computador em estudos de língua portuguesa', *Congresso*, II, 194–99, and J. A. Ferreira, 'A versão portuguesa do Fuero Real de Afonso X estudada ao computador', *ib.*, 417–26, discuss computer applications to modern and medieval text corpora. More of the NURC database is published in *A linguagem falada culta na cidade de São Paulo*, SPo, Queiroz — FAPESP, ii, *Diálogos entre dois informantes*, ed. Ataliba Teixeira de Castilho and Dino Preti, 1987, 264 pp., iii, *Entrevistas*, ed. Dino Preti and Hudinilson Urbano, 1988, 164 pp., iv, *Estudos*, ed. Dino Preti and Hudinilson Urbano, 1990. S. Elia, 'O Brasil e a língua portuguesa', *Congresso*, ii, 203–21, continues to fight the battle for Luso-Brazilian unity. D. M. C. de Castro Duarte, 'Aspectos dialectales del portugués contemporáneo', *Homenaje Zamora Vicente*, ii, 53–68, gives a convenient summary of European–Brazilian contrasts.

Carlos Alberto Faraco, *Lingüística Histórica*, SPo, Ática, 136 pp., is a basic introduction to diachronic linguistics, with exemplification from Portuguese. Rosa Virgínia Mattos e Silva, *Estruturas Trecentistas. Elementos para uma gramática do português arcaico*. L, 1989, 870 pp., is the long-awaited complete study (previewed in 'Gramática do português arcaico. Estruturas trecentistas', *Congresso*, ii, 413–16) of the late 14th-c. text of which S. has published many partial analyses. There is much more usable syntactic information than in other comparable studies, over half the volume being devoted to morphosyntactic data, with statistics of occurrence thoughtfully deployed. The same author extends her data base in 'Caminhos de mudanças sintático-semânticas no português arcaico', *CEL*, 20:59–74, outlining developments in *ser* and *estar*, *ter* and *haver*, and verb concord. L. F. L. Cintra, 'Sobre o mais antigo texto não–literário português: A Notícia do Torto (leitura crítica, data, lugar de redacção e comentário linguístico)', *BF*, 31, 1986–87 [1990]:21–77, finally publishes his own edition and study, comparing it with that of Costa (see *YWMLS*, 43:445). M. F. Xavier, 'Factos de sintaxe histórica', *3° Encontro*, 401–15, explains parallel developments in English and Portuguese in terms of the directionality of syntactic government. J. Brandão de Carvalho, ' "Cantabrie and Mozarabic": de quelques divergences entre espagnol et portugais', *La Linguistique*, 27:61–73, sees North–South differences as more important than the speed of Reconquest. M. I. G. G. A. da Costa, 'Um aspecto da grafia portuguesa no século XVI — a duplicação de vogais', *Diacritica* 5, 1990:43–51, finds little consistency in orthographic double vowels. B. Schäfer, 'Sprachtheorie und –beschreibung in der "Theoria do Discurso" von António Leite Ribeiro', *Variatio Linguarum*, 253–60, introduces a 19th-c. philosophical grammar. M. Brea, 'La partícula galego-portugués *ar/er*', *Homenaje Zamora Vicente*, i, 45–58, gives documentation and discusses its derivation from the prefix *re-*.

2. PHONETICS AND PHONOLOGY

M. H. M. Mateus *et al.*, *Fonética, fonologia e morfologia do português*, L, Universidade Aberta, 1990, 518 pp., is a thorough introduction to

Portuguese and general phonetics with less substantial sections on other components. Dinah Callou and Yonne Leite, *Iniciação à fonética e à fonologia*, R, Jorge Zahar, 1990, 125 pp., embed some interesting observations on Brazilian Portuguese in a very sketchy introduction. M. S. S. de Aragão, 'O significante linguístico – as formas de expressão na língua portuguesa: os meios fonémicos', *Pottier Vol*, I, 67–79, gives a Pottier-style outline of Brazilian Portuguese phonemics, without depth or discussion. M. Ploae Hanganu, 'Propunere pentru descriera sistemului vocalic galician', *SCL*, 40, 1989:227–82, gives an elementary comparison of Galician, Castilian, and Portuguese vowel systems (apparently unaware of Veiga). M. A. Freitas, 'Fonologia das partículas: um modelo em duas versões', *4° Encontro*, 167–76, compares analyses of diachronic processes of vowel contraction. Nasality is as usual in the forefront. M. Drenska, 'Análise acústica das vogais nasais em português e búlgaro', *ib.*, 139–65, remarks on the length of nasal vowels and the relative infrequency of postvocalic consonantal segments. W. L. Wetzels, 'Contrastive and allophonic properties of Brazilian Portuguese vowels', Wanner and Kibbee, *New Analyses*, 77–99, an important study in a non-linear framework, explains the range of nasal offglides as realizations of an unmarked nasal element in the nucleus, assimilation patterns being governed by the Obligatory Contour Principle; the restrictions on mid-vowel contrasts reflect the feature [±ATR], which is only contrastive in stressed syllables. O. R. Kelm, 'Acoustic characteristics of oral vs nasalized /a/ in Brazilian Portuguese: Variation in vowel timbre and duration', *His(US)*, 72, 1989:853–61, confirms that /ɐ/ is higher and more fronted than /a/; his duration measurements are vitiated by false assumptions about segmentation. D. S. Fagan, 'Notes on diachronic nasalization in Portuguese', *Diachronica*, 5, 1988:141–57, finds support for the thesis that nasal glides are insertions rather than retentions. E. d'Andrade and A. Kihm, 'Fonologia autosegmental e nasais em Português', *3° Encontro*, 51–60, give a schematic account of the distribution of nasal vowels, oral vowels, and nasal consonants by identifying nasality as a floating autosegment which may attach to the nucleus or the onset (depending on morphological structure), and deletes if not attached. S. R. Parkinson, 'Portuguese nasal vowels: phonology and morphology', *Congresso*, II, 11–16, warns against casual conflation of formally similar rules with different (morphological or phonological) conditioning, with reference to diphthongization, nasalization, vowel contraction and vowel quality changes. J. B. de Carvalho, 'L'origine de la terminaison -*ão* du portugais: une approche phonétique nouvelle du probleme', *ZRP*, 105, 1989:148–60, makes a lot of sense in proposing that Old Port. /ã/ was [ãŋ] and /ãa/ was [ãŋa], which puts the traditional views of diphthongization and contraction in a new light. Id., 'L'évolution des sonantes ibéro-romains et la chute de -n-, -l- en gallaïco-portugais', *RLiR*, 53, 1989:159–88, hypothesizes convincingly that intervocalic sonorants were in fact syllable-final, which allows him to explain their deletion and the reduction of geminates by a single lenition process of syllable-final weakening. Stress and the atonic vowel pattern are also well covered. E. d'Andrade, 'O acento da palavra em português', Staczek, *Linguistics*, 17–38, gives a metrical account of morphologically-based rules of stress assignment, with heavy reliance on extrametricality. E. d'Andrade and M. C. Viana, 'Ainda sobre o acento e o ritmo em português', *4° Encontro*, 3–15, correlate grid-based analyses of degrees with relative length; no more than three degrees of stress are justified. J. B. de Carvalho, 'Marques segmentales des hiérarchies prosodiques: la contraction vocalique en portugais', *BSLP*, 84, 1989:163–99, shows how different levels of prosodic structure interact to produce previously observed degrees of *crase*. Id., 'Phonological conditions on Portuguese clitic placement: on syntactic evidence for stress and rhythmical patterns', *Linguistics*, 27, 1989:405–36, shows that differences in clitic placement reflect proclisis and the existence of syllabic weight contrasts in European Portuguese, compared with enclisis in the non-quantitative Brazilian system. A. Brakel, 'O nível gramatical e o grau de abstracção da regra de redução vocálica do português euro-africano padrão', *Congresso*, II, 43–54, relates vowel reduction to abstract underlying forms (an analysis developed at greater length in chronologically later work published more speedily, see *YWMLS*, 48:439). M. A. C. Miguel, 'Alternância da vogal fria com a vogal zero em núcleos pretónicos', *5° Encontro*, 119–25 (preceded by a brief exposition of the theoretical background by J. Kaye and M. A. C. Miguel, 'Proper Government, the cold vowel [ɨ] and Portuguese', *ib.*, 109–10) assumes a non-gradient alternation of /ə/ and zero, to bring it into the orbit of Government and Charm phonology. L. Bisol, 'Harmonização vocálica, uma regra variável', *Congresso*, II, 17–42, and 'Vowel harmony: A variable rule in Brazilian Portuguese', *LVC*, 1, 1989, 115–43, identify phonological and social variables in the distinctive process of Brazilian unstressed vowel assimilation. S. M. Bortoni *et al.*, 'Um estudo preliminar do /e/ pretônico', *CEL*, 20:75–90, show a predominance of phonological over social factors, in raising and lowering of pretonic /e/ in Alagoas and Brasília. M. Drenska, 'Tem razão Gonçalves Viana?', *3° Encontro*, 139–56, reports perception test results to show that distinctions between final atonic vowels are neither perfectly clear to native speakers nor totally imperceptible to non-natives, following this with 'Notas sobre a elisão das vogais finais átonas precedidas de vogal no português europeu', *5° Encontro*, 65–71, claiming spectrographic evidence for a general elimination of /u a/ in final unstressed /ia/, /iu/. A. I. M. da Silva, 'Ditongos crescentes do português: análise acústica', *3° Encontro*, 379–400, claims spectrographic evidence for the regular semivocalization of unstressed /i u/ in hiatus. P. Caruso, 'As vogais átonas finais e o português do Brasil', *Alfa*, 33, 1989: 163–69, sees the occurrences of atonic final [e o] in Brazilian as a reflection of 16th-c. pronunciation. B. Comrie, 'The phonology of Brazilian Portuguese hypocoristic kin terms', *Variatio Linguarum*, 63–66, analyses the reduplication process behind *vovó*. A. P. Palácio, 'Um caso de permuta consonântica no dialecto do Recife', Carvalho, *Português culto*, 25–33, discusses the appearance of [h] as neutralization fricative. I. W. Garcia, 'Um estudo sobre a entoação da frase interrogativa na língua portuguesa culta: uma comparação entre dois tipos de elocução', *ib.*, 35–54. M. J. Freitas, 'Elementos para um estudo do tempo real no discurso', *3° Encontro*, 229–43, identifies three classes of pause, whose distribution relates to syntactic structure and style of delivery. I. Pereira and M. J. Freitas, 'Valores do silêncio: contributo para o estudo da pausa na delimitação do grupo entoacional em português', *5° Encontro*, 171–86, is an inconclusive quantitative study. R. E. Hoyos-Andrade, 'O "Alfonia", um pré-alfabeto que deu certo', *Alfa*, 32, 1988: 69–77, describes a Brazilian phonetic teaching alphabet. F. V. Peixoto da Fonseca, 'A linguagem de duas crianças portuguesas até aos dois anos', *Miscellanea Gasca Queirazza*, II, 815–36, brushes the dust off notes on the early speech of his children: useful data for phonological study.

3. SYNTAX

Maria Henriqueta Costa Campos and Maria Francisca Xavier, *Sintaxe e semântica do português*, L, Universidade Aberta, 386 pp., is a thoroughly approachable introduction, with a much-needed clear exposition of X-bar syntax for Portuguese, and good coverage of Case Theory, θ-roles and, as is to be expected from the main author, tense, aspect, and mood. Ana Maria Barros de Brito, *A sintaxe das orações relativas em português*, O, INIC, 279 pp., has a useful overview of Government and Binding theory as applied to Portuguese, as a preliminary to a discussion of restrictive, non-restrictive, and free relatives.

Pronouns, a central concern of Government and Binding syntax, are understandably prominent. C. Galves, 'Algumas diferenças entre português de Portugal e português do Brasil e a teoria de regência e vinculação', *Congresso*, II, 55–65, explains Brazilian uses of *ele* (non-contrastive subject and *lembrete*). M. E. L. Duarte, 'Clítico acusativo, pronome lexical e categoria vazia no Português do Brasil', Tarallo, *Fotografias*, 19–34, finds syntactic and social conditioning for the use of alternatives to object clitics. D. P. Oliveira, 'O preenchimento, a supressão e a ordem do sujeito e do objeto em sentenças do Português do Brasil: um estudo quantitativo', *ib.*, 51–63, links null subjects and objects (overwhelmingly anaphoric) and word order. E. P. Raposo, *'Prepositional infinitival constructions in European Portuguese', Jaeggli and Safir, *The Null Subject Parameter*, 277–305. E. Ranchhod, 'Alguns tipos de referência pronominal restritiva', *Congresso*, ii, 66–71, notes the effects of verb valency and prepositional phrases (*acerca de, de parte de*) on the possible referents of pronouns. J. Lemos Monteiro, 'Variação no uso dos pronomes pessoais no português do Brasil', *Verba*, 17, 1990:145–57, does little more than outline areas for pronoun research. C. M. B. de Souza, 'A concordância sujeito/verbo num dialeto baiano', Castilho, *Português culto*, 89–101, and J. Mota and S. Cardoso, 'Concordância verbal no português do Brasil: caracterização de casos localizados', Ferreira, *Diversidade*, 171–78, give accounts of non-standard agreement in Brazilian dialects. E. J. Martins, 'Pronomes pessoais complementos de 3ª pessoa', Castilho, *Português culto*, 103–19. Christoph Petruck, *Sprachregister und Pronominalgebrauch im Portugiesichen*, Münster, Klenheinrich, ix + 296 pp. F. Oliveira, *'Cadeias anaforicas: que referência?'*, *RFLUP*, 4, 1987:125–35. On word order and topicalization. R. A. Berlinck, 'A construção V SN no português do Brasil: uma visão diacrônica do fenômeno da ordem', Tarallo, *Fotografias*, 95–112, argues that the restriction of VS orders to intransitives is a product of the elimination of object clitics; M. B. N. Decat, 'Construções de tópico em português: uma abordagem diacrônica à luz do encaixamento no sistema pronominal', *ib.*, 113–39, sees the disappearance of clitics contributing to the reanalysis of topics as subjects; I. S. Duarte, 'A construção da topicalização no português europeu: alguns argumentos a favor de uma teoria de princípios e parametros', *3° Encontro*, 157–65, identifies Topicalization in Portuguese as left-adjunction to the Inflection or Complementizer nodes, subject to independent Government and Binding principles. M. L. Braga, 'Discurso e abordagens quantitativas', Tarallo, *Fotografias*, 269–82, finds OSV orders conditioned by discourse factors. M. A. F. Rocha, 'Complementizadores no Português do Brasil: uma abordagem inter- e intra-sistêmica', *ib.*, 141–63, investigates the range of complementizers and argues for a specifier position in the Comp node; M. M. Âmbar, 'Sobre a posição do sujeito, movimento do verbo e estrutura da frase', *5° Encontro*, 369–99, uses a profusion of Specifiers to develop the theory that inversion in *qu-* interrogatives is verb raising, and in 'Flutuação do quantificador e subida de flexão', *3º Encontro*, 17–38, ingeniously explains the preverbal and postverbal positions of the quantifier *todos* referring to the subject, by deriving them from verb-initial sentences in which the subject NP is moved with or without its quantifier. M. T. R. C. da Seabra, 'Algumas observações acerca dos locativos em português', *Congresso*, II, 72–83, classifies spatio-temporal adverbs as complement-types.

J. M. Nunes, '*Se* apassivador e *se* indeterminador: o percurso diacrónico no português brasileiro', *CEL*, 20:33-58, charts the gradual disappearance of the *se*-passive, and the resulting extension of deletion of *se*. R. E. L. Moino, 'Passivas nos discursos oral e escrito', Tarallo, *Fotografias*, 35–50, emphasizes the marginality of syntactic passives. M. J. A. Carvalho, 'Um tipo de passivas no português oral de Moçambique? (1ª parte)', *3º Encontro*, 105–13, notes the predominance of agentless passives in Mozambican Portuguese, and a tendency to passive indirect objects which may be substrate-related. G. A. Matos, 'Elipse do SV em estruturas predicativas com ser e estar', *4º Encontro*, 41–67, compares Portuguese and English VP-deletion strategies, in the context of her analysis of copulas as raising verbs which case-mark small clauses. H. S. Alves, 'Ser ou estar: eis a questão', *3º Encontro*, 3–16, invokes Relevance Theory to explain the value of 'marked' uses of *estar*. Elisabete Marques Ranchhod, *Sintaxe dos predicados nominais com Estar*, L, INIC, 1990, 477 pp., gives full data on *estar* as a support verb, from which she extracts 'Lexique-grammaire du portugais: prédicats nominaux supportés par *estar*', *LInv*, 13, 1989:351–67, tabulating *estar* Prep N constructions; in 'Predicate nouns and negation', *ib.*, 387–97, she provides interesting data on negation of nominal predicates.

Tense, aspect, and mood are well served. M. H. C. Campos, 'O Pretérito perfeito composto: um tempo presente', *3º Encontro*, 75–85, emphasizes values of the perfect which represent absolute present time (more so than the present tense?) and contrasts them with the Galician compound past tense. H. B. Fernandes, 'Expressão perifrástica da categoria verbal *aspecto* em português contemporâneo', *Diacrítica*, 5, 1990:21–42, distinguishes five degrees of grammaticalization. M. H. C. Campos, 'Ambiguidade lexical e representação metalinguística', *BF*, 30, 1985[1989]:113–31, distinguishes two aspectual values of *acabar de*. M. L. Painter, 'The inflected infinitive in Brazilian Portuguese', *LQ*, 29:1–46, attributes differences between Brazilian and European to the presence or absence of a CP in IP, and compares the standard hypotheses of origins in terms of their compatibility with the Case Filter. J. M. Lipski, 'In search of the Spanish personal infinitive', Wanner and Kibbee, *New Analyses*,

201–20, finds NP + Infinitive constructions in Portuguese creoles as well as non-standard Spanish. F. Oliveira, 'Modais e condicionais', *5° Encontro*, 145–61, comments on rules of inference. A. Franco, 'Partículas modais do português', *RFLUP*, 7, 1990:175–96, distinguishes modal particles from phrasal adverbs.

The centrality of verbs is fully recognized. Francisco Silva Borba *et al.*, *Dicionário gramatical de verbos do Português culto do Brasil*, SPo, UNESP, xxi + 1373 pp., is a compendium of valency information, introduced by F. S. Borba, 'A montagem de um dicionário gramatical de verbos do português contemporâneo', *Congresso*, II, 146–72; F. S. Borba, M. H. M. Neves and O. G. L. A. S. Campos, 'Dicionário gramatical de verbos do português contemporâneo do Brasil', *Actes* (Trier), VII, 499–502; and M. H. M. Neves *et al.*, 'A técnica de elaboração de um dicionário de regência verbal', *Congresso*, II, 173–87. R. Chociary, 'O verbo *deparar* e seus problemas de regência verbal', *Alfa*, 34, 1990:175–85, provides additional materials. M. F. Xavier, 'Do léxico à sintaxe com *escrever/write* e *destruir/destroy*', *4° Encontro*, 25–39, makes obvious remarks on valency. A. Múrias, 'Comment améliorer la description des *verba dicendi* du portugais dans le cadre d'un dictionnaire de la valence', *Actes* (Trier), IV, 308–19, classifies speech act verbs according to the number of participants and their semantic roles. M. Vilela, 'Contribution à l'étude des verbes de déplacement: approche sémantique et syntaxique', *RFLUP*, 6, 1989:9–41. M. C. Almeida, 'Co-agencialidade ou instrumentalização?: relações semânticas entre o Agente e outro ser humano em português e alemão', *5° Encontro*, 5–15, proposes a class of co-agents. M. E. de Macedo, 'Complementos locativos: sua caracterização', *ib.*, 127–33, lists different approaches to locatives as arguments and complements. E. M. Ranchhod, 'Frozen adverbs — comparative forms *como C* in Portuguese', *LInv*, 15:141–70, catalogues a range of verbal and adjectival idioms.

P. Gonçalves, 'A fixação do sistema de marcação casual do português em Moçambique', *5° Encontro*, 73–90, shows Bantu influence on case-marking: *a* and associated pronouns act as markers of human objects, while second objects do not receive morphological case (and can thus be passivized). J. Ramos, 'O emprego de preposições no português do Brasil', Tarallo, *Fotografias*, 83–93, studying pre-20th-c. Brazilian, correlates the use of *a* as a Case marker with movement of NPs.

The noun phrase is not totally neglected. L. F. Bulger, 'Interferência linguística: o adjectivo descritivo em português', *Congresso*, II, 800–06, draws obvious lessons from Portuguese–English differences in adjective position. J. Fonseca, 'Aspectos da sintaxe do adjectivo em português', *RFLUP*, 6, 1989:43–57. On the use of articles in

396 *Portuguese Studies*

Brazilian, A. P. Palácio *et al.*, 'O artigo, normas e usos', Castilho, *Português culto*, 57–65, and A. T. R. de Castilho, 'O artigo no português culto falado em São Paulo', *ib.*, 67–87. S. Cardoso, 'O genitivo em português: contributos para uma sintaxe e semântica da preposição *de*', *RFLUP*, 5, 1988 : 19–100, dourly catalogues the functions of *de*. M. Axt, 'Estruturas possessivas em português — uma análise transformacional', Castilho, *Português culto*, 121–46, on possessives in relative clauses. N. F. Carvalho, 'A natureza do gênero em português', *Alfa*, 33, 1989 : 55–88, discusses the interaction of the lexical matrices of nouns with the grammatical matrices of NPs in gender marking. J. A. Peres and A. H. Branco, 'O todo e as suas partes como objectos de referência', *5º Encontro*, 187–99, state the conditions for holistic and distributive readings of *todo*.

On discourse, A. T. de Castilho, 'Para o estudo das unidades discursivas no português falado', Castilho, *Português culto*, 249–79, looks at markers of discourse units in Brazilian Portuguese, while L. A. Marcishi, 'Marcadores conversacionais do português brasileiro: formas, posições e funções', *ib.*, 281–321, is concerned with interactional markers. M. H. M. Neves, 'Palavras fóricas: alguns pronomes e os artigos definidos', *Alfa*, 34, 1990 : 85–100, shows how grammatical class and textual function do not match. On the discourse functions of conjunctions there is a major study by Eduardo Guimarães, *Texto e argumentação. Um estudo de conjunções do português*, Campinas, Pontes, 1987, 200 pp. C. A. Barros explores the same area synchronically in 'A propósito de morfemas contrastivas em português: um *mas* de excepção/provocação', *RFLUP*, 5, 1988 : 269–75, and diachronically in 'Porém: um caso da deriva conclusiva-contrastiva', *ib.*, 101–17, where she finds 13th-c. cases of concessive *porém*. S. P. F. de Matos, '*Agora*: da "deixis" temporal à argumentação', *RFLUP*, 5, 1988 : 119–36. E. G. V. de Figueiredo, 'Coesão textual, sistema verbal e tradução,' *3º Encontro*, 219–28, highlights the literary use of the synthetic pluperfect as an alternative preterite (and vice versa of the preterite as a pluperfect) and shows the disastrous effects on cohesion of ignoring them in translation. M. S. Risso, 'A recorrência da informação como fator de coesão do diálogo', *Alfa*, 34, 1990 : 75–84, studies one NURC dialogue for cohesion. J. Fonseca, 'Coerência de texto', *RFLUP*, 5, 1988 : 7–18. M. C. Fernandes, M. G. Ferreira and M. L. Almeida, 'Enunciados condicionais, contrastivos-concessivos e explicativos-causais: uma visão pragmática', *3º Encontro*, 201–17. L. C. Bastos, 'Construções truncadas e a sua relação com Tópico/Comentário', *ib.*, 61–73, identifies breaches of cohesion in student essay-writing. M. C. Fernández, 'Anáforas Ø em textos discursivos: um estudo preliminar', *ib.*, 187–200, identifies pragmatic factors in zero anaphora. D. A. Koike, 'Markedness and its application to pragmatics: Brazilian Portuguese directives', Staczek, *Linguistics*, 211–25, shows the operation of a hierarchy of politeness. L. C. C. Martine, 'Análise da constituição e reprodução do discurso médico-paciente: uma abordagem sociolingüística interacional', Tarallo, *Fotografias*, 239–68, looks at mothers' interaction with doctors. M. L. D. Sousa, 'Contributos para a caracterização do discurso pedagógico na aula de português', *5° Encontro*, 341–62, analyses the discourse functions of teachers' questions. *Duas línguas em contraste. Português e alemão*, ed. António Franco (*RFLUP* anexo 3) O, Faculdade de Letras, 1989, 209 pp., contains H. Thun, '*Sou eu o que pago/paga — Ich bin derjenige, der zahlt*. A construção convergente e divergente em português e alemão' (9–28); E. Koller, '*Nicht — Não*: Uma equivalên-cia problemática' (29–42); M. C. Almeida, 'Transitividade, intran-sitividade e valores aspectuais em português e alemão' (65–74); W. Roth, 'Composiçao e adjectivos de relação: um desafio ao dicionário alemão-português' (75–85); B. Sieberg, 'Adjektivkomposita im Deut-schen und portugiesischen und Vorschläge ihrer Didaktisierung' (87–110); C. Müller, 'Flexionsmorpheme und Kongruenz des Adjektivs' (111–22); T. Harden, 'Ausdruckweisen der deontischen Modalität im Deutschen und Portugiesischen' (123–36); C. Silva-Joaquim, 'Lugares' (137–45) on *a* and *para*; A. Franco, 'A gramática de valências como modelo para a contrastação alemão-português' (171–89). M. E. Malheiros-Poulet, 'La rélativité de la valeur sémantique des expressions d'intensité (exemples en Portugais du Brésil)', *Pottier Vol*, II, 527–37, comments on contextualization and accumulation of intensifiers, counting seven different types in *Puxa! mas é bem pequenininho mesmo*. J. L. A. de Campo, 'Untersuchungen zu den Phrascoschablonen im Portugiesischen — eine Beispielsamm-lung aus der Erzahlung "Justiça" von M. Torga', *BRP*, 27, 1988:283–90. P. Laranjcira, 'A gramaticalidade [sic] e redundância na informação radiofónica, sob o signo de Camões', *Congresso*, II, 535–41, analyses the pleonasm and repetitiveness (*agramaticalidade* in a specific sense) of a commemorative news broadcast.

4. LEXIS

A. G. Cunha, 'Pontos negros na lexicografia da língua portuguesa', *Actes* (Trier), IV, 13–19, gloomily contemplates the task ahead, while M. Vilela, 'O dicionário do século XX (em comparação com os dicionários até agora existentes)', *Congresso*, II, 133–45, is more optimistic. Mauro Villar, *Dicionário Contrastivo Luso-Brasileiro*, R, Guanabara, 1989, 318 pp., is a useful compendium of differences, without constituting an original or systematic study. C. Lupu, 'Vocabularul representativ si galiciana', *SCL*, 40, 1989:365–67, studies Galician and Portuguese terms in the *Vocabularul representativ al limbilor romanice* and finds few significant divergences. P. Teyssier, 'La méthode statistique dans l'étude des premiers dictionnaires de la langue portugaise', *Actes* (Trier), IV, 360–70, identifies phonological and morphological patterns in the 16th-c. bilingual dictionaries of Jerónimo Cardoso. D. Messner, 'Un aperçu du lexique portugais des XVIIIe et XIXe siècles', *RLiR*, 53, 1989:189–94, suggests sources for re-dating 18th- and 19th-c. borrowings. M. H. M. Mateus adds L–O and P–Q to the ongoing 'Glossário da *Vida e Feitos de Júlio César*', *BF*, 30, 1985 [1989]:167–213, and 31, 1986–87 [1990]:197–236 (see *YWMLS*, 46:414). P. de Silveira, 'Acerca de alguns vocábulos dentro ou ainda fora dos dicionários', *ib.*, 187–95, gives notes on some *açorianismos*.

T. M. Stephens, 'Color terms as racial identifiers in American Spanish and Brazilian Portuguese', *HisL*, 3, 1989–90:219–38, lists colour terms with racial connotations (not many surprises here) noting that such connotations are weaker in South America than in North America. L. C. Bastos, M. G. D. Pereira and M. C. L. O. Fernández, 'Coisas sobra a palavra *coisa*', Staczek, *Linguistics*, 150–59, distinguish lexical, anaphoric, and empty uses. Castilho, *Português culto*, contains M. C. R. Costa. 'O léxico de "profissões e ofícios"' (199–245) and E. del Carratore, 'Nota prévia ao léxico de freqüência do português contemporâneo de São Paulo' (169–98). M. V. M. Rego, 'Francisco da Holanda e a formação do vocabulário das belas-artes em Portugal', *Technische Sprache*, 152–72, analyses the loanwords of a seminal artistic treatise of the 16th c. Word-formation attracts much attention. Antônio José Sandmann, *Formação de palavras no português brasileiro contemporâneo*, Curitiba, Scientia et Labor, 1989, xiv + 185 pp., is the Portuguese version of a dissertation originally published in German (see *YWMLS*, 49:397). A. Li Ching, 'Alguns aspectos características da composição assindética no português contemporâneo', *Congresso*, II, 118–32, assembles noun compounds in Portuguese, as do M. Brea, 'Sobre palabras compostas do tipo pararraios', *Verba*, 17, 1990:405–14, and J. Marques Valea, 'Notas sobre palabras compostas: unidades formadas por máis de dous elementos', *ib.*, 415–19, for Galician. E. G. Pezatti, 'A gramática da derivação sufixal: três casos exemplares', *Alfa*, 33, 1989:103–14, and 'A gramática da derivação sufixal: os sufixos formadores de substantivos abstratos', *ib.*, 34, 1990:153–74, describes the occurrence of suffixes in two groups: *–oso*, *-ento* and *-udo* (arranged in a scale of pejorative value) and the larger set of abstract nominals. M. P. Frota, 'A expressãao do pejorativo em construções morfológicas', Staczek, *Linguistics*, 83–90, takes *-udo* and *-ice* as exemplars. M. C. Rosa and A. Villalva, 'A produtividade das regras de formação de palavras',

3° Encontro, 363–78, reflect on the apparently increasing productivity of *-udo*. On word-formation and neologism-creation, Ieda Maria Alves, **Neologismo. Criacão lexical*. SPo, Ática, 96 pp.; M. T. R. F. Lino, 'Banco de neologismos do português contemporâneo — balanço de uma experiência', *4° Encontro*, 177–94; M. C. C. Mocho, 'Neologia formal por sufixação — alguns aspectos', *ib.*, 195–210; M. R. V. Costa, 'Aspectos da neologia no vocabulário da economia', *ib.*, 211–27; M. M. C. Ferreira, 'Algumas particularidades da prefixação na neologia do português contemporâneo', *ib.*, 239–47; I. M. Alves, 'Empréstimos lexicais na imprensa política brasileira', *Alfa*, 32, 1988: 1–14. A. C. M. Lopes, 'O valor semântico dos antropónimos no texto proverbial', *4° Encontro*, 69–81, has obvious examples of proper names used generically. Reinhard Kiesler, **Sprachliche Mittel der Hervorhebung in der modernen portugiesischen Umgangsprache*, Heidelberg, Winter, 1989, xviii + 370 pp. is a catalogue of forms of emphasis. G. M. O. S. Rio-Torto, 'Estruturas léxicas de intensificação no português contemporâneo', *Congresso*, II, 87–113, compares analytic and synthetic forms of emphasis. E. G. Pezatti, 'A ambiguidade na linguagem da propaganda', *Alfa*, 32, 1988:85–93, studies persuasive and humorous uses of ambiguity.

5. SOCIOLINGUISTICS AND DIALECTOLOGY

SOCIOLINGUISTICS

BRAZIL. E. d'A. Magalhães, 'Os estudos sobre o português do Brasil nas três últimas décadas', *Congresso*, II, 222–28, is a rather dated overview, giving stylistics more weight than dialectology and sociolinguistics. Castilho, *Português culto*, contains two articles on the NURC project: C. Cunha, 'Objectivos do Projeto NURC' (11–14); M. B. da Silva, R. V. Mattos e Silva, and N. Rossi, 'O Projeto NURC e o Nordeste' (15–22), and two lexical studies, S. S. Ferreira and J. A. Mota, 'Léxico urbano e faixa etiária' (149–56) and D. Preti, 'Norma e variedade lexicais urbanas' (157–68). S. A. M. Cardoso, 'Sociolingüística e diatopia: empréstimos no português do Brasil', *CEL*, 20:139–61, finds French loanwords retained in rural speech and eliminated in urban areas. Tarallo, *Fotografias*, contains A. S. Chaves, 'A ordem VS no português da fronteira' (65–79) showing Spanish interference in the speech of Paraguayan immigrants; S. M. Bortoni, 'A migração rural-urbana no Brasil: uma análise sociolingüística' (167–80) summarizing her work on networks; J. Adant, 'Difusão dialetal: o caso dos alagoanos em Brasília' (181–97) studying the variation in conservation of Northern features, (notably unpalatalized dental stops and lowered pretonic vowels); T. Nawa, 'Bilingüismo e mudança de código: uma proposta de análise com os nipo-brasileiros residentes em Brasília' (199–215) who finds code-switching used to define social roles, and M. M. P. Scherre, 'Sobre a atuação do princípio da saliência na concordância nominal' (301–32) who argues for the continued relevance of saliency, and attempts to factor out phonological and morphological elements in number inflection. A. J. Naro and M. M. P. Scherre, 'Variação e mudança lingüística: fluxos e contrafluxos na comunidade da fala', *CEL*, 20:9–16, reanalyse data on subject-verb agreement, to show fluctuations along the age dimension, with education a significant factor in the re-establishment of concord. M. M. Azevedo, 'Vernacular features in educated speech in Brazilian Portuguese', *His(US)*, 72, 1989:862–72, shows how the grammatical simplifications of colloquial Brazilian have penetrated other registers. A. T. Macedo, 'Mundança lingüística no paradigma verbal do português: o caso do futuro do subjuntivo', Staczek, *Linguistics*, 135–49, shows the elimination of a future subjunctive distinct from the personal infinitive to be a change in progress. W. Ferreira Netto, 'As entrevistas abertas: uma técnica para verificar variação linguística entre os locutores', *Alfa*, 34, 1990:129–42, takes incomprehension as a pointer to variation. J. M. Poersch and J. V. da Silva, 'Estudo do contato linguístico na fronteira do Brasil com os países do Prata', *5° Encontro*, 201–24, report preliminary results on Brazilian–Argentinian language contact.

PORTUGAL. M. F. R. Matias, 'Bibliographie sociolinguistique des pays europeens pour 1985 — Portugal', *Sociolinguistica*, 1987: 153–54, and I. H. Faria and I. S. Duarte, 'O paradoxo da variação: aspectos do português europeu', *RILP*, 1, 1989:21–27, give overviews of European varieties.

GALICIA. Bochmann, *Regionalsprachen*, 151–63, is a useful digest of information on the Galician language situation. X. Alonso Montero, 'Do estado da lingua: algunhas cuestións', *Grial*, 28, 1990:275–93, raises political issues. X. Bouzada Fernández and A. M. Lorenzo Suárez, 'A lingua galega nas actividades económicas e comerciais', *ib.*, 317–34, X. F. Rubial, 'Lingua galega e relixión', *ib.*, 335–57, X. Monteagudo, 'A oficialidade da lingua galega: o marco legal', *ib.*, 387–98 and D, García Ramos, 'A lingua galega na administración da xustiza', *ib.*, 399–402, survey the use of Galician in different spheres of activity. X. Alonso Montero, 'Prehistoria da Academia Galega. Á procura da norma culta de 1875 a 1905', *ib.*, 26, 1988:8–18, reviews published discussions of the proposed Academy. H. Monteagudo, 'Sobre a polémica da Normativa do Galego', *ib.*, 28, 1990:294–316, plots the linguistic background to the elaboration of a norm, as does C. A. Cáccamo, 'Variaçom lingüística e o factor social na Galiza', *HisL*, 2, 1988–89:253–98, who attempts to give social and contextual variation as much importance as geographical variation in a broad-brush study of varieties of Galician infused with criticisms of current standardization proposals. M. P. García Negro, 'Algunhas consideracións sobre as relacións Galego/Português na Galiza de hoxe', *Congresso*, II, 649–52. advocates reintegration without fusion. X. H. Costas González, 'O trazo entre o verbo e o pronome átono enclítico', *Grial*, 26, 1988:192–98, rejects hyphens as a recent Portuguese invention. J. L. Pensado, 'O galego no século da Ilustración', *ib.*, 27, 1989:183–98, and D. Blanco Pérez, 'A lingua oral e o estudio do galego no século XVIII', *Verba*, 17, 1990:93–115, fill in the history of Galician.

DIALECTOLOGY

BRAZIL. M. do S. S. de Aragão, 'La situation de la géographie linguistique au Brésil', *Géolinguistique*, 3, 1987–88:89–114, and 'Atlas linguístico do Paraíba', *Congresso*, II, 236–47, survey the surveys. Ferreira, *Diversidade*, has a series of studies based on the *Atlas Prévio dos Falares Baianos* and the *Atlas Lingüístico de Sergipe*, including 'Retrospectiva' (13–18) on the surveys themselves, phonological studies from J. Mota and N. Andrade, 'Neutralização /n/ — /ñ/ em Sergipe' (33–41); C. Ferreira and V. Rollemberg, 'Neutralização do traço continuidade em área brasileira (Bahia e Sergipe)' (93–102); V. Rollemberg, 'Realizações palatais de /k/ e /g/ em área sergipana' (109–12); J. Mota, 'Variação entre *ei* e *e* em Sergipe' (143–48); V. Rollemberg, 'Nasalidade e empréstimo' (149–53); lexical work from S. Cardoso and V. Rollemberg, 'A vitalidade de *sarolha* nos falares baianos' (43–52); R. V. Silva, 'Uma leitura da Carta 99 do *Atlas prévio dos falares baianos*' (53–66); C. Ferreira and J. Freitas, 'Junho e julho em Sergipe' (67–72); J. Mota and N. Andrade, 'Sobre latitude semântica em um dialecto rural (Sergipe)' (73–78); C. Ferreira, 'Polimorfismo e léxico (*rótula* em Sergipe)' (103–06); C. Ferreira, J. Mota and V. Rollemberg, 'Sergipe e Bahia: algumas diferenças lexicais' (113–26); S. Cardoso, 'Designações para "cria da ovelha" e a história do português do Brasil' (127–42). On creole elements in Brazilian, W. M. Megenney, 'Influências africanas na língua brasileira dos terreiros', *His(US)*, 74:627–36, finds Yoruba the principal source of vocabulary of the *candomblé* and *umbanda*.

EUROPE. Pride of place goes to *Atlas lingüístico galego*, I, *Morfoloxía verbal*, ed. Constantino García *et al.*, Corunna, ILG — Fundación Pedro Barrié de la Maza, 1990, 838 pp., a splendid beginning complemented by Francisco Fernández Rei, **Dialectologia da lingua galega*, Vigo, Edicions Xerais de Galicia, 1990. M. González González, 'L'Atlas Linguistique Galicien', *Géolinguistique*, 3, 1987–88: 17–30. C. A. Maia, 'Antecedentes medievais do seseo galego',

402 *Portuguese Studies*

Homenaje Zamora Vicente, I, 33–43, gives early documentation of sibilant confusion. C. Pedreira Lopez *et al.*, 'Nomenclatura das aves do concello de Ames', *Verba*, 17, 1990:117–44, find 185 words corresponding to 65 species, showing the retreat of *seseo* and *gheada*. M. X. Lopez Castro, 'O léxico do cultivo tradicional do liño en Sarria', *ib.*, 421–26. U. Herrmann, 'Zu einigen Besonderheiten des Galicischen gegenüber dem Portugiesischen und dem Kastilischen', *BRP*, 28, 1989:359–62. Maria Luísa Segura da Cruz, *O Falar de Odeleite*, L, INIC, xxiv + 398 pp., is an unrevised 1969 dissertation on an Algarve dialect, rich in detail. G. Vitorino, 'L'Atlas Linguístico do Litoral Português (ALLP) — I. Fauna e Flora. Essai d'analyse dialectometrique', *Géolinguistique*, 4, 1988–89:14–91, identifies a loosely associated Northern area and a closely-knit Southern one. B. F. Head, 'Relações históricas entre variedades rurais da língua portuguesa em Portugal e no Brasil', *3º Encontro*, 261–91, demonstrates *pace* Cintra the preservation of Northern Portuguese features of pronunciation in conservative rural Brazilan dialects.

6. ETYMOLOGY AND ONOMASTICS

Y. Malkiel, 'Carolina Michaelis' Forgotten sketch of an unfinished monograph on E(N)–ZEBRA "wild donkey"', *BF*, 30, 1985 [1989]:1–11, credits Dona Carolina with first intuiting the connection between *zebra* and *enzebra*. A. Monjour, '-ção oder -zão. Zur lautlichen Entwicklung von lateinisch -tione im Portugiesischen', *RJ*, 40, 1989:265–79, reviews a long-standing issue. G. Colón, 'Es *volcà* un lusisme internacional?', *RLiR*, 55:319–37, points to the absence of Portuguese *vulcão* in 16th-c. texts. J. M. Piel, 'A propósito de elementos primitivos, castiços, do léxico galaico-português', *Congresso*, II, 409–12, entertains with texts laden with vocabulary of varying historical origins. M. L. Carvalhão Buescu, 'Em torno do dicionário Histórico de Tupinismos: os paradigmas de uma estratégia', *ib.*, 229–35, reflects on an early grammar of Tupi. C. García, 'Derivados do latín *nebula* e outras palabras afíns no galego de hoxe', *Homenaje Zamora Vicente*, II, 81–89, expands on *néboa/nebra* and pre-Roman *brétema*, and their local alternatives. J. G. Herculano de Carvalho, *'Tres notas filológicas a D. Francisco Manuel de Melo', *RPF*, 19, 1988:235–48. C. García, 'Notas léxicas gallegas', *Verba*, 16, 1989:387–95, expands on *amoar, carafío, cartafol, fírgoa, gurrar, langran*, and *prea*. F. V. P. Fonseca, 'Alguns elementos pré-romanos e gregos no onomástico do português arcaico', *Actes* (Trier), IV, 571–77, finds 54 pre-roman and Greek names, almost all well known, in PMH *Scriptores*. A. Veiga Arias, 'Patronímicos en -z y otros estudios de onomástica gallega', *Verba*, 16, 1989:5–30, identifies two forms of patronymics, relating them to other forms of surname; neither Miguez (<AMICI), Luz (<LUCII) nor Feles (<FELIX) incorporate patronymic suffixes. J. M. Piel, 'Três esboços de antropo-toponímia galego-portuguesa', *BF*, 31, 1986–87 [1990] : 185–86, derives the toponym *Gulfián* from *Wulfila*, the surname *Condesso* from *codesso* contaminated by *condessa*, and throws in *ervilhar* < REBELLIARE. N. Ares, 'Gransimonde, Labesén e Xurix/Oxuriz: Notras histórico-etimológicas', *Grial*, 27, 1988:277–80. M. V. G. Ferreira, 'Antroponímia do Algarve. Reflexo da toponímia local', *Actes* (Trier) IV, 560–70, discusses the etymology of placenames used as surnames — *Loulé* is Arabic, *Alfarrobeira* might not be, *Ovanha* < Eulalia, and *Tor* possibly Celtic. Two useful local monographs are Firmino Aires, *Toponímia Flaviense*, Chaves, Câmara Municipal, 1990, 390 pp., and E. Campos, *Toponímia Abrantina*, Abrantes, Câmara Municipal, 1989, 238 pp. J. Piel, 'O bem e o mal na tradição toponímica portuguesa', *BF*, 30, 1985 [1989] : 13–15, collects toponyms incorporating *bem* and *mal*.

7. PORTUGUESE OVERSEAS

AFRO-PORTUGUESE

R. G. Hamilton, 'Lusofonia, Africa and matters of language and letters', *His(US)*, 74:610–17, remarks on the implications of the concept of African co-ownership of Portuguese, in a similar vein to M. Ferreira, 'Numa perspectiva sociocultural. Que futuro para a língua portuguesa em Africa?', *Congresso*, II, 248–72, observing the appropriation of Portuguese by African nations. J.-M. Massa *et al.*, 'La lusographie africaine — Un projet de dictionnaire bilingue de particularités en Afrique de langue portugaise (écrite)', *ib.*, 188–93, gives little detail. P. Gonçalves, 'A variação do português dentro do português', *RILP*, 1, 1989:15–20, is on African varieties. G. Firmino, 'Desvios à norma no português falado em Moçambique', *4° Encontro*, 97–116, documents contrastive and non-contrastive 'errors'. Maria José Albarrán Carvalho, **Aspectos sintactico-semânticos dos verbos locativos no português oral de Maputo*, L, ICALP, 152 pp. M. A. F. de Oliveira, 'Quimbundismos no português literário do século XVIII nas áreas angolana e brasileira', *Congresso*, II, 273–91, extracts loan-words from a history of Angola.

CREOLES

M. Perl, 'Zur Präsenz des Kreolisierten Portugiesische in der Karibik — ein Beitrag zur Dialektologie des Karibischen Spanisch', *BRP*, 28, 1989:131–48, explores Portuguese influences on Spanish-based

Portuguese Studies

creoles. *Beiträge zur Afrolusitanistik und Kreolistik ed. Matthias Perl, Bochum, Brockmeyer, 1989, 148 pp., includes studies on a range of creoles.

CABO VERDE. D. Fanha, 'Aspectos do contacto entre o português e o croulo de Cabo Verde', Congresso, II, 292–310, outlines the forces favouring and inhibiting decreolization, with reference to the Tense-Aspect-Mood system; the same author continues to promote Caboverdiano in 'Falar crioulo e falar português em Cabo Verde', RILP, 1, 1989:11–14, and 'Crioulo de Cabo Verde: proposta de grafia', ib., 2, 1989:41–48. J. Lang, 'A categoria número no crioulo caboverdiano', Papia, 1, 1990:15–25, drawing data from a modern creole novel, shows number marked only on the first available element in the NP, and never with quantifiers; possessives mark number of the possessor.

GUINÉ-BISSAU. Benjamin Pinto-Bull, *O Crioulo de Guiné-Bissau. Filosofia e sabedoria, L, ICALP — Bissau, INEP, 1989, 352 pp., is previewed by Id., 'O português, presente nas estruturas gramaticais do crioulo de Guiné-Bissau', Congresso, II, 311–22, emphasizing the Portuguese base. H. H. Couto, 'Política e planejamento lingüístico na Guiné-Bissau', Papia, 1, 1990:47–58, highlights the tension between the national languages (creole and Portuguese) and the sixteen native African languages; the problem is one of national identity. H. H. Couto, *O crioulo guineense em relação ao português e às línguas nativas', Lingüística, 29, 1989:107–28; F. Macedo. *'O problema das línguas na Guiné-Bissau', Humanidades, 6, no. 22, 1989:34–38. Jean-Louis Rougé, *Petit Dictionnaire étymologique du kriol de Guinée-Bissau et Casamance, Bissau, INEP, 1988, 163 pp.

ANNOBÓN. G. de Granda, 'Retenciones africanas en la fonética del criollo português de Annobón', Papia, 1, 1990:26–37, identifies 13 African features (by now familiar). Id., 'Procesos de aculturación léxica en el criollo portugués de Annobón', Homenaje Zamora Vicente, II, 145–56, shows Spanish lexical items replacing Portuguese.

CURAÇAO (PAPIAMENTU). Philippe Maurer, *Les Modifications temporelles et modales du verbe dans le papiamento de Curaçao (Antilles Néerlandaises), (Kreolische Bibliothek, 9) Hamburg, Buske, 1988, 443 pp.

SÃO TOMÉ. J. Pontífice, 'Os meandros da cumplicidade crioula', RILP, 1, 1989:52–55, describes the suppression of the Forro of S. Tomé in schools. L. I. Ferraz, 'Uma avaliação lingüística do angolar', Papia, 1, 1990:38–46, argues for a common source to Angolar and São-Tomense, though the former has a higher Bantu lexical content, including most of the numerals.

INDO-PORTUGUESE. I. C. Clements, 'The Indo-Portuguese creoles: languages in transition', His(US), 74:637–46, gives an overview of Indo-Portuguese, with a study of Korlai. M. C. de Matos, 'Para uma análise sistémica das inter-relações do português e o «gujarati» no território de Damão (atraves de espécimes folclóricos ali recolhidos)', *Congresso*, II, 323–49, and K. D. Jackson, 'Indo-Portuguese cantigas: oral traditions in Ceylon Portuguese verse', *His(US)*, 74:618–26, provide documentation. I. Wherritt, 'Portuguese language shift: about town in Goa, India', *ib.*, 72, 1989:385–91, shows elderly Catholic women to be the last bastion of Portuguese in retreat. I. Wherritt, 'Portuguese loan-words in Konkani', *ib.*, 873–81.

MALACCA (KRISTANG). M. C. Rosa, 'As categorias TEMPO, MODO e ASPECTO em kristang', *5° Encontro*, 321–39, neatly analyses the four Kristang particles in terms of one modal opposition (± real) and one aspectual one (± completive). A. Baxter, 'Some observations on verb serialization in Malacca Creole Portuguese', *BF*, 31, 1986–87 [1990]:161–84, exemplifies a wide range of types of verb serialization, and argues that the process has multiple sources, convergence with Malay being as important as the operation of creole universals.

LANGUAGE CONTACT. Jin Guo Ping, 'Alguns dados sobre léxico chinês de origem portuguesa e lexicografia sino-portuguesa e vice versa', *Congresso*, II, 361–79, lists Portuguese loanwords and bilingual dictionaries. K. M. S. Horta, 'O léxico português numa ilha remota da Oceânia — Alguns exemplos de palavras portuguesas enraizadas em tetum — lingua franca de Timor-Leste', *Congresso*, II, 350–63.

ÉMIGRÉS. Eduardo Mayone Dias, *Falares emigreses — uma abordagem ao seu estudo*, L, BB, 172 pp., gives an overview of emigrant communities and varieties, with a useful glossary of *emigresismos*. T. M. Stephens, 'Language maintenance and ethnic survival: the Portuguese in New Jersey', *His(US)*, 72, 1989:716–20, is on the Portuguese of Newark. U. M. S. P. Bendiha, 'Problemas de bilinguismo e interferência em trabalhadores emigrados em França (influência do francês no português)', *Congresso*, II, 390–95, gives examples of the penetration of French loanwords, in greater quantities than M. C. Vilhena, 'O falar do emigrante português em França', *ib.*, 380–89.

MEDIEVAL LITERATURE

POSTPONED

LITERATURE 1500 TO THE PRESENT DAY

POSTPONED

VII.   LATIN AMERICAN STUDIES

SPANISH-AMERICAN LITERATURE
THE COLONIAL PERIOD

By PETER T. BRADLEY, *Lecturer in Spanish and Latin American Studies
in the University of Newcastle upon Tyne*

1.   GENERAL

1492–1992: Re-Discovering Colonial Writing, ed. R. Jara and N. Spadaccini, Minneapolis, Prisma, 1989, 472 pp., is a somewhat unfocused set of individually worthy articles on Oviedo, Las Casas, the chroniclers, and Indian writers. *Dieciocho*, 13, 1990, covers a wide variety of topics: L. Leal traces the occurrence of fables in Mexico but finds little originality (21–35); H. C. Woodbridge writes brief notes on works published since 1950 on Carrió de la Vandera (50–57); R. A. Zapata stresses the impact of the Bourbon reforms on the latter's *El lazarillo de ciegos caminantes* (58–70); M. A. Salgado explains the changing influences on a list of mainly undistinguished 18th-c. Mexican poets (71–83); J. Williams delights in the 'laudatory verses' of a tribute to Philip V written in Lima in 1707 (90–109); R. Heredia Correa scratches the surface of Matías de Escobar's religious chronicle *Americana Thebaida* (110–18); J. H. Kaimowitz translates into English the apologetical essay appended to Alegre's *Alexandriad* (135–48); A. L. Kerson uses textual analysis to display Landívar's use of mock-heroic mode (149–64); and I. Osorio Romero points out the 'helenismo' of Villerías y Roel in original and translated epigrams (171–80). Worthy of note is R. Chang-Rodríguez, **El discurso disidente: ensayos de literatura colonial*, Lima, U. Católica, 282 pp.

2.   PRE-COLUMBIAN

H. Treiber, *LAILJ*, 6, 1990:167–79, offers insights on the Paris Codex, whereas *ib.*, 7, contains: L. M. Burkhart with a preliminary report of her research on the earliest extant Nahuatl religious drama (*c.* 1590) (153–71); R. Gubler scouring the *Book of Chilam Balam of Nah* for mention of herbal cures (192–214); and E. Quiñones Keber on the portrayal of gods (especially Xolotl) as animals in various codices (229–39). A. Segala, *RevIb*, 57:649–55, urges that the time for revision is upon us in studying Nahuatl literature, but offers few ideas. J. A. Flores Martos, 'Un ritual de magia amorosa maya-yucateca', *CHA Los Complementarios*, 7–8:7–19, interprets 'Kay-nicté'. J. J. Himelblau, *Quiché Worlds in Creation. The 'Popol Vuh' as a Narrative Work of Art*,

Culver City, Labyrinthos, 1989, 67 pp., again addresses some of the open questions about the text and its copyist. *The Huarochirí Manuscript: A Testament of Ancient and Colonial Andean Religion*, ed. and trans. F. Salomon and G. L. Urioste, Austin, Texas U.P., xiv + 273 pp., is a most welcome text. *Testimonios de la antigua palabra*, ed. M. León-Portilla and L. Silva Galeana (Crónicas de América, 56), M, 1990, 253 pp., is a valuable bilingual edition of the *huehuehtlahtolli*.

3. HISTORIANS

B. Scharlau, *RCLL*, 16, 1990: 365–75, detects some 'new trends in the study of colonial Latin American chronicles'. Garcilaso *el Inca* features largely in *RHA*, 110, 1990: G. Prado Galán rather laboriously draws attention to 'magia solar' in the *Comentarios reales* (5–18); J. L. González Martínez with some originality re-works the old theme of *mestizaje* (19–35); on the basis of the anonymous pilot story in the *Comentarios reales*, G. Vargas Martínez claims that Garcilaso was the first American to deny Columbus the title 'discoverer' (37–44); and A. González Acosta compares his response to the conquest with that of Alvarado Tezozómoc (45–63). N. Weygómez, *RCLL*, 17:7–31, discusses the formation of a transcultural discourse, and R. González Echevarría, *Myth and Archive: A Theory of Latin American Narrative*, Cambridge U.P., 1990, xiv + 245 pp., in search of the multiple and non-literary origins of the novel, persuasively uses the *Comentarios reales* to demonstrate its links with legal discourse. Cultural aspects of Cortesian historiography in Spain are reviewed by I. Arenas Frutos, *RIndM*, 50, 1990:277–88. M. Glantz, *Hispamérica*, 19, 1990:165–74, briefly discusses the portrayal of Mexico City in the *Cartas de relación*, whereas D. A. Boruchoff, *MLN*, 106:330–69, more ponderously contrasts how Cortés and Díaz del Castillo express realities never before encountered. Less expected is the comparison of the latter's *Historia verdadera* with I. Allende's *La casa de los espíritus*, as chronicles of a disappearing world, by V. Cortínez, *HR*, 59:317–27. Note also A. Mendiola Mejía, *Bernal Díaz del Castillo: verdad romanesca y verdad historiográfica*, Mexico, U. Iberoamericana, 146 pp. 'Trabajos de la guerra y del hambre' are deemed to be essential traits of chronicles of the conquest of Chile by L. Invernizzi Santa Cruz, *RCL*, 36, 1990:7–15, and F. Aguilera, *ib.*, 105–12, summarily passes in review the events of Góngora Marmolejo's chronicle. S. Cro writes on the roots of the 'noble savage' in Pedro Mártir and Montaigne, *RIndM*, 50, 1990:665–85, F. Delpino on Acosta, *ib.*, 861–78, and E. C. Frost on Olmos and Zurita, *ib.*, 51:169–78. P. Thibon-Morey, 'Sur les pas de Sahagún au XVII siècle', *CMHLB*, 56:5–13, traces the survival

408   *Latin American Studies*

and evolution of religious rites as recorded by H. Ruiz de Alarcón. Ten studies are collected in *Bernardino de Sahagún*, ed. A. Hernández de León-Portilla, Mexico, FCE, 1990, 351 pp. F. L. Lisi, *Hispamérica*, 19, 1990: 175–85, discusses 'orality and literacy' in the chronicle of Cieza de León, of which there is a partial new edition, *Crónica del Perú. Cuarta parte, vol. I: La guerra de las Salinas*, ed. P. Guibovich Pérez, Lima, U. Católica, xlv + 437 pp. S. Herman, *REH*, 23, 1989: 32–52, delves into the 'mystery' of Freile's use of the word 'carnero', proposing that it be translated as 'morgue', and G. Perissinotto, *Iberoromania*, 30, 1989: 70–78, examines names given to American products in Cuneo's account of Columbus's second voyage. Noteworthy amongst the latest crop of new editions are: brief selections from F. Huamán Poma de Ayala, *Nueva corónica y buen gobierno*, ed. C. Araníbar, Lima, 123 pp.; B. Cobo, *Inca Religion and Customs*, ed. R. Hamilton, Austin, Texas U.P., 1990, 264 pp.; P. de Valdivia, *Cartas*, ed. M. Rojas-Mix, B, Lumen, 292 pp.; another in the series edited by F. Carrillo, *Cronistas indios y mestizos I*, Lima, Horizonte, 258 pp.; and additions to the series *Crónicas de América*, including the *Relación de Michoacán*, ed. L. Cabrero; M. de Barco, *Historia natural de la antigua California*, ed. M. León-Portilla; B. de Sahagún, *Historia general de las cosas de la Nueva España*, ed. J. C. Temprano; and P. de Ondegardo, *El mundo de los incas*, ed. L. González and A. Alonso.

3. POETRY

With reference to Sor Juana's *Primero sueño*, J. C. Nanfito concludes that 'the fundamental scheme of the symbolic structure is the willful ascent through the element of air', *REH*, 23, 1989: 53–65, and likewise sees the poem as a 'dream of height' transporting the reader 'to the domain of the imaginary, to the cosmic realm of the infinite', *MLN*, 106: 423–31. B. L. Lewis, *RoN*, 32 : 3–10, draws enlightening parallels with *Dios* of Justo Sierra. See also A. Sánchez Robayna, *Para leer 'Primero sueño'*, Mexico, Tierra Firme, 218 pp. M. R. Fort, *RCLL*, 17 : 33–45, discusses the love sonnets of Sor Juana, and there is a new edition, *Poesía amorosa*, ed. E. Kalepis, Mexico, Premiá, 1990, 139 pp. New volumes include: G. H. Tavard, *Juana Inés de la Cruz and the Theology of Beauty*, Notre Dame U.P., 224 pp., and V. Urbano, *Sor Juana Inés de la Cruz: amor, poesía, soledumbre*, Potomac, Scripta Humanistica, 200 pp. Sor Juana is included in E. Bergmann, *Women, Culture and Politics in Latin America*, Berkeley, California U.P., 1990, xi + 269 pp., and in the pioneering bilingual anthology, *Untold Sisters: Hispanic Nuns in their own Words*, ed. E. Arenal and S. Schlau, Albuquerque, New Mexico U.P., 1989, 450 pp. F. J. Cevallos demonstrates that Ercilla has a critical view of most Indians, alongside the heroes who are a product of epic poetic tradition, *REH*, 23, 1989: 1–20. J. Durán Luzio, *RevIb*, 57: 591–96, uses the occasion of a new 'definitive' bilingual edition of Landívar's *Rusticatio mexicana* to make notes on the background to composition and the themes, and A. Lorente Medina, *RIndM*, 50, 1990: 585–92, lists new documents relevant to the biography of Valle Caviedes. Two substantial additions are: M. Rosas de Oquendo, *Sátira hecha a las cosas que pasan en el Perú*, ed. P. Lasarte, Madison, 1990, cxvii + 181 pp., and *Poesía colonial hispanoamericana*, ed. H. J. Becco (Biblioteca Ayacucho, 154), Caracas, 1990, xxxix + 419 pp.

4. THEATRE

J. M. Williams, *REH*, 23, 1989: 21–35, studies the origins and targets of specific acts of censorship in early Mexican theatre. To help bridge the gap between readings and stagings, C. Larson, *BC*, 42, 1990: 179–98, examines stage directions in Sor Juana's *Los empeños de una casa*. Note J. Inés de la Cruz and A. de Salazar y Torres, *La segunda Celestina. Una comedia perdida de Sor Juana*, ed. G. Schmidhuber, Mexico, Gabinete Literario, 1990, 225 pp.

5. PROSE

A. Fernández Insuela, *BH*, 92, 1990: 847–56, puzzles over 'las 4 PPPP de Lima' in Carrió de la Vandera's *El lazarillo de ciegos caminantes*. J. G. Johnson, *REH*, 23, 1989: 67–85, assesses the pleas for reform in Espejo's satiric art, especially *El nuevo Luciano*. C. de Sigüenza y Góngora, *Los infortunios de Alonso Ramírez*, ed. E. Irizarry, Río Piedras, Cultural, 1990, 247 pp., is an impressive edition, using the statistical results of computer analysis to estimate the extent of the proposed dual authorship.

THE NINETEENTH CENTURY

By Annella McDermott, *Lecturer in Hispanic Studies,*
University of Bristol

1. General

A. Arrufat, 'El nacimiento de la novela en Cuba', *RevIb*, 56,
1990:747–57, attempts to explain why the birth of the genre in Cuba
took place in the 1830s. Antonio Cussen, *Poetry and Politics in the
Spanish American Revolution: Bello, Bolívar and the classical tradition*,
Cambridge U.P. B. Frederick, 'In Their Own Voice: The Women
Writers of the Generación del 80 in Argentina', *His(US)*, 74:282–89,
focuses on eight women writers, with the aim of correcting the
impression given by anthologies and histories that the generation
consisted entirely of male writers. *Contextos: Literatura y Sociedad
Latino-americanas del siglo XIX*, ed. E. P. Garfield and I. A. Schulman,
Illinois U.P., 128 pp. Cedomil Goic, *Historia y crítica de la literatura
hispanoamericana*, vol. 2: Del Romanticismo al Modernismo. B, Crítica, 1990, 776 pp. R. Sánchez, '*Don Junípero*, vehículo del costum-
brismo en Cuba', *RevIb*, 56, 1990:759–68, examines the cultural role
played by this satirical newspaper. Doris Sommers, *Foundational
Fictions: the national romances of Latin America*, California U.P. G. M.
Yeager, 'Women and the intellectual life of Nineteenth-Century
Lima', *IARB*, 40, 1990:361–93, explores the work of 18 women who
were editors or writers or held literary salons in the last quarter of the
century.

2. Individual Authors

BORRERO, JUANA. E. Rivero, 'Pasión de Juana Borrero y la crítica',
RevIb, 56, 1990:829–39, attempts to understand the reality behind the
myth of the virginal, almost ethereal figure, created by her critics.

CASAL, JULIÁN DEL. E. de Armas, 'Julián del Casal y el modernismo', *ib.*, 781–91, points to C.'s ambiguous position, not clearly a
'patriotic' poet, and yet significant in the formation of a Cuban
national identity. J. M. Tolentino, 'Las opiniones literarias de Julián
del Casal', *La Torre*, 17:19–55, examines C.'s reactions to other
writers, the literature of certain countries, and literature, art, and
criticism in general.

DELMONTE, DOMINGO. L. Otero, 'Delmonte y la cultura de la
sacarocracia', *RevIb*, 56, 1990:723–31, examines D.'s role as the
animator of a literary and intellectual *tertulia*.

GÓMEZ DE AVELLANEDA, GERTRUDIS. N. Araújo, 'Constantes ideo-
temáticas en la Avellaneda', *ib.*, 715–22, examines her interest in
marginalized figures, such as women, slaves, artists, and bandits.

HEREDIA, JOSÉ MARÍA.   A. Augier, 'José María Heredia. Novela y realidad de América Latina', *ib.*, 733–46, refers to H.'s awareness of the sufferings of Latin America and Cuba (*realidad*), coupled with his dreams of freedom and justice (*novela*).

MARTÍ, JOSÉ.   A. Arpini y L. Giorgis, 'El Caribe: "Civilización" y "barbarie" en Hostos y Martí', *IARB*, 41:49–62, concentrates on the nuances given to these terms by the nature of Caribbean history, particularly the existence of slavery and the late achievement of independence by Cuba. A. E.-P. del Campo, 'Bécquer y Martí: poetas de la claridad/poetas de la vaguedad', *RHM*, 44:18–28, demonstrates how there is in both poets a harmonization of these opposite values. C. Leante, 'Martí y el destierro', *RevIb*, 56, 1990:823–37. A. M. Teja, 'El origen de la nacionalidad y su toma de conciencia en la obra juvenil de José Martí', *ib.*, 793–822, explores M.'s significance in the cultural 'decolonization' of Latin America.

MERA, JUAN LEÓN.   T. O. Bente, '*Cumandá* y *Tabaré*: dos cumbres del indianismo romántico hispanoamericano', *IARB*, 41:15–23, compares and contrasts these two works, by M. and Juan Zorrilla de San Martín, in their presentation of nature, characterization of white and Indian figures and ideological content.

MEZA, RAMÓN.   R. Arenas, 'Meza, el precursor', *RevIb*, 56, 1990:777–79, is a short note on *Mi tío el empleado*, emphasizing its development of certain techniques still used in modern fiction.

ROA BÁRCENA, JOSÉ MARÍA.   P. Lasarte, 'José María Roa Bárcena y la narración fantástica', *Chasqui*, 20.1:10–16, focuses on the short story *Lanchitas*.

SARMIENTO, DOMINGO FAUSTINO.   Juan P. Esteve, **Creación y egocentrismo en la obra de Sarmiento*. M, Pliegos, 122 pp. J. O. Pellicer, 'Vicente Fidel López y *Facundo*', *BHS*, 67:489–501, demonstrates that López was influential in forming S.'s ideas on the connections between geography and culture. A. A. Roig, 'El discurso civilizatorio en Sarmiento y Alberdi', *IARB*, 41:35–49, focuses particularly on *Facundo* and *Conflicto y harmonía de las razas en América*.

VILLAVERDE, CIRILO.   A. Benítez-Rojo, 'Cirilo Villaverde, fundador', *RevIb*, 56, 1990:769–76, concentrates on *Excursión a Vueltabajo*, which is seen as one of the earliest attempts to define Cuban culture.

ZENEA, JUAN CLEMENTE.   C. Vitier, 'Zenea y el romanticismo cubano', *ib.*, 703–13, shows that Z.'s poetry, though strongly influenced from Europe, was the expression of an independent culture.

THE TWENTIETH CENTURY

By D. L. SHAW, *Professor of Spanish American Literature in the
University of Virginia*, and G. M. MARTIN,
Professor of Latin American Studies in the University of Portsmouth

1. GENERAL

D. E. Marting, *Spanish American Writers*, Westport, Greenwood, 1990,
300 pp. is a comprehensive bibliography. R. Boland and A, Kenwood, *War and Revolution in Hispanic Literature*, Melbourne, Voz
Hispánica, 1990, 248 pp., include 10 articles on Spanish American
writers. I. Rodríguez, *El hombre y las metáforas de Dios en la literatura
hispanoamericana*, Miami, Universal, 144 pp. F. Alegría and J. Ruffinelli (eds), *Paradise Lost or Gained*, Houston, Arte Público, 1990, has
nine essays on exile writing. Various authors, *Escritura y sexualidad en
la literatura hispanoamericana*, M, Fundamentos, 1990, 346 pp. D. W.
Foster, *Gay and Lesbian Themes in Latin American Writing*, Austin, Texas
U.P., 178 pp., a 20th-c. survey. N. Lindstrom, 'Dependency and
Autonomy', *IAr*, 17:109–44, reviews dependency theory and Latin
American literature. On women writers: S. Bassnett, *Women Writers
of Latin America*, London, Zed, 1990, 202 pp. D. E. Marting, *Spanish
American Women Writers*, Westport, Greenwood, 1990, 645 pp., gives
bibliographies of 50. S. Messinger (ed.), *Women Authors of Latin
America*, Metuchen, Scarecrow, 1990, 156 pp. N. Erro Orthman and
J. C. Mendizábal, *La escritora hispánica*, Miami, Universal, 1990,
295 pp. has essays on Garro, Puga, Allende, Valenzuela, etc. C.
Berenguer *et. al.*, *Escribir en los bordes*, Santiago, Cuarto Propio, 1990,
sundry papers on feminine writing. L. P. Condé and S. M. Hart,
Feminist Readings on Spanish and Latin American Literature, Lewiston,
Mellen. R. Moore, 'Our Women Don't Write', *RIAB*, 40, 1990:416–
20, was a complaint on bibliographical difficulties. By contrast,
LALR, 37:189–218 contains a handy bibliography of feminism and
general criticism of women prose writers. J. Mandrell, 'The Prophetic
Voice in Garro, Morante and Allende', *CL*, 42, 1990:227–46, is on
female historical writing. J. Beverley and M. Zimmerman, *Literature
and Politics in the Central American Revolutions*, Austin, Texas U.P., 1990,
256 pp. is on revolutionary writing. Beverley edits *RCLL*, 36, a special
number on *testimonio*. See also his 'Thoughts on Testimonio',
Boundary 2, 18, no. 2:1–21, an important reconsideration. E. Sklodowska, 'Hacia una bibliografía sobre el testimonio hispanoamericano', *Chasqui*, 20, no. 1:108–16. G. Videla, *Direcciones del vanguardismo
hispanoamericano*, Mendoza, Cuyo U.P., 1990, 2 vols, 315 and 251 pp.,
contains essays and documentary material. M. H. Foster and K. D.
Jackson, *Vanguardism in Latin American Literature*, Westport,

Greenwood, 1990, 214 pp., is an exemplary bibliographical guide. J. Schwartz, *Las vanguardias latinoamericanas*, M., Cátedra, 1990, 698 pp. H. Wentzlaff-Eggebert, *Las literaturas hispánicas de vanguardia*, Frankfurt, Vervuert, 229 pp., has more than 3000 bibliographical entries including many on our field. His 'Sieben Fragen zur Avantgarde in LateinAmerika', *Iberoromania*, 33:125–39, is rather general. J. Alcina Franch, *Indianismo e indigenismo*, M, Alianza, 1990, 344 pp. A. de Toro, 'Postmodernidad y Latinoamérica', *RevIb*, 155–56:441–67, attempts an explanation. G. Yudice, 'El conflicto de postmodernidades', *NTC*, 7:19–34, explores the problem.

POETRY. J. Sefamí, *Contemporary Spanish American Poets*, Westport, Greenwood, 272 pp., is a major bibliographical guide. *Iberoromania*, 34, carries seven articles on recent poetry in seven Latin American countries. F. W. Murray, *Aesthetics of Contemporary Spanish American Social Poetry*, Lewiston, Mellen, 1990, 224 pp. F. G. Flores, *Rostros de la poesía latinoamericana*, BA, Corregidor, 224 pp., is on Borges, Vallejo, Paz, Cardenal, and Neruda, etc. M. Rojas *et al.*, *Las poetas del buen amor*, Caracas, Monte Ávila, 149 pp., is on Agustini, Ibarbourou and Storni.

FICTION. M. Gálvez, *La novela hispanoamericana hasta 1940*, M, Taurus, 236 pp. R. Martínez, *Para una relectura del Boom*, M, Pliegos, 1990, 135 pp. *Antípodas*, III, is a special number on the contemporary novel with items by Fuentes and Vargas Llosa and sundry articles. K. Brower, *Contemporary Latin American Fiction*, Englewood Cliffs, Salem, 1990, 200 pp. D. Medina, *Técnicas narrativas de la novela latinoamericana contemporánea*, Guadalajara U.P., 1990, 141 pp. H. Bloom (ed.), *Modern Latin American Fiction*, NY, Chelsea House, 1990, 352 pp. E. Sklodowska, *La parodia en la nueva novela hispanoamericana*, Amsterdam, Benjamins, 219 pp., examines 25 novels 1960–85. *Paunch* (Buffalo) 65–66, was on the body and sex in modern Latin American fiction with excellent essays. J. Franco surveys pastiche in contemporary Latin American fiction in *STCL*, 14, 1990:95–107. H. Hermans and M. Steenmeijer, *La nueva novela histórica hispanoamericana*, Amsterdam, Foro Hispánico, 142 pp. *CA*, 28, has six essays on the modern historical novel. R. Antelo, 'La reconstrucción de los hechos', *NTC*, 7:35–42, also on this theme. B. Torres Caballero, 'El deporte en la narrativa latinoamericana', *HR*, 59:401–20, too descriptive on Agustín, Sábato, Skármeta, and Goldemberg. On more than one author: M. L. Puga, *Lo que le pasa al lector*, Mexico, Grijalbo, 188 pp., has essays on Fuentes, Vargas Llosa, del Paso, Poniatowska, etc. A. Rivero Potter, *Autor/lector*, Detroit, Wayne State U.P., 184 pp., has essays on Borges, Huidobro, Fuentes, and Sarduy. F. Alegría, *Creadores en el mundo hispánico*, Santiago, A. Bello, 1990, 184 pp., has essays on Borges, Mistral, Neruda, Parra, García Márquez, etc. A. de Toro, *Texto-mensaje-recipiente*, BA, Galerna, 1990, 220 pp., has essays on García Márquez, Rulfo, and Vargas Llosa. C. Fuentes, *Valiente mundo nuevo*, B, Mondadori, 1990, 288 pp., has essays on Carpentier, Rulfo, García Márquez, etc. B. Espejo, *Palabra de honor*, Tabasco, Gobierno, 1990, 156 pp., has essays on Usigli, Yáñez, Cortázar, Arreola, etc. J. Díaz, *La aventura de la palabra*, BA, Corregidor, 158 pp., has essays on Borges, N. Guillén, and Asturias. C. Perelli, **La mujer en Carpentier y García Márquez*, Tucumán U.P., 1990, 271 pp. *CAm*, 183, had a section on Olga Harmony, Nellie Campobello, and Elena Garro and other feminine topics. M. Palencia-Roth, 'Memory in García Márquez and Vargas Llosa', *MLN*, 105, 1990:351–66, is on its effect on writing. A. Zubizarreta, 'Triunfos del narrador oral', *RCLL*, 34:81–104, is on this technique in Alegría and García Márquez.

DRAMA.   See *Modern Drama*, 34:231–52, for many items not listed here. P. Meléndez, **La dramaturgia hispanoamericana contemporánea*, M, Pliegos, 1990, 189 pp. G. Luzuriaga, *Introducción a las teorías latinoamericanas del teatro*, Mexico, UAP, 1990, 212 pp., treats Usigli, Pavlovsky, Boal, etc. O. Pellettieri, 'Teatro latinoamericano de los 20', *RevIb*, 155–56:635–42, is too schematic. D. Taylor, *Theater of Crisis*, Lexington, Kentucky U.P., 277 pp., covers 1965–70. M. Pianca surveys *El teatro en nuestra América 1959–89*, Minneapolis, Institute for Ideologies and Literature, 1990, 408 pp. See also her **Testimonios de teatro latinoamericano*, BA, GEL, 265 pp. S. J. Albuquerque, *Violent Acts*, Detroit, Wayne State U.P., 297 pp., is on theatre violence 1960–80. L. E. Lasso, *Identidad en la cuentística hispanoamericana*, Bogotá, Universidad Nacional, 1990, 246 pp., deals with the theme in Borges, Cortázar, García Márquez, etc. J. M. Oviedo, **Breve historia del ensayo hispanoamericano*, M, Alianza, 1990, 162 pp. A. Avellaneda, J. Ruffinelli and J. A. Epple, examine the state of criticism in Argentina, Uruguay and Chile in *Hispamérica*, 56–57, 1990:11–45.

2.   INDIVIDUAL COUNTRIES

ARGENTINA.   F. Herrera (ed.), **Erotismo en la literatura argentina*, BA, Fraterna, 1990, 351 pp. B. Frederick, 'Women Writers of the Generación del 80', *His(US)*, 74:262–89, examines their view of women. J. M. Otero, **30 años de revista literarias argentinas*, BA, Catedral, 1990, 240 pp. J. Delgado, *Alfonsina Storni*, BA, Planeta, 1990, 183 pp., is biographical. L. Porto Buciarelli, **Las montañas de oro*, Macerata U.P., 1990, 73 pp. O. Juzyn-Amestoy, 'Girondo o las versiones poéticas del cambio', *RevIb*, 155–56:543–56, is on poems from *Espantapájaros*. On prose: R. Spiller (ed.), *La novela argentina de los*

80, Frankfurt, Vervuert, 324 pp., is on Puig, Posse, Saer, etc. N. Ulla, *Identidad rioplatense 1930*, BA, Torres Aguero, 1990, 329 pp., has essays on Borges, Arlt, Hernández, and Onetti. R. A. Borello, **El peronismo en la narrativa argentina*, Ottawa U.P., 267 pp. N. S. Sternbach, 'Race, Class and Gender in *La gloria de don Ramiro*', *His(US)*, 74:269–81, is on female characters. L. A. Jiménez, *Literatura y sociedad en Gálvez*, BA, Pena Lillo, 1990, 171 pp., is on the role of the bourgeoisie and the proletariat. J. Walker, 'Otra etapa en la evolución ideológica de Gálvez', *RLEH*, 15, 1990:140–48, is on *La tragedia de un hombre fuerte*. F. Colla, **Marechal*, Córdoba, Alción, 159 pp. M. E. de Miguel, *Norah Lange*, BA, Planeta, 225 pp., is, like the next three items, biographical: C. Piña, *Alejandra Pizarnik*, BA, Planeta, 254 pp.; M. A. Vásquez, *Victoria Ocampo*, BA, Planeta, 239 pp.; E. Osorio, *Beatriz Guido*, BA, Planeta, 221 pp. On BORGES: E. Fishburn and P. Hughes, *Dictionary of Borges*, London, Duckworth, 1990, 284 pp., very informative. I. Agheana, **Thematic Dictionary of the Prose of Borges*, Hanover NH, 1990, 387 pp. P. Standish, *A Concordance to the Works of Borges*, (vol. 1 of 7), Lewiston, Mellen, 1990, 500 pp., very thorough. P. Pellicer, **Borges*, M, Pórtico, 287 pp. J. Pickenhayn, **Borges total*, BA, Corregidor, 174 pp. M. S. Stabb, **Borges Revisited*, Boston, Twayne, 151 pp. E. Lapidot, **Borges y la inteligencia artificial*, M, Pliegos, 161 pp. F. Merrell, **Unthinking Thinking: Borges, Mathematics and the New Physics*, West Lafayette, Purdue U.P., 300 pp. M. R. Menocal, **From Borges to Boccaccio*, Durham, Duke U.P., 223 pp. M. Morello-Frosch, 'Borges y los nuevos', *RCLL*, 34:105–20, relates him to successors. M. Ferreira Pinto, 'La narrativa cinematográfica de Borges', *RevIb*, 155–56:495–506 examines montage, ellipsis, and visuality. D. Balderston, 'Historical Situations in Borges', *MLN*, 105, 1990:331–50, is on 'El jardín . . .' and 'Pierre Menard'. J. T. Irwin, 'The Journey to the South', *Virginia Quarterly Review*, 67:416–32, is chiefly on Borges, Poe, and Faulkner. V. Sabido Rivero, *Concordancia de "El Aleph"*, Granada, TAT, 1990, 256 pp., a handy tool. G. Williams, '"La muerte y la brújula"', *RCEH*, 15:295–304, is once more on ironic inversion. N. E. Alvarez, '"La Casa de Asterión"', *RevIb*, 155–56:507–18, is dull. H. Méndez-Ramírez, '"Tres versiones de Judas"', *RIAB*, 40:194–206, is on the tale's structure. W. Rosa, '"El jardín de senderos que se bifurcan"', *RevIb*, 155–56:597–606, is on its binary technique. On other writers: T. Barrera, **Bioy Casares*, M, Cooperación Iberamericana, 104 pp. **Bioy Casares, Premio Cervantes*, M, Anthropos, 224 pp., in the annual series. G. Yovanovich, **Cortázar's Longer Fiction*, Toronto U.P., 225 pp. B. Anderson Córdova, **Cortázar*, M, Pliegos, 1990, 140 pp. E. S. Triff, 'Improvisación musical y discurso literario en Cortázar', *RevIb*, 155–56:657–63, uses the model of jazz. M. C. Rosenblat, **Poe y Cortázar*, Caracas, Monte Avila, 1990, 156 pp.

M. R. Axelrod, *Style in Balzac, Beckett and Cortázar*, London, Macmillan. S. Simpkins, '*Hopscotch*', *JMMLA*, 23, no. 1, 1990:61–74, is on textual games. J. Jones, 'Paris in *Rayuela*', *RCEH*, 15:223–34, is on the impossible quest. L. Madrid, 'La Maga', *ib.*, 328–33, is vaguely feminist. R. Ferré, 'Cortázar ante la crítica', *La Torre*, 17:1–17, very informative. P. Standish, 'La segunda persona en los cuentos de Cortázar', *MLN*, 66:432–40, privileges 'Vd. se tendió a su lado'. L. P. Vranckx, 'Mauricio, aquel otro perseguidor', *CAm*, 182:113–16, compares a tale by Rodolfo Walsh. S. Lago, 'R. Walsh'. *CAm*, 184:56–69, good general study. V. Cohen Imach, '"Variaciones en rojo" de Walsh', *Hispamérica*, 58:3–15, is on his literary stance. *Co-Textes*, 19–20, 1990, was a Sábato number. L. Diamond-Nigh, '*Sobre héroes y tumbas*: a Romance?', *Hispanófila*, 103:47–59, applies Frye. J. M. García Ramos, *Puig*, M, Cooperación Iberoamericana, 120 pp. P. Jessen, *La realidad en Puig*, M, Pliegos, 152 pp. *RCF*, 11, no. 3, has a Puig section with a dozen articles and an interview. C. Kozak, 'Una política del género', *CA*, 25:163–81, was on Puig's first two novels. S. Pellarolo, 'El narrador ausente en *Boquitas pintadas*', *ETL*, 19, no. 2:67–77, is on narrative manipulation. M. M. Velasco, '*El beso de la mujer araña*', *CA*, 25:182–93, obvious on male/female dichotomy. R. Hernández Novás, 'El reto de la mujer araña', *CAm*, 184:70–76, a sympathetic interpretation. P. Bacarisse, '*Sangre de amor correspondido*', *RevIb*: 155–56:469–79, defines its quality. R. Gnutzman, '*Respiración artificial* de Piglia', *RIAB*, 40, 1990:351–60, is on history and literature. J. Corbatta, '*En la zona*', *RevIb*, 155–56:557–67, is on this first work of J. J. Saer. C. Tompkins, 'La postmodernidad de *Como en la guerra* de Valenzuela', *NTC*, 7:169–74, is mainly on 'la difusión del ego'. L. García-Moreno, 'Other Weapons, Other Words', *LALR*, 38:7–22, is on oppression of women in *Cambio de armas*. O. Steinberg, '*Libro de navíos y borrascas* de D. Moyano', *RevIb*, 155–56:617–23, is on it as an allegory of Argentina. K. Kohut, *Un universo cargado de violencia*, Frankfurt, Vervuert, 1990, 226 pp., is on Giardinelli. C. S. Mathieu, '*El amor no es amado*, de Bianchiotti', *RevIb*, 155–56:625–33, comments on this 1963 novel. F. Reati. 'La novelística de E. Sosa López', *ib.*, 643–47, a brief survey. H. R. Morell, 'La narrativa de Gambaro', *ib.*, 481–94, discusses *Dios nos quiere contentos*. On drama: O. Pelletieri, *Cien años de teatro argentino*, BA, Galerna, 184 pp., a sociological approach. *LATR*, 24.2, is a special number on contemporary Argentine theatre. P. Roster, 'Generational Transition in Argentina', *LATR*, 25.1:21–40, is on theatre 1956–85. R. Szmetan, '*Sobre las ruinas*', *RIAB*, 40, 1990:212–17, tries to revive Payró's reputation. D. W. Foster, 'E. Castelnuovo's *Vidas proletarias*', *RoN*, 32:41–45, is on its Socialist Realism. O. Pelletieri, 'El patio de la Torcaza', *LATR*, 25.1:51–61, is on Maggi and the 60's theatre.

CHILE.   S. Bianchi, 'Una suma necesaria', *RCL*, 36, 1990:49–62, reviews Chilean literature 1973–90. J. Giordano, 'Censura (etc.) en la literatura chilena', *RCLL*, 34:165–72, is on the Pinochet period. J. A. Piña, *Conversaciones con la poesía chilena*, Santiago, Pehuén, 1990, 233 pp., interviews six poets. M. N. Alonso *et al.*, 'Poesía en Concepción 1965–73', *RCL*, 36, 1990:63–77, situates four poets. S. Macías, '16 años de poesía chilena', *CHA*, 482–83:177–98, a handy survey. C. Marral, **Mistral*, B, Labor, 1990, 233 pp. C. Hernández, 'Del mito al misticismo', *La Torre*, 18:157–69, is on Mistral's religious evolution. M. L. Gazarian-Gautier, 'La prosa de Mistral', *RCL*, 36, 1990:17–27, descriptive. S. Benko, **Huidobro y el cubismo*, Mexico, FCE. A. Rivero Potter, 'Gómez de la Serna y Huidobro', *HR*, 59:437–50, refutes a critique by the former. L. Neghme Echeverría, '*Ecuatorial*', *RIAB*, 40:400–15, is on the 1918 poems. L. Poirot, **Neruda*, New York, Norton, 1990, 190 pp. J. Rovira, *Para leer a Neruda*, M, Palas Atenea, 198 pp., a fine general survey. F. Velasco Núñez, **Los rostros de Neruda*, Santiago, Nueva Voz, 1990, 159 pp. *CHA*, 482–83:5–73, a homage to Neruda by Luis Rosales. H. Loyola, 'El joven Neruda ingresa en la modernidad', *CAm*, 182:7–35, is on the early verse. M. L. Fischer, 'El *Canto general* de Neruda y Lihn', *RevIb*, 155–56:569–76, is on Lihn's *El Paseo Ahumada*. I. Carrasco, **Parra*, Santiago, CONICYT, 1990, 259 pp. M. N. Alonso and G. Treviños, 'Poesía par/ra desorientar', *Nueva Atenea*, 461, 1990:89–101, makes Parra seem more constructive than usual. N. Núñez, **Pablo de Rokha*, Ottawa, Girol, 216 pp. H. R. May, **La poesía de Gonzalo Rojas*, M, Hiperión, 500 pp. S. Bianchi, 'La poesía de Gonzalo Millán', *Nueva Atenea*, 461, 1990:115–54, stresses detail and intensity. J. A. Epple interviews Jaime Quesada, *RCL*, 36, 1990:129–40, with interesting results. R. A. Campos, 'El poema concreto,' *La Torre*, 17:57–76, examines Raúl Zurita's *Purgatorio* and *Anteparaíso*. J. A. Piña, *Conversaciones con la narrativa chilena*, Santiago, Los Andes, 254 pp., interviews Donoso, Allende, Skármeta, Edwards, Alegría, Blanco, and Eltit. S. Millares and A. Madrid, 'Ultima narrativa chilena', *CHA*, 482–83, 1990:113–22, is general on the short story. S. Mummuch, **La dulce niebla*, Santiago, Universitaria, 118 pp., a female reading of Bombal. J. R. Lagunas, 'Bibliografía de y sobre Lillo', *RCL*, 37:141–96, very useful. O. Sarmiento, 'El arte de la palabra', *ib.*, 67–76, examines a poem in this novel by Lihn. M. Adelstem, **Studies on Donoso*, Lewiston, Mellen, 1990, 208 pp. E. Luengo, '*El obsceno pájaro de la noche*', *Chasqui*, 20, no. 1:23–33, is interesting on technique. C. de Vallejo, '*El lugar sin límites*', *RCEH*, 15:283–94, applies Greimas. P. Meléndez-Páez, 'Autoridad narrativa en *Casa de campo*', *RCL*, 36, 1990:39–47, examines the narrator. C. Genovese, 'El espacio escénico', *LATR*, 25.1:41–50, is on staging Donoso's *Sueños de mala muerte*. V. Cortínez, 'La construcción del pasado', *HR*, 59:317–27, is good on Allende's use of prolepsis. M. Lemaitre, *Skármeta, una narrativa de la liberación*, Santiago, Pehuén, 149 pp., is rather disconnected. J. Incledon, 'Liberating the Reader', *Chasqui*, 20, no. 1:95–107, interviews Dorfman. J. A. Epple, 'Alegría y la narrativa chilena actual', *CAm*, 182:117–22, assesses his *biografías noveladas*. C. Boyle, **Chilean Theatre since 1973*, Rutherford, Fairleigh Dickinson, 1990. M. Hurtado, 'Teatro chileno durante el gobierno militar', *CHA*, 482–83, 1990:149–60, a useful survey. P. Bravo Elizondo, **Raices del teatro popular en Chile*, Guatemala City, Impresos D & M, 162 pp. J. R. Varela, 'M. A. de la Parra', *RCEH*, 15, 1990:81–90, on sado-masochism and social crisis.

COLOMBIA. R. Spitaletta and M. Escobar, *Reportajes a la literatura colombiana*, Medellín, Antioquia U.P., 145 pp., interviews with contemporary writers. M. M. Jaramillo, *Y las mujeres*, Medellín, Antioquia U.P., 503 pp., chiefly on women writers. E. Thomas, '*La vorágine*', *RCL*, 37:97–104, examines *mise en abîme*. *RIAB*, 40, no. 4, 1990, is a special number on Arciniegas. M. Canfield, **Gabriel García Márquez*, Bogotá, Procultura, 128 pp. G. Bell-Villada, **Gabriel García Márquez*, Chapel Hill, North Carolina U.P. R. L. Sims, *El primer García Márquez*, Rockville MD, Potomac, 152 pp., is on the early journalism. P. Swanson, *Cómo leer a García Márquez*, M, Júcar, 152 pp., a brilliant guide. I. Rodríguez Vergara, **El mundo satírico de García Márquez*, M, Pliegos, 1990, 262 pp. H. R. Cohen, 'Decay in *El Coronel no tiene quien le escriba*', *RIAB*, 40, 1990:189–93, useful on symbolism. M. E. and M. J. Valdés (eds), **Teaching One Hundred Years of Solitude*, New York, M. L. A., 1990, 156 pp. R. Janes, **One Hundred Years of Solitude*, Boston, Twayne, 136 pp. D. F. Chamberlin, 'The Temporal Dimension of *Cien años de soledad*', *RCEH*, 15, 1990:123–29, not very original. L. M. Jaeck, '*Cien años de soledad*', *His(US)*, 74:50–56, follows Derrida on the ending. K. C. King, 'Voices in *Crónica de una muerte anunciada*', *CL*, 43:305–25, relates it to *Oedipus Tyrannus*. I. Alvarez Borland, 'Interior Texts in *El amor en los tiempos del cólera*', *HR*, 59:175–86, is on self-reflexivity. M. Zemskov, 'Metamorfosis del amor', *América Latina*, 91, no. 4:79–88, is on love in the same text. M. Maraña, '*Love in the Time of Cholera*', *STCL*, 14, 1990:27–43, sees it reflecting the drama of modernity. M. E. Davis, 'Sophocles, García Márquez and Power', *RHM*, 44:108–23 is on fate in *El general en su laberinto*. R. Prada Oropeza, 'Teoría y recepción', *CAm*, 182:143–53, is on the critical reception of *El general* . . . . R. González Echeverría, 'García Márquez y la voz de Bolívar', *CA*, 28:63–76, applies his archive theory to *El general* . . . . M. Palencia-Roth, 'García Márquez, Labyrinths of Love and History', *WLT*, 65:54–58, is descriptive on the last two novels. N. J. McCarty, 'Temas narrativas en A. Duque López', *ETL*, 19, no. 2:78–88, introduces this new novelist. E. Torres

Cárdenas, *El teatro en Colombia*, Tunja, Universidad, 1990, 96 pp. M. M. de Velasco, 'Nuevas perspectivas en el teatro colombiano', *LATR*, 25.1:95–105, surveys current groups. F. González Cajiao, 'El Teatro Taller de Colombia', *ib.*, 73–76, praises its influence.

CUBA. J. A. Martínez, *Dictionary of 20th Century Cuban Literature*, Westport, Greenwood, 1990, 537 pp., very useful and unbiased. E. Bejel, *Escribir en Cuba*, Río Piedras, Puerto Rico U.P., 402 pp., 26 interviews with writers. M. Rivas, *Literatura y esclavitud*, Seville, Estudios Hispanoamericanos, 1990, 317 pp., on modern treatments. *RevIb*, 152–53, 1990, has some 40 essays on 19th- and 20th-c. Cuban literature. *RevIb*, 154, is on Lezama, Carpentier, Cabrera Infante, Sarduy and Arenas, with good essays. I. Phaf, *Novelando La Habana*, M, Orígenes, 1990, 320 pp. A. Camacho, *La cosmovisión de Lezama Lima*, Miami, Universal, 169 pp., mainly thematic on his novels. C. Caisso, '"Oda a Casal" de Lezama Lima', *Hispamérica*, 56–57, 1990:155–63. P. Collard, *Cómo leer a Carpentier*, M, Júcar, 1990, 136 pp., a general guide. O. Velayos Zurdo, *Historia y utopía en Carpentier*, Salamanca U.P., 1990, 188 pp. F. F. Goldberg, 'Patterns of repetition in *The Kingdom of This World*', *LALR*, 38:23–34, again on Eternal Return. M. M. Carrión, 'La aprendiz de brujo de Carpentier', *REH*, 25, no. 1:49–67. D. Balderston, *'La deformación en Gombrowicz y Piñera'*, *ETL*, 19, no. 2, is on *Pequeñas maniobras*. J. Ortega *et al.*, *Cabrera Infante*, M, Fundamentos, 1990, 253 pp. M. V. García Serrano, 'La advertencia de *Tres triste tigres*', *Hispanófila*, 101:87–92, a re-interpretation. C. Espinosa interviews R. Arenas in *Quimera*, 101:54–61, with useful material. P. Rozencvaig, 'Arenas' Last Interview', *Review*, 44:78–83, very important. *Quimera* 102:28–44, has an interview with Sarduy and other items by and on him. F. López Sacha, 'Jesús Díaz y la interrogación', *CAm*, 182:49–59, is on the individual and history in his work.

ECUADOR. A. Sacoto, *Novelas claves de la literatura ecuatoriana*, Cuenca U.P., 1990, 432 pp. D. Gerdes, *'La cofradía del mullo'*, *LALR*, 36, 1990:50–57, examines this 1985 novel by A. Yáñez Cossío. M. E. Angulo interviews Yáñez Cossío in *Hispamérica*, 58:45–54, with interesting declarations. C. L. Montáñez, 'El desencuentro de Fernando Tinajero', *ETL*, 19, no. 2:42–47.

GUATEMALA. L. Cardoza y Aragón, *Miguel Angel Asturias, casi novela*, Mexico, Era, 248 pp., fundamental. M. A. Arango, 'El surrealismo en *Leyendas de Guatemala* y *El señor Presidente*', *Thesaurus*, 45, 1990:472–81, is not on its title topic.

MEXICO. K. Kohut (ed.), *Literatura mexicana hoy*, Frankfurt, Vervuert, 268 pp., is on post-1968 writing. J. F. Vélez, *Escritores mexicanos*, Mexico, Compañía Editorial, 1990, 200 pp., interviews with Sainz, Leñero, Poniatowska, etc. F. Garrido, *Tierra con memoria*, Guadalajara

U.P., 1990, 149 pp., essays on Azuela, Rulfo, López Velarde, etc. C. Ferman, 'México en la posmodernidad', *NTC*, 7:157–67, is on urban-setting texts of the 80s. L. Palomera, **La nocturnos de Villaurrutia*, Guadalajara U.P., 1990, 73 pp. G. Appendini, **López Velarde*, Mexico, FCE, 1990. J. Prats Sariol, *Pellicer*, Tabasco, Instituto de Cultura, 1990, 146 pp., chiefly on his imagery. R. Chrisalita, 'Pellicer, la insistencia de la mirada', *CAm*, 182:36–48, is on the quest for spiritual communion. J. Malpartida, **José Gorostiza*, *CHA*, 479, 1990:81–88, very general. M. Mejía Valera, 'La poesía de Alí Chumacero', *CA*, 27:86–95, is workmanlike. A. Ruy Sánchez, **Introducción a Paz*, Mexico, Mortiz, 1990, 126 pp. Various authors, **Paz, Premio Cervantes*, B, Anthropos, 1990, 142 pp. E. González Rojo, **El rey va desnudo*, Mexico, Posada, 1990, 306 pp., is on Paz's politics. *Insula*, 532–33, is a homage to Paz. *CA*, 26, similarly. A. González Acosta, *'Petrificada petrificante de Paz'*, *RevIb*, 155–56:519–31, is chiefly thematic. N. Kluhn reviews recent Mexican poetry in *STCL*, 14, 1990:81–93. On prose: S. Menton, *Narrativa mexicana*, Mexico, Puebla and Tlaxcala U.P., 175 pp., essays on writers from Azuela to del Paso. V. F. Torres, *Esta narrativa mexicana*, Mexico, UNAM, 270 pp., discusses 16 recent writers. I. Chia-Olivares, **La novela mexicana contemporánea*, M, Pliegos, 1990, 140 pp. M. Graniela Rodríguez, *El papel del lector en la narrativa mexicana contemporánea*, Rockville MD, Potomac, 230 pp., is on Pacheco and Elizondo. J. Bruce Novoa, 'La novela de la revolución mexicana', *His(US)*, 74:36–44, is on its unity of vision. C. C. D'Lugo, *'Al filo del agua'*, *ib.*, 860–67, is on reader involvement. C. Duncan, 'Castellanos' "La tregua" and Revueltas' "El lenguaje de nadie"', *ib.*, 868–75, is on language barriers in these tales. L. Guerra Cunningham, 'La historia en *Oficio de tinieblas'*, *ETL*, 19, no. 2:37–41, is on Catalina. W. O. Muñoz, 'Locura en "Los convidados de agosto"', *Hispanófila*, 101:77–86, is on the mother figure. F. Antolín, **Los espacios de Rulfo*, Miami, Universal, 148 pp. Y. Jiménez, **Rulfo*, Mexico, FCE, 1990, 294 pp. J. Estrada, **El sonido en Rulfo*, Mexico, UNAM, 1990, 142 pp. G. Mora, '"El llano en llamas"', *RCLL*, 34:121–34, a challenging new reading. J. Ortega, *'Pedro Páramo'*, *STCL*, 14, 1990:21–26, is abstruse on Preciado's personality. C. Cosgrove, *'Pedro Páramo'*, *MLR*, 86:79–88, is on its language. E. Parra's interesting 1979 interview with Rulfo is republished in *Quimera*, 103–04:112–17. J. G. Alonso, 'Susana San Juan', *RCEH*, 15:209–21, is on her structural role. M. van Delden, *'La región más transparente'*, *CL*, 43:326–45, is on Fuentes' view of the revolution. L. A. Gyurko, 'Fuentes, Guzmán and the Mexican Political Novel', *IAr*, 16, 1990:545–610, compares *La sombra del caudillo* and *La cabeza de la hidra*. L. Rodríguez Carranza, **Un teatro de la memoria*, Louvain

U.P., 1990, 286 pp., is on *Terra Nostra*. D. A. Carillo, 'Arabesques in *Cristóbal Nonato*', *REH*, 25, no. 3:1–14, goes back to Sterne. L. A. Gyurko, 'Self and Double in *Gringo viejo*', *IAr*, 17:175–244, digs deep into characterization. J. Roy, '*Gringo viejo*', *RCLL*, 34:147–64, a good background analysis. V. Cabrera, '"En la playa" y otras historias', *RIAB*, 40, 1990:394–99, is on Elizondo's cinematic technique. A. K. Stoll (ed.), *Elena Garro*, Lewisburg, Bucknell, U.P., 1990, collects ten articles. J. Jones, 'Garro's *Reencuentro de personajes*', *CRCL*, 18:41–50, is on her shift from victim to author. L. Kerr, 'Poniatowska's *Hasta no verte, Jesús mío*', *MLN*, 106:370–94, is on her 'gestures of authorship'. A. Pérez, 'La mujer en la narrativa mexicana', *CHA*, 498:129–34, is on the same novel. C. Steele, '*Cerca del fuego*', *STCL*, 14, 1990.61–80, describes J. Agustín's 1986 novel. A. González, 'Neobarroco y carnaval en *Palinuro de Mexico*', *His(US)*, 74:45–49, is Bahktinian. C. Fell, '*Noticias del Imperio*', *CA*, 28:77–89, sees del Paso's novel as polyphonic. B. B. Aponte, '*Noticias del Imperio*', *ETL*, 19, no. 2:16–28, is on the treatment of history. J. Sefaní, '*Muchacho en llamas*', *RCEH*, 15, 1990:130–39, introduces this 1987 novel by Sainz. G. Gliemmo, '*Crónica de la intervención*', *Hispamérica*, 58:17–27, examines this 1982 novel by J. García Ponce. Various authors, *Te lo cuento otra vez*, Mexico, Tlaxcala U.P., 152 pp., is on recent short fiction. C. Schaffer-Rodríguez, 'Embedded agendas'. *LALR*, 38:62–76, is original on literature and journalism. On drama: J. F. Vélez, *Dramaturgos mexicanos*, Mexico, Compañía Editorial Impresora, 1990, 119 pp., carries 15 interviews. F. C. Vevia Romero, **La sociedad mexicana en Usigli*, Guadalajara U.P., 1990, 185 pp. T. G. Compton, 'Usigli's *Jano es una muchacha*', *LATR*, 25.1:63–71, is on illusion and reality. M. S. Gann, 'El teatro de V. H. Rascón Borda', *ib.*, 77–88, is on this new playwright of *hiperrealismo*. L. Rojas-Trempe, '*Por las tierras de Colón*', *ib.*, 115–22, is on this 1987 play by G. Schmidhuber. W. Feliciano, 'El mundo mítico de Solórzano', *RevIb*, 155–56:577–88, is on his anti-religious attitude. See too his '3 Plays by Solórzano', *LATR*, 25.1:123–33, on *Los fantoches*, *El crucificado*, and *Las manos de Dios*. H. Perea, **España en la obra de A. Reyes*, Mexico, FCE, 708 pp. J. W. Robb, 'Reyes y el indio Jesús', *RHM*, 44:138–43, discusses *Silueta del indio Jesús*. See too his 'Reyes: una bibliografía selecta', *RevIb*, 155–56:691–736, very full.

NICARAGUA. *RevIb*, 157, has 15 essays on modern Nicaraguan literature. T. R. Williams, 'Cardenal's *El estrecho dudoso*', *RCEH*, 15, 1990:111–21, is mainly on the quest theme.

PARAGUAY. *Augusto Roa Bastos, Premio Cervantes*, B, Anthropos, 1990, 142 pp., has sundry useful essays. R. Bañuelos *et al.*, **Acercamiento crítico a "Yo el Supremo"*, Guadalajara U.P., 1990. S. M.

Fischer, 'La voz indígena en *Yo el Supremo*', *RHM*, 44:93–107, is on its absence. M. Méndez-Faith interviews Roa on his tale 'La flecha y la manzana', *Puro Cuento*, 22, 1990:2–5.

PERU. C. Toro Montalvo, **Manual de literatura peruana*, Lima, AFA, 1990, 884 pp. R. González Vigil, *El Perú es todas las sangres*, Lima, Fondo Editorial, 419 pp., has essays on Arguedas, Alegría, Mariátegui, Vargas Llosa and others. J. Higgins, *Vallejo en su poesía*, Lima, Seglusa, 1989, 164 pp., brilliantly analyses individual poems. J. Guzmán, *Contra el secreto profesional*, Santiago U.P., 1990, 188 pp., is too general. M. Martos and E. Villanueva, **Las palabras de "Trilce"*, Lima, Seglusa, 1990, 375 pp. S. Yurkievich, 'Aptitud humorística en *Poemas humanos*', *Hispamérica*, 56–57, 1990:3–10, categorizes techniques. C. von Buelow, 'Vallejo and Darwinian Risk', *STCL*, 14, 1990:9–19, is on *Las coynas*. A. M. Gazzolo, 'J. Sologuren', *CHA*, 498:7–34, is introductory. C. Toro Montalvo, **Poesía peruana del 70*, Lima, La Tortuga Ecuestre, 102 pp. On prose: G. Gutiérrez *et al.*, **Arguedas*, Lima, Edaprospo, 1990, 91 pp. G. F. González, *Amor y erotismo en Arguedas*, M, Pliegos, 1990, 188 pp., is on his sexual neurosis. M. Lienhard, **La última novela de Arguedas*, Lima, Horizonte, 1990. A. M. Aldaz, **Manuel Scorza*, New York, Long, 1990, 192 pp. R. Forgues, **La estrategia mítica de Scorza*, Lima, Textos Universitarios, 174 pp. J. Yviricu, 'Dos personajes de *La guerra silenciosa*', *RCLL*, 34:249–59, and F. Schmitt, 'Redoble por Rancas', *ib.*, 235–49, are both unremarkable. J. M. Lassu, 'Une "Noticia" inédite de Scorza', *Caravelle*, 56:53–74, links him to Huamán Poma. J. Higgins, *Cambio social y constantes humanos*, Lima, Universidad Católica, 176 pp., is on Ribeyro's short fiction. S. Castro Klarén, **Understanding Vargas Llosa*, Columbia, S. Carolina U.P., 1990, 165 pp. R. A. Kerr, **Vargas Llosa*, Rockville MD, Potomac, 1990, 117 pp. D. Sobrevilla, 'Teoría de la novela en Vargas Llosa', *CHA*, 496:59–71, is on its evolution. J. A. Payne, '*La ciudad y los perros*', *Chasqui*, 20, no. 1:43–49, is mechanically Jungian. S. Menton, 'La guerra de Vargas Llosa contra el fanatismo', *CA*, 28:50–62, exalts *La guerra del fin del mundo*. P. Meléndez, '*Kathie y el hipopótamo*', *RCEH*, 15, 1990:34–41, is on transgression of dramatic rules. B. Angvik, '*Historia de Mayta*', *Imprévue*, 1990–92:63–98, is too prolix. R. Geisdorfer Feal, 'Eroticism in *Elogio de la madrastra*', *RCEH*, 24, 1990:87–106, is chiefly on the pictures. P. Standish, 'Vargas Llosa's Parrot', *HR*, 59:143–51, is on *El hablador*. C. R. Perricone, '*El hablador*', *South Eastern Latin Americanist*, 35, no. 1:1–10, relates it to his work generally. F. Lafuente, **Bryce Echenique*, M, Cultura Hispánica, 120 pp. L. Scholtz, '*Tantes veces Pedro*', *RevIb*, 155–56:533–42, is excellent on the theme of vacuity. R. J. Slawson, 'El Teatro Nacional Popular', *LATR*, 25.1:89–95, is on cultural policy in the 70's.

PUERTO RICO. J. Ortega, *Reapropriaciones*, Río Piedras, Puerto Rico U.P., 252 pp., is on new writing. Y. Montalvo, '*La víspera del hombre*', *Imprévue* 1990–92 : 27–32, is on Marqués' novel as a *Bildungsroman*. M. del C. Cerezo, '*La guaracha del Macho Camacho*', *ETL*, 19, no. 2 : 48–59, is on its negative message. J. Netchinsky, 'Ferré's Ballet', *REH*, 25, no. 3 : 103–28, is on *La bella durmiente*.

URUGUAY. A. Trigo, *Literatura, historia e ideología en el Uruguay*, Gaithersburg, Hispamérica, 1990, 276 pp. See too his 'Una olvidada página sociológica de Herrera y Reissig', *HR*, 59 : 25–36, reproducing a chapter from an unpublished essay. B. Amestoy Leal, *Poética de lo imaginario*, Montevideo, Trilce, 80 pp., is on woman in Herrera y Reissig. I. Jiménez Faro, *Delmira Agustini*, M, Torremozas, 111 pp. O. G. de León, *Novela y exilio*, Montevideo, Signos, 1990, 280 pp., is on Benedetti, Moyano, Aínsa, and others. W. Lookhart, *Felisberto Hernández*, Montevideo, Arca. S. Rojas, 'El gaucho en Amorim', *RoQ*, 38 : 85–93, is on his social protest. R. Chao, *Onetti*, Paris, Plon, 1990, apparently contains interviews. Various authors, *La obra de J. C. Onetti*, M, Fundamentos, 1990, 284 pp. J. Stavans, 'Onetti, el teatro y la muerte', *LATR*, 25.1 : 107–13, is on *Un sueño realizado*. J. Murray, *Ideological Subversion in Kafka, Céline and Onetti*, Stanford, U.P., 288 pp. M. Robles, 'Estatismo en *El astillero*', *RCL*, 36, 1990 : 121–27, is on stagnation. B. L. Lewis, '*Juntacadáveres*', *Chasqui*, 20, no. 1 : 17–22, is on existence, identity, and art. E. Salinas interviews Onetti in *Quimera*, 103–04 : 22–25, not too interestingly.

VENEZUELA. A. Rama, *Ensayos sobre literatura venezolana*, Caracas, Monte Avila, 1990, 228 pp. M. Milanca Guzmán, *Gallegos*, Caracas, Fundarte, 1990, 160 pp. A. de Falgirolles *et al.*, *"Las lanzas coloradas" ante la crítica*, Caracas, Monte Avila, 177 pp. R. Gnutzman, 'Uslar Pietri: *El camino de El Dorado*', *RCLL*, 34 : 135–46, examines his view of Lope de Aguirre. A. M. Bilbao, *S. Garmendia*, Caracas, Bolívar U.P., 1990, 101 pp., discusses three novels. D. Bohórquez Rincón, *Bernardo Núñez*, Caracas, Casa de Bello, 1990, 121 pp. F. J. Lasarte, '*Abrapalabras*', *RevIb*, 155–56 : 665–71, examines this prize-winning novel by L. Britto García.

BRAZILIAN LITERATURE

POSTPONED

VIII.   ITALIAN STUDIES

LANGUAGE

By M. MAIR PARRY, *Lecturer in Italian,*
University of Wales, Aberystwyth

1.   GENERAL

A topical publication, Lo Cascio, *Lingua*, contains many surveys by renowned linguists on subjects such as the image and use of Italian in Italy and abroad (H. Stammerjohann, R. Simone, A. Tosi, N. Dittmar, A. Sobrero, F. Sabatini); the Italian contribution to lexicography (G. Nencioni, V. Lo Cascio) and to philosophical linguistics (L. Formigari); the current flourishing state of Italian linguistic research in Europe (A. L. and G. Lepschy, T. De Mauro, L. Renzi, G. Nencioni, M. Pfister, G. Holtus–M. Metzeltin–C. Schmitt, C. Schwarze, J. Brunet), as well as specific analyses of linguistic topics. The position of Italian in the world, and especially within the European Community, is also discussed in G. Lepschy, 'L'italiano visto dall'estero', *LIt*, 23:66, while E. Zuanelli, 'Italian in the European Community: An educational perspective on the national language and new language minorities', Coulmas, *Language Policy*, 291–99, considers the educational implications for Italian of its 'minor' language status within the EC context. The achievements and future prospects of Italian linguistics are reviewed by linguists of international standing from Italy and abroad in a stimulating collection of contributions to *La linguistica italiana oggi. Atti del XXII Congresso Internazionale di Studi. Anacapri, 3–5 ottobre, 1988*, ed. Alberto Vàrvaro, Ro, Bulzoni, vi + 204 pp.

Other important conference proceedings are *Atti* (Lecce), *Atti* (Padua), *Atti* (Bergamo), *Atti* (Perugia), *Atti* (Messina), and the proceedings of the first conference of the Società Internazionale di Linguistica e Filologia Italiana: Giannelli, *Rinascimento*, which is divided into two sections devoted to Italian linguistic study during the Renaissance and to the analysis of contemporary Italian and the dialects of Italy, and Còveri, *L'italiano*, dedicated in the main to the fortunes of Italian abroad, with a special final section dealing with the official use of Italian in the Hapsburg Empire.

Those who wish to find their bearings amid the recent spate of publications on the linguistic varieties spoken in Italy will find in Žarko Muljačić, *Scaffale italiano. Avviamento bibliografico allo studio della lingua italiana*, F, La Nuova Italia, 374 pp. a concise and very readable bibliographical survey, indispensable for specialists as well as lay readers. The discursive section (15–263) presents a personal yet balanced critique of all the major areas of linguistic study. M.'s intimate knowledge of other language areas enables him to make pertinent comparisons and to draw attention to topics poorly represented on the Italian scene, while references to work in the press and in preparation add to the value of this excellent guide. Exhaustive coverage was not intended and any omissions (for example, the lack of reference to recent interest in the clitic SI) are more than compensated by the wealth of easily accessible information packed into a reasonably priced volume. The important contributions to Italian linguistics and dialectology of four renowned scholars are commemorated in *Cortelazzo Vol.*, which contains 39 items, many relating to Italian and the dialects; in **Fest. Pellegrini*; in vol. 31 of *Linguistica*, dedicated to Pavao Tckavčić, which includes studies on Rheto-romance as well as general Romance topics, and in Salvatore Gemelli, **Gerhard Rohlfs: una vita per l'Italia dei dialetti: la prima biografia del grande scienziato tedesco e la sua bibliografia*, Ro, Gangemi, 1990, 290 pp.

Giovanni Nencioni, 'La Crusca per voi', *LIt*, 21:55, announces the publication of a regular pamphlet containing short articles on linguistic topics as well as a question-and-answer section in which well-known linguists will seek to resolve various problems, not with the prescriptivism of old, it is claimed, but with the flexibility required by an awareness of language variation. 'Italian' in Campbell, *Compendium*, vol. 1, 645–50, consists of a brief sociolinguistic and historical comment followed by a skeleton grammar, but the data are unreliable. 'Humanities computing in Italy', **Computer and the Humanities*, 24.5–6, 1990:337–494, ed. Giacinta Spinelli, contains some articles relating to Italian. E. Borello, 'Sintesi vocale da testo a voce. Un processore linguistico per l'italiano', *QDLF*, 1, 1990:1–13, discusses several linguistic problems confronting voice synthesizers.

2. EARLY TEXTS, DIACHRONIC STUDIES, AND HISTORY OF THE LANGUAGE

N. Marini, 'Costituzioni per monache benedettine. Edizione e commento linguistico', *ID*, 53, 1990(1991):87–161, examines an early text from the Aquila region, while M. Arcangeli, 'Per una dislocazione tra l'antico veneto e l'antico lombardo (con uno sguardo alle aree contermini) di alcuni fenomeni fono-morfologici', *ib.*, 1–42, offers a useful list of features to aid the localization of early texts. Detailed analysis of Latin legal documents from 12th-c. Umbria in A. Mariotti, 'Le più antiche carte dell'abbazia di S. Maria Val di Ponte', *ib.*, 163–205, reveals the influence of the vernacular on the Latin of the period. The difficulties of interpretation and localization posed by early *scripta* are given more ample treatment in a round table discussion recorded in *Actes* (Trier), III, Section 8, devoted to non-literary texts, and introduced by A. Castellani, 'Problèmes concernant la notion de *scripta* et problèmes concernant le rapport entre graphèmes et phonèmes' (695–99), who stresses the need for constant vigilance regarding the latter point, while A. Vàrvaro, 'Sull'origine della polimorfia nella *scripta*' (710–15), is a timely reminder that, since variation is an integral part of language, no simple formula is available for the interpretation of polymorphy in medieval *scripta*. A. M. Compagna Perrone Capano, 'Testi documentari: utilizzazione delle copie nella ricerca linguistica' (723–37). D. Rocco, '*Scripta* siciliana/*scriptae* italo-meridionali' (738–50), tackles the problem of the correct temporal and geographical identification of early texts. The relationship between *scripta* and *koinè* forms part of a fascinating debate on the concept of *koinè* included in *Koinè in Italia dalle origini al Cinquecento. Atti del Convegno di Milano e Pavia, 25–26 settembre 1987*, ed. Glauco Sanga, Bergamo, Lubrina, 1990, 365 pp. The vol. is also a rich source of documentation regarding the various regions of Italy, e.g. northern Italy (M. A. Grignani and P. Benincà), the Centre (I. Baldelli), the south (A. Vàrvaro), Lombardy (G. Sanga), Veneto (G. B. Pellegrini), Piedmont (A. Cornagliotti), and the Ticino area (S. Bianconi), while Ž. Muljačić, 'Sul ruolo delle *koinè* nell'elaborazione linguistica' (185–94), refers to various theoretical models in his discussion of the crucial role of *koinès* in the rise of standard languages. P. Benincà develops her argument again in 'Discussione preliminare sull'esistenza di una *koinè* medioevale nell'Italia settentrionale', *QDLC*, 3:71–80, skilfully drawing on textual evidence and extrapolations based on modern sociolinguistic data, as well as the striking testimony of Dante. Dante's linguistic sensitivity is also crucial in the argumentation of F. Bruni, 'Fra *Lombardi, Tusci* e *Apuli:* osservazioni sulle aree linguistico-culturali', in Gensini, *Le Italie*, 227–56. This interesting article documents medieval awareness of linguistic variation and diversity, and language attitudes and loyalty, as well as the role of the courts in the adoption of a supra-regional variety (Tuscan). I. Hijmans-Tromp, 'Per il testo dell'Elegia Giudeo-italiana', *LN*, 51:97–99, proposes a number of corrections to the text. Enrico Testa, **Simulazione di parlato: fenomeni dell'oralità nelle novelle del Quattro-Cinquecento*, F, Accademia della Crusca, 247 pp. Lupo de Spechio, **Summa dei re di Napoli e Sicilia e dei re d'Aragona*, Napoli, Liguori, 355 pp., is a critical edition by A. M. Compagna Perrone Capano of a 15th-century text.

M. Cennamo, 'La nascita di un nuovo sistema di voce in italiano antico', *Actes* (Trier), III, 243–62, contains a detailed analysis of SI constructions in early Florentine texts that comes down in favour of the theory (Ronconi) that the impersonal constructions with intransitive verbs, adjectival complements, and reflexive verbs (*si parte, si è allegri*, and *ci si pente*) are the most recent stages of development. Concording with this view, M.-G. de Boer, 'L'uso di *si* nell'italiano rinascimentale, opposto a quello di oggi', *ib.*, 263–72, argues that only the reflexive and passive SI constructions existed in Renaissance Tuscan. Florentine syntax is also the subject of L. Renzi, *'Per una storia della struttura della frase in italiano: il fiorentino del Cinquecento', *Linguistica*, 31:201–10, and Id., 'Per la storia del fiorentino: i pronomi personali soggetto nelle commedie dello Zannoni', Giannelli, *Rinascimento*, 165–78. F. Franceschini, 'Note sull'anafonesi in Toscana occidentale', Giannelli, *ib.*, 259–72, examines both modern and historical data in an attempt to resolve the problem of the source of the phenomenon.

Gianfranco Folena, *Il linguaggio del caos. Studi sul plurilinguismo rinascimentale*, To, Bollati Boringhieri, xviii + 291 pp., brings together important essays on a theme which was of considerable interest to this major Italian philologist and linguist: the inventive, hedonistic, and anti-classical linguistic experimentation of writers such as Paolo Giovio and Ruzante; not unexpectedly, the Veneto features prominently in the volume. P. Cherchi, 'Lingua barbarana', *LN*, 51:106–07, rescues from oblivion a secret language devised by Leonardo Fioravanti in the 16th century. Paolo D'Achille, *Sintassi del parlato e tradizione scritta della lingua italiana. Analisi di testi dalle origini al secolo XVIII*, Ro, Bonacci, 1990, 388 pp., is a valuable in-depth study of the lineage of a number of features found in spoken Italian and traditionally castigated by grammarians, but which today are gaining acceptability as part of the 'new' standard: left and right dislocation, polyvalent *che, ci* with *avere*, etc., agreement *ad sensum*, conditional use of the imperfect indicative, use of oblique third person pronouns. The data adduced confirm the thesis of F. Sabatini (e.g. in 'Una lingua ritrovata: l'italiano parlato', Lo Cascio, *Lingua*, 260–76) that these are not new phenomena, and the study documents their distribution according to the genre and register, as well as the social and geographical characteristics, of approximately 100 texts. In a detailed review of the book in *L'Indice*, 7.4:24, M. Voghera points out that the lack of a clear formulation of what distinguishes the spoken from the written language precludes a systematic analysis of the relationship between speech and the features investigated.

Sebastiano Vecchio, *Democrazia linguistica: il dibattito in Francia e in Italia tra Settecento e Ottocento*, Palermo, Dharba, 1990, 158 pp. I.

Bonomi *et al.*, **Il lessico della stampa periodica milanese nella prima metà dell'Ottocento*, F, La Nuova Italia, 1990, viii + 654 pp. *Atti* (Trento), of particular interest to sociolinguists, contains four sections: 1. 'Aspetti teorici dei processi di standardizzazione', in which illuminating comparisons are drawn between the Italian and other European processes of linguistic standardization, as in Ž. Muljačić, 'Il caso italiano vs altri casi europei: prolegomeni alla standardologia storica comparata'; 2. 'Vicende e problemi dell'italiano nella regione trentina'; 3. 'L'italianizzazione dei nuovi immigrati: l'apprendimento spontaneo dell'italiano L2'; 4. 'Punti di crisi e di rinnovamento nella storia linguistica d'Italia', which focuses on particular cases and features of the diffusion of an Italian standard, past and present.

3. HISTORY OF LINGUISTIC THEORY

The impressive *Storia della Linguistica*, vol. 2, ed. Giulio C. Lepschy, Bo, Il Mulino, 1990, 395 pp., contains sections particularly relevant to the development of linguistic thought in Italy: for example, M. Tavoni, 'La linguistica rinascimentale' (169–312), and R. Simone, 'Seicento e Settecento' (313–95), afford new insights into early Italian grammatical activity, the *Questione della Lingua*, and Vico by placing them in a European context. Giannelli, *Rinascimento* (9–161), contains 11 contributions on the linguistic ferment of the Renaissance, introduced by G. Nencioni, 'La vivente eredità della linguistica rinascimentale' (11–22). G. Skytte, **Il concetto di storia della lingua* nell'opera grammaticale di Benedetto Buonmattei', *Linguistica*, 31:279–89. M. T. Ward, 'Benedetto Varchi and the social dimensions of language', *Italica*, 68:76–94, argues that although Varchi was 'undeniably elitist in matters of culture' the *Ercolano* 'demonstrates an awareness of social differentiation significantly greater than that reflected in other Cinquecento dialogues'. Gianni Maritati, **Parola e linguaggio in Manzoni: riflessioni sulla linguistica manzoniana*, Ro, Città Nuova, 1990, 142 pp. Manzoni's linguistic ideology is the subject of contributions by T. Matarrese, S. Gensini, D. Russo, R. Simone, T. De Mauro, and G. Nencioni to *IO*, 1991, no. 3.

4. PHONOLOGY

Certamen Phonologicum II. Papers from the 1990 Cortona Phonology Meeting, ed. Pier Marco Bertinetto, Michael Kenstowicz, and M. Loporcaro, T, Rosenberg and Sellier, 360 pp., contains many contributions either relating to Italian or the dialects, or using these for exemplification; in particular: I. Vogel, 'Level ordering in Italian lexical phonology?' (81–101); B. E. Bullock, 'Mora-bearing consonants in coda position and related quantity effect' (105–20); A. Calabrese and

C. Romani, 'Syllable structure in aphasia: a case study' (147–71); M. Kenstowicz, 'Enclitic accent: Latin, Macedonian, Italian, Polish' (175–85); A. Andalò and L. Bafile, 'On some phonomorphological alternations in Neapolitan dialect' (247–57); J. Hajek, 'The hardening of nasalized glides in Bolognese' (259–78); M. Loporcaro, 'Compensatory lengthening in Romanesco' (279–307); J. Trumper *et al.*, 'Double consonants, isochrony and *raddoppiamento fonosintattico*: some reflections' (329–60). Another contribution to the growing body of literature seeking to identify the factors that govern the occurrence of RF is A. De Dominicis, 'Fenomeni di "cadenza" melodica e raddoppiamento fonosintattico in alcuni dialetti di area italiana', *ID*, 53:43–86, which adds intonation to the list, suggesting that variation be attributed to sociolinguistic factors. A. Andalò, 'Il raddoppiamento sintattico nel dialetto di Napoli', Giannelli, *Rinascimento*, 241–51, argues on the basis of data from non-Tuscan varieties, in which consonantal doubling is caused not by phonological but by morphological factors only, in favour of making a clear distinction between the two types of *raddoppiamento*.

L'interfaccia tra fonologia e fonetica. Atti del Convegno di Padova, 15 dicembre 1989, ed. Emanuela Caldo Magno and Paola Benincà, Padua, Unipress, xxiii + 186 pp., includes an important discussion by the editors of the crucial interrelationship between the two disciplines in the light of recent major developments, as well as studies relating specifically to Italian, e.g. A. Falaschi, 'Analisi di fenomeni di risillabificazione vocalica' (173–86), or to other linguistic systems found in Italy, e.g. P. Benincà and L. Vanelli, 'La fonologia autosegmentale come interfaccia tra morfologia e fonetica: saggio di analisi del friulano' (3–18); G. Marotta and L. M. Savoia, 'Diffusione vocalica in un dialetto calabrese. Alcuni parametri fonologici' (19–42); J. Trumper *et al.*, 'Vowel systems and areas compared: definitional problems' (43–72). Giannelli, *Rinascimento*, also contains several phonological studies: G. Marotta, 'Innovazione e continuità nella struttura sillabica: italiano e latino a confronto' (179–93); M. Vayra, 'Appunti su un fenomeno di "centralizzazione" nel vocalismo dell'italiano standard' (195–212); A. Batinti, 'Ricerche statistiche sul sistema grafico e fonologico dell'italiano nel lessico basico' (213–31); M. Maiden, 'Armonia regressiva di vocali atone nell'Italia centro-meridionale: la sua importanza per la teoria della fonologia prosodica' (233–39), which highlights the asymmetric prosodic structure of many Italian dialects in a stimulating and theoretically relevant discussion. M. Voghera, 'Gruppi tonali e strutture sintattiche nell'italiano parlato spontaneo', *The Italianist*, 10:175–203, conducts a probing examination of the relationship between syntax and intonation, a sadly neglected area of linguistics.

5. MORPHONOLOGY AND MORPHOLOGY

A significant contribution to the topical debate on the validity of
'morphonology' as a theoretical domain prefaces M. Maiden,
Interactive Morphonology. Metaphony in Italy, London, Routledge,
xi + 295 pp., which contains a timely systematic study of the
relationship between phonetic processes and morphology as evidenced in metaphony, a phenomenon that has characterized at least
some stage of the evolution of most Italian dialects. The volume,
refreshingly clear in presentation and style, is particularly welcome in
so far as it provides a detailed dialect overview, an approach that is all
too scarce in Italo-Romance studies. Id., 'On the phonological
vulnerability of complex paradigms: beyond analogy in Italo- and
Ibero-Romance', *RPh*, 44:284–305, convincingly argues on the basis
of data drawn from southern Italian dialects, Ticinese, and Galician-
Portuguese that 'characteristic morphonological, and particularly
vocalic, alternation in verbal stems and conjugation markers confers
on the verbal system as a whole a peculiar susceptibility to
phonological innovation.'

   Atti (Bergamo) includes many interesting contributions concerning the linguistic varieties of Italy and reflecting recent renewed
interest in morphology. They are divided into five sections: theory
and typology, diachronic evolution, morphological questions bearing
on other levels of analysis, specific subsystems, and language
acquisition and loss. M. Berretta, 'Sulla presenza dell'accusativo
preposizionale in italiano settentrionale: note tipologiche', *VR*, 48,
1989 (1991):13–37, (an amplified version of her *Atti* (Bergamo)
article) presents a detailed functional analysis of a phenomenon that
appears to be on the increase in the regional varieties of Italian (its
absence in northern dialects, however, precludes substratum influence on northern varieties of Italian). A sector of morphology in
which Italian is particularly productive is subjected to scrutiny in
Maria Lo Duca, *Creatività e regole: studio sull'acquisizione della morfologia
derivativa dell'italiano*, Bo, Il Mulino, 1990, 225 pp., which analyses the
acquisition of rules of word formation, especially of agentive nouns,
and draws interesting parallels with popular registers of Italian.
Word-formation is also the subject of Jaqueline Brunet, *Grammaire
critique de l'italien*, 10/11, Paris, Vincennes U.P., 320 pp., devoted to
Les Suffixes. Sergio Scalise, **Morfologia e lessico. Una prospettiva
generativista*, Bo, Il Mulino, 1990, 353 pp. A. M. Thornton, 'Sui
deverbali italiani in *-mento* e *-zione*, 1', *AGI*, 75:169–207, tests the
principles of Natural Morphology in a systematic analysis of forms
relating to 'actions' and rejects certain formation rules proposed by
Scalise and Dardano; while the sequel, *AGI*, 76:79–102, introduces

psycholinguistic considerations and confronts the problem posed by the fact that the evolution of Italian reveals a less than complete obedience to 'natural' formation processes; this is ascribed to external circumstances: the predominantly written nature of Italian and the constant influence of the Latin model.

6. SYNTAX AND SEMANTICS

The eagerly awaited second volume of *Grande grammatica di consultazione. I sintagmi verbale, aggettivale, avverbiale. La subordinazione*, ed. Lorenzo Renzi and Giampaolo Salvi, Bo, Il Mulino, 943 pp., displays, as did the first vol. (*YWMLS*, 50:475), a wealth of detail and exemplification, subjected to rigorous analysis broadly based on the principles of generative grammar. Sections such as that of P. M. Bertinetto on time, mood, and aspect in the verb represent the synthesis of pioneering studies, while social, regional, and situational variation is taken into account. Unfortunately still lacking is an alphabetical index for rapid consultation and for alerting one to the fact that a topic may be dealt with in more than one section, e.g. infinitival subordinate clauses (in chapters 9 and 13). The recent spate of important grammatical activity has inspired numerous review articles comparing the various grammars of Italian that have appeared, e.g. G. Berruto, 'Italiano. Terra nunc cognita? Sulle nuove grammatiche dell'italiano', *RID*, 14, 1990 (1991):157–75; G. Lepschy, 'L'italiano visto dall'estero', *LIt*, 21:56. *Le nuove grammatiche italiane*, ed. Edgar Radkte, Tübingen, Narr, viii + 153 pp., contains the proceedings of a whole conference dedicated to this theme.

Guglielmo Cinque, *Teoria linguistica e sintassi italiana*, Bo, Il Mulino, 323 pp., brings together important essays by one of the most influential Italian linguists on noun phrases, relatives, word order, dislocation, and *mica*. A. Belletti introduces *Generalized Verb Movement. Aspects of Verb Syntax*, T, Rosenberg and Sellier, 1990, 152 pp., with a brief, lucid exposition of X-bar syntax, followed by stimulating analyses of verb movement in Italian tensed and infinitival clauses (the discussion includes comparison with French and a detailed typology of different classes of adverb) and of Italian past participles used absolutely (involving crucial theoretical issues such as case assignment and verbal agreement). Also within the Government and Binding framework, M. Saltarelli, 'VP-Nominative constructions in Italian', Wanner and Kibbee, *New Analyses*, 313–34, offers a principled explanation of the different surface structure properties displayed by verbs such as *piacere*, in comparison with transitive predicates such as *amare*, despite apparently similar argument structures. Piero Bottari, *Strutturabilità lessicale della nominalizzazione*,

Pisa, Giardini, 1990, 120 pp., draws on numerous Italian examples to raise important theoretical questions in the generative context about the relationship between derived nouns and syntax. P. Acquaviva, 'Un'analisi della complementazione dei predicati fattivi', *RGG*, 15, 1990 (1991):3–28, applies the most recent theories of Giorgi/ Longobardi and Rizzi to explain the weak insularity of factitive predicates. L. Lonzi, 'Which adverbs in Spec, VP?', *ib.*, 141–60, tackles puzzling differences in the position of adverbs in Italian, differences that have important consequences for the representation of surface structure. M. Mazzoleni analyses *Costrutti concessivi e costrutti avversativi in alcune lingue d'Europa*, F, La Nuova Italia, 1990, 187 pp., and in 'Costrutti condizionali in *casus realis, possibilis* ed *irrealis:* un paradigma da ridefinire', Giannelli, *Rinascimento*, 357–64, points to the shortcomings of the traditional classification (both M. and Lonzi make significant contributions to the Renzi and Salvi grammar). Giannelli, *Rinascimento*, contains A. Colombo, '*Come, quanto* e le frasi comparative' (305–18); T. Miklić, 'La forma verbale e la sua funzione nel testo: *servigi testuali* del *trapassato del congiuntivo*' (319–30); L. Dezsó, 'Caratteristiche del sistema italiano di reggenze e problemi connessi alla compilazione di un dizionario di reggenze' (331–39); L. Briganti, 'Strutture avverbiali e strutture aggettivali dell'italiano' (341–56); J. C. Smith, 'Problemi dell'accordo del participio passato coll'oggetto diretto nei tempi composti coniugati con *avere* in italiano, con speciale riferimento ai dialetti' (365–71), which neatly explains extensive data variation by means of a hierarchy of thematic prominence, showing that perceptual factors may block the loss of a no longer motivated pattern of agreement; C. Bazzanella, 'Il passivo personale con e senza cancellazione d'agente: verso un approccio multidimensionale' (373–85), which is based on the statistical analysis of contemporary texts and oral usage. E. Suomela-Härmä, 'Appunti per una classificazione degli avverbi frastici in italiano', *Actes* (Trier), II, 162–74, applies a series of syntactic tests, while M. Skubić, 'Appunti sulla costruzione del periodo nella prosa contemporanea italiana', *ib.*, III, 273–81, examines the ordering of subordinate clauses relative to main clauses.

Linguistica, 31, includes G. Ineichen, 'L'italiano nel paragone contrastivo' (171–76); T. Miklić, 'Presenza e valori del passato remoto in riassunti di opere letterarie' (249–58); I. Klajn, 'Pronomi, avverbi e preposizioni' (259–67); R. Sornicola, 'Sui pronomi di prima e seconda plurale in italiano' (269–78); and C. A. Mastrelli, 'Denominatori, divisori e multipli' (291–94). E. Manzotti, 'Aspetti della negazione restrittiva in italiano e in francese', Lo Cascio, *Lingua*, 220–50, compares the use of *non . . . che* with Fr. *ne . . . que*. G. Genot, 'Analisi logico-semantica e descrizione sintattica del verbo', *ib.*,

251–59. G. Graffi, 'Concetti "ingenui" e concetti "teorici" in sintassi', *LS*, 26:347–63, uses Italian as well as English exemplification. Marica de Vincenzi, *Syntactic Parsing Strategies in Italian* (Studies in Theoretical Psycholinguistics, 12), Dordrecht, Kluwer, 256 pp., referring to new developments in psycholinguistics and syntactic theory, offers evidence that syntactic parsing strategies apply in a null subject language with a far less rigid word order than English.

7. PRAGMATICS AND DISCOURSE

L. Vanelli, 'Dimostrativi e articoli: deissi e definitezza', *Cortelazzo Vol.*, 369–81, considers the principle of saliency or pragmatic prominence in relation to the linguistic and extralinguistic context. P. M. Bertinetto, 'Avverbi pseudodeittici e restrizioni sui tempi verbali in italiano', Giannelli, *Rinascimento*, 280–301, is a detailed systematic examination of the narrative use of *ora/adesso; fra, fa; ieri, oggi, domani;* etc., that reveals previous hypotheses regarding use and function to have been too restrictive. According to B. the forms preserve residual deictic value and express a sense of psychological proximity to the events related. R. Veland, 'L'influence modale des verbes d'opinion en italien contemporain: étude d'un corpus', *SN*, 63:209–20, presents an interesting statistical analysis of journalistic data that supports a stylistic, rather than a syntactico-semantic, explanation for the still infrequent use of the indicative with *credere* and *ritenere*. Vincenzo Lo Cascio, *Grammatica dell'argomentare. Una tipologia di testi argomentativi, le strategie e i tipi di argomenti più adoperati, i meccanismi dell'argomentazione fallace, i linguaggi speciali (politico, scientifico, giuridico, pubblicitario)*, F, La Nuova Italia, 448 pp., is not a public-speaking manual but a systematic theoretical study drawing on the pragmatic, textual, and syntactic analysis of Italian data to present 'il primo tentativo di definire una grammatica testuale che analizzi l'argomentazione dal punto di vista linguistico e in particolare sintattico'. Susan George, *Getting Things Done in Naples: Action, Language and Context in Discourse Description*, Bo, CLUEB, 1990, xiii + 217 pp., is a very readable volume that rejects a rigid empiricist approach to discourse description and shows, through an analysis of recorded texts, how much language use depends on 'social context, social knowledge and speaker purpose'; attention is drawn to differences between Neapolitan and northern Italian as well as English usage. Differences in attitude between Italy and other European countries emerge in A. Cardinaletti and Giuliana Giusti, 'Il sessismo nella lingua italiana. Riflessioni sui lavori di Alma Sabatini', *RILA*, 23, 2:169–89, which evaluates proposals made by A. Sabatini for altering the Italian language so as to avoid causing offence by using forms deemed to be sexist. G. Lepschy, 'Language and Sexism', Barański, *Women*, 117–38, an amplified and modified version of 'Sexism and the Italian language', *The Italianist*, 7, 1987:158–69, is rather more sceptical. Daniela Zorzi Calò, **Parlare insieme: la co-produzione dell'ordine conversazionale in italiano e in inglese*, Bo, CLUEB, 1990, x + 123 pp. L. Giannelli, 'Sul valore comunicativo della pausa', *QDLF*, 1, 1990:33–59, uses Tuscan varieties of Italian for exemplification. The seventh chapter of Anna Wierzbicka, *Cross-Cultural Pragmatics: The Semantics of Human Interaction*, Berlin, Mouton De Gruyter, xiii + 502 pp., entitled 'Italian reduplication: its meaning and its cultural significance' (255–84), is a rigorous case-study of a characteristically Italian pragmatic device, *zitto zitto, appena appena*, in which insightful comparisons are made with various English structures. O. Lurati, *'Perché le locuzioni non siano trattati quali banalità. L'ideologia religiosa e i suoi riflessi sul discorso ripetuto (*chiamar chiesa, far Cristo, far Giacomo Giacomo)*', *Fest. Pellegrini*, 251–61.

8. LEXIS

Lessico, strutture e interpretazione, ed. Rodolfo Delmonte, Padua, Unipress, 1990, 257 pp., in the new series *Studi Linguistici Applicati*, contains several articles that use Italian as the language of exemplification: Id., 'Verbi irregolari: una analisi computazionale' (3–59), and Id., 'From subcategorization frames to thematic roles' (167–211); L. Brugè, 'Alcune considerazioni sulla classe dei verbi inaccusativi e dei verbi psicologici in un lessico di frequenza sottocategorizzato' (61–129); R. Dolci, 'La derivazione dei riflessivi attraverso regole lessicali' (215–57). Stefano Urbani, *Le forme del verbo italiano*, Ro, Bonacci, 1990, 282 pp., is an exhaustive guide to verb formation and interpretation, particularly useful regarding the choice of auxiliary. Aldo Duro, *Vocabolario della Lingua Italiana, III*** (*Pe-R*), has appeared. A. L. and G. Lepschy, 'L'italiano visto dall'estero', *LIt*, 22:60, compares Italian–English bilingual dictionaries, suggesting that the public would be better served by fewer publications, greater collaboration, and more attention to detail. New dictionaries of synonyms continue to appear regularly: in Emidio De Felice, *Dizionario critico dei sinonimi italiani*, Venice, Marsilio, xviii + 285 pp., only pages 3–195 are dedicated to actual lemmata, which contain a clear indication of the contexts allowing substitution (information considered vital by the author, given the non-existence of complete synonymity). Less helpful in this respect but far more comprehensive is *Dizionario Garzanti dei sinonimi e dei contrari: con generici, specifici, analoghi, inversi e 207 inserti di sinonimia ragionata*, ed. Pasquale Stoppelli,

Mi, Garzanti, 815 pp. Except in the case of the 207 especially detailed sections, some detail and exemplification had to be sacrificed in order to accommodate the over 45,000 entries (with antonyms and other related terms) in a compact and up-to-date volume (recent loans, e.g. *floppy disk, video* are included); in conjunction with a traditional dictionary this will be a powerful linguistic tool. Italian equivalents for English loan forms may be found in the useful bilingual specialized dictionary, Roberto Lesina, *Software & Hardware: dizionario dei termini informatici italiano–inglese, inglese–italiano*, Bo, Zanichelli, 416 pp. However, well-established loans, e.g. *mouse*, are not translated, while both options are given in the case of oscillation in usage, e.g. *copia di sicurezza/copia di backup* for 'backup copy' and *baco, buco, bug, errore di programma* for 'bug'. Presentation is very clear, with definitions (in Italian) provided in the first section only. Another interesting Zanichelli publication, *La donzelletta vien dalla donzella: dizionario di forme alterate della lingua italiana*, ed. Claudia Alberti *et al.*, v + 366 pp., is devoted to an area of word-formation in which Italian is particularly rich: diminutives, augmentatives, terms of endearment, and pejoratives. Full derivational information is supplied and 'impostors' are revealed: *maggiolino* is not a diminutive of *maggio*, although its etymological link is marked by a star; *ottone* is not related to *otto*, but *ladrone* is synchronically speaking an augmentative of *ladro*.

Two dictionaries concerned with neologisms are A. Forconi, *Dizionario delle nuove parole italiane, Mi, Sugarco, 1990, 222 pp., and A. Frescaroli, *Dizionario delle parole difficili nell'italiano attuale: le parole specialistiche entrate nel linguaggio comune, Mi, De Vecchi, 1990, 246 pp. F. Vian investigates 'Il lessico politico di Pietro Nenni. Coniazioni, neologismi, retrodatazioni (1921–1945), 1', *LN*, 52:57–62. F. Marri, 'Scavi nel lessico contemporaneo', *ib.*, 62–73, pays particular attention to linking neologisms with earlier uses of the terms. R. Simone, 'Parole spia, 5. *Trasparenza*', *LIt*, 21:58, considers its political and journalistic usage. The contribution of the Anglo-Saxon world attracts attention as usual: *Prestiti linguistici dal mondo anglofono: una tassonomia*, ed. A. Amato, Francesca Maria Andreoni, and Rita Salvi, Ro, Bulzoni, 1990, 279 pp., alphabetically lists loans (followed by context and source) grouped according to the various newspaper sections from which they were culled during 1987; G. Folena, 'Anglismi e anglofilia del Pindemonte', *LN*, 52:10; M. L. Fanfani, 'Sugli anglicismi nell'italiano contemporaneo', 1, *ib.*, 11–24, and 11, *ib.*, 73–89, include additions and observations on G. Rando, *Dizionario degli anglicismi nell'italiano postunitario*, F, Olschki, 1987; R. C. Melzi, 'L'italiano che commercia con l'anglo-americano', *IO*, 5, 1990:131–35. Paolo Zolli, *Le parole straniere*, ed. Flavia Ursini, Bo, Zanichelli, x + 246 pp., is a revised, more user-friendly second edn of the very successful 1976 vol., considerably amplified with recent borrowings into Italian and fuller etymological observations that draw on Z.'s experience as one of the compilers of the authoritative *DELI*. L. De Anna, 'Dalla *stufa* alla *sauna*. La nomenclatura italiana riguardante il bagno a vapore di origine finnica', *QDLF*, 1, 1990:125–52. P. Giannoni, '*Mondolo* ("spazzaforno") e correlati: una questione areale ed etimologica', *ib.*, 165–84.

Aimed at the general public, Gianfranco Lotti, *Perché si dice così*, Mi, Rizzoli, 218 pp., is dedicated to relatively common terms with an interesting etymology, ranging from recent neologisms or loans (*ufologia, yuppie*) to more mundane words (*faccenda, ufficio*). Fascinating lexical histories abound in Ernesto Ferrero, *Dizionario storico dei gerghi italiani. Dal Quattrocento a oggi*, Mi, Mondadori, xxvii + 442 pp., a most welcome amplification and updating of his successful 1972 vol., *I gerghi della malavita dal Cinquecento a oggi*. Fascicules 31, 32, and 33 bring Max Pfister, *Lessico etimologico italiano*, up to *aureatus*, the last fasc. containing the first part of a detailed alphabetical index of vols 1–3. Id., *Lessico etimologico italiano: supplemento bibliografico con la collaborazione di R. Coluccia e altri. Analisi, progettazione informatica ed elaborazione dati a cura di M. Linciano*, Wiesbaden, Reichert, 271 pp., replaces the 1979 version. A. Stefanelli, *'Dal lessico latino al lessico italiano'*, *Linguistica*, 31:177–84, and G. Ernst, *'Latinismen des Italienischen in DELI und LEI'*, *ib.*, 185–200. G. Colussi, *Glossario degli antichi volgari italiani*, reaches vol. 16.2 (*Sceda-Sdurre*), 504 pp. P. Lärson, 'Preistoria dell'italiano *-esco*', *AGI*, 75:129–68, carefully examines early medieval Latin texts, in which he finds support for F. Sabatini's theory that the origins of the suffix are Germanic and its diffusion in Italy due largely to the prestige of the Franks. E. Radtke, *'Zur Wortgeschichte von venet./friul. pringhes und it. brindisi'*, *Fest. Pellegrini*, 317–27. *LN*, as usual, contains observations on numerous individual lexical items: 15th-c. *gambillo* 'cammello', *televisione, matinée*, in *LN*, 51:99–106, 109–19, 122, respectively; *vispo, antologia*, and *crestomazia; estivo; assacchiare; berzo; segno/segnale; imbalzare, imbalzato; bafore, baforetto, baforina; surmenage*, in *LN*, 52:1–4, 33–44, 44–52, 52–53, 54–55, 55, 56, 89–90, 90, respectively.

The sumptuously-bound Giuliano Gasca Queirazza *et al.*, *Dizionario di toponomastica. Storia e significato dei nomi geografici italiani*, T, UTET, 1990, 748 pp., is the first comprehensive dictionary of Italian toponyms, covering all *comuni* and regions as well as major islands, mountains, rivers, and seas. The alphabetically-listed entries include precise geographical location, references to early attestations, and a historical and etymological summary. Giovan Battista Pellegrini, *Toponomastica italiana. 10.000 nomi di città, paesi, frazioni, regioni, contrade, fiumi, monti, spiegati nella loro origine e storia*, Mi, Hoepli, 1990,

Ernesto Giammarco, *TAM, Toponomastica abruzzese e molisana*, 1990, lvi + 416 pp. H. Glättli, 'Der Ortsname *Intragna*', *VR*, 48, 1989 (1991):38–40, contains an etymological discussion of a place-name in the Ticino. S. Aprosio, 'L'antico nome locale savonese: Ivarium/Viarium', *AMSSSP*, 26, 1990:7–22. P. Merkù, *'Onomastica tergestina nel Trecento', *Linguistica*, 31:317–24. W. Schweickard, *'Semantische und morphologische Entwicklungsformen von Eth-nika (am Beispiel von it. *veneziano*)', *Fest. Pellegrini*, 345–54. A. Marrale, *L'infamia del nome: i modi della soprannominazione a Licata: con un repertorio etnografico–linguistico dei soprannomi delle persone e dei natanti*, Palermo, Gelka, 1990, 350 pp. V. Valente, 'Nomi di uccelli. Proposte interpretative', *LN*, 52:5–7, focuses on regional terms.

Anna Muru Porcu, *Il dizionario universale della lingua italiana di F. D'Alberti di Villanova*, Ro, Bulzoni, 376 pp., is a systematic analysis of an important landmark in the history of Italian lexicography; comparisons with the fourth edn of the *Vocabolario della Crusca* reveal the advances made in lexical coverage as well as in the annotation, definition, and exemplification of the items. Mirella Sessa, *La Crusca e le Crusche: il vocabolario e la lessicografia italiana del Sette-Ottocento*, F, Accademia della Crusca, 306 pp. P. Manni, 'Note sull'idea di lessico nei primi vocabolari italiani', Giannelli, *Rinascimento*, 69–79.

9. SOCIOLINGUISTICS

The kaleidoscopic range of linguistic varieties that flourish in Italy lends itself to classificatory studies: Ž. Muljačić, 'L'italien est-il une langue polynomique?', *Colloque Corti 90. Actes du Colloque international des langues polynomiques, Université de Corse, 17–22 septembre 1990*, (Publications Universitaires de Linguistique et d'Anthropologie, Université de Corse, 3/4, 1991, pp. 338–43), answers in the affirmative, incorporating the concept into his own 'relativistic' model, while A. M. Mioni, 'Osservazioni sui repertori linguistici in Italia', *Cortelazzo Vol.*, 421–30, is an interesting typological study that seeks to embrace all possible permutations. Variation within Italian has given rise to numerous social, situational, sectional, and regional varieties, which constitute a very productive area of current research. Despite the delay, the publication of *Atti* (Padua) is most welcome, given the paucity of general works on regional varieties of Italian. Most articles include some bibliographical updating, while some, naturally, express views that have in the meantime found expression elsewhere. The majority of the contributions, many by well-known Italian linguists, refer to the present and deal mainly with the oral repertoire, but included are also papers referring to written texts and past centuries, e.g. T. Poggi Salani, 'Italiano regionale del passato:

questioni generali e casi particolari' (327–54). Approaches vary from the descriptive to the more theoretical, with many contributions raising important methodological issues. G. B. Pellegrini's useful overview of research in the field, 'Tra italiano regionale e coinè dialettale' (5–23), is complemented by L. Canepari's description of the new series of monographs on the Italian of the regions (89–104). F. Sabatini's article posits his *italiano dell'uso medio* (75–78), G. Berruto discusses code-switching and code-mixing in Italy (105–28), phenomena that have still not received the attention they deserve, while many contributions contain detailed analyses relating to specific areas of Italy and particular linguistic phenomena. Ž. Muljačić, 'Regionalismi nelle lettere private di Alberto Fortis', *Fest. Pellegrini*, 269–84, eloquently demonstrates that there is a fund of valuable information about regional variation in the past to be gleaned from the largely untapped source of private correspondence. T. Stehl, *'Il concetto di *italiano regionale* dell'italiano nelle regioni', *ib.*, 385–402.

Sprachlicher Substandard III. Standard, Substandard und Varietäten-linguistik, ed. Günter Holtus and Edgar Radtke, Tübingen, Niemeyer, 1990, includes G. Berruto, 'Semplificazione linguistica e varietà substandard'; E. Radtke, 'Substandardsprachliche Entwicklungstendenzen im Sprachverhalten von Jugendlichen im heutigen Italien'; E. Blasco Ferrer, 'Italiano popolare a confronto con altri registri informali: verso una tipologia del substandard'; T. Stehl, 'Ansätze einer strukturalistischen Beschreibung der Variation im Französischen und Italienischen'. Clara Mavellia, *Die Sprache der Jugendlichen in Mailand. Untersuchungen zur Semantik und Wortbildung des aktuellen Italienischen*, Frankfurt, Lang, 1991. *La lingua degli studenti universitari*, ed. Cristina Lavinio and Alberto A. Sobrero, F, La Nuova Italia, vi + 215 pp., comprises eight essays, four on 'Forme di scrittura' and four on 'Fenomeni del parlato', which make a significant contribution, over and above their obvious pedagogical value, to the scientific description of the current linguistic usage of educated young Italians. A. A. Sobrero, 'La lingua degli studenti universitari', *LIt*, 22:54–55, highlights their inappropriate use of register, whilst thought-provoking observations are also found in Id., 'La lingua dei giovani', *LIt*, 23:61. D. Musumeci, *'Ciao, Professoressa!* A study of forms of address in Italian and its implications for the language classroom', *Italica*, 68:434–56, finds that certain predictions made in 1960 and 1975 are not borne out and that the system of pronominal address has become more complex and personal, in so far as it is governed by situation more than by age and status. Interesting details regarding oscillation in the use of pronouns of address during the Fascist period are found in Paola Micheli, *Il cinema di Blasetti, parlò così* . . . *: un'analisi* *linguistica dei film (1929–1942)*, Ro, Bulzoni, 1990, 134 pp. The linguistic analysis of each film in turn reveals the increasing influence of Fascist ideology as well as the uncertainty as to which regional variety of Italian was considered most prestigious. Mario Medici and Sonia Cappelluzzo Springolo, **Il titolo dei film nella lingua comune*, Ro, Bulzoni, 1991, 127 pp. Lorenzo Castellana, **La lingua dello sport in Italia è ancora fascista*, Manduria, Lacaita, 1991, 189 pp. The scientific use of Italian is analysed by Maria Luisa Altieri Biagi in **L'avventura della mente. Studi sulla lingua scientifica*, Na, Morano, 1990, 399 pp., and 'Il linguaggio scientifico italiano in Europa', Lo Cascio, *Lingua*, 119–34. F. Casadei, 'Strutture sintattiche e morfosintattiche dell'italiano scientifico', Giannelli, *Rinascimento*, 411–19, calls into question the classification of scientific language as a 'sottocodice', since there is far more to it than a specialized lexis.

Ramón Volkart-Rey, *Atteggiamenti linguistici e stratificazione sociale. La percezione dello status sociale attraverso la pronuncia. Indagine empirica a Catania e a Roma*, Ro, Bonacci, 1990, 212 pp., describes in detail a rigorous matched-guise study designed to test the correlation between language variety (regional variation is excluded) and perceived social status. The results confirm that speakers of standard Italian are judged highest on the socio-economic and socio-cultural scales, although the most positive judgements regarding personal characteristics are accorded to slightly marked regional varieties. Reference to stereotypes is found to be an integral part of the evaluation process. M. A. Pinto and P. Frassu, 'Interferenze fonologiche e identificazione culturale', *RILA*, 22:43–62, reveals the complexity of this relationship in a study of the linguistic behaviour of Sardinian immigrants in Rome. R. Saladino, ***'Language shift in standard Italian and dialect: a case study', *LVC*, 2, 1990:57–70. In a stimulating article that considers, among other phenomena, code-switching and code-mixing, A. A. Sobrero, 'L'innovazione nei dialetti italiani. Dinamiche recenti e problemi di metodo', *Atti* (Messina), 159–70, challenges traditional and merely sociolinguistic approaches to the study of linguistic innovation, arguing on the basis of concrete examples for more complex and flexible models 'per muovere *dalla linguistica della variazione verso la pragmatica e l'antropologia della variazione*'. Id., 'Immagine e percezione dei dialetti', *LIt*, 24:59, deplores the recent increase in anti-dialect prejudice stemming from racist intolerance and the unfortunate association with separatist movements. Y. Le Clézio, ***'Dialectes et modernité: la situation linguistique en Italie en 1990', *La linguistique*, 27.1:59–74. *Mehr als eine Sprache: zu einer Sprachstrategie in Südtirol/Più di una lingua: per un progetto linguistico in Alto Adige*, ed. Franz Lanthaler, Merano, Alpha e Beta, 1990, 93 pp., contains three important essays for understanding the

440   *Italian Studies*

complex and uneasy linguistic situation in the Alto Adige: A. M. Mioni, 'Bilinguismo intra- e intercomunitario in Alto Adige/Südtirol: considerazioni sociolinguistiche' (13–35); K. Egger, 'Sprachlernen in Südtirol: Antrieb und Zugang' (37–55); F. Lanthaler, 'Dialekt und Zweisprachkeit in Südtirol' (57–93). The papers include theoretical observations but focus on language attitudes and policy. B. Moretti, 'Varietà del repertorio linguistico e fenomeni lessicali nel Baby Talk', *RID*, 14, 1990 (1991): 139–55, analyses Ticinese phenomena, drawing comparisons with unrelated languages, e.g. Walbiri, and making some important generalizations about the role of Baby Talk in the generational transmission of language and especially language attitudes. Claudio Marazzini, *Il Piemonte e la Valle d'Aosta*, T, UTET, 285 pp., is a highly promising inauguration of a new series, *L'italiano nelle regioni*, ed. Francesco Bruni. This broad sociolinguistic study traces the fascinating story of the relationship in this border area between, on the one hand, the Tuscan vernacular, and later, Italian, and, on the other, Piedmontese, as well as French. The vol. also contains a rich and very useful anthology of annotated texts (123–256). C. Grassi and T. Telmon, 'Sulla trasferibilità di morfemi fra sistemi linguistici: il caso dei microsistemi dei possessivi in contatto nell'Italia nord-occidentale', *Atti* (Bergamo), 193–205, draws on a wealth of dialect data to highlight the crucial role of speakers' attitudes towards their language in the transfer of morphemes. F. Albano Leoni and P. Maturi, 'Le occlusive sorde nell'italiano di Nusco', Giannelli, *Rinascimento*, 253–58, has recourse to an instrumental analysis in an attempt to resolve descriptive divergencies regarding consonantal pronunciation in southern regional Italian. F. Cocciolo and I. Tempesta, 'Ai poli della lingua. Il lessico in testi scritti del Salento', *RID*, 14, 1990 (1991): 93–112, analyses schoolchildren's exercises that reveal tensions deriving from the dual pressure of colloquial varieties of Italian and dialect from below and from normative and special varieties of Italian from above.

10. Dialectology

Indice delle voci della rivista 'L'Italia dialettale', prima serie, voll. 1–23, ed. Tristano Bolelli, Pisa, Giardini, x + 1419 pp. P. Benincà, 'Note introduttive a un atlante dialettale sintattico', *Cortelazzo Vol.*, 11–17, makes important preliminary observations on a major project, suggesting that Italian dialects form two groups from the syntactic as well as from the phonological point of view, with the division running just south of the La Spezia–Rimini line, so that Florentine is part of the northern group. *Lavorando al NADIR: un'idea per un atlante linguistico*, ed. A. A. Sobrero *et al.*, Galatina, Congedo, 139 pp., deals with the *Nuovo atlante del dialetto e dell'italiano per regioni*. H. Goebl, *'Una classificazione gerarchica di dati geolinguistici tratti dall'AIS. Saggio di dialettometria dendografica', *Linguistica*, 31:341–52. G. A. Plangg, *'Romanische Relikte im Dreiländereck A–CH–I', *ib.*, 353–60. J. Haiman, 'From V/2 to subject clitics: evidence from northern Italian', Traugott, *Approaches*, 135–57, is a stimulating paper assigning a key role to pragmatic factors in the reduction of personal pronouns to bound affixes. These are deemed to have originated in interrogative inverted word order, with the second person singular pronoun, the sole compulsory subject clitic in all the northern Italian dialects, as the vehicle of the change. E. F. Tuttle, 'Considerazione pluristratica sociale degli esiti di AU e AL + alveodentale nell'Italia settentrionale', *Actes* (Trier), iii, 571–83, argues convincingly on the basis of a masterly array of comparative data for taking into account sociolinguistic factors to solve a long-standing puzzle of Romance evolution. Nasalization in the northern Italian dialects has proved a popular topic of enquiry: Id., *'Nasalization in northern Italy: syllabic constraints and strength scales as developmental parameters', *RivL*, 3:23–92; J. Hajek, 'La nasalizzazione ed il bolognese: aspetti fonologici', Giannelli, *Rinascimento*, 273–79, and J.-P. Montreuil, 'Effetti di località in gallo-italico', *ib.*, 281–88. Id., 'Length in Milanese', Wanner and Kibbee, *New Analyses*, 37–47, considers various analyses relating to both consonants and vowels.

VII Rëscontr antërnassional dë studi an sla lenga e la literatura piemontèisa, Alba, 12–13 magg 1990, ed. Gianrenzo P. Clivio and Censin Pich, Alba, Famija Albèisa, 292 pp., considerably larger than previous vols, has an appreciable linguistic component that includes an important debate on the language of what has traditionally been considered as the first Piedmontese text. H. J. Wolf, 'La langue des *Sermoni subalpini*' (237–54), contains harsh criticisms of M. Danesi's 1976 study, arguing that the language is not only heavily influenced by French and Provençal but that the Gallo-Italian element is not necessarily Piedmontese: 'La langue des *Sermons* est donc un franco-italien'. M. Danesi, 'The language of the *Sermoni Subalpini* revisited: a reply to Wolf' (255–62), resolutely rejects W.'s methodological criticisms, but agrees that the text requires further study. H. Lüdtke, 'Le leggi universali del mutamento linguistico con applicazione al piemontese' (83–88), comments briefly on the evolution from Latin. K. Gebhardt, 'De Carmagnola/Piémont à la *carmagnole* française: histoire du mot' (89–100). G. Gasca Queirazza, 'Documenti del piemontese di Poirino alle soglie dell'Ottocento' (129–44), continues his very useful linguistic analyses of Piedmontese texts. T. Burat, 'Lenga piemontèisa e parlada local ant la literatura bielèisa' (181–235), chronicles the diglossia that developed within one Piedmontese area and which is of particular relevance to current sociolinguistic issues (B. advocates the promotion of standard Piedmontese and not the local dialect). B. Villata, 'L'avnì dle lenghe regionaj e dël piemontèis an particolar' (263–82), draws interesting parallels with the situation of Italian in Montreal. A. Cornagliotti, 'I francesismi nel *Vocabolario piemontese* di Maurizio Pipino (1783)', *StP*, 20:313–20, hopes to encourage others towards a neglected area of research, namely French influence on the dialects, and concludes from the evidence of Pipino's dictionary that, contrary to common belief, Piedmontese was not affected significantly more than other northern dialects or Tuscan. The dialect of a small industrial town on the Piedmontese-Ligurian border provides material for two studies by M. M. Parry: 'L'evoluzione di un dialetto', *RID*, 14, 1990 (1991):7–39, a statistical analysis of the relationship between sociological variables and dialect variation (phonological, morphological, syntactic, and lexical), and 'Le système démonstratif du cairese', *Actes* (Trier), III, 625–31, which examines from both a synchronic and diachronic viewpoint the unusual demonstrative system derived entirely from Latin IPSE. R. Caprini, 'I nomi della "montagna" tra Liguria e Provenza', *ib.*, 461–64, draws on her experiences as contributor to the *Atlas Linguarum Europae* to comment on the wealth of terminology and make methodological observations. W. Forner, *'Relikte sigmatischer Pluralmarkierung und *i*-Umlaut im ligurisch-okzitanischen Übergangsgebiet', *Fest. Pellegrini*, 81–102. S. Aprosio, 'In margine all'Anonimo Genovese: "borchan"', *AMSSSP*, 23–26; Id., 'I bravi di Don Rodrigo', *ib.*, 27–34, and 'Ligure "bunetu", berretto', *ib.*, 35–39, offer interesting Ligurian data which could help resolve etymological problems relating to other Romance varieties also. Attilo Spiller, *Guida ai dialetti lombardi*, Mi, Sugarco, 1991, 220 pp. G. Bonfadini, 'Il dialetto bresciano: modello cittadino e varietà periferiche', *RID*, 14, 1990 (1991):41–92, is a useful classificatory study based on phonetic, morphological, and lexical criteria. R. Bracchi, 'Curiosità etimologiche bormine', *ID*, 53, 1990 (1991): 217–35. O. Lurati, 'Per un'analisi semantica del gergo. A proposito di un recente libro', *ZRP*, 107:443–49, enthusiastically reviewing Bracchi's 1987 book, *Parlate speciali a Bormio*, Roma, Accademia Nazionale dei Lincei, makes valuable observations and a few suggestions for alternative etymologies. F. Spiess, 'La congiunzione *che* da elemento lessicale a segno di subordinazione', *Actes* (Trier), III, 645–49, comments on the pronounced analytical tendencies shown by conjunctions in Ticinese. P. Cordin, 'Il raddoppiamento del dativo in Trentino', Giannelli, *Rinascimento*, 399–410, reviews the Trentino data in the light of similar phenomena in other languages (attention is drawn to parametric variation governed by morphological, lexical, semantic, and thematic features of the NP involved) and considers two hypotheses that seek to resolve the apparent contradiction with case and theta theories. M. Pfister, *'Il popolamento del Trentino settentrionale e del Sudtirolo prima dell'anno Mille', *Fest. Pellegrini*, 285–307. G. B. Pellegrini, 'Breve storia linguistica di Venezia e del Veneto', in *Adunanza solenne di chiusura del 152° anno accademico. Palazzo Ducale, 10 giugno 1990, Venezia*, Venice, Istituto Veneto di Scienze, Lettere ed Arti, 1990, 20–36. In addition to its undeniable artistic merit, Luigi Meneghello, *Maredè, maredè . . . : sondaggio nel campo della volgare eloquenza vicentina*, Mi, Rizzoli, 316 pp., is an exciting sensual journey into the dynamic realm of dialect and language: 'nei diglotti (f/m) accanto a fenomeni di interferenza c'è un continuo insorgere di nuove possibilità espressive, un lievito linguistico che fa fermentare il discorso . . .' (22) and, despite the author's modesty, the *Note di morfologia elementare* (225–67) are certainly of interest to linguists (male and female!). M. Cortelazzo, *'Etimologie venete', *Linguistica*, 31:295–98; A. Zamboni, *'Due etimologie venete ed istriane', *ib.*, 299–302; V. Glavinić, *'Vocabolarietto dell'istro-veneto della città di Pola', *ib.*, 303–17. Ž. Muljačić, 'Sullo status linguistico dell'istrioto medievale', *ib.*, 155–70, uses his 'relativistic' classificatory model to clarify the relationship between local and Venetian varieties in the Middle Ages. S. Kowallik, *'Zur Phonologie der früheren italienischen Mundart von Zara', *Fest. Pellegrini*, 207–25. Fabio Foresti, *Le parole del lavoro: lessici dialettali e culture materiali*, Bologna, CLUEB, 1990, viii + 306 pp., comprises ethnolinguistic essays (some previously published) that record fast-disappearing specialized dialect vocabulary relating to numerous occupations and aspects of rural life in Emilia-Romagna.

   M.-J. Stefanaggi considers 'Les corrélations de sonantes en Corse', *Actes* (Trier), III, 496–507, from the points of view of synchronic typology, diachronic evolution, and linguistic geography. *L'Umbria nel quadro linguistico dell'Italia mediana: incontro di studi, Gubbio, 18–19 giugno 1988*, ed. Luciano Agostiniani *et al.*, Na, Edizioni Scientifiche Italiane, 1990, xvi + 244 pp. G. Mastrangelo Latini, 'Vocaboli di etimo non latino in un dialetto abruzzese', *Actes* (Trier), III, 688–92, examines four terms from the dialect of Martinsicuro. F. Fanciullo, 'Italiano meridionale *guaglione* "ragazzo"', probabile francesismo d'epoca angioina', *ZRP*, 107:398–410, convincingly argues that *guaglione/guagnone* can be traced back via French to the Germanic *WAIDANJAN 'to work on the land', as Sp. *gañán*. G. B. Mancarella, 'Sistemi vocalici della Lucania e classificazione linguistica', *Actes* (Trier), III, 508–16, seeks to introduce order on seemingly chaotic variation. Maria Teresa Greco, *Dizionario dei dialetti di Picerno e Tito*, Na, Edizioni Scientifiche Italiane, 1990, xxiii + 490 pp., is an important work on two Gallo-Italian dialects of Lucania, containing phonetic and morphological data in addition to a wealth of lexical detail. A new series dedicated to Lucania and southern Italy in general and edited by Nicola De Blasi and Franco Fanciullo acknowledges the significant contribution made to dialect study by non-specialists, particularly with regard to the recording of dialects rapidly being transformed by contact with Italian and modern international culture. The first vol., Luigi De Blasi, *Dizionario dialettale di San Mango sul Calore (Avellino)*, Potenza, Il Salice, 112 pp., includes a grammatical description that highlights the conservative features of this dialect in comparison with modern Neapolitan. Antonio Vincelli, *Vocabolario ragionato del dialetto di Casacalenda*, Campobasso, Enne, 267 pp. Giuseppe Forestiero, *Proposta per una grammatica calabrese*, Ro, Accademia degli Incolti, 1989, 50 pp. P. Martino, 'Due esiti di un grecismo bizantino in Calabria', *ID*, 53, 1990 (1991):207–15, discusses terms from the semantic field of 'stupidity'. Pasquale Piemontese, *L'uso del verbo nel 'Trattato di igiene e dietetica' di Anonimo Tarentino*, Siponto, Centro Residenziale di Studi Pugliesi, 1989, 140 pp. Antonio Garrisi, *Dizionario leccese–italiano*, 2 vols, Cavallino di Lecce, Capone, 1990, 845 pp., and Id., *Glossario italiano–leccese*, Cavallino di Lecce, Capone, 1990, 246 pp. Lucio Cristoforo Scobar, *Il vocabolario siciliano–latino*, (16th-c. text) ed. Alfonso Leone, Palermo, CSFLS, 1990, lvii + 323 pp. *La Sicilia linguistica oggi*, ed. Franco Lo Piparo *et al.*, Palermo, CSFLS, vol. 1, 1990, 338 pp. G. Tropea, 'Su alcuni aspetti dell'italianizzazione lessicale in Sicilia', *Atti* (Messina), 171–99, identifies a number of synonymic patterns as well as the particular sociolinguistic factors contributing to the Italianization of the dialect lexis.

11. ITALIAN ABROAD

C. Bettoni, 'Italiano e dialetti fuori d'Italia', *RID*, 14, 1990 (1991):267–82, a useful survey of research on Italian and Italian dialects abroad, provides a rich bibliography. Còveri, *L'italiano*, contains many lexical studies relating to the influence of Italian on various languages of the world: English (G. Brincat, 7–14); American English (H. W. Haller, 15–24); Australian English (G. Rando, 25–32); German (G. Basile, 33–46); Dutch (S. Vanvolsem, 47–58); French (O. Martinez, 59–77); Spanish (M. T. Navarro Salazar, 79–92); Albanian (A. Landi, 93–105); Finnish (E. Suomela and J. Härmä, 107–15); Somalian (A. Costantini, 117–27); while A. Benucci *et al.*, 'L'italiano nei due mondi' (129–53) is a comparative study of the linguistic behaviour of Italian immigrants. The Appendix, 'Premesse per uno studio dell'italiano come lingua nazionale sotto la monarchia austrungarica', introduced by C. Grassi, comprises two articles: W. Forsthofer, 'La terminologia burocratica italiana nel Regno Lombardo-Veneto (1814–1866)' (163–69), and R. Weilguny, 'Il linguaggio settoriale dell'amministrazione scolastica nel Trentino (1867–1918)' (171–80). J. Hajek, *'Parlaree:* etymologies and notes', *SpR*, 6, 1990:87–105, is a fascinating attempt to ascertain exactly which slang forms constitute *Parlaree*, strictly defined here as 'that lexicon of Italian items that entered into English slang between 1840 and 1900'; 40–45 words are eventually accepted as *Parlaree* forms. G. Cartago, **Ricordi d'italiano: osservazioni intorno alla lingua e italianismi nelle relazioni di viaggio degli Inglesi in Italia*, Bassano, Ghedina and Tassotti, 1990, 252 pp. H. W. Haller, 'Intorno alla varietà alta parlata fra gli emigrati italo-newyorchesi', *Atti* (Lecce), 127–32, presenting a brief morphosyntactic description of the heavily dialectalized Italian that serves as a *lingua franca*, is pessimistic regarding the future of Italian in the immigrant community. B. Villata, 'Heritage language and bilingualism in Montreal', *Crosiere*, 1, 2:81–86, uses a statistical study of the linguistic behaviour of young Montrealer trilinguals to demonstrate that competence in the language spoken at home correlates with competence in French, English, and mathematics: improved performance in these subjects provides a strong case for instruction in the heritage language. C. Bettoni and J. Gibbons, 'L'influenza della generazione e della classe sociale sugli atteggiamenti linguistici degli Italiani in Australia', *RID*, 14, 1990 (1991):113–37, draws not too optimistic conclusions concerning the future of Italian in Australia from a series of matched-guise experiments. V. O'Rourke, 'Una noterella sull'italiano in Sud Africa', *LN*, 51:119–22, examines the terms *nero* and *colorato*, whose particular semantic development in the context of apartheid is ascribed to English influence. G. Berruto, **'Note sul repertorio linguistico degli emigrati italiani in Svizzera tedesca', Linguistica*, 31:61–79. G. Berruto *et al.*, 'Interlingue italiane nella Svizzera tedesca. Osservazioni generali e note sul sistema dell'articolo', *Atti* (Trento), 204–28. Ž. Muljačić, 'Innovazioni lessicali irradiatesi dall'Italia nel mondo. Per uno studio comparato degli italianismi nelle bocche e nelle menti europee, maghrebine e vicino-orientali', *Atti* (Perugia), 519–31.

12. SARDINIAN

C. Lavinio, 'Retorica e italiano regionale: il caso dell'antifrasi nell'italiano regionale sardo', *Atti* (Padua), 311–24. E. Blasco Ferrer, 'Linguistica storica e sociolinguistica. L'evoluzione dei dialetti sardi nel medioevo attraverso lo studio della società e della storia', *Actes*

(Trier), III, 282–317, demonstrates the importance of socio-historical information for an accurate understanding of the development of the various Sardinian dialect groups. Id., 'Romania Germanica II: Sardegna, Addenda e corrigenda', *ZRP*, 107:104–40, presents fascinating new data that call into question traditional views on Germanic influence on Sardinian. Two forms examined in detail, *istunda* and *ammayáre*, are considered as having developed directly from Gothic *STUNDA and *MAGAN respectively; their history can also throw light on various Catalan and Spanish etymological problems. H. J. Wolf, 'Orgosolo und das dialektologische Ungemach', *ZRP*, 107:411–17, severely criticizes the inaccuracies in M. T. Atzori, *Sardegna*, in the series *Profilo dei dialetti italiani*, Pisa, Pacini, 1982, and to a lesser extent in M. Contini, *Étude de géographie phonétique et de phonétique instrumentale du sarde*, Alessandria, Orso, 1987.

DUECENTO AND TRECENTO I

DANTE

POSTPONED

DUECENTO AND TRECENTO II

(EXCLUDING DANTE)

By JENNIFER PETRIE, *College Lecturer in Italian, University College, Dublin*

1. GENERAL

Interest in theatre studies has extended to early Italian drama, occasioning a number of surveys. S. Sticca, 'Italy: liturgy and christocentric spirituality', Simon, *Theatre*, 169–88, gives a full account of recent research on liturgical and religious drama. Doglio, *Teatro scomparso*, contains surveys of dramatic *laudi* on the theme of Mary at the foot of the Cross (35–59) and the conflict between soul and body (213–27), both seen in the context of medieval Latin and vernacular traditions; medieval Latin 'elegiac comedies' in Italy (161–81); the colourful entertainments at the court of Frederic II (183–98); the significance and use of masks and disguises in medieval drama in general (199–211). P. Armour, 'Comedy and the origins of Italian theatre around the time of Dante', *McWilliam Vol.*, 1–31, while concerned mainly with Dante, provides a survey of dramatic practices in medieval Italian society as well as attitudes to drama. On poetry and rhetoric, Roberto Gigliucci, *Oxymoron amoris: retorica dell'amore irrazionale nella lirica italiana antica*, Ro, De Rubeis, 1990, 137 pp., examines the figure of oxymoron (distinguished from antithesis as involving a sharp juxtaposition of genuinely contradictory opposites) in medieval Italian lyric after preliminary chapters on its occurrence in Latin and Provençal. On prose narrative, Alessandro Linguiti, *Sulla novella italiana: genesi e generi*, Lecce, Milella, 1990. On Arthurian literature in Italy, Marie-José Heijkant, *La tradizione del 'Tristan' in prosa in Italia e proposte di studio sul 'Tristano Riccardiano'*, Nijmegen, Katholieke Universiteit te Nijmegen, 1989, is given a detailed review article by F. Zambon, *MedRom*, 16:247–53; see also Boccaccio section. On religious literature, C. Delcorno, 'Le *Vitae Patrum* nella letteratura religiosa medievale (secc. XIII–XV)', *LItal*, 43:187–207, provides a general survey of the extensive influence of this work and its Italian versions and adaptations. *Laude fiorentine*, 1: *Il Laudario della Compagnia di San Gilio*, ed. Concetto Del Popolo, F, Olschki, 1990, 2 vols, viii + 696 pp. + 10 pls. On travel narrative,

Pellegrini scrittori: viaggiatori toscani del Trecento in Terra Santa, ed. Antonio Lanza and Marcellina Troncarelli, F, Ponte alle Grazie, 1990, 342 pp.; M. Ciccuto, 'Storia e mito del *Milione*', *LItal*, 43: 153–70, contains a survey of encyclopaedic travellers' tales and crusade literature and considers how *Il Milione* became a book of marvels; F. R. Camarota, 'Dalla *Relatio* di Odorico da Pordenone al *De rebus incognitis*', *RLI*, 95.1–2: 31–39, compares the Latin and Italian version of the account of a Franciscan's journey to China: the first having a missionary and ascetic spirit, the Italian having a more secular emphasis on the marvellous. On 14th-c. Rome, Massimo Miglio, *Scritture, scrittori e storia*, Manziana, Vecchiarelli, 182 pp.

2. BOCCACCIO

Francesco Bruno, *Boccaccio: l'invenzione della letteratura mezzana*, Bo, Il Mulino, 1990, 521 pp., is concerned with B.'s 'double idea' of culture, according to which his vernacular aims (a 'letteratura mezzana') differ from his Latin ones. The main emphasis is on the former, and on the *Decameron* in particular. A shorter introductory study of the *Decameron* is David Wallace, *Boccaccio: 'Decameron'*, CUP, 128 pp., in the useful 'Landmarks of World Literature' series. Corradina Caporello-Szykman, *The Boccaccian Novella: The Creation and Waning of a Genre*, NY, Lang, 157 pp., sees the novella as a distinctive medieval and Renaissance genre invented by Boccaccio, who adapted norms of classical rhetoric; an essential feature is the *cornice*, with its unifying and rhetorical function. Daniela Delcorno Branca, *Boccaccio e le storie di Re Artù*, Bo, Il Mulino, 165 pp., contains three already published articles concerned with the dissemination of Arthurian literature in Italy, B.'s own familiarity with it (not confined to Italian texts), and the presence of this literature in B.'s own works, in particular the *Decameron*. On manuscripts of the *Decameron*, Vittore Branca, *Tradizione delle opere di Giovanni Boccaccio*, II: *Un secondo elenco di manoscritti e studi sul testo del 'Decameron': con due appendici*, Ro, Storia e Letteratura, 584 pp. Also on the *Decameron*, G. Velli, 'Seneca nel *Decameron*', *GSLI*, 168: 321–34, argues that B.'s classical culture is present in the work, especially in the rhetorical use made of Seneca on such topics as fortune and nature. C. Grassi, 'Di Lippo Topo presunto pittore', *ib.*, 271–73, finds references to this character as proverbial for his laziness, but no evidence that he was a painter. J. Usher, 'Simona and Pasquino: "Cur moriatur homo cui salvia crescit in horto?"', *MLN*, 106: 1–14, sees the novella as playing with and subverting a Latin rhyme on the healing properties of sage. N. Jonard, 'Le *Decameron* et la "légende de la bourgeoisie"', *StB*, 18, 1989 (1990): 347–68, questions the notion of a bourgeois or mercantile ethic in the work, suggesting that Boccaccio as an intellectual assumed a mediating role between the generally prevailing Christian and courtly ethic and the mentality of the new, more mercantile society. G. Fermetti, 'Ancora su Ghinozzo Allegretti. Collazione del Ms. Bodmer 38: III', *ib.*, 1–64, continues from earlier issues. E. L. Giusti, 'La novella di Cesca e "intenderlo come si conviene" nella sesta giornata del *Decamerone*', *ib.*, 319–46, takes Cesca, one person who does not learn from the well-chosen words of another, as a starting point for a reading of the sixth day according to the relation between speaker and hearer. P. F. Watson, 'On seeing Guido Cavalcanti and the houses of the dead', *ib.*, 301–18, gives an art historian's reading of the novella, examining its topography, and comparing Cavalcanti's role to that of Mercury on a typical sarcophagus. The relation between literature and iconography has become a fruitful area of interest in Boccaccio studies. There are further additions to the study of V. Branca *et al.*, 'Boccaccio visualizzato, IV', *ib.*, 167–280 + 30 pls, which consists of V. Branca, 'Ancora manoscritti figurati' (167); C. Reynolds, 'Illustrated Boccaccio manuscripts in the British Library (London). Additional list' (169–74); M.-H. Tesnière, '"Lectures illustrées" de Boccace, en France, au XVe siècle. Les manuscrits français du *De casibus virorum illustrium* dans les bibliothèques parisiennes' (175–280). This last is the most substantial, with its discussion of the relations between illustration and translation or adaptation, and of the themes mainly chosen for illustration. Similarly concerned with illustration in relation to reception is B. Buettner, 'Les affinités sélectives. Image et texte dans les premiers manuscrits des *Clères femmes*', *ib.*, 281–99 + 13 pls, according to which the pictures are often to be seen as giving legitimacy to the translator's work. T. Hankey, 'Un nuovo codice delle *Genealogie deorum* di Paolo da Perugia (e tre manualetti contemporanei)', *ib.*, 65–161, discusses medieval genealogies of the gods before Boccaccio, and in particular an illustrated manuscript made for Queen Joanna of Naples. A further bibliographical study, P. Cherchi, 'Codici boccacciani nella biblioteca aragonese', *ib.*, 163–65, draws on the 16-c. inventory of the University Library of Valencia, which obtained large parts of the dispersed Biblioteca Aragonese of Naples. V. Zaccaria, 'Boccaccio e Plinio il Vecchio', *ib.*, 389–96, considers the various periods at which B. may have had access to a manuscript of Pliny, and the uses or use he made of it. G. B. Perini, 'Note esegetiche e testuali al *Bucolicum carmen* del Boccaccio', *ib.*, 369–88, discusses various textual problems relating to B.'s Latinity. On the *Corbaccio*, A. Illiano, '*Corbaccio*: precisazioni e proposte su autobiografismo, età, datazione', *Italianistica*, 19, 1990:239–52, does not favour a strictly autobiographical reading, and discusses the significance of the narrator's age and situation. Id., *Per l'esegesi del 'Corbaccio'*, Na, Federico & Ardia, 102 pp. G. Padoan, 'Il *Corbaccio* tra spunti autobiografici e filtri letterari', *REI*, 37:21–37, favours a qualified biographical interest and points out parallel themes in other later works of B.; the work could be seen as a satire in the manner of Juvenal. P. M. Forni, 'Boccaccio retore', *MLN*, 106:189–201, a review article, discusses interpretations of the *Corbaccio*. On the Griselda story and its fortunes, M. M. Pelen, 'Irony in Boccaccio's *Decameron* and in Chaucer's "Clerk's Tale"', *FMLS*, 27:1–22, considers the way in which different narrators control the stories in each case; also *Atti del convegno 'Modi dell'intertestualità: la storia di Griselda in Europa'*, L'Aquila, Japadre, 1990, 264 pp. P. Boccardo, 'Un inedito imitatore di Boccaccio: Jacopo Serminocci autore del *Libro di difinizioni'*, *RLI*, 95.1–2:40–52, discusses the 15th-c. author of a narrative poem which draws widely on several of B.'s Italian works.

3. PETRARCH

Marjorie O'Rourke Boyle, *Petrarch's Genius: Pentimento and Prophecy*, Berkeley, California U.P., ix + 216 pp., is a stimulating, if at times tendentious, interpretation of the whole of P.'s poetry, Latin and Italian, in the light of his 'theological' claims for poetry. Apollo is a figure of Christ, Laura represents an ecstatic poetic-prophetic vocation; the *Secretum* records a self-definition against a standard hostile to poetry and the imagination, represented by Augustine; to speak, like Freccero or Durling, of a 'poetics of idolatry' is to misread the *Canzoniere*. Other works favour the poetics of idolatry, such as Kathleen Anne Perry, *Another Reality: Metamorphosis and the Imagination in the Poetry of Ovid, Petrarch, and Ronsard*, NY, Lang, ix + 260 pp., especially the chapter 'The triumph of subjectivity in Petrarch's *Rime sparse*' (79–132): metamorphosis is P.'s means of 'expressing the fragmented knowledge that is the domain of poetic imagery' and represents the confusion and flux of subjective self-awareness, so implying an abandonment of the poet's prophetic role. Jill Robbins, *Prodigal Son/Elder Brother: Interpretation and Alterity in Augustine, Petrarch, Kafka, Levinas*, Chicago U.P., viii + 182 pp., has a chapter entitled 'Petrarch reading Augustine: "The ascent of Mont Ventoux"' (49–70) in which she sees P.'s conversion narrative as claiming 'a closure and self-reflexivity, which amounts to an absolute autonomy', confirming the view that 'Petrarch's portrayal of himself as idolatrous serves to vindicate his literary autonomy'. Other books: Amedeo Quondam, *Il naso di Laura: lingua e poesia lirica nella tradizione del classicismo*, Ferrara, Panini, 337 pp.; G. Orelli, *Il suono dei sospiri: sul Petrarca volgare*, T, Einaudi, 1990. Also Domenico De Venuto, *Il*

Bucolicum carmen di Francesco Petrarca: edizione diplomatica dell'autografo Vat. Lat. 3358, Pisa, ETS, xlvi + 176 pp. F. Finotti, 'Rassegna petrarchesca (1985–1990)', *LItal*, 43:412–55, a detailed survey, draws particular attention to the picture of P.'s culture which emerges from recent work. C. Berra, 'La canzone cxxvii nella storia dei "frammenti" petrarcheschi', *GSLI*, 168:161–98, using a detailed rhetorical and lexical analysis, places the poem in relation to predecessors and genres; she sees a 'contaminazione fra poesia stilnovistica e poesia per la donna pietra', constituting part of P.'s project to 'trasporre l'autobiografia ideale nelle forme e nei modi della tradizione poetica'. J. Leclercq, 'Temi monastici nell'opera del Petrarca', *LItal*, 43:23–49, looks at P.'s place in the context of humanist writing on the religious life; he sees his culture as closer to monastic writings of antiquity than to scholasticism, and linked to a reform movement. N. Costa-Zalessow, 'The personification of Italy from Dante through the Trecento', *Italica*, 68:316–31, analyses variations on the topos of Italy as a female victim; whereas minor Trecento poets followed Dante rather than P., later the reverse was true. Also on later influences, P. A. Miller, 'Sidney, Petrarch, and Ovid, or imitation as subversion', *ELH*, 58:499–522, in an article mainly concerned with Sidney, relates the sonnet sequence to a 'highly self-reflective lyric subjectivity'. R. W. Dasenbrock, 'Petrarch, Leopardi, and Pound's appreciation of the Italian past', *ib.*, 215–32, argues that despite his hostility to P., Pound was in several respects closer to him than to Dante or Cavalcanti; this was partly the result of his receiving the Italian tradition as mediated by Leopardi. Also J. Weiss, '*La affección poetal virtuosa*: Petrarch's sonnet 116 as poetic manifesto for fifteenth-century Castile', *MLR*, 86:70–78; Maria Cristina Cabani, **Fra omaggio e parodia: Petrarca e petrarchismo nel Furioso*, Pisa, Nistri-Lischi, 1990, 301 pp.

4. Due-Trecento

Elena Landoni, *Il 'libro' e la 'sentenzia': scrittura e significato nella poesia medievale: Iacopone da Todi, Dante, Cecco Angiolieri*, Mi, Vita e Pensiero, 1990, 198 pp., contains detailed analyses of the poetry of Jacopone: 'Iacopone da Todi e la trasgressione del linguaggio cortese' (19–55), and of Cecco: 'Note su Cecco Angiolieri: antistilnovismo o antipoesia?' (141–78). She argues that while early Italian poetry made formal borrowings from Provence, its originality lay in the content. Both Jacopone and Cecco, in different ways, make use of courtly or *stilnovo* devices, but in order to distance themselves from this tradition; in the case of Cecco, his habit of stylistic and thematic negation seems to amount to a denial of poetry altogether. There is also Alvaro

Cacciotti, *Amor sacro e amor profano in Jacopone da Todi*, Ro, Antonianùm, 1989, 324 pp. On the Sicilians, A. Fratta, 'Correlazioni testuali nella poesia dei Siciliani', *MedRom*, 16:189–206, looks at intertextual relations in a group of five Sicilian poets (Guido delle Colonne, Jacopo Mostacci, Pier delle Vigne, Rinaldo d'Aquino, Ruggeri d'Amici). Research on Guittone has been stimulated by a critical edition of his letters: Guittone d'Arezzo, *Lettere*, ed. Claude Margueron, Bo, Commissione per i Testi di Lingua, 1990, lxii + 396 pp.; there is a review article by L. Banfi, *GSLI*, 168:452–58. M. Marti, 'Della lettera xxxv di Guittone (a "ser Jacopo suo") e di altre Guittonerie', *ib.*, 401–10, suggests some alternative readings to those of Margueron. L. Banfi, 'Il ricupero dugentesco del *Detto della Vergine*', *Italianistica*, 19, 1990:215–37, gives the text of a fragment of a poem existing in two versions, which supports the longer version and allows for possible elucidations of the text. L. Cassata, 'Per il testo delle *Rime* di Guido Cavalcanti. (Contributi a una nuova edizione critica)', *ib.*, 271–318, offers a careful and detailed criticism of the edition of De Robertis. S. Botterill, 'Autobiography and artifice in the medieval lyric: the case of Cecco Nuccoli', *ISt*, 46:37–57, argues that an embarrassment on the part of critics with the homosexual content has prevented a reading of Nuccoli's sonnets as serious lyric poetry. Franca Brambilla Ageno has produced an edition of Franco Sacchetti, *Il libro delle Rime*, F, Olschki — Perth, W. Australia U.P., 1990, 536 pp.

HUMANISM AND THE RENAISSANCE

By E. Haywood, *College Lecturer in Italian, University College, Dublin*
and P. L. Rossi, *Lecturer in Italian Studies, Lancaster University*

1. General

John Stephens, *The Italian Renaissance. The Origins of Intellectual and Artistic Change before the Reformation*, London, Longman, 1990, xviii + 248 pp., comes to the conclusion that, by cancelling the Investiture contest and sanctifying the world anew, the Italian Renaissance, which emerged from the 12th- to 14th-c. collapse of imperial and papal power and the 'hunger for moral improvement awoken by the friars', let princes and educated laymen of the 16th c. break into the armoury of the Church, enabling them to fight it with its own arms. A section on humanism traces the development of 'humanist concerns' from Petrarch through his successors, thanks to whom the 15th-c. laity arrogated to itself the moral authority of priests, while the 'Achievement of the Italian Renaissance' illustrates how the humanists 'let four dynamic ideas loose upon early modern Europe: a belief in man's intellectual and moral capacity; the judging of its proper limits by reference to the human condition; a finely tuned sense of history and a highly sophisticated inductive method'. Two useful collections of documents are: *Venice Portrayed: A Documentary History 1450–1630*, ed. D. Chambers, B. Pullan, J. Fletcher, Oxford, Blackwell, xxiv + 484 pp., and *Culture and Belief in Europe, 1450–1600*, ed. D. Englander *et al.*, Oxford, Blackwell, 1990, xvii + 486 pp. Konrad Eisenbichler, Lesley B. Cormack, Jacqueline Murray, *International Directory of Renaissance and Reformation Associations and Institutes*, Toronto, Centre for Reformation and Renaissance Studies, 1990, 79 pp., is an extremely useful directory which lists 214 institutions and their facilities, with an index. *Renaissance Linguistic Archive 1350–1700. A Third Print-Out from the Secondary-Sources Data-Base*, ed. J. Flood and M. Tavoni, Ferrara, Istituto di Studi Rinascimentali, 1990, xiv + 316 pp. (first print-out 1987, second 1988). *Crisi e rinnovamenti nell'autunno del Rinascimento a Venezia*, ed. V. Branca and C. Ossola, F, Olschki, vii + 516 pp. Christian Bec *et al.*, *L'Italie de la Renaissance. Un monde en mutation, 1378–1494*, Paris, Fayard, 1990, 398 pp. For a reassessment of late 19th-c. historiography see: Felix Gilbert, *History, Politics or Culture. Reflections on Ranke and Burckhardt*, Princeton U.P., 1990, 109 pp.; *Renaissance und Renaissancismus von Jacob Burckhardt bis Thomas Mann*, ed. A. Buck, Tübingen, Niemeyer, 1990, 103 pp., comprises the seven papers read to a 1989 Villa Vigoni conference on the reception of the Italian Renaissance in the second half of the 19th c. and the first half of the 20th c. *Le Corps à la*

454   *Italian Studies*

Renaissance, ed. J. Céard, M.-M. Fontaine, J.-C. Margolin, Paris, Aux Amateurs de Livres, 502 pp. Manfredi Piccolomini, *The Brutus Revival: Parricide and Tyrannicide during the Renaissance*, Carbondale, S. Illinois U.P., xiv + 142 pp. *Art and Politics in Late Medieval and Early Renaissance Italy, 1250–1500*, ed. C. M. Rosenberg, Notre Dame U.P., 1990, 320 pp. John R. Hale, *Artists and Warfare in the Renaissance*, New Haven, Yale U.P., 1990, ix + 278 pp. Peter Thornton, *The Italian Renaissance Interior 1400–1600*, London, Weidenfeld and Nicolson, 407 pp. V. Shrimplin-Evangelidis, 'Sun-symbolism and cosmology in Michelangelo's Last Judgement', *SCJ*, 21, 1990:607–43, is a rather unconvincing interpretation of M.'s Last Judgement, bringing together the Catholic reformation, Neoplatonic symbolism, and Copernican heliocentricity. J. Dundas, 'The *Paragone* and the art of Michelangelo', *ib.*, 21, 1990:87–92, analyses M.'s conversations with Francisco de Hollanda concerning *disegno*, poetry, and the imitation of nature. P. Emison, '*Grazia*', *RenS*, 5:427–60, discusses the concept of *grazia* in the visual arts, and particularly in Raphael, and sees it as an analogue of divine power. *Du Pô à la Garonne: recherches sur les échanges culturels entre l'Italie et la France à la Renaissance*, ed. J. Cubelier de Beynac and M. Simonin, Agen, Centro Matteo Bandello, 1990, 441 pp. Paul Oskar Kristeller, *Renaissance Thought and the Arts: Collected Essays. An Expanded Edition with a New Afterword*, Princeton U.P., 1990, xiv + 266 pp. Ernesto Travi, *Lingua e vita tra Quattrocento e Cinquecento*, Mi, Vita e Pensiero, 1990, 173 pp. Mario Sanfilippo, *Dentro il medioevo: il 'lungo' tardo medioevo dell'Italia comunale e signorile*, F, La Nuova Italia, 1990, vi + 224 pp. The question of the family is explored by: F. Furlan, 'Pour une histoire de la famille et de l'amour à l'époque de l'humanisme', *REI*, 36, 1990:89–104, who makes a case for expanding the sources as currently used and discusses the difficulties facing a new evaluation of the family; Philip Gavitt, *Charity and Children in Renaissance Florence. The Ospedale degli Innocenti 1410–1536*, Ann Arbor, Michigan U.P., 1990, 330 pp., chronicles the concerns and ambivalence of parents who abandoned children and demonstrates how hospitals deliberately duplicated the structure and values of the Florentine family within the hospital walls. Starting, by way of illustration, with Bradamante's admiring of the wall-paintings in the Rocca di Tristano, which show that Ariosto saw both poetry and painting as having the same, rhetorical, nature, Clark Hulse, *The Rule of Art. Literature and Painting in the Renaissance*, Chicago U.P., 1990, xv + 215 pp., proposes an 'archaeology of artistic knowledge' which reveals how visual knowledge is defined, how it is related to other forms of knowledge, especially poetic knowledge, and how, in Renaissance Italy, thanks in particular to L. B. Alberti, to the humanist circle of Raphael, to Gianfrancesco Pico della Mirandola, and to Ludovico Dolce, artistic history comes, for the first time, to stand independent of the schemes of natural or political history. Drawing on an anthropological study of the Indian caste system, J. Lecointe, 'Structures hiérarchiques et théorie critique à la Renaissance', *BHR*, 52, 1990:529–60, traces the stages by which the traditional 'pensée critique hiérarchisante', which postulates a totalitarian view of the world and only defines individuality by default, is slowly eroded during the Renaissance: from Boccaccio, for whom the divinely inspired man-of-letters, in conflict with the world and his father, is outside the hierarchical order, through Ficino, who redefines genius in terms of melancholy and individuality, to Poliziano, who stresses the specificity of geniuses at the expense of the universality of genius, and the importance of spontaneity, improvisation, and subjectivity. Bernard F. Scholz *et al.*, *The European Emblem*, Leiden, Brill, 1990, viii + 190 pp. Mauda Bregoli-Russo, *L'impresa come ritratto del Rinascimento*, Na, Loffredo, 1990, 272 pp., on imprints, devices, and emblematic literature. Nancy G. Siraisi, *Medieval and Early Renaissance Medicine. An Introduction to Knowledge and Practice*, Chicago U.P., 1990, xiv + 250 pp. *Medicine at the Courts of Europe, 1500–1837*, ed. V. Nutton, London, Routledge, 1990, x + 301 pp., has an essay by R. Palmer, 'Medicine at the papal court in the sixteenth century' (49–78).

PRINTING AND PUBLISHING. Martin J. C. Lowry, *Nicholas Jensen and the Rise of Venetian Publishing in Renaissance Europe*, Oxford, Blackwell, 1990, 300 pp., the most important book in this section, includes a valuable analysis of the length of print-runs and the price of books, though the conclusions about the actual number of works commissioned and financed by private patrons are debatable. Fernanda Ascarelli and Marco Menato, *La tipografia del '500 in Italia*, F, Olschki, 1989, 497 pp. + 65 pls, is a list of over 1200 printers and editors in 130 centres set out in chronological order with biographical details and most important editors' and printers' marks. *Les commentaires et la naissance de la critique littéraire: France/Italie (XIVe–XVIe siècles)*, ed. G. Mathieu-Castellani and M. Plaisance, Paris, Aux Amateurs de Livres, 1990, 272 pp. A. Pallotta, 'Venetian printers and Spanish literature in 16th-c. Italy', *CL*, 43:20–39, assesses the reception of Spanish culture by looking at what Spanish texts publishers published and why. S. Giombi, 'Le biblioteche di ecclesiastici nel Cinquecento italiano. Rassegna di studi recenti e prospettive di lettura', *LItal*, 43:291–307, after a survey of studies on the libraries of ecclesiastics discusses the library of Marcello Cervini, to conclude by offering a methodology for a new survey taking into account the changing historical and religious circumstances that influenced the formation of such libraries. R. Bianchi, 'Per la biblioteca di Angelo Colocci', *Rinascimento*, 30, 1990:271–82, finds the library, now in the

Biblioteca Apostolica Vaticana, of the early 16th-c. Roman humanist to reveal an interest in literary history, archaeology, and epigraphy. D. Nebbiai-Dalla Guarda, 'Les livres et les amis de Gerolamo Molin (1450–1458)', *La Bibliofilia*, 93:117–75, assesses the activity and cultural milieu of this Venetian printer, using the *Alphabetum Librorum* in the archives of the Procuratori di S. Marco. Stefano Pillinini, *Bernardino Stagnino. Un editore a Venezia tra Quattrocento e Cinquecento*, Ro, Jouvence, 1989, 128 pp., a bibliographical analysis, places Stagnino (Bernardino Giolito de' Ferrari) in the context of university publishing in the 15th c. and gives a catalogue of editions. C. Fahy, 'Tecniche di stampa cinquecentesche', *EL*, 15.1, 1990:3–16. A. Contò, 'Alle origini della tipografia friulana del Cinquecento', *EL*, 15.2, 49–66. L. Perini, 'La stampa in Italia nel '500: Firenze e la Toscana', *ib.*, 17–48. Gianni Barachetti and Carmen Palamini, 'La stampa a Bergamo nel Cinquecento', *Bergomum*, 84.4, 1989, is a catalogue of holdings at the Biblioteca Civica Angelo Mai and other Bergamo libraries. Anna Modigliani, *Tipografi a Roma prima della stampa. Due società per fare libri con le forme (1466–1470)*, Ro, Roma nel Rinascimento, 1989, 104 pp., the third volume of a series, concentrates on the workshop of Ulrich Han. Z. Baruchson, 'Money and culture. Financing sources and methods in the Hebrew printing shops in Cinquecento Italy', *La Bibliofilia*, 92, 1990:23–39, considers the great expansion of Jewish printing in the 16th c. and the realities of large-scale investment, risk-taking, and money-making deals that made this possible. E. Barbieri, 'Le edizioni illustrate della Bibbia volgare (1490–1517): appunti sulle immagini di traduttori', *ib.*, 1–21, deals with the iconography of the image of the translator: D. Fattori, 'Per la storia della tipografia veronese: Giovanni da Verona', *ib.*, 269–81. Leila Avrin, *Scribes, Script and Books: The Book Arts from Antiquity to the Renaissance*, Chicago, American Library Association, 1991, 388 pp. + 30 pls. Mahmoud Salem Elsheikh, *Medicina e farmacologia nei manoscritti della Biblioteca Riccardiana di Firenze*, Manziana, Vecchiarelli, 1990, 173 pp. Stanley Morison, *Early Italian Writing-Books: Renaissance–Baroque*, Verona, 1990, 218 pp. Paolo Trovato, *Con ogni diligenza corretti: la stampa e le revisioni editoriali dei testi letterari italiani, 1470–1570*, Bo, Il Mulino, 410 pp., considers early printing and editing of literary texts. C. Tidoli, 'Stampa a corte nella Firenze del tardo Cinquecento: Giorgio Marescotti', *NRS*, 20, 1990:605–31. M. worked all his life in the workshop of the official printer to the Grand Duke, yet failed in his attempts to be nominated ducal printer. U. Rozzo, 'Gli *Hecatommithi* all'Indice', *La Bibliofilia*, 93:21–51, reviews the career of Giovan Battista Giraldi Cinthio and the reasons why he appeared in the lists of prohibited books. Id., 'In margine agli *Indici dei libri proibiti* italiani del 1549 e 1554', *ib.*, 92, 1990:311–21, is an overdue review article commenting on the critical stance taken in J. M. De Bujanda and P. F. Grendler, *Index de Venise 1549. Venise et Milan 1554*, Sherbrooke, Éditions de l'Université–Geneva, Droz, 1987. L. Balsamo, 'Venezia e l'attività di Antonio Possevino (1553–1606)', *ib.*, 43:53–92. Mario Santoro, **Il libro a stampa. I primordi*, Na, Liguori, 1990, xiv + 410 pp.

BIBLIOGRAPHY. J. E. Everson, 'A new edition of *Il Mambriano* of Francesco Cieco da Ferrara: the Venice edition of 1512 now in the Beinecke Library', *PBSA*, 84, 1990:168–78, has a full bibliographical description of the 1512 edition, identifies the printer as Giovanni Tachuino da Trin and sets out a new canon of editions. A.-M. van Passen, 'Lodovico Guicciardini, *L'Hore di Ricreatione*. Bibliografia delle edizioni', *La Bibliofilia*, 92, 1990:145–214. **La Biblioteca del Convento dell'Osservanza di Siena*, ed. G. Rossi, Siena, 141 pp. Paul Oskar Kristeller, *Iter Italicum*, v: *Alia Itinera III and Italy III. Sweden to Yugoslavia, Utopia, Supplement to Italy (A–F)*, Leiden, Brill, 1990, xxii + 641 pp. Francesco Barbaro, **Epistolario*, ed. C. Griggio, vol. 1: *La tradizione manoscritta e a stampa*, F, Olschki, viii + 412 pp. Alan Bullock, **Il Fondo Tordi della Biblioteca Nazionale di Firenze. Catalogo delle appendici*, F, Olschki, 1991, 180 pp. *Carteggio universale di Cosimo I de' Medici, Archivio di Stato di Firenze. Inventario V (1551–1553): Mediceo del Principato, filze 404–415*, ed. C. Giabblanco and D. Toccafondi, *Inventario IX (1556–1559), Mediceo del Principato, filze 461–475*, ed. M. Morviducci, F, Giunta Regionale Toscana, 1990, 527 and 526 pp. Craig Kallendorf, **A Bibliography of Venetian Editions of Virgil, 1470–1599*, F, Olschki, 1991, 201 pp. **I Codici Ashburnhamiani della Biblioteca Medicea Laurenziana di Firenze*, I: *Indici*, ed. R. Pintaudi and A. R. Fantoni, Ro, Libreria dello Stato, 404 pp. Marco Paoli, **Le edizioni del Quattrocento in una raccolta toscana: gli incunaboli della Biblioteca Statale di Lucca. Catalogo descrittivo*, I: A–L, Lucca, Pacini Fazzi, 1990, 425 pp.

2. HUMANISM

The Impact of Humanism on Western Europe, ed. A. Goodman and A. MacKay, London, Longman, 1990, xv + 292 pp., is a survey of the present position on humanism, including chapters by P. Burke on the spread (domestication) of Italian humanism, P. Matheson on humanism and Reform movements (Catholic, Lutheran, and Reformation renewals of Church piety, praxis, and doctrine, which are inconceivable without the impact of humanist tools, skills, and perspectives), R. Tuck on humanism and political thought, the Renaissance marking 'the emancipation of the Romans from their Greek tutelage' and Machiavelli standing as an example of 'the dangers, from a Christian point of view, of over-faithful

Ciceronianism', and S. Anglo on humanism and other Court arts, the Court altering the status of the fine arts to the point where humanism was 'itself as much a casualty of the change as was chivalry'; A. Grafton, on humanism, magic, and science, explores the influence of humanists on the social impact and responsibility of science; G. Holmes, on humanism in Italy, reviews the achievements of Italian humanist writers and artists; the volume includes humanism in the Low Countries, the Iberian Peninsula, and England. Three collections deal with the relationship between culture and science. *New Perspectives on Renaissance Thought. Essays in the History of Science, Education and Philosophy in Memory of Charles B. Schmitt*, ed. J. Henry and S. Hutton, London, Duckworth, 1990, 324 pp., includes M. J. B. Allen, 'Marsilio Ficino, Hermes Trismegistus and the Corpus Hermeticum' (38–47); L. Panizza, 'Italian humanists and Boethius: was philosophy for or against poetry?' (48–67); N. G. Siraisi, 'Medicine, physiology and anatomy in early sixteenth-century critiques of the arts and sciences' (214–29); V. Nutton, 'Medicine, diplomacy and finance: the prefaces to a Hippocratic commentary of 1541' (239–43). In *Science, Culture and Popular Belief in Renaissance Europe*, ed. S. Pumfrey, P. L. Rossi, M. P. Slawinski, Manchester U.P., 331 pp., of Italian relevance are M. P. Slawinski, 'Rhetoric and science/rhetoric of science/rhetoric as science' (71–99), and P. L. Rossi, 'Society, culture and the dissemination of learning' (143–75). In *Reappraisals of the Scientific Revolution*, ed. D. C. Lindberg and R. S. Westman, CUP, 1990, 529 pp., of particular interest is W. Eamon, 'From the secrets of nature to public knowledge' (333–66). Francesco Tateo, **I miti della storiografia umanistica*, Ro, Bulzoni, 1990, xix + 300 pp. R. Witt, 'The origins of Italian humanism: Padua and Florence', *Centennial Review*, 34, 1990:92–108. Riccardo Fubini, *Umanesimo e secolarizzazzione da Petrarca a Valla,* Ro, Bulzoni, 1990, xxi + 412 pp. On language and rhetoric the most important contribution is Dilwyn Knox, *Ironia: Medieval and Renaissance Ideas on Irony*, Leiden, Brill, 1989, xviii + 238 pp., the first part of which examines the various meanings of the term from classical times to 1600, while the second is concerned with the Renaissance recovery of *ironia socratica* and how this was regarded as urbane and witty. The one defect is a tendency to take as a fixed theory what were in fact a number of diverse ideas. S. I. Camporeale, 'Lorenzo Valla: the transcending of philosophy through rhetoric', *Renaissance Notes*, 30, 1990:269–84. A. Wesseling, 'Poliziano and ancient rhetoric: theory and practice', *Rinascimento*, 30, 1990:175–90, an investigation into rhetorical theory as seen in the *Panepistemon*, traces P.'s debt to Martianus Capella's textbook on the liberal arts. John D. Lyons, *Exemplum: The Rhetoric of Example in Early Modern France and Italy,*

Princeton U.P., 1989, xiii + 317 pp., has a chapter on Machiavelli's treatment of exemplary material, which explores his emphasis on distance in time, on violent examples, and his basic ambivalence as to the efficacy of relying on examples. D. D. Martin, 'The *Via Moderna*, humanism and the hermeneutics of late medieval monastic life', *JHI*, 51, 1990:179–97, examines the rhetorical and metaphysical theology of the Carthusians in their struggle to renew the Church and theology in the 15th c. J. M. McManamon, 'Marketing a Medici regime: the funeral oration of Marcello Virgilio Adriani for Giuliano de' Medici (1516)', *RQ*, 44:1–41, discusses the Latin eulogy delivered by A., First Chancellor of Florence, as an example of how epideictic rhetoric was used to impart the political message that Florence needed an aristocratic regime under Medici leadership. The text of the oration is included. L. Gualdo Rosa, 'Chi ha paura della filologia classica? In margine ad un recente articolo di Riccardo Fubini', *ASI*, 148, 1990:933–41, is a reply to 'L'umanista: ritorno di un paradigma? Saggio per un profilo storico da Petrarca ad Erasmo', *ASI*, 147, 1989:435–508. J. Monfasani, 'In praise of Ognibene and blame of Guarino: Andronicus Contoblacas's invective against Niccolò Botano and the citizens of Brescia', *BHR*, 52, 1990:309–21, is a study of the *Dialogus invectus*, where C. accuses G. of abolishing the three traditional oratorial *genera dicta* of the low, middle, and high styles and replacing them with a scheme of poetic genres. An appendix contains the text of the dialogue. I. Vignali, 'La lingua di Jacopo Caviceo nel *Peregino*', *SPCT*, 40, 1990:69–147, is a detailed morphological analysis of C.'s work. E. Niccolini, 'Ventiquattro lettere di Francesco Vettori', *GSLI*, 167, 1990:546–89, gives the text of letters from the Florentine Archivio di Stato and Biblioteca Nazionale, written between 1513 and 1531 during V.'s stay in Rome after the fall of Soderini to the end of the siege of Florence. B. Vickers, 'Leisure and idleness in the Renaissance: the ambivalence of *otium*', *RenS*, 4, 1990:1–37 and 107–54. G. Ianziti, 'Storiografia e contemporaneità. A proposito del *Rerum suo tempore gestarum commentarius* di Leonardo Bruni', *Rinascimento*, 30, 1990:3–28, deals with B.'s attempt (1440–41) to discuss his own historical period, missing from the *Historia florentini populi*. F. Bacchelli, 'Palingenio e Postel', *ib.*, 309–15. In *The Transmission of Culture in Early Modern Europe*, ed. A. Grafton and A. Blair, UPP, 1990, vii + 326 pp., an interesting collection of essays ranging from the 15th c. to the 19th c., of particular interest are A. Grafton on Annius of Viterbo and antiquities and L. Jardine on the political nature of Erasmus's stated indebtedness to other humanists. Anthony Grafton, *Forgers and Critics: Creativity and Duplicity in Western Scholarship*, Princeton U.P., 1990, x + 157 pp. Id., *Defenders of the Text: The Traditions of Scholarship in an Age of Science, 1450–1800*, Cambridge,

Mass., Harvard U.P., 330 pp. *Leonardo Bruni cancelliere della Repubblica di Firenze*, ed. P. Viti, F, Olschki, 1990, xvi + 424 pp. *Knowledge, Goodness and Power: The Debate over Nobility among Quattrocento Humanists*, ed. A. Rabil Jr, MRTS, comprises translations of 13 works on nobility. *Martino Filetico umanista e maestro di vita*, ed. B. Valeri and M. T. Valeri, Casamari, 1990, 235 pp. *Homo sapiens, Homo humanus*, ed. G. Tarugi, F, Olschki, 1990, vol. 1, *La cultura italiana tra il passato ed il presente in un disegno di pace universale* and *La pienezza del significato 'homo sapiens' e la necessaria ricerca del significato 'homo humanus'*, lii + 248 pp., includes E. Coturri, 'L'idea della "Libertas Italiae" e quella della "Civitatis libertas" in Coluccio Salutati ed in alcuni suoi contemporanei toscani' (17–23); Id., 'Coluccio Salutati: la sua concezione della "Civitatis libertas" e il *De Tyranno*' (157–66); L. Valcke, '"Homo contemplator": il doppio distacco dell'umanesimo pichiano' (233–45); R. Belladonna, 'Aonio Paleario e Bartolomeo Carli Piccolomini: aspetti e momenti dell'evangelismo italiano del primo Cinquecento' (133–42). Vol. 2, *Letteratura, arte e scienza nella seconda metà del Quattrocento*, and *Individuo e società nei secoli XV e XVI*, 473 pp., contains 34 essays on topics that concern Cosimo and Lorenzo de' Medici, Poliziano, Pico della Mirandola, Ariosto, Machiavelli, Leonardo Bruni. A. Brown, 'Hans Baron's Renaissance', *HJ*, 33, 1990:441–48, a review of B.'s *In Search of Florentine Civic Humanism*. D. Robin, *Filelfo in Milan. Writings 1451–1477*, Princeton U.P., 397 pp., a fascinating study, reveals Filelfo as a misfit at court who was prone to criticizing his patrons. L. d'Ascia, 'Galeazzo Flavio Capello traduttore di Erasmo', *LItal*, 42, 1990:66–88, is an analysis of the *Anthropologia* and the importance of E. for the literary taste behind its composition. M. Billanovich, 'Intorno alla *Iubilatio* di Felice Feliciano', *IMU*, 22, 1989:351–58, centres on the description of a journey made in the company of Mantegna and others along the western shores of Lake Garda in search of classical inscriptions. D. Zancani, 'L'*apparere* di Francesco Sforza in una disputa tra il dottore e il milite', *Schede umanistiche*, 1991, no. 2:5–23, discusses an early contribution to the famous debate, which, it is claimed, is significant because it contains the views of an actual prince on the matter. The lesser-known activities of Sebastiano Fausto da Longiano, who also wrote on arms and letters and edited Petrarch, are recorded in G. Frasso, 'Sebastiano Fausto editore e volgarizzatore di storici medioevali e umanistici', *Aevum*, 64, 1990:363–75. Claude V. Palisca, *Humanism in Renaissance Musical Thought*, New Haven, Yale U.P., 1990, 471 pp.

INDIVIDUAL CENTRES. *City and Countryside in Late Medieval and Renaissance Italy: Essays presented to Philip Jones*, ed. T. Dean and C. Wickham, London, Hambledon, 1990, xv + 197 pp. Christiane

Klapisch-Zuber, *La Maison et le Nom: stratégies et rituels dans l'Italie de la Renaissance*, Paris, EHESS Press, 1990, 388 pp. Fabio Benzi, *Sisto IV Renovator Urbis: architettura a Roma 1471–1484*, Ro, Officina, 1990, 318 pp. Giorgio Simoncini, *'Roma Restaurata'. Rinnovamento urbano al tempo di Sisto V*, F, Olschki, 1990, 240 pp. + 24 pls. Charles Burroughs, *From Signs to Design: Environmental Process and Reform in Early Renaissance Rome*, Cambridge, Mass., MIT Press, 1990, xii + 394 pp. Ilaria Ciseri, *L'ingresso trionfale di Leone X in Firenze nel 1515*, F, Olschki, 1990, vii + 330 pp. Paula C. Clarke, *The Soderini and the Medici: Power and Patronage in Fifteenth-Century Florence*, Oxford, Clarendon, 304 pp. For Tuscany see the comprehensive review article by A. Molho, 'Recent works on the history of Tuscany: fifteenth to eighteenth centuries', *Journal of Modern History*, 62, 1990:57–77. *1598: A Year of Pageantry in Late Renaissance Ferrara*, ed. Bonner Mitchell, MRTS, 1990, xiv + 162 pp.., illustrates the end of nearly four centuries of Este rule in 1598 when the city was taken over by the papacy. This change involved six grand entries, the printed descriptions of which are the subject of this volume. It investigates the nature and purpose of these accounts (Livrets) and includes a detailed bibliography of all contemporary Livrets and other sources involving pageantry at Ferrara in 1598. Facsimiles of five representative Livrets are included. In M. Feldman, 'The Academy of Domenico Venier, music's literary muse in mid-Cinquecento Venice', *RQ*, 44:476–512, the transference of literary ideals to music and the treatment of secular genres give an insight into the informal salons of Venice. The Court continues to receive attention. E. S. Welch, 'The image of a fifteenth-century court: secular frescoes for the Castello di Porta Giovia, Milan', *JWCI*, 53, 1990:163–84, uses the written programmes for two fresco cycles, and the accompanying estimate of the cost, to assess the intentions and ambitions of the patron, Galeazzo Maria Sforza. *Le Muse e il Principe: arte di corte nel Rinascimento padano*, ed. A. Mottola Molfino and M. Natale, 2 vols, Modena, Panini, 390 + 516 pp. *La corte a Ferrara e il suo mecenatismo 1441–1598. The Court of Ferrara and its Patronage*, ed. M. Pade, L. Waage Petersen, D. Quarta, Copenhagen, Museum Tusculanum–Ferrara, Panini, 1990, 36 pp. Two works on iconography deal with texts and programmes: Luciano Cheles, *Lo studiolo di Urbino. Iconografia di un microcosmo principesco*, Modena, Panini, 120 pp., and J. Kliemann, 'Programme, Inschriften und Texte zu Bildern. Einige Bemerkungen zur Praxis in der profanen Wandermalerei des Cinquecento', in *Acta* (Reisensburg), 79–95. *Guglielmo Ebreo da Pesaro e la danza nelle corti italiane del XV secolo*, ed. M. Padovan, Pisa, Pacini, 1990, 343 pp. Alvise Zorzi, *La vita quotidiana a Venezia nel secolo di Tiziano*, Mi, Rizzoli, 1990, vi + 434 pp. Pier Giovanni Fabbri, *Cesena tra Quattro e*

Cinquecento: dai Malatesta a Valentino a Giulio II. La città, le vicende, le fonti, Ravenna, Longo, 1990, 188 pp. C. Bitossi, **Il Governo dei Magnifici: patriziato e politica a Genova fra Cinque e Seicento*, Genoa, ECIG, 1990, 329 pp. V. A. Melchiorre, **Il Ducato Sforzesco di Bari*, Bari, Adda, 1990, 201 pp. Alan Ryder, **Alfonso the Magnanimous, King of Aragon, Naples, and Sicily, 1396–1458*, Oxford, Clarendon, 1990, 468 pp. Lorenzo Fabbri, **Alleanza matrimoniale e patriziato nella Firenze del Quattrocento. Studio sulla famiglia Strozzi*, F, Olschki, xvii + 240 pp. More and more is coming to light about the indigenous features of humanism in the south of Italy. Lucia Miele, *Modelli e ruoli sociali nei 'Memoriali' di Diomede Carafa*, Na, Federico & Ardia, 1989, 155 pp., gives a reading of the *Memoriali* (written 1460s–70s) from the perspective of the emblematic figures of Neapolitan society at the time: the Prince (who must lead by his example, show *mutua caritas*, generosity, justice, and concern himself with money, 'molla di ogni rapporto politico e sociale', and through whose figure C. is said to formulate a practical concept of absolute monarchy), the Courtier (not perfect, but successful: who must show respect and obedience), the Man of Arms (the captain must show foresight and prudence, the soldier obedience, courage, and strength, the army be determined and prepared — money being paramount, firearms important), the Lady (whose figure, as woman and wife, is compared to L. B. Alberti's and F. Barbaro's ideal woman), and the Antagonists (destiny, spies, and detractors). D. Defilippis, 'Per Belisario Acquaviva Conte di Conversano e Duca di Nardò', *Studi di storia pugliese in memoria di Maria Marangelli*, Brindisi, Schena, 1990, pp. 163–82, provides an introduction to the life and works of A., 'uomo d'arme' and 'letterato' (author of four treatises on the ideal prince published at Naples in 1519 and an exposition of the *Pater Noster*, Naples, 1522), whose position as one of the leading figures of southern/feudal humanism is now fully recognized. On Acquaviva's friend and protégé, Antonio De Ferrariis Galateo, see Antonio Iurilli, **L'opera di Antonio Galateo nella tradizione manoscritta. Catalogo*, Na, Istituto Studi Rinascimento Meridionale, 1990, 250 pp. For the religious side of southern humanism, see M. A. Mastronardi, 'Persuasione e mimesi. Modelli retorici e prassi omiletica nella predicazione di Roberto Caracciolo', *Lares*, 56, 1990:59–81, studying the style, in particular the rhetorical devices, used by C. in his *Quaresimale volgare*, the first collection of vernacular sermons ever written (second half 15th c.), and Id., 'Tradizione retorica e 'actio' giullaresca in un sermone semidrammatico del Quattrocento', *Lares*, 56, 1990:587–602, analysing one of his sermons and showing how it is faithful to Franciscan models, using techniques of the 'giullari' and the 'letteratura dei cantari'. *EL*, 16.2–3, is entirely dedicated to Mario Santoro and therefore a must for anyone interested in southern humanism.

PHILOSOPHY AND HERMETICISM. L. Bianchi, 'Un commento umanistico ad Aristotele. L'*Espositio super libros Ethicorum* di Donato Acciaiuoli', *Rinascimento*, 30, 1990:29–55, charts the success and influence of A.'s work, attested by numerous MS copies and expensive folio editions, and also traces the sources in Albertus Magnus, Averroes, Duns Scotus, Walter Burley. Id., '*Interpretes Aristotelis*. Una cinquecentesca "bibliografia aristotelica"', *RSF*, 47, 1990:303–25, publishes the text, with notes and introduction, of a late 16th-c. bibliography of Aristotle's works and their commentators to illustrate the continuity of the Aristotelian tradition and to show how Renaissance Aristotelianism, like its medieval predecessor, was an international phenomenon. A. L. Puliafito, 'Filosofia aristotelica e modi dell'apprendere. Un intervento di Agostino Valier su *Qua ratione versandum sit in Aristotele*', *Rinascimento*, 30, 1990:153–72. A. Ghisalberti, **La filosofia della natura di Bernardino Telesio e le sue fonti*, Cosenza, Busento, 1990, 28 pp. L. Pierozzi and E. Scapparone, 'Il volgarizzamento del *De rerum natura* di Bernardino Telesio a opera di Francesco Martelli', *GCFI*, 69, 1990:160–81. G. Aquilecchia, 'Bruno e la matematica a lui contemporanea. In margine al *De minimo*', *ib.*, 151–59. Id., 'Bruno's mathematical dilemma in his poem *De minimo*', *RenS*, 5:315–26. Id., 'Ramo, Patrizi e Telesio nella prospettiva di Giordano Bruno', *Discorsi*, 9, 1989:27–40. J. Hankins, 'The myth of the Platonic Academy of Florence', *RQ*, 44, 1991:429–75, reassesses the evidence for the existence and activities of this 'academy', to conclude that Ficino, rather than founding an institution, should be seen as a private tutor who taught philosophy as well as other subjects. Id., 'Cosimo de' Medici and the "Platonic Academy"', *JWCI*, 53, 1990:144–62, refutes the idea that Ficino implied that C. founded an institution called either the Florentine, Platonic, or Careggian Academy. Id., *Plato in the Italian Renaissance*, 2 vols, Leiden, Brill, 1990, xxxi + 847 pp., is a brilliant study with exemplary use of primary and secondary sources. Marsilio Ficino, *Lettere*, 1: *Epistolarum familiarum liber I*, ed. S. Gentile, F, Olschki, 1990, ccc + 324 pp., is an important work with a full critical apparatus. S. Gentile, 'Sulle prime traduzioni dal greco di Marsilio Ficino', *Rinascimento*, 30, 1990:57–104, points out F.'s early difficulty with Greek and the resulting poor translations which he was anxious not to have circulated, and also examines the attractions of magical/mystical texts for the young philosopher. Marsilio Ficino, *De Vita*, ed. A. Biodo and G. Pisani, Pordenone, Biblioteca dell'Immagine, xxxv + 501 pp., is the first complete Italian translation, in parallel with the Latin text. *I Guicciardini e le scienze occulte. L'oroscopo di Francesco Guicciardini. Lettere di alchimia, astrologia e cabala a Luigi Guicciardini*, ed. R. Castagnola, F, Olschki, 1990, vii + 397 pp. F. L. Borchardt, 'The *magus* as Renaissance man', *SCJ*, 21, 1990:57–76, puts forward the view that the individuals involved in European magic formed a tight network and that they eventually expressed a disappointment in the efficacy of this magic. The language of magic is shown to have been esoteric and essentially elitist. Paola Zambelli, **L'ambigua natura della magia: filosofi, streghe, riti nel Rinascimento*, Mi, Il Saggiatore, xvii + 345 pp. C. Vasoli, 'La storia della filosofia del Rinascimento: verso la storia della cultura', *RPLit*, 13, 1990:279–91. **Il dialogo filosofico nel Cinquecento europeo*, ed. D. Bigalli, G. Canziani, Mi, Angeli, 1990, 255 pp. Paolo Getrevi, *Le scritture del volto: fisiognomica e modelli culturali dal Medioevo ad oggi*, Mi, Angeli, 251 pp., sheds light on physiognomy in the works of Gaurico, Lomazzo, and Della Porta. G. B. Della Porta, *Metoposcopia, ed. G. Aquilecchia, Na, Ist. Suor Orsola Benincasa, 1990, xvi + 154 pp. G. Aquilecchia, '*In facie prudentis relucet sapientia*. Appunti sulla letteratura metoposcopica tra Cinque e Seicento', in *G. B. Della Porta nell'Europa del suo tempo*, Na, Guida, 1990, pp. 199–228.

RELIGIOUS THOUGHT AND THE CHURCH. Peter Partner, *The Pope's Men: The Papal Civil Service in the Renaissance*, Oxford, Clarendon, 1990, xii + 276 pp., is without doubt the most important study of papal administration to date. It deals with the recruitment, rewards, attitudes, and origins of papal servants, and provides an excellent analysis of the way early modern governments used bureaucracy, and the political price paid to the oligarchies from which these governments recruited their senior officials. **Gli Sforza, la chiesa lombarda, la Corte di Roma: strutture e pratiche beneficiarie nel Ducato di Milano, 1450–1535*, ed. G. Chittolini, Na, Liguori, xxi + 398 pp. Ivan Cloulas, **Jules II: le pape terrible*, Paris, Fayard, 1989, 392 pp. A. Manfredi, 'Primo umanesimo e teologi antichi. Dalla grande Chartreuse alla Biblioteca Papale', *IMU*, 32, 1989:155–203, concerns collecting works of the Church Fathers by Ambrogio Traversari, Niccolò Niccolì, and Tommaso Parentucelli (Nicholas V). *Christianity and the Renaissance: Image and Religious Imagination in the Quattrocento*, ed. T. Verdon, J. Henderson, Syracuse U.P., 1990, xix + 634 pp., is a handsome book full of fascinating information, consisting of 24 chapters by different authors divided into four sections: the monastic world; the religious world of the laity, mainly confraternities; the world of the Christian humanist; a 'coda on method'. It deals mainly with Florence, mostly with the 15th c. or earlier, and largely with imagery. It will certainly put paid to any notion that the Renaissance was pagan, and it successfully debunks Burckhardt's view, as it sets out to do, that Renaissance Christianity was 'an affair of the individual and of his personal feeling', by illustrating its social dimension. It shows how sometimes religion and humanism worked hand in hand, sometimes against each other and sometimes in spite of each other. The great continuity in religious beliefs and practices from the Middle Ages to the Renaissance should lead us, once again, to question the very concept of 'Renaissance' and, to a lesser extent, of 'humanism'. Of particular relevance to students of literature are three articles on Savonarola: by D. R. Lesnick on his preaching, which emerged naturally from a 'long standing marriage of Dominicanism and civicism' (208–25); by M. B. Hall on his lack of preaching style (nevertheless much influenced by humanism) paralleled by a similar absence of style in the art executed under his influence (493–522); by E. Garin on his influence on Gian Francesco Pico della Mirandola, whose *Examen* (1520) is one of the most important philosophical works of the century, defending faith against every prevarication of reason, thanks to the strength of its critical force and its radical skepsis (523–32). M. M. Bullard (467–92) charts the changing relationship between Marsilio Ficino and the Medici, suggesting that the classical models chosen by humanists were not unrelated to the inner requirements of their relationships with their patrons; R. F. E. Weisman (250–71) highlights similarities between confraternities and intellectual sodalities, which were born of the same impulse to get organized into groups and for whom oratory was of paramount importance, and shows how new meanings were infused into traditional beliefs by humanist preachers familiar with Platonic texts; S. Camporeale (445–66) sketches the shift in the writings of the Dominican friar and humanist G. Caroli from pessimism (crisis of monasticism, decline in the quality of civic life) to optimism (privilege of monastic life, reconciliation to the legitimacy of the Medicean oligarchy). E. Ferri, *Luigi Gonzaga: 1568–1591*, T, Paoline, 253 pp. Francesco C. Cesareo, *Humanism and Catholic Reform: The Life and Work of Gregorio Cortese (1483–1548)*, NY, Lang, 1990, xviii + 203 pp. Lowell Gallagher, *Medusa's Gaze: Casuistry and Conscience in the Renaissance*, Stanford U.P., i + 331 pp. Ullrich Langer, *Divine and Poetic Freedom in the Renaissance: Nominalist Theology and Literature in France and Italy*, Princeton U.P., 1990, ix + 215 pp. I. Polverini Fosi, 'Pietà, devozione e politica: due confraternite fiorentine nella Roma del Rinascimento', *ASI*, 149: 119–61, concerns the birth, early years, and significance for the Florentine *nazione* of the Confraternita di S. Giovanni dei Fiorentini and the Confraternita di S. Giovanni Decollato. Ludovica

Sebregondi, *Tre confraternite fiorentine: Santa Maria della Pietà, detta Buca di San Girolamo, San Filippo Benizi, San Francesco Poverino*, F, Salimbeni, xiv + 214 pp. L. Zanette, 'Tre predicatori per la peste 1575–1577', *LItal*, 42, 1990:431–59, traces the attitudes of Carlo Borromeo and Gabriele Paleotti to the sermons of the Franciscan theologian (Girolamo) Francesco Panigarola. In J. Weinberg, 'The voice of God: Jewish and Christian responses to the Ferrara earthquake of November 1570', *ISt*, 46:69–81, the tracts, letters, official reports written on the earthquake are used to explore the cultural concerns of the time. The impact of prophecy is attested by Marjorie Reeves, *Prophetic Rome in the High Renaissance Period*, Oxford, Clarendon, 440 pp.; *Il profetismo gioachimita tra Quattrocento e Cinquecento*, ed. G. L. Podestà, Genoa, Marietti, 520 pp.; Francesco D'Elia, *Gioachino da Fiore, un maestro della civiltà europea. Antologia di testi gioachimiti tradotti e commentati*, Soveria Mannelli, Rubbettino, 191 pp. Riccardo Calimani, *Storie di Marrani a Venezia*, Mi, Rusconi, 197 pp. R. Dotta, *Guglielmo Baldessano: storico della Chiesa nell'età della Controriforma*, Carmagnola, Arktos-Oggero, 190 pp. P. Scaramella, *Le Madonne del Purgatorio: iconografia e religione in Campania tra Rinascimento e Controriforma*, Genoa, Marietti, xi + 377 pp. *Bellarmino e la Controriforma*, ed. R. De Maio *et al.*, Sora, Centro Studi 'V. Patriarca', 1990, xxiv + 1016 pp. *Domenico Scandella detto Menocchio: i processi dell'Inquisizione (1583–1599)*, ed. A. Del Col, Pordenone, Biblioteca dell'Immagine, 1990, cxxxii + 260 pp., contains the original text. *Forme e destinazione del messaggio religioso: aspetti della propaganda religiosa nel Cinquecento*, ed. A. Rotondò, F, Olschki, xii + 401 pp. In M. T. Walton and P. J. Walton, 'In defense of the Church Militant: the censorship of the Rashi Commentary in the *Magna Biblia Rabbinica*', *SCJ*, 21, 1990:385–400, censorship of R.'s commentary on the *Pentateuch* is taken as evidence of the Church's fear that Jewish interpretations could give possible support to Protestant teachings. Sergio Pagano, *Il processo di Endimio Calandra e l'Inquisizione a Mantova nel 1567–1568*, Città del Vaticano, Biblioteca Vaticana, xxi + 406 pp.

WOMEN'S STUDIES. The current healthy state of research on women and the place of women in society is attested by a number of studies. Constance Jordan, *Renaissance Feminism: Literary Texts and Political Models*, Ithaca, Cornell U.P., 1990, xi + 320 pp., surveys feminist 'pro-women' argument in a wide variety of Renaissance printed texts in the vernacular: histories, conduct books, treatises on government, letters, popular and courtly dialogues, prose romances, from Italy, France, and England; in the introduction pride of place, besides Scripture, Aristotle, and Erasmus, is given to Boccaccio, Francesco Barbaro, and L. B. Alberti; in 'Women and the natural law', Italian authors discussed include Bruni, Palmieri, Lodovico

Dolce, Trissino, Galeazzo Flavio Capella, Equicola, and especially
Castiglione; in 'Sex and gender', Ortensio Lando, Niccolò Gozze,
Alessandro Piccolomini, G. M. Bruto, Tasso, Ludovico Domenichi,
Guazzo, Speroni, Bernardo Trotto, Ruscelli, Dardano, D. Bruni. The
conclusion is that Renaissance defences of women, while 'successful
in providing the substance of political debate, had no standing at all
as the pretext for a social revolution'. F. Furlan, 'L'idea della donna e
dell'amore nella cultura tardo-medievale e in L. B. Alberti', *Intersezioni*, 10, 1990:211–38, argues that A.'s hostile attitude to women,
which is to be found in all his writings with the exception perhaps of
Della famiglia, is typical of the misogynism of the humanists, but it is to
be seen in the context of A.'s view of the human condition, in which
love is symptomatic of disorder and irrationality. *Refiguring Woman:
Perspectives on Gender and the Italian Renaissance*, ed. M. Migiel and J.
Schicsari, Ithaca, Cornell U.P., viii + 285 pp. J. Murray, 'Angelo
Firenzuola on female sexuality and women's equality', *SCJ*, 20:199–
213, discusses F.'s *Delle bellezze delle donne* (1548), comparing it with
other Renaissance treatises on women and love by Boccaccio,
Castiglione, Ficino, Leone Ebreo, and focusing on F.'s discussion of
lesbian love; exceptional for his time, he appears as unique in
unequivocally asserting the equality of women and men. His work is
completely devoid of the 'double-standard', 'back-handed' praise of
women by Boccaccio and Castiglione, the indifference of Ficino, or
the disdain of Leone Ebreo, and stresses 'the value of sexuality
independent of its reproductive function'. A. J. Schutte, 'Irene di
Spilimbergo: the image of a creative woman in late Renaissance
Italy', *RQ*, 44:42–61, discusses the memorial volume edited by
Dionigi Atanagi, which contained 279 Italian and 102 Latin poems
written by 143 named authors for the female painter who died in 1559
at the age of 21, an early example of a genre which was to become
common for the celebration of women. G. Pozzi, 'Maria tabernacolo',
IMU, 32, 1989:263–326, is a provocative interpretation of the
iconography of the body of Mary as a spiritual concept and as a
tabernacle from which emerged the body of Christ. *Playing with
Gender: A Renaissance Pursuit*, ed. J. R. Brink and M. C. Horowitz,
Baltimore, Illinois U.P., 168 pp., *Rinascimento al femminile*, ed. O.
Niccoli, Bari, Laterza, xxvii + 240 pp.

3. POETRY

NARRATIVE POETRY

GENERAL. Of particular significance is R. Bizzocchi, 'Culture
généalogique dans l'Italie du 16ème siècle', *Annales*, 46:789–805,
according to whom to say that the many unlikely genealogies of the

16th c. (e.g. by Ariosto, Tasso, Pigna, Francesco Sansovino) are patently false, and to wonder therefore how people could believe in them and how it is that they escaped the scrutiny of philologists, is the wrong way of looking at the question, since they were not born 'd'un besoin d'anoblissement, mais de documentation' in a culture which took it for granted ('La culture nobiliaire est une culture du présupposé') that there was a necessary link between nobility and history, that history belonged to the nobility, for who else, after the fall of the Roman Empire, could have fought off the barbarians between Venetia and Emilia but the ancestors of the Estensi, and who else could have been descended from the Trojans? Also important: *Ritterepik der Renaissance*, ed. K. W. Hempfer, Stuttgart, Steiner, 1989, xiii + 361 pp., which contains a series of Italian and German conference papers (Berlin, 1987), whose titles all speak clearly: A. Quondam, 'La tipografia e il sistema dei generi. Il caso del romanzo cavalleresco' (1–13), M. Beer, 'Il libro di cavalleria: produzione e fruizione' (15–33), C. Ivaldi, 'Cantari e poemetti bellici in ottava rima: la parabola produttiva di un sottogenere del romanzo cavalleresco' (35–46), A. Prosperi, 'Il *miles christianus* nella cultura italiana tra '400 e '500' (47–60), G. Baldassari, 'Tradizione cavalleresca e trattatistica sulle imprese. Interferenze, uso sociale e problemi di committenza' (61–76), P. Orvieto, 'Sul rapporto *Morgante–Orlando laurenziano*' (145–53), M. Mancini, 'I "cavalieri antiqui": paradigmi dell'aristocratico nel *Furioso*' (211–42), C. Vasoli, 'Francesco Patrizi e il dibattito sul poema epico' (315–32); the German papers are on: poetry and truth, the legitimacy of fiction in 16th-c. poetics (A. Kablitz: 77–122), *Morgante* XXII, 215–XXIII, 48 in the context of the 'poema cavalleresco toscano' (R. Ankli: 123–43), inter- and intratextual references in the *Furioso* (F. Penzenstadler: 155–84), Alberti's *Somnium* and Astolfo's journey to the moon (B. Häsner: 185–210), the appearance of beauty and the beauty of appearance in the *Furioso* (K. Stierle: 243–76), deconstruction of sense-constituting systems in the *Furioso* (K. Hempfer: 277–98), the poetics of unity and the exemplarity of history in Tasso's *Rinaldo* (G. Regn: 299–314). Also relevant must be *Chivalry in the Renaissance*, ed. S. Anglo, Woodbridge, Boydell, 1990, 262 pp., Aldo Scaglione, *Knights at Court. Courtliness, Chivalry and Courtesy from Ottonian Germany to the Italian Renaissance*, Berkeley, California U.P., 440 pp., and *War, Literature and the Arts in Sixteenth-Century Europe*, ed. J. R. Mulryne and M. Shewring, London, Macmillan, 1989, xii + 210 pp., which includes a chapter on Italian poetry by C. P. Brand. Comparisons of poets can be found in Paolo Baldan, *L'intrigo e l'avventura (tra Ligurio e Orlando)*, Alessandria, Orso, 1990, xii + 176 pp., which is about Boiardo and Ariosto (as well as Machiavelli); D. L. Hoffman, 'Merlin in Italy', *PQ*, 70:261–75, who traces the history of Merlin in Italian literature (where he is favoured as a prophet) from his first appearance in Godfrey of Viterbo's *Pantheon* (1191) to Boiardo and Ariosto (who 'reconciles the prophetic Merlin and the romance Merlin'), after which he all but disappears; M. Günsberg, '*Donna liberata*? The portrayal of women in the Italian Renaissance epic', in *Women and Italy: Essays on Gender, Culture and History*, ed. Z. Barański and S. W. Vinall, London, Macmillan, pp. 173–208, who analyses the portrayal of women and the construction of the feminine in the *Furioso* and the *Liberata*, concluding that, despite their differences, 'both poems fundamentally reinforce the dominant ideology of fixed gender attributes and the subordination of the feminine'; L. Waage Petersen and D. Quarta, who provide 'Appunti sul duello in Ariosto e in Tasso', *RevR*, 25, 1990:414–27, focusing on the three duels in *Orlando furioso* 1 and Argante and Tancredi's duel in *Gerusalemme liberata* VI; M. Bastiaensen, 'Pompeo Caimo e la controversia tassiana', *GSLI*, 167, 1990:71–81, who argues that the *Discorso del paragone fra Messer Lodovico Ariosto e Messer Torquato Tasso* by an Udine physician and professor (1568–1631) is an interesting indication of how the polemic between 'ariostisti' and 'tassisti' had by then degenerated to a mere rhetorical exercise; G. Bàrberi Squarotti, 'Venere e Marte: le allegorie della pace', *LItal*, 43:517–46, who traces the development of a theme from Lucretius (the pacifist utopia of the love of Mars for Venus) in Poliziano's *Stanze* (where it becomes erotic and decorative), Tasso's *Gerusalemme* (where peace is an 'opera di magia', an aberration in a war poem) and the *Adone* of Marino (who 'esaurisce il tema nel novellistico, nell'erotismo teatrale'); Silvia Longhi, **Orlando insonniato: il sogno e la poesia cavalleresca*, Mi, Angeli, 1990, 96 pp.

ARIOSTO. Influences on the *Orlando furioso* are discussed by Barbara Pavlock, *Eros, Imitation and the Epic Tradition*, Ithaca, Cornell U.P., 1990, xi + 230 pp., in the chapter 'A. and Roman epic values' (147–86), which looks at A.'s 'interplay with the classics' in two episodes, the 'abandoned female' Olimpia (from Ovid, with Catullus and Virgil) and the 'night raid' of Medoro and Cloridano (Virgil and Statius), and concludes that A. rewrites classical epic values in a personalized key, Olimpia 'wilfully acting out a private notion of *fede* to the detriment of family and country' and Cloridano and Medoro 'transforming *fede* and *pietà* on the political and social level into private values'; W. Feinstein, *'Ariosto's parodic rewriting of Virgil in the episode of Cloridano and Medoro', *SAR*, 55, 1990:17–34; Sergio Zatti, **Il 'Furioso' fra epos e romanzo*, Lucca, Pacini Fazzi, 1990, 216 pp.; Maria Cristina Cabani, **Fra omaggio e parodia: Petrarca e petrarchismo nel 'Furioso'*, Pisa, Nistri-Lischi, 1990, 301 pp. The afterlife of the *Furioso* is considered by Daniel Javitch, **Proclaiming a Classic:*

The Canonization of 'Orlando furioso', Princeton U.P., 1991, x + 205 pp.; L. Waage Petersen, 'Calvino lettore d'Ariosto', *RevR*, 26:230–46, who traces the presence of A. in C., which is linked to three main themes: 'trasfigurazione fantastica', 'struttura molteplice', and 'leggerezza'; C. Segre, 'Pio Rajna: le fonti e l'arte dell'*Orlando Furioso*', *StCrit*, 5, 1990:315–27, who argues that R.'s *Le fonti* is not only a 'capolavoro filologico' but also a 'capolavoro letterario' (with artful 'sovrapposizione di linee narrative') and a 'capolavoro della critica' (R.'s interpretation of his data also being a 'giudizio critico sui procedimenti della composizione ariostesca') which has stood the test of time and still serves as a 'guida e modello'; and P. Coccia, 'Le illustrazioni dell'*Orlando Furioso* (Valgrisi 1556) già attribuite a Dosso Dossi', *La Bibliofilia*, 93:279–307, who suggests that the beautiful illustrations are probably by Donato Bertelli, but in any case mark 'una tappa fondamentale nella illustrazione del libro veneziano del '500.' On the structure of the poem, see Maria Cristina Cabani, *Costanti ariostesche. Tecniche di ripresa e memoria interna nell'Orlando furioso*, Pisa, Scuola Normale, 1990; and A. Rizzo, 'Similitudini e comparazioni nell'*Orlando furioso*', *RLI*, 94.3, 1990:83–88, who argues that similes and comparisons are not a 'semplice espediente retorico' but an 'elemento di rilevante importanza' in the narrative structure of the *Furioso*. On the role of the writer in society see: J. Guidi, 'Le statut ambigu de l'écrivain de cour: les *Satires* de l'Arioste', in *Écrire à la fin du Moyen-Âge: le pouvoir et l'écriture en Espagne et en Italie, 1450–1530*, Aix, Provence U.P., 1990, pp. 79–91, which has more to say about St John's speech to Astolfo on the moon, and where it is argued that A. is caught between two stools: he is compromised by the court society which he questions and, envisaging the emancipation of the writer, but far from being emancipated himself, can only express himself fully through a Utopian world of fable; C. Ross, 'Ariosto's fable of power: Bradamante at the Rocca di Tristano', *Italica*, 68:155–75, interprets the episode as a reflection of the political crisis of the time, and of A.'s personality, and thus in terms of a conflict between individuals and institutions, with 'the *practice* of submission' as its theme. On the part of the reader, E. Haywood, 'Would you believe it? A tall story from A. (*Orlando furioso*, 28)', *Italian Storytellers*, ed. E. Haywood et al., Dublin, Irish Academic Press, 1989, pp. 111–49, argues that the story of Fiammetta is not a 'dirty' interlude but indispensable to a proper understanding of the *Furioso*, raising as it does the question of the nature of fiction and allowing Rodomonte (the reader's *alter ego*, responsible for the meaning of the story he is told) to be cured and keep the 'spirit of fiction' alive until the end of the poem. On the subject of women, according to S. Kolsky, 'Male descriptions, female inscriptions (*Orlando furioso* XLII, 73–96)', *RoN*, 31, 1990:155–60, the description of the statues of famous Este women (viewed by Rinaldo) are further proof that women in A. are subordinated 'to the concerns and preoccupations of men'. According to N. Ordine, 'Vittoria Colonna nell'*Orlando furioso*', *SPCT*, 42:55–92, V.C. is introduced into the third edition of the poem and assigned a privileged position, as 'moglie fedele' and 'grande scrittrice', just as the myth about her is beginning to emerge in Italy and women poets beginning to come into their own, her figure also lending itself 'al sottile gioco di rinvii e rimandi disseminato nel poema' (especially with regard to the questions of the fidelity of women and the veracity of literature).

BOIARDO. On how the *Orlando innamorato* has been handed down to us, see: Neil Harris, *Bibliografia dell'"Orlando innamorato'*, II: *Saggio analitico, illustrazioni, indici*, Ferrara, Panini, 310 pp.; P. Luparia, 'Rassegna boiardesca', *GSLI*, 167, 1990:82–135, who gives a detailed critical review of several recent editions and studies; M. Dorigatti, 'Concordanze, rimario e testo critico: il caso del B.', *SPCT*, 40, 1990:51–67, which presents M.M.B., *Orlando Innamorato. The Machine-Readable Text, Microfiche Concordance and Rhyme Dictionary with Related Statistical Data* (ed. D. Robey and M. Dorigatti, O.U. Computing Service, 1990), highlighting interesting features of B.'s language revealed by the study. On the structure of the poem, see Marco Praloran, *Meraviglioso artificio: tecniche narrative e rappresentative nell'"Orlando innamorato'*, Lucca, Pacini Fazzi, 1990, 150 pp.; on B.'s sources, C. Montagnini, 'Fra mito e magia: le *Ambages* dei cavalieri boiardeschi', *RLettI*, 8, 1990:261–85, who illustrates how B. 'contaminates' the stories of his knights with elements from the stories of Theseus and Ariadne, Hercules, the Garden of the Hesperides, etc., using classical myths (especially from Ovid) and contemporary rewritings of those myths in a puzzle-like manner and with 'dissonanze rispetto alla tradizione'.

PULCI. *Morgante*'s sources are the subject of M. P. Ratti, ' "Avaler la tradition": sul bestiario del *Morgante*', *LItal*, 42, 1990:264–75, which is a sample survey of how P. uses sources of animal themes: the topos of the tent description (Luciana's 'padiglione': *Morg.* XIV, 44–86) is expanded 'a dismisura', with borrowings from the bestiary tradition and P.'s own experience; a 'dissacrante' note is struck in passages dealing with the feats of Morgante and Margutte (beasts as food to be gobbled down); a literary topos with recognized symbolical meanings is presented in such a way as to 'depistare il lettore' in the episode of Rinaldo's encounter with the dragon and lion (IV, 7 ff.). The structure of the poem is discussed by E. Vincenti, 'I protagonisti del P.', *FC*, 15, 1990:521–32, who illustrates how it is organized around groups of two or three protagonists and argues that this is the only way to analyse the poem, since it appears to have no central theme. One theme is surveyed by M. G. Di Paolo, 'Osti e osterie nel *Morgante* del P.', *FoI*, 24, 1990:80–93, who tries to show how P. manages to capture the spirit of the common people of 14th-c. Florence, focusing on the inn of 'il Dormi' (XVIII–XIX) and on the episode of the innkeeper Chiarione (XX–XXI) which is said to be 'più consono allo spirito dei poemi cavallereschi.'

TASSO. General studies include *StT*, 38, 1990, which contains the 'Rassegna bibliografica degli studi tassiani' for 1986 and 1987 and the fifth instalment of the 'Appendice alla Bibliografia tassiana "Luigi Locatelli"'; Franco Di Carlo, **Invito alla lettura di Torquato T.*, Mi, Mursia, 1990, 176 pp.; Giovanna Scianatico, **L'arme pietose. Studi sulla 'Gerusalemme Liberata'*, Venice, Marsilio, 1990, 225 pp.; also of interest to T. scholars is Torquato T., **Rinaldo, ed. critica sulla II ed. del 1570 con varianti della 'princeps' (1562)*, ed. M. Sherberg, Ravenna, Longo, 1990, 332 pp. The message of the *Liberata* is the subject of D. Quint, 'L'allegoria politica della *Gerusalemme liberata*', *Intersezioni*, 10, 1990:35–57, who argues that T.'s poem, which was written in the wake of the accession to the throne of Philip II and Mary Tudor, and in which Goffredo has to wage war on two fronts (within his own ranks and against the Infidel), celebrates the triumph of the imperial papacy of the Counter-Reformation and the victory of Catholicism, with Goffredo representing the authority of the pope, Argillano's revolt the revolt of the Protestants, Rinaldo's submission to Goffredo standing for the idealized submission of the House of Este to the pope as his 'privilegiati servitori armati', and the *Liberata* thus voicing the official propaganda of the Estensi, while at the same time expressing T.'s ambiguity towards his masters. The importance of the religious message is also explored by Timothy Hampton, *Writing from History: The Rhetoric of Exemplarity in Renaissance Literature*, Cornell U.P., 1990, xiii + 309 pp., which is about 'the rhetorical value of the representation of the past in literature' from the early Renaissance to the onset of absolutism, with chapters on Budé, Erasmus, Machiavelli; Tasso; Montaigne, Shakespeare; Cervantes — Machiavelli (*Il principe*) being the pivotal figure in the development of Renaissance exemplarity: 'His demystification of historical repetition shows us the limitations of the exemplar theory of history'. H. sees T. (*Discorsi, Liberata, Conquistata*) as trying 'to accommodate aspects of humanist exemplarity to the new ideological exigencies of the Counter-Reformation' by substituting martyrdom for earlier heroic models. G. Aquilecchia, **'Scheda tassiana: Solimano e Palinuro'*, *FC*, 14, 1989, 121–23. According to L. Scancarelli Seem, 'The limits of chivalry: T. and the end of the *Aeneid*', *CL*, 42, 1990:116–25, the two versions of the Turnus–Aeneas duel in the *Liberata* (c. VII, Argante vs Raimondo, and c. XIX, Argante vs Tancredi) are T.'s attempt to provide a solution to the criticisms then being levelled against Virgil (unnecessarily cruel and incomplete ending of the *Aeneid*) in the light of the current discussions about the duel and honour, and 'while T. defends V.'s ending, he also attempts to go beyond him by closing his poem with a Christian act of mercy towards a defeated enemy'. Not religion but phallocracy is the message, according to J. T. Chiampi, 'T.'s Rinaldo in the body of the text', *RR*, 81, 1990:487–503, who leads us on a 'critical journey' through the Armida episode, in which Rinaldo, existing for his own sake, falls into a 'psycho-political sleep of androgyny' from which he is awoken by gazing at 'phallic weaponry' so that he may fulfil his appointed task (to found the Este line, 'which will not tolerate intermingling with pollution, darkness, nor, it seems, woman') and become 'the subservient sign of a sign' (i.e. of Goffredo's success at fulfilling the task set him by God), satisfying the yearning of T.'s text 'to identify the logocentric as phallocentric'. On the same episode see too M. L. Rondi Cappelluzzo, **Il giardino di Armida. Momenti magici ed ermetici in Torquato T.*, Parma, Zara, 1990, 65 pp. 'Is there a message?' has to be the subject of Claudio Scarpati and Eraldo Bellini, **Il vero e il falso dei poeti. Tasso, Tesauro, Pallavicino, Muratori*, Mi, Vita e Pensiero, 1990, xii + 241 pp., who consider whether poetry tells the truth or lies, beginning with T.'s reflections on the links between poetry and reality. The mixture of fact and fantasy is discussed by M. Gori, 'La geografia dell'epica tassiana', *GSLI*, 167, 1990:161–204, who compares the geography of the *Liberata* — where, in spite of a mixture of scientific precision and conjecture, the world is nevertheless recognizable, with a centre (the Mediterranean), fringes (N. Europe, Africa, the New World) and magical regions (Ascalon, Saron, land of Armida) — and that of the *Conquistata* where, because of the addition of fantastical and mythological elements, the 'orditura geografica' becomes 'soffocata', combining 'la vita interiore, il bisogno di verità storica ed il sentimento religioso del poeta, le cognizioni scientifiche e le fantasie di un'epoca in transizione.'

OTHER NARRATIVE POETS. BOLOGNETTI is the subject of Albert N. Mancini, **I 'Capitoli' letterari di Francesco Bolognetti: temi e modi della letteratura epica fra l'Ariosto e il Tasso*, Na, Federico & Ardia, 1989, 213 pp.; FOLENGO of M. Chiesa, 'Schede folenghiane', *GSLI*, 168:274–84, which contains notes on the text of the final version of *Baldus*; TASSONI of **'La secchia rapita'. Atti del Convegno (Modena, 1990)*, Modena, Panini, 87 pp., and Alessandro T., **La secchia rapita*, II: *Redazione definitiva*, ed. O. Besomi, Padua, Antenore, 1990, c + 452 pp.

OTHER POETRY

BOIARDO. G. Mazzacurati, 'Le carte del Boiardo (giochi d'amore e di tarocchi)', in *Écrire à la fin du Moyen-Âge* (see ARIOSTO above), pp. 269–300 argues that, just as B.'s *Amores* are the 'canzoniere più disciplinato e geometrico dell'intera tradizione post-petrarchesca', so the *Trionfi* he composed for Tarot cards show the same disposition for 'ordine geometrico e sequenze sistematiche', both works being typical of the playful mood of the poetry of the age, 'lontana, ancora, da ogni investitura "teologica"'. Also of interest: Matteo Maria B., *Can-zoniere (Amorum libri), ed. C. Micocci, Mi, Garzanti, 1990, xxxvi + 252 pp.

GIORGIO (ZORZI). According to E. Scapparone, 'Temi filosofici e teologici nell'*Elegante Poema* di Francesco G. Veneto', *RSF*, 45, 1990:37–80, Zorzi, in his unpublished poem of the first half of the 16th c., like Ficino and Pico fused Platonism and the Hermetic and Cabalistic traditions in order to elaborate a 'pia philosophia' capable of uniting men in the same faith. His last work, a close commentary on the *Elegante Poema* written just before his death in 1540, in which the Hermetic and Cabalistic traditions are also the main inspiration, is discussed in L. Pierozzi, 'Intorno al *Commento sopra il poema* di Francesco G. Veneto', *Rinascimento*, 30, 1990:283–307.

MICHELANGELO. Paul Barolsky, *M.'s Nose. A Myth and its Maker*, University Park, Pennsylvania State U.P., 1990, xx + 169 pp., is a book about both M. (poet, but mainly sculptor, painter, and architect) and Vasari, which argues that M. is his own greatest masterpiece: he consciously created an image of himself as Socratic satyr or silene, ugly without (broken *nose*) but wise and virtuous within, a Biblical saint, an Homeric hero (influenced by Poliziano), a new Dante (epic poet, poet as hero, subject of his own work) and a new Virgil, with a touch of Machiavelli's Prince. He thus became the first fully autobiographical artist in the modern world, seeing his works as symbolically portraying the great deeds of his own life. These, having been dictated by M. to Ascanio Condivi, were then assimilated and embellished by Vasari, who developed an allegory of the history of art along the lines of the *Comedy*, with M. as the epitome of perfection. The *Lives* thus became M.'s 'autobiography', through which he became 'pivotal in the history of Romanticism' (see also under VASARI below). N. Jonard, 'Péché et culpabilité chez Michel-Ange', *REI*, 36, 1990:27–41, looks at M.'s melancholy from a Freudian perspective, playing down the influence of historical contingencies, and of Savonarola's sermons, and seeing M.'s Neopla-tonism as an alibi for what was the manifestation of a 'névrose collective de culpabilité' and of a 'déséquilibre intime' brought about by the early death of his beloved mother, which became more acute with the passing of time. In *Protrepticon: studi di letteratura classica ed umanistica*, ed. S. Prete, Mi, Istituto Petrarca, 1989, 140 pp., L. Rotondi Secchi Tarugi, 'L'ansia di Dio nell'opera poetica ed artistica di M.' (109–15) highlights 'l'intimo anclito di spiritualità' in the poetry, sculpture, and painting of M. A. Schiavo, *Michelangelo nel complesso delle sue opere, Ro, Libreria dello Stato, 1990; James M. Saslow, *The Poetry of Michelangelo: An Annotated Translation, New Haven, Yale U.P., xii + 559 pp.

POLIZIANO. P.'s versality as a poet is illustrated by the edition: Angelo P., *Rime, ed. D. Delcorno Branca, Venice, Marsilio, 1990, 112 pp.; by J. L. Charlet, 'Le thrène de Politien pour la mort du Magnifique', Protrepticon (see MICHELANGELO), pp. 29–34, who analyses the poem; by A. Bettinzoli, *A proposito delle 'Sylvae' di A.P.: questioni di poetica, Venice, IV, 1990; by M. Javion, 'La "giostra" florentine de 1475', in Écrire à la fin du Moyen-Âge (see ARIOSTO), pp. 95–105, who describes the joust, more 'ludus' than 'certamen', of which P. sings in the Stanze; by S. Carrai, 'Implicazioni cortigiane nell'Orfeo di Poliziano', RLettI, 8, 1990:9–23, who argues that Orfeo has several Carnival features (particularly the killing of Orpheus, which is like the Shrove Tuesday 'killing' of a puppet personifying Carnival) and that, although it was written at the request of Gonzaga and performed at his Roman residence, it was also intended to be performed contemporaneously during the Medici Carnival festivities, with Tirsi representing P. himself and Aristeo Lorenzo, or more probably Giuliano, de' Medici. His importance as a philologist is represented by Angelo P., *Commento inedito alle 'Georgiche' di Virgilio, ed. L. Castano Musicò, F, Olschki, 1990, xvi + 282 pp., and illustrated by the venom of his detractors: according to M. Danzi, 'Novità su Michele Marullo e Pietro Bembo', Rinascimento, 30, 1990:205–33, the one poem in Italian attributed to Marullo (and included here, with explanatory notes) is indeed by him, belongs to the genre 'in obtrectatores', and was part of a many-pronged attack against P.'s Miscellanea. (The article also presents from the same Tedaldi MS, 'silloge privata e familiare', a sonnet, perhaps by G. A. Augurello, which is an early witness to Bembo's future greatness.) According to C. Vecce, 'Multiplex hic anguis. Gli epigrammi di Sannazaro contro P.', Rinascimento, 30, 1990:235–55, who gives the text of the epigrams with a commentary, S. attacked P.'s Miscellanea in order to defend 'un metodo che egli vedeva seriamente minacciato dalla nuova filologia di P.'.

SANNAZARO. Iacopo S., Arcadia, ed. F. Erspamer, Mi, Mursia, 1990, 247 pp., is an affordable and usable edition with copious notes, a comprehensive bibliography, and a lively introduction, which looks in particular at the sources, structure, language, and composition of a work designed to be 'equivoca, aperta' and to stimulate 'la curiosità esegetica, il piacere di ascoltare e di capire, di osservare dentro al romanzo, da fuori come attraverso una finestra' and which is above all 'un'opera di fantasia' and a 'testo allegorico' (allegory of S.'s life, of the links between poetry and society, of the social and political events of the Kingdom of Naples at the time, and of culture and human knowledge). M. Deramaix, 'La genèse du *De partu virginis* de I.S. et trois églogues inédites de Giles de Viterbe', *MEFR*, 102, 1990:174–273, shows that G. of V. not only had a hand in the 1526 revision of the *De partu* but was also responsible for the whole undertaking, as can be seen from the hitherto unknown poems by him published with a commentary in the article.

TASSO. V. Martignone, 'Un segmento delle rime tassiane: gli inediti del codice chigiano nelle stampe 27, 28 e 48', *SFI*, 48, 1990:81–105, examines the relationship between the said MS and the 1586 and 1587 Venice and the 1586 Genoa editions; there are two other detailed studies of MSS of T.'s *Rime* in *StT*, 38, 1990: L. Milite, 'I manoscritti E_1 ed F_2 delle *Rime* del T.' (41–70), and V. Martignone, 'La struttura narrativa del codice chigiano delle *Rime tassiane*' (71–128). The issue also includes a study of Gesualdo's settings of some of T.'s 'intrinsically musical' poems: M. Mazzolini, 'T. e Gesualdo, ovvero del suono dei pensieri' (4–40), where G. is said to have attempted to remain faithful both to the musicality and to the sense of the texts. L. Freedman, 'Melancholy in T.'s poetry', *Neophilologus*, 35:94–101, looks at some of T.'s madrigals and what T. himself wrote (or did not write) about them, concluding that, though most probably unintentionally, T. 'was one of the very first poets to let his poems speak for his inner self'. There is more about melancholy in J. Schiesari, *'Mo(u)rning and melancholia: T. and the dawn of psychoanalysis', *QI*, 11, 1990:13–27. L. Panizza, 'Torquato T.'s *Il mondo creato* and Boethius, a neglected model', *RenS*, 5:301–14, is one of the nine items forming a special issue of *RenS* devoted to 'Philosophical and scientific poetry in the Renaissance'. C. Scarpati, *'Petrocchi e il *Mondo creato* del T.', *CLett*, 18, 1990:63–68.

TEBALDEO. M. Castoldi, 'Nello scrittoio del T.: tra resistenze cortigiane e classicismo bembiano. Tre sonetti inediti: note e varianti', *Italianistica*, 20:55–66, examines how T.'s revisions of three sonnets show him to be torn between Bembian classicism and attachment to the cultural environment of the court of Mantua where he was formed. Antonio T., *Rime*, ed. T. Basile, J.-J. Marchand, Modena, Panini, 238 pp.

OTHER MEN POETS. G. Tanturli, 'Le ragioni del libro: le *Rime* di Giovanni Della Casa', *SFI*, 48, 1990:15–41, highlights C.'s endeavours to achieve 'decoro' and 'altezza formale' in a body of vernacular poetry which is thematically coherent and (in homage to Lucretius) substantial, and which responds to the aspirations 'di una ritrovata spiritualità e di una religiosità severa', unlike most of the literature produced in the shadow of the recently convened Council of Trent. S. Gatti, 'Su *La umanità del Figliuolo di Dio* di Teofilo Folengo',

GSLI, 168: 1–53, is a detailed study of the language, style, and content of F.'s paraphrase of the Gospel accounts of the life of Christ. Published at Venice in 1533, this was not simply a penance, written 'al solo scopo di ottenere la riammissione nel chiostro', but a work of art in its own right, to which F. was deeply committed and which is to be seen in the cultural, literary, and theological context of the time: an example of 'letteratura sacra in volgare', an important genre but hitherto much neglected by scholars. L. Quaquarelli, '"Intendendo di poeticamente parlare": la *Bella mano* di Giusto de' Conti tra i libri di Feliciano', *La Bibliofilia*, 93: 177–98, discusses why G.'s *canzoniere* in its *editio princeps* (1472) came to be given that title, as well as the career of its 'publisher', Felice Feliciano. G. Battista Pigna, *Gli amori*, Orazio Magnanimi, *Discorso sopra 'Gli amori'*, ed. D. Nolan, rev. A. Bullock, Bo, Commissione per i Testi di Lingua, lxii + 257 pp., gives, with a 16th-c. commentary, the authoritative test of P.'s 'real' *Amori*, explaining their *fortuna* before they were rediscovered, and discussing their (still uncertain) date and whether they are a 'raccolta di versi scritti con intenzioni utopistiche' or a 'trasfigurazione ideale' of P.'s love for Lucrezia Bendidio.

WOMEN POETS. Ann R. Jones, *The Currency of Eros: Women's Love Lyric in Europe, 1540–1620*, Indianapolis, Indiana U.P., 1990, xi + 242 pp., analyses the poetry of four pairs of Renaissance women poets ordered along a continuum going from most adaptive to most oppositional positions in relation to the male-centred conventions of the love lyric: (1) Isabella Whitney and Catherine des Roches (2) Pernette du Guillet and Tullia d'Aragona, whose sonnets 'explore the erotics of fame rather than the conventions of passion' in a strategy of self-representation which 'not only recognizes the otherness of the man but appropriates his difference' (3) Gaspara Stampa, who 'manipulated the pastoral convention in order to articulate a critique of the amatory conventions and the social hierarchies of her time', and Mary Wroth (4) Louise Labé and Veronica Franco, who, in her poetry, claims equality with men and writes about sexual pleasure as sexual pleasure. R. Nobbio Mollaretti, *Vittoria Colonna e Michelangelo nel V centenario della sua nascita (1490–1990)*, F, Atheneum, 1990.

PASQUINO. '[Perché] sonci più coglion d'uomini al mondo?' is the memorable last line of a 'pasquinata' by Giovanni della Casa, one of the very few extant attributable ones, published, together with two by a philosopher-rival of C., and a commentary, in E. Scarpa, 'La corrispondenza burlesca fra Giovanni della C. e Antonio Bernardi della Mirandola', *FC*, 15, 1990:88–111. *Pasquino e dintorni. Testi pasquineschi del Cinquecento*, ed. A. Marzo, Ro, Salerno, 1990, 232 pp. C. Rendina, *Pasquino statua parlante: quattro secoli di pasquinate*, Ro, Newton Compton.

'REGIONAL' AND 'HISTORICAL' POETRY. Events in Tuscany are the subject of two studies. F. Battera, 'L'edizione Miscomini (1482) delle *Bucoliche elegantissimamente composte*', *SPCT*, 40, 1990:149–85, claims that this anthology of Florentine and Sienese poets is 'fra le più importanti operazioni culturali' of the second half of the 15th c., a '*pendant* bucolico' of the *Raccolta aragonese*, which was intended to underline Florence's supremacy in this area too and may have been a declaration of support, against the background of the war which followed the Pazzi conspiracy, for one part of the Buoninsegni family, exiled from Siena, against the other part which had sought the protection of the King of Naples. A. Matucci, 'Note per l'edizione della *Storia fiorentina* di Piero Parenti. Il sonetto sulla "Recuperazione della libertà"', *Rinascimento*, 30, 1990:257–60, discusses the three redactions of this poem on the fall of the Medici and the 1494 return of liberty, its place in the *Storia*, and the significance of its historical and religious themes. Also of Tuscan interest are G. Biancardi, 'Un inedito testo senese del Quattrocento: l'ecloga *Hor che gli uccelli fra l'ombrose frondi*', *SPCT*, 42:33–54, which gives a brief introduction to the annotated text of a hitherto unknown work said to illustrate the important part played by 15th-c. Sienese poets in the formal codification of the vernacular eclogue and the 'piena affermazione, in ambito curtense, del genere bucolico', and Claudia Peirone, **Storia e tradizione della terza rima. Poesia e cultura nella Firenze del Quattrocento*, T, Tirrenia, 1990, 127 pp. Events in Rome figure in D. Diamanti, 'La *Presa di Roma* di Eustachio Celebrino da Udine', *Italianistica*, 19:331–49, concerning a 'poemetto' in *ottava rima*, first published 1528 and republished many times before 1547, in which the author fuses the two ways of presenting the Sack of Rome current at the time: as God's punishment of the Church and Rome and as a denunciation of the atrocities committed by the Imperial troops — whereas Marco Guazzo, in his prose imitation of it in the 1546 *Historie*, shifts the attention of the narrative to the invincibility of Charles V and the supremacy of Spanish power. Milan is featured in A. Gandia, 'La biblioteca latina del poeta milanese Lancino Corte (1462–1512)', *La Bibliofilia*, 43:221–77, which illustrates the classical erudition of a Renaissance poet, and in Simone Albonico, **Il ruginoso stile: poeti e poesia in volgare a Milano nella prima metà del Cinquecento*, Mi, Angeli, 1990, 376 pp., and the South in Carlo De Frede, **Galeazzo di Tarsia: poesia e violenza nella Calabria del Cinquecento*, Na, Liguori, 1991.

COURT POETRY. P. Vecchi Galli, 'In margine ad alcune recenti pubblicazioni sulla poesia di corte nel Quattrocento. Linee per una rassegna', *LItal*, 43:105–15, draws together various points emerging as a result of the renewed interest in the genre, which it is now possible to study without 'pregiudizi e schematismi'. S. D. Kolsky, 'The courtier as critic: Vincenzo Calmeta's *Vita del facondo poeta vulgare Serafino Aquilano'*, *Italica*, 67, 1990: 161–72, highlights the main points of the *Vita*, contrasting them with the views of Bembo on poets and poetry. The work, where 'poetry is regarded not solely as textual analysis, but also as a social process', is said to offer the scholar 'a rare opportunity to study a contemporary account of the manner in which a poet operated within the patronage system'.

THE POETICAL CANON. The Renaissance concern for the styles and rules of poetry emerges from the following: R. Cardini, 'Landino e Dante', *Rinascimento*, 30, 1990: 175–90, an invitation to study anew L.'s commentary on D., following its two 'chiavi', linguistic ('primato linguistico di D.' and 'fiorentinità della lingua di D.') and ideological/methodological (Platonism and moral allegory); B. Richardson, 'The two versions of the "Appendix aldina" of 1514', *The Library*, 13: 115–25, which compares to Aldo Manuzio's first edition of Petrarch's *Rerum vulgarium fragmenta* and *Trionfi* (1501, ed. Bembo) his second edition of 1514, for which M. assumed the role of editor as well as printer, thus making 'a major editorial contribution to the study of the Italian lyric tradition and to vernacular philology'; Amedeo Quondam, *Il naso di Laura: lingua e poesia lirica nella tradizione del classicismo*, Modena, Panini; Roland Greene, *Post Petrarchism: Origins and Innovations of the Western Lyric Sequence*, Princeton U.P., xi + 292 pp.; L. G. Clubb and W. G. Clubb, 'Building a lyric canon: Gabriel Giolito and the rival anthologists, 1545–1590', *Italica*, 68: 332–44, the first part of a 'brief history' of the most important of the earliest printed anthologies of lyric verse; Roberto Fedi, *La memoria della poesia: canzonieri, lirici e libri di rime nel Rinascimento*, Ro, Salerno, 1990, 388 pp.; Olimpia Pelosi, *Satira barocca e teoriche sul genere dal Cinquecento all' Ottocento*, Na, Federico & Ardia.

LATIN AND GREEK POETRY. In *Protrepticon* (see MICHELANGELO above) S. Prete takes issue with Burckhardt's thesis that the Renaissance was a period of religious indifference and argues that there was both 'erudizione' and 'sincerità di sentimento' in 'La poesia latina nel Quattrocento' (pp. 101–08). I. Thomson, 'The scholar as hero in Ianus Pannonius' panegyric on Guarinus Veronensis', *RQ*, 44: 197–212, analyses the methods and rhetorical devices used by I.P. (1434–72), one of Guarino's pupils, in his *Panegyricus in Guarinum* (a poem 'classical in meter, grammar, syntax and diction', dedicated to G. as a parting gift), concluding that 'G. fulfills the major criteria of heroism found in the ancient classical myths, the heroic epics, and even the Christian lives of saints, except that his weapon is not the sword or the Cross, but the pen'. In R. Friedman, 'A "lost" Pontano manuscript in the Pierpont Morgan Library (M.867)', *LItal*, 42, 1990: 276–86, a version of P.'s Latin love poems leads to an investigation of the provenance and cultural context of its production. G. L. Gigliotti, 'The Alexandrian Fracastoro. Form and meaning in the myth of Syphilis', *RenR*, 14, 1990:261–69, is a sketchy 'literary study' of F.'s Latin hexameter poem on the 'French disease' which shows him to be well versed in the narrative and poetic techniques of Virgil and other Roman poets in the Alexandrian tradition. *Latin Poetry and the Classical Tradition: Essays in Medieval and Renaissance Literature*, ed. P. Godman and O. Murray, Oxford, Clarendon, 1990, xi + 243 pp. I. Gallo, *'Pomponio Gaurico e la poesia umanistica meridionale in lingua greca', *RPLit*, 13, 1990:93–100.

4. THEATRE

COMEDY

GENERAL.   L. Bottoni, 'La tradizione del comico: letteratura e teatro', *Intersezioni*, 11:135–59, discusses the seminal importance of Borsellino's *La tradizione del comico* (1989) and its implications for a proper understanding of, *inter alia*, Renaissance comedy. Antonio Stäuble, *'Parlar per lettera': il pedante nella commedia del Cinquecento e altri saggi sul teatro rinascimentale*, Ro, Bulzoni, 230 pp., contains some articles not previously published. *Théâtre en Toscane. La comédie (XVIᵉ, XVIIᵉ, XVIIIᵉ siècles)*, ed. M. Plaisance, St-Denis, Vincennes U.P., 191 pp., is on unknown or little known comedies. P. D. Stewart, *'Per una lettura "teatrale" delle commedie italiane del Cinquecento', *YIS*, 9:80–95. R. A. Andrews, *'Written texts and performed texts in Italian Renaissance Comedy', *McWilliam Vol.*, 75–94. J. E. Everson, *'"Fare il becco all'oca" (*Il Mambriano*, canto II): novella per dramma', *ib.*, 53–74.

ARIOSTO.   J. D'Amico, 'Planes of action and fluid space: *I Suppositi* and *The Taming of the Shrew*', *FoI*, 24, 1990:230–46, shows how these two plays are conditioned by different representations of space (fixed/hierarchical vs indeterminate, where space is the creation of language and action), order and unity in A. being the logical outcome for a world of 'fixed points of reference', whereas it spreads outwards from the inner world in Shakespeare.

ARETINO.   M. Lettieri, *'L'Orazia di Pietro A.: riflessioni sulla scelta del testo-base', *QI*, 11, 1990:102–10.

BIBBIENA.   J. D'Amico, *'Drama and the court in La Calandria', *TJ*, 43:93–106.

BRUNO.   G. Aquilecchia, *'Saggio di un commento letterale al testo critico del Candelaio', *FC*, 16:91–126.

MACHIAVELLI.   Antonio Sorella, *Magia, lingua e commedia nel M.*, F, Olschki, 1990, 264 pp.; see also P. Baldan (under NARRATIVE POETRY, GENERAL).

RUZANTE. Linda L. Carroll, *Angelo Beolco (Il Ruzante)*, Boston, Twayne, 1990, xii + 145 pp., provides a chronological play-by-play account of R.'s work (with summary and analysis of each plot, and discussion of dating problems and of the views of other critics). She sees the plays as reflecting R.'s personal circumstances, as well as the political and social context of the time, and interprets them anthropologically as changing from 'liminal' to 'liminoid' entertainment, with R. striving to restructure society through theatre, 'a forum that allowed him to appeal directly to the common humanity of his audience'. Mario Baratto, *Da Ruzante a Pirandello: scritti sul teatro*, Na, Liguori, 1990, 233 pp.

TRAGEDY

DELLA VALLE. P. Trivero, 'Il congegno teatrale dell'*Adelonda di Frigia* di Federico della V.', *Italianistica*, 19, 1990:371–84, argues that this play (performed at the Savoy Court in 1595 to celebrate the passage through Turin of Cardinal Archduke Albert of Savoy) is not to be read simply as a text, but studied in the context of the 'scenografia della tragicommedia' of the time, which reveals the hidden harmony of its structure and its 'felicità di congegno teatrale agli albori del trionfo barocco'.

GIRALDI. By studying apocopation in the autograph and the *editio princeps* of G.'s *Egle*, and comparing it to Bembo, Ariosto, Boiardo, and Petrarch, C. Molinari, 'Caratteri del Boiardo lirico nella verseggiatura tragico-satirica di G.B.G.', *SFI*, 48, 1990:43–80, reveals G.'s 'mentalità pragmatica, tutta volta a sperimentare le molteplici potenzialità del volgare', and sees in his choice of a model 'del tutto estravagante' like Boiardo the affirmation of his 'propria ineludibile padanità'.

NEGRI. F. Millocca, 'La tragedia *Libero arbitrio* di Francesco N. Bassanese (sec. XVI)', *EL*, 16.1:51–64, is an introduction to this 'tragedia soprattutto da leggere' (first published in 1546, twice reprinted, translated into French, Latin, and English, and put on the Index), with a biographical sketch of its author (an ex-Benedictine Protestant sympathizer from Bassano).

TASSO. M. Pastore Passaro, '*Il Re Torrismondo* del T.', *StT*, 38, 1990:129–41, argues that this is a tragedy not only about incest but about love and friendship, its 'elemento basilare' being the choruses at the end of each act, noteworthy for their lyrical beauty.

TRISSINO. C. Musumarra, 'La *Sofonisba*, ovvero della libertà', *Italianistica*, 20:67–75, is a critical study of the play, which concludes that Trissino 'come letterato si dichiarò ossequiente alle regole, ma come poeta fu un trasgressivo'.

SOUTHERN ITALY. Anna Cerbo, **Il teatro dell'intelletto. Drammaturgia di tardo Rinascimento nel Meridione*, Na, Ist. Univ. Orientale, 1990, vii + 243 pp.

PASTORAL (AND COMMEDIA DELL'ARTE)

GUARINI. M. Pieri, 'Il *Pastor Fido* e i comici dell'Arte', *Biblioteca teatrale*, 17, 1990: 1–15, maintains that the acrimonious debate which greeted the *Pastor fido* when it was first performed had nothing to do with its 'Aristotelian legitimacy', but arose from the fact that G. was accused of having stolen many elements from the repertoire of the *comici dell'arte*, which induced him to counter-attack, in defence of court theatre and against those 'attori infami, sordidi, scandalosi, scomunicati e sbanditi' — though ironically the success of his play was to depend, in the long run, on the performances and adaptations of the *comici dell'arte*.

INGEGNERI. Angelo I., *Della poesia rappresentativa e del modo di rappresentare le favole sceniche*, ed. M. L. Doglio, Modena, Panini, 1989, xxxix + 53 pp., is a late 16th-c. treatise which reflects both the current discussions on poetics and the author's direct experience of staging (pastoral) plays.

SCALA. The famous *comico dell'arte* Flaminio S. is the subject of S. Jansen, 'Cos'è, nella fattispecie, il canovaccio? Appunti sul *Teatro delle favole rappresentative* di Flaminio S.', *RevR*, 25, 1990:341–55, who argues that S.'s scenarios are not just stage directions but also 'testi drammatici a pieno diritto', to be read and studied as one would any text by, say, Goldoni or Pirandello.

TASSO. D. Chiodo, 'Partenope in Arcadia. Alle radici dell'ispirazione bucolica in T.', *StT*, 38, 1990:143–62, sees Naples and Ferrara, 'capitali della poesia pastorale italiana', as having contributed in equal measure to formulating 'la celebrazione di Eros che pervade l'*Aminta*'.

RELIGIOUS

THE SACRA RAPPRESENTAZIONE. In two contrasting interpretations of the function of *sacre rappresentazioni* in Florence, G. Ulysse, 'L'image du pouvoir dans la *sacra rappresentazione* florentine', *Écrire à la fin du Moyen-Âge* (see NARRATIVE POETRY, ARIOSTO), pp. 185–221, argues that they were used for political purposes and were 'le lieu privilégié de l'expression et de la réflexion politique' in a city fascinated by politics; whereas N. Newbigin, 'The Word made flesh: the *Rappresentazioni* of mysteries and miracles in 15th-c. Italy', in *Christianity and the Renaissance* (see HUMANISM), pp. 361–75, argues that those put on by confraternities between 1430–78, with a great sense of spectacle and using all the visual media available, were performed because of a typical Renaissance concern with the purpose of the Incarnation and for sheer enjoyment. C. Salvadori Lonergan, *'"A Lorenzo il leon d'oro?" A global look at the *Rappresentazione di San Giovanni e Paolo'*, *McWilliam Vol.*, 53–74.

LAUDE. Several important editions of this form of spectacle, which is attracting more and more attention, have come out: *Laude fiorentine*, I: *Il Laudario della Compagnia di San Gilio*, ed. C. Del Popolo, F, Olschki, 1990, 2 vols, viii + 696 pp.; *Il Laudario 'Frondini' dei Disciplinati di Assisi (sec. XIV)*, ed. F. Mancini, F, Olschki, 1990, ii + 376 pp. Also relevant is R. Rabboni, *Laudari e canzonieri nella Firenze del Quattro- cento: scrittura privata e modelli nel Vat. lat. 3679*, Bo, CLUEB, 1991.

MISCELLANEOUS. Beatrice Del Sera, *Amor di virtù*, ed. E. Weaver, Ravenna, Longo, 1990, is a 1548 spiritual verse play in five acts.

5. PROSE

B. Porcelli, 'Les Cent Nouvelles nouvelles nel Cinquecento italiano', *Italianistica*, 19, 1990:253–70, asks whether, since Celio Malespini at the end of the Cinquecento took 96 of his *Duecento novelle* from *Cent nouvelles nouvelles*, the work was known in Cinquecento Italy, and answers: very little, and only from the second half of the century, and only to authors who, unlike M., wrote very short stories with moralistic intentions. M. Olsen, *Amore, virtù e potere nella novellistica rinascimentale*, Na, Federico & Ardia, 1990, 224 pp. Jeannine Basso, *Le Genre épistolaire en langue italienne, 1538–1662. Répertoire chronologique et analytique*, 2 vols, Ro, Bulzoni–Nancy U.P., 1990, 740 pp. *Le Pouvoir monarchique et ses supports idéologiques aux XIVᵉ–XVIIᵉ siècles*, ed. J. Dufournet, A. C. Fiorato, A. Redondo, Paris, Sorbonne Nouvelle, 1990, iii + 282 pp., includes essays on Machiavelli (M. Marietti), S. Oddi (D. Boillet), Cellini (A. Fontes Baratto). *La scrittura della storia*, ed. E. Scarano, D. Diamanti, Pisa, Ed. Pisana, 1990, 333 pp., includes essays by M. Palumbo on Guicciardini (115–40); by D. Diamanti on Marco Guazzo (141–58); by G. Mazzoni on Camillo Porzio (159–70); by A. Caleca on Vasari (187–98). Antonio Lanza, *Primi secoli. Saggi di letteratura italiana antica*, Ro, Izzi, 273 pp., has three essays of interest: 'Il doppio nel Rinascimento', 'Storia della parola Umanista', 'Il *Diario Fiorentino* del Landucci'. S. Razzi, *La vita in Abruzzo nel Cinquecento: diario di un viaggio in Abruzzo negli anni 1574–1577*, Cerchio, Polla, 1990, 169 pp. Marco Bardini, *Borbone occiso. Studi sulla tradizione storiografica del Sacco di Roma del 1527*, Pisa, Ed. Pisana, 256 pp., charts the history of the changes in the descriptions of the Sack. In *Il nuovo mondo tra storia e invenzione: l'Italia e Napoli*, ed. G.

B. De Cesare, Ro, Bulzoni, 1990, 428 pp., two essays should be noted: G. Bellini, 'Colombo nell'opera di Pietro Martire' (19–43), and A. Caracciolo Aricò, 'Cristoforo Colombo nelle lettere di Angelo Trevisan' (45–52). *Bartolommeo Cederni and his Friends. Letters to an Obscure Florentine*, ed. G. Corti and F. W. Kent, F, Olschki, vi + 128 pp., explores the meanings of *amicizia* and *clientelismo*. B. Richardson, 'Editing the *Decameron* in the sixteenth century', *ISt*, 45, 1990:13–31, argues that in the middle of the 16th c. the *Decameron* began to be seen as a model of prose style preferable to B.'s earlier works. It concentrates on the textual scholarship of the editors and their attempts to clarify the text for their readers. It provides an excellent account of the effect the different editing policies in Venice and Florence had on the fortune of the *Decameron* and for the future of the Italian language built on Tuscan foundations. Giorgio Petrocchi, *Saggi sul Rinascimento italiano*, F, Le Monnier, 208 pp., has essays on Michelangelo, Folengo, Aretino, and Tasso. *Stefano Guazzo e la civil conversazione*, ed. G. Patrizi, Ro, Bulzoni, 1990, 407 pp. S. Prandi, 'L'albero, il gioco, la morte. Un aspetto del tema umanistico della follia attraverso il Cinquecento', *LItal*, 42, 1990:287–93, charts the gradual taming of the power of folly, its expulsion from the 'corpo sociale', and the weakening of its 'statuto gnoseologico', with reference to less well-known and some better-known *Cinquecento* works. Luciana Borsetto, *Il furto di Prometeo: imitazione, scrittura, riscrittura nel Rinascimento*, Alessandria, Orso, 1990, 288 pp., a well-documented study of the metamorphoses of literary images, includes Castiglione, Muzio, Dolce, Colonna, Matraini, Stampa. *Il tema della fortuna nella letteratura francese e italiana del Rinascimento. Studi in memoria di Enzo Giudici*, F, Olschki, 1990, xix + 547 pp. Pasquale Guaragnella, *Le maschere di Democrito e di Eraclito: scritture e malinconie tra Cinque e Seicento*, Fasano, Schena, 1990, 472 pp. *Lettere di cortigiane del Rinascimento*, ed. A. Romano, Ro, Salerno, 1990, 175 pp.

ALBERTI. Roberto Cardini, *Mosaici: il 'nemico' dell'Alberti*, Ro, Bulzoni, 1990, 89 pp. Mark Jarzombeck, *On Leon Baptista A.: His Literary and Aesthetic Theories*, Cambridge, Mass., MIT Press, 1989, xvi + 262 pp., discusses A. in historical context, as architect, art theorist, man of letters, and especially as a theorist of writing: a stimulating discussion of A.'s principal works marred by many misprints and mistranslations. Id., 'The structural problematic of Leon Battista A.'s *De Pictura*', *RenS*, 4, 1990:273–86, is an investigation into the tripartite structural division of the treatise *De Pictura*, linking its organization to concepts from medieval texts such as Hrabanus Maurus's *De Universo*. R. Watkins, 'L.B.A. in the mirror: an interpretation of the *Vita* with a new translation', *ItO*, 117, 1989:5–27, gives the text of A.'s *Vita* with a commentary that interprets the work in terms of narcissistic disorder. J. H. Whitfield, 'A. in the *Intercoenali*', *ISt*, 46:58–68, analyses the *Defunctus* to rescue A. from an unjust accusation of pessimism and emphasizes the festive element. G. Skytte, 'Dall' A. al Forniciari: formazione della grammatica italiana', *RevR*, 25, 1990:268–78. S. F. Baxendale, 'Exile in practice: the A. family in and out of Florence 1401–1428', *RQ*, 44:720–56, explains the consequences of the long and unusual banishment of the A. family from Florence. Ennio Concina, *Navis. L'umanesimo sul mare (1470–1740)*, T, Einaudi, 1990, xviii + 220 pp., takes as its starting point works by the humanist Vettor Fausto and the lost Alberti MS.

ARETINO. Angelo Romano, **Periegesi aretiniane: testi, schede e note biografiche intorno a Pietro A.*, Ro, Salerno, 161 pp. Pietro A., *Sei giornate*, ed. A. Romano, Mi, Mursia, 370 pp.

BANDELLO. D. Maestri, 'B. e Machiavelli: interesse e riprovazione', *LItal*, 43:354–73, explores the presence of the character M. in B.'s novelle and how B. invents a story by M. in a subtle game with his readers.

BEMBO. Pietro B., **Lettere*, II: *1508–1528*, ed. E. Travi, Bo, Commissione per i Testi di Lingua, 1990, 601 pp.

BEROALDO. G. Zappella, 'Un antico mito e la sua interpretazione: la favola di *Amore e Psyche* nel commento di Filippo B. il Vecchio', *Esposito Vol.*, 167–78. F. La Branca and S. Fabrizio-Costa, 'Un maître provincial précurseur de la grande Europe: pour une édition de l'epistolario de Filippo B. l'ancien', *REI*, 37:89–102, charts the intellectual interest of B., the European dimension of his correspondence, his interest in letter-writing as evidence of friendship, and his belief in the language as communication. Appendix I has a description of the correspondence in the Museum Regni Bohemiae in Prague, Appendix II the text of letters to Poliziano.

BIONDO. Ottavio Clavuot, **Biondos 'Italia illustrata': Summa oder Neuschöpfung? Über die Arbeitsmethoden eines Humanisten*, Tübingen, Niemeyer, 1990, vii + 406 pp.

BRUNI. **Per il censimento dei codici dell'Epistolario di Leonardo B.*, ed. L. Gualdo Rosa and P. Viti, Ro, Ist. Storico Italiano per il Medioevo, ix + 198 pp.

BRUNO. Giovanni Aquilecchia, **Le opere italiane di Giordano B. Critica testuale e oltre*, Na, Bibliopolis, 108 pp. + 84 pls. R. Sturlese, 'Il *De imaginum, signorum et idearum compositione* di Giordano B. ed il significato filosofico dell'arte della memoria', *GCFI*, 69, 1990:182–203, highlights the importance of the art of memory in B.'s thought. S. Ricci, 'Infiniti mondi e mondo nuovo. Conquista dell'America e critica della civiltà europea in Giordano B.', *ib.*, 204–21. In C. Ossola, 'Dei legami di senso e dell'analogia in Giordano B.: studi recenti', *LItal*, 43:244–49, B.'s attempts to reduce the description of the universe to signs, and the importance of signs at the end of the 16th c., are examined in the context of the theories of Foucault and Yates. Maurilio Frigerio, *Invito al pensiero di Giordano B.*, Mi, Mursia, 214 pp. John Bossy, *Giordano B. and the Embassy Affair*, New Haven, Yale U.P., xix + 294 pp.

CASTIGLIONE. Elisabetta Soletti, *Parole ghiacciate, parole liquefatte: il secondo libro del 'Cortegiano'*, Alessandria, Orso, 1990, 122 pp. N. Jonard, 'C. moraliste sans morale', *LNL*, 84. 4, 1990:51–66. J. R. Woodhouse, *From C. to Chesterfield. The Decline in the Courtier's Manual*, Oxford, Clarendon, 18 pp., shows how elegance, subtlety, and seriousness are reflected in both the form and contents of the *Cortegiano*.

CELLINI. Marcello Vannucci, *Benvenuto C. 'maledetto fiorentino'*, Ro, Newton Compton, 1990, 254 pp., is a disappointing journalistic survey of C.'s career, with a complete lack of any critical apparatus.

CERRETANI. Biagia C., *'Dialogo della mutatione di Firenze'. Edizione critica secondo l'apografo magliabechiano*, ed. R. Mordenti, Ro, Storia e Letteratura, 1990, cix + 156 pp., is a text published for the first time.

CORAZZA. Bartolomeo del C., *Diario fiorentino*, ed. R. Gentile, Anzio, De Rubeis, 85 pp.

CORNAZZANO. Antonio C., *Vita di Bartolomeo Colleoni*, ed. G. Crevatin, Manziana, Vecchiarelli, 1990, xlvi + 213 pp.

DA BARBERINO. G. Allaire, 'Due testimoni sconosciuti di Andrea da B. nel Codice Barberiniano Latino 4101 della Biblioteca Vaticana', *Pluteus*, 6–7, 1988–89:121–30, presents a discovery of two new witnesses of the *Ugone d'Avernia*, which could belong to a second branch of the textual tradition or represent an author's variant.

DE' MEDICI. Lorenzo de' M., *Lettere*, v: *1480–1481*, and *Lettere*, vi: *1481–1482*, ed. M. Mallett, 1990, F, Giunti-Barbéra, 1990, xxiv + 360 pp., xvi + 384 pp.

EQUICOLA. *Un'apologia per l'E.: le due redazioni della 'Pro Gallis apologia' di Mario E. e la traduzione francese di Michel Roté*, ed. Carlo Vecce, Na, Ist. Univ. Orientale, 1990, 181 pp. Stephen Kolsky, *Mario E.: The Real Courtier*, Geneva, Droz, 341 pp., takes previous historians to task for presenting too negative a picture of E.'s activity in Mantua.

FRANCO. Matteo F., *Lettere*, ed. G. Frosini, F, Accademia della Crusca, 1990, 280 pp.

GARZONI. P. Cherchi and B. Collina, 'Esplorazioni preparatorie per un'edizione della *Piazza universale* di Tomaso G.', *LItal*, 43:250–66, reviews the problems of editing an edition of such a multi-disciplinary work.

GIANNOTTI. Donato G., *La Republica fiorentina; a critical edition and introduction*, ed. G. Silvano, Geneva, Droz, 1990, 263 pp., establishes the text for the first time according to the autograph in the Florence

Biblioteca Nazionale. The comprehensive introduction deals with the MS tradition, the historical context, the text, political vocabulary, and constitutional theory.

GRADENIGO. Giorgio G., *Rime e lettere*, Ro, Bonacci 185 pp.

GUICCIARDINI. G. Silvano, 'Gli "uomini da bene" di Francesco G.: coscienza aristocratia e repubblica a Firenze nel primo '500', *ASI*, 148, 1990:845–92.

LEONARDO DA VINCI. R. J. Rodoni, 'The weight of words: L. and the anxiety of language', *PQ*, 70:277–87, reflects on L.'s 'life-long preoccupation with the nature of language' and on his style, and concludes that his language 'standing between poetic exhilaration and scientific precision is a beacon for the sustained lyricism of Galileo'.

MACHIAVELLI. Karl Mittermaier, *M.: Moral und Politik zu Beginn der Neuzeit*, Gernsbach, Katz, 1989, 528 pp. *Niccolò M.: An Annotated Bibliography of Modern Criticism and Scholarship*, ed. S. Ruffo-Fiore, Westport, Greenwood Press, 1990, 824 pp., contains books, articles, and reviews written between 1935–85, arranged chronologically by year and alphabetically in each year, plus an annotated appendix of works published after 1985. M. Sherberg, 'The problematics of reading in M.'s *Discourses*', *MP*, 89:175–95. E. Garin, 'Polibio e M.', *Quaderni di storia*, 16, 1990:5–22. V. Kahn, 'Habermas, M. and the humanist critique of ideology', *PMLA*, 105, 1990:464–76. A. J. Parel, 'M.'s use of civic rhetoric', *Rhetorica*, 8, 1990:119–36. Id., 'M.'s use of *umori* in the *Prince*', *QI*, 11, 1990:91–101. Andrea Matucci, *M. nella storiografia fiorentina. Per la storia di un genere letterario*, F, Olschki, xiv + 278 pp. Filippo Grazzini, *M. narratore: morfologia e ideologia della novella di Belfagor con il testo della 'Favola'*, Bari, Laterza, 1990, 192 pp., is an excellent study of the novella *Favola* in the context of M.'s other literary works, and includes a new edition of the *Favola*. B. Laeng, *Interpretazione e stile in M.: il terzo libro delle 'Istorie'*, Ro, Bulzoni, 1990, 191 pp. Robert Bireley, *The Counter-Reformation Prince: Anti-Machiavellianism or Catholic Statecraft in Early Modern Europe*, Chapel Hill, N. Carolina U.P., 1990, xii + 309 pp. Perez Zagorin, *Ways of Lying: Dissimulation, Persecution and Conformity in Early Modern Europe*, Cambridge, Mass., Harvard U.P., 1990, xii + 337 pp., includes a section on M. *M. and Republicanism*, ed. Gisela Bock *et al.*, CUP, 336 pp. G. Borghi, *La politica e la tentazione tragica: la modernità in M., Montaigne e Gracian*, Mi, Angeli. Alessandro Guetta, *Invito alla lettura di Niccolò M.*, Mi, Mursia, 172 pp.

MALASPINA. Torquato Malaspina, *Dello scrivere le vite*, ed. V. Bramanti, Bergamo, Moretti e Vitali, 92 pp.

MUZIO. L. Borsetto, 'Lettere inedite di Girolamo M. tratte dal Codice Riccardiano 2115', *RLI*, 94.1–2, 1990:99–178, covers the publishing history of M.'s works, including the letters, and gives the text of the letters.

PETRUCCI. *Tra politica e cultura nel primo Quattrocento senese: le 'Epistole' di Andreuccio P., 1426–1443*, ed. P. Pertici, Siena, Accademia degli Intronati, 1990, 192 pp.

PIUS II. S. C. Honegger, 'L'edizione del 1584 dei *Commentarii* di Pio II e la duplice revisione di Francesco Bandini (analisi del libro primo)', *ASI*, 149:585–612, suggests that the book was edited in an apologetic key, to show a less political, more spiritual Church and a less personalized and more pope-like (non-conciliar) Pius.

POLIZIANO. Angelo P., *Commento inedito ai 'Fasti' di Ovidio*, ed. F. Lo Monaco, F, Olschki, xxxviii + 554 pp. P. Paolini, 'Note sui *Detti piacevoli* attribuiti al P.', *Italianistica*, 19, 1990:319–29, offers reflections on the literary value of the *Detti*, which are by P. and were presumably jottings from readings or, especially, the oral tradition, waiting to be re-used orally amongst friends or, to a lesser degree, in writing.

ROMEI. Stefano Prandi, *Il 'Cortegiano' ferrarese. I 'Discorsi' di Annibale R. e la cultura nobiliare del Cinquecento*, F, Olschki, 1990, 248 pp., evaluates the literary and philosophical traditions that lie behind this important testament to elite culture.

SABADINO DEGLI ARIENTI. Marzia Minutelli, *La 'miraculosa acqua': lettura delle 'Porretane Novelle'*, F, Olschki, 1990, 263 pp.

SFRANZE. Giorgio S., *Cronaca*, ed. R. Maisano, Ro, Accademia Nazionale dei Lincei, 1990, xiv + 276 pp.

SPERONI. J.-L. Fournel, *Les 'Dialogues' de Sperone S.: libertés de la parole et règles de l'écriture*, Marburg, Hitzeroth, 1990, 415 pp. *Sperone S.*, Padua, Ed. Programma, 1989, 371 pp., is a collection of 11 articles.

TASSO. S. Prandi, 'Sul dibattito critico intorno ai *Dialoghi* di T. Tasso', *LItal*, 42, 1990:460–66, gives an overview of different critical approaches to T.'s dialogues. G. Corti, 'Un autografo inedito di T. Tasso', *LItal*, 42, 1990:294–95. Torquato T., *Dialoghi*, ed. B. Basile, Mi, Mursia, 264 pp.

TORELLI. Pomponio T., *Il Polidoro*, ed. V. Guercio, F, La Nuova Italia, 1990, xcviii + 213 pp.

VASARI. P. Rubin, 'What men saw: V.'s Life of Leonardo da Vinci and the image of the Renaissance artist', *Art History*, 13, 1990:34–46, argues that V.'s evaluation of L. was not in terms of traditional social and professional categories but of his genius and the inspiration of his work. In a sequel to *Michelangelo's Nose* (see MICHELANGELO above), Paul Barolsky, *Why Mona Lisa Smiles and Other Tales by V.*, University Park, Pennsylvania State U.P., xiv + 128 pp., maintains that if the Renaissance still lingers in our imagination as a sort of Paradise it is largely thanks to V., who has himself endured primarily thanks to his extraordinary gifts as a storyteller which have given us the *Lives*, a work of art in its own right, in which V. not only records but invents, creating his own poetry out of Dante, playfully parodying Petrarch, transforming the novella into biography, as he reworks stories from Boccaccio, Sacchetti, and others. The work is also the story of V.'s own life and occupies an important place in the history of autobiography.

VILLANI, G. Giovanni V., *Nuova cronica. Edizione critica*, I: *Libri I-VIII*, III: *Libri XII-XIII*, ed. G. Porta, Parma, Fond. P. Bembo–Guanda, 1990–91, lxx + 733, lix + 691 pp.

SEICENTO

By MAURICE SLAWINSKI, *Lecturer in Italian Studies, Lancaster University*

I. GENERAL

LITERARY HISTORY, CRITICISM, POETICS.   *Letteratura genovese e ligure (profilo storico e antologia)*, ed. Fiorenzo Toso, II: *Cinquecento e Seicento*, Genoa, Marietti, 1989, 224 pp., deals with the dialect production of the area; the *Seicento* section, prefaced by a brief introduction (pp. 27–52), is chiefly dedicated to the poems of Gian Giacomo Cavalli (*c.* 1590–1658), whose humorous transposition of baroque lyric topoi to the vernacular, though not exceptionally original, enjoyed considerable local popularity right through to the 19th c.; among the other selections three stand out for their authors' renown in 'Tuscan' letters: one by A. G. Brignole Sale and two attributed to Chiabrera. F. Piselli, 'Filosofia e poesia nel pensiero estetico italiano', *Testo*, 19, 1990:92–100, is a rapid summary of views as to their respective concerns and mutual relations, which includes brief comments on 17th-c. criticism from the theory of the conceit to Vico, but oddly omits any reference to Italian theorists between Pontano and Tesauro. Also on the relationship between literature and the 'sciences', E. Bellini, 'Agostino Mascardi fra "Ars poetica" e "Ars historica"', *StSec*, 32:65–136, examines the *Arte istorica*'s concessions to the poetics of narrative, pointing out how despite the insistence on the separateness of literature and history Mascardi gives considerable scope to literary-rhetorical techniques in the writing of history at the levels of *inventio* and *dispositio* (in the limited sense of choice and arrangement of subject-matter and arguments), and even the rejection of the wilder flights of poetic *elocutio* may be seen more as a manifestation of Mascardi's 'baroque classicism' than as an outright rejection of poetic ornament. On a related topic, Jon R. Snyder, *Writing the Scene of Speaking. Theories of Dialogue in the Late Italian Renaissance*, Stanford U.P., 1989, 320 pp., outlines the theories of dialogue of G. B. Manso and Sforza Pallavicino, both as literary genres and as vehicles for scientific-philosophical investigation, but fails in my view to take into account how the shift from 'Ciceronian' forms (where authorial views emerge between the lines of the dialogue, and writing is itself part of the heuristic process) to 'dialogues of instruction' (whose function is to expound a body of previously determined authorial views through one or more of the interlocutors) relates to changes in the ways and places in which culture is produced; in fact the author shows scant knowledge of the intellectual context of the 17th-c. debate, ignoring even the most obvious and closely-related concerns (such as Tesauro's 'cavillazione urbana'). Concerning this most important of *Seicento* critic-theorists, P. Frare, 'Il *Cannocchiale aristotelico* da retorica della letteratura a letteratura della retorica'. *StSec*, 32:33–63, argues that Tesauro's work should be seen as a practical literary demonstration of rhetoric, even more than as an 'opera metaretorica', confirming the 'vulgata opinione della parentela [con] *L'Adone*', since both are encyclopaedic demonstrations of a signifying process which is constantly confronted with the 'passaggio in atto da un mondo ordinato gerarchicamente, un *cosmos*, ad un *caos* ingovernabile che si sottrae ad ogni tentativo assiologico': a reading which certainly contains more than a grain of truth, but which perhaps begs more than one question about the very different attitudes of the two authors to the challenges posed by epistemological relativism, and glosses over the reservations and omissions in Tesauro's vindication of Marino; also on Tesauro, S. Briossi, *'Il mondo come segno e come gioco. Su Emanuele Tesauro', *AFLFUS*, 10, 1989:171–85. Finally, G. P. Maragoni, 'Furti in barocco (epicedio per un eroe)', *EL*, 16.4:83–88, is a brief, amused (and amusing) peep into how much of this supposed 'secolo senza poesia' has in fact, wittingly or no, crept into subsequent writers' stylistic tics and mental habits.

THEMES AND TOPICS. *Il nuovo mondo tra storia e invenzione: l'Italia e Napoli*, ed. G. B. De Cesare, Roma, Bulzoni, 1990, 428 pp., contains two essays documenting the impact of the discovery of the new world on *Seicento* literature. F. Liberatori, 'Cristóbal Colón de descubridor a conquistador en el *Mondo nuovo* de Tommaso Stigliani' (53–72); T. Cirillo, 'La scoperta dell'America nei letterati meridionali tra Cinque e Seicento' (203–33).

LIBRARIES, PUBLISHING, MANUSCRIPTS, BIBLIOGRAPHY. Two omissions from previous surveys must be rectified: V. Spini and E. Sandel, *Le edizioni bresciane del Seicento. Catalogo cronologico delle opere stampate a Brescia e Salò*, Mi, Ed. Bibliografica, 1988, xxii + 231 pp., lists no less than 976 editions printed at Brescia and a further 35 from Salò; Saverio Franchi, *Drammaturgia Romana*, Roma, Storia e Letteratura, 1988, 450 pp., lists 1280 published plays and other theatre-related texts which appeared in Rome and the Lazio region in the course of the century, an extraordinary testimony to the vast output of *letterati*, public and private theatres, and printing-houses. Further evidence of the vast scale of *Seicento* publishing, and its permeation of substantial 'middle' strata of readers, is provided by L. Callegari, G. Sartini, G. Bersani Berselli, *La librettistica bolognese nei secoli XVII e XVIII*, Roma, Torre d'Orfeo, 1989, xli + 350 pp., which contains parallel chronological and alphabetical title lists of 1327 libretti (450 for the *Seicento*), accompanied by a wealth of indexes (by author, composer, genre, place of performance, publisher) and computer-generated statistical data. Best of all in many respects, and a very welcome innovation, the chronological list includes the names of each publication's dedicatee(s). Faced with such riches, it seems almost ungrateful to have to note that summary bibliographical descriptions of the texts are not provided. An even more 'popular' (and ephemeral) level of production is documented by P. Bellettini, 'Gli annali ravennati della stamperia Dandi (1694–1698)', *StSec*, 32:269–314, which catalogues 25 titles ('fogli volanti', periodical news sheets and short pamphlets largely relating to local social events) published at Ravenna by a printing-house more normally associated with Forlì (1671–84) and Rimini (1686–1734): a brief, but not uninteresting chapter on the chronological, geographic, and literary margins of the *Seicento*. Jeannine Basso, *Le Genre épistolaire en langue italienne, 1538–1622. Répertoire chronologique et analytique*, 2 vols, Ro, Bulzoni–Nancy U.P., 1990, 750 pp., is an invaluable guide to a particularly rich source of information on literary relations (though the cut-off date seems a little arbitrary, given that the popularity of letter collections continued unabated throughout the *Seicento*).

Two essays provide comprehensive documentation of the contents of substantial private libraries (now dispersed). A. Mirto, *La biblioteca del cardinal Leopoldo de' Medici*, pref. C. Vasoli, F, Olschki, 1990, 484 pp., is based on the *Catalogo* compiled by Leopoldo's librarian Magliabechi some 40 years after his former master's death (1675) and records approximately 2500 volumes, pamphlets, and broadsheets (almost half of them printed outside Italy), dominated by civil and criminal law, natural sciences and astrology, and (as one might expect of a Cardinal) assorted religious works (theology, canon law, homilies, hagiography, church history, Catholic–Protestant controversies), but also containing significant collections of contemporary political works and vernacular poetry, including the major *concettisti* from Marino to Ciro di Pers. Mirto's introduction, which one might have wished more extensive, gives useful information on Leopoldo himself, his role in promoting the Accademia del Cimento, Magliabechi's librarianship, the growth of the collection, and the various channels by which the Cardinal's library was supplied. In R. Lefevre, 'Il principe Agostino Chigi e la sua "Libraria di campagna" in Ariccia (fine secolo XVII)', *ASRSP*, 112, 1989:341–452, the manuscript catalogue of a 'leisure' collection overwhelmingly dedicated to plays, librettos, and accounts of spectacles of every sort, is reproduced with introductory remarks on its history and some biographical information concerning its proprietor.

A. Serrai, 'Historia literaria. I cataloghi ('500 e '600)', *Il Bibliotecario*, 27–28:1–271, is an extensive full-title list of published catalogues (not exclusively Italian), subdivided into those of printers and booksellers, private libraries, institutions, and even (shades of Borges!) 'fantastic' catalogues and those including books from more than one library; to the indefatigable Serrai we also owe listings of 'Bibliografie degli ordini religiosi', *ib.*, 25, 1990: 1–29.

Anna Nicolò, *Il carteggio di Cassiano dal Pozzo. Catalogo*, F, Olschki, 323 pp., catalogues Dal Pozzo's own correspondence and the letters of others which came into his possession, giving detailed descriptions of the form and contents of the numerous manuscript volumes (from the Library of the Accademia dei Lincei 41 which formerly belonged to the Dukes of Aosta, three from the École de Médecine, Montpellier, one in the Vatican Archives); this is followed by indexes of correspondents and addressees, and (perhaps most useful of all) a chronological list of the 7000-odd letters catalogued. I also note L. Pelizzoni and S. Pelizzoni, 'Per l'identificazione degli autografi di Federico Borromeo', *Aevum*, 64, 1990: 387–94, which discusses the authenticity of MSS in the Biblioteca Ambrosiana; R. E. Pepin, 'The satires of "Sectanus" and the Spinelli Archive', *Yale University Library Gazette*, 65, 1990: 20–25; A. Bartòla, 'Alessandro VII e Athanasius Kircher S. J. Ricerche ed appunti sulla loro corrispondenza erudita e sulla storia di alcuni codici chigiani', *MBAV*, 3, 1989, pp. 7–105.

COURTS, ACADEMIES, INTELLECTUALS, ORGANIZATION OF CULTURE (but see section 5 for the Lincei Academy). Pierpaolo Merlin, *Tra guerre e tornei. La corte sabauda di Carlo Emanuele I*, T, SEI, xvi + 324 pp., covers the crucial years when Turin was established as the capital of a geographically and culturally Italian 'absolutist' state and the Piedmontese nobility replaced that of Savoy as the chief support of the dynasty. The study is chiefly concerned with their transformation from a feudal army to a class of office-holders, and with the commerce of wealth, power, and influence between the Duke and his nobles, but also touches on the politics of the court, split between pro-French and pro-Spanish factions, and on the 'cultural fall-out' of the new regime, from the hired pens of poets and historians to the 'anthropology' of court display. But the subject's potential is not, alas, fulfilled: a vast amount of useful information is put on display, but in its raw state, with no overall design, and often no clear indication whether a particular fragment of the puzzle is to be attributed exemplary value or is merely an isolated instance; nor is its retrieval made any easier by the absence of an index. Particularly disappointing from the point of view of literary studies is the final chapter, on the cultural and propaganda programmes of the dynasty, which is the least new in content and the most superficial in interpretation. Renata Ago, *Carriera e clientela nella Roma barocca*, Bari, Laterza, 1990, 190 pp., deals with Curial careers of the latter part of the century and is drawn mainly from extant correspondence of the Santacroce, Spada, and Corsini families; *letterati* figure only in passing, and invariably in their extra-literary guises, but the account is nevertheless of some interest in clarifying the context in which they operated.

To the most common courtly-professional activity of the *letterati* is devoted Tommaso Costo and Michele Benvenga, *Il segretario di lettere*, ed. S. S. Nigro, Palermo, Sellerio, 114 pp., consisting of the text of two 'trattati di segreteria' written in 1602 and 1681 respectively; a brief introduction underlines their different approaches, with Costo earnestly emphasizing the minutest details of his 'arte' and seeking to salvage what he can of the humanist ethic of court service, while Benvenga's brief, metaphor-laden collection of aphorisms bespeaks the most complete ethical disengagement.

In *Patronage and Institutions: Science, Technology, and Medicine at the European Court, 1500–1750*, ed. B. T. Moran, Woodbridge, Boydell, 272 pp., W. Eamonn, 'Court, academy and printing house: patronage and scientific careers in late-Renaissance Italy' (25–50), actually focuses on the early 17th c., summarizing the findings of what has become an increasingly fruitful branch of *Seicento* studies, though its own analysis and conclusions are perhaps a little general and superficial; P. Findlen, 'The economy of scientific exchange in early modern Italy' (5–24), is more narrowly focused, concentrating on the system of obligations which underpinned relations between intellectuals and between an intellectual and his patrons; perhaps for that reason it is more informative and stimulating than the previous contribution, though in the absence of a precise theoretical model of such relations it remains excessively impressionistic, as compared, for example, to the theoretical rigour of the recent article by M. Biagioli (*YWMLS*, 52:479). Also on the subject of patronage, D. Conrieri, 'Quattro lettere di Francesco Fulvio Frugoni', *StSec*, 32:3–31, discusses three letters (1678–79) to the Regent Duchess Maria of Savoy-Nemours, and one of 1678 to the Bolognese senator Carlo Luigi Scappi, in the context of Frugoni's patronage strategies.

A brief but significant addition to our understanding of the role of universities in promoting social mobility and training cadres for 'absolutist' administrations is M. C. Toniolo Fascione, 'Il Collegio della Sapienza di Pisa nella Toscana del Seicento: provenienza culturale, sociale e geografica delle richieste di ammissione', *I collegi universitari in Europa tra il XIV e il XVIII secolo. Atti del Convegno di Studi, Siena–Bologna, 16–19 maggio 1988*, ed. D. Maffei and H. De Ridder-Symoens, Mi, Giuffrè, vii + 208 pp., pp. 33–45.

LANGUAGE.   Maria Luisa Altieri Biagi, *L'avventura della mente. Studi sulla lingua scientifica*, Na, Morano, 1990, 400 pp., includes essays on Galileo's syntax, the dialogue form in scientific writing, and the development of scientific language from 17th to 19th c., an issue also addressed by M. T. Frattegiani, 'Caratteristiche del linguaggio scientifico rintracciabili negli scritti di Galileo, Redi e Volta', *AUSP*, 15, 1990:209–46. M. Slawinski, 'Siamo tutti gesuiti? Lingua, cultura e ideologia dal Seicento a oggi', *AFLFUP* (*SLL*), 24, 1986–87 (1989):197–224, traces the development of stylistic models from Bembian petrarchism to Jesuit rhetoric, arguing that the latter continues to condition the (largely unconscious) choice of tropes and figures in modern Italian.

TRAVELLERS, INTERNATIONAL RELATIONS. Lorenzo Magalotti, *Diario di Francia dell'anno 1668*, ed. M. L. Doglio, Palermo, Sellerio, 210 pp., reproduces the text of 40 letters to the future Cosimo III, written during a Parisian visit on the vaguest of diplomatic business (the letters themselves, purposely intended as a kind of princely correspondence course on French politics and *mores*, appear to have been the chief objective of the mission), which Doglio's introduction shrewdly describes as sliding 'dall'*institutio* al ragguaglio', testimony to a 'modo di vedere per il principe' which bespeaks the definitive decline of the humanist ideal of *cortegianeria*. I. Klein and C. Kleinhenz, 'The Order of Santo Stefano in the Levant: an unpublished account of a voyage in 1627', *Viator*, 21, 1990:323–47, includes both a transcription of the original hitherto unpublished text, and an English translation, with brief prefatory remarks; the work may be of some interest to students of the *romanzo*, as well as to those of popular writing and autobiography.

M. Milato, 'Henri de Rohan e Maiolino Bisaccioni: sull'interesse dello stato', *PenP*, 24:143–64, summarizes the hitherto unnoticed manuscript 'Consideration del Marchese Maiolino Bisaccioni sopra l'Interesse dello Stato del Duca di Roano', which Milato dates around 1639, its main interest residing in a 'moderate', if somewhat piecemeal, critique of the Protestant soldier-politician's maxims, viewed from the standpoint of 'uno scrittore . . . preoccupato e fiero dell' "italianità" ' (though what this term might really mean in a 17th-c. context Milato does not make clear). R. Duso, 'Sulla diffusione delle *Lettere Provinciali* di Blaise Pascal nel Sei-Settecento veneto', *AtV*, 132, 1989:71–79, makes brief remarks concerning circulation and known readers, and provides a list of early editions found in Veneto libraries. I also note *I. M. Battafarano, '*Epitaphia ioco-seria*: Loredano und Hallman', *Beiträge zur Aufnahme der italienischen und spanischen Literatur in Deutschland im 16. und 17. Jahrhundert*, ed. A. Martino, Amsterdam, Rodopi, 1990, pp. 133–50.

MISCELLANEOUS CONTRIBUTIONS. Two articles, D. Raines, 'Pouvoir ou privilèges nobiliaires: le dilemme du patriciat vénitien face aux agrégations du XVIIe siècle', *Annales*, 46:827–47, and P. L.

Rovito, 'Strutture cetuali, riformismo ed eversione nelle rivolte apulo-lucane di metà seicento', *ASPN*, 106, 1988 (1989):241–308, may be of some interest to anyone seeking to read *Seicento* literature in the context of class tensions, as well as providing background material for contemporary histories of Venice's wars against the Turk and Masaniello's Neapolitan revolt.

Inquisitorial proceedings are the subject of Giuseppe Farinelli and Ermanno Paccagnini, *Processo per stregoneria a Caterina de Medici, 1616–1617*, Mi, Rusconi, 1989, 380 pp., which consists of a long essay by Paccagnini, '"In materia de stregharie"', surveying the history of witchcraft prosecutions, in Lombardy and beyond, from the late middle ages to the abolition of the Milanese Inquisition (1764), and the record of Caterina's trial, edited by Farinelli with his own substantial introduction; but the essays are similarly old-fashioned in their view of witchcraft trials and inquisitorial procedures, ignoring the substantial rewriting of these subjects which has taken place over the last twenty years, while the edition of the trial documents is really little more than a slavish transcription, with all the mannerisms of 'micro-history' but little sense of what their significance might really be. A similar enterprise (though I cannot comment on its quality) is *La confessione di una strega. Un frammento di storia della controriforma*, ed. L. Sambenazzi, introd. A. Foa, Ro, Bulzoni 1989, 160 pp. Some of the most important recent writings in this field have now been re-issued in John Tedeschi, *The Prosecution of Heresy: Collected Studies on the Inquisition in Early Modern Italy*, MRTS, xxii + 417 pp., which brings together revised versions of Tedeschi's indispensable contributions; bibliographical material has been updated, and a new essay on 'Inquisitorial sources and their uses' is also included. A second interesting addition to the study of the Inquisition is Romano Canosa, *Storia dell'Inquisizione in Italia dalla metà del Cinquecento alla fine del Settecento*, v: *Napoli e Bologna. Le procedure inquisitoriali*, Mi, Sapere 2000, 1990, 200 pp., though this is more a collection of documents organized by topic than a history, and is chiefly concerned with legal practice rather than the content of trials (the author is a serving judge); it contains no really new material but provides useful summaries and an extensive bibliography (but again, alas, no index); earlier volumes, previously unrecorded, but published from 1986 on, had dealt with Modena (I), Venice (II), Turin and Genoa (III), Milan and Florence (IV). A further book on witchcraft, Estella Galasso Calderara and Carla Sodini, *Abratassà. Tre secoli di stregherie in una libera repubblica*, Lucca, Pacini Fazzi, 1989, 322 pp., is concerned with the attitudes of lay magistrates: it examines archival records of witchcraft prosecutions in Lucca (where there was no Church inquisition) for a period from 1571 to 1743, and concludes that the Lucca courts were notably lenient (and occasionally sceptical), contradicting current orthodoxy which tends to emphasize the greater severity (and laxer attitude to legal form) of the secular arm.

A different kind of state control, but more directly connected with literary production, is investigated in L. Braida, 'L'affermazione della censura di stato in Piemonte dall'editto del 1648 alle costituzioni per l'università del 1772', *RSI*, 102, 1990:717–95, though it is to be hoped that future research might work back to the pre-history of the first formal edicts of 1648–49 (promulgated by the regent Madama di Francia and her son Carlo Emanuele II) to cover the reign of Carlo Emanuele I and the first expansion of literary patronage and printing in Piedmont.

G. Bino, 'Sensibilità religiosa e mentalità popolare nel XVII secolo. Il culto di un santo in terra d'Otranto nella pubblicistica coeva', *ArSP*, 43, 1989:169–82, examines the cult of S. Oronzio in the second half of the century, as manifested in local ritual and in devotional literature.

M. P. Balbi, 'Il paesaggio come immagine. Per una storia dell'idea di paesaggio attraverso le descrizioni dell'alta valle Pesio tra XV e XIX secolo', *BSSAAPC*, 103.2, 1990:57–87, is largely (pp.63–77) devoted to two 17th-c. accounts: that to be found in the *Theatrum Sabaudiae* of 1682 and the unpublished 'Descrizione del Piemonte' written earlier in the century by F. A. Della Chiesa.

2. POETRY

Two important new editions of major 'Marinist' poets span the extremes of editorial practice: both are perfectly justifiable and each has its merits and weaknesses. What is now perhaps needed, in view of the number of modern editions of 17th-c. texts published, is renewed debate on the criteria to be employed, and it is as a brief preliminary contribution to such debate that the following comments should be taken.

Claudio Achillini, *Poesie*, ed. A. Colombo, Parma, Zara, 378 pp., collates the early editions (basically that of the 1632 *Poesie*, with additions from the 1644 and 1650 *Rime* constituting two separate appendices) and notes all significant variants, including those from manuscript sources and collections of occasional poems preceding the *princeps*: only minimal orthographic alterations have been carried out (modern accents, 'v' for 'u', 'ed' or 'et' for '&'), while the original punctuation and capitalization have been retained. The result is certainly interesting, though occasionally punctuation is heavier than perhaps absolutely necessary, and capitalization at the beginning of the line a little inconsistent (it has been preserved only after a full-stop or where otherwise deemed significant). This, however, is a text for specialists, which the 'common reader' (if such there still is) may find a little strange. Very full descriptions are also given of printed and manuscript sources, while a brief but pithy introduction seeks to place A.'s verse in the dual context of *concettismo* and his own principal career as courtier-lawyer. The edition has the effect of qualifying somewhat earlier views of his poetry, including those in the editor's own preliminary work (*YWMLS*, 50:556): with the whole *opus*, rather than anthologized titbits, before us it is much clearer just how different A.'s style is from that of either Marino or the so-called *pre-marinisti* (more monumental and grandly epideictic, baroque in its hyperbole rather than the quality and quantity of its conceits) and how its themes and contents are almost invariably connected to some courtly or professional function, very remote from the concept of literature as an autonomous discourse that was at the heart of Marino's production.

By contrast Giuseppe Battista, *Opere*, ed. G. Rizzo, Galatina, Congedo, 624 pp., is unashamedly modernizing, seeking to produce a text more immediately accessible to today's reader, though like Colombo, Rizzo has quite correctly retained the full, sometimes quite lengthy, description preceding each poem rather than opting for the simplified versions to be found in past anthologies. The result is by and large successful, though just occasionally the 'thinning out' of punctuation (on the basis of sense sequences rather than reading pauses) has the effect of making it difficult, at first glance, to 'hear' how the verse should be read. Faced with a much larger body of work than Achillini's, the editor has opted to give us the complete text of only the first and fourth parts of the *Poesie meliche*, with short selections from the third and fifth parts, as well as from the *Epicedi eroici* and the *Lettere* (32 letters to G. B. Manso, undisputed arbiter of Neapolitan literary life and chief anchor of B.'s patronage strategy, plus the letter, to A. Bassi, announcing his death). An excellent introduction reconstructs B.'s role in the literary culture of mid-*Seicento* Naples, relates his poetry to the dominant 'Marinist' model, and emphasizes its strong moralizing vein, though reading through the poems I am struck by the no less strong element of what one might call his 'social realism', the piecemeal daily chronicle of the habits and rituals of Neapolitan (upper-class) society, especially evident in the sections published in their entirety. This is perhaps its clearest distinguishing feature, not only when compared with its major model, Marino, whose depiction of social mores almost always operates at a level of idealized generality, but also in relation to older 'Marinist' contemporaries such as Maia Materdona. Two small reservations concerning Rizzo's 'apparato': the absence of detailed bibliographical descriptions of the main editions of B.'s works (these are listed and their contents noted, but a little more information would have been welcome in view of the patchy state of *Seicento* bibliography), and the lack of any explanation as to Rizzo's selection criteria (whereas the notes, glossary, and inventory of proper names, running to over 150 pages, occasionally verge on the superfluous, as when the editor deems it necessary to remind us who Prometheus was).

Giambattista Basile, *Le opere napoletane*, I: *Le muse napolitane*, ed. O. S. Casale, Ro, Benincasa, 1989, xxxii + 280 pp., is a splendidly produced edition of Basile's nine dialect 'egroche' (the essentially urban attitudes of the interlocutors might rather suggest the term 'anti-eclogue') accompanied by an Italian prose translation. On a more modest scale, Ludovico Lepòreo, *Amante imperversato*, ed. A. Lora-Totino and S. M. Martini, Na, 'Terra del fuoco' (a supplement to the review of that name), 1989, 80 pp., reproduces 56 'nonsense' sonnets from the 1682 edition of L.'s poems, with an introduction making a less than convincing case for their status as proto-modernist 'denudazione del corpo poetico'.

A thematic approach to the reading of the baroque lyric is taken by V. Bonito, 'Gli orologi della poesia: meccanica e barocco', *Intersezioni*, 11:261–81, which hints at new depths to be explored in the rich seam of 17th-c. 'clock poems' and calls on modern luminaries from Benjamin to Foucault to point the way, but a patchwork of fashionable quotations, interspersed with his own somewhat portentous theorizing ('Nell'orologio il tempo scorre, è lo spazio dove concettualmente il movimento è il primo aspetto da considerare'), and the rather perfunctory discussion of familiar texts which follows (Ciro, Paoli, Sempronio, Battista, Lubrano) do not add up to a convincing re-reading of this popular topos. S. Rizzolino, 'Alcune figure teologiche mariane nella poesia dell'ultimo cinquecento e del Seicento', *StSec*, 32:231–66, seeks to demonstrate Counter-Reformation devotional literature's adherence to the developing body of Marian theology and its dogmatic expression, though his examples and analysis rather suggest that the authors considered were better mariologists than poets. M. Capucci, 'Due poemetti estensi di Marco Boschini', *ib.*, 213–29, deals with eulogies 'in morte' of Almerigo and Alfonso IV d'Este (dated respectively 1661 and 1663) written by a picture-dealer connected with several North-Italian courts in what would appear to my untutored ear to be a watered-down Venetian dialect (but oddly, Capucci does not comment on this aspect). I also record G. Cavallini, 'Breve nota sull'edizione critica delle opere di Pirro Schettino', *Italianistica*, 19, 1990:153–55 (for which edition see *YWMLS*, 51:486).

GRILLO. Elio Durante and Anna Martellotti, *Don Angelo G.,
O.S.B., alias Livio Celiano, poeta per musica del secolo decimosesto*, F, SPES,
1989, 429 pp., deals with the erotic poetry of Tasso's often-referred-to
but little-studied friend (whose 'cover' the authors were the first to
'blow' in their *Cronistoria del concerto delle dame principalissime di
Margherita Gonzaga d'Este*, F, SPES, 1979), but perhaps its most
notable interest lies in the reconstruction of G.'s biography. The
monograph is the starting-point for G. Raboni, 'Il madrigalista
genovese Livio Celiano e il benedettino Angelo G.', *StSec*, 32 : 137–88,
which contrast the two poetic careers of the 'Abate di S. Paolo', asks
(without providing wholly satisfactory answers) what the poetic
relationship between them might be, and makes some interesting and
useful preliminary remarks concerning the theological and rhetorical
strategies of the devotional poems.

MARINO. A. Colombo, 'Versi autografi del M. per Ranuccio
Farnese e Margherita Aldobrandini (1599)', *LItal*, 43:374–88, publishes the text and discusses the context of an extremely interesting
finding: two sonnets written while the poet was still in Naples, which
suggest that well before his move to Rome he had set in motion the
patronage strategy which three years later would lead to his entry into
the household of Cardinal-nephew Pietro Aldobrandini. G. Bàrberi
Squarotti, 'Venere e Marte: le allegorie della pace', *ib.*, 517–46, traces
the vernacular fortunes of this Platonist topos from Poliziano,
through Tasso (Rinaldo and Armida as a careful reversal of the values
of the original) to *L'Adone* XIII: here the comic 'imborghesimento' of
the protagonists is well observed, though the critic perhaps underesti-
mates the underlying seriousness of Mars's part in a 'poema di pace'
where the presence of war is less marginal than might at first sight
appear. F. Luoni, 'Un nouveau monde pour Psyche', *DSS*, 43:143–
61, compares La Fontaine's treatment of Apuleius's fable to that of
M. (*L'Adone* IV), though the point of the comparison escapes me. M.
Slawinski, 'The poet's senses: G. B. M.'s epic poem *L'Adone* and the
new science', *CC*, 13:51–81, attempts to suggest some of the ways in
which the 'itinerary' of *L'Adone* parallels those of 17th-c. natural
philosophy. P. Frare, 'M. postmoderno? (A proposito di due recenti
studi mariniani)', *Italianistica* 20:139–49, is essentially a sympathetic
review of two volumes, respectively written and edited by F.
Guardiani (*YWMLS*, 51:487–89), which does more than justice to
their virtues, but scarcely justifies its own catchy title, and does not
significantly advance discussion.

WORDS AND MUSIC. *I musicisti e la lirica di Gabriello Chiabrera*, ed. S.
Volta, Savona, supplement to *Agenda*, 9, 1990, 64 pp.

3. DRAMA

Silvia Carandini, *Teatro e spettacolo nel Seicento*, Bari, Laterza, 1990, 288 pp., is an 'opera divulgativa' (in a series stretching from the Middle Ages to the present) but none the worse for that, especially since its wide-ranging references imply a solid scholarly grasp of the period; its emphasis is on performance rather than texts, and in addition to covering the main aspects (economic and social as well as artistic) of the subject, from court and academic theatre to church spectacles and the *commedia dell'arte*, it rightly stresses the deeper, 'spectacular' nature of baroque society (though falling short of saying how it might differ from medieval and Renaissance pageants, or of seeking out its root causes). Nicola Mangini, *Alle origini del teatro moderno e altri saggi*, Modena, Mucchi, 1989, 302 pp., opens with three essays (all of which have previously appeared in periodicals and conference proceedings) on theatre in the Veneto at the turn of the century, the Paduan stage at the time of C. de' Dottori, and early attempts at a 'reform' of the theatre at the close of the century.

DRAMATIC LITERATURE. The recent Chiabrera celebrations (*YWMLS*, 52:472) have led to a modest revival of interest in the poet's theatrical activities, which in the past have figured little in critics' perception but were certainly a major aspect of his 'professional' activities as a writer: Marzia Pieri, '"Artificio", "vanità" e "onesti diletti": il teatro di Gabriello Chiabrera', *RLI*, 95.1–2:5–20, points out the extent of Chiabrera's theatrical activities (spanning orthodox dramatic genres, new hybrid ones, and texts for other forms of court spectacle), which engaged him throughout a long career, though scarcely with the same attention as his lyric and epic production, and concludes that the results are what might be expected of such indifferent commitment; F. Vazzoler, 'Il poeta, l'attrice, la cantante. A proposito di Chiabrera nella vita teatrale e musicale del XVII secolo', *TeSt*, 11:305–33, concerns the poet's dealings with Isabella Andreini and their influence on his theatrical output.

D. Romei, 'Il papa "comico". Sui melodrammi di Giulio Rospigliosi (Clemente IX)', *ParL*, 482, 1990:43–62, is a brief sketch of the future Pope's play-writing career under the aegis of his Barberini patrons: interesting from the viewpoint of Curial patronage, though a little skimpy when it comes to the importance or otherwise of Rospigliosi's dramas of martyrdom either as literary texts or in the development of opera. M. L. Mayer-Modena, 'A proposito di una scena "all'ebraica" nella *Schiavetta* dell'Andreini', *Acme*, 43.3:73–81, analyses fragments of a 'Judeo-Italian dialect' in a scene from this comedy of 1612. L. Donadio, 'Filippo Caetani: note per una biografia', *AION(SR)*, 31, 1989:173–90, adds to the information concerning the life and theatrical activities of this Roman amateur playwright contained in an earlier article by the same scholar (*YWMLS*, 52:473).

COMMEDIA DELL'ARTE. An omission which must be corrected is Thomas H. Hack, *Commedia dell'Arte. A Guide to the Primary and Secondary Literature*, NY, Garland, 1988, xiv + 450 pp., an extremely rich bibliography with annotated subject entries in sections including *scenari*, improvisation techniques, actors, machines, iconographical evidence, and the *commedia* abroad (by country); for rapid consultation there are also a title index of *scenari* and an alphabetical short-title list. Virginia Scott, *The Commedia dell'Arte in Paris 1644–1697*, Charlottesville, Virginia U.P., 1990, 459 pp., documents the history of the 'comédie italienne' from the establishment of the first permanent company (after a century of regular visits by itinerant players), with a wealth of material concerning its theatres, patrons, finances, personnel, and repertoire, as well as tracing its gradual 'Frenchification' (though new players continued to be imported directly from Italy for most of the century) and the shift from the spectacle and *lazzi* which dominated its early performances to sentimental comedy and a measured dose of social realism. *Viaggi teatrali dall' Italia a Parigi tra '500 e '600. Atti del Convegno Internazionale, Torino 6–7–8 Aprile 1987*, ed. R. Alonge, Genoa, Costa & Nolan, 1989, 256 pp., deals chiefly with the early 17th c., including S. Mamone, 'Il viaggio di Maria, regina di Francia, da Firenze a Lione a Parigi (1600)' (63–108); R. Tessari, 'O Diva, o "Estable à tous chevaux". L'ultimo viaggio di Isabella Andreini' (128–42); G. Davico Bonino, 'Riccoboni a Parigi: l'utopia di un teatro d'arte' (143–48); L. Sozzi, 'Molière, l'Aretino e la Commedia dell'Arte' (149–61); C. Burattelli, 'L'emigrazione di un testo dell'Arte: da *L'Inavertito* di Barbieri a *L'Etourdi* di Molière' (182–99); F. Taviani, '*Centaura*' (234–49), about a play of 1622 by G. B. Andreini.

G. Cecchi, 'Dal carteggio tra Flaminio Scala e Don Giovanni de' Medici (1616–1621). Riflessioni e proposte di ricerca', *BTe*, 17, 1990:75–86, discusses a collection of 96 letters documenting the player-patron relationship and raising interesting questions for the story of the *commedia*; M. Marigo, 'Angiola D'Orso comica dell'arte e traduttrice', *ib.*, 18, 1990:65–94, traces the theatrical and literary career of this player, who corresponded with the Farnese and Bentivoglio in the period 1650–70 and translated contemporary Spanish texts; Marzia Pieri, 'Maschere italiane e Carnevali del Nord', *ib.*, 21:1–19, makes the portrayal of *commedia* figures in a 17th-c. genre painting the starting point for some observations on the *comici dell'arte*'s travels and the establishment of an internationally recognized iconographic tradition quite distinct from direct experience of their work. Other contributions include G. Cecchi, 'Sulle tracce di Domenico Bruni Comico Confidente', *ib.*, 21:47–62; S. Jansen, 'On the clauses in a scenario of Flaminio Scala', *QI*, 11, 1990:175–96.

COURT FESTIVALS, PUBLIC SPECTACLES. G. Cirillo and G. Godi, *Il trionfo del Barocco*, Parma, Albertelli, 1989, 355 pp. (with additional contributions by G. Marchetti and G. Nello Vetro), deals with the 1687 celebrations for the wedding of the heir to the Duchy of Parma, Odoardo, under the direction of the Bibiena brothers. Ivano Cavallini, *Musica, cultura e spettacolo in Istria tra '500 e '600*, F, Olschki, 1990, xviii + 244 pp., is principally concerned with the musical tradition of this multi-lingual frontier region, but also contains some information on the theatrical activities of the Accademia Palladia, and on public festivities and popular entertainments. C. Di Luca, 'Tra "sperimentazione" e "professionismo" teatrale: Pio Enea II Obizzi e lo spettacolo nel Seicento', *TeSt*, 11:257–303, reconstructs the 'multi-media' productions (involving tournaments, ballet, and musical theatre) of this aristocratic 'writer-director' who would appear almost single-handedly to have continued the Ferrarese tradition of court spectacle in the period immediately following the departure of the Este. Florentine court festivals continue to attract the attention of theatre historians: R. Guardenti, 'Un profilo di Maria de' Medici, regina di Francia e impresaria teatrale', *BTe*, 12, 1989:114–23, is a (chiefly descriptive) review article of the previously overlooked Sara Mamone, *Firenze e Parigi, due capitali dello spettacolo per una regina: Maria de' Medici*, Mi, Silvana, 1987, 279 pp. Also by S. Mamone, 'Foto di gruppo: i Medici in scena alle nozze di Maria', *ib.*, 19–20, 1990:63–97, discusses the significance of official paintings of court festivals both as historical evidence and as contemporary propaganda. A lesser Medici theatrical is recorded by D. Landolfi, 'Su un teatrino mediceo e sull'Accademia degli Incostanti a Firenze nel primo Seicento', *TeSt*, 10:57–88.

OPERA. Paolo Fabbri, *Il secolo cantante: per una storia del libretto d'opera nel Seicento*, Bo, Mulino, 1990, 350 pp., concentrates on Venetian 'commercial' theatre, though the opening chapter deals with Florentine and Roman *intermezzi*, and early *melodramma*, and the penultimate ranges further afield, to the theory and practice of the *libretto* in the rest of Italy in the second half of the century; both the socio-economic and the literary aspects of the form are discussed, and what emerges is the librettists' very considerable, self-conscious, concern with literariness and literary propriety. Tim Carter, *Iacopo Peri (1561–1633). The Life and Works*, 2 vols, NY, Garland, 1989, 519 pp., is of general interest because of Peri's role in the early development of opera, but also contains a series of appendices of more specifically literary and theatrical import, including the text of S. Rosselli's mock-serious commentary on F. Ruspoli's 'sonnettaccio' against Peri, descriptions of Florentine *intermedi*, and letters from G. de' Bardi to M. Buonarroti the younger.

I also note Laura Pistolesi, *Del recitar cantando. Per uno studio comparativo dell' 'Euridice' di Jacopo Peri e dell' 'Euridice' di Giulio Caccini*, ed. C. Terni, Mi, Associazione Amici della Scala, 1990, 152 pp.; **Il diletto della scena e dell'armonia. Teatro e musica nelle Venezie dal '500 al '700. Atti del III ciclo dei Corsi Estivi di Musicologia del Conservatorio 'A. Buzzolla', Adria 1986–88*, ed. I. Cavallini, Adria, 1990, 324 pp.

4. PROSE

NARRATIVE.   A major addition to the growing body of modern editions of *Seicento* narrative is Tommaso Costo, *Il fuggilozio*, ed. C. Calenda, Roma, Salerno, 1989, xlv + 746 pp., one of the best-known *novellieri* of the period and perhaps the most successful work of this literary conservative. Further reminders that the novella tradition neither disappeared nor was simply subsumed into the sub-plots and digressions of the *romanzi* are B. Porcelli, 'Struttura macro e micro-testuale e letterarietà nelle "Duecento novelle" del Malespini', *Italianistica*, 18, 1989:47–72, and Id., 'La cronologia nelle novelle del Malespini', *EL*, 15.1, 1990:17–29, which apply techniques Porcelli has already used to good effect on Marino's *Adone* to this *novelliere* of 1609; see also, concerning the fortunes of the most famous 17th-c. *novelliere*, V. Kröker, 'Basile und die Kinder. Zur Rezeptionsgeschichte des *Pentamerone* und seiner Bearbeitungen für Kinder', *ConLet*, 15:3–34.

The uncertain dividing-line between the two narrative genres is the starting-point for M. A. Cortini, 'Narrativa barocca tra romanzo e novella: le tecniche della "amplificatio" ne *La fuggitiva* di G. Brusoni', *Ragioni retoriche di discorsi letterari. Retorica e letteratura tra narrativa, poetica, oratoria sacra e politica*, ed. G. Ledda, Ro, Bulzoni, 1990, 280 pp., pp. 77–105, which deploys the tropes and figures of rhetoric to demonstrate how B. vastly expands what in terms of its main narrative is little more than a novella, to a full-length *romanzo*, a point perhaps a little too self-evident to require so long an analysis, though passing remarks on the superfluousness of many episodes and the associated failure of causality are interesting and bear interesting parallels (not developed) with other *Seicento* texts, starting with *L'Adone*. R. Funara, 'I romanzi "meravigliosi"', *AASLAP*, 8, 1987–88 (1989):79–111, is a general survey which does not seem to me greatly to add to the body of research which has been gradually building up over the last twenty years. M. Corradini, 'La parabola letteraria di

Anton Giulio Brignole Salc', *Aevum*, 64, 1990:387–94, suggests a contrast, or evolution, between B.S.'s 'avant-garde' *Instabilità dell' Ingegno* (1635) and the later *Satirico innocente* (1648), and attributes it to the influence of the 'moderate baroque' views of Matteo Pellegrini, who moved to Genova in 1637; to my mind the argument is somewhat vitiated by the failure to re-examine the terms of a debate which had everyone, from Marino down, criticizing the excesses of *concettismo*, to be identified (of course) with everyone's work but their own. H. Albani, 'Un roman baroque oublié. *L'Ormondo* de Francesco Pona (1635) entre nouveauté et conformisme,' *EL*, 14.4, 1989:37–57, focuses on the tensions between presumed libertinism and orthodoxy, a subject also touched on by R. Funara, '*L'Ormondo* di Francesco Pona', *AASLAP*, 8, 1987–88 (1989):283–317, chiefly devoted to a somewhat aimless narratological analysis. Neither essay, however, quite explains why we should attend to this 'frantumato romanzo'.

BIOGRAPHY, AUTOBIOGRAPHY.   Cecilia Ferrazzi, *Autobiografia di una santa mancata, 1609–1664*, cd. A. Jacobson Schutte, Bergamo, Lubrino, 1990, 113 pp., is a curious and intriguing document, also touching on popular faith, inquisitorial practices, and popular literacy; its author, who had previously kept a hostel for 'putte pericolanti', dictated it to a friar, by way of exculpation, while a prisoner of the Venetian inquisitors, who had arrested her on a charge of laying false claims to sanctity. S. Adorini Braccesi, 'L'esilio e la memoria. Vincenzo Burlamacchi (Ginevra 1598–1682) e il "Libro dei ricordi degnissimi della nostra famiglia"', *CSt*, 28:31–76, describes a family record (begun in 1622 and preserved in manuscript in the Geneva public library) which chiefly details the 16th-c. fortunes of a Protestant family from Lucca who took refuge north of the Alps towards the close of that century. G. C. Amoretti, 'La *Vita di Gabriello Chiabrera da lui stesso descritta* nella tradizione testuale ligure. Contributo per l'edizione critica', *LItal*, 43:587–92, makes rather heavy weather of the supposed editorial questions posed by this brief though interesting text, the most reliable extant version of which, the 1654 edition correctly identified by Amoretti, was overlooked by Chiabrera's modern editor, Franco Croce.

CHURCH ORATORY.   S. Fabrizio-Costa, 'Quelques emplois du personnage de Marie-Madeleine dans l'art oratoire italien de l'âge baroque', *ChrI*, 27:53–84.

5.   THOUGHT

PHILOSOPHY, THEOLOGY, NATURAL PHILOSOPHY.   *Cristina di Svezia: scienza ed alchimia nella Roma barocca*, Bari, Dedalo, 1990, 272 pp., contains, as well as essays dedicated to Cristina herself and her

Swedish background, two contributions concerned with Roman scientific and philosophical culture at the close of the century, W. Di Palma, 'Gli scienziati alla corte di Cristina di Svezia', and T. Bovi, 'Il *Salotto* di Cristina di Svezia e la cultura scientifica della seconda metà del '600 a Roma'. P. Redondi, 'Teologia ed epistemologia nella rivoluzione scientifica', *Belfagor*, 45, 1990:613–36, uses examples drawn largely, though not exclusively, from early 17th-c. Italy to make a convincing case for the need to replace the traditional adversarial model of the interaction between theological and scientific discourses with a more fluid account of the ways in which theologians and natural philosophers (not infrequently, as in the case of the Collegio Romano, the very same people!) continually responded to, and were affected by, the 'rival' practice. P. Findlen, '"Quanto scherzevole la natura"'. La scienza che gioca dal Rinascimento all'Illuminismo', *Intersezioni*, 10, 1990:413–36 (also, in English, in *RQ*, 43, 1990:292–331), seeks to demonstrate how the science of the period moved 'among the various philosophical approaches to knowledge, combining intellectual categories and experimental data in ways that now seem inherently conflictual' and argues that 'lusus provides an interesting opening into the social, cultural, and philosophical systems of the sixteenth and seventeenth centuries'. By the same author, 'From Aldrovandi to Algarotti: the contours of science in early modern Italy', *BJHS*, 24:353–60, is a review essay devoted in part to B. Basile, *L'invenzione del vero* (*YWMLS*, 50:560). P. Gozza, 'Atomi, "spiritus", suoni: le *Speculationi di musica* (1670) del "galileiano" Pietro Mengoli', *Nuncius*, 5.2, 1990:75–98, draws attention to Mengoli's atomistic theory of sound and his 'straordinaria fisiologia dell'udito': though the work referred to dates from half a century later, there are some interesting considerations to be derived from such views for Marino's Garden of the Senses in *L'Adone* VI–VIII. J. Tribby, 'Cooking (with) Clio and Cleo: eloquence and experiment in seventeenth-century Florence', *JHI*, 52:417–39, is an extremely intriguing, if not in every detail convincing, discussion of the interplay of 'scientific' experiment and the 'art' of *civile conversazione* in Redi's *Osservazioni intorno alle vipere* (1664). I. Truci, 'Acquisto di due manoscritti Magalotti di provenienza Ginori-Venturi', *Nuncius*, 6.1:171–74, announces the purchase, by the Florence Istituto e Museo di Storia Naturale e della Scienza of a 'Scrittura intorno al paragone degli occhiali di S[ua] A[ltezza] S[erenissima]', and a 'Miscellanea di cose fisiche non stampate del Galileo e altri' (including letters by G. to F. Ingoli and by V. Cesarini to G.

BELLARMINO. **Roberto B., arcivescovo di Capua, teologo e pastore della riforma cattolica. Atti del convegno internazionale di studi, Capua 28 settembre–1 ottobre 1988*, I: *Teologia, pastorale*, II: *Filosofia, scienza,* *iconografia*, Capua, Arcidiocesi di Capua–Istituto Superiore di Scienze Religiose, 1990, 930 pp.

CAMPANELLA. *Mathematica*, ed. and trans. A. Brissoni, Ro, Gangemi, 1989, 188 pp., is the first modern edition/translation of an incomplete text (only the first book was written) composed by C. for his disciples in 1619 while imprisoned in Naples. Germana Ernst, *Religione, ragione e natura: ricerche su Tommaso C. e il tardo Rinascimento*, Mi, Angeli, 288 pp., brings together a number of important essays on C.'s astrology, political philosophy, and theology in particular, as well as related essays on witchcraft and astrology in Cardano, Della Porta, Vanini; all have already appeared, or are due to appear, separately in article form, but collectively they constitute a coherent and extensive treatment of C.'s chief, interlocking concerns. The results of E.'s further researches not included in the above volume are to be found in her 'Cristianesimo e religione naturale. Le censure all'*Atheismus triumphatus* di Tommaso C.', *NRLett*, 9.1–2, 1989:137–200. I also note *Gaetano Currà, *Il falso profeta Lutero negli scritti di Tommaso C.*, Cosenza, Progetto 2000, 1989, 184 pp. A. Ruschioni, 'La poesia filosofica di Tommaso C.', *Testo*, 19, 1990:70–91, sets out to show how C.'s poetry is not merely an ably versified philosophy but 'la poesia stessa della filosofia': what we get, however, is neither an exposition of the philosophy nor a close reading of the poetic text (postponed to 'studi nuovi e più approfonditi'); instead we are offered a collage of quotations interspersed with earnest assurances as to their combined philosophical and poetic worth but bearing no real sense of a creative tension between language and ideas. L. Bolzoni, 'Un modo di commentare alla fine dell'Umanesimo: i *Commentaria* del C. ai *Poëmata* di Urbano VIII', *ASNP*, 19, 1989:289–311, is a reprint of an article which has also appeared, under a different title, in *Rinascimento* (*YWMLS*, 51:483). Other contributions to C. studies include J. M. Headley, 'Tommaso C. and the end of the Renaissance', *JMRS*, 20, 1990:157–74; M. Mönnich and D. Müller-Jahncke, 'Medicine and magic between tradition and progress in Tommaso C.', Conti, *Medicina*, 15–23; S. Calomino, 'Mechanism, diversity and social progress: emblems of scientific reality in C.'s *La città del sole*', pp. 29–41 of *Utopian Vision, Technological Innovation and Poetic Imagination*, ed. K. L. Berghahn, R. Grimm, H. Kreuzer, Heidelberg, Winter, 1990, 130 pp.

CARAMUEL. The proceedings of a tricentenary conference for this extraordinary Spanish-Flemish nobleman, cleric, and polymath, bishop of Vigevano and last great exponent of Catholic encyclo-paedism (whose influence on Italian culture may have been consider-able but remains to be ascertained), have finally appeared: *Le meraviglie del probabile: Juan C., 1606–1682. Atti del convegno internazionale di studi, Vigevano 29–31 ottobre 1982*, ed. P. Pissavino, introd. C. Vasoli, Vigevano, Comune di Vigevano, 1990, 146 pp., includes papers by D. Pastine, 'C. nel sui tempo'; M. Torrini, 'Monsignor Juan C. e l' Accademia napoletana degli Investiganti'; J. R. Armogathe, 'Probabilisme et libre arbitre: la théologie morale de C. y Lebkowitz'; P. Pissavino, 'Immagini e silenzi della politica in Juan C.'; L. Garcia, 'C. e la critica a Descartes'; I. Golub, 'Juan C. nelle pagine del diario di Alessandro VII'; M. Battlori, 'C. e la tradizione del Lullismo'; A. Pérez de Laborda, 'C. y el cálculo matemático'; P. Barbieri, 'Gli ingegnosi cembali e "violicembali" inventati da Juan C. Lebkowitz per Ferdinando III (*c.* 1650): notizie inedite dal manoscritto *Musica*'; W. Oechslin, 'C. architetto'; I. Golub, 'Juray Krizanic e Juan C.'; F. Pavesi, 'Il "Fondo C." dell'archivio capitolare della Chiesa Cattedrale di Vigevano'. Sadly, the conference paper most directly concerned with literature, Giovanni Pozzi's, 'Poesia anomala di Juan C.', has not been published.

CESI AND THE LINCEI. S. De Renzi, 'Il progetto e il fatto. Nuovi studi sull'Accademia dei Lincei', *Intersezioni*, 9, 1989:501–17, surveys books and articles appearing over the last ten years, but suggests that these have tended to play down the importance of C.'s project, which, after the extravagant claims of progressive patriotic schools of historians, revisionist historiography has reassessed 'col senno di poi', highlighting its limited achievements, rather than the radical enterprise it was in its early 17th-c. Roman context; G. B. Marini-Bettolo, 'Un'enciclopedia di storia naturale nel XVII secolo', Cónti, *Medicina*, 181–91, discusses the publication by C. of Francisco Hernández's *Rerum medicarum thesaurus Novae Hispaniae* (1651); A. Alessandrini, 'Il medico Giovanni Heckius Linceo: personaggio emblematico nella grande svolta della cultura tra '500 e '600', *ib.*, 148–79.

DE DOMINIS. F. P. Raimondi, 'Documenti inediti sul D. (1616–1620)', *BSF*, 9, 1986–89:314–63.

GALILEO. W. R. Shea, *Copernico, G., Cartesio. Aspetti della rivoluzione scientifica*, Ro, Armando, 1989, 283 pp., brings together in the section devoted to G. (the greater part of the volume) Italian versions of articles which have appeared over the last 15 years, but also includes an essay (though it might be better described as a series of 'sketches'), 'G. astronomo al lavoro' (159–86), which had not previously been published in any language; similarly, *G. e Copernico: alle origini del pensiero moderno*, ed. C. Vinti, Assisi, Porziuncola, 1990, 251 pp., is mainly devoted to G., with essays by F. Barone, 'Il copernicanesimo di G.', V. Tonini, 'Misura del tempo, relatività e verità monologica in G.', L. Valdrè, 'Nuovi sistemi e nuovo umanismo', C. Vinti, 'Koyré lettore di Copernico e G.', P. Pizzamiglio, 'Le biblioteche di Copernico e G.', L. Conti, 'Francesco Stelluti, il copernicanesimo dei

Lincei e la teoria galileiana delle maree', W. Mincer, 'G. nell'illuminismo polacco'. I also record the volumes *G.: fede nella ragione,
ragioni della fede*, Bo, Studio Domenicano, 1990, 186 pp., and Paolo
Scandaletti, *G. privato*, Mi, Camunia, 1989, 275 pp.

D. A. Wojciehowski, 'G.'s two chief world systems', *SIR*, 10:61–80,
seeks to show how G. 'helped invent' a new 'concept of science as
mathematical, and therefore as literal and non-rhetorical', by
contrasting earlier logocentric theories of meaning with the one W.
extrapolates from G.'s work; this is accompanied by a 'rhetoric of
difference' by which G. seeks to persuade of the superiority of the new
epistemological model; the article concludes that 'the study of
Galilean rhetoric is tremendously important to an understanding of
the origins of the scientific revolution, but even more importantly,
perhaps, to an awareness of how discourses in any culture rise and
fall'. W. does seem to imply, however, that it is possible clearly to
distinguish in G.'s work between scientific procedures aimed at
discovering objective truths and rhetorical ones seeking popular
acceptance of those truths, a view challenged in M. Slawinski,
'Rhetoric and science/rhetoric of science/rhetoric as science', pp. 71–
99 of *Science, Culture and Popular Belief in Renaissance Europe*, ed. S.
Pumfrey, P. L. Rossi, and M. Slawinski, Manchester U.P., 331 pp. E.
Reeves, 'Augustine and G. on reading the heavens', *JIII*, 52:563–79,
argues that G.'s attempt, in the *Lettera alla Gran Duchessa Cristina*, to
reinterpret Joshua 10, 12–14 in (literally) the light of Copernican
astronomy seeks obliquely to engage the Augustinian interpretation
of the Biblical text and the underlying exegetical assumptions: a
generally acceptable view, though its demonstration relies in part on
rather marginal linguistic evidence which would need to be subjected
to more thorough philological scrutiny. Id., 'Daniel 5 and the *Assayer*:
G. reads the handwriting on the wall', *JMRS*, 21:1–27, explores G.'s
use of Bible stories in his polemic with Grassi. H. Margolis, 'Tycho's
system and G.'s *Dialogue*', *SHPS*, 22:259–75, seeks political explanations for G.'s strange failure to debate the Tychonic model of the
cosmos, and finds them in his manoeuvres to obtain an *imprimatur*. W.
Bernardi, 'G., il microscopio e le "metafisiche biologiche" del
Seicento', Conti, *Medicina*, 195–208, argues, a little confusedly, for
links and parallels between G.'s thought and contemporary interest
in genetics and embryology. I also note M. L. Altieri Biagi, *'Postille
al *Dialogo sopra i massimi sistemi*', *Alma Mater Studiorum*, 3.1, 1990:1–46.

The debate concerning G.'s trial and condemnation, revived by P.
Redondi, *G. eretico* (1985), continues: M. Segre, 'Redondi's theory
and new perspectives in Galilean studies', *AIHS*, 40, 1990:3–10,
agrees with R.'s thesis to the extent of arguing that atomism figured
more prominently among the concerns of G.'s circle than has

generally been supposed. E. Festa, 'Galilée hérétique?', *RHSc*, 44:91–115, concurs to the extent that he identifies atomism as a growing preoccupation among theologians and church-aligned natural philosophers, but qualifies this, very plausibly, with the observation that there is no substantial evidence, other than the mysterious document unearthed by Redondi and attributed by him to Orazio Grassi (though almost certainly *not* in his hand), to suggest that atomism was a key concern in 1632–33: against which Festa points to the far greater and better-documented role, in G.'s condemnation, of Christoph Scheiner who, in a letter of 1633 to Grassi in which he reiterates his condemnation of Copernicanism, also sings the unqualified praises of the scientific achievements of a leading exponent of atomism, Pierre Gassendi. Other interventions include M. A. Finocchiaro, 'Recent interpretations of the G. affair', *Science and Religion/Wissenschaft und Religion*, ed. by A. Bäumer and Manfred Büttner, Bochum, Brockmeyer, 1989, pp. 110–18; R. N. D. Martin, 'The trouble with authority: the G. affair and one of its historians', *Modern Theology*, 6, 1989:3–9.

Other, more technical, contributions on G.'s physics include Silvio A. Bedini, *The Pulse of Time: G. Galilei, the Determination of Longitude and the Pendulum Clock*, F, Olschki, xiv + 132 pp.; M. Segre, 'G., Viviani and the Tower of Pisa', *SHPS*, 20, 1989:435–51; S. Drake, 'G.'s gravitational units', *Physics Teacher*, 27, 1989:432–36; A. De Pace, 'G. lettore di Girolamo Borri', pp. 3–69 of *De motu. Studi di storia del pensiero su G., Hegel, Huygens e Gilbert* (Quaderni di Acme, 12), Mi, Univ. degli Studi, 1990, xxv + 182 pp. (Borri was one of G.'s teachers at Pisa, an Aristotelian whose works on motion figured in G.'s library).

VANINI. *Opere*, ed. F. P. Raimondi, introd. G. Papuli, Cosenza, Galatina, 1990, 628 pp., contains the Latin text of V.'s published works, *Amphitheatrum aeternae providentiae* (1615) and *De admirandis Naturae Reginae Deaeque mortalium arcanis* (1616), whose possible influence on his contemporaries (notably Marino) is only now beginning to be investigated. The introduction places V.'s philosophy in its historic context and seeks to dispel earlier views as to its derivative (not to say plagiarized) contents.

SETTECENTO

By G. W. SLOWEY, *Lecturer in Italian, University of Birmingham*

1. GENERAL

BIBLIOGRAPHY, LIBRARIES, PUBLISHING. Stefano Pillinini, *Il 'Veneto governo democratico' in tipografia. Opuscoli del periodo della Municipalità Provvisoria di Venezia (1797) conservati presso la biblioteca della Deputazione di Storia Patria per le Venezie*, Venice, Comune di Venezia, 1990, 98 pp., describes 500 items, probably collected by L. Bassaglia, who added notes expressing opposition to the events of 1797. Marco Bona Castellotti, **Collezionisti a Venezia nel Settecento. Giovanni Battista Visconti, Gian Matteo Pertusati, Giuseppe Pozzobonelli*, F, Olschki, xi + 127 pp. M. Infelise, **L'editoria veneziana del Settecento*, Mi, Angeli, 1989, 421 pp. B. Dooley, 'L'unificazione del mercato editoriale: i libri contabili del giornalista Apostolo Zeno', *Società e storia*, 53:579–620, draws on books kept by Z. over five years in his capacity as entrepreneur and literary agent, when he was responsible for widespread distribution of books; this activity was originally financed by his opera libretto sales, and the article documents the business acumen which enabled him to make money to finance such works as Scipione Maffei's *Giudizio sopra le poesie liriche del sig. Carlo Maria Maggi* (1706) and his involvement in the *Giornale de' letterati d'Italia*. S, Adorni Fineschi and C. Zarrilli, **Legge, magistrature, archivi. Regesto di fonti normative ed archivistiche per la storia della giustizia criminale a Siena nel Settecento*, Mi, Giuffrè, 1990, x + 354 pp. C. Fahy, 'A printer's manual from Bodoni's Parma: the "Istruzioni pratiche" of Zefirino Campanini (1789)', *The Library*, 13:97–114.

LITERARY HISTORY AND BACKGROUND. Gioacchino Gargallo di Castel Lentini, *Storia della storiografia moderna*, 1: *Il Settecento*, Ro, Bulzoni, 1990, 347 pp., is a new edition of a useful work covering various aspects of the period, including cultural history, philological questions, etc. Brendan Dooley, **Science, Politics and Society in Eighteenth-Century Italy: The 'Giornale de' letterati d'Italia' and its World*, NY, Garland, iv + 207 pp. **L'Italia nella Rivoluzione, 1789–99*, ed. G. Benassati and L. Rossi, Bo, Grafis, 1990, 398 pp. M. Rosa, 'Il giurisdizionalismo borbonico a Napoli nella seconda metà del Settecento', *Società e storia*, 51:53–76, deals with the points of conflict and agreement between church and state, looking at the writings of Antonio Genovesi, Bernardo Tanucci, and also examining the role of the Camera di Santa Chiara. It notes the development of the southern *borghesia*, not along revolutionary lines, but 'all'ombra del feudo . . . anche all'ombra della chiesa'. Francesco Lomonaco, **Rapporto al*

*cittadino Carnot. Dall'illusione alla denuncia: la rivoluzione napoletana del
1799*, ed. G. G. Libertazzi, Venosa, Osanna, 1990, 131 pp. G.
Ricuperati, 'Gli strumenti dell'assolutismo sabaudo: segreterie di
stato e consiglio delle finanze nel XVIII secolo', *RSI*, 102, 1990:796–
873, discusses the way in which certain figures operated in the context
of an apparently absolutist state and examines the role of 'nobiltà
civile' in creating a government and military culture linked with
'modernization' of the state, which had as its price stricter state
censorship, more limited development of public opinion, and a
greater unwillingness to assimilate Enlightenment ideas. Gian Paolo
Romagnoni, *Prospero Balbo intellettuale e uomo di stato*, II: *Da Napoleone a
Carlo Alberto*, T, Deputazione Subalpina di Storia Patria, 1990,
705 pp. Jean-Claude Waquet, *Le Grand-duché de Toscane sous les derniers
Médicis: essai sur le système des finances et la stabilité des institutions dans les
anciens États italiens*, Paris, Bibliothèque des Écoles Françaises
d'Athènes et de Rome, 1990, 657 pp., deals extensively, as its sub-title
indicates, with Medici finance under Cosimo III and Gian Gastone,
but also Francis of Lorraine, showing the different political and
cultural implications of his regime. M. Orlando, 'Massoneria e
massoni in alcune lettere di Giuseppe Maria Pujati', *RSCI*, 45:140–
54, looks at P., who was a noted religious figure linked with the
Jansenist movement for renewal in the church and also connected
with masonic and pro-Austrian parties, though his letters to his
brother make it clear that he was not himself a Freemason. The report
on the Freemasons which he was asked to produce for the Inquisition
(1785) mentions negatively their notions on the rights of man and
describes them as deists. The article also illustrates his disillusionment in the post-revolutionary period when he sees his dreams of
church reform gradually disappear. R. Ajello, 'I filosofi e la regina. Il
Governo delle Due Sicilie da Tanucci a Caracciolo (1776–1786)', *RSI*,
103:398–454, is the first part of a detailed analysis which traces
differences in government by Tanucci and Caracciolo, particularly in
relation to acceptance of Enlightenment influence, e.g. in the field of
law, though the central administration was frequently in a crisis of
credibility because of political ham-fistedness and scandals attached
to the regime. A. Drigani, 'La "potestas dispensandi Episcopi" negli
*Atti dell'Assemblea degli Arcivescovi e Vescovi di Toscana tenuta a Firenze
nell'anno 1787*', *ASI*, 149:163–84, examines events surrounding this
Assembly and the attempts by Leopold of Austria to establish a
division between the Tuscan bishops and Rome. Vittorio Giuntella,
*La religione amica della democrazia: i cattolici democratici del triennio
rivoluzionario (1796–1799)*, Ro, Studium, 1990, 322 pp., gathers
together writings by various authors, including Pietro Paolo Bacini,
Riccardo Bartoli, and Gaetano Palmieri, and introduces them in a

substantial essay which analyses some of the important points at issue at this critical moment. *La chiesa italiana e la rivoluzione francese*, ed. D. Menozzi, Bo, Ediz. Dehoniane, 1990, 359 pp., contains a number of contributions on church policy, on religious reformism in Italy, on the precarious plight of emigré clergy once Rome fell into French hands, including D. Menozzi on pastoral letters and other similar documents (121–79), A.-M. Valenti who highlights the position of the Italian hierarchy after 1793 against the revolution (181–232), M. Caffiero who has an eschatological theme, highlighting how Rome is seen as Babylon and the Revolution as a sign of the imminent millennium (287–357). P. Stella, ' "Quo primum tempore": progetto di bolla pontificia per la condanna del Sinodo di Pistoia (1794)', *RSCI*, 45:1–41, illuminates the defensive and intransigent attitudes which prevailed in Curial circles towards the Synod of Pistoia (1786), analysing the draft which became the papal bull *Auctorem fidei* of 1794. R. Targhetta, 'Secolari e religiosi nel Veneto prima e dopo la legislazione antiecclesiastica (1765–84)', *SV*, 1990:171–84, begins with Labia's *Arringa al Senato sul decreto di abolizione dei frati dell'anno 1767* and examines the consequences and purpose of the legislation, particularly in relation to the intentions of Andrea Tron. V. Di Flavio, 'Ecclesiastici francesi accolti a Rieti durante la rivoluzione (1792–1800)', *RSCI*, 45:450–83, is a well-documented study of some of the thousands of church people who sought asylum in Italy. Rieti was already an area categorized by its bishop as of 'sangue rivoltoso', so the arrival of these emigrés was not always welcome. Umberto Rosso, *Studi sul Settecento in Abruzzo*, Chieti, Solfanelli, 1990, 128 pp. Antonio Trampus, *Tradizione storica e rinnovamento politico. La cultura nel litorale austriaco e nell'Istria tra Settecento e Ottocento*, Gorizia, Ist. Giuliano di Storia, Cultura e Documentazione, 1990, 252 pp. E. Bonora, 'Letteratura dialettale e letteratura nazionale prima dell'Unità', *GSLI*, 167, 1990:481–504, shows the strength of feeling in literary circles about the importance of dialects, using as its first example Parini's *Al padre d. Paolo Onofrio Branda* which was his reply to Branda's *Della lingua toscana* of 1759; it then moves on to Algarotti's centralizing view of literature and theatre which implicitly excluded any development of dialects, a theme continued by Bettinelli, who argued against Italy's cultural division in the second of his *Lettere inglesi* and later writings, and who looked to France as a political and cultural model. M. G. Accorsi and E. Graziosi, 'Da Bologna all'Europa: la polemica Orsi-Bouhours', *RLI*, 93.3, 1989:84–136, is another substantial contribution to work on the controversy, beginning with a summary of Bouhours's anti-Italian stance in *La manière de bien penser dans les ouvrages d'esprit* and of Orsi's *Considerazioni*, written in reply; the article does not concern itself with the history of the quarrel, but with the problem of language and critical method which lie at its centre; it analyses B.'s claims for a single language, good for all literary genres, rejecting in the process *Aminta* and *Pastor fido*, and pressing the claims of the moderns, particularly Racine; O.'s academic stance with 'tutte le sue persistenze barocche' was overtaken by Eustachio Manfredi and other defenders of the Italian language such as Muratori and Martello, who asserted the capacity of Italians to coin their own autonomous language of tragedy. For other figures in this polemic, see the following entry. E. Graziosi, 'Montani e Magalotti: storia di un plagio', *GSLI*, 168:85–127 and 228–70, begins with a summary of the Orsi-Bouhours dispute, in which Montani became embroiled with his *Lettera toccante* of 1709, where he attacked Orsi's position; it would appear that the letter was originally to have been sent to Magalotti in 1705, but had remained in Montani's papers, and it clearly reflects many of Magalotti's ideas, particularly those which strove for a kind of 'nobile sprezzatura' in literary writing; as a consequence, Montani was accused of plagiarism of Magalotti. As Graziosi says, 'Plagi dunque, ma ben provvisti di originalità'. She talks of the controversy as a crossroads in the literary history of Arcadia and refers to 'il progressivo provincializzarsi della cultura toscana', and the article finishes with an appendix of some unpublished letters from Magalotti to Montani. D. Generali, **'Pier Caterino Zeno e le vicende culturali del Giornale de' letterati d'Italia attraverso il regesto della sua corrispondenza'*, *Scienza, filosofia e religione tra Seicento e Settecento in Italia*, ed. M. V. Predaval Magrini, Mi, Angeli, 119–202. L. Braida, 'L'affermazione della censura di stato in Piemonte. Dall'editto del 1648 alle costituzioni per l'università del 1722', *RSI*, 102, 1990:716–95, although beginning with Maria Cristina's edict of 1648 which introduced the requirement for books to be approved by the authorities, is mostly dedicated to tracing the effects of such censorship in the 18th c., particularly highlighting the way in which it was part of a process aimed at reducing the power of the Inquisition in Piedmont. B. also talks of the 'rinnovamento culturale' under Vittorio Amedeo II in the second two decades of the century through the reform of university education. After the middle of the 1720s, the anti-Curial stance of the rulers was somewhat moderated, which led to a tightening of censorship regulations. The article continues with an important section on the Stamperia Reale and its gradual dominance not only in book production but also in the dissemination of information through its publication of journals and gazettes. The article finally deals with the case of Carlo Denina, removed from his post at Turin university for his publication in 1777 of *Dell'impiego delle persone*. Carlo Brisighella, *Descrizione delle pitture e sculture della città di Ferrara*, ed. M. A. Novelli, Ferrara, Spazio Libri,

1990, xx + 834 pp., is a hefty volume which traces the fortunes of B.'s book through the manipulations and additions carried out by Baruffaldi and its further alterations at the hands of Barotti. It follows an interesting line through an examination of local history in the context of a cultural world adorned with riches which have in the last two hundred years been ruthlessly dispersed. L. Spera, 'Una proposta editoriale d'Oltralpe: la *Bibliothèque universelle des romans*', *RLI*, 95, 1–2:66–71, concerns a project printed in Milan in 1790 by Giuseppe Galeazzi, although according to Spera, the whole operation demonstrates only poor understanding of the theoretical basis on which such an undertaking ought to have been based. Giovanni Luseroni, *Cronache della rivoluzione francese. La 'Gazzetta universale' del 1789*, Mi, Angeli, 1990, 207 pp., looks at the *Gazzetta universale* of Florence and points out how, unlike many other chronicles of the period, it initially followed a pro-revolutionary line, one of its collaborators being Filippo Buonarroti, although it later reverted to an anti-revolutionary stance, sacking Buonarroti. The work has an appendix of brief but useful notes covering 36 numbers of the *Gazzetta*.

2. POETRY, DRAMA, THOUGHT

Alessandra Di Ricco, *L'inutile e meraviglioso mestiere: poeti improvvisatori di fine Settecento*, Mi, Angeli, 1990, 271 pp., taking its title from Metastasio's description of the art of poetic improvisation, looks at two poets, Francesco Gianni and Teresa Bandettini, the former perhaps better known as an adversary of Monti (cf. *Bassvilliana*). The book contains useful chapters on the background to the phenomenon of improvisation, starting with Bandettini's career as a dancer and singer and continuing with an examination of her attempts to bring a dimension of classical imitation to her improvisation. It looks at Gianni's concern to move his improvisation away from a mere display of technical ability. The book has appendices of contemporary documents, including Bandettini's autobiography. Carmelo Alberti, *La scena veneziana nell'età di Goldoni*, Ro, Bulzoni, 1990, 266 pp., ranges widely over the theatrical world before and during Goldoni's time. The first section runs from Cristoforo Ivanovich's writings on the theatre in Venice, printed in 1681, to the establishment of the Teatro S. Luca on a firm basis by the Vendramin family. Section II is devoted mainly to Goldoni and *La bottega del caffè*, *Il bugiardo*, and *Le donne gelose*. Section III looks at Goldoni plays which are rarely republished or performed, such as *La sposa persiana* and even *Le donne de casa soa*, to which A. devotes one of his longer analyses. Section IV looks at *I rusteghi* and *Le baruffe chiozzotte*. There is an appendix containing documents and scenes covering theatrical background from the end of the 17th to the first part of the 18th c. Michael Talbot, *Tomaso Albinoni: the Venetian composer and his World*, Oxford, Clarendon, 1990, 300 pp., has its longest chapters on A.'s operas and serenatas with material on the social and economic context of 18th-c. opera in Italy. Id., 'Vivaldi in the sale-room: a new version of *Leon feroce*', *Informazoni e studi vivaldiani*, 12 : 5–16, looks at the MS version of this Vivaldi aria and discusses, amongst other things, the authorship of the text, ascribed to Claudio Nicola Stampa. C. Vitali, 'I fratelli Pepoli contro Vivaldi e Anna Girò. Le ragioni di un'assenza', *ib.*, 19–45, looks at the reasons why V. was not used after 1734 by Sicinio Pepoli, artistic director at the Teatro Malvezzi in Bologna, and concludes with documentation on Pietro Morigi and Castore Castori, two noted castrati of the day. J. Herczog, 'Tendenze letterarie e sviluppo musicale dell'oratorio italiano nel Settecento tra Vienna e il paese d'origine', *NRMI*, 25 : 217–30, examines the work of Zeno and Metastasio, claiming Zeno's *Tobia* (1720) as 'il culmine letterario dell'oratorio italiano'. He points out that M.'s concept of oratorio was very different from Z.'s, since M. found the requirements of dogma in conflict with his dramatic instincts, particularly in the limited scope for women characters and for plot development. In L. Lindgren, 'Musicians and librettists in the correspondence of Giovanni Giacomo Zamboni', *Research Chronicle*, 24 : 1–194, a single-subject issue devoted to Z., who lived for more than forty years in London, the author takes a wide perspective on Italian music and its poetry in the first half of the 18th c. *Mozart, Padova e la 'Betulia liberata': committenza, interpretazione e fortuna delle azioni sacre metastasiane nel '700. Atti del convegno internazionale di studi, 28–30 settembre 1989*, ed. P. Pinamonti, F, Olschki, 436 pp., although containing substantial and interesting articles on the purely musical aspect, devotes much of the space to more obviously literary discussions. M. G. Accorsi, 'Le azioni sacre di Metastasio: il razionalismo cristiano' (3–26), examines M.'s Cartesian line of thought in relation to knowledge of God and self, pointing out that M. is closer to Malebranche in that he questions the possibility of knowing either oneself or the thoughts of others sufficiently. The article shows how M.'s proof of the existence of God in *Betulia liberata* uses reason to convince the non-believer and how M.'s position on questions of sin and punishment is closer to the Jesuits' than the Jansenists', though there remains 'il pessimismo metastasiano sulla condizione umana'. G. Gronda, 'La *Betulia liberata* e la tradizione viennese di componimenti sacri' (27–42), points to the differences between this and other texts by Metastasio, not least in the graphic, not to say macabre, on-stage presentation of Holofernes' head. The author also considers the compositions of Pietro Pariati (for whom see also her book noted below under PARIATI), wondering whether his use of the macabre might not be considered as undermining the texts it draws on. E. Sala Di Felice, 'Betulia come Casa d'Austria' (43–63), sees the work as having political significance at a time of crisis for the Habsburgs during the War of the Polish Succession, and also has sections devoted to the structural organization of sacred drama and music-drama, concluding with a comment about M.'s ability to construct a text which offered the maximum to actors and musicians. J. Joly, 'Atalia e Gioas tra religione, potere e teatro' (65–72), looks at Zeno's *Gioaz* as 'una buona riduzione librettistica' of Racine's *Athalie*. P. Pinamonti, '"Il ver si cerchi/non la vittoria": implicazioni filosofiche nel testo della *Betulia* metastasiana' (73–86), analyses the theological confrontation between Ozìa and Achior in part II of *La Betulia liberata*, seeing it as one of the elements which ensured the success of the work. G. Mangini, '*Betulia liberata* e *La morte d'Oloferne*: momenti di drammaturgia musicale nella tradizione dei *Trionfi di Giuditta*' (145–69), looks at other dramatic and musical versions of the Judith story and compares the Metastasio version with that set by Pietro Guglielmi in 1791. A. Morelli, 'Oratorii ovvero sacre musicali tragedie?' (275–87), takes as its starting point Arcangelo Spagna's *Discorso dogmatico sopra gli oratorii* of 1706 to examine the links between oratorio and tragedy. F. Piperno, 'Drammi sacri in teatro (1750–1820)' (289–316), examines the 1776 Florence performance of *Betulia liberata* at the Teatro della Pergola (the use of a theatre for a religious performance was a new departure for Florence) and concludes with a list of Italian theatres and religious musical performances. F. Rossi, 'La presenza delle azioni sacre nelle biblioteche veneziane' (329–54). R. Strohm, '"Tragédie" into "Dramma per musica", IV', *Informazioni e studi vivaldiani*, 12:47–74, compares Corneille's *Le comte d'Essex* (1678) and Antonio Salvi's *Amore e maestà* (1715) to show how Salvi altered in particular the minor characters, e.g. in strengthening in dramatic terms the matrimonial struggle between Rosmiri and Mitrane. The article also examines the staging and dramatic setting, and concludes with the suggestion that Salvi's work was important in beginning the differentiation between drama and opera. M. Montanile, *'Spettacolo e opinione pubblica nei progetti inediti per un teatro nazionale (Milano 1797–98)', *EL*, 15.3, 1990:85–95. Beatrice Alfonzetti, *Il capo di Cesare. Percorsi di una catastrofe nella tragedia del Settecento*, Modena, Mucchi, 1989, 266 pp., examines the way in which Shakespeare's *Julius Caesar* was treated by various French and Italian writers (e.g. Luigi Riccoboni and Pier Jacopo Martello), particularly in removing the assassination scene, which was thought to be politically problematic. G. Checchi, 'Interventi scenografici di Lorenzo Quaglio: elementi italiani nella Germania del tardo Settecento', *BTe*, 19–20,

1990:141–50, discusses the career of Q. who worked for much of his theatrical life in Mannheim and Munich, where he was responsible for the design of the first performance of Mozart's *Idomeneo* in 1781. *Pulcinella. Una maschera tra gli specchi*, ed. F. C. Greco, Na, Ed. Scientifiche Italiane, 1990, 592 pp., contains a number of items touching on our period. F. Cotticelli, 'Rileggendo gli scenari: l'Arlecchino di Domenico Biancolelli e il Pulcinella della raccolta casamarciana' (169–90), talks of the 'professionismo autonomo di Dominique' and the 'tenace oggettivazione dell'attore/maschera nel personaggio Pulcinella' as indications of the recognition which would be accorded in future to the importance of theatre practice. R. De Maio, 'Pulcinella e l'Illuminismo' (221–34), is a rapid glance at Pulcinella in various French, English, and Italian reincarnations in the 18th c. D. Cialoni, 'Sui "Pulcinella" di Pier Leone Ghezzi' (259–73), considers particularly those famous sketches in the Burcardo collection in the Vatican Library. M. L. Quinn, 'The comedy of reference: the semiotics of commedia figures in eighteenth-century Venice', *TJ*, 43:70–92, examines attempts 'to bring the commedia figures into a more authentic relation to social life', throughout the history of the masks but with particular reference to Goldoni, and it also looks at Pietro Longhi's paintings as a debunking of conventional images, as well as at Carlo Gozzi's reworking of traditional figures to support traditional Venetian values.

G. Gaspari, 'Letteratura e scienza tra illuminismo e romanticismo', *Cenobio*, 40:327–38, examines the ways in which the notions of 'filosofia' and 'filosofo' were seen by such writers as Pietro Verri, Vico, and Filangieri. The author points out the international dimension of Muratori and other thinkers who were Fellows of the Royal Society, including Paolo Frisi who was omitted by Diderot and d'Alembert from the *Encyclopédie*. Lia Formigari, *L'esperienza e il segno: la filosofia del linguaggio tra Illuminismo e Restaurazione*, Ro, Ed. Riuniti, 1990, is a collection of fifteen previously published articles covering 18th-c. philosophical debates on the origin of languages, and discussions on the use of language and dialect, and making particular reference to Muratori and Galiani. M. De Zan, **L'Accademia delle Scienze di Bologna: l'edizione del primo tomo dei Commentarii (1731)'*, *Scienza, filosofia e religione tra Seicento e Settecento in Italia*, ed. M. V. Predaval Magrini, Mi, Angeli, 203–59. M. Di Bono, **Un secolo di astronomia a Pisa nelle vicende della Specola (1735–1833): il primo osservatorio del Granducato di Toscana: la Specola pisana (1735–1808)'*, *BSP*, 59, 1990:49–89. Alessandro Dini, **Vita e organismo: le origini della fisiologia sperimentale in Italia*, F, Olschki, 214 pp. Ilario Tolomio, **I fasti della ragione: itinerari della storiografia filosofica nell'illuminismo italiano*, Padua, Antenore, 1990, 346 pp. M. Affek, 'Il pensiero giuridico di Cesare Beccaria e di Giacinto Dragonetti nella Polonia del Settecento', *StS*, 32:111–36, discusses the reception of the thought of B. and D. in Poland by Ostrowski, Bogusławski, Kołłataj, and others. The author asserts that the Italian contribution to penal law in Poland was 'un gioiello impagabile', giving invaluable support to the processes of reform. **Gaetano Filangieri e l'Illuminismo europeo*, ed. L. D'Alessandro, Naples, Guida, 582 pp. S. Giuntini, **'Una corrispondenza fra Gabriello Manfredi e Giovanni Poleni', *Bollettino di storia delle scienze matematiche*, 10, 1990:99–125. A. Kleinert, **'Maria Gaetana Agnesi und Laura Bassi: zwei italienische gelehrte Frauen im 18. Jahrhundert', *Frauen in den exakten Naturwissenschaften*, ed. W. Schmidt and C. Scriba, Stuttgart, Steiner, 1990, 71–85.

3. AUTHORS

ALGAROTTI. Francesco A., **Viaggi di Russia*, ed. W. Spaggiari, Parma, Fond. P. Bembo–Guanda, lvii + 202 pp. F. Arato, 'Il "secolo delle cose": il newtonianismo di Francesco A.', *GSLI*, 167:505–45, examines the background to the material contained in A.'s *Il newtonianismo per le dame* of 1737 and at the daring method of dialogue presentation. Arato shows A.'s wide interests, pointing also to other works, such as his *Saggio sopra il gentilesimo* (published posthumously) on religion, to demonstrate the importance of A. in the renewal of Italian culture through the popularization of science and the emphasis on free speech and experimental methods.

ALFIERI. Vittorio A., *La virtù sconosciuta*, ed. A. Di Benedetto, T, Fogola, 96 pp., is A.'s celebration of his friend Francesco Gori Gandellini, published in 1788, and includes the five sonnets which appeared in the first edition. Vittorio A., *Panegirico di Plinio a Trajano. Parigi sbastigliato. Le mosche e le api*, ed. C. Mazzotta, Bo, CLUEB, 1990, 176 pp., contains the three items which A. had published at Paris during the period August–October 1789 and which inevitably reflect something of A.'s judgements of events, though the *Panegirico*, calling on the sovereign voluntarily to renounce power, had been drafted as early as 1785. The third work seems to foreshadow A.'s later anti-French sentiments as in fable form it seems to deny the ability of the French to achieve any worthwhile solutions. Daniele Gorret, *Il poeta e i mille tiranni*, Salerno, Laveglia, 167 pp., is a detailed and scholarly examination of A.'s *Misogallo*: France is said to have become, for A., the 'necessary enemy' 'grazie a cui si può riconoscere e riaffermare . . . la propria "sacrosanta" individualità di pensatore e di poeta'. Gorret also analyses A.'s language in the *Misogallo*, particularly his creation of neologisms, and shows how the abnormal and exceptional character of the book's structure is paralleled by the 'carattere abnorme ed eccezionale del suo linguaggio'. O. Besomi, 'Minima alfieriana', *GSLI*, 168:411–16, looks at textual variants (from Maggini's 1954 critical edition of A.'s *Rime*) in autograph MSS of sonnets 153 and 154 found recently in Vienna. A. Battistini, *'Vittorio A., le "mosche" francesi e le "api" inglesi', *La Rivoluzione francese in Inghilterra*, ed. L. M. Crisafulli Jones, Na, Liguori, 1990, 399–419.

ANGIOLINI. Luigi A., *Lettere sopra l'Inghilterra e la Scozia*, ed. Michèle and Antonio Stäuble, Modena, Mucchi, 1990, xxxi + 275 pp., shows the great admiration that A., later to become a career diplomat in the service of the Grand Dukes of Tuscany, evinced for Britain and its institutions, steeped as he was in Enlightenment notions. The book contains the two volumes which documented A.'s journey to Britain in 1787–88, rich in fascinating glimpses of his views on things British, from freedom of the press (where A. finds it odd 'che questa libertà non esista per legge fondamentale come in America') to the customs of the Highland Scots.

ANSALDI. A. Rizzacasa and R. Gatti, *'Momenti di un dibattito nell'illuminismo italiano: "anatomia" ed "etica" in C. I. Ansaldi', Conti, *Medicina*, 289–302.

BANDINI. A. D. Thompson, 'Sallustio Antonio B.: moral philosophy and the agrarian economy in early eighteenth-century Tuscany', *BJECS*, 14.1:31–43, takes a look at this archdeacon of Siena who wrote his *Discorso economico sopra la Maremma di Siena* in 1737, though it was not published until after his death. He was concerned to present the case for socially just prices in the context of the freedom of movement of goods in order to address some of the economic and social ills of the Maremma.

BARETTI. E. Bonora, 'B. e la Spagna', *GSLI*, 168:335–74, although obviously dealing with B.'s various journeys in Spain, reflects on a wider scale his general interest in people and his realistic descriptions of the countryside.

BASSI. A. Elena, '"In lode della filosofessa di Bologna": an introduction to Laura B.', *Isis*, 82:510–18, discusses this innovative experimenter and science teacher in Bologna, best known perhaps for poetry published in several 18th-c. collections, but who worked extensively in the natural sciences.

BECATTINI. M. A. Morelli Timpanaro, 'Su Francesco B. (1743–1813), di professione poligrafo', *ASI*, 149:279–374, is a long essay on this critic of the Grand Duchy of Tuscany, who spent much of his life in exile, author of very minor poetic, dramatic, and historical works, of which perhaps the one most likely to be known is *Vita pubblica e privata di Pietro Leopoldo d'Austria Granduca di Toscana poi Imperatore Leopoldo II* of 1796, recently (1987) republished.

BECCARIA. *Cesare B. tra Milano e l'Europa. Convegno di studi per il 250° anniversario della nascita*, ed. S. Romagnoli and G. D. Pisapia, Mi, Cariplo–Bari, Laterza, 1990, xii + 668 pp.

BIRAGO. C. Caverzasio, 'Un meneghino alla scuola del Maggi: Girolamo B.', *ASL*, 6, 1989:207–52, discusses this lawyer and *letterato* who wrote in Milanese dialect and was praised by Parini because he showed that the dialect 'non è per se medesimo goffo e scipito'.

CALZABIGI. M. Piscitelli, 'I libretti napoletani di Ranieri de' C.', *CLett*, 19:327–40, examines C.'s return to Naples after 1780, when his notions on theatre reform seemed to have fallen on deaf ears, referring especially to *Elfrida* and *Elvira*, historical *melodrammi* written for Paisiello, in which C. 'non perde di vista l'ideale ma, con spirito ironico e distaccato, tenta il compromesso con il reale'. E. Cantini, 'Calzabigi: alcune tradizioni e un dibattito sul sublime', *LS*, 26:223–42, discusses in particular C.'s reading of English authors and his interest in Burke's *Philosophical enquiry into the origins of our ideas of the sublime and beautiful* of 1757 with its analysis of the value of the picturesque. The article also considers C.'s relations with Alfieri and his letter to Alfieri of 1783, where he addresses the problem of the tragic theatre in Italy, seeing Alfieri, in tragedies which C. much admired, as 'poeta-pittore'.

CHIARI. M. L. Bonatti, *'I romanzi teatrali dell'abate C.', *Italian Culture*, 8, 1990:293–305.

CRUDELI Tommaso C., *Poesie con appendice di prose e lettere*, ed. G. Milan, Poppi, Comune di Poppi, 1989, xxxix + 214 pp. Id., *Opere*, ed. M. Catucci, Ro, Bulzoni, 1989, 272 pp. Id., *L'arte di piacere alle donne e alle amabili compagnie*, ed. M. Cerruti and M. Catucci, Ro, Bulzoni, 1989. C., whose sources are clearly to be found in French libertine writing, died in 1745 having published nothing nor even gathered his writings together. As a consequence, the first two of these items are quite different, and Catucci actually disputes C.'s authorship of the third, which does appear in Milan's edition.

DENINA. A. Patrucco Becchi, 'D. segreto. Intorno al secondo volume delle *Lettere brandeburghesi*', *CLett*, 19:543–66, attempts to identify the second volume of this work, the first volume of which came out in Berlin in 1786. It has usually been thought that there was no second volume, but the author claims to have identified a possible candidate in a German translation of 1788.

DI BLASI. Corrado Rosso, *'Un martyr des Lumières: Francesco Paolo di B.', *Aspects inédits du XVIII° siècle: de Montesquieu à la Révolution*, Pisa, Goliardica.

FAGIUOLI. F. Decroisette, 'Le rôle de l'aparté dans le dialogue de Giovan Battista F.', *Théâtre en Toscane: la comédie*, ed. M. Plaisance, Saint-Denis, Vincennes U.P., 157–88, examines the role of the professional actor and, while considering that F. has perhaps been unfairly dismissed in the past, looks particularly at the technique of asides in F.'s plays. The author concludes that F. was clearly part of the school of thought which saw the possibility of adapting the world of the theatre to the idea of the renewal of civic society.

GALIANI. Ferdinando G., *Sentenze e motti di spirito*, ed. M. Catucci, Ro, Salerno, 168 pp., is a collection, under various headings, of sayings, anecdotes, etc., covering about forty years of G.'s writings. W. Brauer, *'Ferdinando G. über den Wert der Dinge und das Gelt in seinem Werk *Della moneta libri cinque* (1751)', *Jahrbuch für Wirtschaftsgeschichte*, 1991 : 57–74.

GOLDONI. Carlo G., *Teatro*, ed. M. Pieri, 3 vols, T, Einaudi, 449 + 515 + 457 pp., is a selection in the *Teatro italiano* series. B. Mulinacci, 'Aspetti della drammaturgia goldoniana negli *Innamorati*', *RLI*, 95.1–2 : 53–65, discusses G.'s fascination with performance practice and, in the analysis of *Gli innamorati*, concludes that it is precisely the 'disagi' of the lovers which leads us to question the system of values that are their cause 'insieme all'assurdità di un rapporto infantile ed immaturo'.

GOZZI. C. Perrone, 'In margine ad un'edizione della *Turandot* di Carlo G.', *FC*, 16 : 127–34, compares the MS in the Marciana with two early editions, pointing out that the Zanardi edition of 1801 cannot be taken as a reflection of G.'s final wishes. Carlo G., *Turandot*, ed. C. Perrone, Ro, Salerno, 1990, 108 pp., is effectively a transcription of the 1772 edition with an introduction setting it in its literary context.

GRAVINA. Gian Vincenzo G., **Della ragion poetica*, ed. G. Izzi, Ro, Archivio Guido Izzi, 172 pp.

MAGALOTTI. Walter Moretti, *M. ritrattista e altri studi magalottiani*, Modena, Mucchi, 125 pp., is a collection of essays all previously published with the exception of 'M. ritrattista' (99–107), which looks at M.'s portrayal of Charles II of England.

MARTELLO. I. Magnani Campanacci, 'Il *Davide in corte* di Pier Jacopo M.: dal dramma regale alla commedia eroica', *SPCT*, 43 : 103–57, looks at the notion of 'commedia eroica' derived from Corneille and his drama *Don Sanche d'Aragon*, though M. queries Corneille's own description of his play as 'comédie héroique'. M.'s own play fits his definition because the virtues and passions of the protagonists are those of private citizens rather than princes. The author points out the 'ideazione poetica' and the pastoral echoes, and also looks at the figure of Micol as 'moderna coquette', underlining M.'s ironic view, 'tanto da far dubitare della sua adesione ideologica all'*exemplum* messo in campo'.

MONTI. Vincenzo M., *Lettera di Francesco Piranesi al Signor Generale D. Giovanni Acton*, ed. R. Caira Lumetti, Palermo, Sellerio, 264 pp., is a letter which M. wrote secretly in 1795 to help P. exculpate himself from accusations of complicity in the attempted assassination of Armfelt, a principal supporter of Gustav III of Sweden. The volume also includes the two accounts of the imprisonment of Vincenzo Mori and Pietro Pasquini, who were arrested in connection with the crimes of which P. was accused. P. Ariatta, 'L'ultimo "Brindisi" di Vincenzo M. per l'onomastico della sua donna', *GSLI*, 168:528–32, publishes a MS birthday greeting for his wife Teresa Pikler. V. Giannantonio, 'Inediti poetici del M. e il Fondo Grossi', *CLett*, 19:45–75, analyses M.'s language, looking at the problem of compromise between written and everyday language, and examines in particular M.'s use of adjectives. It also examines and publishes early autograph drafts, from the Fondo Grossi of the Biblioteca Civica di Treviglio and from the Braidense in Milan, of three poems contained in the Carducci edition (1858).

PARIATI. Giovanna Gronda, *La carriera di un librettista. Pietro P. da Reggio di Lombardia*, Bo, Il Mulino, 1990, 752 pp., contains a wealth of valuable material on P.'s career in Venice and Vienna; B. Dooley, 'Pietro P. a Venezia' (15–44), looks at the period in P.'s career when most of the *intermezzi* were written, including his collaboration with Zeno. Dooley sees P. as typifying the history of a generation where new-found prosperity broadened the social and cultural basis of society; H. Seifert, 'Pietro P. poeta cesareo' (45–71), turns the focus on to P.'s *melodrammi* after his arrival in Vienna in 1714; R. Strohm, 'Pietro P. librettista comico' (73–111), sees tragicomedy as the only genre in which P. had been able to assert his poetic autonomy; G. Gronda, 'Il mestiere del librettista' (113–65), sees P. as 'uno spirito ribelle', able by his choice of tragicomedy to indulge his inclination to parody and irony. There are extensive sections of bibliographical information on P.'s writings and more than half the book is devoted to tracing the development and fortune of *Arianna e Teseo* in its myriad 18th-c. manifestations.

TANZI. Carlo Antonio T., *Le poesie milanesi*, ed. R. Martinoni, Pistoia, Can Bianco Niccolai, 1990, xxviii + 324 pp., has translations, good notes, and a glossary. The poems were first published in 1766, probably with Parini as co-editor, and his introductory presentation is included in this volume.

TIRABOSCHI. Michele Mari, **Il genio freddo. La storiografia letteraria di Girolamo T.*, is a special issue of *Bergomum*, 85, 1990, 372 pp.

VALLISNERI. R. Rappaport, **'Italy and Europe; the case of Antonio V. (1661–1730)'*, *HistS*, 29:73–98.

VERRI. Alessandro V., *Le avventure di Saffo poetessa di Mitilene*, ed. A. Cottignoli, Ro, Salerno, 208 pp.

VICO. Giambattista V., *Principi d'una Scienza Nuova d'intorno alla comune natura delle nazioni (1730)*, ed. M. Sanna and F. Tessitore, Na, Morano, xiii + 480 pp., is a facsimile of the 1730 Naples edition. Marco Veneziani, *Indici e concordanze delle 'Orazioni inaugurali' di Giambattista V.*, F, Olschki, xxxviii + 462 pp. Donald Phillip Verene, *The New Art of Autobiography. An Essay on the 'Life of Giambattista V. Written by Himself'*, Oxford, Clarendon, ix + 263 pp., considers V.'s *Vita* as perhaps his most underrated work, looking at it in the context of the writing of the *Scienza nuova*, and seeing that in Vichian terms 'autobiography is the centre of the problem of philosophising in the modern world'. Verene sees it as a philosophical work, not just an account of his life, and demonstrates in a detailed analysis of the opening paragraph of the *Vita* how V. effectively constructs himself: 'V.'s self-panegyric is carefully built on his principles for understanding a historical *corso* that he takes from the *New Science*'. J. M. Levine, 'Giambattista V. and the quarrel between the ancients and the moderns', *JHI*, 52:55–79, talks of the young men of the new generation (Paolo Mattia Doria, Pietro Giannone, and V. himself) and of V.'s interest in issues raised by the quarrel, both philosophical and literary, as can be seen in his series of inaugural lectures, where he examines both ancient and modern ideas to see what is best in each. Leon Pompa, *Human Nature and Historical Knowledge: Hume, Hegel and V.*, CUP, 1990, 234 pp., has a section (133–91) discussing interpretation of V. in a purely Hegelian light as 'incorrect' and showing how V. differs from Hegel in areas such as the interpretation of the heroic age. P. also talks of the 'inherently dynamic relationship' in V.'s notions of the science of the development of man's humanity between man as he is and man as he ought to be. Id., *V.: A Study of the 'New Science'*, CUP, 1990, xv + 251 pp., is a new edition of the original of 1975, with an important new chapter on V.'s conception of principles which govern the development of law and another on interpretations of V. by Berlin, Verene, and Haddock, discussing differences in interpreting the way in which human insight plays its part in V.'s 'science'. A. D. Hornstein, *'From oracle to echo: the development of law and justice in V.'s Nuova Scienza'*, *Law and History Review*, 8, 1990:129–37. G. Miuccio, *'Hercules and the passage from nature to culture in V.'s La scienza nuova'*, *Diogenes*, 151, 1990:90–103.

OTTOCENTO

POSTPONED

NOVECENTO

By B. C. MERRY, *James Cook University of North Queensland*

1. GENERAL AND PROSE

Two very valuable research tools are: *Letteratura italiana. Gli autori: dizionario biobibliografico e indici*, ed. A. Asor Rosa, 2 vols, T, Einaudi, 1990–91, xxvi + 985, xxvii + 1864 pp., and *Lettere italiane: indice trentennale. I (1949)–XXX (1978)*, ed. Nella Giannetto, F, Olschki, xxxv + 567 pp. *YIS*, 9, brings the journal to its thirtieth year.

Lezioni sul Novecento: storia, teoria e analisi letteraria, ed. Stefano Agosti and Andrea Marino, Mi, Vita e Pensiero, 1990, 269 pp., has a pref. by the Montale scholar Claudio Scarpati. G. Baroni (ed.), 'Per una definizione di "critica". Inchiesta (1)', *ON*, 14.5, 1990:5–54, gathers answers to a series of formulated questions on the canons and tools of modern criticism by Aurelio Benevento, Enza Biagini, Anna Clara Bova, Antonio Carrannante, Lorenzo Catania, Giorgio Cavallini, Angelo Colombo, Corrado Donati, Alberto Frattini, Fernando Gioviale, Angelo Marchese, Antonio Mazza Tonucci, Andrea Rondini, Romolo Runcini, Antonio Samonà, Luigi Scorrano and Vittorio Spinazzola. R. Luperini, 'Tendenze attuali della critica in Italia', *Belfagor*, 46:365–76, surveys critical trends from the birth of post-modernism to the Gulf War, which is seen as being (like Fascism) not an error *against* culture, but an error *of* culture. *Gruppo '63: la recente avventura del dibattito teorico letterario in Italia*, ed. Filippo Bettini and Francesco Muzzioli, Lecce, Manni, 1990, 150 pp. Ezio Raimondi, *Ermeneutica e commento: teoria e pratica dell'interpretazione del testo letterario*, F, Sansoni, 1990, 165 pp., illustrates the common practice of rehashing university class material. Elio Gioanola, *Psicanalisi, ermeneutica e letteratura*, Mi, Mursia, 446 pp., stresses the value of biographical details for accounts of the work of a main triptych of clinical cases, Gadda, Svevo, Pirandello, and of several lesser authors such as Deledda, Tozzi, Noventa, Boine, and Sanguineti. Luca Orsenigo, *L'ossessione dell'assoluto: l'epifania del sacro nella letteratura italiana contemporanea*, T, Tirrenia, 1990, 142 pp., includes essays on D. Campana, C. Pavese, S. D'Arrigo, and C. Coccioli. Marcello Ciccuto, *L'immagine del testo: episodi di cultura figurativa nella letteratura italiana*, Ro, Bonacci, 1990, 481 pp., is a wide-ranging collection of lit. essays incorporating subjects from our period, namely Palazzeschi, Campana, Tozzi, Mario Luzi, and Vittorio Giotti. C. Di Biase, 'Nel "labirinto" del Novecento', *EL*, 16.2–3:171–82, assesses the intellectual choices and author preferences expressed by M. Santoro in his 1981 essays on modern Italian lit., *L'uomo nel labirinto*. R. Frattarolo,

'Santoro e il Novecento', *ib.*, 183–92. Lorenzo Cantatore, *Bibliografia di Giacomo Debenedetti*, Ro, Carucci, 1990, 50 pp., is indispensable for our period. *Il Novecento di Debenedetti*, ed. R. Tordi, Mi, Fondazione Mondadori, 359 pp., prints the proceedings of the Rome conference (Dec. 1988). Giacomo Debenedetti, *Saggi critici*, vol. 2, introd. W. Pedullà, Venice, Marsilio, 1990, 324 pp.

Alberto Cadioli, *Le muse e la sirena: gli scrittori e l'industria culturale nel primo Novecento in Italia*, Mi, Arcipelago, 1990, 147 pp. S. Pautasso, 'Aspetti della cultura letteraria italiana del Novecento: appunti storiografici e critici sugli anni Trenta', *REI*, 36, 1990:19–25, considers the generally unexciting panorama and political conditioning of the 30s, with comments on extremist affirmations in journals such as *L'Italiano, Il Selvaggio*, and even *'900*, and the reception of Kafka and Joyce by Italian intellectuals of the period. N. Trotta, '"Son bell'e stufo di fare il lombardo". Tre lettere di Carlo Linati a Enzo Ferrieri', *StCrit*, 15:405–16, prints three letters from critic and writer L. to F., editor and inspirer of the Milanese journal *Il Convegno* (1920–39); from 1921 F. organized a publishing house 'Il Convegno Editoriale', and F.'s archive, containing letters by more than 200 writers, including celebrities like Ungaretti, Svevo, Montale, Saba, Pirandello, Marr, Joyce, Valéry, and Pound, is now in the Fondo Manoscritti of the University of Pavia. E. Raponi, 'Vita letteraria e intellettuale tra Italia e Germania nei primi anni del Novecento: su alcune lettere toscane di Rudolf Borchardt a Tommaso Gallarati Scotti (1904–1907)', *ON*, 14.5, 1990:87–122. G. Contini, *Lettere all'editore (1945–1954)*, ed. P. Di Stefano, T, Einaudi, 1990, xviii + 90 pp., an edition displaying many aspects of immediate post-war lit. reconstruction, includes letters to M. Mila, D. Ponchiroli, G. Einaudi, C. Pavese, and G. Bollati. Rocco Capozzi, *Scrittori, critici e industria culturale dagli anni Sessanta ad oggi*, Lecce, Manni, 173 pp., with contributions by such *aguerriti* critics as Guido Almansi, is a set of interviews with contemporary lit. figures. Giuseppe Cassieri, *Regine di brezza*, Bari, Dedalo, 1990, 202 pp., offers an ironic and at times sacrilegious deflating of the contemporary lit. climate of *case editrici* and the media, with their critics and operators such as Edoardo Sanguineti: '. . . non lascia in pace anima viva, da Moravia a Bobbio'. G. Fofi, *Prima il pane: cinema, teatro, letteratura, fumetto e altro nella cultura italiana tra anni Ottanta e Novanta*, Ro, Edizioni e/o, 1990, 158 pp., is lively and informative. Sergio Pautasso, *Gli anni Ottanta e la letteratura*, Mi, Rizzoli, 331 pp., is a guide to Italian lit. life in the last decade, with a serviceable bibliography.

La Rosa di Gèrico: la Sicilia fantastica da Linares a Brancati, ed. Rita Verdirame, Chieti, Solfanelli, 1990, 193 pp., presents selected Sicilian short story writers from the *Ottocento* to the present. Rosario

Contarino, *L'umorismo e il comico e altri studi di letteratura siciliana*, Rovito, Marra, 242 pp. Natale Tedesco, *La scala a chiocciola: scrittura novecentesca in Sicilia*, Palermo, Sellerio, 116 pp., is a convenient anthology of Sicilian *saggi*. *La noia e l'offesa: il fascismo e gli scrittori siciliani*, ed. Leonardo Sciascia, Palermo, Sellerio, 214 pp., is a handy up-date, and further evidence, as it were, of Sciascia's extraordinary 'posthumous productivity' (Goethe). *C'era una volta* ... *: le più belle fiabe abruzzesi*, pref. U. Palanza, Cerchio, Polla, 1990, 135 pp., draws on the Antonio De Nino collection. Giuseppe Marci, *Romanzieri sardi contemporanei*, Cagliari, CUEC, 217 pp.

Scrittrici d'Italia, ed. Alma Forlani and Marta Savini, Ro, Newton Compton, 265 pp., is an anthology of women's literature in prose and verse, from saints and heroines of the early centuries through to the present day. A. Santoro, 'Ricerca e lettura delle scritture delle donne in Italia, II: La lettrice', *EL*, 16.1: 99–106, assesses the different modes in which a female reader recuperates lit. texts and responds to 'language of the body' and to her own 'reticence in verbalization'. P. Zambon, 'Leggere per scrivere. La formazione autodidattica delle scrittrici tra Otto e Novecento: Neera, Ada Negri, Grazia Deledda, Sibilla Aleramo', *StN*, 16, 1989:287–324, compares and contrasts the pictures of family, personal regrets, flowers, and private aspirations in the main autobiographical prose works of four of the most influential Italian women writers. *Tuttestorie: racconti, letture, trame di donne*, Ro, Firmato Donna, is a new journal, launched in 1990, on feminist aspects of our area.

G. Gramigna, 'Le istituzioni del romanzo', *Merope*, 1, 1989:5–26, inaugurating another new lit. journal, considers Svevo in relation to other major novelists and Stefano Agosti's critical category 'the operative figure of parallelism' in plot construction. **40 anni di narrativa italiana, vol. I: 1940–1954*, introd. Geno Pampaloni, pref. Walter Pedullà, Mi, Mondadori, liii + 557 pp. R. Ceserani, 'Rassegna di narrativa', *Nuova corrente*, 37, 1990:323–57, assesses new writers with glances at Bompiani's new series *Panta: i nuovi narratori*, and appraisal of Francesco Guccini, Michele Serra, Pierangelo Selva, Andrea De Carlo, Athos Bigongiali, Maurizio Maggiani, among others. C. Toscani, 'Recentiora: cronaca narrativa degli ultimi vent'anni, III: 1973–1975', *ON*, 14.6, 1990:161–212, considers a wide range of bestselling authors, includes two texts by Luigi Santucci, also P. Volporri, Stefano D'Arrigo, Luciano Della Mea, and gives a long account of Giuliano Gramigna's prose criticism in his *Il testo del racconto* (1975). Id., 'Recentiora: cronaca narrativa degli ultimi vent'anni, V: 1977–1978', *ON*, 15.2:201–29, ranges over 20 commercially successful prose texts of a two-year sample, considering authors from Arpino and Bevilacqua to M. Cantele and Flora Vincenti.

Italiana: antologia dei nuovi narratori, Mi, Mondadori, 432 pp., is a collection of already published short stories by such contemporary authors as Edoardo Albinati. V. Spinazzola, *L'offerta letteraria*. *Narratori italiani del secondo Novecento*, Na, Morano, 1990, 269 pp.

2. POETRY

C. Federici, 'On self-reflectiveness and the modern Italian lyric', *Italica*, 67, 1990:440–52, examines, in the light of Linda Hutcheon's categories, the self-proclaiming and deliberately self-dismembering attitudes in modern texts, particularly the works of Zanzotto and Porta. *Poeti in piemontese del Novecento*, ed. Giovanni Tesio and Albina Malerba, T, Centro Studi Piemontesi, 1990, 505 pp., comes together with Italian translations. Nevio Spadoni, *A caval dagli ór: con 12 disegni inediti di Silvano D'Ambrosio*, Ravenna, Longo, 101 pp., contains poems in the dialect of Romagna, with an Italian translation. *Da Leopardi a Montale: aggiornamenti di letteratura otto-novecentesca e testimonianze di scrittori contemporanei*, ed. Paola Paganuzzi and Pierangelo Rabozzi, Brescia, Grafo, 1990, 227 pp. Pier Vincenzo Mengaldo, *La tradizione del Novecento: terza serie*, T, Einaudi, xi + 397 pp., is a collection of his already published essays. G. Lopez, 'Il topos del giardino abbandonato', *StN*, 17, 1990:85–102, considers how a common theme in E. Mencioni and G. D'Annunzio was developed in some early *Novecento* poets, particularly C. Gioveni, G. P. Cucini, and Gozzano, and in the modern writer Moretti's *Hortus incultus*. Remo Pagnanelli, *Studi critici: poesia e poeti italiani del secondo Novecento*, ed. Daniela Marcheschi, Mi, Mursia, 243 pp. Lorenzo Renzi, *Come leggere la poesia: con esercitazioni su poeti italiani del Novecento*, Bo, Il Mulino, 165 pp. A. Briganti, 'Forma chiusa e modernità', *CLett*, 18, 1990:411–18, considers the waning of traditional metrical forms in verse from the 60s onwards and closes with a brief review of recent and late 80s poets such as Sergio Calzone, Nanni Cagnone (*Vaticinio*, 1984), A. Cioni, Michelangelo Coriello, Gabriele Frasca, Gianni Rosati, Roberto Nanetti, Beppe Salvia, Vivian Lamarque, Antonio Ciuffa, and Sebastiano Vassalli's original and highly intertextual *Ombre e destini* (1983). E. Zarniarra, 'Evidenziature stilistiche: la parola "vita" nella lirica italiana dell'ultimo secolo', *CLett*, 18, 1990:513–42, affords a fascinating excursus into actual definitions or characterization of 'life' in poets from G. Gozzano, E. Clementelli, C. Rèbora, C. Govoni, E. Montale, G. Vigolo, U. Saba, C. Pavese, S. Solmi, G. Giudici, S. Corazzini, to such moderns as A. Zanzotto, C. Betocchi, M. Luzi, Pasolini, G. Orelli, Penna, and Luciano Erba. P. Baldan, *Novecento in controcanto. Modi e timbri in Gozzano, Campana, Noventa, Sereni*, Ravenna, Essegi, 1990, 175 pp. Aurelio Benevento, *Primo Novecento: Campana Sbarbaro Rèbora*, Loffredo, 1990, 167 pp., is a useful volume, containing sections on critical fortune, an astute biography, and a detailed analysis of primary texts for the first two of the three authors treated, and closes with a brief critical survey of Clemente Rèbora's works. Donato Valli, *Assaggi di poetica contemporanea*, Cavallino di Lecce, Capone, 1990, 148 pp., collects eight essays, two of which have not previously been published. P. Civitareale, 'Tra testo e contesto: poeti romagnoli del secondo Novecento', *LetP*, 79, 1990:9–19, accounts for the new 'felibrismo' that has boosted the fortunes of dialect poetry in contemporary Italy (tracing it back to 1942, the date of Pasolini's *Poesie a Casarsa*) and introduces a monographic number of the journal devoted to dialect poets of Emilio-Romagna, with articles on Nino Pedretti, Raffaello Boldini, Giuseppe Bellosi, Gianni Fucci, Walter Galli, Tonino Guerra, and Sante Pedrelli, among others. A general review of modern poetry and its prospects is conducted in 'Inchiesta mondiale sulla poesia', *L'informazione bibliografica*, 17:216–40, with *interventi* by Ugo Betti, Massimo Bontempelli, B. Corra, L. Folgore, C. Govoni, F. T. Marinetti, E. Montale, S. Quasimodo, and G. Ungaretti.

3. FUTURISM

I futuristi: i manifesti, la poesia, le parole in libertà, i disegni e le fotografie di un movimento rivoluzionario che fu l'unica avanguardia italiana della cultura europea, ed. Francesco Grisi, Ro, Newton Compton, 1990, 415 pp., includes a 45 page introduction by the editor. G. Grana, 'Scienze e letteratura di avanguardia: il Futurismo', *RSII*, 7, 1989:1–14. P. Rozzi, 'Futurist cinema', *ItQ*, 117, 1989:43–54, emphasizes tricks of screenplay and some Russian influences on the futurists' 'photo-dynamism'. Luciano Folgore, *Crepapelle: risate con una misurazione futurista di F. T. Marinetti*, Montepulciano, Grifo, 1990, 130 pp. Matteo D'Ambrosio, *Emilio Buccafusca e il futurismo a Napoli negli anni Trenta*, Na, Liguori, 1990, 677 pp. Id., *Nuove verità crudeli: origini e primi sviluppi del futurismo a Napoli*, Na, Guida, 1990, xvi + 580 pp., is an illus. anthology on Naples's contribution. Anna Maria Ruta, *Il futurismo in Sicilia. Per una storia dell'avanguardia letteraria*, Marina di Patti, Pungitopo, 310 pp. Santi Correnti, *Il futurismo in Sicilia e la poetessa catanese Adele Gloria*, Catania, CUECM, 1990, 119 pp. Gianni Eugenio Viola, *Gli anni del futurismo: la poesia italiana nell'età delle avanguardie*, Ro, Studium, 1990, 260 pp., has some previously unpublished futurist texts.

4. PERIODICALS

'Il Convegno' di Enzo Ferrieri e la cultura europea dal 1920 al 1940. Manoscritti, immagini e documenti, ed. Angelo Stella, Pavia, Università

degli Studi, 256 pp. E. Zinato, '"Il menabò di letteratura": la ricerca letteraria come riflessione razionale', *StN*, 17, 1990:131–54, notes the mixture of Soviet constructivism, American travel myths, and Italian values of the journal *Il Menabò*, and its relationship to the more avant-garde values of the 'Gruppo '63'. D. Cofano, 'Per una storia delle riviste: *Humanitas* di Piero Delfino Pesce (1911–1924)', *ON*, 15.1:43–56, rapidly charts the story of a Pugliese journal which combined strong 'United Europe' and theosophical tendencies with rationalist and Mazzinian undertones. Romano Luperini, *Gli esordi del Novecento e l'esperienza della Voce*, Bari, Laterza, 1990, 127 pp. E. Ghidetti, 'Bonsanti e il destino di *Solaria*', *RLI*, 94.1–2, 1990:64–75, traces the competition faced by the journal during the parallel contemporary progress of *'900* and *L'Italiano*, stressing A. Bonsanti's editorial sponsorship of young, European, and experimental writers. Vittoria Corti, *Il mondo di 'Solaria' e la vita letteraria a Firenze nel 1919–1920*, S. Eustachio di Mercato S. Severino, Il Grappolo, 1990, 69 pp.

5. THEATRE

Silvio D'Amico, *Le finestre di piazza Navona*, Casale Monferrato, Piemme, viii + 229 pp., pref. by S. D'Amico, theatre critic, is the first complete edition, with prologue, of a work planned as part of a tetralogy never completed. Posthumously titled, it was published in abridged form in 1961. Sandro Camasio, *Addio giovinezza! Commedia in tre atti*, ed. Pier Massimo Prosio, T, Centro Studi Piemontesi, 85 pp. M. Doria, 'Teatro e politica durante il fascismo', *ON*, 15.2:179–83, stresses the interest of archival material, both cabinet papers and police records, for E. Scarpellini's work of theatre organization in the Fascist period. Roberto Trovato, *Il teatro di Vico Faggi*, Forlì, Forum, 1989, 38 pp., on Alessandro Orengo, known as Vico Faggi. *Con Baldini 'teatrevolmente'*, ed. Alfredo Barbina, Ro, Palombi, 1990, 144 pp., is an interesting account of the acerbic theatre column and personal tastes of B. Eduardo De Filippo, *L'arte della commedia. Atti del convegno di studi sulla drammaturgia di Eduardo, Teatro Ateneo 21 settembre 1988*, ed. Antonella Ottai and Paola Quarenghi, in collaboration with Centro Teatro Ateneo, and the music and drama department of Rome University, Ro, Bulzoni, 1990, 161 pp. Giuliana Gargiulo, *Con Eduardo: Diario*, Na, Colonnese, 1989, 109 pp. Anna Barsotti, *Futurismo e avanguardia nel teatro italiano fra le due guerre*, Ro, Bulzoni, 1990, 240 pp. *Autori e drammaturgie: enciclopedia del teatro italiano. Il dopoguerra 1950–1990*, ed. Enrico Bernard, pref. Giorgio Prosperi, Ro, Ed. Associati, 396 pp. Mario Baratto, *Da Ruzante a Pirandello: scritti sul teatro*, Na, Liguori, 1990, 233 pp.

6. Authors

ALERAMO. M. Angelone, *Difesa della donna. La condizione femminile in 'Una donna' di Sibilla A. Fortuna del romanzo nel mondo anglosassone*, Na, Conti, 1990, 208 pp., is a collection of essays, some of which have been already published. Sibilla A., *Dialogo con psiche*, ed. B. Conti, Palermo, Novecento, 59 pp.

ARFELLI. L. B. Sforza, 'Su Dante A.: la narrativa dei superflui', *LetP*, 81:45–55, proposes analysis of one of the forgotten Italian novelists of the 40s and 50s, when he enjoyed a 'sfolgorante stagione di successi'.

BACCHELLI. *Riccardo B.: lo scrittore, lo studioso. Atti del Convegno di studi, Milano 8–10 ottobre 1987*, Modena, Mucchi, 1990, 303 pp.

BANTI. L. Desideri, 'Bibliografia degli scritti di Anna B.', *ParL*, 490, 1990:73–123, covers everything published by the writer between 1919 and 1985, the year of her death, arrayed under the headings 'Opere' and 'Scritti vari'. G. Testori, 'Ritratto di Anna B.', *ib.*, 13–21, and also R. Guerricchio, 'I racconti di Anna B.', *ib.*, 22–55. In this special number of the journal there is an interesting pref. by the editor, Giulio Cattaneo, suggesting that perhaps only Croce published an appreciation of Lucia Lopresti (i.e. Anna B.) in terms of her art criticism.

BASSANI. E. Neppi, 'La figura del sopravvissuto in un racconto di B.', *FoI*, 25:103–19, looks at several short stories or episodes in the Ferrara novels and points to the use of emblematic, hard-earned definitions, by name, ethnos, or proclivity, in several of B.'s fictional heroes/heroines.

BERNARDI. A. Bernardi, *Il vetro del ricordo*, pref. G. Bàrberi Squarotti, Ravenna, Longo, 110 pp.

BIGONGIARI. M. C. Papini, 'Per Piero B.', *Paradigma*, 9, 1990:3, introduces a special issue of the journal (founded by B. in 1977) to mark his 75th birthday. It includes A. Noferi, 'Piero B.: "una ressa di opposti"' (5–12) on the poet's whole production as a conclusion to the surviving heritage of symbolism, G. Luti, 'Nel delta poetico di B.' (19–22), and G. Chiarini, 'Ipotesi sull'*usus scribendi* di Piero B.' (23–29). Also L. Balducci collects (31–45) 'Sei pezzi facili . . .', which concern B. in varying degrees, while S. Ramat (47–58) considers rhyme, structure, and lexicon in two poems about Lucca, and M. Feo analyses the poet's image of Greece in his poetry (59–75).

BILENCHI. R. Pepi, 'Da Spazzapan a "Società"', *Belfagor*, 46:187–96, assembles the text of B.'s responses and reminiscences (not tape-recorded) in a 1977 interview in which he assessed Welso Mucci and the journals of lit. circles in the 1930s and his own relation to anti-Fascist groups; it constitutes an extremely valuable biographical addendum now that B. is dead.

532   *Italian Studies*

BODINI.   *Mancino, Bodini*, Ro, Il Ventaglio, 30 pp., is a special vol. to commemorate the conference on B. and M. (1991).

BONAVIRI.   *Giuseppe B.*, ed. Sarah Zappulla Muscarà, Catania, Maimone, 258 pp.

BONTEMPELLI.   Massimo B., '*522*'. *Racconto di una giornata*, Ro, Lucarini, xxvii + 84 pp., pref. Marinella Galateria. Elena Urgnani, *Sogni e visioni: Massimo B. fra surrealismo e futurismo*, Ravenna, Longo, 154 pp.

BRANCATI.   M. Romanelli, 'L'equivoco di B.', *StN*, 17, 1990: 155–69, insists on the comparative scarceness of *gallismo* in the overall context of B.'s fiction and examines the reality of the mature work, almost completely 'sessuofobico'.

BUSI.   Aldo B., *Vita standard di un venditore provvisorio di collant*, Mi, Mondadori, 488 pp., with postface by Andreina Del Vecchio.

BUZZATI.   A. Colombo, 'B. fra parodia e critica: sul manzonismo di *Peste motoria*', *SPCT*, 42: 175–89, considers specific passages in Manzoni parodied in one of the *Sessanta racconti*.

CALVINO.   Annalisa Ponti, *Come leggere 'Il sentiero dei nidi di ragno' di Italo C.*, Mi, Mursia, 173 pp. Italo C., *Romanzi e racconti*, Mi, Mondadori, ed. Mario Barenghi and Bruno Falcetto, 1400 pp., introd. Claudio Milanini, has a dense pref. (pp. xi–xxxii) by Jean Starobinski which seems to annul recent bibliography, including the *Atti* of the Florence congress in 1988. The pref. shows a strong preference for sources already taken for granted by C. scholars, but fails to mention Leopardi and seems designed for non-Italian consumers, quoting disproportionately from the *Lezioni americane*. G. B. Bronzini, 'Dai Grimm a C. e la fiaba nel duemila', *CeS*, 115, 1990: 53–61, shows some of the sources, in the Grimm brothers' *Fairy Tales*, for C.'s interests and literary anthropology in his intended Harvard 1985 lectures and his *Fiabe italiane*. Italo C., *I libri degli altri: lettere 1947–1981*, ed. Giovanni Tesio, T, Einaudi, x + 658 pp., contains a selection of letters from the archives of the publishing house. *ItQ*, 115–16: 1989, collects a literary symposium of twelve articles on different aspects of C.'s fiction (pp. 5–123) and several reviews of recent, mainly American, monographs on him. F. Lanza, 'Bilanci calviniani: le parole e le scienze', *ON*, 15.2: 185–89, considers the stance of recent C. criticism, particularly in the light of the 1986 San Remo conference, proceedings of which are now published in *Italo C.: la letteratura, la scienza, la città*, ed. G. Bertone, Genoa, Marietti, 1988. K. Siegel, 'Italo C.'s *Cosmicomics*: Qfwfq's postmodern autobiography', *Italica*, 68: 43–59, is on the whimsicality, paradox, and apparently random ordering of events and identities in the creation and history sequence. Ruggero Puletti, *Un millenarismo improbabile: le lezioni americane di Italo C.*, pref. Anna Andreoli, Ro, Lucarini, xiii + 208 pp. P. Harris, 'Italo C.: the code, the chinamen and cities', *Mosaic*, 23.4, 1990:67–85, compares the desire for storytelling to mapmaking, noting that the weaving of Marco Polo and the Khan's intentions in *Le città invisibili* is like a mathematical raising to a higher power of literature's possibilities. B. Guthmüller, 'C.s Partisanen-erzählungen', *RF*, 102, 1990:228–54, adopts an early interpretation of C.'s fiction, seeing his realism as emerging entirely from the horror and vitality of remembered partisan-fighting experiences. A. De Vivo, 'C.: politica e segni letterari', *FoI*, 25:40–56, strongly empha-sizes the case for considering social message as the pre-eminent function in Calvino's fiction, with particular reference to 'Il nome, il naso', the story that opens *Sotto il sole giaguaro*.

CAMPANA.   M. Bulgarelli, 'Note campaniane. Il poeta biografato', *LetP*, 80:29–42, compares different approaches in writing up the poet's unfortunate illness and partially recorded travels, including a duel with an editor (G. Banti) already identified in 1950 by F. Matacotta. A. Capodaglia, **Un'idea di poetica: nuovo saggio su Dino C.*, Galatina, Congedo, 85 pp.

CAMPANILE.   Caterina De Caprio, **Achille C. e l'alea della scrittura*, Na, Liguori, 1990, 167 pp.

CAPRONI.   S. Veronesi, 'La domanda della formica', *NArg*, 34, 1990:5–6, and F. Sanvitale, 'Il cacciatore e il suo bersaglio', *ib.*, 6–13, form an 'Omaggio a C.', together with the publication of two 'minipoesie' by the author, *ib.*, 14. E. Fumi, 'Per Lei . . .?', *ParI*, 480, 1990:59–68, reconsiders the form/content disparity noticed by some in C.'s *Seme del piangere* and attempts to seek a connection between its 'andamento cantante' and the funeral theme. S. Pastore, 'Frammen-tazione e continuità nella poesia di C.', *RLettI*, 8, 1990:111–31, emphasizes certain difficulties in establishing recurring forms in C.'s poetry, but notes the tendency for syntactic period to match the containing measure of simple strophes; individual metrical patterns are not found to carry any particular mood or message. *Giorgio C.*, ed. Antonio Barbuto, Caltanissetta, Sciascia, 1990, 191 pp. Giorgio C., *Res amissa*, ed. Giorgio Agamben, Mi, Garzanti, 228 pp., is a collection of poems published for the first time.

CASATI.   **Carteggio Alessandro C.–Giuseppe Prezzolini*, ed. Dolores Continati, pref. Vittorio Enzo Alfieri, 2 vols, Ro, Storia e Letteratura, 1990, xxxi + 511 pp.

CASSOLA.   R. Bertacchini, 'L'opera di Carlo C.: convegno a Firenze, novembre 1989', *CeS*, 115, 1990:334–37, in reviewing the conference, assesses the reasons for the undeserved decline of C.'s public image from 1976 to his death in 1987.

CHIUSANO.   C. Toscani, 'A Italo A. C. per *Konradin*', *ON*, 14.5, 1990:204–07, interviews the successful novelist and feminist on his fictional rendering (1990) of the story of the German pretender executed in 1268 at the age of sixteen for trying to assert his claim to the throne of the Kingdom of Sicily. C. Toscani and R. Bresciani, 'Italo Alighiero C. fra storia e invenzione', *ON*, 15.2:197–204, assesses six C. novels, emphasizing their powerfully in-built historicism.

CONTINI. P. V. Mengaldo, 'Preliminari al dopo Contini', *ParL*, 480, 1990:3–16, assesses the problem of accounting for the critical methodology of a writer who discussed his techniques and reading comparatively little.

CORTI. C. Varese, 'Maria Corti: da *L'ora di tutti* a *Il canto delle sirene*', *StN*, 16, 1989:325–42, measures C.'s novel against some of the critical canons for fiction expressed in her generally far more influential criticism and also attempts, perhaps too indulgently, to isolate Dantesque or epic elements in her description of contemporary America, as well as in the book's isolation of mythic elements, such as the supernatural revelatory powers of the forest.

CROCE. T. Iermano, 'Lettere inedite di Benedetto C. a Dino Provenzal (1909–1928)', *FoI*, 24, 1990:189–207, prints 16 letters from C. to the scholar and Dante editor (1877–1972). These are to be found in the very full Provenzal *fondo* of the Labronica library's 'Sala Livorno'. About half are written on headed paper from C.'s journal *La Critica*. They contain interesting reflections by C. on Freemasons, on the personal justifications for a religious conversion, and on academic recommendations. In F. Finotti, 'Ritratto, maschera, fisionomia. Il genere epistolare e il carteggio C.–Prezzolini', *LItal*, 43:88–104, the 1990 edition of this important correspondence becomes chiefly an opportunity to explain the fascination exercised by C. on Italian intellectuals of the early *Novecento* and the contrast of temperament between correspondents both impatient not to repeat lit. ground already gone over, especially by contributors to *Il Leonardo*.

D'ARRIGO. F. Gatta, 'Semantica e sintassi dell'attribuzione in *Horcynus Orca* di Stefano D'Arrigo', *LS*, 26:483–95, posits that the distribution and choice of significant epithets permit the interpreter to make a kind of preliminary reconnaissance of this notoriously 'dense and sensual' narrative.

DE DONNO. W. De Nunzio-Schilardi, 'Il dialetto, la lingua della poesia di Nicola D.', *CLett*, 18, 1990:683–717, presents a Salentine (Lecce) dialect poet born in 1920 and quotes many of his sonnets.

DELFINI. M. Facchinetti, 'Gli atti del convegno modenese del 1983 su Antonio D.', *ON*, 15.2:191–95.

D'ERAMO. Luce D., *Deviazione*, Mi, Rizzoli, 1990, vi + 362 pp., has an introd. by Mario Spinella.

ECO. T. Stander, '*Il pendolo di Foucault*: l'autobiografia segreta di Umberto E.', *LetP*, 80:3–21, surveys the ambiguous reception of the novel in Germany and examines the tenuous link with Michel Foucault of the text, sources, epiphanies, referential games, and structure of the book, noting that in an interview Eco refused to admit a connection between the ending of the story and his own personal convictions. D. Parker, 'The literature of appropriation: E.'s use of Borges in *Il nome della rosa*', *MLR*, 85, 1990:842–49, considers several Borgesian situations in the novel but relates them to a specific lit. task, which was to create an arbitrary fictive *persona*. Valeria Chimenti *et al.*, *Da Verga a E.: strutture e tecniche del romanzo italiano*, ed. Gabriele Catalano, Na, Pironti, 640 pp. E. Liddelow, 'E., thinking and faith', *Meanjin*, 50:120–28, proposes the challenge to fresh thinking in E.'s work while discussing the ragged edges and anti-linear progress of *Il pendolo di Foucault*, where all conventions are eventually dissolved in the view of an outsider (*métèque*) who can already see through a system, E.'s typical hero. M. Viano, 'Ancora su *Il pendolo di Foucault*', *FoI*, 25:152–61, an astute assessment, notes some traditional anti-feminist elements in the book's plotting and several mystificatory and erudite trends that deliberately remove it from the area of universal appeal enjoyed by its predecessor *Il nome della rosa*. An indispensable addition to Eco bibliography.

FENOGLIO.   *Beppe F. oggi*, ed. Giovanna Ioli, Mi, Mursia, 302 pp., includes an introd. by Gian Luigi Beccaria and concerns the conference proceedings of San Salvatore Monferrato, 1989. Franco Vaccaneo, *Beppe F.: le opere, i giorni, i luoghi*, Cavallermaggiore, Gribaudo, 1990, 262 pp. *Langhe: memorie, testimonianze, racconti*, ed. Ugo Roello, T, Einaudi, vi + 196 pp., is an anthology of writings and poems about the Langhe area in Piedmont. Ettore Canepa, *Per l'alto mare aperto: viaggio marino e avventura metafisica da Coleridge a Carlyle, da Melville a F.*, Mi, Jaca Book, 160 pp.

FONTANELLA.   M. Bertone, 'La ricerca poetica di Luigi F. da *Simulazione di reato* (1974) a *Stella saturnina* (1989)', *ON*, 15.1:143–52, adds a short bibliography of the poet's collections and footnotes his main critics.

FORTINI.   A. Girardi, 'Schegge d'utopia. I *Nuovi saggi italiani* di Franco F.', *StN*, 16, 1989:343–63, stresses a strong shift in F.'s interest from prose to poetry in this latest edition of essays, noting the pre-eminence of Vittorio Sereni in F.'s pantheon of favourites and the 'sforzo assolutamente unico', the 'serratissima controperizia', of this presentation of S.'s poetics.

GADDA.   Carlo Emilio G., *Saggi, giornali, favole e altri scritti*, ed. Liliana Orlando, Clelia Martignoni, and Dante Isella, Mi, Garzanti, v + 1369 pp. Bruno Basile, *Il tempo e le forme: studi letterari da Dante a G.*, Modena, Mucchi, 1990, 285 pp. F. Pedriali, 'Uno studio in nero: *La passeggiata autunnale* di C.E.G.', *SpR*, 6, 1990:7–18, emphasizes the wide-ranging and almost Odyssean elements of Gadda's very early long short story (written 1918, publ. 1963); see also longer version in *ParL*, 486, 1990:27–40. G. Papponetti, 'G. scrittore "abruzzese"', *LIC*, 11, 1990:303–16, picks out a series of places and themes in G. that link him to other Italian writers who have dealt with Teramo, Marsica, and its pontiff, Celestine V. Marina Fratnik, *L'Écriture détournée: essai sur le texte narratif de C.E.G.*, pref. Carlo Ossola, T, Meynier, 1990, xvii + 317 pp. Maurizio De Benedictis, *La piega nera: groviglio stilistico ed enigma della femminilità in C.E.G.*, Anzio, De Rubeis, 213 pp. N. Spinosi, 'Un racconto di G.: *La casa*', *ParL*, 486, 1990:41–47. With Pedriali's piece, these items establish the context and individual circumstances of two topographically detailed and context-specific stories by G. The former was written in a prison camp in the First World War, the latter in 1932, and they were only recently published in collections which reduce their sparkling unusualness.

GALLIAN.   Marcello G., *Nascita di un figlio ed altri scritti*, introd. Massimo Bontempelli, Montepulciano, Grifo, 1990, 45 pp. P. Luxardo Franchi, 'Marcello G.', *StN*, 16, 1989:207–64, considers the seventeen novels, four short story collections, art criticism, and ideological propaganda of a now completely forgotten writer of the Fascist era, suggesting caution in accepting the obliteration of his memory in the near-universal tendency to exorcise the demons of the whole period by overlooking its representatives.

GINZBURG.   V. Barani, 'Il "latino" polifonico della famiglia Levi nel *Lessico famigliare* di Natalia G.', *ON*, 14.6, 1990:147–57, lists various techniques of dialectal and idiolect deformation which coalesce to form the family idiosyncrasies in the speech of G.'s novel. Alan Bullock, *Natalia G.: Human Relationships in a Changing World*, NY, Berg, 1991, viii + 261 pp.

GOZZANO.   Guido G., *Albo dell'officina*, ed. Nicoletta Fabio and Patrizia Menichi, F, Le Lettere, xxxviii + 168 pp., contains material that has been published for the first time. Gigliola De Donato, *Lo spazio poetico di Guido G.*, Ro, Ed. Riuniti, 159 pp. U. Pirotti, 'Postille gozzaniane', *SPCT*, 42:161–74, makes a series of suggestions and hypotheses for sources based on the Sanguineti commentary on G.'s *Poesie* (T, Einaudi, 1990).

GRAMSCI.   S. Caprioglio, 'G. e l'URSS. Tre note nei *Quaderni del carcere*', *Belfagor*, 46:65–75, attempts an exegesis of three otherwise obscure notes in the *Quaderni* by reference to passages from Russian texts or Russian linguistic features. G. Mastroianni, 'Per una rilettura dei *Quaderni del carcere* di Antonio G.', *Belfagor*, 46:485–509, proposes a cautious reappraisal of necessarily ill-referenced, inadequately researched articles in the *Prison Notebooks*, exemplified by showing some arbitrary judgements involuntarily recirculated in the centenary of G.'s birth. Giuseppe Fiori, *G., Togliatti, Stalin*, Bari, Laterza, 206 pp.

GIUDICE. Giovanni G., *Il paradiso: perché mi vinse il lume d'esta stella. Satira drammatica*, pref. F. Brioschi, Genoa, Costa & Nolan, 96 pp., appears just after Giovanni G., *Poesie (1953–1990)*, Mi, Garzanti, 484 pp.

LANDOLFI. Oreste Macrì, *Tommaso L.: narratore poeta critico artefice della lingua*, F, Le Lettere, 1990, 229 pp., considers the four aspects of the author's activity expressed in the sub-title in a study in part prompted by the April 1989 conference at Trento. Tommaso L., *Des mois*, ed. Idolina Landolfi, Mi, Rizzoli, 178 pp., is a new ed. of the author's diary. In N. Ginzburg, 'Lettura di L.', *ParL*, 484, 1990:3–13, the writer, then aged about 20, recalls meeting L. in a station café at Florence in winter '36 or '37. G. remains characteristically pale, clumsy, envious in her response to the author, whom she already considered radically different from Svevo and Moravia, and her own authorial models at that period. She notes the mixture of strangeness and sheer wittiness in L.'s stories, how he loved 'ardently' the unreal worlds of Kafka, considering them real in the extreme, and how for a while she came to appreciate L.'s intense love of the individual word.

LEVI. *Conversazione con Primo L.*, ed. Ferdinando Camon, Mi, Garzanti, 75 pp. L. Fontanella, 'Il poeta come testimone: per una lettura della poesia di Primo L.', *LIC*, 11, 1990:361–67, notes the ambitious range of L.'s predominantly naturalist verse, slight in quantity over its long period of composition (1943–87). Giuseppe Varchetta, *Ascoltando Primo L.: organizzazione, narrazione, etica*, Mi, Guerini, 107 pp. *Primo Levi as Witness. Proceedings of a symposium held at Princeton University, April 30–May 2 1989*, ed. Pietro Frassica, Fiesole, Casalini, 1990, xi + 131 pp.

LIALA. Aldo Busi, *L'amore è una budella gentile: flirt con L.*, Mi, Leonardo, 1990, 170 pp.

LUCINI. Domenico Cofano, *Il crocevia occulto: L., Nazariantz e la cultura del primo Novecento*, Fasano, Schena, 1990, 209 pp.

LUZI. G. Mazzotta, 'Mario L.: poesia e pensiero della creazione', *ON*, 15.1:133–42, comments on the trend in this poet to measure himself constantly against 'le grandi idee'. G. Cavallini, 'Mario L. e più di quarant'anni di poesia', *CLett*, 18, 1990:79–82, assesses Giorgio Petrocchi's interpretation of L.'s 'signals and messages' in his verse. G. Taffon, 'Metateatro e rapporto teatro-vita: una lettura di *Hystrio* di Mario L.', *CLett*, 18, 1990:587–97, discusses the poet's fourth play (after *Ipazia, Il messaggero*, and *Rosales*), published in 1987 and staged in the theatre season of 1988–89. S. Agosti, 'L. e la lingua della "verità": dal "Canto salutare" ad "Avvento notturno"', *StCrit*, 66:173–94, offers a balanced exposition of the poet's so-called 'hermetic' period (of compositions that can be dated to 1936–39) emphasizing the 'scotomizzazione' of the poet and the sense of a world registered in terms of dark, blindness, dazzle, and obscurity.

MAGRELLI.   Valerio M., 'Scrittura e percezione: appunti per un itinerario poetico', *Il Verri*, 1990:185–202, presents the text of a lecture on his own poetry and the subsequent discussion by a group of university researchers and their *docenti*.

MALAPARTE.   A. Colombo, 'Memoria per una rilettura dei *Santi maladetti* di Curzio M.', *CLett*, 18, 1990:497–511, analyses M.'s 1920 text on the significance to Italy of the October 1917 events, suggesting some comparison with other patriotic accounts of Italy's First World War effort, e.g. Piero Jahier, Carlo Emilio Gadda.

MALERBA.   J. Cannon, 'The search for the missing plot: M.'s *Il pianeta azzurro*', *FoI*, 25:90–102, presents a detailed account of the analysis of the crime and spy thriller conventions within the text of M.'s 1986 novel, with its strong universalizing and its enigmatic affinities to U. Eco's *Il pendolo di Foucault* (1988). The book is a combination of the random and the plotted, of neat closure and artistic non-determinacy.

MARAINI.   G. Weinberg, 'All'ombra del padre: la poesia di Dacia M. in *Crudeltà all'aria aperta*', *Italica*, 67, 1990:453–65, investigates the ambiguous and heart-rending workings of love for father in the early poetry, considered highly erotic, of the successful playwright and novelist. C. De Michelis, 'Dacia M.: *La lunga vita di Marianna Ucria*', *NArg*, 36, 1990:84–86, calls M.'s eighth novel a strange and worrying historical study with its powerful mixture of autobiographical hints; notes the source in an 18th-c. portrait of a deaf-dumb woman shown to the writer by her aunt.

MARINETTI.   Marzia Rocca, *L'oasi della memoria: estetica e poetica del secondo M.*, Na, Tempi Moderni, 1990, 138 pp.

MICHELSTAEDTER.   A. Benevento, '*La persuasione e la rettorica* di M. e la "concretezza artistica"', *ON*, 15.1:119–28, highlights the original-ity of the author's 'tesi di laurea' with its myriad quotations from the Greek 'masters of persuasion' and classical theoreticians, and its autonomous narrative inserts.

MONTALE.   Giorgio Taffon, *L'atelier di M.: sul poeta, sul prosatore, sul critico*, Ro, Ateneo, 1990, 137 pp. Eugenio M., *Diario postumo. Prima parte: 30 poesie*, ed. R. Bettarini, postface by Annalisa Cima, Mi, Mondadori, 52 pp., is another of the curious posthumous editions of verse which Montale chose to prepare 'ready-made' before his death. Mario Martelli, *Le glosse dello scoliasta: pretesti montaliani*, F, Vallecchi, 110 pp. Franco Croce, *Storia della poesia di Eugenio M.*, Genoa, Costa & Nolan, 126 pp., has interesting black and white illus. P. Cataldi, **M.*, Palermo, Palumbo, 276 pp. Rina Sara Virgillito, *La luce di M.: per una rilettura della poesia montaliana*, Cinisello Balsamo,

Paoline, 1990, 135 pp. R. Rinaldi, 'L'arca di Babele: M. e le bestie', *LIC*, 11, 1990:259–74, presents the collection of animals in M.'s later poetry as both a symbol of travel and a kind of salvation by way of the Ark. It also relates to a myth of flood and destruction in M.'s verse, with salvation in a Babel's tower of language flashes. *La tavolozza color foglia secca di Eugenio M.*, ed. Giuseppe Marcenaro, Genoa, SAGEP, 57 pp., incorporates paintings by the poet. F. Leruth, 'Les premières lectures françaises d'Eugenio M.', *LR*, 44, 1990:47–72, makes particularly rich use of the *Quaderno genovese* to trace M.'s early reading programmes or summaries of French literature, including both Goncourt brothers, A. Bertrand, E. Rod, P. Lotti, P. Fort, F. Jammes among several of the standard 19th-c. authors. A. Di Benedetto, 'Intertestualità montaliane: "Forse un mattino . . ." (vecchie e nuove note)', *ON*, 14.6, 1990:135–40, considers a passage from Tolstoy's *Adolescence* as well as a Zen saying and a fragment by O. Weininger as combined sources for the celebrated M. 'osso'. Dario Bellezza, 'Sul caso M.', *NArg*, 34, 1990:15–17, registers the shock felt in the Italian literary world at the revelation that many of M.'s literary articles were written for him by Henry Furst, that Maria Luisa Spaziani composed 'his' articles on German literature, and that many of his translations were 'bought' from L. Rodocanachi, and compares this with Sandro Penna's claim that M.'s 'Imitazioni' were copied from his 1930s verse rejected by *Solaria*. C. Federici, 'Spiritual conceptualization in M.'s later poetry', *FoI*, 24, 1990:176–88, applies some insights from Juri Lotman, concerning interior and exterior space as traversed by the poetic mind, to M.'s *Satura* and *Diari*, and reviews many recent English language critics, noting arguments on paradox, oxymoronic play, the time zones of the verse and the enigmas of past experience. A. Casadei, 'Lettere di M. a Cecchi', *RLettI*, 8, 1990:155–75, prints eight letters out of the 55 from M. to Emilio C. (dated from 1924 through to 1957), which were part of C.'s heirs' bequest to the Regione Toscana in 1982 and are now located in the State Archive. R. Bo, 'Tra cielo e terra: viaggio attraverso i simboli animali della donna nella *Bufera* di M.', *StN*, 17, 1990:103–29, attempts to sort out some of the female or male qualities of the eel, fish, and rooster symbolism of some poems in M.'s third main collection. G. Barfoot, 'Eugenio M. and Thomas Hardy', *Italianistica*, 19, 1990:131–43, proposes a set of coincidences, at best part of the common emotional state of poets who had recently lost their wives at 68 and 71, between M.'s *Xenia* and a series of Thomas Hardy poems. R. Lampugnani, 'Immanenza e transcendenza in M.: l'esempio di Bergson', *SpR*, 6, 1990:57–75, shows how M. operated an alternating and varied allegiance to Bergson in the metaphysics of his poetry. L. Blasucci, 'M., Govoni e l'"oggetto povero"', *RLI*, 94.1–2, 1990:43–63, examines the tendency of M. criticism to trace literary reminiscence in his *œuvre* to the 'high' tradition and argues that, on the contrary, the relationship with humble themes and icons from G. has been conspicuous since the 1983 publication of M.'s *Quaderno genovese*, dating back to his very earliest years (1917).

MORANTE. S. Wood, 'The bewitched mirror: imagination and narration in Elsa M.', *MLR*, 86:310–21, attempts to show how critical response may have been squeamish in responding to M.'s attempt to transfigure the universe, rather than merely depict it. E. Zago, 'Il carattere di stampa come segno ne *Lo scialle andaluso* di Elsa M.', *LetP*, 81:33–40. Graziella Bernabò, *Come leggere 'La storia' di Elsa M.*, Mi, Mursia, 158 pp.

MORAVIA. *Per M. Press book della sua morte*, ed. Jader Jacobelli, Ro, Salerno, 1990, 190 pp., is devoted to commemorative articles. More are to be found in *Nuovi argomenti*, 37, where several short pieces by well-known Italian writers, Enzo Siciliano, Dario Bellezza ('4000 giorni con M.', pp. 6–9), Renzo Paris, F. Sanvitale, also Rocco Carbone and Eraldo Affinati, yield pride of place to T. Tornitore, '*Gli indifferenti* e la critica: prolegomeni ad una futura indagine' (60–98), which analyses the complete critical fortune of the novel and discusses whether its inclusion on the Index led, even after the latter's abolition, to the novel's absence from school syllabuses. This issue also carries (15) a 1988 letter to M. from Stephen Spender and, perhaps as a curiosity, prints (16–17) a letter to Sergio Vacchi, presumably the last thing that M. wrote as it was found in his jacket pocket on the day he died in 1990. S. Torresani, 'M. e il suo teatro', *Sipario*, 510:89–91, assesses rather negatively *La mascherata* and *Beatrice Cenci* (1954, 1957) and concludes that in his third tragedy, *Il dio Kurt*, a full and completely theatrical text, M.'s plays (see also *La vita è gioco*, *La cintura*) effectively have their apex and summation. Dacia Maraini, 'Nota di Dacia Maraini', in '900 moraviano', *NArg*, 39:15–30, prints early travel letters sent fortnightly by the writer to, surprisingly, his mother and reassesses the highly ambiguous fascination with maternal figures in M.'s early fictional pictures of other mature women.

NOVARO. E. Villa, 'Per Mario N. poeta', *Italianistica*, 19, 1990:399–407, examines the relative lack of background information on this mystical poet and energetic cultural organizer of the early *Novecento*: manager, editor, even censor, and occasional user of pseudonyms to reject contributions to *La Riviera Ligure*.

NOVENTA. *'Il Castogallo' e altri scritti, 1922–1959*, ed. Franco Manfriani, Venice, Marsilio, 1990, cxciii + 314 pp., is a collection of writings most of which are here published for the first time.

ORTESE. L. Clerici, 'Anna Maria O.', *Belfagor*, 46:401–17, presents a generous and systematic rehabilitation of the writer, together with select bibliography and a useful account of her travels, foreign journalism, financial rescue by the so-called 'Legge Bacchelli' of 1986, and literary awards; the article pays particular attention to the theme of 'home' and the technique of 'unreality' which dominates her seventeen novels (published between 1937 and 1988).

PAGANO. M. Tondo, 'Proposta di lettura dei *Privilegi del povero* di V. P.', *MC*, 76–77, 1990:55–78.

PALAZZESCHI.   Anthony J. Tamburri, *Of 'Saltimbanchi' and 'Incendiari': Aldo P. and Avant-Gardism in Italy*, CUP, 1990, 229 pp. Laura Lepri, *Il funambolo incosciente: Aldo P. 1905–1914*, F, Olschki, 157 pp.

PALUMBO.   D. Cerullo, 'Il tormentato laboratorio di Nino P., *FoI*, 25:57–80, considers the writer's social engagement and the different titles proposed for *Il mio piccolo mondo* (1964), noting how different textual variants suggest altering degrees of strength for the act of memory. S. Martelli, 'Nell'officina appartata di Nino P.: progetti e realizzazioni', *MC*, 74–75, 1990:73–98, is one of the longest of a collection of fifteen essays gathered in a single number of the journal to honour P., seven years after his death. See also M. David, 'Osservazioni su *Il serpente malioso*' and 'Appendice: lettere di Nino P. ad Alberto Pescetto e Michel David', *ib.*, 21–48 and 50–71 respectively, and G. Bàrberi Squarotti, 'L'esperienza del *Giornale* nella narrativa di Nino P.', *ib.*, 13–19; the journal reproduces a national seminar on the author held on 19 March 1988 at Rapallo.

PARISE.   R. Bertacchini, 'P. a Parigi: mostre e convegni', *CeS*, 115, 1990:330–33, summarizes the December 1989 conference and exhibition on P.'s work, mentioning the publication by Climatats (Montpellier) of *Arsenico*, part of a novel started by the author in 1962 and then abandoned; mentions the negative evaluation by R. De Ceccady of P.'s Japanese travel writing, while noting his choice of 'hot spots', Chile, China, Biafra, Arab countries, and testimony of his involvement in Vietnam by colleagues and witnesses of his work there, B. Valli and S. Viola.

PASOLINI.   *Il realismo impopolare di Pier Paolo P.*, Foggia, Bastogi, 100 pp. M. Del Serra, 'P.: il grembo civile', *LIC*, 11, 1990:275–301, reviews a whole series of devices and artifices in the civic poetry to conclude that P.'s main heritage was a purged and radical recognition of a complete 'sintimint de la vida', a dialect version of Homer's or Verga's global account of a civilization at work and play. Stefano Casini, *P.: un'idea di teatro*, Udine, Campanotto, 1990, 188 pp. A. Banda, 'Appunti sul leopardismo di P.P. P.', *StN*, 17, 1990:171–95, a close comparison of passages from Leopardi and P. confirms the insight, quoted in *Zibaldone*, that 'prose is the nursemaid to verse'. Giorgio Bàrberi Squarotti, *Le maschere dell'eroe: dall'Alfieri a P.*, Lecce,

Milella, 1990, 377 pp. A. Banda, 'L'uso di categorie retoriche nelle interpretazioni di P.: problemi e prospettive', *FoI*, 24, 1990:163–75, notices how a large group of P.'s unwitting detractors tend to quote his gamut of rhetorical devices as negative elements for his poetry; this detracting mode is compared to the positive evaluation in R. Barilli of P.'s renovation of an *ars loquendi* and of antithesis as a capital *figura sententiae* round which his whole poetic corpus could be seen to rotate.

PAVESE.   C. Dionisotti, 'Per un taccuino di P.', *Belfagor*, 46:1–10, offers a less drastic judgement on the politically vacillating, ambiguously semi-Fascist P. revealed in the 'secret' notebook published by L. Mondo in *La Stampa* of 8 August 1990. Cesare P., Ernesto De Martino, *La collana viola: lettere 1945–1950*, ed. Pietro Angelini, T, Bollati Boringhieri, 221 pp., reveals the genesis, editorial decisions, and eclecticism behind the famous series of books on ethnology, magic, and history of religion on which the two correspondents advised (and bickered with) other Einaudi staff. D. Duncan, 'Naming the narrator in *La luna e i falò*', *MLR*, 86:592–601, consider P.'s problematic treatment of first person narrative in what is a symbolically artificial autobiography, where the narrator constructs a text which repeats the past rather than narrating it. Maria de las Nieves Muñiz Muñiz, *Poetiche della temporalità: Manzoni, Leopardi, Verga, P.*, Palermo, Palumbo, 1990, 242 pp. W. Musolino, 'P., Camus and the myth of Sisyphus: among peasants and the stones of life', *SpR*, 6, 1990:35–55, argues that some of P.'s portraits of impoverished peasants in *La luna* correspond to that of C.'s enslaved hero, Sisyphus. Franco Lanza, *Esperienza letteraria e umana di Cesare P.*, Modena, Mucchi, 1990, 31 pp. F. Secchieri, 'Il monologhismo essenziale del dialogo letterario. Sui *Dialoghi con Leucò* di Cesare P.', *LS*, 26:429–47, analyses the structure of the dialogues, seeing them as part of the writer's 'ininterrotto dialogare con l'irrappresentabile'. M. R. Lacalle Zalduendo and Roberto Pellerey, 'La narrazione di Cesare P. Memoria del tempo e ricordo dei luoghi in *Il diavolo sulle colline*', *REI*, 36, 1990:71–84, adapt a (puzzling) notion of 'abductive interference' from semiotics in order to elucidate the text in question, trying to show how temporal references influence all spatial movements of the characters in this least plot-bound of the novelist's books; they also show how places change meaning according to the different stages of their presentation in the novel.

PAZZI.   F. Ricci, 'Intervista con Roberto P.', *ItQ*, 117, 1989:55–66, presents detailed questioning of the novelist (born 1946) said to be foremost among Italy's 'young writers'. Id, 'Beyond tautology: the cosmo-conception of time in Roberto P.'s *La malattia del tempo*', *Italica*,

68:13–28, attempts to re-write the plot of a complex novel in order to interpret anew the gnomic symbolism of P.'s fusing of Napoleon, Edmund Halley, and the themes of *Genesis*.

PENNA. Sandro P., *Appunti di vita*, ed. Elio Pecora, Mi, Electa, 1990, 165 pp. C. Garboli, 'P. postumo', *ParL*, 488, 1990:3–12. G. Luti, 'Sandro P. o della felicità contraddetta', *RLI*, 95.1:21–30.

PIRANDELLO. Nino Borsellino, *Ritratto e immagini di P.*, Bari, Laterza, 270 pp. A. Mozza, 'Una lettera inedita di P. alla figlia Lietta', *ON*, 14.6, 1990:111–13, quotes an original letter held by Delfina Pettinati (1903–90), poet and lit. journalist. Luigi P., *La vita che ti diedi; Ciascuno a suo modo*, ed. Corrado Simioni, Mi, Mondadori, iv + 155 pp. Elio Providenti, *Archeologie pirandelliane*, Catania, Maimone, 1990, 255 pp. *Effetto Sterne: la narrazione umoristica in Italia da Foscolo a P.*, ed. G. Mazzacurati, Pisa, Nistri-Lischi, 1990, 439 pp. Carmelina Sicari, *Profezie di modernità: saggio sui miti di P.*, Cosenza, Pellegrini, 1989, 91 pp. *La 'persona' nell'opera di Luigi P. Atti del XIII Convegno Internazionale*, Mi, Mursia, 1990, 316 pp. Michele Federico Sciacca, *L'estetismo, Kierkegaard, P.*, Palermo, L'Epos, 1990, 334 pp. Pietro Frassica, *A Marta Abba per non morire: sull'epistolario inedito tra P. e la sua attrice*, Mi, Mursia, 132 pp. Giorgio Pullini, *P. e il teatro del Novecento*, Modena, Mucchi, 1990, 41 pp. *P. fra penombre e porte socchiuse: la tradizione scenica del 'Giuoco delle parti'*, T, Rosenberg & Sellier, 183 pp. *Colloquio internazionale sull'opera di Luigi P.*, ed. Giovanna Finocchiaro Chimirri, Catania, CUECM, 1990, 164 pp. L. Aurigemma, 'P.: alcuni lineamenti della teoria linguistica e della prassi scrittoria dei romanzi', *CLett*, 18, 1990:735–56, discusses *inter alia* how the novels reproduce some of the intonations of middle-class speech. N. Mineo, 'Ipotesi per i *Sei personaggi*', *ib.*, 397–403, suggests that the play poses the most romantically extreme reading of a profoundly bourgeois stratification of relationships. A. L. Lepschy, 'The treatment of antefact in P.'s theatre-in-the-theatre trilogy', *McWilliam Vol.*, 129–43. J. R. Dashwood, 'P. and dream theatre', *ib.*, 145–64. C. Di Lieto, 'La coscienza del Nulla ne *L'uomo dal fiore in bocca*', *MC*, 76–77, 1990:45–54.

PIZZUTO. Antonio P., *Lezioni del maestro: lettere inedite e scritti rari*, ed. Antonio Pane and Alessandro Fo, Mi, Scheiwiller, 130 pp.

PORTA. Mario Moroni, *Essere e fare: l'itinerario poetico di Antonio P.*, Rimini, Luisè, 133 pp.

PRATOLINI. R. Bassi, 'Colloquio con Vasco P.', *LetP*, 81:41–43, prints an interview dating from Dec. 1980, settling the small mystery of why P. reprinted *Il tappeto verde* and why he had published nothing significant between 1967 and 1980. A. Costantini, 'Rilettura de *La costanza della ragione*', *MC*, 76–77, 1990:79–89.

PRAZ. D. O'Grady, 'P.'s perversity', *Overland*, 120, 1990:16–20, outlines aspects of P.'s lit. personality with special ref. to articles, written in 1965 for the Roman daily *Il Tempo*, which were more acerbic than those submitted to its competitor, *Il Messaggero*, by Gabriele Baldini from an Australian journey in the same period.

PREZZOLINI. Giuseppe P., *L'arte di persuadere*, introd. Alberto Asor Rosa, Na, Liguori, 113 pp.

QUASIMODO. Salvatore Q., *Notturni del re silenzioso*, pref. Gesualdo Bufalino, ed. Giovanna Musolino, Messina, Sicania, 1989, 209 pp.

RAMAT. P. Poletto, 'Le corrispondenze letterarie ed i raccordi testuali di Silvio R.', *FoI*, 24, 1990:208–12, proposes an analysis of the guiding choices behind a critic's collection of contemporary essays, linking his interest in M. Luzi and V. Sereni to Leopardi and D'Annunzio.

RAPISARDI. *Mario Rapisardi*, ed. Sarah Zappulla Muscarà, Catania, Maimone, 159 pp.

RICEPUTI. A. Ceccaroni, 'La poesia è il crepitare dello spirito. Note e divagazioni sulla poesia di Luigi R.', *LetP*, 80:43–52.

RIPELLINO. A. Pane, 'Il "primo tempo" di Angelo Maria R.', *LIC*, 11, 1990:317–37, reviews the poetic output and critical prose of this scholar and writer, noting also his early review notices on theatre and film, but finding his main aesthetic nucleus in iconographic studies (Matisse, Chagall, Michetti, Daumier, Whistler); closes by printing five poems by R. from 1940.

RIPPO. C. Di Biase, 'Venti anni dopo, 1970–1990: significato e valore del *Canzoniere* di Vincenzo M.R.', *ON*, 14.5, 1990:221–26.

RODARI. Carmine De Luca, *Gianni R.: la gaia scienza della fantasia*, Catanzaro, Abramo, 164 pp.

RUGGIERO. Maria Grazia Lenisa, *La congettura e le ipotesi: sulla poesia di Giovanni R.*, Foggia, Bastogi, 1990, 105 pp.

SABA. Umberto S., *Lettere sulla psicoanalisi: carteggio con Joachim Flescher (1946–1949): con gli scritti di S. sulla psicoanalisi, le lettere di S. a Edoardo Weiss, due lettere di Weiss a Linuccia S.*, ed. Arrigo Stara, T, SEI, 126 pp. P. M. Sipala, 'Lo "strano filo" nell'ultimo S.', *Problemi*, 91:184–96, proposes a hypothesis for the identification of the author's and his family's friends in the names of persons variously referred to in the poet's *Canzoniere*, and assesses the language of pederasty in his novel *Ernesto*.

SABLONE. W. Mauro, 'Benito S. fra parola e scrittura', *FoI*, 25:81–89, considers the wide anthropological net cast by S.'s verse, with its cogent and modernizing Christian conventions.

SANGUINETI. Antonio Pietropaoli, *Unità e trinità di Edoardo S. Poesia e poetica*, Na, Edizioni Scientifiche Italiane, 205 pp. Fausto Curi, *Struttura del risveglio: Sade, S., la modernità letteraria*, Bo, Il Mulino, 232 pp.

SANMINIATELLI. Floriano Romboli, *Le ragioni della natura: un profilo critico di Bino S.*, introd. Fausto Pettinelli, Chieti, Solfanelli, 111 pp.

SAVINIO. N. Spinosi, 'L'anima ingannata: note su Alberto S.', *ParL*, 486, 1990:95–103. V. Valenti, 'Alberto S. tra letteratura dell'"informe" e "forma" del teatro', *Sipario*, 514:25–27, examines the dramatist's polymorphous activity, his deliberate dilettantism, rejection of *verismo*, and experiments with the writing of the absurd, and his long apprenticeship to Surrealism. M. Regosa, 'Alberto S. e la critica teatrale', *ib.*, 28–29, considers the richness of S.'s theatre reviews and the background of his published *Palchetti romani*. S. Pegoraro, 'Alchimie del riso: Alberto S. tra ironia e parodia', *Il Verri*, 1991:59–90.

SBARBARO. Camillo S., *Trucioli: 1920*, ed. Giampiero Costa, Mi, Scheiwiller, 1990, 425 pp. In B. Centovalli, '"D'un solitario revocatc carte". Cinque lettere di Camillo S. agli amici', *StCrit*, 66:249–59, the scholar adds a 1943 letter to Signora E. Labò and two each to Giovanni Giudici (1955, 1956) and Giorgio Caproni (1959, 1965). G. Savoca, *Concordanze delle poesie di Camillo S.*, introd. M. Guglielminetti, F, Olschki, 1990, xliv + 310 pp.

SCHEMBARI. Saverio Saluzzi, *La poesia di Emanuele S.*, Modica, SETIM, 30 pp.

SCIASCIA. S. Briziarelli, 'Of valiant knights and labyrinths: Leonardo S.'s *Il cavaliere e la morte*', *Italica*, 68:1–12, discusses the elaborate detective novel conventions woven into S.'s 1988 novel, pinpointing its originality within the genre, namely the shooting of the detective at the end, as well as the fact that he is ill with cancer. Onofrio Lo Dico, *La fede nella scrittura: Leonardo S.*, Caltanissetta, Sciascia, 1990, 236 pp. Piero Carbone, *Il mio S.: tópoi e riflessioni*, Palermo, Grifo, 1990, 49 pp. G. Giudice, 'Le citazioni di Leonardo S.', *Belfagor*, 46:329–32, picks out the wit of S.'s literary allusions, which draw on literary/philosophical memorization of writers spanning a millennium. V. Paladino, 'L'ultimo S. Il senso del limite', *CLett*, 18,1990:719–31, notes how *Una storia semplice* did not effectively dissimulate a growing sense of satiety, of over-employment, in the author's return to criminal and parochial themes; also compares him to Vitaliano Brancati, and especially to C. E. Gadda and Pirandello, seeing them all as elegant and deliberate 'spoilers' (*guastatori*).

SERENI. Alfredo Luzi, *Introduzione a S.*, Bari, Laterza, 1990, 189 pp., provides detailed and chronologically sequential treatment, with select bibliography in the manner of this handy series 'Gli scrittori'. N. Lorenzini, 'S. e la poesia "a portata di sensi"', *Il Verri*, 1990:135–52, is a bold and sympathetic essay on S.'s production, characterizing his verse as a recension of 'proposte del mondo', and identifying prolific moments in the natural surroundings, physical material, space, and everyday objects.

SERRA. Renato S., *Scritti critici*, ed. Ivanos Ciani, Ro, Libreria dello Stato, 1990, liii + 175 pp.

SINIGAGLIA. C. Carena, 'Lettura postuma di Sandro S.', *ParL*, 484, 1990:105–15, endeavours to re-evaluate the recently deceased author of three comparatively little-known collections, who was admired by G. Contini, F. Portinari, M. Corti, and others.

SINISGALLI. Giancarlo Borri, *Il poeta ingegnere e la civiltà delle macchine*, T, Piazza, 1990, 148 pp.

SILONE. R. C. Lumetti, 'Petrocchi e S.: l'incontro di due moralità', *CLett*, 18, 1990:69–78, demonstrates how Petrocchi consistently returned to all S.'s major works in reviews or essays, seeing him as a piercingly sincere, almost Franciscan moral commentator on the age. *Centro Studio 'Ignazio Silone', 1980–1990. Dieci anni di attività a Parma*, Parma, Battei, 1990, 88 pp.

SLATAPER. A. Benevento, '*Passato ribelle*: un dramma dimenticato di S.', *ON*, 14.5, 1990:215–19. Giampaolo Chiarelli, *Scipio S. scrittore e giornalista*, Udine, Campanotto, 1989, 85 pp.

SOLDATI. S. Verdino, 'Nel mondo di S.', *Nuova corrente*, 37, 1990:215–48, makes an interesting attempt to organize a 'sistema dei luoghi' running through the entire narrative corpus of S., examining his allegiance to Genoa, Liguria, and America, but considering Turin his 'city of nostalgia and order'; also evokes the consistent network of a 'fitta onomastica geografica' in his writing and manages to look at the mechanics of the so-called 'desiring glance' and its 'repentinità' in S.'s prose.

SOLMI. A. M. Vezzosi, 'Sergio S.: lungo il corso della memoria, soluzioni irrepetibili di scrittura', *LetP*, 81:5–22, is a balanced reassessment of S.'s essays and verse ten years on from his death. In L. Betocchi, 'Con Sergio S. alla banca commerciale', *ib.*, 23–32, the author, a nephew of Carlo Betocchi, recalls S.'s mixing of work and literature in the offices of the bank where they both worked. Renato Turcio (*ib.*, 3–4) has a useful bibliography of S., entitled 'Omaggio a Sergio S.'.

SVEVO. Angela Guidotti, *Zeno e i suoi doppi: le commedie di S. Seconda edizione corretta e ampliata*, Pisa, ETS, 1990, 204 pp. Eduardo Saccone, *Commento a 'Zeno': saggio sul testo di S.*, Bo, Il Mulino, 267 pp. L. Benedetti, 'Vivere ed essere vissuti: Amalia in S.'s *Senilità*', *Italica*, 68:204–16, compares S.'s structural techniques in his handling of single or plural female protagonists in the cast of his novels, especially the Amalia of *Senilità*. Giorgio Luti, *L'ora di Mefistofele: studi sveviani vecchi e nuovi (1960–1987)*, F, La Nuova Italia, 1990, x + 210 pp. G.

Savelli, ' "Ogni riferimento è puramente casuale": il lettore nel finale della *Coscienza di Zeno*', *StCrit*, 67 : 457–77, suggests that the impossible 'atomic' bomb of the novel's closing paragraphs requires that the meaning of a text be seen as also lying outside that text and in a pool of inter-actions between the text and all of its possible readers. Id., 'Microstrategie dell'ironia e dell'umorismo nella *Coscienza di Zeno*', *LS*, 26 : 393–428, analyses the ambiguity and irony in S.'s game of witty cross-reference to the reader and the characters, with particular reference to ten passages excerpted from the fifth chapter of this novel. A. Cavaglion, 'Così fan tutti', *Belfagor*, 46 : 462–66, views some witty connections between Da Ponte's stay in Friuli, with an infatuation over the manageress of a *locanda*, the 'Della Lisert', and Svevo's Friulan sojourn and an analogous passion of the Triestine novelist for the 'paffuta contadinella' Teresina. B. Moloney, 'Riduzioni drammatiche: two dramatizations of S.'s *La coscienza di Zeno*', *McWilliam Vol.*, 165–79.

TABUCCHI. J. Francese, 'T.: una conversazione plurivoca', *SpR*, 6, 1990 : 19–34, analyses some of the Montalian references in T.'s collection of short fiction, *I volatili del Beato Angelico* (1987). A. Sempoux, 'Antonio T.: des frontières incertaines', *LR*, 44, 1990 : 357–63, identifies the adventure element in T.'s recent fiction success as a complex reversal and mirror process, also following a kind of neo-Pythagorean rule of the figure nine.

TOBINO. G. Magrini, 'Mario T. e lo stile della comunità', *ParL*, 488, 1990 : 20–32, emphasizes that a significant portion of T.'s writing had to do with dynamic modern models of community living. G. Nava, 'I modi del racconto in T.', *ib.*, 20–32, applies some Russian Formalist analysis to seven of the critic's narrative texts. V. Pardini, 'Omaggio a Mario T.', *NArg*, 35, 1990 : 118–22, explains the greatness of single scenes, and of portraits of individual figures, in the writing of our author, not fully appreciated in newspaper and television treatment on his eightieth birthday, in January 1989.

TOZZI. Federigo T., *Tre croci*, introd. Giuseppe Nicoletti, Mi, Garzanti, 105 pp. Id., *Gli egoisti*, introd. Claudio Toscani, Mi, Mondadori, 154 pp.

TUROLDO. David Maria T., *O sensi miei*, introd. Andrea Zanzotto and Luciano Erba, Mi, Rizzoli, 1990, xxii + 706 pp.

ULIVI. C. Toscani, 'Intervista a Ferruccio U. per *Storie bibliche e d'amore* e *L'anello*', *ON*, 15.1 : 103–10, contains comments by the novelist on the end of 70 years of communism and its depiction in lit., also commenting on the degree of nihilism and significance of the suicide in his 1990 text *L'anello*.

UNGARETTI. Emerico Giachery, *Vita d'un uomo: itinerario di Giuseppe U.*, Modena, Mucchi, 1990, 37 pp. Anna Vergelli, *Un uomo di prim'ordine: Giuseppe U. Documenti e altra corrispondenza inedita*, Ro, Bulzoni, 1990, 152 pp. F. M. Sansoni, 'Petrarca e U. Il recupero e l'invenzione di una tradizione', *RLI*, 94, 1–2, 1990:231–41. B. Carle, 'U. and Valéry: from intertextuality to hypertextuality', *Italica*, 68:29–42, is a close study of intertextual relations and some analogies in the poet's development. C. Annoni, 'U. "allegro"', *LIC*, 11, 1990:233–58, compares the 'sweetness' of Leopardi with U.'s 'allegria'; also notes the poeticity of *L'Allegria*, as a parallel to the passing of great orchestral music (Wagner, Puccini) in the contemporary imagination; makes interesting 'intertextual' leaps to Foscolo's *Grazie* and *Sepolcri*. Marco Forti, *U. girovago e classico*, Mi, All'Insegna del Pesce d'Oro, 196 pp. F. Livi, 'Présentation', *REI*, 35, 1989:5–6, introduces a special number of the journal devoted to U. on his centenary (Feb. 1988) and discusses French conferences held in the year: articles include G. Luti, 'U. e il "mito" della Francia' (7–15), also in *RLI*, 94.1–2, 1990:223–30, P. Bigongiari on U.'s relation to André Bréton and P. Reverdy (16–25), and essays by D. De Robertis, Mario Petrucciani, G. Genot, Luciano Rebay, and Gemma-Antonia Dadour. Livi also adds valuable 'Ungarettiana. Notes bibliographiques' (146–55) which offer a preliminary exploration of the whole revival of U. studies during the 1980s, here called 'l'achèvement de travaux de longue haleine: éditions de textes, publication d'inédits, études critiques'.

VITTORINI.　Sebastiano Saglimbeni, *Il fiore e l'intenso: Il Garofano di Elio V.*, Verona, Ed. Paniere, 67 pp. P. Kuon, '"Ehm! Perché ehm?" — Kommunikationsstörungen und Sinnkonstitution in V.'s *Conversazione in Sicilia*', *RF*, 102, 1990:207–27, examines the resolution of the various allegorical motifs from V.'s novel in the bronze war memorial with the naked woman's lubriciously attractive form. Elio V., *Le città del mondo*, introd. Edoardo Esposito, Mi, Mondadori, 333 pp. E. Esposito, 'Di *Autografo* in *Autografo*', *Belfagor*, 46:583–85, comments on the monographic 22nd number of *Autografo*, devoted to V. and marking a change of publisher: the issue comprises essays on V.'s fiction and journalism and a catalogue of the V. papers in the Pavia Centro di Ricerca sulla Tradizione Manoscritta di Autori Contemporanei.

VIVANTI.　B. Pischedda, 'Annie V.', *Belfagor*, 46:45–64, concentrates on the rise and fall of V. (G. Carducci's unlikely *protegée*), who appeared as a kind of gypsy in the gathering cultural industry of the period; also adds a list of her poems, novels, generally 'failed' plays, and children's books, with a select bibliography.

VOGHERA.　A. Focaccia, 'Giorgio V.', *StN*, 17, 1990:7–53, deals at length with the prolific journalist and travel-writer: a victim of the racial laws in the 1940s, since his retirement in 1962 he has translated from Hebrew as well as French, German, and English.

ZANZOTTO. Luigi Tassoni, *Il sogno del caos: microfilm di Z. e la genericità del testo*, Bergamo, Moretti & Vitali, 1990, 113 pp. Maria Grazia Lenisa, *Il segno trasgressivo: Giorgio Bàrberi Squarotti e Andrea Z*, Foggia, Bastogi, 1990, 115 pp. V. Hand, 'Undermining logocentric thought in Andrea Z.'s *La Beltà* (1961–67)', *IS*, 46:82–101, sets out the undermining of language and lack of politicization in Italy's now fully canonized contemporary poet; draws attention to the mixture of programmatic constructive and parallel destructive elements in his verse and notes some of the pure pleasure of oral articulation, especially via 'petel', the maternal babble that is commonly trotted out to infants. M. Munaro, 'Andrea Z. o la poesia in bicicletta', *Il Verri*, 1990:153–65, is one of rather few articles on Z.'s recent critical success frankly to admit the total obscurity of this congeries of fragments, of broken, unreflecting mirrors and contradictory antitheses.

IX. ROMANIAN STUDIES*

LANGUAGE†

By GLANVILLE PRICE, *University of Wales, Aberystwyth*

GENERAL. Gilbert Fabre, *Parlons roumain: langue et culture*, Paris, L'Harmattan, 204 pp. + audio cassette. Ion Coteanu, *Gramatică. Stilistică. Compoziție*, 1990, Ed. Științifică. Cristina Hoffman, *Romanian Grammar*, NY, Hippocrene, 1991, vii + 100 pp., is a highly compressed summary. Marina Ciolac, '"Umgangssprache" dans le roumain actuel: plaidoyer et repères pour une approche possible', *RRL*, 36: 169–79, takes account of phonetic, morphosyntactic, and lexical features. Klaus Heitmann discusses 'Limba și literatura română în Basarabia și Transnistria (așa-numita limbă și literatură moldovenească)', *RLȘL*, 1991, 4: 79–90 and 5: 56–69 (to be continued).

RRL, 35.4–6, 1990, a special issue devoted to 'Le roumain, idiome roman', includes *inter alia*: Jana Balacciu-Matei, 'Le roumain *mire* est-il le descendant du latin *miles*?' (271–77) (the answer seems to be 'maybe'); Corina Cilianu-Lascu, 'Notes sur la structure thématique de la phrase en roumain' (279–84); Janeta Drăghicescu, 'Remarques sur la construction "gerunziu cu acuzativ"' (303–07) (specifically on Romanian); E. P. Hamp, 'Rom. *tureac, tureatcă*' (311–12); Maria Manoliu-Manea, 'Ethno-syntax and discourse. Inalienability and topicality in Romanian' (323–29); and H. Meier, 'Betrachtungen zur romanischen Etymologie. Von der Kopfbinde bis zur Capa' (331–40); on contrastive items and others covering more than one Romance language, see pp. 11–12 above.

LiR, 39.5–6, 1990 (1991), a homage issue for Ion Coteanu, includes *inter alia*: A. Avram, 'Despre relevanța stilistică a lungimii consoanelor în limba română' (369–72); Gh. Bolocan, 'Toponimie și dialectologie' (379–82); L. Brad-Chisacof, 'Momente de contact în formarea limbilor literare română și neogreacă' (383–88); Gh. Brâncuș, 'Sensul "legere" al verbului *a cînta*' (389–90); M. Dobre, 'Elemente de terminologie geografică populară din Oltenia' (391–93); C. Dominte, 'Originea adverbului *azi-noapte*' (395–99); K. Dumitrașcu, 'Benkő József despre interferențele lingvistice din Transilvania' (401–04); V. Guțu Romalo, 'Preferințe lexicale: *dialog*' (405–08); D. Negomireanu, 'Relații semantice în structura comparației' (417–18); L. Pop,

---

*The place of publication of books is Bucharest unless otherwise stated.

†I am grateful to the Central University Library, Bucharest, for supplying most of the books and periodicals on which this survey is based.

'Identificarea — presupoziție pragmatico-semantică pentru expresii "definite" în limba română' (429–36); and I. Toma, '"Etimologia de grup" în toponimie' (447–51).

HISTORY OF THE LANGUAGE. D. Urițescu, 'Sur quelques formes dialectales dans le latin populaire danubien', *Actes* (Trier), III, 318–28, re-examines the evolution of Latin *i* in Romanian. N. Raevschi, 'Referitor la unele trăsături comune aromâniei și limbilor Romaniei occidentale', *RLȘL*, no. 4:61–68, argues that the sub-Danubian ancestor of Aromanian must have maintained links with the western Romance-speaking area longer than the northern Romanian area. V. Barbu's survey of early attestations to Romanian (see *YWMLS*, 52:524) continues, under the modified overall title 'Mărturii străine despre limba română', with 'II. Secolul al XV-lea (2)', *LiR*, 40:285–90. Gh. Chivu, *ib.*, 45–47, argues that *pentru* and *printru* were already distinct prepositions in the 16th c. M. J. Elson, 'The origin of the present subjunctive of *fi* "be" in standard Romanian', *SN*, 63:113–20, speculates somewhat pointlessly.

TEXTS. A. Avram, 'Valoarea fonetică a literei *e* în *Fragmentul Todorescu* și problema închiderii lui [e] în poziție nazală', *LiR*, 40:5–10; V. Barbu, 'Preliminării la studiul naționalizării serviciului divin: principalele versiuni românești ale *Simbolului credinței* (1650–1713)', *ib.*, 25–31; V. Guruianu, 'Datarea celui mai vechi manuscris românesc al *Fiziologului*', *ib.*, 49–55; G. Nussbächer, 'Tipărituri românești menționate într-un act de partaj din 1585', *ib.*, 73–77; A Șerbănescu, 'Structuri retorice și organizare sintactică în *Manuscrisul de la Ieud*', *ib.*, 85–90. V. Barbu, 'Asupra izvoarelor *Îndreptării legii* (Tîrgoviște, 1652) (3)', *SCL*, 41, 1990:135–44, 269–78, 475–81. N. A. Ursu, 'Concordanțe lingvistice și stilistice între prefețele mitropolitului Teodosi, *Istoria țării rumânești* atribuită Stolnicului Constantin Cantacuzino și *Foletul novel*', *ib.*, 42:231–49, develops his previously argued case for attributing to T. the two texts in question. Ladislau Gyémánt edits, with an introduction co-signed by Ștefan Pascu, a translation, and notes, an important text for the debate about the origins of the Romanian people and language, viz. Ion Budai-Deleanu, *De originibus populorum Transylvaniae/Despre originile popoarelor din Transilvania*, 2 vols, Ed. Enciclopedică, xci + 336 + 559 pp. Petru Maior's *Istoria pentru începutul românilor în Dachia* (1812) is edited with a substantial *postfață* by G. Istrate, Iași, Junimea, 1990, 342 pp.

PHONETICS AND PHONOLOGY. Andrei Avram, *Nazalitatea și rotacismul în limba română*, Ed. Academiei Române, 1990, 247 pp., has synchronic, diachronic, and dialectal dimensions. Id., 'Cu privire la statutul fonologic al semivocalelor, semiconsoanelor și pseudovocalelor în limba română', *SCL*, 42:213–29, defends his previously expressed views against counter-analyses proposed by a number of other scholars. L. Dascălu-Jinga, *SCL*, 42:19–31, studies the intonation of elliptical exclamatory clauses introduced by *de, dacă, să, cînd*, and, *RRL*, 36:183–91, deals with the intonation associated with superlative constructions of the types *era o vreme! e ceva!* and (verb) + *la* + indefinite noun.

ORTHOGRAPHY.   Mioara Avram, *Ortografie pentru toţi*, Ed. Academiei Române, 1990, 168 pp., discusses thirty potential difficulties, each affecting a wide range of words (e.g. *e* or *ie*, the presence or absence of non-syllabic final *-i*, *x* or *cs*, *gz*, the use of hyphens).

GRAMMAR.   M. A. Gabinski, *Din problemele gramaticii şi derivării române*, Chişinău, Ştiinţa, 131 pp. (in Cyrillic), contains four studies, viz. 'Gerundiul şi o evoluţie recentă pe baza lui' (6–71), 'Formaţii supraconfixale în română (tipul *de neclintit*)' (72–104), 'Genitivul şi dativul românesc privite tipologic' (105–16), and 'Cvasitautologiile neoinfinitivale în română' (117–22). J. Felix, *SCL*, 41, 1990:433–46, proposes a classification of Romanian words on the basis of their morphemic structure.

A. Şerbănescu, 'Abordări moderne ale pronumelui românesc', *SCL*, 42:273–78, reviews articles by L. Tasmowski-De Ryck and others. Daniela Stoianova, 'O încercare de interpretare a modelului complementului dublat', *ib.*, 133–50, deals with clitic-copying of the direct object, mainly (but not exclusively) with reference to Romanian. C. Dobrovie-Sorin, 'Clitic doubling, *Wh*-movement and quantification in Romanian', *LI*, 21, 1990:351–97. D. Manea, 'Probleme ale transitivităţii în limba română. (I). Verbele cu complement intern', *SCL*, 41, 1990:447–61; '(II). Verbele cu două obiecte', *ib.*, 42:33–44. W. Moortgat publishes for the second time, *RevR*, 26:25–53, his article on 'le passif plein' and 'le passif réfléchi' (see *YWMLS*, 52:525). D. Stoianova, 'Observaţii cu privire la sensurile temporal-aspectuale ale formelor nominale ale verbului în româna contemporană', *SCL*, 42:201–11, argues that temporal-aspectual values apply to the gerund, past participle, and supine as well as to the infinitive. Sanda Golopenţia discusses 'Verbs for locutionary acts in Romanian', *RRL*, 35:119–40. M.-L. Rivero, **'Exceptional case marking effects in Rumanian subjunctive complements', Wanner and Kibbee, *New Analyses*, 273–98. L. Pop, '"Incidenţa" incidentelor', *SCL*, 42:73–87, takes a discourse analysis approach to interpolated clauses. D. Stoianova and M. Almahel, 'Analiza semantico-sintactică a unui grup de sintagme nominale alcătuite din două substantive în limbile bulgară şi română', *SCL*, 41, 1990:463–74, consider (for Romanian) nouns linked by *de*. Andrea Şerbănescu, 'Despre statutul lui *uite* vs. *uită-te*', *SCL*, 42:151–65, distinguishes between them on the syntactic, semantic, and pragmatic levels. L. Dascălu-Jinga, 'Romanian exclamative *unde* ("where")', *RRL*, 36, 85–89, considers syntax and intonation.

Language   553

LEXICOGRAPHY AND LEXICOLOGY. Laura Vasiliu, *Sufixele. Derivarea verbală*, Ed. Academiei, 1989, 191 pp., is vol. 3 of A. Graur and Mioara Avram (eds), *Formarea cuvintelor în limba română*. S. Drincu, *LiR*, 40:237–40, surveys N. Drăganu's theory (1906) of compound words in Romanian. L. Vasiliu, 'Sufixele -*ară* şi -*are*', *ib.*, 91–95. G. Druţa, 'Formarea şi utilizarea unor neologisme', *RLŞL*, no. 3:43–48, discusses, *inter alia*, forms in -*manie* or -*fobie* and derivatives of *mancurt*. After a long interval, publication of *Dicţionarul limbii române* (see *YWMLS*, 46:578) is resumed with *vol. x, part 3, pp. 691–1041, Universul, 1990, covering SEMN–SÎVEICĂ. Marin Bucă and Onufrie Vinţeler, *Dicţionar de antonime al limbii române*, Ed. Enciclopedică, 1990, 325 pp., is a totally different work from their *Dicţionar de antonime* of 1974 (see *YWMLS*, 36:510), not only containing some 2400 entries (as opposed to 784 in the earlier work) but being entirely reorganized. Within its necessarily restricted scope Andrei Bantaş, *Dicţionar român–englez*, Teora, 294 pp., is well done. W. Schweickard, 'Normverstöße im Gegenwartsrumänischen', *ASNS*, 227, 1990:146–49, is based on Al. Graur's *Dicţionar al greşelilor de limbă* (see *YWMLS*, 45:555). M. Avram, 'Un vechi sens religios al verbelor (*a*) *semna*, (*a*) *însemna* şi etimologia lui (*a se*) *sineca*', *LiR*, 40:11–18. I. Ionescu discusses 'Termeni de cultura creştină daco-română', *ib.*, 157–63, concluding that they illustrate 'aportul factorului cultural-istoric creştin determinant "în procesul de romanizare de la originea poporului român"'. M. Sala, *ib.*, 79–84, argues that *leu* is an inherited word and not a loan-word. Maria Purdela Sitaru, *SCL*, 42:125–31, draws attention to Latin words for 'illness, ill' inherited by Romanian. E. C. Hamp argues, *RRL*, 36:91–92, that *douăzeci*, etc., and probably also *unsprezece*, etc., are calques not on Slavic but on an autochthonous pre-Latin Albanoid language. Id., 'Rom. *păstra*', *ib.*, 181–82, takes issue with M. Ferrand. V. C. Ioniţă, *LiR*, 40:262–63, provides etymological notes on thirteen words for which *DLR* offers either no etymology or else an unsatisfactory one. Rejecting other (somewhat fanciful) suggested origins recently advanced for the word *ler*, I. Ionescu, *ib.*, 265–68, defends the etymology *alleluia* proposed by D. Dan and supported by Al. Rosetti. V. Guţu Romalo, *ib.*, 270–74, discusses recent uses of the verb *a manipula*, and L. Mareş, *ib.*, 274–75, uses of *a debuta*. I. Robciuc, 'Etimologii româneşti', *ib.*, 369–71, discusses *desétnic*, *mésiţă*, *scupós* and *volóhi* on the basis of historical and geographical criteria. V. Drimba studies 'Împrumuturi româneşti detaşate din sintagme determinative turceşti', *SCL*, 41, 1990:305–11. Francisc Kiraly, *Contacte lingvistice. Adaptarea fonetică a împrumuturilor româneşti de origine maghiara*, Timişoara, Facla, 1990.

ONOMASTICS. G. Bolocan discusses 'Modele sinonimice în toponimie', *LiR*, 40:275–83.

DIALECTOLOGY. *Dicţionarul subdialectului bănăţean*, *vol. 4, BICA–BUZUNAR, ed. Maria Purdela Sitaru, Univ. of Timişoara, Fac. of Philology, 1988 (1989?), 243 pp. Sever Pop's *Chestionarul atlasului lingvistic român* is in course of publication, ed. Doina Grecu and others, vol. I, Univ. of Cluj, 1989, xxi + 149 pp. V. Zagaevschi, 'Particularităţi dialectale în flexiunea adjectivului', *RLŞL*, no. 4:69–75, deals with Moldavian dialects. E. P. Hamp, 'Dialectal dynamics in Maramureş', *RRL*, 36:181, identifying a conservative west and an innovating south-east, reconstructs an old name for the inhabitants of the area. E. Vasiliu, *SCL*, 41, 1990:425–27, discusses the origins of the phonemic split between /z/ and /d̦/ in some dialects. N. Saramandu, *ib.*, 429–31, argues on the basis of an Aromanian subdialect that -*ll*- became -*u̦*- and that forms like *stea*, etc., did not precede *steaua*, etc. Id., 'Probleme ale studierii substratului aromânei', *ib.*, 42:119–23, briefly surveys the views of I. I. Russu, C. Brâncus, T. Capidan, C. Poghirc and others.

CONTRASTIVE STUDIES. D. Stojanova writes (in Bulgarian) on functional-semantic parallels in the use of dative pronominal clitics with possessive meaning in Bulgarian and in Romanian, *ConL, 14, 1989:121–28.

LITERATURE

POSTPONED

X. ROMANSH STUDIES

By KENNETH H. ROGERS, *University of Rhode Island*

(This survey covers the years 1990 and 1991)

1. BIBLIOGRAPHICAL AND GENERAL

Giovan Battista Pellegrini, *La genesi del retoromanzo (o ladino)* (*ZRP*, Beiheft 238), Tübingen, Niemeyer, 71 pp., again takes up the theme of his article 'The sociolinguistic position of central Rhaeto-Romance (Ladin)', *RPh*, 40, 1987:287–300, to trace in detail the history of the positing of the unity of Rheto-Romance. P. castigates (1) Romance scholars who have not fully read or understood the works of Salvioni or Battisti (2) those put off by a perceived Italian nationalist bias in Battisti's denial of RR unity (3) Dolomitic Ladin nationalists and teachers who advocate autonomy on spurious linguistic grounds, and (4) politicians who yielded to these nationalists by creating autonomous regions. While conceding that the Sella dialects constitute a special group of 'periferal and archaic' survivals (p. 47), P. again affirms his denial of RR unity and of the status of Ladin separate from northern Italian dialects. P. returns to this theme in 'Qualche considerazione sul "reto-romanzo"', *Linguistica* (Ljubljana), 31:331–39. C. K. Kamprath, 'Rheto-Romance', *Comparative Romance Linguistics Newsletter*, 40:49–52. K. Widmer, *'Publicaziuns 1989: Tscherna bibliografica', *Annalas de la Società Retorumantscha*, 103, 1990:193–98.

2. LANGUAGE

GENERAL. P. Benincà, 'La variazione linguistica del Friuli e la linguistica romanza: la posizione del friulano occidentale', *Ce fastu?*, 66, 1990:219–32, asserts that, in most respects, phonological and morphosyntactic differences within Friulan are surface distinctions, and that Friulan as a whole is characterized by features, such as obligatory pronoun subjects in verbs, which characterize northern Italian and even French, but which do not always characterize Dolomitic Ladin. P. Swiggers, 'Su alcuni principi della grammaticografia latino-volgare: i frammenti grammaticali latino-friulani', *Linguistica* (Ljubljana), 31:325–29, deals with some theoretical linguistics insights as seen in 14th-century pedagogical treatises. A. Widmer, *'Il romontsch alla Scola Claustrala de Mustér', *Annalas de la Società Retorumantscha*, 103, 1990:23–28. L. Vanelli, *'Le varietà friulane occidentali: tra conservazione e innovazione', *Ce fastu?*, 66, 1990:233–55.

PHONOLOGY.   J. I. Hualde, *'Compensatory lengthening in Friulian', *Probus*, 2, 1990:31–46.

MORPHOSYNTAX.   I. Winzap, *'Aspects e problems dalla conjugaziun dils verbs romontschs sursilvans', *Annalas de la Società Retorumantscha*, 103, 1990:29–41.

LEXIS.   Two important dictionaries of Swiss Rheto-Romance varieties deserve mention, both by Theodor Ebneter, *Wörterbuch der Verben des gesprochenen Surselvischen (Oberländischen)*, Tübingen, Niemeyer, xiv + 189 pp., and *Wörterbuch der Verben des gesprochenen Unterengadinischen*, Tübingen, Niemeyer, xv + 183 pp. E. gives German translations for the verbs and provides usage samples, also with translations; unfortunately, no morphophonological information, such as inflectional peculiarities or variants, is included. And the 114th fascicule of the *Dicziunari Rumantsch Grischun* has appeared, containing the articles from *inculpar* to *indrizzar*. G. Taggart, *Dicziunari dal vocabulari fundamental: Rumantsch ladin vallader–frances et frances–rumantsch ladin vallader/Dictionnaire du vocabulaire fondamental: Romanche ladin vallader–français et français–romanche ladin vallader*, Chur, Lia Rumantscha, 1990.

ONOMASTICS.   W. Dahmen, *'La recherche onomastique dans les Grisons', *Dictionnaire historique des noms de famille romans*, ed. D. Kremer, Tübingen, Niemeyer, 1990, pp. 29–31. G. Fran, *'Antroponimia friulana', *ib.*, 40–45. J. Kramer, *'I nomi di persona in Alto Adige fra italiano e tedesco', *ib.*, 32–39. C. Marcato, *'Il castello, il borgo, il territorio di Strassoldo attraverso lo studio degli elementi toponomastici', *Ce fastu?*, 66, 1990:17–33.

SOCIOLINGUISTICS AND LANGUAGES IN CONTACT.   K. Holker, 'Peut-on sauver le romanche des Grisons? Développement et avenir du rumantsch grischun', *RLaR*, 94, 1990:97–119, summarizes the current fragile status of Romansh in the Grisons canton, past efforts at creating a unified language, and the current proposal by the Zürich Romance scholar Heinrich Schmid. H. enumerates the principles which guided Schmid in his language corpus planning, noting S.'s use of the Sursilvan and Vallader varieties as the basis for the 'Fusionsprache' and of the Surmiran variety as arbiter where Sursilvan and Vallader disagree. H.'s comparison of preservation attempts in Romansh with those in Norwegian lead him to a guarded prognosis concerning the fate of the former. O. Gsell, 'Die Kirchen und die romanischen Minderheiten von Graubünden bis Friaul', in *Die romanischen Sprachen und die Kirchen: Romanistisches Kolloquium III*, ed. W. Dahmen *et al.*, Tübingen, Narr, 1990, pp. 125–43. W. Dahmen, '"Romontsch sursilvan da messa — Romontsch sursilvan da priedi": Zur Herausbildung und Entwicklung zweier Orthographiesysteme im Surselvischen', *ib.*, 145–71. M. Betz, *'Das Rätoromanische

Graubündens als Minoritätensprachc', in *Nationalism in Literature —
Literarischer Nationalismus: Literature, Language and National Identity*, ed.
H. Drescher and H. Völkel, Frankfurt, Lang, 1989, pp. 367–72. E.
Diekmann, *'Sprachkontakt, Sprachkonflikt, Sprachsymbiose und
Sprachfrieden(?) im traditionell rätoromanischen Sprachgebiet
Graubündens, beurteilt aus der Perspektive einer Umfrage zum
"Rumantsch Grischun"', in *Language Conflict and Minorities/
Sprachkonflikte und Minderheiten*, ed. P. H. Nelde, Bonn, Dümmler,
1990, pp. 189–211. H. Goebl, *'Methodische Defizite im Bereich der
Rätoromanistik. Kritische Bemerkungen zum Stand der sozio-
linguistischen Diskussion rund um das Dolomitenladinische',
Sociolinguistica, 4, 1990:19–49. C. Soler, *'Germanisierung dcr
Romanischsprecher am Hinterrhein: Sprachwechsel–Sprach-
wandel', in *Language Conflict and Minorities*, 175–87.

3

CELTIC LANGUAGES

I. WELSH STUDIES

LANGUAGE

By DAVID THORNE, *Senior Lecturer in Welsh Language and Literature,
St David's University College, Lampeter*

1. GENERAL

Brynley F. Roberts, 'Y Tywysog Louis-Lucien Bonaparte (1813–
1891)', *Y Traethodydd*, 146:146–61, is an account of the linguistic
interests of Bonaparte and an assessment of his contribution to Celtic
studies. David Thorne, 'Cymreigyddion y Fenni a dechreuadau
ieitheg gymharol yng Nghymru', *NLWJ*, 27:97–107, describes an
attempt to introduce comparative linguistic scholarship to Wales at
the Cymreigyddion eisteddfod of 1842. 'Celtic Languages', Campbell, *Compendium*, 274–77, presents a general introduction to the origin
of Celtic expansion and gives some account of the P-Celtic, Q-Celtic
split. 'Welsh', *ib.*, 1444–51, consists of a brief historical introduction
to Welsh language literature followed by a potted commentary on
phonology and syntax.

2. GRAMMAR

Peter Wynn Thomas, 'The Brythonic consonant shift and the
development of consonant mutation', *BBCS*, 37, 1990:1–42, proposes
an alternative theory of the development of word- and phrase-
internal Brythonic plosives as presented by Kenneth Jackson in
Language and History in Early Britain; T. argues that the developments
in question should be regarded as part and parcel of a single
consonant shift common to the three neo-Brythonic languages, but
generating similar results only word-internally. Bob Morris Jones,
'Linguistic causes of change in pronominalization in children's
Welsh', *ib.*, 43–70, is the latest in a series of significant papers
analysing children's speech patterns; the current discussion argues
that internal grammatical influences, together with sociolinguistic
material, must be considered when examining the pattern of linguistic change. Rhian M. Andrews, '*Yssym, yssit*', *ib.*, 71–88, demonstrates
that, although these verbal forms have a copula as an initial element,

they are used to express being; it is also suggested that they were accentuated on the ultima. Toby D. Griffen, 'Old Welsh *ll* and *rh*', *ib.*, 89–103, continues his discussion, based on dynamic analysis, of the process of eclipsis in the Welsh consonant system. Joseph F. Eska, 'Syntactic notes on the great inscription of Peñalba de Villaster', *ib.*, 104–07, seeks to interpret points of syntax in the text of the Hispano-Celtic inscription. Jenny Rowland, *ib.*, 119–20, has a note on the orthography of Awdl XLV in the 6th-c. poem *Y Gododdin*. *Britain 400–600: Language and History*, ed. Alfred Bammesburger and Alfred Wollmann, Heidelberg, Carl Winter, Universitätsverlag, 485 pp., has a series of contributions on the prehistory of the Celtic languages in Britain: Karl Horst Schmidt, 'Late British' (121–48), reviews the sources available for the study of the neo-Brittonic languages and discusses the date of the emergence of the languages as well as the causes of structural change and the relative speed of change in Early Brittonic; D. Ellis Evans, 'Insular Celtic and the emergence of the Welsh language' (149–77), notes the problems involved in the study of the transition from Old Celtic to Neo-Celtic and concludes that, despite the healthy state of scholarship in this area, it is not possible to demonstrate, as yet, how and when the Welsh language emerged from an earlier Insular form of Celtic; John T. Koch, '*Cothairche, Esposito's theory and Neo-Celtic lenition' (179–202), discusses the evidence which shows that Patrick belongs to a period between the mid 4th and early 5th c. during which period archaic Christian borrowings entered Irish: K. argues that the phonetic reality of these loanwords realizing Old Celtic lention is still reflected in the living Neo-Celtic languages; P. Y. Lambert, 'Welsh *Caswallawn*: the fate of British *au' (203–15), examines the phonetic history of the *u*-diphthongs in the Brittonic languages and argues the case in favour of I.E. *au* developing as a long open $\bar{\rho}$ in Brittonic; Patrick Sims-Williams, 'Dating the transition to Neo-Brittonic: phonology and history, 400–600' (217–61), surveys the evidence and argues that the transition from British to Neo-Brittonic could have been completed early in the 6th c.; Stefan Zimmer, 'Dating the loanwords: Latin suffixes in Welsh (and their Celtic congeners)' (263–81), uses Welsh suffixes borrowed from Latin as a means of dating some words and word groups. Paul Russell, *Celtic Word-Formation: The Velar Suffixes*, Dublin Institute for Advanced Studies, 242 pp., traces the development and productivity of a group of adjectival suffixes having a velar consonant from the earliest Celtic evidence through to the Insular languages. Robert A. Fowkes, 'Verbal noun as "equivalent" of finite verb in Welsh', *Word*, 42:19–29, describes a construction in which a verb-noun adopts the role of a finite verb. Joseph F. Eska, 'The deictic pronominal *ḱEY in Celtic', *Celtica*, 21:153–55, is a discussion of the

Indo-European **key* in the Celtic dialects. David Green, 'Celtic', in Gvozdanović, *Numerals*, 497–554, explores the numeral systems of the Insular Celtic languages. L. Fleuriot, 'Celtoromanica in the light of the newly discovered Celtic inscriptions', *ZCP*, 44:1–35, examines the influence of Celtic on Romance languages in the light of the evidence of the Celtic inscriptions discovered during the last decades. Eric P. Hamp, 'A simplicity metric: Welsh prepositions', *ib.*, 236–38, reconsiders and adds another dimension to an attempt by Martin J. Ball to account for the developments of the inflected prepositions from literary Welsh to modern spoken Welsh.

3. ETYMOLOGY AND LEXICOGRAPHY

Eric P. Hamp, *BBCS*, 37, 1990:111, has a note on *carn*; G. R. Isaac, *ib.*, 111–13 discusses the name Mynyddawg Mwynfawr; Fredrik Otto Lindeman, *ib.*, 113–15, writes on the early Middle Welsh forms *rwy* and *nwy*; Jenny Rowland, *ib.*, 118–19, examines the forms *allan, ymaes*, in the poem 'Seitheinin sawde allan', from the Black Book of Carmarthen; R. L. V. Tersmette, *ib.*, 120–23, tentatively proposes a Dutch connection for *lol*. Lauran Toorians, 'Wizo Flandrensis and the Flemish settlement in Pembrokeshire', *CMCS*, 20:99–118, explores the background of any such connection. *Collins Spurrell Welsh Dictionary*, ed. Anne Convery in collaboration with D. A. Thorne *et al.*, Glasgow, HarperCollins, xii + 372 pp., is a revised and updated edition of the best-selling Welsh dictionary. Part 41 of *GPC* (ed. G. A. Bevan) covers NAF–OBO. Patrick Sims-Williams, 'Cú' Chulainn in Wales: Welsh sources for Irish onomastics,' *Celtica*, 21:620–33, shows how three Welsh literary and documentary sources have a potential value for students of Irish onomastics and the analysis of Irish emigration in the Middle Ages. J. E. Caerwyn Williams, *ib.*, 670–78, has notes on *Wysg, hwysgynt, rhwysg*. J. F. Eska, 'The demonstrative stem, **isto-* in Continental Celtic', *ZCP*, 44:70–73, is a review of the prehistory of the demonstrative stem **isto-* in Continental Celtic.

4. SOCIOLINGUISTICS

Jean Lyon, 'Patterns of parental language use in Wales', *JMMD*, 12:165–81, records the language use of a sample of mothers of new-born babies and their partners on Anglesey in an attempt to discover the factors which influence language choice; the study of the impact of gender on language use/choice in the home suggests that the father may have the greater influence. Christine M. Jones, 'The Ulpan in Wales: a study in motivation', *ib.*, 183–93, explores the motives of participants attending a Welsh immersion course. Harold

Carter, 'Patterns of language and culture: Wales 1961–1990', *THSC*, 1990:261–80, updates a whole series of earlier discussions on the geographical distribution of Welsh and the changes that are shaping its future. John Walter Jones, *ib.*, 311–28, 'Cymraeg a Bwrdd yr Iaith Gymraeg: Welsh and the Welsh Language Board', records the steps that led to the setting up of the Welsh Language Board and comments on the Board's aims and functions. Colin H. Williams (ed.), *Linguistic Minorities, Society and Territory*, Clevedon, Multilingual Matters Ltd., 330 pp., is a series of studies in geolinguistics outlining the opportunities and tensions facing linguistic minorities in their attempt to influence the modern state and presents a synthesis of the relationship between territorial identity and social and economic change in multilingual societies; although the situation in Wales is not explored in depth a series of relevant references occur in contributions by Colin Williams, John Ambrose, Paul White, Humphrey Lloyd Humphreys, Kenneth MacKinnon. Glyn Williams, *The Welsh in Patagonia*, Cardiff, Univ. of Wales Press, 285 pp., is a broad-based sociological study of the Welsh community established in the 1860s in the Chubut Valley of Patagonia in Argentina; the analysis of the social structure and relationship with the larger state provides an additional dimension to the valuable work of R. O. Jones on the Welsh dialects of Patagonia.

EARLY AND MEDIEVAL LITERATURE

POSTPONED

LITERATURE SINCE 1500

By DAVID R. JOHNSTON, *Lecturer in Welsh in the University of Wales,*
College of Cardiff

D. J. Bowen, 'Lewis Morgannwg, Gruffudd Hiraethog a William Salesbury', *LlC*, 16:385–89, consists of four bibliographical notes on the work of the first generation of Welsh Humanists. E. J. Jones, 'Y berthynas rhwng Salmau William Salesbury a Salmau'r Esgob William Morgan', *ib.*, 225–37, discusses differences between the two earliest Welsh versions of the Psalms, noting the varying ways in which the two translators handled their sources. J. G. Jones, 'William Morgan, clerigwr, esgob a chyfieithydd yr Ysgrythurau', *ib.*, 238–72, is a detailed study of M.'s career in the church and the contribution of his translation to the Protestant cause in Wales. Id., 'Braint, awdurdod a chyfrifoldeb uchelwriaeth: agweddau ar waith Syr Philip Sidney (1554–86) a Beirdd yr Uchelwyr', *ib.*, 212–24, goes beyond the circumstantial links between Sidney and Wales to consider the common Renaissance ideals found in his *Arcadia* and the Welsh praise poetry of the period, noting in particular the ideal of the virtuous nobleman as the basis for the well-being of the state. M. T. Burdett-Jones, '"Catalogus authorum Britannicorum" Thomas Wilicms', *NLWJ*, 27:109–11, prints a manuscript list of sources for W.'s Latin–Welsh dictionary. R. G. Gruffydd, 'Thomas Salisbury o Lundain a Chlocaenog: ysgolhaig-argraffydd y Dadeni Cymreig', *ib.*, 1–19, shows how S. conformed to the pattern of the scholar-printer by promoting Humanism and Puritanism in the four books which he published and in others intended for publication. M. Wynn Thomas, *Morgan Llwyd: Ei Gyfeillion a'i Gyfnod*, Cardiff, Univ. of Wales Press, xi + 198 pp., is a collection of eight papers (three previously published) on Ll.'s cultural background and interaction with his fellow Puritans, including Peter Sterry; particularly noteworthy are his analysis of the rhetorical techniques which Ll. acquired from his grammar-school education, and the illuminating comparison with two 'Anglo-Welsh' contemporaries, Henry and Thomas Vaughan. M. Hughes, 'Agweddau ar feddylfryd y Piwritaniaid', *Y Traethodydd*, 146:127–34, argues that personal experience of the Holy Spirit formed the basis for the 'tribal idiom' of the Welsh Puritans. *Gweledigaethau y Bardd Cwsg*, ed. Patrick J. Donovan and Gwyn Thomas, Cyfeillion Ellis Wynne, 163 pp., is a new edition of Wynne's classic with modernized orthography and explanatory notes. *Blodeugerdd Barddas o Gerddi Rhydd y Ddeunawfed Ganrif*, ed. E. G. Millward, Barddas, 338 pp., is a substantial selection of 18th-c. free-metre poetry, including several previously unknown items, with useful introduction and an essay by Phyllis Kinney on the relationship between words and melodies. D. W. Wiliam, 'Ceraint a hynafiaid Wiliam Morris', *Anglesey Antiquarian and Field Club Transactions*: 45–66, sheds further light on the Morris brothers' social background.

The bicentenary of the death of William Williams Pantycelyn has produced a number of studies. The most academically substantial are those in the collective volume, *Meddwl a Dychymyg Williams Pantycelyn*, ed. Derec Llwyd Morgan, Llandysul, Gomer, 199 pp. The influence of Puritanism is discussed in general terms by G. T. Hughes (31–54), and with specific reference to the experience of conversion by M. Evans (55–81); D. Ll. Morgan deals with the relationship between W. and his audience, arguing that in his emphasis on learning he can be seen as heir to the Welsh Humanists (82–101); the principal motifs of the hymns are analysed by K. Jenkins (102–21); B. L. Jones provides a detailed reading of four hymns, noting English influences, metrical sophistication, and the combination of Biblical and spoken language (121–33); W. I. C. Williams interprets W.'s work in the light of modern theological thought (134–58). The October issue of *Y Traethodydd*, 146, is devoted to Williams Pantycelyn. D. Ll. Morgan considers W.'s interest in science in the context of his theology (175–91); K. Jenkins sets out the principles of W.'s hymn-writing on the basis of the introductions to two of his published collections (192–207); R. M. Jones seeks to define W.'s mysticism by analysing 'Bywyd a marwolaeth Theomemphus' (208–20); G. T. Hughes attempts to reconstruct the contents of W.'s library, showing the breadth of his learning and stressing that it was centred on the works of the Puritans (221–31); M. Evans discusses the melodies of the eight moral poems known as 'caniadau duwiol' (232–45). G. T. Hughes, 'Dylanwad Williams Pantycelyn', *Taliesin*, 73:44–52, considers the reception of W.'s hymns and their influence on early 20th-c. poetry. K. Jenkins, '*Chums* â'r Arglwydd', *ib.*, 53–59, discusses W.'s hymns as an expression of the subject's relationship with Christ. B. Jones, 'Tipyn o garwr', *Barddas*, 168:9–13, 169:8–13, 170:10–14, is a stimulating discussion of W.'s hymns ranging over various stylistic and theological topics, most notable for its observations on the ways in which syntax reflects religious feeling. D. Ll. Morgan, 'Daniel Rowland (?1711–1790) pregethwr diwygiadol', *Y Traethodydd*, 146:72–88, reconsiders R.'s place in the Methodist movement, discussing the portrayal of him in the works of Williams Pantycelyn. D. B. Rees, 'Pregethau Daniel Rowland', *ib.*, 89–94, attempts to explain the distinctive quality of R.'s sermons. A. M. Allchin, *Praise Above All: Discovering the Welsh Tradition*, Cardiff, Univ. of Wales Press, xii + 173 pp., pursues the thesis that praise of God's creation is the essential impulse of the Welsh poetic tradition, and seeks to identify 'the specifically Celtic vision of the relationship between God and his creation'. A selective account of the tradition is supplemented by case-studies on the early Methodist hymn-writers and a number of modern poets.

E. G. Millward has two notes explaining references in the interludes, 'Twm o'r Nant a Neli'r Clos', *LlC*, 16:389, and 'Cyfei-riadau Twm o'r Nant at ferched main eu llygaid', *ib.*, 390–91. G. M. Ashton, 'Rhai sylwadau ar hynt y Beibl Cymraeg, 1801–25', *ib.*, 273–91, focuses on the work of the British and Foreign Bible Society, casting considerable light on the book trade in Wales. Geraint and Zonia Bowen, *Hanes Gorsedd y Beirdd*, Barddas, 472 pp., is an account of the development of the *Gorsedd* and its relationship to the *Eisteddfod* from its inception in 1792 to the present day, including its offshoots in Cornwall and Brittany. The wealth of detail and indexes will make this an invaluable reference book. T. Jones, 'Baledi a balcdwyr y bedwaredd ganrif ar bymtheg', in *Cof Cenedl*, vi, ed. Geraint H. Jenkins, Llandysul, Gomer, 101–34, focuses on 'gallows literature', of which there are some 200 examples amongst 19th-c. ballads, more than half dealing with murders committed outside Wales. Glyn Tegai Hughes, *Daniel Owen and the Nature of the Novel*, Mold, Daniel Owen Memorial Room Committee, 16 pp., deals with O.'s reading of English novels, showing that he knew much more about current theories of fiction than is generally supposed. A real-life model for one of O.'s characters is suggested by E. G. Millward, 'Nansi'r Nant a Nancy Connah/Cunnah', *LlC*, 16:391–92. M. Ellis, '*Llan Cwm Awen*, nofel-gyfres gan Ellis Roberts (Elis Wyn o Wyrfai) a ymddangosodd yn *Yr Haul*, Ionawr 1891 — Rhagfyr 1892', *ib.*, 292–362, gives a detailed summary of a little-known novel, with commentary inter-preting its social significance as a portrayal of clerical life in North Wales. *Emrys ap Iwan: Tair Darlith Goffa*, ed. Haydn H. Thomas, Mold, Clwyd County Council, 64 pp., contains two items of impor-tance: D. Glyn Jones, 'Traddodiad Emrys ap Iwan' (1–17), offers a useful list of E.'s most influential principles, and places him in a tradition of political writing about Wales extending back to the early Middle Ages; G. A. Jones, 'Teithi meddwl Emrys ap Iwan' (41–64), is noteworthy for the attention given to contemporary criticism of E.'s ideas. *Llythyrau Syr O. M. Edwards ac Elin Edwards 1887–1920*, ed. Hazel Walford Davies, Llandysul, Gomer, xxxi + 552 pp., contains a wealth of detail about E.'s personal life, and, as the perceptive introduction shows, reveals a new aspect of his skill as a writer.

Alan Llwyd, *Gwae Fi Fy Myw: Cofiant Hedd Wyn*, Barddas, 437 pp., is an exceptionally detailed account of H. W.'s life, showing his role as poet of his local community, and the importance of the *Eisteddfod* in his development. The two chapters devoted to discussion of his poetry

566 *Welsh Studies*

offer a new interpretation of his last poem, 'Yr Arwr', showing the influence of Shelley's *The Revolt of Islam* in addition to the better known source, *Prometheus Unbound. Yr Hen Ganrif: Beirniadaeth Lenyddol W. J. Gruffydd*, ed. Bobi Jones, Cardiff, Yr Academi Gymreig and Hughes a'i Fab, x + 156 pp., gathers together the most important of G.'s essays on 19th-c. literature, including an unpublished piece on literary criticism. B. L. Jones, 'Mae un sy'n Parry-Williams', *Taliesin*, 74:18–31, explores similarities between the careers of R. Williams Parry and T. H. Parry-Williams, noting how the more radical style of the younger cousin influenced the later work of the elder. *The World of Kate Roberts: Selected Stories 1925–1981*, ed. and trans. Joseph P. Clancy, Philadelphia, Temple U.P., xxii + 372 pp., makes available a substantial amount of R.'s work in English translation for the first time, including sections from her autobiography and her two short novels in addition to a large number of short stories. R.'s own response to the first translations of her stories, published by the Penmark Press in 1946, is recounted by J. Harris, 'A long slow sigh across the waters', *Planet*, 87:21–29. One of R.'s early experiments with form, the first *nouvelle* in Welsh, is discussed by G. W. Jones, '*Deian a Loli*', *Taliesin*, 73:20–38, including useful analysis of her technique.

Ioan Williams, *A Straitened Stage: A Study of the Theatre of J. Saunders Lewis*, Bridgend, Poetry Wales Press, 213 pp., is the first full-length study of L.'s theatre. His use of the conventions of Naturalism, contrary to the main trends in modern European theatre, is held to derive from his belief that humanity can only fulfil itself through inter-personal relations. Analysis of the major plays (culminating in *Cymru Fydd*) focuses on 'the exceptionally narrow definition of his stage', its ideological basis and the practical problems it entails. Id., *Y Bom Atom ar y Llwyfan*, Llys yr Eisteddfod, 19 pp., takes the same approach a step further by contrasting L.'s unfinished play about the nuclear physicist Nils Bohr with the absurdist vision of Dürrenmatt's *Die Physiker*. Harri Pritchard Jones, *Saunders Lewis: A Presentation of his Work*, Springfield, Templegate, 1990, 227 pp., contains translations of a wide selection of L.'s poetry, plays, essays, and letters, with introduction presenting him above all as a Christian existentialist. B. M. Hughes, 'Merched yn llenyddiaeth y pumdegau', *Taliesin*, 75:101–9, contrasts L.'s portrayal of female characters with that found in the work of Kate Roberts and Islwyn Ffowc Elis, making the interesting suggestion that *Siwan* represents L.'s views on the need for women to reaccept the constraints of patriarchal society after the freedom of the war years.

Monographs on three modern authors have been published in the 'Writers of Wales' series: Elwyn Evans, *Alun Llywelyn-Williams*, Cardiff, Univ. of Wales Press, 91 pp., a study which makes good use of personal acquaintance to illuminate Ll.-W.'s work; John Emyr, *Bobi Jones*, Cardiff, Univ. of Wales Press, 125 pp., a sympathetic interpretation of the centrality of Calvinism in J.'s many-faceted work; Donald Evans, *Rhydwen Williams*, Cardiff, Univ. of Wales Press, 80 pp., presents W. primarily as celebrator of the industrial communities of his native Rhondda. B. Jones, 'Donald', *Barddas*, 167:18–22, interprets the poetry of Donald Evans as a combination of traditionalism and modernism, in contrast to more conservative strict-metre poets such as Gerallt Lloyd Owen. S. Brynach, 'Tu hwnt i'r Dirfawr Wag: Job ynteu Seffaneia?', *Taliesin*, 74:97–108, delineates the nihilism which derives from the prophetic stance typical of Alan Llwyd's latest poems. D. George, 'Llais benywaidd y nofel Gymraeg gyfoes', *LlC*, 16:363–82, considers the depiction of the sexes in the modern novel, demonstrating the development of feminist attitudes by means of a contrast between two novelists of the inter-war years, Elena Puw Morgan and Kate Roberts, and two contemporary writers, Eigra Lewis Roberts and Jane Edwards.

II. BRETON AND CORNISH STUDIES

By HUMPHREY LLOYD HUMPHREYS, *School of Modern Languages, Saint David's University College, Lampeter*

1. BRETON

The article on Breton in Campbell, *Compendium*, pp. 220–26, contains some inaccuracies apart from the insufficiently considered generalizations which are characteristic of this genre; this work is immensely handy, but dangerous if accorded too authoritative a status. Individually misspelt words will do less harm in a work of this sort than failure to mention the superlative form of the adjective, which could easily lead to typological misclassification, while careless glossing implies that the analytic and synthetic present, in fact mutually exclusive syntactic variants, are semantically differentiated. A.-J. Raude, 'La palatalisation des consonnes vélaires en breton et en britto-roman', *BrL*, 5, 1988–89 (1991): 129–36, is well documented and generally clear and convincing. H. Pilch, 'Breton phonetics: a new analysis', *Studia Celtica Japonica*, n.s., 3 (1990): 9–50, is mainly concerned with stress and contains a number of useful suggestions. There are marked stylistic incompatibilities, however, between his very authoritative formulations and somewhat slipshod data. G. T. Stump, 'A paradigm-based theory of morphosemantic mismatches', *Language*, 67:675–725, includes some discussion of the pluralization of compound nouns and diminutives in Breton. J.-Y. Urien, 'Le syntagme "existentiel" en breton: définition syntaxique et sémantique $(X + zo/n'eus\ ket + X)$', *BrL*, 5:179–95, provides the usual well documented and carefully elaborated analysis.

J. Le Dû and Y. Le Berre, 'La créativité lexicale en breton', *Cahiers de l'ERLA*, 2, 1988–89:71–89, surveys the lexical history of Breton, highlighting the Latin element established by the time the language emerged in writing and puristic selection and creation in modern times. J.-M. Ploneis, 'Le paysan et ses animaux — quelques aspects linguistiques', *BrL*, 5:69–76, presents the vocabulary, expressions, and sayings relating to domestic animals in Berrien. R. Hincks, *Geriadur kembraeg–brezhoneg*, Lesneven, Hor Yezh, lxv + 194 pp., a Welsh–Breton dictionary containing 10,500 headwords, is generally competent. The Breton, however, tends to be puristic and play down dialectal variation, whereas the Welsh readily admits variants and anglicisms, so that the glossing involves frequent stylistic discrepancies.

P. Le Guirriec, 'La nomenclature des termes de référence en Bretagne', *BrL*, 5:51–56, examines as a sociologist traditional

Breton and Cornish Studies 569

non-official naming systems relating individuals to their father, spouse or farm. H. Tremblay-Couédel, 'Remarques sur le parler roman et les noms de lieu du nord-ouest de la Loire-Atlantique', *BrL*, 5:57–67, discusses Gaulish, *-ac*, *-ay*, *-é* and the Breton element in toponymy. P.-Y. Lambert, 'La situation linguistique de la Bretagne dans le Haut Moyen-Âge', *BrL*, 5:139–51, re-examines the Breton migrations, the geographical situation and the discovery of Old Breton, expressing doubts as to substantial Gaulish survival and puzzlement as to the precise significance of the presence of place-names in *-ac*. See also Le Menn, below.

M. McDonald, *We are not French! — Language, Culture and Identity in Brittany*, London, Routledge, 1989, 384 pp., is the work of a sympathetically sceptical social anthropologist. Its four parts deal with the history of Breton in schools, Breton particularism, *Diwan* (both the movement and its schools), and, finally, attitudes towards Breton, Bretonness, and Bretonism in a rural Breton-speaking district. Although documentary material is fully represented, anecdotes are what leave the strongest impression, both as evidence of first-hand experience and for the perceptive commentaries, only occasionally spoilt by inaccuracies and exaggeration. Kl. an Du, *Histoire d'un interdit: le breton à l'école*, Lesneven, Hor Yezh, 317 pp., gives an account of the exclusion of Breton from the schools of Côtes-d'Armor through interviews and official documents. J. Ropars, 'L'enfant et l'école: une expérience caractéristique', *BrL*, 5:153–77, examines through an ethnotext the early impressions school had on a monoglot child in the 20s. S. Le Rouzic, *BrL*, 5:103–09, examines the transition from Breton to French in seasonally migrant wood-cutting families from Camors (Morbihan). H. Ll. Humphreys, 'The geolinguistics of Breton', in C. H. Williams, *Linguistic Minorities: Society and Territory*, Clevedon/Philadelphia/Adelaide, Multilingual Matters, pp. 96–120, presents the distribution of Breton speaking against the geographical, historical, demographic and sociocultural background; it includes three maps. F. Broudic, 'Ar brezoneg hag ar vrezonegerien en deiz a hirie', *Brud Nevez*, 143:20–60, reports the results of a survey carried out by TMO Ouest on a representative sample of 1000 from Breton-speaking Brittany, using the author's questionnaire. 55.5% of the total population claimed to understand Breton, of which fewer than half (21%) had active competence in the language. These figures are lower, the second very much so, than those of the 1983 RBI survey analysed by Broudic (see *YWMLS*, 49:560; used in Humphreys, above), though many other characteristics of the sample appearing in a further 20 diagrams are similar. It should be stressed that the two sets of data are not strictly comparable and that, in this latest survey, those who claimed to be Breton speakers were actually interviewed in person.

D. Carré, 'Pa vehemp bet du-hont', *Hor Yezh*, 186–87, 122 pp., consists of ethnotexts recorded from seasonal migrants from Pluvigner (Morbihan), transcribed in a semi-standardized spelling. B. Corne, *Mélanie: ur vuhe e Groay*, Lesneven, Hor Yezh, vi + 116 pp., reflects pronunciation more systematically by using a modified version of Martinet's *Alfonic*. It is important in providing a substantial corpus from one of the last native-speakers of the Île de Groix; a few pages explain the transcription, draw attention to some of the more prominent features of the dialect, and discuss gallicisms.

G. Le Menn, 'Langue et culture bretonnes', in Y. Pelletier, *Histoire générale de la Bretagne et des Bretons*, Paris, Nouvelle Librairie de France, 1990, vol. 2, pp. 465–591, is concerned mainly with literature, the sections dealing with the period 1450–1900, abundantly illustrated from the texts, being the most solid. References to the historical and social background are scrappy, while pp. 474–76, purporting to present the characteristic features of the language, are a veritable desert: the important matter of the sources of Breton vocabulary, a subject of interest to the general reader and relatively easy to present, is dismissed in just two lines. F. Favereau, *Littérature et écrivains bretons depuis 1945*, Morlaix, Skol Vreizh, 83 pp., contains an excellent survey of themes and genres (in French), followed by a catalogue (in Breton) of practically everyone who has written in Breton down to 1990. The biobibliographic summaries make it possible to classify them chronologically, geographically, and socially, as well as by the nature of their literary production. Some seventy of these (out of a total of 650) could, on the basis of the volume and the regularity of their publications, be considered 'writers'. J. Guillôme, *Livr el labourer/Géorgiques bretonnes* (1849), Brest, CRBC — Univ. de Bretagne Occidentale, contains a photographic reproduction of the 229 pp. of the original bilingual edition, preceded by a 149-page study of the work and its author by Y. Le Berre. This is an enthusiastic and penetrating piece of literary criticism applied to a personal creation, unusual if not unique in a century dominated otherwise by standard devotionalism or Bretonism. Cl.-M. Le Laé, 'Ar Hi' [ar C'hy], *Brud Nevez*, 150:11–42, is a transcription into *orthographe universitaire* of a satirical poem of 552 lines written in 1772 by a Lannilis law student; it is accompanied by a short preface by Y. Le Berre.

2. CORNISH

Campbell, *Compendium*, London, Routledge, pp. 343–48, gives a generally accurate enough outline of the unified version of revived Cornish. R. R. M. Gendall, *A Student's Grammar of Modern Cornish*, Menheniot, Cornish Language Council, viii + 169 pp., is based exclusively on extant written testimony from the 16 c. to the 18 c., using unaltered examples with source references. It performs an important service in making available for general perusal a very substantial sample from a fragmented and inaccessible corpus. Id., *A Student's Dictionary of Modern Cornish*, Pt I, *English–Cornish*, Menheniot, Cornish Language Council, xxv + 136 pp., under some 14,000 headwords, presents a substantial corpus of Cornish lexical material from the same period equally meticulously, though in small, disagreeably prickly sans-serif type. Interpretation of spelling, with its wide range of variation, is discussed at some length in pp. ix–xxii.

III. IRISH STUDIES

EARLY IRISH

POSTPONED

MODERN IRISH

By Nollaig Mac Congáil, *Department of Modern Irish,*
University College, Galway

LANGUAGE

1. General

T. de Bhaldraithe, 'Notes on the diminutive suffix *-ín* in Modern Irish', *Fest. Hamp*, 85–95, discusses the productive modern Irish suffix *-ín* in both the spoken and written language, its various connotations, the consonant and vowel changes it brings about in the words to which it is suffixed and the extension of its application beyond nouns only. S. Donnelly, '*Cranngha(i)l* "a sound or effect in music"', *Celtica*, 22 : 16–17, postulates that this particular meaning for *cranngha(i)l* is attested in a poem by Ó Bruadair which, he feels, was mistranslated by Ó B.'s editor. B. Ó Cuív, 'Vowel hiatus in early modern Irish,' *Fest. Hamp*, 96–107, discusses the evidence for vowel hiatus in Irish in the period 1200–1650 relying heavily on that provided by syllabic verse and, to a lesser extent, on the occurrence of word forms that contain unusual vowel clusters and the relevant comments made by medieval grammarians. The process of hiatus filling is also briefly discussed. Breandán Ó Conchúir, *Clár Lámhscríbhinní Gaeilge Choláiste Ollscoile Chorcaí*, Dublin, DIAS, xi + 201 pp., catalogues 77 MSS, formerly the property of the Revd James E. H. Murphy, professor of Irish in Trinity College, Dublin, but acquired by Univ. College, Cork, in 1926. An index and detailed history of this collection will be published at a later date. C. Ó Háinle, 'The *Pater noster* in Irish: Reformation texts to *c.* 1650', *Celtica*, 22 : 145–64, examines in detail Carsuel's and Ó Cearnaigh's 16th-c. Irish versions of the *Pater noster*, paying particular attention to the actual translations themselves and the sources upon which they were based. He also discusses their importance *vis-à-vis* the versions of the *Pater* in use in the 17th c. Pádraig Ó Macháin, *Catalogue of Irish Manuscripts in Mount Melleray Abbey, Co. Waterford*, Dublin, DIAS, vi + 128 pp., catalogues MSS dating from the early 18th c. until the mid 19th c. and some papers of a former abbot, Fr Maurus Ó Faoláin, dating from the 1880s until 1910. Details of two other MSS once included in

this collection are also supplied. The Ó F. material is of particular
interest for the information it sheds on the Irish language movement
at the end of the last c. Id., 'The early modern Irish prosodic tracts
and the editing of bardic verse', Tristram, *Metrik*, 273–87, examines
the scanty evidence available relating to the poet's attitude to the
written text in bardic poetry and the implications this has for editors
of such poetry. G. Stockman, *'Nodaire'*, *An tUltach*, 68, 5:17, explains
how the Rathlin word *nodaire* derives from the Latin *momentum* by a
combined process of dissimilation and metathesis. Id., *'Iúl, umhail'*,
ib., 10:14, demonstrates why the words *umhail* and *iúl*, listed
separately in earlier dictionaries, are now both erroneously listed
under *iúl* in the most recent Irish–English dictionary. Id., *'Faoi, fá, ó,
bho'*, *ib*., 9:21, looks at the meaning, origin, and distribution of these
prepositions in modern Irish noting, however, that *bho* is not officially
recognized.

2. DIALECT STUDIES

P. Ó Casaide, 'Cainteoirí dúchais Fhearnmhaí agus a gcanúint', *An
tUltach*, 68, 9:22–24, recalls some of the last native speakers of Irish in
Farney, describes the sounds of the dialect spoken there and appends
a story recorded by Scosamh Laoide in the area. H. Wagner, N.
McGonagle, 'Phonetische texte aus Dunquin', *ZCP*, 44:200–35, edit
with phonetic transcription, English summaries and folklore notes,
further Irish texts originally recorded by Wagner in this Kerry
Gaeltacht.

3. SOCIOLINGUISTICS

Birgit Bramsbäck and Ailbhe Ó Corráin, in *Procs* (Uppsala), 11–50,
trace various aspects of the history of Irish Studies/Celtic languages
at Uppsala univ. from 1941 until 1989. Diarmuid Breathnach and
Máire Ní Mhurchú, *1882 1982, Beathaisnéis a Dó*, An Clóchomhar,
1990, 152 pp., provide this second part in the series of short
biographies of those people connected with the Gaelic world in
Ireland during the last c. L. M. Cullen, 'Patrons, teachers and
literacy in Irish: 1700–1850', in Mary Daly and David Dickson (eds),
*The Origins of Popular Literacy in Ireland: Language Change and Educational
Development 1700–1920*, 1990, Department of Modern History, T.C.D.,
Department of Modern History, U.C.D., (henceforth *OPLI*), 15–44,
examines in detail the connection between schooling, patronage,
literacy, printing, and the decline of the Irish language, relying
heavily on information gleaned from those MSS of 18th-c. Irish
poetry by less well-known figures which are heavily glossed with

valuable marginalia. M. E. Daly, 'Literacy and language change in the late nineteenth and early twentieth centuries', *ib.*, 153–66, highlights and explains the marked difference at the beginning of the c. in Gaeltacht areas in counties Galway and Donegal as regards knowledge of English and literacy. S. de Barra, 'Athbheo', *Comhar*, 50, 10:26–28, 11:30–34, takes a new look at various aspects of the Gaelic League over the years, particularly during the early period, and at the thoughts and actions of those connected, directly or indirectly, with the movement. G. Fitzgerald, 'The decline of the Irish language 1771–1871', *ib.*, 59–69, extracts evidence from the censuses of 1851, 1861, 1871, and 1881 to shed light on the position of Irish throughout the country by barony as far back as the last quarter of the 18th c. Illustrative maps are appended. Risteárd Giltrap, *An Ghaeilge in Eaglais na hÉireann*, Cumann Gaelach na hEaglaise, 1990, 151 pp., surveys the contribution made by various members of the Church of Ireland to the Irish language movement over several centuries until the present day. T. Hickey, 'Léamh na Gaeilge: fadhbanna na bpáistí', *Oghma*, 3:82–92, explores the difficulties children have with reading Irish and recommends several remedies which would involve greater efforts from teachers, parents and publishers as well as all the technical backup currently available. Liam Mac Mathúna, *Dúchas agus Dóchas: Scéal na Gaeilge i mBaile Átha Cliath*, Glór na nGael, 91 pp., traces the varied history of the Irish language, literature, learning, culture and society in the city and county of Dublin from early Christian times until the present day. Gabrielle Maguire, *Our Own Language: An Irish Initiative*, Clevedon, Multilingual Matters, 66, vii + 256 pp., details the history of an Irish-speaking community in Belfast, the experiences and views of the children who were part of it with particular reference to their own brand of Irish which is linguistically analysed here. She also examines how successful this community has been in promoting interest in Irish locally and on a wider basis. O. Munch-Pedersen, 'Holger Pedersen's visit to Aran in 1895', in *Procs* (Uppsala), 75–83, traces the history of Pedersen's study of the Celtic languages from the Continent to the Aran islands, discusses his sojourn in the latter and assesses the importance of the work he carried out there in linguistic and folklore terms. Í. Ní Dheirg, *Teangeolas*, 29:11–24, edits a diverse range of papers from many areas of the educational spectrum on the problems of Irish reading. K. E. Nilsen, 'Mícheál Ó Broin agus lámhscríbhinní Gaeilge ollscoil Wisconsin', *Celtica*, 22:112–18, presents additional interesting information on the people who originally supplied the Irish MSS presently housed in Wisconsin Univ. and on their involvement with the Irish language and culture movement in New York at the end of the last c. S. Ó Buachalla, 'Polasaí an Phiarsaigh i leith na Gaeilge:

ceachtanna don am i láthair', *Comhar*, 50, 4:7–12, assesses Pearse's policy *vis-à-vis* Irish in the light of a reappraisal of his writings and his achievements in this area in the Gaelic League, St Enda's, and the Gaeltacht. He illustrates how Pearse's views on the subject have not been incorporated into State educational policy during this century and advocates strongly that they still should be implemented. S. Ó Catháin, 'Nordiska forskare inom keltisk folklore och filologi', in *Procs* (Uppsala), 53–74, discusses the nature and extent of the contribution made by Scandinavian Celtic scholars during this century in the fields of folklore and philology in particular. R. Ó Ciaráin, 'An léachtóir gan mhiç léinn', *An tUltach*, 68, 7:8–9, gives a short account of the life, work, and achievements of John O'Donovan who made an enormous contribution at many levels to public awareness of all things Irish. É. Ó Ciosáin, 'I dtreo athbheochan idé-eolaíocht na Gaeilge', *Comhar*, 50, 5:18–21, examines the various contemporary forces which help to militate against the Irish language and calls for a sound ideology on the whole subject to be revived. N. Ó Ciosáin, 'Printed popular literature in Irish 1750–1850: presence and absence', in *OPLI*, 45–57, outlines the nature of and reasons for the limited tradition of printing in Irish in the 18th and 19th cs and discusses the many implications this had for the development of Irish as an official language throughout the country. C. Ó Coigligh, 'Pádraig Mac Piarais oideachasóir', *An tUltach*, 68, 12:4–16, outlines Patrick Pearse's experience of, interest in, and views on, the educational system in Ireland at the beginning of the c. with particular reference to the Irish language which, he believed, held the key to the salvation of Irish. Ciarán Ó Duibhín, *Irish in County Down since 1750*, Cumann Gaelach Leath Chathail, 40 pp., examines many aspects of the Irish language in County Down since the mid-18th c., especially the recorded history of its decline, its literature, and the salient dialect features found in it. Risteárd Ó Glaisne, *Dúbhglas de h-Íde (1860–1949) Ceannródaí Cultúrtha 1860–1910*, Conradh na Gaeilge, x + 382 pp., recalls the early part of Hyde's life: his student days in T.C.D., his early and subsequent scholarly interest in folklore, his involvement with all aspects of the Revival and the numerous sterling qualities he exhibited in the process. This is an important contribution to our knowledge of Hyde and the role he played in the early history of the Gaelic League. Id., 'Criostóir Mac Aonghusa', *Feasta*, 44, 9:7–13, surveys the life of the writer and language enthusiast C. Mac Aonghusa who was held in high regard by the best-known Gaeltacht writers in his day. B. Ó hEithir, 'Tuarascáil ar staid láithreach na Gaeilge', *Comhar*, 50, 6:6–16, evaluates the contemporary situation of the Irish language. He details how Irish has been eroded drastically in his own lifetime, examines critically the

Irish Studies

attempts being made to revive it and recommends several schemes which could be implemented immediately to assist it. Donncha Ó Súilleabháin, *Na Timirí i Ré Tosaigh an Chonartha* 1893–1927, Conradh na Gaeilge, 1990, x + 117 pp., introduces the *timirí* and *múinteoirí taistil* employed by the Gaelic League from 1899 onwards to promote all aspects of the League's activities throughout the country. This represents an important contribution to the early history of the Gaelic League. M. A. G. Ó Tuathaigh, *The Development of the Gaeltacht as a Bilingual Entity*, Inst. Teangeolaíochta Éireann, 1990, 20 pp., traces the history of and reasons for the decline of the Irish language, the emergence of limited designated Gaeltacht areas in this c. and the various economic, educational, and religious factors militating against their survival. J. E. Rekdal, 'Norwegian linguists in the field of Celtic Studies', in *Procs* (Uppsala), 85–95, surveys the considerable contribution made by Norwegian linguists to Celtic scholarship, in particular the work of Marstrander and Sommerfelt in the field of Irish dialectology. P. Ua Cnáimhsí, 'An tOideachas i nGaeltacht Thír Chonaill san aois seo caite', *An tUltach*, 68, 4:4–15, 17, examines the report of schools' inspector P. J. Keenan on primary schools in the Donegal Gaeltacht in 1856, highlighting its importance as a source of information on the standard of literacy in the English language there after the Famine.

4. FOLKLORE

G. Downey and G. Stockman, 'From Rathlin and the Antrim Glens: Gaelic folktales in translation', *Ulster Folklife*, 37:71–96, edit and translate Irish folk material from Rathlin and Antrim which was originally collected and published earlier this c. An example of the Irish original is included in one instance. J. Henigan, 'Sean-nós in Donegal: in search of a definition', *ib.*, 97–105, discovers from her research in Donegal that *sean-nós* singing cannot be expressed fully by a single definition but involves a multiplicity of functions, takes many shapes and, most importantly, is closely aligned to life which is never static. A. J. Hughes, 'Ulster Scots gowk storm Ulster Gaelic (s)gairbhshíon na cuaiche', *ib.*, 107–08, adds to our linguistic and folklore knowledge of the Cuckoo Storm throughout Ireland. Éilís Ní Dhuibhne-Almqvist and Séamas Ó Catháin (eds), *Viking Ale: Studies on Folklore Contacts between the Northern and the Western Worlds*, Aberystwyth, Boethius Press, xxx + 304 pp., edit a selection of folklore studies by Bo Almqvist which include 'The Viking ale and the Rhine gold', 'The uglier foot', and 'The fish of life and the salmon of life.' Irish material with English translations is included as appendices. M. Ó Briain, 'The horse-eared kings of Irish tradition and St

Brigit', in Benjamin T. Hudson and Vickie Ziegler (eds), *Crossed Paths: Methodological Approaches to the Celtic Aspect of the European Middle Ages*, Univ. Press of America, 83–113, examines an oral tradition of how St Brigit cured a king who was afflicted with horse-ears. He also attempts to discover how and why such tales were told about the saint. Dáithí Ó hÓgáin, *Myth, Legend and Romance: An Encyclopaedia of the Irish Folk Tradition*, London, Ryan Publishing, 1990, 453 pp., provides an important reference work which encompasses folklore, myth, legend, and romance literature. The entries are arranged in alphabetical order on the basis of designations which are mostly names of famous characters but some general entries are also included. The appropriate stories are summarized under each entry, complete with discussion, list of editions of original texts and short critical bibliography. Several indexes and a short guide to Irish and its pronunciation are included. Id., 'Folklore and literature: 1700–1850', in *OPLI*, 1–13, discusses in detail the cross-fertilization between the literature and folklore of the 18th and 19th cs which is greatly complicated by the fact that two different languages and literary traditions are involved. B. Ó Madagáin, 'Gaelic work-songs', *Ireland*, 40, 2:29–32, demonstrates how various songs were closely connected with virtually all aspects of life and work in Gaelic-speaking Ireland. P. Ua Cnáimhsí, 'Biddí Chaitlíne agus na dánta diaga', *An tUltach*, 68, 11:20–22, recalls the life of a woman from Arranmore who was famous for her repertoire of *dánta diaga* which she used to sing at wakes. The words of one of her songs, originally recorded by the Revd C. Quin in the forties, is appended. Id., 'Na dánta diaga', *ib.*, 12:18–20, explains how, why, when, and where *dánta diaga* were recited or sung in former times in Ireland, referring in detail to a renowned local exponent of this art. One poem is appended by way of illustration.

LITERATURE

P. A. Breatnach, 'Die Entwicklung und Gestaltung des neuirischen rhythmischen Versmasses', in Tristram, *Metrik*, 289–99, discusses the origin of the *amhrán* metres first attested in the 16th c., disagreeing with the view that the *amhrán* was a development of earlier native verse forms. The metrical correspondences between the *amhrán* forms and medieval Latin, French, English, and German verse forms lead him to conclude that the Irish forms are of international origin and that their dissemination was aided by music. A. Breeze, 'Two bardic themes: the Trinity in the Blessed Virgin's womb, and the Rain of Folly', *Celtica*, 22:1–15, presents studies of two international themes in Irish bardic poetry, the first being the motif of the Trinity in the

Virgin Mary's womb and the second the fable of the Wise Men and
the Rain of Folly. M. Cronin, 'Babel's suburbs: Irish verse translations in the 1980s', *IUR*, 21.1:15–27, notes the great upsurge in
literary translation from Irish during the last decade, discusses the
reasons for it and its many implications. Gearóid Denvir, *An Dúil is
Dual*, Cló Iar-Chonnachta, 77 pp., analyses Ó Flaitheartaʼs collection
of stories *Dúil* and discovers a unifying chord in theme and technique
running through all the stories. Id., 'Ál an fhathaigh', *Comhar*, 50,
12:22–36, surveys the work of the generation of Irish writers from
Galway who have appeared in the wake of and as a result of the
influence of Ó Cadhain and assesses the influence he has had on their
writing. Louis de Paor, *Faoin mBlaoisc Bheag Sin*, Coiscéim, 378 pp.,
analyses the stories of M. Ó Cadhain, paying particular attention to
the connection between their psychological content and the narrative
technique used. He traces the development of Ó C.'s style of writing
as he progressed in his acquaintance with and knowledge of
humanity. Appended is an analysis of the narrative technique
Ó C. used in his stories at different points of time. S. Donnelly and
S. Ua Súilleabháin, ' "Music has ended": the death of a harper',
Celtica, 22:165–75, edit, with translation, detailed textual notes and
background information on all parties concerned, a lament for
Conchubhar Mac Conghalaigh who was harper to Domhnall Ó
Donnabháin, chief of Clann Chathail from 1584 until 1639. Gareth
W. Dunleavy and Janet E. Dunleavy (eds), *Selected Plays of Douglas
Hyde with Translations by Lady Gregory*, Gerrards Cross, Colin Smythe,
and Washington, DC, Catholic Univ. of America Press, 192 pp., edit
Hyde's Gaelic plays with Gregory's original translations, set out the
history of their composition, evaluate their contribution to Gaelic and
Irish drama and examine the complex nature of the translations.
Short biographical sketches, appropriate to the work in question, are
included. É. Greenwood, 'Crainn', *An tUltach*, 68, 5:24–25, discovers
that the motif of entwining branches on trees growing in lovers' graves
found in Ó Searcaigh's poem *Crainn*, is also found in medieval Celtic
literary sources. R. Hannan, 'An ball uaigneach seo: attachment to
place in Gaelic literature', *Éire–Ireland*, 26, 2:19–31, demonstrates
how meticulously and frequently attachment to place has been
expressed in Irish literature from earliest times until the present day.
Patrick L. Henry, *Dánta Ban: Poems of Irish Women Early and Modern*,
Mercier, 217 pp., presents a historical anthology of Irish poems, with
his own translations, which reflect the status and role of women from
ancient to contemporary times. A short description of this corpus of
literature is also supplied in English. A. J. Hughes, 'Coincheap na
Gaeltachta in aigneadh Shéamuis Uí Ghrianna', *An tUltach*, 68,
11:4–15, discusses Ó Grianna's experience and perception of the

Gaeltacht, the great importance it assumed for him and his portrayal of
it in his writings. J. F. Killeen, 'Influence of ballads on *Caoineadh Airt
Uí Laoghaire?*', *ZCP*, 44:190–99, remarks that there are many
similarities between O'Leary's *caoineadh* and Scottish ballads thus,
possibly, leading to some speculation about the authorship and
literary pedigree of this work. I. Mac Aodha Bhuí, 'Cá raibh an
t-úrscéal nár mhaisigh an bás é?', *An tUltach*, 68, 1:21–23, examines
how D. Ó Súilleabháin treats the theme of death, noting considerable
development in his handling of it in his later works. Id., 'Tarlach Ó
hUid 1917–1990: an scríbhneoir', *ib.*, 5:4–10, contends that although
Ó hUid was one of the first Irish writers to treat in detail the theme of
Northern violence, he is overshadowed by later writers who have
discussed it in a more accurate, convincing, and artistic fashion. M.
Mac Craith, 'The saga of James Mac Pherson's Ossian', *Linen Hall
Review*, 8.2/3:5–9, recalls the history of Mac Pherson's Ossian
deceptions but illustrates that their influence in many spheres, not
least literary and academic, may have been much greater than had he
adhered to the truth and proper scholarly codes. This same article
with some further material added appears under the title 'From
Morven to Oostende: the fate of Macpherson's Ossian', in *Het Europa
van De Dichter/L'Europe des Poètes/A Poet's Europe*, 13, Special Issue,
246–61. C. Mac Giolla Léith, '"Is cuma faoin scéal": gné d'úrscéa-
laíocht na Gaeilge', *LCC*, 21:6–26, examines the question of realism
in the Irish novel during the first half of this c.: its foreign literary
pedigree, its adoption and implementation into Irish novels and the
emphasis placed on it by critics. He also mentions that a completely
different picture emerges in the Irish novel during the second half of
this c. Máirtín Mac Niocl15, *Seán Ó Ruadháin: Saol agus Saothar*, An
Clóchomhar, 199 pp., surveys the life of the Mayo writer S. Ó
Ruadháin and analyses in detail his original creative work which
includes a novel, stories and essays, and scrutinizes his translated
work. A complete bibliography of his works is also appended. A. Mag
Shamhráin, 'Íde na leabhar is na mban', *Oghma*, 3:72–77, contends
that realism should not be overemphasized in literary appreciation
although it can enhance the enjoyment of a work. He goes on to
discuss the female characters in two of P. Ua Maoileoin's works to
discover a great similarity in their portrayal, contrary to what was
formerly thought. T. Mac Síomóin, 'Stoirm scéine agus dún Uí
Dhireáin', *Comhar*, 50, 12:48–62, demonstrates from his personal
acquaintance of Ó Direáin and his knowledge of his work that Ó D.
prized craftsmanship above all else in poetry and that he regretted the
dearth of themes and lack of variety in his own work. He also links his
neurotic anxiety with his poetry. D. Marshall, 'Cathal Ó Searcaigh: a
bheatha agus a shaothar', *An tUltach*, 68, 12:56–65, explores the

themes in Ó Searcaigh's poetry and assesses his development as a poet of stature during the past decade. A brief biographical sketch is also included. M. Mc Kenna, 'A textual history of *The Spiritual Rose*', *Clogher Record*, 14:52–73, discusses the editorial history of this popular text which was first published in Monaghan in 1800, its structure, the English/Latin versions of material in it and also an oral version of it. Appended is a useful chronological list of devotional works printed in Irish from 1571 onwards. D. Mitchell, 'Alienations: a survey of poetry in Irish', *Krino*, 11:104–08, surveys several recent bilingual collections of Gaelic poetry to discover in them an extensive range of subject matter expressed in a vibrant, varied language. C. Ní Bhaoighill, 'An drámaíocht Ghaeilge 1954–89', *IMN*: 131–61, traces the history and fortunes of Gaelic drama throughout the country from the founding of Club Drámaíochta Ghael Linn in Dublin in the 1950s until the present day. She also discusses those elements and conditions necessary to promote drama but which seldom existed *in toto* in the case of Gaelic drama. V. Ní Bhroin, '*Cré na Cille* mar aoir', *ib.*, 56–104, delves into the many aspects of satire in general and applies them to Ó Cadhain's *Cré na Cille* which she concludes qualifies fully to be classed as a satire. M. Nic Eoin, 'An litríocht mar athscríobh na staire: *L'Attaque* agus *Dé Luain* le hEoghan Ó Tuairisc', *LCC*, 21:27–76, examines in detail how Ó Tuairisc as a conscious literary artist deals with historical events and personages in his historical novels as compared to how modern historians treat them. E. Ní Chionnaith, 'An Rómánsachas i scríbhneoireacht Uí Chonaire', *An tUltach*, 68, 3:4–13, 4:27–37, explores many aspects of Romanticism and demonstrates how and why it is so prevalent in the writings of Ó Conaire. A. Ní Dhonnchadha, '*Caoimhghín Ó Cearnaigh*: úrscéal de chuid na hAthbheochana', *LCC*, 21:154–74, discusses various aspects of the novel *Caoimhghín Ó Cearnaigh* (1913) by L. P. Ó Riain in the context of Gaelic literature at the time, noting that it was, in many respects, an interesting and innovative work for its time. Caoilfhionn Nic Pháidín (ed.), *An Chaint sa tSráidbhaile*, Comhar Teo., 233 pp., edits a selection of the best of Breandán Ó hEithir's writing from *Comhar* during the period 1956–90. Also included are a biographical essay on Ó hE. by Liam Mac Con Iomaire and a preliminary bibliography of his works compiled by Máire and Bríd de Grás. S. Ní Fhoghlú, 'Eithne Strong: scríbhneoir agus file', *Comhar*, 50, 9:14–16, conducts a detailed and wide-ranging interview with this bilingual writer who was one of the early feminist poets in Irish. I. Ó Caoimh, 'An t-athrá mar ghléas liteartha', *ib.*, 3:36–40, 4:28–30, demonstrates how repetition has been employed as a literary device with great and varying effect in different *genres* of modern Irish literature. É. Ó Ciosáin, 'Litir ó Sheosamh Mac Grianna', *ib.*, 2:19–21, publishes, with background information, a forgotten letter by Mac Grianna which appeared in the Communist paper *The Worker's Voice* in 1933 and is of importance for the light it sheds on Mac G.'s views on religion, the Gaelic League and the Revolutionary Struggle. M. Ó Cróinín, 'Cumann luathchleasaíochta na nGael: Séamas Mac Annaidh agus cluiche na scríbhneoireachta', *Oghma*, 3, 48–55, examines the important role played by games, playing and fun in Mac A.'s work and in his attitude to life and literature generally. B. Ó Doibhlin, 'Glasnost nó perestroïka? Inspioráid agus ceird an úrscéalaí Ghaeilge', *LCC*, 21:139–53, maintains that Irish novelists will have to return to the roots of their imagination to extract a new vision and perspective which will enable them to assess the reality of contemporary life better. He further states that new forms of language and techniques will be required to translate this new insight. G. Ó Dúill, 'Dán agus díolaim', *Oghma*, 3:3 16, surveys various collections of Irish poetry in the original as well as in translation, questions the criteria used by editors for selecting or excluding poets, mentions the dearth of explanatory criticism of Irish poetry and, finally, criticizes what nowadays often passes for translation. T. Ó Dúshláine, 'Tríocha bliain ag fás', *LCC*, 21:105–38, surveys many aspects of the modern Gaelic novel, noting how it has progressively succeeded in breaking free from the various impediments which restricted its development since the founding of the State. Pádraig Ó Fiannachta (ed.), *Ár bhFilí (Iris na hOidhreachta* 3), Oidhreacht Chorca Dhuibhne, 183 pp., edits a collection of articles by various scholars on the poetic tradition of Corca Dhuibhne from earliest times until the present day, including accounts of specific poets and the folklore collector who was instrumental in preserving so much of the poets' work. Id., 'Ag cogarnaíl le cara', *IMN*: 105–20, examines An tAth. Peadar's correspondence with Séamas Ó Dubhghaill during the years 1899 1911 to illustrate the former's great love and knowledge of native Irish speech and his vehement promotion of it in spite of the efforts of the Gaelic League grammarians. Id., 'Oidhreacht theanga Thiobrad Árann', *ib.*, 121–30, surveys the Gaelic literary tradition of County Tipperary from early times until the 20th c., illustrating its continuity, richness and variety over the centuries. Id., 'Méscéal Gaeltachta', *LCC*, 21:175–83, asserts that *Fiche Blian ag Fás* should not be regarded simply as an autobiography but rather as an autobiographical novel produced by a fecund, creative imagination. Id., 'The poetic warrant', *Studia Celtica Japonica*, 4:1–13, discusses the popular genre of poetic warrant or *barántas* of the 18th and 19th cs, its history, nature, content, and function. R. Ó Glaisne, 'Eithne Strong', *An tUltach*, 68, 10:21–24, surveys the life and work of the female writer E. Strong who has composed a considerable *corpus* of poetry in both

English and Irish. Diarmaid Ó Gráinne, *An Dá Mháirtín*, Comhar, 47 pp., illustrates how Máirtín Ó Cadhain developed as a short story writer in terms of style and technique without glossing over the weaknesses of the earlier and posthumous stories. He maintains, however, that Ó Cadhain's language was his greatest asset. D. Ó Muirí, 'An t-úrscéal turgnamhach — anailís chriticiúil ar *Cuaifeach Mo Lon Dubh Buí*', *LCC*, 21:77–104, looks at the various ways in which Mac Annaidh's *Cuaifeach Mo Lon Dubh Buí* qualifies as an experimental, anti-novel of the type written by Joyce and Flann O'Brien, a fact of which Mac Annaidh was well aware. N. Ó Murchadha, 'Gearrscéalaíocht Thomáis Bairéad 1893–1973', *IMN*: 162–89, categorizes and examines the themes of T. Bairéad's stories to discover that traditional, rural life is affectionately portrayed while urban life is depicted as hostile and brutal. He further demonstrates that, in terms of technique, Bairéad takes his cue from oral, narrative tales rather than from the modern sophisticated short story. S. Ó Tuama, 'Twentieth century poetry in Irish', *Krino*, 11:26–31, highlights, with appropriate corroborative examples, the volume, diversity and quality of modern poetry in Irish which is all the more remarkable when viewed against the general linguistic and cultural decay of Irish during the last century. L. Prút, 'Máirtín Ó Direáin agus an fhírinne', in Eilís Ní Thiarnaigh and Diarmuid Ó Laoghaire (eds), *Machnamh*, Fás, 21–34, re-examines Ó Direáin's poetry to discover that his language is not simply the community language but his own private language, and that he himself is not a community poet but a private, individual poet, contrary to what has been widely believed. Alan Titley, *An tÚrscéal Gaeilge*, An Clóchomhar, 631 pp., presents an exhaustive analysis of the Gaelic novel from the beginning of the Revival until the present day, proving that, contrary to the common belief which was reinforced by critical bias, the novel is not the weak link in the modern Irish literary chain. He groups the novels under special headings rather than chronologically or by individual author and discusses them in those contexts. This exhaustive work on the novel represents an important milestone in the history of modern Irish literary criticism. Id., 'Modern Irish prose: a necessary introduction for the uninitiated', *Krino*, 11:5–12, gives a lively account of the varied fortunes of Irish prose during the present c., according due credit to the significant contribution made by literary critics to the quality of that literature. Id., 'Mála an éithigh', *LCC*, 21:184–206, rejects any narrow, restrictive definition of the novel which would admit only very few of what are generally regarded as novels. He holds that some hundred and fifty Irish works should be considered in this *genre* and discusses many interesting aspects of their history and development. Id., 'An breithiúnas ar *Cúirt an*

Mheán-Oíche', *SH*, 25 : 105–33, maintains that the fact that the *Cúirt* is widely found in MSS, in the oral tradition, has been edited and translated many times and has been dramatized is proof that it is a vibrant piece of literature and should be treated as such by critics and others.

IV. SCOTTISH GAELIC STUDIES

By DERICK S. THOMSON, *Emeritus Professor of Celtic,*
University of Glasgow

There were two notable lexicographical publications in 1991. The first related to one of the most famous landmarks in Gaelic lexicography, Edward Dwelly's *Illustrated Gaelic–English Dictionary*. Dwelly had continued his collection after the dictionary was finally published in 1911, and in 1991 his notes were finally published in *Appendix to Dwelly's Gaelic–English Dictionary*, ed. Douglas Clyne (mainly) and Derick Thomson, Glasgow, Gairm, viii + 134 pp. Additional lexical information is especially concentrated on the early letters of the alphabet, showing the reaction of correspondents to the early publication in parts. Valuable detail is given of usage in places (e.g. Perthshire) where Gaelic is now in terminal decline. A different sort of landmark is provided by Richard A. V. Cox, *Brìgh nam Facal*, Univ. of Glasgow, Dept of Celtic, 442 pp. This is the first Gaelic-to-Gaelic dictionary to be published. It was basically intended for school use, but will have a much wider relevance. It includes between nine and ten thousand head-words, with full grammatical description and a good range of examples of usage. Dialectal alternatives, with cross-references, are included.

Donald E. Meek, 'Language and style in the Scottish Gaelic Bible (1767–1807)', *Scottish Language*, 9, 1990: 1–16, gives a lively and succinct account of this historic translation, showing how it relates to the earlier Gaelic literary language and to vernacular Gaelic, and noting how its richness subsequently influenced Gaelic discourse and writing. He cites e.g. parallel versions from translation in Kirk's Bible of 1690 and the Gaelic Old Testament of 1801. James Gleasure, 'The evolution of the present/future tense in Scottish Gaelic', *SGS*, 16, 1990: 181–89, examines divergences between Scottish Gaelic and Irish, concluding that while Sc. G. innovates in its largely effective merging of present and future tenses, it has also 'preserved the shape of the original Old Irish verb'. His paper suggests that there is much linguistic ground of a similar nature to be explored. Bruce Walker, in *Vernacular Buildings*, 13, 1989: 47–61, edits notes made by Åke Campbell and Calum Maclean, on such topics as shielings, blackhouses, crucks, and outbuildings; Gaelic terminology for the survey, made in 1948, was noted down by Calum Maclean. Campbell, *Compendium*, 1202–09, has a generally accurate summary of Scottish Gaelic phonology and morphology, though it is cavalier in its use of accents.

Richard A. V. Cox, 'The origin and relative chronology of *shader*-names in the Hebrides', *SGS*, 16:95–113, suggests that these Hebridean names derive from O.N. *sǽtr* rather than *setr*, but that the Norse word may well have been used in the more general sense of 'seat, residence' rather than the more specific sense of 'shieling'. He gives a listing of these *shader*-names with suggested etymologies. Donald MacKillop, 'Rocks, skerries, shoals and islands in the Sounds of Harris and Uist and around the island of Berneray', *TGSI*, 56:428–502, gives a valuable listing of these names, many of them unmapped and in danger of being completely lost. Although some of the etymologies are risky, there is much explanatory material in this paper that clarifies the origins of the names. John Kerr, 'The Robertsons of Glen Errochty', *ib.*, 382–427, discusses in the by-going some North Perthshire place-names. Eric P. Hamp, 'Varia', *SGS*, 16:191–95, gives short notes on a number of place-name etymologies and lexical items.

Seán Duffy, 'The Bruce brothers and the Irish Sea world, 1306–29', *CMCS*, 21:55–86, examines various connections the Bruces had with Ireland, including Edward Bruce's 'invasion' of 1315; he suggests that the Bruces' Gaelic credentials are to be taken seriously, and he develops the thesis that in the later Middle Ages the idea of a pan-Gaelic region embracing Scotland and Ireland and Man is very much a political reality. Kenneth Nicholls, 'Notes on the genealogy of Clann Eoin Mhoir', *West Highland Notes and Queries*, Nov. 1991:11–24, uses some little-known MS sources, e.g. from Lambeth Palace Library and Trinity College Dublin, to expand and correct accounts of the descendants of John (brother of Donald Lord of the Isles) Lord of Duniveg and of the Glens of Antrim. An *Index to Notes and Queries of the Society of West Highland and Isles Historical Research*, nos 1–30, provides a valuable key to this series. John Bannerman, 'The clàrsach and the clàrsair', *Scottish Studies*, 30, 1–17, discusses the earliest references to the harp and to harpers, suggesting that *clàrsach* always refers to a triangular stringed instrument and is a later term than *cruit*. Though only minimally attested before the 15th c., Bannerman surmises that it must be much older, since it had been borrowed widely into Scots; he wonders if the word originated in Scotland, though later attested in Ireland. He discusses a wide range of references to harpists, including several of the Galbraith family of Lèim in Gigha, and also an interesting list of harpists (from many parts of Scotland) in the Book of the Dean of Lismore. He argues that the three earliest surviving examples of the *clàrsach* (one of them in Ireland) were all made in Scotland, probably in Knapdale, and that harp-music was an important ancestor of *ceòl mòr*, the classical pipe music developed in Scotland.

Charles W. J. Withers, 'Gaelic speaking in urban Lowland Scotland: the evidence of the 1891 census', *SGS*, 16:115–48, continues with his detailed investigation and mapping of Highland migration and resulting Gaelic colonies, here concentrating on Aberdeen, Dundee, Perth, and Stirling. Kenneth MacKinnon, 'Language-maintenance and viability in Gaelic-speaking communities: Skye and the Western Isles in the 1981 census', *ib.*, 149–80, sets out the census evidence with reference to civil parishes, age-ranges, sex, etc. Id., *Gaelic, A Past and Future Prospect*, Edinburgh, Saltire, 205 pp., provides an update of his 1974 book, *The Lion's Tongue*. Horvàth Làszlò, 'An Ungair agus cànan na dùthcha', *Gairm*, 156:317–25, while chiefly concerned with the rehabilitation of Hungarian as the national language of Hungary, makes some interesting comparisons with the Scottish Gaelic situation.

Ossian Revisited, ed. Howard Gaskill, Edinburgh U.P., lx + 250 pp., includes a variety of essays, dealing with Ossianic influence on German writing (Uwe Böker), and on the poetry of Wordsworth, Scott, Byron, and Tennyson (Fiona Stafford), and an analysis of Hugh Blair's *Dissertation* (Steve Rizza). Some of the writers are handicapped by lack of Gaelic expertise: not so Donald Meek, who discusses the history of heroic verse in Ireland and Scotland, touching briefly on areas of overlap between this and Macpherson's writings. Howard Gaskill, 'What did James Macpherson really leave on display at his publisher's shop in 1762?', *SGS*, 16:67–89, does not succeed in settling this awkward question, but allows himself a number of risky conjectures about Macpherson's methods. J. F. Killeen, 'Influence of ballads on *Caoineadh Airt Uí Laoghaire*', *ZCP*, 44:190–99, discussing the motif of a woman drinking her loved one's blood after his death, refers to an instance in the Scots ballad 'The dowie houms of Yarrow', and wonders in passing if this shows some Gaelic influence on the Lowland ballads. He does not seem to be aware of specific instances of this motif in Gaelic song. John Macinnes, 'Gleanings from Raasay traditions', *TGSI*, 56:1–20, discusses some songs and stories collected in Raasay, including the song 'Oran mòr Sgorabreac', for which he supplies some additional stanzas he heard *c.* 1950. Colm Ó Baoill, 'Bàs Iain Luim', *SGS*, 16:91–94, questions whether Iain Lom composed the song against the Union of 1707, and thinks he may have died some years earlier. William Gillies, 'Gaelic songs of the Forty-Five', *Scottish Studies*, 30:19–58, discusses the range of attitudes shown in these songs: 'bardic' praise, various kinds of political belief or dogma, emotional intensity whether of a political or a personal nature, even doubt and hesitancy over the possible outcome of the war. He adds some notes on later songs which recall the '45. Derick S. Thomson, 'Alasdair Mac

Mhaighstir Alasdair's political poetry', *TGSI*, 56:185–213, describes and attempts to date this body of verse, mostly composed from *c.* 1725 to *c.* 1750, showing how heavy the concentration is in the years on both sides of the '45 Rising. Poetry by some 18th- and 19th-c. members of the famous MacMhuirich family (the Cowal branch) is edited by Ruaraidh MacThòmais in 'Bàrdachd le Cloinn Mhuirich Chòmhghaill is Ghlinn-da-Ruadhail', *Gairm*, 155:230–36, and 156:312–16. Donald A. MacDonald, 'The Balranald elopement in fact and fiction', *TGSI*, 56:52–112, gives a detailed account of this famous elopement of 1850, and shows how the story blossomed in Uist and Harris lore. Donald E. Meek, 'The role of song in the Highland land agitation', *SGS*, 16:1–53, summarizes the ways in which popular verse reflected current views and fuelled political campaigns in the 19th c., and particularly in the 1870s and 1880s. He gives texts and translations of the songs. Seumas Grannd, 'Three songs of the land agitation period from South Argyll', *ib.*, 55–65, edits songs by a Jura bard from the same period (1860–85), supplementing Meek's account. Ian A. Bell, 'The Celtic front?: Scottish studies in Wales', *Scottish Literary Journal*, 18:87–91, making moan about the neglect of such studies in Wales, might have noticed that a good deal of modern Gaelic poetry has been translated into Welsh by John Stoddart, and that Welsh has been extensively studied at Glasgow University in particular over the last forty years. The *Gairm* series of literary re-assessments is continued in *Maoilios Caimbeul*, 'An dàrìribh agus mire na h-ealain', *Gairm*, 154:140–46, and 156:338–46, where he tries to identify the ways in which new attitudes and sensibilities have transformed Gaelic poetry in the last half-century. Iain Crichton Smith, 'The internationalism of twentieth-century Gaelic poetry', *Scottish Literary Journal*, 18:82–86, writes approvingly of this aspect of Gaelic poetry, quoting various examples.

4

GERMANIC LANGUAGES

I. GERMAN STUDIES

LANGUAGE

By Charles V. J. Russ, *Reader in the Department of Language and Linguistic Science, University of York*

1. General
SURVEYS, COLLECTIONS, BIBLIOGRAPHIES

The first linguistic fruits of German unification can be gathered from *Duden. 1. Die deutsche Rechtschreibung*, ed. G. Drosdowski *et al.*, 20th edn, Mannheim, Bibliographisches Institut — F. A. Brockhaus, 832 pp., which is the first all-German *Duden* since 1947. Those forms which were characteristic of the GDR are now labelled as formerly in the GDR. Detailed studies will no doubt reveal how many GDR forms have survived. A wide-ranging study is H. D. Schlosser, *Die deutsche Sprache in der DDR zwischen Stalinismus und Demokratie. Historische, politische und kommunikative Bedingungen*, Cologne, Verlag Wissenschaft und Politik, 1990, 232 pp., which emphasizes the close connection maintained between language and history. S. covers the period immediately after 1945 and 1945–49, and then takes a thematic approach. He deals with language in the constitutions of the GDR, in the socialist economy and education, the mass media, literature and films and language use in everyday life. Each chapter has illustrative material in the shape of chronological tables, diagrams, e.g. that of the organization of a school giving all the different names for teachers and administrators, text extracts, and a map illustrating dialect use. S. sees old regional constellations being filled with new life, the North Germans and Central Germans in East and West finding themselves again. There is a list of all the words mentioned in the text. This is a work which is full of examples and will be of interest to a wide audience. The subject of normalization gets an airing in B. Henn-Memmesheimer, 'Normtheorie oder Praxeologie zur Erklärung sprachlicher Varianz', in *Sprachnorm und Sprachnormierung. Deskription — Praxis — Theorie*, ed. W. Settekorn, Wilhelmsfeld, Egert, pp. 153–64, who sees norms working in many fields of culture. G. Simon, 'Die Bemühungen um Sprachämter und ähnliche Instanzen in Deutschland der letzten hundert Jahre', *ib.*, pp. 69–84, traces the attempts to watch over German from H. Riegel to the Institut für deutsche Sprache. C. V. J. Russ, 'The norms of German and their metamorphosis', *The Federal Republic of Germany. The End of an Era*, ed. E. Kolinsky, New York — Oxford, Berg, pp. 323–32, shows how norms evolve, using examples from pronunciation and syntax. The following articles appeared in *SpLit*, 22, dealing with questions after the unification of Germany: G. Stötzel, 'Entzweiung und Vereinigung. Antworten der Sprache auf die deutsche Frage', 2–20; G. Drosdowski, 'Deutsch — Sprache in einem geteilten Land', 21–35; A.-K. Hess and H. Ramge, 'Der "andere Teil Deutschlands" in Zeitungskommentaren zum "17.Juni"', 36–47; C. H. Good, 'Der Kampf geht weiter oder die sprachlichen Rettungsversuche des SED-Staates', 48–55. Also noted on this topic: U. Esser, 'Neues Denken — neue Sprache?', *DaF*, 28:45–47; B. Wojtak, 'Rede– "Wendungen" in "Wende"–Reden', *ib.*, 47–51; J. Schröder, 'Gesellschaftlicher Wandel und sprachliche Reaktionen', *ib.*, 51–44; J. Salmons, 'Youth language in the German Democratic Republic: its diversity and distinctiveness', *AJGLL*, 3:1–30, which is much more differentiated than hitherto supposed; and G. Helbig, 'Zu Entwikklung der germanistischen Grammatikforschung in der ehemaligen DDR (ein Rückblick)', *DaF*, 28:67–76. The linguistic situation in Namibia is treated by M. Pütz, '"Südwesterdeutsch" in Namibia. Sprachpolitik, Sprachplanung und Spracherhalt', *LBer*, 136:455–76. The features of German in an area where it now no longer exists is treated in E. Kobolt, *Die deutsche Sprache in Estland am Beispiel der Stadt Pernau* (Schriften der baltischen historischen Kommission, 2), Lüneburg, Vlg Nordostdeutsches Kulturwerk, 1990, 330 pp. A map would have been useful to locate this town, now called Pärnu, in Estonia on the gulf of Riga. The volume comprises a short historical introduction, a section on pronunciation, and grammar, but the main part is a dictionary with etymologies. Many words are of Russian and Estonian origin. There are also a number of texts from the 16th c. onwards. The original Low German of the Middle Ages has given way to High German. Since most of the German speakers left before World War II there is uncertainty for the reader as to where the informants came from. An interesting work which, due to circumstances, leaves some questions unanswered.

Articles on individual scholars include W. Sanders, 'Jacob Grimm und die Sprachtheorie', *Fest. Engler*, 242–59, and U. Maas, 'Die erste Generation der deutschsprachigen Sprachwissenschaftlerinnen', *ZPSK*, 44:61–69. Finally, the following deal with advice services on German usage: W. Scholze-Stubenrecht, 'Die Sprachberatungsstelle der Dudenredaktion', *DSp*, 19:178–82, and R. Brons-Albert and S. Höhne, 'Probleme mit der deutschen Sprache. Anfragen von

Deutschen und Ausländern an das Sprachservice-Telefon der
Heinrich-Heine-Universität Düsseldorf', *ib.*, 257–69.

E. Schmider, *Werbedeutsch in Ost und West*, Berlin, Arno Spitz, 1990,
128 pp., is a fascinating comparison. It may come as a surprise to
some that advertising, even for commercial products, existed in
former East Germany. There was even a handbook on the subject. S.
deals with how advertising is judged, how it arises and how it differs in
East and West. The language of advertising uses elements from
nearly all the sub-sets of German. It has three characteristics: it is
short, needs-orientated, and easily remembered. The linguistic
analysis consists of examining a corpus of 400 slogans from East and
West which are listed in an appendix. The rhetorical figures used at
sentence and word level show that the most frequent are exaggeration
and plays on words, both of which figure more in West texts. There is
a noticeable shift in those slogans used to attract Western business as
opposed to those for internal consumption. This is a fascinating book
for all those connected with German. Also noted: G. Szagun,
'Psychologische Perspektiven zum Erwerb von Wortbedeutungen',
DUS, 43:63–77; J. Dittmann, 'Gesprächssituation und Situationsin-
terpretation. Normale und pathologische Prozesse', *Fest. Steger*,
223–36.

Translation and related matters feature in H. Spraul, 'Konfron-
tative Grammatik und Übersetzen. Zum Problem der Analyseebenen
beim Sprachvergleich Deutsch–Russisch', *Fest. Wilss*, 405–15, and J.
Klein, 'Possibilités et limites de la contrastivité dans l'apprentissage
de l'opération traduisante (illustrées par la traduction de l'allemand
vers le français)', *ib.*, 416–29. The language of sermons is the subject
of T. Funk, *Sprache der Verkündigung in den Konfessionen. Tendenzen
religiöser Sprache und konfessionsspezifische Varianten in deutschsprachigen
Predigten der Gegenwart* (EH, 1, 1245), 391 pp. Language and politics,
always a popular combination, appear in *Sprache statt Politik?
Politikwissenschaftliche Semantik- und Rhetorikforschung*, ed. M. Opp *et al.*,
Opladen, Westdeutscher Vlg, 279 pp., and W. Holly, *Politiker-
sprache. Inszenierungen und Rollenkonflikte im informellen Sprachhandeln eines
Bundestagsabgeordneten*, Berlin, de Gruyter, 1990, xi + 406 pp. The
many linguistic facets of teaching German are dealt with in W.
Abraham, 'Die Logik der Lehre des "Deutschen als Fremdsprache
(DaF)', *Papiere zur Linguistik*, 44–45:131–57; E. Diehl *et al.*, *Ler-
nerstrategien im Fremdsprachenerwerb. Untersuchungen zum Erwerb des
deutschen Deklinationssystems* (RGL, 114), xi + 89 pp.; B. Hufeisen,
Englisch als erste und Deutsch als zweite Fremdsprache. Empirische

Untersuchung zur fremdsprachlichen Interaktion (EH, XXI, 95), 220 pp.; N. Dittmer, 'Berliner Längsschnittsstudie zum Deutscherwerb von polnischen Migranten', *LBer*, 131:37–44; C. W. Pfaff, 'Turkish in contact with German: Language maintenance and loss among immigrant children in Berlin (West)', *IJSL*, 90:97–129; and A. di Luzio, 'On some (socio)linguistic properties of Italian foreign workers' children in contact with German', *ib.*, 131–57. The acquisition of German as a first language appears in H. Pishwa, 'Variability in the acquisition of the German agreement rule in syntactic contexts', *Papiere zur Linguistik*, 44–45:29–47.

GENERAL LINGUISTICS, PRAGMATICS, AND
TEXTLINGUISTICS

A general description is J. Feuillet, **Linguistique synchronique de l'allemand* (Contacts, Ser. 3, 13), Berne, Lang, 728 pp. The linguistic organization and analysis of texts feature in W. Heinemann and D. Viehweger, *Textlinguistik. Eine Einführung* (RGL, 115), 310 pp.; D. Gabler, 'Die geschriebene Form eines Rundtischgesprächs', *ZGer*, n.F., 1:110–16; U. Püschel, 'Stilistik: Nicht Goldmarie — nicht Pechmarie. Ein Sammelbericht', *DSp*, 19:50–67; and H. L. Kretzenbacher, 'Rekapitulation. Analyse einer Textsorte der wissenschaftlichen Fachsprache', *ZGL*, 19:49–70. Aspects of spoken language appear in *Discourse Particles. Descriptive and Theoretical Investigations on the Logical, Syntactic and Pragmatic Properties of Discourse Particles*, ed. W. Abraham (Pragmatics and Beyond, n.s., 12), Amsterdam, Benjamins, vi + 338 pp.; E. Luge, 'Perloktionäre Effekte', *ib.*, pp. 71–81; G. Brünner, 'Redewiedergabe in Gesprächen', *DSp*, 19:1–15; and W. Boettcher, 'Beratungsgespräch und Gesprächsberatung. Von der schwierigen Beziehung zwischen Gesprächsanalyse und Weiterbildung', *ib.*, 239–56. Also noted: R. Kischkel, 'Die Behandlung sprachtheoretischer Fragen in den sogenannten "Soldaten-Beleidigungs"-Urteilen', *SpLit*, 22:56–65; U. Pörksen, 'Ist die Sprache ein selbständiger Faktor der Wissenschaftsgeschichte? Über Beispiele unerwarteter Sprache als Grund der Apperzeptionsverweigerung' *Fest. Steger*, 107–24; K. Jakob, 'Naive Techniktheorie und Alltagssprache', *ib.*, 125–36.

2. HISTORY OF THE LANGUAGE

A long awaited volume is P. von Polenz, *Deutsche Sprachgeschichte vom Mittelalter bis zur Gegenwart*, 1 (Sammlung Göschen, 2237), Berlin, de Gruyter, 380 pp., which contains such new elements as the influence of the media in the history of German. Both internal and external changes are treated as well as general theoretical questions. There is also a very useful index of topics. The interest in the linguistic history of the 19th c. is well represented by I. Schikorsky, *Private Schriftlichkeit im 19. Jahrhundert. Untersuchungen zur Geschichte des alltäglichen Sprachverhaltens 'kleiner Leute'* (RGL, 107), 1990, ix + 482 pp., who examines 20 texts from 18 authors from 1802 to 1905. These texts are all written by non-professional writers from a number of motives, for themselves and different kinds of audiences. S. deals with their social and educational background as well as their intentions. This pragmatic information is then complemented by an analysis of linguistic features, types of adjectives, orthography, relative pronouns, dative -*e* etc. The analysis is illustrated by tables and diagrams. A development to a period of stability is discernible in the texts examined. Extracts are presented in an appendix. A fascinating study which points the way to more investigations of a period which is becoming increasingly important in the history of German. Complementary to the last work is *'Denn das Schreiben gehört nicht zu meiner alltäglichen Beschäftigung.' Der Alltag kleiner Leute in Bittschriften. Briefen und Berichten aus dem 19. Jahrhundert. Ein Lesebuch*, ed. S. Grosse *et al.*, Bonn, Vlg J. H. W. Dietz Nachf., 1989, 192 pp., which is a source book of texts, arranged according to themes. It ranges from requests to authorities, through private correspondence in letters and postcards, to war memoirs of old soldiers. Facsimiles and pictures are included as well as commentaries and an introduction on the period. A useful book. Other general items also noted: P. von Polenz, 'Mediengeschichte und deutsche Sprachgeschichte', *Fest. Steger*, pp. 1–18; R. Müller, 'Ergänzende Gedanken zur Entstehungsgeschichte der Sprache, die wir Neuhochdeutsch nennen', *ib.*, 61–76; G. Newton, 'C. J. Wells and histories of the German language', *GLL*, 44:165–83; U. Kriegesmann, **Die Entstehung der neuhochdeutschen Schriftsprache im Widerstreit der Theorien* (GASK, 14), 1990, xi + 311 pp.; and W. U. Wurzel, 'Faktoren des Sprachwandels', *Papiere zur Linguistik*, 44–45:159–73.

R. Hiersche, *Deutsches etymologisches Wörterbuch*, Heidelberg, Winter, 1990, continues with the first fascicule of *D*, *da* — *demolieren*, 80 pp. which includes a good number of foreign words. This is clearly presented work with separate entries for words of the same form but different meaning, *e.g. Dame* has four entries. For most compounds, however, one will have to consult other dictionaries. The syntactic development of German comes under consideration in *Neuere Forschungen zur historischen Syntax des Deutschen*, ed. A. Betten (RGL, 103), 1990, xxix + 452 pp., which is a state of the art report. Different models of syntax are presented, no trees however, and the emphasis is on the material investigated. Different types of texts such as newspapers feature in the analyses. The embedding of syntax in textual and social contexts is given full weight. The book contains the following articles: W. Admoni, 'Die Entwicklung des Gestaltungssystems als Grundlage der historischen Syntax' (1–13); A. Lötscher, 'Variation und Grammatisierung in der Geschichte des erweiterten Adjektiv- und Partizipialattributes des Deutschen' (14–28); R. Grosse, 'Funktionen des Pronomens *iz* im Althochdeutschen' (29–38); G. Schreiter, 'Wie ermittelt man diachronische Veränderungen seltener lexiko-syntaktischer Erscheinungen? Über das Schwanken zwischen Trennbarkeit und Untrennbarkeit bei Verbalkomposita' (29–38); K. Keinästö, 'Über ingressive und egressive Infinitivkonstruktionen im mittelhochdeutschen Prosa-Lancelot' (56–70); V. Vaišnoras, 'Ableitung von Infinitivkomplementen in frühneuhochdeutschen Texten' (71–81); H.-W. Eroms, 'Zur Entwicklung der Passivperiphrasen im Deutschen' (82–97); K. Donhauser, 'Moderne Kasuskonzeptionen im Althochdeutschen. Überlegungen zur Stellung des Objektsgenitivs im Althochdeutschen' (98–112); W. Huber, 'Kasusdarstellungen im Rahmen der Relationalen Grammatik' (113–23); W. Abraham, 'Zur heterogenen Entfaltung der Modalpartikel im Ahd. und Mhd.' (124–38); R. Schrodt, 'Reanalysen bei mhd. *dô* und *doch*?' (139–52); J. Schildt, 'Modalwörter im Frühneuhochdeutschen. Die Entwicklung ihres Bestandes' (153–62); G. Brandt, 'Soziolinguistisch orientierte Forschungen zur Syntax der frühneuzeitlichen deutschen Literatursprache (Satz, erweiterte Substantivgruppe, Text)' (182–95); R. Bentzinger, 'Besonderheiten in der Syntax der Reformationsdialoge 1520–1525' (196–204); H. Kästner, E. Schütz, and J. Schwitalla, '"Dem gmainen Mann zu guttem Teutsch gemacht." Textliche Verfahren der Wissensvermittlung in frühneuhochdeutschen Fachkompendien' (205–23); H. Ebert, 'Bemerkungen zur Syntax frühneuhochdeutscher Bittbriefe' (224–38); U. Demske-Neumann, 'Charakteristische Strukturen von Satzgefügen in den Zeitungen des 17. Jahrhunderts' (239–52); J. Korhonen, 'Zu Verbphrasemen in Zeitungstexten des frühen 17. Jahrhunderts' (253–68); D. Cherubim, 'Rituell formalisierte Syntax in Texten des 16. und 19. Jahrhunderts' (269–85); K. J. Mattheier, 'Formale und funktionale Aspekte der Syntax von Arbeiterschriftsprache im 19. Jahrhundert' (286–99); S. Grosse, 'Zu Syntax und Stil in der deutschen Sprache des 19. Jahrhunderts' (300–09); S. Sonderegger, 'Syntaktische Strukturen gesprochener Sprache im 'alteren Deutschen' (310–23); A. Betten, 'Zur Problematik der Abgrenzung von Mündlichkeit und Schriftlichkeit bei mittelalterlichen Texten' (324–35); M. Giesecke, 'Syntax für die Augen — Strukturen der beschreibenden Fachprosa aus medientheoretischer Sicht' (336–51); T. Wilbur, 'Bourgeois respectability: its origin and final triumph' (352–64); K. Gärtner, 'Das

Verhältnis von metrischer und syntaktischer Gliederung in mittelhochdeutschen Verstexten um 1200' (365–78); B. Stolt, 'Redeglieder, Informationseinheiten: *Cola* und *commata* in Luthers syntax' (379–92); D. Neuendorff, 'Überlegungen zu *comma, colon* und *periodus* in den Predigten Bertholds von Regensburg' (393–405); M. Rössing–Hager, 'Leitprinzipien für die Syntax deutscher Autoren um 1500 — Verfahrensvorschläge zur Ermittlung zeitspezifischer Qualitätsvorstellungen, ihrer Herkunft und Verbreitung' (406–21); F. Hundsnurscher, 'Syntaxwandel zur Gottsched-Zeit' (422–38); and B. Naumann, 'Die "dependenzgrammatischen" Überlegungen Johann Werner Mieners (1723–1789)' (439–50). Also noted: R. Lühr, 'Die deutsche Determinansphrase aus historischer Sicht', *BGDSL*, 113:195–211. The productivity of the study of the history of German is further evidenced by *Deutsche Sprachgeschichte. Grundlagen, Methoden, Perspektiven: Festschrift für Johannes Erben zum 65. Geburtstag*, ed. W. Besch, Berne, Lang, 1990, 485 pp., which contains the following articles on different topics: H. Brinkmann, 'Sprachgeschichte und Sprachsystem in Erinnerung und Gegenwart' (11–20); I. Reiffenstein, 'Interne und externe Sprachgeschichte' (21–29); S. Sonderegger, 'Grundsätzliche Überlegungen zu einer literarischen Sprachgeschichte des Deutschen' (31–49); R. Schützeichel, 'Probleme der Erforschung des Althochdeutschen' (51–58); K. Hyldgaard-Jensen, 'Methodisches zur linguistischen Erforschung des Verhältnisses Althochdeutsch-Altniederdeutsch-Altnordisch' (59–66); Klaus J. Mattheier, 'Otfrid als Orthographiereformer? Überlegungen zu den Bemerkungen Otfrids von Weissenburg über den Gebrauch der Buchstaben <z> und <k> im Evangelienbuch' (67–83); R. Bergmann, 'Probleme und Aufgaben einer althochdeutschen Wortbildungslehre' (85–92); R. Grosse, 'Lexik und Syntax im Althochdeutschen' (93–101); K. P. Wegera, 'Mittelhochdeutsche Grammatik und Sprachgeschichte' (103–13); H. J. Solms, 'Das System der Präfixverben in der frühesten Überlieferung des Hartmannschen "Gregorius" (Hs. A aus dem Alemannischen des 13. Jahrhunderts' (115–28); E. Koller, 'Nu müez iuch got bewarn, fruot unde geil gesparn! Zur Geschichte des Wortfelds "gesund"' (129–40); O. Reichmann, 'Sprache ohne Leitvarietät vs. Sprache mit Leitvarietät: ein Schlüssel für die mittelalterliche Geschichte des Deutschen?' (141–58); A. Betten, 'Die Bedeutung von Textsyntax und Textlinguistik für die Sprachgeschichtsforschung' (159–65); B. Stolt, 'Die Bedeutung der Interpunktion für die Analyse von Martin Luthers Syntax' (167–80); R. P. Ebert, 'Zur Einbettung des Syntaxwandels in der städtischen Gesellschaft des 15. und 16. Jahrhunderts' (181–86); F. Simmler, 'Makrostrukturelle Veränderungen in der Tradition des frühneuhochdeutschen Prosaromans' (187–200);

A. Schwob, 'Die Edition der Lebenszeugnisse Oswalds von Wolkenstein als Basis für sprachwissenschaftliche Untersuchungen des Frühneuhochdeutschen' (201–08); R. Bentzinger, 'Zur Verwendung von Adjektivsuffixen im Frühneuhochdeutschen. Ein Beitrag zur Diskussion der historischen Wortbildung' (209–15); H. P. Prell, 'Luthers Übersetzung des NT in protestantischer Tradition im 17. Jahrhundert. Zu Wortbildung und Syntax der frnhd. Bibelsprache' (217–25); A. Masser, 'Zwischen Sprachbeherrschung und Unvermögen. Bemerkungen zur ersten Übersetzung der "Germania" des Tacitus durch Eberlin von Günzberg (1526)' (227–38); G. A. R. de Smet, 'Humanistische deutsche Lexikographie und Sprachgeschichte' (239–47); F. Hartweg, 'Zu "außlendigen wörter(n) auff unser teutsch"' (249–57); H. Wellmann, 'Textbildung (nach der Frühzeit des Buchdrucks)' (259–72); G. Kettman, 'Das 17. Jahrhundert; (Ausgewählte) Ansatzpunkte zur Beschreibung seines graphematischen Entwicklungsstandes' (273–80); G. Fritz, 'Zur Sprache der ersten periodischen Zeitungen im 17. Jahrhundert' (281–88); G. Bellmann, 'Eine Quelle der deutschen Sprachgeschichte des 17. und 18. Jahrhunderts' (289–300); W. Besch, '"... und überhaupt die ganze Schreibart nach dem nun einmal in ganz Deutschland angenommenen Sprachgebrauche einzurichten." (Zürcher Bibel 1772)' (301–11); M. Schebben-Schmidt, 'Studien zur Diminution in der deutschen Schriftsprache des 18. Jahrhunderts' (313–21); S. Grosse, 'Überlegungen zur deutschen Sprache im 19. Jahrhundert' (323–28); H. Ebert and M. Krieger, 'Syntaktisch-stilistische Untersuchung des Bittens in Bergarbeiterbriefen des 19. und frühen 20. Jahrhunderts. Mit einem Vergleich frühneuhochdeutscher Bittbriefe' (329–36); H. Moser, 'Vom Agenten zum Trader — Österreichische Stellenanzeigen 1900 und heute' (337–51); L. Saltveit, 'Die Mundart als Ergänzung zu den alten Texten bei der sprachgeschichtlichen Formerfassung im verbalen Bereich' (353–61); P. Valentin, 'Ausdrucksseite und Inhaltsseite in der Entwicklung des deutschen Modussystems' (363–69); E. Erämetsä, 'Über einige diskontinuierliche Strukturen ("Wo hat er die Pistole her?")' (371–80); W. Admoni, 'Die semantische Präsenz der grammatisch negierten Redegebilde. Zum Problem des Ungenauen in der Sprache' (381–86); H. H. Munske, 'Über den Wandel des deutschen Wortschatzes' (387–401); P. Wiesinger, 'Zur Periodisierung der deutschen Sprachgeschichte aus regionaler Sicht' (403–14); J. Schildt, 'Zur Rolle von Texten/Textsorten bei der Periodisierung der deutschen Sprachgeschichte' (415–20); N. R. Wolf, 'Über eine textlinguistische Sprachgeschichte' (421–29); P. von Polenz, 'Anfänge sprach(en)politischen Verhaltens in Deutschland' (431–41); H. Beck, '"Deutsch" in den Anfängen der Germanistik'

(443–53); and H. Penzl, 'Zum Stand der Forschung in der deutschen Sprachgeschichte' (455–65).

Germanic linguistic studies, including Gothic, are represented by S. Suzuki, 'A Germanic *Verschärfung*: a syllabic perspective', *JIES*, 19:163–90; G. L. Fullerton, 'Reduplication and the prosody of ancient Germanic', *BGDSL*, 113:1–21; C. M. Barrack, 'PGmc. *–VCiV–* revisted', *AJGLL*, 3:119–44; D. P. Quinlin, 'The accentuation and development of PGmc. */ga-/*', *ib.*, 145–59; F. Kortlandt, 'The Germanic seventh class of strong verbs', *NOWELE*, 18:97–100; T. Vennemann, 'The relative chronology of the High German consonant shift and the West Germanic anaptyxis', *Diachronica*, 8:45–57; M. Salm, *Analogie im Germanischen. Historisch-morphologische Studien zum Ablautsystem der e-Verben anhand des Deutschen und Schwedischen kontrastiv dargestellt* (ZGS, 20), 185 pp.; H. Beifuss, *Diachrone Betrachtungen zur Wortbildung im Germanischen; Eine Studie zur Herkunft, Verbreitung und Weiterentwicklung der germanischen -opu/-oðu-Bildungen* (Information und Interpretation, 5), Frankfurt, Lang, ix + 224 pp.; and E. A. Ebbinghaus, 'Further thoughts on Gothic *boka*', *AJGLL*, 3:51–56.

Old High German features in J. Splett, 'Die Strukturen der althochdeutschen Wortfamilien und die Probleme ihrer Formalisierung im Rahmen von Datenbanksystemen', *Beiträge* (Trier), 113–28; R. Bergmann, *Rückläufiges morphologisches Wörterbuch des Althochdeutschen*, Tübingen, Niemeyer, xii + 740 pp.; J. Voyles, 'A history of OHG *i*-umlaut', *BGDSL*, 113:159–94; and A. Bammesberger, 'Das Präteritum der verba pura und ahd. *ier-/eor-/er-*', *BGDSL*, 113:22–27. ZDP, 110, contains several articles dealing with MHG: P. Wiesinger, 'Zur Reimgrammatik des Mittelhochdeutschen. Methodik — Anwendung — Perspektiven' (56–93); N. R. Wolf, 'Mittelhochdeutsche Hss. II: Zur Adjektivflexion' (93–110); H. J. Solms, 'Zur Wortbildung der Verben in Hartman von Aues "Iwein" (Hs. B) und "Gregorius" (Hs. A): Das Präfix ge- im System der verbalen Präfigierung. Zugleich zur Diskussion historischer Wortbildung' (110–40); U. Schulze, 'Komplexe Sätze und Gliedsatztypen in der Urkundensprache des 13. Jahrhunderts' (140–70); and H. Penzl, 'Zu mhd. Dialekten als Gegenstand der Forschung' (170–82).

Early NHG continues to flourish, as is evidenced by W. J. Jones, 'Regional variation in fifteenth-century German lexis: some new perspectives', *MLR*, 86:89–108; G. Fritz, 'Deutsche Modalverben 1609 — Epistemische Verwendungsweisen', *BGDSL*, 113:29–52; I. Rauch, 'Early NHG *e*-plural', *ib.*, 367–83; J. Barke, *Die Sprache der Chymie. Am Beispiel von vier Drucken aus der Zeit zwischen 1574–1761*

(RGL, III), vii + 582 pp.; *Linguistische Beitrage zur Müntzer-Forschung*, ed. H. O. Spillman, Hildesheim, Olms, x + 346 pp.; Claudine Moulin, *Der Majuskelgebrauch in Luthers deutschen Briefen (1517–1546)* (Germanische Bibliothek. Reihe 3: Untersuchungen), Heidelberg, Winter, 1990, xxxiii + 462 pp.; I. T. Piirainen, 'Möglichkeiten und Grenzen der EDV bei der Untersuchung frühneuhochdeutscher Texte in der Slowakei', *Beiträge* (Trier), 267–73; K. P. Wegera, 'Erfahrungen bei der computergestützten Erarbeitung der frühneuhochdeutschen Flexionsmorphologie', *ib.*, 274–75; and M. Rössing-Harder, 'EDV-gestützte Untersuchungen zum Gebrauch von Verbalsubstantiven in frühneuhochdeutschen Texten', *ib.*, 276–319.

The 18th and 19th cs feature in A. Gardt *et al.*, 'Sprachkonzeptionen in Barock und Aufklärung: Ein Vorschlag für ihre Beschreibung', *ZPSK*, 44:17–33; G. Lerchner, 'Die Kommunikationskultur des 18. Jahrhunderts aus der Sicht Wielands im "Teutschen Merkur"', *ZPSK*, 44:52–66; M. Fauser, *Das Gespräch im 18, Jahrhundert. Rhetorik und Geselligkeit in Deutschland*, Stuttgart, Metzler — Poeschel, 507 pp.; Astrid Jahreiss, *Grammatiken und Orthographielehren aus dem Jesuitenorden. Eine Untersuchung zur Normierung der deutschen Schriftsprache in Unterrichtswerken des 18. Jahrhunderts* (Germanische Bibliothek, Reihe 3: Untersuchungen), Heidelberg, Winter, 1990, 276 pp.; and M. Grimberg, 'Führte die Immigration polnischer Arbeiter in das Ruhrgebiet (1880–1914) zu deutsch-polnischen Interferenzen?', *DSp*, 19:33–49.

The 20th c. is represented by *'Gift, das du unbewußt eintrinkst ...' Der Nationalsozialismus und die deutsche Sprache*, ed. W. Bohleber and J. Drews, Bielefeld, Aisthesis, 133 pp., tracing the unconscious element in the language of National Socialism. The volume contains the following articles: K. Podak, 'Spiegel des Unheils. Hitlers "Mein Kampf": Annäherung an ein Buch, das es nicht gibt' (16–24); U. Maas, 'Sprache im Nationalsozialismus: Macht des Wortes oder Lähmung der Sprache' (25–37); D. Ohlmeier, 'Nazifaschistische Züge in der Sprache heutiger Psychoanalysen' (38–47); J. S. Kafka, 'Anmerkungen zur Emigratensprache' (48–60); M. Kütemeyer, 'Die Sprache der Psychosomatik im Nationalsozialismus' (61–82); K. Bochmann, 'Die Kritik an der Sprache des Nationalsozialismus. Eine kritische Bestandsaufnahme der in der DDR erschienenen Publikationen' (83–100); K. Vondung, 'Angst vor dem Untergang und Sehnsucht nach Erlösung — ein deutsches Syndrom' (101–13); and J. Drews, 'Das Tabu der Aggressivität und Kritik. Zu einer verborgenen Kontinuität der deutschen Literatur vor und nach 1945' (114–31). The articles are general and could be complemented by a detailed linguistic study. They represent one more valuable step towards a full linguistic evaluation of the period.

3. ORTHOGRAPHY

Despite the discussions on the reform of German orthography this year has been an extremely meagre one for orthographical studies. *Zu einer Theorie der Orthographie. Interdisziplinäre Aspekte gegenwärtiger Schrift- und Orthographieforschung*, ed. C. Stetter (RGL, 99), ix + 220 pp., is a general work in this area.

4. PHONETICS AND PHONOLOGY

This seems to have been a sparse year. Among the offerings are the following dealing with phonetics for foreign learners: W. König, 'Welche Aussprache soll im Unterricht "Deutsch als Fremdsprache" gelehrt werden? Ein Plädoyer für umgangssprachenorientierte Lehrnormen', *DSp*, 19:16–32, and H. Dicling, 'Nicht bagatellisieren. Phonetische Fehler im Fremdsprachenunterricht', *DaF*, 28:111–15. The affricates figure in M. Prinz and R. Wiese, 'Die Affrikaten des Deutschen und ihre Verschriftung', *LBer*, 133:165–89, and T. A. Hall, 'Affrikatenstatus von Plosiv- und Frikativsequenzen im Deutschen', *ib.*, 310–13. Also noted: A. P. ten Cate and P. Jordans, **Phonetik des Deutschen. Eine kontrastive deutsch-niederländische Beschreibung für den Zweitsprachenerwerb*, Dordrecht, Foris, 1990, viii + 123 pp.

5. MORPHOLOGY

P. Gallmann, *Kategoriell komplexe Wortformen* (RGL 108), 1990, x + 363 pp., is a modern attempt, based on the latest Chomskyan grammar, to treat the relationship between morphology and syntax in German. Technical terms are defined as they are introduced and the work contains clear diagrams. The starting level is that of basic linguistics which is quickly increased to state of the art linguistics. G.'s emphasis is on the noun phrase and its inflections. He also deals with apposition. There is useful index of terms and words. It is a work that will repay close study. The vast, complicated waters of derivational morphology are skilfully navigated by B. E. Oberle, *Das System der Ableitungen auf -heit, -keit und -igkeit in der deutschen Gegenwartssprache*, Heidelberg, Winter, 1990, 492 pp., who examines 5,086 words. O. uses the *Wörterbuch der deutschen Gegenwartsprache* and *Duden: Das Große Wörterbuch* as her main sources. After outlining the history of the suffixal variants she analyses their structure, concentrating chiefly on the morphological patterns. The semantics are, according to her, too vague. Each type is portrayed in a structural formula. This is a careful, detailed study. In an introduction she discusses some theoretical approaches, deciding to favour a combination of different approaches, particularly those based on the lexicalist hypothesis. This has the virtue of making the book accessible to a large number of readers. However, she gives a rather static view of word formation. There are two historical studies from the Bonn stable. M. Walch, *Zur Formenbildung im Frühneuhochdeutschen* (Sprache — Literatur und Geschichte, 5), Heidelberg, Winter, 1990, 96 pp., is a treatment of general principles of morphological development illustrated by the pronoun system (see *YWMLS*, 50:661). The typology of changes is the one developed by H. Penzl. Graphic illustrations are used to chart the development of the forms which are then discussed. Most of the changes were completed by 1500 but some non-NHG forms are still around by 1700. One of the most frequent changes is the addition of *-en*. Towards the end of ENHG when grammarians are active there seems no real difference between norm and usage. Two main reasons are advanced for the acceptance of forms in NHG: the areal spread of a form and its structural disposition, e.g. maintaining case distinctions. There is plenty of meat for the historical linguist to chew on. This also applies to H.-J. Solms and K.-P. Wegera, *Grammatik des Frühneuhochdeutschen*. VI. *Flexion der Adjektive*, Heidelberg, Winter, 351 pp. This volume covers the rather neglected area of adjective endings in attributive and predicative position, nominalized adjectives, comparative forms, and the status of the adjective as a word class. The coverage is detailed and systematic, including statistics of adjective use. The material is treated according to the different endings and also according to their different functions. A final section suggests that the development of adjective inflection has been characterized by emphasizing the marking for gender and case. Also the rules for agreement have developed from a meaning-based system to a more mechanical rule-based system. The adjective has also consolidated its position as a discrete word class. The treatment makes a dry subject come alive. A modern theoretical approach to word formation is represented by two articles by Susan Olsen, '*Ge*-Präfigierungen im heutigen Deutschen. Ausnahmen der "Righthand Head Rule"', *BGDSL*, 113:333–66, and 'Empty heads as the source of category change in word structures', *Papiere zur Linguistik*, 44–45:109–30. Inflectional morphology features in H. Albrecht and I. Zoch, 'Fehler bei der Adjektivdeklination', *DaF*, 28:116–17, and C. Blackshire-Belay, *Language Contact: Verb Morphology in German of Foreign Workers* (TBL, 356), xii + 451 pp. Lexical morphology is represented by G. Siebert-Ott, 'Wortbildung und sprachliche Kreativität', *SpLit*, 22:83–99; W. Schindler, 'Reduplizierende Wortbildung im Deutschen', *ZPSK*, 44:597–613; H. Kubczak, 'Beobachtungen zur Sexusopposition im Wortschatz', *Sprachwissenschaft*, 16:398–416; J. Schröder, 'Wieder einmal:

BE–Verben', *DaF*, 28:27–31; and Id., 'Zur Beschreibung von ER–Verben', *ib.*, 95–100. Compounds feature in B. Wolf, **Nominalkompositionen im Deutschen und Französischen.* Eine Untersuchung der französischen Entsprechungen zu deutschen Nominalkomposita aus verschiedenen fachsprachlichen Sachbereichen* (Münstersche Beiträge zur romanischen Philologie, 5), Münster, Kleinheinrich, 1990, 187 pp. Also noted: E. Meineke, 'Springlebendige Tradition. Kern und Grenzen des Kompositums', *Sprachwissenschaft*, 16:27–88, and R. Bloomer, 'The role of token frequency in the polymorphy among the strong and irregular participial simplexes of Modern German', *ZPSK*, 44:344–50.

6. SYNTAX

An important work to appear this year is *Hammer's German Grammar and Usage*, rev. M. Durrell, London, Edward Arnold, xvi + 544 pp., which is systematic in its coverage. Other general works are E. Hentschel and H. Weydt, *Handbuch der deutschen Grammatik*, Berlin, de Gruyter, 1990, x + 451 pp.; W. Flämig, *Grammatik des Deutschen. Einführung in Struktur- und Wirkungszusammenhänge. Erarbeitet auf der theoretischen Grundlage der 'Grundzüge einer deutschen Grammatik'*, Berlin, Akademie, 640 pp.; and J. Macheiner, *Das grammatische Varieté oder die Kunst und das Vergnügen, deutsche Sätze zu bilden* (Die andere Bibliothek, 74), Frankfurt am Main, Eichborn, 405 pp. Theoretical studies include K. M. Köpcke and K. U. Panther, 'Kontrolle und Kontrollwechsel im Deutschen', *ZPSK*, 44:143–66; P. R. Lutzeier, *Major Pillars of German Syntax. An Introduction to CRMS–Theory* (LA, 258), ix + 404 pp.; and D. P. Zaun, **Probleme der links-assoziativen Parsings deutscher Sätze* (Fokus, 2), Trier, Wissenschaftlicher Vlg, 1990, iii + 168 pp. The interchange between grammar and lexicon as well as contemporary syntactic changes feature in R. Lühr, 'Veränderungen in der Syntax des heutigen Deutsch', *ZDP*, 110:12–35; W. Abraham, 'The grammaticization of the German modal particles', *Approaches to Grammaticalization*, ed. E. C. Traugott and B. Heine, 2, Amsterdam, Benjamins, pp. 331–80; and C. Lehmann, 'Grammaticalization and related changes in contemporary German', *ib.*, pp. 493–535. Sentences and clauses figure in W. Oppenrieder, *Von Subjekten, Sätzen und Subjektsätzen. Untersuchungen zur Syntax des Deutschen* (LA 241), ix + 366 pp.; U. Scholz, *Wünschsätze im Deutschen. Formale und funktionale Beschreibung: Satztypen mit Verberst- und Verbletztstellung* (LA 265), xi + 316 pp.; and M. Brandt, **Weiterführende Nebensätze. Zu ihrer Syntax, Semantik und Pragmatik* (LGF, 57), 1990, 141 pp.

General word order and gapping occur in C. Küper, 'Geht die Nebensatzstellung im Deutschen verloren? Zur pragmatischen

Funktion der Wortstellung in Haupt- und Nebensätzen', *DSp*, 19:133–58; S. Dentler, *Verb und Ellipse im heutigen Deutsch. Zum 'Fehlen' verbalhängiger Bestimmungen in Theorie und Praxis* (GGF, 31), 1990, 106 pp.; V. Ágel, 'Lexikalische Ellipsen. Fragen und Vorschläge', *ZGL*, 19:24–48; P. Auer, 'Vom Ende deutscher Sätze', *ZGL*, 19:139–57; F. Patocka, 'Vorschläge zu einem korpustauglichen Satztypen und Feldermodell', *DSp*, 19:120–32.

Contrastive studies continue to be popular: K. Lu, *Die Passivkonstruktionen des Deutschen und des Chinesischen. Eine kontrastive grammatische und pragmatische Untersuchung.* Bad Honnef, Bock & Herchen, 1990, 190 pp.; U. Kautz, *Aktiv und Passiv im Deutschen und Chinesischen. Eine konfrontativ- übersetzungswissenschaftliche Studie* (Sinolinguistica, 1), Heidelberg, Groos, xii + 198 pp.; J. Zhu, *Das adnominale Attribut im Deutschen und im Chinesischen. Eine kontrastive Untersuchung* (EH, XXI, 100), 200 pp.; *Studien zum Deutschen aus kontrastiver Sicht*, ed. A. Katny (EH, XXI, 86), 1990, 205 pp.; E. Butulussi, *Studien zur Valenz kognitiver Verben im Deutschen und Neugriechischen* (LA, 262), xx + 344 pp.; K. H. Lie, *Verbale Aspektualität im Koreanischen und im Deutschen. Mit besonderer Berücksichtigung der aspektuellen Verbalperiphrasen* (RGL, 255), ix + 244 pp.; and S. Stojanova-Jovceva, 'Adversative Nebensätze in der deutschen und bulgarischen Gegenwartssprache', *Fest. Wilss*, 466–75. Interest in the noun phrase remains strong as is evidenced by *'DET, COMP und INFL.' Zur Syntax funktionaler Kategorien und grammatischer Funktionen*, ed. S. Olsen and G. Fanselow (LA, 263), vi + 202 pp.; G. Kolde, 'Zur Lexikologie der akkusativzuweisenden Adjektive des Deutschen', *CFS*, 44, 1990:95–121; J. Kunze, *Kasusrelationen und semantische Emphase* (Studia Grammatica, 32), Berlin, Akademie, 225 pp.; *Syntax und Semantik der Substantivgruppe*, ed. I. Zimmermann (Studia Grammatica, 33), Berlin, Akademie, 225 pp.; G. Starke, 'Modelle substantivischer Wortgruppen im Deutschen', *DaF*, 28:22–27; J. Zhu, 'Die adnominalen Attribute des Deutschen als Problem des DaF-Unterrichts', *DaF*, 108–11; S. Dallmann, 'Immer noch: Der Infinitiv als Subjekt', *DaF*, 28:31–35; C. Knobloch, 'Bemerkungen zur Nomination und zur Nominalphrase im Deutschen', *ZPSK*, 44:80–92; C. Römer and S. Henne, 'Über den Zusammenhang von Satzakzentuierung und Konstituentenreihenfolge', *DaF*, 28:35–40; K. Kostov, 'Zum Gebrauch des selbständigen appositionellen Dativs im Schriftdeutschen der Gegenwart', *DaF*, 28:41–43; and S. Chakroun, *Stufung und Reihung als Verbindung attributiver Adjektive in der Nominalklammer*, Munich, Tuduv, 209 pp. Questions receive attention in R. Pasch, 'Überlegungen zur Syntax und semantischer Interpretation von *w*-Interrogativsätzen', *DSp*, 19:193–212, and M. Reis, 'Was konstruiert *w*- Interrogativsätze? Gegen Paschs Überlegungen zur Syntax und semantischer

Interpretation von *w*-Interrogativkonstruktionen', *ib.*, 213–38. The many facets of the verb are treated in J. O. Askedal, ' "Ersatzinfinitiv/ Partizipersatz" und Verwandtes. Zum Aufbau des verbalen Schluß-feldes in der modernen Standardsprache', *ZGL*, 19:1–23; O. Leirbukt, '*Nächstes Jahr wäre er 200 Jahre alt geworden.* Über den Konjunktiv Plusquamperfekt in hypothetischen Bedingungsgefügen mit Zukunftsbezug', *ZGL*, 19:158–93; A. Lötscher, 'Der Konjunktiv II bei Modalverben und die Semantik des Konjunktiv II', *Sprachwissenschaft*, 16:334–64; B. Ulvestad, 'Zur "objektiven" Epistemik des Modalverbs *müssen*', *ib.*, 365–75; and R. Pasch, 'Satzmodus und explizite Performativität von Satzäußerungen', *ZPSK*, 44:568–84. Particles feature in U. Brausse, 'Nicht-propositionales *nicht* oder Modalpartikel?', *ZPSK*, 44:439–53. Also noted: L. Hoffmann, 'Anakoluth und sprachliches Wissen', *DSp*, 19:97–119; R. Lötzsch, 'Grammatische Germanismen im Esperanto', *ZPSK*, 44:695–703; I. Hyvärin, 'Sachverhaltsbeschreibende Finalkonstruktionen. Angaben, Attribute, Ergänzungen?', *Sprachwissenschaft*, 16:302–33; M. Weiss, 'Ein früher Ansatz moderner Sprachbeschreibung Joel Löwes (1762–1802). Vorschläge zur Analyse des Passivs und der periphrastischen Tempora im Deutschen', *ib.*, 376–97; and R. Lühr, 'Zur Subklassifizierung von Abstrakta. Wert und Grenzen operationaler Verfahren', *ib.*, 417–52.

7. SEMANTICS AND LEXIS

General theory and description figure in: V. Âmšanova, 'Die instrumentale semantische Kategorie', *DaF*, 28:91–95; C. Knoblauch, 'Wie man semantisch mit Abstand am besten fährt', *DUS*, 43:5–20; and D. Busse, 'Angewandte Semantik. Bedeutung als praktisches Problem in didaktischer Perspektive', *ib.*, 42–61. A general item on semantic change is T. Schippan, 'Bedeutungswandel', *ZPSK*, 44:93–101. Individual words and word families feature in the following studies. II.-J. Becker, *Das Feld um alt* (Monographien zur Sprachwissenschaft, 16), Heidelberg, Winter, 275 pp., starts by reviewing the literature on structural and lexical field theories. B.'s starting point is not denotation but meaning. B., therefore, using a corpus, starts with a basic word and describes its meaning variants, 19 in the case of *alt*! In every case clear exemplification is given. He then proceeds to divide the semantic characteristics into two blocks, *Eigenalter* and *zeitliche Relation*. This remains his basic framework at the end and the promised archilexeme does not seem to materialize. On the basis of meaning he arrives at a group of primary lexemes: *alt, antik, frisch, greis, jung, klein, groß, neu*. Those 'gaps' in the field can be filled with derived forms and compounds. Finally a definition of a word field is presented. A carefully worked book. A different kind of study is D. N. Yeandle, *Frieden im 'Neuen Deutschland'. Das Vokabular des 'Friedenkampfes'*, Heidelberg, Winter, xx + 407 pp., who uses a corpus from *Neues Deutschland* and categories set up by H. H. Reich. This is a computer-age study with over half the book taken up by tables, lists, and graphics which give information about the frequency of many more words than *Frieden*. This is not only a synchronic study but also shows diachronic change. There has been a subtle change of meaning from a neutral term to a propagandistic one. The term itself belonged to the five most frequent concepts of East German Communist thinking. There has also been an increase in the number of compounds, collocations, and phrases with *Frieden*. Y. admits that his work has been overtaken by events but it will still be useful as a detailed historical study. Also noted: B. Carstensen, 'Wörter des Jahres 1990', *SpLit*, 21, 1990:100–06; W. Klein, 'Raumausdrücke', *LBer*, 131:77–114; H. Dupuy-Engelhardt, **La saisie de l'audible. Étude lexématique de l'allemand* (TBL 346), 1990, xiii + 414 pp.; T. Roelcke, 'Das Eineindeutigkeitspostulat der lexikalischen Fachsprachense-mantik', *ZGL*, 19:194–208; S. Wachter, *Fach- und laiensprachliche Semantik des substantivischen Wortschatzes im Bereich 'Buchhandel und Verlagswesen'* (GASK, 15), xiii + 215 pp.; S. Wichter, *Zur Compu-terwortschatzausbreitung in die Gemeinsprache. Elemente der vertikalen Sprachgeschichte einer Sache* (GASK, 15), viii + 151 pp.; and D. N. Yeandle, 'Der Einsatz von Microcomputern bei Wortschatzunter-suchungen. Dargestellt am Beispiel der Entwicklung von *schame* im Alt- und Mittelhochdeutschen', *Beiträge* (Trier), 177–91.

Metaphor features in B. Henn-Memmesheimer, 'Metapher', *DUS*, 43:21–39; M. Strietz, 'Lexikoneintrag und Metaphorisierung', *ZGer*, n.F., 1:117–23; and W. Walther, 'Faktoren für die Übersetzung von Metaphern (Englisch-Deutsch)', *Fest. Wilss*, 440–52. Borrowing again figures strongly. The multifarious relationship between French and German is examined in *Das Galloromanische in Deutschland*, ed. J. Kramer and O. Winkelmann, Wilhelmsfeld, Egert, 1990, 236 pp. The articles span a wide range of topics, showing how the French influence in the Rhineland dialects and Berlin is very strong. The historical aspects are well covered. This work covers some new ground and should stimulate research in these areas. The volume contains: J. Kramer and O. Winkelmann, 'Recherches sur les vestiges gallo-romans an Allemagne' (1–9); M. Pfister, 'Die Moselromania und die romanischen Reliktzonen im Hochwald-Mittelrheingebiet und im Schwarzwald' (11–32); H. J. Schmitt, 'Lexikalische Unter-suchungen an französischen Waldenserakten aus dem deutschen Refuge' (33–57); B. von Gemmingen, 'Das *Lexique François-Allemant* (1631) des Moritz von Hessen' (59–76); U. Helfrich, 'Sprachliche

Galanterie?! Französisch-deutsche Sprachmischung als Kennzeichen der "Alamodesprache" im 17. Jahrhundert' (77–88); J. Kramer, 'Zur französischen Sprachpolitik im Rheinland 1794–1814' (89–102); R. Windisch, 'Französischer Wortschatz im Rheinischen aus der Napoleonischen Besatzungszeit (1794–1815)' (103–15); A. Greive, 'Französische Wörter in der Kölner Stadtmundart: Aspekte in ihrer Integration' (117–24); O. Winkelmann, 'Französische Elemente in der Stadtmundart Mannheims' (125–39); S. Kowallik, 'Französische Elemente im Siegerländer Wortschatz' (141–92); P. Stein, 'Französisches in einer hessischen Mundart' (193–203); R. Schlösser, 'Französisches in Berlin' (205–15). There is a useful index of words to end the book. Also noted: A. W. Stanforth, 'English linguistic influences on post-war German', Kolinsky, *Eva*, 333–40, and M. Lehnert, **Anglo-amerikanisches im Sprachgebrauch der DDR*, Berlin, Akademie, 1990, 270 pp.

Lexicography is another fruitful area of research and study as is evidenced by *Studien zum deutschen Wörterbuch von Jacob Grimm und Wilhelm Grimm*, ed. A. Kirkness, P. Kühn, and H. E. Wiegand (Lexicographica, Ser. Maior, 33, 34), 2 vols, Tübingen, Niemeyer, lxi + 767 pp.; M. Schlaefer, 'EDV–Einsatz in der Arbeitsstelle Göttingen des Deutschen Wörterbuchs von Jacob und Wilhelm Grimm', *Beiträge* (Trier), 29–32; G. Augst, 'Bedeutung(sangaben) im Wörterbuch', *DUS*, 43:78–95; and G. Harras *et al.*, *Wortbedeutungen und ihre Darstellung im Wörterbuch* (Schriften des Instituts für Deutsche Sprache, 3), Berlin, de Gruyter, vi + 292 pp. K.-D. Ludwig, *Markierungen im allgemeinen einsprachigen Wörterbuch des Deutschen. Ein Beitrag zur Metalexikographie* (Lexicographica, Ser. Maior, 38), Tübingen, Niemeyer, viii + 365 pp., deals with the so-called 'stylistic' labels. L. examines the history of such labels in the past and their usage in seven modern German dictionaries. The exposition is clear and illustrated with copious charts and diagrams. In chapter 4 he makes his own suggestion as how to label words and in chapter 5 illustrates it with reference to 'taking food'. L. separates pragmatic from linguistic information. The knowledge that a word is appropriate or not appropriate in a given context is pragmatic knowledge of the speaker. Style is replaced by communicative predisposition. Those words that belong to the general core of the language are 'neutral' and other words are either above neutral or below neutral. The latter are subdivided into *umgangssprachlich*, *salopp*, and *derb*. There are other markers such temporal, regional, etc. L.'s suggestions seems plausible but could run into difficulties when regional colloquialisms need to be taken into account. An interesting book which combines East and West German scholarship. *Collins German Dictionary*, ed. P. Terrell *et al.*, 2nd edn, Glasgow, Harper Collins, xxvi + 902 pp., does not yet take cognizance of German unification. As well as an increase in entries there are a number of extra bilingual pages giving phrases denoting suggestions, advice, permission, apologies etc., as well as information and models on correspondence, essay writing, and the telephone. Only regular usage will test how effective the range of words is.

8. DIALECTS

S. Moosmüller, *Hochsprache und Dialekt in Österreich* (Sprachwissenschaftliche Reihe, 1), Böhlau, Vienna, 212 pp., is a detailed empirical, sociolinguistic study, using the theory of natural phonology. M. investigates not only speech production but also speech perception of academics in the public and private sector, politicians, and newsreaders. She uses interviews, containing questions about attitudes to language as well as those designed to obtain linguistic data. The best German seems to be that of educated academics from Vienna and Salzburg. A variety of phonological variables are examined. The attitude to dialect tends to be negative. Newsreaders are positively judged whereas politicians are not. There is a great deal of detail to be disentangled in this work which is not made easy by the extremely small print. This also affects the diagrams. The use of the IPA in the transcriptions is to be welcomed. *Studien zur Wortgeographie der städtischen Alltagssprache in Hessen*, ed. H. J. Dingeldein (Hessische Sprachatlanten, Kleine Reihe, 2), Tübingen, Francke, xv + 344 pp. Hesse is rapidly becoming the most cartographed German dialect area. To elicit word geographical items D. administered a questionnaire to a large number of informants all over Hesse. The result is the analysis of 60 lexical maps (*Flächenkarten*) and then as isogloss maps, with four isoglosses to each map. The result is a division of Hesse into three areas: the north, south and an intermediate central area. By examining all the heteronyms and giving them indexical values for their occurrence or non-occurrence in major modern dictionaries as well as for their deviation in phonetic shape from standard forms D. shows that the south has a larger percentage of non-standard forms. A diachronic comparison with the *Deutscher Sprachatlas* and the *Deutscher Wortatlas* confirms the advance of standard forms from the north and a decrease in the number of heteronyms. The picture of Hesse also reflects the wider north–south difference. This work is extremely well organized, with terms being defined and goals set out. The material involved is large and much time is needed to do it full justice. Other general items noted: L. Najdič, 'Viktor Maksimovič Žirmunskij als Dialektologe', *ZDL*, 58:131–46; **Wortatlas der kontinentalgermanischen Winzerterminologie*, ed. W. Kleiber and S. Bingenheimer, Tübingen,

Niemeyer, 1990, 242 pp.; and B. Kelle, 'Dialekt und Dialog, Beobachtungen zu Wortgeographie und geschlechtsspezifischer Verwendung der Sprechersignale *nicht wahr, nicht, gelt, oder* und *wissen Sie*', Fest. Steger, 237–54. Items on Alemannic include *Alemannische Dialektologie im Computerzeitalter*, ed. M. Philipp (GAG, 535), 1990, 323 pp.; R. Lippi-Green, 'The development of the directional adverb *hin* in an Alemannic dialect: From sociolinguistic marker to stereotype', *AJGLL*, 3:31–50; F. Krier, 'Modalpartikeln im spontan gesprochenen Walliser Alemannischen', *ZDL*, 58:147–74; and P. Gardner-Chloros, *Language Selection and Switching in Strasbourg* (Oxford Studies in Language Contact), Oxford, Clarendon, xv + 218 pp. A semi-popular work on the dialects in Bavaria is *Bayerns Mundarten*, ed. W. König *et al.*, Munich, TR–Verlagsunion, 287 pp., with an accompanying cassette. The volume includes a description of the areal structure of the dialect with colour maps and a discussion of the status and use of dialect. There then follow extracts illustrating different dialects. After a discussion of where they belong, each extract is given in a lay transcription with a commentary on interesting forms and a High German version. This is an interesting Cook's tour but it must be remembered that not all the dialects are Bavarian in the dialectological sense. The East Franconian dialects in Bavaria feature in A. R. Rowley, 'Die Adjektivflexion der Dialekte Nordostbayerns. Morphologische Staffelung in einem ostfränkisch-bairischen Kontaminationsraum', *ZDL*, 58:1–23, and E. Koller, *Fränggsch gschriim? Eine fehleranalytische Untersuchung unterfränkischer Schüleraufsätze* (RGL, 110), xiv + 230 pp. The Rhineland continues to be a fruitful area of dialect investigation as is evidenced by *Das rheinische Platt — eine Bestandsaufnahme. Handbuch der rheinischen Mundarten*, ed. G. Cornelissen, P. Honnen, and F. Langensiepen (Rheinische Mundarten, 2), Pulheim, Rheinland Vlg, 1989, 667 pp., and M. Gross, *Das Moselfränkische von Huttersdorf* (Beiträge zur Sprache im Saarland 10), Saarbrücken, SDV Saarbrücker Druckerei und Verlag, 1990, 453 pp. An important work is R. Post, *Pfälzisch. Einführung in eine Sprachlandschaft*, Landau, Pfälzische Verlagsanstalt, 1990, 360 pp., a very detailed account, containing many maps and illustrations. There is also a full, commentated bibliography on Palatinate dialectology. Topics include the delimitation of the dialect, its phonological, grammatical and lexical structure, its spread in other lands, and its history. The *Pfälzisches Wörterbuch* is presented and there is a section on recommendations for writing dialect. This work combines scholarship with accessibility to a wider public. All those concerned with this area will welcome it. Also noted on Pfälzisch: K. M. Frank-Cyrus, *Subjektive Varietätenwahl in pfälzischen Dorfgemeinschaften. Unter besonderer Berücksichtigung geschlechtsspezifischer*

Dialektverwendung, Frankfurt, Haag & Herchen, v + 246 pp. Speech islands feature in K. Wild, 'Zur Satzgliedstellung in den "Fuldaer" deutschen Dialekten Südungarns', *ZDL*, 58:23–43. Two studies by M. L. Huffines are 'Acquisition strategies in language death', *Studies in 2 Language Acquisition*, 3:43–55, and 'Translation: a vehicle for change? Evidence from Pennsylvania German', *AJGLL*, 3:175–93. Items on dialect-based *Sondersprachen* are K. Siewert, 'Masematte. Zur Situation einer regionalen Sondersprache', *ZDL*, 58:44–56, and H. Franke, 'Zur inneren und äußeren Differenzierung deutscher Sondersprachen', *ib.*, 57–62. The following item on Yiddish was noted: J. D. Weissberg, 'Der Aspekt in abgeleiteten jiddischen Verben. Dargestellt anhand der korrelierenden Konverben *iber-* und *ariber-*. Eine kontrastive jiddisch-deutsch-slawische Darstellung', *ZDL*, 58:175–95.

The following dictionary continues on its way: *Preußisches Wörterbuch*, vol. 4, fasc. 5, *Plempermilch — purzeln*, fasc. 6, *Purzknochen — reden*, cols 641–768. The frequent use of word maps make this an extremely interesting work. Customs and technical terms are explained and illustrated nicely by pictures and diagrams. *Nordsiebenburgisch-sächsisches Wörterbuch*, ed. G. Richter, vol. 2, *D — G*, Cologne — Vienna, Böhlau, 1990, xvii + 1440 cols, treats a German dialect area in Romania, in northern Transylvania, north-east of Cluj/Klausenburg. The entries are based on material gathered some years ago. The entries contain headwords in High German, except in the case of loans from Romanian and Hungarian or dialectal words far removed in form from High German. The transcription follows the Teuthonista system. The different forms for different places are given but there are no maps, which might have been interesting. The oblique forms of words such as pronouns are given under the headword itself and there is no cross-referencing. Synonyms, however, are cross-referenced to other headwords. The etymology, particularly in the case of loan words, is given and even in the case of loan translations. The volume is nicely printed. An important work of a variety which may soon no longer exist. A Bratschi and R. Trüb, *Simmentaler Wortschatz*, Thun, Ott, xxi + 578 pp., is an exemplary work on an Alpine Swiss dialect in the Bernese Oberland. B. did not live to see his collection completed. T. and others have worked hard to produce this work. It comprises a grammatical introduction, a dialect–High German section, with head words in dialect script and containing many illustrations of tools, etc. The vocabulary is predominantly rural. After this main part there is a High German–dialect index, a list of *Sachgruppen*, e.g. professions, parts of the body, exclamations, etc., then lists of phrases and proverbs. It is a very thorough lexicographical picture of a dialect. Other dictionaries noted: **Wörterbuch Hochdeutsch-Kölsch*, ed. I. Nitt and V. Gröbe, vol. 1, *Uns Famillich*, Cologne, Bachem, 1990, 152 pp.; F. Hiller, **Mundartwörterbuch der deutschen Sprachinselgemeinde Schöllschitz bei Brünn. Nebst grammatischer Einleitung* (Beiträge zur Sprachinselforschung, 7), Vienna, YWGÖ, 1990, 220 pp.; and B. Suchner, **Schlesisches Wörterbuch. Ein kleines mundartliches Lexikon*, Leer, Rautenberg, 1990, 237 pp.

9. ONOMASTICS

M. Gyger, *Namen-Funktionen im historischen Wandel* (*BNF*, Beiheft 33), Heidelberg, Winter, 244 pp., breaks new ground in examining the functional use of names. The work has three parts. First, G. establishes that names have a special position with regard to meaning. Their meaning in fact varies. Secondly, since she wishes to examine the use of names in newspapers, the communicative framework of newspapers has to be established. Thirdly, she examines a corpus of events from three newspapers, *Neue Zürcher Zeitung, Frankfurter Allgemeine*, and *Die Presse* in four periods, 1865–88, 1890–1914, 1919–38, and 1953–81. The material she divides into three groups: *Referenzfixierungshandlungen*, e.g. *Ministerpräsident Grotewohl*, *Identifikationshandlungen*, e.g. *Wernher von Braun*, and *Appelative Referenzhandlungen*, e.g. *der deutsche Bundeskanzler*. Each type can be realized in certain ways. Several trends can be traced over time, for instance the growth of the first type at the expense of the second. Perhaps this can be paralleled in social and political developments such as the loss of monarchs and emperors. The future will tell if this approach can be fruitfully taken on board by historical linguistics. Other articles include L. Reichardt, **Ortsnamenbuch der Kreises Göppingen* (Veröffentlichungen der Kommission für geschichtliche Landeskunde in Baden-Württemberg, Reihe B, 1120), Stuttgart, Kohlhammer, 1989, vii + 284 pp.; H. Aschenberg, **Eigennamen im Kinderbuch. Eine textlinguistische Studie* (TBL, 351), xiii + 152 pp.; N. Wagner, 'Der Alemannenname *Hortarius*', *Historische Sprachforschung*, 103 : 108–12; F. Debus, 'Namen in der Literatur des Mittelalters', *Proceedings of the XVIIth International Congress of Onomastic Sciences, Helsinki 13–18 August, 1990*, ed. E. M. Närhi, University of Helsinki, 1, 256–64; and C. V. J. Russ, 'Internationale Einwohnernamen und ihre Bildung im Deutschen', *BNF*, 26 : 5–23.

MEDIEVAL LITERATURE

By DAVID A. WELLS, *Professor of German at*
Birkbeck College, University of London

1. GENERAL

Lexikon des Mittelalters, 5, Munich, Artemis, viii + 2220 cols, continues
from *Hiera-Mittel* to *Lukanien*. Wilhelm Volkert, *Adel bis Zunft. Ein
Lexikon des Mittelalters*, Munich, Beck, 307 pp., is an imaginatively
designed encyclopaedia with some 170 alphabetically arranged
articles on many aspects of medieval civilization, although the
emphasis falls heavily on the social, mercantile, and legal fields at the
expense of things of the mind (*Messe* receives a strictly commercial
interpretation). Although intended primarily for the general reader
who is invited to distinguish between similar terms easily confused,
and between the modern usage of words and their medieval
connotations, the information is soundly founded upon a good basic
scholarly bibliography of the topics reviewed, and much useful
background information can be gleaned from articles such as
Gerichtsbarkeit, Vogt, and many others. Ernst and Erika von Borries,
*Deutsche Literaturgeschichte. 1. Mittelalter, Humanismus, Reformationszeit,
Barock* (DTV, 3341), DTV, 432 pp., is the first of a planned
12-volume history of German literature, intended to be 'popular' in
the sense of eschewing theoretical and abstract formulations in favour
of the narrative and visual. Brief introductions on the social, political,
and linguistic background are followed by interpretations of a
representative selection of works seeking to identify the features
particularly characteristic of their periods. The substantial quotations are accompanied by translations. All the major works and
authors are treated, and many lesser ones besides. *Dichtung des
europäischen Mittelalters. Ein Führer durch die erzählende Literatur*, ed. Rolf
Bräuer, Munich, Beck, 576 pp., is a useful handbook from B.'s school
of literary history intended for specialist and layman alike. A vast
range of European (including Slavonic) narrative literature, together
with many lesser-known works, is introduced on the basis of short
details of authorship and background followed by extended summaries of content and fundamental bibliographical aids. The major
subdivisions include the heroic and popular epic of the chief
languages, epic on Classical and Oriental themes respectively,
Arthurian romance, romances of love, legendary works, late-
medieval allegorical poetry, and parodistic and satirical works.
German literature receives a higher profile than is usual in works of
this type. There is a full index, making this a convenient work of first
recourse for basic information. Besides B., the team of 18 authors

includes C. Baufeld, K. Cieslik, S. Heimann, U. Müller, U. M. Schwob, and E. Walter. Fritz Martini and Angela Martini-Wonde, *Deutsche Literaturgeschichte. Von den Anfängen bis zur Gegenwart*, 19th rev. edn (KTA, 196), viii + 765 pp., is a useful reissue of this standard history. The new editor has expanded both text and bibliography. Some of the comments in the quite full section on the medieval period are beginning to have a somewhat outmoded ring, and there is a case for rather more radical reworking in future editions. *Deutsche Literatur in Schlaglichtern*, ed. Bernd Balzer and Volker Mertens, Mannheim, Meyer, 1990, 516 pp., is a chronologically arranged survey of German literature in 22 chapters covering 21 periods. By focusing on 'highlights' the aim is to present a text which can be read in sequence and also form a work of reference. The Middle Ages is well served, with six chapters spanning the beginnings to 1400 by V. Mertens, and one on the 15th c. by U. Schulze, who also covers the 16th c. The presentation, while vivid, remains anchored in accurate factual detail.

Deutsche Literatur. Eine Sozialgeschichte. I. Aus der Mündlichkeit in die Schriftlichkeit: Höfische und andere Literatur 750–1320, ed. Ursula Liebertz-Grün, 1988. II. *Von der Handschrift zum Buchdruck: Spätmittelalter — Reformation — Humanismus 1320–1572*, ed. Ingrid Bennewitz and Ulrich Müller (rororo Handbuch, 6250–51), Reinbek, Rowohlt, 470, 539 pp., is an introductory literary history with chapters by a good team of specialists, including, in volume I, F. G. Gentry (the Carolingian period), V. Mertens (reception of French courtly literature), U. Müller (music and literature, also Wolfram von Eschenbach), I. Kasten (Minnesang), K. Grubmüller (Arthurian romance), J. Bumke (Walther von der Vogelweide), H. Wenzel (Gottfried von Strassburg), U. Schulze (*Nibelungenlied*), A.-D. von den Brincken (historiography), A. M. Haas (the female mystics); in volume II, E. Klesatschke (Meistergesang), W. M. Bauer (drama), I. Bennewitz (prose romance), H. Wenzel (autobiography and travelogue), H.-J. Bachorski (Heinrich Wittenwiler), W. M. Bauer (humanism), P. Schmitt (clerical prose), S. Füssel (Luther), and D. Seitz (Reformation pamphlets). The scholarship is not new, but there is full documentation, with time-charts, bibliographies, and indexes. Peschel-Rentsch, *Skizzen*, is a collection of recent essays on various authors and works of the period, beginning with a discursive essay on number symbolism, truth, and lying in Augustine, and concluding with a study of the miniatures of Bartholomaeus van Eyck. Paul Zumthor, *Oral Poetry: An Introduction*, trans. Kathryn Murphy-Judy, pref. Walter J. Ong (Theory and History of Literature, 70), Minneapolis, Minnesota U.P., 1990, xii + 264 pp., is a translation of the seminal *Introduction à la poésie orale* (see *YWMLS*, 45:35).

Hugo Blank, *Kleine Verskunde. Einführung in den deutschen und romanischen Vers*, Heidelberg, Winter, 1990, 104 pp., is an admirably clear introduction which draws the fundamental distinction between quantitative and accented verse and then focuses upon the essential problems of German, French, Italian, and Spanish verse forms, with many clear examples from the literary canon. In the opening chapters the basic terminology of versification is explained, together with the principal rhetorical figures of speech. Bernhard Sowinski, *Stilistik. Stiltheorien und Stilanalysen* (SM, 263), xii + 247 pp., is a new title in the series which makes an excellent attempt at covering a vast field within the traditional format. There are sections on definition and the relationship to neighbouring disciplines, the history of stylistics which includes a cursory survey of the standard Classical and medieval works, a review of the current state of stylistics in different countries, and an account of the different aspects of stylistic analysis. B. Nagel, *Fest. Wisniewski*, 377–98, includes some medieval examples in a study of poetic imagery. W. Berschin, *ib.*, 191–200, gives a broad outline of 13th-c. translation from various languages into Latin. *Frühe deutsche Literatur und lateinische Literatur in Deutschland 800–1150*, ed. Walter Haug and Benedikt Konrad Vollmann (Bibliothek des Mittelalters, 1), DKV, 1599 pp., packs a very wide range of works: pp. 9–1013 are occupied by texts and translations on facing pages. Among others, the German works, for which Haug is responsible, include the *Hildebrandslied*, a selection of the shorter OHG liturgical texts, *Wessobrunner Gebet*, *Muspilli*, *Petruslied*, *Georgslied*, *Christus und die Samariterin*, *Psalm 138*, *Ludwigslied*, and *De Heinrico*; excerpts, often substantial, from the *Isidor*, *Heliand*, Otfrid, Notker, *Wiener Genesis*, the later *Physiologus*, and *Kaiserchronik*; together with *Ezzolied*, *Annolied*, a substantial selection of charms and shorter Early MHG religious poems. Vollmann is responsible for the complete texts of *Waltharius*, the *Ecbasis cuiusdam captivi per tropologiam*, and *Ruodlieb*. The remainder of the book consists of brief introductions to each work and detailed annotation and bibliographical leads. While it is useful to have so much readily available in a single volume, the presentation inevitably suffers from a certain lack of overall coherence. Kissling, *Epochen*, is a fine anthology which aims to emphasize the artistic view of literature and is organized according to the major genres. A substantial section on the Middle Ages (pp. 17–87), the texts accompanied by translations or notes on difficult vocabulary, covers the whole period from the Merseburg charms to Oswald von Wolkenstein with some surprising omissions (Hartmann and Gottfried) but also some items relatively unusual in works of this type. The *Ackermann aus Böhmen* and *Narrenschiff* are represented in the Humanism and Reformation section. *Die vier Jahreszeiten. Gedichte*, ed. Eckart Klessmann (UB,

40009), 291 pp., is an unusual thematic lyric anthology of texts arranged according to the four seasons. There is nominal representation of the medieval period by Walther von der Vogelweide. *Deutsche Balladen*, ed. Hartmut Laufhütte (UB, 8501), 647 pp., is an attractive anthology of about 270 texts with full documentation of sources and an introductory essay. The book deserves mention in this section as a mine of examples of the reception of medieval themes. With the same title, *Deutsche Balladen. Von den Anfängen bis zur Gegenwart*, ed. Hans Fromm (SPi, 1380), 415 pp., has about half the number of texts found in Laufhütte's anthology, and a 'Nachwort' which surveys the German tradition in rather more sketchy terms. More is made of the conception of anonymous 'Volksballaden', and a short bibliography of previous collections and of critical literature is included.

W. Haug, *GGF*, 11, 1989:78–88, gives a theoretical discussion of the evaluation of medieval German literature in terms of an 'anti-classical' aesthetic, while Haug's approach to medieval literature (see also *YWMLS*, 51:626) is appraised by W. Schröder, *ZRP*, 107:160–66. E. Nährlich-Slateva, *Euphorion*, 85:409–22, defends M. M. Bakhtin against the attack on his theory of the carnivalesque by D.-R. Moser (see *YWMLS*, 52:596), but Moser is supported by A. J. Gurevich, *ib.*, 423–29, who sees B.'s theory as a reductive over-simplification. Moser replies, *ib.*, 430–37. M. Siller, *Sprachwissenschaft*, 16:227–44, identifies a sociolinguistic dimension to medieval German literature. P. Meyvaert, *Speculum*, 66:743–63, in the course of a study of medieval attitudes to national differences, touches on the mutual views of each others' languages held by German and Romance speakers in the early Middle Ages. In *Vorträge* (Liverpool), D. Huschenbett (1–13) introduces a collection of essays on travel and experience of the world in medieval and Renaissance German literature, and N. R. Wolf (14–23) surveys the vocabulary used in travel contexts, while D. Rocher (24–34) is concerned with the problem of linguistic communication on foreign travel, and N. H. Ott (35–53) discusses some iconographic aspects of the subject. In *VB*, 9–10, 1987–88 (1991), K. Kirchert studies the philological and exegetical basis of medieval Bible translation (13–33), J. Splett focuses on the treatment of Matthew 13. 44–52 (34–58), E. Timm notes the relevance of Bible translation for the distinction between Yiddish and German (59–75), H. Härtel documents Bible study in Lower Saxon monasteries (76–96), and S. Lorenz comments on the understanding of Psalm 37(38). 8 (107–14). Karin Wilcke, *Christi Himmelfahrt. Ihre Darstellung in der europäischen Literatur von der Spätantike bis zum ausgehenden Mittelalter*, Heidelberg, Winter, 505 pp., is an ambitious Wuppertal dissertation which fills a gap by surveying the literary treatment of the Ascension in its totality. Biblical epic, hymnography, and the drama naturally occupy a substantial part of the study, and besides Latin, Greek, and Old English treatments those in Old High German together with the *Heliand* receive due attention in the first half. Early MHG is represented by Frau Ava, *Ezzolied, Friedberger Christ, Rede vom Glouben*, Wernher vom Niederrhein, *Anegenge*, and *Veronica*, but the attempt to classify such works into categories such as 'Evangeliendichtung', 'Lehrgedichte', 'Legendendichtung', and so on seems highly tenuous, and results in epic works from the 10th c. on in quite different language areas being mixed up together; the chapter on the drama, however, subdivides the texts according to language groups. There is a brief survey of post-medieval examples to illustrate the continuation of the poetic tradition into the 19th c. and a concluding survey of the chief motifs. While the poetic emphasis is valuable, it leads inevitably to a neglect of comparison with the theological and exegetical background. There is a welcome index of themes; it is a pity that the copious bibliography, though supplied with some cross-references, is not classified in any way. H. Brunner, *Fest. Hoffmann*, 309–33, considers the religious and literary background to a range of political texts spanning the whole period.

R. A. Wisbey, *Beiträge* (Trier), 346–61, makes a spirited survey of over 40 years of computer applications to literary and linguistic tasks, and adds some pointers to the future. Many of the texts produced by Wisbey in machine-readable form at the University of Cambridge Literary and Linguistic Computing Centre are among the first 20 machine-readable floppy discs of medieval German texts in a new series, 'Halbgraue Reihe zur historischen Fachinformatik. Serie C: Datenbasen als Editionen', ed. Manfred Thaller, produced by the Max-Planck-Institut für Geschichte, Göttingen, in conjunction with Dansk Data Arkiv, Campusvej 55, 5230 Odense M, Denmark, from where they are obtainable. Each disc is accompanied by English and German versions of technical preliminaries by Astrid Reinecke who has revised and standardized the series, an introduction by Wisbey to his own texts with information on the specific work and on available concordances. Also in *Beiträge* (Trier), W. A. Slaby, 104–12, outlines in general terms the forms of data-bank available for humanities research, while W. Ott, 129–39, and T. Stadler, 140, discuss computer systems applicable to the field. R. Bräuer, 250–55, considers a computerized motif dictionary to medieval European epic literature, and H. P. Pütz, 238–44, describes a computerized onomastic project for medieval German literature, while D. N. Yeandle, 177–91, investigates the development of *schame* in OHG and MHG in a computer-aided study.

StM, 3.4, is devoted to the reception of the German Middle Ages, with a general survey of the subject by F. G. Gentry and U. Müller, the Arthurian legend in 1980s German literature (W. Wunderlich), anti-Semitism in medieval and recent literature (W. Frey), medievalism in 19th-c. national festivals (F. G. Gentry), J. Grimm's Romantic nationalism (F. R. Jacoby), Wagner's Meistersinger (E. R. Haymes), and medievalism in Jugendstil book production (R. Dépas). The authors constantly refer to the MHG literary tradition. J. Janota, *Akten* (Tokyo), x, 332–37, studies the regional aspect of medieval reception. Also on reception is *Medien, Politik, Ideologie, Ökonomie. Gasammelte Vorträge des 4. Internationalen Symposions zur Mittelalter- Rezeption an der Universität Lausanne 1989*, ed. Irene von Burg (GAG, 550), ix + 549 pp.

U. Wyss, *Fest. Conrady*, 73–88, discusses the 19th-c. origin of medieval literary studies, and U. Hunger, *ib.*, 89–98, the early collection of medieval texts. O. Ehrismann, *Fest. Engels*, 83–104, investigates the approach of the Romantics to the translation of medieval poetry. In *Fest. Conrady*, N. Wegmann, 113–26, records the discussions by early philologists about the unity of the discipline, and R. Kolk, 127–40, focuses on J. Grimm and Lachmann, while J.-D. Müller, 141–64, writes on M. Haupt, and U. Meves, 165–93, on the growth of an official framework for *Germanistik*. K. von See, *ZDA*, 119, 1990:379–96, discusses A. Heusler's correspondence. *'In Ihnen begegnet sich das Abendland.' Bonner Vorträge zur Erinnerung an Ernst Robert Curtius*, ed. Wolf-Dieter Lange, Bonn, Bouvier, 1990, 294 pp., is a wide-ranging collection of essays on the life and background to the work of C. and on both the scope and the detail of his scholarship. There are studies dealing with his relationships with intellectual contemporaries and with all the regional aspects of his view of medieval European literature, including R. P. Lessenich on his conception of philology, W. Ross on the fictive border between literary scholarship and criticism in his work, and C. Cormeau on the rights and wrongs of the 'ritterliches Tugendsystem' debate.

The *Katalog der deutschsprachigen illustrierten Handschriften des Mittelalters*, Munich, Beck, concludes its first volume with a substantial fifth fascicle. The entry on *Artes liberales* is briefly concluded and the remaining text is entirely occupied by the treatment of *Astrologie/ Astronomie*, divided into an introduction and the documentation of Johannes de Sacrobosco's *Sphaera mundi*, the Alsatian astrological texts, Lazarus Beheim's *Puech von der astronomien*, and collective works. The appendix of illustrations brings to 231 the total for the volume, and there is a full bibliography followed by detailed indexes of illustrations, MSS, prints, names, and iconographical themes. H. Meyer, *FmSt*, 25:315–39, examines the indexing of medieval encyclopaedia manuscripts, and R. Neumüllers-Klauser, *Fest. Zimmermann*, 173–84, maintains the recent interest in the problem of epigraphic forgeries. T. Berg and U. Bodemann, *BW*, 24, 1990:1–35, print and discuss the list of books bequeathed by Frederick the Victorious of Bavaria (d. 1476), and J. L. Flood, *ZDA*, 120:325–30, documents the medieval manuscripts bequeathed to the University of London Institute of Germanic Studies by A. Closs. F. P. Knapp, *ÖGL*, 34, 1990:156–62, reviews books on late-medieval Austrian literature published in the 1980s. *Fotographische Sammlungen mittelalterlicher Urkunden in Europa. Geschichte, Umfang, Aufbau und Verzeichnungsmethoden der wichtigsten Urkundenfotosammlungen, mit Beiträgen zur EDV-Erfassung von Urkunden und Fotodokumenten*, ed. Peter Rück (Historische Hilfswissenschaften, 1), Sigmaringen, Thorbecke, 1989, 163 pp., has surveys, technical descriptions, and occasionally more ambitious attempts to provide statistical analyses of important collections of photographs of early documents, including those at Marburg, Vienna, Bonn, Graz, Munich, Constance, Prague, and Budapest, besides some English, French, and Italian sources. The use of computer technology in classification is a recurring theme throughout the well-designed book. N. F. Palmer, *BGSDL*, 113:212–50, discusses the palaeographical and literary implications of K. Schneider's *Gotische Handschriften in deutscher Sprache* (see *YWMLS*, 50:681). Other work of codicological importance includes *Deutsche Staatsbibliothek Berlin. Handschriften, Sammlungen, Autographen: Forschungen aus der Handschriftenabteilung*, ed. U. Winter (Beiträge aus der deutschen Staatsbibliothek, 8), Berlin, Deutsche Staatsbibliothek, 1990, 124 pp.; H. Spilling, *Die datierten Handschriften der Württembergischen Landesbibliothek Stuttgart. 1. Ehemalige Hofbibliothek Stuttgart* (Datierte Handschriften in Bibliotheken der Bundesrepublik Deutschland, 3), Stuttgart, Hiersemann, 1990, xviii + 390 pp.; *Die illuminierten Handschriften und Inkunabeln der Österreichischen Nationalbibliothek*, 7, ed. G. Schmidt (Österr. Akad. der Wiss., phil.–hist. Kl. Denkschriften, 212; Veröffentlichungen der Kommission für Schrift- und Buchwesen des Mittelalters, ser. 1), Vienna, 1990; *Die mittelalterlichen Handschriften der Wissenschaftlichen Stadtbibliothek Soest. Mit einem kurzen Verzeichnis der mittelalterlichen Handschriftenfragmente*, ed. Bernd Michael, Tilo Brandis, and Gerhard Köhn, Wiesbaden, Harrassowitz, 1990, 383 pp.; *Die Handschriften der kleinen Provenienzen und Fragmente*, ed. Hans Thurn and Werner Williams-Krapp (Die Handschriften der Universitätsbibliothek Würzburg, 4), Wiesbaden, Harrassowitz, 1990, xix + 364 pp.; *Die ältesten Klever Stadtrechtshandschriften*, ed. W. R. Schleidgen (Klever Archiv, 10), Kleve, Stadtarchiv, 1990, 242 pp.; and Wolfgang Borm, *Incunabula Guelferbytana (IG), Blockbücher und Wiegendrucke der Herzog August Bibliothek Wolfenbüttel. Ein Bestandsverzeichnis* (Repertorien zur Erforschung der frühen Neuzeit, 10), Wiesbaden, Harrassowitz, 1990, xxiv + 564 pp.

OTHER WORKS

Pergament: Geschichte — Struktur — Restaurierung — Herstellung, ed. Peter Rück (Historische Hilfswissenschaften, 2), Sigmaringen, Thorbecke, 480 pp., is a sumptuous collection containing an account by the editor of the current state of research followed by 33 further specialist essays, classified according to the history and application of parchment, its scientific structure, aspects of restoration and conservation, its modern production, and the iconography of its manufacture and trade from the 10th to the 18th c. The book concludes with a classified bibliography of 909 titles. While the work abounds with information of background interest for medievalists in general, two contributions deserve special mention in this contribution: E. Eisenlohr's analysis of the St Gall records of the 8th–10th cs, and F. M. Bischoff's study of the design, manufacture, and structure of the Evangeliary of Henry the Lion and the other Helmarshausen gospel books. *Rhetorik*, ed. Michael F. Loebbert (Arbeitstexte für den Unterricht; UB, 15021), 152 pp., consists of 18 brief texts from Classical sources including Isocrates, Aristotle, Cicero, and Quintilian, by way of Augustine and Luther to modern authors, accompanied by introductions and suggestions for further study. *Rhetorik*, ed. Josef Kopperschmidt. II. *Wirkungsgeschichte der Rhetorik*, WBG, vii + 464 pp., concludes this work of which the first volume appeared last year (*YWMLS*, 52:599). A substantial introductory essay in which K. places the rehabilitation of rhetoric in its historical context is followed by 20 previously published essays from the period 1949–84. These include several standard studies of aspects of Classical and medieval rhetoric.

Ehlert, *Haushalt*, contains a range of contributions on subjects relating to home management and domestic economy in the latter part of our period, of which those including specifically literary documentation are itemized separately. Clarissa W. Atkinson, *The Oldest Vocation. Christian Motherhood in the Middle Ages*, Ithaca — London, Cornell U.P., xiii + 274 pp., covers a wide range of texts, almost entirely theological, from the Church Fathers to Luther, incorporating views of motherhood or stories about it, and preceded by an account of the understanding of the physiology of reproduction. There are substantial sections on different aspects of sexuality, on individual women of note, and on Marian piety. Although the book is well written and replete with interesting material which is merged into a lucid text, it is questionable whether the vast range of literary register and chronological difference which is the chief characteristic of most of the examples cited really adds up to a homogeneous 'history of motherhood'. *Auf der Suche nach der Frau im Mittelalter. Fragen,*

Quellen, Antworten, ed. Bea Lundt, Munich, Fink, 307 pp., is a collection of essays, all with a feminist orientation, on a wide range of topics. After a survey of earlier approaches by L. there are chapters by C. Opitz (widows in late-medieval society), and on women in various contexts by S. Burghartz (the Zurich town court), R. Habermas (miracle stories), E. Schraut (art in Nuremberg), M. Bussmann (views of Augustine and Aquinas), H. Sciurie (artistic portrayal of couples), U. Liebertz-Grün (political power), H. Reimöller (late-medieval calendars), D. Müller (beguine mysticism), B. Lundt (Melusine), I. Kasten (Cundrie and other ugly women in late-medieval literature), and F. Hassauer (Heloise). *Women in Medieval History and Historiography*, ed. Susan Mosher Stuard, UPP, 1987, xvi + 203 pp., is not in any way, as the title suggests, an account of women in medieval historiographical writing, but rather a series of surveys of medieval histories written in the 19th and 20th cs, classified according to the major national traditions and almost without exception directed to highlighting the absence of interest in women. M. Howell is chiefly responsible for the chapter on 'Germanic', i.e. German, historiography of the period (101–31), a useful bibliographical review. *Heloise und ihre Schwestern. Acht Frauenporträts aus dem Mittelalter*, ed. Ferruccio Bertini, Munich, Beck, 259 pp., is a translation of *Medioevo al femminile* (Rome — Bari, 1989), with biographies of eight medieval women including Egeria and Dhuoda (F. Cardini), Hrotsvitha (F. Bertini), Heloise and Hildegard of Bingen (M. F. B. Brocchieri), and Catherine of Siena (C. Leonardi). Régine Pernoud, *Heloise und Abaelard. Ein Frauenschicksal im Mittelalter*, Munich, Kösel, 280 pp., is yet another retelling of the story which combines the literary and historical evidence, carefully documented, with romantic speculation. It is difficult to avoid the impression that the thesis, that H. inspired A.'s work, is taken for granted at the outset.

Donat de Chapeaurouge, *Einführung in die Geschichte der christlichen Symbole*, 3rd rev. edn, vii + 160 pp. + 48 pls, is a welcome reissue of the fundamental and practical handbook which first appeared in 1984 (see *YWMLS*, 46:660–61). The revisions, however, are modest. Henning Graf Reventlow, *Epochen der Bibelauslegung. I. Vom Alten Testament bis Origenes*, Munich, Beck, 1990, 224 pp., is a clear and concise account of the beginnings of Christian Bible exegesis and the establishment of the forms of thought fundamental to the Middle Ages. R. goes well beyond a narrow concentration on the role of allegory and typology to emphasize the wider dimension of the prophecy-fulfilment pattern, the significance of the Jewish and Hellenistic traditions, and the importance of translation as a medium of interpretation. In *LiLi*, 80, 1990, W. Haubrichs, 7–13, introduces a group of essays on forms of medieval piety, and P. Dinzelbacher,

14–34, sets up a detailed typology of religiosity for the period. F. Neiske, 35–48, considers the large numbers of masses in the commemoration of the dead, I. Grübel, 49–60, the figure of Lucifer, and H. Unterreitmeier, 72–92, the relationship of literature to the liturgy. *Images of Sainthood in Medieval Europe*, ed. Renate Blumenfeld–Kosinski and Timea Szell, Ithaca — London, Cornell U.P., x + 316 pp., contains a wide-ranging collection of essays on hagiography and on the presentation and 'image' of sainthood in historical and literary texts, with noticeable variations in the general quality of the writing. The first section on hagiography and history includes a solid account of lay sanctity in the 12th and 13th cs (A. Vauchez), and studies of the illustrations in MSS of the *Vita sancti Albini* and a life of St Radegund (M. Carrasco). In the second section on the language of religious discourse, E. B. Vitz places the *Legenda aurea* of Jacobus a Voragine at the centre of comments on the oral and written components in hagiography, and there are specific studies of English and French texts and an attempt by D. Damrosch to isolate some of Bernard of Clairvaux's imagery as specifically feminine. The feminist dimension takes over in the final group of essays, where R. Kieckhefer sounds a salutary note of caution about the difficulties created by studies which deliberately set out to differentiate forms of piety on the basis of sex. *Die Weisheit der Heiligen. Ein Brevier*, ed. Johanna Lanczkowski (UB, 40010), 272 pp., is an anthology of brief excerpts in translation from a wide range of saints, many from the Middle Ages. While ostensibly for devotional use the book includes an appendix of informative dates, lives, and sources.

There is much on the role of feasts in the background to the period. In *Mediaevistik*, 2, 1989 (1991), H.-W. Goetz, 123–71, studies Church feasts in the everyday life of the early Middle Ages, while H.-D. Heimann, 173–84, focuses on feasts and festivals in the later Middle Ages, and R. Sprenger, 215–24, concentrates on peasant feasts in Germany. *Symposion* (Paderborn) includes important and interesting work on the background to feasts and celebration in the period. G. Althoff (29–38) considers the link between feasts and political and social alliances, and N. Bulst (39–51) the significance of feasts for family occasions, while H.-W. Goetz (53–62) studies the place of Church feast-days in the later Middle Ages, K. Graf (63–69) the commemoration of battles, H. Kühnel (71–85) the general religious, political and social purposes of feasts in the period, and P. Johanek (525–40) their importance as a focus for social cohesion. P. Bange (125–32) studies evidence of sumptuary laws relating to women and childbirth, and T. Zotz (201–13) the feasts of civic associations. The celebration of Easter forms an important section of the book, with work on aspects of the liturgical background by G. Beyreuther, G.

Björkvall, A. Haug, R. Jacobsson, and H. Möller, while D.-R. Moser
(359–76) is concerned with the liturgical opposition of Shrove
Tuesday and Corpus Christi. C. Lecouteux, *Mediaevistik*, 1,
1988 (1990):87–99, documents the theme of the fairies' banquet on a
comparative basis. Other miscellaneous work of background interest
includes R. Schmidt-Wiegand, *FmSt*, 25:283–99, on the legal gestures
relating to 'mit Hand und Mund' and similar formulae, P. Dinzelbacher, *Mediaevistik*, 2, 1989 (1991):43–79, on the sources available
for the study of high-medieval armour, and H. Kästner, *ZDP*,
110:68–97, on the role of the giant Theuton in German myths of
origins from the 12th c. on.

Urs Bitterli, *Die 'Wilden' und die 'Zivilisierten'. Grundzüge einer Geistes-
und Kulturgeschichte der europäisch-überseeischen Begegnung*, 2nd rev. edn,
Munich, Beck, 498 pp., is a new edition of the highly informative
work first published in 1976 (see *YWMLS*, 44:730). Text and notes
are unchanged, but a brief appendix has been added giving an
excellent critical survey of the most recent literature in the field.
Maria Rosa Menocal, *The Arabic Role in Medieval Literary History. A
Forgotten Heritage*, UPP, 1987, xvii + 178 pp., is the work of a Romance
scholar who has learned Arabic, and consists chiefly of polemic
against the neglect of Arabic culture and influence in historical and
philological treatments of the period. While M. provides food for
thought, her ignorance of Wolfram von Eschenbach and of the names
of German-language writers on this subject makes the study very
one-sided. *Zum Bild Ägyptens im Mittelalter und in der Renaissance.
Comment se représente-t-on l'Égypte au Moyen Âge et à la Renaissance?*, ed.
Erik Hornung (Orbis Biblicus et Orientalis, 95), Fribourg U.P. –
Göttingen, Vandenhoeck & Ruprecht, 1990, vi + 241 pp. + 11 pls,
contains several contributions of both immediate and indirect interest
for the late-medieval travelogue. E. Graefe (9–28) studies Wilhelm
von Boldensele's account of the pyramids of 1335, to which the
account by U. Haarmann (29–58) of Pharaonic Egypt by medieval
Islamic writers forms an interesting counterpart. P. Bleser (59–141)
translates Arnold von Harff's pilgrimage narrative into modern
French, with an introduction and original woodcuts; this is followed
by a translation (143–70) of Lupold von Wedel's travelogue of
1561–1606. Finally, C. Traunecker (171–241) introduces and prints
the accounts of the journey of the Franciscans Giacomo d'Albano and
Joseph of Jerusalem to Upper Egypt in 1691. Norbert Ohler, *Reisen im
Mittelalter* (dtv, 11374), DTV, 456 pp., is a welcome paperback
reprint of the vivid and detailed treatment of the topic which first
appeared in 1986 (see *YWMLS*, 48:672–73).

Codex Justinianus, ed. and trans. Gottfried Härtel and Frank-
Michael Kaufmann (UBL, 1368), 349 pp., contains a selection of

extracts from the seminal legal source in modern translation, each passage easily identified by the inclusion of Latin incipit and full reference to the standard edition of P. Krüger. The editors build on older work for their version, and the reader is guided by introductions to each of the 12 books and a substantial body of notes and indexes. The general introduction explains the late Classical and early medieval legal background and, as befits a work completed in Leipzig in 1988, makes much of Marx, Engels, and a slave society. *The Laws of the Salian Franks*, trans. and introd. Katherine Fischer Drew, UPP, ix + 256 pp., contains a translation, with notes, of two versions of the *Lex Salica*: the *Pactus Legis Salicae* and the 9th-c. *Lex Salica Karolina*. There are brief but informative introductory chapters on the historical background to the early Frankish period, Roman, and Germanic law and the relationship between them, and the picture of early Frankish society which emerges from the texts. G. Koziełek, *GeW*, 92:21–31, writes on references to German–Polish relations in early chronicles. Pierre Riché, *Die Karolinger. Eine Familie formt Europa* (dtv, 4559), DTV, 480 pp., is a translation of the French work, *Les Carolingiens. Une famille qui fit l'Europe*, which appeared in 1983. The book is a vivid political history, tracing the course of events leading to the collapse of the Carolingian Empire and the rise of the nation states, focusing on personalities rather than institutions. A final chapter deals with the Church, the nature of sacral kingship, and the court as a centre of cultural life; the monastic and the vernacular achievements receive inadequate attention. *Fest. Zimmermann* is a monumental collection of 46 essays including a few items of specifically literary interest recorded below and the rest of significance for the historical background to the period. They are broadly classified into (a) basic disciplines and source studies, including K.-E. Petzold on annals and historiography, E. Zöllner on the history of the name *Österreich*, H. Wunder on the Austrasian Mayor of the Palace Pippin, H. Mordek on a list of Irish saints connected with Carolingian reliquaries, and other work on late-medieval records; (b) papal and ecclesiastical history, including R. Hiestand on evidence of high medieval attacks on the papacy; (c) Church and Empire in the Ottonian and Salic periods, including K.-U. Jäschke on Wipo's comments on contemporary rulers, and T. Struve on the view of Rudolph of Swabia in contemporary historiography; and (d) the late-medieval Church and Empire, including R. Schneider on centripetal and centrifugal forces in Cistercian education, G. Baaken on the Imperial contest at the Fourth Lateran Council (1215), K. Walsh on Johannes Siwart, Wyclif's opponent at Vienna, and other work on the 15th c. Uta-Renate Blumenthal, *The Investiture Controversy. Church and Monarchy from the Ninth to the Twelfth Century*, UPP, 1988, xxi + 191 pp., is a translation, by the author, of her *Der Investiturstreit*, Stuttgart, Kohlhammer, 1982. The work is excellent background reading for the period and is accompanied by substantial recent bibliography. *Die abendländische Freiheit vom 10. bis zum 14. Jahrhundert. Der Wirkungszusammenhang von Idee und Wirklichkeit im europäischen Vergleich*, ed. Johannes Fried (Vorträge und Forschungen, 39), Sigmaringen, Thorbecke, 528 pp., is a collection which understands the concept of freedom on a broad basis, so that the primarily historical interest is complemented by the work of legal and linguistic specialists besides philosophers. Among the 20 articles which follow F.'s introductory study of the concept, K. Flasch studies the theme of free will; G. von Olberg, the use of vernacular vocabulary to express ideas of freedom; M. Kerner, John of Salisbury; J. Ehlers, the polarity between free will and predestination in medieval historiography; J. Miethke, the concept of freedom in the establishment of the universities; R. Köhn, and F. Graus, aspects of the concept of freedom in relation to the peasants.

Die Salier und das Reich. I. *Salier, Adel und Reichsverfassung.* II. *Die Reichskirche in der Salierzeit.* III. *Gesellschaftlicher und ideengeschichtlicher Wandel im Reich der Salier*, ed. Stefan Weinfurter, Helmuth Kluger, Frank Martin Siefarth, and Hubertus Seibert, 3 vols, Sigmaringen, Thorbecke, x + 577, viii + 569, viii + 616 pp., are three magisterial volumes of essays by 48 authors designed to accompany the Speyer 1991 exhibition on the Salians but which, together with several other sumptuous publications, mark a significant advance in knowledge of the 11th-c. and 12th-c. historical background in their own right. This notice can do no more than draw attention to some of the items of particular interest for literary scholarship. Besides articles touching on the subject of kingship and authority (K. Schmid, S. Weinfurter), volume I, which deals with numerous aspects of Salian government and territory, includes H.-W. Goetz on the place of the hereditary duchy in Salian historiography, with discussions of chronicles including Adam of Bremen, Lampert von Hersfeld, Frutolf von Michelsberg, and related authors and works. Volume II includes substantial work on the episcopal history of Cologne, Mainz, Speyer and other sees, on the conception of papal authority (H. Beumann), on the Imperial monastic foundations of Corvey, Fulda, and Hersfeld (T. Vogtherr) among others, and on Saxon female monasticism (M. Parisse). Volume III is of particular interest for the cultural and intellectual background, with work on the rise of the *ministeriales* (T. Zotz), the peasants (W. Rösener), Cologne (H. Stehkämper), Strasbourg (P. Dollinger) and other major towns; on the political theory of kingship (T. Struve); the role of Julius Caesar in the origin of German historical awareness and the use of *teutonicus*, with references to Otfrid and the *Annolied* among other sources (H. Thomas); the presentation of conflict, war, and peace (H. Vollrath, T. Reuter); the Bamberg schools (C. Märtle); bishops' *vitae* (S. Coué); and on legal topics, including the background to the *Sachsenspiegel* (G. Theuerkauf), legal authority (W. Hartmann), and changes in legal conceptions in the period (H. Dickerhof). Mechthild Schulze-Dörrlamm, *Die Kaiserkrone Konrads II. (1024–1039). Eine archäologische Untersuchung zu Alter und Herkunft der Reichskrone* (Römisch–Germanisches Zentralmuseum. Forschungsinstitut für Vor- und Frühgeschichte. Monographien, 23), Sigmaringen, Thorbecke, 145 pp., is one of nine further impressive volumes accompanying the Speyer exhibition. With an array of sumptuous plates, many in colour, the author subjects every detail of the Crown to minute analysis with constant reference to archaeological techniques, and reaches the conclusion that it dates essentially from the time of Konrad II rather than from the 11th-c. Ottonian period. In contrast, Reinhart Staats, *Die Reichskrone. Geschichte und Bedeutung eines europäischen Symbols*, Göttingen, Vandenhoeck & Ruprecht, 141 pp., does not attempt to compete with the established scholarly works on the symbolism of the Imperial Crown, but rather reinterprets its significance against the background of German history, especially in the present century. A survey of the chief places and dates associated with the Crown is followed by an exposition of the contrast between its role as a Christian symbol and the myth of the *Reich*. This proves to be the chief thesis which binds the study together; however, a proportionately large number of pages are devoted to the orphan stone and its significance in the context of Walther von der Vogelweide's references. The bibliography embraces the chief literature on the subject. Other work from the Speyer source includes Bernd Kluge, *Deutsche Münzgeschichte von der späten Karolingerzeit bis zum Ende der Salier (ca. 900 bis 1125)* (Römisch-Germanisches Zentralmuseum. Monographien, 29), Sigmaringen, Thorbecke, 302 pp. With a magnificent array of 29 maps and 528 illustrations of coins the handbook is a complete numismatic guide to Germany in the period, with information of relevance for much of the rest of Europe besides. The detailed text, accompanied by marginal references to the illustrations, includes, besides chapters on the organization and distribution of coin production and on the developments within each reign of the period, a detailed assessment of the text, inscriptions, and illustrations of the coins. The latter include, besides rulers, much of hagiographical and architectural interest. There are substantial bibliographies and lists of data, making this a standard and up-to-date source of historical and other source material. Antje Kluge-Pinsker, *Schach und Trictrac. Zeugnisse mittelalterlicher Spielfreude in salischer Zeit* (Römisch-Germanisches Zentralmuseum. Monographien, 30), Sigmaringen, Thorbecke, 223 pp., is divided more or less equally between chess and backgammon, and abundantly illustrates the role of board games in the 11th and 12th cs in the context of everyday life. A finely illustrated descriptive and analytical catalogue of all the archaeological finds relating to these games is preceded by a full account of their early history down to the 12th c. and interpretations of the more elaborate examples with a full survey of research and consideration of the relationship to other art forms. There is much of interest here for literary imagery in this area, as well as for Christian and secular iconography, especially in the field of animal symbolism. Karl Bosl, *Gesellschaft im Aufbruch. Die Welt des Mittelalters und ihre Menschen*, Regensburg, Pustet, 251 pp., focuses on the period from the 11th to the 14th c. and on the basis of a survey of a wide range of sources identifies the chief social trends of what is seen as an essentially turbulent period. B. views creative literature as an important source for the understanding of the mentality of the Middle Ages, and in this context the chapters on the lay piety and religious movements of the 12th c. and on courtly love are of central importance, even though B.'s judgements on literary matters (e.g. his association of Gottfried von Strassburg with heretical movements) are less than orthodox when compared with those of mainstream literary scholarship. *Mentalität und Alltag im Spätmittelalter*, ed. Cord Meckseper and Elisabeth Schraut (Kleine Vandenhoeck-Reihe, 1511), 2nd impr., Göttingen, Vandenhoeck & Ruprecht, 131 pp., is a welcome reissue of this scholarly but unconventional set of introductory essays on the late-medieval background which first appeared in 1985 (see *YWMLS*, 47:647–48). There are minor revisions and corrections.

2. GERMANIC AND OLD HIGH GERMAN

Allan A. Lund, *Zum Germanenbild der Römer. Eine Einführung in die antike Ethnographie*, Heidelberg, Winter, 1990, 100 pp., has the virtue of combining a broadly based Classical perspective with detailed factual information and judgements founded soundly on the textual evidence. The opening chapters deal concisely but thoroughly with the ethnographic contrast in Greek and Roman authors between themselves and foreign barbarians, and the basis and nature of the perceived differences. Tacitus and Julius Caesar then form the focus of the analysis which leads to the conclusion that the term *Germani*, like the Celts, covers a range of different peoples across the Rhine and was probably coined by Caesar to denote their geographical and cultural peculiarities. An excellent complement to this work is the

Frankfurt dissertation of Eve Picard, *Germanisches Sakralkönigtum? Quellenkritische Studien zur Germania des Tacitus und zur altnordischen Überlieferung* (Skandinavistische Arbeiten, 12), Heidelberg, Winter, 243 pp., concerned with the more specific issue of the existence or otherwise of a Germanic sacral kingship which coloured much research well into the present century. On the basis that the Norse evidence has been subjected to *interpretatio christiana*, P. reverts to Tacitus, and reaches the sceptical conclusion that T. incorporates none of the essential features of sacral kingship; comparison of his statements about the Germanic peoples with those about others, such as the Jews, shows that his treatment of religious practices must be understood as subject to Roman conceptions.

Gerhard Köbler, *Neuhochdeutsch-gotisches Wörterbuch. Neuenglisch-gotisches Wörterbuch. Griechisch-gotisches Wörterbuch. Lateinisch gotisches Wörterbuch* (Arbeiten zur Rechts- und Sprachwissenschaft, 35–38), Giessen, Arbeiten zur Rechts- und Sprachwissenschaft Vlg, 1990, vi + 98 + 160 + 88 + 62 pp., continues his useful series of reference works. P. Scardigli, *Fest. Wisniewski*, 419–37, comments on the Giessen Gothic fragments, and E. A. Ebbinghaus, *Neophilologus*, 75:311–13, reviews the evidence for the date of Wulfila's ordination, while H. Löwe, *Fest. Zimmermann*, 17–30, discusses the sparse evidence of Gothic traditions in Cassiodorus and Jordanes. Edgar C. Polomé, *Essays on Germanic Religion* (Journal of Indo-European Studies, Monograph 6), Washington, D.C., Institute for the Study of Man, 1989, vi + 148 pp., includes previously published essays and new studies. A. Quak, *ABÄG*, 34:19–21, discusses a newly discovered Old Frisian runic inscription. H. Vierck, *Symposion* (Paderborn), 115–22, records the archaeological evidence of feasting and drinking in the early Germanic period, and S. Žak, *ib.*, 481–87, the imitation of exemplary courts in early festival music. C. Lofmark, *Trivium*, 26:65–80, studies the theme of fame after death in a range of Germanic poetry, and W. Haubrichs, *ZGer*, 1:521–32, considers the structural and functional changes of early medieval heroic tradition. Beatrice La Farge, *'Leben' und 'Seele' in den altgermanischen Sprachen. Studien zum Einfluß christlich-lateinischer Vorstellungen auf die Volkssprachen* (Skandinavistische Arbeiten, 11), Heidelberg, Winter, 448 pp., is an illuminating comparative semantic study of the terms for 'life' and 'soul' in the older periods of the Germanic languages which is firmly anchored in the tradition of translation of the biblical Vulgate and related texts. The author deals in turn with the conceptions of 'life principle' (exemplified by Genesis 2.7); the seat of life, including metonymic uses such as *sanguis* for *anima*; life as a condition; life as a period of time; and the condition and manner of life. The starting-point of the study is an attempt to explain the disappearance of MHG *verch* and its analogues, and the conclusion convinces as a result of the judicious comment on a very large range of relevant texts; these are generally cited *in extenso*, making the argument all the easier to follow. Birgit Marschall, *Reisen und regieren. Die Nordlandfahrten Kaiser Wilhelms II.* (Skandinavistische Arbeiten, 9), Heidelberg, Winter, 270 pp., is an interesting Frankfurt dissertation concerned with Kaiser Wilhelm II's journeys to Scandinavia, involvement in Nordic politics, and, of primary importance for this section, the cultural and ideological background. This is revealed as an important chapter in the history of the reception of an archaizing, romantic view of the early Germanic past and its fusion with racial theories.

Rolf Bergmann, *Rückläufiges morphologisches Wörterbuch des Althochdeutschen. Auf der Grundlage des 'Althochdeutschen Wörterbuchs' von Rudolf Schützeichel*, Tübingen, Niemeyer, xii + 740 pp., brings to fruition a major development in OHG lexicography announced by B. in a detailed monograph in 1984 (see *YWMLS*, 46:669). The value of a reverse index of forms for students of OHG can scarcely be doubted. The material is wholly based upon the fourth edition of Schützeichel's dictionary (1989); B. convincingly justifies the exclusion of other works, for example the dictionary of glosses, on the grounds of their specialized nature and the impossibility of harmonization. The introduction explains the principles of the work in great detail. The conception of the morpheme has been reduced to the basic morpheme and the word-formational morpheme. Accordingly there are two basic dictionaries: the first is the actual reverse index in which, with suffixes included, the words are classified according to parts of speech. The second dictionary lists the basic morphemes in alphabetical order, and is accompanied by a brief reverse index of lemmata. Finally, a prefix dictionary in alphabetical order makes words containing prefixes easily identifiable. Used in combination, the three dictionaries give easy access to a great range of data and effectively resolve one of the greatest practical problems which have beset traditional OHG lexicography. J. Splett, *Beiträge* (Trier), 113–28, explains a scheme for establishing a data-bank of OHG word families. Also on grammar: Mary Michele Wachope, *The Grammar of the Old High German Modal Particles thoh, ia, and thanne* (Berkeley Insights in Linguistics and Semiotics, 7), Berne, Lang, xii + 205 pp.

Rudolf Schützeichel, *Addenda und Corrigenda (III) zum althochdeutschen Wortschatz* (SA, 12), 406 pp., is the third such supplement (see *YWMLS*, 45:530; 48:676–77) and continuing testimony to the great advances in the coverage of OHG lexis by S. and his pupils. Following the substantial bibliographical record of earlier work in the field S. supplies a monograph of almost 100 pages in which the research of his lexicographical school is introduced and placed in its historical and scholarly context. Attention is then directed in turn to the major literary monuments and the corpora of glosses and legal documents, which are passed in review with illustrations of how recent research has improved knowledge of the textual foundations. A short section on onomastic problems is followed by almost 250 further pages in which the dynamic growth of the subject is vividly illustrated in 11 articles of varying length by R. Bergmann, D. Ertmer, B. Meineke, K. Siewert, S. Stricker, and B. Wulf. These are chiefly concerned with the glosses, while other prominent topics include the question of an OHG translation of Alcuin's *De virtutibus et vitiis* (D. Ertmer) and of an OHG *epistula vulturis* (B. Meineke) for both of which the evidence proves largely negative, and the importance of the *Tatian* variants of Oxford, Bod. Lib., MS Junius 13 (B. Wulf). R. Schützeichel, *Fest. Wisniewski*, 9–17, tackles a number of problems of semantic detail in OHG, while J. C. Wells, *Beiträge* (Trier), 33–39, describes projected computerized dictionaries of Latin and OHG glosses. Birgit Meincke, *Althochdeutsches aus dem 15. Jahrhundert. Glossae Salomonis im Codex Lilienfeld Stiftsbibliothek 228* (SA, 16), 1990, 86 pp., is another contribution from R. Schützeichel's OHG dictionary project in Göttingen which follows the by now wholly familiar format of this series. M. has discovered a hitherto unknown MS of the *Glossae Salomonis* tradition. The description of the MS and edition of the material leads to the identification of 429 vernacular words and the evidence that, in comparison with other MSS of the tradition, the Lilienfeld MS has omitted or distorted many glosses. There are full indexes of the vernacular, Latin, and Greek vocabulary. By the same hand, Birgit Meineke, *Althochdeutsche -scaf(t)-Bildungen* (SA, 17), 219 pp., exploits the dictionary material as providing more substantial evidence than hitherto with which to reconsider the problem of the relationship of the common –*scaft* ending, and its older form *scaf*, to their numerous compounds and the question of their original role as nouns in their own right. M. supplies an alphabetically ordered catalogue of 37 OHG compound nouns with full documentation from the literary monuments and the glosses. Three further instances are established on the basis of later evidence, and another six abstract verbal derivatives distinct from the compound forms. The subsequent historical and semantic analysis provides much support for establishing the basic meanings of *scepfen* as fundamental to the development of the highly productive suffix, the MHG range of which is then tabulated in a concluding chapter. The presentation and indexing of M.'s work fully meets the high standards of this now well-established series. In *Sprachwissenschaft*, 16:459–69, B. Meineke describes a MS with glosses from Ochsenhausen, now in Prague, while E. Langbroek, *ABÄG*, 33:25–38, continues her studies of the glosses of Edinburgh

Adv. MS 18.5.10. Stefanie Stricker, *Die Summarium-Heinrici-Glossen der Handschrift Basel ÖBU. B X 18* (SA, 15), 1990, 178 pp., is conceived as a sequel to S.'s earlier study of the Basel MS B IX 31 (see *YWMLS*, 51:636–37). The present MS, its glossary also not treated in R. Hildebrandt's edition of the *Summarium Heinrici*, is subjected to a full description followed by an edition of the folia recognizably related to the *S.H.* tradition. There follows a catalogue of the 156 glosses and a linguistic analysis which establishes them as generally Upper German forms from the late OHG period. Comparison of both Latin and vernacular content with other evidence of the tradition assigns the MS to the early branch of the transmission. The study impresses as no less methodical and thorough than its predecessor. In *Sprachwissenschaft*, 16:453–58, S. defends her work against the criticism of R. Hildebrandt, while D. Gottschall, *ZDA*, 119, 1990:397–403, finds evidence in a library catalogue to support the early, 11th-c., dating of the *Summarium Heinrici*, against W. Wegstein.

A. N. Doane, *The Saxon Genesis. An Edition of the West Saxon 'Genesis B' and the Old Saxon Vatican 'Genesis'*, Madison, Wisconsin U.P., xvi + 464 pp., takes issue with the artificial demarcation which has led to Germanists treating the OS *Genesis* as an inferior appendage to the *Heliand* and the OE *Genesis B* as a footnote to both, and to Anglicists regarding the latter as an independent part of the OE poetic corpus. Hence he aims to present 'the first edition to treat both texts on the same footing' and 'to integrate them historically and critically'. The edition of the sole MSS is broadly conservative, suggestions for emendation, however persuasive, being confined to a manageable apparatus. The very substantial introduction (pp. 3–180) covers the history of the discovery of the relationship between the texts, the MSS, language, composition, dating, the parallel text, metrics, style, influence, and the literary and theological background, particular attention being paid to the treatment of Satan, Adam and Eve, Cain, Enoch, and Abraham. There is a full bibliography and further substantial commentary (pp. 255–356) on a range of linguistic, metrical, and thematic matters, and complete parsed glossaries to the two works, with full references or total frequencies and modern translations. The appendices contain additional grammatical and metrical information. With its wealth of detail the book is essential for all future study of the works. Dietrich Hofmann, *Die Versstrukturen der altsächsischen Stabreimgedichte Heliand und Genesis. i. Textband. ii. Verslisten*, 2 vols, Heidelberg, Winter, 247, 294 pp., shows a remarkable resurgence in metrical studies which, unlike the previous work of F. Kauffmann dating from 1887 before the discovery of the *Genesis* fragments, has the benefit of modern computer technology. This has enabled, in contrast to earlier metrical studies which usually cited only a few examples, the whole second volume to be filled with printed lists of verses in which the metrical structures are classified according to types and supplied with a full index. The first volume deals in detail with earlier research down to the most recent theories about alliterative verse, H. reaffirming that this form, with its greater identification with the structure of the language, predates rhyming verse. Specialists in the field will find full justification for the typology adopted and a copious body of statistical and diagrammatical analyses, including comparisons with *Beowulf*. G. Ronald Murphy, *The Saxon Savior. The Germanic Transformation of the Gospel in the Ninth-Century Heliand*, OUP, 1989, xiii + 129 pp., returns to the thesis of a 'Germanized' gospel but places it on an altogether more subtle and sensitive basis than the older writers whose works are reviewed in the first chapter. The book is particularly good in its confrontation of the *Heliand* with early annalistic and legal sources. There are separate chapters on the treatment of the themes of birth and fate, Peter, and the emphasis on water. Ingeniously argued but more speculative, being based on essentially non-Continental sources, are the suggestions that Christ with the dove on his shoulder is intended to transcend Woden with his ravens and the Lord's Prayer to replace pagan runes, not to mention the equation of the themes of loyalty and betrayal at the arrest of Christ with *Beowulf* and the *Battle of Maldon*. D. A. Krooks, *A JGLL*, 3: 161–74, returns to the 'hero on the beach' typescene in the *Heliand*, and M. Swisher, *Neophilologus*, 75:232 38, interprets the miracles of the stilling of the storm and the walking on the water in the work.

Die Kultur der Abtei Sankt Gallen, ed. Werner Vogler, Zurich, Belser, 1990, 223 pp., is followed by an English edition, *The Culture of the Abbey of St. Gall. An Overview*, ed. James C. King and Werner Vogler, Zurich, Belser, 252 pp. The German-language material in this concise but scholarly and well-illustrated introduction to the subject has been translated by King. It contains chapters with summaries of the research of a galaxy of leading specialists, including W. Vogler (historical survey), D. Geuenich (the monastic confraternity), I. Auf der Maur (liturgy), J. Duft (music), W. Berschin (palaeography, and Latin literature), C. Eggenberger (codicology), J. Duft (Irish influences), P. Ochsenbein (education), S. Sonderegger (vernacular literature), H. Horat (medieval architecture), H. M. Gubler (baroque architecture), R. McKitterick (charters and literacy), and J. C. King (the background of monasticism in the British Isles). Johannes Duft, *Die Abtei St. Gallen. II. Beiträge zur Kenntnis ihrer Persönlichkeiten. Ausgewählte Aufsätze in überarbeiteter Fassung*, Sigmaringen, Thorbecke, 311 pp. incl. 40 pls, complements the first volume issued last year (see *YWMLS*, 52:597). Whereas the first volume focused on codicology, the 19 essays reprinted here deal with Saints Gallus and Otmar, various bishops, abbots, monks, and pilgrims associated with St Gall, the chronicler Ekkehart and his namesakes, and the three famous Notkers, including a new article which succinctly surveys the documentary evidence of the life of Notker Labeo. J. Peeters, *ABÄG*, 34:33–48, interprets the failings of the Guntharius of *Waltharius*, and Peschel-Rentsch, *Skizzen*, 58–90, studies aspects of *Ruodlieb*, while S. Stricker, *Sprachwissenschaft*, 16:116–41, comments on the vernacular aspects of the same text.

H. Tiefenbach, *ib.*, 99–115, writes on the vocabulary of the Old Bavarian *Paternoster*, and H. Kolb, *Fest. Wisniewski*, 19–38, rejects the view that the translation of Isidore of Seville's *De fide catholica* was intended to counter the Adoptionist heresy; rather the authority of the author reinforced Frankish ecclesiastical orthodoxy. B. Murdoch, *LJb*, 32:11–37, illuminates the OHG charms by comparing them with Latin examples, and B. Kratz, *ABÄG*, 34:23–31, reinterprets the *Pro nessia* charms. W. Schröder, *ZDA*, 120:249–56, pungently attacks W. Haug's structuralist interpretation of the *Hildebrandslied* in the context of other approaches, and H. Pörnbacher, *Fest. Hoffmann*, 19–29, reviews problems relating to the *Wessobrunner Gebet*. W. Haubrichs, *Symposion* (Paderborn), 133–43, cites Otfrid, *Petruslied*, and *Georgslied* in the course of a study of the early medieval performance of songs for saints' feasts, and V. Schupp, *ZDA*, 120:452–55, comments on the *Kicila* of the *Georgslied*. Also noted: Terukazu Takahaši, *Studien zum althochdeutschen Georgslied* (Publications of Okayama University Faculty of Letters, 4), Okayama U.P. (Japanese with German summary). G. A. Henrotte, *Procs* (Kalamazoo), 1–11, interprets Otfrid's neumatic signs as evidence of how the text sounded in performance. M. F. van Gelderen, *ABÄG*, 33:39–79, studies Notker's treatment of the ablative absolute in his translation of Boethius, and E. Hellgardt, *Vorträge* (Liverpool), 54–68, reviews the geographical and astronomical knowledge displayed in Notker's works.

3.   MIDDLE HIGH GERMAN

GENERAL

In *Beiträge* (Trier), F. Hundsnurscher, 40–50, explains the problems encountered in a projected dictionary of MHG on the basis of semantic fields, and W. Wegstein, 85–90, describes a project for a modern German dictionary of the meanings given in Lexer's dictionary, while K. M. Schmidt, 192–204, describes a data-bank system for a conceptual dictionary of the MHG epic. In *ZDP*, 110, *Sonderheft*, T. Klein, 3–32, considers the data-processing of all extant

MIIG MS sources for the purpose of grammatical evaluation, and P. Wiesinger, 56–93, describes and illustrates a method for establishing a grammar of rhyme forms. N. R. Wolf, 93–110, argues that an analysis of attributive adjectival inflexions reveals that existing grammatical descriptions do not reflect the linguistic reality, and H. Penzl, 170–82, points to gaps in knowledge of MHG dialects, especially in the case of texts in Hebrew orthography. U. Müller, *Beiträge* (Trier), 96–103, points to the immense space-saving possibilities of storing MHG texts and related illustration in CD-ROM format, and W. J. Jones, *ZDP*, 110:384–406, reports a computerized analysis of the MHG rhymed couplet, with provisional results, while E. Morlicchio, *ib.*, 1–11, analyses sentence length and frame in 13th-c. documents, and F. Ohly, *ib.*, 321–36, places the study of MHG terms for *desperatio* on a close semantic basis. B. Krause, *Fest. Hoffmann*, 373–96, considers the MHG use of *lîp/mîn lîp/ich* and its philosophical implications. J. A. Asher, *Fest. Wisniewski*, 325–35, discusses principles guiding the emendation of medieval texts, and B. J. P. Salemans, *LB*, 79, 1990:427–68, the theoretical basis of Lachmann's textual criticism, among others. E. Hellgardt, *VB*, 9–10, 1987–88 (1991):400–13, documents the devotional rubrics in psalters from the 12th to the 16th cs. R. Warnock, *Beiträge* (Trier), 141, and W. Windolph, *ib.*, 51–59, report projects involving the computerization of Old and West Yiddish texts respectively.

Der Helden minne, triuwe und êre: Literaturgeschichte der mittelhochdeutschen Blütezeit. Von einem Autorenkollektiv, ed. Rolf Bräuer, Berlin, Volk & Wissen, 1990, 923 pp., is a spirited and well-illustrated literary history from B.'s Greifswald school. While B. can claim the lion's share of the authorship, substantial chapters are also written by C. Baufeld, R. Bentzinger, K. Cieslik, H.-J. Gernentz, W. Heinemann, R. Krolop, O. Müller, U. Müller, W. Spiewok, and I. ten Venne, while B. Bartels has assembled a bibliography occupying pp. 841–908 for the years 1975–85 and designed to supplement the standard East German *Internationale Bibliographie zur Geschichte der deutschen Literatur*. The definition of the period as *feudalklassisch* and the occasional intrusion of related jargon does not detract from the essential value of the work, which gives good introductions to the subject-matter and literary problems of all the great texts of the period and a very wide range of lesser works also. Besides the expected treatments of Hartmann, Gottfried, Wolfram, the *Nibelungenlied*, and the Minnesang to Neidhart, there are chapters on the social and linguistic background, the early court epic, *Kudrun* and *Ortnit*, the beast epic, Rudolf von Ems and several 'epigonal' poets, a range of didactic literature, the drama to the middle of the 13th c., historiographical and legal works, and *artes* literature. All this has the effect of placing the great masterpieces in a wider context than is usually the case. Richard J. Berleth, *The Orphan Stone. The Minnesinger Dream of Reich* (Contributions to the Study of World History, 15), Westport, Connecticut, Greenwood Press, 1990, xviii + 285 pp., is explicitly a 'derivative work' intended to initiate 'general readers' in the English-speaking world into the literature and history of the German Middle Ages. The thesis propounded is that in the 11th and 12th cs 'the minnesinger of German lands were the conscience and social arbiters of Central Europe'. B. admits to a 'broad brush, sacrificing some detail and complexity'. The book begins with a characterization of Otto of Freising and subsequent chapters each focus on a date of importance during the MHG classical period and loosely link most of the great poets and works with historical events. The whole is written in a gushing, journalistic style. H. Tervooren, *ZDA*, 110:113–20, affirms the importance of Ida of Boulogne as a literary patroness. B. Wachinger, Haug, *Autorentypen*, 1–28, poses some fundamental questions about literacy and the conception of authorship and transmission from the high Middle Ages on, and U. Peters, *ib.*, 29–49, compares the court cleric, town clerk, and female mystic as three specific types of author, while P. Johanek, *ib.*, 50–68, contrasts the type of the princely historiographer with the town chronicler. In *Exempel und Exempelsammlungen*, ed. Walter Haug and Burghart Wachinger (FV, 2), viii + 317 pp., F. P. Knapp approaches the vexed question of narrative genres in the light of scholastic poetics, and sets up a system of classification (1–22), and the theoretical rhetorical basis of conversational speech acts is explored by P. von Moos (23–57), while K. Grubmüller stays closer to the text in his treatment of the symbolic basis of the fable in relation to similar *exempla* (58–76), and C. Daxelmüller surveys the educative role of the *exemplum* in the early modern period (77–94). R. Newhauser studies and supplies the basis for a critical edition of Peter of Limoges's *Tractatus moralis de oculo* (95–136), and N. F. Palmer describes and documents the *Compilatio exemplorum anglicorum* which proves to be of major importance for 14th-c. Anglo-German literary relations (137–72), while B. Weiske uses a comparison with Hugo von Trimberg's *Solsequium* to date the *Gesta Romanorum* to before 1284 (173–207), and W. Williams-Krapp introduces the *Seelenwurzgarten* of 1466–67 (208–22). V. Mertens discusses the relationship of gloss and exemplum in Adam Petri (223–38), B. Wachinger, the use of the Decalogue as the structural basis for collections of *exempla* (239–63), and W. Haug, the use of a narrative frame for such compilation (264–87). Finally, J. Berlioz adds a different perspective to the subject-matter with a survey and bibliography of research in France 1966–88 (288–317). *Deutsche Fabeln aus neun Jahrhunderten*, ed. Karl Wolfgang Becker, illus. Rolf Münzner,

Leipzig, Reclam, 552 pp., is a substantial anthology of chronologically arranged fables which begins with a selection from the
Kaiserchronik, Spervogel, Konrad von Würzburg, Der Marner, Gerhard von Minden, Hugo von Trimberg, Heinrich von Mügeln, the
Magdeburg *Äsop*, Ulrich Boner, Heinrich Steinhöwel, Anton von
Pforr, and Sebastian Brant, partly in modern translation. There is full
documentation of authors and sources and a 'Nachwort'. Of interest
for the Alexander legend is Walter von Châtillon, *Alexandreis*. *Das Lied
von Alexander dem Großen*, introd., comm., and trans. Gerhard Strek-
kenbach, Heidelberg, Schneider, 1990, 332 pp. *Das Buch von Alexander,
dem edlen und weisen König von Makedonien mit den Miniaturen der Leipziger
Handschrift*, ed. Wolfgang Kirsch, Leipzig, Reclam, 223 pp., is an
attractively presented and very fluent modern translation of the
Orosius recension of the *Historia de preliis Alexandri Magni*, following A.
Hilka's text. A particularly welcome feature is the inclusion, in good
colour reproduction, of all the miniatures of the Leipzig MS. In
Symposion (Paderborn), T. Ehlert (391–400), studies marriage festivals — and their absence — in literature of the 12th and 13th cs, and
E. Nellmann (145–52) examines the evidence for village festivals in
Neidhart and the *Bayerischer Landfrieden* of 1244. In the same volume,
vernacular chronicle literature is also cited in a more general study of
peasant festivals by W. Rösener (153–63), and in accounts of the
feasts of the Welf aristocracy in the 13th c. by B. Schneidmüller
(165–80), of late-medieval instances of anti-Semitism by M. J.
Wenninger (323–32), and of the royal *adventus* in late-medieval
Imperial cities by A. Niederstätter (491–500), while H. Wolter
(193–99) studies the political significance of the Mainz Festival of
1184. Royal wedding feasts are the subject of F.-R. Erkens (401–21).
H. Boockmann (217–27) discusses the evidence for minstrels and
itinerant entertainers in records of the Teutonic order from the early
15th c. W. Röcke, *Neohelicon*, 17.1, 1990:203–31, writes on the
carnival and the transformation of social norms in late-medieval
literature. J. Jarnut, Ehlert, *Haushalt*, 119–28, cites the *Kaiserchronik*
and *Seifried Helbling* in the course of a survey of dietary and clothing
regulations, and T. Ehlert, *ib.*, 153–56, refers to vernacular texts
mentioning the roles of the master and mistress of the household.
  Torsten Haferlach, *Die Darstellung von Verletzungen und Krankheiten
und ihrer Therapie in mittelalterlicher deutscher Literatur unter gattungsspezifi-
schen Aspekten*, Heidelberg, Winter, x + 259 pp., is a Kiel dissertation
of particular interest, being the work of a qualified medical practi-
tioner. H. emphasizes the broad medieval conception of sickness —
indeed, decapitation of enemies is treated under the heading of
surgical procedure! — and of therapy, the final chapters being
devoted to the different types of healer. In the body of the study the

selected texts, almost 80 in all, are treated according to genre. There is an introductory survey of the Classical, Arabic, and popular background to medieval medicine, which draws on the insights of recent research on vernacular medical texts. Love-sickness is included and there is a substantial section on Iwein's madness, which warns against reading modern and psychoanalytical conceptions into the text. Wolfram's *Parzival*, however, emerges as the richest single source for the subject. W. McConnell, *Procs* (Kalamazoo), 23–37, notes the benefits and dangers of psychological interpretations of medieval literature, and J. A. Schultz, *Speculum*, 66:519–39, uses the absence of a concept of adolescence in Middle High German texts to argue against cultural historians who defend its psychological, physiological, and lexical reality as a distinct life stage in medieval thinking. Wolfgang Beutin, *Sexualität und Obszönität. Eine literaturpsychologische Studie über epische Dichtungen des Mittelalters und der Renaissance*, Würzburg, Königshausen & Neumann, 1990, 482 pp., makes a wide range of modern historical and psychological studies the basis of a comprehensive monograph on a subject which has been arousing ever more interest in recent years. In view of the great number of relevant texts, B. usually supplies brief summaries of content to replace quotation in the original. The first half of the book surveys the portrayal of sexuality in the chief genres, with a section on vocabulary and symbolism. The second half has substantial discussions, with numerous examples, of topics such as sex roles and their exchange, transvestitism, Amazonian women, attitudes to women in general, descriptions of genitalia and copulation, marital attitudes and behaviour, adultery, widowhood, perversions, incest, and castration. Lydia Miklautsch, *Studien zur Mutterrolle in den mittelhochdeutschen Großepen des zwölften und dreizehnten Jahrhunderts* (ES, 88), viii + 284 pp., is understood as a contribution to knowledge of the literary presentation of familial relationships and their reflection of high-medieval social reality. It is probably inherent in the subject-matter that the work consists of relatively independent studies of different maternal roles and situations; M. succeeds in drawing into the argument all the most important epic works with relevant subject-matter, classifying them conveniently as Arthurian romances, *Brautwerbungsromane*, romances of love and adventure, and romances on Classical themes. *Parzival* emerges as by far the most fertile source of insights for this topic. There is an index of mothers. D. Rocher, *Parenté*, 247–55, points to the position of the married lady between two families in medieval narrative, and M. Schleissner, *Akten* (Tokyo), xi, 67–74, surveys wild women in the MHG epic. B. Horacek, *Fest. Wisniewski*, 355–76, comments on R. Wagner's reception of aspects of love from MHG literature, and K. Speckenbach,

Medieval Literature

635

Fest. Hoffmann, 421–42, considers the figurative and allegorical implications of fictive dreams in the period. Id., Vorträge (Liverpool), 125–40, surveys the German examples of visionary otherworld journeys. T. R. Jackson, Akten (Tokyo), VII, 263–74, studies the image of Ireland in the German Middle Ages, and H. Brunner, ib., IX, 346–51, the view of foreigners presented in late-13th-c. Austrian works. Lindemann, Spinnen, includes texts on the subject of spiders by Der Meissner, Berthold von Regensburg, Hugo von Trimberg, Konrad von Megenberg, Hans Folz, and from Reinfried von Braunschweig and Der Judenknabe.

H.-J. Behr, ZDP, 110:373–84, reasserts his view, against W. Schröder, of the relationship between literature and the legitimacy of power. F. P. Knapp, Fest. Hoffmann, 277–89, studies attitudes to the ruler displayed in Der Stricker, Bruder Wernher, and the Buch von Bern. Hartmut Semmler, Listmotive in der mittelhochdeutschen Epik. Zum Wandel ethischer Normen im Spiegel der Literatur (PSQ, 122), 314 pp., takes up the problem of deception and worldly-wise behaviour in epic literature of the period 1150–1300, pointing to the ambivalent moral judgement as the justification for the importance of the problem. The value of the study lies — unlike some earlier work in this area — in its concentration upon the texts themselves and the analysis of the many different forms and expressions of deceit employed; at the same time the business of defining precisely what is meant by list is not without problems. Not surprisingly, Gottfried's Tristan, with over 40 deceptions, is seen as occupying a special place in the tradition. There is also a chapter on the theological and philosophical treatment of worldly wisdom. This focuses on the definition of true and false prudentia but neglects the role of the less refined morality of popular sententious literature which must have played a part here. In similar vein, H. Mettke, GGF, 11, 1989:123–37, writes on parvenus, flatterers, and bad counsellors in Wolfram's Parzival, Otte's Eraclius, and some 13th-c. didactic texts. R. Fisher, Akten (Tokyo), VII, 256–62, studies the exotic dimension in Veldeke and Hartmann, and H.-W. Schäfer, ib., XI, 58–66, the Knights Templar and their significance in Parzival and the Jüngerer Titurel. Werner Schröder, Text und Interpretation III. Zur Kunstanschauung Gottfrieds von Straßburg und Konrads von Würzburg nach dem Zeugnis ihrer Prologe (Sitzungsberichte der Wiss. Gesell. an der J. W. Goethe-Univ. Frankfurt a. M., 26, no. 5), Stuttgart, Steiner, 1990, 53 pp., starts with Konrad von Würzburg's apparently anachronistic statement 'mir selben üebe ich mine kunst' (Trojanerkrieg, 185), and develops an interesting comparison between Gottfried's Tristan prologue, seen as K.'s model, and his prologues to the Trojanerkrieg and to Partonopier und Meliur and other statements about the poet's function and self-image and his conception of his audience, these texts being accompanied by detailed interpretative translations. S. indulges in some characteristically pungent polemic against fashionable sociological approaches to postclassical MHG literature, and sees K. as the poet with the highest degree of reflection about the nature of his art apart from Gottfried and Rudolf von Ems. G. L. Strauch, *Procs* (Kalamazoo), 13–22, points to the importance of Arabic sources as background to the medieval crusading epic, and D. Buschinger, *GeW*, 92:45–53, notes the references to Poland in MHG literature.

EARLY MIDDLE HIGH GERMAN

B. Haupt, *Akten* (Tokyo), VII, 285–95, studies Alexander's journey to the Orient in the *Straßburger Alexander*. H. Szklenar, *Fest. Wisniewski*, 39–56, interprets the San Zeno Maggiore, Verona, sculptures associated with the Roland legend, while sadistical aspects of the narrative of the *Rolandslied* are identified by Peschel-Rentsch, *Skizzen*, 91–102. *Herzog Ernst D (wahrscheinlich von Ulrich von Etzenbach)*, ed. Hans-Friedrich Rosenfeld (ATB, 104), xxxii + 199 pp., is an important new edition, the history of which goes back to the early 1930s: a preface outlines its tortuous progress. The substantial introduction describes the unique MS in detail and then proceeds to assess the importance of the Old Czech *Vévoda Arnošt*, which appears to date at least from the mid-14th c., one of the factors which delayed the appearance of the new text for so long; a useful translation from the Czech work is added in the notes to fill a lacuna in the MS. R. also surveys the recent controversy about the authorship, inclining to accept Ulrich von Etzenbach on the grounds of the linguistic and stylistic affinities with his known works. The text itself is, not surprisingly, more radical than current fashions permit, but succeeds in its aim of presenting the work in the literary language of the late 13th c., with full documentation of editorial emendations. A. Classen, *Euphorion*, 85:292–314, points to textual resemblances between *Herzog Ernst B* and *Tristan* and *Willehalm*, dating the former to c. 1200–30.

R. Andraschek-Holzer, *ABÄG*, 33:81–87, emphasizes the heterogeneity of the possible clerical authors and of the audiences for Early MHG religious poetry, and F. Ohly, *Euphorion*, 85:235–72, includes the *Ezzolied* and *St. Trudperter Hohes Lied* in a survey of the theological imagery of the providential role of the stars. E. Schwarz, *WW*, 40, 1990:304–12, suggests that strophes 1–7 of the *Annolied* were originally conceived as an independent poem, and D. A. Wells, *ZDA*, 120:369–92, studies the tradition of the Fates of the Apostles and its relevance for the lists of apostles in the *Annolied, Mittelfränkische Reimbibel*, and premendicant sermons. K. Gärtner, *ZDP*, 110, *Sonderheft*: 23–55, sees the MSS of Williram von Ebersberg's commentary on the Song of Songs, distributed over the whole Germanspeaking area, as a unique basis for a grammar of Early MHG. B. Murdoch, *ABÄG*, 33:89–115, comments in detail on the 'Scopf von dem lône', and B. Plate, *VB*, 9–10, 1987–88 (1991):181–215, adds to knowledge of the long tradition of the Early MLG Apocalypse translation from the 12th c. on. E. Gössmann, *Akten* (Tokyo), x, 193–200, studies the feminine in Frau Ava, Hrotsvitha von Gandersheim, and Hildegard von Bingen. Fabio Chávez Alvarez, *'Die brennende Vernunft.' Studien zur Semantik der 'rationalitas' bei Hildegard von Bingen* (MGG, i, 8), 282 pp., is a philosophical and theological study of wider general interest than its specialized title might suggest, for, besides focusing on the unique aspects of Hildegard's work in her own time, the whole first half of the book (pp. 22–130) consists of a detailed review of the possible sources of the concept of *rationalitas* in Hellenistic, patristic, and medieval tradition, culminating in 12th-c. usage in the schools of Laon, Chartres, and Bernard of Clairvaux. The second part reveals the importance of the concept as a key term in H.'s writing; in a third, briefer, section her visionary literature is drawn into the argument, so that human *rationalitas* is seen to be the ultimate expression of the divine *logos* of St John's Gospel. J. T. Schnapp, *Exemplaria*, 3·267–98, characterizes Hildegard's imaginary language.

MIDDLE HIGH GERMAN HEROIC LITERATURE

Arthur Thomas Hatto, *Eine allgemeine Theorie der Heldenepik* (Rheinisch-Westfälische Akademie der Wissenschaften. Vorträge, G 307), Opladen, Westdeutscher Vlg, 38 pp., expounds in a short space his view of the heroic epic, in which the conception of epic moments plays a central role. The essay ranges over an astonishing range of Classical and Oriental sources, and concludes with the fall of the Burgundians in the *Nibelungenlied*. The record of the debate by a panel of experts occupies almost as much space as the lecture, and is much more illuminating than the printed text of most such discussions. O. Ehrismann, *GeW*, 92:33–44, surveys references to Poland in German heroic literature, and T. M. Andersson, *Akten* (Tokyo), i, 76–86, examines proto-nationalism in the *Nibelungenlied* and elsewhere, while E. S. Dick, *Procs* (Kalamazoo), 53–64, relates the problem of the genre of the *Nl.* to its reception, and T.-U. Hur, *Akten* (Tokyo), vi, 202–09, focuses on the legitimization of political power in the *Nl.* A. Classen, *IASL*, 16.1:1–31, interprets the work in terms of the eclipse of a matriarchal society, and S. Samples, *Procs* (Kalamazoo), 103–12, studies maternal loyalty in the *Nl.* and *Kudrun.* H. den Besten, *ABÄG*, 33:117–30, criticizes J. Janota for failing to take H. Ritter-Schaumburg's arguments seriously. R. Wisniewski, *Fest. Hoffmann*, 55–69, suggests that the Sigemund episode in *Beowulf* reflects the origins of the Siegfried legend, and O. Ehrismann, *Akten* (Tokyo), x, 320–31, views Brünhild as an alien at court, while H.-F. Rosenfeld, *Fest. Hoffmann*, 71–95, studies Ortlieb's death in different MSS of the *Nl.*, and U. Schwab, *Fest. Wisniewski*, 77–122, the metaphorical uses made of the fiddler and his musical technique in the *Nl.* and other works. The imagery of death and destruction in the structure of the *Nl.* is the subject of Peschel-Rentsch, *Skizzen*, 103–28.

H. C. Seeba, *Fest. Conrady*, 57–71, considers the 19th-c. view of the *Nl.* as a national monument. Heinzle, *Nibelungen*, vividly illustrates the astonishing range of the modern reception of the Nibelungen legend, with an introduction by Heinzle and articles on the national ideology it evoked (K. von See), Karl Simrock's translation (Heinzle), its place in education (W. Wunderlich), and in Göring's speech on the Battle of Stalingrad (P. Krüger), followed by four essays on artistic portrayal, and others on the relevant works by Hebbel, Wagner, and more recent authors and films. Japanese reception is the subject of S. Kishitani, *Fest. Hoffmann*, 97–114. M. Egerding, *Euphorion*, 85:397–408, analyses the action and motivation of the *Eckenlied*, and G. L. Strauch, *Exemplaria*, 3:67–94, studies the Jewish context of *Dukus Horant.*

THE COURTLY ROMANCE

Joachim Bumke, *Courtly Culture: Literature and Society in the High Middle Ages*, trans. Thomas Dunlap, Oxford — Berkeley, California U.P., ix + 771 pp., is an impressive and useful translation of *Höfische Kultur* (see *YWMLS*, 48:681–82). Based on the pragmatic assumption that even the idealization of literature has a basis in reality, B. uses an intimate knowledge of the texts to survey in detail the fundamental aspects of the society which produced it. The absence of jargon-ridden theorizing, such a notable feature of B.'s German style, assists D. in the production of a thoroughly readable English translation of rare quality. What makes this book so remarkable is that with its copious and accurate documentation it serves as a work of reference for the specialist scholar but at the same time can be recommended to students as the best general introduction to the period, or simply read for pleasure. In contrast to the densely printed two-volume paperback format of the original the text now receives the handsome layout it richly deserves. *Curialitas. Studien zu Grundfragen der höfisch-ritterlichen*

Kultur, ed. Josef Fleckenstein (Veröffentlichungen des Max-Planck-Instituts für Geschichte, 100), Göttingen, Vandenhoeck & Ruprecht, 1990, 500 pp., includes introduction and conclusion by F. and studies by P. G. Schmid (the Latin sources of *curia/curialitas*, 15–26), U. Mölk (the Romance adaptation of the same terms, 27–38), P. Ganz (*hövesch* and *hövescheit* in MHG, 39–54), L. Fenske (the education and role of the squire, 55–127), E. Orth (the forms and functions of knightly investiture, 128–70), W. Rösener (the courtly lady, 171–230), R. Schnell ('courtly' love as a 'courtly' discourse about love, 231–301), J. Fleckenstein (knights and clerics at court, 302–25), S. Krüger (the polarities *clerici-milites* and *litterati-illitterati*, 326–49), T. Szabó (the medieval court poised between criticism and idealization, 350–91), and T. Zotz (the medieval conception of *urbanitas*, 392–451). Aldo Scaglione, *Knights at Court. Courtliness, Chivalry, and Courtesy from Ottonian Germany to the Italian Renaissance*, Berkeley — Los Angeles — Oxford, California U.P., xi + 490 pp., is an impressively detailed study of the historical development of the courtly ethos and the values associated with it, taking a broadly sociological approach and repeatedly exemplifying the fact that the medieval literary monuments supply the best evidence for the subject-matter. The focus falls on France, Germany, and Italy. There are chapters on the early relationship between knighthood and nobility, the origins of the courtly codes, their literary transformations in the lyric and epic genres in France and Germany, the situation in Italy down to the Renaissance, and the courtier in the age of absolutism. All the major German classical works are drawn into the argument; the definition of courtliness is broad, so that the genetically archaic features of the *Nibelungenlied* and Gottfried's *Tristan* receive less recognition than in orthodox *Germanistik*. Although the vast, interdisciplinary scope of the field means that the treatment is inevitably selective and the arguments are sometimes only partly convincing for that reason, S. deploys large numbers of texts with ease and everywhere makes challenging statements about the social and cultural background which specialists in the different subjects will have to take seriously. N. Henkel, *Atken* (Tokyo), IX, 334–45, details the educational assumptions relevant to the background to the rise of the courtly romance, and P. Strohschneider, *ZDA*, 120:419–39, highlights abridged versions of courtly romances as a specific class of text.

In *Acta* (Louvain), D. Brewer surveys current trends in Arthurian scholarship (3–18), and A. Stones includes the Iwein murals at Rodenegg in a review of iconography (21–78), while I. Henderson, *Procs* (Kalamazoo), 123–49, comments on the Arthurian iconography in some 15th-c. MSS. T. Yamada, *DB*, 86:12–23, notes mythological aspects of the grail legend, and A. G. Martin, *Acta* (Louvain), 172–85, considers the 'rules' relating to magical episodes in *Parzival, Wigalois, Diu Crone*, and other romances. *An den Grenzen höfischer Kultur. Anfechtungen der Lebensordnung in der deutschen Erzähldichtung des hohen Mittelalters*, ed. Gert Kaiser (FGÄDL, 12), 266 pp., contains six interesting and imaginatively conceived studies of topics relating to the dangerous margins of courtly civilization. U. Küsters (9–75) looks at figures of sorrow and mourning and their behaviour in different situations in a wide range of courtly literature, while in an equally fruitful essay, B. Haupt (77–113) examines the theme of the healing of wounds. H. Brall (115–65) has a greater theoretical concern in his study of the strange and foreign (*altérité*), but still has good examples from the *Kaiserchronik*, Hartmann's *Erec* and *Iwein* (the wild man), and Wolfram's *Parzival* (Cundrie). P. Giloy-Hirtz (167–209) is on well-trodden paths in an account of monstrous beings, while A. Lehmann (211-36) has a more original subject, danger, fear and the overcoming of the latter. Finally, D. Matejovski (237–63) discusses the treatment of suicide in the context of its religious taboo. C. Lecouteux, *EG*, 46:293–304, surveys the sites forming the settings for adventurous incident, and J. P. McDonald, Chickering, *Chivalry*, 473–90, comments, at an elementary level, on chivalric education in *Parzival* and *Tristan*, while K. Grubmüller, Haug, *Positionen*, 1–20, considers the consequences of Guinevere's abduction for the figure of King Arthur in a number of romances, and R. Pérennec, *Acta* (Louvain), 230–35, examines the view of knighthood and kingship in *Erec* and the slaying of Ither in *Parzival* as comments on the texts from which they are 'adapted'. Also noted: Peter Meister, *The Healing Female in the German Courtly Romance* (GAG, 523), 1990, 186 pp. M. Wynn, *Fest. Engels*, 105–23, compares the crises of Iwein and Parzival with those of the heroes of Thomas Mann and Emily Brontë.

Silvia Brugger-Hackett, *Merlin in der europäischen Literatur des Mittelalters* (HS, S8), xii + 368 pp., is an extremely useful Stuttgart dissertation which fills an important gap in the German Arthurian tradition. The correct perspective is obtained on a figure largely unknown to the classical MHG authors by adopting an essentially interdisciplinary approach, so that there are substantial introductory chapters on Geoffrey of Monmouth and the reception and translation of his work, and on the incorporation of the Merlin figure in the Romance grail cycle. The Dutch, Low German, and Ripuarian works and fragments form an essential background to the understanding of the belated introduction of Merlin into MHG literature, in which the *Jüngerer Titurel* and Ulrich Füetrer prove the most significant names before a concluding treatment of other relevant texts from the 15th and early 16th cs. *Der Rheinische Merlin. Text, Übersetzung. Untersuchungen der 'Merlin'- und 'Lüthild'- Fragmente. Nach der Handschrift Ms.*

germ. qu. 1409 der Staatsbibliothek Preußischer Kulturbesitz Berlin, ed. Hartmut Beckers (Schöninghs mediävistische Editionen, 1), Paderborn, Schöningh, 160 pp., inaugurates a new series by publishing the recently rediscovered 324-line fragmentary text, with a translation on facing pages, of a largely unknown Lower Rhineland narrative which associates Merlin with an obscure local saint, Lüthild. There is a full codicological and linguistic analysis, and the text is accompanied by a complete facsimile print. The second part of the book, pp. 65–160, consists of studies by G. Bauer, T. Ehlert, H. Gillmeister, W. Herborn, T. Klein, P. Konietzko, R. Lüddecke, M. Newels, and K. Trimborn. These focus on the relationship of the fragment to the Merlin tradition as a whole, the historical background leading to a dating of the subject-matter to *c.* 1250–1300, and the affinity with other legendary works which identifies the fragment as a 'Legende'. Also on Merlin, see pp. 661–62 below.

  Tristan und Isolde im europäischen Mittelalter. Ausgewählte Texte in Übersetzung und Nacherzählung, ed. Danielle Buschinger and Wolfgang Spiewok (UB, 8702), 367 pp., is an attractive presentation of ten of the most important representative texts in the form of selected passages in translation interspersed with summaries of the content of the rest. The German tradition is represented by Eilhart, Gottfried, and the prose romance. Dagmar Mikasch-Köthner, *Zur Konzeption der Tristanminne bei Eilhart von Oberg und Gottfried von Straßburg* (HS, S7), 135 pp., makes occasional reference to the French sources but is chiefly concerned to compare and contrast the treatment by Eilhart and Gottfried respectively of the themes and episodes relevant to the conception of love. The study is concise but at the same time laboured; considering the quantity of earlier literature on this subject the bibliography is slight, and from the first page on the author focuses on the views of T. Tomasek on Gottfried (see *YWMLS*, 47:664), with which her own are explicitly said to converge (p. 106). Gottfried's failure to resolve the problem of love and society is, however, seen as having less future potential than Eilhart's radical reappraisal of existing values. The German Tristan romances are also treated comparatively by Silvia Grothues, *Der arthurische Tristanroman: Werkabschluß zu Gottfrieds 'Tristan' und Gattungswechsel in Heinrichs von Freiberg Tristanfortsetzung* (EH, 1, 1202), 175 pp., and by R. E. Brown, *Neophilologus*, 75:321–26, who discusses pregnancy, or rather its absence, in extramarital relations in the Tristan legend and in Classical literature, while W. Hoffmann, *Fest. Wisniewski*, 57–76, contrasts the different figures of Marke, and W. C. McDonald, *ZDA*, 120:393–418, studies the Marke figure in the Eilhart tradition, emphasizing his penance and remorse. R. Cormier, *ABÄG*, 34:67–76, points to the individual treatment of several motifs in Eilhart's version of the Tristan legend, and D. Buschinger, *Actes* (Amiens), 63–72, speculates on Eilhart and his work. Marion Mälzer, *Die Isolde-Gestalten in den mittelalterlichen deutschen Tristan-Dichtungen. Ein Beitrag zum diachronischen Wandel*, Heidelberg, Winter, viii + 293 pp., is a Kiel dissertation of which the major part consists of a comparison of the heroines in Eilhart and Gottfried; Ulrich von Türheim and Heinrich von Freiberg, and the other Isoldes, receive substantially less attention. The chief interest of the work is the review of the relatively dominant, active, and sexually independent role of women in the primitive Irish and Pictish societies in which the legend developed: M. argues that this aspect is still reflected in Eilhart's heroine before she leaves Ireland, but thereafter she is subordinated to the courtly Christian ideal of submissive womanhood. Gottfried's independent treatment shows parallels to the archaic, Celtic conception, while the continuations of Ulrich and Heinrich return to the Christian moralizing view with their warning against worldly passion. M. is less than wholly conversant with recent critical literature and it is questionable whether the topic can be adequately treated independently of the French texts, but this is a welcome and stimulating approach notwithstanding.

J. Goossens, *ZDA*, 120:1–65, edits and studies the Munich fragments of Veldeke's *Servatius*, and M. Dobozy, *Mediaevistik*, 2, 1989 (1991):81–96, comments on the interpretation of history in Veldeke's *Eneide*, while J. Bumke, *ZDA*, 119, 1990:404–34, supplies a diplomatic print of the 13th-c. fragments of Herbort von Fritzlar's *Liet von Troye*, continuing the study *ib.*, 120:257–304, and suggesting that the juxtaposition of two parallel versions is the rule rather than the exception for court epic in the 13th c. L. M. Gowans, *Acta* (Louvain), 79–86, associates the Arthurian scene in Modena with Ulrich von Zatzikhoven's *Lanzelet*.

Moderne Artus-Rezeption 18.–20. Jahrhundert, ed. Kurt Gamerschlag (GAG, 548), vi + 328 pp., contains 15 essays on reception in France, Germany, and the English-speaking world.

HARTMANN VON AUE

L. Okken, *ABÄG*, 34:77–109, supplies textual annotations on the latest edition of *Erec* (see *YWMLS*, 47:658–59), and R. Brandt, *ib.*, 153–55, also contributes to the debate on the text, while B. Edrich, *Beiträge* (Trier), 331–45, provides a computerized analysis of the Ambras MS, and R. A. Boggs, *ib.*, 205–13, explores a computer program for studying the epithets in Hartmann's *Erec*. E. M. Jacobson, *Seminar*, 27:121–35, sees both the language and the events of *Erec* as reflecting a Christian dualism, and G. See, *ib.*, 39–54, focuses on the sudden changes in the hero's behaviour as evidence of his immaturity. H. B. Willson, *Acta* (Louvain), 164–71, emphasizes *triuwe* and *staete* as key concepts in the portrayal of Enite, and M. Wis, *NMi*, 92:269–80, suggests that H. reveals personal knowledge of contemporary Hohenstaufen politics with his reference to Conne (*Erec* 2007: 'Iconium'). M. E. Kalinke, *BGDSL*, 113:67–88, shows the relationship of *Gregorius auf dem Stein* to the *Gregorius saga biskups*, and H.-J. Solms, *ZDP*, 110, *Sonderheft*: 110–40, studies the use of the verbal prefix *ge-* in *Gregorius* and *Iwein*. Corinna Dahlgrün, *Hoc fac et vives (Lk 10₂₈)* — *'vor allen dingen minne got'. Theologische Reflexionen eines Laien im 'Gregorius' und in 'Der arme Heinrich' Hartmanns von Aue* (HBG, 14), iv + 277 pp., sees H.'s intentions, though a layman, as paranetic and pastoral, and supplies a masterly survey of the chief aspects of 12th-c. theology and of the numerous biblical allusions in the works, leading to a definition of the particular characteristics of H.'s piety. A. Wolf, *Fest. Hoffmann*, 205–25, compares H.'s conception of the *mære* in *Iwein* with that of Chrétien, and R. Schnell, *DVLG*, 65:15–69, argues that Iwein's behaviour should be judged not according to objective moral norms but on the basis of Abelard's ethic of intention, while A. Masser, *Fest. Hoffmann*, 183–204, links Laudine's hasty marriage to Ascalon's slayer to H.'s crusade and the similar story of Princess Isabella of Jerusalem and Henry of Troyes, Count of Champagne.

WOLFRAM VON ESCHENBACH

Joachim Bumke, *Wolfram von Eschenbach* (SM, 36), 6th rev. edn, x + 301 pp., has almost doubled in size compared to the previous edition of 1981, and is an essential replacement. The additions are less striking in the bibliographical sphere — although vast tracts of recent literature have been included — than in the admirably detailed 'Handlungsanalysen' with which the chapters on each of the three great epics now commence, constituting an entirely new feature of the already indispensable handbook. W. Spiewok, *Actes* (Amiens), 255–73, discusses W.'s personality and poetic intentions, while W.'s authorial persona and its development in *Parzival* is studied by Peschel-Rentsch, *Skizzen*, 158–79. Chrétien de Troyes, *Le Roman de Perceval ou Le Conte du Graal. Der Percevalroman oder Die Erzählung vom Graal, Altfranzösisch/Deutsch*, trans. and ed. Felicitas Olef-Krafft (UB, 8649), 683 pp., is a most useful addition to the Reclam series: the complete text of W. Roach's edition with German prose translation on facing pages, a solidly informative section of notes occupying 120 pages, and bibliography which will take W. scholars straight into the essential literature. The only jarring note is struck by the 'Nachwort' which surveys the chief schools of interpretation but over-emphasizes the fashionable psychoanalytical approach of Lacan and others. W. Haug, *Acta* (Louvain), 236–58, argues that in *Parzival* W. consciously builds on and develops the model supplied by Chrétien, and S. Shitanda, *Akten* (Tokyo), V, 249–58, compares, very reductively, the cognitive structure of *P*.with that of Chrétien. Bernd Ulrich Hucker, *Kaiser Otto IV.* (Monumenta Germaniae Historica. Schriften, 34), Hanover, Hahn, 1990, xc + 760 pp. + 32 pls, includes *P*. among works allegedly written in the ambience of the Welf court of Otto IV. J.-M. Pastré, *GGF*, 11, 1989:116–23, associates W.'s stylistic *obscuritas* with Classical 'Asianism'; Id., *Parenté*, 233–45, studies indicators of kinship in *P*. D. Buschinger, *GGF*, 11, 1989:111–15, surveys the views of *minne* in the work, and A. Kruse and G. Rössler, *Fest. Wisniewski*, 123–50, review the semantic content and function of *triuwe*, while R. Weick, *Mediaevistik*, 2, 1989 (1991):255–69, discusses some ornithological details, and T. E. Hart, *Euphorion*, 85:342–86, analyses *P*. 114, 5 — 116, 4 and 337, 1–30, in terms of proportional and numerological structure. A. Groos, *BGDSL*, 113:384–414, interprets Cundrie's announcement (781–82), emphasizing its metaphysical and mythical dimension, and E. Schmid, *GRM*, 72:46–60, studies the Obie-Obilot episode in relation to Chrétien's version, while B. D. Haage, *Mediaevistik*, 1, 1988 (1990):39–59, shows how W. must have known alchemical sources. Id., *Fest. Hoffmann*, 149–69, links W.'s cosmological and medical learning to the school of Chartres, and J.-M. Pastré, *Le 'Cuer'*, 261–71, writes on the heart of the unicorn and the cure of Anfortas. H. Brunner, *GRM*, 72:369–84, comments on the structure of the conclusion of *P*., and J. Bumke, *DVLG*, 65:236–64, interprets the new subject-matter (Feirefiz, Prester John, Lohengrin) introduced at the conclusion in terms of an 'open ending'.

Wolfram von Eschenbach, *Willehalm. Nach der Handschrift 857 der Stiftsbibliothek St. Gallen. Mittelhochdeutscher Text, Übersetzung, Kommentar. Mit den Miniaturen aus der Wolfenbütteler Handschrift und einem Aufsatz von Peter und Dorothea Diemer*, ed. Joachim Heinzle (Bibliothek des Mittelalters, 9), DKV, 1293 pp. + 28 pls, supplies a complete text with line-by-line translation on facing pages. The edition will have a resonance greater than other titles in this prestigious series, for H. has used the occasion to present his own text according to recently propounded principles, here repeated in detail. There is no fundamental disagreement with Schröder to the extent that the adherence to the St Gall MS as the *Leithhandschrift* goes even further than in S.'s edition, but there are substantial differences in relatively superficial matters of presentation in an endeavour to align the new edition to the norms of classical MHG in appearance (long vowels are marked) and metre. The introductory material and annotations (pp. 789–1092) are sufficiently detailed to amount to a substantial commentary. The list of variants, a complete index of names, bibliography, and the essay of P. and D. Diemer on the MS illustrations, also reproduced, occupy the remainder of the enterprising volume. John Greenfield, *Vivianz. An Analysis of the Martyr Figure in Wolfram von Eschenbach's 'Willehalm' and in his Old French Source Material* (ES, 95), 263 pp., takes Carl Lofmark's study of Rennewart as its model and after defining the concept of martyrdom places Vivianz soundly against the background of the historical development of the Vivien figure of the possible sources, W.'s treatment of these in general leading to some observations of wider interest, as does the view that, notwithstanding the 'tolerance' idea, the ethical norms of *Willehalm* cannot be judged against the yardstick of *Parzival*. Both the action of the work involving Vivianz, and W.'s figure himself, are subjected to detailed analysis in the main body of the thesis. Christian Kiening, *Reflexion — Narration. Wege zum 'Willehalm' Wolframs von Eschenbach* (Hermaea, n.F., 63), Tübingen, Niemeyer, x + 276 pp., is a timely study which, following a period of detailed textual and thematic commentary on *Willehalm*, seeks to focus on the wider perspectives which constitute the narrative process of a work seen as highly complex. After chapters on the prologue in its relation to other courtly prologues and on the narrator and the audience, the 'horizons' of narrative reflection are explored under the headings literary, linguistic, communicative, and thematic. K. strikes a good balance between textual analysis and more theoretical generalization, convincingly illustrating the polarities between the archaic, alien subject-matter and the need to recast it for a German courtly audience, and between the narrative surface structure and the narrator's departure from this into personal comment and excursus. J. A. Rushing, *ZDA*, 120: 304–14, argues persuasively that *Willehalm* 3, 4–5 means that the hero risked the double death of both soul and body, and must therefore have risked damnation. J. Heinzle, *Fest. Hoffmann*, 171–82, studies the onomastics of *Willehalm*.

Albrecht Classen, *Utopie und Logos. Vier Studien zu Wolframs von Eschenbach 'Titurel'*, Heidelberg, Winter, 1990, 157 pp., contains four chapters originally conceived as separate essays, but inevitably with some interdependence; in any case all are of quite recent date, and all provide much food for thought. If provocative, the contention that W. drew on Andreas Capellanus's *De Amore* is not out of line with recent work on other MHG texts. It is for consideration whether the thesis is clarified by its subsequent association with the theories of R. Barthes. The wider problem of source, fictionality, and authority is then treated with Marie de France as a starting point, in a chapter which draws in many other works. The final chapter, which gives the book its title, is the broadest of all, and touches on fundamental questions of reading and understanding in the period. The thesis relating to Andreas Capellanus is also propounded by C. in *Procs* (Kalamazoo), 65–77.

W. Schröder, *ZDA*, 120:140–56, sets out prolegomena to a new edition of *Tristan*, and P. Sappler and W. Schneider-Lastin, *Beiträge* (Trier), 19–28, describe a computerized dictionary to the work, while Peschel-Rentsch, *Skizzen*, 108–206, focuses on Gottfried's authorial self-consciousness, and O. Ehrismann, *Fest. Hoffmann*, 115–34, shows how contemporary attitudes have conditioned the interpretation of *T*. J.-M. Pastré, *Actes* (Amiens), 217–33, notes the significance of John Scotus, Richard of St Victor and others as mediators of G.'s Neoplatonic ideas on perfection and beauty, and P. A. Thomas, *Neohelicon*, 15.2, 1988:187–206, refers to G. in the course of a survey of the medieval literary erotic tradition, while G. Schweikle, *Fest. Hoffmann*, 135–48, reconsiders the significance of the love-potion, and D. J. Levin, *NGR*, 5–6, 1989–90:56–74, studies the theme of recounting origins in the work. W. Lenschen, *Akten* (Tokyo), VI, 210–16, focuses on the importance of the father-figure, and W. C. McDonald, *NMi*, 92:159–78, associates the boar image with Tristan himself, while L. Okken, *ABÄG*, 33:131–36, compares *T*. 18965–19548 with passages from St Augustine's *Confessions*, and P. Strohschneider, *DVLG*, 65:70–98, studies the continuations to G.'s work and their significance for its reception. Dieter Kuhn, *Tristan und Isolde des Gottfried von Straßburg. Ulrich von Türheim. Tristan. Eine Fortsetzung*. Lambertus Okken, *Mitarbeit*, Frankfurt, Insel, 648 pp., tackles Gottfried in the imaginative manner characteristic of his earlier 'trilogy' on MHG poets, and is a no less interesting experiment. A 70-page biographical novel focuses on what can be assumed of G. on the basis of his work and likely social and educational background. There follows a complete translation, with which L. Okken has assisted, of both G.'s work and the continuation of Ulrich von Türheim. This is in unrhymed verse, following as far as possible the line-numbering of the original (which is included) and its syllable-count. There is a concluding essay on K.'s view of translation.

W. Fritsch-Rössler, *Fest. Hoffmann*, 227–54, interprets *Moriz von Craûn*, and J.-M. Pastré, *Procs* (Kalamazoo), 89–102, writes on the portrayal of Amurfina in Heinrich von dem Türlîn's *Diu Crône*, while M. Schilling, *Euphorion*, 85:273–91, places Stricker's *Daniel von dem blühenden Tal* against the background of the Vienna court, and A. Classen, *ABÄG*, 33:167–92, interprets the work as marking the transition of the Arthurian romance to the early modern novel of entertainment and didacticism. Monika Unzeitig-Herzog, *Jungfrauen und Einsiedler. Studien zur Organisation der Aventiurewelt im 'Prosalancelot'*, Heidelberg, Winter, 1990, 184 pp., is dedicated to the principle that the various *Prose Lancelot* texts in different languages form part of a tradition which must be studied in its totality and in relation to Chrétien's verse romance. The work is primarily concerned with the relationship of the major and minor figures, and begins with a comparative study of the episode of the cart, in which the reduction of the female minor figures is contrasted with their vast expansion in the prose version as a whole. There follow close comparative analyses of many other episodes and themes in the different books, attention being paid to the reader's expectations and perspective. The conclusions point to the superior knowledge of the female figures in their guiding role, this replacing the chance adventure of the verse romance. C. Huber, Haug, *Positionen*, 21–38, surveys the precarious unity of the *Prosa Lancelot*, and O. S. H. Lie, *Acta* (Louvain), 404–18, argues that the 15th-c. Blankenheim translation of part of its textual tradition points to a lost, fourth, Middle Dutch exemplar. M. Egerding, *ABÄG*, 34:111–25, makes conflict and crisis the basis of an interpretation of Konrad von Stoffeln's *Gauriel von Muntabel*. K. Nyholm, *Akten* (Tokyo), VII, 275–84, studies the presentation of the Orient in Albrecht's *Jüngerer Titurel*, and A. Lorenz, *Vorträge* (Liverpool), 162–72, considers the place of journeys between the Orient and Occident in the work, while L. Miklautsch, *GRM*, 72:214–23, writes on the figures of Arnive and Klingsor. W. Schröder, *BNF*, 26:282–96, records the onomastic connection of the *Göttweiger Trojanerkrieg* with Konrad von Würzburg's *Trojanerkrieg*.

Haug, *Positionen*, includes studies of several lesser-known late-medieval romances, including C. Cormeau on Der Pleier's *Tandareis und Flordibel* (39–53), B. K. Vollmann on Ulrich von Etzenbach's *Alexander* (54–66), D. Ohlenroth on *Reinfried von Braunschweig* (67–96), B. Wachinger on Heinrich von Neustadt's *Apollonius von Tyrland* (97–115), B. Weiske on the Apollonius version of the *Gesta Romanorum* (116–22), G. Vollmann-Profe on Johann von Würzburg's *Wilhelm von Österreich* (123–35), P. Sappler on *Friedrich von Schwaben* (136–45), M. G. Scholz on the lost *Johann aus dem Baumgarten*, with a transcription of the Middle Dutch *Joncker Jan wt den vergiere* (146–232), and F. Schanze on Hans von Bühel's *Die Königstochter von Frankreich*, with a facsimile print of the version of Cyriacus Schnauss (233–327). At the end of the book, which inaugurates what promises to be an important new series, W. Haug surveys and summarizes in broad outline the problems of postclassical narrative fiction. K. Cieslik, *GGF*, 11, 1989:102–10, writes on the LG *Flos unde Blankeflos*, and in *Actes* (Amiens), 73–84, considers the authors and patrons of *Mai und Beaflor* and Hans von Bühel's *Die Königstochter von Frankreich*, while P. Delorme, *ib.*, 95–103, comments similarly on *Wilhelm von Wenden*. S. Heimann, *Daphnis*, 20:703–09, describes a projected edition of *Malagis* from the Charlemagne epic cycle. Brigitte Schöning, *'Friedrich von Schwaben.' Aspekte des Erzählens im spätmittelalterlichen Versroman* (ES, 90), ix + 252 pp., is a Vienna dissertation which marks a substantial advance in work on this neglected late romance. S. revises the older judgements which associated it with the 'epigonal' cliché, while not falling into the trap of claiming the text is other than mediocre. Particularly important is the rejection of L. Voss's argument about MS interpolation, so that the text can now be interpreted as an entity, to which the themes of time and of political power and weakness lend support. S. also favours a dating to the late 14th or early 15th c. E. G. Fichtner, *ColGer*, 23, 1990:115–33, detects a numerological structure in Ulrich Füetrer's *Trojanerkrieg*.

LYRIC POETRY

The *Repertorium der Sangsprüche und Meisterlieder des 12. bis 18. Jahrhunderts*, Tübingen, Niemeyer, continues with volumes 6, 1990, 7, 1990, and 5. B. Schludermann and H. Bück, *Beiträge* (Trier), 75–84, discuss the problems of alphabetization created in the manufacture of computerized reference works by the mixture of MHG and Middle Dutch in the Hague Song MS. W. Hoffmann, *Mediaevistik*, 2, 1989 (1991):185–202, studies Minnesang in the urban environment, and G. Eifler, *Fest. Engels*, 1–22, refers to Gottfried in a treatment of the lyrical and artistic roles in the Minnesang, while A. Classen, *Mediaevistik*, 2, 1989 (1991):7–42, cites some examples from the Minnesang in a comparative study of the imagery of the game of love and life. Volker Held, *Mittelalterliche Lyrik und 'Erlebnis'. Zum Fortwirken romantischer Kategorien in der Rezeption der Minnelyrik* (Abhandlungen zur Sprache und Literatur, 23), Bonn, Romantischer Vlg, 1989, 246 pp. I. Kasten, *Vorträge* (Liverpool), 69–84, surveys the different approaches to travel in the medieval lyric, including the metaphorical journeys of life and death, and H.-J. Behr, *ib.*, 85–95, illustrates the element of asseveration which accompanies such lyric references. Hermann Apfelböck, *Tradition und Gattungsbewußtsein im deutschen Leich. Ein Beitrag zur Gattungsgeschichte mittelalterlicher musikalischer 'discordia'* (Hermaea, n.F., 62), Tübingen, Niemeyer, viii + 209 pp., marks a fundamental reappraisal of both the terminology and the genre of the *leich*. Beginning with the discrepancy between the thesis of the *leich* as essentially a borrowing of the Romance *lai*, and theories of its continuity from Old High German times. A. follows a review of previous work with a full investigation of the semantic evidence, which suggests that *leich* indicates a musical type of conflict or *discordia*. This leads to a revision of the various models proposed for the form: apart from the *Georgslied* the supposed Old and Early MHG examples are found to be unsuited to the new definition, which however reveals itself as the convincing basis for a substantial corpus of instances in the MHG epic (*Nibelungenlied*, *Parzival*) and throughout the later lyric tradition. This important work will certainly meet with a resonance in future scholarship. Norbert Haas, *Trinklieder des deutschen Spätmittelalters. Philologische Studien an Hand ausgewählter Beispiele* (GAG, 533) 344 pp.

E. Ukena-Best, *Fest. Wisniewski*, 151–66, interprets Albrecht von Johansdorf, MF 93, 12, and H. Heinen, *Procs* (Kalamazoo), 39–51, sees the E version of Rudolf von Fenis 84, 37, as Walther's reworking of the song, while the poetic persona in a range of lyrics of Morungen is the subject of Peschel-Rentsch, *Skizzen*, 129–57. Helmut Tervooren, *Reinmar-Studien. Ein Kommentar zu den 'unechten' Liedern Reinmars des Alten*, Stuttgart, Hirzel, 277 pp., marks an important stage in the understanding of the 25 neglected songs attributed to Reinmar. T. deals in turn with those only found under R.'s name, those attributed both to him and to others, and the unique case of 'Swel wîp wil, daz man si niht enzîhe' ascribed to R. only in scholarship since the 19th c. The commentary form, which T. explains as appropriate in order to collect, arrange, and compare the scholarly literature more objectively, is admirably justified in the present instance: indeed, it results in a work which will be indispensable for future research in the field. A particularly welcome feature is the inclusion of a translation of each song. The book also contains general comments on the problems of authentication and an essay in which T. seeks to draw the threads together and reach general conclusions, which on the whole support the recent re-evaluation of R. against the image of the literary histories.

S. K. Gertz, *Exemplaria*, 3 : 189–219, claims that Walther criticism is still dogged by biographical consideration, and seeks to focus on his attitude to the limits of conventions, while in similar vein C. Edwards, *Vorträge* (Liverpool), 96–109, argues that the documentation allegedly relating to Walther's travels is wholly inadequate for the construction of an itinerary. Theodor Nolte, *Walther von der Vogelweide. Höfische Idealität und konkrete Erfahrung*, Stuttgart, Hirzel, 363 pp., takes issue with the conventional critical dichotomy between the W. of the love-lyrics and the author of the didactic and political songs, and seeks to resolve this with an interpretation focusing on the poet's response to his real professional experience. The heart of the study is formed by detailed interpretation of the later political and religious songs and of the love-songs from the period of the *Preislied*. The relationship between poet, patron, and audience is seen as crucial, and among the many detailed themes which recur in the course of the study there is a welcome emphasis on W.'s self-image and on the importance of sarcasm, irony, and parody in his work. H. Wenzel, *StM*, 3:453–66 + 19 pls, studies the comparative iconography of the 'thinker' of the illustration of Walther in the Manesse MS and elsewhere, and U. Baltzer, *ZDA*, 120:119–39, examines W.'s strategies of persuasion in his didactic and political songs, while H. Brinkmann, *Arntzen Vol.*, 67–72, interprets the ironic dimension of L. 73, 23 'Die mir in dem winter', and H. Gummerer, *ÖGL*, 34, 1990:338–43, writes on the background to the 1889 W. monument in Bozen, the political and ideological significance of which is also the subject of *Walther. Dichter und Denkmal*, ed. Oswald Egger and Hermann Gummerer, Vienna, Per Procura, 1990, 155 pp.

U. Müller, *Acta* (Basel), 1–6, briefly surveys the problems of oral and written tradition fundamental to the Neidhart transmission, and S. Kotake, *DB*, 86:24–34, studies the Neidhart memorial in Vienna, while M. Curschmann, *Traditio*, 44, 1988:145–69, mentions Reinmar von Zweter's allegory of the ideal man in a study of text and image in the works of 12th-c. German theologians, and U. Kühne, *BGDSL*, 113:251–56, interprets a passage in a Latin strophe of Der Marner. K.-F. Kraft, *Fest. Wisniewski*, 167–90, interprets the imagery of Der Meissner's snake strophe (VIII, 2), and K. Stackmann, *Beiträge* (Trier), 4–18, describes the Frauenlob dictionary project, while H. J. Gernentz, *GGF*, 11, 1989:48–58, mentions Wizlaw III of Rügen in a study of the literature of Mecklenburg and Vorpommern, and I. Elter, *ZDA*, 120:65–73, investigates a newly-discovered late *Tagelied*. *Die Schulordnung und das Gemerkbuch der Augsburger Meistersinger*, ed. Horst Brunner, Waltraud Dischner, Eva Klesatschke, and Brian Taylor (Studia Augustana, 1), Tübingen, Niemeyer, x + 234 pp., for the first time presents the text of two documents of major importance in the history of the Meistersinger which complement the similar but more extensive records from Nuremberg. Taylor edits the *Schulordnung* of 1611; his brief but highly informative introduction both explains the history of the text and places the edition in the context of earlier research. The *Gemerkbuch* spanning the years 1610–1701 is edited by the other three authors whose tabulated history in the introduction vividly demonstrates the florescence and decline of the art. There are full indexes of names, melodies, and biblical passages.

DIDACTIC, DEVOTIONAL, AND RELIGIOUS LITERATURE

J.-M. Pastré, *Reinardus*, 4:147–55, finds a Baudouin to equate with the Baldewîn of *Reinhart Fuchs*. Helmut Herles, *Von Geheimnissen und Wundern des Caesarius von Heisterbach. Ein Lesebuch*, 2nd edn, Bonn, Bouvier, vi + 309 pp., is a handy translation of the *Dialogus miraculorum*. There is a substantial introduction, popularizing but at the same time detailed and informative, covering the Cistercian movement and some of its foundations, the background to Heisterbach and to the life of C., and an analysis of the work. A. Koeppel and P. W. Tax, *BGDSL*, 113:53–66, present a new Psalter fragment with MHG glosses. Konrad von Heimesfurt, '*Diu urstende*', ed. Kurt Gärtner and Werner J. Hoffmann. *Studienausgabe* (ATB, 106), ix + 86 pp., follows the new edition of Konrad's works (see *YWMLS*, 51:659), taking over the text, apparatus, and notes unabridged. While the reader needs the earlier edition for information on sources, codicology, and transmission, this text includes an introduction with the indispensable minimum required for practical study. In *Beiträge* (Trier), 148–54, G. and H. describe the computerized method used in their editing. K. Düwel, *Fabula*, 32:67–93, analyses the male and female literary models recorded by Thomasin von Zerclaere in his *Welscher Gast*. Both H. Beckers, *ZDA*, 120:314–22, and K. Klein, *ib.*, 202–09, document hitherto unknown fragments of Rudolf von Ems's *Barlaam und Josaphat*, while W. Hofmeister, *Sprachkunst*, 22:1–24, studies the *Winsbecke* parody. Ursula Will, *Der verschriftlichte Vortragsvers. Untersuchungen zur Metrik dreier Überlieferungen der 'Goldenen Schmiede' Konrads von Würzburg* (ES, 86), 226 pp., builds on the insight that the majority of the MSS of this work represent adaptations for functions remote from that intended for K.'s original text, and accordingly compares different versions with a view to establishing above all how metrical variations reflect the different functions, and especially oral or written reception. No direct development in the influence of the written form on the metre can be detected, but rather orthography and metre reflect the varying uses of literacy in the 13th, 14th, and 15th cs respectively. Reinhard Bleck, *Konrad von Würzburg: 'Der Welt Lohn'. In Abbildung der gesamten Überlieferung, synoptische Edition, Untersuchungen* (LittK, 112), xii + 167 pp.

Rudolf Weigand, *Vinzenz von Beauvais. Scholastische Universalchronistik als Quelle volkssprachiger Geschichtsschreibung* (GTS, 36), x + 378 pp., has a substantial introductory chapter on V.'s life and works which is of great value in its own right. The body of the study is introduced by a treatment of the ambivalent genre of the *Speculum Historiale*, characterized as both chronicle and encyclopaedia. The analysis of the content and structure of the work in its different versions is a prerequisite for an account of its transmission in Germany and the neglected vernacular tradition. The surprisingly limited dissemination of direct translations is explained by the nature of the work: unsuited to wholesale rendering in the vernacular, it rather maintained its status as a major Latin compendium from which German writers could draw on a piecemeal basis for whatever detailed information was required in a given context. K. Gärtner, *Acta* (Basel), 7–14, outlines the editorial problems presented by a projected new edition of the *Christherre-Chronik*, and U. Liebertz-Grün, *GeW*, 92:55–60, characterizes the Polish dimension of Ottokar von Steiermark's *Steirische Reimchronik*, while R. Sprandel, *DAEM*, 46, 1990:132–63, studies the *Kölner Weltchronik* and the chronicle of Albert Stuten, and O. J. Zitzelsberger, *AJGLL*, 3:57–96, a newly-discovered text relating to the Livonian Rhymed Chronicle. R. W. Leckie, *Euphorion*, 85:315–41, writes on Heinrich von Lammesspringe's *Magdeburger Schöppenchronik*, arguing that his view of the Black Death was modelled upon Orosius, while A.-D. von den Brincken, *Fest. Zimmermann*, 91–101, studies the chronicle of Martin von Troppau, and P. Hilsch, *ib.*, 103–15, the German translation of the Czech Dalimil chronicle. Joachim Schneider, *Heinrich Deichsler und die Nürnberger Chronistik des 15. Jahrhunderts* (Wissensliteratur im Mittelalter, 5), Wiesbaden, Reichert, 368 pp., is a substantial monograph on D. and his historiography.

B. A. Zimmermann, *FZPT*, 38:175–91, surveys recent work on Mechthild von Magdeburg. Mechthild von Magdeburg, *'Das fließende Licht der Gottheit.' Nach der Einsiedler Handschrift in kritischem Vergleich mit der gesamten Überlieferung herausgegeben*, ed. Hans Neumann. 1. *Text*, ed. Gisela Vollmann-Profe (MTU, 100), 1990, xxviii + 314 pp., is the first of two volumes of the major new edition which occupied N. for much of his lifetime. V.-P. has revised the text and added prefatory material including an account of the MSS and transmission, a broad review of the chief editorial problems and organization of the edition, an updating of the bibliography, and an index of proper names. The text is clearly laid out and easy to read against the apparatus, which is restricted to the diplomatic rendering of variants and the sources of accepted emendations to the text; the numerous other detailed suggestions for textual improvement are reserved for the notes and studies to appear in the second volume. K. Ruh, *ZDA*, 120:322–25, identifies the Dominican Wichmann von Arnstein (d. 1270), quoted by Mechthild and named by Johannes Tauler, and N. Largier, *Akten* (Tokyo), IX, 268–80, discusses the themes of alienation and self-discovery in Mechthild and in Hadewijch. Sabine B. Spitzlei, *Erfahrungsraum Herz. Zur Mystik des Zisterzienserinnenklosters Helfta im 13. Jahrhundert* (MGG, 1, 9), 201 pp., is a Freiburg dissertation treating the mysticism expressed in the works of Gertrude the Great and Mechthild of Hackeborn, in which the heart imagery plays a central role. S. emphasizes throughout that the subject-matter, which is inherently difficult to present in conventional logical terms — she describes it as 'spiral' rather than linear or circular — is nevertheless rooted in the daily life and practice of the 13th-c. Cistercian convent. There is substantial documentation of the background to the Helfta community, and its foundation, relationship to the other orders, and cultural and educational programme. The biblical and liturgical tradition is shown to be essential to an understanding of the *Legatus divinae pietatis* and the *Liber specialis gratiae*, and S. tackles squarely the problem of the alleged dichotomy between conventional linguistic formulation and the supposed 'originality' of mystical thought. This clarifies the attempt to depict the inner dimension of the piety of the convent, in which the meanings and functions of the heart form the focus of a sensitively and lucidly portrayed exposition of the depiction of the relations between man and God in the surviving works. Niklaus Largier, *Bibliographie zu Meister Eckhart* (Dokimion, 9), Fribourg U.P., 1989, xi + 153 pp., contains 1,491 items. Meister Eckhart, *Mystische Schriften*, ed. and trans. Gustav Landauer (IT, 1302), 204 pp., reissues an old, but still readable, translation of excerpts, with a very brief introduction and notes. The great majority of the texts are from the sermons. J. Margetts, *FMLS*, 27:113–25, comments on Eckhart's views on eternity, '*Die Blume der Schauung*', ed. Kurt Ruh (KDPM, 16), 99 pp., is the first edition since 1881 of an early-14th-c. tract of speculative theology in scholastic form. R. sees the particular importance of the neglected work in the fact that the author takes issue with the views of Meister Eckhart, who is referred to by name. There is a full codicological introduction, an analysis of the contents, and the text, occupying 42 pages, is accompanied by full annotations and followed by an apparatus of variant readings. W. Williams-Krapp, *LiLi*, 80, 1990:61–71, considers the Dominican rejection of mystical experience in the 15th c.

V. Mertens and H.-J. Schiewer, *Editio*, 4, 1990:93–111, discuss a programme for a repertory of late-medieval sermons accompanied by selected texts, and H. Kästner and E. Schütz, *Fest. Steger*, 19–46, place the *Buch der Rügen* at the centre of a study of new forms of late-medieval sermon. J. Knape, *Vorträge* (Liverpool), 141–61, studies the topographical implications of the *Historia apocrypha* of the *Legenda aurea* and the Ebstorf *mappa mundi*, and E. Feistner, *ZDP*, 110:337–48, associates Helwig's *Märe vom heiligen Kreuz* with the anti-Semitism of the Teutonic Order, while J. Goheen, *Procs* (Kalamazoo), 79–87, analyses the social distinctions and ethical norms in Hugo von Trimberg's *Der Renner*, and C. Huber, *Vorträge* (Liverpool), 110–24, studies his references to travel. R. H. Lawson, *Procs* (Kalamazoo), 113–21, characterizes Brother Hermann's *Leben der Gräfin Iolande von Vianden*, and G. J. Lewis, *Akten* (Tokyo), x, 201–11, records the authors of 14th-c. nuns' *vitae*, while E. Tipka, *Mediaevistik*, 2, 1989 (1991):225–53, writes on the same kinds of text, and the South German convents and their letters are also the subject of D. L. Stoudt, *MedS*, 53:309–26.

W. van Anrooij, *Spiegel van ridderschap. Heraut Gelre en zijn ereredes*, Amsterdam, Prometheus, 1990, 316 pp., includes the study of 14th-c. German heraldic and encomiastic literature. Work on a variety of 14th-c. topics includes D. Schmidtke, *Fest. Wisniewski*, 277–90, on the theme of melancholy in Hadamar von Laber's *Die Jagd*, K. Gärtner, *VB*, 9–10, 1987–88 (1991):97–106, on the translation of the Psalms in Heinrich von Mügeln's Psalm commentary, I. Heitel, *Daphnis*, 20:487–504, on Niklaus de Dybin's *Tractatus de rithmis*, and U. Störmer, 'Zur Autorschaft an dem Johann von Vippach zugeschriebenen Fürstenspiegel *Katherina divina* für Katharina, Markgräfin von Meißen', *Jb. für Regionalgeschichte*, 13, 1986:282–87. P. Assion, *Fest. Wisniewski*, 255–75, treats dogma and superstition on Purgatory and the spirits of the dead in late-medieval literature, and C. L. Gottzmann, *ib.*, 229–53, edits and studies a newly-discovered text of the *Heltauer Marienlied*, suggesting the work dates from before the 15th c.

The adaptation of theology to lay piety in the 15th c. is the subject of C. Burger, pp. 400–20 of *Lebenslehren und Weltentwürfe im Übergang vom Mittelalter zur Neuzeit. Politik — Bildung — Naturkunde — Theologie. Bericht über Kolloquien der Kommission zur Erforschung der Kultur des Spätmittelalters 1983 bis 1987*, ed. Hartmut Boockmann, Bernd Moeller, Karl Stackmann, and Ludger Grenzmann (AAWG, 179), 1989, 589 pp., a volume with a number of important studies of the cultural background. In *VB*, 9–10, 1987–88 (1991), N. F. Palmer (273–96) defines and classifies late-medieval lectionaries 'glossed' with sermons, H. Beckers (297–313) studies a Ripuarian pericope MS, G. Hayer (314–24) records German evangeliaries in the library of St Peter, Salzburg, and N. Henkel (325–35) documents an example from St Zeno, Reichenhall. G. Kornrumpf (115–31) studies the anonymous 'Klosterneuburger Evangelienwerk', while K. Gärtner and B. Schnell (155–71) point to newly-discovered textual evidence of the work, as does F. Löser (132–54) for the 'Schlierbach Old Testament'. W. J. Hoffmann (216–72) edits an East Middle German translation of the *Evangelium Nicodemi*, and N. Henkel (172–80) studies the translation of the Apocalypse in the 15th c., while M. Wallach-Faller (336–49) examines Bible citations in the oldest German prose legendary (Solothurn Codex S 451), and C. Wulf (385–99) analyses the titles, summaries, and editorial accompaniment to pre-Lutheran

Bible translations. G. Kornrumpf (350–74) comments on two Austrian 14th-c. *Historienbibeln*, and C. Brandt (375–84) analyses the form and function of their transmission of the Book of Daniel, while U. von Bloh (450–70) studies the relationship between text and illustration in the genre. K.-A. Wirth (471–533) makes the *Biblia pauperum* the basis for a study of the tradition of the Queen of Sheba. Christine Wulf, *Eine volkssprachige Laienbibel des 15. Jahrhunderts. Untersuchung ind Teiledition der Handschrift Nürnberg, Stadtbibliothek, Ms. Solg. 16.2°* (MTU, 98), xii + 264 pp., a Göttingen dissertation from the school of Karl Stackmann, has a concise but admirably detailed introduction to the prose Bible translations of the 14th and 15th cs, within which the importance of the chosen MS is identified: it contains Joshua, Judges, and Ruth, the text of each book based on the Mentel Bible but accompanied by a prologue and illustrations. Comparisons are made with a substantial number of MSS and early prints, the prologues and illustrations are studied in detail, and conclusions are drawn about the function of a partial Bible in German designed for lay use. The edited text is accompanied by fairly detailed notes. Taken together, the whole body of material conveys an excellent impression of the dissemination of the Bible in the vernacular at the end of the Middle Ages. I. Schröder, *Kbl*, 98:24–26, comments on the language of a MLG Bible translation of *c.* 1480, and K.-E. Geith, *Fest. Steger*, 47–59, discusses techniques of translation in 15th-c religious literature.

V. Honemann, Haug, *Autorentypen*, 69–88, characterizes the life and work of Johannes Rothe in Eisenach, and H. Meyer, *ZDA*, 119, 1990:434–53, studies an encyclopaedic work of *c.* 1440 at Klosterneuburg, while H. D. Schlosser, *Fest. Hoffmann*, 291–308, finds a political dimension in Hermann of Sachsenheim's *Mörin*. Ute Obhof, *Das Leben Augustins im 'Niederrheinischen Augustinusbuch' des 15. Jahrhunderts. Überlieferungs- und Textgeschichte. Teiledition*, Heidelberg, Winter, 211 pp., is a Heidelberg dissertation conceived as merely the prolegomena to a full edition of a 15th-c. life of St Augustine found in German and Dutch translations of a Latin *vita*. O. supplies a full account of the MSS, their relation to the Latin, and transmission, with specimens of the text, and also includes much interesting literary information on the evidence for the background to the MSS and their function. Approximately half the study is concerned with the editorial problems and an edition covering about 12 per cent of the Lower Rhine version. P. E. Webber, *Procs* (Kalamazoo), 151–61, surveys the contents of the 15th-c. devotional anthology in the Huntington Library, MS HM 195. Gunhild Roth, *Sündenspiegel im 15. Jahrhundert. Untersuchungen zum pseudo-augustinischen 'Speculum peccatoris' in deutscher Überlieferung* (DLA, 12), vii + 260 pp., clarifies the confusion surrounding the title of this body of texts, distinguishing them from comparable works with a catechetical basis, and places the related scholarship on a completely new footing. R. documents 532 MSS of the Latin text and 43 with German versions, besides those with translations into other languages. There is much valuable information on the dating and attribution of different MSS and their relation to the original, the audience and the reception of the material, and — of particular interest for the literary context — a comparison with similar contemporary works such as Heinrich von Langenstein's *Erchantnuzz der sund* and *De veer utersten*. Specimen texts of the German and Latin are added and there are full indexes. Dorothee Esser, '*Ubique Diabolus* — *Der Teufel ist überall.*' *Aspekte mittelalterlicher Moralvorstellungen und die Kulmination moralisierender Tendenzen in deutschen und niederländischen Weltgerichtsbildern des 15. Jahrhunderts* (ES, 87), x + 248 pp., is essentially a study of the interaction of 15th-c. text and iconography relating to the Last Judgement. The emphasis falls more heavily on painting, but a discussion of *Des Teufels Netz* is central to a review of the chief forms of literary expression relevant to the theme. The symbolic representation of virtues and vices is prominent in the pictorial analysis which culminates in Hieronymus Bosch and records the shifting attitudes created by the rise of humanism. *Nicholas of Cusa: In Search of God and Wisdom. Essays in Honor of Morimichi Watanabe by the American Cusanus Society*, ed. Gerald Christianson and Thomas M. Izbicki (Studies in the History of Christian Thought, 45), Leiden, Brill, xvi + 298 pp., is accompanied by E. Methuen, pp. 421–29 of *Lebenslehren und Weltentwürfe* (see p. 654 above), studying Nicholas's Germany journey in 1451–52. *Heinrich Hallers Bibelzitate*, ed. Erika Bauer, Heidelberg, Winter, 508 pp., continues her long-standing publication on this author with a complete compendium of the translations from the Bible found in H.'s works. B. emphasizes that H. translated directly from his immediate sources independently of other German translations, and that his renderings are spontaneous to the extent that he translates the same quotation anew on each successive occasion. At the same time the work is intended as a contribution to the history of pre-Lutheran German Bible translation. The text occupies pp. 41–262; it is arranged in straightforward biblical order for ease of reference. It is followed by German–Latin and Latin–German word indexes, and reverse indexes of forms. The introduction includes substantial analysis of H.'s linguistic practice in his Bible translation. B. once again writes on H.'s translation activity, pp. 212–19 of *Die Ausbreitung kartäusischen Lebens und Geistes im Mittelalter* (Analecta Cartusiana, 63), I, 1990, 250 pp.

    DRAMA. H. Linke, Simon, *Theatre*, 207–24, surveys medieval German dramatic texts. C. van den Wildenberg-de Kroon, *ABÄG*,

34:143–51, divides MSS of religious plays into those intended for performance and those intended for reading. Dorette Krieger, *Die mittelalterlichen deutschsprachigen Spiele und Spielszenen des Weihnachtsstoffkreises* (BSDL, 15), 1990, x + 472 pp. U. Hennig, *Fest. Wisniewski*, 211–27, notes the participation of women in Easter rites in Germany, England, and France. *Das Brandenburger Osterspiel. Fragmente eines neuentdeckten mittelalterlichen geistlichen Osterspiels aus dem Domarchiv in Brandenburg/Havel*, ed. and comm. Renate Schipke and Franzjosef Pensel (Beiträge aus der Deutschen Staatsbibliothek, 4), Berlin, Deutsche Staatsbibliothek, 1986, iv + 98 pp. H. Linke, *BGDSL*, 113:415–25, rejects the conception of a Vorau Easter Play, and M. Stevens, *NLH*, 22:317–37, mentions the Lucerne Easter Play in a study of the affinities of medieval art and drama, while C. Dauven-van Knippenberg, *ZDA*, 120:439–51, analyses the different traditions of the piercing of Christ's side in the Passion plays, and J. Nowé, *Fest. Verbeeck*, 159–75, discusses dramatic and stage technique in the Alsfeld Passion Play. W. McConnell and I. Henderson, 'Das Weltgerichtsspiel der Sammlung Jantz mit der Donaueschinger Variante Handschrift Nr. 136', *JWGV*, 92–93, 1988–89:223–321, supply introduction, edition, and notes. K. K. Polheim, *Editio*, 3, 1989:41–75, exemplifies the problems of editing religious folk dramas, affirming the need to treat them like medieval plays.

I. ten Venne, *GGF*, 11, 1989:89–102, points to the realistic features of secular drama. M. Siller, *Beiträge* (Trier), 256–66, outlines a project for the computerized analysis of *Fastnachtspiel* texts. E. Simon, *Akten* (Tokyo), VII, 322–28, identifies Turkish polemic in the *Fastnachtspiel* after 1453, and I. ten Venne, *Actes* (Amiens), 335–45, writes on Hans Folz's examples of the genre.

SCIENTIFIC AND SPECIALIZED LITERATURE

Nigel F. Palmer and Klaus Speckenbach, *Träume und Kräuter. Studien zur Petroneller 'Circa instans'- Handschrift und zu den deutschen Traumbüchern des Mittelalters* (Pictura et poesis, 4), Cologne, Böhlau, 1990, x + 318 pp., present detailed studies of a collective MS from Petronell (Hainburg) which includes the mid-12th-c. pharmacological herbarium 'Circa instans' besides three different types of dream book, a type of text otherwise only associated in a similar way in a 16th-c. printed book. There is an introduction to the Petronell MS and its relationship to two other illustrated MSS in the same hand; a study of the herbarium and partial edition; a classification of the different types of German dream book, and comments on their reception; a study and edition of the German prognosticative texts of the Petronell MS, with conclusions; and a facsimile of the German print of 1537. The material is attractively presented and accompanied by full biblio-graphy and indexes. B. Schnell, *ZDA*, 120:184–202, studies the *Prüller Kräuterbuch*, the earliest herbarium in German. In Ehlert, *Haushalt*, M. Lemmer (181–91) reviews the approach to the house-hold and family in works of domestic economy, and E. Barlösius (207–18) cites cookery books on the role of the cook, while H.-J. Raupp (245–68) studies an interesting collection of illustrations to works dealing with domestic matters, and G. Keil (219–43) docu-ments the tradition of works such as Ortolf von Baierland's *Arzneibuch* intended to give guidance on medicine in the home. O. Riha and W. Fischer, *Mediaevistik*, 1, 1988 (1990):175–83, consider editorial prob-lems in the new edition of Ortolf von Baierland's *Arzneibuch*, and P. Stahl, *Beiträge* (Trier), 142–47, applies computerized editorial tech-niques to the same treatise. G. Keil, *ZDA*, 119, 1990:453–54, ejects the supposititious medical author 'Hasso Schertlin' from the first edition of the *Verfasserlexikon*, and C. Baufeld, *GGF*, 11, 1989:29–34, discusses the syntactical usage in UB Greifswald, 8° MS 875, a collection of largely medical texts, while U. Schulze, *ZDP*, 110, *Sonderheft*: 140–70, studies 13th-c. documents as evidence of syntac-tical structures, and G. Roth, *Vorträge* (Liverpool), 228–39, illustrates the trading journeys undertaken by Breslau merchants in the 15th and 16th cs on the basis of legal texts. I. T. Piirainen, *Beiträge* (Trier), 267–73, considers the possibility of the computerized analysis of Early NHG legal and other documents in Slovakia.

OTHER LATER MEDIEVAL LITERATURE

R. Krohn, *Fest. Hoffmann*, 255–76, traces the changing conception of knighthood in the German fabliaux. H. Linke, *Fest. Engels*, 23–45, studies the textual transmission of Stricker's *Pfaffe Amis*, while there is a new edition, *Der Pfaffe Amis. Ein Schwankroman aus dem 13. Jahrhundert in zwölf Episoden von dem Stricker*, ed. and trans. Hermann Henne (GAG, 530), 149 pp. A. Classen, *NMi*, 92:105–22, argues that the attitudes to women in Stricker's fabliaux are far from the traditional misogynistic ones. *Gesta Romanorum. Lateinisch/Deutsch*, ed. and trans. Rainer Nickel (UB, 8717), 275 pp., has a selection of 45 stories with translations on facing pages, largely following H. Oesterley's text, variants from which are listed. There is an excellent short introduc-tion which characterizes the technique of the texts, including their use of allegory and number symbolism.

Rolf Ulbrich, *Der alttschechische 'Tkadleček' ('Der Weber')*. *In deutscher Übersetzung*, Berlin, 1990, 109 pp. (available from Corneliusstr. 3, 1000 Berlin 46), is a useful *samizdat* publication which for the first time makes available in a lucid translation the Czech text of *c*. 1407 of evident importance for the study of the *Ackermann aus Böhmen*. U. includes a brief introduction to the work and its background and notes on particular difficulties. There is work on the *Ackermann aus Böhmen* by P. Walther, *GGF*, 11, 1989:137–44 (interpretation of the basis of the widower's complaint), A. Classen, *ZDP*, 110:348–73 (Renaissance features), and C. Kiening, *Akten* (Tokyo), VI, 183–95 (reception). Heinrich Wittenwiler, *Der Ring. Frühneuhochdeutsch/ Neuhochdeutsch. Nach dem Text von Edmund Wiessner*, trans. and ed. Horst Brunner (UB, 8749), 696 pp., is an important addition to the Reclam series which fully matches the expectations aroused by medieval titles added in the past few years. The translation on pages facing W.'s text, which includes an indication of the red and green marginal lines, is a lucid prose intended to be accurate but also to be readable without reference to the original. Text and translation of *Der Bauernhochzeitsschwank* are included, together with a body of notes, bibliography, 'Nachwort', and index of proper names; the importance of Eckart Conrad Lutz's recent study (see *YWMLS*, 52:635) is everywhere apparent. M. Dallapiazza, Ehlert, *Haushalt*, 167–80, places W. at the centre of a survey of texts relating to the discussion of problems of domestic management, and J. M. Ogier, *Seminar*, 27:1–11, studies his satirical view of astrology, while C. Händl, *ZDP*, 110:98–112, examines the literary function of Neidhart's appearance at the peasants' tournament.

G. F. Jones, *Beiträge* (Trier), 245–49, surveys the 'text word analyser' program applied to Oswald von Wolkenstein and other later-medieval authors, and A. Schwob, *Fest. Zimmermann*, 159–72, shows how recently discovered documents confirm the realism of the detailed references to his life and background in O.'s songs, while U. M. Schwob, *ib.*, 607–21, also refers to O. in the course of a study of Georg Stubier, Bishop of Brixen (1437–43). W. Neuhauser, *Der Schlern*, 65:491–503, links O. to Tyrolean bibliographical history, and E. C. Lutz, *LJb*, 32:39–79, identifies structural patterns in his work. *Johann Hartliebs 'Alexander'*, introd. and ed. Reinhard Pawis (MTU, 97), viii + 367 pp., is a timely replacement of Richard Benz's modernizing edition of 1924, following hard on R. Schnell's edition of the Latin text (*YWMLS*, 51:629–30) which is virtually identical with H.'s source. The codicological evidence points to the St Gall Cod. 625 as the MS closest to the author's original, and there is much of interest on the background to the MS dissemination of the work in the narrow period 1454–77, following which printed versions are traced to as late as 1670. The edition occupies pages 96–338: it follows the *Leit-handschrift*, the apparatus indicating significant variants besides a concordance with the Latin text. Ingeborg Spriewald, *Literatur zwischen Hören und Lesen. Wandel von Funktion und Rezeption im späten*

Mittelalter. Fallstudien zu Beheim, Folz und Sachs, Berlin — Weimar, Aufbau, 1990, 276 pp., contains three substantial interpretative essays on each of the three poets, seen as representative of the three generations in the century from 1450 on, and focusing primarily on the *Reimpaardichtung* as the expression of a form of reception poised between orality and literacy. Supplementary material includes 12 plates and the texts of Folz's *Pestspruch* with its source and of Johann Ohnsorg's *Hausratspruch*. W. J. Jones, *MLR*, 86:89–108, comments on the *Liber ordinis rerum*, *Vocabularius Ex quo*, and other 15th-c. lexicographical works, while H.-J. Stahl, *Beiträge* (Trier), 214–37, documents the applications of computer technology to the *Vocabularius Ex quo* edition (*YWMLS*, 50:714; 51:661), and E. Bremer and K. Ridder, *ib.*, 168–76, make the *Vocabularius optimus* edition (see *YWMLS*, 52:632) the basis of a discussion of computerized editorial methods. Also noted: Robert Damme, *Das Stralsunder Vokabular. Edition und Untersuchung einer mittelniederdeutsch-lateinischen Vokabularhandschrift des 15. Jahrhunderts* (NdS, 34), 1988 (1989), vii + 524 pp. K.-E. Geith, *Akten* (Tokyo), XI, 75–84, discusses the presentation of the Armagnac invaders of Alsace in 1439 and 1444–45.

Work on travel literature abounds. Klaus Ridder, *Jean de Mandevilles 'Reisen'. Studien zur Überlieferungsgeschichte der deutschen Übersetzung des Otto von Diermeringen* (MTU, 99), xi + 421 pp., has an introductory chapter on the generic classification of late-medieval travel literature in general and of M.'s narrative in particular. The body of the thesis is a full textual history of the most influential of the three translations current in Germany and the Low Countries. Descriptions of MSS, fragments, and early printed versions occupy 117 pages. Comparison with the possible source-versions emphasizes the fluid nature of the text, and the translator is identified as a member of a well-attested family from Metz. The problems of his intentions and the function of the translation are placed in the linguistic, literary, and cultural context of Lorraine in the late 14th c., and the wider historical significance of the work is developed by the study of its subsequent reception. X. von Ertzdorff, *Fest. Engels*, 46–63, discusses the German reception of Marco Polo in the 14th and 15th cs, and A. Simon, *Vorträge* (Liverpool), 173–84, examines the experience of travel in 15th-c. pilgrimage reports, while V. Honemann, *ib.*, 306–26, studies the attitudes displayed by Hans Rot in his account of his pilgrimage to the Holy Land (1440). P. A. Jorgensen and B. M. Ferré, *ZDP*, 110:406–21, establish a stemma of the MSS of Arnold von Harff's travelogue, the Breton vocabulary of which is examined by K. Siewert. *ZCP*, 44:239–72. Further examples of interest in pilgrimage literature and travelogues are to be found in *Akten* (Tokyo), VII, with contributions by D. Huschenbett (the problem of tradition, 296–306),

H. Kästner (the marvels of Egypt, 307–16), D. Wuttke (humanism and the age of discovery, 317–21), and M. E. Kalinke (Iceland, 329–38).

Bodo Gotzkowsky, *'Volksbücher': Prosaromane, Renaissancenovellen, Versdichtungen und Schwankbücher. Bibliographie der deutschen Drucke. 1. Drucke des 15. und 16. Jahrhunderts* (Bibliotheca Bibliographica Aureliana, 125), Baden-Baden, Koerner, 603 pp., seeks to update and replace the 1924 bibliography of Heitz and Ritter; not surprisingly, in view of the survey of subsequent literature in the introduction, large numbers of texts are included which were wholly unknown to the earlier work. G. distances himself from the problems of definition relating to the 'Volksbuch', classifying the material into seven major divisions: adaptations from Italian models; from French; from Humanist Latin and Classical sources; *exempla* and similar didactic literature; adaptations of medieval German works; works on 'German' themes, including *Faustbuch* and *Fortunatus*; and 20 collections of fabliaux. Within each section the works are numbered and supplied with introductions, following which the individual prints are numbered chronologically. The bibliographical descriptions are informative and clearly laid out. Id., *GJ*, 66:157–71, summarizes the locations of 15th-c. and later chapbooks, and F. Simmler, *Daphnis*, 20:457–86, studies the generic development of the prose romance on the basis of linguistic theory. Besides a lengthy linguistic study of Ingrid Baumann-Zwirner, *Der Wortschatz Augsburger Volksbuchdrucke der Inkunabelzeit im Vergleich mit dem südwestdeutscher Paralleldrucke* (EH, 1, 1215), 604 pp., the reception of German chapbooks in Scandinavia is the subject of H. Seelow, *Akten* (Tokyo), xi, 385–92, while L. Petzoldt, *Fest. Engels*, 64–82, discusses the transmission of the Griseldis theme, and *Pontus und Sidonia* is studied by Reinhard Hahn, *'Von frantzosischer zungen in teütsch.' Das literarische Leben am Innsbrucker Hof des späteren 15. Jahrhunderts und der Prosaroman 'Pontus und Sidonia' (A)* (Mikrokosmos, 27), Frankfurt, Lang, 1990, 248 pp.; Id., *Vorträge* (Liverpool), 215–27, surveys the geography and topography of the work; and by M. Zimmermann, *Acta* (Louvain), 388–96, who examines the fate of the Arthurian elements.

Melusine emerges this year as a proto-feminist. Thüring von Ringoltingen, *Melusine. In der Fassung des Buchs der Liebe (1587)*, ed, Hans-Gert Roloff (UB, 1484), 176 pp., again makes available a text first issued in this form in 1969. It is accompanied by woodcuts, bibliography, and supplementary material in which R. surveys the textual, historical, and literary background to the work. Bea Lundt, *Melusine und Merlin im Mittelalter. Entwürfe und Modelle weiblicher Existenz im Beziehungs-Diskurs der Geschlechter. Ein Beitrag zur Historischen Erzählforschung*, Munich, Fink, 376 pp., a Bochum dissertation, is not the first feminist study to transform Melusine from a demonic seductress to the major medieval 'Symbolgestalt für weibliche Selbstbestimmung jenseits gesellschaftlicher Normen'. Merlin is seen as her counterpart, a male intellectual confronted by the heroic ideal. L. devotes short chapters to each of the chief literary manifestations of these figures, including the relevant works of Marie de France, Walter Map, Konrad von Würzburg, Egenolf von Staufenberg, Thüring von Ringoltingen, Johann Fischart, Geoffrey of Monmouth, Robert de Boron, Johann von Würzburg, and Ulrich Füetrer. The summaries of content are useful but reinforce the general tendency to read much of the psychology of folklore into widely differing literary treatments; when L. diagrees with the more conventional treatments of earlier critics or of the medieval authors themselves, all alike are dismissed as products of their own age. One might suppose that contemporary women academic writers of this ilk are merely parading their own psychological difficulties of reconciling 'Lernen und Lieben'. A. Mühlherr, Haug, *Positionen*, 328–37, considers the historical and literary background to Thüring von Ringoltingen's *Melusine*, arguing that the notion of a radical shift in perspective in comparison with the source must be revised, and G. S. Williams, *Daphnis*, 20:81–100, comments on sexuality and magic in *Melusine* and in Paracelsus. *Undinenzauber. Geschichten und Gedichte von Nixen, Nymphen und anderen Wasserfrauen*, ed. Frank Rainer Max, introd. Eckart Klessmann, Stuttgart, Reclam, 432 pp., is an attractive collection of 35 texts dealing with mermaids and similar watersprites, all female. Although Paracelsus's *Liber de nymphis* is the earliest work cited and the book takes Fouqué's *Undine* as its literary point of departure, the introductory material traces the form back to the medieval Melusine legend, the reception of which is again the subject of Matthias Vogel, *'Melusine . . . das läßt sich aber tief blicken.' Studien zur Gestalt der Wasserfrau in dichterischen und künstlerischen Zeugnissen des 19. Jahrhunderts* (EH, XXVIII, 101), 1989, 235 pp.

D. Wuttke, *Gymnasium*, 97, 1990:232–54, characterizes the natural sciences in German Renaissance humanism, and P. Weinig, *ZDA*, 120:73–82, draws attention to a contemporary translation of Aeneas Silvius Piccolomini's *De curialium miseriis*, while G. Dicke, *ib*., 156–84, contributes to the biography of Heinrich Steinhöwel, and K. Wende, *BW*, 24, 1990:139–253, traces the genesis of the text and illustrations of S.'s printed prose translation of Aesop's fables. G. Bauer, *Fest. Hoffmann*, 351–71, documents Geiler von Kaysersberg's use of paired synonyms, while H. Brunner, Haug, *Autorentypen*, 89–103, compares Johann von Soest and Willibald Pirckheimer as types of author of their period, and G. Satzinger, *ib*., 104–29, studies the evidence of Dürer's development from craftsman to artist. K. Schuh, *Imagination*, 6.2:26–29, introduces Hartmann Schedel's universal chronicle, and

W. Spiewok, *GeW*, 92:61–73, outlines its portrayal of Poland, while P. Zahn, *GJ*, 66:177–213, studies the 1509 print of the work, and B. Schnell, *Sudhoffs Archiv*, 75:44–57, discusses Hartmann and Hermann Schedel together with Johannes Hartlieb as medical practitioners with literary interests.

Manfred Vischer, *Bibliographie der Zürcher Druckschriften des 15. und 16. Jahrhunderts erarbeitet in der Zentralbibliothek Zürich* (Bibliotheca Bibliographica Aureliana, 124), Baden-Baden, Koerner, 558 pp., arose in connection with a recataloguing of the library. The material is organized chronologically according to the earliest dates recorded for the activity of the different printers. V. emphasizes the relative paucity of printing activity in 15th-c. Zurich, confined to Sigmund Rot; a preface explains the background to the rise of printing in the Reformation period. The indexes, essential to this standard reference work, give full information on authors and titles of works, subsidiary authors, editors, translators, and printers, the provenance of the Zurich copies of the books, and dedicatees and owners. *Printing the Written Word. The Social History of Books, circa 1450–1520*, ed. Sandra Hindman, Ithaca — London, Cornell U.P., xiii + 333 pp., contains ten essays which together form an admirably illuminating account of the cultural background to the period of early printing. The German printers are prominent in several of the studies, including those of S. Edmunds on the scribes who became printers, M. Tedeschi on the career of Lienhart Holle in Ulm, E. König on the development of illuminated imprints in Mainz, L. Hellinga on the importation into England of books printed on the Continent, P. Saenger and M. Heinlen on the implication for the understanding of 15th-c. reading habits of incunable description, and T. Nellhaus on the blockbook versions of the *Biblia pauperum*. Otherwise the focus of the volume, which is richly and relevantly illustrated, tends to fall on Paris and Venice. A. Fujii, *Akten* (Tokyo), III, 49–59, discusses the printer Günther Zainer's graphemic usage. Silvia Pfister, *Parodien astrologisch-prophetischen Schrifttums 1470–1590. Textform — Entstehung — Vermittlung — Funktion* (Saecula Spiritalia, 22), Baden-Baden, Koerner, 1990, 684 pp., a Bamberg dissertation, is the first comprehensive study of the parodistic and satirical literature, mostly but not exclusively in the form of broadsheets and pamphlets, evoked by the different kinds of almanac literature of the period. There is a useful introductory review of the implications of the terminology of parody, satire, the comic, the grotesque, etc., and the classification of the 'genuine' and 'receptive' or derivative forms occupies a lengthy but necessary second chapter which touches on many familiar authors and texts from the *Narrenschiff* on. An account of the origin, diffusion, and influence of the parodies is followed by an attempt to analyse their function, which varies from the fundamental satirical purpose of moral improvement by way of attacks on meddlers in medicine and astrology to downright religious confessional polemic. A final chapter focuses on the background to the particular problem of astrology, its history and its association with *curiositas* and superstition. There is a new facsimile text, *Malleus Maleficarum von Heinrich Institoris (alias Kramer) unter Mithilfe Jakob Sprengers aufgrund der dämonologischen Tradition zusammengestellt. Wiedergabe des Erstdrucks von 1487 (Hain 9238)*, ed. André Schnyder (LittK, 113), 24 + 6 + 258 pp. Brigitte Schulte, *Die deutschsprachigen spätmittelalterlichen Totentänze. Unter besonderer Berücksichtigung der Inkunabel 'Des dodes dantz', Lübeck 1489* (NdS, 36), 1990, ix + 330 pp., is an excellent dissertation from Münster which effectively places a global study of the subject within a scholarly framework. The first half of the book surveys numerous aspects of the historical, social, and cultural background of the phenomenon and its relationship to late-medieval theology, besides its psychological significance. The second half reviews what is known of the medieval textual witnesses to the tradition, culminating in a more detailed study of the Lübeck text of 1489 which is seen as exemplary of the genre. Irmgard Jaeger, *'Speygel des dodes.' Der spätmittelalterliche Totentanz von Lübeck (1489)* (ES, 81), 1989, iv + 280 pp., is an Aachen dissertation which begins with brief chapters on the historical, social, and artistic background and consists for the most part of a piecemeal commentary on the clerical and secular rulers, civic and female representative figures, and their respective confrontations with Death, with separate sections on the prologue and epilogue. J. focuses on a range of parallels and putative sources in late-medieval didactic literature. Thomas Wilhelmi, *Sebastian Brant. Bibliographie* (AMDLS, 18, 3), 1990, xiii + 349 pp., competes with the new bibliography of J. Knape and D. Wuttke (see *YWMLS*, 52:638), and F. Hartweg, *Beiträge* (Trier), 91–95, announces a plan for a computerized dictionary of Brant's German works, while S. Heimann, *Vorträge* (Liverpool), 264–76, analyses the perception and interpretation of travel in his *Narrenschiff*. Also noted from the end of the period: Sabine Heimann, *Begriff und Wertschätzung der menschlichen Arbeit bei Sebastian Brant und Thomas Murner. Ein Beitrag zur Bestimmung des historischen Standortes der Autoren hinsichtlich ihres Verhältnisses zur frühbürgerlichen Entwicklung in Deutschland an der Wende vom 15. zum 16. Jahrhundert* (SAG, 225), 1990, 234 pp., and Rita Schlusemann, *Die hystorie van Reynaert die vos und The History of Reynard the Fox. Die spätmittelalterlichen Prosabearbeitungen des Reynaert-Stoffes* (EH, 1, 1248), 243 pp.

THE SIXTEENTH CENTURY

POSTPONED

THE SEVENTEENTH CENTURY

By JILL BEPLER, *Herzog August Bibliothek, Wolfenbüttel*

1. GENERAL

The first of a projected series of volumes entitled *Die Deutsche Akademie des 17. Jahrhunderts: Fruchtbringende Gesellschaft*, ed. Martin Bircher and Klaus Conermann, appeared this year. *Briefe der Fruchtbringenden Gesellschaft und Beilagen: Die Zeit Herzog Augusts von Sachsen-Weißenfels 1667–1680*, ed. M. Bircher, Tübingen, Niemeyer, 435 pp., contains extremely heterogeneous materials relating to the final phase of the society's activities, most being formal letters of recommendation or application and acceptance of membership. Each document is extensively commented upon, and succeeding volumes will give bio-bibliographical information on members, but it is hard to identify a real common purpose linking the later members of this most important of German language societies, or indeed a literary or cultural policy pursued by its head, Duke August, in Halle. It is therefore very welcome that this documentation is supplemented by the full text of a Breslau school play directed by Georg Wende with a long poem by Quirinus Kühlmann, celebrating the 'Fruchtbringende Gesellschaft' and in particular its Silesian members, and providing an insight into the contemporary view both of the society's significance and its aims. One of the co-editors, G. Henkel, gives a survey of the documentation of day-to-day court life at the seat of the society's head in Halle in 'Die Hoftagebücher Herzog Augusts von Sachsen-Weißenfels', *WB*, 18:75–114. These diaries have survived in many versions and differing segments in several archives, and the original plan to edit them has wisely been dropped in favour of providing accurate information on their contents and their location in order to make them accessible to those interested in the history of the society and court culture. See also under PRAUN. Dealing with the treatment of literary texts during the first and most productive phase of the society's history, under Ludwig of Anhalt-Köthen, D. Merzbacher, 'Conversatio und Editio. Textkorrektur in der Fruchtbringenden Gesellschaft und editorische Wiedergabe aufgezeigt an zwei Texten Christoph von Dohnas (1582–1637)', *Acta* (Basel), 35–51, demonstrates the communal nature of textual production within the framework of the society. This sheds important light on our understanding of the subordinate role of the individual author in the 17th c. and the importance of the concept of 'conversatio' with regard to literary production, whether in a court or civic context. Jane O. Newman, *Pastoral Conventions. Poetry, Language, and Thought in 17th-Century*

Nuremberg, Baltimore, Johns Hopkins U.P., 1990, xiv + 313 pp., gives a highly theoretical analysis of the work of the Pegnischer Blumenorden in Nuremberg. Indebted to 'new historicism' and other current critical trends of thought, N. coins the term 'institution' in an attempt to describe the 'inaugural' and 'monumental' aspects of the texts produced by the Order. Having established her critical apparatus in the first chapter, O. gives a very good survey of European and German academies in the Early Modern period and the evolution of the language theories propounded by the German societies, which saw German as an 'Ursprache' and as a 'Natursprache'. The next two sections of the book deal with the poetics produced by the Nuremberg authors and with the pastoral poetry which was their hallmark. Both genres are seen as attempts to establish traditions and norms for vernacular poetry, doomed, however, to become blind alleys because of their extreme localization and the restriction of the impetus for renewal to the Nuremberg poets alone. This is not an easy book to read, but it contains many interesting points which seem obscured rather than revealed by the array of critical terminology deployed here. It represents, however, a first venture into the fields of deconstruction already so seminal to critical theory of English Renaissance texts. M. Reinhardt, 'Poets and politics: the transgressive turn of history in 17th-c. Nürnberg', *Daphnis*, 20:198–229, also deals with the Nuremberg poets, looking at their social standing and evidence in their works of their attempts to counterbalance efforts by the patrician-oligarchy of the city to legislate against the upward mobility of the intelligentsia. Parente, *Empire*, contains the proceedings of a conference held at Yale in 1987 which set out to examine the cultural and political background of German literary production in a European context. Setting the timespan between 1555 and 1720 the volume attempts to overcome the problematical and limiting effects of the 'periodization' of 17th-c. German culture by demonstrating its continuity with the preceding and succeeding centuries and by relating it to its historical background. Several essays deal with general themes, the model for an interdisciplinary approach being provided by A. Grafton, 'Humanism and science in Rudolphine Prague: Kepler in context', *ib.*, 19–45, who examines the philological and poetic basis of the scientist's work. F. van Ingen, 'Zum Selbstverständnis des Dichters im 17. und frühen 18. Jahrhundert', *ib.*, 206–24, looks at the changing relationship between scholarship and poetic inspiration in the self-fashioning of early modern poets. Taking us beyond the confines of the literary text and conventional genres, D. Breuer, 'Der Zensor als Literaturkritiker: Die Approbationsvermerke im frühneuzeitlichen Buch als literarhistorische Quelle', *ib.*, 126–41, calls attention to the hitherto unnoticed data contained in Catholic works in the texts of the censors' approbations often printed in prefaces. B. points out that the brief of the censor extended beyond moral, religious or political evaluation to include literary judgement on style and content, providing us with additional insight into the aesthetic criteria of the period.

2. POETRY

INDIVIDUAL AUTHORS

GREIFFENBERG. H. Laufhütte, 'Der Oedenburgische Drach. Spuren einer theologischen Kontroverse um die Ehe der Catharina Regina von Greiffenberg', *Daphnis*, 20:355–402, throws fresh light on what has always been seen as the central biographical impulse for much of G.'s poetry, her reluctant marriage to her middle-aged step-uncle and the ensuing legal and religious problems which exacerbated her experience of religious persecution as a Lutheran in re-Catholicized Austrian territories.

GRYPHIUS. N. Lohse, '"Diss Leben kömmt mir vor alss eine Renne Bahn." Poetologische Anmerkungen zu einem Sonett-Zyklus des Andreas Gryphius', *ZDP*, 110:161–80, gives a close reading of G.'s most famous sonnet cycle. In deliberate contrast to what he terms the current positivistic and historical modes of Baroque literary criticism with its concentration on superficial allegorical and emblematic interpretations, L.'s poetological approach identifies 'transition' as the main poetical mode of the sonnets.

HEINOLD. B. Neugebauer, 'Agnes Heinold (1642–1711) — ein Beitrag zur Literatur von Frauen im 17. Jahrhundert', *Daphnis*, 20:601–702, gives us an introduction to the life and work of a female author as yet unmentioned in reference works. Parallel to the larger works of another unnoticed author, Sibylle Schuster, H. wrote occasional poetry and prose eclogues for the Oettingen court, where she was the wife of the court preacher, and for the city of Esslingen where she lived in her widowhood. Although the poetry itself is hardly better or worse than other contemporary occasional verse, the case of H. shows how incomplete our view of the role of women in civic and court culture still is.

HOFFMANNSWALDAU. Veronique Helmridge-Marsillian, *The Heroism of Love in Hoffmannswaldau's 'Heldenbriefe'* (SDL, 113), vii + 269 pp., sets out to provide an ethical rehabilitation of H.'s verse epistles, seeing them not as immoral outpourings in the 'gallant' style, but as a plea for the emancipation of love from social constraint. H.-M. gives a concise survey of the varied history of critical attitudes to H.'s work, setting it in the context of the development of the genre of the heroid and relating it to its direct models, Ovid and Drayton, and its successors, Lohenstein and Besser. Comparison of the manuscript sources leads H.-M. to establish her own chronology of the cycle. Her interpretation of H.'s work as 'the brilliant apogee' of the genre of the heroid is underpinned by the search for evidence of H.'s genius and originality, identified in his propagation of 'the humanistic heroism of love'. The characters in the heroids are seen as representatives of 'moral independence freeing them of political intrigue, sexual prejudices, and religious doctrine'. The seemingly uncritical empathy of the author with the characters of the *Heldenbriefe* is likely to estrange the critical reader. A nagging doubt remains about the basic hypothesis that H. saw these characters, who act only in accordance with the dictates of the emotions, in a purely positive light. Surely there was a consensus between the author and his contemporaries as to what constituted moral behaviour which obviated the necessity for explicit condemnation, making terms such as 'moral independence' difficult to apply here. The almost exclusive concentration on the text of the *Heldenbriefe* and its characters in most sections of the book leaves one wishing for more detailed analysis of the philosophical, social, and political context in which H. composed this extraordinary work.

KUHLMANN. A. Menhennet, '"Wir tunken ein unseren Kil in die Ewikeit"': Quirinus Kuhlmann's experience of eternity', *FMLS*, 27:159–68, looks at the quality of K.'s mystical experience of transcendence and the role of the self within that experience as compared to similar passages in the works of Boehme.

LOGAU. Heidrun Ludolf, *Kritik und Lob am Fürstenhof. Stilunterschiede in den Epigrammen Friedrich von Logaus* (GTS, 39), 198 pp., concentrates, as the title of this dissertation suggests, on stylistic analysis of L.'s epigrams, differentiating between the poet's satirical and occasional verse and pointing to the coexistence of panegyric and criticism of court life in his work. The study stays very much on the surface and often uses vague critical terms. L.'s poetry is never convincingly placed in the poetical context of other texts of the time, either stylistically or thematically. Particularly worrying is the conclusion that L. excluded his longer occasional poems from his published collections because he recognized that they were simply 'bad poetry' (pp. 94–104). Too little is known about L.'s lost poetry for such sweeping statements. U. Seelbach, 'Unbekannte Gedichte Friedrichs von Logaus in den Abdankungsreden des Christoph von Reydeburg', *Daphnis*, 20:531–46, provides us with just such evidence of another facet of L.'s poetical talent. Funeral orations by his friend von Reydeburg contain extracts quoted from epicedia by L. which were not included in his published works, but which provide an important correlative to his satirical poetry. These funerary poems have not survived in manuscript or printed form, but the extracts published here give an impression of the power of L.'s religious verse.

LOHENSTEIN. M. Metzger, 'Of princes and poets: Lohenstein's verse epistles on the divorce of the Elector Palatine Carl Ludwig', Parente, *Empire*, 159–76, looks at the historical and poetic texts providing sources for L.'s verse epistles, posthumously published in the Neukirch collection in 1709.

MÜHLPFORT. Heinrich Mühlpfort, *Teutsche Gedichte. Poetische Gedichte Ander Theil. Neudruck der Ausgabe Breslau und Frankfurt am Main 1686/87*, ed. Heinz Entner (TFN, 8), lxiv + 996 pp., makes available the long-neglected poetical works of one of the major Silesian poets of the second half of the 17th c., put on a par with Lohenstein, Gryphius, and Titz by contemporaries. M.'s forte was funeral poetry, obviously an important source of income for the Breslau archivist. E.'s succinct introduction explores M. as a representative of the 'galanter Stil' in his other poetry, seeing M.'s German verse as exemplary of the occasional poetry produced in a civic context. Both the German and Latin editions of M.'s collected poetry were published posthumously, culled from the various occasional publications in which they had first been printed. *Heinrici Mühlpforti Poemata. Neudruck der Ausgabe Breslau und Frankfurt am Main 1686*, ed. Lutz Claren and Joachim Huber (TFN, 7), xxxi + 404 pp., forms a necessary pendant to M.'s better-known German poetry. Taken together these two volumes provide us with over 20 years of literary production in Breslau, reflecting the cultural network of the city, where poetry emanated from the pens of the city officials, teachers, lawyers, and doctors.

RIST. G. Dammann, 'Johann Rist als Statthalter des Opitzianismus in Holstein. Aspekte seiner literaturpolitischen Strategie anhand der Widmungsbriefe und Vorreden', *Literaten in der Provinz — Provinzielle Literatur? Schriftsteller einer norddeutschen Region*, ed. A. Ritter, Heide, Boyens, 47–66, looks at the tensions between local and national aspirations at work in R.'s markedly autobiographical prefaces, seeing them as R.'s means of establishing himself as the foremost poet in Holstein. By claiming to be the only poet in the region to fulfil the dictates of Opitzian reform, R. managed to retain his position for over 20 years, carrying on a fierce polemical battle against the innovatory Zesen and innumerable occasional poets of the age. In the battle for regional supremacy and national acclaim the fact that the parish of Wedel and Rist himself were so closely linked with Hamburg was decisive. The role of prefaces for the self-stylization of Baroque authors is also explored by U. Maché, 'Author and patron: On the function of dedications in 17th-c. German literature', Parente, *Empire*, 195–205.

SPEE.   Martina Eicheldinger, *Friedrich Spee — Seelsorger und poeta doctus. Die Tradition des Hohenliedes und Einflüsse der ignatianischen Andacht in seinem Werk* (SDL, 110), x + 369 pp., provides an authoritative analysis of S.'s two main works, his manual of devotion *Das Güldenene Tugendbuch* and his posthumously published volume of poetry *Trutznachtigall*. The first part of the study is a detailed examination of the various sources for S.'s popular handbook of devotion, in particular the way in which S. built on the main model, the spiritual exercises of Ignatius Loyola, and provided guidance for individual meditation and exercises in the form of a dialogue between the spiritual pupil and the confessor. E. concentrates on the rhetorical and theological concepts which follow S.'s manual, showing how he relied not only on the spiritual exercises of Ignatius but also on popular Jesuit catechisms and lay prayer books as sources for his own meditational exercises. She demonstrates how S.'s manual was part of the mainstream of the flood of Counter-Reformation literature of its day, employing highly emotional and sensual imagery to maximize its effects on the reader. In contrast, S.'s *Trutznachtigall* with its partial adaptation of Protestant models of language and poetics and the conciliatory confessional stance of its verse is seen as a potential source of conflict with the Jesuit order. E. traces the Classical and Biblical sources of inspiration for S.'s poetry in the Song of Songs and in the Petrarchistic and pastoral verse of his day and his reworkings of these themes. The erotic imagery used as an allegory of spiritual love so foreign to the modern reader of Baroque religious poetry provided the contemporary reader, Protestant and Catholic alike, with an intensification of the mystical experience mapped out in the manual of devotions.

OTHER WORK

The publication of the final volume of *Herrn von Hoffmannswaldau und andrer Deutschen auserlesener und bißher ungedruckter Gedichte Siebender Theil. Nach dem Druck vom Jahre 1727*, ed. E. A. and M. M. Metzger (Neudrucke deutscher Literaturwerke, n.F., 43) Tübingen, Niemeyer, civ + 588 pp. provides us with the complete edition of this most important anthology of Baroque poetry, but also takes us beyond the chronological scope of the present review. As the editors point out, the seventh volume, published nearly 20 years after the sixth, marks a radical change in style, for here changes in taste dictated by the early Enlightenment and the shift from Silesia to Saxony as a cultural centre can be observed. Highlighting the controversial discussion of the uses of poetry which was culminating in 1727, the editors append the anonymous Silesian polemical tract

Poetischer Staar-Stecher, a defence of the poetical ethos of the earlier volumes of the anthology. W. Kühlmann, 'Kunst als Spiel: das Technopaegnium in der Poetik des 17. Jahrhunderts', *Daphnis*, 20:505–29, investigates the negative attitude towards 'Figurenge-dichte' evinced in the poetical treatises of the Baroque, which generally condemned their unserious nature as 'armselige Erfindungen' and discussed them not in the context of imagery and emblematics, but as a verse form. Only Hellwig's *Nymphe Noris* (1650) contains a defence of visual poetry. As K. points out, the fact that no collections of such poems were published in Germany means that there are no prefaces which might have entered into a discussion on the relative merits of pattern poetry, such as we have for the controversial novel. He shows, however, the importance of the long entry in Alsted's Latin encyclopaedia (1630) on the topic, which takes most of its examples from a work by the Italian mannerist poet Bonifacio, who sees the creator of visual poetry as painter and poet in one. P. Rypson, '17th-c. visual poetry from Danzig', *GJ*, 66:269–304, gives a survey of 56 pattern poems contained in volumes of occasional poetry from the Danziger Ratsbibliothek now in the library of the Academy of Sciences there. Giving examples and examining the context in which this occasional poetry was written, R. distinguishes between three main types of visual poems: the outline poem, the labyrinth poem, and the grid poem.

3. PROSE

INDIVIDUAL AUTHORS

BEER.   Johann Beer, *Sämtliche Werke. Band 5. Weiber-Hächel, Jungfer-Hobel, Bestia-Civitatis, Narren-Spital*, ed. Ferdinand van Ingen and Hans-Gert Roloff (Mittlere Deutsche Literatur, 5) Berne, Lang, 236 pp., contains B.'s novels from the years 1680 and 1681. J. Krämer, *Johann Beers Romane. Poetologie, immanente Poetik und Rezeption 'niedere' Texte im späten 17. Jahrhundert* (Mikrokosmos, 28), Berne, Lang, 341 pp., is an extremely readable study of B.'s novels, which combines methods of intertextual study and empirical 'Rezeptions-forschung'. Instead of concentrating just on the prefaces to the novels K. looks at both prefaces and text for statements, whether direct or implicit, on how the novelist sees the genre of the low novel, which audience he is addressing, what his intended impact on the reader is, and how he himself defines satire. In contrast to earlier studies K. does not try to group the novels thematically, but compares their underlying narrative structures. He shows how the apparent chaos of the narrative, which the narrator explains as the realistic depiction of the unpredictability of human existence and which has led many critics since Alewyn to criticize B. for being unable to sustain a 'story-line', is in fact a conscious strategy. One of the most important aspects of B.'s novels is seen to be the intense reflection on narrative and story-telling, satire, and reading which they contain. K. shows how B.'s novels reflect upon their role as low literature and posit their greater worth in contrast to unrealistic high literature, which merely serves to dupe the reader. Another part of K.'s study looks at evidence of book ownership which might indicate what audience these works actually found and how they themselves might have been responding to market forces. This year's volume of *Simpliciana*, 13, 492 pp., contains the proceedings of the Marburg conference 'Johann Beer und Grimmelshausen. Deutsche Prosasatire an der Wende vom 17. zum 18. Jahrhundert'. Most contributions steer well clear of fruitless realism-naturalism debate and seek to examine B. and his work in a broader historical and cultural context. R. Jacobsen, *ib.*, 47–80, re-examines B.'s social status at the Weissenfels court and the possible reasons for his ceasing to write novels, showing how since Alewyn the esteem in which B. was believed to have been held at the Weissenfels court has been overestimated, as have the cultural initiatives open to him within the discourse of court culture. Various contributions (W. Neuber, K. Gurtner, van Ingen) discuss the importance of biography within B.'s narratives and the thematic role of readers, narrators, and authors and texts within the novels. D. Breuer, '"Lindigkeit." Zur affekt-psychologische Neubegründung satirischen Erzählens in Johann Beers Doppelroman', *ib.*, 81–96, draws parallels between B.'s narrative strategies and those of the *roman comique*, where the objective is not unity of plot but confusion, disjunction, and incoherence. He also shows how the narrative and moral perturbation which characterizes B.'s novels must be seen in relationship to contemporary moral treatises such as Schottel's *Ethica*. E. Locher, 'Dimensionen der "Kurtzweil" in Johann Beers Narrenspital-Erzählung', *ib.*, 275–301, also looks for extra-literary sources to shed light on B.'s satirical 'programme', viewing it in the context of the contemporary controversies on the moral value of recreation as such, and also of reading as entertainment (especially with a view to advent of journals and newspapers). He shows how B. parodies the strategies of verbal and non-verbal wit extolled by handbooks for courtiers from Castiglione to Julius Bernhard von Rohr. H. Jaumann, 'Satire zwischen Moral, Recht und Kritik. Zur Auseinandersetzung um die Legitimität der Satire im 17. Jahrhundert', *ib.*, 15–28, calls for a new approach to the theory of satire in the period by looking not at normative poetics, but at satirical texts themselves and handbooks and compendia. J. J. Berns, 'Policey und Satire im 16. und 17. Jahrhundert', *ib.*, 423–41, reflects on the connection between the political legislation on printing in early modern Germany and the activities of satirical authors. Other contributions deal among other things with illustrations to B.'s works and his work as a composer.

GRIMMELSHAUSEN. 'Text and image: representation in Grimmelshausen's *Continuatio*', *GQ*, 64: 138–48, studies the central importance of visual images, both of the frontispiece illustrations and the actual images mentioned in the text, as a theme in the novel. S. concentrates on the *Continuatio* and links between the description of Simplicius and his surroundings on the island and well-known devotional pictures of Saint Onophrius and the emblematical connections between the palm tree, the phoenix, and the monster of the frontispiece. L. E. Feldman, 'The rape of "Frau Welt": transgression, allegory and the grotesque body in Grimmelshausen's *Courasche*', *Daphnis*, 20:61–80, examines the so-called 'narrative ventriloquism' of the novel, in which Courasche offers the reader 'masculine' apologetics for her own various rapes. F. sees the rape of Courasche, an allegory of feminine-irrational-material-chaos, as a figurative means of imposing masculine order on feminine disorderliness. W. Kühlmann, '"Syllogismus practicus." Antithese und Dialektik in Grimmelshausens *Satyrischem Pilgram*', *Simpliciana*, 13:391–406, examines G.'s first work, showing how the structure of these short moral satires, in which pro and contra of some aspect of human existence are expounded and then 'resolved' by the author, prefigure the development of the hero in *Simplicissimus*, who in the face of the ambiguous nature of the world around him learns that moral responsibility rests with the individual. See also under BEER above.

HARSDÖRFFER. Three reprints serve to broaden our understanding of H.'s *œuvre*. Georg Philipp Harsdörffer, *Nathan und Jotham: das ist Geistliche und Weltliche Lehrgedichte. Neudruck der Ausgabe Nürnberg 1659*, ed. Guillaume van Gemert (TFN, 4), xxxvii + 398 + 422 pp., is an example of the overtly didactical element of much of H.'s work. The volume consists of over 600 short prose pieces, 'parables' taken from biblical and fictional sources, concluding in each case with the moral to be drawn from the tale. G.'s introduction stresses the two-tier structure of each piece and shows that the 'Rätsel' which end the work are in fact parables in which it is left to the reader to draw the moral, an exercise for which he or she has been trained in the first two parts of the work. All H.'s works must be understood as material with which the reader was expected to actively engage, either in discussion or in meditation. *Nathan* is to be seen in the context of the devotional literature for which H. and other Nuremberg poets were renowned. Its appendix of sayings taken from the works of Teresa de Ávila highlights the importance of Catholic traditions for Protestant devotional works in Germany in the period. A second work to be reprinted this year belongs not to H.'s corpus of devotional texts, but to the realm of courtly and political rhetoric. *Ars Apophthegmatica. Das ist: Kunstquellen Denckwürdiger Lehrsprüche und Ergötzlicher Hofreden. Neudruck der Ausgaben Nürnberg 1655 und 1656*, ed. Georg Braungart (TFN, 2), 35 + 752 + 721 pp., is perhaps one of the most inaccessible works by the Nuremberg author for modern readers. Following the Classical tradition of the apophthegm or witty maxim cultivated by Plutarch, the 16th c. saw the flowering of this genre with the collections published by Erasmus. The founder of the vernacular German tradition was Zincgref, whose *Der Teutschen Scharpfsinnige kluge Sprüch* appeared in 1626. B.'s informative introduction shows how H. developed the genre, and unlike Zincgref provided the reader not with polished, rounded maxims to be admired, but with a wealth of source material to be tapped and used for creative purposes, whether in writing or in conversation. Thus the *Kunstquellen* must be read as supplementary to such works as H.'s own *Frauenzimmer–Gesprächspiele* and understood in the courtly and societal context of the age. Yet another aspect of H.'s intellectual concerns is reflected in a mathematical and technical compendium reprinted in the same series, George Philipp Harsdörffer and Daniel Schwenter, *Deliciae Physico-Mathematicae oder Mathematische und Philosophische Erquick-stunden. Neudruck der Ausgaben Nürnberg 1636 und 1651*, ed. Jörg Jochen Berns (TFN, 3), xliv + 586 + 647 + 652 pp. Schwenter, professor of Oriental languages and mathematics at Altdorf, died in 1636 before the publication of the first volume of the *Deliciae*. H. decided to build on his very successful recipe, adding two volumes of his own material to the original work. B.'s excellent introduction deals briefly with the myth that the two men had at any time worked together during H.'s student days. He shows the dependence of Protestant technological and scientific works on Jesuit scholarship and the central importance to both of the Bible as a point of reference for geological, cosmological, and biological data. Central to H.'s epistemological theories is seen to be his reading of *Nova Atlantis* by the English philosopher Francis Bacon. B. points out that, whereas Bacon's main concern was to create experiments which would verify scientific observations, H.'s interest lay in the games and illusions which science could offer. The *Erquickstunden* demonstrate yet another side of the 'recreational' literature through which H. supplied his ideal circle of conversationalists with material. The publication of the proceedings of a conference dealing with a variety of aspects of H.'s œuvre, *Georg Philipp Harsdörffer. Ein deutscher Dichter und europäischer Gelehrter*, ed. I. M. Battafarano (Forschungen zur europäischen Kultur, 1), Berne, Lang, 396 pp., provides new impulses for a deeper understanding of his literary production, although many contributions deal with the better-known works. L. W. Forster, 'Zu Harsdörffers *Specimen philologiae germanicae*' (9–22), sees H.'s relatively neglected work as directed to an international audience and demonstrating H.'s interest in medieval German literature. J. J. Berns, 'Gott und Götter. Harsdörffers Mythenkritik und der Pan-Theismus der Pegnitzschäfer unter dem Einfluß Francis Bacons' (23–82), reassesses the controversial role of pagan gods and mythological figures for the Christian poet in the works of the 'Pegnitzschäfer' and other Baroque poets. He points in particular to the hitherto unnoticed influence of Bacon on H.'s understanding of mythology and poetry and the development of the pantheistic programme of the 'Pegnitzschäfer', especially in the joint programmatical text *Pegnesisches Schäfergedicht*. Several contributions in the volume try to come to terms with the communicative and didactic aspects of H.'s texts. D. Breuer, 'Einübung ins allegorische Verstehen. Zur Funktion des Erzählens in Harsdörffers *Gesprächspielen*' (127–42), shows how identification with the role models of the individual speakers in the *Gesprächspiele* gradually trains the reader in modes of interpretation. H. Jaumann, 'Die Kommunikation findet in den Büchern statt. Zu Harsdörffers Literaturprogramm in den *Gesprächspielen*' (163–79), sees the critical faculty which H. wishes his readers to attain not as judgemental in the sense of achieving a qualitative verdict, but as deliberative. The aim is to be able to perceive and weigh arguments rather than reach a decision, and thus the element of 'play' which enters into all of H.'s work. Both R. Drux, 'Sprachspiele gegen den Kreig. Ein Beitrag zur europäischen Nachahmung bei Harsdörffer' (83–104), and I. Höpel, 'Harsdörffers Theorie und Praxis des dreiständigen Emblems' (195–234), deal with imagery and emblems in H.'s work. E. Locher, 'Harsdörffers Deutkunst' (243–65), examines gesture as the fourth communicative means available to H.'s ideal reader alongside speech, the written word, and imagery. Two contributions treat the influence of Italian and French culture and sources on H. J.-D. Krebs, 'Harsdörffer als Vermittler des *honnêteté*-Ideals' (287–311), and I. M. Battafarano, 'Harsdörffers italianisierender Versuch, durch die Integration der Frau das literarische Leben zu verfeinern' (267–86).

GRYPHIUS. Christian Gryphius, *Gedächtnisschriften. Neudrucke der Ausgabe Leipzig 1702*, ed. James Hardin (TFN, 5), xxviii + 240 pp. The funeral orations contained in this edition allow us to study a neglected literary form brought to perfection by G.'s father, Andreas, in his 'Abdankungen'. This 1702 selection of orations from C. G.'s vast output of funerary works in prose and poetry for burghers and aristocrats in the Glogau region covers 25 years and reflects a development in the use of rhetorical strategies and emblematic imagery.

MESSERSCHMID. G. van Gemert, 'Georg Friedrich Messerschmid als Übersetzer. Zur Rezeption italienischer Literatur im frühen 17. Jahrhundert', *Daphnis*, 20:265–310, sheds light on the work of one of the earliest of the many unknown translators of Italian works into German. M. specialized in translations of Italian satirical works in the *facetia* tradition of humorous satire, which were so influential in the development of authors like Harsdörffer. Having examined the five translations as yet identified, G. goes on to posit the possibility that M. could in fact be the translator of Garzoni's *Piazza Universale*, one of the most influential works to be translated from Italian into German in the 17th c.

PRAUN. A. Herz, 'Zwischen Fruchtbringender Gesellschaft und Reichspublizistik. Michael Paun d.J. (1632–1695)', *WB*, 18:115–40, gives an account of the life and writings of one of the later members of this society. P., a native of Nuremberg and friend of S. von Birken, was a court official and prolific author of political and legal treatises. Like many Protestant political theorists, despite the Counter-Reformation policies of the Emperor, P. saw the German Imperial constitutional system as the guarantee of stability. He represents the non-literary tendency of the 'Fruchtbringende Gesellschaft' in its final phase, but his works and his defence of the German vernacular as the appropriate means of courtly and diplomatic communication add an interesting dimension to the introduction of German into the universities by Thomasius.

VEIRAS. Denis Veiras, *Eine Historie der Neu-gefundenen Völcker Sevarambes genannt 1689*, ed. Wolfgang Braungart and Jutta Golawski-Braungart (Deutsche Neudrucke Reihe Barock, 39), Tübingen, Niemeyer, 1990, 362 + 220 pp., reminds us of the European context in which many authors of the 17th c. wrote. This first part of this Utopian novel by the French Huguenot V. was written in English and published in London in 1675. V. was an acquaintance of Pepys and his work shows the influence of Shaftesbury and Locke. The novel describes an ideal state happened upon by shipwrecked sailors. It concentrates on the depiction of manners, morals, and the political system of the Sevarambes, a state founded on the principles of reason and love. As a whole the novel was first published in French in 1679 in Paris. This (anonymous) German translation, which adheres very closely to the original, appeared ten years later and was published in Sulzbach, a court famous for its connections with the most progressive German thinkers of the day (Leibniz, Helmont, Knorr von Rosenroth) and for its religious tolerance towards Jews. The excellent afterword by the editors of the reprint does justice both to the original and to the translation, giving a fascinating tentative biography of V. himself. An analysis of the structural differences between the translation and the original shows how the German version was more concerned to guide the reader didactically by introducing chapter headings and marginalia, rather than allowing him or her to be swept away by the fictional illusion of the Utopian society presented in the novel. The history of the reception of *Savarambes* shows that the novel was generally well received, but that it was soon subjected to criticism on religious grounds. The editors have included reproductions and extracts from many sources commenting on the novel, which show how critical attitudes to the work varied from its publication until well up to the end of the 18th c. This translation provides us with an important link between the German Utopian tradition of the early 17th c. (Andreae) and Schnabel's *Insel Felsenburg*, reminding us how important literature in translation was in supplying new impulses to an emergent vernacular German literature.

OTHER WORK

The first number of *Daphnis*, 20, is again a collection of essays edited by Lynne Tatlock. Entitled 'Writing on the line. Transgression in early modern German literature', the volume contains expanded versions of papers from a conference concerned with the interpretation of 'flagrant transgression', whether social, political, sexual, moral, formal, or hermeneutic, in literary texts. A. Solbach, 'Transgression als Verletzung des Decorum bei Christian Weise, J. J. Chr. v. Grimmelshausen und in Johann Beers *Narrenspital*', ib., 33–60, looks at literary examples of trangressions and inversions of normal order as defined in recent interpretations of Bakhtin's concept of the carnivalesque. In various novels he traces the conservative way in which the infringements of divine or social order are seen by the respective authors not as creating areas of freedom in which that order is satirized or destabilized, but as fundamentally threatening phenomena deserving of exemplary punishment. In Beer's work he points to the importance of the ultimately religious stance of the narrative, which reveals the seeming individuality and emancipation of the transgressions of the main figures as damnatory. Other contributions to this volume are noted under the relevant headings.

4. DRAMA
INDIVIDUAL AUTHORS

GRYPHIUS. Andreas Gryphius, *Dramen*, ed. E. Mannack (Bibliothek deutscher Klassiker, 67), DKV, 1321 pp., provides a superb annotated edition of the complete dramatic works of G. (excluding translations) based on the 'Ausgabe letzter Hand', rectifying the unfortunate decision of the prior editors of the complete works, Powell and Szyrocki, to base their volumes on the texts of first editions. Mannack provides an excellent critical apparatus in an afterword of over 450 pages, giving a general introduction to each play and illuminating annotations to individual passages, highlighting in particular the biblical and emblematic references which infuse G.'s text and were so apparent to contemporary readers and spectators. T. W. Best, 'Gryphius's *Cardenio und Celinde* in its European context: a new perspective', Parente, *Empire*, 60–77, while not denying the importance of contemporary Italian and Spanish exemplary novels as sources for the plot of G.'s drama, points to similarities and counterpoint in structure and character with works by the Classical authors Plautus and Euripides.

LOHENSTEIN. G. Gillespie, 'Passion, piety, and politics: Lohenstein's *Ibrahim Sultan* and Tristan L'Hermite's *Osman*', Parente, *Empire*, 78–88, shows the differing underlying positions of the two dramas, despite their related subject matter. G. sees the French work, which L. knew but did not take as his model, as broadly psychological, whereas L.'s text reveals an intense knowledge of the Turkish political and historical background which he uses to demonstrate the workings and disintegration of a whole social system.

STIELER. J. Aikin, 'Authorial self-consciousness in the theater of Caspar Stieler', Parente, *Empire*, 247–58, highlights the way in which the staging of S.'s plays in the intimate atmosphere of the small courts at which he worked allowed him directly and indirectly to introduce his own persona as figure of fun into his dramas.

WEISE. Christian Weise, *Sämtliche Werke. Band 2. Historische Dramen*, ed. Hans-Gert Roloff (Ausgaben deutscher Literatur des XV. bis XVIII. Jahrhunderts, 140) Berlin, de Gruyter, 667 pp., contains four school dramas by W. performed in Zittau in 1684 and 1685, three of which are dramas of state, the other a comedy. Two of the dramas, *Regnerus* and *Prinzeβin Ulvilda*, have been published here for the first time from extant manuscript copies. On the performance of such works, see P. Skrine, 'German Baroque drama and 17th-c. European theatre', Parente, *Empire*, 49–59.

THE CLASSICAL ERA

By M. L. DAVIES, *Lecturer in German, University of Leicester**

1. GENERAL

In a year which sees the inception of yet another Goethe edition (DKV), now as a precision-made, techno-commodity (see the publishers' brochure), it is high time to praise the 'Kleines Archiv des achtzehnten Jahrhunderts', St. Ingbert, Röhrig, for letting hitherto barely audible voices speak again in these modest paperback pamphlets. Christoph Weiss and his co-editors must be congratulated on their venture, encouraged to spend further hours of research in libraries, and earnestly thanked for restoring to words long neglected the gleam of something new. But the rest is pedagogy (exemplified by the strangely blinkered series 'Poeten als Pädagogen'), the 'eternal recurrence' of historical exegesis which, given the forests of paper and the pitch of 'retroactive energy' it requires, needs to be borne with a similar superhuman fortitude. What stand out, be they concise articles or adventurous monographs, are those thoughtful essays which do not presume upon their subjects, but engage them in dialogue and, by means of a political, anthropological, psychoanalytical, or sociological reflection, establish a point of vital intellectual relevance.

BIBLIOGRAPHY, REFERENCE. *Internationale Bibliographie zur Deutschen Klassik 1750–1850*, ed. Hans Henning, Günther Mühlpfordt, and Heidi Zeilinger (Folge, 35, 1988), 2 vols, Weimar, Nationale Forschungs- und Gedenkstätten der Klassischen Deutschen Literatur, 1990, 616 pp., continues to be a quite indispensable resource. Herbert Kraft, *Editionsphilologie*, WBG, 1990, 314 pp., is a well documented survey of methods and problems in textual criticism in essays by several authors, supplemented by a comprehensive bibliography. Hahn, *Vorfeld*, explores those areas of philology where textual criticism and literary interpretation overlap, in essays mainly on Goether and Schiller, but also on Herder, Heine, Fontane, Nietzsche, H. Mann, and Brecht, as well as on general methodology; but in advocating a methodological pluralism it really only ensures the continuing monopoly of historical-philological procedures. Relevant contributions are noted, where apposite, below.

GENERAL STUDIES AND ESSAY COLLECTIONS. Eberhard Lämmert, *Das überdachte Labyrinth. Ortsbestimmungen der Literaturwissenschaft*

*I would like gratefully to acknowledge the financial assistance of the Arts Faculty Research Committee, Leicester University.

1960–1990, Stuttgart, Metzler, xviii + 306 pp., is a collection of essays on two broad themes: the institutional organization and cultural or didactic purpose of *Germanistik* as a human science; and then its social and economic dimension (e.g. the social responsibility of the writer, the organization of libraries and archives, the relationship between author and publisher). These essays are impressive not only in their scope and consistency, but also in their current relevance. The tendency of *Germanistik* to reflect on itself follows a precedent set by the literary criticism of the Classical period. Here reviewing the purpose of studying German literature and language, L. touches on such issues as scholarship, teaching, and vocational applications. Against a discipline based on nationally ordered philologies yet ramifying into eclecticism, L. argues for a *Literaturwissenschaft* in which literature, as a verbal construct, is a context for human experience illuminated by the co-ordinated efforts of the social and human sciences — a proposal which, though as much as three decades old, would seem barely on the agenda of British *Germanistik*. Complementary to this is *Autoren damals und heute. Literaturgeschichtliche Beispiele veränderter Wirkungshorizonte*, ed. Gerhard P. Knapp (*ABNG*, 31–33), which reflects on the formation of the canon of modern German literature from Justus Möser to Unica Zürn, proposing alternatives to it, reasssessing neglected authors for their contemporary relevance, and suggesting 'eine literaturhistorische Methodik neuer Art': a useful contribution to the contemporary debate. (Relevant individual articles are noted below.)

A further contribution to the reception of the 18th c. is Eva Adelsbach, *Bobrowskis Widmungstexte an Dichter und Künstler des 18. Jahrhunderts: Dialogizität und Intertextualität* (SBL, 19), St. Ingbert, Röhrig, 1990, 187 pp., consisting of detailed studies of B.'s poems and prose pieces on 18th-c. figures (including Klopstock, Hamann, Bach, Buxtehude, Mozart, Lenz). Drawing on Bakhtin's dialogic theory, elaborated in a climate of political oppression, supplemented by related theories of intertextuality and reader reception (Kristeva, Iser), A. shows how Bobrowski's poetic 'conversations' with figures in the past becomes a form of resistance to the conditions of life and authorship in the GDR, though her theoretical postulates are more illuminating than her rather prosaic comments on the poetry. G.-L. Fink, 'Vom Alamodestreit zur Frühaufklärung. Das wechselseitige deutsch-französische Spiegelbild 1648–1750', *RG*, 21:3–47.

PERIODS. On the Enlightenment this year the most noteworthy contribution is three volumes of essays by G. S. Rousseau, two of which were supplied for review: *Enlightenment Crossings: Pre- and Post-Modern Discourses, Anthropological*. Manchester U.P., xv + 259 pp.; *Perilous Enlightenment: Pre- and Post-Modern Discourses, Sexual Historical,* Manchester U.P., xv + 336 pp. Published over the last 20 years or so, R.'s essays are reissued here with illuminating prefaces explaining the context of their first publication and outlining their place in the development of his thinking on the anthropological, sociological, medical, psychological, philosophical, literary, historical issues they raise. Drawing closely on historical documentation they evoke the 'feel' of the 18th c. and yet they never succumb to antiquarianism, nor to the doctoral fallacy that objectivity means explaining an issue in its own unproblematized terms, as they are illuminated by the conceptual frameworks established by the post-1968 reorganization of knowledge. These exemplary essays demonstrate that postmodern reconceptions, as evinced particularly in the crossings of the borders of the conventionally organized disciplines, subversive though they may appear to be of certain intellectual and cultural habits, are remarkably fruitful in reconstructing the discourses of the Enlightenment and reinvigorating the current dialogue with them. Rather than conventionally assuming a simple historical descendence or causal succession from epoch to epoch, they provide a model of how the present, aware of its unprecedented difference from the past, explores in the available 18th-c. artefacts an ambivalent sense of deep affinity. By contrast Roy Porter, *The Enlightenment* (Studies in European History), London, Macmillan, 1990, ix + 95 pp, illustrates well the problems of working with historical convention: that its formulations have to be so simple (for all the author's misgivings) that, despite the earnestness and the questionable assertions of relevance ('We remain today the children of the Enlightenment', p. 75), even the uninitiated reader might well wonder (as does the final section) whether the Enlightenment matters. Besides a crucial misquotation of the title of Kant's essay on the *question* of Enlightenment (p. 1), the unclear description of Adorno and Horkheimer as 'modern' philosophers (p. 8), the identification of the Enlightenment with secularization in which it culminated rather than 'decisively launched' (p. 72), the central issue, the Enlightenment, is simply normatized within a chronologically structured past as something which is past, whereas, e.g. with Mendelssohn (absent here), it is at least as justifiable to say that it has not yet even begun. With a similar pedagogical intention, H.-D. Weber, 'Einleitende Bemerkungen über die Aufklärung in Deutschland', *DUS*, 43.6:5–19, offers a reflection of a higher order. Combining a definition of the 'Aufklärung' in its own time with the subsequent reception of the movement, it affirms its continuing applicability to the constitution of a pluralistic, tolerant society and thus avoids purely historical explanation: 'Nur einem dialektisch gefaßten Aufklärungsbegriff

682 *German Studies*

erschließt sich die deutsche Literatur der zweiten Hälfte des 18. Jahrhunderts als literarische Epoche, deren Gegenwärtigkeit unabgeschlossen ist' (p. 19). This conclusion is further supported by D. Barnouw, 'Modernity and Enlightenment thought', *Slessarev Vol.*, 1–14, which surveys the reception of the Enlightenment from Adorno and Horkheimer to Habermas. Still on the theme of continuing relevance: T. J. Reed, 'Coming of age in Prussia and Swabia: Kant, Schiller, and the Duke', *MLR*, 86:613–26, which regards S.'s escape from the Karlsschule in terms of the fulfilment of K.'s premiss that the natural, social, and political aim to think for oneself has an inherently emancipatory function: a lucid essay which demonstrates in K.'s later essays and in S.'s early poetic and medical works both the compromises the Enlightenment had to make with absolutism and the inherent capacity for dissent in literary and philosophical reflection; and J. Derrida, 'Interpretations at war: Kant, the Jew and the German', *NLH*, 22:39–95, which offers a complex reflection on the German-Jewish tradition in two different manifestations (H. Cohen and K. Rosenzweig), and on the exemplary character of German and Jewish nationhood, topoi originating with Kant, the Enlightenment and emancipation. Another work on the Enlightenment as a process of social modernization is Thomas Kempf, *Aufklärung als Disziplinierung. Studien zum Diskurs des Wissens in Intelligenzblättern und gelehrten Beilagen der zweiten Hälfte des 18. Jahrhunderts*, Munich, Iudicium, 268 pp., which would belong to those dialectical reflections on the interdependence of knowledge and power initiated by Adorno and Horkheimer and, more recently, Foucault. K. valuably focuses on specific 'Intelligenzblätter' (printed in their integrity in an appendix) which mediate knowledge to the agents of juridical, medical, and governmental institutions responsible for public order and well-being. Yet the still unremarkable conclusion that knowledge was used as an instrument of public order is only surprising when it offsets the Enlightenment's 'Utopian', emancipatory aims. K. had only to consider either former Communist Europe to see that knowledge and power can be fatal when they combine; or free-market capitalism to realize that its social and economic power is unthinkable without its vast resources of knowledge. Thus this study reveals its narrow academic origins in not contextualizing its conclusions which need, therefore, to be offset by B. Becker-Cantarino, 'Foucault on Kant: Deconstructing the Enlightenment', *Slessarev Vol.*, 27–33, which argues that 'F. takes the Kantian position merely as a [. . .] challenge to develop a new critical ontology of ourselves' (p. 31). A comprehensive survey of the vulgarization of knowledge which produced the modernization of 18th-c. society is provided by Holger Böning, *Die Genese der Volksaufklärung und ihre Entwicklung bis 1780*, Stuttgart,

Frommann-Holzboog, 1990, liv + 846 pp., which constitutes the first volume of Holger Böhning and Reinhart Siegert, *Volksaufklärung: Biobibliographisches Handbuch zur Popularisierung aufklärerischen Denkens im deutschen Sprachraum von den Anfängen bis 1850*. In a not unrelated vein, K. K. Walther, 'Ausgang aus der Unmündigkeit — Flugschriften des 17. Jahrhunderts im Vorfeld der Aufklärung', Garber, *Barock*, 317–26, regards the content, style, and political intention of broadsheets around 1700 as anticipating Kant's celebrated 1783 response to the issue of the Enlightenment. The theme of Enlightenment and revolution is explored in several essays, as in the following altercation: W. Albrecht, 'Aufklärung, Reform, Revolution oder "Bewirkt Aufklärung Revolution?" Über ein Zentralproblem der Aufklärungsdebatte in Deutschland', *LY*, 22, 1990 (1991): 1–75; T. P. Saine, 'Mainz revisited: or, was this really a revolution to be admired? A response to Wolfgang Albrecht', *ib.*, 77–90; W. Albrecht, 'Der schwierige, aber nötige Anfang eines Diskurses über Zentralprobleme der deutschen Spätaufklärung. Nicht nur eine Duplik auf Thomas P. Saine', *ib.*, 91–95; and in W. D. Wilson, 'Shades of the Illuminati Conspiracy. Koselleck on Enlightenment and revolution', *Slessarev Vol.*, 15–25. Ulrich Rose, *Poesie als Praxis: Jean Paul, Herder und Jacobi im Diskurs der Aufklärung*, Wiesbaden, Deutscher Universitäts Vlg, 246 pp., intends to show how these three authors, conventionally regarded as opposing Classicism and Kantian philosophy, are a part of the broader Enlightenment, since they too reflect on the legitimacy of reason, on the dichotomy between subject and object, and on the problem of subjectivity. The key figure is Jean Paul whose work (says R.) explores these issues practically through the act of writing. However, these themes are hardly novel, either in Jean Paul criticism or in terms of the concept of Enlightenment. An unexceptional study which derives from an academic problem of categorization in literary history rather than from critical discourse analysis. The Italian reception of the Enlightenment is the theme of *Aufklärung*, 5.1, ed. S. Carboncini, and addressed in C. de Pascale, 'Das Bild der Aufklärung in der italienischen Forschung des 20. Jahrhunderts', *ib.*, 5–24. On Classicism, A. Phelan, 'Deconstructing Classicism — Goethe's *Helena* and the need to Rhyme', Sheppard, *Germanistik*, 192–210, illuminatingly considers its preoccupation with the centred subject from the decentred standpoint of deconstruction; while K. S. Guthke, ' "Gipsabgüsse von Leichenmasken"? Goethe und der Kult des letzten Worts', *JDSG*, 35: 73–95, is a study in dying words for which G. acts as a 'Kristallisationsfigur' (p. 83), one of the most thought-provoking essays of the year, and — on reflection — a most suitable epigraph for literary-historical scholarship *per se*.

GENRES.   This year there are substantive volumes on methods and techniques of literary reflection. Titzmann, *Modelle*, confronts the paradox that though literary philology deals with historical phenomena, it has not developed models which adequately explain the transformation of literary genres. Focusing on the intrinsic literarity of the literary work, the volume attempts to rectify this deficit both in theoretical discussions drawing on literary theory, social science, evolutionary theory, and the history of science, and in case studies from English, German, Romance, and Slavonic literature. A stimulating volume and a necessary corrective to the usual literary history. Ueding, *Rhetorik*, is a comprehensive survey of the history, discipline, and application of rhetoric from Antiquity to the present day, not only in literature but also in music, architecture, public life, and television. The variety of the contributions, ordered under five main rubrics: 'Rhetorik als System', 'Rhetorikgeschichte als Problem der Rhetorikforschung', 'Rhetorik und künstlerische Ausdrucksformen', 'Rhetorik und Hermeneutik', 'Felder der ange-wandten Rhetorik', demonstrates the central idea of the volume: that rhetoric has always been understood 'als ein die Fachgrenzen des Wissens überschreitendes Beziehen, als Vermitteln der Erkenntnisse aus den Wissenschaften mit den Kategorien des allgemeinen gesell-schaftlichen Bewußtseins' (p. 2). Particularly relevant for the Classical period are: J. Dyck, 'Überlegungen zur Rhetorik des 18. Jahrhunderts und ihrer Quellenlage', 99–101, which sketches out a research plan for discovering the role of rhetoric in the formation of 18th-c. bourgeois culture; and B. Asmuth, 'Seit wann gilt die Metapher als Bild? Zur Geschichte der Begriffe "Bild" und "Bildlich-keit" und ihrer gattungspoetischen Verwendung', 299–309, which considers mainly 19th-c. definitions of image, metaphor, and symbol in order to clarify the relation between them and to suggest their possible genre-specific functions. Thomas Rathmann, '. . . *Die Sprach will sich ändern.' Zur Vorgeschichte der Autonomie von Sprache und Dichtung*, Munich, Fink, 150 pp., begins with the Moritz's categorical state-ments on the self-sufficient perfection of beauty and on the autonomy of art; proceeds, within a conceptual framework largely derived from the philosophy of Hans Blumenberg, to show the development of this idea in the literature and thought of the Middle Ages and the Baroque; and thus charts the transformation of the poet as imitator of nature into a quasi-divine creator. With chapters on the development of the autonomy of language, from the development of a vernacular to the epistemology both of the nominalists and rationalists, and of the humanists and of Nicholas of Cusa, along with a chapter on poetry, the fine arts and the abandonment of the principle of *mimesis*, the book culminates in a study on Fischart which shows how the literary work gcncrates the aesthetic experience of a world of its own making. A useful study in modern aesthetics. In a similar vein there is B. Fischer, 'Von der Ars zur ästhetischen Evidenz. Überlegungen zur Entwikklung der Poetologie von Gottsched bis Lessing', *ZDP*, 109, 1990: 481–502, which draws on Gottsched, Bodmer, Breitinger, Klopstock, Lessing, Mendelssohn, and Moritz to give a social-historical account of the decline of normative poetics and the emergence of the concept of the autonomous work; similarly, G. Hillen, 'Wertskala und Wertumbrüche im 18. Jahrhundert', *Slessarev Vol.*, 35–41; E. Kleinschmidt, 'Entregelte Poetik. Zum dichtungstheoretischen Sprachaufbruch im 18. Jahrhundert', *Fest. Steger*, 77–91, which valuably summarizes and illustrates in detail a key issue in Enlightenment discourse, the 'sprachliche Defiziterfahrung' (p. 79) between new ways of thinking and feeling and the available literary norms and rhetorical resources in which to express them; Id., ' "Begreif-Welt." Zur fiktionalen Raumerfahrung in der deutschen Literatur des 18. Jahrhunderts', *GRM*, 41:145–56, which traces the process of the internalization of the concept of space in 18th-c. narrative, with reference to Garve, Herder, Lessing, Moritz, Hölderlin, Kant, and Jean Paul. H. Langer, 'Literatursatire an der Wende vom 17. zum 18. Jahrhundert', Garber, *Barock*, 303–15, is a narrowly focused review of the controversy around 1700 between C. Wernicke, C. F. Hunold, and Postel on the use of imagery in poetry.

Deutsche Balladen, ed. Hartmut Laufhütte, Stuttgart, Reclam, 647 pp., is an anthology chronologically grouped according to author from Johann Gleim to Ulla Hahn with almost one fifth of the volume devoted to Classical authors (including Löwen, Pfeffel, Schiebeler, Herder, Bürger, Hölty, Goethe, and Schiller), but by far the major part to the 19th and early 20th cs. Bibliographical details (dates of composition, first publication, and the edition used) are given for each text, along with a bibliography of ballad anthologies and secondary literature, and a most useful 'Nachwort' reviewing critical concepts of the ballad form, proposing a generic model (pp. 619–20) and reassessing its 18th-c. origins in order to affirm its modernity. The six-volume history of poetry, Hans-Georg Kemper, *Deutsche Lyrik der frühen Neuzeit*, Tübingen, Niemeyer, continues with vol. 5/1, *Aufklärung und Pietismus*, xi + 180 pp., and vol. 5/2, *Frühaufklärung*, x + 248 pp., Vol. 5/1 reaffirms the significance of Pietism for 18th-c. poetry and philosophy with chapters on 'Pietismus und Aufklärung' (covering the problem of earthly happiness, the pietistic struggle against the world, and pietistic melancholy); on 'Pietismus, Aufklärung und Mystik' (covering mysticism and alchemy, animism and mechanism, the 'chain of being'); and 'Pietistisches Autonomiestreben: Selbstvergottung und Androgynie (Arnold)'. Authors surveyed include Leibniz, Spener, Francke, Hunold, Moritz, Stahl, Thomasius, while the final chapter offers an appreciation of Arnold's religious verse. Vol. 5/2 argues for a positive re-evaluation of the poetry of the early Enlightenment given that recent research tends to stress its regional variations rather than to contextualize it by reference to France or Britain. The period is covered in two sections: 'Autonomiestreben im Zeichen der Natur' which comprises the following chapters: 'Zum Stil- und Funktionswandel in der Lyrik um 1700', 'Die Auflösung der Harmonie zwischen Vernunft und Offenbarung', and 'Poetisierung des Naturrechts', and deals with philosophy and literary theory (Leibniz, Gottsched, Lessing, Canitz, Wolff, Reimarus, Pufendorf); and 'Poesie als "Dollmetsch" der Natur' which comprises the following sections: 'Poetischer Gottesdienst (Brockes)', 'Lehrdichtung als Aufklärungskritik (Haller)', '"Und glücklich macht uns die Natur" — Poesie als Selbstmedikation (E. Chr. v. Kleist)', and 'Die tugendhafte Aufklärung und ihr anakreontischer Sündenfall', covering Hagedorn, Baumgarten, Meier, Gleim, Uz, and Götz. In short, both volumes are comprehensive, accessible and informative. Similarly, U.-K. Ketelsen, 'Innovation und Transformation: von der Entstehung aufklärerischer Lyrik im Verfall der barocken Poetik', *Slessarev Vol.*, 43–53. Burkhard Moennighoff, *Intertextualität im scherzhaften Epos des 18. Jahrhunderts* (P, 293), 174 pp., studies various kinds of mock heroic epic: the parodistic, exemplified by Zachariä's 'Der Renommiste' (1774); the romantic, by Wieland, *Der neue Amadis* (1771/94); the travesting, by Blumauer's *Virgils Aeneis travestirt* (1782); the Hudibrastic, by Kortum's *Jobsiade* (1784); with an introduction setting out various dimensions of intertextuality (e.g. graphical, phonological, lexical, metrical), and a conclusion on the role of intertextuality in the development of the genre. Those who feel it anachronistic to interpret a Neo-Classical form by recourse to a postmodern technique might reconsider that M.'s study is less an 'approach' to the texts than a response to their inherent literary quality. So well does this book vindicate its methodology that its final, brief accommodation to literary history comes as a disappointment. H. Rölleke, 'German fable poetry in the context of the French Revolution', *The French Revolution: German Responses*, *SMLS*, Special Issue: 5–22.

R. Möhrmann, 'Von der Schandbühne zur Schaubühne: Friederike Caroline Neuber als Wegbereiterin des deutschen Theaters', *Slessarev Vol.*, 61–71; R. Schade, 'An early enlightenment comedy: Bach's "Kaffee-Kantate" (1734–35)', *ib.*, 55–60; C. Zelle, 'Alte und neue Tragödie — Mythos, Maschine, Macht und Menschenherz. Beiträge zur Querelle des Anciens et du Modernes von Saint-Évremond, Lenz, Molitor, Robert und Kürnberger', *GRM*,

41:284–300. This year there is renewed interest in the German reception of English drama (see below: SCHILLER, KOTZEBUE), reflected also in H. Poppelmann, '"To enlarge the province of the graver kind of poetry." Dramentheoretische Überlegungen zu George Lillos *The London Merchant*', *Arntzen Vol.*, 109–22, which examines the literary and social reasons — particularly the imperative to link the Enlightenment and the world of commerce — for L.'s play becoming a precedent for 18th-c. drama. The value of anthropological reconception as opposed to the historical approach is demonstrated in G. Flaherty, 'The art of dying on stage', *LY*, 21, 1989 (1990):103–21, which surveys 18th-c. attitudes to death and dying and their representation in contemporary drama; and in Jutta Greis, *Drama Liebe. Zur Entwicklungsgeschichte der modernen Liebe im Drama des 18. Jahrhunderts*, Stuttgart, Metzler, 271 pp., which constitutes an exemplary reflection on symbolic forms. Rather than rehearsing yet again a social historical interpretation of 18th-c. drama or refining detailed points in existing interpretations, the book presents (in Foucault's term) an 'archaeology' of love as a *topos* of modern culture: 'es bleibt die Frage zu klären, wie im 18. Jahrhundert die Liebessemantik zu einer entscheidenden Tiefenstruktur unserer Kultur wurde' (p. 2). G.'s survey of comedies, tragedies, and historical dramas from Gottsched to Schiller, from 'Empfindsamkeit' to Classicism, demonstrates the articulation of a discourse about love which organizes, though not unproblematically, individual, interpersonal, and social behaviour. She concludes that the connection made in this discourse between love and marriage, love and personal security, love and existential truth, persists into contemporary attitudes and experience. Not unrelated, R. Zeller, 'Gesetzmäßigkeiten literarischen Wandels am Beispiel des Dramas in der zweiten Hälfte des 18. Jahrhunderts', Titzmann, *Modelle*, 89–102, on the basis of Czech and Russian structuralism and formalism, gives a concise and illuminating account of the evolution of 18th-c. drama without relying on the conventional periodizations. Similarly T. Salumets, 'Unterwanderte Normendestruktion. Zur Poetologie des Sturm-und-Drang-Dramas', *Euphorion*, 85:70–84.

G. R. Hoyt, 'Rezeption des Barockromans in der frühen Aufklärung', Garber, *Barock*, 351–64, argues that, ideological and cultural differences apart, German novelists up to 1760 (e.g. Wieland) sought continuity with their Baroque predecessors. *Reflection and Action: Essays on the Bildungsroman*, ed. James Hardin, Columbia, South Carolina U.P., xxvii + 504 pp., contains the following essays: F. Martini, 'Bildungsroman — term and theory', 1–25; J. L. Sammons, 'The Bildungsroman for non-specialists: an attempt at clarification', 26–45; M. Swales, 'Irony and the novel: reflections on the German Bildungsroman', 46–68; H. Steinecke, 'The novel and the individual: the significance of Goethe's *Wilhelm Meister* in the debate about the Bildungsroman', 69–96; D. F. Mahoney, 'The apprenticeship of the reader: the Bildungsroman of the "Age of Goethe"', 97–117; T. P. Saine, 'Was *Wilhelm Meisters Lehrjahre* really supposed to be a Bildungsroman?', 118–41; J. K. Brown, 'The theatrical mission of the *Lehrjahre*', 142–62; E. Bahr, '*Wilhelm Meisters Wanderjahre, oder die Entsagenden* (1821–1829): from Bildungsroman to archival novel', 163–94; E. T. Bannet, 'Rewriting the social text: the female Bildungsroman in eighteenth-century England', 195–227; W. Koepke, '*Bildung* and the transformation of society: Jean Paul's *Titan* and *Flegeljahre*', 228–53; M. Minden, 'The place of inheritance in the Bildungsroman: *Agathon, Wilhelm Meisters Lehrjahre*, and *Der Nachsommer*', 254–92; besides others on Eichendorff, Hoffmann, Rilke, Mann, Hesse, and Wolf. These major studies of individual examples of the genre within its German cultural context provide definitions which attempt to normatize the wider applications of the term as a theoretical concept applicable in non-German literary traditions. But though this volume will surely become a standard work on the subject, it lacks a certain radical self-reflection on its own conceptualizations, in contrast to H. Laufhütte, '"Entwicklungs- und Bildungsroman" in der deutschen Literaturwissenschaft. Die Geschichte einer fehlerhaften Modellbildung und ein Gegenentwurf', Titzmann, *Modelle*, 299–313, which offers a critique of the genre itself based not on the historical origins of its definition (see Morgenstern and Schleiermacher) or (see Hardin) on exceedingly problematic normatization. Instead L. argues from formalistic premisses: 'Gattungen sind als nur in ihren Darbietungs- und Argumentationsstrukturen (rhetorischen Grundstrukturen) feste, in allen anderen Bestandteilen auf verschiedenen Ebenen synchron und diachron variable Darstellungs- und Argumentationsmodelle faßbar' (p. 310). Hence the 'Bildungsroman' is but one manifestation of 'exemplificatory biographical and autobiographical narrative' which also comprises *inter alia* the picaresque novel, the 'Entwicklungsroman', and the 'Künstlerroman'. This is a most useful essay in demystification. *Der deutsche soziale Roman des 18. und 19. Jahrhunderts*, ed. Hans Adler (WF, 630), 1990, 473 pp., contains a well chosen selection of critical essays on the genre from the late Enlightenment to Naturalism, together with an introduction (pp. 1–14) on its scope and changing functions during this time from revealing subjectivity to dealing increasingly with social issues, and a section (pp. 15–19) anthologizing programmatic definitions from 1844 to 1886. The first two sections dealing respectively with the social novel in the Enlightenment and with *Wilhelm Meisters Wanderjahre*, a precedent for the genre in the 19th c., comprise: M. Beaujcan, 'Philanthropie und Gesellschaftskritik im Trivialroman des 18. Jahrhunderts', 23–45; G. Cepl-Kaufmann and M. Windfuhr, 'Aufklärerische Sozialpädagogik und Sozialpolitik. Zu Pestalozzis Erziehungsroman *Lienhard und Gertrud*', 46–98; G. Häntzschel, 'Christian Gotthilf Salzmanns *Carl von Carlsberg oder über das menschliche Elend*', 99–126; G. Radbruch, 'Goethe: Wilhelm Meisters sozialistische Sendung', 129–56; P.-P. Sagave, *'Wilhelm Meisters Wanderjahre* und die sozialistische Kritik', 157–70.

Die Frau im Dialog: Studien zu Theorie und Geschichte des Briefes, ed. Anita Runge and Lieselotte Steinbrügge, Stuttgart, Metzler, 242 pp. (a companion volume to *Brieftheorie des 18. Jahrhunderts*, see *YWMLS*, 52:674), aims to raise the profile of the epistolary genre within 'Literaturwissenschaft' and to demonstrate its significance for specifically female forms of writing as a test-case for the relevance of gender to the interpretation of literature. Ranging over the early 18th c., the 19th c. with Schumann and Reventlow, down to Rilke, Heidegger and Bachmann, the contributions include: R. Nörtemann, 'Die "Begeisterung eines Poeten" in den Briefen eines Frauenzimmers. Zur Korrespondenz der Caroline Christiane Lucius mit Christian Fürchtegott Gellert', 13–32; H. Schwarz, 'Poesie und Poesiekritik im Briefwechsel zwischen Clemens Brentano und Sophie Mercau', 33–50; E. Bettinger, 'Women of letters. Die politische Briefliteratur von Aphra Behn, Dalrivier Manley and Eliza Haywood', 53–76; L. Steinbrügge, 'Kritische Briefe zur Kultur der Aufklärung. Madame Riccobonis *Lettres de Milord Rivers*', 77–92; A. Runge, 'Die Dramatik weiblicher Selbstverständigung in den Briefromanen Caroline Auguste Fischers', 93–114; U. Scholvin, '"... diese Entfernung wird dir mehr geben als oft meine Gegenwart." Zur Poetologie von Goethes *Italienische Reise*', 173–92. These informative essays should give a new impetus to gender-based literary reflection.

The necessary theoretical and general remarks on travel-writing are to be found in Fischer's book on Forster (see below, p. 715) as well as in U. Hentschel, 'Die Reiseliteratur am Ausgang des 18. Jahrhunderts. Vom gelehrten Bericht zur literarischen Beschreibung', *IASL*, 16.2:51–83; Id., '"ein unabsehbares Meer des Krieges." Ein Beitrag zur Geschichte der Reiseliteratur am Ausgang des 18. Jahrhunderts', *WW*, 41:378–88; and N. Salnikow, 'Einige Anmerkungen zu N. M. Karamzins Bildungsreise 1789–1790 durch Deutschland, die Schweiz, Frankreich und England', *Fest. Mayer*, 237–45. Johann Michael Afsprung, *Reise durch einige Cantone der Eidgenossenschaft*, ed. Thomas Höhle, Leipzig, Koehler & Amelang, 1990, 144 pp., a delightful book, illustrated with reproductions of contemporary prints, which gives the integral text of the first (and only) 1784 edition, together with notes and a postface summarizing

A.'s life and works. For A., as for other German republicans and democrats of the late Enlightenment, the travelogue is a vehicle for political opinions.

The development of history as a genre and as a discipline continues to be explored. Ulrich Muhlack, *Geschichtswissenschaft im Humanismus und in der Aufklärung. Die Vorgeschichte des Historismus*, Munich, Beck, 460 pp., considers such topics as the pre-history of historicism; the purpose of history; the theory of historical knowledge; the subject of history including particular histories as well as 'Universalgeschichte', space and time, the history of institutions and cultural phenomena; historical interpretation; and historical method. It thus traces the process, which can be located quite precisely in the late 18th c., whereby history and historical methods became the main means of understanding immanent human reality. However, that this detailed and discriminating reflection of a discipline on its origins, which even recognizes its structural solipsism (p. 435), should reaffirm, rather than critically analyse the controlling *topoi* of its discourse, is surprising. Covering very much the same ground is Horst Walter Blanke, *Historiographiegeschichte als Historik* (FH, 3), 809 pp., which begins by setting out the guiding concepts in the history of historicism, as derived from Kuhn and Rüsen; then, with a wealth of empirical data, examples of historiography from the late Enlightenment onwards, reconstructs the scientific paradigms by which historicism reflects on itself. A major contribution to the social construction of reality which repays careful reading, even though it is debatable whether history, for all its theoretical underpinning, thus becomes more reliable. See also H. W. Blanke, 'Historismus als Wissenschaftsparadigma. Einheit und Mannigfaltigkeit', *Fest. Conrady*, 217–31, and J. Fohrmann, 'Deutsche Literaturgeschichte und historisches Projekt in der ersten Hälfte des 19. Jahrhunderts', *ib.*, 205–15 (cf. *YWMLS*, 52:683).

THEMES. V. Riedel, 'Aristoteles, Lessing, Goethe und Fragen der modernen Wirkungsästhetik', *WB*, 36, 1990:1329–40. G. Flaherty, 'Archaic forms of ecstasy in eighteenth-century aesthetics', *Slessarev Vol.*, 85–90. W. Mauser, 'Poesie der Erscheinung: Zur Rhetorik des "glückseligen Körpers" in der Aufklärungsliteratur. Ein Versuch', *ib.*, 73–84, considers the image of women in the 18th c. C. Rudnik, 'Literarische Exzerpte Charlotte von Schillers — ein Beitrag zur Rezeptionsgeschichte um 1800. Versuch einer summarischen Auswertung der Quellen aus dem Goethe- und Schiller Archiv', Hahn, *Vorfeld*, 140–46, offers a case-study of a woman's intellectual horizons in the late 18th c. S. Lange, 'Über epische und dramatische Dichtung Weimarer Autorinnen. Überlegungen zur Geschlechtsspezifika in der Poetologie', *ZGer*, n.F., 1:341–45, examines Caroline von

Wollzogens 'Der leukadische Fels' (1792), Charlotte von Stein's tragedy 'Dido und Amalia' (1794), and Amalia von Imhoff's epic poem 'Die Schwestern von Lesbos' (1800) to explore these writers' search for a poetics relevant to female experience not to be dismissed as dilettantism by Schiller and Goethe. Similar themes are developed in *'Der Menschheit Hälfte blieb noch ohne Recht': Frauen und die Französische Revolution*, ed. H. Brandes, Wiesbaden, Deutscher Universitäts Vlg, 204 pp., comprising the following: S. Petersen, 'Frauen in der Französischen Revolution', 9–27; I. Modelmog, 'Die Frau aus der Fremde. Portrait einer anderen Revolution: Germaine de Staël', 28–63; B. Becker-Cantarino, 'Poetische Freiheit, Revolution und Patriarchat: Über Therese Hubers Roman *Die Familie Seldorf*', 64–73; D. von Hoff, 'Zwischen Enischluß und Befreiung. Das weibliche Drama um 1800 am Beispiel der Dramatikerin und Schauspielerin Elise Bürger (1769-1833)', 74–87; E. Süllwold, '*Charlotte Corday* in Hamburg. Christine Westphalens Drama von 1804', 88–112; L. Licher, '"Der Völker Schicksal ruht in meinem Busen." Karoline von der Günderrode als Dichterin der Revolution', 113–32; U. Böhmel Fichera, 'Das Frauen*zimmer* und die Manns*person*. Politik in literarischen Frauenzeitschriften des ausgehenden 18. Jahrhunderts', 133–45; H. Brandes, '"Ueber die Revolutionssucht deutscher Weiber." Frauenbilder in der deutschen Publizistik um 1800', 146–63; F. Hoffmann, '". . . nahm sie statt der Flöte das Schwert." Über den Zusammenhang von bürgerlicher Revolution und musikalischer Bewegungsfreiheit von Frauen', 164–84; M. Mies, 'Die Französische Revolution kann für Frauen nicht nachgeholt werden', 185–99. These reflective essays show that even though women were involved in the Revolution and far from unaffected by contemporary political issues, they benefited little from its claims for emancipation. See also: M.-C. Hoock-Demarle, 'Female readings of the French Revolution: the reception of the Revolution in German women's novels of the time', *The French Revolution: German Responses*, SMLS, Special Issue: 5–22. But perhaps the most eloquent testimony of the situation of women at this time is *Die Liebe der Günderode. Ein Roman in Briefen*, ed. Josef Görtz (SPi, 1229), 263 pp., which contains the correspondence of the unhappy love-affair between F. Creuzer and G. which culminated in her suicide. That the female voice is not even heard is here graphically illustrated by the fact that while C.'s letters fill some 220 pp., only 11 pp. of G.'s desperate outpourings survive. See also: M. E. Goozé, 'The seduction of Don Juan: Karoline von Günderrode's Romantic rendering of a Classic story', *Slessarev Vol.*, 117–19. Gender issues are further considered in *Frauenfreundschaft — Männerfreundschaft: Literarische Diskurse im 18. Jahrhundert*, ed. Wolfram Mauser and Barabara Becker-Cantarino, Tübingen, Niemeyer, x + 342 pp., containing: E. Meyer-Krentler, 'Freundschaft im 18. Jahrhundert. Zur Einführung in die Forschungsdiskussion', 1–22; W. Barner, 'Gelehrte Freundscaft im 18. Jahrhundert. Zu ihren traditionalen Voraussetzungen', 23–45; B. Becker-Cantarino, 'Zur Theorie der literarischen Freundschaft im 18. Jahrhundert am Beispiel der Sophie La Roche', 47–74; V. Ehrich-Haefeli, 'Gestehungskosten tugendempfindsamer Freundschaft: Probleme der weiblichen Rolle im Briefwechsel Wieland-Sophie La Roche bis zum Erscheinen der *Sternheim* (1750–1771)', 75–135; W. Fahs, 'Zum Verhältnis Goethe — Schiller', 137–40; M. Heuser, '"Das beständige Angedencken vertritt die Stelle der Gegenwart." Frauen und Freundschaften in Briefen der Frühaufklärung und Empfindsamkeit', 141–65; W. Kehn, '"Die Schönheiten der Natur gemeinschaftlich betrachten." Zum Zusammenhang von Freundschaft, ästhetischer Naturerfahrung und "Gartenrevolution" in der Spätaufklärung', 167–93; B. Leuschner, 'Freundschaft als Lebensgestaltung bei Therese Heyne: Schwärmen und gut handeln', 195–212; W. Mauser, 'Freundschaft und Verführung. Zur inneren Widersprüchlichkeit von Glücksphantasien im 18. Jahrhundert. Ein Versuch', 213–35; U. Prokop, 'Die Freundschaft zwischen Katharina Elisabeth Goethe und Bettina Brentano — Aspekte weiblicher Tradition', 237–77; B. A. Sørensen, 'Freundschaft und Patriarchat im 18. Jahrhundert', 279–92; F. Vollhardt, 'Freundschaft und Pflicht. Naturrechtliches Denken und literarisches Freundschaftsideal im 18. Jahrhundert', 293–309, together with a bibliographical essay. In exploring the theme of friendship in terms of social history and social psychology, this innovating volume compares its literary and philosophical discourse with records of actual interpersonal behaviour: e.g. its stress on the study of friendship between women is particularly significant since friendship was then defined as an exclusively male virtue. Hence this collection of exemplary essays in cultural history further vindicates both the need to elucidate literature with concepts from other disciplines and the conception of literature as a symbolic form of social anthropology. Gender-based interpretations of individual works include: G. K. Hart, 'Voyeuristic star-gazing: authority, instinct and the women's world of Goethe's *Stella*', *Monatshefte*, 82:408–20, which argues that the play 'is an important vehicle of patriarchal ideology [. . .] because it attempts to seduce women into the service of love and [. . .] provides a new type of reassurance for patriarchal anxieties' (p. 417), and also, 'A family without women: the triumph of the sentimental father in Lessing's *Sara Sampson* and Klinger's *Sturm und Drang*', *LY*, 22, 1990 (1991):113–32; B. Prutti, 'Das Bild des Weiblichen und die Phantasie des Künstlers: Das Begehren des Prinzen in Lessings *Emilia Galotti*', *ZDP*, 110:481–505;

W. S. Davis, '"Frauenzimmerliche Handarbeiten." Reflections on
Goethe's poem "Magisches Netz"', *JIG*, 22, 1990 (1991):58–80,
which argues that 'G. celebrates a woman's experience not with
clichés of femininity [. . .] but with a tribute to women's struggle for
power within the salon' (p. 76); B. Greiner, 'Weibliche Identität und
ihre Medien: zwei Entwürfe Goethes (*Iphigenie auf Tauris*, 'Bekenntnisse einer schönen Seele'), *JDSG*, 35:33–56.
  Ernst Cassirer, *Rousseau, Kant, Goethe*, ed. Rainer A. Bast
(PBib, 440), xxxvii + 204 pp., makes widely available for the first
time the original texts of C.'s now classic essays, 'Kant und Rousseau'
(1939), and 'Goethe und die Kantische Philosophie' (1944), first
published in English in 1945, along with two other already published,
but little-known essays, 'Kant und Goethe' (1924) and 'Rousseau'
(1939). Hence this carefully edited and bibliographically informative
volume helps (as B. rightly argues) to repair the inexcusable neglect
from which C., as one of the key thinkers of the 20th c., suffered as a
result of anti-Semitic discrimination and enforced exile. For lending
further impetus to the necessary (even if belated) revival of interest in
C.'s philosophy, this volume is, therefore, doubly welcome. D.
Henrich, 'Die Französische Revolution und die klassische deutsche
Philosophie', *GJb*, 107, 1990:102–14, succinctly summarizes the
reorientation in German thinking provoked by its response to the
events in France. The philosophical issue of understanding is
broached from several perspectives: K. H. Göttert, 'Ringen um die
Verständlichkeit: Ein historischer Streifzug', *DVLG*, 65:1–14, which
succinctly reviews the criteria of intelligibility in literary and
philosophical discourse from Erasmus to Luhmann with reference to
Descartes, D'Alembert, Wieland, Garve, Kant, F. Schlegel, and
Schleiermacher; M. Morton, '*Verum est factum*: critical realism and the
discourse of autonomy', *GQ*, 64:149–65, a well-informed essay which
considers with reference to Lessing's ring parable the human capacity
to establish the integrity of fact and the stability of meaning; W.
Mauser, 'Billigkeit. Zum Konzept der Modernität im 18. Jahrhundert', *RG*, 21:49–77, which discusses this concept in Gellert, Lessing,
and Sophie von La Roche as central to the development of the ethics
of individual autonomy; K. Weimar, 'Zur neuen Hermeneutik um
1800', *Fest. Conrady*, 195–204, which both summarizes the growing
autonomy and inner coherence of the process of understanding as a
response to the cult of originality after 1770, and the ever-diminishing
deference to traditional rhetorical norms of sense and meaning; A.
Käuser, 'Die Physiognomik des 18. Jahrhunderts als Ursprung der
modernen Geisteswissenschaft', *GRM*, 41:129–44, a stimulating
essay which argues that the study of physical appearance anticipates
the cognitive and social functions of modern visual media

(photography, film, and video); T. Althaus, 'Geistige Syntax. Einige Sätze zur Entwicklung des Essays im 18. Jahrhundert, zu einer möglichen Theorie der Gattung und zu Friedrich Schlegels Essay "Über die Unverständlichkeit"', *Arntzen Vol.*, 159–71, which reviews the role of the essay in maintaining a form of reflection beyond the jurisdiction of science: 'der Essay weist durch die in ihm realisierten Möglichkeiten auf die Defizienz des reglementierten und reglementierenden Sprachgebrauchs von Wissenschaft hin' (p. 161); and J. M. Van Der Laan, 'Forster's "Leckereyen" and Mösers "Harlekin": medium and message of the essay', *LY*, 21, 1989 (1990): 157–69. Manfred Frank, *Selbstbewußtsein und Selbsterkenntnis. Essays zur analytischen Philosophie der Subjektivität*, Stuttgart, Reclam, 485 pp., with contributions on 'Subjektivität und Individualität: Überblick über eine Problemlage'; 'Individualität und Innovation'; 'Identität und Subjektivität'; 'Sprachanalytische und neostrukturalistische Theorie des Selbstbewußtseins'; 'Ist Selbstbewußtsein ein propositionales Wissen?'; 'Hat Selbstbewußtsein einen Gegenstand?'; 'Subjektivität und Intersubjektivität', argues, on the basis of classical German philosophy and its subsequent ramifications, for reinstating the concept of subjectivity against postmodern theories proposing the end, or the decentred state of the subject. Whatever one's position in this debate, these essays are required reading.

Samuel Pufendorf, *On the Duty of Man and Citizen According to Natural Law*, ed. James Tully, trans. Michael Silverstone, CUP, xliii + 183 pp., a translation of the 1673 treatise *De officio hominis et civis juxta legem naturalem*, offers in modern English, prefaced with a succinct discussion of its historical and theoretical context, one of the key texts on the theory of natural rights which underpins the *Weltanschauung* of the Enlightenment and Classical periods. The editor and translator are to be congratulated for making available a work which should be required reading not just for students of political theory, but also for those interested in 18th-c. culture in general. Also on this theme, see F. Vollhardt, 'Die Kritik der anthropologischen Begründung barocker Staatsphilosophie in der deutschen Literatur des 18. Jahrhunderts (J. M. von Loen und J. A. Eberhard)', Garber, *Barock*, 377–95, which examines how the notion of the inherent sociability of human beings is transformed from a response to their natural vulnerability into a means of fulfilling the moral imperative of perfectibility, which eventually subverted the state system of absolutism; and M. A. Cattaneo, 'Die Strafrechtsphilosophie der deutschen Aufklärung', *Aufklärung*, 5.1, 1990:25–56. T. Mueller, '"Handlungen, deren sich Cannibalen sich schämen würden" — das Phänomen der Masse in der deutschen Literatur um 1800', *CGP*, 19:37–50, considers the Enlightenment's wariness of the irrational power of crowds in Hölderlin (*Hyperion*), Goethe (*Götz, Egmont*) and Wieland (in his reactions to the French Revolution). Y.-G. Mix, 'Guillotinen aus Papier. A. G. F. Rebmanns, *Obscuranten-Almanach* (1798–1800) and H. A. O. Reichards, *Revolutions-Almanach* (1793–1804)', *WNB*, 16:22–28, examines in these two contrasting responses to the French Revolution the reasons why Reichard's anti-revolutionary journal was so much more popular than its Jacobin counterpart edited by Rebmann. Also on this theme: Edmund Burke and Friedrich Gentz, *Über die Französische Revolution. Betrachtungen und Abhandlungen*, ed. Hermann Klenner, Berlin, Akademie, 802 pp., containing G.'s 1793 translation of B.'s *Reflections* together with five essays of his own on the same theme, plus notes to the texts, a chronology, a bibliography, and a thankfully trenchant essay by K. on 'Burke, Gentz und die Geburt des bürgerlichen Konservatismus' which discusses B.'s influence in Germany, the origins of modern conservatism and its inherent duplicities, and the difference between Burke's ideas and the more reductive thinking in present-day neo-conservatism: a timely edition, in more senses than one. M. Beetz, 'Negative Kontinuität. Vorbehalte gegenüber barocker Komplimentierkultur unter Altdeutschen und Aufklärern', Garber, *Barock*, 281–301, traces how informality and naturalness in social manners became identified with bourgeois culture in contrast to the courtly formality and intricacy of social etiquette in the Baroque period. *Vom alten zum neuen Bürgertum. Die mitteleuropäische Stadt im Umbruch 1780–1820*, ed. Lothar Gall (Stadt und Bürgertum, 3) Munich, Oldenbourg, 678 pp., consists of historical and sociological accounts of the formation of bourgeois culture in Bremen, Göttingen, Münster, Dortmund, Aachen, Cologne, Wetzlar, Wiesbaden, Frankfurt am Main, Heidelberg, Karlsruhe and Mannheim, Heilbronn, Augsburg, and Munich — case studies which provide the literary scholar with useful insights into the everyday life of the Enlightenment, thus relativizing its self-image in literature and philosophy. See also the more theoretical essay, K. von Schilling, 'Bürgerlichkeit. Zum Status einer Kulturwissenschaftlichen Kategorie', *Fest. Mayer*, 465–514. A further contribution to 18th-c. social history is *Volksunruhen in Württemberg 1789–1801*, ed. Axel Kuhn et al. (Aufklärung und Revolution, 2), Stuttgart-Bad Canstatt, Frommann-Holzboog, 369 pp., which contains ten case-studies of popular unrest in South German communities, preceded by an introductory essay. The volume aims to represent everyday life at the time of the French Revolution, and to demonstrate that the German public was by no means as quiescent as is generally believed. However, it abstains from making direct comparisons with the French Revolution: this unrest stemmed from local protests and did not produce programmatic statements on civic rights even if the Revolution itself was a precedent.

Aufklärung, 4.2, 1989, ed. Günther Birtsch, 142 pp., is entitled *Patriotismus* and — besides the introduction, G. Birtsch, 'Erscheinungsformen des Patriotismus', 3–5 — comprises the following surveys of this problematic 18th-c. phenomenon: M. Stolleis, 'Reichspublizistik und Reichspatriotismus vom 16. zum 18. Jahrhundert', 7–23; K. O. Freiherr von Aretin, 'Reichspatriotismus', 25–36; H. Klueting, '"Bürokratischer Patriotismus". Aspekte des Patriotentums im theresianisch-josephinischen Österreich', 37–52; H. Zückert, 'Republikanismus in der Reichsstadt des 18. Jahrhunderts', 53–74; C. Wiedemann, 'Zwischen Nationalgeist und Kosmopolitanismus. Über die Schwierigkeit der deutschen Klassiker, einen Nationalhelden zu finden', 75–101. Further essays on local history are: K. Gerteis, 'Zur Thematik der Alltagsgeschichte im Zeitalter der Aufklärung', *Aufklärung*, 5.2, 1990:3–8, which introduces an entire issue on the subject; A. Gestrich, 'Politik im Alltag. Zur Funktion politischer Information im deutschen Absolutismus des frühen 18. Jahrhunderts', *ib.*, 9–27; U. Puschner, 'Verzögerte Aufklärung. Lesegesellschaften in Kurbayern', *ib.*, 29–48. Perhaps the most ingenious study of the emergence of the bourgeois world, part social history, part discourse analysis, part literary criticism, is Friedrich A. Kittler, *Dichter — Mutter — Kind*, Munich, Fink, 271 pp., which consists of several studies, some of them published as articles from 1977–80, on the development of the family as a social unit and on the discourse, both fictional and social, which controls it: 'Lessing: Erziehung ist Offenbarung', 19–45, on the 'bürgerliches Trauerspiel'; 'Schiller: Archäologie der Psychologie des bürgerlichen Dramas', 47–98, a veritable collage of text extracts from Schiller to the 20th c. on forms of family behaviour; 'Goethe I: Lullaby of Birdland', 103–18, which, starting from 'Wandrers Nachtlied', is about lullabies, lyrical poetry, and the calming parental voice; 'Goethe II: Ottilie Hauptmann', 119–48, on social modernization in the early 19th c., together with essays on Novalis: 'Die Irrwege des Eros und die "absolute Familie"', 148–95; on Hoffmann: 'Eine Detektivgeschichte der ersten Detektivgeschichte', 197–218, and on Bettina von Arnim, 219–55. What makes this work, which repays careful reading, particularly stimulating, is that here literature is presented in its proper social-anthropological context as an agent of social processes. Essays on German-Jewish issues include: H. G. Göpfert, 'Friedrich Alexander Bran (1767–1831) Publizist und Verleger. Ein Hinweis', *AGB*, 36:351–64, a tribute to the journalist and advocate of Jewish emancipation, editor of various *Goethezeit* journals, most notably *Minerva* on the death of Archenholz; C. A. Lea, 'Tolerance unlimited:

"The noble Jew" on the German and Austrian Stage (1750–1805)',
GQ, 64: 166–77, on the development of this stereotype until its demise
in the upsurge of nationalist reaction to the Napoleonic invasion;
S. M. Lowenstein, 'Two Silent Majorities — Orthodox Jews and Poor
Jews in Berlin 1770–1823', *LBIYB*, 36: 3–25, a necessary complement
and counterbalance to the preoccupation with the Jewish Enlightenment, a sociological study of these neglected groups which helps 'put
into perspective the actual shape of events which took place between
1770 and 1830 in Berlin' (p. 3).

In recent years under the impulse provided by interest in
German-Jewish history, gender studies, and sociological theories,
Salon culture has increasingly become a field of research, as in the
compendious Petra Wilhelmy, *Der Berliner Salon im 19. Jahrhundert
(1780–1914)* (Veröffentlichungen der Historischen Kommission zu
Berlin, 73), Berlin, de Gruyter, 1989, 1030 pp. Peter Gradenwitz,
*Literatur und Musik im geselligem Kreise: Geschmacksbildung, Gesprächsstoff
und musikalische Unterhaltung in der bürgerlichen Salongesellschaft*,
Stuttgart, Steiner, 284 pp. + 24 pls, attempts to define the indefin-
able: the ethos of salon sociability, by attempting to reconstruct from
documentary and literary evidence the inherently evanescent conversation, music, and behaviour of this matrix which fostered late-
Enlightenment and Classical culture. This is a most informative
work, a mosaic of all (the sometimes obscure) personalities and
relationships which maintained this unique institution. On the
politics of publishing there are: H. K. Caspart, *Michael Hermann
Ambros. Ein österreichischer Journalist zwischen Aufklärung und Reaktion.
Ein Beitrag zur österreichischen Mediengeschichte* (Dissertationen der
Universität Wien, 221), 2 vols, Vienna, VWGO, 547 pp.; H. Böning,
'Vielfalt der literarische Formen. Alltag und "Volk" in Publizistik
und Gebrauchsliteratur der deutschen Aufklärung', *WB*, 36,
1990: 1754–67; J. D. Popkin, 'The German press and the Dutch
patriot movement, 1781–1787', *LY*, 22, 1990 (1991): 97–111.

*Appelation an das Publikum . . . Dokumente zum Atheismusstreit um Fichte,
Forberg, Niethammer Jena 1798/99*, ed. Werner Röhr, Leipzig, Reclam,
622 pp., the second, revised edition of the volume published in 1987,
provides a substantial, even if not exhaustive, documentary survey of
this controversy, symptomatic of the late Enlightenment, involving
Fichte and Forberg, beginning with the articles which provoked it,
and followed by the accusations of atheism in the *Philosophisches
Journal*, Fichte's *Appelation an das Publikum*, reactions to it from a host
of contemporary sources, legal depositions, documents pertaining to
the Weimar court's decision to dismiss Fichte, student petitions on
behalf of Fichte, contemporary reactions to Fichte's dismissal, and
finally its further reverberations. A further commentary section

includes a chronology of events, as well as an essay on the significance of the controversy, together with annotations, a bibliography of contemporary pamphlets on the affair, and an index. F. M. Eybl, '"P. Abrahams und Kochems Wust." Zur Ausgrenzung der populären geistlichen Literatur in der Aufklärung', Garber, *Barock*, 239–48, deals with the reception of Abraham and Cochem in the 18th c. to show the means by which the Enlightenment was able to integrate popular expressions of apparently outmoded religious themes into its own canon of taste and relevance.

This year sees two key works on the history of medicine. *The Languages of Psyche. Mind and Body in Enlightenment Thought*, ed. G. S. Rousseau (Clark Library Lectures, 12), California U.P., xix + 480 pp., consists of essays grouped under four rubrics: 'Theories of mind and body' which sets out the 18th-c. philosophical aspects of the mind-body problem in essays by G. S. Rousseau, R. Porter, and P. Foot; 'Mind and body in practice: physiology, literature, medicine', with contributions from R. G. Frank, Jr, C. H. Flynn, and A. Luyendijk-Elshout; 'The politics of mind and body: radical practitioners and revolutionary doctors', with essays on 'Enlightenment and natural philosophy', on de Sade, and on the birth of psychiatry by S. Schaffer, D. B. Morris, and D. B. Weiner respectively; and 'The Jewish question', with an essay on medicine, racism, and anti-Semitism by R. H. Popkin. As with the Rousseau essay collections mentioned earlier, these essays too are required reading. They illustrate a feature of 18th-c. discourse which cannot be emphasized enough: that issues of mind and body have a crucially constitutive role to play in it. *The Medical Enlightenment of the Eighteenth Century*, ed. Andrew Cunningham and Roger French, CUP, 1990, xi + 330 pp., consists of eleven contributions covering the politics, professional organization, and ethics of medical theory and practice in 18th-c. England, France, and Germany, including J. Geyer-Kordesch, 'Georg Ernst Stahl's radical Pietist medicine and its influence on the German Enlightenment', pp. 67–87, and R. French, 'Sickness and the soul: Stahl, Hoffman and Sauvages on pathology', pp. 88–110. These studies give a well-documented historical profile of 18th-c. medicine; that they helpfully provide a survey of its heterogeneous character counteracts their aroma of antiquarianism which always attaches to this subject when it is devoid of a theoretical armature drawn from the philosophy or sociology of knowledge. See also H. Schipperges, 'Konzepte der Lebenskunst in Aufklärung und Romantik. Orthobiotik — Makrobiotik — Kalobiotik', *JFDH*, 90–108; S. Seifert, '"Historia literaria" an der Wende zur Aufklärung. Barocktradition und Neuansatz in Morhofs *Polyhistor*', Garber, *Barock*, 215–28, which rightly underlines M.'s significance for contributing both to the organization and theory of science and learning and to founding the culture of critical rationalism in the 18th c.; H. F. Fullenwider, 'Die Rezeption der jesuitischen *argutia-*Bewegung bei Weise und Morhof', *ib.*, 229–38; and R. Stichweh, 'Bildung, Individualität und die kulturelle Legitimation von Spezialisierung', *Fest. Conrady*, 99–112, on the political, social, cultural, and psychological conditions in which knowledge in the latter part of the 18th c. became organized into specialized disciplines promoted by individual scientists and scholars. S. shows how this modern conception asserted itself against feudal class-structures, while the notion of 'Bildung' acted as a compensation against partiality and fragmentation endemic to this process, with the result that philosophy as a unifying discipline was eventually replaced by the concerted interaction of the disciplines of human knowledge. H. Kleindienst, 'Gottesbeweis anhand der Anatomie. Zur Typologie der anatomisch argumentierenden Physikotheologie im 18. Jahrhundert', *Das achtzehnte Jahrhundert*, 15:20–30. Two essays consider continuities between 18th-c. and contemporary attitudes: L. Schiebinger, 'The anatomy of difference: race and sex in eighteenth-century science', *ECS*, 23, 1990:387–405, drawing on a wide range of sources, in particular Soemmerring and Blumenbach, thus showing how conceptions of race and gender were constructed by reference to the biological norms established by the European male scientist, provides further evidence of how the dubious sciences of the 19th c. — in this case eugenics — arose from the anthropocentric idealism of the Enlightenment; H. Detering, 'Die ökologische Nemesis: Zu Carl von Linnés *Iter Dalekarium*', *DVLG*, 65:593–608, discusses an Enlightenment, ecological critique by the celebrated scientist of environmental pollution in the mining region around Falun. M. Komorowski, 'Gelehrte Nachrichten aus Spanien in den *Göttingischen Anzeigen von gelehrten Sachen* am Ende des 18. Jahrhunderts (1780–1800)', *LitL*, 2:90–99.

2. GOETHE

BIBLIOGRAPHY, EDITIONS, AND CORRESPONDENCE. H. Henning, 'Goethe-Bibliographie 1988', *GJb*, 107, 1990:295–338. *Goethe–Bibliographie. Literatur zum dichterischen Werk*, ed. Helmut G. Hermann, Stuttgart, Reclam, 327 pp., with its selection of 3,000 titles from 1773 to April 1990 is a paperback list of secondary literature on G.'s works, life, and personality. That it aims to provide something for everyone: from introductory works suitable for the uninitiated or for pedagogical purposes to the demands of the most differentiated research topics; and to reflect the variable aesthetic and ideological reception of G.'s works by citing publications from authors and critics beyond the academic sphere, is enough to raise the suspicion of ulterior motive. That bibliography is a useful stimulus cannot be denied: but this one is dubious not just because one could never read to the end of this book of books, nor because it proposes accessible information as a surrogate for knowledge, but because it implies that the scientization of the literary understanding is the sole, valid response to the poetic voice. H.'s bibliography is a text-book illustration of how the extension of the culture of expertise feeds commercial enterprise. Having given generations convenient editions of G.'s (finite) works and (not so finite) interpretations of his works, Reclam now sets up a demand for a work of works about works (ad infinitum). This year G.'s *Sämtliche Werke nach Epochen seines Schaffens*, ed. Karl Richter *et al.*, Munich, Hanser, continues with vol. 7: *Leben des Benvenuto Cellini. Diderots Versuch Über Malerei. Rameaus Neffe*, ed. Norbert Miller and John Neubauer, 1181 pp., and vol. 20.1: *Briefwechsel zwischen Goethe und Zelter in den Jahren 1799 bis 1832. Text 1799–1827*, ed. Hans-Günther Ottenburg und Edith Zehm *et al.*, 1088 pp. (with vol. 20.2, containing the remaining letters to 1832 and notes and apparatus, still to come). It also sees the launch of *Sämtliche Werke. Briefe, Tagebücher und Gespräche*, ed. Karl Eibl *et al.*, DKV. The first of the 40 volumes to be published is vol. 3: *Italien — Im Schatten der Revolution. Briefe, Tagebücher und Gespräche vom 3. September 1786 bis 12. Juni 1794*, 1144 pp. + 16 pls, and belongs to the *2. Abteilung: Briefe, Tagebücher und Gespräche*, ed. Karl Eibl *et al.*, in which the material is arranged in chronological order, hence in a manner similar to the Munich edition. The commentary and apparatus otherwise follow the DKV format. Scholars will debate the merits of yet another Goethe edition; the sceptic cannot but wonder if the periodical reinvention of editorial principles is not just a ploy to market the same commodity, which only exacerbates the wide discrepancy between the Rolls-Royce end of the scholarly enterprise and the editions most mortals can actually afford (cf. Martens, below). Other editions include: Johann Wolfgang Goethe, *Unterhaltungen deutscher Ausgewanderten*, ed. Leif Ludwig Albertsen, Stuttgart, Reclam, 147 pp., a carefully modernized text from the Jubiläums-Ausgabe, here presented not only in terms of G.'s aesthetic and moral intentions as revealed in these narratives, but also in terms of the derivation of the genre in late Roman literature, in e.g. Petronius and Apuleius; Johann Wolfgang Goethe, *Aus meinem Leben. Dichtung und Wahrheit*, ed. Walter Hettche, 2 vols, Stuttgart, Reclam, 843, 423 pp., which contains a carefully modernized text of the 'Akademie-Ausgabe' in vol. 1, and in vol. 2 the textual apparatus comprising a list of variants and problematic passages; a new, detailed line-by-line commentary based on the Hamburger Ausgabe but also drawing on later editions and on manuscripts; a bibliography, a postface which outlines the place of the work in G.'s own life as well as its composition and structure, and indexes. Two English editions this year are eloquent reminders of W. Benjamin's insight that translation furthers the continuing survival of the original work: Johann Wolfgang von Goethe, *Faust. Part One*, trans. David Luke, OUP, lxiv + 176 pp., offers a translation of really poetic quality, preceded by an informative introduction and a most useful synopsis of the various stages of composition of the drama. *Goethe's 'Wilhelm Meister's Travels'*, trans. Thomas Carlyle with an introduction by James Hardin (SGLLC, 56), xvi + 352 pp., offering C.'s text preceded by his essay on G., is prefaced by an introduction which stresses the modernity of the novel, summarizes C.'s reception of G., and outlines the publication history of the novel. This reissue is most welcome: for over and above having available for the non-Germanist an English version of this novel, C. remains an exemplary mediator of Classical German culture in the English speaking world, not least because the resources of his language seem so responsive to the dynamics of the original. Various essays deal with editorial issues: W. Hagen, '"Wüßten Sie was ich dieses Jahr gelitten habe . . ." Anlaß und Hintergrund für Goethes Brief an Sulpiz Boisserée vom 3. Februar 1826', Hahn, *Vorfeld*, 58–74, deals with G.'s negotiations with Cotta over the publication of the Ausgabe letzter Hand; E. Nahler, 'Johann Peter Eckermann und Friedrich Wilhelm Riemer als Herausgeber von Goethes literarischem Nachlaß', *ib.*, 75–84; S. Schäfer, 'Zur Erschließung der Registratur der bei Goethe eingegangenen Briefe. Die Einbeziehung der Vorarbeiten zu Goethes *Tag- und Jahresheften* in die Redaktion der ersten Bände der Regestaufgabe *Briefe an Goethe*', *ib.*, 85–107; I. Schmid, 'Goethes Briefregistratur — eine Quelle zu den *Tag- und Jahresheften*', *ib.*, 108–25; Id., 'Auf dem Wege zu einer Gesamtausgabe der Briefe Goethes', *ZDP*, 110:515–29; G. Martens, 'Der wohlfeile Goethe. Überlegungen zur textphilologischen Grundlegung von Leseausgaben', *Fest. Zeller*, 72–91, which surveys, with reference to *Werther*, available paperback editions to test the reliability of the texts in which G. is most widely read. It concludes that publishers, by false economy, generally fail to draw on the philological knowledge available in historical-critical editions.

GENERAL STUDIES AND ESSAY COLLECTIONS. W. Daniel Wilson, *Geheimräte gegen Geheimbünde: Ein unbekanntes Kapitel der klassisch-romantischen Geschichte Weimars*, Stuttgart, Metzler, 391 pp., an absorbing study, which aims to demystify Goethe's endorsement of absolutism by examining his, and Carl August's, involvement in the Illuminati as a means of surveillance. The book thus questions G.'s liberalism by examining the consequences for the literary establishment (Herder, Wieland, Fichte, and Schlegel) of his often secret political activity in the service of a repressive system. Noting that totalitarianism took hold in those countries in the grip of enlightened absolutism in the 18th c., it even suggests that G.'s mentor relationship with Carl August set a precedent for Heidegger's involvement with National Socialism. A study which dissents from G. as exemplary personality, thus contrasting totally with Ludwig Fertig, *Johann Wolfgang von Goethe der Mentor* (Poeten als Pädagogen), WBG, 212 pp., a curious example of a literary intention at odds with its subject, as the preface, acknowledging that G. had no official teaching duties, intimates. In chapters pointing out that G. was generally reserved towards pedagogical institutions, surveying his own private education, evaluating his relationship with Carl August, recognizing the problems of his son and grandsons in coping with his prominence, and, finally, considering the pedagogical aspects of the *Wilhelm Meister* novels, F. goes off in pursuit of the rather obsolete ideal of the artist as existential role-model, oblivious to the fact that in the crassest way he is reducing G.'s significance to a single intention. If F. wished seriously to consider G. as a mentor, he might have mentioned the contemporary impact of *Werther* and then stumbled across the tricky concept of moral responsibility, something which always embarrasses quaintly complacent hagiography. Similarly Roger Paulin, *Goethe, The Brothers Grimm, and Academic Freedom*, CUP, 30 pp., which examines in relation first to Goethe's role in the dismissal of Fichte and Oken from Jena and then to the dismissal of Jacob and Wilhelm Grimm from Göttingen 'how university and state collided in their separate interests and how this typifies the intellectual climate of Germany in [. . .] its golden age' (p. 6). A study far less shrewd than Wilson's, its smaller scope notwithstanding. Since it fails to consider teaching and the development of knowledge as forms of political activity as such, let alone in the Classical era, its interest remains essentially antiquarian. H. Schanze, 'Goethes Rhetorik', Ueding, *Rhetorik*, 139–47, detects three phases in G.'s reception of rhetoric: a 'postmodern' reading of Quintilian, then contempt for it as in *Faust I*, finally its reformulation according to the aesthetic premisses of 'Weltliteratur', so that, in the end, it permits G. to establish Classical criteria for different art forms and to define his own individual literary procedures.

VERSE. This year the validity of the concept of 'Erlebnislyrik' is again being challenged, as in M. Wünsch, 'Die frühe Lyrik Goethes in ihrem literatur- und denkgeschichtlichen Kontext', *Christiana Albertina*, 32, April 1991:5–14, which argues that G.'s early lyric poetry is not 'Erlebnisdichtung' but fragmentary expressions of a literarily self-conscious attempt to establish via fictional and rhetorical techniques moments of harmony between self and nature. An illuminating essay with important implications for poetics in general. H. Geulen, 'Marginalien zu Goethes Gedicht "Ein zärtlich iugendlicher Kummer . . .", *Arntzen Vol.*, 137–46, comments on this 1772 poem to argue for its humanistic concerns as opposed to accepting it as a solipsistic expression of experience. U. Gaier, 'Vom Mythos zum Simulacrum: Goethes "Prometheus"–Ode', *Lenz-Jahrbuch*, 1:147–67, rehearses the social, metaphysical, and aesthetic implications of this key poem of the late 18th c. G. Schmid, 'Die Handschriften zu Goethes *Venezianischen Epigrammen*. Prolegomena zur Analyse und Auswertung einer unausgeschöpften Quelle', Hahn, *Vorfeld*, 35–43. D. Barry, '"Sollte der herrliche Sohn uns an der Seite nicht stehen?" Priapus and Goethes *Römische Elegien*', *Monatshefte*, 82, 1990:421–34, finds a source for the significance of Priapus in R. P. Knight, *A Discourse on the Worship of Priapus and its Connection with the Mystic Theology of the Ancients* (1786). Peter Morgan, *The Critical Idyll: Traditional Values and the French Revolution in Goethe's 'Hermann und Dorothea'* (SGLLC, 54), 1990, 183 pp., analyses the social and political dimensions of the work as well as its literary precedents and Enlightenment context, to consider the challenge to German national self-identity by the consolidation of the Revolution in France after 1792. A detailed analysis which culminates in a justifiable *aporia*: 'The contradictory images of the revolutionary intellectual and the patriotic *Bürger* are presented as a paradox, an irresolvable contradiction in reality, which can be resolved only through irony in the work of literature' (p. 138). Id., 'Aufklärung, Revolution und Nationalgefühl: Der Topos des Jakobiners und die Frage deutscher Identität in Goethes *Hermann und Dorothea*', *ZGer*, n.F. 1:533–43; Y. A. Esaghe, 'Der Schluss von Goethes *Hermann und Dorothea* aus entstehungsgeschichtlicher Sicht', *JDSG*, 35:57–72.

DRAMA (other than *Faust*). I. H. Solbrig, 'The theater, theory, and politics: Voltaire's *Le Fanatisme ou Mahomet Le Prophète* and Goethe's *Mahomet* adaptation', *MGS*, 16.1:21–44, discusses the cultural and political background of G.'s version. H. Detering, 'Die Heilung des Verliebten. Pathologie und Poetologie in Goethes Schäferspiel', *JFDH*, 1–20; K. Mommsen, 'Der politische Kern von Goethes "Elpenor"', *ib.*, 21–56; K. Mickel, *'Die natürliche Tochter* oder: Goethes soziologischer Blick', *GJb*, 107, 1990:56–70; K. F. Gille, *'Die natürliche Tochter*. Zu Goethes Versuch einer Kritik der Krise', *ZGer*, n.F. 1:352–63. K. Ermann, 'Goethes Shakespeare-Bild', *GJb*, 107, 1990:217–42.

FAUST. Hans Kaufmann, *Goethes 'Faust' oder Stirb und werde*, Berlin — Weimar, Aufbau, 315 pp., is a series of reflections dating from the final years of the GDR: on the reception of the drama ('Wozu auf *Faust* zurückkommen?'; 'Bild und Begriff'. 'Der "nationale Faust" in der frühen DDR'); on various themes ('Die Tat als Intention'; 'Helena und das Vorgefühl des Tatgenusses'; 'Arbeit und Freiheit — Herr und Knecht'; 'Goethe und seine Faust-Figur'; 'Die späten Szenen und der Wettausgang'); on stylistic and formal issues (on the intended audience, on the non-classical form of the drama; on allegory and symbol); on G.'s concept of beauty; and concluding with a speculation on Rosa Luxemburg as a reader of *Faust*. Far from aiming at a systematic examination, these essays are rather meditative readings, their insights the outcome of a long familiarity with the work, hence of inspired serendipity. See also R. Geissler, 'Goethes *Faust* als mythopoetische Darstellung der Neuzeit', *LitL*, 2:67–79; K. F. Gille, '*Faust als nationaler Mythos*', *WB*, 37:541–57. J. Göres, '*Faust*: Vers 11091 bis Vers 11115', Hahn, *Vorfeld*, 30–34, considers the implications for the interpretation of these lines arising from a variant unknown to the Weimarer Ausgabe and subsequent editions. Finally, *Doktor Johannes Faust*, ed. Günther Mahal, Stuttgart, Reclam, 132 pp., contains Simrock's four-act version of the puppet play together with the two-part Ulmer Puppentheater version. A brief postface surveys the various forms of the Faust legend from the 16th c. onwards.

NARRATIVE. A. Käuser, 'Das Wissen der Anthropologie: Goethes Novellen', *GJb*, 107, 1990:158–68, which contends rather self-evidently: 'die zeitgenössische Wissenschaft der Anthropologie ist der dann epistemologische Gehalt, den Goethes Novellen als Sinn und Bedeutung innehaben' (p. 160). S. W. Strickland, 'Flight from the given world and return to the new: the dialectic of creation and escape in Goethe's *Leiden des jungen Werther*', *GQ*, 64:190–206, is an allegorical reading based on Fredric Jameson's narrative theory. C. Träger, 'Goethes *Unterhaltungen deutscher Ausgewanderten* als Ausdruck eines novellistischen Zeitbewußtseins', *GJb*, 107, 1990:144–57, covers similar ground to Albertsen's postface to his edition (see above); G. von Wilpert, 'Revolution als Krankheit? Goethes Prokurator-Novelle und die *Cent nouvelles nouvelles*', *Arcadia*, 26:72–76. Theo Elm, *Johann Wolfgang Goethe: Die Wahlverwandtschaften* (Grundlagen und Gedanken zum Verständnis erzählender Literatur), Frankfurt am Main, Diesterweg, 107 pp., is a guide to the novel, placing it in the context of G.'s life and of natural science around 1800, providing a rather sketchy 'Wort- und Sachkommentar' to the text, outlining narrative structure, listing and commenting on themes and characters and concluding with a section on critical reception and a bibliography. A concise, comprehensive introduction but which unconsciously demonstrates how far literary interests are being assimilated to pedagogical intentions: for what would the putative reader who requires a gloss on 'Magnetnadel' or 'Frauenzimmer' make of the comparatively esoteric extracts from Benjamin, Walzel or Kittler? J. Noyes, 'Die blinde Wahl. Symbol, Wahl und Verwandtschaft in Goethes *Die Wahlver-wandtschaften*', *DVLG*, 65:132–51, considers the problem of interpreting the meaning of the novel by reference to the interplay within it between the treacherous, semiological conception of the world in which the characters make erroneous choices and G.'s underlying symbolic order of reality and nature. See also D. Farrelly, 'Die Gestalt einer Heiligen. Zur Figur der Ottilie in Goethes Roman *Die Wahlverwandtschaften*', *ZGer*, n.F. 1:364–78. Benedikt Jessing, *Konstruktion und Eingedenken. Zur Vermittlung von gesellschaftlicher Praxis und literarischer Form in Goethes 'Wilhelm Meisters Wanderjahre' und Johnsons 'Mutmassungen über Jakob'*, Wiesbaden, Deutscher Universitäts Vlg, 259 pp., is an essay in the sociology of the novel: it considers not just how the texts themselves represent society but how they exist in the society they represent. As a study in literary technique understood as a metonymy for social production techniques — in G.'s case the manufacture of textiles and the beginnings of capitalism, in Johnson's, the beginnings of socialist production methods in the GDR — it is in fact an ingenious illustration of one of its key points of reference: Benjamin's essay 'Der Autor als Produzent'. R. Gould, 'The function of the non-literary quotation in Part 4 of *Dichtung und Wahrheit*', *GLL*, 44:291–305, considers the problem of autobiographical self-presentation for the older Goethe. W. Baumgart, '"Südliche Beleuchtung." Der Träumer Eckermann', *Euphorion*, 85.111–24, arguing that it is unjust to regard E. as subaltern to G., evaluates him as a *Goethezeit* author in his own right.

THEMES. Ernst Osterkamp, *Im Buchstabenbilde: Studien zum Verfahren Goethescher Bildbeschreibungen*, Stuttgart, Metzler, x + 442 pp. + 29 pls, contains everything one needs to know — about Goethe's descriptions of paintings (but not sculpture or architecture) as a contribution to the as yet unwritten history of the genre of 'Bildbeschreibungen' (p. 5) — but hardly dared ask. Hence it is not a treatise on art history, nor does it enquire into the further resonances of G.'s essays as a genre, nor does it address directly the crucial issue of the literary reception and evaluation of the fine arts in the 'Kunstperiode' — largely because the work itself arose for a far more urgent reason: as an advanced thesis topic. So much erudition appears naïve: 'produktive Rezeptionsleistungen', 'hermeneutische Leistung', 'Relevanzgraden', 'kunstpolitische Gesamtkonstellation', 'Maßgabe des sich wandelnden Problembewußtseins', 'aktuelle künstlerische Konfliktkonstellationen' — the very vocabulary suggests that everything can be reckoned up, nothing left out of account: Bloch's commodity thinking ['Denkform Ware'] in its unreconstructed form. But when it all comes together, the bluffing is evident: 'so führte die Suche nach

23

einem Beschreibungsverfahren, das den Bildern in ihrer materialbe-
dingten Eigenart gerecht werden konnte, zu einer immer stärkeren
Durchtheoretisierung der Wahrnehmung und Normierung des
Urteilssystems, so daß wiederum die Werkindividualität zusehends
mehr durch werkexterne, universal gültige theoretische Muster
heteronom überformt wurde' (p. 182). This is surely not how G.
thought, rather how O. — here hostage to his own normatizing
mentality — thinks G. should have thought. G. (as O. intimates
(p. 1)) might well have concurred with Valéry's rhetorical reservation: 'Mais comment parler peinture?' The answer? Never ever like
this. On a similar theme is E. Gombrich, 'Goethe and the history of
art. The contribution of Johann Heinrich Meyer', *PEGS*, 60,
1989–90: 1–19, essentially a self-conscious anecdotal *gesture* of its
author's own eminence. J. P. Strelka, '"Da strahlt der Mythos von
Alltäglichkeit . . ." ' Zur Entwicklung Arkadiens als geistiger Landschaft bei Theokrit, Vergil, Goethe und Gottfried Keller', *Fest. Weber*,
149–68, traces the theme of the poeticization of ordinary life. W.
Bunzel, 'Das gelähmte Genie. Zu Goethes "Der Adler und der
Taube"', *WW*, 41: 1–14, regards this fable as unique in G.'s 'Sturm
und Drang' period in that it represents G.'s growing reserve towards
the concept of autonomous genius, hence signals his ambivalence
towards the 'Geniebewegung'. A. Corkhill, 'Zum Sprachdenken
Goethes in beziehungsgeschichtlicher Hinsicht', *Neophilologus*,
75: 239–51.

The theme of Goethe and the French Revolution still resonates:
Ruth I. Cape, *Das französische Ungewitter. Goethes Bildersprache zur
Französischen Revolution* (BNL, 109), 155 pp., is a conscientious work
which isolates G.'s metaphors as a form of figuration in their own
right, informing the higher, more stable sphere of symbol and allegory
in his works. It starts with G.'s conception of metaphor and symbol;
describes his attitude to the Revolution; surveys his early dramas on
the Revolution; and compares them with similar dramas by Iffland
and Kotzebue. There are further chapters on 'Das Märchen' and
Hermann und Dorothea, on *Die natürliche Tochter*, on *Faust II*, and, finally,
on G.'s 'Revolutionsbegriff'. C. concludes that G.'s metaphors,
largely drawn from nature, express his anxiety about the uncontrolled
force of the event while they also attempt to objectivize it historically.
In particular, *GJb*, 107, 1990, is almost entirely devoted to this issue,
as in H.-G. Werner, 'Revolution in Frankreich — Goethe und die
Literatur in Deutschland', 11–26; T. J. Reed, 'Revolution und
Rücknahme: *Wilhelm Meisters Lehrjahre* im Kontext der Französischen
Revolution', 27–43; P. Weber, 'Vom Rom nach Venedig. Bestätigung
und Korrektur "klassischer" Positionen durch den Ausbruch der
Französischen Revolution', 44–55; P. Grappin as well as G.-L. Fink

write on 'Goethe und Napoleon', 71–80, and 81–101, respectively; K.-D. Müller, 'Goethes *Campagne in Frankreich* — Innenansicht eines Krieges', 115–26; K. Richter, 'Das "Regellose" und das "Gesetz"'. Die Auseinandersetzung des Naturwissenschaftlers Goethe mit der Französischen Revolution', 127–43; H. Hamm, 'Der Einfluß der Französischen Revolution auf Goethes Arbeit am *Faust* von 1797 bis 1801', 169–78; L. Ehrlich, 'Goethes Revolutionskomödien', 179–99. Similarly: R. H. Stephenson, 'The place of revolution in Goethe's thinking: the case of *Wilhelm Meister*', *The French Revolution: German Responses*, *SMLS*, Special Issue: 5–22, which argues, in contrast to Reed, that G. does assimilate the Revolution's political implications.

Gerhard Wild, *Goethes Versöhnungsbilder. Eine geschichtsphilosophische Untersuchung zu Goethes späten Werken*, Stuttgart, Metzler, 175 pp., establishes a generative or interpretative framework for Goethe's later works, for his poetry ('Um Mitternacht'; 'Trilogie der Leidenschaft'; 'Dämmrung senkte sich von oben . . .'), for his *Novelle*, for narrative fiction (*Wilhem Meisters Wanderjahre*), and for *Faust*. Initial misgivings that this is yet another example of the literary specialist's obsession with historical categorizations quickly fade, since the main theme is G.'s reaction to the process of social modernization in the early 19th c. The chief characteristic of this process is a form of duplicity: the dichotomy between man and nature (Rousseau); between subject and object, consciousness and nature (Schelling); between the individual and its place in the economic process which culminates in alienation (Smith, Sartorius). W. argues that through poetic and aesthetic means G.'s later works seek forms of reconciliation reaffirming love and nature which are repressed by early modernism but which reassert the wholeness of human experience in the face of the possibility of its fragmentation. A stimulating, thoughtful study. A. Pöthe, 'Goethes Bilder von Kindheit. Überlegungen zu einem Thema der literarischen Öffentlichkeit im 18. Jahrhundert', *ZGer*, n.F. 1:330–40. Marie-Luise Kahler and Gisela Maul, *Alle Gestalten sind ähnlich. Goethes Metamorphose der Pflanzen*, Klassikerstätten zu Weimar, 104 pp., contains the text of G.'s *Versuch die Metamorphose der Pflanzen zu erklären* (pp. 82–101), preceded by an introduction reviewing G.'s interest in botany and evaluating his work (pp. 5–31), but by far the largest portion (pp. 33–82) comprises 53 plates of contemporary scientific drawings of botanical specimens selected from G.'s collection to illustrate his essay. A brilliantly conceived volume which could not be more Classical in its combination of knowledge and beauty. The proximity of the aesthetic and the scientific is also evinced in H. Dressler, 'Goethes Ansätze für eine Analogie von Farbe und Ton und deren Bestätigung aus heutiger Sicht', *GJb*, 107, 1990:243–52. Similarly, Wolfgang Buchheim, *Der*

Farbenlehrstreit Goethes mit Newton in wissenschaftsgeschichtlicher Sicht (Sitzungsberichte der Sächsichen Akad. der Wiss. zu Leipzig, math.-nat. Klasse, 123, 1), Berlin, Akademie, 15 pp., vindicates G.'s opposition to Newton by demonstrating that his insistence on colour as an experience from which the perceiving eye may not be excluded was later endorsed by (amongst others) Carus, Helmholtz, and Virchow in the mid-19th c., by quantum physics and Planck around 1900, and by Heisenberg and Born in the 1960s. Similarly, R. Wild, 'Der Narziß und die Natur. Bemerkungen zu Goethes Ballade "Der Fischer"', *Lenz-Jahrbuch*, 1:168–87, which sees the poem as a reflection on the relationship between human economic needs and the exploitation of nature, an issue which G. was confronting in the Ilmenau mines. W. argues (p. 182) that this is the first poem in which G. searches for a view of nature in which there is no dichotomy between human subject and natural object. Also, on the convergence of scientific method and composition of the scientific works, particularly on botany and zoology, see D. Kuhn, 'Der Arbeitsvorgang bei Goethes naturwissenschaftlichen Studien. Erkenntnisse aus dem nachgelassenen Arbeitsmaterial', Hahn, *Vorfeld*, 44–57.

INFLUENCE, RECEPTION. E. Friedrichsmeyer, 'Keller's *Spiegel, das Kätzchen*: A eudemonist answer to Goethe's Faust', *Slessarev Vol.*, 131–38. A. Pöllinger, 'Die Gründung des Goethebundes 1900. Ein Beitrag zum literarischen Leben im wilhelminischen Deutschland', *Buchhandelsgeschichte*, no. 3:89–98. Two essays on Thomas Mann's reception of Goethe: H. Koopmann, 'Aneignungsgeschäfte. Thomas Mann liest Eckermanns *Gespräche mit Goethe*', *Fest. Wysling*, 21–47, and H. Siefken, 'Goethe "spricht". Gedanken zum siebenten Kapitel des Romans *Lotte in Weimar*', *ib.*, 224–48. J. Hibberd, 'Wedekind und Goethe', *PEGS*, 60, 1989–90 (1991):21–38. W. Düsing, 'Goethe in ironischer Beleuchtung. Zur Klassik-Rezeption in Musils *Mann ohne Eigenschaften*', *JDSG*, 35:257–74. E. Middell, 'Hans Mayers Sicht auf Goethe', *ZGer*, n.F., 1:135–9.

BIOGRAPHY. Nicholas Boyle, *Goethe. The Poet and the Age*. 1. *The Poetry of Desire*, OUP, xx + 807 pp., is indeed a 'synthesis of syntheses' (p. x), already much acclaimed, balance-sheet of the life and works in their historical, social, and political context. It confirms that 'the definitive biography, English-style, is among the most admirable genres of historiography [. . .] it is rather as though the colourless light of historical time were [. . .] refracted by the prism of a great character so that in the resulting spectrum a complete unity of life and world were achieved' (H. Arendt). But in B.'s assertion that 'with G.'s œuvre the biographical approach has great analytical power' (p. xi), it tests Arendt's contention that the genre is 'unsuitable [. . .] for the lives of artists [. . .] whose significance lies chiefly in their works, the artefacts they added to the world, not in the role they played in it'. For the genre itself, a blend of various levels of argument and analysis, far from eliminating 'ideological preconceptions and conventional judgements' (p. xi) raises legitimate issues about the validity of its own conventions: about the nature of biographical truth in the light of Freud's contention (cited by R. Nägele) that it 'cannot be had and if one had it, it would be of no use'; about the reliability of 'historical contexts' constructed *post festum* with the 'cognitive asymmetry' of historical explanation *per se*. Undoubtedly this will be the standard biography for years to come, but that is no reason for ignoring that its narrative is generically determined by irony, i.e. by the trope of incongruity (here between subjective response and historical order, between existential issues and calendrical time) which controls its constant resort to the 'effet du réel': e.g. p. 3: 'When G. was born in the free city of Frankfurt on the Main on 28 August 1749, the Holy Roman Empress Maria Theresa had just [. . .] confirmed her right to rule Austria' (as though this observation did not apply to everyone born at that time); p. 294: 'Even so, G. was not prepared for the brutal opening of the second and [. . .] tragic phase of his early Weimar period'; p. 345: 'When he finally visited Weimar for twelve days in 1784, G. "went pale with joy" at the meeting'; pp. 648–49: 'he had taken the first steps to carrying it [i.e. the plan to return to Italy] out in January 1790, by dropping his hint to Einsiedel, the day after he posted off the manuscript to *Faust. Ein Fragment*'. Julius Voigt, *Goethe und Ilmenau*, ed. Karl-Heinz Hahn and Rosalinde Gothe, Leipzig, Reprintverlag, 1990, 392 + xiv pp., a reprographic reprint of the Leipzig, Xenien, 1912 edition, is a well-documented history of G.'s personal attachment to and administrative activities in this mining region so central to his life and work. Hahn's and Gothe's accompanying remarks respectively stress the value of this study for first drawing attention to G. as an administrator and contextualize it in relation both to other similar studies and to V.'s own life. H. Claussen, ' "Gegen Rondanini über . . ." Goethes römische Wohnung', *GJb*, 107, 1990: 200–16, argues for the restoration of 'eine der bedeutendsten Lokalitäten der deutschen Kultur- und Geistesgeschichte im Ausland' (p. 216). C. Michel, 'Goethe redivivus? Zu einem unbezeichneten Porträt Angelika Kaufmanns', *JFDH*, 57–67. Johann Heinrich Tischbein, *Zeichnungen aus Goethes Kunstsammlung*, ed. Margarete Oppel, Weimar, Klassiker-stätten, 80 pp., consists of 57 drawings from more than 250 in G.'s collection, selected to represent the forty-year relationship between artist and poet in commemoration of the 240th anniversary of T.'s birth. The drawings are ordered in accordance with the three main periods of T.'s association with G.: T.'s sojourn in Zurich and his second Roman period; T.'s personal contact with G. in Italy; and T. as an illustrator of G.'s works. With a brief, informative introduction, quotations from G.'s works accompanying the drawings, and iconographical and bibliographical information, the book provides intriguing examples of the artistic background to the Classical era.

3. Schiller

EDITIONS, LETTERS, AND REFERENCE WORKS. I. Hannich-Bode, 'Schiller-Bibliographie. 1987–1990 und Nachträge', *JDSG*, 35:387–459. *Schillers Werke, Nationalausgabe*, Weimar, Böhlau, continues with vol. 2, Teil IIA, *Gedichte (Anmerkungen zu Band 1)*, ed. Georg Kurscheidt and Norbert Oellers, 668 pp., which is one half of two volumes of textual apparatus to S.'s poetry and covers those works published in vol. 1 of the *Nationalausgabe*, i.e. up to the *Musen-Almanach für das Jahr 1799*. Because of the extent of the material, the plan to confine the apparatus to one volume had (as the editors explain) to be abandoned; hence their general appraisal of S.'s verse will be held over for inclusion in vol. 2, Teil IIB. For each poem are listed the date of composition, provenance of the manuscript and first publication details, variants and, where appropriate, explanatory notes indicating the literary-historical and biographical contexts, matters of versification, as well as commentaries on allusions and resonances in individual lines. There are also concordances for the manuscripts and published versions of the *Tabulae votivae* and the *Xenien*. This product of painstaking scholarship will clearly be a crucial philological resource. Other volumes which have appeared are: vol. 22, *Vermischte Schriften*, ed. Herbert Meyer, 524 pp., a reprographic reprint of the 1958 edition, supplemented by general and name indexes, which contains S.'s early Stuttgart writings mostly on medicine; journalism up to *Die Horen*; and literary criticism and reviews; and vol. 34, Teil I, *Briefwechsel. Briefe an Schiller 1.3.1790 — 24.5.1794 (Text)*, ed. Ursula Naumann, 398 pp., which conveys, refracted through his correspondents' reactions, the key personal and intellectual preoccupations of these years: his marriage, birth of his son, his illnesses, his interest in Kant and aesthetics. Friedrich Schiller, *Hundert Gedichte*, ed. Walter Lewerenz, Berlin, Neues Leben, 326 pp., actually the second edition of a collection published in 1988, is an anthology of well-known verse with accompanying sentimental illustrations.

GENERAL STUDIES AND ESSAY COLLECTIONS. This year there are three monographs on the life and works. First, T. J. Reed, *Schiller (Past Masters)*, OUP, 120 pp., is a sensitive appreciation of both S.'s historical and theoretical writings and his dramas. Because it is precisely the aesthetic view which produces a radical analysis of the actual conditions of human existence, of the relationship between ideals and reality, purpose and effect, and which has proved to be a fruitful legacy explored and developed by subsequent German thinkers and poets, S.'s work is viewed as ' "central" to human concerns', an appraisal which is 'a sober act of location'. A book to be regarded less as an 'introduction' to S., than as a stimulus, to return to the texts and read again. (The relevance of S.'s thinking is pursued further in Id., 'Hope in history: Schiller and the twentieth century', *BJECS*, 14: 125–38, where R. argues that S.'s philosophy of history — in his essays as well as in his dramas — was not characterized by a naïve optimism, but rather reflected a determined desire to find some coherent pattern to human action, and concludes with a parallel between the allegedly utopian revolt in *Wilhelm Tell* and the 'velvet revolutions' in Eastern Europe in 1989–90 to propose that the notion of hope in history has an objective basis.) Secondly, Lesley Sharpe, *Friedrich Schiller. Drama, Thought and Politics* (Cambridge Studies in German), CUP, xiii + 389 pp., is an exercise in biographical criticism, the coherence of the life and the coherence of the work complementing each other. This intellectual construction is articulated through informed and perceptive accounts of the dramas and theoretical essays, arranged chronologically and finished with a brief survey of S.'s reception in Germany. Though covering similar ground to Reed and stressing S.'s relevance, it fails to give the same sense of the implications of his thought. But it will surely become a standard work: it fulfils admirably the requirements of its genre. Thirdly, Sheila Benn, *Pre-Romantic Attitudes to Landscape in the Writings of Friedrich Schiller*, Berlin, de Gruyter, xii + 242 pp., with its conclusion (p. 208) 'that S.'s love of nature is [. . .] revealed by [. . .] his conviction that contact with nature could cure the ills of the moderns and help them attain their ideal potential', evinces the studied amnesia required to produce a work which neither realizes that 'nature' is an ideologically charged word from the 18th to 20th cs, nor problematizes its own terms by wondering what this conclusion means in the contemporary, post-atomic world in which (to quote Lawrence Durrell) we are all 'orphans of nature'. Academic in more ways than one. K. Manger, 'Schillers gebrauchter Barock', Garber, *Barock*, 419–34, starts with the Baroque influences to which S. would have been exposed at the Karlsschule and the court of Karl Eugen and proceeds to indicate Baroque motifs in his drama and poetry.

GENRES. C. Bruckmann, ' "Freude! sangen wir in Thränen, | Freude! in dem tiefsten Leid." Zur Interpretation und Rezeption des Gedichts *An die Freude* von Friedrich Schiller', *JDSG*, 96–112. S. Nienhaus, ' "Nichts sey ohne Ernst und Scherz." Achim von Arnims

Gedicht-Collage "Die Glockentaufe" und Schillers "Lied von der Glocke"', *WW*, 41:357–63, compares S.'s poem with A.'s parody to underscore the ultimately political differences between the two authors. D. Peyrache, 'Le sublime et le crime (Autour des *Brigands* de Schiller)', *RLC*, 259:277–88, considers the sublime as a form of modern heroism which links self-aggrandizement, abjection, and aestheticism. H. Nahler, 'Zur Entstehung der Mannheimer Bühnenbearbeitung von Schillers *Fiesko*', Hahn, *Vorfeld*, 126–33. H. Kraft, 'Schillers *Kabale und Liebe*. Über die Schranken des Unterschieds', *Fest. Verbeeck*, 99–107, discusses the play in terms of its representation of bourgeois consciousness of class distinctions. J.-F. Dwars, 'Dichtung im Epochenumbruch. Schillers *Wallenstein* im Wandel von Alltag und Öffentlichkeit', *JDSG*, 35:150–79, discusses the drama's subtext which invites reflection on the audience's part, leading them to assume responsibility for their action in everyday life to produce a more just society. D. C. Martin, 'Historical fact *versus* literary fiction: members of the House of Liechtenstein occurring in Schiller's *Wallenstein* and Grillparzer's *König Ottokar*', *MLR*, 86:337–48. R. C. Ockenden, '*Wilhelm Tell* as political drama', *OGS*, 18, 1989–90 (1991):23–44. B. Bauer, 'Friedrich Schillers "Maltheser" im Lichte seiner Staatstheorie', *JDSG*, 35:113–49, discusses S.'s fragment as an agent for Rousseauistic republicanism.

THEMES. Hans-Georg Werner, *Schillers literarische Strategie nach der Französischen Revolution* (Sitzungsberichte der Akad. der Wiss. in Berlin, Jg 1990, 7G), Berlin, Akademie, 35 pp., is an illuminating essay on the transformation in S.'s aesthetics and philosophy and its implications for the moral and political aims of his dramatic work. It argues, in particular, that S.'s recourse to ideal auxiliary constructions was a means of coming to terms with the anachronistic situation of German intellectuals (p. 26). M. Hoffmann, 'Ästhetische Erziehung und Ästhetik des Widerstands. Kunstautonomie und Engagements des Kunstwerks bei Schiller, Marcuse und Peter Weiss', *WB*, 37:819–38, considers the relationship between aesthetics and history; T. Cadete, 'Schillers Ästhetik als Synchronisierung seiner anthropologischen und historischen Erkenntnisse', *ib.*, 839–52. D. Pugh, '"Die Künstler": Schiller's philosophical programme', *OGS*, 18, 1989–90 (1991):13–22, argues that it is possible to see in the poem 'the entire architecture of S.'s idiosyncratic philosophical system' (p. 22). B. Bräutigam, '"Generalisierte Individualität." Eine Formel für Schillers philosophische Prosa', *Arntzen Vol.*, 147–58, discusses S.'s philosophy of language and his aim to give poetic concretization to the language of philosophy in order to establish an original link between human beings, language and beauty, thus producing a reflective form of communication rather than an esoteric, abstract metalanguage. N. Oellers, 'Die Heiterkeit der Kunst. Goethe variiert Schiller', *Fest. Zeller*, 92–103, compares S.'s *Wallenstein* prologue delivered at the opening of the new Weimar theatre on 12 October 1798 as amended by Goethe with the original and subsequently published version to reveal S.'s and Goethe's divergent conception of 'Heiterkeit' as applied to art and to nature. A. and J. Golz, '"Ernst ist das Leben, heiter sey die Kunst" — Goethe als Redakteur des *Wallenstein*-Prologs', Hahn, *Vorfeld*, 17–29, reaches similar conclusions to Oellers but evaluates their implications for textual criticism of the works of G. and S.

INFLUENCE, RECEPTION. G. Stilz, 'Robbers, Borderers, Millers and Men: Englische Räuberstücke zwischen Revolutionstragödie und melodramatischer Restauration', *DVLG*, 65:117–31, surveys, with reference to the reception of S.'s *Die Räuber* in England from Wordsworth to Pocock, the social and political conditions which brought about the 'Transformation des Räubermotivs von der Revolutionstragödie ins restaurative Melodrama' (p. 131). Similarly, H. W. Drescher, '"Account of *The Robbers*, a German Tragedy. By Mr. Friedrich Schiller." Text und Verfasserschaft einer zeitgenössischen Besprechung von 1792', *Fest. Mayer*, 270–89, provides an introduction to, and the text of, Henry Mackenzie's review which appeared in *The Sentimental and Masonic Magazine*, 1 (December 1792), 540–47. C. Schulz, 'Sentimentalisches Dichtungsverständnis und poetische Struktur. Zu einigen Aspekten der Schillerschen Ästhetik im Werk Dostoevskijs', *ZGer*, n.F. 1:510–20, centres on D.'s reception of 'Über naive und sentimentalische Dichtung', translated into Russian by D.'s brother Mikhail in the 1840s. L. Schulte-Sasse, 'National Socialism's aestheticization of genius. The case of Herbert Maisch's *Friedrich Schiller — Triumph eines Genies*', *GR*, 66:4–15, offers a critical analysis of the ideological appropriation of the younger Schiller in the 1940 propaganda film. *Schiller spielen: Stimmen der Theaterkritik 1946–1985, eine Dokumentation*, ed. Ferdinand Piedmont, WBG, 1990, 313 pp., comprises 'eine repräsentative Auswahl von Rezensionen bemerkenswerter Inszenierungen der am häufigsten aufgeführten Werke des Dramtikers' (p. xiii), i.e. *Die Räuber, Kabale und Liebe, Don Carlos, Wallenstein, Maria Stuart, Wilhelm Tell*, plus a notice on the *Demetrius* fragment, and an essay by A. Rossmann, 'Kalenderdenken als Rezeptionsmuster. Zu Tradition und Praxis der Schiller-Ehrungen in der DDR: Auch ein Beitrag zum 225. Geburtstag des Dichters', 283–87. P.'s introduction argues that, whether productions remain faithful to the text or depart from it in response to contemporary concerns, both types testify to the continuing resonance of Schiller's moral ideals in the modern world. Hans Georg

Müller, *Mit Wilhelm Tell um den Vierwaldstätter See* (Literaturreisen — Wege, Orte, Texte), Stuttgart, Klett, 1990, 224 pp., is evidence that for the literary person the world itself becomes a text: Schiller's play, offset by Max Frisch's adaptation, overlain by further extracts from Schiller's sources and other contemporary writings (all in blue print) are complemented (in black print) by topographical descriptions, plans, maps, travel information, and illustrations. A fascinating opportunity for the informed tourist to see reality transformed on the spot by the dramatic imagination.

BIOGRAPHY. V. Wahl, '"... daß ihm, zu seiner Aufmunterung, eine Professio Philosophiae ordinaria honoraria conferiret werde." Friedrich Schillers Ernennung zum ordentlichen Honorarprofessor an der Universität Jena. Ein biographisches oder universitätsgeschichtliches Problem?', Hahn, *Vorfeld*, 134–39, outlines the political and economic background to S.'s appointment.

4.   INDIVIDUAL AUTHORS

(EXCLUDING GOETHE AND SCHILLER)

ABBT.   H. E. Bödeker, 'Thomas Abbt (1738–1766)', *Aufklärung*, 14.2:103–05, is a brief biography.

BECK.   Thomas Ludolf Meyer, *Das Problem eines höchsten Grundsatzes der Philosophie bei Jacob Sigismund Beck* (El, 54), 257 pp., reassesses this now almost forgotten contemporary of the first generation of neo-Kantian philosophers, who in the wake of Kant's epistemological relativism sought to rediscover a fundamental basis for knowledge. Put very simply, B. postulated a primary, conscious intuition as the synthetic unity of consciousness. M.'s survey of B.'s philosophy makes a worthwhile contribution to understanding the modern problem of knowledge.

BERTUCH.   S. Seifert, 'Der Bertuch-Nachlaß als Quelle für kultur- und sozialgeschichtliche Forschungen. Das Beispiel des *Allgemeinenen Repertoriums der Literatur 1785 bis 1800*', Hahn, *Vorfeld*, 260–67.

BÜRGER.   I. Schelstraete, 'G. A. Bürgers *Lenore*: Volks- oder Kunstdichtung', *SGG*, 25, 1990:9–46, argues that despite his 'großen "populären" Instinkt' B. required all the techniques of poetry to produce the ballad.

CLAUDIUS.   W. von Meding, 'Matthias Claudius 1740–1815: Narr am Hof der regierenden Aufklärung', *LWU*, 24:3–16, argues with reference to the *Wandesbecker Boten* that C.'s work has an indirect impact which needs to be elicited from the 'Zuordnungen der Bauelemente' (p. 16). W. Martens, 'Gegen den Zeitgeist gerichtet: Matthias Claudius Gedicht "Der Mensch"', *ZDP*, 110, 505–14, considers C.'s critique of Enlightenment optimism.

COLLIN. P. Skrine, 'Collin's *Regulus* reconsidered', pp. 48–72 of *Bristol Austrian Studies*, ed. Brian Keith-Smith (BGP, 2), 1990, xvi + 274 pp., re-evaluates the play which made the reputation of this forgotten dramatist, by relating his — for the time — unconventional Roman theme of stoicism to contemporary art and music, differentiating it from Weimar Classicism, and regarding him, in terms of Austrian theatrical traditions, as a precursor to Grillparzer. It argues that its concern with such issues as the nature of society and the ethos of citizenship contributed to its contemporary success and ensures its continuing relevance.

DOHM. H. Mühleisen, 'Christian Wilhelm von Dohm (1751–1820)', *Aufklärung*, 5.1, 1990: 117–18.

EHRMANN. H. S. Madland, 'An introduction to the works and life of Marianne Ehrmann (1755–95): writer, editor, journalist', *LY*, 21, 1989 (1990): 171–96.

ESCHENBURG. M. Maurer, 'Johann Joachim Eschenburg und das Barock. Ein Beitrag zur Problematik der Kontinuität vom 17. zum 18. Jahrhundert', Garber, *Barock*, 337–49. L. Adey, '"Cursing cries and deep exclaims": Eschenburg's translation of *Richard III* (1776)', *OGS*, 18, 1989–90 (1991): 1–12.

FORSTER. *Georg Forsters Werke. Sämtliche Schriften, Tagebücher, Briefe*, ed. Akad. der Wiss. in Berlin, Zentralinstitut für Literaturgeschichte, Berlin, Akademie, continues with vol. 8: *Kleine Schriften zu Philosophie und Zeitgeschichte*, ed. Siegfried Scheibe, 552 pp. + 20 pls, the second edition of the volume first published in 1974, demonstrating the range of F.'s interests in biography and history, anthropology, biology, philosophy and politics in essays and fragments which in the best Enlightenment manner are pithy, thoughtful and engaging. There is a comprehensive apparatus which includes an introductory commentary on each essay, variants, annotations, and an index. Rotraut Fischer, *Reisen als Erfahrungskunst. Forsters 'Ansichten vom Niederrhein'* (AML), Frankfurt am Main, Hain, 1990, 368 pp., is based on the notion of travel as a form of experience, hence as a form of discourse, which comes into its own in the 18th c. The first part of the study outlines concepts of time, space and movement, as well as historical precedents for travel-writing; the second deals with the aesthetic experience of travel; the third with the ordering and evaluating of the travellers' experience. A thoughtful and stimulating work which co-ordinates a multiplicity of perspectives and vindicates the Classical status of Forster himself.

FREDERICK II. Friedrich der Grosse, *Der Antimachiavell oder Untersuchung von Machiavellis 'Fürst' bearbeitet von Voltaire*, ed. and trans. Helga Bergmann, Leipzig, Reclam, 150 pp., is an edition which both marks the 250th anniversary of its first publication and, in references to the power of the people to remove cynical politicians (p. 124) and the need for a 'Verantwortungspolitik' (p. 145), is also mindful of another, more recent historical milestone. A German translation of the 1740 text is accompanied by annotations, a short bibliography, and a commentary which considers F.'s motivations for writing it, Voltaire's influence and F.'s subsequent forsaking of his youthful political ideals.

GELLERT. E. Schön, 'Aufklärung der Affekte — Christian F. Gellerts *Leben der Schwedischen Gräfin von G****', *DUS*, 43.6:31–41, is a study of the structure and moral intention of the novel.

GOTTSCHED. G.'s importance as a mediator of Baroque culture for the 18th c. is assessed in W. Kühlmann, 'Frühaufklärung und Barock. Traditionsbruch — Rückgriff — Kontinuität', Garber, *Barock*, 187–214, which describes the intention of G.'s literary and cultural criticism to establish the institutions of bourgeois culture through a critique of more exclusive Barock values; in P.-A. Alt, 'Traditionswandel des Allegoriebegriffs zwischen Christian Gryphius und Gottsched', *ib.*, 249–70, which shows how the allegorical style after Gottsched became obsolete even though there is implicit recourse to it in, e.g., Jean Paul, Goethe and Schiller; and in F. Leibrock, 'Das Interesse an der Barockliteratur bei Gottsched und den Schweizern', *ib.*, 327–35. See also: B. Bräutigam, 'Fabelhafte Poesie in optimaler Welt. Gottscheds Literaturbegriff im Spiegel der Theodizee', *Fest. Schumacher*, 35–51; A. B. Gerken, *Die sprachtheoretische Differenz zwischen Gottsched und Gellert* (AD, 27), 1990, iv + 169 pp.

GROSSE. Carl Grosse, *Über das Erhabene*, ed. Carsten Zelle (Kleines Archiv des achtzehnten Jahrhunderts, 9) St Ingbert, Röhrig, 1990, 89 pp., is a timely reissue of the anonymous Göttingen — Leipzig 1788 edition in view of current renewed interest in the sublime in postmodernist criticism. Z.'s commentary, while admitting that this treatise lacks the intellectual penetration of Kant or Schiller, suggests that its subjective, sensual conception of the sublime and the beautiful marks its specific contribution to the contemporary debate while its amoral aestheticism is symptomatic of the end of the Enlightenment.

HAGEDORN. Alfons Klein, *'Die Lust, den Alten nachzustreben.' Produktive Rezeption in der Dichtung Friedrich von Hagedorns* (SBL, 25) St. Ingbert, Röhrig, 324 pp., considers this topic under six headings: a theatrical section on reception theory, a review of recent research, H. in the context of the contemporary reception of Classical antiquity, a survey of its reception in H.'s works, followed by a review of Classical motifs reworked by H., concluding with a section on H. and Horace. A comprehensive and detailed study.

HALLER. *The Correspondence between Albrecht von Haller and Horace-Bénédict de Saussure*, ed. Otto Sonntag (Studia Halleriana, 3), Berne,

Huber, 1990, 507 pp., discusses mainly scientific matters. K. S. Guthke, 'Bekenntnisse eines schweizerischen Opiumessers. Hallers Briefe an Pringle', *Das achtzehnte Jahrhundert*, 15:15–19. W. Preisendanz, 'Die äquivalenz von Rhetorik und poetischem Sprechen in Albrecht von Hallers *Die Alpen*', *DUS*, 43.6:21–29, discusses the style and form of didactic poetry.

HAMANN. B. Weissenborn, 'Erbe und Auftrag: Zur Editionsgeschichte der *Biblischen Betrachtungen* Johann Georg Hamanns', *DVLG*, 65:449–85, takes issue with Josef Nadler's standard edition of the work. Y. Kawanago, 'Hamann und das Alte Testament, "Golgotha und Schlebimini"', *DB*, 87:12–22. Helmut Weiss, *Johann Georg Hamanns Ansicht zur Sprache. Versuch einer Rekonstruktion aus dem Frühwerk*, Münster, Nodus, 1990, 203 pp.

HEBEL. Ludwig Fertig, *Johann Peter Hebel der Schulfreund* (Poeten als Pädagogen), WBG, viii + 121 pp., explores the relationship between H.'s pedagogical praxis and his literary activity. A far more successful study than the Goethe volume in this series, since H. was a teacher and his writings, as a matter of principle, were meant to edify and instruct.

HEIM. Ernst Ludwig Heim, *Tagebücher und Erinnerungen*, ed. Wolfram Körner, Leipzig, Koehler & Amelang, 1989, 406 pp., is a selection from H.'s copious diaries together with his memoirs. Given the extent of the original material, selecting the extracts must have been difficult. Hence a volume which might have provided invaluable insights into the working life of a late 18th-c. doctor, turns out to be of little more than antiquarian interest.

HEINSE. M. Dick, 'Die Suche nach dem verlorenen Leben. Zur Beziehung zwischen Natur, Kunst und Revolution in den Schriften Wilhelm Heinses', *Fest. Mayer*, 21–37.

HERDER. Tino Markworth, *Johann Gottfried Herder. A Bibliographical Survey 1977–1987*, Hürth-Efferen, Gabel, 1990, 97 pp. G. Arnold, 'Ideale und reale Bedingungen für Editionen und die geplante Fortführung der Herder-Briefausgabe', *Fest. Zeller*, 53–61, argues against the normatization of correspondence editions by contrasting the ideal criteria on which normatization could be based with the actual conditions of editorial work which, as illustrated by both the virtues and the ideological drawbacks of the Weimar, Böhlau edition of H.'s correspondence, defy these criteria; Id., 'Erkenntnisgewinn aus handschriftlichen Überlieferungen an Beispielen der Herder-Briefausgabe', Hahn, *Vorfeld*, 147–58, reiterates these issues. Current editions of works are: *Johann Gottfried Herder. Werke in zehn Bänden*, ed. Martin Bollack *et al.*, DKV, which continues with vol. 7, *Briefe zu Beförderung der Humanität*, ed. Hans Dietrich Irmscher, 1192 pp., which, besides the text, comprises a commentary on the genesis of the work as a response to the events in France in 1792–93, on its epistolary form and its structure, as well as a concise summary of H.'s concept of 'Humanität' and its influence, together with some 300 pages of explanatory annotations to the text and a comprehensive index. Works on aesthetics include Robert E. Norton, *Herder's Aesthetics and the European Enlightenment*, Ithaca, Cornell U.P., 1991, xiii + 258 pp., which discusses H.'s attempts to create a unified philosophy of aesthetics. But this year much more attention is paid to Herder's conception of history, as in P. J. Burgard, 'Literary history and historical truth: Herder — "Shakespeare" — Goethe', *DVLG*, 65:636–52, which compares the different views on literary history in H.'s and G.'s Shakespeare essays; B. Fischer, 'Das Ende der Kunst und die Krise der Aufklärung. Zur Entwicklung der spätaufklärerischen Geschichtsphilosophie Johann Gottfried Herders', *JFDH*, 68–69, which reflects on *Ursachen des gesunknen Geschmacks* [. . .] (1775) and *Auch eine Philosophie* [. . .] (1774); but principally, *Johann Gottfried Herder. Language, History, and the Enlightenment*, ed. Wulf Koepke (SGLLC, 52), 1990, 292 pp., which concentrates on 'this primary concern with the implications of H.'s unique idiom' (p. 8). Though the introduction describes H.'s work in the context of the Enlightenment, the Enlightenment itself is presented simplistically: e.g. its concern for natural law does not detract (as Koepke believes) from its revolutionary impact; Kant can hardly be adequately labelled a 'conservative revolutionary'; the systematic nature of German philosophy is neither caused by its remoteness from political action nor does it preclude it. More stimulating and varied than the volume's editorial framework are the essays it comprises: K. Müller-Vollmer, 'From sign to signification: the Herder-Humboldt controversy', 9–24; R. S. Leventhal, 'Progression and particularity: Herder's critique of Schlözer's Universal History in the context of the early writings', 25–46; K. Menges, 'Erkenntnis und Sprache. Herder und die Krise der Philosophie im späten achtzehnten Jahrhundert', 47–70; M. M. Morton, 'Discourse and gesture: the poetic dialectics of *On Diligence in Several Learned Languages*', 71–86; W. D. Wetzels, 'The Herder-Nicolai controversy', 87–97; R. Critchfield, 'Herder's *Journal meiner Reise*', 98–107; J. M. Van Der Laan, 'Herder's essayistic style', 108–23; H. Owren, '"Gewalt über die Worte": Eine Untersuchung zu Herders Wortgebrauch', 124–37; M. Bunge, 'Text and reader in Herder's interpretations of the New Testament', 138–50; E. A. Menze, 'On Herder as a translator and on translating Herder', 151–62; W. Koepke, 'Das Verhältnis individueller und kollektiver Kräfte in Herders Geschichtsauffassung', 162–74; S. B. Knoll, 'The experience denied: Herder abroad', 175–95; K. J. Fink, 'Tithonism, Herder's concept of literary revival', 196–208; E. Knodt, 'Dramatic illusion in the making of the past: Shakespeare's impact on Herder's philosophy of history', 209–23; W. Malsch, 'Herders Schrift über die Skulpturkunst in der Geschichte der Unterscheidung des Plastischen und Malerischen oder Musikalischen in Kunst und Literatur', 224–35; J. Boening, 'Herder and the White Man's Burden: the *Ideen zur Philosophie der Geschichte der Menschheit* and the shaping of British colonial policy', 236–45; L. Frank, 'Herder, Jauß, and the New Historicism: a retrospective reading', 246–88. See also Donald Lüttgens, *Der "Ursprung" bei Johann Gottfried Herder* (EH, I, 1260), 290 pp., which is a study of *Älteste Urkunde des Menschengeschlechts* so descriptive and narrowly focused as to negate its cognitive value — a conclusion reinforced by its unbelievably primitive standard of presentation: e.g. the liberal use of 'Sperrdruck' (e.g. pp. 30–31) which explodes the text into a senseless grid of letters redolent of a pop-art graphic. A. Horning Marschall, 'Oral poetry — written prose: throwing light on Johann Gottfried Herder's *Von den Lebensaltern einer Sprache*', *MGS*, 16.1, 1990: 1–20, deals with the relationship between H. and Condillac and argues that H. did know of C.'s *Essai sur l'origine des connoissances humaines* (1746) prior to writing his own essay.

HIPPEL. J. Kohnen, 'Hippel und die Juden', *RG*, 21:77–95, a well-researched article, considers the anti-Semitism of this reputedly enlightened author.

HUMBOLDT, ALEXANDER VON. Alexander von Humboldt, *Studienausgabe*, WBG, continues with vol. 4, *Mexico-Werk. Politische Ideen zu Mexico. Mexicanische Landeskunde*, ed. Hanno Beck with Wolf-Dieter Grün *et al.*, 578 pp. + 17 pls, a fine tribute to the editor's scholarship and to his commitment to his author and his work. The clear text and maps are supplemented by a commentary which not only illuminates H.'s pioneering and still unparalleled intellectual achievement in uniting history, natural geography, social geography, and statistics, but also offers a concise treatise on the history of geography as a science. E. Weigl, '"So wurde das Neue heimisch wieder." Alexander von Humboldts Integration fremder Naturerfahrung im "Naturgemälde"', *DB*, 87:57–66, is a further essay from a stimulating historian of ideas (cf. *YWMLS*, 52:683) who combines literary and scientific perspectives.

HUMBOLDT, WILHELM VON. K. Amegan, 'Das Reformwerk Wilhelm von Humboldts', *Études Germano-Africaines*, 8, 1990:21–23. J. Wohlleben, 'Wilhelm von Humboldt und die deutsche Griechen-Rezeption', *Fest. Schumacher*, 77–101.

KANT. Immanuel Kant, *Bemerkungen in den 'Beobachtungen über das Gefühl des Schönen und Erhabenen'*, ed. Marie Rischmüller (Kant-Forschungen, 3), Hamburg, Meiner, xxiv + 294 pp. + 5 pls, corrects inadequacies in previous editions and even in the Akademie Ausgabe with an introduction, the texts of K.'s handwritten comments, along with a full critical apparatus and commentary. Given the resonance of the concept of the sublime and the beautiful in the Classical period, given also that K.'s comments were not primarily meant for a re-edition of his essay but are reflections on both personal and philosophical issues in the pre-critical period, this volume gives a valuable insight into K.'s manner of thinking (even though it would have been more illuminating to have provided the text of the original essay for those who do not have the Akademie Ausgabe to which it refers, close to hand). Further studies on this theme include W. Menninghaus, 'Zwischen Überwältigung und Widerstand. Macht und Gewalt in Longinus und Kants Theorie des Erhabenen', *Poetica*, 23: 1–19, which argues that K. stresses the power of speech to resist the superior forces of nature that deprive the subject of its freedom; and Paul Crowther, *The Kantian Sublime. From Morality to Art*, Oxford, Clarendon, 1989, 178 pp., which is an attempt to clarify the sublime 'in the context of possible tensions and distortions forced upon it by the broader philosophical position embodied in Kant's aesthetics and ethics' (p. 3) — an account which may appear less novel to those who come to it from German Classicism than from analytical philosophy. But this is a clear exposition of the origins of the concept in Addison and Burke, of its ethical dimension, and of the aesthetics of the sublime. It is a pity that the valuable ideas of the conclusion were not expressed more forcibly and developed further. The extension of the sublime to the experience of works of art, to the realization of the awesome scope of political power structures, as well as being conducive to the institution of human solidarity demonstrates both the implications of K.'s concept and the relevances of aesthetic attitudes in social praxis — a thoughtful work.

On the theme of ethics the following have appeared. Immanuel Kant, *The Metaphysics of Morals*, introd., trans. and ann. Mary Gregor, CUP, xii + 307 pp., is a complete English translation of the *Metaphysik der Sitten* with extensive annotations on Kant's terminology and a useful introductory essay on Kant's moral philosophy; Henry E. Allison, *Kant's Theory of Freedom*, CUP, xii + 304 pp., explores the notion 'that, at bottom, Kant's critical philosophy is a philosophy of freedom', focusing particularly on the 'problematic conception of transcendental freedom' (p. 1). The work links epistemology, psychology, and rational and moral agency to conclude that 'K.'s theory of freedom is [. . .] the most profound and sustained attempt to deal with this problem in the history of Western philosophy' (p. 249). In particular it deals with objections to K.'s theory in Hegel and in Schiller whose aesthetic works are briefly illuminated here by the method of analytical philosophy (pp. 180–84). Last but not least (despite its ostensibly disconcerting title), N. Hinske, 'Kants "höchstes moralisch-physisches Gut"'. Essen und allgemeine Menschenvernunft', *Aufklärung*, 5.2, 1990:49–58, regards table-conversation as the realization of the Enlightenment ideal of practical reason.

Two studies deal with psychological issues: Patricia Kitcher, *Kant's Transcendental Psychology*, OUP, 1990, xiii + 296 pp., is a closely argued study of K.'s psychology which defines the continuing relevance of the *Kritik der reinen Vernunft* in terms of its contribution to cognitive psychology. This valuable work, which re-evaluates key areas of K.'s epistemology, also shows how his theories far surpassed the contemporary understanding of psychology but also anticipate current theories of cognition. Closely related is Wayne Waxman, *Kant's Model of the Mind. A New Interpretation of Transcendental Idealism*, OUP, x + 306 pp., a concisely argued study of the types and functions of imagination in K.'s theory of knowledge to show how it is central to K.'s concepts of space and time as well as to understanding and cognition. Similarly, P. Pimpinella, 'Reluctantia subiectiva und repugnantia obiectiva in der Inauguraldissertation Kants', *Aufklärung*, 5.1, 1990:57–80, which looks at the relationship between this work and the first Critique; Wilhelm Metz, *Kategoriendeduktion und produktive Einbildungskraft in der theoretischen Philosophie Kants und Fichtes* (Spekulation und Erfahrung, II, 2), Stuttgart-Bad Cannstatt, Frommann-Holzboog, 408 pp., which examines an issue Waxman summarily dismisses (p. 15), namely the relationship between the concepts of imagination in Kant and Fichte and its cognitive role, but otherwise covers very much the same ground and reaches similar conclusions, though places them more in the German philosophical context; and Reinhard Brandt, *Die Urteilstafel. Kritik der reinen Vernunft A67–76; B92–101* (Kant-Forschungen, 4), Hamburg, Meiner, vi + 129 pp., which is a detailed analysis of the categories and logic of the understanding and an enquiry into their origins and justification, hence a contribution to the development of K.'s main work. Id., *D'Artagnan und die Urteilstafel. Über ein Ordnungsprinzip der europäischen Kulturgeschichte (1,2,3/4)*, Stuttgart, Steiner, 180 pp., is a highly original work which repays sustained reflection in that starting from Kant's categories of understanding (and alluding also to other authors of the Classical period) it widens out to conjecture a sequential system of intelligible order in the deep structure of Western thinking. A thought-provoking work which has far-reaching implications for the methodology of the human sciences in general. Similarly Ulrike Dünkelsbühler, *Kritik der Rahmen-Vernunft, Parergon-Versionen nach Kant und Derrida*, Munich, Fink, 187 pp., which, in a dialogue with Kant, Sophocles, and post-structuralist theory, explores topoi of framing, prefacing, translating and related issues of presence and absence, sublimity and mourning: as Derrida points out in his 'preface', a singular and artfully subversive study of aspects of modern rationality. Max-Otto Lorenzen, *Metaphysik als Grenzgang. Die Idee der Aufklärung unter dem Primat der praktischen Vernunft in der Philosophie Immanuel Kants*, Hamburg, Meiner, ix + 376 pp., offers a systematic survey of Kant's philosophy with chapters dealing with 'Philosophie als Aufklärung', on the vindication of freedom and individual autonomy through philosophical criticism; 'Geschichtsphilosophie', on the issues of progress, culture, judgement and their possible purpose; and 'Ethik und Religionsphilosophie', on ethics, the categorical imperative and problems of evil, guilt, and political force. This study, conceived as an 'Einführung in die Grundstruktur des strebenden Bewußtseins' (p. ix), premissed on K.'s conviction that human beings can only strive towards autonomy (as opposed to simply attaining it), re-examines this postulate now that both in Marxist and capitalist terms its underlying concept of progress seems highly questionable. K. H. Kiefer, 'Zur Definition aufklärerischer Vernunft. Kants "Was ist Aufklärung?"', *WW*, 41:1, 15–27, is an illuminating and closely argued analysis of the relationship between theory and practice in Enlightenment reason, deriving from the premiss that K.'s celebrated essay is a perlocutionary speech act. M. Mori, 'Aufklärung und Kritizismus in Kants Geschichtsphilosophie', *Aufklärung*, 5.1, 1990:81–102.

KAYSER.　Albrecht Christoph Kayser, *Adolfs gesammelte Briefe*, ed. Gerhard Sauder (Kleines Archiv des achtzehnten Jahrhunderts, 8), St. Ingbert, Röhrig, 1990, 90 pp., reissues the first edition (1778) of this key, but long since unavailable novel of the 'Empfindsamkeit'/'Sturm und Drang' period which was held in some quarters to be even more dangerous than *Werther*. S.'s postface gives a concise account of the author's life and works.

KLOPSTOCK.　K. M. Kohl, '"Wir wollen weniger erhoben und fleissiger gelesen sein"': Klopstock's sublime aspirations and their role in the development of German poetry', *PEGS*, 60, 1989–90 (1991):39–62.

KNIGGE.　This year sees the inception of an important initiative, the publication of Adolph Freiherr Knigge, *Ausgewählte Werke in zehn Bänden. Im Auftrag der Adolph Freiherr-von-Knigge-Gesellschaft zu Hannover*, ed. Wolfgang Fenner, Hanover, Fackelträger, with vol. 1: *Romane I: Geschichte Peter Clausens*, 409 pp., and vol. 2: *Romane II: Die Verirrungen des Philosophen oder Geschichte Ludwigs von Seelberg*, 360 pp. The edition will include novels, drama, philosophical and political writings as well as a biography and correspondence. In the case of vols 1 and 2, the modernized text follows the last editions published in K.'s lifetime. Adolph Freiherr Knigge, *Über den Umgang mit Menschen*, ed. Karl-Heinz Göttert, Stuttgart, Reclam, 480 pp., is, with its accompanying select bibliography, another useful modern edition of this celebrated work which discloses key insights into the *mœurs* of the late Enlightenment. G.'s *Nachwort* justifiably argues that K. intended to promote a practical, utilitarian social ethic (contrasting directly with Kant's explicitly juridical conception) based not on traditional etiquette but on direct experience. A further sign of renewed interest in K. is Pierre-André Bois, *Adolph Freiherr Knigge (1752–1796). De la 'nouvelle religion' aux Droits de l'Homme. L'itinéraire politique d'un aristocrate allemand franc-maçon à la fin du dix-huitième siècle* (Wolfenbütteler Forschungen, 50), Wiesbaden, Harrassowitz, 1990, 656 pp., a revised 'doctorat d'état', which re-evaluates K.'s life and work on the basis of the most recent philological evidence. The first part describes K.'s early life and aristocratic milieu; the second, K.'s involvement with secret societies, the Freemasons, and the Illuminati; the third his reactions to the French Revolution, including his political writing and thought, together with a list of primary manuscript and printed sources and a bibliography of secondary literature. This indispensable study, which sees reflected in K. all the various dimensions of the Enlightenment, concludes by regarding him as an advocate of freedom whose career 'marque pour l'Allemagne l'entrée des intellectuels dans la politique.' (p. 602.)

KOTZEBUE. Publications this year focus on K.'s reception in England: August von Kotzebue, *Lovers' Vows*, adapted by Elizabeth Inchbald 1798, Oxford — NY, Woodstock, 1990, unpaginated + iv + 92 pp., is a facsimile reprint of I.'s English version of K.'s *Das Kind der Liebe*. L. Fietz, 'Zur Genese des englischen Melodramas aus der Tradition der bürgerlichen Tragödie und des Rührstücks: Lillo — Schröder — Kotzebue — Sheridan — Thompson — Jerrold', *DVLG*, 65:99–116, traces, in the various British and German adaptations of Lillo's *The London Merchant* (1731), the growing self-confidence of the bourgeoisie and the concomitant transformation of the 'bürgerliche Tragödie' into the 'bürgerliches Rührstück' which explores the conflicts between personal ideals and the necessities of the wider world. K., whose plays were translated by Sheridan and Thompson, plays a central role in this transformation of the genre.

KRAUSE. Enrique M. Ureña, *K. C. F. Krause: Philosoph, Freimaurer, Weltbürger. Eine Biographie* (Spekulation und Erfahrung, II,2), Stuttgart-Bad Canstatt, Frommann–Holzboog, 690 pp., is — unlike the case with Schiller and Goethe — an example of biography as redemption, to establish the coherence of the life and thought of a prolific and original thinker whose subsequent obscurity in his own

724 *German Studies*

land was, and largely still remains, as great as his continuing relevance in Hispanic culture, particularly in current South American politics. U. has performed a massive task: tracing K.'s numerous works on diverse philosophical, political, moral, and aesthetic issues, charting their emergence against an unsettled existence, and assessing their reception in Hispanic culture. A valuable contribution both to the subsequent reception of Kantian philosophy and to the international ramifications of German philosophy of the Classical period.

LAROCHE. B. Spies, 'Sophie von La Roches *Geschichte des Fräuleins von Sternheim* und die moderne Trivialliteratur. Das moralische Vorbild als psychologische Kompensation', *LiL*, 2:80–89. L. K. Worley, 'Sophie von La Roche's *Reisejournale*: reflections of a travelling subject', *Slessarev Vol.*, 90–103. J. Blackwell, 'Sophie von La Roche and the black slave poet Feuerbach: a study in sentimentality, Enlightenment, and outsiderdom', *ib.*, 105–15.

LAVATER. Horst Weigelt, *J. K. Lavater. Leben, Werk und Wirkung* (Kleine Vandenhoeck-Reihe, 1556), Göttingen, Vandenhoeck & Ruprecht, 132 pp., comprising sections on L.'s life, on his religious thought, on his poetical works along with his writings on education, physiology and psychology, and politics, as well as an assessment of his influence, is an essentially descriptive introduction to this author which concludes with his contribution to the development of modern subjectivity. Rather more politically relevant is: R. Gray, 'Die Geburt des Genies aus dem Geiste der Aufklärung. Semiotik und Aufklärungsideologie in der Physiognomik Johann Kaspar Lavaters', *Poetica*, 23:95–138, which concludes: 'Lavaters Kampagne gegen jede Form der Zufälligkeit im menschlichen Leben [. . .] entspricht dem Wunsch der Aufklärung, [. . .] die Welt auf das Sinnvolle zu reduzieren, und das heißt jede Form der Kontingenz und Unberechenbarkeit auszuschließen' (p. 137). C. Zelle, 'Physiognomie des Schreckens im achtzehnten Jahrhundert. Zu Johann Caspar Lavater und Charles Lebrun', *LY*, 21, 1989 (1990):89–92, continues a series of informative essays by Z. on aesthetics and physiology. Edmund Heier, *Studies on Johann Caspar Lavater (1741–1801) in Russia* (SH, 37), 179 pp.

LEIBNIZ. Samuel Clarke, *Der Briefwechsel mit G. W. Leibniz von 1715/1716*, ed. Ed Dellian (PBib, 423), cxxvi + 183 pp., is a new edition of this work which is not easily available and yet crucial for understanding not merely the development of science in the 18th c. but also a fundamental dichotomy in the Enlightenment, between experimental science and positivistic philosophy on the one hand, and rationalism and systematic philosophy on the other. A lengthy, demanding but, therefore, informative introduction explores these issues on the basis of the most recent research and precedes a translation based on Clarke's 1717 text and on L.'s subsequently revised French text from the Gerhardt edition. Erhard Holze, *Gott als Grund der Welt im Denken des Gottfried Wilhelm Leibniz* (Studia Leibnitiana, Sonderheft 20), Stuttgart, Steiner, 204 pp., with its sections on 'Gott als Grund seiner Selbst', 'Gott als Grund der Welt', 'Gott als Grund der Harmonie der Welt', 'Gott als Grund der Güte der Welt', is a systematic exploration of L.'s philosophy of religion and metaphysics and — given L.'s influence — a useful, even if demanding, treatment of the theocentric structure of the 18th-c. world. L. C. Madonna, 'Gewißheit, Wahrscheinlichkeit und Wissenschaft in der Philosophie von Leibniz', *Aufklärung*, 5.1, 1990:103–16.

LENZ. This year sees the inaugural volume of the *Lenz-Jahrbuch. Sturm-und Drang-Studien*, ed. Matthias Luserke, Christoph Weiss, and Gerhard Sauder, devoted to L. as one of the most significant writers of the latter part of the 18th c. and (according to the editors) one of the most radical of his generation, but who, on account of the prevailing Classical norms, has not received due recognition. But the editors' recourse to W. Benjamin on the need for (materialistic) history to subvert the conformity of received traditions is a disingenuous legitimation of their own ('bourgeois') aim to add L. to the prevailing canon by means of the conventional resources of philology. Contributions include: P. Petersen and H.-G. Winter, 'Lenz-Opern. Das Musiktheater als Sonderzweig der produktiven Rezeption von J. M. R. Lenz' Dramen und Dramentheorie', 9–58; M. Luserke and C. Weiss, 'Arbeit an den Vätern. Zur Plautus-Bearbeitung "Die Algierer" von J. M. R. Lenz', 59–91, which contains the text of the play (77–91); M. Rector, 'Anschauendes Denken. Zur Form von Lenz' "Anmerkungen übers Theater"', 92–105; R. Scholz, 'Zur Biographie des späten Lenz', 106–34; G. Vonhoff, 'Kunst als "fait social". Lenz' "Dido" — auch eine Kritik am Melodrama', 135–46. But the editors' complaints about lack of academic recognition for L. should in any case be offset by the fascination of his life for subsequent authors, as evinced by P. Pütz, 'Peter Schneiders *Lenz*. Von der Agitation zur Reflexion', *Fest. Verbeeck*, 195–207, which considers the figure of L. in terms of the poetological self-reflection in present-day literature. H. Gersch and S. Schmalhaus, 'Die Bedeutung des Details: J. M. R. Lenz, Abbadona und der "Abschied". Literarisches Zitat und biographische Selbstinterpretation', *GRM*, 41:385–412, attempts to reconstruct Lenz's now lost letter of 7 February 1778, presumably to Charlotte von Stein written during a stay with J. F. Oberlin. J. Guthrie, 'Revision und Rezeption: Lenz und sein *Hofmeister*', *ZDP*, 110:181–201.

LESSING. D. Kuhlis, '"Er verlangt, ihm nachzudenken." Zum neuen Band der Weimarer Lessing-Bibliographie', *LY*, 21, 1989 (1990):19–28. Studies of L.'s drama include: H. A. Glaser, 'Von der Comédie larmoyante zum Bürgerlichen Trauerspiel oder: Diderot versus Lessing', *Arntzen Vol.*, 99–108, which deals with the precedents set by D. and L. in finding a confident dramatic form for the presentation of bourgeois virtue in a feudal society; U. Gaier, 'Das Lachen des Aufklärers. Über Lessings *Minna von Barnhelm*', *DUS*, 43.6:42–56, which discusses the play both in terms of the effectiveness of laughter as a moral corrective to instrumental reason and dogmatism, and as a reflection on its appropriateness to confront or compensate for human misfortune; S. G. Donald, '"An officer and a gentleman": *Minna von Barnhelm* and the rhetoric of class and gender', *FMLS*, 27:43–69, a stimulating study in the sociological and cultural sub-texts in the play; H. Scheuer, '"Theater der Vorstellung" — Lessings *Emilia Galotti* und Schillers *Kabale und Liebe*', *DUS*, 43.6:58–74, which rehearses the issue of the portrayal of the tension between courtly and bourgeois society and considers the extent to which the bourgeoisie is presented as being duped by its own class ideology; and R. Simon, 'Nathans Argumentationsverfahren: Konsequenzen der Fiktionalisierung von Theorie in Lessings Drama *Nathan der Weise*', *DVLG*, 65:609–35, which concludes: 'der *Nathan* [stellt] die fortgeschrittene Gestalt von Lessings Theoretisieren dar' (p. 635). But only two essays rise above this fairly predictable level of discussion to argue a vital relevance: K. S. Calhoon, 'The education of the human race: Lessing, Freud and the savage mind', *GQ*, 64:178–89, which sees L.'s treatise as a precursor of Freud's Oedipal theory and of Lévi-Strauss's concept of the 'cerebral savage' to explore the relationship between violence and virtue, thus tracing a theme of Enlightenment desire which L. already problematizes in the depiction of paternal authority in *Emilia Galotti*; and J. A. Kowalik, '*Nathan der Weise* as Lessing's work of mourning', *LY*, 21, 1989 (1990):1–17, which, reviewing the theme of paternity, is an essay of compelling psychological insight into the motivations of L.'s thought and writing. More general essays include W. E. Bender, '"Eloquentia corporis": Rhetorische Tradition und Aufklärung bei Lessing', *ib.*, 45–53; A. Ohage, 'Von Lessings "Wust" zu einer Wissenschaftsgeschichte der Physiognomik im 18. Jahrhundert', *ib.*, 55–87, which discusses L., Lavater, and the development of anthropology in the 18th c. D. Hill, '"Es ist nicht wahr, daß die kürzeste Linie immer die grade ist" — Eine Quelle', *Euphorion*, 85:98–101, finds a precedent for this quotation from *Die Erziehung des Menschengeschlechts* in contemporary theories of optics. W. Barner, 'Das europäische 17. Jahrhundert bei Lessing und Herder', Garber,

Barock, 397–417, assesses both Lessing's (in Wolfenbüttel) and Herder's research into the 17th c. and traces their increasingly distanced attitude towards it in their work — a small contribution to the far more interesting topic which B.'s philological perspective ignores, i.e. how the past constructs its *own* past. On L. in his own time and as received by subsequent authors there are the following: *Da Vienna a Napoli in carrozza. Il viaggio di Lessing in Italia*, ed. Lea Ritter Santini, 2 vols, Hanover, Herzog August Bibliothek, Wolfenbüttel, 724 pp. which is the catalogue of an exhibition on Lessing and Italy held in Naples. It covers in well-researched articles not only Lessing's travels, but also his responses to Italian culture. Containing numerous illustrations, including colour plates, maps and town plans, this is a major resource on this aspect of Lessing's life and works; J. Pizer, 'Lessing's reception of Charles Batteux', *LY*, 21, 1989 (1990):29–43; C. E. Schweitzer, 'Heinrich Zscholle's *Jonathan Frock* as Lessing reception, especially of *Die Juden*', *LY*, 22, 1990 (1991):133–41; S. Wilke, '"Auf Kotsäulen [ruht] der Tempel der Vernunft": Heiner Müllers Lessing', *ib.*, 143–57.

LEVIN VARNHAGEN. L. Weissberg, 'Stepping out: the writing of difference in Rahel Varnhagen's letters', *NGC*, 53:149–62, is a sensitive case-study of the growth of Jewish self-awareness within the context of emergent 19th-c. German nationalism. H. Patsch, '"Als ob Spinoza sich wollte taufen lassen." Biographisches und Rechtsgeschichtliches zu Taufe und Trauung Rahel Levins', *JFDH*, 149–78, is a detailed biographical study based on documentary evidence.

LICHTENBERG. Georg Christoph Lichtenberg, *Aphorismen. Schriften. Briefe*, ed. Wolfgang Promies with Barbara Promies, Munich, Hanser, 669 pp., though announced as new, is actually a reissue of the 1974 edition and contains a selection of aphorisms, well-known essays, and letters, together with annotations to the text and a postface. *Taschenbuch zum Nutzen und Vergnügen für das Jahr 1781. Mit Kupfern von Chodowiecki nebst den neuesten Frauenzimmer-Moden in Kupfer. Nebst Göttinger Taschenkalender von 1781*, ed. Wolfgang Promies, Mainz, Dieterich, 1989, unpaginated + 136 pp., is a facsimile reprint of almanacs edited by L. In the postface P. argues that they demonstrate L.'s ability to combine entertainment with useful information and enlightening knowledge. J. Manthey, 'Der große Herr Gerneklein. Lichtenberg, die Französische Revolution und der vierte Stand', *Merkur*, 45:24–33.

MENDELSSOHN. Moses Mendelssohn, *Gesammelte Schriften. Jubiläumsausgabe*, ed. I. Elbogen, J. Guttmann, E. Mitwoch, A. Altmann, and E. J. Engel, Stuttgart-Bad Canstatt, Frommann-Holzboog, continues with vol. 5, 1: *Rezensionsartikel in Briefe, die neueste Litteratur betreffend (1759–1765)*, ed. Eva J. Engel, lxxxiv + 696 pp., and vol. 5,2: *Rezensionsartikel in Allgemeine deutsche Bibliothek (1765–1784)*. *Literarische Fragmente*, ed. Eva J. Engel, lxix + 327 pp. Each volume contains an informative introduction on the provenance of M.'s articles, and on their context both in his work and in terms of the journals in which they appeared, thus offering concise accounts of the Enlightenment in Berlin as much as commentary on M. as critic and reviewer. There follows in each volume the text of the first edition, together with a schematic overview of M.'s contributions to the journals by year and issue number, and an index of proper names. What is impressive about these volumes, besides the painstaking scholarship of their editor, is that they incontrovertibly confirm Mendelssohn's significance not just for the Jewish community, but for German society as a whole in contributing decisively to the establishment of a German literary culture in the 18th c. — a fact which, as the fraught history of the *Jubiläumsausgabe* itself demonstrates, could never be taken for granted. E. Engel Holland, 'The world of Moses Mendelssohn', *LBIYB*, 36:27–43, reconstructs the geographical and intellectual horizons of M.'s world from published and recently discovered correspondence: a moving appreciation of a humane thinker whose integration into the life of his age is at odds with his problematic relation to German history. Two essays which illustrate M.'s interest in civic and political issues are H. Mühleisen, 'Moses Mendelssohn und die preußische Rechtsreform', *Aufklärung*, 5.2, 1990:131–36, and A. Košenina, '"Zur Reform des Judeneides": Ein unpublizierter Brief von Johann Jakob Engel an Moses Mendelssohn', *LY*, 22, 1990 (1991):159–67.

MERCK.   G. Sauder, '"Wunderliche Großheit." Johann Heinrich Merck (1741–1791)', *Lenz-Jahrbuch*, 1:207–27; and A. Grieger, 'Johann Heinrich Merck 1741–1791', *Das achtzehnte Jahrhundert*, 15:31–34, both offer appreciations of his life and works.

MORITZ.   Alo Allkemper, *Ästhetische Lösungen: Studien zu Karl Philipp Moritz*, Munich, Fink, 1990, 296 pp.; Id., 'Der Schein der Rettung oder die Phantasie vom guten Zufall. Zu Karl Philipp Moritz' Drama *Blunt oder der Gast*', *LY*, 21, 1989 (1990):123–39. Corinna Fricke, *Zwischen Leibniz und Humboldt: Zur Stellung des sprachwissenschaftlichen Werkes von Karl Philipp Moritz im geistigen Leben des ausgehenden 18. Jahrhunderts* (Linguistische Studien; Reihe A: Arbeitsberichte, 201), Berlin, Akad. der Wiss. der DDR Zentralinstitut für Sprachwissenschaft, 1990, iv + 140 pp., has much to say about the modern relevance of M.'s ideas, his stress on the internal dynamic of language development as well as on language as an expression of the individual. But, since F. places M. 'in die Reihe dieser aufklärerisch gesinnten bürgerlichen Beamten' (p. 13), hence as representing conservative bourgeois values in an anachronistic feudal system, a description belied by M.'s biography if nothing else, this study fails to appreciate M.'s reflections on language in the context of his radical critique of contemporary culture. For this, it is necessary to turn to J. Pustevjosky, 'Moritz, deafmutes and the myth of the sign', *LY*, 21, 1989 (1990): 141–55, a thoughtful essay on M.'s resistance to Enlightenment optimism.

MÖSER. Noteworthy here is *Möser Forum*, 1, 1989, the first issue of a bi-annual or possibly tri-annual, publication intending to focus on, and promote interest in M., and his life, works, thought, and their Osnabrück context. This inaugural issue contains contributions under five headings — 'M. als Autor und Herausgeber'; 'M. und die Zeitgenossen'; 'Ms ämtliche Tätigkeit'; 'Editionsprobleme bei M.'; and 'Arbeitsergebnisse der Möser-Dokumentationsstelle', as follows: J. Moes, 'Geschichte als Wissenschaft und als politische Waffe bei M.', 3–27; Id., 'Pariser Luft in Osnabrück. Französische Sprache und Literatur in Justus Ms Briefen an Johann Heinrich von dem Bussche-Hünnefeld', 119–38; R. Stauf, 'Justus Ms *Arminius* und die Frage der deutschen Identität um 1850', 28–45; W. Martens, 'M. als Wochenschriftschreiber', 46–63; U. Sheldon, 'Drei Gelegenheitsgedichte von J.M.', 64–75; Id., 'Die Briefe der Johanna Friederika von Bar an J.M. Zur "Bürgerlichkeit" einer adligen Frau. Eine Fallstudie', 139–55; G. Wagner, 'Zum Publikumsbezug in M.'s Beiträge für die *Wöchentlichen Osnabrückischen Anzeigen*', 76–87; K. H. Rengstorf, 'M. und der Toleranzbegriff', 88–98; H. Beckers, 'J M. und die beginnende Wiederentdeckung der mittelalterlichen deutschen Literatur im 18. Jahrhundert', 99–116; W. Gödden, '"Eine gefüllte Rose auf einem wilden Stocke." J.M. und Anton Mathias Sprickmann', 156–75; R. Brand, 'Kant und M.', 176–91; W. Woesler, '"[...] ob unsere Art der Kultur der fremden vorzuziehen sei?" — J.M. antwortet Friedrich II.', 192–207; A. Schindling, 'Osnabrück, Nordwestdeutschland und das Heilige Römische Reich zur Zeit Ms', 211–22; K. II. L. Welker, 'Behandlungskontrakt statt Eigengebung: Erbpacht statt Eigenbehörigkeit', 223–56; B. Plachta, 'Ms Handexemplar der Osnabrückischen Geschichte', pp. 259–72; R. Renger, 'Probleme einer Edition der amtlichen Schriften J.Ms', 273–79, an issue also treated by W.Woesler, 'Edition und Kommentierung eines dienstlichen Briefes an J.M.', *Fest. Zeller*. pp. 62–71, which argues that an author's works deriving from their official capacity need to be edited with regard to considerations other than those applicable to original writings; and B. Erker, M. Goltz, M. Siemsen, and W. Woesler, 'Zwei Jahre M. Dokumentationsstelle (1985/86). Ein Arbeitsbericht', 283–302. Similarly, W. A. von Schmidt, 'J.M.: Advokat eines historisch-organischen und partikularistischen Kulturbewußtseins', *ABNG*, 31–33: 7–28, discusses the question of the continuing relevance of M. to argue, on the grounds of his notion of the responsibility of the individual, that his works should be more widely known.

MÜLLER. Maler Müller, *Kleine Gedichte zugeeignet dem Herrn Canonicus Gleim. Nach der Handschrift im Freien Deutschen Hochstift/ Frankfurter Goethe-Museum*, ed. Rolf Paulus, Christoph Weiss, and Gerhard Sauder (Kleines Archiv des achtzehnten Jahrhunderts, 10), St. Ingbert, Röhrig, 1990, 101 pp., is an edition of a hitherto unpublished manuscript collection of M.'s early anacreontic poetry. The collection, written mostly around 1773, was (S. remarks) never sent to Gleim for publication and is only indirectly influenced by his verse. This edition reflects the intention to lend a new impetus to research on Müller, with a particular emphasis on little-known and hitherto unpublished works and documents, and which is more programmatically articulated in *Maler Müller in neuer Sicht. Studien zum Werk des Schriftstellers und Malers Friedrich Müller (1749–1825)*, ed. Gerhard Sauder, Rolf Paulus, and Christoph Weiss (SBL, 24), St. Ingbert, Röhrig, 1990, 250 pp., which contains the following contributions: R. Böschenstein, 'Grotte und Kosmos. Überlegungen zu Maler Müllers Idyllen-Mythologie', 9–29; V. Ehrich-Haefeli, 'Maler Müller: Körper — Sprache — Dichtung', 31–48; Y.-G. Mix, '"Komm schöne Galatee!/Die Lämmer ruhn im Klee ..." Zum Problem des Realismus in Friedrich (Maler) Müllers Idylle *Die Schafschur*', 49–63; J. Mahr, '"Er ist, er ist herabgesunken,/Der Silbermond, ins Wonnethal!" Maler Müller und Friedrich Gottlieb Klopstock', 65–83; R. Paulus, '"Alles verdunkelnde Nacht, gibt mir nur helleren Schein." Die ungedruckte Odensammlung Maler Müllers (1792)', 85–100; G. Mahal, 'Ein Kerl in Shakespeares Manier', 101–11; U. Leuschner, 'Traum und Erwachen. Das Nachspiel in Maler Müllers metrischem *Faust*', 113–24; G. Sauder, 'Maler Müllers lyrisches Drama *Niobe*', 125–34; I. S. Bernardini, 'Maler Müller und der römische Kunstbetrieb, parodiert im *Kunstantiquariat*', 135–50; S. Thös-Kössel, 'Maler Müllers *Schriften zur Kunst*', 151–73; A. Stahl, 'Rhetorik und Spontaneität. Zu den Liebesbriefen Maler Müllers', 175–92; J.-U. Fechner, 'Die deutsche Übersetzung der Rhein-Reisebeschreibung Bertòlas: eine unberücksichtigte Arbeit von Maler Müller?', 193–209; C. Weiss, '"Critik unter aller Critik" oder "die kleine Execuzion".' Friedrich Müllers Kotzebue-Polemik', 211–24; G. Sauder, 'Romantisches Interesse am Sturm und Drang (Maler Müller, Lenz, Goethe)', 225–42; and R. Paulus 'Auswahlbibliographie zur neueren Maler-Müller-Forschung', 243–50.

MUSÄUS. H. Hox, 'Johann Karl August Musäus und die *Volksmärchen der Deutschen*', *SGG*, 25, 1990:47–70, regards M.'s work as complementing the popular fairy-tale of oral tradition with its values derived from the literary Enlightenment.

NICOLAI. Friedrich Nicolai, *Das Leben und die Meinungen des Herrn Magister Sebaldus Nothanker. Kritische Ausgabe*, ed. Bernd Witte, Stuttgart, Reclam, 616 pp. + 22 illus., is an edition which ought effectively to scotch a still pervasive view of Nicolai as the pedant *par excellence* of the Classical period. The novel, complemented by reproductions of Chodowiecki's illustrations, is also accompanied by a selection of texts demonstrating the favourable, contemporary reception of the work, as well as by helpful notes to the text and a concise bibliography. On the premiss that the novel is 'das deutendste Prosabuch der deutschen Aufklärungsliteratur', W.'s succinct *Nachwort* portrays N. as a committed advocate of Enlightenment ideals and shrewd critic of prevailing cultural and social attitudes, and his novel as a worthy representative of the genre in the 18th c.

PESTALOZZI. Johann Heinrich Pestalozzi, *Politische Schriften*, ed. Ruedi Graf (Birkhäuser Klassiker), Basel, Birkhäuser, 464 pp., contains writings from 1782 to 1815 on political, economic, educational, and constitutional issues. The editor argues that P.'s pedagogical interests derived from a political standpoint which adapted itself by turns to absolutism, revolution, and restoration, the deeper coherence of which can be traced to a political idealism which developed from P.'s conception of the 14th-c. Swiss Confederation.

PFEFFEL. W. E. Schäfer, 'Pfeffels späte Episteln. Zugleich Vorüberlegungen zu einem Repertorium der Briefe Pfeffels', *RG*, 21:177–88.

REINHOLD. Alexander von Schönborn, *Karl Leonhard Reinhold. Eine annotierte Bibliographie*, Stuttgart-Bad Canstatt, Frommann-Holzboog, 135 pp., usefully contributes to the understanding of a much neglected, pragmatic thinker who, in practice as in theory, could be regarded as the 'Idealtypus des Aufklärers' (p. 10), and who with his intellectual interests and his many personal contacts was a central figure of the age. The long introduction (pp. 9–64) traces R.'s intellectual development, regrets the lack of scholarly interest, assesses R.'s significance as a thinker, suggests areas and problems for future research ranging from biographical issues to R.'s relevance to contemporary analytical philosophy, and most crucially gives an account of the problems involved in establishing a bibliography of R.'s works.

SCHICKANEDER. H. Aust, 'Emanuel Schickaneders "Kreis der Schöpfung"', *ABNG*, 31–33:59–89, is an appreciation of S.'s works.

SCHLEGEL, DOROTHEA. W. Schmitz, '". . . nur eine Skizze, aber durchaus in einem großen Stil": Dorothea Schlegel', *ABNG*, 31–33:91–131, is — as one might expect from its author — an exceedingly informative appreciation of the life and work of a figure still too much in her husband's shadow.

SCHUBART. H. Dedert, 'Schubarts Anekdote vom verlorenen Sohn: "Zur Geschichte des menschlichen Herzens"', *Lenz-Jahrbuch*, 1 : 188–206.

SEUME. Johann Gottfried Seume, *Mein Leben. Nebst der Fortsetzung von G. J. Göschen und C. A. H. Clodius*, ed. Jörg Drews, Stuttgart, Reclam, 216 pp., reissues the text of the G. J. Göschen, 1813 edition, supplemented by a biographical sketch in a letter to Wieland (no date given), together with an explanation of why it is impossible to publish the original manuscript text, and, in accordance with the Reclam format, a section of annotations and a bibliography. D.'s postface outlines the literary and historical context of this important, yet untimely figure.

STOLBERG. M. Wichelhaus, 'Der Freiheitsgesang des Grafen Friedrich Leopold zu Stolberg', *Arntzen Vol.*, 123–35, comments on this 1775 ode to conclude that S. was one of the first to harness Protestant convictions of divine revelation to German nationalist aspirations.

VARNHAGEN VON ENSE. Karl August Varnhagen von Ense. *Schriften und Briefe*, ed. Werner Fuld, Stuttgart, Reclam, 363 pp., is a very modest selection of V.'s journalism and memoirs, literary reviews (here on Heine, Goethe, and Keller) and from his correspondence (here with von Arnim, Jean Paul, Goethe, Cotta, A. von Humboldt, Gutzkow, Metternich, Tieck, Heine, Fontane and others) together with an appreciative introduction which underlines V.'s significance for the political and cultural life of the 19th c. However, this edition does not address the problem of how in principle V. can be made available to a wider public, given the vastness of the *Nachlaß*, the occasional nature of V.'s writings, and the restrictions of the paperback format. The resulting texts here seem fragmentary and arbitrary, the correspondence, already selective, is in many cases reduced to extracts without any indication of what, and how much has been omitted. In short, it tries to do too much. If V. is as significant a witness to the age as F. claims, why not (e.g. as with Goethe) produce several volumes, each devoted to his different areas of activity?

WAGNER. Heinrich Leopold Wagner, *Phaeton, eine Romanze*, St. Ingbert, Röhrig, 1990, unpaginated (16 pp.), a facsimile reprint of the Saarbrücken, Hofer, 1774 edition, is (as Christoph Weiss's postface points out) a witty and thinly veiled satire on the person and the court of the Prince of Nassau in which W. gives vent to his frustration with their parochiality.

WEZEL.   H. A. Pausch, '"Vergessene" Autoren bei Arno Schmidt: Das Beispiel Johann Carl Wezel. Über den Grad der Wahrheitsfindung', *ABNG*, 31–33:29–57. H.-C. Koller, 'Destruktive Arbeit: Zur Auseinandersetzung mit der philanthropischen Arbeitserziehung in J. K. Wezels *Robinson Krusoe*', *LY*, 22, 1990 (1991):169–97.

WIELAND.   H. Schelle, 'Nachträge und Ergänzungen zur Wieland-Bibliographie 6', *LY*, 21, 1989 (1990), 197–209, and 'Nachträge und Ergänzungen zur Wieland-Bibliographie 7', *LY*, 22, 1990 (1991): 219–28. Ludwig Fertig, *Christoph Martin Wieland der Weisheitslehrer* (Poeten als Pädagogen), WBG, viii + 245 pp., examines W.'s pedagogical activity in both his life and as a theme in his works as a means of elaborating a picture of the role of the teacher around 1800. An initial chapter on 'Lehrende Literaten' emphasizes the number of 18th-c. writers who were also teachers, but gives no conceptual clarity about the aim of this volume which (like the others) is an essay in old-fashioned biographical criticism. Since it addresses neither the economic, psychological nor ethical premises of this pedagogical activity, and assumes a continuity between 18th-c. and modern educational theories, this volume mystifies more than it informs. S. A. Jørgensen, 'Vom Fürstenspiegel zum *Goldenen Spiegel*', Garber, *Barock*, 365–75, draws on comparisons and contrasts with the political novels of P. von Zesen and H. A. von Sigler to argue that W.'s novel follows the tradition of fictionalized treatises on the education of princes and which deal with the problematic legitimation of princely power. K. Schaefer, 'Wielands Beitrag zur Revolutionsdebatte in der Endfassung seines Romans *Die Geschichte des Agathon* (1794)', *ZGer*, n.F. 1:323–29. E. Shookman, 'Intertextuality, *Agathon*, and *Ion*: Wieland's novel, Euripides' tragedy, Plato's dialogue', *LY*, 22, 1990 (1991):199–217, is a further example of the fruitfulness of the intertextual approach for 18th-c. works. D. Martin, 'Wielands letzte Auftragsarbeit für Bodmer. Ein unbekannter Druck', *JDSG*, 35:5–11, discusses the 1759 publication of W.'s translation of Mary Jones, 'The story of Jacob and Rachel attempted'. F. Dieckmann, 'Eine Zauberflöte aus Dschinnistan. Wielands Sammlung und Schickaneders Text', *NDL*, 468:135–45, discusses the relationship between the story in W.'s anthology of folk-tales and the libretto for Mozart's opera.

WINCKELMANN.   *Johann Joachim Winckelmann. Neue Forschungen. Eine Aufsatzsammlung*, ed. Winckelmann Gesellschaft (Studien der Winckelmann-Gesellschaft, 11), Stendal, Winckelmann-Gesellschaft, 1990, 157 pp. + 51 pls, contains mostly descriptive essays on W.'s sources and reception, only alluding to much wider issues: M. Kunze, 'Winckelmanns Sicht der griechischen Denkmäler', 8–21; Id., 'Der Winckelmann-Übersetzer Michael Huber an Chr. C.

Murr — ein unbekannter Brief in der Berliner Antikensammlung', 105–09; S. Gerrit-Breuer, 'Die Wirkung Winckelmans in der Geschichte der klassischen Archäologie', 21–26; A. Allrogen-Bedel, 'Winckelmann und die Archäologie im Königreich Neapel', 27–46; E. Schröter, 'Antiken der Villa Medici in der Betrachtung von Winckelmann, Anton Raphael Mengs und Johannes Wiedewelt', 47–66; B. Andreae, 'Die Laokoon-Gruppe in neuem Licht', 67–72; M. Käfer, 'J. J. Winckelmann — ein Ancien', 73–78; S. Neumeister, 'Winckelmann und Madame de Staël: Vom Kunstideal zur Kunstwissenschaft', 79–87; H. J. Herrmann, 'Zu Methoden des Studiums der Geschichte in der Zeit Winckelmanns', 88–92; G. Heres, 'Winckelmanns Beschreibung der Dresdener Gemäldegalerie', 93–97; H. Henning, '"Ueber Winckelmanns Charakter und Jugendgeschichte" (1787)', 98–100; J. Irmscher, 'Giacomo Casanova und Johann Joachim Winckelmann', 101–04; M. L. Bäumer, 'Winckelmanns Wirkung auf Thomas Jefferson und die Staatsarchitektur der frühen amerikanischen Republik', 110–23; D. M. Sweet, 'Walter Paters Winckelmann', 124–29; W. von Wangenheim, 'Winckelmann als Held', 130–47; V. Riedel, 'Winckelmanns Gedankengut in Erich Arendts Bildbändchen zur Welt des Mittelmeers', 148–57. Gerald Heres, *Winckelmann in Sachsen. Ein Beitrag zur Kulturgeschichte und zur Biographie Winckelmanns*, Berlin, Koehler & Amelang, 186 pp. + 52 pls, is, with its concepts of 'Schicksal', 'Vorbereitung' (i.e. the years in Saxony) and 'Erfüllung' (i.e. in Italy), a decidedly hagiographical account of the significance of Dresden for the formation of W.'s aesthetic theories. Acknowledging the sparsity of documentary evidence, it draws on previous biographical studies and complements them by setting W.'s life in an art-historical context. A detailed and factual essay in historical reconstruction.

THE ROMANTIC ERA

By NICHOLAS SAUL, *Lecturer in German, Trinity College Dublin*

I. GENERAL STUDIES

A major new yearbook takes pride of place this time: *Athenäum. Jahrbuch für Romantik*, ed. Ernst Behler, Alexander von Bormann, Jochen Hörisch, and Günter Oesterle, Paderborn, Schöningh, 292 pp. As the preface, 'Das Athenäum — (k)eine Renaissance', pp. 7–11, shows, the editors are well aware of the task set in claiming to follow the precedent of the Schlegels, Schleiermacher, Novalis *et al.* The enterprise grows from a sense of Romanticism's contemporary relevance, but — despite the dehistoricization implied by sub-title's lack of definite article before the substantive 'Romantik' — they see Romanticism in fact as possessing only 'widersprüchliche Aktualität': being simultaneously modern and anachronistic. Thus they take on only parts of the Schegels' mission: the mixture of genre, form, theme and style, the desire to rescue intellectual culture in the age of mass (in this case visual) media and, primarily, the dominance of provocative radical criticism, including self-criticism and the acceptance of constitutive provisionality which that implies. What they produce is however basically a work by (incidentally male-only) academics and for academics. Non-aesthetic themes are limited to K. Mueller-Vollmer, 'Mutter Sanskrit und die Nacktheit der Südseesprachen: Das Begräbnis von Humboldts Sprachwissenschaft', pp. 109–33, a trenchant reconstruction and condemnation of the way Wilhelm von Humboldt's individualistic philological paradigm was colonized by Bopp's uniformitarian comparative Indo-Germanic studies. Poetic contributions (in the narrow sense) are restricted to J. Hörisch, ' "Sein ist gut." Ein Jenaer Geistergespräch vom Mai 1795 in Hause Niethammer mit Fichte, Hölderlin und Hardenberg', pp. 279–89. For the rest, we have learned articles, strongly interdisciplinary, on literature and the arts (the Schlegels, Hoffmann, Brentano, the *Fragment*, Friedrich, W. von Müller/Schubert, Wagner), extensive reviews, plus brief miscellaneous reports. Judged on this basis the *Athenäum* is of a very high scholarly standard, fills a gap in the market, and is correspondingly welcome. See below for comments on individual articles.

THEMES. As usual in recent years three linked themes dominate: Romanticism and modernity, women in Romanticism, and Romanticism and the sciences. The status and function of women has been a major focus of interest, particularly the construction of a reading standpoint adequate to writing which by definition resists classification in received categories. Bürger, *Leben*, contains eight essays on six women writers. B. sees them as marginalized by gender-specific aesthetic norms and forced into a discursive ghetto, 'die mittlere Sphäre', where their fundamentally autobiographical writing is granted status neither as high nor as trivial literature, neither life nor work. Against this background B. examines their various strategies of self-negation, self-invention and self-expression. Runge, *Frau*, is the excellent newest instalment of the FU Berlin project *Der Brief als kommunikatives und literarisches Faktum* and has essays on several women writers' correspondence: H. Schwartz, 'Poesie und Poesiekritik im Briefwechsel zwischen Clemens Brentano und Sophie Mereau', pp. 33–50, shows how Brentano's attempts to integrate Mereau into his 'poetische Existens' through the letters involve a manipulative communicative strategy which violates her identity and independence; A. Runge, 'Die Dramatik weiblicher Selbstverständigung in den Briefromanen Caroline Auguste Fischers', pp. 93–114, is a fine analysis of perspectivist technique in the epistolary novels *Die Honigmonathe*, *Der Günstling*, and *Margarethe*, which shows how Fischer dramatizes non-communication between the sexes in the cause of emancipation. The novels are in fact a creative feminist experiment in the long-despised 'women's' genre. Stephan, *Frauen*, has I. Stephan, 'Weibliche und männliche Autorschaft. Zum *Florentin* von Dorothea Schlegel und zur *Lucinde* von Friedrich Schlegel', pp. 83–98, which contrasts the presentation of the heroes and notes fundamental contradictions in the realization of the androgynous ideal; also D. Böck, 'Caroline de la Motte-Fouqué. Sie hätte "eine deutsche Stael werden können". . .', pp. 139–48, a portrait of Fouqué's wife as a social and literary Don Quixote; and C. Bürger, 'Schriften, die nicht Werke sind. Zu Carolines Briefen', pp. 162–66, which examines a miniature *Charakteristik* of Bettina in Caroline Schlegel's letters and interprets the latter's writings as ironic rejections of received norms. *Bitter Healing. German Women Writers 1700–1830. An Anthology*, ed. Jeannine Blackwell and Susanne Zantop (European Women Writers Series), Lincoln — London, Nebraska U.P., 1990, 538 pp., is a set of translations designed for the comparative literature market (a purpose it serves well), but also makes a contribution to the subject *per se*. In fact the title is a mild misnomer (women writers aligning themselves with Classicism being excluded), so that the book divides into two equal halves of Enlightenment and Romantic authors. Thus we have in the second half texts from C. Schlegel-Schelling, H. Herz, D. Schlegel, C. A. Fischer, S. Mereau, R. Varnhagen, Günderode, and B. von Arnim. S. Zantop, 'Trivial pursuits? An introduction to German women's writing from the Middle Ages to 1830', pp. 9–50, is not at all unfocused and a useful exposition of the latest analytical categories. The choice of material is also good, being designed to offer representative variety across genres, and we especially welcome Fischer's *William der Neger*. Lyric poetry is represented in the original with verse translations, and the volume is rounded off by a concise general bibliography in addition to Zantop's very full annotations. Lehmann, *Clarissa*, constructs a model (with variants) of the 'Verführungsroman' on the basis of Richardson's novel: a virtuous middle-class young and unmarried woman is seduced by an aristocratic sensualist; instead of reaping praise for her commitment to love the woman is punished by death for her expression of sensuality; the man escapes scot-free. Several novels are analysed within the terms of this framework. In particular *Lucinde* is seen as an essay in false emancipation, offering women emancipation of the senses à la Gutzkow in the service of male sexuality, rather than social and legal freedom. Also noted: M.-C. Hoock-Demarle, 'Female readings of the French Revolution: the reception of the Revolution in German women's novels of the time', *SMLS*, *Special Issue*: 23–38.

The interest in Romanticism and modernity is still strong. Manfred Frank, *Einführung in die frühromantische Ästhetik. Vorlesungen*, Frankfurt, Suhrkamp, 1989, 466 pp., has 22 lectures covering a vast range of material from Plato and Aristotle to the pre-Kantian Enlighteners, Kant, Schiller, Hölderlin, Novalis, the Schlegel brothers, Tieck and the deconstructivist philosophers. F. develops here his familiar arguments. Early Romantic speculative philosophy (particularly Novalis) confers upon poetic discourse something radically new in a Western tradition seen as disadvantaging mimesis: epistemological dignity. This derives from (primarily Novalis's) rigorous logical analysis of the origin of identity in a pre-reflexive 'Gefühl' of absolute being, which whilst inaccessible to philosophical discourse also regulates the thinking of identity. Thus ironic aesthetic discourse, seeking to express the otherwise inexpressible, takes over where philosophy, in the search for identity, falls short. Tieck's allusive and transparent musical style is offered as the paradigm of Romantic Irony. In the notion of the ego as a field of reflexive tension never identical with itself lies for F. the relevance of Romanticism to contemporary thought and literature, yet, in keeping with his well-known commitment to the dignity of the subject, he is careful to point out that even this radical interpretation of Romantic literary philosophy offers no foundation for modernity understood as the 'Tod des Subjekts'. These lectures, which retain even in digressions their spontaneous character, are elegantly written expositions of often complex thought which, in keeping with their argument for the primacy of aesthetic utterance, conclude with extended analyses of Tieck lyrics. They will fulfil their function not only' for German students. *Romantik — eine lebenskräftige Krankheit. Ihre literarischen*

Nachwirkungen in der Moderne, ed. Erika Tunner (ABNG, 34), 243 pp., offers the oxymoronic metaphor in the title to account for the continuing irresistible attraction of the Romantic achievement for diverse modern writers. It is odd that Goethe's denunciation of Romanticism should be given a positive accentuation, and this unresolved ambiguity extends to the contributions, which waver between celebration and condemnation. J. F. Fetzer, 'Mediation as medication for the Romantic malady? John Erpenbeck's *Heillose Flucht*', pp. 63–85, is a perceptive study of the modern *Novelle* about Brentano's experiences at Emmerick's bedside, which generally commends Erpenbeck for his perspicuity in rendering Brentano's character and problem (the self-defeating urge to achieve unmediated vision). He sees Erpenbeck himself, philosopher and scientist become poet, as a modern Romantic. U. H. Peters, 'Morbide Theorien zur seelischen Gesundheit. Einige romantische Wurzeln der gegenwärtigen Psychiatrie bei E. T. A. Hoffmann', pp. 5–35, sees the presentation of psychopathological cases in Hoffmann's works as not merely implying modern psychiatric theory and typology, but as actually containing 'die Theorien [. . .] bereits weitgehend in ihrer heutigen Form'. M. Kesting, 'Das imaginierte Kunstwerk. E. T. A. Hoffmann und Balzacs *Chef d'œuvre inconnu*, mit einem Ausblick auf die gegenwärtige Situation', pp. 37–62, sees basic issues in Hoffmann, such as the conflict of art and life or art and woman as a quintessentially Romantic and modern disease of art, and, although she comes to contradictory conclusions, suggests that Balzac used Hoffmann's work for his own story. J. De Vos, '"Du knüpfest zwischen Nationen/Aus noch getrennten, fernen Zeiten/Ein heiliges, geweihtes Band." Novalis und Hölderlin in der Lyrik der ehemaligen DDR', pp. 87–120, analyses painstakingly four poems on Novalis and Hölderlin by Hilbig, Czechowski and Braun, suggesting that their reception of Romantics serves the purpose of emotional or political protest by individuals against the collective rather than serious engagement with Romanticism *per se*. C. Albert, 'Eine verunglückte Bettine. Romantik-Rezeption in der Nachfolge Christa Wolfs', pp. 121–33, sees the way in which Helga Schütz's *In Annas Namen* indulgently foregrounds individual suffering as typical for the exploitation of the 'Projektionsraum Romantik' in the GDR. G. Kurpanik-Malinowska, 'Stil und Traditionsbezüge gehören zusammen: Zu Christa Wolfs Aufarbeitung der deutschen Romantik', pp. 135–44, argues that Christa Wolf's representation of Günderode is to be seen in the light of the positive reception of Romanticism in 1970s GDR *Germanistik*. J. Lajarrige, 'Wahnsinn mit Gänsefüßchen. Zur Rehabilitierung Heinrich von Kleists in Günter Kunerts *Ein anderer K.*', pp. 145–58, shows how the inquisition into

Kleist's death in the radio play is a model of Kunert's own conflict with official ideology. M. Krajenbrink, '"Romantiker der elektronischen Revolution"? Zur Verwendung romantischer Elemente in Botho Strauß' *Der junge Mann*', pp. 159–85, sees the function of the Romantic elements in this novel as encouraging an often un-Romantic serious play with time and tradition. S. Burka, '"Vorsicht Lebensgefahr." Die Spätfolgen der Romantik bei Botho Strauß', pp. 187–208, sees Strauss's reception of Romanticism in *Der junge Mann* as a radicalization of F. Schlegel's irony, resulting in the dissolution of text and author. Since the analysis refers far more to de Man, Derrida, Lacan, etc., than to Schlegel, one wonders here whether the genealogical 'Spät*folgen*' is in fact justified. K. Bartsch, 'Affinität und Distanz. Ingeborg Bachmann und die Romantik', pp. 209–34, is the only essay here to approach the problem of Romanticism and modernity analytically. Bartsch polemicizes against categorizations of Bachmann as a Romantic and demonstrates how she distances herself from Romantic material in her works. E. Tunner, 'Fabelhafte Begegnungen. Aus den Papieren eines reisenden Enthusiasten', pp. 234–43, is a fictive conversation between Hoffmann, Gogol, Kafka, and Anna Seghers. Knapp, *Autoren*, contains 31 essays on authors from the 18th to the 20th c. in terms of differing terms of reception, including three on authors of our period. Claudia Becker, *Zimmer-Kopf-Welten. Motivgeschichte des Intérieurs im 19. und 20. Jahrhundert*, Munich, Fink, 1990, 195 pp., is an updated prizewinning Bochum dissertation of 1987. This fine work of comparative literary history and 'Geistesgeschichte' traces the changing meaning and function of the motif of the interior, from its role as sign of spiritual withdrawal from social and political alienation to its role as sign of ultimate, non-referential disorientation of inner and outer worlds. *Des Vetters Eckfenster* and *Des Lebens Überfluß* stand for the place of late Romanticism in this process. In the Hoffmann the interior signifies withdrawal into the aesthetic ego, with final inability to create connoting renunciation of Romantic subjectivism as a principle of art. Thus observation of reality takes its place, and the window stabilizes the new relation of inner and outer. In the Tieck the interior connotes the same Romantic artificial paradise; yet here the burning stair connotes the danger of isolation in the fantasy-world, and the return to city life connotes a similar renunciation of early Romantic poetics.

The relationship between Romanticism and the natural sciences/ 'Naturphilosophie' is intensively investigated. Saul, *Wissenschaften*, contains 14 papers from a symposium at Trinity College, Dublin, which focus less on reconstructing the by now well-known Romantic theorems than on analysing the function of scientific material in the poetic text in writers ranging from A. von Humboldt to Wackenroder, Brentano, Hoffmann, Chamisso, and Kleist. R. Görner, 'Schattenrisse und andere Ansichten vom Ich. Zur Identitätsproblematik als ästhetischem Gegenstand romantischen Bewußtseins', pp. 1–18, takes the silhouette as a metaphor for Romantic approaches to resolving the problematic relation of 'Ich' and 'Nicht-Ich': the outline is given with positively scientific precision yet partial, the aesthetic substance is wholly rendered yet dark. He sees the Romantic text (the *Chronika* and *Peter Schlemihl*) as the experimental attempt to integrate these scientific and aesthetic modes of understanding self and world. M. L. Davies, 'Zwischen Eros und Thanatos: Zur Wissenschaftsauffassung der Romantik', pp. 19–43, sees Romantic identity as an irreducible dualism of narcissism and death-wish, which he interprets as a reaction to the epistemic crisis of the age, and which seeks resolution without success in aestheticism. N. Saul argues in the 'Nachwort', pp. 306–18, that the Romantic text criticizes the scientism of the age by reference to holistic paradigms of science from pre-modern epochs, with the meaning-creating function of the poetic text seen as last line of defence against nihilism. H. Schipperges, 'Konzepte der Lebenskunst in Aufklärung und Romantik. Orthobiotik — Makrobiotik — Kalobiotik', *JFDH*: 90–108, is the text of a lecture, reprinted without notes, reconstructing briefly medicinal principles of health regulation, life prolongation, and beautiful living in such as Hufeland, Novalis, and Goethe.

Other themes are a mixed bag. Andreas Schumann, *Nation und Literaturgeschichte. Romantik-Rezeption im deutschen Kaiserreich zwischen Utopie und Apologie* (Cursus. Texte und Studien zur deutsche Literatur, 1), Munich, Iudicium, 309 pp., is a reworked Munich dissertation of 1984. It uses the concept of a discursive framework (derived from Foucault) to describe the dominant self-understanding of the age (1871–1913), which is seen as the basic consensual common denominator of all communication; its chief terms are 'Volk', 'Nation', 'Einheit', 'Größe'. Within this frame the various tendencies of literary historiography (Roman Catholic, Protestant, for women, etc.) are located, as elements of a discursive grid. What these 'Teilsdiskurse' say about Romanticism is then measured against the above set of basic consensual assumptions. The conclusion is that all the partial discourses (irrespective of apparent confessional or other ideological differences) are so dominated by value-laden terms like 'Nation' that they reduce the investigated phenomenon (whatever it may be) to not much more than central value. Thus for example early Romantic philosophy and cosmopolitan ethics are excluded. The only observable shift is from the propounding of the nationalist Utopia to its apologetic defence. From this the author derives the lesson that such dominant discursive myths are to be avoided by scholars. This book often arouses the suspicion that it is concerned more with the elaboration of theoretical frameworks than actual analysis, and its style is mannered and loquacious, yet it is well worth reading. See also P. Régnier, 'La question romantique comme enjeu national: critique française et littérature allemande autour de 1830', *Romantisme*, 73:29–42. U. Wyss, 'Der doppelte Ursprung der Literaturwissenschaft nach 1800', *Fest. Conrady*, 73–88, sees a dialectic (originating at this time) between textual immediacy and contextual mediation as constitutive for the relationship of scholars with the literary text. Tieck's *Minnelieder* exemplify on the one hand an attempt to revive the immediate experience of the text as text, an approach which Lachmann's commentary-less philology (paradoxically) continues. A. W. Schlegel's synthetic, modernizing re-writing of *Tristan* exemplifies the opposite pole: highly mediated reception of the text. J. Grimm however goes his own anarchic way, rejecting both paths in favour of a 'wild' methodology. W. concludes that literary scholarship, whilst not needing to follow the idealist attempt at synthesizing textual immediacy and historical contextualization, must none the less even today recognize that both approaches to the text must necessarily complement each other.

Poesie der Apokalypse, ed. Gerhard R. Kaiser, Würzburg, Königshausen & Neumann, 318 pp. (the proceedings of the 1990 conference of the Deutsche Gesellschaft für Allgemeine und Vergleichende Literaturwissenschaft) contains a number of useful essays on this central Romantic theme. W. Braungart, 'Apokalypse und Utopie', pp. 64–102, is a wide-ranging essay which recognizes the creative as well as destructive implications of the apocalypse, and thus can identify its affinity with the Utopia topos. He interprets the motif of the ruin in Kleist, Jean Paul, and C. D. Friedrich in this light. I. Oesterle, 'Romantische Poesie der Poesie der Apokalypse. Neue Kunst, neue Mythologie und Apokalyptik in der Heidelberger Romantik und im Spätwerk Friedrich Schlegels', pp. 103–28, sees the creative-destructive function of apocalyptic imagery in Romantic writing as expressing reactions to the religious and poetic crisis. The imagery is applied either to the critique of modern poetry (in F. Schlegel's 'Das Hieroglyphenlied oder Anklänge und Bilder der Zeit und Zukunft'), or dissolved (in Görres's contribution to *BOGS, der Uhrmacher*) into the new syncretic mythology. C. Becker, 'Der Traum der Apokalypse — die Apokalypse ein Traum? Eschatologie und/ oder Ästhetik im Ausgang von Jean Pauls *Rede des toten Christus*', pp. 129–44, examines the poetic function of apocalytic imagery in Jean Paul's *Rede* and notes how it gradually become reduced in its reception in 19th-c. France to a thesaurus of disposable images for self-referential lyricism. There is a good section relating the historical sense of the *Rede* to its genesis during the French Revolution, Herder's *Shakespear*, and Jacobi's philosophy of religion. Udo Dickenberger, *Liebe, Geist, Unendlichkeit. Die Inschriften des Stuttgarter Hoppenlau-Friedhofs und die poetische Kultur um 1800* (GTS, 34), 1990, 268 pp., is a semi-popular work collecting headstone inscriptions and listing their provenance in the poetic literature of the age. There is a very large quantity of material here but almost no analysis. The same author's *Der Tod und die Dichter. Scherzgedichte in den Musenalmanachen um 1800. Eine Sammlung von 220 Spottgrabinschriften* (GST, 35), 118 pp., looks at another neglected genre, but also restricts itself to material-gathering and popular commentary.

   Debatten und Kontroversen. Literarische Auseinandersetzungen in Deutschland am Ende des 18. Jahrhunderts, ed. Hans-Dietrich Dahnke and Bernd Leister, 2 vols, Berlin—Weimar, Aufbau, 1989, 539, 431 pp., is concerned — against the background of stifled public discussion in the ex-GDR — to reconstruct in refreshingly unideological manner the processes of literary debate which formed public opinion in our epoch. All the essays are thorough if top-heavy with (often repeated) information and drearily chronological in structure, and there is little evaluation of the exposed processes of debate. Vol. II, which is relevant here, has J. Golz, 'Jean Pauls "Poesie in Prose" und das klassische Kunstkonzept. — Aspekte kontroverser Literaturauffassungen in den Jahren 1796/97', pp. 72–153, which reconstructs the communicative situation and aesthetic function of the humoristic narrator and explores its consequences for the shadowy controversy between Jean Paul and Weimar Classicism; W. Beyer, 'Der Atheismusstreit um Fichte', pp. 154–245, reconstructs at length the 'Atheismusstreit', including the pamphlet war that followed, and shows its importance for the Berlin phase of Fichte's system; H. Härtl, '*Athenaeum*-Polemiken', pp. 246–357, reconstructs in detail the at once esoteric and popularist communicative strategy of this organ, and analyses its consequences for the polemics against Schiller, Wieland, Jean Paul and late Enlightenment figures, with useful analysis in this context of *Über die Unverständlichkeit*; and W. Albrecht, 'Friedrich Nicolais Kontroversen mit den Klassikern und Frühromantikern (1796–1802)', pp. 9–71, which has sections on Nicolai's attacks against Tieck, the Schlegels, and Fichte.

   L. Puchalski, 'Europäischer Patriotismus und nationales Bewußtsein. Zur Europa-Idee in der deutschen und polnischen Romantik', *Arcadia*, 26: 141–71, compares and contrasts the different versions and functions of the idea of Europe in two cultural contexts. He shows how radically different they were and how the differences are conditioned by political situation and historical experience. C.

McClanahan, *European Romanticism: Literary Societies, Poets and Poetry* (AUS, III, 31) 1990, 245 pp.

GENRES. Ernst Weber, *Lyrik der Befreiungskriege (1812–1815). Gesell-schaftspoetische Meinungs- und Willensbildung durch Literatur* (GerAb, 65), viii + 391 pp., is a Regensburg *Habilitationschrift* of 1989. In eight chapters and an excursus the author reviews the work done hitherto, presents the socio-historical situation and literary traditions, the literary forms used, their re-application for political purposes, interprets the political lyrics in Prussia, Hessen, and the 'Rheinbund-staaten', and, finally, assesses the further development of the genre so defined at crucial points in the 19th c. The strength of the book is its differentiated analysis of work which has suffered too much from ideologized treatment. W. shows in enormous detail how the ostensibly aesthetic genre of the lyric took on during this epoch the publicistic role of forming public opinion, not just offering informa-tion, but channelling collective experience, changing self-understanding, and exhorting to action. Typical of the richness is the chapter on Prussia, with its careful shadings of content, audience, and function between Arndt's nationalistic lyrics of 1813 with their calculated call to *lèse-majesté*, Jahn's volunteer-collections (including Körner's more personal and psychological works) with their educa-tive and democratizing function, and the patriotic Prussian writings located in 18th-c. traditions of absolutist loyalty to the person of the King. This book is set to become the standard work on an important theme.

Frederick Burwick, *Illusion and the Drama. Critical Theory of the Enlightenment and Romantic Era*, University Park, Pennsylvania, Penn State Press, ix + 326 pp., offers a history of the idea of dramatic illusion from the Enlightenment to the early Romantic era in France, Germany, and Britain. In seven chapters B. argues that in the 18th c. illusion, as lever of emotional affect, was seen in the Enlightenment as the primary goal of dramatic aesthetics. Sources of illusion were traced in turn to various functions of the players, the audience, the stage and the play *qua* dialogue. In the Romantic epoch consciousness of illusion became however a problem, which was then thematized by the plays themselves, so that 'metadramatic' effects on various levels predominated. The last two chapters contrast works which sup-posedly exemplify opposite reactions to the phenomenon: Goethe's *Faust* and Hugo's *Hernani* seek to reintegrate alienated material into non-naturalistic illusion; Coleridge's *Remorse* and Tieck's *Der ge-stiefelte Kater* emphasize disintegration and reversal of expectation within the illusion. Romantic drama's play with 'the phenomenon of illusion', says B. finally, offers 'insight into the ambiguities of knowledge and the frail and fallible access we have to self, others and the world'. Unfortunately the book is far too long, virtually all of it consisting in accurate but laborious restatements of others' arguments, and the chronological-generic disposition of material is poor: Coleridge and Tieck both surface twice, and far too little interest is focused on the metadramatic dramas themselves. More fundamentally, once the extensive material supporting the book's predictable thesis has been expounded, the results are not evaluated save in the single sentence cited above, so that we do not know what they mean — a major defect in so large and ambitious a work. H. Steinecke, 'Die fürstliche Bibliothek Corvey. Eine "Sudelbibliothek" als "Schatzkammer" romantischer Literatur', *Athenäum*, 1:233–42, contains in the main the text of S.'s paper on the holdings of this library to a symposium on the subject at Paderborn in 1990. The library, where Hoffmann von Fallersleben worked for 14 years, promises soon to be one of the major centres of research on the Romantic novel and drama: it contains 67,000 books in English, French, and German, mainly from 1800–34, with large numbers of *rarissima* and *unica*, and will be the basis of DFG projects on '*Der deutsche Roman 1815–1830*' and '*Das deutsche Drama 1805–1832*'. Most relevant works have already been duplicated on microfiche.

T. Althaus, 'Geistige Syntax. Einige Sätze zur Entwicklung des Essays im 18. Jahrhundert, zu einer möglichen Theorie der Gattung und zu Friedrich Schlegels Essay *Über die Unverständlichkeit*', *Arntzen Vol.*, 159–71, sees the genre as hybrid, spanning 'Poesie' and 'Prosa', its virtue being that — by contrast to systematic logic — the essay enacts the very process of argumentation. It thus expresses a fundamental linguistic fact of life, according to A., namely the inadequate relation of language and logic. S.'s essay, with its careful avoidance of logical referents and thematization of the process of argument, exemplifies the definition and functions as a provocation of the reader.

E. Ostermann, 'Der Begriff des Fragments als Leitmetapher der ästhetischen Moderne', *Athenäum*, 1:189–205, is a cool analysis of the role of the fragment in aesthetic and philosophical theory from the Romantic age to post-modernity. Three possibilities of interpreting the necessarily fragmentary character of art — as a still attainable ideal of aesthetic totality (Goethe, Schiller, F. Schlegel); as the negative token of a still thinkable Utopia (Benjamin, Bloch, Adorno); as the destruction of a totality seen as illusion (Nietzsche, Foucault, Derrida) — are identified and contrasted in terms of subject, language, and historical process. Jürgen Wertheimer, '*Der Güter Gefährlichstes, die Sprache.' Zur Krise des Dialogs zwischen Aufklärung und Romantik*, Munich, Fink, 1990, 269 pp., is not about the relation between two opposing schools of thought. Instead, it links problems of genre and communication, using the contrasting theoretical frameworks of Lyotard, Bakhtin and Kopperschmidt to identify and describe a crisis in communication related to the self-understanding of the subject over this period, which is exemplified in the development of the dialogue both as philosophical genre and as element of the poetic genres. A model of communication is allotted to the early Enlightenment. Its criticism, continuous reconstitution, and final destruction by (primarily) Diderot, Rousseau, Lessing, and Hölderlin are retraced in perceptive analyses of the progressive distortion, refusal, and monologization of communication in their dialogical texts, especially *Hyperion*, *Empedokles*, and the later hymns and elegies. This is an important and innovative book. Also noted: M.-C. Hoock-Demarle, 'Un lieu d'interculturalité franco-allemande: le réseau épistolaire de Coppet', *Romantisme*, 71 : 19–28; and H. Rölleke, 'German fable poetry in the context of the French Revolution', *SMLS*, *Special Issue*: 57–78.

2. INDIVIDUAL AUTHORS

ARNIM, BETTINA VON. C. Bürger, 'Bettina/Bettine — Die Grenzgängerin', Bürger, *Leben*, 133–57, portrays B.'s personality as dualistically 'zerrissen', eroded by inner emptiness and vacillating on the border of fantasy and understanding, nature and culture, poetic vocation and conformism to role. Overcoming the poetic resignation imposed by marriage only after Arnim's death, her later work is a search for self-realization, so that the image of the child Bettine in *C.Bs Frühlingskranz* connotes a kind of fleeting, epiphatic reinvention of self. K. Rudert, 'Die Breslauer Kasematten. B. v. A. als Rezipientin des schlesischen Frühsozialisten Wilhelm Wolff', *JFDH*: 139–48, looks at a modified extract from the *Breslauer Zeitung* which B. made for the *Armenbuch*, identifies the author of the original as the Utopian socialist Wilhelm Wolff, and reinterprets the extract's intended function in B.'s book. A. Neuhaus-Koch, 'Bettine von Arnim im Dialog mit Rahel Varnhagen, Amalie von Helvig, Fanny Tarnow und Fanny Lewald', *Fest. Windfuhr*, 103–18, is a brisk reconstruction of B.'s relationships, written and personal, with the individuals concerned, which whilst interesting offers no evaluation of the material. The *Internationales Jb. der B.v.A.-Gesellschaft*, 4, 1990, 229 pp., has W. Schmitz, '"Experimentum Medietatis": Lebensmythen bei C. und B.B.' (17–44), which compares and contrasts *Godwi* and *C.Bs Frühlingskranz* in terms of self-creation and the mythical ideal of family; also K. Bäumer, 'Margaret Fuller (1810–1850) and B.v.A.: An encounter between American Transcendentalism and German Romanticism' (47–69), which reconstructs and interprets a transatlantic relationship with two unpublished letters; U. Landfester,

' "Da, wo ich duldend mich unterwerfen sollte, da werde ich mich rächen" — Mignon auf dem Weg zur Revolte' (71–97), is fine essay analysing how Mignon came to have a dualistic reception among men and women writers. She sees the cause of the problem in a chance remark of Goethe's on Mme de Staël, which appears to authorize an interpretation of Mignon (contrary to his intention) as no longer an asexual androgyne and ideal of natural creativity, but as a distinctly female figure, whose fate marks woman as creature of nature and excludes her from the cultural sphere of aesthetic creativity in 'archivierbare Form'. Eichendorff's and Immermann's Mignon figures in *Ahnung und Gegenwart* and *Die Epigonen* show how male authors reinforce this link of poetics and gender-theory; Marianne von Willemer's life and especially B.'s famous Mignon letter in *Goethe's Briefwechsel mit einem Kinde* exemplify the alternative possibility of the original, namely to rewrite the image from a distinctly female viewpoint and use it as instrument of resistance to determination by masculine discursive norms; S. Lesser, 'B.v.A. — Psychologisches um eine ungewöhnliche Frau' (99–124), is a psychological analysis of B.'s personality on the basis of her biography; W. Maierhofer, 'Einfühlen, Einvernahme und Mißverstehen, Rilke und B.v.A.' (125–50), reconstructs the readings of B.'s work (mainly *Goethe's Briefwechsel mit einem Kinde*) in *Malte* and elsewhere, and charts a series of appropriations and misunderstandings, notably that Rilke saw the literary works as mere biography; finally H. Hirsch, ' "Dieses Buch gehört Hoffmann von Fallersleben" ' (151–52); Theodor Fontane, '*An Bettina (bei der Lesung ihres König-Buches)*' (153); and U. Lemm, 'B.v.A. Köthener Straße 44, 2 Treppen' (154–57).

ARNIM, LUDWIG ACHIM VON. A.v.A., *Erzählungen*, ed. Gisela Henckmann (UB, 1505), 384 pp., is a useful edition of the seven best-known *Novellen* but also including *Raphael und seine Nachbarinnen*. There are short notes explaining references and glossing usages, brief good bibliographies on Arnim in general and the individual stories, and a concise afterword emphasizing Arnim's use of semitic material, his interest in animal magnetism, and the unusual strength of his women characters. Particularly useful here are the perceptive comments on form and the list of leading categories which link the disparate selection of texts together in a common focus. L.A.v.A., *Armut, Reichtum, Schuld und Buße der Gräfin Dolores*, ed. Hans-Georg Werner (ATV, 15), 603 pp., reprints the text of the Hanser edition (1962), with a brief afterword and note. The afterword does reflect the latest tendencies of Arnim research, and so defends the novel against the charge of wilful formlessness, and the notes make this edition useful for students. Christof Wingertszahn, *Ambiguität und Ambivalenz im erzählerischen Werk A. v. As. Mit einem Anhang unbekannter Texte aus As*

Nachlaß (SBL, 23), 1990, 699 pp., sees itself as the first extensive study of A.'s narratives. Its main purpose is to undermine any notion of fixed, pre-existent authorial meaning which the texts subsequently express. This is achieved by the use of complementary analytical categories ambiguity and ambivalence, the former connoting (not necessarily binary) plurality or irreducibility of meaning, the latter at bottom a psychoanalytic category connoting the simultaneous coexistence of opposite emotions. That ambiguity describes A.'s implicit poetics adequately is demonstrated convincingly with a mass of documentation, and particularly so in the discussion of the function of the reflective frame and perspectival interpretation in *Der Wintergarten*. That ambivalence is equally fundamental is not demonstrated quite so convincingly, although the analysis of *Der tolle Invalide* is illuminating. The appendix contains some 37 short as yet unpublished texts, including an interesting review of Fiorillo's *Geschichte der zeichnenden Künste*. **Neue Tendenzen der Arnim-Forschung: Edition, Bibliographie, Interpretation, mit unbekannten Dokumenten*, ed. Roswitha Burwick and B. Fischer (GSA, 60), 1990, 321 pp. P. Sprengel, 'Triumph und Versammlung. Strukturen des Festspiels in Klassik und Romantik. Mit einem ungedruckten Text A. v. As *Plan zu einem Festspiel beym Feste des allgemeinen Friedens*', *Aurora*, 50, 1990:1–26, publishes the A. text for the first time and contrasts effectively 'Festspiele' by Goethe and A., Schiller and Brentano around the events of 1813–14. He shows how a fundamental tension between A.'s political conception and the traditional form of the feudal genre underlies the aesthetic failure of A.'s work, whereas Brentano's *Victoria*, using the alternative model of 'bürgerlich' celebration offered by Schiller's *Tell* and *Wallenstein*, anticipates 19th-c. forms. M. Andermatt, 'Produktive Rezeption. Vergleich, Metapher und Allegorie in der zeitgenössischen A.-Kritik', *Aurora*, 50, 1990:219–29, looks at the type of metaphor applied to A.'s work in its reception by his peers, from Goethe to Bettina, Eichendorff and Wilhelm Grimm, concluding that they tended to apply a classicistic yardstick which is inadequate to its object. B. Plachta, 'Die Darstellung der Französischen Revolution in A.v.As Novelle "Melück Maria Blainville"', *LWU*, 23:299–310, analyses the representation of the Revolution in this story, notes that the tension between individual and general is consistently present, and concludes that Melück symbolizes the role of the individual as source of renewal on the post-Revolutionary age. See also Jaynie Anderson, '"Die geniale Bettina": Giovanni Morelli in conversation with B.v.A.', *OGS*, 18–19, 1989–90:45–59.

BRENTANO, CLEMENS. *C. B. Sämtliche Werke und Briefe*, ed. Jürgen Behrens, Wolfgang Frühwald, Detlev Lüders, Christoph Perels, and Hartwig Schultz. Vol. 31. *Briefe*. III. *1803–1807*, ed. Lieselotte Kinskofer, Stuttgart, Kohlhammer, 752 pp., contains 218 letters, diplomatically edited in the usual meticulous fashion, with a brief commentary plus indexes of addressees, poems, and persons. Erika Tunner, 'Bs Mitarbeit an den "Berliner Abendblättern"', *KlJb*, 1990:127–34, notes that B. published his appreciation of Runge *Andenken eines trefflichen Deutschen Mannes und tiefsinnigen Künstlers* in the *Berliner Abendblätter* and uses the occasion to reconstruct B.'s relationships with Kleist and Runge. Beyond the conclusion that B. functioned here as a 'Brückenbauer' seeking to mediate Runge's art to a wider audience she however adds little to what is already known. Petra Maisak and Hartwig Schultz, 'Verschiedene Empfindungen bei enem Berliner Ausstellungsbesuch. Ungedruckte Texte aus dem Nachlaß C. Bs', *JFDH*: 109–30, takes up another strand of B.'s poetic art-criticism, and publishes for the first time three *Bildgedichte* of his relating to works by C. D. Friedrich, the Kügelgen twins and Kretschmar exhibited at the Berlin exhibition of 1810. They are located in the wider context of other reviews in the *Berliner Abendblätter* and the narrower one of B.'s lyric responses to fine art. A. Ammer, 'Betrachtung der Betrachtung in einem Zeitungsartikel über die Betrachter eines Bildes, worauf der Betrachter einer Landschaft. (*Mönch am Meer* — Friedrich, B., Arnim, Kleist, Ernst usw.)', *Athenäum*, 1:135–62, is a semiological analysis about the implications for author, signified and medium of (primarily) B.'s and Arnim's reactions to the Friedrich. N. Saul, 'Predigt und predigende Rede bei C.B.', Saul, *Wissenschaften*, 125–55, uncovers B.'s fascination with homiletics and parodistic sermons in all phases of his career and interprets the frequent later occurrences as esoteric compensation for his exoteric renunciation of poetry. H. Rölleke, '"Warteinweil". Zur Genealogie eines überirdischen Begriffs', *JFDH*: 131–38, traces in his inimitable style the descent of the expression and place name which occurs in *Des Knaben Wunderhorn*, B.'s *Geschichte und Ursprung des ersten Bärnhäuters* and *Herzliche Zueignung* of *Gockel, Hinkel und Gackeleia* to a work of Jakob Frey (1556) and, finally, the apocryphal Gospel of Nicodemus, where it connotes limbo. A. Lorenczuk, 'Die Fetthenne, eine kühn-fromme Kräuter-Allegorie. Zur Spätfassung des Märchens "Gockel, Hinkel und Gackeleia" von C. B. — Eine Miszelle —', *Aurora*, 50, 1990:231–35, decodes the name 'Grasette Fetthenne' as an allusion to Anna Katharina Emmerick and links it both with her function of relieving suffering and B.'s stylistic tendency to reveal and conceal. P. Hasubek, 'Spielraum des Humors. Humoristisch–komische Strukturen in C.Bs Erzählung "Die mehreren Wehmüller und ungarischen Nationalgesichter"', *Fest. Windfuhr*, 71–101, examines humoristic structures here in terms of 'angewandte Phantasie' or the discrepancy between forms and contents, concentrating on the *Doppelgänger* motif, the language of humour, the conclusion and the contemporary context of humour theory. He concludes by seeing Wehmüller positively, as a figure designed to signal B.'s increasing distance from early Romantic aesthetics. Also A. Krättli, '*Der schiffbrüchige Galeerensklave vom todten Meer — Zauberer, Poet, wortverliebt und unbesonnen*', *SchwM*, 69, 1989:613–21.

CAROVÉ. C. E. Schweitzer, 'Friedrich Wilhelm C., Autor eines einzigartigen Kunstmärchens', Knapp, *Autoren*, 133–53, pleads for C.'s place in literary history (as well as Hegel and Runge scholarship) on the basis of a singular *Kunstmärchen, Kinderleben* (1830), amongst his relatively modest literary production.

CHAMISSO. C. J. Wickham, 'Narrative strategies of experience, fact and fantasy in C.'s *Peter Schlemihl*', *Fest. Grimm*, 229–39, relates scientific material and fantasy in the tale to the theme of discovering identity in the synthesis of the two realms.

EICHENDORFF, JOSEPH VON. P. U. Hohendahl, 'Konservatismus oder Romantik? Überlegungen zu Es historischem Ort', *Fest. Grimm*, 23–42, investigates the relationship between conservatism and Romanticism in E.'s historical and political writings. Analysis shows that the terms are to be used only in a highly differentiated and individual sense: E.'s conservatism predates his involvement with Romanticism and is not uncritically identified therewith; nor does his conservatism, as his involvement in the Prussian reform movement suggests, necessitate his identification with restorative monarchists. E. is therefore a 'Romantiker "with a difference"'. K. K. Polheim, 'Interpretation und Textgenese. Es Gedicht "Götterdämmerung"', *Fest. Zeller*, 124–41, publishes 'Was klingt mir so heiter' and 'Von kühnen Wunderbildern' which appeared both separately and in *Das Marmorbild*. He reconstructs their genesis, interpreting the texts in each phase. Thus he shows how carefully E. composed, how concerned he was to establish symmetric and semantic weighting and to guarantee the reflexive function in the *Novelle*. *Aurora*, 50, 1990, contains mainly the proceedings of the 1990 conference on 'Schiller und die Romantik', and these essays are reviewed where appropriate elsewhere, but there are also a number of essays on E. H.-J. Pott, 'Schillers spekulative Gattungspoetik und Es Poesie', *Aurora*, 50, 1990:87–101, reinterprets Schiller's naïve and sentimental poetics as a dialectic rather than a polar opposition, makes out of that an historical progression akin to the one in F. Schlegel's *Studium* essay, interprets the dialectic as prescribing the role of poetry in restoring anthropological wholeness, and sees the scheme satiric-elegaic-idyllic under this aspect as exemplified in some of E.'s writings. H.-J. Lüthi, 'Es Heimat', *ib.*, 145–64, see E.'s poems on this theme as constituted by a tension between Venus as mythical origin of poetry and Christianity, so that the destruction of the bond with the former is the condition of E.'s adherence to the latter. F. Heiduk, 'E. und Theodor Opitz. Des Dichters letzter Brief an den Übersetzer Alexander Puschkins', *ib.*, 165–76, reconstructs E.'s relationship with the translator of Pushkin and Lermontov, and publishes anew (and amended) E.'s letter to him. G. Reichard, 'Das Motiv des Wahnsinns bei E. Zum Verhältnis von Literatur und psychopathologischer Forschung im frühen 19. Jahrhundert', *ib.*, 177–94, uncovers a theme well-treated in numerous Romantic authors but until now not E. He shows how well-read E. was in contemporary psychopathology, especially the Romantic tendency of Schelling and Steffens, so that *Die Zauberei im Herbste*, *Das Marmorbild*, and *Dichter und ihre Gesellen* can all be shown to utilize the latest scientific theory for the portrayal of poetological problems associated with fantasy. C. Rodiek, "Und die Welt hebt an zu singen." Es Beitrag zu einem deutschen Calderón', *ib.*, 195–205, is a subtle analysis and evaluation of E.'s principles of translation, concluding that, whilst superficially true to the content and even the imagery of the *autos*, E. none the less uses stylistic means to romanticize his author. Thus the goals of the literary-historical and the translation projects are identical: the propagation of an outdated image of Calderón as *the* Romantic. See also: V. Stein, 'Bericht über den 10. Internationalen Kongreß der E.-Gesellschaft vom 5. bis 8. Juli 1990 in Marbach', *ib.*, 236–44; I. Holtmeier, 'E.-Bibliographie', *ib.*, 245–51. Michael Perraudin, '"Das Baumbesteigen nimmt . . . kein Ende." Tree-climbing in E.', *GLL*, 44:103–09, traces the developing meaning of the motif in E., concluding that the tree-top is 'a place for [. . .] escape and salvation, for awareness and clarity, for open-hearted longing. But above all or altogether [. . .] a place for the apprehension of God'. Günther Debon, *Das Heidelberger Jahr J. v. Es*, Heidelberg, Guderjahn, 275 pp., is a popular study foregrounding the role of the city in E.'s life and work at this time, with brief chapters on friends, academic life, excursions, and Käthchen Förster, plus lengthier chapters emphasizing the reflection of Heidelbergiana in E.'s works during and after the year. The book is distinguished by numerous splendid illustrations and a reprint of Görres's comments on Runge's *Vier Zeiten*. See also S. J. Richter, 'Under the sign of Venus: E.'s *Marmorbild* and the erotics of allegory', *SAR*, 56:59–71. M. Sauter, 'Marmorbilder und Masochismus. Die Venusfiguren in Es *Das Marmorbild* und in Sacher-Masochs *Venus im Pelz*', *Neophilologus*, 75:119–27. G. Pflüger, **Die Komponentenanalyse und das Problem der ästhetischen Wertung: Eine wissenschaftshistorische und literaturtheoretische Diskussion anhand ausgewählter Dichtungen von J.v.E.* (BNE, 11), 1990, 156 pp.

    FICHTE. J. G. F., *Gesamtausgabe*, ed. Reinhard Lauth and Hans Gliwitzky. Vol. 1, 8. *Werke 1801–1806*, ed. Reinhard Lauth, Hans

Gliwitzky, *et al.*, Stuttgart — Bad Cannstatt, Frommann-Holzboog, x + 493 pp., contains *inter alia* the would-be popular works from F.'s first Berlin and Erlangen period: *Die Grundzüge des gegenwärtigen Zeitalters* and *Ueber das Wesen des Gelehrten*, plus (as an *incertum*) the *Philosophie der Maurerei*, which was strongly contaminated by Fessler and Fischer, and several sonnets. The volume maintains the high standards set by the edition as a whole, with model introductions to each work describing the work, its genesis, and contemporary reception. *J.G.F. im Gespräch. Berichte der Zeitgenossen*, ed. Erich Fuchs, Reinhard Lauth, and Walter Schieche. Vol. 5. *1812–1814*. *J.G.F.-Chronik* (Specula 1, 5), Stuttgart—Bad Cannstatt, Frommann-Holzboog, xiv + 436 pp., is a first-class volume containing reactions to F.'s activities from contemporaries and successors as diverse as Marheineke (whose funereal oration is reproduced in full), Crabbe Robinson, Zacharias Werner, Arndt, Schopenhauer, and Ranke. This mine of valuable information covers issues such as F.'s character and system, his retirement as Rector of the Berlin University, illness, and death. It is complemented by full bibliographies of works used and indexes of F.'s works referred to both here and in the indispensable chronicle of his life. Peter Rohs, *J.G.F.* (BsR, 521), 195 pp., is an extremely useful introduction to a philosopher whose importance for literary Romanticism, once generally recognized, has become obscured in recent years by the intensive work done in particular on Schelling in this context. The author's clear and sober exposition of F.'s system in its development (through 15 different versions) focuses our attention away from the off-putting 'Manie des "Deduzierens"' on its surface and reveals sympathetically and in its context F.'s true achievement as an inheritor of the Kantian project, who sought to put its implications about subjectivity into rigorous and coherent form. In this he sees F.'s major and lasting philosophical achievement. Rohs attacks the absolutist presuppositions of Schelling's and Hegel's — at the time crippling — F. critiques, and thus denies that a logical line leads from Kant through F. to Hegel. Many of Rohs's detailed expositions of less well-known texts (*Der geschlossene Handelsstaat, Die Anweisung zum seligen Leben, Reden an die deutsche Nation, Die Grundzüge des gegenwärtigen Zeitalters, Die Bestimmung des Menschen*) also reveal F. unexpectedly as a practical thinker, who in the context of property, ecological ethics, the theory of communicative action and the critique of writing (but not in that of women's rights) adopted positions widely held today. That Rohs should devote only one sketchy page to the reception of F. by Novalis and F. Schlegel thus offers scholars of literary Romanticism the chance to explore the links between these writers, increasingly seen as 'modern', and those hitherto neglected dimensions of F.'s thought. There are useful bibliographies, a potted biography exposing the religious roots of F.'s philosophical stance, and a chronology.

FISCHER, CAROLINE AUGUSTE. Wilhelmine Karoline von Wobeser, *Elisa oder das Weib wie es sein sollte*, ed. Lydia Schieth (Frühe Frauenliteratur in Deutschland, 8), Hildesheim, Olms, 1990, 351 + 96 + 39 pp., also contains Christian August Fischer, *Über den Umgang der Weiber mit Männern*, a response to *Elisa* by Fischer's husband, plus a short afterword by the editor, briefly locating the texts in their context. See also A. Runge, p. 736 above.

FOUQUÉ. F. de la M. F., *Sämtliche Romane und Tagebücher*, ed. Wolfgang Möhring. 13. *Mandragora. Fata Morgana. Erzählungen und Novellen*, ed. Wolfgang Möhring, Hildesheim, Olms, 319, 107, 184 pp., reprints texts from 1827, 1830, and 1833 editions respectively, a valuable addition to libraries but with no scholarly apparatus. B. bei der Wieden, 'Zu Fouqués *Galgenmännlein*', *ASNS*, 227, 1990:323–27.

GRIMM, JACOB, AND WILHELM. James M. McGlathery, *Fairy Tale Romance. The Grimms, Basile and Perrault*, Urbana — Chicago, Illinois U.P., xii + 226 pp., is a study of that unusual thing, author-intentionality in the folk fairy tale. The thesis is that there is such a genre; its *raison d'être* for the collective authors is to express erotic passion, which they experience as problematic, in a more-or-less veiled mode, for entertainment and instruction. The means by which the thesis is elaborated is therefore neither folkloristic nor structuralist, anthropological or psychoanalytic, but literary. McG. discusses fully problems of authorship and oral tradition, settles for the literized text (in the Grimms' case the last edition of their own hand) from each collection, and discusses the corpus so established in a deliberately ahistorical and context-free way, isolating six fields of figural tension, between brother and sister, beauty and the beast, father and daughter, hag/witch and daughter, brides and husbands, husbands and brides. From the frequency of these occurrences in the corpus is derived the above conclusion about intentionality. Perhaps it is because of the relative blandness of the conclusion that the introduction and conclusion, abandoning the established method, set the typology so derived once more into the general context of patriarchal social values, relating the degree of frankness to the historical development of a given society. Brüder G., *Volkslieder. Aus der Handschriftensammlung der Universitätsbibliothek Marburg*, ed. Charlotte Oberfeld, Peter Assion, Ludwig Deneke, Lutz Röhrich, and Heinz Rölleke. 2. *Kommentar*, Marburg, Elwert, 1989, viii + 343 pp., is the companion to the texts in vol. 1. In addition to L. Deneke and C. Oberfeld, 'Die Bedeutung der "Volkspoesie" bei J. und W. G.', pp. 1–23, an oddly organized but instructive exposition of the concept and its application, and P. Assion, 'Die Volksliedersammlung der Brüder G. und ihre Bedeutung für das Land Hessen', pp. 24–33, a learned analysis of their achievement in and for Hessen, it contains detailed commentary section by section by luminaries such as H. Rölleke on the previously edited material from many different cultures. Roger Paulin, *Goethe, the Brothers G. and Academic Freedom*, CUP, 30 pp., is the Inaugural Lecture of 1990 and shows how notions of organic unity and freedom underlie the Romantic concept of *Wissenschaft*. This, when applied to the creation of the modern German university system around 1810, fostered an academic culture of resistance to state interference exemplified in the cases of Fichte, Oken and the Gs, which Paulin sees as a major achievement of Romanticism. Miljan Mojašević, *Jacob G. und die serbische Literatur und Kultur* (MSG, 14), 1990, 212 pp., is a part-translation of a Serbo-Croat monograph of 1983 which reconstructs G.'s (and Goethe's) work on Serbian philology and 'Volkspoesie', whilst also pointing up the contribution of Serbian contemporaries. There is much material here but relatively little analysis. B. Koch-Häbel, 'Erinnerungen an einen "Garten alter Poesie". Zu den *Kinder- und Hausmärchen* der Brüder G.', *Arntzen Vol.*, 237–45, reads the tales as continuations of early Romantic aesthetics: as prose reflections of absolute *Poesie* which embody the story of *Poesie* in ever new epic actualizations. The infinite narrative potential of language is seen as condensed into the 'Es' of every tale's first sentence, but what 'Es' is can only be remembered and re-presented in and as language. *Schneewittchen* is the example: the daughter — her name being significant — is the expression of desire for unity with nature, her death and rebirth the symbol of poetry's power to recall that lost unity in language. Thus the Grimms preserve in the modern world the function of *Poesie* as medium for criticizing everyday consciousness and morality. Wolfgang Frühwald, '*Von der Poesie im Recht*. Über die Brüder G. und die Rechtsauffassung der deutschen Romantik', *Saul, Wissenschaften*, 282–305, reconstructs the link of law and culture in Savigny's and Jacob G.'s concepts of legal scholarship, identifying immediacy of linguistic expression of a common body of values as the mediating term. Both scholars are seen to project a lost paradise of legal-poetic myth into the past and future as the foundation of their theory.

GÜNDERODE. K.v.G., **Sämtliche Werke. Historisch-kritische Ausgabe*, ed. Walter Morgenthaler, 3 vols, Frankfurt, Roter Stern, 1200 pp. M. E. Goozé, 'The seduction of Don Juan: K.v.G.'s romantic rendering of a classic story', *Slessarev Vol.*, 117–29, locates the romance in literary tradition and shows in a careful analysis that the text plays with point of view, including contamination of narrative standpoint, in order to express the gender conflicts G. experienced without resolving them.

HEBEL. Ludwig Fertig, *J.P.H. Der Schulfreund* (Poeten als Pädagogen), WBG, viii + 121 pp., is a history of H.'s career as pedagogue, which looks back at his schooldays and uncovers the contradictory picture of a man who was committed to his profession and sought repeatedly to reform it, yet who complained constantly about his duties, read almost no pedagogical literature, and also refused a promotion to his own parish which entailed no such teaching duties. The last chapter investigates the function of *Der Rheinische Hausfreund* as 'Volksaufklärung'. Wolfgang Ritzel, *J.P.H. Briefschreiber. Proteuser. Naturforscher. Poet. Hausfreund. Mann der Kirche*, Waldkirch, Waldkircher Vlg, 182 pp. is a general study, as the author charmingly says, without scholarly ambition. None the less this handsome book is a worthy attempt to see H. in the round, with chapters on each facet of his activities save teaching, and the reconstruction of his Protean theory is commendable. D. G. Bond, 'Two ships: correspondences between Uwe Johnson and J.P.H.', *GQ*, 64:313–24, uses insights gained from a similarity of motif in Johnson and H. to support a reading of Johnson and identifies further parallels: the standpoint of the little people, the multiplicity of text-types, the subtlety of moral didacticism, the deliberate provinciality of the situation. K. Roland, 'Johann Peter Hebel und die Juden', *GerLux*, 2:45–72, analyses the image of the Jews in the *Kalendergeschichten*, pointing up H.'s accentuation of positive as well as negative features (the image of Mendelssohn as wise man, the recognition of the religious achievement of the nation) as instruments of the appeal for Christian tolerance and socio-cultural integration. See also D. Arendt, 'Dialektpoesie als Weltliteratur. J.P.H *Alemannische Gedichte*', *SchwM*, 69, 1989:219–34.

HOFFMANN. Alfred Hoffmann, *E.T.A.H. Leben und Arbeit eines preußischen Richters*, Baden-Baden, Nomos, 1990, 251 pp., is a Freiburg legal dissertation which seeks to reconstruct and evaluate H.'s legal career. The bulk of the book looks at four cases in which H. was crucially involved, all of them well-known to literary scholars: the murderer Schmolling, the counterfeiter Schnallenberger, the demagoguery issue between von Mühlenfels and Kamptz, and the copyright issue between Leidesdorf and Weber. The author emphasizes H.'s great talent, courage and skill in his civil profession and concludes that, far from stifling his literary career, H.'s legal work actually furthered it. The reconstructions of the cases are painstaking and we have an improved transcript of H.'s submission in the counterfeiting case, but the dimension of literary analysis is sadly lacking. This is not the next contribution to the important interdisciplinary debate currently dominating H. scholarship. G. Oesterle, 'Arabeske, Schrift und Poesie in E.T.A.Hs Kunstmärchen *Der goldne*

Topf', *Athenäum*, 1:69–107, is a masterly discussion of the function of this tale as Romantic arabesque: as an interim, synthetic art-form designed to restore poetic quality to written literature. Not the least interest of the essay is the linking of the motifs of Anselmus's copying, the figure of Serpentina and the arabesque style to Hogarth and Raphael. J. Harnischfeger, 'Das Geheimnis der Identität. Zu E.T.A.Hs *Die Elixiere des Teufels*', *Mitteilungen der E.T.A.H.– Gesellschaft*, 36, 1990:1–14, is another Freudian interpretation of the story, which rejects the significance of the *Künstlerroman* dimension and reduces Medardus's problem of identity to the unresolved Oedipus-conflict. B. M. Dreike, 'Die Serapionsbrüder und der Pyramidendoktor. Marginalien zu E.T.A.Hs Kritik an der zeit-genössischen Therapie', *ib.*, 15–23, looks at H.'s reception of physical illness and medicine in several tales, concluding that he regarded contemporary therapy with scepticism; also K. L. Barkhausen, 'John Hardman, Bernhard S. Ingemann und E.T.A.H.', *ib.*, 24–35; B. F. Cothran, 'Der "Einbruch der E. T. A. Hoffmannschen Welt" in dem Werk von Leo Perutz', *ib.*, 36–47; H. J. Koning, 'E.T.A.H. in Holland. Zur Rezeption im 20. Jahrhundert', *ib.*, 48–78; G. All-roggen, 'Zur Nachahmung empfohlen: Aufführung der *Undine* durch das Theater der Stadt Koblenz', *ib.*, 112–14; Hans Neubauer, '*Aurora*. E.T.A.Hs Oper in der Originalfassung in Bamberg konzertant aufgeführt', *ib.*, 115–16; H.-D. Holzhausen, 'Die Berliner H.-Freunde 1987–1990', *ib.*, 117–18. M. Kohlenbach, 'Ansichten von der Nacht-seite der Romantik. Zur Bedeutung des animalischen Magnetismus bei E.T.A.H.', Saul, *Wissenschaften*, 209–33, interprets this tale as an aesthetically formulated attack on that most Romantic science, animal magnetism. The tale shows that this ostensibly liberating therapy in fact exploits suggestion in order to establish a power-relation. H.'s Romantic critique of Romanticism is however comple-mented and contradicted by the form of the tale itself, with its own structure of suggestion imposed on the reader. D. T. Wright, 'Masochism, mourning, melancholia. A Freudian interpretation of E.T.A.H.'s tale *The Mines of Falun*', *GN*, 21, 1990:49–55, is just that, seeing Elis as transformed into a masochistic suicide by the shock to his Oedipal psyche at the deaths of father and mother. The descent to the mines is a self-punishment for the figures of father and mother, which are projected on to the super-ego as Miner and Queen of Nature. W. Pleister, 'E.T.A.Hs Affe Milo und Fipps der Affe. Ein literarhistorischer Vergleich', *Busch-Jb.*, 56, 1990:44–59, compares and contrasts the two apes. The analogy between Milo and Hegelian dialectic here does seem implausible. A. Dumont, 'Die Einflüsse von Identitätsphilosophie und Erfahrungsseelenkunde auf E.T.A.Hs *Elixiere des Teufels*', *ZGer*, n.F., 1:37–48, is not, as expected, a treatment of H.'s Schelling reception; instead it argues that H. uses his knowledge of Moritz and Schubert as the basis for narratological games, and these are interpreted as undermining any possible Christian reading of the text's apparently positive conclusion. See also S. M. Schröder, 'Die Heimkehr des Elis Fröbom. E.T.A.H. im Norden nach frühen Rezeptionszeugnissen', *Skandinavistik*, 21 : 30–52. P. Küchler-Sakellariou, **Implosion des Bewußtseins. Allegorie und Mythos in E.T.A.Hs Märchenerzählungen* (BBNDL, 12), 1989, 305 pp. Michael Rohrwasser, **Coppelius, Caliostro und Napoleon. Der verborgene politische Blick E.T.A.Hs. Ein Essay*, Frankfurt, Roter Stern, 120 pp. Gerhard Weinholz, **E.T.A.Hs Erzählung 'Die Automate'. Eine Kritik an einseitiger naturwissenschaftlich-technischer Weltsicht vor zweihundert Jahren* (Literaturwissenschaft in der Blauen Eule, 8), Essen, Blaue Eule, 72 pp.

HÖLDERLIN. F.H., **Sämtliche Werke. 'Frankfurter Ausgabe'*, *Historisch-kritische Ausgabe*, ed. D. E. Sattler. Vol. 17. *Frühe Aufsätze und Übersetzungen*, ed. Michael Franz, Hans Gerhard Steimer, and D. E. Sattler, Frankfurt, Roter Stern, 660 pp. The *Internationale H.-Bibliographie (IHB) auf der Grundlage der Neuerwerbungen des H.-Archivs der Württembergischen Landesbibliothek 1984–1988. Quellen und Sekundärliteratur. Rezeption und Rezensionen.* I. *Erschließungsband.* II. *Materialband*, ed. Hölderlin-Archiv, Werner Paul Sohnle and Marianne Schütz, 2 vols, Stuttgart, Bad Cannstatt, Frommann-Holzboog, xxiv + 337, 327 pp., documents over 2,300 titles with admirable thoroughness. The systematic and alphabetical indexes in vol. I provide easy access to the well-organized material in vol. II. This indispensable tool will be updated every two years. Mark Ogden, *The Problem of Christ in the Works of F.H.* (MHRA Texts and Dissertations, 33; BSD, 16), viii + 183 pp., is a radical piece of work which aims to show that the 'problem of Christ', as he defines it, is fundamental for the understanding not only of the late hymns but of all H.'s major works, so that the received notion of a late return to Christ is a misapprehension. Christology in O.'s sense is a basic if latent feature of H.'s response to the exclusion of sensual experience from religion by Kant: he sees a version of Platonic beauty as instantiating the absolute in empirical experience and identifies this with the transforming power of Christ (*qua* incarnation, baptism). This response dates from his days at the Tübinger Stift (so neglected by scholars) and is located in the reception of Kant by his *Repetenten*. In powerful analyses of the Tübingen sermon and hymns, *Hyperion*, *Empedokles*, and 'Friedensfeier' O. traces the development of this 'concealed Christology' through variations of social, political, and eschatological functionality. Stefanie Roth, *F.H. und die deutsche Frühromantik*, Stuttgart, Metzler, x + 425 pp., is a Hildesheim dissertation of 1989–90 which finally asks in systematic fashion why H. the great outsider is not grouped in terms of epoch or school with the Jena early Romantics. She concludes that he should be, since he shares with them basic convictions, procedures, and goals, even if transcending them in formal coherence. The crux, she argues, is the project of synthesis derived from their shared experience of fragmentation and Spinozan critique of Fichte common to H., Schelling, F. Schlegel, and Novalis, which generates the concept 'intellectuale Anschauung' and the demand to poeticize philosophy. The plausible argument is further strengthened by analyses of the concepts of love, mythology, and the Golden Age. Especially praiseworthy is the case for investigating the Romantic reception of Leibniz. Anselm Haverkamp, *Laub voll Trauer. Hs späte Allegorie,* Munich, Fink, 123 pp., collects deconstructive readings of Haller and (mainly) H.'s 'Mnemosyne', 'Andenken', and 'Der Kirchhof' (the latter also published separately in *Fest. Verbeeck*, see below), the basic thrust of which is to confer on the late hymns the status of mourning in Benjamin's sense: they are seen as empty allegories which function as H.'s form of memory. Bernhard Böschenstein, *'Frucht des Gewitters.' H.s Dionysos als Gott der Revolution,* Frankfurt, Insel, 1989, 221 pp., is a collection of essays, most of them previously published and reviewed here, which consist in close readings supporting the central thesis of the title. There are two new essays, '"Was nennst du Glück, was Unglück?". Heinse in Hs Dichtung', pp. 91–113, which uncovers the poetic image of Heinse as father-figure of 1796, in 'Der Rhein' and 'Brod und Wein'; and 'Hs Dionysos-Hyme "Wie wenn am Feiertage ..."', pp. 114–36, which glosses the text strophe by strophe and sets it in the developing context of H.'s hymns. '"Lang ist die Zeit ..." Zu Hs Hymne "Mnemosyne"', pp. 187–204, is published for the first time in German. The *H.-Jb.*, 1990–91, concentrates on myth. M. Frank, 'H. über den Mythos' (1–31), analyses how H.'s concept of myth as expression of the divine moment of unification in poetic discourse emerges from two of the three early phases of H.'s philosophical development (1794–95, 1796–97) which F. distinguishes; E. Jüngel, 'Die Wahrheit des Mythos und die Notwendigkeit der Entmythologisierung' (32–50), links Bultmann's notion of demythologization all too briefly with H.; L. Kempter, 'Herder, H. und der Zeitgeist. Zur Frühgeschichte eines Begriffs' (51–76), provides an extensive collection of more or less plausible references to Herder's conception of this term in H.'s lyric poetry; M. Behre, 'Dionysus oder die Begierde. Deutung der *Weisheit der Alten* bei Bacon, Hamann und H.' (77–99), reconstructs the genealogy of an idea or, better, method, namely the naturalistic approach to myth and Dionysus in especial characteristic of Bacon's scientific method. Hamann and H. are shown to be Bacon's successors in their use of mythopoetic discourse for the understanding of nature. H. Gaskill, 'H. und Ossian' (100–30), attacks those who have ignored traces of Ossian in H.'s works and argues that H. not only sustained his interest in Ossian right up to the catastrophe, but also that a self-identification with the lonely, melancholic and unheard bard lies behind the relationship; R. Böschenstein, 'Hs Œdipus-Gedicht' (131–51), decides that this text is entirely by H. and also not a fragment but a complete and finished tripartite poem; from the standpoint of her subtle theological interpretation the text's hermeneutic centre is 'Reflexion des Menschen auf sich selbst', a reflexion which unfolds 'in der Dreiheit des Blicks: auf die orientierende Zeichensprache des Himmels; auf die maßgebende Idee; auf das Spiegelbild'; M. Franz, 'Jupiter Befreier' (152–54), finds a plausible source, in Conz's translation of Tacitus, for the appeal of Empedokles in the first version of the drama, and suggests a line of interpretation; Id., '*Quantum distat ab illo*' (155–58), locates a further, equally plausible second source (after Ovid) in Virgil's *Aeneid* for Gerning's description of H.'s external appearance during the visit to Bad Homburg v.d.H. in 1804; H. Kaulen, 'Der unbestechliche Philologe. Zum Gedächtnis Norbert von Hellingraths' (182–209), is an affectionate but also scholarly portrait of a distinguished editor of H., with fascinating documentation on the D. Phil.; also U. Brauer, 'Landgraf Friedrich V. von Hessen-Homburg (1766–1820): Einiges zu den politischen Ansichten und zur Person. Mit Materialien: den politischen Aufsätzen, einer autobiographischen Skizze, einem autobiographischen Gedicht und einem Brief des Hofraths F. W. Jung an die Landgräfin Caroline' (210–62); C. Prignitz, '"Der würdige Sinclair." Eine zeitgenössische Stellungnahme zum Hochverratsprozeß gegen Isaak von Sinclair' (262–74); and W. P. Sohnle and M Schütz, 'Ein System für H. Die neue H.-Bibliographie: Was will und kann sie leisten?' (274–95); K. Kaspers, '"Der arme H.". Die stilisierte Dichterfigur in der Rezeption der Romantik' (159–81), analyses and contrasts the image of H. and his work in Arnim, Clemens Brentano, and Bettina, which she sees as consisting in various combinations of self-identification with the poet, intellectual analysis of the work, or egocentric appropriation of the work. B. Allemann, 'Beim Wiederlesen von Hs *Hyperion*', *Fest. Verbeeck*, 15–29, points up hidden potentialities of the narrative situation, mainly by contrast to *Werther*. A. Haverkamp, 'Späte Allegorie. Der Name des Vaters und das Bild des ewigen Friedens in Hs "Der Kirchhof"', *ib.*, 81–98, sees the poem as deconstructivist discourse: the cemetery, with its 'Holunder' trees signifying the name of the father, is H.'s last reckoning with allegorical-psychoanalytical structures of meaning, and is reduced to a pure empty signifier. B. Philipsen, 'Herz aus Glas. H., Rousseau und das "blöde" Subjekt der

Moderne', *Fest Verbeeck*, 177–94, sees traces of Rousseau on his island in parts of 'Rheinhymne', and suggests that H. overcomes in the poem Rousseau's empty, 'supplementary' intuitions of selfhood. T. Mueller, '"Handlungen, deren sich Cannibalen schämen würden" — das Phänomen der Masse in der deutschen Literatur um 1800', *CGP*, 19:37–50, looks at the portrayal of the masses in the failed revolution of *Hyperion*, select plays of Goethe and dialogues of Wieland, and establishes that these authors are using the term to reflect aesthetically upon the causes of the French Revolution. He concludes that in each case the causation is reduced inadequately to individual rather than mass psychology and the remedy, just as inadequately, to individual education, for which he makes the discourse of Enlightenment responsible. See also C. Albert, 'H. im Exil', *WB*, 37:723–36; H. Gaskill, '"Diss ist die Zeit der Könige nicht mehr"': H. and Republicanism', *SMLS*, *Special Issue*: 39–56; M. Ogden, 'H.'s wager on transcendence', *CC*, 12, 1990:273–81; Roland Reuss, *'. . ./Die eigene Rede des andern.' H.s 'Andenken' und 'Mnemosyne'*, Frankfurt, Roter Stern, 1990, 786 pp.; and Gerhard Weinholz, *Zur Genese des 'Wahnsinns' bei F.H. Ein Erklärungsmodell aus dem Kontext seines Lebens und seiner Zeit* (Literaturwissenschaft in der Blauen Eule, 2), 2nd edn, Essen, Blaue Eule, 235 pp.

HUMBOLDT, A. VON. T. E. Bourke, 'Der Wissenschaftler als Dichter. Betrachtungen zur Ästhetik der Expeditionsberichte Georg Forsters und A.v.Hs', *Saul*, *Wissenschaften*, 103–24, compares the interaction of aesthetics and science in the travel literature of the two, seeing Forster as a forerunner of Romanticism and H.'s style as in key respects (precision, transparency, totality) similar to that of Novalis.

KLEIST. A bumper year of course. H.v.K., *Sämtliche Werke. 'Berliner/Brandenburger Ausgabe', Historisch-kritische Ausgabe*. Vol. 1, 4. *Amphitryon*, ed. Roland Reuss and Peter Staengle, Frankfurt, Roter Stern, 148 pp. H.v.K., *Dramen 1802–1807*, ed. Ilse-Marie Barth, Hinrich C. Seeba and Hans Rudolf Barth (DKV), 1011 pp., is vol. 1 of the projected four-volume *Sämtliche Werke und Briefe* and contains *Die Familie Schroffenstein*, *Robert Guiskard*, *Der zerbrochne Krug* and *Amphitryon* as well as fully reproduced early versions of the former. As usual with this house high standards are set. The commentary is in proportion to the primary texts far longer than is usually the case. All parts of the scholarly apparatus show that attention to language was the editors' major concern: the commentary, always sober but, unusually, often suggestive of interpretation, skilfully points up links with other works in K.'s *œuvre*, notes references to his putative sources, glosses linguistic peculiarities of his highly characteristic usage (including prosodic and grammatical aspects), and also highlights indicators of aesthetic structures (including stage directions). Seeba has provided not only illuminating interpretations of the texts, but also a stimulating programmatic essay 'Erscheinung eines Dichters', which sees epistemological uncertainty as to knowledge of self and world as the central problem of all K.'s writings and the non-referentiality of language, of which the 'Kant-Krise' is but one reflection, as the locus of that uncertainty. The arguments justifying the editors' minimalistic modernizations of spelling and punctuation within the house-conventions (potentially of great controversial value) are acceptable. H. Sembdner, 'Die Doppelgänger des Herrn von K.' *JDSG*, 35: 180–95, notes that K. is the most frequent name in the Prussian army and draws out the negative consequences of this for the biographical side of K. research: travelling Kleists are not always H.v.K. In particular he attacks the aspect of the Samuel-Brown thesis about K.'s journeys from Mainz to Paris in 1803–04. K. Hilliard, '"Rittergeschichte mit Gespenst": The narration of the subconscious in K.'s *Das Bettelweib von Locarno*', *GLL*, 44:281–90, is an unequalled close reading of this formidably resistant text as a drama of repressed guilt inexorably rising to consciousness. Highly crafted silences of the text representing the Marchese's experience of the four replays are the technique used to reveal and conceal the dynamics of repression. Hilliard concludes that this technique is not 'modern', but rather places the text in the tradition of the 19th-c. *Novelle*.

The *KlJb* looks at K. and Romanticism in Berlin and Dresden. E. Osterkamp, 'Das Geschäft der Vereinigung. Über den Zusammenhang von bildender Kunst und Poesie im "Phöbus"', *KlJb*, 1990:51–70, uncovers the synaesthetic ambitions implicit in the title of *Phöbus*, and examines, through a contrastive interdisciplinary analysis of the relation between Hartmann's title-plate, K.'s programmatic distichs and Müller's aesthetic reflections, how the arts were to be unified in it. He shows that an un-Romantic notion of each art-form remaining within its own limits informs the structure of material presented, so that any unification follows from the deliberate opposition of Classical picture and Romantic poem in the spirit of the 'Lehre vom Gegensatz'. R. Vierhaus, '"Man muß sich mit seinem ganzen Gewicht in die Waage der Zeit werfen." Die Zeit, der Dichter und die Tat', *ib.*, 71–85, examines the failed project of the *Berliner Abendblätter* in the context of Prussian patriotism and K.'s suicide, and concludes that its failure was due more to K.'s inability to identify himself with any such cause than government interference. F. Strack, 'Suchen und Finden. Romantische Bewußtseinsstrukturen im Werk H. v. Ks?', *ib.*, 86–112, is a masterly discussion of K.'s ambivalent relationship to Romanticism proper structured around the motif of seeking and finding from Novalis and K.'s *Der Findling*, which shows that K. shared many of the Romantics' basic concerns but only in his unique, sceptical transformation, so that the story is to be seen as a virtual travesty of *Hyacinth und Rosenblüthchen*. Where Strack uses the definition of a 'Findling' as a rock found inexplicably remote from its presumed geological origins to identify Klara as the found child and hope for the future, I. Wagner, '"Der Findling": Erratic signifier in K. and geology', *GQ*, 64:281–95, puts forward the same ingenious geological thesis, also of interest to students of 'Fachsprache' history and this time linked to the tale through a reconstruction of K.'s studies with Wünsch, in order to suggest why Nicolo is called 'Findling' rather than 'Findelkind'. Like the rock in the theory of geology, he disrupts irredeemably any attempt to find coherent meaning in the text.

G. Schulz, 'Todeslust bei K. und einigen seiner Zeitgenossen', *KlJb*, 1990:113–25, offers a brief canter through selected authors around 1800, contrasting K.'s images of death mainly with Werner's *Wanda* and the Kitsch of Theodor Körner, concluding that K. offers an alternative transcendence of death through states of self-consciousness analogous to Hegel's *Phänomenologie des Geistes*. U. H. Peters, 'Somnambulismus und andere Nachtseiten der menschlichen Natur', *ib.*, 135–52, covers much familiar terrain in his overview of the importance of Mesmerism and animal magnetism for Romantic theory, and concludes with a survey of magnetic symptoms displayed by the heroine of *Das Käthchen von Heilbronn*. S. R. Huff, 'The *Holunder* motif in K.'s *Das Käthchen von Heilbronn* and its nineteenth-century context', *GQ*, 64:304–12, explains why K. situated Käthchen's magnetic dreams under this tree: the plant was commonly associated in folk belief with dream, subliminal states of mind, eroticism and the like, as well as healing. This essay also has a valuable brief history of the motif. H. J. Kreutzer, 'K. in der Nähe der Romantik. Ein neu gefundener Brief an Georg Andreas Reimer', *KlJb*, 1990:153–57, publishes for the first time a note from K. requesting F. and J. Riepenhausen's *Geschichte der Mahlerei in Italien* (1810) on loan from the bookseller and locates it in the context of K.'s late preoccupation with the Christian and, particularly, apocalyptic themes prominent in Romantic art. K. E. Laage, 'Zwei K.-Raritäten aus dem Storm-Nachlaß', *ib.*, 158–64, retraces the history of Storm's taste for Kleistiana. D. Görne, '"Aber überhaupt steht der Sachse auf einem höhern Grad der Kultur, als unsre Landleute?" Zum Dresdner Theater um 1800', *ib.*, 14–29. H. Börsch-Supan, 'Dresden 1803–1809. Bildende Kunst zwischen Alter und Jugend', *ib.*, 30–50. C. C. Bentzel, 'Knowledge in narrative: The significance of the swan in K.'s *Die Marquise von O . . .*', *GQ*, 64:296–303, finds another plausible source, this time linking the count's dream to Kosegarten's 'Die Unschuld', in order to plead against critics who use psychoanalytic methods to interpret the dream as his unconscious confession of guilt, and so settle the question of paternity. Such critics in fact, dominated by their desire to know definitively, falsify the point of the entire tale. M. Rhiel, 'The author function as security agent in Rohmer's *Die Marquise von O . . .*', *ib.*, 6–16, is an interesting exposure of significant differences in the narrative technique of K. and Rohmer, which concludes that R. falsifies K.'s basic concerns and glosses over the fundamental 'sexual crisis' of the *Novelle*. O. Lorenz, 'Experimentalphysik und Dichtungspraxis. Das "geheime Gesetz des Widerspruchs" im Werk Hs v. K.', Saul, *Wissenschaften*, 72–90, plausibly identifies nothing less than a basic principle of K.'s writings, derived from his reading of Wünsch and Müller. A self-dissolving process of continuous reactive antagonism analogous to positive and negative in electricity is argued to be applicable to thought-processes and actions, and leads to the characteristic sequences of creation and destruction of his work. A. Stephens, '"Gegen die Tyrannei des Wahren." Die Sprache in Ks *Hermannsschlacht*', *Arntzen Vol.*, 175–95, raises the issue of ethical indifferentism. He rejects any attempt to discover humane values in the text, but instead focuses on the linguistic rather than conceptual dimension. The play is a propagandistic work — as such an exception in K.'s *œuvre* — but it is distinguished from mere propaganda in that it lacks a Utopian vision at the close and ends in a vision of destruction. The identification of language usage with the exercise of power reflects the (in K.'s works) unparalleled lack of interest in the search for truth in a poetic medium. As such its conclusion may be seen as an attempted provocation of the contemporary mentality.

J oachim Pfeiffer, *Die zerbrochenen Bilder. Gestörte Ordnungen im Werk H. v. Ks* (Ep, Reihe Literaturwissenschaft, 45), 1989, 188 pp., takes as his theme the omnipresence of contradictory structures in K., which he sees as the works' paradoxical structural principle and mark of their radical modernity. A non-biographical refinement of the Freudian method is used to analyse this constitutive centrifugality in chapters focusing on language, the family, the idyll and objects. A fundamental deep structure of fantasy is seen as latent in all the texts, which does not, as Freud sometimes seems to imply, connote regressive escapism, so much as a degree of resistance to the order of reality imitated in the text. It is not clear how the radical destabilization of meaning presupposed by P. harmonizes with the fixity of the Freudian system of reference basic to his method of analysis. Mary Howard, *Vom Sonderling zum Klassiker. Hundert Jahre K.-Rezeption in Großbritannien* (PSQ, 119), 1990, 210 pp., an updated Munich dissertation of 1982, is in more senses than one a model analysis, which uses the process of K. reception in Britain from 1828 to 1928 to develop the theory of *Rezeptionsgeschichte*. H. shows that K. reception in Britain over this period was characterized by sheer discontinuity, which she — disregarding as a factor the contradictory meaning-structures of the texts themselves — argues can only be due to the variables of the receptive situation in each given epoch. The first phase is characterized by mediation of K. and his writings through English metatexts on which readers were totally dependent. Since the mediatory texts lacked any serious engagement with the German cultural context, the image of K. here was largely a British myth. In the second phase mediatory literature derives generally from German secondary work and, against the background of increased knowledge of German, encourages reading of K.'s texts, which are discussed as such. Yet even in this phase the K. reception is hierarchically centred on critic and nation, from which H. concludes that the stability of cultural tradition functioned in this case as a more important factor in the constitution of meaning than the texts themselves. This book is a mine of information on intercultural literary relations and should be recommended reading for all those who attack the legitimacy of university German Studies. Ingeborg Harms, *Zwei Spiele Ks um Trauer und Lust. 'Die Familie Schroffenstein' und 'Der zerbrochne Krug'*, Munich, Fink, 1990, 259 pp., is a decidedly 'werkimmanent' reading of the two plays and *Über das Marionettentheater*, which concentrates on expounding how mythical categories of origin and end, unity and division are present in the (generally biblical) imagery and plot or argument structure of the texts in question, focusing mainly on the cave-scene in *Die Familie Schroffenstein* and Eve's evidence in the 'Variant'. Harms's K. is a surprisingly positive figure, whose texts always seek to transcend finiteness and fragmentation, whether this be evidenced as gender, genre (hence the title), nation or history. H. Koopmann, 'Schiller und K.', *Aurora*, 50, 1990: 127–43, rectifies the image of K. and Schiller as two quite unconnected phenomena. Taking up recent research he shows that K. extensively read and often cited Schiller, especially around 1801, and identifies a tendency: the correction of Schiller's general pessimism through a restitutive moment he sees in K.'s tales and dramas. Klaus-Michael Bogdal, *H. v. K.: 'Michael Kohlhaas'* (UTB, 1027; Text und Geschichte. Modellanalysen zur deutschen Geschichte), 125 pp., is the reissue of a book which first appeared in 1981. Whilst the material and the analysis are still useful, the terminology is now often outdated, and the bibliographies have not been updated. Mathieu Carrière, *für* [sic] *eine Literatur des Krieges, K.* (FT, 10159), 1990, 118 pp., is the unaltered reissue of a work first published in 1981. It has lost nothing since then in capriciousness of argument and unconventionality of form, but still contains none the less occasional stimulating insights. See also P.

Goldammer, 'Mit mehr als fünfzigjähriger Verspätung. Ein unbekanntes Standardwerk der K.-Forschung soll endlich veröffentlicht
werden: "H.v.Ks Teilnahme an den politischen Bewegungen der
Jahre 1805–1809." Von Richard Samuel', *WB*, 37:692–704; S.
Lange, 'K.: *Penthesilea*', *ib.*, 705–22; L. Dietrick, 'Immaculate conceptions: the Marquise von O . . . and the swan', *Seminar*, 27:317–30;
W. C. Reeve, 'K.'s *Hermannsschlacht* and the Brandenburger Tor', *ib.*,
95–101; I. Stipa, 'K.'s *Penthesilea*: From misapprehension to madness', *ib.*, 113–25; R. Ergetowska, 'Polnische Übersetzungen des
Dramas *Das Käthchen von Heilbronn*', *Beiträge zur K.-Forschung*,
1990:57–61; P. Foley, **H.v.K. und Adam Müller: Untersuchung zur
Aufnahme idealistischen Gedankenguts durch H.v.K.* (EH, I, 1209), 1990,
254 pp.; and Christiana Schreiber, **'Was sind das für Zeiten!' H.v.K.
und die preußischen Reformen* (GASK, 18), 414 pp.

MEREAU, SOPHIE.   C. Bürger, 'S. M. oder die sinnliche Gewißheit',
Bürger, *Leben*, 19–31, relates in interesting discussions the centreless-
ness and impressionistic fixation of M.'s lyric and epic writing to her
acceptance willy-nilly of institutionalized aesthetic norms which
exclude her particularity as woman. See too H. Schwartz, p. 736
above.

MÜLLER, WILHELM VON.   J. Hörisch, '"Fremd bin ich eingezogen."
Die Erfahring des Fremden und die fremde Erfahrung in der
Winterreise', *Athenäum*, 1:41–67, analyses Schubert's song-cycle and
M.'s texts, especially *Der Wegweiser*. He concludes that not love, so
much as the search for an ultimate sense of things (*qua* transcendental
signified), is that from which the wanderer takes his leave, and sees
the cycle in this as a watershed in the history of mentality. H. Wetzel,
'"Fremd zieh' ich wieder aus." Fragen an W.M.', Knapp, *Autoren*,
173–210, is a potted literary biography, suggesting that M.'s lyric
cycles are in fact structured by conscious role-play rather than
experience. W.M., **Rom, Römer und Römerinnen*, Berlin, Rütten &
Loening, 392 pp.

NACHTWACHEN VON BONAVENTURA.   H. L. Gumpert, 'Georg
Christoph Lichtenberg und Ernst Theodor Amadeus Hoffmann als
Konkurrenten für die Verfasserschaft der 1804 unter dem Pseudo-
nym "B." erschienenen *Nachtwachen*', *Lichtenberg-Jb.*, 1990:224–27.

NOVALIS.   An extraordinarily thin year. Thomas Grosser, *Identität
und Rolle. Kontext, Konzept und Wirkungsgeschichte der Genieästhetik bei N.*,
Opladen, Westdeutscher Vlg, 251 pp., is an impressive work which
focuses systematically for the first time on the several utterances
where N. describes his concept of identity as paradoxically plural in
number and aesthetic in character. G. sees this as a fundamental
feature of N.'s thinking of the self, and interprets it as his response to
the increasing diversity of fields of experience (such as the division of

labour or scientific specialization) confronting and threatening the individual at the end of the 18th c. The ego is thus for N. not a substance so much as a 'flexibles Integrationszentrum' or disposition to adopt specific roles in given concrete encounters with self, society or scientific material. Aesthetic discourse, suggestively projecting wholeness into past and future, integrates the centrifugal moments, and this describes the intended relationship of *Die Lehrlinge zu Sais* and *Das allgemeine Brouillon*. In this specific feature of his thinking lies not so much N.'s modernity as his relevance for postmodern discussion in philosophy and sociology. G. also gives us a short reconstruction of the reception of this feature of N. in Dilthey and Simmel. This is an important if, alas, reader-unfriendly work. H. Uerlings, 'N. und die Weimarer Klassik', *Aurora*, 50, 1990: 27–46, reconstructs the relationship between N., Schiller and Goethe as a web of continuities as well as discontinuities, and in each dimension (notably in the notions of the absolute and Utopia) sets accents which are subtly different from much received wisdom. U. Stadler, 'N. — ein Lehrling Friedrich Schillers?', *ib.*, 47–62, explores primarily the treatment of the goddess at Sais in Alxinger, Schiller, and N., in order to assess the quality of N.'s mature Schiller reception. The recuperation of Rosenblüthchen can be read as a sentimental recovery of the naïve, so that Hyacinth as a figure in fact applies lessons of *Über naive und sentimentalische Dichtung* against Schiller himself, thus exemplifying N.'s ambiguous attitude to his former teacher. K. Reinfrank-Clark, 'Novalisbild im Wandel. Neuansätze in der Romantik- und Aufklärungsforschung der DDR', *Slessarev Vol.*, 155–60, sketches the familiar path of literary scholarship in the ex-GDR, from portraying N. as bogeyman of fantasy to humanistic critic of Enlightenment rationalism, and locates this in the context of the general shift in approach. W. M. Sepasgosarian, **Der Tod als romantisierendes Prinzip des Lebens: Eine systematische Auseinandersetzung mit der Todesproblematik im Leben und Werk des N.* (EH, I, 1229), 275 pp.

OKEN. W. Pross, 'Lorenz Oken — Naturforschung zwischen Naturphilosophie und Naturwissenschaft', Saul, *Wissenschaften*, 44–71, reconstructs O.'s concept of *mathesis* as a theoretical stratum designed to mediate between empirical and speculative levels of natural science.

PLATEN. W. Heck, 'A.v.P.: *Tristan:* Ein Gedicht und seine (Be-)Deutung', *FHL*, 11: 5–52.

RICHTER, JEAN PAUL. *'Standhafte Zuschauer ästhetischer Leiden.' Interpretationen und Lesarten in J.Ps 'Hesperus'*, ed. Hans Geulen and Andreas Gössling (Münsteraner Beiträge zur Deutschen und Nordischen Philologie, 4), Münster, Kleinheinrich, 1989, 270 pp., is a valuable *vademecum*. It offers not commentary so much as extensive explication and interpretation of the text, chapter by chapter, with special focus on the unfolding of narrative structures and their function plus reference to other works of J.P. and major thematic concerns therein. References are throughout to the standard edition of Norbert Miller (J.P., *Sämtliche Werke*, 6 vols, Munich, Hanser, 1960 ff.). There is a useful bibliography and summary of J.P.'s not-so-trivial plot. Gustav Lohmann, *J.P.s 'Flegeljahre' gesehen im Rahmen ihrer Kapitelüberschriften*, Würzburg, Königshausen & Neumann, 1990, 131 pp., explains the function of the references to 'Kabinettstücke' in the chapter-headings of *Flegeljahre*. They signal the chapter content, usually referring to a particular figure who dominates the chapter, and can also, according to the properties of the mineral or fossil adduced, be grouped around social classes or types of behaviour which they characterize. Thus patterns can be recognized in the chapter-sequence, and this leads to discussion of the relationship between J.P., Walt, and Vult. In the novel as a whole the headings serve also to emphasize the humoristic narrative presence of J.P. himself. L. does however look at only 33 of 64 chapters and notes that one possible source, Webel's *Enzyklopädisches Wörterbuch*, was not available to him. Günter de Bruyn, *Das Leben des J. P. F. R. Eine Biographie*, Frankfurt, Fischer, 410 pp., is the well-known work originally issued in 1975 (Halle/Saale, Mitteldeutscher Vlg). It has not been updated, so that we still hear of the 'Bezirk Leipzig' and find Marx and Engels in the bibliography, yet the reissue is welcome for its beautiful style and quality of personal response. The *Jb. der J.P.-Gesellschaft*, 25, 1990, 174 pp., has B. Hahn, ' "Geliebtester Schriftsteller". Esther Gads Korrespondenz mit J.P.' (7–42), which edits for the first time the full correspondence according to the MSS. in Cracow and suggests a feminist framework for its interpretation; W. Köpke, 'Abschied von der Poesie. *Flegeljahre* und die Auseinandersetzung mit Herder' (43–60), is an extension of Neumann's well-known argument relating the German Plato to Herder. The modalities of J.P.'s self-identifications with Walt and Vult as poet and satirist are linked to the changing status of the Plato-Herder-vision in the plot's development. Walt's increasing distance from reality is interpreted as J.P.'s increasing distance from Herder, and to such an extent that Herder is linked with the 'poetische Nihilisten', so that the entire text can be seen as a question to Herder; M. Dörries, 'Ent-setzter Apotheker. Ein Naturwissenschaftler als Metapher in J.Ps *Komet*' (61–73), sees this work as composed of polarities (body–soul, alchemy–science, middle class–aristocratic). The language of alchemy, but also of a modern science such as animal magnetism, is used by J.P. symbolically, as part of his project to poeticize reality and harmonize the opposites; M. Schmitz-Emans, 'Georg Christoph Lichtenberg und der Maschinen-Mann. Zur

Interferenz von literarischer Phantasie und naturwissenschaftlicher Modellbildung' (74–111), is a splendid and useful account of L. as a precursor of the Romantic obsession with the automaton, which is here located in the context of natural scientific models and interpreted as an interface between literature and science in their parallel drives to understand human nature. L.'s ambivalent attitude to the mechanical model of humanity itself — as at once of great explicative power and yet also threatening to identity — is seen to have strong echoes in J.P., Tieck, and E. T. A. Hoffmann; K. Viëtor, '"J.P." Mitgeteilt von Carsten Zelle' (112–33), is a newly discovered MS of unknown date on an author hitherto not known to have interested Viëtor greatly. It paints a portrait of J.P. as poet of *Innerlichkeit*, incapable of grasping external reality like Goethe or Schiller, yet none the less never allowing his inwardness to culminate in Romantic contempt for reality; P. Sprengel, 'Schwanengesang der Innerlichkeit. Viëtors J.-P.-Vortrag im Kontext der Wirkungsgeschichte' (134–39), locates the paper on the basis of internal evidence in the context of the jubilee 1925–26, and sees it as Viëtor's attempt to counter the arguments of Alt and Walter Harich with the more historical concept of 'Innerlichkeit', whilst it also contains germs of a sociological and psychological approach; and T. de Quincey, 'John Paul Frederick Richter' (140–52), which is a translation of the English. P. H. Neumann, 'Vorgriffe auf die Unsterblichkeit. Über das Scheintod-Motiv bei J.P.', *Aurora*, 50, 1990:207–17, is a subtle exploration of the motif as an experiment with immortality, culminating in interpretation of the Castor and Pollux image in the Ministergattin of Scheerau, Walt/Wult and Siebenkäs/Leibgeber as a synthetic compromise between mortality and immortality. T. J. Casey, 'Der tolle Mensch in der Pfarrhausstube. J.Ps Stellung zu der Gretchenfrage und seine Auseinandersetzung mit der Theologie', Saul, *Wissenschaften*, 156–76, reconstructs J.P.'s search for religious truth in instructive comparisons with Nicolai and Kanne, concluding that he takes refuge in the irreducibility of dialogical poetic forms. J. Barkhoff, 'Allsympathie im magnetischen Geiste. J.P. und der animalische Magnetismus', *ib.*, 177–208, is a rich essay which locates J.P.'s use of animal magnetism in the tradition of alchemical and hermetic theory, arguing that he sees in the phenomenon a solution to the anthropological mind-body-problem preoccupying the age. In *Der Komet* the emancipatory trances of the Ledermensch are shown to be of magnetic character; his dual personality, which confronts both rationalistic and holistic-magnetic paradigms of humanity, is the instrument of J.P.'s critique of the age. The novel also functions, like Goethe's late works, as a storehouse of lost wisdom in bad times. P. Krahé, '"The Empty Altar". Zum Einfluß J.Ps auf Thomsons *City of*

Dreadful Night', *Sprachkunst*, 21, 1990:325–34, shows plausibly that Canto xiv of the Thomson is inspired by the *Rede des toten Christus*. T. Yamada, 'Auf der Suche nach Wirklichkeit. Zur Poetik J.Ps', *DB*, 85, 1990:142–49, examines the problem of imitation of reality in J.P. He concludes that the highest reality is to be found in fantasy. This the texts imitate, and it serves as a model for transforming reality. See also B. Achenbach, 'Eine Antwort auf Lichtenbergs *Orbis pictus:* J.Ps Erstling *Verteidigung des BedientenStandes, von einem Bedienten entdeckt'*, *Lichtenberg-Jahrbuch*, 1990:7–12, and M. Thibaut, **Sich-selbst-Erzählen: Schreiben als poetische Lebenspraxis. Untersuchungen zu diaristischen Prosatexten von Goethe, J.P., Dostojewski, Rilke und anderen* (SAG, 239), 223 pp.

SCHLEGEL, AUGUST WILHELM.   Ulrike Schenk-Lenzen, *Das ungleiche Verhältnis von Kunst und Kritik. Zur Literaturkritik A.W.Ss* (Studien zur Literatur- und Kulturgeschichte, 3), Würzburg, Königshausen & Neumann, 352 pp., is a Münster dissertation of 1989 which interprets, with heavy dependence on Walter Benjamin's well-known dissertation, S.'s theory and practice of criticism as a synthesis of critical, theoretical, and historical energies. The main focus of the book is a painstaking reconstruction of the method's genesis in S.'s critical writings on Schiller and Bürger in their development from enthusiasm to ambiguous rejection. Schiller is argued to have been highly influential. The exposition of allegory in the *Divine Comedy* — with proof that he knew and used Dante's self-interpretation in the dedication to Con Grande della Scala — is in conclusion argued to be S.'s major contribution to his brother's formulation of Romantic poetic theory. This work is very thorough, so far as it goes, but is hampered by its lack of development beyond its immediate, rather modest, goals. W. Schmitz, 'Schillers ungeschriebenes Romgedicht und A.W.Ss "Rom"-Elegie. "Moderne" und Historismus in der Stilkonkurrenz des Klassischen und Romantischen um 1800', *Aurora*, 50, 1990:103–26, contrasts in these texts the use of the Rome motif as a symbol of the role of antique values in the historical process. R. Paulin, 'Die romantische Übersetzung: Theorie und Praxis', Saul, *Wissenschaften*, 250–64, offers an instructive broad survey of contemporary theories. He sees Romantic translation as a particular tendency. In the field of theory, the Romantics are torn between the notion of translation as subservient to the original and that of translation as an autonomous new original. A.W.S.'s translations are seen as representing the former tendency and as the major achievement in practice.

SCHLEGEL, CAROLINE VON.   C. Bürger, 'Luziferische Rhapsodien. Cs Briefwerk', Bürger, *Leben*, 81–107, as ever in this volume, sees C.'s assertion of her femininity in her paradoxical refusal to write in a literary mode recognized as a canonical 'Werk'. This realization of identity-in-negativity she locates in C.'s letters, which are not to be read as biographical documents but instead as rhapsodic prose in F. Schlegel's sense: generally formless, they yet contain frequent masterpieces in miniature literary forms such as anecdote and (especially) portrait, and enact in language her Luciferian autonomy as woman. C. emerges in fact as possessor of a very undivided and self-assured, un-Romantic ego, so that we are surprised to hear her letter-work at the last suggested, because of its generic plurality, to be the best contemporary approximation to the ideal type of the Romantic novel. See also C. M. Craig, 'A.W.S.'s reading of Shakespearean wordplay', *MGS*, 15, 1989:215–25.

SCHLEGEL, DOROTHEA. W. Schmitz, '"... nur eine Skizze, aber durchaus in einem großen Stil": D.S.', Knapp, *Autoren*, 91–131, is a long essay in literary biography, which reconstructs D.S.'s literary and social contribution to the various environments in which F. Schlegel operated. Her activities are seen as continuously focused on the role of woman in poetry and history, and interpreted as Utopian Romantic or Catholic expressions of rejection of banal public life. See also R. D. Richardson, 'D. Mendelssohn Veit S.'s 1801 novel *Florentin:* a religion of the feminine ideal', *New Athenaeum/Neues Athenaeum*, 2:81–100, and I. Stephan, p. 736 above.

SCHLEGEL, FRIEDRICH. Ulrike Zeuch, *Das Unendliche. Höchste Fülle oder Nichts? Zur Problematik von F.Ss Geist-Begriff und dessen geistesgeschichtlichen Voraussetzungen* (Ep. Reihe Literaturwissenschaft, 69), iv + 268 pp., is a Mainz dissertation of 1990 which reconstructs the origin and purpose of S.'s concept of insight into the infinite, initially 'systemimmanent' on the basis of his own, mainly philosophical writings, then, as foil, in contrast with Giordano Bruno and Nicholas of Cusa. Finally the consequences of S.'s project for his art (it is seen as necessitating aesthetic utterance) and the influence of the theory (Proust, Broch, Benn, etc.) are sketched. All too briefly. The strength and value of this work is in the dimension of philosophical ideas, and the author is refreshingly sober in her judgements. E. Behler, 'Die Poesie in der frühromantischen Theorie der Brüder S.', *Athenäum*, 1:14–40, reconstructs by contrast the origin, evolution and purpose of the brothers' central concern not in epistemological problems, but primarily in their engagement with Kant's *Verstand*-orientated definition of aesthetic experience in the *Kritik der Urteilskraft*. There is enlightening detailed discussion of their attempts to ground the concept of autonomous *Poesie* as 'differentielle Einheit' in analyses of Shakespeare, Goethe, and the classics. The essay, having reached Romantic irony, is to be continued. Id., 'F.Ss *Letztes Wort über Goethe*', *ib.*, 207–32, publishes from the forthcoming vol. 17 of the Kritische

25

Friedrich–Schlegel–Ausgabe from S.'s notebooks *Zur Poesie und Literatur* from 1823 which illuminate the later S.'s attitude to Goethe. S. sees his work as lacking a central focus in the divine and thus falling prey to dualism; as therefore calling forth a dualistic reception; and as failing to integrate the ideal and the real other than in a language of reflection. G. Niggl, 'Die Anfänge der romantischen Literaturgeschichtsschreibung: F. und August Wilhelm S.', Saul, *Wissenschaften*, 265–81, looks at this in the context of the Enlightenment achievement. He shows how organological metaphors replaced mechanistic ones in literary-historical narratives, how primarily F.S., following Winckelmann, established epochal divisions, and how gradually philosophical and nationalistic perspectives replaced purely aesthetic ones. See also T. Althaus, p. 744 above.

SCHLEIERMACHER. **S. und die wissenschaftliche Kultur des Christentums*, ed. Günter Meckenstock, Berlin, de Gruyter, xv + 521 pp. K. Weimar, 'Zur neuen Hermeneutik um 1800', *Fest. Conrady*, 195–204, reconstructs the paradigm of hermeneutics around 1800 as a structure of equivalence in writer and readers based naïvely on a presupposed semantic unity. As this erodes a new creative hermeneutic emerges, however S.'s work involves a return to the old model. M. L. Davies, 'Sociability in practice and theory: Henriette Herz and Friedrich S.', *New Athenaeum/Neues Athenaeum*, 2 : 18–59, analyses the *Salon* as a social and ideological phenomenon, a kind of aestheticized, compensatory and unstable compromise between private aspirations and public realities, the theory of which is given by S., and the demise of which the 19th c. would rue. See also D. Boer, 'Gespannt zwischen Hegel und S.: Für S.', *ib.*, 1–17; W. von Meding, 'S. als Zeuge gegen die Todesstrafe', *ib.*, 60–68; H. Patsch, 'S. und die Bestattung Rahel Varnhagens. Eine kommentierte Briefedition', *ib.*, 69–80; and P. Weiss, 'Ss Religionsbegriff in seiner gesellschafts-politischen Relevanz', *ib.*, 109–30.

SCHUMANN, R. Christina E. Brantner, **Robert Schumann und das Tonkünstler-Bild der Romantiker* (SMGL, 32), 196 pp.

TIECK. L.T., *Schriften 1789–1794*, ed. Achim Hölter (DKV), 1298 pp., is vol. 1 of the projected 13-volume edition of selected *Schriften*. It unfortunately contains only a selection of T.'s early works, both poetical (1789–93) and critical-historical, including adaptations (1792–94). Previously unedited works are *Das Märchen vom Roßtrapp* and the *Ur-Berneck* 'Orest in Ritterzeiten'. The 39 *Kupferstiche nach der Shakespearschen Galerie in London* are helpfully reproduced and *Über das Erhabene* is a greatly amended version of a work first edited by Erwin H. Zeydel (*PMLA*, 50, 1935 : 537–40). Reasons for the relative paucity of previously unedited works, to which we had looked forward, are given in the introductory essay 'Der junge T.': the house guidelines forced the principle of representativeness upon the editor, and the large quantity of literary-historical notes are still too dispersed and uncollated to be usable in the present edition. The principle of representativeness forces awkward compromises: the general focus of interest in the text selection and the commentary is T.'s use of received source-material, in particular Shakespeare; yet *Das Buch über Shakespeare*, as H. acknowledges, is not reproduced, on the grounds of its easy accessibility elsewhere. This does not however preclude republishing H.'s own edition of *Soll der Maler [. . .]?*, which appeared as recently as 1985. The essay also contains, however, useful leading categories for interpretation and biographical material, both locating T. in his late Enlightenment context and his early work in the context of his entire *œuvre*. Particularly in this and in the exposure of the young T.'s contradictory enthusiastic yet scholarly leanings through the masterly commentaries this edition is none the less a valuable contribution to the re-appraisal of T. and German Romanticism, without however explaining 'alles [. . .], was die rätselhafte Vielschichtigkeit des Phänomens in Deutschland ausmacht'. T. Unger, '"Romantisierte Welt" als ästhetische Überwindung des Gartens: Überlegungen zum Gartenmotiv in den Rahmengesprächen von L. Ts *Phantasus*', *JEGP*, 90:467–90, is a painstaking analysis of the aesthetics of landscape garden in the framework dialogue and descriptions of *Phantasus*. U. discovers that T. is in fact not merely a strangely anachronistic admirer of the French geometric garden, rather, this style is already perceived by the participants through Romantic eyes and located in the wider context of Romantic nature, which thus transcends the category of garden altogether. Still a further type, the naïve peasant garden is added, and the author concludes that T. has no fully developed theory, yet nevertheless his own, context-dependent position in the question of garden choice.

TIECK, SOPHIE. *'Bei aller brüderlichen Liebe.' The Letters of S. T. to her Brother Friedrich*, ed. James Trainer (QFSK, 97 (221)), 314 pp., contains 126 letters to the sculptor Friedrich T. between 1810 and 1830 published (mainly) for the first time. The letters themselves are diplomatically edited, with the commentary however indicated by footnotes, the numbers of which intrude into the otherwise pristine text. The commentary is a model of discreet informativeness, as is the brief, generally biographical introduction, which does not conceal S.'s unsympathetic personality. There is a good index of names and a select bibliography to round off a beautifully presented volume.

VARNHAGEN VON ENSE. K. A. V. v. E., *Schriften und Briefe*, ed. Werner Fuld (UB, 2657), 363 pp., is a welcome edition for students and other newcomers to V., that key figure in the social and political history of the Restoration. There is a long, interesting and learned biographical introduction, a good annotated curriculum vitae, a useful bibliography, and even an 11-page index of persons. The text selection is thoughtful, with literary reviews as well 'as his better-known biographical sketches and memoirs, plus letters to his wide acquaintance. The introduction attempts a polemical defence of V. against the numerous critics of his integrity and accuracy down the decades, and will itself draw fire, but the pleas for the precious *Nachlaß* to be included in some future cultural exchange, and for more of V.'s writings to be edited from it, are laudable.

VARNHAGEN, RAHEL (LEVIN). C. Bürger, 'Ich R.', Bürger, *Leben*, 109–32, sees R.'s writing as informed by her rejection of the dominant aesthetic which separates life and work. Whereas her life consists in sheer deficit, she creates her identity anew by writing through figures of negation and hypostasis of self, in the medium of letters. Clemens Brentano features as gender assassin, V. emerges in a positive light. H. Patsch, '"Als ob Spinoza sich wollte taufen lassen." Biographisches und Rechtsgeschichtliches zu Taufe und Trauung R. L.s', *JFDH:* 149–78, reconstructs the baptism and marriage preparations and ceremonies of R. (which he takes as exemplary), with several fascinating newly published documents. L. Weissberg, 'Stepping out: the writing of difference in R.V.'s letters', *NGC*, 53:149–62, uses a close analysis of metaphor and narrative structure in the letters to modify Arendt's thesis that the genesis of anti-Semitism is coincident with the rise of the concept of the German nation. Barbara Hahn, **Antworten Sie mir, R.L.V Briefwechsel*, Frankfurt, Roter Stern, 1990, 240 pp.

WACKENRODER. A milestone this year. W.H.W., *Sämtliche Werke und Briefe. Historisch-kritische Ausgabe*, ed. Silvio Vietta and Richard Littlejohns, 2 vols, Heidelberg, Winter, 506, 672 pp. The first Romantic has at last received the accolade of a modern edition on sound principles. Vol. I contains *Werke*, vol. II primarily *Briefe*, *Reiseberichte*, and *Philologische Arbeiten*. There is much that is new and praiseworthy. All texts are authentically reproduced for the first time on the basis of the best available source. Where this is printed, exhaustive comparison has been made of existing editions. Authoritative attributions are made for the *Herzensergießungen* and the *Phantasien*. The philological works are printed complete for the first time, there are two completely new letters (to Sophie Tieck), and one new in part. Many of the known letters contain material corrections on the basis of the MSS, all are printed here for the first time in strict chronological order, and Tieck's responses have been included as aids to understanding. The texts previously printed as letters from Franconia have been plausibly reclassified as *Reiseberichte* and allocated a section of their own, which also includes Tieck's contemporaneous reports. W.'s translation of Warner's *Netley Abbey* has been reproduced in full together with the first chapter of the original for comparison. The major achievement is however in the dimension of commentary, for in this the contours of a new W. image become evident. Following the example of Samuel's and Mähl's work on Novalis, the editors have uncovered much source-material for W.'s texts. They record this in their commentary and sometimes reprint it synoptically in a documentary appendix, so that W.'s mode of reception can be appreciated fully for the first time. The major conclusion is to demolish the image of the naïve and pious youth, which is replaced by insights into the semi-fictive, interdisciplinary character and purpose of much of his work, his pedantic and scholarly mode of working, his gift of observation, competence and keen sense of the transitional character of the age. Each section is preceded by masterly introductions, which offer full orientation without pre-forming interpretation, and the new standard edition is rounded off by *Lebenszeugnisse* and a chronology of W.'s life. R. Littlejohns, 'Frühromantische Kunstauffassung und wissenschaftliche Kunstgeschichte', Saul, *Wissenschaften*, 234–49, sees the Romantic achievement in this field as the foundation of modern art history. Especially W., Tieck and the Schlegels overcome the twin Enlightenment prejudices of identifying beauty with the Classical inheritance and/or with mere aesthetic pleasure. After rejecting Enlightenment theory they are pioneers in rediscovering older, more adequate paradigms of the aesthetic in Quad von Kinkelbach, Sandrart, and Vasari (but also Fiorillo), which involve concepts of historicity and contextuality. See also R. Köhler, **Poetischer Text und Kunstbegriff bei W.H.W.: Eine Untersuchung zu den 'Herzensergießungen eines kunstliebenden Klosterbruders' und den 'Phantasien über die Kunst'* (BSDL, 13), 1990, 221 pp., and P. Thewalt, **Die Leiden der Kapellmeister: Zur Umwertung von Musik und Künstlertum durch W.H.W. und E.T.A. Hoffmann* (BSDL, 20), 184 pp.

WAIBLINGER. W.W., *Mein flüchtiges Glück, Tagebücher, Briefe, Prosa*, ed. Wolfgang Hartwig (ATV, 32), 589 pp., reprints an edition of 1974 (Berlin, Rütten & Loening), including *Friedrich Hölderlins Leben*, some of the more important letters and *Erklärung der Kupfer*, plus an afterword and commentary.

WERNER. H. Reinhardt, 'Das "Schicksal" als Schicksalsfrage. Schillers Drama in romantischer Sicht: Kritik und Nachfolge', *Aurora*, 50, 1990:63–86, sees W.'s work, with remarkably few limiting conditions, as the practical realization of Solger's critique of Schiller's fate-concept. Thus, Schiller is attacked at once for alleged fatalism and excessive emphasis on human freedom, whereas Romantic drama should emphasize Christian mythology. *Der 24. Februar* is taken as representative of W.'s dramas and argued to be itself a drama of fatalism, with little Christian content.

LITERATURE, 1830–1880

By JOHN GUTHRIE, *Fellow of New Hall, University of Cambridge*

1. GENERAL

REFERENCE. Klemm, *Romanführer*, covers the major novels of the period with robust summaries, if with also perhaps a few less clues to the diversity of possible interpretations and to further reading than Kindler's *Literatur-Lexikon*, but its virtues are a wide, up-to-date coverage with succinct and down-to-earth entries. 'Austrian writers of the Enlightenment and Biedermeier: A biographical directory', *ASt*, 2:161–67, provides concise biographical information on some of the less well-known writers referred to in articles in the second volume of this new and welcome periodical.

BIBLIOGRAPHY. **Internationale Bibliographie zur deutschen Klassik 1750–1850*, Weimar, Nationale Forschungs- und Gedenkstätten der klassischen deutschen Literatur in Weimar, vol. 34, 1987. *Mit Nachträgen zu den früheren Jahren*, ed. Günther Mühlpfardt and Heidi Zeilinger, 1990, 528 pp. *Deutsche Staatsbibliothek in der Stiftung Preußischer Kulturbesitz. Verzeichnis der lieferbaren Veröffentlichungen. Catalogue of Publications Available*, Berlin, 27 pp.

THEMES. Two important books this year take us from creation to nihilism and should not be overlooked by those interested in the period. A broad approach to the problem of poetic inspiration and creativity is taken by Günter Blamberger, *Das Geheimnis des Schöpferischen oder: ingenium est ineffabile*, Stuttgart, Metzler, 216 pp. The point of departure is, after Kleist, the psychology of creativity and its failure to address itself to the question of the origins of the creative process. Nietzsche provides more fruitful ground, as do Warburg and Panofsky, principly the latter, whence the concept of 'Grammatographie' with its three stages (study of motifs, tropes and topoi, iconological interpretation) which are to be applied to literary works. Not a job to be undertaken by the individual scholar, we are advised, and a polyphonic chorus of researchers is suggested. Plenty of 'Totalitätsanspruch' here then. But the immediate aim is more modest, the (tentative, iconological) interpretation of a handful of 'Künstlernovellen'. Before that, though, an attack on Foucault, an explanation of the relevance of radical constructivism (postmodernist cognition theory), a sketching-in of Edward Young's and Kant's respective positions on genius. Via A. W. Schlegel and Hegel and the unsatisfactory accounts of creativity given in the *Goethezeit* we are led towards our period. The first 'Künstlernovellen' and 'Künstlerromane' are more interested in the depiction of a way of life than the artist *per se*. The questions raised prior to an examination of specific works are: that as to the relevant subjective theory of the origin of the creative; the reasons for the fascination with the problem of origins and the function of the creative model; the question of the readability and describability of distinctive features of the artist/creator or of the ineffable base of creativity; congruence of theory and practice, use of traditional mythological as opposed to new patterns of expression; the social and cultural anchoring of the creative process. Besides Novellen by Hoffmann and Thomas Mann, the second half of this book examines Mörike's *Mozart auf der Reise nach Prag* and Storm's *Ein stiller Musikant*. It is hardly necessary to add that the light thrown on each of these two works is powerful and new. B. engages many well-known critical views. He succeeds in showing the appropriateness of the Novelle to the depiction of the creative process, and its development is seen in a wider context. This is a meaty, original, and stimulating book. The other book is Bruno Hillebrand, *Ästhetik des Nihilismus. Von der Romantik zum Modernismus*, Stuttgart, Metzler, 237 pp., which sees nihilism as one of the obverse sides of idealism, but like Marxism, only one side and a diverse phenomenon whose aesthetic is that of perspectivism, relativism and negativism without which Modernism is incomprehensible. A limpid panoramic survey is followed by a chapter on the 'bold' school of the Romantics as precursors. The path to Nietzsche is prepared by Büchner. Writing as philosopher-cum-historian of ideas H. is inclined to neglect the poetic context. Thus Danton's words to Camille at the beginning of Act 2, Scene 1 of *Dantons Tod* (no reference is given!) are taken to be Büchner's own insight into fundamental nihilism, a view long since overhauled in the literature on B., though the paradox, that the nihilistic insights of his characters is a pleasurable experience does point back to the Romantics and forward to Nietzsche. A progression is made clear; the dualism and paradox of Nietzsche's position is emphasized (nihilistic insights followed by their overcoming, nihilism as the axis of revaluation). Before moving on to Futurism and Dada in the second half of his book H. considers the misunderstandings sown by Nietzsche's interpreters (especially by Thomas Mann). This is a compellingly written book, always provocative, and the reader will not want to look only at those sections directly concerned with our period.

Other studies take us from reading societies to photography and the visual arts and to acts of arson. Rosel Müller, *Von Patrioten, Jakobinern und anderen Lesehungrigen. Lesegesellschaften der 'Intelligens'-Stadt Marburg*, Marburg, Hitzeroth, 199 pp., focuses on the structure and composition of reading societies in Marburg, beginning in the 18th c. and moving forward to the mid-19th c. and their politicization and decline. The detailed scrutiny of one town, based on archival research, offers many insights into social and literary life of the period. *Der photographierte Dichter, MaM*, 51, 1989, ed. Michael Davidis and Mathias Michaelis, features many authors of our period in daguerrotypes, and in addition has excerpts from Ludwig Pfau and F. W. Hackländer relevant to the history of photography. Achim Ricken, *Panorama und Panoramaroman. Parallelen zwischen der Panorama-Malerei und der Literatur im 19. Jahrhundert dargestellt an Eugène Sues Geheimnissen von Paris und Karl Gutzkows 'Rittern vom Geist'* (EH, 1, 1253), iii + 365 pp., illus. Virginia L. Lewis, *Flames of Passion, Flames of Greed. Acts of Arson in German Prose Fiction* (STML, 2), xvi + 251 pp. Important light is also shed on the cultural life of the period by Fliegner's study of Mörike (see below, p. 800). Other themes figuring this year in major studies relating to the period are marriage and the family (see under BUSCH), and illness (book by Kubik, under BÜCHNER, and by Fliegner, under MÖRIKE).

Thematic studies in article form this year range from ideological consensus to culinary concerns. R. C. Holub, 'Rewriting an ideological consensus: institutions, nationalism, and the function of literature', *MLN*, 106:699–711. M. G. Ward, '"Only an elephant can bear an elephant's burden": German Realism — the limits and limitations of liberal reading', *NGS*, 16:71–92. W. Hinderer, 'Deutsches Theater der Französischen Revolution', *GQ*, 64:207–19, deals *inter alia* with Büchner and Griepenkerl. W. Scheffler, '". . . und jauchzten Freiheitslieder". Gedankengut der Französischen Revolution im schwäbischen Dichterkreis', *GeW*, 80, 1990:267–82. H. Kirchner, 'Reflexe der Französischen Revolution im Deutschen Vormärz', *Runa*, 11–12, 1989(1991):109–26. M. Botzenhart, 'Das Bild der Französischen Revolution in der liberalen Geschichtsschreibung des deutschen Vormärz', pp.179–92 of *Revolution und Gegenrevolution 1789–1830*, ed. Roger Dufraisse, Munich, Oldenbourg, 274 pp. H. Brandt, 'Die Julirevolution (1930) und die Rezeption der "principes de 1789" in Deutschland', *ib.*, pp.225–35. Roger Paulin, *Goethe, The Brothers Grimm and Academic Freedom. Inaugural Lecture Delivered 9 May 1990*, CUP, 30 pp., addresses the issue of academic freedom at German universities in the 19th c. and takes one of his examples from 1840. I. Schikorsky, 'Zwischen Privatheit und Öffentlichkeit. Autobiographische Texte von Handwerken', Wimmer, *Wurzeln*, 223–49. D. Arendt, 'Der verwachsene Mensch im Kunst-spiegel der Literatur oder: Orandum est, ut sit mens sana in corpore sano', *Universitas*, 45, 1990:53–70. W. Frühwald, 'Die Entdeckung des Leibes. Über den Zusammenhang von Literatur und Diätetik in der deutschen Literatur des 18. und 19. Jahrhunderts', *MBA*, 10:13–23. C. Jolles, 'Lukullisches und "Kochbuchliches". Zum Kulinarischen in der

Erzählkunst des Realismus', *Fest. Mayer*, 117–35. R. Paulin, 'The Biedermeier anomaly. Cultural conservatism and technological progress', *ASt*, 2:88–101. Austrian studies are prominent once again. Hans Heinz Hahnl, *Hofräte. Revoluzzer. Hungerlieder: vierzig verschollene österreichische Literaten*, Vienna, Wiener Journal Zeitschriften Vlg, 1990, 243 pp., contains short sketches of forgotten authors whose works contained a political message, many of them falling into our period. W. G. Sebald, *Unheimliche Heimat. Essays zur österreichischen Literatur*, Salzburg — Vienna, Residenz, 195 pp., collects together previously published essays by S., adding an introduction. The first two essays are of particular interest here, on Charles Sealsfield, and on ghetto-stories (dealing with Kompert, Franzos, Sacher-Masosch and others). E. Timms, 'National memory and the 'Austrian Idea' from Metternich to Waldheim', *MLR*, 86:898–910. R. J. W. Evans, 'Josephinism, "Austrianness", and the Revolution of 1848', *ASt*, 2:145–60. H. Lengauer, 'Literarisch-politische Opposition aus Prag. Ein Beitrag zur österreichischen Vormärzliteratur', *PhP.*, 33, 1990:7–16. G. Sebestyén, 'Der Anspruch auf den großen Roman. Über das Wesen der österreichischen Literatur', *MAL*, 24:1–12, touches marginally on Stifter.

Relations with the New World in this period continue to attract the attention of scholars. Peter J. Brenner, **Reisen in die neue Welt. Die Erfahrung Nordamerikas in deutschen Reise- und Auswandererberichten des 19. Jahrhunderts* (STSL, 35), 580 pp. M. Stoljar, 'Die frühe Rezeption der deutschen Literatur in Australien am Beispiel der kolonialen Presse', Schulz, *Literatur*, 113–40, asks what German literature was read in Australia up to 1860. M. Jurgensen, 'Deutsche Literatur in Australien — die historische Perspektive', *ib.*, pp. 333–47. Other reception studies include H. J. Koning, 'Niederländische Autoren des 19. Jahrhunderts als Rezipienten deutscher Literatur', *Arcadia*, 25, 1990:255–69.

Aspects of the history of our discipline and the formation of ideas in relation to it are the focus of interest in a number of essays: *Fest. Conrady*, has, of particular relevance, H. C. Seeba, 'Nationalbücher. Zur Kanonisierung nationaler Bildungsmuster in der frühen Germanistik' (57–71); R. Kolk, 'Zur Professionalisierung und Disziplinentwicklung in der Germanistik' (127–40); J.-D. Müller, 'Moriz Haupt und die Anfänge der *Zeitschrift für deutsches Altertum*' (141–64); U. Meves, '"Wir armen Germanisten . . ." Das Fach *deutsche Sprache und Literatur* auf dem Weg zur Brotwissenschaft' (165–93); J. Fohrmann, 'Deutsche Literaturgeschichte und historisches Projekt in der ersten Hälfte des 19. Jahrhunderts' (205–15); H. W. Blanke, 'Historismus als Wissenschaftsparadigma. Einheit und Manningfaltigkeit' (217–31), and many other references to the history of our

778 *German Studies*

subject in the period. M. Werner, '(Romanische) Philologie in Frankreich? Zu Geschichte und Problematik eines deutsch-französischen Wissenschaftstransfers im 19. Jahrhundert', *Fest. Zeller*, 31–43. R. Berbig, 'R. E. Prutz' Berufsentwicklung und Theoriebildung vor 1848', *ZGer*, 11, 1990:543–56. H.-M. Kruckis, 'Mikrologische Wahrheit. Die Neugermanistik des 19. Jahrhunderts und Heinrich Düntzer', *GRM*, 41:270–83. Relation to the canon is the concern of essays in *ABNG*, 31-33, 1990–91, with the following from our period treated in separate articles: Alexis, Franzos, Hille-brand, Fanny Lewald, Temme, Sealsfield. (See under INDIVIDUAL AUTHORS.) This volume also contains J. Bark, 'Zwischen Hoch-schätzung und Obskurität. Die Rolle der Anthologien in der Kanonbildung des 19. Jahrhunderts' (441–57). See also under LASSBERG.

GENRES. NARRATIVE PROSE. *Erzählte Kriminalität*, ed. Jürg Schönert (STSL, 27), collects papers from an interdisciplinary collo-quium in Hamburg in 1985. The main focus was the period 1850–80. As the editor notes in his foreword, the coming together of legal and literary scholars has produced many new perspectives in recent years, and detective fiction is no longer a marginal sub-genre. Here is a major contribution to research in the area which no scholar will be able to ignore. The book contains Schönert's introduction providing a general orientation to the subject area and the interdisciplinary approach. Section 1 has three general essays dealing with hermeneu-tic and pragmatic aspects of the theme. The increasing factualization through the processes of criminal law and criminal law proceedings in the 19th c. is surveyed by W. Naucke; T.-M. Seibert examines narrative as a social construction of criminality; L. Hoffmann looks at linguistic patterns for the description and reviewing of facts in the courtroom. Section 2 concerns the period 1770–1830, while Section 3 concerns ours. The contributions here are: J. Rückert, 'Zur Rolle der Fallgeschichte in Juristenausbildung und juristischer Praxis zwischen 1790 und 1880'; J. Linder, 'Deutsche Pitavalgeschichten in der Mitte des 19. Jahrhunderts. Konkurrierende Formen der Wis-sensvermittlung und der Verbrechensdeutung'; J. Henning, 'Ger-ichtsberichterstattung in den deutschen Tageszeitungen 1850–1890'; K. Marxen, 'Zum Verhältnis von Strafrecht und Gerichtsberichter-stattung in der zweiten Hälfte des 19. Jahrhunderts'; K. Imm, 'Der Fall Chorinsky/Ebergenyi: Der Weg vom Geschehen zu den Geschichten'; R. Schröder, 'Hegels Rechtsphilosophie im realisti-schen Roman. Zu *Hammer und Amboß* von Friedrich Spielhagen'; K. Lüdderssen, 'Der Text ist klüger als der Autor. Kriminologische Bemerkungen zu T. Fs Erzählung *Unterm Birnbaum*'; K. Imm, 'Kaspar Hauser: Kriminalisierung und Historisierung'. Section 4 concerns the 20th c., but the 19th c. resurfaces in the conclusion ('"Verfachlichung" als kennzeichnende Kategorie für den geschichtlichen Prozeß des 19. Jahrhunderts in der Strafrechtspflege'), with a contribution by J. Rückert. A rich volume. Mark Lehrer, *Intellektuelle Aporie und literarische Originalität. Wissenschaftsgeschichtliche Studien zum deutschen Realismus: Keller, Raabe und Fontane* (NASNCGL, 8), 168 pp., builds on some aspects of recent *Realismus* research in a clever and stimulating book. L. begins by noting that the experience of a reality showing opposition between subject and the outside world is typical of the novel of European Realism, but that the use of paradox to depict this is peculiar to the three authors he has chosen. He aims to show common features of their writing and the relation between their work and wider issues on the intellectual horizon. Disillusionment of the hero is crucial to Realism and Cervantes's recipe for parody is seen as operative. L. shows the link between literary originality and non-literary patterns of thought; the modification or rejection of myth-laden plot and narrative structures. Keller's 'anthropological' Realism for example shows the cultural relativity of social patterns of behaviour and related clichés of *Trivialliteratur*. Demythologization is the link between these writers; their originality is closely linked to their desire to show the limitations of contemporary ideas. Raabe's and Fontane's late work is seen to be linked by the desire to show causalities behind the thought and action of their characters, with Raabe emphasizing more the psychological, Fontane more the social factors. None of the three opted for mechanistic solutions. Keller's early prose is shown to reveal his anthropological picture of man, derived from Rousseau and Feuerbach. The conflict between 'Schein' and 'Sein' in his work is seen as linked to the contemporary scientific question of determination and freedom. In *Kleider machen Leute* he shows the anthropological paradox of the producer as opposed to the produced, though, ultimately, the scientific perspective gives way to that of the moralist, bound to the values of his society. Before analysing Raabe's and Fontane's works, L. sketches in philosophical and literary currents between 1770 and 1900, emphasizing the role played by theories of causality. Raabe is considered in relation to Darwinism. The paradox of individual development is seen to have formal consequences in the 'Antientwicklungsromane'. Raabe and Fontane are also considered in relation to Dilthey, and Fontane, finally, in relation to 'Enthüllungspsychologie', enabling us to see how the debate over blind determinism and freedom is thematized once again. No cosy, provincial realists here, but complex, original writers, grappling with vital philosophical questions on the same level as other major European realists. This is a tightly argued, refreshing book, with much food for thought.

Der deutsche soziale Roman des 18. und 19. Jahrhunderts, ed. H. Adler (WF, 630), vii + 473 pp., has an introduction by the editor, followed by a section with definitions of the social novel between 1844–86. The introduction gives a survey of the social novel in Germany, much neglected in literary histories, emphasizing its 18th-c. beginnings, and the first two sections of this book are devoted to the earlier phase of its history. This is followed by two sections relevant to our period: 'Literatur und soziale Frage — Der soziale Roman des Vormärz', which contains 'Kritische Gastrollen II' (1845) by Dingelstedt, 'Proletarierpoesie in Deutschland (1846) by Marggraff, and four (previously published) articles representative of recent scholarship, by E. Edler (on Dronke), F. Wagner (on Weerth), J.-W. Goette and R. Schloesser (on Weerth), and H. Adler (on literature and social criticism). Section IV, 'Formen des sozialen Romans im Realismus und im Naturalismus', contains Wilhelm Heinrich Riehl, 'Der soziale Roman' (1851), and again, important articles published in recent years by R.-E. Boetcher Joeres (social commentary in novels by German women writers, 1850–70), W. Müller-Seidel (on the art of the social novel), and by H.-H. Reuter (on *Die Poggenpuhls*). Mirosław Ossowski, *Der Berliner Roman zwischen 1880 und 1990*, Rzeszów, 1989, is also relevant to our period. Waltraud Maierhofer, *'Wilhelm Meisters Wanderjahre' und der Roman des Nebeneinander*, Bielefeld, Aisthesis, 1990, 331 pp., has a very dense introduction on the theory of novel-writing 1820–50, theoretically very sound and up to date, considering various perspectives on the novel in this period. In the forefront are the theory and practice of the novel in the late *Goethezeit*, its relation to contemporary reality, the distinction between *Zeitroman* and *Entwicklungsroman*. Gutzkow's theory and practice of novel-writing is discussed, and the structure of *Die Ritter vom Geiste* analysed in detail. A further chapter is devoted to a similar treatment of Immermann's *Die Epigonen* and the remainder of this study to a structural analysis of Goethe's novel and a comparison between it and the 'Roman des Nebeneinander'. Immermann's work is placed in a wider context than before, and seen as a forerunner of Realism. This is a well-researched book on an interesting topic, providing many new insights into two authors in particular, but also into the diverse reactions to the *Wanderjahre*. J.-J. Eckhardt, *Angriff, Rückzug und Zuversicht: satirisches Erzählen bei Bonventura, Jean Paul, E. T. A. Hoffmann, Heinrich Heine und Georg Weerth* (NYUOS, 35), 1989, 207 pp. A report on a conference in Magdeburg, 1990, on the 18th-c. and 19th-c. novel is given by N. Pohlmann and C. Köppe in *ZGer*, 11, 1990:607–09.

Reception studies also figure in relation to the novel. *Quellen zur Rezeption des englischen und französischen Romans in Deutschland und*

Österreich des 19. Jahrhunderts, ed. Norbert Bachleitner (STSL, 31), 614 pp., is a compilation of views on English and French novels expressed by writers and critics, major and minor, from the length and breadth of Germany and Austria in review and article form throughout our period. There are eight chapters: the first deals with commentaries on translations, the second with publishers, the third with the censorship of English and French literature in Austria, 1815–48, while the fourth lists and comments on the novels published in the Viennese *Zeitungs-Feuilleton*. The rest of the book presents reviews of novels: by a cross-section of (mostly, apart from Scott) social novelists (chapter five) and of Dickens, Eugène Sue, and Zola (a chapter each). The relevant material is introduced analytically and there are tables, a bibliography, and index. This volume will be of interest not only to those studying Anglo-German or Franco-German literary relations, it will also be a major source book for study of the reception of novel-literature in Europe, and of the importance of novel reading in shaping literary taste and cultural life. The volume's format facilitates the study of the various stages of the reception process. Many neglected documents come to the fore. It is certainly a step in the right direction and will open up many doors. Hildegunde Nuth, **Die Figur des Unternehmers in der Phase der Frühindustrialisierung in englischen und deutschen Romanen. Ansätze eines Vergleichs* (EH, XIV, 240), 2 vols, xlvi + 894 pp. E. O. McInnes, **'Eine untergeordnete Meisterschaft?' The Critical Reception of Dickens in Germany, 1837–1870*, Frankfurt, Lang, 195 pp. Id., 'Realism, history and the nation. The reception of the "Waverley" novels in Germany in the nineteenth century', *NGS*, 16:39–51. N. Bachleitner, '"... der so nachteiligen Romanen-Lektüre ein Ende zu machen." Der historische Roman und die österreichische Zensur im Vormärz, am Beispiel von Walter Scotts *Woodstock*', *Sprachkunst*, 22:35–48.

Shorter fiction is dealt with in several studies. See the book by Blamberger, p. 774. Du Gyu Kim, *Volkstümlichkeit und Realismus: Untersuchungen zu Geschichte, Motiven und Typologien der Erzählgattung 'Dorfgeschichte'*, Bielefeld, Aisthesis, 207 pp., surveys the genre from the middle of the 19th c. On travel literature see M. Maurer, 'Der Anspruch auf Bildung und Weltkenntnis. Reisende Frauen', *Lichtenberg-Jb.*, 1990:122–58. See also under GOLTZ, PFEIFFER, PÜCKLER-MUSKAU.

GENRES. DRAMA. *Texte zur Theorie des Theaters*, ed. Klaus Lazarowicz and Christopher Balme (UB, 8736), 703 pp., has a wide range of texts divided thematically into general and specific aspects of theory of the theatre. The latter is broken down into texts on the art of acting, directing, the play, stage and scene, intratheatrical communication, folk theatre, political theatre, and para-theatre. Our period is represented by excerpts from the writings of August Lewald, Schopenhauer, Nietzsche, and Wagner. This is a very handy volume, with index and introduction, particularly useful if a comparative approach to the theatre is pursued by the reader. *Die aristotelische Katharsis. Dokumente ihrer Deutung im 19. und 20. Jahrhundert*, ed. Matthias Luserke (Olms Studien, 30), Hildesheim, Olms, 443 pp., presents selected key texts relevant to the debate on catharsis. From our period we find texts by Henri Weil ('Über die Wirkung der Tragödie nach Aristoteles', 1847), and by Leonhard Spengel, ('Über die ΚΑΘΑΡΣΙΣ ΤΩΝ ΠΑΘΗΜΑΤΩΝ, ein Beitrag zur Poetik des Aristoteles', 1858), besides much other material of general interest.

GENRES. LYRIC POETRY. *Deutsche Balladen*, ed. Hartmut Laufhütte (UB, 8501), 647 pp. In contrast to the earlier volume in the same series edited by Nussbächer, this one omits earlier folk ballads and begins in the mid-18th c. There is thus more room for ballads from the 19th c. and they are generously represented by a wide selection of poets. The scholarly afterword is up to date and to be recommended without reservation.

Gerhard Kaiser, *Geschichte der deutschen Lyrik von Heine bis zur Gegenwart*, Frankfurt, Suhrkamp, 3 vols, 930 (vols 1–2), 314 pp., is the continuation of the first part of this ambitious history of German lyric poetry, *Geschichte der deutschen Lyrik von Goethe bis Heine* (see *YWMLS*, 50:828), using individual texts as a starting point for interpretation (collected together in the third volume), synthesized by comparison and contrast and examination of historical conditions. K. develops psycho-historical categories, taking account of Nietzsche's emphasis on aesthetic experience, emphasizing the positive value of the 'Problematisierung des Ichs' for modern poetry. The roots of those modern developments are of course to be found in our period and they receive detailed examination here. This dual role of lyric poetry after Goethe's death is emphasized (exclusivity on the one hand, increase of *Trivialliteratur* on the other), and a broad view is taken of literary developments embracing traditional '-isms'. Poets like Droste-Hülshoff and Keller are seen to be conscious of the status quo, but not as going beyond it, with a real break coming only in 1890 and the impact of historical developments making themselves fully felt. The diversity of poetic developments in our period and distinct reactions to the same historical phenomena are emphasized; the self-reflective poem at its outset as the last stage in the development of 'Erlebnislyrik' from the previous epoch; from here the transformations of 'Erlebnislyrik' to the recent dominance of new subjectivity are traced; from there the criticism of reality and its reconstitution in recent poetry are studied. The European context is not neglected in this account of the development of the German lyric whose main emphasis is thus on the emergence of Modernism. K.'s is a fresh approach, with many close, stimulating new readings of individual poems, and the benefit of an accessible style. H. Koopmann, 'Die Vorliebe des Sprachverfalls. Zur Sprache der Lyrik im 19. Jahrhundert', Wimmer, *Wurzeln*, 307–24.

LITERARY JOURNALS. Helga Brandes, *Die Zeitschriften des Jungen Deutschland: Eine Untersuchung zur literarisch-publizistischen Öffentlichkeit im 19. Jahrhundert* (Kulturwissenschaftliche Studien zur deutschen Literatur), Opladen, Westdeutscher Vlg, 306 pp., treats mainly, from the mass of journals in this period, those edited by Gutzkow, Wienbarg, Laube and Mundt, and the gradual progress of these journals towards the 'Revue'. They are seen within the framework of a process of social communication, i.e. 'kommunikations-geschichtlich', broken down into production, analysis of the medium itself, and reception. The study relies, as befits the vastness of material, on selective analysis of representative journals. The Enlightenment legacy is seen as important in shaping these journals, but the new aspect of professional journalism is emphasized, and its diversity and development from political to literary highlighted, as mass production ensues. U. Püschel, 'Journalistische Textsorten im 19. Jahrhundert', Wimmer, *Wurzeln*, 428–47. M. Thormann, 'Heinrich von Kleist und der programmatische Realismus. Zur liberalen Kleist-Rezeption in den *Grenzboten*', *Beiträge zur Kleist-Forschung*, 1988 (1989); 24–30. H. O. Horch, '"Auf der Zinne der Zeit." Ludwig Philipson (1811–1899) der "Journalist" des Reformjudentums. Aus Anlaß seines 100. Todestages am 29. Dezember 1989', *BLBI*, 86:5–21. See also the article by J. Henning in the volume by Jörg Schönert, p. 778 above.

LETTERS. Reinhard M. G. Nickisch, *Brief* (SM, 260), 259 pp., adds to the increasing number of studies considering the contribution of the letter to literary life, and attempts a survey. A theoretical chapter on the nature of epistolary communication is followed by chapters approaching the subject historically. Analysis then switches to examples of different formal elements, aspects of reception, and the social, legal, and cultural implications. This wide-ranging volume is rounded off with a chapter attempting to show the way forward for research. Our period is dealt with specifically in two chapters besides the many references to individual writers to be found *passim*. The importance of the 19th c. for letter-writing is emphasized and the two new evolving tendencies, objectivity and politicization, highlighted. Types of letters and their models are also briefly dealt with. What a vast, fascinating and barely tapped area reveals itself here in this volume, incidentally twice the length of most in the series. See B. Borchard on Clara Schumann as editor of her husband's letters in *Die*

Frau im Dialog, Studien zu Theorie und Geschichte des Briefs, ed. Anita Runge and Lieselotte Steinbrügge, Stuttgart, Metzler, 242 pp., and E. Czucka, 'Wissenschaftsprosa — Sprachgewalt und Tatkraft. Notizen zu Justus Liebigs "Chemischen Briefen"', *Arntzen Vol.*, 257–68. See also under PÜCKLER-MUSKAU, DROSTE-HÜLSHOFF (book by Walther Gödden, article by B. Plachta), STORM (article by Krummacher).

2. INDIVIDUAL AUTHORS

ALEXIS. C. Grawe, 'Preußen 1803 bis 1813 im "vaterländlischen Roman"': W.A., George Hesekiel, Theodor Fontane', Schulz, *Literatur*, 141–79. L. Tatlock, 'Gendering fashion and politics in the fatherland: W. As "Doppelroman" *Die Hosen des Herrn von Bredow*', *ABNG*, 31–33, 1990–91:231–55.

BÖRNE. M. Rauschenberg, **'La Balance' oder die Kunst des Lebens: zur Integration von Sozialkritik und Ästhetik in L. Bs Schriften* (EH, I, 1144), 1989, 199 pp. I. Rippmann, '"Haben Sie Geld zum prosaischen Honorar?" Ein unbekannter Brief L.Bs an den Buch- und Kunsthändler Friedrich König', *Heine-Jb.*, 30.

BÜCHNER. T. M. Mayer, 'G. B.: Shakespeare-, Goethe- und Follen-Zitate aus dem letzten Schulheft von 1831', *G. B. Jb.*, 7, 1988–89 (1991):9–44. T. M. Mayer, **G. B.: Woyzeck. Gezeichnet von Dino Battaglia*, Berlin, Altamira, 1990. (For some comments on this edition, see K. Kanzog, *Fest. Zeller*, 6–7.) G. B., *Woyzeck*, ed. Henri Poschmann, illus. Alfred Hrdlička, Munich, Beck, 256 pp., does well to use Poschmann's text, printing it in large and lavish format interspersed with H.'s pastel drawings, which however, despite the blurb's claim, do little to enhance our understanding of the drama.

Reiner Niehoff, *Die Herrschaft des Textes. Zitattechnik als Sprachkritik in G. Bs Drama 'Dantons Tod' unter Berücksichtigung der 'Letzten Tage der Menschheit' von Karl Kraus* (UDL, 57), 245 pp., is a clever exposure of B.'s text from the point of view of what has loosely been termed 'Zitatmontage'. Building on T. M. Mayer's edition of the play (1980) and finding the two poles of criticism (those stressing the striving for authenticity and those stressing a new aesthetic concept) a hindrance, N. is particularly concerned with the meaning of a 'literal' quotation in the text, and the thrust of his detailed study is in the opposite direction to much recent research that has been intent on locating and listing sources, or noting B.'s deviations from them without analysing the reasons for this. Comparisons with Schiller's technique form the springboard of this carefully argued and illuminating book. One *aperçu* illustrates the trend: 'Die Sprache der französischen Revolution ist der Motor des dramatischen Textes' (p. 20), and this helps to get to

Literature, 1830–1880   785

the heart of the text. Though there have been previous studies of B.'s
technique of using quotations (by Helbig, Siess), N. covers new
ground, not least by virtue of the breadth of reference to other writers,
the awareness of modern critical theory, and his development of Karl
Kraus's notion of language and negativity in respect of B.'s works. In
so doing, he is awakening interest in areas which have been less
treated in recent research. The same is true of Sabine Kubik, *Krankheit
und Medizin im literarischen Werk G. Bs.* Stuttgart, M & P Vlg, 319 pp., a
dissertation which establishes in its first section the importance of
illness and medicine in each of B.'s works, and proceeds to an
examination of these thematic concerns in relation to their historical
context in its second. A third section analyses the paradigm of the
patient-doctor relationship in the literary works against the background of the basic positions adopted in B.'s thinking, while, finally,
K. deals with the depiction of illness and the image of the physician in
B.'s works in relation to literary history and the history of science. K.
builds on Burghard Dedner's view that all B.'s texts are 'Chronik von
Erkrankungen' and provides some perceptive analysis of the texts
before moving on to the context and wider issues. The main virtue of
this study is that it combines those two elements, which have for too
long been separately pursued. Eward McInnes, *B.: Woyzeck*
(GIGGL, 9), 52 pp., is an introduction to the play for students, with
chapters on 'B. and the German dramatic tradition', 'The genesis of
the play: the Woyzeck case and the Clarus reports', 'Analysis of the
dramatic action', and 'Social insight and tragic awareness: the
imaginative world of *Woyzeck*'. M. gets many essential points about
the play across well. Good are the analysis of dramatic structure, the
explanation of the social theme and the nature of tragedy, presenting
clearly the opposing points of view in the critical literature. The
section on the tragic hero and the historical Woyzeck is also nicely
done, offering as it does the crux of the interpretation here: that B.'s
Woyzeck is not as downtrodden as his historical counterpart and that
his love 'for Marie appears as an act of gigantic defiance'. B.'s
exploratory technique and searching ambivalence are emphasized.
Naturally one could wish, in view of M.'s acknowledgement of the
work of recent scholars in the area of textual criticism, that he had also
been able to endorse Schmid's or Poschmann's text, and discussed
more fully some of the textual aspects, but this little volume has much
to recommend it. *Der widerständige Klassiker: Einleitungen zu Büchner von
Nachmärz bis zur Weimarer Republik*, ed. Burghard Dedner, Frankfurt,
Athenäum, 1990, 575 pp., bears witness to the enormous amount of
useful spade-work being done in relation to this author by the
'Forschungsstelle G. B.–Literatur und Geschichte des Vormärz' in
Marburg, and adds to the increasing number of reception studies of

B. The authors dealt with here are Ludwig Büchner, Karl Emil Franzos, Paul Landau, Wilhelm Hausenstein, Arnold Zweig, and Adam Kuckhoff. As D. points out in his preface, this is a particularly useful exercise in the case of B., whose works have been subjected to such conflicting interpretations. D. is able to pinpoint recurrent features and phases, historical and ideological bias as well as new insights in the history of B. reception over a period of 80 years. The detailed introduction examines the limited amount of factual knowledge available to these authors, whose reception is then examined in turn. The notes are copious and careful, with painstaking attention to detail, which is also true of the index. A full assessment of the determining factors in B. reception in the 19th c. still awaits us; the task is made easier by the appearance of this volume. Rodney Taylor, *History and the Paradox of Metaphysics in Dantons Tod* (AUS, v, 100), 1990, 277 pp.

G. B. Jb., 7, 1988–89 (1991), has F. Vollhardt, 'Straßburger Gottesbeweise. Adolf Stoebers, *Idées sur les rapports de Dieu à la Nature* (1834) als Quelle der Religionskritik G. Bs'; I. Nagel, 'Seuche, Vulkan, Überschwemmung: Saint-Just als Naturforscher'; I. Diersen, 'Bs *Lenz* im Kontext der Entwicklung von Erzählprosa im 19. Jahrhundert'; H. H. Hiebel, 'Das Lächeln der Sphinx. Das Phantom des Überbaus und die Aussparung der Basis: Leerstellen in Bs *Leonce und Lena*'; B. Dedner, 'Die Handlung des *Woyzek*: wechselnde Orte — "geschlossene Form"'; T. M. Mayer, 'Zu einigen neuen Lesungen und zur Frage des "Dialekts" in den *Woyzeck*-Handschriften'; E. Bockelmann, 'Von Bs Handschrift oder Aufschluß, wie der *Woyzeck* zu edieren sei'; M. Kuhnigk, 'Kometen, Sternkunde und Politik. Zur astronomischen Metaphorik in G. Bs *Kato*-Rede'; I. Fellrath, '"Der Freiheit einer Gasse!" Eine stoff- und wirkungsgeschichtliche Anmerkung zu *Dantons Tod*'; A. Kühnlenz, '"Wie den Leuten die Natur so nahtrat . . ." Ludwig Tiecks *Der Runenberg* als Quelle für Bs *Lenz*'; R. Pabst, 'Kurze Notiz zu Freiligrath und B.'; E.-U. Pinkert, 'Schwedens "Marat" als Übersetzer von *Dantons Tod*. Zur ersten skandinavischen B.–Übersetzungen (Malmö, 1889)'; W. Karbach, '"Ich lebte geräuschlos dahin." Erste Hinweise auf Bs Bedeutung für Heinar Kipphardts Ästhetik und Werk'; U. Kaufmann, '"Noch immer rasiert Woyzeck seinen Hauptmann . . ." Zum Problem des Fragmentarischen bei G. B. und Heiner Müller'; R. Pabst, 'Zwei unbekannte Berichte über die Hinrichtung Johann Christian Woyzecks'; U. Walter, 'Der Fall Woyzeck. Eine Quellen-Dokumentation. (Repertorium und vorläufiger Bericht)'; J.-C. Hauschild, 'Bs letzte Stunden. Ein unbekannter Brief von Wilhelm Baum'; T. M. Mayer and S. Rink, 'Das Inventar und die Versteigerung des Nachlasses von Friedrich Ludwig und Amalie Weidig'; R.

Pabst, 'Ein unbckannter Bericht Luise Bs über die Zürcher B.–Feier 1875'; a bibliography for 1988–89 and list of performances and reviews of B.'s plays for the 1985–86 season through to 1988–89. L. Lamberechts, 'Zur sozialen Grundlage der Idealismuskritik in G. Bs *Woyzeck*', *Fest. Verbeeck*, 109–21. K. v. Delft, ' "Setzt die Leute aus dem Theater auf die Gasse . . .!" ' G. Bs *Dantons Tod* aus südafrikanischer Sicht', *AGJSG*, 20, 1990:9–26. H. Gersch and S. Schmalhans, 'Die Bedeutung des Details: J. M. R. Lenz, Abbadona und der "Abschied" ', *GRM*, 41:385–412, is relevant to a study of B.'s sources. M. Perraudin, 'Towards a new cultural life: B. and the "Volk" ', *MLR*, 86:627–44. M. Durzak, 'Die Modernität G.Bs. *Lenz* und die Folgen', *L'80*, 45, 1988:132–46. W. Hinderer, 'Festschrift-liche Bemerkungen zur Codierung von Liebe in Bs Dantons Tod', *Fest. Grimm*, 151–65. G. Kurz, 'Guillotinenromantik. Zu Bs *Dantons Tod*', *ZDP*, 110:550–74. T. Dorst, 'Phantasie über ein verlorenge-gangenes Theaterstück von G. B. Dankrede', *JDASD*, 1990:121–30. See also book by Hillebrand, p. 775 above.

BUSCH. Michael Hetzner, *Gestörtes Glück im Innenraum. Über Ehe und Familie bei W. B.*, Bielefeld, Aisthesis, 251 pp., investigates the techniques used by B. to depict marital problems in his works. H. studies the prose as well as the better known works and places them in their literary context, emphasizing the contrast between the con-temporary ideal picture of family life and the reality of it, which B.'s work reveals. B.'s cartoon stories, the poetry, and the narrative prose are examined in turn. The realism and modernity of the prose is stressed, in comparison with the relatively harmless, popular verse, with the cartoon poetry seen as occupying the middle ground. The *W. B.-Jb.*, 56, has five contributions of interest. J. Lieskounig, 'Die Odysee eines späten Taugenichts. W. Bs Erzählung "Der Schmetter-ling" ', *WW*, 41:405–16.

DROSTE-HÜLSHOFF. A.v.D.-H., *Historisch-kritische Ausgabe, Werke, Briefwechsel*, ed. Winfried Woesler, Tübingen, Niemeyer, has pro-duced vol. III, 2, *Epen. Dokumentation*, ed. Lothar Jordan, 1035 pp. A brief general introduction deals with the genre of the verse epic and an extensive section with the publication history of the *Gedichte*, 1838, in which the epics, so crucial for D.'s development as a poet, appeared. Each of the longer verse epics (and the early one, *Walther*) has a separate introduction dealing with textual history, sources, genesis, in some cases writing and revision, and reception. Valuable are the explanatory notes for each work. There is an enormous amount of detail here, an extraordinary number of variants and different versions, all presented with great clarity. As Jordan himself notes in an article devoted to an aspect of the editing of these epics, it will be some time before literary scholarship comes to terms with the sheer amount of material here; see L. Jordan, 'Titel literarischer Werke, historisch-kritisch betrachtet. Das Beispiel der Epen A.v.D.-Hs', *Fest. Zeller*, 142–49. B. Plachta, 'Das Manuskript und seine Legende. Die Widmungsgedichte A.v.D.-Hs an Levin Schücking', *ColGer*, 23, 1990:134–45. Walter Gödden, *Die andere Annette. A.v.D.-H. als Briefschreiberin*, Paderborn, Schöningh, 262 pp., is a most interesting book from the editor of Droste's letters, whose dissertation, a painstaking chronology of D.'s life, prepared the ground for this study. By studying some of the letters in the context of the entire output and their 'Adressatenbezogenheit', a daunting task long avoided by scholars, G. aims to get behind the traditional sentimental image of the dreamy young aristocratic woman. The first section of this illuminating study examines the Biedermeier custom of letter-writing in relation to D. from a number of different points of view. Basic questions such as what went into the making of a good letter in D.'s view and the importance attached to different types of letters are discussed; humour and conversational elements are analysed. Two strands of correspondence emerge: that with relatives and that with friends, each with different characteristics. Through his analysis of her letters G. puts paid to many a cliché about D., for example that she was not *au fait* with political issues or uncritical of her own class. New light is thrown on her view of herself as a writer: we find an important element of conscious, willed withdrawal. She is often a very tactical correspondent. This is shown in detail in the second section of G.'s book, which analyses separately the correspondence with Sprickmann, Schlüter, and Schücking, throwing new light on the important relationships that D. had with each of them. G. also looks at the posthumous fate of D.'s letters (censorship and manipulation) and aspects of editing them, as well as at the nature of postal connections and idiosyncrasies of handwriting. The reader seeking information about letter-writing in the Biedermeier should turn to this book, but the D. specialist will not be able to ignore it, for this is one of the most important books on D. to appear in recent years, revealing a much more complex, contradictory, multi-layered personality than heretofore assumed. B. Plachta, '"Le papier ne rougit pas." Gefühl und Kalkül in Briefen an A.v.D.-H.', *EG*, 46:141–60.

EBNER-ESCHENBACH. M.v.E.-E., *Kritische Texte und Deutungen*, ed. Karl Konrad Polheim, Tübingen, Niemeyer, has added *Tagebücher* II. *1871–1878*, ed. Karl Konrad Polheim *et al.*, 674 pp. (see *YWMLS*, 51:767). This volume has roughly 600 pp. of text, with an entry for almost every day of the year. There are three more volumes to come. E. Sagarra, 'M.v.E.-E. and the tradition of the Catholic Enlightenment', *ASt*, 2:117–31.

FALLERSLEBEN. H. v. Jürgen Borchert, *H. v. F. Ein deutsches Dichterschicksal*, Berlin, Vlg der Nation, 239 pp., is a not surprising publication in the early days of reunification. It is written in a fairly chatty style and traces the author's own travels and tribulations in search of F. the poet and Germanist, refreshing, if not of major scholarly importance.

FELDER. 'F. M. F., der Dichter einer vorindustriellen österreichischen Provinzgesellschaft', *ÖGL*, 35: 147–54.

FONTANE. G. Effler edits F.'s correspondence with Joseph Kürschner in *F. Blätter*, 51. W. Hettche, 'Strümpfe und Schopenhauer. Ein bisher unbekannter Brief T. Fs an Karl Ferdinand Wiesike', *ib.*, 4–6. G. Gerler, 'T. F. Die Dörfer im Ruppinischen', *ib.*, 7–14. Two fine volumes complete the new edition of the *Wanderungen*. These are the 60 or so texts related to the *Wanderungen* that F. did not include in the original four-volume edition and many of them are published here for the first time. They constitute T.F., *Wanderungen durch die Mark Brandenburg*, ed. Gotthard Erler and Therese Erler, Berlin, Aufbau. 6. *Dörfer und Flecken im Lande Ruppin. Unbekannte und vergessene Geschichten aus der Mark Brandenburg I*, 748 pp.; 7. *Das Ländchen Friesack und die Bredows Unbekannte und vergessene Geschichten aus der Mark Brandenburg II*, 498 pp., containing together sketches and the pieces F. rejected, essays thematically related to the *Wanderungen*, F.'s reviews relating to Brandenburg and Berlin and to the treatment of historical and geographical subjects. Apart from their intrinsic value the writings in these volumes offer many insights into F.'s working methods and they have been well edited here. T.F., *Die Poggenpuhls* (IT, 1271), 141 pp.

Rolf Zuberbühler, *'Ja, Luise, die Kreatur.' Zur Bedeutung der Neufundländer in Fs Romanen* (UDL, 60), 88 pp., is not as narrow as its title might suggest. Starting with the importance of 'Natürlichkeit', Z. progresses to the centrality of the canines, showing how neglected they have been. A brief survey of the dog in 19th-c. literature and painting follows and F.'s distance from *Genremalerei* noted; Landseer's influence is pinpointed, faithfulness seen as the most important characteristic of man's best friend. The central chapters analyse the role of these wonderful Newfoundlanders in different novels and the conclusion is reached that through them F. portrays 'das Natürlich-Gute', with a notable absence of irony. A development towards indirectness is also persuasively argued for. F.'s world remains anthropocentric, but with another dimension added. Winfried Jung, *Bildergespräche: zur Funktion von Kunst und Kultur in T. Fs 'L'Adultera'*, Stuttgart, M & P, 278 pp., uses as his point of departure F.'s anticipation of Freud's notion of man's dependence on art in an all too complex world, noting how F.'s characters frequently use works of art and pictures as points of reference. *L'Adultera* is used as an example of a novel in which the aesthetic realm influences the course of the plot.

Iser's theories are invoked for the analysis of strategies for reader manipulation; the study pursues a discussion of the wider question of the relation between the individual, reality and art in F.'s social novels; the use of art as model is seen, with Marcuse, as a social and political problem. J.'s close and illuminating reading of the text takes place within the context of a discussion of the theme of 'Kunst und Kultur' in F. research. Gabriele Althoff, *Weiblichkeit als Kunst. Die Geschichte eines kulturellen Deutungsmusters*, Stuttgart, Metzler, 176 pp., has a chapter on F.'s *L'Adultera*, another on the sociology of the bourgeois adultress, and looks at the social function of images of women in their historical context. Christine Lehmann, *Das Modell Clarissa. Liebe, Verführung, Sexualität und Tod der Romanheldinnen des 18. und 19. Jahrhunderts*, Stuttgart, Metzler, 217 pp., touches on *Effi Briest*. C. Liebrand, **Das Ich und die anderen. Fs Figuren und ihre Selbstbilder* (Rombach Wissenschaft Reihe Litterae), Freiburg, Rombach, 1990, 341 pp. Luise Burg-Ehlers, **T. F. und die Literaturkritik: zur Rezeption eines Autors in der zeitgenössischen konservativen und liberalen Berliner Tagespresse*, Bochum, Winkler, 1990, xiii + 338 pp. Susanne Konrad, **Die Unerreichbarkeit von Erfüllung in T. Fs 'Irrungen, Wirrungen' und 'L'Adultera'* (EH, 1, 1265), 186 pp. See also the book by Mark Lehrer, p. 779 above.

F. Blätter, 51, includes a lecture by Charlotte Jolles on the occasion of the founding of the T. F. Gesellschaft on 15 December in Potsdam, 1990, P. Wruck on national songs and hymns at the thirteenth 'Stiftungsfest' of the 'Tunnel über der Spree' (1840), M. Thuret on patriotic and political poetry in the same society around 1848, K. Hannusch analysing its membership, G. Friedrich on F.'s literary borrowings in *Ellernklipp*, F. Gebauer on the 'Vaterländische Reiterbilder' and F.'s attitudes to Bismarck, O. Keiler's essay on *Vor dem Sturm* (also published in the volume edited by Grawe, see below), H. Nürnberger on artists and their world as a theme in F.'s poems, C. Grawe on time in F.'s novels, A. Graf on the genesis and structure of *Quitt* (F. Möllhausen and Friedrich Karl in Dreilinden). Helga Schütz writes on F. from the perspective of a modern writer and the volume concludes with reviews, bibliographies and an index for vols 1–50 of the journal. *F. Blätter*, 52, also has B. Plette, 'Tintensklaven mit Kronenorden. Diagnose, Travestie und Kritik in Fs "Dichtergedichten"'; G. Friedrich, 'Die Witwe Schmolke. Ein Beitrag zur Interpretation von Fs Roman *Frau Jenny Treibel*'; P. A. Anderson, 'Der Durchbruch mit Grete Minde. Ein Probekapitel aus Fs Biographie'; M. Masanetz, '"Awer de Floh, de ist dull!" Fs *Unwiederbringlich* — das Weltuntergangsspiel eines postmodernen Realisten'; G. Kerekes, 'Gragger, F. und die Fakten'; U. Berger, 'Klang der Hoffnung'; H. Nürnberger, 'Einführende Worte zur ersten Jahresversammlung der

F.-Ges. am 27.9.1991 in Gildenhall'; E. Sagarra, 'Fs Roman: *Der Stechlin*'; reports, reviews, bibliographies, etc. *Interpretationen: Fs Novellen und Romane*, ed. C. Grawe (UB, 8416), 304 pp., is a collection of interpretative essays by various F. specialists on 11 of the novels. H. Ester, 'Die Fontaneforschung im Wandel der Zeiten', *DK*, 40, 1990:19–32. H. Poser, 'Katholisierende Elemente bei T.F.', *ib.*, 461–69. H. Ohl, 'Zeitgenossenschaft. Arthur Schnitzler und T.F.', *JFDH*:262–307. P. Peters, 'Sozialisation als Denaturierung. Anmerkungen zum zivilisationskritischen Potential in T.Fs Ellernklipp', *LitL*:31–45. H. Blumenberg, 'Lebensgedichte. Einiges aus T.Fs Vielem', *Akzente*, 38:7–28. G. Kerekes, 'Der Weg durch die Wüste — T.Fs Dramentheorie', *ALitH*, 31, 1989 (1990). N. Mecklenburg, 'Figurensprache und Bewußtseinskritik in Fs Romanen', *DVLG*, 65:674–94. H. Aust, 'Das "wir" und das "töten". Anmerkungen zur sprachlichen Gestaltung des Krieges in Fs Kriegsbüchern', *WW*, 41:199–211. See also under ALEXIS, STIFTER (article by P. Howe), and the article by K. Lüderssen in the vol. by Jörg Schönert, p. 778 above.

FRANÇOIS, LOUISE VON. T. C. Fox, 'L. v. F. rediscovered', *ABNG*, 31–33, 1990–91:303–19.

FRANZOS. Carl Steiner, *K. E. F., 1848–1904. Emancipator and Assimilationist* (NASNCGL, 5), x + 230 pp. Id., 'Deutscher und Jude. Das Leben und Werk des K.E.F. (1814–1904)', *ABNG*, 31–33, 1990 91:367–87. See also under THEMES.

FREILIGRATH. Ernst Fleischhack, *Fs Gedichte in Lied und Ton*, Bielefeld, Aisthesis, 163 pp., is a bibliography listing settings to music of F.'s poems. See the article by D. Hellfaier on F. MSS, *Grabbe-Jb.*, 10, which also has: W. Büttner, 'Wie F. zum politischen Dichter wurde'; B. Plachta, 'F.F. und Amerika'; E. Fleischhack, 'Gottesglaube und Mitmenschlichkeit. Zum religiösen Hintergrund im Werk und Leben F.Fs'; H. Wipperfürth, 'F., John Keats und die soziale Lyrik'.

GOLTZ. M. Maher, 'Sprachliche Besonderheiten des Orient-Reiseberichts am Beispiel von B.G.' Buch *Ein Kleinstädter in Aegypten*', *Arntzen Vol.*, 247–55.

GOTTHELF. J. Rankin, 'One level removed: narrative framing as a didactic device in the 'Rahmennovellen' of J.G.', *ColGer*, 23, 1990:253–71.

GRABBE. **Grabbe über seine Werke, C.D.Gs Selbstzeugnisse zu seinen Dramen, Aufsätzen und Plänen*, ed. L. Löb, Frankfurt, Lang, 338 pp. *G.-Jb.*, 10, contains M. Vogt, '"'s ist ja doch alles Komödie' — Gs metapoetisches Frühwerk. Mit einem Exkurs über ein zeitgenössisches Arminiusdrama'; M. Porrmann, G. — Detmold: Traumpaarung oder Klischee? Kursorische Anmerkungen zum Umgang mit Gs Biografie in fiktionalen Texten der achtziger Jahre'; J. Fauser, '*Café Grabbe*. Mit bio-bibliographischen Anmerkungen'; E. Meyer-Krentler, 'Willkomm und Abschied im Detmolder Zuchthaus. Lichtbild-Vortrag zur Eröffnung des G.-Hauses in Detmold am 22. Dezember 1990'; D. Hellfaier, 'G. und Freiligrath-Autographen. Neuerwerbungen der Lippischen Landesbibliothek 1984–1991'.

GREGOROVIUS. F.G., *Idyllen vom baltischen Ufer*, ed. Eugen Thurnher, DBO, 153 pp., is a delightful volume, also with *Idyllen vom lateinischen Ufer* and *Die Insel Capri*, using first edition texts and having an afterword by the editor.

GRILLPARZER. Arno Dusini, *Die Ordnung des Lebens. Zu F.Gs '*Selbstbiographie*'* (UDL, 61), 156 pp., draws on recent work in the area of autobiography for this stylistic, structural, and thematic analysis of G.'s autobiography. Beginning with an analysis of the depiction of physical surroundings and G.'s father, this study moves into the area of psycho-biography, locating the 'real' father in Goethe. A chapter on Kafka's reception of G. concludes this readable and illuminating study. Masato Ikuta, **Geschichte und Individuum in Gs dramatischer Welt* (EH, I, 1205), 240 pp. *Jb. der G.-Ges.*, 17, has R. Mühler, 'G. — Metternich — Napoleon'; A. Barthofer, '*Die Ahnfrau* und Freuds Grillparzerdeutung'; W. Lux, 'Der Krug als zentrales Symbol in Gs *Des Meeres und der Liebe Wellen*'; S. Jones, 'Werte und Menschlichkeit in *Weh dem, der lügt*'. *GLL*, 44, has one issue devoted to G., containing: A. Menhennet, 'G., Shakespeare and historical drama' (208–20); B. Mullan, 'Characterisation and narrative technique in G.'s *Der arme Spielmann* and Storm's *Ein stiller Musikant*' (187–97); I. F. Roe, 'G. and the language of quietism' (221–35); S. P. Scheichl, 'Atalus: ein unaufgelöster Widerspruch in *Weh dem, der lügt*' (198–207); M. G. Ward, 'The structure of G.'s thought' (236–52). H. Unterreitmeier, 'Das falsche Spiel mit dem lieben Gott. Natur, Moral und Politik in Gs Trauerspiel *Die Jüdin von Toledo*', *LiB*, 23:36–39. D.-R. Moser, 'Feuchtwanger gegen G. *Die Jüdin von Toledo*', *ib.*, 26–35. G. Fuchs, '"Unser G." Zur G.-Rezeption im Dritten Reich', *ÖGL*, 35:91–118. G. D. C. Martin, 'Historical fact versus literary fiction: members of the house of Liechtenstein occurring in Schiller's *Wallenstein* and G.'s *König Ottokar*', *MLR*, 86:337–48.

GROTH. The *Jahresgabe der K.-G.-Ges.*, 33, has appeared, with a range of items of interest to G. scholars.

GUTZKOW. See book by Ricken under THEMES, that by Maierhofer under GENRES, and the article by F. Mende in *Heine-Jb.*, 30.

HEBBEL. V. Schulz, 'Zwei neue H.-Briefe', *H.-Jb.*: 157–61. M.-M. Langner, 'Ein neuer Brief von Christine H.' *ib.*, 163–69. A. T. Alt, 'H.-Briefe, Berlin 1989. Addenda und Corrigenda' *ib.*, 171–72. Volker Nölle, *Hs dramatische Phantasie. Versuch einer kategorialen Analyse*,

Berne, Francke, 1990, 506 pp., approaches H. from Kant, Feuerbach, and Sartre with the help of intersubjective categories. The categories are 'Blick', 'Entzug', 'Abstand', 'Kontingenz' and 'Reflexivität'. They are theoretically expounded and systematically pursued. In search of the deep structures, the specific grammar of H.'s dramas, N. has written a theoretically rigorous, readable, and reasonable study, paying particular attention to dramatic situation. He is able to show that certain basic patterns are used over again in the dramas. The study is not without a certain abstractness; however, many new insights into the specific nature of Hebbel's dramas are to be had. An awareness of the main directions of research in recent decades is another feature of this impressive contribution. Heinze Stolte, *Im Wirbel des Seins. Erkundungen über H.*, Heide, Boyens, 552 pp., collects over 20 pieces by this seasoned H. scholar and President of the H.-Ges., most having been previously presented in the form of lectures for the society and published in the *H.-Jb.* The essays are grouped into two sections, those relating to H.'s 'world' and those dealing with aspects of his work. *H.-Jb.*, has K. Kratzsch, '"Das große Rad ging über sie hinweg". Agnes Bernauer bei H. und Orff"; C. Pilling, '"Unsere Kinder sind die Armen". Von der Wohltätigkeit der bürgerlichen Gesellschaft in Hs "Mutter und Kind"'; H. Müller-Dietz, 'Tagebuch und Recht — am Beispiel F.Hs'; A. Stumpf, 'Masken des Erzählens. Zur Illusionskritik in zwei Prosa-Texten F Hs· "Der Schneider Nepomuk Schlägel" und "Schnock"'; F. Schlee, 'F.Hs äußere Erscheinung'; L. Lütkehaus, 'Die Wiederkehr F.Hs. Von der Aktualität eines (fast) vergessenen Dichters'; H. Grundmann, '"Ich sah des Sommers letzte Rose stehn..." Hinweise zu einem der bekanntesten Gedichte F.Hs'. H. A. Glaser, 'Ein deutsches Trauerspiel. F.Hs Nibelungen', Heinzle, *Nibelungen*, 333–50. A. S. Coulson, 'Die Rolle der Zaubermacht in IIs *Gyges und sein Ring* und Nestroys *Der Talisman*', *Arntzen Vol.*, 197–219.

HEINE. The HKA, ed. Manfred Windfuhr (see *YWMLS*, 52:763 for last vol.), has produced vol. 14,2, *Lutezia*. II. *Apparat 59–61. Artikel und Anhang*, ed. Volkmar Hansen, 839–1736 pp. H.H., *Der Doktor Faust. Ein Tanzpoem nebst kuriosen Berichten über Teufel, Hexen und Dichtkunst*, ed. Joseph A. Kruse (UB, 3605), 116 pp., uses the text of the first edition (Voigt's printing) with H.'s own 'Erläuterungen', collated with the Düsseldorf edition. The afterword treats the genesis, sources, reception, and interpretation of H.'s 'Faust-ballet', which seems well worth another run. H.H., **Briefe aus Berlin*, ed. Joseph A. Kruse (IT, 1322), 120 pp. Karlheinz Fingerhut, *H. H. Der Satiriker. Eine Darstellung mit Texten und Erläuterungen*, Stuttgart, Metzler, 182 pp., will be useful, especially for teaching purposes. It has a generous selection of texts interspersed with commentaries placing the texts chosen to illustrate H.'s importance as satirist in their literary, thematic, and historical context. The selections and analytical sections are so organized as to illustrate H.'s own concept of himself as satirist and the development of his satirical style in prose and poetry, which reveals three stages: satire of the philistine (ch. 2), political satire of the 'Vormärz' writer (ch. 3), the satirical dealings with the topsy-turvy world of the Restoration period (ch. 4). The illustrations are by Hermann Burkhardt, who discusses aspects of illustrating H.'s satirical texts in ch. 6. A well-researched and well-presented volume. See also the essay by F. on H. as satirist in the volume of essays ed. G. Höhn, below.

Jeffrey L. Sammons, *H.H.* (SM, 261), 160 pp., replaces the earlier volume by Eberhard Galley in this series. The volume's growth in size compared with its predecessor is symptomatic of the critical attention H. has received in recent years, a phenomenon in itself, as S. notes. Here is one of the most elegantly written 'Realienbände' to have appeared in recent years, distinguished by crisp and reliable value judgements backed up by a vast knowledge of H. and of H. research. There are three main sections ('Germany 1797–1831', 'France 1831–48', 'Matrazengruft 1848–56'), each with chapters dictated by biographical or political events or by major works. A section on the reception is also included. The work of Anglo-Saxon scholars is given a good hearing. Naturally a volume of this kind can only hint at some of the many unsolved questions relating to H.'s life and works: an admirable coverage of them is given. In his conclusion S. warns of the danger of seeing H. too much with his own eyes and, with a plea for close textual analysis, suggests a new look at the (dualistic rather than dialectical) nature of his irony, a revision of our notions of his political views and historical position, the establishment of a more complete picture of the reception, a more objective one of his relation to France. With these questions to guide research and the useful division of information here, this is likely to become an indispensable research tool for H. scholars, exemplary in its balance. Ursula Hofstaetter, *Langeweile bei H.H.* (BNL, 110), 324 pp., notes the pervasiveness of boredom in the 'Vormärz'. Scattered throughout H.'s works as his confrontations with the problem of boredom are, they are an underlying theme of his work. His various attitudes are here gathered together and carefully analysed. The endorsement of the principle of 'Bewegung' as an antipode to boredom is seen as crucial, and H.'s reaction to the July Revolution reflected in his emphasis on the role of boredom and lethargy in society. The differences between H.'s attitudes and those of admirers of Goethe, the Romantics, the Swabian poets and Platen, the influence of life on philosophy and art and the problem of autonomy of art are treated. A further section is devoted to Kant, Schopenhauer, and Kierkegaard. II.'s attitudes to England, his political views, his early depiction of states of boredom in relation to 'Weltschmerz', his Utopian visions in relation to his fear of monotony are scrutinized. This is a clear-headed and illuminating study using close textual analysis without too narrow a focus. Johann Jokl, *Von der Unmöglichkeit romantischer Liebe. H.Hs 'Buch der Lieder'* (Kulturwissenschaftliche Studien zur deutschen Literatur), Wiesbaden, Westdeutscher Vlg, 282 pp., shows the complex, contradictory nature of H.'s first cycle, its 'Zerrissenheit' as opposed to its Romanticism. The contradictions are seen not only as part of the poet's personality, but as characteristic of the period. This view is corroborated by a broad-based approach to the text, relating critical insights to literature of the period and the reception of the cycle. Notably, 'Vereinigungsphilosophie' and Hegel's phenomenology are related to parts of the cycle and the whole. Walter Hinck, **Die Wunde Deutschland. H.Hs Dichtung im Widerstreit von Nationalidee, Judentum und Antisemitismus*, Frankfurt, Insel, 1990, 305 pp. *Paul Peters, *H.H. 'Dichterjude.' Die Geschichte einer Schmähung*, Frankfurt, Hain, 1990, 271 pp. Jost Hermand, **Mehr als ein Liberaler, Über H.H.*, ed. Helmut Kreutzer and Karl Riha (FLK, 31), 211 pp.

Three volumes of essays should be noted. *H.H. im Spannungsfeld von Literatur und Wissenschaft*, ed. W. Gössmann and M. Windfuhr, Essen, Hobbing, 1990, 226 pp., contains papers from an interdisciplinary colloquium on the occasion of the renaming of the University of Düsseldorf after H.H. The contributions are wide-ranging and emphasize the relevance of H.'s œuvre to many different disciplines: W. Gössmann, 'Die Herausforderung der Wissenschaft durch die Literatur'; M. Windfuhr, 'Kritische Wissenschaft, fröhliche Wissenschaft. H. als Anreger der Wissenschaften'; J.-C. Hauschild, 'Professor H.? Von den Lockungen einer akademischen Karriere'; W. Hogrebe, 'Die II.-Frage. Brouillon zur dichterischen Semantik'; H. Boldt, 'H. im Zusammenhang der politischen Ideen seiner Zeit'; J. A. Kruse, '"Die wichtigste Frage der Menschheit" — H. als Theologe'; S. Bierwirth, 'Sänger, Märtyrer und Befreiungskämpfer. Hs Selbstverständnis im Spiegel seiner Dichterbilder'; A. Waschinsky, 'H. und die Kunstkritik'; A. Neuhaus–Koch, 'H. als Faust-Philologe und Erneuerer der volksliterarischen Tradition'; H. Anton, 'Hs "Venus-Mythologie"'; K.-H. Roth, 'Sprachreflexion bei H.H.'; L. Schrader, 'H.H. als Leser des "Quijote"'; H.-G. Pott, 'H. und die "Romantische Schule" Eichendorffs'; H. Friedl, 'H.H. und Friedrich Nietzsche'. *H.H.: ästhetisch-politische Profile*, ed. G. Höhn (Suhrkamp Taschenbuch Materialien, 2112), 342 pp., contains 17 contributions, wideranging, all except two of them written for this volume: K. Briegleb, 'Abgesang auf Geschichte? Hs jüdisch-poetische Hegelrezeption'; H. Heissenbüttel, 'Materialismus und Phantasmagorie im Gedicht.

Anmerkungen zur Lyrik H.Hs' (previously published, 1972); P. Stein, '"Prototyp einer Denk- und Schreibweise". H.Hs *Reisebilder* als Auftakt zur "Julirevolution der deutschen Literatur"'; G. Höhn, 'H.H. und die Genealogie des modernen Intellektuellen'; F. Mende, 'H.H., "Sohn der Revolution"'; W. Preisendanz, 'Der Ironiker H. Ambivalenzerfahrung und kommunikative Ambiguität'; N. Altenhofer, 'Chiffre, Hieroglyphie. Vorformen tiefenhermeneutischer und intertextueller Interpretation im Werk Hs' (previously published, 1979); R. Hosfeld, 'Welttheater als Tragikomödie. Ein denkbarer Dialog Hs mit der Moderne'; H. Pepperle, 'H.H. als Philosoph'; G. Höhn, '"Blutrosen" der Freiheit. H.Hs Geschichtsdenken'; B. Kortländer, 'Poesie und Lüge. Zur Liebeslyrik des *Buchs der Lieder*'; J. Hermand, 'Von Buch der Lieder zu den *Verschiedenen*. Hs zweimalige Partnerverfehlung'; K. Fingerhut, 'H. der Satiriker'; J. A Kruse, 'H.H. — Der Lazarus'; M. Windfuhr, 'Der Erzähler H. *Der Rabbi von Bacherach* als historischer Roman'; W. Werner, 'Der Journalist H.'; R. C. Holub, 'H. als Mythologe'. The third volume of essays derives from an international symposium at Cornell University in 1988: *H.H. and the Occident. Multiple Identities, Multiple Receptions*, ed. Peter Uwe Hohendahl and Sander L. Gilman, Lincoln — London, Nebraska U.P., 235 pp. It contains an introduction by the editors stressing the varying reception of H.'s multifaceted work in European countries and in the Americas; J. Hermand, 'One identity is not enough; H.'s legacy to Germans, Jews, and Liberals'; M. Werner, 'Crossing borders between cultures; on the preconditions and function of H.'s reception in France'; E. Schwarz, 'H., *Don Quijote*, and the generation of 1898'; L. Zagari, 'Permanence in change: H.'s reception in Italian culture through two centuries'; S. Zantop, 'Colonialism, cannibalism, and literary incorporation: H. in Mexico'; H. Steinecke, '"The lost cosmopolite": H.'s images of foreign cultures and peoples in the historical poems of the late period'; T. J. Reed, 'History in nutshells: H. as a cartoonist'; J. A. Kruse, 'The diversity of H.'s reception in Western European and American art'; R. A. Berman, 'Poetry for the Republic: H. and Whitman'.

H-Jb., 30, has P. Hasubek, 'Dreiecksverhältnis: Campe — Immermann — H. mit 28 unveröffentlichten Briefen Julius Campes an Immermann'; G. Söhn, 'Von gereizter Höflichkeit zu gehässiger Gegnerschaft. Zum Verhältnis Wolfgang Menzel — H.H.'; P. L. Rose, 'H. and Wagner revisited: art, myth and revolution'; K. Kranke, 'Richard von Zychlinski. Biographische Entdeckungen zu H.Hs letzten Sekretär'; P. Peters, 'Die Abbildung des Bildlosen. Zu H.Hs "Morphine"'; U. Pongs, 'Was ist klassisch? Zur Antike-Rezeption H.Hs'; A. Dorschel, 'Stilisierte Simplizität. Hs "Ich stand in dunkeln Traümen" in Schuberts Kompositionen'; F. Mende,

'"Schufterle" in der "Livree der Tagesidee". Zum Streit H. — Gutzkow'; G. Pauls, '"Deutsche und französische Frauen". Zu einem Heineschen Fragment'; H. Henning, 'Gobineaus Urteil über Hs "Deutschland ein Wintermärchen" aus dem Jahre 1844'. Other items include speeches by Marion Gräfin Dönhoff, Ralf Dahrendorf, Max Frisch, Christoph Hein, reviews, bibliographies, etc. A. Gleber, 'Briefe aus Berlin: H.H. und eine Ästhetik der Moderne', *Monatshefte*, 82:452–66. R. Geissler, 'H., der Dichter', *LitL*:46–62. C. Perels, '"Wahlverwandte Farbtöne". H.Hs Lyrik im Licht seiner Schrift *Französische Maler*', *JFDH*:179–206. H. Rölleke, '"Das Grauen". Georg Trakl und H.H.?', *WW*, 41:163–65. R. Anglade, 'Mignons emanzipierte Schwester. Hs kleine Harfenistin und ihre Bedeutung', *GRM*, 41:301–21. D. Arendt, 'Die Maskerade der Weltgeschichte oder "Dieser [...] Karneval beginnt und endet mit dem ersten Januar und endigt mit dem einundreißigsten Dezember"', *LitL*, 147–66. K. Narayana Chandron, 'A portmanteau allusion to Arnold — H. in Henry James's "London"', *ASNS*, 1990:327–29.

HENSEL, LUISE. Oskar Köhler, *'Müde bin ich, geh' zur Ruh': die hell-dunkle Lebensgeschichte L.Hs*, Paderborn, Schöningh, 132 pp., is an engaging account of the life. A. J. Harper, 'L.H.: Profile of a Romantic poetess', pp. 35–51 of *Women Writers in the Age of Goethe*, III, ed. M. C. Ives (Occasional Papers in German Studies, 3), Lancaster University, 52 pp., offers a concise, useful introduction to the life and works.

HERWEGH. M. Krausnick, *Die eiserne Lerche. G. H. Dichter und Rebell*, Baden Baden, Signal, 176 pp.

HESEKIEL. See under ALEXIS.

HEYSE. The reprint edition of P.H., *Gesammelte Werke*, 15 vols, Stuttgart 1924, is now complete with the appearance of section 3, vol. 5, *Hadrian. Alkibiades. Gedichte*, Hildesheim, Olms, 817 pp.

HILLEBRAND. G. Marahrens, 'Über den problematischen humanistischen Idealismus von K.H.', *ABNG*, 31–33, 1990–91:321–66. W. Maurer, 'K. Hillebrand. Revolutionär, Grenzgänger, Europäer', *Germanica*, 7, 1990:15–25.

IMMERMANN. K. I., *Der Karneval und die Somnambule: aus den Memoiren eines Unbedeutenden: Erzählung. Mit einem Nachwort von Fritz Böttger*, Berlin, Vlg der Nation, 1989, 129 pp. *K.I. 1796–1840. Ein Dichter zwischen Poesie und sozialer Wirklichkeit. Ausstellung des Heinrich-Heine-Instituts*, Düsseldorf, Heinrich-Heine-Institut, 1990, 68 pp. See article by P. Hasubek in *Heine-Jb.*, 30, with unpublished correspondence of Campe to I., and book by Maierhofer, p. 780 above.

KAISER. Jeanne Bernay, *F.K. Gesamtprimärbibliographie seiner dramatischen Produktion zwischen 1835–1874 (Nachlaß 1875)*, Berne, Lang, lv + 396 pp.

KELLER. *'Du hast alles, was mir fehlt . . .' G.K. im Briefwechsel mit Paul Heyse*, ed. Fridolin Stähli, Zurich, Gut, 1990, 311 pp., completes this elegant four-volume set of K.'s correspondence. (See *YWMLS*, 51 : 777, for the last volume.) This one collects not only K.'s 50 letters to Heyse and Heyse's 43 letters to K., but also postcards, telegrams, watercolours, sketches, and photographs. It is a great boon to have this important correspondence complete here in such a nicely produced volume, with an introduction sketching in the lives of the writers and their relationship, and evaluating the correspondence. There are also copious annotations and an index. G.K., *Sieben Legenden. Das Sinngedicht. Martin Salander*, ed. Dominik Müller, DKV, 1208 pp., is vol. 6 of G.K., *Sämtliche Werke*. (See *YWMLS*, 51 : 776–77; 52 : 765.) This edition is distinguished by the thoroughness and clear structure of its critical apparatus. A brief introduction to K.'s later work argues that the novel is both response to the story cycles and linked by common techniques. Editorial principles are explained. Each work is dealt with from the point of view of genesis, different versions where relevant (the early versions of the *Sieben Legenden* are included), the author's view of his work and his exchange of views with other writers, reception, structure and content, text, and sources. Explanatory notes to the text are provided. Once again, although this is not a historical-critical edition, praise for its fine appearance and excellent apparatus cannot be too high. G.K., *Die Jugenddramen*, ed. Laurence A. Rickels, Zurich, Amman, 1990, 179 pp. Bruno Weber, *G.K. Landschaftsmaler*, Zurich, Vlg Neue Zürcher Zeitung, 1990, 194 pp., with illustrations and facsimiles, is glossy but good. Jeanlouis Cornuz, *G.K.*, Lausanne, Favre, 1990, 286 pp. Theo Loosli, **Fabulierlust und Defiguration. 'Phantastische' Spiele der Ein-bildungskraft im Prosawerk G.Ks* (EH, I, 1251), 411 pp. See also the book by Mark Lehrer, p. 779 above.

An indication of the interest in K. on this side of the channel is the volume of lively essays edited by John L. Flood and Martin Swales, *G.K. 1819–1890. London Symposium 1990* (SAG, 256), 161 pp., which contains K. Pestalozzi, 'K.'s Gedicht "Rosenglaube"'; M. Minden, '*Der grüne Heinrich* and the legacy of *Wilhelm Meister*'; M. Swales, 'Reflectivity and realism. On K.'s *Der grüne Heinrich*'; B. A. Rowley, 'Views of society implied in *Die Leute von Seldwyla*'; T. M . Holmes, '*Romeo und Julia auf dem Dorfe*: the idyll of possessive individualism'; D. Jackson, '*Kleider machen Leute*: literary outfitters by appointment to the muses or to the paying public?'; M. Jacobs, 'The art of allusion in K.'s fiction'; L. Adey, "Göttlicher Unsinn und unbeschränkter Mut-willen": K. and the concept of comedy'; E. Mason, 'Two views on *Bürgerlichkeit* in G.K.'s *Die Leute von Seldwyla*'; E. Swales, 'Dead end(ings) in K.'. Different versions of the articles by M. and E. Swales appeared in the volume edited by Hans Wysling from the Zurich colloquium (see *YWMLS*, 52:765–66). On that, see '"Gefährlich mit Worten und Fäusten." Versuch über das G.K.–Kolloquium vom 13./14. Juli 1990 an der Universität Zürich', *SchM*, 70, 1990:716–29. P. Faessler, 'Ks *Fähnlein* — eine rhetorische Deutschstunde', *ib.*, 733–41. H. Bänziger, 'Das Tabernakel des Pfarrers von Schwanau. Zur Kritik des religiösen Liberalismus in Ks Novelle *Das verlorene Lachen*', *ib.*, 529–35. P. Utz, 'Heimatträume. Risse im literarischen Film der Schweiz bei G.K., Robert Walser und Thomas Hürlimann', *ib.*, 71:913–25. M. Stern, 'G.Ks Apotheker und Heine', *Sprachkunst*, 22:49–59. G. Dönni, 'Der Teufel bei L. Th. Kosegarten und in G.Ks *Sieben Legenden*', *ib.*, 61–79. G. Cattaneo, 'König David in G.Ks "Tanzlegendchen"', *ib.*, 71–91. A. Maas, 'Verborgenes Grün. Zu einem Motiv bei G.K.', *Fest. Weber*, 486–97, 537–38. E. Friedrichsmeyer, 'Ks *Spiegel, das Kätzchen*: as eudemonist answer to Goethe's *Faust?*', *Slessarev Vol.*, 131–38. I. Fickel, 'Die Gestaltung von Widerspruch und Konflikt in G.Ks Novelle *Kleider machen Leute*', *NFT*, 18, 1989:31–47.

KERNER.   M. Zybura, '"...die schlechte Revolution." Über J.Ks Verhältnis zum Revolutionsgeschehen in Frankreich', *GeW*, 80, 1990:283–90.

KINKEL, JOHANNA.   J.K., *Hans Ibeles in London. Ein Roman aus dem Flüchtlingsleben*, ed. Ulrike Helmer, Frankfurt, Helmer, 410 pp., is a nicely produced reading edition of this novel with afterword and notes by the editor.

KOHL.   J.G.K., *Reisen durch das weite Land: nordwestdeutsche Skizzen, 1864*, ed. Geert Demarest, Berlin, Neues Leben, 1990, 375 pp., illus., facs.

KOMPERT.   See under THEMES.

LASSBERG.   Martin Harris, *J. M. C. Freiherr v. L. 1770–1855. Briefinventar und Prosopographie. Mit einer Abhandlung zu Ls Entwicklung zum Altertumsforscher* (Beihefte zum *Euphorion*, 25), Heidelberg, Winter, 407 pp., is an impressive piece of compilatory work combined with a detailed examination of L.'s career. The third section, the 'Prosopographie', has 374 alphabetically arranged articles on figures who came into contact with this remarkable man .

LAUBE.   M. Huesmann, '"... sie wissen nicht was sie tun." "Jungdeutsches" Bildungsbewußtsein und bürgerliche Krisenerfahrung als biographische Grundlagen H.Ls', *WW*, 41:27–47.

LENAU.   *Reimregister zu N.Ls Versepen*, ed. Heinrich P. Delfosse, Karl Jürgen Skrodzki and Michael Trauth, Tübingen, Niemeyer, xx + 180 pp., links up with the earlier volume in the series, the 'synoptic concordance' to the verse epics (see *YWMLS*, 51:778), and is divided into alphabetical rhyme list showing frequency and source, list of word stems, distribution list, rhyming pair list to show vowel length, a table showing length of rhyme words and one showing length of syllables. The explanatory introduction has other statistics.

LEWALD, FANNY. I. Stocksieker Di Maio, 'Jewish emancipation and integration: F.Ls narrative strategies', *ABNG*, 31–33, 1990–91:273–301.

MEYER. The projected 15-volume edition, C.F.M., *Sämtliche Werke*, historisch-kritische Ausgabe, ed. H. Zeller and A. Zäch, Berne, Benteli, has produced volume 7, *Die Gedichte aus dem Nachlaß*, 814 pp. Beth L. Mugge-Meiburg, **Words Chiseled into Marble. Artworks in the Prose Narratives of C.F.M.* (NASNCGL, 9), 226 pp. H. Koopmann, 'Grün oder blau? Zu C.F.Ms poetischen Farben', *Fest. Zeller*, 150–58. B. Boeschenstein, 'Anmerkungen zu C.F.Ms "Zwiegespräch"', *ib.*, 159–68. B. Boeschenstein, 'Das Gespräch mit der Muse. Zu C.F.Ms Gedichten', *JFDH*:207–37. T. V. Laane, 'Static and dynamic images as thematic motifs in C.F.M.'s *Die Versuchung des Pescara*', *MGS*, 16, 1990:44–67. H. Kaiser, 'Tod, Erinnerung, Geschichte. Zur Kritik des historischen Bewußtseins in Ms "Huttens letzte Tage" und Storms "Zur Chronik von Grieshuus"', *DUS*, 43:20–31.

MÖRIKE. Susanne Fliegner, *Der Dichter und die Dilettanten: E.Ms Lyrik und die bürgerliche Geselligkeitskultur des 19. Jahrhunderts* (GerAb, 68), 210 pp., is a rich and interesting book, taking its cue from Gerhart von Graevenitz's study of M. (*E.M. Die Kunst der Sünde*, 1978). F. investigates M. from the context of cultural history, showing how the poetry relates to the world it was written for. The starting point is M.'s hypochondria (seen in relation to contemporary medical thinking), and the search for therapeutic preoccupations. The early Tübingen friendships, concern with the Goethe–Schiller correspondence, the attraction to folk-song and progression towards a *poeta doctus*, are all given new emphasis here. Motifs and figures are seen to be anchored in contemporary attitudes: historicism, mythology and the search for stability. M.'s poetic production is seen in relation to the social function of various types of poetry (notably occasional and remembrance poetry), and we are shown how M.'s poetic preoccupations were closely related to the cultural pastimes of his contemporaries (mass dilettantism, musical societies, the cult of the memorial). The Swabian poet's activities as translator and editor, and as collector of artefacts, are placed in their historical and cultural context and used as a basis for explaining important themes and motifs in his poetry. Thus there is no narrow literary perspective here. This is an important book, carefully researched and well written, rewarding with regard to M. and his historical position, but also the cultural life of the Biedermeier in general. Doris Hennemann,

Individuation oder Integration? Ms *Weg zur zweiten Fassung des 'Maler Nolten'* (EH, I, 1216), 146 pp. G. Österle, 'Eingedenken und Erinnern des Überholten und Vergessenen. Kuriositäten und Raritäten in den Werken Goethes, Brentanos, Ms und Raabes', Schulz, *Literatur*, 81–111. H.-G. Gadamer, 'Gesang Weylas', *Fest. Weber*, 169–73, 512. A. Holusch, 'Wem leuchtet Ms "Lampe"?', *ZDP*, 110:574–93.

MUNDT. L. Tatlock, 'Grim wives' tales: M.'s Stieglitz, Stieglitz's Goethe', *Monatshefte*, 82:467–86.

NESTROY. G. Baumbach, 'Fund eines Briefes und einer Zeichnung in Leipzig', *Nestroyana*, 10, 1990:81–84. J. Hein, 'Neue N. Funde: Studiennotizen zu Höllenangst und zwei bislang unbekannte Gedichte', *ib.*, 85–92. H. Stroszeck, **Heilsthematik in der Posse. Über J.Ns 'Der Talisman'*, Aachen, Alano, 1990, 100 pp. *Nestroyana*, 10, 1990, also has M. Rogers, 'Handwerker und Fabrikarbeiter. Die Launen des Komikers' (68–78); R. Theobald, 'N. am Alexanderplatz. Die Berliner Erstaufführung von *Zur ebener Erde und erster Stock*' (55–67); W. E. Yates, 'Nachträge und Berichtigungen zum Band *Stücke 34* der historisch-kritischen Nestroyausgabe ("Nur keck!")' (79–80). *Nestroyana*, 11, has G. Baumbach, 'Vorstellung zweier Welten und das Prinzip der Verkehrung' (7–15); J. Hein, 'Nur Gutes! — Nur Böses! Raimund, Nestroy und die Metaphysik des Wiener Volkstheaters' (19–24); W. Obermaier, 'Ein unbekannter Bericht zur Premiere von *Robert der Teuxel*' (25–29); H. J. Koning, 'Louis Ferron und N.' (32–34). W. Häusler, '"Wart's Gourmanninen!" Vom Essen und Trinken in Ns Possen und in Ns Zeit', *ÖGL*, 35:217–41. F. Walla, 'J.N. im Urteil und Vorurteil der Kritik', *ib.*, 242–62. M. Kastl, 'Beobachtungen zur barocken Predigttradition bei N.', *Jb. der Grillparzer-Gesellschaft*, 17. C. Decker, 'The hermeneutics of democracy: N., Horváth, Turrini and the development of the "Volksstück"', *Seminar*, 27:219–32. See article by A. S. Coulson under HEBBEL.

NIETZSCHE. The N. HKA founded by Giorgio Colli and Mazzino Montinari and continued by Wolfgang Müller-Lauter and Karl Pestalozzi has produced vol. IV, 4, *Nachbericht zum ersten Band der sechsten Abteilung: Also sprach Zarathustra*, Berlin, de Gruyter, 985 pp. F.N., '*Dionysos — Dithyramben*', ed. Wolfram Groddeck, Berlin, de Gruyter, has 2 vols: *Textgenetische Edition der Vorstufen und Reinschriften*, lvi + 156 pp. + 142 pp. pls, and *Die 'Dionysos-Dithyramben'; Bedeutung und Entstehung von Ns letztem Werk*, xxii + 484 pp. Keith May, **N. and the Spirit of Tragedy*, Basingstoke, Macmillan, 216 pp. Alan White, *Within N.'s Labyrinth*, London, Routledge, 1990, xiv + 187 pp. *N. and Modern German Thought*, ed. Keith Ansell-Pearson, London, Routledge, 314 pp., contains a number of articles of philosophical interest. W. Wiley Richards, **The Bible and Christian Traditions. Keys to*

Understanding the Allegorical Subplot of N.'s Zarathustra (AUS, VII, 75), 1990, 425 pp. Greg Whitlock, *Returning to Sils-Maria. A Commentary to N.'s 'Also sprach Zarathustra'* (AUS, V, 87), xx + 328 pp. *N.-Studien*, 20, has appeared with a wide range of articles. W. Groddeck, '"Gedichte und Sprüche". Überlegungen zur Problematik einer vollständigen, textkritischen Ausgabe von Ns Gedichten', *Fest. Zeller*, 169–80. J. L. Pettey, 'The stranger's return: Strindberg, Kierkegaard, and N.', *OL*, 46 : 13–26. G. Merlio, 'Erlösung vom Erlöser. Ns Weg von Wagner zu sich selbst', *TI*, 5, 1990 : 155–77. R. Reschke, 'Einspruch gegen "abgeirrte Cultur". Zu einigen Konturen Nietzschescher Kultur-kritik', *WB*, 37 : 165–85. J. Lungstrum, 'Kafka, N. and creativity', *Seminar*, 27 : 102–20. V. P. Pecora, 'N. genealogy, critical theory', *NGC*, 53 : 104–30. R. Grimminger, 'Offenbarung und Leere. N., Freud, Paul de Man", *Merkur*, 45 : 387–402. S. Grgas, 'Tragic affirmation in Yeats and N.', *OL*, 46 : 165–79. B. A. Sørensen, 'Laura Marholm, Fr. N. und G. Hauptmanns *Einsame Menschen*', *OL*, 46 : 52–62. E. Herity, 'Robert Musil and N.', *MLR*, 86 : 911–23. T. J. Howell, 'Early and late deconstructions: N.'s surviving role in the philosophy of literature and psychology', *Literature and Psychology*, 37 : 45–58. See also book by Hillebrand, p. 775 above.

PFEIFFER, IDA.   H. S. Watt, 'I.P.: a nineteenth-century woman travel writer', *GQ*, 64 : 339–52.

PÜCKLER-MUSKAU.   P.-M., *Briefe eines Verstorbenen*, ed. Günter J. Vaupel, 2 vols, Frankfurt, Insel, 857, 751 pp., is an attractive reading edition of these letters, presented, as the author intended, back-to-front, that is with the earlier letters (called Parts III and IV) in vol. 1. Included are selected letters from P.-M.'s *Nachlaß* relevant to the published letters, with those written in French and English having been translated. The edition includes contemporary illustrations (from English and French editions) and there are notes and an afterword by the editor. The editions of 1836 (for Part I and II) and 1837 (for Parts II and IV) have been compared with the first editions of 1830 and 1832 respectively.

RAABE.   W.R., *Holunderblüte*, ed. Dieter Arendt (UB, 8485), 60 pp., follows the edition by Karl Hoppe *et al.* (1962). *R.-Jb.* has G. Köpf's W. R. Prize Speech (1990), and the following: F. Henrich, '"Wunsidel und die Gründung des Deutschen Nationalvereins." Polarität und Komplexität in W.Rs "Gutmanns Reisen"'; E. Meyer-Krenter, 'Elektronische Einsicht, Neue Zugänge zu Rs Tagebuch'; R. Noltenius, 'Die Einheit Deutschlands unter einem Schriftsteller als Führer. Rs Schiller-Gedicht 1859 als politische Glaubensbekenntnis'; A. Schweimler, 'Tumurkieland Albert Dulk — ein mögliches Vorbild für Leonhard Hagebucher?'; S. Diebitz, '"Wiederlesen im eigenen Lebensbuche." W.Rs "Alte Nester", interpretiert als Palimpsest auf

"Die Kinder von Flikerode"'; R. Schillemeit, 'Der berüchtigte Vers in "Hermann und Dorothea"'; F. Krobb, '"Ganz vertraut und fremd." Jakob Julius David über W.R.'; F. Schüppen, 'Ein Hauch vom ganzen Fontane: "Was ich wollte, was ich würde . . ."'; and an extensive review section and bibliography for the current year. B. O. Peterson, 'Refunctioning history, R. bowdlerized, or *Unseres Herrgotts Kanzlei* as a "myth of descent"', *GQ*, 64:353–67. W. Hanson, 'Florinchen and "die dicke Dame" — the function of female figures in Rs Prinzessin Fisch', *GLL*, 44:306–16. See also the book by Mark Lehrer, p. 779 above, and the article by G. Österle under MÖRIKE.

RAIMUND. Yong-Ho Kim, *Der Ernst von F.Rs Spielen. Unter besonderer Berücksichtigung der Traditionsbezüge und der gesellschaftlichen Funktion seines Theaters* (EH, I, 1269), vi + 254 pp. H. Aust, 'Der tragisch-komische Sinn des Bösen in Rs Schauspielen', *Nestroyana*, 11:16–18. C. N. Jones, 'F.R. and Ödön von Horváth: The *Volksstück* as negation and utopia', *GQ*, 64:325–38. See also article by J. Hein under NESTROY.

ROSENKRANZ. K.R., *Königsberger Skizzen*, ed. Hermann Dembowski, DBO, 189 pp., has the author's foreword (slightly shortened), and 17 of these sketches, based on the text of the first edition (1842), providing the widest selection since then in a pleasantly produced reading edition, with a useful afterword by the editor.

RÜCKERT. S. Taraman, 'Die Funktion des "fremden Wortes" in der arabisch-deutschen Übersetzung des 19. Jahrhunderts', *KGS*, 4, 1989:7–31.

SAAR. Herbert Klauser, *Ein Poet aus Österreich. F.v.S. — Leben und Werk*, Vienna, Literas — Universitätsvlg, 1990. See also the article by P. Howe under STIFTER.

SACHER-MASOCH. L.S.-M., *Das schwarze Kabinett und soziale Schattenbilder*, ed. Karl Emmerich, Berlin, Vlg Neues Berlin. R. Felski, 'The counter discourse of the feminine in three texts by Wiede, Huysmans, and S.-M.', *PMLA*, 106:1094–1105. See also under THEMES.

SEALSFIELD (KARL POSTL). C.S., *Sämtliche Werke*, ed. Karl J. Arndt, Hildesheim, Olms, has added two more volumes: 24, *Journalistik und vermischte Schriften. Christophorus Bärenhäuter. Die Grabesschuld*, ed. Karl Arndt; and 27, *Katalog der Sealsfieldiana in der Zentralbibliothek Solothurn*, ed. Denise Steinmann, which is vol. 3 of the *Supplementreihe 'Materialien und Dokumente'*. J. L. Sammons, 'C.S. A case of non-canonicity', *ABNG*, 31–33, 1990–91:155–72. See also under THEMES.

SPIELHAGEN. Henrike Lamers, *Held oder Welt? Zum Romanwerk F.Ss*, Bonn, Bouvier, 261 pp., emphasizes the poles of individual and society in five novels by S. and the increasing disorientation of the individual which is revealed in them. L. studies the novels from the point of view of the intersection they represent between 'Bildungsro-man' and 'Zeitroman'. She includes a section on S.'s biography and the reception of his works, previous scholarship is summarized, and this worthwhile study concludes by raising the question of S.'s literary reputation anew, stressing his importance for an understand-ing of the development of the novel in the 20th c. Rosa-Maria Zinken, *Der Roman als Zeitdokument. Bürgerlicher Liberalismus in F.Ss 'Die von Hohenstein' (1863/64)* (KSL, 4), 295 pp. See also the article by K. Imm in the volume by Jörg Schönert, p. 778 above.

STIFTER. A.S., *Die kleinen Dinge schreien drein. 59 Briefe,* ed. Werner Welzig, Frankfurt, Insel, 231 pp., is a reliably edited selection of S.'s letters designed to illustrate the tensions within S.'s life. Brigid Haines, *Dialogue and Narrative Design in the Works of A.S.* (BSD, 17; MHRA Texts and Dissertations, 34), London, MHRA, 158 pp., is an extremely useful study of the 'crucial interplay' between dialogue and narrative in S.'s works. H. is aware that estimations of S.'s art depend to a large extent on what we make of the handling of dialogue in them and sets about a systematic analysis of three works. Not the least important aspect of this thesis is that it confidently enters the theoretical discussion on dialogue and narrative, setting up the kind of solid and clearly defined critical concepts which have been sadly lacking in previous discussions of dialogue in S. Three works are examined in detail (*Der beschriebene Tännling, Der Nachsommer, Die Mappe meines Urgroßvaters*), and there is a close focus on the nuts and bolts of dialogue. The study profits from a comparison of different versions of these texts where relevant and highlights the importance of dialogue for the structure and meaning of the works. A refreshing view is taken of the stylization of dialogue in these later works. Stefan Braun, *'Lebenswelt' bei A.S.* (FLK, 29), 148 pp. Karen Danford, *The Family in A.S.'s Moral and Aesthetic Universe. A Rarefied Vision* (NASNCGL, 7), 190 pp. Carola Salm, *Reale und symbolische Ordnungen in Ss Nachsommer* (EH, 1, 1254), 219 pp. *VASILO,* 39.3–4, has M. Beckmann, 'Die ästhetische Funktion des Weg-Motivs in Ss *Nachsom-mer*' (3–23); E. Grimm, 'Vorspiel zum Glück. Heinrich Drendorfs *Nachsommer*' (25–39); 'A.-S.-Bibliographie' (41–69); 'Presse-Echo' (70–86). E. Mason, 'S. and the Enlightenment', *ASt,* 2:102–16. R. G. Rogan, 'S.'s *Brigitta*: the eye to the soul', *GSR,* 13, 1990:243–51. M.-C. Méry, 'La description dans *Der Nachsommer* de S. Peinture de genre ou trompe-l'œil?', *TI,* 5, 1990:129–53. J. Louzil, 'F. T. Bratraneks Beitrag zum A.-S.-Verständnis', *PhP,* 33, 1990:20–28. P. Howe, 'Faces and fortunes: ugly heroines in S.'s *Brigitta*, Fontane's *Schach von Wuthenow* and Saar's *Sappho*', *GLL,* 44:426–43.

STORM. *T.S. — Otto Speckter. T.S. — Hans Speckter. Briefwechsel — Kritische Ausgabe,* ed. Walter Hettche, Berlin, Schmidt, 216 pp., 10 pls, documents the relationship between S. and these two artists in the years 1859–87, offering insights into S.'s life and the interplay of art and literature. Most of the 92 letters edited here (using the MSS) were unpublished. This edition also includes an excerpt from Auguste Speckter's family chronicle and Hans Speckter's autobiography, his obituary of Morgenstern as well as his own obituary. As with previous volumes (this is vol. 12), the notes are copious and the critical apparatus is of a high standard. A delight to use. Hans-Heinrik Krummacher, 'Lebensrückblick im Brief. Eine unbekannte Korrespondenz T.Ss mit seinem einstigen Lübecker Mitschüler Marcus von Heise-Rotenburg', *Fest. Mayer*, 61–116. Gertrud Storm, **T.S. Ein Bild seines Lebens*, 2 vols, 2nd edn, Berlin 1912–13, ed. Walter Zimorski, Hildesheim, Olms, 490 + 36 pp., is a useful reprint of this early biography. E. Downing, 'Repetition and realism: the "Ligea" impulse in T.S.'s *Viola tricolor*', *DVLG*, 65:265–303. A. Stolpe, '"Matthias Claudius" und T.Ss Vorstellungen von Leben und Tod', **Wandsbek zu Hause. Essays zur Würdigung des 'Wandsbecker Boten' Matthias Claudius im Gedenkjahr 1990*, ed. G.-W. Röpke, Hamburg, Heinevetter, 1990, 159 pp. See also the articles by B. Mullan under GRILLPARZER and by P. Howe under MEYER.

TEMME. W. Freund, 'Demokrat, Richter, Kriminalautor. Eine Wiederbegegnung mit Jodokus Donatus Hubertus T.', *ABNG*, 31–33, 1990–91:257–71.

WAGNER. Two books using very different approaches to W deserve special mention this year: Andrea Mork, *R.W. als politischer Schriftsteller: Weltanschauung und Wirkungsgeschichte*, Frankfurt, Campus, 280 pp., takes up the old chestnut of W.'s influence on the Third Reich, telling us that a good deal of aesthetic whitewashing has gone on and that we need to focus clearly once again on W. as precursor. W.'s vision of a nationalistic consciousness unfolding itself according to the principles of art is the point of departure, and the political dimension of his mythology is in the foreground. The book's argument proceeds vigorously, thus: an examination of the influences on W.'s thought; W. is seen as anti-Enlightenment, anti-political thinker, embracing the notion of the German 'Sonderweg'; his mythology, an alternative plan for his middle-class society, is shown as the dream of a return to pre-modern forms of consciousness and social life, leading to anti-democratic models of order. W.'s ideal of German identity is developed by Wagnerians into a racist mythology, Bayreuth's role in the Third Reich is re-examined. Finally we see how W.'s ideas were used and adapted by the National Socialists, the large role of aestheticized means of control being possible because their philosophy is a conglomerate of myths. Mork's study is provocative and she is careful: she aims to show how the 'völkisch-rassistisch[er]

Nationalismus' in W.'s writings became what it did. She shows that W. cannot be seen as the unpolitical figure he thought he was or others saw him as. Her book is a significant contribution to the continuing debate on W.'s political meaning which is reflected in the discussion on how to produce his operas. In her introduction M. quotes Brecht's phrase about the hollow heroism of W.'s characters. Just how complex and interesting the relationship between Brecht and Wagner proves to be on closer inspection is revealed by Hilda Meldrum Brown, *Leitmotiv and Drama. W, Brecht, and the Limits of the 'Epic' Theatre*, Oxford, Clarendon, 217 pp. B. is concerned to refute accepted notions of discontinuity in the German dramatic tradition and brings to the fore neglected links between W. and Brecht, in particular the latter's exploitation of leitmotiv networks. A theoretical introduction (suggesting overemphasis on narrative in recent theory and disregard of intrinsic perspectivism) is followed by an examination of W.'s antecedents (Lessing, Schiller), a section insisting on the dramatic (as opposed to epic) nature of leitmotiv, and the role of reflection and intuition. A reinterpretation of Brecht's theories and their relation to his dramatic practice follows, with four exemplary chapters, which provide close readings of plays. It is particularly the distinction between *Grundmotiv* and *Nebenmotiv* which is found to be relevant to Brecht's plays. In this original and firmly argued study, B. throws new light not only on the theory and practice of W.'s music drama but also Brecht's relation to it. An important book. William O. Cord, *The Teutonic Mythology of R.W.'s the 'Ring of the Nibelung'*, 3 vols, Lewiston, Edwin Mellen Press, consists of vol. 1, *Nine Dramatic Properties*, 1989, 176 pp., vol. 2, *The Family of Gods*, 1990, 225 pp., and vol. 3, *The Natural and Supernatural Worlds* 1991, 607 pp. Elizabeth Magee, **Richard Wagner and the Nibelungs*, OUP, 1990, 224 pp. L. J. Rather, **Reading Wagner: A Study in the History of Ideas*, Louisiana State U.P., 1990, 368 pp.

B. Coghlan, ' "Was deutsch und echt" — Was deutsch und recht? Gedanken zum Bild des deutschen Meisters im deutschen Musiktheater (R. W., Hans Pfitzner, Paul Hindemith)', Schulz, *Literatur*, 181–217. B. Laroche, ' "Merkt auf die Wort." Die Porträt-rezeption im *Fliegenden Holländer* von R.W.', *Arntzen Vol.*, 220–36. P. O. Brønsted, 'R.W.'s Siegfried and the ancient satyr drama', *Edda*: 40–44. T. Koebner, 'Minne Macht. Zu R.Ws Bühnenwerk Der Ring des Nibelungen', Heinzle, *Nibelungen*, 309–32. M. Poster, 'What does Wotan want?: Ambivalent feminism in Wagner's Ring', *NGC*, 53: 131–48. See also article by P. L. Rose in *Heine-Jb.*, 30.

LITERATURE, 1880–1945

By MALCOLM HUMBLE, *Lecturer in German in the University of St Andrews*

I. GENERAL

LITERARY HISTORIES AND SURVEYS. Hermann Boeschenstein, *A History of Modern German Literature*, ed. Rodney Symington (CSGLL, 40), 292 pp., is a survey from Nietzsche to the present with the emphasis on the continuity of the humanistic tradition in the modern era. A large number of authors receive attention in a fluent and easily digested narrative. Raymond Furness and Malcolm Humble, *A Companion to Twentieth Century German Literature*, London, Routledge, 305 pp., contains about 200 entries on authors of the period active in the major genres, with basic biographical facts, information on involvement in literary groups, movements, and political developments.

MOVEMENTS AND PERIODS. K. Roper, *German Encounters with Modernity: Novels of Imperial Berlin*, Humanities Press International, Atlantic Highlands, N.J., 280 pp. Id., 'Novels of Imperial Berlin. In search of the German revolution', Brude-Firnau, *Fact*, 123–34. Hans-Joachim Eberhard, *Intellektuelle der Kaiserzeit* (EH, I, 1200), 144 pp. James W. Jones, *We of the Third Sex. Literary Representations of Homosexuality in Wilhelmine Germany* (GLC, 7), 348 pp. *Deutsche Dichtung um 1900. Beiträge zu einer Literatur im Umbruch*, ed. Robert Leroy and Eckart Pastor, Berne, Lang, 450 pp. Marianne Wünsche, *Die fantastische Literatur der frühen Moderne (1890–1930)*, Munich, Fink, 264 pp. Heide Eilert, *Das Kunstzitat in der erzählenden Dichtung. Studien zur Literatur um 1900*, Stuttgart, Steiner, 378 pp., is a *Habilitationsschrift* which documents and analyses references to works of fine art, dramas, operas, music, and novels in the narrative works of Heinrich and Thomas Mann, Rilke, Schnitzler, Wasserman, Keyserling, Carl Hauptmann and a number of minor writers of the turn of the century. The emphasis is placed on dramatic performance and some of the material will be familiar to readers of Koppen and Furness on Wagner's influence. The scale and thoroughness of this study, supported by numerous reproductions of the paintings discussed, make it much more than an illumination of *fin-de-siècle* aestheticism; its main value lies in the way connections are made between the meaning of the art and the psychological development of the characters and their relationships. J. M. Fischer, 'Jahrhundert-dämmerung. Kleines Glossar des Fin de siècle', *Merkur*, 44, 1990:999–1005. P. Schünemann, 'Rückkehr in die Zukunft. Skizzen zum Expressionismus', *NRu*, 102.1:159–69. R. J. Murphy, 'The

Expressionist revolution: the re-writing of the discursive world', *GQ*, 64:464–74. Manfred Gierke, **Probleme der Epochenkonstituierung des Expressionismus* (BSDL, 22), 437 pp. Hans-Georg Schmidt-Bergmann, **Die Anfänge der literarischen Avantgarde in Deutschland — Über Anverwandlung und Abwehr des italienischen Futurismus. Ein literarischer Beitrag zum expressionistischen Jahrzehnt*, Stuttgart, M & P Vlg, 474 pp. J. Hermand, 'Die sogenannten Zwanziger Jahre. Ein kritischer Rückblick auf die Kultur der Weimarer Republik', *Fest. Grimm*, 3–22. M. A. Weiner, 'Urwaldmusik and the borders of German identity: Jazz in literature of the Weimar Republic', *GQ*, 64:475–87. K. Petersen, 'Legalität oder Legitimität? Die Justizkrise um 1918 aus der Sicht der Literatur', Brude-Firnau, *Fact*, 165–72. G. D. Feldman, 'Weimar writers and the German inflation', *ib.*, 173–84. A. Todorow, 'Frauen im Journalismus der Weimarer Republik', *IASL*, 16, 2:84–103. D. Mayer, '"Die Weltbühne", ein Forum linksbürgerlichen Denkens', *LitL*, no. 2:100–14. D. Schiller, 'Europa-Ideen der literarischen Linken. Demokratische Europa-Konzepte und deutsch-französische Beziehungen in der deutschen Literatur der 20er und 30er Jahre', *WB*, 37:186–95. Manfred Altner, **Kinder- und Jugendliteratur der Weimarer Republik* (Studien zur Germanistik und Anglistik, 9), Frankfurt, Lang, 294 pp. Edelgard Spaude-Schulze, **Macht das Maul auf! Kinder- und Jugendliteratur gegen den Krieg in der Weimarer Republik* (Ep, 66), 182 pp. H. Haarmann, '"... nur meines Kummers Gewalt sänftigen können sie nicht./Seit ich die Heimat verließ .." Exil, Exilliteratur und Exilpublizistik', *IASL*, 16:79–93. D. Schiller, 'Diskussionen um den Freiheitsbegriff im englischen Exil 1944/45', *Exil*, 11:93–99. W. Koepke, 'The exiles' view of France', Pfanner, *Der Zweite Weltkrieg*, 53–62. C. Eykman, 'Der Krieg in Frankreich: Drei Perspektiven', *ib.*, 63–72. **Autour du 'front populaire allemand': études. Einheitsfront — Volksfront*, ed. Michel Grunwald and Frithjof Trapp (Contacts, ser. III. Études et Documents, 9), Berne, Lang, 1990, 363 pp. E. Loewy, 'Zum Paradigmawechsel in der Exilliteraturforschung', *Exilforschung* 9:208–17. **Rückkehr aus dem Exil. Emigranten aus dem Dritten Reich in Deutschland nach 1945. Essays zu Ehren von Ernst Loewy*, ed. Thomas Koebner and Erwin Rotermund, Marburg, 1990, 175 pp. A. Reiter, 'Literature and survival: the relationship between fact and fiction in concentration camp memoirs', *JES*, 21:259–79. L. Bluhm, **Das Tagebuch zum Dritten Reich: Zeugnisse der Inneren Emigration von Jochen Klepper bis Ernst Jünger*, Bonn, Bouvier, 320 pp.

    AUSTRIA, PRAGUE, AND SWITZERLAND. **Vermittlungen. Texte und Kontexte österreichischer Literatur und Geschichte im 20. Jahrhundert*, ed. Walter Weiss and Ernst Hanisch, Salzburg, Residenz, 1990, 280 pp. Jacques Le Rider, *Das Ende der Illusion. Die Wiener Moderne und die Krisen der Identität*, Vienna, Österreichischer Bundesverlag, 1990,

496 pp. W. Pöckl, 'Österreichische Schriftsteller als Übersetzer François Villons', Pöckl, *Dichter*, 187–210. K. Brzovic, 'Towards a reassessment of Fin-de-Siècle Vienna', *OL*, 46:257–75. Gerald Stieg, *Frucht des Feuers*. *Canetti, Doderer, Kraus und der Justizpalastbrand*, Vienna, Österreichischer Bundesverlag, 1990, 237 pp. *Austria and the Thirties: Culture and Politics*, ed. K. Segar and J. Warren, Riverside, California, Ariadne, 384 pp., contains 18 contributions which trace the development from democracy through the Austro-Fascist corporate state to the *Anschluß* in publishing, the theatre, the cinema, philosophy, and in the work of Bronnen, S. Zweig, Auernheimer, F. Braun, Horváth, Kramer, Soyfer, Freud, and Kraus. *Eine schwierige Heimkehr. Österreichische Literatur im Exil 1938–1945*, ed. Johann Holzner, Sigurd Paul Scheichl and Wolfgang Wiesmüller, Innsbruck, Institut für Germanistik, 560 pp., covers all aspects of its subject in 24 contributions, in which lesser-known figures, e.g. Anna Gmeyner, Lili Körber, Ernst Lothar, Hermynia zur Mühlen, are represented. Karl Müller, *Zäsuren ohne Folgen. Das lange Leben der literarischen Antimoderne Österreichs seit den 30er Jahren*, Salzburg, Müller, 1990, 376 pp., concentrates on Waggerl, Spunda, Schreyvogl and Mell. J. P. Stern, 'Über Prager deutsche Literatur', *Merkur*, 45:1–10. *Berlin und der Prager Kreis*, ed. Margarita Pazi and Hans Dieter Zimmermann, Würzburg, Königshausen & Neumann, 303 pp., has 20 contributions on a wide range of Prague authors, including not only Werfel, Kornfeld, Brod, Kafka, Ernst Weiss, Urzidil, and Kisch, but also lesser-known figures. **Prager Profile: vergessene Autoren im Schatten Kafkas*, ed. Hartmut Binder, Berlin, Gebrüder Mann, 1990. Maria Klanska, *Problemfeld Galizien. Zur Thematisierung eines nationalen und politisch-sozialen Phänomens in deutschsprachiger Prosa 1846–1914*, Cologne, Böhlau, 232 pp. *Unerkannt und (un)bekannt. Deutsche Literatur in Mittel- und Osteuropa*, ed. Carola Gotzmann (Edition Orpheus, 5), Tübingen, Francke, 400 pp., surveys the literature of all the German-speaking minorities of Eastern Europe in 12 contributions. Klaus Pezold *et al.*, *Geschichte der deutschsprachigen Schweizer Literatur im 20. Jahrhundert*, Berlin, Volk & Wissen, 363 pp.

THEMES AND TECHNIQUES. Thomas Keck, **Der deutsche 'Baudelaire'*, I. *Studien zur übersetzerischen Rezeption der 'Fleurs du Mal'*. II. *Materialien* (BNL, 112), 2 vols, 244, 210 pp. Walter Grünzweig, **Walt Whitman. Die deutschsprachige Rezeption als interkulturelles Phänomen*, Munich, Fink, 315 pp. F. Weber, 'Die Nietzsche-Rezeption im George-Kreis', *DK*, 40. 3–4, 1990, 3–18. C. Diethe, 'The dance theme in German Modernism', *GLL*, 44:330–52. Ulrich Ott, **Amerika ist anders. Studien zum Amerika-Bild in deutschen Reiseberichten des 20. Jahrhunderts*, Frankfurt, Lang, 479 pp. Ursula Sampath, *Kaspar Hauser: A Modern Metaphor* (SGLLC, 67), 163 pp., is probably the fullest account in any language of the legend's literary treatment and allows broad changes in the conception of the foundling to emerge clearly. A. D. White, 'Modernism in German literature: a review article', *MLR*, 86:924–28. H. Ochm, 'Künstlerische Avantgarde und ästhetischer Totalitätsbegriff bei Einstein, Brecht und Benjamin', *Fest. Schumacher*, 153–74. R. Nägele, 'Ornamente des Lebens. Leben und Kunst bei Benjamin und Lukács', *Fest. Verbeeck*, 135–58. Bettina Kümmerling-Meibauer, *Die Kunstmärchen von Hofmannsthal, Musil und Döblin* (KGS, 32), x + 297 pp. R. Alter, *Necessary Angels: Tradition and Modernity in Kafka, Benjamin and Scholem*, Cambridge, Mass., Harvard U.P., 131 pp. *Akten* (Tokyo), I–XI, has over 60 papers relevant to the period; in accordance with the congress's overall theme ('Begegnung mit dem "Fremden"') the authors most commonly represented are those with exotic interests and special links with the Far East (Döblin, Dauthendey, Hesse, Feuchtwanger) and the exiles of the Third Reich.

2. Drama

Drama und Theater der Jahrhundertwende, ed. Dieter Kafitz (MFDT, 5), 313 pp. J. Hein, 'Unbewältigte Realität und Verstummen des Dialogs. Bemerkungen zum Volksstück um 1930', *Arntzen Vol.*, 501–12. *Exiltheater und Exildramatik 1933–1945*, ed. Edita Koch and Frithjof Trapp (*Exil*, Sonderband 2). H. Kreuzer, '"Ostfront" 1941. Ein dramatisches Thema in drei Variationen von Herbert Reinacker, Johannes R. Becher und Heiner Müller', *Eggert, Geschichte*, 330–52.

3. Poetry

Jürgen Froehlich, *Liebe im Expressionismus. Eine Untersuchung der Lyrik in den Zeitschriften Die Aktion und Der Sturm von 1910–1914* (SMGL, 38), 214 pp. L. Olschner, '"In Widerwärtigkeit des Kriegs", oder: Variationen über keine Heimkehr in der Lyrik der Exildichter', *Pfanner, Der Zweite Weltkrieg*, 239–53.

4. Prose

Klemm, *Romanführer*, summarizes in varying detail all the major novels of the period and supplies pertinent comments on form, theme, place in literary history, and intertextuality. D. Roberts, 'The German historical novel in the twentieth century: continuities and discontinuities: I — theoretical questions', *Roberts, Novel*, 49–58. H. Müller, 'Possibilities of the historical novel in the nineteenth and twentieth centuries', *ib.*, 59–70. Heidy M. Müller, *Töchter und Mütter in deutschsprachiger Erzählprosa von 1885 bis 1935*, Munich, Iudicium,

403 pp. Angela Schmitt-Gläscr, *Politik und Roman. Der Zeitungsroman in der 'Münchner Post' als Zeugnis der kulturpolitischen Verbürgerlichung der SPD. Eine Untersuchung für das Jahr 1930* (MSLKD, 11), xiv + 301 pp. A. von Bormann, 'Der deutsche Exilroman in den Niederlanden. Formsemantische Überlegungen', Onderdelinden, *Exil*, 225–49. Georg Pichler, *Der Spanische Bürgerkrieg (1936–1939) im deutschsprachigen Roman. Eine Darstellung* (EH, 1, 1239), 517 pp. Erna Kritsch Neuse, *Der Erzähler in der deutschen Kurzgeschichte* (SGLLC, 60), 94 pp. Burkhard Spinnen, *Schriftbilder. Studien zu einer Geschichte emblematischer Kurzprosa* (LS, 9), vi + 337 pp., concentrates on Altenberg, Kraus, and Benjamin.

5. INDIVIDUAL AUTHORS

ANDREAS-SALOMÉ, LOU. B. Haines, 'L.A.–S.'s *Fenitschka*: a feminist reading', *GLL*, 45:416–25.

ARENDT, ERICH. S. Schlenstedt, 'Dic Rückkehr E.As aus dem Exil', *Exilforschung*, 9:81–89.

BAHR, HERMANN. S. Brantly, 'Ushering in the 1890s: the letters from Ola Hansson and Laura Marholm to H.B.', *MAL*, 24.1:23–42.

BECHER, JOHANNES R. M. Mieth, '"Der Mensch, der nicht gcschunden wird, wird nicht erzogen." J.R.B. und die Gewalt des Stalinismus', *WB*, 37:764–72. J. E. Michaels, 'Two views of the eastern front: J.R.B.'s *Schlacht um Moskau* and Theodor Plievier's *Stalingrad*', Pfanner, *Der Zweite Weltkrieg*, 123–32.

BENJAMIN, WALTER. Bettine Menke, *Sprachfiguren. Name — Allegorie — Bild bei Walter Benjamin* (TGLSK, 81), 448 pp. Rudolf Speth, *Wahrheit und Ästhetik: Untersuchungen zum Frühwerk Walter Benjamins* (Ep, 64), 322 pp. *Leib- und Bildraum. Lektüren nach Benjamin*, ed. Sigrid Weigel, Colognc, Böhlau, 190 pp. I. Camartin, 'Ibiza Arcadia 1932. Zu W.Bs "In der Sonne"', *Fest. Weber*, 441–50. Y. Furuya, 'Die Sprache als das Fremde. Zu W.Bs "Die Aufgabe des Übersetzers"', *DB*, 87:96–107. C. Kambas, 'Bulletin de Vernuches. Neue Quellen zur Internierung W.Bs', *Exil*, 10, 1990:5–30. G. Smith, '"Das Jüdische versteht sich von selbst": W.Bs frühe Auseinandersetzung mit dem Judentum', *DVLG*, 65:318–34. R. Zschachlitz, 'Waren, Zeichen, Warenzeichen, Allegorien, Huren — In den Pariser Passagen WBs', *EG*, 46:179–202. J.P. Reemtsma, 'Der Bote. W.B. über Karl Kraus', *SuF*, 43:104–15. *MLN*, 106.3, has four articles, by I. Balfour on his view of history, by A. G. Düttmann on his politics of language, by R. Nägele on his monadology, and by T. Schestag on asphalt.

BENN, GOTTFRIED. Mark William Roche, *G.B.'s Static Poetry: Aesthetic and Intellectual-Historical Interpretations* (UNCSGL, 112),

140 pp. W. Buddecke, '"Alles möglich" — Zum Thema Frauen und Liebe in der Lyrik G.Bs', *ZDP*, 110:593–618. R. Grimm, 'The eye of the hurricane: G.B.'s paradox of a historical novel', Roberts, *Novel*, 109–26. H. Müller, 'G.Bs paradoxer Antihistorismus. Einige Überlegungen über Zusammenhänge zwischen ästhetischem Absolutismus und faschistischem Engagement', Eggert, *Geschichte*, 182–95.

BINDING, RUDOLF. J. Margetts, 'Ride a cock horse . . . to see two fine ladies: on the contradictions in R.G.B.'s *Der Opfergang*', *GLL*, 44:110–21.

BORCHARDT, RUDOLF. K. Schumacher, 'Der messianische Liebhaber R.B.', *JDSG*: 234–56.

BRECHT, BERTOLT. Hilda Meldrum Brown, *Leitmotiv and Drama. Wagner, B., and the Limits of 'Epic' Theatre*, Oxford, Clarendon, 217 pp., courageously challenges the consensus on B.'s theory of epic theatre; whatever doubts one may have about the author's theoretical claims, one must acknowledge the insights into particular plays provided by the application of her view of the leitmotiv technique. Kenneth Fowler, *Received Truths: Bertolt Brecht and the Problem of Gestus and Musical Meaning* (AMS Studies in German Language and Culture, 1), NY, AMS Press, 88 pp. H. Heinze, 'Bedeutung und Verfremdung, B~ Semantikmodell gestischer Zeichen', *LiLi*, 21:37–52. J. Kolkenbrock-Netz, 'Geschichte und Geschichten in Bs "Trommeln in der Nacht" (1922/53)', Eggert, *Geschichte*, 172–81. E. Schumacher, 'Brandstiftung am "Hotel zum Reichen Mann". Gedanken nach der zweiten deutschen Novemberrevolution 1989 zur Oper "Aufstieg und Fall der Stadt Mahagonny" von B./Weill', *SuF*, 43:358–72. T. Kuhn, 'The politics of the changeable text: *Furcht und Elend des Dritten Reiches* and the new B. edition', *OGS*, 18–19, 1990:132–49. S. Onderdelinden, 'Der aufhaltsame Aufstieg der Parabelform: B.Bs "Arturo Ui"', Onderdelinden, *Exil*, 250–66. K.-H.J. Schoeps, 'The absent hero and the fall of France: sources of B.B.'s *The Visions of Simone Machard*', *Fest. Grimm*, 201–12. R. Jaretzky, '"Der Sieg der Fünften Kolonne", Frankreich-Kritik in literarischen Werken von B.B. und Lion Feuchtwanger', Pfanner, *Der Zweite Weltkrieg*, 73–85. N. Brough and R. J. Kavanagh, 'But who is Azdak? The main source of B.'s *Der kaukasische Kreidekreis*', *Neophilologus*, 75:573–80. R.Jost, 'Über die Fragwürdigkeit von Bildern — Bs "Kriegsfibel" im gegenwärtigen Kontext', *DD*, 22:231–39. G. Seidel, 'Anerkennung durch Aneignung? Ein Sonett Margarete Steffins, bearbeitet von B.B.', *Fest. Zeller*, 181–85. W. Woesler, 'Bs Kinderlied "Der Schneider von Ulm (Ulm 1952)"', *Euphorion*, 85:182–91. *Lernen im Dialog. Untersuchungen zu B.Bs 'Flüchtlingsgesprächen'*, ed. Gerd Bräuer (Reihe Sprach- und Literaturwissenschaft, 21), Pfaffenweiler, Centaurus, 207 pp. D. Ignasiak, 'Historisches Sujet und aktuelle Bezüge. Zu B.Bs

Erzählung "Die Trophäen des Lukullus" (1939)', *SGP*, 14, 1990:49–64. K. R. Achberger, '"Kunst als Veränderndes"': Bachmann und B.', *Monatshefte*, 83:7–16. D. Scheunemann, 'Montage in theatre and film: observations on Eisenstein and B.', *Avantgarde*, 5–6:109–35. *Brecht Yearbook*, 16, includes, besides three articles on B.'s influence in the Soviet Union, P. Horn, '"Doch die am ärgsten brennen/ Haben keinen, der drum weint." Die Verleugnung der Emotion in den frühen Gedichten Bs' (2–23); C. Kinzer, 'B., the "fable", and the teaching of directing' (24–37); Vera Stegmann, 'Strawinsky, B. und Weill: Stationen des epischen Theaters' (74–96); and H. Teschke, 'Im Dickicht der Städte das Gespenst aus der Zukunft' (132–38).

BROCH, HERMANN. Giscla Roethke, *Zur Symbolik in H.Bs Werken. Platons Höhlengleichnis als Subtext* (Edition Orpheus, 4), Tübingen, Francke, 150 pp. M. Roesler, 'H.Bs Romanwerk: ein Forschungsbericht', *DVLG*, 65:502–87. P. Morgan, 'The artist within and beyond language: art and history in H.B.'s *The Death of Virgil'*, Roberts, *Novel*, 127–44. D. Horrocks, 'The novel as parable of National Socialism: on the political significance and status of H.B.'s *Bergroman'*, *MLR*, 86:361–71. R. Koester, 'H.B. in Amerika. Rezeption eines Exilanten und seiner Werke', *Arntzen Vol.*, 439–52.

CANETTI, ELIAS. Richard H. Lawson, *Understanding Elias Canetti*, Columbia, S.C., South Carolina U.P., 113 pp. *Elias Canetti. Londoner Symposion*, ed. Adrian Stevens and Fred Wagner (SAG, 245), 157 pp., includes contributions on the fantastic aphorism (P. von Matt), C., Kraus and China (E. Timms), the autobiographies (A. Doppler, H. Reiss), *Die Blendung* (A. Stevens, N. Thomas), the dramas (R. Furness). D. Darby, '"'Esse percipi', Sein ist wahrgenommen werden." Perception und Perspective in Berkeley und C.', *Neophilologus*, 75:425–32. J. G. Pankau, 'Körper und Geist. Das Geschlechtsverhältnis in E.Cs Roman *Die Blendung'*, *ColGer*, 23, 1990:146–70. Jutta Paal, *Die Figurenkonstellation in E.Cs Roman 'Die Blendung'*, Würzburg, Königshausen & Neumann, 116 pp. H. Wanninger, 'E.Cs Übersetzungen von Upton Sinclair', Pöckl, *Dichter*, 103–22. N. Thomas, 'E.C.'s *Die Blendung* and Robert Musil's *Der Mann ohne Eigenschaften'*, Hickman, *Musil*, 247–62.

CAROSSA, HANS. *Hans Carossa. Dreizehn Versuche zu seinem Werk*, ed. Hartmut Laufhütte, Tübingen, Niemeyer, 290 pp., has 12 contributions on a representative selection of his work in prose and poetry.

CHRIST, LENA. Ghemela Adler, *Heimatsuche und Identität. Das Werk der bairischen Schriftstellerin Lena Christ* (EH, 1, 1261), 355 pp.

CSOKOR, FRANZ THEODOR. *Immer ist Anfang. Der Dichter Franz Theodor Csokor*, ed. Joseph P. Strelka, Berne, Lang, 193 pp., contains ten contributions on C.'s work in all three major genres.

DÄUBLER, THEODOR.   Carl Schmitt, *Theodor Däublers Nordlicht. Drei Studien über die Elemente, den Geist und die Aktualität des Werkes (1916)*, Berlin, Duncker & Humblot, 74 pp. T. Rietzschel, 'Dichtung des Mythos — Mythos der Dichtung. Ein Hinweis auf T.D.', *ABNG*, 31–33:513–25.

DÖBLIN, ALFRED.   *Internationales Alfred-Döblin-Kolloquium Lausanne 1987*, ed. Werner Stauffacher (*JIG*, A 28), 188 pp. J. Balve, *Ästhetik und Anthropologie bei A.D. Vom musikphilosophischen Gespräch zur Romanpoetik*, Wiesbaden, Deutscher Universitätsverlag, 1990, 270 pp. M. Prangel, 'A.Ds Konzept von der geistigen Erneuerung des Judentums', Onderdelinden, *Exil*, 162–80. W. Schäffner, 'Psychiatrisches Schreiben um 1900. Dr. A.D. in Karthau-Prüll', *JDSG*, 35:12–29. Zheng Fee, *Alfred Döblins Roman 'Die drei Sprünge des Wang-lun'* (RBDSL, B 49), 224 pp. B. Hüppauf, 'The historical novel and a history of mentalities: A.D.'s *Wallenstein* as an historical novel', Roberts, *Novel*, 71–96. K. R. Scherpe, '"Ein Kolossalgemälde für Kurzsichtige" — Das Andere der Geschichte in A.Ds "Wallenstein"', Eggert, *Geschichte*, 226–41. Ursula Elm, *Literatur als Lebensanschauung. Zum ideengeschichtlichen Hintergrund von A.Ds 'Berlin Alexanderplatz'*, Bielefeld, Aisthesis, 264 pp., is an abstract and verbose investigation of D.'s relation to 'Lebensphilosophie' in all its ramifications; the final chapter sets other authors of the first quarter of the century against the same intellectual background. Although the formal features of the novel are studied, more light is shed on D.'s philosophy than on the novel. Otto Keller, *Döblins Berlin Alexanderplatz. Die Großstadt im Spiegel ihrer Diskurse*, Berne, Lang, 1990, 171 pp., applies methods drawn from semiotics and structuralist narratology to the many forms of communication which form D.'s epic montage. R. Hillman, 'D.'s "symphony of the big city": *Berlin Alexanderplatz* and the historical novel', Roberts, *Novel*, 97–108. Jürgen Blume, *Die Lektüren des Alfred Döblin. Zur Funktion des Zitats im Novemberroman* (EH, I, 1235), ii + 204 pp. D. Schiller, 'D. Feier. Zu einem Briefwechsel Ds mit Hans Siemsen', *ZGer*, n.F., 1:145–55.

DODERER, HEIMITO VON.   K. Hopf, 'Die Funktion der Tagebücher H. von Ds', *MAL*, 24.1:79–98.

EBNER-ESCHENBACH, MARIE VON.   E. Sagarra, 'M. von E.-E. and the tradition of the Catholic enlightenment', *ASt*, 2:117–31.

EINSTEIN, CARL.   T. Krämer, *Carl Einsteins Bebuquin: Romantheorie und Textkonstitution* (Ep, 63), 232 pp.

EISNER, KURT.   R. Sheppard, 'K.E.'s literary remains: a forgotten check-list from the 1930s', *GLL*, 44:253–70.

FALLADA, HANS.   G. Bartram, '"Wenn das auch alles nicht stimmt und nur Kientopp ist, . . ."': some observations on the cinema episode in F.'s *Kleiner Mann — was nun?*', *MLR*, 86:929–38.

FEUCHTWANGER, LION. *Das Buch Bayern: Lion Feuchtwanger als Chronist der Zeitgeschichte,* ed. W. Schmitz and R. Weber (Stauffenburg Kolloquium, 20), Tübingen, Stauffenberg, 320 pp. Karl Kröhnke, *Lion Feuchtwanger — Der Ästhet in der Sowjetunion. Ein Buch nicht nur für seine Freunde,* Stuttgart, Metzler, 350 pp. Doris Rothmund, **Lion Feuchtwanger und Frankreich. Exilerfahrung und deutsch-jüdisches Selbstverständnis* (EH, I, 1212), 380 pp.

FLEISSER, MARIELUISE. C. Albert, 'Lust an der Gewalt. Opfer und Täter in M.Fs Roman "Eine Zierde für den Verein"', *LitL,* no. 1:18–30.

FRANK, BRUNO. A. Lukomska-Woroch, 'Das historische Prosawerk von B.F.', *SGP,* 14, 1990:35–48.

FRIEDELL, EGON. Roland Innerhofer, *Kulturgeschichte zwischen den beiden Weltkriegen: Egon Friedell* (LGGL, 20), 177 pp.

GEORGE, STEFAN. Melchior Lechter und S.G., *Briefe. Kritische Ausgabe,* ed. Günter Heintz, Stuttgart, Hiersemann, 548 pp. Dominik Jost, *Blick auf Stefan George. Ein Essay,* Berne, Lang, 115 pp., considers G.'s nine volumes of poetry as a single work, avoiding analysis in favour of an illumination of essential aspects. D. Heimbockel, 'Anspruch und Wirklichkeit. Theodor W. Adornos Beitrag zur "Rettung" S.Gs', *CP,* 196–97:70–79. K. Kluncker, 'Zur neueren G.-Literatur', *ib.,* 86–93. W. Frommel, 'Templer und Rosenkreuz. Ein Traktat zur Christologie S.Gs', *ib.,* 198–200:3–315. F. Paepcke, 'Geglücktes Übersetzen von Dichtung', *NBGF,* 16:4–23. E. Thieme, 'Johannes von Guenther — Er brachte G. nach Rußland', *ib.,* 27–32.

GLAUSER, FRIEDRICH. M. Haldemann, **Die Mutter und die Wüste: Friedrich Glausers Roman 'Gourrama' und die Deutschschweizer Fremdenlegionliteratur* (ZGS, 21), 273 pp.

GOLL, IWAN. S. Schlenstedt, '"Johann Ohneland steuert den letzten Hafen an": I.G. im amerikanischen Exil', Pfanner, *Der Zweite Weltkrieg,* 43–52.

GURK, PAUL. I. E. Hunt, 'Die Berlin-Romane P.Gs: Mythos Stadt, Mythos Mensch', *ABNG,* 31–33:547–70.

HABE, HANS. R. K. Zachau, '"Gute Europäer in Amerikas Uniform": H.H. und Stefan Heym in der Psychological Warfare', Pfanner, *Der Zweite Weltkrieg,* 177–86. H. Peitsch, 'Das Jahr, in dem Alfred Andersch Hitler "eine Chance gab": H.H. und Alfred Döblins Erlebnisberichte über den Krieg in Frankreich', *ib.,* 273–94.

HASENCLEVER, WALTER. C. H. Helmetag, 'W.H.: a playwright's evolution as a film writer', *GQ,* 64:452–63. H. Denkler, 'Zeugnisse einer Lebensfreundschaft. W.Hs Widmungen für Kurt Pinthus', *Fest. Schumacher,* 175–84.

HAUPTMANN, GERHART. *Gerhart Hauptmann. Autor des 20. Jahrhunderts,* ed. Krzysztof A. Kuczynski and Peter Sprengel, Würzburg,

Königshausen & Neumann, 220 pp., has ten contributions including two on *Till Eulenspiegel*, one on *Die Insel der großen Mutter*, and one on *Vor Sonnenuntergang*. Dong-Youl Jeon, **Mitleid als poetologische und sozialkritische Kategorie beim frühen dramatischen Werk Gerhart Hauptmanns* (EH, I, 1255), v + 273 pp. P. Mellen, 'Through a glass darkly: glass as symbol in G.H.'s view of ideality', *ColGer*, 23:272–87. R. Whitinger, 'G.H.'s metadramatic use of "Das Blutgericht" in "Die Weber" and its relation to Heine and Brecht', *GR*, 46:141–47.

HERMANN, GEORG. L. Nussbaum, 'Verliebt in Holland: ein wichtiges und wechselndes Verhältnis in G.Hs reiferen Jahren', Onderdelinden, *Exil*, 181–98.

HESSE, HERMANN. C. I. Schneider, *Hermann Hesse* (Autorenbücher, 620), Munich, Beck, 230 pp., covers the entire range of H.'s activities and the temporal phases and full geographical spread of his critical reception. Kyung Yang Cheong, **Mystische Elemente aus West und Ost im Werk Hermann Hesses* (EH, I, 1217), 206 pp. *Hermann Hesses weltweite Wirkung. Internationale Rezeptionsgeschichte*, III, Frankfurt, Suhrkamp, 309 pp. Peter Huber, *Hermann Hesse und das Theater* (Ep, 71), 255 pp. R. G. Helt, 'H.Hs Notturni as a body of his early poetry', *GSR*, 14:11–22.

HEYM, GEORG. Patrick Bridgwater, *Poet of Expressionist Berlin. The Life and Work of Georg Heym*, London, Libris, 312 pp., is a major contribution to H. studies, outstanding above all for the skill with which it penetrates the poet's psychology, situates him in an artistic milieu which only with reservations can be described as Expressionist, and relates him to the authors (Hölderlin, Nietzsche, Merezhkovsky, Baudelaire, Rimbaud, Poe *et al.*) and artists (Van Gogh, Hodler *et al.*) to whom he is indebted.

HILLE, PETER. R. Bernhardt, 'Asket oder Voyeur? Der Wanderer zwischen den Welten P.H.', *ABNG*, 31–33:389–418.

HIRSCH, KARL JAKOB. H. F. Pfanner, 'K.J.H.: Schriftsteller, Maler, Musikexperte und Humanist', *ABNG*, 31–33:665–88.

HOFMANNSTHAL, HUGO VON. A special issue of the French journal *Sud* (1990) contains some ten articles on H., including three on the Chandos letter and one on *Elektra*. K. Pestalozzi and M. Stern, *Basler Hofmannsthal-Beiträge*, Würzburg, Königshausen & Neumann, 281 pp., consists of 19 articles, all previously published in *Festschriften* and journals. S. Takahashi, 'Das "Fremde" bei H. Seine Produktivität und Drohung"', *DB*, 87:76–85. F. Schröder, 'Materialien zu Hs Casanova-Lektüre', *MAL*, 24.1:13–22. M. Mayer, "Hs Elektra: Der Dichter und die Meduse", *ZDP*, 110:230–46. L. van Vaerenbergh, 'Leben und Tod. Grundbegriffe im Werk H. von Hs. Ein Vergleich der frühen Dramoletten mit dem Salzburger *Jedermann*', *Fest. Verbeeck*, 265–82. M. Stern, 'Nur Wiener Aristokraten-Deutsch? Zur Funktion der Französismen in H. von Hs Lustspiel *Der Schwierige*', *RG*, 21:109–19. I. Graham, 'Auch ein Schattenriß des Ganzen? Ein Versuch zu Hs Komödie *Der Unbestechliche*', *JFDH*: 308–26. C. Morgan, 'H. and the quatrain', pp. 177–204 of *Bristol Austrian Studies*, ed. Brian Keith-Smith (BGP, 2), 1990, xvi + 274 pp. Jost Bomers, **Der Chandosbrief. Die Nova Poetica Hofmannsthals*, Stuttgart, Metzler, viii + 255 pp. R. Steinlein, 'H. von Hs "Reitergeschichte". Versuch einer struktural-psychoanalytischen Lektüre', *ZDP*, 110:208–29. R. Vilain, '"Wer lügt, macht schlechte Metaphern." Hs "Manche freilich . . ." und Walter Pater', *DVLG*, 65:717–54. B. Keith-Smith, '"Muß der Titel einer Tatsache entsprechen?" H. v. H.'s "Prolog zu dem Buch ANATOL"', *Bristol Austrian Studies* (see above), pp. 206–28.

ÖDÖN VON HORVÁTH. *Horváth auf der Bühne 1926–1938. Eine Dokumentation*, ed. Traugott Krischke, Vienna, Vlg der österreichischen Staatsdruckerei, 398 pp. Christian Schnitzler, *Der politische Horváth* (MSG, 11), 291 pp. C. N. Jones, 'Ferdinand Raimund and Ö. von H.: the Volksstück and Utopia', *GQ*, 64:325–38. E. Krückeberg, 'Vom "Leben in der Lüge" zum "Leben in der Wahrheit". Zu Ö. von Hs Roman *Jugend ohne Gott*', *Arntzen Vol.*, 483–500.

HUCH, RICARDA. *Ricarda Huch. Studien zu ihrem Leben und Werk*, 3, ed. Hans-Werner Peter, Brunswick, pp–Vlg, 144 pp., includes contributions by G. Ueberschlag on the Bakunin study, A. E. Ratz on *Der letzte Sommer* and on the image of the Jew in H.'s work, B. Balzer on the relation between biography and work. K.-H. Hahn, 'Stadt der Jugend, der Freiheit und der Hoffnung oder Frühling in der Schweiz. Erinnerungen von R.H.', *Fest. Weber*, 395–408.

JAHNN, HANS HENNY. E. A. Nickelsen, 'Kuckuckskinder. H.H.Js "Fluß ohne Ufer"', *GSI*, 15.3:161–73. K. Brynhildsvoll, 'Dichtung und Wirklichkeit im Urrland-Kapitel des Romans "Fluß ohne Ufer"', Askedal, *Ingerid Dal*, 97–114.

JOHST, HANNS. W. Pache, 'Karriere eines deutschen Dichters', *LiB*, 23:14–22.

JUNG, FRANZ. H.-J. Schulz, 'Utopie des Herzens: F.J. zwischen Expressionismus und proletarischer Literatur', *ABNG*, 31–33:599–638.

JÜNGER, ERNST. Peter Koslowski, *Der Mythos der Moderne. Die dichterische Philosophie Ernst Jüngers*, Munich, Fink, 160 pp. J. P. Stern, 'E.Js Zwischenkrieg', *Arntzen Vol.*, 465–82.

KAFKA, FRANZ. *'Hochlöblicher Verwaltungsausschuß!' Amtliche Schriften*, ed. Klaus Hermsdorf, Frankfurt, Luchterhand, 456 pp. Gisbert Kranz, **Kafkas Lachen und andere Schriften zur Literatur 1950–1990, mit einer Kranz-Bibliographie*, ed. Elmar Schenkel (Literatur und Leben, 42), Cologne, Böhlau, xx + 455 pp. R. F. Goebel, 'Kafka, der Poststrukturalismus und die Geschichte', *ZGer*, n.F., 1:70–81. H.

818 German Studies

Steinmetz, 'Vergangenheit, Gegenwart und Geschichte bei Kafka', Onderdelinden, *Exil*, 12–25. H. Arie-Gaifman, 'Milena, Odradek, Samsa. Zur tschechischen Etymologie einiger Eigennamen bei Kafka', *GRM*, 41:95–100. Herbert Kraft, *Someone like K.: K.'s Novels*, Würzburg, Königshausen & Neumann, 204 pp., interprets the novels as a 'trilogy of resistance' in which the protagonists, despite their failures, point by their increasingly assertive challenge to authority to a social condition in which the free man exists; it therefore rejects not only the tendency to see the texts as metaphysical allegories, but also a view of them as testimonies of Kafka's psychological vulnerability and complex inner life. K. Hermsdorf, 'Schuld und Schuldbewußtsein in F.Ks "Der Proceß"', *ZGer*, n.f., 1:581–87. M. Reddy, 'K. muß scheitern. Zur Psychologie der Hauptfigur des Romans *Der Prozeß* von F.K.', *GSI*, 15.1–2:29–40. J. Hawes, 'Revanche and radicalism: the psychology of power in *Der Proceß* and *Der Untertan*', *OGS*, 18–19, 1990:119–31. H.-J. Deppisch, *Hypothese und Appell. Franz Kafka und seine Romane 'Der Proceß' und 'Das Schloß'* (WHNDL, 12), 612 pp. E. R. Miller, 'Without a key: the narrative structure of *Das Schloß*', *GR*, 46:132–40. E. Filhol, 'L'autre procès ou La lettre au père de K.', *Neophilologus*, 75:128–38. E. Schwarz, 'Katze und Maus: Ist die Fabel wirklich aus? Reflexionen zu Ks Tierfabeln', *Fest. Grimm*, 213–28. Ralf Nicolai, *Kafkas 'Beim Bau der chinesischen Mauer' im Lichte themenverwandter Texte*, Würzburg, Königshausen & Neumann, 112 pp. E. Boa, 'K.'s "Auf der Galerie". A resistant reading', *DVLG*, 65:486–501. R.-H. Steinmetz. 'Ks neuer Advokat', *WW*, 41:72–80. R. Murphy, 'Semiotic excess, semantic vacuity and the photograph of the imaginary: the interplay of realism and the fantastic in K.'s "Die Verwandlung"', *DVLG*, 65:304–17. J. Hibberd, 'Uncertain perspectives on knowledge, hope and belief: K.'s notebook entry "Das entscheidend Charakteristische dieser Welt"', pp. 229–60 of *Bristol Austrian Studies*, ed. Brian Keith-Smith (BGP, 2), 1990, xvi + 274 pp. F. Pilipp, 'Der Wahrheitsbegriff bei Kafka und Bachmann', *MAL*, 24.1:43–58. J. Lungstrum, 'Self-constructs of impermanence: Kafka, Nietzsche and creativity', *Seminar*, 27:102–20. J. Zilcovsky, 'Kafka approaches Schopenhauer's castle', *GLL*, 44:353–69. E. Moonen, 'Kafka and Steiner. Der Schneefall und das Schnapsglas', *Fest. Verbeeck*, 1990:123–34.

KÄSTNER, ERICH. Johan Zonneveld, *Erich Kästner als Rezensent 1923–1933* (EH, I, 1256), 503 pp. L. Springman, 'A "better reality": the enlightenment legacy in E.K.'s novels for young people', *GQ*, 64:518–30.

KESSLER, HARRY GRAF. A. Hölter, 'H.G.K. liest Samuel Butler d. Ä.', *WW*, 41:416–24.

KESTIEN, KÄTHE. A. Tramitz, '"Vom stillen Heldentum der deutschen Frau im Weltkrieg." K.K. und ihr autobiographischer Roman', *Krieg und Literatur*, 5–6 : 310–18.

KEUN, IRMGARD. G. Kreis, *'Was man glaubt, gibt es.' Das Leben der Irmgard Keun*, Zurich, Arche, 302 pp. Doris Rosenstein, *Irmgard Keun: das Erzählwerk der dreißiger Jahre* (FLK, 28), 387 pp. R. J. Horsley, '"Warum habe ich keine Worte? . . . Kein Wort trifft zutiefst hinein." The problematics of language in the early novels of I.K.', *ColGer*, 23, 1990:297–313. J. M. Ritchie, 'I.K.'s Weimar girls', *PEGS*, 40:63–79.

KEYSERLING, EDUARD VON. Angela Schulz, *Ästhetische Existenz im Erzählwerk Eduards von Keyserling* (EH, I, 1231), 258 pp.

KLUGE, KURT. Rainer Drewes, *Die Ambivalenz nichtfaschistischer Literatur im Dritten Reich — am Beispiel Kurt Kluges* (EH, I, 1218), 234 pp.

KOKOSCHKA, OSKAR. G. Frink, 'Zur Geschlechtsbeziehung in O.Ks Einakter *Mörder, Hoffnung der Frauen*', Kohn-Waechter, *Flammen*, 95–111.

KOLB, ANNETTE. S. Bauschinger, '"Ein Kind ihrer Zeit": A.K.', *ABNG*, 31–33:459–88.

KOLMAR, GERTRUD. E. Wizisla, 'Deine Teilnahme wäre eine viel tiefere', *SuF*, 43:125–28. M. Shafi, 'G.K.: "Niemals 'die Eine' immer 'die Andere'." Zur Künstlerproblematik in G.Ks Prosa', *ABNG*, 31–33:689–712. Id., '"Mein Ruf ist dünn und leicht." Zur Weiblichkeitsdarstellung in G.Ks Zyklus "Weibliches Bildnis"', *GR*, 66:81–88.

KÖLWEL, GOTTFRIED. Ingrid Girlinger, *Gottfried Kölwel. Studien zu seinem erzählerischen Werk* (RBDSL, B 50), 457 pp.

KRACAUER, SIEGFRIED. *NGC*, 54 (Fall), contains 12 contributions on all aspects of K.'s work, including his literary criticism, film theory, and conception of history.

KRAUS, KARL. *Karl Kraus. Diener der Sprache — Meister des Ethos*, ed. Joseph P. Strelka (Edition Orpheus, 1), Tübingen, Francke, 356 pp., contains 18 contributions in five thematic groups (questions of genre, language and style, satire, relations to other authors, including Brecht, Bahr, Shakespeare, Nietzsche and Wittgenstein, and reception). V. Dürr, 'K.K.: Sprachmystik, Kabbala und die deutsche Sprache als "Haus des Seins". Zum Essay "Heine und die Folgen"', *Arntzen Vol.*, 375–90. F. Jenaczek, 'K.K.: "Daß die Gedanken aus der Sprache kommen"', *ib.*, 391–412. K. Pestalozzi, 'Vom Hören einer K.-K.-Platte', *ib.*, 413–22. F. Baron, 'Albert Blochs Bedeutung für die Germanistik. Bemühungen eines Künstlers um die Rezeption von K.K. und Georg Trakl in den USA', *ib.*, 423–30. H. Zohn, 'Das (mitunter verfremdete) Wort als Waffe. Zur Übersetzbarkeit von K.K. und Kurt Tucholsky', *ib.*, 431–37. U. Lang, 'Schnitzler-Feier.

Ein Kommentar', *MBA*, 9, 1990:37–47. S. P. Scheichl, 'Von der Männerschwäche und der Weihe der Kraft. Über praktische Probleme des Kommentierens von K.K.', *ib.*, 28–37. E. Wimmer-Webhofer, 'Albert Bloch und K.K.: Gedichte', *ib.*, 48–54. G. Marahrens, 'Die Erfassung der Ursachen und des Wesens des Erstens Weltkriegs durch die dichterisch-kulturgeschichtlichen Kategorien in der Weltkriegs-Aphoristik von K.K.', Brude-Firnau, *Fact*, 1990:147–64. G. Blaikner-Hohenwart, 'K.K. als "Übersetzer" von Shakespeares *Troilus und Cressida*', Pöckl, *Dichter*, 81–102. G. J. Carr, 'Zum Briefwechsel K.Ks mit O. Stoessl', *WW*, 41:62–71.

LANGGÄSSER, ELISABETH.   K. Müller, 'Poesie und Glaube. Grenzen und Möglichkeiten christlicher Dichtung im 20. Jahrhundert am Beispiel E.Ls', *Fest. Kienecker*, 126–50. J. Bossinade, 'Zwischen Heldentum und Hadeswelt. Eine Suche nach dem Doppelleben der Antigone-Figur anhand einer Erzählung von E.L.', Kohn-Waechter, *Flammen*, 173–92.

LASKER-SCHÜLER, ELSE.   Ruth Schwertfeger, *Else Lasker-Schüler. Inside this Deathly Solitude*, Oxford, Berg, 116 pp., which studies her relation to Expressionism, her identity as a woman, her consciousness of being Jewish and her struggle in exile, consists largely of anecdotal biographical information and translations by the author of numerous poems, and presents her as elusive, eccentric, and exotic, but also as vulnerable, death-fearing and of precarious identity.

LE FORT, GERTRUD.   L. Bossle, 'Europa — die geistige Heimat G. von L.Fs', *Fest. Kienecker*, 50–57. A. Bungert, 'Muse und Sibylle, zwei Schwestern. Reflexionen über ein Gedicht G. von L.Fs', *ib.*, 15–21. J. Pottier, 'G. von L. F. Eine biographische Skizze', *ib.*, 22–49.

LEHMANN, WILHELM.   V. Kobel-Bänninger, 'W.L. und Paul Valéry: — Ein Beispiel deutsch-französischer Literaturbeziehungen im 20. Jahrhundert', *MLN*, 106:172–89.

LERSCH, HEINRICH.   N. Voorwinden, 'H.Ls "Siegfried"-Roman. Zur Nibelungen-Rezeption im Interbellum', Onderdelinden, *Exil*, 126–39.

LUDWIG, EMIL.   **Für die Weimarer Republik und Europa. Ausgewählte Zeitungs- und Zeitschriftenartikel 1919–1932*, ed. Franklin C. West (Trouvaillen, 11), Berne, Lang, 270 pp.

MAASS, JOACHIM.   D. Sevin, 'Moralist in "apokalyptischer Zeit": J.Ms schwieriger Weg zum Erfolg', *ABNG*, 31–33:731–60.

MANN, ERIKA.   R. Kieser, 'Die Legende von der Pfeffermühle', Pfanner, *Der Zweite Weltkrieg*, 13–22. I. von der Lühe, 'Gegen den Alltag — Erzählungen aus dem Alltag: E.M.'s *The Lights Go Down*', *ib.*, 159–68.

MANN, HEINRICH.   M. M. Nunes, **Die Freimaurerei: Untersuchungen zu einem literarischen Motiv bei Heinrich und Thomas Mann*, Bonn, Bouvier,

260 pp. A. Stephan, 'H.M. Die FBI-Akte', *WB*, 37:866–79. A.A.A. Hasha, 'Die literarische Darstellung der Moral in H.Ms "Der Untertan" (1917) und Jussuf Idris' "Das Verbot" (1953)', *Arntzen Vol.*, 287–95. R. Dziergwa, 'H.Ms historischer Roman *Henri Quatre* in der polnischen Rezeption 1936–1985', *SGP*, 14, 1990:65–80. H. Lehnert, 'H.Ms "Eine Liebesgeschichte" und der Prozeß Possehl', *HMJb*, 8, 1990:1–16. C. Albert, 'Der Dichter im Exil: Goethe und Victor Hugo in H.Ms Klassikerporträts', *ib.*, 17–32. A. Riemen and U. Rosenkranz, '"L'heure décisive pour l'Allemagne." H.Ms Artikel für die Dépêche de Toulouse in den Jahren 1931 und 1932', *ib.*, 33–58. E. Wolffheim, '"Heinrich Mann war leider nicht auf dem Kongreß." Deutsche Exilautoren als Gäste auf dem "Ersten Allunionskongreß der Sowjetschriftsteller" in Moskau im Jahre 1934', *ib.*, 59–80. R. Critchfield, 'H.M.'s view of history and the allied leaders in *Ein Zeitalter wird besichtigt*: visions of utopia', Pfanner, *Der Zweite Weltkrieg*, 221–28.

MANN, KLAUS. U. Naumann, 'Mit den Waffen des Geistes: K.M. im zweiten Weltkrieg', *ib.*, 209–21.

MANN, THOMAS. *Tagebücher 1949–1950*, Frankfurt, Fischer, 960 pp. *Jahre des Unmuts. Thomas Manns Briefwechsel mit René Schickele 1930–1940*, ed. Hans Wysling and Cornelia Bernini (TMS, 10), 420 pp. *Briefwechsel T.M. — Kurt Martens*, II, ed. H. Wysling, *TMJb*, 4:185–260. Peter de Mendelssohn, *Der Zauberer: das Leben des deutschen Schriftstellers Thomas Mann. Jahre der Schwebe: 1919 und 1933. Nachgelassene Kapitel, Register*, Frankfurt, Fischer, 460 pp. '*Die Beleuchtung, die auf mich fällt, hat . . . oft gewechselt': Neue Studien zum Werk Thomas Manns*, ed. H. Wisskirchen, Würzburg, Königshausen & Neumann, 184 pp., contains contributions on *Vision* (J. Rossellit), *Wälsungenblut* and *Schwere Stunde* (F. Orlik), *Der Zauberberg* (R. Scheer and A. Seppi), *Joseph und seine Brüder* (H. Wisskirchen), and *Doktor Faustus* (U. Hofstaetter). C. Grimm, **Zum Mythos Individualstil: mikrostilistische Untersuchungen zu Thomas Mann*, Würzburg, Königshausen & Neumann, 312 pp. K. W. Böhm, **Zwischen Selbstsucht und Verlangen: Thomas Mann und das Stigma der Homosexualität. Untersuchungen zu Frühwerk und Jugend* (Studien zur Literatur- und Kulturgeschichte, 2), Würzburg, Königshausen & Neumann, 408 pp. Theo Stammen, **Thomas Mann und die politische Welt*, Freiburg, Rombach, 192 pp. Kurt Sontheimer, 'T.M.'s political engagement', Brude-Firnau, *Fact*, 185–96. E. Sauermann, 'T.M. und die Deutschnationalen. Otto Grautoff als Faktor der Rezeptionssteuerung von T.Ms Frühwerk', *IASL*, 16:57–78. Bernhard J. Dotzler, *Der Hochstapler. Thomas Mann und die Simulakren der Literatur* (Materialität der Zeichen), Munich, Fink, 110 pp., relates Felix Krull the sublime simulator to modern literature as a paradigm of simulation. F. Hoffmann, 'Die "kalten Morde" T.Ms', *GerLux*,

2:73–107. W. Emrich, 'T.M. spricht. Ein kritischer Beitrag zur Krise des Bürgertums', *Arntzen Vol.*, 297–300. U. Karthaus, 'Überlegungen zur Sprache T.Ms', *ib.*, 301–10. K. Abels, 'Pädagogen und Humanisten im Werk T.Ms', *ib.*, 311–22. G. Debon, 'T.M. und der chinesische Geist', *HMJb*, 8, 1990:145–70. M. Dierks, 'Traumzeit und Verdichtung. Der Einfluß der Psychoanalyse auf T.Ms Erzählweise', *Fest. Wysling*, 111–37. V. Hansen, 'Die Kritik der Modernität bei T.M.', *TMJb*, 4:145–60. W. Frizen, '"Venus Anadyomene"', *Fest. Wysling*, 189–223. S. Lenz, '*Buddenbrooks*', *TMJb*, 4:21–28. L. Furst, 'Re-reading *Buddenbrooks*', *GLL*, 44:317–29. M. Swales, 'Symbolic patterns or realistic plenty? T.M.'s *Buddenbrooks* and the European novel', *PEGS*, 40:80–95. U. Weinzierl, 'Die "besorgniserregende Frau". Anmerkungen zu *Luischen*, T.Ms "peinlichste Novelle"', *TMJb*, 4:9–20. F. Orlik, 'T.Ms Skizze "Das Wunderkind"', *WW*, 41:48–61. T. Hake, 'Theaterwelt und "tiefes Reich": Beobachtungen zur Erzähl- und Bedeutungsstruktur von T.Ms Novelle *Wälsungenblut*', *LWU*, 24:287–306. H. Karasek, '*Königliche Hoheit*', *TMJb*, 4:29–44. R. Sheppard, '*Tonio Kröger* and *Der Tod in Venedig*: from bourgeois realism to visionary modernism', *OGS*, 18–19, 1990:92–108. J. Suzuki, 'Narziß und Narzißmus im "Tod in Venedig"', *DB*, 87:86–95. H.-J. Sandberg, '"Der fremde Gott" und die Cholera. Nachlese zum *Tod in Venedig*', *Fest. Wysling*, 66–110. Herbert Lehnert and Eva Wessell, *Nihilismus der Menschenfreundlichkeit. Thomas Manns 'Wandlung' und sein Essay 'Goethe und Tolstoy'* (TMS, 9), 256 pp. Brigitte Schmitz, *'Gedankenfreiheit' in T.Ms 'Der Zauberberg'*, Essen, Die blaue Eule, 289 pp. M. Kamata, 'Erzählender Geist oder reflektierte Subjektivität? Zu T.Ms "Zauberberg" und Robert Musils 'Mann ohne Eigenschaften"', *Arntzen Vol.*, 323–34. T. Tholen, 'Neues vom Dunkelmann Naphta', *HMJb*, 8, 1990:81–100. G. Bridges, 'T.M.'s *Mario und der Zauberer*: "Aber zum Donnerwetter! Deshalb bringt man doch niemand um!"', *GQ*, 64:501–17. J. Hillesheim, 'Der Schritt ins Exil. T.Ms Rede "Leiden und Größe Richard Wagners"', *Exil*, 11:30–40. H. Lehnert, 'Das Chaos und die Zivilisation, das Exil und die Fiktion: T.Ms "Meerfahrt mit Don Quijote"', *Fest. Wysling*, 152–71. P. Pütz, 'Verwirklichung durch "lebendige Ungenauigkeit". *Joseph* von den Quellen zum Roman', *ib.*, 173–89. H. Siefken, 'Goethe "spricht". Gedanken zum siebenten Kapitel des Romans *Lotte in Weimar*', *ib.*, 224–48. E. Heftrich, 'Potiphars Weib im Lichte von Wagner und Freud. Zu Mythos und Psychologie im *Josephsroman*', *TMJb*, 4:58–74. R. Baumgart, 'Joseph in Weimar — Lotte in Aegypten', *ib.*, 75–88. E. Scheiffele, 'Die Joseph-Romane im Lichte heutiger Mythos-Diskussion', ib., 161–83. H. R. Vaget, '*Germany: Jekyll and Hyde.* Sebastian Haffners Deutschlandbild und die Genese von *Doktor*

Faustus', *Fest. Wysling*, 249–71. H.F. Fullenwider, 'Adrian Lever-kühn's corrupt diction in T.M.'s *Doktor Faustus'*, *Neophilologus*, 75:581–90. M. Travers, 'T.M., *Doktor Faustus* and the historians: the function of "anachronistic symbolism"', Roberts, *Novel*, 145–60. *Thomas Mann's Doctor Faustus. A Novel at the Margin of Modernism*, ed. Herbert Lehnert and Peter C. Pfeiffer (SGLLC, 49), 224 pp., consists of an English version of the essays collected in *TMJb*, 2, and responses to them. Christiane Walter, **Zur Psychopathologie der Figuren in Thomas Manns Roman 'Doktor Faustus'* (EH, 1, 1267), ii + 227 pp. D. W. Adolphs, '"Wenn der gegenwärtig tobende Krieg, so oder so, sein Ende gefunden hat . . .": Die Bedeutung der Kriegsthematik in T.Ms Doktor Faustus', Pfanner, *Der Zweite Weltkrieg*, 229–38. E. Heftrich, 'Vom höheren Abschreiben', *Fest. Wysling*, 1–20, is on *Die Entstehung des Doktor Faustus*. H. Kurzke, 'Dostojewski in den *Betrachtungen eines Unpolitischen*', *ib.*, 138–51. M. Reich-Ranicki, '*Der Erwählte*', *TMJb*, 4:99–108. J. Spering, 'Die dämonische Familie in T.Ms "Erwähl-tem" und Dostojewskis "Brüdern Karamasow"', *HMJb*, 8, 1990:101–44. F. A. Lubich, '"Fascinating Fascism": T. Ms "Das Gesetz" und seine Selbst(de)montage als Moses-Hitler', *LiLi*, 20:129–33, and *GSR*, 14:553–74. D. Runge, '*Die Betrogene*', *TMJb*, 4:109–18. H. Wysling, 'T.Ms unveröffentlichte Notizbücher', *ib.*, 119–35. R. Wimmer, 'Die altdeutschen Quellen im Spätwerk T.Ms', *Fest. Wysling*, 272–99. H. Koopmann, 'Aneignungsgeschäfte. T. M. liest *Gespräche mit Goethe'*, *ib.*, 31–48. T. J. Reed, 'Einfache Verulkung, Manier, Stil: die Briefe an Otto Grautoff als Dokument der frühen Entwicklung T.Ms', *ib.*, 48–65.

MORGENSTERN, CHRISTIAN. M. S. Zach and O. W. Johnston, 'Deconstructing the metaphysics of love: C.M.'s and Ernst Toch's parody of Goethe and Mozart', *Seminar*, 27:331–46.

MÜHSAM, ERICH. D. Sheppard, 'The dramas of E.M.', *ABNG*, 31–33:525–46.

MÜLLER, ROBERT. G. Helmes, '"Er hatte sich mit Urkräften ringen sehen und blätterte beschriebenes Papier um." Einführendes zu Leben und Werk des Wiener Expressionisten, Literaturmanagers und Aktivisten R.M. (1887–1924)', *ABNG*, 31–33:571–99. Stephanie Heckner, **Die Tropen als Tropus. Zur Dichtungstheorie Robert Müllers* (LGGL, 21), 203 pp. A. Servranckx, 'R.M.: das literarische Werk', Hickman, *Musil*, 53–71.

MUSIL, ROBERT. *Robert Musil and the Literary Landscape of his Time*, ed. Hannah Hickman, Department of Modern Languages, University of Salford, 285 pp. contains contributions on M. and 'primitive mentality' (R. Robertson), *Die Vollendung der Liebe* (L. Huber), *Vereinigungen* (D. Midgley), the plays (R. Zeller, D. Goltschnigg), *Der Mann ohne Eigenschaften* (C. Lavin), *Törleß* (R. Schröder-Werle), visual compulsion in M.'s works (A. Webber), M.'s relationship to Csokor and O. M. Fontana (A. Daigger), the diaries (P. Payne). M. Wagner-Egelhaaf, '"Wirklichkeitserinnerungen." Photographie und Text bei R.M.', *Poetica*, 23:217–56. B. Hüppauf, 'M. in Paris. R.Ms Rede auf dem Kongreß zur Verteidigung der Kultur (1935) im Zusammenhang seines Werks', *ZGer*, n.F., 1:55–69. A. Frise, 'Mißdeutungen und Fehlschlüsse. Wie R.M. bisweilen von der Kritik gesehen wird', *Arntzen Vol.*, 365–74. C. Asendorf, 'Hinter Glas. Wohnform und Raumerfahrung bei M.', *Fest. Schumacher*, 185–96. H. Lahme-Gronostaj, *Einbildung und Erkenntnis bei Robert Musil und im Verständnis der 'Nachbarmacht' Psychoanalyse*, Würzburg, Königshausen & Neumann, 216 pp. C. Erhart, **Der ästhetische Mensch bei Robert Musil. Vom Ästhetizismus zur schöpferischen Moral* (IBKG, 43), 337 pp. B. Cetti Marinoni, **Essayistisches Drama: Die Entstehung von Robert Musils Stück 'Die Schwärmer'* (Musil-Studien, 21), Munich, Fink, 200 pp. Gerhard Meisel, **Liebe im Zeitalter der Wissenschaften vom Menschen. Das Prosawerk Robert Musils*, Wiesbaden, Westdeutscher Vlg, 306 pp. M.-L. Roth, 'Ein Kommentar zur "Vollendung der Sprache" am Beispiel einer unbekannten handschriftlichen Vorstufe zu R.Ms Novelle "Grigia"', *Arntzen Vol.*, 343–52. J. Lungstrum, 'Conceiving the text: Nietzschean inspiration in M.'s "Tonka"', *GQ*, 64:488–501. R. Svandrli, 'Selbstopfer und Selbsterniedrigung in R.Ms Erzählung "Die Vollending der Liebe"', Kohn-Waechter, *Flammen*, 112–28. W. Düsing, 'Goethe in ironischer Beleuchtung. Zur Klassik-Rezeption in Ms *Mann ohne Eigenschaften*', *JDSG*: 257–74. R. G. Renner, 'Transformatives Erzählen. Ms Grenzgang im "Mann ohne Eigenschaften"', *GR*, 66:70–80. G.-T. Tewilt, 'Bewegung und Geschichte in R.Ms "Nachlaß zu Lebzeiten"', *Arntzen Vol.*, 353–64. M. Wagner-Egelhaaf, '"Anders ich" oder: Vom Leben im Text. R.Ms Tagebuch-Heft 33', *DVLG*, 65:152–73. E. Herity, 'R.M. and Nietzsche', *MLR*, 86:911–23. J. LeRider, 'M. et Nietzsche', *Europe*, 741–42:45–49. F. Maier-Solgk, 'M. und die problematische Politik. Zum Verhältnis von Literatur und Politik bei R.M., insbesondere zu einer Auseinandersetzung mit Carl Schmitt', *OL*, 46:340–63.

NORDAU, MAX. H.-P. Soder, 'Disease and health as contexts of modernity: M.N. as a critic of fin-de-siècle modernism', *GSR*, 14:473–88.

NOSSACK, HANS ERICH. G. Baumgaertel, 'H.E.N.: Die frühen Dramen (1925–1934)', *Euphorion*, 85:147–67.

OSSIETZKY, CARL VON. *C. von O. und die politische Kultur der Weimarer Republik. Symposion zum 100. Geburtstag*, ed. Gerhard Kraiker and Dirk Grathoff (Schriftenreihe des Fritz-Küster-Archivs), Oldenburg.

PANNWITZ, RUDOLF. M.-O. Thirouin-Deverchere, 'L'engagement d'un allemand en faveur des tschèques: la découverte de la Bohème par R.P.', *RLC*, 65:409–28.

PISCATOR, ERWIN. Hermann Haarmann, *Erwin Piscator und die Schicksale der Berliner Dramaturgie. Nachträge zu einem Kapitel deutscher Theatergeschichte*, Munich, Fink, 192 pp., traces P.'s career from the Weimar Republic to 1955 with the aid of previously unpublished material and incidental comparisons with the work of Brecht and Friedrich Wolf.

POLLAK, FELIX. K. Berghahn, 'Von der Hinfälligkeit des Körpers und dem Triumph des Geistes. Anmerkungen zu F.Ps "Galileo"', *Fest. Grimm*, 139–50. R. Grimm, 'Ein Aphoristiker im Gehäus: Neues aus dem Nachlaß von F.P.', *MAL*, 24.3–4:17–42.

REMARQUE, ERICH MARIA. Hans Wagener, *Understanding Erich Maria Remarque*, Columbia, S.C., South Carolina U.P., 141 pp.

REUTER, GABRIELE. G. Rahaman, 'G.R.'s *Aus guter Familie* in the light of Klaus Theweleit's concept of "Entlebendigung"', *GLL*, 45:459–68. L. K. Worley, 'G.R.: reading women in the "Kaiserreich"', *ABNG*, 31–33:419–41. Id., The body, beauty, and woman: the ugly heroine in stories by Therese Huber and G.R.', *GQ*, 64:368–78.

RILKE, RAINER MARIA. Renate Breuninger, *Wirklichkeit in der Dichtung Rilkes* (EH, I, 1224), 316 pp. V. Kaiser, 'Die Katastrophe der Repräsentation. Überlegungen zum figurativen Sprechen in Rs Dichtung', *DVLG*, 65:695–716. B. Schreurs, 'Das Abenteuer der Bedeutung. Ein R.-Gedicht aus Lacanscher Sicht', *Fest Verbeeck*, 221–40. H. Schwall, 'Le graphe du désir. R. und die "Kubisten" — Des Malers Denkmäler', *ib.*, 241–58. A. Stahl, 'Rs Rede über den Tod', *Perspektiven des Todes*, ed. Reiner Marx and Gerhard Stegner, Heidelberg, Winter, 1990. U. Bieber, 'Rs *Igorlied*-Übersetzung', Pöckl, *Dichter*, 57–80. L. Sergo, 'R. als Übersetzer Michelangelos', *ib.*, 335–60. A. Larcati, 'Rs Übersetzungskunst am Beispiel von zwei Leopardi-Übertragungen. Mit einem Übersetzungsvergleich', *ib.*, 361–402. P. Walther, '"Wie ein Fähnrich zum Feldwebel wird." Grenzen der Offenheit in Rs "Cornet"', *WB*, 37:130–36. T. Nolden, 'Portrait of the artist as a young soldier: R.M.R.'s cornet', *GQ*, 64:443–51. *Rilke Blätter*, 16–17, 1989–90 (1991), contains contributions on R.'s relation to Sweden, Denmark, and Venice.

ROSEGGER, PETER. Wolfgang Hölzl, *'Der Großdeutsche Bekenner.' Nationale und nationalsozialistische Rosegger-Rezeption* (EH, I, 1236), 271 pp. Karl Wagner, *Die literarische Öffentlichkeit der Provinzliteratur. Der Volksschriftsteller Peter Rosegger* (STSL, 36), 430 pp.

ROTH, JOSEPH. Reinhard Baumgart, *Auferstehung und Tod des Joseph Roth. Drei Ansichten*, Munich, Hanser, 124 pp. *Co-existent Contradictions. Joseph Roth in Retrospect*, ed. Helen Chambers, Riverside, California, Ariadne, 246 pp., contains 12 contributions on reception, journalism, and fiction, including D. Turner on R.'s journey to Russia, K.

Rossbacher on 'Der Merseburger Zauberspruch', H. Chambers on women in R.'s works, J. Sachsleiner on R.'s views on war, J. Beug on the frontier as a topos, J. Sonnenleitner on the early fiction, R. Robertson on *Hiob* and ghetto fiction, A. Barker on the last novels and Ernst Weiss. I. von Sültemeyer-von Lips, 'J.Rs Reiseberichte besonderer Art. "Die weißen Städte" und "Der Antichrist"', *GM*, 33:3–16. U. Reidel-Schrewe, 'Im Niemandsland zwischen Indikativ und Konjunktiv. J.Rs Radetzkymarsch', *MAL*, 24.1:59–78. Luc Spielmann, *La marche de Radetzky de Joseph Roth. Essai d'Interpretation*, Paris, Éditions du CNRS, 1990, 312 pp. M. Rietra, '"Muß man dann immer postwended Geld senden, um überhaupt mit ihnen verkehren zu dürfen?" J.R. und Barthold Fles in Briefen', Onderdelinden, *Exil*, 199–224.

SALTEN, FELIX   W. Lehnemann, '"Judelnde Hasen". F.Ss Roman "Fünfzehn Hasen"', *Arntzen Vol.*, 453–64.

SCHAFFNER, JAKOB.   H. Bänziger, 'Literarische Konsequenzen einer nationalistischen Utopie: J.S.', *ABNG*, 31–33:489–512.

SCHAUMANN, RUTH.   *Fest. Kienecker* contains four contributions on S., including J. Pottier, 'Wiedergelesen: R.Ss Roman *Elise*. Ein Beitrag zur Wesensbestimmung des Widerstandes der deutschen christlichen Dichter gegen das Dritte Reich', 101–25.

SCHICKELE, RENÉ.   *René Schickele aus neuer Sicht. Beiträge zur deutsch-französischen Kultur* (Auslandsdeutsche Literatur der Gegenwart — Beiträge zur Literatur- und Kulturgeschichte, 24), Hildesheim, Olms, 289 pp. G. Holtz, 'Das Erbe am Rhein. Mythos, Glaube und europäische Vision im Werk R.Ss', *RG*, 21:161–76.

SCHIROKAUER, ARNO.   H. Heinze, 'Faktographie romancée — ein erster Blick auf das literarische Werk A.Ss (1899–1954)', *ABNG*, 31–33:713–30.

SCHNITZLER, ARTHUR.   Ellen Butzko, *Arthur Schnitzler und die zeitgenössische Theaterkritik* (German Studies in Canada, 1), Frankfurt, Lang, xv + 160 pp. D. Azuelos, 'S. et la question juive', *Austriaca*, 31, 1990:37–48. M. Levene, 'The duel in the plays of A.S.', pp. 159–76 of *Bristol Austrian Studies*, ed. Brian Keith-Smith (BGP, 2), 1990, xvi + 274 pp. M. Squercina, 'History and fiction in a drama on revolution: A.S.'s *Der grüne Kakadu*', *NGR*, 5–6, 1989–90:98–109. E. Offermanns, 'A.Ss Schauspiel "Der Gang zum Weiher"', *Arntzen Vol.*, 277–86. T. Eicher, 'Deformierte Märchen. Zum Märchenbegriff in den frühen Erzählungen A.Ss', *Sprachkunst*, 22.1:81–92. W. C. Donohue, 'The role of the Oratorium in S.'s *Leutnant Gustl*', *NGR*, 5–6, 1989–90:29–42. Maya Kündig, *Arthur Schnitzlers 'Therese'. Erzähltheoretische Analyse und Interpretation* (Narratio, 5), Berne, Lang, 203 pp. H. Ohl, 'Zeitgenossenschaft. A.S. und Theodor Fontane', *JFDH*: 262–307. M. Levene, 'Erlebte Rede in S.'s *Frau Berta Garlan*', Hickman, *Musil*, 228–46.

SCHREYER, LOTHAR. Brian Keith-Smith, *Lothar Schreyer: ein vergessener Expressionist. Achtzehn Aufsätze über Leben und Werk mit unveröffentlichten Texten* (SAG, 151), 1990, 432 pp.

SCHWITTERS, KURT. Lambert Wiesing, **Stil statt Wahrheit. Kurt Schwitters und Ludwig Wittgenstein über ästhetische Lebensformen*, Munich, Fink, 148 pp.

SEGHERS, ANNA. S. Bock, 'Sprechen in Andeutungen. Bemerkungen zu A.S.', *TK. Sonderband Literatur in der DDR*, 72–84. J. Barkhoff, 'Erzählung als Erfahrungsrettung. Zur Ich-Perspektive in A.Ss Exilroman "Transit"', *Exilforschung*, 9:218–35. H. A. Doane, 'Die Dialektik der Moral: Vorbereitung auf Krieg und Widerstand in A.Ss Roman *Das siebte Kreuz*', Pfanner, *Der Zweite Weltkrieg*, 85–96.

SIEMSEN, HANS. M. Föster, 'Verbotene Liebe im Exil. Einige Schwierigkeiten beim Finden der Wahrheit über H.S. und andere Autoren', Kalveram, *Homosexualitäten*, 37–51. J. Meve, '"Homosexuelle Nazis." Zur literarischen Gestaltung eines Stereotyps des Exils bei Ludwig Renn und H.S.', *FHL*, 11:79–100. J. W. Joncs, '"Gegenwartsbewältigung": the male homosexual character in selected works about the Fascist experience', Pfanner, *Der Zweite Weltkrieg*, 303–10.

SOYFER, JURA. *Zwischenwelt. Die Welt des Jura Soyfer*, ed. Jura-Soyfer-Gesellschaft, Vienna, Vlg für Gesellschaftskritik, 255 pp.

SPENGLER, OSWALD. J. Farrenkopf, 'S's "Der Mensch und die Technik": an embarrassment or a significant treatise?', *GSR*, 14:533–52.

SUDERMANN, HERMANN. L. Tampi, 'Die Frau mit Schatten: Künstlerin und Bürgerwelt in H.Ss "Heimat"', *GSI*, 15.3:112–37.

THIESS, FRANK. H. Schwerte, 'Auflösung einer Republik. Über einen Roman von F.T.: *Der Zentaur*, 1931', *JDSG*: 275–93.

TOLLER, ERNST. P. K. Tyson, 'E.T.'s *Die Maschinenstürmer*: an Expressionist historical drama', *OL*, 46:294–304.

TRAKL, GEORG. **The Dark Flutes of Fall. Critical Essays on Georg Trakl*, ed. Eric William (SGLLC, 50), vii + 292 pp. J. de Vos, '"An Novalis." Überlegungen zu Ts Romantik-Rezeption', *SGG*, 24:175–94. H. Rölleke, '"Das Grauen." G.T. und Heinrich Heine?', *WW*, 41:163–65.

TRAVEN, BEN. K. S. Guthke, 'Rassentheorien von links: Der Fall B.T.', *ColGer*, 23, 1990:288–96.

TUCHOLSKY, KURT. Antje Bonitz and Thomas Wirtz, *Kurt Tucholsky. Ein Verzeichnis seiner Schriften*, 3 vols, Marbach, Deutsches Literaturarchiv, 1288 pp. *Tucholsky heute. Rückblick und Ausblick*, ed. Irmgard Ackermann and Klaus Hübner, Munich, Iudicium, 242 pp.

UHSE, BODO. R. von Hanffstengel, 'Einige mexikanische Erzählungen von B.U. am Rande von Wunsch und Wirklichkeit des Widerstands im Exil', Pfanner, *Der Zweite Weltkrieg*, 115–22.

WALDEN, HERWARTH. P. Sprengel, 'Institutionalisierung der Moderne: H.W. und *Der Sturm*', *ZDP*, 110:247–80.

WALSER, ROBERT. Joachim Strelis, **Die verschwiegene Dichtung. Reden, Schweigen, Verstummen im Werk Robert Walsers* (EH, I, 1250), 163 pp. A. Gabrisch, 'R.W. und die Fee', *Akzente*, 38:250–65. B. von Matt, 'Der stehende Tänzer. Zu R.W.', *Fest Weber*, 220–27. H. Bloemen, 'Durch die "inneren Gemächer" geführt: Zur Lektüre von R.Ws *Jakob von Gunten*', *Fest. Verbeeck*, 51–66. Andreas Gössling, **Kommentar zu Robert Walsers 'Geschwister Tanner', mit einem Anhang unveröffentlichter Manuskriptvarianten des Romans* (Kommentare und Studien zu Robert Walsers Romanen, I), Würzburg, Königshausen & Neumann, 234 pp. A. Starck, '*Geschwister Tanner* de R.W. ou le roman du regard', *RG*, 21:97–108. Thomas Bolli, **Inszeniertes Erzählen. Überlegungen zu Robert Walsers 'Räuber'-Roman*, Berne, Francke, 128 pp.

WEDEKIND, FRANK. A. Wilder-Mintzer, 'Die Beziehung der Geschlechter bei F.W.', *Fest. Schumacher*, 129–34. J. Hibberd, 'W. and Goethe', *PEGS*, 40:20–38.

WEINHEBER, JOSEF. S. Marx, 'J.W.: Übersetzer von Francesco d'Assisi und Cecco Angiolieri', Pöckl, *Dichter*, 301–34.

WEISS, ERNST. Sabine Adler, **Vom 'Roman experimental' zur Problematik des wissenschaftlichen Experiments: Untersuchungen zum literarischen Werk von Ernst Weiß* (EH, I, 1207), 266 pp. A. P. Diereck, 'Heilige und Dämonen: Die expressionistischen Erzählungen von E.W.', *Seminar*, 27:233–48.

WERFEL, FRANZ. *Franz Werfel im Exil: International Franz Werfel Conference, Los Angeles, Oktober 1990*, ed. W. Nehring and H. Wagener, Bonn, Bouvier, 240 pp. R. Taylor, 'The concepts of reality and transcendental being in F.W.'s *Das Lied von Bernadette*', *ABNG*, 31–33:639–64. J. C. Davidheiser, 'From premonition to portrayal: F.W. and World War II', Pfanner, *Der Zweite Weltkrieg*, 13–22. *MAL*, 24.2, is a special issue on W., with contributions on the poetry (H. Binder and K. Klinger), *Höret die Stimme* (J. C. Davidheiser), *Der Tod des Kleinbürgers* (E. Bahr), the exile correspondence (L. B. Steiman), and W.'s relation to Stefan Zweig.

WIECHERT, ERNST. B. Niven, 'E.W. and his role between 1933 and 1945', *NGS*, 16:1–20. F. von Ingen, 'Zwischen "Totenwolf" und "Totenwald". E.W. und die völkische Literatur', Onderdelinden, *Exil*, 140–41.

WOLFSKEHL, KARL. F. Voit, 'Tomi heißt auf Englisch Auckland. Zum Leben und Werk von K.W. im neuseeländischen Exil', *Exil*, 11:23–29.

ZECH, PAUL. G. Rademacher, 'Avantgardist oder Schein-Avantgardist? Zur Marginalisierung des Lyrikers P.Z. (1881–1946) in der allgemeinen und sektoriellen Literaturgeschichtsschreibung nach 1945', *WW*, 43:454–70. H. W. Panthel, 'Ein schwacher Revancheakt. P.Zs dramtische Skizze *Brot*', *ASNS*, 142, 1990:276–81. D. G. Daviau, 'P.Z.'s anti-Fascist drama "Die drei Gerechten. Eine tragische Episode": a tribute to three German heroes of the resistance', Pfanner, *Der Zweite Weltkrieg*, 97–106.

ZUCKMAYER, CARL. Margot Finke, *Carl Zuckmayer's Germany*, Frankfurt, Haag & Herchen, 1990, 297 pp. William Grange, *Partnership in the German Theatre. Zuckmayer and Hilpert, 1925–1961* (SMGL, 43), xviii + 241 pp.

ZWEIG, ARNOLD. Wilhelm von Sternburg, *Arnold Zweig*, Frankfurt, Hain, 272 pp. P. Huys, 'A.Z. Een introductie in het licht van het A.Z.-colloquium 1991', *SGG*, 24:195–210. A. Wolf, 'A.Zs Zionismus. Einiges über Zs zionistische Gesinnung und sein aktives zionistisches Engagement', *HMJb*, 8, 1990:171–88. S. Thielking, '"Er warb nicht mehr um mich, er kommandierte . . ." Zu A.Zs Roman *Junge Frau von 1914*', *Krieg und Literatur*, 5–6:298–309. H. Schreckenberger, 'Gefangen im Geisterreich der Ideen: Das Unvermögen des deutschen Bildungsbürgertums in A.Zs *Das Beil von Wandsbek* (1938–1944)', Pfanner, *Der Zweite Weltkrieg*, 149–58.

ZWEIG, STEFAN. R. Reisinger, 'S.Z. als Übersetzer Verhaerens: Zum Selbstverständnis eines poètc-traducteur und zu seinen Übersetzungsverfahren im Bereich der lyrischen Bildwelt', Pöckl, *Dichter*, 239–66. J. B. Berlin, '"Wie unwichtig sind ja überhaupt jetzt alle unsere Bücher und das, was wir machen!" The unpublished correspondence between S.Z. and Felix Braun during the Anschluß year 1938', *GRM*, 41:322–48. H. W. Panthel, 'Aushalten als Gebet der Stunde: Ein unbekannter Brief S.Zs an Paul Zech', *MAL*, 24.1:125–28.

LITERATURE FROM 1945 TO THE PRESENT DAY

By MARGARET LITTLER, *Lecturer in German, University of Manchester*

1. GENERAL

M. Bansleben, 'Betroffenheit und Aufklärung: Die Auseinander-setzung mit dem Nationalsozialismus im Jugendbuch', *GR*, 26:182–87. A. Barsch, '"Populäre Literatur" als Forschungsproblem einer empirischen Literaturwissenschaft', *WW*, 41:101–19. *Das chinesische Deutschlandbild der Gegenwart*, ed. Wolfgang Bauer, Chang Peng, and Stephan von Minden (Münchener Ostasiatische Studien, 56), Stuttgart, Steiner, lvi + 792 pp., is a bibliography which reflects the opening-up of Chinese intellectual life to the West since the mid-1980s. It contains 799 entries on literature and shows the radical shift from an exclusive focus on GDR literature to an interest in the German-speaking capitalist West. C. Baumann, 'Das Gespräch als Existenzform der Menschlichkeit. Zur Rolle gesamtdeutscher Antho-logien der fünfziger Jahre im Kampf um die Einheit Deutschlands', *HSWSL*, 17, 1989:75–86. W. Biechele, 'Das neue Deutschland und seine Dichter. Vom schwierigen Weg zur Vereinigung der beiden deutschen Literaturen', *DeutUB*, 10:153–65. E. Boa, 'Women, life and letters: An introduction', *GLL*, 44:387–91. B. Bobrowski, 'Literatur und Zukunft. Ein Kolloquium zur Literatur der Bundesre-publik in Rostock', *WB*, 37:462–65. K.-M. Bogdal, 'Wer darf sprechen? Schriftsteller als moralische Instanz — Überlegungen zu einem Ende und einem Anfang', *WB*, 37:597–603. A. von Bormann, 'Anarchismus und Literatur: eine anarchistische Literatur? Zum Buch von Walter Fähnders: "Anarchismus und Literatur"', *Avant-garde*, 3, 1989:99–106. F. V. Bülow, 'Wenn die schweigende Mehrheit zu schreiben beginnt ... Zwei Jahrzehnte "Werkkreis Literatur der Arbeitswelt" in München', *LiB*, 22, 1990:52–53. *Der deutsch-deutsche Literaturstreit oder 'Freunde, es spricht sich schlecht mit gebundener Zunge'*, ed. Karl Deiritz and Hannes Kraus (SL, 1002), 176 pp., documents the controversy unleashed by C. Wolf's *Was bleibt*, also addressing the broader issue of the relationship between *Geist und Macht* in the GDR. It is discussed both from East German perspectives and in the context of West German *Vergangenheitsbewältigung*, the *Historikerstreit*, and the Gulf War, and is seen as symptomatic of a crisis of the left-wing liberal consensus in the West. A final section presents the views of four Germanists from Poland, Czechoslovakia, Italy, and Britain. G. Ecker, 'Der Kritiker, die Autorin und das "allgemeine Subjekt". Ein Dreiecksverhältnis mit Folgen', Stephan, *Frauen*, 43–56. B.

Dolle-Weinkauf, *Comics. Geschichte einer populären Literaturform in Deutschland seit 1945*, Weinheim, Beltz, 1990, 390 pp. Andreas Dybowski, *Endstation, Wartesaal oder Schatzkammer für die Zukunft. Die deutsche Exilliteratur und ihre Wirkung und Bewertung in der westdeutschen Nachkriegsrepublik* (EH, I, 1138), 1989, 278 pp. *Die Gruppe 47 in der Geschichte der Bundesrepublik*, ed. Justus Fetscher, Eberhard Lämmert, and Jürgen Schütte, Würzburg, Königshausen & Neumann, vi + 251 pp., arose out of a Berlin symposium (1988) and presents a composite view on the nature and significance of Gruppe 47. Contributions include general assessments of the impact on publishing of the currency reform, the influence of French writing and the significance of group identity as a form of retrospective *résistance*. Two essays treat the group's relationship to exile writers, and there are individual contributions on A. Andersch, H. E. Nossack, P. Handke, G. Eich, and I. Bachmann. With an essay on the *Hörspiel* in the 1950s and Heinrich Vormweg's concluding discussion of the group's critical practices, it is seen as having played a significant role in bringing literature and literary criticism into the media age. Forsås-Scott, *Liberation*, is an ambitious attempt to map out the construction and radicalization of female consciousness in women's writing in Eastern and Western Europe, Russia, Scandinavia, and Turkey. Of particular interest is C. Weedon's chapter on German feminist writers from the liberal beginnings early in the century to the politicization of gender in second-wave feminist writing since 1968. The emergence of *Frauenliteratur* in the West is placed in the context of New Left politics and *Neue Subjektivität*, both of which failed adequately to address the politics of gender. The contradictions between public and private female roles in the GDR provide the context for the separate discussion of East German women's writing, and overall the lack of Utopian perspectives and continuity of themes is attributed to the enduring nature of patriarchal power structures. *Deutsche Literatur 1990. Jahresüberblick*, ed. Franz-Josef Görtz, Volker Hage, and Uwe Wittstock, Stuttgart, Reclam, 322 pp., is organized in three sections: the first chronicles major publications and cultural events, the second lists new publications, with selected reviews of works such as Grass's *Deutscher Lastenausgleich*, L. Harig's *Weh dem, der aus der Reihe tanzt*, and B. Kronauer's *Die Frau in den Kissen*. A third section treats major debates of the year, primarily that over Christa Wolf's *Was bleibt* and the 'Deutscher Literaturstreit'. D. Göttsche, 'Stilkrise und Krisenstile. Überlegungen zur Stilistik der "Sprachkrise" in der erzählenden Prosa um 1970', *JIG*, 22.2, 1990:33–55. U. Greiner-Kemptner, *Subjekt und Fragment: Textpraxis in der (Post-)Moderne. Aphoristische Strukturen in Texten von Peter Handke, Botho Strauss, Jürgen Becker, Thomas Bernhard, Wolfgang Hildesheimer, Felix Ph. Ingold und André v. Heiz*

(SAG, 240), 1990, 298 pp. J. Hörnisch, 'Das Vergehen der Gegen-wartsliteratur', *Merkur*, 45:88–93. J. Jabłkowska, 'Das Groteske in der heutigen Katastrophenliteratur', *KN*, 36, 1989 (1990):349–60. A. Huyssen, 'After the wall: the failure of German intellectuals', *NGC*, 52:109–43. C. Karolak, 'Deutsche Literatur nach dem Dritten Reich. Die fünfziger Jahre im "toten Winkel" der Geschichte', *SGP*, 14, 1990:81–104. S. Knauss, 'Literatur oder Frauenliteratur: Instrumente zur Frauenförderung', *PSGAS*, 3.3:48–54. U. Landfester, 'Die Spuren des Lesers. Überlegungen zur intertextuellen Rezeption im modernen deutschen Kriminalroman', *Poetica*, 22, 1990:413–35. *Spätmoderne und Postmoderne. Beiträge zur deutschsprachigen Gegenwarts-literatur*, ed. Paul Michael Lützeler, Frankfurt, Fischer, 266 pp., consists of 18 essays, three general profiles of German literature and consequences of reunification, the remaining 15 devoted to individual works: H. M. Enzensberger's *Ach Europa!*, TORKAN's *Tufan: Brief an einen islamischen Bruder*, S. Nadolny's *Die Entdeckung der Langsamkeit*, P. Süskind's *Das Parfum*, B. Strauss's *Paare, Passanten*, P. Handke's *Die Geschichte des Bleistifts*, *Das Gewicht der Welt* and *Phantasien der Wiederholung*, F. Mayröcker's *Mein Herz mein Zimmer mein Name*, K. Hoffer's *Bei den Bieresch*, B. Kronauer's *Rita Münster*, L. Harig's *Der kleine Brixius*, T. Bernhard's *Auslöschung*, G. Grass's *Die Rättin*, C. Wolf's *Störfall*, C. Hein's *Drachenblut*, and V. Braun's poem 'Tagtraum'. Daniela Magill, **Literarische Reisen in die exotische Fremde. Topoi der Darstellung von Eigen- und Fremdkultur* (EH, I, 1150) 1989, 131 pp. Hannelore Mundt, **'Doktor Faustus' und die Folgen. Kunstkritik als Gesellschaftskritik im deutschen Roman seit 1947*, Bonn, Bouvier, 1989, 176 pp. G. Müller, 'Deutschland nach 1945 — Rückkehr aus dem Exil?', *Exil*, 10.1, 1990:77–79. R. J. Murphy, 'Russian formalism and German reception theory: a reconsideration. Continuities in the methodologies of Victor Shklovsky and Wolfgang Iser', *GSL*, 6, 1990:339–49. *Philosophie der Gegenwart in Einzeldarstellungen von Adorno bis V. Wright*, ed. Julian Nida-Rümelin, Stuttgart, Kröner, xxvi + 659 pp., is a useful, compact reference work containing entries on over 130 20th-c. Western philosophers. While the bias is towards German thought, the range of continental philosophers included will make this an invaluable aid to all those grappling with the ideas underlying poststructuralism (Derrida), postmodernism (Lyotard, Vattimo) or feminist theories (Kristeva, Irigaray). J. Quack, 'Die hektische Grimasse der Zeit. Literatur und Terrorismus im letzten Jahrzehnt', Quack, *Identifikation*, 133–54. Id., 'Gegenwartsliteratur, alexandrinisch', *ib.*, 155–72. S. Parkes, '"Leiden an Deutschland": some writers' views of Germany and the Germans since 1945', Williams, *Literature*, 187–206. Wolfgang Paulsen, *Das Ich im Spiegel der Sprache. Autobiographisches Schreiben in der deutschen Literatur des 20.*

Jahrhunderts (UDL, 58), viii + 264 pp., traces the development of autobiographical writing from Neo-Romanticism through Expressionism and *Neue Sachlichkeit* to exile in the 1930s and 1940s and the post-war period. The ambitious scope of the study and its attempts to detect large-scale continuities are pursued at the expense of detail and accuracy. The charting of a trend towards fictionalized autobiography and the renewed popularity of confessional forms in the 1970s and 1980s produces a rather undifferentiated view of the genre, whilst acknowledging its various impulses in the Students' Movement, feminism and *Neue Subjektivität*. J. Preece, '"1968": literary perspectives in political novels from East and West', Williams, *Literature*, 299–320. K. Riha, 'Zur Literatur der achtziger Jahre. Ein Situationsbericht', Kreuzer, *Pluralismus*, 225–41. G. Rohr, 'Die Rezeption der Exilliteratur nach 1945 in Deutschland', *SLWU*, 21.2, 1990:16–28. K. R. Scherpe, 'Literaturgeschichte im sozialen und kulturellen Zusammenhang. Eine Revision und ein Prospekt', *ZGer*, n.F., 1:257–69. D. Scheunemann, '"Fiktionen — auch aus dokumentarischem Material". Von Konstruktionen der Geschichte in Literatur und Film seit den sechziger Jahren', Eggert, *Geschichte*, 296–314. H. Schlaffer, 'Die Schauseite der Poesie. Über literarische Ausstellungen und den literarhistorischen Fernsehfilm', *ib.*, 365–71. R. Schmidt, 'Theoretische Orientierungen in feministischer Literaturwissenschaft und Sozialphilosophie', *WGY*, 7:79–89. Schmidt, 'The concept of identity in recent East and West German women's writing', Williams, *Literature*, 429–47. R. Schnell, 'Das fremde Geschlecht. Männerbilder in der neueren deutschsprachigen Frauenliteratur', *Akten* (Tokyo), x, 267–74. G. Schulz, 'Anmerkungen zum Verschwinden des Autors und zum Erscheinen der Autorin', Stephan, *Frauen*, 57–62. Heimo Schwilk, *Wendezeit-Zeitwende. Beiträge zur Literatur der achtziger Jahre*, Bonn, Bouvier, 220 pp., is a collection of critical essays on German literature of the 1980s which detect beneath the surface stability and affluence of the Western *Literaturbetrieb* an apocalyptic mood similar to that evident in the GDR. The sense of cultural crisis in the West is examined in works by C. Amery, E. Jünger, G. Heidenreich, and F. Dürrenmatt. One section is devoted to attitudes to German identity in East and West, including those who called for unification (M. Walser, B. Strauss) and those who declared the German nation state obsolete (H. J. Ortheil, J. M. Simmel). J. P. Stern, 'Über Prager deutsche Literatur', *Merkur*, 45:88–93. *Romantik — Eine lebenskräftige Krankheit. Ihre literarischen Nachwirkungen in der Moderne*, ed. Erika Tunner (ABNG, 34), v + 243 pp., comprises 11 essays, including two on E. T. A. Hoffmann and modern psychoanalytic theory, one on J. Erpenbeck's fictional treatment of Clemens Brentano in *Heillose Flucht*, and on Novalis and Hölderlin reception in

GDR poetry. Two contributions survey the use of Romantic themes by and after Christa Wolf, whilst G. Kunert's rehabilitation of Kleist is explored in *Ein anderer K*. While the main emphasis is on GDR writers, there are two studies of the influence of the *Jenaromantik* on B. Strauss, and one on I. Bachmann's Romanticism reception from 'Undine geht' to *Todesarten*. Jochen Vogt, '*Erinnerung ist unsere Aufgabe.*' *Über Literatur, Moral und Politik 1945–1990*, Opladen, Westdeutscher Vlg, 191 pp., is largely a collection of essays published or broadcast in the 1980s on *Vergangenheitsbewältigung* in West German literature. After an introduction to psycho-sociological and historical debates on the topic there is an account by B. Meier of the controversy surrounding the reconstruction of the 'Goethehaus' in Frankfurt. The author's own essays include discussions of oppositional voices in novels of the Adenauer era, literature and the Student Movement, and the writings of Böll, Weiss, and Bernward Vesper. The conclusion outlines the recent critical debate around the moral-critical function of literature in the Federal Republic. Id., 'Langer Abschied von der Nachkriegsliteratur. Aus Anlaß der letzten westdeutschen und ersten gesamtdeutschen Literaturdebatte', *WB*, 37:452–61. Volker Wehdeking and Günter Blamberger, *Erzählliteratur der frühen Nachkriegszeit (1945–1952)*, Munich, Beck, 1990, 239 pp., focuses on the period in which the polarization of German literature was taking place. Starting with background to social and cultural policies in East and West, it moves on to more detailed discussion of contemporary cultural debates, and a third section offers textual analysis including works by Andersch, Koeppen, Rinser, Böll, Hermlin, Becher, Seghers, Heym, and Loest. Each section contains extensive bibliographic information. V. Wehdeking, 'Literarische Programme der frühen Nachkriegszeit', *SLWU*, 21.2, 1990:2–15. Waltraud Wende-Hohenberger, *Ein neuer Anfang? Schriftsteller-Reden zwischen 1945 und 1949*, Stuttgart, Metzler, 1990, vi + 333 pp., is a socio-historical study of writers' statements on Germany's political and cultural regeneration between the end of the war and the founding of two German states. The speeches analysed include E. Wiechert's 'Rede an die deutsche Jugend', Johannes R. Becher's speeches on the founding of the 'Kulturbund zur demokratischen Erneuerung Deutschlands', A. Andersch's 'Deutsche Literatur in der Entscheidung', F. von Unruh's 'Rede an die Deutschen', and T. Mann's 'Ansprache im Goethejahr 1949'. J. Wigmore, 'The emergence of women's writing since 1945 in the German-speaking area', Brassloff, *Insights*, 247–61.

WEST GERMANY, AUSTRIA, SWITZERLAND. *Das Schreiben der Frauen in Österreich seit 1950*, ed. Walter Buchebner Gesellschaft, Vienna, Cologne, Böhlau, 120 pp., begins by addressing the conditions of literary production for women in Austria immediately after the war, seeking to explain the emergence and subsequent obscurity of a generation of young women writers (I. Aichinger, I. Bachmann , M. Haushofer, Hertha Kräftner). The rediscovery by feminist critics of Haushofer and Bachmann is reaffirmed in readings of their works which highlight their extraordinary anticipation of feminist debates of the 1970s and 1980s. The volume also includes detailed essays on F. Mayröcker, I. Aichinger, and E. Jelinek, and concludes with a comparison of recent works by Mayröcker, Jelinek, and M.-T. Kerschbaumer which reveals beneath the stylistic diversity some of the common concerns of Austrian women's writing today. *Rejection and Emancipation. Writing in German-Speaking Switzerland 1945–1991*, ed. Michael Butler and Malcolm Pender, Oxford, Berg, viii + 257 pp., charts the development of post-war Swiss German literature in 14 essays, the first two providing political and economic background, and assessing the impact of Frisch and Dürrenmatt on traditional cultural representations of Swiss national identity. The social criticism of the second generation is explored in individual essays on O. F. Walter, P. Bichsel, A. Muschg, H. Loetscher, and K. Marti, and their influence detected in turn on the next generation, represented here by E. Y. Meyer, C. Geiser, and H. Burger. Their rejection of comfortable notions of affluence and stability coincides with the emergence in the 1970s of women writers such as G. Leutenegger and M. Schriber with their specifically feminist critique. The radical individualism and environmental concerns of the fourth generation publishing since the 1980s are presented in discussion of works by L. Hartmann, R. Niederhauser, R. Hänny, B. Sterchi, M. Zschokke and others. The emphasis is not on a specifically 'Swiss' literature as much as the contribution of Swiss writers since 1945 to the development of a broader German literary culture. H. Ehlers, 'Erinnerungsarbeit gegen Vergessen und "Entsorgung". On the treatment of the experience of German fascism in prose works of the last decade in the Federal Republic', Williams, *Literature*, 225–42. M. Hall, 'Verleger in Österreich oder österreichische Verleger?', *AION(T)*, 33.1–2, 1990:147–61. J. Holzner, 'Drei Bemerkungen zur österreichischen Gegenwartsliteratur', *ModSpr*, 84, 1990:120–29. M. Huter, 'Erinnerung an das Unbekannte. Zur Konjunktur der österreichischen Moderne in Italien', *Sprachkunst*, 20, 1989(1990):271–303. R. Krämer, 'Die gekaufte "Zukunft". Zu Produktion und Rezeption von Science Fiction in der Bundesrepublik Deutschland nach 1945', *AGB*, 34, 1990:117–265. H. Kreuzer, 'Pluralismus und Postmodernismus. Zur Literatur und Literaturwissenschaft der 80er Jahre im westlichen Deutschland', Kreuzer, *Pluralismus*, 7–22. Andrea Kunne, *Heimat im Roman: Last oder Lust? Transformationen eines Genres in der österreichischen Nachkriegsliteratur* (APSL, 95), viii + 342 pp., devotes an initial section to the development of the *Heimatroman* from the 19th-c. *Dorfgeschichte* through the *Heimatkunst* of the 1930s to the post-war period, when it attained a greater literary respectability. Social critical, experimental, and postmodern aspects of the genre are then examined in works by F. Innerhofer, H. Lebert, M. Maetz, R. P. Gruber, G. Jonke, G. Roth, and J. Winkler. E. Lämmert, 'Patterns beneath the gloss: The Federal Republic in its fiction', Kolinsky, *Era*, 275–96. R. W. McCormick, *Politics of the Self: Feminism and the Postmodern in West German Literature and Film*, Princeton U.P., 283 pp. E. Naganowski, 'Von Stefan Zweig zu Robert Musil. Ein Bericht über die Verbreitung der österreichischen Literatur im heutigen Polen', *Musil-Forum*, 4, 1990:5–13. O. Nicolai, 'Experiment und Engagement. Überlegungen zur Veränderung experimenteller Schreibweisen in der österreichischen Literatur nach 1945', *Germanistisches Jahrbuch DDR–RU*, 9, 1990:146–53. Markus Paul, *Sprachartisten — Weltverbesserer: Bruchlinien in der österreichischen Literatur nach 1960*, Innsbruck, Institut für Germanistik, 297 pp., explores the debate between literary realism and avant-garde in Austria as mirroring that between Marxism and anarchic individualism. The ideas of the avant-garde are traced from O. Wiener and the Wiener Gruppe to the columns of *manuskripte* and exemplified in works of writers such as E. Jandl, F. Mayröcker, and R. Priessnitz. Those of the realist tendency are presented with reference to M. Scharang, the 'Arbeitskreis österreichischer Literaturproduzenten' and the journal *Wespennest*, and considered in works by P. Turrini, H. Zenker, G. Wolfengruber, and F. Innerhofer. Helmut Peitsch, *'Deutschlands Gedächtnis an seine dunkelste Zeit'. Zur Funktion der Autobiographik in den Westzonen Deutschlands und den Westsektoren von Berlin 1945 bis 1949*, Berlin, Sigma, 1990, 478 pp., documents a chronological development from accounts of exile and resistance towards memoirs of *Innere Emigration*, relating this to the intensification of the Cold War. Analysis of reception shows up patterns of interpretation clearly shaped by Western Cold War attitudes. In particular the role of journals is highlighted in promoting the more conservative, apologetic accounts of the administrative and military élites in the Third Reich, and helping to shape the collective memory. This process of 'selective memory' served to legitimate the restoration and alignment with the capitalist liberal Western Alliance. Id., 'West German reflections on the role of the writer in the light of reactions to 9 November 1989', Williams, *Literature*, 155–86. Klaus Pezold *et al.*, *Geschichte der deutschsprachigen schweizer Literatur im 20. Jahrhundert*, Berlin, Volk & Wissen, 363 pp., is an impressive piece of collaborative scholarship by a Marxist collective, which combines comprehensive coverage with detailed textual analysis and contextual discussion of cultural debates. The neglected Swiss literature between Keller and Frisch is here rediscovered in detailed sections on the early decades of the century, Expressionism in Switzerland, and the works of authors such as C. Spitteler, F. Glauser, R. Walser, A. Zollinger, and M. Inglin. After a chapter on Frisch and Dürrenmatt, there is extensive analysis of developments since the 1960s in prose, lyric poetry, and drama, including discussion of dialect literature, multilingualism, and writers' organizations and publishing in Switzerland since 1945. W. Pöckl, 'Österreichische Schriftsteller als Übersetzer François Villons', Pöckl, *Dichter*, 187–209. *Wesen und Wandel der Heimatliteratur: am Beispiel der österreichischen Literatur seit 1945*, ed. K. K. Pohlheim, Berne, Lang, 1989, 263 pp. K. R. Scherpe, 'Von der Moderne zur Postmoderne? Einige Entwicklungslinien westdeutscher Literatur und Kulturindustrie in den achtziger Jahren, polemisch nachgezeichnet', *WB*, 37:356–71. S. P. Schleichl, '"Zu wenig österreichverbunden." Bemerkungen zu kulturpolitischen Positionen im österreich der Nachkriegszeit', *AION(T)*, 33.1–2, 1990:163–81. W. G. Sebald, *Unheimliche Heimat: Essays zur österreichischen Literatur*, Salzburg, Residenz, 250 pp. *Vermittlungen. Texte und Kontexte österreichischer Literatur und Geschichte im 20. Jahrhundert*, ed. Walter Weiss and Ernst Hanisch, Salzburg, Residenz, 1990, 280 pp. D.-S. Winkler, 'Ideologische Ziele der "Wiener Gruppe" und ihre Bedeutung für die Gegenwartsliteratur', *ZGer*, n.F., 1:588–99.

GDR. *'Es geht nicht um Christa Wolf.' Der Literaturstreit im vereinten Deutschland*, ed. Thomas Anz, Munich, Spangenberg, 270 pp., gives a good impression of the complexities of the ongoing 'deutscher Literaturstreit' which erupted on the publication of C. Wolf's *Was bleibt*. In eight chapters, each introduced by the author, prominent writers and critics present their conflicting and often passionately argued views on the debate. The discussion points beyond the specific case of Wolf's text to the broader issues of the relationship of GDR writers to the state, the moralizing triumphalism of Western critics, and the implications for left-wing intellectuals throughout Europe of the end of the Cold War. *Literatur in der DDR. Rückblicke*, ed. Heinz Ludwig Arnold and Frauke Meyer-Gosau (TK Sonderband), 307 pp., attempts to present a differentiated view of the writers, debates, and institutions which made up the complex literary landscape of the GDR. It includes essays on A. Seghers, F. Fühmann, Erich Köhler, F. R. Fries, E. Erb, and Heiner Müller, as well as covering more general tendencies from Socialist Realism to the Prenzlauer Berg avant-garde. It also addresses the material and ideological conditions of literary production and criticism, with essays on *Sinn und Form*, the Leipzig 'Johannes R. Becher Institut', state censorship, and literary identity. GDR literature emerges as more than a product of the strategies of SED *Kulturpolitik*, but as a crucial agent in complex cultural debates and one with continuing significance for the intellectual life of the reunited Germany. *Die andere Sprache. Neue DDR-Literatur der 8oer Jahre*, ed. Heinz Ludwig Arnold and Gerhard Wolf (TK Sonderband), 1990, 258 pp., gives a vivid impression of the anarchic impulses in GDR literature in the 1980s, exemplified in texts by 19 prominent contemporary writers. Individual critical essays focus on linguistic innovation as the signal of a new autonomy in the work of B. Papenfuss-Gorek, R. Schedlinski, and G. Neumann. Other contributors help to locate these within the broader cultural landscape of the GDR, with essays on Prenzlauer Berg, the journal *ariadnefabrik* and the theatre company 'Zinnober'. U.-H. Bader, 'Stofflich-thematische Neuerungen und Transformationserscheinungen in der niederdeutschen Literatur der DDR', *GGF*, 11, 1989:58–64. D. Bathrick, 'The end of the wall before the end of the wall', *GSR*, 14:297–311. H. J. Bernhard, 'Identität im Widerstand. Anschreiben gegen die Beliebigkeit in der zeitgenössischen Literatur', *WB*, 37:402–11. G.-J. Berendse, 'Gruppenbild mit Endler. Die "sächsische Dichterschule" in lyrischer Korrespondenz', *JLitDDR*, 6, 1987 (1988):95–118. Id., 'Outcast in Berlin. Opposition durch Entziehung bei der jüngeren Generation', *ZGer*, n.F., 1:21–27. W. Biechele, 'Literatur als positive Provokation. Der Schriftsteller als engagierter Autor in der DDR-Literatur der achtziger Jahre', *Germanistisches Jahrbuch DDR-RU*, 9, 1990:9–18. T. Buck, 'The German "October Revolution" in the GDR and the writers', Williams, *Literature*, 21–46. R. Buhtz, 'Kolloquium "Subjektivität-Geschichte-Erzählen. Zur DDR-Literatur der letzten Jahrzehnte", 8. bis 10. Mai 1990, Veliko Târnovo (Bulgarien)', *ib.*, 391–95. F. Cambio, 'Ästhetik der Erinnerung und Geschichtsbewußtsein in der DDR-Literatur der achtziger Jahre', *ib.*, 19–27. P. Collini, '"Gräßlicher Fatalismus der Geschichte." Passato e presente nella letteratura della DDR', *Belfagor*, 45, 1990:637–52. *Dissidenten. Texte und Dokumente zur DDR–'Exil'–Literatur*, Berlin, Volk & Wissen, 144 pp., is a tribute to the work of writers who were expatriated from the GDR. Without editorial comment it gives brief biographical details and records the circumstances of each case through letters, newspaper reports, and official documents, including also samples of the 'dissident' writing itself. The 14 authors include W. Biermann, J. Fuchs, R. Kunze, B. Jentzsch, G. Kunert, R. Loewig, R. Kunze, and H. J. Schädlich. I. Dölling, 'Alte und neue Dilemmata: Frauen in der ehemaligen DDR', *WGY*, 7:121–36. *Dialog ohne Grenzen. Beiträge zum Bielefelder Kolloquium zur Lage von Linguistik und Literaturwissenschaft in der ehemaligen DDR*, ed. Jörg Drews and Christian Lehmann, Bielefeld, Aisthesis, 174 pp., records the proceedings of one of the first united German conferences which brought together Germanists from the old and new *Bundesländer* in November 1990. The resulting volume is somewhat one-sided, all contributions being from invited academics from the East, but they cover a broad range of topics and challenge some Western prejudices about GDR scholarship: there is discussion of GDR literary history and the *Kulturerbe*, as of GDR *Literaturpsychologie*, English, and American Studies. There are also essays on Romance linguistics, theoretical grammar, *Deutsch als Fremdsprache* and *Auslandsgermanistik*. T. Eberlein, 'Happy few?! Zur DDR-Kinder- und Jugendliteratur mit Gegenwartsthematik', *Germanistisches Jahrbuch DDR-RU*, 9, 1990:40–51. M. Ebersbach, 'Kriminalliteratur in der DDR', *DaF*, 27, 1990:18–20. W. Emmerich, 'Affirmation-Utopie-Melancholie: Versuch einer Bilanz von vierzig Jahren DDR-Literatur', *GSR*, 14:325–44. W. Gabler, 'Wieder eine verlorene Generation? Zur Literatur junger DDR-Autoren der 80er Jahre', *ib.*, 28–39. *Neue Ansichten. The Reception of Romanticism in the Literature of the GDR*, ed. Howard Gaskill, Karin McPherson, and Andrew Barker (*GDR Monitor* Special Series, 6), Amsterdam, Rodopi, 1990, 236 pp., comprises 14 essays on a wide range of topics, based around a broad definition of both 'reception' and 'Romanticism'. There is analysis of the particular appeal of the language and institutions of Romanticism, whether in the marginal discourses of irrationality in the early literature of the GDR or in the interest in Berlin literary salons as sites of solidarity and dissent. Other contributors treat the themes of sickness and the *Märchen* in GDR writing, or focus on the influence of specific writers (e.g. E.T.A. Hoffmann in the works of C. Wolf and F. Fühmann). Women's writing is represented by studies of S. Damm, C. Moog, B. Struzyk, and I. Morgner, and there are four essays on the poetry of the GDR. G. Giesenfeld, 'Die Literatur der DDR: ein Nachruf?', *Universitas*, 45, 1990:764–75. K.-D. Hähnel, ' "Weltweite Moderne" in der Lyrik der DDR', *Akten* (Tokyo), x, 47–54. T. Hartung, 'Science fiction in der DDR', *DaF*, 27, 1990:33–36. Id., 'Erik Simon, Olaf R. Spittel. Die science fiction der DDR. Autoren und Werke: Ein Lexikon', *WB*, 37:151–55. P. Herminghouse, 'Confronting the "Blank spots of history"': GDR culture and the legacy of Stalinism', *GSR*, 14:345–65. U. Heukenkamp, 'Das Frauenbild in der antifaschistischen Erneuerung der SBZ', Stephan, *Frauen*, 3–13. W. Hildebrandt, 'Die Mühen der Emanzipation. Expressionismus und kulturelles Erbe in der DDR', *Universitas*, 45, 1990:373–97. S. Hoefert, 'Stoff- und Motivwandlungen bei DDR-Schriftstellern. Zur Gestalt des Fremden bei Günter Kunert, Helga Königsdorf und Heiner Müller', *Akten* (Tokyo), x, 71–77. A. Hollis, 'The portrayal of war and fascism in the literature of East Germany', Brassloff, *Insights*, 215–32. T. Honnef,

840 German Studies

'"Wir haben schon wieder weiße Flecken." Die Anfangsjahre der DDR in Werken Loests, Heyms und Heins', *GLL*, 44:143–64. F. Hörnigk, 'Verlust von Illusionen — Gewinn an Realismus', *GSR*, 14:313–24. W. Jens, 'Plädoyer gegen die Preisgabe', *SuF*, 42, 1990:859–67. *Socialism and the Literary Imagination. Essays on East German Writers*, ed. Martin Kane, Oxford, Berg, xii + 256 pp., examines the many responses of GDR writers to the political ideology of their state, whilst seeking to avoid applying only the criterion of relative dissidence in evaluation of their works. The 15 essays span three generations from J. R. Becher to Prenzlauer Berg. They chart the optimism of the *Gründergeneration* (A Seghers, S. Heym, Erwin Strittmatter) to the generation born in the Third Reich (F. Fühmann, C. Wolf, J. Becker) and finally those born in the GDR (H. Königsdorf, V. Braun, C. Hein). A diverse picture emerges, including many variations on Marxist notions of historical progress, from the traditionalist nostalgia of J. Bobrowski to H. Müller's anarchic postmodernism and the exploration of fantastic and Utopian scenarios in the work of I. Morgner. E. Kaufmann, 'DDR-Schriftstellerinnen, die Widersprüche und die Utopie', *WGY*, 7:109–20. G. Kerekes, 'In der Opposition vereint — aber was nun?', *DeutUB*, 10:143–52. A. Krättli, 'Schwierigkeiten mit der "Wende". Die Schriftsteller in der DDR', *SchwM*, 70, 1990:26–29. B. Leistner, '"... im Entfernten nah." Kleist in der neueren DDR-Literatur', Leistner, *Beckmesser*, 221–53. H. Lenk, 'Rock für die Revolution. Zur Artikulation von Wirklichkeitserfahrung in DDR-Rockmusiktexten der späteren 8oer Jahre', *Ginkgobaum*, 10:163–93. Hans Mayer, *Der Turm von Babel. Erinnerung an eine Deutsche Demokratische Republik*, Frankfurt, Suhrkamp, 272 pp., makes no claims to academic status but constitutes an important contribution to the literary history of the GDR. Going back to the origins of the state and focusing on key personalities and events of the 1950s, this volume serves as a timely reminder of the anti-fascist consensus on which the GDR was based, whilst also exploring its failure to generate a democratic socialist political culture. The last three chapters deal specifically with the relationship of GDR writers to the state, looking in particular at U. Johnson, H. Kant, and V. Braun. M. Pulkenat, 'Geschichten der Töchter. Autobiographisch geprägte Erzählprosa von DDR-Autorinnen in den 8oer Jahren', *WB*, 36, 1990:1185–92. Marcel Reich-Ranicki, *Ohne Rabatt. Über Literatur aus der DDR*, DVA, 288 pp., is an expanded version of the 1974 volume of the same name, containing 37 critical essays (1961–91) on 18 GDR writers. While categorically denying GDR literature an independent identity at the outset, it points to the author's personal contribution to its serious reception in the West since the early 1960s. In addition to positive evaluation of works by F. Fühmann, H. J. Schädlich, and S. Kirsch, there is characteristically outspoken criticism of writers such as A. Seghers, Erwin Strittmatter, and C. Wolf. D. J. Rosenberg, 'Learning to say "I" instead of "we". Recent works on women in the former GDR', *WGY*, 7:161–68. R. Rosenberg, 'Zur Geschichte der Literaturwissenschaft in der DDR', *ZGer*, n.F., 1:247–56. Günther Rüther, *'Grief zur Feder, Kumpel.' Schriftsteller, Literatur und Politik in der DDR 1949–1990*, Düsseldorf, Droste, 221 pp., is another exploration of the relationship between *Geist und Macht* throughout the literary history of the GDR. It traces this chronologically from the ideologically legitimating role of literature in the new state to its increasingly oppositional function in the totalitarian regime, finally attributing to it a significant part in the *sanfte Revolution* of 1989. D. Schlenstedt, 'Träume. Beobachtungen an der neueren Literatur in der DDR', Gerber, *Studies*, 105–33. K.-W. Schmidt, 'Grenzüberschreitungen. Über Leben und Literatur ehemaliger DDR-Autoren in der Bundesrepublik. Eine Bestandsaufnahme. Kulturpolitische Folgen der Biermann-Ausbürgerung', Kreuzer, *Pluralismus*, 151–92. B. Spies, 'Von der schwierigen Zeitgenossesnschaft der DDR-Literatur. Eine Vorbemerkung', *LitL*, 1990:61–68. F. Trommler, 'The literature of the German Democratic Republic. An assessment in 1990: A symposium — introduction', *GSR*, 14:293–95. I. Wallace, 'Literature, censorship and glasnost in East Germany', Brassloff, *Insights*, 233–45.

MINORITY LITERATURE. G. Aescht, 'Kreation und Administration. Zur rumäniendeutschen Kurzprosa der Jahre 1962–1973', *ZSL*, 12, 1989:118–23. H. Avenary, 'Orale judendeutsche Volkspoesie in der Interaktion mit literarischer Überlieferung', *BLBI*, 87, 1990:5–17. G. Baur, 'Die alemannische Mundartliteratur in Südbayern nach 1945', Baur, *Mundartliteratur*, 13–56. H. Block, 'Plattdeutsche Literatur im Radio, zum Beispiel "Bökor-Schapp"', *Quickborn*, 80, 1990:311–16. L. Bodi, 'Zur Frage der deutschsprachigen Literatur in Australien', Rosenthal, *Literatur*, 67–82. N. J. Dornheim, 'Die deutschsprachige Literatur in Argentinien', *ib.*, 119–35. N. Feinäugle, 'Schwäbische Mundartdichtung seit 1945', *ib.*, 57–78. H. Fischer, 'Ethnische Stereotypen in der gegenwärtigen Volkserzählung', *Fabula*, 31, 1990:262–71. Id., 'Gegenwärtiges Erzählen. Neue Sagen im "Volksmund"', *VRM*, 9, 1990:11–19. M. Fleischer, 'Die deutschbrasilianische Literatur', Rosenthal, *Literatur*, 101–18. R. Goltz, 'Ein Hauch von Rosen zwischen Strandhafer und Heidekraut. Versuche über die niederdeutsche Literatur von 1945 bis 1989', *DBl*, 42, 1990:109–38. G. M. Gugelberger, 'Rethinking Germanistik', *Monatshefte*, 83:45–58, is on German–Third World literary relationships. E. Guntz, 'Zum Stand der deutschsprachigen Literatur in

Elsaß seit 1945', Rosenthal, *Literatur*, 11–23. D. Huck, 'Mundartdichtung in Elsaß nach 1945. Formen — Entwicklungen — Tendenzen', *ib.*, 79–97. R. Nethersole, 'Die deutschsprachige Literatur im südlichen Afrika', *ib.*, 25–46. J. Nieraad, 'Deutschsprachige Literatur in Israel', *ib.*, 83–100. M. Rankl, 'Ost- und westpreußische Literatur seit 1945. Vorüberlegungen zu einer Literaturgeschichte Ost- und Westpreußens von 1945 bis zur Gegenwart', *ABor*, 4, 1990:264–87. G. Richardt, 'Platter als Platt oder neue Vielfalt? Die achtziger Jahre und die niederdeutsche Literatur in der DDR', *Quickborn*, 81 : 112–24. K. V. Riedel, 'Der niederdeutsche Autorenwettbewerb 1989', *ib.*, 80, 1990:203–11. W. Riedel, 'Zur Literatur der deutschsprachigen Kanadier', Rosenthal, *Literatur*, 47–65. C. Schmid-Cadalbert, 'Entwicklungen und Tendenzen der neuen Mundartliteratur der deutschen Schweiz', Baur, *Mundartliteratur*, 99–125. D. Simonides, 'Zur Methodologie der Sammlung zeitgenössischer populärer Erzählungen', *Fabula*, 31, 1990:279–83. M. B. Stein, 'Transit: a narrative of travel across the two Germanys', *ib.*, 289–96. A. Unterkircher, 'Tiroler Literatur 1890–1990. Versuch eines ersten Überblicks', *MBA*, 9, 1990:81–87. J. Wirrer, 'Die niederdeutsche Kulturszene als Gegenstand der empirischen Literaturwissenschaft', *NdJb*, 113, 1990:44–69.

2. LYRIC POETRY

G.-J. Berendse, 'Zu neuen Ufern: Lyrik der "sächsischen Dichterschule" im Spiegel der Elbe', Gerber, *Studies*, 197–212. A. Bushell, **The Emergence of West German Poetry from the Second World War into the Early Post-War Period: A Study in Poetic Response* (EH, 1, 1120), 1989, 305 pp. W. Emmerich, 'Von der "durchgearbeiteten Landschaft" zur *nature morte*. Alte und neue Landschaftslyrik von Volker Braun, Wulf Kirsten und anderen', *LitL*, 1990:69–83. *Ein Molotow-Cocktail auf fremder Bettkante. Lyrik der siebziger/achtziger Jahre von Dichtern aus der DDR*, ed. Peter Geist, Leipzig, Reclam, 408 pp., is an anthology which reflects a basic consensus about poetry's oppositional function in the last two decades of the GDR's existence. The *Nachwort* outlines major developments and impulses of the period, including the abandonment of the integrated subject, increasing linguistic virtuosity, rhetorical urgency, and an anthropological and mythological urge to transcend historical pessimism. A. Goodbody, '*Deutsche Ökolyrik*: comparative observations on the emergence and expression of environmental consciousness in West and East German poetry', Williams, *Literature*, 373–400. W. Hartinger and K. Werner, 'DDR-Lyrik der siebziger und achtziger Jahre. Thesen', *WB*, 36, 1990:1986–92. H. Hartung, 'Placebos, Kwehrdeutsch, Vaterlandkanal. Anmerkungen zur jungen Lyrik', *Merkur*, 45:1145–52.

Wolfgang Haas, **Sprachtheoretische Grundlagen der konkreten Poesie* (SAG, 233), 1990, 294 pp. K. Leeder, '"*Poesie ist eine Gegensprache*": young GDR poets in search of a political identity', Williams, *Literature*, 413–27. H. Witt, 'Leipziger Dichterschule', *StZ*, 28, 1990:321–29. Joachim Wittowski, *Lyrik in der Presse. Eine Untersuchung der Kritik an Wolf Biermann, Erich Fried und Ulla Hahn* (Ep, 67), 339 pp., takes as its premise the crisis of bourgeois culture in 1968, which signalled a politicization of literary criticism and consequent elevation of the status of journalistic press reviews. It is also assumed that lyric poetry was the genre most radically affected by this development. The three case studies investigated here provide a contrastive analysis of press reaction to the Biermann affair in East and West, reception of Fried's *und* VIETNAM *und* (1966) and the role of the press for the emergence of a younger generation of poets exemplified by Ulla Hahn. The volume concludes with an attempted summary of the aesthetic and ideological criteria employed by the Austrian, East and West German press in their literary reviews.

3. Drama

Kurz bevor der Vorhang fiel. Zum Theater der DDR, ed. John Flood (*GDRMonitor* Special Series, 7), Amsterdam, Rodopi, 1990, 104 pp., records the proceedings of a London symposium held in 1988, and its eight contributions include comments on the development of GDR drama from the perspective of the theatre critic and director as well as *Germanistik*. It includes essays on comedy and *Kabarett* as well as individual studies of Christoph Hein and Heiner Müller. H. Haider-Pregler, 'Willkommene Heimkehrer? Die Rezeption des schweizer Exiltheaters in Österreich', Jauslin, *Schweiz*, 183–209. Pia Kleber and Colin Visser, **Re-interpreting Brecht: his Influence on Contemporary Drama and Film*, CUP, 1990, xiii + 220 pp. U. Profitlich, 'Literarische Geschichtsvermittlung als Thema deutschsprachiger Nachkriegsdramatik', Eggert, *Geschichte*, 315–29. H. Schneider, 'Exildramatik auf Bühnen der sowjetischen Besatzungszone Deutschlands', Jauslin, *Schweiz*, 132–55. M. Töteberg, '"Ich möchte hier den Vorhang des Schweigens herunterlassen." Über die Darstellung des Dritten Reiches in Schauspielermemoiren. Mit einem Exkurs über den Theaterkritiker Herbert Jhering', Mierendorff, *Aufsätze*, 121–48.

4. Prose

Wolfgang Ferchl, *Zwischen 'Schlüsselroman', Kolportage und Artistik: Studien zur gesellschaftskritisch-realistischen Romanliteratur der 50er Jahre in der Bundesrepublik Deutschland in ihrem sozialgeschichtlichen und poetologischen Kontext* (APSL, 93), 319 pp., looks at the attempts of left-wing

844 *German Studies*

intellectuals in the 1950s to develop a synthesis of liberalism and socialism and steer a middle course in the Cold War rhetoric of the day. It identifies a form of 'unmittelbar-veristischer Realismus' in the novel corresponding to this political ideal, and considers its realization in works by Kolbenhoff, Ledig, Kuby, Meischner, Drewitz, Bender, Wiesenborn, Frank, Arno Schmidt, and Martin Walser, seeing in *Ehen in Philippsburg* the highest achievement of realism in the 1950s. Michaela Holdenried, *Im Spiegel ein anderer. Erfahrungskrise und Subjektdiskurs im modernen autobiographischen Roman* (BNL, 114), xii + 552 pp., bases its analysis of texts by P. Weiss, T. Bernhard, Georges-Arthur Goldschmidt, and F. Innerhofer on an extensive historical and theoretical section, which relates the contemporary autobiographical novel to 20th-c. theories on autobiography and literary debates on the subject since the 'death of the author'. The aestheticization of existence in the texts under consideration is seen principally as a response to the post-modern crisis of the subject. M. Kraus, 'Zwischen Autonomie und Solidarität. Anmerkungen zum Bildungsroman der Studentenbewegung', *WW*, 40, 1990:394–407. Erna Kritsch Neuse, *Der Erzähler in der deutschen Kurzgeschichte* (SGLLC, 60), xii + 94 pp., is an attempt to test the author's own hypothesis that the short story can be defined as a genre by the length of 'erzählte Zeit' relative to 'Erzählzeit'. Adopting Franz Stanzel's distinction between 'Erzählerfiguren' and 'Reflektorfiguren' it proceeds to describe in detail the distinct forms taken by 'auktorial', 'personal', and 'Ich-Erzählsituation' in the short story, but finds none of these particularly dominant, and thus upholds, if only by default, the initial definition. L. Lamberechts, 'Zwischen Anomie und Inszenierung. Die deutschsprachige Prosa der Gegenwart in kultursoziologischer Sicht', *SGG*, 24.2:211–28. Jozef A. Modzelewski, **Das Pandämonium der achtziger Jahre. Kurzprosa des Jahres 1983* (SMGL, 37), 1990, xiv + 313 pp. H. Peitsch, '"Auf Sand gebaut?" Die Bundesrepublik in der Prosa der frühen fünfziger Jahre', *GLL*, 44:370–86. Id., 'Built on sand? Prose writings in the fifties and sixties', Kolinsky, *Era*, 297–322. D. Roberts, 'The German historical novel in the twentieth century: continuities and discontinuities. II. The postwar generation', Roberts, *Novel*, 171–80. H. Scheuer, 'Biographische Romane der 70er Jahre — Kunst und Wissenschaft', *DUS*, 43.4:32–42. R. Schnell, 'Zwischen Geschichtsphilosophie und "Posthistoire". Geschichte im deutschen Gegenwartsroman', *WB*, 37:342–55. Joachim Scholl, *In der Gemeinschaft des Erzählers: Studien zur Restitution des Epischen im deutschen Gegenwartsroman* (BNL, 105), 1990, 243 pp., outlines 20th-c. debates about the novel from Benjamin and Adorno to Enzensberger's pronouncement of the 'death of literature' and Martin Walser's *Fiction*. The second part of the study examines fictional responses to theoretical questions of narrative in G. Grass's *Danziger Trilogie* and U. Johnson's *Jahrestage*. Friedrich H. Schregel, *Die Romanliteratur der DDR. Erzähltechniken, Leserlenkung, Kulturpolitik*, Opladen, Westdeutscher Vlg, 367 pp., sets out to evaluate narrative technique in GDR writing according to aesthetic as well as political criteria, taking into account cultural policy, literary and cultural debates, and the material conditions of literary production. After an introductory chapter on reception theory, the analysis proceeds decade by decade, tracing the development of literature's role from ideological mouthpiece of the party to autonomous site of public debate. The emphasis is on the years until the mid-1970s, by which time GDR literature is deemed to have developed narrative techniques comparable to those used in the West, and cultural debates focused increasingly on socialist politics rather than socialist aesthetics. H. C. Sceba, 'Erfundene Vergangenheit: zur Fiktionalität historischer Identitätsbildung in den Väter-Geschichten der Gegenwart', *GR*, 26:176–82. Oliver Sill, *Zerbrochene Spiegel. Studien zur Theorie und Praxis modernen autobiographischen Erzählens*, Berlin, de Gruyter, xiv + 537 pp., devotes a long theoretical section to the analysis of autobiography in the light of the loss of an overall coherent system of thought since the Enlightenment, and fragmentation of the self since the First World War. This is seen reflected in the wide variety of autobiographical forms in the 20th c. which defy all normative attempts to define the genre in formal terms. The second half of the study illustrates this thesis in discussion of six autobiographies of the 1970s: E. Canetti's *Die gerettete Zunge*, Curd Jürgens's '. . . und kein bißchen weise*', P. Schneider's *Lenz*, Urs Jaeggi's *Brandeis*, P. Härtling's *Zwelte*, and Helga Novak's *Die Eisheiligen*.

5. INDIVIDUAL AUTHORS

AICHINGER, ILSE. J. P. Bier, 'Unsinn und Sinnbedürfnis. Ein Erzählproblem bei I.A.', *Fest. Verbeeck*, 31–49.

AMÉRY, JEAN. *Über J.A.*, ed. Irène Heidelberger–Leonard (BNL, 102), 1990, 130 pp., contains eight essays, all of which underline the prophetic significance of A.'s work. Individual contributions treat the question of A.'s Jewish identity, his linking of the themes of history's victims with the responsibility of the survivors, his linguistic critique of the 'jargons' of the Marxist dialectic, structuralism and postmodernism, his anticipation of the *Historikerstreit* in his views on history and the subject, the autobiographical self-examination in *Unmeisterliche Wanderjahre* and *Örtlichkeiten*, and the French sources of his essay 'Über das Altern'. There is also an interpretation of his 'Roman Essay' *Charles Bovary. Landarzt* and a comparison with Primo Levi. P. Süss, 'Autobiographische Essayistik bei J.A.', *GM*, 32, 1990:3–14.

ANDERS, GÜNTHER. T. H. Macho, 'Die Kunst der Verwandlung. Notizen zur frühen Musikphilosophie von G.A.', *Merkur*, 45:475–84.

ANDERSCH, ALFRED. D. Horrocks, 'On teaching A.'s *Sansibar oder der letzte Grund*', *German Teaching*, 2.1:24–31. M. Liebe, **A.A. und sein 'Radio essay'* (EH, I, 1185), 1990, 253 pp. Margaret Littler, *A.A. (1914–1980) and the Reception of French Thought in the Federal Republic of Germany*, Lewiston, Edwin Mellen, xii + 390 pp., is a reassessment of the influence of French Existentialism on A.'s work and literary aesthetic. In detailed analysis of the treatment of perception in his autobiographical writing, his novels, short stories and travelogues, a consistent philosophical position emerges which is more akin to the Phenomenology of Maurice Merleau-Ponty than to any notions of Sartrean commitment. M. Littler, '"Drei Schwierigkeiten für die Frau, die Andersch liest ..."': A reassessment of the portrayal of women in the work of A.A.', *GLL*, 44:443–58. B. Murdoch '"Überhaupt nichts los"': some comments on A.A. and Dylan Thomas', *Neophilologus*, 75:11–20. J. Quack, '"Beschreiben Sie die Sahara!" Zum Prosaverständnis A.As', Quack, *Identifikation*, 74–88.

AUSLÄNDER, ROSE. Claudia Beil, *Sprache als Heimat. Jüdische Tradition und Exilerfahrung in der Lyrik von Nelly Sachs und R.A.*, Munich, tuduv, v + 436 pp., looks at the interaction of Jewish and German cultural traditions in the works of the two poets. First they are located in a tradition of German Jewish exile writing (Heine), and then of Jewish mysticism, as assimilated into German culture by the *Frühromantik* (Jakob Böhme, Novalis). Their works are then interpreted in the light of their debt to this cabbalistic tradition as mediated through German Romanticism. For both of them it is the German language and literary heritage which, more than their Jewish origins, offers a substitute for the lost homeland. *R.A. Materialien zu Leben und Werk*, ed. Helmut Braun, Frankfurt, Fischer, 292 pp., includes a biographical introduction, four essays by R.A. from the years 1920–73, and five personal tributes. Three critical essays on her poetry focus on the notion of *Heimat* and the significance of the Jewish philosophical heritage in her writing. The volume is completed by 16 reviews and tributes, authors including M. L. Kaschnitz, K. Krolow, H. Bender, and G. Kunert.

BACHMANN, INGEBORG. K. R. Achberger, 'Kunst als Veränderndes: B. und Brecht', *Monatshefte*, 83:7–16. C. Baehr, 'I.Bs Übersetzung von Gedichten der Sammlung "Allegria" von Guiseppe Ungaretti', Pöckl, *Dichter*, 403–95. E. Boa, 'Unnatural Causes: modes of death in Christa Wolf's *Nachdenken über Christa T.* and I.B.'s *Malina*', Williams, *Literature*, 139–54. D. G. Bond, '"Gedanken über die ganze Bildungsstufe der Männer." Firc imagery in thc work of I.B.', *FMLS*, 27:238–54. J. Bossinade, '"Erklär mir Liebe" von I.B. Reflexionen über eine erweiterte Poetik', *Sprachkunst*, 20, 1989 (1990):177–97. G. Dolei, 'La parola nel "regno del perfetto". Sulla lirica di I.B.', *AION(T)*, 29, 1986 (1990):319–34. I. Dusar, 'Identität und Sprache. I.Bs Erzählung "Simultan"', *Fest. Verbeeck*, 67–79. S. Hamen, 'Espaces circulaires et temps cyclique dans l'œuvre d'I.B.', *TI*, 5, 1990:235–53. Andreas Hapkemeyer, *I.B. Entwicklungs-linien in Werk und Leben*, Vienna, Vlg der Österr. Akad. der Wiss., 169 pp., is a strictly biographical, chronological approach to B.'s work which does little to challenge the popular myths of B. reception. It traces her development from philosophy studies in post-war Vienna through her literary debut with Gruppe 47 to her travels between Italy, the USA, the FRG and Austria, and her relationships with Hans Werner Henze, Max Frisch, and Pierre Evrard. Discussion of her work focuses on linguistic/philosophical issues, taking little account of her reception by feminist criticism since the late 1970s. H. Kaulen, 'Zwischen Engagement und Kunstautonomie: I.Bs letzter Gedichtzyklus *Vier Gedichte* (1968)', *DVLG*, 65:755–76. G. Kohn-Waechter, '"... ich liebte ihr Herunterbrennen." Das Zerschreiben der Opferfaszination *Gespräch im Gebirg* von Paul Celan und *Malina* von I.B.', Kohn-Waechter, *Flammen*, 219–40. Kohn-Waechter, 'Das "Problem der Post" in *Malina* von I.B. und Martin Heideggers *Der Satz vom Grund*', Runge, *Frau*, 225–42. H Mahrdt, 'I.B. Es geht ein Riß durch die Welt. Zu I.Bs Geschlechter- und Öffentlichkeitskritik', *Rapial*, 1:8–10. M. T. Mandalari, '"Mantenete le distanze da me, o morirò ..."; I.B.', *Belfagor*, 44, 1989:437–49. M. Oberle, **Liebe als Sprache und Sprache als Liebe. Die sprachutopische Poetologie der Liebeslyrik I.Bs* (EH, 1, 1243), 1990, 309 pp. M. L. Punte, 'Die Bedeutung des Weiblichen im Werk von I.B.', *Akten* (Tokyo), x, 275–81. Saskia Schottelius, **Das imaginäre Ich: Subjekt und Identität in I.Bs Roman 'Malina' und Jacques Lacans Sprachtheorie* (EH, 1, 1184), 1990, 187 pp. S. Thiele, 'Die Selbstreflexion der Kunst in I.Bs Roman *Malina*', *GR*, 26:58–69. I. Vemmelund, '"Ein Ende mit der Schrift. Ein andrer Anfang." Über die Sprach- und Strukturproblematik bei I.Bs *Der Fall Franza* und Christa Wolfs *Kassandra*', *Ginkgobaum*, 10:81–102. See also DUDEN, ANNE.

BECKER, JUREK. G. Kerekes, '"Warnung vor dem Schriftsteller." J.Bs Frankfurter Vorlesungen zur Poetik im Sommersemester 1989', *Germanistisches Jahrbuch DDR-RU*, 9, 1990:366–72. A. Simpson, 'The production of meaning in J.B.'s *Schlaflose Tage*', *Seminar*, 27:153–68.

BECKER, THORSTEN. M. Kane, 'Was the wall a laughing matter? Some reflections on T.B.'s *Die Bürgschaft*', Williams, *Literature*, 359–71.

BERNHARD, THOMAS.   L. Bodi, 'Annihilating Austria: T.B.'s *Auslö-schung. Ein Zerfall*', Roberts, *Novel*, 201–16. Id., 'Österreicher in der Fremde — Fremde in Österreich. Zur Identitäts- und Differenzerfahrung in T.Bs *Auslöschung. Ein Zerfall* (1986)', *Akten* (Tokyo), x, 120–25. D. G. Daviau, 'T.B.s *Heldenplatz*', *Monatshefte*, 83:29–44. W. Hackl, 'Unterhaltung und Provokation. T.B. als Satiriker des österreichischen Kulturbetriebs: *Holzfällen*. Eine Erregung', *Germanistisches Jahrbuch DDR-RU*, 9, 1990:132–45. U. Kinzel, 'Am Ursprung des Erzählens. Zeit und Erzählen bei Moritz, Büchner, Benn und B.', *Schiller Jb.*, 34, 1990:364–92. Christian Klug, *T.Bs Theaterstücke*, Stuttgart, Metzler, xiv + 321 pp., is a comprehensive study of B.'s dramas, focusing on the notion of *Todeskrankheit* in the light of B.'s reception of Pascal's, Schopenhauer's, and especially Kierkegaard's philosophy. It analyses the rhetorical function of fragmentary speech in the plays as indicative of a fundamental philosophical stance. The philosophical model is applied to central concepts and metaphors such as 'Finsternis', 'Isolation', and 'Musikalität', and is exemplified in detailed textual analysis of *Der I. und der W.* and *Die Jagdgesellschaft*. M. Madel, *Solipsismus in der Literatur des 20. Jahrhunderts: Untersuchungen zu T.Bs Roman 'Frost', Arno Schmidts Erzählung 'Aus dem Leben eines Fauns' und Elias Canettis Roman 'Die Blendung'* (EH, 1, 1190), 1990, viii + 329 pp. Eva Marquardt, *Gegenrichtung. Entwicklungstendenzen in der Erzählprosa T.Bs*, Tübingen, Niemeyer, 1990, 198 pp., rejects the tendency to use B.'s autobiographical works as the key to all his fictional writing, and treats *Korrektur* and *Die Ursache. Eine Andeutung* as objects of literary interpretation in their own right. The author begins by analysing the antithetical narrative structures of B.'s prose works from the early 1950s to *Auslöschung*. The second section examines locality in relation to the narrative subject in B.'s works, only then looking at the autobiographical texts as stages in the development of a narrative universe in which fiction and reality are indistinguishable, and thus in tune with a European Modernist tradition based on the impossibility of representation. G. Melzer, 'Das Wien T.Bs', *AION(T)*, 33.1–2, 1990:257–70. G. Plow, 'The affliction of prose: T.B.'s critique of self-expression in *Korrektur, Ja* und *Der Stimmenimitator*', *GLL*, 44:133–42. J. Quack, 'Figuren der Polemik, Gesten der Empörung. Am Beispiel T.B. and Rolf Dieter Brinkmanns', Quack, *Identifikation*, 89–100. Marcel Reich-Ranicki, *T.B.*, Zurich, Ammann, 1990, 113 pp., is a collection of the author's essays and talks on B.'s prose since 1967 and a testimony to a lasting fascination. Individual essays discuss B.'s treatment of madness in the novel *Verstörung*, his use of Austrian locality in *Ungenach* and other stories collected in the volume *Prosa* (1967), his macabre tales of murder, madness and despair, and his autobiographical novels. A welcome note of optimism is detected in *Wittgensteins Neffe*, *Breton*, *Holzfällen*, and *Auslöschung*, and Reich-Ranicki asserts 'B. wird von Buch zu Buch menschlicher'. U. Wienzerl, 'B. als Erzieher: T.Bs *Auslöschung*', *GQ*, 63, 1990:445–61.

BICHSEL, PETER. *P.B. Texten, Daten, Bilder* (SL, 997), 180 pp., contains 12 texts by B., largely speeches and articles reprinted here for the first time, an illustrated biographical section, and nine essays on his work. These include discussions of *Jahreszeiten*, his *Kindergeschichten*, and the essay volume *Der Leser. Das Erzählen*. There are also contributions on the question of B.'s Swiss identity, his political commitment and a final section is devoted to his journalistic writing. D. de Vin, 'Erzähl mir eine Geschichte. P.B.', *SGG*, 2:229 54.

BIENEK, HORST. H. Ortowski, 'Zur Bedeutung Eichendorffs in den Romanen von H.B.', *SGP*, 14, 1990:105–17. A. Reif, 'Der Verständigungsprozeß kann nur "von unten" geführt werden. Gespräch mit dem Schriftsteller H.B.', *Universitas*, 45, 1990:513–22.

BIERMANN, WOLF. J. Drews, 'Oj, oj, B!', *Merkur*, 45:1174–79. See also p. 843 above.

BOBROWSKI, JOHANNES. *Sarmatische Zeit. Erinnerung und Zukunft. Dokumentation des J.B. Kolloquiums 1989 in der Akademie Sankelmark*, ed. Alfred Kelletat, Sankelmark, Akademie Sankelmark, 1990, 143 pp., contains nine essays, several of which focus on geographical locality in B.'s poetry, the significance of the Memelland and Russian influences, and his concept of a 'Sarmatischer Divan'. There are also considerations of his reception in the GDR, Poland, and Lithuania, as well as his evocation in prose of a tradition of oral literature. Alex Stock, *Warten, ein wenig. Zu Gedichten und Geschichten von J.B.*, Würzburg, Königshausen & Neumann, 71 pp. J. Wieczorek, 'Questioning philosemitism: the depiction of Jews in the prose works of J.B.', *GLL*, 44:122–32. A. Williams, '"Aber wo befinde ich mich?"': the narrator's location and historical perspective in works by Siegfried Lenz, Günter Grass and J.B.', Williams, *Literature*, 255–71.

BÖLL, HEINRICH. B. Balzer, *B: Die verlorene Ehre der Katharina Blum*, Frankfurt, Diesterweg, 1990, 72 pp. R. A. Berman, 'The rhetoric of citation and the ideology of war in H.B.'s short fiction', *GR*, 26:155–60. S. Güstrau, *Literatur als Theologieersatz: H.B. 'Sie sagt, ihr Kuba ist hier und auch ihr Nicaragua'*, Berne, Lang, 1990, iii + 113 pp. K. Kovács, 'Historismus und Transzendenz in H.Bs *Billard um Halbzehn*', *NFT*, 18, 1989:99–111. O. Lappalainen, 'B. und "deutscher Kitsch". Zur Rezeption von H.Bs (1917–1985) letzten Romanen', *TeK*, 16, 1988 (1990):172–80. *H.B. Was soll aus dem Jungen bloß werden?*, ed. J. H. Reid (MNGT), vi + 153 pp., places B.'s autobiographical account of schooldays under National Socialism in its historical and literary context. The introduction offers background information to B.'s life and work, the Third Reich and its youth organizations, as well as an introduction to theories of autobiography and some detail on the contemporary political and cultural context of 1981. The 'Arbeitsteil' provides the opportunity of comparison of B.'s text with the abridged version first published in the *FAZ* in April 1981. Dorothee Römhild, **Die Ehre der Frau ist unantastbar. Das Bild der Frau im Werk H.Bs*, Pfaffenweiler, Centaurus, vii + 228 pp.

BORN, NICOLAS. Heinrich Bosse and Ulrich A. Lampen, *Das Hineinspringen in die Totschlägerreihe. N.Bs Roman 'Die Fälschung'*, Munich, Fink, 127 pp., is a psychological and existentialist reading of *Die Fälschung* (1979), B.'s third and last novel, the story of a journalist's attempt to cope with reporting on war-torn Beirut by constructing a barrier of inauthenticity between himself and his experience. This is discussed in chapters which focus on central themes and motifs, on struggle, writing, the gaze, love, and killing.

BRAUN, VOLKER. G.-J. Berendse, '25 Jahre politische Poesie von V.B.', *WW*, 41:425–35. D. Goltschnigg, 'Utopie und Revolution. Georg Büchner in der DDR-Literatur: Christa Wolf, V.B., Heiner Müller', *ZDP*, 109, 1990:571–96. C. Klotz, 'V.B. oder Wir haben die Morgenröte entrollt, um in der Dämmerung zu wohnen', *LitL*, 1990:107–21. G. Shaw, 'Kast *resurrectus*: V.B.'s *Bodenloser Satz*', Williams, *Literature*, 85–96. D. Wolff, '"Entweder würden sie in den mächtigen eisernen Bedingungen verschwinden, oder sie müßten sie zerbrechen" — Gedanken zur Gestaltung des Verhältnisses Leiter-Geleiteter im Hinze-Kunze Roman von V.B.', *Germanistisches Jahrbuch DDR-RU*, 9, 1990:63–76. See also p. 842 above.

DE BRUYN, GÜNTER. *G.d.B. Materialien zu Leben und Werk*, ed. Uwe Wittstock, Frankfurt, Fischer, 247 pp., contains nine essays on de B.'s work: two discussions of marriage in *Buridans Esel* and essays on *Märkische Forschungen*, on *Preisverleihung, Neue Herrlichkeit, Lesefreuden*, and his biography of Jean Paul. The critical essays are supplemented by five interviews, three appreciations by other authors (F. R. Fries, M. Walser, C. Wolf), and four essays by de B. himself on aspects of writing and publishing in the GDR.

BURMEISTER, BRIGITTE. A. Gargano, 'Ein visueller Flaneur: B.Bs *Aufenthalt in der Fremde*', *AION(T)*, 33.3, 1990:103–18.

BUSTA, CHRISTINE. W. Wiesmüller, 'Das Gedicht als Predigt. Produktions- und rezeptionsästhetische Aspekte biblischer Motivik in Gedichten von C.B.', *Sprachkunst*, 20, 1989 (1990):199–226.

CELAN, PAUL. M. M. Anderson, 'The "impossibility of poetry": C. and Heidegger in France', *NGC*, 53:3–18. M. Braun, 'Interpretation und ihr Text. Zu Derridas und Gadamers Umgang mit Gedichten von P.C.', *LitL*:8–17. P.C. *'Atemwende': Materialien*, ed. Gerhard Buhr and Roland Reuss, Würzburg, Königshausen &

Neumann, 371 pp., is in three sections, the first comprising six interpretations of individual poems, the second nine, largely comparative, discussions of the anthology, including its relation to Goethe's *West-östlicher Divan*, to the Russian poet Osip Mandel'shtam, the baroque, and to his own earlier poetry. Other contributors discuss the seafaring metaphors and the musical setting of 'Fadensonnen'. Five essays concern the interpretation of C.'s work as a whole, addressing broader methodological issues such as the 'hermetic' poem, phenomenological and semantic approaches, and the use of symbol and allegory. Amy Colin, *P.C.: Holograms of Darkness*, Indianapolis — Bloomington, Indiana U.P., xxviii + 211 pp., approaches C.'s work through readings of his earliest German and Romanian texts 1938–47, situating them in the tradition of the German Yiddish, Ukrainian, and Romanian literature of the Bukovina, and relating them to German Expressionism and Franco-Romanian Surrealism. In close textual analysis the author seeks to show how C. exploded these traditions in the attempt to articulate a response to the holocaust. A. Fioretos, 'Nothing: reading P.C.'s "Engführung"', *CLS*, 27, 1990:158–68. E. Hünnecke, 'Die "spätere" Zeit. P.Cs Gedicht "Kristall"', *RG*, 20, 1990:181–93. M. Ossar, 'The malevolent God and P.C.'s "Tenebrae"', *DVLG*, 65:174–97. V. Piredda, 'Dido und "Der Andere"'. Guiseppe Ungaretti — P.C.: Beobachtungen zu einer Übertragung aus dem Italienischen', Pöckl, *Dichter*, 497–508. E. Polt-Heinzl, 'P.C. (1920–1970)', *ZDNÖL*, 13, 1990:10–12. J. Roelans, 'Auseinandergeschrieben. Lesenotizen zu C.'s "Engführung" und "Muschelhaufen"', *Fest. Verbeeck*, 209–20. G. Schank, 'Gitter der Sprache und Gitter des Geistes: zu P.Cs "Sprachgitter". Ein ergänzender Vorschlag', *Pörnbacher Vol.*, 321–32. E. Schreiner, 'P.Cs Übertragung von Valérys "La Jeune parque"', Pöckl, *Dichter*, 267–300. Arnold Stadler *Das Buch der Psalmen und die deutschsprachige Lyrik des 20. Jahrhunderts. Zu den Psalmen im Werk Bertolt Brechts und P.Cs*, Cologne — Vienna, Böhlau, 1989, x + 341 pp. R. Zschachlitz, *Vermittelte Unmittelbarkeit im Gegenwort: P.Cs kritische Poetik* (Literarhistorische Untersuchungen, 15), Berne, Lang, 1990, 248 pp. Y. Yokitani, 'Vieldeutigkeit des Textes — Vielfältigkeit der Interpretationen. Über P.Cs Gedicht "Blume"', *Doitsu Bungaku-ronko*, 32, 1990:75–92. See also BACHMANN, INGEBORG.

CSOKOR, FRANZ THEODOR. *Immer ist Anfang: der Dichter F.T.C.*, ed. J. P. Strelka, Berne, Lang, 1990, 193 pp.

CZECHOWSKI, HEINZ. I. Hilton, 'The darkened face of nature', Williams, *Literature*, 401–12.

CZURDA, ELFRIEDE. E. Tunner, 'Einiges über Grenz-Verrückungen. Eindrücke beim Lesen von E.Cs Texten "Diotima oder die Differenz des Glücks" und "Signora Julia"', *Germanica*, 7, 1990:109–14.

DAMM, SIGRID.   K. Sager, 'Der Schattenriß einer Frau', *Ginkgobaum*, 10:155–62.

DISCHE, IRENE.   W. Winkler, 'Wie funktioniert ein Dosenöffner? I.Ds Erzählungen', *Merkur*, 45:1157–59.

DODERER, HEIMITO VON.   K. Hopf, 'Die Funktion der Tagebücher H. von Ds', *MAL*, 24:231–49. M. Loew-Cadonna, 'Suspense in Ds Erzählen', *Sprachkunst*, 21, 1990 (1991):231–49.

DOMIN, HILDE.   W. Hinck, 'Fluchtwohnungen – Zufluchtwohnungen. Zur Lyrik H.Ds', *Fest. Rathofer*, 509–17. M. Titze, 'Frau mit Schirm. Von der Gunst des Gedichts. Eine Begegnung mit H.D.', *SuF*, 43:286–94.

DORST, TANKRED.   Peter Bekes, *T.D. Bilder und Dokumente*, Munich, Spangenberg, 94 pp., provides an attractively illustrated introduction to D.'s life and work for stage and film. It charts his career from the early 'Revolutionsdrama' *Toller* through the realism of the *Deutsche Stücke* to the Utopian themes of the 1980s and the dream visions of his most recent works *Karlos*, *Korbes*, and *Nach Jerusalem*. The volume includes the text of T.D.'s Büchnerpreis-Rede 1990.

DREWITZ, INGEBORG.   Yvonne-Christiane Fischer-Lüder, *An den Rand gedrückt — zum Opfer gemacht — Subjekt geworden. Die Entwicklung der Frauenfiguren in den Romanen von I.D.* (EH, I, 1172), 1990, 298 pp. M. Schafe, 'Die überfordete Generation: Mutterfiguren in Romanen von I.D.', *WGY*, 7:23–42.

DUDEN, ANNE.   M. Brügmann, 'Verstoßene Väter — verstörte Töchter. Faschismus als Schibboleth im Werk von Wolf, Bachmann und D.', *Akten* (Tokyo), x, 261–66. E. Dangel, 'Übergang und Ankunft. Positionen neuerer Frauenliteratur. Zu A.Ds "Übergang" und Verena Stefans "Wortgetreu ich träume"', *JIG*, 22.2, 1990:80–94.

DÜRRENMATT, FRIEDRICH.   Heinz Ludwig Arnold, *Querfahrt mit D.*, Göttingen, Wallstein, 1990, 110 pp., is a collection of the author's essays on D., ranging from the affectionately anecdotal to the text-analytical and presenting an impression of the breadth of D.'s talent as dramatist, philosopher, and artist. There is discussion of *Der Mitmacher*, *Justiz*, and *Durcheinandertal* and his project 'Stoffe', with a separate essay devoted to the autobiographical chapter of vol. 2 of this work entitled 'Querfahrt'. Identifying D.'s two main themes as 'Labyrinth' and 'Rebellion' A. attempts to define the non-Brechtian revolutionary nature of his dramatic art, becoming more radical until its culmination in the play *Achterloo* (1988). P. A. Bloch, 'F.D.: Entwürfe und Stoffe. Fragmente eines Gesprächs', *SchwM*, 71:43–50. E. S. Dick, 'Ds Dramaturgie des Einfalls. *Der Besuch der alten Dame* und

Der Meteor', Mainusch, *Komödie*, 389–95. G. Fritsch, 'Labyrinth und
großes Gelächter — die Welt als "Durcheinandertal". Ein Beitrag zu
F.Ds grotesker Ästhetik', *DD*, 21, 1990:652–70. R. Heikkilä, 'Die
finnische Diskussion über schweizerische Dramen: F.D. und Max
Frisch als Seher und Propheten', *JFinL*, 23:297–303. A. Krättli, 'Die
Vision verführt mich zum Schreiben. Im Blick auf "Turmbau,
Stoffe IV — IV"', *SchwM*, 71:35–42. M. Misch, 'Zu Ds *Der Besuch der
alten Dame'*, *DUSA*, 22.1:16–29. F. Piedmont, 'Der Besuch der alten
Dame in Wallensteins Lager: D. im Dialog mit Schiller', *ZDP*,
110:281–94. Alexander Ritter, *F.D.: Die Physiker. Erläuterungen und
Dokumente*, Stuttgart, Reclam, 243 pp., comprises a detailed commen-
tary of the language of the play, followed by sections on origins,
influences, and reception. In addition to biographical and socio-
political context it is located within the German theatrical comic
tradition and contemporary debates around scientific research,
nuclear technology, and political power. I. F. Roe, 'D.'s *Die Physiker*:
"Die drei Leben des Galilei"?', *FMLS*, 27:255–67. F. Sammern-
Frankenegg, 'Exit Strindberg. Zur Eliminierung Strindbergs in F.Ds
Play Strindberg', *SN*, 63:89–93. K. Whitton, 'F.D. (1921–1990). An
appreciation', *German Teaching*, 2.1:32–35. M. Wright, 'Teaching
D.'s *Die Physiker'*, *ib.*, 2.4:20–25.

ЕІСН, GÜNTER.   M. Oppermann, '"Das Jahr Lazertis", oder: G.Es
Begriff der "hergestellten Wirklichkeit"', *ZDP*, 109, 1990:538–51.

EISENDLE, HELMUT.   J. Potgieter, 'H.E.: *Exil oder der braune Salon.*
Der Essay als Motor des Romangeschehens', *MAL*, 24.1:113–23.

ENDE, MICHAEL.   D.-R. Moser, 'Das Ende der Geschichte . . .
Bundesgerichtshof gab M.E. recht', *LiB*, 22, 1990:26–27.

ENZENSBERGER, HANS MAGNUS.   P. M. Lützeler, 'Bachmann und
Bernhard an Böhmens Strand. Schriftsteller und Europa oder die
Entdeckung des Homo Europaeus Enzensbergensis' (on *Ach
Europa!*), *NRu*, 102.1:23–35. Holger-Heinrich Preusse, **Der politische
Literat H.M.E.: politische und gesellschaftliche Aspekte seiner Literatur und
Publizistik* (EH, 1, 1164), 1990, 234 pp. B. A. Watson, 'Reception as
self-definition: H.M.E.'s edition of *Der hessische Landbote* (1965)',
Mills, *Büchner*, 227–45.

ERB, ELKE.   G. Wolf, 'Die selbst erlittene Geschichte mit dem Lob
— zur Verleihung des Heinrich–Mann–Preises 1990 an E.E. und
Adolf Endler', *MAKDDR*, 28.5, 1990:8–12.

FASSBINDER, RAINER WERNER.   R. Grimm, 'Juden als Wanzen: der
Fall des R.W.F.', *AION(T)*, 29, 1986 (1990):335–97. Id., 'Der reiche
Jude, zum Fall des R.W.F.', *AUGIAS*, 40, 1990:5–19. Id., 'The Jew,
the playwright, and trash: West Germany's F. controversy',
Monatshefte, 83:17–28.

FICHTE, HUBERT. H. Böhme, '"Eine Schematisierung der Zerstückelungsphantasien." Über einen Ursprung der Fichte'schen Literatur', *FHL*, 10, 1990:5–21. *Leben, um eine Form der Darstellung zu erreichen: Studien zum Werk H. Fs*, ed. Hartmut Böhme and Nicolaus Tiling, Frankfurt, Fischer, 266 pp., contains 13 essays which treat sources, influences, and themes of F.'s work. These include considerations of his transition from the medium of radio to literature, significant literary relationships such as that with Hans Henny Jahnn, and influences from Classical antiquity to the Marquis de Sade. Several of the contributors focus on intercultural and ethnographic aspects of his work and on issues of formulating a homoerotic aesthetic. Bertil Madsen, *Auf der Suche nach einer Identität. Studien zu H.Fs Romantetralogie 'Das Waisenhaus', 'Die Palette', 'Detlevs Imitationen "Grünspan"', 'Versuch über die Pubertät'*, Stockholm, Almquist & Wiksell, 1990, x + 352 pp., aims to relate the textual complexity of H.F.'s tetralogy (1965–74) to its central theme: the acquisition of masculine sexual identity. The author rejects attempts to classify F.'s work as 'homosexuelle Literatur', claiming that sexuality, for F., is a social construct. In the first two novels the construction of an 'outsider' position is analysed narratologically, thematically, and linguistically, while the psychological/relational nature of the subject is explored in a chapter entitled 'Generationsbeziehungen'. The struggle of the fatherless half-Jewish hero to assert his independent ego against almost totalitarian matriarchal power is traced throughout the tetralogy remaining unresolved even in the fourth novel in which F. experiments with first person narrative to investigate the complex relationship between narrator, author, protagonist, and reader. W. Popp, '"Weibliches Schreiben" — "männliches Schreiben". Geschlechtsidentität und literarische Authentizität am Beispiel von Christa Wolf, Hans Henny Jahnn und H.F.', Kalveram, *Homosexualitäten*, 123–32. T. Vollhaber, 'Das Nichts — die Angst — die Erfahrung. Untersuchung zur zeitgenössischen schwulen Literatur', *ib.*, 133–43.

FRIED, ERICH. W. Görtschacher, 'Nur die Schattseite des Dichters? E.F. als Übersetzer von Dylan Thomas', Pöckl, *Dichter*, 123–86. Volker Kaukoreit, **Vom Exil bis zum Protest gegen den Krieg in Vietnam. Frühe Stationen des Lyrikers E.F. Werk und Biographie 1938–1966*, Darmstadt, Jürgen Häusser, 560 pp. Volker Kaukoreit and Heidemarie Vahl, **Einer singt aus der Zeit gegen die Zeit. E.F. 1921–1988. Materialien und Texte zum Leben und Werk*, Darmstadt, Jürgen Häusser, 124 pp. See also p. 843 above.

FRIES, FRITZ RUDOLF. W. F. Schoeller, 'Flugrouten des Ironikers. F.R.F. Romancier aus Petershagen', *NRu*, 102.3:134–41.

FRISCH, MAX. J. Barkhoff, 'Zur erzähltheoretischen Tiefenstruktur in M.Fs *Homo Faber*', *WW*, 41:212–27. W. Konrad, **M.F.* '*Die chinesische Mauer*': *ein Paradigma für seine Oswald-Spengler-Rezeption*, Berne, Lang, 1990, 103 pp. Manfred Leber, *Vom modernen Roman zur antiken Tragödie. Interpretation von M.Fs* '*Homo Faber*', Berlin, de Gruyter, 1990, xii + 201 pp., examines F.'s novel as a significant contribution to the history of tragedy, and a work which transcends the tradition of the novel. The author compares technology as universal structure of modern life to the function of the gods of Classical antiquity. The novel is first placed in the context of contemporary debates on technology and a contradiction is identified between technology as all-encompassing closed system and as a dominant symbolic mode of signification. The subsequent discussion of the text demonstrates a convergence of scientific and mythological terms of reference and focuses on the incest theme, pointing to direct parallels with Euripides' *Oedipus*. F. A. Lubich, **M.F.* '*Stiller*', '*Homo Faber*' *und* '*Mein Name sei Gantenbein*', Stuttgart, UTB, 1990, 151 pp. Marcel Reich-Ranicki, *M.F. Aufsätze*, Zurich, Ammann, 125 pp., is Reich-Ranicki's personal tribute to F. as 'Klassiker inmitten unserer Gegenwart' in seven essays collected here for the first time. Subjects include the fragmentation of identity in *Stiller* and in F.'s *Tagebuch 1946–1949*, a defence of *Mein Name sei Gantenbein* against the critique of Hans Mayer, F.'s attitude to literary commitment, his relationship to Switzerland, an enthusiastic reception of *Montauk* and more measured but still positive assessment of *Blaubart*. K. Reschke, **Life as a Man: Contemporary Male–Female Relationships in the Novels of M.F.* (SMGL, 34), 1990, 409 pp. C. Sisegrist, 'Ein großer Autor — im Werk und im Widerspruch. Zum Tod des Schriftstellers M.F.', *SchwM*, 71:403–12. A. D. White, 'Reality and imagination in *Mein Name sei Gantenbein*', *OGS*, 18–19, 1989–90:150–64.

FRISCHMUTH, BARBARA. S. Ogawa, 'Offenes Denken bei F. Über *Die Mystifikationen der Sophie Silber*', *Doitsu Bungaku-ronko*, 32, 1990:93–110.

FRISÉ, ADOLF. *Musil-Forum*, 16, 1990 (*Festschrift für A.F.*) includes 80th birthday tributes by F. Aspetsberger, U. Karhaus, H. Ledig-Rowohlt, as well as P. Payne, 'A.F. — a view from across the Channel', 28–31, and G. Vogt, '"Einer literarischen Mode folge ich nicht." Der Schriftsteller A.F.', 22–27.

FRITSCH, GERHARD. J. Sonnleitner, 'Zwischen Geschichtshaß und -verlangen. Zum Roman *Fasching* von G.F.', *AION(T)*, 33.1–2, 1990:183–98.

FÜHMANN, FRANZ. U. Elsner, 'Wandlung und Erfahrung im Erbeverständnis F.Fs: dargestellt am Beispiel seiner Homer-Rezeption', *Germanistisches Jahrbuch DDR-RU*, 9, 1990:86–98. U.

Meyszies, 'Die Analyse von Makrostrukturen im literarischen Erzähltext am Beispiel von "Kameraden"', *HSWSL*, 15, 1988:56–68. D. Tate, '"Subjective authenticity" in F.F.'s early prose writing', Gerber, *Studies*, 135–50. Id., 'The sufferings of "Kamerad Fühmann"': a case of distorted reception in both German states', Williams, *Literature*, 285–98. Irmgard Wagner, **F.F. Nachdenken über Literatur*, Heidelberg, Winter, 1989, 167 pp.

GAISER, GERD. J. Lieskounig, '"An ihren Körpern sollt ihr sie erkennen?"': Funktionen und Rolle der Körperdarstellung in zwei zeitkritischen Romanen der fünfziger Jahre', *Seminar*, 27.1:12–26, deals with G. and Koeppen.

GLAUSER, FRIEDRICH. E. Pulver, '"Wahrheit hat mit Worten nichts zu tun." Ein Leitmotiv im Leben und im Werk F.Gs', *SchwM*, 69, 1989:821–31.

GOETZ, RAINALD. W. Delabar, 'G., Sie reden wirres Zeug. R.G. und sein Wahnsinns-Ritt in die Literaturszene', *Juni*, 4.4, 1990:68–78.

GRASS, GÜNTER. S. Anderson, 'Lies and more lies: fact and fiction in G.G.'s *Die Rättin*', *GR*, 26:106–12. G. Cepl-Kaufmann, 'G.G.: *Die Rättin*', *GeW*, 81, 1990:49–70. I. Diersen, '"Ein Zeitgenosse, der sich einmischt." Zu G.G' Roman *Die Rättin*', *WB*, 36, 1990:1821–27. K.C. Gopa, 'Das Asienbild in *Kopfgeburten oder Die Deutschen sterben aus*', *GSI*, 14, 1990:91–94. F.J. Görtz, 'Apokalypse im Roman: G.G' *Die Rättin*', *GQ*, 63, 1990:462–70. G. A. Guidry, 'Theoretical reflections on the ideological and social implications of mythic form in G.'s *Die Blechtrommel*', *Monatshefte*, 83:127–46. N. Honsza, 'Vom Geniestreich zur Erkenntnis-Depression', *GeW*, 81, 1990:37–48. K. R. Ireland, 'Doing very dangerous things: *Die Blechtrommel* and *Midnight's Children*', *CL*, 42, 1990:335–61. Thomas W. Kniesche, *Die Genealogie der Post-Apokalypse. G.G' 'Die Rättin'*, Vienna, Passagen, 223 pp., adopts a psychoanalytical and intertextual approach to G.'s novel, locating it firstly in the context of contemporary apocalyptic literature, then analysing it as a critique of rationalism and as a contribution to German *Vergangenheitsbewältigung*. A detailed analysis of the novel as 'Traumtext', drawing on Freud, Nietzsche, and Derrida is then used to characterize it as post-apocalyptic, its primary signifier being the figure of the Great Mother. S. Lohr, 'Literatur-kritik aus Autorenperspektive. G. G. im Gespräch', *DUS*, 43.1:69–73. M. McAnear, 'A Benjaminian reading of G.G.'s *Katz und Maus*', *NGR*, 5–6, 1989–90:90–97. J. Mizinski, 'G.G. — eine katastrophale Zukunftsvision. Zu einigen Aspekten des Romans *Die Rättin*', *GeW*, 81, 1990:117–26. H.-C. Graf von Nayhauss, 'G.G.' *Rättin* im Spiegel der Rezensionen', *GeW*, 81, 1990:81–115. V. Neuhaus, 'Das Meißner Tedeum — G.G. als Koautor eines liturgischen Textes', *Fest. Rathofer*,

491–97. *Die Danziger Trilogie von G.G. Texte, Daten, Bilder*, ed. Volker Neuhaus and Dorothea Hermes, Frankfurt, Luchterhand, 243 pp. J. Papiór, 'Um "fünf nach zwölf" beginnt der qual- und hoffnungsvolle Traum von einer [post]humanen [Ratten]Zivilisation', *GeW*, 81, 1990:71–80. K. Pezold, 'G.G' *Blechtrommel* in der Literaturgeschichte', *ib.*, 9–18. M. P. Savarino, 'La prospettiva del ratto. Sul romanzo *Die Rättin* di G.G.', *AION(T)*, 32.1–2, 1989 (1990):227–37. M. Scofield, 'Drama, politics and the hero: *Coriolanus*, Brecht and G.', *CDr*, 24, 1990–91:322–41. D. Stolz, '"Deutschland — ein literarischer Begriff": G.G. and the German question', Williams, *Literature*, 207–24. M. Szyrocki, '*Adebar*. Offene Gedichtinterpretation', *GeW*, 81, 1990:19–23. P. Thomson, 'History-writing as hybrid form: G.G.'s *From the Diary of a Snail*', Roberts, *Novel*, 181–90. A. Wierlacher, 'Die Mahlzeit auf dem Acker und die Schwarze Köchin. Zum Rachemotiv des Essens in Grass' *Die Blechtrommel*', *GeW*, 81, 1990:25–36. J. Wittmann, 'The GDR and G.G.: East German reception of the literary works and public persona', Williams, *Literature*, 273–84. L. Zyliński, 'G.G' nationale Sendung', *GeW*, 81, 1990:133–40. See also BOBROWSKI, JOHANNES.

GRÜN, MAX VON DER. A. Bushell, 'M.v.d.G.: "Stellenweise Glatteis"', *German Teaching*, 2.4:16–19. *M.v.d.G.: Texte, Daten, Bilder*, ed. Stephan Reinhardt (SL, 931), 1990, 175 pp.

HACKS, PETER. H. Hartung, 'Remontage der Lyrik. Anmerkungen zu Lyrik und Lyriktheorie bei P.H.', *JLitDDR*, 6, 1987 (1988):11–26. T. Honnef, '"Was nie anwendbar war, wird es nicht mehr." P.H. und die Romantik', *GR*, 26:122–31. A. Jaeger, 'Das Glück der Mühen. Individuum und Gesellschaft in Adam und Eva von P.H.', *JLitDDR*, 6, 1987 (1988):43–58. B. Leistner, 'Der gegenwärtige Klassiker. Goethe im Werk von P.H.', Leistner, *Beckmesser*, 202–20. C. Lubkoll, '"Diese Heiden-Eva hat seit Urzeiten zwei Gesichter . . .". Der Mythos von Pandora bei Goethe und Peter Hacks', *JLitDDR*, 6, 1987 (1988):59–77. W. Pallus, 'Parodie und Aktualisierung des Mittelalters in *Rosie träumt* von P.H.', *GGF*, 11, 1989:172–79. U. Profitlich, '"Menschen unserer Zeit". Zu P.H' *Die Sorgen und die Macht*', *JLitDDR*, 6, 1987 (1988):27–42. P. Schütze, 'König Chilperich oder das Hoftheater ohne Hof. Etwas zum Wesen der Gattung bei H.', *ib.*, 78–94.

HAHN, ULLA. See p. 843 above.

HAMBURGER, MICHAEL. Walter Eckel, *Von Berlin nach Suffolk. Zur Lyrik MHs* (Ep, 62), 220 pp., is the first study devoted to H.'s own poetry as opposed to his critical and translation work. As primary influences the author identifies Hölderlin and Huchel, while the most significant landscapes are London and Berlin. At the same time a constant tension is identified between city and rural life, manifesting itself in an ecological consciousness long before this became a fashionable theme.

HAMMER, FRANZ. G. von Prittwitz, 'F.H. — "Aktivist des kulturellen Aufbaus"', *WB*, 36, 1990:1915–30.

HANDKE, PETER. A. Bürge, 'Aischylos, "Prometheus, gefesselt" — übertragen von P.H.', Pöckl, *Dichter*, 9–55. D. Caldwell and P. W. Rea, 'H.'s and Wenders' "Wings of Desire": transcending postmodernism', *GQ*, 64.1:46–54. E. Fischer-Lichte, 'Vom "Theatertheater" zurück zum Theater. Aufführungsanalyse von Hs *Kaspar* in einer Inszenierung des Theaters der Landeshauptstadt Mainz', Floeck, *Theater*, 119–33. G. Fuchs, 'Das Theater P.Hs unter besonderer Berücksichtigung des *Kaspar*', *ib.*, 99–117. I. Fulde, 'Sprache ohne Leidenschaft. Die sexuellen Beziehungen in P.Hs *Der kurze Brief zum langen Abschied*', Cremerius, *Literatur*, 153–72. A. Gellhaus, 'Das allmähliche Verblassen der Schrift. Zum Prosa von P.H. und Christoph Ransmayr', *Poetica*, 22, 1990:106–42. B. L. Knapp, 'P.H.'s *Kaspar*: the mechanics of language — a fractionating schizophrenic theatrical event', *STCL*, 14, 1990:241–59. M. Mixner, 'Die alten Maße — Hs Genauigkeit im Erzählen', Müller, *Aporie*, 149–61. H. Müller, 'Die Augenhöhe als Maß der Erzählung. Zu P.Hs Bildsprache', *ib.*, 175–94. P. O'Neill, 'The role of the reader: signs and semiosis in P.H.'s *Angst des Tormanns beim Elfmeter*', *Seminar*, 27:283–300. M. Scharang, 'Heilige Schriften. Über die Feierlichkeit in der Gegenwartsliteratur am Beispiel H.', Müller, *Aporie*, 215–25. G. Sergooris, 'Das Ich endet, wo die Sprache beginnt. Zum Sprachfetischismus in P.Hs *Kaspar*', *ib.*, 195–213. M. Tabah, **Vermittlung und Unmittelbarkeit: die Eigenart von P.Hs fiktionalem Frühwerk, 1966–1970* (EH, 1, 1159), 1990, 360 pp. C. Terhorst, **P.H.: Die Entstehung literarischen Ruhms. Die Bedeutung der literarischen Tageskritik für die Rezeption des frühen P.H.* (EH, 1, 1206), 1990, xii + 382 pp. E. Tunner, 'Unordnung bewirkt die Empörung aller anständig denkenden Menschen. Noch einmal *Kaspar* von P.H.', Müller, *Aporie*, 163–74. Jürgen Wolf, *Visualität, Form und Mythos in P.Hs Prosa*, Opladen, Westdeutscher Vlg, 248 pp., is a study of the phenomenological world-view in H.'s prose works, focusing mainly on literary representations of time, space, and perception in *Langsame Heimkehr*, and *Die Lehre der Sainte Victoire*, but also tracing the genesis of this model in previous works and in H.'s reception of Robbe Grillet. A final section draws parallels with Italian paintings of the 'Transavanguardia', especially three works of Enzo Cucchi from the 1980s. Common to both is their proposal of a mythological alternative to contemporary beliefs in reason and progress. A. Wallas, '"Und ich gehöre mit meinem Spiegelbild zu diesem Volk." P.H. als Schöpfer eines slovenischen Mythos. Zu Hs Roman *Die Wiederholung*', *ÖGL*, 33,

1989:332–38. W. Weiss, 'Religiöse Motive. Poetik des Fragments bei P.H.', *Sprachkunst*, 20, 1989 (1990):227–35. K. Zeyringer, 'Meistern wir nicht die sagenhaftesten Sager? Literatur mit und gegen Sprachformeln. Zu P.H., Alois Brandstetters *Zu Lasten der Briefträgers* und H. C. Artmanns *Nachrichten aus Nord und Süd*', *ÖGL*, 33, 1989:314–31. See also STRAUSS, BOTHO.

HARIG, LUDWIG. Petra Lanzendörfer-Schmidt, **Die Sprache als Thema im Werk L.Hs. Eine sprachwissenschaftliche Analyse literarischer Schreibtechniken*, Tübingen, Niemeyer, 1990, ix + 201 pp.

HÄRTLING, PETER. A. Binder, 'Zum "Elend unserer Jugendliteratur." Kritische Bemerkungen zu Büchern von P.H., Gudrun Pausewang und Janosch', *DD*, 22:271–85. I. Huish, 'The adult writer in a child's world: some reflections on P.H. and the *Kinderroman*', Williams, *Literature*, 243–53. J. Quack, 'Die wiedergefundene Wirklichkeit', Quack, *Identifikation*, 101–22. H. Schmidt-Bergmann, 'Über die Gegenwärtigkeit von Literatur in literarischen Werken. Leben und Werk Lenaus als Modell für Ferdinand Kürnberger, P.H. und Gernot Wolfgruber', *Lenau-Forum*, 16, 1990:77–84. **P.H. im Gespräch* (SL, 912), 1990, 210 pp. H.-G. Winter, 'Ausbruchsversuche. Veränderung und Selbstveränderung in Romanen der achtziger Jahre von Dieter Wellershoff, Urs Jaeggi und P.H.', *WB*, 37:390–401.

HAUSHOFER, MARLEN. H. Caviola, 'Behind the transparent wall. M.H.'s novel *Die Wand*', *MAL*, 24.1:100–12. C. Schmidjell, 'M.H. (1920–1970)', *ZDNÖL*, 13, 1990:12–13. E. Wessel, ''Ich werde schreiben bis es dunkel wird ...'' Über M.Hs Roman *Die Wand*', Askedal, *Ingerid Dal*, 115–28.

HEIN, CHRISTOPH. *C.H.* (TK, 111), 107 pp., includes two essays on *Drachenblut*, analysis of H.'s historical materialism in *Horns Ende* and in his dramas, and of narrative perspective and identity in his prose works. Other contributions consider H.'s position in GDR literature: the problems he posed for theatre critics and his public statements since the *Wende*. The volume is completed by an illuminating interview with C.H. **C.H.: Texte, Daten, Bilder*, ed. L. Baier (SL, 943), 1990, 192 pp. Bernd Fischer, *C.H.: Drama und Prosa im letzten Jahrzehnt der DDR*, Heidelberg, Winter, 1990, ii + 154 pp., begins with a discussion of H.'s theoretical statements on the function of art and literary criticism, relating his views to Walter Benjamin's cultural critique. Individual chapters treat H.'s works from the early plays (*Cromwell, Lassalle fragt Herrn Herbert nach Sonja* and *Schlötel oder Was solls*) to *Die Ritter der Tafelrunde* (1989), and his prose works from the volume *Einladung zum Lever Bourgeois* (1980) to *Der Tangospieler* (1989). H. emerges as a prophet of the demise of the GDR, with his tragi-comic representations of the failure of intellectuals throughout the history of socialism. J. Marquardt, 'Ästhetik der Toten — tote

Ästhetik? Der neuere (glücklichere) Umgang mit Kleists Erbe in C.Hs Variation auf "Michael Kohlhaas"', *Beiträge zur Kleist-Forschung*, 1988 (1989):17–35. J. Saavedrová, 'Linguostilistische Betrachtungen zur Erzahlstruktur von C.Hs Novelle *Der fremde Freund*', *BEDS*, 10:61–71.

HEIN, MANFRED PETER. M. Gratz, 'H. in Greifswald, DDR', *Ginkgobaum*, 10:38–42. A. F. Kelletat, 'Annäherung an das Gedicht M.P.Hs', *ib.*, 9–34.

HEINISCH, PETER. C. Decker, 'Photographic eye, narrative I: P.H.'s *Die kleine Figur meines Vaters*', *Monatshefte*, 83:147–60.

HEINRICH, REINHART. C. Gansel, 'Leistungen und Defizite. Nachdenken über das literarkritische Echo auf R.Hs Roman *Jenseits von Babel*', *WB*, 37:140–51.

HENSEL, KERSTIN. K. Hammer, 'Gespräch mit K.H.', *WB*, 37:93–110.

HERBURGER, GUNTER. *G.H.: Texte, Daten, Bilder*, ed. Klaus Siblewski (SL, 1005), 235 pp., begins with a selection of H.'s own statements on literature, followed by an illustrated biographical section. The volume includes personal tributes and an essay on H.'s problematic relationship to cinema and mass culture. Critical essays include discussions of his novels, in particular the *Thuja*-trilogy, his short stories and his children's writing (both the BIRNE stories and his poetry). P. Hamm and A. Chiarloni write on H.'s poetry, K. Franke on his radio plays, and there is a discussion between H. and Peter Bichsel.

HEYM, STEFAN. C. Gansel, I. Hanke, *et al.*, 'Nachruf von S.H. (Für und Wider)', *WB*, 37:213–33. G. Kerekes, 'Anmerkungen zu S.H.', *Germanistisches Jahrbuch DDR-RU*, 9, 1990:77–85. J. Milfull, 'The wandering Jew and the sense of history: S.H. and the ahasveric principle', Roberts, *Novel*, 191–200. R. Smith, 'S.H.: a question of identity', Williams, *Literature*, 47–64.

HILDESHEIMER, WOLFGANG. Dietmar Goll-Bickmann, **Aspekte der Melancholie in der frühen und mittleren Prosa W.Hs*, Münster, Literatur Vlg, 1989, ix + 503 pp. I. Hilton, 'Die absurde Welt von W.H. The English connection', *Akten* (Tokyo), x, 140–45. V. Jehle, **W.H.: Werkgeschichte* (STM, 2109), 1990, 485 pp.

HOCHHUTH, ROLF. R.H., **Panik im Mai: Sämtliche Gedichte und Erzählungen. Mit Essays von Karl Krolow, Herbert Reinoß und Gert Ueding*, Reinbek, Rowohlt, 773 pp.

HONIGMANN, BARBARA. M. S. Fries, 'Text as locus, inscription as identity: on B.H.'s *Roman von dem Kinde*', *STCL*, 14, 1990:175–93.

JAHNN, HANS HENNY. K. Brynhildsvoll, 'Dichtung und Wirklichkeit im Urrland-Kapitel des Romans *Fluß ohne Ufer*', Askedal, *Ingerid Dal*, 97–114.

JANDL, ERNST. G. Conradt, 'E.J., meine Verehrung. Anmerkungen zur Inszenierung von J.-Gedichten', *InfD*, 14.4, 1990:120–22. R. Koch, 'Die geliebte Freude. Zu zwei Theaterstücken der 80er Jahre — E.J.: *Aus der Fremde*, Botho Strauss: *Die Fremdenführerin*', Kreuzer, *Pluralismus*, 117–30. M. Schmitz-Emans, 'Poesie als Sprachspiel. Überlegungen zur Poetik E.Js', *ZDP*, 109, 1990:551–71. M. Schmitz-Emans, '"Ich habe nichts zu sagen/und ich sage es . . .". E.Js produktive Auseinandersetzung mit John Cages Ästhetik', *Sprachkunst*, 21, 1990:285–312.

JELINEK, ELFRIEDE. Dirk Baecker, Rembert Hüser, and Georg Stanitzek, *Gelegenheit. Diebe. 3 x Deutsche Motive*, Bielefeld, Haux, 166 pp., consists of three very varied responses to the notion of a unified Germany, one of which is based on J.'s essay for performance in the theatre, *Wolken. Heim.* Just as J.'s text defies classification, so this volume blurs the distinction between creative and critical writing. Dirk Baecker's essay 'Die Leute' reflects on German identity, Rembert Huser's 'Wale malen' is a cultural odyssey through recent German film, literature, history and the feuilleton of the *FAZ*. Georg Stanitzek's 'Kuckuck' is an exploration of J.'s 'Deutschland collage' with its quotations from Hölderlin, Hegel, Heidegger, Fichte, Kleist and the correspondence of RAF terrorists 1973–77, proposing a cultural identity based on repetition and quotation. *E.J.*, ed. Kurt Bartsch and Günther A. Höfler (Dossier, 2), Graz, Droschl, 316 pp., contains an interview with J., contemporary reviews of all her major works, and a biographical essay and comprehensive bibliography by E. Spanlang. In eight critical essays there are discussions of J.'s work from feminist perspectives, in terms of its cultural critique of Austrian society, of her use of realism and satire. There is also analysis of her use of mimicry and montage in *Wolken. Heim*, her treatment of sexuality and her screenplay for Werner Schroeter's film of *Malina*. D. Burdorf, '"Wohl gehn wir täglich, doch wir bleiben hier." Zur Funktion von Hölderlin-Zitaten in Texten E.Js', *SLWU*, 21.2, 1990:29–36. A. Fiddler, 'Problems with porn. Situating E.J.'s *Lust*', *GLL*, 44:404–15. R. Schneider, 'Diese Liebe ist im Kern Vernichtung. Zu E.J.', *Argument*, 33:361–71.

JENS, WALTER. T. Lichtmann, 'Utopische Vision oder Zeitroman? Über W.J.' Roman *Nein. Die Welt der Angeklagten*', *Germanistisches Jahrbuch DDR-RU*, 9, 1990:110–20. H. Thiel, 'Republikanisches Engagement und das Streben nach Brillanz und "Witz" (in Lessings Sinn) schließen einander nicht aus. Gespräch mit W.J.', *DD*, 22:245–48.

JOHNSON, UWE. D. G. Bond, 'Two ships: correspondences between U.J. and Johann Peter Hebel', *GQ*, 64:313–24. R. Krems,

'"Nachrichten über die Lage." Zum Realismusbegriff U.Js', *Germanistisches Jahrbuch DDR-RU*, 9, 1990:121–31. N. Mecklenburg, 'U.J. als Autor einiger deutscher Literaturen', *LitL*:1–7. P. O'Neill, 'The system in question: story and discourse in U.J.'s *Zwei Ansichten*', *GQ*, 64:531–43. Siegfried Unseld and Eberhard Fahlke, *U.J.: 'Für wenn ich tot bin'*, Frankfurt, Suhrkamp, 144 pp., is the first in the U.-J.-Archiv series, introduced by J.'s publisher, friend, and heir, S. Unseld. J.'s papers are collected in a Frankfurt archive, the contents of which are outlined in an essay by its custodian, E. Fahlke, to demonstrate how the archive might be used by researchers to arrive at J.'s unique literary profile. D. Weber, 'Ein Haus. Zu einem Lyrismus in U.Js *Jahrestagen*', *Fest. Rathofer*, 499–508.

KANT, HERMANN. G. Hammarskjöld, *Schuldlos schuldig sein: zur Schuld und Freiheit in H.Ks Roman 'Der Aufenthalt'* (LGF, 56), 1989, 172 pp.

KASCHNITZ, MARIE LUISE. J. Østbø, '"Im Angesicht des Todes ..."' Zu den existentiellen Bezügen der motivischen Tiefenstruktur von M.L.Ks Kurzgeschichten in der Sammlung *Das dicke Kind und andere Erzählungen*', Askedal, *Ingerid Dal*, 129–53.

KASER, NORBERT. S. Klettenhammer, '"der gemeinplatz ausgewalzt zur heimat." Motiv und Thema "Heimat" in der Lyrik N.C.Ks und Gerhard Koflers', *MBA*, 9, 1990:64–80. H. Obermair, 'Eine Art K.-Abwicklung. Aspekte der K.-Verwaltung, oder: wie zähmt man ein Werk?', *Distel*, 39–40, 1989:44–47. A. Pfeiffer, 'Eiertänze. Ein Plädoyer für Respektlosigkeit', *ib.*, 48–49.

KEMPOWSKI, WALTER. V. Ladenthin, 'Versuch, W.K. mit der Hilfe Arno Schmidts besser zu verstehen', *WW*, 41:436–43.

KERSCHBAUMER, MARIE-THÉRÈSE. H. Höller, 'Leben und Werk. Zur Prosa M.-T.Ks', *LK*, no. 257–58:39–42. G. Moser, '"Mir ist es so gegangen wie dem Fraulein Pöllinger." Gespräch mit M.-T.K.', *ib.*, 34–38.

KIPPHARDT, HEINAR. T. Lindner, *Die Modellierung des Faktischen: H.Ks 'Bruder Eichmann' im Kontext seines dokumentarischen Theaters*, Berne, Lang, 1990, 296 pp. W. Karbach, 'Produzieren wider die Verhältnisse: H.Ks ästhetische Positionen', *DVLG*, 65:335–87.

KIRCHHOFF, BODO. G. Rupp, 'Literarische Postmoderne und ihre Diskurse im Spannungsfeld empirischer Rezeption', *Akten* (Tokyo), x, 416–24.

KIRSCH, RAINER. A. Visser, 'Gespräch mit R.K.', *DeutB*, 20, 1990:241–59.

KIRSCH, SARAH. Christine Cosentino, *'Ein Spiegel mit mir darin.' S.Ks Lyrik*, Tübingen, Francke, 1990, viii + 181 pp., charts the course of K.'s life and work from East to West in detailed exploration of her poetic imagery. Devoting one chapter to each of the anthologies to date, the author tries to account for the uniqueness of the 'Sarah Sound', always locating her work in the context of German-German relations and in contemporary debates around *Frauenliteratur*. F. Eigler, '"Verlorene Zeit, gewonnener Raum." S.Ks Abschied von der DDR in *Allerlei-Rauh*', *Monatshefte*, 83:176–89. P. Graves, 'East-West memories of a lost summer: Christa Wolf and S.K.', Williams, *Literature*, 129–38. Id., 'S.K. Some comments and a conversation', *GLL*, 44:271–80. B. Mabee, '"Im Totenspiegel ungewisser Bedeutung". Antirassistische Assoziationsraüme in der Lyrik von S.K.', *JLitDDR*, 6, 1987 (1988):143–61. C. von Maltzan, '"Man müßte ein Mann sein." Zur Frage der weiblichen Identität in Erählungen von K., Morgner und Wolf', *AGJSG*, 20, 1990:141–55.

KLUGE, ALEXANDER.   T. Corrigan, 'The commerce or auteurism: a voice without authority', *NGC*, 49, 1990:43–57. G. Koch, 'A.K.'s phantom of the opera', *ib.*, 79–88. W. Menninghaus, 'Geschichte und Eigensinn. Zur Hermeneutik-Kritik und Poetik A.Ks', Eggert, *Geschichte*, 258–72. E. Rosentochler, 'Remembering not to forget: a retrospective reading of K.'s *Brutality in Stone*', *NGC*, 49, 1990:23–41. H. Sander, '"You can't always get what you want": the films of A.K.', *ib.*, 59–68. H. Schlüppmann, 'Femininity as productive force: K. and critical theory', *ib.*, 69–78.

KNOBLOCH, HEINZ.   S. Heerich, 'Durch das Labyrinth abseitiger Genauigkeiten. H.Ks Feuilletons — Perspektiven der "kleinen Form" in der Literatur der DDR', *TI*, 5, 1990:155–72.

KOEPPEN, WOLFGANG.   C. Friederici-Brink, **W.K.: die Stadt als Pandämonium* (EH, 1, 1148), 1990, 188 pp. B. Widdig, 'Melancholie und Moderne: W.Ks *Der Tod in Rom*', *GR*, 26:161–68. See also GAISER, GERD.

KÖNIGSDORF, HELGA.   J. Clausen, 'Resisting objectification: H.K.'s Lise Meitner', Gerber, *Studies*, 165–80. B. Haines, '"Aber jetzt wird ausgeplaudert." H.G. and the "sanfte Revolution"', *PSGAS*, 3.3:55–60. E. Kaufmann, 'Spielarten des Komischen. Zur Schreibweise von H.K.', Stephan, *Frauen*, 177–84. N. A. Laukner, 'The treatment of the past and future in H.K.'s *Respektloser Umgang*: "Sich der Erinnerung weihen oder für die Zukunft antreten? Mit der Vergangenheit im Bunde"', Gerber, *Studies*, 151–63.

KROETZ, FRANZ XAVER.   C. Decker, '". . . und den Kasten zusammenhauen": televisual questions and the dramas of F.X.K.', *GQ*, 64.1:25–34. G. Thierot, 'Rédemption ou lutte des classes? De l'utilisation de certains motifs chrétiens dans le "Volksstück critique"', *TI*, 5, 1990:219–33. Ingeborg C. Walther, **The Theatre of F.X.K.* (SMGL, 40), 1990, xi + 276 pp.

KRONAUER, BRIGITTE.   *B.K.*, ed. Heinz Ludwig Arnold (TK, 112), 91 pp., contains two essays on the relationship of aesthetic theory to literary practice in K.'s work, one on Utopian aspects of her work and one on her portrayal of 'Alltag'. The significance of the gaze is investigated in the novels *Rita Münster, Berittener Bogenschütze* and *Die Frau in den Kissen,* while another contributor compares this trilogy with Bachmann's *Todesarten.* With her 'literarisches Programm aus dem Geist der Melancholie' her writing is further compared to that of Peter Handke. B. Clausen, 'Ein staunenswerter Fall, und Aufstieg. Zur Prosa B.Ks', *Merkur,* 45:442–47.

KUBA. A. Hartmann, 'Ks "Gedicht vom Menschen" und die sowjetische Poemtradition', *WB,* 36, 1990:1430–48.

KUNERT, GÜNTER. *G.K* (TK, 109), ed. Heinz Ludwig Arnold, 95 pp., includes examples of K.'s short prose and poetry, as well as ten essays which explore his reception in the GDR, aspects of modernism and antimodernism in his writing, the belief in progress expressed in 'Aufbruch eines bedeutenden Tieres' (1966), and its disappearance in the 1970s. The influence of travel is examined in his representations of Berlin, Italy, and the USA, as in the experience of travel itself in the search for identity. K. is further located within a literary tradition ranging from Montaigne to Kleist. A. Reif, 'Mit geschlossenen Augen vor der unerträglichen Wahrheit. Gespräch mit dem Schriftsteller G.K.', *Universitas,* 45, 1990:484–95.

LANGGÄSSER, ELISABETH. J. Bossinade, 'Zwischen Heldentum und Hadeswelt. Eine Suche nach dem Doppelleben der Antigone-Figur anhand von E.L.', Kohn-Waechter, *Flammen,* 173–92.

LENZ, SIEGFRIED. H. Glade and P. Bukowski, 'Der Traditionalist S.L.: ein sowjetischer Bestseller', *GSL,* 6, 1990:351–63. Rachel J. Halverson, **Historiography and Fiction. S.L. and the 'Historikerstreit',* Berne, Lang, 190, 173 pp. Ming-Jong Kuo, **Das Romanwerk von S.L. Unter besonderer Berücksichtigung des Romans 'Das Vorbild',* Berne, Lang, 346 pp. Trudis Reber, **S.L.,* Berlin, Colloquium, 112 pp. See also BOBROWSKI, JOHANNES.

LOETSCHER, HUGO. R. Zeller, 'Vielsprachigkeit und Verfremdung im Werk H.Ls', *SchwM,* 69, 1989:1035–43.

LUDWIG, PAULA. U. Längle, '"Tausend Winter durchmaß ich mit meinen Schritten." P.L. (1900–1974), Dichterin aus Vorarlberg', *Allemende,* 10.30–31:116–43.

MARGINTER, PETER. C. Pawlowitsch-Hussein, 'Zur Variierung der Märchenmotive in P.Ms Roman *Der Baron und die Fische*', *KGS,* 4, 1989:159–70.

MARON, MONIKA. T. Beckermann, '"Die Diktatur repräsentiert das Abwesende nicht": Essay on M.M., Wolfgang Hilbig und Gert Neumann', Williams, *Literature,* 97–116. M.-F. Demet, 'Die Themen der Flucht und der Grenze als Wiederkehrende Motive in Prosawerken von M.M. und Hartmut Lange', *Germanica,* 7, 1990:123–33. A.

Reiter, '"Ein schwierges Gespräch": the correspondence between M.M. and Joseph von Westphalen', Williams, *Literature*, 321–38.

MARTI, KURT. *K.M.: Texte, Daten, Bilder*, ed. Christof Mauch (SL, 897), 230 pp., includes personal tributes to the Swiss Protestant writer and clergyman which show the fascination he holds for feminist theologians, readers, and critics in East and West alike. A section of critical essays looks in detail at his position in contemporary Swiss literature, his poems both in High German and dialect, the religious and ludic dimensions of his writing, his novel *Die Riesin*, and his short stories. An interview with C. Mauch and an illustrated biographical section complete the volume. Christof Mauch, **Poesie — Theologie — Politik: Studien zu K.M.* (SDL, 118), 230 pp. W. Sedelnik, 'K.M.: Satire und Barmherzigkeit', *Germanistisches Jahrbuch DDR-RU*, 9, 1990:164–70.

MAYRÖCKER, FRIEDERIKE. B. Alms, 'Eine nie vollendete Liebeszene. Zu F.Ms Schreiben', *Die Horen*, 35.1, 1990:149–54. Sara Barni, 'Gespräch mit F.M.', *AION(T)*, 32.3, 1989 (1990):73–85. M. Beyer, 'F.M. Eine Bibliographie 1947 bis 1990', *ZDNÖL*, 14:9–10. D. Riess-Meinhardt, 'Auslösung der Textarbeit. Einige Überlegungen zu F.Ms Prosa', *ÖGL*, 34, 1990:251–58.

MITTERER, ERIKA. J. Wigmore, '"Vergangenheitsbewältigung" in Austria: the personal and the political in E.M.'s *Alle unsere Spiele* and Elisabeth Reichart's *Februarschatten*', *GLL*, 44:477–87.

MONIKOVA, LIBUŠE. S. Cramer, 'Lobrede auf L.M.', *Akzente*, 28:229–35.

MORGNER, IRMTRAUD. K. Hauser, 'Weiblicher Teiresias oder trojanisches Pferd im Patriarchat? Geschlechtertausch bei I.M. und Christa Wolf', *Argument*, 33:373–81. M. Meier, 'Konzerte der Redevielfalt. Die Walpurgisnacht. Darstellung in der *Amanda* I.Ms', *LitL*, 1990:213–27. See also KIRSCH, SARAH.

MUCKE, DIETER. P. D. Bartsch, 'Gespräch mit D.M.', *WB*, 36, 1990:1628–40.

MUELLER, HARALD. F. Horst, 'Aufführungsanalyse von H.Ms *Bolero* in einer Inszenierung des Hessischen Stadttheaters Wiesbaden', Floeck, *Theater*, 151–60. D. Kafitz, 'Sprachrealismus und Zeichenspiel in den Dramen H.Ms', *ib.*, 135–49.

MÜLLER, HEINER. 'Der Fall H.M. Dokumente zur "Umsiedlerin"'. Protokolle, Gutachten, Briefe, Kommentare', *SuF*, 43:435–86. R. von Dassanowsky-Harris, 'The dream and the scream: "Die deutsche Misere" and the unrealized GDR in H.M.'s *Germania Tod in Berlin*', *NGR*, 5–6, 1989–90:15–28. Horst Domdey, '"Ich lache über den Neger." Das Lachen des Siegers in H.Ms Stück *Der Auftrag*', *JLitDDR*, 6, 1987 (1988):220–34. N. O. Eke, '"Der Neger schreibt ein andres Alphabet." Anmerkungen zu H.Ms dialektischem

Denk-Spiel *Anatomie Titus Fall of Rome. Ein Shakespearekommentar'*, *ZDP*, 110:294–315. *Spiele und Spiegelungen von Schrecken und Tod. Zum Werk von H.M. Sonderband zum 60. Geburtstag des Dichters*, ed. Paul Gerhard Klussmann and Heinrich Mohr (*JLitDDR*, 7), Bonn, Bouvier, 1990, ii + 228 pp., includes literary tributes by S. Kirsch, R. Schedlinski, D. Grünbein, K. Bartsch, B. Struzyk, and F. Mirau, in addition to 12 critical essays which focus mainly on *Bildbeschreibung*, *Wolokolamsker Chaussee I–V* and *Der Lohndrücker*, both the texts, their sources and recent productions. Other contributions discuss M.'s poetry, his Büchner-Preis-Rede 'Die Wunde Woyzeck', executions in his plays, and his artistic collaboration with his wife Inge Müller. H. Kreuzer, '"Ostfront" 1941. Ein dramatisches Thema in drei Variationen von Herbert Reinicker, Johannes R. Becher und H. M.', Eggert, *Geschichte*, 330–52. M. Mieth, 'Zur Rezeption von H.M. in DDR und BRD. Eine Erinnerung an das Verhältnis von politischer und ästhetischer Wertung', *WB*, 37:604–14. **Zur Lage der Nation. H.M. im Interview mit Fritz Raddatz*, Berlin, Rotbuch, 1990, 99 pp. P. Pavis, '"Malaise dans la civilisation." La représentation de la catastrophe dans le théâtre franco-allemand contemporain', Floeck, *Theater*, 79–96. Frank-Michael Raddatz, *Dämonen unterm Roten Stern. Zur Geschichtsphilosophie und Ästhetik H.Ms*, Stuttgart, Metzler, vi + 214 pp., traces a development from M.'s autobiographical prose texts *Der Vater* (1958) and *Die Todesanzeige* (1975–76) to the central themes of the 1970s: Germany, European concepts of revolution, and women's liberation. These are explored in detailed analysis of individual plays, positing a shift of emphasis from social criticism to a critique of Western civilization and notions of progress, thus locating M. close to Benjamin's catastrophe theory. A. Schalk, '"Deutschland — Dia/Lektish": H.M. and the German question', Williams, *Literature*, 65–84. J. Schmitt-Sasse, 'Die Kunst aufzuhören. Der Nibelungen-Stoff in H.Ms *Germania Tod in Berlin*', Heinzle, *Nibelungen*, 370–96. M. Streisand, '"Experimenta 6 — H.M." in Frankfurt/Main', *WB*, 36, 1990:1670–75. M. Streisand, 'Chronik einer Ausgrenzung. Der Fall H.M. Dokumente zur *Umsiedlerin*', *SuF*, 43:429–34. M. Streisand, '"Mein Platz, wenn mein Drama noch stattfinden würde, wäre auf beiden Seiten der Front, zwischen den Fronten, darüber." Über das Arbeitsprinzip der Gleichzeitigkeit bei H.M.', *WB*, 37:485–508. H.-C. Stillmark, 'Entscheidungen um und bei H.M. Bermerkungen zu *Wolokolamsker Chaussee III–V*', *Germanistisches Jahrbuch DDR-RU*, 9, 1990:52–62. Y. Tawada, 'Frauengestalten im Werk H.Ms und im Nō-Theater', *Akten* (Tokyo), x, 300–06. H.-D. Weber, 'H.Ms Geschichtsdrama — die Beendigung einer literarischen Gattung', *DUS*, 43.4:43–57.

MÜLLER, HERTA. N. Barry, 'Grenze — Entgrenzung in H.Ms Prosaband *Der Mensch ist ein großer Fasan auf der Welt*', *Germanica*, 7, 1990:115–21.

MURR, STEFAN. K. Feilchenfeldt, 'Ganghofer-Enkel sah literarisch den Golfkrieg voraus. 1984 — von Orwell zu den *Toten der Nefud*', *LiB*, 23:3–10.

NADOLNY, STEN. L. Schäfer, 'Die langsame Entdeckung. Nachüberlegungen zu S.N.', *DUS*, 43.1:45–52.

NICK, DAGMAR. M. Basse, 'Medea — ein Monolog. Gespräch mit D.N. über Medea, Kassandra und die Arbeit am Mythos', *NDH*, 36, 1989:390–402. Sabine Friedrich, **Traditionsbewußtsein als Lebensbewältigung. Zu Leben und Werk der D.N.* (EH, 1, 1181), 1990, 199 pp.

NIZON, PAUL. *P.N.*, ed. Heinz Ludwig Arnold (TK, 110), 99 pp., contains new texts by N. and an interview, as well as essays on his life and work which demonstrate the difficulty of classifying his writing formally or thematically. Contributions include an interpretation of N.'s *Canto* in the light of his views on modern art and film, a reading of *Untertauchen. Protokoll einer Reise*, and a reader-response to *Stolz*. There is an essay on the city in N.'s work, the metaphor of the 'Mantel', and the autobiographical self-reflexive nature of his writing. The tone of all contributors reflects their enthusiastic response to a talent which defies conventional critical discourses of evaluation and categorization. Roland Jerzewski, **Zwischen anarchischer Fronde und revolutionärer Disziplin. Zum Engagement-Begriff bei Walter Benjamin und P.N.*, Stuttgart, Vlg für Wissenschaft und Forschung, vii + 347 pp.

NOSSACK, HANS ERICH. G. Baumgaertel, 'H.E.N.: Die späten Dramatisierungen', *WW*, 41:444–53.

PAPENFUSS-GOREK, BERT. E. Grimm, 'Der Tod der Ostmoderne oder die BRDigung des DDR-Untergrunds: Zur Lyrik B.P.-Gs', *ZGer*, n.F., 1:9–20.

PEDRETTI, ERICA. H. F. Schafroth, 'Fliegen — Flunkern — Fliehen. Literarische Grenzüberschreitungen bei E.P., Jürg Laederach, Margrit Baur', *Germanica*, 7, 1990:77–86.

PETRI, WALTHER. W. Bartsch, 'Alex-Wedding-Preis 1990 an W.P.', *MAKDDR*, 28.5, 1990:13–15.

PLESSEN, ELISABETH. P. M. Bagley, 'The death of a father: the start of a story. Bereavement in E.P., Brigitte Schwaiger and Jutta Schutting', *NGS*, 16, 1990–91:21–38.

RANSMAYR, CHRISTOPH. P. Bachmann, 'Die Auferstehung des Mythos in der Postmoderne. Philosophische Voraussetzungen zu C.Rs Roman *Die letzte Welt*', *DD*, 21, 1990:639–51. H. Bernsmeier, '"Keinem bleibt seine Gestalt": Rs *Letzte Welt*', *Euphorion*, 85:168–81. D. Gorše, 'Einige Aspekte der Metaphorik im Roman *Die letzte Welt* von C.R.', *ANeo*, 23, 1990:75–86. C. de Groot, 'Es lebe Ovid — Ein

Plädoyer für die ars longa. C.Rs Roman *Die letzte Welt* (1988)',
Neophilologus, 75 : 252–69. See also HANDKE, PETER.

RATHENOW, LUTZ.   A. Reif, '"Mit zwanghaft hochgehaltenem
guten Glauben in den Abgrund." Gespräch mit dem ostberliner
Schriftsteller L.R.', *Universitas*, 45, 1990 : 1037–47.

REICH-RANICKI, MARCEL.   **Betrifft Literatur: über M.R.R.*, ed. Peter
Wapnewski, DVA, 1990, 280 pp.

REINIG, CHRISTA.   M. L. Gansberg, 'C.R.: "Müßiggang ist aller
Liebe Anfang" (1979). 'Ästhetische Taktlosigkeit als weibliche
Schreibstrategie', Stephan, *Frauen*, 185–94.

RICHARTZ, WALTER E.   J. Quack, 'Abschied von der Wissenschaft.
Über W.E.R.', Quack, *Identifikation*, 123–32.

RINSER, LUISE.   G. Gill, **Die Utopie Hoffnung bei L.R.: eine sozio-
psychologische Studie* (AUS, 1, 92), vii + 232 pp. C. Zacharias, '"Liebe
pur war nie ein Thema meiner Bücher"', *BDB*, 158 : 1556–58. E.
Zeile, 'Liebe und tu, was du willst. Gedanken zu L.Rs Erzählung *Jan
Lobel aus Warschau*', *LitL*, 1989 : 213–20.

ROSEI, PETER.   R. Stöckli, '"Wo ich bin ist *Amerika*": Zu P.Rs
Ulenspiegel Amerika', *Eulenspiegel-Jb.*, 29, 1989 : 73–85. D. Wiedling,
'Vom Drehbuch zum literarischen Werk: P.Rs Übertragung von
"Zabriskie Point"', Pöckl, *Dichter*, 509–36.

RÜHMKORF, PETER.   T. Verweyen and G. Wittig, '*Leslie Meiers
Lyrik-Schlachthof* oder über das Verhältnis des literarischen zur
wissenschaftlichen Kritik', *H.-Mann-Jb.*, 8, 1990 : 203–30.

SACHS, NELLY.   G. Überschlag, 'Der Weg der N.S. von der
furchtbaren zur fruchtbaren Entgrenzung', *Germanica*, 7, 1990 : 57–66.

SAEGER, UWE.   A. Jaeger, 'Der Schrecken der Selbstbegegnung.
Zwei Novellen von U.S.', *LitL*, 1990 : 94–106.

SCHÄDLICH, HANS JOACHIM.   C. Kleiber, 'Die "schlechten Wörter"
des H.J.Ss', *Germanica*, 7, 1990 : 135–39.

SCHIRMER, BERND.   S. Kleinteich, '"Algerien ist mein Grunderleb-
nis". Ein Interview mit dem Autor B.S.', *DaF*, 27, 1990 : 102–05.

SCHMIDT, ARNO.   F. Becker-Bertau, 'xxxxxxx"-: king!" xxxxxxxxx
The opening of A.S.'s *Zettels Traum* and Poe's poem "Dreamland"',
BaB, 145, 1990 : 15–17. 'Desiderateliste "Joyce bei Schmidt"',
ib., 148, 1990 : 14. **A.S. (1914–1979); Materialien zu Leben und Werk*, ed.
Axel Dunker, TK, 1990, 160 pp. Id., '"Njus fromm hell." Dualisti-
sche Prinzipien in Ss Erzählung *Caliban über Setebos*', *BaB*, 146–47,
1990 : 3–26. Id., '"Man begeht kein Plagiat an sich selbst." Zur
Transformation der Werke von James Joyce und Heinrich Albert
Oppermann in A.Ss Erzählung *Großer Kain*', *ib.*, 152–53 : 3–20. H.
Fischer, '"Oh, das müßte doch auch näher untersucht werden" —
einige Anmerkungen zu dem Radioessay "Die Meisterdiebe"', *ib.*,
146–47, 1990 : 26–30. 'Gesellschaft der A.S.-Leser e.V.', *Schauerfeld*,

3.3, 1990:8–12. J. Huerkamp, 'Brief an Frau Schmitter', *BaB*, 151:10–13. J. Huerkamp, 'Brief an Frau Schmitter', *ib.*, 10–13. D. Kuhn, 'Erläuterungen zu Ss *Gadir*', *ib.*, 149–50, 1990:15–33. A. Kupka, 'Der Wärme in der Kälte. *Bürgerlicher Abend* als Geworfenheitsausdruck', *Schauerfeld*, 3.3, 1990:13–16. T. Lautwein, 'Des Meeres und der Liebe Wellen. Über eine Stelle in A.Ss *Kosmas* und ihre Beziehung zu Eichendorffs "Nachtblume"', *BaB*, 152–53:3–20. B. Leistner, '"... der tapfere dünne Lärm zwischen den Felsenzähnen des Daseins." Zu A.Ss antigermanistischen Funkessays', Leistner, *Beckmesser*, 173–201. W. Martynkewicz, '"Fremdeste Welten würden sich auftun." Die Entscheidung für das Imaginäre beim frühen A.S.', *BaB*, 149–50, 1990:3–15. Id., **Selbstinszenierung. Untersuchungen zu psychosozialen Habitus A.Ss*, TK, 256 pp. H. A. Pausch, '"Vergessene" Autoren bei A.S.: das Beispiel Johann Carl Wezel. Über den Grad der Wahrheitsfindung', *ABNG*, 31–33:29–57. H. G. Pott, **Neue Theorie des Romans. Sterne — Jean Paul — Joyce — Schmidt*, Munich, Fink, 1990, 272 pp., contains an analysis of *Brands Haide*. H. Radspieler, 'Wer taufte Zettel? Zum Titel von *Zettels Traum*', *BaB*, 154–55:25–29. **Zettelkasten. 8. Aufsätze und Arbeiten zum Werk A.Ss*, ed. F. Rathjelm, Frankfurt, Bangert & Metzler, 1990, 308 pp. Id., 'Planwagen und Wolffstage. Trivia Zetteliana 2.', *BaB*, 148, 1990:10–11. Id., 'Portland → Paris. Weltreisen für A.S.', *Schauerfeld*, 4.2:2–4. D. P. Rudolph, 'Das Große — Ganze und die Einzelheiten. Zwei Autoren lesen ein Buch', *ib.*, 10–14. *A.S.: Leben — Werk — Wirkung*, ed. Michael Schardt and Hartmut Vollmer, Reinbek, Rowohlt, 1990, 349 pp., aims to provide a comprehensive picture of S.'s literary *œuvre* in 17 essays, one biographical, three on reception and research, and the remaining 13 on aspects of his work. These include four studies of his early work, two on the works of his 'middle phase' in the 1960s (*Kaff auch mare crisium* and *Kühe im Halbtrauer*), and two considerations of his work in the 1970s. In addition there is an assessment of his essays and critical writing, his cultural and religious critique, his treatment of sexuality, his appropriation of literary tradition, and a consideration of his position in German post-war literature. C. Schillow, 'KAFF auch SCHMÛN und anderswo. Aegyptiaca in A.Ss *Kaff*, oder: Nachweis und Spekulation', *BaB*, 154–55:3–24. T. Spreckelsen, '"Lassen Sie mich lieber weiter Menzel zitieren." A.Ss *Der Vogelhändler von Imst*', *ib.*, 151:3–9. R. Schweikert, 'Wenn zwei Gleiches erzählen, ist es noch lange nicht dasselbe: Witz und Anekdote bei Hans Reimann und A.S., insbesondere in dessen Juvenilium "Die Fremden" (1942)', *ib.*, 148, 1990:3–9. Id., 'Über A.S. in einem andern "Boten". Bibliographische Notiz', *ib.*, 152–53:31–32. Id., 'Andeutungen über Architekturphantasien und "archaische Ideenamalgame" bei A.S.',

Schauerfeld, 4.1:2–19. E.-D. Steinwender, '"ICH bin doch bloß KLEIN = DOWI!" Versuch über *Zettels Traum*', *BaB*, 145, 1990:3–15. H. Wollschläger, 'A.S. und Karl May', *Jb. der Karl-May-Gesellschaft*, 1990:12–29. See also BERNHARD, THOMAS, and KEMPOWSKI, WALTER.

SCHNEIDER, PETER. P. Pütz, 'P.Ss *Lenz*. Von der Agitation zur Reflexion', *Fest. Verbeeck*, 195–207.

SCHUTTING, JUTTA. B. Molinelli-Stein, 'J. (Justus) *Julian Schutting*: what's in a name? Oder: welchen Geschlechtes die Kunst sei', *Akten* (Tokyo), X, 288–99. See also PLESSEN, ELISABETH.

SCHÜTZ, HELGA. D. Dodds, '"Die Mauer stand bei mir im Garten": Interview with H.S.', *WGY*, 7:137–50.

SCHWAIGER, BRIGITTE. D. C. Lorenz, '"Hoffentlich werde ich taugen." Zu Situation und Kontext von B.S./Eva Deutsch, *Die Galizianerin*', *WGY*, 7:1–25.

SEGHERS, ANNA. G. Gutzmann, 'Zum Stellenwert des Spanischen Bürgerkriegs in A.S' Romanen *Die Entscheidung* und *Das Vertrauen*', Stephan, *Frauen*, 195–210. See also WOLF, CHRISTA.

SEIDEL, GEORG. I. Diersen, '"Wir haben allen wohl anders geträumt." Zum Werk G.Ss', *WB*, 37:509–26.

SEIDEMANN, MARIA. C. Baumann, 'Gespräch mit M.S.', *WB*, 36, 1990:1782–92.

SIMMEL, JOHANNES MARIO. W. Bialik, 'Zwischen fragwürdiger Historiosophie und utopischen Entwicklungsperspektiven: das weltanschauliche Angebot der beiden ersten Romane von J.M.S.', *SGP*, 14, 1990:119–38.

SPECHT, KERSTIN. H. S. Macher, 'Tradition des Volkstheaters. Gespräch mit K.S.', *LiB*, 22, 1990:33–35.

SPERBER, MANÈS. K. Wenzel, *M.Ss Romantrilogie: 'Wie eine Träne im Ozean'* (EH, I, 1232), v + 272 pp.

SPIEL, HILDE. B. Z. Schoenberg, 'In memoriam H.S.', *MSL*, 24. 1:184–89. W. Strickhausen, 'H.Ss historischer Roman *Die Früchte des Wohlstands*. Ein erster Reflex der Erfahrungen von Nationalsozialismus, Krieg und Exil', *Exil*, 10.1, 1990:27–42.

SPYRI, JOHANNA. H. Müller, 'Pädagogik in J.Ss Heidi-Büchern. Literaturgeschichtliche Koordinaten eines "Bildungsromans"', *SchwM*, 69, 1989:921–32.

STRAUSS, BOTHO. Sigrid Berka, *Mythos-Theorie und Allegorik bei B.S.*, Vienna, Passagen, 250 pp., locates S.'s work in the context of the 1980s renaissance of mythology, not simply on a thematic level, but in its theoretical basis. Drawing on Freud's psycho-mythological theory, Adorno and Horkheimer's *Dialektik der Aufklärung*, Blumenberg's *Arbeit am Mythos* and Lévi Strauss's notion of *bricolage* as well as modern film theory and intertextuality, S.'s allegorical, symbolic and mythological writing is characterized as postmodern, in contrast to the retrospective nostalgia of Romantic appropriations of mythology. S. Berka, 'Spätzeit des Mythos in B.Ss *Der Park*: Terror und Poesie', *NGR*, 5–6, 1989–90:1–14. J. Förster, 'Subjekt-Geschichte-Sinn. Postmoderne, Literatur und Lektüre', *DUS*, 43.4:58–79. Katrin Kazubko, *Spielformen des Dramas bei B.S.*, Hildesheim, Olms, 1990, 200 pp., departs from classical dramatic categories of 'Rede', 'Szene', and 'Handlung', placing instead 'Spiel' at the centre of its formal and thematic study of S.'s work. Drawing on ideas from Huizinga, Callois and Detweiler among others, a theory of 'play' is developed and the ludic aspects of S.'s dramas discussed under four headings: montage, the play within a play, mimicry, and play with the audience. Walter Rügert, *Die Vermessung des Innenraumes. Zur Prosa von B.S.*, Würzburg, Königshausen & Neumann, 294 pp. K. Schwind, 'Verflüchtigung von Satire im gleich-wertigen Allerlei? Anmerkungen zu Wirkungspotentialen "satirischer Texte" unter der Bedingung der "Postmoderne" am Beispiel von B.Ss *Kalldewey, Farce*', *Neohelicon*, 16, 1989:129–59. C. Sommerhage, 'Odeon oder der verschollene Krug. Über B.S' romantische Poetik der Erinnerung', *SuF*, 43:177–96. A Williams, 'B.S.: from identity crisis to German *ennui* — whither the poet?', Williams, *Literature*, 449–70. C. Winkelmann, *Die Suche nach dem 'großen Gefühl': Wahrnehmung und Weltbezug bei B.S. und Peter Handke* (EH, I, 1157), 1990, 241 pp. See also JANDL, ERNST.

STRITTMATTER, EVA. A. Holshuh, 'Frau E.S.', *LWU*, 24:91–111.

TIELSCH, ILSE. C. Kleiber, 'I.T's Grenzüberschreitungen', *Germanica*, 7, 1990:87–96.

TURRINI, PETER. C. Decker, 'The hermeneutics of democracy: Nestroy, Horváth, T., and the development of the "Volksstück"', *Seminar*, 27:219–32.

VALENTIN, KARL. *Kurzer Rede langer Sinn. Texte von und über K.V.*, ed. Helmut Bachmaier, Munich, Piper, 1990, 409 pp.

VETTER, ANNA. W. Gröner, 'Schneerose. Über A.V.', *Allmende*, 28–29, 1990:3–5.

WALLRAFF, GÜNTER. *G.W. Der Aufmacher. Der Mann, der bei Bild Hans Esser war*, ed. John Sandford (MNGT), x + 158 pp., maintains the high standard set by this series, with its excellent introduction, abridged text with detailed notes, and imaginative *Arbeitsteil*. It offers a balanced account of the background to the text, the author and his various campaigns, while addressing the ethical issues raised by some of W.'s methods. There is probing analysis of the role and significance of the *Bild Zeitung* in the history of the FRG, and pertinent discussion of the freedom of the press. Finally, the text is located within a German tradition of political literary reportage, and a variety of possible critical approaches are suggested.

WALSER, MARTIN. Frank Pilipp, *The Novels of M.W.: A Critical Introduction* (SGLLC, 64), xii + 152 pp., is a comprehensive study of W.'s prose works and critical essays 1976–88, detecting in the abandonment of first person narrative a disintegrating sense of identity, contrasting with the tendency of *Neue Subjektivität* in the 1970s. Adopting Herbert Marcuse's psycho-political social theory, the analysis of the novels looks at their socio-critical aspects in relation to the psychological interplay between protagonist and outside world. J. Schote, 'M.Ws Novelle *Ein fliehendes Pferd*', *OL*, 46. 1 : 52–63. A. Talarczyk, 'Revolutionsfimmel der "gebrannten Kinder". M.W. — "Ein Kinderspiel"', *Skamandros*, 1988 : 256–77.

WALTHER, JOACHIM. R. Andress, 'Feudalabsolutisches Barock und DDR-Literatur-Verhältnisse: Johann Christian Günther in J.Ws Roman *Bewerbung bei Hofe*', Gerber, *Studies*, 181–95.

WEIGEL, HANS. H. Fröhlich, 'Empfohlene Aufbrauchsfrist abgelaufen? Bemerkungen zu H.Ws Molière Übersetzung', Pöckl, *Dichter*, 211–37.

WEISS, PETER. Christian Bommert, *P.W. und der Surrealismus: poetische Verfahrensweisen in der 'Ästhetik des Widerstands'*, Opladen, Westdeutscher Vlg, 195 pp., constructs a theory of the significance of dream in W.'s work on the basis of his reception of French Surrealism and Freud's *Traumdeutung*. This is seen as central to W.'s notion of the relationship between art and politics and hence to his literary commitment, and is explored in his theatrical and film work in addition to *Ästhetik des Widerstands*. Kuibert Erbel, **Sprachlose Körper und körperlose Sprache. Studien zu 'innerer' und 'äußerer' Natur in 'Die Ästhetik des Widerstands' von P.W.*, St. Ingbert, Röhrig, 198 pp. Ian Hilton, **W: Die Verfolgung und Ermordung Jean Paul Marats dargestellt durch die Schauspielgruppe des Hospizes zu Charenton unter Anleitung des Herrn de Sade* (CGGT, 12), 1990, 113 pp. W. Hinderer, 'Deutsches Theater der Französischen Revolution', *GQ*, 64 : 207–19, writes on *Marat/Sade*, Büchner and Griepenkerl. M. Hofmann, 'Ästhetische Erziehung und Ästhetik des Widerstands. Kunstautonomie und Engagement des Kunstwerks bei Schiller, Marcuse und P.W.', *WB*, 37 : 819–38. Andreas Huber, *Mythos und Utopie. Eine Studie zur 'Ästhetik des Widerstands' von P.W.*, Heidelberg, Winter, 1990, 416 pp., analyses W.'s trilogy as an exposure of 'abstrakte Vernunft' as a modern myth employed in the service of power. In contrast to other postmodern critiques it also proposes a positive alternative, that of 'integrale Vernunft' based on a de-centred notion of the self and a new language defined in terms of Bakhtinian and feminist linguistic theories. Individual sections treat such topics as the construction of the subject, aesthetic experience as alternative to political rationality, and the notions of mythology, Utopia, and androgyny in the texts.

P.W. Life and Work, ed. Gunilla Palmsticrna-Wciss and Jürgen Schutte, Frankfurt, Suhrkamp, 345 pp., is a beautifully illustrated bilingual volume based on the exhibition to mark the deposition almost ten years after W.'s death of his *Nachlaß* in Berlin 1991. 21 German and Swedish writers and critics pay tribute to W. as artist, dramatist, film-maker, and novelist. Contributions range from literary critical analysis of his writing and political reassessments of his work to the more personal reminiscences of H. Müller and C. de Seynes. In a concluding essay, the author's widow reflects on their 30 years of marriage and collaboration, and on the recent radical transformation of the political landscape which he knew.

WELLERSHOFF, DIETER. *D.W. Studien zu seinem Werk*, ed. Manfred Durzak, Keith Bullivant, *et al.*, Cologne, Kiepenheuer & Witsch, 1990, 394 pp., comprises 14 essays on W.'s novels, radio, and television dramas, including studies of *Sirene*, *Einladung an alle*, *Glücksucher*, *Flüchtige Bekanntschaften*, *Phantasten*, and *Der Sieger nimmt alles*. It also includes an assessment of his contributions in the 1950s to the *Deutsche Studentenzeitung* and one on his editorial and critical work. Two contributors consider aspects of dream and the unconscious in his prose, while others look at the significance of isolation and of locality. J. Jaeger, **Realismus und Anthropologie: eine Studie zum Werk D.Ws* (EH, 1, 1180), 1990, iii + 312 pp. H. Peitsch, '"Ein schöner Tag." D.W. zum 65. Geburstag', *Juni*, 4, 1990:113–36. Jan Sass, *Der magische Moment: Phantastestrukturen im Werk D.Ws*, Tübingen, Stauffenberg, 1990, 346 pp., situates W.'s work within the literary landscape of his time, but is as concerned with his theory of literature as with his works themselves. His 'neuer Realismus' is placed in the context of the 1960s politicization of literature but differentiated from Enzensberger's position, as also from the 'Erfahrungsliteratur' of 1970s *Neue Subjektivität*. W.'s central notion of 'productive' and 'reproductive' imagination is elucidated with reference to Freud, and his debts to reception theory, Siegfried Kracauer, Maurice Blanchot, the *nouveau roman* and Russian Formalism are illustrated with reference to characters in *Einladung an alle* and *Bau einer Laube*. The significance of mythological motifs and locality is further discussed with reference to characters from *Ein schöner Tag*, *Die Schönheit der Schimpansen*, *Der Sirene*, and *Der Sieger nimmt alles*. See also HÄRTLING, PETER.

WERBER, MARKUS. M. Ebel, 'Laudatio auf M.W. anläßlich der Verleihung des alemannischen Literaturpreises in Waldshut-Tiengen am 19. Mai 1990', *Allmende*, 28–29, 1990:230–38. G. Mack, '"Aufrecht durch den Nebel gehen." Ein Gespräch mit dem Schaffhauser Autor M.W.', *Allmende*, 28–29, 1990:216–29.

WIENER, OSWALD. G. Pichler, 'Das Kreative selbst ist ein Mechanismus. Gespräch mit O.W.', *manuskripte*, 113:67–70.
WOLF, CHRISTA. K. H. Biedenkopf, 'C.W.: Soziale Marktwirtschaft, Kultur und Utopie', *SuF*, 42, 1990:1037–57. A. Bohm, 'C.W.'s *Störfall* and Chinzig Aitmatov's *I dol'she veka dlitsia den'*: technology and history', *GSL*, 6, 1990:323–38. C. Brink-Friederici, 'Von der Selbstfremdheit zur Selbstwerdung. Dargestellt am Beispiel von C.Ws Erzählung *Kassandra*', *Akten* (Tokyo), x, 282–87. J. Dalemans, 'Kassandra und Panthoos. Ein Beitrag zur Interpretation von C.Ws Erzählung *Kassandra*', *Neophilologus*, 75:433–44. Rainer Gerdzen and Klaus Wöhler, *Matriarchat und Patriarchat in C.Ws 'Kassandra'*, Würzburg, Königshausen & Neumann, 144 pp., interprets W.'s novel as an attempt to understand contemporary society by retracing its origins to the transition from matriarchal to patriarchal culture in Classical antiquity. It presents a definition of matriarchy and patriarchy and the textual evidence of transition in W.'s depiction of Trojan culture. In detailed textual analysis, this reading of *Kassandra* points to recurring triadic structures around which the narrative is organized, in which it departs from the dualistic world view associated with patriarchal thought. K. Hauser, 'Literatur in politisierten Verhältnissen. C.W.: Selbstaussage und Werkinterpretationen', *Argument*, 32, 1990:895–904. S.-Y. Kim, 'Untersuchung über die Literaturtheorie und die literarische Praxis bei C.W. — dargestellt am Beispiel von *Nachdenken über Christa T.*', *Büchner und moderne Literatur*, 3, 1990:127–55. U. Klingmann, 'Entmythologisierter Mythos: die Problematik des Wissens in C.Ws *Kassandra*', *ZGer*, n.F., 1: 270–79. V. Langbehn, 'Vom Feminismus zum Post-Marxismus? C.Ws *Nachdenken über Christa T.*', *NGR*, 5–6, 1989–90:43–55. H. Lehnert, 'Fiktionalität und autobiographische Motive. Zu C.Ws Erzählung *Was bleibt*', *WB*, 37:423–44. J. Lieskounig, 'Gescheiterte Anverwandlung? Zu C.Ws Erzählung *Kein Ort. Nirgends*', *AGJSG*, 20, 1990:129–40. S. Lohr, 'Ein Sommerstück — Die C.W. Kontroverse im Juni 1990', *DUS*, 43. 1:77–104.. M. Love, '"A little susceptible to the supernatural?" On C.W.', *WGY*, 7:1–22. F. Meyer-Gosau, 'Am Ende angekommen. Zu C.Ws Erzählungen *Störfall*, *Sommerstück* und *Was bleibt*', *LitL*, 1990:84–93. G. Müller-Waldeck, 'C.Ws *Sommerstück* — jetzt gelesen', *WB*, 37:136–40. A. Neusinger, 'Zum Verständnis von Literatur und Utopie bei C.W. sowie zum utopischen Potential ihres literarischen Schaffens zwischen 1959 und 1989', *KGS*, 4, 1989:171–87. H. Mundt, 'Ordnung und Chaos, Zeitlosigkeit und Vergänglichkeit: zur Symbolik in C.Ws *Juninachmittag*', *Monatshefte*, 83:161–75. J. Pischel, 'The end of utopia? The current discussion on GDR literature and the controversy surrounding C.W.', Williams, *Literature*, 117–27. W. H.

Rey, '"Wo habt ihr bloß alle gelebt?" C.Ws Dilemma in ihrem Verhältnis zur DDR', *GR*, 66:89–95. R. Schmidt, 'Die Dialektik zwischen Wort und Wirklichkeit, dem Selbst und dem Fremden in C.Ws *Sommerstück*', *GLL*, 44:469–76. K. Schumann, 'Blickwechsel: C.W. und Ingeborg Bachmann: drei Begegnungen', *ANeo*, 23, 1990:63–74. R. Waldeck, '"Hitler hat Deutschland kaputtgemacht." Ein deutscher Opfermythos, aufgeklärt mit Hilfe von C.Ws *Kindheitsmuster*', Kohn-Waechter, *Flammen*, 241–58. S. Wilke, '"Rückhaltlose Subjektivität." Subjektwerdung, Gesellschafts- und Geschlechtsbewußtsein bei C.W.', *WGY*, 6, 1990:27–45. Wilke, '"Worüber man nicht sprechen kann, darüber muß man allmählich zu schweigen aufhören": Vergangenheitsbeziehungen in C.Ws *Kindheitsmuster*', *GR*, 26:169–76. C. Zehl Romero, '"Erinnerung an eine Zukunft." Anna Seghers, C. W. und die Suche nach einer weiblichen Tradition des Schreibens in der DDR', Stephan, *Frauen*, 211–24. See also BACHMANN, INGEBORG; BRAUN, VOLKER; DUDEN, ANNE; FICHTE, HUBERT; KIRSCH, SARAH; KÖNIGSDORF, HELGA; MORGNER, IRMTRAUD.

WOLLSCHLÄGER, HANS. U. Benzenhöfer, '"Herzgewächse oder Der Fall Adams." Bemerkungen zu einem Roman H.Ws', *Ärzteblatt Baden-Württemberg*, 10, 1990:650–54.

ZECH, PAUL. H. W. Panthel, 'Ein schwacher Revancheakt: P.Zs dramatische Skizze *Brot*', *ASNS*, 227, 1990:276–82.

ZELLER, EVA. E. Martin, 'Patriarchy, memory, and the Third Reich in the autobiographical novels of E. Z.', *WGY*, 6, 1990:47–62.

ZEPLIN, ROSEMARIE. I. Wallace, 'Gespräch mit R.Z.', *DeutB*, 21:1–8.

ZODERER, JOSEPH. G. Riedmann, 'J.Z. oder Der unaufhaltsame Abschied von der (deutschen) Sprache', *Sprachkunst*, 21, 1990:313–24. A. Tetter Saxalber and I. Hubert, '"Man versteht die unverständliche Welt am besten mit einer unverständlich guten Literatur." Ein Gespräch mit J.Z.', *DD*, 22:209–15.

ZÜRN, UNICA. M. Eifler, 'U.Z.: Surreale Lebensbeschreibung', Knapp, *Autoren*, 775–93.

II. DUTCH STUDIES

LANGUAGE

By ROEL VISMANS, *Department of Dutch Studies, University of Hull*

1. GENERAL

Jaarboek van de KANTL 1989–90, 108 pp.; *VMKA*, 1989, no. 3, 198 pp.; *VMKA*, 1990, nos. 1, 150 pp., and 2, 126 pp., and *VMKA*, 1991, no. 1, 147 pp., survey KANTL's activities with in addition many contributions by its members. *Liber Amicorum Kåre Langvik-Johannessen*, ed. K. Portemann and K. E. Schöndorf, Leuven, Peeters, 1989, 314 pp., celebrates the 70th birthday and retirement of the first Professor of Dutch at Oslo University, with contributions on Dutch linguistics (five articles) and literature (13), and Austrian Literature (5), another of L.-J.'s specialities. T. Janssen and B. Triesscheijn, *Gebruik, inhoud en effectiviteit van taal- en literatuurmethoden in Nederland en Vlaanderen*, The Hague, Stichting Bibliographia Neerlandica, 1990, 119 pp., reports on a study of the available courses in Dutch language and literature at primary and secondary schools in the Netherlands and Belgium. Little is known about how teachers use courses and how effective they are. Course content is evaluated critically, concluding that many courses are traditional, lacking in clear structure and irrelevant to students' needs. P. Van Hauwermeiren and F. Simonis, *Waar Nederlands de voertaal is. Nederland- en Vlaanderenkunde*, Lier, Van In, 1990, 195 pp., is a Low Countries *Landeskunde* coursebook. In 19 chapters it introduces its readers to aspects of the Low Countries like geography, politics, media, and a 28-page potted history. Most chapters divide their attention equally between the two countries.

2. LINGUISTICS

R. Salverda, *Linguistics and the Dutch*, London, University College, 1990, 26 pp., is S.'s inaugural lecture as Professor of Dutch Language and Literature at UCL. It surveys the contribution made to linguistics by Dutch scholars past and present, concluding that their strengths have been and remain 'the accumulation of diverse linguistic materials, the concentration of high quality scholarship and the availability of a well established publishing trade working for the linguistic world market'. *The Berkeley Conference on Dutch Linguistics. Issues and Controversies, Old and New*, ed. T. F. Shannon and J. P. Snapper, Lanham, UPA, 205 pp., contains a variety of papers on the history of the language (substrate words in Dutch by E. C. Polomé, submorphemic attraction in Early Dutch by G. W. Davis, the 'linguistic lineage of the dialects of the Northeastern Netherlands' by J. Goossens, the 'Veldeke problem': did he write in Dutch or German? by H. Penzl, the diphthongization of Middle Dutch long *i* by R. B. Howell), language contact (the influence of Dutch on American English and Indonesian by J. de Vries, language shift in Belgium, Switzerland and Canada by R. Willemyns), syntax (R. S. Kirsner on the indirect object with or without *aan*), and phonology (tone segments in the description of Dutch intonation by C. Gussenhoven, word stress assignment by M. Trommelen, morphology and syllable structure by T. S. Shannon).

Jaarboek van de Stichting Instituut voor Nederlandse Lexicologie. Overzicht van het jaar 1990, Leiden, Stichting Instituut voor Nederlandse Lexicologie, 134 pp., is the 1990 annual report of the Institute for Dutch Lexicology containing three academic studies: R. Landheer on the interaction between lexical and textual semantics; R. Tempelaars on nicknames; and M. C. van den Toorn on the language during the Second World War. *H. J. Pos (1898–1955). Taalkundige en geëngageerd filosoof*, ed. S. Daalder and J. Noordegraff, Amsterdam, Huis aan de Drie Grachten, 1990, 227 pp., is a collection of essays on the philosopher and linguist Pos. Apart from a section on his political philosophy there are essays on his linguistic philosophy by R. Salverda and S. Daalder, his structuralism by P. Desmet and P. Swiggers, semantics by F. Balk-Smit Duyzentkunst, P.'s work as linguistic historian by J. Noordegraaf, and his relationship with Karl Bühler by F. Vonk.

A. Neijt, *Universele fonologie. Een inleiding in de klankleer*, Dordrecht, Foris, x + 188 pp., is an introduction to phonology with Dutch as starting point, but with a universal perspective. Of its 11 chapters, the first three are introductory, followed by chapters on articulatory phonetics, phonological rules, syllable structure, intonation, and accent. The last three chapters are about (Dutch) spelling. J. de Caluwe, *Nederlandse nominale compositsa in functionalistisch perspectief*, The Hague, SDU, xii + 240 pp., diss., studies nominal compounds in a 'functionalistic' framework. The compounds in question are noun-noun and verb-noun, and C. is particularly interested in the relationship between *determinans* (the first part of the compound) and *determinatum* (the head word) which is very rich and relatively unrestricted, lending itself easily to a functional approach. The last chapter on idiomaticity and compounds concludes that a compound is only idiomatic when the relationship between it and its individual members is opaque. W. Haseryn, *Syntactische normen in het Nederlands. Een empirisch onderzoek naar volgordevariatie in de werkwoordelijke eindgroep*,

Nijmegen, diss., 1990, xii + 401 pp., is an empirical study of native speaker norms for order in the verbal cluster at the end of the (subordinate) clause. A well-known problem is for example whether the order should be past participle-auxiliary or *vice versa*. H.'s study is based on elicitation tests carried out amongst native speakers from various regions, of differing socio-economic backgrounds. The results confirm earlier studies, in that there is a large consensus, in terms of both judgement and behaviour, on the various possible word-order patterns and that a number of tendencies can be distinguished which are influenced by linguistic factors such as rhythm, form, function, and meaning. However, there are clear regional differences and certain (professional) groups show particular preferences. Jan Model, *Grammatische analyse. Syntactische verschijnselen van het Nederlands en het Engels*, Dordrecht, ICG Publication, xii + 450 pp., written by a collective studying grammatical models under the pseudonym *John Model*, is not a comparative study of Dutch and English syntax (as the title suggests), but a non-technical introduction to the syntax of mainly Dutch, and occasionally English. Written in a Chomskyan vein, it offers the student an overview of the main syntactic phenomena in 11 chapters. F. Devos, R. De Muynck, and M. Van Herreweghe, *Nederlands, Frans en Engels in contrast. 1. De nominale constituent*, Leuven, Peeters, xvi + 262 pp., on the other hand, is contrastive. It is the first of a projected three-part series, parts two and three covering the clause and the verbal constituent. The idea is to offer a contrastive grammar of the two main foreign languages (for Flemish learners at any rate) starting from the native language. The grammar is not exactly prescriptive but nevertheless clearly written with a pedagogical purpose in mind, avoiding theoretical niceties. Each phenomenon is explained first, followed by an indication as to what extent it exists in the three languages concerned. There are eight appendices, e.g. lists of several categories of *pluralia tantum* in the three languages, and a trilingual list of grammatical terms. A number of popular books on Dutch include two by J. Welling (*Vishandel Hein Graat en andere taalcuriosa*, Weert, Uitgeverij M & P, 1990, 96 pp., and *Taxibedrijf antiloop en andere taalcuriosa, ib.*, 95 pp.), discussing homonymy, toponymy, spelling problems, etc. *'Een slipje van de sluier.' Een opmerkelijke collectie taalkronkels verzameld door het Genootschap Onze Taal, ib.*, 111 pp., is a collection of Malapropisms. R.-H. Zuidinga, *Eroticon. Het ABC van de erotiek*, The Hague, BZZTôH, 1990, 128 pp., is a collection of 26 accounts of erotic language. It covers technical but more commonly colloquial expressions. A similar collection of texts about linguistic phenomena from shipping is to be found in J. Berns, *We zien wel waar het schip strandt. Zee- en scheepvaarttermen in het dagelijks gebruik, ib.*, 93 pp., lacking an index.

3. History of the Language

In *Beiträge* (Trier), W. J. J. Pijnenburg reports on progress of the *Vroegmiddelnederlands Woordenboek (1200–1300)*, a project undertaken at the Institute for Dutch Lexicology whose aim is to produce a dictionary of Early Middle Dutch by the end of the decade to supplement the *Middelnederlands Woordenboek* (1280–1550). L. Peeters, *Taalopbouw als renaissance-ideaal. Studies over taalopvattingen en taalpraktijk in de zestiende en zeventiende eeuw*, Amsterdam, Buijten en Schipperheijn, 204 pp., consists of ten previously published articles about standardization in Early Modern Dutch as seen in, for example, the so-called *Trivium* tradition. Looking at this process from various angles it shows an interesting insight into language attitudes of the period. L. Van Durme, *Toponymie van Velzeke-Ruddershove en Bochoute*, II (2), Ghent, KANTL, 356 pp., diss., is part two of the glossary of this extensive toponymical study of an area of East Flanders (see *YWMLS*, 49:818 and 50:916). The 65th birthday and retirement of D. P. Blok, Emeritus Professor of toponymy at the University of Amsterdam, is celebrated in *Feestbundel D.P. Blok*, ed. J. B. Berns *et al.*, Hilversum, Verloren, 1990, 197 pp., with 35 contributions from J. Daan, R. A. Ebeling, H. J. T. Miedema, and A. Weijnen, among others.

4. Sociolinguistics and Dialectology

A. Weijnen, *Vergelijkende klankleer van de Nederlandse dialecten*, The Hague, SDU, xlviii + 318 pp., illustrated by 102 maps, consists of a diachronic and a phonological (synchronic) part. The diachronic part sketches the development of the sounds of Dutch dialects with Proto-Germanic as its starting point. C. Hoppenbrouwers, *Het regiolect. Van dialect tot algemeen Nederlands*, Muiderberg, Coutinho, 1990, 252 pp., describes a phenomenon that H. perceives in the transition from dialect use to the use of the standard language. Whereas in earlier periods there may have been incidental interference of the standard in dialects, these days contact between the two varieties leads to structural changes in dialects. The first three chapters form a general introduction to the opposition between standard and dialect, and dialect change. Chapter 4 defines the term 'regiolect' itself and is followed by three chapters setting out phonological, morphological, and lexical aspects of regiolect formation. The last three chapters discuss sociolinguistic aspects of the phenomenon: language use in school, attitudes, and standardization in general. H. Bloemhoff, *Fonologie en morfologie van het Stellingwerfs: een toetsing van de natuurlijke generative fonologie*, Groningen, Sasland, 341 pp., diss., English and German summaries, is a critical study of

Natural Generative Phonology based on empirical data collected
from the dialect of Stellingwerf in the eastern Netherlands. D. Gorter,
L. G. Jansma, and G. H. Jelsma, *Taal yn it Grinsgebiet. Undersyk nei de
taalferhâldings en de taalgrins yn it Westerkertier yn Grinslân*, Leeuwarden,
Fryske Akademy, 1990, 295 pp., with a summary in Dutch, studies
the linguistic frontier between Frisian and the eastern Dutch dialect
in the Westerkwartier area of Groningen. The language mix here
consists of Frisian, Groningen dialect and (standard) Dutch. The
study concludes that, although the border between Frisian and Dutch
in the Westerkwartier cannot be said to be shifting, Frisian is
receding. The Groningen dialect is also far from stable, because there
is a strong tendency towards Dutchification in the nothern provinces
of the Netherlands. The authors give suggestions for further research.
T. Beintema, *Moai sa Sikke/Goed zo Sicco. Frysk sprekwurdeboek met
Nederlânske oersetting, ferklearring of taljochting/Fries spreekwoordenboek met
Nederlandse vertaling, verklaring of toelichting*, Drachten, Osinga, 1990,
152 pp., is a collection of 1,000 Frisian proverbs with Dutch translations or explanations. The term proverb has been applied loosely, as
other idiomatic expressions are included.

C. Swanenberg, *Jikkes merante! Sprokkelen in Brabantse spreuken*, Den
Bosch, Heinen, 1990, 94 pp., is a collection of 28 essays describing
idiomatic expressions from Brabants dialect under certain 'themes'
like 'the potato', 'eyes and ears', etc. Again, the word proverb has
been interpreted liberally and there is no index. R. Van Alboom, *De
Verbeulemansing van Brussel*, Brussels, BRT-Instructieve Omroep,
295 pp. + map, is a well-presented and richly illustrated book
sketching the Gallicization of Brussels over the centuries. The four
chapters follow the chronology: pre-1830, 1830–1900, 1900–60,
post-1960. Each chapter, apart from the first which is purely
historical, puts the process in its economic, political and social
context (e.g. industrialization, federalization, demography). A. Verbiest, *Het gewicht van de directrice. Taal over, tegen en door vrouwen*,
Amsterdam, Contact, 134 pp., discusses sexism in language under
four headings: language used about, towards and by women, and
listeners' reactions to women. The author's ideological point of view
is clear, but the argument is well-founded and meticulously
researched.

Taal voor welzijn, ed. C. Fahner, Kampen, Kok, 128 pp., looks at the
role language can play in welfare. It is perhaps a vague concept, but is
illustrated by A. Eppink's article on language and cross-cultural aid
and counselling. In welfare work, too, it is important to be aware of
the codes used by people from different backgrounds. Two opening
articles discuss purely linguistic issues and are followed by four
welfare-orientated ones. M. C. van den Toorn, *Wij melden u den nieuwen*

tijd. Een beschouwing van het woordgebruik van de Nederlandse nationaal-socialisten, The Hague, SDU, viii + 412 pp., is a thorough study of the linguistic behaviour of the Dutch National Socialists before and during the Second World War. The first three chapters define National Socialism in the Dutch context, describe the use of NS propaganda, and sketch the means used for this. The next six chapters detail the various usages of the NS vocabulary. Chapter 10 is an attempt to discern a specific NS style, but concludes that it is mostly a matter of vocabulary. A final chapter looks at NS literature. *Taal en Omroep*, ed. L. Beheydt, The Hague, Stichting Bibliographia Neerlandica, 131 pp., treats language and broadcasting. The purpose of this collection is to make a start with a discussion of the language of the media, so that the *Nederlandse Taalunie* can integrate the media in its policies. Eight articles cover programmes about language on radio and television, the vocabulary of television news and football reports, and linguistic developments in the Flemish media.

5. APPLIED LINGUISTICS

W. A. van Loon-Vervoorn and I. J. van Bekkum, *Woordassociatie lexicon*, Lisse, Swets & Zeitlinger, iii + 240 pp., on word associations, includes associations of words that are acquired relatively late and have a low imageability. A brief introduction explains the methodology followed by a list of 1,199 stimuli plus detailed information about their associations. H. Lammers, *Taal in tweevoud. Communicatieve competentie, taalvaardigheid & het onderwijs in het Nedertlands*, De Lier, Academisch Boeken Centrum, 289 pp., diss., with summary in English, is a study about mother-tongue teaching in relation to the perceived confusion between communicative competence and language skills. The author tries to disentangle these two concepts, opening the way for improved language teaching. H. Bakkes-Rennes and E. Plantinga-Veldhuizen, *Moedertaal in de basiseducatie*, Amersfoort, Stichting SVE, 194 pp., contains the objectives of mother-tongue education for adults, plus models for observation and analysis. W. Burgers, *Correct Nederlands. Spellingsadviezen voor de media*, Rijswijk, Elmar, 68 pp., is a reference work for journalists in seven chapters covering writing words together, preferred (i.e. official) spelling, etc. P. J. van der Horst, *Leestekenwijzer. Praktische handleiding voor het gebruik van leestekens en andere tekens*, The Hague, SDU, 1990, xvi + 132 pp., supplements *Schrijfwijzer* (*YWMLS*, 52:839). Whereas the latter advises on general issues of writing, *Leestekenwijzer* deals exclusively with punctuation and other textual marks. Books like this are by their nature prescriptive and often selective. This one is carefully written and virtually complete. K. Groeneboer, *Het ABC voor Indië. Bibliografie van leermiddelen Nederlandse taal voor Nederlands-Indië*, Leiden, KITLV, viii + 136 pp., is a bibliography of Dutch language teaching material used in the Dutch East Indies between *c.* 1840 and 1950. Its importance is that Dutch was first taught as a foreign language in Indonesia and this material should give many insights into language teaching methodology. The introduction sketches the history of teaching Dutch in Indonesia. The bibliography itself is divided into two periods: pre-1900 and post-1900. The period post-1900 is further divided into primary and secondary education, and for each of these three sections the material is divided into teaching and reading materials.

J. van der Toorn-Schutte, *Maatwerk. Onderwijs toegesneden op allochtone leerlingen*, Apeldoorn, Auctor, 125 pp., is a handbook for teachers involved with ethnic minorities in the Netherlands. It first deals with the available facilities, followed by three chapters on Dutch as a second language including one describing briefly the differences between Dutch and ten languages spoken by ethnic minorities and refugees. A short chapter on test design is followed by two detailing cultural differences and religion. The last chapter argues strongly for the integration of intercultural education at all levels. P. Broeder, *Talking about People. A Multiple Case Study on Adult Language Acquisition*, Lisse, Swets & Zeitlinger, iv + 198 pp., on the acquisition of the Dutch pronoun system at word and discourse level by two Turkish and two Moroccan adults, also refers to the acquisition of German by Turkish and Italian immigrants. J. Kurvers, *In de ban van het schrift. Over analfabetisme en alfabetisering in een tweede taal, ib.,* 1990, 309 pp., studies literacy and illiteracy in the Netherlands, in particular amongst ethnic minorities. Part I discusses some general aspects of literacy and defines it. Part II describes the acquisition of literacy in a second language in a non-intensive and an intensive course with the intensive course scoring consistently higher. The last chapter gives some practical tips for teaching second-language literacy. *Etnische minderheden en geletterdheid*, ed. L. Verhoeven, *ib.,* 1990, 222 pp., has contributions to a symposium on literacy among ethnic minorities with four themes: literacy and society, primary education, adult education, and policy developments. M. Boogaard *et al., De Nederlandse taalvaardigheid van Nederlandse en allochtone kleuters. Peiling van de taalvaardigheid in het Nederlands van Surinaamse, Antilliaanse, Marokkaanse, Turkse en Nederlandse leerlingen aan het einde van de kleuterperiode, ib.,* 1990, iv + 168 pp., compares the language skills of Dutch six-year-olds with those of children from ethnic minorities. In general, children from West Indian backgrounds score lower than native children, and Turkish and Moroccan children lower still. Teachers have a good idea of the skills of their pupils, although a minority (*c.* 25%) are overestimated, especially their vocabulary. The amount of attention given to pupils with lower skills is generally quite high.

Y. Timman, *De sleutels van de taal. Idiomatische en andere vaste uitdrukkingen in tweede taalverwerving*, Amsterdam, Instituut voor Algemene Taalwetenschap, 1989, vi + 138 pp., discusses the role of idiomatic expressions in second language acquisition. T.'s position is that much of linguistic science is analytical, leaving little room for idiom. Its cultural and communicative importance, and ways of integrating its acquisition in second language teaching are discussed. The so-called *Delftse methode* of teaching Dutch as a foreign language has existed since 1984. F. Lo Cascio and L. Heerkens, *Docentenhandleiding Nederlands voor buitenlanders. De Delftse methode*, Meppel, Boom, 108 pp., is its teacher manual. L. Beheydt, *Elementair woordenboek Nederlands*, Lier, Van In, 123 pp., lists the 1,000 most elementary words in Dutch for foreigners and is set out in the same way as the *Basiswoordenboek Nederlands* (*YWMLS*, 45:819), i.e. each entry gives grammatical information and (syntactic) context(s), but no direct meaning. There is a useful appendix with numerals, measures, etc. F. Kuiken and A. van Kalsbeek, *Code Nederlands*, 2, Amsterdam, Meulenhoff Educatief, is part two of this communicative language course (see *YWMLS*, 52:839–40 for part 1) consisting of a textbook (191 pp), teacher manual (166 pp.), and exercises (190 pp). I. de Bakker *et al.*, *Lezen las gelezen. 1. Leescursus voor volwassen anderstaligen*, Leiden, Martinus Nijhoff, iv + 206 pp., is a reading course for intermediate students based around eight graded themes (e.g. politics, the economy, technology).

6. Dictionaries

After a dictionary of proverbs (*YWMLS*, 50:920) and an etymological dictionary (*YWMLS*, 51:836–37), Van Dale have now published a dictionary of synonyms: P. G. J. van Sterkenburg *et al.*, *Groot Woordenboek van Synoniemen en andere betekenisverwante woorden*, Utrecht, Van Dale Lexicografie, xxv + 1215 pp. Where necessary, meaning differences are indicated in the margin and other associative meaning relations are given, like antonyms and hyponyms. M. Grauls, *Bintje en Kalasjnikov. Het Eponiemen Boek*, Zonhoven, Uitgeverij Boek, 300 pp., is a dictionary of eponyms. *Polytechnisch Handwoordenboek* in two volumes (Dutch–English, 315 pp. and English–Dutch, 320 pp.), Deventer, Kluwer, is a technical dictionary with over 24,000 entries from all fields of science, technology, and engineering. D. Van Hoof, *Dictionary for Foreign Trade and International Co-operation*, Antwerp, Maklu, 1052 pp. is a quadrilingual dictionary (English, Dutch, French, German) with *c.* 25,000 entries based on a large number of sources (many from the EC) dealing with areas like customs, transport, and arbitration. J. van der Eijk, *Woordenboek voor de Beurs*, Amsterdam, Balans, 85 pp., is a dictionary with terms from the stock exchange and banking. *Engels Marketing Lexicon*, Eeserveen, Sifra, 256 pp., is an English–Dutch marketing dictionary with *c.* 3,000 entries. P. Marechal, *Woordwijzer Ecologie*, Lisse, Reaal Uitgevers, 320 pp., is a specialist ecological dictionary, also containing a large number of less usual names from flora and fauna. C. Uitert and A. M. Kaspers, *Verklarend Informatica Woordenboek*, Alphen an den Rijn, Samsom, 1989, 1063 pp., is the second completely revised edition of an IT dictionary with sections on Dutch, English–Dutch, and acronyms. A. Gillissen and P. Olden, *Het eerste Nederlandse studenten woordenboek*, Amersfoort, Novella, 89 pp., is a dictionary of student slang with *c.* 1,000 entries with local variants playing an important part. D. De Bleeker *et al.*, *Lik op stuk. Nieuw Woordenboek van Agressief Taalgebruik*, Tielt, Lannoo, 1990, ix + 135 pp., is a dictionary of terms of abuse.

Dutch Studies 885

LITERATURE

By ELSA STRIETMAN, *Lecturer in Dutch, University of Cambridge*

1. GENERAL

Professor R. P. Meijer, or P. M. Reinders, as many will know him from his long-standing presence as a literary critic for the NRC, was honoured on the occasion of his retirement from the Chair of Dutch Language and Literature at University College, London (1971–88) by *Standing Clear. A Festschrift for Reinder P. Meijer*, ed. Jane Fenoulhet and Theo Hermans (Crossways, 1), London, University College, Centre for Low Countries Studies, 237 pp. Contributions include articles on G. Reve's *Werther Nieland* (M. H. Schenkeveld), W. Elsschot's *Kaas* (L. Gilbert), S. Vestdijk (J. Fenoulhet), M. Nijhoff (W. Woods), the poet G. J. Resink (K. Snoek), J. van der Noot (K. Bostoen), Dutch Renaissance approaches to translations (T. Hermans), Dutch 17th-c. genre painting and drama (P. K. King), J. C. Weijerman (T. Broos), Dutch influence on Indonesian (J. W. de Vries), the linguist H. J. Pos (R. Salverda), R. P. Meijer's persona as the literary chronicler P. M. Reinders (D. Boukema), G. Achterberg's poetry (F. Balk-Smit Duyzentkunst). A tribute to another literary critic-cum-academic is Kees Fens, *Voetstukken, een keuze uit de essays 1964–1982*, Amsterdam, Querido, 191 pp.; a welcome reprint of some of F.'s most memorable essays; often these have given the impetus for further discussion and research, such as in the case of W. Elsschot, Nescio, W. F. Hermans, and G. Achterberg. Besides these there are essays about K. van de Woestijne, J. van Oudshoorn, T. Thijssen, S. Vestdijk, G. Reve, S. Carmiggelt, A. Koolhaas, A. Alberts, and T. S. Eliot. A, sadly posthumous, tribute honours a scholar whose most important work was in 18th-c. studies: *Accidentia. Taal en letteroefeningen voor Jan Knol*, ed. J. Noordegraaf, R. Zemel et al., Amsterdam, Stichting Neerlandistiek VU, 248 pp., is a collection which ranges far and wide. Of literary interest specifically are contributions about I. da Costa (J. Noordegraaf), *Ferguut* (Th. A. J. M. Janssen), *Fergus* (R. Zemel), P. C. Hooft (H. Duits), C. Huygens (J. A. van Leuvesteyn, A. Leerintveld), evaluation of literary texts (D. Schram), G. Achterberg (T. van Loon), J. Kuyper (A. Zuiderent), L. van Deyssel (J. W. van der Weij). Carel Peeters, *Echte Kennis. Essays over filosofie en literatuur*, Amsterdam, de Harmonie, 212 pp., writes from the desire to uncover the inherent secret agenda in terms of philosophical beliefs and conviction in some important authors. P. scrutinizes amongst others A. Kellendonk, W. F. Hermans, N. Claus, P. Sloterdijk, and G. Komrij, and pays attention to the up-and-coming generation of Dutch authors, such as D. van Weelden, C. Palmers, M. Möhring, and M. Brouwers.

Another foray into the many adjacent disciplines which can shed light on literature is *De Verleiding van de overvloed. Reflecties op de eigenheid van de cultuurgeschiedenis*, ed. R. Sanders *et al.*, Amsterdam, Rodopi, 116 pp.; it is not difficult to find justification for the literary scholar or historian to dabble in the realm of cultural history, but the present volume tries both to illustrate the usefulness of cultural history as an applied science (A. T. van Deursen, P. Perrot), and to proclaim its standing as an independent academic discipline (R. Sanders, B. Mesters, W. Frijhoff, R. Kramer, K. Thomas, A. Corbin, M. Winders). The history of reading culture is addressed in *Omzien met een glimlach. Aspecten van een eeuw Protestantse leescultuur*, ed. R. G. K. Kraan *et al.*, The Hague, 339 pp. It traces the development of a Protestant reading culture in the 19th c. and discusses the plight of Protestant authors and poets, often too unorthodox for the Church and not unorthodox enough to make their name in the canon of literature. An interesting study of secularization. B. van Selm, *Inzichten en vergezichten; zes beschouwingen over het onderzoek naar de geschiedenis van de Nederlandse boekhandel*, ed. H. van Goinga and P. Hoftijzer, Amsterdam, De Buitenkant, is another example of useful research applicable to and illuminating for literary history and reception history. More directly useful is *De teksteditie in theorie en praktijk*, ed. M. de Smedt *et al.*, Gelrode, Contactgroep 19de eeuw — F. A. Snellaertcomité. This is a reprint from *Spektator* 19.3, 1990, and the result of a 1989 Louvain colloquium. In view of the desire for more and better text editions this collection addresses some interesting and useful issues: editing letters, such as those by J. F. Willems and F. A. Snellaert (A. Deprez), those of Thorbecke (G. J. Hooykaas), a theoretical discussion of printing techniques and their consequences for editing (M. Mathijsen), a general survey of editing problems (M. de Smedt), the non-differences between reading-editions and academic text-editions (H. T. M. van Vliet). More directly bearing on the literary text is Odile Heinders, *De verbeelding van betekenis. Vooronderstellingen en praktijk van deconstructieve lezingen: teksten van Paul Celan en Gerrit Achterberg*, Leuven — Apeldoorn, Garant, 338 pp.; a theoretical work discussing deconstructionist readings of literature, its strategies and its implications for literary criticism. It also offers an extensive deconstructionist reading of some of Achterberg's and other modernist poetry. A.'s poetry is here largely seen as coherent in its thematic issues but the author aims to show in her analysis that there is greater complexity than has commonly and hitherto been thought.

Verslagen en Mededelingen, Nieuwe Reeks, Ghent, KANTL, 147 pp., discusses amongst others the 'Beekwater' theme in G. Gezelle's poetry (C. d'Haen), the literary heritage of Gery Helderenberg (R. van de Perre), L. Couperus's *De boeken der kleine zielen* (E. Wessel), a fragment of J. van Maerlant's *Spieghel Historiael* (M. Vandecasteele), the Ulenspieghel legend (W. Spillebeen). Its *Jaarboek 1989–1990*, Ghent, KANTL, 108 pp., has its usual useful list of publications by members, many literary contributions among them. *Jaarboek 1990–1991*, Ghent, KANTL, 149 pp., contains contributions about Jacobus van Cruitrode's *Speculum* (J. Reynaert), letters by J. F. Willems (A. Deprez, M. De Smedt), F. van Eeden and F. Timmermans (A. Keersmaekers), Marnix Gijsen (M. Janssens), Herwig Hensen (R. van de Perre), Paul van Ostaijen and Vincent van Gogh (M. Janssens), and letters by A. A. Angillus to F. A. Snellaert (M. Carlier).

De canon onder vuur. Nederlandse literatuur tegendraads gelezen, Amsterdam, Van Gennep, 259 pp., is an original contribution to literary criticism and history: it aims to re-evaluate some of the 'sacred' texts, to stimulate the ideological-critical reading of canonized male authors, and to discuss how such literature functions in its cultural context. It fortunately avoids mere 'deconstruction' for the sake of it, but adds fresh insights to Dutch literature, such as *Lanseloet van Denemarken* (J. Koekman), G. A. Bredero (M. Spies), C. Huygens (A. J. Gelderblom), Gorter's *Mei* (T. Stevens), L. Couperus (J. van Luxembourg), Nescio's *Dichtertje* (A. van Doggenaar). Other contributions include H. Marsman, F. du Perron, F. Bordewijk, W. Elsschot, H. Mulisch, and A. M. G. Schmidt. M. J. G. de Jong, *Literatuur: een spel zonder grenzen*, Leiden, Dimensie, 154 pp., equally aims to expand one's consciousness and question one's received notions. J. always writes with deceptive ease, but he truly practises comparative criticism to a very high degree; here he does not confine himself to Dutch literature alone, but includes essays relevant with regard to the medieval mystic texts by Suster Bertken, and the poetry of W. Bilderdijk and G. Gezelle. Another publication which looks beyond the frontiers of Dutch studies is *Van aangezicht tot aangezicht, modelinterpretaties moderne lyriek*, ed. R. Duhamel, Leuven — Apeldoorn, Garant, 222 pp.; a very useful general essay about the interpretation of poetry (R. Duhamel) is preceded by an interesting selection of poets: J. Werumeus Buning (P. Pelckmans), Hugo Claus (G. Wildemeersch), Rutger Kopland (D. de Geest), H. C. Pernath (J. Gerits), Hans Faverey (M. van Buuren), Anton Korteweg (H. Brems), Eddy van Vliet (A. M. Musschoot), Stefan Hertmans (B. Vervaeck).

A number of useful reference works have appeared. The latest issues of the excellent *Lexikon van Literaire Werken*, Groningen, Wolters-Noordhoff, occupies itself with L. Couperus, F. van Eeden,

G. Gossaert, M. Nijhoff, H. C. Pernath, F. de Pillecijn, K. van de Woestijne, G. Achterberg, L. P. Boon, J. Cremer, C. C. S. Crone, H. S. Haasse, D. A. Kooiman, and G. Krol. As always the essays are succinctly written, full of information and with a good mixture of older and modern literature, canonized and up-and-coming authors. *Sleutelwoorden. Kernbegrippen uit de hedendaagse literatuurwetenschap*, ed. W. van Peer and K. Dijkstra, Leuven — Apeldoorn, Garant, 239 pp., is a useful book, more than a set of definitions. Instead a number of concepts and fields of investigation are treated in essays, amongst many others: avant-garde, *écriture féminine*, catharsis, genre, reception, metaphor. G. J. Janssens and H. J. Vanisselroy, *Retour Brussel-Amsterdam*, Groningen, Wolters-Noordhoff, 1990, 221 pp., is a quick-reference book, providing up-to-date information on the Netherlands and Flanders, more for teachers of ab initio courses than for beginning students, since it is in Dutch. Cees van der Zalm, *Prisma van de Letterkunde*, Utrecht, Spectrum, 306 pp., is more like a reference dictionary and quite useful. L. Goosen, *Van Andreas tot Zacheus. Thema's uit het Nieuwe Testament en de apocriefe literatuur in religie en kunsten*, Nijmegen, SUN, 334 pp., is the marvellous successor to the same author's *Van Abraham tot Zacharia*, which deals with Old Testament themes and figures; both are indispensable and enjoyable aids to the teaching of literature and very helpful in making connections between the visual arts and literature. *Handelingen Elfde Colloquium Neerlandicum*, ed. T. Hermans, T. A. J. M. Janssen, and P. G. M. de Kleijn, Woubrugge, Internationale Vereniging voor Neerlandistiek (IVN), contains contributions to the IVN Utrecht 1991 Colloquium, divided in sections: language didactics, phraseology, translation, literature and the visual arts, land, and people. Specifically of literary interest are the opening address by W. P. Gerritsen about J. van Maerlant and J. van Boendale's poetics, Karel van Mander (H. Miedema), 17th-c. poetry and painting (K. Porteman), Vestdijk's poetry (T. van Deel), experimental painting and literature (H. Brems), representation of Old Testament stories in painting and literature (I. M. Veldman). *De Franse Nederlanden/Les Pays Bas Français*, 16, ed. J. Deleu, Rekkem, Stichting Ons Erfdeel, 255 pp., contains no strictly literary articles this year, but much that is of interest to Dutch studies. *Verslagen en Mededelingen*, 1990. 2, Ghent, KANTL, 276 pp., contains amongst others an interesting article about new fragments of H. van Veldeke's *Sente Servaes* (J. Goossens). *Contemporary fiction of the Low Countries*, ed. J. Goedegebuure and A. M. Musschoot, Rekkem, Stichting Ons Erfdeel, 127 pp., introduces a number of Dutch and Flemish authors who made their name after the Second World War; a brief introduction is followed by a short profile of each author. A bibliography of secondary literature in English and a bibliography of English translations concludes this very useful publication.

Voortgang, Jaarboek voor de Neerlandistiek, 11, 1990, 268 pp., contains an obituary for L. Strengholt (H. Duits), and articles about A. L. G. Bosboom-Toussaint (E. J. Folkers-Loosjes, H. Reeser), the poetry of Tesselschade Roemers (A. A. Sneller, N. van der Blom), documents relating to Groot-Nederland (S. J. A. van Faassen), a new edition of *Dystorie van Saladine* (G. H. M. Claassens), and anthologies (A. Zuiderent).

2. THE MIDDLE AGES

F. P. van Oostrom *et al.*, *Misselike tonghe. De Middelnederlandse letterklunde in interdisciplinair verband*, Amsterdam, Prometheus, 245 pp., is the result of an extremely succesful 1990 Leiden symposium which addressed a number of important issues relating to the interrelationships between Middle Dutch literature and the medieval literature of neighbouring countries, as well as the possibilities of interdisciplinary research between the various literary and other disciplines, such as history and cultural history, French, German, and English medieval studies, medieval Latin, theology, history of science, and bibliographical studies. Dutch medievalists were encouraged to partake more in the international theoretical discussions at present and to publish more in languages other than Dutch. Historical linguistics and codicology were shown to be potentially extremely helpful aids in medieval literary studies, as well as important disciplines in themselves. Historiographical texts with literary content too were shown to be valuable documents in cultural and literary historical research. A very rich publication, giving much food for thought and for research, a stimulating combination. Although so much of Middle Dutch literature is connected with Old French literature, the reception of the latter in the Low Countries is still an area in which much research is needed. A. T. Bouwman, *Reinaert en Renart. Het dierenepos 'Van den Vos Reynaerde' vergeleken met de Oudfranse 'Roman de Renart'*, 2 vols, Amsterdam, Prometheus, 427, 229 pp., is one of the outstanding contributions to medieval studies this year. Though the reception of the *Renart* as such is not addressed in this dissertation, the extremely complex and interesting adaptation technique of the Dutch author shows how the French material was 'made ready' for a Dutch audience. This valuable study is made even more useful by the parallel edition of the Old French and the Middle Dutch texts. As welcome as the comparative study of *Reinaert/Renart* is that of R. M. T. Zemel, *Op zoek naar Galiene. Over de Oudfranse Fergus en de Middelnederlandse Ferguut*, 1, Amsterdam, Schiphouwer en Brinkman,

403 pp.; this volume deals mostly with the French text, but includes a comparison with the Dutch work; vol. II will concentrate on that part of the *Ferguut* which seems to be an adaptation rather than a translation of the original (ll. 2593 ff.) Each *Fergus* chapter is followed by a comparative chapter about the *Ferguut*. Thus the texts are discussed as Arthurian romances; in comparison with Chrétien's *Conte del Graal*; in their use of setting and space; in their relationship of original and translation. The *Ferguut*'s method of translation is investigated as well as the various MSS and editions; the *Ferguut* is considered as an abbreviated translation. This is a monumental study and vol. II is eagerly awaited. After the important study of literature at the court of Holland around 1400 by F. P. van Oostrom (1987) which will shortly be available in an English translation, T. Meder, *Sprooksprekers in Holland. Leven en Werk van Willem van Hildegaersberch c. 1400*, Amsterdam, Prometheus, concentrates on one of the main personalities in the literary circle of that court. It centres on the content and function of H.'s impressive *œuvre* and on the audience for whom it was intended. What makes this study particularly interesting is the attention given to H.'s efforts to marry urban bourgeois morality with the mentality of court aristocracy at a time that shifts in power caused destabilization in which a different society came slowly into being. Urban literature and bourgeois morality are very much at the centre of *Op belofte van profijt. Stadsliteratuur en burgermoraal in de Nederlandse letterkunde van de Middeleeuwen*, ed. H. Pleij *et al.*, Amsterdam, Prometheus, an excellent collection. *Europees Toneel van Middeleeuwen naar Renaissance*, ed. M. Gosman, Groningen, Boekwerk, 455 pp., is an extremely useful collection of medieval and Renaissance plays in English, French, Spanish, Dutch, German, and Italian, with the original texts facing English translations. The Dutch contribution is the delicious play *Hoe Mars en Venus tsaemen bueleerden* (*c.* 1500), ed. F. Boersma and H. van Dijk. *Het Esbatement van den Appelboom* has been translated into English before by N. Denny and E. Morgan, but these are not easily available. A new English translation has now appeared: *The Apple Tree*, trans. J. Cartwright, *Dutch Crossing*, 44: 76–101, and can be welcomed as a reliable and representative rendering of the original as well as a text for performance. It does take liberties but in the main translates the spirit if not always the letter. Interesting from a comparative point of view is the edition of the English version of *Mariken van Nieumeghen: Mary of Nimmeghen*, ed. M. M. Raftery (Medieval and Renaissance Texts), Oxford, Blackwell, 81 pp., a meticulous edition. S. M. Murk Jansen, *The Measure of Mystic Thought. A Study of Hadewijch's Mengeldichten* (GAG, 536), 252 pp., is an excellent study of this hitherto rather neglected collection of poems attributed to Hadewijch. Not only does it address the conventional

issues of manuscript evidence, aspects of the vocabulary and poetics, as well as authorship, but also provides a re-evaluation of the theology and mysticism of the *Mengeldichten*. This study especially ventures into new territory in the use of statistics in literary research, here applied to the *Mengeldichten* with the *Strofische Gedichten*. Chapters 3 and 4 as well as Appendices II and III are devoted to this, whilst Appendix I gives a meticulous description of the five MSS involved. *Een school spierinkjes. Kleine opstellen over Middelnederlandse artes literatuur*, ed. W. P. Gerritsen, A. van Gijsen, and O. S. H. Lie (Middeleeuwse studies en bronnen, 26), Hilversum, Verloren, 192 pp., is a follow-up of the seminal work of R. Jansen-Sieben's *Repertorium van de Middelnederlandse artes-literatuur*, Utrecht, HES, 1989. The present collection addresses the use and usefulness, and the composition, of the *Repertorium*. Discussions about the definition of *artes* literature and the connections between the *artes* and various fields of knowledge, science, and culture are included; possible additions to the *Repertorium* are scrutinized and a number of articles address specific *artes* texts and particular approaches and problems, illustrating altogether the many-sided interest and methodical pluriformity of *artes* research.

   Beatrijs. Ingelei en van taalkundige aantekeninge voorsien, ed. R. Schutte and G. J. de Klerk, Pretoria, Haum-Literêr, 127 pp., is the second in a series of Middle Dutch texts for South African readers, after *Elckerlijc* (1987), and with the promise of *Mariken van Nieumeghen* as the third. It has an introduction about medieval literature in general and Middle Dutch in particular, about the transmission of older texts, the 12th-c. Renaissance, courtly literature and culture, and then a more specific background introduction to *Beatrijs*. It also has an up-to-date bibliography and extensive linguistic notes. The role of the British Library and its staff in the dissemination of Dutch literary culture is an important one, and there is evidence of this in J. P. Gumbert, *The Dutch and their Books in the Manuscript Age. The Panizzi Lectures 1989*, London, The British Library, 93 pp., which has many illustrations in black and white and even some in colour. It ranges from the 11th to the 15th c., with two out of three chapters specifically devoted to the 15th c.: Dutch books of the 15th c., and the Dutch and their books in the 15th c. Thus a host of issues, technical, decorative, are addressed, as well as production, transmission, reception, audience, reading public, scribes, and scriptoria. A book worthy of the Panizzi tradition. L. Jongen, *ABÄG*, 34:127–41, surveys source references in late-medieval Dutch hagiographies.

3. The Renaissance

M. B. Smits-Veldt, *Het Nederlandse Renaissance toneel*, Utrecht, HES, 155 pp., investigates the genesis and development of Dutch

Renaissance drama. It emphasizes the 'modernity' of this renascent classical drama and its didactic aims. It includes the dramatic activity of D. V. Coornhert, J. van Hout, and J. Duym, as well as P. C. Hooft, G. A. Bredero, and J. van den Vondel and ends with the foundation of *Nil Volentibus Arduum* and its French classicist drama. These well-known names however form no more than a small part of the enormous production of plays at the time and this study pays attention to this much wider field as well. The work ends with an extremely useful survey about the study of Renaissance drama, past and present. One of the most powerful of 17th-c. tragedies has been beautifully translated: Joost van den Vondel, *Lucifer*, trans. N. Clark, Bath, Absolute Press, 69 pp. The two translators of P. C. Hooft, *The Tragedy of Geeraert van Velsen*, trans. T. Hermans and Paul Vincent, *Dutch Crossing*, 45: 105–83, are by now well known and here they perform a double act of considerable skill. This translation is a philological rendering, keeping more or less to the iambic beat; rhyme is restricted to the choruses; it has integrity and the characteristic elegance of H. and V. Two 17th-c. plays come to our attention in the same periodical: *Willem de Baudour, Edipes en Antigone (1618)*, ed. Lesley Gilbert, *ib.*, 5–103, is an Anglicized Dutchman's version of Robert Garnier's *Antigone* (1580). G. provides us in effect with a monograph about the play, a very interesting account, presenting us with questions of transmission and reception of classical material in three cultures, French, Dutch, and English in the transition period around the turn of the 17th c. when those societies themselves experienced tremendous changes and upheaval. Central here are the two authors and a close analysis and comparison of the texts. It also sheds light on French influence on Dutch drama in the early part of the century when interrelations in the Amsterdam literary world were particularly complex due to the founding of the Nederduytsche Academie. J. de Lange, *P. C. Hooft's Reisheuchenis, naar de autograaf uitgegeven, ingeleid en toegelicht* (APSL, 97), 280 pp., is the first edition of this text with an introduction; it also gives a new transcription of the autograph, since the first and only edition by J. van Vloten (1856) contains many mistakes. This text is of prime importance for the knowledge of Hooft's development as a young man and the European experience which formed him as a poet, historian, playwright, and administrator.

M. A. Schenkeveld, *Dutch Literature in the Age of Rembrandt. Themes and Ideas*, Amsterdam, Benjamins, 215 pp., is a handsomely produced and illustrated book with a challenging title. Dutch literature has never been well known outside the Low Countries and the literature of this period in particular has to compete against the overwhelming popularity of the painting which has become synonymous with the

Dutch Golden Age. Though not intended as a literary history this work however is a unique, much-encompassing survey of a literary period which is every bit as rich as the painting overshadowing it. There is of course, the small obstacle of the language, but here too S. tempts the non-Dutch-speaking reader with elegant translations of various poems and a bibliography in which that reader will also find much in other languages. The themes and ideas include politics, religion, daily life, and nature; there is a special chapter on the many connections between poetry and painting and one which shows how the traders of the Republic were matched with literary traders too. This is a wonderfully convincing and substantial piece of evidence for the richness and importance of Dutch literature and every library should have it. One of the most difficult poets in this century is the subject of Tineke Ter Meer, *Snel en dicht. Een studie over de epigrammen van Constantijn Huygens* (APSL, 96), 206 pp., which aims to redress the often negative evaluations of H. as an epigrammatical poet. Many of the epigrams exist in autographs and part of the investigation concentrates on reconstructing H.'s method of working; the corpus, the sources and themes form the subject of the rest of this study. J. Duijkerius, *Het leven van Philopater en Vervolg van 't leven van Philopater. Een spinozistische sleutelroman uit 1691/1697*, ed., introd., and ann. Geraldine Maréchal, Amsterdam — Atlanta, Rodopi, 215 pp., shows the other side of the Republic's much-praised tolerance. The two novels here presented are an attempt to explain Spinoza's theories, on the Index since 1653, by means of a satirical fictional account of the divisions within the Reformed Church in the Republic, and, secondly, by the development of the novels' hero, Philopater, from a Cartesian to a Spinozist. The author, once exposed, got ten years hard labour and his books were placed on the Index. The reception history of Spinozism in the Republic but also the stratagems to which the literary work could be put are particularly illuminated by this study. Another not-so-usual investigation is conducted in Jelle Koopmans and Paul Verhuyck, *Een kijk op anekdotencollecties in de zeventiende eeuw. Jan Zoet. Het leven en bedrijf van Clément Marot*, Amsterdam — Atlanta, Rodopi, 385 pp., which opens up a fairly unknown literary genre and field of investigation, that of the Kluchtboeken, enormously popular from the 16th to the 19th c. but now not often easily available for research. They are clearly very much part of the early modern reading culture and of interest for the social aspects of literary history in particular. The present study concentrates on Jan Zoet's fictional biography of the French poet C. Marot and on a collection of anecdotes ascribed to this court poet. The image of M. presented in the collection poses interesting questions with regard to the comic epic concentration around a well-known, serious author. After the charting of late-medieval *Trivialliteratur* which got under way in the last 20 years, this study opens up a similar path for a later period.

Poetry and music are still very much connected in the 17th c. and this leads to the inclusion here of L. P. Grijs, **Het Nederlandse lied in de Gouden Eeuw. Het mechanisme van de contrafactuur*, Amsterdam, Publi-katies van het P. J. Meertens Instituut, which is first and foremost a musicological study but of interest also for the fact that so many of the most important authors were set to music. *Across the Narrow Seas. Studies in the History and Bibliography of Britain and the Low Countries. Presented to Anna E. C. Simoni*, ed. Susan Roach, London, The British Library, 223 pp., is a beautifully produced and illustrated book honouring this scholar and bibliographer who has done so much for cultural and historical research into Dutch material. All of the essays are interesting, but specifically of interest for Dutch literary studies are those about post-incunabula (J. A. Gruys), the Dutch book trade (B. van Selm), the poet G. Kiliaen (E. Cockx-Indestege), the printer Henrick van Haestens at Louvain (C. Coppens, M. de Schepper), the bookseller Jan Claesz. van Dorp (T. Bögels), the Dutch translator of *The Parliament of Women* (C. van Heertum), early printed Dutch books in German libraries (D. Paisey), and the publisher of Hobbe's Dutch *Leviathan* (A. J. Gelderblom). *The Catalogue of Books from the Low Countries 1601–1621 in the British Library*, ed. Anna E. C. Simoni, London, The British Library, xviii + 842 pp., is evidence enough for the monumental contribution to Dutch book studies this scholar has made. Although such a brief period is covered in comparison with the earlier Dutch *STC*, ed. A. W. Pollard and G. R. Redgrave (London, 1926), which it follows chronologically, it is nevertheless an extremely productive time for the printing presses and of course it includes the period of the Twelve Years Truce, of which the voluminous pamphlet literature, so important in the political and religious conflicts and squabbles, is here recorded also. Not only books wholly or partly in Dutch are here included, but also those in other languages which were printed or published in the Low Countries. The definition of the area takes into account the present-day Netherlands, Belgium, and Luxembourg, with the areas then under Spanish rule, but later belonging to France. A monumental work in every respect.

The Renaissance in National Context, ed. Roy Porter and Mikulas Teich, CUP, 239 pp., demonstrates and investigates the diversity of Europe's Renaissance; whilst giving due attention to 'the uses of Italy', it surveys the contributions and the particular aspects of a number of national renaissances and includes countries which are sometimes overlooked, such as Hungary, Poland, Bohemia, and Moravia; the Low Countries have found their deserved place here too

(E. Strictman). The prize for the most monumental contribution to 17th-c. studies must surely go to J. Six van Chandelier, *Gedichten. Studie-uitgave met inleiding en commentaar*, ed. A. E. Jacobs (Monumenta Literaria Neerlandica, 5), 2 vols, Assen — Maastricht, Van Gorcum, 939, 626 pp. J. has brought together all known poems, except for the psalm versions. The major part of Six's *œuvre* existed in an edition of 1657 and there were therefore hardly any transmission problems, but what made this study so monumental was the need for an exceedingly detailed and extensive commentary both for content and language. Six has always found appreciation, with his contemporaries and later, but his readers consisted of a small, select band, prepared to persist in the unravelling of these at times extremely hermetic poems. J. has tackled this enormous task with exemplary care and it will now be possible, for instance, to include Six in a curriculum with more than the few anthologized selections of his poetry, although this edition is in the first place geared to a community of literary scholars. J. identifies in her introduction a number of areas which invite further research. This is a monumental book also in that it is beautifully produced with a particularly nice lettertype.

4. THE EIGHTEENTH CENTURY

P. J. Buynsters, *Spectatoriale geschriften*, Utrecht, HES, 120 pp., is a study in the framework of the Enlightenment. The spectatorial journals comprised a great variety of writings and debates and were enormously popular in 18th-c. Europe. They were truly international too in their attention for other cultures, witness the many borrowings and translations. This is as yet a little known field of investigation in the Netherlands and B.'s tireless efforts on its behalf are admirably fruitful as is clear from the present study. As widespread as the journals were the literary societies, which form the subject of C. B. F. Singeling, *Gezellige schrijvers. Aspecten van letterkundige genootschappelijkheid in Nederland, 1750–1800*, Amsterdam — Atlanta, Rodopi, 353 pp. The literature of the Netherlands in the 18th c. was as dominated by these societies as the 15th and 16th cs by the Rhetoricians. Here we are provided with a chronological description of the various kinds of societies and with an analysis of their organization, membership and activities. S. also charts the reasons for their immense popularity as well as for their subsequent demise. He aims to dispel the traditional image of such societies in their narrowest and most parochial, and therefore often ridiculed, form, that of the poetry-writing clubs, which were largely discredited by the early 19th c. This study thus also ventures into the realm of literary evaluation of the past, of reception, of the emergence of views on and theories of literature. Hence this work is part of the 'rehabilitation' of the 18th c. currently in process at the Netherlands and of far wider interest than its title might lead one to suppose. Joannis Franciscus Cammaert, *Straf ende dood van Balthassar, Koning der Chaldeen, benevens de kronige van Darius, koning van Meden, blij-eijndig treurspel*, ed. K. Langvik-Johannessen and W. Waterschoot, 2 parts, Brussels, Studiecentrum 18de eeuwse Zuidenederlandse Letterkunde, FUSL, 58, 50 pp., provides a careful and interesting introduction, a facsimile text, glossary, and annotations of these plays.

5. THE NINETEENTH CENTURY

De briefwisseling van Guido Gezelle met de Engelsen, 1854–1899, ed. B. de Leeuw, P. de Wilde, K. Verbeke, and A. Deprez, 3 vols, Ghent, KANTL, 370, 301, 463 pp., is a voluminous but not terribly exciting edition of letters by and to Gezelle. Most of these have not been published before. Not all G.'s letters in English are here, only those to and from his English correspondents, such as students and ex-students, their families and the British colony in Bruges. We encounter G. here in particular in his role as educator and moral guardian and in that respect this edition adds substantially to our picture of the poet. Dr J. van Iseghem, *Guido Gezelle's 'Vlaemsche dichtoefeningen' (1858). Een benadering van de dichter en het werk*, Ghent, KANTL, has been given the KANTL prize for literature and is reviewed in *Jaarboek*, Ghent, KANTL. Olf Praamstra, *Gezond Verstand en Goede Smaak*, Amstelveen, Ernst, 476 pp., is a massive, impressive study of the influential critic and man of letters Conrad Busken Huet. H.'s literary theories are embedded in reviews of authors and works and the present study analyses these, departing from questions with regard to H.'s literary views in literary historical terms, from where he derived his views on literature and criticism and what his significance for Dutch literature has been. The chapters deal with H.'s activities *vis-à-vis* moralistic literature, literature before the 19th c., his contributions to *De Gids*, his activities in the Dutch Indies, in Paris; his critical pursuit of Bilderdijk; the influences he integrated in his work, and his literary views in terms of Romanticism and Realism. A careful account of the method of research and the methodology of this study is included. H. H. J. de Leeuwe, *Bilderdijk, het drama en het toneel*, Utrecht, Pressa Traiectina, 1990, discusses the theatricality, the themes, the moral and political aims of *Floris de vijfde* (1808), *Kormak* (1808), and B.'s theoretical essay *Het treurspel* (1808) and his didactic poem *Het Tooneel* (1808). B.'s interest in and awareness of the actual staging of plays is stressed as are his attempts to familiarize himself with many different dramatic genres. The other great romantic Dutch author is the subject of *Multatuli, Max Havelaar of de koffieveilingen der Nederlandsche Handelmaatschappij. Historisch-kritische uitgave*, ed. A. Kets-Vree (Monumenta Literaria Neerlandica, VI, 1, 2), Assen— Maastricht, Van Gorcum, 288, 500 pp., contains a carefully edited text, based on the last edition Multatuli himself directed (1881) with a survey of the textual changes in the *Max Havelaar* during M.'s life (1859; 1860–71; 1875; 1881). The question of 'autobiography' or 'autohagiography' is extensively discussed as is the socio-cultural context of the novel, as well as the relationship between historical facts and M.'s fiction. The MS and its vicissitudes are investigated, the relationship between M. and his publisher as well as the conflicts. A monumental study about one of the monuments of Dutch literature.

Thorbecke op de romantische tour, ed. G. J. Hooykaas, Amsterdam, Querido, Griffioenseries, 76 pp., contains letters from T. to his parents about his encounter with German Romanticism and philosophy during an academic educational journey interesting for T.'s development and for the mores of the period in terms of expectations, preferences and taste in literature, music and philosophy. Some solid preparatory work has now been done in respect of the correspondence of an extremely prolific letter-writer, Mrs A. L. G. Bosboom-Toussaint (1812–86). She is a good subject since she herself and her husband, the painter J. Bosboom, had widespread contacts in the literary, artistic political, and publishing world. *Repertorium op de briefwisseling van A. L. G. Bosboom-Toussaint*, ed. H. Reeser, Amsterdam, Stichting Neerlandistiek VU, 219 pp., has thus become more than just a reference work, since it provides a wealth of biographical material about a host of people. Clearly, the time is now ripe for an edition of B.'s letters, which will put the flesh on the bones of this study.

6. 1880 TO 1945

One of the best-known authors of this period is well-represented this year, for instance in Luc Dirikx, *Louis Couperus en het decadentisme. Een thematologische confrontatie*, diss. Univ. of Louvain, Neerpelt, De Roosen 3, Belgium, L. Dirikx, which fits in well with the renewed interest in decadence and *fin de siècle* studies. F. Bastet, *De wereld van Louis Couperus*, Amsterdam, Querido, 208 pp., visualizes in particular the The Hague environment which C. portrayed so unforgettably. This is more than a coffee-table book, as is to be expected from the meticulous C. biographer which B. has proved to be. Frans de Jonghe, *Eline Vere bij de psychiater*, Bloemendaal, Aramith, 94 pp., is a very lucidly written description and analysis of Eline Vere as a 'patient'. It increases, if possible, one's admiration for Couperus who created this character so sensitively and convincingly without having had the benefit of Freud. It also helps to dispel the image of Eline as a time-and-place-bound character, and 'universalizes' her. An illuminating study. Would this could be done for *De Boeken der kleine zielen*! *Couperus-catalogus*, Deventer, Stads- of Athenaeumbibliotheek, provides all the information about the W. M. S. Pitlooy Van Rooyen-Couperuscollection. J. S. de Ley and B. Luger, **Over Van Eeden*. *Walden in droom en daad*, HDG, illuminates Van Eeden's fundamental vision as a reformer of society, so important for his literary work as well. A. H. Den Boef, **Musil? Ken ik niet*. *Ter Braak en Du Perron over Modernisme en epigonen*, Leiden, Dimensie, throws itself into the fray with regard to whether *Forum*, Ter Braak, and Du Perron can properly be seen as belonging to modernism. The author arrives at the conclusion that they do not, quite the opposite of the recent judgement of D. Fokkema and E. Ibsch, *Modernist Conjectures* (see *YWMLS*, 50:201), who consider them as quite obviously representing modernism in the Netherlands. Clearly more scope here for further research. The man who made it into modernism this year however is a painter: Griselda Pollock, 'Van Gogh, Nationalism and Modernism' *Dutch Crossing*, 44:45—49, quite usefully places the painter in the international modernist tradition, relocating him as a Dutch artist with the aim of 'the exploration of the historical and the culturally particular, to undo the effacement of history which has been the effect of both modernism and art history in general'. D. van der Meulen, **E. du Perron. Een korte biografie*, The Hague, SDU, explores a bit of 'het land van herkomst' of the subject. Not exclusively relevant for Dutch literature, but interesting amongst others for its chapter on E. du Perron's *Het land van Herkomst* as a modernist(!) novel is Hans van Stralen, *Onbestemd verblijf. Een onderzoek naar het semantische veld 'bewustzijn' in modernistische literatuur*, Nijmegen, Quine, 1990, 192 pp. Central here is the theme of the Prodigal Son in modernism and the important role of aspects of this theme such as doubt, cosmopolitanism, introspection, and detachment in modernism. P. Kralt, *Stem en Tegenstem. De structuur van de bundel 'Verzen' van S. Vestdijk*, Leiden, Dimensie, 80 pp., discusses these poems in terms of subject categories: poems about art, poetic and pictoral; poems with portraits, friends and magicians; poems about relationships, love and destruction; about time, history, youth; and in this diversity it shows the thematic and structural coherence of the collection. S. Bakker, *Ik ben maar een dilettant. F. Bordewijk 1884–1965*, Nijmegen, Quine, 70 pp., is a catalogue of the 1991 Bordewijk exhibition in Nijmegen, containing a short biography and two chapters about the cultural, literary, and historical-topographical content of B.'s work. **Verzameld Werk van*

Nescio, ed. L. Frerichs, Amsterdam, Van Oorschot, is a long-awaited publication, delayed because the rights to N.'s work were divided over two publishers. Now however a historical-critical edition of the literary texts, N.'s letters and some diaries will appear in the usual beautiful Collected Work format of Van Oorschot. *Omtrent Anna-Maria. Jaarboek 1990 van het Felix Timmermans Genootschap*, ed. L. Vercammen, Lier, I. van In, 232 pp., discusses T.'s novel *Anna-Maria* as well as more general aspects of his work. *Mededelingen van het Cyriel Buysse Genootschap*, 6, 1990, and 7, ed. A. M. Musschoot, Ghent, Cyriel Buysse Genootschap, 131, 219 pp., contain respectively articles about B.'s relationship with *Van Nu en Straks*, his political views, his relationship with *Groot-Nederland*, the role of fate in his novels and the characters in *Het gezin Van Paemel* in its film version, and a survey of events and publications with regard to B.; B. and L. van Deyssel open vol. 7, followed by a contribution about B. and Saint-Simonism; the perspective in *'tBolleken*; an edition of *De levenskring*; an essay about *De biezenstekker/Driekoningenavond* and a stage performance; and the usual chronicle.

7. 1945 TO THE PRESENT DAY

H. Brems and D. de Geest, *Opener dan dicht is toe. Poezie in Vlaanderen 1965–1990*, Leuven — Amersfoort, Acco, 267 pp., is an extremely useful study and original presentation of 25 years of Flemish poetic creativity. An extensive survey is followed by a chronological anthology together with a number of reactions, positive and negative, on the various poets and their *œuvre*. A third part lets some of the poets speak for themselves, about their poetic creativity, activities and involvement in various movements and trends. Hugo Brems, 'Dutch poetry since 1950', *Dutch Crossing*, 44:18–44, is a useful and sensitive survey of recent poetry in both the Netherlands and Belgium, as useful as the regular contributions by T. Hermans about recent Dutch and Flemish poetry in *Neerlandica Extra Muros*, Lier, I. van In, and by R. P. Meijer about recent Dutch prose in the same periodical. R. van de Perre, *Het land van de wortelstok. Over de poezie van Anton van Wilderode*, Leiden, Dimensie, 55 pp., introduces this much-honoured Flemish poet to an audience in the Netherlands, where he is too little known. In his neo-classicism and as priest-poet W. seems almost anachronistic, but this study shows his creativity and his mastery over the language and gives us an insight in the rich subject-matter of his poetry. Much material, biographical and otherwise has been released for study this year about the poet Hans Lodeizen and we can expect a number of publications making use of that new material. *Over Hans Lodeizen, Tussen de regels, De sprong van Münchhausen, Op het twijgje der indigestie. Verzamelde essays en kritieken*, ed. Paul Rodenko, Amsterdam, Meulenhoff, vol. 1, 600 pp., is the first of four volumes. Another

Flemish poet is the subject of Frans Depeuter, *De zwarte doos van Icarus. Een studie over het leven en de poezie van Paul Snoek*, Hilversum — Antwerp, De Koofschep, 293 pp., which was given a prize in 1987 by KANTL but only now finds a publisher. D.'s interpretation of S. as an experimental poet has provoked some severe criticism, but now provokes new research and assessment of this nearly forgotten poet. The bibliography of this book is not precise and it would have been helpful to have the quotes identified. Snoek is also the subject of a new series *Dichters van nu. Paul Snoek*, ed. H. Leus, Ghent, Poeziecentrum, 206 pp.; the first volume was devoted to another Flemish writer and poet: *Dichters van nu. Hugo Claus*, ed. F. de Vree, Ghent, Poeziecentrum, 216 pp. *Schrijfsters in de jaren vijftig*, ed. M. Prinssen and L. T. Vermij, Amsterdam, Van Gennep, 212 pp., rescues some writers from oblivion and places better known ones in the particular context of the 1950s, including Aya Zikken, Dola de Jong, Nel Noordzij, Clare Lennart, and Ellen Warmond. Frans Ruiter, *De receptie van het Amerikaanse postmodernisme in Duitsland en Nederland*, Leuven — Apeldoorn, Garant, 403 pp., aims to chart the reception of this elusive and much-abused literary concept which gained ground in the Netherlands and Germany very slowly and belatedly. Neither country has very much responded in their literary production, though the theoretical discussion has become a lively one and R. investigates extensively the possible reasons for this and also gives a very readable account of postmodernism thus far. *Het plezier van de tekst. Vijf letterkundige bijdragen*, ed. S. Bakker *et al.* (Nijmeegse Reeks, 3), Nijmegen, Quine, 109 pp., contains five investigations into the field of Modern Dutch literature which make the reader share in the pleasure of the text. They include Vestdijk's essay-writing (H. Bekkering), the significance of the word 'vrouw' in Gerrit Krol's work (I. Bulte), W. F. Hermans's recent novel *Een heilige van de horlogerie* (S Bakker), the vitalist aspects of L. P. Boon's *Vergeten Straat* (A. Schmitz), and an analysis of Ida Gerhardt's *Dolen en Dromen* (I. Bulte). A new periodical, *De Kantieke Schoolmeester*, Kortenhoef, Louis Paul Boon Genootschap, aims to bring new research, bibliographical and biographical material, personalia, and reviews. It also provides some monographs and special issues of periodicals, such as the 'Sicnummer' and 'L. P. Boon, Brussel een oerwoud', *Dilbeekse Cahiers*, 1989, and the *Louis Paul Boon Catalogus*, 1989. A useful reference book is J. Zandbergen, *Schippers naast God. Wie is wie in de belletrie 1965–1990*, Amsterdam, Prometheus, 176 pp. Two further bibliographical publications are *Bibliografie van de tijdschriften in Vlaanderen en Nederland. De tijdschriften verschenen in 1988*, ed. H. van Assche and H. Baeyens, Antwerp, Rob. Roemansstichting, and *De tijdschriften verschenen in 1989*, ed. H. van Antwerp, Rob. Roemansstichting, 519 pp.

III. DANISH STUDIES*

By BENTE ELSWORTH, *Lector in Danish, School of Modern Languages and European History, University of East Anglia*

LANGUAGE

1. GENERAL

Moscow University Press has published summaries of the papers given at the 11th All-Union conference on the study of the history, economics, literature, and languages of the Scandinavian countries and Finland. *Procs* (Moscow), includes in the section on linguistics (323–97) the following contributions which deal specifically with Danish: L. M. Lokshtanova, 'К типологической характеристике глагольных систем датского языка в сопоставлении с немецким и английским' (325–27); Iu. K. Kuz'menko, 'Изменения в датских диалектах Ютландии и тенденции развития германских языков' (333–34); E. V. Krasnova, 'Эволюция датского безударного [ə]' (343–44); E. I. Miachinskaia, 'Вокализация согласных в условиях корреляции усечения слога (на материале датского и английского языков)' (345–46); A. I. Uskov, 'Опыт норвежского языкового планирования и проблемы датской орфографии' (351–52); F. M. Chekalina, 'Семантика футуральных конструкций в датском и шведском языках' (361–63); L. L. Galenko and L. M. Lokshtanova 'О нормах употребления глагольных форм и придаточных дополнителъных в датском и немецком языках' (363–64); E. B. Krylova, 'О передаче значения неочевидности высказывания в датском и немецком языках' (365–66); N. V. Safonova and A. N. Livanova, 'К вопросу о категории падежа в датских и норвежских диалектах' (376–77); and B. S. Zharov, 'Датская научно-техническая лексикография' (396–97). Two of the papers in the section on the history of the Scandinavian languages (398–427) are concerned specifically with Danish: E. V. Babushkina, 'Типы безличных конструкций в древнейших датских рукописных памятниках и в датском языке XVI века' (404–05); and A. V. Savitskaia, 'К истории развития группового генитива в датском и шведском языках' (414–15). *Auditorium X. Dansk før, nu — og i fremtiden? En antologi om moderne sprogforskning*, ed. Erik Hansen, Inge Lise Pedersen, and Ib Poulsen, Amanda, 251 pp., contains a series of public lectures given by Institut for Nordisk Filologi and Institut for Dansk Dialektforskning in the spring of 1990: P. Lindegård Hjorth,

---

* The place of publication of books is Copenhagen unless otherwise indicated.

'Den historiske baggrund' (11–30), which outlines the development of the Danish language; E. Hansen, 'Rigtigt og forkert dansk' (31–47), which discusses the prescription of linguistic norms, its aim and possible consequences; I. L. Pedersen, 'Dagligsproget — lokalsprog eller klassesprog' (48–71), which is concerned with Danish dialects and offers the view that while dialects in the past signalled place of origin, today they are indicative of social circumstances; J. E. Andersen, 'Sprogets takt og tone' (72–99), which deals with polite language, what it shows and what it hides regarding the relationship between the people involved; K. Lund, 'Dansk med mange accenter — dansk som fremmed- og andetsprog' (100–21); I. Poulsen, 'Sproget i radio og fjernsyn' (122–36); O. Togeby, 'Semantik, forståelse og maskiner' (137–57), which discusses the increased interest in semantics that computer translation has occasioned; H. Ruus, 'Fælles danske ord' (158–80); E. Møller, 'Lad talesproget komme til orde!' (181–204), which deals with the problems that research into spoken language encounters; K. Kjøller, 'Sprog og politik' (205–29); and F. Gregersen, 'Dansk i 90'erne — et oplæg til diskussion' (230–51), which looks to the future and asks the questions whether Danish can survive the strong influence of English/American or whether it will become smothered in the EC. *Det danske sprogs status år 2001 — er dansk et truet sprog?*, ed. J. Normann Jørgensen, Danmarks Lærerhøjskole, 142 pp. Tore Kristiansen, *Udtalenormering i skolen. Skitze af en ideologisk bastion*, Gyldendal, 1990, 303 pp.

2. History of the Language, Morphology, Syntax, and Semantics

F. Hansen, 'Brugen af konj. *unz* og synonyme temporalsyntagmer i norrønt sprog', *ANF*, 105, 1990:81–105. *3. Møde om Udforskningen af Dansk Sprog: Aarhus Universitet, 11–12 oktober 1990*, ed. Mette Kunøe and Erik Vive Larsen, Århus U.P., 259 pp. Klaus Kjøller, *Politisk argumentation. En teori om offentlig politisk argumentation i et velfærdsdemokrati*, Copenhagen U.P., 273 pp. Frans Gregersen, *Sociolingvistikkens (u)mulighed. Videnskabshistoriske studier i Ferdinand de Saussures og Louis Hjelmslevs strukturalistiske sprogteorier*, 2 vols, Tiderne Skifter, iii + 304, 316 pp. J. C. Bang and J. Døør, *Deixis, text & sex: to essays om syntaktiske, semantiske & pragmatiske aspekter af skønlitterære texter* (Sprogteori, 5), Odense U.P., 42 pp.

3. Dialects, Contrastive Linguistics, and Bilingualism

Danske Folkemål, 33, contains the proceedings of *4. Nordiske Dialektologkonference, Askov Højskole, 12.–16. august, 1990*. It is divided into six subgroups, and the following contributions discuss Danish dialects: 1. 'Sprog og identitet': F. Gregersen, 'Afvigeren og gruppen, gruppen og klassen, klassen og normen: Om stil og identitet' (36–50), which continues the discussion in Id., 'Hvordan undersøger man københavnsk?', *TsSk*, 10, 1989:38–58; T. Kristiansen, 'Sprogholdninger hos folkeskolelærere, unge mennesker og personalechefer på Næstvedegnen' (51–62), which examines the role of the individual's attitude to the regional dialect, the Copenhagen dialect and R.P. in the ongoing change of the language spoken in Næstved; I. L. Pedersen, 'Højskolen og dialekterne — og dialektologerne' (75–86), which deplores the fact that dialectology has become a structural description of the most archaic and 'pure' form of a dialect instead of a study of a permanent process of adaptation and borrowing. II. 'Metoder til indsamling og bearbejdning af talesprogsdata': E. Møller, 'Tal som du plejer — om indsamling af talesprog' (99–110), which contends that since linguistic differences are mainly socially determined the collection of data to establish language variation must consider representativeness in terms of the individual's social norm; K. M. Pedersen, 'Selvrapportering — kan man bruge det til noget?' (111–21). III. 'Regionalsprog. Dialektblanding': J. Normann Jørgensen and K. Kristensen, 'Stød i moderne (syd)sjællandsk talesprog' (135–45); M. Nyberg, 'Unge sønderjyders rigsmålstilegnelse' (159–68). IV and V deal only with Norwegian and Swedish dialects. VI. 'Ord. Ordforråd. Orddannelse': T. Arboe Andersen, 'Tyske, frisiske og hollandske låneord i jyske dialekter — på grundlag af *Jysk Ordbog*, afsnit a-butting' (289–300); T. Ejskjær, 'Haletudsens skandinaviske navne set i lyset af galloromanske og vestgermanske betegnelser for samme dyr' (331–42); A. Gudiksen, 'Tre suffikser i danske dialekter. En dialektgeografisk skitse' (343–52), which deals with the suffixes *-vorn*, *-agtig*, and *-et/-ig*. The subgroups are followed by V. Sørensen and T. Arboe Andersen, 'Demonstration af Jysk Ordbogs edb-programmel — database og kortlægningsprogram til udnyttelse af spørgelistebesvarelser' (353–56). *Ord og Sag*, 9, ed. Viggo Sørensen, Inst. for Jysk Sprog- og Kulturforskning, Århus Univ., 1989, has the following contributions: B. Daugaard Jørgensen, 'Englefedt og pukkelblå — et kapitel af narrestregernes historie' (4–6), which deals with meaningless words and expressions used to send somebody on a wild-goose chase; T. Arboe Andersen, 'Kan man brodde en klæpning? På sporet af en jysk tærske-terminologi' (7–19); S. Andresen and V. Sørensen, 'Fra den yderste forpost mod syd — det danske sprog i Læk' (20–29), which deals with the linguistic situation in Læk, 15 km. south of the border with Germany; M. Bjerrum, 'Det tostavede *grebe* (=hank) i danske dialekter' (30–33); O. Rasmussen, 'Vredne bukser' (34–42), which is concerned with dialect words for *klejner*; and V. Sørensen, 'Brød og kage — og hvad dét betyder på jysk' (43–56). *Ord og Sag*, 10, 1990: I. L. Pedersen, 'Fra klenodie til pisallik

— grovkornede navne på finbrød' (5–12); A. Espegaard, 'En grammatik i støbeskeen' (13–19), which describes differences between the dialects of Læsø, Hirtsholmen, Vendsyssel, Østerhanherred and the northern part of Østhimmerland and their development from a presumed common dialect in the Middle Ages; K. M. Pedersen and V. Sørensen, 'Legetøj, syltetøj, troldtøj og andet tøjeri — om en sproglig joker i vore dialekter' (20–36), which discusses the meaning of (-)*tøj* in Danish dialects; A. Gudiksen, 'Meget liner som på Sælland. Afledningsendelserne -*et*, -*ig* og -*eret* i jysk' (37–46); J. Nielsen and V. Sørensen, 'Dernede fra grænsen — om sprog og liv i Højer' (47–56); and T. Arboe Andersen, 'Låning — et frisisk låneord i jysk' (57–60). Bent Jul Nielsen and Karen Margrethe Pedersen, **Danske talesprog: dialekter, regionalsprog, sociolekter*, Gyldendal, 85 pp. **Bornholmsk ordtøj. Ordsprog, talemåder, leveregler, udtryksformer, skældsord*, comp. and ed. Leif Henriksen, Rønne, William Dams Boghandel, 1990, 95 pp. Anne Holmen, **Udviklingslinier i tilegnelsen af dansk som andetsprog*, Danmarks Lærerhøjskole, 1990, 222 pp. K. Sørensen, 'Engelsk indflydelse på det danske sprog: en oversigt', *TsSk*, 11, 1990:60–71. E. Dittmer, 'Erfahrungen aus der Praxis einer Aarhuser Projektarbeit über deutsch-dänische Synonyme', *Procs* (Svendborg), 23–40.

4. Lexicography, Grammars, and Phonology

Lexicon Mediae Latinitatis Danicae — Ordbog over dansk middelalderlatin, ed. Franz Blatt *et al.* Århus U.P., vol. 3: *Continentia-evinco*, 1990, pp. 167–262. **Rapport om 'Møde om leksikografisk forskning og ordbogsarbejde i Danmark', Fuglsøcenteret, 8.–10. juni, 1988*, ed. Henrik Holmboe, Århus, Handelshøjskolen, 149 pp. H. Basbøll, 'Nyt om moderne rigsdansk prosodi: stød, tryk, intonation', *Procs* (Svendborg), 11–22. K. Gregersen, 'Hollandsk udtræk — eller essensen af et undervisningsforløb i dansk udtale', *TsSk*, 11, 1990:72–80. Eli Fischer-Jørgensen, **A Phonetic Study of the Stød in Standard Danish*, Turku U.P., 1989, 215 pp.

5. Onomastics

Vibeke Dalberg, *Stednavneændringer og funktionalitet. Analogisk stednavneomdannelse, epexegetisk stednavnedannelse og stednavneskifte belyst ved danske toponymer* (Navnestudier, udgivet af Institut for Navneforskning, 33), C. A. Reitzel, 273 pp. **Studia Onomastica. Festskrift till Thorsten Andersson den 23. februari 1989*, ed. Lena Pedersen, Stockholm, Almqvist & Wiksell, 1989, xxiv + 454 pp., contains contributions on Germanic and Scandinavian names.

LITERATURE

1. GENERAL

An anthology of texts by female writers spanning 300 years is intended to rescue from oblivion literary works that have been excluded from authoritative reference books and collections. *Nordiske forfatterinder fra Leonora Christina til Else Gress*, ed. Lise Busk-Jensen, Gyldendal, 1990, 400 pp., contains a selection of texts with introductions which approach the works through recent feminist literary criticism. In the introd. B.-J. expresses the hope that the anthology will show a pattern of lines connecting the women writers, who share gender-defined conditions of life, and also display their involvement in their time and literature in the broadest sense. Johan E. de Mylius, **Anskuelsesformer. Træk af dansk litteraturhistorie*, 1 (OUSSLL, 21), 326 pp. T. Bredsdorff, 'Nogen skrev et sagn om "Agnete og Havmanden", hvem, hvornår og hvordan', *Fund og Forskning*, Det kongelige Bibliotek, 30:67–80, examines the consequences of two assumptions made by recent research concerning the dating of the ballad and the legend, in Jørn Piø's *Nye veje til folkevisen* (1985) and Peter Meisling's *Agnetes latter* (1988). The assumptions are that the ballad may have been composed as late as 1770 and that the prose version is a faked legend, more recent than the ballad. The hypothesis is put forward that Poul Martin Møller created the legend to play a trick on Just Mathias Thiele. P. Meisling, 'De sympatiske havmænd — en lille replik til Thomas Bredsdorff', *Fund og Forskning*, Det kongelige Bibliotek, 30:81–86, concurs in B.'s supposition. The likelihood that the pseudo-legend was composed at the beginning of the 19th c. is substantiated by M.'s view of its theme, which he sees as the tragic split between Christianity and humane ethics, between social and natural values, typical of the Romantics' use of demonic material. E. Bredsdorff, 'Danish literature as seen through British and American eyes before 1900', *Fest. Mitchell*, 119–26. *Uriasposten*, 10, ed. Aage Jørgensen, Mårslet, CUK/Center for Undervisning og Kulturformidling, includes: Aa. Jørgensen, 'Dansk litteraturhistorisk bibliografi 1989 (udkast)' (5–59); 'Tilføjelser til numrene i "Dansk litteraturhistorisk bibliografi 1965–1986"' (60–62); and 'Tilføjelser til numrene i "Dansk litteraturhistorisk bibliografi 1987" og "Dansk litteraturhistorisk bibliografi 1988"' (63–65). *Uriasposten*, 11: 'Thomas Bredsdorff. Bibliografi 1960–1991' (4–10); 'Erik M. Christensen, Bibliografi 1943–1990' (11–21); 'Jørgen Elbek. Bibliografi 1953–1991' (22–31); 'Wilhelm Friese. Verzeichnis der gedruckten Schriften, 1955–1990' (32–41); 'Bo Hakon Jørgensen. Produktionsliste

1969–1991' (42–45); 'Johan de Mylius. Bibliografi 1970–1991' (46–55); and Aa. Jørgensen, 'Bidrag til en P. L. Møller-bibliografi' (56–59).

2. THE MIDDLE AGES

L. Søndergaard, 'Fastelavnsspil i Skandinavien i 1400-tallet og det tidlige 1500-tal', *Procs* (Svendborg), 77–95. P. Meisling, 'Danske folkeviser i tysk tradition', *ib.*, 191–205. *Latin og nationalsprog i Norden efter reformationen. Konference 1.–5. august, 1987, Biskops-Arnö*, ed. Marianne Alenius *et al.*, Museum Tusculanum, 328 pp. B. Baldwin, '*Jammersminde* remembered. A new look at the status of history and literature', *ScSt*, 62, 1990:266–79, argues that to read *J.* only as a historical account is to miss much of its literary dimension. Rather than ask whether or not Leonora Christina tells the truth, B. suggests a different approach, i.e. an examination of the relationship between telling the truth and the dissolution of identity which threatens L.C. in her imprisonment.

3. THE EIGHTEENTH CENTURY

J.-U. Fechner, 'Helfrich Peter Sturz auf dem Weg zum deutschen Stilisten. Ein Hinweis auf eine vergessene dänische Zeitschrift', *Fest. Mitchell*, 64–77, deals with the periodical, *Choix de nouveaux opuscules*, publ. in Copenhagen 1771–72.

BAGGESEN, J.   O. Oberholzer, 'Jens Baggesen: *Oceania*. Streifzug in Baggesens poetischen Werken in deutscher Sprache', *Fest. Mitchell*, 78–87.

EWALD, J.   A. Holstein-Rathlou, 'Den dulmende latter', *Kritik*, 94:59–79, is concerned with what in H.-R.'s opinion are inconsistencies in Peer E. Sørensen's *Håb og erindring. Johannes Ewald i Oplysningen* (1989). The incompatibility between new ideas and the language of neo-classicism led to parody, and E.'s art is the fusion of diagnostics, criticism and Utopian vision. But according to H.-R., Sørensen reads *Levned og Meninger* not merely as a text about writing, but considers that the interpretation of the work hinges on what is not expressed (the absent tragedy). In addition H.-R. concludes that S.'s view that the ultimate symptom of modernism is inexpressibility undermines his grounds for defining E.'s work as modern, since inexpressibility has been the theme of philosophical debate since the pre-Socratics.

HOLBERG, L.   S. Eegholm-Pedersen, 'Holberg og "Die europäische Fama". En kildestudie til Holbergs første bøger', *Fund og Forskning*, Det kongelige Bibliotek, 30:50–66, shows that *Die europäische Fama*, a German monthly publ. in Leipzig 1702–35, was a principal source for

H.'s accounts of contemporary European wars, citing a series of instances of H.'s use of the Leipzig journal in various chapters of *Introduktion til de fornemste Europæiske Rigers Historier* (1711) and in the following work, *Anhang* (1713). F. J. Billeskov Jansen, 'Ludvig Holberg and Human Rights', *Fest. Mitchell*, 57–63, compares H.'s notion of the natural rights of an individual, which are expressed in *Natur- og Folkeret* (1716), with later declarations of human rights in America, France, the UN charter, and the Helsinki protocol.

4. THE NINETEENTH CENTURY

The prevalent opinion that Grundtvig and Kierkegaard did not affect each óther's views and beliefs is challenged by Otto Bertelsen who in *Dialogen mellem Grundtvig og Kierkegaard*, C. A. Reitzel, 1990, 131 pp., aims to establish that a dialogue actually took place which influenced both. Aa. Jørgensen, 'Fordækt seksualitet og fortrængt lidenskab', *Bogens Verden*, Danmarks Biblioteksforening, 1990:422–29, which deals with this theme in Danish Golden Age literature. S. M. Schröder. 'Die Heimkehr des Elis Fröbom. E. T. A. Hoffmann im Norden nach frühen Rezeptionszeugnissen', *Skandinavistik*, 21:30–50, investigates the main features of the reception of Hoffmann in Scandinavia and analyses individual texts to show not so much what they have in common as differences, the dialogue between them. Peter B. Valore, **Sophie Ørsted og digterne*, Bakkehusmuseet, 143 pp.

ANDERSEN, H. C. A.'s language forms the topic of Torben Brostrøm and Jørn Lund, *Flugten i sproget. H. C. Andersens udtryk*, Gyldendal, 157 pp. The ambiguous title refers to A.'s artistic expression, language in flight, and to his escape into creativity to keep loneliness at bay, flight into language. I. York Möller-Christensen, 'Eventyr og historier. En læsning af H. C. Andersens *Hyldemor*', *Nordica*, 8:149–59, offers the view that *H.* is a poetic illustration of the relationship between the two genres, between 'eventyret', the synthesizing romantic form, and 'historien', which reflects a modern feeling of alienation in A.'s *œuvre*. J. L. Greenway, '"Reason in Imagination is Beauty". Oersted's acoustics and H. C. Andersen's *The Bell*', *ScSt*, 63:318–25, discusses the aesthetic role that Ørsted's physics of sound and light plays in *Klokken*. T. Barfoed Møller, 'Tre udkast af H. C. Andersen til en ny ballonvise i "Meer end Perler og Guld"', *Fund og Forskning*, 30:87–103, dates the three draft versions on the basis of references in the texts to current events. Two were written in the period December 1857 to February 1858, prompted by rumours that *Meer end Perler og Guld* (1849) was to be performed in 1858, and the third was intended for the production in 1872. 'Splash! Six views of "The Little Mermaid"', *ScSt*, 63:140–63, includes U. Thomsen, 'A structuralist approach'; S. Soracco, 'A psychoanalytic approach'; N. and F. Ingwersen, 'A folktale/Disney approach'; G. Nybo, 'A synopsis'; and P. Dahlerup, '"The Little Mermaid" deconstructed'. Lotte Eskelund, *Da Andersen var i Wien. H. C. Andersens rejser i Østrig i årene 1834–1872*, Spectrum, 329 pp. Heinrich Detering, *Åndelige amfibier: homoerotisk camouflage i H. C. Andersens forfatterskab — Intellectual amphibia: Homoerotic Camouflage in Hans Christian Andersen's Works*, Odense U.P., 72 pp., trans. Birgit Fussing from German into Danish and English. E. Sønderholm, 'Hans Christian Andersen als Opernlibrettist. Eine textkritische Untersuchung', *Fest. Mitchell*, 138–54. V. Stybe, 'At illustrere H. C. Andersen, Den grimme ælling, Svinedrengen og Kejserens nye klæder', *TsSk*, 11, 1990:32–49. H. Detering and H. Depenbrock, 'Der Tod der Dryade und die Geburt der neuen Muse', *Procs* (Svendborg), 366–90. L. I. Tarashvili, 'Датская традиция в символике сказки Х.К. Андерсена "Стойкий оловянный солдатик"', *Procs* (Moscow), 287–88.

BANG, H.   P. Bjørby, 'Herman Bang's "Franz Pander": Narcissism, self and the nature of the unspoken', *ScSt*, 62, 1990:449–67, argues that B.'s work speaks by means of the unspoken, through the intimation of an absence. B.'s response to the authoritative discourse of the masculine position and standards of the Modern Breakthrough was *Franz Pander*, a story about a modern Narcissus, about emptiness of soul. Bjørby reads this story as a truly modernist work destabilizing the reigning ideology. Franz's self-love, in spite of its effeminate veiling, can be seen as a direct reflection of masculine self-love, of a heterosexually masculine ideology that is deeply homoerotic. A. Heitman, 'Herman Bang, *Det hvide Hus* — eller: Hvad er egentlig en selvbiografi', *Edda*:144–53, is a contribution to the debate on the genre of autobiography. The normative prescriptions of this genre, according to H., are referentiality and representation of identity. A discussion of whether *Det hvide Hus* and *Det graa Hus* are autobiographical works concludes that taken together the two texts represent a bankrupt autobiographical project. In *DhH* the boy is identifiable, but his unique individuality cannot be represented because of the similarity between the boy and his mother and his adoption of her language. The impossibility of creating a positive identity is overcome in *DgH* where the narrator becomes another and can no longer be identified with Bang. A. Wischmann, 'Herman Bangs "Haabløse Slægter" — Inszenierung einer Autobiographie?', *Procs* (Svendborg), 244–51, argues in favour of an autobiographical reading of *HS*. The tendencies to dramatization do not preclude this view, rather a suggestive ambivalence seems, in W.'s opinion, to be intended with the aim of encouraging the reader to form conjectures regarding the relationship between fiction and truth.

BERGSØE, V. D. Lohmeier, 'Im Vorfeld des modernen Durch-
bruchs. Adolf Strodtmanns Briefe an Vilhelm Bergsøe', *Fest.
Mitchell*, 155–68, is the first publication of the letters written by S., B.'s
German translator, to B. These letters express S.'s attempts to
rekindle the exchange of ideas between Germany and Denmark that
had been curtailed by the wars of 1848–50 and 1864.

BRANDES, G. *Georg Brandes. Selected Letters*, ed. and trans. W. Glyn
Jones, Norwich, Norvik Press, 1990, 275 pp.

CLAUSSEN, S. L. J. Onslev, 'Antonius og Malte i storbyen', *Nordica*,
8 : 181–203, sees C.'s *Antonius i Paris* (1896) and Rainer Maria Rilke's
Die Aufzeichnungen des Malte Laurids Brigge (1910) as attempts at a
revaluation of the aesthetic norms inherent in 19th-c. bourgeois
morality. O. contends that the city environment (Paris) has a crucial
influence on the narrative technique in both novels. The main
characters cease to be the organizing principle and the realistically
depicted characters change into synthetic figures that psychologically
and empirically no longer constitute valid identities. This illustrates
what, according to O., is the new position of modernism: instead of
integrated elements in the plot, moods and sense perceptions precede
and engender the narrative.

GOLDSCHMIDT, M. A. K. H. Ober, '"Med saadanne Følelser
skriver man en Roman." Origins of Meïr Goldschmidt's *En Jøde*',
ScSt, 30 : 25–39, carries out a close, detailed inspection of G.'s
treatment of an apparently insignificant sub-tale in *En Jøde*: 'Simon
Abeles', a story which was included in Hermann Schiff's *Hundert und
ein Sabbat* (1842). O. shows the painstaking care with which G.
reproduced and reworked the original and argues that the inclusion of
the Simon Abeles story was essential to G.'s novel. It constitutes a
miniature core containing the essence of the novel's tragedy and
foretelling the entire development of the work.

GRUNDTVIG, N. F. S. Peter Balslev-Clausen, *Det vingede ord: om
N. F. S. Grundtvigs salmedigtning*, Materialecentralen, 144 pp.

JACOBSEN, J. P. Bengt Algot Sørensen, **Jens Peter Jacobsen*,
Munich, Beck, 134 pp. B. Algot Sørensen, 'Naturalisme og naturfilo-
sofi. Om J. P. Jacobsen, Darwin og Ernst Haeckel', *Edda* : 359–67,
discusses the dependence of European naturalism on the scientific
principles of positivism and empiricism. An analysis of *Mogens* leads
to the conclusion that the view of nature expressed here has little in
common with Darwinism, but much with Ernst Haeckel's philosophy
of nature. The whole of J.'s work, according to S., is based on the view
that man and nature are united by sharing a universal soul, and it
deals with the existential problem of man's longing for fusion with
nature. Erik Falsig, **Jens Peter Jacobsen bibliografi: fortegnelse over hans
skrifter på dansk og oversat til germanske og romanske sprog med en indledning
af Erland Munch-Petersen*, Danmarks biblioteksskole, 1990, 147 pp.

JØRGENSEN, J. A. V. Sergeev, 'Йоханнес Йоргенсен и проб-лемы датского символизма', *Procs* (Moscow), 294–95. B. Glienke, 'Sommer des Blütengifts oder Winter der Wahrheitsmacht? Der symbolistische Durchbruch in Dänemark laut Johannes Jørgensens Romankunst und Autobiographik', *Procs* (Svendborg), 281–94.

KIERKEGAARD, S. Wilfried Greve, **Kierkegaards maieutische Ethik: von 'Entweder/Oder II' zu den 'Stadien'*, Frankfurt, Suhrkamp, 1990, 353 pp. Bruce H. Kirmmse, *Kierkegaard in Golden Age Denmark*, Bloomington, Indiana U.P., 1990, 558 pp., deals with K.'s political orientation. J. Risum, "Kierkegaard og skuespillerne', *Kritik*, 94:81–91, brings together comments made by K. on dramatic art and argues that K.'s views could have had an innovative effect on contemporary theatre criticism. J. Carson Pettey, 'The stranger's return: Strindberg, Kierkegaard and Nietzsche', *OL*, 46:13–26, traces and identifies in *Till Damaskus I* the importance of *Gjentagelsen* for the theme of the stranger's return. Carl Henrik Koch, *En flue på Hegels udødelige næse eller Om Adolph Adler og Søren Kierkegaards forhold til ham*, C. A. Reitzel, 1990, 240 pp., is a monograph on the theologian and philosopher A. P. Adler (1812–69), who exercised a strong influence on K.'s views on Christianity.

MØLLER, P. M. Gunnar Jakobsen, **Opfattelsen af mennesket i Poul Martin Møllers 'Strøtanker': pessimistisk eller optimistisk?*, Danmarks Lærerhøjskole, 59 pp.

PALUDAN-MÜLLER, F. *Dandserinden*, ed. and ann. Berit Ziegler (Danske klassikere), for DSL, Borgen, 157 pp.

5. THE TWENTIETH CENTURY

GENERAL

J. Kondrup, 'Selvbiografien og det ubevidste. En skitze', *Edda*:134–43, discusses the relationship between the remembering conscious-ness and the unconscious level of the remembered life in three Danish autobiographies: Elsa Gress's *Mine mange hjem* (1965), in which the memory remains autocratic, all-embracing, and confident; Thorkild Hansen's *Søforhør* (1982), which is in the form of a dialogue between H., the psychoanalyst, and H., the writer, with the aim of challenging H.'s understanding of himself through provocative questions; and Jacob Paludan's *Lidt af en livsregistrering* (1973–76), which abandons the classic autobiographical task of establishing connections and patterns and instead records spontaneous ideas, associations and dreams that originate in the unconscious. In the concluding section K. refers to Thorkild Bjørnvig's autobiographical work, which is still in progress, and argues that this displays a possible harmony between the conscious and the unconscious. The controlling consciousness and the Freudian view of the id have been replaced by receptiveness and celebration of the unconscious. P. Dahlerup, 'Hvad er modernisme', *Kritik*, 94:98–108, defines modernism as literature written in spite of the presupposition that both transcendence and immanence have lost their existential validity. Modernism is the situation when language can neither denote nor represent anything. Henrik Norbrandt's *Rosen fra Lesbos* (1979) and Inger Christensen's *Jeg* (*Lys*, 1962) are analysed in an attempt to answer the questions: *what* do they mean? and *how* do they mean?

ANDERSEN NEXØ, M. Henrik Yde, *Det grundtvigske i Martin Andersen Nexøs liv*, 2 vols, Vindrose, 408, 358 pp. Vol. 1 describes N.'s meeting with G.'s views in the 1890s and follows their impact on this development, while vol. 2 focuses on the mature N.'s attempts at mediating between G.'s thoughts on education and socialist pedagogical opinions. Id., *Et venskab: venskabet mellem Martin Andersen Nexø og Johan Borup belyst gennem samtidige dokumenter*, Vindrose, 71 pp. Børge Houmann, *Venskab og revolution: Martin Andersen Nexøs og Marie Nielsens venskab og politiske virke 1918–24*, Selskabet til forskning i arbejderbevægelsens historie, 1990, 276 pp.

BLIXEN, K. D. C. Riechel, 'Isak Dinesen's "Roads round Nietzsche"', *ScSt*, 63:326–50, explores reflections and adaptations of N.'s philosophy in B.'s work. Although there are comparatively few direct references to N. in her writings, R. suggests that a Nietzschean interpretation of art unfolds in the structure of B.'s stories, in the interreferentiality of text and metatext. B.'s irony allows her to entertain an un-Nietzschean 'metaphysical need' for divine intention while at the same time displaying a Nietzschean desire to shape life into beautiful significance. M. Johns Blackwell, 'The transforming gaze, identity and sexuality in the works of Isak Dinesen', *ScSt*, 63:50–66, investigates B.'s deployment of mirror and sight imagery as means of establishing identity. Blackwell argues that while mirrors reflect men's intellectual, psychological, and philosophical complexity, women see only their sexuality. Man is worthy of God's transforming gaze, whereas woman is deserving only of man's transforming gaze. Blackwell rejects the various scholarly attempts to claim B. for feminism as, in her opinion, B.'s vision of the world is fundamentally androcentric. S. Maksymiuk, '"Tro imod Historien"? Karen Blixen's *Det ubeskrevne Blad* and the limits of literary realism', *Edda*:32–39, is concerned with the methodology of literary realism. M. contends that the illusion of 'authenticity' depends on acquiescent readers who accept as unambiguous and true the text's ideas and concepts and create fictional worlds from these. The clean sheet in B.'s short story undermines the story-teller's control of meaning in her text, as it offers a plurality of meaning and draws the audience into the fictional process as each reader inscribes the blank page with his interpretation. M. concludes that the clean sheet speaks ultimately to the reader about the role he has to play in the textual strategy of literary realism.

CHRISTENSEN, I. H. Depenbrock, ' "Alle Verdinglichung ist ein Vergessen." Inger Christensens *alfabet*', *Skandinavistik*, 21:1–29, argues that *alfabet* can be read not only as an outline of man's cognitive development, but also as a model for the recording of a world that is becoming more and more complex. Man's making sense of the world is compared to the reading of a text, during which the assimilation of new data is carried out through existing concepts and definitions, a process which is sequential, cyclic, and hierarchic. *Alfabet* is a deposit of existing knowledge, a necessary tool for the widening of man's intellectual horizon. It is also, H. argues, intended as a cognitive structure with the aim of influencing this process. J. Olov Ullén, 'Del av labyrinten. Anteckningar kring Inger Christensen', *BLM*, 59, 1990:86–88, deals with the meaning of the expression 'at nå frem', which appears in the last line of *De hænder at* . . . (1988). U. suggests that in C.'s fictional world 'arriving' means experiencing the world as a place one has always known and not a bewildering labyrinth. U. puts forward the view that *Det hænder at . . .* can be read as a metaphor for the process of reading any text by C. Her systems and alphabets ensure that there is clarity behind the apparently labyrinthine surface.

DITLEVSEN, T. A. van hees, 'Død og digtning i Tove Ditlevsens roman *Vilhelms værelse*', *Procs* (Svendborg), 344–54.

GRESS, E. **Nærværende: en bog om Else Gress*, ed. Michael Cotta-Schønberg and Helga Vang Lauridsen, Glydendal, 1990, 245 pp.

HANSEN, M. A. Bjarne Nielsen Brovst, **Martin A. Hansen. Bondesøn og digter*, Viby J., Centrum, 375 pp.

HANSEN, T. J. Kondrup, 'Den skeptiske autobiografi. Thorkild Hansens *Søforhør* som eksempel', *Procs* (Svendborg), 355–65. H. van der Liet, 'På sporet af det fortabte individ. Om Thorkild Hansens arktiske oplevelser', *Nordica*, 8:213–35, deals with the fictional work *Jens Munk* (1965), the scientific report *Jens Munks Minde-ekspedition* (1965), and the diary *Vinterhavn* (1972; written during the expedition in 1964), examining how H. arranged the same material in three different genres. In the second part the existential view expressed in the works is compared to the cultural discussion in *Sidste sommer i Angmagssalik* (1978) in order to determine whether any development took place between the two visits to the Arctic.

HEINESEN, W. W. Glyn Jones, 'Cultural perspectives in the late works of Wilhelm Heinesen', *Fest. Mitchell*, 206–14.

JACOBSEN, J.-F. M. B. Matveeva, 'Творчество Йоргена-Франца Якобсена', *Procs* (Moscow), 300–01.

JENSEN, J. V. I. P. Kupriianova, 'Культурно-историческая концепция Йоханнеса В. Йенсена. Эпопея "Долгий путь"', *Procs* (Moscow), 296–97.

JENSEN, T. Jens Andersen, **Thit — den sidste valkyrie*, Gad, 1990, 307 pp. *'Jeg længes . . .'. Fra Thit Jensens dagbøger 1891–1927*, ed. and ann. Jens Andersen, Gad, 208 pp.

KRISTENSEN, T. Bent Haugaard Jeppesen, *Orfeus i underklassen. Tom Kristensens proletardæmoni*, Århus U.P., 1990, 237 pp. Aage Jørgensen, *Litteratur om Tom Kristensen. En bibliografi*, 2nd rev. edn, Mårslet, CUK/Center for Undervisning og Kulturformidling, 27 pp.

NORBRANDT, H. H. Strand, 'En billedteoretisk tilgang til systemmodernistisk metaforik — eksemplificeret med en analyse af Henrik Norbrandts digt "Violinbyggernes by"', *Nordica*, 8:81–110, argues that in *Vb* a play between the words' concrete and transferred meanings emerges gradually as the various sections of the poem combine. The concluding river scene can be read (and should be read according to the rules of the poem) as concrete and present as well as a metaphor for the absent and inexpressible. Defining systemic metaphorics, S. puts forward five criteria, which can be summarized by 'reflexivity' and 'reciprocity'.

SKOU-HANSEN, T. E. M. Christensen, 'Kan Holger Mikkelsen skrive?', *Procs* (Svendborg), 334–43.

SØRENSEN, V. M. Krysztofiak, 'Krigssyndromet i det modernistiske verdensbillede i Villy Sørensens novelle "Koncerten"', *Nordica*, 8:205–12.

STANGERUP, H. H. van der Liet, 'Fjenden i teksten. Om Henrik Stangerups selvbiografiske roman "Fjenden i forkøbet"', *Procs* (Svendborg), 318–33, is a revaluation of S.'s autobiographical project. H.'s view that the modern autobiography is not so much an account of the process of individuation as the very process of self-realization, is applied to S.'s work, and the conclusion is drawn that *Fif* is not a painful and failed report of an existential crisis, but an interesting autobiographical novel.

TAFDRUP, P. C. Engberg, 'Læseren i tekstanalysen — om køn, tekst og læsning i forbindelse med Pia Tafdrups digt "Mørkeglans"', *TsSk*, 11, 1990:81–91. I Frandsen-Roger, 'Strukturer, temaer og billedsprog i Pia Tafdrups digtsamlinger 1981–1988', *Procs* (Svendborg), 419–29.

THORUP, K. C. S. Gray, 'Identity and narrative structure in Kirsten Thorup's novels', *ScSt*, 63:214–20.

914 *Germanic Languages*

IV. NORWEGIAN STUDIES*

LANGUAGE AND EARLY LITERATURE

By Erling Georg Larsen, *Senior Lecturer in Norwegian Language at Rogaland Regional College, Stavanger, Norway*

1. General

Media and Communication, ed. Helge Rønning and Knut Lundby, Norwegian U.P. (distributed outside Scandinavia by OUP), 382 pp., is a substantial contribution to communication research, reflecting a variety of theories and methods. The volume is intended as an attempt to map this variety of approaches within an interdisciplinarity framework, and is above all a documentation of the quality of communication studies, including a hermeneutic approach, as it has developed in Norway in the last decade. The range of topics covered in 23 essays by 24 contributors includes theories of interpersonal communication, empirical studies of the media in Norway, as well as rhetorics, textual analysis, and linguistic theories. *Det umuliges kunst. Om å oversette*, ed. Per Qvale *et al.*, Aschehoug, 338 pp., is a comprehensive presentation, by 24 contributors, of translation strategies, focusing on Norwegian, and reflecting individual experiences, often problematic, together with useful theoretical introductions. The translator's creativity in its confrontation with the original text is given serious consideration. Political manipulation and objectionable influences in journalism are highlighted, on a general basis, in Jan Inge Sørbø, *Offentleg samtale. Innføring i presse-etiske grunnspørsmål*, Det Norske Samlaget, 249 pp. The insight into classical rhetoric in its true sense, combined with the knowledge of genre theories, is said, in this well-documented study, to be a prerequisite for the appropriate linguistic and rhetorical forms. A systematically convincing textbook on Norwegian *bokmål*, above elementary level, appealing to foreigners, is Anders Martin Kvam, *Noen emner i norsk for utlendinger*, Trondheim, Tapir, 1990, 260 pp. Focusing on pronunciation, grammar, and exercise texts, areas creating particular difficulties for foreign learners have been explained in detail. Tape-recordings are available from the publisher. Two useful bibliographies should be noted here: Johan A. Schulze, *Skrifter og talar av Marius Hægstad*, Novus, 1990, 48 pp., and Id., *Skrifter av Per Nyquist Grøtvedt*, Målførearkivet, Univ. of Oslo, 35 pp. These surveys are concerned with two scholars primarily famous for their investigations of Old and Middle Norwegian dialects. Campbell, *Compendium*, 1035–40, introduces a survey of Norwegian, not without mistakes.

*The place of publication of books is Olso unless otherwise stated.

2. HISTORY OF THE LANGUAGE AND LINGUISTIC DISPUTE

Partly philosophizing, always eloquent, is Eigil Lehmann, *Reise det som velt er. Um norrøn målbygnad og målbunad*, Bergen, Norsk Bokreidingslag, 1990, 82 pp., a collection of articles, primarily taken up with the preservation of the Norse linguistic heritage. With reasonable arguments L. deplores that Ivar Aasen did not exclusively found his *nynorsk* on the dialects of the central west Norwegian area, i.e. the county of Hordaland. A bibliography of L.'s important publications and an assessment of his lexicographical works have been added by J. Bondevik. A similar defence of the New Norwegian language is Jostein Krokvik, *Mål og vanmæle. Frå soga um norsk offentleg skriftmål*, Bergen, Norsk Bokreidingslag, 139 pp., perspicaciously attacking the official regulations of *nynorsk* in the last hundred years. Some largely unknown aspects of the linguistic dispute are revealed. Peter Hallaråker, *The Nynorsk Language in the United States*, Norwegian U.P., 164 pp., presents the use of and the debate on *nynorsk* in the USA from the pioneer period until the present time. After a survey of the development of *nynorsk* in Norway, the language situation in the Norwegian immigrant communities is clarified, and the debate on the language from among the immigrants is summarized. L. Groven in *MM*, nos 1–2:85–91, outlines the approximation to dialects in the writing of New Norwegian. It especially applies to idiomatic usage and orthophone spelling. In this respect attention is drawn to the unbroken connection between Olaus Fjørtoft in the 1870s and Olav Duun in the first half of this century. H. Perridon, *ABÄG*, 34:5–18, discusses the Reistad runic inscription and the chronology of certain Proto-Scandinavian sound changes.

3. LEXICOGRAPHY, ONOMASTICS, DIALECTS

A weighty contribution to lexicography, with the object of presenting the central vocabulary of modern Norwegian, is *Aschehoug og Gyldendals Store Norske Ordbok*, ed. Tor Guttu, Kunnskapsforlaget, x + 692 pp., comprising moderate *bokmål* and *riksmål*. The book, impressive also for its layout and binding, is concerned with orthography, inflection, pronunciation, as well as definitions, examples, and, as an interesting additional information, etymology.

Olav Veka, *Namneboka*, Det Norske Samlaget, 175 pp., contains more than 3,000 Norwegian first names, together with commonly accepted interpretations. The book gives a good overview and has much updated information for the general public, e.g. the recently introduced name-day calendar list. *Den 5. nasjonale konferansen i namnegransking*, ed. Botolv Helleland and Kristoffer Kruken,

Department of Onomastics, Univ. of Oslo, 150 pp., contains 12 papers and reports of discussions from the conference in Oslo in November 1988, where the main topic was written and oral regulations on place names. The book includes the new statute on place names, passed by the Norwegian Parliament in 1990, together with official commentaries and statute provisions. Published by the Department of Onomastics, Univ. of Oslo, is also *Den 6. nasjonale konferansen i namnegransking*, ed. Botolv Helleland and Anne Svanevik, 146 pp., containing 18 papers and reports of discussions from the Oslo conference of November 1990, where the main concern was a presentation of various impressive projects for onomastic research. From the same publisher is *Avdeling for namnegransking. Årsmelding 1990*, 14 pp. *Namn og nemne* (Norsk namnelag), Øvre Ervik, Alvheim & Eide, 7, 1990, containing articles by V. Antonesen (official Norwegian nomenclature for birds contrasting with the zoological system), E. Fure (the influx of new first names in the 19th c. as a possible expression of a new spirit of the times), O.-J. Johannessen (a discussion of the names of 11 country settlements in the district of Nordhordland in the Middle Ages, as well as their ancient geographical localization), K. Kruken (an interpretation of a few place names, mainly from the section of Trøndelag, which are said to be based on ON *skurð(f.), etymologically related to *skera* infinitive), and H. B. Randsborg (old rural customs indicating whom a child should be named after). In addition, O. Nes, *ib.*, 103–22, has printed an almost unknown account from 1897, by the great place name researcher Oluf Rygh, on the lines laid down when collecting and interpreting Norwegian farm names a century ago. To keep abreast of the increasing onomastic research in Norway, with the manifold activities implied, one needs *Nytt om namn* (Norsk namnelag), ed. Botolv Helleland and Kristoffer Kruken, Department of Onomastics, Univ. of Oslo, which has so far appeared with fascs 13 and 14. A consecutive, practically complete, bibliography on this research is included. B. Helleland in *Probleme der älteren Namenschichten. Leipziger Symposion (1989)*, Heidelberg, Winter, pp. 199–211, has collected and systematized about 100 river names from the area of Hardangervidda in western Norway, making attempts to estimate which names belong to the oldest stratum.

Concerned with sociolinguistic dialect geography within an urban area is Aage Evensen and Tone Tveit, *TÅG. Talemålsvariasjon åt gjøvikensere*, Novus, 1990, 171 pp. The investigation, carried out by the help of quantitative methods, applies to the spoken language of the town of Gjøvik, in the county of Oppland, and is focused on a spoken variation where the surrounding rural dialect, the East Norwegian folk idiom, and standard East Norwegian are taken into account.

From social variables it is concluded that with regard to the surrounding dialect forms these are to a greater extent used by men, and by speakers belonging to the secondary trades. Edited for Målførearkivet, Univ. of Oslo, in the series Norske studiar, is Sigurd Sandvik, *Suldalsmålet. Mållæra, ord og vendingar*, Bergen, Norsk Bokreidingslag, 326 pp. It contains a short grammar of the dialect of Suldal in the county of Rogaland, and above all a list of words, 5000 in all (pp. 45–326) interestingly exemplified in sentences reflecting ancient modes of living, rural methods of work, as well as an abundance of old phrases and sayings. The yearly publication *Talatrosten*, Målførearkivet, Univ. of Oslo, includes stimulating short articles by J. Øverby (Johan Storm's centennial phonetic symbols, the so-called Norvegia transcription, now adapted for computerized printing), K. Kruken (the exceedingly rare male name 'Pros'), J. A. Schulze (the lexicographer Hans Ross), and A. Borg (Atlas Linguarum Europae and samples of Norwegian vocabulary).

4. SEMANTICS, STYLISTICS, MORPHOLOGY, SYNTAX

Intended for the teaching of foreigners and immigrants in Norway is Svein Lie, *Kontrastiv grammatikk — med norsk i sentrum*, Novus, 1990, 113 pp., which surveys differences between Norwegian and a large number of other languages, with regard to phonology, morphology, and syntax. The various categories discussed in the book are seen from the point of view of Norwegian. Reflecting efforts made by the State to ameliorate and simplify the language of laws and regulations is *Språket i lover og annet regelverk*, ed. Finn-Erik Vinje, Tano, 1990, 134 pp. This book, containing articles by five contributors, is certainly the most comprehensive account so far of this special aspect of written Norwegian. As an example the problem of ambiguity and vagueness in legal language is elucidated. Grammatical errors as expressed in modern written or spoken Norwegian are discussed against the background of the equivalent correct expressions in Olav Vesaas and Finn-Erik Vinje, *Språkrøret*, Scanbok, 189 pp. The book, highly entertaining and certainly also containing much information on present-day usage, is based on a long series of radio programmes where questions from listeners were answered. E. Bruaas in *Norskrift*, 64: 1–86, Nordic Department, Univ. of Oslo, penetratingly analyses the structure of a problematic complex like 'hjelpsom som han var' in the sentence 'hjelpsom som han var, lå aldri nei i hans munn'. It is concluded that we have a relative complex, not a comparative one, and that it should be semantically assessed as a free predicative. Light is further shed on a few special cases of free predicative, with their various aspects, partly unmentioned in previous research, or in contrast with it. H. Uri, *ib.*, 86–105, outlines various communication strategies employed towards and by speakers suffering from aphasia. Ed. by O. Øyslebø, *ib.*, 67, are ten analyses by students at Nordic Inst., Oslo, on the perception gained through a combination of textual and visual information, embracing layout, illustrations, and media pictures. M. Sandvik, *ib.*, 68 : 1–33, values oral examination in Norwegian as a secondary language. It is perceived as a communicative situation, where the partners participate in a non-symmetrical relation as it is the teacher who conducts the reciprocal language functions. J. Svennevik, *ib.*, 68 : 33–57, concludes that the dialogue in Ibsen's *Vildanden* mostly satisfies the demands of oral conversation. As the dialogue nevertheless seems to be idealized, this is due to an ambiguity in the communicative situation: in addition to the situation on the stage, the text is to function in front of a reader, i.e. in a written communication. H. T. H. Nilsen, *ib.*, 68 : 57–75, presents to modern readers A. Western, *Norsk riksmåls-grammatikk*, 1921, and estimates it to be a valuable source for scholars even today. V. Leira, *ib.*, 68 : 75–83, discusses the syntagmatic type 'hjelpsom som han var', cf. Bruaas above, claiming that it is, in the context concerned, an adverbial, not a free predicative. T. K. Solberg, *ib.*, 69, gives an interesting semantic-pragmatical analysis of the six modality particles 'vel', 'visst', 'nok', 'da', 'jo', and 'nå', based on the hypothesis that these particles constitute informative elements of communication. H. T. H. Nilsen, *ib.*, 70, distinguishes between aspect and so-called 'aksjonsart', analysing their respective use in connection with finite forms of 'være' and 'bli'. J. R. Hagland in *MM*, nos 1–2 : 77–85, analyses semantic contents in designations of persons in H. J. Wille's dialect word list from the county of Telemark *c.* 1785, a collection full of designations of both sexes. A complex system of semantic structures within a limited lexical field has in this way been studied synchronically. It appears that the attitude towards sex has been of minor importance in the semantic creation at the epoch concerned. *Edda*, 91 : 3–32, contains contributions at the doctoral disputation at the Univ. of Oslo in March 1990 on Geir Mork, *Den reflekterte latteren. På spor etter Arne Garborgs ironi*. Relevant in this context is the stimulating discussion of the conception of various forms of irony. M. E. Halse, *ib.*, 91 : 45–56, philosophizes on teaching writing as a process in a broader perspective: combined with a literary science fruitfully rooted in critical hermeneutics and poststructuralist text theories. *NLT*, 9, contains well informed articles, mostly on syntax, by O. C. Dahl (the existence of sandhi between words, in East Norwegian and Madagascan), K. Venås (free relative clauses versus interrogative subordinate clauses), K. K. Christensen (Scandinavian existential-presentative sentences from the point of view of the

Government and Binding theories), T. Trosterud (locality cases and prepositions in Finnish, Sámi, and Norwegian), E. Papazian (main classification of sentences). H. Lødrup (syntactic differences between complement clauses in English and Norwegian), F. Hertzberg (methodological principles for the classification of grammars), and B. Mæhlum (a historical survey concerning the question whether it is the language of the individual or that of the collectivity which should be the object of research).

5. PHONETICS AND PHONOLOGY

Hanne Gram Simonsen, *Barns fonologi: System og variasjon hos tre norske og ett samoisk barn*, Inst. of Linguistics and Philosophy, Univ. of Oslo, 1990, 345 pp. + apps, is a doctoral thesis on phonological development in children. The treatise primarily gives a thorough description of consonant phonology in some Norwegian children aged 2–4 years. The object is furthermore to throw light on the possible regularity of development from step to step. The description is at the same time meant to be applicable to languages which differ phonologically, with a view to disclosing possible universal features in the phonological development. The same model is consequently used in the description of the phonology in a Samoan child speaking a Polynesian language, after which the results are compared. The analysis *inter alia* discloses distinct differences between initial, medial, and final word systems in the Norwegian children. As to the adult language, it has more phonemes in final than in initial position, the opposite being the case in Norwegian children. The phonological development seems to take place in connection with some phonetic variation. An interesting aspect applies to the acquisition of liquids in Samoan and Norwegian, the liquids being among the latest acquired phonemes.

6. TEXTUAL STUDIES

Particularly valuable, not only for the history of language, is Kjell Venås, *Den fyrste morgonblånen. Tekster på norsk frå dansketida*, Novus, 1990, 635 pp., which is meant to be a complete collection of poetic works founded on diversified rural dialects before the end of the Danish-Norwegian union in 1814, the oldest text of which is from the 16th c. Some of the texts appear in printed form for the first time. Ancient dialect texts from Trøndelag, already published, have not been included (cf. *YWMLS*, 47:897). In the present diplomatic edition, the specific genre of folk songs has been omitted. The editor has supplied comprehensive commentaries, pp. 401–616. Edited for Kjeldeskriftfondet, under the direction of Riksarkivet, is *Fra Amerika til Norge. Norske utvandrerbrev 1838–1857*, ed. Orm Øverland and Steinar Kjærheim, Solum, 496 pp. Written by the first Norwegian immigrants into the USA, these preserved letters are informative linguistic as well as historical documents. Orthography and syntax, scrupulously reproduced in this diplomatic edition, reflect individual variants of Danish-Norwegian, or rather wavering attempts at writing what may be called an alien written language. A.-M. Hamre, in *Historisk tidsskrift*, 70:357–73, highlights the genesis of Bishop Eysteinn's cadastre, also called the Red Book, which constitutes the register of lands and rights belonging to the churches within the diocese of Oslo, mainly in the 1390s.

7. EARLY LITERATURE AND FOLKLORE

There will be a warm welcome for *Norroena et Islandica. Utvalde artiklar av Hallvard Magerøy*, ed. E. F. Halvorsen, F. Hødnebø, E. Mundal, and V. Ólason, Øvre Ervik, Alvheim & Eide, xvi + 297 pp., which marks M.'s 75th birthday, primarily presenting his research on Old Norse prose literature. From among sagas treated in this collection of manifold articles, 18 in all, may be mentioned *Bandamanna saga*, *Ljósvetninga saga*, and *Bǫglunga sǫgur*. There is a complete bibliography of his works. Comprising history as well as Old Norse philology is Claus Krag, *Ynglingatal og Ynglingesaga. En studie i historiske kilder*, Norwegian U.P., 286 pp. K. argues, remarkably, that crucial parts of *Ynglingatal* show the influence of concepts that cannot be dated before 900, but reflect the ideas of a Christian age, most likely the 12th c. He further attempts to show how the Yngling tradition took shape, not in ancient lore but as a result of conscious reconstruction by the medieval historians. Attention is drawn to Gro Steinsland, *Det hellige bryllup og norrøn kongeideologi. En undersøkelse av hierogami-myten i Skírnismál, Ynglingatal, Háleygjatal og Hyndluljóð*, Univ. of Oslo, 1989, 657 pp., a doctoral thesis, which *inter alia* maintains that the prototypical ruler in pre-Christian culture was the offspring of a god and a giantess; this is the key to a deeper understanding of mythical elements in Norse literary sources. Childhood and related aspects as they are described in Old Scandinavian, especially Old Norse, literature, are accounted for in Gert Kreutzer, *Kindheit und Jugend in der altnordischen Literatur. 1. Schwangerschaft, Geburt und früheste Kindheit*, Münster, Kleinheinrich, 1987, 388 pp. As a solid documentation there are numerous quotations from relevant texts, also rendered in German translation. O. E. Haugen in *MM*, nos 1–2:1–25, gives an uncommonly thorough review and a laudatory assessment of *Barlaams ok Josaphats saga*, ed. Magnus Rindal, Oslo, 1981 (cf. *YWMLS*, 43:1010). The diplomatic edition is claimed as an accurate linguistic document, enabling scholars to penetrate with more precision into Old Norwegian language history and grammar. There is a proposed etymology by W. B. Lockwood, *ib.*, 25–29, of Old Norse *fljóð*, *sprund*, and *víf*, poetic terms for woman. The Norse words, highly stylized, are said to lack vulgarity in an epoch with other values, an unexpected facet of literary taste at the beginning of the recorded ON literature. M. Rindal, *ib.*, 29–59, surveys the 50 years' history, 1940–90, of the Department of Lexicography for Old Norwegian, at the Univ. of Oslo. H. Pálsson, *ib.*, 59–77, explains, in a detailed investigation, the influence of the Latin Middle Ages on *Sverris saga*. Such influence generally took place through Latin readers studied by Norwegians and Icelanders in the 12th and 13th cs. *ANF*, 105, includes important articles, mostly on literature, by O. Grønvik (two ON words of importance for the understanding of the runic inscription of Rök: *gjalda* infinitive, and *minni* neuter), K. E. Gade (the phrase *gǫfugt dýr* in *Fáfnismál*, strophe 2, explained as an onomastic pun indicating a circumlocution for an alternative form of *Sigurðr*), S. Bagge (the relationship between *Konungs skuggsiá* and *Stjórn*), F. Hansen (the use of the ON conjunction *unz* and synonymous phrases), A. Jakobsen (the insignificant part played by King Arthur and his Round Table in ON literature), M. Malm (a discussion of the term *sannkenning* in skaldic poetry), E. A. Rowe (elements in *Páttr Sveins ok Finns* in *Flateyjarbók* borrowed from the legend of St Christopher, and the *páttr* author's intention in doing so), K. Wolf (the sources of *Gyðinga saga*), E. Salberger (a certain connection between the Eddic poem *Guðrúnarkviða II* and the runic inscription of Sigtuna), and G. Holm (objections to H. Bjorvand's explanation of such ON plural forms as *Húsar*, *Holtar*, *Nesjar*, cf. *YWMLS*, 51:879). R. Kroesen, *ABÄG*, 33:137–48, writes on the usurpation of land as a motif in the *Laxdæla saga*; K. Wolf, *ib.*, 149–66, discusses the Old Norse renderings of Peter Comestor's *Historia Scholastica* with special emphasis on *Gyðinga saga* and the Joshua section in *Stjórn* III; H. H. Dörner, *ib.*, 34:49–66, interprets Óðinn's announcement of his names in *Grímnismál*; and H. Perridon, *ABÄG*, 34:5–17, discusses the runic inscription on the Reistad stone. H. Fix, *Beiträge* (Trier), 155—68, discusses various forms of ON text edition, focusing on the computer-aided 1989 edition of the Old Icelandic *Elucidarius*.

A well-informed contribution to knowledge of folklore, intended for scholars as well as the general public, is *Scandinavian Folk Belief and Legend*, ed. Reimund Kvideland and Henning K. Sehmsdorf, Norwegian U.P. (distributed outside Scandinavia, the USA, Canada, and Japan by OUP), xxii + 430 pp. It is a rich compendium of hundreds of legends, stories, beliefs, and magic from preindustrial Scandinavia, all translated into straightforward English. The extensive introduction also discusses the various categories of folk-loric forms, and explains their cultural function. The series of publications from Norsk Folkeminnelag on folklore and popular traditions has now reached no. 133 with *Tippoldemors oppskrifter*, ed. Velle Espeland, Aschehoug, 1990, 95 pp., presenting recipes and culinary art from the upper classes more than a century ago. B. Rogan, *Norveg*, 34:47–66, Norwegian U.P., discusses the custom of giving names to houses, cars, and boats. A common characteristic of such named artefacts is said to be the investment of more meaning than most artefacts possess, with all the personal associations that individuals put into them. People thereby take control, cognitively and emotionally, of their neutral or incomprehensible surroundings. This process may contain symbolic and even metaphysical elements. C. Eike, *ib.*, 153–70, analyses, on the background of experiences, the interview as a method of collecting information in ethnological and folkloric research. The importance of indirect information is empha-sized. U. Palmenfelt, *ib.*, 197–208, accounts for jokes in inter-Scandinavian relations. The telling of such jokes, which are a sort of folklore, is interpreted as a continuous discussion about one's cultural identity. *Tradisjon. Tidsskrift for folkeminnevitskap*, 21, is dedicated to the folklorist Bente Gullveig Alver on the occasion of her 50th birthday. A bibliography of her publications accompanies ten articles by women colleagues, the common denominator of which in most cases applies to gender roles. Attention is further drawn to a discussion by A. H. B. Skjelbred, pp. 5–15, of the essence of folklore, which is suggestively defined as a language of feeling, expressing something fundamental to human mentality: through folklore we gain self-understanding as human beings.

LITERATURE SINCE THE REFORMATION

POSTPONED

V. SWEDISH STUDIES*

LANGUAGE

By KERSTIN PETERSSON, *Lecturer in Swedish, University of East Anglia*

(This survey covers the years 1990–91)

1. GENERAL

Språket som kulturspegel: Umeforskare berättar: symposium och språklärardagar, Umeå 5–6 november 1990, ed. Karl Johan Danell, Gunnar Persson, and Astrid Stedje (USH, 100), 203 pp. In addition to teaching and research Swedish university teachers are expected to give information about their work to the general public. This volume is an attempt to fulfil this task. It contains papers from a symposium for a group of language teachers, collected under the following sub-headings: language, social attitude and ideological influence; intercultural differences; different cultures — same language; language — a living archive. The book includes B. Odenstedt, 'Samhällssyn och sociala roller i grammatikexempel' (11–14); U. Sedlacek, 'Språkligt beteende i tyska och svenska (41–46); C. Heldner, 'Pippi Långstrump i fransk tvångströja' (63–74); P. Sedlacek, 'Idrottsspråk som kulturspegel' (72–82); and H. Jerke, 'Vad svenska och tyska månadsnamn berättar' (165–78). *Sammankomst for att dryfta frågor rörande svenskans beskrivning*, 17, 1989, ed. Erik Andersson and Marketta Sundman, Åbo, Åbo Akademi, 1990, 433 pp., is a collection of papers from one of the regular conferences on topics related to the description of modern Swedish. *Språket i bibeln — bibeln i språket*, ed. Christer Åsberg (SSSN, 76), 254 pp., contains articles on the language used in the Bible and also on biblical language and biblical references in general usage. *Svenska skrivregler* (SSSN, 4), the normative guidelines for punctuation and style in written Swedish, has appeared in a new edition. Bengt Sigurd, **Språk och språkforskning*, Lund, Studentlitteratur, 176 pp.

2. RUNOLOGY

Bengt Odenstedt, *On the Origin and Early History of the Runic Script: Typology and Graphic Variation in the Older Futhark* (Acta Academiae Regiae Gustavi Adolphis, 59), 181 pp., is the first monograph on the development and geographic distribution of runic forms in the older futhark, *c*. AD 200–700. The early Scandinavian inscriptions use more archaic forms and the late ones more innovations than the ones in

*The place of publication of books is Stockholm unless otherwise indicated.

England and on the Continent. Runic script was used earlier and for a longer period in Scandinavia than elsewhere. The author has attempted to find the original form for each rune and gives detailed explanation of the derivation of each one. Svante Lagman, *De stungna runorna: användning och ljudvärden i runsvenska steninskrifter* (Runrön, 4), 202 pp., diss. with English and German summaries, is a study of the use of the 'dotted' runes and the phonetic sounds they represented in Swedish stone inscriptions. Conny Petersson, *Rökstenen — Varins besvärjelse*, Borensberg, Noteria, 101 pp., is a contribution to the interpretation of the famous stone at Rök, Östergötland. Thorgunn Snædal, *Från Järnatullen till Gårdarike: en bok om Södertäljetraktens runinskrifter*, Täljebygden, 1990–91, 80 pp., deals with the runic inscriptions from the region round Södertälje, just south of Stockholm. Helmer Gustavsson, *Runstenar i Vallentuna* (Vallentuna kulturnämnds skriftserie, 7), 200 pp., describes the rune stones in the community of Vallentuna, just north of Stockholm. Ingrid Cederquist, *Tio utflykter till runristningar i Uppland*, Folkuniversitetets förlag, 80 pp., is a guide to runic inscriptions in the Uppland region, including a linguistic and historical commentary for the amateur. Olof Eriksson, *Runstenar/Rune Stones*, Malmö, Ed. Eriksson, 119 pp., is a beautifully produced picture book of selected rune inscriptions with a text commentary by Jan Paul Strid.

3. PHONETICS AND MORPHOLOGY

David House, **Tonal Perception in Speech* (Travaux de l'Institut de Linguistique de Lund, 24), 1990, 169 pp., diss. Anders Eriksson, **Aspects of Swedish Speech Rhythm* (Gothenburg Monographs in Linguistics, 9), 234 pp., diss. Pia Norell, *Native-Speaker Reactions to Swedish Pronunciation Errors in English: Recognition, Intelligibility and Attitude* (Stockholm Studies in English, 79), 181 pp., diss., aims to account how 11 different Swedish pronunciation errors were received by native speakers of British English. The results show that there is little agreement among the informants as to the 'typically Swedish' error, but there is overwhelming agreement considering intelligibility. An account is also given of informants' reaction to different perceived accents. The informants were much influenced by which accent they believed they heard when evaluating the speech samples. The informants' reactions were also related to various social characteristics, i.e. age, sex, occupation. Gerd Eklund, *Vrist — brist — rist: utvecklingen av gammalt uddljudande wr i nordiska, särskilt svenska, dialekter* (Skrifter utgivna genom Dialekt- och folkminnesarkivet i Uppsala. Ser. A, 17), 254 pp. This dissertation is a study of the five word initial sounds and sound combinations *rw*, *r*, *w*, *br*, and *vr*, all developments of the Germanic combination *wr* which has not survived in any standard language. The aim has been to describe the occurrence of these sound combinations and to explain their age and origin. Gösta Holm, *Uppkomsten av de neutrala verbabstrakterna på -ande* (Scripta Minora Regiae Societatis Humaniorum Litterarum Lundensis 1990–91, no. 1), 39 pp. After Fredrik Tham's idea in 'Tränne tyska ändelser' from 1878 all Swedish scholars were of the opinion that 'talande' came from Middle Low German. The author investigates another possibility: the Swedish *-ande* could be derived from Scandinavian verbal abstracts in *-an*, originally feminine, but developing into neuter.

4. SYNTAX, SEMANTICS, AND COMMUNICATION THEORY

Kent Larsson, *Svenska brev: några bidrag till studiet av en texttyps historia* (USH, 102), 214 pp., is a study of correspondence and the letter as a text type, including a historical perspective. Björn Melander, **Innehållsmönster i svenska facktexter* (Skrifter utgivna av institutionen för nordiska språk vid Uppsala universitet, 28), 272 pp., diss. with English summary, is a study of content patterns in factual, non-fictional texts. Sheila Dooley Collberg, *Comparative Studies in Current Syntactic Theories* (Working Papers, Lund University, Department of Linguistics, General Linguistics, Phonetics, 37), 160 pp., diss. Sven-Göran Malmgren. *Adjektiviska funktioner i svenskan* (Nordistica Gothoburgensia, 13), 1990, 231 pp., is a diss. with English summary, dating from 1984. It is a contribution to the study of adjectival functions in Swedish. As the term indicates, a combination of semantic and syntactic aspects is taken into account. Elsie Wijk-Andersson, *Bara i fokus: en semantisk-syntaktisk studie av bara och dess ekvivalenter i nysvenskt skriftspråk* (Skrifter utgivna av institutionen för nordiska språk vid Uppsala universitet, 27), 200 pp., diss. with English summary, describes the use of 'bara' and its equivalents from Old Swedish to the 1970s.' The aim is to account for the distribution and versatility of 'bara', the degree of synonymity between the variants, and the effect of different positions of the 'bara' variants relative to the focused element. Per Jansson, *Säkerhetspolitikens språk: myt och metafor i säkerhetspolitisk diskurs 1919–1939* (Lund Political Studies, 68), 170 pp., uses the constructivist perspective in communication theory, suggesting that language is instrumental in creating as well as transmitting meaning. The author opposes the process model of communication which claims that a message always has an unambiguous meaning, making language a passive medium for the transmission of ideas. The aim of this interesting study is to show that the function of metaphor goes far beyond mere rhetorical adornment. *Samtal och språkundervisning: Studier till Lennart Gustavssons minne*, ed. Ulrika Nettelbladt and

Gisela Håkansson (Linköping Studies in Art and Science, 60), 238 pp., contains 14 articles largely focused on discourse analysis and various aspects of dialogue. In his 'Konversasjon i Ibsens dokkehus' (1–24), Ragnar Rommetveit uses Lennart Gustavsson's and Per Linell's IR (initiative-response) model for his analysis of a theatrical dialogue sequence. Per Linell contributes 'Om gruppsamtalets interaktionsstruktur' (39–54). Ulrika Nettelbladt and Kristina Hansson investigate the influence of the adult as conversation partners with children in 'Samtalspartnerns inverkan på barns språk' (87–104). The language used in class-room teaching generally and the teaching of a second language in particular is the subject of articles like 'Vilket språk ska vi lära ut? Om talspråk och skriftspråk hos Sv2–lärare' by Gisela Håkansson (211–20), and Lennart Gustavsson, 'Ta talspråket på allvar! Om talspråksnormer och skriftspråksnormer i Sv2-undervisning' (221–34).

5. FIRST AND SECOND LANGUAGE ACQUISITION, LANGUAGES IN CONTACT

Ulf Teleman, *Lära svenska: om språkbruk i modersmålsundervisning* (SSSN, 75), 126 pp., deals with the usage in the teaching of Swedish as a mother tongue. Rune Ingo, *Frå källspråk till målspråk*, Lund, Studentlitteratur, 284 pp., is an introduction to translation studies, a revised version of the original publication in Finnish. Kenneth Hyltenstam and Christopher Stroud, *Språkbyte och språkbevarande: om samiskan och andra minoritetsspråk*, Lund, Studentlitteratur, 175 pp., deals with sami and other minority languages in the context of language preservation and code switching. *Flerspråkighet i och utanför Norden / Multilingualism in the Nordic Countries and Beyond*, ed. Kjell Herberts and Christer Laurén (Institutet för finlandssvensk samhällsforskning, 13), 376 pp., is a collection of papers from the 6th Nordic conference on bilingualism held in June 1990 in Vasa, Finland. The motto for the volume is 'Bilingualism — a resource' and the topics include the bilingual city, language and school, bilingualism in the family, and threatened language communities.

6. DIALECTOLOGY

The first part of a Swedish dialect dictionary, *Ordbok över Sveriges dialekter*, ed. Vidar Reinhammar (Arkivet för Ordbok över Sveriges dialekter, Uppsala), fasc. 1, 80 pp., covers *A — andtäppt*. Lars Levander and Stig Björklund, *Ordbok över folkmålen i övre Dalarna* (Skrifter utgivna genom Dialekt- och folkminnesarkivet i Uppsala. D, Dialektordböcker från Dalarna, Gotland och andra landskap, 1), has reached volume 4, fasc. 30, *S - Skata*, pp. 2056–134. Gösta Sjöstedt, *Ordbok över folkmålen i Västra Göinge härad* (Skrifter utgivna genom Dialekt- och ortnamnsarkivet i Lund, 1), vol. 3, *Lön — Smörösta*, pp. 380–562. *Västgötska dialektord från Södra Redväg*, comp. David Haldorson and Harald Filipsson, Blidberg, Blidbergs hembygdsförening, 141 pp. Bengt af Klintberg, *En tjottablängare mellan lysmaskarna* (Höjerings Stockholmianaserie, 29), 51 pp., is a book about the role of Stockholm slang and local idioms in fiction and folklore. Hugo Enström and Sven Söderström, *Enångersmålet: ordlista över en dialekt i Hälsingland* (Skrifter utgivna genom Dialekt- och folkminnesarkivet i Uppsala, Ser. A, Folkmål, 16), 1990, 123 pp. Anna Westerberg, *Utvecklingen av gammalt kort a framför ld och nd i svenska dialekter* (Skrifter utgivna genom Dialekt- och folkminnesarkivet i Uppsala, Ser. A, Folkmål, 19), 2 vols, 179, 20 pp. (text and maps), shows the development of short a preceding *ld* and *nd* in Swedish dialects.

7. ONOMASTICS

Claes Garlén. *Svenska ortnamn: uttal och stavning*, Norstedt, 108 pp., is an inventory of Swedish place names, including details on pronunciation and spelling. It has been published under the auspices of Lantmäteriverket and Svenska språknämnden and replaces the older work, *Svenska ortnamn med uttalsuppgifter*, by Jöran Sahlgren and Gösta Bergman. Svante Strandberg, **Studier över Sörmländska sjönamn* (Skrifter utgivna genom ortnamnsarkivet i Uppsala, Ser. B. Meddelanden, 8), 300 pp., diss., with an English summary, on Swedish lake names, investigates the formation of the names, their etymology, and their morphological development. Gunilla Harling-Kranck, **Namn på åkrar, ängar och hagar* (Skrifter utgivna genom Svenska litteratursällskapet i Finland, 565), 1990, 384 pp., diss., is a study of the naming of fields, meadows, and pastures. Margareta Svahn, *Finnskägg, tåtel och sia* (Skrifter utgivna av Dialekt- ortnamns- och folkminnesarkivet i Umeå, Ser. A. Dialekter, 8), diss. with English summary, deals with popular names for grasses. It includes a study of the etymology and geographical spread of the individual plant names. But another aim of the investigation is to determine the way in which popular botany systematizes the plants. The popular classification indicated by the dialect words can then be compared to the systems used in scientific botany. Mats Rydén, 'Den mångtydiga maskrosen (The multifaceted dandelion)', *Svensk botanisk tidskrift*, 84, Lund, 1990:267–77, is another study in popular botany, focusing on the different Swedish names for the dandelion in a historical perspective, i.e. the acceptance and diffusion of the standard Swedish name, as reflected in the botanical handbooks of the 19th c. *Analogi i navngivning*, ed. Gordon Albøge, Eva Villarsen Meldgaard, and Lis Weise (NORNA-rapporter, 45), 244 pp., contains papers from an onomastics symposium held in Brandbjerg in 1989. The symposium in Gilleleje, 1990, resulted in the volume *Sakrale navne*, ed. Gillian Fellows-Jensen and Bente Holmberg (NORNA-rapporter, 48), 294 pp. Bror Lindén, *Ortnamnen i Kopparbergs län. Mora kommun: bebyggelsenamn* (Skrifter utgivna genom ortnamnsarkivet i Uppsala. A. Sveriges ortnamn, 10), 131 pp., and Gösta Franzén, *Ortnamnen i Östergötlands län. Lösings härad: bebyggelsenamn* (*ib.*, 15), 90 pp., deal with settlement names.

8. Lexicography

The Swedish Academy's *Ordbok över svenska språket*, Lund, Svenska Akademien, continues with fascs 324–28, cols 12037–804, *Stod — Strutshår*. Göran Walter, *Bonniers synonymordbok*, Bonnierfakta, 372 pp., is also available on disc with the title *Svensk synonymorbok för PC*, Walters Lexikon. *Prismas främmande ord*, 3rd edn, Prisma, 1990, 550 pp., contains 25,000 entries with explanations and derivations. It is modelled on the Danish Gyldendals fremmedordbog and translated from the Danish by Sven Brüel. *Nordisk förvaltningsordbok* (Nord, 1991, 24), 423 pp., is a dictionary of terms in local and national government, published by the Nordic Council, with Swedish, Danish, Finnish, Icelandic, and Norwegian text. Natanael Beckman. *Norsksvenska ordboken*, ed. Leif Mæhle and Bengt Sigurd, 3rd rev. edn, Norstedt, 210 pp., has Norwegian entries in both *bokmål* and *nynorsk*. Vincent Petti, *English–Swedish and Swedish–English Dictionary*, Norstedt, 747 pp., has a supplementary handbook on business language and terminology. Norstedt have also published similar dictionaries, including the supplement on business terminology, for French and German.

9. Bibliography

S. Fries, D. Kornhall, B. Pamp, and C. Platzack, 'Litteraturkrönika 1989', *ANF*, 105, 1990:189–227. S. Fries, B. Pamp, and C. Platzack, 'Litteraturkrönika 1990', *ANF*, 106:175–218. *Språk i Norden*, 1990, includes 'Ny språklitteratur' (125–64), and 'Nye ordbøker og ordlister' (165–75).

LITERATURE

By PETER GRAVES, *Lecturer in Swedish in the University of Edinburgh*

1. GENERAL

The first thing to be said is that the quality of article in *Dictionary of Scandinavian Literature*, ed. Virpi Zuck, Chicago, St James Press, 1990, 792 pp., is good — the reader is given as much as can be expected in the space, along with good references and bibliographies. Nor is there any great criticism of the authors considered worthy of an entry: the coverage is fair if inevitably a little hit and miss in the contemporary period. (But why no Gustav III, Flygare-Carlén, Elsa Grave, Stig Claesson or Torgny Lindgren, to mention just five of the several dozen names I missed?) In other respects, however, the volume shows insufficient thought and planning and general articles seem to have been included or omitted according to principles I could not perceive: no entries on genre (but one on theatre), no entries on periods (but one on history of criticism), an entry on sagas (but nothing on eddic and scaldic poetry or ballads) and so on. Gunnar Hansson, *Vem gör litteraturens historia?*, Linköping University, 1990, 110 pp., argues for a historiography based on what is actually read rather than on what, for instance, a Schück thinks should be read; of recent works he finds Algulin essentially in the right direction whereas *Den svenska litteraturen* is only partly so. Johan Svedjedal, 'Skyltfönster mot bokmarknaden', *BLM*, 60.2:29–35, traces histories of Swedish literature from Atterbom's *Svenska siare* to *Författarnas litteraturhistoria*. Jan-Erik Pettersson, 'Sven Delblanc håller ihop bygget', *ib.*, 36–43, works his way through *Den svenska litteraturen* and suggests that the whole is marred by volume 6, which should be replaced by a volume more in keeping with the aims and ambitions of the earlier volumes. Britt Dahlström, 'Åter till biografin', *BLM*, 60.3:30–35, considers literary biographies as a genre and discusses a number of past and recent examples. Johan Svedjedal, 'De svenska författarna och staten. En essay i det goda litteratursamhället', *BLM*, *ib.*, 14–19, assesses the advantages and dangers brought to literature by state support. Walter Baumgartner, '"Centrallyrik" — ein obskurer Begriff im skandinavischen Diskurs über Lyrik', *Edda*:334–44, attempts, with some justified irony, to trace the origin, history, and import of this term that has been applied to poets as various as Egil Skallagrímsson and Leonard Cohen. He suggests that in current Swedish critical practice it means little more than the presence of the pronoun 'jag'. Christina Sjöblad, 'Dagboken — dokument, vän och samtalspartner. Om dagboken i det litterära systemet', *Edda*:167–75, includes Viktoria Benediktsson, Queen Hedvig Elisabeth Charlotta, Sven Lindquist, and Helena Reenstierna in her wide-ranging survey of the genre and its sub-types. *Procs* (BASS), contains many papers of Swedish interest, itemized below.

2.   FROM THE RENAISSANCE TO THE GUSTAVIAN AGE

In *SBR*, no. 1:34–46, Peter Graves discusses and compares Carl Linné and Jacob Wallenberg as travel writers and examines some of the problems of translation. Bernt Olsson, 'Folkböckerna — forna tiders trivialliteratur', *TidLit*, 20.2:39–44.

DALIN, OLOF VON.   Gunnar Bäck, 'En gammal succé', *Edda*: 56–65, studies D.'s drama *Brynilda* in an attempt to ascertain what made it so successful with contemporary audiences. He argues that the rhetorical ideals necessary to an appreciation of the play have been in disrepute during the centuries of dominance by more or less realistic drama and concludes, pointing in the direction of opera and Oriental drama, that such might not always remain the case.

3.   THE NINETEENTH CENTURY

Yvonne Leffler, *I skräckens lustgård. Skräckromantik i svenska 1800-talsromaner* (SLIGU, 21), 223 pp., is an excellent if slightly bitty study of the Gothic tradition as it affects the Swedish novel. L. begins by establishing criteria for the Gothic novel, admits that few Swedish examples of the pure form exist, and goes on to examine the influence of the Gothic and its use and adaptation by writers of serious literature. There are excellent chapters, for instance, on Rydberg's *Singoalla* and Lagerlöf's *Herr Arnes penningar*. L.'s thesis succeeds in its aims of both showing the origins and development of the Gothic in Sweden and of demonstrating the importance of the tradition but, more than that, it both informs and stimulates thought about the development of the Swedish novel in general.

HAMMARSKÖLD, LORENZO.   Tomas Sikström, 'En romantikens banerförare', *FT*:62–66, assesses H.'s contribution as author, translator, critic, and publisher.

LAGERLÖF, SELMA.   Vivi Edström, *Selma Lagerlöf*, Natur och Kultur, 187 pp., is a readable and excellent monograph that concentrates on a relatively small number of major works rather than plodding through the *opus*. E. is at pains to continue the demolition of the image of L. as being 'snäll', 'naiv' and 'en moralistisk sagotant'; she is also the first to use the 2,000 letters from L. to Sophie Elkan that became available in 1990. Although clearly intended as an introductory monograph, it is a very worthwhile addition to the literature on L.

Linda Schenk, 'Reading Selma Lagerlöf anew: reconsideration and retranslation', *Procs* (BASS), 243–51, offers a stimulating discussion of the recurrent need to retranslate older texts in the light of critical reconsideration; S. considers that L.'s *Löwensköldska ringen* is a prime example of a novel where feminist readings have opened up layers in the text that were concealed to earlier translators. Lisbeth Larsson, 'Bortom moderniteten. Det tredje kontraktet i *Gösta Berlings saga*', *OB*, no. 4:45–52.

NYBLOM, HELENA. Eva Nordlinder, *Sekelskiftets svenska konstsaga och sagodiktaren Helena Nyblom* (SSB, 41), Bonniers, 281 pp., falls into two parts. Firstly, Nordlinder defines the genre and fits it into both the literary history and sociology of literature of the turn of the century. The second section, devoted to Nyblom, is partly biography and partly analysis concentrated on three of N.'s 80 or more literary fairy-tales. The joins between the various sections are not neatly patched but, in general, the book provides both a thorough survey and convincing arguments for viewing Nyblom as a writer of tales a good deal more complex than most of the 627 stories Nordlinder has excavated.

RUNEBERG, JOHAN LUDVIG. *Konkordans över J. L. Runebergs lyrik (Dikter I–III)*, ed. Lars Huldén, Kerstin Forslund, and Helena Solstrand-Pipping (SSLF, 566), Helsinki, 1990, 239 pp., is the result of work at the Helsinki *Archiv för litterär svenska* (which also holds material on Södergran, Gunnar Björling, and Bellman). R.'s poetic vocabulary runs to some 15,500 words and we might note, for instance, that he used *hydda* 25 times compared with *hus* five times and *slott* three. The work is thorough, the organization clear, and the book simple to use.

STRINDBERG, AUGUST. Egil Törnqvist, *Transposing Drama. Studies in Representation*, Basingstoke Macmillan, 216 pp., takes *Spöksonaten* as one of his four example plays and, in addition to referring to it in passing, devotes Chapter 4 (95–138) to a detailed discussion of the problems of transposing it to the screen mass media. Hans-Göran Ekman, *Klädernas magi. En Strindbergstudie*, Gidlunds, 206 pp., is a chronologically organized survey of S.'s use of costume throughout his writings and is far more useful and thought-provoking than such a topic might seem at first sight. Carla Waal, *Harriet Bosse: Strindberg's Muse and Interpreter*, Carbondale, Southern Illinois U.P., 1990, 298 pp., traces B.'s long theatrical career emphasizing the S. roles she inspired and acted: the volume is also an excellent history of 50 years of Swedish theatre. *Strindbergiana* (Sjätte samlingen utgiven av Strindbergssällskapet), Atlantis, 175 pp., contains, along with notes on recent productions and events, the following papers: Åke Åberg (17–47), in view of S.'s own importance for the popular education

movement, assesses the young Strindberg's views on popular education, particularly on the subject of public libraries; Göran Söderström
(48–60) introduces a recently discovered scenography for *Till
Damaskus* that suggests how S. himself wished the play to be
produced; Margareta Wirmark (61–94) interprets *Carl XII* as an
early modern drama or 'pre-absurd text' in that it fulfils most of the
criteria for modern drama proposed by John Peter; Thomas Gilek
(95–112) analyses S.'s philosophical world as revealed in *En blå bok*;
Gösta Werner (113–20) suggests that the change in S.'s dramatic
writing marked by *Till Damaskus* coincides with and may even reflect
the early development of film; Freddie Rokem (121–39) views the
productions of the 1987–88 season with special emphasis on the
directors' use of the play of light and dark. Jan Myrdal, 'August
Strindberg and his Tradition in Swedish Literature', *Scandinavica*,
30:5–23, argues that it is not useful to view S. from a European
perspective: he is 'a paradigm of Swedish writing', both the product
and the renewer of a democratic literary tradition that is uniquely
Swedish. Christine Banér, 'Some observations on translating August
Strindberg's *The Father*', *Procs* (BASS), 37–54, makes useful comparisons of the Michael Meyer and John Osborne translations of the play.
Ulf Olsson, 'I textens ursprung — en läsning av Strindbergs *I
havsbandet*', *TidLit*, 20.2:65–80, argues that S.'s text has an allegoric
intention. Lutz Rühling, 'Realitätsanpassung und Sinnbewahrung.
Zur Darstellung des Modernisierungsprozesses in Strindbergs
Roman *Hemsöborna*', *Skandinavistik*, 21:100–15, suggests that the
pragmatic and uncritical view of industrialization and commerciali-
zation visible in *Hemsöborna* is unusual both for S. and for his
contemporary writers.

SÖDERBERG, HJALMAR. Bure Holmbäck, *Hjalmar Söderberg och
passionerna*, Natur och Kultur, 159 pp., aims to adjust the balance of
the standard image of S. away from 'coolness' and 'control' by
viewing his work as a whole rather than by separating off his social
and political writings and his later period of interest in the history and
philosophy of religion from his purely literary works. Viewed from
such a perspective, H. argues, the passionate 'engagemangslinje'
apparent in S.'s non-literary production can also be traced in the
literary work. As one has come to expect from H.'s many earlier books
on S., this volume is readable, knowledgeable, and convincing. Hans
Holmberg, 'Hjalmar Söderberg speglad i några brevfragment', *NT*,
67:11–14.

4. THE TWENTIETH CENTURY

Pia Lamberth, 'Som ensamma fyrar i natten?', *TidLit*, 20.3:31–42, is
a mainly quantitative investigation of women writers in the period

1900–49: her purpose is to ascertain the actual numbers — given the relatively small number of women discussed in literary histories — as well as to discover how much they wrote and which genres they favoured. L. demonstrates that the numbers are much greater than might have been suspected and suggests that there exists a great 'stream of women's writings with its own traditions and sources of inspiration'. She wonders whether established literary history has failed to integrate this women's tradition for fear of losing its own identity. In *SBR*, no. 1 : 53–58, George Schoolfield reviews in detail a number of recent translations of Finland-Swedish literature and has some perceptive points to make both about that literature and its translation. Siv Storå, 'Katalogen *Finlandssvenska böcker* läst som följetong', *FT*: 183–95, surveys the usefulness of the publication at the end of its first five years. Carl Olov Sommar, 'Vad visste Fredrik Böök om Apollinaire?', *BLM*, 60.6:60–68, wonders why literary modernism took so long to be known and accepted in Sweden. Patricia Crampton, 'Swedish children's books in English', *Procs* (BASS), 86–96, surveys the changing fashions of the last 25 years and highlights some problems of cultural adaptation. Kay Glans, 'Skräckellitteratur', *BLM*, 60.1:6–12, offers a thought-provoking essay on violence and fiction with particular reference to the works of Stig Larsson, Magnus Dahlström, and Carina Rydberg. Per Ringby, 'Värde och värderingar i metakritiken. Synpunkter på mottagandet av antologin *Samtida* i svensk dagkritik 1990', *TidLit*, 20.1:82–90. Björn Widegren, 'Ett dimmight landskap. Litteraturen i Sverige 1990', *NT*, 67:405–13.

BÄCK, TOMAS MIKAEL. Michel Ekman, 'Det drunknande jaget eller Vad menar Tomas Mikael Bäck?', *FT*: 160–67.

BERGMAN, INGMAR. 'Rewriting God's plot: Ingmar Bergman and feminine narrative', *ScSt*, 63:1–29, examines 'how the process of exorcising God on the thematic level is accompanied by an attempt to transfer discursive control from male to female'. Birgitta Steene, 'Ingmar Bergmans *Bilder* och den självbiografiska genren', *FT*:274–86, suggests that *Bilder* and *Laterna magica* may be seen as the same life narrated from different angles.

DAGERMAN, STIG. Laurie Thompson, 'Dagerman's Daily Dose', *Procs* (BASS), 275–84, assesses D. as a lyric poet and finds him wanting. His 'dagsverser', on the other hand, show him to be a master rhymester when it comes to producing apt and witty verse commentaries on the news of the moment.

DELBLANC, SVEN. Irene Scobbie, 'The Delblancs in Canada', *Procs* (BASS), 252–62, investigates the biographical background to *Kanaans land* and assesses, in particular, the impact of the tension between father and mother.

DICKSON, WALTER. Richard Estreen, 'Sagoberättaren och dadaisten', *BLM*, 60.5:46–53.

EKELÖF, GUNNAR. Reidar Ekner, 'Ekelöf Alexander', *BLM*, 60.1:24–34, views E.'s 'Alexander' poems as elements in an autobiographical search.

EKMAN, KERSTIN. In *SBR*, no. 1:11–13, Rochelle Wright discusses narration as transformative power in E.'s *Rövarna i Skuleskogen*.

ENCKELL, RABBE. Mikael Enckell, — *dess ljus lyse!*, Helsinki, Söderström, 257 pp., is the second volume of Mikael Enckell's biography of his father. It covers the years 1937 to 1950, years of great personal tension in E.'s life and, clearly, eventful years in Finland. M.E.'s approach is probing (he is, among other things, a psychoanalyst) rather than definite, and what emerges is a low-key portrait in which, one feels, the author (himself an actor in the story by this stage) has been overly careful to be fair. E.'s poetry is frequently discussed but almost invariably in order to cast light on the biography.

ENQUIST, PER OLOV. Thomas Bredsdorff, *De svarta hålen. Om tillkomsten av ett språk i P.O. Enquists författarskap*, Norstedts, 263 pp., analyses E.'s works from his debut to *Kapen Nemos bibliotek*. B. is interested solely in the texts — mainly the novels, though there is some treatment of the dramas — and excludes everything external, including the man. An early chapter of the work is devoted to Pound, Hemingway and imagism: B.'s argument is that it is, above all, the imagist method that E. has developed and refined from novel to novel and that that method reaches its Swedish culmination in E.'s writings. It is in every way a stimulating book: closely argued, lucid, and free of jargon — as an example of the systematic yet sympathetic application of a methodology it should be recommended to postgraduates whatever their topic. Crister Enander, 'Mannen på stranden', *BLM*, 60.5:24–35, argues that E.'s work is driven by the tension between two ambitions: the political — to deal with social problems, and the personal — to overcome painful memories from childhood.

ESPMARK, KJELL. Peter Krameus, 'Vägar in i ett landskap. En tematisk läsning av Kjell Espmarks senare poesi', *Samlaren*, 111, 1990 (1991):33–44.

GUILLOU, JAN. Lisbeth Larsson, 'Det svenska 80-talets Manlige Agent', *TidLit*, 20.2:28–37, studies the recipe that has made G.'s books the bestsellers of the late 1980s.

GYLLENSTEN, LARS. Gavin Orton, 'St Antony in Värmland: Lars Gyllensten's *Grottan i öknen*', *Scandinavica*, 30:41–62, suggests that the problem of how to act with commitment in a world without obvious meaning lies at the heart of G.'s works. In *Grottan i öknen* the mystic's aim is to achieve a level of self-denial that will prevent the ego from

Literature 935

excluding 'that which is not egoistic if it should bother to reveal itself'. St Antony in his asceticism achieves this and is rewarded with visions. In the reconstructed life of Johannes Elfberg in modern Värmland, however, G. offers us a much less certain Antony, in a 'more modern tradition, a hero of our unheroic time'. Johan Frostegård, 'Gud bevare oss för Ordets paradis. Gyllenstens experiment', *BLM*, 60.4:8–13.

HERNE, TORD. Erik Andersson, 'En prosakonstnär. En introduktion till Tord Herne och *Janus kallad*', *OB*, no. 4:19–26.

HERTZMAN-ERICSON, GURLI. Britt Dahlström, 'Gurli', *BLM*, 60.5:13–16, reintroduces H.-E.'s now forgotten writings.

HÖIJER, BJÖRN-ERIK. Christer Eriksson, 'Tack och lov för Höijer', *BLM*, 60.3:20–24, offers a reassessment of H. and suggests he has been unjustly put to the side.

JANSSON, TOVE. Suvi Ahola, 'Towards the empty page', *Books from Finland*, 25:131–37, examines the psychoses, sexual ambiguity and concern for personal freedom central to J.'s *Mumin* books.

JOHNSON, EYVIND. Bo G. Jansson, *Självironi, självbespegling och självreflexion: den metafiktiva tendensen i Eyvind Johnsons diktning* (SLIUU), 1990, 208 pp.

LAGERKVIST, PÄR. Ulf Lagerkvist, *Den bortvändes ansikte. En minnesbok*, Brombergs, 192 pp., is a memoir of his father. *Pär Lagerkvist. Brev i urval*, ed. Ingrid Schöier, Bonniers, 224 pp. Henning Howlid Waerp, 'Kubisme og litteratur. Om Pär Lagerkvists kunstmanifest *Ordkonst och bildkonst* fra 1913', *NLÅ*:93–111, aims to place L.'s programme in the aesthetic tradition of cubism, to assess how far cubism can be transferred to literature, and to examine whether cubist principles are visible in L.'s literary works. Sven Linnér, 'Pär Lagerkvist, Småland och evigheten', *FT*:316–23, suggests that L.'s Småland och evigheten', *FT*:316–23, suggests that L.'s Småland should be seen as 'en poetisk provins, och denna provins hör hemma i en litterär tradition'. Örjan Lindberger, 'Kring 100-årsminnet av Pär Lagerkvists födelse', *NT*, 67:328–29, discusses a number of recent books on L.

LO-JOHANSSON, IVAR. *SBR*, Supplement, is a special number devoted to L.-J. It contains the usual range of translations and information as well as a number of articles: Rochelle Wright (5–10) offers personal memories of L.-J. that are a good deal more penetrating and thought-provoking about the man and the works than the usual run of memoir; Philippe Bouquet (10–15) discusses L.-J.'s position as a working-class writer, as well as discussing the essence and uniqueness of Swedish proletarian literature; Rochelle Wright (15–20) examines L.-J.'s repeated reworking of autobiographical material at different stages of his life; Peter Graves (20–25) considers L.-J.'s contributions to the short story during the 1930s and again during the 1970s; W. E. Ottecrans (25–27) discusses the nature of L.-J.'s theory of realism as expounded in his last book of essays *Till en författare*. Peter Graves, 'Ivar Lo-Johansson and proletarian writing in Sweden', *Planet*, 85:35–46, discusses L.-J. in the context of the history of working-class writing.

MARTINSON, HARRY. Brita Green, 'Harry Martinson and other Modernists. A comparison of linguistic innovations', *Procs* (BASS), 118–31, tests statistically the subjective statements concerning M.'s innovative noun compounds and finds that the figures support the suppositions. The statistics also support the view that the Finland-Swedish Modernists — particularly Diktonius — were an important formative source of M.'s linguistic fertility.

NYMAN, VALDEMAR. J. O. Tallqvist, 'Valdemar Nyman, Ålands apostel', *Bokvännen*, 46:93–97, introduces N.'s writing, particularly his historical novels, and speculates that N.'s omission from many modern literary handbooks has to do with the difficulty of fitting in a Christian author.

NORÉN, LARS. Gunilla Anderman, 'The drama of the closed room: Some observations on Lars Norén's plays', *Procs* (BASS), 24–36.

RYDSTEDT, ANNA. Bengt Höglund, 'Har jag ett ansikte?', *BLM*, 60.4:18–28, seeks beyond the label 'naivism' that is usually attached to R.

THOURSIE, RAGNAR. Ragnar Thoursie, 'Fyrtiotalisten som kom tillbaka', *Kungälv 1990 Konferencerapport*, Kungälv, Nordiska språk- och informationscentret Nordspråk, 118 pp., introduces his work in general and his come-back volume *Kråkorna skrattar* in particular.

TRANSTRÖMER, TOMAS. Torsten Rönnerstrand, '"Sanningen finns på marken." Om Tomas Tranströmers "Air Mail" och 80-talets språkdebatt', *TidLit*, 20.3:43–57.

WÄGNER, ELIN. Helena Forsås-Scott, 'Swedish "literature of preparedness" and feminist pacifism: the example of Elin Wägner', *Procs* (BASS), 97–111, offers close analyses of W.'s *Mannen vid min sida* and *Vändkorset* in order to make important distinctions between feminist pacifist texts of the 1930s and the largely male-produced 'literature of preparedness'. The feminist texts take a firm stance against Hitler and fascism but they also point to the connections between fascism and the prevailing patriarchy. The feminist texts thus call for a complete transformation of values rather than a mere defence of general democratic ideals. It is a very stimulating paper and a useful contribution to the more nuanced picture of the inter-war period being produced by feminist critics.

WIK, INGA-BRITT. Birgitta Steene, 'Man måste leva nära orden. En studie i Inga-Britt Wiks författarskap', *FT*:168–82.

5

SLAVONIC LANGUAGES*

I. CZECH STUDIES

LANGUAGE

POSTPONED

LITERATURE†

By K. BRUŠÁK, *Visiting Lecturer in Czech and Slovak at the University of Cambridge*

(This survey covers the years 1989, 1990 and 1991)

1. GENERAL

The works registered in the present survey belong, with a few exceptions, to a period of transition that began in the middle of the 1980s and came into full swing after 1989. L. Doležel, 'Strukturální tematologie a sémantika možných světů. Případ Dvojníka', *ČL*: 1–11, observing the situation from abroad, states: 'The liquidation of the totalitarian regime in Czechoslovakia created the conditions for a revival of theoretical thinking generally and consequently for the revival of Czech literary theory. [. . .] The question is, which way should it go?'. After recommending giving attention to the results of the Prague School of the thirties and applying them to versology and thematology, D. distinguishes two methodologically different modes of thematics, the traditional selective *Stoffengeschichte* and the structural thematology, and tests the latter on the traditional theme of the double. He distinguishes three types: a character with a definite identity existing in two or several fictitious worlds, whom he calls Orlando; two different characters with identical physical features existing in one fictitious world, whom he calls Amphitryon; one single character existing in one single fictitious world, the double in the proper sense. The interest in structuralism, recommended by Doležel, is pursued by several authors. Its main concepts such as aesthetic function, sign, semantic gesture, foregrounding, and

* For languages using the Cyrillic alphabet names are transliterated according to the Library of Congress system, omitting diacritics and ligatures.

† The place of publication of books is Prague unless otherwise indicated.

automatization are recapitulated in H. Schmidová, '"Třífázový model" českého literárněvědného strukturalismu', *ČL*: 193–219, and M. Červenka, 'Základní kategorie pražského literárněvědného strukturalismu', *SLit*, 1990: 305–26, while M. Petříček, 'Francouzský poststrukturalismus a tradice českého strukturalismu', *ČL*: 385–91, points out that some elements in Derrida's deconstruction have been anticipated in Mukařovský's dynamic conception of structure, and M. Grygar, '"Tupý smysl" a "nezáměrnost". Poznámky k semiotice R. Barthesa a J. Mukařovského', Grygar, *Czech Studies*, 173–202, discusses the coincidences and differences in the concept of the artistic sign of Mukařovský and Barthes. The concept of 'semantic gesture' is analysed and supported by V. Svatoň, 'Vztah pojmu struktura a sémantické gesto v historické poetice', *Slav*, 1990: 28–34, and Id., 'O struktuře a sémantickém gestu', *SLit*, 1990: 276–82, while in W. F. Schwarz, 'Mukařovského "sémantické gesto" — chiméra alebo prakticky využitelný pojem? K problematike vývinu a operacionalizácie jednej literárnosemiotickej koncepcie', *ib.*, 1989: 459–72, it is criticized as a 'terminological metaphor' which should be replaced by some other terms denoting the process by which the author expresses reality. M. Červenka and M. Jankovič, 'Dva příspěvky k předmětu individuální stylistiky v literatuře', *ČL*, 1990: 212–34, deals with Mukařovský's conception of individual style and aesthetic function. M. Jankovič, *Nesamozřejmost smyslu*, ČSp, 223 pp., analyses *Švejk* and some Hrabal texts on the principle of the semantic gesture. M. Červenka, 'Mukařovského "fónická linie" a rozbor veršové intonace', *ČL*: 242–68, summarizes M.'s contribution to versology and Id., *Styl a význam*, ČSp, 280 pp., is a structuralist study of the verse of Březina, Bezruč, Gellner, Hora, and J. Kolář. D. Hodrová, *Hledání románu*, ČSp, 1989, 280 pp., provides an important contribution to the study of the novel, which it considers as a genre transgressing all the genres, distancing itself from its past and from itself, and the changes in which are not dependent on changes in society but primarily on its own dynamism. 'Text jako místo s tajemstvím', *ČL*: 14–27, by the same author, discusses the text as a motif of the novel and deals with the magic potentiality of the text to influence reality. Jiří Pechar, *Od příběhu k románu: K poetice výpravné prózy*, ČSp, 1989, 114 pp., follows the narrative transformations leading to the emergence of the novel form, while J. Nejedlá, *Balada v proměně doby*, ČSp, 1989, 250 pp., traces the history of the ballad. P. Jiráček, 'Fonologická expresivita českého básnického jazyka', *ČL*: 289–312, gives the result of a psychosemantic experiment with ten groups of 40 people, seeking to assess the symbolism of individual Czech phonemes. Jan Czech, *Filozofie dramatu*, Scéna, 80 pp., maintains that drama provides a unique opportunity to teach knowledge which cannot be acquired by a theoretical approach: it constitutes the truth, prerequisite to understanding. This truth has to embrace the spiritual structure of the world and, in particular, the meaning of the relationship between Man and the world, the mutual relationship between human beings, the meaning of history, the freedom and value of human life and its aim.

2. EARLIER LITERATURE UP TO THE NATIONAL REVIVAL

J. Vlášek, 'Staroslověnský *Život Metodějův* jako dílo velkomoravské literární školy', *Slav*: 300–07, supports the view that the work was composed in Moravia *c.* 885. J. Vintr, 'Styl dvou vrcholných děl nejstarší české duchovní lyriky — *Ostrovské písně* a *Kunhutiny modlitby*', *ČL*: 313–28, is a careful analysis supporting the hypothesis that the author of the *Kunhutina modlitba* was Canon Beneš, the librarian at the St George convent. M. Šváb, 'Besermené a ti druzí v české *Alexandreidě*', *LFil*, 1990: 146–50, infers on the evidence of the use of the Latin form Bezzermini in chronicles and diplomatic documents in Bohemia between 1260–79 that the work was written at the end of the 13th c. Radko Šťastný, *Tajemství jména Dalimil*, Melantrich, 349 pp., summarizes all the theories concerning the chronicle and its presumed author and ventures a hypothesis that the work was composed by Peter I of Rosenberg (1282–1347) who spent his youth and old age in Vyšší Brod (Hohenfurth) monastery, was the Chancellor of Bohemia and later in the service of John of Luxembourg. Id., 'Dalimilovy ideje v husitství', *ČL*, 1989: 385–89, examines the impact of the chronicle on Hussitism. A. Thomas, 'Czech-German relations as reflected in Old Czech literature', pp. 199–215 of *Medieval Frontier Societies*, ed. R. Bartlett and Angus MacKay, Oxford, Clarendon Press, 1989, is useful for its enumeration of instances of anti-German animosity in Czech literary works from the early 13th to the beginning of the 14th c., but its exposition of the political and economic situation is oversimplified and its conclusion that 'hostility towards the Germans constituted an important part of a more extensive political-religious upheaval culminating in the Hussite wars' cannot be substantiated. J. Tříska, *Předhusitské bajky*, Vyšehrad, 1990, 232 pp., provides a historical and literary interpretation of the genre and its authors and propounds that the *Quadripartitus* was composed by Řehoř z Uherského Brodu (Gregorius de Hungaricali Broda). T. also maintains that the name Smil Flaška, used to denote the author of *Nová rada*, is a literary fiction, a sobriquet denoting 'an immoral drunkard', and has no connection with the historical Smil Flaška of Pardubice. Jan Lehár, *Česká středověká lyrika*, Vyšehrad, 1990, 408 pp., presents the most comprehensive collection of Czech medieval lyrics and summarizes all research on the subject to date. L. offers several original suggestions, in particular on the Czech lyrics with courtly love elements, the source of which he sees in the late German *minnesang* of the 14th and 15th cs. F. Šmahel, 'Stärker als der Glaube. Magie, Aberglaube und Zauber in der Epoche des Hussitismus', *Bohemia*, 32. 2:316–37, which traces these features in the Czech literature of the 14th and beginning of the 15th c., includes an excellent bibliography of the subject. P. Voit, 'K českému básnictví předbělohorské doby — *Život a putování sv. Kryštofa*', *ČL*, 1990:419–24, proves that this composition by Tobiáš Mouřenín dating from 1601 is an adaptation of the work of Nicodemus Frischlin (1547–90). J. Fiala, 'Barokní balady a morytáty', *ČL*, 1990:295–305, discusses the broadsides describing criminal acts; A. Fechtnerová and L. Sochorová, 'Česká hra o kněžně Ludmile na Mělníce roku 1722', *ib.*, 1989:457–67, presents considerable information on J. J. Dukát, the little-known author of the play based on Hájek's chronicle. P. Čornej, 'Poznámky k vydávání starších česky psaných listů', *ib.*, 1–15, proposes a new classification for editing Czech documents of the 14th to 16th cs, dividing them into (a) manifestos and public letters, (b) credentials, mandates and safe-conducts, (c) diplomatic notes.

INDIVIDUAL AUTHORS

HUS.   P. Freitinger, 'K otázce Husova překladu bible', *Časopis Národního Musea. Řada historická*, 158.3–4, 1989:136–56, compares the texts of the Wolfenbüttel and Moscow Bibles with quotations from H.'s *Postile* and concludes that he was the author of the third translation of the Bible. J. Boubín and E. Fialová, 'K otázce autorství údajně Husova traktátu *De Peccato Originali*', *Český časopis historický*, no. 2:239–45.

KOMENSKÝ.   F. Všetečka, 'Komposice Komenského písně *Ó ve všech svých divný nám skutcích, Bože*', *LFil*, 1990:200–03. M. Kopecký, 'John Amos Comenius as a theoretician of literature', *ACo*, no. 9:99–111, bases his study on K.'s views expressed in his *Zpráva o naučení o kazatelství* and *O poezi české*.

LOMNICKÝ ŠIMON.   Petr Voit, *Šimon Lomnický z Budče a exempla v kontextu jeho mravněvýchovné prózy*, AUCP, Philosophica et Historica, Monographia cxxvii, 148 pp.

3.   FROM THE NATIONAL REVIVAL TO THE END OF THE NINETEENTH CENTURY

The works in this section are mostly devoted to individual authors. Amongst the few exceptions are J. Střítecký, 'Die tschechische nationale Wiedergeburt: Mythen und Denkanstösse', *Bohemia*, 31.1,

1990:38–54, which takes a broader look at the Revival. Questions of style and metre are discussed in L. Merhaut, '"Tvůrčí" stylizace jako jeden z případů stylizace v literárním díle', *ČL*:403–23, which examines the characteristic features of paraliterary confections produced and published around the 1890s (mostly at their own expense) by eccentrics with philosophical or poetical ambitions, such as J. Hron, S. Mráz, and A. Racek, and in M. Červenka, 'Polymetrie v české epice 19. století' *WSJ*, 1988:7–43 and *ib.*, 1989:7–47.

INDIVIDUAL AUTHORS

BŘEZINA. J. Med, 'K interpretaci symbolismu u O.B.', *Slav*, 1989:79–81.

DOBROVSKÝ. G. Ziegengeist, 'Neue Zeugnisse über J.D. und die deutsch-tschechischen Wissenschaftsbeziehungen', *ZSl*, 1990:3–34.

ERBEN. F. Vodička, 'K vývojovému postavení Erbenova díla v české literatuře', *ČL*, 1990:385–404.

HOSTINSKÝ. R. Kalivoda, 'O Otakaru Hostinském, estetické teorii a estetickém programu', *ČL*, 1990:194–234.

F. KAVÁN. F.K., *Přesýpání nálad. Básně z konce století*, ed. J. Kudrnáč, Jindřichův Hradec, Kruh, 1989, 213 pp., is a first edition in book form of poems and essays by this well-known painter (1886–1941).

KOLLÁR S. Nagayo, 'Japonské motívy v poéme *Slávy dcera* Jána Kollára', *SL*, 1989:264–72.

V. M. KRAMERIUS. O. Hausenblas, 'Interpretace druhořadosti literárního díla', *ČL*, 1989:441–46.

MÁCHA. A. Thomas, 'Ztracený lidstva Ráj. Language and loss in Mácha's *Máj*', *Bohemia*, 30.1, 1989:71–83, is a psychoanalytical study à la Lacan, based on an unsubstantiated claim that the central theme of the poem is the Oedipus complex. R. B. Pynsent, 'Characterization in Mácha's *Máj*', Grygar, *Czech Studies*, 229–64, maintains that 'most characters in *Máj* are simply vehicles for M.'s irony'. M. Červenka, 'Polymetrie Máje', *ČL*, 1989:413–30. O. Králík, 'K strukturalistické interpretaci Máchy', *ČL*:269–76, presents a criticism of Mukařovský's interpretation of the poem; it is opposed by M. Jankovič, 'Strukturalismus a interpretace', *ib.*, 277–85.

MASARYK. L. Nový, 'Literatura v Masarykově myšlení', *ČL*, 1990:405–18.

MAYER. V. Křivánek, 'Mayerův "dech noci"', *ČL*, 1989:289–300.

NĚMCOVÁ. H. Sobková, 'Nová fakta o školní docházce Boženy Němcové', *ČL*, 1989:81–88, tries to prove that N. was born in 1817 and that she was not the daughter of Terezie and Jan Pankl.

NERUDA. E. Hermanová, '"Kletba žurnalismu" v *Povídkách malostranských'*, *ČL*, 1989:16–32. M. Otruba, 'Nerudova povídka *U tří lilií'*, *ČL*:87–131, discusses the impact of other than aesthetic values on the reception of a literary work. F. Všetička, 'Kompozice Nerudova fejetonu', *WSJ*, 1990:151–59.

SCHAUER. D. Dvořáková, 'H.G.S. a jeho koncepce národní literatury', *ČL*, 1989:496–514.

VRCHLICKÝ. J. Janáčková, 'Z geneze *Meče Damoklova'*, *ČL*, 1990:235–43.

ZEYER. Z. Hrbata, '*Karolínská epopeja* jako Zeyerovo gesto', *ČL*, 1990:494–505.

4. THE TWENTIETH CENTURY UP TO 1945

One of the main questions preoccupying Czech critics looking for a new orientation in the changed climate is the examination and re-evaluation of the past including former contacts with the West. Contacts with France were the subject of two conferences held by Collegium Carolinum at Bad Wiessee from 28–30 November 1986 and 20–22 November 1987, the proceedings of which are published in *Frankreich und die böhmischen Länder im 19. und 20. Jahrhundert*, ed. F. Seibt and M. Neumüller, Munich, Oldebourg, 1990, 312 pp. The French influence in the field of culture is discussed by several authors: F. Seibt, 'Frankreich und die böhmischen Länder. Zur Einführung' (8–13), pays special attention in a concise summary to contacts in the 14th and 15th cs, while J. Janoušek, 'Die Rezeption französischer Kunst und Kultur bei den Tschechen im 19. und 20. Jahrhundert. Reales Vorbild oder Illusion?' (15–38), gives a comprehensive and well documented survey of the French contribution to the formation of Czech thought, literature and arts from the period of the Revival to that of the 1930s; whilst recognizing the seminal role of France in helping the Czechs to overcome their isolation and provincialism and discover their own identity by combining French inspiration with the native tradition, he is not blind to the less beneficial effects of francophilia. The impact of French avant-garde movements on Czech writers and artists in the inter-war years is examined in detail by H. Voisine-Jechová, 'Interpretation und Spuren des französischen Kubismus in der tschechischen Kritik und Dichtung' (77–90), and the influence of new trends in the French theatre on Czech dramatists by J. Hoensch, 'Der französische Einfluß auf die Entwicklung des modernen tschechischen Theaters' (67–75). M. Blahynka, 'Surrealismus', *ČL*, 1989:235–46, whilst still maintaining the former timidly defensive manner, points out that Surrealism, although an exclusive episode producing no important poet apart from Nezval, had a great influence on poetic imagination. A critical approach to former relations between Western and Czech literatures is taken by V. Kudělka, 'Česká meziválečná literatura ve světovém kontextu', *ib.*, 1990:41–52, who argues that these relations were out of tune with the political and cultural situation in Bohemia: 'to the slightest sneeze in the West we reacted with a zealous anxiety not to be left behind and not to be thought out of date'. The historical novel is analysed by B. Dokoupil, 'Prostředky místní lokalizace a kategorie prostředí v českém historickém románě 20. století', *ib.*, 1989:147–55, dealing with, amongst others, the works of Vančura, Fábera, and Kratochvíl, while K. Hausenblas, 'Zur Norm des Reims in der tschechischen Poesie', *ZSl*, 1989:850–54, and F. Valouch, 'Česká poezie v době Mnichova', *ČL*, 1989:206–26, discuss the poetry of Nezval, Biebl, Seifert, Halas, Holan, and Orten. Pavel Janoušek, *Rozměry dramatu*, Panorama, 1989, 308 pp., which analyses drama as a specific literary form with regard to its authorial subject and changes in its poetics, traces its development in Bohemia from the drama of social conflict and attempts at tragedy to the collective drama, and includes an invaluable chronological survey of plays written and produced between 1918 and 1939.

INDIVIDUAL AUTHORS

BEZRUČ. Z. Pešat, 'Poetika *Slezských písní*', *ČL*:495–511.

ČAPEK. S. V. Nikolskij, 'Man, pseudo-man and anti-man in the writings of K.Č.', *PhP*, 72, 1990:123–26. J. Paštčka, 'La vision grotesque et tragique dans le théâtre de Č.', *ib.*, 148–54. H. Janaszek-Ivaničková, 'K.Č. and post-modernism', *ib.*, 137–40. R. B. Pynsent, 'K.Č.'s nostalgia and women', *ib.*, 134–37, affirms that 'the attitude to women in Č.'s works is puerile and any serious consideration of love is glibly avoided'. V. Heftrich, 'K.Č.'s Auseinandersetzung mit Henri Bergson', *ZSP*, 1990:354–87, deals with *Povětroň*. J. Klein, 'K.Č. als Reiseschriftsteller', *ib.*, 1988:372–92. M. Heinemann, 'Sprachkomik bei K.Č.', *ZSl*, 1990:72–75. I. Seehase, 'K.Č.'s Umgang mit Huxleys *Brave New World*', *ib.*, 56–65. Z. Kožmín, 'Čapkova transpozice motivů', *ČL*:512–25. P. Steiner, 'Opomíjená sbírka: Čapkova kniha apokryfů jako alegorie', *ib.*, 1990:306–20. P. Janoušek, 'Mezi problémovým dramatem a groteskou', *ib.*, 1989:193–205. M. Podhorský, 'K.Č. novinář, 1926–1931', *ib.*, 227–34. J. Magnuszewski, 'O Karolu Čapku — rozważania jubileuszowe', *PrzH*, 1990, no. 12:1–10.

DURYCH. E. Strohsová, 'J.D. (Pokus o portrét)', *ČL*:132–44.

HAŠEK. J. Chalupecký, 'Podivný Hašek', *ČL*:28–40, brings to our attention some hitherto neglected facts about H., such as his ambition to produce 'real literature' when writing *Švejk*, and his homosexuality.

J. HAVLÍČEK. F. Všetička, 'Románová iniciativa Jaroslava Havlíčka', *ČL*: 61–66.

HOLAN. I. Hroudová, 'Mlčení a jeho reflexe v poezii Vladimíra Holana', *ČL*: 55–60.

HOSTOVSKÝ. V. Vaněk, 'Vedlejší postavy v románech Egona Hostovského', *ČL*: 526–38.

LANGER. 'Jak jsem psal *Bronzovou rapsodii*', *ČL*: 178–82.

NEZVAL. I. V. Inov, 'Žánrová specifičnost prózy V. Nezvala', *ČL*, 1989: 301–14.

NOVÁK. J. Štěpánková, 'Literárněhistorické dílo mladého Arne Nováka', *ČL*, 1989: 481–95.

REYNEK. J. Hradec, 'Blázen jsem ve své vsi', *Proglas*, Brno, no. 1: 58–72.

TOMAN. P. Blažíček, 'Karel Toman a antika', *ČL*, 1990: 245–53.

5. THE TWENTIETH CENTURY SINCE 1945

Although primarily intended as a textbook for grammar schools, Aleš Haman, *Česká literatura po roce 1945 z ptačí perspektivy*, Fortuna, 1990, 109 pp., is the first serious attempt at a judicious and unbiased presentation of Czech literature which 'during the past 45 years has been interpreted by the ruling ideology as the way to Socialist Realism, i.e. as an instrument for the defence of the existing and historically the only possible social system, i.e. the political regime of one party' (p. 9). It replaces the former monological concept of literature by a pluralist and dialogical concept, recognizes the indivisibility of literature and provides an invaluable survey of the most important Czech works produced since 1945, whether published in the country or abroad or unpublished formerly for political reasons. Other important surveys are M. Jungmann, 'Česká próza v normalizační tísni', *ČL*: 145–58, P. Janoušek, 'Súčasná česká próza z pohľadu pešiaka', *SlPoh*, 1989, no. 3: 57–67, and Květoslav Chvatík, *Pohledy na českou literaturu z ptačí perspektivy*, Pražské imaginace, vol. 176, 176 pp., which also contains an informative interview on Czech structuralism, Vladimír Pistorius, *Stárnoucí literatura (Česká literatura 1969–1989)*, StPN, 111 pp., is a sharply critical assessment of the last two decades. P. maintains that authors attempted to cover paucity of thought by exploiting linguistic devices and introducing exaggerated psychological details. Both the authors and their ideas are superannuated; out of 108 of the most important writers 34 have remained in exile, 31 have died and only seven are under 40 years old. J. Čulík, 'Česká a slovenská literatúra v zahraničí', *Romboid*, 25.2, 1990: 91–102, surveys works published abroad either because they could not appear at home or were written in exile, but it is weak on

Slovak literature. An excursion into thematology along conventional lines is provided by R. B. Pynsent, 'Chápanie viny v súčasnej českej a slovenskej literatúre', *Romboid*, 24.10, 1989:87–96. Starting from the assumption that 'the main theme of literature is love and after love guilt', P. presents a great number of *explications de texte* on the strength of three arbitrary categories of guilt and concludes that by using the device of guilt authors avoid the solution of the problem of good and evil.

INDIVIDUAL AUTHORS

L. FUKS. L. Merhaut, 'Nelchká cesta za poznáním zla', *ČL*, 1989:398–412, discusses *Myši Natálie Mooshabrové*.

GRUŠA. R. Huff, 'Bassompierre pays another visit: an episode from Jiří Gruša's *Questionnaire* and its indebtedness to Goethe and Hofmannsthal', *GSl*, 1990, no. 5:285–98.

HAVEL. J. Holý, 'V.H.: *Zahradní slavnost, ČL*:167–71.

HRABAL. I. Štorcová, 'K problematice jednoho Hrabalova textu', *SaS*, 1989:278–87, on *Taneční hodiny pro starší a pokročilé*. I. Bock, 'Bohumil Hrabals Frühwerk und seine Metamorphosen in den offiziellen Ausgaben der 1960er Jahre', *ZSP*, 1989:97–115.

J. KOSTRHUN. L. Machala, 'Dvě svatby a jedna láska Jana Kostrhuna', *Romboid*, 26.9:29–37.

KUNDERA. M. Němcová-Banerjee, *Terminal Paradox. The Novels of M.K.*, London, Faber and Faber, 294 pp.

LUSTIG. M. Mravcová, 'A.L.: *Démanty noci*', *ČL*:159–66.

O. MIKULÁŠEK. J. Trávníček, 'Moravská inspirace v poezii Oldřicha Mikuláška a Jana Skácela', *ČL*, 1990:337–46. J. Opelík, 'Zaumné verše v poezii O.M.', *ib.*, 321–36.

PETERKA. I. Seehase, 'Josef Peterkas philosophisches Poem *Autobiografie vlka / Autobiografie člověka*', *ZSl*, 1989:833–40.

SKÁCEL. See O. MIKULÁŠEK.

ŠKVORECKÝ. K. Chvatík, 'Velký vypravěč J.Š.', *ČL*:41–53.

ŠOTOLA. J. Hoffmanová, 'Komunikační konflikt a dramatický text', *SaS*:264–72, analyses *Cesta Karla IV. do Francie a zpět*.

L. VACULÍK. V. Karfík, 'Deník jako román', *ČL*:255–65, discusses *Český snář*.

J. WEIL. E. Štědronová, 'Dialektika umělecké metody a reality v díle Jiřího Weila', *ČL*, 1990:126–40.

Z. ZAPLETAL. M. Nekula, 'Typizace v Zapletalových *Půlnočních běžcích*', *SaS*:285–90.

II. SLOVAK STUDIES

LANGUAGE

By JAMES NAUGHTON, *Lecturer in Czech and Slovak, Taylor Institution, University of Oxford*

1. BIBLIOGRAPHIES

Marie Nováková, Zlata Lešková, *Bibliografie české lingvistiky*, volume for 1988, Prague, ČSAV, Ústav pro jazyk český, 1990, 281 pp., contains items on Slovak, pp. 86–88. L. Dvonč has compiled some personal bibliographies: in *SR*, 56: for Jozef Mistrík, covering 1980–89 (37–50), Ján Žigo, covering 1936–46 (51–52), Ján Holly, covering 1941–90 (180–86), and František Ruščák, covering 1970–90 (330–33); in *SlSl*, 26: for Dezider Kollár, covering 1954–89 (69–74), Štefan Švagrovský, covering 1957–89 (76–82), and Pavol Sima, covering 1957–89 (83–88). *WSlA*, 25–26, 1990:13–30, contains a list of the publications of Ľubomír Ďurovič, including a couple of current items not yet in print.

2. HISTORY OF THE LANGUAGE

A very important arrival on the scene, both for the history of the language in general and its lexicology in particular, is the long-awaited historical dictionary of Slovak, *Historický slovník slovenského jazyka*, vol. 1 (A–J), ed. M. Majtán *et al.*, Bratislava, Veda, 536 pp. M. Greenberg, *Obdobja* (Ljubljana, Univerza Eduarda Kardelja, Filozofska fakulteta), 10, 1989:215–28, discusses 'Jer vocalization in Slovene, Serbo-Croatian and Slovak'. H. Birnbaum, *WSlA*, 25–26, 1990:89–99, presents 'More on the place of Slovak among the Slavic languages'. V. Blanár, *ib.*, 101–09, discusses the conditions and preconditions for the development of Literary Slovak. G. Shevelov, *ib.*, 411–19, considers the origin of Slovak *(i)hneď* 'at once' (and its Czech equivalent). K. Lifanov, *SR*, 56:160–69, analyses the Slovakized Czech of Peter Benický's *Verše slovenské* of 1652, focusing on competing morphological and phonological units, and also, *SlSl*, 26:51–61, the same aspects of František Buľovský's MS translation from the 1660s of J. A. Comenius's *Janua linguae latinae*. E. Jóna, *KS*, 25:109–12, presents a study of Daniel Krman's *Rudimenta grammaticae Slavicae* of 1704 (basically a Czech grammar). G. Sabo, *WSlA*, 25–26, 1990:379–96, looks at 'Lenten sermons by Slovak Franciscans of the eighteenth century'. L. Smirnov, pp. 221–28 of *Studia Slavica: языкознание, литературоведение, история, история науки. К 80-летию Самуила Борисовича Бернштейна*, ed. R. V. Bulatova *et al.*, Mw, AN, Inst. slavianovedeniia i balkanistiki, 372 pp., is a study of Štúr's conception of Literary Slovak. E. Jóna, *SR*, 56:65–78, examines Štúr's grammar. F. Gregor, *ib.*, 3–14, provides an interesting study of the second edition, 1863, of Štefan Jančovič's two-volume Slovak-Hungarian and Hungarian-Slovak dictionary (first edition, 1848); he discusses a number of Hungarian lexical parallels, e.g. *rušeň* 'locomotive' (Hungarian *mozdony*), as well as some Hungarian-inspired compounds, e.g. *sviňorilosť* (Hungarian *disznótúrás*), *síkorkochlopka (czinkefogó)*, *mrazoboťka (fagypont)*. K. Palkovič, *ib.*, 53–55, also examines this first lexicographer of Štúr's Slovak. J. Horecký, *KS*, 25:42–45, looks at the poet Ján Smrek's views on Slovak, and also, *SAS*, 19, 1990:139–50, at language policy from 1948 to 1988.

3. LEXICOLOGY

Some small-scale word studies include J. Pavlovič, *KS*, 25:88–90, on the religious terms *ruženec* and *pátričky*, and also, *ib.*, 180–81, biblical senses of the term *poznať* 'to know'. I. Masár, *ib.*, 127–28, attempts to distinguish the overlapping terms *veterinárny* and *veterinársky*. J. Dolník, *SAS*, 19, 1990:47–70, discusses polysemantic words in Slovak, material related to his book **Lexikálna sémantika*, Bratislava, Univerzita Komenského, 1991, 304 pp. A. Habovštiak, *Slavia*, 60:145–53, examines some features of Slovak and East Slav vocabulary (see also section 11 below).

TERMINOLOGY. K. Hegerová, *KS*, 25:46–52, looks at some terms from the field of cosmetics. I. Masár, *ib.*, 76–81, provides some discussion of religious terminology in the form of correspondence received in 1968–69 from Stanislav Polčin in Rome, translator into Slovak of documents from the Second Vatican Council. J. Kačala, *ib.*, 85–86, discusses the legal senses for the purposes of language law of the terms *úradný* and *verejný* ('official' and 'public'). A. Petrovský, *ib.*, 148–75, provides a list of terminology relating to the law of the sea. J. Nižnanský, *SR*, 56:79–87, discusses beekeeping terminology in the writings of Juraj Fándly (1750–1811). J. Horecký, *WSlA*, 25–26, 1990:201–04, examines 'terminologization' and 'determinologization' in Slovak. Also noted, Ivan Masár, **Príručka slovenskej terminologie*, Bratislava, Veda, 240 pp.

PHRASEOLOGY. J. Mlacek, *KS*, 25:14–21, studies phrasemes containing ordinal numerals; also, *SAS*, 19, 1990:223–39, journalistic phraseology in Slovak.

4. ONOMASTICS

V. Blanár, in *Reader zur Namenkunde. I. Namentheorie (GermL*, 98–100), ed. Friedrich Debus and Wilfried Seibicke, Hildesheim, Olms, 1989,

450 pp., examines 'Der linguistische und onomastische Status des Eigennamens'. V. Uhlár, *SR*, 56:14–19, looks at work on onomastic evidence concerning the ethnogenesis of the Slavs and Slavonic speech from P. J. Šafárik up to O. N. Trubachov. Amongst a number of studies of individual names, B. Varsik, *ib.*, 106–09, examines the origin of the place name *Prestavlky*. V. Uhlár, *ib.*, 147–60, studies the settlement of Liptov county and local names ending in -*any* and -*ovany*. Š. Ondruš, *ib.*, 229–32, returns to the question of the origin of the river name *Poprad*. K. Palkovič, *ib.*, 238–39, discusses the origin of the place name *Plavecký hrad*. I. Kutlík-Garudo, *ib.*, 222–29, in the context of increased public discussion of the Romany Gypsies, discusses their term for themselves, and pronounces in favour of a short vowel *o* in the Slovak term *Rom*, sometimes given as *Róm*. R. Ondrejková, *ib.*, 323–27, discusses the Slovak ethnic term *Cigáň* 'Gypsy', its origin, meaning, and derivatives. K. Habovštiaková, *SAS*, 19, 1990:113–26, examines the subject of Slovak surnames. Š. Švagrovský, *ib.*, 355–66, discusses the settlement names associated with Slovaks living in (now former) Yugoslavia. Also noted, in **Onomastyka, historia języka, dialektologia. Księga pamiątkowa ku czci prof. dr. Henryka Borka (1929–1986)* (*ZNWSPO*. Językoznawstwo 13), two relevant articles: V. Blanár on the surname *Goga* (97–100) and M. Majtán on the words *bor, borovica*, and *sosna* in Slovak place names (233–36).

5. WORD CLASSES

NOUNS. K. Palkovič, *SR*, 56:27–34, examines secondary prefixes, mainly in nouns. J. Trnková, *ib.*, 87–95, studies the derivation of diminutives. A. Škapincová and P. Odaloš, *ib.*, 318–23, discuss the somewhat parallel journalistic noun formations in -*gate* and the suffix -*iáda*. They cite delightful recent terms such as *Tatragate, Budajgate, Dunajgate* and *Sachergate*, along with *klausiáda, palachiáda* and *čalfiáda*, all what you might call linguistic spin-offs of the 'Velvet Revolution'.

VERBS. M. Pisárčiková, *KS*, 25:9–13, looks at the semantically very close perfective verbs *ukončiť, skončiť, dokončiť, zakončiť* 'to end, finish', and also, *ib.*, 71–76, 102–09, synonyms for verbs with the prefix *u*-. J. Horecký, *ib.*, 22–23, notes the new verb *stržniť, stržňovať* 'to marketize'. P. Žigo, *SAS*, 19, 1990:379–90, discusses the expression of the category of time in Slovak.

OTHERS. E. Tibenská, *SR*, 56:294–305, discusses synonymy in adjectives; J. Horecký, *ib.*, 315–17, the form of adjectives of the type *jednorazový*. J. Šikra, *JČ*, 42:22–38, looks at adverbials in Slovak, part of a wider thorough study of the Slovak adverb, published as *Sémantika slovenských prísloviek* (*JazŠ*), Bratislava, Veda, 150 pp. J. Pavlovič, *SR*, 56:203–09, discusses the use of the preposition *bez* 'without' as a means of grammatical negation. E. Bajzíková, *SAS*, 19, 1990:15–24, discusses the classification of pronouns in Slovak.

6. SYNTAX AND TEXT

Ľ. Ďurovič, *SR*, 56:20–37, studies the question of the Slovak passive and the relationship between constructions using the verbs 'to be' and 'to have'. F. Kočiš, *ib.*, 129–39, studies word-order tendencies in Slovak syntax. Ľ. Kralčák, *ib.*, 140–46, studies some semantic-syntactic relations between principal and subordinate clauses. J. Glovňa, *ib.*, 209–13, examines the elision of the verb or parts of it in sentence clauses. J. Kačala, *SAS*, 19, 1990:165–76, looks at grammatical features of the word as the starting point for grammatical structure of the clause. J. Pekarovičová, *ib.*, 257–87, looks at clause models in specialist communication. J. Horecký, *KS*, 25:65–71, studies the rhetoric of the journalistic interview. O. Schulzová, *RSl*, 62, 1990:367–76, examines 'Les procédés paralinguistiques de l'énonciation en langue slovaque'.

7. PHONETICS. PHONOLOGY. PRONUNCIATION

L. Dvonč, *SR*, 56:170–78, looks at the diphthong *ô* in standard Slovak, and also, *SAS*, 19, 1990:83–95, paired alternations of vowels. S. Ondrejovič, *ib.*, 241–56, discusses speech at the Slovak National Theatre. J. Sabol, *ib.*, 321–31, describes his synthetic phonological theory as applied to the sounds of Slovak. This theory is expounded in book form in his *Syntetická fonologická teória*, Bratislava, Jazykovedný ústav Ľ. Štúra SAV, 1989, 253 pp.

8. STANDARD LANGUAGE. ORTHOGRAPHY. STYLE

J. Kačala, *KS*, 25:3–9, discusses the definition of language sovereignty, and, *ib.*, 33–42, the position of Slovak hitherto and in the future; also, *ib.*, 97–102, the state of research into Slovak at the Academy of Sciences. M. Sokolová, *SR*, 56:305–14, examines the morpheme analysis of Slovak from the teaching point of view. On orthography, I. Horňanský, *KS*, 25:52–58, considers the ticklish business of where to write capital letters in geographical names consisting of more than one word. J. Pavlovič, *ib.*, 112–17, reopens the question of whether *Boh* 'God' and its adjectives *Boží* 'God's' and *Božský* 'divine' are allowed capital letters. L. Dvonč, *SR*, 56:95–99, considers the proper usage of the letter *x* in loan-words.

USAGE. Amongst a number of brief articles picking up on contemporary points of usage and symptomatic points of codificatory uncertainty, Ľ. Sičáková, *KS*, 25:24–25, wonders whether *sanitárny* or *sanitačný deň* is correct for 'sanitary (cleaning) day'. J. Horecký, *ib.*, 59–60, considers vowel length in *bahaizmus* from *bahá'í*, which ends in a long vowel. M. Pisárčiková, *ib.*, 63–64, considers the relative correctness of the time phrases in 'Druhý deň/Druhým dňom zasadá parlament'. M. Považaj, *ib.*, 87–88, looks at the vogue political term *konzensus* 'consensus'. I. Masár, *ib.*, 91–94, reviews language usage in Slovak church missals published in Rome in 1981 and Trnava in 1952. J. Šikra, *SR*, 56:257–62, describes a language questionnaire distributed in late 1989 and early 1990, sociolinguistic data from which are analysed by K. Buzássyová, *ib.*, 262–76, on doubt in animate/inanimate masculine usage; M. Nábělková, *ib.*, 276–87, on contextual usage of identical-rooted adjectives with varying suffixes; and A. Oravcová, *ib.*, 288–94, on attitudes to linguistic polling.

9. Dialects and Varieties

V. Uhlár, pp. 298–315 of *Okres Topoľčany. Historicko-vlastivedná monografia*, ed. V. Uhlár, Bratislava, Obzor, 1988, 463 pp., discusses the dialects and dialect boundaries in the Topoľčany area. A. Habovštiak, *Slovenský národopis*, 38, 1990:103–10, discusses the secret language of Upper Orava cloth merchants.

10. Languages in Contact

Contacts between Czech and Slovak are a perennial happy hunting ground. K. Hegerová, *KS*, 25:31–32, discusses the non-existent Slovak verb *uťať se* as it appears in the phrase borrowed from Czech 'Aj majster tesár sa utne'. A lot of this must be going on. I. Masár, *ib.*, 119–21, also inspects some Czechisms, reporting on discussions with editors of the daily newspaper *Práca*. M. Pisárčiková, *ib.*, 125–26, condemns the Czech-influenced use of the prepositions *po* and *na* instead of *od* in phrases meaning 'to want something from somebody' ('chciet' od niekoho/*po niekom/*na niekom niečo'). V. Budovičová, *SAS*, 19, 1990:25–46, discusses Slovak-Czech bilingual communication and taboo expressions. Z. Sochová, *NŘ*, 74:124–31, takes a good look at Czech-Slovak confrontational lexicography. I. Ripka, *SAS*, 19, 1990:289–303, examines Slovak language in the United States. J. Horecký, *KS*, 25:86–87, notes the Hungarian background of some Slovak financial and legal terms, e.g. *účastina* 'share' (cf. Hungarian *részvény* with its parallel suffix -*vény*, contrasting with Czech *akcie*, which gives the Slovak synonym *akcia*); similarly *daňový kľúč* (Hungarian *adó kulcs*) and *hlavný slúžny* (Hungarian *föispán*), contrasting with Czech *míra daně* (German *Steuermass*) and *vrchní soud* (German

Obergericht). B. Valehrach-Schaefer, *SR*, 56:100–06, reconsiders the problem of transcribing foreign names in literary translations. M. Čarnogurská, *ib.*, 214–22, discusses the transcription of Chinese characters and names in Slovak. M. Čabala, **JZ*, 7, 1986 (1989):93–98, looks at Russian adjectives formed from Slovak geographical names.

11. COMPARATIVE STUDIES

There is a good deal of inevitable overlap between Slovak-Czech contact studies and pure comparison. L. Dvonč, *KS*, 25:139–43, discusses sporting terms in *-bal* and *-bol* in Slovak and Czech. O. Schulzová, *SAS*, 19, 1990:333–44, compares some greetings in the two languages. E. Ružičková, *ib.*, 305–19, compares the system of prepositions of time in Slovak and English, while O. Škvareninová, *ib.*, 345–53, looks at Slovak as a foreign language against the background of English. A. Jarošová, *SlSl*, 26:12–25, confronts some aspects of Russian and Slovak lexis, and J. Benkovičová, *ib.*, 38–50, examines the methods of confrontational lexicology, based on Russian and Slovak material. A. Habovštiak, *ib.*, 62–67, examines Slovak names for livestock in the overall Slav context (see also section 3 above). M. Mika, **JZ*, 7, 1986(1989):39–42, studies noun determination in Russian and Slovak. J. Opalková, *ib.*, 67–72, examines synonymy and antonymy in phraseology involving animals. Not previously noted, **Studia Linguistica Polono-Slovaca*, 1, Wrocław etc., 1988, over 215 pp., with 18 articles on comparative Slovak-Polish topics by Slovak and Polish authors; likewise *ib.*, 2, Bratislava, 1990, over 268 pp., with 17 comparative articles; and *ib.*, 3, Wrocław etc., 1990, over 236 pp., with 28 miscellaneous articles, some comparative.

LITERATURE*

By K. Brušák, *Visiting Lecturer in Czech and Slovak at the University of Cambridge*

(This survey covers the years 1989, 1990 and 1991)

1. General

The efforts to come to terms with the remnants of Socialist Realism (cf. *YWMLS*, 50:1003) have persisted most notably in *Program a tvorba*, ed. D. Hajko, SlSp, 1989, 176 pp., a collection of 11 studies by theoreticians and aestheticians of the Literary Institute of the Slovak Academy. The authors argue that Socialist Realism is not an aesthetic doctrine but an ideological programme that 'has become the appropriate style of the present epoch'. But as one of the contributors admits, 'those who were expecting a definition of the attributes of Socialist Realism as a style will be disappointed'. Karol Rosenbaum, *Vzťahy slovenskej a českej literatúry 19. a 20. storočia. Koncepcie a riešenia*, Obzor, 1989, 392 pp., another study which echoes the past, when analysing the relations between these two literatures since the Revival from the Marxist-Leninist standpoint, finds that they were 'integrative, differentiative and complementary'. A new approach is taken by Vladimír Petrík, *Proces a tvorba*, SlSp, 1990, 428 pp.; dealing with Slovak prose written in the 1970s and 1980s, it states that it has used notions which have been superseded by developments and that it used to express 'a social and cultural perspective which is obviously behind us'. Peter Zajac, *Tvorivosť literatúry*, SlSp, 1990, 248 pp., examines the crisis of modernism in the last 25 years during which changes in the general situation have brought about a new combination of reality, the notions of the author and the text, resulting in literature becoming 'a dynamic category'. The problems of the literary genre are discussed from the historical standpoint in D. Ďurišin, 'Modifikácia žánru v medziliterárnom procese', *Romboid*, 24.4, 1989:62–70, and in R. Burgan, 'Ontologický štatút a funkcie literárneho žánru', *ib.*, 24.6, 1989:44–53, which rejects the concept of genre as a historical model or as an autonomous entity. B. Hochel, 'Problémy súčasnej slovenskej najadológie', *ib.*, 24.2, 1989:73–76, surveys Slovak studies in this field and recommends intensified investigation of the frequency of the naiad motif in Slovak folklore and literature. *Text a textológia*, ed. I. Kusý, E. Tkáčiková *et al.*, Veda, 1989, 160 pp., defines the tasks of textology in editing literary works.

---

*The place of publication of books is Bratislava unless otherwise stated.

Literature 953

2. EARLIER LITERATURE UP TO THE END OF THE NINETEENTH
CENTURY

J. Minárik, 'K problematice staršej slovenskej literatúry', *SLit*,
1990:172–94, suggests the periodization of older Slovak literature
into medieval (800–1500), Renaissance (1500–1650) and Baroque
(1650–1780). V. Marčok, 'Romantici a folklór', *ib.*, 1989:228–35,
discusses broadsheets as a source of inspiration for the Slovak
Romantics, and G. Gáfriková, 'Príspevok k figurálnej poézii
slovenského baroka', *ib.*, 1989:357–67, publishes and discusses two
figural poems, one in the form of a lily and another in the form of a
rose, composed at the end of the 17th c. in pre-literary Slovak and
showing elements of courtoisie and religious symbolism. M. Hamada,
'Zrod osvietenskej kultúry na Slovensku', *ib.*, 1990:393–427, deals
with M. Bel and A. F. Kollár as the last representatives of humanism
in the Reformation period, and Id., 'K zrodu novodobej slovenskej
kultúry', *SlPoh*, 1989, no. 3:61–77, discusses the work of Hugolín
Gavlovič. *Antológia slovenskej literatúry v období klasicizmu a romantizmu*,
ed. and introd. H. Urbancová and E. Hleba, SIPN, 1989, 337 pp.,
contains an important introduction evaluating the importance of
Classicism and pre-Romanticism for the formation of Slovak literature. E. Fordinálová, 'Idea bratstva v našej osvietenskej poézii pred
Velkou francúzskou revolúciou', *SLit*, 1989:513–25, discusses the
impact of Rousseau and Voltaire on the social thought of A. Doležal
and I. Bajza, while the same author, 'Idey, ideály a revolúcia', *ib.*,
1990:42–55, traces the echoes of the French Revolution in the
writings of Bernolák, Bajza, Fándly, Hollý and Tablic. Z. Hegedüsová, 'Recepcia G. G. Byrona na Slovensku', *ib.*, 1989:137–47, and P.
Vongrej, 'Recepcia G. G. Byrona v slovenskom romantizme', *ib.*,
1989:473–76, discuss the attitudes of Kollár and Štúr to Byron.
Amongst the many works concerned with the history of Slovak
literary criticism those deserving mention are Rudolf Chmel, *Dejiny
slovenskej literárnej kritiky*, Tatran, 427 pp., C. Kraus, 'K počiatkom
slovenskej literárnej kritiky', *Romboid*, 25.2, 1990:62–68, and 25.3,
1990:77–83; Id., 'Glosy k vývinu kritiky v slovenskom literárnom
klasicizme a romantizme', *SLit*: 194–206; Id., *Začiatky slovenskej kritiky.
Literárna kritika v slovenskom klasicizme a romanizme*, Veda, 281 pp., and
E. Panovová, 'Počiatky formovania slovenskej literárnej kritiky a
ruská literatúra', *SLit*, 1990:464–72. Slovak historical prose of the
19th c. is surveyed by Viera Žemberová, *Próza a čas*, Košice,
Východoslovenské nakľadatelstvo, 1990, 112 pp., and contacts
between Polish and Slovak literatures by Josef Hvišč, *Slovensko-poľské
literárne vzťahy 1815–1918*, Veda, 240 pp.

INDIVIDUAL AUTHORS

BERNOLÁK. Ján Považan, *Bernolák a Bernolákovci*, Osveta, 1990, 304 pp.

CHALUPKA. V. Mikula, 'Chalupkov zverinec', *SlPoh*, no. 10:106–112, discusses his *Bendeguz*.

DOHNÁNY. O. Čepan, 'Vizionár praxe M. D.', *SLit*: 1–20.

FÁNDLY. J. Tibenský, 'J. F. a slovenské národné obrodenie', *Historický časopis*, 39. 1:49–78.

HOLLÝ. K. Palkovič, 'J. H. a Bulhari', *SlSl*, 25, 1990:179–85. M. Hamada, 'J.H. — tvorca spevníka', *SLit*:66–72. F. Štraus, 'Rytmická štruktúra hexametra Hollého *Svatopluka*, *ib.*, 1990:131–51. E. Fordinálová, 'Dobové zápasy a ideály v Hviezdoslavovej básni J. H.', *ib.*, 1989:236–49.

HROBOŇ. V. Kovalčík, 'S. B. H. — prekliaty básnik, predchodca modernej poézie', *Romboid*, 25.11, 1990:68–73.

KOLLÁR. K. Rosenbaum, 'Odraz európskych revolučných myšlienok v diele mladého Jána Kollára', *SLit*, 1989:526–34.

J. KRÁĽ. O. Čepan, 'Kráľov slovanský princíp', *SLit*: 169–93, discusses the unfinished allegorical poem *Strom nesmrtelnosti*.

ŠTÚR. Štefan Drug, *Štúrov program na našich zástavách*, Smena, 1990, 288 pp. Z. Sojková, 'Staré i nové motivy básníka Štúra roku 1840', *ČL*:74–82.

TAJOVSKÝ. M. Mináriková, 'Textologicko-štylistická problematika poviedok Jozefa Gregora Tajovského', *SLit*, 1990:350–69.

VAJANSKÝ. I. Kusý, 'Zmysel vajanského postáv v *Suchej ratolesti*', *SLit*:50–64.

3. THE TWENTIETH CENTURY UP TO 1945

The treatment of native themes and the inspiration derived from the European novel are discussed in J. Števček, 'Traditionen des slowakischen Romans und ihre Wirkung in der Gegenwart', *ZSl*, 34, 1989:821–25, and D. Slobodník, 'Cesty a rázcestia moderného románu', *Romboid*, 24.8, 1989:91–99, 24.10:108–16. E. Panovová, 'Slovenský vzťah k sovietskej porevolučnej literárnej reflexii', *SlSl*, 24, 1989:110–16, admits that although Slovak poets were influenced by Soviet views on the mission of the poet in society, they had no sympathy for the poetry of the masses, leaning rather towards Symbolism, and that Slovak critics were following the formalist trends condemned in the USSR.

INDIVIDUAL AUTHORS

HRONSKÝ. J. Sabol, 'Jozef Cíger-Hronský, majster textovej skice a jej kolorovania', *SlPoh*, no. 12:155–59. Id., 'Dvojrozmernosť textu

Jozefa Cígera-Hronského', *KS*, no. 9:289–92. Marta Patáková, *Kompozičná variabilnosť prózy. Kompozičné postupy v románovej tvorbe J. C. Hronského*, Nitra, Pedagogická fakulta, 1990, 211 pp. JESENSKÝ. P. Petrus, 'Autorské kontexty v typologických súradniciach. K prozaickému dielu J. Jesenského a A. P. Čechova', *SlSl*, 25, 1990:137–49. M. Gáfrik, 'Modernistické tendence v novelách Janka Jesenského', *SLit*:21–48. RÁZUS. M. Gáfrik, 'Expresionizmus v próze mladého Rázusa', *SlPoh*, no. 7:67–75.

4. THE TWENTIETH CENTURY SINCE 1945

Hodnoty desaťročia, ed. and postscript Vladimír Petrík, *SlSp*, 1989, 340 pp., a collection of essays by S. Šmatlák, P. Winczer, J. Hvič, B. Truhlář, K. Tomiš and Z. Rampák, provides a serious analysis of Slovak poetry, prose and drama which, during the 1970s, accepted again class and Party criteria, began once more to serve 'the socialist character of society on Leninist principles', and abandoned 'experimentation, subjectivism and scepsis for reality and optimism'. V. Petrík, 'Štátnosť a slovenská literatúra (po roku 1945)', *SLit*, 1989;1–9, in surveying the relations between the Czechs and Slovaks in the common state since 1945 as reflected in Slovak literature, argues that the specific character of Slovak prose during the 1970s and 1980s marked the culmination of the struggle for national identity, whilst J. Mistrík, 'Funktionelle Arhythmien in der modernen slowakischen Prosa', *ZSl*, 34, 1989:879–81, after examining the distortion of the prose rhythm in the novels of Mináč, Ballek, Jaroš and Chudoba, arrives at the rather dubious conclusion that it is not only a formal means of expression but has a great impact on the content. T. Žilka, 'Postmodernismus v próze', *Romboid*, 24.9, 1989:18–24, discusses characteristic features of the prose of Vilikovský, Bútora and Sloboda such as absurd reality and radical irony, whilst V. Macura, 'Podnet žánru pásma v českej a slovenskej poézii z prelomu 50. a 60. rokov', *ib.*, 24.7, 1989:33–39, deals with the influence of Apollinaire's *Zone*, and P. Koprda, 'Taliansky neorealizmus a slovenská literárna kritika v rokoch 1945–1956', *SLit*: 112–27, and Vladimír Oleríny, *Poludníky literatúry*, Tatran, 1989, 152 pp., with that of Italian neo-Realism and Latin-American magical Realism on contemporary Slovak prose and criticism. Slovak literary works published abroad are surveyed in P. Winczer, 'Slovenská poézia vydaná v Ríme a jej domáce korene', *SLit*:128–39, and Ľ. Petraško, 'Národ v malom — slovenská literatúra v exile', *Romboid*, 26.10:3–12.

INDIVIDUAL AUTHORS

BALLEK. U. Raßloff, 'Das Ende der Linearität', *ZSl*, 34, 1989:841–49. Id., 'Pohľad na dejiny cez postavy v Ballekových *Agátoch*', *SLit*, 1990:105–12. R. B. Pynsent, 'Ballek a Vilikovský', *Romboid*, 25.12, 1990:120–28.

BARČ-IVAN. J. Vanovič, 'Katastrofické povojnové drámy Júliusa Barča-Ivana', *SLit*:81–92.

BEDNÁR. K. Buzássyová, 'Pokus o sociolinguistickú analýzu románu Alfonza Bednára *Ako sme sušili bielizeň*', *SLit*, 1989:45–60.

DILONG. J. M. Rydlo, 'Bibliografia knižných prác Rudolfa Dilonga', *SLit*:140–55.

DUŠEK. Z. Stanislavová, 'Fenomén detstva a dospelosti v Dušekovom *Pravdivom príbehu o Pačovi*', *SLit*, 1989:335–41.

FABRY. P. Winczer, 'Fabryho *Ja je niekto iný* — tradície a súdobé súvislosti', *SLit*, 1990:1–26, 120–33.

FELDEK. Z. Rampák, 'Poetika divadelných hier Ľubomíra Feldeka', *SLit*, 1989:27–44.

HABAJ. Ľ. Machala, 'K poetike prozaického diela Ivana Habaja', *Romboid*, 24.1, 1989:50–55.

KARVAŠ. L. Hensel, 'Karvašov a Mrožkov pohľad na svet', *SlSl*, 25, 1990:293–301.

MIHALKOVIČ. F. Matejov, 'Básnický text ako konštruovanie sveta', *SLit*, 1989:10–26.

MITANA. Z. Prušková, 'O dvoch možnostoch tematizácie konfliktu v krátkej próze D. Mitanu a J. Puškáša', *SLit*, 1990:224–39.

ONDRUŠ. V. Krupa, 'Prejavy rečovej tvorivosti v poézii Jána Ondruša', *SLit*, 1990:105–112.

PUŠKÁŠ. See MITANA.

SLOBODA. I. Sulík, 'Erotický motív v próze Rudolfa Slobodu', *Romboid*, 26.1:3–9.

ŠIKULA. V. Fulka, 'Svet hudby v prózach Vincenta Šikulu', *Romboid*, 24.7, 1989:57–62.

TATARKA. P. Petro, 'Tatarkova trúfalosť', *Romboid*, 25.4, 1990:3–8.

VILIKOVSKÝ. I. Hrubaničová, 'K synonymii v umeleckom texte', *KS*, no. 6:201–08. See also BALLEK.

III. POLISH STUDIES

LANGUAGE

By NIGEL GOTTERI, *University of Sheffield*

1. APPRECIATIONS AND SURVEYS

H. Borek (1929–86) is honoured in *ZNWSPO*. Językoznawstwo, 13, which begins with papers on B. and his work, followed by M. Wojtkiewicz, 'Bibliografia prac Henryka Borka' (53–72). J. Chojak and A. Nagórko, 'Profesor Jadwiga Puzynina — podwójny jubileusz', *PJ*: 147–52, is an appreciation, followed by a list of over 140 of P.'s publications (153–59). A. Pasoń, 'Działalność naukowa i pedagogiczna Salomei Szlifersztejnowej', *PFil*, 35: 7–14, includes a bibliography (13–14). J. Rokoszowa, 'Doktor Irena Żwak (1939–1988)', *JPol*, 70, 1990: 223–24. General surveys: M. Fleischer, 'Die Polonistik in der Bundesrepublik Deutschland (eine statistische Analyse)', *ASP*, 20, 1990: 103–21, and H. Rybicka, 'Aus der Geschichte der polnischen Linguistik', *ZSl*, 36: 99–106.

2. PHONETICS AND PHONOLOGY

Z. Adamiszyn, 'O niektórych fonetycznych wyznacznikach tekstu potocznego', *ZNWSPO*. Językoznawstwo, 13: 349–57; A. Bańkowski, '*Świeboda, swoboda, śleboda, słoboda*', *SlOc*, 44, 1987 (1990): 1–12; B. Nykiel-Herbert, 'Sekwencje samogłoskowe w procesie przyswajania zapożyczeń w języku polskim', *Polonica*, 14, 1989 (1990): 167–74; W. Sobkowiak, 'On spoonerisms', *Word*, 41, 1990: 277–92, draws some evidence from the Polish gra półsłówek; Id., 'On tongue twisters', *PSCL*, 25, 1990: 23–36.

3. MORPHOLOGY AND WORD-FORMATION

Greville Corbett, *Gender*, CUP, xx + 363 pp., is an excellent study in which Polish examples frequently feature. Andrew Spencer, *Morphological Theory: An Introduction to Word Structure in Generative Grammar*, Oxford, Blackwell, xviii + 512 pp., makes extensive use of data from Polish and Russian, the most common languages, with English and Chukchee, of exemplification. J. Bień, 'Koncepcja słownikowych tablic morfologiczncyh (na przykładzie rzeczownika)', *PrIJP*, 70. Studia Gramatyczne, 9, 1990: 115–34; A. Bogusławski, 'Polski sufiks *-utki*', *PJ*: 174–79. K. Długosz-Kurczabowa, 'Pochodzenie, produktywność i funkcje formantu *-as* w języku polskim', *PFil*, 35: 53–58, and by the same author, 'Formant *-tor*', *ib.*, 245–62; M. Domaradzki, 'Nieosobowe nazwy subiektów cech z formantem <*-eć*> w polszczyźnie XIV–XVIII wieku', *AUNCFP*, 31. Językoznawstwo, Nauki Humanistyczno-Społeczne, 192, 1990:189–216; I. Kamińska-Szmaj, 'Charakterystyka statystyczno-stylistyczna części mowy (na materiale polskiego słownika frekwencyjnego)', *Polonica*, 14, 1989 (1990):87–120; K. Kowalik, 'Morfonologiczny aspekt derywacji przymiotników w języku polskim — system spółgłoskowy (w porównaniu z językiem słowackim)' *SLPS*, 1, 1988:49–62; M. Kucała, 'Dlaczego męskie nazwiska na *-o* mają odmianę żeńską?', *ZNWSPO*. Językoznawstwo, 13:211–18. Li Jin Tao, 'Propozycja nowej systematyzacji polskiej koniugacji', *PrIJP*, 70. Studia Gramatyczne, 9, 1990:99–114; N. Markar'ian, 'Семантико-стилистические особенности флективного *-у* в становлении современных норм польского именного склонения', *PFil*, 35:105–111, is on *zuchy, druhowie*, etc. H. Mieczkowska, 'Rozwój kategorii żeńskich nazw osobowych w języku polskim i słowackim mających odpowiedniki w rodzaju męskim', *SLPS*, 1, 1988:63–82; H. Mieczkowska, 'Rozwój nazw abstrakcyjnych z sufiksem *-ość/-osť* w języku słowackim i polskim', *ib.*, 2, 1990:59–79; N. Nübler, 'Zum Begriff der Subsumptionspräfixe in der Aspektforschung', *ASP*, 20, 1990:123–34; M. Papierz, 'Adwerbializacja w języku słowackim i polskim', *SLPS*, 3, 1990:107–10; A. Pasoń, 'Z zagadnień liczby rzeczowników zwanych singularia tantum w polszczyźnie XVI wieku', *PFil*, 35:263–71; R.S., 'Problemy fleksyjne (IV)', *PJ*, 1990:704–07, is about the dative singular of *anioł* and *dzień*; Id., 'Václav Havel w Hradcu Králové', *PJ*:62–65, treats problems of declining other-Slav names, e.g., is the genitive form *Havla* or *Havela*? W. Śmiech, 'Uwagi o klasyfikacji derywacji w języku polskim', *RKJŁ*, 35, 1989 (1991):179–90; K. Waszakowa, 'O wartościowaniu w słowotwórstwie', *PJ*:180–87; and her 'Sufiks *-ant* jako formant międzynarodowy', *JPol*, 70, 1990:32–39; E. Willim, 'On case marking in Polish', *PSCL*, 25, 1990:203–18; A. Wróbel, 'Antroponimiczne formacje feminatywne w XVII– i XVIII–wiecznym Chełmnie', *AUNCFP*, 31. Językoznawstwo, Nauki Humanistyczno-Społeczne, 192, 1990:285–310; M. Zarębina, 'Stosunek wzajemny wołacza i mianownika', *SlOc*, 44, 1987 (1990):89–102.

4. Syntax

Polish data feature frequently in Robert D. Borsley, *Syntactic Theory. A Unified Approach*, London, Arnold, xii + 238 pp., e.g., in the final exercise of the book (p. 212), but Polish is hardly mentioned in Liliane Haegeman, *Introduction to Government and Binding Theory*, Oxford,

Blackwell, xx + 618 pp. Анна Siewierska, *Functional Grammar*, London, Routledge, xxii + 279 pp., is a clear introduction to the grammatical theory associated with the name of Simon Dik; after English, Polish is the language most frequently used for exemplification. G. Walczak, 'Klasyfikacja zdań złożonych w języku polskim', *PFil*, 35:291–400, is a monograph within a periodical, delayed since 1977 for reasons beyond its author's control.

S. Dyła, 'Two counterexamples to the resolution principle?', *Linguistics*, 29:261–72, argues that *przed i po kolacji* contains two co-ordinated prepositional phrases, the first containing an intransitive preposition. Id., 'Quantified NPs as subjects in Polish', *ASEES*, 5:91–101, argues that there is nothing impersonal or subjectless about constructions like *Tam czekało kilku studentów*. G. Greenberg and S. Franks, 'A parametric approach to dative subjects and the second dative in Slavic', *NZSJ*:71–97, looks at a phenomenon, even more common in Russian than in Polish, seen in the default situation in *Dobrze jest iść samemu*. R. Grzegorczykowa, 'Jeszcze o bezosobowych konstrukcjach z *się*', *PFil*, 35:75–81; A. Kałkowska, 'Morfologiczne uwarunkowania przekształceń składni czasownika (Uwagi o składni czasowników staropolskich)', *Polonica*, 14, 1989 (1990):175–82; D. Kopcińska, 'Założenia opisu strukturalnego zdań współczesnej polszczyzny pisanej ze składnikiem realizującym akomodującą frazę nominalną', *PrIJP*, 70. Studia Gramatyczne, 9, 1990:73–86; M. Krauz, 'Tematyczno-rematyczne rozczłonkowanie zdania inicjalnego', *WSPRRNDFP*. Prace Językoznawcze, 20/72, 1990:25–46; B. Nykiel-Herbert, 'Jeszcze raz o uniwerbizacji', *Polonica*, 14, 1989 (1990):193–203; J. Podracki, 'Związki zgody, rządu i przynależności w dydaktyce szkolnej', *PFil*, 35:141–46. Z. Saloni, 'O konstrukcji *ile ludzi* po dwudziestu latach', *ib.*, 161–70, goes back to Id., 'Czy należy mówić "ile ludzi"?', *PJ*, 1965:247–50, which was answered at the time by W. Doroszewski, 'Dyskusja z pedagogiem (młodym)', *ib.*, 250–52. T. Skubalanka, 'Historia języka a gramatyka stylistyczna', *JPol*, 70, 1990:18–25; S. Szpakowicz and M. Świdziński, 'Formalna definicja równorzędnej grupy nominalnej we współczesnej polszczyźnie pisanej', *PrIJP*, 70. Studia Gramatyczne, 9, 1990:9–54; P. Tajsner, 'Scrambling and the Polish word order. An alternative hypothesis', *Further Insights into Contrastive Analysis*, LLSEE, 30, 1990:37–42; E.W., '*Oszczędzać czego, oszczędać co*', *PJ*:66–67; M. Wiśniewski, 'Czy liczebnik może być uznany za nadrzędnik dystrybucyjny szeregu rzeczownikowego?', *PrIJP*, 70. Studia Gramatyczne, 9, 1990:87–98; Id., 'Czy ciągi typu *wobec tego, że* są spójnikami?', *AUNCFP*, 31, Językoznawstwo, Nauki Humanistyczno-Społeczne, 192, 1990:63–74; Id., 'Formalno-gramatyczny opis leksemów *to*. 2. Słowo *to* w funkcji spójnika, partykuły, czasownika niewłaściwego', *ib.*, 75–90; Id., 'Status gramatyczny tzw. przysłówków odprzymiotnikowych typu *duszno, wolno, nieprzyjemnie*', *Polonica*, 14, 1989 (1990): 183–92.

5. LEXICOLOGY AND PHRASEOLOGY

English–Polish dictionaries are appearing in some profusion; Janina Jaślan and Henryk Jaślan, *Słownik terminologii prawniczej i ekonomicznej angielsko-polski*, Wa, WP, 714 pp., is an example. Andrzej Marciniak and Michał Jankowski, *Słownik informatyczny angielsko-polski*, Wa-Pń, PWN, 670 pp., is intended to be more informative about English than about Polish, as the bibliography (669–70) and Wiktor Jassem's phonetic transcriptions of the English show. The authors provide notes rather than glosses for some English terms: if Polish terms subsequently come into existence to fill these gaps in the specialized vocabulary, this volume will be of assistance in dating the neologisms. Monika Woytowicz-Neymann, Roman Kozierkiewicz and Mieczysław Puławski, *Słownik handlowy angielsko-polski*, Wa, Państwowe Wyd. Ekonomiczne, 880 pp., is equally informative about English and Polish, and contains a short bibliography (p. 879).

M. Ampel-Rudolf, 'Z semantyki predykatywów *jasn- ciemn-*', *WSPRRNDFP*. Prace Językoznawcze, 20/72, 1990:99–110. J. Bartmiński, '*Prawica — lewica*. Sposoby profilowania pojęć', *PJ*: 160–66, is a historical study of the connotations of the two terms. J. Biniewicz, 'Językowe i symboliczne oznaczenia związków chemicznych', *ZNWSPO*. Językoznawstwo, 13:373–80; D. Buttler and H. Satkiewicz, 'Prasa jako źródło w badaniach innowacji słownikowych współczesnej polszczyzny', *SLPS*, 3, 1990:63–70. S. Bąba, 'Warianty zwrotu *oddać niedźwiedzią przysługę*', *PJ*:238–42, exemplifies and discusses *oddać/wyświadczyć/wyrządzić/zrobić/czynić niedzwiedzią przysługę*, of which *oddać* and *zrobić* are colloquial, and *wyświadczyć/wyrządzić/czynić* are rather more elevated; *wyrządzić*, possibly leading the way, is often used in the sense of simply harming, regardless of intention. Id., 'Między bajki włożyć', *JPol*, 71:155–58; E. Breza, 'Etymologiczne objaśnienie wyrazów i terminów pochodzenia grecko-łacińskiego w pracach naukowych', *ib.*, 70, 1990:39–45; A. Dobaczewski, 'Próba interpretacji semantycznej leksemów *no*', *PJ*:1–9; Maria Frankowska, 'Monografie syntaktyczne. 7. Czasownik *dbać* w historii polszczyzny', *AUNCFP*, 31. Językoznawstwo, Nauki Humanistyczno-Społeczne, 192, 1990:149–88; W. Gruszczyński *et al.*, 'Stopień dokładności opisu słownikowego jako problem językoznawczy', *PrIJP*, 70. Studia Gramatyczne, 9, 1990:135–74; H. Jadacka, 'Dwie wartości, dwa gniazda (o prawdzie i fałszu)', *PJ*:163–73; M. Karamańska, 'Słownictwo aktorskie', *JPol*,

70, 1990:88–100; K. Kleszczowa, 'Mechanizmy przekształceń znaczeniowych czasowników mówienia w historii języka polskiego', *SLPS*, 3, 1990:217–30; S. Kochman, 'Z dziejów terminologii filozoficznej w języku polskim: *postęp, postępowy*', *ZNWSPO*. Językoznawstwo, 13:415–20; R. Lipczuk, 'Znaczenie leksykalne w świetle semantycznej teorii użycia', *Polonica*, 14, 1989 (1990):5; J. Puzynina, 'Słownictwo eucharystyczne w historii języka polskiego', *ZNWSPO*. Językoznawstwo, 13:479–86; R. S., 'Sejm, senat, parlament', *PJ*: 37–41.

Z. Saloni, 'Co i jak poprawiać w *Słowniku języka polskiego* pod red. W. Doroszewskiego (Ankieta leksykograficzna Polskiego Towarzystwa Językoznawczego)', *JPol*, 70, 1990:56–66; J. Sambor, 'Struktura kwantytatywna wyrazów polisemicznych w słowniku, czyli o tzw. prawie Kryłowa (na materiale języka polskiego i rosyjskiego)', *Polonica*, 14, 1989 (1990):13–32; Id., 'Prawdopodobieństwo subiektywne wyrazów i tzw. słownik umysłowy człowieka (uwagi na marginesie *Podstawowego słownika frekwencyjnego języka polskiego*)', *ib.*, 77–86; T. Skubalanka, 'Problematyka gramatyczno-stylistyczna neologizmu', *SLPS*, 3, 1990:31–38; T. Smółkowa, 'Rola modeli nazwotwórczych w rozwoju słownictwa', *ib.*, 55–62; B. Wołowik, '*Borkarnia* — zapomniany synonim *bursy*', *ZNWSPO*. Językoznawstwo, 13:507–10; J. Wronicz, 'O etymologii *otrąb* i zjawisku reinterpretacji', *JPol*, 70, 1990:46–62, with a note by W. Smoczyński (52–53); K. Wróblewski, '*Fan* – moda czy językowa konieczność?', *PJ*:142–45, mentions not only *fan*, but also *fanka*, and notes that young people use *fani* in speech, while *fanowie* is used chiefly in official texts such as fan-clubs' communications to members; J. Zieniukowa, 'Czy polski wyraz *kipiątek* "wrzątek, ukrop" jest zapożyczeniem wschodniosłowiańskim i regionalizmem kresowym?' *ZNWSPO*. Językoznawstwo, 13:531–53.

6. SEMANTICS AND PRAGMATICS

A. Bednarek, 'O *reasumuję*. Rozważania semantyczne', *AUNCFP*, 31. Językoznawstwo, Nauki Humanistyczno-Społeczne, 192, 1990:3–12, and Id., 'Charakterystyka składniowo-znaczeniowa wyrażeń typu *czyli* w podręcznikach składni polskiej', *ib.*, 13–36; A. Bogusławski, 'Nieorzecznikowa fraza *cokolwiek* z referencją indywiduową', *PFil*, 35:23–33. B. Boniecka, 'Strategia konwersacji', *PJ*:24–37, discusses a non-questioning way of inviting an answer in radio and television interviews. W. Boryś, 'Etymologie polskie 4. dial. *spótek*, kasz. *spółk*, *špól* "szufla do wylewania wody z łodzi"', *JPol*, 71:110–15; D. Buttler, 'Przenośnie polszczyzny potocznej', *PFil*, 35:39–46; J. Chojak and Z. Zaron, '*Ten cały* c a ł y. Refleksja na temat znaczenia', *PJ*:206–11; M. Danielewiczowa, 'Pytania rozstrzygnięcia a pytania uzupełnienia (o kryteriach podziału)', *ib.*, 103–09; A. Dobaczewski, 'Próba interpretacji semantycznej leksemów *no*', *ib.*, 1–9; M. Frankowska, 'Zmiany językowe a funkcja pragmatyczna (na przykładzie konstrukcji z *zamiast* (stp. *miasto*)', *PrIJP*, 70. Studia Gramatyczne, 9, 1990:175–90; M. Grochowski, 'Pojęcie zazdrości. Próba eksplikacji semantycznej', *AUNCFP*, 31. Językoznawstwo, Nauki Humanistyczno-Społeczne, 192, 1990:37–50; Id., 'Meble: zakres pojęcia a hiperonimy nazw denotowanych obiektów', *ib.*, 51–62; Id., '"Obojętność" i "zło" w strukturze semantycznej wyrażenia *byle*', *PJ*:201–05; Id., 'O pojęciu groźby', *Polonica*, 14, 1989 (1990):33–44; R. Grzegorczykowa, 'Składniki znaczeń leksemów a interpretacja semantyczno-pragmatyczna wypowiedzi', *PJ*:87–95, and her 'Obelga jako akt mowy', *ib.*, 193–200.

E. Kozarzewska, 'Elementy wartościujące w wypowiedzeniach oznaczających zachowania językowe', *PJ*:188–92; E. Masłowska, 'Zjawiska desemantyzacji wyrazów w procesie nominacji ekspresywnej' *SLPS*, 3, 1990:199–208. L. A. Grenoble, 'Variation in colloquial speech: Russian and Polish verbs of motion', pp. 121–42 of *Topics in Colloquial Russian*, ed. Margaret H. Mills, NY, Lang, 1990, xii + 203 pp., shows the Polish distribution of indeterminate/determinate verbs to differ from Russian in some contexts. The remarks about Polish are preliminary and tentative. T. Minikowska, 'Miłosierdzie w ujęciu językoznawczym', *AUNCFP*, 31. Językoznawstwo, Nauki Humanistyczno-Społeczne, 192, 1990:217–58; M. Mycawka, 'O modyfikacji znaczeniowej wyrazu *filozofia*', *JPol*, 81:98–105; J. Reszka, 'Cechy semantyczne i składniowe wybranych wyrażeń komunikujących niezadowolenie z istniejącego stanu rzeczy (*narzeka, utyskuje, skarży się, żali się*)', *Polonica*, 14, 1989 (1990):45–66; K. Siekierska, 'Brunatne fiołki', *PFil*, 35:179–86; A. Tombińska, 'Z zagadnień semantyki galicyzmów', *Polonica*, 14, 1989 (1990):143–56; K. Waszakowa, 'O wyznaczoności w polskich derywatach imiennych', *PJ*:110–18; M. Wojtyła-Świerzowska, 'Nieco inaczej o semantyce godła', *JPol*, 71:17–22; Z. Topolińska, 'Z semantyki tzw. przymiotników i przysłówków właściwych', *PFil*, 35:229–37; D. Zdunkiewicz, 'Problem referencji grup nominalnych w tekstach propagandy politycznej', *PJ*:119–23.

7. SOCIOLINGUISTICS AND DIALECTOLOGY

Socjolingwistyka, 10, Ww, ZNiO, includes: M. Brzezina, 'Sytuacja języka ukraińskiego w świetle polskich utworów literackich XIX i XX w.' (97–104); K. Długosz, 'Uwagi o potocznym słownictwie medycznym' (91–96); E. Kuryło, 'Wartościowanie w leksyce potocznej' (21–38); T. Rittel, 'Z badań nad słownictwem społeczno-moralnym studentów (podejście socjolingwistyczne)' (59–70); K. Urban, 'Wzorce językowe w opinii społecznej' (7–20); U. Żydek-Bednarczuk, 'Analiza syntaktyczno-semantyczna i pragmatyczna mówionych tekstów dialogowych' (39–58); and Id., 'Pojęcie spójności w mówionych tekstach dialogowych' (71–90). *BSZJPS*, 81, 1990, includes: M. Biolik, 'Substytucje leksykalne pruskich nazw wodnych z terenu Polski' (41–52); S. Dubisz, 'Relikty bałtyckiego substratum językowego w nazewnictwie roślinnym gwar ostródzko-warmińsko-mazurskich' (87–94); S. Glinka, 'Lituanizmy fonetyczne w gwarach białoruskich i polskich Białostocczyzny' (117–28); A. Gołąbek, 'Wpływy litewskie na polszczyznę okolic Puńska' (129–40); K. Morkunas, 'К вопросу о диалектологических исследованиях на территории литовско-польского пограничья' (291–96). Comments on American-printed Polish vary from the highly favourable, such as M. Kucała, 'Chicagoski "Głos nauczyciela"', *JPol*, 71:143–46, to the highly critical B. Szydłowska Ceglowa, 'Uwagi językowe o książkach', *ib.*, 153–58, and M. Kucała, 'Język niby-polski w amerykańskim poradniku', *ib.*, 142–43.

J. Bartmiński, 'Styl potoczny jako centrum systemu stylowego języka', *PJ*:10–23; D. Buttler and H. Satkiewicz, 'Dynamism i zmienność współczesnej polszczyzny a polityka kodyfikacyjna', *PJ*, 1990:672–79; V. Fegl, 'O pewnych cechach dialogów w audycjach radiowych', *PJ*:82–86; S. Grabias, 'Kultura słowa a sprawności komunikacyjne', *Polonistyka*, 44:419–29; A. Kowalska, 'Ludowe słownictwo ekspresywne a polszczyzna ogólna', *SLPS*, 3, 1990:175–82; B. Kreja, 'Kaszubskie i innosłowiańskie przymiotniki typu *małuszki* "maluśki"', *JPol*, 71:115–19; J. Kwiek-Osiowska, 'Tendencje rozwojowe współczesnej polszczyzny w nauczaniu szkolnym', *ib.*, 127–35, and her 'Wpływ zmian zachodzących w Polsce w latach 1988/89 na język (Na wybranych przykładach)', *ib.*, 153–55; H. Makówczyńska-Góźdź, 'Teksty gwarowe 80. Z Dębna w woj. kieleckim', *ib.*, 46–52; J. Puzynina, 'Kultura słowa w oczach członków Towarzystwa naukowego Warszawskiego', *PJ*, 1990:640–71; E. Rzetelska-Feleszko, 'Czy język łużycki przeżyje?', *JPol*, 71:120–26.

R. Sussex, 'The Slavonic literary languages: complementary and conflicting parameters for language-hood', *ASEES*, 5:105–22, looks at Isačenko's polyvalency, standardization, obligatoriness and codification, Stewart's standardization, autonomy, historicity, and vitality, and Picchio's norma and dignitas, touching on unproblematic Polish and problematic Kashubian. Z. Łapiński, 'Elegia na odejście nowomowy', *TD*, 1990, no. 4:1–4, in a volume also containing A. Wierzbicka, 'Język antytotalitarny w Polsce' (5–30); M. Głowiński, 'Trzy głosy' (31–33); E. Tabakowska, 'Niezawodne zwierciadło'

964   *Polish Studies*

(34–38); J. Bralczyk, 'Antytotalitarny metajęzyk' (45–46); S. Balbus, 'Słowa i desygnaty czy akty i gatunki mowy?' (47–55); and A. Wierzbicka, 'Odpowiedzi autorki' (56–59). D. Bieńkowska, 'Analiza tekstów polszczyzny mówionej Łodzi i Radomska', *RKJŁ*, 35, 1989 (1991):5–12, and in the same volume, her 'O niektórych rodzajach ekspresiwów w polszczyźnie mówionej Łodzi' (13–18); K. Dejna and S. Gala, 'Z prac nad częstochowskim wycinkiem "Atlasu gwar polskich"' (69–86); G. Habrajska, 'Typy słowotwórcze rzeczowników występujących w gwarze wsi Masłońskie (woj. częstochowskie)' (87–110); M. Hemmert-Udalska, 'Teksty gwary polskiej mieszkańców Istvánmajor na Węgrzech' (111–16); M. Kamińska, 'Wybrane cechy stylu polszczyzny mówionej Łodzi' (125–32), and her 'Lustracje dóbr gnieźnieńskich jako źródło do znajomości polszczyzny XVII wieku' (133–42).

H. Nowak, 'Charakterystyka fonetyczna gwar okolic Borku Wielkopolskiego (w południowej Wielkopolsce). Część II: Konsonantyzm', *SlOc*, 44, 1987 (1990):29–72; J. Damborský, 'Z badań nad słownictwem polonijnym: *Wyraz polonijny* — próba definicji', *PFil*, 35:47–52; W. Kupiszewski, 'Z zagadnień gwary uczniowskostudenckiej', *ib.*, 91–95; H. Satkiewicz, 'Z obserwacji nad językiem polskich emigrantów w Belgii', *ib.*, 171–77. I. Bajerowa, 'Nadawca — wydawca — ewolucja języka', *ZNWSPO*. Językoznawstwo, 13:357–66, in a volume also containing A. Basara and J. Basara, '*Cuscuta trifoolii*, czyli *kanianka koniczynowa* (nazwy i ich zasięg geograficzny)' (367–72); A. Brożek, 'Język a świadomość narodowa zbiorowości polskich w diasporze' (381–86); M. Choroś, 'Nazwy czynności i stanu z formantem *-aczka* w dialektach śląskich' (403–06); A. Kowalska, 'Polszczyzna literacka na Śląsku w dobie średniopolskiej' (429–36); B. Kreja, 'Zdrobnienia na —'*(ecz)ek* typu *chłopieczek* w gwarach i historii języka polskiego (na tle słowiańskim)' (437–46); W. Kupiszewski, '*Księżyc w lisiej czapie* (ze słownictwa gwarowego)' (447–52); J. Miodek, 'Germanizmy w gwarze śląskiej' (463–68); H. Popowska-Taborska, 'Archaiczny kaszubski przymiotnik *grądi*' (473–78); J. Treder, 'Nowa dziedzina badawcza: frazeologia gwarowa' (501–06); Z. Zagórski, 'O *Małym atlasie językowym województwa gorzowskiego*' (519–30). G. Rytter, 'Prasłowiańskie **gomyla* → dialektyczne (północne) **mogyla* "pogański nasyp nagrobny"', *SlOc*, 46–47, 1989–90 (1991):155–66; E. Siatkowska, 'Język literacki czy regionalny? (Porównanie języków grup etnicznych z zachodniej Słowiańszczyzny nie posiadających politycznej autonomii)', *ib.*, 185–96; Z. Sobierajski, H. Nowak, and M. Hasiuk, 'Tematyka nagrań gwarowych i etnograficznych z lat 1965–1969. Katalog taśmoteki Zakładu Dialektologii Polskiej Uniwersytetu A. Mickiewicza w Poznaniu (cz. VII)', *ib.*, 279–300; Z. Zagórski,

'Materiał słownikowy z kilku wsi krajniackich w okolicach Złotowa (województwo pilskie) (cz. I)', *ib.*, 327–37.

8. INDIVIDUALS. INDIVIDUAL WORKS. STYLISTICS

ARGIGLOBYN. W. R. Rzepka and B. Walczak, 'Właściwości językowe wielkopolskiego rękopisu Jerzego Argiglobyna (Poznańczyka) z połowy XVI wieku', *ZNWSPO*. Językoznawstwo, 13:167–84; W. R. Rzepka, 'Uwagi o słownictwie rękopisu Jerzego Argiglobyna (Poznańczyka) połowy XVI w.', *ib.*, 487–94.

BAUDOUIN. I. Łuczków, 'Problemy polsko-rosyjskiego językoznawstwa konfrontatywnego w pracach Jana Baudouina de Courtenay', *SlaW*, 56:93–102.

BERNATOWICZ. J. Brzeziński, 'O słownictwie *Nierozsądniczych ślubów* Feliksa Bernatowicza', *ZNWSPO*. Językoznawstwo, 13:387–94.

BIBLE AND LITURGY. K. Długosz-Kurczabowa, 'Onomastyka *Nowego Testamentu*', *SlOc*, 46–47, 1989–90 (1991):71–88; E. Breza, 'Polszczyzna "Ojcze nasz" i "Zdrowaś Maryjo"', *JPol*, 71:2–9; S. Urbańczyk, 'Glosy do Modlitwy Pańskiej i Pozdrowienia anielskiego', *ib.*, 9–17; M. Jurkowski, '"Na początku było Słowo" — z zagadnień przekładu tekstów biblijnych', *PJ*:212–16.

BRÜCKNER. W. Kośny, 'Aleksander Brückner — ein polnischer Slavist in Berlin als "Dolmetscher der Geister"', *ZSl*, 96:381 91.

DZIENNIK CHICAGOSKI. M. Maliborska, 'Z zagadnień słowotwórczej adaptacji wyrazów amerykańskopolskich (na materiale "Dziennika Chicagoskiego" 1921–31)', *PFil*, 35:113–28.

GDACJUSZ. B. Wyderka, 'Sugestywność w kazaniach Adama Gdacjusza', *ZNWSPO*. Językoznawstwo, 13:511–18.

GOMBROWICZ. P. Kupiszewski and W. Kupiszewski, 'Uwagi o języku dramatu Witolda Gombrowicza *Iwona księżniczka Burgunda*', *PJ*:225–33.

HERBERT. M. Nowotna, 'La crise du vouloir: analyse sémio-linguistique du poème de Zbigniew Herbert, *Monsieur Cogito de la position debout*', *RSl*, 63:351–65, examines the poem *Pan Cogito o postawie wyprostowanej*, looking at the contrast between *nie chcą* on the one hand and *chciałby/chce* on the other.

JARUZELSKI. D. Zdunkiewicz, 'Język w służbie stanu wojennego (o przemówieniu gen. Wojciecha Jaruzelskiego z 13 grudnia 1981r.)', *PJ*:38–46.

JUNGMANN. E. Mańczak-Wohlfeld, 'Zapożyczenia angielskie w słowniku Josefa Jungmanna', *ZNWSPO*. Językoznawstwo, 13:115–20; T. Z. Orłoś, 'Leksyka słowiańska w przekładach Josefa Jungmanna', *ib.*, 133–42.

KOCHANOWSKI. J. Kobylińska, 'Analiza stylistyczno-językowa *Trenów* Jana Kochanowskiego (na przykładzie Trenu IV)', *Polonistyka*, 44:3–10; M. Foltmann, '"Fraszki nieprzepłacone ..."'. Kilka uwag o dowcipie językowym *Fraszek* Jana Kochanowskiego', *WSPRRNDFP*. Prace Językoznawcze, 20/72, 1990:149–70; J. Lizak, 'Wypowiedzenia pytajne w funkcji ekspresywnej w *Pieśniach* Jana Kochanowskiego', *ib.*, 171–200.

LEKARZ WIEJSKI. H. Rybicka-Nowacka, '*Lekarz wiejski* z roku 1788 wobec oryginału francuskiego', *PFil*, 35:287–90, concludes that *Dykjonarz powszechny medyki, chirurgii i sztuki hodowania bydląt* represents a reworking rather than a translation of its French 'original'.

ŁOZIŃSKI. S. Tomaszewska, 'Funkcje nazw własnych w "Zaklętym dworze" Walerego Łozińskiego', *RKJŁ*, 35, 1989 (1991):191–204.

MACIEJ Z MIECHOWA. W. Decyk, 'O kilku wyrazach ruskich w *Tractatus de duabus sarmatiis* Macieja z Miechowa', *PFil*, 35:239–44.

MICKIEWICZ. Ł. M. Szewczyk, 'Nazwy własne w "Grażynie" Adama Mickiewicza', *AUNCFP*, 31. Językoznawstwo, Nauki Humanistyczno-Społeczne, 192, 1990:259–84; M. Zarębina, 'Funkcje osobowych nazw własnych w *Panu Tadeuszu*', *ZNWSPO*. Językoznawstwo, 13:325–32; Ł. M. Szewczyk, 'Funkcje artystyczne nazewnictwa biblijnego w "Dziadów cz. III" Adama Mickiewicza', *Onomastica*, 35, 1990:91–102.

MŁODZIANOWSKI. T. Sokołowska, 'Kultura mówienia i nauka o języku w XVII–wiecznych *Kazaniach i homiliach* Tomasza Młodzianowskiego', *PFil*, 35:209–16.

MRONGOWIUSZ. E. Czerniakowska, 'Kaszubskie nazwy miesięcy w słownikach Krzysztofa Celestyna Mrongowiusza', *SlOc*, 44, 1987 (1990):13–18.

NORWID. R. Pawelec, 'Normy w tekstach publicystycznych Cypriana Norwida', *PFil*, 35:279–86, looks at *powinien, trzeba, należy, może, godzi się* etc. Id., 'Sztukmistrz Norwid i jego sztuka', *PJ*:217–24, discusses what the word *sztuka* meant for Norwid. J. Puzynina, 'Z badań nad składnią poezji Norwida', *PFil*, 35:147–571, points out that deviant syntax helps to account for the existence of competing interpretations. See also her 'Semantyka i pragmatyka w analizie tekstu literackiego (na materiale wiersza C. Norwida *Czy ten ptak kala gniazdo, co je kala*', *PJ*:96–102, and 'Język Cypriana Norwida', *Polonistyka*, 44:266–83, on Norwid's unique poetic idiolect.

NOWAKOWSKI. E. Pajewska, 'Charakterystyka elementów składniowo-stylistycznych w wybranych opowiadaniach Marka Nowakowskiego', *PFil*, 35:273–78.

PASEK. A. Holvoet, 'O pewnych osobliwościach użycia aspektu w *Pamiętnikach* Jana Chryzostoma Paska', *PFil*, 35:83–89.

PRZYJACIEL LUDU. K. Długosz, 'Nazwy własne i ich formy pochodne w *Przyjacielu Ludu*', *SlOc*, 46–47, 1989–90 (1991):59–70.

SLOVO O POLKU IGOREVE. J. Kunińska, 'Ze studiów nad epitetami w polskich przekładach "Słowa o wyprawie Igora"', *ZNUJ*, 962. Prace Językoznawcze, 101, 1990:35–44.

SZELBURG-ZAREMBINA. C. Kosyl, 'Nazwy własne w literaturze dla dzieci (na przykładzie prozy Ewy Szelburg-Zarembiny)', *ZNWSPO*. Językoznawstwo, 13:201–10.

SZPAKOWICZ. M. Bańko, 'Niektóre problemy oceny adekwatności gramatyk (na przykładzie fragmentu gramatyki Szpakowicza)', *PrIJP*, 70. Studia Gramatyczne, 9, 1990:55–72.

ŚRZODKA. A. Bańkowski and W. Wydra, 'Słowniczek Tomasza Śrzodki. Editio secunda', *ZNWSPO*. Językoznawstwo, 13:275–78.

TORUŃ CANTIONAL. B. Bartnicka, 'Na marginesie reedycji *Kancjonalu toruńskiego*', *PFil*, 35:15–22.

WAŁĘSA. J. Bralczyk, 'O języku Wałęsy', *TD*, 1990, no. 4:60–81; M. Czyżewski and S. Kowalski, 'Retoryka Wałęsy', *ib.*, 82–92.

ZEGADŁOWICZ. E. Malinowska, 'O słownictwie Emila Zegadłowicza powieściopisarza', *ZNWSPO*. Językoznawstwo, 13:453–62.

ŻEROMSKI. W. Kupiszewski, 'Z zagadnień języka "Syzyfowych prac" S. Żeromskiego', *Polonistyka*, 44:575–84, stresses the importance of foreign words, especially Russianisms for colouring. T. Ampel and J. Litwin, 'Kategoria czasu w prozie artystycznej', *WSPRRNDFP* Prace Językoznawcze, 20/72, 1990:5–24.

POSITIVISM. K. Strycharz, 'O tematycznych wskaźnikach nawiązania między akapitami w nowelach pozytywistycznych', *WSPRRNDFP*. Prace Językoznawcze, 20/72, 1990:47–60.

REPORTAGE. J. Litwin, 'Przytoczenie i parenteza w reportażu', *WSPRRNDFP*. Prace Językoznawcze, 20/72, 1990:61–78.

TRANSLATION. H.J. Kamińska, 'Język i sprawa autorstwa przekładu *Pasji* z 1643 roku', *WSPRRNDFP*. Prace Językoznawcze, 20/72, 1990:127–48; S. Barańczak, 'Mały lecz maksymalistyczny Manifest translatologiczny albo: Tłumaczenie się z tego, że tłumaczy się wiersze również w celu wytłumaczenia innym tłumaczom, iż dla większości tłumaczeń nie ma wytłumaczenia', *TD*, 1990, no. 3:7–66; E. Tabakowska, 'Językoznawstwo kognitywne a poetyka przekładu', *ib.*, 97–113.

FUNCTIONAL STYLISTICS. M. Čechová, 'Metody stylistyki funkcjonalnej' *PJ*:71–75.

ACAPITS. H. Hrdličková, 'Akapit jako jednostka tekstowa (z punktu widzenia językoznawczo-dydaktycznego)', *PJ*:76–81.

CONTEMPORARY POETRY. E. Dąbrowska, 'Przeciwstawienie a spójność tekstu (na materiale polskiej poezji współczesnej)', *ZNWSPO*. Językoznawstwo, 13:407–14; A. Starzec, 'Ścisłość jako cecha stylowa tekstu naukowego i popularnonaukowego', *ib.*, 495–500.

9. POLISH AND OTHER LANGUAGES

J. Kriššáková, 'Zmeny v systéme laterál v goralských nárečiach z aspektu slovensko-poľských jazykových kontaktov', *SLPS*, 1, 1988:7–14, in a volume also containing A. Zaręba, 'Z polsko-słowackich stosunków językowych. Szkic głosowni gwary oszczadnickiej' (15–40); F. Buffa, 'O deminutívach v poľštine a slovenčine' (41–48); M. Pančíková, 'Zložené substantíva v poľštine a slovenčine a ich produktívne typy' (83–92); E. Orwińska, 'Wartość badań konfrontatywnych dla teorii części mowy' (93–110); M. Papierz, 'Słowackie i polskie modulanty — ich rola w procesia fokalizacji' (111–18); A. Ferenčíková, 'O jednom zhodnom slovensko-poľskom syntaktickom prostriedku (Časové vety so spájacím výrazom *kedy/kiedy*' (119–24); M. Honowska, 'Polski bezokolicznik na tle słowackiego' (125–40); A. Habovštiak, 'Zo slovanskej lexikálnej problematiky *Borievka obyčajná* (Juniperus communis) v západoslovánských jazykoch' (141–54); M. Majtánová, 'Názvy húb z rodu Lycoperdon v českých, slovenských a poľských nárečiach' (155–64); I. Ripka, 'O niektorých slovenských a poľských prirovnaniach (Príspevok k porovnávacej frazeológii)' (175–82); M. Servátka, 'Významové asociácie a konotácie pri vnímaní lexiky cudzieho jazyka (na slovenskom a poľskom jazykovom materiáli)' (183–88).

J. Kriššáková, 'Fonologický systém goralských nárečí z aspektu slovensko-poľských kontaktov', *SLPS*, 2, 1990:3–21, in a volume also containing M. Servátka, 'Prejavy fonetickej interferencie v rámci slovensko-poľských kontaktov' (22–35); K. Holly, 'O słowackich wpływach językowych w gwarze Żywiecczyzny' (36–45); M. Pančíková, 'Nové pomenovania miesta v slovenčine a poľštine' (46–58); P. Žigo, 'Vyjadrenie konečnej hranice deja časovou vedľajšou vetou v predspisovnej slovenčine a poľštine' (80–97); M. Papierz, 'Interiekcjonalizacja w języku słowackim i polskim' (98–105); F. Buffa, 'O slovensko-poľskej medzijazykovej homonymii' (124–40); A. Habovštiak, 'Slovenská nárečová lexika v západoslovanskom kontexte' (141–61); Z. Sobierajski, 'Z polskiej i międzysłowiańskiej terminologii hodowlanej na Spiszu polskim i słowackim' (62–84); K. Habovštiaková, 'Zhody a kontrastivity v názvoch členov rodiny a príbuzenstva v slovenčine a v poľštine' (185–97); E. Krošláková, 'Zhody a kontrastivity medzi slovenskou a poľskou frazeológiou' (251–67).

M. Zarębina, 'Przyczyny zmian w systemie leksykalnym. Wzajemny stosunek wyrazów wychodzących z użycia i nowo powstałych', *SLPS*, 3, 1990:23–30, in a volume also containing B. Falińska, 'Z badań nad przysłówkami w gwarach północnowschodniej Polski' (119–28); J. Okoniowa, 'O pewnych tendencjach rozwojowych polskich przymiotników gwarowych' (129–34); J. Reichan, 'Słownictwo gwarowe w przestrzeni i czasie' (135–42); R. Lebda, 'O socjolingwistyczną metodę w badaniach dialektologicznych (na przykładzie zapożyczeń niemieckich w gwarze Kobylorzy na Opolszczyźnie)' (143–54); M. Servátka, 'Lexikálna interferencia na multilingvickom teritóriu Spiša v PĽR' (155–62); M. Pančíková, 'Neologizácia v slovenčine a poľštine (Porovnanie substantiv)' (191–98); K. Handke, 'Język familijny i jego rola w kształtowaniu potocznej polszczyzny' (209–16); B. Rejakowa, 'Inwencja a schemat (czynniki indywidualne i systemowe w przekładach związków frazeologicznych z języka słowackiego na polski i z polskiego na słowacki)' (230–45).

S. F. Kolbuszewski, 'Znaczenie języka łotewskiego dla etymologii słowiańskiej (pol. *piegża*: łot. *spiêdze*)', *ABS*, 19, 1990:35–38; I. S. Tikhonovich, 'Роль Виленского университета (1578–1842) в распространении польского языка на земли Литвы, Белоруссии и Украины', *ib.*, 179–92; M. Szybińska, 'Formy adresatywne w języku polskim i serbochorwackim (wybrane zagadnienia)', *JPol*, 71:35–41; N. Popowska-Taborska, 'Analiza polskich zapisów w tak zwanym Słowniku Zinowa', *BSZJPS*, 81, 1990:299–306; Z. Zinkiavichius, 'O личных именах литовского происхождения в *Słowniku polskich nazw osobowych*', *ib.*, 389–97; A. S. Aksamitau, 'Zu einigen Besonderheiten der belorussischen Phraseologie im Vergleich zur russischen, bulgarischen und polnischen', *ZSl*, 36:271–81. J. Podracki, 'Słowo polskie czy obce?', *Polonistyka*, 44:518–25, gives an overview of borrowings in Polish. T. Piotrowska-Małek, 'Wybrane prefiksy rzeczownikowe w języku czeskim i polskim', *PJ*:124–29; V. Mitrinović, 'Fonctionnement de l'aspect dans les verbes d'emprunt en polonais et en serbo-croate', *RSL*, 63:887–97; W. Morawski, 'Adaptacja angielskich elementów leksykalnych w języku polskim emigrantów w Stanach Zjednoczonych i Kanadzie do polskiego systemu fleksyjnego', *PFil*, 35:129–34; H. Rybicka and R. Sinielnikoff, 'Predykatywne funkcje czasowników *widać*, *słychać* i ich odpowiedników w języku rosyjskim i czeskim', *ib.*, 159–65; M. Strybel, 'O budowie morfologicznej polonijnych pożyczek leksykalnych pochodzących ze złożeń amerykańskoangielskich', *ib.*, 217–27.

10. ONOMASTICS

Kazimierz Rymut, *Nazwiska Polaków*, Ww, ZNiO, 316 pp., begins with material on linguistic, historical, etymological, orthographical and legal aspects of surnames, including a section on Polish surnames of foreign origin (60–70). Exemplification follows, a selected list of groups of interrelated surnames from Abel to Żyżel (73–309). There are three full pages of 'basic' bibliography (310–12). J. Piotrowski, 'O etymologii nazwy osobowej *Kościół*, *JPol*, 70, 1990:53–56; H. Kunstmann, 'Poln. *Gdańsk*, russ. *Gdov*, kroat. *Gacka* und verwandtes. Zwei unbeachtete slavische Lauterscheinungen', *WSl*, 36:314–29. K. Rymut, 'O potrzebie rekonstrukcji prasłowiańskiego systemu antroponimicznego', *Onomastica*, 35, 1990:5–15, in a volume also containing A. Cieślikowa, 'Problemy derywacji paradygmatycznej w antroponimii' (17–29); U. Bijak, 'Nazwy zestawione typu *Boguty-Augustyny* na Mazowszu i Podlasiu' (31–54); Z. Gołąb, 'Czy *Warszawa* (starsze Warszewa) rzeczywiście pochodzi od pomorskiego imienia *Warsza-Warcisława*?' (55–65), which connects Warsaw's name with the surname *Warsz*, from *vъršь 'dzik [wild boar]'; K. Holly, 'Nazwy terenowe Żywiecczyzny' (67–90); A. and D. Galasińscy, 'Nazwy biur matrymonialnych' (103–11). J. Chojnacki, 'Nazwy terenowe środkowej części gminy Kazimierz Biskupi w województwie konińskim', *SlOc*, 46–47, 1989–90 (1991):33–58; M. Borejszo, 'Staropolskie nazwy miesięcy', *ib.*, 19–32; J. Nalepa, '*Pokój* i *wojna* w staropolskich imionach (cz. I)', *JPol*, 71:87–97; D. Kopertowska, 'Związek toponimii z rozwojem przestrzennym Kielc', *SlOc*, 46–47, 1989–90 (1991):107–14; A. Pospiszylowa, 'Wspólne typy bazy semantycznej w nazwach geograficznych staropruskich, niemieckich i polskich z obszaru południowej Warmii', *ib.*, 143–54; A. Bańkowski, 'Toponimy ziemi krakowskiej w zapiskach sądowych z lat 1394–1397', *ZNWSPO. Językoznawstwo*, 13:83–92, in a volume also containing I. Bily, 'Rekonstrukcja starołużyckich wyrazów pospolitych na podstawie nazw miejscowych' (93–96); E. Breza, 'Pomorskie nazwiska od imion z członem *borzy-* i *bor-*' (101–08); K. Długosz, 'O polskich przezwiskach od niemieckich podstaw' (109–21); S. Gajda, 'Znaczenie nazw własnych a lingwodydaktyka' (125–34); S. Gala, 'System antroponimiczny imion, przezwisk, nazwisk' (135–42); M. Gruchmanowa, 'Nazwiska śląskie w Independence Wisconsin w USA' (143–54); K. Handke, 'Nazwy typu *Sułkowskie, Ordynackie* w toponimii, miejskiej' (155–62); K. Hengst, '*Trebula* — ein theophores Toponym in West-slavischen?' (163–74); E. Jakus-Borkowa, 'Terminy geograficzne mikropola "wody stojące" a hydronimy ogólnopolskie' (175–82); Ł, Jarczak, 'Nazwiska w urbarzu rybnickim z 1614 r.' (183–94); M. Kamińska, 'O kształtowaniu się nazwisk mieszczańskich w centralnej Polsce (na przykładzie Łasku)' (195–200); W. Lubaś, 'Kodyfikacja egzonimów z punktu widzenia potrzeb komunikacyjnych' (219–24); R. Mrożek, 'O systemie mikrotoponimicznym polsko-czeskiego pogranicza językowego XVIII w.' (245–50); K. Nowik, 'Baza *g(v)ozdъ* w polskiej toponimii', (251–59); F. Pluta, 'Przezwiska ludowe z okolic Głogówka' (259–66); E. Rzetelska-Feleszko, 'Nazwy rezerwatów przyrody' (271–78); W. P. Schmidt, '*Skawa*' (279–82); S. Sochacka, 'Polskie nazwy terenowe na XIX-wiecznych mapach katastralnych powiatu lublinieckiego' (283–90); W. Śmiech, '*Isep* (i pochodne) — polska nazwa terenowa i miejscowa'·(301–06); J. Udolph, '*Mała Panew/Malapane*' (307–12); S. Warchoł, 'Uwagi w sprawie genezy i funkcji formantu *-*itjo*- w nazwach osobowych i w apelatywach' (313–20); J. Węgier, 'Współczesne użycie formantów tworzących nazwiska żon i dzieci w wybranych środowiskach miejskich i wiejskich' (321–24); K. Zierhoffer, 'Jeszcze raz o nazwie *Śrem*' (333–38); Z. Zierhofferowa, 'Terminy osadnicze i ich funkcje w toponimii (na podstawie materiału nazewniczego z obszaru dawnego województwa kaliskiego)' (339–46). R.S., 'Związek Radziecki czy Związek Sowiecki?', *PJ*: 234–37, cites a number of views from writers in the Polish press in 1990.

11. POLISH AND THE COMPUTER

T. Woźniak, 'Próba automatyzacji transkrypcji tekstu staropolskiego — propozycja metody', *JPol*, 71 : 42–46.

LITERATURE

By Ursula Phillips, *Assistant Librarian, School of Slavonic and European Studies, University of London*

1. General

There has been very little published this year on Polish literature prior to Romanticism. Interest, especially that of West European scholars, concentrates as in previous years on 20th-c. writing. The 19th c., however, is reasonably well represented. *Słownik literatury polskiej XIX wieku* (Vademecum Polonisty), ed. Józef Bachórz and Alina Kowalczykowa, Ww, ZNiO, 1112 pp., provides a general introduction to the period and complements, in the same series, the earlier *Słownik literatury staropolskiej: Średniowiecze, Renesans, Barok*, ed. Teresa Michałowska, Barbara Otwińska and Elżbieta Sarnowska-Temeriusz, 1990, 976 pp. *Fakty i interpretacje: szkice z historii literatury i kultury polskiej*, ed. Tomasz Lewandowski, Wa, PWN, 397 pp., is a collection of essays dedicated to Jarosław Maciejewski by pupils and colleagues and covers all periods. There have been several collections of essays by well-known critics: Jan Kott, **Pisma wybrane*, ed. Tadeusz Nyczek, Wa, Krąg, 3 vols, 334, 422, 485 pp.; Artur Sandauer, **Byłem . . .*, Wa, PIW, 149 pp.; M. Fik, 'Burzliwa pogoda — z oddalenia', *Dialog*, 36.5–6:181–90, provides an overview of Konstanty Puzyna's collections of critical essays. Specifically on the 20th c.: **W pejzażu ojczyzny i obczyzny: studia i szkice o literaturze polskiej XX wieku* (PNUS, 1201), ed. Włodzimierz Wójcik, Katowice U.P., 104 pp.; Jacek Łukasiewicz, **Oko poematu*, Ww, Wyd. Dolnośląskie, 349 pp., which deals with poetry only. There have also been a number of contributions on more specific aspects of poetry. Love in pastoral and folk poetry is the theme of Dobrosława Weżowicz-Ziółkowska, **Miłość ludowa: wzory miłości wieśniaczej w polskiej pieśni ludowej XVIII–XX wieku*, Ww, Polskie Towarzystwo Ludoznawcze, 203 pp. A. Nasiłowska, 'Kamienie', *Twórczość*, 47.1:68–81, speculates on the symbolism of stones in Polish poetry. W. Dynak, 'Łowiectwo w poezji polskiej', *PL(W)*, 82.1:3–22, similarly encompasses all periods. More theoretical is S. Wysłouch, 'Od Lessinga do Pryzbosia: teoria i kompozycja opisu', *ib.*, 82.4:5–26, which examines the close relationship between art and poetry, putting the philosophical background in a general context but drawing most of the practical examples from Polish poetry.

Maria Janion, *Projekt krytyki fantazmatycznej* (Biblioteka Tekstów, 4), Wa, Wyd. PEN, 219 pp., treats the function of the imagination and of fantasies in literature and the double reality this sometimes causes writers to live in. The main focus is Polish Romanticism, especially Mickiewicz, as well as the work of Tadeusz Konwicki and his interpretation of Mickiewicz; his film *Lawa* is discussed. Also included is an essay on revolution in Krasiński's *Nie-Boska Komedia*, S. I. Witkiewicz's *Szewcy* and Gombrowicz's *Operetka*. *Zwierciadła północy: związki i paralele literatur*, ed. Maria Janion, Nils Åke Nilsson and Anna Sobolewska, Wa, IBL, 228 pp., covers literary links with Scandinavian writers from and including Romanticism up to and including the interwar period. C. Miłosz and T. Venclova, 'Rozmowa o Litwie: autorzy dyskusji z prowadzącym spotkanie Janem Błońskim', *Odra*, 31.1:23–33, is an interesting discussion of the Lithuanian connection. *PL(L)*, 16, continues the Italian theme of last year's volume dealing with the reception of Polish culture in Italy. Of particular interest to literary scholars are: J. Żurawska, 'Awangarda i futuryzm polski we Włoszech powojennych' (8–18); R. K. Lewański, 'Literatura podróżnicza' (23–28); M. Calore, 'Recepcja powojennej dramaturgii polskiej we Włoszech' (58–69). *TD*, nos 1–2, provides a retrospective review of some of the highlights of émigré writing, whilst no. 5 is devoted to the treatment of economic problems in literature.

Włodzimerz Bolecki, *Pre-teksty i teksty: z zagadnień związków międzytekstowych w literaturze polskiej XX wieku* (IBL), Wa, PWN, 235 pp., is an interesting collection of articles written over several years and grouped here thematically into chapters. The work includes material on Berent (60–101), Miłosz (159–95) and Barańczak (196–225), as well as a chapter on the links between Młoda Polska and the literature of the interwar period, entitled 'Od potworów do znaków pustych. Z dziejów groteski: Młoda Polska i Dwudziestolecie Międzywojenne' (102–58).

2. FROM THE MIDDLE AGES UP TO ROMANTICISM

A number of works emphasize the importance of Italian influences on Polish literature in both the Renaissance and Baroque periods: Jan Ślaski, **Wokół literatury włoskiej, węgierskiej i polskiej w epoce Renesansu: szkice komparatystyczne* (RUW, 135), Wa U.P., 329 pp.; Sante Graciotti, **Od Renesansu do Oświecenia*, trans. Wojciech Jekiel *et al.*, Wa, PIW, 2 vols, 400, 486 pp.; L. Gambacorta, '"Arkadia": model włoskiej kultury arkadyjskiej a polska kultura literacka', trans. J. Łukaszewicz, *PL(W)*, 82.3:3–14; Dorota Gostyńska, *Retoryka iluzji: koncept w poezji barokowej*, Wa, IBL, 259 pp. This last is very general, but contains important background to the period as well as commentary on M. K. Sarbiewski and J. A. Morsztyn. On the religious theme: Jacek Sokolski, **Staropolskie zaświaty* (AUW, 1160), Ww U.P., 1990,

264 pp.; Krzysztof Obremski, *Obraz Boga w polskiej liryce religijnej XVII wieku* (Prace Wydziału Filologiczno-filozoficznego, 32.2), Toruń, TNT, 1990, 104 pp. Janina Abramowska, *Polska bajka ezopowa* (Seria Filologia Polska, 51), Pń, UAM, 379 pp., surveys the classical and general European background to the fable before discussing the work of M. Rej, W. Potocki, K. Niemirycz, J. S. Jabłonowski, and I. Krasicki. Hanna Dziechcińska, *O staropolskich dziennikach podróży*, Wa, IBL, 121 pp., is an interesting study though not exclusively literary.

INDIVIDUAL WRITERS

BAKA. Aleksander Nawarecki, *Czarny karnawał: "Uwagi śmierci niechybnej" księdza Baki — poetyka tekstu i paradoksy recepcji* (Rozprawy literackie, 67), Ww, ZNiO, 377 pp.

KOCHANOWSKI. Wiktor Weintraub, *Nowe studia o Janie Kochanowskim* (Biblioteka Studiów Literackich), Kw, WL, 240 pp.

KOŹMIAN. P. Zbikowski, '"Ziemiaństwo polskie" Kajetana Koźmiana jako poemat dydaktyczny: próba tożsamości gatunkowej', *PL(W)*, 82.3:15–30.

PASEK. *O języku i stylu 'Pamiętników' Jana Chryzostoma Paska*, ed. Halina Rybicka-Nowacka, Wa U.P., 1989, 263 pp.

W. POTOCKI. Dariusz Rott and Renata Sadło, *Bibliografia prac magisterskich dotyczących twórczości Wacława Potockiego*, part 1 (1956–78), Katowice, Instytut Literatury i Kultury Polskiej Uniwersytetu Śląskiego, 8 pp.

ROŹDZIEŃSKI. Jerzy Piaskowski, *Walenty Roździeński i jego poemat hutniczy 'Officina ferraria'*, Katowice, Museum Śląskie, 161 pp.

S. RZEWUSKI. K. Maksimowicz, 'Seweryn Rzewuski i okolicznościowa poezja polityczna doby Sejmu Czteroletniego', *PL(W)*, 82.4:124–41.

SKARGA. H. Fros, 'Źródła "Żywotów Świętych" Piotra Skargi', *PL(W)*, 82.3:172–94.

TRZECIESKI. J. Snopek, 'Nieznane wierszy Andrzeja Trzecieskiego', *PL(W)*, 82.1:158–66.

3. ROMANTICISM

Anna Kowalczykowa, *Czym był romantyzm?*, Wa, LSW, 1990, 189 pp., discusses the specifically Polish features of Romanticism against the wider European background and is a useful overview rather than an in-depth study. Waleria Szydłowska-Brykczyńska, *Egzystencjalistyczne królestwo albo romantyzm na wyganiu*, Chotomów, Verba, 115 pp., analyses Mickiewicz's *Dziady*, Słowacki's *Kordian* and Wyspiański's *Wyzwolenie*. Jerzy Pietrkiewicz, *Messianic Prophecy: A Case for*

Reappraisal, London, School of Slavonic and East European Studies, 51 pp., is the text of the fifth Grabowski Memorial Lecture and is published as a parallel text in English and Polish. Zbigniew Przychodniak, *U progu romantyzmu: przemiany warszawskiej krytyki teatralnej w latach 1815–1825* (Źródła do historii polskiej krytyki teatralnej, 1), Ww, Wiedza o Kulturze, 205 pp., discusses theatre criticism in the light of political and social values prevalent in the Kingdom of Poland, including the impact of the new Romantic movement. A chapter is devoted to Kazimierz Brodziński and his views on theatre.

INDIVIDUAL WRITERS

FREDRO. Bogdan Zakrzewski, **Śląskie przygody Aleksandra Fredry*, Ww, ZNiO, 127 pp.

KRASIŃSKI. Andrzej Fabianowski, *Myśl polityczna Zygmunta Krasińskiego* (Ciechanowskie Studia i Materiały, 36), Ciechanów, Ciechanowskie Towarzystwo Naukowe, 138 pp. L. Kolankicwicz, 'Notatki po spektaklu: "Nie-Boska Komedia"', *Dialog*, 36.8:94–101; this is a review of Maciej Prus' recent production, but the emphasis is on the interpretation of the play and the relevance for today of K.'s views on history and revolution.

KRASZEWSKI. Jerzy Jarowiecki, **O powieści historycznej Józefa Ignacogo Kraszewskiego* (Prace Monograficzne, 129), Kw, WSP, 231 pp.

MICKIEWICZ. Jan Walc, *Architekt Arki*, Chotomów, Verba, 259 pp., covers the creative years of M.'s life (1822–34) and constitutes something of a personal crusade against the received wisdom of 'mickiewiczologia' which Walc believes has undergone little re-examination since Kleiner and which has failed to confront and illuminate major issues raised by M.'s work. M. Strzyzewski, 'Przeklęte zwycięstwo Wallenroda', *Twórczość*, 47.8:91–102, is a long review article of Maria Janion, *Życie pośmiertne Konrada Wallenroda*, Wa, PIW, 1990, 707 pp. (see *YWMLS*, 52:934). M. Masłowski, 'Kto jest bohaterem "Dziadów"?', *PrzH*, 35.2:23–31. N. Taylor, 'The folklore origins of Mickiewicz's "Dziady": Olimpia Swianiewiczowa's interpretation', *OSP*, 23, 1990:39–60. M. Masłowski, 'Wiara i historia: dynamiczny model religii wcielania w dziele Adama Mickiewicza', *PL(W)*, 82.3:31–54. Dorota Siwicka, **Ton i bicz: Mickiewicz wśród towiańczyków* (IBL), Ww, ZNiO, 1990, 228 pp. Jarosław Marek Rymkiewicz, *Baket*, Wa, Niezależna Oficyna Wydawnicza, 251 pp., is a sequel to his *Żmut* and covers M.'s life at Vilnius University. D. Świerczyńska, 'Zapomniane relacje o pobycie Mickiewicza w Burgas', *PL(W)*, 81.4, 1990:217–28, discusses accounts of the last weeks of M.'s life not so far considered by his biographers. See also SŁOWACKI.

NORWID. Mieczysław Inglot, *Cyprian Norwid* (Biblioteka 'Polonistyki'), Wa, WSP, 487 pp. *Cyprian Norwid — w setną rocznicę śmierci poety: materiały z sesji poświęconej życiu i twórczości C. Norwida (27–29 października 1983)*, ed. Stanisław Burkot, Kw, WL, 278 pp. Krzysztof Raczyński, *Słowa i brzmienia: studia o prozie i warsztacie pisarskim C. Norwida* (Studia i Monografie, 171), Opole, WSP, 87 pp. Marek Adamiec, *Oni i Norwid: problemy odbioru twórczości Cypriana Norwida w latach 1840–1883* (Rozprawy Literackie, 66), Ww, ZNiO, 245 pp. J. Zach-Błońska, 'Norwid: "Mowa, dlatego że jest mowa, musi być nieodzownie dramatyczną!"', *PL(W)*, 82.2:3–16, discusses N.'s deliberations on the function of speech and on the importance of silence. C. S. Kraszewski, 'Norwid's "Quidam" as heroic literature', *PolR*, 36.3:309–22. *The Mature Laurel* (details under 1945 TO THE PRESENT DAY) contains two pieces on N.: B. Czaykowski, 'The place of the author of "Vade-Mecum" in the context of nineteenth-century European poetry and his relevance for Modernism' (17–33); G. Hyde, 'Cyprian Kamil Norwid: "Yesterday-and-I"/"Wczora-i-ja"' (91–94).

H. RZEWUSKI. A. Waśko, '"Pamiątki Soplicy" na tle programowych wypowiedzi Henryka Rzewuskiego', *PL(W)*, 82.1:60–85.

SKARBEK. K. Bartoszyński, 'Ekonomia — historia — literatura: na marginesie twórczości Fryderyka Skarbka', *TD*, no. 5:25–44.

SŁOWACKI. *PL(W)*, 82.1 contains two articles on S.: M. Saganiak, 'Czytelnik idealny pism mistycznych Juliusza Słowackiego' (23–38), which is largely about *Król-Duch*, and P. Jarmocik, 'Sprawa sztana i sprawa Kanclerza: antynomie etyczne w "Samuelu Zborowskim" Juliusza Słowackiego' (39–59). S. Makowski, '"Dziady" Mickiewicza — "Dziady" Słowackiego', *PrzH*, 35.2:33–50, also analyses *Król-Duch*. A. Kowalczykowa, '"Genezis z Ducha" Słowackiego — czy na pewno rok 1844?', *PL(W)*, 81.4, 1990:209–15.

4. FROM REALISM TO NEO-REALISM

H. Markiewicz, 'Spór o przełom pozytywistyczny', *TD*, nos 5–6, 1990:62–79, questions whether 1863 was really the turning point between Romanticism and Positivism. W. Olkusz, 'Orientalizm w poezji doby pozytywizmu', *PL(W)*, 82.2:17–59, demonstrates how poets in this period carried on the exotic themes and imagery of the Romantics whilst anticipating, thanks to their interest in Indian culture, the philosophical and emotional concerns of the Modernists. *PL(W)*, 81.4, 1990, contains two articles on Young Poland: L. Tatarowski, 'Sielanka wiejska w literaturze Młodej Polski' (37–91);

W. Gutowski, 'Hedonizm młodopolskiej erotyki' (93–118). Also on Young Poland: Tadeusz Linkner, *Mitologia słowiańska w literaturze Młodej Polski* (Rozprawy i Monografie, 162), Gd U.P., 254 pp.; Jean Lajarrige, *La Jeune Pologne et les lettres européennes (1890–1910)*, Wa, PWN, 549 pp. K. Stępnik, 'Opowiadania o Legionach (1914–1917)', *PL(W)*, 82.2 : 55–73, discusses the fiction and some poetry of the war years.

INDIVIDUAL WRITERS

ASNYK. Antoni Baczewski, *Poezja Adama Asnyka*, Rzeszów, WSP, 194 pp.
BRZOZOWSKI. M. Głowiński, 'Wielka parataksa: o budowie dyskursu w "Legendzie Młodej Polski" Stanisława Brzozowskiego', *PL(W)*, 82.4 : 43–70.
DYGASIŃSKI. *O twórczości i życiu Adolfa Dygasińskiego: materiały z sesji naukowej w 150 rocznicę urodzin pisarza*, ed. Helena Wolny, Kielce, Centrum Doskonalenia Nauczycieli/Oddział w Kielcach, 1990, 225 pp.
IRZYKOWSKI. M. Bukowska-Schielman, 'Teatr i kino w krytyce Karola Irzykowskiego', *Dialog*, 36.2 : 146–52.
LEŚMIAN. *The Mature Laurel* (details under 1945 TO THE PRESENT DAY) contains an article on L.: B. Czaykowski, 'From rhythm and metaphysics to intonation, experience and gnosis: the poetry of Bolesław Leśmian, Aleksander Wat and Czesław Miłosz' (35–87).
MICIŃSKI. D. Jagła, 'Czerwone białe plamy', *Odra*, 31.2 : 77–80, deals with the mystery surrounding M.'s murder in 1918.
PRUS. Tadeusz Budrewicz, *'Lalka': konteksty stylu* (Prace Monograficzne WSP, 113), Kw, WSP, 1990, 230 pp. J. Bachórz, '"Polska zwyciężyła Niemców pod Grunwaldem, a — co z tego?": o ekonomii politycznej Bolesława Prusa', *TD*, no. 5 : 45–61.
REYMONT. F. Ziejka, 'Władysława Stanisława Reymonta droga na francuski Parnas', *PL(W)*, 82.4 : 71–94.
SIENKIEWICZ. M. J. Mikoś, 'Sienkiewicz's "Trilogy" according to Jeremiah Curtin: materials from the Milwaukee County Historical Society', *PolR*, 36.4 : 421–34.
SZYMAŃSKI. Bogdan Burdziej, *Inny świat ludzkiej nadziei: 'Szkice' Adama Szymańskiego na tle literatury zsyłkowej*, Toruń, the Author, 252 pp.
ŚWIĘTOCHOWSKI. Bogdan Mazan, *Wczesne dramaty Aleksandra Świętochowskiego: Niewinni, Ojciec Makary, Piękna: zarys monograficzny*, Łódź U.P., 198 pp.
WYSPIAŃSKI. Rafał Węgrzyniak, *Wokół 'Wesele' Stanisława Wyspiańskiego*, Ww, ZNiO, 201 pp.

5. FROM 1918 TO 1945

Jerzy Kwiatkowski, *Literatura Dwudziestolecia* (IBL), Wa, PWN, 1990, 477 pp., is a general but thorough survey of the literary movements, poetry, prose and drama of the interwar years. **Szkice i interpretacje* (Skamander, 8; PNUS, 1170), ed. Ireneusz Opacki, Katowice U.P., 148 pp., discusses Baliński, Iwaszkiewicz, Lechoń, and Tuwim. K. Stępnik, 'Literatura polska roku 1920', *Odra*, 31.11–12:63–70, shows how contemporary events, especially the war against the Bolsheviks, were reflected in literature.

RSl, 63:293–579, 'Contre une vérité exclusive: littérature polonaise 1939 à 1989', ed. Hélène Włodarczyk, is a major contribution to the study of Polish writers of this period and of the post-1945 period. The essays, covering both poetry and prose, almost all focus on individuals and will therefore be listed below under individual writers.

INDIVIDUAL WRITERS

BACZYŃSKI. Jerzy Święch, **Wiersze Krzysztofa Kamila Baczyńskiego* (Biblioteka Analiz Literackich, 68), Wa, WSP, 160 pp.

BOBKOWSKI. J. Zieliński, 'Wielki Spokój', *TD*, nos 1–2:96–108. Two articles by S. Stabro: '"Polska usiadła nam na mózgach": o Andrzeju Bobkowskim', *Odra*, 31.1:34–41; 'Andrzej Bobkowski — contre la tradition', *RSl*, 63:457–66.

CZERNIK. Zbigniew Andres, **Stanisław Czernik: autentystyczny rodowód twórczości*, Rzeszów, WSP, 1990, 237 pp.

CZUCHNOWSKI. W. Ligęza, 'Uczta instynków i lekcja historii: o twórczości Mariana Czuchnowskiego', *PL(W)*, 82.1:86–104.

GOMBROWICZ. *RSl*, 63 includes three contributions on G.: M. Tomaszewski, 'La formation de la réalité dans la "Pornographie" et "Cosmos" de Gombrowicz' (419–28); M. Smorąg, 'La reconstruction de la réalité ou l'affirmation de soi dans l'oeuvre de Gombrowicz' (429–37); M. Legierski, 'Généalogie et variétés des doubles chez Gombrowicz' (439–55). *TD* also contains three articles: L. Neuger, 'Polskość jako cel', nos 1–2:5–23; L. Neuger, 'Witold Gombrowicz w Sztokholmie', *ib.*, 204–09; J. Margański, 'Filozof Gombrowicz', no. 5:106–18. E. Baniewicz, '"Pod krzakiem losu naszego"', *Twórczość*, 47.8:74–83, is about the various recent stagings, and hence the various interpretations and receptions, of *Ślub* in the new political climate in Poland. M. Głowiński, *'Ferdydurke' Witolda Gombrowicza* (Biblioteka Analiz Literackich, 71), Wa, WSP, 118 pp. H. Berressem, 'Witold Gombrowicz: "Cosmos": the case of the hanged sparrow', *PolR*, 36.2:145–59.

Literature

HAUPT.   K. Rutkowski, 'Mizdra i lico czyli o Hauptcie', *Twórczość*, 37.6:82–84, is mainly biographical. *TD*, nos 1–2, contains two pieces: K. Rutkowski, 'W stronę Haupta' (109–25); M. Tomaszewski, 'Nad Seretem, czyli w Europie: o prozie Zygmunta Haupta' (126–32).

HERLING-GRUDZIŃSKI.   *Etos i artyzm: rzecz o Herlingu-Grudzińskim*, ed. Seweryna Wysłouch and Ryszard K. Przybylski, Pń, Wyd. a–5, 256 pp., is a collection of essays by a number of leading critics: T. Burek, W. Bolecki, M. Wyka, R. Nycz. Other books: Ryszard K. Przybylski, *Być i pisać: o prozie Gustawa Herlinga-Grudzińskiego*, Pń, Wyd. a–5, 148 pp.; Zdzisław Kudelski, *Pielgrzym Świętokrzyski: szkice o Herlingu-Grudzińskim*, Lublin, Fis, 157 pp. *TD*, nos 1–2, contains two articles: R. Nycz, '"Zamknięty odprysk świata": o pisarstwie Gustawa Herlinga-Grudzińskiego' (35–46); T. Burek, 'Cały ten okropny świat: sztuka pamięci głębokiej a zapiski w "Innym Świecie" Herlinga-Grudzińskiego' (46–57). *Odra*, 31.4, also has two articles: M. Wyka, 'Nasz wiek według Herlinga-Grudzińskiego (51–57); B. Zielińska, '"Dziennik pisany nocą" jako portret epoki' (58–62).

IWASZKIEWICZ.   S. Kryński, 'W poszukiwaniu samego siebie: dylematy tożsamości oraz inicjacji artystycznej w powieści Iwaszkiewicza "Księżyc wschodzi"', *PL(W)*, 82.3:98–119.

JAWORSKI.   J. Kopciński, 'Antymodernistyczne parodia i groteska: "Wesele hrabiego Orgaza" Romana Jaworskiego', *PL(W)*, 82.3:74–97.

KOZARYNOWA.   J. Zieliński, 'Anioł paradoksu', *ZL*, 9.33:89–93.

LECHOŃ.   *Szkice o twórczości Jana Lechonia* (Skamander, 7; PNUS, 1150), ed. Ireneusz Opacki, Katowice U.P., 129 pp. M. Wyka, '"Dziennik" Jana Lechonia — autoterapia, sny, przepowiednie', *TD*, nos 1–2:191–97.

PEIPER.   T. Kłak, 'Tadeusz Peiper i jego odbiorcy', *PL(W)*, 81.4, 1990:119–43.

PIGOŃ.   S. Dąbrowski, 'Wspominkowy cykl sachsenhausenowski Stanisława Pigonia', part 2, *PL(W)*, 82.3:120–34.

PRZYBOŚ.   *Juliana Przybosia najmniej słów: analizy i interpretacje: praca zbiorowa*, ed. Stanisław Makowski, Wa, WSP, 192 pp.

SCHULZ.   *PolR*, 36.2, contains three pieces on S.: T. Robertson, 'Bruno Schulz and comedy' (119–26); A. Schönle, '"Cinnamon shops" by Bruno Schulz: the apology of "tandeta"' (127–44); C. Shmeruk, 'Isaac Bashevis Singer on Bruno Schulz' (161–67).

TROCZYŃSKI.   Two articles by S. Dąbrowski: 'Od doktoratowego szkicu ku rozwiniętej doktrynie teoretycznoliterackiej: logika i dynamika drogi naukowej Konstantego Troczyńskiego', *PL(W)*, 82.1:105–30; 'Konstanty Troczyński "Dynamika literatury": wstępny szkic problematyki', *PrzH*, 35.2:51–59.

WAT. J. Zychowicz, 'Medytacje o świecie bez wzoru: o figurach poezji Aleksandra Wata', *Poezja*, 35.4–6, 1990: 73–82. K. Rutkowski, 'Słowo o Wacie', *Twórczość*, 47.2: 82–88. M. Szpakowska, 'Diabeł, poeta i plebs', *ib.*, 47.4: 97–105, is a review article of *Mój wiek* on the occasion of the Czytelnik edition, 1990. M. Baranowska, 'Poeta mimo woli', *TD*, nos 1–2: 185–90, discusses *Ciemn świecidło*. See also LEŚMIAN.

WIERZYŃSKI. A. Nasiłowska, 'Późna młodość Wierzyńskiego', *Odra*, 35.1: 42–47.

WIKTOR. Anna Niewolak-Krzywda, **Twórczość literacka Jana Wiktora*, Rzeszów, WSP, 217 pp.

S. I. WITKIEWICZ. Anna Micińska, *Witkacy — Stanisław Ignacy Witkiewicz: życie i twórczość*, Wa, Interpress, 367 pp., is largely on painting and theatre, and there are also editions in English and French from the same publisher.

6.   1945 TO THE PRESENT DAY

Most of the material produced on this period concerns poetry. *The Mature Laurel: Essays on Modern Polish Poetry*, ed. Adam Czerniawski, Bridgend, Seren Books, xii + 325 pp., contains many contributions by English scholars and critics (George Hyde, John Bayley, John Pilling, Neil Ascherson), whose main field is not necessarily Poland, as well as articles by poets themselves (A. Alvarez, Tom Paulin, Edwin Morgan). Many contributions are on individuals and have been listed as such. Of the more general essays especially worthy of note is D. P. A. Pirie, 'Engineering the people's dreams: an assessment of socialist realist poetry in Poland 1949–1955' (133–59). The book also contains a good bibliography (307–13), which includes 'Anthologies devoted wholly or in part to Polish poetry', 'Individual volumes' and 'Critical studies'. M. Głowiński, 'Poezja i rytual: wiersze na sześćdziesiąte urodziny Bolesława Bieruta', *TD*, no. 6: 5–26, fits well with the theme of the Pirie article, as does *Paranoja: zapis choroby*, ed. Andrzej Roman, Wa, Editions Spotkania, 1990, 200 pp., which is an anthology of texts displaying enthusiasm for Stalinism. The book is not directly about literature but the texts are important for understanding the context within which literature was forced to operate; it includes texts of this ilk from 1968 and some from the Sejm in 1982, as well as 50 plates of illustrations.

   Marian Stala, *Chwile pewności: 20 szkiców o poezji i krytyce*, Kw, Znak, 281 pp., covers Miłosz, Szymborska, Herbert, Krynicki, Barańczak, Kornhauser, Połkowski and Maj. S. Stabro, '"Teraz" ... po latach', *Odra*, 31.11–12: 71–78, reassesses the group of poets of that name, which included Kornhauser, Kronwald, Piątkowski, Stabro himself,

Wit Jaworski, and Zagajewski. Also on poetry: K. Pisarkowa, 'O kodach współczesnej liryki krajowej: szkic', *RSl*, 62:333–49; B. Sharratt, 'Reflections of Martial Law in Polish literature of the 1980s', *NZSJ*: 101–12.

Józef Wróbel, *Tematy żydowskie w prozie polskiej 1939–1987*, Kw, Universitatis, 189 pp., tackles the Jewish theme, whilst D. Patkaniowska, 'Kultura nieżalezna', *Odra*, 31.3:17–24, presents an interesting point of view about the 'independent' literary journals of the 1980s. She mentions many more journals of the 'second circulation' than the one specifically referred to in the title, questions their ideological — and emotional — sympathies and asks whether they were in fact as independent as they claimed to be in the views they promoted.

INDIVIDUAL WRITERS

BARAŃCZAK. T. Nyczek, 'Ocalone w tłumaczeniu', *ZL*, 9.34:118–26, is a review article of *Tablica z Macondo*, London, Aneks, 1990. J. Drzewuski, 'Stanisław Barańczak i ten drugi', *Twórczość*, 47.3:82–95, is a review article of *159 wierszy (1968–1988)*, Kw, Znak, 1990.

BIAŁOSZEWSKI. H. Konicka, 'Être poète et ne pas être fier: rotations des choses de Miron Białoszewski', *RSl*, 63:329–49. Half of *TD*, no. 6, is devoted to B. The issue includes the full text of his 'Listy do Eumenid' (83–136), written to Maria Janion during the last months of his life, a short commentary on the letters by T. Sobolewski (137–42), and a memoir of B., 'Miron widziany przeze mnie' (143–53) by J. J. Lipski.

CZERNIAWSKI. Marian Kisiel, *U podstaw twórczości Adama Czerniawskiego*, Gliwice, Wokół Was, 125 pp.

GŁOWACKI. S. Chwin, '"Wallenrodowie" w Sierpniu', *TD*, no. 6:27–38, analyses *Moc truchleje*.

GROCHOWIAK. M. Delaperriére, 'Stanisław Grochowiak, poète de la dissonance', *RSl*, 63:311–27.

HERBERT. J. Łukasiewicz, 'Krajobraz czyli sposób bycia: noty o Herbercie', *Odra*, 31.2:41–46. *The Mature Laurel* (details above) contains four pieces on H.: J. Pilling, 'Zbigniew Herbert: "Mr. Cogito and the imagination"/"Pan Cogito i wyobraźnia"' (119–23); T. Paulin, 'Zbigniew Herbert: "Elegy of Fortinbras"/"Tren Fortynbrasa"' (124–30); A. Alvarez, 'Noble poet' (163–71); P. Coates, 'Gardens of stone: the poetry of Zbigniew Herbert and Tadeusz Rożewicz' (175–88).

HŁASKO. A. Grudzińska, 'La parole et sa force: la prose de Marek Hłasko et la sortie du réalisme socialiste: étude comparée d'extraits de

"Sur le chantier" de Tadeusz Konwicki et des "Ouvriers" de Marek Hłasko', *RSl*, 63:481–88. Zyta Kwiecińska, **Opowiem Wam o Marku*', Ww, Wyd. Dolnośląskie, 150 pp., discusses H.'s memoirs.

KARPOWICZ. A. Falkiewicz, 'Metafora metafor: o poezji Tymoteusza Karpowicza', *TD*, no. 3:75–87.

KONWICKI. A. Sobolewska, 'Współczesna powieść inicjacyjna: Konwicki, Walpole, Vesaas', *Twórczość*, 47.5:73–87, includes an analysis of K.'s little known *Zwierzoczłekoupiór* as well as of *Wniebowstąpienie*. *RSl*, 63 contains two articles on K.: S. Eile, '"Bohin" de Tadeusz Konwicki et le postmodernisme' (529–45); M. Masłowski, 'Tadeusz Konwicki ou le mythe du Juif errant' (547–59). B. Zielińska, 'W trzecim wymiarze', *Odra*, 31.3:56–58, is another analysis of *Bohin*. M. Tomaszewski, 'Magiczna triada Tadeusza Konwickiego', *PL(W)*, 82.3:135–49, explores the literal and symbolic use in K.'s work of three key elements — the valley, the river, the forest. See also HŁASKO.

KOSIŃSKI. Gloria L. Cronin and Blaine H. Hall, *Jerzy Kosinski: An Annotated Bibliography* (Bibliographies and Indexes in American Literature, 15), NY, Greenwood Press, xviii + 104 pp., is a thorough listing of primary and secondary sources including recordings and interviews, criticism and reviews.

LEM. Ryszard Handke, **Ze Stanisławem Lemem na szlakach fantastyki naukowej* (Biblioteka Analiz Literackich, 70), Wa, WSP, 138 pp. Two articles have appeared by J. Jarzębski: 'Intertextualité et connaissance dans l'oeuvre de Stanisław Lem', *RSl*, 63:561–76; 'Przygody rycerzy św. Kontaktu', *Odra*, 31.9:32–39.

MACKIEWICZ. Włodzimierz Bolecki, *Ptasznik z Wilna: o Józefie Mackiewiczu*, Kw, Arka, 520 pp., is a very thorough study though Bolecki is keen to point out, given the controversy which always surrounds M., that it is 'a guide and only a guide' to the facts of M.'s biography and to the problems raised by his literary works; he describes it as a 'Mackiewicz Baedecker'.

MAREK. T. Karpowicz, 'Le souverain de l'île de la Conscience pure: sur la poésie de Zdzisław Marek', *RSl*, 63:367–417.

MIŁOSZ. Jolanta Dudek, **'Gdzie wschodzi słońce i kędy zapada': europejskie korzenie poezji Czesława Miłosza* (Rozprawy Habilitacyjne, 213), Kw, Uniwersytet Jagielloński, 284 pp. *TD*, nos 1–2, contains two articles: M. P. Markowski, 'Miłosz: dylematy autoprezentacji' (24–34); M. Zaleski, 'Miłosz: piosenki niewinności i doswiadczenia' (81–95). See also LEŚMIAN.

MROŻEK. H. Włodarczyk, 'Le vertige de la circularité: lecture de l'oeuvre de Sławomir Mrożek, *RSl*, 63:505–27.

T. NOWAKOWSKI. A. Fiut, 'Polskie piekiełko', *TD*, nos 1–2:169–76, examines *Obóz Wszystich Świętych*.

ODOJEWSKI. W. Tomasik, 'Odojewski: literatura bliska wyczerpania', *TD*, nos 1–2 : 133–53.

PARNICKI. K. Uniłowski, 'Metaliteratura w pisarstwie Parnickiego', *PL(W)*, 82.2 : 90–122.

RÓŻEWICZ. J. Łukasiewicz, 'Płaskorzeźba', *Odra*, 31.10 : 55–69. *The Mature Laurel* (details above) contains several contributions on R. including: E. Morgan, 'Tadeusz Różewicz: "Following the guide"/ "Za przewodnikiem"' (98–104); J. Osborne, 'Tadeusz Różewicz: "Pigtail"/"Warkoczyk"' (105–11); J. Lucas, 'Tadeusz Różewicz: "A tale of old women"/"Opowiadanie o starych kobietach"' (112–18). See also HERBERT.

J. M. RYMKIEWICZ. A. Poprawa, '"Jesteśmy przypisami"', *Odra*, 31.3 : 59–61, is a short analysis of *Baket*.

STACHURA. B. Gautier, 'Edward Stachura — donner un sens', *RSl*, 63 : 489–503.

J. J. SZCZEPAŃSKI. M. Orski, 'Umrzeć za Polskę', *Odra*, 31.3 : 51– 55, is an analysis of *Ikar*.

SZCZYPIORSKI. Leszek Bugajski, **Szczypiorski* (Sylwetki Współczesnych Pisarzy), Wa, Agencja Autorska, 44 pp.

SZYMBORSKA. K. Karasek, 'Mozartian joy: the poetry of Wisława Szymborska', *The Mature Laurel* (details above), 191–98. *TD*, no. 4, is devoted to S. and includes articles by J. Łukasiewicz, Cz. Miłosz, E. Balcerzan, G. Borkowska, W. Ligęza, S. Barańczak.

TWARDOWSKI. Waldemar Smaszcz, **Jan Twardowski: kapłan-poeta*, Białystok, Filia Uniwersytetu w Białymstoku/Wydział Humanistyczny, 32 pp.

WOJTYŁA. Krzysztof Dybciak, **Karol Wojtyła a literatura*, Tarnów, Biblos, 164 pp.

IV. RUSSIAN STUDIES*

GENERAL REFERENCE AND BIBLIOGRAPHICAL WORKS

By D. L. L. Howells, *Taylor Institution Library, Oxford*

(This survey covers the years 1990 and 1991)

1. Archives and Libraries

E. Matthes, *Katalog der slavischen Handschriften in Bibliotheken der Bundesrepublik Deutschland*, Wiesbaden, Harrassowitz, 1990, xxvi + 247 pp., lists and describes 233 MS codices in 28 West German and Berlin libraries. The three largest collections are kept in the Staatsbibliothek Preussischer Kulturbesitz in Berlin (59 MSS), the Bayerische Staatsbibliothek in Munich (56 MSS), and the Slavische Institut of Heidelberg University (34 MSS). The MSS date from the late 13th to the early 20th cs and are written in all the Slavonic languages. The catalogue is a much needed and useful contribution to Russian and Slavonic studies, and provides nearly three times as much material as that contained in Kurt Günther's 'Slawische Handschriften in Deutschland' (*ZSl*, 5, 1960:317–55).

2. Congresses

Первый Всесоюзный съезд советских писателей 1934: стенографический отчет, ed. I. K. Luppol *et al.*, SovP, 1990, 714 + vi pp., is a reprint of the edition published in 1934, which has long since been a bibliographical rarity. It is accompanied by a supplementary volume compiled by S. S. Lesnevskii, *Первый Всесоюзный съезд советских писателей 1934: стенографический отчет. Приложения*, 172 pp., containing short biographical details of members of the Congress. It is noteworthy that of the 372 full members (члены с решающим голосом), 152 were subsequently arrested. Only 28 of these survived the experience, the remainder being shot or otherwise dying in prison or the camps.

3. Dissertations

Research on Russia and Eastern Europe: a Catalogue of Doctoral Dissertations 1984–1991, Godstone, Surrey, University Microfilms International, 50 pp., continues the listing of North American doctoral dissertations of which copies are available from the publishers either as xerographic reprints or microfilms.

---

*The place of publication of all books in the Russian section is Moscow, unless otherwise stated.

4. ÉMIGRÉ LITERATURE

The growing awareness of, and interest in, the intellectual output of Russian émigré communities of all periods is reflected in several recent publications. T. Ossorguine-Bakounine, *L'Emigration russe en Europe: catalogue collectif des périodiques en langue russe 1855–1940*, 2nd rev. and expanded edn (BRIES, 40/1), 1990, 354 pp., updates the work first published in 1976 with the addition of 41 titles (pp. 349–54) in 40 French and one Swiss libraries. As Marc Raeff points out in his introduction (p. 5), the work is the principal reference book for material of this kind. Iu. Abyzov, *Русское печатное слово в Латвии 1917–1944 гг.: биобиблиографический указатель* (*SSS*, 3), 4 vols, Stanford, 1990–91, traces the progress of Russian-language publishing in Latvia during its independence and under German occupation. Editions of the works of Soviet writers, many of whom were published in Latvia, especially during the 'twenties, are included, but biographical information is given only for Russians living in Latvia. The list of abbreviations (vol. 1, pp. 417–37) provides a useful list of Russian émigré publishing houses and periodical titles. Two union catalogues of Russian émigré serials and periodicals are provided by D. L. L. Howells, *Russian Émigré Serials 1855–1990 in Oxford Libraries: Materials for a Union Catalogue*, Oxford, W. A. Meeuws, 1990, x + 43 pp., and M. A. Ovsiannikova *et al.*, *Материалы к сводному каталогу периодических и продолжающихся изданий российского зарубежья в библиотеках Москвы (1917–1990 гг.)*, GPIB, GBL, 87 pp. Howells's catalogue is simply a finding-list. Its 234 entries are presented in two alphabetical sequences: 1–222 (pp. 1–40); Addenda, 223–34 (pp. 40–43). The extent of a series and its terminal dates are given where known together with the location and shelf-mark or class-mark in one or other of six Oxford libraries, five of which are part of the University. The three major Oxford repositories of this material are the Taylor Institution Library (129 titles), the Bodleian Library (97 titles) and St Antony's College Russian Centre (62 titles). Ovsiannikova's catalogue includes 593 titles, also arranged in alphabetical order, but including subtitles and the names of editors and publishers where known. The basic list is followed by indexes of issuing bodies and places of publication.

5. ENCYCLOPEDIAS

Without any doubt the most exciting encyclopedic work to be published last year is the suppressed and long-lost tenth volume of the *Литературная энциклопедия. 10. Романов-Современник*, Munich,

Sagner, 938 columns. The book is a remake of what the publishers call the only existing makeup copy. It complements vols 1–9, 11 published by A. V. Lunacharskii *et al.* (1930–39) of the Literary Encyclopedia, and publishes for the first time the entry '*Русская литература*' (columns 88–397). The copy is slightly damaged in several places, and contains a number of proofmarks and misprints. These do not, however, detract in any way from its value. One would love to know how on earth the publishers obtained it. *Русские писатели: биобиблиографический словарь*, 2 vols, ed. P. A. Nikolaev, Prosveshchenie, 1990, contains more than 300 articles on Russian writers and critics of the 19th and early 20th cs. The biographical articles are full and helpful, and each is followed by a short bibliography of the most important editions of a writer's works and secondary literature on him. *Лингвистический энциклопедический словарь*, ed. V. N. Iartseva, SE, 1990, 683 pp., is partly a dictionary of linguistic terms, partly an encyclopedia of ancient and modern world languages. It also contains articles on Russian and Soviet linguistic movements, e.g. 'Новое учение о языке' (on Marrism), 'Московская фортунатовская школа', etc. The only articles devoted to individuals are 'Ленин В.И. о языке' (pp. 263–64), and 'Маркс К., Энгельс Ф. о языке' (pp. 286–87). Stalin's intervention in the Marrist controversy (1950) is also mentioned (p. 335). The articles are followed by short bibliographies.

6. ENGLISH-LANGUAGE PUBLICATIONS

C. R. Proffer, R. Meyer, *Nineteenth-Century Russian Literature in English: A Bibliography of Criticism and Translations*, Ann Arbor, Ardis, 1990, 188 pp., includes works published between the 1890s and 1986 covering general topics and 69 writers. Bibliographies of individual writers are divided into translations and criticism. Works already mentioned in R. C. Lewanski's *The Literatures of the World in English Translation: a Bibliography. II. The Slavic Literatures* (NY, 1967) are not included. The bibliography includes articles published in journals and Festschriften, but not review articles. It is based on material collected before his death in 1984 by Proffer, and has been updated by Meyer. G. M. Terry, *East European Languages and Literatures. V: A Subject and Name Index to Articles in English-language Journals, Festschriften, Conference Proceedings and Collected Papers, 1988–1990*, Nottingham, Astra, 150 pp. (Astra Soviet and East European bibliographies, 11), continues the invaluable series begun by the author in 1978 which provides a comprehensive overview of English-language scholarship on Eastern Europe and the Slavs since the beginning of this century.

7. FOLK LITERATURE

T. G. Ivanova, *Русский фольклор: библиографический указатель 1881–1900*, Ld, BibAN, 1990, 500 pp., is the seventh volume in the bibliographical series *Русский фольклор* which began publication in 1961, compiled, until his death, by M. Ia. Mel'ts, and continued since by T. G. Ivanova. It now provides coverage of Russian and Soviet works on Russian folklore for the period 1881–1980. The present volume includes over 5000 studies on, and editions of, folk literature. The inclusion of 'lubochnye izdaniia' (pp. 366–455) of popular stories is a new departure, not attempted in the previous volume covering the pre-Revolutionary period (i.e. 1901–16, publ. 1981), although such works continued to be published until 1918 when they were banned by the new Soviet government. The most popular of these stories during the last quarter of the 19th c. was clearly *Frantsel' Ventsian* (40 editions), a story which is ultimately derived from the 15th-c. French tale of Paris and Vienne by Pierre de la Cypède.

8. LINGUISTICS

Linguistic bibliographies include W. Birkenmaier and I. Mohl, *Bibliographie zur russischen Fachsprache*, Tübingen, Gunter Narr Verlag, 1990 (*Forum für Fachsprachen-Forschung*, 12), 652 pp. The material is grouped into three main sections: Allgemein, which treats technical language in general by linguistic level (grammar, vocabulary, word-formation, semantics etc.); individual sciences and technologies; technical dictionaries. The main sections are followed by a list of abbreviations (pp. 597–605) and an index of personal names (pp. 606–52). A. E. Mamatov, *Библиографический указатель работ по культуре речи и языковой норме*, 2 vols, Tashkent, Samarkandskii meditsinskii institut, 1990, includes books, articles in books and series, reviews and dissertation abstracts published in the Soviet Union 1920–89 in Russian and other Soviet languages, a total of 4678 items. Each volume has an index of authors.

9. MEMOIRS

Советское общество в воспоминаниях и дневниках: аннотированный библиографический указатель книг, публикаций в сборниках и журналах. II, ed. V. Z. Drobizheva, KP, 1990, 356 pp., continues the series begun in 1987. The present volume is divided into two parts. The first contains memoirs on the creation of the state apparatus, especially of the armed forces, in the period 1921–40, concentrating on international affairs, e.g. the Soviet intervention in the Chinese and Spanish civil wars and the Soviet–Finnish War of 1939–40 (pp. 1–56; 271 entries). The second part contains memoirs on the war period 1941–45 in general, and individual campaigns for the period June 1941–November 1942.

10. POETRY

Русские советские писатели. Поэты: библиографический указатель. 13: *М. Львов — Н. Матвеева.* КР, 1990, 598 pp., and 14: *В. В. Маяковский. 1: Произведения В. В. Маяковского,* КР, 269 pp., continue the series which, since it began in 1977, has provided bibliographical coverage of the works of 114 Soviet Russian poets. The important and encouraging difference between this and previous volumes is the inclusion, for the first time, of Western editions of, and studies on, the works of the writers covered. Thus, Mandel′shtam's works begin (p. 117) with the important *Собрание сочинений,* edited by Struve and Filippov (Washington etc., 1967–81, 4 vols). The notorious poem 'Мы живем, под собою не чуя страны' is included (pp. 124, 144), and the bibliography of secondary literature to 1988 (pp. 153–207) must be the most complete available listing so far produced anywhere. Other poets included in the volume are M. D. L′vov (1917–88), N. P. Maiorov (1919–42), M. D. Maksimov (1918–86), A. B. Mariengof (1897–1962), L. N. Martynov (1905–80), S. Ia. Marshak (1887–1964), and N. N. Matveeva (1934–). Secondary literature on Maiakovskii will be included in volume 14(2). V. V. Bazanov (comp.), 'Поэзия 1917–1922 годов: материалы к библиографии', *У истоков русской советской литературы 1917–1922,* ed. N. A. Groznova *et al.,* Ld, Nauka, 1990, pp. 63–129, is the most complete bibliography available to date of separately published books of poetry, especially for the period 1917–20, which has always presented great problems to bibliographers. The bibliography includes books by single authors and anthologies. Anthologies of prose and poetry are included if the poetry component is thought to be significant.

11. SCIENCE FICTION

'Библиография библиографий фантастики: указатель библиографических пособий по научной фантастике и литературы по проблемам библиографии и пропаганды жанра, изданных в СССР за 1917–1988 гг.', pp. 199–216 of A. N. Osipov, *Библиография фантастики: опыт историко-аналитической и методико-теоретической характеристики,* Mw PI, 1990, lists 300 bibliographies of works of science fiction and studies on them published in the period.

12. TITLES

B. M. Vishnevetskaia *et al.*, *Указатель заглавий произведений художественной литературы 1801–1975. IV. М-О*, GBL, 1990, 430 pp., continues the series begun in 1985, giving the titles of literary works, and their authors, published in Russian in Russia and the Soviet Union since the beginning of the 19th c. The titles include both original works and translations into Russian.

LANGUAGE

By PETER MAYO, *Senior Lecturer in Russian and*
Slavonic Studies, University of Sheffield

1. COLLECTIVE VOLUMES

Slavistische Linguistik 1989. Referate des XV. Konstanzer Slavistischen
Arbeitstreffens Bayreuth 18.–22.9.1989 (SB, 260), ed. Walter Breu, 1990,
contains the following papers relating to Russian language: W. Girke,
'Zum Valenzrahmen evaluativer Prädikate (Am Beispiel von *važnyj*)'
(67–89); P. Kosta, 'Zur formalen Lizensierung und inhaltlichen
Determination leerer Subjekte im Russischen' (117–65); H. Mehlig,
'Überlegungen zur Thema-Rhema-Gliederung' (189–236); R. Rathmayr, '*Не влезай, убьет*: Sprachliche und pragmatische Strukturen
öffentlicher Aufschriften' (237–57); T. Reuther, 'Semantik und
Situation: Zur Bedeutung einiger russischer Verben der
Fortbewegung' (259–67); R. Růžička, 'Leere Kategorien und Ver-
stehensprinzipien partizipieller Adjunkte (Deepričastija) des Russischen' (269–84); D. Weiss, 'Satverknüpfung und Textverweis' (285–
312).

2. HISTORY OF THE LANGUAGE

G. A. Khaburgaev, **Очерк исторической морфологии русского языка.*
Имена, Mw U.P., 1990, 296 pp. Id., 'Проблема диглоссии и
южнославянских влияний в истории русского литературного
языка', *VIa*, no. 2:111–25, is a lengthy review article on B. A.
Uspenskii's *История русского литературного языка (XI–XVII вв.)*
(see *YWMLS*, 51:945). M. L. Remneva, 'О грамматической норме
языка книжнославянской и деловой письменности Древней
Руси', *FilN*, no. 2:53–61, is a general survey. H. Birnbaum, *ScSl*, 36,
1990:115–30, argues that the proper classification of Old Church
Slavonic is both polygenealogical and polytypological in nature. As a
tribute to Anders Sjöberg, Id. offers 'Reflections on the language of
medieval Novgorod', *RLing*, 15:195–215, while A. A. Zalizniak, *ib.*,
217–45, replies to the objections by Sjöberg (*WSlA*, 25–26, 1990:421–
26) and J. I. Bjørnflaten (*RLing*, 14, 1990:315–38) to his thesis that
there are present in the Old Novgorod dialect a series of features
which do not allow this dialect to be regarded as a late offshoot of a
single proto-East-Slavonic language. F. Kortlandt, 'On methods of
dealing with facts and opinions in a treatment of the progressive
palatalization of Slavic', *FLinHist*, 9.2, 1988:3–12, is a restrained
reply to H. G. Lunt's splenetic criticism of K.'s work on the same

topic in *ib.*, 7.2, 1987:251–90. Meanwhile Lunt himself, *ib.*, 10.1–2, 1989:35–59, continues his attempt to substantiate his case for the progressive palatalization predating the two regressive ones.

W. Vermeer, 'The mysterious North Russian nominative singular ending *-e* and the problem of the reflex of Proto-Indo-European **-os* in Slavic', *WSl*, 36:271–95, offers a convincing account of the phonetic shape of this ending and its distribution. V. S. Efimova, *SovSl*, no. 3:71–80, treats OCS adverbs in -ѣ derived from adjectives. Short active participles in Russian OCS of the 11th–13th cs are examined by S. V. Petrova, *RLing*, 15.53–78. G. Hentschel, *ib.*, 31–51, investigates the role of formal differentiation patterns in the historical development of substantival flexion in Russian. E. V. Kravets, 'Книжная справа и переводы Максима Грека как опыт нормализации церковнославянского языка XVI века', *ib.*, 247–79. A. S. Gerd, *SovSl*, no. 3:64–70, demonstrates the richness and variety of word formation even in late (14th–16th cs) OCS. The dual number is the subject of an article by M. L. Remneva and O. N. Kiianova, *VMUF*, no. 1:23–33. Also noted: R. Aitzetmüller, 'Beobachtungen zur Endung *-a* in masc. Appellativen und Völkernamen in Altrussischen', *ASP*, 20, 1990:63–74; A. V. Barandeev, 'Статус географической терминологии в русском литературном языке XVI–XVII вв.', *FilN*, no. 5:54–61; D. B. Zakhar'in, 'О немецком влиянии на русскую грамматическую мысль', *RLing*, 15:1–29; H. Keipert, 'Die "Wiener Anleitung" in der slavischen Grammatikographie des ausgehenden 18. Jahrhunderts', *ZSP*, 51:23–59.

L. Sadnik, 'Wortschatzstudien XI–XII', *ASP*, 20, 1990:1–8, continues her series of word studies with a look at OCS *istęsknǫti*, *istęsklъ* ... and *debelъ*. On the names of birds in Old Russian see an article by the suitably named I. O. Sokol, *Mov*, no. 5:57–62. Finally, E. I. Zinov'eva, *VLUllaL*, no. 2:64–71, analyses set expressions involving colour adjectives in 16th–17th-c. Russian.

3. PHONETICS AND PHONOLOGY

P. Cubberley, *ASEES*, 5.2:19–29, analyses the hard vs soft pronunciation of consonants before the vowel phoneme /e/ in foreign words on the basis of various synchronic descriptions from the last 20–30 years, but finds no evidence of a clear trend. N. K. Pirogova, *VMUF*, no. 3:19–25, looks at sociolinguistic factors influencing Russian's orthoepic norm. T. Berger, 'Zur typologischen Einordnung des russischen Akzents', *WSl*, 35, 1990:370–80, deals with Russian stress position in its role as differentiator of otherwise homonymous forms. R. F. Kasatkina, *VIa*, no.2:65–73, studies the reflexes of **ě* in the dialects of the Arkhangel'region.

4. Morphology and Word-Formation

A thin year. I. S. Ulukhanov, 'Об изучении закономерностей ударения в русском словоизменении (правила переноса ударения на префикс)', *RIaR*, no. 4:76–81, gives useful rules and a summary table. V. F. Ivanova, *RIa*, no. 1:69–77, writes on some current problems in Russian orthography. C. V. Chvany, *SEEJ*, 34, 1990:421–38, takes another look at 'the two-stem nature of the one-stem verb system'. On the relationship between simple imperfective, secondary imperfective and the perfective of limit, see V. N. Obukhova, *FilN*, no. 3:67–72. Also on the verb: O. E. Kalašnikova, 'Grundlegende verbale Kategorien des russischen Adverbialpartizips und Hypothese eines Funktionmodells in der russischen Gegenwartsprache', *WSJ*, 36, 1990:49–59; N. E. Shershakova, 'Метонимическая деривация глагола', *RIa*, no. 3:69–71. M. F. Lukin, *FilN*, no. 1:73–83, considers broad and narrow interpretations of the concept 'adjective' in Russian grammar. V. I. Chuglov, *RIa*, no. 2:79–82, writes on the classification of possessive pronouns, while V. N. Nemchenko, *ib.*, 91–94, discusses the variants их/них etc. after certain prepositions, adverbs, and comparative adjectives.

O. P. Ermakova and E. A. Zemskaia, *RLing*, 15:105–16, attempt to refine word-derivation relationships in Russian. N. A. Pugieva, *FilN*, no. 6:64–73, writes on the positional status of derivational morphemes and their neutralization in the structure of the derived word. O. E. Ol'shanskaia, *ib.*, 55–64, examines the simplification of composite words in Russian. L. I. Osipova, *ib.*, no. 5:61–69, analyses univerbation by means of the suffix -ка on the basis of recent editions of *Новое в русской лексике. Словарные материалы* and other publications giving new words that have appeared over the last two decades. L. P. Krysin, *RIa*, no. 2:74–78, describes the stages through which foreign elements pass in the process of assimilation into Russian. Also noted: E. I. Litievskaia, 'Агглютинация и фузия на морфемном шве в современном русском языке', *VMUF*, no. 1:67–73.

5. Syntax. Semantics and Pragmatics

A belated mention for I. Fougeron, **Prosodie et organisation du message. Analyse de la phrase assertive en russe contemporain*, Paris, Librairie C. Klincksieck, 1989, 487 pp. Two articles in *RLing*, 15, deal with interrogative sentences: H. R. Mehlig, 'Экзистенциальные и экспликативные вопросы' (117–25) and N. I. Golubeva-Monatkina, 'Русские вопросы-кентавры' (127–38), the latter concerned with interrogative phraseology. By the same author, 'Классификационное исследование вопросов и ответов диалогичекой речи',

VIa, no. 1:125–34. Also on the interrogative, see M. H. Mills, 'The performance force of the interrogative in colloquial Russian: from direct to indirect speech acts', *SEEJ*, 35:553–69 (note that an earlier version of the same article, *ib.*, 98–114, contains numerous uncorrected compositor's errors). One aspect of negation is treated by N. A. Lutsenko, 'Отрицание при глаголе в придаточной части, вводимой союзом "чтобы"', *RIa*, no. 3:72–75. Sentence homonymy is considered by P. Adamec, *RLing*, 15:139–52. A. V. Bondarko, *VIa*, no. 5:27–41, examines the various elements which serve as vehicles of predicative meaning. O. M. Chupasheva, *RIa*, no. 2:82–87, looks at the theory and changing practice of punctuation in conjunctionless compound sentences. Also noted: T. Lilova, 'Система глагольных предикатов-авторизаторов в русском языке', *BR*, no. 4:42–49.

C. V. Chvany, 'Verbal aspect, discourse saliency, and the so-called "perfect of result" in modern Russian', pp. 213–35 of *Verbal Aspect in Discourse*, ed. Nils B. Thelin, Amsterdam, Benjamins, 460 pp., concludes that Russian sentence grammar does not encode in the perfective aspect a difference between action and result. L. Grenoble, 'Deixis, point of view, and the prefixes *po-* and *pri-* in Russian', *WSl*, 36:254–70, demonstrates the semantic and aspectual changes between Old Russian and CSR in the verbs идти, пойти, прийти, приходить. There are two articles on the sememic analysis of the prefix по- by A. A. Karavanov: 'Семный состав ингрессивных глаголов и проблема генезиса ингрессивной приставки *по-*', *VMUF*, no. 3:11–18, and 'Семный состав ограничительных глаголов с приставкой *по-*', *FilN*, no. 3:57–66. Also noted: Iu. P. Kniazev, **Акциональность и статальность: их соотношение в русских конструкциях с причастиями на -н, -т* (SPS, 81) 1989, 271 pp..

J. E. Levine, 'Pragmatic implicatures and case: the Russian dative revisited', *RLJ*, 44, nos 147–49, 1990:9–27, examines the pragmatic implications associated with the use of the dative case in two constructions: in combination with the instrumental case of a predicate nominal denoting a kinship term, and when used to express possession (in place of the possessive pronoun). Also on the dative, G. R. Greenberg and S. Franks, *SEEJ*, 35:71–97, use parametric theory to elucidate dative subjects and the second dative firstly in Russian and then across the spectrum of the Slavonic languages as a whole, where they find a 'surprising consistency in the range of phenomena that exist in each language'. A. B. Kopeliovich, *FilN*, no. 3:40–49, sets the gender-sex correlation in Russian nouns in the context of Indo-European languages generally. T. Wade, 'Prepositional triads: constructions with под', *Rusistika*, 2, 1990:35–40, shows how the triadic principle and semantic progression can help to overcome 'arbitrariness' in prepositions. Also noted: W. Lehfeldt, 'Zum gegenwärtigen Stand von Definition und Beschreibung der Kongruenz im Russischen', *ZSP*, 51:21–22; K. Liukkonen, 'Русские конструкции типа *ум хорошо*', *SSFin*, 8:159–83; V. P. Musienko, 'Функціонально-семантична категорія міри в російській мові', *Mov*, no. 2:43–48.

6. Lexicology and Phraseology

B. Cooper continues his series of studies of Russian botanical terms (see also *YWMLS*, 50:1030, 51:951, 52:954) with a look at onions and garlic, *TPS*, 89:197–220, and bilberries, cowberries, and cranberries, *NZSJ*:81–100. A. Room, 'Russian Rockspeak', *Rusistika*, 2, 1990:41–44, is a brief look at neology in the area of popular music. The theme of new borrowings and, in particular, their phonetic and orthographical assimilation is continued by G. G. Timofeeva in two articles: 'Письменная фиксация иноязычных слов в ситуации заимствования на материале новой лексики английского происхождения', *ib.*, 3:33–39, and 'Письменная фиксация иноязычных слов в ситуации заимствования', *VLUIIaL*, no. 3:40–45. Among the very few studies of individual words are J. Reinhart, 'Slavisch *zajęcь*', *WSJ*, 35, 1989:155–58, and, a more substantial piece, H. Kunstmann, 'Der russische Fluß- resp. Stadtname *Moskva* und sein hydronymisches Umfeld. Onomastisches zur Frühgeschichte der Slaven in Raum Moskau', *WSl*, 36:140–65.

On the development of emotive meanings in phraseological units, see V. N. Vakurov, *FilN*, no. 6:74–82. Also noted: I. V. Pavlovich, 'Парадигмы образов в русском поэтическом языке', *VIa*, no. 3:104–17; N. I. Iatmanova, *RIa*, no. 1:80–82, on the polysemy of adjectives in Kataev's *Белеет парус одинокий*. Finally, the publication of *Русско-японский словарь*, ed. M. Togo *et al.*, Tokyo, 1988, 2764 pp., prompts L. P. Kalakutskaia, *VIa*, no. 1:91–115, to part with some thoughts on Russian lexicography in general.

7. Languages in Contact and in Contrast

Christine D. Tomei, *The Structure of Verse Language: Theoretical and Experimental Research in Russian and Serbo-Croatian Syllabo-Tonic Versification* (SB, 246), 1989, 192 pp., describes an experiment undertaken by the author for her doctoral dissertation and has rather more to say about Serbo-Croat than about Russian. A rare comparison of Russian and Slovene is offered by A. Derganc, *SlavRev*, 39:277–83, who deals with the various semantic properties of nouns denoting fruit, vegetables, berries, etc. She notes the prevalence in Russian of non-countable mass nouns as against countable nouns in Slovene, though the latter show a marked tendency for transition to a dual role in the singular. *BR* has its usual crop of Russian–Bulgarian comparisons, including N. Kovacheva, 'Лексическая пара в грамматике' (no. 1:69–74); T. Chalykova, 'Фонетическая реализация болгарских мягких согласных (в сопоставлении с русскими)' (no. 3:48–51), and, by the same author, 'О некоторых особенностях болгарской артикуляторной базы (в сопоставлении с русской)' (no. 4:63–67); A. Karlovska, 'Толкование лексического значения и сопоставительный семантический анализ' (no. 3:52–61), which compares Russian принести, отнести, привезти, отвезти with Bulgarian донеса, занеса, докарам, закарам; I. Chongarova, 'Русско-болгарские апроксиматы. Межъязыковые лексические соответствия омонимического характера' (no. 4:50–56); T. Tancheva, 'О семантическом тождестве русских и болгарских слов, заимствованных из французского языка' (no. 4:57–62); G. Mishevska, 'Семантический анализ русской и болгарской спортивной лексики, заимствованной из английского языка' (no. 4:68–74). M. Zatovkaňuk, *SlSl*, 26:26–37, shows that 77% of deverbal nouns in Russian and Ukrainian are formed by different means and that Ukrainian deverbatives more consistently differentiate aspect than do their Russian counterparts.

Russian and German are contrasted in a monograph by G. Freidhof, 'Dialoganalyse, Gliederungspartikeln und Übersetzen (mit Belegen aus dem Slavischen, insbesondere Russischen, und dem Deutschen)', *ZSP*, 51:225–90; and, more briefly, by A. A. Kul'bakin, 'Русский глагол в зеркале немецкого (на материале макрополя аспектуальности)', *RIaR*, no. 4:63–70. Finally, a relatively unusual comparison of Russian and Spanish: S. G. Vorkachev, 'Хотеть — желать vs querer — desear: сопоставительный анализ употребления русских и испанских глаголов', *ib.*, no. 3:75–82.

8. MISCELLANEOUS

W. Lehfeldt *et al.*, 'Das Verhältnis von Literatursprache (Standardsprache) und nichtstandardsprachlichen Varietäten in der russischen Gegenwartssprache', *WSl*, 36:1–71, is a monograph-length presentation of seven papers from the fifth Deutsche Slavistentag. H. H. Keller, *RLJ*, 44, nos 147–49, 1990:61–68, argues that the impressive storage capabilities and versatile display possibilities of the computer are equal to the complexities of 'problem verbs' in Russian, while J. E. Brown, *ib.*, 69–87, looks to the future of CALL in the context of Russian. Comparing *Pravda* editorials in 1979 and 1988–89, R. Pyykkö, *SSFin*, 8:184–96, suggests that the increase in readability is based not so much on the content as on the shortening of clauses and sentences, more frequent use of finite verb forms and less frequent use of passive constructions.

Finally, the irritating number of inconsistencies of transliteration (я appears variously as *ja, ya*, and *'a)* and other inaccuracies (e.g. *ktoraja, ko nam*) in the Russian section of Campbell, *Compendium*, 1170–77, cause one to question the value of such a work.

LITERATURE, FROM THE BEGINNING TO 1700

By R. M. CLEMINSON, *Senior Lecturer in Russian, Portsmouth University*

1. GENERAL

This year has seen the appearance of an attempt to provide a unitary theoretical framework for the whole of Old Russian literature, viz. I. P. Smirnov, *O древнерусской культуре, русской национальной специфике и логике истории* (*WSlA*, Sonderband 28), 196 pp. This work displays a remarkable depth of knowledge of both eastern and western scholarship, but suffers from the fact that it treats Russian literary activity as a closed system, and tends to operate at a theoretical altitude from which the texts themselves are sometimes barely visible. More limited in scope, but also more down to earth, is the survey of social attitudes as expressed in Old Russian writings provided by the authors of the collection entitled *Древнерусская литература: изображение общества*, Nauka. Some useful contributions to the question of genres come from L. Boeva, *SBL*, 25–26: 38–44, who concentrates on the position of the author in respect of the type of text he is writing, and M. L. Ferazzi, *EO*, 9: 7–21, who traces the varying meanings of the term *povest'* from the earliest times to the present day. L. Sazonova, *RL*, 29: 471–88, examines the idea of the journey in early pilgrimages, Afanasii Nikitin, Avvakum and 17th-c. fiction, and not surprisingly discovers that it is different in each. Even less substantial are the contributions of R. Řežábek in *ČRu*, 35: 20–25 and 158–65, who discovers philosophical views in original literature of the Kievan period, and renaissance elements in the Aristotelian quotations in the florilegia! *Методические рекомендации по описанию славяно-русских рукописных книг*, vol. 3, AN SSSR, 1990, as well as the expected material on watermarks and calendars, contains articles by I. V. Dergacheva on *synodica*, B. M. Kloss on the Lives of SS Sergius and Nicon of Radonezh, M. S. Fomina on the *Zlatostrui*, T. V. Chartoritskaia on the *Panegyricon*, and B. M. Pudalov on the *Zlatoust* and *Izmaragd*.

CHRONICLES. Ia. S. Lur'e, *TODL* 44: 185–95, writes on general problems of the study of the chronicles, while individual chronicles are the subject of articles by other contributors to the same volume: V. V. Morozov on the Nikon Chronicle as a forerunner of the *Litsevoi svod* (246–68) and Ia. G. Solodkin on the Piskarev Chronicle and its authorship (387–96). As ever, though, the Primary Chronicle received the lion's share of attention. P. Rolland, *SlO*, 38: 301–09, studies the legend of St Andrew's journey through Russia, while

J. Dębski, *SlO*, 38:294–300, studies the evidence it provides for the early penetration of Christianity into Rus'. The stories relating to Olga are examined by I. Chekova, *SBL*, 23–24:77–98, who reveals their connection with folklore, and M. Gyóni, *Századok*, 123:298–342, discusses the chronicle's references to *volokhi* and their identity. Finally, those interested in historical writing in the late 16th and early 17th cs may find useful gleanings in Igumen Feofilakt's work on St Job, first Patriarch of Moscow, *BT*, 30:200–40.

BIBLIOGRAPHY. The *TODL* continue to publish *Иссле-дователъские материалы для 'Словаря книжников и книжности Древней Руси'*, and vol. 44:3–160 contains 17th-c. writers from Averkii to Kurakin Ivan Semenovich. *RusMed*, 6, fasc. 2, consists of an annotated bibliography of works published 1978–82 relevant to medieval Russia, including a substantial section on literature. F. B. Poljakov, *WSl*, 36:298–313, supplements the 1988 catalogue of the Pogodin MSS with additional bibliographical information, and there are accounts (by N. V. Shukhtina-Savelieva and A. V. Voznesenskii and A. A. Saveliev) of archaeographical expeditions to the Russian North in *TODL*, 44:480–89 and 490–92. There is a bibliography of the works of A-E. N. Tachiaios in *SovSl*, no. 6:120–24, and one of O. V. Tvorogov in *TODL*, 44:497–506, while D. S. Likhachev's 85th birthday prompts an appreciation in *ISLIa*, 50:486–90.

2. PRE-MONGOLIAN LITERATURE

TRANSLATED LITERATURE. The *Izbornik* of 1073 is the subject of an article by M. V. Bibikov, *VV*, 51:92–102, which gives a detailed comparison of its contents and those of Byzantine compendia of a similar type, while J. Johannet, *RSl*, 63.1:55–111, gives parallel texts in Greek and Slavonic of those sections containing 'philosophical definitions'. Another source for the *Izbornik* of 1076 is provided by D. M. Bulanin, *TODL*, 44:161–78, and D. S. Likhachev, *ib.*, 179–84, discusses the purpose for which it was compiled. O. V. Tvorogov, *ib.*, 196–226, continues his study of other early anthologies, this time examining the hagiographical works contained in them. A. Minche-va's work on the Slavonic version of St Isaac the Syrian's *Ascetica*, *Pal*, 14.3:19–38, is chiefly concerned with the process of translation, and compares a Middle Bulgarian and an Old Russian MS of the text with the original Greek. The transmission of the Slavonic translation of the *Ladder* of St John Climacus is discussed by T. Mostrova, *ib.*, 15.3:70–90, while G. M. Prokhorov, *TODL*, 44:226–45, continues his publication of the Slavonic version of John Cantacuzenus' Dialogues. T. Slavova, *Pal*, 15.3:57–69, discusses the origin of the

Tolkovaia Paleia and its relationship with various hexaemera, and E. Tomova, *ib.*, 15.2:54–67, explores the position of the Warsaw MS of the *Zlatostrui* in its textual transmission.

ORIGINAL LITERATURE. Metropolitan Ilarion has received a considerable amount of attention. *AlBi*, 26, is largely devoted to him, printing the text of his works (after MS Sin. 591), a translation into modern Russian and nine articles about him. Myroslav Labunka, *Митрополит Іларіон і його писання* (Editiones Universitatis Catholicae Ucrainorum S. Clementis Papae, 80), Rome, 1990, provides a Ukrainian translation of the works and a popular introduction, but is most useful for its facsimile of the relevant parts of Sin. 591. G. Brogi Bercoff, *EO*, 9:37–57, claims to find structural parallels between the *Sermon on Law and Grace* and the Life of Peter and Fevronia and Afanasii Nikitin's *Khozhenie*, while R. Picchio, *ib.*, 23–36, finds elements of the *povest'* in the Sermon (as he does in the *Slovo o polku Igoreve*). F. J. Thomson, *RSl*, 63.1:19–54, vindicates Ilarion, together with St Methodius and other early Slavonic Christians, from the charge of Arianism. Simon Franklin, *Sermons and Rhetoric of Kievan Rus'*, Harvard U.P., provides not only an English translation of the *Sermon on Law and Grace*, but also significant introductory material. He provides a similar service for the works of Kirill of Turov and Klim Smoliatich. Kirill is also the subject of works by I. Ferincz, *SSH*, 35:149–55, who compares his rhetorical technique with that of Epifanii Premudryi, and S. V. Kozlov, pp. 19–36 of *Литературный процесс и творческая индивидуальность*, Kishinev, Ştiinţa, 1990, who argues for originality in his use of imagery.

Although Iu. A. Isichenko, *Києво печерський патерик у літературному процесі кінця XVI — початку XVIII ст. на Україні*, Kiev, ND, 1990, focuses on the baroque period, it contains a fair amount of material on the work's earlier history. F. J. Thomson, *ASP*, 20:15–62, is primarily concerned with quotations from the Slavonic version of St Ephraim the Syrian's *Paraenesis* in Simon of Vladimir's Epistle to Polycarp, but in fact ranges much wider in his consideration of the textological significance of quotation. The Kiev Caves Monastery, or rather an icon of the Mother of God therein, is also studied by V. Putsko, *SBL*, 23–24:57–62, who traces references to it in the Life of Feodosii.

Apart from L. A. Dmitriev's closely-reasoned demolition of L. E. Makhnovets's theory of the authorship of Prince Vladimir Iaroslavich of Galicia, *RusL*, no. 1:88–103, this year's contributions on the *Slovo o polku Igoreve* are mostly concerned with very narrow questions: N. M. Dylevskii, *BR*, no. 2:3–21, on the meaning of *хинове* and *буесть*; L. V. Sokolova, *TODL*, 44:325–62, on *Troian* and J. V. Pavlík; *ScSl*, 36:173–84, on Cuman battle tactics as recorded by Czech chronicles.

Finally, O. Anisimova, *SlO*, 38:477–95, sees Daniil Zatochnik as a sort of Kievan goliard, while V. Konzal, *Slavia*, 60:232–47, defends the theory of a Bohemian origin for the *Prayer to the Trinity* — probably Sázava in the 1090s.

3. Literature of the Later Middle Ages

HISTORICAL WRITING.   A number of historical stories have come in for attention. G. Dell'Agata, *EO*, 9:59–79, discusses the origin of the Russian redaction of the *Повесть о взятии Царьграда*, while the *Сказание о Мамаевом побоище* is the subject of two studies, by G. Brogi Bercoff, *RSl*, 63.1:161–73, and D. Cavaion, *EO*, 9:81–105. I. A. Evseeva-Lobakova, *TODL*, 44:370–77, discusses a particular redaction of the *Повесть о разорении Рязани Батыем*, and I. P. Sbriziolo, *EO*, 9:107–23, examines the Russian accounts of the Council of Florence-Ferrara. Much more substantial is M. L. Ferrazzi's study of the *Казанская история*, *EO*, 9:125–59, covering its origin and place in the development of Russian historical writing. M. Taube, *RSl*, 63.1:113–22, reveals the source for the story of the Seventy-Two Translators in the *Trinity Chronograph*, viz. the *Dialogue of Timothy and Aquila*, which he prints in parallel Greek and Slavonic versions.

HAGIOGRAPHY.   M. Pliukhanova, *Rossiia*, 7:3–21, discusses the *topos* of the saint who carries his severed head — Mercurius of Smolensk and Ivan of Kazan' are the two Russian examples, but the article ranges much more widely on the symbolic significance of the head and decapitation in Old Russian religious literature. A. Fałowski, *SlO*, 39:27–34, raises the question of what Fevronia used to heal Peter in the story concerning them, and comes to a rather unpleasant conclusion.

VARIOUS.   Later copyists' modifications of the *Повесть о Дракуле* are discussed by M. Di Salvo, *EO*, 9:161–70. N. Doncheva-Panaiotova, *ZhMP*, no. 9:53–56, gives us a rather uncritical account of the life and literary activity of Metropolitan Cyprian. C. Zuckerman, *Byzantinoslavica*, 50:193–96, demonstrates that the *Vita Constantini* was a source for Joseph of Volokolamsk's *Просветитель*, thus also demonstrating that the *Vita* was known in Russia by the end of the 15th c. The *Vita Constantini*, incidentally, is also studied by G. Ziffer, *SovSl*, no. 3:59–63, who gives a summary of its *Überlieferungsgeschichte*, and by M. Capaldo, *EO*, 541–644, in a brilliant and extensive textological analysis centred upon the inscription on the cup of Solomon.

4. Seventeenth-Century Literature

Seventeenth-century verse has received a fair amount of attention. L. V. Sazonova, *TODL*, 44:300–24, discovers that Evfimii Chudovskii was also a poet, and prints some of his verses. The same author, *RicS*, 37:385–404, looks at the persistence of medieval preoccupations in the work of Simeon Polotskii, Silvester Medvedev, and Karion Istomin. Simeon Polotskii is also the dominant figure in V. K. Bilibin's study of metrical paraphrases of liturgical texts, *ib.*, 367–83, while A. A. Iliushin, *SovSl*, 1990, no. 1, 89–95, embarks upon the remarkable project of translating Simeon's Polish verse into the 'slavenorusskii' language of his Muscovite period. O. Dolskaya-Acherley's study of 17th-c. MS songbooks, *ASEES*, 5.1:1–14, is more concerned with their musical than literary content. L. A. Petrova, pp. 37–43 of Книга в России, XVI — середина XIX в., Ld, 1990, provides a general survey of the 183 texts so far identified in the genre of penitential verses.

Ia. G. Solodkin, *ib.*, 44–52, traces literary influences on the *Vremennik* of Ivan Timofeev, while another historical composition of the same period, the so-called Летописная книга of the Time of Troubles, is examined by I. Iu. Serova, *TODL*, 44:269–83. Повесть о боярыне Морозовой, ed. N. S. Demkova, pref. A. M. Panchenko, *KLL*, 158 pp., includes not only the *Povest'* (printed from GPB MS O.1.341 with corrections after A. I. Mazurin's edition of 1979), but also correspondence between Morozova, Avvakum, and E. P. Urusova, and Avvakum's О трех исповедницах слово плачевное. N. V. Ponyrko, *TODL*, 44:397–402, prints two documents relating to Avvakum's son Afanasii. Much wider in scope is B. A. Uspenskii's work on the cultural conflicts surrounding the Old Believer schism, *RicSl*, 37:424–58, which examines attitudes on both sides of the divide.

N. Anashkina, *SlO*, 38:497–510, re-examines the life and works of Ivan Andreevich Khvorostinin and suggests Socinian influence. L. I. Alekhina, *RusL*, no. 1:142–44, attempts to elucidate some obscure passages in the Повесть о Горе-Злочастии, while A. Iu. Fedorov, *TODL*, 44:284–99, investigates its connection with the folk-tale and S. Garzonio, *EO*, 9:171–91, connects it with metrical folk genres. The interrelation between 17th-c. *povesti* and folklore is also dealt with by E. Malek, *ib.*, 193–210. Finally, D. Ecklund Farrell traces the representations of medieval humorous tales in 18th-c. *lubki*.

LITERATURE, 1700–1820

By N. J. CROWE, *Junior Research Fellow in Russian,*
St John's College, Oxford

1. GENERAL

One turns to *SGECRN*, 18, 1990, to discover a scholarly medley of the expected highest standards. Among the contributions to this issue are a note by A. G. Cross on Catherine II's *Oleg*, a 'lawless' balletic and theatrical spectacle with pretensions to Shakespeare (10–17); a résumé by I. K. Lilly of 18th-c. themes and motifs in modern Russian verse, notably in the area, increasingly attractive to researchers, of Petersburg poetry (30–34); and a survey review by W. Gareth Jones which examines the 'updating' of the 18th c. by editors and publishers in Russia who are anxious to ally *perestroika* with culturally inspired 18th-c. forms (49–53). In *ib.*, 19, one finds a higher than average proportion of literary/'cultural' contributions, conspicuous among which are A. Lentin on 'Shcherbatov and science' (3); F. Wigzell on 'Printed dream books and divinatory literature in Russia before 1825' (4–5); N. Crowe, 'Pastoral opéra-comique in 18th-century Russia' (6–8); G. Andreeva, 'Итальянские встречи. Русские и британские живописцы в Риме во второй половине XVIII века' (9–12); and G. Seaman, 'Catherine the Great and musical enlightenment' (13–14).

Russia in the Age of Enlightenment, ed. Roger Bartlett and Janet M. Hartley, London, Macmillan, 1990, 253 pp., is a *Festschrift* for Professor Isabel de Madariaga which properly contains a number of items of literary interest. There is a piece by I. Serman examining National Consciousness (40–56) which takes in not only political and state activists but authors (Kantemir, Lomonosov, Sumarokov, Novikov, Radishchev and others). W. Gareth Jones, writing about the image of the 18th-c. Russian author, and beginning with Simeon of Polotsk and Feofan Prokopovich, takes the line up to Novikov and Derzhavin — politically iconoclastic but still without the tone of voice, individualistic and distinct from the vocabulary of state, of a Karamzin (57–74). A. G. Cross, 'Catherine the Great: views from the distaff side' (203–21) assesses the perennially fascinating salacious image of the Empress preserved in the popular western imagination, arguing that the wealth of serious and authentic material about her which is now available makes this approach look even more tawdry and frivolous. A. Erokhin, 'Столетье безумно и мудро', *AlBi*, 25, 1989: 165–74, provides a brief, illustrated survey of the Hermitage's catalogue of the 1987 'Russia–France. The Age of Enlightenment' exhibition. A rather different attempt at a transcultural essay is made by R. F. Iusufov, *ISLIa*, 49, 1990 : 119–25, whose diffuse argument establishes the predominance of the classicism-feudalism relationship in the literary cultures of the Urals, North Caucasus and Southern Siberia. The suggestion is that the dynamic was just as in 'high' culture. N. N. Skatov, 'Начало всех начал. Об особенностях русской литературы начала прошлого века', *LSh*, 1990, no. 1 : 3–17, brings together various materials from the late 18th and early 19th cs, including comparative analyses of the lexis of the 'classical' and the 'Krylovian' fable, to show that the period contained the essential kernel of Russian literature.

ANTHOLOGIES. J. Sullivan and C. L. Drage have contributed substantially to the understanding of the early 18th-c. love song with their impressive three-volume edition, *Russian Love Songs in the Early Eighteenth Century: A Manuscript Collection*, publ. the authors, London, 1988–89; vol. 1, *The Text of the Manuscript*, 187 pp.; vol. 2, *Notes to the Song-Book*, 260 pp.; vol. 3, *Photographic Reproduction of the Manuscript*, 160 folios. This is a piece of scholarship much required, and a similar need for the re-presentation of forgotten or neglected areas of literature is thankfully being supplied too by native Russian specialists, most notably by the two following publications. N. D. Kochetkova supplies a 20-page introduction to, and has in collaboration with numerous others edited, an important anthology of lyrics, *Русская литература. Век XVIII, Лирика*, KhL, 1990, 736 pp. The lyrical range is broad, running from Feofan to Dmitriev, relocating some poets under the lyrical sign, and bringing others back into recollection — the likes of I. P. Maksimovich, E. V. Kheraskova, Ia. V. Orlov, M. L. Magnitskii, and others. All genres approximating to the lyric are covered, and the working definition of the form seems to be conciseness and musicality. The second volume in what is setting itself up as a multi-volume series appeared in the following year from the same publishers. *Трагедия*, 719 pp., is a worthy companion. The introductory article is by Iu. V. Stennik, who supplies the background of such included tragedians as Sumarokov, Lomonosov, Kheraskov, and Kniazhnin. Even better, the volume laudably collects examples from Rzhevskii, Maikov, Nikolev and Plavil'shchikov. The desire for compendious representation which these volumes evince is an auspicious sign for the future.

PERIODS, GENRES, AND THEMES. The 18th-c. section of Fridlender, *Революция*, includes Iu. M. Lotman on the political thinking of Karamzin and Radishchev, Iu. V. Stennik on the impact of the Revolution on conservative publicistic thought in the 1790s, and A. S. Ianushkevich on Zhukovskii. There are contributions dealing with Pushkin's relationship to the revolutionary events, and the volume moves thereafter into the 19th c. and more recent literature. In S. A. Kibal'nik's study, *Русская антологическая поэзия первой трети XIX века*, Ld, 1990, the 'anthologizing' framework which structures this useful reading of (pre-)Romantic poetry is devoted primarily to the reception of the Greek Anthology, but other typologies (e.g. *Anacreontea*) find a place. Another literary form, likewise not quite a 'genre', and one deserving considerably greater attention, is that of cadenced prose. S. I. Kormilov, *RusL*, 1990, no. 4:31–44, analyses and assesses the importance of what he calls 'prozostikh' at the end of the 18th and beginning of the 19th c. in the light of its great usefulness to subsequent stylists, concluding, perhaps lamely, that one ought not to seek a definition of what this amorphous mood is. A different form, this time more difficult still to isolate in literary evidence, is brought to the fore by L. S. Sarkisian, 'Об одном "несостоявшемся" жанре русской лирики конца XVIII-начала XIX в. Карамзин и Державин', *ib.*, 196–201. The article describes these authors' interest in, but failure to develop coherently, the sub-genre of the 'historico-epic romance'. More traditional historiographical assessments are still to be found in other places. A. A. Takho-Godi, *LitU*, 1990, no. 4:139–50, has assembled from amongst the papers of the late A. F. Losev a brief but informative survey of *klassitsizm* in Russia and the rest of Europe with particular reference to western trends, figures, sources, and influences. A follow-up piece on Romanticism, identically presented, appears in *ib.*, 1990, no. 6:139–45. Stephen Lessing Baehr has collated an enormous amount of research material, familiar hitherto only in the form of articles, with his study of *The Paradise Myth in Eighteenth-Century Russia. Utopian Patterns in Early Secular Russian Literature and Culture*, Stanford U.P., xiv + 308 pp. The work is a thorough investigation, extending in fact beyond the 18th c. in both directions, of the uses to which paradisiac iconography has been put in the service of panegyric utopianism. This is related to the urgent need to construct supporting cultural models which no longer, by the beginning of the 'iron age' at the start of the 19th c., held any water for authors and readers alike. The reality undercut all too painfully the eulogistic intention of culture. The idea is that literature can be read as the most important epiphenomenon of these cultural events. The civic, panegyric, and didactic uses of literature are discussed by L. I. Sazonova, *Поэзия русского барокко (вторая половина XVII — начало XVIII века)*, Nauka, 261 pp. The author has set about a comprehensive analysis of the poetry, drama, rhetoric, and emblematism of the baroque period, with an eye to the work that they could be made to do. The volume contains a very fine polyglossal bibliography.

　　COMPARATIVE STUDIES.　S. Garzonio continues his sound scholarly investigations of Russo-Italian cultural links with 'Малоизвестные русские переводы Петрарки в XVIII веке', *SSH*, 35.1–2, 1989:19–31, which takes as its subject versions of Petrarch by, *inter alia*, Tin'kov, N. A. L'vov, Murav'ev, Derzhavin, and Batiushkov in the latter part of the century. A predilection for statistics, with an underpinning of 13 scientific tables, is evidenced in Garzonio's piece on 'Стих русских поэтических переводов итальянских оперных либретто. XVIII век', pp. 107–32 of *Russian Verse Theory* (UCLA Slavic Studies, 18), Columbus, Ohio, Slavica, 1989. Still within the sphere of influence of Romance languages, 18th-c. translations of Cervantes are briefly examined by O. Kašpar, 'Ruské překlady Cervantesova Dona Quijota a Příkladných Novel v 18 století', *ČRu*, 35, 1990:268–72. Apart from the two works in the title, translations made in the 1780s and 1790s of *Galatea* and *Persiles and Sigismunda* are referred to. Moving on to Anglo-Russian literary relations, *SEER*, 68, 1990:217–33, publishes a revised version of the lecture delivered in London by Iu. D. Levin in 1988, the year of his honorary Oxford D.Litt. The broad purchase on scholarly resources, and equal breadth of literary erudition which were applauded at that ceremony are evident in this article, an account of 'Translations of Henry Fielding's works in eighteenth-century Russia'. There is a translation by M. S. Shatz of '"Western Influence in Russia After Peter the Great" by V. O. Kliuchevskii', *CanSS*, 24, 1990:431–55. This careful translation comprises lectures three and four of the original. The first two lectures in Shatz's version appeared in *ib.*, 20, 1986:467–84. II. Schmidt, *ZSl*, 35, 1990:334–41, has analysed literary tropes, motifs, and types of required commitment in France and Russia, as a comparative study, from the time of the French Revolution up to 1825. He claims, curiously, that the Revolution and the 'European' Enlightenment have not been properly studied in terms of their mutual impact. Broader artistic links (music, theatre, plastic arts) in the Russo-Czech context have been methodically studied, from the end of the 18th to the middle of the 19th c., by L. N. Titova, *SovSl*, 1990, no. 1:42–48. An even broader investigation of cultural cross-overs is entertainingly provided by A. G. Cross, *OSP*, 24:34–59, who collates and assesses images of the Russian *bania* as seen by foreign travellers and artists. The contours of the subject are fleshed out by a number of reproductions of engravings and paintings, essential to the article, which convey all the bathing and disporting but conceal the licence and squalor of the institution. Ironic interpretations of 'cleanness' are amusingly implied.

PRINTING, PUBLISHING, AND LIBRARIES.   There is much of interest in P. I. Khoteev's most recent study, *Книга в России в середине XVIII в. Частные книжные собрания*, Ld, Nauka, 1989, 142 pp. Chapters are devoted to imperial holdings, the collections of the nobility and the clergy, and to the libraries of scholars and physicians generally. In this latter category new publications were still written predominantly in Latin rather than Russian. The scantiness of evidence of book ownership among other estates (particularly the upwardly mobile peasantry) is lamented by the author. *Книга в России XVI — середины XIX в. Материалы и исследования*, ed. A. A. Zaitseva, Ld, BibAN, 1990, 193 pp., is a workmanlike collection of articles on the book trade and book ownership. Of the nine pieces devoted specifically to the 18th c., the contributions dealing with books in the libraries of Empress Elizaveta Petrovna and of V. N. Tatishchev contain interesting new matter.

CULTURE AND THOUGHT.   SSR has recently published two articles of note on the important 'Scots in Russia' theme: M. M. Page, 'Admiral Samuil Karlovich Greig: a Scot in the service of Catherine the Great', 15, 1990:7–18, and A. G. Cross, 'In Cameron's shadow: Adam Menelaws, stonemason turned architect', 17:7–20. P. R. Roosevelt, *SRev*, 49, 1990:335–49, analyses 'Tat'iana's Garden' as a focus for discussion of estate park design generally in the light of, among other things, A. T. Bolotov's articles on gardening, and work as an estate landscaper. Another subject is tackled by D. E. Farrell: 'Medieval popular humor in Russian eighteenth-century *lubki*', *ib.*, 50:551–65, takes these prints (reproducing four well-known examples) to reveal an 'archaic premodern humor', which is presumably still amusing. There is one linguistic piece whose specific relevance to literary studies is marked: V. M. Zhivov, **Культурные конфликты в истории русского литературного языка XVIII — начала XIX в.*, IRIa AN SSSR, 1990, 271 pp. Zhivov examines the development of the Russian literary language in the context of a 'hybrid', russified and weakened form of Church Slavonic which could be used, in baroque literature, for panegyric purposes or to bolster a perceived identification of sacred and profane in literary culture. Some engaging and useful work has been done in bringing out more discursive anthologies of essays on diverse cultural themes. *Очерки русской культуры XVIII века. Часть четвертая*, ed. B. A. Rybakov, Mw U.P., 1990, 382 pp., the concluding volume of this successful series, comprises eight liberally illustrated contributions, focusing on the decorative and plastic arts, with a particularly interesting piece by V. S. Dediukhina (220–51) on the culture of aristocratic homes and estates. An additional essay by M. M. Gromyko (299–356), taking as its subject the cultural life of peasants, charts the degeneration of ritual in the countryside into desacralized ritualistic form. *Русская мысль в век просвещения*, ed. N. F. Utkin and A. D. Sukhov, Nauka, 278 pp., provides a good deal of new and interesting material on general themes in intellectual history, including scholastic philosophy,

absolutism, Lomonosovian *Naturphilosophie*, Freemasonry, utopianism, 'free thought', Shcherbatov and Radishchev, in a concise and
sharp account. *Безвременье и временщики. Воспоминания об 'эпохе
дворцовых переворотов' (1720-е — 1760-е годы)*, ed. E. Anisimova, Ld,
KhL, 367 pp., is a collection of more or less unvarnished memoirs
which includes contributions from Natal'ia Borisovna Dolgorukaia
(daughter of B.P. Sheremet'ev) and Mikhail Vasil'evich Danilov,
'artillery major'. A pleasing work of anecdotal reminiscence.

2. INDIVIDUAL AUTHORS

AKSAKOV, S. T. M. Lobanov, *MG*, 9:247–55, supplies a brief
introduction to A. and an argument for the importance of his writings,
in readiness for the bicentennial celebrations.

BOLOTOV. I. I. Pshenichnikova, 'К истории морально-
эстетической лексики (честь, достоинство в текстах XVIII–XIX
вв.)', *VLUIIaL*, 1990, no. 4:39–43, analyses, very briefly, these
lexical qualities as one finds them, chiefly, in the pages of B.'s
memoirs.

CATHERINE II. The Empress's activities as author continue to
provoke flurries of more or less serious academic interest. *Сочинения
Екатерины II*, ed. O. N. Mikhailov, SR, 1990, 384 pp., forms part of a
spate of reprintings organized, it sometimes seems, without too much
regard for scholarly propriety, and preferring the more sensational
aspects of Catherine's character and personal life. This work is solid,
and among noted reprints of primary and secondary sources one finds
A. V. Khrapovitskii, **Памятные записки*, Soiuzteatr, 1990, and a
volume of *Записки Императрицы Екатерины II*, Nauka, 1990,
278 pp., a facsimile of Herzen and Ogarev's 1859 London edition. A
piece by I. S. Sharkova, 'Подписка Екатерины II на иностранные
периодические издания в годы Великой французской
революции', *RusL*, 1990, no. 3:130–36, approaches the Catherine-
and-the-French-Revolution theme obliquely by tabulating the
Empress's subscription lists from, primarily, Königsberg and Memel.
Also noted is O. N. Mikhailov's shorter work, straightforward and
unprovocative, on Catherine as 'Empress, writer and memoirist',
Moskva, 1990, no. 4:199–207.

DASHKOVA. A. Woronzoff-Dashkov has produced an extremely
stimulating piece on 'Disguise and gender in Princess Dashkova's
Memoirs', *CanSP*, 33:62–74. The argument is that the Princess,
though a woman, was able also to attain eminence in well-defined
male roles by dint of skilful manipulation of gender codes, including
those of dress and language. The point is well put.

DEL'VIG.   R. G. Nazar'ian, *RusL*, 1990, no. 4:202–07, throws new light on the familiar corpus of D.'s notebooks as a possible source for a biography of Kiukhel'beker, in this minor but interesting contribution to 'Golden Age' literary associations.

DERZHAVIN.   B. Belov, 'Поэтическое завещание Г. Р. Державина', *AlBi*, 25, 1989:112–31, presents a historical assessment of D., for those whose expertise in the subject is not outstanding, from the cue of a newly discovered autograph on the flyleaf of the first volume of *Сочинения Державина*.

FEOFAN PROKOPOVICH.   O. M. Buranok, *FilN*, no. 2:20–28, on folkloric motifs and inspirations in the work of F., argues for the extended importance, across the century, of such themes in addition to the more familiar 'School' erudition and didacticism. The starting point is the 1705 tragicomedy *Vladimir*.

FONVIZIN.   W. Berelowitch, 'Le "Discours sur les lois" de Fonvizin: une éthique subversive', *CMRS*, 30.3–4:193–206, analyses F.'s 'Рассуждение о непременных государственных законах' in the context created by Montesquieu, Rousseau and the philosophy of German natural law as 'un jalon important dans la préhistoire du radicalisme révolutionnaire russe'.

KANTEMIR.   There has been considerable interest in K. of late, of which the weightiest representation might be said to be M. Baracchi Bavagnoli, *Le origini del poema epico russo La Petrida di A. Kantemir*, Milan, Guerini e Associati, 1990, 138 pp. The author is on familiar ground when locating K. firmly within the tradition of scholarly enlightenment as represented by Feofan, but then goes on to examine the 'theatricality' of the *Petrida* from inside the heritage of Latin/Italian epic literature, and that of Boileau and Voltaire. Parallelism with the latter's *Henriade*, indeed, is shown to be the consistent policy which clearly it is. Readers who wonder at Russia's inability to produce epics should pause here. The French connections are traced also by G. Hüttl-Folter, *ZMS(Sl)*, 38, 1990:97–110, who re-examines K.'s translation of Fontenelle, *Entretiens sur la pluralité des mondes*, as a stage in the normalization of some western linguistic norms in the 'new' literary language.

KARAMZIN.   Gitta Hammarberg's interests in K. and the idyllic mode have come to a major culmination with her book, *From the Idyll to the Novel: Karamzin's Sentimentalist Prose*, CUP, xiii + 334 pp. This account of K.'s sentimentalism, having paid obeisance to the theoretical creeds of Bakhtin, Voloshinov, Doležel and speech-act philosophy, traces the course of idyll motifs through the *povesti* and prose fragments. The picture which emerges is one of conventional idyllicism rather than ideological pastoralism. K.'s ambivalence towards his heroes and heroines is manifested by a tone of voice made flexible by resulting ironic distance. Presumably it was the latter element of the rubric of *RRe* (a 'scholarly-popular journal') which accounted for I. N. Vrubel''s 800-word essay on K.'s life and work, *RRe*, no. 6:70–72.

KIUKHEL'BEKER. A presentation and analysis of the 'Estonian pages' in K.'s biography, known but not well-known, is provided by R. G. Nazar'ian and M. G. Salupere, *RusL*, 1990, no. 1:156–63.

KRYLOV. S. V. Nikol'skii, *ISLIa*, 50:151–55, takes K.'s fables as masterpieces of sound-patterning and *instrumentovka*, and subjects them to an analysis of internal phonetic affinities.

LEVASHOV. P. Perminov, 'Пасынок фортуны', *AlBi*, 25, 1989:154–64, provides the bare essentials of L.'s diplomatic and literary career in a context which historians of the 18th c. will find indispensable. Another figure due, it may seem, for resuscitation.

LOMONOSOV. G. N. Moiseeva, 'Из истории архива М. В. Ломоносова', *RusL*, 1990, no. 2:171–75, presents the archive story as chequered, and has to conclude with questions: is all the archive now known? Where is L.'s home and foreign correspondence? Given the heightened interest in L. in recent years, Moiseeva suggests, these are spaces that ought to be filled. I. P. Shcheblykin's rather more run-of-the-mill article for L.'s 280th anniversary, '"Гряди, Российская отрада ... Поставь опасностям конец"', *LSh*, no. 4:64–78, takes in a conspectus of L.'s life and heroic works in order to conclude, naturally, that he is a champion of 'national spirit'.

RADISHCHEV. The vatic and courageous intensity of R.'s prose and verse, with particular regard to his attitudes to the French Revolution, is celebrated by L. Boeva, *BR*, 1990, no. 5:3–12. A different side of the great activist, conceived in terms of a retreat into folklore from the struggle and torment of the end of his life, is provided by Л. Bacheva, '"Бова" А. Н. Радищева в контексте русской ироикомической поэзии XVIII в.', *ib.*, 13–19. Also noted is Tania Galcheva, 'О некоторых особенностях коммуникативной ситуации в главе "Тверь" (*Путешествие из Петербурга в Москву* А. Н. Радищева)', *ib.*, 20–26. A rather summarily constructed article by G. I. Zhuravleva, *RRe*, 1990, no. 3:3–7, uses the analysis of rhetorical tropes in R.'s 'Liberty' ode to celebrate the bicentenary of the first publication of the *Puteshestvie*.

SUMAROKOV. The history of Boileau's influence on S., in terms both of the mediation of the antique classical and of a newly 'European' fluency in the literary language is continued by J. Klein, 'Sumarokov und Boileau. Die Epistel "Über die Verskunst" in ihrem Verhältnis zur "Art Poétique": Kontextwechsel als Kategorie der vergleichenden Literaturwissenschaft', *ZSP*, 50, 1990:254–304. S.'s relationship with Lomonosov in the 1740s, coloured by his mocking attitude towards Trediakovskii, is concisely summarized by M. Sh. Grinberg and B. A. Uspenskii, *AIPS*, 24, 1990:113–24.

TATISHCHEV.   Notable here is *Василий Никитич Татищев. За-писки, письма, 1717–1750 гг.* (Nauchnoe nasledstvo, 14), ed. A. I. Iukht, Nauka, 1990, 440 pp. The broadness of T.'s interests is manifest in these 276 letters, many of them showing his heavy involvement with official service, state, military and civil, but there is also much of interest for those inclined to *personalia*, represented here from emperors to foreign artisans.

TREDIAKOVSKII.   Scholarship on T. has been looking up, and his very neglect is now the subject of monographs. There has been an important contribution from Irina Reyfman, *Vasilii Trediakovsky. The Fool of the 'New' Russian Literature*, Stanford U.P., 1990, viii + 316 pp. The image of T. as a buffoon and a drudge, the laughing-stock of the century, is submitted to careful scrutiny in its contemporary context and also as a defining characteristic of later attitudes. This re-examination of mid-century polemics argues that T.'s status as canonical failure arose from a need for a mythological jester-figure to counterbalance the majesty of Lomonosov's intellect and deeds. T. happened to be cast as a sort of 'Holy Fool' in the antinomian dialectic. Reyfman concludes that the 'real' and admirable T., historically available from the time of Pushkin onwards, is still less useful than his status as a polemical tool and focus of ineptitude. None the less, if the literature is a reliable guide, the course has been set for rehabilitation. C. Carrier, *ZSP*, 50, 1990:167–79, continues the not unfamiliar story of T.'s importance in the work of V. S. Shefner by analysing the latter's cycle of lyrics addressed to T. The article includes a brief run-through of T.'s major works. Also noted is Carrier's *Trediakovskij und die 'Argenida'*, Munich, Otto Sagner, 330 pp. T.'s religious and theological involvements have come in for some attention, An academic edition of his *Psalter*, *Vasilij Kirillovic Trediakovskij, Psalter 1753*, ed. A. Levitsky, Paderborn–Munich–Vienna–Zurich, 1989, is fairly favourably assessed, in an important review, by V. M. Zhivov, *ISLIa*, 50:551–55. B. A. Uspenskii and A. B. Shishkin, *Simvol*, 23, 1990:105–264, write on the subject of T. and the Jansenists. This implies a reference to T.'s dealings with Abbé Jacques Jubé de la Cour, the personal confessor of Princess Irina Dolgorukaia. The piece concludes by reiterating that whilst to 18th c. eyes T.'s behaviour was reminiscent of something from a picaresque novel, it was perfectly possible in the following century to see him as a typical *intelligent-raznochinets*. There are an exceptionally good biblio-graphy and notes.

ZAGOSKIN.   I. P. Shcheblykin, *LSh*, 1990, no. 3:3–14, provides a short article for Z.'s 200th anniversary year (although he was actually born in 1789) which comes to the laudable though hardly surprising decision that after so much time, and on the basis of his 29 volumes of prose, 17 plays and one vaudeville, Z. would benefit from some critical enthusiasm.

LITERATURE, 1820–1880

POSTPONED

LITERATURE, 1880–1917

By DAVID N. WELLS, *Research Fellow, Department of Politics,*
La Trobe University, Melbourne

ABBREVIATIONS. In the text of this section the following works are referred to in the abbreviated forms in parentheses: *Горький и его эпоха. Исследования и материалы*, vyp. 1, ed. B. A. Bialik, Nauka, 1989, 280 pp. (Bialik, *Горький*); *L'Avant-garde russe et la synthèse des arts*, ed. Gerard Conio, Lausanne, L'Age d'homme, 1990, 281 pp. (Conio, *Avant-garde*); *Александр Блок: исследования и материалы*, ed. Iu. K. Gerasimov *et al.*, Ld, Nauka, 344 pp. (Gerasimov, *Блок*); *L'avantguardia letteraria russa*, ed. Marzio Marzaduri, Daniela Rizzi and Michail Evzlin, Università di Trento, Dipartimento di Storia della Civiltà Europea, 1990, 342 pp. (Marzaduri, *Avantguardia*); *Михаил Кузмин и русская литература XX века. Тезисы и материалы конференции 15–17 мая 1990 г.*, ed. G. A. Morev, Ld, AN SSSR, 1990, 258 pp. (Morev, *Кузмин*).

1. GENERAL

The appearance of previously unpublishable material continues, though perhaps at a slower rate than during the last few years. As in previous reports an attempt has been made to cover at least the most significant examples of these. The focus of critical attention is varied, but a tendency can be observed in Russian criticism to pay noticeably more attention than in the past to erotic, philosophical, and religious topics.

Писатели советуются, негодуют, благодарят. О чем думали и что переживали русские писатели XIX — нач. XX в. при издании своих произведений. По страницам переписки, ed. A. E. Mil'chin, Kniga, 1990, 416 pp., is an anthology of writers' comments on their profession. E. Etkind, Etkind, *Letteratura*, 13–33, writes on the unity of the Silver Age. *DI*, no. 3, is a special issue on the Silver Age and refers throughout to writers of the period. Berdiaev's *Русская идея* is published in *RusL*, 1990, no. 2:85–133, no. 3:67–102 and no. 4:59–111, and is followed by a discussion of its themes by V. A. Kotel'nikov, no. 4:112–19. *Glossarium der russischen Avantgarde*, ed. Aleksander Flaker, Graz, Droschl, 1989, 548 pp., contains articles on key topics in the study of the avant-garde movement; C. Leclanche-Boulé, Conio, *Avant-garde*, 137–51, discusses Futurist typography. M. Marzaduri, Marzaduri, *Avantguardia*, 9–20, surveys the study of the movement in Italy. On *zaum'* see V. Shklovskii, *ib.*, 253–59; and O. Ronen, *LitO*, no. 12:40–43. Alexander Ocheretiansky, **Literature and*

Art of Avant-Garde Russia 1890–1930, Newtonville, Mass., ORP, 1989, 270 pp., is a useful bibliographical work. On Constructivism see especially pp. 113–48 of François Albera, *Eisenstein et le constructivisme russe*, Lausanne, L'Age d'homme, 1990, 289 pp. Renate Lachmann devotes pp. 354–71 of her *Gedächtnis und Literatur: Intertextualität in der russischen Moderne*, Frankfurt, Suhrkamp, 1990, 555 pp., to a discussion of the Acmeists' cultural philosophy. On Acmeism see also A. G. Mets, *TCh*, 5, 1990:111–30. N. Sal'ma, *SSH*, 35, 1989:355–73, explores the intellectual context of Symbolism. V. M. Tolmachev, *VMUF*, no. 5:18–28, offers a characterization of Decadence. There are several works on the role played by religious thought in writing of the period. P. von Maidel, *UZTarU*, 917 (Блоковский сборник, 11):67–81, writes on aspects of anthroposophy and revolutionary thought; pp. 119–46 of Valentin Boss, *Milton and the Rise of Russian Satanism*, Toronto U.P., 276 pp., covers writers of the period; De Michelis, *Avversario*, 53–76, considers the Antichrist theme; E. A. D'iakova, *ISLIa*, 50:414–25, looks at Christianity and revolution among the 'Scythians'. Also on the Scythian movement is V. G. Belous, *Zv*, no. 10:158–66. Elisabeth Dobringer, *Der Literaturkritiker R. V. Ivanov-Razumnik und seine Konzeption des Skythentums* (SB, 271), 254 pp., considers the work of an important critic of the period. I. P. Foote, *OSP*, 24:60–120, examines the work of the St Petersburg Censorship Committee, 1828-1905. Henrietta Mondry, pp. 47–97 of her *The Evaluation of Ideological Trends in Recent Soviet Literary Scholarship* (SB, 255), 1990, 134 pp., examines the recent treatment of previously unpublished 19th- and 20th-c. writers. J. Orłowski, *SlaW*, 55, 1990:71–86, surveys post-war Polish criticism of Russian literature 1850–1917.

POETRY. Bristol, *Poetry*, has sections on the *fin de siècle*, 1890–1905 (167–85), Symbolist idealism, 1905–12 (186 201), Acmeism (205–23), and Futurism (224–48). Aage A. Hansen-Löve, *Der Russische Symbolismus: System und Enthaltung der poetischen Motive. I Band: Diabolischer Symbolismus*, Vienna, Verlag der österreichischen Akademie der Wissenschaften, 1989, 561 pp., is the first part of what promises to be a comprehensive treatise on Symbolist poetics. There is a book by Inna Broude, *От Ходасевича до Набокова: ностальгическая тема в поэзии первой русской эмиграции*, Tenafly, New Jersey, Ermitazh, 1990, 160 pp., which treats several authors of the period. G. V. Zykova, *VMUF*, no. 6:11–14, looks at reminiscences of Lermontov in the poetry of the late 19th c. T. V. Krivoshchapova, *FilN*, no. 2:28–35, examines the verse fable in the late 19th and early 20th c. Also of interest is *Poetry and Revolution in Russia 1905–1930: An Exhibition of Books and MSS*, ed. Lazar Fleishman, Stanford University Libraries, 1989, 63 pp.

THEATRE.   Several books are noted on the theatre of the period: K. L. Rudnitskii, *Русское режиссерское искусство 1898–1907*, Nauka, 1989, 384 pp.; Id., *Русское режиссерское искусство 1908–1917*, Nauka, 1990, 280 pp.; Sharon Marie Carnicke, *The Theatrical Instinct: Nikolai Evreinov and the Russian Theatre of the Early Twentieth Century*, NY, Lang, 1989, xiii + 247 pp.; Daniela Rizzi, **La rifrazione del simbolo: Teorie del teatro nel simbolismo russo*, Padua, Edizioni GB , 1989, 202 pp., which has chapters on Blok, Ivanov, and Belyi; and *Theatre in Revolution: Russian Avant-Garde Stage Design*, ed. Nancy van Norman Baer, London, Thames and Hudson, 208 pp. D. Kšicová, *WSJ*, 36, 1990:95–112, discusses the theme of secession in Russian and Austrian drama of the period. Senelick, *Theatre*, 317–42, reviews the period 1812–98.

2.   INDIVIDUAL AUTHORS

ANDREEV.   The second volume of A., *Собрание сочинений в шести томах*, KhL, 1990, 559 pp., covers the stories and plays of 1904–07 and contains 50 pages of commentary by A. V. Bogdanov. L. A. Es'kina edits and introduces the First World War story *Ночной разговор* in *Mos*, no. 6: 105–21, and correspondence from 1918–19 in *ib.*, no. 3: 198–208. A. Barratt discusses the circumstances surrounding the composition of A.'s story *Тьма* and its reception by Gor'kii and others in Luker, *Short Story*, 73–97. S. Iu. Iasenskii considers the historical and cultural context of *Так было* in Fridlender, *Революция*, 397–406.

ANNENSKII.   *Произведения И. Ф. Анненского на русском языке: библиографический указатель*, comp. A. I. Cherviakov, Ivanovo U. P. 1989, 108 pp., contains 534 items. M. V. Trostnikov writes on recurrent motifs in A.'s verse in *ISLIa*, 50:328–37, and on the symbolism of the colour yellow in *RRe*, no. 4: 15–17. C. Cardone, *RicSl*, 36, 1989:303–25, considers the influence of Euripedes in *Меланиппа-философ*. L. M. Borisova, *VRL*, 56, 1990: 11–18, looks at the Dionysian and the Apollonian in *Фамира-кифаред*. A. E. Anikin continues his work on A. and Akhmatova in *Ахматова и Анненский: заметки к теме*, vols 6 and 7, preprint, Novosibirsk, AN SSSR, 1990, 53 and 53 pp. The theme of A. and Pushkin is investigated by N. V. Fridman in *ISLIa*, 50:338–49; that of A. and Mandel'shtam by A. Barzokh in *Zv*, no. 11:161–65. M. L. Gasparov, *Сборник научных труд Московского государственного института иностранных языков им. Мориса Тореза*, 347, 1989:61–69, investigates A. as a translator of Aeschylus. See also Anikin under BLOK, Id., Morev, *Kuzmin*, 70–74, and J. Dewey, Marsh and Rosslyn, *Culture*, 47–59.

ARTSYBASHEV. N. Luker, 'Studies in Instability: Artsybashev's *Etiudy* (1910)', Luker, *Short Story*, 99–128, is a revised version of his earlier article.

BAL'MONT. B., *Стихотворения*, KhL, 1990, 397 pp., introd. (3–20) and ed. L. Ozerov. B., **Ашвагхоша. Жизнь Будды. Ашвагхоша. Драмы. Калидаса*, KhL, 1990, 573 pp., contains B.'s translations from Indian languages and three essays by G. Bongard-Levin on B.'s approach to India and to translation (6–27, 33–41, 263–67). B.'s 1925 essay 'Звуковой зазыв' is reprinted in *SovM*, no. 3:89–91. K. M. Azadovskii and E. M. D'iakonova, *Бальмонт и Япония*, Nauka, 190 pp., offers a detailed study of B.'s approach to Japan.

BELYI. There are several editions of B.'s works, most notably, B., *Сочинения в двух томах*, KhL, 1990, vol. 1 (poetry), 703 pp., and vol. 2 (prose), 671 pp., introd. (1, 5–42) and ed. V. Piskunov. S. I. Timina introduces B., *Москва*, SR, 1989, 768 pp. (3–16); A. V. Lavrov introduces B., *Симфонии*, Ld, KhL, 528 pp. (5–34). Other publications noted are B., *Antichrist: Abbozzo di un misterio incompiuto*, ed. and comm. Daniela Rizzi, Università di Trento, Dipartimento di Storia della Civiltà Europea, 1990, 91 pp., and B., 'Душа самосознающая (из кн. "История самосознающей души")', ed. G. F. Parkhomenko, pp. 278–310 of *Laterna magica* (details under ROZANOV). B.'s letters to A. A. Blok, the poet's mother, are in Gerasimov, *Блок*, 281–335.

The Andrej Belyj Society Newsletter, 9, 1990, contains a current bibliography 1989–90, comp. J. Graffy (51–64), and includes articles by A. V. Lavrov (9–13, B. and autobiography), M. Carlson (14–15, *Серебряный голубь*), J. M. Copper (16–18, *Котик Летаев*), and M. Wessels (29–37, *Петербург* and syphilis). B.'s prose is discussed in Jochen Becker, *Andrej Belyjs Prosa und seine ästetisch weltanschaulichen Schriften*, Cologne, no publisher given, 1990, 189 pp.; by O. Muller Cooke in Rancoeur-Laferrière, *Psychoanalysis*, 263–84 (pathological patterns in B.'s works); by S. P. Il'ev, *WSlA*, 27:109–18 (the symbolic meaning of proper nouns); and by S. Kormilov, *RusL*, 1990, no. 4:30–44 (metrical prose). R. Lachmann, pp. 88–125 of *Gedächtnis und Literatur* (details under GENERAL), discusses intertextuality in *Петербург*. *Петербург* is also examined by L. N. Tselkova, *FilN*, no. 2:11–20 (the poetics of the subject), and P. Pesonen, *Semiotica*, 87:349–68 (the myth of St Petersburg). M. Cymborska-Leboda, *SSR*, 15, 1990:43–58, discusses *Пришедший*. B. and other writers are considered by S. V. Poliakova, *UZTarU*, 917 (*Блоковский сборник*, 11):82–89 (B.'s response to Gogol''s *Hoc*), N. Kauchtchi-schwili, *EO*, 6, 1987:95–134 (B. and Solov'ev), and S. M. Gargolina, *RL*, 30:431–53 (B. and Mandel'shtam). J. E. Malmstad, *SSR*, 15,

1990:59–102, presents the second part of his article on B. and Serafim of Sarov. See also P'ianykh under BLOK, Il'ev under BLOK, Rizzi under THEATRE, and Bryś under IVANOV.

BLOK. *Александр Блок. Андрей Белый. Диалог поэтов о России и революции*, ed. M. F. P'ianykh, VysSh, 1990, 687 pp., is an anthology of the two poets' reflections on national and revolutionary themes. Gerasimov, *Блок* contains several articles of a general or biographical nature, notably pieces by K. G. Isupov (3–21) and L. A. Il'iunina (41–48), both on B. and history; K. A. Kumkan (151–57, B. and the ancient world); E. V. Ivanova (198–212, B. and B. V. Nikol'skii); and materials on B. and P. I. Karpov, ed. K. M. Azadovskii (234–80).

There are several works on *Двенадцатъ*: A. D. P. Briggs, *A Comparative Study of Pushkin's 'The Bronze Horseman', Nekrasov's 'Red-Nosed Frost', and Blok's 'The Twelve': The Wild World*, Lewiston, NY, Edwin Mellon Press, 1990, 276 pp.; E. Ivanova, *Mos*, no. 8:191–96 (on the ending of the poem). A. E. Anikin, *RRe*, no. 5:15–20, compares *Незнакомка* with Annenskii's *Баллада*. S. Iu. Iasenskii, Gerasimov, *Блок*, 64–77, discusses allusion in *Ночная фиалка*; L. Allain, *ib.*, 189–97, considers the question of genre in *Возмездие*; D. White, *SRev*, 50:779–91, examines *Нечаянная радостъ*; B. van Sambeek-Weideli, *Brang Vol.*, 327–39, examines key words in B.'s essays.

Numerous works consider B. and other writers. Avramenko, *Блок* has chapters on B. and Zhukovskii (13–60), B. and Fet (61–131), B. and Grigor'ev (132–55), B. and Baratynskii and Tiutchev (156–212), and B. and Lermontov (213–43). Gerasimov, *Блок* includes articles by S. P. Il'ev (22–40, comparing 'На поле куликовом' and Belyi's *Петербург*); N. Iu. Griakalova (49–63, on B., Polonskii, and Solov'ev); A. M. Gracheva (78–100, B. and Novikov); N. V. Vulikh (142–50, B. and Ovid); and N. V. Skvortsova (158–64, B. and Khomiakov). E. I. Belkin, *ib.*, 101–24, considers B. as a reader of Pushkin; A. N. Shustov, *ib.*, 125–41, looks at B. in the life and work of E. Iu. Kuz'mina-Karavaeva. A. P. Iulova, *FilN*, 1990, no. 6:97–101, considers B. and Hauptmann; D. M. Magomedova, *UZTarU*, 917 (*Блоковский сборник*, 11):39–49, compares B. and Voloshin. K. Taranovsky, *Van der Eng Vol.*, 563–69, discusses the influence on B. of a romance by the Grand Duke Konstantin. V. Molodiakov, *Pro*, no. 1:107–11, considers B. and G. E. Zinov'ev. T. Kozhevnikova, *Poez*, 55, 1990:171–79, examines B.'s reception in Italy, and O. Panchenko, *ib.*:138–47, looks at B. and Akhmatova. Also noted are M. Carlson, *InSS*, 5, 1990:1–10, on B. and the myth of the 'Great National Poet'; M. Banjanin, *ASEES*, 4.1–2, 1990:1–20, on echoes of the *Commedia dell'arte* in B.'s work; H. Gemba, *WSl*, 36:166–200, on B.'s treatment of space; P. Basinskii, *VL*, 1990, no. 6:104–26 (the 'music of the revolution' and the fate of the intelligentsia); and E. Iu. Kukushkina, *PSL*, 1985–87 (1989):246–60 (syntactical repetition). *LitU*, 1990, no.6:93–103, reprints an article attributed to P. Florenskii on B. and Christianity. This is followed by a reply by N. Berdiaev (104–05), and by an article on the debate by E. Ivanova (106–14). V. Radzivshevskii, *LitG*, 31:11 and 34:11, considers the deaths of B., Gumilev, and Tsvetaeva. See also A. V. Lavrov, 'Маргиналии к блоковским текстам', Gerasimov, *Блок*. 165–88; Iu. Lotman, *LitG*, 23:11; P. P. Suvchinskii, *VMUF*, no.3:53–68; G. A. Smirnova, pp.156–65 of *Поэтика и стилистика: 1988–1990*, Nauka, 244 pp.; Rizzi under THEATRE, and Bryś under IVANOV.

BOBORYKIN.   Kirsten Blanck, *P. D. Boborykin: Studien zur Theorie und Praxis des naturalistischen Romans in Russland*, Wiesbaden, Harrassowitz, 1990, xi + 268 pp.

BRIUSOV.   B., *Среди стихов: 1894–1924: манифесты, статьи, рецензии*, SovP, 1990, 720 pp., has an introduction by N. A. Bogomolov (3–32) and extensive notes. 'Erotopaegnia. Переводы Валерия Брюсова', *ILen*, no.4:18–27, presents B.'s translations from the Latin poets. There is a general article by M. A. Shapovalov, *LSh*, no.3:19–27. N. A. Bogomolov, *TCh*, 5, 1990:100–11, examines B.'s use of the term 'decadent'. E. N. Kolesnikova, *RusL*, no.3:197–204, writes on the play *Диктатор*. See also T. Klimowicz, 'Briusowowskie *miscellanea*', *SlaW*, 52, 1990:67–77.

CHEKHOV.   E. M. Sakharova introduces (5–20) and edits the reminiscences of members of Ch.'s family in *Вокруг Чехова*, Pravda, 1990, 656 pp. There is a letter of 1899 to I. S. Vologdin in *SA*, no.6:81–82. H. Tolstoy, *SRev*, 50:590–600, considers Ch. in 1886–87. B. Lishchinskii, *DV*, 1990, no.7:156–60, discusses Ch.'s trip to Vladivostok. Critical work on Ch. is reviewed by Charles W. Meister, *Chekhov Criticism: 1880 through 1986*, Jefferson, North Carolina, McFarland, 1988, x + 350 pp., which has separate sections on the reception of the stories (20–161), *Чайка* (210–28), *Дядя Ваня* (229–44), *Три сестры* (245–64), and *Вишневый сад* (265–85). *Anton P. Čechov. Werk und Wirkung. Vorträge und Diskussionen eines internationalen Symposiums in Badenweiler im Oktober 1985*, ed. Rolf-Dieter Kluge, Wiesbaden, Harrasowitz, 1990, 2 vols, xix + 1270 pp., contains 76 articles on all aspects of Ch.'s work, including his reception in Russia (806–946) and Germany (1108–1242).

General works noted on the stories include Roswitha Hoffrichter, *Natur und Raumdarstellungen in A. P. Čechovs Erzählungen 1895–1902* (Beiträge zur Slavistik, 12), Frankfurt, Lang, 1990, 206 pp.; E. I. Romanova, *VRL*, 56, 1990:75–81, which discusses the imagery of works of the 1880s; N. M. Fortunatov, *BCh*, 14, 1990:91–100, which considers the effect of the *reprise* in Ch.'s prose; R. E. Lapushin, *VBDU*, 1990, no. 2:15–17 (on works of the 1880s and 1890s); and M. F. Kuntysh, *ib.*, 37–41. V. Erofeev, Erofeev, *В лабиринте*, 402–19, compares Ch. and Maupassant. P. G. Christensen, *SAR*, 54.4, 1989:51–62, considers the role of Ch. in the work of the poets Howard Moss and Denise Levertov. There is a book by V. P. Rynkevich, **Путешествие к дому с мезонином*, KhL, 1990, 319 pp. P. Eremin, *VL*, no. 4:93–123, examines *Скрипка Ротшильда*. There are three articles on *Дама с собачкой*: Y. Greenberg, *MLR*, 86:126–30 (on Ch.'s presentation of the unconscious); B. Creaseman, *SSF*, 27, 1990:257–60 (Gurov's flights of emotion); and A. A. Bragina and R. A. Budagov, *FilN*, no. 1:23–31. R. L. Jackson, *RL*, 29:427–38, looks at the metaphor of space in *Степь*; J. L. Conrad, *SSR*, 16:47–63, discusses *Жена*; there are articles by A. Durkin, *InSS*, 5, 1990:31–42, on narrative structure in the *Человек в футляре — Крыжовник — О любви* trilogy; C. F. Dowsett, *RLJ*, 147–49, 1990:151–61, on characterization in *Палата № 6*; A. R. Durkin, *ASJ*, 8, 1990:1–11, on *Моя жизнь*. There are articles on *Черный монах* by S. D. Abramovich, *VRL*, 56, 1990:81–89; F. Raskol'nikov, *RLJ*, 147–49, 1990:163–81; and M. I. Gorelikova, *FilN*, no. 5:33–45. G. McVay, Luker, *Short Story*, 1–21, discusses Ch.'s last stories, *Архиерей* and *Невеста*. *Архиерей* is also examined by C. J. G. Turner, *MLR*, 86:131–36.

There is a book on Ch.'s one-act plays: S. V. Zubkova, *Драматический характер в одноактной комедии А. П. Чехова*, Kiev, Lybid', 1990, 108 pp. An article by L. Senelick, *Te*, no. 1:91–100, examines the origins of Ch.'s dramaturgy. C. Marsh, Marsh and Rosslyn, *Culture*, 17–29, writes on Ch.'s 'Modernist' theatre. There are many articles on individual plays. *Te*, no. 1:73–83, contains comments by Nabokov on Ch., the greater part of which focus on *Чайка*. On *Чайка* see also V. Ja. Zvinjackovskij, *RSl*, 63:587–605 (the polemic function of Treplev and Trigorin). On *Дядя Ваня* see P. Dolzhenkov, *Te*, no. 1:83–91. On *Три сестры* see R. B. Bennett, *CLS*, 28:156–77, which compares Ch.'s use of the theme of the golden age with that of Shakespeare in *Henry IV. Part II*; D. G. Stenberg, *ISS*, 10, 1989 (1991):41–46 (linguistic opposition); C. S. Tufts, *ModD*, 32, 1989:485–501 (literary allusion); G. McVay, *Rusistika*, 3:2–7. On *Вишневый сад* see A. G. F. van Holk, 'The syntax of sale in Chekhov's *The Cherry Orchard*', SH, 33, 1989:433–46; G. Anderson, *ModD*, 34:340–50 (textual repetition); V. Mil'don, *Te*, no. 1:106–13 (spatial imagery); D. Stenberg, *Rusistika*, 3:14–17 (linguistic markers of disintegration).

There are several articles dealing with the foreign reception of Ch. as dramatist. V. Gottlieb, pp. 163–72 of *The Play Out of Context: Transferring Plays from Culture to Culture*, ed. Hanna Scolnicor and Peter

Holland, NY, CUP, 1989, viii + 227 pp., looks at British productions of Ch.'s plays; E. Fischer-Lichte, *ib.*, 173–85, considers the adaptation of *Три сестры* by Suzuki Tadashi; *SSR*, 16:103–21, presents various reports of Ch. productions in Britain, Ireland, and Russia; D. Allen, *NTQ*, 17, 1989:52–66, discusses a 1976 production of *Три сестры* by Jonathan Miller. On filming *Три сестры* see C. Hollosi, *SSH*, 35, 1989:349–54; and on staging *Вишневый сад*, C. Marsh, *Rusistika*, 3:8–13; T. Proskurnikova, *Te*, no. 2:106–20, considers Ch. in France; and the Czech director Otomar Krejča gives his view of Ch. in *Te*, no. 1:119–31 and no. 2:69–76. M.-C. Pasquier, pp. 77–83 of *Eugene O'Neill and the Emergence of American Drama*, ed. Marc Maufort, Amsterdam, Rodopi, 1989, 205 pp., compares the relationship of Ch. to the Moscow Arts Theatre with that of O'Neill to the Provincetown Players. D. W. Gunn, *ModD*, 33, 1990:313–21, considers Ch.'s influence on Tennessee Williams. Also noted are articles by Z. Papernyi, *LitG*, no. 3:11; M. Petrovskii, *Te*, no. 1:100–05; V. Kataev, *ib.*, 114–19; L. Garon, *Te*, no. 2:76–85; A. Iniakhin, *ib.*, 85–96; G. Kholodova, *ib.*, 96–106.

ESENIN. E., *Собрание сочинений в двух томах*, SR, 1990, 480 and 384 pp., is edited and introduced (1, 5–22) by Iu. Prokushev. D. F. Ditts, *Есенин в Петрограде-Ленинграде*, Ld, Lenizdat, 1990, 269 pp., charts E.'s involvement with that city. Another biographical work is Jessie Davies, *Isadora Duncan's Russian Husband or Child of the Terrible Years*, no place, no date [1991?], 286 pp. *Научные труды Литвийского университета*, 550, 1990, is devoted entirely to E. *Пугачев* is treated in Poliakova, *Поэзия*, 62–74, and by G. Tsukanov, *LRia*, 1990, no. 5:239–69. Zuev, *Жизнь*, devotes two chapters to E.: one on the philosophy of nature and man in E.'s lyrics (172–94), the other on *Анна Снегина* (195–207). V. I. Khazan, *FilN*, 1990, no. 6:3–10, discusses biblical quotations and reminiscences in E.'s poetry; A. Plitchenko, *SO*, 1990, no. 10:167–76, examines E.'s use of imagery; O. Hasty, *SRev*, 50:836–46, compares Tsvetaeva's responses to the suicides of E. and Maiakovskii.

GIPPIUS. There are poems in *Ko*, no. 8:194–96. *Da*, no. 1:63–79, no. 2:58–80, and nos 3–4:176–92, publishes G.'s 'Petersburg Diaries' with notes and an introduction by M. Pavlova. N. Bogomolov introduces extracts from G.'s *Дмитрий Мережковский* in *VL*, 1990, no. 5:219–48. There are documents relating to G.'s life in Paris in *Ok*, no. 9:160–78. S. J. Rabinowitz, *OSP*, 24:121–44, presents materials concerning G.'s relationship to Akim Volynskii. See also Pavlova under ROZANOV, and pp. 55–85 of Pachmuss under MEREZHKOVSKII, which compares G.'s and Merezhkovskii's metaphysics.

GUMILEV. Three more editions of G.'s work are noted: *Избранное*, SR, 1989, 496 pp., introd. L. A. Smirnova (5–30); *Стихи. Письма о русской поэзии*, KhL, 1989, 447 pp., introd. V. V. Ivanov (5–32); and *Драматические произведения. Переводы. Статьи*, Ld, Iskusstvo, 1990, 405 pp., introd. D. Zolotnitskii (3–38). Vera Luknitskaia, *Николай Гумилев. Жизнь поэта по материалам домашнего архива семьи Лукницких*, Ld, Lenizdat, 1990, 302 pp., is a biographical work of major importance. There are articles by T. M. Nikolaeva, *RL*, 30:343–56, on G.'s *Охота* and Akhmatova's *Сероглазый король*; Iu. Medvedev, *Av*, no. 11:127–33, on G.'s translation of Baudelaire's 'Une Martyre'; E. Gollerbakh, *Zv*, no. 8:188–94, on Lenin as a reader of G.; and I. Kurlandskii, *NN*, no. 1:36–38, who presents a report written by G. while serving in France during the First World War. See also Radzivshevskii under BLOK and Ivanov under KHLEBNIKOV.

IVANOV, VIACHESLAV. I., *Эрос*, Kniga, 102 pp., is a reprint of the 1907 volume and contains an afterword on 14 unnumbered pages by V. Shirokov. There is an essay on Pushkin in *LSh*, no. 3:15–18; an essay ('Наш язык') in *RRe*, no. 1:43–48, with an introductory article by L. M. Granovskaia (39–42) on I. as essay writer; and three letters to V. A. Merkuraeva from 1921–22 in *RusL*, no. 1:176–80. *LitG*, no. 34:11, has 1949 appreciations by F. Stepun and G. Ivanov. G. Bryś, *SlaW*, 52, 1990:79–102, examines the motif of the rose in I.'s cycle 'Rosarium'; and Id., *ib.*, 56:45–63, investigates the role of minerals in the work of I., Belyi and Blok. I. V. Koretskaia, Bialik, *Горький*, 169–84, considers the theme of I. and Gor'kii; A. Shishkin, *VRKhD*, 160, 1990:118–40, writes on I. and Pavel Florenskii; B. Merzhvinskite, *Научные труды вузов Литовского ССР*, 32.3, 1990:19–28, on Lithuanian themes in I. See also *SMu*, 1990, no. 5:42–47, Rosenthal under MEREZHKOVSKII and Rizzi under THEATRE.

KAMENSKII. K., *Сочинения*, Kniga, 1990, 591 pp., includes the collections of 1914, 1916, and 1918.

KHLEBNIKOV. There is a book by R. V. Duganov, *Велимир Хлебников. Природа творчества*, SovP, 1990, 350 pp.; and articles by V. V. Ivanov, *RL*, 29:409–26, comparing the treatment of Africa in Kh.'s *Ka* and Gumilev's African poems; J.-C. Lanne, Conio, *Avant-garde*, 49–95, on Kh. and the city; and Id., *Essais sur le discours soviétique, russe . . . et autres discours slaves*, 9, 1990:141–65, on *zaum'*. See also V. V. Kravets', *SiCh*, 1990, no. 9:62–66, on Kh. and Shevchenko; G. McVay, *ISS*, 11, 1990 (1991):91–97, which presents two forgotten obituaries of Kh. by Shershenevich and Mariengof; G. A. Levinton, Morev, *Кузмин*, 86–89; A. E. Parnis, *ib.*, 156–65 (Kh. in Kuzmin's diary); and the materials in *ISLIa*, 50:43–57.

KHODASEVICH. Kh., *Собрание сочинений*. II, *Статьи и рецензии 1905–1926*, ed. J. Malmstad and R. Hughes, AAA, 1990, 574 pp., is a valuable resource. *Zn*, no. 12:178–92, contains letters to M. V. Vishniak, the draft of an unfinished story and an essay ('О "Жизни

Арсеньева"'); *Smena*, no. 4:161–66, has a 1931 article on Del'vig; M. Z. Dolinskii and I. O. Shaitanov, *Ok*, no. 4:180–200, introduce *Парижский альбом* and two essays. There is an article by D. M. Magomedova, *FilN*, 1990, no. 6:17–22, on the symbol of the 'soul' in *Тяжелая лира*; and a bibliographical note by I. Tolstoi, *Zv*, no. 4:206–07. See also Broude under POETRY.

KLIUEV.   K., *Стихотворения и поэмы*, KhL, 351 pp., has an introduction by K. Azadovskii (3–26). There are poems in *Слово*, no. 4:64–66; *NN*, no. 1:113–17; poems and a memoir by V. Manuilov in *ILen*, 1990, no. 8:21–29. There are poems in *Zv*, no. 3:157–64; and a lost *poema* (*Песнь о Великой Матери*) is introduced by V. Shentalinskii, *Zn*, no. 11:3–44 (3–4). There are two books on Kliuev: V. G. Bazanov, *С родного берега: о поэзии Николая Клюева*, Ld, Nauka, 1990, 244 pp., written in the 1970s, but published now for the first time; and K. Azadovskii, *Николай Клюев: путь поэта*, Ld, SovP, 1990, 336 pp. There is an article by L. K. Shvetsova, Bialik, *Горький*, 204–24, on K. and Gor'kii. See also B. N. Kravchenko, *NN*, no. 1:117–25; K. M. Azadovskii, *ILen*, 1990, no. 8:121–26.

KOMAROVSKII.   There are poems in *Pro*, no. 6:114–18; and poetry and prose in *Iu*, no. 12:66–71.

KOROLENKO.   K.'s diaries from 1917–21 are presented in *VL*, 1990, no. 5:193–218, no. 6:207–25, and no. 8:195–217. There are letters to Kh. G. Rakovskii from 1919–21 in *VIst*, 1990, no. 10:3–39, and fragments of diaries and letters from 1919–20 in **LKuz*, 1990, no. 2:93–108. There are publications of K.'s journalistic writing in *Vo*, no. 1:124–39; *RusL*, 1990, no. 4:45–58; and *LitG*, no. 27:11. Articles are noted by L. L. Pil'd, *UZTarU*, 917 (*Блоковский сборник*, 11):6–22, on K.'s aesthetic position; and S. N. Dmitriev, *LSh*, no. 1:15–28, on K. in Poltava.

KRUCHENYKH.   There is correspondence in Marzaduri, *Avantguardia*, 129–50; and memoirs by O. Setnitskaia, *ib.*, 151–99. There are articles by N. Khardzhiev, *ib.*, 207–13, on literary polemics involving K.; S. Sigov, *ib.*, 215–25; R. Vroon, *SRev*, 50:359–70, on *Разбойник Ванька-Каин* and the literary politics of LEF; A. Sola, *CMRS*, 31, 1990:579–86 (the logic of sounds); and A. Hansen-Löve, *Van der Eng Vol.*, 291–308 (antisymbolism).

KUPRIN.   There are letters to K. from the Grand Duchess Ol'ga Aleksandrovna in *Iu*, no. 11:72–74. R. Rischin, Luker, *Short Story*, 23–52, writes on K.'s 1904 story *Жидовка*. See also Iu. A. Kozlovskii, *UM*, 1990, no. 10:91–92 (K. in Ukraine).

KUZMIN.   K., *Избранные произведения*, Ld, KhL, 1990, 576 pp., ed. and introd. A. Lavrov and R. Timenchik (3–16), contains verse and prose and includes 70 pages of notes. There are letters in *NZh*, 183:358–64. *LitU*, 1990, no. 6:115–20, contains notes by K. on

reading and life and is followed by a comment by N. A. Bogomolov
(120–21). Morev, *Kuzmin* contains articles and archive material
relating to many aspects of K.'s life and work, including V. V. Ivanov
(13–16, postsymbolism and K.), V. N. Toporov (17–24, K. and
Petersburg), I. G. Vishnevetskii (25–27, K. and St Francis), Iu. F.
Freidin (28–31, K. and Mandel′shtam), V. K. Kondrat′ev (32–36,
K. and the new poetry), K. Kharer (37–38, Крылья), S. I. Gindin
(39–42, K. and Maeterlinck), T. V. Tsiv′ian (43–46, 'Фузий в
блюдечке'), V. M. and M. L. Gasparov (47–49, 'Олень изольды'),
and P. V. Dmitriev (61–64, K. and opera). There is also an article by
A. Pasquinelli, *CMRS*, 32:369–78, comparing K., Nabokov, and
Chinnov. See also A. Remizov, *LitU*, 1990, no. 6:121–24; and a 1936
article by N. Kannegiser, *ILen*, 1990, no. 9:65–67.

LIVSHITS. V. Ia. Morderer, 'Бенедикт Лившиц. "Игра в
слова"', Morev, *Кузмин*, 90–95.

MAMIN-SIBIRIAK. There are articles by A. Jaekel, 'D. N. Mamin-
Sibirjak — Schöpfer einer humanistischen Kinderliteratur', Bussevitz, *Jugendliteratur*, 111–17, and N. Aleksandrov, *DL*, 1990, no. 9:73–
75, 79, on the stories *Вертел* and *Приисковый мальчик*.

MEREZHKOVSKII. Several further publications are noted, in particular vols 3 and 4 of *Христос и Антихрист*, Kniga, 1990, 431 and
638 pp., with copious notes by Z. G. Mints. M., *Избранное*, Kishinev,
1989, 544 pp., contains *Петр и Алексей* as well as verse and other
prose pieces. M., *Воскресшие боги. Леонардо да-Винчи*, KhL, 1990,
640 pp., has an afterword by D. Panchenko (629–39). *Тайна Запада.
Атлантида-Европа* is contained in *Ko*, no. 1:35–87, no. 2:51–71,
no. 3:49–85, no. 4:43–78, no. 5:35–71, no. 6:72–115, and no. 7:6–
36. The essay 'Россия будет (интеллигенция и народ)' is in *DN*,
no. 4:204–13. T. Pachmuss edits M. and Z. Gippius, *Dante. Борис
Годунов — киносценарии*, NY, Gnozis Press, 1990, 195 pp. M.'s
notebooks, 1919–20 are in *Вильнюс*, 1990, no. 6:130–43.

The most important work to appear on M. is Temira Pachmuss, *D.
S. Merezhkovsky in Exile: The Master of the Genre of Biographie Romancée*,
NY, Lang, 1990, xvi + 338 pp. There are articles by L. A. Kolobaeva,
ISLIa, 50:445–53, on M. as novelist; L. G. Frizman, *ib.*, 454–58, on
M.'s conception of Pushkin; B. G. Rosenthal, *SEEA*, 6.2, 1990:33–50,
on parallels between M. and Viacheslav Ivanov; and G. M.
Ponomareva, *RRe*, no. 4:18–19, on intertextuality in *Петр и Алексей*.
See also the reprint of I. A. Il′in's 1934 lecture in *Zv*, no. 6:198–205;
and M. V. Koz′menko, *ISLIa*, 50:380–83.

NARBUT. There are poems in *Ko*, no. 7:188–91.

PARNOK. D. L. Burgin, *SEEJ*, 35:214–27, discusses P.'s poetic
dialogue with Tsvetaeva.

REMIZOV. R., *Избранное*, Ld, Lenizdat, 608 pp., contains works of the period 1908–18 and includes an essay by A. A. Danilevskii on R.'s prerevolutionary writing (596–607). The stories *Царь Додон* and *Чудесный урожай* are in *LitO*, no. 11 : 75–79. There are selections from *Иверень* in *Se*, no. 3 : 64–86, and no. 4 : 54–72, introduced by V. Bondarenko (no. 3, 64–66). Correspondence with S. P. Remizova-Dovgello is in *EO*, 6, 1987 : 237–310. There are two articles on the erotic in R.'s work: G. N. Slobin, Luker, *Short Story*, 53–72, and S. N. Dotsenko, *LitO*, no. 11 : 72–75. C. Dowsett, *MLR*, 86 : 372–86, considers the originality of *Часы* and its context within Symbolist fictional poetics. K. Szőke, *SSH*, 35, 1989 : 385–92, analyses *Пятая язва*. See also V. Sosinskii, *VL*, no. 6 : 167–207.

ROZANOV. There are two book publications of R.'s critical writings: R., *Мысли о литературе*, Sovremennik, 1989, 607 pp., is introduced by A. Nikoliukin (5–40) and has 50 pages of notes; R., *Несовместимые контрасты жития: литературно-эстетические работы разных лет*, Iskusstvo, 1990, 605 pp., has an introduction by V. V. Erofeev (6–36). There are essays in *LitO*, no. 9 : 68–74; in *Ko*, no. 5 : 161–75; in *RusL*, no. 1 : 105–23, ed., introd. and ann. M. M. Pavlova; and in *Ko*, no. 4 : 136–57, with an afterword by A. M. Kuznetsov (157–58). There are three letters to Gippius in *LitO*, no. 11 : 67–71, ed. M. Pavlova; and correspondence with M. O. Gershenzon, *NovM*, no. 3 : 215–42, ed. V. Proskurin. V. Iu. Grishin and L. A. Riazanova edit extracts from Prishvin's diaries relating to R., *Контекст*, 1990 : 161–218. V. Sukach, *Mos*, no. 10 : 135–76, is a biographical compilation written during the second half of the 19th c. There is a general work by A. N. Nikoliukin, *Василий Васильевич Розанов: писатель нетрадиционного мышления*, Znanie, 1990, 64 pp. (*Литература*, 1990, no. 8). V. Erofeev writes on R. in pp. 102–20 of *Laterna magica. Альманах*, Prometei, 1990, 360 pp., and in Erofeev, *В лабиринте*, 102–37. Iu. Ivask's introduction to the 1956 New York edition of R., *Избранное*, is reprinted in *Vo*, no. 5 : 119–42.

SEVERIANIN. S., *Сочинения*, Tallinn, Eesti Raamat, 1990, 544 pp., contains original verse, translations and prose, and is introduced by S. Isakov (5–34). S., *Стихотворения и поэмы 1918–1941*, Sovremennik, 1990, 493 pp., has an afterword by Iu. Shumakov on S. and Estonia (430–39). There is an article by V. Linetskii, *S*, 30 : 85–91, on S. and Solzhenitsyn.

SOLOGUB. There are two editions of *Творимая легенда: Творимая легенда. Роман*, Sovremennik, 574 pp., ed. and introd. A. I. Mikhailov (5–14), and *Творимая легенда*, KhL, 2 vols, 494 and 302 pp., with a biographical appendix and essay by L. Sobolev (vol. 2, 260–79). S., *Голодный Блеск. Избранная проза*, Kiev, Dnipro, 511 pp., has an introduction by V. Keldysh (5–24). A newly discovered translation from Rimbaud is published in *InL*, 1990, no. 9:175–83. There are articles by Iu. N. Kukushkina, *UZTarU*, 917 (Блоковский сборник, 11):23–38, on intertextuality in the verse collections *Родине* and *Пламенный круг*; V. Erofeev, Erofeev, *В лабиринте*, 79–100, on *Мелкий бес* and Realism; K. Hansen-Löve, *RL*, 30:109–33, on the 1907 short story *В толпе*; and M. A. Nikitina, Bialik, *Горький*, 185–204, on S. and Gor′kii.

SOLOV′EV. S., *Избранное*, SR, 1990, 496 pp., contains prose works and is introduced by A. V. Gulyga (5–40). S., '*Неподвижно лишь солнце любви . . .*' *Стихотворения. Проза. Письма. Воспоминания современников*, MosR, 1990, 445 pp., ed. and introd. A. Nosov (3–16). There are letters to Dostoevskii in *NN*, no. 6:68–69, followed by Rozanov's essay on the breach between Dostoevskii and S., *ib.*, 70–72. On S.'s biography the most important publication is S. M. Luk′ianov. *О Вл. С. Соловьеве в его молодые годы: материалы*, 3 vols, Kniga, 1990, 447, 566, and 382 pp. This is reprinted from the original (1916–21) edition and contains in vol. 3 an essay by A. Nosov on Luk′ianov as biographer of S. (297–316), and an article by R. Gal′tseva and I. Rodnianskaia on S.'s life and fate (317–40). On S.'s life see also N. V. Davydov's memoirs in *Pro*, no. 11:171–76; and I. N. Golenishchev-Kutuzov, 'Владимир Соловьев и его югославские друзья', *VRKhD*, 160, 1990:141–54. Critical articles are noted by J. D. Kornblatt, *SRev*, 50:487–96, on S. and the Kabbalah; C. Emerson. *ib.*, 663–71, on S., Tolstoi and Bakhtin; B. A. Nikitin, *RV*, 53:84–112, and G. Przebinda, *SlO*, 38, 1989:611–22, both on S. and Nikolai Fedorov; A. F. Losev, Losev, *Страсть*, 102–225, covering S.'s life and symbolic system; N. F. Utkina, pp. 74–90 of *Русская философская мысль в 80–х гг. XIX в. О будущем России*, ed. N. F. Utkina, AN SSSR, Institut Filosofii, 1990, 117 pp.; P. Ch. Born, *VF*, 1990, no. 9:27–36 ('Три разговора'); A. Gulyga, *DV*, 1990, no. 5:119–23; and G. Mastroianni, *Belfagor*, 44, 1989:94–97 (S. and the Antichrist). See also the interview with A. F. Losev, *Poez*, 55, 1990:196–204; *LitG*, no. 37:13; Kauchtchischwili under BELYI, and Griakalova under BLOK.

USPENSKII. G. Goes, 'Die Ideen und das Wirken der Narodniki als Künstlerlische Botschaft', *WZUJ*, 38, 1989:23–26, compares U. with Garshin and Tolstoi.

VOLOSHIN. V., *Киммерия. Стихотворения*, Kiev, Molod′, 1990, 128 pp., ed. and introd. (9–22) I. T. Kupriianov, also contains numerous reproductions of V.'s watercolours. *Воспоминания о Максимилиане Волошине*, ed. V. P. Kupchenko and Z. D. Davydov, SovP, 1990, 720 pp., includes 85 pages of notes and an introduction by L. Ozerov (5–26). The preface to *Протопопу Аввакуму* is published for the first time in *Se*, 1990, no. 2:154–56. There is correspondence with O. K. and S. A. Tolstaia in *Zv*, no. 6: 175–79; and a biographical note by V. Kupchenko in *ib.*, no. 10:152–57. *SovM*, 1990, no. 3: 115–17, has documents from 1916. There are articles by V. Adamantova, *RSl*, 63:607–19, on V.'s translation of Verhaeren's 'Au nord'; and V. Kupchenko, *Ko*, 1990, no. 12:173–83, on V. and G. A. Shengeli. See also Iu. Arishkin and L. Katsis, *LitO*, no. 9:66–67, and Magomedova under BLOK.

ZDANEVICH. There are letters from O. I. Leshkova, Marzaduri, *Avanguardia*, 33–108, and other archive materials, *ib.*, 109–19. M. Marzaduri writes on *41°*, *ib.*, 121–27, and on the play *Янко круль албанский*, *ib.*, 21–23. R. Gayraud, Conio, *Avant-garde*, 113–18, writes on Z. and synaesthesia.

LITERATURE FROM 1917 TO THE PRESENT DAY

By DAVID GILLESPIE, *Senior Lecturer in Russian,*
School of Modern Languages and International Studies, University of Bath

ABBREVIATIONS. In the text of this section the following abbreviations of collective and general works supplement those listed in the Abbreviations section at the end of this volume: Adibaev, *Стиховедение: Проблемы стиховедения и поэтики*, resp. ed. Kh. A. Adibaev *et al.*, Alma-Ata, Kazakhskii PI, 1990, 183 pp.; Gerasimova, *История: Проблемы развития советской литературы. История и современностъ*, resp. ed. L. E. Gerasimova *et al.*, Saratov U.P., 1990, 155 pp.; Golubkov, *Поэтика: Поэтика советской литературы двадцатых годов*, resp. ed. S. A. Golubkov *et al.*, Kuibyshev GPI, 1989, 144 pp.; Grinfel'd, *Проблемы: Проблемы изображения материального мира в художественной прозе*, resp. ed. T. Ia. Grinfel'd, Syktyvkar U.P., 1989, 155 pp.; Gura, *Жанр: Жанр и творческая индивидуальностъ*, ed. V. V. Gura, Vologda GPI, 1990, 162 pp.; Miliavskii, *Критика: Критика в художественном тексте*, resp. ed. B. L. Miliavskii *et al.*, Dushanbe GPI, 1990, 130 pp.; Ognev, *О жанре: О жанре и стиле советской литературы*, resp. ed. A. V. Ognev *et al.*, Kalinin U.P., 1990, 147 pp.; Oskotskii, *Взгляд: Взгляд. Сборник. Критика. Полемика. Публикации. Выпуск 3*, comp. V. D. Oskotskii and E. A. Shklovskii, SovP, 496 pp.; Smirnov, *Изучение: Изучение поэтики реализма*, resp. ed. A. S. Smirnov *et al.*, Murmansk/Vologda, Murmansk GPI, 1990, 132 pp.; Subbotin, *Опыт: Художественный опыт советской литературы. Стилевые и жанровые процессы*, resp. ed. A. S. Subbotin *et al.*, Sverdlovsk, Urals U.P., 1990, 126 pp.; Volkova, *Советская: Советская литература в прошлом и настоящем*, ed. I. F. Volkova, Mw U.P., 1990, 159 pp.; Zakharov, *Композиция: Жанр и композиция литературного произведения*, resp. ed. V. N. Zakharov, Petrozavodsk U.P., 1989, 177 pp.

1. GENERAL

Iu. M. Gal'perin, *Дорисовывая портреты. Из 'литературных вечеров'*, SovP, 315 pp., discusses Berggol'ts, Chukovskii, Abramov, Shergin, Shklovskii, Simonov and Shukshin, while V. E. Kovskii, *Реалисты и романтики. Из творческого опыта русской советской классики*, KhL, 1990, 381 pp. concentrates on Briusov, Maiakovskii, Tolstoi, Grin, and Paustovskii. Iu. M. Oklianskii, *Счастливые неудачники. Биографические повести и рассказы о писателях*, SovP,

1990, 474 pp., looks at Abramov, Trifonov, Slutskii, Erenburg, and Panova. Another book of memoirs and portraits is Iraklii Andronnikov, *Все живо . . . Рассказы. Портреты. Воспоминания*, SovP, 1990, 496, where Gor'kii, Marshak, Chukovskii, Kazakevich, Eikhenbaum, Shklovskii, Tynianov, Zabolotskii, Kataev, and Mikhoels are among those recalled. See also Ts. S. Vol'pe, *Искусство непохожести. Б. Лифшиц, А. Грин, А. Белый, Б. Житков, М. Зощенко*, SovP, 316 pp. *Из творческого наследия советских писателей*, resp. eds N. A. Groznova and V. V. Timofeeva, Ld, Nauka, 331 pp., contains materials by Klychkov, Lunts, Pasternak, Prokof'ev, Gumilev, Briusov. Also of interest are M. B. Isakovskii, *Письма о литературе*, comp. A. I. Isakovskaia, SovP, 1990, 239 pp., and V. Sosinskii's writings on Remizov, Alekhin and others, *VL*, no. 6: 167–207. V. Kurbatov, pp. 44–59 of Oskotskii, *Взгляд*, looks at literary Petersburg in the 20th c. A seminal study is Andrew Baruch Wachtel, *The Battle for Childhood: Creation of a Russian Myth*, Stanford U.P., 1990, 262 pp., which reads Gor'kii's trilogy as a subversion of Lev Tolstoi's vision of childhood, and also has a chapter on Bunin. Iu. Karabchievskii, *Улица Мандельштама. Эссе*, Orange, Connecticut, Antiquary, 1989, 198 pp., is a collection of essays from the 1970s and 1980s on Mandel'shtam, Bitov, Okudzhava, Galich, and modern literature in general.

LITERARY HISTORY. A. Skaldin's *Странствия и приключения Никодима Старшего* (1917) is in *Iu*, no. 9. 4–23, no. 10: 34–44, no. 11: 33–63. Korolenko's diaries, 1917–21, are continued in *VL*, 1990, no. 8: 195–217, no. 10: 174–206; on this period see also R. Russell, 'The arts and the Russian Civil War', *JES*, 20, 1990: 219–40. *Русский литературный авангард. Материалы и исследования*, ed. M. Marzaduri *et al.*, Trento U.P., 1990, 342 pp., has articles and materials on Zdanevich, Kruchenykh and I. Terent'ev, and Bal'mont letters, 1909–34, are discussed by L. P. Lapteva, *RusL*, 1990, no. 3: 169–79. V. N. Nosov, pp. 88–96 of *Литературный процесс и творческая индивидуальность*, resp. ed. G. E. Ionkis, Kishinev, Shtiintsa, 1990, 172 pp., assesses 'sociological' literary criticism of the 1920s. Among the 'Constructivist' novels of the 1920s discussed by A. Flaker, *RL*, 29: 47–56, are *Мы, Голый год, Зависть, Вор*, and others. J.-Ph. Jaccard, *WSlA*, 27: 229–47, publishes a story by and essay on L. Lipavskii (pen-name Savel'ev). On OBERIU, see A. Nikitaev, *Te*, no. 11: 4–7, and L. Zhukova, *ib.*, 8–9 (a memoir from 1983). A. V. Bliumbaum and G. A. Morev, *WSlA*, 28: 263–69, relate the history of the non-appearance in 1929 of the almanac *Ванна Архимеда*, with contributions by OBERIU members as well as Formalist critics. There are letters from the 1920s by Shmelev, Voloshin and Serafimovich to Lunacharskii, *SA*, no. 5: 87–91. Also on the 1920s, see V. Voronov,

LSh, no. 2:25–33, and E. S. Romanicheva, *ib.*, 103–09. Iu. Shul'man, *Se*, no. 12:142–48, discusses Shergin, and there are poems by Savinkov, *Iu*, no. 5:70–71. L. Levin, *VL*, 1990, no. 10:36–76, assesses RAPP and its leading personalities. R. Giaquinta, pp. 377–413 of *Russica. Studi e Richerche sulla Russia contemporanea*, ed. A. Masoero and A. Venturi, Milan, Franco Angeli, 1990, xiv + 510 pp., discusses Leningrad writers of the 1920s and 1930s. These years as recalled by Nadezhda Mandel'shtam and Lidiia Ginzburg are the subject of an article by J. M. Négrignat, *CMRS*, 32:323–35. Noted is *Добычинские чтения*, no ed., Daugavpils PI, 113 pp., and see O. I. Aleksandrova, pp. 47–57 of Golubkov, *Поэтика*, on Malyshkin. Kuzmin letters from the 1930s are in *NZh*, 183:358–62, and V. Shentalinskii, *IC*, 20, no. 8:3–49, discusses writers repressed in the 1930s, with texts by Babel', Platonov, Bulgakov, Kliuev, and Mandel'shtam. Ewa M. Thompson, 'Russian writers and the Soviet invasion of Poland in 1939', pp. 158–66 of *The Search for Self-Definition in Russian Literature*, ed. E. M. Thompson, Houston, Rice U.P., 220 pp., offers insights into hitherto little-known areas. Of interest to some will be *Традиции и новаторство А. П. Гайдара*, resp. ed. N. I. Rybakov *et al.*, Gor'kii GPI, 1989, 93 pp. E. Dobrenko, *DN*, no. 2:249–71, analyses the national self-consciousness of late Stalinist culture, and Ol'ga Berggol'ts's 1949 (May–October) diaries are published in *Zn*, no. 3:160–72. I. Butenko, *Библиотекарь*, no. 5:11–13, juxtaposes mass reading during the thaw and *perestroika*. Chivilikhin diaries and letters are in *MG*, no. 10:92–128, 161–86, no. 11:163–94, and V. Frolov, *VL*, 1990, no. 9:211–44, publishes a memoir of Panferov and *Октябрь* during the 1950s. I. Sokolov-Mikitov's notes, 1955–62, are in *NovM*, no. 12:164–78. A. I. Kondratovich, *Новомирский дневник, 1967–1970*, SovP, 524 pp., offers excellent insights into literary life of the period, and is discussed by I. Dedkov, *DN*, 1990, no. 9:197–205. Jelena Milojković-Djurić, pp. 19–30 of her *Aspects of Soviet Culture: Voices of Glasnost', 1960–1990*, Boulder, East European Monographs, vi + 190 pp., looks at Tvardovskii and *Новый мир*, and further, pp. 31–49, surveys Soviet literature in the 1960s and 1970s, and pp. 62–89, in the 1980s. Also on Tvardovskii and *Новый мир*, see the detailed essay-memoir of V. Ognev, *K*, 69:263–313. A. Arkhangel'skii, *NovM*, no. 2:225–41, assesses *Огонек* and *Наш современник* as 'mirrors of social awareness', 1986–90. On the vagaries of literary history, see V. Oskotskii, *VL*, no. 4:158–87, and D. Gillespie, *Русистика*, 4:2–5. A. Suetnov, *Solanus*, 5:143–52, relates the history of *samizdat*, 1952–90.

THEMES. M. Ziolkowski, *SRev*, 50:59–69, looks at some literary Stalins (by Rybakov, Solzhenitsyn, Shatrov and Maksimov), as does E. Dobrenko, *VL*, 1990, no. 9:3–34 (image of 'the great leader' in

Soviet literature). Village prose is being reassessed in the light of contemporary developments. There is a book, T. A. Nikonova, *Прощания. Размышления над страницами 'деревенской' прозы,* Voronezh, Tsentro-Chernozemnoe kn. iz-vo, 1990, 142 pp., and articles by K. Parthé, *SCC* 23, 1990:161–76 (images of rural transformation); M. Levina, *VL*, nos 9–10:3–29 (village prose as seen today); E. Shcheglova, *Ne*, no. 10:171–84 (national and moral aspects); G. A. Tsvetov, pp. 125–34 of Grinfel′d, *Проблемы* (village prose in the 1950s and 1960s); A. Ognev, *MG*, no. 6:250–64 (the village in life and literature); D. Gillespie, *FMLS*, 27:70–84 (village prose and *glasnost'*). N. Pereiaslov, *Ok*, no. 9:154–59, assesses spiritual searchings in modern prose. O. Dark, *DN*, no. 4:257–69, looks at 'women's prose', as does E. Gessen, *VM*, 114:203–17; a related topic is that of B. Iukht, *LitO*, nos 9–10:24–28 (eroticism in literature). On science fiction, see T. Stepnovska, *BR*, no. 2:38–45; I. Oswald, *Ost*, 41:393–405; E. M. Neelov, pp. 167–76 of Zakharov, *Композиция*; M. V. Shekhtman, pp. 100–09 of Miliavskii, *Критика*.

THE CONTEMPORARY SCENE. Vladislav Krasnov, *Russia beyond Communism: A Chronicle of National Rebirth*, Boulder, Westview, xxii + 356 pp., contains the debates and ideas of writers and critics on Russia's future, with examples taken from Rasputin, Solzhenitsyn, Soloukhin, Zalygin, Latynina and others. A companion piece is A. N. Latynina, *За открытым шлагбаумом. Литературная ситуация конца 80-х гг*, SovP, 335 pp. *Советская литература второй половины восьмидесятых годов и ее осмысление в критике*, resp. ed. M. S. Shtern *et al.*, Omsk, no publisher, 1990, 62 pp., contains 30 very short papers on recent Soviet and 'returned' literature. E. Bich, *Zv*, no. 2:181–86, discusses Viktor Erofeev's 'wake' for Soviet literature (published in *Апрель*, no. 1:274–82; *Glas: New Russian Writing*, no. 1:224–34). Prose published in journals in 1990 is surveyed by E. Shklovskii, *LitO*, no. 2:10–18. C. Engel, *Ost*, 41:140–49, 831–46, looks at Russian literature over the last three years, and see also M. Epshtein and I. Dedkov, *Zn*, no. 1:217–40; S. Chuprinin, *ib.*, no. 3:218–33; and L. Heller, *SST*, 40, 1990:189–204. N. Ivanova, *Zn*, no. 8:211–23, writes on modern prose, and, *Ok*, no. 10:179–92, on the novel. R. Kireev, *Zn*, no. 8:224–26, gives examples of 'untraditional' prose. G. Gorbovskii, *Zv*, no. 4:99–150, no. 5:97–124, no. 6:114–44, publishes a writer's notes; there are materials and texts by O. V. Volkov, *LSh*, no. 5:45–58, an interview with V., *K*, 69:366–73, and criticism by N. L. Krupina, *ib.*, 109–19 (there is a V. letter to Sholokhov from 1957 in *Zv*, no. 5:158–60). S. Chuprinin, *Zn*, no. 10:220–34, discusses Russian literature after *perestroika*, and see also Id., pp. 10–43 of Oskotskii, *Взгляд* (the struggle of ideas in modern literature). Also of interest is M. Zolotonosov, *Ok*, no. 4:

166–79 ('post-socialist realism'), and M. T. Choldin, *Solanus*, 5:130–42 (censorship under Gorbachev). R. Pittman, *Русистика*, 4:22–25, brings us up to date with an account of writers and their role in the 1991 coup.

On Astaf'ev, see M. Shneerson, *K*, 62, 1990:273–86. J. Woodhouse, *SEER*, 69:601–20, analyses Bek's *Новое назначение*, while the work of Borodin is discussed by S. Kuniaev, *LSh*, no. 2:56–62 (*Третья правда*) and V. P. Pavliukevich, *ib.*, 113–21 (short stories). On Dudintsev, see N. Kuznetsova, *LSh*, no. 1:77–83 (from 1988: see *YWMLS*, 50:1103); G. Gachev, *ib.*, 83–92; and A. P. Kuznetsova, *ib.*, 114–18. E. Steffensen, *Svantetit*, 14, 1990:101–14, discusses Granin's *Зубр*; Ia. Dukhan, *BR*, no. 2:46–59, looks at the war prose of Viacheslav Kondrat'ev; A. Mikhailov, *Mos*, no. 7:177–84, analyses Lichutin's *Душа неизъяснимая*. J. Hansen, *Svantetit*, 14, 1990:35–48, looks at the work of Tolstaia, Makanin, and Kim; also on M., see C. Dowsett, *ASEES*, 4, 1990:21–36 (*Утрата*); E. Gessen, *VM*, 111, 1990:155–67, and *G*, 161:144–59. L. Anninskii, pp. 60–74 of Oskotskii, *Взгляд*, discusses P'etsukh. On Evgenii Popov, see S. Borovikov, *DN*, no. 12:231–40. A. Mashevskii, *Zv*, no. 3:176–79, responds to Narbikova's *Около эколо . . .* , and see also N. Kolesnikoff, *CanSP*, 32, 1990:444–56 (the narrative structure of Petrushevskaia's short stories). M. Shneerson, *K*, 62, 1990:286–97, discusses Soloukhin.

THE EMIGRATION. There is a major collection: *Under Eastern Eyes: The West as Reflected in Recent Russian Émigré Writing*, ed. A. McMillin, Basingstoke, Macmillan, xii + 163 pp., with contributions on individual authors as well as broader themes. Of more general interest are G. Belaia, pp. 1–11 (the East–West theme in Soviet and émigré criticism), and J. Graffy, pp. 115–57 (Soviet journals and the émigré experience of the West). Of lesser scholarly interest is *Literature in Exile*, ed. John Glad, Durham and London, Duke U.P., 1990, xvi + 175 pp., with contributions by various émigré writers, but no criticism or analysis. A. Blium, *NZh*, 183:264–82, looks at the émigré press through the eyes of the GPU and Glavlit in the 1920s. *RusL*, no. 2:68–103, publishes essays by N. I. Ul'ianov. O. Mikhailov, *LSh*, no. 5:28–44, writes on the 'unnoticed generation' of the first emigration. A. G. Sokolov, *VMUF*, no. 5:11–17, relates the problems of studying émigré literature.

Chirikov materials are in *NSo*, no. 9:66–94, and Dovlatov materials in *LitO*, no. 4:71–73. On D., see A. Zverev, *ib.*, 65–70; on Gladilin, see N. Buhks, pp. 84–90 of *Under Eastern Eyes*; on Gorenshtein, see A. Zverev, *LitO*, no. 12:16–22; and on Limonov, see R. Porter, pp. 62–75 of *Under Eastern Eyes*, and V. Linetskii, *S*, 28, 1990:118–25 (L.'s latest novel . . . *У нас была Великая Эпоха*). *Mos*, no. 5:69–83, contains stories by P. Murav'ev. There are Shakhovskaia materials in *Слово*, no. 4:23–26, *NovM*, no. 7:231–39 and *ib.*, no. 9:183–86. Memoirs by Stepun are in *Vo*, no. 8:131–44, no. 9:125–56, no. 10:132–53, no. 12:148–69 (extracts in *IK*, no. 10:19–31, no. 11:6–17). Teffi's memoirs are in *Слово*, no. 12:56–61, and *VM*, 111, 1990:225–41, Weidlé materials are in *VL*, 1990, no. 7:97–128; *RRe*, no. 3:29–42; and *NZh*, 183:364–70.

2. THEORY

A new book of interest to theorists: V. V. Eidinova, *Стиль художника. Концепция стиля в литературной критике 20-х гг.*, KhL, 284 pp. N. I. Glushkov, pp. 4–16 of Ognev, *О жанре*, looks at Socialist Realism. There are chapters on Russian literary theory in Steven Cassedy, *Flight from Eden: The Origins of Modern Literary Criticism and Theory*, Berkeley, California U.P., 1990, x + 254 pp. (the Russian tradition from Potebnia to Shklovskii, 39–63; Iakobson, 121–32; Futurists, 162–80). Lubomir Doležel, pp. 134–46 of his *Occidental Poetics: Tradition and Progress*, Lincoln, Nebraska U.P., 1990, x + 262 pp., discusses Russian Formalism and especially the work of Propp. Also on Formalism, see V. Cherednichenko, *LGr*, no. 6:150–60. R. J. Murphy, *GSl*, 6, 1990:339–49, seeks continuities in the methodologies of Shklovskii and Wolfgang Iser. On Lidiia Ginzburg, see A. Mashevskii, *Ne*, no. 8:84 88, and Iu. Kublanovskii, *VRKhD*, 158, 1990:266–74.

BAKHTIN. There are two books on B.: *Mikhail Bakhtin and the Epistemology of Discourse*, ed. C. Thomson, Amsterdam, Rodopi, 1990, 207 pp., contains 13 papers on B.; David K. Danow, *The Thought of Mikhail Bakhtin: From Word to Culture*, Basingstoke, Macmillan, viii + 160 pp., is the latest of a number of monographs. See also the major study by Allan Reid, *Literature as Communication and Cognition in Bakhtin and Lotman*, NY, Garland, 1990, x + 210 pp. Also on B., C. Emerson, *WSlA*, 27:33–44, links B., Freud, and Dostoevskii, and also, *SRev*, 50:663–71, Solov'ev, the late Tolstoi and B. on the problem of shame and love. V. E. Khalizev, *FilN*, no. 5:3–13, analyses B.'s legacy and the classical vision of the world. C. Lock, *Literature and Theology*, 5:68–82, discusses B. and Orthodox theology with reference to carnival. D. Bak, *VL*, nos 9–10:259–70, looks at B. today, and E. Gvozdeva, *ib.*, 270–79, considers B.'s work on Rabelais. N. Vasil'ev, *LitO*, no. 9:38–43, discusses B. and Voloshinov; there are biographical materials on B.'s arrest and exile, 1928–30, in *VL*, no. 3:128–41.

THE CONTEMPORARY SCENE. On the current state of literary criticism and theory, see A. Nemzer, *LitO*, no. 2:26–37, and S.

Carsten, *SSR*, 17:61–85 (current literary polemics). N. Kuznetsova, *K*, 66:305–21, analyses the work and thought of the critic Lev Anninskii.

3. DRAMA

I. Vishnevskaia, *SD*, no. 1:150–59, no. 2:176–85, no. 3:114–21, attempts an ambitious reassessment of the history of Soviet theatre. S. D. Balukhatyi, *Вопросы поэтики. Сборник статей*, Ld U.P., 1990, 320 pp., contains chapters on drama theory (17–79). K. Stanislavskii, *Мое гражданское служение России*, Pravda, 1990, 654 pp., is an important edition. I. Malinovskaia, *Te*, no. 7:58–68, discusses S.'s opera productions, and G. Brodskaia, *ib.*, no. 10:89–107, looks at relations between S. and Gor'kii. See also the collection *The Moscow Art Theatre Letters*, ed. and trans. J. Benedetti, London, Methuen, xvi + 378 pp. (on post-1917 theatre, pp. 315–60). Iu. Aikhenval'd, *NZh*, 183:244–63, exposes the Maly Theatre's use of convict labour, 1920–22. An important and overdue study is Michaela Böhmig, *Das russische Theater in Berlin, 1919–1931*, Munich, Sagner, 1990, 324 pp.

On the theatre of OBERIU, see M. Meilakh, *Te*, no. 11:173–79, and Iu. Girba, *ib.*, 180–91 (the latter on OBERIU plays performed in the 1980s–1990s). Iu. Dmitriev, *ib.*, no. 10:107–13, relates the history of theatrical criticism in the late 1920s–early 1930s. There are fragments from Iu. Elagin, *Темные аллеи*, on Meierkhol'd, in *SD*, no. 5:235–44 (assessed by A. Tomashevskii, *ib.*, 229–30, and M. Chekhov, *ib.*, 231–34). M. Chekhov's letters to M. V. Dobuzhinskii, 1938–51, are in *ib.*, no. 6:91–120. There are eight letters from Mikhoels to S. Radlov, 1929–35, in *K*, 68:264–86. T. Gnedich's play, *Мистерия*, from 1943, is published in *Av*, no. 2:114–30. N. Agisheva, *Te*, no. 5:49–65, relates the history of the Sovremennik theatre.

THE CONTEMPORARY SCENE. Of considerable interest is I. V. Zborovets, *Русская советская историко-революционная драматургия 70–80-х годов*, Kharkov, Osnova, 1990, 133 pp. On Shatrov, see N. I. Gorelova, pp. 104–17 of Gerasimova, *История*. V. Liubimov, *NovM*, no. 4:233–38, surveys the theatre, 1985–90, as does K. Bjørnager, *Svantetit*, 14, 1990:63–78. B. Zingerman, *Te*, no. 1:37–61, discusses Liubimov at considerable length; on the fate of L.'s production of *Владимир Высоцкий*, there are extracts from the play, *SD*, no. 2:155–74, as well as the text (tape-recorded) of the revealing meeting in August 1980 of the Taganka theatre's artistic council. V. Dmitrievskaia, *ib.*, no. 3:134–42, analyses the repertoire of *perestroika*; A. Svobodin, *LitO*, no. 10:89–93, discusses the state of the theatre today, and N. Starosel'skaia, *ib.*, no. 2:45–52, looks at the 1990 theatrical season.

4. Poetry

Bristol, *Poetry*, contains a substantial section (205–309) on post-1917 poetry. There are three other general books: M. N. Epshtein, *Природа, мир, тайник вселенной* ... *Система пейзажных образов в русской поэзии*, VSh, 1990, 303 pp., with a section on the Soviet period (245–79) that extends from Maiakovskii and Esenin to Kushner and Chukhontsev; O. G. Chaikovskaia, *Соперники времени. Опыт поэтического восприятия прошлого*, SovP, 1990, 366 pp.; S. L. Strashnov, *Молодеет и лад баллад. Баллада в истории русской советской поэзии*, Sovremennik, 155 pp. Svetlana Boym, *Death in Quotation Marks. Cultural Myths of the Modern Poet*, Cambridge, Mass., Harvard U.P., vii + 291 pp., looks at Tsvetaeva and Maiakovskii as Russian suicide poets but also discusses poets from other countries.

On the past, articles include E. A. D'iakova, *ISLIa*, 50:414–25 (the Scythians, 1917–19); R. Vroon, *SRev*, 50:359–70 (Kruchenykh's *Разбойник Ванька-Каин* and the literary politics of LEF); A. Pasquinelli, *CMRS*, 32:369–79 (Kuzmin, Nabokov, Chinnov as Alexandrian poets); A. Alekseev-Gai, *VL*, 1990, no. 10:268–81 (memoir of Mandel'shtam, Maiakovskii, Burliuk). V. A. Zaitsev, *VMUF*, no. 5:3–11, laments the 'tragic humanism' of Soviet poetry, 1945–46. See also V. Kulakov, *VL*, no. 3:3–45 (the Lianozovo group of poets in Moscow in the 1950s–1960s). S. V. Poliakova, *WSlA*, 28:259–62, writes on the poetry of Nikolai Oleinikov, and in *Zv*, no. 5:3–5, there are poems by V. Shchirovskii. Daniil Andreev's *Изнанка мира* is in *ILen*, no. 3:66–85; on the poetry of A., see G. Pomerants, *Ok*, no. 8:157–62. There are Aseev materials in *VL*, no. 4:133–57, and Burliuk poems in *Смена*, no. 3:138–43. On Gorodetskii, see L. Pavlova, pp. 132–34 of Adibaev, *Стиховедение* (*Ярь*). On Kirsanov, see V. I. Dolgalakova, *ib.*, 135–36. There are poems by B. Koplan in *Pro*, no. 5:153–57, and by E. Kuz'mina-Karavaeva, *Mos*, no. 1:117–18. On Lugovskoi, see O. M. Varzatskaia, pp. 73–83 of Subbotin, *Опыт*; on Shershenevich, see L. Kuklin, *VL*, nos 9–10:51–83. There are poems by M. Tarlovskii, *Ok*, no. 2:122–26, and by M. Zenkevich, *NovM*, no. 3:134–36.

THE CONTEMPORARY SCENE. G. Aigi and S. Biriukov, *VL*, no. 6:3–15, hold a dialogue on the avant-garde. V. A. Red'kin, pp. 73–84 of Ognev, *О жанре*, looks at the modern historical long poem. See also A. L. Krupchanov, pp. 131–44, and G. N. Malysheva, pp. 120–30, respectively, of Volkova, *Советская*. There are also three new books: I. M. Sheveleva, **Песнь о родном (Поэты наших дней)*, Prometei, 1990, 67 pp.; V. V. Avdonin, **Советская поэзия 1960–1970-х годов и научно-техническая революция*, Tashkent, Fan, 1990, 89 pp.; V. I. Slavetskii, *Возвращение Марии (Современная поэзия. Пути,* *тенденции, проблемы)*, Sovremennik, 174 pp. A. Ageev, *Zn*, no. 2:221–31, rails against modern 'patriotic' poetry (especially Kuniaev); he is countered by V. Khatiushin, *MG*, no. 1:258–75, who attacks Evtushenko, Akhmadulina and Voznesenskii, while praising V. Smirnov and Iu. Kuznetsov. V. A. Zaitsev, *FilN*, no. 1:3–12, surveys new tendencies in modern poetry. See also I. Shaitanov, pp. 127–40 of Oskotskii, *Взгляд*; A. Pikach, *LitO*, no. 2:19–25; G. Margovskii, *ib.*, no. 9:19–24; M. Tetzlaff, *Svantetit*, 14, 1990:23–34; D. Bobyshev, *Zv*, no. 6:190–97; V. Kulakov, *Zn*, no. 12:222–29 (the 'new wave'). M. Aizenberg, *Te*, no. 4:98–118, relates the recent history (1960s–1970s) of 'alternative' poetry.

INDIVIDUAL POETS. Anna Barkova is another 'returned name', and there are materials and poems in *LitO*, no. 8:7–12, and *Vo*, no. 3:78–80 (with essay by A. Ageev, 66–78). On the poetry of A. Eremenko, see V. Kuritsyn, *DN*, no. 9:264–68, and Evtushenko's *19 августа* is discussed by A. D. P. Briggs, *Русистика*, 4:26–29. Also on E., see V. P. Prishchepa, *Поэма в творчестве Е. А. Евтушенко и А. А. Вознесенского (1960–1965)*, Krasnoiarsk U.P., 1990, 154 pp. (On V., see Prishchepa above; also P. E. Suvorova, pp. 137–38 of Adibaev, *Стиховедение*, and P. Gaidarska, *BR*, no. 4:25–30 (*O*).) Timur Kibirov is discussed by M. Zolotonosov, *Iu*, no. 5:78–81; V. Krivulin is discussed by O. Sedakova, *DN*, no. 10:258–66. G. Gamper, *Zv*, no. 7:197–200, writes about Andrei Kryzhanovskii. On Martynov, see S. V. Savchenko, pp. 51–56 of Adibaev, *Стиховедение*. There is a Rein memoir, *Zv*, no. 12:188–95; on him, see M. Iasnov, *K*, 68:351–56, and Brodskii, *Zn*, no. 7:180–84. Poems by the scholar S. Petrov are published in *DN*, no. 1:165–68. There is a new book on Rozhdestvenskii: A. Mal'gin, *Роберт Рождественский. Очерк творчества*, KhL, 1990, 203 pp. Samoilov poems are in *Ne*, no. 3:41–43; *Av*, no. 4:3–8; *Zn*, no. 6:86–89; *Ok*, no. 9:125–31. On S., see S. D. Abisheva, pp. 115–18, and D. Bel'skaia, pp. 4–13, respectively, of Adibaev, *Стиховедение*. Gleb Semenov is published, *Zv*, no. 2:106–09. There are Slutskii poems in *ib.*, no. 1:82–85; *NovM*, no. 1:156–58; *NSo*, no. 2:163–68; *LKirg*, no. 2:79–83; *Ne*, no. 6:53–54; *DN*, no. 9:112–15. On S., see Kuniaev, *NSo*, no. 2:156–63. There are Arsenii Tarkovskii letters, *Don*, no. 8:170–72, and on T. see E. Taratuta, *Iu*, no. 7:82–83, and Iu. Neiman, *VL*, no. 4:225–33.

THE EMIGRATION. Jan Paul Hinrichs, *Verbannen muze: Vijftien essays over schrijvers van de Russische emigratie*, Leiden, Slavische Stichting, 1990, 192 pp., contains essays on Viacheslav Ivanov, Bunin, Khodasevich, Nesmelov, Tsvetaeva, Georgii Ivanov, Viacheslav Lebedev, Nabokov, Dovid Knut, Vera Lur'e, Poplavskii, Pereleshin, Shteiger, Elagin, Nikolai Morshen, but may now be out of date in its concentration on the emigration as a literary concern separate from poetry written in Russia. More thematically inclined is I. Broude, *От Ходасевича до Набокова. Ностальгическая тема в поэзии первой русской эмиграции*, Tenafly, New Jersey, Ermitazh, 1990, 160 pp. Poems by Nabokov, G. Ivanov, and Bozhnev are published in *RusL*, no. 1:229–52; also on early émigré poets, see O. N. Mikhailov, *LSh*, no. 1:65–68. V. Sinkevich, *G*, 160:149–72, discusses Irina Saburova and Lidiia Alekseeva. On Galich, see A. G. Frizman, *RRe*, no. 3:23–28, and Iu. Karabchievskii, *Ne*, no. 1:170–76. Vadim Kreid, *G*, 159:129–46, discusses Aleksandr Kondrat'ev; there are Kondrat'ev letters, 1930–32, to A. V. Amfiteatrov in *NZh*, 181:139–72. On Kublanovskii, see S. Lipkin, *Zn*, no. 10:43–45. I. Chinnov, *NZh*, 184–85:604–13, recalls Odoevtseva; E. Shtein, *ib.*, 621–29, discusses Pereleshin. On the poetry of Ratushinskaia, see E. Dobrenko, *LitO*, no. 12:8–15. E. Dubnov, *G*, 160:301–11, considers Liia Vladimirova.

5. INDIVIDUAL AUTHORS

ABRAMOV. There are more stories from the *Трава-мурава* cycle, *Se*, no. 7:3–19, and a new book, Iu. M. Oklianskii, *Дом на угоре. О Ф. Абрамове и его книгах*, KhL, 1990, 208 pp.

AITMATOV. Two new books: A. A. Akmataliev, **Чингиз Айтматов и взаимосвязи литератур*, Bishkek, Adabiat, 182 pp.; L. I. Shevchenko, *Чингиз Айтматов*, Kiev, Dnipro, 210 pp. Articles include A. Bohm, *GSl*, 6, 1990:323–38 (*И дольше века длится день* and Christa Wolf's *Störfall*); also on the novel, see K. A. Rublev, pp. 163–66 of Zakharov, *Композиция* (the novel as science fiction). On *Плаха* see the following: J. B. Woodward, *SEER*, 69:201–20; R. Jacquenoud, *RSl*, 63:691–704; K. B. Jørgensen, *Svantetit*, 14, 1990:79–100.

AKHMATOVA. *The Speech of Unknown Eyes: Akhmatova's Readers on her Poetry*, ed. Wendy Rosslyn, Nottingham, Astra Press, 1990, 2 vols, vii + 169 pp., viii + 342 pp., is a major collection, comprising 22 papers; likewise, *RL*, 30:273–403, contains ten papers, all from the 1989 Moscow conference. Noted is **Воспоминания об Анне Ахматовой*, comp. V. Ia. Vilenkin and V. A. Chernykh, SovP, 718 pp. Articles include D. Bobyshev, *Zv*, no. 2:177–81 (A. in the emigration); V. S. Baevskii, pp. 13–24 of Gerasimova, *История* (A.'s poetics), and M. P. Belova, *ib.*, pp. 24–32 (A.'s works published in the late 1980s); L. I. Bronskaia, pp. 120–30 of Gura, *Жанр* (A.'s early work); W. Rosslyn, pp. 69–87 of Marsh and Rosslyn, *Culture* (*Поэма без героя*); S. Kaji, *JSEES*, 12:45–60, and A. E. Anikin, *RRe*, no. 1:23–28 (both general). There is an A.-Mandel'shtam 'bio-bibliography' in *SBib*, no. 2:86–100, with a memoir of A. by E. S.

Shal′man, *ib.*, 101–03, and S. Lipkin, pp. 377–85 of Oskotskii, *Взгляд*, recalls conversations with A.

AKSENOV.   Two articles by A. McMillin: pp. 50–61 of *Under Eastern Eyes* (details under GENERAL), and *ISS*, 10, 1989:1–16.

ALDANOV.   Texts include A.'s historical portraits, *NN*, no. 4:78–94; in *SD*, no. 1, there is an Adamovich memoir of him (208–39) and (206–08) an essay by A. Chernyshev (theatre in A.'s work). For general discussion, see O. N. Mikhailov, *LSh*, no. 2:34–42.

BABEL′.   S. Povartsov, *VL*, no. 6:48–66, discusses B.'s 'posthumous' fate. On *Конармия* see D. K. Danow, *MLR*, 86:939–53 (non-dialogic aspect); N. I. Khimukhina, *VMUF*, no. 3:26–32 (genre); N. Leiderman, *LitO*, no. 10:11–18.

BELOV.   Articles include A. I. Korolenok, pp. 145–54 of Gura, *Жанр* (*Лад*); T. N. Andreeva, pp. 114–20 of Ognev, *О жанре* (*Кануны*).

BITOV.   Articles include E. Chances, *SRev*, 50:400–09 (*Жизнь в ветреную погоду*); G. Ritz, *ZSPh*, 50, 1990:337–53 (*Человек в пейзаже*); W. Schmid, *WSlA*, 27:5–12 (B.'s award of the Pushkin Prize).

BLOK.   S. Nebol′sin, *NSo*, no. 8:176–84, demonstrates how B. has been distorted in Soviet editions. I. S. Prikhod′ko, *ISLIa*, 50:426–44, examines the image of Christ in *Двенадцать*, while A. M. Mikeshin, pp. 100–19 of Gura, *Жанр*, interprets the work as a romantic poem. L. and V. Vil′chek, *Zn*, no. 11:219–28, provide a modern reading of the poem.

BONDAREV.   *Игра* is discussed by V. V. Kompaneets, pp. 104–14 of Ognev, *О жанре*. On his new novel *Искушение*, see N. Fed′, *MG*, no. 4:247–77, and N. Rogoshchenkov, *Se*, no. 8:138–42.

BRODSKII.   A major book: *Brodsky's Poetics and Aesthetics*, ed. L. Loseff and V. Polukhina, Basingstoke, Macmillan, 1990, xii + 211 pp., contains documentary materials, B.'s Nobel Prize lecture, and nine studies of B.'s poetry. Other studies include G. S. Smith, pp. 17–24 of *Under Eastern Eyes* (details under GENERAL), and Loseff, *ib.*, pp. 25–41; D. Bethea, *RusL*, no. 3:167–75 (butterfly imagery in B. and Nabokov); K. Verheul, *Zv*, no. 8:195–98 (*На выставке Карла Виллинка*); N. Galatskaia, *ScSl*, 36, 1990:69–85 (*Ночной полет*); Iu. Kolker, *G*, 162:93–152 (general).

BULGAKOV.   Not surprisingly, given the centenary year, B. has been exercising the minds of Russian and Western critics and scholars more than any other writer. Vol. III of B.'s *Собрание сочинений в пяти томах* (for details and previous vols, see *YWMLS*, 51:997) contains the plays. *Гудок* texts from 1923–26 are in *VL*, 1990, no. 10:255–67, and there are documentary materials, *Te*, no. 5:14–47. There are also biographical sketches by M. Chudakova, *Iu,* no. 5 : 72–76, and B. Sokolov, *MG*, no. 5 : 74–79. The centenary has seen a wealth of publications on B. General and biographical books include *Mikhail Bulgakov in English: A Bibliography 1891–1991*, comp. G. M. Terry, Nottingham, Astra Press, 32 pp., and J. A. E. Curtis, *Manuscripts Don't Burn. Mikhail Bulgakov: A Life in Letters and Diaries*, London, Bloomsbury, xiv + 306 pp. *Дневник Елены Булгаковой*, comp. V. Losev and L. Ianovskaia, KP, 1990, 398 pp., and L. E. Belozerskaia-Bulgakova, *Воспоминания*, KhL, 1990, 221 pp., both offer excellent first-hand accounts. Iu. G. Vilenskii, *Доктор Булгаков*, Kiev, Zdorov'ia, 256 pp., traces the influence of medicine on B.'s work. A. Konchalovskii and D. Malakov, *Киев Михаила Булгакова*, Kiev, Mystetstvo, 1990, 284 pp., include a map of Kiev in 1911 and many photographs, as well as an account of the development of Kiev, 1890–1919.

Collections noted are **Украинские республиканские булгаковские чтения*, resp. ed. not indicated, Chernovtsy, publisher not indicated, 128 pp.; *Литературные традиции в поэтике Михаила Булгакова*, no ed., Kuibyshev GPI, 1990, 161 pp., which contains 12 papers; **Творчество Михаила Булгакова. Исследования. Материалы. Библиография*, resp. eds N. A. Groznova and A. I. Pavlovskii, Ld, Nauka, 445 pp. The whole of *LitO*, no. 5, is given over to B., and contains 18 articles, including contemporary responses to *Дни Турбиных* and *Белая гвардия* (by Adamovich and Khodasevich respectively), as well as more recent studies, by Soviet, émigré and Western scholars. Also noted is V. A. Chebotareva, **Рукописи не горят*, Baku, Iazychny, 143 pp.

On *Мастер и Маргарита, NN*, no. 3 : 58–86, contains documentary and archival materials, including early versions of the novel. There are also early versions in *Mos*, no. 5 : 178–201, together with critical articles. On the novel, there are no fewer than four new books. George Krugovoy, *The Gnostic Novel of Mikhail Bulgakov. Sources and Exegesis*, Lanham, University Press of America, x + 316 pp.; Edward E. Ericson, Jr., *The Apocalyptic Vision of Mikhail Bulgakov's 'The Master and Margarita'*, Lewiston, Edwin Mellon, 204 pp.; B. V. Sokolov, *Роман М. Булгакова 'Мастер и Маргарита'. Очерки творческой истории*, Nauka, 173 pp.; Riitta H. Pittman, *The Writer's Divided Self in Bulgakov's 'The Master and Margarita'*, Basingstoke, Macmillan, x + 211 pp. Also on the novel, see N. Gavriushin, *VL*, no. 8 : 75–88 (biblical aspects); E. Olonová, *SlSl*, 26 : 161–68 (Faust theme); M. F. Oja, *SRev*, 50 : 144–49 (ironic parallels between Margarita and Afranius); and G. Nivat, pp. 95–116 of Etkind, *Litteratura* (the novel and Nabokov's *Дар* as 'mirrors' of the 1930s). Other studies of the novel include I. Zolotusskii, *LitU*, no. 2 : 147–65 (the novel and *Белая гвардия* juxtaposed); E. Ia. Iablokov, *FilN*, no. 4 : 33–42 (a

comparative analysis of the novel and Grin's *Блистающий мир*); L. F.
Kiseleva, *ib.*, no. 6:3–11 (dialogue of good and evil); C. Testa, *CSS*,
24, 1990:257–78; L. Ianovskaia, *Ok*, no. 5:182–201; P. Palievskii,
Библиотекарь, no. 5:58–62; L. A. Levina, *FilN*, no. 1:12–23; A. K.
Kiselev, *LSh*, no. 1:102–08; V. Losev, *Слово*, no. 4:15–17; A.
Korablev, *VL*, no. 5:35–54; and see under PASTERNAK.

   On *Белая гвардия*, see the following: L. P. Fomenko, pp. 47–56 of
Ognev, *О жанре*; R. Urbán Nagy, *ALitH*, 30, 1988:273–92, 31,
1989:273–82 (motifs of crime-guilt-punishment in the novel and
Бег); V. I. Nemtsev, pp. 72–98 of Golubkov, *Поэтика*. There is in *Te*,
no. 12:82–102, a history of the ban and then authorization of *Дни
Турбиных* in MKhAT. On B.'s plays, see V. P. Petrov, pp. 98–111 of
Golubkov, *Поэтика* (B.'s and Maiakovskii's comedies of the 1920s);
Iu. V. Nevodov, pp. 54–65 of Gerasimova, *История*; and O.
Iumasheva and I. Lepikhov, *IK*, no. 5:132–40. Other studies include
A. Ninov, *Te*, no. 7:39–57 (*Батум*); S. Ioffe, *Слово*, no. 1:18–23
(*Собачье сердце*); V. B. Petrov, pp. 28–39 of Subbotin, *Опыт*
(*Зойкина квартира*); E. Ransome, *RSl*: 63:631–56 (*Жизнь господина
де Мольера*); Iu. M. Smirnov, pp. 56–65 of Miliavskii, *Критика*
(*Театральный роман*); M. Petrovskii, *VL*, no. 5:3–34 (B. and
Сатирикон); Ia. S. Lur'e, *RusR*, 50:203–10 (B. between Mark Twain
and Lev Tolstoi); Id., *Zv*, no. 9:168–74 (B. and Il'f and Petrov); M.
Iovanovich, *SSH*, 35, 1989:107–15 (B. and Dante); A. V. Zaitsev,
VMUF, no. 6:19–23 (moral searches of the intelligentsia in B.'s early
work). L. Milne (pp. 89–99 of Marsh and Rosslyn, *Culture*) and M.
Jones (*ib.*, 101–09), argue as to whether B. is a modernist.

   More general appreciations are noted as follows: V. Gudkova, *DN*,
no. 5:262–70; V. G. Boborykin, *LSh*, no. 1:52–65; I. Belza, *VL*,
no. 5:55–83; M. Zolotonosov, *DN*, 1990, no. 11:247–62; A. Shindel',
Zn, no. 5:193–208; E. G. Babaev and O. A. Podgaets, *RRe*, no. 3:8–
22; A. Ninov, *ILen*, no. 5:12–16; P. Palievskii, *NSo*, no. 9:178–82. As
part of the centenary celebrations, there are critical comments and
reviews from the 1920s collected in *Vo*, no. 5:164–74.

   BUNIN.   Major editions of B.'s diaries: *Лишь слову жизнь дана . . .* ,
SR, 1990, 368 pp., contains diaries 1881–1953, an introd. by O. N.
Mikhailov (pp. 5–20), and copious notes; *Окаянные дни. Вос-
поминания. Статьи*, SovP, 1990, 416 pp., contains diaries, 1917–18,
Окаянные дни, and recollections of Gor'kii, Maiakovskii, Kuprin,
Voloshin and others. Diaries, 1918–20, are in *Ne*, no. 5:121–29,
no. 6:142–55 (with archival materials). Poems not republished since
1896 are in *MG*, no. 1:36–37. There are letters from the 1940s to K. G.
Shemetillo, *RusL*, 1990, no. 4:223–28. Criticism includes a book,
Andrea Meyer, *Die Sonnetdichtung Ivan Bunins*, Wiesbaden, Harrassowitz, 1990, xiv + 328 pp., and an article by O. N. Semenova,
pp. 46–67 of Grinfel'd, *Проблемы* (*Темные аллеи*).

BYKOV.   There is a new book: I. Dedkov, *Василь Быков. Повесть о человеке, который выстоял*, SovP, 1990, 308 pp.

CHUKOVSKII.   Ch.'s 1922 diary is in *NovM*, no. 5:160–93 (see also 1990, nos 7–8); Correspondence from the 1930s–1960s with Moscow linguists is in *RRe*, no. 5:27–53, no. 6:35–43.

DOMBROVSKII.   There are unpublished texts, *K*, 67:7–40, and for reflections on D. see Ia. S. Lur'e, *Zv*, no. 3:171–76, and V. Nepomniashchii, *NovM*, no. 5:234–40.

ERENBURG.   There is an unpublished text in *Zv*, no. 1:129–31, followed by a portrait of E. by B. Paramonov, 132–50. A major new edition of *Люди, годы, жизнь*, 3 vols, SovP, 1990, 640, 448, 496 pp., contains material not previously published, as well as photographs and illustrations by E. himself (some also published for the first time). Each volume is served with copious notes. There are no fewer than four new books on E.: Ewa Bérard, *La vie tumultueuse d'Ilya Ehrenbourg. Juif, russe et soviétique*, Paris, Ramsay, 375 pp.; M. Klimenko, *Ehrenburg. An Attempt at a Literary Portrait*, NY, Lang, 1990, x + 273 pp.; J. L. Laychuk, *Ilya Ehrenburg: An Idealist in an Age of Realism*, NY, Lang, x + 486 pp.; A. I. Rubashkin, *Илья Эренбург. Путь писателя*, Ld, SovP, 1990, 526 pp. Rubashkin discusses *Оттепель*, *Av*, no. 1:120–26.

EROFEEV, VENEDIKT.   There are unpublished texts and materials, *Te*, no. 9:59–73; *K*, 67:285–317; *NZh*, 182:47–58. There is a memoir by I. Avdiev (Chernousyi), *K*, 67:318–23. On *Москва-Петушки* see C. Simmons, *CSS*, 24, 1990:155–68.

ESENIN.   New books include S. Koshechkin, *Весенней гулкой ранью . . . Этюды-раздумья о Сергее Есенине*, Minsk, Iunatstva, 1989, 239 pp.; L. L. Bel'skaia, *Песенное слово. Поэтическое мастерство С. Есенина*, Prosveshchenie, 1990, 142 pp.; A. D. Panfilov, **Нинесе. Поиски, исследования, находки*, *SBib*, 1990, 191 pp.; **Славянская филология. Творчество С. А. Есенина. Традиции и новаторство*, resp. eds D. D. Ivlev *et al.*, Riga, Latvian U.P., 1990, 151 pp. A continuation of the conspiracy theory is provided in *Убийство Есенина. Новые материалы*, no ed., Makhachkala, Dagestanskoe kn. izd–vo, 152 pp. For further criticism, see N. N. Zaitsev, pp. 36–46 of Ognev, *О жанре*; V. I. Khazan, pp. 32–48 of Gerasimova, *История*; I. I. Stepanchenko, pp. 105–07 of Adibaev, *Стиховедение*. An essay by R. Gul' on E. abroad is reproduced, *Слово*, no. 4:81–84.

FEDIN.   Articles include A. M. Khusikhanov, pp. 72–80 of Gerasimova, *История* (the trilogy), and N. I. Kuznetsov, pp. 84–95 of Ognev, *О жанре* (F.'s work during the 1940s).

GOR'KII.   The 1922 article *Русская жестокость* is reprinted, *Памир*, 1990, no. 10:174–80, with commentary by M. Saidova, 181–88, and a 1921 letter to Helsinki Professor J. J. Mikola is in *ScSl*,

37:101–07. There are biographical materials, *Vo*, no. 8:190–91, and K. Zelinskii's 1932 diary (on his meetings with G.), *VL*, no. 5:144–70. Biographical books include E. N. Pozdnin, *Друзья молодого Горького*, Gor'kii, Volgo-Viatskoe kn. izd-vo, 1990, 110 pp.; Nikolaus Katzer, *Maksim Gorkijs Weg in die russische Sozialdemokratie*, Wiesbaden, Harrassowitz, 1990, 259 pp.; *M. Горький и революция*, resp. ed. I. K. Kuz'michev, Nizhnii Novgorod, Volgo-Viatskoe kn. izd-vo, 219 pp. On G.'s work, books include *Поэтика художественной прозы M. Горького*, resp. eds I. K. Kuz'michev *et al.*, Gor'kii GPI, 1989, 122 pp., which contains six papers on both general themes and individual works; see also V. I. Baranov, *Огонь и пепел костра. M. Горький: творческие искания и судьба*, Gor'kii, Volgo-Viatskoe kn. izd-vo, 1990, 365 pp. On G.'s early work, see pp. 244–301 of Balukhatyi, *Вопросы поэтики* (details under DRAMA). The reassessment of G.'s place in Russian literature continues with P. Basinskii, *VL*, no. 2:129–54, who muses on G.'s 'tragedy' and his losing touch with reality, and N. Primochkina, *MG*, no. 3:258–68, who relates G.'s 'mistake' in his attitude to the peasantry, collectivization and the peasant poets. See also A. B. Udodov, *LSh*, no. 4:79–87. A. Barratt and E. W. Clowes, *SovS*, 43:1123–42, summarize the 'death of a cultural superhero' under *glasnost'* and *perestroika*. I. F. Eremina, *ScSl*, 37:69–83, in similar fashion assesses G.'s romanticism in the context of today. I. Serman, pp. 55–93 of Etkind, *Letteratura*, discusses G.'s search for the hero of his time. Also on his work, see S. A. Iezuitov, pp. 34–47 of Smirnov, *Изучение* (*Егор Булычев и другие*); G. Mitin, *LSh*, no. 1:28–52 (*Несвоевременные мысли*); N. V. Kornienko, pp. 93–101 of *Жанрово-стилевое единство художественного произведения*, resp. eds Iu. V. Shatin *et al.*, Novosibirsk GPI, 1989, 127 pp. (*Городок Окуров*); M. M. Girshman, *ib.*, 102–08, and B. Scherr, *RL*, 29:455–69 (both on *По Руси*); S. Vaiman, *LitO*, no. 12:26–33 (*Мать*). Also on *Мать*, see A. Siniavskii, pp. 80–92 of *Избавление от миражей. Соцреализм сегодня*, comp. E. A. Dobrenko, SovP, 1990, 413 pp. (the novel as an early example of Socialist Realism). Other articles noted include L. M. Borisova, *VRL*, 1990, no. 1:76–83 (*Мещане* in the context of the struggle of ideas in the early 20th c.; L. Kolobaeva, *VL*, 1990, no. 10:162–73 (G. and Nietzsche), and N. Primochkina, *ib.*, no. 7:241–48 (G. and Pavel Radimov); see also Brodskaia under DRAMA.

GRIN.   General articles noted include I. V. Potapova, pp. 72–84 of Volkova, *Советская*; A. O. Lopukhova, pp. 142–48 of Zakharov, *Жанр*; and M. V. Saidova, pp. 50–56 of Miliavskii, *Критика*. See also Iablokov under BULGAKOV.

GROSSMAN.   An important new book: S. Lipkin, *Жизнь и судьба Василия Гроссмана*, Kniga, 1990, 269 pp. M. Shneerson, *G*,

160:107–48, considers the relationship between *За правое дело* and *Жизнь и судьба*. Also on *Жизнь и судьба*, see A. G. Kovalenko, *FilN*, no. 5:25–32; I. Zakharieva, *BR*, no. 4:3–9; J. Garrard, *SRev*, 50:336–46; and E. A. Dobrenko, pp. 95–106 of Subbotin, *Опыт*. L. E. Gerasimova and V. V. Pugachev, pp. 145–54 of Gerasimova, *История*, discuss *Все течет*. A. Bocharov, pp. 386–406 of Oskotskii, *Взгляд*, looks at the 'creative affinity' of G. and Platonov.

IL′F AND PETROV. Iu. Shcheglov, *Da*, 7–8:142–77 (the novels); see also Lur′e under BULGAKOV.

IVANOV, GEORGII. Vadim Kreid, *Петербургский период Георгия Иванова*, Tenafly, New Jersey, Ermitazh, 1989, 192 pp., takes in the years 1909–22. The essay *Распад атома* (1937) is in *LitO*, no. 2:86–93, followed by an essay on it by I. Prokhorova, 93–94. A. Ar′ev, *Zv*, no. 9:174–79, discusses I.'s early poetry.

IVANOV, VSEVOLOD. There are archival materials and texts from 1943, *Смена*, no. 2:48–63.

KAVERIN. G. Kern, *RLT*, 24:439–63 (general), and E. G. Elina, pp. 65–71 of Gerasimova, *История* (K.'s critical method).

KAZAKOV. I. M. Sukhareva, pp. 96–106 of *Литературный процесс и творческая индивидуальность* (details under GENERAL).

KHARMS. A very good year for Kh. studies. There is a major publication of texts and materials in *Te*, no. 11:10–79 (poems and unfinished plays as well as criticism). J.-Ph. Jaccard and A. Ustinov, *WSlA*, 27:159–228, publish important new texts and documents, and V. I. Glotser, *RusL*, no. 1:204–09, publishes documents relevant to Kh.'s arrest and death. An important collection is *Daniil Kharms and the Poetics of the Absurd: Essays and Materials*, ed. N. Cornwell, Basingstoke, Macmillan, xvi + 282 pp., which contains 15 papers, texts, bibliography, and memoirs. C. Müller-Scholle, pp. 57–92 of *Russische Avantgarde 1917–1934: Kunst und Literatur nach der Revolution*, ed. Bodo Zelinsky, Bonn, Bouvier Vlg, 146 pp., looks at Kh., Vvedenskii and the theatre of the absurd.

KRIUKOV. There is a short story, *Mos*, no. 2:56–77. On the continuing *Тихий Дон* controversy, there is a book: M. P. Astapenko, *Его называли автором 'Тихого Дона'*, Rostov-na-Donu, Edinstvo, 107 pp. Also on K., see F. G. Biriukov, *LSh*, no. 2:13–24.

KUPRIN. There are texts from 1920–22, *Слово*, no. 3:71–77.

LEONOV. A new book: G. G. Isaev, *Леонид Леонов — литературный критик и публицист*, Tomsk U.P., 327 pp. Isaev writes on *Вор*, pp. 94–100 of Miliavskii, *Критика*; T. V. Fanina, *VMUF*, no. 6:23–30, on *Унтиловск*; and see also V. V. Khimich, pp. 51–63 of Subbotin, *Опыт* (general).

LUNACHARSKII. There are two new books: S. G. Isaev, *Поэтика А. В. Луначарского*, Tashkent, Fan, 105 pp.; V. V. Efimov, *Мастерство*

A. B. Луначарского — литературного критика (1917–1933 гг.),
Dushanbe, Donish, 1990, 325 pp. Also on L., see Efimov and N.
Trifonov, *VL*, no. 1:226–40.

MAIAKOVSKII.   New books include A. A. Mikhailov, *Мир Маяковского (Взгляд из восьмидесятых)*, Sovremennik, 1990, 462 pp.; and
Iu. A. Karabchievskii, *Воскресение Маяковского*, SovP, 1990, 222 pp.
V. Katanian, *Слово*, no. 7:59–63, publishes an extract from his book
on M.'s last days. I. Iu. Iskrzhitskaia, *VMUF*, no. 4:3–12, writes
curiously on M.'s 'return'. B. Jangfeldt, *ScSl*, 37:26–34, relates details
of M.'s romantic liaison in the USA, which produced a child. On M.'s
poetry, see T. A. Sokolova, pp. 48–53 of Gerasimova, *История*; M. L.
Gasparov, *ISLIa*, 50:531–38; K. Iu. Postoutenko, *ib.*, pp. 521–30 (M.
and Shengeli). Z. V. Ibragimova, pp. 80–87 of Miliavskii, *Критика*,
looks for Gogolian influences in *Баня*; see also Petrov under
BULGAKOV. T. A. Sokolova, pp. 48–54 of Gerasimova, *История*, looks
at M.'s use of metaphor. General articles include B. L. Miliavskii,
pp. 65–80 of Miliavskii, *Критика*; G. A. Baranova, pp. 174–76 of
Adibaev, *Стиховедение*; A. Mikhailov, *LSh*, no. 2:43–51; and V. N.
Terekhina, *SBib*, no. 2:60–71. Perhaps the most interesting discussion is by Mikhailov, pp. 256–73 of Oskotskii, *Взгляд*, who attempts a
contemporary reassessment of M.'s place in Russian literature.

MANDEL'SHTAM.   The centenary, not surprisingly, has seen some
major publications. There are texts: *VL*, no. 1:241–54 (poems); *Av*,
no. 1:18–25 (poems and a letter from 1928); *LitU*, no. 1:149–81
(letters to Zamiatin and memoirs); *ILen*, no. 1:54–56 (extract from
Шум времени); *Zn*, no. 1:193–203 (correspondence with Nadezhda
Iakovlevna, 1936–38); and *NN*, no. 1:62–76 (unpublished extracts
from *Египетская марка*). The centenary is marked by the publication
of a major book: B. L. Sarnov, *Заложник вечности. Случай
Мандельштама*, KP, 1990, 214 pp. Other books include Petra Hesse,
*Mythologie in moderner Lyrik: Osip E. Mandel'štam vor dem Hintergrund des
'Silbernen Zeitalters'*, NY, Lang, 1989, 377 pp.; Sof'ia M. Margolina,
Мировоззрение Осипа Мандельштама, Marburg/Lahn, Blaue
Hörner Vlg, 1989, 210 pp.; **Творчество Мандельштама и вопросы
исторической поэтики*, resp. ed. V. I. Tiupa *et al.*, Kemerovo U.P.,
1990, 142 pp. The whole issue of *LitO*, no. 1, is devoted to M., with 14
articles by Soviet, Western, and émigré scholars and writers; likewise,
RL, 30:405–530, contains studies of M.'s work, six papers in all.
There are four articles in *ISLIa*, 50: V. V. Musatov, 236–47 (early
lyric poetry); V. I. Khazan, 248–57 (theme of death and apocalypse
in M.'s poetry of the 1930s); I. V. Koretskaia, 258–62 (*Ламарк*); D. I.
Cherashniaia, 263–68 (*Разговор о Данте*). *RusL*, no. 1:42–87, contains articles by A. V. Makedonov and I. Stanishich, and also
publishes M.'s article *Скрябин и христианство*; *VL*, no. 1:9–76,

contains articles by G. Freidin, P. Nerler, and I. Feinberg. There are memoirs by G. Adamovich, *Ok*, no. 2:194–99; E. Tager, *Zv*, no. 1:151–67; P. Luknitskii, *ib.*, no. 2:110–29. A. Parnis, *LitO*, no. 6:25–30, publishes materials on M. in Petrograd, 1915–16; H. Meyer, *WSl*, 36 (n.f. 15):72–98, looks at M. in the 'mute' years, 1925–30. There is further appreciation in *VRKhD*, 160, 1990:187–257. The year sees some major individual studies: D. Myers, *SEER*, 69:1–39 (*Нашедший подкову*); S. Boym, *SRev*, 50:118–26 (M.'s challenge to Bakhtin); Živa Benčić, *RL*, 29:25–45 (M. and oxymoron); D. I. Cherashniaia, pp. 15–22 of Subbotin, *Опыт* (*Камень*); M. S. Pavlov, *FilN*, no. 6:20–30 (*Как светотени мученик Рембрандт*); I. Mess-Baehr, *RL*, 29:243–393 (Aesopian language in M.'s poetry of the 1930s); E. Nevzgliadova, *Ne*, no. 1:167–69 (M.'s use of metaphor). Furthermore, H. Meyer, *WSlA*, 28:107–47, interprets M.'s Acmeism as Neoclassicism. General articles include L. A. Kolobaeva, *VMUF*, no. 2:3–14; L. L. Bel'skaia and E. A. Obukhova, *RRe*, no. 1:10–22; E. Toddes, *LitO*, no. 3:30–43; I. Putlina, *VL*, no. 5:220–37; L. K. Polikarpik, *FilN*, no. 6:12–20; E. P. Berenshtein, *LSh*, no. 6:31–45. See also A. Barzakh, *Zv*, no. 11:161–65 (M. and Annenskii); E. M. Breido, pp. 74–76 of Adibaev, *Стиховедение* (M. and Vvedenskii); B. L. Borukhov, *Vo*, no. 2:177–85; B. Kats, *ILen*, no. 1:44–53; S. Makovskii, *Ok*, no. 2:187–94. There is also an article by V. Gofman from 1926, *Zv*, no. 12:175–87. See also under AKHMATOVA.

MEREZHKOVSKII. An important new study: T. Pachmuss, *D. S. Merezhkovsky in Exile: The Master of the Genre of Biographie Romancée*, NY, Lang, 1990, xvi + 338 pp., concentrates on M.'s post-1917 prose and in particular his biographies of historical and religious figures. There are archival materials about the early years of emigration in *NZh*, 180, 1990:173–202.

MOZHAEV. M.'s collected works: vol. II, 1989, 574 pp., contains short works; vol. III, 1990, 623 pp., contains the better known *povesti* and Book One of *Мужики и бабы*; vol. IV, 1990, 543 pp., contains Book Two as well as articles (for details and vol. 1: *YWMLS*, 51:1008).

NABOKOV. Texts include short stories in *Zv*, no. 3:9–28, and *Pro*, no. 4:32–37; a poem from *Бледный огонь* translated into Russian, *Av*, no. 1:93–119; and archival materials, *NN*, no. 1:109–12. The second volume of Brian Boyd's excellent biography is published: *Vladimir Nabokov: The American Years*, London, Chatto and Windus, xvi + 784 pp. There are two full-length studies of N.: Vladimir E. Alexandrov, *Nabokov's Otherworld*, Princeton U.P., xi + 270 pp., has chapters on seven novels as well as general and concluding sections; Tony Sharpe, *Vladimir Nabokov*, London, Arnold, xii + 116 pp., is a much more general study. A major collection is contained in *RLT*, 24, most of which is devoted to N.: there are 12 articles on his prose, five on poetry, with texts and an interview with Vera and Dmitrii Nabokov. Further issues of *The Nabokovian* are 24 and 25 (1990), which contain translations, notes, letters, bibliographies, and articles on N. in the USSR; 26 contains materials on the late Vera Nabokova and abstracts; 27 contains articles by Boyd on the N. archives and an article by D. B. Johnson on *Ада*.

Shorter studies include M. T. Naumann, *RL*, 29:229–42 (N. and Pushkin); M. Medarić, *ib.*, 29:79–100 (N. and the 20th-c. novel); J. B. Foster Jr, *CLS*, 28:51–67 (revisionary modernism in *Pale Fire*); G. Diment, *ib.*, 27:285–97 (N. and Strachey); S. Pol'skaia, *ScSl*, 36, 1990:101–13 (E. T. A. Hoffman in *Облако, озеро, башня*); G. Diment, *ISS*, 12:11–26 (N. and Joyce); I. Tolstoi, *G*, 159:147–56 (*Лик*); G. K. Vasil'ev, *FilN*, no. 3:33–40 (linguistic analysis of an extract from *Весна в Фиальте*); see also under BRODSKII and BULGAKOV. There are general articles by O. N. Mikhailov, *LSh*, no. 3:42–52; N. Prikhod'ko, *ib.*, pp. 53–59; and V. Stark, *ILen*, no. 3:17–25.

NAGIBIN.   There is a new book: V. F. Kholopova, *Парадокс любви. Новеллистика Ю. Нагибина*, Sovremennik, 1990, 250 pp. M. Sendich, *RLJ*, 147–49, 1990:183–213, also discusses N.

NEVEROV.   *Гуси-лебеди* is discussed by A. R. Zaitseva, pp. 33–47 of Golubkov, *Поэтика*.

OLESHA.   Victor Peppard, *The Poetics of Yury Olesha*, Gainesville, Florida U.P., 1989, xi + 164 pp., is a major study, concentrating on the application of Bakhtin's theory of carnival to the study of *Зависть*. Also on the novel, see M. Ehre, *SRev*, 50:601–11 (utopia and dystopia).

OSORGIN.   There are texts in *RRe*, no. 2:33–41, *SBib*, no. 2:127–35, *Слово*, no. 3:79–80; and letters to M. Vishniak, 1926–38, *NZh*, 178, 1990:277–303.

OSTROVSKII.   L. Anninskii, *LSh*, no. 1:69–76, continues his re-evaluation of O.

PASTERNAK.   Another good year for P. studies. Further volumes of the collected works (for details of vol. I see *YWMLS*, 51:1010–11) are as follows: vol. II, 1989, 703 pp. (poems 1931–59, translations); vol. III, 1990, 734 pp. (*Доктор Живаго*); vol. IV, 909 pp. (prose, drama, critical articles). New texts published include a letter to P. Kogan, *VRKhD*, 158, 1990:226–30. On P.'s correspondence with P. P. Suvchinskii, see V. Kozovoï, *RSl*, 63:657–89. New books include Z. A. Maslennikova, *Портрет Борис Пастернака. Записки скульптора*, SR, 1990, 286 pp.; Daša Šilhánková Di Simplicio, *La nascità di un poeta. Boris Pasternak*, Naples, Liguori Editore, 1990, 220 pp.; **Пастернаковские чтения*, ed. R. V. Kozhina *et al.*, Perm' U.P., 1990, 107 pp. A curious addition to P. studies is Zina Gimplevich-Schwartzmann, *Boris Pasternak: What M Is Out There?*, NY, Legas, 1990, 164 pp., which juxtaposes Мастер и Маргарита and Доктор Живаго. Collections noted are *Boris Pasternak*, ed. K. Szöke, Szeged U.P., 1988, 345 pp.; Поэтика Пастернака, ed. A. Majmieskułow, Bydgoszcz, Zeszyty Naukowe Wyższej Szkoły Pedagogiczney, 1990, 221 pp., which contains seven papers.

On Доктор Живаго, there is a book: 'Доктор Живаго' Бориса Пастернака. С разных точек зрения, ed. L. V. Bakhnov and L. B. Borodin, SovP, 1990, 285 pp., contains most of the articles on the novel that appeared in the Soviet press, 1988–89, as well as protocols from 1958. Also on the novel, see P. M. Waszink, *WSlA*, 28:149–89 (the novel's 'literariness'); D. K. Danow, *SRev*, 50:954–64 (as governed by a dialogic poetics); V. Strada, pp. 117–42 of Etkind, *Letteratura* (as a historical novel); I. P. Smirnov, *WSlA*, 27:119–36. L. Fleishman, *ISLIa*, 50:114–23, traces P.'s path from Записки Патрика to Живаго.

Other works: E. Glazov, *ib.*, 137–58, and A. Ljunggren, *RL*, 29:489–99, examine Детство Люверс. Other articles noted include J. Faryno, *SEER*, 69:418–57 (Pushkin in Тема с вариациями); A. K. Zholkovskii, *ISLIa*, 50:20–34 (Мне хочется домой в огромности . . .); A. Parin, *VRKhD*, 158, 1990:231–45 (P. and Maiakovskii); B. Paramonov, *Zv*, no. 4:198–205 (P. against Romanticism). See also T. A. Burtseva, pp. 114–15, and A. L. Zhovtis, pp. 158–60, of Adibaev, Стиховедение. Felix Dreizin, *The Russian Soul and the Jew: Essays in Literary Ethno-centrism*, Lanham, Maryland, University Press of America, 1990, xviii + 246 pp., includes an intriguing chapter on P. (127–51). See also N. Perlina and K. Moss, *SRev*, 50:371–84, on Ol'ga Freidenburg.

PAUSTOVSKII. Critical articles noted include L. O. Achkasova, pp. 56–62 of Ognev, О жанре (general), and S. Ollivier, *BR*, no. 2:22–28 (stories of the 1940s).

PIL'NIAK. Texts include letters to Gor'kii, 1920–28, *RusL*, no. 1:180–89. I. Shaitanov, *LitO*, no. 6:19–25, no. 7:4–11, writes on P. and Zamiatin, and again on P., *VL*, 1990, no. 7:35–73. Articles noted include M. A. Nicholas, *SRev*, 50:422–32 (P. and modernism); N. Moranjak-Bamburać, *RL*, 29:101–12 (Штосс в жизнь); O. O. Geintse, pp. 122–35 of Golubkov, Поэтика (P. in the 1920s).

PLATONOV. The year has seen some important publications: texts and materials, *Ok*, no. 10:194–206, *NovM*, no. 1:130–55; the novel Счастливая Москва (1932–36), *ib.*, no. 9:9–76. There is a new book: O. A. Kuz'menko, Андрей Платонов. Призвание и судьба, Kiev, Lybid', 229 pp., and an updated and substantially amended edition of V. V. Vasil'ev, Андрей Платонов. Очерк жизни и творчества, Sovremennik, 1990, 285 pp. Articles on P. include E. A. Iablokov, pp. 55–71 of Volkova, Советская (nature in P. and Prishvin in the

1920s–1930s); S. A. Golubkov, pp. 112–21 of Golubkov, *Поэтика (Город Градов)*; G. V. Galas'eva, pp. 78–94 of Grinfel'd, *Проблемы* (poetics of nature in P.'s prose of the 1920s); L. P. Grigor'eva, pp. 94–102 of *ib.*, (P.'s early Utopias); A. I. Pavlovskii, *RusL*, no. 1:21–41, and V. G. Bobylev, *RIa*, no. 2:62–71 (both on *Котлован*); Per-Arne Bodin, *ScSl*, 37:5–25 (*Джан*); A. Trinko, *Se*, no. 3:150–60 (general). See also Bocharov under GROSSMAN.

POPLAVSKII. Texts published this year include poems, *RusL*, no. 2:239–48, and *MG*, no. 12:181–83, the novel *Аполлон Безобразов*, *Iu*, no. 1:2–17, no. 2:38–56, and the novel *Домой с небес*, *ib.*, no. 10:56–75. There are materials (biographical essay by A. Bogoslavskii, P.'s 1934 diaries, texts) also in *VRKhD*, 158, 1990:246–65. On P., see O. N. Mikhailov, *LSh*, no. 4:22–24.

PRISHVIN. P.'s 1940 diary is continued in *DN*, 1990, no. 9:217–55; his diary from 1918 is in *LitU*, no. 3:116–28, no. 4:63–108. There are also diaries from 1930–32, pp. 410–58 of Oskotskii, *Взгляд*, and P.'s views on Rozanov, with diaries from the 1920s–1940s, and correspondence between the two wives from 1969 is published, pp. 161–218 of *Контекст 1990. Литературно-теоретические исследования*, resp. ed. A. V. Mikhailov, Nauka, 1990, 264 pp. L. A. Riazanova, *LSh*, no. 6:45–51, talks about the diaries. Remizov, Vsevolod Ivanov, Inber and Iashin are among those who recollect P. in *Воспоминания о Михаиле Пришвине*, comp. Ia. Z. Grishina and L. A. Riazanova, SovP, 368 pp. Criticism noted includes G. P. Klimova, pp. 27–36 of Ognev, *О жанре (Кащеева цепь)*; T. Ia. Grinfel'd, pp. 113–24 of Grinfel'd, *Проблемы* ('light' and 'shadow' in P.'s artistic world); A. L. Kiselev, pp. 57–72 of Golubkov, *Поэтика* (P.'s works of the 1920s). See also under PLATONOV.

RASPUTIN. A new book offers as yet the most detailed study of R.'s work as a writer: Günther Hasenkamp, *Gedächtnis und Leben in der Prosa Valentin Rasputins*, Wiesbaden, Harrassowitz, 1990, vii + 302 pp., contains substantial chapters on each of the *povesti*, and covers both the early and later short stories. L. G. Dorofeeva, pp. 111–19 of Volkova, *Советская*, examines *Живи и помни*. On *Прощание с Матерой* see R. Porter, *LHum*, no. 1:211–20, and Kathleen Parthé's foreword, pp. vii–xxiii of V. Rasputin, *Farewell to Matyora*, trans. A. V. Bouis, Evanston, Illinois, Northwestern U.P., xxiv + 227 pp. M.-L. Magnusson, *Svantetit*, 14, 1990:115–44, discusses *Пожар*. V. K. Sigov, pp. 95–104 of Ognev, *О жанре*, offers an overview, and see also E. G. Shik, pp. 115–27 of Subbotin, *Опыт*.

RUBTSOV. There are poems, *ILen*, no. 1:42–44; *Слово*, no. 1:16–17, 51–52; *LSh*, no. 3:99–106. On R., see A. Z. Dmitrovskii, pp. 97–102 of *Сюжет и фабула в структуре жанра*, resp. ed. V. I. Greshnykh, Kaliningrad U.P., 1990, 111 pp.; V. N. Barakov, *LSh*, no. 3:60–68; N. Panina, *ib.*, 92–99; V. Safonov, *Слово*, no. 1:45–50; V. A. Red'kin, pp. 83–95 of Subbotin, *Опыт*.

RYBAKOV.   On *Дети Арбата* see S. McLaughlin, *SRev*, 50:90–99, and L. Bakhnov, *DN*, no. 12:252–57.

SEMIN.   M. V. Kul'gavchuk, pp. 101–10 of Volkova, *Советская* (*Семеро в одном доме*).

SEVERIANIN.   A major publication is *Письма к Августе Барановой, 1916–1938*, comp. B. Jangfeldt and R. Kruus, Stockholm, Almqvist and Wiksell International, 1989, 166 pp. For criticism, see I. A. Vasilevskaia, *RIa*, no. 6:47–52.

SHALAMOV.   There are materials (notes, essays, memoirs), *Ok*, no. 7:169–85. Criticism includes L. Timofeev, *ib.*, no. 3:182–95 (*Колымские рассказы*), and E. Shklovskii, *DN*, no. 9:254–63.

SHMELEV.   Sh. materials from 1917 are in *Слово*, no. 12:78–82. Criticism noted includes R. M. Goriunova, *FilN*, no. 4:25–32 (*Солнце мертвых*) and L. N. Dudina, *RRe*, no. 4:20–25 (*Богомолье*).

SHOLOKHOV.   There are four new books on Sh.: E. A. Kostin, *Художественный мир писателя как объект эстетики. Очерк эстетики М. Шолохова*, Vil'nius U.P., 1990, 270 pp.; *Творчество М. А. Шолохова и современная литература. Шолоховские чтения*, resp. ed. N. I. Glushkov, Rostov-na-Donu U.P., 1990, 135 pp., which contains 27 short papers; G. Ia. Sivovolov, *'Тихий Дон'. Рассказы о прототипах. Заметки литературного краеведа*, kn. izd-vo Rostova-na Donu, 347 pp.; L. I. Zalesskaia, *Шолохов и развитие советского многонационального романа*, Nauka, 266 pp. The controversy over the authorship of *Тихий Дон* rages on: V. Vasil'ev, *MG*, no. 11:239–63, no. 12:225–35, sees the campaign against Sh. as instigated by Russia's enemies, and castigates particularly Solzhenitsyn; L. Kolodnyi, *Mos*, no. 10:191–97, refutes the suggestion of plagiarism and supports Sh.'s authorship; the discussants (M. Mezentsev, F. Biriukov. H. Ermolaev, E. Vertel', L. Aksenova) in *VL*, no. 2:3–81, have divided opinions. See also under KRIUKOV. L. V. Krzhivinskaia, *LSh*, no. 2:109–13, rereads *Поднятая целина* positively; V. Litvinov, *VL*, nos 9–10:30–50, attempts to reclaim the novel for literature, and laments that it has lately become a 'weapon in the political skirmish'. E. Sharfavi, pp. 135–42 of Golubkov, *Поэтика*, relates Sh.'s treatment at the hands of Czech critics. M. M. Sholokhov, *Дон*, no. 5:155–62, continues his recollections of his father.

SHUKSHIN.   There is a new book on Sh.: V. F. Gorn, *Василий Шукшин. Личность. Книги*, Barnaul, Altaiskoe kn. izd-vo, 1990, 284 pp. Articles noted include L. Morgan, *ASEES*, 5:59–76 (allegorical elements in the short stories); L. A. Posadskaia, pp. 117–28 of Gerasimova, *История* (*Точка зрения*); I. A. Spiridonova, *RusL*, no. 4:18–30 (Sh.'s Stephan Razin). See also Zalygin under TRIFONOV.

SHVARTS.　Iu. Aikhenval'd, *VM*, 113:121–39, relates the history of *Дракон* in performance; T. Zarubina, *Ne*, no. 10:202–08, recalls Sh.

SINIAVSKII.　*Прогулки с Пушкиным* is discussed by L. Batkin, *Ok*, no. 1:164–93, and by several contributors in *VL*, 1990, no. 10:77–153, while M. Rozanov, *ib.*, 154–61, outlines the book's history (the work itself is in *ib.*, 1990, no. 7:155–75, no. 8:81–111, no. 9:146–78). Articles noted include M. Levitt, *CanSP*, 32:46–61 (*Голос из хора* as alternative autobiography); B. Holmgren, *SRev*, 50:965–77 (Terts transfiguring context); V. Linetskii, *Ne*, no. 4:161–74.

SOLZHENITSYN.　Two important new books are P. Palamarchuk, *Александр Солженицын. Путеводитель*, Stolitsa, 96 pp. (comprising the 1989 publications in *Mos* and *Ku*: see *YWMLS*, 51:1018); James F. Pontuso, *Solzhenitsyn's Political Thought*, Charlottesville, Virginia U.P., 1990, xii + 272 pp. A. Gorlov, *Ne*, no. 5:130–44, no. 6:156–93, publishes a memoir of S. in the early 1970s (and written at that time). S.'s ideas for rebuilding Russia are discussed by Korzhavin, L. Batkin, and A. Tsipko, *Ok*, no. 4:146–65, and S. is discussed generally by V. Kondrat'ev, Iskander, Bitov, V. Sokolov, and I. Efremov, *LitO*, no. 2:64–66. V. Bondarenko, pp. 96–105 of Oskotskii, *Взгляд*, is generally positive about S.'s 'return', as is A. Latynina, *ib.*, 106–26. M. Lifshits, *VL*, 1990, no. 7:74–83, discusses *Один день Ивана Денисовича* and the manuscript of *В круге первом*. Other articles noted include S. Ollivier, *ISS*, 12:27–39 (the world of detention in S. and Dostoevskii); A. McConnell, 'Solzhenitsyn's quest for faith', *Soviet Union/Union Soviétique*, 16, 1989:145–61; J. G. Harris, *EPoet*, 16. 1:24–42, and T. V. Telitsyna, *FilN*, no. 5:14–24 (both on *The Gulag Archipelago*); N. Pervukhin, *SEEJ*, 35:489–502 (Chekhov's *Сахалин* and *The Gulag Archipelago*). See too F. Dreizin, pp. 153–98 of his *The Russian Soul and the Jew* (details under PASTERNAK). L. Pol'skii, *Don*, no. 1:168–72, offers a general overview, and L. Kopelev, *VL*, 1990, no. 7:84–96, recalls Marfino.

TOLSTOI, A. N.　Noted is *А. Н. Толстой. Проблемы творчества*, resp. ed. P. A. Borozdina, Voronezh U.P., 1990, 151 pp. Articles include L. S. Pushkareva, pp. 67–78 of Grinfel'd, *Проблемы* (T.'s early prose); E. M. Kiriukhina, pp. 3–33 of Golubkov, *Поэтика* (T.'s work 1917–21).

TRIFONOV.　Two new books of major benefit to T. studies: Nina Kolesnikoff, *Yury Trifonov: A Critical Study*, AAA, 154 pp.; Josephine Woll, *Invented Truth: Soviet Reality and the Literary Imagination of Iurii Trifonov*, Durham, North Carolina, Duke U.P., x + 170 pp. The latter in particular places T. in the forefront of Soviet writers. Articles include S. P. Zalygin, 'Трифонов, Шукшин и мы', *NovM*, no. 11:221–30; K. Kustanovich, *SRev*, 50:978–88 (T. and prose of the last decade); D. Gillespie, *ASEES*, 5:45–58 (*Опрокинутый дом*); G.

S. Levinskaia, *FilN*, no. 2:3–11 ('T.'s concept of 'home'); J. B. Woodward, *WSl*, 36 (n.F. 15):330–46 (*Время и место*). R. Uzunova and V. Kinov, *LitMis*, nos 5–6:156–63, recall a conversation with T.

TSVETAEVA. *Кедр* is published in *NovM*, no. 7:162–76, and there is a text in *RusL*, no. 3:163–67. Her correspondence with A. Bakhrakh, 1923–28, is in *LitO*, no. 8:97–109, no. 9:102–12, no. 10:100–12 (also *NZh*, 180, 1990:214–53; 181, 1990:98–138). There are also letters and materials in *NZh*, 183:211–25; and *NN*, no. 4:45–53. A major collection is *Marina Tsvetaeva: Actes du Ier colloque international (Lausanne 30.VI.–3.VII.1982)*, ed. R. Kemball *et al.*, Bern, Lang, 514 pp., which contains 45 papers, materials, texts, and translations. Other new books include: L. V. Zubova, *Поэзия Марины Цветаевой. Лингвистический аспект*, Ld U.P., 1989, 264 pp.; I. V. Kudrova, *Версты, дали ...: Марина Цветаева, 1922–1939*, SR, 368 pp. (a biography). O. Hasty, *SRev*, 50:836–46, discusses Ts. on Esenin and Maiakovskii; O. G. Revzina, pp. 172–92 of *Поэтика и стилистика, 1988–1990*, resp. ed. V. P. Grigor'ev, Nauka, 238 pp., looks at Ts.'s use of personal names; A. Pavlovskii, *LSh*, no. 3:32–41, is a general study.

TVARDOVSKII. Materials include a letter from 1968 to Nadezhda Mandel'shtam, *Ne*, no. 2:188–89, and a stenogram of the discussion on *Родина и чужбина* in 1947 in the editorial offices of *Литературная газета*, *VL*, nos 9–10:188–226. P. Spivak, *ib.*, no. 4:3–35, discusses T. and *Новый мир*, and A. V. Makedonov, *RusL*, no. 3:175–80, discusses T.'s letters on *По праву памяти*. I. Murav'eva, *K*, 68:287–304, celebrates T.'s eightieth birthday. Literary analysis includes N. B. Abdalova, *RIa*, no. 3:55–59 (key words in *Страна Муравия*); V. V. Il'in, pp. 155–63 of Gura, *Жанр* (T.'s formative environment); K. A. Rublev, pp. 177–78 of Adibaev, *Стиховедение* (*Теркин на том свете*); T. A. Snigireva, pp. 63–73 of Subbotin, *Опыт* (general).

TYNIANOV. There is a book: *Тыняновский сборник (Четвертые Тыняновские чтения, 1988)*, resp. ed. M. O. Chudakova, Riga, Zinatne, 1990, 335 pp. Articles noted include A. Nemzer, *DN*, no. 6:241–52 (*Смерть Вазир-Мухтара*); G. A. Levinton, *RusL*, no. 2:126–30 (the novels).

VAGINOV. There are poems, *Te*, no. 11:171–73. O. Shindina, *ib.*, 161–71, relates the theatrical adaptation of *Козлиная песнь*.

VAMPILOV. There are two short stories, *Zv*, no. 8:180–87 (with essay by G. Nikolaev), and a new book: E. M. Gushanskaia, *Александр Вампилов. Очерк творчества*, Ld, SovP, 1990, 318 pp. See also L. L. Ivanova, pp. 22–33 of Smirnov, *Изучение*.

VASIL'EV. G. Tiurin, *Pro*, no. 3:101–11, gives details of V.'s arrest and execution. Articles noted are L. Chashchina, *VL*, no. 6:16–47, and S. Kuniaev, *Mos*, no. 3:187–97.

VOINOVICH. D. Rancour–Laferrière, *SRev*, 50:36–47 (V.'s picture of Stalin as castrated leader), is, to say the least, challenging. A. Nemzer, pp. 215–36 of Oskotskii, *Взгляд*, looks at both V. and Vladimov in the USSR.

VVEDENSKII. Alongside that of Kharms, there is a major publication of texts and memoirs in *Te*, no. 11:80–122. For criticism and analysis, see G. Roberts, *EPoet*, 16.2:24–49; E. Faryno, *WSlA*, 28:191–258 (*Купрянова и Наташа*). See also Breido under MANDEL'SHTAM and Müller-Scholle under KHARMS.

VYSOTSKII. An interesting publication is V. S. Vysotskii, *O времени, о себе*, Dushanbe, Soiuzteatr, 1990, 86 pp., which comprises poems, interviews, and an autobiographical essay. V.'s diary is in *Ok*, no. 6:194–200, and there are poems, *Av*, no. 7:26–29. New books on V. include L. Georgiev, *Владимир Высоцкий. Встречи, интервью, воспоминания*, Iskusstvo, 266 pp.; L. V. Abramova, *Факты его биографии. Л. Абрамова о В. Высоцком*, Izd-vo tsentra 'Rossiia molodaia', 110 pp.; V. B. Smekhov, *Живой, и только. Воспоминания о Высоцком*, Mezhdunarodnoe sovmestnoe predpriiatie 'Interkontakt', 1990, 108 pp. Smekhov was a fellow-actor at the Taganka; another was V. Zolotukhin, whose diary on V. is in *LitO*, no. 3:75–87, no. 4:80–89. On V.'s work, see A. Kolchakova, *BR*, no. 3:38–47.

ZABOLOTSKII. Nikita Zabolotskii, *Te*, no. 11:153–56, relates Z.'s activities after the completion of *Столбцы* at the end of the 1920s–early 1930s. On *Столбцы* see S. Brudermüller, pp. 42–56 of *Russische Avantgarde 1917–1934* (details under KHARMS). Further criticism includes I. A. Vasil'ev, pp. 131–40 of Ognev, *О жанре*, and pp. 39–51 of Subbotin, *Опыт* (both on Z.'s early work); E. V. Krasil'nikov, pp. 165–72 of *Поэтика и стилистика* (details under TSVETAEVA) (general).

ZAITSEV. There are letters, *Слово*, no. 4:19–23; and *LitU*, no. 5:141–45 (correspondence with Adamovich, 1968–72). For criticism, see A. M. Liubomurov, *RusL*, no. 3:112–21 (*Преподобный Сергий Радонежский*).

ZALYGIN. L. N. Dar'ialova, pp. 81–88 of *Сюжет и фабула в структуре жанра* (details under RUBTSOV), reads *После бури* as a philosophical novel.

ZAMIATIN. E. E. Deviataikin, pp. 39–54 of Volkova, *Советская* (Z.'s pre-1917 prose); see also Shaitanov under PIL'NIAK.

ZINOV'EV. *Зияющие высоты* is published in the USSR (in part), *Ok*, no. 1:30–97, no. 2:23–82, no. 3:59–81; other texts include *Иди на Голгофу*, *Смена*, no. 1:14–58, no. 2:82–124, no. 3:68–135; and *Живи*, *Zv*, no. 10:23–106. M. Kirkwood, pp. 102–14 of *Under Eastern Eyes* (details under GENERAL), examines Z.'s view of the West.

ZOSHCHENKO. *Вспоминая Михаила Зощенко,* comp. Iu. B. Tomashevskii, Ld, KhL, 1990, 512 pp., has contributions by Chukovskii, Fedin, Kaverin, Granin, Nagibin, Admoni, Mariengof and others. Articles include Ia. Vezhbin'ski, *BR*, no. 4:31–41 (Z.'s language and style).

V. UKRAINIAN STUDIES*

By V. Swoboda, *Honorary Research Fellow at the School of Slavonic and East European Studies in the University of London*

GENERAL

S. Bilokin', *SiCh*, no. 11:82–87, surveys the state of Ukrainian bibliography and points out important defects in *Джерела українознавства* (*YWMLS*, 52:1037). Ia. Dashkevych, *Dz*, no. 8:114–19, writes on the fate of the NTSh library. L. Lazechko, *ib.*, no. 10:146–48, surveys the holdings of M. Vozniak's library. V. Iashchun, *'Вибране із славістики'*, *ZNTSh*, 216, 319 pp. V. Skurativs'kyi, *Dni*, no. 2:183–92, is apprehensive about the fate of Ukrainian culture. V. Chabanenko *et al.* survey V. Hnatiuk's work, *Mov*, no. 2:61–68; *SiCh*, no. 5:31–36; *UM*, no. 5:91–93. Ia. Dashkevych *et al.* write on Hrushevs'kyi's life and work, *SiCh*, no. 9:18–24; *Dz*, no. 9:137–40; *UM*, no. 9:74–77; *LiU*, nos 28, 39. H.'s letters, *ZNTSh*, 221, 1990:326–38; *SiCh*, no. 9:25–31; *Vit*, no. 12:174–76. See also *LiU*, no. 22.

LANGUAGE

1. GENERAL. HISTORY OF THE LANGUAGE

S. Bevzenko, **Історія українського мовознавства. Історія вивчення української мови*, *VySH*, 231 pp. M. Zhovtobriukh, *Mov*, no. 5:63–69, writes on Ie. Tymchenko's achievement. B. Mykhailyshyn, *ib.*, no. 1:61–66, surveys I. Svientsits'kyi's contribution to the study of Ukrainian; an article by S. on early Ukrainian is reprinted, *ib.*, 66–69. G. Y. Shevelov, *In and around Kiev*, Heidelberg, Winter, vi + 412 pp.: collected articles. Ia. Isaievych, *ZSl*, 36:40–52, shows the role of printing in the development of literary languages in 16th–17th-c. Ukraine. L. Kots'-Hryhorchuk, *ZNTSh*, 221, 1990:210–36 (medieval inscriptions). V. Skliarenko, *Mov*, no. 5:14–19, traces the history of stress in gerunds. I. Sokol, *ib.*, no. 5:57–62, studies old names of birds. T. Chernysh, *ib.*, no. 6:25–31, reconstructs Old Slavonic relics in agricultural vocabulary. V. Shul'hach, *ib.*, no. 1:57–60, offers etymologies of шкарваток, взяти на крам, лузавий, кайдан ('boat').

---

*The place of publication of books is Kiev unless otherwise indicated.

2. MODERN UKRAINIAN

GENERAL. PHONETICS. MORPHOLOGY. WORD FORMATION. SYNTAX

O. Ponomariv *et al.*, **Сучасна українська мова*, Lybid´, 312 pp. M. Pliushch and N. Hrypas, **Українська мова. Довідник*, RSh, 1990, 225 pp. 'Ukrainian', Campbell, *Compendium*, 1413–18, has some errors (e.g. *i* for *ι* [y]). A. Zahnitko, *Mov*, no. 5:7–14, discusses the fundamentals in the evolution of grammatical categories. Id., **Дієслівні категорії в синтагматиці і парадигматиці*, Donetsk U.P., 1990, 129 pp. D. J. Birnbaum, *HUS*, 14, 1990:268–92, studies the stress of *a-* stem nouns. V. Vynnyts´kyi, *Mov*, no. 6:19–25, examines the stress of suffixed adjectives. I. Borysiuk, **Форми і функції інтонації українського спонтанного мовлення*, ND, 1990, 202 pp. O. Pokyd´ko, *Mov*, no. 1:33–38, studies the intonation of emphatic particles. N. Klymenko, **Як народжується слово*, RSh, 288 pp. Id. and Ie. Karpilovs´ka, *Mov*, no. 4:10–21, write on the computerized study of morphology. O. Bondar, *ib.*, no. 6:51–55, studies the morphological means of expressing 'real time' relationships. V. Horpynych, *UM*, no. 9:38–42, discusses multiple nominative attributes. K. Shul´zhuk, *Mov*, no. 3:49–52, writes on multicomponent compound sentences.

LEXICOGRAPHY. SEMANTICS. PHRASEOLOGY. ORTHOGRAPHY. STYLISTICS. SOCIOLINGUISTICS

N. Danyliuk, *Mov*, no. 5:70–75, writes on lexicography with regard to Kryms´kyi's 1924–33 Ukrainian–Russian dictionary. H. Matsiuk and T. Pan´ko, *ib.*, no. 6:3–11, trace Hrushevs´kyi's views on the language of scholarship. N. Ozerova, **Лексическая и грамматическая семантика существительного*, ND, 1990, 192 pp., deals with Russian and Ukranian. M. Muravitskaia, *VIa*, no. 1:116–24, analyses lexical homonymy. A. Pys´mychenko, *Mov*, no. 6:46–51, compares building terms in Ukrainian and Russian. V. Manakin, *ib.*, no. 5:30–37, compares Ukrainian meterological vocabulary with that of other Slavonic languages. H. Myronova, *ib.*, no. 4:21–30, studies East Slavonic terms relating to windows and their parts. I. Kononenko, *ib.*, no. 5:42–46, writes on the semantics of the adjective. V. Frydrak, *UM*, no. 10:51–55, systematizes adjectives of colour. V. Uzhchenko and L. Avksent´iev, **Українська фразеологія*, Kharkov, Osnova, 1990, 167 pp. V. Kononenko, *Mov*, no. 6:30–36, studies the semantic structure of phraseological units. M. Dems´kyi, *ib.*, no. 2:36–43, writes on phraseological synonyms. *Ураїнський правоп ис*, 3rd edn, ND, 1990, 239 pp.; discussed, *UM*, no. 8:4–9; *LiU*, nos 33, 52; *VSh*, 44:1501–05. V. Nimchuk, *Mov*, 1990, no. 6:3–10; 1991, no. 1:9–18; no. 2:18–24; no. 3:12–21, traces the history of r and the [g]/[h] dichotomy from the 10th c. to the abolition of r in 1933, its post-war restoration attempts, and imperfect reinstatement in the above *правопис*. M. Pylyns'kyi *et al.*, **Взаємодія художнього і публіцистичного стилів української мови*, ND, 1990, 216 pp. Z. Franko, *Mov*, no. 1:3–9, surveys the functioning of Ukrainian in the Soviet period. N. Babych, **Основи культури мовлення*, Lvov, Svit, 1990, 232 pp. O. Tkachenko, *Mov*, no. 2:14–18, discusses the problem of linguistic stability. V. Zhaivoronok, *ib.*, no. 3:22–30, writes on Ukrainian and politics. O. Tykhyi's unpublished 1972 article on the plight of Ukrainian, *SiCh*, no. 4:54–62. Also *VSh*, 44:341–49.

3. DIALECTS. ONOMASTICA. LANGUAGES IN CONTACT

I. Dzendzelivs'kyi, *Mov*, no. 2:24–36, writes on I. Zilyns'kyi's pioneering work in linguogeography, and, *ZNTSh*, 221, 1990:249–61, on the study of dialectal vocabulary. P. R. Magocsi, **Carpatho-Rusyn Studies. An Annotated Bibliography*, I, *1975–1984*, NY, 1989, 141 pp. **Общекарпатский диалектологический атлас*, introd. fasc., Skopje, 1987, 184 pp.; fasc. 1, Chişinaü, Ştiinţa, 1989, 196 pp. N. Varkhol and A. Ivchenko, **Фразеологічний словник лемківських говірок Східної Словаччини*, Bratislava, SlPN, 1990, 159 pp. Iu. Zhluktenko, **Українська мова на лінгвістичній карті Канади*, postscript R. Zorivchak, ND, 1990, 175 pp. D. Buchko, **Походження назв населених пунктів Покуття*, Lvov, Svit, 1990, 143 pp. Ia. Pura, **Походження назв населених пунктів Ровенщини*, Svit, 1990, 143 pp. I. Zheliezniak, *Mov*, no. 6:11–19, traces toponyms deriving from Common Slavonic **(s)val*. V. Tsymbaliuk and Iu. Pasichnyk, *UM*, no. 11:45–51, survey toponyms of the Skvyr area. Iu. Marynovs'kyi, *Mov*, no. 4:62–65, opposes M. Ponomarenko (*YWMLS*, 50:1134) regarding Черкаси. Iu. Saplin, *ib.*, no. 3:42–49, writes on vocabulary interaction in bilingualism. A. Vincenz, *ib.*, no. 5:37–41, discusses Ukrainian-Polish language contacts. Ie. Slups'kyi, *ib.*, no. 4:34–40, traces lexical calques from English in Canadian Ukrainian.

LITERATURE

1. GENERAL. LITERATURES IN CONTACT

*Українська літературна енциклопедія (see *YWMLS*, 51:1028), vol. 2 (Д—К), 1990, 575 pp. S. Kvit, *SiCh*, no. 11:23–28, surveys the study of the history of Ukrainian literature over the last 100 years. M. Tarnawsky, **Ukrainian Literature in English. Books and Pamphlets, 1890–1965. An annotated bibliography*, Edmonton, CIUS, 1988, 127 pp.

M. Syvachenko, *Сторінки історії української літератури і
фольклористики*, ND, 1990, 302 pp. *Хрестоматія української
релігійної літератури*, vol. 2, book 1, *Поезія*, ed. and introd. I.
Kachurovs'kyi, Munich, Naukovyi kongres v tysiacholittia khresh-
chennia Rusi-Ukrainy, 1988, 552 pp. Iu. Boiko, *Вибране*, vol. 4,
Heidelberg, Winter, 1990, 328 pp. O. Bilets'kyi, **Літературно-
критичні статті*, ed. and ann. M. Honcharuk, Dnipro, 1990,
254 pp. V. Shevchuk, **Дорога в тисячу років. Роздуми, есе*, RP, 1990,
411 pp. Id., **Із вершин та низин. Книга цікавих фактів із історії
української літератури*, Dnipro, 1990, 446 pp. S. Iefremov's 1916
article on the 18th–20th-c. suppression of Ukrainian print, *Ky*,
no. 5 : 121–27. T. Borysiuk, *SiCh*, no. 9 : 3–12, publishes Drahomanov's *Про волю віри*. D., 'Малоруський інтернаціоналізм', *Ky*,
no. 8 : 108–15. Also on D., P. Fedenko, **М. Д.*, Dnipro; Ia. Dashkevych *et al.*, *SiCh*, no. 10 : 3–6; 1990, no. 7 : 36–41; *UM*, no. 9 : 77–82;
no. 11 : 52–54; *Mov*, no. 4 : 66–74; *Vit*, no. 9 : 152–56; *Dz*, no. 10 : 137–
45; *Dni*, nos 11–12 : 124–29; *LiU*, no. 38. V. Matviishyn, **Українсько-
французькі літературні зв'язки XIX — початку XX ст.*, Lvov, 1989,
166 pp. A. Kondratiuk, *SiCh*, no. 8 : 71–73, writes on Skovoroda and
the Turkmen poet Makhtumkuli.

2. Early Literature

F. E. Sysyn, *HUS*, 14, 1990 : 593–607, places the Cossack chronicles in
the context of the development of modern Ukrainian culture. A.
Makarov, *SiCh*, no. 7 : 44–54; *Dz*, no. 5 : 130–38, discusses the Ukrain-
ian Baroque. A round table on it, *Dni*, no. 2 : 90–105. M. Trofymuk,
ZNTSh, 221, 1990 : 21–32, traces Martial's influence on 17th–18th-c.
Ukrainian scholastic literature. B. Krysa, *ib.*, 33–46, writes on
Christmas and Easter verse of that period. Also *SiCh*, no. 5 : 71–76;
no. 11 : 8–12.

INDIVIDUAL AUTHORS AND WORKS

MAZEPA. Ia. Slavutych, *Ky*, no. 3 : 97–103 (M.'s poetry).

PRIMARY CHRONICLE. **Повість врем'яних літ*, transl., comm.
and postscript V. Iaremenko, RP, 1990, 558 pp.

SKOVORODA. A. Pashuk, *ZNTSh*, 222 : 181–200, writes on 'the real
man' in S.'s philosophy. M. Skrynnyk, *ib.*, 201–15, sees S. as the
source of Ukrainian Romanticism. N. Pylypiuk, *HUS*, 14, 1990 : 551–
83, studies S.'s theology and poetics. R. Hantula, *ib.*, 343–49
(Song 29).

SLOVO O POLKU IGOREVE. O. Tolochko, *SiCh*, 1990, no. 12 : 63–66,
discusses textual problems.

VYSHENS'KYI. H. Goldblatt, *HUS*, 15 : 7–34, examines V.'s beliefs
on language.

3. The Nineteenth Century

G. G. Grabowicz, *ZNTSh*, 221, 1990:13–20, traces the functions of genre and style in the formation of Ukrainian literature. S. Pavlychko *et al.*, *SiCh*, no. 6:10–29, offer a feminist view of Ukrainian literature; see also I. Dziuba, *ib.*, no. 8:26–33.

INDIVIDUAL AUTHORS

FRANKO. S. Kvit, *SiCh*, no. 1:61–70 (F. and Hrushevs'kyi). M. Shalata, *Dni*, no. 3:141–45, introduces the banned *Пролог*. Ia. Hrytsai, *'... Дух, що тіло рве до бою ...'. Спроба політичного портрета І. Ф.*, Lvov, Kameniar, 1990, 176 pp. O. Serbens'ka, *ZNTSh*, 221, 1990:237–48 (views on language). M. Moroz, *ib.*, 108–22, 265–82 (*Зів'яле листя*). N. Zabuzhko, *UM*, no. 9:21–32 (*Мойсей*). I. Bazhynov, *SiCh*, no. 9:13–17, attributes the 1897 anonymous article on F. in *Вестник Европы* to Drahomanov. I. Denysiuk, *ib.*, 1990, no. 10:56–61; no. 11:13–22, fills in 'blank spots' in the F. study. Also M. Kuchyns'kyi *et al.*, *UM*, no. 5:66–72; *SiCh*, 1990, no. 8:37–42; and SHEVCHENKO below.

KOSTOMAROV. M. K., 'Книги Битія українського народу', introd. V. Ianivs'kyi, *Ky*, no. 10:3–8. 'Чернігівка', introd. B. Hrinchenko, *Dni*, no. 4:4–92.

KOTSIUBYNS'KYI. A letter, *SiCh*, no. 11:54–55. M. Mohylians'kyi's 1941 MS on K., *ib.*, 1990, no. 12:48–62.

KULISH, P. O. Hnidan and N. Os'mak, *UM*, no. 10:22–29, write on K.'s world view. Also *Vit*, nos 4–6.

MARTOVYCH. O. S. Ilnytzkyj, *HUS*, 14, 1990:350–63, discusses the psychologism of M.'s prose.

NECHUI-LEVYTS'KYI. M. Tarnawsky, *HUS*, 14, 1990:608–22, contrasts N.-L.'s populism and realism. N. Zinchenko, *SiCh*, no. 8:42–47 (the intelligentsia in N.-L.'s works).

SHEVCHENKO. D. Krasyts'kyi, *SiCh*, no. 5:85–90 (Sh.'s genealogy). D. Chub, **Живий Шевченко*, 3rd rev. edn, Melbourne, Lastivka, 1987, 152 pp. **Питання текстології. Т. Г. Ш. Збірник наукових праць*, ND, 1990, 199 pp. V. Rusanivs'kyi, *SiCh*, 1990, no. 11:60–64; *Mov*, no. 2:3–7; no. 4:3–9, writes on Sh.'s language. S. Hrytsa, *SiCh*, no. 7:55–59, surveys F. Kolessa's study of poetry, especially that of Sh. M. Kotsiubyns'ka, **Етюди про поетику Шевченка*, RP, 1990, 272 pp. G. G. Grabowicz, *HUS*, 14, 1990:313–42, examines the theme of writing in Sh.'s poetry. Ia. Isaievych, *ZNTSh*, 221, 1990:47–56 (Sh. and history). V. Miiakovs'kyi, *ib.*, 70–92 (Sh. and the Cyril-Methodius Brotherhood). V. Swoboda, *ib.*, 93–107 (Sh. and Belinskii). S. Holunenko, *SiCh*, no. 2:54–58 (the

Перебендя image). N. Chamata, *ib.*, no. 3:49–54 (*Розрита могила*). O. Pavliv, *ib.*, no. 6:67–73; T. Komarynets', *ZNTSh*, 221, 1990:57–69 (*Великий льох*). H. Avrakhov, *SiCh*, no. 9:59–61 (*Мені однаково*). Ia. Rozumnyi, *Su*, no. 3:25–41; *SiCh*, no. 11:57–63 (*Москалева криниця*). O. Fenenko, *UM*, no. 5:62–66 (*Сліпий*). O. Sydorenko and H. Hrytsiuta, *SiCh*, no. 12:68–78 (*Близнецы*). Petliura's early article on Sh. is reprinted, *ib.*, no. 3:40–49; *LiU*, no. 27; and, with one on Franko, *Ky*, no. 2:124–27, 132–40. Also V. Shubravs'kyi *et al.*, *UM*, no. 3:79–85, 70–72; no. 4:79–88; no. 5:57–61; *SiCh*, 1990, no. 8:31–36; no. 9:12–16, 52–55, 62–66; *Vit*, no. 3:203–05; no. 5:142–48; no. 6:178–87; no. 12:157–66, 176–84; *Ky*, no. 1:85–87; *Dni*, no. 3:82–89; no. 7:140–50; *Su*, no. 3:74–84; *VSh*, 44:829–44; *LiU*, nos 10, 11.

STARYTS'KYI. 'Руїна', *Ky*, no. 6:61–111; no. 7:36–106.

UKRAINKA. L. Zelins'ka *et al.*, *UM*, no. 2:18 29 (life and work). S. Iermolenko and L. Stavyts'ka, *Mov*, no. 2:7–14, write on U.'s language. Correspondence, *SiCh*, no. 2:8–14; no. 3:24–27; no. 5:14–20, 37–48. L. Kostenko, *LiU*, no. 39, discusses the nature of U.'s genius. P. Odarchenko and I. Betko, *VSh*, 44:1223–31, 1380–90, 1487–94; *SiCh*, no. 3:28–36, examine the Bible as inspiration in U.'s work. M. Leonova and T. Luk"ianchuk, *UM*, no. 8:76–79 (*Дим*). P. Fylypovych's 1928 article on the Prometheus image is reprinted, *ib.*, no. 9:84–88. O. Slon'ovs'ka, *ib.*, no. 12:26–30 (*Бояриня*'s historical background). O. Stavyts'kyi, *SiCh*, no. 8:59–60, corrects some errors in publications on U. Also *ZNTSh*, 221, 1990:283–307; *Su*, no. 2:29–37; *Vit*, no. 2:181–86; *VSh*, 44:464–69; *LiU*, nos 8, 31.

4. THE FIRST THIRD OF THE TWENTIETH CENTURY

Ia. Rudyk, *SiCh*, no. 6:83–85, decodes several pseudonyms of writers from the Zakhidna Ukraina publishing house. O. Halych, *Vit*, no. 4:164–68 (writers' diaries). F. Pohrebennyk, *SiCh*, no. 10:22–28, surveys the émigré literature of the late 19th and early 20th cs. M. Zhulyns'kyi *et al.*, *LiU*, no. 9; *Dni*, no. 8:107–22 (Ukrainian writers in the RSFSR). **20-і роки. Літературні дискусії, полеміки*, Dnipro, 366 pp. N. Shumylo, *UM*, no. 11:62–68 ('populism'). N. Bieliaieva, *SiCh*, 1990, no. 10:30–35, discusses Symbolism in *Музагет*. M. Il'nyts'kyi, *ZNTSh*, 221, 1990:156–70 (West Ukrainian poets). **Розсипані перли. Поети 'Молодої музи'*, ed., introd. and ann. Id., Dnipro, 709 pp.; also V. Pohrebennyk, *SiCh*, 1990, no. 9:56–61. I. Betko, *UM*, no. 10:64–70, traces biblical motifs in poetry. More on poetry, *ib.*, no. 8:79–81, 85–91. Iu. Kuznetsov, *ib.*, no. 2:30–35 ('psychologism' in prose). L. Senyk, *ZNTSh*, 221, 1990:123–35 (Futurist novel); also under KHVYL'OVYI. O. Sydorenko, *SiCh*, no. 8:61–63, writes on *Зоря* (1906), the first Ukrainian-language literary journal in Russia. N . Zrazhevs'ka and N. Khuzakhmetova, *ib.*, no. 8:34–41; *UM*, no. 3:88–91, trace the evolution of the journal *Критика* (1928–40). Also *Dni*, no. 8:129–32.

INDIVIDUAL AUTHORS

ALCHEVS'KA.   N. Hryshaienko, *UM*, no. 4:89–93; L. Kovalets', *ib.*, no. 11:84–87 (life and work).

ANTONENKO-DAVYDOVYCH.   B. A.-D., **Твори*, 2 vols, Dnipro, 746, 623 pp. Id., **Як ми говоримо*, augmented edn, Lybid', 252 pp. Letters to V. Briuhhen, *SiCh*, 1990, no. 10:36. P. Kravchuk reminisces, *LiU*, no. 29.

ANTONYCH.   T. Kul'chyns'ka and N. Graider, **Б. І. А. Покажчик друкованих матеріалів та автографів*, Lvov, Naukova biblioteka im. Stefanyka, 1989, 140 pp. M. Il'nyts'kyi, **Б. І. А.*, RP (life and work).

BAHRIANYI.   I. B., **Тигролови*, Molod', 261 pp.; also *Dni*, no. 1:4–51. 'Гуляй-Поле', *ib.*, no. 6:81–91. 'Огненне коло', *Ky*, no. 3:3–37, 95–96; no. 4:6–43. M. Zhulyns'kyi *et al.*, *SiCh*, no. 10:7–17; *Dz*, no. 5:94–95; *LiU*, no. 41 (life and work).

BAZHAN.   Letters, *LiU*, no. 33. G. Mihaychuk, *HUS*, 14, 1990:461–81, re-evaluates *Сліпці*. Also *Vit*, no. 12:148–51.

BEN.   V. Polishchuk writes on B. and the Neoclassicists, *SiCh*, 1990, no. 10:52–55.

CHAIKOVS'KYI.   I. Prodan *et al.*, *UM*, no. 6:58–62; *LiU*, no. 51; *SiCh*, 1990, no. 11:82–89 (life and work).

CHERKASENKO.   O. Myshanych, *SiCh*, no. 7:19–29; N. Kopylenko, *UM*, no. 10:85–87 (life and work).

CHUMAK.   V. Ch., **Червоний заспів*, Dnipro, 363 pp. S. Kryzhanivs'kyi, *SiCh*, no. 1:18–23 (life and work).

DNIPROVS'KYI.   N. Kuziakina, *SiCh*, no. 7:35–38, publishes D.'s letters to Lev Tolstoi.

DOSVITNII.   V. Aheieva, *SiCh*, no. 11:13–16; T. Lysenko, *UM*, no. 11:88–92 (prose). See OLES' below.

DRAI-KHMARA.   O. Asher, *SiCh*, no. 9:45–48 (language).

FYLYPOVYCH.   V. Kapusta *et al.*, *SiCh*, no. 9:32–35; *UM*, no. 9:83–88; *Vit*, no. 2:172–80 (life and work).

HADZINS'KYI.   T. Lysenko, *SiCh*, no. 3:55–62 (life and work).

HOLOVKO.   Unpublished prologue to *Мати*, *Ky*, no. 1:61–70.

IVCHENKO.   Documents on imprisonment in the 'SVU' affair, *SiCh*, 1990, no. 8:52–54. Diary, *Su*, no. 4:93–101.

KHVYL'OVYI.   M. Kh., **Твори*, ann. P. Maidanchenko, 2 vols, Dnipro, 1990, 650, 925 pp., is fuller than the New York edition (*YWMLS*, 50:1141). O. S. Ilnytzkyj, *ZNTSh*, 221, 1990:135–55 (Kh.

and the Futurists). R. Kharchuk, *SiCh*, no. 6:74–80 (M. Shapoval and Kh.). V. Aheieva, *ib.*, 1990, no. 10:3–9 ('superfluous people'). Also *Vit*, no. 7:152–57.

KRYMS'KYI. Correspondence, *SiCh*, no. 1:8–13. Folklore notes, *UM*, no. 7:26–33; no. 9:50–53; no. 10:44–46; no. 11:38–45; no. 12:75–76. V. Rybalkin, *Mov*, no. 2:68–74 (K. as an Arabist).

KULISH. M. N. Kuziakina, *Ky*, no. 11:130–35, publishes a KGB file on K.'s beliefs. L. Zales'ka-Onyshkevych, *SiCh*, no. 9:48–53 (the role of Easter in *Патетична соната*).

LEPKYI. Letters to Shchurat, *ZNTSh*, 221, 1990:339–48.

LYPA. L. Cherevatenko, *Dni*, no. 4:147–58 (poetry).

MALANIUK. 'Нариси з історії нашої культури', *Dni*, no. 1:146–77. 'Книга спостережень', *Ky*, no. 7:107–19. Article on Gogol', *SiCh*, no. 8:3–15. Letters, *ib.*, 16–20. Also Iu. Lavrinenko *et al.*, *UM*, no. 1:59–66; *ib.*, no. 10:56–64; *Dz*, no. 7:138–41.

OLES'. N. Surovtsova, reminiscences of O., Kjotkevych and Dosvitnii, *SiCh*, 1990, no. 7:88–94; no. 9:76–82.

PANCH. V. Donchyk, *SiCh*, no. 7:59–66, introduces the banned *Зелена трясовина*. Diary, *Vit*, no. 8:166–80; *LiU*, no. 27.

PIDMOHYL'NYI. V. Mel'nyk, *Vit*, no. 1:150–58, publishes archive data on P.'s death. Letters, *SiCh*, no. 2:20–27; *LiU*, no. 5. 'З життя будинку N° 29', *Dni*, no. 2:176–82. M. Tarnavs'kyi *et al.*, *SiCh*, no. 5:56–70; *ib.*, 1990, no. 11:23–33 (*Місто*). Also V. Shevchuk, *UM*, no. 2:70–78.

PLUZHNYK. M. Taiha, *Dni*, no. 1:178–80 (P.'s death in Solovki). Also *Vit*, no. 8:152–60 (prose and drama).

RYL'S'KYI. 1931 prison depositions from the KGB archives, *Ky*, no. 2:79–101. Also *Vit*, no. 3:199–201.

SENCHENKO. M. Mar"ianivs'kyi, *UM*, no. 2:85–89; M. Hnatiuk, *LiU*, no. 8 (life and work).

SLISARENKO. V. Aheieva, *SiCh*, no. 3:36–39 (life). Also M. Naienko *et al.*, *UM*, no. 3:85–88; *LiU*, no. 22.

SOSIURA. M. Tkachuk, *Vit*, no. 9:157–62 (*Мазепа*).

STARYTS'KA-CHERNIAKHIVS'KA. Letters to Iavornyts'kyi, *SiCh*, no. 7:30–34; to Hrushevs'kyi, *Vit*, no. 10:166–76.

STEFANYK. Letters to Sheptyts'kyi, *ZNTSh*, 221, 1990:308–25; to V. Kostashchuk, *LiU*, no. 21. Also M. Stepanenko *et al.*, *VSh*, 44:1079–92, 1232–38; *SiCh*, no. 5:26–31; *UM*, no. 5:89–91; *Vit*, no. 5:2–3, 149–66.

SVIDZYNS'KYI. Reminiscences, *SiCh*, 1990, no. 10:46–52.

TYCHYNA. *3 архіву П. Г. Т.*, ND, 1990, 601 pp. Letters, *SiCh*, 1990, no. 9:42–49; *LiU*, no. 4. D. Stepovyk and V. Kostenko reminisce, *Su*, no. 2:18–28; *UM*, no. 1:53–59. S. Tel'niuk, *Молодий я, молодий ...'. Поетичний світ П. Т. (1906–1925)*, Dnipro, 1990,

424 pp. Id. *Dni*, no. 1:181–97, refutes 'T.'s conformism' thesis. I. Mykhailyn, *SiCh*, no. 9:80–85, reinterprets *Відповідь землякам* (1922). Also *Su*, no. 2:46–60; *SiCh*, no. 1:14–18; *UM*, no. 9:89–93.

VORONYI, MYKOLA. A. Tkachenko, *SiCh*, no. 12:8–12 (life and work). Also *UM*, no. 3:43–52; *LiU*, nos 11, 50.

VYNNYCHENKO. Letters, *SiCh*, no. 8:21–25; *ib.*, 1990, no. 8:22–30. 'Між двох сил', *Vit*, no. 2:20–63. 'Відродження нації', parts 2–3, *Dni*, nos 1–8. I. Hryshyn-Hryshchuk, *SiCh*, no. 1:83–86; no. 2:59–70 (reminiscences). O. Bilyi, *ib.*, no. 6:39–48 (*Записки кирпатого Мефістофеля*). O. Koval'chuk, *UM*, no. 1:30–36 (early stories). Iu. Barabash, *Ky*, no. 8:120–26 (V. and Lenin). Also H. Kostiuk *et al.*, *SiCh*, 1990, no. 7:12–26; *ib.*, 1991, no. 11:55–56; *UM*, no. 2:62–68.

VYSHNIA. I. Zub, *О. В. Риси творчої індивідуальності*, ND, 169 pp. N. Surovtsova, *SiCh*, no. 8:74–76; S. Mostepanov, *ib.*, 1990, no. 11:92–93 (reminiscences).

ZEROV. M. Zubryts'ka, *SiCh*, no. 9:54–58, writes on the problem of dialogue with the reader. Also *UM*, no. 12:64–68; *SiCh*, 1990, no. 10:89–91.

5. The Rest of the Twentieth Century

I. Koshelivets', **Літературний процес дещо з віддалі*, Paris, NTSh. S. Hrechaniuk, **На тлі XX століття. Літературно-критичні нариси*, RP, 1990, 311 pp. P. Serdiuk, **Невичерпність пізнання. Літературно-критичні статті*, RP, 1989, 235 pp. P. Movchan, **Ключ розуміння. Есе, літературно-критичні статті*, RP, 1990, 357 pp. O. Semashko, *SiCh*, no. 3:68–74, offers a sociological profile of Ukrainian writers. Iu. Tsekov, *ib.*, no. 10:79–86, writes on Ukrainian literature in market conditions. V. Dibrova, *ib.*, no. 3:15–23, discusses Ukrainian literature and the problem of preserving national identity under totalitarianism; also *Vit*, no. 4:172–76; *Ky*, no. 4:112–20; *Dni*, no. 9:162–72; no. 10:163–70; nos 11–12:197–204; *LiU*, no. 29:6. P. Maidachenko, *SiCh*, 1990, no. 8:43–48, chronicles the 'rehabilitation' of writers. R. Kupchyns'kyi's reminiscences of the September 1939 Soviet Ukrainian writers' visit to Lvov, *Dz*, no. 10:133–36. Iu. Bacha, **За і проти. Про умови розвитку української літератури в Чехо-Словаччині після 1945 р.*, Bratislava, SlPN, 1990, 149 pp. M. Roman, *SiCh*, 1990, no. 8:16–21, surveys Ukrainian literature in Czecho-Slovakia. M. Osadchyi, *VSh*, 44:1362–72 (literature of resistance). V. Donchyk and L. Drazhevs'ka, *SiCh*, no. 10:19–22, 28–34, write on the literature of the diaspora; also *Vit*, no. 6:2–29. T. Salyha, **Продовження*, Lvov, Kameniar, 252 pp., is on poetry. E. Solovei, **Поезія пізнання. Філософська лірика в сучасній літературі*, Dnipro, 271 pp. I. Fizer *et al.*, *SiCh*, no. 9:37–44, examine contemporary poetry; *ib.*, 1990, no. 8:78–86; *LiU*, no. 34; *Vit*, no. 7:21–22; *Dni*, no. 9:175–79. H. Hordasevych, *Силуети поетес. Літературні портрети*, RP, 1989, 246 pp. O. Chepurko, *UM*, no. 4:71–79, surveys the theme of collectivization in the prose of the 1970s–1980s, while Ia. Slavutych, *SiCh*, no. 7:10–18, does this regarding the 1933 famine in Ukrainian literature in the West. S. Andrusiv, *ib.*, no. 2:48–53, writes on the historical novel. L. Masenko and O. Koval′chuk, *Mov*, no. 1:26–33; *SiCh*, 1990, no. 7:42–47, discuss химерний роман. N. Bilotser-kivets′, *ib.*, no. 1:42–52, writes on the Neoavantgarde of 1989. M. Pavlyshyn and M. Tkachenko, *ib.*, no. 4:27–40, examine the Chor-nobyl′ theme. T. Sverbilova and V. Zhenzhera, *ib.*, no. 5:49–55; no. 10:92–95, survey recent drama. B. Minchyn, *ib.*, no. 12:38–40, writes on satire in Бібліотека Перця. H. Syvokin′, *Від аналізу до прогнозу. Літературно-художній пошук і позиція критика*, Dnipro, 1990, 446 pp. Id., *SiCh*, no. 10:69–71, discusses his work. M. Slaboshpyts′kyi, *UM*, no. 8:93; *LiU*, no. 34, writes on H. S. Ia. Pelens′kyi and M. Zhulyns′kyi, *SiCh*, no. 12:43 48; *LiU*, no. 31, discuss I. Dziuba's work; see also I. D., *SiCh*, 1990, no. 8:76–77. Also on criticism, N. Cherchenko, *Vit*, no. 12:152–56; M. Kotsiubyns′ka, *SiCh*, no. 9:75–79.

INDIVIDUAL AUTHORS

BARKA. D. Stepovyk, *LiU*, no. 32 (life and work).

HONCHAR. M. Zhulyns′kyi, *UM*, no. 11:55–61; no. 12:53–59, views H.'s work as his 'destiny'. Also *Su*, no. 4:22–39; *Vit*, no. 12:145–48; *LiU*, no. 10.

HORDYNS′KYI, S. H., *І переливи барв, і динамічність ліній*, ed. and introd. V. Luchuk, Lvov, Kameniar, 265 pp. I. Lozyns′kyi reminisces, *Dz*, no. 7:144–47.

KHARCHUK. Unpublished stories, *Ky*, no. 1:9–18. H. Syvokin′ *et al.* reminisce, *UM*, no. 9:59–69; *Dz*, no. 9:141–44.

KLEN. Iu. Kovaliv, *SiCh*, no. 4:41–54, writes on K.'s life and work and introduces a selection of his poetry and a part of Думки на дозвіллі. Also *Dni*, nos 11–12:101–23; *LiU*, no. 41.

KOSTENKO. M. Naidan *et al.*, *CanSP*, 32:119–76 (poetry).

KRASIVS′KYI. Life, poetry, *VSh*, 44:1465–66, 1481–86.

KUNDZICH. V. Polishchuk, *SiCh*, no. 11:48–54, writes on K.'s banned works.

OREST. S. Pavlychko, *SiCh*, no. 11:29–36, writes on O.'s life and work and introduces a selection of his poetry. Also *LiU*, no. 23.

PALII. V. Kyryliuk, *LiU*, no. 35 (life and work).

PAVLYCHKO.   N. Hryshaienko, *UM*, no. 1:69–73; M. Tkachuk, *Dz*, no. 9:145–47 (poetry).

RUDENKO.   M. R., 'Орлова балка', *Vit*, no. 1:64–151. M. Kudriavtsev, *SiCh*, no. 10:64–68 (*На дні морському*).

SAMCHUK.   U. S., 'Волинь', *Dni*, nos 6–9. S. Pinchuk, *LiU*, no. 3 (life and work).

SAPELIAK.   O. Bilyk, *SiCh*, no. 5:14–19 (*Житіє*).

SNIEHIR'OV.   Diary and poems, *Ky*, no. 1:22–41.

STUS.   Camp notes, *Dni*, no. 9:72–80. Ie. Sverstiuk, *Ky*, no. 10:121–23, introduces the transcript of S.'s 1971 talk on M. Vorobiov's poetry. M. Kotsiubyns'ka, *SiCh*, no. 5:3–13, introduces S.'s 1970–71 article on Svidzins'kyi, returned from KGB files in December 1990, and, *ib.*, no. 11:37–47, L. Pliushch's article on S.'s poetry. Prosecution files, *Vit*, no. 8:141–81. H. Harmash, *SiCh*, no. 5:20–25 (poetry). Also *ib.*, 1990, no. 10:74; *Dz*, no. 7:131–37; *Dni*, no. 6:177–79; *LiU*, no. 39.

SVITLYCHNYI.   I. S., *Серце для куль і рим: Поезії, поетичні переклади, літературно-критичні статті*, introd. I. Dziuba, RP, 1990, 581 pp. Article on Kalynets', *SiCh*, 1990, no. 7:27–35. See also *Vit*, no. 1:200–08.

SYMONENKO.   S. Tel'niuk reminisces, *SiCh*, no. 1:38–41.

TARNAVS'KA.   R. Zorivchak, *Dz*, no. 5:12–16 (poetry).

TELIHA.   Iu. Kovaliv, *SiCh*, no. 6:30–38, introduces T.'s article on feminism in Ukrainian literature. Another three articles, *Dni*, no. 3:148–61. Also *LiU*, no. 34.

TIUTIUNNYK, HRYHIR.   Letters, *SiCh*, no. 12:12–23. M. Slaboshpyts'kyi *et al.* reminisce, *UM*, no. 12:3–8; *Ky*, no. 11:125–29; *LiU*, no. 49. I. Semenchuk, *SiCh*, no. 12:24–29 (life and work). T. Avrakhov, *ib.*, no. 3:62–67 (*Поминали Маркіяна*).

VI. BELORUSSIAN STUDIES*

By JAMES DINGLEY, *School of Slavonic and East European Studies,*
University of London

LANGUAGE

1. HISTORY OF THE LANGUAGE

Этымалагічны слоўнік беларускай мовы, 7, NT, 315 pp., covers the
letters М–Н. Ia. Stankevich's pioneering article on Belorussian
Muslims and Belorussian literature in Arabic script, originally
published Vilnia 1933, has been reprinted as a brochure, Belaruskae
kooperatsyina-vydavetskae tavarystva, 33 pp. For a study of adjectival endings in the reports written by F. Kmita in the 16th c. see M.
Krutalevich, *BML*, no. 2 : 61–64. L. Vyhonnaia, *ib.*, nos 7–8 : 63–66,
writes on the history of the words збожжа, дабро, жыта.

2. MODERN BELORUSSIAN

V. Lastouski, Падручны расійска-крыўскі (беларускі) слоўнік, NT,
832 pp., is a facsimile reprint of the Kaunas 1924 edition. See also
below under LITERATURE. 2. INDIVIDUAL AUTHORS. V. Starychonak, Слоўнік амонімаў беларускай мовы, VSh, 255 pp. N. Haurosh, Слоўнік эпітэтаў беларускай мовы, NA, 175 pp. I. Mametau has
a 1100-word list of Belorussian and Crimean Tatar in *Bairam*, the
quarterly journal of the Zhurtavanne tatarau-musul'man na Belarusi
(al'–Kitab), nos 2–3 : 71–74. A. Kalashnikava, *VANB*, no. 4 : 110–17,
writes on the principles behind the compilation of phraseological
dictionaries. A facsimile reprint of the fifth edition of B. Tarashkevich's Беларуская граматыка для школ (Vilnia 1929) has appeared,
NA, 132 + iv pp. On the 100th anniversary of T.'s birth
see T. Novikava, *BML*, no. 12 : 61–66. See also below under
LITERATURE. 2. INDIVIDUAL AUTHORS.

L. Vyhonnaia, Ад гук да літары, NA, 78 pp., is an elementary
book on the relationship between spoken and written forms of
Belorussian. On language 'culture', Пытанні культуры пісьмовай
мовы, ed. A. Padluzhny, NA, 175 pp.; see also A. Kaurus, *Po*,
no. 9 : 232–38. A. Klyshka continues his Belorussian language course
in *Mal*, no. 1 : 151–57; no. 2 : 150–54; no. 3 : 153–57; no. 4 : 144–48;
no. 5 : 152–56; no. 6 : 155–57; no. 10 : 155–59; no. 11 : 156–59.

---

*The place of publication of books is Minsk unless otherwise indicated.

Матчына слова, comp. U. Paulau, MLit, 335 pp., is an anthology of poetry and prose about the Belorussian language. N . Mordas, *BML*, nos 7–8 : 55–58, writes on the Belorussian words for precious stones; U. Sodal', *ib*., 98–100, on the preposition 'з'.

H. Bieder on the first and second rebirth of Belorussian language and culture, pp. 405–51 of *Georg Mayer zum 60. Geburtstag*, ed. U. Bieber and A. Woldan, Munich, Sagner. V. Picheta's important article of 1923, *Белорусский язык как фактор национально-культурный*, has been reprinted as a separate publication, NT, 31 pp. P. Buzuk's 1926 paper on the position of Belorussian among the other Slavonic languages is reproduced in *BML*, nos 7–8 : 83–89. A. Sprynchan, *Mal*, no. 2 : 125–29, on the policy of Belorussification in the 1920s. U. Konan has a characteristically sharp article on the politics of Russification in the linguistic and cultural spheres in *Po*, no. 8 : 229–41; R. Shkraba, *ib*., no. 7 : 198–213, writes on the same subject. T. Mikulich has an article on bilingualism as a national fact of life in *VANB*, no. 1 : 85–90, and, *ib*., no. 4 : 91–96, on ethnolinguistic processes and national self-awareness among the Belorussians. V. Viachorka, *Sp*, no. 4 : 2–10, deals with the history of Belorussian orthography. On the reform of the orthography: P. Stsiatsko, *BML*, no. 1 : 7–11; A. Padluzhny, *ib*., no. 3 : 3–6; no. 4 : 6–9.

To commemorate the 130th anniversary of the birth of Ia. Karski: *Шануючы спадчыну Я. Карскага . . . Другія навуковыя чытанні*, ed. Z. Danil'chyk and M. Kaniushkevich, Hrodna, Hrodzenski dziarzhauny universitet imia Ianki Kupaly, 101 pp., and a number of brief articles in *BML*, no. 1 : 12–20.

CONTRASTIVE STUDIES (BELORUSSIAN-RUSSIAN). Z. San'ko, *Малы руска-беларускі слоўнік прыказак, прымавак і фразем*, NT, 218 pp., is an excellent contrastive phraseological dictionary demonstrating the lexical wealth of Belorussian. Very similar is I. Lepeshau, *З народнай фразеалогіі. Дыферэнцыяльны слоўнік*, VSh, 110 pp. A. Mikhnevich, *Русско-белорусский разговорник*, VSh, 335 pp., has a useful survey of contrastive points and a reader. Mikhnevich and A. Hirutski, *Вазьмі маё слова*, NT, 1990, 88 pp., examine the mutual lexical influence of Belorussian and Russian. V. Krachek, *VBDU*, no. 1 : 21–25, contrasts syllable structure in the two languages. Machine-building terminology in Belorussian and Russian is the subject of an article by V. Zakharava, *VANB*, no. 4 : 106–10. I. Ratnikava, *BML*, no. 12 : 70–72, writes on certain controversial aspects of patronymic formation in Belorussian on the basis of comparison with Russian. The bibliography of Belorussian-Russian linguistic contacts by I. Germanovich and P. Shuba continues in *RIaMS*, 11 : 151–57.

3. Dialects. Onomastics

A wordlist of the Stoubtsy dialect, compiled by Ia. Kamarouski and E. Miatsel'skaia, appears in *Po*, no. 11:226–35. M. Danilovich, *VANB*, no. 1:115–20, writes on collocations involving personal names in the dialects of the Hrodna region. P. Stiatsko has an article on the declension of surnames in *Po*, no. 6:237–44. Exotic views on the possible Komi origins of some Belorussian surnames are expounded by I. Laskou, *ib.*, no. 8:204–28. V. Shur on proper names, *BML*, nos 7–8:60–63. H. Mezenka, *VANB*, no. 2:119–23, writes on urban toponyms, and, *Sp*, no. 1:56–57, on historical toponyms. H. Kantsavaia, *VANB*, no. 1:110–15, on tautological constructions in Belorussian oral epic poetry.

LITERATURE

1. General

Прадмовы і пасляслоўі паслядоўнікаў Францыска Скарыны, ed. A. Mal'dzis, NT, 309 pp., brings together a valuable collection of literary texts covering the period 1562–1641. For the background to the early history of Belorussian literature, see *Памятники философской мысли Белоруссии XVII — первой половины XVIII в.*, comp. S. Podokshin, NT, 391 pp. V. Iatsuk and V. Krautsova, *BLit*, 18:3–10, deal with the relations between philosophy and literature from the mid-14th to the beginning of the 16th cs. A. Kalubovich's work on the destruction of early Belorussian literature appears in Russian translation in *Ne*, no. 7:133–51.

Of particular importance for the study of Belorussian writing in the early years of this century is the facsimile reprint of the first Belorussian newspaper, *Наша Доля*, NT. A. Loika, *Po*, no. 1:215–40, is an important article on the periodization of Belorussian literature. A. Bialiatski, *Літаратура і нацыя*, Art Geyser, 103 pp., examines Belorussian literature at the beginning of the 20th c. from the point of view of today. B. Sachanka's articles on Belorussian émigré literature have been brought together and extended in *Беларуская эміграцыя*, 2nd edn, Holas Radzimy, 111 pp.

T. Hramadchanka, *Перад праўдай высокай і вечнай*, NT, 144 pp., deals with modern Belorussian prose writing. P. Dziubaila, *Po*, no. 9:192–209, is an article on the same subject. On prose by young writers: U. Damashevich, *Mal*, no. 2:130–32. On modern poetry: U. Hnilamiodau, *Po*, no. 2:220–49; no. 3:227–47; no. 4:225–41; and poetry by young writers: A. Bel'ski, *BML*, no. 2:50–60; no. 3:42–53; no. 4:60–68; Id., *BLit*, 18:10–21, on the countryside in Belorussian poetry from Chachot to Bahushevich; V. Makarevich, *Mal*, no. 2:133–35. Modern drama is the subject of P. Vasiuchenka, *Драматургія і час*, NT, 144 pp. U. Niafiod, *Po*, no. 8:172–85, has an article on I. Buinitski and the origins of Belorussian theatre. Historical themes in Belorussian drama form the subject of an article by H. Niafahina, *BML*, no. 6:50–56. On the history of the Belaruski Teatr im. Ia. Kupaly, see V. Nikifarovich, *Po*, no. 9:174–91. V. Kavalenka, *Po*, no. 7:207–13, marks the 60th anniversary of the Institute of Literature of the Belorussian Academy of Sciences. On Belorussian–Polish literary relations in the first half of the 19th c., U. Markhel', *Прадвесце*, NT, 112 pp.

2. Individual Authors

ABUKHOVICH, A. (1840–98). *Творы*, MLit, 61 pp., comp., pref. and comm. R. Rodchanka.

ADAMCHYK, V. N. Suddzeva on *І скажа той, хто народзіцца*, *BLit*, 18:134–43.

ALIAKHNOVICH, F. (1883–1944). *У капцюрох ГПУ*, *Po*, no. 1:149–214.

AROL, M. (1890–1917). *Творы*, MLit, 182 pp., ed. and comm. Ia. Salamevich; this is the first major published collection of works by A.

ARSENNEVA, N. Poems and *3 майго жыццяпісу*, with an introduction by B. Sachanka, *Mal*, no. 4:149–59.

BAHDANOVICH, M. (1891–1917). The 100th anniversary of B.'s birth has inevitably been marked by a spate of publishing activity. *Зорка Венера*, MLit, 460 pp., is a new anthology of his work with an introduction by A. Klyshka. New biographical studies include H. Kakhanouski, *А сэрца ўсё імкне да бацькаўскага краю*, MLit, 77 pp. See also Id., *Po*, no. 8:186–203; no. 9:155–73. Other articles noted: I. Bahdanovich, *Mal*, no. 11:137–45; A. Barakhovich, *BML*, no. 9:70–79; S. Belaia on B. in Iaroslavl', *Polatsak*, no. 3:36–42; no. 4:44–48; T. Chaban on *Вянок*, *Po*, no. 12:193–212; V. Kachatkova, *BML*, nos 7–8:80–82; T. Karotkaia, *ib.*, no. 11:68–71; A. Klyshka, *Po*, no. 6:226–36; U. Konan, *ib.*, no. 11:236–47 and *Ne*, no. 12:159–65; V. Lastouski, *BML*, nos 7–8:121–25 (notes by V. Mikuta); Ia. Liosik, *Po*, no. 12:177–92 (article of 1923, notes by I. Bahdanovich); A. Maiseichyk, *BLit*, 18:49–57, on B. and the Belorussian folktale epic; H. Malazhai, *BML*, no. 4:50–53; L. Mazanik, *VANB*, no. 4:106–10, on textological issues; V. Mikuta, *BML*, nos 7–8:116–20; M. Mushynski, *Po*, no. 10:235–42; U. Rahoisha, *BD*, no. 1:2–7; U. Sodal', *BML*, no. 10:66–69; no. 11:72–76; *Po*, no. 10:226–34; L. Voitsikava (Zos'ka Veras), *Mal*, no. 12:7–12; V. Zuionak, *Po*, no. 6:223–25. Much of *BML*, no. 12 is given over to short articles on B.

BAHUSHEVICH, F. (1840–1900). U. Sodal', *BML*, no. 9:66–69 and *Mal*, no. 10:136–39.

BUILO, K. H. Prybytka, *BML*, no. 10:72–74.

CHORNY, K. (1900–44). S. Svirydau, *Po*, no. 7:197–206; I. Kivel', *BML*, no. 12:67–69, on *Лявон Бушмар*.

CHYHRYNAU, I. A. Martsinovich, *BML*, no. 4:53–59; no. 5:58–64; no. 9:59–62.

CHYKVIN, IA. M. Siadniou, *Polatsak*, no. 3:43–45.

DRAZDOVICH, IA. (1888–1954). The diaries of this artist and sculptor have much of interest for a study of Belorussian literature in the 20th c.: *Mal*, no. 5:117–28; no. 6:101–07; no. 10:113–30; no. 11:101–12.

DUBOUKA, U. (1900–76). H. Kharoshka, *BLit*, 18:69–78, on D.'s dramatic poems.

DUNIN-MARTSINKEVITCH, V. (1807–84). Ia. Ianushkevich, *Беларускі дудар*, MLit, 143 pp., deals with problems of Slavonic tradition and influences in D.-M.'s work. V. Atrakhovich, *BLit*, 18:43–49, on autobiographical elements in D.-M.'s work. I. Bykhavets, *BML*, no. 9:53–59.

DVARCHANIN, I. (1895–1937). See below under SKARYNA.

HARETSKI, M. (1893–1939). E. Karnilovich, *Mal*, no. 2:120–24.

HARUN, A. (1887–1920). *Сэрцам пачуты звон*, MLit, 359 pp., comp., introd., and comm. U. Kazbiaruk, contains all works by H. discovered so far — poetry, prose, drama, journalism. H.'s journalistic writings are also to be found in *Sp*, no. 1:25–32; no. 2:23–28. Iu. Harbinski, *BML*, no. 1:46–53; no. 11:43–55 (with bibliography).

HAURUSIOU, S. V. Makarevich, *Po*, no. 5:229–40.

IADVIHIN SH. (1869–1922). N. Niamkovich, *BML*, nos 7–8:96–98.

KALIUHA, L. (1909–37). Ia. Letska, *Po*, no. 9:210–31.

KARATKEVICH, U. (1930–84). A. Rusetski, *Уладзімір Каратксовіч: праз гісторыю ў сучаснасць*, MLit, 287 pp. From *BLit*, 18: E. Sadaunichy and M. Malchanava on K.'s plays, 101–09; V. Shynkarenka on folklore elements in K., 109–17; L. Prashkovich on the image of the writer and time in K.'s posthumously published works, 117–25.

KARYTSKI, M. (1714–81?). Ia. Paretski, *Міхаіл Карыцкі*, Universitetskae, 142 pp.

KAZ'KO, V. See below under MELEZH.

KOLAS, IA. (1882–1956). V. Zhurauliou, *Якуб Колас і паэтыка беларускага рамана*, NT, 208 pp. M. Zhyhotski, *Po*, no. 7:187–96, on the factual background to *Дрыгва*. T. Salauiova on K. and music, *BML*, no. 3:57–61; T. Shamiakina, *ib.*, no. 2:42–50.

KRAPIVA, K. (1896–1991). P. Navumenka, *BML*, no. 3:36–41; Id., *BLit*, 18:78–84, on *Мядзведзіны*.

KUDRAVETS, A. See below under MELEZH.

KULAKOUSKI, A. (1913–86). A. Martsinovich, *Po*, no. 10:211–26, on problems with the publication of *Дабрасельцы*.

KUPALA, IA. (1882–1942). I. Kurbeka has a biographical note on K.'s wife, U. Lutsevich, in *BD*, no. 1:80–83.

LASTOUSKI, V. (1883–1938). Impressions of his visit to the Belorussian Soviet Socialist Republic in 1926 and his story *Лабірынты*, *Mal*, no. 1:86–127, with an introduction by Ia. Letska. See also above under LANGUAGE. 2. MODERN BELORUSSIAN and BAHDANOVICH.

LIOSIK, IA. (1884–1940). A selection of short stories introduced by A. Zhynkin, *Sp*, no. 2:44–63.

LUTSKEVICH, A. (1884–1946). Diary, notes by A. Sidarevich, *Po*, no. 4:205–24; no. 5:168–92.

MAKAIONAK, A. V. Iatsukha, *BLit*, 18:127–34, on M.'s one-act plays.

MALIAUKA, M. K. Kameisha, *Mal*, no. 12:148–54.

MELEZH, I. (1921–76). Previously unpublished diary excerpts, *Po*, no. 2:209–24; A. Zhuk, *ib.*, 225–28. Iu. Nestserau, *BLit*, 18:93–101, on *Палеская хроніка* in the context of Soviet prose about collectivization. V. Niachai, *BML*, no. 10:49–54, on M. and the younger writers A. Kudravets (*Сачыненне на вольную тэму*) and V. Kaz'ko (*Неруш*). Brief articles to celebrate the 70th anniversary of his birth, *Mal*, no. 2: 136–49.

MURASHKA, R. (1902–44). Z. Sudnik, *BLit*, 18:62–69.

PALTARAN, V. S. Kukharau, *Po*, no. 11:204–11.

PAZ'NIAK, IA. (1897–1939). Journalistic writings with an introduction by I. Bahdanovich, *Sp*, no. 6:47–53.

PUSHCHA, IA. (1902–64). M. Mishchanchuk, *BML*, no. 2:25–32.

SALAHUB, A. (1906–41?). P. Prudnikau, *Sp*, no. 6:54–56.

SALAVEI, A. (1922–78). *На хуткіх крыльлях вольнага Пегаса*, *Sp*, no. 5:24–32.

SERBANTOVICH, A. (1941–70). K. Kameisha, *Po*, no. 5:241–45.

SERHIEVICH, IU. (1910–76). Verses from the archive in *Po*, no. 7:145–48.

SHAMIAKIN, I. Interview with Sh. by A. Kamarouski, *Mal*, no. 1:144–49; U. Kavalenka on *Зеніт*, *BLit*, 18:84–93; V. Smal', *BML*, no. 1:60–65, on Sh. and the cinema.

SKARYNA, F. (1486?–1551?). *Францыск Скорина и Вильнюс*, comp. L. Sudavichene, Izd-vo Vil'niusskogo Universiteta, 146 pp., contains the proceedings of a conference. I. Dvarchanin, *Францішак Скарына як культурны дзеяч і гуманіст на беларускай ніве*, NT, 187 pp., is a translation by T. Karotkaia from Czech of D.'s doctoral thesis. Iu. Labyntsau, '*Зерцало жития*' — *з літаратурнай спадчыны*

Францыска Скарыны, MLit, 220 pp., contains reproductions of a selection of S.'s work. *Падарожная кніжка Скарыны*, comp. S. Paniznik and V. Dyshynevich, Iunatstva, 1990, 326 pp., is an anthology of writings about S. for young people. See also A. Iaskevich, *Po*, no. 6:214–22.

TANK, M. *На зорных шляхах*, MLit, 335 pp., is a collection of translations by T.

TARASHKEVICH, B. (1892–1939). *Выбранае*, ML, 319 pp., offers a selection of T.'s political and journalistic writing. See also above under LANGUAGE. 2. MODERN BELORUSSIAN.

TSIOTKA. (1876–1916). V. Kouton, *Po*, no. 7:214–45; M. Novik, *BML*, nos 7–8:91–95.

VERAS, Z. (1892–1991). For an article written under her married name L. Voitsikava see above under BAHDANOVICH.

VIALIUHIN, A. A. Hurskaia, *BML*, nos 7–8:69–79.

VITKA, V. E. Hurevich, *Po*, no. 5:218–28.

ZARETSKI, M. (1901–41). M. Mushynski, *Нескароны талент. Праўдзівая гісторыя жыцця і творчасці Міхася Зарэцкага*, MLit, 294 pp. Id. on *Ракавыя жаронцы*, *BML*, no. 1:43–46. T. Dasaeva, *ib.*, no. 10:43–48.

ZIAZULIA, A. (1878–1921). Ia. Salamevich, *BML*, nos 7–8:140–48 (with a selection of poems).

ZUIONAK, V. L. Harelik, *BML*, nos 7–8:69–79.

3. FOLKLORE

On one of the first Belorussian ethnographers: H. Piatrouskaia, *Пачынальнік беларускага народазнаўства М. Я. Нікіфароўскі* NT, 72 pp. A. Fiadosik, *Ілюзорнасць і сапраўднасць*, NT, 77 pp., deals with 'blank spots' in the history of Belorussian folklore studies in the 1920s and 1930s; see also Id., *Po*, no. 3:198–226. U. Vasilevich, *Збіральнікі*, NT, 189 pp., deals with hitherto little-known collectors of Belorussian folklore. Z. Dołęga-Chodakowski is the subject of a book by A. Aksamitau and L. Malash, *3 душой славяніна*, Polymia, 151 pp. T. Sheliahovich, *BML*, no. 2:75–78, writes on A. Bahdanovich.

A. Nenadavets, *BLit*, 18:143–49, writes on folklore customs connected with death; Id., *VANB*, no. 1:102–09, on the mythological sources of the cock and the cuckoo as folklore characters; M. Matsiukh, *ib.*, no. 3:85–92, on parallelism in wedding songs; H. Kaliada, *ib.*, no. 4:84–90, on plant and tree symbolism in folk songs and dances.

VII. SERBO-CROAT STUDIES

LANGUAGE

By TREVOR PRESTON, *Research Student, School of Slavonic and East European Studies, University of London*

1. GENERAL

D. Vukomanović, *KJ*, 38:479–82, discusses the process of language acquisition among young children and the 'substandard' features which they absorb from peer groups in school. M. Popović, *ib.*, 315–34, examines the Amsterdam School of Functional Grammar with special reference to Serbo-Croat, Old Church Slavonic, Hungarian, and English. H. Keipert, *ZSP*, 51:23–59, considers the composition and aims of the earliest Slavonic grammars published in Vienna, concentrating on Avram Mrazović's *Rukovodstvo kъ slavenstěj grammaticě*.

2. HISTORY OF THE LANGUAGE

An etymological examination of the Croatian toponym Gacka (*Gъdьsk–?) and its relationship to Polish Gdańsk and Russian Gdov is contributed to *WSl*, 36:314–29, by H. Kunstmann. G. Rytter, *SlOc*, 46–47:155–66, examines the etymology of Slav *mogyla/*gomyla (Serbo-Croat *mògila/gòmila*). Two etymological studies are offered in *Slav*, 60: I. Janyšková, 275–83, considers Slavonic words for 'oak', specifically Serbo-Croat *hrâst, dûb, gòrun*; E. Havlová and Ž. Šarapatková discuss Serbo-Croat *òba* 'both' and *òdar* 'catafalque'. A. Loma, *ib.*, 99–139, writes on the pre-Slav substratum in Serbian toponymy, including hydronyms (e.g. Dunav, Morava) and oronyms (e.g. Tara). Winter's Law and Slavic diphthongal bases are considered by S. Young, *SEEJ*, 35:245–53; Russian and especially Serbo-Croat are selected as representatives of Slavonic in general. An analysis of a transliteration of the 15th-c. Aljamiado is contributed to *ZB*, 27:133–56, by W. Lehfeldt. J. Lindstedt, *ScSl*, 37:108–22, remarks on a general lack of interest among many Slavists in Proto-Slavonic accentology and discusses various shortcomings in the traditional system of notation devised for Common Slavonic. S. Vukomanović, *KJ*, 38:1–11, discusses in general terms the development of the Serbo-Croat vocalic and consonantal systems. Lastly, V. Šaur, *Slav*, 60:122–33 and 287–99, considers the Slavic 'prothetic j-' in such words as Serbo-Croat *jàgnje, jêž, jèzik et al.*

3. MODERN SERBO-CROAT

A number of grammatical studies has appeared. Lj. Popović, *KJ*, 38:38–53, examines the agreement of adjectives and verbs with the 'polite' personal pronoun *vî* and establishes a hierarchy of honorific agreement. M. Kovačević, *ib*., 285–95, offers an exposition of subordinate clauses with *da*, concentrating on 'necessitative-final' clauses of the type *da bi se to postiglo, potrebna je veća briga društva*. O. Buchholz, *ZB*, 27:83–100, considers sentences of the type *(on je to uradio) što je bolje moguće '*. . . as well as he could' and . . . *sve bolje* 'better and better' and compares them structurally with corresponding expressions in other Balkan languages. The narrative use of verb tenses in Russian and Serbo-Croat is examined by M. Belyavski-Frank, *SEEJ*, 35:115–32. G. Greenberg and S. Franks, *ib*., 71–97, compare sentences of the type *nemamo šta ovde da radimo* with their corresponding Russian (impersonal) constructions (нам здесь нечего делать).

Morphological studies are provided by H. Muratagić-Tuna, *KJ*, 38:200–04, who discusses peculiarities of nouns in the works of Ćamil Sijarić; by B. Čigoja, *ib*., 233–37, who treats the accusative singular of masculine animate nouns and cites special circumstances where the expected ending (formally = genitive singular) does not appear; and by B . Ćorić, *ib*., 296–304, who considers the difficulties posed by the inflection of anthroponyms, especially those of foreign origin.

There are several articles dealing with semantic themes. G. Schubert, *ZB*, 27:62–67, compares individual proverbs in Balkan languages (including Osmanli) and assesses the degree of coincidence and the different applications to everyday life. K. Zakrajšek, *KJ*, 38:366–70, discusses the meanings and usage of Slovene *dežela* (broadly 'country, state') and the degree to which it has been absorbed into standard Serbo-Croat. B. Ćorić, *ib*., 73–77, examines the terms *dijàlekat, gòvor*, and *nárečje* in the standard language.

Lastly, J. Hlavač, *WSlA*, 28:281–97, treats, on the basis of research conducted with native speakers, the gender of recent loanwords and loan-translations in Serbo-Croat.

4. DIALECTS

P. Houtzagers, *WSl*, 36:201–53, analyses a kajkavian tale from Hidegség (translation in German provided) and discusses the phonemic inventory of the dialect. D. Ćupić, *KJ*, 38:407–18, examines in general terms the differences between the two standard variants of štokavski, and considers the growing tendency to regard Croatian as a separate language. Finally, M. Okuka, *WSlA*, 28:271–80, writes on some of the differences between the two official variants of Serbo-Croat.

LITERATURE

By DAVID A. NORRIS, *Lecturer in Serbo-Croat, University of Nottingham*

1. GENERAL

I. Lokos, 'Hrvatsko-Madžarske književne veze u vrtlozima stoljeća', *Forum*, 61:335–50, is a survey of literary links from the 16th to the 20th cs. J. Vončina, *ib.*, 62:263–70, considers the use which I. Mažuranić must have made of Ardelio Della Bella's *Dizionario italiano, latino, illirico*, (1st edn, Venice, 1728; 2nd edn, Dubrovnik, 1785) in completing Gundulić's epic poem *Osman*. D. Ćupić, *KJ*, 38:407–18, examines differences in the literary language between the western and eastern variants of Serbo-Croat. M. Jenihen, *Jugoslavis-tičke teme: Analize i sinteze*, VZ, offers a series of articles on Serbian and Croatian literature from Romanticism to the post-war period. *Bajron i bajronizam u jugoslovenskim književnostima*, ed. S. Kabiljo–Šutić, Iku, 332 pp., contains 27 essays mainly covering Byron's influence in the development of Serbian and Croatian Romanticism. The sixth edition of M. Pavlović's *Antologija srpskog pesništva*, SKZ, 1990, xxxvi + 365 pp., contains a new introduction on the history of Serbian poetry from the Middle Ages to today.

2. FROM THE MIDDLE AGES TO THE END OF THE EIGHTEENTH CENTURY

K. Nemec, *Forum*, 61:5–22, addresses the beginnings of the novel in Croatia from the 14th to 16th cs. K. Pavić, *ib.*, 62:13–23, examines the first secular writers to appear in Slavonia from the 1690s to the publication of Relković's *Satir* in 1762. D. Fališevac, *Stari pisci hrvatski i njihove poetike*, Z, Liber, 1990. C. M. MacRobert, 'The systems of supplementary penitential texts in the Psalter MSS Peć 68, Belgrade 36, and Plevlja 80', *OSP*, 24:1–22.

INDIVIDUAL WRITERS

Đ. BRANKOVIĆ.   J. Ređep, *Grof Đorđe Branković i usmeno predanje*, Novi Sad, Institut za jugoslovenske književnosti i opštu književnost, offers a study of B.'s chronicle of medieval Serbian history and its relationship to folk poetry.

M. DRŽIĆ.   D. Fališevac, *Republika*, 47.5–6:214–32, examines hum-our and comedy in D.'s work drawing on theories from H. R. Jauss, Aristotle, and S. Freud.

3. CROATIAN LITERATURE IN THE NINETEENTH AND TWENTIETH CENTURIES

K. Nemec, *Forum*, 61:569–79, examines A. Kovačić's parody of I. Mažuranić's *Smrt Smail-age Čengića* as the subversion of a literary canon with broad ideological implications. D. Jelčić, *ib.*, 62:5–12, discusses the role of I. Kukuljević-Sakcinski in the Croatian national renaissance of the 19th c. T. Sabljak, 'Ideologija u teatru: Teze i belješke o kazalištu NDH', *ib.*, 276–82. K. Nemec, *ib.*, 770–87, offers a survey of the history of the Croatian novel from the end of the 18th c. to the middle of the 19th. N. Dragojević *et al.*, *Republika*, 47.1–2:120–45, survey the publication of translations according to genre and source language for their contribution to the intercultural development of literature in post-war Croatia. I. Perić, *ib.*, 47.7–8:176–81, discusses the role of the newspaper *Crvena hrvatska* in the cultural and artistic life of Dubrovnik in the 1890s. D. Dajmić, *ib.*, 47.9–10:214–19, considers the appearance of women writers in the Croatian *Moderna* of the 1890s to the First World War. M. Stančić, 'Recepcija Friedricha Nietzschea u hrvatskoj "moderni"', *ib.*, 47.9–10:220–27. T. Maštrović, *Drama i kazalište hrvatske moderne u Zadru*, Z, Nakladni zavod Matice Hrvatske, 1990. N. Ivanišin, *Fenomen književnog ekspresionizma (o hrvatskom književnom ekspresionizmu)*, Z, Školska knjiga, 1990.

INDIVIDUAL WRITERS

J. KAŠTELAN. B. Vuletić has two articles in *UR*, 35: 'Odrazi. O plošnom/prostornom ustrojstvu pjesništva Jure Kaštelana', 7–21; 'Glasovno ustrojstvo pjesništva Jure Kaštelana. Asonance i aliteracije', 203–19.

A. KOVAČIĆ. V. Brešić, 'Literatura kao ideologem: Ante Kovačić i pravaštvo', *UR*, 35:47–53.

M. KRLEŽA. S. Lasić, 'Kritička literatura o Miroslavu Krleži od 1945 do 1989', *Republika*, 47.7–8:15–31; 47.9–10:30–48, examines criticism of K. which focuses on political rather than artistic criteria. I. Vidan, 'Što je Hamlet Krleži?', *UR*, 35:305–34. A. Flaker, 'Der Erasmische Konflikt: Miroslav Krleža und Erasmus von Rotterdam', *RL*, 30:21–28. R. Bogert, *The Writer as Naysayer: Miroslav Krleža and the Aesthetic of Interwar Central Europe* (UCLA Slavic Studies, 20). Columbus, Ohio, Slavica, 266 pp.

I. MAŽURANIĆ. N. Batušić, *Republika*, 47.7–8:162–75, writes on M.'s contribution to Croatian theatre in the 19th c. P. Pavličić, 'Kojoj književnoj vrsti pripada *Smrt Smail-age Čengića*?, *UR*, 35:187–201.

z. MRKONJIĆ. C. Milanja, 'Mrkonjićeve poetičke mijene', *Republika*, 47.7–8:39–55.

s. NOVAK. *Republika*, 47.3–4, is a thematic issue covering N.'s work and its place in the development of Croatian literature and it includes an interview (3–29), the publication of some poems (31–49), and multiple articles (50–234).

i. SLAMNIG. P. Pavličić, 'Ogled o kratkoj prozi Ivana Slamniga', *Republika*, 47.7–8:32–38.

a. ŠOLJAN. P. Pavličić, *Republika*, 47.1–2:105–18, offers an interpretation of Š.'s poem 'Mjesečina u Novom Zagrebu'.

d. TADIJANOVIĆ. J. Skok, *Republika*, 47.3–4:118–23, covers T.'s poems on childhood, 'Tadijanovićeva poezija i poetika detinjstva'.

d. UGREŠIĆ. J. Lukić, *Književnost*: 938–50, analyses the narrative structure of U.'s *Forsiranje romana-reke*, focusing on intertextuality.

a. UJEVIĆ. *Izraz*, 68:429–60, publishes a series of papers from the conference held in Sarajevo on U.'s life and work; some of the papers are also published in *Književnost*: 794–813.

i. VRKLJAN . C. Hawkesworth, 'I. Vrkljan: Marina, or about biography', *SEER*, 69:221–31.

4. SERBIAN LITERATURE IN THE NINETEENTH AND TWENTIETH CENTURIES

G. Tešić, *Srpska avangarda u polemičkom kontekstu (dvadesete godine)*, Novi Sad, Svetovi, 384 pp., discusses different views on the impact of the avant-garde in Serbian literature and culture. P. Palavestra, *Književnost — kritika ideologije*, SKZ, 353 pp., examines the work of a number of modern prose writers including Andrić, Ćosić, Selimović, Velmar-Janković, Pavić, Kiš. Following the death of Vasko Popa, *Književnost*, no. 3, was given over to reprints of articles about his work and of his poems published in the journal. M. Pantić has a series of articles, 'Čitanje pesme', *Književnost*: 511–14, 716–20, 965–69, with commentaries on modern poets. *Književnost*, no. 6, commemorates the death of M . Bulatović by republishing those of his works which appeared in the journal and A. Ilić's article 'Sazdati noć', 745–60. M. Egerić, *Dela i dani (III)*, Novi Sad, Matica srpska, 1990, has published a new collection of his essays on Andrić, Crnjanski, Ćosić, Koš, Njegoš, etc. M. Maticki, 'Nastanak epskog istorijskog romana: Istorijska proza o ustanku', *LetMS*, 448:832–47. D. Živković, *KI*, 83–84, 1990:63–68, discusses genre distinctions in the short story of the 19th c. M. Radulović, *LetMS*, 448:639–68, examines the relationship of modern poetics to national cultural values in contemporary literature.

Literature

1075

INDIVIDUAL WRITERS

1. ANDRIĆ. T. Brajović, 'Skrivena simbolika *Proklete avlije*', *Književnost*: 217–28. *RL*, 30, features articles by M. Begić (1–20) on A.'s aesthetics; Ž. Juričić (29–42) on A.'s Berlin writings and (43–54) on A.'s views on love.

M. BEĆKOVIĆ. S. Vuksanović, 'Poeme Matije Bećkovića', *Književnost*: 711–15, 957–64.

M. CRNJANSKI. D. Norris, Marsh and Rosslyn, *Culture*, 113–21, discusses interpretations of M.'s poem 'Pesma'. Id., *ReMS*, 34:97–114, applies a Bakhtinian approach to discuss the status of character and the theme of exile in C.'s novel *Roman o Londonu*. D. Ivanić discusses variations in different editions of C.'s *Seobe* and *Druga knjiga Seoba* in his essay at the end of the first critical edition of those novels, 'O izvorima i izdanju *Seoba*', pp. 801–12 of *Seobe: Druga knjiga Seoba*, Be, Zadužbina Miloša Crnjanskog, 814 pp.

R. DRAINAC. N. Ješić, *Književnost*: 970–1014, gives an introduction to D.'s contribution to the Serbian avant-garde of the 1920s and includes some of his lesser known texts.

J. DUČIĆ. *Književnost*: 99–129, features a series of short articles on D. and closes with some of D.'s reports written while working as a diplomat.

M. JOSIĆ-VIŠNJIĆ. *Književnost*: 473–84, publishes a series of short articles on J.-V.'s novel *Odbrana i propast Bodroga u sedam burnih godina*, winner of the NIN prize for novel of the year. S. Gardić has an article on the same novel in *LetMS*, 448:826–31. 'Slovo na tribini "Francuska 7"', *Dometi*, 64:35–50, is the transcription of a discussion by V. Ribnikar, Lj. Jeremić, Đ. Vuković on J.-V.'s novel and is followed *ib.*, 51–61, by a bibliography of J.-V.'s works and criticism of them.

V. ST. KARADŽIĆ. 1. Prijma, *KI*, 83–84, 1990:31–40, discusses K. as a literary critic and his links with, among others, Herder.

L. KOSTIĆ. *Književnost*: 302–76, and *LetMS*, 447:202–86, both feature numerous articles on K. M. Topolovački, 'Dramski torzo Laze Kostića', *ib.*, 448:269–300.

D. MAKSIMOVIĆ. S. Marković, 'Letopis poezije i pesnička misao Desanke Maksimović', *KJ*, 38:275–84.

T. MLADENOVIĆ. M. Mirković, *Književnost*: 130–36, analyses form in M.'s poetry.

P. NJEGOŠ. V. Milinčević, *KJ*, 38:427–37, discusses heroism, lyricism and humour in Nj.'s *Gorski vijenac*.

M. PAVIĆ. There is an interview with P. in *Književnost*: 733–38. J. Delić, *Hazarska prizma: Tumačenje proze Milorada Pavića*, Be, Prosveta, 319 pp.

v. pavković.   M. Orlić, *LetMS*, 447:318–23, considers P.'s book of stories *Monstrumi i druge fikcije*, beginning with Barthes' notion of the pleasure of the text.

m. pavlović.   *Braničevo*, nos 1–2, contains an interview with P., and the remainder is made up of nine articles about his work.

b. pekić.   P. Pijanović, *Poetika romana Borislava Pekića*, Be, Prosveta.

r. petrović.   S. Boškovic, *Izraz*, 69:69–83, discusses P.'s *Burleska gospodina Peruna boga groma* from a Bakhtinian perspective on carnival.

v. pištalo.   There are three articles on P.'s new collection of short stories *Kraj veka* in *Književnost*: 914–26.

v. popa.   D. Antonijević, 'Igra smrti: *Nepočin polje* Vaska Pope', *LetMS*, 447:962–82; 448:98–119.

v. radović.   V. Ribnikar, *Književnost*: 162–67, discusses the style of R.'s short stories, a writer who is otherwise better known as a playwright.

s. ranković.   S. Veličković, 'Dokumentarna osnova proze Svetolika Rankovića', *KJ*, 38:12–19.

s. selenić.   R. Mikić, *Književnost*:137–39, discusses the figure of Stojan Blagojević in S.'s *Timor mortis*.

m. selimović.   M. Nedić, 'Pripovetke Meše Selimovića: Forma i značenje', *Književnost*:229–35.

a. šantić.   A. Peco, 'Nad Šantićevom patriotskom poezijom', *KJ*, 38:419–26.

d. vasiljev.   A. Vraneš, 'Dušan Vasiljev: Skica života i rada', *KJ*, 38:219–27.

s. velmar-janković.   *Književnost*: 489–502, features a series of articles on V.'s novel *Lagum*. A. Peco, 'Neke jezičke osobine u romanu *Lagum* Svetlane Velmar-Janković', *ib.*, 951–56.

j. veselinović.   V. Cvetanović, 'Književni svet Janka M. Veselinovića', *KJ*, 38:460–69.

s. vinaver.   *Književno delo Stanislava Vinavera*, ed. G. Tešić, IKU, 1990, 490 pp.

5.   Folk Literature

Lj. Milosavljević, 'Gresi, njihova ispaštanje i iskupljenja u Vukovoj zbirci narodnih pesama', *Gradina*, 26.1:95–102. N. Milošević-Đorđević edits a collection of essays about different aspects of the Kosovo cycle, *Kosovska epika*, Be, Zavod za udžbenike i nastavna sredstva, 1990. *KI*, 83–84, 1990, has two articles on folk poetry: H. Krnjević (3–30) on folk lyrics from the region of Kosovo, and J. Delić (41–61) on the appearance of Kraljević Marko in Vuk Karadžić's dictionary and an analysis of his qualities as an epic hero. J. Foley, *Immanent Art: From Structure to Meaning in Oral Epic*, Bloomington, Indiana U.P., xvi + 278 pp., has two sections on the Moslem tradition in Serbo-Croat folk poetry (61–95), and on the Christian tradition (96–134).

VIII. BULGARIAN STUDIES*

By Thomas Henninger, *London*

LANGUAGE

1. Lexicography and Lexicology

There is a dictionary of linguistic terms by I. Kasabov, *Семантичен речник-минимум: филологически науки, езикознание*, KO, 1990, 227 pp. The first bilingual dictionary of modern business terms has appeared, *Английско-български Българско-английски търговско-икономически речник*, ed. I. Petrova-Vuteva, Veliko Turnovo [?], Vega–3, 255 pp. M. Kurpacheva, *BulEz*, 41:379–89, introduces approximatization and approximative dictionaries in connection with a newly completed **Речник на полско-българските апроксимати*. Russian-Bulgarian approximates of a homonymous character are introduced by I. Chongarova, *BR*, 17.4:50–56. V. Kiuvlieva-Mishaikova, *BulEz*, 41:55–62, reviews the uncompleted Bulgarian-Russian dictionary by K. Petkovich of 1848, while R. Bitsaeva-Stoianova, *BR*, 17.4:3–9, traces the history of the one-language dictionaries by V. I. Dal' and N. Gerov. A linguistic working thesaurus is suggested by M. Kurpacheva, *BulEz*, 41:158–76.

G. Mishevska, *BR*, 17.4:68–74, analyses the semantics of Russian and Bulgarian sports terminology borrowed from English, while T. Tancheva, *ib.*, 57–62, focuses on the semantic identity of French loan-words in Russian and Bulgarian. T. Henninger, *CanSP*, 1990, 32.1:3–17, researches into the elimination of Turkisms from the lexis of the National Revival. The origin of some popular names of plants is targeted by L. Dimitrova-Todorova, *BulEz*, 41:340–43. M. Nikolova, *ib.*, 43–44, returns to the etymology of *кук, кукер*. The old synonyms *трева/сено* in Daniil's *Четириезичен речник* are highlighted by K. Kostov, *ib.*, 48–50. A. Kocheva, *ib.*, 131–32, analyses /*ne/vĕmь* in Old Bulgarian . G. Rikov, *ib.*, 225–27, explains Proto-Slavonic **gāliti sę* 'to clear up (of the sky)'.

2. History of the Language

V. Šaur, *BulEz*, 41:117–20, investigates Proto-Slavonic *-zъč->щ*, while O. Mladenova, *ib.*, 220–25, highlights the development of the Proto-Slavonic conjugation types in *-i-* and *-i-/-ĕ-* in the modern language. In the field of morphology, T. Todorov, *ib.*, 30–38, and I. Kharalampiev, *ib.*, 38–42, deal with the origin and development of

---

*The place of publication of books is Sofia unless otherwise stated.

some third-person personal pronouns in the accusative. Syntactic features in the language of I. Bogorov are treated by M. Deianova, *ib.*, 354–58.

Patriarch Evtimii's orthographic reform is targeted by I. Talev, *ib.*, 120–27. The history of the literary language is further the object of a monograph by R. Gyllin, *The Genesis of the Modern Bulgarian Literary Language*, Uppsala U.P., 122 pp. The 19th c. is focused on in a monograph by G. K. Venediktov, *Болгарский литературный язык эпохи Возрождения. Проблемы нормализации и выбора диалектной основы*, Moscow, Nauka, 1990, 206 pp. D. Ivanova, *EzLit*, 46.2 : 48–55, considers issues of codification in the third quarter of the 19th c., based on material from the periodical *Читалище* (1870–75).

3. MODERN BULGARIAN

Issues of speech realization, intonation, and sociolinguistics are investigated by several scholars. Urban speech is highlighted in a monograph by M. Videnov, *Съвременната българска градска езикова ситуация: теоретически и методологически проблеми на нейното проучване*, KO, 1990, 525 pp. R. Kurlova and L. Levkova, *BulEz*, 41 : 3–12, research into the connection between stress and syllable as components of the rhythmic organization of speech, while M. Khristov and P. Sotirov, *ib.*, 62–67, introduce an undescribed type of pronunciation as a linguistic variant. D. Milieva, *ib.*, 67–71, observes the intonational formation of speech, while P. Georgieva, *ib.*, 139–44, compares issues of paralinguistics in conversational and stage speech. Kh. Totev, *EzLit*, 46.1 : 103–06, looks into forms of the future-tense particle used in the conversational speech of the capital.

Morphology is dealt with by a number of contributions. I. Tabakova, *BulEz*, 41 : 367–69, focuses on the use of the definite article in medical terms. S. Burov, *ib* ., 13–21, deals with asymmetry of form and meaning in the number paradigm of abstract nouns, while M. Veleva, *ib.*, 204–11, looks at the relation between gender and sex in nouns designating persons. M. Almalekh, *ib.*, 373–78, deals with word formation of two nouns without a preposition. Occasional word formation is treated by V. Radeva, *EzLit*, 46.1 : 76–82. A. Kocheva, *BulEz*, 41 : 42–43, considers the popular basis of deadjectival adverbs. The verbal system is focused on by M. Dimitrova, *ib.*, 132–39, on the semantics of prefixes expressing the beginning of a verbal action; by N. Pavlova, *ib.*, 252–55, on the contracted present-tense type in -м; and by M. Bozhilova, *ib.*, 369–72, on the issue of verbal aspect in verbs of foreign origin ending in *-(из)ирам*. V. Šaur, *EzLit*, 46.1 : 32–40, considers the impact of Turkish upon the Bulgarian verb system.

Issues of syntax are treated by M. Lakova in a monograph, *Местоименни въпросителни изречения в съвременния български език*, BAN, 294 pp., and also in *BulEz*, 41:320–24. I. Tisheva, *EzLit*, 46.2:60–63, describes features of indirect questions. R. Kurshakova, *BulEz*, 41:22–29, highlights the construction of statements in scientific texts. S. Savova, *ib.*, 212–19, surveys compound sentences with a disjunctive element. I. Nedev, *ib.*, 325–39, focuses on types of sentences without conjunction, and, *EzLit*, 46.1:57–67, looks into the combination of predicative units without conjunction. L. Uhlířová, *SlSl*, 26:3–11, characterizes Bulgarian word order.

Comparative studies draw parallels with several languages. The second volume of a Bulgarian–Polish comparative grammar has appeared, *Българско-полска съпоставителна граматика*. 2. *Семантичната категория определеност/неопределеност*, resp. eds V. Koseska-Tosheva, S. Ivanchev, I. Penchev, BAN, 1990, 182 pp. T. Chalukova, *BR*, 17.3:48–51, compares the phonetic realization of the Bulgarian soft consonants with the Russian, and further certain features of Bulgarian articulation with the Russian, *ib.*, 17.4:63–67. A. Karlonska, *ib.*, 17.3:52–61, considers Russian and Bulgarian causative verbs of displacement, while A. Kitina, *BulEz*, 41:101–09, researches into the concept of 'irreality' of the Bulgarian future tense in the past and its Russian equivalents. I. Chobanov, *BR*, 17.3:69–76, studies the abbreviations of male proper names consisting of two stems in both Bulgarian and Russian. Bulgarian–Greek parallels are highlighted in joint contributions by S. Petrova and F. Angelieva, *BulEz*, 41:256–61, on the forms of the imperative, and *ib.*, 350–54, on the future particles *ще/θa*.

4. DIALECTS AND ONOMASTICA

The main dialectal features are summarized by I. Kochev, *BulEz*, 41:307–10. Phonological issues are presented by E. Khristova, *ib.*, 50–54, on palatal consonants in the dialect of the village of Leshko, Blagoevgrad area, and by G. Mitrinov, *EzLit*, 46.1:115–19, on the combinations of *a, e* with the nasal consonant *n* in the Momchilgrad area. Aspects of morphology in the dialects are investigated by E. Kiaeva, *BulEz*, 41:243–52, on Nomina attributiva with the suffix -*ак*, while T. Todorov, *ib.*, 232–38 and *EzLit*, 46.1:83–91, focuses on various aspects of the third-person personal pronouns. The linguistic situation in the Lovech area is introduced by B. Baichev, *BulEz*, 411:239–43. G. Rikov, *ib.*, 44–45, derives *клинкам* from Proto-Slavonic **klypāti, klypājǫ*.

General aspects of onomastic semantics are treated by S. Georgiev, *ib.*, 96–100. Ts. Ivanova, *ib.*, 182–83, considers adjectival formations from the names of foreign geographical objects. Toponyms are the target of several contributions. B. Krustev and S. Vitlianov, *EzLit*, 46.2:64–73, analyse ancient elements in the Preslav area, while M. Nikolova, *BulEz*, 41:128–31, focuses on pre-Slavic elements in the Vidin area. I. Elenin, *ib.*, 345–46, investigates the village name Семчиново, and N . Kovachev, *EzLit*, 46.2:129–30, the reserve name Боатин. Anthroponyms are surveyed by I. Elenski, *ib.*, 46.1:12–19, on historic aspects of male proper names in the dialect of the village of Komarevo, Pleven area. Bulgarian anthroponymy in the (former) USSR is examined by T. Balkanski, *BulEz*, 41:346–50.

LITERATURE

1. GENERAL. GENRES

An introduction to the study of Bulgarian literature is given in a monograph by T. Zhechev, *Въведение в изучаването на новата българска литература*, BP, 1990, 445 pp. New approaches towards literature after the political changes are initiated by O. Saparev, *LitMis*, 35.1:30–40, on the social content of present-day literature, and *ib.*, 35.3:3–33, on ideologization of trivial elements under the auspices of 'Socialist Realism'. B. Nichev, *ib.*, 35.1:5–10, suggests a new reading of contemporary literature, while S. Stefanov, *ib.*, 35.3:133–41, settles accounts with the unsuccessful attempt of mass culture during the period of the personality cult. B. Bogdanov, *ib.*, 35.1:11–29, reflects on the limits of language in Bulgarian literature. Literary criticism is the subject of two monographs: by B . Bozhilov, *Критика и образи*, BP, 1990, 212 pp., on a large number of writers, and by I. Tsvetkov, *Преломно време: студии, очерци, портрети*, BP, 1990, 204 pp., including also selected Russian authors.

The novel is focused on by D. Peneva, *EzLit*, 46.2:40–47, on the issue of personality and human behaviour in the present-day novel. The image of the village in poetry is presented in a monograph by A. Mochurov, *Разорани сънища: опит върху селската поезия 1958–1983*, BP, 1990, 211 pp. R. Likova, *LitMis*, 35.5–6:41–93, gives an account of poetry in 1991.

2. LITERATURES IN CONTACT. LITERARY HISTORY

The interest of the intelligentsia in the Russian novel of the first half of the 19th c. is considered by A. Anchev, *BR*, 17.1:37–52 (continuation of *ib.*, 16.6, 1990:36–44), while I. Petrova, *ib.*, 17.3:3–9, surveys the presence of A. Fet in the cultural consciousness of the Bulgarians. B. Mirchev, *LitMis*, 35.7:41–51, reflects on the selection of present-day translations from the German.

The National Revival is the target of several contributions. Zh. Avdzhiev, *EzLit*, 46.1 : 3–11, follows the literary traditions laid by Sofronii Vrachanski up to the end of the 19th c., while L. Mikhova, *LitMis*, 35.3 : 90–107, researches into the status of popular literature. N. Aretov, *ib.*, 35.4 : 67–87, surveys translated prose fiction and the formation of a genre system, and further focuses on the reception of foreign cultures, *ib.*, 35.7 : 21–40.

Literary criticism versus mass readership during the decades following the Liberation is analysed by K. Bechev, *ib.*, 35.3 : 108–23. S. Beliaeva, *ib.*, 35.1 : 78–102, surveys the conflict between the editor of the periodical *Нов път* and its contributors in the 1920s.

Modernism is dealt with by K. Krustev, *ib.*, 35.5–6 : 3–23.

3. Individual Writers

M. BELCHEVA. (1868–1937). A. Purvanova, *EzLit*, 46.2 : 124–28, surveys B.'s poetry.

KH. BOTEV (1848–76). B. Baier, *LitMis*, 35.2 : 77–94, considers B.'s poem *До моето първо либе*.

CHUDOMIR (1890–1967). N. Georgiev, *ib.*, 35.4 : 3–40, investigates the aspect of foreignness in Ch.'s stories.

A. DALCHEV (b. 1904). R. Stoianov, *ib.*, 35.7 : 115–27, deals with the reception of D.'s poetry in Brazil.

ELIN PELIN (1887–1949). L. Boeva, *ib.*, 35.5–6 : 24–40, approaches E.'s story *На оня свят* from the viewpoint of a medievalist.

I. IOVKOV (1880–1937). M. Dimieva, *EzLit*, 46.2 : 79–83, focuses on semantic fields and space limitation in I.'s *Постолови воденици*.

G. KARASLAVOV (b. 1904). A. Panov, *LitMis*, 35.4 : 41–66, considers the aspect of man and property in K.'s novel *Снаха*.

S. KH. KARASLAVOV (b. 1932). K. Popov, *EzLit*, 46.1 : 20–32, analyses folk elements in K.'s lyric poetry.

T. KUNEV (1880–1954). D. Avramov, *LitMis*, 35.1 : 63–77, surveys K.'s folk lyrics.

PAISII KHILENDARSKI (1722–73). R. Zaimova, *ib.*, 35.2 : 44–54, investigates elements of West European historiography in P.'s *История славянобългарска*.

I. RADOSLAVOV (1880–1969). I. Sestrimski, *EzLit*, 46.2 : 34–39, remembers R.

N. RAINOV (1889–1954). V. Trendafilov, *LitMis*, 35.8 : 31–93, considers R.'s personality. Ia. Milchakov, *ib.*, 101–26, investigates rhythm and meaning in R.'s rhythmic prose *Градът. Поема на тайните*.

P. P. SLAVEIKOV (1866–1912). S. Tsoneva, *BulEz*, 41 : 150–58, analyses some syntactic peculiarities in S.'s works.

P. R. SLAVEIKOV (1827–95). There is a monograph by K. Topalov, *Петко Р. Славейков*, NM, 1990, 328 pp.

KH. SMIRNENSKI (1898–1923). A. Panov, *LitMis*, 35.1:41–55, considers the myth of the creation of the world in S.'s poetry.

E. STANEV (1907–79). P. Dimitrov, *ib.*, 35.2:13–33, deals with historic myth in S.'s prose fiction .

R. SUGAREV (b. 1941). V. Ruseva, *ib.*, 35.5:94–104, researches into the dimension of the 'unclear meaning' in S.'s prose fiction.

I. VAZOV (1850–1921). Different aspects of V .'s *Чичовци* are treated by N. Genkova, *EzLit*, 46.1:41–48, and D. Iugova, *ib.*, 49–56. A. Khranova, *LitMis*, 35.3:67–89, deals with triviality in V .'s poem *Аз съм българче*.

4.   FOLK LITERATURE

S. Petkova, *EzLit*, 46.1:107–14, investigates the image of the plague in folk aphorisms. V. Manolov, *ib.*, 46.2:105–10, reflects on the song *Крали Марко освобождава три синджира роби*. V. Nikolova, *LitMis*, 35.4:88–112, researches into the theme of the 'immured bride'.

ABBREVIATIONS

I. ACTA, FESTSCHRIFTEN AND OTHER COLLECTIVE AND GENERAL WORKS

Acta (Basel): *Textkonstitution bei mündlicher und bei schriftlicher Überlieferung. Basler Editoren-Kolloquium 19.–22. März 1990, autor- und werkbezogene Referate*, ed. Martin Stern, Beatrice Grob, Wolfram Groddeck and Helmut Puff (Beihefte zu *Editio*, 1), Tübingen, Niemeyer, x + 225 pp.

Acta (Louvain): *Arturus Rex*. II. *Acta Conventus Lovaniensis 1987*, ed. Willy Van Hoecke, Gilbert Tournoy, and Werner Verbeke (Mediaevalia Lovaniensia, I, 17), Louvain University Press, xi + 527 pp.

Acta (Reisensburg): *Text und Bild, Bild und Text. DFG-Symposion 1988*, ed. Wolfgang Harms (Germanistische Symposien Berichtsbände, 11), Stuttgart, Metzler, 1990, ix + 523 pp. + 179 pls.

Actas (Alcalá): *Actas del segundo coloquio internacional de la Asociación de Cervantistas (Alcalá de Henares, 6–9 noviembre, 1989) (II-CIAC)*, Barcelona, Anthropos, 783 pp.

Actas (Berlin), I, II: *Actas del IX Congreso de la Asociación Internacional de Hispanistas. 18–23 agosto 1986 Berlin. Ibero-Amerikanisches Institut Preußischer Kulturbesitz. Freie Universität Berlin Institut für Romanische Philologie*, ed. Sebastian Neumeister, 2 vols, Frankfurt, Vervuert, 1989, xx + 700, 749 pp.

Actas (Brown): *Actas do segundo congreso de estudios galegos (Brown University, novembro 10, 12 — 1988). Homenaxe a José Amor y Vázquez*, ed. Antonio Carreño, Vigo, Galaxia, 501 pp.

Actas (Lisbon), I: *Actas do Congresso da Associação Hispánica de Literatura Medieval*. I. *Sessões Plenárias*, Lisbon, Cosmos, 135 pp.

Actes (Amiens): *Figures de l'écrivain au moyen âge. Actes du Colloque du Centre d'Études Médiévales de l'Université de Picardie, Amiens 18–20 mars 1988*, ed. Danielle Buschinger (Göppinger Arbeiten zur Germanistik, 510), Göppingen, Kümmerle, 388 pp.

Actes (Barcelona), I, II: *Actes du XIᵉ Congrès International de la Société Rencesvals* (Memórias de la Real Academia de Buenas Letras de Barcelona, 21–22), 2 vols, Barcelona, Real Academia de Letras, 1990, 431, 456 pp.

Actes (Dakar): *Montaigne penseur et philosophe (1588–1988). Actes du congrès de la littérature française tenu en ouverture à l'année de la francophonie les 20, 21 et 22 mars 1989 à Dakar organisé par les départments de Lettres modernes et de Philosophie*, ed. Claude Blum (Études Montaignistes, 5), Paris, Champion, 1990, 233 pp.

Actes (Montpellier): *Vers un 'thesaurus' informatisé: topique des ouvertures narratives avant 1800. Actes du Quatrième Colloque International SATOR, Université Paul-Valéry — Montpellier III, 25–27 octobre 1990*, ed. Pierre Rodriguez and Michèle Weil, Montpellier, Centre d'Étude du Dix-Huitième Siècle, 449 pp.

Actes (Mulhouse): *La liberté de conscience (XVIᵉ–XVIIᵉ siècles). Actes du Colloque de Mulhouse et Bâle (1989)*, ed. Hans R. Guggisberg, Frank Lestringant, and Jean-Claude Margolin (Études de Philologie et d'Histoire, 44), Geneva, Droz, 375 pp.

Actes (Strasbourg): *La Cour au miroir des mémorialistes (1530–1682). Actes du Colloque du Centre de Philologie et de Littérature Romanes de Strasbourg, Strasbourg, 16–18 novembre 1989*, ed. Noémi Hepp, Paris, Klincksieck, 213 pp.

Actes (Trier), II: *Actes du XVIIIᵉ Congrès International de Linguistique et de Philologie Romanes, Université de Trèves (Trier) 1986*. II. *Section III. Linguistique théorique et linguistique synchronique*, ed. Dieter Kremer, Tübingen, Niemeyer, xi + 670 pp.

Actes (Trier), III: *Actes du XVIIIᵉ Congrès International de Linguistique et de Philologie Romanes, Université de Trèves (Trier) 1986*. III. *Section V. Grammaire diachronique et histoire de la langue. Section VIII. Dialectologie et géographie linguistique. Section XIII. Textes non-littéraires*, ed. Dieter Kremer, Tübingen, Niemeyer, xii + 785 pp.

Actes (Trier), IV: *Actes du XVIIIᵉ Congrès International de Linguistique et de Philologie Romanes, Université de Trèves (Trier) 1986*. IV. *Section VI. Lexicologie et lexicographie. Section VII. Onomastique*, ed. Dieter Kremer, Tübingen, Niemeyer, 1989, xi + 682 pp.

Actres (Trier), v: *Actes du XVIII Congrès International de Linguistique et de Philologie Romanes, Université de Trèves (Trier) 1986.* v. *Linguistique pragmatique et linguistique sociolinguistique,* ed. Dieter Kremer, Tübingen, Niemeyer, 1988, vii + 400 pp.

Actes (Trier), vii: *Actes du XVIII Congrès International de Linguistique et de Philologie Romanes, Université de Trèves (Trier) 1986.* vii. *Section XIV. Histoire de la linguistique et de la philologie romanes. Section XV. Philologie romane et langues romanes: prise de conscience ou: la philologie pour quoi faire? Section XVI. Travaux en cours,* ed. Dieter Kremer, Tübingen, Niemeyer, 1989, xi + 565 pp.

Actes (Zaghouan): *Actes du IV Symposium International d'Études Morisques sur: Métiers, vie religieuse et problématiques d'histoire morisque,* ed. Abdeljelil Temimi, Zaghouan, Centre d'Études et de Recherches Ottomanes, Morisques, de Documentation et d'Information, 1990, 365 + 43 pp.

Akten (Tokyo), i–xi: *Begegnung mit dem 'Fremden'. Grenzen — Traditionen — Vergleiche. Akten des VIII. Internationalen Germanisten-Kongresses Tokyo 1990,* ed. Eijirō Iwasaki and Yoshinori Shichiji, 11 vols, Munich, Iudicium, 182, 306, 289, 540, 329, 402, 502, 291, 498, 424, 544 pp.

Alluin, *Nouvelle: La Nouvelle: définitions, transformations,* ed. Bernard Alluin and François Suard (Collection UL3. Coordonnée par le Conseil Scientifique de l'Université Charles de Gaulle — Lille III), Presses Universitaires de Lille, 1990, 227 pp.

Anglada, *Cambio: El cambio lingüístico en la Romania,* ed. Emília Anglada and Maria Bargalló, Lérida, Virgili & Payès, 1990, 126 pp.

Apter, *Fetish*: Emily Apter, *Feminizing the Fetish: Psychoanalysis and Narrative Obsession in Turn-of-the-Century France,* Ithaca, Cornell University Press, xviii + 273 pp.

Arac, *Macropolitics: Macropolitics of Nineteenth-Century Literature: Nationalism, Exoticism, Imperialism,* ed. Jonathan Arac and Harriet Ritvo, Philadelphia, Pennsylvania University Press, 309 pp.

Arntzen Vol.: 'Die in dem alten Haus der Sprache wohnen.' Beiträge zum Sprachdenken in der Literaturgeschichte. Helmut Arntzen zum 60. Geburtstag, ed. Eckehard Czucka, Thomas Althaus, and Burkhard Spinnen, Münster, Aschendorff, x + 609 pp.

Atti (Bergamo): *Morfologia/Morphologie. Atti del V Incontro Italo-Austriaco della Società di Linguistica Italiana a Bergamo, 2–4 ottobre, 1989,* ed. M. Berretta, Piera Molinelli, and Ada Valentini (Parallela, 4), Tübingen, Narr, 1990, xi + 349 pp.

Atti (Lecce): *Dialettologia urbana: problemi e ricerche. Atti del 16. Convegno del C.S.D.I. (Lecce, 1–4 ottobre 1986),* Pisa, Pacini, 1989, 255 pp.

Atti (Messina): *Innovazione e conservazione nelle lingue. Atti del Convegno della Società Italiana di Glottologia, Messina, 9–11 novembre 1989,* ed. V. Orioles, Pisa, Giardini, 214 pp.

Atti (Padua): *L'italiano regionale. Atti del XVIII Congresso internazionale di studi Padova-Vicenza, 14–16 settembre 1984,* ed. Michele A. Cortelazzo and Alberto M. Mioni, Rome, Bulzoni, 1990, xi + 452 pp.

Atti (Perugia): *Lingua e cultura italiana nel mondo oggi. Atti del 13. Congresso A.I.S.L.L.I. Perugia, 30 maggio — 3 giugno 1988,* ed. Ignazio Baldelli and Bianca Maria Da Rif, 2 vols, Florence, Olschki, xi + 730 pp.

Atti (Trento): *Storia dell'italiano e forme dell'italianizzazione. Atti del XXIII Congresso Internazionale di Studi Trento-Rovereto, 18–20 maggio 1989,* ed. Emanuele Banfi and Patrizia Cordin, Rome, Bulzoni, 1990, vi + 468 pp.

Avramenko, *Блок*: A. P. Avramenko, *А. Блок и русские поэты XIX века,* Moscow University Press, 1990, 248 pp.

Barański, *Women: Women and Italy. Essays on Gender, Culture and History,* ed. Zygmunt G. Barański and Shirley W. Vinall, Basingstoke, Macmillan, 1990, xi + 304 pp.

Baur, *Mundartliteratur: Alemannisch-schwäbische Mundartliteratur nach 1945. Formen — Entwicklungen — Tendenzen diesseits und jenseits des Rheins,* ed. Gerhard W. Baur, Bühl, Konkordia, 1989, 125 pp.

Beiträge (Trier): *Maschinelle Verarbeitung altdeutscher Texte IV. Beiträge zum Vierten Internationalen Symposion Trier 28. Februar bis 2. März 1988,* ed. Kurt Gärtner, Paul Sappler, and Michael Trauth, Tübingen, Niemeyer, x + 399 pp.

Bevan, *Génétique: Sur la génétique textuelle,* ed. D. G. Bevan and P. M. Wetherill, Amsterdam, Rodopi, 1990, 205 pp.

Blum, *Montaigne*: *Montaigne. Apologie de Raimond Sebond. De la 'Theologia' à la 'Théologie'*, ed. Claude Blum (Études Montaignistes, 6), Paris, Champion, 1990, 362 pp.

Bochmann, *Regionalsprachen*: Klaus Bochmann, *Regional- und Nationalitätensprachen in Frankreich, Italien und Spanien*, Leipzig, Enzyklopädie Verlag, 1989, 219 pp.

Bosque, *Indicativo*: *Indicativo y subjuntivo*, ed. Ignacio Bosque, Madrid, Taurus, 1990, 464 pp.

Bouché, *Le Rire*: *Le Rire au Moyen Âge dans la littérature et dans les arts. Actes du colloque international des 17, 18 et 19 novembre 1988*, ed. Thérèse Bouché and Hélène Charpentier, Presses Universitaires de Bordeaux, 1990, 376 pp.

Brang Vol.: *'Прими собрание пестрых глав.' Slavistische und slavenkundliche Beiträge für Peter Brang zum 65. Geburstag*, ed. Cartsen Goehrke, Robin Kemball, Daniel Weiss, and Monika Bankowski-Züllig (Slavica Helvetica, 33), Berne — Frankfurt — New York — Paris, Lang, 1989, 748 pp.

Brassloff, *Insights*: *European Insights. Post-War Politics, Society and Culture*, ed. Audrey Brassloff and Wolfgang Brassloff, Amsterdam — New York — Tokyo, Elsevier, vii + 309 pp.

Bristol, *Poetry*: Evelyn Bristol, *A History of Russian Poetry*, New York, Oxford University Press, ix + 354 pp.

Brown, *Writers*: *Women Writers of Contemporary Spain: Exiles in the Homeland*, ed. Joan L. Brown, Newark, Delaware University Press — London, Associated University Presses, 292 pp.

Brownlee, *New Medievalism*: *The New Medievalism*, ed. Marina S. Brownlee, Kevin Brownlee, and Stephen G. Nichols, Baltimore, Johns Hopkins University Press, vi + 330 pp.

Brude-Firnau, *Fact*: *Fact and Fiction. German History and Literature 1848–1942*, ed. Gisela Brude-Firnau and Karin J. MacHardy (Edition Orpheus, 2), Tübingen, Francke, 1990, 216 pp.

Bürger, *Leben*: Christa Bürger, *Leben Schreiben. Die Klassik, die Romantik und der Ort der Frauen. (Bettina von Brentano, Charlotte von Kalb, Sophie Mereau, Caroline Schlegel, Johanna Schopenhauer, Rahel Varnhagen)*, Stuttgart, Metzler, 1990, viii + 203 pp.

Bussevitz, *Jugendliteratur*: *Zeitgenössische sowjetische Kinder- und Jugendliteratur: Entwicklungstendenzen und Traditionen*, ed. Wolfgang Bussevitz, Potsdam, Pädagogische Hochschule 'Karl Liebknecht', 1989, 216 pp.

Campbell, *Compendium*: George L. Campbell, *Compendium of the World's Languages*, 2 vols, London — New York, Routledge, xxvi + 1–828, 829–1574 pp.

Cerrón-Palomino, *Temas*: *Temas de lingüística amerindia. Primer Congreso Nacional de Investigaciones Lingüístico-filológicas*, ed. Rodolfo Cerrón-Palomino and Gustavo Solís Fonseca, Lima, 1990, 315 pp.

Chai, *Aestheticism*: Leon Chai, *Aestheticism. The Religion of Art in Post-Romantic Literature*, New York, Columbia University Press, 1990, xiv + 269 pp.

Chickering, *Chivalry*: *The Study of Chivalry. Resources and Approaches*, ed. Howell Chickering and Thomas H. Seiler, Kalamazoo, Michigan, Western Michigan University Medieval Institute Publications for The Consortium for the Teaching of the Middle Ages, Inc., 1988, x + 700 pp.

Colloque (Fordham): *Colloque de la S.A.T.O.R. à Fordham. Actes du Troisième Colloque international de la S.A.T.O.R., Université de Fordham (25–28 juillet 1989)*, ed. J. Macary (Biblio 17, 61), Paris — Seattle — Tübingen, Papers on French Seventeenth Century Literature, 217 pp.

Colloque (Las Vegas): *Théorie dramatique, Théophile de Viau, Les Contes de Fées. XXIIe Colloque de la North American Society for Seventeenth Century French Literature, University of Nevada, Las Vegas (1–3 mars 1990)*, ed. M.-F. Hilgar (Biblio 17, 60), Paris — Seattle — Tübingen, Papers on French Seventeenth Century Literature, 230 pp.

Condé, *Readings*: *Feminist Readings on Spanish and Latin-American Literature*, ed. L. P. Condé and S. M. Hart, Lewiston, Edwin Mellen, xvi + 197 pp.

Conti, *Medicina*: *Medicina e biologia nella rivoluzione scientifica*, ed. L. Conti, Assisi, Porziuncola, 1990, 302 pp.

Corfield, *Language*: *Language, History and Class*, ed. Penelope J. Corfield, Oxford, Blackwell, viii + 320 pp.

Cortelazzo *Vol.*: *Dialettologia e varia linguistica. Per Manlio Cortelazzo*, ed. Gianluigi Borgato and Alberto Zamboni, Padua, Unipress, 1989, x + 430 pp.

Corvin, *Théâtre*: Michel Corvin, *Dictionnaire encyclopédique du théâtre*, Paris, Bordas, 942 pp.

Coulmas, *Language Policy*: *A Language Policy for the European Community. Prospects and Quandaries*, ed. Florian Coulmas, Berlin, Mouton de Gruyter, 311 pp.

Còveri, *L'italiano*: *Atti del Primo Convegno della Società Internazionale di Linguistica e Filologia Italiana, Siena, 28–31 marzo 1989*. II. *L'italiano allo specchio. Aspetti dell'italianismo recente*, ed. Lorenzo Còveri, Turin, Rosenberg & Sellier, 164 pp.

Cremerius, *Literatur*: *Literatur und Sexualität*, ed. Johannes Cremerius (Freiburger literaturpsychologische Gespräche, 10), Würzburg, Königshausen & Neumann, 315 pp.

Criado de Val, *Literatura*: *Literatura hispánica. Reyes Católicos y Descubrimiento. Actas del Congreso Internacional sobre literatura hispánica en la época de los Reyes Católicos y el Descubrimiento*, ed. Manuel Criado de Val, Barcelona, Promociones y Publicaciones Universitarias, 1989, x + 595 pp.

De Jean, *Displacements*: *Displacements*, ed. Joan De Jean and Nancy K. Miller, Baltimore, Johns Hopkins University Press, xiii + 336 pp.

De Michelis, *Avversario*: Cesare G. De Michelis, *I nomi dell'avversario: il 'papa-anticristo' nella cultura russa*, Turin, Meynier, 1989, 113 pp.

Desan, *Humanism*: *Humanism in Crisis: The Decline of the French Renaissance*, ed. Philippe Desan, Ann Arbor, University of Michigan Press, viii + 323 pp.

D'haen, *Convention*: *Convention and Innovation in Literature*, ed. Theo D'haen, Rainer Grübel, and Helmut Lethen (Utrecht Publications in General and Comparative Literature, 24), Amsterdam — Philadelphia, Benjamins, 1989, xxii + 434 pp.

Didier, *Penser*: *Penser, classer, écrire. De Pascal à Pérec*, ed. Béatrice Didier and Jacques Neefs, Vincennes University Press, 1990, 208 pp.

Doglio, *Teatro scomparso*: Federico Doglio, *Il teatro scomparso. Testi e spettacoli fra il X e il XVII secolo*, Rome, Bulzoni, 1990, 444 pp.

Eggert, *Geschichte*: *Geschichte als Literatur. Formen und Grenzen der Repräsentation der Vergangenheit*, ed. Hartmut Eggert, Ulrich Profitlich, and Klaus Scherpe, Stuttgart, Metzler, 1990, x + 423 pp.

Ehlert, *Haushalt*: *Haushalt und Familie in Mittelalter und früher Neuzeit. Vorträge eines interdisziplinären Symposions vom 6.–9. Juni 1990 an der Rheinischen Friedrich-Wilhelms-Universität Bonn*, ed. Trude Ehlert, Sigmaringen, Thorbecke, 304 pp.

Emelina, *Comique*: Jean Emelina, *Le Comique: essai d'interprétation générale*, Paris, Société d'Éditions d'Enseignement Supérieur, 212 pp.

Energeia und Ergon, I, II, III: *Energeia und Ergon. Sprachliche Variation — Sprachgeschichte — Sprachtypologie. Studia in honorem Eugenio Coseriu*, ed. Jörn Albrecht, Jens Lüdtke, and Harald Thun (Tübinger Beiträge zur Linguistik, 300), 3 vols, Tübingen, Narr, 1988, xliii + 416, xiv + 577, viii + 536 pp.

Erofeev, В лабиринте: Viktor Erofeev, *В лабиринте проклятых вопросов*, Moscow, Sovetskii pisatel', 1990, 448 pp.

Esposito *Vol.*: *Per le nozze di corallo (1955–1990) di Enzo Esposito e Citty Mauro*, Ravenna, Longo, 1990, 185 pp.

Estudios Ruiz-Fornells: *Estudios en homenaje a Enrique Ruiz-Fornells*, ed. Juan Fernández Jiménez, José J. Labrador Herraiz, and L. Teresa Valdivieso, Erie, Pennsylvania, ALDEEU, 1990, xxvi + 706 pp.

Estudis Lafont: *Per Robert Lafont. Estudis oferts a Robert Lafont per sos collègas e amics*, Montpellier — Nîmes, 1990, xiv + 313 pp.

Etkind, *Letteratura*: *La letteratura russa del novecento: problemi di poetica*, ed. Efim Etkind *et al.*, Naples, Istituto Suor Orsola Benincasa, 1990, 144 pp.

Fenoaltea, *Ladder*: *The Ladder of High Designs. Structure and Interpretation of the French Lyric Sequence*, ed. Doranne Fenoaltea and David Lee Rubin, Charlottesville, Virginia University Press, xiii + 205 pp.

Ferrer, *L'Écriture: L'Écriture et ses doubles. Genèse et variation textuelle*, ed. Daniel Ferrer and Jean-Louis Lebrave, Paris, Centre National de la Recherche Scientifique, 216 pp.

Fest. Conrady: Wissenschaft und Nation. Zur Entstehungsgeschichte der deutschen Literaturwissenschaft. [*Karl Otto Conrady zum 65. Geburtstag gewidmet*], ed. Jürgen Fohrmann and Wilhelm Vosskamp, Munich, Fink, 240 pp.

Fest. Engels: Festschrift für Heinz Engels zum 65. Geburtstag, ed. Gerhard Augst, Otfrid Ehrismann, and Hans Ramge (Göppinger Arbeiten zur Germanistik, 561), Göppingen, Kümmerle, 380 pp.

Fest. Engler: Sprachtheorie und Theorie der Sprachwissenschaft. Geschichte und Perspektiven. Festschrift für Rudolf Engler zum 60. Geburtstag, ed. Ricarda Liver, Iwar Werlen and Peter Wunderli (Tübinger Beiträge zur Linguistik, 355), Tübingen, Narr, 1990, viii + 337 pp.

Fest. Flasche: Homenaje a Hans Flasche. Festschrift zum 80. Geburtstag am 25. November 1991, ed. Karl-Hermann Körner and Günther Zimmermann, Stuttgart, Steiner, 695 pp.

Fest. Grimm: 'Was in den alten Büchern steht . . .': Neue Interpretationen von der Aufklärung zur Moderne. Festschrift für Reinhold Grimm, ed. Karl-Heinz J. Schoeps and Christopher J. Wickham (Forschungen zur Literatur- und Kulturgeschichte, 32), Frankfurt, Lang, xiv + 261 pp.

Fest. Hamp: Celtic Language, Celtic Culture. A Festschrift for Eric P. Hamp, ed. A. T. E. Matonis and Daniel F. Melia, Van Nuys, California, Ford & Bailie, 1990, 415 pp.

Fest. Hoffmann: Uf der mâze pfat. Festschrift für Werner Hoffmann zum 60. Geburtstag, ed. Waltraud Fritsch-Rössler and Liselotte Homering (Göppinger Arbeiten zur Germanistik, 555), Göppingen, Kümmerle, 447 pp.

Fest. Kienecker: Deutsche christliche Dichterinnen des 20. Jahrhunderts. Gertrud von Le Fort, Ruth Schaumann, Elisabeth Langgässer. Festschrift für Friedrich Kienecker aus Anlaß seines 70. Geburtstages, ed. Lothar Bossle and Joël Pottier, Paderborn, Creator, 1990, 150 pp.

Fest. Mayer: Interdisziplinarität. Deutsche Sprache und Literatur im Spannungsfeld der Kulturen. Festschrift für Gerhart Mayer zum 65. Geburtstag, ed. Martin Forstner and Klaus von Schilling (FAS. Publikationen des Fachbereichs Angewandte Sprachwissenschaft der Johannes Gutenberg-Universität Mainz in Germersheim, A, 15), Frankfurt, Lang, 514 pp.

Fest. Mitchell: Grenzerfahrung — Grenzüberschreitung. Studien zu den Literaturen Skandinaviens und Deutschlands. Festschrift für P. M. Mitchell, ed. Leonie Marx and Herbert Knust, Heidelberg, Winter, 1989, xv + 259 pp.

Fest. Pellegrini: Sive Padi ripis Athesim seu propter amoenum. Studien zur Romanität in Norditalien und Graubünden. Festschrift für Giovan Battista Pellegrini, ed. Johannes Kramer, Hamburg, Buske, 435 pp.

Fest. Rathofer: Architectura poetica. Festschrift für Johannes Rathofer zum 65. Geburtstag, ed. Ulrich Ernst and Bernhard Sowinski (Kölner germanistische Studien, 30), Cologne, Böhlau, 1990, xii + 543 pp.

Fest. Schumacher: Spiegelungen. Festschrift für Hans Schumacher zum 60. Geburtstag, ed. Reiner Matzker, Petra Küchler-Sakellariou, and Marius Babias, Frankfurt am Main, Lang, 251 pp.

Fest. Steger: Erscheinungsformen der deutschen Sprache. Literatursprache, Alltagssprache, Gruppensprache, Fachsprache. Festschrift zum 60. Geburtstag von Hugo Steger, ed. Jürgen Dittmann, Hannes Kästner and Johannes Schwitalla, Berlin, Schmidt, xxii + 264 pp.

Fest. Verbeeck: Bild-Sprache. Texte zwischen Dichtern und Denken. Festschrift für Prof. Dr. Lude Verbeeck, ed. Luc Lamberechts and Johan Nowé (Symbolae. Ser. D, Litteraria, 5), Leuven University Press, 1990, 311 pp.

Fest. Wandruszka: Wege in die Sprachwissenschaft. Vierundvierzig autobiographische Berichte. Festschrift für Mario Wandruszka, ed. Hans-Martin Gauger and Wolfgang Pöckl (Tübinger Beiträge zur Linguistik, 362), Tübingen, Narr, 259 pp.

Fest. Weber: Verlust und Ursprung. Festschrift für Werner Weber. Mit Beiträgen zum Thema 'Et in Arcadia ego', ed. Angelika Maass and Bernhard Hinser, Zurich, Ammann, 1989, 548 pp.

35

Fest. Wilss: Übersetzungswissenschaft. Ergebnisse und Perspektiven. Festschrift für Wolfram Wilss zum 65. Geburtstag, ed. Reiner Arntz and Gisela Thome (Tübinger Beiträge zur Linguistik, 354), Tübingen, Narr, 1990, xx + 562 pp.

Fest. Windfuhr: 'Stets wird die Wahrheit hadern mit dem Schönen.' Festschrift für Manfred Windfuhr zum 60. Geburtstag, ed. Gertrude Cepl-Kaufmann, Winfried Hartkopf, Ariane Neuhaus-Koch, and Hildegard Stauch, Cologne, Böhlau, 1990, xi + 513 pp.

Fest. Wisniewski: Geist und Zeit. Wirkungen des Mittelalters in Literatur und Sprache. Festschrift für Roswitha Wisniewski zu ihrem 65. Geburstag, [ed. Carola L. Gottzmann and Herbert Kolb], Frankfurt, Lang, 459 pp.

Fest. Wysling: Thomas Mann und seine Quellen. Festschrift für Hans Wysling, ed. Eckhard Heftrich and Helmut Koopmann, Frankfurt, Klostermann, x + 319 pp.

Fest. Zeller: Edition und Wissenschaft. Festschrift für Hans Zeller, ed. Gunter Martens and Winfried Woesler (Beihefte zu *Editio*, 2), Tübingen, Niemeyer, 199 pp.

Fest. Zimmermann: Ex ipsis rerum documentis. Beiträge zur Mediävistik. Festschrift für Harald Zimmermann zum 65. Geburtstag, ed. Klaus Herbers, Hans Henning Kortüm, and Carlo Servatius, Sigmaringen, Thorbecke, xvi + 664 pp.

Floeck, *Theater: Zeitgenössisches Theater in Deutschland und Frankreich. Théâtre contemporain en Allemagne et en France*, ed. Wilfried Floeck (Mainzer Forschungen zu Drama und Theater, 3), Tübingen, Francke, 1989, xvi + 275 pp.

Forsås-Scott, *Liberation: Textual Liberation: European Feminist Writing in the Twentieth Century*, ed. Helena Forsås-Scott, London, Routledge, x + 342 pp.

Fothergill-Payne, *Drama: Parallel Lives: Spanish and English National Drama 1580–1680*, ed. Louise and Peter Fothergill-Payne, Lewisburg, Bucknell University Press — London and Toronto, Associated University Presses, 329 pp.

Fothergill-Payne, *Theater: Prologue to Performance: Spanish Classical Theater Today*, ed. Louise and Peter Fothergill-Payne, Lewisburg, Bucknell University Press — London and Toronto, Associated University Presses, 167 pp.

Fridlender, *Революция: Великая французская революция и русская литература*, ed. G. M. Fridlender, Leningrad, Nauka, 1990, 408 pp.

Garber, *Barock: Europäische Barock-Rezeption*, ed. Klaus Garber, Ferdinand van Ingen, Wilhelm Kühlmann and Wolfgang Weiss (Wolfenbütteler Arbeiten zur Barockforschung, 20), 2 vols, Wiesbaden, Harrassowitz, xiv + 1–838, vi + 839–1365 pp.

Gensini, *Le Italie: Le Italie del tardo medioevo*, ed. Sergio Gensini, Pisa, Pacini, 1990.

Gerber, *Studies: Studies in GDR Culture and Society*, 10, ed. Margy Gerber, Lanham, University Press of America, viii + 214 pp.

Gervers, *Conversion: Conversion and Continuity: Indigenous Christian Communities in Islamic Lands, Eighth to Eighteenth Centuries*, ed. Michael Gervers and Ramzi Jibran Bikhazi (Papers in Mediaeval Studies, 9), Toronto, Pontifical Institute of Medieval Studies, 1990, xi + 559 pp.

Giannelli, *Rinascimento: Atti del Primo Convegno della Società Internazionale di Linguistica e Filologia Italiana, Siena, 28–31 marzo 1989. 1. Tra Rinascimento e strutture attuali. Saggi di linguistica italiana*, ed. Luciano Giannelli *et al.*, Turin, Rosenberg & Sellier, 380 pp.

Glaudes, *Personnage: Personnage et histoire littéraire*, ed. Pierre Glaudes and Yves Reuter, Université de Toulouse-Le Mirail, 258 pp.

González-del-Valle, *Essays: Critical Essays on the Literatures of Spain and Spanish America*, ed. Luís T. González-del-Valle and Júlio Baena (*Anales de la Literatura Española*, Añejo), Boulder, Colorado, Society of Spanish and Spanish-American Studies, viii + 243 pp.

Grigsby Vol.: Continuations. Essays on Medieval French Literature and Language. In Honor of John L. Grigsby, ed. Norris J. Lacy and Gloria Torrini-Roblin, Birmingham, Alabama, Summa, 1989, 328 pp.

Grillo, *Dominant Languages*: R. D. Grillo, *Dominant Languages. Language and Hierarchy in Britain and France*, Cambridge University Press, 1989, ix + 261 pp.

Grygar, *Czech Studies: Czech Studies. Literature, Language, Culture*, ed. Mojmir Grygar, Amsterdam — Atlanta, Georgia, Rodopi, 1990, 336 pp.

Gvozdanović, *Numerals: Indo-European Numerals*, ed. Jadranka Gvozdanović (Trends in Linguistics: Studies and Monographs, 57), Berlin — New York, Mouton de Gruyter, x + 943 pp.

Hahn, *Vorfeld: Im Vorfeld der Literatur. Vom Wert archivalischer Überlieferung für das Verständnis von Literatur und ihrer Geschichte. Studien*, ed. Karl-Heinz Hahn, Weimar, Böhlau, 316 pp.

Harris and Vincent, *Romance Languages: The Romance Languages*, ed. Martin Harris and Nigel Vincent, London, Croom Helm, 1988, xii + 500 pp.

Harvey Vol.: Cultures in Contact in Medieval Spain. Historical and Literary Essays Presented to L. P. Harvey, ed. David Hook and Barry Taylor, London, King's College, 1990, xv + 216 pp.

Haug, *Autorentypen: Autorentypen*, ed. Walter Haug and Burghart Wachinger (Fortuna Vitrea, 6), Tübingen, Niemeyer, viii + 176 pp.

Haug, *Positionen: Positionen des Romans im späten Mittelalter*, ed. Walter Haug and Burghart Wachinger (Fortuna Vitrea, 1), Tübingen, Niemeyer, viii + 365 pp.

Heinzle, *Nibelungen: Die Nibelungen. Ein deutscher Wahn, ein deutscher Alptraum. Studien und Dokumente zur Rezeption des Nibelungenstoffs im 19. und 20. Jahrhundert*, ed. Joachim Heinzle and Anneliese Waldschmidt (Suhrkamp Taschenbuch, 2110), Frankfurt, Suhrkamp, 408 pp.

Hickman, *Musil: Robert Musil and the Literary Landscape of his Time*, ed. Hannah Hickman, Department of Modern Languages, University of Salford, 286 pp.

Holtus, *Lexikon: Lexikon der Romanistischen Linguistik.* v, 2. *Okzitanisch, Katalanisch*, ed. Günter Holtus, Michael Metzeltin, and Christian Schmitt, Tübingen, Niemeyer, xxii + 310 pp. + map.

Holzner, *Heimkehr: Eine schwierige Heimkehr. Österreichische Literatur im Exil 1938–1945*, ed. Johann Holzner, Sigurd Paul Scheichl, and Wolfgang Wiesmüller, Innsbruck, Institut für Germanistik, 560 pp.

Homenaje Barceló Jiménez: Homenaje a Juan Barceló Jiménez, Murcia, Academia de Alfonso X el Sabio, 1990, 679 pp.

Homenaje Criado de Val: Imago Hispaniae. Lengua, literatura, historia y fisonomía del español. Homenaje a Manuel Criado de Val, ed. Angel Montero Herrero et al., Kassel, Reichenberger, 1989, xi + 693 pp.

Homenaje Gallego Morell, I–III: *Homenaje al Profesor Antonio Gallego Morell*, ed. C. Argente del Castillo and A. Sánchez Trigueros, 3 vols, Granada University Press, 1989, 587, 513, 514 pp.

Homenaje Lapesa: Homenaje al Profesor Lapesa. XI Curso de Lingüística Textual. Murcia 25–29 Abril 1988, University of Murcia, 1990, 236 pp.

Homenaje Marichal: La voluntad de humanismo. Homenaje a Juan Marichal, ed. Biruté Ciplijauskaité and Christopher Maurer, Barcelona, Anthropos, 1990, 270 pp.

Homenaje Porqueras Mayo: Varia hispania. Homenaje a Alberto Porqueras Mayo, ed. Joseph L. Laurenti and Vern Williamsen, Kassel, Reichenberger, 1989, viii + 693 pp.

Homenaje Rubio, I–III: *Homenaje al profesor Luis Rubio*, ed. J. Hernández Serna (Estudios Románicos, 4–6), 3 vols, Murcia University Press, 1987–89, 675, x + 677–1504, viii + 1505–1837 pp.

Homenaje Ubieto Arteta: Homenaje al Profesor Emérito Antonio Ubieto Arteta (Aragón en la Edad Media, 8), Universidad de Zaragoza, Facultad de Filosofía y Letras, Departamento de Historia Medieval, Ciencias y Técnicas Historiográficas y Estudios Arabes e Islámicos, Saragossa University Press, 1989, 727 pp.

Homenaje Vilanova, I–II: *Homenaje al profesor Antonio Vilanova*, ed. Adolfo Sotelo Vázquez and Marta Cristina Carbonell, Barcelona University Press, 1989, 866, 838 pp.

Homenatge García Díez: Miscel.lània. Homenatge García Díez, ed. Angel López García and Evangelina Rodríguez Cuadros, Valencia, Universitat de València — Conselleria de Cultura, Educació i Ciència de la Generalitat Valenciana, 594 pp.

Homenatge Roca-Pons: Homenatge a Josep Roca-Pons. Estudis de llengua i literatura, ed. Jane White Albrecht, Janet Ann DeCesaris, Patricia V. Lunn, and Joseph Miquel Sobrer, Montserrat, Abadia de Montserrat — Indiana University, 318 pp.

Hommage Payen: *Farai chansoneta novele: essais sur la liberté créatrice au moyen âge*. *Hommage à J.-Charles Payen*, Université de Caen, 1989, 462 pp. + 10 pls.

Hommage Pottier: *Hommage à Bernard Pottier*, [ed. J.-L. Benezech *et al.*], 2 vols, Paris, Klincksieck, 454, 455–862 pp.

Hunt, *Eroticism*: *Eroticism and the Body Politic*, ed. Lynn Hunt, Baltimore, Johns Hopkins University Press, 243 pp.

Hunter, *Topos*: *Towards a Definition of Topos: Approaches to Analogical Reasoning*, ed. Lynette Hunter, Basingstoke, Macmillan, 256 pp.

Jaeggli and Safir, *The Null Subject Parameter*: *The Null Subject Parameter*, ed. Osvaldo Jaeggli and Kenneth J. Safir, Dordrecht, Kluwer, 1989, 320 pp.

Jauralde, *Actas*: *La edición de textos. Actas del I Congreso Internacional de Hispanistas del Siglo de Oro*, ed. Pablo Jauralde, Dolores Noguera, and Alfonso Rey, London, Tamesis, 1990, 495 pp.

Jauslin, *Schweiz*: *Ausgangspunkt Schweiz — Nachwirkungen des Exiltheaters*, ed. Christian Jauslin and Louis Naef (Schweizer Theaterjahrbuch, 50), Willisau, Theaterkultur-Verlag, 1989, 319 pp.

Jones-Davies, *Renaissance*: *Langues et nations au temps de la Renaissance*, ed. M. T. Jones-Davies, Université de Paris-Sorbonne: Société Internationale de Recherches Interdisciplinaires sur la Renaissance S.I.R.I.R. Centre de Recherches sur la Renaissance, Paris, Klincksieck, 256 pp.

Juden Vol: *Ideology and Religion in French Literature: Essays in Honour of Brian Juden by Pupils, Colleagues and Friends*, ed. Harry Cockerham and Esther Ehrman, Camberley, Porphyrogenitus, 1989, xviii + 359 pp.

Jurkowski, *Écrivains*: Henryk Jurkowski, *Écrivains et marionnettes: quatre siècles de littérature dramatique*, Charleville-Mézières, Institut International de la Marionnette, 409 pp.

Kalveram, *Homosexualitäten*: *Homosexualitäten — literarisch. Literaturwissenschaftliche Beiträge zum internationalen Kongreß 'Homosexuality, which homosexuality?' Amsterdam 1987*, ed. Maria Kalveram and Wolfgang Popp, Essen, Die Blaue Eule, 146 pp.

Kenny, *Fictions*: *Philosophical Fictions and the French Renaissance*, ed. Neil Kenny (Warburg Institute Surveys and Texts, 19), London, University of London, The Warburg Institute, 137 pp

Kissling, *Epochen*: *Deutsche Dichtung in Epochen. Ein literaturgeschichtliches Lesebuch*, ed. Walter Kissling, Achim Block, Helmut Hoffacker, Peter Kohrs, Paul Schmitt, and Ulrich Vossen, Stuttgart, Metzler, 1989, 799 pp.

Klemm, *Romanführer*: *Deutscher Romanführer*, ed. Imma Klemm (Kröners Taschenausgabe, 370), Stuttgart, Kröner, xiv + 527 pp.

Knapp, *Autoren*: *Autoren damals und heute. Literaturgeschichtliche Beispiele veränderter Wirkungshorizonte* (Amsterdamer Beträge zur neueren Germanistik, 31–33), Amsterdam, Rodopi, 793 pp.

Knapp, *Exile*: Bettina L. Knapp, *Exile and the Writer. Exoteric and Esoteric Experiences. A Jungian Approach*, Philadelphia, Pennsylvania State University Press, 253 pp.

Kohn-Waechter, *Flammen*: *Schrift der Flammen. Opfermythen und Weiblichkeitsentwürfe im 20. Jahrhundert*, ed. Gudrun Kohn-Waechter, Berlin, Orlanda, 309 pp.

Kolinsky, *Era*: *The Federal Republic of Germany: The End of an Era*, ed. Eva Kolinsky, Oxford, Berg, 384 pp.

Kreuzer, *Pluralismus*: *Pluralismus und Postmodernismus. Beiträge zur Literatur- und Kulturgeschichte der 80er Jahre*, ed. Helmut Kreuzer, Berne, Lang, 1989, 248 pp.

Kritzman, *Signe*: *Le Signe et le Texte. Études sur l'écriture au XVIᵉ siècle en France*, ed. Lawrence D. Kritzman (French Forum Monographs, 72), Lexington, Kentucky, French Forum, 1990, 187 pp.

Lagorio and Day, *Arthur*, I, II: *King Arthur through the Ages*, ed. Valerie M. Lagorio and Mildred Leake Day (Garland Reference Library of the Humanities, 1269, 1301), 2 vols, New York, Garland, 1990, xix + 327, xxxii + 335 pp.

Le 'Cuer': *Le 'Cuer' au Moyen Âge (Réalité et Sénéfiance)* (Sénéfiance, 30), Aix-en-Provence, Université de Provence, Publications du CUER MA, 472 pp.

Lehmann, *Clarissa*: Christine Lehmann, *Das Modell Clarissa. Liebe, Verführung, Sexualität und Tod der Romanheldinnen des 18. und 19. Jahrhunderts*, Stuttgart, Metzler, 217 pp.

Leistner, *Beckmesser*: Bernd Leistner, *Sixtus Beckmesser. Essays zur deutschen Literatur*, Berlin — Weimar, Aufbau, 1989, 263 pp.

Lindemann, *Spinnen: Lauter schwarze Spinnen. Spinnenmotive in der deutschen Literatur. Eine Sammlung*, ed. Klaus Lindemann and Raimar Stefan Zons (Bouviers Bibliothek, 9), Bonn, Bouvier, 1990, iv + 303 pp.

Livingston, *Literature*: Paisley Livingston, *Literature and Rationality: Ideas of Agency in Theory and Fiction*, Cambridge University Press, x + 256 pp.

Lo Cascio, *Lingua: Lingua e cultura italiana in Europa*, ed. Vincenzo Lo Cascio, Florence, Le Monnier, 1990, xlvii + 540 pp.

Losev, *Страстъ*: А. F. Losev, *Страстъ к диалектике: литературные размышления философа*, Moscow, Sovetskii pisatel', 1990, 320 pp.

Luker, *Short Story: The Short Story in Russia 1900–1917*, ed. Nicholas Luker, Nottingham, Astra, xvi + 182 pp.

Mainusch, *Komödie: Europäische Komödie*, ed. Herbert Mainusch, Darmstadt, Wissenschaftliche Buchgesellschaft, 1990, vii + 449 pp.

Marsh and Rosslyn, *Culture: Russian and Yugoslav Culture in the Age of Modernism*, ed. Cynthia Marsh and Wendy Rosslyn, Nottingham, Astra, xvi + 168 pp.

Mascaró, *Grammar: Grammar in Progress. Glow Essays for Henk van Riemsdijk*, ed. J. Mascaró and M. Nespor, Dordrecht, Foris, 1990, x + 461 pp.

McWilliam Vol.: Writers and Performers in Italian Drama from the Time of Dante to Pirandello. Essays in Honour of G. H. McWilliam, ed. J. R. Dashwood and J. E. Everson, Lampeter, Mellen, xii + 186 pp.

Mélanges Bec: Mélanges de langue et de littérature occitanes en hommage à Pierre Bec par ses amis, ses collègues, ses élèves, Poitiers, Centre d'Études Supérieures de Civilisation Médiévale, 625 pp.

Mélanges Chouillet: L'Encyclopédie, Diderot, l'esthétique: mélanges en hommage à Jacques Chouillet, ed. S. Auroux, D. Bourel, and C. Porset, Paris, Presses Universitaires de France, 334 pp.

Mélanges Deloffre: Langue, littérature du XVIIᵉ et du XVIIIᵉ siècle: mélanges offerts à M. le Professeur Frédéric Deloffre, ed. Roger Lathuillère, Paris, SEDES, 1990, 771 pp.

Mierendorff, *Aufsätze*: Marta Mierendorff and Walter Wicclair, *Im Rampenlicht der 'dunklen Jahre'. Aufsätze zum Theater im 'Dritten Reich', Exil und Nachkrieg*, ed. Helmut G. Asper, Berlin, Sigma, 1989, 153 pp.

Mills, *Büchner: Georg Büchner — Tradition and Innovation. Fourteen Essays*, ed. Ken Mills and Brian Keith-Smith (Bristol German Publications, 1), Bristol University Press, 1990, 268 pp.

Miscellanea Gasca Queirazza: Miscellanea di studi romanzi offerta a Giuliano Gasca Queirazza per il suo 65° compleanno, ed. Anna Cornagliotti et al., 2 vols, Alessandria, Edizioni del Orso, 1988, xxiv + 1124 pp.

Mouillaud-Fraisse, *Littérature: Littérature et double culture/Literatura y doble cultura*, ed. Geneviève Mouillaud-Fraisse and José María Fernández Cardo (Actes Noésis / Actas Noesis, 3), Noesis, 1989, 287 pp.

Müller, *Aporie: Aporie und Euphorie der Sprache. Studien zu Georg Trakl und Peter Handke. Akten des internationalen Europalia-Kolloquiums Gent 1987*, ed. Heidi M. Müller, Louvain, Peeters, 1989, xi + 230 pp.

Newton, *Romance*: Ruth Newton and Naomi Lebowitz, *Dickens, Manzoni, Zola, and James: The Impossible Romance*, Columbia, Missouri University Press, 1990, 236 pp.

Niderst, *Pastorale: La Pastorale française. De Rémi Belleau à Victor Hugo*, ed. A. Niderst (Biblio 17, 63), Paris — Seattle — Tübingen, Papers on French Seventeenth Century Literature, 156 pp.

Niederehe, *Linguistics*, I, II: *History and Historiography of Linguistics. ICHOLS IV, Trier, 24–28 August, 1987*, ed. Hans-Josef Niederehe and Konrad Koerner (Studies in the History of the Language Sciences, 51), 2 vols, Amsterdam — Philadelphia, Benjamins, 1990, 873 pp.

Onderdelinden, *Exil: Interbellum und Exil*, ed. Sjaak Onderdelinden (Amsterdamer Publikationen zur Sprache und Literatur, 90), Amsterdam, Rodopi, vi + 293 pp.

Papers (Cambridge): *New Studies in Latin Linguistics. Selected Papers from the 4th International Colloquium on Latin Linguistics, Cambridge, April 1987*, ed. Robert Coleman (Studies in Language Companion Series, 21), Amsterdam — Philadelphia, Benjamins, x + 478 pp.

Papers (Leningrad): *Language Typology 1988. Typological Models in Reconstruction. Papers from the Linguistic Typology Symposium. Leningrad, 13–15 June 1988*, ed. Winfried P. Lehmann and Helen-Jo Jakusz Hewitt (Current Issues in Linguistic Theory, 81), Amsterdam — Philadelphia, Benjamins, vi + 182 pp.

Papers (Trier): *History and Historiography of Linguistics. Papers from the Fourth International Conference on the History of Language Sciences (ICHOLS IV). Trier, 24–28 August 1987*, ed. Hans-Josef Niederehe and Konrad Koerner, 2 vols, Amsterdam — Philadelphia, Benjamins, 1990, xxxv + 876 pp.

Parenté: Les Relations de parenté dans le monde médiéval (Sénéfiance, 26), Aix-en-Provence, Publications du CUER MA, 1989, 605 pp.

Parente, *Empire: Literary Culture in the Holy Roman Empire, 1555–1720*, ed. James A. Parente, Jr, Richard Erich Schade, and George C. Schoolfield (University of North Carolina Studies in Germanic Languages and Literatures, 113), Chapel Hill — London, University of North Carolina Press, 290 pp.

Pelckmanns, *Monde*: Paul Pelckmanns, *Concurrences au monde. Propositions pour une poétique du collectionneur moderne*, Amsterdam, Rodopi, 1990, 150 pp.

Peschel-Rentsch, *Skizzzen*: Dietmar Peschel-Rentsch, *Gott, Autor, Ich. Skizzen zur Genese von Autorbewußtsein und Erzählerfigur im Mittelalter* (Erlanger Studien, 89), Erlangen, Palm & Enke, 258 pp.

Pfanner, *Der Zweite Weltkrieg: Der Zweite Weltkrieg und die Exilanten / World War II and the Exiles*, ed. Helmut F. Pfanner (Studien zur Literatur der Moderne, 21), Bonn, Bouvier, 324 pp.

Pöckl, *Dichter*: *Österreichische Dichter als Übersetzer. Salzburger komparatistische Analysen*, ed. Wolfgang Pöckl (Österreichische Akademie der Wissenschaften, phil.-hist. Klasse, Sitzungsberichte, 571; Veröffentlichungen der Kommission für Literaturwissenschaft, 12), Vienna, Verlag der Österreichischen Akademie der Wissenschaften, 536 pp.

Poirion, *Contexts*: *Contexts: Style and Values in Medieval Art and Literature*, ed. Daniel Poirion and Nancy Freeman Regalado (*Yale French Studies*, Special Issue), Binghamton, NY, Vail-Ballou, 290 pp.

Poirion, *Styles*: *Styles et valeurs pour une histoire de l'art littéraire au moyen âge*, ed. D. Poirion, Paris, SEDES, 1990, 212 pp.

Poliakova, *Поэзия*: Larisa Poliakova, *Поэзия и современность: 'за' и 'против'*, Moscow, Sovremennik, 1989, 302 pp.

Pörnbacher Vol.: Grenzgänge: Literatur und Kultur im Kontext, ed. Guillaume van Gemert and Hans Ester (Amsterdamer Publikationen zur Sprache und Literatur, 88), Amsterdam — Atlanta, Georgia, Rodopi, 1990, vi + 478 pp.

Porter, *Desire*: Dennis Porter, *Haunted Journeys: Desire and Transgression in European Travel Writing*, Princeton University Press, 334 pp.

Procs (BASS): *Proceedings of the Ninth Biennial Conference of the British Association of Scandinavian Studies*, ed. Janet Garton, Norwich, University of East Anglia School of Modern Languages and European History, 316 pp.

Procs (Kalamazoo): *Von Otfrid von Weißenburg bis zum 15. Jahrhundert. Proceedings from the 24th International Congress on Medieval Studies, May 4–7, 1989*, ed. Albrecht Classen (Göppinger Arbeiten zur Germanistik, 539), Göppingen, Kümmerle, iii + 171 pp.

Procs (Moscow): *XI Всесоюзная конференция по изучению истории, экономики, литературы и языка скандинавских стран и Финляндии*, ed. A. O. Chubar'ian, Moscow University Press, 1989, 451 pp.

Procs (Munich), I–V: *Proceedings of the XIIth Congress of the International Comparative Literature Association. Actes du XIIe Congrès de l'Association Internationale de Littérature Comparée. München 1988 Munich*, ed. Roger Bauer, Douwe Fokkema, and Michael de Graat, 5 vols, Munich, Iudicium, 1990, 251, 606, 509, 651, 415 pp.

Procs (Svendborg): *Deutsch-Nordische Begegnungen. 9. Arbeitstagung der Skandinavisten des deutschen Sprachgebiets 1989 in Svendborg*, ed. Kurt Braunmüller and Mogens Brøndsted, Odense University Press, 472 pp.

Procs (Teruel): *Actas de las II Jornadas Internacionales de Cultura Islámica Teruel, 1988*, [*Aragón vive su historia.*] *Entidades Patrocinadoras: Excmo. Ayuntamiento de Teruel, Banco Arabe Español. Teruel, 22 al 25 de septiembre 1988*, Madrid, Al-Fadila (Instituto Occidental de Cultura Islámica), 1990, 324 pp.

Procs (Uppsala): *Societas Celtologica Nordica. Proceedings of Inaugural Meeting and First Symposium 26 May 1990 at Uppsala University*, ed. Birgit Bramsbäck and Ailbhe Ó Corráin (Acta Universitatis Upsaliensis; Studia Anglistica Upsaliensia, 76), Uppsala, 100 pp.

Quack, *Identifikation*: Josef Quack, *Die fragwürdige Identifikation*, Würzburg, Königshausen & Neumann, 207 pp.

Quinones, *Cain*: Ricardo J. Quinones, *The Changes of Cain. Violence and the Lost Brother in Cain and Abel Literature*, Princeton University Press, viii + 284 pp.

Ramond, *Figures*: *Les Figures de l'autre*, ed. Michèle Ramond (Collection Hespérides, 5), Toulouse, Presses Universitaires du Mirail, 204 pp.

Rancœur-Laferrière, *Psychoanalysis*: Daniel Rancœur-Laferrière, *Russian Literature and Psychoanalysis*, Amsterdam, Benjamins, 1990, 485 pp.

Rees, *Drama*: *Leeds Papers on Hispanic Drama*, ed. Margaret A. Rees (Leeds Iberian Papers), Leeds, Trinity and All Saints College, 181 pp.

Rees, *Saint John*: *Leeds Papers on Saint John of the Cross: Contributions to a Quatercentenary Celebration*, ed. Margaret A. Rees (Leeds Iberian Papers), Leeds, Trinity and All Saints College, 237 pp.

Roberts, *Novel*: *The Modern German Historical Novel*, ed. David Roberts and Philip Thomson, Oxford, Berg, 368 pp.

Rodriguez, *Thesaurus*: *Vers un 'thesaurus informatisé': topique des ouvertures narratives avant 1800. Actes du quatrième colloque international Sator*, ed. P. Rodriguez and M. Weil, Montpellier, 449 pp.

Rosenthal, *Literatur: Deutschsprachige Literatur des Auslandes*, ed. Erwin Theodor Rosenthal, Berne, Lang, 1989, 170 pp.

Roudaut, *Villes*: Jean Roudaut, *Les Villes imaginaires dans la littérature française: les douze portes*, Paris, Hatier, 1990, liv + 191 pp.

Runge, *Frau*: *Die Frau im Dialog. Studien zu Theorie und Geschichte des Briefes*, ed. Anita Runge and Lieselotte Steinbrügge (Ergebnisse der Frauenforschung, 21), Stuttgart, Metzler, 242 pp.

Sareil Vol.: *Voltaire, the Enlightenment and the Comic Mode: Essays in Honor of Jean Sareil*, ed. M. G. Cutler, New York, Lang, 1990, 270 pp.

Saul, *Wissenschaften*: *Die deutsche literarische Romantik und die Wissenschaften*, ed. Nicholas Saul (Publications of the Institute of Germanic Studies, 47), London, University of London Institute of Germanic Studies, viii + 318 pp.

Schulz, *Literatur*: *Literatur und Geschichte 1788–1988*, ed. Gerhard Schulz, Tim Mehigan, and Marion Adams (Australian and New Zealand Studies in German Language and Literature, 15), Berne, Lang, 1990, 350 pp.

Senelick, *Theatre*: *National Theatre in Northern and Eastern Europe 1746–1900*, ed. Laurence Senelick, Cambridge University Press, xxx + 480 pp.

Sheppard, *Germanistik*: *New Ways in Germanistik*, ed. Richard Sheppard, Oxford, Berg, 1990, 336 pp.

Simon, *Theatre*: *The Theatre of Medieval Europe. New Research in Early Drama*, ed. Eckehard Simon (Cambridge Studies in Medieval Literature, 9), Cambridge University Press, xxii + 311 pp.

Slessarev Vol.: *The Enlightenment and its Legacy. Studies in German Literature in Honor of Helga Slessarev*, ed. Sara Friedrichsmeyer and Barbara Becker-Cantarino, Bonn, Bouvier, 227 pp.

Staczek, *Linguistics*: *On Spanish, Portuguese, and Catalan Linguistics*, ed John J. Staczek, Washington, D.C., Georgetown University Press, 1988, 239 pp.

Stephan, *Frauen*: *'Wen kümmert's, wer spricht.' Zur Literatur und Kulturgeschichte von Frauen aus Ost und West*, ed. Inge Stephan, Sigrid Weigel, and Kerstin Wilhelms, Cologne, Böhlau, xii + 229 pp.

Stoll, *Women*: *The Perception of Women in Spanish Theater of the Golden Age*, ed. Anita K. Stoll and Dawn L. Smith, Lewisburg, Bucknell University Press — London and Toronto, Associated University Presses, 276 pp.

Stone Vol.: Lapidary Inscriptions. Renaissance Essays for Donald A. Stone, Jr, ed. Barbara C. Bowen and Jerry C. Nash (French Forum Monographs, 74), Lexington, Kentucky, French Forum, 205 pp.

Symposion (Paderborn): *Feste und Feiern im Mittelalter. Paderborner Symposion des Mediävistenverbandes*, ed. Detlef Altenburg, Jörg Jarnut, and Hans-Hugo Steinhoff, Sigmaringen, Thorbecke, 551 pp.

Technische Sprache: *Technische Sprache und Technolekete in der Romania. Romanistisches Kolloquium*, II, ed. Wolfgang Dahmen, Günter Holtus, Johannes Kramer and Michael Metzeltin (Tübinger Beiträge zur Linguistik, 326), Tübingen, Narr, 1989, xiv + 395 pp.

Tindall, *Countries*: Gillian Tindall, *Countries of the Mind: The Meaning of Place to Writers*, London, Hogarth Press, ix + 254 pp.

Titzmann, *Modelle*: *Modelle des literarischen Strukturwandels*, ed. Michael Titzmann (Studien und Texte zur Sozialgeschichte der Literatur, 33), Tübingen, Niemeyer, vi + 440 pp.

Traugott, *Approaches*: *Approaches to Grammaticalization*, II, ed. Elizabeth Closs Traugott and Bernd Heine, Amsterdam — Philadelphia, Benjamins, 556 pp.

Tristram, *Metrik*: *Metrik und Medienwechsel / Metrics and Media*, ed. Hildegard L. C. Tristram, Tübingen, Narr, 319 pp.

Ueding, *Rhetorik*: *Rhetorik zwischen den Wissenschaften. Geschichte, System, Praxis als Probleme des 'Historischen Wörterbuchs der Rhetorik'*, ed. Gert Ueding (Rhetorik-Forschungen, 1), Tübingen, Niemeyer, vii + 379 pp.

Van der Eng Vol.: The Semantic Analysis of Literary Texts: To Honour Jan van der Eng on the Occasion of his 65th Birthday, ed. Eric de Haard *et al.*, Amsterdam, Elsevier, 1990, xii + 647 pp.

Varley Vol.: Golden Age Spanish Literature: Studies in Honour of John Varey by his Colleagues and Pupils, ed. Charles Davis and Alan Deyermond, London, Westfield College, 247 pp.

Variatio Linguarum: *Variatio Linguarum. Beiträge zu Sprachvergleich und Sprachentwicklung. Festschrift zum 60. Geburtstag von Gustav Ineichen*, ed. Ursula Klenk, Karl-Hermann Körner and Wolf Thümmel, Stuttgart, Steiner, 1989, xvii + 332 pp.

Vergers et jardins: *Vergers et jardins dans l'univers médiéval* (Sénéfiance, 28), Aix-en-Provence, Publications du CUER MA, 1990, 420 pp.

Vorträge (Liverpool): *Reisen und Welterfahrung in der deutschen Literatur des Mittelalters. Vorträge des XI. Anglo-deutschen Colloquiums 11.–15. September 1989 Universität Liverpool*, ed. Dietrich Huschenbett and John Margetts (Würzburger Beiträge zur deutschen Philologie, 7), Würzburg, Königshausen & Neumann, x + 362 pp.

Wanner and Kibbee, *New Analyses*: *New Analyses in Romance Linguistics. Selected Papers from the XVIII Linguistic Symposium on Romance Languages Urbana-Champaign, April 7–9, 1988*, ed. Dieter Wanner and Douglas A. Kibbee (Amsterdam Studies in the Theory and History of Linguistic Science. IV. Current Issues in Linguistic Theory, 69), Amsterdam — Philadelphia, Benjamins, xviii + 406 pp.

Wardropper Vol.: Studies in Honor of Bruce W. Wardropper, ed. Dian Fox, Harry Sieber and Robert ter Horst, Newark, New Jersey, Juan de la Cuesta, 1989, xx + 377 pp.

Wasserman, *Sign*: *Sign, Sentence, Discourse. Language in Medieval Thought and Literature*, ed. Julian N. Wasserman and Lois Roney, Syracuse University Press, 1989, xxi + 318 pp.

Watson, *Patterns*: *Patterns of Evolution in Nineteenth-Century French Poetry*, ed. Lawrence Watson and Rosemary Lloyd, Deddington, Tallents Press, 1990, 288 pp.

Wentzlaff-Eggebert, *Langage*: *Le Langage littéraire au XVIIe siècle: de la rhétorique à la littérature*, ed. C. Wentzlaff-Eggebert (Études Littéraires, 50), Tübingen, Narr, 306 pp.

Whinnom Vol.: *The Age of the Catholic Monarchs, 1474–1516. Literary Studies in Memory of Keith Whinnom*, ed. Alan Deyermond and Ian Macpherson (Bulletin of Hispanic Studies, Special Issue), Liverpool University Press, 1989, xii + 211 pp.

Williams, *Literature*: *German Literature at a Time of Change 1989–1990. German Unity and German Identity in Literary Perspective*, ed. Arthur Williams, Stuart Parkes, and Roland Smith, Berne, Lang, 494 pp.

Wimmer, *Wurzeln*: *Das 19. Jahrhundert. Sprachgeschichtliche Wurzeln des heutigen Deutsch*, ed. Rainer Wimmer (Institut für Deutsche Sprache, Jahrbuch, 1990), Berlin, de Gruyter, 509 pp.

Wotjak, *Verbo*: *La descripción del verbo español*, ed. Gerd Wotjak and Alexandre Veiga (Verba. Anuario Galego de Filoloxía, Anejo 32), Santiago de Compostela University Press, 1990, 285 pp.

Wright, *Latin*: *Latin and the Romance Languages in the Early Middle Ages*, ed. Roger Wright, London — New York, Routledge, ix + 262 pp.

Zuev, *Жизнь*: Nikolai Zuev, '*Жизнь и поэзия — одно.*' *Очерки о русских поэтах XIX–XX вв.*, Moscow, Sovremennik, 1990, 303 pp.

II. GENERAL

abbrev., abbreviation, abbreviated to.
Acad., Akad., Academy, Academia, etc.
ann., annotated (by).
anon., anonymous.
appx, appendix.
Arg., Argentinian (and foreign equivalents).
arkh., архив, архивный, etc.
Assoc., Association (and foreign equivalents).
bel., беларускі, etc.
B.L., British Library.
B.M., British Museum.
B.N., Bibliothèque Nationale, Biblioteka Narodowa, etc.
bull., bulletin.
c., century.
c., circa.
col., column.
comm., commentary (by).
comp., compiler, compiled (by).
diss., dissertation.
ed., edited (by), editor (and foreign equivalents).
edn, edition
fac., facsimile.
fasc., fascicle.
Fest., Festschrift, Festskrift.
Fr., France, French, Français.
fr., français.
Ger., German(y).
glav., главный, etc.
Gmc, Germanic.
IE, Indo-European.
illus., illustrated, illustration(s).
impr., impression.
incl., including, include(s).
Inst., Institute (and foreign equivalents).
inst., институт.
introd., introduction, introduced by, introductory.
izd., издание.
izd-vo, издательство.
Jb., Jahrbuch.
Jg, Jahrgang.

Jh., Jahrhundert.
Jo., Journal.
kn., книжный, etc.
lit., literature, literary (and foreign equivalents).
MS, manuscript.
m-vo, министерство.
n.d., no date.
n.F., neue Folge.
no., number (and foreign equivalents).
n.s., new series.
obl., областной, etc.
PGmc, Primitive Germanic.
pl., plate.
pref., preface (by).
Proc., Proceedings.
publ., publication, published (by).
ref., reference.
repr., reprint(ed).
resp., responsible.
Rev., Review, Revista, Revue.
rev., revised (by).
s., siècle.
ser., series.
Slg, Sammlung.
Soc., Society (and foreign equivalents).
supp., supplement.
Trans., Transactions.
trans., translated (by), translation.
Univ., University (and foreign equivalents).
univ., университет.
unpubl., unpublished.
U.P., University Press (and foreign equivalents).
upr., управление.
Vlg, Verlag.
vol., volume.
vs, versus.
wyd., wydawnictwo.

* before a publication signifies that it has not been seen by the contributor.

III. PLACE NAMES

B, Barcelona.
BA, Buenos Aires.
Be, Belgrade.
Bo, Bologna.
C, Coimbra.
F, Florence.
Gd, Gdańsk.
Kw, Kraków, Cracow.
L, Lisbon.
Ld, Leningrad.
M, Madrid.
Mi, Milan.
Mw, Moscow.

Na, Naples.
NY, New York.
O, Oporto.
Pń, Poznań.
R, Rio de Janeiro.
Ro, Rome.
SPo, São Paulo.
T, Turin.
V, Valencia.
Wa, Warsaw.
Ww, Wrocław.
Z, Zagreb.

IV. PERIODICALS, INSTITUTIONS, PUBLISHERS

AA, Antike und Abendland.
AAA, Ardis Publishers, Ann Arbor, Michigan.
AAA, Archivio per l'Alto Adige.
AAASS, American Association for the Advancement of Slavic Studies.
AAL, Atti dell'Accademia dei Lincei.
AAM, Association des Amis de Maynard.
AAPN, Atti dell'Accademia Pontaniana di Napoli.
AAPP, Atti Accademia Peloritana dei Pericolanti. Classe di Lettere Filosofia e Belle Arti.
AASB, Atti dell'Accademia delle Scienze dell'Istituto di Bologna.
AASF, Annales Academiae Scientiarum Fennicae.
AASLAP, Atti dell'Accademia di Scienze, Lettere ed Arti di Palermo.
AASN, Atti dell'Accademia di Scienze Morali e Politiche di Napoli.
AAST, Atti dell'Accademia delle Scienze di Torino.
AAVM, Atti e Memorie dell'Accademia Virgiliana di Mantova.

AAWG, Abhandlungen der Akademie der Wissenschaften in Göttingen, phil.-hist. Kl., 3rd ser., Göttingen, Vandenhoeck & Ruprecht.
AB, Analecta Bollandiana.
ABa, L'Année Balzacienne.
ABAG, Amsterdamer Beiträge zur älteren Germanistik.
ABB, Archives et Bibliothèques de Belgique — Archief– en Bibliotheekswezen in België.
ABDB, Aus dem Antiquariat. Beiträge zum Börsenblatt für den deutschen Buchhandel.
ABDO, Association Bourguignonne de Dialectologie et d'Onomastique, Fontaine lès Dijon.
ABHL, Annual Bulletin of Historical Literature.
ABI, Accademie e Biblioteche d'Italia.
ABN, Anais da Biblioteca Nacional, Rio de Janeiro.
ABNG, Amsterdamer Beiträge zur neueren Germanistik, Amsterdam, Rodopi.
ABor, Acta Borussica.
ABP, Arquivo de Bibliografia Portuguesa.
ABR, American Benedictine Review.

ABr, Annales de Bretagne et des Pays de l'Ouest.
ABS, Acta Baltico-Slavica.
AC, Analecta Cisterciensa, Rome.
ACer, Anales Cervantinos, Madrid.
ACo, Acta Comeniana, Prague.
Acme, Annali della Facoltà di Filosofia e Lettere dell'Università Statale di Milano.
ACP, L'Amitié Charles Péguy.
ACUA, Anales del Colegio Universitario de Almería.
AD, Analysen und Dokumente. Beiträge zur Neueren Literatur, Berne, Lang.
ADA, Anzeiger für Deutsches Altertum und Deutsche Literatur.
AE, Artemis Einführungen, Munich, Artemis.
AE, L'Autre Europe.
AEA, Anuario de Estudios Atlánticos, Las Palmas.
AEd, Arbeiten zur Editionswissenschaft, Frankfurt, Lang.
AEF, Anuario de Estudios Filológicos, Cáceres.
AEL, Anuario de la Escuela de Letras, Mérida, Venezuela.
AEM, Anuario de Estudios Medievales.
AESC, Annales. Économies—Sociétés—Civilisations.
AF, Anuario de Filología, Barcelona.
AFA, Archivo de Filología Aragonesa.
AFF, Anali Filološkog fakulteta, Belgrade.
AFH, Archivum Franciscanum Historicum.
AFHis, Anales de Filología Hispánica.
AfL, L'Afrique Littéraire.
AFLE, Annali della Fondazione Luigi Einaudi.
AFLFUB, Annali della Facoltà di Lettere e Filosofia dell'Università di Bari.
AFLFUC, Annali della Facoltà di Lettere e Filosofia dell'Università di Cagliari.
AFLFUG, Annali della Facoltà di Lettere e Filosofia dell'Università degli Studi di Genova.

AFLFUM, Annali della Facoltà di Lettere e Filosofia dell'Università di Macerata.
AFLFUP(SF), Annali dellà Facoltà di Lettere e Filosofia dell'Università di Perugia. 1. Studi Filosofici.
AFLFUP(SLL), Annali della Facoltà di Lettere e Filosofia dell'Università di Perugia. 3. Studi Linguistici-Letterari.
AFLFUS, Annali della Facoltà di Lettere e Filosofia dell'Università di Siena.
AFLLS, Annali della Facoltà di Lingua e Letterature Straniere di Ca' Foscari, Venice.
AFLN, Annales de la Faculté des Lettres et Sciences Humaines de Nice.
AFP, Archivum Fratrum Praedicatorum.
AFrP, Athlone French Poets, London, The Athlone Press.
AG, Anales Galdosianos.
AGB, Archiv für Geschichte des Buchwesens.
AGI, Archivio Glottologico Italiano.
AGJSG, Acta Germanica. Jahrbuch des Südafrikanischen Germanistenverbandes.
AGP, Archiv für Geschichte der Philosophie.
AH, Archivo Hispalense.
AHAW, Abhandlungen der Heidelberger Akademie der Wissenschaften, phil.-hist. Kl.
AHCP, Arquivos de História de Cultura Portuguesa.
AHDLMA, Archives d'Histoire Doctrinale et Littéraire du Moyen Âge.
AHF, Archiwum Historii Filozofii i Myśli Społecznej.
AHP, Archivum Historiae Pontificae.
AHR, American Historical Review.
AHRF, Annales Historiques de la Révolution Française.
AHSJ, Archivum Historicum Societatis Jesu.
AI, Almanacco Italiano.
AIBL, Académie des Inscriptions et Belles-Lettres, Comptes Rendus.

AIEM, Anales del Instituto de Estudios Madrileños.

AIEO, Association Internationale d'Études Occitanes.

AIFMUR, Annali dell'Istituto di Filologia Moderna dell'Università di Roma.

AIFUF, Annali dell'Istituto di Filosofia dell'Università di Firenze.

AIHI, Archives Internationales d'Histoire des Idées, The Hague, Nijhoff.

AIHS, Archives Internationales d'Histoire des Sciences.

AILLC, Associació Internacional de Llengua i Literatura Catalanes.

AION(FG), Annali dell'Istituto Universitario Orientale, Naples: Sezione Germanica. Filologia Germanica.

AION(SF), Annali dell'Istituto Universitario Orientale, Naples: Studi Filosofici.

AION(SL), Annali dell'Istituto Universitario Orientale, Naples: Sezione Linguistica.

AION(SR), Annali dell'Istituto Universitario Orientale, Naples: Sezione Romanza.

AION(SS), Annali dell'Istituto Universitario Orientale, Naples: Sezione Slava.

AION(T), Annali dell'Istituto Universitario Orientale, Naples: Sezione Germanica. Studi Tedeschi.

AIPHS, Annuaire de l'Institut de Philologie et de l'Histoire Orientales et Slaves.

AIPS, Annales Instituti Philologiae Slavica Universitatis Debreceniensis de Ludovico Kossuth Nominatae — Slavica.

AIV, Atti dell'Istituto Veneto.

AJ, Alemannisches Jahrbuch.

AJCAI, Actas de las Jornadas de Cultura Arabe e Islámica.

AJFS, Australian Journal of French Studies.

AJGLL, American Journal of Germanic Linguistics and Literatures.

AJL, Australian Journal of Linguistics.

AJP, American Journal of Philology.

AKG, Archiv für Kulturgeschichte.

AKML, Abhandlungen zur Kunst-, Musik- und Literaturwissenschaft, Bonn, Bouvier.

AL, Anuario de Letras, Mexico.

AlAm, Alba de América.

ALB, Annales de la Faculté des Lettres de Besançon.

AlBi, Альманах библиофила, Moscow.

ALE, Anales de Literatura Española, Alicante.

ALEC, Anales de Literatura Española Contemporánea.

ALet, Armas y Letras, Universidad de Nuevo León.

ALEUA, Anales de Literatura Española de la Universidad de Alicante.

ALH, Acta Linguistica Academiae Scientiarum Hungaricae.

ALHA, Anales de la Literatura Hispanoamericana.

ALHa, Acta Linguistica Hafniensia.

ALHisp, Anuario de Lingüística Hispánica.

ALit, Acta Literaria, Chile.

ALitH, Acta Litteraria Academiae Scientiarum Hungaricae.

ALLI, Atlante Linguistico dei Laghi Italiani.

ALM, Archives des Lettres Modernes.

ALMA, Archivum Latinitatis Medii Aevi (Bulletin du Cange).

ALUB, Annales Littéraires de l'Université de Besançon.

AM, Analecta Musicologica.

Am, Américas.

AMAA, Atti e Memorie dell'Accademia d'Arcadia.

AMAASLV, Atti e Memorie dell'Accademia di Agricultura, Scienze e Lettere di Verona.

AMal, Analecta Malacitana.

AMAP, Atti e Memorie dell'Accademia Patavina di Scienze, Lettere ed Arti.

AMAPet, Atti e Memorie dell'Accademia Petrarca di Lettere, Arti e Scienze, Arezzo.

AMAT, Atti e Memorie dell'Accademia Toscana di Scienze e Lettere, La Colombaria.

AMDLS, Arbeiten zur Mittleren Deutschen Literatur und Sprache, Berne, Lang.

AMDSPAPM, Atti e Memorie della Deputazione di Storia Patria per le Antiche Province Modenesi.

AMGG, Abhandlungen der Marburger Gelehrten Gesellschaft, Munich, Fink.

AmH, American Hispanist.

AMid, Annales du Midi.

AML, Athenäums Monographien Literaturwissenschaft, Frankfurt, Athenäum.

AmIn, América Indígena, Mexico.

AMSSSP, Atti e Memorie della Società Savonese di Storia Patria.

AN, Академия наук.

AN, Americana Norvegica.

ANABA, Asociación Nacional de Bibliotecarios, Arquiveros y Arqueólogos.

AnAlf, Annali Alfieriani.

ANeo, Acta Neophilologica, Ljubljana.

ANF, Arkiv för nordisk filologi.

AnI, Annali d'Italianistica.

AnL, Anthropological Linguistics.

AnM, Anuario Medieval.

AnN, Annales de la Normandie.

AnnM, Annuale Medievale.

ANQ, American Notes and Queries.

AnS, Annals of Science.

ANTS, Anglo-Norman Text Society.

AnVi, Antologia Vieusseux.

ANZSGLL, Australian and New Zealand Studies in German Language and Literature, Berne, Lang.

AÖAW, Anzeiger der Österreichischen Akademie der Wissenschaften.

AP, Aurea Parma.

APIFN, Актуальные проблемы истории философии народов СССР.

APK, Aufsätze zur portugiesischen Kulturgeschichte, Görres-Gesellschaft, Münster.

APL, Associação Portuguesa de Linguística, Lisbon.

APPP, Abhandlungen zur Philosophie, Psychologie und Pädagogik, Bonn, Bouvier.

APr, Analecta Praemonstratensia.

APS, Acta Philologica Scandinavica.

APSL, Amsterdamer Publikationen zur Sprache und Literatur, Amsterdam, Rodopi.

APUCF, Association des Publications de la Faculté des Lettres et Sciences Humaines de l'Université de Clermont-Ferrand II, Nouvelle Série.

AQ, Arizona Quarterly.

AR, Archiv für Reformationsgeschichte.

ARAJ, American Romanian Academy Journal.

ARAL, Australian Review of Applied Linguistics.

ARCA, ARCA: Papers of the Liverpool Latin Seminar.

ArCCP, Arquivos do Centro Cultural Português, Paris.

ArFil, Archivio di Filosofia.

ArI, Arthurian Interpretations.

ARL, Athlone Renaissance Library.

ArL, Archivum Linguisticum.

ArLit, Arthurian Literature.

ArP, Археографски прилози.

ArSP, Archivio Storico Pugliese.

ArSPr, Archivio Storico Pratese.

ArSt, Archivi per la Storia.

ART, Atelier Reproduction des Thèses, Univ. de Lille III, Paris, Champion.

AS, The American Scholar.

ASAvS, Annuaire de la Société des Amis du vieux-Strasbourg.

ASB, Archivio Storico Bergamasco.

ASEES, Australian Slavonic and East European Studies.

ASELGC, 1616. Anuario de la Sociedad Española de Literatura General y Comparada.

ASGM, Atti del Sodalizio Glottologico Milanese.

ASI, Archivio Storico Italiano.

ASJ, Acta Slavonica Japonica.

ASL, Archivio Storico Lombardo.

ASNP, Annali della Scuola Normale Superiore di Pisa, Bologna.

ASNS, Archiv für das Studium der Neueren Sprachen und Literaturen.

ASocRous, Annales de la Société J.-J. Rousseau.

ASP, Anzeiger für slavische Philologie.

ASPN, Archivio Storico per le Province Napoletane.

ASPP, Archivio Storico per le Province Parmensi.

ASRSP, Archivio della Società Romana di Storia Patria.

ASSO, Archivio Storico per la Sicilia Orientale.

ASSUL, Annali del Dipartimento di Scienze Storiche e Sociali dell'Università di Lecce.

AST, Analecta Sacra Tarraconensia.

ASt, Austrian Studies.

ASTic, Archivio Storico Ticinese.

AŞUI, (e), (f), Analele Ştiinţifice ale Universităţii 'Al. I. Cuza' din Iaşi, secţ. e, Lingvistică, secţ. f, Literatură.

AT, Athenäums Taschenbücher, Frankfurt, Athenäum.

ATB, Altdeutsche Textbibliothek, Tübingen, Niemeyer.

Ate, Nueva Atenea, Universidad de Concepción, Chile.

ATS, Arbeiten und Texte zur Slavistik, Munich, Sagner.

ATV, Aufbau Taschenbuch Verlag, Berlin, Aufbau.

AtV, Ateneo Veneto.

AUBLLR, Analele Universităţii Bucureşti, Limba şi literatura română.

AUBLLS, Analele Universităţii Bucureşti, Limbi şi literaturi străine.

AUC, Anales de la Universidad de Cuenca.

AUCP, Acta Universitatis Carolinae Pragensis.

AUL, Acta Universitatis Lodziensis.

AUL, Annali della Facoltà di Lettere e Filosofia dell'Università di Lecce.

AUML, Anales de la Universidad de Murcia: Letras.

AUMLA, Journal of the Australasian Universities Modern Language Association.

AUN, Annali della Facoltà di Lettere e Filosofia dell'Università di Napoli.

AUNCFP, Acta Universitatis Nicolai Copernici. Filologia Polska, Toruń.

AUPO, Acta Universitatis Palackianae Olomucensis.

AUS, American University Studies, Berne — New York, Lang.

AUSP, Annali dell'Università per Stranieri di Perugia.

AUSSSR, Acta Universitatis Stockholmiensis. Stockholm Studies in Russian Literature.

AUSSSS, Acta Universitatis Stockholmiensis. Stockholm Slavic Studies.

AUTŞF, Analele Universităţii din Timişoara, Ştiinţe Filologice.

AUUSRU, Acta Universitatis Upsaliensis. Studia Romanica Upsaliensia.

AUW, Acta Universitatis Wratislaviensis.

Av, Аврора.

AVen, Archivio Veneto.

AvT, L'Avant-Scène Théâtre.

AWR, Anglo-Welsh Review.

BA, Bollettino d'Arte.

BAAA, Bulletin de l'Association des Amis d'Alain.

BAAG, Bulletin des Amis d'André Gide.

BAAJG, Bulletin de l'Association des Amis de Jean Giono.

BAAL, Boletín de la Academia Argentina de Letras.

BaB, Bargfelder Bote.

BAC, Biblioteca de Autores Cristianos.

BACol, Boletín de la Academia Colombiana.

BÄDL, Beiträge zur Älteren Deutschen Literaturgeschichte, Berne, Lang.

BADLit, Bonner Arbeiten zur deutschen Literatur, Bonn, Bouvier.

BAE, Biblioteca de Autores Españoles.

BAFJ, Bulletin de l'Association Francis Jammes.

BAG, Boletín de la Academia Gallega.

BAIEO, Bulletins de l'Association Internationale d'Études Occitanes.

BAJR, Bulletin des Amis de Jules Romains.

BAJRAF, Bulletin des Amis de Jacques Rivière et d'Alain-Fournier.

BALI, Bollettino dell'Atlante Linguistico Italiano.

BALM, Bollettino dell'Atlante Linguistico Mediterraneo.

BAN, Българска Академия на Науките, Sofia.

BAR, Biblioteca dell'Archivum Romanicum.

BARLLF, Bulletin de l'Académie Royale de Langues et de Littératures Françaises de Bruxelles.

BAWA, Bayerische Akademie der Wissenschaften. Phil.-hist. Kl. Abhandlungen, n.F., Munich, Beck.

BB, Biblioteca Breve, Lisbon.

BB, Bulletin of Bibliography.

BBB, Berner Beiträge zur Barockgermanistik, Berne, Lang.

BBCS, Bulletin of the Board of Celtic Studies.

BBGN, Brünner Beiträge zur Germanistik und Nordistik.

BBib, Bulletin du Bibliophile.

BBL, Bayreuther Beiträge zur Literaturwissenschaft, Frankfurt, Lang.

BBMP, Boletín de la Biblioteca de Menéndez Pelayo.

BBN, Bibliotheca Bibliographica Neerlandica, Nieuwkoop, De Graaf.

BBNDL, Berliner Beiträge zur neueren deutschen Literaturgeschichte, Berne, Lang.

BBSANZ, Bulletin of the Bibliographical Society of Australia and New Zealand.

BBSIA, Bulletin Bibliographique de la Société Internationale Arthurienne.

BBSMES, Bulletin of the British Society for Middle Eastern Studies.

BBUC, Boletim da Biblioteca da Universidade de Coimbra.

BC, Bulletin of the 'Comediantes', University of Wisconsin.

BCB, Boletín Cultural y Bibliográfico, Bogatá.

BCEC, Bwletin Cymdeithas Emynwyr Cymru.

BCél, Bulletin Célinien.

BCh, Болдинские чтения.

BCLSMP, Académie Royale de Belgique: Bulletin de la Classe des Lettres et des Sciences Morales et Politiques.

BCMV, Bollettino Civici Musei Veneziani.

BCRLT, Bulletin du Centre de Romanistique et de Latinité Tardive.

BCS, Bulletin of Canadian Studies.

BCSM, Bulletin of the Cantigueiros of Santa Maria.

BCSS, Bollettino del Centro di Studi Filologici e Linguistici Siciliani.

BCSV, Bollettino del Centro di Studi Vichiani.

BCZG, Blätter der Carl Zuckmayer Gesellschaft.

BD, Беларуская думка.

BDB, Börsenblatt für den deutschen Buchhandel.

BDBA, Bien Dire et Bien Aprandre.

BDP, Beiträge zur Deutschen Philologie, Giessen, Schmitz.

Be, Беларусь.

BEC, Bibliothèque de l'École des Chartes.

BEDS, Beiträge zur Erforschung der deutschen Sprache.

BelL, Беларуская лінгвістыка.

BelS, Беларускі сьвет.

BEP, Bulletin des Études Portugaises.

BEPar, Bulletin des Études Parnassiennes et Symbolistes.

BEzLit, Български език и литература.

BF, Boletim de Filologia.

BFC, Boletín de Filología, Univ. de Chile.

BFE, Boletín de Filología Española.

BFF, Bulletin Francophone de Finlande.

BFFGL, Boletín de la Fundación Federico García Lorca.

BFLS, Bulletin de la Faculté des Lettres de Strasbourg.

BFo, Biuletyn Fonograficzny.

BFPLUL, Bibliothèque de la Faculté de Philosophie et Lettres de l'Université de Liège.

BFR, Bibliothèque française et romane, Paris, Klincksieck.

BFR, Bulletin of the Fondation C.F. Ramuz.

BFr, Börsenblatt Frankfurt.

BG, Bibliotheca Germanica, Berne, Francke.

BGB, Bulletin de l'Association Guillaume Budé.

BGDSL, Beiträge zur Geschichte der deutschen Sprache und Literatur, Tübingen.

BGKT, Беларускае грамадска-культуральнае таварыства.

BGLKAJ, Beiträge zur Geschichte der Literatur und Kunst des 18. Jahrhunderts, Heidelberg, Winter.

BGP, Bristol German Publications, Bristol U.P.

BGT, Blackwell German Texts, Oxford, Blackwell.

BH, Bulletin Hispanique.

BHR, Bibliothèque d'Humanisme et Renaissance.

BHS, Bulletin of Hispanic Studies.

BI, Bibliographisches Institut, Leipzig.

BibAN, Библиотека Академии наук СССР.

BIDS, Bulletin of the International Dostoevsky Society, Klagenfurt.

BIEA, Boletín del Instituto de Estudios Asturianos.

BIHBR, Bulletin de l'Institut Historique Belge de Rome.

BIHR, Bulletin of the Institute of Historical Research.

BJA, British Journal of Aesthetics.

BJCS, British Journal for Canadian Studies.

BJECS, The British Journal for Eighteenth-Century Studies.

BJHS, British Journal of the History of Science.

BJL, Belgian Journal of Linguistics.

BJR, Bulletin of the John Rylands University Library of Manchester.

BL, Brain and Language.

BLAR, Bulletin of Latin American Research.

BLBI, Bulletin des Leo Baeck Instituts.

BLe, Börsenblatt Leipzig.

BLFCUP, Bibliothèque de Littérature Française Contemporaine de l'Université Paris 7.

BLI, Beiträge zur Linguistik und Informationsverarbeitung.

BLi, Беларуская літаратура. Міжвузаўскі зборнік.

BLJ, British Library Journal.

BLL, Beiträge zur Literatur und Literaturwissenschaft des 20. Jahrhunderts, Berne, Lang.

BLM, Bonniers Litterära Magasin.

BLR, Bibliothèque Littéraire de la Renaissance, Geneva, Slatkine–Paris, Champion.

BLR, Bodleian Library Record.

BLVS, Bibliothek des Literarischen Vereins, Stuttgart, Hiersemann.

BMCP, Bollettino del Museo Civico di Padova.

BML, Беларуская мова і літаратура ў школе.

BMo, Беларуская мова. Міжвузаўскі зборнік.

BNE, Beiträge zur neueren Epochenforschung, Berne, Lang.

BNF, Beiträge zur Namenforschung.

BNL, Beiträge zur neueren Literaturgeschichte, 3rd ser., Heidelberg, Winter.

BNP, Beiträge zur nordischen Philologie.
BOCES, Boletín del Centro de Estudios del Siglo XVIII, Oviedo.
BOP, Bradford Occasional Papers.
BP, Български писател.
BPTJ, Biuletyn Polskiego Towarzystwa Językoznawczego.
BR, Болгарская русистика.
BRA, Bonner Romanistische Arbeiten, Berne, Lang.
BRABLB, Boletín de la Real Academia de Buenas Letras de Barcelona.
BRAC, Boletín de la Real Academia de Córdoba de Ciencias, Bellas Letras, y Nobles Artes.
BRAE, Boletín de la Real Academia Española.
BRAH, Boletín de la Real Academia de la Historia.
BRIES, Bibliothèque Russe de l'Institut d'Études Slaves, Paris, Institut d'Études Slaves.
BRJL, Bulletin ruského jazyka a literatury.
BrL La Bretagne Linguistique.
BRP, Beiträge zur romanischen Philologie.
BS, Biuletyn slawistyczny, Łódź.
BSAM, Bulletin de la Société des Amis de Montaigne.
BSAMPAC, Bulletin de la Société des Amis de Marcel Proust et des Amis de Combray.
BSBS, Bollettino Storico–Bibliografico Subalpino.
BSCC, Boletín de la Sociedad Castellonense de Cultura.
BSD, Bithell Series of Dissertations — MHRA Texts and Dissertations, London, Modern Humanities Research Association.
BSDL, Bochumer Schriften zur deutschen Literatur, Berne, Lang.
BSDSL, Basler Studien zur deutschen Sprache und Literatur, Berne, Francke.
BSE, Галоўная рэдакцыя Беларускай савецкай энцыклапедыі.

BSF, Bollettino di Storia della Filosofia.
BSHPF, Bulletin de la Société de l'Histoire du Protestantisme Français.
BSIS, Bulletin of the Society for Italian Studies.
BSLLW, Bulletin de la Société de Langue et Littérature Wallonnes.
BSLP, Bulletin de la Société de Linguistique de Paris.
BSLV, Bollettino della Società Letteraria di Verona.
BSM, Birmingham Slavonic Monographs, University of Birmingham.
BSOAS, Bulletin of the School of Oriental and African Studies.
BSP, Bollettino Storico Pisano.
BSPC, Bulletin de la Société Paul Claudel.
BSPia, Bollettino Storico Piacentino.
BSPN, Bollettino Storico per le Province di Novara.
BSPSP, Bollettino della Società Pavese di Storia Patria.
BsR, Beck'sche Reihe, Munich, Beck.
BSRS, Bulletin of the Society for Renaissance Studies.
BSSAAPC, Bollettino della Società per gli Studi Storici, Archeologici ed Artistici della Provincia di Cuneo.
BSSCLE, Bulletin of the Society for the Study of the Crusades and the Latin East.
BSSP, Bullettino Senese di Storia Patria.
BSSPHS, Bulletin of the Society for Spanish and Portuguese Historical Studies.
BSSV, Bollettino della Società Storica Valtellinese.
BSZJPS, Bałtosłowiańskie związki językowe. Prace Slawistyczne.
BT, Богословские труды, Moscow.
BTe, Biblioteca Teatrale.
BTH, Boletim de Trabalhos Historicos.
BulEz, Български език.
BW, Bibliothek und Wissenschaft.
BySt, Byzantine Studies.

CA, Cuadernos Americanos.

CAAM, Cahiers de l'Association Les Amis de Milosz.

CAB, Commentari dell'Ateneo di Brescia.

CAC, Les Cahiers de l'Abbaye de Créteil.

CAG, Cahiers André Gide.

CAIEF, Cahiers de l'Association Internationale des Études Françaises.

CalLet, Calabria Letteraria.

CAm, Casa de las Américas, Havana.

CAm, Casa de las Américas, Havana

CanJL, Canadian Journal of Linguistics.

CanL, Canadian Literature.

CanSP, Canadian Slavonic Papers.

CanSS, Canadian–American Slavic Studies.

CARB, Cahiers des Amis de Robert Brasillach.

CAT, Cahiers d'analyse textuelle, Liège, Les Belles Lettres.

CatR, Catalan Review.

CAVL, Cahiers des Amis de Valery Larbaud.

CB, Cuadernos Bibliográficos.

CC, Comparative Criticism.

CCe, Cahiers du Cerf XX.

CCend, Continent Cendrars.

CCF, Cuadernos de la Cátedra Feijoo.

CCMe, Cahiers de Civilisation Médiévale.

CCol, Cahiers Colette.

CCU, Cuadernos de la Cátedra M. de Unamuno.

CD, Cuadernos para el Diálogo.

CdA, Camp de l'Arpa.

CDB, Coleção Documentos Brasileiros.

CDr, Comparative Drama.

CDs, Cahiers du Dix-septième, Athens, Georgia.

CDU, Centre de Documentation Universitaire.

CE, Cahiers Élisabéthains.

CEAL, Centro Editor de América Latina.

CEC, Conselho Estadual de Cultura, Comissão de Literatura, São Paulo.

CEcr, Corps Écrit.

CEDAM, Casa Editrice Dott. A. Milani.

CEG, Cuadernos de Estudios Gallegos.

CEL, Cadernos de Estudos Lingüísticos, Campinas, Brazil.

CEM, Cahiers d'Études Médiévales, Univ. of Montreal.

CEPL, Centre d'Étude et de Promotion de la Lecture, Paris.

CER, Cahiers d'Études Romanes.

CERoum, Cahiers d'Études Roumaines.

CeS, Cultura e Scuola.

CESCM, Centre d'Études Supérieures de Civilisation Médiévale, Poitiers.

CET, Centro Editoriale Toscano.

CEtGer, Cahiers d'Études Germaniques.

CF, Les Cahiers de Fontenay.

CFLA, Cuadernos de Filología. Literaturas: Análisis, Valencia.

CFM, Cahiers François Mauriac.

CFMA, Collection des Classiques Français du Moyen Âge.

CFol, Classical Folia.

CFS, Cahiers Ferdinand de Saussure.

CFSLH, Cuadernos de Filología: Studia Linguistica Hispanica.

CFTM, Classiques Français des Temps Modernes, Paris, Champion.

CG, Cahiers de Grammaire.

CGD, Cahiers Georges Duhamel.

CGFT, Critical Guides to French Texts, London, Grant & Cutler.

CGGT, Critical Guides to German Texts, London, Grant & Cutler.

CGP, Carleton Germanic Papers.

CGS, Colloquia Germanica Stetinensia.

CGST, Critical Guides to Spanish Texts, London, Támesis, Grant & Cutler.

CH, Crítica Hispánica.

CHA, Cuadernos Hispano-Americanos.

CHB, Cahiers Henri Bosco.

ChrI, Chroniques Italiennes.
ChrL, Christianity and Literature.
ChS, Champs du Signe.
CHum, Computers and the Humanities.
CHP, Cahiers Henri Pourrat.
CI, Critical Inquiry.
CiD, La Ciudad de Dios.
CIDO, Centre International de Documentation Occitane, Béziers.
CIF, Cuadernos de Investigación Filológica.
CIH, Cuadernos de Investigación Historica.
CILF, Conseil International de la Langue Française.
CILH, Cuadernos para Inverstigación de la Literatura Hispanica.
CILL, Cahiers de l'Institut de Linguistique de l'Université de Louvain.
CIMAGL, Cahiers de l'Institut du Moyen Âge Grec et Latin, Copenhagen.
CIRVI, Centro Interuniversitario di Ricerche sul 'Viaggio in Italia', Moncalieri.
CIt, Carte Italiane.
CIUS, Canadian Institute of Ukrainian Studies, Edmonton.
CivC, Civiltà Cattolica.
CJb, Celan-Jahrbuch.
CJC, Cahiers Jacques Chardonne.
CJIS, Canadian Journal of Italian Studies.
ČJL, Český jazyk a literatura.
CJNS, Canadian Journal of Netherlandic Studies.
CJP, Cahiers Jean Paulhan.
CJR, Cahiers Jules Romains.
CL, Cuadernos de Leiden.
CL, Comparative Literature.
ČL, Česká literatura.
CLAJ, College Language Association Journal.
CLCC, Cahiers de Littérature Canadienne Comparée.
CLE, Comunicaciones de Literatura Española, Buenos Aires.
CLe, Cahiers de Lexicologie.

CLEAM, Coleción de Literatura Española Aljamiado–Morisca, Madrid, Gredos.
CLESP, Cooperativa Libraria Editrice degli Studenti dell'Università di Padova, Padua.
CLett, Critica Letteraria.
CLF, Cahiers de Linguistique Française.
CLHM, Cahiers de Linguistique Hispanique Médiévale.
CLin, Cercetări de Lingvistica.
CLit, Cadernos de Literatura, Coimbra.
CLO, Cahiers Linguistiques d'Ottawa.
ClP, Classical Philology.
CLS, Comparative Literature Studies.
CLSl, Cahiers de Linguistique Slave.
CLTA, Cahiers de Linguistique Théorique et Appliquée.
CLTL, Cadernos de Lingüística e Teoria da Literatura.
CLUEB, Cooperativa Libraria Universitaria Editrice Bologna.
CM, Classica et Mediaevalia.
CMA, Cahier Marcel Aymé.
CMCS, Cambridge Medieval Celtic Studies.
CMERSA, Center for Medieval and Early Renaissance Studies, State University of New York at Binghamton. Acta.
ČMF (PhP), Časopis pro moderni filologii: Philologica Pragensia.
CMHLB, Cahiers du Monde Hispanique et Luso-Brésilien.
CMi, Culture Milano.
CML, Classical and Modern Literature.
ČMM, Časopis Matice Moravské.
CMP, Cahiers Marcel Proust.
CMRS, Cahiers du Monde Russe et Soviétique.
CN, Cultura Neolatina.
CNat, Les Cahiers Naturalistes.
CNor, Los Cuadernos del Norte.
CNRS, Centre National de la Recherche Scientifique.
CO, Camera Obscura.
CoF, Collectanea Franciscana.
COK, Centralny Ośrodek Kultury, Warsaw.

ColA, Colóquio Artes.
ColGer, Colloquia Germanica.
ColH, Colloquium Helveticum.
ColL, Colóquio Letras.
ComB, Communications of the International Brecht Society.
ComGer, Comunicaciones Germánicas.
CompL, Computational Linguistics.
ConL, Contrastive Linguistics.
ConLet, Il Confronto Letterario.
ConLit, Contemporary Literature.
ConS, Condorcet Studies.
CP, Castrum Peregrini.
CPL, Cahiers Paul Léautand.
CPR, Chroniques de Port-Royal.
CPUC, Cadernos PUC, São Paulo.
CQ, Critical Quarterly.
CR, Contemporary Review.
CRAC, Cahiers Roucher — André Chénier.
CRCL, Canadian Review of Comparative Literature.
CREL, Cahiers Roumains d'Études Littéraires.
CRI, Cuadernos de Ruedo Ibérico.
CRIAR, Cahiers du Centre de Recherches Ibériques et Ibéro-Américains de l'Université de Rouen.
CRIN, Cahiers de Recherches des Instituts Néerlandais de Langue et Littérature Françaises.
CRQ, Cahiers Raymond Queneau.
CRR, Cincinnati Romance Review.
CRRI, Centre de Recherche sur la Renaissance Italienne, Paris.
ČRu, Československá rusistika.
CS, Cornish Studies.
ČSAV, Československá akademie věd.
CSDI, Centro di Studio per la Dialettologia Italiana.
CSem, Caiete de Semiotică.
CSFLS, Centro di Studi Filologici e Linguistici Siciliani, Palermo.
CSG, Cambridge Studies in German, Cambridge U.P.
CSGLL, Canadian Studies in German Language and Literature, Berne — New York — Frankfurt, Lang.

CSIC, Consejo Superior de Investigaciones Científicas, Madrid.
CSJP, Cahiers Saint-John Perse.
CSl, Critica Slovia, Florence.
CSM, Les Cahiers de Saint-Martin.
ČSp, Československý spisovatel.
CSS, California Slavic Studies.
CSSH, Comparative Studies in Society and History.
CST, Cahiers de Sémiotique Textuelle.
CSt, Critica Storica.
CT, Christianity Today.
CTC, Cuadernos de Teatro Clásico.
CTE, Cuadernos de Traducción e Interpretación.
CTe, Cuadernos de Teología.
CTH, Cahiers Tristan l'Hermite.
CTh, Ciencia Tomista.
CTL, Current Trends in Linguistics.
CUECM, Cooperativa Universitaria Editrice Catanese Magistero.
CUP, Cambridge University Press.
CUUCV, Cultura Universitaria de la Universidad Central de Venezuela.
CWPWL, Cardiff Working Papers in Welsh Linguistics.

Da, Даугава, Riga.
DAEM, Deutsches Archiv für Erforschung des Mittelalters.
DaF, Deutsch als Fremdsprache.
DalR, Dalhousie Review.
DanU, Dansk Udsyn.
DaSt, Dante Studies.
DB, Дзяржаўная бібліятэка БССР.
DB, Doitsu Bungaku.
DBl, Driemaandelijkse Bladen.
DBO, Deutsche Bibliothek des Ostens, Berlin, Nicolai.
DBR, Les Dialectes Belgo-Romans.
DBr, Doitsu Bungakoranko.
DCFH, Dicenda. Cuadernos de Filología Hispánica.
DD, Diskussion Deutsch.
DDG, Deutsche Dialektgeographie, Marburg, Elwert.
DDJ, Deutsches Dante-Jahrbuch.
DegSec, Degré Second.

DESB, Delta Epsilon Sigma
Bulletin, Dubuque, Iowa.
DeutB, Deutsche Bücher.
DeutUB, Deutschungarische
Beiträge.
DFC, Durham French Colloquies.
DFS, Dalhousie French Studies.
DgF, Danmarks gamle Folkeviser.
DHA, Diálogos Hispánicos de
Amsterdam, Rodopi.
DHR, Duquesne Hispanic Review.
DhS, Dix-huitième Siècle.
DI, Deutscher Idealismus,
Stuttgart, Klett-Cotta Verlag.
DI, Декоративное искусство.
DIAS, Dublin Institute for
Advanced Studies.
DiL, Dictionnairique et
Lexicographie.
DisA, Dissertation Abstracts.
DisSlSHL, Dissertationes Slavicae:
Sectio Historiae Litterarum.
DisSlSL, Dissertationes Slavicae:
Sectio Linguistica.
DK, Duitse Kroniek.
DkJb, Deutschkanadisches
Jahrbuch.
DKV, Deutscher Klassiker Verlag,
Frankfurt.
DL, Детская литература.
DL, Детская литература.
DLA, Deutsche Literatur von den
Anfängen bis 1700, Berne —
Frankfurt — Paris — New York,
Lang.
DLit, Discurso Literario.
DLM, Deutsche Literatur des
Mittelalters (Wissenschaftliche
Beiträge der Ernst-Moritz-Arndt-
Universität Greifswald).
DLR, Deutsche Literatur in
Reprints, Munich, Fink.
DMTS, Davis Medieval Texts and
Studies, Leiden, Brill.
DN, Дружба народов.
Dni, Дніпро.
DNT, De Nieuwe Taalgids.
DosS, Dostoevsky Studies.
DoV, Дошкольное воспитание.
DPL, De Proprietatibus Litterarum,
The Hague, Mouton.
DpL, День поэзии, Leningrad.
DpM, День поэзии, Moscow.
DR, Drama Review.

DRLAV, DRLAV, Revue de
Linguistique.
DS, Diderot Studies.
DSEÜ, Deutsche Sprache in Europa
und Übersee, Stuttgart, Steiner.
DSL, Det danske Sprog- og
Litteraturselskab.
DSp, Deutsche Sprache.
DSS, XVIIᵉ Siècle.
DSt, Deutsche Studien,
Meisenheim, Hain.
DSt, Danske Studier.
DT, Deutsche Texte, Tübingen,
Niemeyer.
DteolT, Dansk teologisk Tidsskrift.
DtL, Die deutsche Literatur.
DTM, Deutsche Texte des
Mittelalters, Berlin, Akademie.
DTV, Deutscher Taschenbuch
Verlag, Munich.
DUB, Deutschunterricht, East
Berlin.
DUJ, Durham University Journal
(New Series).
DUS, Der Deutschunterricht,
Stuttgart.
DUSA, Deutschunterricht in
Südafrika.
DV, Дальний Восток.
DVA, Deutsche Verlags-Anstalt,
Stuttgart.
DVLG, Deutsche
Vierteljahresschrift für
Literaturwissenschaft und
Geistesgeschichte.
Dz, Дзвін.

E, Verlag Enzyklopädie, Leipzig.
EB, Estudos Brasileiros.
EBal, Etudes Balkaniques.
EBTch, Études Balkaniques
Tchécoslovaques.
EC, El Escritor y la Crítica,
Colección Persiles, Madrid,
Taurus.
EC, Études Celtiques.
ECan, Études Canadiennes.
ECent, The Eighteenth Century,
Lubbock, Texas.
ECentF, Eighteenth-Century Fiction.
ECF, Écrits du Canada Français.
ECI, Eighteenth-Century Ireland.

ECIG, Edizioni Culturali
   Internazionali Genova.
ECla, Les Études Classiques.
ECon, España Contemporánea.
ECr, Essays in Criticism.
ECS, Eighteenth Century Studies.
EdCat, Ediciones Cátedra, Madrid.
EDESA, Ediciones Españolas S.A.
EDHS, Études sur le XVIIIᵉ Siècle.
EDL, Études de Lettres.
EDT, Edizioni di Torino.
EE, Erasmus in English.
EEQ, East European Quarterly.
EF, Erträge der Forschung,
   Darmstadt, Wissenschaftliche
   Buchgesellschaft.
EF, Études Françaises.
EFE, Estudios de Fonética
   Experimental.
EFF, Ergebnisse der
   Frauenforschung.
EFil, Estudios Filológicos, Valdivia,
   Chile.
EFL, Essays in French Literature,
   Univ. of Western Australia.
EFR, Éditeurs Français Réunis.
EG, Études Germaniques.
EH, Europäische
   Hochschulschriften, Berne–
   Frankfurt, Lang.
EH, Estudios Humanísticos.
EHF, Estudios Humanísticos.
   Filología.
EHN, Estudios de Historia
   Novohispana.
EHQ, European History Quarterly.
EHR, English Historical Review.
EHS, Estudios de Historia Social.
EHT, Exeter Hispanic Texts,
   Exeter.
EIA, Estudos Ibero-Americanos.
EIP, Estudos Italianos em Portugal.
EL, Esperienze Letterarie.
El, Elementa, Würzburg,
   Königshausen & Neumann
   –Amsterdam, Rodopi.
ELA, Études de Linguistique
   Appliquée.
ELF, Études Littéraires Françaises,
   Paris, J.-M. Place — Tübingen,
   Narr.
ELH, English Literary History.
ELit, Essays in Literature.

ELLC, Estudis de Llengua i
   Literatura Catalanes.
ELLF, Études de Langue et
   Littérature Françaises, Tokyo.
ELR, English Literary Renaissance.
ELu, Estudios Lulianos.
EM, English Miscellany, Rome.
EMus, Early Music.
En, Енисей.
ENC, Els Nostres Clàssics,
   Barcelona, Barcino.
ENSJF, École Nationale Supérieure
   de Jeunes Filles.
EO, Europa Orientalis.
EOc, Estudis Occitans.
EP, Études Philosophiques.
Ep, Epistemata, Würzburg,
   Königshausen & Neumann.
EPESA, Ediciones y Publicaciones
   Españolas S.A.
EPoet, Essays in Poetics.
ER, Estudis Romànics.
ERab, Études Rabelaisiennes.
ERB, Études Romanes de Brno.
ER(BSRLR), Études Romanes
   (Bulletin de la Société Roumaine
   de Linguistique Romane).
ERL, Études Romanes de Lund.
ErlF, Erlanger Forschungen.
EROPD, Ежегодник рукописного
   отдела Пушкинского дома.
ERR, European Romantic Review.
ES, Erlanger Studien, Erlangen,
   Palm & Enke.
ES, Estudios Segovianos.
EsC, L'Esprit Créateur.
ESk, Edition Suhrkamp, Frankfurt,
   Suhrkamp.
EspA, Español Actual.
ESt, English Studies.
EstE, Estudios Escénicos.
EstG, Estudi General.
EstH, Estudios Hispánicos.
EstL, Estudios de Lingüística,
   Alicante.
EstR, Estudios Románticos.
EStud, Essays and Studies.
ET, L'Écrit du Temps.
EtCan, Études Canadiennes.
ETJ, Educational Theatre Journal.
ETL, Explicación de Textos
   Literarios.
EtLitt, Études Littéraires, Quebec.

EUDEBA, Editorial Universitaria de Buenos Aires.

EUNSA, Ediciones Universidad de Navarra, Pamplona.

EUS, European University Studies, Berne, Lang.

EzLit, Език и литература.

FAL, Forum Academicum Literaturwissenschaft, Königstein, Hain.

FAPESP, Fundação de Amparo à Pesquisa do Estado de São Paulo.

FAR, French-American Review.

FAS, Frankfurter Abhandlungen zur Slavistik, Giessen, Schmitz.

FBAN, Фундаментальная бібліятэка Акадэміі навук БССР.

FBG, Frankfurter Beiträge zur Germanistik, Heidelberg, Winter.

FBS, Franco-British Studies.

FC, Filologia e Critica.

FCE, Fondo de Cultura Económica, Mexico.

FCG — CCP, Fondation Calouste Gulbenkian — Centre Culturel Portugais, Paris.

FCS, Fifteenth Century Studies.

FDL, Facetten deutscher Literatur, Berne, Haupt.

FEI, Faites entrer l'infini. Journal de la Société des Amis de Louis Aragon et Elsa Triolet.

FEK, Forschungen zur europäischen Kultur, Berne, Lang.

FemSt, Feministische Studien.

FFM, French Forum Monographs, Lexington, Kentucky.

FGÄDL, Forschungen zur Geschichte der älteren deutschen Literatur, Munich, Fink.

FH, Fundamenta Historica, Stuttgart-Bad Cannstatt, Frommann-Holzboog.

FH, Frankfurter Hefte.

FHL, Forum Homosexualität und Literatur.

FHS, French Historical Studies.

Fi, Filología, Buenos Aires.

FIDS, Forschungsberichte des Instituts für Deutsche Sprache, Tübingen, Narr.

Fil, Filosofia, Turin.

FilMod, Filologia Moderna, Udine –Pisa.

FilN, Филологические науки.

FilR, Filologia Romanza.

FilS, Filologické studie.

FilZ, Filologija, Zagreb.

FiM, Filologia Moderna, Facultad de Filosofía y Letras, Madrid.

FinS, Fin de Siglo.

FIRL, Forum at Iowa on Russian Literature.

FLG, Freiburger literaturpsychologische Gespräche.

FLin, Folia Linguistica.

FLinHist, Folia Linguistica Historica.

FLK, Forschungen zur Literatur- und Kulturgeschichte. Beiträge zur Sprach- und Literaturwissenschaft, Berne, Lang.

FLS, French Literature Series.

FLV, Fontes Linguae Vasconum.

FM, Le Français Moderne.

FMLS, Forum for Modern Language Studies.

FmSt, Frühmittelalterliche Studien.

FMT, Forum Modernes Theater.

FNT, Foilseacháin Náisiúnta Tta.

FoI, Forum Italicum.

FP, Folia Phonetica.

FR, French Review.

FrA, Le Français aujourd'hui.

FranS, Franciscan Studies.

FrCS, French Cultural Studies.

FrF, French Forum.

FrP Le Français Préclassique.

FS, Forum Slavicum, Munich, Fink.

FS, French Studies.

FSB, French Studies Bulletin.

FSlav, Folia Slavica.

FSSA, French Studies in Southern Africa.

FT, Fischer Taschenbuch, Frankfurt, Fischer.

FT, Finsk Tidskrift.

FUE, Fundación Universitaria Española.

FV, Fortuna Vitrea, Tübingen, Niemeyer.

FZPT, Freiburger Zeitschrift für Philosophie und Theologie.

G, Грани.

GA, Germanistische Arbeitshefte, Tübingen, Niemeyer.

GAB, Göppinger Akademische Beiträge, Lauterburg, Kümmerle.

GAG, Göppinger Arbeiten zur Germanistik, Lauterburg, Kümmerle.

GAKS, Gesammelte Aufsätze zur Kulturgeschichte Spaniens.

GANDLL, Giessener Arbeiten zur neueren deutschen Literatur und Literaturwissenschaft, Berne, Lang.

GAS, German-Australian Studies, Berne, Lang.

GASK, Germanistische Arbeiten zu Sprache und Kulturgeschichte, Frankfurt, Lang.

GBA, Gazette des Beaux-Arts.

GBL, Государственная библиотека СССР им. В. И. Ленина.

GCFI, Giornale Critico della Filosofia Italiana.

GDRMon, GDR Monitor, Dundee.

GerAb, Germanistische Abhandlungen, Stuttgart, Metzler

GerLux, Germanistik Luxembourg.

GermL, Germanistische Linguistik.

GeW, Germanica Wratislaviensia.

GF, Giornale di Fisica.

GFFNS, Godišnjak Filozofskog fakulteta u Novom Sadu.

GG, Geschichte und Gesellschaft.

GGF, Göteborger Germanistische Forschungen, University of Gothenburg.

GGF, Greifswalder Germanistische Forschungen.

GGVD, Grundlagen und Gedanken zum Verständnis des Dramas, Frankfurt, Diesterweg.

GGVEL, Grundlagen und Gedanken zum Verständnis erzählender Literatur, Frankfurt, Diesterweg.

GHT, Göteborgs Handelstidning.

GIF, Giornale Italiano di Filologia.

GIGFL, Glasgow Introductory Guides to French Literature.

GIGGL, Glasgow Introductory Guides to German Literature.

GJ, Gutenberg-Jahrbuch.

GJb, Goethe Jahrbuch.

GK, Goldmann Klassiker, Munich, Goldmann.

GL, Germanistische Lehrbuchsammlung, Berne, Lang.

GL, General Linguistics.

GLC, German Life and Civilisation, Berne, Lang.

GLL, German Life and Letters.

GLML, The Garland Library of Medieval Literature, New York –London, Garland.

GLR, García Lorca Review.

GLS, Grazer Linguistische Studien.

Glyph, Glyph: Johns Hopkins Textual Studies, Baltimore.

GM, Germanistische Mitteilungen.

GN, Germanic Notes.

Go, Горизонт.

GPB, Государственная публичная библиотека им. М. Е. Салтыкова-Щедрина.

GPI, Государственный педагогический институт.

GPIB, Государственная публичная историческая библиотека.

GPSR, Glossaire des Patois de la Suisse Romande.

GQ, German Quarterly.

GR, Germanic Review.

GRLH, Garland Reference Library of the Humanities, New York — London, Garland.

GRLM, Grundriss der romanischen Literaturen des Mittelalters.

GRM, Germanisch-Romanische Monatsschrift.

GrSt, Grundtvig Studier.

GSA, Germanic Studies in America, Berne–Frankfurt, Lang.

GSI, German Studies in India.

GSl, Germano-Slavica, Ontario.

GSLI, Giornale Storico della Letteratura Italiana.

GSR, German Studies Review.

GSSL, Göttinger Schriften zur
Sprach– und
Literaturwissenschaft, Göttingen,
Herodot.
GSU, Годишник на Софийския
университет. Факултет по
славенски филологии, Bulgarian
Academy of Sciences, Sofia.
GTN, Gdańskie Towarzystwo
Naukowe.
GTS, Germanistische Texte und
Studien, Hildesheim, Olms.
GY, Goethe Yearbook.
GZPI, Государственный заочный
педагогический институт.

H, Hochschulschriften, Cologne,
Pahl-Rugenstein.
HAHR, Hispanic American
Historical Review.
HB, Horváth Blätter.
HBA, Historiografía y Bibliografía
Americanistas, Seville.
HBG, Hamburger Beiträge zur
Germanistik, Berne, Lang.
HDG, Huis aan de Drie Grachten,
Amsterdam.
HEI, History of European Ideas.
HES, Histoire, Économie et Société.
HeyJ, Heythrop Journal.
HF, Heidelberger Forschungen,
Heidelberg, Winter.
HI, Historica Ibérica.
HIAR, Hamburger Ibero-
Amerikanische Reihe.
HICL, Histoire des Idées et Critique
Littéraire, Geneva, Droz.
His, Hispania, Madrid.
HisJ, Hispanic Journal, Indiana–
Pennsylvania.
HisL, Hispanic Linguistics.
HistL, Historiographia Linguistica.
HistS, History of Science.
His(US), Hispania, Los Angeles.
HJ, Historical Journal.
HJb, Heidelberger Jahrbücher.
HKADL, Historisch-kritische
Arbeiten zur deutschen Literatur,
Frankfurt, Lang.
HKZMTLG, Handelingen van de
Koninklijke Zuidnederlandse
Maatschappij voor Taalen,
Letterkunde en Geschiedenis.

HL, Hochschulschriften
Literaturwissenschaft,
Königstein, Hain.
HL, Humanistica Lovaniensia.
HLB, Harvard Library Bulletin.
HLQ, Huntingdon Library
Quarterly.
HMJb, Heinrich Mann Jahrbuch.
HPS, Hamburger Philologische
Studien, Hamburg, Buske.
HPSl, Heidelberger Publikationen
zur Slavistik, Frankfurt, Lang.
HPT, History of Political Thought.
HR, Hispanic Review.
HRel, History of Religions.
HRev, Hrvatska revija.
HS, Helfant Studien, Stuttgart,
Helfant.
HS, Hispania Sacra.
HSLA, Hebrew University Studies
in Literature and the Arts.
HSlav, Hungaro-Slavica.
HSMS, Hispanic Seminary of
Medieval Studies, Madison.
HSp, Historische Sprachforschung
(Historical Linguistics).
HSS, Harvard Slavic Studies.
HSSL, Harvard Studies in Slavic
Linguistics.
HSt, Hispanische Studien.
HSWSL, Hallesche Studien zur
Wirkung von Sprache und
Literatur.
HT, Helfant Texte, Stuttgart,
Helfant.
HT, History Today.
HTh, History and Theory.
HTR, Harvard Theological Review.
HUS, Harvard Ukrainian Studies.
HZ, Historische Zeitschrift.

IÅ, Ibsen-Årbok, Oslo.
IAP, Ibero-Americana Pragensia.
IAr, Iberoamerikanisches Archiv.
IARB, Inter-American Review of
Bibliography.
IASL, Internationales Archiv für
Sozialgeschichte der deutschen
Literatur.
IASLS, Internationales Archiv für
Sozialgeschichte der deutschen
Literatur: Sonderheft.
IB, Insel-Bücherei, Frankfurt, Insel.

IBKG, Innsbrucker Beiträge zur Kulturwissenschaft. Germanistische Reihe.

IBL, Instytut Badań Literackich PAN, Warsaw.

IBLe, Insel-Bücherei, Leipzig, Insel.

IBS, Innsbrücker Beiträge zur Sprachwissenschaft.

IC, Index on Censorship.

ICALP, Instituto de Cultura e Língua Portuguesa, Lisbon.

ICALPR, Instituto de Cultura e Língua Portuguesa. Revista.

ICC, Instituto Caro y Cuervo, Bogotá.

ID, Italia Dialettale.

IDF, Informationen Deutsch als Fremdsprache.

IDL, Indices zur deutschen Literatur, Tübingen, Niemeyer.

IdLit, Ideologies and Literature.

IEC, Institut d'Estudis Catalans.

IEI, Istituto dell'Enciclopedia Italiana.

IES, Institut d'Études Slaves, Paris.

IF, Impulse der Forschung, Darmstadt, Wissenschaftliche Buchgesellschaft.

IF, Indogermanische Forschungen.

IFC, Institutión Fernando el Católico.

IFEE, Investigación Franco-Española. Estudios.

IFiS, Instytut Filozofii i Socjologii PAN, Warsaw.

IFR, International Fiction Review.

IG, Informations Grammaticales.

IHE, Índice Histórico Español.

IHS, Irish Historical Studies.

II, Information und Interpretation, Frankfurt, Lang.

IIa, Институт языкознания.

III, Институт истории искусств.

IJ, Italian Journal.

IJAL, International Journal of American Linguistics.

IJCS, International Journal of Canadian Studies.

IJL, International Journal of Lexicography.

IJP, International Journal of Psycholinguistics.

IJSL, International Journal for the Sociology of Language.

IJSLP, International Journal of Slavic Linguistics and Poetics.

IK, Искусство кино.

IKU, Institut za književnost i umetnost, Belgrade.

IL, L'Information Littéraire.

ILASLR, Istituto Lombardo. Accademia di Scienze e Lettere. Rendiconti.

ILen, Искусство Ленинграда.

ILing, Incontri Linguistici.

IML, Институт мировой литературы имени А. М. Горького.

IMN, Irisleabhar Mhá Nuad.

IMU, Italia Medioevale e Umanistica.

InfD, Informationen und Didaktik.

INLF, Institut National de la Langue Française.

INIC, Instituto Nacional de Investigação Científica.

INION, Институт научной информации по общественным наукам Академии наук СССР.

InL, Иностранная литература.

INLE, Instituto Nacional del Libro Español.

INSS, Indiana Slavic Studies.

InstEB, Inst. de Estudos Brasileiros.

InstNL, Inst. Nacional do Livro, Brasilia.

IO, Italiano e Oltre.

IPL, Istituto di Propaganda Libraria.

IR, L'Immagine Riflessa.

IRAL, International Review of Applied Linguistics.

IRIa, Институт русского языка.

IRIaP, Институт русского языка АН СССР. Проблемная группа по экспериментальной и прикладной лингвистике. Предварительные публикации, Moscow.

IrR, The Irish Review.

IRSH, International Review of Social History.

IRSL, International Review of Slavic Linguistics.

IS, Институт славяноведения.

IS, Iberian Studies.

Is, Искусство.

ISLIa, Известия Академии наук СССР. Серия литературы и языка.

ISOAN, Известия сибирского отделения АН СССР, Novosibirsk.

ISP, International Studies in Philosophy.

ISS, Irish Slavonic Studies.

ISSA, Studi d'Italianistica nell'Africa Australe: Italian Studies in Southern Africa.

ISt, Italian Studies.

IT, Insel Taschenbuch, Frankfurt, Insel.

ITL, ITL. Review of Applied Linguistics, Instituut voor Toegepaste Linguistiek, Leuven.

ItQ, Italian Quarterly.

ITsK, Известия ЦК КПСС.

ItStudien, Italienische Studien.

Iu, Юность.

IUJF, Internationales Uwe-Johnson-Forum.

IUP, Irish University Press.

IUR, Irish University Review.

IuU, Южный Урал.

IV, Istituto Veneto di Scienze, Lettere ed Arti.

IVAS, Indices Verborum zum altdeutschen Schrifttum, Amsterdam, Rodopi.

IVN, Internationale Vereniging voor Nederlandistiek.

JAAC, Journal of Aesthetics and Art Criticism.

JAE, Journal of Aesthetic Education.

JAMS, Journal of the American Musicological Society.

JAOS, Journal of the American Oriental Society.

JanL, Janua Linguarum, The Hague, Mouton.

JAPLA, Journal of the Atlantic Provinces Linguistic Association.

JARA, Journal of the American Romanian Academy of Arts and Sciences.

JATI, Association of Teachers of Italian Journal.

JazA, Jazykovědné aktuality.

JazŠ, Jazykovedné štúdie.

JAZU, Jugoslavenska akademija znanosti i umjetnosti.

JBS, Journal of Byelorussian Studies.

JBSP, Journal of the British Society for Phenomenology.

JČ, Jazykovedný časopis, Bratislava.

JCanS, Journal of Canadian Studies.

JCL, Journal of Child Language.

JCS, Journal of Celtic Studies.

JDASD, Deutsche Akademie für Sprache und Dichtung: Jahrbuch.

JDF, Jahrbuch Deutsch als Fremdsprache.

JDSG, Jahrbuch der Deutschen Schiller-Gesellschaft.

JEGP, Journal of English and Germanic Philology.

JEH, Journal of Ecclesiastical History.

JEL, Journal of English Linguistics.

JES, Journal of European Studies.

JF, Južnoslovenski filolog.

JFDH, Jahrbuch des Freien Deutschen Hochstifts.

JFinL, Jahrbuch für finnisch-deutsche Literaturbeziehungen.

JFL, Jahrbuch für fränkische Landesforschung.

JFLS, Journal of French Language Studies.

JFR, Journal of Folklore Research.

JG, Jahrbuch für Geschichte, Berlin, Akademie.

JGO, Jahrbücher für die Geschichte Osteuropas.

JHA, Journal for the History of Astronomy.

JHI, Journal of the History of Ideas.

JHispP, Journal of Hispanic Philology.

JHP, Journal of the History of Philosophy.

JHS, Journal of the History of Sexuality.

JIAS, Journal of Inter-American Studies.

JIES, Journal of Indo-European Studies.

JIG, Jahrbuch für Internationale Germanistik.

JIL, Journal of Italian Linguistics.

JILS, Journal of Interdisciplinary Literary Studies.
JIPA, Journal of the International Phonetic Association.
JJQ, James Joyce Quarterly.
JJS, Journal of Jewish Studies.
JL, Journal of Linguistics.
JLAL, Journal of Latin American Lore.
JLAS, Journal of Latin American Studies.
JLH, Journal of Library History.
JLitDDR, Jahrbuch zur Literatur in der DDR.
JLS, Journal of Literary Semantics.
JLSP, Journal of Language and Social Psychology.
JMH, Journal of Medieval History.
JML, Journal of Modern Literature.
JMLat, Journal of Medieval Latin.
JMMD, Journal of Multilingual and Multicultural Development.
JMMLA, Journal of the Midwest Modern Language Association.
JModH, Journal of Modern History.
JMP, Journal of Medicine and Philosophy.
JMRS, Journal of Medieval and Renaissance Studies.
JNT, Journal of Narrative Technique.
JONVL, Een Jaarboek: Overzicht van de Nederlandse en Vlaamse Literatuur.
JOWG, Jahrbuch der Oswald von Wolkenstein Gesellschaft.
JP, Journal of Pragmatics.
JPC, Journal of Popular Culture.
JPCL, Journal of Pidgin and Creole Languages.
JPh, Journal of Phonetics.
JPol, Język Polski.
JPR, Journal of Psycholinguistic Research.
JQ, Jacques e i Suoi Quaderni.
JRH, Journal of Religious History.
JRIC, Journal of the Royal Institution of Cornwall.
JRMA, Journal of the Royal Musical Association.
JRMMRA, Journal of the Rocky Mountain Medieval and Renaissance Association.

JRUL, Journal of the Rutgers University Libraries.
JRuS, Journal of Russian Studies.
JS, Journal des Savants.
JSEES, Japanese Slavic and East European Studies.
JSFWUB, Jahrbuch der Schlesischen Friedrich-Wilhelms-Universität zu Breslau.
JSH, Jihočeský sborník historický.
JSHR, Journal of Speech and Hearing Research.
JSS, Journal of Spanish Studies: Twentieth Century.
JTS, Journal of Theological Studies.
JU, Judentum und Umwelt, Berne, Lang.
JUS, Journal of Ukrainian Studies.
JVF, Jahrbuch für Volksliedforschung.
JVLVB, Journal of Verbal Learning and Verbal Behavior.
JWBS, Journal of the Welsh Bibliographical Society.
JWCI, Journal of the Warburg and Courtauld Institutes.
JWGV, Jahrbuch des Wiener Goethe-Vereins, Neue Folge.
JWH, Journal of World History.
JZ, Jazykovedný zborník.

К, Континент.
KANTL, Koninklijke Akademie voor Nederlandse Taal- en Letterkunde.
KASL, Kasseler Arbeiten zur Sprache und Literatur, Frankfurt, Lang.
KAW, Krajowa Agencja Wydawnicza.
KAWLSK, Koninklijke Academie voor Wetenschappen, Letteren en Schone Kunsten van België, Brussels.
KB, Književni barok.
KBGL, Kopenhagener Beiträge zur germanistischen Linguistik.
Kbl, Korrespondenzblatt des Vereins für niederdeutsche Sprachforschung.
KDPM, Kleine deutsche Prosadenkmäler des Mittelalters, Munich, Fink.

KGOS, Kultur- und geistesgeschichtliche Ostmitteleuropa-Studien, Marburg, Elwert.

KGS, Kölner germanistische Studien, Cologne, Böhlau.

KGS, Kairoer germanistische Studien.

KH, Komparatistische Hefte.

KhL, Художественная литература.

KhTLP, Художественное творчество и литературный процесс, Tomsk.

KI, Književna istorija.

KIM, Книга. Исследования и материалы.

KiW, Książka i Wiedza.

KJ, Književnost i jezik.

KK, Kirke og Kultur.

KlJb, Kleist-Jahrbuch.

KLWL, Krieg und Literatur: War and Literature.

KMS, Кирило-Методиевски студии.

KMZh, Культура мовы журналіста.

KN, Kwartalnik Neofilologiczny.

KnK, Kniževna kritika.

KO, Университетско издателство 'Климент Охридски'.

KO, Книжное обозрение.

Ko, Кодры.

KP, Книжная палата.

Kr, Крыніца.

KRA, Kölner Romanistische Arbeiten, Geneva, Droz.

KS, Kúltura slova.

KSDL, Kieler Studien zur deutschen Literaturgeschichte, Neumünster, Wachholtz.

KSL, Kölner Studien zur Literaturwissenschaft, Frankfurt, Lang.

KSt, Kant Studien.

KTA, Kröners Taschenausgabe, Stuttgart, Kröner.

KTRM, Klassische Texte des romanischen Mittelalters, Munich, Fink.

KU, Konstanzer Universitäts-reden.

Ku, Кубань.

KUk, Коммунист Украины.

KUL, Katolicki Uniwersytet Lubelski, Lublin.

KuSDL, Kulturwissenschaftliche Studien zur deutschen Literatur, Opladen, Westdeutscher Verlag.

KVS, Коммунист вооруженных сил.

Ky, Київ, Kiev.

KZG, Koreanische Zeitschrift für Germanistik.

KZMTLG, Koninklijke Zuidnederlandse Maatschappij voor Taal- en Letterkunde en Geschiedenis, Brussels.

KZMTLGH, Koninklijke Zuidnederlandse Maatschaapij voor Taal- en Letterkunde en Geschiedenis. Handelingen.

LA, Linguistische Arbeiten, Tübingen, Niemeyer.

LA, Linguistic Analysis.

LAbs, Linguistics Abstracts.

LaF, Langue Française.

LAILJ, Latin American Indian Literatures Journal.

LaLi, Langues et Linguistique.

LALR, Latin-American Literary Review.

LaM, Les Langues Modernes.

LangH, Le Langage et l'Homme.

LArb, Linguistische Arbeitsberichte.

LARR, Latin-American Research Review.

LaS, Langage et Société.

LATR, Latin-American Theatre Review.

LatT, Latin Teaching, Shrewsbury.

LAz, Литературный Азербайджан.

LB, Leuvense Bijdragen.

LBer, Linguistische Berichte.

LBIYB, Leo Baeck Institute Year Book.

LBR, Luso-Brazilian Review.

LC, Letture Classensi.

LCC, Léachtaí Cholm Cille.

LCh, Literatura Chilena.

LCrit, Lavoro Critico.

LCUTA, Library Chronicle of the University of Texas at Austin.

LD, Libri e Documenti.

LDan, Lectura Dantis.

LDanN, Lectura Dantis Newberryana.

LEA, Lingüística Española Actual.
LebS, Lebende Sprachen.
LenP, Ленинградская панорама.
LetA, Letterature d'America.
LetD, Letras de Deusto.
LETHB, Laboratoires d'Études Théâtrales de l'Université de Haute-Bretagne. Études et Documents, Rennes.
LetMS, Letopis Matice srpske, Novi Sad.
LetP, Il Lettore di Provincia.
LetS, Letras Soltas.
LevT, Levende Talen.
LF, Letras Femeninas.
LFil, Listy filologické.
LFQ, Literature and Film Quarterly.
LGF, Lunder Germanistische Forschungen, Stockholm, Almqvist & Wiksell.
LGGL, Literatur in der Geschichte, Geschichte in der Literatur, Cologne–Vienna, Böhlau.
LGL, Langs Germanistische Lehrbuchsammlung, Berne, Lang.
LGP, Leicester German Poets, Leicester U.P.
LGPI, Ленинградский государственный педагогический институт им. Герцена.
LGr, Литературная Грузия, Tbilisi.
LGW, Literaturwissenschaft —Gesellschaftswissenschaft, Stuttgart, Klett.
LH, Lingüística Hispánica.
LHum, Litteraria Humanitas, Brno.
LI, Linguistic Inquiry.
LiB, Literatur in Bayern.
LIC, Letteratura Italiana Contemporanea.
LIE, Lessico Intellettuale Europeo, Rome, Ateneo.
LiL, Limbă și Literatură.
LiLi, Zeitschrift für Literaturwissenschaft und Linguistik.
LingAk, Linguistik Aktuell, Amsterdam, Benjamins.
LingBal, Балканско езикознание – Linguistique Balkanique.
LingCon, Lingua e Contesto.

LingLett, Linguistica e Letteratura.
LíngLit, Língua e Literatura, São Paulo.
LINQ, Linq [Literature in North Queensland].
LInv, Linguisticae Investigationes.
LiR, Limba Română.
LIT, Literature Interpretation Theory.
LIt, Lettera dall'Italia.
LitA, Литературная Армения.
LitAP, Literární archív Památníku národního písemnictví.
LItal, Lettere Italiane.
LitB, Literatura, Budapest.
LitC, Littératures Classiques.
LitG, Литературная газета, Moscow.
LItL, Letteratura Italiana Laterza, Bari, Laterza.
LitL, Literatur für Leser.
LitLing, Literatura y Lingüística.
LitM, Literární měsíčník.
LitMis, Литературна мисъл.
LitO, Литературное обозрение, Moscow.
LitP, Literature and Psychology.
LitR, Литературная Россия.
LittB, Litteraria, Bratislava.
LittK, Litterae, Lauterburg, Kümmerle.
LittS, Litteratur og Samfund.
LittW, Litteraria, Wrocław.
LitU, Литературна учеба.
LiU, Літературна Україна.
LJA, Ljetopis Jugoslavenske Akademije.
LJb, Literaturwissenschaftliches Jahrbuch der Görres–Gesellschaft.
LK, Literatur-Kommentare, Munich, Hanser.
LK, Literatur und Kritik.
LKirg, Литературный Киргизстан.
LKol, Loccumer Kolloquium.
LKuz, Литературный Кузбасс.
LL, Langues et Littératures, Rabat.
LLC, Literary and Linguistic Computing.
LlC, Llên Cymru.
LLit, Литва литературная.
LlLi, Llengua i Literatura.

LLS, Lenguas, Literaturas, Sociedades. Cuadernos Hispánicos.

LLSEE, Linguistic and Literary Studies in Eastern Europe, Amsterdam, Benjamins.

LM, Le Lingue del Mondo.

LN, Lingua Nostra.

LNB, Leipziger namenkundliche Beiträge.

LNL, Les Langues Néo-Latines.

LNouv, Les Lettres Nouvelles.

LoP, Loccumer Protokolle.

LOS, Literary Onomastic Studies.

LOs, Литературная Осетия.

LP, Lingua Posnaniensis.

LPen, Letras Peninsulares.

LPh, Linguistics and Philosophy.

LPLP, Language Problems and Language Planning.

LQ, Language Quarterly, University of S. Florida.

LR, Linguistische Reihe, Munich, Hueber.

LR, Les Lettres Romanes.

LRev, Linguistic Review.

LRI, Libri e Riviste d'Italia.

LRia, Литературный Рязань.

LS, Literatur als Sprache, Münster, Aschendorff.

LS, Lingua e Stile.

LSa, Lusitania Sacra.

LSc, Language Sciences.

LSh, Литература в школе.

LSil, Linguistica Silesiana.

LSNS, Lundastudier i Nordisk Språkvetenskap.

LSo, Language in Society.

LSp, Language and Speech.

LSty, Language and Style.

LSW, Ludowa Spółdzielnia Wydawnicza.

LTG, Literaturwissenschaft, Theorie und Geschichte, Frankfurt, Lang.

LTI, Лингво-типологические исследования, Moscow U.P.

ŁTN, Łódzkie Towarzystwo Naukowe.

LTP, Laval Théologique et Philosophique.

LU, Literarhistorische Untersuchungen, Berne, Lang.

LVC, Language Variation and Change.

LW, Literatur und Wirklichkeit, Bonn, Bouvier.

LWU, Literatur in Wissenschaft und Unterricht.

LY, Lessing Yearbook.

M, Meddelelser, Universitet i Oslo, Slavisk-Baltisk Institutt.

M, Московские новости.

MA, Moyen Âge.

MACL, Memórias da Academia de Ciências de Lisboa, Classe de Letras.

MAe, Medium Aevum.

MAKDDR, Mitteilungen der Akademie der Künste der DDR.

MAL, Modern Austrian Literature.

Mal, Маладосць, Minsk.

MaM, Marbacher Magazin.

MAPS, Medium Aevum. Philologische Studien, Munich, Fink.

MAST, Memorie dell'Accademia delle Scienze di Torino.

MatSl, Matica Slovenská.

MBA, Mitteilungen aus dem Brenner-Archiv.

MBAV, Miscellanea Bibliothecae Apostolicae Vaticanae.

MBMRF, Münchener Beiträge zur Mediävistik und Renaissance-Forschung, Bachenhausen, Arbeo.

MBRP, Münstersche Beiträge zur romanischen Philologie, Münster, Kleinheinrich.

MBSL, Mannheimer Beiträge zur Sprach- und Literaturwissenschaft, Tübingen, Narr.

MC, Misure Critiche.

MCV, Mélanges de la Casa de Velázquez.

MD, Musica Disciplina.

MDan, Meddelser fra Dansklærerforeningen. (Kursiv.)

MDG, Mitteilungen des deutschen Germanistenverbandes.

MDL, Mittlere deutsche Literatur, Berne, Lang.

MDr, Momentum Dramaticum.

MEC, Ministerio de Educação e Cultura, Rio de Janeiro.

MedH, Medioevo e Umanesimo.

MedLR, Mediterranean Language Review.

MedRom, Medioevo Romanzo.

MedS, Medieval Studies.

MEFR, Mélanges de l'École Française de Rome, Moyen Age.

MerP, Mercurio Peruano.

MERSL, The Modern Encyclopedia of Russian and Soviet Literatures, ed. Harry B. Weber, Gulf Breeze, Florida, Academic International Press.

MF, Mercure de France.

MFDT, Mainzer Forschungen zu Drama und Theater, Tübingen, Francke.

MFS, Modern Fiction Studies.

MG, Молодая гвардия.

MG, Молодая гвардия.

MGB, Münchner Germanistische Beiträge, Munich, Fink.

MGG, Mystik in Geschichte und Gegenwart, Stuttgart-Bad Cannstatt, Frommann-Holzboog.

MGPI, Московский государственный педагогический институт им. Ленина.

MGS, Michigan Germanic Studies.

MGSL, Minas Gerais, Suplemento Literário.

MH, Medievalia et Humanistica.

MHLS, Mid-Hudson Language Studies.

MHRA, Modern Humanities Research Association.

Mi, Минувшее, Paris.

MichRS, Michigan Romance Studies.

MILUS, Meddelanden från Institutionen i Lingvistik vid Universitetet i Stockholm.

MINS, Meddelanden från institutionen för nordiska språk vid Stockholms universiteit, Stockholm U.P.

MiscBarc, Miscellanea Barcinonensia.

MiscEB, Miscel·lània d'Estudis Bagencs.

MiscP, Miscel·lània Penedesenca.

MJ, Mittellateinisches Jahrbuch.

MK, Maske und Kothurn.

MKH, Deutsche Forschungsgemeinschaft: Mitteilung der Kommission für Humanismusforschung, Weinheim, Acta Humaniora.

MKNAWL, Mededelingen der Koninklijke Nederlandse Akademie van Wetenschappen, Afd. Letterkunde, Amsterdam.

ML, Mediaevalia Lovaniensia, Leuven U.P.

ML, Modern Languages.

MLAIntBibl, Modern Language Association International Bibliography.

MLit, Мастацкая літаратура.

MLit, Miesięcznik Literacki.

MLJ, Modern Language Journal.

MLN, Modern Language Notes.

MLQ, Modern Language Quarterly.

MLR, Modern Language Review.

MLS, Modern Language Studies.

MM, Maal og Minne.

MMS, Munstersche Mittelalter-Schriften, Munich, Fink.

MN, Man and Nature. L'Homme et la Nature.

MNGT, Manchester New German Texts, Manchester U.P.

ModD, Modern Drama.

MoL, Modellanalysen: Literatur, Paderborn, Schöningh–Munich, Fink.

MolK, Молодой коммунист.

MON, Ministerstwo Obrony Narodowej, Warsaw.

MOPI, Московский областной педагогический институт им. Н. Крупской.

Mos, Москва, Moscow.

MosR, Московский рабочий.

Mov, Мовознавство.

MoyFr, Le Moyen Français.

MP, Modern Philology.

MPI, Мінскі педагагічны інстытут.

MQ, Mississippi Quarterly.

MQR, Michigan Quarterly Review.

MR, Die Mainzer Reihe, Mainz, Hase & Koehler.

MR, Medioevo e Rinascimento.

MRLCST, Modern Russian
Literature and Culture. Studies
and Texts, Berkeley, Berkeley
Slavic Specialties.

MRo, Marche Romane.

MRS, Medieval and Renaissance
Studies.

MRTS, Medieval and Renaissance
Texts and Studies, Binghamton,
NY, Renaissance Society of
America.

MS, Marbacher Schriften, Stuttgart,
Cotta.

MS, Moderna Språk.

MSC, Medjunarodni slavistički
centar, Belgrade.

MSG, Marburger Studien zur
Germanistik, Marburg,
Hitzeroth.

MSL, Marburger Studien zur
Literatur, Marburg, Hitzeroth.

MSLKD, Münchener Studien zur
literarischen Kultur in
Deutschland, Frankfurt, Lang.

MSM, Michigan Slavic Materials,
Ann Arbor, Michigan U.P.

MSMS, Middeleeuse Studies —
Medieval Studies, Johannesburg.

MSNH, Mémoires de la Société
Néophilologique de Helsinki.

MSŞFLA, Academia Republicii
Socialiste România, Memoriile
Secţiei de Ştiinţe Filologice,
Literatură şi Arte.

MSSp, Münchener Studien zur
Sprachwissenschaft, Munich.

MTCGT, Methuen's Twentieth-
Century German Texts, London,
Methuen.

MTG, Mitteilungen zur
Theatergeschichte der Goethezeit,
Bonn, Bouvier.

MTNF, Monographien und Texte
zur Nietzsche-Forschung, Berlin,
New York — de Gruyter.

MTU, Münchener Texte und
Untersuchungen zur deutschen
Literatur des Mittelalters,
Munich, Artemis.

MUP, Manchester University Press.

MusL, Music and Letters.

MusP, Museum Patavinum.

N, Nachbarn, Bonn, Kgl.
Niederländische Botschaft.

N, Неделя.

NA, Народная асвета.

NA, Nuova Antologia.

NaAs, Народная асвета.

NAFMUM, Nuovi Annali della
Facoltà di Magistero
dell'Università di Messina.

NArg, Nuovi Argomenti.

NASNCGL, North American
Studies in Nineteenth-Century
German Literature, Berne, Lang.

NAWG, Nachrichten der Akademie
der Wissenschaften zu Göttingen,
phil.-hist. Kl., Göttingen,
Vandenhoeck & Ruprecht.

NBGF, Neue Beiträge zur George-
Forschung.

NC, New Criterion.

NCA, Nouveaux Cahiers
d'Allemand.

NCF, Nineteenth-Century Fiction.

NCFS, Nineteenth-Century French
Studies.

NCo, New Comparison.

NCSRLL, North Carolina Studies in
the Romance Languages and
Literatures, Chapel Hill.

ND, Наукова думка.

NDH, Neue deutsche Hefte.

NdJb, Niederdeutsches Jahrbuch.

NDL, Nachdrucke deutscher
Literatur des 17. Jahrhunderts,
Berne, Lang.

NDL, Neue deutsche Literatur.

NdS, Niederdeutsche Studien,
Cologne, Böhlau.

NDSK, Nydanske Studier og almen
kommunikationsteori.

NdW, Niederdeutsches Wort.

NE, Nueva Estafeta.

Ne, Нева.

NEL, Nouvelles Éditions Latines,
Paris.

Nem, Неман.

NFF, Novel: A Forum in Fiction.

NFS, Nottingham French Studies.

NFT, Német Filológiai
Tanulmányok. Arbeiten zur
deutschen Philologie.

NGC, New German Critique.

NGFH, Die Neue Gesellschaft/
Frankfurter Hefte.

NGR, New German Review.
NGS, New German Studies, Hull.
NH, Nuevo Hispanismo.
NHLS, North Holland Linguistic
Series, Amsterdam.
NHVKSG, Neujahrsblatt des
Historischen Vereins des Kantons
St Gallen.
NI, Наука и изкуство.
NIMLA, NIMLA. Journal of the
Modern Language Association of
Northern Ireland.
NiR, Наука и религия.
NJ, Naš jezik.
NJL, Nordic Journal of Linguistics.
NKB, Новыя кнігі БССР.
NKT, Norske klassiker-tekster,
Bergen, Eide.
NL, Nouvelles Littéraires.
NLÅ, Norsk Litterær Årbok.
NLD, Nuove Letture Dantesche.
NLH, New Literary History.
NLi, Notre Librairie.
NLLT, Natural Language and
Linguistic Theory.
NLN, Neo-Latin News.
NLT, Norsk Lingvistisk Tidsskrift.
NLWJ, National Library of Wales
Journal.
NM, Народна младеж.
NMi, Neuphilologische
Mitteilungen.
NMS, Nottingham Medieval
Studies.
NN, Наше наследие.
NNH, Nueva Narrativa Hispano-
americana.
NOb, Народное образование.
NOR, New Orleans Review.
NovM, Новый мир.
NovR, Nova Renascenza.
NOWELE, North-Western
European Language Evolution.
Nowele.
NP, Народна просвета.
NQ, Notes and Queries.
NR, New Review.
NR, Naše řeč.
NRE, Nuova Rivista Europea.
NRF, Nouvelle Revue Française.
NRFH, Nueva Revista de Filología
Hispánica.
NRL, Neue russische Literatur.
Almanach, Salzburg.

NRLett, Nouvelles de la République
des Lettres.
NRMI, Nuova Rivista Musicale
Italiana.
NRP, Nouvelle Revue de
Psychanalyse.
NRS, Nuova Rivista Storica.
NRSS, Nouvelle Revue du Seizième
Siècle.
NRu, Die Neue Rundschau.
NS, Die Neueren Sprachen.
NSc, New Scholar.
NSD, На Севере Дальнем.
NSh, Начальная школа.
NSL, Det Norske Språk- og
Litteraturselskap.
NSlg, Neue Sammlung.
NSo, Наш современник . . .
Альманах.
NSP, Nuovi Studi Politici.
NSS, Nysvenska Studier.
NSt, Naše stvaranje.
NT, Навука і тэхніка.
NT, Nordisk Tidskrift.
NTBB, Nordisk Tidskrift för Bok-
och Biblioteksväsen.
NTC, Nuevo Texto Crítico.
NTE, Народна творчість та
етнографія.
NTg, Nieuwe Taalgids.
NTI, Научно-техническая
информация. Серия 2.
Информационные процессы и
системы, Moscow.
NTQ, New Theatre Quarterly.
NTSh, Наукове товариство ім.
Шевченка.
NTW, News from the Top of the
World: Norwegian Literature
Today.
NU, Narodna umjetnost.
NV, Новое время.
NyS, Nydanske Studier/Almen
Kommunikationsteori.
NYSNDL, New Yorker Studien zur
neueren deutschen
Literaturgeschichte, Berne,
Lang.
NYUOS, New York University
Ottendorfer Series, Berne,
Lang.
NZh, Новый журнал.
Nzh, Наука и жизнь.

NZJFS, New Zealand Journal of French Studies.

NZSJ, New Zealand Slavonic Journal.

OB, Ord och Bild.

Ob, Обозрение, Paris.

OBS, Osnabrücker Beiträge zur Sprachtheorie.

OBTUP, Universitetsforlaget Oslo–Bergen–Tromsø.

ÖBV, Österreichischer Bundesverlag, Vienna.

OC, Œuvres et Critiques.

OCP, Orientalia Christiana Periodica, Rome.

OCS, Occitan/Catalan Studies.

Og, Огонек, Moscow.

ÖGL, Österreich in Geschichte und Literatur.

OGS, Oxford German Studies.

OH, Ottawa Hispánica.

Ok, Октябрь, Moscow.

OL, Orbis Litterarum.

OLR, Oxford Literary Review.

ON, Otto/Novecento.

OPI, Overseas Publications Interchange, London.

OPL, Osservatore Politico Letterario.

OPRPNZ, Общество по распространению политических и научных знаний.

OPSLL, Occasional Papers in Slavic Languages and Literatures.

OR, Odrodzenie i Reformacja w Polsce.

ORP, Oriental Research Partners, Cambridge.

OSP, Oxford Slavonic Papers.

Ost, Osteuropa.

OT, Oral Tradition.

OUP, Oxford University Press.

OUSL, Odense University Studies in Literature.

OUSSLL, Odense University Studies in Scandinavian Languages and Literatures, Odense U.P.

OZ, Onomastický zpravodaj.

P, Palaestra, Göttingen, Vandenhoeck & Ruprecht.

PA, Présence Africaine.

Pa, Память, Paris.

PAGS, Proceedings of the Australian Goethe Society.

Pal, Palaeobulgarica — Старобългаристика.

PAN, Polska Akademia Nauk, Warsaw.

PaP, Past and Present.

PapBSA, Papers of the Bibliographical Society of America.

PAPhS, Proceedings of the American Philosophical Society.

ParL, Paragone Letteratura.

PartR, Partisan Review.

PaS, Pamiętnik Słowiański.

PAX, Instytut Wydawniczy PAX, Warsaw.

PB, Д–р Петър Берон.

PBA, Proceedings of the British Academy.

PBib, Philosophische Bibliothek, Hamburg, Meiner.

PBLS, Proceedings of the Annual Meeting of the Berkeley Linguistic Society.

PBSA, Publications of the Bibliographical Society of America.

PC, Problems of Communism.

PCh, Природа и человек.

PCLS, Proceedings of the Chicago Linguistic Society.

PCP, Pacific Coast Philology.

PD, Probleme der Dichtung, Heidelberg, Winter.

PDom, Институт русской литературы (Пушкинский дом).

PDV, Проблемы Дальнего Востока.

PE, Poesía Española.

PEGS(NS), Publications of the English Goethe Society (New Series).

PenP, Il Pensiero Politico.

PerM, Perspectives Médiévales.

PFil, Prace Filologiczne.

PFPS, Z problemów frazeologii polskiej i słowiańskiej, ZNiO.

PFSCL, Papers on French Seventeenth Century Literature.

PGIG, Publikationen der Gesellschaft für interkulturelle Germanistik, Munich, Iudicium.

PH, La Palabra y El Hombre.

PhilosQ, Philosophical Quarterly.

PhilP, Philological Papers, West Virginia University.

PhilR, Philosophy and Rhetoric.

PHol, Le Pauvre Holterling.

PhonPr, Phonetica Pragensia.

PhP, Philologica Pragensia.

PhR, Phoenix Review.

PHSL, Proceedings of the Huguenot Society of London.

PI, педагогический институт.

PId, Le Parole e le Idee.

PIGS, Publications of the Institute of Germanic Studies, University of London.

PiH, Il Piccolo Hans.

PIMA, Proceedings of the Illinois Medieval Association.

PIW, Państwowy Instytut Wydawniczy, Warsaw.

PJ, Poradnik Językowy.

PK, Палата книгописная.

PKNO, Памятники культуры. Новые открытия. Письменность, искусство, археология, Leningrad.

PLing, Papers in Linguistics.

PLit, Philosophy and Literature.

PLL, Papers on Language and Literature.

PL(L), Pamiętnik Literacki, London.

PLRL, Patio de Letras/La Rosa als Llavis.

PL(W), Pamiętnik Literacki, London.

PM, Pleine Marge.

PMLA, Publications of the Modern Language Association of America.

PMPA, Publications of the Missouri Philological Association.

PMZh, Проблемы метода и жанра, Tomsk.

PNR, Poetry and Nation Review.

PNUS, Prace Naukowe Uniwersytetu Śląskiego, Katowice.

Po, Полымя.

POb, Политическое образование.

Pod, Подъем.

PoetT, Poetics Today.

Poez, Поэзия, Moscow.

PolR, Polish Review.

PortSt, Portuguese Studies.

PP, Prace Polonistyczne.

PPNCFL, Proceedings of the Pacific Northwest Conference on Foreign Languages.

PPr, Papers in Pragmatics.

PPU, Promociones y Publicaciones Universitarias, S.A., Barcelona.

PQ, The Philological Quarterly.

PR, Podravska Revija.

Pra, Прапор.

PraRu, Prace Rusycystyczne.

PRF, Publications Romanes et Françaises, Geneva, Droz.

PRH, Pahl-Rugenstein Hochschulschriften, Cologne, Pahl–Rugenstein.

PrHlit, Prace Historycznoliterackie.

PrHum, Prace Humanistyczne.

PRIA, Proceedings of the Royal Irish Academy.

PrIJP, Prace Instytutu Języka Polskiego.

Prilozi, Prilozi za književnost, jezik, istoriju i folklor, Belgrade.

PrilPJ, Prilozi proučavanju jezika.

PrLit, Prace Literackie.

Pro, Простор.

PRom, Papers in Romance.

PrRu, Przegląd Rusycystyczny.

PrzH, Przegląd Humanistyczny.

PS, Проблеми слов'янознавства.

PSCL, Papers and Studies in Contrastive Linguistics.

PSGAS, Politics and Society in Germany, Austria and Switzerland.

PSL, Проблемы структурной лингвистики, Moscow.

PSML, Prague Studies in Mathematical Linguistics.

PSQ, Philologische Studien und Quellen, Berlin, Schmidt.

PSRL, Полное собрание русских летописей.

PSS, Z polskich studiów slawistycznych, Warsaw, PWN.

PT, Pamiętnik Teatralny.

PTLP, Проблемы типологии литературного процесса, Perm'.

PUC, Pontifícia Universidade Católica, São Paulo.
PUF, Presses Universitaires de France, Paris.
PUMRL, Purdue University Monographs in Romance Languages, Amsterdam — Philadelphia, Benjamins.
PUStE, Publications de l'Université de St Étienne.
PW, Poetry Wales.
PWN, Państwowe Wydawnictwo Naukowe, Warsaw, etc.
PY, Phonology Yearbook.
PZ, Полярная звезда.

QALT, Quaderni dell'Atlante Lessicale Toscano.
QCFLP, Quaderni del Circolo Filologico Linguistico Padovano.
QDLC, Quaderni del Dípartimento di Linguistica, Università della Calabria.
QDLF, Quaderni del Dipartimento di Linguistica, Università degli Studi, Florence.
QDLLSMG, Quaderni del Dipartimento di Lingue e Letterature Straniere Moderne, Università di Genova.
QDSL, Quellen zur deutschen Sprach- und Literaturgeschichte, Heidelberg, Winter.
QFCC, Quaderni della Fondazione Camillo Caetani, Rome.
QFESM, Quellen und Forschungen zur Erbauungsliteratur des späten Mittelalters und der frühen Neuzeit, Amsterdam, Rodopi.
QFGB, Quaderni di Filologia Germanica della Facoltà di Lettere e Filosofia dell'Università di Bologna.
QFIAB, Quellen und Forschungen aus italienischen Archiven und Bibliotheken.
QFLR, Quaderni di Filologia e Lingua Romanze, Università di Macerata.
QFSK, Quellen und Forschungen zur Sprach- und Kulturgeschichte der germanischen Völker, Berlin, de Gruyter.

QI, Quaderni d'Italianistica.
QIA, Quaderni Ibero-Americani.
QILLSB, Quaderni dell'Istituto di Lingue e Letterature Straniere della Facoltà di Magistero dell'Università degli Studi di Bari.
QILUU, Quaderni dell'Istituto di Linguistica dell'Università di Urbino.
QJS, Quarterly Journal of Speech, Speech Association of America.
QLII, Quaderni di Letterature Iberiche e Iberoamericane.
QLL, Quaderni di Lingue e Letterature, Verona.
QLLSP, Quaderni di Lingua e Letteratura Straniere, Facoltà di Magistero, Università degli studi di Palermo.
QLO, Quasèrns de Lingüistica Occitana.
QM, Quaderni Milanesi.
QP, Quaderns de Ponent.
QPet, Quaderni Petrarcheschi.
QQ, Queen's Quarterly, Kingston, Ontario.
QRP, Quaderni di Retorica e Poetica.
QS, Quaderni di Semantica.
QSF, Quaderni del Seicento Francese.
QSGLL, Queensland Studies in German Language and Literature, Berne, Francke.
QSt, Quaderni Storici.
QStef, Quaderni Stefaniani.
QSUP, Quaderni per la Storia dell'Università di Padova.
QT, Quaderni di Teatro.
QuS, Quebec Studies.
QV, Quaderni del Vittoriale.
QVen, Quaderni Veneti.
QVer, Quaderni Veronesi di Filologia, Lingua e Letteratura Italiana.

R, Родник, Riga.
RA, Romanistische Arbeitshefte, Tübingen, Niemeyer.
RA, Revista Agustiniana.
RAA, Rendiconti dell'Accademia di Archeologia, Lettere e Belle Arti.

RABM, Revista de Archivos, Bibliotecas y Museos.

Rad, Rad Jugoslavenske akademije znanosti i umjetnosti.

RAE, Real Academia Española.

RAF, Research in African Literatures.

Ra(K), Радуга, Kiev.

RAL, Revista Argentina de Lingüística.

RAPL, Revista da Academia Paulista de Letras, São Paulo.

RAR, Renaissance and Reformation.

Ra(T), Радуга, Tallinn.

RB, Revue Bénédictine.

RBC, Research Bibliographies and Checklists, London, Grant & Cutler.

RBDSL, Regensburger Beiträge zur deutschen Sprach- und Literaturwissenschaft, Frankfurt–Berne, Lang.

RBGd, Rocznik Biblioteki Gdańskiej PAN (Libri Gedanenses).

RBKr, Rocznik Biblioteki PAN w Krakowie.

RBL, Revista Brasileira de Lingüística.

RBLL, Revista Brasileira de Lingua e Literatura.

RBN, Revista da Biblioteca Nacional.

RBPH, Revue Belge de Philologie et d'Histoire.

RC, Le Ragioni Critiche.

RCat, Revista de Catalunya.

RCAV, Rozpravy Československé akademie věd, Prague, ČSAV.

RCB, Revista de Cultura Brasileña.

RCCM, Rivista di Cultura Classica e Medioevale.

RCEH, Revista Canadiense de Estudios Hispánicos.

RCEN, Revue Canadienne d'Études Néerlandaises.

RCF, Review of Contemporary Fiction.

RCL, Revista Chilena de Literatura.

RCLL, Revista de Crítica Literaria Latino-Americana.

RCSF, Rivista Critica di Storia della Filosofia.

RCVS, Rassegna di Cultura e Vita Scolastica.

RDE, Recherches sur Diderot et sur l''Encyclopédie'.

RDM, Revue des Deux Mondes.

RDsS, Recherches sur le XVIIᵉ Siècle.

RDTP, Revista de Dialectología y Tradiciones Populares.

RE, Revista de Espiritualidad.

RedLet, Red Letters.

REE, Revista de Estudios Extremeños.

REH, Revista de Estudios Hispánicos, Poughkeepsie, New York.

REHisp, Revista de Estudios Hispánicos, Puerto Rico.

REI, Revue des Études Italiennes.

REJ, Revista de Estudios de Juventud.

REL, Revue des Études Latines.

RELA, Revista Española de Lingüística Aplicada.

RelCL, Religion in Communist Lands.

RELing, Revista Española de Lingüística, Madrid.

RelLit, Religious Literature.

ReMS, Renaissance and Modern Studies.

RenD, Renaissance Drama.

RenP, Renaissance Papers.

RenR, Renaissance and Reformation.

RenS, Renaissance Studies.

RES, Review of English Studies.

RESEE, Revue des Études Sud-Est Européennes.

RESS, Revue Européenne des Sciences Sociales et Cahiers Vilfredo Pareto.

RevA, Revue d'Allemagne.

RevAuv, Revue d'Auvergne.

RevF, Revista de Filología.

RevG, Revista de Girona.

RevIb, Revista Iberoamericana.

RevL, Revista Lusitana.

RevLM, Revista de Literatura Medieval.

RevLR, Revista do Livro.

RevPF, Revista Portuguesa de Filosofia.

RevR, Revue Romane.

RF, Romanische Forschungen.

RFE, Revista de Filología Española.

RFHL, Revue Française d'Histoire du Livre.

RFLSJ, Revista de Filosofía y Lingüística de San José, Costa Rica.

RFLUL, Revista da Faculdade de Letras da Universidade de Lisboa.

RFLUP, Revista da Faculdade de Letras da Universidade do Porto.

RFN, Rivisti di Filosofia Neoscolastica.

RFo, Ricerca Folklorica.

RFP, Recherches sur le Français Parlé.

RFR, Revista de Filología Románica.

RFr, Revue Frontenac.

RG, Recherches Germaniques.

RGand, Romanica Gandensia.

RGG, Rivista di Grammatica Generativa.

RGL, Reihe Germanistische Linguistik, Tübingen, Niemeyer.

RH, Reihe Hanser, Munich, Hanser.

RH, Revue Hebdomadaire.

RHA, Revista de Historia de America.

RHAM, Revue Historique et Archéologique du Maine.

RHCS, Rocznik Historii Czasopiśmiennictwa Polskiego.

RHDFE, Revue Historique de Droit Français et Étranger.

RHE, Revue d'Histoire Ecclésiastique.

RHEF, Revue d'Histoire de l'Église de France.

RHel, Romanica Helvetica, Berne, Francke.

RHFB, Rapports — Het Franse Boek.

RHI, Revista da Historia das Ideias.

RHis, Revue Historique.

RHL, Reihe Hanser Literaturkommentare, Munich, Hanser.

RHLF, Revue d'Histoire Littéraire de la France.

RHLP, Revista de História Literária de Portugal.

RHM, Revista Hispánica Moderna.

RHMag, Revue d'Histoire Maghrébine.

RHMC, Revue d'Histoire Moderne et Contemporaine.

RHPR, Revue d'Histoire et de Philosophie Religieuses.

RHR, Réforme, Humanisme, Renaissance.

RHRel, Revue de l'Histoire des Religions.

RHS, Revue Historique de la Spiritualité.

RHSc, Revue d'Histoire des Sciences.

RHSt, Ricarda Huch. Studien zu ihrem Leben und Werk.

RHT, Revue d'Histoire du Théâtre.

RHTe, Revue d'Histoire des Textes.

RI, Rassegna Iberistica.

RIA, Rivista Italiana di Acustica.

RIa, Русский язык.

RIa, Русский язык в школе.

RIAB, Revista Interamericana de Bibliografía.

RIaMS, Русский язык. Межведомственный сборник.

RIaN, Русский язык в национальной школе.

RIaR, Русский язык за рубежом.

RicSl, Ricerche Slavistiche.

RID, Rivista Italiana di Dialettologia.

RIE, Revista de Ideas Estéticas.

RIEB, Revista do Instituto de Estudos Brasileiros.

RIL, Rendiconti dell'Istituto Lombardo.

RILA, Rassegna Italiana di Linguistica Applicata.

RILCE, Revista del Instituto de Lengua y Cultura Españoles.

RILP, Revista Internacional da Língua Portuguesa.

RIM, Rivista Italiana di Musicologia.

RIndM, Revista de Indias.

RInv, Revista de Investigación.

RIO, Revue Internationale d'Onomastique.

RIP, Revue Internationale de Philosophie.

RITL, Revista de Istorie şi Teorie Literară, Bucharest.

RivL, Rivista di Linguistica.
RJ, Romanistisches Jahrbuch.
RKHlit, Rocznik Komisji Historycznoliterackiej PAN.
RKJŁ, Rozprawy Komisji Językowej Łódzkiego Towarzystwa Naukowego.
RKJW, Rozprawy Komisji Językowej Wrocławskiego Towarzystwa Naukowego.
RL, Russian Literature, Amsterdam.
RLA, Romance Languages Annual.
RLaR, Revue des Langues Romanes.
RLB, Recueil Linguistique de Bratislava.
RLC, Revue de Littérature Comparée.
RLD, Revista de Llengua i Dret.
RLet, Revista de Letras.
RLettI, Rivista di Letteratura Italiana.
RLF, Revista de Literatura Fantástica.
RLFRU, Recherches de Linguistique Française et Romane d'Utrecht.
RLH, Revista de Literatura Hispanoamericana.
RLI, Rassegna della Letteratura Italiana
RLing, Russian Linguistics.
RLiR, Revue de Linguistique Romane.
RLit, Revista de Literatura.
RLJ, Russian Language Journal.
RLM, Revista de Literaturas Modernas, Cuyo.
RLMC, Rivista di Letterature Moderne e Comparate.
RLMed, Revista de Literatura Medieval.
RLMod, Revue des Lettres Modernes.
RLModCB, Revue des Lettres Modernes. Carnets Bibliographiques.
RLSer, Revista de Literatura Ser, Puerto Rico.
RLŞL, Revistă de Lingvistică şi Ştiinţă Literară.
RLT, Russian Literature Triquarterly.
RLTA, Revista de Lingüística Teórica y Aplicada.
RLV, Revue des Langues Vivantes.

RM, Romance Monograph Series, University, Mississippi.
RM, Remate de Males.
RMAL, Revue du Moyen Âge Latin.
RMH, Recherches sur le Monde Hispanique au XIXe Siècle.
RMM, Revue de Métaphysique et de Morale.
RMRLL, Rocky Mountain Review of Language and Literature.
RMS, Reading Medieval Studies.
RNC, Revista Nacional de Cultura, Carácas.
RO, Revista de Occidente.
Ro, Родина.
RoczH, Roczniki Humanistyczne Katolickiego Uniw. Lubelskiego.
RoczSl, Rocznik Slawistyczny.
ROl, Rossica Olomucensia.
RoM, Rowohlts Monographien, Reinbek, Rowohlt.
ROMM, Revue de L'Occident Musulman et de la Méditerranée.
RoN, Romance Notes.
RoQ, Romance Quarterly.
RORD, Research Opportunities in Renaissance Drama.
RoS, Romance Studies.
RP, Радянський письменник.
RP, Revista de Portugal.
RPA, Revue de phonétique appliquée.
RPac, Revue du Pacifique.
RPF, Revista Portuguesa de Filologia.
RPFE, Revue Philosophique de la France et de l'Étranger.
RPh, Romance Philology.
RPL, Revue Philosophique de Louvain.
RPl, Río de la Plata.
RPLit, Res Publica Litterarum.
RPP, Romanticism Past and Present.
RPr, Raison Présente.
RQ, Renaissance Quarterly.
RQL, Revue Québécoise de Linguistique.
RR, Romanic Review.
RRe, Русская речь.
RRL, Revue Roumaine de Linguistique.
RS, Reihe Siegen, Heidelberg, Winter.
RS, Revue de Synthèse.
RSC, Rivista di Studi Canadesi.

RSCI, Rivista di Storia della Chiesa in Italia.
RSF, Rivista di Storia della Filosofia.
RSH, Revue des Sciences Humaines.
RSh, Радянська школа.
RSI, Rivista Storica Italiana.
RSJb, Reinhold Schneider Jahrbuch.
RSL, Rusycystyczne Studia Literaturoznawcze.
RSl, Revue des Études Slaves.
RSLR, Rivista di Storia e Letteratura Religiose.
RSPT, Revue des Sciences Philosophiques et Théologiques.
RSR, Rassegna Storica del Risorgimento.
RSt, Research Studies.
RStI, Rivista di Studi Italiani.
RTAM, Recherches de Théologie Ancienne et Médiévale.
RTLiM, Rocznik Towarzystwa Literackiego im. Adama Mickiewicza.
RTUG, Recherches et Travaux de l'Université de Grenoble III.
RUB, Revue de l'Université de Bruxelles.
RUC, Revista de la Universidad Complutense.
RuLit, Ruch Literacki.
RUM, Revista de la Universidad de Madrid.
RUMex, Revista de la Universidad de México.
RUOt, Revue de l'Université d'Ottawa.
RUS, Rice University Studies.
RusH, Russian History.
RusL, Русская литература, ПД, Leningrad.
RusM, Русская мысль.
RusMed, Russia Medievalis.
RusR, Russian Review.
RUW, Rozprawy Uniwersytetu Warsawskiego, Warsaw.
RV, Русское возрождение.
RVB, Rheinische Vierteljahrsblätter.
RVF, Revista Valenciana de Filología.
RVQ, Romanica Vulgaria Quaderni.
RVV, Romanische Versuche und Vorarbeiten, Bonn U.P.

RVVig, Reihe der Villa Vigoni, Tübingen, Niemeyer.
RyF, Razón y Fe.
RZLG, Romanistische Zeitschrift für Literaturgeschichte.
RZSF, Radovi Zavoda za slavensku filologiju.

S, Синтаксис, Paris.
SA, Studien zum Althochdeutschen, Göttingen, Vandenhoeck & Ruprecht.
SA, Советские архивы.
SAB, South Atlantic Bulletin.
Sac, Sacris Erudiri.
SAG, Stuttgarter Arbeiten zur Germanistik, Stuttgart, Heinz.
SANU, Srpska akademija nauka i umetnosti.
SAOB, Svenska Akademiens Ordbok.
SAR, South Atlantic Review.
SAS, Studia Academica Slovaca.
SaS, Slovo a slovesnost.
SASc, Studia Anthroponymica Scandinavica.
SATF, Société des Anciens Textes Français.
SAV, Slovenská akadémia vied.
SAVL, Studien zur Allgemeinen und Vergleichenden Literaturwissenschaft, Stuttgart, Metzler.
SB, Slavistische Beiträge, Munich, Sagner.
SB, Studies in Bibliography.
SBAW, Sitzungsberichte der Bayerischen Akad. der Wissenschaften, phil-hist. Kl., Munich, Beck.
SBib, Советская библиография.
SBL, Saarbrücker Beiträge zur Literaturwissenschaft, Frankfurt, R. G. Fischer.
SBL, Старобългарска литература.
SBR, Swedish Book Review.
SBVS, Saga-Book of the Viking Society.
SC, Studia Celtica.
SCC, Studies in Comparative Communism.
SCen, The Seventeenth Century.

SCES, Sixteenth Century Essays and Studies, Kirksville, Missouri, Sixteenth Century Journal.

SCFS, Seventeenth-Century French Studies.

SchG, Schriftsteller der Gegenwart, Berlin, Volk & Wissen.

SchwM, Schweizer Monatshefte.

SCJ, Sixteenth Century Journal.

SCL, Studii şi Cercetări Lingvistice.

SCl, Stendhal Club.

ScM, Scripta Mediterranea.

SCN, Seventeenth Century News.

SCR, Studies in Comparative Religion.

ScRev, Scandinavian Review.

ScSl, Scando-Slavica.

ScSt, Scandinavian Studies.

SD, Sprache und Dichtung, n.F., Berne, Haupt.

SD, Современная драматургия.

SdA, Storia dell'Arte.

SDG, Studien zur deutschen Grammatik, Tübingen, Narr.

SDL, Studien zur deutschen Literatur, Tübingen, Niemeyer.

SDLNZ, Studien zur deutschen Literatur des 19. und 20. Jahrhunderts, Berne, Lang.

SdO, Serra d'Or.

SDS, Sydsvenska Dagbladet Snällposten.

SDv, Sprache und Datenverarbeitung.

SE, Советская энциклопедия.

SE, Série Estudos, Uberaba.

Se, Север, Petrozavodsk.

SeC, Scrittura e Civiltà.

SECC, Studies in Eighteenth-Century Culture.

SEDES, Société d'Éditions d'Enseignement Supérieur.

SEEA, Slavic and East European Arts.

SEEJ, The Slavic and East European Journal.

SEER, Slavonic and East European Review.

SEES, Slavic and East European Studies.

SEI, Società Editrice Internazionale, Turin.

SEN, Società Editrice Napoletana, Naples.

SEP, Secretaría de Educación Pública, Mexico.

SeS, Serbian Studies.

SEz, Съпоставително езикознание.

SF, Slavistische Forschungen, Cologne — Vienna, Böhlau.

SFAIEO, Section Française de l'Association Internationale d'Études Occitanes, Montpellier.

SFI, Studi di Filologia Italiana.

SFIS, Stanford French and Italian Studies.

SFKG, Schriftenreihe der Franz Kafka–Gesellschaft, Vienna, Braumüller.

SFL, Studies in French Literature, London, Arnold.

SFL, Studi di Filologia e Letteratura.

SFPS, Studia z Filologii Polskiej i Słowiańskiej PAN.

SFR, Stanford French Review.

SFr, Studi Francesi.

SFS, Swiss-French Studies.

SFUŠ, Sborník Filozofickej Fakulty Univerzity P. J. Šafárika, Prešov.

SG, Sprache der Gegenwart, Düsseldorf, Schwann.

SGAK, Studien zu Germanistik, Anglistik und Komparatistik, Bonn, Bouvier.

SGECRN, Study Group on Eighteenth-Century Russia Newsletter.

SGEL, Sociedad General Española de Librería.

SGesch, Sprache und Geschichte, Stuttgart, Klett-Cotta.

SGF, Stockholmer Germanistische Forschungen, Stockholm, Almqvist & Wiksell.

SGG, Studia Germanica Gandensia.

SGI, Studi di Grammatica Italiana.

SGLLC, Studies in German Literature, Linguistics, and Culture, Columbia, S.C., Camden House.

SGP, Studia Germanica Posnaniensia.

SGS, Stanford German Studies, Berne, Lang.

SGS, Scottish Gaelic Studies.

SGU, Studia Germanistica Upsaliensia, Stockholm, Almqvist & Wiksell.

SH, Slavica Helvetica, Berne, Lang.

SH, Studia Hibernica.

SHAW, Sitzungsberichte der Heidelberger Akademie der Wissenschaften, phil.-hist. Klasse, Heidelberg, Winter.

SHPF, Société de l'Histoire du Protestantisme Français.

SHPS, Studies in History and Philosophy of Science.

SHR, The Scottish Historical Review.

SI, Sprache und Information, Tübingen, Niemeyer.

SI, Семиотика и информатика.

SIAA, Studi di Italianistica nell'Africa Australe.

SiCh, Слово i час.

SIDES, Société Internationale de Diffusion et d'Édition Scientifiques, Antony.

SIDS, Schriften des Instituts für deutsche Sprache, Berlin, de Gruyter.

Siglo XX, Siglo XX/20th Century.

SILTA, Studi Italiani di Linguistica Teorica ed Applicata.

SiN, Sin Nombre.

SINSU, Skrifter utgivna av institutionen för nordiska språk vid Uppsala universitet, Uppsala U.P.

SIR, Stanford Italian Review.

SIsp, Studi Ispanici.

SISSD, Società Italiana di Studi sul Secolo XVIII.

SJLŠ, Slovenský jazyk a literatúra v škole.

SK, Сводный каталог русской книги гражданской печати XVIII века. 1725–1800, 5 vols and supp., Moscow, 'Книга', 1962–75.

SK, Советская культура.

SkFil, Скандинавская филология (Scandinavica).

SkSb, Скандинавский сборник.

SkSt, Skandinavistische Studien.

SKZ, Srpska književna zadruga, Belgrade.

SL, Sammlung Luchterhand, Darmstadt, Luchterhand.

SL, Studia Linguistica.

SLÅ, Svensk Lärarföreningens Årsskrift.

SlaG, Slavica Gandensia.

SlaH, Slavica Helsingensia.

SlaL, Slavica Lundensia.

Slav, Slavia, Prague.

SlavFil, Славянска филология, Sofia.

SlavH, Slavica Hierosolymitana.

SlavLit, Славянските литератури в България.

SlavRev, Slavistična revija.

SlaW, Slavica Wratislaviensia.

SLeg, Studium Legionense.

SLeI, Studi di Lessicografia Italiana.

SLESPO, Suplemento Literário do Estado de São Paulo.

SLF, Studi di Letteratura Francese.

SLG, Studia Linguistica Germanica, Berlin, de Gruyter.

SLI, Società di Linguistica Italiana.

SLI, Studi Linguistici Italiani.

SLIGU, Skrifter utgivna av Litteraturvetenskapliga institutionen vid Göteborgs universitet, Gothenburg U.P.

SLit, Schriften zur Literaturwissenschaft, Berlin, Dunckler & Humblot.

SLit, Slovenská literatúra.

SLitR, Stanford Literature Review.

SLIUU, Skrifter utgivna av Litteraturvetenskapliga institutionen vid Uppsala universitet, Uppsala U.P.

SLK, Schwerpunkte Linguistik und Kommunikationswissenschaft.

SLL, Skrifter utg. genom Landsmålsarkivet i Lund.

SLM, Studien zur Literatur der Moderne, Bonn, Bouvier.

SLO, Slavica Lublinensia et Olomucensia.

SlO, Slavia Orientalis.

SlOc, Slavia Occidentalis.

SlOth, Slavica Othinensia.

SlPN, Slovenské pedagogické nakladateľstvo.

SlPoh, Slovenské pohľady.

SlPr, Slavica Pragensia.

SLPS, Studia Linguistica Polono-Slovaca.

SLR, Second Language Research.

SLS, Studies in the Linguistic Sciences.

SlSb, Slezský sborník.

SlSl, Slavica Slovaca.

SlSp, Slovenský spisovateľ.

SLWU, Sprach und Literatur in Wissenschaft und Unterricht.

SM, Sammlung Metzler, Stuttgart, Metzler.

SM, Studi Medievali.

Sm, Страна и мир, Munich.

SMC, Studies in Medieval Culture.

SMer, Студенческий меридиан.

SMGL, Studies in Modern German Literature, Berne — Frankfurt — New York, Lang.

SMLS, Strathclyde Modern Language Studies.

SMRT, Studies in Medieval and Reformation Thought, Leiden, Brill.

SMS, Sewanee Medieval Studies.

SMu, Советский музей.

SMV, Studi Mediolatini e Volgari.

SN, Studia Neophilologica.

SNL, Sveučilišna naklada Liber, Zagreb.

SNM, Sborník Národního muzea.

SNov, Seara Nova.

SNTL, Státní nakladatelství technické literatury.

SO, Сибирские огни.

SÖAW, Sitzungsberichte der Österreichischen Akademie der Wissenschaften, phil.-hist. Klasse.

SoCR, South Central Review.

SOH, Studia Onomastica Helvetica, Arbon, Eurotext: Historisch-Archäologischer Verlag.

SoK, Sprog og Kultur.

SopL, Sophia Linguistica, Tokyo.

SoRA, Southern Review, Adelaide.

SoRL, Southern Review, Louisiana.

SovEt, Советская этнография.

SovM, Советская музыка.

SovP, Советский писатель.

SovS, Soviet Studies.

SovSl, Советское славяноведение.

SP, Sammlung Profile, Bonn, Bouvier.

SP, Studies in Philology.

Sp, Спадчына.

SPat, Studi Patavini.

SpC, Speech Communication.

SPCT, Studi e Problemi di Critica Testuale.

SPES, Studio per Edizioni Scelte, Florence.

SPFB, Sborník Pedagogické fakulty v Brně.

SPFFBU, Sborník prací Filosofické fakulty Brněnské University.

SPFHK, Sborník Pedagogické fakulty, Hradec Králové.

SPFO, Sborník Pedagogické fakulty, Ostrava.

SPFOl, Sborník Pedagogické fakulty, Olomouc.

SPFUK, Sborník Pedagogické fakulty Univerzity Karlovy, Prague.

SPGS, Scottish Papers in Germanic Studies, Glasgow.

SPi, Serie Piper, Munich, Piper.

SPIEL, Siegener Periodicum zur Internationalen Empirischen Literaturwissenschaft.

SpLit, Sprache und Literatur.

SpMod, Spicilegio Moderno, Pisa.

SPN, Státní pedagogické nakladatelství.

SPol, Studia Polonistyczne.

SPR, Slavistic Printings and Reprintings, The Hague, Mouton.

SpR, Spunti e Ricerche.

SPRF, Société de Publications Romanes et Françaises, Geneva, Droz.

SPS, Specimina Philologiae Slavicae, Munich, Kubon & Sagner.

SPS, Studia Philologica Salmanticensia.

SPSO, Studia Polono–Slavica–Orientalia. Acta Litteraria.

SpSt, Spanish Studies.

SR, Советская Россия.

SR, Slovenská reč.

SRAZ, Studia Romanica et Anglica Zagrabiensia.

SRev, Slavic Review.

SRF, Studi e Ricerche Francescane.
SRL, Studia Romanica et
 Linguistica, Frankfurt, Lang.
SRLF, Saggi e ricerche di letteratura
 francese.
SRo, Studi Romanzi.
SRom, Studi Romeni.
SRoP, Studia Romanica
 Posnaniensia.
SRP, Studia Rossica Posnaniensia.
SRU, Studia Romanica Upsaliensia.
SS, Symbolae Slavicae, Frankfurt–
 Berne–Cirencester, Lang.
SS, Syn og Segn.
SSB, Skrifter utgivna av Svenska
 barnboksinstitutet.
SSB, Strenna Storica Bolognese.
SSCJ, Southern Speech
 Communication Journal.
SSE, Studi di Storia
 dell'Educazione.
SSF, Studies in Short Fiction.
SSFin, Studia Slavica Finlandensia.
SSGL, Studies in Slavic and General
 Linguistics, Amsterdam, Rodopi.
SSH, Studia Slavica Academiae
 Scientiarum Hungaricae.
SSh, Семья и школа.
SSL, Studi e saggi linguistici.
SSLF, Skrifter utgivna av Svenska
 Litteratursällskapet i Finland.
SSLP, Studies in Slavic Literature
 and Poetics, Amsterdam, Rodopi.
SSMP, Stockholm Studies in
 Modern Philology.
SSR, Scottish Slavonic Review.
SSS, Slavic and Soviet Series, Tel
 Aviv.
SSS, Stanford Slavic Studies.
SSSAS, Society of Spanish and
 Spanish-American Studies,
 Boulder, Colorado.
SSSlg, Sagners Slavistische
 Sammlung, Munich, Sagner.
SSSN, Skrifter utgivna av Svenska
 språknämnden.
SSSP, Stockholm Studies in
 Scandinavian Philology.
SSSRVP, СССР — Внутренние
 противоречия, Benson,
 Vermont.
SST, Studies in Soviet Thought.
SSt, Slavic Studies, Hokkaido.

ST, Suhrkamp Taschenbuch,
 Frankfurt, Suhrkamp.
ST, Советская торговля.
St, Стрелец, New York–Paris.
StB, Studi sul Boccaccio.
STC, Studies in the Twentieth
 Century.
StCJ, Studia Celtica Japonica.
STCL, Studies in Twentieth Century
 Literature.
StCL, Studies in Canadian
 Literature.
StCrit, Strumenti Critici.
STD, Союз театральных деятелей.
StD, Studi Danteschi.
StF, Studie Francescani.
StFil, Studia Filozoficzne.
STFM, Société des Textes Français
 Modernes.
StG, Studi Germanici.
StGol, Studi Goldoniani.
StH, Studies in the Humanities.
StI, Studi Italici, Kyoto.
STiurk, Советская тюркология.
StL, Studium Linguistik.
StLa, Studies in Language,
 Amsterdam.
StLI, Studi di Letteratura Ispano-
 Americana.
StLM, Studies in the Literary
 Imagination.
StLo, Studia Logica.
StM, Studies in Medievalism.
STM, Suhrkamp Taschenbuch
 Materialien, Frankfurt,
 Suhrkamp.
STML, Studies on Themes and
 Motifs in Literature, New York,
 Lang.
StMon, Studia Monastica.
StMus, Studie Musicali.
StMy, Studia Mystica.
StN, Studi Novecenteschi.
StNF, Studier i Nordisk Filologi.
StO, Studium Ovetense.
StP, Studi Piemontesi.
StPet, Studi Petrarcheschi.
StPN, Státní pedagogické
 nakladatelství.
StR, Studie o rukopisech.
StRLLF, Studi e ricerche di
 letteratura e linguistica francese.
StRo, Studi Romani.
StRom, Studies in Romanticism.

StRu, Studia Russica, Budapest.
StS, Studi Storici.
StSec, Studi Secenteschi.
StSk, Studia Skandinavica.
StSet, Studi Settecenteschi.
STSL, Studien und Texte zur
  Sozialgeschichte der Literatur,
  Tübingen, Niemeyer.
StT, Studi Tassiani.
StV, Studies on Voltaire and the 18th
  Century.
STW, Suhrkamp Taschenbücher
  Wissenschaft, Frankfurt,
  Suhrkamp.
StZ, Sprache im technischen
  Zeitalter.
SU, Studi Urbinati.
Su, Сучасність, Munich.
SUBBP, Studia Universitatis Babeş-
  Bolyai, Philologia, Cluj.
SUDAM, Editorial Sudamericana,
  Buenos Aires.
SuF, Sinn und Form.
SUP, Spisy University J. E.
  Purkyně, Brno.
SupEz, Съпоставително
  езикознание, Sofia.
SV, Studi Veneziani.
SZ, Studia Zamorensia.

TAm, The Americas, Bethesda.
TB, Tempo Brasileiro.
TBL, Tübinger Beiträge zur
  Linguistik, Tübingen, Narr.
TC, Texto Critico.
TCBS, Transactions of the
  Cambridge Bibliographical
  Society.
TCERFM, Travaux du Centre
  d'Études et de Recherches sur
  François Mauriac, Bordeaux.
TCh, Тыняновские чтения.
TCL, Twentieth-Century Literature.
TCLN, Travaux du Cercle
  Linguistique de Nice.
TD, Teksty Drugie.
Te, Театр.
TEC, Teresiunum Ephemerides
  Carmeliticae.
TeK, Text und Kontext.
TELK, Trouvaillen — Editionen
  zur Literatur- und
  Kulturgeschichte, Berne, Lang.

TeN, Terminologies Nouvelles.
TeSt, Teatro e Storia.
TE(XVIII), Textos y estudios del
  siglo XVIII.
TF, Texte zur Forschung,
  Darmstadt, Wissenschaftliche
  Buchgesellschaft.
TFN, Texte der Frühen Neuzeit,
  Frankfurt am Main, Keip.
TGLSK, Theorie und Geschichte
  der Literatur und der Schönen
  Künste, Munich, Fink.
TGSI, Transactions of the Gaelic
  Society of Inverness.
THL, Theory and History of
  Literature, Manchester U.P.
THM, Textos Hispánicos
  Modernos, Barcelona, Labor.
THR, Travaux d'Humanisme et
  Renaissance, Geneva, Droz.
THSC, Transactions of the
  Honourable Society of
  Cymmrodorion.
TI, Le Texte et l'Idée
TidLit, Tidskrift för
  Litteraturvetenskap.
TILAS, Travaux de l'Institut
  d'Études Latino-Américaines de
  l'Université de Strasbourg.
TILL, Travaux de l'Institut de
  Linguistique de Lund.
TJ, Theatre Journal.
TK, Text und Kritik, Munich.
TKS, Търновска книжевна школа,
  Sofia.
TL, Theoretical Linguistics.
TLF, Textes Littéraires Français,
  Geneva, Droz.
TLit, Travaux de Littérature.
TLP, Travaux de Linguistique et de
  Philologie.
TLQ, Travaux de Linguistique
  Québécoise.
TLTL, Teaching Language Through
  Literature.
TM, Les Temps Modernes.
TMJb, Thomas Mann-Jahrbuch.
TMo, O Tempo e o Modo.
TMS, Thomas Mann–Studien,
  Berne, Francke.
TN, Theatre Notebook.
TNA, Tijdschrift voor Nederlands en
  Afrikaans.

TNT, Towarzystwo Naukowe w Toruniu.

TODL, Труды Отдела древнерусской литературы Института русской литературы АН СССР.

TP, Textual Practice.

TPLP, Творчество писателя и литературный процесс, Ivanovo.

TPS, Transactions of the Philological Society.

TQ, Theatre Quarterly.

TR, Телевидение и радиовещание.

TRCTL, Texte-Revue de Critique et de Théorie Littéraire.

TRI, Theatre Research International.

TrK, Трезвость и культура.

TrL, Travaux de Linguistique.

TS, Theatre Survey.

TSDL, Tübinger Studien zur deutschen Literatur, Frankfurt, Lang.

TsGALI SSR, Центральный государственный архив литературы и искусства СССР.

TSJ, Tolstoy Studies Journal.

TSL, Trierer Studien zur Literatur, Frankfurt, Lang.

TSLL, Texas Studies in Literature and Language.

TSM, Texte des späten Mittelalters und der frühen Neuzeit, Berlin, Schmidt.

TsNTL, Tijdschrift voor Nederlandse Taal- en Letterkunde.

TSRLL, Tulane Studies in Romance Languages and Literature.

TsSk, Tijdschrift voor Skandinavistiek.

TsSV, Tijdschrift voor de Studie van de Verlichting.

TSWL, Tulsa Studies in Women's Literature.

TT, Tekst en Tijd, Nijmegen, Alfa.

TT, Travail Théâtral.

TTAS, Twayne Theatrical Arts Series, Boston–New York.

TTG, Texte und Textgeschichte, Tübingen, Niemeyer.

TUGS, Texte und Untersuchungen zur Germanistik und Skandinavistik, Frankfurt, Lang.

TV, Третья волна, Paris — New York.

TWAS, Twayne's World Authors Series, Boston–New York.

TWQ, Third World Quarterly.

UAC, Universidad de Antioquia, Colombia.

UAM, Uniwersytet Adama Mickiewicza, Poznań.

UB, Universal-Bibliothek, Stuttgart, Reclam.

UBL, Universal-Bibliothek, Leipzig, Reclam.

UCPL, University of California Publications in Linguistics.

UCPMP, University of California Publications in Modern Philology.

UDL, Untersuchungen zur deutschen Literaturgeschichte, Tübingen, Niemeyer.

UDR, University of Dayton Review.

UFRGS, Univ. Federal do Rio Grande do Sul (Brazil).

UGE, Union Générale d'Éditions.

UGFGP, University of Glasgow French and German Publications.

UL, Українське літературознавство, Lvov U.P.

UM, Українська мова і література в школі.

UMCS, Uniwersytet Marii Curie-Skłodowskiej, Lublin.

UMov, Українське мовознавство.

UNAM, Universidad Nacional Autónoma de Mexico.

UNC, Univ. of North Carolina.

UNCSGL, University of North Carolina Studies in Germanic Languages and Literatures, Chapel Hill.

UNED, Universidad Nacional de Enseñanza a Distancia.

UNESP, Universidade Estadual de São Paulo.

UNMH, University of Nottingham Monographs in the Humanities.

UPP, University of Pennsylvania Press, Philadelphia.

UQ, Ukrainian Quarterly.

UR, Umjetnost riječi.

Ur, Урал.

USCFLS, University of South Carolina French Literature Series.

USFLQ, University of South Florida Language Quarterly.

USH, Umeå Studies in the Humanities, Stockholm, Almqvist & Wiksell International.

USLL, Utah Studies in Literature and Linguistics, Berne, Lang.

USP, Universidade de São Paulo.

UTB, Uni-Taschenbücher.

UTET, Unione Tipografico-Editrice Torinese.

UTPLF, Università di Torino, Pubblicazioni della Facoltà di Lettere e Filosofia.

UTQ, University of Toronto Quarterly.

UVAN, Українська Вільна Академія Наук, Winnipeg.

UZAz, Ученые записки Азербайджанского педагогического института русского языка и литературы.

UZGU, Ученые записки Горьковского университета.

UZKu, Учены записки Курского педагогического института.

UZLPI, Ученые записки Ленинградского педагогического института.

UZLU, Ученые записки Ленинградского университета.

UZMOPI, Ученые записки Московского областного педагогического института.

UZTarU, Ученые записки Тартуского государственного университета, Tartu.

UZUU, Ученые записки Уральского государственного университета им. А. М. Горького, Sverdlovsk.

VAM, Vergessene Autoren der Moderne, Siegen U.P.

VAN, Вестник Академии наук СССР.

VANB, Весці Акадэміі навук БССР. Серыя грамадскіх навук.

VAS, Vorträge und Abhandlungen zur Slavistik, Giessen, Schmitz.

VASILO, Vierteljahresschrift des A. Stifter-Instituts des Landes Oberösterreich.

VASSLOI, Veröffentlichungen der Abteilung für Slavische Sprachen und Literaturen des Osteuropa-Instituts (Slavistiches Seminar) an der Freien Universität Berlin.

VB, Vestigia Bibliae.

VBDU, Веснік Беларускага дзяржаўнага ўніверсітэта імя У. І. Леніна. Серыя IV.

VCT, Les Voies de la Création Théâtrale.

VDASD, Veröffentlichungen der Deutschen Akademie für Sprache und Dichtung, Darmstadt, Luchterhand.

VF, Вопросы философии.

VGBIL, Всесоюзная государственная библиотека иностранной литературы.

VH, Vida Hispánica, Wolverhampton.

VI, Военно издателство.

VI, Voix et Images.

Vla, Вопросы языкознания.

Vid, Віднова, Munich.

VIKP, Вопросы истории КПСС.

VIN, Veröffentlichungen des Instituts für Niederländische Philologie, Erftstadt, Lukassen.

ViSH, Вища школа.

VIst, Вопросы истории.

Vit, Вітчизна.

VKP, Всесоюзная книжная палата.

VL, Вопросы литературы.

VLet, Voz y Letras.

VLNSSSR, Вопросы литературы народов СССР.

VLUIIaL, Вестник Ленинградского университета. Серия 2. История, языкознание, литературоведение.

VM, Время и мы, New York — Paris — Jerusalem.

VMKA, Verslagen en Mededelingen, Koninklijke Academie voor Nederlandse Taal- en Letterkunde.

VMUF, Вестник Московского университета. Серия IX, филология.

VMUFil, Вестник Московского университета. Серия VII, философия.

Vo, Волга.

Voz, Возрождение.

VP, Встречи с прошлым, Moscow.

VPen, Vita e Pensiero.

VR, Vox Romanica.

VRIaL, Вопросы русского языка и литературы, Erevan.

VRKhD, Вестник Русского христианского движения.

VRL, Вопросы русской литературы.

VRM, Volkskultur am Rhein und Maas.

VS, Вопросы семантики.

Vs, Всесвіт, Kiev.

VSAV, Vydavateľstvo Slovenskej akadémie vied.

VSh, Вышэйшая школа.

VSh, Визвольний шлях.

VSSH, Вечерняя средняя школа.

VSt, Вопросы стилистики, Saratov.

VV, Византийский временник.

VVM, Vlastivědný věstník moravský.

VVSh, Вестник высшей школы.

VWGÖ, Verband der Wissenschaftlichen Gesellschaften Österreichs.

VySh, Вища школа.

VysSh, Высшая школа.

VyV, Verdad y Vida.

VZ, Vukova zadužbina, Belgrade.

WAB, Wolfenbütteler Arbeiten zur Barockforschung, Hamburg, Hauswedell.

WADL, Wiener Arbeiten zur deutschen Literatur, Vienna, Braumüller.

WAGAPH, Wiener Arbeiten zur germanischen Altertumskunde und Philologie, Vienna, Halosar.

WAiF, Wydawnictwa Artystyczne i Filmowe, Warsaw.

WaT, Wagenbachs Taschenbücherei, Berlin, Wagenbach.

WB, Weimarer Beiträge.

WBG, Wissenschaftliche Buchgesellschaft, Darmstadt.

WBN, Wolfenbütteler Barock-Nachrichten.

WF, Wege der Forschung, Darmstadt, Wissenschaftliche Buchgesellschaft.

WGY, Women in German Yearbook.

WHNDL, Würzburger Hochschulschriften zur Neueren Deutschen Literaturgeschichte, Frankfurt, Lang.

WHR, The Welsh History Review.

WKJb, Wissenschaftskolleg. Institute for Advanced Study, Berlin. Jahrbuch.

WL, Wydawnictwo Literackie, Cracow.

WŁ, Wydawnictwo Łódzkie.

WLub, Wydawnictwo Lubelskie.

WLT, World Literature Today.

WNB, Wolfenbütteler Notizen zur Buchgeschichte.

WNT, Wydawnictwa Naukowo-Techniczne.

WoB, Wolfenbütteler Beiträge.

WP, Wiedza Powszechna, Warsaw.

WPFG, Working Papers in Functional Grammar, Amsterdam U.P.

WRM, Wolfenbütteler Renaissance Mitteilungen.

WS, Wort und Sinn.

WSA, Wolfenbütteler Studien zur Aufklärung, Heidelberg, Schneider.

WSiP, Wydawnictwa Szkolne i Pedagogiczne, Warsaw.

WSJ, Wiener Slavistisches Jahrbuch.

WSl, Die Welt der Slaven.

WSlA, Wiener Slawistischer Almanach.

WSP, Wyższa Szkoła Pedagogiczna.

WSp, Word and Spirit.

WSPRRNDFP, Wyższa Szkoła Pedagogiczna w Rzeszowie. Rocznik Naukowo-Dydaktyczny. Filologia Polska.

WuW, Welt und Wort.
WW, Wirkendes Wort.
WZHUB, Wissenschaftliche Zeitschrift der Humboldt-Universität, Berlin: gesellschafts- und sprachwissenschaftliche Reihe.
WZPHP, Wissenschaftliche Zeitschrift der pädagogischen Hochschule Potsdam. Gesellschafts- und sprachwissenschaftliche Reihe.
WZUG, Wissenschaftliche Zeitschrift der Ernst-Moritz-Arndt- Universität Greifswald.
WZUH, Wissenschaftliche Zeitschrift der Martin-Luther-Universität Halle-Wittenberg: gesellschafts- und sprachwissenschaftliche Reihe.
WZUJ, Wissenschaftliche Zeitschrift der Friedrich-Schiller-Universität Jena/Thüringen: gesellschafts- und sprachwissenschaftliche Reihe.
WZUL, Wissenschaftliche Zeitschrift der Karl Marx Universität Leipzig: gesellschafts- und sprachwissenschaftliche Reihe.
WZUR, Wissenschaftliche Zeitschrift der Universität Rostock: gesellschafts- und sprachwissenschaftliche Reihe.

YaIS, Yale Italian Studies.
YB, Ysgrifau Beirniadol.
YCC, Yearbook of Comparative Criticism.
YCGL, Yearbook of Comparative and General Literature.
YEEP, Yale Russian and East European Publications, New Haven, Yale Center for International and Area Studies.
YES, Yearbook of English Studies.
YFS, Yale French Studies.
YIS, Yearbook of Italian Studies.
YJC, Yale Journal of Criticism.
YPL, York Papers in Linguistics.
YR, Yale Review.
YSGP, Yearbook. Seminar for Germanic Philology.

YWMLS, The Year's Work in Modern Language Studies.

ZÄAK, Zeitschrift für Ästhetik und allgemeine Kunstwissenschaft.
Zap, Запісы, Belorussian Institute of Arts and Sciences, New York.
ZB, Zeitschrift für Balkanologie.
ZBL, Zeitschrift für bayerische Landesgeschichte.
ZbS, Zbornik za slavistiku.
ZCP, Zeitschrift für celtische Philologie.
ZD, Zielsprache Deutsch.
ZDA, Zeitschrift für deutsches Altertum und deutsche Literatur.
ZDL, Zeitschrift für Dialektologie und Linguistik.
ZDNÖL, Zirkular. Dokumentationsstelle für neuere österreichische Literatur.
ZDP, Zeitschrift für deutsche Philologie.
ZFKPhil, Zborník Filozofickej fakulty Univerzity Komenského. Philologica.
ZFL, Zbornik za filologiju i lingvistiku.
ZFSL, Zeitschrift für französische Sprache und Literatur.
ZGer, Zeitschrift für Germanistik.
ZGKS, Zeitschrift der Gesellschaft für Kanada-Studien.
ZGL, Zeitschrift für germanistische Linguistik.
ZGS, Zürcher germanistische Studien, Berne, Lang.
ZhMP, Журнал московской патриархии.
ZK, Zeitschrift für Katalanistik.
ZL, Zeszyty Literackie, Paris.
ZMS(FL), Zbornik Matice srpske za filologiju i lingvistiku.
ZMS(KJ), Zbornik Matice srpske za književnost i jezik.
ZMS(Sl), Zbornik Matice srpske za slavistiku.
Zn, Знамя.
ZNiO, Zakład Narodowy im. Ossolińskich, Wrocław.
ZnS, Знание — сила.
ZNTSh, Записки наукового товариства ім. Шевченка.

ZNUG, Zeszyty Naukowe Uniw. Gdańskiego, Gdańsk.

ZNUJ, Zeszyty Naukowe Uniw. Jagiellońskiego, Cracow.

ZNWHFR, Zeszyty Naukowe Wydziału Humanistycznego. Filologia Rosyjska.

ZNWSPO, Zeszyty Naukowe Wyższej Szkoly Pedagogicznej w Opolu.

ZO, Zeitschrift für Ostforschung.

ZOR, Записки Отдела рукописей, гос. орд. Ленина библиотеки СССР им. В. И. Ленина.

ZPSK, Zeitschrift für Phonetik, Sprachwissenschaft und Kommunikationsforschung.

ZPŠSlav, Zborník Pedagogickej fakulty v Prešove Univerzity Pavla Jozefa Šafárika v Košiciach-Slavistika, Bratislava.

ZR, Zadarska revija.

ZRAG, Записки русской академической группы в США.

ZRBI, Зборник радова византолошког института, Belgrade.

ZRL, Zagadnienia Rodzajów Literackich.

ZRP, Zeitschrift für romanische Philologie.

ZS, Zeitschrift für Sprachwissenschaft.

ZSJ, Zápisnik slovenského jazykovedca.

ZSK, Ze Skarbca Kultury.

ZSL, Zeitschrift für Siebenbürgische Landeskunde.

ZSl, Zeitschrift für Slawistik.

ZSP, Zeitschrift für slavische Philologie.

ZSVS, Zborník Spolku vojvodinských slovakistov, Novi Sad.

ZV, Zeitschrift für Volkskunde.

Zv, Звезда.

ZvV, Звезда востока.

ZWL, Zeitschrift für Württembergische Landesgeschichte.

INDEXES

I. SUBJECTS

Absurd, theatre of,
  and D. I. Kharms, 1041
Academic freedom,
  in 19-c. Germany, 753, 776
Acmeism,
  Russian, 1013, 1043
Adolescence,
  in med. German lit., 634
Advertising,
  in East and West Germany, 591
Aesthetics,
  and science,
  med. Arabic, 301
  Danish, 19-c., 909
  French, 18-c., 145, 146, 157
  French, 19-c., 180–81, 188, 199, 200, 203
  German, Classical era, 690, 716, 724, 734
  German, Romantic era, 744, 753, 759,
    760, 764–65, 769–70
  German (since 1945), 684–85, 863–64
  Italian, 18-c., 521
  of J. W. von Goethe, 707–08
  of Gottfried von Strassburg, 646
  of J. G. Herder, 718
  of I. Kant, 719–20
  of the Pléiade, 88
  of F. Schiller, 711, 712–13
Air,
  in 16-c. French lit., 84
Alchemy,
  in 16-c. French lit., 92
  in J. P. Richter, 766, 767
  in J. Verne, 203
Alienation,
  in H. C. Andersen, 907
Allegory,
  in med. French lit., 75
  in 17-c. French lit., 100
  in 20-c. French lit., 220
  in med. German lit., 650, 658
  in German Classical lit., 716
  in med. Latin lit., 10
  in C. Baudelaire, 185
  in W. Benjamin, 811
  in P. Calderón de la Barca, 317
  in *Divine Comedy*, 768
  in E. T. A. Hoffmann, 756
  in F. Hölderlin, 757, 758
  in F. Nietzsche, 802
  in B. Pascal, 119

  in I. Sannazaro, 475–76
  in A. Strindberg, 932
  in T. Tasso, 472
  in G. Vasari, 474
  in E. Vittorini, 548
Alliteration,
  in med. German poetry, 629
Almanacs,
  med. German, 663
  German, 18-c., 727
Alterity,
  in 20-c. French lit., 209, 216
  in med. German lit., 640
Ambiguity,
  in med. French lit., 77
  in med. Latin lit., 6
  in med. Occitan poetry, 262
  in L. A. von Arnim, 747
  in I. Svevo, 547
Anagrams,
  in med. French lit., 74–75
Analogy,
  in 16-c. French lit., 90
  in 20-c. French lit., 225
Anarchy,
  in mod. German lit., 830
Androgyny,
  in German Romantic lit., 736, 746
  in V. Hugo, 175
  in E. Pardo Bazán, 334
Anecdotes,
  Dutch, 17-c., 893
Animal magnetism,
  in German Romantic lit., 761, 766, 767
  in E. T. A. Hoffmann, 755
Animals, animal imagery,
  bear, in med. Latin lit., 5
  beaver, in French lit., 59
  boar, in Gottfried von Strassburg,
    646
  dog, in 19-c. German lit., 789
  fox, in med. French lit., 65–67
  lion, in fable, 103
  in 16-c. French lit., 84
  in 17-c. French lit., 103
  in med. German lit., 624
  in med. Latin lit., 3
  in G. de Maupassant, 201
  in M. de Montaigne, 96
  in E. Montale, 539

in B. Pérez Galdós, 336
in L. Pulci, 471–72
Anthropology,
  18-c., 726
  and G. Keller, 779
Anti-monasticism,
  in med. Latin lit., 5
Anti-Nazism,
  French, 208
Anti-Petrarchism,
  French, 16-c., 87
  French, 17-c., 101
Anti-Semitism,
  and 18-c. medicine, 698
  in med. Germany, 633, 653
  in German Classical lit., 719
  in 19-c. Germany, 772
  in mod. Germany, 693
Antichrist,
  in 16-c. French lit., 79
  in Russian lit. (1880–1917), 1013
  in V. S. Solov'ev, 1024
Anticlericalism,
  French, 18-c., 151
Antiquarianism,
  in European lit., 192
Apocalypse, Apocalypticism,
  in German Romantic lit., 741–42
  in German lit. (since 1945), 833, 856
  in med. Spanish lit., 296
  in M. A. Bulgakov, 1037
  in P. Claudel, 219
  in O. E. Mandel'shtam, 1042
Apologia,
  French, 16-c., 95–96
Arabs, Arab culture,
  and med. literary history, 620
  and Belorussian lit., 1063
  and Serbo-Croat lit., 1077
  in med. Spain, 300–03
  See also Islam
Archaeology,
  and J. J. Winckelmann, 734
Archaisms,
  in 17-c. French lit., 101
Architecture,
  and art criticism, 181
  French baroque, 97
  Italian Ren., 461
  theatrical, 127
  and 16-c. French lit., 81
  and French Romantic lit., 166
Argot,
  French, 19-c., 205
Arson,
  in 19-c. German lit., 776
Art,
  autonomy of, 684–85
  children in, 99
  and poetry, 209

and politics, in P. Weiss, 872
theory of, in L. B. Alberti, 484
med. Dutch, 891
and Dutch 17-c. lit., 892–93
Dutch (1880–1945), 898
French, 18-c., 132, 136
in French 19-c. lit., 193
French, 20-c., 213–14
and German 19-c. lit., 776
in German lit. (1880–1945), 807
Ren. Italian, 454–55
and Polish poetry, 972
Spanish (1898–1936), 355
in Spanish lit. (1898–1936), 341, 344,
    345, 346, 354
in Spanish lit. (since 1936), 370, 373
and Swedish lit., 935
and Y. Bonnefoy, 236
in H. Broch, 813
and M. Butor, 236
in T. Fontane, 789–90
of F. García Lorca, 346–47, 349
and J. W. von Goethe, 705–06, 709–10
and J. G. Herder, 719
in E. T. A. Hoffmann, 738
of G. Keller, 798
in C. F. Meyer, 800
and M. Proust, 229
of M. de Unamuno, 357
Art criticism,
  French, 19-c., 162, 181–82
  French, 20-c., 219
  Italian, 20-c., 544
  of C. Brentano, 748
  of E. Zola, 203
Art history,
  German, Romantic era, 773
  of G. Vasari, 474, 488–89
Arthurian lit.,
  themes and motifs in, 57
  med. Dutch, 890
  med. French, 55–58, 57, 60, 68
  med. German, 639–42, 661
  in med. Italian lit., 447
  Norwegian, 921
  med. Spanish, 296, 298
  and contemp. Spanish lit., 371
  in G. Boccaccio, 448
Ascension of Christ,
  in med. German lit., 613–14
Astrology,
  med. German, 664
  in med. Latin lit., 6
Atheism,
  French, 16-c., 81
  French, 19-c., 182
  and J. G. Fichte, 697–98, 742
Atomism,
  in 17-c. Italy, 509–10

Authorship, authority,
in med. lit., 51
in med. German lit., 632, 645
Autobiography,
as a genre, 908
Danish, 20-c., 910–11
French, Romantic era, 173
in German novels, 688
in German Romantic lit., 736
in German 20-c. lit., 832–33, 836, 840, 844
mod. Irish, 581
in Italian women writers, 527
in med. Spanish lit., 293
in R. Alberti, 345
in J. Améry, 845–46
in M. Azaña, 355
of T. Bandettini, 515
in H. Bang, 908
in I. Bergman, 933
in T. Bernhard, 848
in G. Boccaccio, 449–50
in H. Böll, 849–50
of E. Canetti, 813
in G. de Céspedes y Meneses, 311
in F. R. de Chateaubriand, 164
of G. Chiabrera, 505
in R. Debray, 237
in V. Dunin-Martsinkevitch, 1067
in F. Dürrenmatt, 852
in U. Eco, 534–35
in G. Ekelöf, 934
of C. Ferrazzi, 505
in G. Flaubert, 195
in J. Goytisolo, 369
of F. Grillparzer, 792
in T. Hansen, 912
in K. Kestien, 819
in I. Lo-Johansson, 935
in P. Loti, 200
in D. Maraini, 538
in Michelangelo, 474
in H. Müller, 866
in Multatuli, 897
in P. Nizon, 867
in C. Nuccoli, 452
in Restif de la Bretonne, 160
in J. Rist, 669
of K. Roberts, 566
in M. Schwob, 202
of J. G. Seume, 732
in C. Simon, 243
in A. D. Siniavskii, 1048
of H. Speckter, 805
in H. Stangerup, 913
in Stendhal, 171, 172
in G. Vasari, 489
of G. Vico, 524
of V. S. Vysotskii, 1050
in C. Wolf, 874

in E. Zeller, 874
See also Diaries; Memoirs; Self-image, self-representation
Automata,
in German Romantic lit., 766–67
Automatism,
in 20-c. French lit., 210, 218
opposition to, 220, 223
Auto sacramental,
and English Eucharist theatre, 315
of P. Calderón de la Barca, 317–18
Autumn,
in 19-c. French poetry, 188
Avant-garde,
Austrian, 836
Czech, 942
French, 210, 215, 225, 942
German, 808
Italian, 529, 530
Latin American, 413
Russian, 1012–14, 1033
Serbian, 1074, 1075

Ballads,
Czech, 938
Danish, 905
med. German, 613
German, Classical era, 714
German, 19-c., 782, 685
Scottish, 579, 586
med. Spanish, 290–91
Welsh, 565
Baroque,
French, 91, 95
Ukrainian, 1055
Battle rhetoric,
medieval, 5, 65
Begging poetry,
med. Latin, 5–6
Bereavement,
in German lit. (since 1945), 867
Bible,
med. exegesis, 618
translation of,
medieval, 940
Old English, 3
med. German, 613, 625, 628–29, 637, 654–55, 656
Italian, 456
Scottish Gaelic, 584
in 16-c. French lit., 85
in med. Latin lit., 2
in med. Spanish lit., 290–91, 293
in Ukrainian lit., 1057
in M. A. Bulgakov, 1037
and Chrétien de Troyes, 59
in S. A. Esenin, 1019
in J. Racine, 126–27, 130
in L. Ukrainka, 1057

Bibliographies, general,
   of *commedia dell'arte*, 502
   of the Crusades, 50
   of fairy-tales, 107
   of picaresque lit., 309
   of sexuality, in med. French lit., 52
   of Breton lit., 570
   Catalan, dialectological, 377
   of Catalan linguistics, 375
   of Danish lit., 905–06
   of Dutch lang. teaching material, 882
   of French 18-c. writers, 137
   of French linguistics, 25
   of French press, 137
   of French publishing, 139
   of German ballads, 685
   of med. German chapbooks, 661
   of German Classical lit., 679
   of German dialectology, 607
   of German lit. (1750–1850), 774
   of mod. German lit., Chinese reaction to,
      830
   of German literary history, 631
   of Italian Inquisition, 496
   of Italian linguistics, 424–25, 444
   of Italian pageantry, 461
   of Italian Ren. lit., 457
   of 17-c. Italian publications, 491–92, 493
   of 18-c. Italian publications, 511
   of Polish onomastics, 970
   of Polish poetry, 980
   of Portuguese linguistics, 388
   of Romance linguistics, 25
   of Russian avant-garde, 1013
   of Russian folklore, 987
   of Russian linguistics, 987
   of early Russian lit., 998
   of Russian lit. (1700–1820), 1004
   of Russian lit. titles, 989
   of Russian poetry, 988
   of Russian science fiction, 988
   of translated Russian lit., 986
   of Slovak linguistics, 946
   of Spanish 20-c. lit., 363
   of Spanish drama, 360, 373
   of Spanish surrealism, 343
   of Spanish-American lit., 412, 413, 419
   of Swedish lit., 928
   of Welsh humanism, 563
   of Zurich printers, 663
Bibliographies, individual,
   of Angélique Arnauld, 118
   of A. Banti, 531
   of C. Baudelaire, 186
   of A. Belyi, 1015
   of G. Boccaccio, 449
   of M. M. Boiardo, 471
   of S. Brant, 664
   of M. A. Bulgakov, 1037
   of I. Calvino, 532

   of A. de Cartagena, 295
   of R. de Castro, 331
   of *La Celestina*, 314
   of N. S. R. Chamfort, 140
   of G. Debenedetti, 526
   of D. Diderot, 146
   of L. Ďurovič, 946
   of Meister Eckhart, 653
   of L. Fontanella, 535
   of F. Freiligrath, 791
   of F. García Lorca, 347, 350
   of A. Gide, 221
   of J. W. von Goethe, 699–700
   of P. N. Grøtvedt, 914
   of M. Hœgstad, 914
   of A. Harun, 1067
   of J. G. Herder, 717
   of F. Hölderlin, 756
   of V. Hugo, 174–75
   of J. P. Jacobsen, 909
   of E. Jelinek, 861
   of M. Josić-Višnjić, 1075
   of F. Kafka, 817
   of F. Kaiser, 797
   of D. Kollár, 946
   of J. Kosiński, 982
   of E. Labiche, 207
   of J. de La Fontaine, 104
   of N. Machiavelli, 487
   of H. Magerøy, 920
   of F. Mayröcker, 865
   of A. Mickiewicz, 975–76
   of J. Mistrík, 946
   of G. de Nerval, 175
   of B. Ó hEithir, 580
   of S. Ó Ruadháin, 579
   of J. O. Picón, 340, 354
   of J. Puzynina, 957
   of K. L. Reinhold, 731
   of F. Ruščák, 946
   of D. A. F. de Sade, 153
   of F. Schiller, 710
   of P. Šima, 946
   of S. Solmi, 546
   of B. Stagnino, 456
   of S. Svagrovský, 946
   of S. Szlifersztejnowej, 957
   of T. Tasso, 472
   of P. Tekavčić, 11
   of O. V. Tvorogov, 998
   of G. Ungaretti, 548
   of J. Žigo, 946
Biographies,
   as a genre, 929
   French, 17-c., 108
   of med. women, 618
   of Russian writers, 986
   of T. Abbt, 714
   of I. Bachmann, 847
   of M. Bahdanovich, 1066

of A. Breton, 217
of Conde de Buelna, 298
of M. A. Bulgakov, 1036–37
of R. de Castro, 331
of C. J. Cela, 368
of L. Celiano (A. Grillo), 500
of B. Cellini, 486
of J.-A.-N. de Condorcet, 140
of T. Dorst, 852
of R. Enckell, 934
of G. Feydeau, 206
of J. G. Fichte, 751
of B. le B. de Fontenelle, 140
of E. Fried, 854
of V. García Escobar, 332
of J. de la Gessée, 92
of J. Giono, 222
of J. W. von Goethe, 708–10
of M. Gor'kii, 1040
of Gottfried von Strassburg, 646
of H. Grégoire, 141
of N. S. Gumilev, 1020
of H. Heine, 794
of L. Hensel, 797
of H. Hesse, 816
of G. Heym, 816
of D. Hyde, 575
of I. Keun, 819
of A. F. Knigge, 723
of K. C. F. Krause, 723–24
of P. Lagerkvist, 935
of Mme de Lambert, 141
of N. Lange, 415
of J. M. C. Lassberg, 799
of R. Levin Varnhagen, 727
of U. Lutsevich, 1068
of C. Mac Aonghusa, 575
of J. Mackiewicz, 982
of F. de Malherbe, 104
of T. Mann, 821
of C. Marot, 85
of W. Morgan, 563
of V. V. Nabokov, 1043
of V. Ocampo, 415
of B. Ó hEithir, 580
of E. du Perron, 898
of P. Picasso, 209
of A. Pizarnik, 415
of M. Praun, 676
of M. Proust, 228, 229
of Rachilde, 202
of J. P. Richter, 766
of A. Rimbaud, 188, 189
of R. Rolland, 230
of P. de Ronsard, 86
of J. J. Rousseau, 148
of F. von Saar, 803
of D. A. F. de Sade, 157
of F. Schiller, 711, 714
of V. S. Solov'ev, 1024

of H. Steinhöwel, 662
of T. Storm, 805
of A. Storni, 414
of Teresa of Avila, 305
of J. H. du T. de Valincour, 143
of F. M. A. de Voltaire, 150–51
of C. M. Wieland, 733
of J. J. Winckelmann, 734
of E. Zola, 203
Birds,
    cock, in Belorussian folklore, 1069
    cuckoo, in Belorussian folklore, 1069
    magpie, in med. lit., 3, 51
    parrot, in C. Baudelaire, 186
    pheasant, vow of, 74
    phoenix, in 16-c. French lit., 80
    pica, in med. Latin lit., 3
    swan, in H. von Kleist, 761
    in B. Pérez Galdós, 339
    in P. Verlaine, 191
Bishops,
    poetry about selection of, 7
Black Death. *See* Plague
Boredom,
    in H. Heine, 794–95
Bride, immured,
    in Bulgarian folk lit., 1083
Broadsheets,
    and Slovak Romanticism, 953
Buddhism,
    in M. Zambrano, 360, 372
Bullfighting,
    and A. Machado, 352
Bureaucracy,
    in Ren. Italy, 464
Butterflies,
    in I. A. Brodskii and V. V. Nabokov,
    1036

Cannibals,
    in 16-c. French lit., 95
Carnival,
    in med. German lit., 613, 633
    in 17-c. German lit., 677
    in Italian Ren. poetry, 475
    in modern Latin American lit., 421
    and M. M. Bakhtin, 1031
    in P. Calderón de la Barca, 319
    in A. Mira de Amescua, 324
    and Iu. K. Olesha, 1044
    and R. Petrović, 1076
Catastrophe,
    in German drama since 1945, 866
Catholicism,
    French, 20-c., 226
Celibacy,
    in 19-c. French lit., 199
Cell poetry,
    med. Latin, 4

Censorship,
  in Austria, of English and French lit., 781
  in Chile, 417
  of 19-c. French drama, 207
  in 17-c. Germany, 666–67
  in East Germany, 841
  in Ren. Italy, 466
  in 17-c. Italy, 497
  in 18-c. Italy, 512, 514
  in 20-c. Italy, 540
  in 19-c. Russia, 1013
  in contemporary Russia, 1030
Chapbooks,
  med. German, 661–62
Characterization,
  in med. French lit., 60
  in 17-c. French drama, 127, 128
Charms,
  med. German, 630
Chastity,
  in med. French lit., 55, 61
Chess,
  in med. Germany, 623–24
Children's lit.,
  Danish, 19-c., 907–08
  German, 808, 830, 839, 859, 860
  Swedish, 933
  See also Fairy-tales
Children, childhood,
  in 16-c. French lit., 83
  in 17-c. French lit., 98–99, 102, 103, 106,
    113, 117
  in 17-c. French drama, 120
  in Old Norse lit., 920
  in J. W. von Goethe, 707
  in M. Gor'kii, 1027
  in D. Tadijanović, 1074
Chivalry, chivalric lit.,
  med., general, 639
  med. French, 57, 59, 74, 77
  German, 658
  Italian Ren., 468, 471, 472–73
  Spanish (1490–1700), 309–10, 311–13
  See also Courtly lit.
Christianity, Christian symbolism
  Ren. imagery of, 464–65, 466
  in 16-c. French lit., 84
  in the French press, 41
  in med. Germany, 618, 623
  in med. Latin lit., 3
  in A. A. Blok, 1036
  in F. X. Kroetz, 863
  in F. Rabelais, 82
Chronicles,
  medieval, Northern, 50
  Cossack, 1055
  Czech, 939, 999
  med. French, 65, 73
  med. German, 622, 633, 651–52, 662–63
  early Russian, 997–98

Serbian, 1072
  med. Spanish, 289, 293, 294–95
  Spanish-American Colonial, 406, 407–08
Cinema,
  German, 713, 836, 863
  Polish, 973
  Spanish, 342, 344, 369
  Spanish-American, 415, 421
  in H. Fallada, 814
  and P. C. de Laclos, 155
  and J.-B. P. Molière, 123
Cistercians,
  and education, 621
  in med. Germany, 651, 653
Cities,
  dead, 202
  and modernism, 210
  in German lit. (since 1945), 857–58, 867
Civility,
  French, 17-c., 123, 124
Classicism,
  medieval, 6
  French, 16-c., 79
  French, 17-c., 104, 105
  German, 683
  Russian (1700–1820), 1003
  Slovak, 953
  Spanish (since 1936), 366
Cliché,
  in 19-c. French lit., 186
  in J. Barbey d'Aurevilly, 193
Clock imagery,
  in 17-c. Italian poetry, 499
Coins,
  med. German, 623
Collectivization,
  in Belorussian prose, 1068
  in Ukrainian prose, 1061
Colonialism,
  French, 20-c., 220, 222
Colour,
  in J. W. von Goethe, 707–08
  in V. Hugo, 163
  in E. Zola, 204
Comedia,
  Spanish (1490–1700), 314–17, 319, 322,
    324
Comedy,
  morality and, 125
  French, 16-c., 93
  French, 17-c., 123–26
  French, 19-c., 206–07
  med. Italian, 447
  Italian Ren., 480–81
  Spanish (1490–1700), 325
  and G. Keller, 798
  in E. Zola, 206
  See also Humour
Comics,
  German (since 1945), 831

Commedia dell'arte,
  French, 17-c., 502
  Italian Ren., 482
  Italian, 17-c., 502–03
  Italian, 18-c., 518
Commemoration,
  in med. French lit., 59
Communication,
  in Spanish lit. (1490–1700), 315
  non-verbal, in 17-c. French drama, 123
  theory of,
    Norwegian, 914
    Swedish, 925–26
Computers,
  in codicology, 616
  in German lit. and ling. studies, 614
  in metrical analysis, 628–29
  in text editing, 14, 287, 409, 651, 658, 660, 921
  in textual analysis, 471, 642, 657, 658, 659
  in translation, 18, 302
  See also Linguistics: *Computer linguistics*
Confraternities,
  Italian, 464, 465–66, 483
Confusion,
  in A. Mira de Amuesca, 324–25
Conservatism,
  German, 695
  in J. von Eichendorff, 749
Conspiracy,
  in 17-c. France, 98
Constraint, formal,
  in R. Queneau, 241
Constructivism,
  Russian, 1013
Conteurs,
  French, 83–84
Cooking, cookery books
  med. French, evolution of, 75
  in med. Germany, 658
  in 19-c. German lit., 776–77
Correspondence,
  Pope Alexander VII — A. Kircher, 493
  B. von Arnim — M. Fuller, 745
  C. Brentano — S. Mereau, 689, 736
  A. Casati — G. Prezzolini, 533
  Champfleury — G. Sand, 194
  B. Croce — G. Prezzolini, 534
  A. von Droste-Hülsoff — C. B. Schlüter, 788
  A. von Droste-Hülsoff — L. Schücking, 788
  A. von Droste-Hülsoff — A. M. Sprickmann, 788
  G. Flaubert — G. Sand, 176, 196
  T. Fontane — J. Kürschner, 789
  J. W. von Goethe — C. F. Zeller, 700
  K. von Günderode — F. Creuzer, 691

  A. von Haller — H.-B. de Saussure, 716–17
  J.-M. de Heredia — G. Moreau, 186
  Hildegard of Bingen — Elisabeth von Schönau, 7
  G. Keller — P. Heyse, 798
  K. Kraus — O. Stoessl, 820
  G. W. Leibniz — S. Clarke, 724–25
  C. C. Lucius — C. F. Gellert, 689
  G. Manfredi — G. Poleni, 519
  T. Mann — K. Martens, 821
  T. Mann — R. Schickele, 821
  F. P. Morozova — Avvakum — E. P. Urusova, 1001
  G. Naudé — J. Mazarin, 107
  B. L. Pasternak — P. P. Suvchinskii, 1044
  J. Paulhan — R. Caillois, 240
  C. Pavese — E. De Martino, 542
  An tAth. Peadar — S. Ó Dubhghaill, 581
  A. M. Remizov — S. P. Remizova-Dovgello, 1023
  J. P. Richter — E. Gads, 766
  R. Rolland — M. Gorkii, 230
  V. V. Rozanov — M. O. Gershenzon, 1023
  F. Scala — Giovanni de' Medici, 502
  to F. Schiller, 710
  H. Sloane — A. J. Bignon, 137
  T. Storm — H. Speckter, 804–05
  T. Storm — O. Speckter, 804–05
  M. I. Tsvetaeva — A. Bakhrakh, 1049
  M. de Unamuno — J. Teixeira de Pascoaes, 357
  W. H. Wackenroder — S. Tieck, 772
  B. K. Zaitsev — G. V. Adamovich, 1050
  S. Zweig — F. Braun, 829
  See also Letters
Cosmography, cosmology
  Renaissance, 79
  Italian, 17-c., 508–09
  in Spanish lit. (1490–1700), 310
  in Michelangelo, 454
Countryside. *See* Landscape
Courage,
  in med. French lit., 58, 61
  in med. Latin lit., 5
Court life, courtly culture
  ballet and, 123, 124
  drama and, 317, 319, 324, 447
  handbooks of, 672
  med. Dutch, 890
  French, 17-c., 97–98, 112
  med. German, 638–39
  German, 17-c., 665
  German, 18-c., 726
  Italian Ren., 461–62
  and Italian Ren. poetry, 478–79
  Italian, 17-c., 493–94, 503

Courtly lit.,
    med. French, 51
    med. German, 638–48
    Spanish, 298
    See also Chivalry; Romance
Creationism,
    Spanish, 341, 347
Creativity,
    depiction of, in German lit. (1830–1880),
    774–75
Criticism. *See* Art criticism; Drama criticism;
    Literary criticism
Cross,
    in med. Latin lit., 3
Crowds,
    fear of, in German Classical lit., 695
Crusades,
    ethos of, 53
    and med. Latin lit., 6, 7
    in med. French lit., 50
Cultural exchange,
    French — German, 163
Curses,
    in 16-c. French lit., 91

Dada,
    French, 215, 217, 235
Dance,
    terminology, in med. French lit., 71
    in 17-c. French drama, 123, 124
    in German lit. (1880–1945), 809
Dance of death,
    in med. French lit., 73
    in med. German lit., 664
    in med. Spanish lit., 299
Dandyism,
    in 19-c. French lit., 181
Darwinism,
    and W. Raabe, 779
Death,
    near-death experiences, 1–2
    pretence of,
        in med. French lit., 65
        in 17-c. French drama, 125
    in Belorussian folklore, 1069
    and 18-c. French medicine, 132
    in French Romantic lit., 166
    in 20-c. French lit., 208–09
    in med. German lit., 638, 648
    in German drama, 687
    in German Romantic lit., 761
    in German lit. (1880–1945), 825
    in med. Latin lit., 1, 6
    in I. Bachmann, 846
    in H. de Balzac, 170
    in P. Calderón de la Barca, 319
    in A. Malraux, 240
    in O. E. Mandel'shtam, 1042
    in Novalis, 765

    in M. Proust, 228
    in D. Ó Súilleabháin, 579
    in M. de Unamuno, 358
    in C. Wolf, 846
    See also Dance of death
Death-wish,
    in German Romantic lit., 740
Debate poetry,
    med. Latin, 3
Decadence,
    French, 19-c., 192, 199
    Russian, 1013
    and L. Couperus, 897
Deceit, deception
    in med. French lit., 50, 77
    in 17-c. French lit., 103
    in med. German lit., 635
Dedications,
    in 17-c. German lit., 669
Desire, sexual,
    in med. French lit., 50
    in 18-c. French lit., 149
    in med. Latin lit., 6–7
    in 19-c. Spanish lit., 329
Destiny,
    in J. Racine, 127
Detective lit. *See* Novel, *mystery*
Devil,
    in med. Latin lit., 1
Dialogue,
    medieval *ars dialogica*, 2
    in scientific lit., 494, 519
    in 20-c. French lit., 233
    in German Enlightenment and Romantic
        lit., 744–45
    theory of, Italian, 490–91
    in med. Spanish lit., 298
    in Spanish lit. (1490–1700), 309
    in P. de Ronsard, 87
    in A. Stifter, 804
Diaries,
    German, 17-c., 665
    Swedish, 929–30
    of O. F. Berggol'ts, 1028
    of I. A. Bunin, 1038
    of V. A. Chivilikhin, 1028
    of K. I. Chukovskii, 1038
    of H. von Doderer, 814
    of Ia. Drazdovich, 1067
    of M. von Ebner-Eschenbach, 788
    of J. W. von Goethe, 700
    of M. Gor'kii, 1040
    of E. L. Heim, 717
    of M. Ivchenko, 1058
    of T. Jensen, 913
    of V. G. Korolenko, 1021, 1027
    of T. Landolfi, 537
    of A. Lutskevich, 1068
    of T. Mann, 821
    of I. Melezh, 1068

of J. Munks, 912
of P. Panch, 1059
of B. Iu. Poplavskii, 1046
of M. M. Prishvin, 1046
of H. Sniehir'ov, 1062
of V. S. Vysotskii, 1050
of V. Zolotukhin, 1050
didactic lit.,
  med. French, 74–77
  French, 17-c., 109, 110, 112, 114
  med. German, 661, 664
  German, 17-c., 673, 675
  med. Latin, 7
  med. Spanish, 294, 299
divorce,
  in Spain, 350
Dominicans,
  in med. Germany, 653
doubles,
  in Czech lit., 937
  in C. Brentano, 748
  in W. Gombrowicz, 978
drama,
  art and, 10
  court plays, 317, 319, 324, 447
  and history, in France, 234
  med., general, 890
  national theatre movement, 177
  and politics, in 18-c. French lit.,
    158
  radio, 128
  religious
    med., general, 127
    med. French, 71–72
    med. German, 657
    med. Italian, 447
    Italian Ren., 482–83
    Italian, 18-c., 516–17
    med. Latin, 7
    Spanish (1490–1700), 315–17
  theory of, B. Brecht's, 812
Belorussian, 1066
Croatian, 1073
Czech, 940, 942, 943
Danish, 19-c., 907
med. Dutch, 890
Dutch Ren., 892
Dutch, 18-c., 896
Dutch, 19-c., 896
English, German reception of, 687
med. French, 65, 71–73
French, 16-c., 93
French, 17-c., 120–30
French, 18-c., 144, 158–60
French, Romantic era, 177–79
French, 19-c., 206–07
French, 20-c., 212–13, 215–16, 234–35,
  237, 238–39
med. German, 656–57
German, 17-c., 677–78

German, Classical era, 686–87, 691, 697,
  703–04, 706, 711, 712, 713–14, 715,
  723, 725, 726, 728
German, Romantic era, 743–44, 759, 773
German, 19-c., 776
German (1830–1880), 781–83, 784–87,
  791–93, 797, 803, 806
German (1880–1945), 806, 807, 810,
  812–13, 816–17, 823–25, 826
German (since 1945), 843, 848, 852–53,
  858, 859, 865–66, 871
mod. Irish, 578, 580
med. Italian, 447
Italian Ren., 480–83
Italian, 17-c., 491, 501–04
Italian, 18-c., 515–18, 521–22, 523
Italian, 20-c., 530, 537, 540, 543, 545,
  546–47
med. Latin, 1
Polish, 19-c., 975
Polish, 20-c., 980
Russian (1880–1917), 1014, 1018–19
Russian (since 1917), 1032, 1038, 1041
med. Spanish, 288, 299
Spanish (1490–1700), 314–25, 330–31
Spanish, 19-c., 326, 330–31, 335
Spanish, 20-c., 335
Spanish (1898–1936), 344, 348, 349–50,
  353, 358, 359, 360–61
Spanish (since 1936), 372–74
Spanish-American, 409, 413, 416, 417,
  418, 419, 421, 422
Swedish, 930, 931–32, 934, 936
Ukrainian, 1061
Welsh, 566
Drama criticism,
  Danish, 19-c., 910
  French, 17-c., 121
  German (1880–1945), 826
  Italian, 20-c., 545
  Polish, 975
  Russian (since 1917), 1032
  Spanish, 19-c., 330, 336
  Spanish (1898–1936), 360–61
  Spanish-American, 20-c., 414
Dreams,
  in med. lit., 7
  in 17-c. French lit., 109, 115
  in 19-c. French lit., 200
  in med. German lit., 635, 657
  in Russian lit. (1700–1820), 1002
  in Spanish lit. (1490–1700), 310
  in 19-c. Spanish lit., 330
  in Spanish lit. (1898–1936),
    343
  in H. de Balzac, 168
  in F. García Lorca, 348
  in H. von Kleist, 761–62
  in P. Weiss, 872
  in D. Wellershoff, 873

Dualism,
  in 19-c. French lit., 167
  in C. Baudelaire, 185
  of R. Descartes, 118
  in G. Sand, 176
Duels,
  in Italian Ren. lit., 469
  in A. Mira de Amuesca, 324
  in A. Schnitzler, 826
Dying words,
  J. W. von Goethe and, 683

Earth,
  in 16-c. French lit., 84
  in 20-c. French lit., 224
Earthquakes,
  Italian, 466
Eating,
  eating habits, med. French, 75
  and sex, in med. French lit., 67
  in 17-c. French lit., 113
  in 17-c. French drama, 125
  in É. Zola, 204
Economics,
  French, and Revolution, 134
  in Polish lit., 973
Education,
  chivalric, 640
  humanist,
  Dutch, 876
  English, med., 4, 8
  French, med., 4
  French, 16-c., 79
  French, 17-c., 104, 110, 120
  French, 18-c., 132, 139, 140, 141, 146
  French, 20-c., 211, 217, 226
  German, med., 621
  German, 17-c., 676
  German, 18-c., 733
  German, 19-c., 753, 776
  mod. Irish, 573, 575, 576
  Italian, med., 10
  Italian, 18-c., 514
  Spanish, med., 295, 301
  Spanish, 16-c., 267
  Spanish, 20-c., 266, 385
Egypt, Egyptomania,
  med. image of, 620
  in 16-c. France, 93
Eisteddfod,
  and *Gorsedd*, 565
Elegies,
  Spanish (1490–1700), 307
Emblem lit.,
  French, 16-c., 81
Émigré lit.,
  Belorussian, 1065
  German (1880–1945), 808, 810, 811, 815,
    821, 828

German (since 1945), 831, 833, 843
  Italian, 17-c., 505
  Jewish, 846
  Polish, 973
  Russian, 985, 1030–31, 1034–35
  Spanish, 20-c., 356–57, 362–63
  Spanish-American, 20-c., 412
  Ukrainian, 1057, 1060
Encyclopaedias,
  of historical linguistics, 986
  of natural history, 17-c. Italian, 507, 508
  med. German, 615, 651–52, 655
  of German Middle Ages, 610
  of Irish folklore, 577
  med. Latin, 8
  of Russian lit., 985–86
  D. Diderot's, 144–47
Enlightenment,
  Catholic, 788, 814
  everyday life of, in Germany, 695
  and revolution, 683
  Dutch, 895
  French, 131, 141, 143, 144, 166
  German, 670, 680–83, 685–86, 694–99,
    716, 718, 722, 728, 770, 804
  Italian, 512, 518, 520
  Jewish, 697
  Russian, 1002–03
Environmentalism,
  German, 842, 858
  C. Linnaeus and, 699
Epic,
  classical, 51
  mock heroic, 686
  med. French, 52–55, 60, 68
  med. German, 637–38
  German (1830–1880), 787–88, 799–800
  Italian Ren., 467–73
  med. Occitan, 263–64
  Russian (1700–1820), 1008
  med. Spanish, 290
  Spanish (1490–1700), 308
Epigrams,
  French, 17-c., 104
  of C. Huygens, 893
  of F. von Logau, 668
  of I. Sannazaro, 475
Epistemology,
  Renaissance, 82
  med. Arabic, 289
  French, 17-c., 108, 109, 119
  French, 20-c., 212
  German, 17-c., 674
  German, Classical era, 693–94,
    714
  German, Romantic era, 737, 760
  of Galileo, 509
  of I. Kant, 720–21
Epitaphs,
  med. Latin, 1

Eroticism,
    in med. lit., 646
    in med. French lit., 57
    in 20-c. French lit., 240
    in German fairy-tales, 752
    in Occitan poetry, 260–61
    in Russian lit. (since 1917), 1029
    in med. Spanish lit., 301
    in Spanish lit. (1490–1700), 322
    in Spanish lit. (since 1936), 368
    and G. Bataille, 216
    in A. Gide, 221
Eschatology,
    in 16-c. French lit., 79, 92
Esoterism,
    French, 19-c., 181
    in G. A. Bécquer, 330
Essays,
    German, Romantic era, 744
    Russian (1880–1917), 1020
Ethics,
    German, Classical era, 693, 723
    of A. Breton, 217
    of I. Kant, 720–21
Ethnography,
    ancient Roman, 624
Eugenics,
    in 19-c. Germany, 699
Europe,
    Romantic concept of, 742
    20-c. concept of, 808
Evangelism,
    in 16-c. French lit., 85
Exemplarity,
    in 17-c. French drama, 121, 122
Exile,
    in French Romantic lit., 164, 166, 167
    in German lit. (1880–1945), 827
    of L. B. Alberti, 485
    in M. Crnjanski, 1075
    in T. Mann, 822
    See also Émigré lit.
Existentialism,
    in Spanish lit. (since 1936), 374
    and A. Andersch, 846
Exoticism,
    French, 19-c., 182
    French, 20-c., 220
    See also Orientalism
Expressionism,
    German, 807–08, 810, 816, 817, 820, 827,
        828, 839, 851
    Swiss, 837
Eyes,
    and heart, in med. French lit., 59
    See also Gaze, the; Seeing

Fable poetry,
    German, 745

Fables,
    medieval, 3
    French, 17-c., 100
    med. German, 632–33
    Russian, 1009, 1013
    in med. Spanish lit., 293
    of Aesop, in German, 662
    in J. W. von Goethe, 706
    of La Fontaine, 102–04
    M.-A. Muret's theory of, 87
Fabliaux,
    Arthurian, 55
    gender in, 50
    med. French, 60, 67
    German, 658, 661
Facetious lit.,
    French, 17-c., 100
Failure,
    in med. French lit., 56
    in 17-c. French lit., 109
Fainting,
    in 18-c. French lit., 155
Fairy-tales,
    French, 17-c., 107, 112, 113 14
    German, 752–53
    Italian, 527, 532
    Swedish, 931
Family,
    in med. German lit., 634
    in German Classical lit., 696
    in Italian Ren. lit., 454
    in A. Stifter, 804
Fantasy,
    in 19-c. French lit., 201
    in German lit. (1880–1945), 807
    in German lit. (since 1945), 840
    in Polish lit., 972–73
    in A. von Chamisso, 749
    in J. von Eichendorff, 750
    in F. Kafka, 818
    in H. von Kleist, 762
    in J. P. Richter, 768
Fascism,
    feminist texts on, 936
    French, 133
    in German lit. (since 1945), 835, 839
    and Italian lit., 438–39, 527, 530
Fatalism,
    in Z. Werner, 773
Fathers, father figure,
    in C. Baudelaire, 185
    in Gottfried von Strassburg,
        646
    in G. E. Lessing, 726
    in M. de Montaigne, 94
    in M. Proust, 227
    in F. Rabelais, 82
    in J. Racine, 128
Faust theme,
    in M. A. Bulgakov, 1037

Fear,
   in med. German lit., 640
Feminism,
   philosophy of, 832
   French, 16-c., 81, 93, 94–95
   French, 18-c., 141
   French, 19-c., 174
   French, 20-c., 220
   med. German, 661–62
   German, 20-c., 831, 736, 769, 833, 836,
      865, 874
   Irish, 580
   in Ren. Italy, 466
   Spanish, 20-c., 367
   Spanish-American, 412
   Swedish, 936
   Ukrainian, 1062
   Welsh, 567
   in R. de Castro, 331
   in F. Lope de Vega Carpio, 320
   in B. Pérez Galdós, 338, 339
   in R. Wagner, 806
   See also Literary criticism, feminist
Festivals, fêtes,
   in med. French lit., 52, 68, 73–74
   French, 17-c., 98
   in 19-c. French lit., 191
   in med. Germany, 619–20, 625, 633
   in German Romantic lit., 747
   Italian, 17-c., 503
   in P. Calderón de la Barca, 319
Fetishism,
   in 19-c. French lit., 181, 192
Feudalism,
   in Russian lit. (1700–1820), 1003
Fiction,
   attitudes toward, in 17-c. French lit., 107
   vs. history, in 16-c. French lit., 81
   theory of, 238
   Spanish-American, 20-c., 413–14
Fictional devices,
   in med. lit., 7
Fire,
   in 16-c. French lit., 80, 84
   in I. Bachmann, 847
Flowers,
   in F. García Lorca, 348
   rose, in V. I. Ivanov, 1020
Folklore, folk-tales, folk lit.
   Belorussian, 1066, 1069
   Bulgarian, 1083
   German, 733
   Irish, 576–77
   Norwegian, 922
   Russian, 987, 998, 1001
   Scandinavian, 921–22
   Serbian, 1076–77
   Slovak, 952
   Ukrainian, 1059
   in F. García Lorca, 347

   and S. Kh. Karaslavov, 1082
   and U. Karatkevich, 1067
   and T. Kunev, 1082
   in E. Pardo Bazán, 334
   and F. Prokopovich, 1008
   and A. N. Radischchev, 1009
Folly,
   in Italian Ren. lit., 484
Food,
   cultural presentation of, med., 51
Fools,
   in med. French lit., 68
Forests,
   in G. Apollinaire, 214
   in T. de Banville, 184
   in M. Corti, 534
   in T. Konwicki, 982
Formalism,
   Russian, 832, 1031
   of P. Valéry, 232
Freedom, concept of,
   in 16-c. French lit., 94
   in med. Germany, 622
   I. Kant's theory of, 720–21
Freedom of conscience,
   in 16-c. French lit., 78, 81, 84, 92
   in 17-c. French lit., 117
Freemasonry,
   in 18-c. Italy, 512
   Russian, 1007
   and A. F. Knigge, 723
   in H. and T. Mann, 820
   and Stendhal, 171, 172
Friendship,
   in med. French lit., 58
   in 17-c. French lit., 101
   in German Classical lit., 691–92
Fury,
   in J. Racine, 129
Futurism,
   Italian, 529, 530
   Russian, 1012, 1013, 1031
   Ukrainian, 1057
   and M. Khvyl'ovyi, 1059

Gallows literature,
   Welsh, 565
Gaming,
   in med. Spanish lit., 290–91
Gardens,
   abandoned, in 20-c. Italian poetry, 52
   in L. Tieck, 771
Gaze, the
   in German lit. (since 1945), 850, 864
   transforming, in K. Blixen, 911
Gender,
   and interpretation of lit., 689
   and language choice, 561
   in med. French lit., 50, 62, 68

in 17-c. French lit., 107, 109
in 18-c. French lit., 148
in 19-c. French lit., 181, 200
in 20-c. French lit., 220
in med. German lit., 637
in German Classical lit., 691–93, 699
in German Romantic lit., 746
in German lit. (1830–1880), 803
in German lit. (since 1945), 831
in Italian Ren. lit., 467, 469
in modern Latin American lit., 416
in 19-c. Spanish lit., 331
in W. Alexis, 784
in C. Baudelaire, 185
in P. Calderón de la Barca, 318
in E. R. Dashkova, 1007
in D. Diderot, 146
in M. Frisch, 855
in F. Garcia Lorca, 349
in K. von Günderode, 753
in V. Hugo, 175
in G. E. Lessing, 726
in A. Mira de Amuesca, 324
in E. Pardo Bazán, 333, 334
in Tirso de Molina, 322–23
in J. A. Valente, 366
in R. del Valle-Inclán, 358–59
in E. Zola, 204
Genealogy,
    in Italian Ren. poetry, 467–68
Geography,
    and A. von Humboldt, 719
Gesture,
    in med. Germany, 620
    in B. Brecht, 812
    in G. P. Harsdörffer, 675
Giants,
    in med. French lit., 61
Gloss,
    in med. Spanish lit., 299
Gold,
    in 16-c. Spanish lit., 304
Gorsedd,
    and *Eisteddfod*, 565
Greek language,
    in med. Latin lit., 4
Grotesque, the,
    in German lit. (since 1945), 832
    in *Don Quixote*, 312
Guillotine,
    in 19-c. French lit., 180
Guilt,
    in Czech lit., 945
    in M. A. Bulgakov, 1037
    in J. Racine, 129

Hagiography,
    of women, 4
    medieval, 246, 619

med. Dutch, 891
med. French, 51, 63–64
med. German, 655
med. Latin, 1, 4, 5
early Russian, 998, 1000
med. Spanish, 295
Hair,
    in *La Celestina*, 314
Hand,
    in 16-c. French lit., 87
Harp,
    in Scottish lit., 585
Head, severed,
    in early Russian lit., 1000
Headstone inscriptions,
    German, Romantic era, 742
Heart,
    in med. French lit., 51, 52, 55, 56, 60, 64,
        68, 70, 75
    in 16-c. French lit., 87
    in med. German lit., 653
Heaven,
    in med. French lit., 50
Heimatliteratur,
    development of, 835–36, 837
    German (since 1945), 846, 862
Hell,
    in med. French lit., 50
    in 16-c. French lit., 91
Heraldry,
    in med. German lit., 654
Herbaria,
    med. German, 657, 658
Hermeticism,
    in Ren. Italy, 463–64, 474
Hermits,
    in med. German lit., 647
Hero, heroism,
    in med. Germany, 625
    in med. Spanish lit., 291
    and G. Guarini, 479
Heroic lit. *See* Epic
Historiography,
    of Middle Ages, 618
    Bulgarian, 1082
    Middle English, 9
    med. French, 52, 73–74
    and 16-c. French poetry, 91, 92
    French, 17-c., 112
    in 17-c. French press, 107
    French, 18-c., 151
    French, Romantic era, 163
    French, 20-c., 180
    med. German, 621, 632, 642
    German, Classical era, 690, 715, 729–30
    Ren. Italian, 459
    Italian Ren., 483
    Italian, 17-c., 490
    med. Latin, 1, 5, 7
    med. Norwegian, 920

early Russian, 998, 1000
Russian, 17-c., 1001
Russian (1700–1820), 1004
Russian (since 1917), 1036
med. Spanish, 288, 294
Spanish (since 1936), 367, 368
Spanish, Colonial, 407
Spanish-American, 20-c., 412
See also Chronicles
History,
  and fiction,
    in 20-c. Spanish-American lit., 421
    in Spanish lit. (since 1936), 367, 368,
      369, 371
    in R. Sender, 357
  philosophy of,
    J. G. Herder's, 718–19
    I. Kant's, 722
    F. Schiller's, 711
  of 18-c. Italy, 511–15
  of Colonial Latin America, 407–08
  in French Romantic lit., 165, 166, 167
  and med. Danish lit., 906
  in German lit. (since 1945), 833, 838,
    845, 849
  in Italian Ren. lit., 468, 472
  in Italian Ren. poetry, 478
  in A. A. Blok, 1016
  in B. Brecht, 812
  in H. Broch, 813
  in A. Chiusano, 534
  in F. Kafka, 817–18
  in S. Lenz, 864
  in G. E. Lessing and J. G. Herder,
    726–27
  in G. Sand, 176
  P. Valéry on, 231–32
  See also Historiography
Holocaust,
  P. Celan and, 851
Homosexuality,
  in German lit. (1880–1945), 807, 827
  in 20-c. Spanish-American lit., 412
  in F. García Lorca, 347
  and A. Gide, 221–22
  and P. Hašek, 943
  of H. von Hofmannsthal, 163
  and T. Mann, 821
  in C. Nuccoli, 452
Honour,
  in med. Spanish lit., 290
Horticulture,
  French, 41
Household, management of,
  in med. Germany, 617, 633, 658, 659
Humanism,
  in med. French lit., 75
  in 16-c. French lit., 78–79
  in 17-c. French lit., 108
  French, 18-c., 143, 144

French, 20-c., 215
German, 20-c., 807, 656, 661, 662, 666
Italian, 453, 457–67
in med. Latin lit., 5
Slovak, 953
in med. Spanish lit., 297, 298
Spanish, 20-c., 363
Welsh, 563
and J. W. von Goethe, 703
in M. de Montaigne, 95, 96
and F. Petrarch, 451
Human nature,
  in med. French lit., 61
Humour,
  in med. French lit., 55, 71
  in early Russian lit., 1001, 1006
  in Sicilian lit., 527
  in C. Brentano, 748–49
  in D. Diderot, 145
  in M. Držić, 1072
  in J. Roubaud, 241–42
  See also Comedy
Hymns,
  German, Romantic era, 756, 757
  by W. Williams Pantycelyn, 564
Hyperbole,
  in J. Racine, 129
Hypochondria,
  and E. Mörike, 800
Hysteria,
  male, in 19-c. French lit., 176–77, 197
  in 19-c. French lit., 204
  in L. Alas, 330

Iconography,
  Arthurian, 639
  of *commedia dell'arte*, 502–03
  of heaven, hell, and purgatory, medieval
    50
  of Last Judgement, 656
  of madness, in med. French lit., 51
  of violence, in med. French lit., 52
  in med. French lit., 62, 68
  in Italian Ren. lit., 461, 464–65
  in G. Boccaccio, 449
  of M. de Montaigne, 95
Idealism,
  and 19-c. science, 699
  French, 18-c., 142, 147
  in French Romantic lit., 161, 165
  in German lit. (1830–1880), 787, 797
  in Spanish lit. (1490–1700), 309
Identity,
  sexual, in German lit. (since 1945),
    854
  in I. Bachmann, 847
  in T. Bernhard, 848
  in K. Blixen, 911
  in Novalis, 764–65

Idyll,
  in N. M. Karamzin, 1008–09
Illness,
  medieval concept of, 633
  in 19-c. French lit., 199
  in G. Büchner, 785
  in E. T. A. Hoffmann, 755
Illusion, dramatic,
  from Enlightenment to early Romantic
    era, 743–44
Illustration,
  of German med. Bibles, 655
  of German med. lit., 615
  Italian Ren., 470
  and reception of G. Boccaccio, 449
  of H. J. C. von Grimmelshausen, 673
  of H. Heine, 794
Imagination,
  in Polish lit., 972–73
  in I. Kant, 721
Imagism,
  in P. O. Enquist, 934
Improvisation,
  in 18-c. Italian lit., 515
Incest,
  in M. Frisch, 855
  in E. Pardo Bazán, 334
  in Tirso de Molina, 322–23
Incipits,
  of 17-c. French novel, 106, 109, 112, 115
  in 18-c. French lit., 156, 158, 160
  of Ronsard's sonnets, 86
Indians,
  in Spanish American lit., 408–09, 411
Individualism,
  and J.-B. P. Molière, 125
Industrialization,
  and A. Strindberg, 932
Infinite, the,
  in F. Schlegel, 769
Inquisition,
  Italian, 496–97, 505, 512, 514
  Spanish, 306
Interior, the,
  in German Romantic lit., 739
Intertextuality,
  Surrealist, 238
  in 16-c. French lit., 88, 92
  in 18-c. French lit., 146, 155
  in 19-c. French lit., 187, 200
  in 20-c. French lit., 218
  in German Classical lit., 686, 733
  in med. Italian poetry, 452
  in med. Latin lit., 10
  in 19-c. Spanish lit., 331
  in A. Belyi, 1015
  in J. Bobrowski, 680
  in J. Guillén, 351
  in S. Lem, 982
  in D. S. Merezhkovskii, 1022

  in F. K. Sologub, 1024
  in D. Ugrešić, 1074
  in G. Ungaretti, 548
Ireland,
  med. German image of, 635
Irony,
  in med. French lit., 71
  in 17-c. French lit., 111, 113
  in French Romantic lit., 165
  in 19-c. French lit., 185
  in 20-c. French lit., 230
  in German Romantic lit., 737
  in med. Italian lit., 458
  in Italian Ren. lit., 458
  in Spanish lit. (since 1936), 364, 366, 369
  in C. Baudelaire, 181
  in G. Boccaccio, 450
  in J. L. Borges, 415
  in B. Pérez Galdós, 337, 338
  in R. Queneau, 241
  in I. Svevo, 547
  in Walther von der Vogelweide, 650
Islam,
  and 16-c. French lit., 78
  in 18-c. French lit., 132, 144
  and Chrétien de Troyes, 59
  See also Arabs, Arab culture

Jansenism,
  and journalism, 137, 138
  in 17-c. French lit., 116, 118
  in 17-c. French drama, 127
  in Italy, 512
  and V. K. Trediakovskii, 1010
Jesuits,
  drama, 17-c., 120–21
  and the Enlightenment, 131
  German, 17-c., 670, 674
  and Italian language, 495
  journalism, 137
  rhetoric,
    and H. de Balzac, 168
Jews, Jewishness,
  and French Revolution, 137
  in German Enlightenment, 682
  in 18-c. Germany, 696–97, 728
  in Ren. Italy, 456
  in 18-c. Italian drama, 501
  in 20-c. Italy, 548
  in Polish 20-c. lit., 981
  in med. Spanish lit., 288
  and J. Améry, 845
  and R. Ausländer, 846
  and W. Benjamin, 811
  and J. Bobrowski, 849
  and R. W. Fassbinder, 853
  and L. Feuchtwanger, 815
  in J. P. Hebel, 754
  and H. Heine, 795

and S. Heym, 860
of H. von Hofmannsthal, 163
in R. Huch, 817
and E. Jabès, 239
and T. Konwicki, 982
and E. Lasker-Schüler, 820
and R. Levin Varnhagen, 727
and B. L. Pasternak, 1045
and N. Sachs, 846
and A. Schnitzler, 826
Journalism,
  and French Revolution, 134, 137–38
  and poetic inspiration, 183
  Belorussian, 1065
  Catalan, 386
  Croatian, 1073
  French, 18-c., 137–39
  French, 19-c., 181
  French, 20-c., 224–25
  German, 18-c., 906–07
  German (1880–1945), 808, 820
  German (since 1945), 849
  Norwegian, 914
  Russian (1880–1917), 1021
  Spanish, 19-c., 326, 327, 336
  Spanish (1898–1936), 355
Journals, personal,
  definition of, 163
  See also Diaries; Memoirs
Justice,
  in J. Racine, 126

Kings, kingship,
  death of, 288
  in med. French lit., 52–53
  in med. Germany, 621, 622, 625
Knight errant,
  in med. French lit., 57
Knighthood. *See* Chivalry
Knowledge,
  and power, in German Enlightenment,
    682
  vulgarization of, 682–83

Labyrinth,
  in 17-c. French drama, 128
Landscape,
  in Belorussian poetry, 1065–66
  in 17-c. Italian lit., 497
  in P. A. de Alarcón, 328
  in G. Apollinaire, 213–14
  in F. Schiller, 711
Language,
  Italian, controversy over, 513–14, 521
  sexist, 434
  theme of, in German lit. (since 1945),
    858, 859
  of Leonardo da Vinci, 487

and power, in H. von Kleist, 762
F. Schiller's philosophy of, 712–13
Language theory,
  German, 17-c., 666
  and Spanish lit. (1490–1700), 314–15
  and Spanish lit. (1898–1936), 350–51
  in J. G. Herder, 718
  of K. P. Moritz, 728–29
  of J.-P. Sartre, 243
Latin quotations,
  in M. de Montaigne, 93–94
Laughter,
  in med. French lit., 68, 69, 73
  in 16-c. French lit., 81
  in 17-c. French lit., 110, 120
  in 19-c. French lit., 175, 191
  in G. E. Lessing, 726
  in F. Rabelais, 82
  in Stendhal, 171
Law,
  criminal, 18-c. French, 140
  language rights, 384–85
  martial, in Polish lit., 981
  natural, and French Revolution, 138
  in med. French lit., 66
  med. German, 620–21, 623
  and 19-c. German lit., 778–79
  Italian, and Polish reform, 519
  and E. T. A. Hoffmann, 754
  and culture, in K. F. Savigny and J.
    Grimm, 753
Legal terminology,
  in A. d'Aubigné, 91
Legend,
  in 20-c. French lit., 211
  of Alexander, 62, 633, 636
  of Apolonio, 296
  of Helen, 87
  of Majnûn, 215
  of Merlin, 468–69
  of Paris, 9
  of Psyche, 103
  of Roland, 54–55, 180, 263, 636
  of Tristan, 60–61, 211
Leisure,
  in Italian Ren. lit., 459
Leitmotiv,
  in B. Brecht, 812
  in R. Wagner, 806
Letter-writing,
  French, 17-c., 100–01, 107
  in 17-c. French drama, 128
  in 19-c. Germany, 783–84, 788
  in P. C. de Laclos and Stendhal, 173
Letters,
  of German Classical era, 689
  of Ital. Ren. courtiers, 484
  of Ren. and 17-c. Italy, 492
  med. Latin, 2
  of Norwegian immigrants in USA, 920

of V. Aleixandre, 345
of L. N. Andreev, 1014
of A. A. Angillus, 887
of B. Antonenko-Davydovych, 1058
of M. Azaña, 355
to H. Bahr, 811
of K. D. Bal'mont, 1027
of H. de Balzac, 168
of T. de Banville, 183
of C. Basire, 139
of G. Battista, 498
of M. Bazhan, 1058
of A. Behn, 689
of A. Belyi, 1015
of P. Bembo, 485
of F. Beroaldo, 485
of M. Białoszewski, 981
of R. Borchardt, 526
of L. Börne, 784
of A. L. G. Bosboom-Toussaint, 897
of L. Bouilhet, 195
of G. Brandes, 909
of C. Brentano, 747–48
of P.-M.-A. Broussonet, 136
of K. Brugmann, 26
of L. Bruni, 485
of I. A. Bunin, 1038
of I. Calvino, 532
of I. de Charrière, 140
of A. P. Chekhov, 1017
of M. Chekhov, 1032
of V. A. Chivilikhin, 1028
of K. I. Chukovskii, 1038
of P. Claudel, 219
of E. B. de Condillac, 140
of B. Constant, 165
of B. Croce, 534
of T. Crudeli, 521
of I. Dniprovs'kyi, 1058
of A. von Droste-Hülshoff, 788
of M. Du Camp, 195
of P. de la Ecosura, 332
of J. von Eichendorff, 750
of J. J. Engel, 728
of G. Flaubert, 194–95, 196, 196
of T. Fontane, 789
of M. Franco, 486
of F. F. Frugoni, 494
of Galileo, 506
of F. García Lorca, 346
of T. Gautier, 174
of S. George, 815
of G. Gezelle, 896
of A. de Gobineau, 198
of J. W. von Goethe, 700, 701
of A. Goudar, 157
of F. M. Grimm, 146
of Guittone d'Arezzo, 452
of A. von Haller, 717
of E. Haywood, 689

of C.-A. Helvétius, 141
of J. G. Herder, 717–18
of Hildegard of Bingen, 7, 8
of M. Hrushevs'kyi, 1052
of V. Hugo, 174–75
of A.-L. de Jussieu, 136
of V. F. Khodasevich, 1020
of H. von Kleist, 761
of A. Kondrat'ev, 1035
of A. E. Kruchenykh, 1021
of A. Kryms'kyi, 1059
of M. A. Kuzmin, 1021, 1028
of S. Lagerlöf, 930
of A. de Lamartine, 175
of M. Lechter, 815
of B. Lepkyi, 1059
of M.-S. Leroyer de Chantepie, 194
of O. I. Leshkova, 1025
of C.-L. L'Héritier, 136
of C. Linati, 526
of A. Lista, 327
of S. Mac Grianna, 581
of L. Magalotti, 495, 514
of Ie. Malaniuk, 1059
of S. Mallarmé, 187
of O. E. Mandel'shtam, 1042
of D. Manley, 689
of T. Mann, 823
of J.-P. Marat, 142
of H. Martineau, 172
of Lorenzo de' Medici, 486
of M. Mendelssohn, 728
of M. Menéndez Pelayo, 333
of S. Mikhoels, 1032
of E. Montale, 539
of V. Monti, 523
of A. Moravia, 540
of A. Morellet, 142
of J. Möser, 729
of G. Muzio, 487–88
of J. Nestroy, 801
of Ol'ga Aleksandrovna, 1021
of J. Ortega y Gasset, 355–56
of M. A. Osorgin, 1044
of N. Palumbo, 541
of E. Pardo Bazán, 333, 334
of B. L. Pasternak, 1044
of V. Pidmohyl'nyi, 1059
of B. A. Pil'niak, 1045
of L. Pirandello, 543
of F. Piranesi, 523
of A. Pizzuto, 543
of C. dal Pozzo, 493
of M. Proust, 228
of H. Pückler-Muskau, 802
of G. M. Pujati, 512
of F. Rabelais, 82
of R. Rolland, 211
of J. J. Rousseau, 148
of V. V. Rozanov, 1023

of U. Saba, 544
of Mme de Sabran, 143
of D. A. F. de Sade, 153
of P. Salinas, 353
of G. Sand, 176
of F. de Saussure, 26
of C. Sbarbaro, 545
of C. von Schlegel, 768–69
of A. S. Serafimovich, 1027
of I. S. Shmelev, 1027
of V. S. Solov'ev, 1024
of L. Staryts'ka-Cherniakhivs'ka, 1059
of V. Stefanyk, 1059
of Stendhal, 171
of A. Stifter, 804
of T. Storm, 805
of A. Strodtmann, 909
of J. B. A. Suard, 143
of A. Tarkovskii, 1034
of V. N. Tatishchev, 1010
of J. R. Thorbecke, 897
of S. Tieck, 771
of A. de Toqueville, 179
of M. I. Tsvetaeva, 1049
of A. T. Tvardovskii, 1049
of P. Tychyna, 1059
of L. Ukrainka, 1057
of P. de Valdivia, 408
of R. Varnhagen, 772
of K. A. Varnhagen von Ense, 732, 772
of F. Vettori, 459
of A. de Vigny, 167
of O. V. Volkov, 1029
of C. Volney, 144
of M. A. Voloshin, 1024–25, 1027
of F. M. A. de Voltaire, 150
of V. Vynnychenko, 1060
of W. H. Wackenroder, 772
of J. F. Willems, 887
of B. K. Zaitsev, 1050
of G. G. Zamboni, 516
of M. Zambrano, 356
of É. Zola, 203, 206
of S. Zweig, 829
See also Correspondence
Lexicography,
  Breton, 660
  Catalan, 376
  Danish, 904
  French, 36–40
  German, 605–06, 625, 626–28, 630, 660
  med. Latin, 7
  Norwegian, 915, 921
  Occitan, 245
  Portuguese, 397–98
  Romanian, 553
  Romansh, 556
  Russian, 994
  Scottish Gaelic, 584
  Spanish, 281–82

Swedish, 928
Ukrainian, 1053
Atlases,
  French, 43
  Galician, 401
  German, 606
  Italian, 440–41
  Occitan, 246, 254, 255, 257
  Romanian, 554
Dictionaries,
  Anglo-Norman, 37
  Bulgarian — English, 1078
  Bulgarian, linguistics, 1078
  Bulgarian — Russian, 1078
  Catalan, etymological, 375
  Catalan, reverse, 378
  Cornish, 571
  Dutch, eponyms, 883
  Dutch, finance, 884
  Dutch, foreign trade terms, 883–84
  Dutch, information science, 884
  Dutch, student slang, 884
  Dutch, synonyms, 883
  Dutch, technical, 883
  Dutch, terms of abuse, 884
  English — Dutch, 884
  English — Polish, 960
  French, 36–38
  French, of allusions, 39–40
  French, electronic, 39
  French, idiomatic, 37–38
  French, onomastic, 42
  French, regional, 43, 44
  French, rhyming, 29
  Gaelic — English, 584
  Old High German, 627
  med. German, 660
  German, 590
  German, dialects, 608–09
  German — English, 605–06
  Italian, altered forms, 435
  Italian — English, 434, 435
  Italian, neologisms, 435
  Italian, onomastic, 436–37
  Italian, slang, 436
  Italian, synonyms, 434–35
  Latin — Welsh, 563
  Occitan, 247
  Occitan — French, 245, 250, 252, 256, 258
  Occitan, toponymic, 253
  Portuguese, 397
  Portuguese, Creole, 404
  Portuguese, linguistics, 388
  Romance, onomastic, 20
  Romanian, 553
  Romanian — English, 553
  Romansh, 556
  Romansh — French, 556

Russian — Bulgarian, approximative, 1078
Russian, linguistics, 986
Scandinavian, government terminology, 928
Scottish Gaelic, 584
Slovak, historical, 946
Slovak — Hungarian, 947
med. Spanish, 268
Swedish, dialect, 926–27
Swedish — English, 928
Swedish, synonyms, 928
Ukrainian — Russian, 1053
Welsh, 561
Welsh — Breton, 568
Thesauruses,
   French, 37
Lexicology,
   Breton, 568
   Bulgarian, 1078
   Catalan, 378, 381
   Dutch, 879
   French, 40–42, 56, 67, 187–88
   German, 603–05
   mod. Irish, 573
   Italian, 434–37
   Occitan, 247–48, 250, 252–53, 254–55, 256, 258–59, 263, 264
   Polish, 960–61
   Portuguese, 397–99
   Romance, 20–23
   Romanian, 553
   Russian, 994
   Slovak, 947
   Spanish, 268–70, 273–75, 281–83
Libertinism,
   in 18-c. French lit., 152, 155
Libraries,
   private,
      French, 137
      in Ren. Italy, 455–56
      in 18-c. Italy, 511
      of A. Chigi, 492
      of Leopoldo de' Medici, 492
      of E. Privat, 246
      of É. Zola, 206
      Russian, 1005–06
   public, and A. Strindberg, 932
   of Romantic lit., 744
   Ukrainian, 1052
Life,
   in med. German lit., 625–26
   in 20-c. Italian poetry, 528, 648
Light,
   in *La Celestina*, 314
   and spiritual darkness, in M. Scève, 86
Linguistics,
   Belorussian, 1063–65
   Breton, 568–70
   Bulgarian, 1078–81

Catalan, 375–87
Cornish, 570–71
Danish, 901–04
Dutch, 876–84
French, 25–49
German, 589–609, 661, 735
mod. Irish, 572–76
Italian, 424–46
Latin, 11, 13, 425–26
Morisco, 302
Norwegian, 914–21
Occitan, 245–59
Polish, 957–71
Portuguese, 388–405
   overseas, 403–05
Romance, 11–24, 425, 839
Romanian, 11–12, 550–54
Romansh, 555–57
Russian, 986, 987, 990–96
Sardinian, 445–46
Scottish Gaelic, 584–86
Serbo-Croat, 1070–71
Slovak, 946–51
Spanish, 266–86
Swedish, 923–28
Ukrainian, 1052–54
Welsh, 559–62
Applied linguistics,
   Dutch, 881–83
   Swedish, 926
Bilingualism,
   general, 24
   in Belorussia, 1064
   in Denmark, 902–04
   in Latin America, 284
   in Nordic countries, 926
   in Russia, 1054
   in Strasbourg, 48
Comparative linguistics,
   Bulgarian — Greek, 1080
   Bulgarian — Polish, 1080
   Bulgarian — Russian, 1080
   Italian — English, 434
   Polish — Slovak, 968
   Russian — Bulgarian, 995
   Russian — Slovene, 994–95
   Russian — Spanish, 995
   Russian — Ukrainian, 995
   Slovak — Czech, 951
   Slovak — Hungarian, 947
   Slovak — Polish, 951
   Slovak — Russian, 951
Computer linguistics,
   German, 614, 630–31
   Italian, 425
   Polish, 971
   Portuguese, 388
   Romance, 18
   Russian, 995
   Ukrainian, 1053

Contact linguistics,
  Breton — French, 569
  French — English, 47
  French — German, 604–05
  French — Spanish, 24
  Italian — German, 592
  Portuguese — Chinese, 405
  Russian — Serbo-Croatian, 994
  Slovak — Czech, 950–51
  Slovak — Hungarian, 950
  Slovak — Polish, 968
  Slovak — Russian, 951
  Turkish — German, 592
  Ukrainian — Polish, 1054
Contrastive linguistics,
  Belorussian — Russian, 1064
  Dutch — French — English, 878
  French — Bulgarian, 49
  French — English, 49
  French — German, 49
  German — Bulgarian, 602
  German — Chinese, 602
  German — mod. Greek, 602
  German — Korean, 602
  Portuguese — Brazilian, 389, 397
  Portuguese — German, 397
  Romanian — Bulgarian, 554
  Romanian — French, 11, 12
  Romanian — Galician, 12
  Romanian — Portuguese, 12
  Russian — German, 995
Dialectology,
  American Spanish, 283–85
  Belorussian, 1065
  Breton, 570
  Bulgarian, 1080–81
  Catalan, 376, 381–82
  Danish, 902–04
  Dutch, 879–80
  Old French, 27
  French, 42–45
    African, 47
    Canadian, 45–47
    Creole, 47–48
  German, 606–09
  mod. Irish, 573, 576
  Italian, 425, 440–46
  Norwegian, 916–17
  Occitan, 250, 253, 255, 257, 258, 259
  Polish, 962–65
  Portuguese, 401–02
  Romance, 23–24
  Romanian, 554
  Serbo-Croat, 1071
  Slovak, 950
  Spanish, 283–86
  Swedish, 926–27
  Ukrainian, 1054
Discourse analysis,
  Catalan, 383

  German, 592
  Italian, 433–34
  med. Latin, 1
  Portuguese, 396–97
  Romance, 19–20
  Swedish, 926
Etymology,
  Bulgarian, 1078
  Occitan, 246
  Portuguese, 402–03
  Romance, 21–23
  Serbo-Croat, 1070
  Welsh, 561
Grammar,
  Cornish, 570–71
  Danish, 904
  French, 30–36
  Old High German, 626
  Middle High German, 631, 637
  Occitan, 257
  Portuguese, 388
  Romanian, 550, 552
  Scottish Gaelic, 584
  Serbo-Croat, 1071
  Welsh, 559–61
Historical linguistics,
  Belorussian, 1063
  Breton, 568, 569
  Bulgarian, 1078–79
  Catalan, 375–77
  Celtic, 559, 560–61
  Danish, 901–02
  Dutch, 877, 879
  French, 28–29
  German, 592–98, 604
  Irish, 574
  Italian, 425–28, 437
  Norwegian, 915
  Occitan, 246, 248
  Portuguese, 388–89
  Romance, 13–15
  Romanian, 551
  Russian, 990–91
  Serbo-Croat, 1070
  Slovak, 946–47
  Spanish, 268–75
  Ukrainian, 1052
  Welsh, 560–61
History of etymology,
  French, 40
History of grammar,
  French, 26–28, 101
  German, 593–95, 600
  Occitan, 245
  Spanish, 294
History of linguistic theory,
  Dutch, 876
  French, 26–28
  Italian, 428, 518
  Polish, 957

Romance, 15, 21, 26
Romansh, 555
Spanish, 266–68
Welsh, 559
Interdisciplinary linguistics,
German, 591–92
Language planning,
Catalan, 387
Morphology,
Bulgarian, 1078–79
Catalan, 376, 378
Danish, 902
Old French, 27
French, 84
German, 599–601, 626
Italian, 430–31
Norwegian, 917–19
Occitan, 249, 257–58
Polish, 957–58
Romance, 16–17
Russian, 992
Scottish Gaelic, 584
Serbo-Croat, 1071
Spanish, 276–77
Swedish, 924–25
Ukrainian, 1053
Morphosyntax,
French, 30
Occitan, 246–47, 249–50, 252, 254, 256
Romance, 16
Romansh, 556
Onomastics, Toponymy,
Belorussian, 1065
Breton, 569
Bulgarian, 1080–81
Catalan, 382–83
Danish, 904
Dutch, 879
French, 42, 66, 250
German, 609
Irish, 561
Italian, 436–37
Norwegian, 915–16
Occitan, 250, 253, 255, 258, 259
Polish, 969–71
Portuguese, 402–03
Romanian, 553
Romansh, 556
Scottish Gaelic, 585
Serbo-Croat, 1070
Slovak, 947–48
Swedish, 927–28
Ukrainian, 1054
Orthography,
Belorussian, 1064
Bulgarian, 1079
French, 29–30
German, 599
Occitan, 249, 256
Romanian, 552

Russian, 992
Slovak, 949
Ukrainian, 1053–54
Phonetics, Phonology,
Breton, 568
Bulgarian, 1080
Catalan, 377–78
Celtic, 560
Danish, 904
Dutch, 877
French, 29
German, 599
Italian, 428–29
Norwegian, 919
Occitan, 249, 252, 257
Polish, 957
Portuguese, 389–92
Romance, 15–16
Romanian, 551–52
Romansh, 556
Russian, 991
Scottish Gaelic, 584
Slovak, 949
Spanish, 275–76
Swedish, 924–25
Ukrainian, 1053
Welsh, 559
Phraseology,
Polish, 960–61
Russian, 994
Slovak, 947
Ukrainian, 1053–54
Pragmatics,
secret languages, 48–49, 427
Catalan, 378–80
French, 30, 48–49
German, 592
Italian, 433–34
Polish, 961–62
Romance, 19–20
Russian, 992–94
Spanish, 280–81
Pronunciation,
Bulgarian, 1079
Slovak, 949
Psycholinguistics,
Italian, 431, 433
Runology,
Scandinavian, 923–24
Swedish, 924
Semantics,
Bulgarian, 1078
Catalan, 378–80
Danish, 902
Dutch, 877
French, 41
Old High German, 627
Middle High German, 630–31, 644
German, 603–06, 625–26
Italian, 431–33

Norwegian, 917–19
Polish, 961–62
Romance, 17–19
Russian, 990, 992–94
Serbo-Croat, 1071
Spanish, 280–81
Swedish, 925–26
Ukrainian, 1053–54
Sociolinguistics,
American Spanish, 283–85
Breton, 569–70
Bulgarian, 1079
Catalan, 376, 383–87
Dutch, 879–81
French, 47, 48–49
German, 589–90, 606
mod. Irish, 573–76
Italian, 428, 437–40
Occitan, 250–51, 253–54, 255–57
Polish, 962–65
Portuguese, 399–401
Romance, 12, 24, 246
Romansh, 556–57
Scottish Gaelic, 586
Slovak, 950
Spanish, 283–86
Ukrainian, 1053–54
Welsh, 561–62
Standard (literary) language,
Bulgarian, 1079
French, 25
Italian, 428
Occitan, 249, 257
Polish, 963
Russian, 1006, 1008
Serbo-Croat, 1072
Slovak, 949–50
Stylistics,
Norwegian, 917–19
Polish, 965–68
Slovak, 949–50
Ukrainian, 1053–54
Syntax,
Breton, 568
Bulgarian, 1079, 1080
Catalan, 378–80
Danish, 902
Dutch, 877–78
French, 31
Middle High German, 658
German, 601–03
Italian, 431–33
Norwegian, 917–19
Occitan, 249, 257–58
Polish, 958–60
Portuguese, 392–97
Romance, 17–19
Russian, 992–94
Slovak, 949
Spanish, 277–80

Swedish, 925–26
Ukrainian, 1053
Welsh, 559
Textual linguistics,
German, 592
Norwegian, 919–20
Romance, 14
Romanian, 551
Slovak, 949
Word classes,
Slovak, 948–49
Word formation,
Bulgarian, 1079
French, 41
Polish, 957–58
Portuguese, 399
Russian, 991, 992
Ukrainian, 1053
Word order,
Portuguese, 393–94
Romance, 11, 20
Word studies,
French, 41–42
Russian, 991
Literacy,
in Carolingian period, 2
in med. Germany, 632, 651
in Ireland, 573–74
Literary borrowing,
in C. Péguy, 226
in Petrarch, 9
in T. Fontane, 790
Literary criticism,
feminist, 76–77, 99, 129, 185, 192, 199,
204, 260, 289–90, 318, 331, 332, 366,
372, 412, 417, 527, 618, 619, 661–62,
766, 811, 835, 861, 905, 931, 1002, 1056
formalist, 342, 547
postmodernist, 80, 525, 681, 686, 694,
716, 872
Bulgarian, 1081, 1082
Dutch, 20-c., 886, 887
French, 18-c., 140
French, Romantic era, 163, 165, 167
French, of German Romantic lit., 741
French, 19-c., 182
German, Classical era, 716
of German Classical lit., 679
German (since 1945), 843, 859
Italian Ren., 455
Italian, 17-c., 490–91
Italian, 20-c., 525–26, 534, 539,
544
Russian (1880–1917), 1023, 1027
Serbian, 1075
Slovak, 953
Spanish (1898–1936), 345–46
of E. Montale, 539
of J.-P. Sartre, 243
in A. W. Schlegel, 768

Literary history,
  Bulgarian, 1081–82
  Croatian, 1072, 1073
  Danish, 905
  Dutch, 886, 887, 893–94
  European, 610–11
  French, 18-c., 137–39
  German, 610–11, 631–32, 680, 684, 718,
    739, 740, 777–78, 780, 782, 807, 833,
    840
  Italian, 490–91, 511–15, 526
  Norwegian, 920
  Russian, 1028
  Serbian, 1072
  Slovak, 952
  Swedish, 929, 931, 933
  Ukrainian, 1054
Literary theory,
  Czech, 937–39
  French, 115, 175, 184
  German, 684, 686, 737, 873. 874
  Russian, 1031–32
  of C. B. Huet, 896
  and D. Owen, 565
Liturgical drama. *See* Drama, religious
Loup-garou,
  in med. French lit., 64
Love,
  conventions of, in med. French lit., 57
  courtly,
    in Czech lit., 940
    in med. Germany, 624, 639
  in med. French lit., 60
  in French Romantic lit., 176
  in 20-c. French lit., 209
  in med. German lit., 634, 641, 648
  in 17-c. German poetry, 667–68
  in German classical drama, 687
  in German Romantic lit., 757
  in Italian Ren. lit., 467
  in Polish poetry, 972
  in Spanish lit. (1490–1700), 311
  in I. Andrić, 1075
  in F. Aragon, 215
  in I. Bachmann, 847
  in B. Constant, 165
  in G. García Márquez, 418
  in V. Hugo, 167
  in G. de Maupassant, 201
  in M. Proust, 228
  in P. de Ronsard, 87
Love-sickness,
  in med. French lit., 51
  in med. German lit., 634
Lullabies,
  German, 696
Lyric poetry,
  early Czech, 939–40
  med. French, 70–71
  med. German, 648–50

German, Romantic era, 737, 757–59, 764
German (1830–1880), 782–83
German (since 1945), 842–43, 857–58
Russian (1700–1820), 1003
med. Spanish, 289–90
Swedish, 929, 933

Madness,
  in med. French lit., 51
  in med. German lit., 634
  in T. Bernhard, 848
  in B. Pérez Galdós, 337
Madrigals,
  French, 17-c., 104
Magic,
  Renaissance, 463–64
  in med. German lit., 640, 662
Mannerism,
  French, 17-c., 101, 105
Marriage,
  as happy ending, convention of, 125
  woman's role in, in med. French lit., 75
  in 19-c. French lit., 200
  in med. Occitan lit., 263
  in med. Spanish lit., 293–94
  in Spanish lit. (since 1936), 373
  in G. de Bruyn, 850
  in W. Busch, 787
  in G. de Maupassant, 201
Marrism,
  Russian, 986
Martyrs, martyrdom,
  in 16-c. French lit., 89–90
  in med. German lit., 645
Marxism,
  in 17-c. French drama, 127
  and J.-B. P. Molière, 125
Masons, Masonic rite. *See* Freemasonry
Materialism,
  in med. French lit., 77
  in 16-c. French lit., 87
  French, 18-c., 131, 141, 144, 153
  in French Romantic lit., 161
  French, 19-c., 182
  French, 20-c., 229
  German, 19-c., 182
Mathematics,
  Italian, 17-c., 507
Matriarchy,
  in C. Wolf, 874
Maxims,
  German, 17-c., 674
Medicine,
  and humanism, 458
  Ren. European, 455
  med. French, 52
  French, 17-c., 108
  in 17-c. French drama, 120
  French, 18-c., 132

French, 19-c., 202
  med. German, 633–34, 658
  German, Classical era, 698
  German, Romantic era, 755
  in German Romantic lit., 740
  Italian Ren., 456
  Italian, 17-c., 507, 508
  med. Occitan, 264
  med. Spanish, 296
  Spanish-American Colonial, 406
  in G. Büchner, 785
Meistersinger,
  records of, 650
Melancholy,
  in med. German lit., 654
  in German lit. (since 1945), 863, 864
  in W. Hildesheimer, 860
Memoirs,
  French, 17-c., 97–98, 100, 114
  Russian (1700–1820), 1007
  Russian, 20-c., 987–88
  of A. P. Chekhov, 1017
  of C. de Gaulle, 100
  of A. de Lamartine, 175
  of O. E. Mandel'shtam, 1042
  of H. Rouy, 181
  of F. Stepun, 1031
  of Teffi, 1031
  of A. I. Vvedenskii, 1050
  See also Autobiography; Diaries
Memory,
  in modern Latin American lit., 414
  in Spanish lit. (since 1936), 367, 368
  in G. Bruno, 485
  in L. R. Des Forêts, 238
  in *Don Quixote*, 312
  in N. Palumbo, 541
  in M. Proust, 229
  in R. del Valle-Inclán, 359
Mermaids,
  in med. German lit., 662
Metamorphosis,
  in P. Calderón de la Barca, 318
  in F. Petrarch, 450
Metaphor,
  of letter-writing, in French lit., 107
  medical, in French lit., 27
  theatrical, in 20-c. French lit., 100
  in 19-c. French lit., 178
  in J. W. von Goethe, 706
  in V. V. Maiakovskii, 1042
  in O. E. Mandel'shtam, 1043
  in H. Norbrandt, 913
Metaphysics,
  French, 16-c., 95
  French, 18-c., 141
  French, Romantic era, 167
  of E. Montale, 539
Metrical analysis,
  of med. French lit., 53

  of 19-c. French poetry, 186
  of med. German poetry, 628–29
  of med. Latin poetry, 2, 8
  of G. Caproni, 533
  of G. Celaya, 365
  of J.-B. P. Molière, 125
Mind-body problem,
  in 18-c. lit., 698
  and J. P. Richter, 767
Minerals,
  in V. I. Ivanov, 1020
Minnesang,
  in urban environment, 648
Minnesinger,
  social role of, 632
Minstrels,
  minstrel MS, myth of, 52
Miracles,
  in med. Spanish lit., 292
Mirrors,
  in 17-c. French lit., 114
  in 18-c. French lit., 155
  in Spanish lit. (since 1936), 370
  in K. Blixen, 911
Misanthropy,
  in 17-c. French lit., 100
Misogyny,
  in med. French lit., 73, 77
  in L. B. Alberti, 467
  in H. de Balzac, 170
  in C. Baudelaire and G. Flaubert, 185
  in F. Lope de Vega Carpio, 320
Mobs,
  in F. Lope de Vega Carpio, 321
Modernism,
  Bulgarian, 1082
  Croatian, 1073
  Danish, 906, 908, 909, 911
  Dutch, 898
  French, 183, 209, 210, 223, 225
  German, 783, 809, 810, 824, 848, 864
  Polish, 976
  Russian, 1044, 1045
  Spanish, 344, 353, 357, 359
  Spanish-American, 410
  Swedish, 933, 936
Monasticism,
  at St. Gall, 629–30
Mongols,
  med. attitudes toward, 8
Monologue,
  in med. French lit., 62
  in P. Valéry, 231
Monsters,
  in med. German lit., 640
  in med. Spanish lit., 288
  in J. Racine, 128–29
Morality,
  bourgeois, 909
  in med. Dutch lit., 890

in 19-c. French lit., 200
in med. German lit., 635
in Spanish lit. (1490–1700), 311
in H. de Balzac, 169
in D. Diderot, 145, 147
and A. Gide, 221
in H. J. C. von Grimmelshausen, 673
in M. de Montaigne, 96
and R. Rolland, 211
Moral lit.,
    med. French, 74–77
Mothers, mother figure,
    in the Middle Ages, 617
    in 16-c. French lit., 90
    in 18-c. French lit., 131–32
    in med. German lit., 634
    in German lit. (1880–1945), 810
    in modern Latin American lit., 420
    in Spanish lit. (since 1936), 367
    in G. Flaubert, 196
    in A. Moravia, 540
Mourning,
    in med. German lit., 640
    in F. Hölderlin, 757
Music,
    Dutch, 17-c., 894
    med. French, 64–65
    in 17-c. French drama, 123
    in German lit. (1880–1945), 808
    German (since 1945), 840
    Italian Ren., 461, 476
    Italian, 17-c., 500, 508
    Italian, 18-c., 516–17
    med. Latin, 1
    Russian, 17-c., 1001
    Scottish, 585
    D. Diderot on, 146
    in M. Proust, 227
    See also Hymns; Lullabies; Opera; Songs
Mysticism,
    med. Dutch, 890–91
    med. German, 652–53
    Jewish, 846
    in Spanish lit. (1490–1700), 305,
        307
    in L. Alas, 330
    in G. Flaubert, 195
    in L. Gyllensten, 934–35
    of Q. Kuhlmann, 668
Mystification,
    in 19-c. French lit., 182
    in 20-c. French lit., 221
Myth,
    classical,
        in Middle Ages, 10, 70–71
        in 17-c. German poetry, 675
        in German Romantic lit., 757
        in Spanish lit. (1490–1700), 307
        and H. de Balzac, 169, 170
        in M. M. Boiardo, 471

in P. Calderón de la Barca, 317,
    319–20
in F. Lope de Vega Carpio, 322
modern cultural, 183
of creation, 1083
of Cupid and Psyche, 218, 485
of Merlin, 640–41
of Oedipus, 220
of Orpheus, 202
of Prometheus, 1057
of Satan, 181
of Venus and Mars, 469, 500
and revolution, 133, 135
in 20-c. French lit., 211, 244
in German lit. (since 1945), 858, 870–71,
    872, 873
in med. Latin lit., 5, 8
in Old Norse lit., 920
in G. Apollinaire, 213
in L. Felipe, 365
in G. P. Harsdörffer, 675
in F. Hölderlin, 757–58
in R. Wagner, 805, 806

Naiad,
    in Slovak lit., 952
Narcissism,
    in 18-c. French lit., 132
    in 19-c. French lit., 201
    in German Romantic lit., 740
    in Spanish lit. (1490–1700), 307
    in L. B. Alberti, 485
    in H. Bang, 908
    in T. Mann, 822
Narration, narrative,
    autofiction, 218
    in med. French lit., 57
    in 16-c. French lit., 83
    in 17-c. French lit., 101, 106
    in 18-c. French lit., 152, 153
    in French Romantic lit., 161–62, 175
    in 20-c. French lit., 224
    in med. German lit., 632, 645
    in German Romantic lit., 762
    in German lit. (since 1945), 845
    in med. Latin lit., 7, 9
    in modern Latin American fiction, 413,
        416, 417
    in Swedish 20-c. lit., 934
    in J. Beer, 671–72
    in T. Bernhard, 848
    in C. J. Cela, 368
    in M. de Cervantes, 312
    in A. P. Chekhov, 1018
    in S. Claussen, 909
    in D. Diderot, 147
    in H. Fichte, 854
    in G. Flaubert, 196
    in C. Hein, 859

in E. T. A. Hoffmann, 756
in S. Mallarmé, 188
in C. Pavese, 542
in B. Pérez Galdós, 336, 337, 338
in J. P. Richter, 742, 766
in R. M. Rilke, 909
in A. Stifter, 804
in R. del Valle-Inclán, 358
See also Epic; Romance
Nationalism,
in Middle Ages, 2–3, 8–9, 613
Catalan, 386
Croatian, 1073
Dutch, 898
in English drama, 315
in med. French lit., 63, 249
in 16-c. French lit., 90
in 20-c. French lit., 208
German, medieval, 622–23, 637
German, Classical era, 697
German, 19-c., 727,
German, Romantic era, 740, 743
Russian, 1002, 1028
and R. Wagner, 805–06
Naturalism,
in 19-c. Danish lit., 909
in 20-c. Italian poetry, 537
in 19-c. Spanish lit., 339, 340
in Welsh drama, 566
in T. Fontane, 789
and É. Zola, 203, 204, 205
Natural rights,
theory of, 694
Nature,
exploitation of, and J. W. von Goethe,
708
and man, in J. W. von Goethe, 707
in S. A. Esenin, 1019
in F. García Lorca, 349
in J. M. de Pereda, 334
in A. P. Platonov, 1045–46
in F. Schiller, 711
Naturphilosophie,
Russian, 1007
Neoclassicism,
French, 166, 177, 178
Russian, 1043
Ukrainian, 1058
Neologisms,
Swedish, 936
in V. Alfieri, 519–20
in R. Barthes, 235
Neoplatonism,
French, 83, 87–88, 151
Italian, 474
in Gottfried von Strassburg, 646
Newspapers. *See* Journalism
New World,
in Italian Ren. lit., 483–84, 485
in 17-c. Italian lit., 491

Nihilism,
in 19-c. German lit., 775
in T. Mann, 822
Nobility,
in Italian Ren. lit., 460, 468
in 16-c. Wales, 563
Nominalism,
in France and Italy, 465
Nonsense poetry,
med. French, 71, 72
Nouvelle,
origin of, 68–69
poetics of, 84
Welsh, 566
Novel,
autofiction, 243
bilingual, 235
origins of, 407
theory of, in 19-c. Germany, 780
Bulgarian, 1081
Croatian, 1072, 1073
Czech, 938, 945
Danish, 19-c., 909
Dutch, 17-c., 893
Dutch, 19-c., 897
Dutch (1880–1945), 897–98, 899
English, 19-c., 780–81
French, 17-c., 106, 676–77
French, 18-c., 134, 144–45, 150, 152–58
French, Romantic era, 161, 168–77
French, 19-c., 192–206, 780–81
French, 20-c., 210–11, 222–25, 227–29,
233, 235–44
German, 17-c., 671–73
German, Classical era, 687–89, 704–05,
731, 733
German (1830–1880), 774–75, 780,
789–91, 798–99, 803–04
German (1880–1945), 807, 810, 813–14,
818, 821–23, 826
German (since 1945), 832, 836, 843–45,
855–57
mod. Irish, 579, 581, 582–83
Italian, 17-c., 504–05
Italian, 20-c., 527–28
Russian, 19-c., 1081
Russian (1880–1917), 1022, 1027
Russian (since 1917), 1035, 1037–38,
1045
Serbian, 1075
Slovak, 954, 955
Spanish (1490–1700), 309–13
Spanish, 19-c., 327–40
Spanish, 20-c., 223
Spanish (since 1936), 365, 367–72
Spanish-American, 19-c., 410–11
Spanish-American, 20-c., 413–23
Swedish, 19-c., 930–31
Swedish, 20-c., 934
Welsh, 565, 566

Bildungsroman,
  German, Classical era, 687–88
  German (since 1945), 844, 870
comic,
  French, 17-c., 106, 114
  French, Romantic era, 171
epistolary,
  French, 17-c., 106, 111
  French, 18-c., 155
  German, Classical era, 689, 722
  German, Romantic era, 736
  Italian Ren., 483
Gothic,
  Swedish, 930
historical,
  Czech, 943
  French, 17-c., 107–08
  French, Romantic era, 168
  German (1880–1945), 810, 812, 814, 821
  German (since 1945), 844, 870
  mod. Irish, 580
  Italian, 20-c., 538
  Spanish-American, 20-c., 413
  Swedish, 20-c., 936
  Ukrainian, 1061
mystery,
  French, 19-c., 193
  German, 19-c., 778–79
  German (since 1945), 832, 839
  Italian, 20-c., 545
picaresque,
  Spanish (1490–1700), 309
  and M. de Cervantes, 312
political,
  German (since 1945), 833
roman à clef,
  French, 17-c., 108, 115
social,
  German, Classical era, 688–89
  German (1830–1880), 780, 790
spy,
  Italian, 20-c., 538
Novella,
  medieval, 448
  Renaissance, 483,
    17-c., 504
Numerals,
  Romance, 20–21

Obesity,
  in 17-c. French lit., 100
Obscenity,
  in med. French lit., 74
  in 17-c. French lit., 101
  in 18-c. French lit., 138
  in med. German lit., 634
  in med. Spanish lit., 289, 293
  See also Pornography

Occultism,
  French, 19-c., 181
Oedipal complex,
  in Czech lit., 941
  in 19-c. French lit., 173, 177, 191, 197
  and G. E. Lessing, 726
  in F. Rabelais, 83
Opera,
  French, 17-c., 103, 122
  German, Classical era, 733
  German, Romantic era, 755
  German, 19-c., 806
  Italian, 17-c., 491–92, 503–04
  Italian, 18-c., 516–17
  Russian (1700–1820), 1002
Optimism,
  in 17-c. French lit., 100
Orality,
  in med. French lit., 56, 70
  in 18-c. French lit., 154
  in med. German lit., 611
  in Italian Ren. lit., 426
  in Spanish lit. (1490–1700), 300, 307
  in J. Bobrowski, 849
  in A. Poliziano, 488
  in A. Zanzotto, 549
Oratory,
  funerary,
    German, 17-c., 675
    German, Romantic era, 751
    in Ren. Italy, 459
  religious,
    Italian, 17-c., 505
    See also Sermons
  in Ren. Italy, 465
Orientalism,
  French, 18-c., 142, 148, 152
  French, 19-c., 176, 184, 188, 190, 196
  in med. German lit., 647
Originality,
  in 19-c. German lit., 779
Oxymoron,
  in O. E. Mandel'shtam, 1043

Pacifism,
  and feminism, 936
Pageantry,
  in Ren. Italy, 461
Pamphlet lit.,
  Dutch, 17-c., 894
  French, 18-c., 137–39, 157
  med. German, 663
  German, 18-c., 683
  German, Romantic era, 742
  Italian, 17-c., 492
Pantheism,
  and G. P. Harsdörffer, 675
Paradise,
  in Russian lit. (1700–1820), 1004

Paranoia,
　in 20-c. French lit., 217
Parchment,
　manufacture and use of, 617
Parody,
　in Croatian lit., 1073
　in med. French lit., 60, 71
　in 18-c. French lit., 155
　in 19-c. French drama, 177
　in med. German lit., 663–64
　in 19-c. Spanish lit., 333
　in Spanish lit. (1898–1936), 360
　in 20-c. Spanish-American lit., 413
　in G. Flaubert, 197, 198
　in Walther von der Vogelweide, 650
Passion plays,
　med. French, 71–72
Pastoral,
　French, 17-c., 102, 120, 122–23
　in 17-c. German poetry, 666
　in Italian Ren. drama, 482
　in Russian lit. (1700–1820), 1002
　in M. de Cervantes, 313
Patriarchy,
　in C. Wolf, 874
Patriotism,
　in 18-c. Germany, 696
　See also Nationalism
Patronage,
　and literacy, in Carolingian period, 2
　in med. Germany, 650
　in Ren. Italy, 461, 465, 479
　in 17-c. Italy, 494
Peasants,
　cultural life of, in Russia, 1006
Peregrinatio,
　Irish tradition of, 3
Performance. *See* Stagecraft
Periodical lit.,
　Bulgarian, 1082
　Danish, 18-c., 906
　Dutch, 18-c., 895
　German, Classical era, 695, 728
　German, 19-c., 783
　German (1880–1945), 811
　Italian, 17-c., 492
　Italian, 18-c., 511, 515
　Italian, 20-c., 529–30, 531
　Polish, 20-c., 981
　Russian, émigré, 985
　Spanish, 341, 362, 364, 368
　Spanish-American, 19-c., 410
　Spanish-American, 20-c., 414
　Ukrainian, 1058
Personification,
　in med. French lit., 75
Phenomenology,
　of 16-c. French poetry, 86
Philosophy,
　medieval, 637

　20-c. Western, 832
　and Belorussian lit., 1065
　Danish, 19-c., 910
　Danish, 20-c., 911
　Dutch, 885–86, 893
　French, 16-c., 78–79, 80–81
　French, 17-c., 116–20
　French, 18-c., 131–32, 141–42, 144,
　　148–50, 151, 156
　French, Romantic era, 162
　French, 20-c., 211–12, 216, 220, 240,
　　242–43
　German, Classical era, 686, 693–94, 698,
　　714, 715, 718, 724, 731
　German, Romantic era, 751, 757–58, 769
　German (1830–1880), 801–02
　German (1880–1945), 811, 814
　Italian Ren., 463–64, 465, 474
　Italian, 17-c., 490–91, 505–10
　Italian, 18-c., 516, 518–19, 524
　Russian (1700–1820), 1008
　Russian (1880–1917), 1019
　Spanish, 20-c., 360, 362–63
　in A. Andersch, 846
　in T. Bernhard, 848
　in P. Handke, 858
　of I. Kant, 719–22
　of G. W. Leibniz, 724–25
　of F. Schiller, 712–13
　See also Epistemology; Metaphysics
Photography,
　German, 19-c., 776
Physiognomy,
　in Italian Ren. lit., 464
Physiology,
　French, 18-c., 132
Pietism, piety
　in med. Germany, 618, 624, 654
　in 18-c. German lit., 685–86, 698
Plagiarism,
　French, 18-c., 144
　and M. A. Sholokhov, 1047
Plague,
　in Bulgarian folk lit., 1083
　med. French historiography of, 74
　in med. German lit., 652
　in med. Spanish lit., 298–99
Plants,
　in Belorussian folklore, 1069
　in J. W. von Goethe, 707
Poetics,
　German, Classical era, 685
　German, Romantic era, 768, 769–70
Poetry,
　Belorussian, 1065–66
　Breton, 570
　Bulgarian, 1081
　Caribbean, 217
　Czech, 19-c., 941, 938, 941, 943, 945
　Danish, 20-c., 913

med. Dutch, 890–91
Dutch, 17-c., 893, 894, 895
Dutch, 19-c., 896
Dutch (1880–1945), 886, 887, 898
Dutch (since 1945), 899–900
Old English, 8
Old French, 7, 8
med. French, 57, 63–64, 69–71, 72, 76
French, 16-c., 85–93
French, 17-c., 101–05
French, 18-c., 145, 160
French, Romantic era, 166–67
French, 19-c., 182–92
French, 20-c., 208–09, 212, 213–15, 217, 218–19, 220–21, 223, 224, 225–27, 235, 236, 241
med. German, 612–13, 625, 635–36, 660
German, 17-c., 666, 667–71
German, Classical era, 685–86, 702–03, 710, 722, 730
German, Romantic era, 741, 743, 749–50
German (1830–1880), 787–88, 790, 791, 793–97, 800–02
German (1880–1945), 810, 811–12, 815, 816–17, 825
German (since 1945), 839, 850–51, 862–63
mod. Irish, 573, 577–82, 586
med. Italian, 447, 450–52
Italian Ren., 467–80
Italian, 17-c., 490, 497–500, 507
Italian, 18-c., 515, 519–21
Italian, 20-c., 528–29, 531–49
med. Latin, 2, 3, 4, 5–6, 7, 8
Norwegian, 919
Occitan, 245, 247, 260–63, 264, 265
Polish, 972, 976, 977, 980–83, 1001
Russian, 17-c., 1001, 988
Russian (1700–1820), 1004
Russian (1880–1917), 1013, 1019, 1021
Russian (since 1917), 1033–35
Scottish, 586–87
Serbian, 1072, 1074
Slovak, 953, 954
med. Spanish, 289–93, 296–97
Spanish (1490–1700), 306–08, 324
Spanish, 19-c., 327, 330, 331, 332, 333
Spanish (1898–1936), 342, 344–53, 358, 359
Spanish (since 1936), 331, 363–66, 368
Spanish-American, 19-c., 410, 411
Spanish-American, 20-c., 413, 414, 417, 420, 422
Spanish-American Colonial, 406, 408–09
Swedish, 19-c., 931
Swedish, 20-c., 933
Ukrainian, 1057, 1060
Welsh, 563, 564–67
autobiographical, med. French, 70
bilingual, med., 5, 9

didactic, classical German, 717
embedded, med. French, 70
epic, Belorussian, 1065
figural, visual,
  German, 17-c., 671
  Slovak, 953
folk, peasant,
  Polish, 972
  Russian, 1040
  Serbian, 1076–77
funerary, memorial,
  German, 17-c., 668–69, 675
  mod. Irish, 578
  Italian, 475, 499
  historical, Russian, 1033
liturgical, religious,
  med. German, 628–29, 636–37, 648–49
  Ukrainian, 1055
of Nuremberg, 666
occasional, German, 17-c., 669, 671
pastoral, Polish, 972
penitential, Russian, 1001
political,
  German, 19-c., 790
  German (since 1945), 850
urban, 349, 350
of World War I, 208, 214
See also Lyric poetry
Poland,
  med. German references to, 636, 637, 663
Polemic,
  in Spanish lit. (1090–1936), 342
  in G. de Berceo, 292
  in J.-B. P. Molière, 126
  in B. Pascal, 119
  in Théophile de Viau, 115
Politics,
  and Nuremberg poets, 666
  scientists and, in 18-c. France, 132–33
  and Surrealism, 209
  in 16-c. French lit., 92–93, 94, 95
  in 17-c. French lit., 102
  in 19-c. French lit., 199
  French, 20-c., 225
  med. German, 621
  German, 17-c., 676
  German, Classical era, 715–16
  in German Classical lit., 694–96, 723, 731
  in 19-c. German lit., 777
  in German lit. (1880–1945), 813, 824
  German (since 1945), 871
  and German lit. (since 1945), 830–45
  in modern Latin American lit., 420
  Russian (1700–1820), 1003
  and Scottish Gaelic poetry, 587
  in Spanish drama, 317
  in med. Spanish lit., 294–95
  in Spanish lit. (1490–1700), 304
  in Spanish lit. (1898–1936), 344
  and Welsh lit., 565

and V. Alfieri, 519
and C. Baudelaire, 184
and I. Calvino, 533
and B. Constant, 165
and R. Descartes, 118–19
in J. von Eichendorff, 749
and H. M. Enzensberger, 853
and J. W. von Goethe, 701–02
and H. Heine, 795
and V. Hugo, 175
and H. von Kleist, 760
in F. Lope de Vega Carpio, 321
and T. Mann, 821
and F. Ortega y Gasset, 356
and B. Pérez Galdós, 334–35, 339, 362
in F. Schiller, 712
and R. Sender, 357
in T. Tasso, 472
and R. Wagner, 805–06
and art, in P. Weiss, 872
Polyglotism,
    in F. Rabelais, 83
Populism,
    Ukrainian, 1056, 1057
    in I. Nechui-Levyts'kyi, 1056
Pornography,
    French, 18-c., 153
    See also Obscenity
Positivism,
    Polish, 976
Postmodernism,
    philosophy of, 832
    Czech, 943
    Dutch, 900
    German, 835, 837, 870–71
    Italian, 532
    Latin American, 413, 416, 420
    Polish, 982
    Slovak, 955
    Spanish, 363, 364, 365, 368,
        370
Poststructuralism,
    philosophy of, 832
Power,
    in French baroque lit., 97
Pragmatism,
    German, Classical era, 731
Pre-Romanticism,
    Slovak, 953
Pregnancy,
    in med. French lit., 50–51
Press. *See* Journalism
Printing,
    in med. Germany, 663
    Italian Ren., 455–57
    in Zurich, 663
Prison,
    poets and, 212
Prodigal Son, theme of,
    and modernist lit., 898

Prophecy,
    in 16-c. French lit., 90
    in Ren. Italy, 466
Prose,
    metrical,
        Bulgarian, 1082
        med. Latin, 6
        Russian, 1004, 1015
        of F. Aragon, 215
    village, Russian, 1029
    Belorussian, 1065
    French, 17-c., 106–16
    French, 18-c., 152–58
    German, 17-c., 671–77
    German (1830–1880), 778–81
    German (1880–1945), 810–11
    German (since 1945), 843–45
    mod. Irish, 578–83
    med. Italian, 447–52
    Italian Ren., 483–89
    Italian, 17-c., 504–05
    Italian, 20-c., 525–28, 531–49
    Old Norse, 920
    Slovak, 955
    med. Spanish, 293–96, 297–99
    Spanish (1490–1700), 309–13
    Spanish (1898–1936), 354–60
    Spanish-American Colonial, 409
Proverbs,
    in med. epic, 264
    in Spanish lit. (1490–1700), 309
Psalms, psalters,
    in England, role of, 4
    German, 654
Psychoanalysis,
    and 20-c. Italian lit., 525
    in Spanish lit. (1898–1936), 352
    and G. Bernanos, 216
    and G. Grass, 856
    and L. Couperus, 897–98
    and E. T. A. Hoffmann, 755, 833
    and P. J. Jouve, 223–24
    and H. von Kleist, 761–62
    and K. H. Mácha, 941
    and J. Racine, 127
Psychology,
    and A. Döblin, 814
    and J. von Eichendorff, 750
    in E. T. A. Hoffmann, 738
    and I. Kant, 721
    in T. Mann, 822
    and M. Walser, 872
Publishing,
    Dutch, 17-c., 894
    of English books, in France, 139
    in 18-c. Germany, 697
    German (since 1945), 831
    Italian Ren., 455–57
    Italian, 17-c., 491–93
    Italian, 18-c., 511, 514–15

Russian (1700–1820), 1006
Russian-language, émigré, 985
Puppet theatre,
　French, 19-c., 206
　German, Classical era, 704
Purgatory,
　in med. French lit., 50
　in med. German lit., 654
Puritanism,
　Welsh, 563, 564

Quietism,
　French, 116–17, 181
Quotation,
　in G. Büchner, 784–85

Race,
　in German Classical lit., 699
Rape,
　in med. French lit., 66, 69
　in P. Calderón de la Barca, 318
　in H. J. C. von Grimmelshausen, 673
Rationalism,
　in 18-c. Germany, 699
Rationalitas,
　in Hildegard von Bingen, 637
Readers, reading,
　female, Italian, 527
　history of, 180
　and picaresque novel, 309
　Protestant reading culture, 886
　in med. Germany, 646
　German reading societies (18-c. and
　　19-c.), 775–76
　in German lit. (since 1945), 858
　in J. Beer, 672
　and I. Christensen, 912
　and F. Ponge, 240–41
Realism,
　French, 18-c., 142, 152
　in 19-c. French lit., 192–93, 194
　in 19-c. Spanish lit., 327, 328
　in 20-c. French lit., 220
　in med. German drama, 657
　German, 19-c., 776, 779, 780
　in German lit. (since 1945), 836, 840,
　　844, 862
　in mod. Irish lit., 579
　Polish, 976
　Russian, 1024
　Slovak, 955
　in 20-c. Spanish-American drama,
　　416
　in L. Alas, 329
　in G. Battista, 498
　and K. Blixen, 911–12
　in I. Calvino, 533
　and I. Lo-Johansson, 936

in I. Nechui-Levyts'kyi, 1056
of D. Wellershoff, 873
Recognition,
　in med. French lit., 65
Religion, religious lit.,
　Breton, 570
　med. French, 51, 52, 53, 63–64, 74–77
　French, 16-c., 92, 93, 94
　French, 17-c., 116–20
　French, 18-c., 136
　French, Romantic era, 161
　French, 19-c., 177
　med. German, 613–14, 618–20, 630, 643,
　　651–57
　German, 17-c., 670, 673–74
　German, Classical era, 698, 717
　German, Romantic era, 770
　German (since 1945), 856, 865
　mod. Irish, 580
　med. Italian, 447
　Italian Ren., 464–66, 472–73, 476–77
　Italian, 17-c., 497, 499
　Polish, 973–74
　early Russian, 999–1000
　Russian, 17-c., 1001
　Spanish (1490–1700), 304–06, 307, 310
　Spanish (1898–1936), 344
　Spanish-American Colonial, 406–07, 408
　Welsh, 564–65
　in G. Büchner, 786
　and B. Constant, 165
　and D. Diderot, 147
　and A. Gide, 211
　in F. García Lorca, 348, 349
　in F. Hölderlin, 756
　and V. Hugo, 167
　in G. W. Leibniz, 725
　and F. Petrarch, 450
　in J. P. Richter, 767
　in F. M. A. de Voltaire, 151
　See also Drama, religious; Poetry,
　　liturgical
Religious orders,
　spread of, 8
Remorse,
　in 19-c. French poetry, 185
Renaissance,
　concept of, 6
　Dutch, 891–95
　European, diversity of, 894–95
　Italian, 453–89
　Spanish, 304
Repetition,
　in med. French lit., 53
　in mod. Irish lit., 580
　in A. Carpentier, 419
　in C. Péguy, 226
　in T. Storm, 805
Revolution,
　changing meaning of concept, 162

French, 132–36, 143, 170
  chronology of, 135
  and Enlightenment, 1005
  myth and, 133
  scientists and, 132–33
  women in, 691
  German reaction to, 695–96, 703, 723,
    759, 776, 784, 799, 872
  Occitan texts of, 135
  in Russian lit. (1700–1820), 1003, 1009
  and Slovak lit., 953
  in L. A. von Arnim, 747
  and J. W. von Goethe, 693, 703,
    706–07
  and F. Schiller, 712
  literature and, in France, 179
  in Polish lit., 973
  Russian, 170
  in Stendhal, 172
Rhetoric,
  battle, med., 5, 65
  general, 612
  history of, 617, 684
  and journalism, 914
  and science, in Italy, 458, 509
  med. French, 51, 56, 65
  French, 16-c., 79, 92
  French, 17-c., 101, 111
  German, 17-c., 674
  in German Classical lit., 684
  in med. Italian lit., 447, 448
  Italian Ren., 458–59
  Italian, 17-c., 491
  med. Latin, 2, 5
  in early Russian lit., 999
  in med. Spanish lit., 297
  Welsh, 563
  J. W. von Goethe and, 702
  in F. Lope de Vega Carpio, 322
  in P. P. Pasolini, 542
  in P. de Ronsard, 87
Rhyme analysis,
  of N. Lenau, 799–800
Ring,
  in med. French lit., 60
Ritual,
  in Russian countryside, 1006
Rivers,
  in T. Konwicki, 982
Romance,
  origins of, 56
  Middle English, 52
  med. French, 51, 55–63, 68–69
  med. German, 638–48, 661
  med. Occitan, 264
  Russian (1700–1820), 1004
  Spanish (1490–1700), 306–07
  in P. Calderón de la Barca, 319
  See also Chivalry; Courtly lit.
Romanticism,
  and modernity, 737–39

  and the natural sciences, 739–40
  women and, 735–37
  Croatian, 1072
  Danish, 907
  Dutch, 896–97
  English, 342, 352
  French, 161–79, 223
  German, 735–73, 833–34, 839, 846, 857,
    897
  Irish, 580
  Polish, 972, 973, 974–76
  Russian, 1004
  Serbian, 1072
  Slovak, 953
  Spanish, 311, 326–27, 328, 333, 337, 342,
    352, 354
  Ukrainian, 1055
  in M. Gor'kii, 1040
  and B. L. Pasternak, 1045

Sacrifice,
  in G. Bataille, 233
Sagas,
  Old Norse, 920, 921
Saints. *See* Hagiography
Salons,
  German, 19-c., 697, 770
  German, 20-c., 839
Samizdat,
  history of, 1028
Sarcasm,
  in Walther von der Vogelweide, 650
Satire,
  in med. French lit., 66
  French, 17-c., 102
  in med. German lit., 663
  in 17-c. German lit., 672–73
  in German Classical lit., 732
  in 17-c. Italian lit., 676
  in med. Latin lit., 9, 10
  in Ukrainian lit., 1061
  in J. Beer, 671–72
  in D. Diderot, 146
  in H. Heine, 793–94
  in F. von Logau, 668
  in M. Ó Cadhain, 580
Scala naturae,
  in M. de Montaigne, 94
  in W. Shakespeare, 318
Scholarship,
  as heroic virtue, 10
Science,
  and European naturalism, 909
  and humanism, 458, 459
  language of, Italian, 494–95
  and patronage, in 17-c. Italy, 494
  and surrealism, 343
  French, 18-c., 132–33
  and 19-c. French lit., 193

med. German, 630, 662
med. German texts, 657–58
German, 17-c., 666
German, Classical era, 699, 707–08, 724–25
in German Romantic lit., 739–40, 759, 765, 766–67
and Italian Ren. poetry, 476
Italian, 17-c., 494–95, 505–06, 507, 508–10
Italian, 18-c., 518, 519, 520, 519, 524
and R. Barthes, 235–36
and G. P. Harsdörffer, 674
Science fiction,
German (since 1945), 835, 839
Russian, 988, 1029
Scythian movement,
Russian, 1013
Sea imagery,
in 17-c. French lit., 97, 102
in A. Enrique, 365
Secession,
in Russian and Austrian drama, 1014
Seeing,
of ideas, 117
and knowledge, 86
and showing, 88
truth and, 90
in 16-c. French lit., 86, 88, 90
in French Romantic lit., 164
in 19-c. French lit., 203
in K. Blixen, 911
in J. M. G. Le Clézio, 239
in J. Racine, 128
in Stendhal, 173
See also Eyes; Gaze, the
Self-consciousness, self-discovery, self-reflection,
in 19-c. German poetry, 782
in 20-c. Italian poetry, 528
in G. García Márquez, 418
in Gottfried von Strassburg, 646
in J.-B. P. Molière, 126
in F. Petrarch, 450, 451
in F. Rabelais and M. de Montaigne, 95
in C. Stieler, 678
See also Identity; Individualism
Self-image, self-representation,
in 16-c. French lit., 86
in 17-c. French lit., 115
in med. German poetry, 635–36
in German Romantic lit., 740
in Spanish lit. (1490–1700), 311
in J. W. von Goethe, 705
in F. Petrarch, 450
in J. Racine, 126
in Walther von der Vogelweide, 650
Semantic gesture,
in Czech lit., 937–38

Semiotics,
of med. French lit., 58–59
of 16-c. French poetry, 85, 87
of French Romantic lit., 165
of Spanish lit. (1490–1700), 310
of A. Gide, 221
of C. Pavese, 542
of P. Salinas, 353
Sensibility,
in 18-c. French lit., 144–45, 158
Serenades,
in 17-c. French drama, 124
Sermons,
medieval, 6
memorial, 8
German, language of, 591
med. German, 653, 654
German, Romantic era, 748
Italian Ren., 462–63, 465, 466
med. Latin, 8, 9
Welsh, 564
Sexuality,
in 19-c. Danish lit., 907
in med. French lit., 50, 52, 57
in French Romantic lit., 166
in 19-c. French lit., 185
in 20-c. French lit., 237
in med. German lit., 634, 662
in German lit. (since 1945), 854
in med. Latin lit., 6
in modern Latin American lit., 413
in J. M. Arguedas, 422
in K. Blixen, 911
in H. Fichte, 854
in E. Jelinek, 861
in G. de Maupassant, 201
in M. de Montaigne, 94
in Tirso de Molina, 322–23
See also Desire, sexual; Gender; Homosexuality; Incest; Obscenity; Rape
Shepherds,
in 17-c. French lit., 108
Short stories,
German, Romantic era, 746–47, 749
German (1830–1880), 781
German (since 1945), 844
mod. Irish, 578, 582
Italian, 20-c., 526, 528
Russian (1880–1917), 1017–18
Serbian, 1074
Sicilian, 526
Swedish, 20-c., 936
Welsh, 566
Sickness. *See* Illness
Signs,
in G. Bruno, 486
Slavery,
18-c., 142–43
in Spanish-American lit., 419

Social history,
of 18-c. Germany, 695–97
Socialism,
P. Leroux's opposition to, 179
Socialist Realism,
Bulgarian, 1081
Czech, 944
Polish, 980, 981–82
Russian, 1031, 1040
Slovak, 952
Societies, learned,
Dutch, 18-c., 895
German, 17-c., 665–66
German, 19-c., 790
Society,
J. W. von Goethe and, 705, 707
Solitude,
in 18-c. French lit., 132, 149–50
Songs,
political, German, 743
Belorussian, 1069
med. French, 64–65
in 16-c. French lit., 84
in 18-c. French lit., 156
med. German, 630
mod. Irish, 577
med. Latin, 4
Russian (1700–1820), 1003
Scottish Gaelic, 586, 587
in É. Zola, 205
See also Ballads; Hymns; Lullabies; Lyric
poetry
Soul,
in med. French lit., 52
in V. F. Khodasevich, 1021
Space,
attachment to, in Irish lit., 578
concept of, in 18-c. German lit., 685
in A. A. Blok, 1016
in A. P. Chekhov, 1018
in C. Pavese, 542
in E. Montale, 539
in L. Ariosto and W. Shakespeare,
480
Spiders, spider webs,
in 19-c. French lit., 193
in med. German lit., 635
Spirit,
in med. French lit., 52
Stagecraft,
of Passion plays, 657
English, 315, 321
French, 20-c., 220, 234
German (1830–1880), 781–82
German (1880–1945), 813
Italian, 18-c., 517
Spanish (1490–1700), 315, 321,
324
Spanish (1898–1936), 361
Spanish, 19-c., 326

modern, of Spanish Golden Age plays,
316, 319
of A. de Musset, 178
State support of lit.,
in Sweden, 929
State symbolism,
medieval, 623
Statistics,
in lit. research, 891
Stones,
in Polish poetry, 972
Structural analysis,
of med. French lit., 59
of G. de Maupassant, 201
of M. Proust, 227
of R. Queneau, 241
Structuralism,
and Czech lit., 937–38, 944
Stylistic analysis,
general, 612
Subconscious,
in H. von Kleist, 760
Subjectivity,
in German Classical lit., 683, 694
in German poetry, 782
in German Romantic lit., 739, 751
Sublime, the,
in German Classical lit., 716, 720
in F. Schiller, 712
Suicide,
in med. German lit., 640
Sun,
in 19-c. French poetry 183
Surgery,
French, 18-c., 132
Surrealism,
definition of, 343
Czech, 942–43
Franco-Romanian, 851
French, 208, 209–10, 217, 218, 223, 230,
235, 238
Italian, 545
Spanish, 343–44, 347, 368
Suspended animation,
in J. P. Richter, 767
Symbolist movement,
Belgian, 183
French, 183, 186, 188, 206, 222, 229
Italian, 531
Russian, 1013, 1023, 1024
Slovak, 954
Ukrainian, 1057
Syphilis,
in Italian Ren. poetry, 480

Tears,
in 16-c. French lit., 81
in Stendhal, 171

Technology,
    and tragedy, in M. Frisch, 855
Teratology,
    and 16-c. French lit., 79
Textual analysis,
    of 17-c. French lit., 99
    of Spanish lit. (1898–1936), 342
Theatre. *See* Drama
Theology,
    and natural philosophy, in 17-c. Italy,
      506
    French, 16-c., 78–79
    Italian Ren., 459
Time,
    in French Romantic lit., 167
    in 20-c. French lit., 244
    in H. de Balzac, 168
    in U. Karatkevich, 1067
    in R. Pazzi, 542–43
    in M. Proust, 228
    in J. Racine, 126
    in E. Zola, 204, 205
Tournaments,
    med. French, 74
Tragedy,
    theory of, 223
    Dutch, 17-c., 892
    French, 17-c., 120, 122, 127–31
    Italian Ren., 481–82
    Italian, 18-c., 521
    Russian (1700–1820), 1003
    Spanish (1490–1700), 321–22
    and M. Frisch, 855
Tragicomedy,
    in 18-c. Italian drama, 523
Transgression,
    in 17-c. German lit., 677
Translation,
    Aljamiado, 302
    computers and, 18, 302
    in Middle Ages, 3, 8, 9, 612
    theory of,
      German, Romantic era, 768
      Norwegian, 914
      med. Spanish, 267, 295
    into Bulgarian, from German, 1081
    Middle Dutch, of Old French, 889–90
    Dutch, Renaissance, 885
    of Finland-Swedish lit., 933
    French, 18-c., 139, 158
    French, Romantic era, 163
    French, 19-c., 175, 356
    French, of G. Boccaccio, 449
    of med. German poetry, 615
    German, 19-c., 184, 591, 662
    Irish, of *Pater noster*, 572
    of Irish lit., 578
    Italian, of Bible, and image of translator,
      456
    Russian, 326

    of Russian lit., into English, 986
    Scottish Gaelic, of Bible, 584
    med. Spanish, 293, 295, 296, 299
    Spanish, 304, 342
    Welsh, of Psalms, 563
    by N. Boileau, of Longinus, 108
    by Y. Bonnefoy, of W. B. Yeats, 236
    of M. de Cervantes, into Russian, 1005
    by J. von Eichendorff, of P. Calderón de
      la Barca, 750
    by J. J. Eschenburg, of Shakespeare, 715
    of H. Fielding, into Russian, 1005
    of B. le B. de Fontenelle, by A. D.
      Kantemir, 1008
    of J. W. von Goethe, into English, 701
    of D. Hyde, by Lady Gregory, 578
    of A. von Kotzebue, into English, 723
    of J. de Mandeville, into German, 660
    by G. F. Messerschmid, of Italian lit.,
      676
    by M. de Montaigne, of R. Sebond, 94
    of A. Rimbaud, into Russian, 1024
    by Théophile de Viau, of Plato, 120
    of D. Veiras, into German, 676–77
    by S. Zweig, of E. Verhaerens, 829
    See also Bible, translation of
Transliteration,
    of Aljamiado, 1070
Travel lit.,
    French, 16-c., 79
    French, 18-c., 143
    French, 19-c., 173, 183, 198, 199
    French, 20-c., 222
    med. German, 613, 620, 626, 660–61
    German, Classical era, 689–90, 715, 724
    German, Romantic era, 759, 772
    German (1830–1880), 781, 789, 799, 802
    German (since 1945), 864
    med. Italian, 447–48
    Italian Ren., 460, 483
    Italian, 17-c., 495
    Italian, 18-c., 519, 520
    Italian, 20-c., 541
    med. Spanish, 288
    Spanish, 19-c., 328
    Spanish (since 1936), 363, 368
    Swedish, 930
    of J. de Mandeville, 660
Trees,
    symbolism of, 761
    in Belorussian folklore,
      1069
    in med. French lit., 62–63
    in mod. Irish lit., 578
    in J. von Eichendorff, 750
    in H. von Kleist, 761
    in C. Simon, 243–44
    See also Forests
Trials, literary,
    in 19-c. French lit., 180

Trojan legend,
  in Old French poetry, 8
Troubadours,
  Occitan, 260–63
Turkish ceremony,
  in 17-c. French drama, 123–24

Unconscious, the,
  in Danish autobiography, 910–11
  in A. P. Chekhov, 1018
Universities,
  Italian, 17-c., social role of, 494
Urban culture,
  med. Dutch, 890
  See also Cities
Urban renewal,
  in Ren. Italy, 461
Utopian lit.,
  Danish, 906
  French, 17-c., 106, 110, 676–77
  French, 18-c., 131, 142, 145
  French, 20-c., 219
  German, 17-c., 677
  German, Romantic era, 741
  German (since 1945), 840, 850, 861, 864,
    868, 872, 874
  Russian (1700–1820), 1004, 1007
  Russian (since 1917), 1044, 1046

Valleys,
  in T. Konwicki, 982
Vampirism,
  in French Romantic lit., 176
Vanguardism,
  Latin American, 412–13
Versification,
  Alexandrine, 190, 261
  Parnassian, 183, 186, 188, 191
  med. French, 65–66
  French, 17-c., 103, 105
  French, 20-c., 213, 229–30
  German and Romance, 612
  Italian Ren., 479
  Italian, 20-c., 528
  med. Occitan, 261
  med. Spanish, 292
Violence,
  in med. French lit., 52
  in med. Latin lit., 6
  in Swedish 20-c. lit., 933
  in J. Racine, 128
Virginity,
  in 19-c. French poetry, 187
Virgin Mary,
  Ren. iconography of, 467
  in Irish poetry, 577–78
  in med. Spanish lit., 292, 294
  in J. de La Ceppède, 118

Vision lit.,
  med. German, 635, 637
  med. Latin, 1, 6
Voice synthesizers,
  and Italian linguistics, 425
Volcanoes,
  in French Romantic lit., 166
  in 19-c. French lit., 198–99
Volkspoesie,
  and the Grimms, 752–53

War,
  in German lit. (since 1945), 870
  in 20-c. Spanish-American lit., 412
  Spanish Civil, 348, 350, 362–63, 363–64,
    368, 373,
  World War I,
    and French lit., 208, 210–11
    Italy and, 538
  World War II,
    and French lit., 224–25
    and German lit., 808, 811, 812, 815,
      821, 823, 827, 828, 829
War poetry, 208, 214
Water,
  in 16-c. French lit., 80, 84
  See also Rivers; Sea
Widowhood,
  in med. French lit., 76
Wild man, wild woman
  in med. German lit., 620, 634, 640
  in med. Latin lit., 5
Windows,
  in 19-c. French lit., 183, 198
Wine,
  in med. Latin lit., 3
Wing imagery,
  in B. Pérez Galdós, 338, 339
Witchcraft trials,
  Italian, 496–97
Women,
  and French Revolution, 133, 138, 691
  heroic, in 17-c. French lit., 112
  language and,
    in the Middle Ages, 50
    in 17-c. French lit., 100
  in the Middle Ages, 617–18
  militancy of, in med. French lit., 75
  and Romanticism, 735–37
  saints, hagiography of, 4, 63, 64
  in troubadour poetry, 260, 261
  in med. French lit., 55, 57, 69, 75–77
  in 16-c. French lit., 80, 87, 95
  in 17-c. French drama, 123
  in 17-c. French lit., 99–100, 112
  in 18-c. French lit., 140, 152, 155, 156,
    159
  in French Romantic lit., 161
  in 19-c. French lit., 179, 187, 192, 199

in 20-c. French lit., 217, 230, 244
in med. German drama, 657
in med. German lit., 634, 640, 642, 647, 658
in 18-c. Germany, 690
in 19-c. German lit., 790
in German lit. (1830–1880), 804
in German lit. (1880–1945), 808, 825
in German lit. (since 1945), 841, 866
in Italian Ren. lit., 462, 466–67, 469
in 20-c. Italian lit., 531, 535
in modern Latin American lit., 414, 415, 416, 423
in Old Norse lit., 921
in med. Occitan lit., 263
in med. Spanish lit., 289–90, 298
in Spanish lit. (1490–1700), 304, 306, 310, 311, 323
in 19-c. Spanish lit., 332
in Spanish lit. (since 1936), 366, 367
and contemp. Spanish drama, 373, 374
in mod. Welsh lit., 566
in A. Andersch, 846
in L. Ariosto, 470–71
in L. A. von Arnim, 746
in H. de Balzac, 168, 169, 170
in C. Baudelaire, 185
in G. Benn, 812
in I. Bergman, 933
in H. Böll, 850
in K. Capek, 943
in M. de Cervantes, 311
D. Diderot and, 147
in I. Drewitz, 852
in J. W. von Goethe, 692, 693
in V. Hugo, 174–75
in F. Lope de Vega Carpio, 320–21
in A. Mira de Amuesca, 325
in W. Raabe, 803
J. J. Rousseau on, 148
in I. Svevo, 546
in P. Ua Maoileoin, 579
in E. Zola, 204
See also Feminism; Misogyny
Women writers,
Belorussian, 1069
Croatian, 1073
Czech, 941
Danish, 20-c., 911–12, 913, 905
Dutch (since 1945), 900
med. French, 61–62, 75–77
French, 16-c., 79–80, 81, 84, 85–86
French, 17-c., 108, 112, 114–15, 116, 117–18

French, 18-c., 141, 143, 149, 154, 157
French, Romantic era, 161, 166, 173, 176–77
French, 19-c., 198, 202
French, 20-c., 233, 242
med. German, 637
German, 17-c., 667
German, Classical era, 686, 689, 690–91, 715, 724, 731–32
German, Romantic era, 736–37, 745–46, 752, 753, 764, 768–69, 771, 772
German (1830–1880), 780, 787–88, 791, 797, 799, 800, 802
German (1880–1945), 811, 813, 814, 815, 819, 820, 825, 826, 827
German (since 1945), 738, 739, 830, 831, 832, 833, 834–35, 839, 845, 846–47, 850, 851–52, 853, 855, 860, 861, 862–65, 867, 868, 870, 871, 874 75
Irish, 578, 580, 581–82
Italian, general, 527
Italian Ren., 477
Italian, 17-c., 505
Italian, 18-c., 515, 519, 520
Italian, 20-c., 529, 531, 534, 538, 540–41, 548
Norwegian, 20-c., 922
Occitan, 260, 264
Russian (1700–1820), 1007
Russian (since 1917), 1034, 1035–36, 1049
Spanish (1490–1700), 323, 325
Spanish, 19-c., 326, 331–32, 333–34
Spanish (1898 1936), 343, 359–60
Spanish (since 1936), 362, 363, 366, 367, 369, 370–71, 372, 373
Spanish-American Colonial, 408
Spanish-American, 19-c., 410
Spanish-American, 20-c., 412, 414, 415, 418, 421
Swedish, 930–31, 932–33, 936
Ukrainian, 1062
Welsh, 566, 567
Working class, portrayal of, in 20-c. French lit., 211
Wounds, in med. German lit., 640

Year 1000, 50

Zionism, and A. Zweig, 829

II. NAMES

Aasen, I., 915
Abad, F., 268
Abad, M., 308
Abba, M., 543
Abbot, H. P., 235
Abbt, T., 714
Abdalova, N. B., 1049
Abelard, P., 7, 618, 643
Abélès, L., 176, 194
Abellán, J. L., 341
Abels, K., 822
Åberg, A., 931–32
Abirached, R., 207
Abisheva, S. D., 1034
Abner de Burgos, 295
Abou Ghannam, A., 167
Abraham, C., 128
Abraham, P., 698
Abraham, W., 591, 592, 594, 601
Abramov, F. A., 1026, 1027, 1035
Abramova, L. V., 1050
Abramovich, S. D., 1018
Abramowicz, M., 64
Abramowska, J., 974
Abreu, G., 106
Abril, P.-S., 267
Abuin, A., 331, 368
Abukhovich, A., 1066
Abyzov, Iu., 985
Acciaiuoli, D., 463
Accorsi, M. G., 513, 516
Achard, C.-F., 256
Achberger, K. R., 813, 846
Achenbach, B., 768
Achillini, C., 497–98
Achkasova, L. O., 1045
Achterberg, G., 885, 886, 888
Acker, L. van, 7
Ackermann, I., 827
Acosta, J. de, 407
Acquaviva, B., 462
Acquaviva, P., 432
Adalbert of Laon, 5
Adam, C., 220
Adam, J. (*Mme*), 175
Adam, M., 118
Adamantova, V., 1025
Adamchyk, V., 1066

Adam de la Halle, 72–73
Adamec, P., 993
Adamiec, M., 976
Adamiszyn, Z., 957
Adam of Bremen, 622
Adamovich, G. V., 1036, 1037, 1043, 1050
Adams, J. N., 16–17
Adamson, D., 161
Adant, J., 399
Addison, J., 720
Adelsbach, E., 680
Adelstem, M., 417
Adenet le Roi, 68
Adey, L., 715, 798
Adibaev, Kh. A., 1026
Adler, A. P., 910
Adler, G., 813
Adler, H., 688, 780
Adler, S., 828
Admoni, V., 1051
Admoni, W., 594, 596
Adolphs, D. W., 823
Adomnán, 3
Adorini Braccesi, S., 505
Adorni Fineschi, S., 511
Adorno, T. W., 99, 681, 682, 744, 815, 844, 870
Adriani, M. V., 459
Aebischer, P., 383
Aedilvulf, 4
Aelfric, 3
Aescht, G., 841
Aeschylus, 1014
Aesop, 113, 292, 662
Afanasii, 1001
Afanasii Nikitin, 997, 999
Affek, M., 518–19
Affinati, E., 540
Afsprung, J. M., 689–90
Agamben, G., 533
Ageev, A., 1034
Agel, V., 602
Ages, A., 147
Agheana, I., 415
Agisheva, N., 1032
Agnesi, M. G., 519
Ago, R., 493–94
Agosti, S., 187, 525, 527, 537–38

Agostiniani, L., 443
Aguilera, F., 407
Aguirano, B., 58
Aguirre, L. de, 423
Agustín, J., 421
Agustini, D., 413, 423
Aheieva, V., 1058, 1059
Ahmed, E., 88
Ahola, S., 935
Ahumada Lara, I., 282
Aichinger, I., 835, 845
Aigi, G., 1033
Aikhenval'd, Iu., 1032, 1048
Aikin, J., 678
Aínsa, F., 423
Aires, F., 403
Aitmatov, Ch. T., 874, 1035
Aitzetmüller, R., 991
Aizenberg, M., 1034
Ajello, R., 512
Akhmadulina, B. A., 1034
Akhmatova, A. A., 1014, 1016, 1020, 1035–36
Akmataliev, A. A., 1035
Aksakov, S. T., 1007
Aksamitau, A. S., 969, 1069
Aksenov, V. P., 1036
Aksenova, L., 1047
Alamanda de Castelnau, 260
Alan of Lille, 7, 59
Alarcón, P. A. de, 327–29
Alas, L., 328, 329–30, 340
Alatorre, A., 270–71
Albani, H., 505
Albano, G. d', 620
Albano Leoni, F., 440
Alba Pelayo, M. A., 357
Albera, F., 1013
Alberdi, J. B., 411
Alberi, M., 4
Albert, C., 191, 738, 759, 815, 821
Albertan, C., 135
Albertan-Coppola, S., 135, 146
Alberti, C., 435, 515–16
Alberti, L. B., 454, 462, 466, 467, 468, 484–85
Alberti, R., 343, 344, 345, 352, 354, 360

Albert of Savoy (*Cardinal Archduke*), 481
Albert Robato, M., 332
Alberts, A., 885
Albertsen, L. L., 700, 704
Albertus Magnus, 7, 463
Albi, E., 250
Albiac, G., 363
Albina, L. L., 142
Albinati, E., 528
Albinoni, T., 516
Albøge, G., 928
Albonico, S., 478
Alborg, C., 370
Albrecht, 647
Albrecht, H., 600
Albrecht, W., 683, 742
Albrecht von Johansdorf, 649
Albuquerque, S. J., 414
Alcalá, A., 306
Alcalá Galiano, A., 327
Alchevs'ka, Kh., 1058
Alcina Franch, J., 413
Alcoba, S., 277
Alcuin, 3, 4, 627
Aldanov, M. A., 1036
Aldaz, A. M., 422
Aldhelmus of Malmesbury, 288
Aldobrandini, M., 500
Aldobrandini, P., 500
Aldrich, M. C., 351
Aldrovandi, U., 506
Alegre, F. J., 406
Alegre, M., 381
Alegría, C., 414, 422
Alegría, F., 412, 413–14, 417, 418
Aleixandre, V., 343–44, 345
Alekhin, A., 1027
Alekhina, L. I., 1001
Aleksandrov, N., 1022
Aleksandrova, O. I., 1028
Alekseeva, L., 1035
Alekseev-Gai, A., 1033
Alemán, M., 309
Alembert, J.-B. le R. d', 140, 518, 693
Alenius, M., 906
Alenyar, M., 384
Aleramo, S., 527, 531
Alessandrini, A., 508
Alewyn, R., 672
Alexander VII (*Pope*), 493, 508
Alexander, R., 255
Alexandrov, V. E., 1043
Alexis (*Saint*), 295, 295
Alexis, W., 784
Alfieri, V., 519–20, 521, 541
Alfieri, V. E., 533
Alfonso V (*King of Aragon*), 462

Alfonso VI (*King of Castile*), 290
Alfonso X (*King of Castile*), 293–94
Alfonso de Cartagena, 295
Alfonso de Valladolid, 295
Alfonzetti, B., 517
Alfred (*King of England*), 3
Algarotti, F., 506, 513, 519
Algulin, I., 929
Aliakhnovich, F., 1066
Alibert, L., 250, 254
Alinei, M., 13, 24
Allain, L., 1016
Allaire, G., 486
Allais, A., 182
Allchin, A. M., 564–65
Alleau, R., 133
Allegra, G., 359
Allegretti, G., 449
Allemann, B., 758
Allen, D., 1019
Allen, J. J., 311, 315
Allen, J. S., 180
Allen, M. J. B., 458
Allen, P., 68
Allende, I., 407, 412, 417, 418
Allières, J., 245–46, 252, 254
Allison, H. E., 720–21
Allkemper, A., 728
Allott, T., 103
Allrogen-Bedel, A., 734
Allroggen, G., 755
Almahel, M., 552
Almalekh, M., 1079
Almansi, G., 526
Almeida, M., 275
Almeida, M. C., 395, 397
Almeida, M. L., 396
Almirall, V., 341
Almqvist, B., 576
Alms, B., 865
Alonge, R., 502
Alonso, A., 345, 408
Alonso, C., 338
Alonso, D., 341, 342, 345–46, 351, 364
Alonso, J. G., 420
Alonso, J. L., 319
Alonso, M. N., 417
Alonso Hernández, J. L., 269
Alonso Montero, X., 400
Alonso Seoane, M. J., 340
Alonso y Padilla, P. J., 304
Alsina, A., 376
Alsina, J., 368
Alsted, J., 671
Alt, A. T., 792
Alt, P.-A., 716, 767
Altenberg, P., 811
Altenhofer, N., 796

Alter, R., 810
Altes, L. K., 244
Althaus, T., 694, 744
Althoff, G., 619, 790
Altieri Biagi, M. L., 439, 494–95, 509
Altman, J. G., 154
Altmann, A., 727
Altner, M., 808
Alvar, C., 287–88, 290, 295–96, 298
Alvar, E., 299
Alvar, M., 269, 274, 285–86, 290, 299
Alvarado, S., 282
Alvarado Tezozómoc, F., 407
Álvarez, A., 980, 981
Álvarez, N. E., 415
Álvarez Barrientos, J., 313
Álvarez Borland, I., 418
Álvarez de Miranda, P., 275
Álvarez de Villasandino, A., 70
Álvarez Osés, J. A., 363
Alvarez Pellitero, A.-M., 299
Alvar Ezquerra, M., 281–82
Álvarez Quintero, J., 270, 335, 360
Álvarez Quintero, S., 270, 335, 360
Alver, B. G., 922
Alves, H. S., 394
Alves, I. M., 399
Alxinger, J. B. von, 765
Amacker, R., 27
Amasuno Sárraga, M. V., 298–99
Amato, A., 435
Ambar, M. M., 393–94
Ambrière, M., 167, 168
Ambros, M. H., 697
Ambrose, J., 562
Ambrosini, R., 13
Amegan, K., 719
Amery, C., 833
Améry, J., 845–46
Amestoy Leal, B., 423
Amezcua, J., 312
Amfiteatrov, A. V., 1035
Amiel, H.-F., 163
Amigó, R., 382–83
Ammer, A., 748
Amoretti, G. C., 505
Amorim, E., 423
Amorós, A., 352
Amós de Escalante, V., 326
Amossy, R., 217
Amour, Joan, 201
Amour, Joël, 201
Ampel, T., 967
Ampel-Rudolf, M., 960

Âmšanova, V., 603
Anahory-Librowicz, O., 306
Anashkina, N., 1001
Anatole, C., 254
Anchev, A., 1081
Andalò, A., 429
Anderman, G., 936
Andermatt, M., 747
Anders, G., 846
Andersch, A., 815, 831, 834, 846
Andersen, H. C., 907–08
Andersen, J., 913
Andersen, J. E., 902
Andersen, T. A., 903, 904
Andersen Nexø, M., 911
Anderson, A. A., 344, 347–48, 350
Anderson, G., 1018
Anderson, J., 747
Anderson, K., 211–12
Anderson, M. M., 850
Anderson, P. A., 790
Anderson, S., 856
Anderson, W., 144
Anderson Córdova, B., 415
Andersson, E., 923, 935
Andersson, T. M., 637
Andrachuk, G. P., 292, 319
Andrade, E. d', 390, 391
Andrade, N., 401
Andraschek-Holzer, R., 636
André, S., 198
Andreae, B., 734
Andreae, J. V., 677
Andreas Capellanus, 6, 50, 645, 646
Andreas-Salomé, L., 811
Andreev, D., 1033
Andreev, L. N., 1014
Andreeva, G., 1002
Andreeva, T. N., 1036
Andreini, G. B., 501, 502
Andreini, I., 501, 502
Andrenio, *see* Gómez Baquero, E.
Andreoli, A., 532
Andreoni, F. M., 435
Andrés, C., 322
Andrès, P., 184
Andres, Z., 978
Andresen, S., 903
Andress, R., 872
Andreu, A. A., 335
Andrew (*Saint*), 60, 997–98
Andrews, R. A., 480
Andrews, R. M., 559–60
Andrić, I., 1074, 1075
Andrieu d'Arras, 64
Andronnikov, I., 1027

Andrusiv, S., 1061
Andueza, M., 365
Aneau, B., 81
Angelico (*Fra*), 229
Angelieva, F., 1080
Angelini, P., 542
Angelone, M., 531
Angillus, A. A., 887
Angiolieri, C., 451
Angiolini, L., 520
Anglade, R., 797
Anglard, V., 237
Anglo, S., 458, 468
Angremy, A., 153
Angulo, M. E., 419
Angvik, B., 422
Anikin, A. E., 1014, 1016, 1035
Anisimova, E., 1007
Anisimova, O., 1000
Ankli, R., 468
Annenskii, I. F., 1014, 1016, 1043
Anne of Austria (*Queen of France*), 98
Anninskii, L. A., 1030, 1032, 1044
Annius of Viterbo, 459
Annoni, C., 548
Annunziata, A., 74
Anrooij, W. van, 654
Ansaldi, C. I., 520
Ansalone, M. S., 156
Anscombre, J.-C., 34, 35
Ansel, Y., 171
Ansell-Pearson, K., 801
Antelo, R., 413
Anthimus, 4
Anthonay, T. d', 200
Antoine, A., 206, 213
Antoine, R., 217
Antolín, F., 420
Anton, H., 795
Antonenko-Davydovych, B., 1058
Antonesen, V., 916
Antonijević, D., 1076
Antonych, B.-I., 1058
Antraigues, E. H. L. A. de L. d' (*comte*), 139
Anz, T., 837
Apel-Muller, M., 215
Apfelböck, H., 648–49
Apollinaire, G., 208, 209, 212, 213–14, 343, 933, 955
Apollonius of Tyre, 1
Aponte, B. B., 421
Apostolidès, J.-M., 99, 144
Appendini, G., 420
Appia, A., 213
Aprosio, S., 437, 442

Apter, E., 181, 192, 202
Apuleius, 103, 218, 500, 700
Aquilano, S., 479
Aquilecchia, G., 463, 464, 472, 480, 485
Arac, J., 177
Aragão, M. S. S. de, 390, 401
Aragon, L., 209, 214–15, 225
Araguas, V., 369
Arango, M. A., 419
Aranguren, J. G., 364
Aranníbar, C., 408
Araquistáin, L., 361
Arato, F., 519
Araújo, N., 194, 410
Arcangeli, M., 425
Archenholz, J. von, 696
Archer, J., 174
Archibald, E., 1
Archpoet, 5
Arciniegas, G., 418
Arcipreste de Hita, 292–93
Arcos, R., 208
Ardemagni, E. J., 292
Arden, H., 59
Arderíus, J., 354
Arellano, I., 308, 325
Arenal, E., 408
Arenas, J., 385
Arenas, R., 411, 419
Arenas Frutos, I., 407
Arencibia, Y., 337
Arendt, D., 754, 772, 776, 797, 802
Arendt, E., 734, 811
Arendt, H., 708–09
Ares, N., 403
Aretin, K. O. von (*Freiherr*), 6
Aretino, P., 480, 484, 485, 502
Aretov, N., 1082
Arfelli, D., 531
Argaya, M., 365
Argens, J.-B. d' (*marquis*), 139, 142, 157
Argente del Castillo, C., 324–
Argiblobyn, J., 965
Arguedas, J. M., 422
Arias Barredo, A., 277
Arias Montano, B., 304–05
Ariatta, P., 523
Arico, S. L., 175
Arie-Gaifman, H., 818
Ariosto, L., 454, 460, 468, 469–71, 473, 480, 481
Arishkin, Iu., 1025
Aristotle, 50, 65, 74, 173, 222, 234, 463, 466, 617, 690, 737, 782, 1072
Ariza, M., 272

Arizmendi, M., 352
Arkhangel'skii, A., 1028
Arkhipoff, O., 134
Arlt, R., 415
Armas, E. de, 410
Armas, F. de, 320
Armfelt, G. M., 523
Armistead, S. G., 291
Armogathe, J.-R., 117–18, 508
Armour, P., 447
Armstrong, A. H., 168, 169
Arnao, A., 332
Arnauld (*abbé*), 98
Arnauld, Agnès, 117–18
Arnauld, Angélique, 118
Arnauld, Antoine, 117, 118, 119
Arnauld, S. (*marquis*), 124
Arnaut Daniel, 263
Arnaut de Marueil, 260
Arndt, E. M., 743, 751
Arndt, K. J., 803
Arniches, C., 360
Arnim, A. von, 711–12, 732
Arnim, B. von, 696, 736, 738, 745–46, 747, 758
Arnim, L. A. von, 746–47, 748, 758
Arnold, G., 685, 686, 717
Arnold, H. L., 837–38, 852, 863–64, 867
Arnold, M., 182
Arnold von Harff, 620, 660
Arnould, J.-C., 01
Arol, M., 1066
Aronstein, S., 57
Arpini, A., 411
Arpino, G., 527
Arredondo, G. de, 292
Arreola, J. J., 414
Arrieta, K., 276
Arrou-Vignod, J.-P., 203
Arrouye, J., 75
Arrufat, A., 410
Arsenneva, N., 1066
Artal, S. G., 310
Artaud, A., 70, 215–16, 234
Artigal, J. M., 256, 385
Artmann, H. C., 859
Artsybashev, M. P., 1015
Arveiller, R., 36
Arvieux, d' (*chevalier*), 124
Asberg, C., 923
Ascarelli, F., 455
Aschenberg, H., 609
Ascherson, N., 980
Ascoli, G., 17
Ascunce Arrieta, J. A., 365
Aseev, N. N., 1033
Asendorf, C., 824
Ashby, W., 28

Asher, J. A., 631
Asher, O., 1058
Ashton, G. M., 565
Askedal, J. O., 603
Askénazi, J., 155
Asmuth, B., 684
Asnyk, A., 977
Asor Rosa, A., 525, 544
Asperti, S., 261
Aspetsberger, F., 855
Assaf, F., 107, 110
Assche, H. van, 900
Asselineau, C., 184
Assion, P., 654, 752–53
Assoun, P.-L., 155
Astaf'ev, V. P., 1030
Astapenko, M. P., 1041
Astraña Marín, L., 312
Asturias, M. A., 414, 419
Aszyk, U., 336, 372
Atanagi, D., 467
Atkinson, C. W., 617
Atrakhovich, V., 1067
Atterbom, P. D. A., 929
Atzori, M. T., 446
Aub, M., 354
Aubailly, J.-C., 73
Aubert, J., 164
Aubignac, F. H. d', 120
Aubigné, A. d', 89–92, 108
Auer, P., 602
Auerbach, N., 332
Auernhelmer, R., 809
Auf der Maur, I., 629
Augendre, J.-C., 172
Augier, A., 411
Augier, E., 180
Augst, G., 605
Augurello, G. A., 475
August (*Duke of Sachsen-Weissenfels*), 665
Augustín, J., 413
Augustine (*Saint*), 450, 509, 617, 618, 646, 655
Auld, L. E., 123
Aulnoy, M.-C. le J. de B. (*comtesse*) d', 108, 113
Aulotte, R., 78, 86, 95
Aurigemma, L., 543
Auroux, S., 252
Ausländer, R., 846
Aust, H., 731, 791, 803
Austin, G., 187
Austin, J. L., 242
Austin, K. O., 337, 338
Austin, L. J., 187
Autrand, M., 124, 207
Ava (*Frau*), 614, 637
Avalle-Arce, J. B. de, 310, 311
Avdiev, I., 1039

Avdonin, V. V., 1033
Avdzhiev, Zh., 1082
Avellaneda, A., 414
Avenary, H., 841
Averkii, 998
Averroes, 463
Avezona, G., 287
Avila, R., 284
Avksent'iev, L., 1053
Avrakhov, H., 1057
Avrakhov, T., 1062
Avram, A., 11, 550, 551
Avram, M., 552, 553
Avramenko, A. P., 1016
Avramov, D., 1082
Avrin, L., 456
Avvakum (*Archpriest*), 997, 1001
Axeitos, X. L., 366
Axelrod, M. R., 416
Axt, M., 396
Ayala, F., 312, 343, 354–55
Ayres-Bennett, W., 26, 27
Azadovskii, K. M., 1015, 1016, 1021
Azaña, M., 341, 355, 371
Azem, L., 41
Azemar lo Negre, 261
Azevedo, M. M., 400
Aznar Soler, M., 361
Azorín, *see* Martínez Ruiz, J.
Azouvi, F., 132, 141
Azuela, M., 420
Azuela, M. C., 291
Azuelos, D., 826
Azzi, M.-D. B., 221

Baaken, G., 621
Bąba, S., 960
Babaev, E. G., 1038
Babel', I. E., 1028, 1036
Babeuf, F. N., 135
Babeuf, G., 134
Babilas, W., 215
Babushkina, E. V., 901
Babych, N., 1054
Bacarisse, M., 342
Bacarisse, P., 416
Baccar, A. B., 97
Bacchelli, F., 459
Bacchelli, R., 531
Bach, J. S., 349, 680, 686
Bach, R., 167
Bacha, Iu., 1060
Bachelard, G., 175, 183, 200
Bacheva, A., 1009
Bachleitner, N., 781
Bachmaier, H., 871
Bachmann, I., 689, 739, 813, 818, 831, 834, 835, 846–47, 852, 853, 864, 875

Bachmann, P., 867
Bachorski, H.-J., 611
Bachórz, J., 972, 977
Bacini, P. P., 512
Baciu, I., 11
Bäck, G., 930
Bäck, T. M., 933
Bacon, F., 674, 675, 757
Baczewski, A., 977
Baczyński, K. K., 978
Bada, J. R., 384
Bader, U.-H., 838
Badia i Margarit, A. M., 20, 376
Badinter, E., 140
Badinter, R., 140
Baecker, D., 861
Baecque, A. de, 138
Baehr, C., 846
Baetens, J., 225, 240
Baevskii, V. S., 1035
Baeyens, H., 900
Báez Montero, I. C., 269
Báez San José, V., 279
Bafaro, G., 155
Bafile, L., 429
Bagaría, A., 359
Bagge, S., 921
Baggesen, J., 906
Baggioni, D., 27
Bagley, P. M., 867
Bahdanovich, A., 1069
Bahdanovich, I., 1066, 1068
Bahdanovich, M., 1066
Bahr, E., 688, 828
Bahr, H., 811, 819
Bahrianyi, I., 1058
Bahushevich, F., 1066, 1067
Baichev, B., 1080
Baier, B., 1082
Baier, L., 859
Baïf, J.-A. de, 93
Bail (*sieur du*), L., 109
Bailey, C., 13
Bailly, G., 29
Bairéad, T., 582
Bajerowa, I., 964
Bajza, I., 953
Bajza, J. I., 953
Bajzíková, E., 949
Bak, D., 1031
Bak, J. M., 51
Baka, J., 974
Baker, A. F., 330, 358
Baker, E., 336
Baker, M., 69
Baker, P., 147
Baker, S. R., 121
Bakhnov, L., 1047
Bakhnov, L. V., 1045

Bakhrakh, A., 1049
Bakhtin, M. M., 83, 115, 169, 172, 193, 226, 324, 348, 366, 370, 421, 613, 677, 680, 745, 872, 1008, 1024, 1031, 1043, 1044, 1075, 1076
Bakker, B. H., 203
Bakker, I. de, 883
Bakker, S., 898, 900
Bakkes-Rennes, H., 881
Bakst, L. N., 229
Bal, W., 20, 25
Balacciu-Matei, J., 550
Balañà, P., 382
Balayé, S., 161
Balbi, M. P., 497
Balbo, P., 512
Balbus, S., 964
Balcerzan, E., 983
Baldan, P., 468, 528
Baldassari, G., 468
Baldelli, I., 426
Balderston, D., 415, 419
Baldessano, G., 466
Baldinger, K., 41–42, 247, 252, 375
Baldini, A., 530
Baldini, G., 544
Baldit, J.-P., 257, 258
Balducci, L., 531
Baldwin, B., 906
Baldwin, J. W., 6, 50
Baldwin, S., 274, 291, 294
Balfour, I., 811
Balibar, R., 226
Balibar-Mrabti, A., 35
Baliński, S., 978
Balkanski, T., 1081
Balk-Smit Duyzentkunst, F., 877, 885
Ball, M. J., 561
Ballabriga, M., 237
Ballano Olano, I., 356
Ballek, Ľ., 955, 956
Ballester, C., 338
Bally, C., 27
Balmas, E., 95
Balme, C., 781–82
Bal'mont, K. D., 1015, 1027
Balsamo, L., 457
Balslev-Clausen, P., 909
Baltrusaitis, J., 288
Baltzer, U., 650
Balukhatyi, S. D., 1032
Balve, J., 814
Balzac, H. de, 114, 147, 161, 162, 163, 168–70, 172, 175, 182, 193, 194, 196–97, 204, 205, 416, 738
Balzer, B., 611, 817, 849

Bamforth, S., 78
Bammesberger, A., 560, 597
Bancquart, M.-C., 198
Banda, A., 541, 542
Bandello, M., 168, 485
Bandello, R., 323
Bandettini, T., 515
Bandier, N., 217
Bandini, F., 488
Bandini, S. A., 520
Banér, C., 932
Bañeres, J., 385, 386
Banfi, L., 452
Bang, H., 908
Bang, J. C., 902
Bange, P., 619
Baniewicz, E., 978
Banjanin, M., 1016
Bańko, M., 967
Bańkowski, A., 957, 967, 970
Banks, B., 200
Bannerman, J., 585
Bannet, E. T., 688
Banniard, M., 200
Bannister, M., 107–08
Bañón Hernández, A.-M., 271
Bansleben, M., 830
Bantaş, A., 553
Banti, A., 531
Bañuelos, R., 421
Banville, T. de, 181, 183–84, 186, 188
Bänziger, H., 799, 826
Baquero Escudero, A. L., 309
Baquiast, P., 183
Bar, J. F. von, 729
Barabash, Iu., 1060
Baracchi Bavagnoli, M., 1008
Barachetti, G., 456
Baradel, Y., 44
Barakhovich, A., 1066
Barakov, V. N., 1046–47
Barańczak, S., 967, 973, 980, 981, 983
Barandeev, A. V., 991
Barani, V., 536
Baranov, V. I., 1040
Baranova, A., 1047
Baranova, G. A., 1042
Baranowska, M., 980
Baranski, Z., 469
Barante, P. de, 161
Baratto, M., 481, 530
Baratynskii, E. A., 1016
Barbagallo Rolanía, A., 352
Barbaro, F., 457, 462, 466
Barberini, M., *see* Urban VIII (*Pope*)
Barberino, A. da, 486

Bàrberi Squarotti, G., 469, 500, 541, 549
Barbey d'Aurevilly, J., 181, 193–94
Barbi, M., 287
Barbier, J., 84
Barbieri, D., 502
Barbieri, E., 456
Barbieri, P., 508
Barbin, C., 102
Barbina, A., 530
Barbu, V., 551, 551
Barbuto, A., 533
Barchilon, J., 113
Barč-Ivan, J., 956
Barclay, J., 108
Barco, M. de, 408
Bardi, G. de', 504
Bardini, M., 483
Barenghi, M., 532
Baretti, G., 520
Barfoed Møller, T., 907
Barfoot, G., 539
Barguillet, F., 149–50
Barguillet, M., 155
Barilli, R., 542
Bark, J., 778
Barka, V., 1061
Barke, J., 597–98
Barker, A., 826, 839
Barkhausen, K. L., 755
Barkhoff, J., 767, 827, 855
Barkova, A., 1034
Barlösius, E., 658
Barner, W., 692, 726–27
Barnett, R.-L., 126
Barni, S., 865
Barnouw, D., 682
Barny, R., 139
Baro, B., 110
Baroja, P., 338, 341, 355, 357, 360
Barolsky, P., 474, 488–89
Baron, A.-M., 168
Baron, F., 819
Baron, H., 460
Barone, F., 508
Baroni, G., 525
Barotti, G., 515
Barra, S. de, 574
Barrack, C. M., 597
Barra Jover, M., 293
Barral, C., 365
Barral, M., 255
Barratt, A., 1014, 1040
Barrault, J.-L., 128, 234
Barrel, Y., 133
Barrenchea, A. M., 268
Barrera, T., 415

Barrera López, J. M., 344, 347, 353
Barrès, M., 168, 194, 208, 210
Barreyre, E., 253
Barrier, P., 258
Barros, C. A., 396
Barros García, P., 282
Barruel, A., 135
Barry, C., 169
Barry, D., 703
Barry, N., 867
Barsch, A., 830
Barsotti, A., 530
Barsòtti, G., 251
Bartels, B., 631
Barth, H. R., 759
Barth, I.-M., 759
Barthès, H., 249
Barthes, R., 121, 130, 167, 188, 212, 235, 645, 938, 1076
Barthofer, A., 792
Bartholomaeus Anglicus, 8
Bartholomaeus van Eyck, 611
Bartlett, R., 939, 1002
Bartmiński, J., 960, 963
Bartnicka, B., 967
Bartòla, A., 493
Bartoli, G., 14
Bartoli, R., 512
Bartoszyński, K., 976
Bartra i Kaufmann, A., 378
Bartram, G., 814
Bartsch, K., 739, 861, 866
Bartsch, P. D., 865
Bartsch, W., 867
Baruchson, Z., 456
Baruffaldi, G., 515
Barugel, A., 290–91
Barzakh, A., 1014, 1043
Basañez, J., 357
Basara, A., 964
Basara, J., 964
Basbøll, H., 904
Basile, B., 506, 535
Basile, G., 444, 499, 504
Basile, G. B., 752
Basile, T., 476
Basinskii, P., 1016–17, 1040
Basire, C., 139
Basnage, J., 118
Bassaglia, L., 511
Bassan, F., 167, 207
Bassani, G., 531
Basse, M., 867
Bassi, A., 498
Bassi, L., 519, 520
Bassi, R., 543
Bassnett, S., 412
Basso, J., 483, 492

Bassompierre, F. de (baron), 97, 98
Bast, R. A., 693
Bastardas, A., 387
Bastardas, J., 377
Bastet, F., 897
Bastiaensen, M., 469
Bastin, J., 70
Bastos, L. C., 396, 398
Bataille, G., 216, 233
Bathrick, D., 838
Batinti, A., 429
Batiushkov, K. N., 1005
Batkin, L., 1048, 1048
Batkin, M., 458
Battafarano, I. M., 495, 674–75
Battera, F., 478
Batteux, C. (abbé), 140, 727
Battista, G., 498–99
Battisti, C., 555
Battistini, A., 520
Battlori, M., 508
Battye, A. C., 18, 35
Batušić, N., 1073
Baude, J.-M., 217
Baudel, Y., 223
Baudelaire, C., 163, 176, 178, 180, 181, 182, 183, 184–86, 239, 351, 809, 816, 1020
Baudorre, P., 205
Baudouin de Courtenay, J., 965
Baudour, W. de, 892
Baudrillard, J., 234, 363
Baudry, H., 84
Bauer, B., 712
Bauer, E., 656
Bauer, G., 641, 662
Bauer, G. H., 235
Bauer, W., 830
Bauer, W. M., 611
Baufeld, C., 611, 631, 658
Baugnet, L., 43
Bauhr, G., 281
Baumann, C., 830, 870
Baumann-Zwirner, I., 661
Baumbach, G., 801
Bäumer, A., 510
Bäumer, K., 745
Bäumer, M. L., 734
Baumgaertel, G., 824, 867
Baumgart, R., 822, 825
Baumgart, W., 705
Baumgarten, A. G., 686
Baumgartner, W., 929
Baur, G., 841
Baur, M., 867
Bauschatz, C. M., 80
Bauschatz, P., 220
Bauschinger, S., 819
Baxendale, S. F., 485

Baxter, A., 405
Bayle, L., 249
Bayley, J., 980
Bayley, P., 129
Bazalgas, G., 245
Bazanov, V. G., 1021
Bazanov, V. V., 988
Bazhan, M., 1058
Bazhynov, I., 1056
Bazzanella, C., 432
Beale, G., 136
Beauchamps, P.-F. G. de, 124
Beauchemin, N., 46
Beauduin, N., 208
Beaujean, M., 689
Beaujour, M., 86
Beaumarchais, P.-A. C. de, 153, 158, 159
Beauvoir, S. de, 233
Beauvy, F., 43
Beauzée, N., 27
Bec, C., 453
Bec, P., 245, 249, 265
Becattini, F., 520
Beccaria, C., 519, 521
Beccaria, G. L., 535
Becco, H. J., 409
Becher, J. R., 810, 811, 834, 837, 840, 866
Bechev, K., 1082
Beck, H., 596, 719
Beck, J. S., 714
Becker, C., 203, 204, 206, 739, 741–42
Becker, H.-J., 603–04
Becker, J., 831, 840, 847, 1015
Becker, K. W., 632–33
Becker, T., 847
Becker-Bertau, F., 868
Becker-Cantarino, B., 682, 691–92
Beckermann, T., 864
Beckers, H., 641, 651, 654, 729
Beckett, S., 233, 234, 235–36, 416
Beckman, N., 928
Beckman, P. E., 309
Beckmann, M., 804
Bećković, M., 1075
Bécquer, G. A., 330, 350, 353, 411
Bécquer, V., 330
Bédard, E., 275
Bédier, J., 14, 287
Bedini, S. A., 510
Bednár, A., 956
Bednarek, A., 961
Beer, A., 235
Beer, J., 671–73
Beer, M., 468

Beers, J., 677
Beethoven, L., 349
Beetz, M., 695
Begić, M., 1075
Béhar, H., 181, 215, 217
Beheim, L., 615
Beheim, M., 70, 660
Beheydt, L., 881, 883
Behiels, L., 337
Behler, E., 735, 769–70
Behn, A., 689
Behr, H.-J., 635, 648
Behre, M., 757–58
Behrens, J., 747
Beifuss, H., 597
Beigbeder, F., 252
Beil, C., 846
Beintema, T., 880
Bejel, E., 419
Bek, A. A., 1030
Bekes, P., 852
Bekkering, H., 900
Bekkum, I. J. van, 881
Bel, M., 953
Belaia, G., 1030
Belaia, S., 1066
Belcheva, M., 1082
Belgrand, A., 204
Beliaeva, S., 1082
Belinskii, V., 1056
Belkin, E. I., 1016
Bell, A., 281
Bell, D. F., 205
Bell, I. A., 587
Belladonna, R., 460
Bellarmine, R. F. R., 466, 506–07
Belleau, R., 88–89
Bellemin-Noël, J., 191
Bellenger, Y., 92
Bellet, R., 133
Belletti, A., 431
Bellettini, P., 492
Bellezza, D., 539, 540
Bellini, E., 473, 490
Bellini, G., 484
Bellman, C. M., 931
Bellmann, G., 596
Bello, A., 266, 410
Bellosi, G., 529
Bell-Villada, G., 418
Belous, V. G., 1013
Belov, B., 1008
Belov, V. I., 1036
Belova, M. P., 1035
Belozerskaia-Bulgakova, L. E., 1037
Bel'skaia, D., 1034
Bel'skaia, L. L., 1039, 1043
Bel'ski, A., 1065–66

Beltrán, R., 298
Beltrán, V., 289, 297
Beltrán de Heredia, P., 334
Belyavski-Frank, M., 1071
Belyi, A., 1014, 1015–16, 1020, 1027
Belza, I., 1038
Bem, J., 121, 178, 180, 201
Bembo, P., 475, 476, 479, 481, 485, 495
Ben, S., 1058
Benabu, I., 319
Benassati, G., 511
Benavente, J., 360
Bénazraf, J., 124
Benčić, Z., 1043
Bender, H., 844, 846
Bender, W. E., 726
Bendidio, L., 477
Bendiha, U. M. S. P., 405
Bendjebbar, A., 158
Benedetti, J., 1032
Benedetti, L., 546
Benedetti, M., 423
Benediktsson, V., 930
Benet, J., 367, 368
Benet, J. M., 342
Benevento, A., 525, 528–29, 538, 546
Beniak, E., 47
Benický, P., 946
Benincà, P., 426, 429, 440, 555
Benítez, R., 332
Benítez-Rojo, A., 411
Benjamin, W., 499, 701, 705, 725, 744, 757, 768, 810, 811, 844, 856, 859, 866, 867
Ben Jemia, M. N., 300
Benko, S., 417
Benkov, E. J., 50, 73
Benkovičová, J., 951
Benn, G., 769, 811–12, 848
Benn, S., 711
Bennett, P., 52, 71
Bennett, R. B., 1018
Bennett, W. A., 29, 34
Bennewitz, I., 611
Benoit of St Maure, 63
Benot, Y., 139, 142
Benrekassa, G., 155
Bensimon-Choukroun, G., 49
Benson, D. K., 353, 366
Bente, T. O., 411
Bentley, G. E., Jr, 158
Bentzel, C. C., 761–62
Bentzinger, R., 594, 596, 631
Benucci, A., 444–45
Benvenga, M., 494
Benz, R., 659
Benzenhöfer, U., 875

enzi, F., 461
eolco, A., *see* Ruzante, il
erard, E., 1039
érard, V., 179
erbig, R., 778
erceo, G. de, 292, 351
erchtold, J., 198
erdiaev, N. A., 1012, 1017
erelowitch, W., 1008
erendse, G.-J., 838, 842, 850
erenguer, C., 412
erenshtein, E. P., 1043
erent, W., 973
erg, T., 275–76, 616
ergal, I., 81
ergamín, J., 360
ergen, J. J., 285
erger, A.-E., 190
erger, G., 107
erger, T., 991
erger, U., 790
ergero, A. J., 343
ergerot, B., 172
erggol'ts, O. F., 1026, 1028
erghahn, K. L., 507, 825
ergman, G., 927
ergman, I., 933
ergmann, E., 408
ergmann, H., 715–16
ergmann, R., 595, 597, 626, 627
ergounioux, P., 195
ergsøe, V., 909
ergson, H., 120, 539, 943
erka, S., 870–71
erkeley, G., 119, 813
erleth, R. J., 632
erlin, I., 524
erlin, J. B., 829
erlinck, R. A., 393
erlioz, J., 632
erman, R. A., 796, 849
ernabé Pons, L. F., 302
ernabò, G., 540
ernadan, P., 135
ernanos, G., 194, 210, 216
ernard, E., 530
ernard Gordon, 296
ernard-Griffiths, S., 133
ernardi, A., 531
ernardi, W., 509
ernardi della Mirandola, A., 477
ernardin de Saint-Pierre, J.-H., 153
ernardini, I. S., 730
ernard of Clairvaux (*Saint*), 5, 619, 637
ernard of Morval, 5
ernard Silvestris, 6, 7

Bernart de Ventadorn, 260, 262
Bernart Marti, 262
Bernat, F., 376
Bernatowicz, F., 965
Bernay, J., 797
Bernhard, G., 253
Bernhard, H. J., 838
Bernhard, T., 831, 832, 844, 848–49, 853
Bernhardt, R., 816
Bernini, C., 821
Bernolák, A., 953, 954
Berns, J. B., 878, 879
Berns, J. J., 672–73, 674, 675
Bernshtein, S. B., 946–47
Bernsmeier, H., 867
Béroalde de Verville, F., 80, 82, 108
Beroaldo, F., 485
Béroul, 60, 211
Berra, C., 451
Berressem, H., 978
Berretta, M., 430
Berrichon, P., 189, 191
Berriot, F., 78
Berriot-Salvadore, E., 79–80
Berroa, R., 349
Berruto, G., 431, 438, 445
Berry, A. F., 83
Bersani Berselli, G., 491–92
Berschin, W., 612, 629
Bertacchini, R., 533, 541
Bertaud, J.-P., 138
Bertaud, M., 97
Bertelli, D., 470
Bertelsen, O., 907
Bertens, H., 369
Berthelot, A., 68
Berthet, R. D., 172
Berthier, F., 133
Berthier, G. F., 151
Berthier, P., 172, 178
Bertho, S., 233
Berthold von Regensburg, 595, 635
Berthonneau, A.-M., 35
Bertière, S., 97
Bertinetto, P. M., 428, 431, 433
Bertini, F., 618
Bertken, 887
Bertolini, V., 71
Bertone, G., 532
Bertone, M., 535
Bertrand, A., 539
Bertrand, D., 110, 115
Bertrand, J.-P., 186, 192
Bertrand, M., 173, 192
Bertrand de Bar-sur-Aube, 53
Bertran de Born, 263
Bertuch, J. F., 714

Bérulle, P. de (*cardinal*), 118
Bery, R.-J., 54
Besch, W., 595, 596
Besomi, O., 473, 520
Besser, J., 668
Bessire, F., 151
Best, J., 207
Best, T. W., 678
Besten, H. den, 638
Bethea, D., 1036
Betko, I., 1057
Betocchi, C., 528, 546
Betocchi, L., 546
Bettarini, R., 538
Betten, A., 593–94, 595
Betti, U., 529
Bettinelli, S., 513
Bettinger, E., 689
Bettini, F., 525
Bettinzoli, A., 475
Bettoni, C., 444, 445
Betz, D. M., 166–67, 176, 184
Betz, M., 556 57
Beug, J., 826
Beugnot, B., 105, 212
Beumann, H., 622
Beutin, W., 634
Bevan, D. G., 211, 225, 227
Beverley, J., 334–35, 412
Bevilacqua, A., 527
Bevzenko, S., 1052
Beyer, M., 235, 865
Beyer, S., 176
Beyer, W., 742
Beyle, H., *see* Stendhal
Beynel, M., 102
Beyreuther, G., 619
Bèze, T. de, 78, 116
Béziau, R., 198
Bezruč, P., 938, 943
Bhaldraithe, T. de, 572
Biagini, E., 525
Biagioli, M., 494
Bialiatski, A., 1065
Bialik, B. A., 1012, 1020
Bialik, W., 870
Białoszewski, M., 981
Biancardi, G., 478
Bianchi, L., 463
Bianchi, R., 455–56
Bianchi, S., 417
Bianchiotti, H., 416
Bianco, J.-F., 146
Biancolelli, D., 518
Bianconi, S., 426
Biard, M., 135–36, 158
Biasi, P.-M. de, 195
Bibbiena, *see* Dorizi, B.
Bibbiena, Ferd. Galli, 503
Bibbiena, Franc. Galli, 503

Bibikov, M. V., 998
Bibolet, J.-C., 61
Bich, E., 1029
Bichard, M.-C., 84
Bichsel, P., 835, 849, 860
Bickerton, D., 255
Bideaux, M., 84, 115
Bieber, U., 825, 1064
Biebl, K., 943
Biechele, W., 830, 838
Biedenkopf, K. H., 874
Bieder, H., 1064
Bieder, M., 334
Biedma, A., 324
Bieliaieva, N., 1057
Bień, J., 957
Bienek, H., 849
Bieńkowska, D., 964
Bier, J. P., 845
Biermann, W., 838, 841, 843, 849
Bieruta, B., 980
Bierwirth, S., 795
Biet, C., 104
Bigalli, D., 464
Bignon, A. J. (*abbé*), 137
Bigongiali, A., 527
Bigongiari, P., 531, 548
Bigot, M., 239
Bijak, U., 970
Bilbao, A. M., 423
Bilderdijk, W., 887, 896
Bilenchi, R., 531
Bilets'kyi, O., 1055
Bilibin, V. K., 1001
Billanovich, M., 460
Billaud-Varenne, J.-N., 140
Billault, A., 93
Billeskov Jansen, F. J., 907
Billoret, J.-L., 134
Bilokin', S., 1052
Bilotserkivets', N., 1061
Bily, I., 970
Bilyi, O., 1060
Bilyk, O., 1062
Binder, A., 859
Binder, H., 809, 828
Bindhoff, E., 217
Binding, R., 812
Bingenheimer, S., 606
Biniewicz, J., 960
Binkley, P., 8
Bino, G., 497
Biodo, A., 463–64
Biolik, M., 963
Bioy Casares, A., 415
Birabent, J.-P., 252
Birago, G., 521
Birchall, I. H., 151
Bircher, M., 665

Bireley, R., 487
Biriukov, F. G., 1041, 1047
Biriukov, S., 1033
Birken, S. von, 676
Birkenmaier, W., 987
Birn, R., 137
Birnbaum, D. J., 1053
Birnbaum, H., 946, 990
Birtsch, G., 696
Bisaccioni, M., 495
Bischoff, F. M., 617
Bishop, M., 219, 235
Bismarck, O., 790
Bismut, R., 159
Bisol, L., 391
Bitossi, C., 462
Bitov, A. G., 1027, 1036, 1048
Bitsaeva-Stoianova, R., 1078
Bitterli, U., 620
Bivort, O., 189, 190, 191
Bizzocchi, R., 467–68
Bjerrum, M., 903
Bjørby, P., 908
Björklund, S., 926–27
Björkvall, G., 620
Björling, G., 931
Bjørnager, K., 1032
Bjørnflaten, J. I., 990
Bjørnvig, T., 910–11
Bjorvand, H., 921
Black, J., 137
Black, M., 343
Blackshire-Belay, C., 600
Blackwell, J., 724, 736
Blahynka, M., 942–43
Blaikner-Hohenwart, G., 820
Blair, A., 459
Blair, H., 586
Blake, R., 272
Blake, W., 158
Blakeslee, M. R., 60
Blamberger, G., 774–75, 834
Blanár, V., 946, 947–48
Blancart-Cassou, J., 206–07
Blanchard, J., 74
Blanchard, M. E., 79
Blanche, J., 228
Blanche-Benveniste, C., 31, 44
Blanchet, P., 44, 256
Blanchot, M., 127, 873
Blanck, K., 1017
Blanco, C., 331, 365
Blanco, G., 417
Blanco Aguinaga, C., 338
Blanco Pérez, D., 401
Blanco Vila, L., 368
Blank, H., 31, 612
Blanke, H. W., 690, 777
Blanqui, A., 136

Blasco Ferrer, E., 273, 438, 445–46
Blasucci, L., 539–40
Blatt, F., 904
Blažíček, P., 944
Bléchet, F., 137
Bleck, R., 651
Blecua, A., 287
Bleich, D., 169
Bleser, P., 620
Bliese, J. R. E., 5, 65
Blium, A., 1030
Bliumbaum, A. V., 1027
Blixen, K., 911–12
Bloch, E., 705, 744
Bloch, A., 819, 820
Bloch, P. A., 852
Bloch, R. H., 55
Block, H., 841
Bloemen, H., 828
Bloemhoff, H., 879–80
Bloh, U. von, 655
Blok, Aleksandra Andreevna, 1015
Blok, Aleksandr Aleksandrovich, 1014, 1016–17, 1020, 1036
Blok, D. P., 879
Blom, N. van der, 889
Blondin, A., 236
Błoński, J., 973
Bloom, A., 148
Bloom, H., 413
Bloomer, R., 601
Blot-Labarrère, C., 223
Blottier, H.-P., 112
Bloy, L., 192, 193, 194, 216
Blue, W. R., 321
Blüher, K. A., 215, 231
Bluhm, L., 808
Blum, C., 86, 94, 95–96
Blumauer, A., 686
Blume, J., 814
Blumenbach, J., 699
Blumenberg, H., 684, 791, 870
Blumenfeld-Kosinski, R., 77, 619
Blumenthal, P., 34
Blumenthal, U.-R., 621–22
Bly, P. A., 335, 336–37, 338
Bo, R., 539
Boa, E., 818, 830, 846
Boak, D., 242
Boal, A., 414
Boase, R., 306
Bobbio, N., 526
Bobillot, J.-P., 213
Bobkowski, A., 978
Boborykin, P. D., 1017
Boborykin, V. G., 1038

Bobrowski, B., 830
Bobrowski, J., 680, 840, 849
Bobylev, V. G., 1046
Bobyshev, D., 1034, 1035
Bocaz, A., 283
Boccaccio, G., 320, 415,
  448–50, 455, 466, 467, 484,
  489
Boccardo, P., 450
Bocharov, A. S., 1041
Bochmann, K., 400, 598
Böck, D., 736
Bock, G., 487
Bock, I., 945
Bock, S., 827
Bockelmann, E., 786
Boddaert, F., 163
Bödeker, H. E., 714
Bodel, J., 6, 50, 65
Bodemann, U., 616
Bodi, L., 841, 848
Bodin, J., 78
Bodin, P.-A., 1046
Bodin, T., 149
Bodini, V., 532
Bodmer, J. J., 685, 733
Bodon, J., 254
Boehme, J., 668
Boendale, J. van, 888
Boening, J., 719
Boer, D., 770
Boer, M.-G. de, 427
Boersma, F., 890
Boeschenstein, B., 800
Boeschenstein, H., 807
Boetcher Joeres, R.-E., 780
Boethius, 9, 458, 476, 630
Boettcher, W., 592
Boeva, L., 997, 1009, 1082
Bofarull i Terrades, M., 382
Bogacki, K., 33
Bogdal, K.-M., 763, 830
Bogdanov, A. V., 1014
Bogdanov, B., 1081
Bögels, T., 894
Bogert, R., 1073
Boggs, R. A., 642
Bogomolov, N. A., 1017, 1019,
  1022
Bogorov, I., 1079
Bogoslavskii, A., 1046
Bogusławski, A., 957, 961
Bohemond I (*Prince*), 7
Böhl de Faber, *see* Caballero, F.
Bohleber, W., 598
Bohm, A., 874, 1035
Böhm, K. W., 821
Böhme, H., 854
Böhme, J., 846
Böhmig, M., 1032

Bohn, W., 213, 343
Bohórquez Rincón, D., 423
Bohr, N., 566
Boiardo, M. M., 468, 469, 471,
  473–74, 481
Boiko, Iu., 1055
Boileau, N., 101, 108, 121,
  1008, 1010
Boillet, D., 483
Boine, G., 525
Bois, G., 50
Bois, P.-A., 723
Boisgontier, J., 44
Boissel, P., 43
Boisserée, S., 701
Boissinot, A., 153
Boisson, M., 213, 214
Boissy, J., 37
Boissy d'Anglas, F. (*comte*), 134
Boiste, P. C. V., 38
Boisvert, L., 46
Boix, C., 368
Böker, U., 586
Bokoam, S., 91–92
Boland, R., 412
Boldini, R., 529
Boldt, H., 795
Boldt, L. A., 169
Boldún y Conde, C., 316
Bolecki, W., 973, 979, 982
Bolelli, T., 440
Bolinger, D., 277
Bolívar, S. de, 418
Böll, H., 834, 849–50
Bollack, M., 717
Bollati, G., 526
Bolli, T., 828
Bolocan, G., 550, 553
Bologne, J.-C., 39
Bolognetti, F., 473
Bolotov, A. T., 1006, 1007
Bolzan, L., 175
Bolzoni, L., 507
Bombal, M. L., 417
Bomers, J., 817
Bommert, C., 872
Bona Castellotti, M., 511
Bonaccorso, G., 156
Bonaparte, L.-L., 559
Bonatti, M. L., 521
Bonaventura, N. von (*pseud.*),
  764, 780
Bonaviri, G., 532
Bond, D. G., 754, 846–47, 861
Bondar, O., 1053
Bondarenko, V., 1023, 1048
Bondarev, Iu. V., 1036
Bondarko, A. V., 993
Bondevik, J., 915
Boner, U., 633

Bonet, L., 328, 346, 364
Bonetto, E., 124
Boney, J., 85–86
Bonfadini, G., 442
Bonfils, C., 155
Bongard-Levin, G., 1015
Bongie, C., 181
Bonhomme, B., 155
Boniecka, B., 961
Boniface (*Saint*), 2
Bonifacio, G. B., 671
Bonifassi, G., 257
Böning, H., 682–83, 697
Bonito, V., 499
Bonitz, A., 827
Bonnaud, P., 258
Bonnefoy, Y., 209, 234, 236
Bonnet, J.-C., 195
Bonomi, I., 428
Bonora, E., 513, 520
Bonsanti, A., 530
Bonte, M., 210
Bontempelli, M., 529, 532, 536
Bonvesin de la Riva, 6
Bony, J., 175
Boo, M. L., 336
Boockmann, H., 633, 654
Boogaard, M., 882–83
Böök, F., 933
Booker, J. T., 170
Boon, L. P., 888, 900
Boons, J.-P., 41
Bopp, F., 735
Bopp, F., 15
Borba, F. S., 395
Borchard, B., 783–84
Borchardt, F. L., 464
Borchardt, R., 526, 812
Borchert, J., 788–89
Bordès, H., 116, 120
Bordeu, T., 132
Bordewijk, F., 887, 898
Bordier, R., 215
Bordier, S., 7
Borejszo, M., 970
Borek, H., 948, 957
Borel, D., 141
Borello, E., 425
Borello, R. A., 415
Borer, A., 188–89
Boretzky, N., 250
Borg, A., 917
Borges, J. L., 327, 413, 414,
  415, 535
Borghi, G., 487
Borgia, C., 462
Borie, J., 199
Borielo, A., 35
Borisova, L. M., 1014, 1040
Bork, H. D., 23

Borkowska, G., 983
Borm, W., 616
Bormann, A. von, 735, 811, 830
Born, M., 708
Born, N., 850
Born, P. Ch., 1024
Börne, L., 784
Borodin, L. B., 1045
Borodin, L. I., 1030
Borovikov, S., 1030
Borozdina, P. A., 1048
Borrego, A., 333
Borrel, A., 229
Borrero, J., 410
Borri, G., 510, 546
Borries, Erika von, 610
Borries, Ernst von, 610
Borromeo, C., 466
Borromeo, F., 493
Borrut, M., 155
Börsch-Supan, H., 761
Borsellino, N., 480, 543
Borsetto, L., 484, 487–88
Borsley, R. D., 958
Bortoni, S. M., 391, 399
Boruchoff, D. A., 407
Borukhov, B. L., 1043
Borup, J., 911
Boryś, W., 961
Borysiuk, I., 1053
Borysiuk, T., 1055
Bosboom, J., 897
Bosboom-Toussaint, A. L. G.,
  889, 897
Bosch, H., 656
Böschenstein, B., 757
Böschenstein, R., 730, 758
Boschini, M., 499
Bošković, S., 1076
Bosl, K., 624
Bosque, I., 280, 281
Bosredon-Tamba, B. I., 35
Boss, V., 1013
Bossé, D., 46
Bosse, H., 850, 931
Bossinade, J., 820, 847, 864
Bossle, L., 820
Bossong, G., 273
Bossuet, J.-B., 108, 117
Bossy, J., 486
Bossy, M.-A., 263
Bostoen, K., 885
Botano, N., 459
Botev, Kh., 1082
Bottari, P., 431–32
Botterill, S., 452
Böttger, F., 797
Bottoni, L., 480
Botzenhart, M., 776
Bou, E., 342, 344

Boubín, J., 940
Bouchard, A., 83
Bouché, T., 74
Boucherie, J.-L., 144
Bouchet, J., 85
Boudou, J., 255
Bougainville, L.-A. de, 230
Bougon, P., 237
Bouhours, D., 513–14
Bouilhet, L., 195
Bouis, A. V., 1046
Boukema, D., 885
Bouloumié, A., 244
Bounin, P., 155
Bounoure, G., 189
Bouquet, P., 935
Bourdaloue, L., 117
Bourdieu, P., 234
Bourdin, P., 28
Bourez, G., 135
Bourez, M.-T., 135
Bourgain, D., 48
Bourgeade, P., 25–26, 38
Bourgeois, L., 108
Bourgeois, R., 100
Bourget, P., 168, 193, 194
Bourgois, C., 169
Bourguet, P., 153
Bourguignon, J., 44, 189
Bourke, T. E., 759
Bourquin, J., 27
Boursier, N., 114
Bouscal, G. de, 108
Bousoño, C., 307
Boutier, M.-G., 36
Bouverot, D., 162
Bouvier, J.-C., 25
Bouwman, A. T., 889
Bouysse, A., 158
Bouzada Fernández, X., 400
Bova, A. C., 525
Bovi, T., 506
Boviatsis, A., 124
Bowen, B. C., 83
Bowen, D. J., 563
Bowen, G., 565
Bowen, Z., 565
Boyd, B., 1043, 1044
Boyer, H., 43, 135, 251, 255,
  383
Boyer, Z., 233
Boyle, C., 418
Boyle, M. O., 450
Boyle, N., 708–09
Boym, S., 183, 1033, 1043
Boyrié-Fénié, B., 253
Bozetto, R., 192
Bozhilov, B., 1081
Bozhilova, M., 1079
Bozhnev, B., 1035

Braak, M. ter, 898
Bracchi, R., 21, 442
Bradby, D., 127, 235
Brad-Chisacof, L., 550
Bradford, C. A., 365
Bradley, D. R., 4
Bradley-Croney, N., 59
Brady, P., 153, 205
Braet, H., 62
Braga, M. L., 393
Bragina, A. A., 1018
Brahe, T., 509
Braida, L., 497, 514
Brajović, T., 1075
Brakel, A., 391
Bralczyk, J., 964, 967
Brall, H., 640
Bramanti, V., 487
Brambilla Ageno, F., 452
Bramsbäck, B., 573
Bran, F. A., 696
Branca, V., 448, 449, 453
Branca-Rosoff, S., 38, 41, 140
Brancati, V., 526, 532, 545
Branco, A. H., 396
Brâncus, C., 554
Brâncuş, Gh., 550
Brand, C. P., 468
Brand, R., 729
Branda, P. O., 513
Brandão de Carvalho, J., 271
Brandes, G., 909
Brandes, H., 691, 783
Brandis, T., 616
Brandstetter, A., 859
Brandt, C., 655
Brandt, G., 594
Brandt, H., 776
Brandt, M., 601
Brandt, R., 642, 721
Branković, Đ., 1072
Brant, S., 633, 664
Brantly, S., 811
Brantner, C. E., 770
Brasillach, R., 212, 216, 220,
  224, 225
Brasseur, P., 45, 46
Bratman, M., 205
Bratranek, F. T., 804
Bratschi, A., 608
Bratu, A., 50
Bräuer, G., 812
Bräuer, R., 610, 614, 631
Brauer, U., 758
Brauer, W., 522
Brault, G. J., 53
Braun, F., 809, 829
Braun, H., 846
Braun, M., 850
Braun, S., 804

Braun, V., 738, 832, 840, 842, 850
Braungart, G., 674
Braungart, W., 676–77, 741
Brausse, U., 603
Bräutigam, B., 716
Bräutigam, G., 712–13
Bravo Elizondo, P., 418
Bravo García, E. M., 269–70, 277
Bray, B., 100, 115
Bray, L., 38
Braybrook, J., 88–89
Brea, M., 389, 398
Bréal, M., 15
Breathnach, D., 573
Breatnach, P. A., 577
Brebier, J., 72
Brecht, B., 151, 359, 679, 806, 810, 812–13, 816, 819, 825, 843, 846, 851, 852, 857
Brécy, R., 182
Bredero, G. A., 887, 892
Bredsdorff, E., 905
Bredsdorff, T., 905, 934
Breeze, A., 577–78
Bregoli-Russo, M., 455
Breido, E. M., 1043
Breitinger, J. J., 685
Bremer, E., 660
Brems, H., 887, 888, 899
Brenan, G., 369
Brenner, P. J., 777
Brentano, B., 692
Brentano, C., 689, 735, 736, 738, 740, 747–49, 758, 772, 801, 833
Bresciani, R., 534
Bresdin, R., 184
Brešić, V., 1073
Bretagne, P.-A., 192
Breteque, F. de la, 65
Breton, A., 209, 210, 217–18, 548
Breton, Y., 134
Bretón de los Herreros, M., 330–31
Breu, W., 990
Breuer, D., 666–67, 672, 675
Breuninger, R., 825
Breva-Claramonte, M., 267
Brewer, D., 639
Breza, E., 960, 965, 970
Březina, O., 938, 941
Briçonnet, G., 85
Bridgeman, T., 200
Bridges, G., 822
Bridgwater, P., 816
Briegleb, K., 795
Briganti, A., 528

Briganti, L., 432
Briggs, A. D. P., 1016, 1034
Bright, W., 12
Brigit (*Saint*), 577
Brignole Sale, A. G., 490, 505
Brincat, G., 444
Brincken, A.-D. von den, 611, 652
Brines, F., 353
Brink, J. R., 467
Brink-Friederici, C., 874
Brinkmann, H., 595, 650
Brinkmann, R. D., 848
Brinsmead, A.-M., 155
Brioschi, F., 537
Briossi, S., 491
Brisighella, C., 514–15
Brissac, (*comte*) de, 108
Brissoni, A., 507
Brissot, J.-P., 140
Bristol, E., 1013, 1033
Britnell, J., 85
Brito, A. M. B. de, 392
Britto García, L., 423
Britton, D., 8
Briuhhen, V., 1058
Briusov, V. Ia., 1017, 1026, 1027
Brix, M., 175–76
Briz, A., 277, 278
Briziarelli, S., 545
Brocchieri, M. F. B., 618
Brocense, El, *see* Sánchez de las Brozas
Broch, H., 769, 813
Brockes, B. H., 686
Brockmeier, P., 9
Brod, M., 809
Brodskaia, G., 1032
Brodskii, I. A., 1034, 1036
Brody, J., 112
Brodziński, K., 975
Broeder, P., 882
Brogan, H., 179
Brogi-Bercoff, G., 999, 1000
Bronnen, A., 809
Brons-Albert, R., 590–91
Bronskaia, L. I., 1035
Brønsted, P. O., 806
Brontë, E., 640
Bronzat, F., 256–57
Bronzini, G. B., 532
Brook, L. C., 62
Brook, P., 316, 319
Brooks, P., 197
Brooks, W. S., 121
Broos, T., 885
Brostrøm, T., 907
Brouard-Arends, I., 131–32
Broude, I., 1013, 1035

Broudic, F., 569
Brough, N., 812
Broussonet, P.-M.-A., 136
Brouwers, M., 886
Brovst, B. N., 912
Brower, K., 413
Brown, A., 132, 460
Brown, C. G., 88
Brown, H. M., 806, 812
Brown, J. E., 995
Brown, J. K., 688
Brown, J. L., 370, 371
Brown, R. E., 50–51, 641
Brown, S., 119
Browning, R., 231
Brownlee, K., 73, 76
Brownlee, M. S., 298
Brownlow, J. P., 336
Brownson, C., 173
Brożek, A., 964
Bruaas, E., 917–18
Bruce, E., 585
Bruce Novoa, J., 420
Bruchner, C., 61
Brucker, C., 30–31
Bruckmann, C., 711
Brückner, A., 965
Bruckner, M. T., 61
Brudermüller, S., 1050
Brüel, S., 928
Brugè, L., 434
Brugge-Hackett, S., 640
Brugmann, K., 26
Brügmann, M., 852
Bruguera, J., 376
Brummel, B., 181
Brun, B., 227
Bruneau, É., 206
Bruneau, J., 194, 195
Brunel, F., 140
Brunel, P., 190
Brunel-Lobrichon, G., 261
Bruner, J., 354
Brunet, F., 183
Brunet, J., 424, 430
Brunetti, G. D. B., 261
Bruni, D., 467, 503
Bruni, F., 426, 440
Bruni, L., 459, 460, 466, 485
Brünner, G., 592
Brunner, H., 614, 635, 644, 650, 659, 662
Bruno, F., 448
Bruno, G., 463, 480, 485–86, 769
Brunon, J.-C., 112–13
Brunot, F., 27, 101
Brusoni, G., 504
Bruto, G. M., 467
Bruyn, G. de, 766, 850

Bruyne, J. de, 283
Bryant, D., 171, 201
Bryce Echenique, A., 422
Brynach, S., 567
Brynhildsvoll, K., 817, 860
Bryś, G., 1020
Bryson, S. S., 158
Brzezina, M., 962
Brzeziński, J., 965
Brzovic, K., 809
Brzozowski, S., 977
Bucă, M., 553
Buccafusca, E., 529
Bucher, G., 241
Buchheim, W., 707–08
Buchholz, O., 1071
Buchko, D., 1054
Büchner, G., 775, 776, 784–87, 848, 850, 872
Büchner, L., 786, 787
Buck, A., 453
Bück, H., 648
Buck, T., 838
Budagov, R. A., 1018
Budai-Deleanu, I., 551
Buddecke, W., 812
Budé, G., 472
Budovičová, V., 950
Budrewicz, T., 977
Buelow, C. von, 422
Buendía López, J. L., 370
Buero Vallejo, A., 353, 359, 372, 373
Buettner, B., 449
Bufalino, G., 544
Buffa, F., 968
Buffard, M., 155
Buffat, M., 146, 243
Buffet, M., 99
Buffier, C., 27
Buffon, G.-L. L. (*comte*) de, 145
Bugajski, L., 983
Bugnion-Secretan, P., 118
Buhks, N., 1030
Bühler, K., 877
Buhr, G., 850–51
Buhtz, R., 838
Builo, K., 1067
Buinitski, I., 1066
Bukdahl, E. M., 144
Bukowska-Schielman, M., 977
Bukowski, P., 864
Bulanin, D. M., 998
Bulatova, R. V., 946–47
Bulatović, M., 1074
Bulgakov, M. A., 1028, 1036–38
Bulgakova, E., 1037
Bulgarelli, M., 533
Bulger, L. F., 395
Bullard, M. M., 465

Bullivant, K., 873
Bullock, A., 457, 477, 536
Bullock, B. E., 428
Buľovský, F., 946
Bülow, F. V., 830
Bulst, N., 619
Bulte, I., 900
Bultmann, R. K., 757
Bumke, J., 611, 638, 642, 643, 644
Bund, K., 8
Bunge, M., 718
Bungert, A., 820
Bunin, I. A., 1027, 1034, 1038
Buñuel, L., 344
Bunzel, W., 706
Buonarotti, P., 135
Buonarroti, F., 515
Buonarroti, M., 504
Buranok, O. M., 1008
Burat, T., 441–42
Burattelli, C., 502
Burckhardt, J., 453, 465, 479
Burdett-Jones, M. T., 563
Burdorf, D., 861
Burdziej, B., 977
Burek, T., 979
Burg, I. von, 615
Burgan, R., 952
Burgard, P. J., 718
Bürge, A., 858
Burg-Ehlers, L., 790
Burger, C., 654
Bürger, C., 735–36, 745, 764, 768–69, 772
Bürger, E., 691
Bürger, G. A., 685, 714
Burger, H., 835
Bürger, P., 343, 351
Burgers, W., 881
Burgess, G., 54
Burghartz, S., 618
Burgin, D. L., 1022
Burgos, J., 214
Buridant, C., 37
Burka, S., 739
Burke, E., 138, 521, 695, 720
Burke, J. F., 290
Burke, P., 457
Burkhardt, H., 794
Burkhart, J. L., 164
Burkhart, L. M., 406
Burkot, S., 976
Burlamacchi, V., 505
Burley, W., 463
Burliuk, D. D., 1033
Burmeister, B., 850
Burnam, B. B., 63
Burnett, C., 8
Burov, S., 1079

Burroughs, C., 461
Burton, R. D. E., 184, 185
Burtseva, T. A., 1045
Burwick, F., 177, 743–44
Burwick, R., 747
Bury, E., 111
Burzio, L., 18
Busby, K., 60
Busch, W., 787
Buschinger, D., 636, 641, 642, 644
Bushell, A., 842, 857
Busi, A., 532, 537
Busk-Jensen, L., 905
Bussche-Hünnefeld, J. H. von dem, 729
Busse, D., 603
Bussmann, M., 618
Bussy-Rabutin, R. de, 98, 109
Busta, C., 850
Busto Cortina, J. C., 300
Butcher, W., 203
Butenko, I., 1028
Butler, M., 835
Butler, R., 168, 206
Butler, S., 818
Butor, M., 236
Bútora, M., 955
Butt, J., 352
Buttler, D., 960, 961, 963
Büttner, M., 510
Büttner, W., 791
Butulussi, E., 602
Butzko, E., 826
Buuren, M. van, 887
Buxtehude, D., 680
Buynsters, P. J., 895
Buysse, C., 899
Buzássyová, K., 950, 956
Buzuk, P., 1064
Buzzati, D., 532
Buzzi, L., 171
Bybee, J., 281
Bygrave, S., 202
Bykhavets, I., 1067
Bykov, V. V., 1039
Byrd, S. W., 350
Byron, G. G. (*Lord*), 164, 357, 586, 953, 1072

Çabal, F., 372
Čabala, M., 951
Caballero, F., 328, 332
Caballero, J., 347
Caballero Escribano, E., 286
Cabaãas Vacas, P., 359
Cabanès, J.-L., 199
Cabani, M. C., 451, 469, 470
Cabré, M. T., 378

Cabrejas, G., 339
Cabrera, V., 313, 421
Cabrera Infante, G., 419
Cabrero, L., 408
Cáccamo, C. A., 400–01
Caccini, G., 504
Cacciotti, A., 452
Cacho Viu, V., 355
Cadete, T., 712
Cadioli, A., 526
Cadiot, P., 35
Caesarius of Heisterbach, 651
Caetani, F., 501–02
Caffiero, M., 513
Cage, J., 861
Cagnone, N., 528
Caillet, B., 155
Cailliot, N., 214
Caillois, R., 240
Caimari Frau, F., 270
Caimbeul, M., 587
Caimo, P., 469
Caira Lumetti, R., 523
Cairasco de Figueroa, B., 317
Caire, G., 134
Caire, P.-L., 249
Cairncross, J., 125
Caisso, C., 419
Calabrese, A., 428–29
Calandra, A., 466
Caldera, E., 331
Calderón de la Barca, P., 316, 317–20, 324, 336, 357, 750
Caldo Magno, E., 429
Caldwell, D., 858
Caleca, A., 483
Calenda, C., 504
Calero, C., 365
Calhoon, K. S., 726
Calimani, R., 466
Calin, W., 55, 57, 265
Callegari, L., 491–92
Calle-Gruber, M., 201, 243
Calles, J. M., 364
Callois, R., 871
Callou, D., 390
Calmet, A. (*dom*), 151
Calmeta, V., 479
Calomino, S., 507
Calore, M., 973
Caluwe, J. de, 877
Calvet, L.-J., 49
Calvi, M. V., 370
Calvin, J., 78
Calvino, I., 470, 532–33
Calvo Carilla, J. L., 328
Calvo Pérez, J., 267, 278
Calvo Sotelo, J., 372
Calzabigi, R. de', 521
Calzone, S., 528

Camacho, A., 419
Camargo, M., 9
Camarota, F. R., 448
Camartin, I., 811
Camasio, S., 530
Cambien, M., 167
Cambio, F., 838
Camenisch, C., 249
Cameron, K., 84
Caminero, J., 304, 310
Cammaert, J. F., 896
Camoens, L. de, 308
Camon, F., 537
Campana, D., 525, 528, 533
Campanella, T., 507
Campanile, A., 533
Campanini, Z., 511
Campbell, A., 584
Campbell, C. E., 93
Campbell, G. L., 12, 249, 266, 388, 425, 568, 570, 584, 914, 996, 1053
Campbell, J., 126, 371
Campbell, R., 348
Campe, J., 796, 797
Campillo, A., 363
Campion, E. J., 120
Campion, P., 197, 236
Campo, A. E.-P. del, 330, 411
Campo, J. L. A. de, 397
Campoamor, R. de, 329, 331
Campobello, N., 414
Camporeale, S. I., 458, 465
Campos, E., 403
Campos, H., 278
Campos, M. H. C., 392, 394
Campos, O. G. L. A. S., 395
Campos, R. A., 417
Camprubí, Z., 351
Camps, C., 44, 255, 264
Camus, A., 233, 236–37, 363, 374, 542
Camus, J.-P., 106, 109
Camus, R., 237
Canard, N.-F., 134
Cañas, D., 349
Canavaggio, J., 311, 313
Candaux, J.-D., 165
Canepa, E., 535
Canepari, L., 438
Canetti, E., 265, 809, 813, 845, 848
Canfield, M., 418
Canitz, F. R. L. von (*Freiherr*), 686
Cannon, J., 538
Cano, J. L., 346
Canonica de Rochemonteix, E., 323
Canosa, R., 496

Cansinos Assens, R., 342
Cantacuzino, C., 551
Cantalausa (L. Combes), 246
Cantatore, L., 526
Cantele, M., 527
Cantenac, (*sieur*) de, 118
Cantini, E., 521
Canziani, G., 464
Capaldo, M., 1000
Çape, R. I., 706
Capek, K., 943
Capello, G. F., 460, 467
Capidan, T., 554
Caplan, J. L., 160
Capodaglia, A., 533
Caporello-Szykman, C., 448
Capozzi, R., 526
Cappelluzzo Springolo, S., 439
Caprini, R., 256, 442
Caprioglio, S., 536
Caproni, G., 533, 545
Capucci, M., 499
Caracciolo, D., 512
Caracciolo, R., 462
Caracciolo Aricò, A., 484
Carafa, D., 462
Caramatie, B., 224
Caramuel y Lebkowitz, J., 507–08
Carancha (Sánchez del Campo, J.), 352
Carandini, S., 501
Carassus, E., 194
Caravaggi, G., 307, 308
Caravaggio, M. da, 111
Caravolas, J., 267
Carboncini, S., 683
Carbone, P., 545
Carbone, R., 540
Carco, F., 211
Cardaillac, L., 302
Cardano, G., 507
Cardenal, E., 413, 421
Cardinal, M., 233
Cardinaletti, A., 433–34
Cardini, F., 618
Cardini, R., 479, 484
Cardona, R., 359
Cardone, C., 1014
Cardoso, J., 398
Cardoso, S. A. M., 393, 396, 399, 401
Cardoza y Aragón, L., 419
Carducci, G., 523, 548
Cardwell, R. A., 188, 332
Carena, C., 546
Carenas, F., 338
Carillo, D. A., 420–21
Carle, B., 548
Carles, P., 204

Carlier, M., 887
Carli Piccolomini, B., 460
Carl Ludwig (_Elector Palatine_), 669
Carlson, M., 234, 1015, 1016
Carlyle, T., 701
Carmiggelt, S., 885
Carnel, A., 49
Carner, J., 351
Carnero, G., 365
Çarnicke, S. M., 1014
Čarnogurská, M., 951
Caro, A., 323
Carofiglio, V., 170
Caroli, G., 465
Caroline (_Landgräfin of Hesse-Homburg_), 758
Carossa, H., 813
Carové, F. W., 749
Carpaccio, V., 229
Carpenter, C. A., 360
Carpenter, H., 73
Carpenter, S., 157
Carpentier, A., 414, 419
Carr, G. J., 820
Carrai, S., 475
Carrannante, A., 525
Carrasco, I., 417
Carrasco, M., 619
Carratore, E. del, 398
Carré, D., 570
Carreão, A., 310, 321, 331, 364
Carrère, B., 202
Carrero Eras, P., 342
Carrete Redondo, C., 306
Carrier, C., 1010
Carrière, M., 763
Carrillo, F., 408
Carrillo Alonso, A., 330
Carrió de la Vandera, A., 406, 409
Carrión, M. M., 419
Carroll, L., 205, 344
Carroll, L. L., 481
Carsten, S., 1032
Carstensen, B., 604
Carsuel, S., 572
Cartagena, A. de, 297
Cartago, G., 445
Cartelier, J., 142
Carter, H., 562
Carter, T., 503–04
Cartier, J., 47
Carton, F., 44
Cartwright, J., 890
Carulla, M., 383
Carus, G. G., 708
Caruso, P., 392
Carvalhão Buescu, M. L., 402
Carvalho, J. B. de, 389, 390–91

Carvalho, J. G. H. de, 402
Carvalho, M. J. A., 394, 403
Carvalho, N. F., 396
Casadei, A., 539
Casadei, F., 439
Casal, J. del, 410, 419
Casale, O. S., 499
Casanova, G., 734, 816
Casanova, J. de S., 154
Casanova, J.-Y., 264
Casares, C., 367
Casares, J., 342
Casas Gómez, M., 281
Casati, A., 533
Cascardi, A. J., 313
Cascardi, A. L., 311
Case, T., 320–21
Casey, T. J., 767
Casini, S., 541
Casona, A., 360
Caspart, H. K., 697
Cassata, L., 452
Cassedy, S., 1031
Cassieri, G., 526
Cassiodorus, 625
Cassirer, E., 693
Cassola, C., 533
Cassou, J., 225
Castagnola, R., 464
Castan, F. M., 264
Castañer Martín, R. M., 286
Castano Musicò, L., 475
Castellana, L., 439
Castellani, A., 14, 16, 426
Castellani, C., 132
Castellanos, R., 420
Castellet, J. M., 346
Castelloza, 260, 261
Castelnuovo, E., 416
Castiglione, B., 467, 484, 486, 672
Castilho, A. T. de, 388, 389, 396
Castillo, A., 352
Castillo, D. A., 335
Castillo, M. del, 36
Castoldi, M., 476
Castori, C., 516
Castrillo Márquez, R., 302
Castro, A., 345
Castro, G. de, 315
Castro, I., 326
Castro, R. de, 328, 331–32, 364
Castro Duarte, D. M. C. de, 389
Castro Klarén, S., 422
Catalano, G., 535
Cataldi, P., 538
Catania, L., 525
Cate, A. P. ten, 599
Cátedra, P. M., 289, 296

Catherine II (_Empress_), 146, 1002, 1006, 1007
Catherine of Siena (_Saint_), 618
Cattaneo, G., 531, 799
Cattaneo, M. A., 694
Catucci, M., 521, 522
Catullus, 469
Çaty, M. P., 186
Čaušev, A., 41
Cavaglion, A., 547
Cavaillac, C., 110
Cavaion, D., 1000
Cavalcanti, G., 451, 452
Cavallero, P. A., 295
Cavalli, G. G., 490
Cavallini, G., 499, 525, 537
Cavallini, I., 503, 504
Cave, T., 83
Caverzasio, C., 521
Caviceo, J., 459
Caviola, H., 859
Cazauran, N., 78, 83
Cazelles, B., 63
Cazenobe, C., 152, 155
Cazotte, J., 154
Céard, J., 78, 79, 86–87, 454
Ceccaroni, A., 544
Cecchi, E., 539
Cecchi, G., 502, 503
Çecco Angiolieri, 828
Čechová, M., 967
Cederni, B., 484
Cederquist, I., 924
Cejador, J., 355
Cela, C. J., 368–69
Celan, P., 847, 850–51, 886
Celaya, G., 347, 365
Celebrino, E., 478
Celestine V (_Pope_), 536
Celeyrette-Pietri, N., 231
Celiano, L., _see_ Grillo, A.
Céline, L.-F., 199, 210, 211, 218, 423
Cellard, J., 37–38, 38
Cellini, B., 474, 483, 486, 700
Celma Valero, M. P., 326, 341
Cendrars, B., 218
Cendré, L., 208
Cennamo, M., 19, 427
Censer, J. R., 137
Centeno, E., 374
Çentovalli, B., 545
Čepan, O., 954
Cepl-Kaufmann, G., 689, 856
Cerbo, A., 482
Cerenza, G. O., 216
Cerezo, M. del C., 423
Cerezo Galán, P., 356
Cernuda, L., 341, 342, 343, 345, 346, 347, 351

Cerquiglini, B., 28
Cerquiglini-Toulet, J., 70
Cerretani, B., 486
Cerrón-Palomino, R., 284
Cerruti, M., 521
Cerullo, D., 541
Cervantes, M. de, 288, 304, 308, 311–13, 354, 365, 472, 779, 1005
Cervenka, M., 938, 941
Cervera Fras, M. J., 301, 303
Cervini, M., 455
Cervoni, J., 34–35
Césaire, A., 217
Cesareo, F. C., 465
Cesarini, V., 506
Ceserani, R., 527
Cesi, F., 508
Céspedes y Meneses, G. de, 270, 311
Cetti Marinoni, B., 824
Cevallos, F. J., 408–09
Chaban, T., 1066
Chabanenko, V., 1052
Chabás, J., 342
Chabut, M.-H., 146, 147
Chacel, R., 343, 369
Chachot, Ia., 1066
Chadwick, C., 191
Chagall, M., 544
Chai, L., 180–81
Chaikovskaia, O. G., 1033
Chaikovs'kyi, A., 1058
Chaillon de Pestain, 293
Chaitin, G. D., 175
Chaitlíne, B., 577
Chakroun, S., 602
Chalas, Y., 133
Challe, R., 106, 109, 154
Chalon, J., 176
Chalukova, T., 1080
Chalupecký, J., 943
Chalupka, J., 954
Chalykova, T., 995
Chamata, N., 1057
Chamberlain, H. S., 187
Chamberlain, N., 352
Chamberlin, D. F., 418
Chamberlin, V. A., 334, 335, 336
Chambers, D., 453
Chambers, H., 825–26
Chambers, R., 170, 185
Chambige, H., 193, 194
Chambon, J.-P., 21, 40, 190, 248, 255, 258, 259
Chamfort, N. S. R. dit de, 140
Chamisso, A. von, 740, 749
Chamorro Martínez, J. M., 274
Champfleury, 176, 192, 194

Champlain, S., 109
Chances, E., 1036
Chang-Rodríguez, R., 406
Chao, R., 423
Chapco, E., 112
Chapeaurouge, D. de, 618
Chaperon, D., 193, 220
Chappuzeau, S., 124
Char, R., 218–19
Chardin, J. B. S., 229
Charlemagne, 2, 4, 54, 55, 263
Charles II (*King of England*), 522
Charles V (*Emperor*), 478
Charles d'Orléans, 70, 71, 212
Charles Emmanuel I (*Duke of Savoy*), 493, 497
Charles Emmanuel II (*Duke of Savoy*), 497
Charlet, J. L., 475
Charnitski, M., 278
Charpentier, F., 82, 84, 85, 91
Charrière, I. de, 140
Charron, P., 118
Chartier, A., 75
Chartier, P., 221
Chartier, R., 133
Chartoritskaia, T. V., 997
Chashchina, L., 1049
Chassignet, J. B., 92
Chastellain, G., 73, 74
Chateaubriand, F.-R. de, 127, 163, 164
Chaucer, G., 9, 450
Chauchadis, C., 288
Chaudenson, R., 26
Chaussée, F. de la, 28
Chaussier, C., 139
Chauveau, J.-P., 101, 102, 120
Chauvin, J., 257
Chaves, A. S., 399
Chávez, R., 312
Chávez Álvarez, F., 637
Chebotareva, V. A., 1037
Checa, J., 311
Checchi, G., 517–18
Chédozeau, B., 116
Chekalina, E. M., 901
Chekhov, A. P., 242, 955, 1017–19, 1048
Chekhov, M., 1032
Chekova, I., 998
Cheles, L., 461
Chemris, C., 308
Chenerie, M.-L., 61
Chenet, F., 214
Chénier, A., 135, 136
Chénier, M.-J., 164
Chennevière, G., 208
Cheong, K. Y., 816

Chepurko, O., 1061
Cherashniaia, D. I., 1042, 1043
Cherchenko, N., 1061
Cherchi, P., 427, 449, 486
Cherednichenko, V., 1031
Cherevatenko, L., 1059
Cherkasenko, S., 1058
Chernykh, V. A., 1035
Chernysh, T., 1052
Chernyshev, A., 1036
Cherpillod, G., 202
Cherubim, D., 594
Cherviakov, A. I., 1014
Chesnaye, N. de la, 93
Chessex, J., 196
Chesterfield, P. D. Stanhope (*4th Earl of*), 486
Chevalier, J.-C., 27, 28
Chevalier, M., 311, 312
Chevallier, M., 116
Chevereau, A., 176
Chiabrera, G., 490, 500, 501, 505
Chiampi, J. T., 473
Chia-Olivares, I., 420
Chiappini, G., 307
Chiarelli, G., 546
Chiari, P., 521
Chiarini, G., 531
Chiarloni, A., 860
Chibnall, M., 63
Chica, F., 344
Chicharro Chamorro, A., 345
Chiesa, M., 473
Chigi, A., 492
Chigi, F., *see* Alexander VII (*Pope*)
Chimenti, V., 535
Ching, B., 115
Chiniac de la Bastide, P. de, 149
Chinnov, I. V., 1022, 1033, 1035
Chiodo, D., 482
Chirikov, E., 1030
Chisick, H., 137
Chitnis, B., 204
Chittolini, G., 464
Chiusano, I. A., 533–34
Chivilikhin, V. A., 1028
Chivu, Gh., 551
Chmel, R., 953
Chobanov, I., 1080
Chocheyras, C., 60
Chocheyras, J., 100
Chociary, R., 395
Chodorow, N., 335
Chodowiecki, D., 727, 731
Choi, J. S., 357
Choisy, F.-T. de (*abbé*), 109

Chojak, J., 957, 961
Chojnacki, J., 970
Choldin, M. T., 1030
Chollet, R., 168
Chomsky, N., 18, 878
Chongarova, I., 995, 1078
Chorny, K., 1067
Choroś, M., 964
Chorpenning, J. F., 298, 310
Chotard, L., 178, 199
Chothia, J., 206
Chouillet, A.-M., 146
Chouillet, J., 143, 145
Chrétien de Troyes, 7, 54, 56, 57, 58–60, 62, 63, 65–66, 643, 644, 647, 890
Chrisalita, R., 420
Christ, G., 41
Christ, L., 813
Christensen, E. M., 905, 913
Christensen, I., 911, 912
Christensen, K. K., 918–19
Christensen, P. G., 1018
Christianson, G., 656
Christina (*Saint*), 64
Christina (*Queen of Sweden*), 505–06
Christine de Pizan, 74, 75, 76–77
Christine of Bourbon (*Duchess of Savoy*), 497
Christmann, H. H., 15, 37
Chub, D., 1056
Chudakova, M. O., 1036–37, 1049
Chudoba, A., 955
Chudomir, 1082
Chuglov, V. I., 992
Chukhontsev, O. G., 1033
Chukovskii, K. I., 1026, 1027, 1039, 1051
Chumacero, A., 420
Chumak, V., 1058
Chupasheva, O. M., 993
Chupeau, J., 112
Chuprinin, S., 1029
Chvany, C. V., 992, 993
Chvatík, K., 944, 945
Chwin, S., 981
Chyhrynau, I., 1067
Chykvin, Ia., 1067
Cialoni, D., 518
Ciani, I., 546
Cicaut (*Saint*), 62
Ciccuto, M., 448, 525
Ciceri, M., 297
Cicero, 22, 58, 297, 458, 617
Cichon, P., 251
Cid Uribe, M., 276
Cieco da Ferrara, F., 457, 480

Cierbide Martinena, R., 247–48
Cieslik, K., 611, 631, 648
Cieślikowa, A., 970
Cieza de León, P., 408
Cifuentes, B., 271
Cifuentes, L. F., 328
Çigada, S., 29
Çigoja, B., 1071
Cilianu-Lascu, C., 550
Cima, A., 538
Cinque, G., 431
Cintra, L. F. L., 389
Cioffi, C. A., 6
Ciolac, M., 550
Cioni, A., 528
Cirillo, G., 503
Cirillo, N. R., 199
Cirillo, T., 491
Cirlot, V., 288
Ciseri, I., 461
Cismaru, A., 239
Citron, P., 168, 222
Citti, P., 210
Ciuffa, A., 528
Civitareale, P., 529
Cixous, H., 233, 330, 366, 372
Claassens, G. H. M., 889
Claesson, S., 929
Claesz van Dorp, J., 894
Claisse, B., 191
Clamurro, W. H., 311
Clancy, J. P., 566
Claren, L., 669
Clarín, *see* Alas, L.
Clark, N., 892
Clarke, A. H., 333, 337
Clarke, P. C., 461
Clarke, S., 724–25
Classen, A., 70, 636, 637–38, 645–46, 647, 648, 658, 659
Claudel, H., 219
Claudel, P., 167, 180, 208, 210, 212, 219
Claudius, M., 714, 805
Claudon, F., 172
Claus, H., 885, 887, 900
Clausen, B., 864
Clausen, J., 863
Claussen, H., 709
Claussen, S., 909
Claval, S., 39–40
Clavel, B., 36
Clavuot, O., 485
Clédat, L., 27
Clej, A., 54
Clement IX (*Pope*), 501
Clément, A., 256
Clément, M., 181
Clementelli, E., 528
Clements, I. C., 404–05

Clénard, N., 267
Clercq, J. de, 26, 27
Clerici, L., 540–41
Clier-Colombani, F., 68
Clivio, G. P., 441
Clodius, C. A. H., 732
Closs, A., 616
Cloulas, I., 464
Clowes, E. W., 1040
Clubb, L. G., 479
Clubb, W. G., 479
Clyne, D., 584
Coates, P., 981
Cobo, B., 408
Cobo, E., 328
Cobos, P. de A., 356
Coca Senande, J., 296
Coccia, P., 470
Coccioli, C., 525
Cocciolo, F., 440
Cochem, 698
Cochin, C.-N., 140
Cochrane, L. G., 133
Cock, J. de, 142
Cockerham, H., 161
Cockx-Indestege, E., 894
Cocteau, J., 220, 233
Cofano, D., 530, 537
Coggio, R., 123
Coghlan, B., 806
Cogman, P. W. M., 185
Cohen, H., 146, 682
Cohen, H. R., 418
Cohen, L., 929
Cohen Imach, V., 416
Cohn, R. G., 187
Coirault, Y., 114
Colatrella, C., 179
Colbois, S., 165
Colecchia, F. M., 348, 350
Coleman, R., 11, 12, 21
Coleridge, S. T., 352, 743, 744
Colet, L., 196
Colette, 185, 210, 220, 233
Coligny, G. de, 90
Colin, A., 851
Colin, J.-P., 38, 49
Colin, R.-P., 180, 203
Colinas, A., 365
Coll, P., 381
Colla, F., 415
Collard, P., 419
Collberg, S. D., 925
Colleoni, B., 486
Colli, G., 801
Collier, P., 190
Collin, H. J. von, 715
Collina, B., 486
Collinet, J.-P., 101, 102, 103
Collini, P., 838

Collinot, A., 38
Collins, K., 105
Collins, M. S., 339
Colliot, R., 60, 68
Collot d'Herbois, J.-M., 136, 158
Colocci, A., 455–56
Coloma, L., 328
Colomb, R., 171
Colombat, A. P., 240
Colombo, A., 432, 497–98, 500, 525, 532, 538
Colomina, J., 377, 381
Colón, G., 21, 402
Colonna, V., 471, 477, 484
Colucci, B., 10
Coluccia, R., 436
Columbus, C., 407, 408, 491
Colussi, G., 436
Combarieau du Gres, M., 55–56
Combarieu, M. de, 65, 247
Combe, D., 224, 243
Combeaud, B., 159
Combet, L., 311
Comenius, *see* Komenský, J. A.
Commynes, P. de, 76, 77
Compagna Perrone Capano, A. M., 426
Compan, A., 256
Company, C., 273
Comparot, A., 84
Compère, D., 202
Compitello, M. A., 368
Compton, T. G., 421
Comrie, B., 392
Comtessa de Dia, 261
Conchado, D., 331
Concina, E., 485
Condé, L. P., 338, 339, 412
Condè, M., 160
Conde, M., 369
Conde Lucanor, 300
Condillac, E. B. de, 140, 719
Condivi, A., 474
Condorcet, J.-A.-N. de C. (*marquis*), 134, 136, 140, 146
Condradt, G., 861
Conejo, D., 140
Conermann, K., 665
Confais, J.-P., 49
Conio, G., 1012
Conley, T., 87
Conlon, P. M., 137
Connolly, J. E., 295
Connon, D. F., 160
Connors, K., 46
Conon de Bethune, 51
Conrad, J., 222
Conrad, J. L., 1018

Conrieri, D., 494
Conroy, P. V., 146
Consarelli, B., 135
Constable, J., 236
Constant, B., 136, 161, 163, 164–65, 180
Constant, J. de, 154
Constant, J.-M., 83
Constant d'Hermenches, D. L. (*baron*), 140
Contarino, R., 527
Contat, M., 171
Conti, B., 531
Conti, G. de', 477
Conti, L., 508, 509
Continati, D., 533
Contini, G., 526, 534, 546
Contini, M., 23, 446
Contò, A., 456
Contoblacas, A., 459
Contreras, F. de, 308
Convery, A., 561
Conz, K. P., 758
Cook, A., 191
Cook, M., 117, 154
Coolput, C.-A. van, 58
Cooper, B., 994
Cooper, B. T., 177, 178
Cooper, R., 80, 82
Coornhert, D. V., 892
Copceag, D., 17
Copeau, J., 212–13, 234
Copernicus, N., 508
Coppens, C., 894
Copper, J. M., 1015
Coquard, O., 142
Corazza, B. del, 486
Corazzini, S., 528
Corbatta, J., 416
Corbett, G., 957
Corbett, N., 47
Corbière, T., 186
Corbin, A., 886
Corbin, D., 40
Corbin, P., 39, 40
Corblin, F., 27
Corcoran, M. C., 262
Cord, W. O., 806
Corday, C., 691
Cordier, M., 192
Cordin, P., 442–43
Cordonier, N., 190
Ćorić, B., 1071
Coriello, M., 528
Corkhill, A., 706
Cormack, L. B., 453
Cormeau, C., 615, 647
Cormier, M., 154
Cormier, R., 641–42
Cornagliotti, A., 426, 442

Cornazzano, A., 486
Corne, B., 570
Corneille, P., 99, 100, 120, 121–22, 123, 127, 130, 226, 523
Corneille, T., 517
Cornej, P., 940
Cornelissen, G., 607
Cornille, J.-L., 187
Cornilliat, F., 86
Cornish, F., 32
Cornud-Peyron, M., 243
Cornuz, J., 798
Cornwell, N., 1041
Corominas, J., 268, 269
Corominas, J. M., 308
Coromines, J., 253, 375, 378, 380, 382
Coronado, C., 332
Corot, J. B. C., 229
Corra, B., 529
Corradini, M., 504–05
Correa, G., 349
Correa Ramírez, A., 284
Correnti, S., 529
Corriente Córdoba, F., 300
Corrigan, T., 863
Corsetti, J.-P., 178, 194
Cortázar, J., 357, 414, 415–16
Corte, L., 478
Cortelazzo, M., 443
Cortés, H., 407
Cortese, G., 465
Cortés Rodríguez, L., 279
Corti, G., 484, 488
Corti, M., 534, 546
Corti, V., 530
Cortínez, V., 407, 417–18
Cortini, M. A., 504
Corum, R. T., Jr, 105
Corvin, H., 206
Cosentino, C., 862–63
Coseriu, E., 41, 280
Cosgrove, C., 420
Cosić, D., 1074
Cosman, M., 76
Cosman, W., 76
Cosset, E., 206
Cossío, J. M. del, 334
Costa, G., 41, 545
Costa, I. da, 885
Costa, J., 338, 355
Costa, M., 297
Costa, M. C. R., 398
Costa, M. I. G. G. A. da, 389
Costa, M. R. V., 399
Costa Ferrandis, J., 369
Costantini, A., 444, 543
Costas Goberno, J. M., 370
Costas González, X. H., 401

Costa-Zalessow, N., 451
Coste, G., 109
Costo, T., 494, 504
Coston, F.-G. de, 172
Coteanu, I., 550
Cothran, B. F., 755
Cotta, J. F., 701, 732
Cotta-Schønberg, M., 912
Cotticelli, F., 518
Cottignoli, A., 524
Cottingham, J., 118, 119
Cottrell, R. D., 85, 96
Cottret, B., 131
Coturri, E., 460
Coué, S., 623
Coulet, H., 106, 156
Coulson, A. S., 793
Coulson, F. C., 7
Couperus, L., 887, 897–98
Couprié, A., 126
Courteline, G., 206
Courtilz de Sandras, G. de, 137
Courtney, C. P., 154, 164, 165
Courtois, B., 39
Court-Perez, F., 178
Coussot, D., 206
Coustau, P., 81
Couto, H. H., 404
Couton, G., 100
Coutreau, J., 331
Couturier, M., 72
Cova, P., 172
Covarrubias, S. de, 266, 267
Còveri, L., 424, 444
Covo, J., 337
Coward, D., 156
Coward, R., 187
Cowling, D., 87
Cox, R. A. V., 584, 585
Cox Davis, N., 309
Craddock, J., 14
Craig, C. M., 769
Craig, G., 212
Cramer, S., 865
Crampé, B., 79
Crampton, P., 933
Cranston, M., 148
Cravens, T. D., 14, 16
Craveri, B., 135
Creaseman, B., 1018
Crébillon, C.-P. J. de, 152
Cremer, J., 888
Crépel, P., 134
Crespin, J., 90
Creutz, G. P., 143
Creuzer, F., 691
Crevatin, G., 486
Crèvecoeur, M. G. J. de, 143
Crévenat-Werner, D., 44
Criado, I., 342

Criado de Val, M., 304, 306
Crisafulli Jones, L. M., 520
Criscenti Grassi, A., 139
Crispin, J., 352
Crist, L. S., 67
Cristando, W., 118
Cristea, T., 11
Critchfield, R., 718, 821
Crnjanski, M., 1074, 1075
Cro, S., 407
Croce, B., 498, 531, 534
Croce, F., 505, 538
Crone, C. C. S., 888
Cronin, G. L., 982
Cronin, M., 578
Cropp, G. M., 247, 261
Cros, C., 186
Cros, S. du, 108
Cross, A. G., 1002, 1005, 1006
Cross, J. E., 3
Crossley, C., 182
Crouzet, M., 172, 198, 225
Crowe, N., 1002
Crowther, P., 720
Crudeli, T., 521
Cruickshank, D. W., 315
Cruitrode, J. van, 887
Cruz, J., 344
Cruz, M. L. S. da, 402
Cruz Casado, A., 310
Cruz Mendizábal, J., 370
Csokor, F. T., 813, 824, 851
Cubberley, P., 991
Cubelier de Beynac, J., 454
Cucchi, E., 858
Cucini, G. P., 528
Cuenca, L. A. de, 364, 365
Cuenca, M. J., 378–79
Cuénin, M., 116
Cuénin-Lieber, M., 97–98
Cuesta Abad, J. M., 345–46
Cueto, R., 305, 348
Cuevas, C., 308
Çuevas García, C., 307
Čulík, J., 944
Cull, J. T., 296, 312
Cullen, L. M., 573
Cummins, B., 118
Cuneo, M. da, 408
Cunha, A. G., 397
Cunha, C., 399
Cunită, A., 11
Cunningham, A., 698
Çunqueiro, A., 369
Čupić, D., 1071, 1072
Curat, H., 32–33
Curi, F., 544
Curial, H., 121
Currà, G., 507
Curros Enríquez, M., 332

Curschmann, M., 650
Curtin, J., 977
Curtis, J. A. E., 1037
Curtius, E. R., 615
Cussen, A., 410
Cvetanović, V., 1076
Cymborska-Leboda, M., 1015
Cyprian (*Metropolitan*), 1000
Cyrano de Bergerac, S. de, 109
Czaykowski, B., 976
Czech, J., 938–39
Czechowski, H., 738, 851
Czerniakowska, E., 966
Czerniawski, A., 976, 977, 980, 981
Czernik, S., 978
Czuchnowski, M., 978
Czucka, E., 784
Czurda, E., 851–52
Czyżewski, M., 967

Daalder, S., 877
Daan, J., 879
Dabit, E., 211
Dąbrowska, E., 967
Dąbrowski, S., 979
D'Achille, P., 427
Dadoun, R., 226
Dadour, G.-A., 548
Dadson, T. J., 306
Dagenais, J., 293
Dagenais, L., 29
Dagerman, S., 933
Dagon, J., 111
Dahan, J.-R., 179
Dahl, O. C., 918
Dahlerup, P., 908, 911
Dahlgrün, C., 643
Dahlström, B., 929, 935
Dahlström, M., 933
Dahmen, W., 556
Dahnke, H.-D., 742
Dahrendorf, R., 797
Daigger, A., 824
Dajmić, D., 1073
Dal', V. I., 1078
Dalbera, J.-P., 246, 256
Dalberg, V., 904
Dalché, P. G., 8
Dalchev, A., 1082
Dalemans, J., 874
Dalençon, J., 183
D'Alessandro, L., 519
Dali, S., 217, 347
Dalin, O. von, 930
Dallapiazza, M., 659
Dallmann, S., 602
Dal Pozzo, C., 493
Daly, M. E., 573–74

Damashevich, U., 1065
Damborský, J., 964
D'Ambrosio, M., 529
D'Amico, J., 480
D'Amico, S., 530
Damm, S., 839, 852
Dammann, G., 669
Damme, R., 660
Damourette, J., 26, 27
Damrosch, D., 619
Dan, D., 553
Danahy, M., 166
Danaly, M., 177
Dancourt, F. C., 107
Dandrey, P., 102, 104, 124
Danélan, C. F., 173
Danell, K. J., 923
Danesi, M., 15, 441
Danford, K., 804
Dangel, E., 852
Dānī, al-, 303
Daniel, J.-L., 258
Daniel, R. R., 186
Daniel, S., 188
Danielewiczowa, M., 961–62
Daniil, 1078
Daniil Zatochnik, 1000
Danil'chyk, Z., 1064
Danilevskii, A. A., 1023
Danilov, M. V., 1007
Danilovich, M., 1065
D'Annunzio, G., 528, 544
Danow, D. K., 1031, 1036, 1045
Dante Alighieri, 15, 263, 426,
    447, 451, 474, 479, 489, 535,
    768, 1022, 1038
Danyliuk, N., 1053
Danzi, M., 475
Da Ponte, L., 547
Darby, D., 813
Darcel, J.-L., 166
Darcos, X., 150, 151–52
Dardano, M., 430, 467
Dardel, R. de, 23
Dar'ialova, L. N., 1050
Darío, R., 351, 353
Dark, O., 1029
Darmon, J.-C., 110
Darmsteter, A., 15
Darnton, R., 139
D'Arrigo, S., 525, 527, 534
Daru, M., 172
Daru, P., 171
Darwin, C., 909
Dasaeva, T., 1069
Dascălu-Jinga, L., 552
D'Ascia, L., 460
Dasenbrock, R. W., 451
Dashkevych, Ia., 1052, 1055
Dashkova, E. R. (*Princess*), 1007

Dashwood, J. R., 543
Dassanowsky-Harris, R. von,
    865
Dassonville, M., 87
Dasté, M.-H., 212
Däubler, T., 814
Daudet, A., 175, 180, 194, 358
Daumal, R., 220
Daumier, H., 544
Dauphiné, C., 202
Dauphiné, J., 92
Dauthendey, M., 810
Dauven-van Knippenberg, C.,
    657
Davaux, J.-B., 133
Daviau, D. G., 829, 848
Davico Bonino, G., 502
David, J.-C., 142, 143
David, J. J., 803
David, M., 541
Davidheiser, J. C., 828
Davidis, M., 776
Davies, C., 331, 367
Davies, G., 188
Davies, G. A., 330–31
Davies, H. W., 565
Davies, J., 108, 1019
Davies, M. L., 740, 770
Davies, P., 255
Davies, S., 150
Davis, C. K., 332
Davis, G. W., 877
Davis, M. E., 418
Davis, W. S., 693
D'Avray, D. L., 8
Davydov, N. V., 1024
Davydov, Z. D., 1024
Dawson, R. L., 139
Daxelmüller, C., 632
Day, L. T., 238
De Agostini, D., 204
Dean, T., 460
De Anna, L., 436
Debauve, J.-L., 157, 186
Debax, M., 291
Debenedetti, G., 526
De Benedictis, M., 536
Debicki, A. P., 366
De Blasi, L., 444
De Blasi, N., 444
De Bleeker, D., 884
Debon, C., 214
Debon, G., 750, 822
Debray, R., 237
Debrie, R., 43
Dębski, J., 998
Debu, J., 88
De Bujanda, J. M., 457
Debus, F., 609, 947–48
De Caprio, C., 533

De Carlo, A., 527
Decat, M. B. N., 393
Décaudin, M., 191, 213–14
De Ceccady, R., 541
De Cesare, G. B., 484, 491
De Cesare, R., 168, 170
Decker, C., 801, 860, 863, 871
Decroisette, F., 521–22
Decyk, W., 966
Dedert, H., 732
Dédéyan, C., 147, 168
Dediukhina, V. S., 1006
Dedkov, I., 1028, 1029, 1039
Dedner, B., 785–86
De Dominicis, A., 429
De Dominis, M., 508
De Donato, G., 536
De Donno, N., 534
Deel, T. van, 888
Dees, A., 14, 28
Defaux, G., 85, 125
Defays, J.-M., 182
De Felice, E., 434
De Ferrariis, *see* Galateo, A.
Deffis de Calvo, E. I., 308
Defilippis, D., 462
De Filippo, E., 530
De Frede, C., 478
Defrenne, M., 128
De Gaulle, C. A. J. M., 100
Degn, I., 244
Deguise, P., 161, 165
Deguy, J., 224
Deguy, M., 297
Deianova, M., 1079
Deichsler, H., 652
Deiritz, K., 830
DeJean, J., 99
Déjean, J.-L., 85
Dejna, K., 964
Delabar, W., 856
Delacroix, D., 187
Delaisement, G., 199
Delaperrière, M., 981
De La Tailhède, R., 208
Delaty, S., 186
Delavouët, M.-P., 265
Delay, P., 254
Delblanc, S., 929, 933
Delbouille, P., 161
Del Col, A., 466
Delcorno, C., 447
Delcorno Branca, D., 448, 475
Delcourt, D., 77
Delcroix, M., 128
Delden, M. van, 420
Deledda, G., 525, 527
Delègue, Y., 90
Deleu, J., 888
Deleuze, G., 240, 349

Delfini, A., 534
Delfosse, H. P., 799–800
Delft, K. von, 787
Delgado, J., 414
D'Elia, F., 466
Delibes, M., 369
Delić, J., 1075, 1076–77
Delille, J., 162
Delisle de la Drévetière, L. F., 142
Della Bella, A., 1072
Della Casa, G., 476, 477
Della Chiesa, F. A., 497
Dell'Agata, G., 1000
Della Mea, L., 527
Della Porta, G. B., 464, 507
Della Porte, G., 126
Della Valle, F., 481
Dellepiane, A. B., 270
Dellian, E., 724–25
Del Litto, V., 171, 172
Delmas, B., 134
Delmas, C., 128
Delmonte, D., 410
Delmonte, R., 434
Deloffre, F., 111, 154
Delomez, G., 192
Delomier, D., 25
Delon, M., 142, 144, 153
Delorme, P., 648
Delpino, F., 407
Del Popolo, C., 483
Del Sera, B., 483
Del Serra, M., 541
De Luca, C., 544
De Luca, G. A. (Mancino), 532
Del Vecchio, A., 532
Del'vig, A. A., 1008, 1021
De Maio, R., 466, 518
Demals, T., 134
Demarest, G., 799
Demarolle, P., 16
De Martino, E., 542
De Mauro, T., 424, 428
Dembowski, H., 803
Dembowski, P., 75
Demerson, G., 82, 92
Demet, M.-F., 864
Demeulenaere, R., 1
De Michelis, C., 538
De Michelis, C. G., 1013
Démier, F., 134
Demkova, N. S., 1001
Democritus, 81
Demske-Neumann, U., 594
Dems'kyi, M., 1053
De Muynck, R., 878
Den Boef, A. H., 898
Dendale, P., 193–94

Dendle, B. J., 326–27, 334, 336, 337, 362
Deneke, L., 752–53
Deniau, X., 26
Denina, C., 514, 521
De Nino, A., 527
Denkler, H., 815
Dennett, D. C., 118
Dennis, N., 343, 363
Denny, N., 890
Dentler, S., 602
Dentzer-Tatin, C., 202
De Nunzio-Schilardi, W., 534
Denvir, G., 578
Denys, A., 144
Denys, H., 144
Denysiuk, I., 1056
Déon, M., 172
De Pace, A., 510
Dépas, R., 615
Depenbrock, H., 908, 912
Depestre, R., 237
Depeuter, F., 900
Deppisch, H.-J., 818
Depreux, J., 238
Deprez, A., 886, 887
De Quincey, T., 767
Deramaix, M., 476
D'Eramo. L., 534
De Renzi, S., 508
Dergacheva, I. V., 997
Derganc, A., 994–95
De Ridder-Symoens, H., 494
Derivière, P., 223
De Robertis, D., 452, 548
Derouin, C., 178
Derréal, H. (*Mère*), 119
Derrida, J., 85, 221, 227, 234, 334, 418, 682, 721–22, 739, 744, 832, 850, 856, 938
Derycke, P.-H., 134
Derynck, P., 23, 43
Derzhavin, G. R., 1002, 1005, 1008
Desan, P., 78, 79, 87, 96
Desaulniers, G., 29
Desbordes-Valmore, M., 166, 173, 185
Descartes, C., 99
Descartes, R., 79, 96, 99, 117, 118–19, 508, 516, 693
Deschamps, E., 71, 75
Descomps, D., 254
Descomps, X., 254
Des Croix, N.-C., 122
Des Escuteaux, 109
Des Forêts, L. R., 237–38
Desgranges, B., 204
Desideri, L., 531
Desjardins, M. C. (*Mlle*), 100

Desjardins-Daude, J., 108
Desmet, P., 877
Desné, R., 145, 150
Desnos, R., 212
Despautère, J., 27
De Spechio, L., 426
Desplat, C., 253
Des Roches, C., 93, 477
Des Roches, M., 93
Dessales, L., 249
Dessert, D., 182
Dessons, G., 178
Detering, H., 699, 703, 908, 908
Detweiler, R., 871
Deug-Su, I., 4–5
Deursen, A. T. van, 886
Deutsch, E., 870
De Venuto, D., 450–51
Deviataikin, E. E., 1050
De Vincenzi, M., 433
De Vivo, A., 533
Devleeshouwer, R., 132
Devos, F., 878
De Vos, J., 738
Devoto, D., 290
Dewey, J., 1014
De Wulf, G., 172
Deyermond, A., 288, 289
Deyssel, L. van, 885, 899
De Zan, M., 518
Dezsó, L., 432
D'haen, T., 369
Dhombres, J., 132
Dhuoda, 2, 618
Dhuygelaere, D., 202
D'iakonova, E. M., 1015
D'iakova, E. A., 1013, 1033
Diamant, N., 227
Diamanti, D., 478, 483
Diamond-Nigh, L., 416
Diane, A., 95
Dias, E. M., 405
Diaz, B., 177
Díaz, J., 373, 414, 419
Diaz, J.-L., 162–63, 163–64, 177
Díaz de Games, G., 298
Díaz del Castillo, B., 407
Díaz de Rivas, P., 308
Díaz de Toledo, F., 299
Díaz Fernández, J., 354
Díaz Roig, M., 291
Di Benedetto, A., 519, 539
Di Biase, C., 525, 544
Di Blasi, F. P., 521
Dibon, H., 264
Di Bono, M., 518
Dibrova, V., 1060
Di Carlo, F., 472
Di Cesare, D., 26
Dichy, A., 238

Dick, E. S., 637, 852–53
Dick, M., 717
Dicke, G., 662
Dickenberger, U., 742
Dickens, C., 204, 781
Dickerhof, H., 623
Dickson, D., 573
Dickson, W., 934
Dictys Cretensis, 9
Diderot, Denis, 131, 142,
  144–47, 152, 158, 170, 230,
  234, 518, 700, 726, 745
Diderot, Denise, 147
Diderot, D.-P., 145, 147
Didier, B., 134, 153, 156, 164,
  192
Di Domenico, M. G., 142
Diebitz, S., 802–03
Dieckmann, F., 733
Diefenbach, D., 171
Diego, G., 341, 344, 345
Diego de Valera, M., 288
Diehl, E., 591
Diekmann, E., 557
Dieling, H., 599
Diemer, D., 645
Diemer, P., 645
Diereck, A. P., 828
Dierks, M., 822
Diersen, I., 786, 856, 870
Dieten, J. L. van, 4
Diethe, C., 809
Dietrick, L., 764
Dietz, D., 315–16
Diez, F., 14, 15, 22
Díez Canedo, E., 361
Díez de Revenga, F. J., 352, 353
Di Flavio, V., 513
Dijk, H. van, 890
Dijkstra, K., 888
Dik, S. C., 959
Diktonius, E., 936
Di Lieto, C., 543
Diller, G. T., 73
Dilong, R., 956
Dilthey, W., 765, 779
Di Luca, C., 503
Diment, G., 1044
Dimieva, M., 1082
Dimitrov, P., 1083
Dimitrova, M., 1079
Dimitrova-Todorova, L., 1078
Diner, J. B., 69
Dingeldein, H. J., 606
Dingelstedt, F., 780
Dini, A., 518
D'Introno, F., 279
Dinzelbacher, P., 618–19, 620
Dionisotti, C., 542
Dionysius the Areopagite, 117

Diosdado, A., 372
Di Palma, W., 506
Di Paolo, M. G., 472
Di Ricco, A., 515
Di Rienzo, E., 135
Dirikx, L., 897
Di Salvo, M., 1000
Dische, I., 852
Dischner, W., 659
Di Simplicio, D. S., 1044
Di Stefano, P., 526
Ditlevsen, T., 912
Dittmann, J., 591
Dittmar, N., 424
Dittmer, E., 904
Dittmer, N., 592
Ditts, D. F., 1019
D'Lugo, C. C., 420
Długosz, K., 962, 967, 970
Długosz-Kurczabowa, K.,
  957–58, 965
Dmitriev, Iu., 1032
Dmitriev, L. A., 999
Dmitriev, P. V., 1022
Dmitriev, S. N., 1021
Dmitrievskaia, V., 1032
Dmitrovskii, A. Z., 1046
Dniprovs'kyi, I., 1058
Doane, A. N., 628
Doane, H. A., 827
Dobaczewski, A., 960, 962
Döblin, A., 810, 814, 815
Dobozy, M., 642
Dobre, M., 550
Dobrenko, E. A., 1028–29,
  1035, 1040, 1041
Dobringer, E., 1013
Dobrovie-Sorin, C., 552
Dobrovský, J., 941
Dobuzhinskii, M. V., 1032
Dobychin, L., 1028
Dobzynski, C., 214–15
Dodds, D., 870
Dodds, J. D., 289
Doderer, H. von, 809, 814, 852
Doggenaar, A. van, 887
Doglio, F., 447
Doglio, M. L., 482, 495
Doglio, M. M., 206
Dohm, C. W. von, 715
Dohnány, M., 954
Dohnas, C. von, 665
Doison, N., 109
Dokoupil, B., 943
Dolan, K. H., 308
Dolce, L., 455, 467, 484
Dolci, R., 434
Dołęga-Chodakowski, Z., 1069
Dolei, G., 847
Dolet, E., 81

Doležal, A., 953
Doležel, L., 937, 1031
Doležel, P., 1008
Dolgalakova, V. I., 1033
Dolgorukaia, N. B., 1007
Dolinskii, M. Z., 1021
Dolle-Weinkauf, B., 831
Dölling, I., 838
Dollinger, P., 622
Dolník, J., 947
Dolskaya-Acherley, O., 1001
Dolzhenkov, P., 1018
Domaradzki, M., 958
Dombrovskii, Iu. O., 1039
Domdey, H., 865
Domenchina, J. J., 342
Domenichi, L., 467
Domin, H., 852
Dominte, C., 550
Donadio, L., 501–02
Donahue, M., 349
Donald, S. G., 726
Donati, C., 525
Doncheva Panaiotova, N., 1000
Donchyk, V., 1059, 1060
Dondaine, C., 44
Dondaine, L., 43
Donhauser, K., 594
Donnan, T. M., 227
Donne, J., 308
Donnelly, S., 572, 578
Dönni, G., 799
Donohue, W. C., 826
Donoso, J., 417
Donovan, P. J., 563
Dooley, B., 511, 523
Døør, J., 902
Doppler, A., 813
Doray, M.-F., 202
Doré, G., 102
Dorfman, A., 418
Doria, M., 530
Doria, P. M., 524
Dorigatti, M., 471
Dorizi, B. (il Bibbiena), 480
Dornbush, J. M., 56
Dörner, H. H., 921
Dornheim, N. J., 841
Dorofeeva, L. G., 1046
Doroszewski, W., 959, 961
Dörries, M., 766
D'Ors, E., 356
Dorschel, A., 796
D'Orso, A., 502
Dorst, T., 787, 852
Dosgilbert, P., 246
Dossi, D., 470
Dostoevskii, F. M., 311, 713,
  768, 823, 1024, 1031, 1048
Dostoevskii, M., 713

Dosvitnii, O., 1058, 1059
Dotoli, G., 100
Dotras, A. M., 369
Dotsenko, S. N., 1023
Dotta, R., 466
Dottin, G., 43
Dottori, C. de', 501
Dotzler, B. J., 821
Doubrovsky, S., 218, 243
Dougherty, D., 359, 360
Doumerc, B., 249
Douvier, C., 98
Dovlatov, S. D., 1030
Downey, G., 576
Downing, E., 805
Dowsett, C. F., 1018, 1023, 1030
Dozy, R., 267
Drăganu, N., 553
Drage, C. L., 1003
Drăghicescu, J., 550
Dragojević, N., 1073
Dragonetti, G., 519
Dragonetti, R., 72–73
Drahomanov, M., 1055, 1056
Drai-Khmara, M., 1058
Drainae, R., 1075
Drake, S., 510
Drayton, M., 667
Drazdovich, Ia., 1067
Drazhevs'ka, L., 1060
Dreike, B. M., 755
Dreizin, F., 1045, 1048
Drenska, M., 390, 391–92
Drescher, H. W., 557, 713
Dressler, H., 707
Dressler, S., 141
Drew, K. F., 621
Drewes, R., 819
Drewitz, I., 844, 852
Drews, J., 598, 838–39, 849
Dreyfus, A., 203, 222, 355
Drieu La Rochelle, P., 220, 225
Drigani, A., 512
Drillon, J., 30
Drimba, V., 553
Drincu, S., 553
Drinkwater, J., 333
Drobizheva, V. Z., 987–88
Droin, A., 208
Droin, R., 38
Droixhe, D., 143
Drölling, M., 168
Drölling, M.-M., 168
Dronke, A., 780
Drosdowski, G., 589, 590
Drost, W., 102
Droste-Hülshoff, A. von, 782, 787–88
Drouet, J., 166–67, 174

Drouin, M., 163, 180, 189
Drug, Š., 954
Drummond, D., 242
Druța, G., 553
Drux, R., 675
Drzewuski, J., 981
Držić, M., 1072
Du, K. an, 569
Duarte, I. S., 393, 400
Duarte, M. E. L., 392–93
Du Bartas, G., 92
Du Bellay, J., 15, 87, 88
Dubisz, S., 963
Dubnov, E., 1035
Dubois, C.-G., 78, 79, 82–83, 90, 91
Dubois, J., 39, 40, 193
Dubois, J. (Sylvius), 78
Dubois-Charlier, F., 39
Du Boscq, J., 110
Dubost, F., 57, 61
Du Bouchet, A., 238
Dubouka, U., 1067
Du Boulay, S., 305
Dubruck, E., 71
Dubský, J., 281
Dubu, J., 126–27, 129
Dubuis, R., 68–69
Du Camp, M., 194, 195
Duchamp, G., 234
Duchatelet, B., 211
Duchêne, R., 101
Duchet, C., 178
Duchet, M., 142
Dučić, J., 1075
Ducis, J.-F., 159
Duconquéré, P., 254
Ducoudray, E., 138
Ducrot, O., 34, 48
Dudek, J., 982
Duden, A., 852
Dudina, L. N., 1047
Dudintsev, V. D., 1030
Duez, D., 48
Du Fail, N., 83–84
Dufaud, J., 259
Dufeu, R., 156
Duffy, S., 585
Dufour, A., 78
Dufour, H., 189
Dufour, P., 197
Dufournet, J., 70, 77, 483
Dufraisse, R., 776
Dufresne, M., 226
Dufresny, C. R., 107
Duft, J., 629–30
Duganov, R. V., 1020
Dugas, A., 39, 46
Duggan, J. J., 56
Duhamel, R., 887

Duijkerius, J., 893
Duits, H., 885, 889
Dukát, J. J., 940
Dukhan, Ia., 1030
Dulac, G., 146
Dulac, L., 76
Dulk, A., 802
Dull, O., 70
Dullin, C., 213
Dulong, G., 45
Dumas, A., 121
Dumas, C., 337
Dumas, M., 171
Dumitrașcu, K., 550
Dumitrescu, D., 19, 277
Dümmler, E., 4
Du Monin, J.-É., 80
Dumont, A., 755–56
Dumont, P., 26
Dumoulié, C., 215
Duncan, C., 420
Duncan, D., 542
Duncan, I., 1019
Dundas, J., 454
Duneton, C., 39–40
Dunin-Martsinkevich, V., 1067
Dünkelsbühler, U., 721–22
Dunker, A., 868
Dunkley, J., 159
Dunlap, T., 638
Dunleavy, G. W., 578
Dunleavy, J. E., 578
Dunn, D., 128
Dunn, K., 118
Dunn, P. N., 309
Duns Scotus, 463
Dunstan (*Saint*), 5
Düntzer, H., 778
Dupèbe, J., 78
Du Perron, E., 887, 898
Du Plaisir (*le sieur*), 106
Dupleich (J.-J.-P. ?), 252
Dupleix, S., 117
Du Plessis-Mornay, *see* Mornay, P. de
Dupont, J., 184
Du Pont de Nemours, P. S., 134
Dupont-Escarpit, D., 98–99
Dupouy, C., 218
Duprat, H., 134
Dupré, M., 99
Dupuit, C., 181
Dupuy, M., 118
Dupuy-Engelhardt, H., 604
Duque López, A., 418
Duracher, M.-H., 158
Durán, A., 333
Durán, G., 349
Durán, M., 306, 348
Durand, F., 329

Durand, T., 146
Durand, Y., 117
Durand de Gros, J.-P., 249
Durand-Sendrail, B., 143, 146, 166
Durán Luzio, J., 409
Durante, E., 500
Duranty, E., 206
Duras, M., 233, 238
Dürer, A., 662
Durišin, D., 952
Durkin, A. R., 1018
Durling, N., 68
Durling, R. M., 450
Duro, A., 434
Durovič, Ľ., 946, 949
Dürr, V., 819
Durrell, L., 711
Durrell, M., 601
Dürrenmatt, F., 566, 833, 835, 837, 852–53
Durruty, B., 135
Durych, J., 943
Durzak, M., 787, 873
Dusar, I., 847
Dušek, D., 956
Düsing, W., 708, 824
Dusini, A., 792
Duso, R., 495
Dust, P. H., 356
Dutertre, E., 104
Düttmann, A. G., 811
Dutton, B., 296, 297
Duun, O., 915
Duval, E. M., 82, 108
Düwel, K., 651
Duym, J., 892
Dvarchanin, I., 1067, 1068
Dvonč, L., 946, 949, 951
Dvořáková, D., 942
Dwars, J.-F., 712
Dwelly, E., 584
Dwyer, R. A., 56
Dybciak, K., 983
Dybowski, A., 831
Dyck, J., 684
Dygasiński, A., 977
Dyła, S., 959
Dylevskii, N. M., 999
Dynak, W., 972
Dynamius (prefect of Marseilles), 2
Dyshynevich, V., 1069
Dzendzelivs'kyi, I., 1054
Dziechcińska, H., 974
Dziergwa, R., 821
Dziuba, I., 1056, 1061, 1062
Dziubaila, P., 1065

Eade, J. C., 6
Eamon, W., 458, 494
Eastridge, T. I., 173
Eaubonne, F. d', 233
Ebbinghaus, E. A., 597, 625
Ebel, M., 873
Ebeling, R. A., 879
Eberenz, R., 271
Eberhard, H.-J., 807
Eberhard, J. A., 694
Eberlein, T., 839
Eberlin von Günzberg, 596
Ebersbach, M., 839
Ebert, H., 594, 596
Ebert, R. P., 595
Ebner-Eschenbach, M. von, 788, 814
Ebneter, T., 556
Ebreo, L., 467
Echegaray, J., 360
Echenique Elizondo, M. T., 271
Eckel, W., 857
Ecker, G., 830
Eckermann, J. P., 701, 705, 708
Eckhardt, C. D., 9
Eckhardt, J.-J., 780
Eckhart (Meister), 653
Eco, U., 111, 534–35, 538
Economou, G. D., 262
Eddington, D., 272
Edelstein, M., 138
Edler, E., 780
Edmiston, W. F., 152
Edmunds, S., 663
Edrich, B., 642
Edström, V., 930
Edwards, C., 649
Edwards, J., 417, 567
Edwards, M., 236
Edwards, O. M. (Sir), 565
Edwards, P. J., 184
Edwards, R., 244
Edwards, R. R., 9
Edwards, T. (Twm o'r Nant), 565
Eeden, F. van, 887, 898
Eegholm-Pedersen, S., 906–07
Effler, G., 789
Efimov, V. V., 1041–42
Efimova, V. S., 991
Efremov, I., 1048
Egenolf von Staufenberg, 662
Egerding, M., 638, 647
Egeria, 618
Egerić, M., 1074
Eggenberger, C., 629
Egger, K., 440
Egger, O., 650
Eggermont, C., 281
Eggs, E., 29

Egido, A., 312
Egido, T., 305
Egil Skallagrímsson, 929
Ehlers, H., 835
Ehlers, J., 622
Ehlert, T., 617, 633, 641
Ehrard, J., 156
Ehre, M., 1044
Ehrich-Haefeli, V., 692, 730
Ehrismann, O., 615, 637, 638, 646
Ehrlich, L., 707
Ehrmann, M., 715
Eibl, K., 700
Eich, G., 831, 853
Eichel, P., 87
Eicheldinger, M., 670
Eichendorff, J. von, 688, 746, 747, 749–50, 795, 849, 869
Eicher, T., 826
Eidinova, V. V., 1031
Eifler, G., 648
Eifler, M., 875
Eigeldinger, M., 182–83
Eigler, F., 863
Eijk, J. van der, 884
Eike, C., 922
Eikhenbaum, B. M., 1027
Eile, S., 982
Eilhart von Oberg, 641–42
Einaudi, G., 526
Einstein, A., 951
Einstein, C., 810, 814
Eisenberg, D., 311, 313
Eisenbichler, K., 453
Eisendle, H., 853
Eisenlohr, E., 617
Eisenstein, E. L., 137
Eisenstein, S. M., 813, 1013
Eisermann, D., 143
Eisner, K., 814
Ejskjær, I., 903
Eke, N. O., 865–66
Ekelöf, G., 934
Ekkehart of St. Gall, 630
Eklund, G., 924 25
Ekman, H.-G., 931
Ekman, K., 934
Ekman, M., 933
Ekner, R., 934
Ekstein, N., 105
Elagin, I., 1034
Elagin, Iu., 1032
Elbek, J., 905
Elbogen, I., 727
Elena, A., 520
Elenin, I., 1081
Elenski, I., 1081
Eley, P., 8, 82
El Greco, 346, 357

Elia, P., 307
Elia, S., 389
Elilert, H., 807
Elina, E. G., 1041
Elin Pelin, 1082
Eliot, T. S., 231, 342, 885
Elis, I. Ff., 566
Elisabeth of Schönau, 7
Elis Wyn o Wyrfai, *see* Roberts, E.
Elizaveta Petrovna (*Empress*), 1006
Elizondo, S., 420, 421
Elkabas, C., 205–06
Elkan, S., 930
Elliot, A., 192
Ellis, M., 565
Elm, T., 704–05
Elm, U., 814
El Saffar, R., 334
Elsheikh, M. S., 456
Elsner, U., 855
Elson, M. J., 551
Elsschot, W., 885, 887
Elter, I., 650
Eltit, D., 417
Eluard, P., 209, 220–21, 225
Éluerd, P., 38
Elyada, O., 138
Emelina, J., 120, 180
Emersön, C., 1024, 1031
Emiliano, A., 268–69
Emison, P., 454
Emmerich, K., 803
Emmerich, W., 839, 842
Emmerick, A. K., 738, 748
Empedokles, 758
Emrich, W., 822
Emrys ap Iwan, 565
Emsel, M., 281
Emyr, J., 567
Enander, C., 934
Encina, J. del, 269
Enckell, M., 934
Enckell, P., 40
Enckell, R., 934
Ende, M., 853
Endler, A., 853
Endress, H. P., 311–12
Engberg, C., 913
Engel, C., 1029
Engel, E. J., 727–28
Engel, J. J., 728
Engel Holland, E., 728
Engelmann, W., 267
Engels, F., 621, 986
England, J., 294
Englander, D., 453
Engling, E., 320
Enninger, W., 251

Ennius, 87
Enquist, P. O., 934
Enrique, A., 365
Enríquez Gómez, A. (F. de Zárate), 323–24
Enström, H., 927
Entner, H., 669
Entwistle, W. J., 376
Enzensberger, H. M., 832, 844, 853, 873
Epalza, M. de, 302
Ephraim the Syrian (*Saint*), 999
Epifanii Premudryi, 999
Eppink, A., 880
Epple, J. A., 414, 417, 418
Epshtein, M. N., 1029, 1033
Epstein, J., 347
Equicola, M., 467, 486
Erämetsä, E., 596
Erasmus, D., 459, 460, 466, 472, 674, 693, 1073
Erb, E., 837, 853
Erba, L., 528, 547
Erbel, K., 872
Erben, K. J., 941
Ercilla y Zúñiga, A. de, 308, 408–09
Eremenko, A., 1034
Eremin, P., 1018
Eremina, I. F., 1040
Erenburg, I. G., 1027, 1039
Ergetowska, R., 764
Erhart, C., 824
Ericson, E. E., Jr, 1037
Erikson, E. H., 352
Eriksson, A., 924
Eriksson, C., 935
Eriksson, O., 36, 924
Erkens, F.-R., 633
Erker, B., 729
Erler, M. C., 76
Erler, T., 789
Ermakova, O. P., 992
Ermann, K., 703
Ermolaev, H., 1047
Ernst, G., 436, 507
Ernst, K., 748
Ernst, U., 51
Erofeev, V., 1018, 1023, 1024
Erofeev, Venedikt, 1039
Erofeev, Viktor, 1029
Erokhin, A., 1002–03
Eroms, H.-W., 594
Erpenbeck, J., 738, 833
Erspamer, F., 475–76
Ertmer, D., 627
Ertzdorff, X. von, 660
Erwin, T., 151
Esaghe, Y. A., 703
Eschenburg, J. J., 715

Eschmann, J., 31
Esclapez, R., 84, 94, 95
Escobar, J., 333
Escobar, M., 418
Escobar, M. de, 406
Escosura, P. de la, 332
Escribano Pueo, M. L., 291
Escrivá, J. R. de, 306, 308
Esenin, S. A., 1019, 1033, 1039, 1049
Eska, J. F., 560–61
Eskelund, L., 908
Es'kina, L. A., 1014
Espagne, M., 163
Espegaard, A., 904
Espejo, B., 414
Espejo, E., 409
Espeland, V., 922
Espert, N., 348
Espina, A., 342
Espinal, M. T., 379
Espinosa, C., 419
Espinosa Elorza, R. M., 274
Espmark, K., 934
Esposito, E., 548
Esposito, M., 560
Espronceda, J. de, 327, 332
Esquenet-Bernaudin, M., 25
Esquier, S., 171
Esser, D., 656
Esser, U., 590
Estang, L., 230
Este, Alfonso IV d', 499
Este, Almerigo d', 499
Estébanez Calderón, D., 332
Ester, H., 791
Esteve, J. P., 411
Estienne, H., 79
Estienne, R. d', 36
Estoile, P. de l', 79
Estrada, J., 420
Estreen, R., 934
Estruch, J., 374
Estruch Tobella, J., 328, 330
Étiemble, R., 25
Etkind, E., 1012
Etner, F., 134
Etreros, M., 310
Eugen, K., 711
Eugène, C., 194
Eulalia (*Saint*), 63–64
Euripides, 127, 678, 733, 855, 1014
Eusebius, 88
Evans, D., 567
Evans, D. E., 560
Evans, E., 566–67
Evans, M., 564
Evans, P., 363
Evans, R. J. W., 777

Evensen, Aa., 916–17
Everson, J. E., 457, 480
Evfimii Chudovskii, 1001
Evrard, É., 2
Evrard, P., 847
Evreinov, N. N., 1014
Evseeva-Lobakova, I. A., 1000
Evtimii (*Patriarch*), 1079
Evtushenko, E. A., 1034
Evzlin, M., 1012
Ewald, J., 906
Eybl, F. M., 698
Eyck, Barthélémy d', 75
Eykman, C., 808
Eyquem, M., 94
Eyquem, P., 94

Faassen, S. J. A. van, 889
Fabbri, L., 462
Fabbri, P., 503
Fabbri, P. G., 461–62
Fábera, M., 943
Fabianowski, A., 975
Fabio, N., 536
Fabra, P., 378
Fabre, G., 550
Fabre, P., 250
Fabre d'Olivet, A., 245
Fabrizio-Costa, S., 485, 505
Fabry, R., 956
Faccarello, G., 134
Facchinetti, M., 534
Faessler, P., 799
Fagan, D. S., 390
Fagiuoli, G. B., 521–22
Fahlke, E., 862
Fähnder, W., 830
Fahner, C., 880
Fahs, W., 692
Fahy, C., 456, 511
Faisant, C., 92
Fajardo, A., 282
Falaschi, A., 429
Falcetto, B., 532
Falcó, J. L., 364
Falcón, L., 372
Falgirolles, A. de, 423
Falicka, K., 194
Falińska, B., 969
Fališevac, D., 1072
Falk, J. N., 18
Falkiewicz, A., 982
Falla, M. de, 344
Fallada, H., 814
Fallersleben, Hoffmann von, *see*
   Hoffmann von Fallersleben
Fallot, G., 27
Fallows, N., 295, 309
Falowski, A., 1000

Falsig, E., 909
Faltenbacher, K. F., 78
Fanciullo, F., 443, 444
Fándly, J., 947, 953, 954
Fanfani, M. L., 435
Fanha, D., 404
Fanina, T. V., 1041
Fanlo, J.-R., 89, 90, 91, 92
Fanselow, G., 602
Fantin-Latour, H., 187
Fantoni, A. R., 457
Faraco, C. A., 389
Faral, E., 70
Farasse, G., 155
Faret, N., 79
Farfantello (H. Dibon), 264
Faria, I. H., 400
Farin, M., 157
Farinelli, G., 496
Farnese, Odoardo II (*Duke of
   Parma*), 503
Farnese, R., 500
Farnetani, E., 377
Farquhar, S., 95
Farrel, E. R., 164
Farrell, D. E., 1001, 1006
Farrell, M. L., 99
Farrelly, D., 705
Farrenkopf, J., 827
Faryno, E., 1050
Faryno, J., 1045
Fassbinder, R. W., 853
Fattori, D., 456
Fauchon, P., 141
Faulhaber, C. B., 14, 287, 314
Faulkner, W., 415
Fauré, G. A., 208
Fauriel, C., 163
Faurisson, R., 190
Fauser, J., 792
Fauser, M., 598
Fausto, S., 460
Fausto, V., 485
Fauvel, M., 238
Favereau, F., 570
Faverey, H., 887
Favre, R., 136
Favre, Y.-A., 188
Feal, C., 352, 353, 358–59
Fechner, J.-U., 730, 906
Fechtnerová, A., 940
Fed', N., 1036
Fedenko, P., 1055
Federici, C., 528, 539
Fedi, R., 479
Fedin, K. A., 1039, 1051
Fedorov, A. Iu., 1001
Fedorov, N., 1024
Fee, Z., 814
Feeney, T., 371

Feeny, T., 355
Fegl, V., 963
Feilchenfeldt, K., 867
Feinäugle, N., 841
Feinberg, I., 1043
Feinstein, W., 469
Feistner, E., 653
Feldek, Ľ., 956
Felder, F. M., 789
Feldman, G. D., 808
Feldman, L. E., 673
Feldman, M., 461
Feldman, S. G., 350
Feldwick, A., 7
Felgine, O., 240
Feliciano, F., 460, 477
Feliciano, W., 421
Felipe II (*King of Spain*), 306
Felipe III (*King of Spain*), 321
Felipe, L., 365
Felix, J., 552
Fell, C., 421
Fellows-Jensen, G., 928
Fellrath, I., 786
Felski, R., 200, 803
Fénelon, F. de S. de la M., 110,
   117
Fenenko, O., 1057
Fenner, W., 722–23
Fenoaltea, D., 81
Fenoglio, B., 535
Fenoulhet, J., 885
Fens, K., 885
Fenske, L., 639
Fenster, T. S., 76
Feo, M., 531
Feofilakt (*Igumen*), 998
Féraud, J.-F. de, 29, 101
Ferchl, W., 843–44
Ferenčíková, A., 968
Ferguson, G., 85
Ferincz, I., 999
Ferman, C., 420
Fermetti, G., 449
Fernandes, H. B., 394
Fernandes, M. C., 396
Fernández, A. M., 357
Fernández, M. C. L. O., 396,
   398
Fernández de Oviedo, G., 309,
   406
Fernández de Urbina, J. M.,
   354
Fernández Fernández, M. J.,
   301
Fernández Gonzáles, J. R., 250
Fernández Insuela, A., 373,
   374, 409
Fernández-Montesinos, M.,
   346

Fernández Pérez, M., 279
Fernández Rei, F., 401
Fernando II (*King of Aragon*), 311
Fernando Lara, L., 282
Fernán Gómez, F., 373
Ferrand, C., 63
Ferrand, M., 553
Ferrando, A., 375–76
Ferraté, J., 346
Ferrater Mora, J., 356
Ferraz, L. I., 404
Ferrazzi, C., 505
Ferrazzi, M. L., 997, 1000
Ferré, B. M., 660
Ferré, R., 416, 423
Ferreira, C., 388, 401
Ferreira, J. A., 388
Ferreira, M., 403
Ferreira, M. G., 396
Ferreira, M. M. C., 399
Ferreira, M. V. G., 403
Ferreira, S. S., 399
Ferreira Pinto, M., 415
Ferreiro-Couso González, K., 273
Ferreras, J. I., 337
Ferrer-Chivite, M., 309
Ferrer i Gironès, F., 386
Ferrero, E., 436
Ferrer Sola, J., 355
Ferreyrolles, G., 108, 124
Ferri, E., 465
Ferrieri, E., 526, 529
Férriz, T., 341, 362
Ferro, J. N., 294–95
Ferron, L., 801
Ferry, J., 230
Fertig, L., 702, 717, 733, 754
Festa, E., 510
Festa, G., 153, 157
Fet, A. A., 1016, 1081
Fetscher, J., 831
Fetzer, J. F., 738
Feuchtwanger, L., 792, 810, 812, 815
Feuerbach, L., 779, 793
Feuillet, J., 592
Feydeau, G., 206–07
Fiadosik, A., 1069
Fiala, J., 940
Fialová, E., 940
Fichera, U. B., 691
Fichte, H., 854
Fichte, J. G., 697–98, 702, 721, 735, 742, 750–52, 753, 757, 861
Fichtner, E. G., 648
Ficino, M., 10, 455, 458, 463–64, 465, 467, 474

Fickel, I., 799
Fiddler, A., 861
Fidler, D. P., 148
Field, F., 208
Field, T. T., 252, 253
Fielding, H., 145, 1005
Fietz, L., 723
Fiévée, J., 161
Figge, U. L., 42
Figueiredo, E. G. V. de, 396
Figueres, J. M., 386
Fik, M., 972
Filangieri, G., 518, 519
Filelfo, F., 460
Filetico, M., 460
Filhol, E., 818
Filippov, B., 988
Filipsson, H., 927
Findlay, L. M., 177
Findlen, P., 494, 506
Fingerhut, K., 793–94, 796
Fink, B., 165
Fink, G.-L., 680, 706–07
Fink, K. J., 718
Finke, M., 829
Finocchiaro, M. A., 510
Finocchiaro Chimirri, G., 543
Finotti, F., 451, 534
Fiorato, A. C., 483
Fioravanti, L., 427
Fioretos, A., 851
Fiori, G., 537
Fiorillo, J. D., 747, 773
Firenzuola, A., 467
Firmino, G., 403
Fischart, J., 662, 684
Fischer, B., 685, 718, 747, 859
Fischer, Caroline A., 689, 736, 737, 751, 752
Fischer, Christian A., 752
Fischer, G.-N., 162
Fischer, H., 841, 868
Fischer, J.-L., 132
Fischer, J. M., 807
Fischer, M. L., 417
Fischer, R., 689, 715
Fischer, S. L., 319
Fischer, S. M., 422
Fischer, W., 658
Fischer-Jørgensen, E., 904
Fischer-Lichte, E., 858, 1019
Fischer-Lüder, Y.-C., 852
Fischler, A., 170
Fishburn, E., 415
Fisher, B., 200
Fisher, R., 635
Fishman, J. A., 24
Fitch, B. T., 237
Fitzgerald, G., 574
Fiut, A., 982

Fix, H., 921
Fizaine, M., 174
Fizer, I., 1060–61
Fjørtoft, O., 915
Flaherty, G., 687, 690
Flaker, A., 1012, 1027, 1073
Flämig, W., 601
Flandrois, I., 138
Flanell-Friedman, D., 202
Flanigan, C. C., 1
Flasch, K., 622
Flaubert, G., 156, 168, 169, 173, 176, 180, 181, 185, 192, 194–98, 199, 205, 218, 222
Flaux, N., 42
Flavio Biondo, 485
Fleckenstein, J., 639
Fleischer, M., 841, 957
Fleischhack, E., 791
Fleischman, S., 12, 17, 19, 30
Fleishman, L., 1013, 1045
Fleisser, M., 815
Fles, B., 826
Flescher, J., 544
Fletcher, J., 29, 453
Fleurance-Rivault, D. de, 79
Fleuriot, L., 561
Fliegner, S., 776, 800
Flikeid, K., 46
Floch, J., 146
Flood, C., 219
Flood, J., 453, 843
Flood, J. L., 616, 798
Flor, F. R. de la, 304
Florenskii, P., 1017, 1020
Flores, F. G., 413
Flores, J. A., 284
Flores García, F., 360
Flores Martos, J. A., 406
Flori, J., 53
Florian, J.-P.-C., 154
Flygare-Carlén, E., 929
Flynn, C. H., 698
Fo, A., 543
Foa, A., 496
Focaccia, A., 548
Fofi, G., 526
Fohrmann, J., 690, 777
Foigny, G. de, 106
Foisil, M., 138
Foix, J. V., 343
Fokkema, D., 898
Fol, M., 206
Folena, G., 427, 435
Folengo, T., 473, 476–77, 484
Foley, J., 1077
Foley, P., 764
Folgore, L., 529
Folkers-Loosjes, E. J., 889
Foltmann, M., 966

'olz, H., 635, 657, 660
'omenko, L. P., 1038
'omina, M. S., 997
'ongaro, A., 191, 209
'onseca, F. V. P. da, 392, 402
'onseca, J., 395, 396
'ontaine, J., 1
'ontaine, M.-M., 81, 454
'ontana, B., 165
'ontana, O. M., 824
'ontane, T., 679, 732, 746, 778, 779, 784, 789–91, 803, 804, 826
'ontanella, L., 535, 537
'ontanella de Weinberg, M. B., 283
'ontenelle, B. le B. de, 117, 140, 1008
'ontes Baratto, A., 483
'ontius, M., 142–43
'onvizin, D. I., 1008
'onyi, A., 201
'oot, P., 698
'oote, I. P., 1013
'orain, J.-L., 190
'orberg, F. K., 697–98
'orconi, A., 435
'ord, P., 87–88
'ordinálová, E., 953, 954
'oresti, F., 443
'orestier, L., 187, 201
'orestiero, G., 111
'orgues, R., 422
'orlani, A., 527
'orman, E. B., 129
'ormigari, L., 424, 518
'ormisano, L., 260
'órneas, J. M., 267
'ornel, M. de, 48
'orner, W., 442
'ornet-Betancourt, R., 356
'orni, P. M., 450
'orniciari, L., 485
'orsås-Scott, H., 831, 936
'orsgren, M., 34
'orslund, K., 931
'orster, G., 689, 694, 715, 759
'örster, J., 871
'örster, K., 750
'orster, L. W., 675
'orsthofer, W., 445
'ort, M. R., 408
'ort, P., 539
'ortassier, P., 191
'orthomme-Nicholson, M., 4
'orti, M., 548
'orti-Lewis, A., 124–25
'ortini, F., 535
'ortis, A., 438
'ortoul, H., 178

Fortunatov, N. M., 1017–18
Fortuny, A., 229
Foscolo, U., 548
Foscolo, V., 543
Fossat, J.-L., 250, 252
Foster, D. W., 412, 416
Foster, J. B., Jr, 1044
Föster, M., 827
Foster, M. H., 412–13
Fothergill-Payne, L., 320
Fouano, R., 194
Foucart, C., 212
Foucault, M., 110, 158, 172, 234, 240, 321, 372, 486, 499, 535, 682, 687, 744
Foucher, E., 190
Foucquet, N., 103
Fougéron, I., 992
Foulet, L., 70
Fouqué, C. de la M., 736
Fouqué, F. de la M., 662, 752
Fourier, C., 162
Fourier, J., 133, 171
Fourier, P. (Saint), 119
Fournel, J.-L., 488
Fournier, G., 135
Fourny, J.-F., 188
Fowkes, R. A., 560
Fowler, K., 812
Fox, A. A., 357–58
Fox, C. A., 46
Fox, T. C., 791
Fracastoro, G., 480
Fradejas Rueda, J. M., 293
Fragonard, M. M., 81, 89, 90, 91
Fraisse, S., 225, 226
Fran, G., 556
Francard, M., 43
France, A., 180, 198
France, H. de, 249
France, P., 129
Franceschini, F., 427
Francese, J., 547
Franchetti, A., 99, 216
Franchi, L., 536
Franchi, S., 491
Francillon, R., 154
Francis I (King of France), 78
Francisco de Hollanda, 454
Francis of Assisi (Saint), 828, 1022
Francis of Lorraine (Grand Duke of Tuscany), 512
Francke, A. H., 686
Franckel, J.-J., 35
Franco, A., 395, 397
Franco, F., 348, 352, 362, 363, 369
Franco, J., 413

Franco, M., 486
Franco, V., 477
François, L. von, 791
François de Sales (Saint), 116, 117, 120
François-Geiger, D., 49
Frandsen-Roger, I., 913
Frank, B., 815
Frank, C., 339
Frank, L., 719, 844
Frank, M., 694, 737, 757
Frank, R. G., Jr, 698
Frank-Cyrus, K. M., 607–08
Franke, H., 608
Franklin, B., 140
Franklin, S., 999
Franko, I., 1056, 1057
Franko, Z., 1054
Frankowska, M., 960, 962
Franks, S., 959, 993, 1071
Franz, M., 756, 758
Franz, T. R., 335, 338–39
Franzén, G., 928
Franzos, K. E., 777, 786, 791
Frappier-Mazur, L., 157
Frare, P., 491, 500
Frasca, G., 528
Fraser, V., 260–61
Frassica, P., 543
Frasso, G., 460
Frassu, P., 439
Fratnik, M., 536
Fratta, A., 452
Frattarolo, R., 525–26
Frattegiani, M. T., 495
Frattini, A., 525
Frauenlob, 650
Frazao, J. A., 115
Freccero, C., 82
Freccero, J., 450
Frederick II (Emperor), 8, 447
Frederick II the Great (King of Prussia), 715–16, 729
Frederick, B., 410, 414
Frederick the Victorious (Count Palatine), 616
Fredro, A., 975
Freedman, L., 476
Freidenburg, O., 1045
Freidhof, G., 995
Freidin, G., 1043
Freidin, Iu. F., 1022
Freiligrath, F., 786, 791, 792
Freire López, A. M., 332, 333
Freitas, J., 401
Freitas, M. A., 390
Freitas, M. J., 392
Freitinger, P., 940
Frémont, P., 141
French, R., 698

Frenk, M., 289, 290
Frerichs, L., 899
Fréron, E., 151
Frescaroli, A., 435
Freud, S., 166, 197, 200, 206, 228, 311, 329, 330, 348, 709, 726, 762, 789, 792, 802, 809, 822, 856, 870, 872, 873, 898, 1031, 1072
Freund, W., 805
Frey, J., 748
Frey, W., 615
Fricke, C., 728–29
Fricke, D., 123, 124, 145
Fridlender, G. M., 1003
Fridman, N. V., 1014
Fried, E., 843, 854
Fried, J., 5, 622
Friedell, E., 815
Friedemann, M.-A., 32
Friederici-Brink, C., 863
Friedl, H., 795
Friedman, E. H., 322
Friedman, L., 74
Friedman, R., 479–80
Friedrich V (*Landgrave of Hesse-Homburg*), 758
Friedrich, C. D., 735, 741, 748
Friedrich, G., 790
Friedrich, S., 867
Friedrichsmeyer, E., 708, 799
Fries, F. R., 837, 850, 854
Fries, M. S., 860
Fries, S., 928
Friese, W., 905
Frigerio, M., 486
Frijhoff, W., 886
Frink, G., 819
Frisch, M., 714, 797, 835, 837, 847, 853, 855
Frischmuth, B., 855
Frisé, A., 824, 855
Frisi, P., 518
Fritsch, G., 853, 855
Fritsch-Rössler, W., 646
Fritz, G., 226, 596, 597
Fritz, J.-M., 68
Frizen, W., 822
Frizman, A. G., 1035
Frizman, L. G., 1022
Froehlich, J., 810
Fröhlich, H., 872
Froissart, J., 70–71, 73–74, 75
Frølich, J., 169, 196
Frolov, V., 1028
Fromentin, E., 181, 198
Fromm, H., 613
Frommel, W., 815
Fros, H., 974
Frosini, G., 486

Frost, E. C., 407
Frostegård, J., 935
Frota, M. P., 398
Frugoni, F. F., 494
Frühwald, W., 747, 753, 776
Frutolf von Michelsberg, 622
Frutos, A. de, 357
Fruyt, M., 23
Frydrak, V., 1053
Frye, N., 416
Fubini, R., 458, 459
Fucci, G., 529
Fuchs, C., 28, 198
Fuchs, E., 751
Fuchs, G., 792, 858
Fuchs, J., 838
Fuente Ballesteros, R. de la, 327–28
Fuente Cornejo, T., 303
Fuente Fernández, F. J., 306
Fuentes, C., 413, 414, 420
Fuentes, V., 335, 354
Fuentes Rodríguez, C., 278
Fuentes Vázquez, T., 347
Füetrer, U., 640, 648, 662
Fühmann, F., 837, 839, 840, 841, 855–56
Fujii, A., 663
Fuks, L., 945
Fukushima, N., 280
Fuld, W., 732, 771–72
Fulde, I., 858
Fulgentius, 6
Fulka, V., 956
Fullenwider, H. F., 699, 823
Fuller, L., 185
Fuller, M., 745
Fullerton, G. L., 597
Fumaroli, M., 103
Fumi, E., 533
Funara, R., 504, 505
Funes, L., 294
Funk, T., 591
Funke, H.-G., 145
Fure, E., 916
Furetière, A., 38, 110, 145
Furlan, F., 454, 467
Furness, R., 807, 813
Furst, H., 539
Furst, L., 822
Furtado, A. L., 58
Furuya, Y., 811
Füssel, S., 611
Fussing, B., 908
Fylypovych, P., 1057, 1058

Gaatone, D., 31, 36
Gabinski, M. A., 552
Gabler, D., 592

Gabler, W., 839
Gabriel, A., 231
Gabriele, J. P., 340, 372, 374
Gabrisch, A., 828
Gachev, G., 1030
Gad, E., 766
Gadamer, H.-G., 801, 850
Gadda, C. E., 525, 535–36, 538, 545
Gade, K. E., 921
Gadet, F., 25
Gáfrik, M., 955
Gáfriková, G., 953
Gaidarska, P., 1034
Gaier, U., 703, 726
Gaiser, G., 856
Gaitet, P., 175, 205
Gajda, S., 970
Gala, S., 964, 970
Galán Font, E., 314
Galantaris, C., 168
Galas'eva, G. V., 1046
Galasiński, A., 970
Galasiński, D., 970
Galasso Calderara, E., 496–97
Galateo, A. (De Ferrariis, A.), 462
Galateria, M., 532
Galatskaia, N., 1036
Galcheva, T., 1009
Galeazzi, G., 515
Galenko, L. L., 901
Galeote, M., 286
Galera Sánchez, M., 340
Galiani, F., 518, 522
Galich, A. A., 1027, 1035
Galilei, G., 487, 494, 495, 506, 508–10
Gall, L., 695
Gallagher, E. J., 198
Gallagher, L., 465
Gallais, P., 62–63, 65
Galland, A., 152, 154
Gallarati, S., 74
Gallarati Scotti, T., 526
Galle, R., 145
Gallego, A., 342
Gallego Roca, M., 325
Gallegos, R., 423
Galley, E., 794
Galli, W., 529
Gallian, M., 536
Gallmann, P., 599
Gallo, I., 480
Gallofré Virgili, M. J., 362
Galluci, J. A., 119
Gallud Jardiel, E., 309
Gallus (*Saint*), 630
Galmés de Fuentes, A., 300, 30
Galmiche, X., 127

al'perin, Iu. M., 1026
al'tseva, R., 1024
alves, C., 392
álvez, M., 413, 415
ambacorta, L., 973
ambaro, G., 416
amboni, D., 162, 181
amerschlag, K., 642
amper, G., 1034
anabi, W. al-, 303
andia, A., 478
anelin, C., 316
anelon, 54, 55
ann, M. S., 421
ansberg, M. L., 868
ansel, C., 860
anz, P. F., 639
aos, J., 362
arapon, R., 102 03, 111, 121, 125
araudy, R., 139
aravini, F., 254, 264
arbini, P., 6
arboli, C., 543
arborg, A., 918
arcía, C., 345, 401, 402
arcía, C. J., 357
arcía, E. C., 272, 284
arcia, I. W., 392
arcia, L., 508
arcía, M., 297
arcía, P., 298
arcia Baena, P., 364
arcía Berrio, A., 345
arcía Castañeda, S., 326
arcía de la Concha, V., 307, 342, 354
arcía de la Torre, J. M., 358
arcía de Santa María, A., 299
arcía-Diego, J. A., 352
arcía Escobar, V., 332
arcía Godoy, M., 324
arcía-Hernández, B., 266
arcía Lorca, F., 344, 346–50, 359, 360
arcía Márquez, G., 414, 418
arcía-Mateo, R., 305
arcía Montero, L., 345, 347, 364
arcía Morales, A., 369
arcía-Moreno, L., 416
arcía Negro, M. P., 401
arcía Padrón, D., 281
arcía-Page, M., 277
arcía Pelegrín, J., 289
arcía Ponce, J., 421
arcía Ramos, D., 400
arcía Ramos, J. M., 416
arcía Riverón, R., 285
arcía Serrano, M. V., 419

García Templado, J., 327
García Viño, M., 330
García Yebra, V., 293
Garci-Gómez, M., 314
Garcilaso de la Vega (*El Inca*), 306–07, 311, 313, 340, 352, 407
Gardes-Tamine, J., 31
Gardić, S., 1075
Gardner-Chloros, P., 32, 48, 607
Gardt, A., 598
Gardy, F., 245
Gardy, P., 43, 135, 264, 265
Garette, F., 127
Garfias, P., 344, 347
Garfield, E. P., 410
Garfitt, T., 224
Gargano, A., 850
Gargett, G., 147, 151
Gargiulo, G., 530
Gargolina, S. M., 1015
Garguilo, R., 204
Garin, E., 465, 487
Garin de Monglane, 55
Garlén, C., 927
Garmendia, S., 423
Garnier, A., 3, 51
Garnier, G., 134
Garnier, R., 892
Garon, L., 1019
Garramiola Prieto, E., 311
Garrard, J., 1041
Garrido, F., 419–20
Garrido, J., 279
Garrido, R. M., 294
Garrisi, A., 444
Garro, E., 412, 414, 421
Garrote Pérez, F., 308
Garshin, V. M., 1024
Gärtner, E., 281
Gärtner, K., 594–95, 637, 651, 652, 654
Garve, C., 685, 693
Gary, R., 238
Gary-Prieur, M.-N., 42
Garzoni, T., 486, 676
Garzonio, S., 1001, 1004–05
Gasarian, G., 185
Gasbarrone, L., 147
Gasca Queirazza, G., 436, 441
Gascón Vera, E., 314, 349
Gasiglia-Laster, D., 174
Gaskill, H., 586, 758, 759, 839
Gaspari, G., 518
Gasparov, M. L., 1014, 1022, 1042
Gasparov, V. M., 1022
Gassendi, P., 510
Gastaldi, J., 174

Gateau, J.-C., 236
Gatta, F., 534
Gatti, A., 234
Gatti, R., 520
Gatti, S., 476–77
Gaudard, F.-C., 185–86
Gaudelman, C., 138
Gaudon, J., 129, 174
Gaudrard, F.-C., 103
Gaujon, J.-P., 178
Gaulmyn, M.-M. de, 31
Gaunt, S., 260
Gaurico, P., 464, 480
Gautier, B., 983
Gautier, J., 198
Gautier, R., 150, 159
Gautier, T., 161, 164, 166, 173, 182, 191, 198
Gautier de Belleperche, 64
Gautier de Coinci, 51
Gauzit, E., 257
Gavarró, A., 379
Gavitt, P., 454
Gavlovič, H., 953
Gavriushin, N., 1037
Gayraud, R., 1025
Gazarian-Gautier, M. L., 417
Gazzolo, A. M., 422
Gdacjusz, A., 965
Geary, J., 292
Gebauer, F., 790
Gebhardt, K., 441
Geckeler, H., 41
Geest, D. de, 887, 899
Geiler von Kaysersberg, J., 662
Geintse, O. O., 1045
Geisdorfer Feal, R., 422
Geiser, C., 835
Geissler, R., 704, 797
Geist, A. L., 343–44
Geist, P., 842
Geistdoerfer, A., 45
Geith, K.-E., 655, 660
Gelderblom, A. J., 887, 894
Gelderen, M. F. van, 630
Gellert, C. F., 689, 693, 716
Gellhaus, A., 858
Gellner, F., 938
Gemba, H., 1016
Gemelli, S., 425
Gemenne, L., 190
Gemert, G. van, 673, 676
Gemmingen, B. von, 38, 604
Gendall, R. R. M., 570–71
Generali, D., 514
Genet, J., 212, 238
Genette, G., 226, 227–28, 234
Genette, J., 368
Gengembre, G., 161, 166
Genkova, N., 1083

Genlis, F.-S. de B. de (*Mme*), 154
Genot, G., 432, 548
Genovese, C., 417
Genovesi, A., 511
Genre, A., 246
Gensini, S., 428
Gentile, R., 486
Gentile, S., 463
Genton, E., 136
Gentry, F. G., 611, 614, 615
Gentz, F., 695
Geoffrey of Monmouth, 7, 9, 56, 58, 640, 662
Geoffrey of Vinsauf, 9
Geoffrin, M.-T. (*Mme*), 136
George, D., 567
George, F., 239
George, S., 433, 809, 815
Georgiev, L., 1050
Georgiev, N., 1082
Georgiev, S., 1080
Georgieva, P., 1079
Gérard, P., 135
Gerasimov, Iu. K., 1012, 1016
Gerasimova, L. E., 1026, 1041
Gerbod, F., 225–26
Gerd, A. S., 991
Gerdes, D., 419
Gerdzen, R., 874
Gerecht, M.-J., 42
Gerhardi, G. C., 123
Gerhardt, I., 900
Gerhard von Minden, 633
Gerits, J., 887
Gerken, A. B., 716
Gerler, G., 789
Germain, J., 25
Germain, J.-P., 195
Germanovich, I., 1064
Gernentz, H.-J., 631, 650
Gerning, 758
Gerov, N., 1078
Gerrit-Breuer, S., 734
Gerritsen, W. P., 888, 891
Gersch, H., 725, 787
Gershenzon, M. O., 1023
Gerteis, K., 696
Gertrude the Great, 653
Gertz, S. K., 649
Gervais, B., 202
Gesner, B. E., 46
Gessée, J. de la, 92
Gessen, E., 1029, 1030
Gestrich, A., 696
Gesualdo, C., 476
Gethner, P., 107
Getrevi, P., 464
Geuenich, D., 629
Geulen, H., 703, 765–66

Gevrey, F., 106
Geyer-Kordesch, J., 698
Gezelle, G., 886–87, 896
Ghelderode, M., 359
Ghezzi, P. L., 518
Ghidetti, E., 530
Ghisalberti, A., 463
Giabblanco, C., 457
Giachery, E., 547
Giacomelli, G., 13
Giammarco, E., 437
Giammarco, M., 183
Giannantonio, V., 523
Giannelli, L., 424, 434
Giannetto, N., 525
Gianni, F., 515
Giannone, P., 524
Giannoni, P., 436
Giannotti, D., 486–87
Giaquinta, R., 1028
Giardina, C., 84, 186
Giardinelli, M., 416
Gibbons, J., 445
Gibert, R., 356
Gibson, W., 100
Gide, A., 210, 211, 212, 221–22
Gidel, H., 206, 207
Gierke, M., 808
Gies, D. T., 333
Giesecke, M., 594
Giesenfeld, G., 839
Gifreu, J., 387
Gigliotti, G. L., 480
Gigliucci, R., 447
Gijsen, A. van, 891
Gijsen, M., 887
Gil, A., 310
Gil, E., 351
Gil, M., 358
Gilabert, J. J., 341
Gil-Albert, J., 344, 347, 365
Gilbert, C., 110, 154
Gilbert, F., 453
Gilbert, L., 885, 892
Gilbert, S., 332
Gilbert, W., 510
Gil de Biedma, J., 346, 364
Gil de Zamora, 294
Gilek, T., 932
Giles of Viterbo, 9, 476
Gill, G., 868
Gille, K. F., 703, 704
Gillespie, D., 1028, 1029, 1048
Gillespie, G., 678
Gilli, P., 75–76
Gilliam, T., 359
Gilliéron, J., 15, 27
Gillies, W., 586
Gillissen, A., 884
Gillmeister, H., 641

Gilman, S., 334, 338
Gilman, S. L., 796
Gilot, M., 132, 135, 137, 156
Giloy-Hirtz, P., 640
Giltrap, R., 574
Gil y Carrasco, E., 332
Giménez Arnau, J. A., 372
Giménez Caballero, E., 343
Giménez-Frontín, J. L., 365
Gimeno, L., 382
Gimeno Casalduero, J., 293
Gimeno Menéndez, F., 285
Gimplevich-Schwartzman, Z., 1044–45
Gindin, S. I., 1022
Ginn, L. H., 193
Ginsburg, M. P., 171
Ginzburg, L., 1028, 1031
Ginzburg, N., 536, 537
Gioanola, E., 525
Giolito, G., 479
Giolito de' Ferrari, *see* Stagnino B.
Giombi, S., 455
Giono, J., 168, 211, 222
Giordani, J., 134
Giordano, J., 417
Giordiano, J., 365
Giorgi, A., 432
Giorgio (Zorzi), F., 474
Giorgis, L., 411
Giotti, V., 525
Giovacchini, D., 155
Giovanni da Verona, 456
Gioveni, C., 528
Gioviale, F., 525
Giovio, P., 427
Gippius, Z. N., 1019, 1022, 1023
Giraldi, G. B., 481
Giraldi Cinthio, G. B., 456
Girard, I., 264
Girardet, A., 133
Girardi, A., 535
Girardot-Soltner, C., 44, 45
Giraud, A., 186
Giraud, Y., 101, 105
Giraudoux, J., 222–23, 354
Giraut de Bornelh, 262, 264
Girba, Iu., 1032
Girke, W., 990
Girlinger, I., 819
Girò, A., 516
Girón Alconchel, J. L., 280
Girondo, O., 414
Girou-Swiderski, M.-L., 135
Girshman, M. M., 1040
Gislain, J.-J., 134
Gitlitz, D. M., 298
Giudici, E., 484

Giudici, G., 528, 537, 545
Giuntella, V., 512–13
Giuntini, S., 519
Giusti, E. L., 449
Giusti, G., 433–34
Glad, J., 1030
Glade, H., 864
Gladilin, A. T., 1030
Glans, K., 933
Glantz, M., 407
Glaser, H. A., 726, 793
Glatigny, A., 186
Glatigny, M., 38
Glättli, H., 437
Glaudes, P., 194, 200, 201
Glauser, A., 86
Glauser, F., 815, 837, 856
Glavinić, V., 443
Glazov, E., 1045
Gleasure, J., 584
Gleber, A., 797
Gleim, J. W. L., 685, 686
Gleim, L., 730
Glenn, K. M., 370
Glessgen, M.-D., 246, 248
Glidden, H. H., 83
Gliemmo, G., 421
Glienke, B., 910
Glinka, S., 963
Gliwitzky, H., 750–51
Gloria, A., 529
Glotser, V. I., 1041
Glovňa, J., 949
Głowacki, J., 981
Głowiński, M., 963, 977, 978, 980
Glushkov, N. I., 1031, 1047
Gmeyner, A., 809
Gnedich, T., 1032
Gnutzman, R., 416, 423
Gobineau, J. A. de (*comte*), 166, 198–99, 797
Godard, H., 218
Godard de Donville, L., 98, 120
Godden, J., 150
Gödden, W., 729, 788
Godefroy de Lagny, 62
Godenne, R., 152
Godfrey of Viterbo, 469
Godi, G., 503
Godinho, H., 265
Godman, P., 6, 480
Godolin, 264
Godwin, D., 106, 115
Godwin, W., 158
Goebel, R. F., 817
Goebl, H., 14, 23, 441, 557
Goedegebuure, J., 888–89
Goes, G., 1024

Goethe, J. W. von, 679, 683, 685, 688, 689, 690, 691, 692, 693, 695, 696, 699–710, 713, 716, 717, 718, 723, 730, 732, 738, 740, 743, 744, 746, 747, 753, 759, 765, 767, 768, 769–70, 776, 780, 784, 794, 800, 801, 821, 823, 824, 828, 851, 857
Goethe, K. E., 692
Goette, J.-W., 780
Goetz, H.-W., 619, 622
Goetz, R., 856
Gofman, V., 1043
Goggi, G., 142
Gogol', N. V., 739, 1015, 1042, 1059
Goheen, J., 653
Gohin, Y., 178
Goic, C., 410
Goinga, H. van, 886
Gołąb, Z., 970
Gołąbek, A., 963
Golawski-Braungart, 676–77
Gold, D. L., 42
Goldammer, P., 764
Goldberg, F. F., 419
Goldblatt, H., 1055
Goldemberg, I., 413
Golder, J., 123
Goldoni, C., 482, 515–16, 518, 522
Goldschmidt, G.-A., 844
Goldschmidt, M. A., 909
Goldstein, J., 197
Goldzink, J., 151, 160, 166
Golenishchev-Kutuzov, I. N., 1024
Goll, I., 815
Goll-Bickmann, D., 860
Gollerbakh, E., 1020
Golopenția, S., 242, 552
Golsan, R. J., 363
Golstein, J., 176
Goltschnigg, D., 823
Goltz, B., 791
Goltz, M., 729
Goltz, R., 841
Golub, I., 508
Golubeva-Monatkina, N. I., 992
Golubkov, S. A., 1026, 1046
Golz, A., 713
Golz, J., 713, 742
Gomberville, M. le R., 97, 110, 116
Gombrich, E., 706
Gombrowicz, W., 419, 965, 973, 978
Gomez, A., 158

Gómez, D. U., 350
Gómez Baquero, E., 342, 361
Gómez Carrillos, E., 336
Gómez de Avellaneda, G., 410
Gómez de Avellaneo, G., 176
Gómez de la Serna, R., 343, 355, 359, 417
Gómez-Ferrer Morant, G., 333
Gómez López, N., 325
Gómez Molina, C., 279
Gómez Moreno, A., 287–88, 292, 299
Gómez Redondo, F., 288
Gómez Solís, F., 269
Gómez Torrego, L., 278
Gonçalves, P., 395, 403
Goncourt, E. de, 192, 193, 195, 199, 204, 539
Goncourt, J. de, 192, 193, 195, 199, 204, 539
Góngora, L. de, 301
Góngora Marmolejo, A. de, 407
Góngora y Argote, L. de, 308, 310, 324
Gonnot, M., 56
Gonzaga, F. (*Cardinal*), 475
Gonzaga, L., 465
González, A., 364, 366, 421
González, B. A., 333–34, 345, 373
González, G. F., 422
González, L., 408
González, M. S., 382
González, N., 279
González Acosta, A., 407, 420
González Bravo, J. G., 327
González Bravo, L., 330
González Cajiao, F., 419
González Calvo, J. M., 277
González-Casanovas, R. J., 297
González-del-Valle, L. T., 358
González de Posada, C., 270
González Echegaray, C., 333
González Echevarría, R., 407, 418
González Fernández de Sevilla, J. M., 308
González García, J. R., 328
González González, M., 401
González Herrán, J. M., 326, 329, 334, 358
González Martín, J. P., 362
González Martínez, J. L., 407
González Muela, J., 352
González Rojo, E., 420
González Vigil, R., 422
Gonzalo, C. R., 280
Good, C. H., 590
Goodbody, A., 842
Goodkin, R. E., 228

Goodman, A., 457
Goodwin, G., 289
Goosen, L., 888
Goosse, A., 30, 44
Goossens, J., 642, 877, 888
Goozé, M. E., 691, 753
Gopa, K. C., 856
Göpfert, H. G., 696
Gorbachev, M. S., 1030
Gorbovskii, G., 1029
Gorcy, G., 39
Gorelikova, M. I., 1018
Gorelova, N. I., 1032
Gorenshtein, F., 1030
Göres, J., 704
Gorgias, 87
Gori, M., 473
Gori Gandellini, F., 519
Göring, H., 638
Goriunova, R. M., 1047
Gor'kii, M., 230, 1014, 1020,
   1021, 1024, 1027, 1032, 1038,
   1039–40, 1045
Gorlov, A., 1048
Gormally, P., 244
Gorn, V. F., 1047
Gornall, J., 291, 306
Görne, D., 761
Görner, R., 740
Gorodetskii, S. M., 1033
Gorostiza, J., 420
Görres, J., 741, 750
Gorret, D., 519–20
Gorše, D., 867
Gorter, D., 880
Gorter, H., 887
Görtschacher, W., 854
Görtz, F.-J., 831, 856
Görtz, J., 691
Göschen, G. J., 732
Gosman, M., 890
Gossaert, G., 888
Gosselin, L., 32
Gossling, A., 765–66, 828
Gössmann, E., 637
Gössmann, W., 795
Gossy, M. S., 304, 313
Gostyńska, D., 973
Gothe, R., 709
Gothot-Mersch, C., 196
Göttert, K.-H., 693, 723
Gottfried von Strassburg, 611,
   612, 624, 631, 635, 636, 639,
   640, 641, 642, 646, 648
Gotthelf, J., 791
Gottlieb, V., 1018–19
Gottschall, D., 628
Göttsche, D., 831
Gottsched, J. C., 685, 686, 687,
   716

Gottzmann, C. L., 654
Götz, J. N., 686
Gotzkowsky, B., 661
Gotzmann, C., 809
Goubert, J.-P., 132
Gouberville, G. de, 79
Goudaillier, J.-P., 49
Goudar, A., 157
Gougenheim, G., 27
Gouges, O. de, 154
Gouiran, G., 246, 247, 248, 261,
   263
Goujon, J.-P., 187, 200
Goulart, S., 92
Goulas, N., 98
Gould, R., 705
Goulding, E., 222
Goulemot, J. M., 153
Goulet, A., 221
Gourc, J., 261
Gourdin-Servenière, G., 203
Gourmont, R. de, 182, 192
Gournay, M. de, 80, 95, 111
Govoni, C., 528, 529, 540
Gowans, L. M., 642
Gower, J., 299
Goytisolo, J., 327, 367, 369
Goytisolo, J. A., 364
Goytisolo, L., 367
Gozza, P., 506
Gozzano, G., 528, 536
Gozze, N. Vito di, 467
Gozzi, C., 518, 522
Gozzoli, B., 229
Grabbe, C. D., 791–92
Grabias, S., 963
Grabowicz, G. G., 1056
Gracheva, A. M., 1016
Gracia, J., 362
Gràcia i Solé, L., 379
Gracián, B., 114, 310–11, 487
Graciotti, S., 973
Gracq, J., 238
Gradenigo, G., 487
Gradenwitz, P., 697
· Grader, W., 139
Graefe, E., 620
Graevenitz, G. von, 800
Graf, A., 790
Graf, K., 619
Graf, R., 731
Graffi, G., 433
Graffigny, F. d'I. d'H. de
   (*Mme*), 154
Graffy, J., 1015, 1030
Gräfin Dönhoff, M., 797
Grafström, Å., 246
Grafton, A., 458, 459, 666
Graham, I., 817
Graider, N., 1058

Gramigna, G., 527, 527
Gramsci, A., 536–37
Grana, G., 529
Granada, L. de (*Fray*), 305, 310
Granados González, C. E., 282
Granda, G. de, 270, 286, 404
Granderoute, R., 135
Grandpré, C. de, 197
Grange, H., 164
Grange, W., 829
Granger, G. G., 198
Graniela Rodríguez, M., 420
Granin, D. A., 1030, 1051
Granja, A. de la, 324, 325
Grannd, S., 587
Granovskaia, L. M., 1020
Grant, R. B., 176
Granville, J. I. G., 169
Grappin, P., 706–07
Grás, B. de, 580
Grás, M. de, 580
Grass, G., 831, 832, 845, 849,
   856–57
Grassi, C., 440, 445, 448
Grassi, M.-C., 134
Grassi, O., 509, 510
Grate, P., 162
Grathoff, D., 824
Gratz, M., 860
Grauls, M., 883
Graur, A., 553
Graus, F., 622
Grautoff, O., 821, 823
Gravdal, K., 66
Grave, E., 929
Graves, P., 863, 930, 935–36
Gravina, G. V., 522
Grawe, C., 784, 790, 791
Gray, C. S., 913
Gray, F., 93–94, 96
Gray, R., 724
Graziosi, E., 513, 514
Grazzini, F., 487
Greco, F. C., 518
Greco, M. T., 443–44
Grecu, D., 554
Green, B., 936
Green, D., 561
Green, J., 36, 223
Green, J. N., 12, 17
Green, R. F., 9
Greenberg, G. R., 953, 959,
   1071
Greenberg, M., 946
Greenberg, W., 166
Greenberg, Y., 1018
Greene, G., 357
Greene, R., 479
Greenfield, J., 645
Greenway, J. L., 907

Greenwood, É., 578
Greer, M. R., 317
Gregersen, F., 902–03
Gregersen, K., 904
Grégoire, H. (*abbé*), 41, 43, 141, 144
Gregor, F., 947
Gregor, M., 720
Gregorio Cirillo, V. de, 204
Gregorovius, F., 792
Gregory, A. (*Lady*), 578
Gregory, S., 55
Gregory of Tours, 1
Greiffenberg, C. R. von, 667
Greig, S. K., 1006
Greimas, A. J., 318, 417
Greiner, B., 693
Greiner-Kemptner, U., 831
Greis, J., 687
Greive, A., 125, 605
Grenaud, P., 147
Grendler, P. F., 457
Grenier, R., 236
Grenoble, L. A., 962, 993
Grenzmann, L., 654
Greshnykh, V. I., 1046
Grésillon, A., 198
Gress, E., 910, 912
Gretz, M., 251
Greve, W., 910
Grevisse, M., 40
Grgas, S., 802
Griakalova, N. Iu., 1016
Grieger, A., 728
Griepenkerl, R., 776, 872
Grieve, P. E., 311
Griffen, T. D., 560
Griffin, R. B., 196
Griffiths, R., 192
Griggio, C., 457
Grignani, M. A., 426
Grigor'ev, A. A., 1016
Grigor'ev, V. P., 1049
Grigor'eva, L. P., 1046
Grijs, L. P., 894
Grillo, A., 500
Grillo, R. D., 251
Grillparzer, F., 712, 715, 792
Grimaldi, D., 140
Grimaldi, J. de, 333
Grimaud, M., 41
Grimberg, M., 598
Grimbert, J. T., 58
Grimm, C., 821
Grimm, E., 804, 867
Grimm, F. M., 146
Grimm, J., 15, 103, 113, 532, 590, 615, 702, 741, 752–53, 776
Grimm, R., 507, 812, 825, 853

Grimm, W., 113, 532, 702, 747, 752–53, 776
Grimmelshausen, J. J. C. von, 672, 673, 677
Grimminger, R., 802
Grin, A. S., 1026, 1027, 1038, 1040
Grinberg, M. Sh., 1010
Grinfel'd, T. Ia., 1026, 1046
Gris, J., 341, 352
Grisé, C., 103
Grishin, V. Iu., 1023
Grishina, Ia. Z., 1046
Grisi, F., 529
Grivel, G., 149
Grmek, M. D., 132
Gröbe, V., 609
Grochowiak, S., 981
Grochowski, M., 962
Groddeck, W., 801, 802
Groeneboer, K., 881–82
Gromyko, M. M., 1006
Gronda, G., 516–17, 523
Gröner, W., 871
Grønvik, O., 921
Groos, A., 7, 644
Groot, C. de, 867–68
Gros, G., 63, 66, 72, 75
Grosclaude, M., 251, 253
Grosholz, E. R., 118
Grosjean, F., 24
Gross, G., 39
Gross, M., 35, 39, 40, 607
Grosse, C., 716
Grosse, R., 594, 595
Grosse, S., 593, 594, 596
Grosser, T., 764–65
Grossman, K. M., 175
Grossman, S., 238
Grossman, V. S., 1040–41
Groth, K., 792
Grothues, S., 641
Grøtvedt, P. N., 914
Groult, F., 233
Groven, L., 915
Groznova, N. A., 988, 1027, 1037
Grübel, I., 619
Gruber, P. P., 836
Grubmüller, K., 611, 632, 640
Gruchmanowa, M., 970
Grudzińska, A., 981–82
Gruffudd Hiraethog, 563
Gruffydd, R. G., 563
Gruffydd, W. J., 566
Grün, M. von der, 857
Grün, W.-D., 719
Grünbein, D., 866
Grundmann, H., 793

Grundtvig, N. F. S., 907, 909, 911
Grunwald, M., 808
Grünzweig, W., 809
Gruša, J., 945
Gruszczyński, W., 960
Gruys, J. A., 894
Grygar, M., 938, 941
Gryphius, A., 667, 669, 675, 677–78
Gryphius, C., 675, 716
Grzegorczykowa, R., 959, 962
Gsell, O., 556
Guadalajara Medina, J., 296
Guaita Martorell, A., 266, 384–85
Gualdo Rosa, L., 459, 485
Guaragnella, P., 484
Guardenti, R., 503
Guardiani, F., 500
Guarini, B., 482, 514
Guarini, G. (Guarino of Verona), 10, 479
Guarino, G. B., 459
Guattari, F., 349
Guazzo, M., 478, 483
Guazzo, S., 467
Gubar, S., 332
Gubler, H. M., 629
Gubler, R., 406
Guccini, F., 527
Gudiksen, A., 903, 904
Gudkova, V., 1038
Guénot, H., 142
Guénoun, S., 127
Guentchéva, Z., 49
Guenther, J. von, 815
Guentner, W. A., 198
Guercio, V., 488
Guérin de la Pinelière, P., 122
Guerlac, S., 216
Guerra, T., 529
Guerra Cunningham, L., 420
Guerra Garrido, A., 370
Guerrero, M., 361
Guerrero Ruiz, P., 345
Guerricchio, R., 531
Guesle, J. de la, 92–93
Guetta, A., 487
Guevarra, C., 237
Gueye, P., 95
Gugelberger, G. M., 841
Gugenberger, E., 284
Guggisberg, H. R., 117
Guglielmi, P., 517
Guglielminetti, M., 545
Guglielmo Ebreo, 461
Guibert, J.-A., 134
Guibert, N., 158
Guibovich Pérez, P., 408

Guicciardini, F., 464, 483, 487
Guicciardini, L., 457, 464
Guichemerre, R., 101–02, 114, 115
Guidi, J., 470
Guidicelli, M.-A., 138
Guido, B., 415
Guido delle Colonne, 452
Guidotti, A., 546
Guidry, G. A., 856
Guigard, J., 227
Guilhamou, J., 133, 136
Guilhem IX of Aquitaine, 260, 261–62
Guillaume, G., 27, 28
Guillaume le Clerc, 62
Guillem de Berguedan, 263
Guillemin, A., 192
Guillén, J., 341, 342, 345, 350–51, 352, 353, 365
Guillén, N., 414
Guillén Acosta, C., 353
Guillén de Segovia, P., 269
Guilleragues, G.-J. de la V., 111
Guillet, A., 39
Guillet, P. du, 477
Guillôme, J., 570
Guillot, R., 92
Guillou, J., 934
Guimarães, E., 396
Guiraud, P., 49
Guiraut de Bornelh, 263
Guiraut Riquier, 263
Guise, R., 168
Guitart, J. M., 281
Guiter, H., 23, 250, 257
Guitton, I., 159
Guittone d'Arezzo, 452
Gul', R., 1039
Gullón, A. M., 329
Gullón, G., 327, 328, 338, 342, 356–57
Gulsoy, J., 376
Gulstad, D. E., 354–55
Gulthmüller, B., 533
Gulyga, A. V., 1024
Gumbert, J. P., 891
Gumbrecht, H. U., 297
Gumilev, N. S., 1017, 1019–20, 1027
Gummerer, H., 650
Gumpert, H. L., 764
Günderode, K. von, 691, 736, 738, 753
Gundulić, I., 1072
Gunn, D. W., 1019
Gunny, A., 132
Günsberg, M., 469
Guntert, G., 312
Günther, J. C., 872

Günther, K., 984
Guntz, E., 841–42
Gura, V. V., 1026
Gurevich, A., 51
Gurevich, A. J., 613
Gurk, P., 815
Gurtner, K., 672
Guruianu, V., 551
Gushanskaia, E. M., 1049
Gussenhoven, C., 877
Gustav III (_King of Sweden_), 143, 523, 929
Gustavsson, H., 924
Gustavsson, L., 925–26
Güstrau, S., 849
Guthke, K. S., 683, 717, 827
Guthrie, J., 725
Gutiérrez, G., 422
Gutiérrez Abelo, E., 344
Gutiérrez Flórez, F., 328
Gutowski, W., 977
Guttmann, J., 727
Guttu, T., 915
Guţu Romalo, V., 550, 553
Gutzkow, F., 732
Gutzkow, K., 737, 776, 780, 783, 792, 797
Gutzmann, G., 870
Guy, A., 306
Guyaux, A., 189, 194, 231
Guyon, A., 193, 211
Guyon, C.-M. (_abbé_), 151
Guyon, M., 238
Guzmán, J., 422
Guzmán, L. W., 337
Guzmán, M. L., 420
Gvozdanović, J., 20
Gvozdeva, E., 1031
Gyémánt, L., 551
Gyger, M., 609
Gyllensten, L., 934–35
Gyllin, R., 1079
Gyóni, M., 998
Gyurko, L. A., 420, 421

Haag, C., 23
Haage, B. D., 644
Haarmann, H., 808, 825
Haarmann, U., 620
Haas, A. M., 611
Haas, N., 649
Haas, W., 843
Haasse, H. S., 888
Habaj, I., 956
Habe, H., 815
Habermas, J., 487, 682
Habermas, R., 618
Habib, C., 148, 174, 192
Habovštiak, A., 947, 950, 951, 968

Habovštiaková, K., 948, 968
Habrajska, G., 964
Hack, T. H., 502
Hackett, C. A., 189
Hackl, W., 848
Hackländer, F. W., 776
Hacks, P., 857
Hadamar von Laber, 654
Haddock, B. A., 524
Hadewijch, 652, 890–91
Hadzins'kyi, V., 1058
Haeckel, E., 909
Haegeman, L., 958–59
Hægstad, M., 914
Haen, C. d', 887
Haestens, H. van, 894
Haferlach, T., 633–34
Haffner, S., 822–23
Hafter, M. Z., 335, 340
Hage, V., 831
Hagedorn, F. von, 686, 716
Hagen, W., 701
Hagland, J. R., 918
Hahn, B., 766, 772
Hahn, K.-H., 679, 709, 817
Hahn, R., 661
Hahn, U., 685, 843, 857
Hähnel, K.-D., 839
Hahnl, H. H., 777
Haider-Pregler, H., 843
Haidu, P., 54
Haiman, J., 441
Haines, B., 804, 811, 863
Hajek, J., 429, 441, 445
Hájek, J., 940
Hajko, D., 952
Håkansson, G., 926
Hake, T., 822
Halas, F., 943
Haldemann, M., 815
Haldorson, D., 927
Hale, J., 229
Hale, J. R., 454
Hall, B. H., 982
Hall, J., 384
Hall, K., 82
Hall, M., 835
Hall, M. B., 465
Hall, T. A., 599
Hall, T. N., 3
Hallaråker, P., 915
Halle, M., 275
Haller, A. von, 132, 686, 716–17, 757
Haller, H., 656
Haller, H. W., 444, 445
Hallman, J. C., 495
Hals, F., 229
Halse, M. E., 918
Halsey, M. T., 373

Halverson, R. J., 864
Halvorsen, E. F., 920
Halych, O., 1057
Hamada, M., 953, 954
Haman, A., 944
Hamann, J. G., 680, 717, 757–58
Hambly, P. S., 186, 188
Hamburger, M., 857–58
Hamen, S., 847
Hamer, K., 227
Hamilton, J., 197
Hamilton, J. F., 167
Hamilton, R., 408
Hamilton, R. G., 403
Hamm, H., 707
Hamm, J.-J., 170, 171
Hamm, P., 860
Hammarberg, G., 1008–09
Hammarskjöld, G., 862
Hammarsköld, L., 930
Hammer, F., 858
Hammer, K., 860
Hamon, P., 172, 203
Hamp, E. C., 553
Hamp, E. P., 550, 554, 561, 585
Hampton, T., 96, 472
Hamre, A.-M., 920
Han, U., 456
Hand, V., 549
Handke, K., 969, 970
Handke, P., 831, 831, 832, 858–59, 864, 871
Handke, R., 982
Händl, C., 659
Hauffstengel, R. von, 827
Hanganu, M. P., 390
Hanisch, E., 808, 837
Hanke, I., 860
Hankey, T., 449
Hankins, J., 10, 463
Hannan, R., 578
Hannich-Bode, I., 710
Hannon, P., 108
Hannoosh, M., 169
Hannusch, K., 790
Hänny, R., 835
Hanon, S., 34
Hansen, E., 901, 902
Hansen, F., 902, 921
Hansen, J., 1030
Hansen, M. A., 912
Hansen, T., 910, 912
Hansen, V., 793, 822
Hansen-Löve, A. A., 1013, 1021
Hansen-Löve, K., 1024
Hanson, W., 803
Hansson, G., 929
Hansson, K., 926
Hansson, O., 811

Hans von Bühel, 647
Hantula, R., 1055
Häntzschel, G., 689
Hapkemeyer, A., 847
Harbinski, Iu., 1067
Hardee, A. M., 122
Harden, T., 397
Hardenberg, F. von, *see* Novalis
Hardin, J., 675, 687, 688, 701
Hardman, J., 755
Hardy, A., 122–23
Hardy, T., 204, 539
Harelik, L., 1069
Haretski, M., 1067
Harich, W., 767
Harig, L., 831, 832, 859
Harlay, A. de, 92
Harleville, C. d', 100
Harling-Kranck, G., 927
Härmä, J., 444
Harmash, H., 1062
Harmony, O., 414
Harms, I., 763
Harnischfeger, J., 755
Haroche, C., 215
Haroche-Bouzinac, G., 107
Harpaz, E., 161, 165
Harper, A. J., 797
Harras, G., 605
Harre, C. E., 16, 272
Harris, C. J., 373
Harris, D., 343, 350
Harris, G. T., 161, 192
Harris, J., 566
Harris, J. G., 1048
Harris, J. W., 275, 276 77
Harris, M., 323, 799
Harris, M. B., 12, 15, 249
Harris, N., 471
Harris, P., 533
Harris, T. A. Le V., 201
Harris-Northall, R., 14
Harrison, A., 71
Harry, M., 210
Harsdörffer, G. P., 673–75, 676
Hart, G. K., 692
Hart, S., 348
Hart, S. M., 372, 412
Hart, T. E., 644
Hart, T. R., 312
Härtel, G., 620–21
Härtel, H., 613
Harth, E., 99
Hartinger, W., 842
Härtl, H., 742
Hartley, J. M., 1002
Hartlieb, J., 659, 663
Härtling, P., 845, 859
Hartmann, A., 864
Hartmann, L., 835

Hartmann, N., 760
Hartmann, P., 111
Hartmann, W., 623
Hartmann von Aue, 597, 612, 631, 635, 640, 642–43
Hartung, H., 842, 857
Hartung, T., 839
Hartweg, F., 27, 49, 596, 664
Hartwig, W., 773
Harun, A., 1067
Harvey, L. P., 289, 301–02
Harvey, P. M., 284
Hašek, J., 943
Hasenclever, W., 815
Hasenkamp, G., 1046
Haseryn, W., 877–78
Hasha, A. A. A., 821
Hasiuk, M., 964
Haskins, C. H., 6
Häsner, B., 468
Hasquin, H., 133
Hassauer, F., 618
Hassine, J., 228
Hasty, O., 1019, 1049
Hasubek, P., 748–49, 796, 797
Hathaway, R. L., 317
Hatto, A. T., 637
Haubrichs, W., 618, 625, 630
Hauck, D., 248
Hauf, A., 375
Haug, A., 620
Haug, W., 612, 613, 630, 632, 644, 647–48
Haugen, E., 25
Haugen, O. E., 920–21
Haupt, B., 636, 640
Haupt, M., 615, 777
Haupt, Z., 979
Hauptmann, C., 807
Hauptmann, G., 802, 815–16, 1016
Haurosh, N., 1063
Haurusiou, S., 1067
Hauschild, J.-C., 786, 795
Hausenblas, K., 943
Hausenblas, O., 941
Hausenstein, W., 786
Hauser, K., 778–79, 809–10, 865, 874
Haushofer, M., 835, 859
Häusler, W., 801
Hausmann, F.-R., 83
Haust, J., 43
Havard, R. G., 348
Havel, V., 945, 958
Haverkamp, A., 757, 758
Haverkate, H., 280–81
Havlíček, J., 944
Havlová, E., 1070
Hawes, J., 818

Hawkesworth, C., 1074
Hawkins, J., 294
Hawkins, J. P., 302
Haxell, N. A., 185
Hay, L., 174
Hayer, G., 654
Hayes, J. C., 158
Hayman, R., 228
Haymes, E. R., 615
Hayward, J., 136
Haywood, E., 470, 689
Hazaël-Massieux, M.-C., 47
Head, B. F., 402
Headley, J. M., 507
Heap, D. J., 285
Hearn, L., 186
Heathcote, O., 161–62
Heather, N., 92
Hebbel, C., 792
Hebbel, F., 638, 792–93
Hebel, J. P., 717, 754, 861
Heck, J., 508
Heck, W., 765
Heckner, S., 823
Hedd Wyn, 565–66
Hedvig Elisabeth Charlotta
    (*Queen of Sweden*), 930
Heene, K., 4
Heerich, S., 863
Heerkens, L., 883
Heertum, C. van, 894
Hees, A. van, 912
Heftrich, E., 822, 823
Heftrich, V., 943
Hegedüsová, Z., 953
Hegel, G. W. F., 162, 188, 216,
    217, 220, 510, 524, 720–21,
    749, 751, 755, 761, 770, 774,
    778, 861, 910
Hegerová, K., 947, 950
Hegyi, O., 301, 302
Heidegger, M., 146, 353, 356,
    689, 702, 847, 850, 861
Heidelberger-Leonard, I.,
    845
Heidenreich, G., 833
Heiduk, F., 750
Heier, E., 724
Heijkant, M.-J., 447
Heikkilä, R., 853
Heim, E. L., 717
Heimann, H.-D., 619
Heimann, S., 611, 648, 664
Heimbockel, D., 815
Hein, C., 797, 832, 840, 843,
    859–60
Hein, J., 801, 810
Hein, M. P., 860
Heinders, O., 886
Heine, B., 601

Heine, H., 163, 326, 679, 732,
    780, 782, 793–97, 799, 816,
    827, 846
Heinemann, E. A., 53
Heinemann, M., 943
Heinemann, W., 592, 631
Heinen, H., 649
Heinesen, W., 912
Heinisch, P., 860
Heinlen, M., 663
Heinold, A., 667
Heinrich, R., 860
Heinrich von dem Türlîn, 646
Heinrich von Freiberg, 641, 642
Heinrich von Lammesspringe,
    652
Heinrich von Langenstein, 656
Heinrich von Meissen, 650
Heinrich von Morungen, 649
Heinrich von Mügeln, 633, 654
Heinrich von Neustadt, 647
Heinrich von Veldeke, 635, 642,
    877
Heinse, W., 717
Heintz, G., 815
Heintze, M., 53
Heinze, H., 812, 826
Heinzelmann, M., 1
Heinzle, J., 638, 644–45
Heiple, D., 320
Heisenberg, W., 708
Heise-Rotenburg, M. von, 805
Heissenbüttel, H., 795–96
Heitel, I., 654
Heitman, A., 908
Heitmann, K., 550
Heitz, P., 661
Heiz, A. von, 831
Helbig, G., 590
Helbig, L. F., 785
Held, V., 648
Helderenberg, G., 887
Heldner, C., 923
Heldris de Cornuälle, 68
Helfrich, U., 604–05
Hélisenne de Crenne, 81
Helkkula-Lukkarinen, M.,
    35–36
Helleland, B., 915–16
Heller, L., 1029
Heller, L. M., 88
Hellfaier, D., 791, 792
Hellgardt, E., 630, 631
Hellinga, L., 663
Hellingrath, N. von, 758
Hellwig, J., 671
Helmer, U., 799
Helmes, G., 823
Helmetag, C. H., 815
Helmholtz, H. von, 708

Helmont, J. B. van, 676
Helmridge-Marsillian, V.,
    667–68
Heloise, 7, 618
Helt, R. G., 816
Helvétius, C.-A., 141, 172
Helvig, A. von, 745
Hemingway, E., 934
Hemingway, M., 337
Hemingway, M. J., 334
Hemmerdinger, B., 179
Hemmert-Udalska, M., 964
Hempfer, K. W., 468
Henckmann, G., 746
Henderson, I., 639, 657
Henderson, J., 464–65
Hendrick, P., 94
Hendrickson, W. L., 55
Hendrup, S., 72
Henein, E., 109
Hengst, K., 970
Henigan, J., 576
Henkel, G., 665
Henkel, N., 639, 654
Henmerdinger, B., 169–70
Henn, D., 333, 368, 369
Henne, H., 658
Henne, S., 602
Hennemann, D., 800–01
Hennequin, J., 98, 119
Henning, H., 679, 699–700,
    734, 797
Henning, J., 778
Henninger, T., 1078
Henn-Memmesheimer, B., 589,
    604
Henri II (*King of France*), 87
Henri III (*King of France*), 98
Henri IV (*King of France*), 81,
    90, 91, 98, 113
Henrich, D., 693
Henrich, F., 802
Henriksen, L., 904
Henri of Navarre, 91
Henrotte, G. A., 630
Henry VIII (*King of England*),
    78
Henry, A., 32, 58, 190
Henry, F., 39
Henry, J., 458
Henry, P. L., 578
Henry of Avranches, 8
Henry of Huntingdon, 8
Henry of Segusio (*cardinal of
    Ostia*), 8
Henry of Troyes (*Count of
    Champagne*), 643
Henry the Lion (*Duke of
    Saxony*), 617
Hensel, K., 860

Iensel, L., 797, 956
Iensen, H., 887
Ientschel, E., 601
Ientschel, G., 991
Ientschel, U., 689
Ienze, H. W., 847
Iepp, N., 98, 121
Ieraclitus, 80, 81, 217
Ieras, G., 372
Ierbert, Z., 965, 980, 981
Ierberts, K., 926
Ierborn, W., 641
Ierbort von Fritzlar, 642
Ierburger, G., 860
Ierczog, J., 516
Ierder, J. G., 679, 683, 685, 702, 717–19, 726–27, 742, 757, 766, 1075
Ierdmann, F., 148
Ieredia, J. M., 411
Ieredia, J.-M. de, 180, 183, 186
Ieredia Correa, R., 406
Ieres, G., 734
Iérilier, C., 259
Ierity, E., 802, 824
Ierles, H., 651
Ierling-Grudziński, G., 979
Ierman, J., 13, 15, 20, 155, 158
Ierman, S., 408
Iermand, J., 795, 796, 808
Iermann (*Brother*), 654
Iermann, G., 816
Iermann of Sachsenheim, 655
Iermanová, E., 942
Iermans, H., 29, 413
Iermans, T., 885, 888, 892, 899
Iermans, W. F., 885, 900
Iermenegildo, A., 299, 319
Iermes, D., 857
Iermes Trismegistus, 9, 458
Ierminghouse, P., 639
Iermlin, S., 834
Iermosilla, M. J., 302
Iermosilla Alvarez, M. A., 355
Iermsdorf, K., 817, 818
Iernández, A., 309
Iernández, C., 417
Iernández, F., 384, 423, 508
Iernández, J., 415
Iernández, M., 346
Iernández, R., 305
Iernández de León-Portilla, A., 408
Iernández García, C., 370
Iernández González, E., 324
Iernández Guerrero, J. A., 346
Iernández Novás, R., 416
Iernández-Pérez, P., 343
Iernández Sacristín, C., 280
Iernanz, M. Ll., 281

Herne, T., 935
Héroët, A., 85
Herraiz de Tresca, T., 309
Herren, M. W., 4
Herrera, F., 414
Herrera, F. de, 307
Herrera Garbarini, M. O., 276
Herreras, J. C., 266
Herrera y Reissig, J., 423
Herrero, J., 348–49
Herrero Moreno, G., 280
Herrero Ruiz de Loizaga, F. J., 272
Herrmann, H. J., 734
Herrmann, U., 402
Herrnstein-Smith, B., 357
Hertmans, S., 887
Hertzberg, F., 919
Hertzman-Ericson, G., 935
Hervás y Panduro, L., 267
Herwegh, G., 797
Herz, A., 676
Herz, H., 736, 770
Herzberger, D. K., 367
Herzen, A. I., 1007
Hesekiel, G. L., 784, 797
Hess, A.-K., 590
Hesse, C., 139
Hesse, H., 688, 810, 816
Hesse, P., 1042
Hettche, W., 700–01, 789
Hetzner, M., 787
Heukenkamp, U., 839
Heusch, C., 295
Heuser, M., 692
Heusler, A., 615
Heym, G., 816
Heym, S., 815, 834, 840, 860
Heyne, T., 692
Heyse, P., 260, 797, 798
Hibberd, J., 708, 818, 828
Hibbert, G., 307
Hickey, T., 574
Hickman, H., 823–24
Hicks, E., 74, 76
Hicks, M. R., 320
Hidalgo, M., 283
Hidalgo-Serna, E., 310
Hiddleston, J. A., 185
Hiebel, H. H., 786
Hiersche, R., 593
Hiestand, R., 621
Higginbotham, V., 349–50
Higgins, J., 422, 422
Higman, F., 78–79
Higuero, F. J., 363
Hijmans-Tromp, I., 426
Hilbig, W., 738, 864
Hilde, C., 366
Hildebrandt, R., 628

Hildebrandt, W., 839
Hildegaersberch, W. van, 890
Hildegard of Bingen (*Saint*), 7, 8, 618, 637
Hildesheimer, W., 831, 860
Hilgar, M.-F., 122–23
Hilka, A., 633
Hill, D., 726
Hille, P., 816
Hillebrand, B., 775
Hillebrand, K., 797
Hillen, G., 685
Hiller, F., 609
Hillesheim, J., 822
Hilliard, K., 760
Hillis Miller, J., 343
Hillman, R., 814
Hilpert, H., 829
Hilsch, P., 652
Hilton, I., 851, 860, 872
Hilty, G., 281
Himelblau, J. J., 406–07
Himy, O., 236
Hinard, F., 124
Hinck, W., 795, 852
Hincker, F., 134
Hincks, R., 568
Hindemith, P., 806
Hinderer, W., 776, 787, 872
Hindman, S., 663
Hindret, J., 29
Hinojosa, J. M., 343
Hinrichs, J. P., 1034–35
Hinske, N., 721
Hippel, T. G. von, 719
Hirdt, W., 204
Hirsch, H., 746
Hirsch, K. J., 816
Hirutski, A., 1064
Hitchcock, A., 228
Hitchcock, R., 289, 304
Hitler, A., 598, 936
Hjelmslev, L., 902
Hłasko, M., 981–82
Hlavač, J., 1071
Hleba, E., 953
Hnatiuk, M., 1059
Hnatiuk, V., 1052
Hnidan, O., 1056
Hnilamiodau, U., 1065
Hobbe, C., 894
Hobbes, T., 149
Hobson, M., 145
Hoccleve, T., 70
Hochel, B., 952
Hochhuth, R., 860
Hodler, F., 816
Hødnebø, F., 920
Hodrová, D., 938
Hoefert, S., 839

Hoensch, J., 942
Hofer, H., 135
Hoff, D. von, 691
Hoffer, K., 832
Hoffman, C., 550
Hoffman, D. L., 468–69
Hoffman, F., 698, 821
Hoffmann, A., 754
Hoffmann, E. T. A., 688, 696, 735, 738, 739, 740, 754–56, 764, 767, 773, 775, 780, 833, 839, 907, 1044
Hoffmann, F., 691
Hoffmann, L., 603, 778
Hoffmann, M., 712
Hoffmann, S., 148
Hoffmann, W., 641, 648
Hoffmann, W. J., 651, 654
Hoffmannswaldau, C. H. von, 667–68
Hoffmann von Fallersleben, A. H., 744, 746, 788–89
Hoffmanová, J., 945
Hoffrichter, R., 1017
Höfler, G. A., 861
Hofmann, D., 628–29
Hofmann, M., 872
Hofmannsthal, H. von, 163, 810, 816–17
Hofmeister, W., 651
Hofstaetter, U., 794–95, 821
Hoftijzer, P., 886
Hogarth, W., 755
Höglund, B., 936
Hogrebe, W., 795
Hohendahl, P. U., 749, 796
Höhle, T., 689–90
Höhn, G., 795, 796
Höhne, S., 590–91
Höijer, B.-E., 935
Holan, V., 943, 944
Holanda, F. da, 398
Holbach, P.-H. T. d' (*baron*), 131, 141
Holberg, L., 906–07
Holdenried, M., 844
Hölderlin, F., 685, 695, 735, 737, 738, 745, 756–59, 816, 833–34, 857, 861
Holk, A. G. F. van, 1018
Holker, K., 556
Holland, P., 1019
Holle, L., 663
Höller, H., 862
Hollingsworth, P. A., 51
Hollis, A., 839
Hollosi, C., 1019
Hollý, J., 946, 953, 954
Holly, K., 968, 970
Holm, C., 28

Holm, G., 921, 925
Holmbäck, B., 932
Holmberg, B., 928
Holmberg, H., 932
Holmboe, H., 904
Holmen, A., 904
Holmes, A., 187
Holmes, D., 220
Holmes, G., 458
Holmes, S., 165
Holmes, T. M., 798
Holmgren, B., 1048
Holovko, A., 1058
Holshuh, A., 871
Holstein-Rathlou, A., 906
Holt, L., 187
Hölter, A., 770–71, 818
Holtmeier, I., 750
Holtus, G., 12, 424, 438
Hölty, L. H. C., 685
Holtz, G., 826
Holub, R. C., 776, 796
Holunenko, S., 1056–57
Holusch, A., 801
Holvoet, A., 966
Holý, J., 945
Holyoake, J., 96
Hölz, K., 306
Holze, E., 725
Holzhausen, H.-D., 755
Hölzl, W., 825
Holzner, J., 809, 835
Homer, 179, 474, 541, 855
Honchar, O., 1061
Honcharuk, M., 1055
Honegger, S. C., 488
Honemann, V., 655, 660
Honigmann, B., 860
Honnef, T., 839–40, 857
Honnen, P., 607
Honowska, M., 968
Honsza, N., 856
Hoock-Demarle, M.-C., 163, 691, 737, 745
Hooff, A. J. L. van, 22
Hooft, P. C., 885, 892
Hooykaas, G. J., 886, 897
Höpel, I., 675
Hopf, K., 814, 852
Hoppe, K., 802
Hoppenbrouwers, C., 879
Hora, J., 938
Horace, 88, 308
Horat, H., 629
Horch, H. O., 783
Hordasevych, H., 1061
Hordyns'kyi, S., 1061
Horecký, J., 947, 948, 949, 950
Horiot, B., 45
Hörisch, J., 735, 764

Horkheimer, M., 681, 682, 870
Horn, P., 813
Horňanský, I., 949
Horne, M., 30
Hörnigk, F., 840
Hörnisch, J., 832
Hornstein, A. D., 524
Hornung, E., 620
Horowitz, M. C., 467
Horpynych, V., 1053
Horrocks, D., 813, 846
Horsley, R. J., 819
Horst, F., 865
Horst, P. J. van der, 881
Horta, K. M. S., 405
Horváth, Ö. von, 801, 803, 809, 817, 871
Horville, R., 100
Hosfeld, R., 796
Hostiensis, *see* Henry of Segusio
Hostinský, O., 941
Hostovský, E., 944
Houbert, O., 230–31, 239
Houin, C., 189
Houle, M. M., 99
Houmann, B., 911
Hourcade, A., 252
Hourcade, P., 112
Hourwitz, Z., 137
House, D., 924
Houston, J. P., 184
Hout, J. van, 892
Houtzagers, P., 1071
Howard, M., 762–63
Howe, E., 231
Howe, P., 804
Howell, M., 618
Howell, R. B., 877
Howell, T. J., 802
Howells, D. L. L., 985
Howells, R. J., 160
Hox, H., 730–31
Hoy, J., 9
Hoyle, A., 339
Hoyos-Andrade, R. E., 392
Hoyos y Vinent, A. de, 270
Hoyt, G. R., 687
Hrabal, B., 938, 945
Hrabanus Maurus, 484
Hradec, J., 944
Hramadchanka, T., 1065
Hrbata, Z., 942
Hrdlička, A., 784
Hrdličková, H., 967
Hrechaniuk, S., 1060
Hrinchenko, B., 1056
Hroboň, S. B., 954
Hron, J., 941
Hronský, J. C., 954–55

Hrotsvitha of Gandersheim, 618, 637
Hroudová, I., 944
Hrubaničová, I., 956
Hrushevs'kyi, M., 1052, 1053, 1056, 1059
Hrypas, N., 1053
Hryshaienko, N., 1058, 1062
Hryshyn-Hryshchuk, I., 1060
Hrytsa, S., 1056
Hrytsai, Ia., 1056
Hrytsiuta, H., 1057
Hualde, J. I., 286, 556
Huamán Poma de Ayala, F., 408, 422
Huarte de San Juan, J., 320
Huber, A., 872
Huber, C., 647, 653–54
Huber, J., 669
Huber, L., 823
Huber, M., 734
Huber, P., 816
Huber, T., 691, 825
Huber, W., 594
Hubert, I., 875
Hübner, K., 827
Hubschmid, J., 21
Huch, R., 817
Huchel, P., 857
Huchet, J.-C., 262, 264
Huchon, M., 78, 84
Huck, D., 842
Hucker, B. U., 644
Huckle, N. M., 188
Hudson, B. T., 577
Hudson, O., 357
Hue, D., 70
Huerga, C. de la, 304
Huerkamp, J., 869
Huerta, E., 330
Huesmann, M., 799
Huet, C. B., 896
Hufeisen, B., 591–92
Hufeland, C. W., 740
Huff, R., 945
Huff, S. R., 761
Huffines, M. L., 608
Hughes, A., 1
Hughes, A. J., 576, 578–79
Hughes, B. M., 566
Hughes, G. T., 564, 565
Hughes, M., 563
Hughes, P., 415
Hughes, R., 1020–21
Hug-Mander, A., 248
Hugo, A., 174
Hugo, V., 161, 163, 164, 166–67, 174–75, 177, 197, 214, 215, 226, 743, 821
Hugo von Montfort, 70

Hugo von Trimberg, 632, 633, 635, 653–54
Huidobro, V., 341, 355, 413, 417
Huish, I., 859
Huizinga, J., 871
Huldén, L., 931
Hulk, A., 36
Hullot-Kentor, O., 99
Hulse, C., 454–55
Humble, M., 807
Humbley, J., 37
Humboldt, A. von, 719, 732, 740, 759
Humboldt, W. von, 26, 718, 719, 728, 735
Hume, D., 119
Humphreys, H. Ll., 562, 569
Hundsnurscher, F., 595, 630
Hunger, U., 615
Hünnecke, E., 851
Hunnius, K., 32
Hunold, C. F., 685, 686
Hunt, I. E., 815
Hunter, G., 202
Huot, H., 27, 27
Huot, S., 70–71
Hüppauf, B., 814, 824
Huppert, G., 79
Hur, T.-U., 637
Hurevich, E., 1069
Hürlimann, T., 799
Hurskaia, A., 1069
Hurtado, A., 285
Hurtado, M., 418
Hus, J., 940
Huschenbett, D., 613, 660
Hüser, R., 861
Huster, F., 178
Hutcheon, L., 357, 360, 528
Hutchison, R., 131
Huter, M., 835
Hüttl-Folter, G., 1008
Hutton, M.-A., 169
Hutton, S., 458
Huxley, A., 943
Huygens, C., 510, 885, 887, 893
Huys, P., 829
Huysmans, J.-K., 180, 181, 192, 193, 194, 199–200, 803
Huyssen, A., 832
Hvič, J., 955
Hviezdoslav, P. O., 954
Hvišč, J., 953
Hyatte, R., 58, 60
Hyde, D., 575, 578
Hyde, G., 976, 980
Hyldgaard-Jensen, K., 595
Hyltenstam, K., 926
Hyvärin, I., 603

Iablokov, E. A., 1045–46
Iablokov, E. Ia., 1037–38
Iacopone da Todi, 451
Iadvihin Sh., 1067
Iakobson, R. O., 1031
Iáñez, E., 327
Ianivs'kyi, V., 1056
Ianovskaia, L., 1037, 1038
Ianushkevich, A. S., 1003
Ianushkevich, Ia., 1067
Ianus Pannonius (*Bishop of Pécs*), 10
Ianziti, G., 459
Iaremenko, V., 1055
Iartseva, V. N., 986
Iasenskii, S. Iu., 1014, 1016
Iashchun, V., 1052
Iashin, A. Ia., 1046
Iaskevich, A., 1069
Iasnov, M., 1034
Iatmanova, N. I., 994
Iatsuk, V., 1065
Iatsukha, V., 1068
Iavornyts'kyi, D., 1059
Ibarbourou, J., 413
Ibn Hazm, 289
Ibragimova, Z. V., 1042
Ibrahim, A., 145–46
Ibsch, E., 898
Ibsen, H., 918
Ibsen, K., 344
Ida of Boulogne, 632
Idris, J., 821
Iefremov, S., 1055
Iermano, T., 534
Iermolenko, S., 1057
Iezuitov, S. A., 1040
Iffland, A. W., 706
Iffland, J., 309
Iglesias, A., 359
Iglesias Feijoo, L., 359
Iglesias Ovejero, A., 368
Ignasiak, D., 812–13
Ignatius (*Saint*), 64
Ignatius of Loyola (*Saint*), 305, 670
Ikuta, M., 792
Ilarion (*Metropolitan*), 999
Il'ev, S. P., 1015, 1016
Il'f, I., 1038, 1041
Ilić, A., 1074
Iliescu, M., 13, 16, 18
Il'in, I. A., 1022
Il'in, V. V., 1049
Il'iunina, L. A., 1016
Iliushin, A. A., 1001
Illiano, A., 449–50
Il'nyts'kyi, M., 1057, 1058
Ilnytzkyj, O. S., 1056, 1058–59
Imbruglia, G., 143

Imhoff, A. von, 691
Imhoff, G., 224
Imm, K., 778–79
Immermann, K. L., 746, 780, 797
Inber, V. M., 1046
Inca, El, *see* Garcilaso de la Vega
Inchbald, E., 723
Incledon, J., 418
Ineichen, G., 16
Infantes, V., 306
Infelise, M., 511
Ingarden, R., 223
Ingegneri, A., 482
Ingemann, B. S., 755
Ingen, F. van, 666, 671, 672, 828
Inglés, J., 383
Inglin, M., 837
Inglot, M., 976
Ingo, R., 926
Ingold, F. P., 831
Ingoli, F., 506
Ingwersen, F., 908
Ingwersen, N., 908
Iniakhin, A., 1019
Iñigo de Mondoza, *see* López de Mendoza
Innerhofer, F., 836, 844
Innerhofer, R., 815
Innocent III (*Pope*), 8
Inov, I. V., 944
Institoris, H., 664
Invernizzi, L., 407
Inzé-Armstrong, M.-S., 205
Ioffe, S., 1038
Iolande von Vianden (*Countess*), 654
Ioli, G., 535
Ionesco, E., 234, 238–39
Ionescu, I., 553
Ioniță, V. C., 553
Ionkis, G. E., 1027
Iordan, I., 11
Iovanovich, M., 1038
Iovkov, I., 1082
Ireland, C. A., 3
Ireland, K. R., 856
Ireland, S., 241–42
Irigaray, L., 330, 832
Irina Dolgorukaia (*Princess*), 1010
Irmscher, H. D., 717–18
Irmscher, J., 734
Irwin, J. T., 415
Irzykowski, K., 977
Isaac, G. R., 561
Isaac the Syrian (*Saint*), 998
Isabeau de Bavière, 73–74

Isabel (*Queen of Castille*), 311
Isabella of Jerusalem (*Princess*), 643
'Isà b. Yàbir, 300
Isačenko, A. V., 963
Isaev, G. G., 1041
Isaev, S. G., 1041
Isaievych, Ia., 1052, 1056
Isakov, S., 1023
Isakovskaia, A. I., 1027
Isakovskii, M. B., 1027
Isbel, J., 166
Iseghem, J. van, 896
Isella, D., 535
Iser, W., 680, 790, 832, 1031
Isichenko, Iu. A., 999
Isidore of Seville (*Saint*), 289, 295, 297, 630
Iskander, F. A., 1048
Iskrzhitskaia, I. Iu., 1042
Iskul, S., 146
Isocrates, 617
Israel-Pelletier, A., 196
Issacharoff, M., 201, 233
Issorel, J., 342
Istrate, G., 551
Isupov, K. G., 1016
Iugova, D., 1083
Iukht, A. I., 1010
Iukht, B., 1029
Iulova, A. P., 1016
Iumasheva, O., 1038
Iurilli, A., 462
Iusufov, R. F., 1003
Ivaldi, C., 468
Ivanchev, S., 1080
Ivanić, D., 1075
Ivanišin, N., 1073
Ivan of Kazan' (*Saint*), 1000
Ivanov, G., 1020, 1034, 1035, 1041
Ivanov, V. I., 1014, 1020, 1022
Ivanov, Viacheslav, 1034
Ivanov, Vsevolod, 1041, 1046
Ivanov, V. V., 1020, 1022
Ivanova, D., 1079
Ivanova, E., 1017
Ivanova, E. V., 1016
Ivanova, L. L., 1049
Ivanova, N., 1029
Ivanova, T. G., 987
Ivanova, Ts., 1080–81
Ivanova, V. F., 992
Ivanovich, C., 515
Ivanov-Razumnik, R. V., 1013
Ivan Timofeev, 1001
Ivask, Iu., 1023
Ivchenko, A., 1054
Ivchenko, M., 1058
Ives, M. C., 797

Ivlev, D. D., 1039
Iwaszkiewicz, J., 978, 979
Izbicki, T. M., 656
Izquierdo Dorta, O., 337
Izzi, G., 522

Jabès, E., 239
Jabłkowska, J., 832
Jabłonowski, J. S., 974
Jaccard, J.-P., 1027, 1041
Jackson, D., 798
Jackson, K., 559
Jackson, K. D., 405, 412–13
Jackson, R. L., 1018
Jackson, T. R., 635
Jacob, M., 212, 223, 225, 239
Jacobelli, J., 540
Jacobi, F., 683
Jacobi, F. H., 742
Jacobs, A. E., 895
Jacobs, H., 28
Jacobs, M., 798
Jacobsen, J.-F., 913
Jacobsen, J. P., 909
Jacobsen, R., 672
Jacobson, E. M., 642
Jacobson Schutte, A., 505
Jacobsson, R., 620
Jacobus a Voragine, 619
Jacoby, F. R., 615
Jacopone, *see* Iacopone
Jacquard, E., 238
Jacquenoud, R., 1035
Jacques-Dalcroze, E., 212
Jadacka, M., 960
Jaeck, L. M., 418
Jaeger, A., 857, 868
Jaeger, I., 664
Jaeger, J., 873
Jaeggi, U., 845, 859
Jaekel, A., 1022
Jaffe, C. M., 338
Jager, P., 135
Jagła, D., 977
Jagueneau, L., 46
Jahier, P., 538
Jahn, F. L., 743
Jahnn, H. H., 817, 854, 860
Jahreiss, A., 598
Jakob, K., 592
Jakobsen, A., 921
Jakobsen, G., 910
Jakus-Borkowa, E., 970
James (*Saint*), 295
James, A. R. W., 161
James, E., 119, 125
James, E. D., 151
James, H., 196, 204, 797
Jameson, F., 351, 363, 704

Jameson, M., 197
Jami, 215
Jammes, F., 539
Janáčková, J., 942
Janaszek-Ivaničková, H., 943
Jančovič, S., 947
Jandl, E., 836, 861
Janés, C., 366
Janes, R., 418
Jangfeldt, B., 1042, 1047
Jänicke, O., 40
Janion, M., 972–73, 975, 981
Jankovič, M., 938, 941
Jankowski, M., 960
Janosch, H. E., 859
Janota, J., 615, 638
Janoušek, J., 942
Janoušek, P., 943, 944
Jansen, S., 482, 503
Jansen, S. M. M., 890–91
Jansen-Sieben, R., 891
Jansma, L. G., 880
Janson, T., 13
Janssen, T., 876
Janssen, T. A. J. M., 885, 888
Janssens, B., 2
Janssens, G. J., 888
Janssens, M., 887
Jansson, B. G., 935
Jansson, P., 925
Jansson, T., 935
Janyšková, I., 1070
Jara, R., 406
Jaramillo, M. M., 418
Jarczak, Ł., 970
Jardiel Poncela, E., 342
Jardine, L., 459
Jaretzky, R., 812
Jarmocik, P., 976
Jarnés, B., 342, 354
Jarnet, M., 172
Jarnut, J., 633
Jaroš, P., 955
Jarošová, A., 951
Jarowiecki, J., 975
Jarry, A., 200
Jaruzelski, W., 965
Jarzębski, J., 982
Jarzombeck, M., 484
Jäschke, K.-U., 621
Jasenas, E. F., 177
Jaślan, H., 960
Jaślan, J., 960
Jassem, W., 960
Jaucourt, L. de (*chevalier*), 144
Jaufre Rudel, 262
Jaumann, H., 672, 675
Jaume II (*King of Aragon*), 376
Jaunet, J.-J., 155
Jauralde Pou, P., 309

Jauss, H. R., 719, 1072
Javier Higuero, F., 363
Javion, M., 475
Javitch, D., 469–70
Jaworski, R., 979
Jaworski, W., 981
Jean Baptiste de la Salle (*Saint*), 120
Jeancolas, C., 189
Jean de Fécamp, 4
Jean de Mandeville, 8
Jean de Meun, 56, 62, 74, 77
Jean de Montreuil, 77
Jean le Bel, 74
Jeanneret, M., 87, 92
Jeanneret, T., 48
Jefferson, T., 734
Jehensen, Y., 312
Jehle, V., 860
Jekiel, W., 973
Jelčić, D., 1073
Jelinek, E., 835, 861
Jelsma, G. H., 880
Jenaczek, F., 819
Jenihen, M., 1072
Jenkins, G. H., 565
Jenkins, K., 564
Jenkyns, R., 12–13
Jens, W., 840, 861
Jensen, F., 247
Jensen, J. V., 913
Jensen, K.-A., 99
Jensen, N., 455
Jensen, T., 913
Jentzsch, B., 838
Jeon, D.-Y., 816
Jeppesen, B. H., 913
Jeremić, Lj., 1075
Jerez-Ferrán, C., 360
Jerke, H., 923
Jerome (*Saint*), 3, 4, 267
Jerzewski, R., 867
Jeschke, C., 123
Jesenský, J., 955
Ješić, N., 1075
Jessen, P., 416
Jessing, B., 705
Jeune, S., 178
Jhering, H., 843
Jida, S., 240–41
Jimack, P., 149
Jiménez, D. J., 364
Jiménez, J. O., 360
Jiménez, J. R., 331, 342, 351
Jiménez, L. A., 415
Jiménez, Y., 420
Jiménez Faro, L., 423
Jiménez Martínez, J., 277
Jiménez-Vera, A., 349
Jiráček, P., 938

Joachim of Fiore, 466
Joanna (*Queen of Naples*), 449
Joan of Arc, 75
Job (*Saint*), 998
Jodelle, E., 89, 93
Johanek, P., 619, 632
Johannes de Sacrobosco, 615
Johannessen, O.-J., 916
Johannet, J., 998
Johann von Soest, 662
Johann von Tepl, 658–59
Johann von Vippach, 654
Johann von Würzburg, 647, 662
John (*King of England*), 53
John (*Lord of Duniveg*), 585
John, S. B., 230
John Cantacuzenus, 998
John Climacus (*Saint*), 998
John of Biclaro, 289
John of Freiburg, 8
John of Garland, 9
John of Gaunt, 9
John of Salisbury, 6, 7, 622
John of the Cross (*Saint*), 305, 307, 341
Johns Blackwell, M., 911
John Scotus, 646
Johnson, A. L., 373
Johnson, B., 185
Johnson, C. B., 311, 313
Johnson, D., 199
Johnson, D. B., 1044
Johnson, E., 935
Johnson, J. G., 409
Johnson, L., 70
Johnson, S., 151
Johnson, U., 705, 754, 840, 845, 861–62
Johnston, O. W., 823
John the Deacon of Rome, 2
Johst, H., 817
Joinville, J. de, 65, 74
Jokl, J., 795
Jolles, C., 776–77, 790
Jolley, N., 119
Joly, A., 28
Joly, J., 517
Joly, M., 312
Jóna, E., 946, 947
Jonard, N., 448–49, 474, 486
Jonasson, K., 42
Jones, A. R., 477
Jones, B., 564, 566, 567
Jones, B. L., 564, 566
Jones, B. M., 559
Jones, C. M., 561
Jones, C. N., 803, 817
Jones, D. F., 125
Jones, D. G., 565
Jones, E. J., 563

Jones, G. A., 565
Jones, G. F., 659
Jones, G. J., 214
Jones, G. W., 566
Jones, H. P., 566
Jones, J., 416, 421
Jones, J. A., 310
Jones, J. F., Jr, 149
Jones, J. G., 563
Jones, J. W., 562, 807, 827
Jones, L. C., 7
Jones, M., 733, 1038
Jones, M. E. W., 370–71
Jones, R. M., 564
Jones, R. O., 562
Jones, S., 792
Jones, T., 565
Jones, W. G., 909, 912, 1002
Jones, W. J., 597, 631, 660
Jong, D. de, 900
Jong, I. J.-F. de, 127
Jong, M. J. G. de, 887
Jongen, L., 891
Jonghe, F. de, 897–98
Jonke, G., 836
Jordan, B., 367–68, 371
Jordan, C., 466–67
Jordan, L., 787–88
Jordanes, 625
Jordans, P., 599
Jordy, J., 160
Jørgensen, Aa., 905, 906, 907
Jørgensen, B. D., 903
Jørgensen, B. H., 905–06
Jørgensen, J., 910
Jørgensen, J. N., 902, 903
Jørgensen, K. B., 1035
Jorgensen, P. A., 660
Jørgensen, S. A., 733
Joseph of Jerusalem, 620
Joseph of Volokolamsk, 1000
Josephs, A., 349
Joset, J., 292–93
Josić-Višnjić, M., 1075
Jost, D., 815
Jost, R., 812
Joubert, J., 162
Joubert, J.-P., 134
Jouffroy, A., 189
Jouhaud, C., 97
Joukovsky, F., 78, 80–81, 88
Jourda, P., 199
Jourde, P., 237
Journeau, B., 337
Joutard, P., 133
Jouve, P. J., 208, 209, 223–24
Jouve, S., 200
Jouvet, L., 213
Joyce, J., 164, 231, 342, 526, 582, 868, 869, 1044

Juana Inés de la Cruz (*Sor*), 308, 311, 325, 408, 409
Juan Bolufer, A. de, 368
Juan Manuel (*Don*), 294
Juaristi, F., 363
Juaristi, J., 364
Jubé de la Cour, J. (*abbé*), 1010
Jubien, A., 207
Juettner, S., 145
Julian (*Emperor*), 177
Julius II (*Pope*), 462, 464
Julius Caesar, 622, 624
Juneau, M., 45
Jung, C. G., 69, 373, 422
Jung, F., 817
Jung, F. W., 758
Jung, M.-R., 264
Jung, R., 39
Jung, W., 789–90
Jüngel, E., 757
Jünger, E., 808, 817, 833
Jungmann, J., 965
Jungmann, M., 944
Junqué, C., 386
Junquera, C., 284
Junyent, S., 373
Jürgens, C., 845
Jurgensen, M., 777
Juričić, Ž., 1075
Jurieu, P., 117
Jurkevich, G., 358
Jurkowski, H., 206
Jurkowski, M., 965
Jurt, J., 194
Jussieu, A.-L. de, 136
Juvenal, 450
Juzyn-Amestoy, O., 414

Kabiljo-Šutić, S., 1072
Kablitz, A., 468
Kačala, J., 947, 949
Kachatkova, V., 1066
Kachurovs'kyi, I., 1055
Kacimi, M., 190
Kaczynski, M., 199
Kaempfer, J., 193, 240
Käfer, M., 734
Kafitz, D., 810, 865
Kafka, F., 218, 423, 450, 526, 537, 739, 792, 802, 809, 810, 817–18
Kafka, J. S., 598
Kafker, F. A., 146
Kahler, M.-L., 707
Kahn, V., 487
Kaimowitz, J. H., 406
Kaiser, F., 797
Kaiser, G., 640, 782–83
Kaiser, G. R., 741

Kaiser, H., 800
Kaiser, V., 825
Kaji, S., 1035
Kakhanouski, H., 1066
Kalakutskaia, L. P., 994
Kalashnikava, A., 1063
Kalašnikova, O. E., 992
Kalepis, E., 408
Kaliada, H., 1069
Kalinke, M. E., 643, 661
Kaliuha, L., 1067
Kalivoda, R., 941
Kałkowska, A., 959
Kallendorf, C., 457
Kalsbeek, A. van, 883
Kalubovich, A., 1065
Kalynets', I., 1062
Kamarouski, A., 1068
Kamarouski, Ia., 1065
Kamata, M., 822
Kambas, C., 811
Kameisha, K., 1068
Kamenskii, V. V., 1020
Kamińska, H. J., 967
Kamińska, M., 964, 970
Kamińska-Szmaj, I., 958
Kamm, L., 169, 205
Kampers-Manhe, B., 33
Kamprath, C. K., 555
Kane, M., 840, 847
Kaneko, M., 187
Kaniushkevich, M., 1064
Kannegiser, N., 1022
Kant, H., 840, 862
Kant, I., 94, 141, 374, 682, 683, 685, 693, 710, 716, 718, 719–22, 723, 724, 737, 751, 756, 760, 769, 774, 793, 795
Kantemir, A. D., 1002, 1008
Kantsavaia, H., 1065
Kanzog, K., 784
Kaplan, J. M., 143
Kapp, V., 123, 161
Kapusta, V., 1058
Karabchievskii, Iu. A., 1027, 1035, 1042
Karadžić, V. St., 1075, 1076–77
Karamańska, M., 960–61
Karamzin, N. M., 689, 1008–09
Karasek, H., 822
Karasek, K., 983
Karaslavov, G., 1082
Karaslavov, S. Kh., 1082
Karatkevich, U., 1067
Karatsinidou, C., 175
Karavanov, A. A., 993
Karbach, W., 786, 862
Karfík, V., 945
Karhaus, U., 855
Karion Istomin, 1001

Karl, F., 790
Karl August (*Duke of Saxe-Weimar*), 701–02
Karl Eugen (*Duke of Württemberg*), 682
Karlovska, A., 995, 1080
Karnilovich, E., 1067
Karolak, C., 832
Karotkaia, T., 1066, 1068
Karp, S., 146
Karpilovs'ka, Ie., 1053
Karpov, P. I., 1016
Karpowicz, T., 982
Karro, F., 123–24
Karski, Ia., 1064
Karst-Matausch, R., 133
Karthaus, U., 822
Karvaš, P., 956
Karytski, M., 1067
Kasabov, I., 1078
Kasatkina, R. F., 991
Kaschnitz, M. L., 846, 862
Kaser, N., 862
Kašpar, O., 1005
Kaspers, A. M., 884
Kaspers, K., 758
Kassier, T. L., 293
Kaštelan, J., 1073
Kasten, I., 611, 618, 648
Kastl, M., 801
Kästner, E., 818
Kästner, H., 594, 620, 653, 661
Kataev, V. I., 994
Kataev, V. P., 1019, 1027
Katanian, V., 1042
Katharina (*Margravine of Meissen*), 654
Katny, A., 602
Kats, B., 1043
Katsis, L., 1025
Katz, D. M., 62
Katz Crispin, R., 352
Katzer, N., 1040
Kauchtchischwili, N., 1015
Kauffman, F., 628
Kaufman, P. H., 136
Kaufmann, A., 709
Kaufmann, E., 840, 863
Kaufmann, F.-M., 620–21
Kaufmann, H., 703–04
Kaufmann, U., 786
Kaukoreit, V., 854
Kaulen, H., 758, 847
Kaurus, A., 1063
Käuser, A., 693–94, 704
Kautz, U., 602
Kavalenka, U., 1068
Kaván, F., 941
Kavanagh, R. J., 812
Kaverin, V. A., 1041, 1051

Kawaguchi, J., 36
Kawanago, Y., 717
Kay, S., 55, 59
Kaye, J., 391
Kayne, R. S., 18, 32
Kayser, A. C., 722
Kazakevich, E. G., 1027
Kazakov, Iu. P., 1041
Kazbiaruk, U., 1067
Kaz'ko, V., 1067, 1068
Kazubko, K., 871
Keats, J., 163, 791
Keck, T., 184, 809
Keenan, P. J., 576
Keersmaekers, A., 887
Kègle, C., 222
Kehn, W., 692
Keil, G., 658
Keiler, O., 790
Keinästö, K., 594
Keipert, H., 991, 1070
Keith-Smith, B., 817, 818, 826, 827
Keldysh, V., 1023
Kelle, B., 607
Kelledonk, A., 885
Keller, G., 706, 708, 732, 779, 782, 798–99, 837
Keller, H.-E., 57, 63, 245, 263, 264
Keller, H. H., 995
Keller, M., 30
Keller, O., 814
Kelletat, A. F., 849, 860
Kelley, E. B., 312
Kelley, M. J., 289, 292
Kellman, S. G., 236–37
Kelly, A., 69
Kelly, D., 51, 57
Kelly, J., 193
Kelm, O. R., 390
Kemball, R., 1049
Kemp, L., 348
Kempchinsky, P., 281
Kemper, H.-G., 685–86
Kempf, T., 682
Kempowski, W., 862
Kempter, L., 757
Kennedy, A., 76
Kennedy, E., 56
Kenny, N., 80, 82, 108
Kenstowicz, M., 428, 429
Kent, F. W., 484
Kenwood, A., 412
Keown, D., 358
Kepler, J., 666
Kerbrat-Orecchioni, C., 35
Kerekes, G., 790, 791, 840, 847, 860
Kerkhof, M. P. A. M., 296

Kermode, F., 339
Kern, G., 1041
Kerner, J., 799
Kerner, M., 622
Kerner, S., 256
Kerr, A. P., 179
Kerr, J., 585
Kerr, L., 421
Kerr, R. A., 422
Kerschbaumer, M.-T., 835, 862
Kerson, A. L., 406
Kesselring, W., 37
Kessler, H. G., 818
Kessler, J. C., 166, 176
Kester, E.-P., 18, 276
Kestien, K., 819
Kesting, M., 738
Ketelsen, U.-K., 686
Kets Vree, A., 897
Kettmann, G., 596
Keun, I., 819
Kevorkian, S., 116
Keyserling, E. von, 807, 819
Khaburgaev, G. A., 990
Khalizev, V. E., 1031
Kharalampiev, I., 1078–79
Kharchuk, B., 1061
Kharchuk, R., 1059
Khardzhiev, N., 1021
Kharer, K., 1022
Kharms, D. I., 1041
Kharoshka, H., 1067
Khatiushin, V., 1034
Khazan, V. I., 1019, 1039, 1042
Kheraskov, M. M., 1003
Kheraskova, E. V., 1003
Khimich, V. V., 1041
Khimukhina, N. I., 1036
Khlebnikov, V. V., 1020
Khodasevich, V. F., 1013, 1020–21, 1034, 1037
Kholodova, G., 1019
Kholopova, V. F., 1044
Khomiakov, A. S., 1016
Khoteev, P. I., 1005–06
Khotkevych, H., 1059
Khranova, A., 1083
Khrapovitskii, A. V., 1007
Khristov, M., 1079
Khristova, E., 1080
Khusikhanov, A. M., 1039
Khuzakhmetova, N., 1058
Khvorostinin, I. A., 1001
Khvyl'ovyi, M., 1058–59
Kiaeva, E., 1080
Kibal'nik, S. A., 1004
Kibbee, D. A., 28–29
Kibédi-Varga, A., 101
Kibirov, T., 1034
Kibler, W. W., 54

Kidd, W., 194, 216
Kieckhefer, R., 619
Kiefer, K. H., 722
Kieffer, H., 168
Kiening, C., 645, 659
Kierkegaard, S., 543, 795, 802, 848, 907, 910
Kieser, R., 820
Kiesler, R., 399
Kihm, A., 390
Kiianova, O. N., 991
Kiliaen, C., 894
Killeen, J. F., 579, 586
Killiam, M.-T., 219
Killick, R., 185, 188
Kim, A. A., 1030
Kim, D. G., 781
Kim, S.-Y., 874
Kim, Y.-E., 195
Kim, Y.-H., 803
Kinder, G., 304
Kindermann, U., 5, 9
King, J. C., 629
King, K. C., 418
King, P. K., 885
King, R., 46
Kingma-Eijgendaal, A. W. G., 190
Kinkel, J., 799
Kinkelbach, Q. von, 773
Kinloch, D., 162
Kinney, P., 563–64
Kinov, V., 1049
Kinskofer, L., 747–48
Kinzel, U., 848
Kinzer, C., 813
Kinzler, C., 121–22
Kipphardt, H., 786, 862
Kiraly, F., 553
Kircher, A., 493
Kirchert, K., 613
Kirchhoff, B., 862
Kirchner, H., 776
Kireev, R., 1029
Kirill of Turov, 999
Kiriukhina, E. M., 1048
Kirkness, A., 605
Kirkness, J., 127
Kirkwood, M., 1050
Kirmmse, B. H., 910
Kirsanov, S. I., 1033
Kirsch, F. P., 249, 264–65
Kirsch, R., 862
Kirsch, S., 841, 862–63, 866
Kirsch, W., 633
Kirschner, T. J., 321
Kirsner, R., 368
Kirsner, R. S., 877
Kirsten, W., 842
Kiš, D., 1074

Kisch, E. E., 809
Kischkel, R., 592
Kiselev, A. K., 1038
Kiselev, A. L., 1046
Kiseleva, L. F., 1038
Kishitani, S., 638
Kisiel, M., 981
Kiss, S., 17
Kissling, W., 612
Kitcher, P., 721
Kite, B., 129
Kitina, A., 1080
Kittler, F. A., 696
Kittler, W., 705
Kiukhel'beker, V. K., 1008, 1009
Kiuvlieva-Mishaikova, V., 1078
Kivel', I., 1067
Kjærheim, S., 920
Kjøller, K., 902
Klajn, I., 432
Kłak, T., 979
Klanska, M., 809
Klapisch-Zuber, C., 461
Klauser, H., 803
Kleber, P., 843
Kleiber, C., 868, 871
Kleiber, G., 31
Kleiber, W., 606
Kleijn, P. G. M. de, 888
Klein, A., 716
Klein, F., 281
Klein, I., 495
Klein, J., 25, 591, 943, 1010
Klein, K., 651
Klein, K. W., 261
Klein, T., 630–31, 641
Klein, T. A.-P., 6, 9
Klein, W., 604
Kleindienst, H., 699
Kleiner, J., 975
Kleinert, A., 137, 519
Kleinhenz, C., 495
Kleinschmidt, E., 685
Kleinteich, S., 868
Kleist, E. C. von, 686
Kleist, H. von, 738–39, 740, 741, 748, 759–64, 774, 783, 834, 840, 860, 861, 864
Klemm, I., 774, 810
Klen, Iu., 1061
Klenk, U., 302
Klenner, H., 695
Klepper, J., 808
Klerk, G. J. de, 891
Klesatschke, E., 611, 650
Klessmann, E., 612–13, 662
Kleszczowa, K., 961
Klettenhammer, S., 862

Kliebenstein, G., 198
Kliemann, J., 461
Klimenko, M., 1039
Klimova, G. P., 1046
Klimowicz, T., 1017
Klim Smoliatich, 999
Klinger, F. M., 692
Klinger, K., 828
Klingmann, U., 874
Klintberg, B. af, 927
Kliuchevskii, V. O., 1005
Kliuev, N. A., 1021, 1028
Kloocke, K., 165
Klopstock, F. G., 680, 685, 722, 730
Kloss, B. M., 997
Klotz, C., 850
Kluck, F., 176
Klueting, H., 696
Klug, C., 848
Kluge, A., 863
Kluge, B., 623
Kluge, K., 819
Kluge, R.-D., 1017
Kluge-Pinsker, A., 623–24
Kluger, H., 622
Kluhn, N., 420
Kluncker, K., 815
Kluppelholz, H., 62
Klussmann, P. G., 866
Klychkov, S. A., 1027
Klymenko, N., 1053
Klyshka, A., 1063, 1066
Kmita, F., 1063
Knabe, P., 145
Knape, J., 653, 664
Knapp, B., 199
Knapp, B. L., 349, 858
Knapp, F. P., 616, 632, 635
Knapp, G. P., 680, 739
Knauss, S., 832
Kniazev, Iu. P., 993
Kniazhnin, Ia. B., 1003
Kniesche, T. W., 856
Knigge, A. von (*Freiherr*), 722–23
Knight, A. E., 65
Knight, R. C., 122
Knight, R. P., 703
Knoblauch, C., 603
Knobloch, C., 602
Knobloch, H., 863
Knodt, E., 718–19
Knoll, S. B., 718
Knox, D., 458
Knut, D., 1034
Knutson, H., 125, 127
Kobel-Bänninger, V., 820
Köbler, G., 625
Kobolt, E., 590

Kobylas, J. G., 339
Kobylińska, J., 966
Koch, C. H., 910
Koch, E., 810
Koch, G., 863
Koch, J. T., 560
Koch, P., 17
Koch, R., 861
Kochanowski, J., 966, 974
Kochetkova, N. D., 1003
Kochev, I., 1080
Kocheva, A., 1078, 1079
Koch-Häbel, B., 753
Kochiwa, M., 336
Kochman, S., 961
Kočiš, F., 949
Kock, J. de, 279
Koebner, T., 806, 808
Koekman, J., 887
Kocpke, W., 688, 718, 808
Koeppel, A., 651
Koeppen, W., 834, 863
Koester, R., 813
Kofler, G., 862
Kofman, S., 124
Kogan, P., 1044
Kohl, J. G., 799
Kohl, K. M., 722
Kohlenbach, M., 755
Köhler, E., 261, 837
Köhler, O., 797
Köhler, R., 773
Kohn, G., 616
Köhn, R., 622
Kohnen, J., 719
Kohn-Waechter, G., 847
Kohut, K., 416, 419
Koike, D. A., 396–97
Kokoschka, O., 819
Kolankiewicz, L., 975
Kolář, J., 938
Kolas, Ia., 1067
Kolb, A., 819
Kolb, H., 630
Kolb, P., 228
Kolbenhoff, W., 844
Kolbuszewski, S. F., 969
Kolchakova, A., 1050
Kolde, G., 602
Kolesnikoff, N., 1030, 1048
Kolesnikova, E. N., 1017
Kolessa, F., 1056
Kolinsky, E., 590
Kolk, R., 615, 777
Kolkenbrock-Netz, J., 812
Kolker, Iu., 1036
Kollár, A. F., 953
Kollár, D., 946
Kollár, J., 941, 953, 954
Koller, E., 397, 595, 607

Koller, H.-C., 733
Kolmar, G., 819
Kolobaeva, L. A., 1022, 1040, 1043
Kolodnyi, L., 1047
Kolsky, S. D., 470–71, 478–79, 486
Kölwel, G., 819
Komarovskii, V. A., 1021
Komarynets', T., 1057
Komenský, J. A., 267, 940, 946
Komorowski, M., 699
Kompaneets, V. V., 1036
Kompert, L., 777, 799
Komrij, G., 885
Konan, U., 1064, 1066
Konchalovskii, A., 1037
Kondrat'ev, A., 1035
Kondrat'ev, V., 1030, 1048
Kondrat'ev, V. K., 1022
Kondratiuk, A., 1055
Kondratovich, A. I., 1028
Kondrup, J., 910–11, 912
Konenko, V., 1053
Konicka, H., 981
Konietzko, P., 641
König, E., 663
König, F., 784
König, W., 599, 607
Königsdorf, H., 839, 840, 863
Koning, H. J., 755, 777, 801
Kononenko, I., 1053
Konrad II (German king), 623
Konrad, S., 790
Konrad, W., 855
Konrad von Heimesfurt, 651
Konrad von Megenberg, 635
Konrad von Stoffeln, 647
Konrad von Würzburg, 633, 635, 647, 651, 662
Konstantin (Grand Duke), 1016
Kontzi, R., 302
Konwicki, T., 973, 982
Konzal, V., 1000
Kooiman, D. A., 888
Koolhaas, A., 885
Koopmann, H., 708, 763, 783, 800, 823
Koopmans, J., 72, 93, 893–94
Kopcińska, D., 959
Kopciński, J., 979
Köpcke, K. M., 601
Kopecký, M., 940
Kopelev, L., 1048
Kopeliovich, A. B., 993
Kopertowska, D., 970
Köpf, G., 802
Kopit, A., 359
Köpke, W., 766
Koplan, B., 1033

Kopland, R., 887
Kopp, R., 194
Köppe, C., 780
Köpperschmidt, J., 617, 745
Koprda, P., 955
Kopylenko, N., 1058
Korablev, A., 1038
Körber, L., 809
Koren, R., 138
Koretskaia, I. V., 1020, 1042
Korhonen, J., 594
Kormilov, S., 1015
Kormilov, S. I., 1004
Kornblatt, J. D., 1024
Körner, C. G., 743
Körner, K.-H., 17, 34
Körner, T., 761
Körner, W., 717
Kornfeld, P., 809
Kornhall, D., 928
Kornhauser, J., 980
Kornienko, N. V., 1040
Kornrumpf, G., 654, 655
Korolenko, A. I., 1036
Korolenko, V. G., 1021, 1027
Kortazar, J., 363
Korteweg, A., 887
Kortländer, B., 796
Kortlandt, F., 597, 990–91
Kortum, K. A., 686
Korzen, H., 34
Korzhavin, N., 1048
Koš, E., 1074
Kosegarten, L. T., 761, 799
Koselleck, R., 683
Košenina, A., 728
Koseska-Tosheva, V., 1080
Koshechkin, S., 1039
Koshelivets', I., 1060
Kosiński, J., 982
Koslowski, P., 817
Kośny, W., 965
Kosta, P., 990
Kostashchuk, V., 1059
Kostenko, L., 1057, 1061
Kostenko, V., 1059
Kostić, L., 1075
Kostin, E. A., 1047
Kostiuk, H., 1060
Kostomarov, M., 1056
Kostov, K., 602, 1078
Kostrhun, J., 945
Kosyl, C., 967
Kotake, S., 650
Kotel'nikov, V. A., 1012
Kotler, E., 91
Kots'-Hryhorchuk, L., 1052
Kotsiubyns'ka, M., 1061, 1062
Kotsiubyns'kyi, M., 1056
Kott, J., 972

Kotzebue, A. von, 687, 706, 723, 730
Koutun, V., 1069
Kovačec, A., 11–12
Kovačević, M., 1071
Kovachev, N., 1081
Kovacheva, N., 995
Kovačić, A., 1073
Kovács, K., 849
Koval'chuk, O., 1060, 1061
Kovalčík, V., 954
Kovalenko, A. G., 1041
Kovalets', L., 1058
Kovaliv, Iu., 1061, 1062
Kovskii, V. E., 1026
Kowalczykowa, A., 974, 976
Kowalik, J. A., 726
Kowalik, K., 958
Kowallik, S., 443, 605
Kowalska, A., 963, 964, 969
Kowalski, S., 967
Kowlaczykowa, A., 972
Koyré, A., 111, 508
Kozak, C., 416
Kozarynowa, Z., 979
Kozarzewska, E., 962
Kozhevnikova, T., 1016
Kozhina, R. V., 1044
Koziełek, G., 621
Kozierkiewicz, R., 960
Kozlov, S. V., 999
Kozlovskii, Iu. A., 1021
Koz'menko, M. V., 1022
Koźmian, K., 974
Kožmín, Z., 943
Kozovoï, V., 1044
Kraan, R. G. K., 886
Kracauer, S., 819, 873
Krachek, V., 1064
Kraft, H., 679, 712, 818
Kraft, K.-F., 650
Kräftner, H., 835
Krag, C., 920
Krahé, P., 767–68
Kraiker, G., 824
Krajenbrink, M., 739
Krajewska, B., 99–100
Král', J., 954
Kralčák, Ľ., 949
Králík, O., 941
Kralt, P., 898
Kramer, J., 556, 604, 605
Krämer, J., 671–72
Krämer, M., 24
Krämer, R., 835
Kramer, R., 886
Krämer, T., 814
Kramerius, V. M., 941
Krameus, P., 934
Kranke, K., 796

Kranz, G., 817
Krapiva, K., 1067
Krasicki, I., 974
Krasil'nikov, E. V., 1050
Krasiński, Z., 973, 975
Krasivs'kyi, Z., 1061
Krasnov, V., 1029
Krasnova, E. V., 901
Krasyts'kyi, D., 1056
Kraszewski, C. S., 976
Kraszewski, J. I., 975
Kratochvíl, M. V., 943
Krättli, A., 749, 840, 853
Kratz, B., 630
Kratzsch, K., 793
Krau, J., 122
Kraus, C., 953
Kraus, H., 830
Kraus, K., 785, 809, 811, 813, 819–20
Kraus, M., 844
Krause, B., 631
Krause, K. C. F., 723–24
Krausnick, M., 797
Krautsova, V., 1065
Krauz, M., 959
Kravchenko, B. N., 1021
Kravchuk, P., 1058
Kravets, E. V., 991
Kravets', V. V., 1020
Krebs, J.-D., 675
Krefeld, T., 17
Kreid, V., 1035, 1041
Kreis, G., 819
Kreja, B., 963, 964
Krejča, O., 1019
Kremer, D., 11, 556
Kremnitz, G., 24, 250–51, 376
Krems, R., 861–62
Kretschmar, J. C. H., 748
Kretzenbacher, H. L., 592
Kreutzer, G., 920
Kreutzer, H., 795
Kreutzer, H. J., 761
Kreuzer, H., 507, 810, 835, 866
Krieger, D., 657
Krieger, M., 596
Kriegesmann, U., 593
Krier, F., 607
Krischke, T., 817
Kriššáková, J., 968
Kristeller, P. O., 454, 457
Kristensen, K., 903
Kristensen, T., 913
Kristeva, J., 233, 366, 680, 832
Kristiansen, T., 902, 903
Kristol, A. M., 249, 253
Kritsch Neuse, E., 811, 844
Kritzman, L. D., 80, 87
Kriukov, F., 1041

Křivánek, V., 941
Krivoshchapova, T. V., 1013
Krivulin, V., 1034
Krizanic, J., 508
Krleža, M., 1073
Krman, D., 946
Krnjević, H., 1076
Krobb, F., 803
Kroesen, R., 921
Kroetz, F. X., 863
Krohn, R., 658
Kröhnke, K., 815
Kröker, V., 504
Krokvik, J., 915
Krol, G., 888, 900
Krolop, R., 631
Krolow, K., 846, 860
Kronauer, B., 831, 832, 863–64
Kronwald, J., 980
Krooks, D. A., 629
Krošláková, E., 968
Kruchenykh, A. E., 1021, 1027, 1033
Krückeberg, E., 817
Kruckis, H.-M., 778
Krugel, L., 177
Krüger, P., 621, 638
Krüger, S., 639
Krugovoy, G., 1037
Kruken, K., 915–16, 917
Krummacher, H.-H., 805
Krupa, V., 956
Krupchanov, A. L., 1033
Krupina, N. L., 1029
Kruse, A., 644
Kruse, J. A., 793, 795, 796
Krustev, B., 1081
Krustev, K., 1082
Krutalevich, M., 1063
Kruus, R., 1047
Krylov, I. A., 961, 1009
Krylova, E. B., 901
Kryms'kyi, A., 1053, 1059
Krynicki, R., 980
Kryński, S., 979
Krysa, B., 1055
Krysin, L. P., 992
Krysztofiak, M., 913
Kryzhanivs'kyi, S., 1058
Kryzhanovskii, A., 1034
Krzhivinskaia, L. V., 1047
Kšicová, D., 1014
Kuba, 864
Kubczak, H., 600
Kubik, S., 785
Kublanovskii, Iu., 1031
Kublanovskii, Iu. M., 1035
Kuby, E., 844
Kucała, M., 958, 963
Küchler-Sakellariou, P., 756

Kuchyns'kyi, M., 1056
Kuckhoff, A., 786
Kuczynski, K. A., 815–16
Kudělka, V., 943
Kudelski, Z., 979
Kudo, S., 246
Kudravets, A., 1068
Kudriavtsev, M., 1062
Kudrnáč, J., 941
Kudrova, I. V., 1049
Kügelgen, G., 748
Kuhlis, D., 726
Kuhlmann, Q., 665, 668
Kühlmann, W., 671, 673, 716
Kuhn, A., 695–96
Kuhn, D., 646, 708, 869
Kühn, P., 605
Kuhn, T., 812
Kuhn, T. S., 690
Kühne, U., 8, 650
Kühnel, H., 619
Kuhnigk, M., 786
Kühnlenz, A., 786
Kuiken, F., 883
Kuizenga, D., 106
Kukharau, S., 1068
Kuklin, L., 1033
Kukuljević-Sakcinski, I., 1073
Kukushkina, E. Iu., 1017
Kukushkina, Iu. N., 1024
Kulakouski, A., 1068
Kulakov, V., 1033, 1034
Kul'bakin, A. A., 995
Kul'chyns'ka, T., 1058
Kul'gavchuk, M. V., 1047
Kulish, M., 1059
Kulish, P., 1056
Kumkan, K. A., 1016
Kümmerling-Meibauer, B., 810
Kundera, M., 945
Kündig, M., 826
Kundzich, O., 1061
Kunert, G., 834, 838, 839, 846, 864
Kunert, H. P., 250
Kunerts, G., 738–39
Kunev, T., 1082
Kuniaev, S., 1030, 1034, 1049
Kunińska, J., 967
Kunne, A., 835–36
Kunøe, M., 902
Kunstmann, H., 970, 994, 1070
Kuntysh, M. F., 1018
Kunze, J., 602
Kunze, M., 733–34
Kunze, R., 838
Kuo, M.-J., 864
Kuon, P., 548
Kupala, Ia., 1068
Kupchenko, V. P., 1024, 1025

Kupchyns'kyi, R., 1060
Küper, C., 601–02
Kupferman, L., 32
Kupiszewski, P., 965
Kupiszewski, W., 964, 965, 967
Kupka, A., 869
Kupriianov, I. T., 1024
Kupriianova, I. P., 913
Kuprin, A. I., 1021, 1038, 1041
Kurakin, I. S., 998
Kurbatov, V., 1027
Kurbeka, I., 1068
Kuritsyn, V., 1034
Kurlandskii, I., 1020
Kurlova, R., 1079
Kürnberger, F., 686, 859
Kurpacheva, M., 1078
Kurpanik-Malinowska, G., 738
Kurscheidt, G., 710
Kürschner, J., 789
Kurshakova, R., 1080
Kurtz, B., 317
Kurvers, J., 882
Kuryło, E., 962–63
Kurz, G., 787
Kurzke, H., 823
Kushner, A. S., 1033
Kustanovich, K., 1048
Küsters, U., 640
Kusý, I., 952, 954
Kütemeyer, M., 598
Kutlík-Garudo, I., 948
Kutz, W., 281
Kuypers, J., 885
Kuziakina, N., 1058, 1059
Kuz'menko, Iu. K., 901
Kuz'menko, O. A., 1045
Kuz'michev, I. K., 1040
Kuzmin, M. A., 1020, 1021–22, 1028, 1033
Kuz'mina-Karavaeva, E. Iu., 1016, 1033
Kuznetsov, A. M., 1023
Kuznetsov, Iu., 1034, 1057
Kuznetsov, N. I., 1039
Kuznetsova, A. P., 1030
Kuznetsova, N., 1030, 1032
Kvam, A. M., 914
Kvideland, R., 921–22
Kvit, S., 1054
Kwiatkowski, J., 978
Kwiecińska, Z., 982
Kwiek-Osiowska, J., 963
Kyd, T., 318
Kyryliuk, V., 1061

Laage, K. E., 761
Laane, T. V., 800
Labanyi, J., 330

Labbé, A., 55, 263–64
Labbé, F., 159
Labé, L., 85, 477
Labesse, J., 155
Labia, A. M., 513
Labib, A., 142
Labiche, E., 180, 207
Lablée, 142
Labò, E., 545
La Boétie, E. de, 94
Labov, W., 286, 384
La Branca, F., 485
Labrosse, C., 134
Labrousse, J.-P., 92
La Bruyère, J. de, 98, 100, 111, 114, 117
Labunka, M., 999
Labyntsau, Iu., 1068–69
Lacalle Zalduendo, M. R., 542
La Calprenède, G. de C. de, 111
Lacan, J., 80, 83, 87, 180, 188, 260, 322, 329, 358, 365, 371, 644, 739, 847, 941
Lacassin, F., 169
Lacenaire, P. F., 179
La Ceppède, J. de, 92, 118
La Charité, R. C., 83
La Châtre, E. de, 97–98
Lachmann, K., 14, 287, 615, 631
Lachmann, R., 1013, 1015
Laclos, P. C. de, 152, 153, 154, 155, 173
Lacomba, A., 255
Lacoste, C., 173
Lacour, C., 252
Lacour, N., 252
Lacour-Gayet, G., 179
Lacroix, J., 153
Lacurne de Sainte-Palaye, J.-B., 245, 264
Lacy, N. J., 58, 68
Ladenthin, V., 862
Laederach, J., 867
Laeng, B., 487
Laeufer, C., 29
Lafage, S., 49
La Fare, C.-A. de, 149
La Farge, B., 625–26
La Fayette, M.-M. de (*Mme*), 106, 112
Lafleur, B., 37
Lafollette Miller, M., 331, 332
Lafon, C., 95
Lafon, H., 156
Lafont, R., 28, 43, 245, 263, 264, 265
La Fontaine, J. de, 100, 101, 102–04, 500
La Force, P. de, 112

Laforet, C., 354, 367, 370
Laforgue, J., 180, 186, 231
Laforgue, P., 167, 177
Lafuente, F., 422
Lagarde, A., 254
La Garde, G. de, 80
Lagerkvist, P., 935
Lagerkvist, U., 935
Lagerlöf, S., 930–31
Lagman, S., 924
Lago, S., 416
Lagunas, J. R., 417
Lahme-Gronostaj, H., 824
Lahurie, M., 51
Laín Martínez, M., 269
Lajarrige, J., 738, 977
Lajarte, P. de, 84
Lakova, M., 1080
Lalouette, J., 182
Lamarque, V., 528
Lamartelière, J.-H.-F., 159
Lamartine, A. de, 167, 175
Lamberechts, L., 787, 844
Lambert, A. T. de (*Mme*), 141
Lambert, J. C., 103
Lambert, P.-Y., 560, 569
Lambert, W., 385
Lamberth, P., 932–33
Lamers, H., 803–04
La Mesnardière, H.-J. P de, 120
La Mettrie, J. O. de, 131, 141
Laming, J., 148
Lamíquiz, V., 279
Lamiroy, B., 19, 32, 40
Lammers, H., 881
Lämmert, E., 679–80, 831, 836
La Morlière, C. J. L. A. R. (dit de), 155
La Mothe Guyon, de (*Mme*), 117
La Mothe le Vayer, F. de, 112, 117
Lampedusa, G. T. di, 172
Lampen, U. A., 850
Lampert von Hersfeld, 622
Lampugnani, R., 539
Lancelot, C., 116
Lanczkowski, J., 619
Landau, P., 786
Landauer, G., 653
Landeira, R., 367
Landero, L., 370
Landfester, U., 745–46, 832
Landheer, R., 877
Landi, A., 444
Landino, C., 479
Landívar, R., 406, 409
Lando, O., 467
Landolfi, D., 503
Landolfi, I., 537

Landolfi, T., 537
Landoni, E., 451
Landre, J., 210
Landry, J., 154
Landseer, E. H., 789
Landucci, L., 483
Landy-Houillon, I., 101
Lang, F., 344
Lang, J., 34, 404
Lang, U., 819–20
Langbehn, V., 874
Langbroek, E., 627–28
Lange, H., 864
Lange, J. de, 892
Lange, S., 690–91, 764
Lange, W.-D., 615
Langensiepen, F., 607
Langer, F., 944
Langer, H., 685
Langer, U., 465
Langgässer, E., 820, 864
Längle, U., 864
Langlois-Berthelot, D., 168
Langner, M.-M., 792
Langslow, D., 22
Languet, H., 78
Langvik-Johannessen, K., 876, 896
Lanly, A., 69–70
Lanne, J.-C., 1020
Lanoue, P. de, 29
Lanthaler, F., 439–40
Lanz, J. J., 364, 365
Lanza, A., 448, 483
Lanza, F., 532, 542
Lanzendörfer-Schmidt, P., 859
Laoide, S., 573
Lapaire, P. G., 237
Lapesa, R., 268
Lapidot, E., 415
La Pierre, C. de (*Mme*), 175
Łapiński, Z., 963
Laporte, E., 39
Laporte, P.-E., 47
Lappalainen, O., 849
Laprade, V. de, 182
Lapteva, L. P., 1027
Lapushin, R. E., 1018
La Quintinie, J. de, 41
Larada, B., 245, 264
Laranjeira, P., 397
Larcati, A., 825
Lardoux, J., 173
Largier, N., 652, 653
Larivey, P. de, 93
Laroche, B., 806
La Roche, S. von, 692, 693, 724
La Rochefoucauld, F. de (*duc*), 100, 109, 112, 114
Larra, M. de, 333, 336, 342

Larrea, J., 341
Larsen, A. R., 80
Larsen, E. V., 902
Larson, C., 314–15, 318, 322, 409
Lärson, P., 436
Larsson, F., 156
Larsson, K., 925
Larsson, L., 931, 934
Larsson, S., 933
Larthomas, P., 153
Lasagabaster, J. M., 355
Lasaga Medina, J., 356
Lasarte, F. J., 423
Lasarte, P., 409, 411
Las Casas, B. de, 406
Las Casas, C. de, 266
Lasić, S., 1073
Lasker-Schüler, E., 820
Laskier Martin, A., 308
Laskou, I., 1065
Lasowski, P. W., 180, 193
Lasowski, R. W., 193
Lassalle, T., 115
Lassberg, J. M. C. von (*Freiherr*), 799
Lasso, L. E., 414
Lassu, J. M., 422
Lastouski, V., 1063, 1066, 1068
Làszlò, H., 586
Latorre, G., 280
Latrubesse, J.-P., 252
Latynina, A. N., 1029, 1048
Laube, H., 783, 799
Laubriet, P., 173
Laude, P., 116–17, 167, 181, 183, 185
Laufhütte, H., 613, 667, 685, 688, 782, 813
Laugaa, M., 112
Laukner, N. A., 863
Launay, E., 199
Launay, M. B. de, 203
Laurén, C., 926
Laurent, E., 190
Laurent, J., 202
Laurent, J.-F., 190
Laurenti, J. L., 309
Lauridsen, H. V., 912
Laurie, H. C. R., 7
Lauth, R., 750–51
Lautréamont, F.-R. de (*comte*), 183, 187, 191
Lautwein, T., 869
Lauvergnat-Gagnière, C., 98
Laval, A. Mathé de, 79
Lavalade, Y., 251, 257–58
Lavandera, B., 281
Lavater, J. K., 724, 726
Lavaud, P., 254

Lavaudant, G., 178
Lavaud-Fage, E., 358
Laverde, G., 326, 333
Lavielle, V., 203
La Vigne, A. de, 99
Lavin, C., 823
Lavinio, C., 438, 445
Lavocat, F., 148
Lavoisier, A. L. de, 134
Lavric, E., 49
Lavrinenko, Iu., 1059
Lavrov, A., 1021
Lavrov, A. V., 1015, 1017
Law, J., 160
Law, V., 2
Lawler, J., 231
Lawrance, J., 304
Lawrence, T. E., 222
Lawson, R. H., 654, 813
Laychuk, J. L., 1039
Lazard, M., 78, 90, 93
Lazarowicz, K., 781–82
Lazechko, L., 1052
Lazzerini, L., 261
Lea, C. A., 696–97
Leadbeater, L. W., 222–23
Leakey, F. W., 184
Leal, C., 340
Leal, R. B., 197
Leante, C., 411
Le Baillif, R., 84
Lebaud, D., 35
Lebda, R., 969
Lebedev, V., 1034
Le Bel, É., 32
Leber, M., 855
Le Berre, Y., 568, 570
Lebert, H., 836
Le Bigot, C., 344, 364
Le Boulay, J.-C., 185
Lebrave, J. L., 198
Le Brun, A., 157
Lebrun, C., 724
Lebsaneft, F., 386
Lecaye, H., 184
Lecce, R. C. da, 462
Lecercle, F., 78
Lechanteur, J., 43
Lechoń, J., 978, 979
Lechter, M., 815
Leckie, R. W., 652
Leclanche-Boulé, C., 1012
Leclerc, P., 142
Leclerc, Y., 167, 180, 195
Leclercq, J., 451
Leclercq-Magnien, A., 83
Leclère, C., 39
Le Clézio, J. M. G., 239
Le Clézio, Y., 439
Lecointe, J., 455

Lecointre, C., 27
Lecointre, S., 145
Lecomte, G., 226
Leconte de Lisle, C.-M.-R.,
  181, 182, 187
Lecouteux, C., 620, 640
Lecoy, F., 42, 60–61
Ledda, G., 504
Ledig, G., 844
Ledig-Rowohlt, H., 855
Le Dù, J., 568
Leduc-Adine, J.-P., 162, 182,
  199, 203, 205
Leeder, K., 843
Leeman, D., 35, 39
Leerintveld, A., 885
Lee Six, A., 369
Leeuw, B. de, 896
Leeuwe, H. H. J. de, 896
Lefebvre, C., 48
Lefebvre, H., 201
Lefevre, R., 492
Leffler, Y., 930
Le Fibure, G.-R., 137
Le Fort, G., 820
Lefrère, J.-J., 190
Legierski, M., 978
Legrand, M.-D., 78, 91
Le Guern, M., 117
Le Guirriec, P., 568–69
Lehár, J., 939–40
Lehfeldt, W., 993–94, 995, 1070
Lehman, A., 40
Lehman, T., 201
Lehmann, A., 640
Lehmann, C., 601, 737, 790,
  838–39
Lehmann, E., 915
Lehmann, W., 820
Lehnemann, W., 826
Lehnert, H., 821, 822, 823, 874
Lehnert, M., 605
Lehrer, M., 779
Leibniz, G. W., 119, 676, 686,
  724–25, 728, 757
Leibrock, F., 716
Leiderman, N., 1036
Leigh, R. A., 148
Leiner, W., 101
Leira, V., 918
Leirbukt, O., 603
Leister, B., 742
Leistner, B., 840, 857, 869
Leite, Y., 390
Leiter, S. L., 234
Lejeune, P., 218
Lejeune, R., 262
Le Laé, C.-M., 570
Le Lay, Y., 201
Lem, S., 982

Lemaire, J., 81
Lemaitre, M., 418
Le Menn, G., 570
Lemm, U., 746
Lemmer, M., 658
Lemonnier, A. C. G., 136
Le Moyne, P., 102, 104, 160
Lenardon, D., 138
Lenardon, J., 137
Lenau, N., 799–800, 859
Leñero, V., 419
Lenet, P., 98
Lengauer, H., 777
Lenin, V. I., 986, 1020, 1060
Lenisa, M. G., 544, 549
Lenk, H., 840
Lennart, C., 900
Le Noble, E., 112
Lenoble Pinson, M., 40
Lenschen, W., 646
Lentin, A., 1002
Lentini, G. G. di C., 511
Lenz, J. M. R., 680, 686, 725,
  730, 787
Lenz, S., 822, 849, 864
Leo X (*Pope*), 461
León, L. de (*Fray*), 305–06,
  307–08, 310
León, M. T., 350
León, O. G. de, 423
Léonard, A.-M., 28
Leonard, C., 372
Léonard, M., 69
Leonardi, C., 618
Leonardo da Vinci, 170, 487,
  488–89
Leone, A., 444
Leonetti Jungl, M., 281
Leonhardt, C., 39
Leonora Christina, 906
Leonov, L. M., 1041
Leonova, M., 1057
León-Portilla, M., 407, 408
Leopardi, G., 451, 528, 532,
  541, 542, 544, 548, 825
Leopold of Austria (*Grand Duke
  of Tuscany*), 512, 520
Lepage, Y. G., 60
Lepape, P., 146
Lepeshau, I., 1064
Le Petit, L., 102
Le Pichon, Y., 229
Lepikhov, I., 1038
Lépinette, B., 38, 253
Lepkyi, B., 1059
Lep reo, L., 499
Lepri, L., 541
Lepschy, A. L., 424, 434, 543
Lepschy, G. C., 424, 428, 431,
  434

Lerat, P., 40
Lerchner, G., 598
Le Rider, J., 163, 808, 824
Lermontov, M. Iu., 750, 1013, 1016
Lerouge, M.-J., 28
Leroux, C.-J., 141
Leroux, P., 179
Le Rouzic, S., 569
Leroy, J.-P., 126
Leroy, M., 168
Leroy, R., 807
Leroyer de Chantepie, M.-S. (*Mlle*), 194
Lersch, H., 820
Leruth, F., 539
Leschemelle, P., 94, 95
Lescou, L., 255
Lescuyer, J., 246
Leshkova, O. I., 1025
Lesina, R., 435
Lešková, Z., 946
Leśmian, B., 977
Lesne-Jaffro, E., 98
Lesnevskii, S. S., 984
Lesnick, D. R., 465
Lespinasse, J. de, 147
Lespy, V., 254
Lessard, G., 170, 171
Lessenich, R. P., 615
Lesser, S., 746
Lessing, F., 690
Lessing, G. E., 685, 686, 692, 693, 696, 726–27, 745, 806, 861, 972
Lessing Baehr, S., 1004
L'Estrange, R. (*Sir*), 113
Lestringant, F., 79, 85, 89–90, 91, 92
Lethbridge, R., 205, 206
Letska, Ia., 1067, 1068
Lettenhove, de, 73
Lettieri, M., 480
Leus, H., 900
Leuschner, B., 692
Leuschner, U., 730
Leutenegger, G., 835
Leuvesteyn, J. A. van, 885
Leva, J., 105
Levander, L., 926–27
Levashov, P. A., 1009
Levene, M., 826
Leventhal, R. S., 718
Lever, M., 106, 153, 157
Levertov, D., 1018
Levi, P., 537, 846
Levillain, H., 181
Levin, D. J., 646
Levin, Iu. D., 1005
Levin, L., 1028

Levina, L. A., 1038
Levina, M., 1029
Levinas, E., 233, 450
Levine, J. E., 993
Levine, J. M., 524
Levine, R., 6
Levinskaia, G. S., 1049
Levinton, G. A., 1020, 1049
Levin Varnhagen, R., *see* Varnhagen (Levin), R.
Lévi-Strauss, C., 113, 726, 870
Levitsky, A., 1010
Levitt, M., 1048
Lévi-Valensi, J., 237
Levkova, L., 1079
Le Vot, G., 261
Levy-Bloch, M., 185
Lewald, A., 782
Lewald, F., 745, 800
Lewandowski, T., 972
Lewanski, R. C., 986
Lewański, R. K., 973
Lewerenz, W., 710
Lewis, B. L., 308, 408, 423
Lewis, G. J., 654
Lewis, H., 209
Lewis, J. S., 566
Lewis, P., 113
Lewis, V. L., 776
Lewis Morgannwg, 563
Lewisohn, I., 349
Lewis-Smith, P., 312
Lexer, M., 630
Ley, J. S. de, 898
Le Yaouanc, M., 168
Lezama Lima, J., 419
L'Héritier, C.-L., 136
Lhoest, B., 41, 77
L'Hospital, M. de, 78
Li, J. T., 958
Liala, 537
Líbano Zamalacárregui, A., 273
Liberatori, F., 491
Libertazzi, G. G., 512
Licher, L., 691
Li Ching, A., 398
Lichtenberg, G. C., 727, 764, 766–67, 768
Lichtenstein, J., 122
Lichtmann, T., 861
Lichutin, V. V., 1030
Liddelow, E., 535
Liddicoat, A., 44
Lie, K. H., 602
Lie, O. S. H., 647, 891
Lie, S., 917
Liebe, M., 846
Liebertz-Grün, U., 611, 618, 652

Liebig, J., 784
Liebrand, C., 790
Lien, E. J., 166
Lienhard, M., 422
Lieskounig, J., 787, 856, 874
Liet, H. van der, 913
Lifanov, K., 946
Lifshits, B., 1027
Lifshits, M., 1048
Ligęza, W., 978, 983
Lihn, E., 417
Likhachev, D. S., 998
Likova, R., 1081
Lillo, B., 417
Lillo, G., 687, 723
Lilly, I. K., 1002
Lilova, T., 993
Lima, R., 316, 349
Limbrick, E., 94
Limonov, E., 1030
Linares, V., 526
Linati, C., 526
Lindberg, D. C., 458
Lindberger, O., 935
Lindegård Hjorth, P., 901–02
Lindeman, F. O., 561
Lindemann, K., 635
Lindén, B., 928
Linder, J., 778
Lindgren, L., 516
Lindgren, T., 929
Lindner, T., 862
Lindquist, S., 930
Lindstedt, J., 1070
Lindstrom, N., 412
Linell, P., 926
Linetskii, V., 1023, 1030, 1048
Linguet, S. N. H., 138
Linguiti, A., 447
Linke, H., 9, 656, 657, 658
Linkner, T., 977
Linnaeus, C., 699, 930
Linnér, S., 935
Lino, M. T. R. F., 399
Lintvelt, J., 201
Lionne, H. de, 124
Liosik, Ia., 1066, 1068
Lioult, J.-L., 206
Lipavskii, L., 1027
Lipczuk, R., 961
Lipkin, S., 1035, 1036, 1040
Lippi-Green, R., 607
Lipski, J. J., 981
Lipski, J. M., 276, 285, 394–95
Lipson, L., 312
Lishchinskii, B., 1017
Lisi, F. L., 408
Lisola, F.-P. de, 123
Lispector, C., 372
Lista, A., 327

Litievskaia, E. I., 992
Little, R., 191
Littlejohns, R., 772–73
Littler, M., 846
Littré, É., 15, 27, 38
Litvak, L., 334
Litvinov, V., 1047
Litwin, J., 967
Liubimov, Iu., 1032
Liubimov, V., 1032
Liubomurov, A. M., 1050
Liukkonen, K., 994
Livanova, A. N., 901
Livi, F., 548
Livingston, P., 205
Livshits, B. K., 1022
Lizak, J., 966
Ljunggren, A., 1045
Llácer, E., 333
Llanos Gutiérrez, V. de, 327
Llazamares, J., 364
Lleal, C., 268, 270, 376
Llinàs i Grau, M., 379
Llobregat, E. A., 382
Llovet, E., 340
Lloyd, H. A., 149
Lloyd, P. M., 13, 15
Lloyd, R., 166, 181, 185
Lloyd, S., 65
Lluis Sirera, J., 306
Llwyd, A., 565–66, 567
Llwyd, M., 563
Llywelyn-Williams, A., 566–67
Löb, L., 791
Lobanov, M., 1007
Lobbes, L., 108
Lo Cascio, F., 883
Lo Cascio, V., 424, 433
Locher, E., 672, 675
Lock, C., 1031
Locke, J., 119, 131, 676
Lockwood, W. B., 921
Lodares, J., 22
Lodares, J. R., 275
Lodeizen, H., 899
Lodge, A., 49, 66
Lodge, R. A., 25
Lo Dico, O., 545
Lødrup, H., 919
Lo Duca, M., 430
Loebbert, M. F., 617
Loen, J. M. von, 694
Loest, E., 834, 840
Loetscher, H., 835, 864
Loeuw, G. van de, 136
Loew-Cadonna, M., 852
Loewig, R., 838
Loewy, E., 808
Lofmark, C., 625, 645
Löfstedt, B., 5

Löfstedt, L., 2
Loft, L., 140
Logan Capuccio, B., 290
Logau, F. von, 668–69
Logé, T., 160
Lohenstein, D. C. von, 668, 669, 678
Lohmann, G., 766
Lohmeier, D., 909
Lohr, S., 856, 874
Lohse, N., 667
Loika, A., 1065
Lois, E., 268
Lo-Johansson, I., 935–36
Lokos, I., 1072
Lokshtanova, L. M., 901
Lom, I., 586
Loma, A., 1070
Lomazzo, G. P., 464
Lombard, J., 137
Lommatzsch, E., 37
Lomnický, S., 940
Lo Monaco, F., 488, 511–12
Lomonosov, M. V., 1002, 1003, 1007, 1009–10
Longespée, William II (d. 1250), 65
Longhi, P., 518
Longhi, S., 469
Longinus, 108, 720
Longnon, A., 70
Longobardi, G., 432
Lonzi, L., 432
Lookhart, W., 429
Loon, T. van, 885
Loon-Vervoorn, W. A. van, 881
Loosli, T., 798
Looze, L. de, 62
Lope Blanch, J. M., 266, 281, 284, 285
Lope de Vega Carpio, F., 301, 308, 315, 320–22, 324, 351
Lopes, A. C. M., 399
López, A., 326, 331
López, G., 284
Lopez, G., 528
López, I. J., 328
López, V. F., 411
López Alonso, C., 280
López-Baralt, L., 301, 307
López-Baralt, M., 335
López Bobo, M. J., 269
López-Casanova, A., 326, 328, 342
Lopez Castro, M. X., 402
López de Abiada, M., 364
López de Ayala, P., 294–95
López de Mendoza, I. (*Marqués de Santillana*), 269, 296

López de Yanguas, H., 300
López Morales, H., 285
López-Morillas, C., 302
López-Morillas, J., 334
López Mozo, J., 372
López Muñoz, A., 324
López Obrero, A., 354
López Rodríguez, M., 282
López Sacha, F., 419
López Velarde, R., 420
Lo Piparo, F., 444
Loporcaro, M., 428, 429
Lopresti, L., *see* Banti, A.
Lopukhova, A. O., 1040
Lora-Totino, A., 499
Loredano, F., 495
Lorenceau, A., 144
Lorenczuk, A., 748
Lorente Medina, A., 409
Lorenz, A., 647
Lorenz, B., 33
Lorenz, D. C., 870
Lorenz, O., 762
Lorenz, S., 33, 613
Lorenzen, M.-O., 722
Lorenzini, N., 545–46
Lorenzo Gradín, P., 289
Lorenzo Maiorano (*Saint*), 10
Lorenzo Suárez, A. M., 400
Lorrain, C., 236
Lorrain, J., 192, 200
Loseff, L., 1036
Löser, F., 654
Losev, A. F., 1004, 1024
Losev, V., 1037, 1038
Loskoutoff, Y., 93
Lothar, E., 809
Loti, P., 181, 200, 539
Lotman, Iu. M., 1003, 1017, 1031
Lotman, J., 539
Lötscher, A., 594, 603
Lotti, G., 436
Lötzsch, R., 603
Lough, F., 357
Lough, J., 136
Louis VII (*King of France*), 6
Louis XI (*King of France*), 70, 77, 108
Louis XIII (*King of France*), 97, 98, 100
Louis XIV (*King of France*), 41, 98, 124, 127
Louis XV (*King of France*), 41
Louis XVIII (*King of France*), 168
Loureiro, A. G., 331
Loustallot, É., 138
Louÿs, P., 187, 200
Loužil, J., 804

Love, M., 874
Löwe, H., 625
Lowe, J., 335, 369
Lowe, L., 196
Löwen, J. F., 685
Lowenstein, S. M., 697
Lowrie, J. O., 147, 170
Lowry, M. J. C., 455
Loyola, H., 417
Lozano-Renieblas, I., 314
Łoziński, W., 966
Lozyns'kyi, I., 1061
Lu, K., 602
Lubaś, W., 970
Lubich, F. A., 823, 855
Lubin, G., 176
Lubkoll, C., 857
Lubomiriski, H. (*Prince*), 168
Lubrano, G., 499
Luca de Tena, I., 372
Lucas, J., 983
Lucena, J. de, 298
Luchuk, V., 1061
Lucini, G. P., 537
Lucius, C. C., 689
Lucretius, 105, 469, 476
Łuczków, I., 965
Lüddecke, R., 641
Lüdderssen, K., 778
Lüders, D., 747
Lüdi, G., 21
Ludolf, H., 668
Ludolf, J., 14
Lüdtke, H., 11, 441
Lüdtke, J., 279, 283
Ludwig (*Prince of Anhalt-Köthen*), 665
Ludwig, E., 820
Ludwig, K.-D., 605
Ludwig, P., 864
Ludwig, R., 47
Luengo, E., 417
Luge, E., 592
Luger, B., 898
Lugovskoi, V. A., 1033
Lühe, I. von der, 820
Luhmann, N., 693
Lühr, R., 595, 601, 603
Luini, B., 229
Luis, L. de, 366
Luján, M., 279
Lukács, G., 810
Łukasiewicz, J., 972, 981, 983
Łukaszewicz, J., 973
Luke, D., 701
Luker, N., 1015
Luk"ianchuk, T., 1057
Luk'ianov, S. M., 1024
Lukić, J., 1074
Lukin, M. F., 992

Luknitskaia, V., 1020
Luknitskii, P., 1043
Lukomska-Woroch, A., 815
Lully, J.-B., 123, 158
Lumetti, R. C., 546
Lumsden, J. S., 48
Luna, J. de, 266
Luna, M.-F., 135
Lunacharskii, A. V., 986, 1027, 1041–42
Luna Selles, M. C., 368
Lund, A. A., 624
Lund, J., 907
Lund, K., 902
Lundby, K., 914
Lundelius, R., 325
Lundt, B., 618, 661–62
Lungstrum, J., 802, 818, 824
Lunt, H. G., 990–91
Lunts, L. N., 1027
Luoni, F., 103, 500
Luparia, P., 471
Luperini, R., 525, 530
Lupiáñez, J., 365
Lupin, A., 63–64
Lupold von Wedel, 620
Luppol, I. K., 984
Lupu, C., 397–98
Lurati, O., 434, 442
Lurbe, P., 141
Lur'e, Ia. S., 997, 1038, 1039
Lur'e, V., 1034
Luria, K. P., 116
Lüsebrink, H.-J., 133–34, 135, 142
Luserke, M., 725, 782
Luseroni, G., 515
Lussy, F. de, 231
Lustig, A., 945
Luther, M., 507, 595, 596, 598, 611, 617
Lüthi, H.-J., 749–50
Lüthild (*Saint*), 641
Luti, G., 531, 543, 546, 548
Lütkehaus, L., 793
Lutsenko, N. A., 993
Lutsevich, U., 1068
Lutskevich, A., 1068
Lüttgens, D., 719
Lutz, E. C., 659
Lutzeier, P. R., 601
Lützeler, P. M., 832, 853
Lux, W., 792
Luxembourg, J. van, 887
Luxemburg, J. van, 329–30
Luxemburg, R., 704
Luyendijk-Elshout, A., 698
Luzi, A., 545
Luzi, M., 525, 528, 537–38, 544
Luzio, A. di, 592

Luz Pimentel, P., 229
Luzuriaga, G., 414
Luzzati, D., 25
L'vov, M. D., 988
L'vov, N. A., 1005
Ly, N., 307
Lydon, M., 228–29
Lyon, J., 561
Lyons, J. D., 122, 458–59
Lyotard, J.-F., 359, 363, 745, 832
Lypa, Iu., 1059
Lysenko, T., 1058

Maas, A., 799
Maas, P., 287
Maas, U., 590, 598
Maass, J., 820
Mabee, B., 863
Mably, B. de, 140
Mac Annaidh, S., 581, 582
Mac Aodha Bhuí, I., 579
Mac Aonghusa, C., 575
Mac Conghalaigh, C., 578
Mac Con Iomaire, L., 580
Mac Craith, M., 579
MacDonald, D. A., 587
MacDonald, R. D., 127
Macedo, A. T., 400
Macedo, F., 404
Macedo, M. E. de, 395
Mac Giolla Léith, C., 579
Mac Grianna, S., 580–81
Mácha, K. H., 941
Machado, A., 331, 350, 352
Machado, M., 344, 352, 354
Machala, Ľ., 945, 956
Machaut, G. de, 70, 71, 74
Maché, U., 669
Macheiner, J., 601
Macher, H. S., 870
Machiavelli, N., 318, 457, 459, 468, 472, 474, 480, 483, 485, 487
Machida, K., 246
Macho, T. H., 846
Macías, S., 417
Maciejewski, J., 972
Maciej z Miechowa, 966
Macinnes, J., 586
Mack, G., 873
MacKay, A., 457, 939
Mackenzie, D., 337
Mackenzie, H., 713
MacKenzie, L., 221
Mackiewicz, J., 982
MacKillop, D., 585
MacKinnon, K., 562, 586
Maclean, C., 584

Maclean, I., 80
Maclean, M., 183
Mac Mathúna, L., 574
Mac Mhaighstir Alasdair, A., 587
Mac Nioclais, M., 579
Macpherson, I., 307
Mac Pherson, J., 579, 586
Mac Piarais, P., *see* Pearse, P.
Macrì, O., 537
MacRobert, C. M., 1072
Macrobius, 6
Mac Síomóin, T., 579
MacThòmais, R., 587
Macura, V., 955
Madariaga, I. de, 1002
Maddox, D., 65
Madel, M., 848
Madland, H. S., 715
Madonna, L. C., 725
Madrid, A., 417
Madrid, L., 416
Madrigal, A. de (*El Tostado*), 267, 295, 297
Madroñal Durán, A., 311
Madsen, B., 854
Madureira, M., 114
Mæhle, L., 928
Mæhlum, B., 919
Maerlant, J. van, 887, 888
Maestri, D., 485
Maeterlinck, M., 181, 1022
Maetz, M., 836
Maeztu, R., 354
Maffei, D., 494
Maffei, S., 511
Magalhães, E. d'A., 399
Magalotti, L., 495, 506, 514, 522
Magaña, J., 283–84
Magee, E., 806
Magerøy, H., 920
Maggetti, D., 218
Maggi, C., 416
Maggi, C. M., 511, 521
Maggiani, M., 527
Maggini, F., 520
Magill, D., 832
Magliabechi, A., 492
Magnani Campanacci, 523
Magnanimi, O., 477
Magnien-Simonin, C., 83, 113
Magnitskii, M. L., 1003
Magnusson, M.-L., 1046
Magnuszewski, J., 943
Magocsi, P. R., 1054
Magomedova, D. M., 1016, 1021
Magrelli, V., 538
Magrini, G., 547

Magritte, R., 344
Mag Shamhráin, A., 579
Maguire, G., 574
Mahal, G., 704, 730
Mahelot, L., 123
Maher, M., 791
Mahieu, R., 193
Mähl, H. J., 773
Mahoney, D. F., 688
Mahr, J., 730
Mahrdt, H., 847
Maia, C. A., 401–02
Maiakovskii, V. V., 988, 1019, 1026, 1033, 1038, 1042, 1045, 1049
Maia Materdona, G. F., 498
Maidachenko, P., 1058, 1060
Maidel, P. von, 1013
Maiden, M., 429, 430
Maierhofer, W., 746, 780
Maier-Solgk, F., 824
Maignien, C., 114
Maikov, V. I., 1003
Maillard, C., 360, 372
Maillard, J., 158
Mailly, (*chevalier de*), 112
Mainer, J. C., 340
Maingueneau, D., 36
Maior, P., 551
Maiorov, N. P., 988
Mairet, J., 97
Maisak, P., 748
Maisano, R., 488
Maisch, H., 713
Maiseichyk, A., 1066
Maistre, J. de, 136, 166
Maj, B., 980
Majmieskułow, A., 1045
Majtán, M., 946, 948
Majtánová, M., 968
Makaionak, A., 1060
Makanin, V. S., 1030
Makarevich, V., 1066, 1067
Makarov, A., 1055
Makedonov, A. V., 1042, 1049
Makhnovets, L. E., 999
Makhtumkuli, 1055
Makino, Y., 186
Makovskii, S., 1043
Makówczyńska-Góźdź, H., 963
Makowski, S., 976, 979
Maksim Grek, 991
Maksimov, M. D., 988
Maksimov, V. E., 1028
Maksimović, D., 1075
Maksimovich, I. P., 1003
Maksimowicz, K., 974
Maksymiuk, S., 911–12
Malachova, T. A., 247
Malakov, D., 1037

Malandain, G., 174
Malaniuk, Ie., 1059
Malaparte, C., 538
Malaret, N., 336
Malarte, C.-L., 112
Malash, L., 1069
Malaspina, T., 487
Malavie, J., 167
Malaxecheverría, C., 354
Malazhai, H., 1066
Malchanava, M., 1067
Maldaut, 139
Malden, M., 16
Maldonado, J., 309
Mal'dzis, A., 1065
Malebranche, N., 117, 119, 516
Malek, E., 1001
Malerba, A., 528
Malerba, L., 538
Malesherbes, C.-G. de L. de, 148
Malespini, C., 483, 504
Malewski, J., *see* Bolecki, W.
Mal'gin, A., 1034
Malheiros-Poulet, M. E., 397
Malherbe, F. de, 101–02, 104
Maliauka, M., 1068
Maliborska, M., 965
Malibran, M., 176
Malicet, M., 219
Malino, F., 137
Malinovskaia, I., 1032
Malinowska, E., 967
Malkiel, Y., 15, 22, 27, 41, 273–74, 291, 402
Mall, L., 127–28
Mal Lara, J. de, 309
Mallarmé, S., 180, 181, 183, 185, 187–88, 228, 231, 239, 351
Mallén, E., 278
Mallet, N., 110
Malleville, C., 104
Mallinson, G., 12
Malm, M., 921
Malmgren, S.-G., 925
Malmstad, J. E., 1015–16, 1020–21
Malo, D., 145
Malory, T. (*Sir*), 58
Malpartida, J., 366, 420
Malraux, A., 239–40, 242
Malsch, W., 719
Maltzan, C. von, 863
Malville, P., 155
Malysheva, G. N., 1033
Malyshkin, A. G., 1028
Mälzer, M., 642
Mamatov, A. E., 987
Mametau, I., 1063

Mamin-Sibiriak, D. N., 1022
Mamone, S., 502, 503
Man, P. de, 185, 334, 739, 802
Manakin, V., 1053
Manardi, G., 82
Mañas, A., 335
Mancarella, G. B., 443
Mancebo de Arévalo, 300, 302
Mancho Duque, M. J., 305, 307
Mancini, A. N., 473
Mancini, F., 483
Mancini, M., 260, 468
Mancino, 532
Mańczak, W., 14, 15
Mańczak-Wohlfeld, E., 965
Mandalari, M. T., 847
Mandelbaum-Reiner, F., 49
Mandel'shtam, N. Ia., 1028, 1042, 1049
Mandel'shtam, O. E., 851, 988, 1014, 1015, 1022, 1027, 1028, 1033, 1035, 1042–43
Mander, K. van, 888
Mandeville, J. de (*Sir*), 660
Mandlove, N. B., 351
Mandrell, J., 307, 329, 332, 340, 412
Manea, D., 552
Manet, É., 184
Manfredi, A., 464
Manfredi, E., 514
Manfredi, G., 519
Manfriani, F., 540
Manger, K., 711
Mangini, G., 517
Mangini, N., 501
Manitius, K., 5
Manley, D., 689
Manley Hopkins, G., 342
Mann, E., 820
Mann, H., 679, 807, 820–21
Mann, J. T., 93
Mann, K., 821
Mann, T., 453, 640, 688, 708, 775, 807, 820, 821–23, 834
Mannack, E., 677–78
Manni, P., 437
Manning, C., 4
Manoliu-Manea, M., 20, 550
Manolov, V., 1083
Manrique, G., 299
Mansau, A., 114, 172
Manso, G. B., 490, 498
Manson, M., 141
Mantchev, K., 28
Mantegna, A., 460
Manteiga, R., 368
Manteiga, R. C., 344
Mantero, M., 366
Manthey, J., 727

Manuel, J., 274
Manuilov, V., 1021
Manuzio, A., 479
Manzoni, A., 204, 428, 532, 542
Manzotti, E., 432
Maragoni, G. P., 491
Marahrens, G., 797, 820
Maraini, D., 538, 540
Maraña, M., 418
Marat, J.-P., 142
Maravall, J., 324
Marazzini, C., 440
Marbeuf, P. de, 102
Marcabru, 260, 261, 262
Marcato, C., 556
Marcenaro, G., 539
March, K. N., 367
Marchal, A., 254
Marchal, R., 141
Marchand, J.-J., 476
Marchand, J. W., 9, 274, 291, 294
Marcheschi, D., 528
Marchese, A., 525
Marchetti, G., 503
Marci, G., 527
Marciniak, A., 960
Marcishi, L. A., 396
Marco, J. M., 355
Marčok, V., 953
Marconot, J.-M., 48
Marco Polo, 660
Marcos Marín, F., 14, 287
Marcotte, G., 191
Marcou, G., 259
Marcus, T., 102
Marcuse, H., 712, 790, 872
Marczuk-Szwed, B., 85
Maréchal, G., 893
Maréchal, M., 248
Marechal, P., 884
Maréchal, S., 135
Marek, Z., 982
Mareş, L., 553
Marescotti, G., 456
Mareste, M. V. de, 171
Margański, J., 978
Margetts, J., 653, 812
Marggraff, H., 780
Marginter, P., 864
Margolin, J.-C., 454
Margolina, S. M., 1042
Margolis, H., 509
Margovskii, G., 1034
Marguerite de Navarre, 80, 84, 85
Margueron, C., 452
Marheineke, P. K., 751
Marholm, L., 802, 811
Mari, M., 523

Maria Cristina of Savoy, 514
Mar″ianivs′kyi, M., 1059
Maria of Savoy-Nemours (*Regent Duchess*), 494
Marías, J., 311
Mariatégui, C., 422
Marie de France, 54, 57, 61, 75, 645, 662
Mariengof, A. B., 988, 1020, 1051
Marietti, M., 483
Marigo, M., 502
Marín, J., 368–69
Marin, L., 97, 99, 171
Mariner, F., 116
Mariner, S., 376
Marinetti, A., 26
Marinetti, F. T., 529, 538
Marini, N., 425
Marini-Bettolo, G. B., 508
Marino, A., 525
Mariño, F. M., 332
Marino, G. B., 103, 104, 105, 469, 491, 492, 498, 500, 505, 506, 510
Marín Pina, M. C., 298, 299, 310
Marion, J.-L., 118
Mariotti, A., 425–26
Mariscal, G., 363
Maristany, J., 306
Maritati, G., 428
Marivaux, P. C. de C. de, 121, 131, 132, 137, 141, 142, 152, 154, 155–56, 160
Mark (*Apostle*), 211
Markar′ian, N., 958
Markhel′, U., 1066
Markhof, W., 251
Markiewicz, H., 976
Marko (*Prince*), 1076–77
Marković, S., 1075
Markowski, M. P., 982
Markworth, T., 717
Marmin, L., 93
Marmontel, J.-F., 153
Marner, Der, 633, 650
Maron, M., 864–65
Marot, C., 85, 893
Marotta, G., 429
Marquardt, E., 848
Marquardt, J., 859–60
Marqués, R., 423
Marques Valea, J., 398
Márquez, H. P., 311
Márquez Torres, F., 313
Márquez Villanueva, F., 311
Marquis, P., 258–59
Marr, I., 526
Marral, C., 417

Marrale, A., 437
Marrero, V., 275
Marri, F., 435
Marschall, A. H., 719
Marschall, B., 626
Marsden, R., 3
Marsé, J., 367, 370
Marsh, C., 1018, 1019
Marshak, S. Ia., 988, 1027
Marshall, B., 237
Marshall, D., 579–80
Marshall, J. H., 261
Marshall, M. M., 48, 257
Marsland, E. A., 208
Marsman, H., 887
Marstrander, C., 576
Martel, C., 25
Martel, F., 249
Martel, P., 135, 264
Martelli, F., 463
Martelli, M., 538
Martelli, S., 541
Martello, P. J., 514, 517, 523
Martellotti, A., 500
Martens, G., 701
Martens, K., 821
Martens, W., 714, 729
Martí, J., 330, 375, 377, 411
Martí, K., 835, 865
Marti, M., 452
Martial, 1055
Martianus Capella, 59, 458
Martignone, V., 476
Martignoni, C., 535
Martin, A. G., 639–40
Martin, C., 200
Martin, D., 733
Martin, D. C., 712
Martin, D. D., 459
Martín, E., 348
Martin, E., 875
Martin, F., 154
Martin, F. R., 264
Martin, G. C., 333
Martin, G. D. C., 792
Martin, J. L., 288
Martin, J.-P., 240
Martin, R., 3, 34
Martin, R. N. D., 510
Martin du Gard, R., 224
Martine, L. C. C., 397
Martine, N., 215
Martineau, F., 30
Martineau, H., 172
Martinell, E., 275
Martinet, A., 187, 570
Martinet, M., 208
Martínez, A., 354
Martínez, C. D., 322
Martínez, J. A., 419

Martinez, O., 444
Martínez, R., 326, 384, 413
Martínez, S., 290
Martínez Ballesteros, A., 372
Martínez Cachero, J. M., 328, 329, 342, 368
Martínez Comeche, J. A., 308
Martínez Cuitiño, L., 347
Martínez de Toledo, 297
Martínez Domene, P. G., 323–24
Martínez Egido, J. J., 302
Martínez Ruiz, J., 342, 354, 360
Martínez Sarrión, A., 364
Martínez Torrón, D., 327
Marting, D. E., 412
Martín Gaite, C., 354, 367, 370
Martín Gil, J. F., 365
Martini, F., 611, 687
Martini, S. M., 499
Martini-Wonde, A., 611
Martin le Franc, 75
Martino, P., 444
Martino Crocetti, M., 318
Martinoni, R., 523
Martín Recuerda, J., 373
Martín Rodríguez, A. M., 280
Martins, E. J., 393
Martín-Santos, L., 354
Martinson, H., 936
Martín Vega, A., 304
Martin von Troppau, 652
Mártir, P., 407
Märtle, C., 623
Martos, M., 422
Martovych, L., 1056
Martsinovich, A., 1067, 1068
Martynkewicz, W., 869
Martynov, L. N., 988, 1034
Maruéjouls, G., 255
Marullo, M., 475
Maružanić, I., 1073
Marx, K., 127, 621, 986
Marx, R., 825
Marx, S., 828
Marxen, K., 778
Mary, G., 219
Marynovs'kyi, Iu., 1054
Mary Tudor (Queen of Spain), 472
Marzaduri, M., 1012, 1021, 1025, 1027
Marzo, A., 477
Masanetz, M., 790
Masaniello, 496
Masár, I., 947, 950
Masaryk, T. G., 941
Mascardi, A., 490
Mascaró, J., 377–78
Mascaró-Passarius, J., 382

Masenko, L., 1061
Mas Ferrer, J., 342
Mashevskii, A., 1030, 1031
Maskell, D., 128, 129
Maslennikova, Z. A., 1044
Masłowska, E., 962
Masłowski, M., 975, 982
Masoero, A., 1028
Masoliver Ródenas, J. A., 371
Mason, E., 798, 804
Mason, H. T., 145, 150
Mason, P., 77
Mason, S., 147–48
Mass, E., 145
Massa, J.-M., 403
Masseau, D., 134
Masser, A., 596, 643
Massip, A., 381
Massol, J.-F., 224
Masson, B., 177, 178
Masson, M., 30
Masson, P., 221
Masters, B. A., 51
Mastrangelo Latini, G., 443
Mastrelli, C. A., 432
Mastroianni, G., 536, 1024
Mastronardi, M. A., 462–63
Maštrović, T., 1073
Matacotta, F., 533
Matarrese, T., 428
Matejov, F., 956
Matejovski, D., 640
Mateo, E., 362
Materna, L. S., 345
Mateus, M. H. M., 388, 389–90, 398
Matfre Ermengaud, 264
Matheson, P., 457
Mathet, M.-T., 197
Mathieu, C. S., 416
Mathieu, J.-C., 210
Mathieu-Castellani, G., 78, 84, 86, 87, 90, 91, 101, 105, 455
Mathieu-Colas, M., 39
Mathijsen, M., 886
Matias, M. F. R., 400
Maticki, M., 1074
Matisse, H., 544
Matlock, J., 181
Matos, G. A., 394
Matos, M. C. de, 405
Matos, S. P. F. de, 396
Matraini, C., 484
Matsiuk, H., 1053
Matsiukh, M., 1069
Matsumuro, S., 187
Matt, B. von, 828
Matt, P. von, 813
Mattheier, K. J., 594, 595
Matthes, E., 984

Matthew of Vendôme, 6, 9
Matthews, J. H., 209–10
Matthieu, P., 108
Mattie, B., 132
Matucci, A., 478, 487
Matucci, M., 142, 156
Maturi, P., 440
Matute, A. M., 367, 370
Matveeva, M. B., 913
Matveeva, N. N., 988
Matviishyn, V., 1055
Matzen, R., 44
Mauch, C., 865
Mauclair, C., 182
Maudich, A., 150
Maufort, M., 1019
Maul, G., 707
Maupassant, G. de, 181, 192, 201, 205, 1018
Maupertuis, P. L. M. de, 142
Mauprat, A., 169
Maurais, J., 47
Maurand, G., 103
Maurel, D., 34
Maurer, C., 346, 349
Maurer, K., 162
Maurer, M., 715, 781
Maurer, P., 404
Maurer, W., 797
Mauriac, F., 210, 224–25
Mauro, W., 544
Maurras, C., 208, 212, 225
Maury, N., 46
Mauser, W., 690, 691–92, 693
Mavellia, C., 438
Max, F. R., 662
May, G., 154
May, H. R., 417
May, K., 801, 870
Mayans Natal, M. J., 367
Mayer, C. A., 85
Mayer, D., 808
Mayer, G., 1064
Mayer, H., 708, 840, 855
Mayer, M., 816
Mayer, R., 941
Mayer, T. M., 784, 786
Mayer-Modena, M. L., 501
Mayhew, J., 350–51, 353, 366
Maynard, F., 101
Maynard, L. de, 178
Mayoral, M., 331, 333, 370
Mayröcker, F., 832, 835, 836, 865
Maza, S., 138
Mazaheri, H., 103
Mazan, B., 977
Mazanik, L., 1066
Mazarin, J. (*cardinal*), 107
Mazepa, I., 1055

Mazière, F., 38
Mazouer, C., 130
Mažuranić, I., 1072, 1073
Mazurin, A. I., 1001
Mazzacurati, G., 473–74, 543
Mazza Tonucci, A., 525
Mazzochi, G., 308
Mazzoleni, M., 432
Mazzolini, M., 476
Mazzoni, G., 483
Mazzotta, C., 519
Mazzotta, G., 537
McAnear, M., 856
McCann, J., 186
McCarty, N. J., 418
McClanahan, C., 743
McClendon, W. E., 204
McConnell, A., 1048
McConnell, W., 634, 657
McCormick, R. W., 836
McDermott, P., 348, 372
McDonald, J. P., 640
McDonald, M., 569
McDonald, W. C., 641, 646
McDonough, D. J., 5
McElveen, N. M., 128
McEnerney, J. I., 4
McGaha, M. D., 320
McGlathery, J. M., 113, 752
McGoldrick, M., 167
McGonagle, N., 573
McGowan, J., 3
McGowan, J. M., 98, 124
McGregor, G., 72
McInnes, E., 785
McInnes, E. O., 781
McKenna, M., 580
McKinley, M., 94
McKitterick, R., 629
McLaughlin, S., 1047
McManamon, J. M., 459
McMillin, A., 1030, 1036
McNamara, M., 197
McPherson, M., 839
McVay, G., 1018, 1020
Meadows, P. A., 193
Meakin, D., 202–03
Mechthild of Hackeborn, 653
Mechthild von Magdeburg, 652
Meckenstock, G., 770
Mecklenburg, N., 791, 862
Meckseper, C., 624
Meɗ, J., 941
Medarić, M., 1044
Meder, T., 890
Medici, Caterina de', 496
Medici, Cosimo I de' (*Grand Duke of Tuscany*), 457, 460, 463

Medici, Cosimo III de' (*Grand Duke of Tuscany*), 495, 512
Medici, Ferdinando III de' (*Grand Duke of Tuscany*), 508
Medici, Gian Gastone de' (*Grand Duke of Tuscany*), 512
Medici, Giovanni de', 502
Medici, Giuliano de' (*Duke of Nemours*), 459, 475
Medici, Leopoldo de' (*Cardinal*), 492
Medici, Lorenzo de', 177, 460, 475, 486
Medici, Maria de' (*Queen of France*), 502, 503
Medici, Mario, 439
Medina, D., 413
Medina Granda, R. M., 246–4
Meding, W. von, 714, 770
Medio, D., 370–71
Medlin, D., 142
Medvedev, Iu., 1020
Medvedev, S., 1001
Meek, D. E., 584, 586, 587
Megenney, W. M., 401
Mehlig, H. R., 990, 992
Mehlman, J., 188
Meiden, W., 63
Meier, B., 834
Meier, G. F., 686
Meier, H., 550
Meier, M., 865
Meierkhol'd, V. E., 1032
Meigret, L., 101
Meijer, M., 96
Meijer, R. P., 885, 899
Meilakh, M., 1032
Meilán García, A. J., 268
Meiller, A., 28
Meillet, A., 14
Mein, M., 211
Meinecke, F., 386
Meineke, B., 627
Meineke, E., 601
Meischner, D., 844
Meisel, G., 824
Meisenburg, T., 249, 255
Meisling, P., 905, 906
Meissner, Der, 635, 650
Meister, C. W., 1017
Meister, P., 640
Mejía Valera, M., 420
Méla, V., 48
Melançon, R., 87, 89
Melander, B., 925
Melara, M., 171
Melchiorre, V. A., 462
Meldgaard, E. V., 928
Meléndez, P., 414, 422
Meléndez-Páez, P., 417

Meléndez Valdés, J., 332
Meleuc, S., 39
Mélezet, J. du, 109
Melezh, I., 1068
Melis, L., 27
Mell, M., 809
Mellen, P., 816
Mellet, S., 26
Melly, G., 210
Mel'nyk, V., 1059
Mel'ts, M. Ia., 987
Melzer, G., 848
Melzi, R. C., 435
Mena, J. de, 296, 297
Ménage, G., 266
Ménager, D., 78, 82, 87, 94
Ménager, S., 229
Ménard, P., 262
Menato, M., 455
Menchacatorre, F., 332
Mencioni, E., 528
Mende, F., 796–97
Mendelssohn, M., 681, 685, 727–28
Mendelssohn, P. de, 821
Méndez-Faith, M., 422
Méndez Ferrín, C., 371
Méndez Ferrín, X. L., 367
Méndez García de Paredes, E., 281
Méndez-Ramírez, H., 415
Mendikoetxea, A., 18
Mendiola Mejía, A., 407
Mendizábal, J. A., 333
Mendizábal, J. C., 412
Mendoza, A. de, 330
Meneghello, L., 443
Meneghetti, M. L., 262
Menelaws, A., 1006
Menéndez Onrubia, C., 326
Menéndez Pelayo, M., 326, 333, 345
Menéndez Pidal, R., 270, 345
Menestrier, C.-F., 124
Mengaldo, P. V., 528, 534
Menges, K., 718
Mengoli, P., 506
Mengs, A. R., 734
Menhennet, A., 668, 792
Menichelli, G. C., 204
Menichi, P., 536
Menke, B., 811
Menninghaus, W., 720, 863
Menocal, M. R., 22, 415, 620
Menozzi, D., 513
Mentel, J., 655
Menton, S., 420, 422
Menze, E. A., 718
Menzel, W., 796
Mera, J. L., 411

Mercier, A., 100
Mercier, L.-S. de, 131, 135, 158
Merck, J. H., 728
Mercurius of Smolensk (*Saint*), 1000
Mercury, F., 182
Mereau, S., 689, 736, 764
Mered, C., 301
Merezhkovskii, D. S., 816, 1019, 1022, 1043
Merhaut, L., 941, 945
Mérimée, P., 171, 201, 358
Mériot, C., 182
Merkù, P., 437
Merkuraeva, V. A., 1020
Merle, R., 135, 249, 256, 257
Merleau-Ponty, M., 353, 846
Merlin, H., 235
Merlin, P., 493
Merlio, G., 802
Merollo, I., 198
Merrell, F., 415
Mertens, V., 611, 632, 653
Mervaud, C., 150, 151
Méry, M.-C., 804
Merzbacher, D., 665
Merzhvinskite, B., 1020
Meschonnic, H., 215, 262
Mesmer, F. A., 132
Mesnard, J., 117, 119, 154
Mesonero Romanos, R. de, 336
Mess-Baehr, I., 1043
Messerschmid, G. F., 676
Messière, P., 155
Messinger, S., 412
Messner, D., 398
Mesters, B., 886
Metastasio, P., 515, 516–17
Methodius (*Saint*), 939, 999
Methuen, E., 656
Mets, A. G., 1013
Metternich, K. L. W. von, 732, 777, 792
Mettke, H., 635
Metz, W., 721
Metzeltin, M., 280, 424
Metzger, E. A., 670–71
Metzger, M. M., 669, 670–71
Meulen, D. van der, 898
Meve, J., 827
Meves, U., 615, 777
Meyer, A., 1038
Meyer, B., 190
Meyer, C. F., 800
Meyer, E. Y., 835
Meyer, H., 8, 615, 655, 710, 1043
Meyer, J. H., 706
Meyer, M., 932
Meyer, P., 41, 67, 248

Meyer, R., 986
Meyer, T. L., 714
Meyer, W. J., 33–34
Meyer-Gosau, F., 837–38, 874
Meyer-Hermann, R., 279, 280, 294
Meyer-Krentler, E., 692, 792, 802
Meyer-Petit, J., 168–69
Meysonnier, S., 134
Meyszies, U., 856
Meyvaert, P., 2, 613
Meza, R., 411
Mezenka, H., 1065
Mezentsev, M., 1047
Mezzatesta, M., 346
Miachinskaia, E. I., 901
Miatsel'skaia, E., 1065
Michael, B., 616
Michaelis, C., 402
Michaelis, M., 776
Michael of Cornwall, 8
Michaels, J. E., 811
Michałowska, T., 972
Michaux, H., 209, 225, 240
Michel, A., 168
Michel, C., 140, 709
Michel, E. J., 54
Michel, P., 201–02
Michelangelo Buonarroti, 454, 474–75, 477, 484, 489, 825
Michelet, J., 163, 179
Michelet, J. (*Mma*), 249
Micheli, P., 438–39
Michelstaedter, C., 538
Michetti, F. P., 544
Michon, P., 189
Micińska, A., 980
Miciński, T., 977
Mickel, K., 703
Mickiewicz, A., 966, 973, 974, 975–76
Micocci, C., 474
Middell, E., 708
Middell, M., 136
Midgley, D., 823
Mieczkowska, H., 958
Miedema, H., 888
Miedema, H. J. T., 879
Miel, J., 113
Miele, L., 462
Mieners, J. W., 595
Mies, M., 691
Mieth, M., 811, 866
Miethke, J., 622
Migeon, G., 102
Migiel, M., 467
Miglio, M., 448
Migozzi, J., 202
Miguel, E. de, 347

Miguel, M. A. C., 391
Miguel, M. E. de, 415
Miguel-Prendes, S., 298
Miguet-Ollagnier, M., 243
Mihalkovič, J., 956
Mihaychuk, G., 1058
Miiakovs'kyi, V., 1056
Mika, M., 951
Mikasch-Köthner, D., 641
Mikeshin, A. M., 1036
Mikhaël, É., 188
Mikhailov, A., 1030
Mikhailov, A. A., 1042
Mikhaïlov, A. D., 168
Mikhailov, A. I., 1023
Mikhailov, A. V., 1046
Mikhailov, O., 1030
Mikhailov, O. N., 1007, 1035,
    1036, 1038, 1044, 1046
Mikhnevich, A., 1064
Mikhoels, S., 1027, 1032
Mikhova, L., 1082
Mikić, R., 1076
Miklautsch, L., 634, 647
Miklić, T., 432
Mikola, J. J., 1039–40
Mikoś, M. J., 977
Mikula, V., 954
Mikulášek, O., 945
Mikulich, T., 1064
Mikuta, V., 1066
Mila, M., 526
Milà i Fontanals, M., 377
Milan, G., 521
Milanca Guzmán, M., 423
Milanesi, C., 132
Milanini, C., 532
Milanja, C., 1074
Milato, M., 495
Milchakov, Ia., 1082
Mil'chin, A. E., 1012
Mil'don, V., 1018
Milfull, J., 860
Milhou, A., 271
Miliavskii, B. L., 1026, 1042
Milieva, D., 1079
Milin, G., 64
Milinčević, V., 1075
Milite, L., 476
Militz, H.-M., 47
Millán, G., 417
Millares, S., 417
Miller, E. R., 818
Miller, E. S., 92
Miller, J., 1019
Miller, N., 700, 766
Miller, N. K., 99
Miller, P. A., 451
Miller, S., 329
Millet, C., 174

Millet, O., 78
Millocca, F., 481
Millot, C., 180
Mills, M. H., 962, 993
Millward, E. G., 563–64, 565
Milman, Y., 243
Milne, L., 1038
Milner, M., 164
Milner Garlitz, V., 359
Milojković-Djurić, J., 1028
Milosavljević, Lj., 1076
Milošević-Đorđević, N., 1076
Miłosz, C., 225, 973, 977, 980,
    982, 983
Milroy, J., 25
Milroy, L., 25
Miltchina, V., 168
Milton, J., 1013
Mináč, V., 955
Minahan, C. D., 243
Miñambres Sánchez, N., 359
Minárik, J., 953
Mináriková, M., 954
Mincer, W., 509
Mincheva, A., 998
Minchyn, B., 1061
Minden, M., 688, 798
Minden, S. von, 830
Mineo, N., 543
Mingelgrün, A., 237
Minikowska, T., 962
Minogue, V., 204
Minter, G., 323
Mints, Z. G., 1022
Minutelli, M., 488
Miodek, J., 964
Mioni, A. M., 437, 440
Miquet, J., 75
Mir, J., 355
Mira, J. F., 386
Mira de Amescua, A., 324–25
Miralles, E., 334
Miranda, A., 292
Mirau, F., 866
Mirbeau, O., 182, 192, 201–02
Mirchev, B., 1081
Mirković, M., 1075
Miró, J., 343
Mirto, A., 492
Misch, M., 853
Mishchanchuk, M., 1068
Mishevska, G., 995, 1078
Misrahi, C., 202
Mistral, G., 414, 417
Mistrík, J., 955
Mitana, D., 956
Mitchell, B., 461
Mitchell, D., 580
Mitchell, H., 138
Mitin, G., 1040

Mitrinov, G., 1080
Mitrinović, V., 969
Mitterand, F., 237
Mitterand, H., 192, 203
Mitterer, E., 865
Mittermaier, K., 487
Mitwoch, E., 727
Miuccio, G., 524
Mix, Y.-G., 142, 695, 730
Mixner, M., 858
Mizinski, J., 856
Mlacek, J., 947
Mladenova, O., 1078
Mladenović, T., 1075
Młodzianowski, T., 966
Mocho, M. C. C., 399
Mochurov, A., 1081
Model, J., 878
Modelmog, I., 691
Modigliani, A., 456
Modzelewski, J. A., 844
Moeller, B., 654
Moennighoff, B., 686
Moes, J., 729
Moeschler, J., 48
Mohl, I., 987
Mohr, H., 866
Möhren, F., 37
Möhring, M., 886
Möhring, W., 752
Möhrmann, R., 686
Mohylians'kyi, M., 1056
Moino, R. E. L., 394
Moiseeva, G. N., 1009
Moix, A. M., 371
Mojašević, M., 753
Mok, Q. I. M., 249–50, 254
Mole, A., 162
Molho, A., 461
Molho, M., 313
Molière, J.-B. P., 49, 100, 101,
    120, 121, 123–26, 213, 226,
    502, 872
Molière d'Essertine, 112–13
Molin, G., 456
Molina Gete, E., 336
Molina Molina, A. L., 288
Molinari, C., 481
Molinaro, N. L., 372
Molinelli-Stein, B., 870
Molinié, G., 29, 111
Molinier, C., 34, 35
Molinos, M. de, 310
Molitor, W., 686
Mölk, U., 260, 261, 639
Moll, F. de B., 375, 383
Mollà, D., 384
Mollà, T., 384
Møller, E., 902, 903
Möller, H., 620

Møller, M., 905
Møller, P. L., 906
Møller, P. M., 910
Möller-Christensen, I. Y., 907
Möllhausen, F., 790 ·
Molodiakov, V., 1016
Moloney, B., 547
Mommsen, K., 703
Moncomble, E., 191
Moncond'huy, D., 104
Mondo, L., 542
Mondot, J., 143
Mondry, H., 1013
Monegal, A., 343, 346
Moner, M., 312
Monestier, J., 258
Monfasani, J., 9–10, 459
Monikova, L., 865
Monjour, A., 43, 402
Monleón, J., 345
Monluc, B. de, 79
Monné, E., 386
Monnet, M. (*Mme*), 135
Mönnich, M., 507
Monson, D. A., 262–63
Mont, E. du, dit Costentin, 93
Montagnini, C., 471
Montaigne, M. de, 79, 80, 81, 88, 93–96, 114, 130, 147, 254, 407, 472, 487, 864
Montale, E., 526, 528, 529, 538–40, 547
Montalvo, Y., 423
Montaner Frutos, A., 300, 303
Montáñez, C. L., 419
Montani, F., 514
Montanile, M., 517
Montchrestien, A. de, 120
Monteagudo, H., 400
Monteagudo, X., 400
Monteiro, J. L., 393
Montenay, G. de, 93
Montero, R., 362, 367, 371
Montero Vallejo, M., 305
Montesquieu, C.-L. de S. de, 131, 136, 147–48, 152, 1008
Montesquiou, R. de, 228
Montfort, S. de, 55
Montgomery, A., 235–36
Montgomery, T., 290
Monti, V., 515, 523
Montinari, M., 801
Montón Puerto, P., 311
Montoro, A. de, 297
Montoya, B., 381–82, 383–84
Montpensier, A. M. L. (*Mlle*), 98
Montreuil, J.-P. Y., 28, 441
Moog, C., 839
Moonen, E., 818

Moore, R., 412
Moore, W. G., 125
Moorman, C., 56
Moortgat, W., 552
Moos, P. von, 2, 6, 632
Moosmüller, S., 606
Mora, G., 420
Mora, J. J. de, 327
Mora de Ubeda, la, 302
Morain, M.-R., 175
Morais, A. P., 110
Moraleda, P., 353
Moralejo, J.-L., 15–16
Morales, A., 285
Morales, A. de, 309
Morales Raya, R., 325
Moran, B. T., 494
Moran, J., 376
Moranjak-Bamburać, N., 1045
Morante, E., 412, 540
Moravia, A., 526, 537, 540
Morawski, W., 969
Mordas, N., 1064
Mordek, H., 621
Mordellet, I., 29
Mordenti, R., 486
Morderer, V. Ia., 1022
Moreau, G., 102, 186
Morel, J., 111, 120, 121, 128, 129, 130
Morcl, M.-A., 25
Morel, R., 128
Morell, H. R., 416
Morellet, A. (*abbé*), 134, 135, 142
Morelli, A., 517
Morelli, G., 345, 747
Morelli Timpanaro, M. A., 520
Morello-Frosch, M., 415
Morelly, E.-G., 142
Moreno Castillo, R., 290
Moreno Villa, J., 341, 342
Morera, M., 274
Moretti, B., 440
Moretti, M., 528
Moretti, W., 522
Moreu-rey, E., 383
Moreux, B., 251, 253, 254
Moreux, C., 253
Morev, G. A., 1012, 1022, 1027
Morgagni, G. B., 132
Morgan, C., 817
Morgan, D. Ll., 564
Morgan, E., 890, 980, 983
Morgan, E. P., 567
Morgan, L., 1047
Morgan, P., 703, 813
Morgan, S. E., 349
Morgan, T. A., 276
Morgan, W., 563

Morgenstern, C., 823
Morgenstern, K. von, 688, 805
Morgenthaler, W., 753
Morgner, I., 839, 840, 863, 865
Morhof, D., 698–99
Mori, M., 722
Mori, V., 523
Morigi, P., 516
Mörike, E., 775, 776, 800–01
Morin', L., 56
Morin, Y.-C., 29, 29
Morison, S., 456
Moritz, K. P., 684, 685, 686, 728–29, 756, 848
Moritz von Hessen, 604
Mork, A., 805–06
Mork, G., 918
Morkunas, K., 963
Morla, B., 347
Morlet, M.-T., 42
Morlicchio, E., 631
Mornay, P. de, 78, 81
Mornet, D., 133
Morocho Gayo, G., 304
Morón Arroyo, C., 306, 307
Moroni, M., 543
Morot-Sir, E., 242–43
Moroz, M., 1056
Morozov, V. V., 997
Morozova, F. P., 1001
Morreale, M., 275, 292, 306, 314
Morris, C. B., 343, 344
Morris, D. B., 698
Morris, W., 564
Morshen, N., 1034
Morsztyn, J. A., 973
Mortier, R., 145
Mortimer, A. K., 170
Morton, M. M., 693, 718
Morviducci, M., 457
Mosele, E., 200
Moser, D.-R., 613, 620, 792, 853
Moser, G., 862
Moser, H., 596
Moser, J., 680, 694, 729–30
Mosher, N. M., 209
Moss, A., 81
Moss, H., 1018
Moss, K., 1045
Mossman, C. A., 165
Mostacci, J., 452
Mostepanov, S., 1060
Mostrova, T., 998
Mota, J. A., 393, 399, 401
Motte, W., 229–30
Motte, W. F., Jr, 241
Motteville, L. de (*Mme*), 98
Mottola Molfino, A., 461

Mouchard, C., 163, 180
Mougenot, M., 152
Mougeon, R., 47
Moulin, C., 598
Moulis, M., 51
Moure, J. L., 295
Moureau, F., 140, 142, 144, 145
Mouřenín, T., 940
Mourin, L., 12, 16
Moutier, L., 249
Moutote, D., 221
Movchan, P., 1060
Moyal, J. D., 119
Moyano, D., 416, 423
Mozart, W. A., 224, 516, 518, 680, 733, 823
Mozet, N., 161
Mozhaev, B. A., 1043
Mozza, A., 543
Mozzoni-Frosconi, A., 168
Mravcová, M., 945
Mráz, S., 941
Mrazović, A., 1070
Mrkonjić, Z., 1074
Mrongowiusz, K. C., 966
Mrożek, R., 970–71
Mrożek, S., 956, 982
Mucci, W., 531
Mucke, D., 865
Mueller, H., 865
Mueller, T., 694–95, 759
Mueller-Vollmer, K., 735
Mugge-Meiburg, B. L., 800
Mugnier, A. (abbé), 190
Mugnier, F. C., 193
Muhlack, U., 690
Mühleisen, H., 715, 728
Mühlen, H. Zur, 809
Mühler, R., 792
Mühlherr, A., 662
Mühlpfordt, G., 679, 774
Mühlpfort, H., 669
Mühsam, E., 823
Muirchú, 3
Mukařovský, J., 938, 941
Mulinacci, B., 522
Mulisch, H., 887
Muljačić, Z., 424–25, 426, 428, 437, 443, 445
Mullally, R., 71
Mullan, B., 792
Müller, A., 764
Müller, A. von, 760, 762
Müller, B., 267, 268
Muller, C., 34, 40, 41, 127
Müller, C., 397
Müller, D., 618, 798
Müller, F. (Maler), 730
Müller, G., 832
Müller, H., 812, 858, 870, 873

Müller, Heiner, 727, 786, 810, 837, 839, 840, 843, 850, 865–66
Müller, Herta, 867
Müller, H. G., 714
Müller, H. M., 810
Müller, I., 866
Müller, J.-D., 615, 777
Muller, K., 141
Müller, K., 809, 820
Müller, K.-D., 707
Müller, O., 631
Müller, R., 593, 775–76, 823
Müller, U., 611, 614, 631, 650
Müller, W. von, 735, 764
Muller Cooke, O., 1015
Müller-Dietz, H., 793
Müller-Jahncke, D., 507
Müller-Lauter, W., 801
Müller-Scholle, C., 1041
Müller-Seidel, W., 780
Müller-Vollmer, K., 718
Müller-Waldeck, G., 874
Mulon, M., 250
Mulryne, J. R., 468
Multatuli, 897
Mummuch, S., 417
Munaro, M., 549
Munch-Pedersen, O., 574
Munch-Petersen, E., 909
Mundal, E., 920
Mundt, H., 832, 874
Mundt, T., 783, 801
Muñiz, C., 373, 374
Muñiz Muñiz, M. de las N., 542
Muñoz, W. O., 420
Muñoz Garrigós, J., 268
Muñoz Seca, P., 360
Munske, H. H., 596
Munsters, W., 162
Münzer, R., 632
Murashka, R., 1068
Muratagić-Tuna, H., 1071
Muratore, M.-J., 113
Muratori, L. A., 473, 514, 518
Murav'ev, P., 1031
Murav'ev, V., 1005
Murav'eva, I., 1049
Muravitskaia, M., 1053
Murdoch, B., 630, 637, 846
Muret, M.-A., 86–87
Murger, H., 168
Murguía, M., 331
Múrias, A., 395
Murner, T., 664
Murphy, C. J., 238
Murphy, G. R., 629
Murphy, J. E. H., 572

Murphy, R. J., 807–08, 818, 832, 1031
Murphy, S., 86, 189, 190, 191
Murphy-Judy, K., 611
Murr, C. C., 734
Murr, S., 867
Murray, B., 138
Murray, F. W., 413
Murray, J., 218, 423, 453, 467
Murray, O., 480
Murray, W. J., 137
Muruáis, J., 334
Muru Porcu, A., 437
Musatov, V. V., 1042
Musäus, J. K. A., 730–31
Muscarà, S. Z., 532
Muschg, A., 835
Mushynski, M., 1066, 1069
Musienko, V. P., 994
Musil, R., 708, 802, 810, 813, 822, 823–24, 836, 898
Musolino, G., 544
Musolino, W., 542
Musschoot, A. M., 887, 888–89, 899
Musset, A. de, 121, 167, 177–78
Musumarra, C., 481
Musumeci, D., 438
Muzio, G., 484, 487–88
Muzzioli, F., 525
Mycawka, M., 962
Myers, D., 1043
Myers, K. A., 311
Mykhailyn, I., 1060
Mykhailyshyn, B., 1052
Mylius, J. E. de, 905, 906
Mylne, V., 145
Myrdal, J., 932
Myronova, H., 1053
Myshanych, O., 1058

Nábělková, M., 950
Nablow, R. A., 131, 150
Nabokov, D., 1044
Nabokov, V. V., 1013, 1018, 1022, 1033, 1034, 1035, 1036, 1037, 1043–44
Nabokova, V., 1044
Nachiavelli, N., 460
Nadasdi, T. J., 45
Nadler, J., 717
Nadler, S., 119
Nadolny, S., 832, 867
Naganowski, E., 836
Nagayo, S., 941
Nagel, B., 612
Nagel, I., 786
Nagel, S., 223, 354
Nägele, R., 709, 810, 811

Nagibin, Iu. M., 1044, 1051
Nagórko, A., 957
Nagy, R. U., 1038
Naharro-Calderón, J. M., 338, 351
Nahler, E., 701
Nahler, H., 712
Nährlich-Slateva, E., 613
Naidan, M., 1061
Naienko, M., 1059
Naigeon, J. A., 146
Naish, C., 157
Najdič, L., 606
Nalepa, J., 970
Nancy, J.-L., 233
Nanetti, R., 528
Náñez Fernández, E., 282
Nanfito, J. C., 310, 408
Nantell, J., 343
Nantet, M.-V., 212
Napoleon I, Bonaparte (*Emperor*), 161, 179, 792
Narayana Chandron, K., 797
Narbikova, V., 1030
Narbut, V. I., 1022
Närhi, E. M., 609
Naro, A. J., 400
Narváez, M. T., 300
Nash, J. C., 81, 86, 88
Nasiłowska, A., 972, 980
Natale, M., 461
Nathan, L., 225
Natta, M.-C., 181
Naucke, W., 778
Naudé, G., 107
Naughton, J., 236
Naugrette, F., 174
Naumann, B., 595
Naumann, M. T., 1044
Naumann, U., 710, 821
Nauton, P., 246
Nava, G., 547
Navajas, G., 363
Navarrete, I., 307
Navarro, M., 284
Navarro Carrasco, A. I., 270
Navarro González, A., 337
Navarro Ledesma, F., 355
Navarro Salazar, M. T., 444
Navas Ruiz, R., 281, 332
Navumenka, P., 1067
Nawa, T., 399-400
Nawarecki, A., 974
Nayhauss, H. C. G. von, 856
Nazar'ian, R. G., 1008, 1009
Nazariantz, H., 537
Ndiaye, A. R., 118
Neaud, P.-M., 172
Nebbiai-Dalla Guarda, D., 456
Nebol'sin, S., 1036

Nebrija, E. A. de, 267
Nechui-Levyts'kyi, I., 1056
Necker, J., 143, 163
Nederman, C. J., 7
Nedev, I., 1080
Nedić, M., 1076
Needham, J. T., 141
Needler, H., 3
Neefs, J., 153, 192
Neelov, E. M., 1029
Neera, 527
Nef, F., 34
Neghme Echeverría, L., 417
Negomireanu, D., 550
Nègre, E., 5, 42, 250, 254
Negri, A., 527
Negri, F., 481
Négrignat, J. M., 1028
Negroni, B. de, 148
Nehring, W., 828
Neidhart von Reuental, 631, 633, 650
Neijt, A., 877
Neiman, Iu., 1034
Neira, J., 343
Neiske, F., 619
Nejedlá, J., 938
Nekrasov, N. A., 1016
Nekula, M., 945
Nelde, P. H., 557
Nellhaus, T., 663
Nellmann, E., 633
Nello Vetro, G., 503
Nelson, D., 77, 292
Nelson, D. H., 64-65
Nemchenko, V. N., 992
Němcová, B., 941
Němcová Banerjee, M., 945
Nemec, K., 1072, 1073
Nemtsev, V. I., 1038
Nemzer, A., 1031, 1049, 1050
Nenadavets, A., 1069
Nencioni, G., 424, 425, 428
Nenni, P., 435
Nepaulsingh, C. I., 274
Nepomniashchii, V., 1039
Népote-Desmarres, F., 113
Neppi, E., 531
Nerler, P., 1043
Nerlich, B., 26
Neruda, J., 942
Neruda, P., 413, 414, 417
Nerval, G. de, 121, 163, 175-76, 184
Nes, O., 916
Nescio, 885, 887, 899
Nesmelov, A., 1034
Nesmy, C.-J. (*Dom*), 210
Nestroy, J., 793, 801, 871
Nestserau, Iu., 1068

Netchinsky, J., 423
Nethersole, R., 842
Nettelbladt, U., 925-26
Netto, W. F., 400
Neu-Altenheimer, I., 386
Neubauer, H., 755
Neubauer, J., 700
Neuber, F. C., 686
Neuber, W., 672
Neuendorff, D., 595
Neugebauer, B., 667
Neuger, L., 978
Neuhaus, V., 856-57
Neuhauser, W., 659
Neuhaus-Koch, A., 745, 795
Neuhoff, T. de, 142
Neumann, G., 838, 864
Neumann, H., 652
Neumann, P. H., 767
Neumeister, S., 96, 310, 318-19, 734
Neumüller, M., 942
Neumüllers-Klauser, R., 615-16
Neusinger, A., 874
Nevares, M. de, 320
Neverov, A. S., 1044
Neves, M. H. M., 395, 396
Nevodov, Iu. V., 1038
Nevzgliadova, E., 1043
Newbigin, N., 482-83
Newels, M., 73, 641
Newhauser, R., 632
Newman, J. C., 373
Newman, J. O., 665-66
Newmark, P. K., 229
Newton, G., 593
Newton, I., 131, 519, 708
Newton, J., 181-82
Newton, R., 204
Nezval, V., 942, 943, 944
Niachai, V., 1068
Niafahina, H., 1066
Niafiod, U., 1066
Niamkovich, N., 1067
Niangouna, A., 47
Ní Bhaoighill, C., 580
Ní Bhroin, V., 580
Niccolì, N., 464
Niccoli, O., 467
Niccolini, E., 459
Nic Eoin, M., 580
Nichev, B., 1081
Ní Chionnaith, E., 580
Nicholas V (*Pope*), 464
Nicholas, M. A., 1045
Nicholas of Cusa, 656, 684, 769
Nicholas of Verona, 71
Nicholls, K., 585
Nichols, S. G., 51

Nick, D., 867
Nickel, C., 358
Nickel, R., 658
Nickelsen, E. A., 817
Nickisch, R. M. G., 783
Nicodemus, 748
Nicodemus Frischlin, 940
Nicolai, F., 718, 731, 742, 767
Nicolai, O., 836
Nicolai, R., 818
Nicolaidis, D., 136
Nicolas de Clamanges, 69
Nicolas de la Chesnaye, 72
Nicole, E., 227
Nicoletti, G., 547
Nicolò, A., 493
Nicon (*Saint*), 997
Nicot, J., 36
Nic Pháidín, C., 580
Nida-Rümelin, J., 832
Niderst, A., 102, 103, 107, 109, 114–15, 117, 121, 140
Ní Dheirg, I., 574
Ní Dhonnchadha, A., 589
Ní Dhuibhne-Almqvist, É., 576
Nie, G. de, 1
Niederehe, H.-J., 46
Niederhauser, R., 835
Niederstätter, A., 633
Niehoff, R., 784–85
Nielsen, B. J., 904
Nielsen, J., 904
Nielsen, M., 911
Niemirycz, K., 974
Nienhaus, S., 711–12
Nieraad, J., 842
Niethammer, 735
Nieto, J. C., 305
Nietzsche, F., 260, 365, 679, 744, 774, 775, 782, 795, 801–02, 809, 816, 818, 819, 824, 856, 910, 911, 1040, 1073
Niewolak-Krzywda, A., 980
Ní Fhoghlú, S., 580
Niggl, G., 770
Nightingale, J. A., 59
Nigro, S. S., 494
Nigro, V. F., 372
Nijhoff, M., 885, 888
Nikifarouski, M., 1069
Nikifarovich, V., 1066
Nikitaev, A., 1027
Nikitin, B. A., 1024
Nikitina, M. A., 1024
Niklaus, R., 146
Niklaus de Dybin, 654
Nikolaev, G., 1049
Nikolaev, P. A., 986, 987
Nikolaeva, T. M., 1020
Nikolev, N. P., 1003

Nikoliukin, A. N., 1023
Nikolova, M., 1078, 1081
Nikolova, N., 1083
Nikol'skii, B. V., 1016
Nikol'skii, S. V., 1009
Nikolskij, S. V., 943
Nikonova, T. A., 1029
Nilsen, H. T. H., 918
Nilsen, K. E., 574
Nilsson, N. A., 973
Nimchuk, V., 1054
Nimetz, M., 313
Ní Mhurchú, M., 573
Ninov, A., 1038
Nitt, I., 609
Nivat, G., 1037
Niven, B., 828
Nivet, J.-F., 201–02
Nizan, P., 225
Nizier du Puitspelu, 45
Nižnanský, J., 947
Nizon, P., 867
Njegoš, P., 1074, 1075
Noailles, A. de, 210
Noailly, M., 31
Nobbio Mollaretti, R., 477
Nodier, C., 176, 179
Noël, F., 119
Noferi, A., 531
Nogrette, P., 173
Noirfontaine, F. de, 138
Nolan, D., 477
Nolden, T., 825
Nølke, H., 34
Nölle, V., 792–93
Nolte, T., 649–50
Noltenius, R., 802
Nondier, G., 102
Nonnotte, F., 151
Noordegraaf, J., 877, 885
Noordzij, N., 900
Noot, J. van der, 885
Nora, E. G. de, 342
Norberg, D., 2
Norbrandt, H., 911, 913
Nordau, M., 824
Nordlinger, E., 931
Nordmann, J.-T., 168, 182
Norell, P., 924
Norén, L., 936
Norman Baer, N. van, 1014
Norris, D., 1075
Nörtemann, R., 689
Northeast, C. M., 131
Norton, R. E., 718
Norwid, C. K., 966, 976
Nosov, A., 1024
Nosov, V. N., 1027
Nossack, H. E., 824, 831, 867
Notker, 612, 630

Notker Labeo, 630
Nouveau, G., 183
Novák, A., 944
Novak, H., 845
Novak, S., 1074
Nováková, M., 946
Novalis, 218, 696, 735, 737, 738, 740, 751, 757, 759, 760, 764–65, 773, 833–34, 846
Novaro, M., 540
Novelli, M. A., 514–15
Noventa, G., 525, 528, 540
Novik, M., 1069
Novikava, T., 1063
Novikov, I. A., 1016
Novikov, N. I., 1002
Nový, L., 941
Nowak, H., 964
Nowakowski, B., 256
Nowakowski, M., 966
Nowakowski, T., 982
Nowé, J., 657
Nowik, K., 971
Nowotna, M., 965, 981
Noyes, J., 705
Nübler, N., 958
Nuccoli, C., 452
Nuez, S. de la, 335, 337
Nunes, J. M., 394
Nunes, M. M., 820
Núñez, B., 423
Núñez, N., 417
Núñez Cedeão, R. A., 276
Núñez Muñoz, F., 286
Nürnberger, H., 790–91
Nurse, P. H., 81, 125
Nussbächer, G., 551
Nussbächer, K., 782
Nussbaum, L., 816
Nuth, H., 781
Nutton, V., 455, 458
Nyan, T., 34, 48
Nyberg, M., 903
Nyblom, H., 931
Nybo, G., 908
Nycz, R., 979
Nyczek, T., 972, 981
Nyholm, K., 647
Nykiel-Herbert, B., 957, 959
Nyman, V., 936

Ó Baoill, C., 586
Ober, K. H., 909
Oberfeld, C., 752–53
Oberholzer, O., 906
Oberle, B. E., 599–600
Oberle, M., 847
Oberlin, J. F., 725
Oberlin, J.-J., 27

Obermaier, W., 801
Obermair, H., 862
Obhof, U., 655
Obizzi, Pio Enea II, 503
Obregón, B., 270
Obremski, K., 974
O Briain, M., 576–77
O'Brien, F., 582
O'Brien, J., 88, 92, 129–30
O Broin, M., 574
O Bruadair, D., 572
O Buachalla, S., 574–75
Obukhova, E. A., 1043
Obukhova, V. N., 992
O'Byrne Curtis, M., 332
O Cadhain, M., 578, 580, 582
Ocampo, F., 279
Ocampo, V., 415
O Caoimh, I., 580
O Casaide, P., 573
O Catháin, S., 575, 576
O Cearnaigh, S., 572
Ocheretiansky, A., 1012–13
Ochoa, J. A., 288
Ochsenbein, P., 629
O Ciaráin, R., 575
O Ciosáin, É., 575, 580–81
O Ciosáin, N., 575
Ockenden, R. C., 712
O Coigligh, C., 575
O Conaire, P., 580
O Conchúir, B., 572
O'Connor, D. J., 336
O'Connor, P. W., 372, 374
O'Connor, T. A., 318
O Corráin, A., 573
O Cróinín, M., 581
O Cuív, B., 572
Odaloš, P., 948
Odarchenko, P., 1057
Oddi, S., 483
Odenstedt, B., 923–24
O Direáin, M., 579, 582
Odoevtseva, I. V., 1035
O Doibhlin, B., 581
Odojewski, W., 983
O Donnabháin, D., 578
O'Donovan, J., 575
O'Donovan, P., 199
Odo of Deuil, 6
Odo of Magdeburg, 6, 9
Odorico da Pordenone, 448
O Dubhghaill, S., 581
O Duibhín, C., 575
O Duibhín, C., 575
O Dúill, G., 581
O Dúshláine, T., 581
Oechslin, W., 508
Oehm, H., 810
Oellers, N., 710, 713
Oesterle, G., 735, 754–55

Oesterle, I., 741
Oesterley, H., 658
O Faoláin, M., 572–73
Offermanns, E., 826
Offord, M. H., 41
O Fiannachta, P., 581
O Flaithearta, L., 578
Ogarev, N. P., 1007
Ogawa, S., 855
Ogden, M., 756, 759
Ogier, J. M., 659
O Glaisne, R., 575, 581
Ognev, A., 1029
Ognev, A. V., 1026
Ognev, V., 1028
Ognibene, S., 459
O'Grady, D., 544
O Gráinne, D., 582
O Grianna, S., 578–79
Ohage, A., 726
O Háinle, C., 572
O hEithir, B., 575–76, 580
Ohl, H., 826
Ohlenroth, D., 647
Ohler, N., 620
Ohlmeier, D., 598
Ohly, F., 631, 636
Ohnsorg, J., 660
O hOgáin, D., 577
O hUid, T., 579
Oja, M. F., 1037
Ojeda Escobar, P., 332
Okamura, H., 314
Oken, L., 702, 753, 765
Okken, L., 642, 646
Oklianskii, Iu. M., 1026–27,
    1035
Okoniowa, J., 969
Okudzhava, B. Sh., 1027
Okuka, M., 1071
Olason, V., 920
Olberg, G. von, 622
Olden, P., 884
O'Leary, A., 579
Olef-Krafft, F., 643–44
Oleinikov, N., 1033
Oleríny, V., 955
Oles', O., 1059
Olesha, Iu. K., 1044
Ol'ga (Princess of Kiev), 998
Ol'ga Aleksandrovna (Grand
    Duchess), 1021
Oliva, C., 373
Oliveira, D. P., 393
Oliveira, F., 393, 395
Oliveira, M. A. F. de, 403
Olivet, see Fabre d'Olivet
Olivier de la Marche, 74
Olkusz, W., 976
Oller, N., 333, 336

Ollivier, S., 1045, 1048
Olmo, L., 372, 373, 374
Olmos, A. de, 407
Olonová, E., 1037
Olschner, L., 810
Olsen, G. W., 5
Olsen, M., 483
Olsen, S., 600, 602
Ol'shanskaia, O. E., 992
Olsson, B., 930
Olsson, U., 932
Oltra, J. M., 369
O Macháin, P., 572–73
Omacini, L., 162
O Madagáin, B., 577
O Muirí, D., 582
O Murchadha, N., 582
Ondegardo, P. de, 408
Onderdelinden, S., 812
Ondrejková, R., 948
Ondrejovič, S., 949
Ondruš, J., 956
Ondruš, S., 948
O'Neill, E., 353, 1019
O'Neill, P., 858, 862
O'Neill, P. P., 4
Onetti, A., 374
Onetti, J. C., 218, 415, 423
Ong, W. J., 611
Onimus, J., 226
Onslev, L. J., 909
Ontañón de Lope, P., 352
Oostrom, F. P. van, 889, 890
Opacki, I., 978, 979
Opalková, J., 951
Opelík, J., 945
Opitz, C., 618
Opitz, T., 750
Opp, M., 591
Oppel, M., 709–10
Oppenrieder, W., 601
Oppermann, H. A., 868
Oppermann, M., 853
Oppici, P., 117
Oppila, 1
Oppy, G., 119–20
Oravcová, A., 950
Orcel, M., 163
Ordine, N., 471
Ordóñez, E. J., 367, 369
Orduna, G., 287, 291
Orduña, L. E. F. de, 310
O'Reilly, T., 305
Orejudo, A., 345
Orelli, G., 450, 528
Orengo, A., 530
Orest, M., 1061
Orff, K., 793
Orgelfinger, G., 74
O Riain, L. P., 580

Oriel, C., 312
Origen, 618
Orlandi, G., 9
Orlandini, A., 18–19
Orlando, L., 535
Orlando, M., 512
Orlić, M., 1076
Orlik, F., 821, 822
Orłoś, T. Z., 965
Orlov, Ia. V., 1003
Orłowski, J., 1013
Oronzio (*Saint*), 497
Orosius, 633, 652
O'Rourke, V., 445
Orrell, J., 315
Orsenigo, L., 525
Orsi, G. G., 513–14
Orski, M., 983
Ørsted, H. C., 907
Ortega, S., 355
Ortega y Gasset, J., 341, 342,
   354, 355–56, 357, 419, 420,
   423
Orten, J., 943
Ortese, A. M., 540–41
Orth, E., 639
Ortheil, H. J., 833
Orthman, N. E., 412
Ortiz, F., 334
Ortiz, L., 371
Ortiz Armengol, P., 336, 337
Ortolf von Baierland, 658
Orton, G., 934–35
Ortowski, H., 849
Ó Ruadháin, S., 579
Orvieto, P., 468
Orwell, G., 867
Orwińska, E., 968
Osadchyi, M., 1060
Osbern of Gloucester, 7
Osborne, J., 932, 983
Ó Searcaigh, C., 578, 579–80
Osipov, A. N., 988
Osipova, L. I., 992
Oskam, J., 362
Oskotskii, V. D., 1026, 1028
Os'mak, N., 1056
Osorgin, M. A., 1044
Osorio, E., 415
Osorio Romero, I., 406
Ossa, T., 349
Ossar, M., 851
Ossian, 579, 586, 758
Ossietzky, C. von, 824
Ossola, C., 453, 485–86, 536
Ossorguine-Bakounine, T., 985
Ossowski, M., 780
Ostaijen, P. van, 887
Østbø, J., 862
Oster, D., 231

Osterkamp, E., 705–06, 760
Österle, G., 801
Ostermann, E., 744
Ostrovskii, N. A., 1044
Ó Súilleabháin, D., 576, 579
Oswald, I., 1029
Oswald von Wolkenstein, 70,
   596, 612, 659
Otero, J. M., 414
Otero, L., 410
Otfrid von Weissenburg, 595,
   612, 623, 630
Otmar (*Saint*), 630
Otruba, M., 942
Ott, N. H., 613
Ott, U., 809
Ott, W., 614
Ottai, A., 530
Otte, 635
Ottecrans, W. E., 936
Ottenburg, H.-G., 700
Ottevaere-van Praag, G., 113
Otto IV (*Emperor*), 644
Ottokar von Steiermark, 652
Otto of Freising, 632
Ó Tuairisc, H., 580
Ó Tuama, S., 582
Ó Tuathaigh, M. A. G., 576
Otwińska, B., 972
Oudart, J., 135
Oudin, C., 38
Oudshoorn, J. van, 885
Ouimette, V., 356
Ouvry-Vial, B., 225
Øverby, J., 917
Øverland, O., 920
Ovid, 9, 68, 71, 73, 102, 105,
   186, 294, 450, 451, 469, 471,
   488, 667, 758, 1016
Oviedo, J. M., 414
Ovsiannikova, M. A., 985
Owen, D., 118, 565
Owen, D. D. R., 62
Owen, G. Ll., 567
Owren, H., 718
Øyslebø, O., 918
Ozaeta, J. M., 305
Ozerov, L., 1015, 1024
Ozerova, N., 1053

Paal, J., 813
Pabst, R., 786, 787
Paccagnini, E., 496
Pache, W., 817
Pacheco, F., 306
Pacheco, J. E., 420, 421
Pachet, P., 163
Pachmuss, T., 1022, 1043
Pacho, E., 307

Paco, M. de, 343, 373
Pade, M., 461
Paden, W. D., 262
Padilla, J. A., 278
Padilla Rivera, J., 280
Padluzhny, A., 1063, 1064
Padoan, G., 450
Padovan, M., 461
Paepcke, F., 815
Paepe, C. de, 347
Pagano, S., 466
Pagano, V., 541
Paganuzzi, P., 528
Pagden, A., 304
Page, M. M., 1006
Pagès, A., 200, 203
Pagnanelli, R., 528
Pailloux, S., 156
Painter, G., 228
Painter, M. L., 394
Paisey, D., 894
Paisiello, G., 521
Paisii Khilendarski, 1082
Paixao, M., 115
Pajewska, E., 966
Pakenham, M., 183, 186, 190,
   191
Palácio, A. P., 392, 396
Palacio Valdés, A., 333
Paladino, V., 545
Palamarchuk, P., 1048
Palamedes, 56
Palamini, C., 456
Palanza, U., 527
Palau de Nemes, G., 351
Palavestra, P., 1074
Palazzeschi, A., 525, 541
Paleario, A., 460
Palencia-Roth, M., 414, 418
Palenque, M., 327
Paleotti, G., 466
Paliersi, C., 138
Palievskii, P., 1038
Palii, L., 1061
Palingenio, A., 459
Palisca, C. V., 460
Palkovič, K., 947, 948, 954
Pallarés, M. del C., 364
Pallavicino, P. S., 473
Pallavicino, S., 490
Pallotta, A., 304, 455
Pallus, W., 857
Palm, L., 42
Palmada, B., 378
Palmenfelt, U., 922
Palmer, N. F., 616, 632, 654,
   657–58
Palmer, R., 455
Palmers, C., 886
Palmieri, G., 523

Palmieri, M., 466
Palmstierna-Weiss, G., 873
Palomera, L., 420
Pálsson, H., 921
Paltaran, V., 1068
Paludan, J., 910
Paludan-Müller, F., 910
Palumbo, M., 483
Palumbo, N., 541
Pamp, B., 928
Pampaloni, G., 527
Panch, P., 1059
Panchenko, A. M., 1001
Panchenko, D., 1022
Panchenko, O., 1016
Pančíková, M., 968, 969
Pandarus, 9
Pandolfi Burzio, Λ. M., 276, 283
Pane, A., 543, 544
Panferov, F. I., 1028
Panfilov, A. D., 1039
Panigarola, F., 466
Panina, N., 1047
Paniznik, S., 1069
Panizza, L., 458, 476
Pankau, J. G., 813
Pan'ko, T., 1053
Pannonius, I., 479
Pannwitz, R., 824
Panofsky, E., 774
Panov, A., 1082, 1083
Panova, V. F., 1027
Panovová, E., 953, 954
Panthel, H. W., 829, 875
Panther, K. U., 601
Pantić, M., 1074
Pantin, I., 92
Paoli, G., 59
Paoli, M., 457
Paoli, P. F., 499
Paolini, G., 333
Paolini, P., 488
Paolo da Perugia, 449
Paor, L. de, 578
Papasogli, B., 102
Papazian, E., 919
Papenfuss-Gorek, B., 838, 867
Papernyi, Z., 1019
Papierz, M., 958, 968
Papini, M. C., 531
Papiór, J., 857
Papon, L., 81
Pappas, J., 140
Papponetti, G., 536
Paquot, A., 46–47
Paracelsus, T. B., 662
Paramonov, B., 1039, 1045
Paravicino, H. F. (Fray), 346
Pardini, V., 547

Pardo Bazán, E., 328, 331, 332, 333–34, 336, 340
Parel, A. J., 487
Parenti, P., 478
Parentucelli, T., see Nicholas V (Pope)
Paretski, Ia., 1067
Pariati, P., 517, 523
Parin, A., 1045
Parini, G., 513, 521, 523
Paris, G., 41
Paris, M., 65
Paris, R., 540
Parise, G., 541
Parish, R., 119, 125, 129
Parisse, M., 622
Parker, A. A., 315
Parker, D., 535
Parkes, S., 832
Parkhomenko, G. F., 1015
Parkinson, S., 12
Parkinson, S. R., 390
Parnicki, T., 983
Parnis, A. E., 1020, 1043
Parnok, S. Ia., 1022
Parr, J. A., 304, 322
Parra, E., 420
Parra, M. A. de la, 418
Parra, N., 414, 417
Parry, M., 210
Parry, M. M., 442
Parry, R. W., 566
Parry-Williams, T. H., 566
Parthé, K., 1029, 1046
Partner, P., 464
Pascal, B., 117, 119–20, 127, 151, 495, 848
Pascal, G., 171
Pascale, C. de, 683
Pasch, R., 602, 603
Pasco, A. H., 164, 169, 170, 173
Pascu, Ş., 551
Pascual, J. A., 376
Pasek, J. C., 966, 974
Pasero, N., 261–62
Pashuk, A., 1055
Pasichnyk, Iu., 1054
Pasky, R., 68
Paso, A. del, 413
Paso, F. del, 420, 421
Pasolini, P. P., 528, 529, 541–42
Pasoń, A., 957, 958
Pasquali, G., 287
Pasquariello, A. M., 372
Pasques, L., 29
Pasquier, M.-C., 1019
Pasquier, P., 120
Pasquinelli, A., 1022, 1033
Pasquini, P., 523
Pasquino, 477

Passy, P., 26
Paštěka, J., 943
Pasternak, B. L., 1027, 1044–45
Pastine, D., 508
Pastor, E., 807
Pastor, M. A., 326, 331
Pastore, S., 533
Pastore Passaro, M., 481
Pastor Milán, M. A., 273
Pastoureau, H., 217
Pastoureau, M., 66
Pastré, J.-M., 644, 646, 651
Patáková, M., 955
Pater, W., 734, 817
Paterson, A. K. G., 320
Paterson, L. M., 263
Patkaniowska, D., 981
Patocka, F., 602
Patrick (Saint), 560
Patrizi, F., 463, 468
Patrizi, G., 484
Patrucco Becchi, A., 521
Patsch, H., 727, 770, 772
Patterson, R., 92–93
Pattison, D. G., 293
Pattison, W. T., 334
Patty, J. S., 186, 206
Paufler, H.-D., 268
Paul, M., 836
Paul, N. H., 212
Paulau, U., 1064
Paulhan, J., 225, 240
Paulin, R., 702, 753, 768, 776, 777
Paulin, T., 980, 981
Pauls, G., 797
Paulsen, W., 832–33
Paulsin, W., 169
Paulus, R., 730
Paupe, A., 172
Paupert, A., 63
Pausch, H. A., 733, 869
Pausewang, G., 859
Paustovskii, K. G., 1026, 1045
Pautasso, S., 526
Pauvert, J.-J., 153, 157
Pavel, T., 318
Pavese, C., 525, 526, 528, 542
Pavesi, F., 508
Pavić, K., 1072
Pavić, M., 1074, 1075
Pavis, P., 207, 350, 866
Pavković, V., 1076
Pavličić, P., 1073, 1074
Pavlík, J. V., 999
Pavliukevich, V. P., 1030
Pavliv, O., 1057
Pavlock, B., 469
Pavlov, M. S., 1043
Pavlova, L., 1033

Pavlova, M., 1019
Pavlova, M. M., 1023
Pavlova, N., 1079
Pavlovič, J., 947, 948–49
Pavlović, M., 1072, 1076
Pavlovich, I. V., 994
Pavlovskii, A., 1049
Pavlovskii, A. I., 1037, 1046
Pavlovsky, E., 414
Pavlovsky, I., 326, 336
Pavlychko, D., 1062
Pavlychko, S., 1056, 1061
Pavlyshyn, M., 1061
Pawelec, R., 966
Pawis, R., 659
Pawlowitsch-Hussein, C., 864
Payeras Grau, M., 373
Payne, J. A., 422
Payne, P., 824, 855
Payró, R., 416
Paz, A. de, 342
Paz, O., 413, 420
Paz, P. N. de la, 360–61
Pazi, M., 809
Paz'niak, Ia., 1068
Pazos, M.-L., 386–87
Pazzi, R., 542–43
Peadar, An tAth., 581
Pearce, E., 30
Pearre, A., 236
Pearse, P., 575
Pecellín Lancharro, M., 305
Pechar, J., 938
Péchoin, D., 37
Peckham, R., 70
Peco, A., 1076
Pecora, E., 543
Pecora, V. P., 233–34, 802
Pedersen, H., 574
Pedersen, I. L., 901, 902, 903–04
Pedersen, J., 105
Pedersen, K. M., 903, 904
Pedersen, L., 904
Pedraza, J. de, 317
Pedreira Lopez, C., 402
Pedrelli, S., 529
Pedrero, P., 373, 374
Pedretti, E., 867
Pedretti, N., 529
Pedriali, F., 535–36
Pedro de Portugal (Don), 297
Pedullà, W., 526, 527
Peer, W. van, 888
Peeters, B., 21–22
Peeters, C., 885–86
Peeters, J., 630
Peeters, L., 879
Pegoraro, S., 545
Péguy, C., 208, 211, 225–26

Peillen, T., 253
Peinador Marín, L. J., 309
Peiper, T., 979
Peire de Gauceran, 263
Peire Vidal, 261
Peirone, C., 478
Peitsch, H., 815, 836, 844, 873
Pekarovičová, J., 949
Pekić, B., 1076
Pelagius (monk), 4
Pelckmanns, P., 192, 887
Pelen, M. M., 450
Pelens'kyi, Ia., 1061
Pelizzoni, L., 493
Pelizzoni, S., 493
Pellarolo, S., 416
Pellegrin, N., 132
Pellegrini, G. B., 426, 436, 438, 443, 555
Pellegrini, L., 543
Pellegrini, M., 505
Pellerey, R., 144, 542
Pelletier, A., 124
Pelletier, Y., 570
Pelletieri, O., 414, 416
Pellicer, D., 271
Pellicer, J. O., 321, 411, 420
Pellicer, P., 415
Pelosi, O., 479
Pemán, J. M., 372
Peña, M. de los R., 326
Penadés Martínez, I., 279
Peñarroja Torrejón, L., 268
Penas, E., 337
Penchev, I., 1080
Pender, M., 835
Peneva, D., 1081
Peng, C., 830
Penke, O., 143
Penna, S., 528, 539, 543
Pennington, E., 373
Penny, R., 269, 270, 272
Pensado, C., 268
Pensado, J. L., 12, 401
Pensado Ruiz, C., 12
Pensel, F., 657
Penzenstadler, F., 468
Penzl, H., 597, 600, 631, 877
Pepi, R., 531
Pepin, R. E., 6, 493
Pepoli, S., 516
Peppard, V., 1044
Pepperle, H., 796
Pepys, S., 676
Percival, A., 338
Perea, H., 421
Pereda, J. M., 326, 328, 333, 334, 336
Pereiaslov, N., 1029

Pereira, A. J., 334
Pereira, I., 392
Pereira, M. G. D., 398
Pereleshin, V. F., 1034, 1035
Perelli, C., 414
Perels, C., 747, 797
Pérennec, R., 640
Peres, J. A., 396
Pérez, A., 421
Perez, C.-P., 240
Pérez, J., 366, 370
Pérez Bazo, J., 342
Pérez de Ayala, R., 354, 361
Pérez de Guzmán, F., 299
Pérez de Laborda, A., 508
Pérez de Oliva, F., 309
Pérez Firmat, G., 370
Pérez Galdós, B., 327, 328, 329, 334–39, 362
Pérez López, M. M., 354
Pérez Magallón, J., 368
Pérez Saldanya, M., 379
Pérez Sánchez, M. A., 323–24
Peri, I., 503–04
Perić, I., 1073
Perini, G. B., 449
Perini, L., 456
Perissinotto, G., 408
Perkins, W., 108
Perl, M., 403–04
Perlina, N., 1045
Perloff, N., 210
Perminov, P., 1009
Pernath, H. C., 887, 888
Pernette du Guillet, 80, 85–86
Pernot, M., 98
Pernoud, R., 618
Perona, J., 266–67
Péronnet, L., 45
Pérouse, G.-A., 84
Perraudin, M., 750, 787
Perrault, C., 99, 113, 752
Perre, R. van de, 887, 899
Perri, D., 348
Perricone, C. R., 422
Perridon, H., 915, 921
Perrier, S., 91, 93
Perrin, P., 122, 123
Perrone, C., 522
Perrot, P., 886
Perry, K. A., 91, 450
Perry, N., 150–51
Pers, C. di, 492, 499
Persson, G., 923
Pertici, P., 488
Pertusati, G. M., 511
Perugi, M., 263
Pérus, J., 230
Perutz, L., 755
Pervukhin, N., 1048

Péry-Woodley, M.-P., 49
Pešat, Z., 943
Pesce, P. D., 530
Peschel-Rentsch, D., 611, 630, 636, 638, 643, 646, 649
Pesonen, P., 1015
Pessin, A., 133
Pessoa, F., 331
Pestalozzi, J. H., 689, 731
Pestalozzi, K., 798, 801, 816, 819
Pestureau, J. F., 86
Pétain, H. P., 219
Peter I (of Rosenberg), 939
Peter, H.-W., 817
Peter, J., 932
Peter Comestor, 921
Peterka, J., 945
Peterkiewicz, J., *see* Pietrkiewicz, J.
Peter Martyr, 484
Peter of Limoges, 632
Peters, P., 791, 795, 796
Peters, U., 632
Peters, U. H., 738, 761
Petersen, K., 808
Petersen, P., 725
Petersen, S., 691
Peterson, B. O., 803
Peterson, C., 924
Peter the Chanter, 6, 50
Petiot, G., 25
Petit, J.-M., 245
Petkova, S., 1083
Petkovich, K., 1078
Petliura, S., 1057
Petrarch, F., 9, 86, 87, 296, 306–07, 450–51, 453, 459, 460, 479, 481, 489, 1005
Petraško, L., 955
Petri, A., 632
Petri, W., 867
Petříček, M., 938
Petrík, V., 952, 955
Petro, P., 956
Petrocchi, G., 476, 484, 537, 546
Petronius, 700
Petrov, E., 1038, 1041
Petrov, S., 1034
Petrov, V. P., 1038
Petrova, I., 1081
Petrova, L. A., 1001
Petrova, S., 1080
Petrova, S. V., 991
Petrova-Vuteva, I., 1078
Petrović, R., 1076
Petrovskii, M., 1019, 1038
Petrovský, A., 947
Petrucci, A., 488

Petrucciani, M., 548
Petruck, C., 393
Petrus, P., 955
Petrushevskaia, L. S., 1030
P'etsukh, V., 1030
Pettersson, J.-E., 929
Pettey, J. C., 910
Pettey, J. L., 802
Petti, V., 928
Pettinati, D., 543
Pettinelli, F., 545
Petzold, K.-E., 621
Petzoldt, L., 661
Peuchet, J., 134
Peylet, G., 181
Peyrache, D., 712
Peyrat, N., 180
Pezatti, F. G., 398, 399
Pezold, K., 809, 836–37, 857
Pfaff, C. W., 592
Pfanner, H. F., 816
Pfau, L., 776
Pfeffel, G. K., 685, 731
Pfeffer, W., 264
Pfeiffer, A., 862
Pfeiffer, H., 182
Pfeiffer, I., 802
Pfeiffer, J., 762
Pfeiffer, P. C., 823
Pfister, M., 247, 248, 424, 436, 443, 604
Pfister, S., 663–64
Pfitzner, H., 806
Pflüger, G., 750
Pforr, A. von, 633
Phaf, I., 419
Phalese, H. de, 199
Phan, C., 263
Pharies, D. A., 22
Phelan, A., 683
Philip II (*King of Spain*), 472
Philipot, J., 9, 117
Philipp, M., 607
Philippe Auguste (*King of France*), 52
Philippe de Mézières, 75
Philipsen, B., 758–59
Philipson, L., 783
Philip the Good (*duc*), 74
Phillips, H., 128, 130
Pianca, M., 414
P'ianykh, M. F., 1016
Piaskowski, J., 974
Piątkowski, J., 980
Piatrouskaia, H., 1069
Piau, C., 154
Piau-Gillot, C., 157
Pic, F., 245, 264
Picallo, C., 280
Picallo, M. C., 379–80

Picano, J., 155
Picard, B., 130
Picard, E., 625
Picard, M., 46
Picasso, P., 209, 308, 357, 368–69
Picat-Guinoiseau, G., 179
Picchio, R., 963, 999
Piccolomini, A., 467
Piccolomini, A. S., *see* Pius II (*Pope*)
Piccolomini, E. S., 10
Piccolomini, M., 454
Pich, C., 441
Pich, E., 187
Picheta, V., 1064
Pichler, G., 811, 874
Pichois, C., 220
Pichon, E., 26, 27
Pichon, J., 27
Pichou, 126
Pickenhayn, J., 415
Pickering, R., 231
Picoche, J., 40
Pico della Mirandola, G., 454, 460, 465, 474
Picón, J. O., 339–40, 354
Picón Garfield, E., 341
Picot, E., 72
Pidmohyl'nyi, V., 1059
Piedmont, F., 713, 853
Piel, J. M., 402, 403
Piemontese, P., 444
Piera, C., 346
Pier delle Vigne, 452
Pieri, M., 482, 501, 502, 522
Pierini, P., 15
Pieros du Ries, 64
Pierozzi, L., 463, 474
Pierrard, M., 32
Pierre, C., 356
Pierre, M., 356
Pierre de la Cypède, 987
Pierrot, R., 168
Pierssens, M., 183
Pietrkiewicz, J., 974–75
Pietro, P. di, 132
Pietropaoli, A., 544
Pigault-Lebrun, C.-A.-G., 156
Piglia, R., 416
Pigna, G. B., 468, 477
Pigoń, S., 979
Piirainen, I. T., 598, 658
Pijanović, P., 1076
Pijnenburg, H., 36
Pijnenburg, W. J. J., 879
Pikach, A., 1034
Pikler, T., 523
Pilawa, J., 252
Pilch, H., 568

Pil'd, L. L., 1021
Pilipp, F., 818, 872
Pillecijn, F. de, 888
Pillepich, A., 172
Pilling, C., 793
Pilling, J., 980, 981
Pillinini, S., 456, 511
Pil'niak, B. A., 1045
Pilström, I., 120
Pimpinella, P., 721
Piña, C., 415
Piña, J. A., 417
Pinamonti, P., 516, 517
Pinchon, J., 25
Pinchuk, S., 1062
Pineau, J., 122
Pineaux, J., 78
Piñera, V., 419
Ping, J. G., 405
Pinget, R., 240
Piniès, J.-P., 250
Pinkernell, G., 70
Pinkert, E.-U., 786
Pinkster, H., 17, 20
Pino, J. M. del, 339
Pintaudi, R., 457
Pinthus, K., 815
Pinto, M. A., 439
Pinto-Bull, B., 404
Piø, J., 905
Piotrowska-Małek, T., 969
Piotrowski, J., 970
Piperno, F., 517
Pipino, M., 442
Pirandello, Lia, 543
Pirandello, Luigi, 482, 525, 526,
    530, 543, 545
Piranesi, F., 523
Pirckheimer, W., 662
Piredda, V., 851
Pirie, D. P. A., 980
Pirogova, N. K., 991
Pirotti, U., 536
Pisani, G., 463–64
Pisapia, G. D., 521
Pisárčiková, M., 948, 950
Pisarkowa, K., 981
Piscator, E., 825
Pischedda, B., 548
Pischel, J., 874
Piscitelli, M., 521
Piselli, F., 490
Pishwa, H., 592
Piskunov, V., 1015
Pissarro, C., 201
Pissavino, P., 508
Pištalo, V., 1076
Pistolesi, L., 504
Pistorius, G., 221
Pistorius, V., 944

Pittas-Herschbach, M., 127
Pittman, R. H., 1030, 1037
Pius II (*Pope*), 10, 488, 662
Pizarnik, A., 415
Pizer, J., 727
Pizzamiglio, P., 508
Pizzorusso, A., 152
Pizzuto, A., 543
Plachta, B., 729, 747, 788, 791
Plaisance, D., 109
Plaisance, M., 455, 480, 521
Planck, M., 708
Plangg, G. A., 441
Plantinga-Veldhuizen, E., 881
Plate, B., 637
Platen, A. von, 765, 794
Plato, 95, 118, 120, 263, 463,
    733, 737, 766, 813
Platonov, A. P., 1028, 1041,
    1045–46
Platzack, C., 928
Plautus, 7, 678, 725
Plavil'shchikov, P. A., 1003
Plavinskaya, N., 146
Pleier, Der, 647
Pleij, H., 890
Pleister, W., 755
Plénat, M., 40, 48–49
Plessen, E., 867
Plessen, J., 190
Plette, B., 790
Plievier, T., 811
Pliny the Elder, 449
Plitchenko, A., 1019
Pliukhanova, M. V., 1000
Pliushch, L., 1062
Pliushch, M., 1053
Ploneis, J.-M., 568
Ploquin, J.-F., 186
Plouzeau, M., 56
Plow, G., 848
Plummer, J. F., 58
Pluta, F., 971
Plutarch, 96
Pluzhnyk, Ie., 1059
Pobel, D., 239
Pociña, A., 331
Pöckl, W., 69, 809, 837
Pocock, J., 713
Podak, K., 598
Podestà, G. L., 466
Podgaets, O. A., 1038
Podhorský, M., 943
Podokshin, S., 1065
Podol, P. C., 373
Podol, P. L., 360, 373
Podracki, J., 959, 969
Poe, E. A., 184, 187, 328, 332,
    415, 816, 868
Poelstra, W., 165

Poersch, J. M., 400
Poghirc, C., 554
Pohl, J., 12
Pohlheim, K. K., 837
Pohlmann, N., 780
Pohrebennyk, F., 1057
Pohrebennyk, V., 1057
Poirier, C., 46
Poirion, D., 73
Poirot, L., 417
Pokyd'ko, O., 1053
Polčin, S., 947
Poleni, G., 519
Polenz, P. von, 592–93, 596
Poletto, P., 544
Polheim, K. K., 657, 749, 788
Poli, S., 106
Poliakova, L., 1019
Poliakova, S. V., 1015, 1033
Polier de Bottens, C. de, 150
Polikarpik, L. K., 1043
Polishchuk, V., 1058, 1061
Poliziano, A., 455, 458, 460,
    469, 474, 475, 485, 488, 500
Poljakov, F. B., 998
Połkowski, J., 980
Pollak, F., 825
Pollard, A. W., 894
Pollard, P., 221
Pöllinger, A., 708
Pollock, G., 898
Polo de Beaudieu, M. A., 64
Polomé, E. C., 625, 877
Polonskii, Ia. P., 1016
Polska, M., 973
Pol'skaia, S., 1044
Pol'skii, L., 1048
Polt-Heinzl, E., 851
Polukhina, V., 1036
Polverini Fosi, I., 465
Polybius, 487
Pombo, A., 371
Pombo, P., 372
Pomeau, R., 144, 145, 150, 153
Pomerants, G., 1033
Pomey, F., 100
Pommier, E., 134
Pommier, R., 121, 125
Pompa, L., 524
Pompeius, 17
Pona, F., 505
Ponchiroli, D., 526
Ponge, F., 211, 212, 227, 240–4
Pongs, U., 796
Poniatowska, E., 413, 419, 421
Ponnau, G., 200
Ponomarenko, M., 1054
Ponomareva, G. M., 1022
Ponomariv, O., 1053
Pons, J. C., 94, 95

'ons, J.-S., 264
'ons d'Ortaffa, 261
'ont, J., 364
'ontano, G., 479–80, 490
'onti, A., 532
'ontifice, J., 404
'ontis, L. de, 98
'ontuso, J. F., 1048
'onyrko, N. V., 1001
'ooley, T., 43–44
'op, L., 550–51, 552
'op, S., 554
'opa, V., 1074, 1076
'ope, R. D., 335
'opin, J., 154
'opkin, J. D., 137, 697
'opkin, R. H., 698
'oplavskii, B. Iu., 1034, 1046
'opolo, C. del, 447
'opov, E., 1030
'opov, K., 1082
'opović, Lj., 1071
'opović, M., 1070
'opowska-Taborska, H., 964
'opowska-Taborska, N., 969
'opp, W., 854
'oppelmann, H., 687
'oprawa, A., 983
'orcelli, B., 483, 504
'örksen, U., 592
'orlán Merlo, R., 342, 353
'örnbacher, H., 630
'orpetta, A., 366
'orret, M., 141
'orrmann, M., 791–92
'orta, A., 528, 543
'orta, G., 489
'orteman, K., 876, 888
'orter, D., 173, 197, 222
'orter, L., 70
'orter, R., 152, 681, 698, 894, 1030, 1046
'ortinari, F., 546
'orto Buciarelli, L., 414
'orzio, C., 483
'os, H. J., 877, 885
'osadskaia, L. A., 1047
'oschmann, H., 784
'oser, H., 791
'osner, R., 13
'ospiszylowa, A., 970
'osse, M., 415
'ossevino, A., 457
'ost, R., 607
'ostel, C. H., 685
'ostel, G., 459
'oster, M., 806
'ostl, K., see Sealsfield, C.
'ostouenko, K. Iu., 1042
'ot, O., 101

Potapova, I. V., 1040
Potebnia, A. A., 1031
Potgieter, J., 853
Pöthe, A., 707
Potocki, J., 156
Potocki, W., 974
Pott, H.-G., 749, 795, 869
Potte, J.-C., 246
Pottier, J., 820, 826
Potts, D. C., 220–21
Potulicki, E., 146
Pouilloux, J.-Y., 95, 241
Poulaille, H., 211
Poulet, D., 44
Poulsen, I., 901, 902
Poumarède, J., 248
Pound, E., 451, 526, 934
Poust, A., 345
Poutet, Y., 120
Povartsov, S., 1036
Považaj, M., 950
Považan, J., 954
Powell, B. J., 223
Powell, H., 678
Powric, P., 218, 220
Pozdnin, E. N., 1040
Pozo Garza, L., 364
Pozzi, G., 467, 508
Pozzobonelli, G., 511
Praamstra, O., 896
Prada Oropeza, R., 418
Prado Galán, G., 407
Pradoo, E., 349, 944, 947
Praetere, T. de, 229
Praloran, M., 471
Prandi, S., 484, 488
Prangel, M., 814
Prashkovich, L., 1067
Prassoloff, A., 177
Prat, M.-H., 90
Pratolini, V., 543
Prats Sariol, J., 420
Pratt, T. M., 167
Praun, M., 676
Praz, M., 544
Préchac, J. de, 112
Predaval Magrini, M. V., 514, 518
Preece, J., 833
Preisendanz, W., 717, 796
Prell, H. P., 596
Prete, S., 479
Preti, D., 389, 399
Preusse, H.-H., 853
Preussner, M., 184
Prévost, A.-F. (abbé), 121, 131, 132, 152, 156
Prévot, J., 109
Prezzolini, G., 533, 534, 544
Price, G., 21, 29

Priessnitz, R., 836
Priest, S., 118
Prignitz, C., 758
Prijma, I., 1075
Prikhod'ko, I. S., 1036
Prikhod'ko, N., 1044
Primochkina, N., 1040
Pringle, J., 717
Prinssen, M., 900
Prinz, M., 599
Prishchepa, V. P., 1034
Prishvin, M. M., 1023, 1045–46
Pritchett, K., 365
Prittwitz, G. von, 858
Privat, É., 246
Privat, S.-P., 246
Prochasson, C., 180
Proclus, 88
Prodan, I., 1058
Protter, C. R., 986
Profitlich, U., 843, 857
Prokhorov, G. M., 998
Prokhorova, I., 1041
Prokof'ev, A. A., 1027
Prokop, U., 692
Prokopovich, F., 1002, 1008
Prokushev, Iu., 1019
Promies, B., 727
Promies, W., 727
Propertius, 105
Propp, V. Ia., 1031
Proschwitz, G. von, 153
Prosdocimi, A. I., 26
Prosio, P. M., 530
Proskurin, V., 1023
Proskurnikova, T., 1019
Prosperi, A., 468
Prosperi, G., 530
Pross, W., 765
Prost, D., 155
Proudhon, P., 136
Proust, M., 114, 200, 204, 210, 211, 227–29, 359, 769
Provenzal, D., 534
Providenti, E., 543
Prudnikau, P., 1068
Prus, B., 977
Prus, M., 975
Prušková, Z., 956
Prút, L., 582
Prutti, B., 692
Prutz, R. E., 778
Prybytka, H., 1067
Przebinda, G., 1024
Przyboś, J., 972, 979
Przybylski, R., 979
Przychodniak, Z., 975
Pseudo-Beda, 5
Pshenichnikova, I. I., 1007
Pucci, A., 70

Pucci, J., 4
Pucci, S. R., 152, 159
Puchalski, L., 742
Pückler-Muskau, H. (*Prince*), 802
Pudalov, B. M., 997
Puech, S., 159
Pufendorf, S., 686, 694
Puga, M. L., 412, 413
Pugachev, V. V., 1041
Pugh, A., 227
Pugh, A. R., 170
Pugh, D., 712
Pugieva, N. A., 992
Puig, A., 252–53
Puig, M., 415, 416
Puig Salellas, J. M., 384
Pujati, G. M., 512
Puławski, M., 960
Pulci, L., 471–72
Puletti, R., 532
Puliafito, A. L., 463
Pulkenat, M., 840
Pullan, B., 453
Pullini, G., 543
Pulver, E., 856
Pumfrey, S., 458, 509
Punte, M. L., 847
Punzi, A., 3
Pura, Ia., 1054
Purdela Sitaru, M., 553, 554
Purvanova, A., 1082
Püschel, U., 592, 783
Puschner, U., 696
Pushcha, Ia., 1068
Pushkareva, L. S., 1048
Pushkin, A. S., 750, 1003, 1014, 1016, 1020, 1022, 1044, 1045
Puškáš, J., 956
Pustevjosky, J., 729
Putlina, I., 1043
Putnam, W. C., 222
Putsko, V., 999
Pütz, H. P., 614
Pütz, M., 590
Pütz, P., 725, 822, 870
Puyau, J.-M., 251–52
Puzyna, K., 972
Puzynina, J., 957, 961, 963, 966
Py, B., 24
Pylyns'kyi, M., 1054
Pylypiuk, N., 1055
Pynsent, R. B., 941, 943, 945, 956
Pys'mychenko, A., 1053
Pyykkö, R., 995–96

Quack, J., 832, 846, 848, 859, 868

Quaglio, L., 517–18
Quainton, M., 88, 92
Quak, A., 625
Quallio, E. B., 135
Quantin, J.-L., 136
Quaquarelli, L., 477
Quarenghi, P., 530
Quarta, D., 461, 469
Quasimodo, S., 529, 544
Queffélec, A., 47
Quemada, B., 40
Queneau, R., 211, 229–30, 241
Quenot, Y., 118
Querleu, P., 192
Quéro, D., 159
Querol, E., 383
Quéruel, D., 69
Quesada, J., 417
Quesnay, F., 142
Quevedo y Villeyas, F. de, 301, 308, 310, 351
Quignard, M.-F., 104
Quilis, A., 284
Quillet, C., 132
Quillien, P.-J., 231–32
Quin, C., 577
Quinault, P., 120, 121
Quinet, E., 133
Quinlin, D. P., 597
Quinn, A., 225
Quinn, M. L., 518
Quinones, R., 182
Quiñones Keber, E., 406
Quint, D., 472
Quint, N., 258
Quintana, A., 384
Quintana Docio, F., 350
Quintero, M. C., 324
Quintilian, 617, 702
Quintin, D., 287
Quirk, R., 20
Quirk, R. J., 334
Quiroga, E., 371
Quondam, A., 450, 468, 479
Qvale, P., 914

Raabe, W., 779, 801, 802–03
Rabadan, M., 300
Rabbe, A., 179
Rabboni, R., 483
Rabelais, F., 80, 81, 82–84, 95, 1031
Rabil, A., Jr, 460
Rabinowitz, S. J., 1019
Raboni, G., 500
Rabozzi, P., 528
Racan, H. de B., 104, 105
Racault, J.-M., 131
Racek, A., 941

Rachilde (*Mme* A. Valette), 200, 202, 210
Racine, J., 99, 101, 120, 121, 126–30, 514, 517
Raczyński, K., 976
Radbruch, G., 689
Raddatz, F., 866
Raddatz, F.-M., 866
Radegund (*Saint*), 619
Rademacher, G., 828–29
Radeva, V., 1079
Radicchio, G., 159
Radimov, P., 1040
Radishchev, A. N., 1002, 1007, 1009
Radkte, E., 431
Radlov, S., 1032
Radoslavov, I., 1082
Radović, V., 1076
Radspieler, H., 869
Radtke, E., 436, 438
Radulović, M., 1074
Radzivshevskii, V., 1017
Raeff, M., 985
Raevschi, N., 551
Rafel, J., 378
Raffaello Sanzio (Raphael), 454, 755
Raftery, M. M., 890
Rague-Arias, M.-J., 372, 373
Rahaman, G., 825
Rahoisha, U., 1066
Raimbaut d'Aurenga, 263
Raimbaut de Vaqueiras, 260
Raimond, M., 168, 194
Raimondi, E., 525
Raimondi, F. P., 508
Raimon Jordan, 261
Raimon Vidal, 247
Raimund, F., 801, 803, 817
Rainaldus, 2
Raine, C., 128
Raines, D., 495
Rainov, N., 1082
Raissen, H., 168
Raitt, A. W., 168, 185, 187, 196–97
Rajna, P., 470
Rakovskii, Kh. G., 1021
Rama, A., 423
Ramajo Caño, A., 267
Ramat, S., 531, 544
Rambaud, H., 29
Rambaud, V., 168, 194
Rameau, J.-P., 146
Ramée, P. de la, 463
Ramge, H., 590
Ramírez, A. J., 285
Ramos, J., 395
Ramos, R. A., 358

Rampák, Z., 955, 956
Ramsey, M., 388
Ramus, P., 79
Ramuz, C.-F., 211
Ranchhod, E. M., 393, 394, 395
Rancour-Laferrière, D., 1015, 1050
Randel, M. G., 306
Rando, G., 435, 444
Randsborg, H. B., 916
Ranger, J.-C., 129
Ranke, L., 453, 751
Rankin, J., 791
Rankl, M., 842
Ranković, S., 1076
Ransmayr, C., 858, 867–68
Ransome, F., 1038
Ranum, O., 97
Raphael, *see* Raffaello Sanzio
Rapin, C., 250
Rapisardi, M., 544
Raponi, E., 526
Raposo, E. P., 393
Rappaport, R., 523
Rasico, P. D., 376
Raskol'nikov, F., 1018
Rasmussen, O., 903
Rasputin, V. G., 1029, 1046
Rassloff, U., 956
Rasson, L., 220
Rathenow, L., 868
Rather, L. J., 806
Rathjelm, F., 069
Rathmann, T., 684–85
Rathmayr, R., 990
Ratnikava, I., 1064
Ratti, M. P., 471
Ratushinskaia, I., 1035
Ratz, A. E., 817
Rauch, I., 597
Raude, A.-J., 568
Rauf de Lenham, 77
Raupp, H.-J., 658
Rauschenberg, M., 784
Ravier, X., 246, 248, 250, 254
Ravis, S., 215
Ray, L., 219
Raymond, F. de, 198
Raymund of Peñaforte, 8
Raynal, G.-T. (*abbé*), 135, 142–43
Raynaud, C., 51–52, 73, 75
Razgonnikoff, J., 158
Rázus, M., 955
Razzi, S., 483
Rea, P. W., 858
Real Ramos, C., 346
Reati, F., 416
Rebay, L., 548
Rebmann, A. G. F., 695

Rebollo Torío, M. A., 270
Rèbora, C., 528, 529
Reboul, A., 48
Reboul, J., 211
Récamier, J., 165
Recasens, D., 276, 377, 381
Recio, R., 267, 295
Rector, M., 725
Reddy, M., 818
Reďep, J., 1072
Redgrave, G. R., 894
Redi, F., 495, 506
Red'kin, V. A., 1033, 1047
Redman, H., 164, 175
Redman, H., Jr, 180
Redmond, J., 128
Redondi, P., 506, 509–10
Redondo, A., 312, 483
Reed, J., 54–55
Reed, M. K., 363
Reed, T. J., 682, 706, 707, 710–11, 796, 823
Reemtsma, J. P., 811
Reenen, P. van, 27, 30, 42–43
Reensticrna, H., 930
Rees, D. B., 564
Rees, M. A., 305, 307, 348
Reeser, H., 889, 897
Reeve, M. D., 5
Reeve, W. C., 764
Reeves, E., 509
Reeves, M., 466
Reginold von Eichstätt, 4
Regn, G., 468
Regnard, J.-F., 130
Régnier, H. de, 188
Régnier, P., 163, 741
Régnier-Bohler, D., 57, 288
Rego, M. V. M., 398
Regosa, M., 545
Regosin, R., 87, 96
Regoyos, D., 355, 357
Řehoř (z Uherského Brodu), 939
Reich, H. H., 604
Reichan, J., 969
Reichard, G., 750
Reichard, H. A. O., 695
Reichardt, L., 609
Reichart, E., 865
Reichmann, O., 595
Reich-Ranicki, M., 823, 840–41, 848–49, 855, 868
Reid, A., 1031
Reid, J. H., 849–50
Reid, M., 170–71, 176, 193, 196
Reidel-Schrewe, U., 826
Reif, A., 849, 864, 868
Reiffenstein, I., 595
Reimann, H., 869

Reimarus, H. S., 686
Reimer, G. A., 761
Reimöller, H., 618
Rein, E., 1034
Reina, M. M., 372, 373
Reincaker, H., 810
Reinders, P. M., *see* Meijer, R. P.
Reinecke, A., 614
Reinfrank-Clark, K., 765
Reinhammar, V., 926
Reinhardt, H., 773
Reinhardt, M., 666
Reinhardt, S., 857
Reinhart, J., 994
Reinheimer-Ripeanu, S., 12
Reinhold, K. L., 731
Reinicker, H., 866
Reinig, C., 868
Reinman von Hagenan, 649
Reinmar von Zweter, 650
Reinoss, H., 860
Reis, M., 602–03
Reisinger, R., 829
Reiss, H., 813
Reiss, T. J., 79, 118
Reisse, J., 132
Reiter, A., 808, 865
Reixach, M., 384
Rej, M., 974
Rejakowa, B., 969
Rejano, J., 341
Rekdal, J. E., 576
Relković, A. M., 1072
Remarque, E. M., 825
Remi-Giraud, S., 31
Remizov, A., 1022
Remizov, A. M., 1023, 1027, 1046
Remizova-Dovgello, S. P., 1023
Remneva, M. L., 990, 991
Renan, E., 181, 182, 226
Renart, J., 6, 50, 62
Rendina, C., 477
René d'Anjou, 75
Renger, R., 729
Rengstorf, K. H., 729
Renn, L., 827
Renner, R. G., 824
Renwick, J., 140
Renzi, L., 424, 427, 431, 528
Repina, T., 12
Repiso Repiso, S., 269, 293
Rescetto, A., 541
Rescher, N., 119–20
Reschke, K., 855
Reschke, R., 802
Resina, J. R., 309, 313
Resink, G. J., 885
Resino, C., 372

Respaut, M., 199
Restif de la Bretonne, N.-E., 131, 153, 156, 158, 160, 197, 218
Reszka, J., 962
Rétat, P., 134, 137
Retz, J. F. P. de G. de (*cardinal*), 98, 100
Reuss, R., 759, 850–51
Reuter, G., 825
Reuter, H.-H., 780
Reuter, T., 623
Reuther, T., 990
Reve, G., 885
Reventlow, F. zu, 689
Reventlow, H. G., 618
Reverdy, P., 347, 548
Revueltas, J., 420
Revzina, O. G., 1049
Rey, A., 37–38, 40
Rey, R., 132, 146–47
Rey, W. H., 875
Rey-Debove, J., 40
Reydeburg, C. von, 668–69
Reyes, A., 421
Reyes Cano, R., 306
Rey-Flaud, H., 262
Reyfman, I., 1010
Reymont, W., 977
Reynaert, J., 887
Reynek, B., 944
Reynolds, C., 449
Reynolds, D., 188
Řežábek, R., 997
Rézeau, P., 39, 40
Rhiel, M., 762
Rhodes, E., 310
Riazanova, L. A., 1023, 1046
Ribbans, G. W., 327, 335–36, 337–38, 357
Ribeiro, A. L., 389
Ribémont, B., 52, 71, 73–74
Ribera, J., 357
Ribeyro, J. R., 422
Ribnikar, V., 1075, 1076
Ricapito, J. V., 323
Ricca, D., 21
Ricci, F., 542–43
Ricci, S., 485
Riccoboni, L., 502, 517
Riccoboni, M.-J. de L. (*Mme*), 157, 689
Riceputi, L., 544
Richard, G., 46, 190
Richard of St Victor, 646
Richard Pluto, 8
Richardson, B., 479, 484
Richardson, J., 209
Richardson, R. D., 769
Richardson, S., 152, 737

Richardt, G., 842
Richartz, W. E., 868
Riché, P., 621
Richelet, C.-P., 38
Richelieu, A. J. du P. de (*cardinal*), 97
Richer, L., 207
Richet, D., 137
Richmond, C., 329, 342–43
Richter, G., 608
Richter, J. P. F., 683, 685, 688, 716, 732, 741–42, 765–68, 780, 850, 869
Richter, K., 700, 707
Richter, S. J., 750
Rickels, L. A., 798
Ricken, A., 776
Ricketts, P. T., 261, 264
Rico, A., 377
Rico, F., 297
Ricoeur, P., 343
Ricuperati, G., 512
Riddel, M. C., 371
Ridder, K., 660
Ridruejo Alonso, E., 273
Riechel, D. C., 911
Riedel, K. V., 842
Riedel, V., 690, 734
Riedel, W., 842
Riedmann, G., 875
Riegel, H., 590
Rieger, A., 260
Rieger, D., 261, 263
Riehl, W. H., 780
Riemen, A., 821
Riemer, F. W., 701
Riepenhausen, J., 761
Riera, C., 365
Riess-Meinhardt, D., 865
Rietra, M., 826
Rietzschel, T., 814
Rieu, J., 92
Riffaterre, M., 88, 218, 227–28, 343, 353
Rigau, G., 380
Rigg, A. G., 8
Rigolot, F., 85, 88, 94–95
Rigosta, J., 250
Riha, K., 795, 833
Riha, O., 658
Rikov, G., 1078, 1080
Riley, E. C., 311, 312
Rilke, R. M., 688, 689, 746, 768, 807, 825, 909
Rimbaud, A., 175, 178, 180, 181, 182, 183, 187, 188–91, 192, 351, 816, 1024
Rimbaud, F., 190
Rimmon-Kenan, S., 358
Rinaldi, R., 539

Rinaldo d'Aquino, 452
Rindal, M., 920–21
Ringby, P., 933
Rini, J., 272
Rink, S., 786
Rinser, L., 834, 868
Rio-Torto, G. M. O. S., 399
Rioual, L., 155
Ripellino, A. M., 544
Ripka, I., 950, 968
Ripoll, B., 304
Rippmann, I., 784
Rippo, V. M., 544
Riquer, I. de, 260
Riquer, M. de, 333
Rischin, R., 1021
Rischmüller, M., 719–20
Risco, A., 358, 359
Rissel, D. A., 284–85
Risselada, R., 20
Risso, M. S., 396
Rist, J., 669
Risum, J., 910
Ritchie, J. M., 819
Rittaud-Hutinet, C., 44
Rittel, T., 963
Ritter, A., 853
Ritter, E., 48
Ritter, F., 661
Ritter-Schaumburg, H., 638
Ritvo, H., 177
Ritz, G., 1036
Ritzel, W., 754
Rivara, A., 152
Rivas (*duque de*), *see* Saavedra, A. de (*duque de Rivas*)
Rivas, E. de, 355, 361
Rivas, M., 419
Rivas Cherif, C. de, 355, 361
Rivero, E., 410
Rivero, M. L., 281
Rivero, M.-L., 552
Rivero-Potter, A., 355, 413, 417
Rivière, C., 133
Rivière, J., 228
Rivière, J.-C., 259
Rivière, M. S., 110, 151, 154
Rivière, N., 34
Rivière, S., 151
Rivière-Chalan, V.-R., 248
Rivkin, L., 329
Rizza, C., 115
Rizza, S., 586
Rizzacasa, A., 520
Rizzi, D., 1012, 1014, 1015
Rizzi, L., 432
Rizzo, A., 470
Rizzo, G., 498–99
Rizzolino, S., 499
Roa Bárcena, J. M., 411

Rua Bastos, A., 421–22
Roach, P., 276
Roach, S., 894
Roach, W., 643
Robb, B. A., 146
Robb, G., 183, 184
Robb, J. W., 421
Robbe-Grillet, A., 233, 241, 858
Robbins, J., 233, 450
Robciuc, I., 553
Roberge, Y., 46
Robert, J.-B., 133
Robert, R., 107, 113
Robert de Boron, 662
Robert de Clari, 52
Robert l'Argenton, F., 49
Roberts, B. F., 559
Roberts, D., 105, 810, 844
Roberts, E. (Elis Wyn o Wyrfai), 565
Roberts, E. L., 567
Roberts, G., 1050
Roberts, K., 566, 567
Robertson, R., 823, 826
Robertson, T., 979
Robertson, W., 143
Robespierre, M. de, 136, 137
Robey, D., 471
Robillard, D. de, 26
Robin, D., 460
Robin, R., 265
Robinet, R., 192
Robinson, C., 751
Robinson-Valéry, J., 231
Robles, M., 423
Robrieux, J.-J., 124
Robson, J., 305
Rocca, M., 538
Roccati, G., 71
Rocco, D., 426
Rocha, M. A. F., 393
Roche, M. W., 811
Rochefort, C., 233
Rochegrosse, G., 184
Rocher, D., 613, 634
Rochet, B., 43
Röcke, W., 633
Rod, E., 539
Rodari, G., 544
Rodchanka, R., 1066
Rodenbach, G., 181, 183, 192, 202
Rodenko, P., 899
Rodgers, E. J., 335, 337, 338
Rodiek, C., 750
Rodin, A., 182
Roditi, E., 179
Rodnianskaia, I., 1024
Rodocanachi, L., 539
Rodoni, R. J., 487

Rodríguez, A., 312, 340
Rodríguez, A. A., 357
Rodríguez, A. R., 334
Rodríguez, I., 412
Rodriguez, L., 46
Rodríguez, R., 285
Rodríguez-Badendyck, C., 321
Rodríguez Baltanás, E. J., 322
Rodríguez Cacho, L., 312
Rodríguez Carranza, L., 420
Rodríguez del Padrón, J., 297
Rodríguez de Montalvo, G., 310
Rodríguez Fer, C., 366
Rodríguez Fischer, A., 343, 370
Rodríguez Freile, J., 408
Rodríguez González, F., 282
Rodríguez Marín, R., 327
Rodríguez Méndez, J. M., 373
Rodríguez Puértolas, J., 297
Rodríguez Rapún, R., 347
Rodríguez Rodríguez, A. R., 333
Rodríguez Rodríguez, J. J., 309
Rodríguez-San Pedro Bezares, L. E., 305
Rodríguez Velasco, J., 297–98
Rodríguez Vergara, I., 418
Roe, I. F., 792, 853
Roe, S. A., 141
Roederer, P. L., 134
Roegiest, E., 11, 18, 19, 278
Roelandt, J., 27
Roelans, J., 851
Roelcke, T., 604
Roellenbleck, G., 78
Roello, U., 535
Rocsler, M., 813
Roethke, G., 813
Rogan, B., 922
Rogan, R. G., 804
Roger, P., 135, 153, 157
Rogers, D. M., 329, 335
Rogers, M., 801
Roget, P. M., 37
Rogge, W., 255
Rogister, M., 230
Roglic, N. V., 35
Rogoshchenkov, N., 1036
Rohan, H. de, 495
Rohlfs, G., 425
Rohmer, F., 762
Rohou, J., 84, 128
Rohr, G., 833
Rohr, J. B. von, 672
Röhr, W., 697–98
Rohrbach, R., 26
Röhrich, L., 752–53
Rohrwasser, M., 756
Rohs, P., 751–52

Roig, A. A., 411
Roig, B., 331
Roig, M., 367
Roigé, D., 383
Rojas, C., 354, 355, 371
Rojas, F. de, 300, 314
Rojas, G., 417
Rojas, M., 413
Rojas, S., 423
Rojas-Mix, M., 408
Rojas-Trempe, L., 421
Rojo, J., 363
Rokem, F., 932
Rokha, P. de, 417
Rokoszowa, J., 957
Roland, 2, 54
Roland, K., 754
Roland, M.-J. (*Mme*), 161
Roll, S., 340
Rolland, P., 997
Rolland, R., 208, 211, 230
Rölleke, H., 686, 745, 748, 752–53, 797, 827
Rollemberg, V., 401
Roloff, H. G., 661, 671, 678
Rolshoven, J., 18
Romagnoli, S., 521
Romagnoni, G. P., 512
Romains, J., 208
Román ('Comendador'), 308
Roman, A., 980
Roman, M., 1060
Romanelli, M., 532
Romani, C., 429
Romanicheva, E. S., 1028
Romano, A., 484, 485
Romanos, M., 308
Romanova, E. I., 1017
Romanowski, S., 147
Romboli, F., 545
Romei, D., 501
Romeli, A., 488
Römer, C., 602
Romero, J. M., 355
Romero, L., 340
Romero Ortiz, A., 332
Römhild, D., 850
Rommelaere, F., 201
Rommeru, C., 155
Rommetveit, R., 926
Rondi Cappelluzzo, M. L., 473
Rondini, A., 525
Ronen, O., 1012
Rönnerstrand, T., 936
Rønning, H., 914
Ronsard, P. de, 80, 86–88, 91, 108, 121, 226, 450
Ronzeaud, P., 106
Room, A., 994
Rooryck, J., 32

Roosevelt, P. R., 1006
Ropars, J., 569
Roper, K., 807
Ropero Núñez, M., 282–83
Röpke, G.-W., 805
Roques, G., 40, 44, 45, 248
Roques, M., 263
Roqueta, M., 264–65
Rorty, A. O., 149
Rosa, A., 174
Rosa, G., 174, 178
Rosa, M., 511
Rosa, M. C., 398–99, 405
Rosa, W., 415
Rosa da Silva, E., 240
Rosales, L., 347, 417
Rosas, Y., 366
Rosas de Oquendo, M., 409
Rosati, G., 528
Rosbottom, R., 132
Ros de Olano, A., 340
Rose, P. L., 796, 806
Rose, U., 683
Rosegger, P., 825
Rosei, P., 868
Rosenbaum, K., 952, 954
Rosenberg, A., 150
Rosenberg, C. M., 454
Rosenberg, D. J., 841
Rosenberg, R., 841
Rosenblat, M. C., 415
Rosenblat, W., 312–13
Rösener, W., 622, 633, 639
Rosenfeld, H.-F., 636, 638
Rosenkranz, K., 803
Rosenkranz, U., 821
Rosenplüt, H., 70
Rosenroth, K. von, 676
Rosenstein, D., 819
Rosenstein, R., 60, 262
Rosenstiehl, A., 189
Rosenthal, B. G., 1022
Rosentochler, E., 863
Rosenzweig, K., 682
Rosetti, A., 366, 553
Rösner, J., 280
Rospigliosi, G., see Clement IX
  (*Pope*)
Ross, A. S. C., 20
Ross, C., 470
Ross, D. P., 20
Ross, H., 917
Ross, W., 615
Rossbacher, K., 826
Rosselli, S., 504
Rossellit, J., 821
Rosset, F. de, 106
Rossi, F., 517
Rossi, G., 457
Rossi, L., 511

Rossi, N., 399
Rossi, P. L., 458, 509
Rossi-Landi, F., 383
Rössing-Harder, M., 595, 598
Rössler, G., 644
Rosslyn, W., 1035
Rossmann, A., 713
Rosso, C., 521
Rosso, U., 513
Rossum-Guyon, F. van, 176,
  177
Rostand, E., 207
Roster, P., 416
Rot, H., 660
Rot, S., 663
Roté, M., 486
Rotermund, E., 808
Rotert, R. W., 359
Roth, G., 655–56, 658, 836
Roth, J., 825–26
Roth, K.-H., 795
Roth, M.-L., 824
Roth, N., 268, 288
Roth, S., 756–57
Roth, W., 397
Rothe, J., 655
Rothmund, D., 815
Rotondi Secchi Tarugi, L.,
  474–75
Rotondò, A., 466
Rotrou, J. de, 120, 130
Rott, D., 974
Roubaud, J., 241–42
Roudaut, F., 92
Roudaut, J., 192
Rougé, J.-L., 404
Rougé, J.-M., 43
Rougemont, M. de, 165
Rougeon, J., 239
Rougerie, R., 253
Roulet, E., 48
Round, N. G., 327, 338
Rouse, R. H., 13
Rousse, M., 84
Rousseau, G. S., 152, 680–81,
  698
Rousseau, J.-J., 131, 136, 139,
  148–50, 157, 159, 168, 693,
  707, 745, 758–59, 779, 953,
  1008
Rousseau, P., 172
Rousseau, T., 311
Rousselot, P.-J., 26, 41
Rousset, J. R. de M., 137
Rouy, H., 181
Rovira, J., 417
Rovito, P. L., 496
Rowan, M. M., 109
Rowe, E. A., 921
Rowland, D., 564

Rowland, J., 560, 561
Rowley, A. R., 607
Rowley, B. A., 798
Rowlinson, W., 31, 32
Roy, B., 76
Roy, G., 242
Roy, J., 230, 421
Royo, J., 383
Royo Latorre, M. D., 328
Royon (*abbé*), 138
Rozanov, M., 1048
Rozanov, V. V., 1023, 1024,
  1046
Roździeński, W., 974
Rozencvaig, P., 419
Rożewicz, R., 983
Rożewicz, T., 981
Rozhdestvenskii, R. I., 1034
Rozumnyi, Ia., 1057
Rozzi, P., 529
Rozzo, U., 456–57
Ruaix i Vinyet, J., 380
Ruano de la Haza, J. M., 316,
  319
Ruat, P., 257
Rubashkin, A. I., 1039
Rubellin, F., 155, 156
Rubenstein, S., 185
Rubial, X. F., 400
Rubin, D. L., 103
Rubin, P., 488
Rubio, F., 366
Rubio Cremades, E., 340
Rubio Jiménez, J., 328
Rubio Vela, A., 269
Rublev, K. A., 1035, 1049
Rubtsov, N. M., 1046–47
Ruck, E. H., 56–57
Rück, P., 616, 617
Rückert, F., 803
Rückert, J., 778, 779
Rudenko, M., 1062
Rudert, K., 745
Rudlin, J., 212
Rudnik, C., 690
Rudnitskii, K. L., 1014
Rudolf (*monk*), 5
Rudolf von Ems, 631, 636, 651
Rudolf von Fenis, 649
Rudolph (*Duke of Swabia*), 621
Rudolph, D. P., 869
Rudolph, G., 132
Rudyk, Ia., 1057
Ruffinato, A., 309
Ruffinelli, J., 412, 414
Ruffo-Fiore, S., 487
Rufinus of Assisi, 6
Rufo, J., 306
Rügert, W., 871
Ruggeri d'Amici, 452

Ruggiero, G., 544
Ruh, K., 652
Rühling, L., 932
Rühmkorf, P., 868
Ruisiñol, S., 355
Ruiter, F., 900
Ruiz, M. C., 294
Ruiz de Alarcón, H., 408
Ruiz de la Peña, A., 333
Ruiz Lagos, M., 369
Ruiz Noguera, F., 345
Ruiz Otín, D., 269
Ruiz Pérez, P., 306, 309
Ruiz Ramón, F., 316, 353
Ruiz Silva, C., 340
Rulfo, J., 414, 420
Runcini, R., 525
Runeberg, J. L., 931
Runge, A., 689, 736, 784
Runge, D., 823
Runge, F. O., 749, 750
Runge, P. O., 748
Runnalls, G. A., 71–72
Runte, H. R., 59
Rupp, G., 862
Rupp, S., 318
Rusanivs'kyi, V., 1056
Ruščák, F., 946
Ruscelli, G., 467
Ruschioni, A., 507
Rüsen, J., 690
Rusetski, A., 1067
Ruseva, V., 1083
Rushing, J. A., 645
Ruspoli, F., 504
Russ, C. V. J., 590, 609
Russell, D., 81
Russell, P., 560
Russell, R., 1027
Russell, R. H., 335
Russo, D., 428
Russu, I. I., 554
Rusticiano da Pisa, 56
Ruta, A. M., 529
Rüther, G., 841
Rutherford, J., 329
Rutkowski, K., 979, 980
Ruus, H., 902
Ruwet, N., 32
Ruy Sánchez, A., 420
Ruyter-Tognotti, D. de, 234
Ruzante, il (A. Beolco), 427, 481, 530
Růžička, R., 990
Ružičková, E., 951
Rybakov, A. N., 1028, 1047
Rybakov, B. A., 1006
Rybakov, N. I., 1028
Rybalkin, V., 1059
Rybicka, H., 957, 969

Rybicka-Nowacka, H., 966, 974
Rychner, J., 53
Rydberg, C., 933
Rydberg, V., 930
Rydén, M., 927–28
Ryder, A., 462
Rydlo, J. M., 956
Rydstedt, A., 936
Rygh, O., 916
Ryl's'kyi, M., 1059
Rymkiewicz, J. M., 975, 983
Rymut, K., 969–70
Rynkevich, V. P., 1018
Rypson, P., 671
Rytter, G., 964, 1070
Rzepka, W. R., 965
Rzetelska-Feleszko, E., 963, 971
Rzewuski, H., 976
Rzewuski, S., 974
Rzhevskii, A. A., 1003

Saachi, S., 188
Saar, F. von, 803, 804
Saavedra, A. de (duque de Rivas), 340
Saavedrová, J., 860
Saba, G., 105
Saba, L., 544
Saba, U., 526, 528
Saba, V., 544
Sabadino degli Arienti, G., 488
Sabatier, E., 987
Sabatier, R., 105
Sabatier de Castres, A., 135
Sabatini, A., 433–34
Sabatini, F., 424, 427, 436, 438
Sábato, E., 413, 416
Sabido Rivero, V., 415
Sabir, K., 332
Sablé, M., de (Mme), 114
Sabljak, T., 1073
Sablone, B., 544
Sabo, G., 946
Sabol, J., 949, 954–55
Sabran, F.-E. de (comtesse), 143
Sabugo Abril, A., 341
Saburova, I., 1035
Sacchetti, F., 452, 489
Sacchi, S., 190
Saccone, E., 546
Sachanka, B., 1065, 1066
Sacher-Masoch, L. von, 200, 750, 777, 803
Sachs, H., 660
Sachs, N., 846, 868
Sachsleiner, J., 826
Sacoto, A., 419
Sadaunichy, E., 1067

Sade, D. A. F. de (marquis), 133, 135, 152, 153, 157, 158, 163, 176, 344, 544, 698, 854
Sadło, R., 974
Sadnik, L., 991
Saeger, U., 868
Saenger, P., 663
Saer, G., 415
Saer, J. J., 416
Šafárik, P. J., 948
Saffrey, H. D., 190
Safonov, V., 1047
Safonova, N. V., 901
Saganiak, M., 976
Sagaro Faci, M., 355
Sagarra, E., 788, 791, 814
Sagave, P.-P., 689
Sager, K., 852
Saglimbeni, S., 548
Sagra, R. de la, 327
Sahagún, B. de, 408
Sahlgren, J., 927
Sahuquillo, A., 347
Saidova, M. V., 1039, 1040
Saine, T. P., 683, 688
Saint-Amand, P., 156
Saint-Amant, M. A. de G. de, 101–02
Saint-Beuve, C. A., 103
Saint-Chéron, P. de, 239
Saint-Denis, M., 213
Sainte-Beuve, C. A., 162, 167, 103
Sainte-Pelaye, see Lacurne de Sainte-Palaye
Saint-Évremond, C. de S.-D. de, 117, 686
Saint-Exupéry, A. de, 230
Saint-Genis, V. de, 76
Saint-Gérand, J.-P., 38
Saint-Guilhem, R., 252
Saint-Jean, A. de, 116
Saint-Just, A. L. I., 143, 786
Saint-Martin, J., 95
Saint-Réal, C. V. de, 114
Saint-Simon, C. H., 136
Saint-Simon, L. de R. de (duc), 98, 114
Sainz, G., 419, 421
Sainz de la Mata, C., 295
Sajous d'Oria, M., 159
Sajus, B., 253
Sakari, A., 251
Sakharova, E. M., 1017
Sala, M., 11, 553
Sala Di Felice, E., 517
Saladino, R., 439
Salahub, A., 1068
Salamevich, Ia., 1066, 1069
Salani, T. P., 437–38

Salauiova, T., 1067
Salavei, A., 1068
Salazar, P.-J., 100, 112, 183
Salazar y Torres, A. de, 409
Salberger, E., 921
Salemans, B. J. P., 631
Salesbury, W., 563
Salesse, J., 164
Salgado, M. A., 406
Salinas, E., 423
Salinas, P., 341, 345, 351, 352–53, 354
Salinas, S., 352
Salinas de Castro, J. de (*Conde*), 306
Salisbury, J. E., 52
Salisbury, T., 563
Salles-Loustau, J., 252
Salm, C., 804
Salm, M., 597
Sal'ma, N., 1013
Salmon, G., 43
Salmon, G.-L., 44–45
Salmons, J., 590
Salnikow, N., 689
Salom, J., 373
Salomon, F., 407
Saloni, Z., 959, 961
Saltarelli, M., 431
Salten, F., 826
Saltveit, L., 596
Salumets, T., 687
Salupere, M. G., 1009
Salutati, C., 460
Saluzzi, S., 545
Salvador, A., 327
Salvadori Lonergan, C., 483
Salvat, J., 254
Salverda, R., 876, 877, 885
Salvi, A., 517
Salvi, G., 431
Salvi, R., 435
Salvia, B., 528
Salvioni, C., 555
Saly, A., 60
Salyha, T., 1060
Salzmann, C. G., 689
Samaras, Z., 95
Sambeek-Weideli, B. van, 1016
Sambenazzi, L., 496
Sambor, J., 961
Samchuk, U., 1062
Sammern-Frankenegg, F., 853
Sammons, J. L., 687, 794, 803
Samoilov, D. S., 1034
Samonà, A., 525
Sampath, U., 809–10
Sampayo Rodríguez, R., 304
Samper Padilla, J. A., 286
Samples, S., 638

Sams, J., 124
Samuel, R., 764, 773
Sánchez, A., 313
Sánchez, D., 317
Sánchez, E. D., 329
Sánchez, R., 410
Sánchez, R. G., 335
Sánchez Cámara, I., 356
Sánchez de las Brozas (El Brocense), F., 267
Sánchez de León, M. J., 326
Sánchez de Lima, M., 306
Sánchez Ferlosio, R., 371
Sánchez Palomino, M. D., 30
Sánchez-Prieto Borja, P., 293
Sánchez Robayna, A., 366, 408
Sánchez Romeralo, A., 307, 351
Sánchez Vázquez, A., 362–63
Sánchez Vidal, A., 344
Sancho IV (*King of Castile*), 294
Sancho Cremades, P., 277
Sand, G., 163, 176–77, 194, 196, 197
Sand, M., 206
Sandauer, A., 972
Sandberg, H.-J., 822
Sandel, E., 491
Sander, H., 863
Sanders, J. B., 206
Sanders, R., 886
Sanders, W., 590
Sandford, J., 871
Sandmann, A. J., 398
Sandrart, J. J. von, 773
Sandras, C. de, 106
Sandvik, M., 918
Sandvik, S., 917
Sanfilippo, M., 454
Sanfiz Fernández, C., 368
Sanga, G., 426
Sanguineti, E., 525, 526, 536, 544
San José Lera, J., 306, 308, 310
San'ko, Z., 1064
Sankovitch, T., 73
Sanminiatelli, B., 545
Sanna, M., 524
Sannazaro, I., 475–76
San Román, G., 313
Sansoni, F. M., 548
Sansot, P., 133
Sansovino, F., 468
Santamarina, A., 388
Santervás, R., 357
Santić, A., 1076
Santillana, *see* López de Mendoza
Santini, L. R., 727
Santoro, A., 527
Santoro, M., 457, 463, 525

Santos Zas, M., 359
Santoyo, J.-C., 267
Santucci, L., 527
Santucci, M., 58, 69
Sanvitale, F., 533, 540
Sanz del Río, J., 338
Sanz Villanueva, S., 371
Saparev, O., 1081
Sapeliak, S., 1062
Saplin, Iu., 1054
Sappler, P., 646, 647
Şaramandu, N., 554
Šarapatková, Ž., 1070
Sarbiewski, M. K., 973
Sardou, V., 207
Sarduy, S., 413, 419
Sargent-Baur, B. N., 59–60, 69
Sarkisian, L. S., 1004
Sarmiento, D. F., 411
Sarmiento, O., 417
Sarmiento, R., 267
Sarnov, B. L., 1042
Sarnowska-Temeriusz, E., 972
Saronak, R., 243–44
Sarrasin, J.-F., 120
Sarraute, N., 242
Sartini, G., 491–92
Sartorius, G., 707
Sartre, J.-P., 188, 195, 196, 222–23, 233, 235, 239, 242–43, 374, 793, 846
Saslow, J. M., 475
Sass, J., 873
Sastre, A., 374
Satie, E., 210
Satkiewicz, H., 960, 963, 964
Sattler, D. E., 756
Satzinger, G., 662
Sauder, G., 722, 725, 728, 730
Sauermann, E., 821
Saul, N., 739–40, 748
Saulnier, V.-L., 81
Šaur, V., 1070, 1078
Saurin, B.-J., 160
Saurin, E., 117
Saussure, F. de, 26, 902
Saussure, H.-B. de, 716–17
Sauter, M., 750
Sauvages, F., 698
Sauvages (de la Croix), P. A. Boissier de (*abbé*), 43
Sauzet, P., 245, 249
Savarino, M. P., 857
Savary, J., 123
Savater, F., 363
Savchenko, S. V., 1034
Savéan, M.-F., 239
Savel'ev, *see* Lipavskii, L.
Saveliev, A. A., 998
Savelli, G., 547

Savigny, K. F., 753
Savini, M., 527
Savinian (*monk*), 254
Savinio, A., 545
Savinkov, B., 1028
Savitskaia, A. V., 901
Savoca, G., 545
Savoia, L. M., 429
Savonarola, G., 474
Savova, S., 1080
Savy, N., 174
Say, J.-B., 134
Sazonova, L. I., 1004
Sazonova, L. V., 997, 1001
Sbarbaro, C., 528, 545
Sbriziolo, I. P., 1000
Scaglione, A., 468, 639
Scala, F., 482, 502, 503
Scalise, S., 430
Scancarelli Seem, L., 472–73
Scandaletti, P., 509
Scandella, D., 466
Scapparone, E., 463, 474
Scappi, C. L., 494
Scaramella, P., 466
Scaramuzzi Vidoni, M. R., 304
Scarano, E., 483
Scarano, L. R., 332, 353, 360, 365
Scarcella, R., 203
Scardigli, P., 625
Scarpa, E., 477
Scarpati, C., 473, 476, 525
Scarpellini, E., 530
Scarron, P., 114
Scemama, R., 239
Scève, M., 80, 86
Schabol, R., 41
Schade, R., 686
Schädlich, H. J., 838, 841, 868
Schaefer, K., 733
Schaeffer, J.-M., 234
Schaetzen, C. de, 39
Schafe, M., 852
Schäfer, B., 389
Schäfer, H.-W., 635
Schäfer, L., 867
Schäfer, S., 701
Schäfer, W. E., 731
Schaffer, S., 698
Schaffer-Rodríguez, C., 421
Schaffner, J., 826
Schäffner, W., 814
Schafroth, H. F., 867
Schalk, A., 866
Schank, G., 851
Schanze, F., 647
Schanze, H., 702
Scharang, M., 836, 858
Schardt, M., 869

Scharlau, B., 407
Schauer, H. G., 942
Schaumann, R., 826
Schebben-Schmidt, M., 596
Schedel, Hartmann, 662–63
Schedel, Hermann, 663
Schedlinski, R., 838, 866
Scheel, C., 193
Scheer, R., 821
Scheffler, W., 776
Schehr, L., 198
Schehr, L. R., 170, 175
Scheibe, S., 715
Scheichl, S. P., 792, 809, 820
Scheiffele, E., 822
Scheiner, C., 510
Scheler, M., 345
Schelle, H., 733
Schelling, F. W. J., 707, 750, 751, 756, 757
Schelstraete, I., 714
Schembari, E., 545
Schenk, L., 931
Schenkel, E., 817
Schenkeveld, M. A., 892–93
Schenkeveld, M. H., 885
Schenk-Lenzen, U., 768
Schepper, E., 31
Schepper, M. de, 894
Scherfer, P., 29
Scherpe, K. R., 814, 833, 837
Scherr, B., 1040
Scherre, M. M. P., 400
Schertlin, H., 658
Schestag, T., 811
Schettino, P., 499
Scheuer, H., 726, 844
Scheunemann, D., 813, 833
Schiavo, A., 475
Schiavo, L., 359
Schichele, R., 230
Schick, C. G., 166
Schickaneder, E., 731, 733
Schickclc, R., 821, 826
Schiebeler, D., 685
Schiebinger, L., 699
Schieche, W., 751
Schiesari, J., 467, 476
Schieth, L., 752
Schiewer, H.-J., 653
Schiff, H., 909
Schiffman, Z. S., 79
Schikorsky, I., 593, 776
Schildt, J., 594, 596
Schillemeit, R., 803
Schiller, C. von, 690
Schiller, D., 808, 814

Schiller, F., 145, 159, 679, 682, 685, 687, 691, 692, 696, 710–14, 716, 720–21, 723, 726, 737, 742, 744, 747, 749, 763, 765, 768, 773, 784, 792, 800, 806, 853, 872
Schilling, K. von, 695
Schilling, M., 646–47
Schillow, C., 869
Schimmelmann, H. E. von, 142
Schindler, W., 600
Schindling, A., 729
Schipke, R., 657
Schippa, N., 149
Schipperges, H., 698, 740
Schirmer, B., 868
Schirokauer, A., 826
Schlaefer, M., 605
Schlaffer, H., 833
Schlau, S., 408
Schlee, E., 793
Schlegel, A. W., 735, 737, 741, 742, 768, 769, 770, 773, 774
Schlegel, C., 735, 736, 742, 768–69, 773
Schlegel, D., 731–32, 735, 736, 742, 769, 773
Schlegel, F., 693, 694, 702, 735, 736, 737, 739, 741, 742, 744, 749, 751, 757, 769–70, 773
Schlegel-Schelling, C., 736
Schleichl, S. P., 837
Schleidgen, W. R., 616
Schleiermacher, F. D. E., 688, 693, 770
Schleiner, W., 313
Schleissner, M., 634
Schlenstedt, D., 841
Schlenstedt, S., 811, 815
Schlieben-Lange, B., 19, 245, 264
Schloesser, R., 780
Schlosser, H. D., 589, 655
Schlösser, R., 605
Schlossman, B., 125
Schlözer, A. L., 718
Schludermann, B., 648
Schlüppmann, H., 863
Schlusemann, R., 664
Schlüter, C. B., 788
Schmalhaus, S., 725, 787
Schmid, E., 644
Schmid, G., 703
Schmid, H., 556
Schmid, I., 701
Schmid, K., 622
Schmid, P. G., 639
Schmid, W., 1036
Schmid-Cadalbert, C., 842
Schmidely, J., 19

Schmider, E., 591
Schmidhuber, G., 409, 421
Schmidjell, C., 859
Schmidová, H., 938 ·
Schmidt, A., 733, 844, 848, 868–70
Schmidt, A.M. G., 887
Schmidt, C., 134
Schmidt, G., 616
Schmidt, H., 1005
Schmidt, J., 47
Schmidt, K. H., 560
Schmidt, K. M., 630
Schmidt, K.-W., 841
Schmidt, P. G., 2, 6, 7
Schmidt, R., 833, 875
Schmidt, W., 519
Schmidt, W. A. von, 729–30
Schmidt, W. P., 971
Schmidt-Bergmann, H., 808, 859
Schmidtke, D., 654
Schmidt-Radefelt, J., 231
Schmidt-Wiegand, R., 620
Schmitt, C., 41, 424, 814, 824
Schmitt, F., 422
Schmitt, H. J., 604
Schmitt, M., 104
Schmitt, P., 611
Schmitt-Gläser, A., 811
Schmitt-Sasse, J., 866
Schmitz, A., 900
Schmitz, B., 822
Schmitz, W., 731–32, 745, 768, 769, 815
Schmitz-Emans, M., 766–67, 861
Schnabel, J. G., 677
Schnapp, J. T., 637
Schnauss, C., 647
Schneider, C. I., 816
Schneider, H., 124, 843
Schneider, J., 652
Schneider, K., 616
Schneider, M. J., 357
Schneider, P., 725, 845, 870
Schneider, R., 621, 861
Schneider-Lastin, W., 646
Schneidmüller, B., 633
Schnell, B., 654, 658, 663
Schnell, R., 639, 643, 659, 833, 844
Schnepf, M. A., 339
Schnitzler, A., 791, 807, 826
Schnitzler, C., 817
Schnyder, A., 664
Schoeller, W. F., 854
Schoenberg, B. Z., 870
Schoeps, K.-H. J., 812
Schöier, I., 935

Scholem, G., 810
Scholl, J., 844–45
Scholtz, L., 422
Scholvin, U., 689
Scholz, B. F., 455
Scholz, M. G., 647
Scholz, R., 725
Scholz, U., 601
Scholze-Stubenrecht, W., 590
Schön, E., 716
Schönborn, A. von, 731
Schöndorf, K. E., 876
Schönert, J., 778
Schöning, B., 648
Schönle, A., 979
Schoolfield, G., 933
Schopenhauer, A., 339, 751, 782, 789, 795, 818, 848
Schøsler, L., 27, 30
Schote, J., 872
Schottel, J. G., 672
Schottelius, S., 847
Schrader, L., 795
Schram, D., 885
Schraut, E., 618, 624
Schreckenberger, H., 829
Schregel, F. H., 845
Schreiber, C., 764
Schreiner, E., 851
Schreiter, G., 594
Schrenck, G., 89, 90, 91, 92
Schreurs, B., 825
Schreyer, L., 827
Schreyvogl, F., 809
Schriber, M., 835
Schröder, F., 816
Schröder, F. L., 723
Schröder, I., 655
Schröder, J., 590, 600–01
Schröder, R., 778
Schröder, S. M., 756, 907
Schröder, W., 613, 630, 635–36, 644, 646, 647
Schröder-Werle, R., 823
Schrodt, R., 594
Schroeter, W., 861
Schröter, E., 734
Schubart, C. D. F., 732
Schubert, F., 735, 764, 796
Schubert, G., 1071
Schubert, G. H., 756
Schuck, E., 181
Schück, H., 929
Schücking, L., 788
Schuerewegen, F., 166, 170, 198–99, 205
Schuh, K., 662
Schulman, I. A., 341, 410
Schulte, B., 664
Schulte-Sasse, L., 713

Schultz, G., 192
Schultz, G. M., 166
Schultz, H., 747, 748
Schultz, J. A., 634
Schulz, A., 819
Schulz, B., 979
Schulz, C., 713
Schulz, G., 761, 833
Schulz, H.-J., 817
Schulz, V., 792
Schulze, J. A., 914, 917
Schulze, U., 597, 611, 658
Schulze-Busacker, E., 249
Schulze-Dörrlamm, M., 623
Schulzová, O., 949, 951
Schumacher, C., 215–16
Schumacher, E., 812
Schumacher, K., 812
Schumann, A., 740–41
Schumann, C., 689, 783–84
Schumann, K., 875
Schumann, R., 770
Schumm, S., 366
Schünemann, P., 807
Schupp, V., 630
Schüppen, F., 803
Schuster, S., 667
Schutte, A. J., 467
Schütte, J., 831
Schutte, J., 873
Schutte, R., 891
Schutting, J., 867, 870
Schütz, E., 594, 653
Schütz, H., 738, 790, 870
Schütz, M., 756, 758
Schütze, P., 857
Schützeichel, R., 595, 626–27
Schwab, U., 638
Schwaiger, B., 867, 870
Schwall, H., 825
Schwartz, H., 736
Schwartz, J., 88
Schwartz Lerner, L., 310
Schwarz, E., 636, 796, 818
Schwarz, H., 689
Schwarz, J., 413
Schwarz, W. F., 938
Schwarze, C., 424
Schweickard, W., 437, 553
Schweikert, R., 869
Schweikle, G., 646
Schweimler, A., 802
Schweitzer, C. E., 727, 749
Schwenter, D., 674
Schwerte, H., 827
Schwertfeger, R., 820
Schwilk, H., 833
Schwind, K., 871
Schwitalla, J., 594
Schwitters, K., 827

Schwob, A., 596, 659
Schwob, M., 192, 193, 202
Schwob, U. M., 611, 659
Sciacca, M. F., 543
Scianatico, G., 472
Sciascia, L., 527, 545
Sciurie, H., 618
Scobar, L. C., 444
Scobbie, I., 933
Scofield, M., 857
Scolnicor, H., 1018–19
Scorrano, L., 525
Scorza, M., 422
Scott, D., 183
Scott, V., 502
Scott, W., 169, 175, 586, 781
Screech, M. A., 81
Scriba, C., 519
Scudéry, G. de, 104
Scudéry, M. de (*Mlle*), 106, 111, 114–15
Scullion, R., 241
Scully, T., 75
Seabra, M. T. R. C. da, 394
Sealsfield, C. (K. Postl), 777, 803
Seaman, G., 1002
Sears, D., 227
Sears, D. E., 241
Sears, T. A., 296
Sebald, W. G., 777, 837
Sebestyén, G., 777
Sebillet, T., 88
Sebold, R. P., 330
Sebond, R., 94, 95
Sebregondi, L., 466
Secchieri, F., 542
Seco, E., 304
Seco de Lucena Vázquez de Gardner, M. E., 348
Sectanus, 493
Sedakova, O., 1034
Sedano, L., 374
Sedelnik, W., 865
Sedlacek, P., 923
Sedlacek, U., 923
Sedulius Scottus, 2
See, G., 642–43
See, K. von, 615, 638
Seeba, H. C., 638, 759–60, 777, 845
Seeger, J., 291
Seehase, I., 943, 945
Seelbach, D., 18
Seelbach, U., 668–69
Seelow, H., 661
Sefamí, J., 413, 421
Segal, N., 172–73, 197
Segala, A., 406
Segalen, V., 230–31

Segar, K., 809
Segarra, M., 262
Seghers, A., 739, 827, 834, 837, 840, 841, 870, 875
Séginger, G., 200
Segrais, J. R. de, 108, 115
Segre, C., 470
Segre, M., 509–10
Seguin, J.-P., 38
Ségur, S. de (*comtesse*), 202
Sehmsdorf, H. K., 921–22
Seibert, H., 622
Seibert, T.-M., 778
Seibicke, W., 947–48
Seibt, F., 942
Seidel, G., 812, 870
Seidemann, M., 870
Seifert, H., 523
Seifert, H.-U., 157
Seifert, J., 943
Seifert, L. C., 107
Seifert, S., 698–99, 714
Seitz, D., 611
Seknadje-Askénazi, E., 155
Selenić, S., 1076
Sclig, K.-L., 144, 312
Selimović, M., 1074, 1076
Sellier, P., 119
Selm, B. van, 886, 894
Selva, P., 527
Semashko, O., 1060
Sembdner, H., 760
Semenchuk, I., 1060
Semenov, G., 1034
Semenova, O. N., 1038
Scmin, V., 1047
Semmler, H., 635
Semonin, L., 44
Sempoux, A., 547
Sempronio, G. L., 499
Sénac, J., 243
Sénac de Meilhan, G., 135
Senchenko, I., 1059
Sender, R. J., 371–72, 356–57
Sendich, M., 1044
Seneca, 6, 448
Senelick, L., 1014, 1018
Senelier, J., 175
Senior, N. W., 179
Senyk, L., 1057
Sepasgosarian, W. M., 765
Seppi, A., 821
Serafim of Sarov, 1016
Serafimovich, A. S., 1027
Sérane, P., 149
Sérant, P., 47
Şerbănescu, A., 551, 552
Šerbantovich, A., 1068
Serbat, G., 17, 22, 252
Serbens'ka, O., 1056

Serdiuk, P., 1060
Sereni, V., 528, 535, 544, 545–46
Serés, G., 297
Sergeev, A. V., 910
Sergius (*Saint*), 997
Sergo, L., 825
Sergooris, G., 858
Serhievich, Iu., 1068
Serman, I. Z., 1002, 1040
Serminocci, J., 450
Serova, I. Iu., 1001
Serper, A., 264
Serra, F. X., 382
Serra, M., 527
Serra, P., 378
Serra, R., 546
Serrai, A., 492–93
Serra i Casals, E., 385
Serralda, V., 4
Serrano, A., 324
Serrano Asenjo, J. E., 344, 355
Serrano Plaja, A., 344
Scrrano Vázquez, M. del C., 355
Serres, M., 241
Serres de La Tour, A. de, 149
Serroy, J., 100, 116
Servátka, M., 968, 969
Servera Baño, J., 307, 341, 358, 365
Servet, P., 93
Servetus, M., 304
Servin, M., 234
Servius, 3
Servodidio, M., 372
Servranckx, A., 823
Sesé, B., 305, 352
Sessa, M., 437
Sestrimski, I., 1082
Setnitskaia, O., 1021
Settekorn, W., 589
Seume, J. G., 722
Severianin, I., 1023, 1047
Sévigné, M. de R.-C. de (*marquise*), 100, 115
Sevin, D., 820
Seybert, G., 176, 177
Seynes, C. de, 873
Sfez, L., 133
Sforza, F., 460
Sforza, G. M., 461
Sforza, L. B., 531
Sfranze, G., 488
Sgard, J., 134, 135, 137
Shafi, M., 819
Shaftesbury, A. (*Earl*), 145, 676
Shaitanov, I., 1034, 1045
Shaitanov, I. O., 1021

Shakespeare, W., 1, 231, 318–19, 321, 328, 365, 472, 480, 517, 703, 718, 719, 730, 769, 771, 784, 792, 819, 820, 857, 866, 1018, 1073
Shakhovskaia, Z., 1031
Shalamov, V. T., 1047
Shalata, M., 1056
Shal'man, E. S., 1036
Shamiakin, I., 1068
Shamiakina, T., 1067
Shannon, T. F., 876–77
Shapoval, M., 1059
Shapovalov, M. A., 1017
Sharfavi, E., 1047
Sharkova, I. S., 1007
Sharpe, L., 711
Sharpe, R., 7
Sharpe, T., 1043
Sharratt, B., 981
Shatin, Iu. V., 1040
Shatrov, M.-F., 1028, 1032
Shatz, M. S., 1005
Shaw, D., 125–26
Shaw, G., 850
Shcheblykin, I. P., 1009, 1010–11
Shcheglova, E., 1029
Shcherbatov, M. M. (Prince), 1002, 1007
Shchirovskii, V., 1033
Shchurat, V., 1059
Shea, W. R., 508
Shefner, V. S., 1010
Shekhtman, M. V., 1029
Sheldon, U., 729
Sheliahovich, T., 1069
Shelley, P. B., 566
Shemetillo, K. G., 1038
Shengeli, G. A., 1025, 1042
Shentalinskii, V., 1021, 1028
Sheppard, D., 823
Sheppard, R., 814, 822
Sheptyts'kyi, A., 1059
Sher, A., 127
Sherberg, M., 472, 487
Sheremet'ev, B. P., 1007
Shergin, B. V., 1026, 1028
Sheridan, R. B., 723
Shershakova, N. E., 992
Shershenevich, V. G., 1020, 1033
Sherzer, W. M., 336
Shevchenko, L. I., 1035
Shevchenko, T., 1056–57
Shevchenko, T. G., 1020
Shevchuk, V., 1055, 1059
Sheveleva, I. M., 1033
Shevelov, G. Y., 946, 1052
Shewring, M., 468

Shik, E. G., 1046
Shindel', A., 1038
Shindina, O., 1049
Shirokov, V., 1020
Shishkin, A., 1020
Shishkin, A. B., 1010
Shitanda, S., 644
Shklovskii, E. A., 1026, 1029, 1047
Shklovskii, V. B., 1012, 1026, 1027, 1031
Shklovsky, V., 832
Shkraba, R., 1064
Shmelev, I. S., 1027, 1047
Shmeruk, C., 979
Shneerson, M., 1030, 1040–41
Sholokhov, M. A., 1029, 1047
Sholokhov, M. M., 1047
Shookman, E., 733
Short, J.-P., 129
Showalter, E., 335
Shrimplin-Evangelidis, V., 454
Shteiger, A. S., 1034
Shtein, E., 1035
Shtern, M. S., 1029
Shuba, P., 1064
Shubravs'kyi, V., 1057
Shukhtina-Savelieva, N. V., 998
Shukshin, V. M., 1026, 1047
Shul'hach, V., 1052
Shul'man, Iu., 1028
Shul'zhuk, K., 1053
Shumakov, Iu., 1023
Shumylo, N., 1057
Shur, V., 1065
Shustov, A. N., 1016
Shvarts, E. L., 1048
Shvetsova, L. K., 1021
Shynkarenka, V., 1067
Siadniou, M., 1067
Siatkowska, E., 964
Sibbald, K. M., 349
Siblewski, K., 860
Sičáková, L'., 950
Sicari, C., 543
Siciliano, E., 540
Sidarevich, A., 1068
Sidney, P. (Sir), 451, 563
Sieberg, B., 397
Siebert-Ott, G., 600
Sieburth, S., 329, 338
Siefarth, F. M., 622
Siefken, H., 708, 822
Siegel, K., 532
Siegel, P. J., 178
Siegert, R., 683
Siekierska, K., 962
Siemsen, D., 814
Siemsen, H., 827

Siemsen, M., 729
Sienkiewicz, H., 977
Sierra, J., 308, 408
Sierra, T., 305
Siess, J., 785
Siewert, K., 608, 627, 660
Siewierska, A., 959
Sieyès, E. J., 136
Sigibaldus (Bishop of Metz), 62
Sigler, H. A. von, 733
Sigov, S., 1021
Sigov, V. K., 1046
Sigüenza, J. de (Fray), 305
Sigüenza y Góngora, C. de, 409
Sigurd, B., 923, 928
Sijarić, C., 1071
Šikra, J., 948, 950
Šikström, T., 930
Šikula, V., 956
Silagi, G., 9
Silberzstein, M., 39
Siles, J., 364, 366
Sill, O., 845
Siller, M., 613, 657
Silone, I., 546
Silva, A. I. M. da, 392
Silva, F. de, 298, 310
Silva, J. V. da, 400
Silva, M. B. da, 399
Silva, R. V. M. e, 389, 399, 401
Silva Galeana, L., 407
Silva-Joaquim, C., 397
Silvano, G., 486–87
Silveira, P. de, 398
Silverman, J. H., 277
Silverstone, M., 694
Šilvestre, J.-C., 168
Sima, P., 946
Simenon, G., 169, 231
Simeon Polotskii, 1001, 1002
Simioni, C., 543
Simmel, J. M., 765, 833, 870
Simmler, F., 595, 661
Simmons, C., 1039
Simon, A., 660
Simon, C., 243–44
Simon, E., 1, 657, 839
Simon, G., 589–90
Simón, M. del C., 363
Simon, R., 726
Simoncini, G., 461
Simone, R., 424, 428, 435
Simonelli, J., 179
Simonetti, A., 6
Simoni, A. E. C., 894
Simoni-Aurembou, M.-R., 41, 45
Simonides, D., 842
Simonin, M., 78, 83, 86, 87, 88, 94

Simon-Ingram, J., 149
Simonis, F., 876
Simon of Vladimir, 999
Simonov, K. M., 1026
Simón Palmer, M. C., 326
Simonsen, H. G., 919
Simpkins, S., 416
Simpson, A., 847
Simrock, K., 638, 704
Sims, R.L., 418
Sims-Williams, P., 560, 561
Sinclair, I. von, 758
Sinclair, K. V., 55, 68
Sinclair, U., 813
Sindou, R., 250
Singeling, C. B. F., 895–96
Singer, I. B., 979
Siniavskii, A. D., 1040, 1048
Sinielnikoff, R., 969
Sinigaglia, S., 546
Sinisgalli, L., 546
Sinkevich, V., 1035
Sinnigen, J. H., 335
Sipala, P. M., 544
Siraisi, N. G., 455, 458
Sironneau, J.-P., 133
Sisegrist, C., 855
Sistac, R., 381
Sivovolov, G. Ia., 1047
Siwart, J., 621
Siwicka, D., 975
Sixtus IV (*Pope*), 461
Sixtus V (*Pope*), 461
Six van Chandelier, J., 895
Sjöberg, A., 990
Sjöblad, C., 929–30
Sjöstedt, G., 927
Skácel, J., 945
Skaldin, A., 1027
Škapincová, A., 948
Skarbek, F., 976
Skarga, P., 974
Skármeta, A., 413, 417, 418
Skaryna, F., 1065, 1068–69
Skatov, N. N., 1003
Skjelbred, A. H. B., 922
Skliarenko, V., 1052
Sklodowska, E., 412, 413
Skok, J., 1074
Skou-Hansen, T., 913
Skovoroda, H., 1055
Skrine, P., 678, 715
Skrodzki, K. J., 799–800
Skrynnyk, M., 1055
Skrzypek, M., 143
Skubalanka, T., 959, 961
Skubić, M., 432
Skurativs'kyi, V., 1052
Škvareninová, O., 951
Škvorecký, J., 945

Skvortsova, N. V., 1016
Skytte, G., 428, 485
Slaboshpyts'kyi, M., 1061, 1062
Slaby, W. A., 614
Slama, B., 192
Şlamnig, I., 1074
Ślaski, J., 973
Slataper, S., 546
Slater, M., 103, 128
Slaveikov, P. P., 1082
Slaveikov, P. R., 1083
Slavetskii, V. I., 1033–34
Slavova, T., 998–99
Slavutych, Ia., 1055, 1061
Slawinski, M. P., 458, 495, 500, 509
Slawson, R. J., 422
Slawysutton, C., 220
Slerca, A., 29
Slisarenko, O., 1059
Sloane, H., 137
Slobin, G. N., 1023
Sloboda, R., 955, 956
Slobodník, D., 954
Slon'ovs'ka, O., 1057
Sloterdijk, P., 885
Słowacki, J., 974, 976
Slups'kyi, Ie., 1054
Slusanski, D., 13
Šlutskii, B. A., 1027, 1034
Šmahel, F., 940
Smal', V., 1068
Şmaszcz, W., 903
Šmatlák, S., 955
Smeaton, W. A., 150
Smedt, M. de, 886, 887
Smeets, J. R., 64
Smekhov, V. B., 1050
Smeloff, M. M., 312
Şmet, G. A. R. de, 596
Šmiech, W., 958, 971
Smil Flaška, 939
Smirnenski, Kh., 1083
Smirnoff, R. de, 168
Smirnov, A. S., 1026
Smirnov, I. P., 997, 1045
Smirnov, Iu. M., 1038
Smirnov, L., 946–47
Smirnov, V., 1034
Smirnova, G. A., 1017
Smirnova, L. A., 1019
Smith, A., 178, 707
Smith, C., 159, 282, 297
Smith, D. L., 321
Smith, G., 811
Smith, G. S., 1036
Smith, I. C., 587
Smith, J. C., 432
Smith, J. H., 236
Smith, M. C., 81, 94

Smith, P. J., 363
Smith, R., 860
Smits-Veldt, M. B., 891–92
Smoczyński, W., 961
Smółkowa, T., 961
Smorąg, M., 978
Smrek, J., 947
Snædal, T., 924
Snaith, G., 128
Snapper, J. P., 876–77
Snellaert, F. A., 886, 887
Sneller, A. A., 889
Sniehir'ov, H., 1062
Snigireva, T. A., 1049
Snoek, K., 885
Snoek, P., 900
Snoek, J., 974
Snow, J. T., 314
Snyder, J. R., 490–91
Soarez, C., 79
Sobejano, G., 330, 363
Sobejano-Morán, A., 329, 363
Sobierajski, Z., 964, 968
Sobková, H., 941
Sobkowiak, W., 957
Sobolev, L., 1023
Sobolewska, A., 973, 982
Sobolewski, T., 981
Sobrero, A., 424
Sobrero, A. A., 438, 439
Sobrevilla, D., 422
Sochacka, S., 971
Sochorová, L., 940
Sochová, Z., 950
Socrate, M., 312
Socrates, 233
Sodal', U., 1064, 1066, 1067
Soder, H.-P., 824
Söderberg, H., 932
Södergard, O., 77
Södergran, E., 931
Soderini, P., 459
Söderström, G., 932
Söderström, S., 927
Sodini, C., 496–97
Soemerring, T., 699
Sofronii Vrachanski, 1082
Söhn, G., 796
Sohnle, W. P., 756, 758
Sojková, Z., 954
Sokalski, A., 143
Sokol, I. O., 991, 1052
Sokolov, A. G., 1030
Sokolov, B. V., 1037
Sokolov, V., 1048
Sokolova, L. V., 999
Sokolová, M., 949
Sokolova, T. A., 1042
Sokolov-Mikitov, I., 1028
Sokołowska, T., 966

Sokolski, J., 973
Sola, A., 1021
Solà, J., 375, 378, 380
Solà Pujols, J., 380
Solbach, A., 677
Solberg, T. K., 918
Solbrig, I. H., 703
Soldati, M., 546
Soldevila-Durante, I., 343, 359, 368
Solé i Camardons, J., 387
Soleillet, P., 190
Soler, C., 557
Soletti, E., 486
Solger, K. W. F., 773
Şoliman Aga, 124
Šoljan, A., 1074
Solmi, S., 528, 546
Solms, H.-J., 595, 597, 600, 643
Solodkin, Ia. G., 997, 1001
Sologub, F. K., 1023–24
Sologuren, J., 422
Solórzano, C., 421
Soloukhin, V. A., 1029, 1030
Solovei, E., 1060
Solov'ev, V. S., 1015, 1016, 1024, 1031
Solstrand-Pipping, H., 931
Solterer, H., 75
Solzhenitsyn, A. I., 1023, 1028, 1029, 1047, 1048
Sommar, C. O., 933
Sommerfelt, A., 576
Sommerhage, C., 871
Sommers, D., 410
Sommers, P., 83
Sonderegger, S., 594, 595, 629
Søndergaard, L., 906
Sønderholm, E., 908
Sonnenfeld, A., 204
Sonnenleitner, J., 826
Sonnleitner, J., 855
Sontheimer, K., 821
Soons, A., 291
Sophocles, 220, 223, 418, 722
Soracco, S., 908
Sørbø, J. I., 914
Sorel, C., 101, 115
Sorella, A., 480
Sørensen, B. A., 692, 802, 909
Sørensen, K., 904
Sørensen, P. E., 906
Sorensen, R., 186
Sørensen, V., 903, 904, 913
Sorgeloos, C., 133
Soria, A., 328–29
Soriano, C., 292
Soriano, M., 113
Soria Olmedo, A., 341, 342, 345, 347, 353

Sornicola, R., 17, 432
Sosa López, E., 416
Sosinskii, V., 1023, 1027
Sosiura, V., 1059
Sotelo Vázquez, A., 330, 355, 370
Şotirov, P., 1079
Šotola, J., 945
Soufas, C. C., Jr, 351
Soufas, T. S., 323
Souffrin-Le Breton, E., 183–84, 186
Soulié, F., 187
Soulié, M., 91
Sourdot, M., 49
Sousa, M. L. D., 397
Souto, E., 371
Souza, C. M. B. de, 393
Sowinski, B., 612
Soyfer, J., 809, 827
Sozzi, L., 502
Spaas, L., 149, 165
Spacagna, A., 160
Spadaccini, N., 406
Spadoni, N., 528
Spaggiari, W., 519
Spagna, A., 517
Spallanzani, L., 132
Spang, K., 331
Spanlang, E., 861
Spanoghe, A.-M., 19, 278
Spaude-Schulze, E., 808
Spaziani, M. L., 539
Spear, F., 146
Spear, T., 218
Specht, K., 870
Speckenbach, K., 634–35, 657–58
Speckter, A., 805
Speckter, H., 804–05
Speckter, O., 804–05
Spee, F., 670
Speiss, S., 124
Spencer, A., 957
Spencer, C., 99, 114
Spencer, M., 162
Spender, S., 540
Spener, P. J., 686
Spengel, L., 782
Spengler, O., 827
Spera, L., 515
Sperber, M., 870
Spering, J., 823
Speroni, S., 15, 467, 488
Spervogel, 633
Speth, R., 811
Spiel, H., 870
Spielhagen, F., 778, 803–04
Spielmann, L., 826
Spies, B., 724, 841

Spies, M., 887
Spiess, F., 442
Spiewok, W., 631, 641, 643, 663
Spilimbergo, I. di, 467
Spillebeen, W., 887
Spiller, A., 442
Spiller, R., 414–15
Spilling, H., 616
Spillmann, H. O., 598
Spinazzola, V., 525, 528
Spinella, M., 534
Spinelli, G., 425
Spini, V., 491
Spinnen, B., 811
Spinosi, N., 536, 545
Spinoza, B., 727, 757, 772, 893
Spiquel, A., 174
Spire, A., 208
Spires, R. C., 371
Spiridonova, I. A., 1047
Spitaletta, R., 418
Spittel, O. R., 839
Spitteler, C., 837
Spitzer, L., 111
Spitzlei, S. B., 652–53
Spivak, P., 1049
Splett, J., 597, 613, 626
Spottorno, R., 355
Sprandel, R., 652
Spraul, H., 591
Spreckelsen, T., 869
Sprengel, P., 747, 767, 815–16, 828
Sprenger, J., 664
Sprenger, R., 619
Sprickmann, A. M., 729, 788
Spriewald, I., 659–60
Springman, L., 818
Sprynchan, A., 1064
Spunda, F., 809
Spyri, J., 870
Squarotti, G. B., 531
Squercina, M., 826
Squires, J., 371
Srzodka, T., 967
Staats, R., 623
Stabb, M. S., 415
Stableford, B., 154
Stäblein, P. H., 263
Stabro, S., 978, 980
Stachura, E., 983
Stackelburg, J. von, 145
Stackmann, K., 650, 654, 655
Stadler, A., 851
Stadler, T., 614
Stadler, U., 765
Städtler, K., 260
Staël, A. de, 161

Staël, G. de (*Mme*), 143, 149,
  161, 162, 163, 164, 166, 198,
  691, 734, 736, 746
Staël-Holstein, E. M. de
  (*baron*), 143
Staengle, P., 759
Stafford, F., 586
Stage, L., 36
Stagg, G., 313
Stagnino, B. (B. Giolito de'
  Ferrari), 456
Stahl, A., 730, 825
Stahl, G. E., 686, 698
Stahl, H.-J., 660
Stahl, P., 658
Stähli, F., 798
Stala, M., 980
Stalin, I. V., 986, 1028–29, 1050
Stamelman, R., 208 09
Stammen, T., 821
Stammerjohann, H., 19, 424
Stampa, C. N., 516
Stampa, G., 477, 484
Stančić, M., 1073
Stander, T., 534–35
Standish, P., 415, 416, 422
Stanev, E., 1083
Stanforth, A. W., 605
Stangerup, H., 913
Stanishich, I., 1042
Stanislavová, Z., 956
Stanislavskii, K., 213, 1032
Stanitzek, G., 861
Stankevich, Ia., 1063
Stankova, B., 33
Stanton, D., 99
Stanzel, F., 844
Stara, A., 544
Starck, A., 828
Stark, V., 1044
Starke, G., 602
Starke, M., 186
Starobinski, J., 224, 532
Starosel'skaia, N., 1032
Stary, S., 169
Starychonak, V., 1063
Staryts'ka-Cherniakhivs'ka, L.,
  1059
Staryts'kyi, M., 1057
Starzec, A., 967–68
Stassi, A., 13
Šťastný, R., 939
Statius, 3, 469
Stäuble, A., 126, 480, 520
Stäuble, M., 520
Stauf, R., 729
Stauffacher, W., 814
Stavans, J., 423
Stavyts'ka, L., 1057
Stavyts'kyi, O., 1057

Stedje, A., 923
Štědronová, E., 945
Steele, C., 421
Steene, B., 933, 936
Steenmeijer, M., 413
Stefan, V., 852
Stefanaggi, M.-J., 443
Stefanelli, A., 436
Stefanov, S., 1081
Stefanyk, V., 1059
Steffenelli, A., 101
Steffens, H., 750
Steffensen, E., 1030
Steffins, M., 812
Stegmann, A., 120–21
Stegmann, V., 813
Stegner, G., 825
Stehkämper, H., 622
Stehl, T., 438
Steiman, L. B., 828
Steimer, H. G., 756
Stein, C. von, 691, 725
Stein, M. B., 842
Stein, P., 605, 796
Stein, R. F., 285
Stein, V., 750
Steinberg, O., 416
Steinbrügge, L., 689, 784
Steinecke, H., 688, 744, 796
Steiner, C., 791
Steiner, P., 134, 943
Steiner, R., 818
Steinfeld, D., 245
Steinhöwel, H., 633, 662
Steinlein, R., 817
Steinmann, D., 803
Steinmetz, H., 818
Steinmetz, J.-L., 188, 189–90,
  217, 218–19
Steinmetz, R.-H., 818
Steinsland, G., 920
Steinwender, E.-D., 870
Stella, A., 529
Stella, P., 513
Stelluti, F., 508
Stenberg, D. G., 1018
Stendhal, 163, 164, 170–73,
  197, 201, 223, 260, 356
Stengaard, B., 21, 268, 273
Stennik, Iu. V., 1003
Stenzel, H., 124
Stepanchenko, I. I., 1039
Stepanenko, M., 1059
Štěpánková, J., 944
Stephan, A., 821
Stephan, I., 736
Stephens, A., 762
Stephens, J., 453
Stephens, T. M., 398, 405
Stephenson, R. H., 707

Stępnik, K., 977, 978
Stepnovska, T., 1029
Stepovyk, D., 1059, 1061
Stepun, F., 1020, 1031
Sterchi, B., 835
Sterkenburg, P. G. J. van, 883
Stern, C., 316–17
Stern, J. P., 809, 817, 833
Stern, M., 799, 816–17
Sternbach, N. S., 415
Sternburg, W. von, 829
Sterne, L., 145, 543, 869
Sterry, P., 563
Stetter, C., 599
Stevček, J., 954
Stevens, A., 813
Stevens, M., 10, 657
Stevens, T., 887
Stevens, W., 351
Stevenson, J., 375
Stevenson, R. L., 192
Stewart, P. D., 480
Stiatsko, P., 1065
Sticca, S., 447
Stichweh, R., 699
Stieg, G., 809
Stieglitz, H., 801
Stieler, C., 678
Stierle, K., 468
Stifter, A., 777, 804
Stigliani, T., 491
Stillmark, H.-C., 866
Stilz, G., 713
Stimm, H., 247
Stipa, I., 764
Stivale, C. J., 193
Stixrude, D. L., 353
Stock, A., 849
Stock, J., 229
Stöckli, R., 868
Stockman, G., 573, 576
Stocksieker Di Maio, I., 800
Stockwell, E., 156
Stoddart, J., 587
Stoebers, A., 786
Stoessl, O., 820
Stoianov, R., 1082
Stoianova, D., 552, 554
Stojanova-Jovceva, S., 602
Stolberg, F. L. (*Graf zu*), 732
Stoljar, M., 777
Stoll, A. K., 321, 421
Stolleis, M., 696
Stolpe, A., 805
Stolt, B., 595
Stolte, H., 793
Stolz, D., 857
Stolz, T., 17, 251
Stone, L., 37
Stone, M., 293–94

Stones, A., 639
Stoppelli, P., 434–35
Ştorǎ, S., 933
Storcová, I., 945
Storm, G., 805
Storm, J., 917
Storm, T., 761, 775, 792, 800, 804–05
Störmer, U., 654
Storni, A., 413
Stötzel, G., 590
Stoudt, D. L., 654
Strabo, 382
Strachey, G. L., 1044
Strack, F., 760–61
Strada, V., 1045
Straka, G., 263
Stralen, H. van, 898
Strancar, N., 174
Strand, C. M., 358
Strand, H., 913
Strandberg, S., 927
Strashnov, S. L., 1033
Stratanovskii, S., 1036
Ştrauch, G. L., 636, 638
Straus, F., 954
Strauss, B., 739, 831, 832, 833, 834, 861, 870–71
Strauss, D. F., 177
Strauss, J., 216
Stravinsky, I., 220, 813
Streckenbach, G., 633
Streisand, M., 866
Streitberg, W., 26
Strelis, J., 828
Strelka, J. P., 706, 813, 819, 851
Strengholt, L., 889
Stricker, Der, 635, 646–47, 658
Stricker, S., 627, 628, 630
Strickhausen, W., 870
Strickland, S. W., 704
Strid, J. P., 924
Strietman, E., 895
Strietz, M., 604
Strindberg, A., 802, 853, 910, 931–32
Střítecký, J., 940–41
Strittmatter, E., 840, 841, 871
Strodtmann, A., 909
Strohm, R., 517, 523
Strohschneider, P., 639, 646
Strohsová, E., 943
Strong, E., 580, 581–82
Strosetzki, C., 117
Stroszeck, H., 801
Stroud, C., 926
Stroud, M. D., 322
Strubel, A., 71
Strugnell, A., 143
Struve, G., 988

Struve, T., 621, 622
Struzyk, B., 839, 866
Strybel, M., 969
Strycharz, K., 967
Stryienski, C., 172
Strzyzewski, M., 975
Stsiatsko, P., 1064
Stuard, S. M., 618
Stubier, G., 659
Stuhlmann, G., 177
Stuip, R., 69
Stump, G. T., 568
Ştumpf, A., 793
Štúr, L., 947, 953, 954
Sturlese, R., 485
Sturm, R., 69
Sturz, H. P., 906
Stus, V., 1062
Stuten, A., 652
Stybe, V., 908
Suard, F., 69
Suard, J. B. A., 143
Suarès, A., 163, 180
Suárez, J. A., 273
Suárez Solí, S., 368
Subbotin, A. S., 1026
Subirats, E., 363
Subirats, M., 384
Subrenat, J., 66
Suchner, B., 609
Sudavichene, L., 1068
Suddzeva, N., 1066
Sudermann, H., 827
Sudnik, Z., 1068
Sue, E., 776, 781
Suetnov, A., 1028
Sueur, J.-P., 31
Sugarev, R., 1083
Sukach, V., 1023
Sukhareva, I. M., 1041
Sukhov, A. D., 1006–07
Sulík, I., 956
Sulivan, J., 244
Sullivan, H. W., 322–23
Sullivan, J., 1003
Sullivan, K., 76–77
Süllwold, E., 691
Sully, M. de B. de (*duc*), 120
Sültemeyer-von Lips, I. von, 826
Sumarokov, A. P., 1002, 1003, 1010
Sundman, M., 923
Suñén, J. C., 364
Suñer, A., 281
Suñer, M., 280
Suomela-Härmä, E., 67, 432, 444
Supple, J. J., 79, 96, 121
Surovtsova, N., 1059, 1060

Surtz, R., 299
Süskind, P., 832
Süss, P., 846
Sussex, R., 963
Sussmann, H., 168
Suvchinskii, P. P., 1017, 1044
Suvorova, P. E., 1034
Suwala, H., 205
Suzuki, J., 822
Suzuki, S., 597
Ṣuzuki, T., 1019
Šváb, M., 939
Švagrovský, S., 946, 948
Svahn, M., 927
Svandrli, R., 824
Svanevik, A., 916
Svatoň, V., 938
Svedjedal, J., 929
Svennevik, J., 918
Sverbilova, T., 1061
Sverstiuk, Ie., 1062
Svevo, I., 525, 526, 527, 537, 546–47
Svidzyns'kyi, V., 1059, 1062
Svientsits'kyi, I., 1052
Svirydau, S., 1067
Svitlychnyi, I., 1062
Svobodin, A., 1032
Swales, E., 798–99
Swales, M., 687–88, 798–99, 822
Swanenberg, C., 880
Swanson, P., 418
Sweet, D. M., 734
Sweetser, M.-O., 69, 100, 104, 122, 127
Şwianiewiczowa, O., 975
Świdziński, M., 959
Święch, J., 978
Świerczyńska, D., 975–76
Świetlicke, C., 307
Świętochowski, A., 977
Swiggers, P., 13, 19, 25, 26, 27, 40, 247, 555, 877
Swisher, M., 629
Switten, M., 263
Swoboda, V., 1056
Sydorenko, O., 1057–58
Sylvester, J., 126
Sylvius, *see* Dubois, J. (Sylvius)
Symington, R., 807
Symonenko, V., 1062
Sysyn, F. E., 1055
Syvachenko, M., 1055
Syvokin', H., 1061
Szabó, T., 639
Szagun, G., 591
Szakács, L., 204–05
Szanto, G. H., 359

Szczepański, J. J., 983
Szczypiorski, A., 983
Szelburg-Zarembina, E., 967
Szell, T., 619
Szewczyk, Ł. M., 966
Szkilnik, M., 58
Szklenar, H., 636
Szlifersztejnowa, S., 957
Szmetan, R., 416
Szőke, K., 1023, 1045
Szpakowicz, S., 959, 967
Szpakowska, M., 980
Szybińska, M., 969
Szydłowska-Brykczyńska, W., 974
Szydłowska Ceglowa, B., 963
Szymański, A., 977
Szymborska, W., 980, 983
Szyrocki, M., 678, 857

Taat, M., 244
Tabah, M., 858
Tabakova, I., 1079
Tabakowska, E., 963–64, 967
Tablic, B., 953
Tabucchi, A., 547
Tachiaios, A.-E. N., 998
Tachuino da Trin, G., 457
Tacitus, 173, 596, 624, 625, 758
Tadié, J.-Y., 210
Tadijanović, D., 1074
Taldrup, P., 913
Taffon, G., 537, 538
Tager, E., 1043
Taggart, G., 556
Taiha, M., 1059
Taille, J. de la, 93
Taillemont, C. de, 81
Taillevent, 75
Taine, H., 168, 180, 182
Tajovský, J. G., 954
Tajsner, P., 959
Takahashi, S., 816
Takahaši, T., 630
Takeuchi, N., 187
Takho-Godi, A. A., 1004
Talarczyk, A., 872
Talbot, L. K., 371
Talbot, M., 516
Talev, I., 1079
Talleyrand-Périgord, C. M. de, 179
Tallqvist, J. O., 936
Talon, G., 239–40
Tamayo y Baus, M., 326
Tamba, I., 252
Tamburri, A. J., 541
Tamim Ad-dar, 301
Tampi, L., 827

Tancheva, T., 995, 1078
Tank, M., 1069
Tanturli, G., 476
Tanucci, B., 511, 512
Tanzi, C. A., 523
Tarallo, F., 388
Taraman, S., 803
Taranovsky, K., 1016
Tarashkevich, B., 1063, 1069
Tarashvili, L. I., 908
Taratuta, E., 1034
Tardieu, J., 209, 225
Targhetta, R., 513
Tarkovskii, A., 1034
Tarlovskii, M., 1033
Tarnavs'ka, M., 1062
Tarnavs'kyi, M., 1059
Tarnawsky, M., 1054–55, 1056
Tarnow, F., 745
Tarsia, G. di, 478
Tarugi, G., 460
Tasende-Grabowski, M., 334
Tasmowski-De Ryck, L., 12, 552
Tassara, G., 283–84
Tasso, T., 114, 263, 467, 468, 469, 472–73, 476, 481, 482, 484, 488, 500, 514
Tassoni, A., 473
Tassoni, L., 549
Tatarka, D., 956
Tatarowski, L., 976
Tate, D., 850
Tateo, F., 458
Tatishchev, V. N., 1006, 1010
Tatlock, L., 677, 784, 801
Taube, M., 1000
Tauler, J., 652
Tavani, G., 376
Tavard, G. H., 408
Taviani, F., 502
Tavoni, M., 428, 453
Tawada, Y., 866
Tax, P. W., 651
Taylor, A., 52
Taylor, B., 288, 295, 308, 650
Taylor, D., 414
Taylor, J., 73
Taylor, N., 975
Taylor, R., 261, 786, 828
Tebaldeo, C., 476
Tedaldi, I., 475
Tedeschi, J., 496
Tedeschi, M., 663
Tedesco, N., 527
Teffi, 1031
Teich, M., 894
Teilhard de Chardin, P., 358
Teja, A. M., 411
Tekavčić, P., 11, 13, 425

Teleman, U., 926
Telesio, B., 463
Teliha, O., 1062
Telitsyna, T. V., 1048
Tellechea Idígoras, J. I., 310
Tellier, C., 36
Telmon, T., 440
Tel'niuk, S., 1059–60, 1062
Temme, J. D. H., 805
Tempelaars, R., 877
Tempesta, I., 440
Temprano, J. C., 408
Tennyson, A. (*Lord*), 586
Teodosi (*Metropolitan*), 551
Terekhina, V. N., 1042
Terent'ev, I., 1027
Teresa of Avila (*Saint*), 305, 310, 329, 673–74
Terhorst, C., 858
Ter Horst, R., 313
Ter Meer, T., 893
Terni, C., 504
Terrell, P., 605–06
Terrell, T. D., 281
Terrón González, J., 269
Terry, G. M., 986, 1037
Tersmette, R. L. V., 561
Terts, A., *see* Siniavskii, A. D.
Tervooren, H., 632, 649
Tesauro, E., 473, 490, 491
Teschke, H., 813
Tešić, G., 1074, 1076
Teskey, G., 528, 532
Tesnière, L., 27
Tesnière, M.-H., 449
Tessari, R., 502
Tessitore, F., 524
Tessonerie, G. de la, 126
Testa, C., 1038
Testa, E., 426
Testori, G., 531
Testud, P., 153
Tetel, M., 86, 89, 95
Tetter Saxalber, A., 875
Tetzlaff, M., 1034
Teulat, R., 249, 254, 264
Teunis, H. B., 63
Tewilt, G.-T., 824
Texeda, J. de, 266
Texeira de Pascoaes, J., 357
Texier, L., 208
Teyssandier-Pichon, F., 201
Teysseire, D., 132
Teyssier, P., 398
Thaller, M., 614
Tham, F., 925
Theile, W., 87
Thelin, N. B., 993
Theobald, R., 801

Theocritus, 706
Theodulf of Orléans, 3
Théophile de Viau, 101,
104–05, 115, 120, 130
Theophilis, J., 374
Théré, C., 134
Theuerkauf, G., 623
Thevenin, N., 178
Thevet, A., 79
Thewalt, P., 773
Theweleit, K., 825
Thibault, B., 242
Thibault, R., 236
Thibault-Delpuech, J.-P., 251
Thibaut, M., 768
Thibon-Morey, P., 407–08
Thiel, H., 861
Thiele, J., 40
Thiele, J. M., 905
Thiele, S., 847
Thielking, S., 829
Thieme, E., 815
Thierot, G., 863
Thierry, A., 90
Thierry, D., 102
Thiess, F., 827
Thiesse, A.-M., 211
Thijssen, T., 885
Thirouin-Deverchere, M.-O.,
824
Thody, P., 130
Tholen, T., 822
Thomas, 56, 58, 60, 61
Thomas, A., 939, 941
Thomas, C., 157
Thomas, C. L., 170
Thomas, D., 846, 854
Thomas, E., 418
Thomas, G., 563
Thomas, H., 623
Thomas, H. H., 565
Thomas, J., 62–63
Thomas, K., 886
Thomas, M. W., 563
Thomas, N., 813
Thomas, P. A., 262, 646
Thomas, P. M., 60–61
Thomas, P. W., 559
Thomas, Y., 197
Thomas Aquinas (*Saint*), 618
Thomas Becket (*Saint*), 7
Thomasin von Zerclaere, 651
Thomasius, C., 686
Thomas of Cantimpré, 8, 288
Thomasseau, J.-M., 178
Thompson, A. D., 520
Thompson, C. P., 307
Thompson, C. W., 175, 191
Thompson, E. M., 1028
Thompson, F., 723

Thompson, I. A. A., 275
Thompson, L., 933
Thompson, P., 165
Thomsen, U., 907–08
Thomson, C., 1031
Thomson, D. S., 584, 586–87
Thomson, F. J., 999
Thomson, I., 10, 479
Thomson, J., 767–68
Thomson, P., 857
Thorbecke, J. R., 886, 897
Thormann, M., 783
Thornasset, C., 52
Thornberry, R., 225
Thorne, D. A., 559, 561
Thornton, A. M., 430–31
Thornton, P., 454
Thorup, K., 913
Thös-Kössel, S., 730
Thoursie, R., 936
Thun, H., 397
Thuret, M., 790
Thüring von Ringoltingen, 661,
662
Thurn, H., 616
Thurnher, E., 792
Tibenská, E., 948
Tibenský, J., 954
Tidoli, C., 456
Tieck, F., 771
Tieck, L., 732, 737, 739, 741,
742, 743, 744, 767, 770–71,
786
Tieck, S., 771, 772, 773
Tiefenbach, H., 630
Tielsch, I., 871
Tietz, M., 142
Tikhonovich, I. S., 969
Tiling, N., 854
Timenchik, R., 1021
Timina, S. I., 1015
Timm, E., 613
Timman, Y., 883
Timmermans, F., 887, 899
Timms, E., 777, 813
Timofeev, L., 1047
Timofeeva, G. G., 994
Timofeeva, V. V., 1027
Tinajero, F., 419
Tinayre, M., 210
Tindall, G., 204
Tin'kov, A., 1005
Tipka, E., 654
Tiraboschi, G., 523
Tirechán, 3
Tirso de Molina, 322–23
Tischbein, J. H., 709–10
Tisheva, I., 1080
Tissier, A., 71
Titley, A., 582–83

Titova, L. N., 1005
Titz, P., 669
Titze, M., 852
Titzmann, M., 684
Tiupa, V. I., 1042
Tiurin, G., 1049
Tiutchev, F. I., 1016
Tiutiunnyk, H., 1062
Tiziano Vecellio (Titian), 461
Tkachenko, A., 1060
Tkachenko, M., 1061
Tkachenko, O., 1054
Tkachuk, M., 1059, 1062
Tkáčiková, E., 952
Tobin, R., 129
Tobino, M., 547
Tobler, A., 15, 37
Toccafondi, D., 457
Toch, E., 823
Tocqueville, A. de, 136, 165,
179
Toddes, E., 1043
Todolí, J., 380
Todorov, T., 1078–79, 1080
Todorow, A., 808
Togeby, O., 902
Togo, M., 994
Tolentino, J. M., 410
Toller, E., 827
Tollis, F., 27–28
Tolmachev, V. M., 1013
Tolochko, O., 1055
Tolomio, I., 519
Tolstaia, O. K., 1025
Tolstaia, S. A., 1025
Tolstaia, T., 1030
Tolstoi, A. N., 1026, 1048
Tolstoi, I., 1021, 1044
Tolstoi, L. N., 539, 1024, 1027,
1031, 1038, 1058
Tolstoy, H., 1017
Toma, I., 551
Toman, K., 944
Tomasek, T., 641
Tomashevskii, A., 1032
Tomashevskii, Iu. B., 1051
Tomasik, W., 983
Tomaszewska, S., 966
Tomaszewski, M., 978, 979, 982
Tombeur, P., 40
Tombińska, A., 962
Tomei, C. D., 994
Tomiš, K., 955
Tomova, E., 999
Tompkins, C., 416
Tondo, M., 541
Tonini, V., 508
Toniolo Fascione, M. C., 494
Tonnemine, de (*père*), 100
Toorians, L., 561

Toorn, M. C. van den, 877, 880–81
Toorn-Schutte, J. van der, 882
Topalov, K., 1083
Topolińska, Z., 962
Topolovački, M., 1075
Toporov, V. N., 1022
Tordi, R., 526
Torelli, P., 488
Torga, M., 397
Torkan, 832
Tornero Poveda, E., 289
Tornitore, T., 540
Törnqvist, E., 931
Toro, A. de, 413, 414
Toro Montalvo, C., 422
Torre, G. de, 342
Torreblanca, M., 271–72
Torreilles, C., 256
Torrejón, A., 283
Torrente Ballester, G., 367, 372
Torrents, N., 367
Torres, J., 376
Torres, V. F., 420
Torres, X., 367
Torres-Alcalá, A., 261
Torresani, S., 540
Torres Caballero, B., 413
Torres Cárdenas, E., 418–19
Torres Nebrera, G., 353
Torrini, M., 508
Torrini-Roblin, G., 57
Tortajada, R., 134
Tortarolo, E., 143
Toscani, C., 527, 533–34, 547
Toscano, N., 357
Tosi, A., 424
Toso, F., 490
Töteberg, M., 843
Totev, Kh., 1079
Toure, A., 95
Tournier, M., 244
Tournon, A., 90, 91
Toussaint, M., 28
Touzot, J., 224
Townsend, D., 5, 7–8
Tozzi, F., 525, 547
Träger, C., 704
Traill, D. A., 6
Traill, N. H., 201
Trainer, J., 771
Trakl, G., 797, 819, 827
Tramitz, A., 819
Trampus, A., 513
Tranströmer, T., 936
Trapero, M., 282
Trapnell, W., 156
Trapp, F., 808, 810
Traugott, E. C., 601
Traunecker, C., 620

Trauth, M., 799–800
Traven, B., 827
Travers, M., 823
Traversari, A., 464
Travi, E., 454, 485
Trávníček, J., 945
Treder, J., 964
Trediakovskii, V. K., 1010
Treiber, H., 406
Tremblay-Couédel, H., 569
Trendafilov, V., 1082
Trethewey, J., 122, 130
Treviños, G., 417
Trevisan, A., 484
Trévisan, C., 174
Triaire, D., 156
Tribby, J., 506
Triesscheijn, B., 876
Triff, E. S., 415
Trifonov, Iu. V., 1027, 1048–49
Trifonov, N., 1042
Trigo, A., 423
Trimborn, K., 641
Tringant, 74
Trinko, A., 1046
Tříska, J., 939
Trissino, G. G., 467, 481
Tristan, F., 172
Tristan l'Hermite, F., 101, 116, 678
Trivero, P., 481
Trnková, J., 948
Troczyński, K., 979
Trofymuk, M., 1055
Trommelen, M., 877
Trommler, F., 841
Tron, A., 513
Troncarelli, M., 448
Tropea, G., 444
Trosterud, T., 919
Trostnikov, M. V., 1014
Trotta, N., 526
Trotto, B., 467
Troubetzkoy, W., 113
Trouille, M., 149
Trousson, R., 149, 155
Trovato, P., 456
Trovato, R., 530
Troyat, H., 242
Trüb, R., 608
Trubachov, O. N., 948
Truci, I., 506
Trueblood, A. S., 308
Truhlář, B., 955
Trujillo, R., 279
Trumper, J., 429
Trzecieski, A., 974
Tsekov, Iu., 1060
Tselkova, L. N., 1015
Tsiotka, 1069

Tsipko, A., 1048
Tsiv'ian, T. V., 1022
Tsoneva, S., 1082
Tsuchiya, A., 336
Tsukanov, G., 1019
Tsvetaeva, M. I., 1017, 1019, 1022, 1033, 1034, 1049
Tsvetkov, I., 1081
Tsvetov, G. A., 1029
Tsymbaliuk, V., 1054
Tucholsky, K., 819, 827
Tuck, R., 457
Tucker, G. H., 189
Tucoo-Chala, S., 138
Tufts, C. S., 1018
Tulard, J., 168
Tulaytuli, al-, 303
Tullia d'Aragona, 477
Tully, J., 694
Tunner, E., 738, 739, 748, 833, 851–52, 858
Turbet-Delof, G., 118
Turchetti, M., 117
Turcio, R., 546
Turgot, A. R. J., 134
Turley, J. S., 274
Turner, C. J. G., 1018
Turner, D., 825
Turner, H. S., 329, 335
Turner, J. M. W., 229
Turoldo, D. M., 547
Turrini, P., 801, 836, 871
Turton, D., 164–65
Turull, A., 382
Tusquets, E., 362, 367, 372
Tuțescu, M., 12
Tuttle, E. F., 13, 441
Tuwim, J., 978
Tvardovskii, A. T., 1028, 1049
Tveit, T., 916–17
Tvorogov, O. V., 998
Twain, M., 1038
Twardowski, J., 983
Twm o'r Nant, *see* Edwards, T.
Tychyna, P., 1059–60
Tykhyi, O., 1054
Tymchenko, Ie., 1052
Tynianov, Iu. N., 1027, 1049
Tyson, P. K., 827

Ua Cnáimhsí, P., 576, 577
Ua Maoileoin, P., 579
Ua Súilleabháin, S., 578
Ubaldo of Saint-Amand (*Saint*), 4–5
Ubersfeld, A., 130, 177, 350
Uc Faidit, 247
Udodov, A. B., 1040
Udolph, J., 971

Ueberschlag, G., 817, 868
Ueding, G., 684, 860
Uerlings, H., 765
Ugalde, S. K., 366
Ughetto, A., 155
Ugrešić, D., 1074
Uhl, P., 71, 262
Uhlár, V., 948, 950
Uhlířová, L., 1080
Uhse, B., 827
Uitert, C., 884
Ujević, A., 1074
Ukena-Best, E., 649
Ukrainka, L., 1057
Ulbrich, R., 658–59
Ul'ianov, N. I., 1030
Ulivi, F., 547
Ulla, N., 415
Ullén, J. O., 912
Ulrich von Etzenbach, 636, 647
Ulrich von Türheim, 642, 646
Ulrich von Zatzikhoven, 642
Ulukhanov, I. S., 992
Ulvestad, B., 603
Ulysse, G., 482
Unamuno, M. de, 341, 351, 354, 357–58, 360, 361
Ungaretti, G., 526, 529, 547–48, 846, 851
Unger, T., 771
Ungvari, T., 162
Uniłowski, K., 983
Unruh, F. von, 834
Unseld, S., 862
Unterkircher, A., 842
Unterreitmeier, H., 619, 792
Unwin, T., 170, 195
Unwin, T. A., 184–85
Unzeitig-Herzog, M., 647
Urban VIII (*Pope*), 507
Urban, K., 963
Urbancová, H., 953
Urbańczyk, S., 965
Urbani, B., 155
Urbani, S., 434
Urbano, H., 389
Urbano, V., 408
Urbina, E., 312
Urdiales, M., 270
Ureña, E. M., 723–24
Urey, D. F., 329, 334, 335
Urfé, A. d', 81
Urfé, H. d', 106, 109, 116
Urgnani, E., 532
Uri, H., 918
Uría, I., 291–92
Urien, J.-Y., 568
Urioste, G. L., 407
Urițescu, D., 551
Urraca (*Queen of Spain*), 371

Ursini, F., 435–36
Ursu, N. A., 551
Urusova, E. P., 1001
Urza, C., 372
Urzainqui, I., 294
Urzidil, J., 809
Usher, J., 448
Usigli, R., 414, 421
Uskov, A. I., 901
Uslar Pietri, A., 423
Uspenskii, B. A., 990, 1001, 1010
Uspenskii, G. I., 1024
Ustinov, A., 1041
Utkina, N. F., 1006–07, 1024
Utrera, R., 342
Utz, P., 799
Uytfanghe, M. van, 1, 246
Uz, J. P., 686
Uzhchenko, V., 1053
Uzunova, R., 1049

Väänänen, V., 13, 15
Vaccaneo, F., 535
Vacchi, S., 540
Vachon, S., 168
Vaculík, L., 945
Vaerenbergh, L. van, 816
Vaget, H. R., 822–23
Vaginov, K. K., 1049
Vahl, H., 854
Vaiman, S., 1040
Vairasse, D., *see* Veiras, D.
Vaišnoras, V., 594
Vaisse, P., 163
Vaissièra, C., 254–55
Vajanský, S. H., 954
Vakurov, V. N., 994
Valbuena Briones, A., 319–20
Valcke, L., 460
Valdés, J. de, 15, 266
Valdés, M. E., 418
Valdés, M. J., 418
Valdivia, P. de, 408
Valdivieso, H., 283–84
Valdrè, L., 508
Valehrach-Schaefer, B., 951
Valente, J. A., 331, 364, 366
Valente, V., 437
Valenti, A.-M., 513
Valenti, V., 545
Valentin, K., 871
Valentin, P., 596
Valenzuela, L., 367, 412, 416
Valera, J., 328, 335, 340
Valeri, B., 460
Valeri, M. T., 460
Valéry, P., 231–32, 342, 351, 526, 548, 706, 820, 851

Valette, B., 201
Valier, A., 463
Valin, R., 28
Valiñas, L., 284
Valincour, J.-H. du T. de, 143
Valis, N. M., 329, 339–40
Valla, L., 458
Valle Caviedes, J. del, 409
Valle-Inclán, R. M. del, 334, 358–59, 360
Vallejo, C., 413, 422
Vallejo, C. de, 417
Vallès, J., 133, 202
Valli, B., 541
Valli, D., 529
Vallisneri, A., 523
Vallois, M.-C., 148
Valls, F., 368
Vallverdú, F., 387
Valore, P. B., 907
Valouch, F., 943
Valverde Azula, I., 365
Vampilov, A. V., 1049
Van Alboom, R., 880
Vance, J., 119
Vančura, V., 943
Vandecasteele, M., 887
Vandel, C., 112
Van Delft, L., 101, 111, 128
Vandeloise, C., 41
Van den Heuvel, J., 150
Van de Pitte, F. P., 119
Van Der Laan, J. M., 694, 718
VanderWolk, W., 195–96
Van de Vyver, G., 132
Van Deyck, R., 28, 70
Van Durme, L., 879
Vaněk, V., 944
Vanelli, L., 429, 433, 555
Van Gogh, V., 215, 816, 887, 898
Van Hauwermeiren, P., 876
Van Herreweghe, M., 878
Van Hoof, D., 883–84
Vanini, G. C., 507, 510
Vanisselroy, H. J., 888
Van Kley, D. K., 139
Vannucci, M., 486
Vanovič, J., 956
Van Passen, A.-M., 457
Van Slyke, G., 176
Van Vleck, A. E., 260
Vanvolsem, S., 444
Vanwelkenhuyzen, G., 192
Vaquero, M., 285, 290
Varaut, J.-M., 212
Varchetta, G., 537
Varchi, B., 428
Varela, J., 327
Varela, J. R., 418

Varese, C., 534
Varey, J. E., 315
Vargas Churchill, A., 350
Vargas Llosa, M., 413, 414, 422
Vargas Martínez, G., 407
Varikas, E., 154
Varkhol, N., 1054
Varloot, J., 145
Varnhagen (Levin), R., 727, 736, 745, 770, 772
Varnhagen von Ense, K. A., 732, 771–72
Varsik, B., 948
Varty, K., 66
Vàrvaro, A., 13, 14, 424, 426
Varzatskaia, O. M., 1033
Vasari, G., 474, 483, 488–89, 773
Vasil'ev, G. K., 1044
Vasil'ev, I. A., 1050
Vasil'ev, N., 1031
Vasil'ev, P. N., 1049
Vasil'ev, V. V., 1045, 1047
Vasileva, A., 49
Vasilevich, U., 1069
Vasilevskaia, I. A., 1047
Vasiliu, E., 554
Vasiliu, L., 553
Vasiljev, D., 1076
Vasiuchenka, P., 1066
Vasoli, C., 464, 468, 492, 508
Vásquez, M. A., 415
Vásquez, M. S., 333
Vassalli, S., 528
Vassevière, J., 160
Vasvari, L. O., 293
Vattimo, G., 363, 832
Vauchez, A., 619
Vaudelin, G. de, 29
Vaugelas, C. F. de, 46
Vaughan, H., 563
Vaughan, T., 563
Vauquelin de La Fresnaye, J., 102
Vauvenargues, L. de C. de (*marquis*), 144
Vayra, M., 429
Vazov, I., 1083
Vázquez, F., 298, 310
Vázquez, M. A., 301
Vázquez, V., 267
Vázquez Montalbán, M., 362
Vázquez Rozas, M. V., 279–80
Vazzoler, F., 501
Vecce, C., 475, 486
Vecchi Galli, P., 478
Vecchio, S., 427
Vedrine, M., 148–49
Vedrire, M., 167
Vega, C., 382

Vega, C. A., 295
Veiga Arias, A., 277, 390, 402–03
Veiras, D., 106, 676–77
Veka, O., 915
Veland, R., 433
Velasco, M. M. de, 416, 419
Velasco Núñez, F., 417
Velayos Zurdo, O., 419
Velázquez, D. Rodríguez de Silva y, 229, 357
Veldeke, H. van, 888
Veldman, I. M., 888
Veleva, M., 1079
Vélez, J. F., 419, 421
Vélez de Guevara, J., 315, 325
Velguth, M., 230
Veličković, S., 1076
Velli, G., 448
Velmar-Janković, J., 1074
Velmar-Janković, S., 1076
Vemmelund, I., 847
Venås, K., 918, 919
Venclova, T., 973
Venediktov, G. K., 1079
Venesoen, C., 111
Venesoen, P., 95
Veneziani, M., 524
Venier, D., 461
Venier, M. E., 309
Venne, I. ten, 631, 657
Vennemann, T., 597
Venosoen, C., 122
Ventura, R., 143
Venturi, A., 1028
Veny, J., 381
Vera Luján, A., 280
Veras, Z., 1066, 1069
Verbeke, K., 896
Verbiest, A., 880
Vercammen, L., 899
Vercier, B., 200
Verdelhan-Bourgade, M., 49
Verdier, G., 106, 107, 115
Verdino, S., 546
Verdirame, R., 526
Verdon, T., 464–65
Verdonk, R. A., 274–75
Verene, D. P., 524
Verga, G., 535, 541, 542
Vergelli, A., 547–48
Vergier de Hauranne, J. du, 118
Vergnaud, J.-R., 275
Verhaeren, E., 208, 1025
Verheugd-Daatzelaar, E., 36
Verheul, K., 1036
Verhoeven, L., 882
Verhuyck, P., 72, 93, 893–94
Verjat, A., 133

Verlaine, P., 166, 180, 181, 183, 187, 191–92
Verlinde, S., 23, 43
Vermeer, J., 229
Vermeer, W., 991
Vermij, L. T., 900
Vernay, H., 20
Verne, J., 181, 192, 202–03
Vernet, J., 147, 151
Vernet, M., 109, 126
Vernière, P., 145
Verny, M.-J., 256
Véron de Fourbonnais, F., 134
Veronesi, S., 533
Verri, A., 524
Verri, P., 518
Verroul, E., 104
Versaille, A., 196
Versé, N. A. de, 117
Versini, L., 147, 152, 153
Vertel', E., 1047
Vervaeck, B., 887
Verweyen, T., 868
Vesaas, O., 917
Vesaas, T., 982
Veselinović, J., 1076
Vesper, B., 834
Vespertino Rodríguez, A., 300, 301, 303
Vestdijk, S., 885, 888, 898, 900
Vet, C., 32
Vetter, A., 871
Vettori, F., 459
Vevia Romero, F. C., 421
Veyne, P., 219
Vezhbin'ski, Ia., 1051
Vezzosi, A. M., 546
Viachorka, V., 1064
Vialiuhin, A., 1069
Vian, F., 435
Viana, A. dos R. G., 380, 391
Viana, M. C., 391
Vian Herrero, A., 298
Viano, M., 535
Viaplana, J., 378, 381
Viard, J., 179
Viart, D., 223–24
Viaut, A., 253
Vicente, A., 360
Vickers, B., 459
Vickers, N., 87
Vico, G., 428, 490, 518, 524
Vico Faggi, *see* Orengo, A.
Victor, L., 215
Vidal, J. C., 363
Vidal, M., 147
Vidal-Collell, M. A., 383
Vidal Tibbits, M., 330
Vidan, G., 143
Vidan, I., 1073

Vidart, L., 334
Videla, G., 412
Videnov, M., 1079
Viehweger, D., 592
Vieillard, F., 62, 63
Vierck, H., 625
Vierhaus, R., 760
Viëtor, K., 767
Vietta, S., 772–73
Vigerie, P., 39
Vignali, L., 459
Vignaud, P., 258
Vignaud, S., 258
Vigneau-Rouayrenc, C., 25
Vigny, A. de, 167, 177
Vigolo, G., 528
Viguera, M. J., 300
Viguier, A., 187
Viguier, M.-C., 251
Vilà, C., 381
Vilain, R., 817
Vilanova, A., 329
Vilar, A., 144–45
Vil'chek, L., 1036
Vil'chek, V., 1036
Vilches de Frutos, M. F., 360, 372–73
Vildrac, C., 208
Vilela, M., 395, 397
Vilenkin, V. Ia., 1035
Vilenskii, Iu. G., 1037
Vilhena, M. C., 405
Vilikovský, P., 955, 956
Villa, E., 540
Villalón, C. de, 266
Villalón, F., 342
Villalva, A., 398–99
Villani, G., 489
Villani, J., 155
Villani, P., 26, 155
Villanueva, D., 330, 359, 369
Villanueva, E., 422
Villanueva, E. de, 306
Villar, M., 397
Villata, B., 442, 445
Villaurrutia, X., 420
Villaverde, C., 411
Villedieu, C. de, *née* Desjardins, 116
Villena, E. de, 296, 299
Villena, L. A. de, 364
Villerías y Roel, J. de, 406
Villiers de l'Isle-Adam, P.-A., 181, 203
Villon, F., 69–70, 77, 809, 837
Vin, D. de, 849
Viña Liste, J. M., 288
Vinall, S. W., 469
Vinaver, E., 129
Vinaver, S., 1076

Vince, S., 186
Vincelli, A., 444
Vincensini, J.-J., 52
Vincent, J.-D., 154
Vincent, N. B., 12, 15, 249
Vincent, P., 892
Vincenti, E., 471
Vincenti, F., 527
Vincent of Beauvais, 8, 651–52
Vincenz, A., 1054
Vinet, A., 164
Vinet, M.-T., 36
Vinje, F.-E., 917
Vinot, B., 143
Vințeler, O., 553
Vinti, C., 508
Vintr, J., 939
Viola, G. E., 529
Viola, S., 541
Virchow, R., 708
Virgil, 2, 3, 4, 9, 105, 228, 457, 469, 473, 474, 475, 480, 686, 706, 758
Virgillito, R. S., 538
Vischer, M., 663
Visconti, G. B., 511
Viselli, S., 148
Vishnevetskaia, B. M., 989
Vishnevetskii, I. G., 1022
Vishnevskaia, I., 1032
Vishniak, M. V., 1020, 1044
Visser, A., 862
Visser, C., 843
Vissière, I., 140
Vissière, J.-L., 139, 140
Vitale, R., 350
Vitali, C., 516
Vitalis, J., 88
Vitez, A., 174
Viti, P., 460
Viti, R. M., 204, 205
Vitier, C., 411
Vitka, V., 1069
Vitlianov, S., 1081
Vitoria, F. de, 304
Vitorino, G., 402
Vittorini, E., 530, 548
Vittorio Amedeo II of Savoy (*King of Sardinia*), 514
Vitz, E. B., 619
Vivaldi, A., 516
Vivant-Denon, D., 158
Vivanti, A., 548
Vivès, J. L., 267
Vives, L., 311
Vivès, R., 39
Viviani, V., 510
Vivier-Boudrier, J., 201
Viviès, J., 142
Vladimirova, L., 1035

Vladimir Yaroslavich (*Prince of Galicia*), 999
Vladimov, G. N., 1050
Vlášek, J., 939
Vliet, E. van, 887
Vliet, H. T. M. van, 886
Vloten, J. van, 892
Vodička, F., 941
Vogel, I., 428
Vogel, M., 662
Voghera, G., 548
Voghera, M., 427, 429
Vogler, W., 629
Vogt, G., 855
Vogt, J., 834
Vogt, M., 791
Vogtherr, T., 622
Voigt, J., 709
Voinovich, V. N., 1050
Voisine-Jechová, H., 942
Voit, F., 828
Voit, P., 940
Voitsikava, L., 1066, 1069
Volkart-Rey, R., 439
Völkel, H., 557
Volkert, W., 610
Volkov, O. V., 1029
Volkova, I. F., 1026
Vollhaber, T., 854
Vollhardt, F., 692, 694, 786
Vollmann, B. K., 612, 647
Vollmann-Profe, G., 647, 652
Vollmer, H., 869
Vollrath, H., 623
Volney, C., 144
Vologdin, I. S., 1017
Voloshin, M. A., 1016, 1024–25, 1027, 1038
Voloshinov (*pseud.*), 1031
Voloshinov, M., 348
Voloshinov, V. N., 1008
Volpe, S., 196
Vol'pe, Ts. S., 1027
Volporri, P., 527
Volta, A., 495
Volta, S., 500
Voltaire, F.-M. A. de, 131, 142, 144, 145, 150–52, 703, 715–16, 953, 1008
Volynskii, A., 1019
Vončina, J., 1072
Vondel, J. van den, 892
Vondung, K., 598
Vongrej, P., 953
Vonhoff, G., 725
Vonk, F., 877
Voorwinden, N., 820
Vorkachev, S. G., 995
Vormweg, H., 831
Vorobiov, M., 1062

Voronov, V., 1027–28
Voronyi, M., 1060
Voros, S. D., 318
Vos, J. de, 827
Vos, W. de, 115
Voss, L., 648
Vovelle, M., 138
Voyles, J., 597
Voznesenskii, A. A., 1034
Voznesenskii, A. V., 998
Vozniak, M., 1052
Vranckx, L. P., 416
Vraneš, A., 1076
Vrchlický, J., 942
Vree, F. de, 900
Vries, J. W. de, 877, 885
Vrkljan, I., 1074
Vrooman, J. R., 150
Vroon, R., 1021, 1033
Vrubel', I. N., 1009
Všetička, F., 940, 942, 944
Vuijlsteke, M. M. R., 263
Vukomanović, D., 1070
Vukomanović, S., 1070
Vuković, Đ., 1075
Vuksanović, S., 1075
Vuletić, B., 1073
Vulikh, N. V., 1016
Vvedenskii, A. I., 1041, 1043, 1050
Vyhonnaia, L., 1063
Vynnychenko, V., 1060
Vynnyts'kyi, V., 1053
Vyshens'kyi, I., 1055
Vyshnia, O., 1060
Vysotskii, V. S., 1050

Waage Petersen, L., 461, 469, 470
Waal, C., 931
Wace, 57, 63, 65
Wachinger, B., 632, 647
Wachope, M. M., 626
Wachs, M., 146, 147, 150
Wachtel, A. B., 1027
Wachter, S., 604
Wack, M. F., 3
Wackenroder, W. H., 740, 772–73
Wade, T., 993
Waelti-Walters, J., 210
Waerp, H. H., 935
Wagener, H., 825, 828
Wager, W., 316
Waggerl, K. H., 809
Wägner, E., 936
Wagner, F., 780, 813
Wagner, G., 729
Wagner, H., 573

Wagner, H. L., 732
Wagner, I., 761, 856
Wagner, J., 137
Wagner, K., 825
Wagner, M. L., 286
Wagner, N., 609
Wagner, R., 211, 228, 615, 634, 638, 735, 782, 796, 805–06, 807, 812, 822
Wagner, R.-L., 17
Wagner-Egelhaaf, M., 824
Wahl, V., 714
Waiblinger, W., 773
Walahfrid Strabo, 4
Walc, J., 975
Walch, M., 600
Walczak, B., 965
Walczak, G., 959
Wald, L., 12
Waldeck, R., 875
Walden, H., 828
Waldheim, K., 777
Wałęsa, L., 967
Walcy, P., 306–07
Walker, B., 584
Walker, D. C., 46
Walker, J., 415
Wall, A., 237–38
Walla, F., 801
Wallace, D., 448
Wallace, I., 841, 875
Wallach-Faller, M., 654
Wallas, A., 850
Wallenberg, J., 930
Wallraff, G., 871
Walpole, H., 982
Walser, M., 833, 844, 850, 872
Walser, R., 799, 828, 837
Walsh, J. K., 350
Walsh, K., 621
Walsh, R., 416
Walsh, T. J., 271
Walter, C., 823
Walter, E., 611
Walter, G., 38, 928
Walter, H., 38, 43, 49
Walter, O. F., 835
Walter, P., 5, 61
Walter, U., 786
Walter Map, 3, 6, 662
Walter of Châtillon, 633
Walters, D. G., 347
Walters, R. L., 150
Walther, I. C., 863
Walther, J., 872
Walther, K. K., 683
Walther, P., 659, 825
Walther, W., 604
Walther von der Vogelweide, 611, 613, 623, 649–50

Walton, M. T., 466
Walton, P. J., 466
Walzel, O., 705
Walzer, M., 91
Wangenheim, W. von, 734
Wannicke, R., 196
Wanninger, H., 813
Wapnewski, P., 868
Waquet, J.-C., 512
Warburg, A., 774
Warchoł, S., 971
Ward, M. G., 776, 792
Ward, M. T., 428
Wardropper, N. P., 310
Warmond, E., 900
Warner, R., 358, 772–73
Warnet, J.-M., 151
Warning, R., 204
Warnock, R., 631
Warren, J., 809
Wartburg, W. von, 21
Waschinsky, A., 795
Waśko, A., 976
Wasserman, J., 807
Wasserstein, D., 275
Waszakowa, K., 958, 962
Waszink, P. M., 1045
Wat, A., 977, 980
Watbled, J.-P., 45
Waterschoot, W., 896
Watkins, R., 484–85
Watriquet de Couvin, 71
Watson, B. A., 859
Watson, P. F., 449
Watson-Williams, H., 242
Watt, H. S., 802
Watteau, A., 132, 183
Watthee-Delmotte, M., 193
Watts, D., 130
Watts, D. A., 98
Waugh, L. R., 19
Waxman, W., 721
Weaver, J., 123
Weaver, E., 483
Webber, A., 824
Webber, P. E., 655
Weber, B., 798
Weber, D., 862
Weber, E., 743
Weber, F., 809
Weber, F. P., 110
Weber, H., 87
Weber, H.-D., 681–82, 866
Weber, M., 336
Weber, P., 706
Weber, R., 815
Webster, J., 321
Wedekind, F., 708, 828
Weedon, C., 831
Weelden, D. van, 886

Weerth, G., 780
Wegera, K.-P., 595, 598, 600
Węgier, J., 971
Wegmann, N., 615
Wegrzyniak, R., 977
Wegstein, W., 628, 630
Wehdeking, V., 834
Wehle, W., 162
Weiand, C., 150
Weick, R., 644
Weidig, A., 786
Weidig, F. L., 786
Weidlé, V., 1031
Weigand, R., 651–52
Weigel, H., 872
Weigel, S., 811
Weigelt, H., 724
Weigl, E., 719
Weij, J. W. van der, 885
Weijerman, J. C., 885
Weijnen, A., 879
Weil, H., 782
Weil, J., 945
Weil, M., 109, 154
Weil, S., 225
Weilguny, R., 445
Weill, I., 55, 68
Weill, K., 812, 813
Weimar, K., 693, 770
Weinberg, F. M., 88
Weinberg, G., 538
Weinberg, J., 466
Weiner, D. B., 698
Weiner, M. A., 808
Weinfurter, S., 622
Weingarten, B. E., 350
Weinheber, J., 828
Weinholz, G., 756, 759
Weinig, P., 10, 662
Weininger, O., 539
Weintraub, W., 974
Weinzierl, U., 822
Weise, C., 677, 678, 699
Weise, L., 928
Weiske, B., 647
Weisman, R. F. E., 465
Weiss, C., 679, 725, 730, 732
Weiss, D., 990
Weiss, E., 544, 809, 826, 828
Weiss, H., 717
Weiss, J., 296, 299, 451
Weiss, M., 603
Weiss, P., 712, 770, 834, 844,
    872–73
Weiss, W., 808, 837, 859
Weissberg, J. D., 608
Weissberg, L., 727, 772
Weissberger, J., 349
Weissenborn, B., 717
Weissenrieder, M., 278

Wekhrlin, W. L., 143
Welch, E. S., 461
Welch, M. M., 112
Welker, K. H. L., 729
Wellershoff, D., 859, 873
Welles, M., 318
Welling, J., 878
Wellington, M., 156
Wellmann, H., 596
Wells, C. J., 593
Wells, D. A., 636–37
Wells, J. C., 627
Welzig, W., 804
Wende, G., 665
Wende, K., 662
Wende-Hohenberger, W., 834
Wenders, W., 858
Wenninger, M. J., 633
Wentzlaff-Eggebert, C., 100,
    105
Wentzlaff-Eggebert, H., 114,
    413
Wenzel, H., 611, 650
Wenzel, K., 870
Werber, M., 873
Werf, H. van der, 64–65
Werfel, F., 809, 828
Werner, G., 932
Werner, H., 31
Werner, H.-G., 706, 712, 746,
    761
Werner, K., 842
Werner, M., 163, 778, 796
Werner, W., 796
Werner, Z., 751, 773
Wernher (*Bruder*), 635
Wernher vom Niederrhein, 614
Wernicke, C., 685
Wertheimer, J., 744–45
Wertmüller, L., 359
Werumeus Buning, J., 887
Wessel, E., 859, 887
Wesseling, A., 458
Wessell, E., 822
Wessels, M., 1015
West, F. C., 820
Westerberg, A., 927
Western, A., 918
Westman, R. S., 458
Westphalen, C., 691
Westphalen, J. von, 865
Westra, H. J., 2
Wetherill, P. M., 161, 192, 227
Wetzel, H., 764
Wetzels, W. D., 718
Wetzels, W. L., 390
Weydt, H., 601
Weygómez, N., 407
Wezel, J. C., 733, 869
Weżowicz-Ziółkowska, D., 972

Wheeler, M. W., 249, 376, 380
Whelan, R., 118
Wherritt, I., 405
Whinnom, K., 298
Whistler, J. A. McN., 181–82,
    229, 544
Whiston, J., 337, 338
Whitaker, M.-J., 178
White, A., 801
White, A. D., 810, 855
White, D., 1016
White, P., 562
Whitenack, J. A., 309
Whiteside, A., 214
Whitfield, J. H., 485
Whitinger, R., 816
Whitlock, G., 802
Whitman, W., 191, 347, 351,
    796, 809
Whitney, I., 477
Whitton, D., 126
Whitton, K., 853
Whobrey, W. T., 3
Wichelhaus, M., 732
Wichmann von Arnstein, 652
Wichter, S., 604
Wickham, C., 460
Wickham, C. J., 749
Wicks-Boisson, B. M., 179
Widdig, B., 863
Widegren, B., 933
Widmer, A., 555
Widmer, K., 555
Wiechert, E., 828, 834
Wieczorek, J., 849
Wiede, F., 803
Wiedemann, C., 696
Wieden, B. bei der, 752
Wiedewelt, J., 734
Wiedling, D., 868
Wiegand, H. E., 605
Wiegers, G., 300
Wieland, C. M., 686, 687, 692,
    693, 695, 702, 732, 733, 742,
    759
Wienbarg, L., 783
Wiener, O., 836, 874
Wienzerl, U., 849
Wierlacher, A., 857
Wierzbicka, A., 434, 963, 964
Wierzyński, K., 980
Wiese, R., 599
Wiesenborn, G., 844
Wiesike, K. F., 789
Wiesing, L., 827
Wiesinger, P., 596, 597, 631
Wiesmüller, W., 809, 850
Wiessner, E., 659
Wietelmann Bauer, B., 327
Wigmore, J., 834, 865

Wigzell, F., 1002
Wijk-Andersson, E., 925
Wik, I.-B., 936
Wiktor, J., 980
Wilbur, T., 594
Wilchard of Lyon, 5
Wilcke, K., 613–14
Wild, G., 707
Wild, K., 608
Wild, R., 708
Wilde, O., 200, 336
Wilde, P. de, 896
Wildemeersch, G., 887
Wildenberg-de Kroon, C. van den, 656–57
Wilder-Mintzer, A., 828
Wilderode, A. van, 899
Wiley Richards, W., 801–02
Wilhelm II (*Emperor*), 626
Wilhelmi, T., 664
Wilhelm of Hirnkofen, 10
Wilhelm von Boldensele, 620
Wilhelmy, P., 697
Wiliam, D. W., 564
Wiliems, T., 563
Wilke, S., 727, 875
Wilkins, C., 325
Wilkinson, H. E., 21
Will, U., 651
Willard, C. C., 75, 76, 77
Wille, H. J., 918
Willem, L. M., 335, 338
Willemart, P., 198
Willemer, M. von, 746
Willems, D., 44
Willems, J. F., 886, 887
Willemyns, R., 877
William, N., 162
Williams, A., 849, 871
Williams, A. V., 209
Williams, C. G. S., 143
Williams, C. H., 562, 569
Williams, D. A., 156, 197, 198
Williams, E., 827
Williams, G., 415, 562
Williams, G. S., 662
Williams, H., 74, 75
Williams, I., 566
Williams, J., 406
Williams, J. E. C., 561
Williams, J. M., 409
Williams, M. E., 305, 348
Williams, R., 567
Williams, T., 1019
Williams, T. R., 421
Williams, W. I. C., 564
Williams, W. (Pantycelyn), 564
Williamsen, A. R., 324
Williams-Krapp, W., 616, 632, 653

Williamson, E., 171
William the Conqueror, 63
Willim, E., 958
Williram von Ebersberg, 637
Willson, H. B., 643
Wilmet, M., 27, 33, 42
Wilpert, G. von, 704
Wilson, E. F., 186–87
Wilson, M., 305
Wilson, W. D., 683, 701–02
Wimmer, R., 823
Wimmer-Webhofer, E., 820
Winckelmann, J. J., 733–34, 770
Winczer, P., 955, 956
Winders, M., 886
Windfuhr, M., 689, 793, 795, 796
Windisch, R., 605
Windolph, W., 631
Wingertszahn, C., 746–47
Winkelmann, C., 871
Winkelmann, O., 253, 604, 605
Winkler, D.-S., 837
Winkler, T., 836
Winkler, W., 852
Winspur, S., 230, 232, 241
Winter, H.-G., 725, 859
Winter, U., 616
Winzap, I., 556
Wipperfürth, H., 791
Wirmark, M., 932
Wirrer, J., 842
Wirth, K.-A., 655
Wirtz, T., 827
Wis, M., 643
Wisbey, R. A., 614
Wischmann, A., 908
Wiśniewski, M., 959–60
Wisniewski, R., 638
Wisskirchen, H., 821
Withers, C. W. J., 586
Witkiewicz, S. I., 225, 973, 980
Witkin, S. C., 173
Witt, H., 843
Witt, R., 458
Witte, B., 731
Wittenwiler, H., 611, 659
Wittgenstein, L., 819, 827
Wittig, G., 868
Wittmann, J., 857
Wittowski, J., 843
Wittstock, U., 831, 850
Wizisla, E., 819
Wizlaw III (*Prince of Rügen*), 650
Wizo Flandrensis, 561
Włodarczyk, H., 978, 982
Wobeser, W. K. von, 752
Woesler, W., 729, 812

Woestijne, K. van de, 885, 888
Wogan-Browne, J., 64
Wöhler, K., 874
Wohlleben, J., 719
Wojciehowski, D. A., 509
Wójcik, W., 972
Wojtak, B., 590
Wojtkiewicz, M., 957
Wojtyła, K., 983
Wojtyła-Świerzowska, M., 962
Woldan, A., 1064
Wolf, A., 643, 829
Wolf, A. de, 75
Wolf, B., 601
Wolf, C., 688, 738, 830, 831, 832, 834, 837, 839, 840, 841, 846, 847, 850, 852, 854, 863, 865, 874–75, 1035
Wolf, F., 825
Wolf, G., 838, 853
Wolf, H. J., 441, 446
Wolf, J., 858
Wolf, K., 921
Wolf, K. B., 7, 289
Wolf, L., 44, 45 46, 246
Wolf, N., 211
Wolf, N. R., 596, 597, 613, 631
Wolfe, K. W., 107, 126
Wolfe, P. J., 107
Wolfengruber, G., 836
Wolff, C., 686
Wolff, D., 850
Wolff, W., 745
Wolffheim, E., 821
Wölfflin, H., 342
Wolfgang, L. D., 59, 61–62, 67
Wolfgruber, G., 859
Wolfram von Eschenbach, 611, 620, 631, 634, 635, 636, 640, 643–46, 649
Wolfskehl, K., 828
Woll, J., 1048
Wollmann, A., 560
Wollschläger, H., 870, 875
Wollstonecraft, M., 149, 158
Wollzogen, C. von, 691
Wolny, H., 977
Wolosky, S., 235
Wołowik, B., 961
Wolter, H., 633
Wood, D. S., 81
Wood, S., 540
Woodbridge, H. C., 406
Woodhouse, J., 1030
Woodhouse, J. R., 486
Woods, W., 885
Woodward, J. B., 1035, 1049
Woodward, L. J., 307
Woodward, S., 206
Woodward, W. J., 278

Woolard, A., 383
Wooldridge, T. R., 36, 258
Woollen, G., 168
Wordsworth, W., 191, 586, 713
Worley, L. K., 724, 825
Woronzoff-Dashkov, A., 1007
Worth, V., 100
Wotjak, B., 277
Wotjak, G., 277, 279, 281
Woytowicz-Neymann, M., 960
Woyzeck, J. C., 786
Woźniak, T., 971
Wright, B., 198
Wright, C. D., 3
Wright, D. T., 755
Wright, J. J., 85
Wright, M., 853
Wright, N., 7
Wright, R., 377, 934, 935
Wright, R. H. P., 13, 14
Wróbel, A., 958
Wróbel, J., 981
Wróblewski, K., 961
Wronicz, J., 961
Wroth, M., 477
Wruck, P., 790
Wucher, M.-N., 215
Wüest, J. T., 253
Wuillermoz, M., 121
Wulf, B., 627
Wulf, C., 654–55
Wulfila, 625
Wulfstan, 3
Wunder, H., 621
Wunderli, P., 261
Wunderlich, W., 615, 638
Wünsch, C. E., 761, 762
Wünsch, M., 702–03
Wünsche, M., 807
Wurzel, W. U., 593
Wuttke, D., 661, 662, 664
Wyclif, J., 621
Wyderka, B., 965
Wydra, W., 967
Wyka, M., 979
Wynn, M., 640
Wynne, E., 563
Wysling, H., 799, 821, 823
Wysłouch, S., 972
Wysłouch, W., 979
Wyspiański, S., 974, 977
Wyss, U., 615, 741

Xavier, M. F., 388, 389, 392, 395
Xirau, J., 362
Xirgu, M., 361

Yagüe Bosch, J., 347
Yaguello, M., 25

Yamada, T., 639, 768
Yáñez, A., 414
Yáñez Cossío, A., 419
Yardeni, M., 138
Yates, F., 486
Yates, W. E., 801
Yde, H., 911
Yeager, G. M., 410
Yeandle, D. N., 604, 614
Yeats, W. B., 236, 802
Ynduráin, D., 305
Yokitani, Y., 851
Yolton, J. W., 131
Yon, B., 116
Yoon, S.-M., 294
Young, E., 774
Young, H. T., 342, 349, 351
Young, S., 1070
Yovanovich, G., 415
Yudice, G., 413
Yurkievich, S., 422
Yviricu, J., 422
Yxart, J., 330

Zabolotskii, N., 1050
Zabolotskii, N. A., 1027, 1050
Zabuzhko, N., 1056
Zaccaria, V., 449
Zäch, A., 800
Zach, M. S., 823
Zachariä, J. F. W., 686
Zacharias, C., 868
Zachau, R. K., 815
Zach-Błońska, J., 976
Zaddy, Z. P., 59
Zagaevschi, V., 554
Zagajewski, A., 981
Zagari, L., 796
Zago, E., 540
Zagorin, P., 487
Zagórski, Z., 964–65
Zagoskin, M. N., 1010–11
Zahareas, A. N., 359
Zahn, P., 663
Zahnitko, A., 1053
Zaimova, R., 1082
Zainer, G., 663
Zaitsev, A. V., 1038
Zaitsev, B. K., 1050
Zaitsev, N. N., 1039
Zaitsev, V. A., 1033, 1034
Zaitseva, A. A., 1006
Zaitseva, A. R., 1044
Zajac, P., 952
Żak, S., 625
Zakharava, V., 1064
Zakharieva, I., 1041
Zakhar'in, D. B., 991
Zakharov, V. N., 1026

Zakrajšek, K., 1071
Zakrzewski, B., 975
Zales'ka-Onyshkevych, L., 1059
Zaleski, M., 982
Zalesskaia, L. I., 1047
Zalizniak, A. A., 990
Zalm, C. van der, 888
Zalygin, S. P., 1029, 1048, 1050
Zamarreño, A. S., 310
Zambelli, P., 464
Zambon, F., 262, 447
Zambon, P., 527
Zamboni, A., 443
Zamboni, G. G., 516
Zambrano, M., 346, 356, 359–60, 362, 372
Zamiatin, E. I., 1042, 1045, 1050
Zanardi, M., 522
Zancani, D., 460
Zandbergen, J., 900
Zanette, L., 466
Zantop, S., 736–37, 796
Zanzotto, A., 528, 528, 547, 549
Zapata, R. A., 406
Zapletal, Z., 945
Zappella, G., 485
Zappulla Muscarà, S., 544
Zárate, F. de, 323–24
Zard, P., 236
Zaręba, A., 968
Zarębina, M., 958, 966, 968–69
Zaretski, M., 1069
Zaring, L., 32
Zarniarra, E., 528
Zaron, Z., 961
Zarrilli, C., 511
Zarubina, T., 1048
Zatlin, P., 371, 373
Zatovkaňuk, M., 995
Zatti, S., 469
Zaun, D. P., 601
Zayas y Sotomayor, M. de, 311, 320, 325
Zayed, G., 191
Zbikowski, P., 974
Zborovets, I. V., 1032
Zdanevich, I. M., 1025, 1027
Zdunkiewicz, D., 962, 965
Zech, P., 828–29, 875
Zegadłowicz, E., 967
Zehl Romero, C., 875
Zehm, E., 700
Zeile, E., 868
Zeilinger, H., 679, 774
Zelins'ka, L., 1057
Zelinskii, K., 1040
Zelinsky, B., 1041
Zelle, C., 686, 716, 724

Zeller, E., 875
Zeller, H., 800
Zeller, R., 687, 823, 864
Zelter, C. F., 700
Zemberová, V., 953
Zemel, R. M. T., 885, 889–90
Zemskaia, E. A., 992
Zemskov, M., 418
Zenea, J. C., 411
Zenker, H., 836
Zenkevich, M., 1033
Zenkine, S., 173
Zeno, A., 511, 516, 517, 523
Zeno, P. C., 514
Zeno of Elea, 228
Zeplin, R., 875
Zeromski, S., 967
Zerov, M., 1060
Zesen, F. von, 669
Zesen, P. von, 733
Zeuch, U., 769
Zeydel, E. H., 770
Zeyer, J., 942
Zeyringer, K., 859
Zhaivoronok, V., 1054
Zharov, B. S., 901
Zhechev, T., 1081
Zheliezniak, I., 1054
Zhenzhera, V., 1061
Zhirmunskii, V. M., 606
Zhitkov, B., 1027
Zhivov, V. M., 1006, 1010
Zhluktenko, Iu., 1054
Zholkovskii, A. K., 1045
Zhovtis, A. L., 1045
Zhovtobriukh, M., 1052
Zhu, J., 602
Zhuk, A., 1068
Zhukova, L., 1027
Zhukovskii, V. A., 1003, 1016
Zhulyns'kyi, M., 1057, 1058, 1061
Zhurauliou, V., 1067
Zhuravleva, G. I., 1009
Zhyhotski, M., 1067
Zhynkin, A., 1068
Ziazulia, A., 1069
Ziegengeist, G., 941
Ziegler, B., 910
Ziegler, R., 202
Ziegler, V., 577
Ziejka, F., 977

Zielińska, B., 979, 982
Zieliński, J., 978, 979
Zieniukowa, J., 961
Zierhoffer, K., 971
Zierhofferowa, Z., 971
Ziffer, G., 1000
Zigo, J., 946
Zigo, P., 948, 968
Zikken, A., 900
Zilcovsky, J., 818
Zilka, T., 955
Zilyns'kyi, I., 1054
Zimmer, S., 560
Zimmerman, M., 412
Zimmermann, B. A., 652
Zimmermann, H. D., 809
Zimmermann, I., 602
Zimmermann, M., 76, 661
Zimmermann, M. C., 376
Zimorski, W., 805
Zinato, E., 530
Zincgref, J. W., 674
Zinchenko, N., 1056
Zingerman, B., 1032
Zink, M., 52, 70, 74
Zinken, R.-M., 804
Zinkiavichius, Z., 969
Zinov'ev, A. A., 1050
Zinov'ev, G. E., 1016
Zinov'eva, E. I., 991
Ziolkowski, E. J., 312
Ziolkowski, J. M., 5
Ziolkowski, M., 1028
Zissman, C., 181
Zitzelsberger, O. J., 652
Živković, D., 1074
Zoch, I., 600
Zoderer, J., 875
Zoet, J., 893
Zohn, H., 819
Zola, É., 169, 175, 179, 180, 181, 182, 192, 193, 194, 198, 202, 203–06, 211, 334, 781
Zolli, P., 435–36
Zollinger, A., 837
Zöllner, E., 621
Zolotnitskii, D., 1020
Zolotonosov, M., 1029–30, 1034, 1038
Zolotukhin, V., 1050
Zolotusskii, I., 1037
Zonneveld, J., 818

Zorivchak, R., 1054, 1062
Zorrilla, J., 329, 340
Zorrilla de San Martín, J., 411
Zorzi, A., 461
Zorzi, F., *see* Giorgio, F.
Zorzi Calò, D., 434
Zoshchenko, M. M., 1027, 1051
Zotos, A., 110
Zotz, T., 619, 622, 639
Zrazhevs'ka, N., 1058
Zschachlitz, R., 811, 851
Zschokke, M., 835
Zscholle, H., 727
Zuanelli, E., 424
Zub, I., 1060
Zuber, H., 98
Zuber, R., 108
Zuberbühler, R., 789
Zubizarreta, A., 414
Zubizarreta, M.-L., 18
Zubkova, S. V., 1018
Zubova, L. V., 1049
Zubryts'ka, M., 1060
Zuck, V., 929
Zuckerman, C., 1000
Zückert, H., 696
Zuckmayer, C., 829
Zuev, N., 1019
Zufferey, F., 246
Zuiderent, A., 885, 889
Zuidinga, R.-H., 878
Zuionak, V., 1066, 1069
Zuloaga, I., 355, 357
Zumthor, P., 53, 57, 611
Zúñiga, D. de (*Fray*), 310
Zúñiga, J. E., 363
Żurawska, J., 973
Zurita, A. de, 407
Zurita, R., 417
Zürn, U., 680, 875
Zverev, A., 1030
Zvinjackovskij, V. Ja., 1018
Żwak, I., 957
Zweig, A., 786, 829
Zweig, S., 230, 809, 828, 829, 836
Zybura, M., 799
Zychlinski, R. von, 796
Zychowicz, J., 980
Żydek-Bednarczuk, U., 963
Zykova, G. V., 1013
Zyliński, L., 857